SCIENCE FICTION AND FANTASY LITERATURE

SCIENCE FICTION AND FANTASY LITERATURE

A Checklist, 1700-1974

with

Contemporary Science Fiction Authors II

R. Reginald

Volume 1:

Author Index
Title Index
Series Index
Awards Index
Ace and Belmont Doubles Index

Editorial Associates:
Douglas Menville, Mary A. Burgess

Assistants:
George Locke, Gordon Johnson, Doris Illes,
Barry R. Levin, Michael Grainey

Gale Research Company • Book Tower • Detroit, Michigan 48226

Acknowledgment of previous·publication of selected material in "Contemporary Science Fictions Authors II" is made to the following publications:

STELLA NOVA: THE CONTEMPORARY SCIENCE FICTION AUTHORS. Copyright © 1970 by Unicorn & Son, Publishers. Used by permission of the publisher.

CONTEMPORARY SCIENCE FICTION AUTHORS, FIRST EDITION. Copyright © 1974 by R. Reginald. Used by permission of the author.

CONTEMPORARY AUTHORS. Copyright © 1961, 1962, 1963, 1964, 1965, 1966, 1967, 1968, 1969, 1970, 1971, 1972, 1973, 1974, 1975, 1976, 1977, 1978 by Gale Research Company. Used by permission of Gale Research Company.

Printed in the United States of America

Published simultaneously in the United Kingdom
by Gale Research International Limited
(An affiliated company of Gale Research Inc.)

For my wife,

Mary

My mistress' eyes are nothing like the sun;
Coral is far more red than her lips' red:
If snow be white, why then her breasts are dun;
If hairs be wires, black wires grow on her head.
I have seen roses damaskt, red and white,
But no such roses see I in her cheeks;
And in some perfumes is there more delight
Than in the breath that from my mistress reeks.
I love to hear her speak, yet well I know
That music hath a far more pleasing sound;
I grant I never saw a goddess go;
My mistress, when she walks, treads on the ground.
    And yet, by heaven, I think my love as rare
    As any she belied with false compare.

     --William Shakespeare

it is at moments after i have dreamed
of the rare entertainment of your eyes,
when (being fool to fancy) i have deemed

with your peculiar mouth my heart made wise;
at moments when the glassy darkness holds

the genuine apparition of your smile
(it was through tears always) and silence moulds
such strangeness as was mine a little while;

moments when my once more illustrious arms
are filled with fascination, when my breast
wears the intolerant brightness of your charms:

one pierced moment whiter than the rest

--turning from the tremendous lie of sleep
i watch the roses of the day grow deep.

     --e. e. cummings

Contents

Introduction

Science Fiction & Fantasy Literature is a continuing bibliography of fantastic literature. The first volume lists 15,884 English-language first editions of books and pamphlets published between 1700 and 1974 in the fields of science fiction, fantasy, and weird supernatural fiction. Approximately 2,000 retitlings are also included. Only prose works are listed; drama and verse are excluded. For a more complete description of how this book was put together and what it contains, please see the Afterword.

The Author Index to the Literature

SF&FL consists of six different indexes. The Author Index is the heart of the bibliography itself. Entries are listed here in alphabetical order by the name under which the author is best known, real or fictitious, with appropriate references where necessary. The author's byline which appears on the majority of his books is underlined in capital letters; the rest of his name, if known, appears in parentheses, followed by the years of his birth and death. A pseudonymous author's name is followed by the word "pseud." or "house pseud." (a penname used by several different authors), and then the author's real name, if known, in brackets. The words "[*biography included*]" refer the reader to the author's biography in *Contemporary Science Fiction Authors II*. Books written by more than one author appear in full under each author's name. Anonymous works appear under their author's names, if known, with references from their titles; anonymous books by authors unknown are listed here under their titles. Library of Congress filing rules are followed throughout, except that names beginning with "Mc" appear in strict alphabetical sequence.

Under each entry, the author's books are listed alphabetically, first under his best-known name, and then sequentially under each successive pseudonym he has employed, each name being listed in alphabetical order. These are followed in turn by collaborations with other authors, listed alphabetically under the name of the collaborator. The books are numbered consecutively from 00001 to provide for easy citation. A typical bibliographical entry contains the following information, in this order: citation number, title (in italics), publisher, city of publication, state or country of publication if the city is little-known, year of publication, number of pages in the main body of the work (the number of pages is followed by a single "p"), format of the book ("Cloth" is loosely defined as stiff covers, "Paper" as limp covers), type (the terms used are: Novel, Coll. [a selection of stories by one author], Anth. [a selection of stories by more than one author], Movie [adaptation], Tele. [TV adaptation], Radio [adaptation], Nonf. [nonfiction], Story [a prose monograph under fifty pages in length], Fiction [a prose work which does not fit the other categories]), series entries (in brackets), bibliographical notes (in brackets). *SF&FL* lists English-language first editions only; where a book has appeared simultaneously in the United States and United Kingdom, or when the true first edition has not been found, both editions are listed, with appropriate bibliographical data. Simultaneously hard- and softcover editions are listed as "Cloth" only. Retitlings appear directly following the first edition of a particular book; the citation number is the same as that of the original work, with the addition of the letters "A," "B," "C," and so forth.

Other Indexes

The Title Index gives title and author only; the reader must refer to the Author Index for complete bibliographical information. The Series Index lists each series under the name by which it is generally known; where no name seems to be in common usage, one has arbitrarily been assigned. A series is considered to be two or more books featuring common characters, settings, or themes, by one or more authors. The series name is followed by the author's name; the books are listed in the order established by the author, or chronologically where no order has been established, with sequence number, title, date of publication, and author's name, where different authors have written parts of a series. The Awards Index includes a listing of world science fiction conventions, officers of the Science Fiction Writers of America, an index of awards by award name and the year given, an index by recipient, and various statistical tables, complete through the end of 1978. The Ace and Belmont Doubles Index includes numerical and chronological indexes of all the books published in each series, with dates of publication, stock numbers, and titles and authors of each two-in-one volume.

Contemporary Science Fiction Authors II is the second edition of a biographical directory first published in 1970 as *Stella Nova: The Contemporary Science Fiction Authors,* and later reprinted with slight revisions as *Contemporary Science Fiction Authors, First Edition* (1975). It includes 1,443 biographies of science fiction and fantasy authors active in the twentieth century, compiled from questionnaires mailed directly to the authors, and supplemented with additional information from *Contemporary Authors.* Each entry includes basic biographical data about the author's life, education, and career, his awards and honors, first professional publication, agent, together with statements solicited on a variety of subjects. Authors are listed in alphabetical order by surname.

The illustrations featured in this volume are intended to provide a representative collection of cover work used by publishers both currently and retrospectively, and are printed with the consent of the publishers. The selection is not meant to be definitive.

List of Abbreviations

Anth.	An anthology of stories by more than one author
Coll.	A collection of stories by one author
cont.	Continued from the previous page
house pseud.	A penname used by more than one author
Movie	An adaptation from a screen or television film
Nonf.	Nonfiction
pseud.	A penname used by one author only
Radio	An adaptation from a radio broadcast or serial
Tele.	An adaptation from a television series

Author Index

A. D. 2000

00001 *A.D. 2000; The Observer prize stories, 1954.*
William Heinemann, London, 1955, 241p,
Cloth, Anth.

A. E., pseud.
see: RUSSELL, GEORGE WILLIAM

A. F. S., pseud.
see: SILVANI, ANITA

A. G. F. B., pseud.
see: B., A. G. F.

A. H. M., pseud.
see: M., A. H.

A. J. O., pseud.
see: OGILVY, ARTHUR JAMES

A. K. H., pseud.
see: HOPKINS, A. K.

A. M. R., pseud.
see: RICHARDS, ANNA MATLOCK

AARONS, EDWARD S(idney), 1916-1975

00002 *Assignment to disaster.* Gold Medal, Greenwich, 1955, 160p, Paper, Novel [Sam Durrell
#1]

THE ABBEY OF KILKHAMPTON
see: CROFT, HERBERT

ABBOT, ANTHONY, pseud.
see: OURSLER, FULTON

ABBOTT, EDWIN A(bbott), 1838-1926

as A. Square, pseud.:

00003 *Flatland; a romance of many dimensions.*
Seeley & Co., London, 1884, 100p, Cloth,
Novel

as Edwin A. Abbott:

00003A *Flatland.* Basil Blackwell, Oxford, 1926, 102p,
Cloth, Novel

ABDULLAH, ACHMED [Ahmad 'Abd Allah Nadir Khan al-Idrisi al-Durrani, 1881-1945 (variously cited as Achmed Abdullah Nadir Khan el-Durani el-Iddrissyeh)]

00004 *The mating of the blades.* James A. McCann,
New York, 1920, 281p, Cloth, Novel
00005 *Mysteries of Asia.* Philip Allan, London,
1935, 256p, Cloth, Coll.

00006 *The thief of Bagdad.* H. K. Fly, New York,
1924, 319p, Cloth, Movie
00007 *Wings; tales of the psychic.* James A. McCann,
New York, 1920, 239p, Cloth, Coll.

with Anthony Abbot:

00008 *The Flower of the Gods.* Green Circle Books,
New York, 1936, 254p, Cloth, Novel

ABÉ, KŌBŌ, 1924-

00009 *Inter ice age 4.* Alfred A. Knopf, New York,
1970, 228p, Cloth, Novel

ABEL, R(ichard) COX, with Charles Barren

00010 *Trivana I.* Panther, London, 1966, 171p, Paper,
Novel

ABLEMAN, PAUL (Victor), 1927- [biography included]

00011 *The twilight of the Vilp.* Victor Gollancz,
London, 1969, 157p, Cloth, Novel

ABOUT, EDMOND (François Valentin), 1828-1885

The lawyer's nose; a story. [see 00014B]
00012 *The man with the broken ear.* Leypoldt & Holt,
New York, 1867, 254p, Cloth, Novel
00013 *A new lease of life; and, Saving a daughter's
dowry.* Vizetelly & Co., London, 1880, 216p,
Cloth, Coll.
00014 *The nose of a notary.* Loring, Boston, 1863,
171p, Cloth, Novel
00014A retitled: *The notary's nose.* Henry Holt,
New York, 1874, 240p, Cloth, Novel
00014B retitled: *The lawyer's nose; a story.* Remington, London, 1878, 208p, Cloth, Novel
00015 *The notary's nose, and other stories.* Vizetelly & Co., London, 1882, 224p, Cloth, Coll.

ABRAHAMS, DORIS CAROLINE
see: BRAHMS, CARYL

ABRAHAMSEN, CHRISTINE
see: CRISTABEL

ABRAMOV, ALEKSANDR (Ivanovich), 1900- [biography included], with Sergei Abramov

00016 *Horsemen from nowhere.* Mir, Moscow, 1969, 304p,
Cloth, Novel

ABRAMOV, SERGEI (Aleksandrovich), 1944- [biography included], with Aleksandr Abramov

00016 *Horsemen from nowhere.* Mir, Moscow, 1969, 304p,
Cloth, Novel

ABRASHKIN, RAYMOND, 1911-1960, with Jay Williams

00017 *Danny Dunn and the anti-gravity paint.* Whit-

ABRASHKIN, RAYMOND, with Jay Williams (cont.)

tlesey House, New York, 1956, 154p, Cloth, Novel [Danny Dunn #1]

00018 *Danny Dunn and the automatic house.* Whittlesey House, New York, 1965, 139p, Cloth, Novel [Danny Dunn #9]

00019 *Danny Dunn and the fossil cave.* Whittlesey House, New York, 1961, 146p, Cloth, Novel [Danny Dunn #6]

00020 *Danny Dunn and the heat ray.* Whittlesey House, New York, 1962, 144p, Cloth, Novel [Danny Dunn #7]

00021 *Danny Dunn and the homework machine.* Whittlesey House, New York, 1958, 141p, Cloth, Novel [Danny Dunn #3]

00021A retitled: *The homework machine.* Brockhampton Press, Leicester, 1960, 120p, Cloth, Novel [Danny Dunn #3]

00022 *Danny Dunn and the smallifying machine.* McGraw-Hill, New York, 1969, 139p, Cloth, Novel [Danny Dunn #11]

00023 *Danny Dunn and the swamp monster.* McGraw-Hill, New York, 1971, 142p, Cloth, Novel [Danny Dunn #12]

00024 *Danny Dunn and the voice from space.* McGraw-Hill, New York, 1967, 157p, Cloth, Novel [Danny Dunn #10]

00025 *Danny Dunn and the weather machine.* Whittlesey House, New York, 1959, 144p, Cloth, Novel [Danny Dunn #4]

00026 *Danny Dunn, invisible boy.* McGraw-Hill, New York, 1974, 154p, Cloth, Novel [Danny Dunn #13]

00027 *Danny Dunn on a desert island.* Whittlesey House, New York, 1957, 159p, Cloth, Novel [Danny Dunn #2]

00028 *Danny Dunn on the ocean floor.* Whittlesey House, New York, 1960, 156p, Cloth, Novel [Danny Dunn #5]

00029 *Danny Dunn, time traveller.* Whittlesey House, New York, 1963, 138p, Cloth, Novel [Danny Dunn #8]

ABROJAL, TULIS, pseud.

00030 *An index finger.* R. F. Fenno & Co., New York, 1898, 382p, Cloth, Novel

ABU NADAAR, pseud.
    see: MORROUGH, E. R.

AN ACCOUNT OF THE STATE OF LEARNING IN THE EMPIRE OF LILLIPUT
    see: ARBUTHNOT, JOHN

THE ACCUSING SPIRIT
    see: PILKINGTON, MARY

ACKERMAN, FORREST J(ames), 1916- [*biography*]

00031 *Best science fiction for 1973.* Ace, New York, 1973, 268p, Paper, Anth.

00032 *The Frankenscience monster.* Ace, New York, 1969, 191p, Paper, Nonf.

00033 *James Warren presents Famous monsters of filmland strike back!* Paperback Library, New York, 1965, 161p, Paper, Nonf.

00034 *James Warren presents Son of Famous monsters of filmland.* Paperback Library, New York, 1965, 162p, Paper, Nonf.

00035 *James Warren presents The best from Famous monsters of filmland.* Paperback Library, New York, 1964, 162p, Paper, Nonf.

with others:

00036 *Science fiction worlds of Forrest J Ackerman & friends.* Powell Publications, Reseda, 1969, 223p, Paper, Coll.

ADAIR, HAZEL, pseud. [Hazel Iris Addis, 1900-   ], with Ronald Marriott

00037 *Stranger from space.* Weidenfeld & Nicolson, London, 1953, 191p, Cloth, Tele.

A'DAIR, JEANNE, with Eleanor Roberts

00038 *Once upon a summertime; a story with lyrics for children.* Exposition Press, New York, 1951, 139p, Cloth, Novel

ADAM, JEAN VILLIERS de L'ISLE
    see: VILLIERS de L'ISLE ADAM, JEAN

ADAM, R. J.
    see: MacTYRE, PAUL

ADAM, RUTH (Augusta), 1907-   [*biography included*]

00039 *War on Saturday week.* J. B. Lippincott, Philadelphia, 1937, 310p, Cloth, Novel; Chapman & Hall, London, 1937, 311p, Cloth, Novel

ADAMS, ARTHUR H(enry), 1872-1936

00040 *A touch of fantasy; a romance for those who are lucky enough to wear glasses.* John Lane, London, 1912, 304p, Cloth, Novel

ADAMS, EUSTACE L(ane), 1891-

00041 *Pirates of the air.* Grosset & Dunlap, New York, 1929, 212p, Cloth, Novel [Andy Lane #5]

ADAMS, FRANCIS A(lexandre), 1874-

00042 *The transgressors; story of a great sin; a political novel of the twentieth century.* Independence Publishing Co., Philadelphia, 1900, 345p, Cloth, Novel

ADAMS, FRED C. (Jr.)

00043 *The chaos spawn.* Shroud Publishers, North Hollywood, 1974, 32p, Paper, Story

ADAMS, FREDERICK UPHAM, 1859-1921

00044 *President John Smith; the story of a peaceful revolution (written in 1920).* Charles H. Kerr, Chicago, 1897, 289p, Paper, Novel

ADAMS, H(enry) C(adwallader), 1817-1899

00045 *Sivan the sleeper; a tale of all time.* Rivingtons, London, 1857, 338p, Cloth, Novel

ADAMS, HAZARD, 1926-

00046 *The truth about dragons; an anti-romance.* Harcourt Brace Jovanovich, New York, 1971, 179p, Cloth, Novel

ADAMS, J.
    see: KUPPORD, SKELTON

ADAMS, JACK, pseud. [Alcanoan O. Grigsby]

00047 *Nequa; or, The problem of the ages, vol. I.* Equity Publishing Co., Topeka, 1900, 387p, Paper, Novel [no more published]

ADAMS, JOHN, pseud.?

00048 *When the gods came.* Badger, London, 1960, 142p, Paper, Novel

ADAMS, RICHARD (George), 1920- [*biography included*]

00049 *Shardik.* Allen Lane in association with Rex Collings, London, 1974, 526p, Cloth, Novel
00050 *Watership down.* Rex Collings, London, 1972, 413p, Cloth, Novel

ADAMS, SAMUEL HOPKINS, 1871-1958

00051 *The flying death.* McClure Company, New York, 1908, 239p, Cloth, Novel
00052 *The world goes smash.* Houghton Mifflin, Boston, 1938, 286p, Cloth, Novel

with Stewart Edward White:

00053 *The mystery.* McClure, Phillips, New York, 1907, 286p, Cloth, Novel [Percy Darrow #]]

ADAMS, W(illiam) (Wheen) S(covell)

00054 *The fourth programme; a fantasia on contemporary themes.* Lawrence & Wishart, London, 1955, 63p, Cloth, Novel

ADAMS, WALTER MARSHAM
    see: MACAULAY, CLARENDON

ADDEO, EDMOND G., with Richard M. Garvin

00055 *The FORTEC conspiracy.* Sherbourne Press, Los Angeles, 1968, 181p, Cloth, Novel

00056 *The Talbott Agreement.* Sherbourne Press, Los Angeles, 1968, 255p, Cloth, Novel

ADDERLEY, JOSEPH (Granville), 1861-1942

00057 *Behold the days to come; a fancy in Christian politics.* Methuen, London, 1907, 243p, Cloth, Novel

ADDIS, HAZEL IRIS
    see: ADAIR, HAZEL

ADDISON, HUGH, pseud. [Harry Collinson Owen, 1882-1956]

00058 *The Battle of London.* Herbert Jenkins, London, 1923, 312p, Cloth, Novel

ADELER, MAX, pseud. [Charles Heber Clark, 1841-1915]

00059 *Transformations, containing Mrs. Shelmire's djinn; and, A desperate adventure.* Ward, Lock, London, 1883, 122p, Cloth, Coll.

"ADELPHOS," pseud.

00060 *Ush; the revelation of Bandobast Wilderness.* John Ouseley, London, 1912, 184p, Cloth, Novel

AN ADEPT, pseud.
    see: JOHNSTONE, CHARLES

ADKINS, P. H.

00061 *Edgar Rice Burroughs; bibliography & price guide.* P.D.A. Enterprises, New Orleans, 1974, 25p, Paper, Nonf.

ADKINSON, ROBERT (K.), with Allen Eyles and Nicholas Fry

00062 *The house of horror; the story of Hammer Films.* Lorrimer Publishing, London, 1973, 127p, Paper, Nonf.

ADLARD, MARK [Peter Marcus Adlard, 1932-   ] [*biography included*]

00063 *Interface; science fiction.* Sidgwick & Jackson, London, 1971, 191p, Cloth, Novel [T-City #1]
00064 *Volteface; science fiction.* Sidgwick & Jackson, London, 1972, 210p, Cloth, Novel [T-City #2]

ADLEMAN, ROBERT H., 1919-

00065 *Annie Deane.* World Publishing Co., Cleveland, 1971, 213p, Cloth, Novel

ADLER, ALLEN A., 1916-

00066   *Mach 1; a story of the planet Ionus.* Farrar,
      Straus & Cudahy, New York, 1957, 212p, Cloth,
      Novel
00066A retitled: *Terror on planet Ionus.* Paperback
      Library, New York, 1966, 160p, Paper, Novel

ADRIEL, JEANNE

00067   *Soaring sunward; woman's initiation.* Pageant
      Press, New York, 1961, 242p, Cloth, Novel

THE ADULT VERSION OF DRACULA
    see: KANTOR, HAL

ADVENTURE

00068   *Adventure in space.* Burke, London, 1964,
      304p, Cloth, Anth. [includes *Captives of
      the Moon*, by Patrick Moore; *Peril on the
      lost planet*, by Angus MacVicar]
00069   *Adventure in time.* American Science Fiction,
      Sydney, 1953, 34p, Paper, Anth.

ADVENTURES IN THE MOON
    see: RUSSELL, JOHN RUSSELL, 1st Earl

THE ADVENTURES OF BARON MUNCHAUSEN
    see: RASPE, RUDOLF ERICH

THE ADVENTURES OF EOVAAI, PRINCESS OF IJAVEO
    see: HAYWOOD, ELIZA

ADYE, Major-General Sir JOHN, 1857-1930

00070   *The golden scarab.* Herbert Jenkins, London,
      1926, 312p, Cloth, Novel

THE AEROBUS

00071   *The aerobus, containing "A thousand miles an
      hour," by Herbert Strang; "The pirate aero-
      plane," by Major Charles Gilson; "A mystery
      of the air," by J. F. C. Westerman.* Oxford
      University Press, London, 1935, 771p, Cloth,
      Anth.

AFTER THE BATTLE OF DORKING

00072   *After the Battle of Dorking; or, What became
      of the invaders!* George Maddick, London,
      1871, 23p, Paper, Story [Dorking sequence]

AGEL, JEROME

00073   *The making of Kubrick's* 2001. Signet, New
      York, 1970, 368p, Paper, Nonf. Anth.

AGRICOLA, pseud.

00074   *How England was saved; the history of the*

years 1910-1925. Swan Sonnenschein, London,
    1908, 172p, Cloth, Novel

AICHINGER, ILSE, 1921-

00075   *The bound man, and other stories.* Secker &
      Warburg, London, 1955, 100p, Cloth, Coll.

AICKMAN, ROBERT (Fordyce), 1914-   [*biography
included*]

00076   *Dark entries.* Collins, London, 1964, 173p,
      Cloth, Coll.
00077   *The eighth Fontana book of great ghost stories.*
      Fontana, London, 1972, 190p, Paper, Anth.
00078   *The fifth Fontana book of great ghost stories.*
      Fontana, London, 1969, 224p, Paper, Anth.
00079   *The Fontana book of great ghost stories.*
      Fontana, London, 1964, 256p, Paper, Anth.
00080   *The fourth Fontana book of great ghost stories.*
      Fontana, London, 1967, 192p, Paper, Anth.
00081   *Powers of darkness.* Collins, London, 1966,
      253p, Cloth, Coll.
00082   *The second Fontana book of great ghost stories.*
      Fontana, London, 1966, 252p, Paper, Anth.
00083   *The seventh Fontana book of great ghost stories.*
      Fontana, London, 1971, 190p, Paper, Anth.
00084   *The sixth Fontana book of great ghost stories.*
      Fontana, London, 1970, 190p, Paper, Anth.
00085   *Sub rosa; strange tales.* Victor Gollancz,
      London, 1968, 256p, Cloth, Coll.
00086   *The third Fontana book of great ghost stories.*
      Fontana, London, 1966, 224p, Paper, Anth.

with Elizabeth Jane Howard:

00087   *We are for the dark; six ghost stories.* Jona-
      than Cape, London, 1951, 285p, Cloth, Coll.

AIKEN, JOAN (Delano), 1924-   [*biography included*]

00088   *Armitage, Armitage, fly away home.* Doubleday,
      Garden City, 1968, 214p, Cloth, Novel
00089   *The green flash, and other stories of horror,
      suspense, and fantasy.* Holt, Rinehart &
      Winston, New York, 1971, 163p, Cloth, Coll.
00090   *The kingdom and the cave.* Abelard-Schuman,
      London, 1960, 162p, Cloth, Novel
00091   *Not what you expected; a collection of short
      stories.* Doubleday, Garden City, 1974, 320p,
      Cloth, Coll.
00092   *Smoke from Cromwell's time, and other stories.*
      Doubleday, Garden City, 1970, 164p, Cloth,
      Coll.
00093   *The Whispering Mountain.* Jonathan Cape, Lon-
      don, 1968, 240p, Cloth, Novel
00094   *The windscreen wipers, and other tales of hor-
      ror and suspense.* Victor Gollancz, London,
      1969, 256p, Cloth, Coll.

AIKEN, JOHN (Kempton), 1913-   [*biography
included*]

as John Paget:

00095   *World well lost.* Robert Hale, London, 1970,
      206p, Cloth, Novel

AIKEN, JOHN (cont.)

as John Aiken:

00095A *World well lost*. Doubleday, Garden City,
         1971, 208p, Cloth, Novel

AIKIN, ANNA L(aetitia), 1743-1825, & J. Aikin

00096 *Miscellaneous pieces in prose*. J. Johnson,
        London, 1773, 219p, Cloth, Coll.

AIKIN, CHARLES

00097 *Forty years with the damned; or, Life inside
         the Earth; a novel*. Regan Printing House,
         Chicago, 1895, 422p, Cloth, Novel

AIKIN, JOHN, 1747-1822, with Anna L. Aikin

00096 *Miscellaneous pieces in prose*. J. Johnson,
        London, 1773, 219p, Cloth, Coll.

AINSBURY, RAY, pseud.
       see: VERRILL, A. HYATT

AINSWORTH, RUTH (Gallard), 1908-   [*biography
included*]

00098 *The phantom cyclist, and other stories*. Andre
        Deutsch, London, 1971, 126p, Cloth, Coll.

AINSWORTH, W(illiam) HARRISON, 1805-1882

00099 *Auriol; or, The elixir of life*. George Rout-
        ledge & Sons, London, 1865, 238p, Cloth,
        Novel
00099A retitled: *The elixir of life*. Four Square
        Books, London, 1966, 122p, Paper, Novel
00100 *Chetwynd Calverley; a tale*. Tinsley Brothers,
        London, 1876, 3vol, Cloth, Novel
       The elixir of life. [see 00099A]
       Herne the hunter. [see 00102A]
00101 *The Lancashire witches; a novel*. Henry Col-
        burn, London, 1849, 3vol, Cloth, Novel
00102 *Windsor Castle; an historical romance*. Henry
        Colburn, London, 1843, 3vol, Cloth, Novel
00102A retitled: *Herne the hunter (Windsor Castle)*.
        Herbert Jenkins, London, 1920, 320p, Cloth,
        Novel

AINSWORTHY, ROY

00103 *Focolor*. Robert Hale, London, 1973, 184p,
        Cloth, Novel

AKERS, ALAN BURT, pseud.
       see: BULMER, KENNETH

AKIRA, pseud. [Erica Maria Moore]

00104 *The amber necklace*. Being Inc., Ojai, Calif.,
        1974, 75p, Paper, Novel

AKUTAGAWA, RYUNOSUKE, 1892-1927

00105 *Kappa*. Akitaya, Osaka, 1947, 154p, Cloth, Coll.
00106 *Rashomon, and other stories*. Charles E. Tuttle,
        Rutland, Vermont, 1951, 95p, Cloth, Coll.
00107 *Tales grotesque and curious*. Hokuseido Press,
        Tokyo, 1930, 144p, Cloth, Coll.

AL ARAWIYAH
       see: ARAWIYAH, AL

ALARCÓN (y Ariza), PEDRO A(ntonio) de, 1833-
1891

00108 *The strange friend of Tito Gil*. A. Lovell,
        New York, 1890, 133p, Cloth, Novel

published anonymously:

00108A retitled: *The friend of death; a fantastic
         tale*. Cassell Publishing Co., New York,
         1891, 163p, Cloth, Novel

ALBAN, ANTONY, pseud. [Antony Allert Thompson]

00109 *Catharsis Central*. Dennis Dobson, London,
        1968, 192p, Cloth, Novel
00110 *The day of the Shield*. Berkley Medallion, New
        York, 1973, 191p, Paper, Novel

ALBANO, Judge M(ichael) W.

00111 *Souls' judgment day*. Lorecraft Publishers,
        Paterson, NJ, 1940, 256p, Cloth, Novel

ALBERT, MARVIN H.

00112 *Goodbye Charlie*. Dell, New York, 1964, 157p,
        Paper, Movie

ALBERTSON, GARRETT V(inton)

00113 *A visit to Mars*. Moody Press, Chicago, 1960?,
        124p, Paper, Novel

THE ALBIGENSES; A ROMANCE
       see: MATURIN, CHARLES R.

ALBRECHT, HOWARD, with Sol Weinstein

00114 *The Exerciser*. Ballantine, New York, 1974,
        147p, Paper, Novel [a parody of *The Exorcist*,
        by William Peter Blatty]
00115 *Jonathan Segal Chicken*. Pinnacle, New York,
        1973, 122p, Paper, Novel [a parody of *Jona-
        than Livingston Seagull*, by Richard Bach]

ALDEN, HENRY MILLS, 1836-1919, with William
Dean Howells

00116 *Shapes that haunt the dusk; Harper's novelettes*.
        Harper & Brothers, New York, 1907, 301p,
        Cloth, Anth.

ALDISS, BRIAN W(ilson), 1925-   [*biography included*]

00117 *An age*. Faber & Faber, London, 1967, 224p, Cloth, Novel

00117A retitled: *Cryptozoic!* Doubleday, Garden City, 1968, 240p, Cloth, Novel

00118 *The airs of Earth; science fiction stories.* Faber & Faber, London, 1963, 256p, Cloth, Coll.

00119 *Barefoot in the head; a European fantasia.* Faber & Faber, London, 1969, 281p, Cloth, Novel

00120 *Best fantasy stories.* Faber & Faber, London, 1962, 208p, Cloth, Anth.

00121 *Best science fiction stories of Brian W. Aldiss.* Faber & Faber, London, 1965, 253p, Cloth, Coll.

00121A retitled: *Who can replace a man? The best science-fiction stories of Brian W. Aldiss.* Harcourt, Brace & World, New York, 1966, 253p, Cloth, Coll.

00122 *Best science fiction stories of Brian W. Aldiss (revised edition).* Faber & Faber, London, 1971, 260p, Cloth, Coll. [different contents from previous edition]

00123 *Billion year spree; the true history of science fiction.* Weidenfeld & Nicolson, London, 1973, 339p, Cloth, Nonf.

00124 *The book of Brian Aldiss.* DAW, New York, 1972, 191p, Paper, Coll.

00124A retitled: *The comic inferno.* New English Library, London, 1973, 159p, Paper, Coll.

00125 *Bow down to nul.* Ace Double, New York, 1960, 145p, Paper, Novel

00125A retitled: *The interpreter.* Digit, London, 1961, 156p, Paper, Novel

00126 *A Brian Aldiss omnibus, containing The interpreter, The primal urge, The saliva tree, The impossible star, Basis for negotiation, Man in his time.* Sidgwick & Jackson, London, 1969, 508p, Cloth, Coll.

00127 *Brian Aldiss omnibus (2).* Sidgwick & Jackson, London, 1971, 585p, Cloth, Coll. [includes *Space, time, and Nathaniel*; *Non-Stop*; *The Male Response*]

00128 *The canopy of time.* Faber & Faber, London, 1959, 222p, Cloth, Coll.

The comic inferno. [see 00124A]

Cryptozoic! [see 00117A]

00129 *The dark light years; a science fiction novel.* Faber & Faber, London, 1964, 190p, Cloth, Novel

00130 *Earthworks; a science fiction novel.* Faber & Faber, London, 1965, 155p, Cloth, Novel

00131 *The eighty-minute hour; a space opera.* Jonathan Cape, London, 1974, 286p, Cloth, Novel

00132 *Equator; a human time bomb from the Moon!* Digit, London, 1961, 160p, Paper, Coll. [includes *Vanguard from Alpha*]

00133 *Frankenstein unbound.* Jonathan Cape, London, 1973, 184p, Cloth, Novel

00134 *Galaxies like grains of sand.* Signet, New York, 1960, 144p, Paper, Coll. [roughly based on *The canopy of time*]

00135 *Greybeard.* Faber & Faber, London, 1964, 237p, Cloth, Novel

00136 *Hothouse; a science fiction novel.* Faber & Faber, London, 1962, 253p, Cloth, Novel

00136A retitled: *The long afternoon of Earth.* Signet, New York, 1962, 192p, Paper, Novel

00137 *Intangibles, Inc., and other stories; five novellas.* Faber & Faber, London, 1969, 198p, Cloth, Coll.

The interpreter. [see 00125A]

00138 *Introducing SF; a science fiction anthology.* Faber & Faber, London, 1964, 224p, Cloth, Anth.

The long afternoon of Earth. [see 00136A]

00139 *The male response; a timely original story!* Galaxy Publishing Corp., New York, 1961, 188p, Paper, Novel

00140 *The moment of eclipse.* Faber & Faber, London, 1970, 215p, Cloth, Coll.

00141 *More Penguin science fiction; an anthology.* Penguin, Harmondsworth, 1963, 236p, Paper, Anth.

00142 *Neanderthal planet.* Avon, New York, 1970, 192p, Paper, Coll. [roughly based on *Intangibles, Inc., and other stories*]

00143 *No time like tomorrow.* Signet, New York, 1959, 160p, Paper, Coll. [roughly based on *Space, time, and Nathaniel*]

00144 *Non-stop.* Faber & Faber, London, 1958, 252p, Cloth, Novel

00144A retitled: *Starship.* Criterion Books, New York, 1959, 256p, Cloth, Novel

00145 *Penguin science fiction; an anthology.* Penguin, Harmondsworth, 1961, 236p, Paper, Anth.

00146 *The Penguin science fiction omnibus; an anthology.* Penguin, Harmondsworth, 1973, 616p, Paper, Anth. [includes *Penguin Science Fiction*; *More Penguin science fiction*; *Yet more Penguin science fiction*]

00147 *The primal urge.* Ballantine, New York, 1961, 191p, Paper, Novel

00148 *Report on probability A.* Faber & Faber, London, 1968, 176p, Cloth, Novel

00149 *The saliva tree, and other strange growths.* Faber & Faber, London, 1966, 232p, Cloth, Coll.

00150 *The shape of further things; speculations on change.* Faber & Faber, London, 1970, 185p, Cloth, Nonf.

00151 *Space opera; an anthology of way-back-when futures.* Weidenfeld & Nicolson, London, 1974, 324p, Cloth, Anth.

00152 *Space, time, and Nathaniel (presciences).* Faber & Faber, London, 1957, 208p, Cloth, Coll.

Starship. [see 00144A]

00153 *Starswarm.* Signet, New York, 1964, 159p, Paper, Coll. [roughly based on *The airs of Earth*]

00154 *Vanguard from Alpha.* Ace Double, New York, 1959, 109p, Paper, Novel

Who can replace a man? [see 00121A]

00155 *Yet more Penguin science fiction; an anthology.* Penguin, Harmondsworth, 1964, 205p, Paper, Anth.

with Harry Harrison:

All about Venus. [see 00165A]

00156 *The Astounding-Analog reader, volume one.* Doubleday, Garden City, 1972, 530p, Cloth, Anth.

00156A retitled: *The Astounding Analog reader, book 1.* Sphere, London, 1973, 291p, Paper, Anth. [abridged]

00156B retitled: *The Astounding Analog reader, book 2.* Sphere, London, 1973, 320p, Paper, Anth. [abridged]

00157 *The Astounding-Analog reader, volume two.* Doubleday, Garden City, 1973, 458p, Cloth, Anth.

00158 *Best SF: 1967.* Berkley Medallion, New York, 1968, 256p, Paper, Anth.

ALDISS, BRIAN W., with Harry Harrison

00158A retitled: *The year's best science fiction no. 1.* Sphere, London, 1968, 207p, Paper, Anth.
00159 *The year's best science fiction no. 2.* Sphere, London, 1969, 207p, Paper, Anth.
00159A retitled: *Best SF: 1968.* G. P. Putnam's Sons, New York, 1969, 245p, Cloth, Anth.
00160 *The year's best science fiction 3.* Sphere, London, 1970, 206p, Paper, Anth.
00160A retitled: *Best SF 1969.* G. P. Putnam's Sons, New York, 1970, 243p, Cloth, Anth.
00161 *The year's best science fiction no. 4.* Sphere, London, 1971, 221p, Paper, Anth.
00161A retitled: *Best SF: 1970.* G. P. Putnam's Sons, New York, 1971, 224p, Cloth, Anth.
00162 *The year's best science fiction no. 5.* Sphere, London, 1972, 239p, Paper, Anth.
00162A retitled: *Best SF: 1971.* G. P. Putnam's Sons, New York, 1972, 253p, Cloth, Anth.
00163 *Best SF: 1972.* G. P. Putnam's Sons, New York, 1973, 254p, Cloth, Anth.
00163A retitled: *The year's best science fiction no. 6.* Sphere, London, 1973, 236p, Paper, Anth.
00164 *Best SF: 1973.* G. P. Putnam's Sons, New York, 1974, 238p, Cloth, Anth.
00165 *Farewell, fantastic Venus! a history of the planet Venus in fact and fiction.* Macdonald, London, 1968, 293p, Cloth, Anth.
00165A retitled: *All about Venus; a revelation of the planet Venus in fact and fiction.* Dell, New York, 1968, 221p, Paper, Anth. [abridged]
00166 *Nebula award stories two.* Doubleday, Garden City, 1967, 252p, Cloth, Anth.

ALDISS, MARGARET (Christie), 1933-   [*biography included*]

as Margaret Manson:

00167 *Item forty-three; Brian W. Aldiss: a bibliography, 1954-1962.* Dryden Press, Birmingham, 1962, 24p, Paper, Nonf.

as Margaret Aldiss:

00168 *Item eighty-three; Brian W. Aldiss: a bibliography, 1954-1972.* SF Horizons, Abingdon, England, 1972, 39p, Paper, Nonf. [expanded version of 00167]

ALETHITHERAS, pseud.
  see: OSBORN, LAUGHTON

ALEXA, pseud.

00169 *The spectre bridegroom; a terrific and interesting tale.* Dean & Munday, London, 1880?, 36p, Paper, Story

ALEXANDER, HOLMES (Moss), 1906-

00170 *The spirit of '76; a political novel of the near future.* Arlington House, New Rochelle, 1966, 396p, Cloth, Novel

ALEXANDER, JAMES B(radun), 1831-

00171 *The Lunarian professor, and his remarkable revelations concerning the Earth, the Moon, and Mars, together with an account of the cruise of the Sally Ann.* no publisher, Minneapolis, 1909, 291p, Cloth, Novel

ALEXANDER, LLOYD (Chudley), 1924-

00172 *The Black Cauldron.* Holt, Rinehart & Winston, New York, 1965, 224p, Cloth, Novel [Prydain Chronicles, Book 2]
00173 *The Book of Three.* Holt, Rinehart & Winston, New York, 1964, 217p, Cloth, Novel [Prydain Chronicles, Book 1]
00174 *The Castle of Llyr.* Holt, Rinehart & Winston, New York, 1966, 201p, Cloth, Novel [Prydain Chronicles, Book 3]
00175 *The cat who wished to be a man.* E. P. Dutton, New York, 1973, 107p, Cloth, Novel
00176 *The foundling, and other tales of Prydain.* Holt, Rinehart & Winston, New York, 1973, 88p, Cloth, Coll. [loosely connected with the Prydain Chronicles]
00177 *The High King.* Holt, Rinehart & Winston, New York, 1968, 285p, Cloth, Novel [Prydain Chronicles, Book 5]
00178 *The marvelous misadventures of Sebastian; grand extravaganza, including a performance by the entire cast of the Gallimaufry-Theatricus.* E. P. Dutton, New York, 1970, 204p, Cloth, Novel
00179 *Taran Wanderer.* Holt, Rinehart & Winston, New York, 1967, 256p, Cloth, Novel [Prydain Chronicles, Book 4]
00180 *Time cat; the remarkable journeys of Jason and Gareth.* Holt, Rinehart & Winston, New York, 1963, 191p, Cloth, Novel

ALEXANDER, ROBERT

00181 *The pendulum of fate; cosmic glimpses of past & future.* C. W. Daniel, London, 1933, 192p, Cloth, Coll.

ALEXANDER, ROBERT WILLIAM
  see: BUTLER, JOAN

ALEXANDER, SIGMUND B(owman)

00182 *The veiled beyond; a romance of the adepts.* Cassell & Co., New York, 1888, 276p, Cloth, Novel

ALFVEN, HANNES
  see: JOHANNESSON, OLOF

ALI MIRDREKVANDI GUNGA DIN
  see: MIRDREKVANDI, ALI

ALICE, TINY
  see: RAMIREZ, ALICE

ALLAN, ANGUS P.

00183 *Thunderbirds are go.* Armada, London, 1966, 127p, Paper, Tele. [Thunderbirds #4]

ALLAN, MABEL ESTHER, 1915-

00184   *A chill in the lane.*   Thomas Nelson, Nashville, 1974, 157p, Cloth, Novel
00185   *Time to go back.*   Abelard-Schuman, London, 1972, 134p, Cloth, Novel

ALLAN, MEA, 1909-   [*biography included*]

00186   *Change of heart.*   George G. Harrap, London, 1943, 288p, Cloth, Novel

ALLEN, ARTHUR BRUCE, 1903-

00187   *The pyromaniac.*   James Blackwood, London, 1938, 211p, Cloth, Novel

ALLEN, BARBARA JO

00188   *The animal convention.*   Vantage Press, New York, 1969, 94p, Cloth, Novel

ALLEN, C(harles) R.

00189   *The ship beautiful; a two-fold tale.*   Frederick Warne, London, 1925, 279p, Cloth, Novel
00190   *Tarry, knight! a study in stained glass.*   John Hamilton, London, 1927, 256p, Cloth, Novel

ALLEN, DAVE

00191   *A little night reading; twenty tales of horror and the supernatural.*   Roger Schlesinger R. H. S., London, 1974, 315p, Cloth, Anth.

ALLEN, DICK [Richard Stanley Allen, 1939-] [*biography included*]

00192   *Science fiction: the future.*   Harcourt Brace Jovanovich, New York, 1971, 345p, Paper, Anth.

with Lori Allen:

00193   *Science fiction: Jules Verne to Ray Bradbury.*   Center for the Humanities, White Plains, NY, 1974, 55p, Paper, Nonf.

ALLEN, EDWARD HERON-
   see: HERON-ALLEN, EDWARD

ALLEN, F. M., pseud.
   see: DOWNEY, EDMUND

ALLEN, (Charles) GRANT (Blairfindie), 1848-1899

00194   *The British barbarians; a hill-top novel.*   John Lane, London, 1895, 202p, Cloth, Novel

with May Cotes:

00195   *Kalee's shrine.*   J. W. Arrowsmith, Bristol, 1886, 196p, Cloth, Novel

ALLEN, HAROLD W. G.

00196   *The edge of the universe; what is our destiny? is there life after death? what incredible secret lies in the depths of space?*   Abbey Book Publishers, Toronto, 1970, 263p, Cloth, Novel [actually released in 1975 by Allen Book Publishing, Downsview, Ontario, Canada, with labels pasted over the original publisher's name]

ALLEN, HENRY FRANCIS

as Pruning Knife:

00197   *The key of industrial co-operative government.*   The Author, St. Louis, 1886, 133p, Cloth, Novel [partly in verse]
00197A   retitled: *A strange voyage; a revision of The key of industrial co-operative government; an interesting and instructive description of life on planet Venus.*   Monitor Publishing Co., St. Louis, 1891, 226p, Cloth, Novel [expanded]

ALLEN, HENRY WILSON, 1912-

00198   *Genesis Five.*   William Morrow, New York, 1968, 256p, Cloth, Novel

ALLEN, JOHANNES, 1916-   [*biography included*]

00199   *Data for death.*   Hogarth Press, London, 1971, 192p, Cloth, Novel

ALLEN, JUDY

00200   *The spring on the mountain.*   Jonathan Cape, London, 1973, 155p, Cloth, Novel

ALLEN, L(ouis) DAVID, 1940-   [*biography included*]

00201   *Science fiction; an introduction.*   Cliffs Notes, Lincoln, 1973, 187p, Paper, Nonf.
00201A   retitled: *Science fiction reader's guide.*   Centennial Press, Lincoln, 1974, 299p, Paper, Nonf.

ALLEN, LORI, with Dick Allen

00193   *Science fiction: Jules Verne to Ray Bradbury.*   Center for the Humanities, White Plains, NY, 1974, 55p, Paper, Nonf.

ALLEN, M(arion) C(ampbell), 1914-   [*biography included*]

00202   *Shock!*   Popular Library, New York, 1965, 144p, Paper, Anth.

ALLEN, RICHARD STANLEY
   see: ALLEN, DICK

ALLEN, ROBERT, pseud. [Allen Robert Dodd, 1887-   ]

00203 *Captain Gardner of the International Police.*
       Dodd, Mead, New York, 1916, 366p, Cloth,
       Novel

ALLEN, VIRGINIA FRENCH

00204 *Times 4; four science-fiction tales.* Falcon
       Press, New York, 1968, 160p, Paper, Anth.

ALLIGHAN, GARRY, 1898-

00205 *Verwoerd--the end; a look-back from the future.*
       Purnell & Sons, Cape Town, 1961, 228p,
       Cloth, Novel

ALLINGHAM, MARGERY (Louise), 1904-1966 [*biography included*]

00206 *The mind readers.* Chatto & Windus, London,
       1965, 256p, Cloth, Novel

ALLINSON, A. A., with F. E. Hotchin

00207 *SF.* Cheshire, Melbourne, 1968, 31p, Paper,
       Nonf.

ALLISON, CLYDE, pseud. [William Knoles]

00208 *The Desdamona affair.* Ember Library, San
       Diego, 1966, 159p, Paper, Novel [Agent 0008
       (Trevor Anderson) #5]
00209 *The desert damsels.* Candid Reader, San Diego,
       1968, 159p, Paper, Novel [Agent 0008 #20]
00210 *For your sighs only.* Ember Library, San
       Diego, 1966, 159p, Paper, Novel [Agent 0008 #9]
00211 *From rapture with love.* Leisure Book, San
       Diego, 1966, 159p, Paper, Novel [Agent 0008
       #16]
00212 *Gamefinger.* Ember Library, San Diego, 1966,
       159p, Paper, Novel [Agent 0008 #6]
00213 *Go-go SADISTO.* Ember Library, San Diego, 1966,
       160p, Paper, Novel [Agent 0008 #4]
00214 *The ice maiden.* Ember Library, San Diego,
       1967, 159p, Paper, Novel [Agent 0008 #17]
00215 *The lost bomb.* Ember Library, San Diego,
       1966, 159p, Paper, Novel [Agent 0008 #10]
00216 *Merciless mermaids.* Leisure Book, San Diego,
       1966, 159p, Paper, Novel [Agent 0008 #11]
00217 *Mondo SADISTO.* Leisure Book, San Diego, 1966,
       159p, Paper, Novel [Agent 0008 #12]
00218 *Nautipuss.* Ember Library, San Diego, 1965,
       160p, Paper, Novel [Agent 0008 #3]
00219 *Our girl from MEPHISTO.* Ember Library, San
       Diego, 1965, 160p, Paper, Novel [Agent 0008
       #2]
00220 *Our man from SADISTO.* Ember Library, San
       Diego, 1965, 160p, Paper, Novel [Agent 0008
       #1]
00221 *Platypussy.* Nightstand Book, San Diego, 1968,
       159p, Paper, Novel [Agent 0008 #19]
05845 *Roburta the conqueress.* Corinth, San Diego,
       1966, 158p, Paper, Novel [Agent 0008 #15]
00222 *SADISTO royale.* Ember Library, San Diego,
       1966, 160p, Paper, Novel [Agent 0008 #7]
00223 *The sex-ray.* Leisure Book, San Diego, 1966,
       159p, Paper, Novel [Agent 0008 #14]

00224 *The sin funnel.* Candid Reader, San Diego, 1967,
       159p, Paper, Novel [Agent 0008 #18]
00225 *0008 meets Gnatman.* Leisure Book, San Diego,
       1966, 159p, Paper, Novel [Agent 0008 #8]
00226 *0008 meets Modesta Blaze.* Leisure Book, San
       Diego, 1966, 159p, Paper, Novel [Agent 0008
       #13]

as Clyde Ames:

00227 *Bang the doll slowly.* Lancer, New York, 1969,
       159p, Paper, Novel
00228 *Gorgonzola, won't you please come home?* Lancer,
       New York, 1967, 159p, Paper, Novel

ALLISON, LEONARD, 1933-   , with Leonard Jenkin and Robert Perrault

00229 *Survival printout.* Vintage, New York, 1973,
       335p, Paper, Anth.

ALLMAN, JAMES

00230 *God's children; a modern allegory.* Charles H.
       Kerr, Chicago, 1903, 113p, Cloth, Novel

ALLONBY, EDITH

published anonymously:

00231 *Jewel sowers; a novel.* Greening & Co., London,
       1903, 345p, Cloth, Novel [Lucifram #1]
00232 *Marigold; a story,* by the author of "Jewel
       Sowers." Greening & Co., London, 1905, 294p,
       Cloth, Novel [Lucifram #2]

ALLOTT, KENNETH, d. 1973, with Stephen Tait

00233 *The rhubarb tree.* Cresset Press, London, 1937,
       293p, Cloth, Novel

ALLUM, TOM

00234 *Emperor of space.* Blackie & Son, London, 1959,
       220p, Cloth, Novel
00234A retitled: *Boy beyond the Moon.* Bobbs-Merrill,
       Indianapolis, 1960, 255p, Cloth, Novel

AL-MODAD, pseud.
   see: MOORE, M. LOUISE

ALPER, GERALD A(rthur)

00235 *My name is Vladimir Sloifoiski.* Curtis, New
       York, 1970, 205p, Paper, Novel

ALTER, ROBERT EDMOND, 1925-1965 [*biography included*]

00236 *Path to savagery.* Avon, New York, 1969, 174p,
       Paper, Novel

AN AMAZING REVOLUTION

00237 *An amazing revolution and after.* George Allen
       & Sons, London, 1909, 165p, Cloth, Novel

AMBER, GRACIE, pseud. [Gerda Koontz]

00238   *Always hard!* Cameo Library, North Hollywood, 1970, 192p, Paper, Novel

AMBLER, ERIC, 1909-

00239   *The dark frontier.* Hodder & Stoughton, London, 1936, 320p, Cloth, Novel

AMELIO, RALPH J., 1939-   [*biography included*]

00240   *HAL in the classroom; science fiction films.* Pflaum Publishing, Dayton, 1974, 153p, Paper, Nonf.

AMERY, L(eopold) (Charles Maurice) S(tennett), 1873-1955

00241   *The stranger of the* Ulysses. Jarrolds Publishers, London, 1934, 163p, Cloth, Coll.

AMES, CLYDE, pseud.
   see: ALLISON, CLYDE

AMES, DELANO (L.), 1906-

00242   *A double bed on Olympus.* Grayson & Grayson, London, 1936, 288p, Cloth, Novel

AMES, ELEANOR MARIA
   see: KIRK, ELEANOR

AMES, JOSEPH BUSHNELL, 1878-1928

00243   *The bladed barrier.* Century, New York, 1929, 393p, Cloth, Novel

AMIS, KINGSLEY (William), 1922-   [*biography included*]

00244   *The green man.* Jonathan Cape, London, 1969, 253p, Cloth, Novel
00245   *New maps of Hell; a survey of science fiction.* Harcourt, Brace & Co., New York, 1960, 161p, Cloth, Nonf.

with Robert Conquest:

00246   *Spectrum; a science fiction anthology.* Victor Gollancz, London, 1961, 304p, Cloth, Anth.
00246A   retitled: *Spectrum I; a science fiction anthology.* Pan, London, 1964, 316p, Paper, Anth.
00247   *Spectrum II; a second science fiction anthology.* Victor Gollancz, London, 1962, 271p, Cloth, Anth.
00248   *Spectrum III; a third science fiction anthology.* Victor Gollancz, London, 1963, 272p, Cloth, Anth.
00249   *Spectrum IV; a science fiction anthology.* Victor Gollancz, London, 1965, 320p, Cloth, Anth.
00250   *Spectrum V; a science fiction anthology.* Victor Gollancz, London, 1966, 272p, Cloth, Anth.

AMOSOFF, N.
   see: AMOSOV, NIKOLAI

AMOSOV, N(ikolai Mikhailovich), 1913-

00251   *Notes from the future,* by N. Amosoff. Simon & Schuster, New York, 1970, 384p, Cloth, Novel

AMPER, DRAX, pseud.

00252   *Far beyond the blue; a science fiction thriller* Gannet Press, London, 1953, 128p, Paper, Novel

ANDERSON, A(ndrew) A., with A. Wall

00253   *A romance of N'Shabé, being a record of startling adventures in South Central Africa.* Chapman & Hall, London, 1891, 366p, Cloth, Novel

ANDERSON, ADRIENNE (Wynne Barton) [*biography included*]

00254   *Wings of the morning.* Robert Hale, London, 1971, 192p, Cloth, Novel

ANDERSON, ANDY, 1932-

00255   *The valley of the gods.* Andoll Publishing Co., Baraboo, Wisc., 1957,   , Paper, Novel

ANDERSON, CHESTER (V. J.), 1932-

00256   *The Butterfly Kid.* Pyramid, New York, 1967, 190p, Paper, Novel [Greenwich Village Trilogy, vol. 1]

with Michael Kurland:

00257   *Ten years to doomsday; a science fiction novel.* Pyramid, New York, 1964, 158p, Paper, Novel

ANDERSON, COLIN

00258   *Magellan; a novel.* Victor Gollancz, London, 1970, 189p, Cloth, Novel

ANDERSON, HELEN VAN
   see: VAN ANDERSON, HELEN

ANDERSON, KATHLEEN
   see: MARY CATHERINE, SISTER

ANDERSON, MARY

00259   *A son of Noah.* Digby, Long, London, 1893, 318p, Cloth, Novel

ANDERSON, OLOF W.

00260   *The treasure vault of Atlantis, giving an account of a very remarkable discovery of an ancient temple of wealth.* Midland Publishing Co., Minneapolis, 1925, 326p, Cloth, Novel

ANDERSON, POUL (William), 1926-   [*biography included*]

00261 *After doomsday.* Ballantine, New York, 1962, 128p, Paper, Novel

00262 *Agent of the Terran Empire.* Chilton, Philadelphia, 1965, 201p, Cloth, Coll. [Future History Series--Dominic Flandry]

00263 *Beyond the beyond.* Signet, New York, 1969, 263p, Paper, Coll.

00264 *Brain wave.* Ballantine, New York, 1954, 166p, Paper, Novel

00265 *The broken sword.* Abelard-Schuman, New York, 1954, 274p, Cloth, Novel

00266 *The byworlder.* Signet, New York, 1971, 160p, Paper, Novel

00267 *A circus of hells.* Signet, New York, 1970, 160p, Paper, Novel [Future History Series-- Dominic Flandry]

00268 *The corridors of time.* Doubleday, Garden City, 1965, 209p, Cloth, Novel

00269 *The dancer from Atlantis.* Nelson Doubleday, Garden City, 1971, 183p, Cloth, Novel

00270 *The day of their return.* Nelson Doubleday, Garden City, 1973, 182p, Cloth, Novel [Future History Series]

00271 *Earthman, go home!* Ace Double, New York, 1960, 110p, Paper, Novel [Future History Series-- Dominic Flandry]

00272 *The enemy stars.* J. B. Lippincott, Philadelphia, 1959, 191p, Cloth, Novel

00273 *Ensign Flandry.* Chilton, Philadelphia, 1966, 205p, Cloth, Novel [Future History Series-- Dominic Flandry]

00274 *Fire Time.* Doubleday, Garden City, 1974, 219p, Cloth, Novel

00275 *Flandry of Terra.* Chilton, Philadelphia, 1965, 225p, Cloth, Coll. [Future History Series--Dominic Flandry]

00276 *Guardians of time.* Ballantine, New York, 1960, 140p, Paper, Coll.

00277 *The high crusade.* Doubleday, Garden City, 1960, 192p, Cloth, Novel

00278 *The horn of time.* Signet, New York, 1968, 144p, Paper, Coll.

00279 *Hrolf Kraki's saga.* Ballantine, New York, 1973, 261p, Paper, Novel

00280 *A knight of ghosts and shadows.* Nelson Doubleday, Garden City, 1974, 184p, Cloth, Novel [Future History Series--Dominic Flandry]

00281 *Let the spacemen beware!* Ace Double, New York, 1963, 98p, Paper, Novel [Future History Series]

00282 *The makeshift rocket.* Ace Double, New York, 1962, 97p, Paper, Novel

00283 *The many worlds of Poul Anderson.* Chilton, Radnor, Pa., 1974, 324p, Cloth, Coll.

00284 *Mayday orbit.* Ace Double, New York, 1961, 126p, Paper, Novel [Future History Series-- Dominic Flandry]

00285 *A midsummer tempest.* Doubleday, Garden City, 1974, 207p, Cloth, Novel

00286 *Nebula award stories four.* Victor Gollancz, London, 1969, 240p, Cloth, Anth.

00287 *No world of their own.* Ace Double, New York, 1955, 158p, Paper, Novel

00288 *Operation Chaos.* Doubleday, Garden City, 1971, 232p, Cloth, Novel

00289 *Orbit unlimited; a science-fiction adventure.* Pyramid, New York, 1961, 158p, Paper, Novel

00290 *The people of the wind.* Signet, New York, 1973, 176p, Paper, Novel [Future History Series]

00291 *Perish by the sword.* Macmillan, New York, 1959, 180p, Cloth, Novel

00292 *Planet of no return.* Ace Double, New York, 1957, 105p, Paper, Novel

00293 *The Queen of Air and Darkness, and other stories.* Signet, New York, 1973, 149p, Paper, Coll.

00294 *The rebel worlds.* Signet, New York, 1969, 141p, Paper, Novel [Future History Series-- Dominic Flandry]

00295 *Satan's world.* Doubleday, Garden City, 1969, 204p, Cloth, Novel [Future History Series-- Nicholas van Rijn]

00296 *Seven conquests; an adventure in science fiction.* Macmillan Co., New York, 1969, 224p, Cloth, Coll.

00297 *Shield.* Berkley Medallion, New York, 1963, 158p, Paper, Novel

00298 *The snows of Ganymede.* Ace Double, New York, 1958, 96p, Paper, Novel

00299 *The Star Fox.* Doubleday, Garden City, 1965, 274p, Cloth, Novel

00300 *Star ways.* Avalon, New York, 1956, 224p, Cloth, Novel

00301 *Strangers from Earth.* Ballantine, New York, 1961, 144p, Paper, Coll.

00302 *Tales of the flying mountains.* Macmillan Co., New York, 1970, 253p, Cloth, Coll.

00303 *Tau zero.* Doubleday, Garden City, 1970, 208p, Cloth, Novel

00304 *There will be time.* Nelson Doubleday, Garden City, 1972, 181p, Cloth, Novel

00305 *Three hearts and three lions.* Doubleday, Garden City, 1961, 191p, Cloth, Novel

00306 *Three worlds to conquer.* Pyramid, New York, 1964, 143p, Paper, Novel

00307 *Time and stars.* Doubleday, Garden City, 1964, 249p, Cloth, Coll.

00308 *Trader to the stars.* Doubleday, Garden City, 1964, 176p, Cloth, Coll. [Future History Series--Nicholas van Rijn]

00309 *The trouble twisters.* Doubleday, Garden City, 1966, 189p, Cloth, Coll. [Future History Series--David Falkayn]

00310 *Twilight world.* Torquil, New York, 1961, 181p, Cloth, Novel

00311 *UN-man, and other novellas.* Ace Double, New York, 1962, 158p, Paper, Coll.

00312 *Vault of the ages.* John C. Winston, Philadelphia, 1952, 210p, Cloth, Novel

00313 *Virgin planet.* Avalon, New York, 1959, 224p, Cloth, Novel

00314 *War of the wing-men.* Ace Double, New York, 1958, 160p, Paper, Novel [Future History Series--Nicholas van Rijn]

00315 *The war of two worlds.* Ace Double, New York, 1959, 108p, Paper, Novel

00316 *We claim these stars!* Ace Double, New York, 1959, 125p, Paper, Novel [Future History Series--Dominic Flandry]

00317 *World without stars.* Ace, New York, 1967, 125p, Paper, Novel

00318 *The worlds of Poul Anderson.* Ace, New York, 1974, 349p, Paper, Coll. [includes *Planet of no return*; *The war of two worlds*; *World without stars*]

with Gordon R. Dickson:

00319 *Earthman's burden.* Gnome Press, New York, 1957, 184p, Cloth, Coll.

with Gordon Eklund:

00320 *Inheritors of Earth.* Chilton, Radnor, Pa., 1974, 190p, Cloth, Novel

ANDERSON, WILLIAM C(harles), 1920-   [*biography included*]

00321 *Adam M-1; a novel.* Crown Publishers, New York, 1964, 255p, Cloth, Novel
00322 *Pandemonium on the Potomac; a novel.* Crown Publishers, New York, 1966, 245p, Cloth, Novel
00323 *Penelope.* Crown Publishers, New York, 1963, 215p, Cloth, Novel [Penelope #1]
00324 *Penelope, the damp detective; a novel.* Crown Publishers, New York, 1974, 188p, Cloth, Novel [Penelope #2]

ANDERSON IMBERT, ENRIQUE, 1910-   [*biography included*]

00325 *The other side of the mirror (El grimorio); short stories.* Southern Illinois University Press, Carbondale, 1966, 226p, Cloth, Coll.

ANDOM, R., pseud. [Alfred Walter Barrett, 1869-   ]

00326 *The enchanted ship; a story of mystery with a lot of imagination.* Cassell, London, 1908, 279p, Cloth, Novel
00327 *The Identity Exchange; a story of some odd transformations.* Jarrold & Sons, London, 1902, 286p, Cloth, Novel
00327A retitled: *The marvellous adventures of me; or, The Identity Exchange.* Jarrold & Sons, London, 1904, 286p, Cloth, Novel
00328 *The magic bowl; and, The blue-stone ring; Oriental tales with Occi(or acci)dental endings.* Jarrold & Sons, London, 1909, 312p, Cloth, Coll.
       The marvellous adventures of me. [see 00327A]

ANDRE, LEE, pseud. [L. R. Andrus]

00329 *Alaric, galactic diplomat.* Exposition Press, Jericho, NY, 1974, 155p, Cloth, Novel

ANDREEV, LEONID (Nikolaevich), 1871-1919 [variously Andreyev or Andreief]

00330 *The red laugh; fragments of a discovered manuscript.* T. Fisher Unwin, London, 1915, 191p, Cloth, Novel; Duffield, New York, 1915, 191p, Cloth, Novel [as Andreief]
00331 *Satan's diary.* Boni & Liveright, New York, 1920, 263p, Cloth, Novel [as Andreyev]
00332 *The seven that were hanged.* Boni & Liveright, New York, 1918, 194p, Cloth, Coll. [includes *The seven that were hanged* (not SF) and *The red laugh*] [as Andreyev]
00333 *The seven that were hanged, and other stories.* Random House, NY, 1958, 249p, Paper, Coll. [different contents from 00332] [as Andreyev]

ANDREIEF, LEONID
    see: ANDREEV, LEONID

ANDRÉOTA, PAUL, 1917-

00334 *The sweet taste of burning.* David McKay, New York, 1973, 161p, Cloth, Novel

ANDREWS, CECILY ISOBEL
    see: WEST, REBECCA

ANDREWS, CLAIRE, 1940-   , with Keith Andrews as Keith Claire

00335 *Duringwitch.* Eyre & Spottiswoode, London, 1968, 208p, Cloth, Novel

ANDREWS, F(rank) EMERSON, 1902-   [*biography included*]

00336 *Grugan's god.* Muhlenberg Press, Philadelphia, 1955, 196p, Cloth, Novel

ANDREWS, J(ames) S(ydney), 1934-   [*biography included*]

00337 *The green hill of Nendrum.* Hawthorn, New York, 1970, 214p, Cloth, Novel
00338 *The man from the sea.* Bodley Head, London, 1970, 154p, Cloth, Novel

ANDREWS, KEITH, 1930-   , with Claire Andrews as Keith Claire

00335 *Duringwitch.* Eyre & Spottiswoode, London, 1968, 208p, Cloth, Novel

ANDREWS, LEWIS M., with Marvin Karlins

00339 *Gomorrah.* Doubleday, Garden City, 1974, 163p, Cloth, Novel

ANDREYEV, LEONID
    see: ANDREEV, LEONID

ANDRUS, L. R.
    see: ANDRE, LEE

ANET, CLAUDE, pseud. [Jean Schopfer, 1868-1931]

00340 *The end of a world.* Alfred A. Knopf, New York, 1927, 268p, Cloth, Novel

ANEX, GUY

00341 *Sex, hypnosis and the infinite.* Ram, Las Vegas, 1969, 216p, Paper, Novel

THE ANGEL AND THE IDIOT

00342 *The angel and the idiot; a story of the next century.* David Stott, London, 1890, 158p, Cloth, Novel

ANGELO, pseud.

00343 *The adventures of an atom, its autobiography by itself,* by the author of "The dancing imps of the wine." Hurst, New York, 1880, 416p, Cloth, Novel

ANGELUCCI, ORFEO M.

00344 *Son of the sun.* DeVorss, Los Angeles, 1959,
        211p, Cloth, Novel

ANGOFF, CHARLES, 1902-   [*biography included*]

00345 *Adventures in Heaven.* Bernard Ackerman, New
        York, 1945, 120p, Cloth, Coll.

ANGUS, JOHN

00346 *The homecoming; a tale of two ages.* Hutchin-
        son, London, 1935, 287p, Cloth, Novel

ANKER LARSEN, J(ohannes), 1874-1957

00347 *The philosopher's stone.* Alfred A. Knopf,
        New York, 1924, 379p, Cloth, Novel

ANNALS OF THE TWENTY-NINTH CENTURY
    see: BLAIR, ANDREW

ANNAN, DAVID

00348 *Cinefantastique; beyond the dream machine.*
        Lorrimer, London, 1974, 132p, Paper, Nonf.

ANNE MARIE, pseud.
    see: MARIE, ANNE

ANNESLEY, MAUDE

00349 *The door of darkness.* John Lane, the Bodley
        Head, London, 1908, 349p, Cloth, Novel
00350 *Shadow-shapes.* Methuen, London, 1911, 312p,
        Cloth, Novel

ANONYM, MON, pseud.

00351 *Flight to fantasy.* Fabian, Los Angeles?,
        1970, 153p, Paper, Novel

ANONYMOUS, pseud.

00352 *Autobiography of a louse, vol. III.* Midwood,
        New York, 1970,   , Paper, Novel

ANONYMOUS, pseud. [Damned]
    see: DORRANCE, ETHEL SMITH

ANONYMOUS, pseud. [El Reshid]
    see: HATCH, DAVID PATTERSON

"ANONYMOUS," pseud. [The president vanishes]
    see: STOUT, REX

ANSLE, DOROTHY PHOEBE
    see: CONWAY, LAURA

ANSON, AUGUST

00353 *When woman reigns.* Pen-in-Hand Publishing Co.,
        Oxford, 1938, 206p, Cloth, Novel

ANSON, CAPT. (Charles Vernon)

00354 *The great Anglo-American war of 1900.* Edward
        Stanford, London, 1896, 88p, Cloth, Novel

ANSTEY, F., pseud. [Thomas Anstey Guthrie,
1856-1934]

00355 *The black poodle, and other tales.* Longmans,
        Green, London, 1884, 269p, Cloth, Coll.
00356 *The brass bottle.* Smith, Elder, London, 1900,
        312p, Cloth, Novel
00357 *A fallen idol.* Smith, Elder, London, 1886,
        334p, Cloth, Novel
00358 *Humour and fantasy; Vice versa; The tinted
        Venus; A fallen idol; The talking horse;
        Salted almonds; The brass bottle.* John
        Murray, London, 1931, 1174p, Cloth, Coll.
00359 *In brief authority.* Smith, Elder, London,
        1915, 413p, Cloth, Novel
00360 *Only toys!* Grant Richards, London, 1903, 260p,
        Cloth, Novel
00361 *Paleface and redskin, and other stories for
        boys and girls.* Grant Richards, London,
        1898, 295p, Cloth, Coll.
00362 *Salted almonds.* Smith, Elder, London, 1906,
        312p, Cloth, Coll.
        The statement of Stella Maberly. [see 00367]
00363 *The talking horse.* J. W. Lovell, New York,
        1891, 298p, Cloth, Coll.
        The time bargain. [see 00365A]
00364 *The tinted Venus; a farcical romance.* J. W.
        Arrowsmith, Bristol, 1885, 192p, Cloth, Novel
00365 *Tourmalin's time cheques.* J. W. Arrowsmith,
        Bristol, 1891, 172p, Cloth, Novel
00365A retitled: *The time bargain; or, Tourmalin's
        cheque book.* J. W. Arrowsmith, Bristol,
        1905, 122p, Cloth, Novel
00366 *Vice versa; or, A lesson to fathers.* Smith,
        Elder, London, 1882, 364p, Cloth, Novel

published anonymously:

00367 *The statement of Stella Maberly, written by
        herself.* T. Fisher Unwin, London, 1896, 251p,
        Cloth, Novel

ANTHEIL, GEORGE, 1900-1959

published anonymously:

00368 *The shape of the war to come.* Longmans, Green,
        New York, 1940, 83p, Cloth, Novel

ANTHONY, BARBARA
    see: BARBER, ANTONIA

ANTHONY, PIERS, pseud. [Piers Anthony Dillingham Jacob, 1934-   ] [*biography included*]

00369 *Chthon.* Ballantine, New York, 1967, 254p,
        Paper, Novel
00370 *Macroscope.* Avon, New York, 1969, 480p, Paper,
        Novel

ANTHONY, PIERS, pseud. (cont.)

00371 *Omnivore.* Ballantine, New York, 1968, 221p,
       Paper, Novel [Omnivore Sequence #1]
00372 *Orn.* Nelson Doubleday, Garden City, 1970,
       247p, Cloth, Novel [Omnivore Sequence #2]
00373 *Prostho plus.* Victor Gollancz, London, 1971,
       190p, Cloth, Novel
00374 *Race against time.* Hawthorn Books, New York,
       1973, 179p, Cloth, Novel
00375 *Rings of ice.* Avon, New York, 1974, 191p,
       Paper, Novel
00376 *Sos, the Rope.* Pyramid, New York, 1968, 157p,
       Paper, Novel [Sos Trilogy, vol. 1]
00377 *Triple detente.* DAW, New York, 1974, 175p,
       Paper, Novel
00378 *Var, the Stick.* Faber & Faber, London, 1972,
       191p, Cloth, Novel [Sos Trilogy, vol. 2]

with Roberto Fuentes:

00379 *The bamboo bloodbath.* Berkley Medallion, New
       York, 1974, 188p, Paper, Novel [Jason Striker
       #3]
00380 *Kiai!* Berkley Medallion, New York, 1974, 191p,
       Paper, Novel [Jason Striker #1]
00381 *Mistress of death.* Berkley Medallion, New
       York, 1974, 192p, Paper, Novel [Jason Striker
       #2]

with Robert E. Margroff:

00382 *The E.S.P. worm.* Paperback Library, New York,
       1970, 159p, Paper, Novel
00383 *The ring.* Ace, New York, 1968, 254p, Paper,
       Novel

ANTICIPATION

00384 *Anticipation; or, The voyage of an American to
       England in the year 1899, in a series of let-
       ters, humourously describing the supposed
       situation of this kingdom at that period.*
       William Lane, London, 1781, 183p, Cloth,
       Novel

ANTONICK, ROBERT J.
  see: KAMIN, NICK

ANTONIORROBLES, pseud. [Antonio Robles Soler,
1897-   ]

00385 *The refugee centaur.* Twayne Publishers, New
       York, 1952, 245p, Cloth, Novel

ANVIC, FRANK, pseud. [Jory Sherman, 1932-   ]

00386 *Bride of Satan.* Brandon, Chatsworth, Cal.,
       1974, 189p, Paper, Novel
00387 *The sex savages.* Barclay House, Chatsworth,
       Cal., 1974, 159p, Paper, Novel

ANVIL, CHRISTOPHER, pseud. [Harry C. Crosby,
Jr.]

00388 *The day the machines stopped.* Monarch, Derby,
       Conn., 1964, 124p, Paper, Novel
00389 *Pandora's planet.* Doubleday, Garden City,
       1972, 233p, Cloth, Novel

00390 *Strangers in Paradise.* Tower Books, New York,
       1970, 170p, Paper, Novel

APERY, HELEN d'
  see: HARPER, OLIVE

APHRODISIAC AFFAIR

00391 *The aphrodisiac affair.* Collectors Publica-
       tions, City of Industry, Cal., 1969, 247p,
       Cloth, Novel

APPEL, BENJAMIN, 1907-1977 [*biography included*

       The death master. [see 00393A]
00392 *The fantastic mirror; science fiction across
       the ages.* Pantheon, New York, 1969, 139p,
       Cloth, Nonf.
00393 *The Funhouse; an eyewitness report of the his-
       toric search for the world's most dangerous
       weapon, the A-I-D...* Ballantine, New York,
       1959, 158p, Paper, Novel
00393A retitled: *The death master.* Popular Library,
       New York, 1974, 189p, Paper, Novel

APPLE, A. E.

00394 *Mr. Chang's crime ray; a detective story.*
       Chelsea House, New York, 1928, 249p, Cloth,
       Novel

APPLEMAN, MARK J(erome), 1917-   [*biography
included*], with Edmund Demaitre

00395 *The liberation of Manhattan.* Doubleday, Gar-
       den City, 1949, 223p, Cloth, Novel

APPLETON, VICTOR, house pseud. [see also
Howard R. Garis]

00396 *Don Sturdy in the temples of fear; or, Destined
       for a strange sacrifice.* Grosset & Dunlap,
       New York, 1932, 202p, Cloth, Novel [Don
       Sturdy #12]
00397 *Tom Swift among the diamond makers; or, The
       secret of Phantom Mountain.* Grosset & Dunlap,
       New York, 1911, 216p, Cloth, Novel [Tom Swift
       #7] [by Howard R. Garis]
00398 *Tom Swift among the fire fighters; or, Battling
       with flames from the air.* Grosset & Dunlap,
       New York, 1921, 214p, Cloth, Novel [Tom Swift
       #24] [by Howard R. Garis]
00399 *Tom Swift and his aerial warship; or, The naval
       terror of the seas.* Grosset & Dunlap, New
       York, 1915, 218p, Cloth, Novel [Tom Swift
       #18] [by Howard R. Garis]
00400 *Tom Swift and his air glider; or, Seeking the
       platinum treasure.* Grosset & Dunlap, New
       York, 1912, 209p, Cloth, Novel [Tom Swift
       #12] [by Howard R. Garis]
00401 *Tom Swift and his air scout; or, Uncle Sam's
       mastery of the sky.* Grosset & Dunlap, New
       York, 1919, 218p, Cloth, Novel [Tom Swift
       #22] [by Howard R. Garis]
00402 *Tom Swift and his airline express; or, From
       ocean to ocean by daylight.* Grosset & Dunlap

APPLETON, VICTOR, house pseud. (cont.)

New York, 1926, 218p, Cloth, Novel [Tom Swift #29] [by Howard R. Garis]

00403 *Tom Swift and his airship; or, The stirring cruise of the Red Cloud.* Grosset & Dunlap, New York, 1910, 216p, Cloth, Novel [Tom Swift #3] [by Howard R. Garis]

00404 *Tom Swift and his big dirigible; or, Adventures over the forest of fire.* Grosset & Dunlap, New York, 1930, 214p, Cloth, Novel [Tom Swift #33] [by Howard R. Garis]

00405 *Tom Swift and his big tunnel; or, The hidden city of the Andes.* Grosset & Dunlap, New York, 1916, 218p, Cloth, Novel [Tom Swift #19] [by Howard R. Garis]

00406 *Tom Swift and his chest of secrets; or, Tracing the stolen inventions.* Grosset & Dunlap, New York, 1925, 216p, Cloth, Novel [Tom Swift #28] [by Howard R. Garis]

00407 *Tom Swift and his electric locomotive; or, Two miles a minute on the rails.* Grosset & Dunlap, New York, 1922, 212p, Cloth, Novel [Tom Swift #25] [by Howard R. Garis]

00408 *Tom Swift and his electric rifle; or, Daring adventures in elephant land.* Grosset & Dunlap, New York, 1911, 212p, Cloth, Novel [Tom Swift #10] [by Howard R. Garis]

00409 *Tom Swift and his electric runabout; or, The speediest car on the road.* Grosset & Dunlap, New York, 1910, 216p, Cloth, Novel [Tom Swift #5] [by Howard R. Garis]

00410 *Tom Swift and his flying boat; or, The castaways of the giant iceberg.* Grosset & Dunlap, New York, 1923, 212p, Cloth, Novel [Tom Swift #26] [by Howard R. Garis]

00411 *Tom Swift and his giant cannon; or, The longest shots on record.* Grosset & Dunlap, New York, 1913, 216p, Cloth, Novel [Tom Swift #16] [by Howard R. Garis]

00412 *Tom Swift and his giant magnet; or, Bringing up the lost submarine.* Grosset & Dunlap, New York, 1932, 216p, Cloth, Novel [Tom Swift #35] [by Howard R. Garis]

00413 *Tom Swift and his giant oil gusher; or, The treasure of Goby Farm.* Grosset & Dunlap, New York, 1924, 210p, Cloth, Novel [Tom Swift #27] [by Howard R. Garis]

00414 *Tom Swift and his great searchlight; or, On the border for Uncle Sam.* Grosset & Dunlap, New York, 1912, 214p, Cloth, Novel [Tom Swift #15] [by Howard R. Garis]

00415 *Tom Swift and his house on wheels; or, A trip to the mountain of mystery.* Grosset & Dunlap, New York, 1929, 216p, Cloth, Novel [Tom Swift #32] [by Howard R. Garis]

00416 *Tom Swift and his motor-boat; or, The rivals of Lake Carlopa.* Grosset & Dunlap, New York, 1910, 212p, Cloth, Novel [Tom Swift #2] [by Howard R. Garis]

00417 *Tom Swift and his motor-cycle; or, Fun and adventures on the road.* Grosset & Dunlap, New York, 1910, 206p, Cloth, Novel [Tom Swift #1] [by Howard R. Garis]

00418 *Tom Swift and his ocean airport; or, Foiling the Haargolanders.* Grosset & Dunlap, New York, 1934, 214p, Cloth, Novel [Tom Swift #37]

00419 *Tom Swift and his photo telephone; or, The picture that saved a fortune.* Grosset & Dunlap, New York, 1914, 216p, Cloth, Novel [Tom Swift #17] [by Howard R. Garis]

00420 *Tom Swift and his planet stone; or, Discovering the secret of another world.* Grosset & Dunlap, New York, 1935, 203p, Cloth, Novel [Tom Swift #38]

00421 *Tom Swift and his sky racer; or, The quickest flight on record.* Grosset & Dunlap, New York, 1911, 207p, Cloth, Novel [Tom Swift #9] [by Howard R. Garis]

00422 *Tom Swift and his sky train; or, Overland through the clouds.* Grosset & Dunlap, New York, 1931, 218p, Cloth, Novel [Tom Swift #34] [by Howard R. Garis]

00423 *Tom Swift and his submarine boat; or, Under the ocean for sunken treasure.* Grosset & Dunlap, New York, 1910, 216p, Cloth, Novel [Tom Swift #4] [by Howard R. Garis]

00424 *Tom Swift and his talking pictures; or, The greatest invention on record.* Grosset & Dunlap, New York, 1928, 216p, Cloth, Novel [Tom Swift #31] [by Howard R. Garis]

00425 *Tom Swift and his television detector; or, Trailing the secret plotters.* Grosset & Dunlap, New York, 1933, 217p, Cloth, Novel [Tom Swift #36]

00426 *Tom Swift and his undersea search; or, The treasure on the floor of the Atlantic.* Grosset & Dunlap, New York, 1920, 218p, Cloth, Novel [Tom Swift #23] [by Howard R. Garis]

00427 *Tom Swift and his war tank; or, Doing his best for Uncle Sam.* Grosset & Dunlap, New York, 1918, 218p, Cloth, Novel [Tom Swift #21] [by Howard R. Garis]

00428 *Tom Swift and his wireless message; or, The castaways of Earthquake Island.* Grosset & Dunlap, New York, 1911, 211p, Cloth, Novel [Tom Swift #6] [by Howard R. Garis]

00429 *Tom Swift and his wizard camera; or, Thrilling adventures while taking moving pictures.* Grosset & Dunlap, New York, 1912, 210p, Cloth, Novel [Tom Swift #14] [by Howard R. Garis]

00430 *Tom Swift circling the globe; or, The daring cruise of the Air Monarch.* Grosset & Dunlap, New York, 1927, 216p, Cloth, Novel [Tom Swift #30] [by Howard R. Garis]

00431 *Tom Swift in captivity; or, A daring escape by airship.* Grosset & Dunlap, New York, 1912, 218p, Cloth, Novel [Tom Swift #13] [by Howard R. Garis]

00432 *Tom Swift in the caves of ice; or, The wreck of the airship.* Grosset & Dunlap, New York, 1911, 214p, Cloth, Novel [Tom Swift #8] [by Howard R. Garis]

00433 *Tom Swift in the city of gold; or, Marvelous adventures underground.* Grosset & Dunlap, New York, 1912, 216p, Cloth, Novel [Tom Swift #11] [by Howard R. Garis]

00434 *Tom Swift in the land of wonders; or, The search for the idol of gold.* Grosset & Dunlap, New York, 1917, 218p, Cloth, Novel [Tom Swift #20] [by Howard R. Garis]

APPLETON, VICTOR II, house pseud.

00435 *Tom Swift and his aquatomic tracker.* Grosset & Dunlap, New York, 1964, 178p, Cloth, Novel [Tom Swift Jr. #23]

00436 *Tom Swift and his atomic earth blaster.* Grosset & Dunlap, New York, 1954, 210p, Cloth, Novel [Tom Swift Jr. #5]

00437 *Tom Swift and his Cosmotron Express.* Grosset & Dunlap, New York, 1970, 180p, Cloth, Novel [Tom Swift Jr. #32]

APPLETON, VICTOR II, house pseud.

00438   *Tom Swift and his deep-sea hydrodome.* Grosset
        & Dunlap, New York, 1958, 184p, Cloth, Novel
        [Tom Swift Jr. #11]
00439   *Tom Swift and his diving seacopter.* Grosset
        & Dunlap, New York, 1956, 214p, Cloth, Novel
        [Tom Swift Jr. #7]
00440   *Tom Swift and his Dyna-4 capsule.* Grosset &
        Dunlap, New York, 1969, 175p, Cloth, Novel
        [Tom Swift Jr. #31]
00441   *Tom Swift and his electronic retroscope.* Gros-
        set & Dunlap, New York, 1959, 184p, Cloth,
        Novel [Tom Swift Jr. #14]
00441A retitled: *Tom Swift in the jungle of the Mayas.*
        Grosset & Dunlap, New York, 1972, 184p, Paper,
        Novel [Tom Swift Jr. #14]
00442   *Tom Swift and his flying lab.* Grosset & Dunlap,
        New York, 1954, 208p, Cloth, Novel [Tom Swift
        Jr. #1]
00443   *Tom Swift and his G-force inverter.* Grosset
        & Dunlap, New York, 1968, 175p, Cloth, Novel
        [Tom Swift Jr. #30]
00444   *Tom Swift and his giant robot.* Grosset & Dun-
        lap, New York, 1954, 211p, Cloth, Novel [Tom
        Swift Jr. #4]
00445   *Tom Swift and his jetmarine.* Grosset & Dunlap,
        New York, 1954, 208p, Cloth, Novel [Tom Swift
        #2]
00446   *Tom Swift and his megascope space prober.* Gros-
        set & Dunlap, New York, 1962, 176p, Cloth,
        Novel [Tom Swift Jr. #20]
00447   *Tom Swift and his outpost in space.* Grosset
        & Dunlap, New York, 1955, 210p, Cloth, Novel
        [Tom Swift Jr. #6]
00448   *Tom Swift and his polar-ray dynasphere.* Gros-
        set & Dunlap, New York, 1965, 177p, Cloth,
        Novel [Tom Swift Jr. #25]
00449   *Tom Swift and his repelatron skyway.* Grosset
        & Dunlap, New York, 1963, 179p, Cloth, Novel
        [Tom Swift Jr. #22]
00450   *Tom Swift and his rocket ship.* Grosset & Dun-
        lap, New York, 1954, 208p, Cloth, Novel [Tom
        Swift Jr. #3]
00451   *Tom Swift and his sonic boom trap.* Grosset &
        Dunlap, New York, 1965, 178p, Cloth, Novel
        [Tom Swift Jr. #26]
00452   *Tom Swift and his space solartron.* Grosset &
        Dunlap, New York, 1958, 183p, Cloth, Novel
        [Tom Swift Jr. #13]
00453   *Tom Swift and his spectromarine selector.* Gros-
        set & Dunlap, New York, 1960, 184p, Cloth,
        Novel [Tom Swift Jr. #15]
00453A retitled: *Tom Swift and the city of gold.*
        Grosset & Dunlap, New York, 1972, 184p,
        Paper, Novel [Tom Swift Jr. #15]
00454   *Tom Swift and his subocean geotron.* Grosset
        & Dunlap, New York, 1966, 178p, Cloth, Novel
        [Tom Swift Jr. #27]
00455   *Tom Swift and his 3-D telejector.* Grosset &
        Dunlap, New York, 1964, 177p, Cloth, Novel
        [Tom Swift Jr. #24]
00456   *Tom Swift and his triphibian atomicar.* Grosset
        & Dunlap, New York, 1962, 188p, Cloth, Novel
        [Tom Swift Jr. #19]
00457   *Tom Swift and his ultrasonic cycloplane.* Gros-
        set & Dunlap, New York, 1957, 182p, Cloth,
        Novel [Tom Swift Jr. #10]
00458   *Tom Swift and the asteroid pirates.* Grosset &
        Dunlap, New York, 1963, 178p, Cloth, Novel
        [Tom Swift Jr. #21]
00459   *Tom Swift and the captive planetoid.* Grosset
        & Dunlap, New York, 1967, 174p, Cloth, Novel
        [Tom Swift Jr. #29]

        Tom Swift and the city of gold. [see 00453A]
00460   *Tom Swift and the cosmic astronauts.* Grosset
        & Dunlap, New York, 1960, 184p, Cloth, Novel
        [Tom Swift Jr. #16]
00461   *Tom Swift and the electric hydrolung.* Grosset
        & Dunlap, New York, 1961, 188p, Cloth, Novel
        [Tom Swift Jr. #18]
00462   *Tom Swift and the galaxy ghosts.* Grosset &
        Dunlap, New York, 1971, 180p, Cloth, Novel
        [Tom Swift Jr. #33]
00463   *Tom Swift and the mystery comet.* Grosset &
        Dunlap, New York, 1966, 178p, Cloth, Novel
        [Tom Swift Jr. #28]
00464   *Tom Swift and the visitor from Planet X.* Gros-
        set & Dunlap, New York, 1961, 184p, Cloth,
        Novel [Tom Swift Jr. #17]
00465   *Tom Swift in the caves of nuclear fire.* Gros-
        set & Dunlap, New York, 1956, 214p, Cloth,
        Novel [Tom Swift Jr. #8]
        Tom Swift in the jungle of the Mayas. [see
        00441A]
00466   *Tom Swift in the race to the Moon.* Grosset &
        Dunlap, New York, 1958, 180p, Cloth, Novel
        [Tom Swift Jr. #12]
00467   *Tom Swift on the phantom satellite.* Grosset &
        Dunlap, New York, 1957, 214p, Cloth, Novel
        [Tom Swift Jr. #9]

AN ARABIAN TALE
    see: BECKFORD, WILLIAM

ARANA-MARINI Y COPPEL, ALFREDO
    see: COPPEL, ALFRED

ARATUS, pseud.

00468   *A voyage to the Moon, strongly recommended to
        all lovers of real freedom.* J. Ridgway,
        London, 1793, 39p, Paper, Novel

ARAWIYAH, AL, pseud. [H. N. Crellin]

00469   *Tales of the caliph.* T. Fisher Unwin, London,
        1887, 234p, Cloth, Coll.

ARBUTHNOT, JOHN, 1667-1735

published anonymously:

00470   *An account of the state of learning in the Em-
        pire of Lilliput, together with the history
        and character of Bullum the Emperor's library
        keeper, faithfully transcribed out of Captain
        Lemuel Gulliver's general description of the
        Empire of Lilliput, mention'd in the 69th
        page of the first volume of his travels.* J.
        Roberts, London, 1728, 37p, Paper, Story
        [Gulliver series]

ARCH, E. L., pseud. [Rachel Ruth Cosgrove
Payes, 1922-   ][*biography included*]

00471   *Bridge to yesterday.* Avalon, New York, 1963,
        192p, Cloth, Novel
00472   *The deathstones.* Avalon, New York, 1964, 192p
        Cloth, Novel
00473   *The double-minded man.* Avalon, New York, 1966
        192p, Cloth, Novel

ARCH, E. L., pseud. (cont.)

00474   *The first immortals.* Avalon, New York, 1965,
        192p, Cloth, Novel
00475   *The man with three eyes.* Avalon, New York,
        1967, 190p, Cloth, Novel
00476   *Planet of death.* Avalon, New York, 1964, 192p,
        Cloth, Novel

ARCHAMBAULT, ALBERIC A., 1887-1950

00477   *The Samsons.* Bruce Humphries, Boston, 1941,
        84p, Cloth, Novel

ARCHER, RON, pseud.
    see: WHITE, TED

ARCOS, J. PACO D'
    see: PACO D'ARCOS, J.

ARDEN, CLIVE, pseud. [Lily Clive Nutt, 1888-]

00478   *The enchanted spring.* Bobbs-Merrill, Indiana-
        polis, 1935, 352p, Cloth, Novel

ARDIES, TOM, 1931-   [*biography included*]

00479   *Their man in the White House.* Macmillan, Lon-
        don, 1971, 190p, Cloth, Novel
00480   *This suitcase is going to explode.* Doubleday,
        Garden City, 1972, 234p, Cloth, Novel

ARDREY, ROBERT, 1908-   [*biography included*]

00481   *Worlds beginning.* Duell, Sloan & Pearce, New
        York, 1944, 244p, Cloth, Novel

ARGAL; OR, THE SILVER DEVIL
    see: HADLEY, GEORGE

ARISS, BRUCE (Wallace Jr.), 1911-   [*biography
included*]

00482   *Full circle.* Avalon, New York, 1963, 224p,
        Cloth, Novel

ARK

00483   *The ark of Mars.* American Science Fiction,
        Sydney, 1954, 34p, Paper, Anth.

ARKWRIGHT, WILLIAM, 1857-1925

00484   *Utinam; a glimmering of goddesses.* John Lane,
        The Bodley Head, London, 1917, 120p, Cloth,
        Novel

ARLEN, MICHAEL [originally Dikrān Kuyumjian],
1895-1956

00485   *Ghost stories.* W. Collins Sons, London, 1932,
        181p, Cloth, Coll.

00486   *Hell! said the duchess; a bedtime story.* Wil-
        liam Heinemann, London, 1934, 181p, Cloth,
        Novel
00487   *Man's mortality; a story.* William Heinemann,
        London, 1933, 379p, Cloth, Novel

ARMATA
    see: ERSKINE, THOMAS

ARMOUR, DONALD

00488   *So fast he ran.* Chapman & Hall, London, 1940,
        319p, Cloth, Novel

ARMOUR, FRANCES J.

00489   *The Brotherhood of Wisdom.* Brown, Langham,
        London, 1908, 320p, Cloth, Novel

ARMOUR, MARGARET, pseud. [Margaret Macdougall,
d. 1943]

00490   *The eerie book.* J. Shiells & Co., London,
        1898, 211p, Cloth, Anth. [includes some nonf.]

ARMOURER'S SON

00491   *The armourer's son; or, The mysteries of the
        Tower of London.* Harkaway House, London,
        1870?, 171p, Paper, Novel

ARMSTRONG, ANTHONY, pseud. [George Anthony
Armstrong Willis, 1897-1976]

00492   *The love of Prince Raameses.* Stanley Paul,
        London, 1921, 256p, Cloth, Novel
00493   *Lure of the past.* Stanley Paul, London, 1920,
        256p, Cloth, Novel
        The naughty princess. [see 00494A]
00494   *The pack of pieces.* Michael Joseph, London,
        1942, 180p, Cloth, Novel
00494A retitled: *The naughty princess.* Macdonald &
        Co., London, 1945, 167p, Cloth, Novel
00495   *The strange case of Mr. Pelham.* Methuen, Lon-
        don, 1957, 224p, Cloth, Novel
00496   *Wine of death.* Stanley Paul, London, 1925,
        288p, Cloth, Novel

with Bruce Graeme:

00497   *When the bells rang; a tale of what might have
        been.* George G. Harrap, London, 1943, 240p,
        Cloth, Novel

ARMSTRONG, (Terence Ian) FYTTON, 1912-

00498   *Full score; twenty-five stories.* Rich & Cowan,
        London, 1933, 295p, Cloth, Anth.

as John Gawsworth:

00499   *Strange assembly; new stories.* Unicorn Press,
        London, 1932, 334p, Cloth, Anth.

ARMSTRONG, MARTIN (Donisthorpe), 1882-1974

00500   *Desert; a legend.* Jonathan Cape, London, 1926,
        252p, Cloth, Novel

ARMSTRONG, WILLIMINA L.
    see: KI DOST, ZAMIN

ARNAC, MARCEL, 1886-1931

00501   *Thirty-six inches of adventure.* Planet Press,
            New York, 1930, 247p, Cloth, Novel

ARNAM, DAVE VAN
    see: VAN ARNAM, DAVE

ARNE, AARON, pseud. [Alf A. Jorgenson, 1899-]

00502   *Feet of clay; a fantasy.* Vantage Press, New
            York, 1958, 276p, Cloth, Novel

ARNESON, D. J.

00503   *Creature reader.* Young Readers Press, New
            York, 1972, 93p, Paper, Coll.

ARNOLD, EDWARD LESTER (Linden), 1857-1935

00504   *Lepidus the centurion; a Roman of to-day.* Cas-
            sell & Co., London, 1901, 342p, Cloth, Novel
00505   *Lieut. Gullivar Jones; his vacation.* S. C.
            Brown, Langham, London, 1905, 301p, Cloth,
            Novel
00505A retitled: *Gulliver of Mars.* Ace, New York,
            1964, 224p, Paper, Novel
00506   *The wonderful adventures of Phra the Phoenician.*
            Harper & Bros., New York, 1890, 329p, Cloth,
            Novel
00506A retitled: *Phra the Phoenician.* George Newnes,
            London, 1910, 182p, Cloth, Novel

ARNOLD, FRANK EDWARD, 1914-

00507   *Wings across time.* Pendulum Publications,
            London, 1946, 118p, Paper, Coll.

ARNOLD, P. W.
    see: LLOYD, JEREMY

ARNOLD, RALPH (Crispian Marshall), 1906-1970

00508   *Hands across the water.* Constable, London,
            1946, 235p, Cloth, Novel

ARNOTHY, CHRISTINE, 1930-

00509   *The captive cardinal; a novel.* Collins, Lon-
            don, 1964, 254p, Cloth, Novel

ARNOUX, ALEXANDRE (Paul), 1884-1973

00510   *Abishag.* Thornton Butterworth, London, 1925,
            286p, Cloth, Novel

ARONIN, BEN, 1904-

00511   *Cavern of destiny.* Behrman's Jewish Book House,
            New York, 1943, 182p, Cloth, Novel [Drale #2]

00512   *The lost tribe, being the strange adventures
            of Raphael Drale in search of the lost tribes
            of Israel.* Simons Press, New York, 1934,
            352p, Cloth, Novel [Drale #1]
00513   *The moor's gold.* Argus Books, Chicago, 1935,
            271p, Cloth, Novel

ARONSTAM, NOAH E(phraim), 1872-1957

00514   *The lost nation.* Duo-art Press, Detroit, 1937,
            92p, Cloth, Novel

AROUET, FRANCOIS MARIE
    see: VOLTAIRE

ARRIGHI, MEL, 1933-   [*biography included*]

00515   *An ordinary man.* Peter H. Wyden, New York,
            1970, 187p, Cloth, Novel

ARTHUR, ROBERT, pseud. [Robert Arthur Feder,
1909-1969]

00516   *Davy Jones' haunted locker; great ghost stories
            of the sea.* Random House, New York, 1965,
            204p, Cloth, Anth.
00517   *Ghosts and more ghosts.* Random House, New York
            1963, 211p, Cloth, Coll.
00518   *Monster mix; 13 chilling tales.* Dell, New York
            1968, 284p, Paper, Anth.
00519   *Thrillers and more thrillers.* Windward Books,
            New York, 1968, 208p, Paper, Anth.

as ghost editor for Alfred Hitchcock:

00520   *Alfred Hitchcock presents: stories not for
            the nervous.* Random House, New York, 1965,
            363p, Cloth, Anth.
00520A retitled: *Alfred Hitchcock presents: more
            stories not for the nervous.* Dell, New York,
            1967, 188p, Paper, Anth. [abridged]

as ghost editor with Thomas Disch for Alfred
Hitchcock:

00521   *Alfred Hitchcock presents: stories that
            scared even me.* Random House, New York,
            1967, 463p, Cloth, Anth.

ARTHUR, RUTH (Mabel), 1905-   [*biography included*]

00522   *The Autumn People.* Atheneum, New York, 1973,
            167p, Cloth, Novel
00523   *A candle in her room.* Atheneum, New York,
            1966, 212p, Cloth, Novel
00524   *Dragon summer.* Hutchinson, London, 1962, 106p,
            Cloth, Novel
00525   *The Saracen lamp.* Victor Gollancz, London,
            1970, 210p, Cloth, Novel
00526   *The whistling boy.* Atheneum, New York, 1969,
            201p, Cloth, Novel

ARTHUR, WALLACE

00527   *The diabolists.* Midwood Private Library Edi-
            tions, New York, 1970, 202p, Paper, Novel

ARTHUR, WILLIAM

00528 *Heroneous in 69.* Greenleaf Classics, San
       Diego, 1970, 176p, Paper, Novel

ARVONEN, HELEN
    see: WORTH, MARGARET

ASBELL, BERNARD
    see: MAX, NICHOLAS

ASBURY, HERBERT, 1891-1963

00529 *The devil of Pei-Ling.* Macy-Massius, New York,
       1927, 284p, Cloth, Novel
00529A retitled: *The crimson rope.* Jarrolds, London,
       1928, 287p, Cloth, Novel
00530 *Not at night!* Macy-Massius, The Vanguard
       Press, 1928, 386p, Cloth, Anth.

ASCHER, EUGENE

00531 *The grim caretaker.* Strothers Bookshops, Lon-
       don, 1944, 50p, Paper, Novel [Lucian Carolus
       series]
00532 *There were no Asper ladies.* Mitre Press, Lon-
       don, 1944, 126p, Paper, Novel [Lucian Caro-
       lus series]
00532A retitled: *To kill a corpse.* World Distribu-
       tors, Manchester, 1959, 160p, Paper, Novel
       [Lucian Carolus series]
00533 *Uncanny adventures; 5 strange thrillers.*
       Everybody's Books, London, 1944, 48p, Paper,
       Coll.

ASH, ALAN

00534 *Conditioned for space.* Ward, Lock, London,
       1955, 192p, Cloth, Novel

ASH, CAY VAN
    see: VAN ASH, CAY

ASH, FENTON, pseud.
    see: AUBREY, FRANK

ASHBEE, C(harles) R(obert), 1863-1942

00535 *The building of Thelema.* J. M. Dent & Sons,
       London, 1910, 361p, Cloth, Novel

ASHBY, R(ubie) C(onstance), 1899-

00536 *Out went the taper.* Macmillan Co., New York,
       1934, 320p, Cloth, Novel; Hodder & Stough-
       ton, London, 1934, 320p, Cloth, Novel

ASHBY, RICHARD

00537 *Act of God.* Leisure Books, North Hollywood,
       1971, 158p, Paper, Novel

ASHE, GEOFFREY (Thomas), 1923-

00538 *The finger and the Moon.* Heinemann, London,
       1973, 262p, Cloth, Novel

ASHLEY, ARTHUR ERNEST
    see: VIVIAN, FRANCIS

ASHLEY, FRED, pseud.
    see: AUBREY, FRANK

ASHLEY, MICHAEL (Raymond Donald), 1948-

00539 *The history of the science fiction magazine,
       part 1, 1926-1935.* New English Library,
       London, 1974, 239p, Cloth, Anth. [includes
       some nonf.]

ASHLEY-BROWN, W(illiam), 1887-1970

00540 *Zaudi (Princess of Abyssinia).* Hutchinson,
       London, 1936, 288p, Cloth, Novel

ASHTON, FRANCIS (Leslie), 1904-

00541 *Alas, that great city.* Andrew Dakers, London,
       1948, 395p, Cloth, Novel
00542 *The breaking of the seals.* Andrew Dakers, Lon-
       don, 1946, 317p, Cloth, Novel

  with Stephen Ashton:

00543 *Wrong side of the Moon.* T. V. Boardman, London,
       1952, 191p, Cloth, Novel

ASHTON, HELEN (Rosaline), 1891-1958

00544 *Belinda Grove.* Victor Gollancz, London, 1932,
       288p, Cloth, Novel

ASHTON, MARVIN, pseud.

00545 *People of Asa.* Curtis Warren, London, 1953,
       159p, Cloth, Novel

ASHTON, ROSABEL H.

00546 *Magog of Arana.* Vantage Press, New York, 1969,
       230p, Cloth, Novel

ASHTON, STEPHEN, with Francis Ashton

00543 *Wrong side of the Moon.* T. V. Boardman, London,
       1952, 191p, Cloth, Novel

ASHTON, WINIFRED
    see: DANE, CLEMENCE

ASHTON-GWATKIN, FRANK
    see: PARIS, JOHN

ASIMOV, ISAAC, 1920-   [biography included]

00547 *Asimov's mysteries.* Doubleday, Garden City, 1968, 228p, Cloth, Coll.

00548 *Before the golden age; a science fiction anthology of the 1930s.* Doubleday, Garden City, 1974, 986p, Cloth, Anth.

00549 *The best of Isaac Asimov.* Sidgwick & Jackson, London, 1973, 336p, Cloth, Coll.

The big sun of Mercury. [see 00584A]

00550 *The caves of steel.* Doubleday, Garden City, 1954, 224p, Cloth, Novel [Lije Baley #1]

00551 *The currents of space.* Doubleday, Garden City, 1952, 217p, Cloth, Novel [Trantorian Empire sequence]

00552 *The early Asimov; or, Eleven years of trying.* Doubleday, Garden City, 1972, 540p, Cloth, Coll.

00552A retitled: *The early Asimov, book one.* Fawcett Crest, Greenwich, 1974, 302p, Paper, Coll. [abridged]

00552B retitled: *The early Asimov, book two.* Fawcett Crest, Greenwich, 1974, 304p, Paper, Coll. [abridged]

00552C retitled: *The early Asimov; or, Eleven years of trying, volume 1.* Panther, St. Albans, 1973, 188p, Paper, Coll. [abridged]

00552D retitled: *The early Asimov; or, Eleven years of trying, volume 2.* Panther, St. Albans, 1974, 237p, Paper, Coll. [abridged]

00552E retitled: *The early Asimov; or, Eleven years of trying, volume 3.* Panther, St. Albans, 1974, 192p, Paper, Coll. [abridged] [00552A and 00552B together constitute the original volume, as do 00552C, 00552D, and 00553E together]

00553 *Earth is room enough; science fiction tales of our own planet.* Doubleday, Garden City, 1957, 192p, Cloth, Coll.

Eight stories from The rest of the robots. [see 00573A]

00554 *The end of eternity.* Doubleday, Garden City, 1955, 191p, Cloth, Novel

00555 *Fantastic voyage; a novel.* Houghton Mifflin, Boston, 1966, 239p, Cloth, Novel

00556 *Foundation.* Gnome Press, New York, 1951, 255p, Cloth, Novel [Foundation Trilogy #1]

00556A retitled: *The 1,000 year plan.* Ace Double, New York, 1955, 160p, Paper, Novel [abridged]

00557 *Foundation and empire.* Gnome Press, New York, 1952, 247p, Cloth, Novel [Foundation Trilogy #2]

00557A retitled: *The man who upset the universe.* Ace, New York, 1955, 254p, Paper, Novel [Foundation Trilogy #2]

00558 *The Foundation Trilogy; three classics of science fiction.* Doubleday, Garden City, 1963, 679p, Cloth, Coll. [Foundation Trilogy #s 1-3]

00558A retitled: *An Isaac Asimov omnibus.* Sidgwick & Jackson, London, 1966, 548p, Cloth, Coll. [Foundation Trilogy #s 1-3]

00559 *The gods themselves.* Doubleday, Garden City, 1972, 288p, Cloth, Novel

00560 *Have you seen these?* NESFA Press (A Boskone Book), Boston, 1974, 94p, Cloth, Coll.

00561 *The Hugo winners.* Doubleday, Garden City, 1962, 318p, Cloth, Anth.

00562 *The Hugo winners, volume 2.* Doubleday, Garden City, 1971, 654p, Cloth, Anth.

00562A retitled: *More stories from The Hugo winners, volume II.* Fawcett Crest, Greenwich, 1973, 320p, Paper, Anth. [abridged]

00562B retitled: *Stories from The Hugo winners, volume 2.* Fawcett Crest, Greenwich, 1973, 320p, Paper, Anth. [abridged]

00562C retitled: *The Hugo winners, volume one, 1963-1967.* Sphere, London, 1973, 363p, Paper, Anth. [abridged]

00562D retitled: *The Hugo winners, volume two, 1968-1970.* Sphere, London, 1973, 365p, Paper, Anth. [abridged] [00562A and 00562B together constitute the original volume, as do 00562C and 00562D together]

00563 *The Hugo winners, volumes one and two.* Nelson Doubleday, Garden City, 1972, 849p, Cloth, Anth. [includes 00561 and 00562]

00564 *I, robot.* Gnome Press, New York, 1950, 253p, Cloth, Coll. [Robot series]

00565 *An Isaac Asimov double; Space ranger; Pirates of the asteroids.* New English Library, London, 1972, 286p, Cloth, Coll. [Lucky Starr #s 1-2]

An Isaac Asimov omnibus. [see 00558A]

An Isaac Asimov second omnibus. [see 00581A]

The man who upset the universe. [see 00557A]

00566 *The Martian way, and other stories.* Doubleday, Garden City, 1955, 222p, Cloth, Coll.

The moons of Jupiter. [see 00585A]

More stories from The Hugo winners, volume II. [see 00562A]

00567 *The naked sun.* Doubleday, Garden City, 1957, 187p, Cloth, Novel [Lije Baley #2]

00568 *Nebula award stories eight.* Harper & Row, New York, 1973, 248p, Cloth, Anth.

00569 *Nightfall, and other stories.* Doubleday, Garden City, 1969, 343p, Cloth, Coll.

00569A retitled: *Nightfall one; science fiction stories.* Panther, London, 1971, 176p, Paper, Coll. [abridged]

00569B retitled: *Nightfall two; science fiction stories.* Panther, London, 1971, 192p, Paper, Coll. [abridged] [00569A and 00569B together constitute the original volume]

00570 *Nine tomorrows; tales of the near future.* Doubleday, Garden City, 1959, 236p, Cloth, Coll.

The oceans of Venus. [see 00586A]

The 1,000 year plan. [see 00556A]

00571 *Opus 100.* Houghton Mifflin, Boston, 1969, 318p, Cloth, Coll.

00572 *Pebble in the sky.* Doubleday, Garden City, 1950, 223p, Cloth, Novel [Trantorian Empire sequence]

Pirates of the asteroids. [see 00587A]

The rebellious stars. [see 00577A]

00573 *The rest of the robots.* Doubleday, Garden City 1964, 556p, Cloth, Coll. [Robot series] [includes 00550, 00567, and misc. stories]

00573A retitled: *Eight stories from The rest of the robots.* Pyramid, New York, 1966, 159p, Paper, Coll. [Robot series] [excludes the two novels]

The rings of Saturn. [see 00588A]

00574 *The robot novels; The caves of steel; The naked sun.* Doubleday, Garden City, 1972, 404p, Cloth, Coll. [Lije Baley #s 1-2; Robot series]

00575 *Second Foundation.* Gnome Press, New York, 1953, 210p, Cloth, Novel [Foundation Trilogy #3]

00575A retitled: *2nd Foundation: galactic empire.* Avon, New York, 1958, 192p, Paper, Novel [Foundation Trilogy #3]

00576 *A second Isaac Asimov double; The big sun of Mercury; The oceans of Venus.* New English Library, London, 1973, 281p, Cloth, Coll. [Lucky Starr #s 3-4]

ASIMOV, ISAAC (cont.)

    Space ranger. [see 00583A]
00577 *The stars, like dust.* Doubleday, Garden City,
      1951, 218p, Cloth, Novel [Trantorian Empire
      sequence]
00577A retitled: *The rebellious stars.* Ace Double,
      New York, 1954, 176p, Paper, Novel [Trantor-
      ian Empire sequence]
      Stories from The Hugo winners, volume 2. [see
      00562B]
00578 *The third Isaac Asimov double; The rings of
      Saturn; The moons of Jupiter.* New English
      Library, London, 1973, 286p, Cloth, Coll.
      [Lucky Starr #s 5-6]
00579 *Through a glass, clearly.* 4 Square Books, Lon-
      don, 1967, 124p, Paper, Coll.
00580 *Tomorrow's children.* Doubleday, Garden City,
      1966, 431p, Cloth, Anth.
00581 *Triangle; The currents of space; Pebble in
      the sky; The stars, like dust.* Doubleday,
      Garden City, 1961, 516p, Cloth, Anth. [Tran-
      torian Empire sequence]
00581A retitled: *An Isaac Asimov second omnibus.*
      Sidgwick & Jackson, London, 1969, 516p,
      Cloth, Coll. [Trantorian Empire sequence]
00582 *Where do we go from here?* Doubleday, Garden
      City, 1971, 441p, Cloth, Anth.
00582A retitled: *Where do we go from here? book 1.*
      Sphere, London, 1974, 192p, Paper, Anth.
      [abridged]
00582B retitled: *Where do we go from here? book 2.*
      Sphere, London, 1974, 200p, Paper, Anth.
      [abridged] [00582A and 00582B together con-
      stitute the original volume]

as Paul French:

00583 *David Starr, Space Ranger.* Doubleday, Garden
      City, 1952, 186p, Cloth, Novel [Lucky Starr
      #1]
00583A retitled: *Space Ranger,* by Isaac Asimov.
      New English Library, London, 1973, 144p,
      Paper, Novel [Lucky Starr #1]
00584 *Lucky Starr and the big sun of Mercury.*
      Doubleday, Garden City, 1956, 191p, Cloth,
      Novel [Lucky Starr #4]
00584A retitled: *The big sun of Mercury,* by Isaac
      Asimov. New English Library, London, 1974,
      143p, Paper, Novel [Lucky Starr #4]
00585 *Lucky Starr and the moons of Jupiter.* Double-
      day, Garden City, 1957, 192p, Cloth, Novel
      [Lucky Starr #5]
00585A retitled: *The moons of Jupiter,* by Isaac
      Asimov. New English Library, London, 1974,
      142p, Paper, Novel [Lucky Starr #5]
00586 *Lucky Starr and the oceans of Venus.* Double-
      day, Garden City, 1954, 186p, Cloth, Novel
      [Lucky Starr #3]
00586A retitled: *The oceans of Venus,* by Isaac Asi-
      mov. New English Library, London, 1974,
      142p, Paper, Novel [Lucky Starr #3]
00587 *Lucky Starr and the pirates of the asteroids.*
      Doubleday, Garden City, 1953, 188p, Cloth,
      Novel [Lucky Starr #2]
00587A retitled: *Pirates of the asteroids,* by Isaac
      Asimov. New English Library, London, 1973,
      144p, Paper, Novel [Lucky Starr #2]
00588 *Lucky Starr and the rings of Saturn.* Double-
      day, Garden City, 1958, 179p, Cloth, Novel
      [Lucky Starr #6]
00588A retitled: *The rings of Saturn,* by Isaac Asi-
      mov. New English Library, London, 1974,
      144p, Paper, Novel [Lucky Starr #6]

with Groff Conklin:

00589 *Fifty short science fiction tales.* Collier,
      New York, 1963, 287p, Paper, Anth.

ASKHAM, FRANCIS, pseud. [Julia Eileen Courtney
Greenwood, 1910-   ]

00590 *The heart consumed; a novel.* John Lane, The
      Bodley Head, London, 1944, 234p, Cloth, Novel

ASPETO, M.

00591 *The misbound volumes; a story of incredibili-
      ties, with a very good moral.* Drane's,
      London, 1924, 301p, Cloth, Novel

ASQUITH, Lady CYNTHIA (Mary Evelyn Charteris),
1887-1960

00592 *The black cap; new stories of murder and mys-
      tery.* Hutchinson, London, 1927, 318p, Cloth,
      Anth.
      A book of modern ghosts. [see 00594A]
00593 *The ghost book; sixteen new stories of the un-
      canny.* Hutchinson, London, 1926, 318p, Cloth,
      Anth.
00594 *The second ghost book.* James Barrie, London,
      1952, 236p, Cloth, Anth.
00594A retitled: *A book of modern ghosts.* Charles
      Scribner's Sons, New York, 1953, 236p, Cloth,
      Anth.
00595 *Shudders; a collection of new nightmare tales.*
      Hutchinson, London, 1929, 287p, Cloth, Anth.
00596 *The third ghost book.* James Barrie, London,
      1955, 302p, Cloth, Anth.
00597 *This mortal coil.* Arkham House, Sauk City,
      1947, 245p, Cloth, Coll.
00598 *What dreams may come.* James Barrie, London,
      1951, 255p, Cloth, Coll. [adapted from 00597,
      with two less stories than the American edi-
      tion, plus one story not included therein]
00599 *When churchyards yawn; fifteen new ghost sto-
      ries; a collection of ghost stories.* Hutch-
      inson, London, 1931, 287p, Cloth, Anth.

ASSOLLANT, (Jean Baptiste) ALFRED, 1827-1886

00600 *The fantastic history of the celebrated Pierrot,
      written by the magician Alcofribas, and trans-
      lated from the Sogdian.* Sampson Low, Marston,
      Low & Searle, London, 1875, 262p, Cloth, Novel

* * * *, pseud.
   see: WATSON, HENRY CROCKER MARRIOTT

******, pseud.
   see: MAUDE, F. N.

ASTERLEY, H(ugh) C(ecil)

00601 *Escape to Berkshire; a novel.* Pall Mall Press,
      London, 1961, 247p, Cloth, Novel

ASTON, B(enjamin) G(william)

00602 *The eye of the god.* Blackie & Son, London, 1927, 223p, Cloth, Novel

ASTOR, JOHN JACOB, 1864-1912

00603 *A journey in other worlds; a romance of the future.* D. Appleton, New York, 1894, 476p, Cloth, Novel

ASTOR, WILLIAM WALDORF, 1st Viscount Astor, 1848-1919

00604 *Pharaoh's daughter, and other stories.* Macmillan & Co., Lodnon, 1900, 235p, Cloth, Coll.

ASTRAEA'S RETURN
    see: MERCIER, LOUIS-SEBASTIEN

ASTURIAS, MIGUEL ANGEL, 1899-1974 [*biography included*]

00605 *The mulatta and Mr. Fly; a novel.* Peter Owen, London, 1967, 304p, Cloth, Novel
00605A retitled: *Mulata.* Delacorte Press (A Seymour Lawrence Book), New York, 1967, 307p, Cloth, Novel

AT THE MOUNTAINS OF MURKINESS
    see: LOCKE, GEORGE

ATHANASSIADES, NIKOS [variously Athanasiadēs], 1904-

00606 *A naked girl.* Orion Press, New York, 1968, 217p, Cloth, Novel

ATHELING, WILLIAM Jr., pseud.
    see: BLISH, JAMES

ATHERTON, GERTRUDE (Franklin), 1857-1948

00607 *Black oxen.* Boni & Liveright, New York, 1923, 346p, Cloth, Novel
00608 *Dido, Queen of hearts.* Horace Liveright, New York, 1929, 384p, Cloth, Novel
00609 *The foghorn; stories.* Houghton Mifflin, Boston, 1934, 198p, Cloth, Coll.
00610 *The white morning; a novel of the power of the German women in wartime.* Frederick A. Stokes, New York, 1918, 195p, Cloth, Novel

ATHEY, HENRY, with A. Herbert Bowers

00611 *With gyves of gold; a novel.* G. W. Dillingham, New York, 1898, 274p, Cloth, Novel

ATHOLL, JUSTIN

00612 *The grey beast.* Everybody's Books, London, 1944, 48p, Paper, Coll.

00613 *Land of hidden death.* Everybody's Books, London, 1944, 50p, Paper, Novel
00614 *The man who tilted the Earth.* Mitre Press, London, 1943, 63p, Paper, Novel
00615 *The oasis of sleep.* Mitre Press, London, 1944, 62p, Paper, Novel

ATKEY, BERTRAM

00616 *The escapes of Mr. Honey; an entertainment comprising the curious adventures of an English author in the Gulf of Bygone.* Macdonald, London, 1944, 174p, Cloth, Novel
00617 *Folk of the wild; a book of the forests, the moors, and the mountains, of the beasts of the silent places, their lives, their doings, and their deaths.* E. Grant Richards, London, 1907, 324p, Cloth, Novel
00618 *Hercules--sportsman; an entertainment.* G. Heath Robinson & J. Birch, London, 1922, 253p, Cloth, Novel

ATKINS, FRANK
    see: AUBREY, FRANK

ATKINS, JOHN (Alfred), 1916- [*biography included*]

00619 *Tomorrow revealed.* Neville Spearman, London, 1955, 254p, Cloth, Novel

ATTERLEY, JOSEPH, pseud. [George Tucker, 1775-1861]

00620 *A voyage to the Moon, with some account of the manners and customs, science and philosophy, of the people of Morosofia, and other Lunarians.* Elam Bliss, New York, 1827, 264p, Cloth, Novel

AUBIN, ETIENNE

00621 *Dracula and the virgins of the undead.* New English Library, London, 1974, 124p, Paper, Novel [Dracula series]
00622 *Terror of the seven crypts.* New English Library, London, 1974, 108p, Paper, Novel

AUBREY, FRANK, pseud. [Frank Atkins]

00623 *The devil-tree of El Dorado; a romance of British Guiana.* Hutchinson, London, 1896, 392p, Cloth, Novel [Monella series]
00624 *King of the dead; a weird romance.* John Macqueen, London, 1903, 292p, Cloth, Novel [Monella series]
00625 *A queen of Atlantis; a romance of the Caribbean Sea.* Hutchinson, London, 1899, 391p, Cloth, Novel [Monella series]

as Fenton Ash:

00626 *The black opal; a romance of thrilling adventure.* John F. Shaw, London, 1915, 320p, Cloth, Novel
00627 *By airship to Ophir.* John F. Shaw, London, 1911, 320p, Cloth, Novel

AUBREY, FRANK (cont.)

as Fenton Ash:

00628 *The radium seekers; or, The wonderful black
         nugget.* Sir Isaac Pitman & Sons, London,
         1905, 348p, Cloth, Novel

00629 *A trip to Mars.* W. & R. Chambers, London,
         1909, 318p, Cloth, Novel

as Fred Ashley:

00630 *The temple of fire; or, The mysterious island;
         a romance of the southern seas.* Sir Isaac
         Pitman & Sons, London, 1905, 332p, Cloth,
         Novel

AUCTOR IGNOTUS, pseud. [?W. Dorr Legg?]

00631 *AE: the open persuader.* One Inc., Los An-
         geles, 1969, 283p, Cloth, Novel

AUDEN, RENEE

00632 *High thrust.* Olympia Press, New York, 1971,
         170p, Paper, Novel

AUGUST, LEO, pseud. [Don Segall]

00633 *Superdoll.* Award, New York, 1969, 152p, Paper,
         Novel

AUGUSTINUS, pseud.

00634 *Paul Rees; a story of the coming reformation.*
         Simpkin, Marshall, Hamilton, Kent, London,
         1899, 126p, Cloth, Novel

00635 *Two brothers; a story of the twentieth century.*
         Chapple & Kemp, Cardiff, 1898, 88p, Paper?,
         Novel

AUGUSTUS, ALBERT JR.
     see: NUETZEL, CHARLES

AUREVILLY, J. BARBEY d'
     see: BARBEY d'AUREVILLY, J.

AUSTIN, ALEX

00636 *The greatest lover in the world.* Rinehart,
         New York, 1956, 278p, Cloth, Novel

AUSTIN, B(enjamin) F(ish), 1850-1932

00637 *Christ or Barabbas; a psychic novel.* Austin
         Publishing Co., Los Angeles, 1921, 142p,
         Paper, Novel

AUSTIN, F(rederick) BRITTEN, 1885-1941

00638 *On the borderland.* Hurst & Blackett, London,
         1922, 279p, Cloth, Coll.

00639 *The war god walks again.* Doubleday, Page,
         Garden City, 1926, 274p, Cloth, Novel; Wil-
         liams & Norgate, London, 1926, 247p, Cloth,
         Coll.

00640 *When mankind was young.* Doubleday, Page, Gar-
         den City, 1927, 282p, Cloth, Coll.

AUSTIN, JANE G(oodwin), 1831-1894

00641 *Moonfolk; a true account of the home of the
         fairy tales.* G. P. Putnam's Sons, New York,
         1874, 205p, Cloth, Novel

AUSTIN, MARY (Hunter), 1868-1934

as Gordon Stairs:

00642 *Outland.* John Murray, London, 1910, 311p,
         Cloth, Novel

as Mary Austin:

00642A *Outland.* Boni & Liveright, New York, 1919,
         306p, Cloth, Novel

AUSTIN, WILLIAM, 1778-1841

00643 *Peter Rugg, the missing man.* F. P. Rice,
         Worcester, Mass., 1882, 64p, Cloth, Novel

AUTHOR OF "A LITTLE PILGRIM" AND "OLD LADY MARY"
     see: OLIPHANT, MRS.(Margaret)

AUTHOR OF "A NEW MARGUERITE," pseud.

00644 *Lotus; a psychological romance.* George Redway,
         London, 1888, 265p, Cloth, Novel

AUTHOR OF "A TIME OF TERROR"
     see: FORD, D. M.

AUTHOR OF "A TRAP TO CATCH A SUNBEAM"
     see: MACKARNESS, M. A.

AUTHOR OF "ADA, THE BETRAYED," "JANE BRIGHT-
WELL," ETC.
     see: RYMER, JAMES MALCOLM

AUTHOR OF "ANNALS OF THE PARISH," "A RINGAN
GILHAIZE," ETC.
     see: GALT, JOHN

AUTHOR OF "ATLANTIS," pseud.

00645 *The emigrants; or, The Island of Esmeralda*, by
         the author of 'Atlantis.' bound with: *The
         Island of Atlantis; a personal narrative of
         the travels and wonderful adventures of Lord
         Arthur A.....y, of Phantom Castle, Ben Nevis.*
         no publisher, London?, 1879/1871, 64p + 59p,
         Cloth, Coll. [*The emigrants* is not SF]

00646 *The Island of Atlantis; a personal narrative
         of the travels and wonderful adventures of
         Lord Arthur A.....y, of Phantom Castle, Ben
         Nevis.* no publisher, London?, 1871, 59p,
         Cloth, Novel [issued anonymously]

AUTHOR OF "BERTRAM, A TRAGEDY," "WOMAN; OR, POUR ET CONTES," ETC.
     see: MATURIN, CHARLES R.

AUTHOR OF DARNLEY
     see: JAMES, G. P. R.

AUTHOR OF DELIA, ROSINA, AND THE SUBTERRANEAN CAVERN
     see: PILKINGTON, MARY

AUTHOR OF FAIR DIANA
     see: WANDERER

AUTHOR OF FRANKENSTEIN
     see: SHELLEY, MARY WOLLSTONECRAFT

AUTHOR OF "FRIENDS IN COUNCIL"
     see: HELPS, ARTHUR

AUTHOR OF GIL BLAS OF SANTILLANE
     see: LE SAGE, ALAIN RENE

AUTHOR OF "GRACE RIVERS; OR, THE MERCHANT'S DAUGHTER"
     see: VARNEY THE VAMPIRE

AUTHOR OF HE
     see: DE MORGAN, JOHN

AUTHOR OF IT, KING SOLOMON'S WIVES, BESS
     see: LANG, ANDREW and POLLOCK, WALTER HERRIES

AUTHOR OF "JANE EYRE"
     see: BRONTE, EMILY

AUTHOR OF "JEWEL SOWERS"
     see: ALLONBY, EDITH

AUTHOR OF "JOHN HALIFAX, GENTLEMAN"
     see: CRAIK, D. M.

AUTHOR OF KILKHAMPTON ABBEY
     see: CROFT, SIR HERBERT

AUTHOR OF KING SOLOMON'S WIVES
     see: DE MORGAN, JOHN

AUTHOR OF "MEPHISTOPHELES IN LONDON"
     see: WILLIAMS, ROBERT FOLKESTONE

AUTHOR OF MIDNIGHT HORRORS, FEMALE PILGRIM, ETC.

00647   *Midnight horrors; or, The bandit's daughter; an original romance.* W. Borradaile, New York, 1823, 45p, Paper, Story [anonymous]

00648   *The spectre mother; or, The haunted tower,* by the author of Midnight horrors, Female pilgrim, &c. W. Borradaile, New York, 1823, 23p, Paper, Story

AUTHOR OF "MISS MOLLY"

00649   *The laws of Leflo.* John Ouseley, London, 1911, 181p, Cloth, Novel

AUTHOR OF "NIGHT AND MORNING," "RIENZI," ETC.
     see: LYTTON, EDWARD BULWER

AN AUTHOR OF OUR NEIGHBORHOOD
     see: GRIFFITH, MARY

AUTHOR OF 'POST MORTEM'
     see: BROOKFIELD, ARTHUR MONTAGU

AUTHOR OF 'RAMESES'
     see: UPHAM, EDWARD

AUTHOR OF "RIENZI"
     see: LYTTON, EDWARD BULWER

AUTHOR OF "SPACE AND SPIRIT"
     see: KENNEDY, R. A.

AUTHOR OF "THE ADVENTURE OF JOHN JOHNS"
     see: CARREL, FREDERIC

AUTHOR OF "THE ADVENTURES OF UNCLE JEREMIAH AND FAMILY AT THE GREAT FAIR"
     see: QUONDAM

AUTHOR OF 'THE BATTLE OF DORKING'
     see: CHESNEY, GEORGE T.

AUTHOR OF "THE DANCING IMPS OF THE WINE"
     see: ANGELO

AUTHOR OF THE LAST MAN
     see: SHELLEY, MARY WOLLSTONECRAFT

AUTHOR OF "THE REALM OF THE ICE KING"

00650   *The North Pole, and Charlie Wilson's adventures in search of it.* Griffith Farran Browne, London, 1875, 284p, Cloth, Novel

AUTHOR OF THE TRUE-BORN ENGLISH MAN
     see: DEFOE, DANIEL

AUTHOR OF "THE TRUTH ABOUT MAN" ["Spinster"]

00651   *Star of the morning; a chronicle of Karyl the Great and the revolt of 1920-22.* Thomas Burleigh, London, 1906, 242p, Cloth, Novel

AUTHOR OF "THE WHITE SLAVE," "REVELATIONS OF RUSSIA," "EASTERN EUROPE AND THE EMPEROR NICHOLAS"
    see: HENNINGSEN, CHARLES FREDERICK

AUTHOR OF THE WILD IRISH BOY
    see: MATURIN, CHARLES ROBERT

AUTHOR OF "THOTH"
    see: NICHOLSON, JOSEPH SHIELD

AUTHOR OF "WAS SHE ENGAGED?"
    see: "JONQUIL"

AUTHOR OF "WORLDS DISPLAYED"
    see: CAMPBELL, JOHN

AUTHORS' CHOICE

    00652 *Authors' choice 2; stories.* Hamish Hamilton, London, 1973, 246p, Cloth, Anth.

AUTHORS OF "READY-MONEY MORTIBOY"
    see: RICE, JAMES and BESANT, WALTER

AUTOBIOGRAPHY

    00653 *The autobiography of a flea.* Erotica Biblion Society of London and New York, London, 1901, 274p, Cloth, Novel [first edition actually published in 1789?]
    00654 *Autobiography of a flea, book two.* Pendulum, Atlanta, 1968, 240p, Paper, Novel
    00655 *Autobiography of a louse.* Tower Books, New York, 1967, 170p, Paper, Novel [The relationship between 00653, 00654, 00655, and others of a similar nature is unclear, although it is apparent that some of these books are modern imitations of an older erotic classic that may date to either the eighteenth or nineteenth century.]

AUTOBIOGRAPHY OF A LOUSE, VOL. III
    see: ANONYMOUS

AUTOMATHES
    see: KIRKBY, JOHN

AUZIAS-TURENNE, RAYMOND, 1861-

    00656 *The last of the mammoths.* Chatto & Windus, London, 1907, 307p, Cloth, Novel

AVALLONE, MICHAEL (Angelo Jr.), 1924-   [biography included]

    00657 *Beneath the planet of the apes; a novel.* Bantam, New York, 1970, 134p, Paper, Movie [Planet of the Apes movie #2]
    00658 *The girl from U.N.C.L.E.; the birds-of-a-feather affair.* Signet, New York, 1966, 128p, Paper, Tele. [Girl from U.N.C.L.E. #1 (British series #2)]

    00659 *The girl from U.N.C.L.E.; the blazing affair.* Signet, New York, 1966, 127p, Paper, Tele. [Girl from U.N.C.L.E. #2]
    00660 *The man from Avon.* Avon, New York, 1967, 127p, Paper, Novel
    00661 *The man from U.N.C.L.E.* [internally: *The thousand coffins affair*]. Ace, New York, 1965, 160p, Paper, Tele. [Man from U.N.C.L.E. #1]
    00662 *Missing!* Signet, New York, 1969, 160p, Paper, Novel
    00663 *Tales of the frightened.* Belmont, New York, 1963, 128p, Paper, Coll.
    00663A retitled: *Boris Karloff presents Tales of the frightened.* Pyramid, New York, 1973, 124p, Paper, Coll.

as Troy Conway, house pseud.:

    00664 *Coxeman #12; had any lately?* Paperback Library, New York, 1969, 160p, Paper, Novel [Coxeman #12]
    00665 *Coxeman #17; the big broad jump.* Paperback Library, New York, 1968, 158p, Paper, Novel [Coxeman #17]
    00666 *Coxeman #19; the blow-your-mind job; an adult novel.* Paperback Library, New York, 1970, 157p, Paper, Novel [Coxeman #19]
    00667 *Coxeman #20; the cunning linguist; an adult novel.* Paperback Library, New York, 1970, 158p, Paper, Novel [Coxeman #20]
    00668 *Coxeman #28; a stiff proposition.* Paperback Library, New York, 1971, 159p, Paper, Novel [Coxeman #28]

as Edwina Noone:

    00669 *The Craghold creatures.* Beagle, New York, 1972, 149p, Paper, Novel [Craghold #3]
    00670 *The Craghold crypt.* Curtis, New York, 1973, , Paper, Novel [Craghold #4]
    00671 *The Craghold curse.* Beagle, New York, 1972, 152p, Paper, Novel [Craghold #2]
    00672 *The Craghold legacy.* Beagle, New York, 1971, 146p, Paper, Novel [Craghold #1]

as Sidney Stuart:

    00673 *The beast with the red hands.* Popular Library, New York, 1973, 192p, Paper, Novel
    00674 *The night walker.* Award, New York, 1964, 139p, Paper, Movie

AVICE, CLAUDE-PIERRE
    see: BARBET, PIERRE

AVIGDOR, ELIM HENRY D'
    see: WANDERER

AVON GHOST READER
    see: WILLIAMS, HERBERT

AYCOCK, ROGER D.
    see: DEE, ROGER

AYLESWORTH, JOHN (B.), 1938-   [*biography included*]

    00675 *Fee, fei, fo, fum.* Avon, New York, 1963, 158p, Paper, Novel

AYLESWORTH, THOMAS G(ibbons), 1927-   [biography included]

00676   *Monsters from the movies.* J. B. Lippincott, Philadelphia, 1972, 160p, Cloth, Nonf.

AYMÉ, MARCEL (André), 1902-1967

00677   *Across Paris, and other stories.* Bodley Head, London, 1957, 254p, Cloth, Coll.
00677A retitled: *The walker-through-walls.* Berkley Medallion, New York, 1962, 191p, Paper, Coll.
00678   *The fable and the flesh.* Bodley Head, London, 1949, 232p, Cloth, Novel
00679   *The green mare.* Fortune Press, London, 1938, 234p, Cloth, Novel
        The magic pictures. [see 00680A]
00680   *Return to the wonderful farm.* Bodley Head, London, 1954, 160p, Cloth, Novel [Wonderful Farm #2]
00680A retitled: *The magic pictures; more about the wonderful farm.* Harper & Bros, New York, 1954, 117p, Cloth, Novel [Wonderful Farm #2]
00681   *The second face.* Bodley Head, London, 1951, 192p, Cloth, Novel
        The walker-through-walls. [see 00677A]
00682   *The wonderful farm.* Harper & Bros., New York, 1951, 182p, Cloth, Novel [Wonderful Farm #1]

AYRTON, MICHAEL, 1921-1975

00683   *The Maze Maker; a novel.* Longmans, London, 1967, 282p, Cloth, Novel
00684   *Tittivulus; or, The verbiage collector.* Max Reinhardt, London, 1953, 138p, Cloth, Novel

B., A. G. F.

00685   *Plus encore d'Angleterre; or, The repulse of the French; a reply to "Plus d'Angleterre; or, The downfall of England."* J. W. Arrowsmith, Bristol, 1888, 16p, Paper, Story [Angleterre #2]

B., B., pseud. [Denys James Watkins-Pitchford, 1905-   ] [biography included]

00686   *The little grey men.* Eyre & Spottiswoode, London, 1947, 188p, Cloth, Novel

B., K.

00687   *Say not good-night.* Peter Davies, London, 1936, 277p, Cloth, Novel

BABCOCK, GEORGE

00688   *Yezad; a romance of the unknown.* Co-operative Publishing Co., Bridgeport, 1922, 463p, Cloth, Novel

BABCOCK, WILLIAM HENRY, 1849-1922

00689   *The brides of the tiger; a tale of adventure when these colonies were new.* Merrill, Higgins, Chicago, 1892, 218p, Cloth, Novel

00690   expanded: *The Tower of Wye; a romance.* Henry T. Coates, Philadelphia, 1901, 330p, Cloth, Novel

BABER, ASA, 1936-   [biography included]

00691   *The land of a million elephants.* William Morrow, New York, 1970, 153p, Cloth, Novel

BACH, RICHARD (David), 1936-   [biography]

00692   *Jonathan Livingston Seagull.* Macmillan, New York, 1970, 93p, Cloth, Novel

BACHELDER, JOHN

00693   *A.D. 2050; electrical development at Atlantis,* by A former resident of "The Hub." Bancroft Company, San Francisco, 1890, 83p, Cloth, Novel

BACHELLER, IRVING (Addison), 1859-1950

00694   *The master of silence; a romance.* Charles L. Webster, New York, 1892, 176p, Cloth, Novel

BACHELOR, GEORGE C.

00695   *Uncanny.* Mitre Press, London, 1945, 32p, Paper, Coll.

BACK AGAIN

00696   *Back again; or, Five years of liberal rule, 1880-5; a forecast.* Sampson Low, Marston, 1880, 32p, Paper, Story

BACON, JOSEPHINE (Dodge) DASKAM, 1876-1961

00697   *Medusa's head.* D. Appleton, New York, 1926, 121p, Cloth, Novel
00698   *The strange cases of Dr. Stanchon.* D. Appleton, New York, 1913, 362p, Cloth, Coll.

BACON, MARTHA (Sherman), 1917-

00699   *The third road.* Little, Brown, Boston, 1971, 188p, Cloth, Novel

BACON, PEGGY, 1895-

00700   *The ghost of Opalina; or, Nine lives.* Little, Brown, Boston, 1967, 243p, Cloth, Novel

BACON, WALTER

00701   *The last experiment.* Robert Hale, London, 1974, 188p, Cloth, Novel

BADGER, JOSEPH E(dward) Jr., 1848-1909

00702   *The Lost City.* Dana Estes, Boston, 1898, 326p, Cloth, Novel

BAERLEIN, ANTHONY

00703 *Daze, the magician.* Arthur Barker, London, 1936, 218p, Cloth, Novel

BAGLEY, JOHN

00704 *Wasp-waisted Arabella.* Herbert Jenkins, London, 1936, 314p, Cloth, Novel

BAGNALL-STUBBS, JAMES

00705 *The order of Isis; a story of mystery and adventure in Egypt.* Skeffington & Son, London, 1900, 302p, Cloth, Novel

BAHNSON, AGNEW H(unter) Jr., 1915-1964?

00706 *The stars are too high.* Random House, New York, 1959, 250p, Cloth, Novel

BAILEY, ANDREW J(ackson), 1840-1927

00707 *The Martian Emperor-President.* William James Ray, Walsall, UK, 1932, 262p, Cloth, Novel

BAILEY, CHARLES W(aldo) II, 1929-   , with Fletcher Knebel [*biography included*]

00708 *Seven days in May.* Harper & Row, New York, 1962, 342p, Cloth, Novel

BAILEY, HILARY, 1936-   , with Charles Platt

00709 *New worlds 7.* Sphere, London, 1974, 213p, Paper, Anth.

BAILEY, J(ames) O(sler), 1903-   [*biography included*]

00710 *Pilgrims through time and space; trends and patterns in scientific and utopian fiction.* Argus Books, New York, 1947, 341p, Cloth, Nonf.

BAILEY, PAUL (Dayton), 1906-   [*biography included*]

00711 *Deliver me from Eva.* Murray & Gee, Hollywood, 1946, 237p, Cloth, Novel

BAILEY, THOMAS, pseud. [Edward Bellamy Partridge, 1877-1960]

00712 *Long night.* Godwin Publishers, New York, 1935, 287p, Cloth, Novel

BAILLIE-SAUNDERS, MARGARET (Elsie), 1873-1949

00713 *The candle virgins.* Hutchinson, London, 1937, 286p, Cloth, Novel

BAIN, F(rancis) W(illiam), 1863-1940

00714 *The ashes of a god.* Methuen, London, 1911, 115p, Cloth, Novel
00715 *Bubbles of the foam.* Methuen, London, 1912, 124p, Cloth, Novel
00716 *The descent of the Sun; a cycle of birth.* James Parker, London, 1903, 109p, Cloth, Novel
00717 *A digit of the Moon; a Hindoo love story.* James Parker, London, 1899, 122p, Cloth, Novel
00718 *A digit of the Moon, and other love stories from the Hindoo.* G. P. Putnam's Sons, New York, 1905, 421p, Cloth, Coll. [includes *A digit of the Moon; A heifer of the dawn; The descent of the Sun; In the great god's hair*]
00719 *A draught of the blue.* James Parker, London, 1905, 87p, Cloth, Novel
00720 *A draught of the blue, together with An essence of the dusk.* G. P. Putnam's Sons, New York, 1907, 245p, Cloth, Coll.
00721 *An essence of the dusk.* James Parker, London, 1906, 88p, Cloth, Novel
00722 *A heifer of the dawn.* James Parker, London, 1904, 75p, Cloth, Novel
00723 *In the great god's hair.* James Parker, London, 1904, 89p, Cloth, Novel
00724 *An incarnation of the snow.* James Parker, Oxford, 1908, 87p, Cloth, Novel
00725 *The livery of Eve.* Methuen, London, 1917, 108p, Cloth, Novel
00726 *A mine of faults.* James Parker, London, 1909, 113p, Cloth, Novel
00727 *The substance of a dream.* Methuen, London, 1919, 150p, Cloth, Novel
00728 *A syrup of the bees.* Methuen, London, 1914, 107p, Cloth, Novel

BAINBRIDGE, OLIVER

00729 *The devil's note book.* Cochrane Publishing Co., New York, 1908, 154p, Cloth, Novel

BAINES, CUTHBERT EDWARD

00730 *The black circle.* Hodder & Stoughton, London, 1921, 316p, Cloth, Novel

BAIR, PATRICK
   see: GURNEY, DAVID

BAIRD, JOHN C(ranmer), 1869-1922

00731 *The traveler and the grapes.* Broadway Publishing Co., New York, 1907, 258p, Cloth, Novel

BAKER, A(rthur) P(onsford)

00732 *A college mystery; the story of the apparition in the Fellows' Garden at Christ's College, Cambridge.* W. Heffer & Sons, Cambridge, 1918, 76p, Cloth, Novel

BAKER, BETTY (Lou), 1928-   [biography inclu-
ded]

00733   Great ghost stories of the old west. Four
        Winds Press, New York, 1968, 126p, Cloth,
        Anth.

BAKER, D. PETERSEN

00734   The apparitional influx. Vantage Press, New
        York, 1974, 91p, Cloth, Novel

BAKER, DENYS VAL, 1917-   [variously cited as:
Val Baker, Denys][biography included]

00735   The face in the mirror. Arkham House, Sauk
        City, 1971, 113p, Cloth, Coll.
00736   Haunted Cornwall; a book of supernatural sto-
        ries. William Kimber, London, 1973, 217p,
        Cloth, Anth.
00737   Worlds without end; a book of short stories.
        Sylvan Press, London, 1945, 168p, Cloth, Coll.

BAKER, EMERSON

00738   When fortune dares; or, Adventures in wild
        places. Street & Smith, New York, 1925,
        , Paper, Novel

BAKER, FRANK (Edgar), 1908-

00739   Before I go hence; fantasia on a novel. Andrew
        Dakers, London, 1946, 233p, Cloth, Novel
00740   The birds. Peter Davies, London, 1936, 246p,
        Cloth, Novel
00741   Miss Hargreaves; a fantasy. Eyre & Spottis-
        woode, London, 1940, 310p, Cloth, Novel
00742   Mr. Allenby loses the way; a novel. Coward-
        McCann, New York, 1945, 262p, Cloth, Novel
00743   Sweet chariot; a romance. Eyre & Spottiswoode,
        London, 1942, 316p, Cloth, Novel

BAKER, G(eorge) P(hilip), 1879-1951

00744   The magic tale of Harvanger and Yolande. Mills
        & Boon, London, 1914, 346p, Cloth, Novel
        [Greenwood #1]
00745   The romance of Palombris and Pallogris (the
        second magic tale). Mills & Boon, London,
        1915, 451p, Cloth, Novel [Greenwood #2]

BAKER, GEORGE
    see: OLEMY, P. T.

BAKER, GEORGE A(ugustus), 1849-1906

00746   Mrs. Hephaestus, and other short stories;
        together with West Point, a comedy in three
        acts. White, Stokes & Allen, New York,
        1887, 211p, Cloth, Coll.

BAKER, GORDON

00747   None so blind. Newman Wolsey, London, 1946,
        207p, Cloth, Novel

BAKER, MARGARET J(oyce), 1918-

00748   The sand bird. Methuen, London, 1973, 156p,
        Cloth, Novel

BAKER, (Robert) MICHAEL (Graham), 1938-   [bio-
graphy included]

00749   The Mountain and the Summer Stars; an old tale
        newly ended. Victor Gollancz, London, 1968,
        96p, Cloth, Novel

BAKER, RUSSELL (Wayne), 1925-   [biography in-
cluded]

00750   Our next president; the incredible story of
        what happened in the 1968 elections. Athene-
        um, New York, 1968, 111p, Cloth, Novel

BAKER, W. HOWARD, pseud. [Wilfred Glassford
McNeilly, 1921-   ] [biography included]

00751   The Guardians. Mayflower, London, 1967, 144p,
        Paper, Novel [Guardians series]

as W. A. Ballinger:

00752   Drums of the dark gods. Mayflower, London,
        1966, 126p, Paper, Novel

as Peter Saxon, house pseud.:

00753   The darkest night. Mayflower, London, 1966,
        157p, Paper, Novel
00754   Satan's child. Mayflower, London, 1967, 127p,
        Paper, Novel
00755   The Torturer. Mayflower, London, 1966, 159p,
        Paper, Novel

BALCHIN, NIGEL (Marlin), 1908-1970

00756   Kings of infinite space. Collins, London,
        1967, 256p, Cloth, Novel

BALDWIN, Mrs. ALFRED [Louisa], 1845-1925

00757   The shadow on the blind, and other ghost sto-
        ries. J. M. Dent & Co., London, 1895, 309p,
        Cloth, Coll.

BALDWIN, BEE

00758   The red dust. Robert Hale, London, 1965, 190p,
        Cloth, Novel

BALDWIN, OLIVER RIDSDALE
    see: HUSSINGTREE, MARTIN

BALINT, EMERY [originally Imre], 1892-

00759   Don't inhale it. Gaer Associates, New York,
        1949, 222p, Cloth, Novel

BALL, BRIAN N(eville), 1932-   [*biography included*]

00760 *Devil's peak.* New English Library, London,
       1972, 156p, Paper, Novel
00761 *Lesson for the damned.* New English Library,
       London, 1971, 127p, Paper, Novel
       The night creature. [see 00771A]
       Night of the robots. [see 00764A]
00762 *Planet probability.* DAW, New York, 1973, 188p,
       Paper, Novel [Frames #2]
00763 *The Probability Man.* DAW, New York, 1972,
       175p, Paper, Novel [Frames #1]
00764 *The Regiments of Night.* DAW, New York, 1972,
       188p, Paper, Novel
00764A retitled: *Night of the robots; science fic-
       tion.* Sidgwick & Jackson, London, 1972,
       235p, Cloth, Novel
00765 *Singularity station.* DAW, New York, 1973,
       176p, Paper, Novel
00766 *Sundog.* Dennis Dobson, London, 1965, 216p,
       Cloth, Novel
00767 *Tales of science fiction.* Hamish Hamilton,
       London, 1964, 159p, Cloth, Anth.
00768 *Timepiece.* Dennis Dobson, London, 1968, 144p,
       Cloth, Novel
00769 *Timepit; a science fiction novel.* Dennis Dob-
       son, London, 1971, 188p, Cloth, Novel
00770 *Timepivot.* Ballantine, New York, 1970, 186p,
       Paper, Novel
00771 *The venomous serpent.* New English Library,
       London, 1974, 126p, Paper, Novel
00771A retitled: *The night creature.* Fawcett Gold
       Medal, Greenwich, 1974, 159p, Paper, Novel

BALL, F(rank) N(orman)

00772 *Metatopia.* Thames Bank Publishing Co., Ips-
       wich, UK, 1961, 244p, Cloth, Novel

BALL, JOHN (Dudley Jr.), 1911-   [*biography
included*]

00773 *The first team; a novel.* Little, Brown, Bos-
       ton, 1971, 422p, Cloth, Novel
00774 *Operation Springboard.* Duell, Sloan & Pearce,
       New York, 1958, 168p, Cloth, Novel
00774A retitled: *Operation Space.* Hutchinson, Lon-
       don, 1960, 208p, Cloth, Novel
00775 *Spacemaster I.* Duell, Sloan & Pearce, New
       York, 1960, 148p, Cloth, Novel

BALL, PATRICIA
    see: SQUIRES, PATRICIA

BALLANTYNE, R(obert) M(ichael), 1825-1894

00776 *The giant of the north; or, Pokings round the
       Pole.* Thomas Nelson, London, 1882, 432p,
       Cloth, Novel

BALLARD, J(ames) G(raham), 1930-   [*biography
included*]

00777 *The atrocity exhibition.* Jonathan Cape, Lon-
       don, 1970, 157p, Cloth, Novel
00777A retitled: *Love and napalm: export, U.S.A.*
       Grove Press, New York, 1972, 156p, Cloth,
       Novel

00778 *Billenium.* Berkley Medallion, New York, 1962,
       159p, Paper, Coll.
00779 *The burning world.* Berkley Medallion, New York,
       1964, 160p, Paper, Novel
00779A retitled: *The drought.* Jonathan Cape, London,
       1965, 252p, Cloth, Novel
00780 *Chronopolis, and other stories.* G. P. Putnam's
       Sons, New York, 1971, 319p, Cloth, Coll.
00781 *The crystal world.* Jonathan Cape, London,
       1966, 221p, Cloth, Novel
00782 *The day of forever.* Panther, London, 1967,
       141p, Paper, Coll.
00783 *The disaster area.* Jonathan Cape, London, 1967,
       206p, Cloth, Coll.
       The drought. [see 00779A]
00784 *The drowned world.* Berkley Medallion, New York,
       1962, 158p, Paper, Novel
00785 *The drowned world; and, The wind from nowhere.*
       Doubleday, Garden City, 1965, 316p, Cloth,
       Coll.
00786 *The four-dimensional nightmare.* Victor Gollancz,
       London, 1963, 208p, Cloth, Coll.
00787 *The impossible man, and other stories.* Berkley
       Medallion, New York, 1966, 160p, Paper, Coll.
       Love and napalm: export, U.S.A. [see 00777A]
00788 *The overloaded man.* Panther, London, 1967,
       158p, Paper, Coll.
00789 *Passport to eternity.* Berkley Medallion, New
       York, 1963, 160p, Paper, Coll.
00790 *Terminal beach.* Berkley Medallion, New York,
       1964, 160p, Paper, Coll.
00791 *The terminal beach.* Victor Gollancz, London,
       1964, 221p, Cloth, Coll. [different from
       00790]
00792 *Vermilion sands.* Berkley Medallion, New York,
       1971, 192p, Paper, Coll.
00793 *The voices of time, and other stories.* Berkley
       Medallion, New York, 1962, 158p, Paper, Coll.
00794 *The wind from nowhere.* Berkley Medallion, New
       York, 1962, 160p, Paper, Novel

BALLINGER, BILL S. [William Sanborn Ballinger,
    1912-   ] [*biography included*]

00795 *The 49 days of death.* Sherbourne Press, Los
       Angeles, 1969, 214p, Cloth, Novel

BALLINGER, W. A., pseud.
    see: BAKER, W. HOWARD

BALLOU, ARTHUR W., 1915-   [*biography included*]

00796 *Bound for Mars.* Little, Brown, Boston, 1970,
       218p, Cloth, Novel [sequel to 00797]
00797 *Marooned in orbit.* Little, Brown, Boston,
       1968, 184p, Cloth, Novel

BALLOU, WILLIAM HOSEA, 1857-1937

00798 *A ride on a cyclone.* Belford, Clarke, Chicago,
       1889, 178p, Cloth, Novel

BALMER, EDWIN, 1883-1959

00799 *Flying Death.* Dodd, Mead, New York, 1927, 198p,
       Cloth, Novel

BALMER, EDWIN (cont.)

with William MacHarg:

00800   *The achievements of Luther Trant.* Small, May-
        nard, Boston, 1910, 365p, Cloth, Novel

with Philip Wylie:

00801   *After worlds collide.* Frederick A. Stokes,
        New York, 1934, 341p, Cloth, Novel [Bronson
        Beta #2]
00802   *When worlds collide.* Frederick A. Stokes, New
        York, 1933, 344p, Cloth, Novel [Bronson Beta
        #1]

BALOGH, BARNARD [variously Bernát]

00803   *The lady of the fjords.* Rider & Co., London,
        1937, 288p, Cloth, Novel

BALSDON, (John Percy Vivian) DACRE, 1901-1977
[*biography included*]

00804   *The day they burned Miss Termag.* Eyre & Spot-
        tiswoode, London, 1961, 251p, Cloth, Novel
00805   *Have a new master.* Eyre & Spottiswoode, Lon-
        don, 1935, 278p, Cloth, Novel
00806   *Sell England?* Eyre & Spottiswoode, London,
        1936, 278p, Cloth, Novel

BALZAC, HONORÉ de, 1799-1850

        The alchemist; or, The house of Claes. [see
        00812B]
        The alkahest; or, The house of Claës. [see
        00812C]
        Balthazar; or, Science and love. [see 00812A]
00807   *Don Juan.* Happy Hour Library, New York, 189?,
        95p, Cloth, Novel
00807A retitled: *Elixir of life.* Macmillan, New York,
        1901, 332p, Cloth, Novel
        The fatal skin. [see 00808D]
        The heartless woman. [see 00808C]
00808   *Luck and leather; a Parisian romance.* Brainerd
        & Co., Boston, 1843, 2vol, Cloth, Novel
00808A retitled: *The magic skin.* Roberts Bros., Bos-
        ton, 1888, 323p, Cloth, Novel
00808B retitled: *The wild ass's skin.* Macmillan,
        New York, 1901, 288p, Cloth, Novel
00808C retitled: *The heartless woman.* Susil Gupta,
        Calcutta, 1945, 203p, Cloth, Novel
00808D retitled: *The fatal skin.* Hamish Hamilton,
        London, 1949, 310p, Cloth, Novel
        The magic skin. [see 00808A]
00809   *The magic skin; Christ in Flanders; Melmoth
        reconciled.* Century Co., New York, 1908,
        344p, Cloth, Coll.
00810   *The magic skin; The hidden masterpiece.* Little,
        Brown, Boston, 1896, 363p, Cloth, Coll.
00811   *The magic skin, The quest of the absolute, and
        other stories.* Dana Estes, Boston, 1901,
        2vol/1, Cloth, Coll.
00812   *The philosopher's stone; a novel.* J. Winches-
        ter, New York, 1844, 77p, Cloth, Novel
00812A retitled: *Balthazar; or, Science and love.*
        Routledge, Warne & Routledge, London, 1859,
        170p, Cloth, Novel
00812B retitled: *The alchemist; or, The house of
        Claes.* Rudd & Carleton, New York, 1861,
        310p, Cloth, Novel

00812C retitled: *The alkahest; or, The house of Claës.*
        Roberts Bros., Boston, 1887, 307p, Cloth,
        Novel
00812D retitled: *The quest of the absolute.* J. M.
        Dent & Sons, London, 1895, 226p, Cloth, Novel
00812E retitled: *The tragedy of a genius.* Greening
        & Co., London, 1912, 303p, Cloth, Novel
        The quest of the absolute. [see 00812D]
00813   *The quest of the absolute, and other stories.*
        Gebbie Publishing Co., Philadelphia, 1897,
        372p, Cloth, Coll.
00814   *The quest of the absolute, and other stories.*
        Colonial Press, Boston, 1901, 386p, Cloth,
        Coll. [different from 00813]
        The tragedy of a genius. [see 00812E]
00815   *The wild ass' skin, and other stories.* Gebbie
        Publishing Co., Philadelphia, 1897, 324p,
        Cloth, Coll.
00816   *The wild ass skin; The quest of the absolute.*
        P. F. Collier & Son, New York, 1900?, 504p,
        Cloth, Coll.
        The wild ass's skin. [see 00808B]

BAMBER, GEORGE (Everett), 1932-   [*biography
included*]

00817   *The sea is boiling hot.* Ace, New York, 1971,
        253p, Paper, Novel

BAMMAN, HENRY (A.), 1918-   [*biography included*], with William Odell and Robert Whitehead

00818   *Bone people.* Benefic Press, Westchester, 1970,
        72p, Cloth, Novel
00819   *Ice men of Rime.* Benefic Press, Westchester,
        1970, 72p, Cloth, Novel
00820   *Inviso man.* Benefic Press, Westchester, 1970,
        72p, Cloth, Novel
00821   *Milky Way.* Benefic Press, Westchester, 1970,
        71p, Cloth, Novel
00822   *Planet of the whistlers.* Benefic Press, West-
        chester, 1970, 72p, Cloth, Novel
00823   *Space pirate.* Benefic Press, Westchester,
        1970, 72p, Cloth, Novel

BANGS, JOHN KENDRICK, 1862-1922

00824   *Alice in Blunderland; an iridescent dream.*
        Doubleday, Page, New York, 1907, 124p, Cloth,
        Novel [Alice series]
00825   *The autobiography of Methuselah.* B. W. Dodge,
        New York, 1909, 185p, Cloth, Novel
00826   *Bikey the skicycle, and other tales of Jimmie-
        boy.* Riggs Publishing Co., New York, 1902,
        321p, Cloth, Coll.
00827   *The enchanted type-writer.* Harper & Bros.,
        New York, 1899, 171p, Cloth, Novel
00828   *Ghosts I have met, and some others.* Harper &
        Bros., New York, 1898, 191p, Cloth, Coll.
00829   *A house-boat on the Styx, being some account of
        the divers doings of the associated shades.*
        Harper & Bros., New York, 1895, 171p, Cloth,
        Novel [House-Boat #1]
00830   *Jack and the check book.* Harper & Bros., New
        York, 1911, 235p, Cloth, Coll.
00831   *Mr. Munchausen, being a true account of some of
        the recent adventures beyond the Styx of the
        late Hieronymus Carl Friedrich, sometime Baro
        Munchausen of Bodenwerder, as originally*

BANGS, JOHN KENDRICK (cont.)

*reported for the Sunday edition of the Ge-
henna Gazette by its special interviewer,
the late Mr. Ananias, formerly of Jerusalem,
and now first transcribed from the columns
of that journal.* Noyes, Platt, Boston,
1901, 180p, Cloth, Novel [Munchausen series]

00832 *Olympian nights.* Harper & Bros., New York,
1902, 224p, Cloth, Novel

00833 *Over the plum-pudding.* Harper & Bros., New
York, 1901, 245p, Cloth, Coll.

00834 *The pursuit of the house-boat, being some further account of the divers doings of the
associated shades, under the leadership of
Sherlock Holmes, Esq.* Harper & Bros., New
York, 1897, 204p, Cloth, Novel [House-Boat
#2]

00835 *A rebellious heroine; a story.* Harper & Bros.,
New York, 1896, 225p, Cloth, Novel

00836 *Shylock Homes; his posthumous memoirs.* Dis-
patch-Box Press, Arlington, VA, 1973, 102p,
Paper, Coll.

00837 *Toppleton's client; or, A spirit in exile.*
Charles L. Webster, New York, 1893, 269p,
Cloth, Novel

00838 *The water ghost, and others.* Harper & Bros.,
New York, 1894, 296p, Cloth, Coll.

published anonymously:

00839 *Mr. Bonaparte of Corsica.* Harper & Bros., New
York, 1895, 265p, Cloth, Novel

with Frank Dempster Sherman:

00840 *New waggings of old tales*, by Two Wags. Ticknor & Co., Boston, 1888, 165p, Cloth, Coll.

BANGSUND, JOHN

00841 *John W. Campbell; an Australian tribute.*
Ronald E. Graham & John Bangsund, Canberra,
1974, 100p, Paper, Nonf. Anth.

BANIM, JOHN, 1798-1842

published anonymously:

00842 *Revelations of the dead-alive.* W. Simpkin &
R. Marshall, London, 1824, 376p, Cloth, Novel

00842A retitled: *London and its eccentricities in
the year 2023; or, Revelations of the dead-
alive.* London, 1845, 376p?, Cloth, Novel

BANIS, VICTOR

as Lynn Benedict:

00843 *A family affair.* Avon, New York, 1973, 156p,
Paper, Novel

00844 *The twisted tree.* Avon, New York, 1973, 158p,
Paper, Novel

as Victor Samuels:

00845 *The vampire women.* Popular Library, New York,
1973, 190p, Paper, Novel [Dracula series]

BANISTER, MANLY (Miles), 1914-   [*biography
included*]

00846 *Conquest of Earth.* Avalon, New York, 1957,
224p, Cloth, Novel

00847 *Eegoboo--a fantasy satire.* The Nekromantikon,
Kansas City, 195?, 24p, Paper, Story

BANKOFF, GEORGE ALEXIS
    see: BORODIN, GEORGE

BANNERMAN, Sir ALEXANDER, Bart., 1871-1934

00848 *Leaders of the blind.* National Review, London,
1921, 352p, Cloth, Novel

BANNET, IVOR

00849 *The Amazons; a novel.* Golden Cockerel Press,
London, 1948, 252p, Cloth, Novel

BANNON, MARK

00850 *The assimilator.* Robert Hale, London, 1974,
191p, Cloth, Novel

00851 *The wayward robot.* Robert Hale, London, 1974,
188p, Cloth, Novel

BANZIE, ERIC de
    see: de BANZIE, ERIC

BARBEAU, CLAYTON C.

00852 *The ikon; a novel.* Coward-McCann, New York,
1961, 255p, Cloth, Novel

BARBER, ANTONIA, pseud. [Barbara Anthony,
1932-   ]

00853 *The ghosts.* Jonathan Cape, London, 1969, 190p,
Cloth, Novel

00853A retitled: *The amazing Mr. Blunden.* Puffin,
Harmondsworth, 1972, 138p, Paper, Novel

BARBER, DULAN (Friar), 1940-   [*biography included*]

00854 *The horrific world of monsters.* Marshall Caven-
dish, London, 1974, 121p, Cloth, Nonf.

00854A retitled: *Monster's who's who.* Crescent Books,
New York, 1974, 121p, Cloth, Nonf.

BARBET, PIERRE, pseud. [Claude-Pierre Avice,
1925-   ] [*biography included*]

00855 *Baphomet's meteor.* DAW, New York, 1972, 144p,
Paper, Novel

00856 *Games psyborgs play.* DAW, New York, 1973, 158p,
Paper, Novel

BARBEY d'AUREVILLY, J(ules) (Amédée), 1808-1888

00857 *Bewitched.* Harper & Bros., New York, 1928,
276p, Cloth, Novel

BARBOR, H(erbert) R(eginald)

00858 *Against the red sky; silhouettes of revolution.*
       C. W. Daniel, London, 1922, 272p, Cloth,
       Novel

BARBUSSE, HENRI, 1874-1935

00859 *Chains.* International Publishers, New York,
       1925, volume I-287p, volume II-303p, Cloth,
       Novel

BARCLAY, ALAN, pseud. [George B. Tait]

00860 *Of Earth and fire.* Robert Hale, London, 1974,
       175p, Cloth, Novel

BARCLAY, FLORENCE L(ouisa) (Charlesworth),
1862-1921

00861 *Returned empty.* G. P. Putnam's Sons, New York,
       1920, 247p, Cloth, Novel
00862 *The Upas tree.* G. P. Putnam's Sons, New York,
       1912, 246p, Cloth, Novel

BARGONE, CHARLES
   see: FARRERE, CLAUDE

BARING, MAURICE, 1874-1945

00863 *The glass mender, and other stories.* James
       Nisbet, London, 1910, 260p, Cloth, Coll.
00864 *Half a minute's silence, and other stories.*
       William Heinemann, London, 1925, 204p,
       Cloth, Coll.

BARING-GOULD, S(abine), 1834-1924

00865 *A book of ghosts.* Methuen, London, 1904, 383p,
       Cloth, Coll.

BARJAVEL, RENÉ (Gustave Henri), 1911-

00866 *Ashes, ashes.* Doubleday, Garden City, 1967,
       215p, Cloth, Novel
00867 *Future times three.* Award, New York, 1970,
       185p, Paper, Novel
00868 *The ice people.* Rupert Hart-Davis, London,
       1970, 205p, Cloth, Novel
00869 *The immortals.* William Morrow, New York, 1974,
       239p, Cloth, Novel

BARK, C. VOSS-
   see: VOSS-BARK, C.

BARKER, ALBERT (W.), 1900-   [*biography included*]

00870 *The Apollo legacy.* Award, New York, 1970,
       156p, Paper, Novel [Reefe King #2]

BARKER, ARTHUR W.

00871 *The light from Sealonia.* Four Seas Co., Bos-
       ton, 1927, 197p, Cloth, Novel

BARKER, ELSA, 1869-1954

00872 *The son of Mary Bethel.* Duffield & Co., New
       York, 1909, 549p, Cloth, Novel

BARKER, GRANVILLE, pseud.
   see: GRANVILLE-BARKER, HARLEY

BARKER, LEONARD NOEL
   see: NOEL, L.

BARKER, NUGENT

00873 *Written with my left hand; twenty-one tales.*
       Percival Marshall, London, 1951, 233p, Cloth,
       Coll.

BARKER, SHIRLEY (Frances), 1911-1965

00874 *Peace, my daughters.* Crown Publishers, New
       York, 1949, 248p, Cloth, Novel
00875 *Swear by Apollo.* Random House, New York, 1958,
       307p, Cloth, Novel

BARLOW, J. SWINDELLS

00876 *A mighty empire.* Ward, Lock, London, 1902,
       311p, Cloth, Novel

BARLOW, JAMES (Henry Stanley), 1921-1973

00877 *One half of the world.* Cassell, London, 1957,
       215p, Cloth, Novel

BARLOW, JAMES WILLIAM, 1826-1913

as Skorpios Antares:

00878 *History of a world of immortals without a god.*
       William McGee, Dublin, 1891, 177p, Cloth,
       Novel

as James William Barlow:

00878A retitled: *The Immortals' great quest, trans-
       lated from an unpublished manuscript in the
       library of a continental university.* Smith,
       Elder, London, 1909, 177p, Cloth, Novel

BARNABY, HUGO
   see: FITZPATRICK, ERNEST HUGH

BARNARD, MARJORIE FAITH, 1897-   , with Flora
Eldershaw as M. Barnard Eldershaw

00879 *Tomorrow and tomorrow.* Georgian House, Mel-
       bourne, 1947, 466p, Cloth, Novel

BARNES, ARTHUR K(elvin), 1911-1969

00880 *Interplanetary hunter*. Gnome Press, New York, 1956, 231p, Cloth, Coll.

BARNES, JAMES, 1866-1936

00881 *The unpardonable war*. Macmillan Co., New York, 1904, 356p, Cloth, Novel

BARNES, WILLIS, 1843-

00882 *Dame Fortune smiled; the doctor's story*. Arena Publishing Co., Boston, 1896, 335p, Cloth, Novel

BARNETT, ADA

00883 *The man on the other side*. George Allen & Unwin, London, 1921, 248p, Cloth, Novel

BARNEY, J(ohn) STEWART, 1868-1925

00884 *L.P.M.; the end of the Great War*. G. P. Putnam's Sons, New York, 1915, 419p, Cloth, Novel

BARNEY, NATALIE CLIFFORD, 1878?-1972

00885 *The One who is legion; or, A.D.'s afterlife*. Eric Partridge, London, 1930, 161p, Cloth, Novel

BARNHOUSE, PERL T.

00886 *My journeys with Astargo; a tale of past, present, and future*. Bell Publications, Denver, 1952, 212p, Paper, Novel

BARON, ANTHONY LE, pseud.
  see: LAUMER, KEITH

THE BARON, pseud.
  see: WORFEL, W. G.

BARON MUNCHAUSEN
  see: RASPE, RUDOLPH ERICH

BARON MUNCHAUSEN'S NARRATIVE OF HIS MARVELLOUS TRAVELS AND CAMPAIGNS IN RUSSIA
  see: RASPE, RUDOLPH ERICH

BARR, DENSIL NEVE, pseud. [Douglas Norton Buttrey, 1918-   ]

00887 *The man with only one head*. Rich & Cowan, London, 1955, 192p, Cloth, Novel

BARR, DONALD, 1921-   [*biography included*]

00888 *Space relations; a slightly gothic interplanetary tale*. Charterhouse, New York, 1973, 249p, Cloth, Novel

BARR, JAMES (Angus Evan Abbot), 1862-1923

00889 *The witchery of the serpent*. Gay & Bird, London, 1907, 315p, Cloth, Novel

BARR, ROBERT, 1850-1912

00890 *From whose bourne?* Chatto & Windus, London, 1893, 277p, Cloth, Coll.

BARR, TYRONE C.

00891 *Split worlds*. Digit, London, 1959, 156p, Paper, Novel
00891A retitled: *The last fourteen*. Chariot, Long Island, 1960, 156p, Paper, Novel

BARRATT, F. LAYLAND
  see: LAYLAND BARRATT, F.

BARREN, CHARLES (MacKinnon), 1913-   [*biography included*], with R. Cox Abel

00010 *Trivana I*. Panther, London, 1966, 171p, Paper, Novel

BARRETT, ALFRED WALTER
  see: ANDOM, R.

BARRETT, EATON STANNARD, 1786-1820

00892 *The heroine; or, Adventures of a fair romance reader*. Henry Colburn, London, 1813, 716p [also issued in 3vol], Cloth, Novel

BARRETT, ETHEL

00893 *Ethel Barrett's Holy war, with apologies to John Bunyan*. G/L Regal Books, Glendale, 1969, 234p, Cloth, Novel

BARRETT, FRANK, 1848-1926

00894 *The justification of Andrew Lebrun; a novel*. William Heinemann, London, 1894, 277p, Cloth, Novel

BARRETT, G(eoffrey) J(ohn), 1928-   [*biography included*]

00895 *The brain of Graphicon*. Robert Hale, London, 1973, 192p, Cloth, Novel

BARRETT, G(eoffrey) J(ohn)   (cont.)

00896 *The lost fleet of Astranides*. Robert Hale,
         London, 1974, 188p, Cloth, Novel
00897 *The tomorrow stairs*. Robert Hale, London,
         1974, 183p, Cloth, Novel

BARRETT, LAURENCE (I.), 1935-   [*biography
included*]

00898 *The mayor of New York*. Doubleday, Garden City,
         1965, 282p, Cloth, Novel

BARRETT, NEAL Jr.

00899 *The gates of time*. Ace Double, New York, 1970,
         140p, Paper, Novel
00900 *Highwood*. Ace Double, New York, 1972, 122p,
         Paper, Novel
00901 *Kelwin*. Lancer, New York, 1970, 223p, Paper,
         Novel
00902 *The leaves of time*. Lancer, New York, 1971,
         205p, Paper, Novel
00903 *Stress pattern*. DAW, New York, 1974, 160p,
         Paper, Novel

BARRETT, WILLIAM E(dmund), 1900-   [*biography
included*]

00904 *The edge of things*. Doubleday, Garden City,
         1960, 336p, Cloth, Coll. [includes *Flight
         from youth*]
00905 *Flight from youth*. J. B. Lippincott, Philadel-
         phia, 1939, 215p, Cloth, Novel
00906 *The fools of time*. Doubleday, Garden City,
         1963, 309p, Cloth, Novel

BARRIE, Sir J(ames) M(atthew), Bart., 1860-1937

00907 *Peter and Wendy*. Hodder & Stoughton, London,
         1911, 267p, Cloth, Novel [Peter Pan #2]
00907A retitled: *Peter Pan & Wendy*. Hodder & Stough-
         ton, London, 1931?, 271p, Cloth, Novel [Peter
         Pan #2]
00907B retitled: *Peter Pan*. Hodder & Stoughton,
         London, 1947, 192p, Cloth, Novel [Peter Pan
         #2]
00908 *Peter Pan in Kensington Gardens*. Hodder &
         Stoughton, London, 1906, 126p, Cloth, Novel
         [Peter Pan #1] [This is an excerpt from an
         earlier novel, *The little white bird* (1902),
         in which Peter Pan's adventures with Maimie
         Mannering are related by the narrator to a
         small friend, as a story within the story.
         The play version of *Peter Pan* was first
         performed in 1904, and published that same
         year by Charles Scribner's Sons.]

BARRINGER, D(aniel) MOREAU, 1900-1962

00909 *And the waters prevailed*. E. P. Dutton, New
         York, 1956, 188p, Cloth, Novel

BARRINGER, LESLIE, 1895-1968

00910 *Gerfalcon*. William Heinemann, London, 1927,
         310p, Cloth, Novel [Neustrian Cycle #1]

00911 *Joris of the Rock*. William Heinemann, London,
         1928, 325p, Cloth, Novel [Neustrian Cycle #2]
00912 *Shy leopardess*. Methuen, London, 1948, 392p,
         Cloth, Novel [Neustrian Cycle #3]

BARRINGTON, E., pseud.
    see: BECK, L. ADAMS

BARRON, D(onald) G(abriel), 1922-

00913 *The Zilov bombs*. Andre Deutsch, London, 1962,
         173p, Cloth, Novel

BARROWS, (Ruth) MARJORIE (Wescott) [*biography
included*]

00914 *The children's hour, volume 16; science fiction
         and reader's guide*. Spencer Press, Chicago,
         1954, 376p, Cloth, Anth.

BARROWS, P. S.
    see: SARBROW, CEPRE

BARRY, IRIS, 1895-

00915 *The last enemy*. Bobbs-Merrill, Indianapolis,
         1929, 320p, Cloth, Novel
00915A retitled: *Here is thy victory*. Elkin Mathews
         & Marriott, London, 1930, 256p, Cloth, Novel

BARRY, RAY, pseud.
    see: HUGHES, DENIS TALBOT

BARRY, RICHARD (Hayes), 1881-

00916 *Fruit of the desert*. Doubleday, Page, Garden
         City, 1920, 245p, Cloth, Novel

BARRY, Rev. WILLIAM (Francis), 1849-1930

00917 *The place of dreams; four stories*. Catholic
         Truth Society, London, 1893, 274p, Cloth,
         Coll.

BARSKY, ARTHUR

00918 *Phantastique*. Vantage Press, New York, 1974,
         138p, Cloth, Novel

BARTER, ALAN FRANK, 1933-   [*biography included*], with Raymond Wilson

00919 *Untravelled worlds; an anthology of science
         fiction*. Macmillan, London, 1966, 168p,
         Paper, Anth.

BARTH, JOHN (Simmons), 1930-   [*biography included*]

00920 *Chimera*. Random House, New York, 1972, 308p,
         Cloth, Novel

BARTH, JOHN (cont.)

00921 *Giles Goat-Boy; or, The revised new syllabus.* Doubleday, Garden City, 1966, 710p, Cloth, Novel

BARTLETT, FREDERICK ORIN, 1876-1945

00922 *The web of the golden spider.* Small, Maynard, Boston, 1909, 354p, Cloth, Novel

BARTLETT, LANDELL

00923 *The vanguard of Venus.* Experimenter Publishing Co., New York, 1928, 24p, Paper, Story

BARTLETT, VERNON (Oldfield), 1894- [*biography included*]

00924 *Tomorrow always comes.* Chatto & Windus, London, 1943, 127p, Cloth, Novel

BARTON, C(atherine) JOSEPHINE, 1857-

00925 *Evangel Ahvallah; or, The white spectrum; a novel whose incidents are linked together by a chain of metaphysical deductions.* The Author, Kansas City, 1895, 430p, Cloth, Novel

BARTON, ERLE, pseud.
    see: FANTHORPE, R. LIONEL

BARTON, LEE, pseud.
    see: FANTHORPE, R. LIONEL

BARTON, SAMUEL

00926 *The Battle of the Swash, and the capture of Canada.* Chas. T. Dillingham, New York, 1888, 131p, Paper, Novel

BARTON, WILLIAM (Renald III), 1950- [*biography included*]

00927 *Hunting on Kunderer.* Ace Double, New York, 1973, 120p, Paper, Novel

BARZEVI, A. H., with Marc F. Keller

00928 *Migrants of the stars, being an account of the discovery of the marvelous land of Niames, and of the secret of its inhabitants.* Classic Press, New York, 1931, 406p, Cloth, Novel

BARZMAN, BEN

00929 *Out of this world.* Collins, London, 1960, 320p, Cloth, Novel
00929A retitled: *Twinkle, twinkle, little star.* G. P. Putnam's Sons, New York, 1960, 261p, Cloth, Novel

00929B retitled: *Echo X.* Paperback Library, New York, 1962, 252p, Paper, Novel

BASIL, OTTO, 1901- [*biography included*]

00930 *The twilight men; a novel.* Meredith Press, New York, 1968, 277p, Cloth, Novel

BASS, T. J., pseud. [Thomas Joseph Bassler, 1932-] [*biography included*]

00931 *The Godwhale.* Ballantine, New York, 1974, 281p, Paper, Novel [Hive #2]
00932 *Half past human.* Ballantine, New York, 1971, 279p, Paper, Novel [Hive #1]

BASSLER, THOMAS JOSEPH
    see: BASS, T. J.

BATCHELOR, JOHN M.

00933 *A strange conflict.* J. S. Ogilvie, New York, 1888, 299p, Paper, Novel
00934 *A strange people.* J. S. Ogilvie, New York, 1888, 312p, Paper, Novel [sequel to 00933?]

BATEMAN, ROBERT (Moyes Carruthers), 1922-1973 [*biography included*]

00935 *The hands of Orlac.* Four Square, London, 1961, 128p, Paper, Movie [an adaptation of the movie, which in turn was based on the novel by Maurice Renard]
00936 *When the whites went.* Dennis Dobson, London, 1963, 183p, Cloth, Novel

BATES, ARLO, 1850-1918

00937 *The intoxicated ghost, and other stories.* Houghton Mifflin, Boston, 1908, 304p, Cloth, Coll.

BATES, H(erbert) E(rnest), 1905-1974

00938 *The seekers.* John & Edward Bumpus, London, 1926, 32p, Cloth, Story

BATES, HARRY
    see: GILMORE, ANTHONY

BATT, LEON

00939 *Formula for power.* Pinnacle Books, Sydney, 1942, 64p, Paper, Novel

BATTLE FOR THE PACIFIC

00940 *The battle for the Pacific, and other adventures at sea.* Harper & Bros., New York, 1908, 238p, Cloth, Anth.

THE BATTLE OF DORKING
    see: CHESNEY, GEORGE

THE BATTLE OF DORKING: A MYTH

00941   *The Battle of Dorking: a myth; England impreg-*
         nable; or, The events that occurred in A.D.
         1871. Style, Exeter, 1871, 31p, Paper,
         Story [Dorking series]

THE BATTLE OF DORKING CONTROVERSY
    see: CLARKE, I. F.

THE BATTLE OF THE IRONCLADS

00942   *The battle of the ironclads; or, England and*
         her foes in 1879. G. J. Palmer, London,
         1871, 32p, Paper, Story

THE BATTLE OF THE MOY

00943   *The Battle of the Moy; or, How Ireland gained*
         her independence, 1892-1894. Lee & Shepard,
         Boston, 1883, 74p, ?Paper, Novel

THE BATTLE OF TO-MORROW

00944   *The battle of to-morrow.* Chappell, London,
         1885, 54p, Paper, Novel

BAUGHMAN, GRACE A.

00945   *The abominable snowman, and other stories;*
         fantasy at its best. Brock Publishing Co.,
         Chico, CA., 1972, 79p, Paper, Coll.
00946   *The disappearance of the 7 teenage Aquarians.*
         Celestial Press, Sacramento, 1971. 51p,
         Paper, Novel
00947   *The exotic swamp plant, and other stories.*
         Central Valley Press, Fresno, 1973, 97p,
         Paper, Coll.
00948   *The tree, and other stories.* Celestial Press,
         Sacramento, 1971, 149p, Paper, Coll.

BAUM, L(yman) FRANK, 1856-1919

00949   *The master key; an electrical fairy tale foun-*
         ded upon the mysteries of electricity and
         the optimism of its devotees. Bowen-Merrill,
         Indianapolis, 1901, 245p, Cloth, Novel

published anonymously:

00950   *The last Egyptian; a romance of the Nile.* Ed-
         ward Stern, Philadelphia, 1908, 287p, Cloth,
         Novel

BAUM, TOM [Thomas]

00951   *Counterparts; a novel.* Dial Press, New York,
         1970, 127p, Cloth, Novel

BAUMAN, CAROLYN BUSEY

00952   *The woman who would not die.* Signet, New York,
         1969, 128p, Paper, Novel

BAUMGARTL, I(sidor), 1860-

00953   *Sea gods; a Japanese fantasy in five parts.*
         Kroch's Bookstores, Chicago, 1937, 139p,
         Cloth, Novel

BAXTER, GREGORY, pseud.
    see: de BANZIE, ERIC and RESSICH, JOHN

BAXTER, JOHN, 1939-   [*biography included*]

         The god killers. [see 00954A]
00954   *The off-worlders.* Ace Double, New York, 1966,
         127p, Paper, Novel
00954A retitled: *The god killers.* Horwitz, Sydney,
         1968, 127p, Paper, Novel
00955   *The Pacific book of Australian SF.* Pacific,
         Sydney, 1968, 180p, Paper, Anth.
00956   *Science fiction in the cinema.* A. S. Barnes,
         New York, 1970, 240p, Paper, Nonf.
00957   *The second Pacific book of science fiction.*
         Pacific, Sydney, 1971, 149p, Cloth, Anth.

BAYLE, MONSIEUR, pseud. [Simon Tyssot de Patot,
1655-   ]

00958   *The travels and adventures of James Massey,*
         being a general criticism upon religion,
         the several arts and sciences, trade, com-
         merce, &c. J. Watts, London, 1733, 318p,
         Cloth, Novel

BAYLEY, BARRINGTON J(ohn), 1937-   [biography
included]

00959   *Annihilation factor.* Ace Double, New York,
         1972, 134p, Paper, Novel
00960   *Collision course.* DAW, New York, 1973, 175p,
         Paper, Novel
00961   *Empire of two worlds.* Ace, New York, 1972,
         157p, Paper, Novel
00962   *The fall of Chronopolis.* DAW, New York, 1974,
         175p, Paper, Novel
00963   *Soul of the robot.* Doubleday, Garden City,
         1974, 206p, Cloth, Novel
00964   *The star virus.* Ace Double, New York, 1970,
         120p, Paper, Novel

BAYLISS, A(lfred) E(dward) M(acDuff), 1892-
1961, with J. C. Bayliss

00965   *Science in fiction.* Pilot Books, University
         of London Press, London, 1957, 191p, Cloth,
         Anth.

BAYLISS, J(ohn) C(lifford), 1919-   [*biography
included*]

with A. E. M. Bayliss:

00965   *Science in fiction.* Pilot Books, University
         of London Press, London, 1957, 191p, Cloth,
         Anth.

as John Clifford:

00966   *Atlantis adventure.* Lutterworth Press, London,
         1958, 143p, Cloth, Novel

BAYLISS, MARGUERITE (Farlee), 1895-

    00967 *Earth eagles.* Henry Holt, New York, 1947, 53p, Cloth, Novel

BAYLY, ADA ELLEN
    see: LYALL, EDNA

BAYNE, CHARLES J(oseph), 1870-

    00968 *The fall of utopia.* Eastern Publishing Co., Boston, 1900, 190p, Cloth, Novel

BAZHOV, P(avel) (Petrovich), 1879-1950

    00969 *The malachite casket; tales from the Urals.* Hutchinson, London, 1944, 192p, Cloth, Coll.

BEACH, CHARLES A., pseud. [Mayne Reid, 1818-1883]

    00970 *Pitzmaroon; or, The magic hammer.* Whitney & Adams, Springfield, 1874, 96p, Cloth, Novel

BEACHCROFT, NINA

    00971 *Well met by witchlight.* Heinemann, London, 1972, 138p, Cloth, Novel

BEACONSFIELD, EARL OF
    see: DISRAELI, BENJAMIN

BEAGLE, PETER S(oyer), 1939- [*biography included*]

    00972 *A fine and private place; a novel.* Viking Press, New York, 1960, 272p, Cloth, Novel
    00973 *The last unicorn; a fantastic tale.* Viking Press, New York, 1968, 218p, Cloth, Novel
    00974 *Lila the werewolf.* Capra Press, Santa Barbara, 1974, 42p, Cloth, Story

BEAL, JOHN ROBINSON, 1906-

    00975 *The secret speech; the failure of Comrade Khrushchev's leadership.* Duell, Sloan & Pearce, New York, 1961, 138p, Cloth, Novel

BEALE, CHARLES WILLING, 1845-1932

    00976 *The ghost of Guir House.* Editor Publishing Co., Cincinnati, 1897, 184p, Cloth, Novel
    00977 *The secret of the Earth.* F. Tennyson Neely, London, 1899, 256p, Cloth, Novel

BEALS, CARLETON, 1893- [*biography included*]

    00978 *Dawn over the Amazon.* Duell, Sloan & Pearce, New York, 1943, 536p, Cloth, Novel

BEAMAN, EMERIC HULME-
    see: HULME-BEAMAN, EMERIC

BEAMISH, NOEL DE VIC [Annie O'Meara de Vic Beamish, 1883-] [*biography included*]

    00979 *The king's missal.* Herbert Jenkins, London, 1934, 312p, Cloth, Novel

    as John Bernard:

    00980 *The new race of devils.* Anglo-Eastern Publishing Co., London, 1921, 188p, Paper, Novel

BEARD, DAN(iel) (Carter), 1850-1941

    00981 *Moonblight; and, Six feet of romance.* Charles L. Webster, New York, 1892, 221p, Cloth, Coll.

BEARD, HENRY N., with Douglas C. Kenney

    00982 *Bored of the Rings; a parody of J. R. R. Tolkien's The Lord of the Rings.* Signet, New York, 1969, 160p, Paper, Novel

BEARD, JOHN R(elly), 1800-1876

    00983 *The autobiography of Satan.* Williams & Norgate, London, 1872, 418p, Cloth, Novel

BEARDSLEY, AUBREY (Vincent), 1872-1898

    00984 *The story of Venus and Tannhäuser, in which is set forward an exact account of the manner of state held by madam Venus, goddess and meretrix, under the famous Hörselberg; and containing the adventures of Tannhäuser in that place, his repentance, his journeying to Rome, and return to the loving mountain; a romantic novel.* Smithers, London, 1907, 88p, Cloth, Novel
    00984A retitled: *Venus and Tannhauser.* Privatly [sic] printed, no place, no date, 48p, Cloth, Novel
    00985 *Under the hill, and other essays in prose and verse.* John Lane, London, 1904, 70p, Cloth, Coll. [includes some verse and nonf.]

BEARNE, C(olin) G(erald), 1939- [*biography included*]

    00986 *Vortex; new Soviet science fiction.* MacGibbon & Kee, London, 1970, 224p, Cloth, Anth.

BEATON, GEORGE, pseud. [Edward Fitz-Gerald Brenan, 1894-]

    00987 *Doctor Partridge's almanack for 1935, with an account of his resurrection from the grave after lying dead in it for 2 centuries, by G. Robinson; also, a brief exposition of his religious & astrological teaching, by Professor Blish.* Chatto & Windus, London, 1934, 65p, Cloth, Novel

BEATTY, JEROME Jr., 1918- [*biography included*]

    00988 *Matthew Looney and the space pirates; a space story.* Young Scott Books, Reading, Mass., 1972, 158p, Cloth, Novel [Matthew Looney #4]

BEATTY, JEROME Jr. (cont.)

00989   *Matthew Looney in the outback; a space story.*
        V. R. Scott, New York, 1969, 223p, Cloth,
        Novel [Matthew Looney #3]
00990   *Matthew Looney's invasion of the Earth; a space
        story.* W. R. Scott, New York, 1965, 155p,
        Cloth, Novel [Matthew Looney #2]
00991   *Matthew Looney's voyage to the Earth; a space
        story.* W. R. Scott, New York, 1961, 131p,
        Cloth, Novel [Matthew Looney #1]

BEATTY, JOHN, 1828-1914

00992   *The Acolhuans; a narrative of sojourn and ad-
        venture among the Mound Builders of the Ohio
        Valley, being a free translation from the
        Norraena of the memoirs of Ivarr Bartholdsson.*
        McClelland & Co., Columbus, 1902, 423p, Cloth,
        Novel

BEATTY, (Rose) **MABEL**, 1879-1932

00993   *The resurrection of Merion Lloyd.* Thornton
        Butterworth, London, 1929, 284p, Cloth, Novel

BEAUCLERK, HELEN (De Vere), 1892-1969

00994   *The green lacquer pavilion.* W. Collins Sons,
        London, 1926, 319p, Cloth, Novel
00995   *The love of the foolish angel.* W. Collins
        Sons, London, 1929, 251p, Cloth, Novel
00996   *The mountain and the tree.* Collins, London,
        1935, 395p, Cloth, Novel

BEAUJON, PAUL, pseud. [Beatrice Lamberton
Warde, 1900-1969]

00997   *Peace under Earth; dialogues from the year
        1946.* Megaw, London?, 1938, 47p, Cloth,
        Story

BEAUMONT, CHARLES, pseud. [Charles Nutt, 1929-
1967] [*biography included*]

00998   *The edge.* Panther, London, 1966, 143p, Paper,
        Coll.
00999   *The fiend in you.* Ballantine, New York, 1962,
        158p, Paper, Anth.
01000   *The hunger, and other stories.* G. P. Putnam's
        Sons, New York, 1957, 234p, Cloth, Coll.
01000A retitled: *Shadow play.* Panther, London, 1964,
        190p, Paper, Coll. [abridged]
01001   *The Magic Man, and other science-fantasy sto-
        ries.* Fawcett Gold Medal, Greenwich, 1965,
        258p, Paper, Coll.
01002   *Night ride, and other journeys.* Bantam, New
        York, 1960, 184p, Paper, Coll.
        Shadow play. [see 01000A]
01003   *Yonder; stories of fantasy and science fiction.*
        Bantam, New York, 1958, 184p, Paper, Coll.

BEAUMONT, DONNA BROOKS
   see: CLAXTON, JOHN G.

BEAUVOIR, SIMONE (Lucie Ernestine Marie Bertrand) de, 1908-   [*biography included*]

01004   *All men are mortal; a novel.* World Publishing
        Co., Cleveland, 1955, 346p, Cloth, Novel

BECHDOLT, JACK [John Ernest], 1884-1954

01005   *The lost Vikings.* Cosmopolitan Book Corp., New
        York, 1931, 267p, Cloth, Novel
01006   *The torch.* Prime Press, Philadelphia, 1948,
        229p, Cloth, Novel

BECHER, DON

01007   *A ticket to nowhere.* Vega Books, Clovis, CA,
        1966, 160p, Paper, Novel

BECK, CALVIN (Thomas), 1930-

01008   *The Frankenstein reader.* Ballantine, New York,
        1962, 159p, Paper, Anth.

BECK, CHRISTOPHER, pseud.
   see: BRIDGES, T. C.

BECK, L(ily) **ADAMS** [Eliza Louisa Moresby Beck,
186?-1931]

01009   *Dreams and delights.* Dodd, Mead, New York,
        1926, 317p, Cloth, Coll.
01010   *The Garden of Vision; a story of growth.* Cos-
        mopolitan Book Corp., New York, 1929, 421p,
        Cloth, Novel
01011   *The house of fulfilment; the romance of a soul,*
        by L. Adams Beck (E. Barrington). Cosmopoli-
        tan Book Corp., New York, 1927, 342p, Cloth,
        Novel
01012   *The key of dreams; a romance of the Orient.*
        Dodd, Mead, New York, 1922, 353p, Cloth, Nove
01013   *The Ninth Vibration, and other stories.* Dodd,
        Mead, New York, 1922, 313p, Cloth, Coll.
01014   *The openers of the gate; stories of the occult,*
        by L. Adams Beck (E. Barrington). Cosmopoli-
        tan Book Corp., New York, 1930, 368p, Cloth,
        Coll.
01015   *The perfume of the rainbow, and other stories.*
        Dodd, Mead, New York, 1923, 324p, Cloth, Coll
01016   *The treasure of Ho; a romance.* Dodd, Mead,
        New York, 1924, 303p, Cloth, Novel
01017   *The way of stars; a romance of reincarnation.*
        Dodd, Mead, New York, 1925, 408p, Cloth, Nove

as Louis Moresby:

01018   *The glory of Egypt; a romance.* Thomas Nelson
        & Sons, London, 1926, 281p, Cloth, Novel

BECK, ROBERT E.

01019   *Literature of the supernatural.* McDougal,
        Littell, Evanston, IL, 1974, 192p, Paper,
        Anth.

BECKER, KURT, 1915-

01020 *Countdown*. Benziger Bros., New York, 1958,
        179p, Cloth, Novel

BECKER, MARY KAY, with Patricia Coburn

01021 *Superspill; an account of the 1978 grounding
        at Bird Rocks*. Madrona Press, Seattle,
        1974, 161p, Paper, Novel

BECKFORD, WILLIAM, 1760-1844

01022 *An Arabian tale*. J. Johnson, London, 1786,
        334p, Cloth, Novel [published anonymously]
01022A retitled: *Vathek*. W. Clarke, London, 1816,
        284p, Cloth, Novel [published anonymously]
01022B retitled: *The history of the Caliph Vathek*.
        Sampson Low, London, 1868, 189p, Cloth,
        Novel
01023 *The episodes of Vathek*. S. Swift, London,
        1912, 207p, Cloth, Coll. [consists of ex-
        cerpts left out of the original edition
        of the novel]
        The history of the Caliph Vathek. [see 01022B]
        Vathek. [see 01022A]
01024 *Vathek, with The episodes of Vathek*. Con-
        stable, London, 1929, 2vol, Cloth, Coll.
01025 *The vision; liber veritatis*. Constable,
        London, 1930, 166p, Cloth, Coll. [includes
        some nonf.]

BEDFORD-JONES, H(enry James O'Brien), 1887-
1949

01026 *The Star Woman*. Dodd, Mead, New York, 1924,
        293p, Cloth, Novel

as Allan Hawkwood:

01027 *The seal of John Solomon*. Hurst & Blackett,
        London, 1924, 283p, Cloth, Novel [Solomon
        series]
01028 *The shawl of Solomon*. Hurst & Blackett, Lon-
        don, 1925, 248p, Cloth, Novel [Solomon ser.]
01029 *The wizard of the Atlas*. Hurst & Blackett,
        London, 1928, 285p, Cloth, Novel

with W. C. Robertson:

01030 *The Temple of the Ten*. Donald M. Grant, Pub-
        lisher, W. Kingston, RI, 1973, 159p, Cloth,
        Novel

BEECHING, JACK [biography included]

01031 *The Dakota Project*. Jonathan Cape, London,
        1968, 256p, Cloth, Novel

BEEDING, FRANCIS, pseud.
    see: PALMER, JOHN and SAUNDERS, HILARY

BEEMISH, CRAGG, pseud.

01032 *Worlds away*. Gannet Press, London, 1953,
        127p, Paper, Novel

BEER, RICHARD C(ameron), 1894?-1959

01033 *The wave that drowned a baby*. Inquirer & Mir-
        ror Press, Nantucket, 1951, 12p, Paper, Story

BEERBOHM, (Sir Henry) MAX(imilian), 1872-1956

01034 *The dreadful dragon of Hay Hill*. William Hein-
        emann, London, 1928, 113p, Cloth, Novel
01035 *Seven men*. William Heinemann, London, 1919,
        219p, Cloth, Coll.
01036 *Seven men, and two others*. William Heinemann,
        London, 1950, 283p, Cloth, Coll.

BEEVER, ROBERT F. VAN
    see: VAN BEEVER, ROBERT F.

BEGBIE, (Edward) HAROLD, 1871-1929
as The man who was warned:

01037 *The day that changed the world*. Hodder &
        Stoughton, London, 1912, 289p, Cloth, Novel

as Harold Begbie:

01037A *The day that changed the world*. Hodder &
        Stoughton, London, 1914, 289p, Cloth, Novel

with J. Stafford Ransome & M. H. Temple as
Caroline Lewis:

01038 *Clara in Blunderland*. William Heinemann, Lon-
        don, 1902, 150p, Cloth, Novel [Clara #1;
        parody of *Alice in Wonderland*]
01039 *Lost in Blunderland; the further adventures of
        Clara*. William Heinemann, London, 1903, 145p,
        Cloth, Novel [Clara #2; parody of *Alice in
        Wonderland*]

BEGOUËN, MAX (Henri), Vicomte

01040 *Bison of clay*. Longmans, Green, London, 1926,
        252p, Cloth, Novel

BEHN, HARRY, 1898-1973 [biography included]

01041 *The faraway lurs*. World Publishing Co., Cleve-
        land, 1963, 190p, Cloth, Novel
01041A retitled: *The distant lurs*. Victor Gollancz,
        London, 1964, 160p, Cloth, Novel

BEITH, JOHN HAY
    see: HAY, IAN

BELASCO, DAVID, 1853-1931

01042 *The return of Peter Grimm*. Andrew Melrose,
        London, 1912, 344p, Cloth, Novel [based upon
        the play of the same name]

BELAYEV, ALEXANDER
    see: BELIAEV, ALEKSANDR

BELIAEV, ALEKSANDR (Romanovich), 1884-1942

01043 *The amphibian.* Foreign Languages Publishing
       House, Moscow, 1959?, 285p, Cloth, Novel
       [by Belyaev]
01044 *The struggle in space; Red dream; Soviet-Ameri-*
       can war. Arfor Publishers, Washington,
       1965, 116p, Cloth, Novel [by Beliayev]

BELL, ELLIS, pseud.
    see: BRONTE, EMILY

BELL, ERIC TEMPLE
    see: TAINE, JOHN

BELL, GEO(rge) W.

01045 *Mr. Oseba's last discovery.* New Zealand
       Times, Wellington, 1904, 225p, Cloth, Novel

BELL, JOHN KEBLE
    see: HOWARD, KEBLE

BELL, NEAL

01046 *Gone to be snakes now.* Popular Library, New
       York, 1974, 158p, Paper, Novel

BELL, NEIL, pseud. [Stephen Southwold, 1887-
1964]

01047 *The disturbing affair of Noel Blake.* Victor
       Gollancz, London, 1932, 280p, Cloth, Novel
       The gas war of 1940. [see 01056B]
01048 *Life and Andrew Otway.* Victor Gollancz, London,
       1931, 495p, Cloth, Novel
01049 *Life comes to Seathorpe; a novel.* Eyre & Spot-
       tiswoode, London, 1946, 302p, Cloth, Novel
01050 *The lord of life.* Collins, London, 1933,
       320p, Cloth, Novel
01051 *One came back; a novel.* Collins, London, 1938,
       416p, Cloth, Novel
01052 *Precious porcelain.* Victor Gollancz, London,
       1931, 351p, Cloth, Novel
       The seventh bowl. [see 01057A]
       Valiant clay. [see 01056A]
01053 *Who walk in fear.* Alvin Redman, London, 1953,
       310p, Cloth, Coll.

as S. H. Lambert:

01054 *Portrait of Gideon Power.* Jarrolds Publishers,
       London, 1944, 168p, Cloth, Novel

as Paul Martens:

01055 *Death rocks the cradle; a strange tale.* W.
       Collins Sons, London, 1933, 254p, Cloth,
       Novel

as "Miles":

01056 *The gas war of 1940.* Eric Partridge, London,
       1931, 302p, Cloth, Novel
01056A retitled: *Valiant clay,* by Neil Bell. Collins,
       London, 1934, 251p, Cloth, Novel
01056B retitled: *The gas war of 1940,* by Neil Bell.
       White Circle, London, 1940, 251p, Paper,
       Novel

01057 *The seventh bowl; a novel.* Eric Partridge,
       London, 1930, 254p, Cloth, Novel
01057A *The seventh bowl,* by Neil Bell. Collins, Lon-
       don, 1934, 252p, Cloth, Novel

BELL, NORMAN (Edward), 1899-   [*biography included*]

01058 *The weightless mother.* Follett Publishing Co.,
       Chicago, 1967, 144p, Cloth, Novel

BELL, PAUL W., with Ralph F. Robinett

01059 *English: target 1, the space visitors.* Har-
       court, Brace & World, New York, 1968, 168p,
       Cloth, Novel

BELL, ROBERT

01060 *In realms unknown; a story of adventure, inven-*
       tion, and romance. Bell Publishing Co.,
       Detroit, 1934, 265p, Cloth, Novel

BELL, THORNTON, pseud.
    see: FANTHORPE, R. LIONEL

BELL, WILLIAM DIXON

01061 *The Moon colony.* Goldsmith Publishing Co.,
       Chicago, 1938, 247p, Cloth, Novel
01062 *The secret of Tibet.* Goldsmith Publishing Co.,
       Chicago, 1938, 251p, Cloth, Novel

BELLAIRS, JOHN, 1938-   [*biography included*]

01063 *The face in the frost.* Macmillan, New York,
       1969, 174p, Cloth, Novel
01064 *The house with a clock in its walls.* Dial
       Press, New York, 1973, 179p, Cloth, Novel

BELLAMY, EDWARD, 1850-1898

01065 *Dr. Heidenhoff's process.* D. Appleton, New
       York, 1880, 140p, Cloth, Novel
01066 *Equality.* D. Appleton, New York, 1897, 412p,
       Cloth, Novel [Julian West #2]
01067 *Looking backward, 2000-1887.* Ticknor & Co.,
       Boston, 1888, 470p, Cloth, Novel [Julian
       West #1]
01068 *Miss Ludington's sister; a romance of immorta-*
       lity. James R. Osgood, Boston, 1884, 260p,
       Cloth, Novel

BELLAMY, FRANCIS RUFUS, 1886-1972

01069 *Atta; a novel of a most extraordinary adventure*
       A. A. Wyn, New York, 1953, 216p, Cloth, Novel

BELLINI, TINA
    see: FOREST, SALAMBO

BELLOC, (Joseph) HILAIRE (Pierre René), 1870-
1953

01070 *But soft--we are observed!* Arrowsmith, London,
       1928, 312p, Cloth, Novel
01070A retitled: *Shadowed!* Harper & Bros., New
       York, 1929, 312p, Cloth, Novel
01071 *A change in the cabinet.* Methuen, London,
       1909, 309p, Cloth, Novel
01072 *The haunted house.* Arrowsmith, London, 1927,
       270p, Cloth, Novel
01073 *The man who made gold.* Arrowsmith, London,
       1930, 296p, Cloth, Novel
01074 *Mr. Clutterbuck's election.* Eveleigh Nash,
       London, 1908, 329p, Cloth, Novel
01075 *Mr. Petre; a novel.* Arrowsmith, London, 1925,
       310p, Cloth, Novel
01076 *Pongo and the bull.* Constable, London, 1910,
       305p, Cloth, Novel
01077 *The postmaster-general.* Arrowsmith, London,
       1932, 286p, Cloth, Novel
       Shadowed! [see 01070A]

BELOVE, B(enjamin), 1880-

01078 *The split atom; last human pair on Earth; the
       whirling of ideas.* Boris Ackerman, Los An-
       geles, 1946, 478p, Cloth, Novel

BENARY-ISBERT, MARGOT, 1889-

01079 *The wicked enchantment.* Harcourt, Brace & Co.,
       New York, 1955, 181p, Cloth, Novel

BENDIX, HANS, 1898-

01080 *The lady who kept her promise.* American Ar-
       tists Group, New York, 1941, 32p, Cloth,
       Story

BENEDICT, LYNN, pseud.
    see: BANIS, VICTOR

BENEDICT, STEWART H(urd), 1924-

01081 *Tales of terror and suspense.* Dell, New York,
       1963, 288p, Paper, Anth.

BENEFICE, pseud. [Frederick U. Worley]

01082 *Three thousand dollars a year: moving forward;
       or, How we got there; the complete libera-
       tion of all the people, abridged from the
       advance sheets of a history of industrial
       and governmental reforms in the United
       States, to be published in the year 2001.*
       J. P. Wright, Printer, Washington, 1890,
       104p, Cloth, Novel

BENEFIELD, (John) BARRY, 1883-

01083 *Eddie and the archangel Mike.* Reynal & Hitch-
       cock, New York, 1943, 310p, Cloth, Novel
01083A retitled: *Texas, Brooklyn, and Heaven.* World
       Publishing Co., Cleveland, 1948, 310p, Cloth,
       Novel

BENÉT, LAURA, 1884-

01084 *Goods and chattels.* Doubleday, Doran, Garden
       City, 1930, 223p, Cloth, Coll.

BENÉT, STEPHEN VINCENT, 1898-1943

01085 *The devil and Daniel Webster.* Farrar & Rine-
       hart, New York, 1937, 61p, Cloth, Novel
01086 *The devil and Daniel Webster, and other stories.*
       Archway, New York, 1967, 120p, Paper, Coll.
01087 *Johnny Pye & the Fool-Killer.* Countryman Press,
       Vermont, 1938, 78p, Cloth, Novel
01088 *The last circle; stories and poems.* Farrar,
       Straus & Co., New York, 1946, 309p, Cloth,
       Coll. [includes some verse]
01089 *Selected stories.* Maurice Fridberg, Dublin,
       1947, 135p, Cloth, Coll.
01090 *Selected works of Stephen Vincent Benét, volume
       two, prose.* Farrar & Rinehart, New York,
       1942, 483p, Cloth, Coll.
01091 *Selected works of Stephen Vincent Benét, volumes
       one-two.* Farrar & Rinehart, New York, 1942?,
       970p, Cloth, Coll. [volume one in this 2 in
       1 volume consists of verse only]
01091A retitled: *The Stephen Vincent Benét Pocket
       book.* Pocket Books, New York, 1946, 414p,
       Paper, Coll. [abridged]
01092 *Short stories of Stephen Vincent Benét--a selec-
       tion.* Editions for the Armed Services, New
       York, 1944, 320p, Paper, Coll.
01093 *Tales before midnight.* Farrar & Rinehart, New
       York, 1939, 274p, Cloth, Coll.
01094 *Thirteen o'clock; stories of several worlds.*
       Farrar & Rinehart, New York, 1937, 305p,
       Cloth, Coll.
01095 *Twenty-five short stories by Stephen Vincent
       Benét.* Sun Dial Press, New York, 1943, 579p,
       Cloth, Coll. [includes 01093 and 01094]

BENFORD, GREG(ory Albert), 1941-   [*biography
included*]

01096 *Deeper than the darkness.* Ace, New York, 1970,
       191p, Paper, Novel

BENHAM, CHARLES

01097 *The fourth Napoleon; a romance.* Herbert S.
       Stone, Chicago, 1897, 600p, Cloth, Novel

BENNET, ROBERT AMES, 1870-1954

01098 *Thyra; a romance of the Polar pit.* Henry Holt,
       New York, 1901, 258p, Cloth, Novel

BENNETT, ALFRED GORDON, 1901-1962

01099 *The demigods.* Jarrolds Publishers, London,
       1939, 384p, Cloth, Novel
01100 *The forest of fear.* T. Fisher Unwin, London,
       1924, 319p, Cloth, Novel
01101 *Whom the gods destroy.* Pharos Books, Colwyn
       Bay, North Wales, 1946, 100p, Paper, Novel

BENNETT, (Enoch) ARNOLD, 1867-1931

01102   *The ghost; a fantasia on modern times.* Chatto
        & Windus, London, 1907, 302p, Cloth, Novel
01103   *The glimpse; an adventure of the soul.* Chap-
        man & Hall, London, 1909, 365p, Cloth, Novel

BENNETT, ARTHUR, 1862-1931

01104   *The dream of a Warringtonian.* "Sunrise" Pub-
        lishing Co., Warrington, UK, 1900, 245p,
        Paper, Novel
01105   *The dream of an Englishman.* "Sunrise" Publi-
        shing Co., Warrington, UK, 1893, 190p, Cloth,
        Novel

BENNETT, DIANA

01106   *Adam and Eve and Newbury.* Hodder & Stoughton,
        London, 1970, 191p, Cloth, Novel

BENNETT, GEOFFREY MARTIN
    see: SEA-LION

BENNETT, GERTRUDE BARROWS
    see: STEVENS, FRANCIS

BENNETT, JAMES CLARK, 1866/67-1942

01107   *Shedding the years.* Capitol Book Co., New
        York, 1925, 383p, Cloth, Novel

BENNETT, JEFF, pseud.

01108   *Cosmic rape.* Orpheus Series, New York, 1974,
        187p, Paper, Novel

BENNETT, JOHN, 1865-1956

01109   *Madame Margot; a grotesque legend of old
        Charleston.* Century Co., New York, 1921,
        110p, Cloth, Novel

BENNETT, KEM(ys Deverell), 1919-

01110   *The wink.* Rupert Hart-Davis, London, 1951,
        227p, Cloth, Novel
01110A retitled: *The fabulous wink.* Pellegrini &
        Cudahy, New York, 1951, 244p, Cloth, Novel

BENNETT, MARGOT (M.), 1903-   [*biography included*]

01111   *The furious masters.* Eyre & Spottiswoode,
        London, 1968, 240p, Cloth, Novel
01112   *The long way back.* Bodley Head, London, 1954,
        206p, Cloth, Novel

BENNETT, RICHARD M., with Granville Hicks

01113   *The first to awaken.* Modern Age Books, New
        York, 1940, 347p, Cloth, Novel

BENOIT, (Ferdinand Marie) PIERRE, 1886-1962

01114   *The Queen of Atlantis.* Hutchinson, London,
        1920, 287p, Cloth, Novel
01114A retitled: *Atlantida (L'Atlantide).* Duffield
        & Co., New York, 1920, 303p, Cloth, Novel

BENSEN, D(onald) R(oynold), 1927-   [*biography
included*]

01115   *The unknown; 11 stories.* Pyramid, New York,
        1963, 192p, Paper, Anth.
01116   *The unknown five; stories of fantasy.* Pyramid,
        New York, 1964, 190p, Paper, Anth.

BENSON, ARTHUR CHRISTOPHER, 1862-1925

01117   *Basil Netherby.* Hutchinson, London, 1927,
        211p, Cloth, Coll.
01118   *The child of the dawn.* Smith, Elder, London,
        1912, 314p, Cloth, Novel
01119   *The hill of trouble, and other stories.* Isbis-
        ter & Co., London, 1903, 398p, Cloth, Coll.
01120   *The Isles of Sunset.* Isbister & Co., London,
        1904, 307p, Cloth, Coll.
01121   *Paul the minstrel, and other stories reprinted
        from The hill of troubles and The Isles of
        Sunset.* Smith, Elder, London, 1911, 443p,
        Cloth, Coll.

BENSON, E(dward) F(rederic), 1867-1940

01122   *Across the stream.* John Murray, London, 1919,
        314p, Cloth, Novel
01123   *"And the dead Spake--"; and, The horror-horn.*
        George H. Doran, New York, 1923, 47p, Cloth,
        Coll.
01124   *The angel of pain.* J. B. Lippincott, Philadel-
        phia, 1905, 364p, Cloth, Novel
01125   *Colin; a novel.* Hutchinson, London, 1923,
        302p, Cloth, Novel [Colin #1]
01126   *Colin II; a novel.* Hutchinson, London, 1925,
        286p, Cloth, Novel [Colin #2]
01127   *David Blaize and the blue door.* Hodder &
        Stoughton, London, 1918, 228p, Cloth, Novel
        [David Blaize #2]
01128   *The horror horn, and other stories; the best
        horror stories of E. F. Benson.* Panther,
        St. Albans, UK, 1974, 205p, Paper, Coll.
01129   *The house of defence.* Macleod & Allen, Toronto;
        Authors & Newspapers Association, New York,
        1906, 318p, Cloth, Novel
01130   *The image in the sand.* William Heinemann, Lon-
        don, 1905, 334p, Cloth, Novel
01131   *The inheritor.* Hutchinson, London, 1930, 286p,
        Cloth, Novel
01132   *More spook stories.* Hutchinson, London, 1934,
        288p, Cloth, Coll.
01133   *Ravens' brood.* Arthur Barker, London, 1934,
        320p, Cloth, Novel
01134   *The room in the tower, and other stories.* Mills
        & Boon, London, 1912, 338p, Cloth, Coll.
01135   *Spook stories.* Hutchinson, London, 1928, 288p,
        Cloth, Coll.
01136   *The Valkyries; a romance founded on Wagner's
        opera.* Dean & Son, London, 1903, 259p, Cloth,
        Novel
01137   *Visible and invisible.* Hutchinson, London,
        1923, 288p, Cloth, Coll.

BENSON, ROBERT HUGH, 1871-1914

01138 *The dawn of all*. Hutchinson, London, 1911,
       320p, Cloth, Novel
01139 *The light invisible*. Isbister, London, 1903,
       250p, Cloth, Coll.
01140 *Lord of the world*. Sir Isaac Pitman & Sons,
       London, 1907, 384p, Cloth, Novel
01141 *A mirror of Shalott, composed of tales told
       at a symposium*. Sir Isaac Pitman & Sons,
       London, 1907, 301p, Cloth, Coll.
01142 *The necromancers*. Hutchinson, London, 1909,
       326p, Cloth, Novel

BENSON, STELLA, 1892-1933

01143 *The awakening; a fantasy*. Lantern Press, San
       Francisco, 1925, 16p, Cloth, Story
01144 *Collected short stories, by Stella Benson*.
       Macmillan & Co., London, 1936, 304p, Cloth,
       Coll.
01145 *Living alone*. Macmillan & Co., London, 1919,
       264p, Cloth, Novel

BENTLEY, JOHN, 1908-

01146 *Where are the Russians?* Doubleday, Garden
       City, 1968, 284p, Cloth, Novel

BENTLEY, NORMAN (S.)

01147 *Armada of the air*. Lothrop, Lee & Shepard,
       New York, 1937, 245p, Cloth, Novel

BENTLIF, SYD

01148 *Horror anthology*. Mayflower-Dell, London,
       1965, 126p, Paper, Anth.

BERARD, FREDERICK B. DE
   see: DE BERARD, FREDERICK B.

BERCKMAN, EVELYN (Domenica), 1900-   [*biography included*]

01149 *The Victorian album*. Doubleday, Garden City,
       1973, 237p, Cloth, Novel

BERESFORD, ELISABETH

01150 *Awkward magic*. Rupert Hart-Davis, London,
       1964, 149p, Cloth, Novel
01150A retitled: *The magic world*. Bobbs-Merrill,
       Indianapolis, 1965, 153p, Cloth, Novel
01151 *Sea-green magic*. Rupert Hart-Davis, London,
       1968, 156p, Cloth, Novel
01152 *Travelling magic*. Rupert Hart-Davis, London,
       1965, 163p, Cloth, Novel
01152A retitled: *The vanishing garden*. Funk & Wag-
       nalls, New York, 1967, 160p, Cloth, Novel
01153 *The Wombles*. Ernest Benn, London, 1968, 189p,
       Cloth, Novel

BERESFORD, J(ohn) D(avys), 1873-1947

01154 *The Camberwell miracle*. William Heinemann,
       London, 1933, 327p, Cloth, Novel
01155 *A common enemy*. Hutchinson, London, 1941,
       208p, Cloth, Novel
01156 *Goslings*. William Heinemann, London, 1913,
       325p, Cloth, Novel
01156A retitled: *A world of women*. Macaulay Co.,
       New York, 1913, 306p, Cloth, Novel
01157 *The Hampdenshire Wonder*. Sidgwick & Jackson,
       London, 1911, 295p, Cloth, Novel
01157A retitled: *The Wonder*. George H. Doran, New
       York, 1917, 311p, Cloth, Novel
01158 *Nineteen impressions*. Sidgwick & Jackson, New
       York, 1918, 226p, Cloth, Coll.
01159 *Revolution; a novel*. W. Collins Sons, London,
       1921, 252p, Cloth, Novel
01160 *Signs & wonders*. Golden Cockerel Press, Wal-
       tham Saint Lawrence, UK, 1921, 151p, Cloth,
       Coll.
01161 *"What dreams may come..."* Hutchinson, London,
       1941, 256p, Cloth, Novel
       The Wonder. [see 01157A]
       A world of women. [see 01156A]

with Esme Wynne-Tyson:

01162 *The riddle of the tower*. Hutchinson, London,
       1944, 152p, Cloth, Novel

BERESFORD, LESLIE

01163 *The second rising; a romance of India*. Hurst
       & Blackett, London, 1910, 328p, Cloth, Novel
01164 *The Venus girl*, by Leslie Beresford ("Pan").
       John Long, London, 1924, 318p, Cloth, Novel

as "Pan":

01165 *The great image*. Odhams Press, London, 1921,
       288p, Cloth, Novel
01166 *The kingdom of content*. Mills & Boon, London,
       1918, 278p, Cloth, Novel

BERESFORD, MARCUS
   see: BRANDEL, MARC

BERGER, THOMAS (Louis), 1924-   [*biography included*]

01167 *Regiment of women; a novel*. Simon & Schuster,
       New York, 1973, 349p, Cloth, Novel

BERGIN, PAUL A.

01168 *Xuan and the girl from the other side*. Tower,
       New York, 1970, 138p, Paper, Novel

BERGLUND, E(dward) P., with Robert E. Weinberg

01169 *Reader's guide to the Cthulhu Mythos, second
       revised edition*. Silver Scarab Press, Albu-
       querque, 1973, 88p, Paper, Nonf.

BERGONZI, BERNARD, 1929-   [*biography inclu-ded*], with H. G. Wells

01170   *The early H. G. Wells; a study of the scienti-fic romances.* University Press, Manchester, 1961, 226p, Cloth, Anth. [includes several stories by Wells, and an extensive critique by Bergonzi]

BERINGTON, SIMON, 1680-1755 [published anony-mously]

01171   *The memoirs of Sign. Gaudentio di Lucca, taken from his confession and examination before the fathers of the Inquisition at Bologna in Italy, making a discovery of an unknown land in the midst of the vast deserts of Africa, as ancient, populous, and civilized as the Chinese, with an account of their antiquity, origin, religion, customs, polity, and the manner how they first got over those vast deserts, interspersed with several most sur-prising and curious incidents.* T. Cooper, London, 1737, 355p, Cloth, Novel

01171A retitled: *The astonishing adventures of Sig. Gaudentio di Lucca, as related in a private examination before that secret and dreadful tribunal, the Inquisition, at Bologna in Italy.* London, no date, 40p, Cloth, Novel [abridged]

01171B retitled: *The adventures of Sigr. Gaudentio di Lucca, being the substance of his examina-tion before the fathers of the Inquisition at Bologna in Italy, giving an account of an unknown country in the midst of the de-serts of Africa, the origine and antiquity of the people, their religion, customs, poli-ty and laws; 2nd edition.* W. Innys & R. Manby & H. S. Cox, London, 1748, 291p, Cloth, Novel

01171C retitled: *The life and adventures of Sig. Gaudentio di Lucca, written by himself, giving an account of a country in the midst of the vast desarts [sic] of Africa, being unknown to any person except Sig. Gaudentio and its inhabitants, altho' as ancient, popu-lous, and civilized as the Chinese; with a particular account of their antiquity, ori-gin, religion, customs, polity, &c.--the man-ner how they first got over those vast des-arts--and their method of travelling, inter-spersed with several most surprizing and curious incidents.* John Trumbull, Norwich, Conn., 1796, 130p, Cloth, Novel

BERK, HOWARD

01172   *The Sun grows cold.* Delacorte Press, New York, 1971, 245p, Cloth, Novel

BERKELEY, EDMUND C(allis)

01173   *Ride the east wind; parables of yesterday and today.* Quadrangle, New York, 1973, 214p, Cloth, Anth.

BERKELEY, REGINALD (Cheyne), 1890-1935

01174   *Cassandra.* Victor Gollancz, London, 1931, 288p, Cloth, Novel

BERMAN, LUCY

01175   *Demon lovers.* Tandem, London, 1970, 192p, Paper, Anth.

BERMAN, RUTH

01176   *Patterns of unification in Sylvie & Bruno.* T-K Graphics, Baltimore, 1974, 23p, Paper, Nonf.

BERMANN, RICHARD ARNOLD
   see: HOLLRIEGEL, ARNOLD

BERMONT, HUBERT (Ingram), 1924-   [*biography included*]

01177   *Jonathan Livingston Fliegle.* Dell, New York, 1973, 56p, Paper, Novel [parody of Richard Bach's *Jonathan Livingston Seagull*]

BERNA, PAUL, 1913-

01178   *Continent in the sky.* Bodley Head, London, 1959, 170p, Cloth, Novel [Michael Jousse #2]
01179   *Threshold of the stars.* Bodley Head, London, 1958, 163p, Cloth, Novel [Michael Jousse #1]

BERNANOS, MICHEL, d. 1964

01180   *The other side of the mountain.* Houghton Miff-lin, Boston, 1968, 107p, Cloth, Novel

BERNARD, CHRISTINE (Ruth), 1926-   [*biography included*]

01181   *The Armada ghost book.* Armada, London, 1967, 159p, Paper, Anth.
01182   *The Fontana book of great horror stories.* Fon-tana, London, 1966, 221p, Paper, Anth.
01183   *The fourth Fontana book of great horror stories* Fontana, London, 1969, 190p, Paper, Anth.
01184   *The second Armada ghost book.* Armada, London, 1968, 127p, Paper, Anth.
01185   *The second Fontana book of great horror stories* Fontana, London, 1967, 221p, Paper, Anth.
01186   *The third Fontana book of great horror stories* Fontana, London, 1968, 188p, Paper, Anth.

BERNARD, JOEL

01187   *The man from U.N.C.L.E., no. 11; the thinking machine affair.* Four Square, London, 1967, 128p, Paper, Tele. [#21 in the Ace series]

BERNARD, JOHN, pseud.
   see: BEAMISH, NOEL de VIC

BERNARD, RAFE

01188   *The Wheel in the Sky.* Ward, Lock, London, 1954, 192p, Cloth, Novel
01189   *The halo highway.* Corgi, London, 1967, 158p, Paper, Tele. [Invaders #1 (UK series)]

BERNARD, RAFE (cont.)

01189A retitled: *Army of the undead; an Invaders adventure.* Pyramid, New York, 1967, 142p, Paper, Tele. [Invaders #3 (US series)]

BERNERS, LORD [Gerald Hugh Tyrwhitt-Wilson, 9th Baron Berners, 1883-1950]

01190 *Count Omega.* Constable, London, 1941, 208p, Cloth, Novel

BERRIAULT, GINA, 1926-

01191 *The descent.* Atheneum, New York, 1960, 183p, Cloth, Novel

BERRIDGE, JESSE

01192 *The stronghold.* Andrew Melrose, London, 1926, 268p, Cloth, Novel

BERRY, BRYAN, 1930-d.

01193 *And the stars remain.* Panther, London, 1952, 112p, Paper, Novel
01194 *Born in captivity.* Hamilton & Co. (Stafford), London, 1952, 192p, Cloth, Novel
01195 *Dread visitor.* Panther, London, 1952, 128p, Paper, Novel
01196 *From what far star?* Panther, London, 1953, 143p, Cloth, Novel
01197 *Return to Earth.* Hamilton & Co. (Stafford), London, 1951, 111p, Paper, Novel
01198 *The venom-seekers.* Panther, London, 1953, 160p, Cloth, Novel

as Rolf Garner:

01199 *The Immortals.* Panther, London, 1953, 159p, Cloth, Novel [Kennet Trilogy #2]
01200 *The indestructible.* Panther, London, 1954, 159p, Cloth, Novel [Kennet Trilogy #3]
01201 *Resurgent dust.* Panther, London, 1953, 160p, Cloth, Novel [Kennet Trilogy #1]

BERRY, D(ouglas) BRUCE
as Morgan Drake:

01202 *Flowers of Hell.* Ophelia, New York, 1970, 192p, Paper, Novel

with Andrew J. Offutt as Jeff Douglas:

01203 *The balling machine.* Orpheus Series, New York, 1971, 192p, Paper, Novel

BERRY, JAMES R.

01204 *Dar Tellum: stranger from a distant planet.* Walker, New York, 1973, 64p, Cloth, Novel

BERRY, JOHN (Edgar), 1915-

01205 *Krishna fluting.* Macmillan, New York, 1959, 266p, Cloth, Novel

BERTHET, ÉLIE (Bertrand), 1818-1891

01206 *The pre-historic world.* Porter & Coates, Philadelphia, 1879, 310p, Cloth, Novel

BERTIGNONO, GIOVANNI
  see: BERTIN, JACK

BERTIN, JACK, pseud. [Giovanni Bertignono, 1904-1963] [*biography included*]

01207 *Brood of Helios.* Arcadia House, New York, 1966, 189p, Cloth, Novel

[by Peter B. Germano, Bertin's executor, under his client's name]:

01208 *The pyramids from space.* Lenox Hill Press, New York, 1970, 192p, Cloth, Novel
01209 *The interplanetary adventurers.* Lenox Hill Press, New York, 1970, 192p, Cloth, Novel

BERTON, PIERRE, 1920-   [*biography included*]

01210 *The secret world of Og.* McClelland & Stewart, Toronto, 1961, 146p, Cloth, Novel

BESANT, WALTER, 1836-1901

01211 *The doubts of Dives; Arrowsmith's Christmas annual, 1889.* J. W. Arrowsmith, Bristol, 1889, 192p, Paper, Novel
01212 *The inner house; Arrowsmith's Christmas annual, 1888.* J. W. Arrowsmith, Bristol, 1888, 198p, Paper, Novel

published anonymously:

01213 *The revolt of man.* William Blackwood & Sons, Edinburgh, 1882, 358p, Cloth, Novel
01213A *The revolt of man*, by Walter Besant. Chatto & Windus, London, 1896, 358p, Cloth, Novel

with James Rice:

01214 *The case of Mr. Lucraft, and other tales*, by the authors of "Ready money Mortiboy." Sampson Low, Marston, Searle & Rivington, London, 1876, 2vol, Cloth, Coll.
01214A *The case of Mr. Lucraft, and other tales*, by Walter Besant and James Rice. Chatto & Windus, London, 1877, 341p, Cloth, Coll.

BESSAND-MASSENET, PIERRE, 1899-

01215 *Amorous ghost.* Elek Books, London, 1957, 126p, Cloth, Novel

BEST, HARRY, pseud.

01216 *The lid comes off.* Darkroom Reader, San Diego, 1970, 159p, Paper, Novel

BEST, (Oswald) HERBERT, 1894-

01217 *The twenty-fifth hour.* Random House, New York, 1940, 321p, Cloth, Novel

THE BEST FROM GALAXY

01218   *The best from Galaxy.* Award, New York, 1972,
        251p, Paper, Anth.
01219   *The best from Galaxy, volume II.* Award, New
        York, 1974, 235p, Paper, Anth.

THE BEST FROM IF

01220   *The best from If.* Award, New York, 1973, 252p,
        Paper, Anth.
01221   *The best from If, vol. 2.* Award, New York,
        1974, 235p, Paper, Anth.

THE BEST GHOST STORIES
    see: FRENCH, JOSEPH LEWIS

THE BEST OF SF

01222   *The best of SF; an international exhibition of
        science fiction literature, May 17-31.* Na-
        tional Book League, London, 1971, 50p, Paper,
        Nonf.

THE BEST TERRIBLE TALES FROM THE FRENCH/GERMAN/
ITALIAN/SPANISH
    see: T., C. J.

BESTER, ALFRED, 1913-   [*biography included*]

01223   *An Alfred Bester omnibus.* Sidgwick & Jackson,
        London, 1967, 710p, Cloth, Coll. [includes
        *The demolished man; Tiger! Tiger!; The dark
        side of Earth*]
01224   *The dark side of Earth.* Signet, New York,
        1964, 160p, Paper, Coll.
01225   *The demolished man.* Shasta Publishers, Chica-
        go, 1953, 250p, Cloth, Novel
01226   *Starburst.* Signet, New York, 1958, 160p,
        Paper, Coll.
        The stars my destination. [see 01227A]
01227   *Tiger! Tiger!* Sidgwick & Jackson, London,
        1956, 232p, Cloth, Novel
01227A retitled: *The stars my destination.* Signet,
        New York, 1957, 197p, Paper, Novel

BETE NOIRE, pseud.
    see: HENRY, PAUL-MARC

BETIERO, T(homas) J(asper)

01228   *Nedoure, priestess of the Magi; an historical
        romance of white and black magic, a story
        that reveals wisdom of the ancient past.*
        W. F. Wohlstein, Seattle, 1916, 247p, Cloth,
        Novel

BETTAUER, HUGO, 1872-1925

01229   *The city without Jews; a novel of our time.*
        Bloch Publishing Co., New York, 1926, 189p,
        Cloth, Novel

BEUF, CARLO (Maria Luigi), 1893-

01230   *The innocence of Pastor Müller.* Duell, Sloan
        & Pearce, New York, 1951, 156p, Cloth, Novel

BEUTTLER, EDWARD
    see: BUTLER, IVAN

BEVAN, C. ELNITH

01231   *A collection of ghosts [eleven Indian fantasies]*
        Morland, Amersham, UK, 1920, 119p, Cloth,
        Coll.

BEVERLEY, BARRINGTON

01232   *The space raiders; a novel.* Philip Allan, Lon-
        don, 1936, 245p, Cloth, Novel

BEVIS, H(erbert) U(rlin), 1902-   [*biography
included*]

01233   *The alien abductors.* Lenox Hill Press, New
        York, 1972, 192p, Cloth, Novel
01234   *Space stadium.* Lenox Hill Press, New York,
        1970, 192p, Cloth, Novel
01235   *The star rovers.* Lenox Hill Press, New York,
        1970, 192p, Cloth, Novel
01236   *The time winder.* Lenox Hill Press, New York,
        1970, 192p, Cloth, Novel
01237   *To Luna with love.* Lenox Hill Press, New York,
        1971, 192p, Cloth, Novel

THE BEWITCHED

01238   *The bewitched.* Master Classic, New York, 1969,
        152p, Paper, Novel

BEYER, WILLIAM GRAY

01239   *Minions of the Moon; a novel of the future.*
        Gnome Press, New York, 1950, 190p, Cloth,
        Novel

BEYMER, WILLIAM GILMORE, 1881-

01240   *12:20 P.M.; a novel.* Whittlesey House, McGraw-
        Hill, New York, 1944, 273p, Cloth, Novel
01240A retitled: *The middle of midnight (12:20 A.M.).*
        Whittlesey House, McGraw-Hill, New York,
        1947, 242p, Cloth, Novel

BEYNON, JOHN, pseud.
    see: WYNDHAM, JOHN

BEYOND
    see: DARDIS, THOMAS A.

BEYOND THE STARS

01241   *Beyond the stars, and other stories.* Satellite,
        London, 1958, 113p, Paper, Anth.

BEYOND THE SUNRISE

01242 *Beyond the sunrise; observations by two travel-
      lers.* John W. Lovell, New York, 1883, 237p,
      Cloth, Novel

BIAGI, L. D., pseud.

01243 *The Centaurians; a novel.* Broadway Publishing
      Co., New York, 1911, 339p, Cloth, Novel

BIAMONTI, FRANCESCO

01244 *Harry Harrison; bibliographia (1951-1965).*
      Editoriale Libraria, Trieste, 1965, 11p,
      Paper, Nonf.

BIBIENA, JEAN GALLI de
    see: GALLI de BIBIENA, JEAN

BIDWELL, BENSON, 1835-

01245 *Flying cows of Biloxi.* Henneberry Press,
      Chicago, 1907, 44p, Cloth, Story

BIEMILLER, CARL L(udwig Jr.), 1912-   [*biography included*]

01246 *Escape from the crater; more adventures of the
      Hydronauts.* Doubleday, Garden City, 1974,
      203p, Cloth, Novel [Hydronauts #3]
01247 *Follow the whales; the Hydronauts meet the
      otter-people.* Doubleday, Garden City,
      1973, 185p, Cloth, Novel [Hydronauts #2]
01248 *The Hydronauts.* Doubleday, Garden City,
      1970, 131p, Cloth, Novel [Hydronauts #1]
01249 *The magic ball from Mars.* William Morrow,
      New York, 1953, 127p, Cloth, Novel [Jonny #1]
01250 *Starboy.* Henry Holt, New York, 1956, 158p,
      Cloth, Novel [Jonny #2]

BIEN, H(ermann) M(ilton), 1831-1895

01251 *Ben-Beor; a story of the anti-Messiah, in two
      divisions; pt. 1, Lunar intaglios: the man
      in the Moon, a counterpart of Wallace's
      "Ben-Hur"; pt. 2, historical phantasmagoria:
      the wandering gentile, a companion romance
      to Sue's "Wandering Jew."* Isaac Frieden-
      wald, Baltimore, 1891, 528p, Cloth, Novel

BIERBOWER, AUSTIN, 1844-1913

01252 *From monkey to man; or, Society in the Terti-
      ary Age; a story of the missing link, show-
      ing the first steps in industry, commerce,
      government, religion, and the arts, with an
      account of the great expedition from Cocoa-
      nut Hill, and the wars in Alligator Swamp.*
      Dibble Publishing Co., Chicago, 1894, 231p,
      Cloth, Novel

BIERCE, AMBROSE (Gwinnett), 1842-1914?

01253 *Can such things be?* Cassell, New York, 1893,
      320p, Cloth, Coll.

01254 expanded: *Can such things be?* Boni & Live-
      right, New York, 1924, 427p, Cloth, Coll.
01255 *The collected writings of Ambrose Bierce.*
      Citadel Press, New York, 1946, 810p, Cloth,
      Coll. [includes some verse and nonf.]
01256 *The complete short stories of Ambrose Bierce.*
      Doubleday, Garden City, 1970, 496p, Cloth,
      Coll.
01256A retitled: *The complete short stories of Am-
      brose Bierce, volume I: the world of horror.*
      Ballantine, New York, 1971, 298p, Paper, Coll.
      [Volume 2 contained all of the non-fantastic
      stories.]
01257 *Eyes of the panther; tales of soldiers and
      civilians.* Jonathan Cape, London, 1928, 282p,
      Cloth, Coll.
01258 *Fantastic fables.* G. P. Putnam's Sons, New
      York, 1899, 194p, Cloth, Coll.
01258A retitled: *Fantastic debunking fables.* Halde-
      man-Julius, Girard, KS, 1926?, 64p, Paper,
      Coll. [abridged]
01259 *Ghost and horror stories.* Dover, New York,
      1964, 199p, Paper, Coll.
01260 *In the midst of life.* Boni & Liveright, New
      York, 1918, 403p, Cloth, Coll.
01261 *In the midst of life, and other tales.* Signet
      Classic, New York, 1961, 256p, Paper, Coll.
      [different contents]
      *In the midst of life; tales of soldiers and
      civilians.* [see 01265A]
01262 *A little book of humor, horror, and the super-
      natural.* Little Paperback Classics, Pyramid
      Books, New York, 1968, 62p, Paper, Coll.
01263 *Tales of ghouls and ghosts.* Haldeman-Julius,
      Girard, KS, 1926?, 64p?, Paper, Coll.
01264 *Tales of haunted houses.* Haldeman-Julius,
      Girard, KS, 1926?, 64p?, Paper, Coll.
01265 *Tales of soldiers and civilians.* E. L. G.
      Steele, San Francisco, 1891, 300p, Cloth,
      Coll.
01265A retitled: *In the midst of life; tales of
      soldiers and civilians.* Chatto & Windus,
      London, 1892, 244p, Cloth, Coll. [different
      from other collections of this title]
01266 *Ten tales.* First Edition Club, London, 1925,
      136p, Cloth, Coll.

THE BIG BOOK OF MYSTERY STORIES

01267 *The big book of mystery stories.* Grosset &
      Dunlap, New York, 1927?, 1001p, Cloth, Anth.
      [includes *The death gong*, by Selwyn Jepson;
      The mystery of the yellow room, by Gaston
      Leroux; *The perfume of the lady in black*, by
      Gaston Leroux]

BIGGLE, LLOYD Jr., 1923-   [*biography included*]

01268 *All the colors of darkness.* Doubleday, Garden
      City, 1963, 210p, Cloth, Novel [Jan Darzek #1]
01269 *The angry espers.* Ace Double, New York, 1961,
      136p, Paper, Novel
01270 *The fury out of time.* Doubleday, Garden City,
      1965, 257p, Cloth, Novel
01271 *The light that never was.* Doubleday, Garden
      City, 1972, 216p, Cloth, Novel
01272 *The metallic muse; a collection of science fic-
      tion stories.* Doubleday, Garden City, 1972,
      228p, Cloth, Coll.
01273 *Monument.* Doubleday, Garden City, 1974, 185p,
      Cloth, Novel

BIGGLE, LLOYD Jr. (Cont.)

01274 *Nebula award stories seven.* Harper & Row,
       New York, 1973, 289p, Cloth, Anth.
01275 *The Rule of the Door, and other fanciful re-
       gulations.* Doubleday, Garden City, 1967,
       206p, Cloth, Coll.
01276 *The still, small voice of trumpets.* Double-
       day, Garden City, 1968, 189p, Cloth, Novel
       [Cultural Survey series]
01277 *Watchers of the dark.* Doubleday, Garden
       City, 1966, 228p, Cloth, Novel [Jan Darzek
       #2]
01278 *The world menders.* Doubleday, Garden City,
       1971, 181p, Cloth, Novel

BIGGS, JOHN Jr., 1895-

01279 *Demigods.* Charles Scribner's Sons, New York,
       1926, 230p, Cloth, Novel

BIGLY, CANTELL A., pseud. [George Washington
Peck, 1817-1859]

01280 *Aurifodina; or, Adventures in the gold region.*
       Baker & Scribner, New York, 1849, 103p,
       Cloth, Novel

BIGNON, JEAN PAUL
    see: SANDISSON, Mr.

BILL, ALFRED H(oyt), 1879-1964

01281 *The wolf in the garden.* Longmans, Green, New
       York, 1931, 287p, Cloth, Novel

BILLINGS, MARIS HERRINGTON [Edith S. Billings]

01282 *An Egyptian love spell.* Central Publishing
       Co., New York, 1914, 64p, Paper, Novel

as Maris Warrington:

01283 *Cleomenes (the new Quo vadis).* John Lane,
       New York, 1917, 378p, Cloth, Novel

BINDER, EANDO, pseud.
    see: BINDER, EARL and BINDER, OTTO

BINDER, EARL ANDREW, d. 1965
with Otto Binder as Eando Binder:

01284 *Enslaved brains.* Avalon, New York, 1965,
       192p, Cloth, Novel

with Otto Binder as John Coleridge:

01285 *Martian martyrs.* Columbia Publications, New
       York, 1942?, 23p, Paper, Story
01286 *The new life.* Columbia Publications, New
       York, 1942?, 23p, Paper, Story

BINDER, OTTO O(scar), 1911-1974 [*biography
included*]

01287 *The Avengers battle the Earth-wrecker.* Bantam,
       New York, 1967, 122p, Paper, Novel [Captain
       America #1]

01288 *The hospital horror.* Popular Library, New York
       1973, 192p, Paper, Novel

as Eando Binder:

01289 *Adam Link in the past.* Fantasy Fiction, Sydney
       1950, 48p, Paper, Story [Adam Link series]
01290 *Adam Link--robot.* Paperback Library, New York,
       1965, 174p, Paper, Novel [Adam Link series]
01291 *The cancer machine.* Bizarre Series, Millheim,
       PA, 1941?, 30p, Paper, Story
01292 *The double man.* Curtis, New York, 1971, 159p,
       Paper, Novel
01293 *Five steps to tomorrow.* Curtis, New York, 1970
       158p, Paper, Novel
01294 *Get off my world.* Curtis, New York, 1971, 144p
       Paper, Novel
01295 *The impossible world.* Curtis, New York, 1970,
       159p, Paper, Novel
01296 *Lords of creation.* Prime Press, Philadelphia,
       1949, 232p, Cloth, Novel
01297 *Menace of the saucers.* Belmont, New York, 1969
       144p, Paper, Novel [Saucer series #1]
01298 *The mind from outer space.* Curtis, New York,
       1972, 159p, Paper, Novel
01299 *Night of the saucers.* Belmont, New York, 1971,
       156p, Paper, Novel [Saucers series #2]
01300 *Puzzle of the space pyramids.* Curtis, New
       York, 1971, 205p, Paper, Novel
01301 *Secret of the Red Spot.* Curtis, New York, 1971
       160p, Paper, Novel
01302 *The three eternals.* Fantasy Fiction, Sydney,
       1949, 48p, Paper, Story
01303 *Where eternity ends.* Fantasy Fiction, Sydney,
       1950, 32p, Paper, Story

with Earl Binder as Eando Binder:

01284 *Enslaved brains.* Avalon, New York, 1965, 192p,
       Cloth, Novel

with Earl Binder as John Coleridge:

01285 *Martian martyrs.* Columbia Publications, New
       York, 1942?, 23p, Paper, Story
01286 *The new life.* Columbia Publications, New York,
       1942?, 23p, Paper, Story

**as Eando Binder, with Jack Williamson, Edmond
Hamilton, Raymond Z. Gallun, and John Russel
Fearn:**

01304 *The great illusion.* Fantasy Booklet, Wallsend,
       UK, 1973, 12p, Paper, Story

BINGFIELD, WILLIAM, pseud.

01305 *The travels and adventures of William Bingfield
       Esq., containing as surprizing a fluctuation
       of circumstances, both by sea and land, as
       ever befel one man, with an accurate account
       of the shape, nature, and properties of that
       most furious and amazing animal, the dog-bird
       printed from his own manuscript.* E. Withers
       & R. Baldwin, London, 1753, Vol. I-296p, Vol.
       II-246p, Cloth, Novel
01305A retitled: *The voyages, shipwreck, travels,
       distresses, strange adventures, and miracu-
       lous preservation of William Bingfield, who,
       with two others, was cast away on a desolated
       island, where they discovered the surprising
       ferocity and tractable disposition of that
       amazing animal called the dog bird; likewise,
       an account of his dispersing an immense mul-
       titude of African cannibals.* S. Fisher &
       T. Hurst, London, 1799, 144p, Cloth, Novel

BINGHAM, CARSON, pseud. [Bruce Bingham Cassiday, 1920-   ] [*biography included*]

01306 *Flash Gordon; the witch queen of Mongo.* Avon, New York, 1974, 143p, Paper, Novel [Flash Gordon #5]
01307 *Gorgo.* Monarch, Derby, Conn., 1960, 141p, Paper, Movie

as Con Steffanson, house pseud.:

01308 *Flash Gordon; the time trap of Ming XIII.* Avon, New York, 1974, 160p, Paper, Novel [Flash Gordon #4]

BINGHAM, ROGER, with Raymond Hawkey

01309 *Wild Card; a novel.* Stein & Day, New York, 1974, 248p, Cloth, Novel

BINNS, JACK, 1884-1959

01310 *The flying buccaneer; a novel of adventure in the skies.* Nicholas L. Brown, New York, 1923, 311p, Cloth, Novel

BINNS, OTTWELL

01311 *Dan Yeo; or, The island of the lost.* Ward, Lock, London, 1929, 315p, Cloth, Novel

BIOY CASARES, ADOLFO, 1914-   [*biography included*]

01312 *Diary of the War of the Pig; a novel.* McGraw-Hill, New York, 1972, 196p, Cloth, Novel
01313 *The invention of Morel, and other stories (from La trama celeste).* University of Texas Press, Austin, 1964, 237p, Cloth, Coll.

BIRD, ARTHUR

01314 *Looking forward; a dream of the United States of the Americas in 1999.* L. C. Childs, Utica, NY, 1899, 234p, Cloth, Novel [reply to Bellamy's *Looking backward*]

BIRD, WILLIAM HENRY FLEMING, 1896-1971 [*biography included*]

as Adrian Blair:

01315 *Cosmic conquest.* Curtis Warren, London, 1953, 159p, Cloth, Novel

as Lee Elliot, house pseud.:

01316 *The Third Mutant.* Curtis Warren, London, 1953, 160p, Cloth, Novel

as Harry Fleming:

01317 *Blast-off into space.* Jonathan Cape, London, 1966, 128p, Paper, Novel

as Rand Le Page, house pseud.:

01318 *War of Argos.* Curtis Warren, London, 1952, 127p, Paper, Novel

as Paul Lorraine, house pseud.:

01319 *Two worlds.* Curtis Warren, London, 1952, 128p, Cloth, Novel

as Kris Luna, house pseud.:

01320 *Operation orbit.* Curtis Warren, London, 1953, 159p, Cloth, Novel

BIRDWELL, RUSSELL

01321 *Mount Horeb.* Robert Speller & Sons, New York, 1972, 74p, Cloth, Novel

BIRKHEAD, EDITH

01322 *The tale of terror; a study of the gothic romance.* Constable, London, 1921, 241p, Cloth, Nonf.

BIRKIN, (Sir) CHARLES (Lloyd), Bart., 1907- [*biography included*]

01323 *Dark menace; thirteen new stories of horror and the macabre.* Tandem, London, 1968, 188p Paper, Coll.
    The haunted dancers. [see 01329A]
01324 *The kiss of death, and other horror stories.* Tandem, London, 1964, 234p, Paper, Coll.
01325 *My name is death, and other new tales of horror.* Panther, London, 1966, 139p, Paper, Coll.
01326 *The smell of evil.* Tandem, London, 1965, 189p, Paper, Coll.
01327 *So pale, so cold, so fair.* Tandem, London, 1970, 191p, Paper, Coll.
01328 *Spawn of Satan.* Award, New York, 1970, 186p, Paper, Coll.
01329 *The Tandem book of ghost stories.* Tandem, London, 1965, 192p, Paper, Anth.
01329A retitled: *The haunted dancers.* Paperback Library, New York, 1967, 159p, Paper, Anth.
01330 *The Tandem book of horror stories.* Tandem, London, 1965, 192p, Paper, Anth.
01330A retitled: *The witch-baiter.* Paperback Library, New York, 1967, 159p, Paper, Anth.
01331 *Where terror stalked, and other stories.* Tandem, London, 1966, 192p, Paper, Coll.
    The witch-baiter. [see 01330A]

BIRKMAIER, ELIZABETH G.

01332 *Poseidon's paradise; the romance of Atlantis.* Clemens Publishing Co., San Francisco, 1892, 305p, Cloth, Novel

BIRNIE, MARY SIMPSON

01333 *The ghost washed white.* Vantage Press, New York, 1959, 62p, Cloth, Novel

BIRNSTINGL, EDGAR M(agnus), 1898-1915

01334 *Destur mobed, and other stories.* Privately printed, Oxford, 1915, 121p, Cloth, Coll.

BIRON, HENRY CHARTRES
    see: RAGGED, HYDER

BIRREN, FABER
    see: LANG, GREGOR

BISBEE, EUGENE SHADE

01335 *The treasure of the ice; a romance.* F. Tenny-
       son Neely, New York, 1898, 280p, Cloth,
       Novel

BISHOP, FARNHAM, 1886-1930, with Arthur Gilchrist Brodeur

01336 *The altar of the legion.* Little, Brown, Bos-
       ton, 1926, 316p, Cloth, Novel

BISHOP, GERALD (Vernon), 1949-   [*biography
included*]

01337 *Isaac Asimov: first visit to Britain, 1974.*
       Aardvark House/Mensa, London, 1974, 20p,
       Paper, Nonf.
01338 *New British science fiction and fantasy books
       published during 1970 & 1971.* Joanne Burger,
       Lake Jackson, TX, 1974, 40p, Paper, Nonf.
01339 *New science fiction books published in Great
       Britain, 1968, 1969.* Joanne Burger, Lake
       Jackson, TX, 1970, 15p, Paper, Nonf.

with Bob Leman:

01340 *Venture science fiction magazine; a checklist
       of the first American series, and the first
       British series, with an index to both of
       these by author and title; also, an index
       of the first three issues of the second
       American series.* Aardvark House, Exeter, UK,
       1970, 28p, Paper, Nonf.

BISHOP, MORCHARD, pseud. [Oliver Stonor,
1903-   ] [*biography included*]

01341 *The star called Wormwood; an investigation of
       the possible reasons for its decline and
       fall, as described in the VIIIth chapter of
       the Apocalypse.* Victor Gollancz, London,
       1941, 279p, Cloth, Novel

BISHOP, MORRIS, 1893-1973 [*biography included*]

01342 *A romantic story book.* Cornell University
       Press, Ithaca, NY, 1971, 309p, Cloth, Anth.

BISHOP, W(illiam) H(enry), 1847-1928

01343 *The garden of Eden, U.S.A.; a very possible
       story.* Charles H. Kerr, Chicago, 1895,
       369p, Cloth, Novel

BISHOP, ZEALIA B(rown)

01344 *The curse of Yig.* Arkham House, Sauk City,
       1953, 175p, Cloth, Coll.

BISS, GERALD

01345 *The door of the unreal.* Eveleigh Nash, London,
       1919, 271p, Cloth, Novel

BISSEROV, GEORGE

01346 *An omnibus of continental mysteries, part I.*
       Juniper Press, New York, 1960, 382p, Paper,
       Anth.

BITZIUS, ALBERT
    see: GOTTHELF, JEREMIAS

BIXBY, (Drexel) JEROME (Lewis), 1923-   [*biography included*]

01347 *Devil's scrapbook.* Brandon House, North Holly-
       wood, 1964, 158p, Paper, Coll.
01347A retitled: *Call for an exorcist.* Brandon Books,
       Chatsworth, 1974, 158p, Paper, Coll.
01348 *Space by the tale.* Ballantine, New York, 1964,
       159p, Paper, Coll.

BLACK, ANGUS

01349 *The devil's coven; classic stories of Scottish
       witchcraft.* New English Library, London,
       1972, 156p, Paper, Anth. [includes some nonf.

BLACK, DOROTHY (Delius), 1899-

01350 *Candles in the dark.* Cassell, London, 1954,
       188p, Cloth, Novel

BLACK, FRANK BURNE

01351 *The Chronicle of Kan-Uk the Kute, being a copy
       of a scroll inscribed to him, what time he
       did travel in his caravan throughout the
       land of Kan-a-Da and of Am-er-Eka in the days
       of the Great War, and now given to the world
       by its finder.* G. P. Putnam's Sons, New
       York, 1918, 102p, Cloth, Novel

BLACK, JAMES (Macdougall), 1879-1949

01352 *The pilgrim ship.* Hodder & Stoughton, London,
       1910, 359p, Cloth, Novel

BLACK, LADBROKE (Lionel Day), 1877-1940

01353 *The Gorgon's head.* Sampson Low, Marston, Lon-
       don, 1932, 250p, Cloth, Novel
01354 *The Poison War.* Stanley Paul, London, 1933,
       288p, Cloth, Novel

BLACK, PANSY E.

01355 *The men from the meteor.* Stellar Publishing
       Corp., New York, 1932, 24p, Paper, Story
01356 *The valley of the great ray.* Stellar Publish-
       ing Corp., New York, 1930, 24p, Paper, Story

BLACK, WILLIAM, 1841-1898

01357 *The magic ink, and other stories*. Sampson
       Low, Marston, London, 1892, 284p, Cloth,
       Coll.

THE BLACK MONK
    see: RYMER, JAMES MALCOLM

THE BLACK PIRATE

01358 *The black pirate; or, The phantom ship; a
       romance*. William Emans, London, 1839,
       710p, Cloth, Novel

BLACK TALES

01359 *Black tales; an anthology*. Corgi, London,
       1965, 158p, Paper, Anth.

BLACKBURN, JOHN (Fenwick), 1923-   [*biography
included*]

01360 *Bury him darkly*. Jonathan Cape, London, 1969,
       191p, Cloth, Novel
01361 *Children of the night*. Jonathan Cape, London,
       1966, 192p, Cloth, Novel
01362 *Devil daddy*. Jonathan Cape, London, 1972,
       191p, Cloth, Novel
01363 *For fear of little men*. Jonathan Cape, Lon-
       don, 1972, 191p, Cloth, Novel
01364 *Nothing but the night*. Jonathan Cape, London,
       1968, 192p, Cloth, Novel
01365 *A scent of new-mown hay*. Secker & Warburg,
       London, 1958, 221p, Cloth, Novel
01366 *A sour apple tree*. Secker & Warburg, London,
       1958, 191p, Cloth, Novel
01367 *The Young Man from Lima*. Jonathan Cape, Lon-
       don, 1968, 190p, Cloth, Novel

BLACKDEN, PAUL

01368 *Adam and Eve, 2020 A.D.* Everest Books, Lon-
       don, 1974, 123p, Paper, Novel

BLACKLEDGE, KATHARINE TREAT, 1866?-1924?

01369 *The Amulet; a tale of the Orient*. Commercial
       Printing House, Los Angeles, 1916, 277p,
       Cloth, Novel
01370 *The jeweled serpent*. Cornhill Publishing Co.,
       Boston, 1922, 258p, Cloth, Novel

BLACKSTOCK, CHARITY, pseud. [Ursula Torday]

01371 *The encounter*. Coward, McCann & Geoghegan,
       New York, 1971, 251p, Cloth, Novel

BLACKSTONE, VALERIUS D., pseud. [J. A. Galpin]

01372 *Auburn; a novel*. F. Tennyson Neely, New York,
       1901, 147p, Cloth, Novel

BLACKWOOD, ALGERNON (Henry), 1869-1951

01373 *Ancient sorceries, and other stories*. Penguin,
       Harmondsworth, 1968, 203p, Paper, Coll.
       Ancient sorceries, and other tales. [see
       01411A]
01374 *Best ghost stories of Algernon Blackwood*.
       Dover, New York, 1974, 366p, Paper, Coll.
01375 *The best supernatural tales of Algernon Black-
       wood*. Causeway, New York, 1973, 526p, Cloth,
       Coll. [adapted from *Strange Stories*]
01376 *The bright messenger*. Cassell, London, 1921,
       349p, Cloth, Coll. [Julius LeVallon #2]
01377 *The centaur*. Macmillan, London, 1911, 347p,
       Cloth, Novel
01378 *The dance of death, and other tales*. Herbert
       Jenkins, London, 1927, 224p, Cloth, Coll.
01379 *Day and night stories*. Cassell, London, 1917,
       332p, Cloth, Coll.
01380 *The doll, and one other*. Arkham House, Sauk
       City, 1946, 138p, Cloth, Coll.
01381 *Dudley & Gilderoy; a nonsense*. Ernest Benn,
       London, 1929, 281p, Cloth, Novel
01382 *The education of Uncle Paul*. Macmillan, London,
       1909, 348p, Cloth, Novel [Uncle Paul #1]
01383 *The empty house, and other ghost stories*. Eve-
       leigh Nash, London, 1906, 316p, Cloth, Coll.
01384 *The extra day*. Macmillan, London, 1915, 358p,
       Cloth, Novel
01385 *The fruit stoners, being the adventures of
       Maria among the fruit stoners*. Grayson &
       Grayson, London, 1934, 287p, Cloth, Novel
01386 *Full circle*. Elkin Mathews & Marrot, London,
       1929, 23p, Cloth, Story
01387 *The garden of survival*. Macmillan, London,
       1918, 168p, Cloth, Novel
01388 *The human chord*. Macmillan, London, 1910, 326p,
       Cloth, Novel
01389 *In the realm of terror; 8 haunting tales*. Pan-
       theon, New York, 1957, 312p, Cloth, Coll.
01390 *Incredible adventures*. Macmillan, London,
       1914, 366p, Cloth, Coll.
       The insanity of Jones, and other tales. [see
       01402B]
01391 *Jimbo; a fantasy*. Macmillan, London, 1909,
       258p, Cloth, Novel
01392 *John Silence, physician extraordinary*. Eve-
       leigh Nash, London, 1908, 390p, Cloth, Coll.
01393 *Julius LeVallon; an episode*. Cassell, London,
       1916, 332p, Cloth, Novel [Julius LeVallon #1]
01394 *The listener, and other stories*. Eveleigh Nash,
       London, 1907, 350p, Cloth, Coll.
01395 *The lost valley, and other stories*. Eveleigh
       Nash, London, 1910, 328p, Cloth, Coll.
01396 *Pan's garden; a volume of nature stories*. Mac-
       millan, London, 1912, 530p, Cloth, Coll.
01397 *A prisoner in Fairyland (the book that 'Uncle
       Paul' wrote)*. Macmillan, London, 1913, 506p,
       Cloth, Coll. [Uncle Paul #2]
01398 *The promise of air*. Macmillan, London, 1918,
       275p, Cloth, Novel
01399 *Sambo and Snitch*. Basil Blackwell, Oxford,
       1927, 89p, Cloth, Novel
01400 *Selected short stories of Algernon Blackwood*.
       Armed Forces Edition, 194?,   , Paper, Coll.
01401 *Selected tales of Algernon Blackwood*. Penguin,
       Harmondsworth, 1942, 173p, Paper, Coll.
01402 *Selected tales of Algernon Blackwood*. John
       Baker, London, 1964, 381p, Cloth, Coll [dif-
       ferent contents from preceding book]

BLACKWOOD, ALGERNON (cont.)

01402A   retitled: *Tales of terror and the unknown.*
E. P. Dutton, New York, 1965, 381p, Cloth,
Coll.

01402B   retitled: *The insanity of Jones, and other
tales.* Penguin, Harmondsworth, 1966, 365p,
Paper, Coll.

01403   *Shocks.* Grayson & Grayson, London, 1935,
300p, Cloth, Coll.

01404   *Short stories of to-day and yesterday.* George
G. Harrap, London, 1930, 284p, Cloth, Coll.

01405   *Strange stories.* William Heinemann, London,
1929, 745p, Cloth, Coll.

01406   *The tales of Algernon Blackwood.* Martin Secker, London, 1938, 684p, Cloth, Coll.
Tales of terror and the unknown. [see 01402A]

01407   *Tales of the mysterious and macabre.* Spring
Books, London, 1967, 400p, Cloth, Coll.

01408   *Tales of the uncanny and supernatural.* Peter
Nevill, London, 1949, 426p, Cloth, Coll.

01409   *Ten minute stories.* John Murray, London,
1914, 271p, Cloth, Coll.

01410   *Tongues of fire, and other sketches.* Herbert
Jenkins, London, 1924, 311p, Cloth, Coll.

01411   *The willows, and other queer tales.* Collins,
London, 1925?, 318p, Cloth, Coll.

01411A   retitled: *Ancient sorceries, and other tales.*
Collins Clear-Type Press, London, 1927,
251p, Cloth, Coll. [abridged]

with Wilfred Wilson:

01412   *The wolves of God, and other fey stories.*
Cassell, London, 1921, 328p, Cloth, Coll.

BLAIN, WILLIAM

01413   *Witch's blood.* Hurst & Blackett, London,
1946, 216p, Cloth, Novel

BLAINE, JOHN, pseud. [Harold Leland Goodwin,
1914-   ] [*biography included*]

01414   *The blue ghost mystery.* Grosset & Dunlap,
New York, 1960, 181p, Paper, Novel [Rick
Brant #15]

01415   *The Caves of Fear.* Grosset & Dunlap, New
York, 1951, 210p, Cloth, Novel [Rick Brant
#8]

01416   *The deadly Dutchman.* Grosset & Dunlap, New
York, 1967, 176p, Cloth, Novel [Rick Brant
#22]

01417   *The Egyptian cat mystery.* Grosset & Dunlap,
New York, 1961, 182p, Cloth, Novel [Rick
Brant #16]

01418   *The electronic mind reader.* Grosset & Dunlap,
New York, 1957, 214p, Cloth, Novel [Rick
Brant #12]

01419   *The flaming mountain.* Grosset & Dunlap, New
York, 1962, 172p, Cloth, Novel [Rick Brant
#17]

01420   *The flying stingaree.* Grosset & Dunlap, New
York, 1963, 176p, Cloth, Novel [Rick Brant
#18]

01421   *The golden skull.* Grosset & Dunlap, New York,
1954, 214p, Cloth, Novel [Rick Brant #10]

01422   *The lost city.* Grosset & Dunlap, New York,
1947, 209p, Cloth, Novel [Rick Brant #2]

01423   *100 fathoms under.* Grosset & Dunlap, New
York, 1947, 209p, Cloth, Novel [Rick Brant
#4]

01424   *The phantom shark.* Grosset & Dunlap, New York,
1949, 206p, Cloth, Novel [Rick Brant #6]

01425   *The pirates of Shan.* Grosset & Dunlap, New
York, 1958, 181p, Cloth, Novel [Rick Brant
#14]

01426   *Rocket jumper.* Grosset & Dunlap, New York,
1966, 177p, Cloth, Novel [Rick Brant #21]

01427   *The rocket's shadow.* Grosset & Dunlap, New
York, 1947, 209p, Cloth, Novel [Rick Brant #1]

01428   *The ruby ray mystery.* Grosset & Dunlap, New
York, 1964, 176p, Cloth, Novel [Rick Brant
#19]

01429   *The Scarlet Lake mystery.* Grosset & Dunlap,
New York, 1958, 184p, Cloth, Novel [Rick
Brant #13]

01430   *Sea gold.* Grosset & Dunlap, New York, 1947,
214p, Cloth, Novel [Rick Brant #3]

01431   *Smugglers' Reef.* Grosset & Dunlap, New York,
1950, 211p, Cloth, Novel [Rick Brant #7]

01432   *Stairway to danger.* Grosset & Dunlap, New
York, 1952, 210p, Cloth, Novel [Rick Brant #9]

01433   *The veiled raiders.* Grosset & Dunlap, New
York, 1965, 178p, Cloth, Novel [Rick Brant
#20]

01434   *The wailing octopus.* Grosset & Dunlap, New
York, 1956, 209p, Cloth, Novel [Rick Brant
#11]

01435   *The whispering box mystery.* Grosset & Dunlap,
New York, 1948, 216p, Cloth, Novel [Rick
Brant #5]

as Blake Savage:

01436   *Rip Foster rides the gray planet.* Whitman,
Racine, 1952, 250p, Cloth, Novel

01436A   retitled: *Assignment in space with Rip Foster.*
Whitman, Racine, 1958, 282p, Cloth, Novel

01436B   retitled: *Rip Foster in ride the gray planet.*
Golden Press, New York, 1969, 253p, Paper,
Novel

with Philip Harkins as John Blaine:

01437   *Danger below!* Grosset & Dunlap, New York,
1968, 178p, Cloth, Novel [Rick Brant #23]

BLAIR, ADRIAN, pseud.
see: BIRD, WILLIAM HENRY FLEMING

BLAIR, ANDREW [published anonymously]

01438   *Annals of the twenty-ninth century; or, The
autobiography of the tenth president of the
World Republic.* Samuel Tinsley, London,
1874, vol. I-260p, vol. II-248p, vol. III-
250p, Cloth, Novel

BLAIR, ERIC ARTHUR
see: ORWELL, GEORGE

BLAIR, HAMISH [Andrew James Fraser Blair, 1872-
1935]

01439   *Governor Hardy.* William Blackwood & Sons,
Edinburgh, 1931, 303p, Cloth, Novel

01440   *The great gesture.* William Blackwood & Sons,
Edinburgh, 1931, 295p, Cloth, Novel

01441   *1957.* William Blackwood & Sons, Edinburgh,
1930, 354p, Cloth, Novel

BLAIR, JOHN HUNTER-
   see: HUNTER-BLAIR, JOHN

BLAIR, PETER (Hunter)

  01442 *The coming of Pout.* Jonathan Cape, London,
       1966, 159p, Cloth, Novel

BLAISDELL, ELINORE (Rosenburg), 1904-

  01443 *Tales of the undead; vampires and visitants.*
       Thomas Y. Crowell, New York, 1947, 372p,
       Cloth, Anth.

BLAKE, EMILIA AYLMER
   see: GOWING, MRS. AYLMER

BLAKE, KEVIN

  01444 *The cocked connection.* Eros Goldstripe, Wil-
       mington, Del., 1974, 182p, Paper, Novel
       [Brandy French #7]

BLAKE, NICHOLAS, pseud. [Cecil Day Lewis,
1904-1972] [*biography included*]

  01445 *The smiler with the knife.* Collins, London,
       1939, 284p, Cloth, Novel

BLAKE, STACEY

  01446 *Beyond the blue; the story of a great adven-
       ture.* Books Ltd., London, 1920, 221p, Cloth,
       Novel

BLAKE, THOMAS (A.)

  01447 *U.N. confidential--A.D. 2000.* Vantage Press,
       New York, 1967, 86p, Cloth, Novel

BLAKEMORE, FELIX J(ohn)

  01448 *The coming hour (?).* Sands & Co., London,
       1927, 226p, Cloth, Novel

BLAMIRES, HARRY, 1916-   [*biography included*]

  01449 *Blessing unbounded; a vision.* Longmans,
       Green, London, 1955, 185p, Cloth, Novel
       [Heaven & Hell #3]
  01450 *Cold war in Hell.* Longmans, Green, London,
       1955, 198p, Cloth, Novel [Heaven & Hell #2]
  01451 *The devil's hunting-grounds; a fantasy.* Long-
       mans, Green, London, 1954, 162p, Cloth,
       Novel [Heaven & Hell #1]

BLANC, MAURICE LE
   see: LE BLANC, MAURICE

BLANCHARD, CHARLES ELTON, 1868-

  01452 *A new day dawns; a brief history of the Altru-
       istic Era (1930 to 2162 A.D.), A.E. 200.*
       Medical Success Press, Youngstown, OH, 1932,
       191p, Cloth, Novel

BLANCHARD, H(enry) PERCY, 1862-1939

  01453 *After the Cataclysm; a romance of the age to
       come.* Cochrane Publishing Co., New York,
       1909, 137p, Cloth, Novel

BLAND, C(harles) A(shwold)

  01454 *Independence; a retrospect, from the "Reminis-
       cences, home and colonial," of C. A. Bland.*
       Harrison & Sons, London, 1891, 56p, Paper,
       Novel

BLAND, T(homas) A(ugustus), 1830-

  01455 *"In the world celestial."* Alliance Publishing
       Co., New York, 1901, 159p, Cloth, Novel

BLATCHFORD, ROBERT, 1851-1943

  01456 *The sorcery shop; an impossible romance.* Clari-
       on Press, London, 1907, 199p, Cloth, Novel

BLATTY, WILLIAM PETER, 1928-   [*biography included*]

  01457 *The exorcist.* Harper & Row, New York, 1971,
       340p, Cloth, Novel
  01458 *I, Billy Shakespeare.* Doubleday, Garden City,
       1965, 89p, Cloth, Novel

BLAUSTEIN, ALBERT P.
   see: DeGRAEFF, ALLEN

BLAVATSKY, H(elena) P(etrovna), 1831-1891

  01459 *Nightmare tales.* Theosophical Publishing House,
       London, 1892, 133p, Cloth, Coll.

with W. Q. Judge:

  01460 *The tell-tale picture gallery; occult stories.*
       International Book House, Bombay, 194?, 218p,
       Cloth, Coll.

BLAYDES, R. O.

  01461 *Lady Eve.* H. S. Crocker Co., San Francisco,
       1899, 28p, Cloth, Story

BLAYN, HUGO, pseud.
   see: FEARN, JOHN RUSSELL

BLAYRE, CHRISTOPHER, pseud.
   see: HERON-ALLEN, EDWARD

BLAZE de BURY, F.
    see: DICKBERRY, F.

BLEACKLEY, HORACE (William), 1868-1931

01462 *Anymoon.* John Lane, The Bodley Head, London,
       1919, 327p, Cloth, Novel

BLECH, AIMÉE, pseud. [Lionel Dalsace]

01463 *Lights and shadows; tales of karma and reincar-
       nation.* Theosophical Publishing House, Lon-
       don, 1928, 144p, Cloth, Coll.

BLEILER, EVERETT F(ranklin), 1920-

01464 *The castle of Otranto, by Horace Walpole; Vat-
       hek, by William Beckford; The vampyre, by
       John Polidori; and a fragment of a novel by
       Lord Byron; three gothic novels.* Dover, New
       York, 1966, 291p, Paper, Anth.
01465 *The checklist of fantastic literature; a bib-
       liography of fantasy, weird, and science fic-
       tion books published in the English language.*
       Shasta Publishers, Chicago, 1948, 455p, Cloth,
       Nonf.
01466 *Five Victorian ghost novels.* Dover, New York,
       1971, 421p, Paper, Anth.

with T. E. Dikty:

01467 *The best science fiction stories, 1949.* Fred-
       erick Fell, New York, 1949, 314p, Cloth, Anth.
01468 *The best science-fiction stories, 1950.* Fred-
       erick Fell, New York, 1950, 347p, Cloth, Anth.
01468A retitled: *The best science fiction stories.*
       Grayson & Grayson, London, 1951, 256p, Cloth,
       Anth. [abridged]
01469 *The best science-fiction stories, 1951.* Fred-
       erick Fell, New York, 1951, 352p, Cloth, Anth.
01469A retitled: *The best science fiction stories,
       second series.* Grayson & Grayson, London,
       1952, 240p, Cloth, Anth. [abridged]
01469B retitled: *The mindworm; a collection of the
       best science fiction stories.* Tandem, Lon-
       don, 1967, 191p, Paper, Anth. [abridged; pub-
       lished anonymously]
01470 *The best science-fiction stories, 1952.* Fred-
       erick Fell, New York, 1952, 288p, Cloth, Anth.
01470A retitled: *The best science fiction stories,
       third series.* Grayson & Grayson, London,
       1953, 256p, Cloth, Anth. [abridged]
01471 *The best science-fiction stories, 1953.* Fred-
       erick Fell, New York, 1953, 279p, Cloth, Anth.
01471A retitled: *The best science fiction stories,
       fourth series.* Grayson & Grayson, London,
       1955, 239p, Cloth, Anth. [abridged]
01472 *The best science-fiction stories, 1954.* Fred-
       erick Fell, New York, 1954, 316p, Cloth, Anth.
01472A retitled: *The best science fiction stories,
       fifth series.* Grayson & Grayson, London,
       1956, 207p, Cloth, Anth. [abridged]
       Category Phoenix. [see 01477A]
01473 *Frontiers in space; selections from The best
       science fiction stories.* Bantam, New York,
       1955, 166p, Paper, Anth. [selections from
       the 1951, 1952, and 1953 series]
01474 *Imagination unlimited; science-fiction and
       science.* Farrar, Straus & Young, New York,
       1952, 430p, Cloth, Anth.

01474A retitled: *Men of space and time.* Bodley Head,
       London, 1953, 221p, Cloth, Anth. [abridged]
       The mindworm. [see 01469B]
01475 *Science fiction omnibus; The best science fic-
       tion stories, 1949, 1950.* Garden City Books,
       Garden City, 1952, 658p, Cloth, Anth. [in-
       cludes 01467, 01468]
01476 *Year's best science fiction novels, 1952.*
       Frederick Fell, New York, 1952, 352p, Cloth,
       Anth.
01476A retitled: *Year's best science fiction novels.*
       Grayson & Grayson, London, 1953, 263p, Cloth,
       Anth. [abridged]
01477 *Year's best science fiction novels, 1953.*
       Frederick Fell, New York, 1953, 317p, Cloth,
       Anth.
01477A retitled: *Category Phoenix.* Bodley Head, Lon-
       don, 1955, 192p, Cloth, Anth. [abridged]
01478 *Year's best science fiction novels, 1954.*
       Frederick Fell, New York, 1954, 318p, Cloth,
       Anth.
01478A retitled: *Year's best science fiction novels,
       second series.* Grayson & Grayson, London,
       1955, 240p, Cloth, Anth. [abridged]

BLEUNARD, A(lbert), 1852-

01479 *Babylon electrified; the history of an expedi-
       tion undertaken to restore ancient Babylon
       by the power of electricity, and how it re-
       sulted.* Gebbie & Co., Philadelphia, 1889,
       304p, Paper, Novel

BLINN, EDITH

01480 *The ashes of my heart.* Mark-Well Publishing
       Co., New York, 1916, 385p, Cloth, Novel

BLISH, JAMES (Benjamin), 1921-1975 [*biography
included*]

01481 *...And all the stars a stage.* Doubleday, Gar-
       den City, 1971, 206p, Cloth, Novel
01482 *Anywhen.* Doubleday, Garden City, 1970, 168p,
       Cloth, Coll.
01483 *Best science fiction stories of James Blish.*
       Faber & Faber, London, 1965, 224p, Cloth,
       Coll.
01484 *Best science fiction stories of James Blish,
       revised edition.* Faber & Faber, London, 1973,
       216p, Cloth, Coll.
01485 *Black Easter; or, Faust Aleph-Null.* Doubleday,
       Garden City, 1968, 165p, Cloth, Novel [After
       Such Knowledge #2]
01486 *A case of conscience.* Ballantine, New York,
       1958, 188p, Paper, Novel [After Such Know-
       ledge #4]
01487 *Cities in flight.* Avon, New York, 1970, 607p,
       Paper, Coll. [includes 01489, 01493, 01514,
       01516]
       A clash of cymbals. [see 01516A]
01488 *The day after judgment; a novel.* Doubleday,
       Garden City, 1971, 166p, Cloth, Novel [After
       Such Knowledge #3]
       ESPer. [see 01492]
01489 *Earthman, come home.* G. P. Putnam's Sons, New
       York, 1955, 239p, Cloth, Novel [Cities in
       Flight #3]
       Fallen star. [see 01490A]

BLISH, JAMES (cont.)

01490 *The frozen year.* Ballantine, New York, 1957, 155p, Cloth, Novel
01490A retitled: *Fallen star.* Faber & Faber, London, 1957, 224p, Cloth, Novel
01491 *Galactic cluster.* Signet, New York, 1959, 176p, Paper, Coll.
01492 *Jack of eagles.* A Corwin Book, Greenberg: Publisher, New York, 1952, 246p, Cloth, Novel
01492A retitled: *ESPer.* Avon, New York, 1958, 190p, Paper, Novel
01493 *A life for the stars.* G. P. Putnam's Sons, New York, 1962, 188p, Cloth, Novel [Cities in Flight #2]
01494 *Midsummer century.* Doubleday, Garden City, 1972, 106p, Cloth, Novel
01495 *Mission to the heart stars.* G. P. Putnam's Sons, New York, 1965, 158p, Cloth, Novel
01496 *Nebula award stories five.* Victor Gollancz, London, 1970, 215p, Cloth, Anth.
01497 *New dreams this morning.* Ballantine, New York, 1966, 190p, Paper, Anth.
01498 *The night shapes.* Ballantine, New York, 1962, 127p, Paper, Novel
01499 *The quincunx of time.* Dell, New York, 1973, 128p, Paper, Novel
01500 *The seedling stars.* Gnome Press, New York, 1957, 185p, Cloth, Novel
01501 *So close to home.* Ballantine, New York, 1961, 142p, Paper, Coll.
01502 *Spock must die!* Bantam, New York, 1970, 118p, Paper, Tele. [Star Trek series]
01503 *The star dwellers.* G. P. Putnam's Sons, New York, 1961, 192p, Cloth, Novel
01504 *Star trek.* Bantam, New York, 1967, 136p, Paper, Tele. Coll. [Star Trek series]
01505´ *Star trek 2.* Bantam, New York, 1968, 122p, Paper, Tele. Coll. [Star Trek series]
01506 *Star trek 3.* Bantam, New York, 1969, 118p, Paper, Tele. Coll. [Star Trek series]
01507 *Star trek 4.* Bantam, New York, 1971, 134p, Paper, Tele. Coll. [Star Trek series]
01508 *Star trek 5.* Bantam, New York, 1972, 136p, Paper, Tele. Coll. [Star Trek series]
01509 *Star trek 6.* Bantam, New York, 1972, 149p, Paper, Tele. Coll. [Star Trek series]
01510 *Star trek 7.* Bantam, New York, 1972, 155p, Paper, Tele. Coll. [Star Trek series]
01511 *Star trek 8.* Bantam, New York, 1972, 170p, Paper, Tele. Coll. [Star Trek series]
01512 *Star trek 9.* Bantam, New York, 1973, 183p, Paper, Tele. Coll. [Star Trek series]
01513 *Star trek 10.* Bantam, New York, 1974, 165p, Paper, Tele. Coll. [Star Trek series]
01514 *They shall have stars; a science fiction novel.* Faber & Faber, London, 1956, 181p, Cloth, Novel [Cities in Flight #1]
01514A retitled: *Year 2018!* Avon, New York, 1957, 159p, Paper, Novel [Cities in Flight #1]
01515 *Titan's daughter.* Berkley Medallion, New York, 1961, 142p, Paper, Novel
01516 *The triumph of time.* Avon, New York, 1958, 158p, Paper, Novel [Cities in Flight #4]
01516A retitled: *A clash of cymbals.* Faber & Faber, London, 1959, 197p, Cloth, Novel [Cities in Flight #4]
01517 *VOR.* Avon, New York, 1958, 159p, Paper, Novel
01518 *The vanished jet.* Weybright & Talley, New York, 1968, 117p, Cloth, Novel
01519 *The Warriors of Day.* Galaxy Novel, New York, 1953, 125p, Paper, Novel

01520 *Welcome to Mars.* G. P. Putnam's Sons, New York, 1967, 160p, Cloth, Novel
       Year 2018! [see 01514A]

as William Atheling, Jr.:

01521 *The issue at hand; studies in contemporary magazine science fiction.* Advent: Publishers, Chicago, 1964, 136p, Cloth, Nonf. Coll.
01522 *More issues at hand; critical studies in contemporary science fiction.* Advent: Publishers, Chicago, 1970, 154p, Cloth, Nonf. Coll.

with Norman L. Knight:

01523 *A torrent of faces.* Doubleday, Garden City, 1967, 270p, Cloth, Novel

with Robert W. Lowndes:

01524 *The duplicated man.* Avalon, New York, 1959, 222p, Cloth, Novel

BLISHEN, EDWARD, 1920-   [*biography included*], with Leon Garfield

01525 *The god beneath the sea.* Longman, London, 1970, 168p, Cloth, Novel
01526 *The golden shadow.* Longman Young Books, Harmondsworth, 1973, 159p, Cloth, Novel

BLISS, DOUGLAS PERCY, 1900-

01527 *The devil in Scotland, being four great Scotish stories of diablerie, along with an introductory essay and thirty-nine original wood engravings.* Alexander Maclehose, London, 1934, 107p, Cloth, Anth.

BLISS, EDGAR JANES

01528 *The peril of Oliver Sargent.* Charles L. Webster, New York, 1891, 177p, Cloth, Novel

BLISSETT, NELLIE K.

01529 *The sea hath its pearls; a phantasy.* Hutchinson, London, 1901, 344p, Cloth, Novel

BLIXEN, KAREN
     see: DINESEN, ISAK

BLOCH, BERTRAM

01530 *The little laundress and the fearful knight.* Doubleday, Garden City, 1954, 122p, Cloth, Novel

BLOCH, CHAYIM, 1881-

01531 *The golem; legends of the ghetto of Prague.* The Golem, Vienna, 1925, 247p, Cloth, Coll.

BLOCH, REGINA MIRIAM

01532 *The book of strange loves.* John Richmond, London, 1918, 293p, Cloth, Coll.
01533 *The swine-gods, and other visions.* John Richmond, London, 1917, 84p, Cloth, Coll.

BLOCH, ROBERT (Albert), 1917-   [*biography included*]

01534 *Atoms and evil*. Gold Medal, Greenwich, 1962, 160p, Paper, Coll.
01535 *Blood runs cold*. Simon & Schuster, New York, 1961, 246p, Cloth, Coll.
01536 *Bogey men; ten tales*. Pyramid, New York, 1963, 159p, Paper, Coll.
01537 *Chamber of horrors*. Award, New York, 1966, 139p, Paper, Coll.
01538 *Dragons and nightmares; four short novels*. Mirage Press (The Voyager Series), Baltimore, 1968, 185p, Cloth, Coll.
01539 *The eighth stage of fandom; selections from 25 years of fan writing*. Advent: Publishers, Chicago, 1962, 176p, Cloth, Nonf. Coll.
01540 *Fear today, gone tomorrow*. Award, New York, 1971, 159p, Paper, Coll.
01541 *Horror-7*. Belmont, New York, 1963, 125p, Paper, Coll.
       The house of the hatchet. [see 01552A]
01542 *It's all in your mind*. Curtis, New York, 1971, 128p, Paper, Novel
01543 *Ladies' day; and, This crowded Earth*. Belmont Double, New York, 1968, 172p, Paper, Coll.
01544 *The living demons*. Belmont, New York, 1967, 156p, Paper, Coll.
01545 *More nightmares*. Belmont, New York, 1962, 173p, Paper, Coll.
       Nightmares. [see 01547A]
01546 *The opener of the way*. Arkham House, Sauk City, 1945, 309p, Cloth, Coll.
01547 *Pleasant dreams--nightmares*. Arkham House, Sauk City, 1960, 233p, Cloth, Coll.
01547A retitled: *Nightmares*. Belmont, New York, 1961, 140p, Paper, Coll. [abridged]
01548 *Sea kissed*. Utopian Publications, London, 1945, 39p, Paper, Coll. [one story co-authored with Henry Kuttner]
01549 *The skull of the Marquis de Sade, and other stories*. Pyramid, New York, 1965, 157p, Paper, Coll.
01550 *Sneak preview*. Paperback Library, New York, 1971, 192p, Paper, Novel
01551 *Tales in a jugular vein*. Pyramid, New York, 1965, 144p, Paper, Coll.
01552 *Yours truly, Jack the Ripper; tales of horror*. Belmont, New York, 1962, 189p, Paper, Coll.
01552A retitled: *The house of the hatchet, and other tales of horror*. Tandem, London, 1965, 190p, Paper, Coll.

BLODGETT, MABEL FULLER, 1869-1959

01553 *At the queen's mercy*. Lamson, Wolffe, Boston, 1897, 261p, Cloth, Novel

BLOODSTONE, JOHN, pseud.
    see: BYRNE, STUART J.

BLOOM, URSULA (Harvey), 1896?-   [*biography included*]

01554 *The judge of Jerusalem*. George G. Harrap, London, 1926, 303p, Cloth, Novel

with Charles Eade as Lozania Prolé:

01555 *Daughter of the devil*. Robert Hale, London, 1963, 192p, Cloth, Novel

BLOOM, WILLIAM, 1948-   [as W∴W∴, pseud.]

01556 *The taming power; the first Qhe adventure*. Mayflower, St. Albans, UK, 1974, 189p, Paper, Novel [Qhe #1]
01557 *White fire*. Mayflower, St. Albans, UK, 1974, 204p, Paper, Novel [Qhe #2]

BLOOMER, J(ames) **M**(oses), 1841-

01558 *D'Mars affinity; romance of love's final test in time and tide*. J. S. Ogilvie Publishing Co., New York, 1903, 342p, Cloth, Novel

BLOOMFIELD, PAUL, 1898-

01559 *Imaginary worlds; or, The evolution of utopia*. Hamish Hamilton, London, 1932, 283p, Cloth, Nonf.

BLORE, Lieut.-Commander TREVOR

01560 *The house of living death*. Francis Aldor, London, 1946, 156p, Cloth, Novel

BLOT, THOMAS, pseud. [William Simpson]

01561 *The man from Mars, his morals, politics, and religion*. Bacon & Co., Printers, San Francisco, 1891, 173p, Cloth, Novel

BLOW, ERNEST J.

01562 *Appointment in space*. Consul, London, 1963, 221p, Paper, Novel

BLUE, PETER, pseud.

01563 *Bend over*. Orpheus Series, New York, 1969, 185p, Paper, Novel

BLUE WOLF, pseud.

01564 *Dwifa's curse; a tale of the stone age*. Robert Scott, London, 1921, 253p, Cloth, Novel

BLUM, EDGAR C.

01565 *Satan's realm*. Rand, McNally, Chicago, 1899, 309p, Cloth, Novel [cover title: *In Satan's realm*]

BLUM, RALPH, 1932-

01566 *The simultaneous man; a novel*. Little, Brown, Boston, 1970, 238p, Cloth, Novel

BLUNDELL, PETER, pseud. [Frank Nestle Butterworth]

01567 *The star of the Incas*. Humphrey Milford, Oxford University Press, London, 1926, 304p, Cloth, Novel

BLUNT, WILFRID (Jasper Walter), 1901- [*bio-graphy included*]

01568 *Omar; a fantasy for animal lovers.* Chapman & Hall, London, 1966, 191p, Cloth, Novel

BLYTH, JAMES, 1864-1933

01569 *The aerial burglars.* Ward, Lock, London, 1906, 255p, Cloth, Novel
01570 *A haunted inheritance; a story of modern mysticism.* F. V. White, London, 1910, 295p, Cloth, Novel
01571 *Ichabod.* John Milne, London, 1910, 316p, Cloth, Novel
01572 *The swoop of the vulture.* Digby, Long, London, 1909, 315p, Cloth, Novel
01573 *The weird sisters.* Ward, Lock, London, 1918, 304p, Cloth, Novel

with Barry Pain:

01574 *The shadow of the unseen.* Chapman & Hall, London, 1907, 295p, Cloth, Novel

BOADEN, JAMES, 1762-1839

published anonymously:

01575 *The man of two lives; a narrative written by himself.* Henry Colburn, London, 1828, 2vol, Cloth, Novel

BOARDMAN, TOM [Thomas Volney Boardman Jr., 1930-] [*biography included*]

01576 *An ABC of science fiction.* Four Square, London, 1966, 207p, Paper, Anth.
01577 *Connoisseur's science fiction; an anthology.* Penguin, Harmondsworth, 1964, 234p, Paper, Anth.
01578 *SF horizons--one.* Dennis Dobson, London, 1968, 189p, Cloth, Anth.
01579 *The unfriendly future.* Four Square, London, 1965, 175p, Paper, Anth.

BODART, ANNE, 1939-

01580 *The blue dog, and other fables from the French.* Houghton Mifflin, Boston, 1956, 48p, Cloth, Coll.

BODELSEN, ANDERS, 1937-

01581 *Freezing point.* Michael Joseph, London, 1971, 175p, Cloth, Novel
01581A retitled: *Freezing down.* Harper & Row, New York, 1971, 179p, Cloth, Novel

BOETZEL, ERIC, with Herbert Clock

01582 *The light in the sky.* Coward-McCann, New York, 1929, 304p, Cloth, Novel

BOEX-BOREL, JOSEPH
     see: ROSNY, J.-H. aîné

BOGGS, D. W.

01583 *Astounding story-key, 1920-1951.* D. W. Boggs, Minneapolis, 1952, 18p, Paper, Nonf.

BOGORAS, WALDEMAR [Vladimir Germanovich Bogoraz, 1865-1936]

01584 *Sons of the mammoth.* Cosmopolitan Book Corp., New York, 1929, 254p, Cloth, Novel

BOGGON, MARTYN

01585 *The inevitable hour.* Tandem, London, 1968, 188p, Paper, Novel

BOIS, GAYLORD DU
     see: DuBOIS, GAYLORD

BOIS, SHIRLEY GRAHAM DU
     see: DU BOIS, SHIRLEY GRAHAM

BOIS, THEODORA DU
     see: DuBOIS, THEODORA

BOIS, WILLIAM PENE DU
     see: DU BOIS, WILLIAM PENE

BOISGILBERT, EDMUND, pseud.
     see: DONNELLY, IGNATIUS

BOK, HANNES (Vajn), 1914-1964

01586 *Beyond the golden stair.* Ballantine, New York, 1970, 209p, Paper, Novel
01587 *The sorcerer's ship.* Ballantine, New York, 1969, 205p, Paper, Novel

with A. Merritt:

01588 *The black wheel.* New Collector's Group, New York, 1947, 115p, Cloth, Novel
01589 *The fox woman; and, The blue pagoda.* New Collector's Group, Denver, 1946, 109p, Cloth, Coll. [*The blue pagoda* is Bok's sequel to Merritt's story, *The fox woman*]

BOILEAU, PIERRE (Louis), 1906- , with Thomas Narcejac

01590 *Choice cuts.* Arthur Barker, London, 1966, 207p, Cloth, Novel

BOLAND, (Bertram) JOHN, 1913- [*biography included*]

01591 *Holocaust.* Orbit, London, 1974, 192p, Paper, Novel
01592 *No refuge.* Michael Joseph, London, 1956, 254p, Cloth, Novel
01593 *White August.* Michael Joseph, London, 1955, 239p, Cloth, Novel

BO'LD, PAUL

01594   *The Temple of Dreams.* W. J. Ham-Smith, London,
        1912, 318p, Cloth, Novel

BOLITHO, (Henry) HECTOR, 1897-1974 [*biography
included*]

01595   *The house in Half Moon Street, and other sto-
        ries.* Cobden-Sanderson, London, 1935, 303p,
        Cloth, Coll.

BOLMER, W(illiam) B(revoort)

01596   *The time is coming.* G. W. Dillingham, New
        York, 1896, 282p, Cloth, Novel

BOLT, DAVID (Michael Langstone), 1927-   [*biography included*]

01597   *Adam; a tone poem.* J. M. Dent & Sons, London,
        1960, 143p, Cloth, Novel

BOLTON, F. H.

01598   *In the heart of the silent sea.* R. T. S.,
        London, 1910, 306p, Cloth, Novel

BOLTON, WILLIAM W(orden), 1900-

01599   *The sexless dynasty.* Dorrance & Co., Phila-
        delphia, 1960, 198p, Cloth, Novel

BOMB, BONNEE du
        see: du BOMB, BONNEE

BOMBAL, MARIA-LUISA, 1910-

01600   *The shrouded woman.* Farrar, Straus & Co.,
        New York, 1948, 198p, Cloth, Novel

BOMBARDMENT OF SCARBRO' BY THE RUSSIAN FLEET
        see: UNTRUTHFUL THOMAS

BOND, J. HARVEY, pseud.
        see: WINTERBOTHAM, RUSS

BOND, MADELEINE

01601   *The blue flower of the goblin peak.* "Child-
        ren's Companion" Office, London, 1926, 175p,
        Cloth, Novel

BOND, MARY BLIGH

01602   *Avernus.* Basil Blackwell, Oxford, 1924, 320p,
        Cloth, Novel

BOND, NELSON (Slade), 1908-   [*biography included*]

01603   *Exiles of time.* Prime Press, Philadelphia,
        1949, 183p, Cloth, Novel
01604   *Mr. Mergenthwirker's lobblies, and other fan-
        tastic tales.* Coward-McCann, New York,
        1946, 243p, Cloth, Coll.
01605   *The monster.* American Science Fiction, Sydney,
        1953, 34p, Paper, Coll.
01606   *Nightmares and daydreams.* Arkham House, Sauk
        City, 1968, 269p, Cloth, Coll.
01607   *No time like the future.* Avon, New York, 1954,
        221p, Paper, Coll.
01608   *The remarkable exploits of Lancelot Biggs,
        spaceman.* Doubleday, Garden City, 1950,
        224p, Cloth, Novel
01609   *The thirty-first of February, with a convey-
        ance of title in fee simple by James Branch
        Cabell.* Gnome Press, New York, 1949, 272p,
        Cloth, Coll.

BONE, J(esse) F(ranklin), 1916-   [*biography
included*]

01610   *The Lani people.* Bantam, New York, 1962, 152p,
        Paper, Novel

BONE, LEON, 1874-

01611   *Naomi, daughter of Ruth.* Pageant Press, New
        York, 1952, 191p, Cloth, Novel

BONHOTE, Mrs. (Elizabeth), 1744-1818

01612   *Bungay Castle; a novel.* W. Lane, The Minerva-
        Press, London, 1796, 2vol, Cloth, Novel

BONNER, RICHARD

01613   *The boy inventors and the vanishing gun.* Hurst
        & Co., New York, 1912, 287p, Cloth, Novel
        [Boy Inventors #2]
01614   *The boy inventors' diving torpedo boat.* Hurst
        & Co., New York, 1912, 313p, Cloth, Novel
        [Boy Inventors #3]
01615   *The boy inventors' electric hydroaeroplane.*
        Hurst & Co., New York, 1914, 292p, Cloth,
        Novel [Boy Inventors #5]
01616   *The boy inventors' flying ship.* Hurst & Co.,
        New York, 1913, 301p, Cloth, Novel [Boy In-
        ventors #4]
01617   *The boy inventors' radio-telephone.* Hurst &
        Co., New York, 1915, 303p, Cloth, Novel [Boy
        Inventors #6]
01618   *The boy inventors' wireless triumph.* Hurst &
        Co., New York, 1912, 293p, Cloth, Novel [Boy
        Inventors #1]

THE BOOK OF ALGOONAH
        see: NEWCOMB, CYRUS

A BOOK OF QUEER STORIES

01619   *A book of queer stories.* University of London
        Press, London, 1950, 157p, Paper, Anth.

BOORMAN, JOHN, 1933-   , with Bill Stair

01620 *Zardoz.* Signet, New York, 1974, 127p, Paper,
       Movie

BOOTH, DUANE A.

01621 *Another war--another world; a novel.* Exposi-
       tion Press, Jericho, NY, 1973, 242p, Cloth,
       Novel

BOOTH, HENRY SPENCER
    see: CRAIG, COLIN

BOOTH, PAT(rick John), 1929-   [*biography included*]

01622 *Long night among the stars.* Collins, London,
       1961, 191p, Cloth, Novel

BOOTHBY, GUY (Newell), 1867-1905

01623 *A bid for fortune; or, Dr. Nikola's vendetta.*
       Ward, Lock & Bowden, London, 1895, 344p,
       Cloth, Novel [Dr. Nikola #1]
01623A retitled: *Dr. Nikola's vendetta; or, A bid
       for fortune.* Arthur Westbrook, Cleveland,
       1908,   , Paper, Novel [Dr. Nikola #1]
01624 *The curse of the snake.* F. V. White, London,
       1902, 312p, Cloth, Novel
01625 *Doctor Nikola.* Ward, Lock, London, 1896, 322p,
       Cloth, Novel [Dr. Nikola #2]
01626 *Dr. Nikola's experiment.* Hodder & Stoughton,
       London, 1899, 340p, Cloth, Novel [Dr. Nikola
       #4]
       Dr. Nikola's vendetta. [see 01623A]
01627 *'Farewell, Nikola!'* Ward, Lock, London, 1901,
       315p, Cloth, Novel [Dr. Nikola #5]
01628 *The lust of hate.* Ward, Lock, London, 1898,
       283p, Cloth, Novel [Dr. Nikola #3]
01629 *Pharos, the Egyptian; a romance.* Ward, Lock,
       London, 1899, 376p, Cloth, Novel

BORDEN, MARY, 1886-1968 [*biography included*]

01630 *Jehovah's day.* William Heinemann, London,
       1928, 491p, Cloth, Novel

BORDEN, WILLIAM (Vickers), 1938-   [*biography
included*]

01631 *Superstoe.* Victor Gollancz, London, 1967,
       255p, Cloth, Novel

BOREL, JOSEPH BOEX-
    see: ROSNY, J. H. aîné

BORGESE, ELISABETH MANN

01632 *To whom it may concern.* MacGibbon & Kee,
       London, 1960, 167p, Cloth, Novel

BORGIA, ANTHONY (V.)

01633 *Beyond this life.* Feature Books, London, 1942,
       125p, Paper, Novel

BORODIN, GEORGE, pseud. [George Alexis Bankoff,
1903-   ; also cited by various authorities
as George Sava or George Alexis Milkomanovich
Milkomane]

01634 *Spurious sun.* T. Werner Laurie, London, 1948,
       282p, Cloth, Novel
01634A retitled: *Threatened people.* Regular Publi-
       cations, London,   , 160p, Paper, Novel

BOSHELL, GORDON

01635 *Dog's life; a satirical novel.* Secker & War-
       burg, London, 1945, 110p, Cloth, Novel
01636 *John Brown's body.* Secker & Warburg, London,
       1942, 176p, Cloth, Novel

BOSSCHERE, JEAN de, 1878-

01637 *Weird islands.* Chapman & Hall, London, 1921,
       210p, Cloth, Novel

BOSTON, L(ucy) M(aria), 1892-

01638 *The children of Green Knowe.* Faber & Faber,
       London, 1954, 157p, Cloth, Novel [Green Knowe
       #1]
01639 *The chimneys of Green Knowe.* Faber & Faber,
       London, 1958, 186p, Cloth, Novel [Green Knowe
       #2]
01639A retitled: *Treasure of Green Knowe.* Harcourt,
       Brace & World, New York, 1958, 185p, Cloth,
       Novel [Green Knowe #2]
01640 *An enemy at Green Knowe.* Harcourt, Brace &
       World, New York, 1964, 156p, Cloth, Novel
       [Green Knowe #5]
01641 *The river at Green Knowe.* Faber & Faber, Lon-
       don, 1959, 144p, Cloth, Novel [Green Knowe #3]
01642 *A stranger at Green Knowe.* Faber & Faber, Lon-
       don, 1961, 158p, Cloth, Novel [Green Knowe #4]
       Treasure of Green Knowe. [see 01639A]

BOSWELL, DIANE

01643 *Posterity; a novel.* Jonathan Cape, London,
       1926, 254p, Cloth, Novel

BOUCHER, ANTHONY, pseud. [William Anthony Parker White, 1911-1968] [*biography included*]

01644 *The best from Fantasy and science fiction,
       fourth series.* Doubleday, Garden City,
       1955, 250p, Cloth, Anth.
01645 *The best from Fantasy and science fiction,
       fifth series.* Doubleday, Garden City, 1956,
       256p, Cloth, Anth.
01646 *The best from Fantasy and science fiction,
       sixth series.* Doubleday, Garden City, 1957,
       255p, Cloth, Anth.

BOUCHER, ANTHONY, pseud. (cont.)

01647   *The best from Fantasy and science fiction,*
        seventh series. Doubleday, Garden City,
        1958, 264p, Cloth, Anth.
01648   *The best from Fantasy and science fiction,*
        eighth series. Doubleday, Garden City,
        1959, 240p, Cloth, Anth.
01649   *The compleat werewolf, and other stories of*
        fantasy and science fiction. Simon & Schus-
        ter, New York, 1969, 256p, Cloth, Coll.
01650   *Far and away; eleven fantasy and science-*
        fiction stories. Ballantine, New York,
        1955, 168p, Cloth, Coll.
        Rocket to the morgue. [see 01653A]
01651   *A treasury of great science fiction, volume*
        one. Doubleday, Garden City, 1959, 527p,
        Cloth, Anth.
01652   *A treasury of great science fiction, volume*
        two. Doubleday, Garden City, 1959, 522p,
        Cloth, Anth.

as H. H. Holmes:

01653   *Rocket to the morgue.* Duell, Sloan & Pearce,
        New York, 1942, 279p, Cloth, Novel
01653A *Rocket to the morgue,* by Anthony Boucher. Dell,
        New York, 1952, 223p, Paper, Novel

with J. Francis McComas:

01654   *The best from Fantasy and science fiction.*
        Little, Brown, Boston, 1952, 214p, Cloth,
        Anth.
01655   *The best from Fantasy and science fiction,*
        second series. Little, Brown, Boston, 1953,
        270p, Cloth, Anth.
01656   *The best from Fantasy and science fiction,*
        third series. Doubleday, Garden City, 1954,
        252p, Cloth, Anth.

BOUIC, FREDERIC VERNON

01657   *Good-bye, white man; a novel of A.D. 2711.*
        Exposition Press, New York, 1953, 241p,
        Cloth, Novel

BOULENGER, E(dward) G(eorge), 1888-1946, with
Percy White

01658   *The centaur passes.* Duckworth, London, 1933,
        303p, Cloth, Novel

BOULLE, PIERRE (Francois Marie Louis), 1912-
[biography included]

01659   *Because it is absurd (on Earth as it is in*
        Heaven). Vanguard Press, New York, 1971,
        190p, Cloth, Coll.
01660   *Desperate games.* Vanguard Press, New York,
        1973, 213p, Cloth, Novel
01661   *The garden on the Moon.* Secker & Warburg, Lon-
        don, 1965, 316p, Cloth, Novel
        Monkey planet. [see 01662A]
01662   *Planet of the apes.* Vanguard Press, New York,
        1963, 246p, Cloth, Novel [Planet of the Apes
        series]
01662A retitled: *Monkey planet.* Secker & Warburg,
        London, 1964, 223p, Cloth, Novel [Planet of
        the Apes series]
01663   *Time out of mind, and other stories.* Secker
        & Warburg, London, 1966, 254p, Cloth, Coll.

BOUMPHREY, GEOFFREY M(axwell), 1894-1969, with
Kenneth M. Walker

01664   *The log of the Ark.* Constable, London, 1923,
        214p, Cloth, Novel
01664A retitled: *What happened in the Ark.* E. P.
        Dutton, New York, 1926, 275p, Cloth, Novel

BOUNDS, S(ydney) J(ames), 1920-

01665   *Dimension of horror.* Panther, London, 1953,
        160p, Cloth, Novel
01666   *The Moon raiders.* W. Foulsham, London, 1955,
        160p, Cloth, Novel
01667   *The robot brains.* Digit, London, 1958, 160p,
        Paper, Novel
01668   *The world wrecker.* W. Foulsham, London, 1956,
        159p, Cloth, Novel

BOURDILLON, FRANCIS WILLIAM, 1852-1921

01669   *Nephelé.* George Redway, London, 1896, 156p,
        Cloth, Novel

BOURNE, ARTHUR M(ason)

01670   *A mystery of the Cordillera; a tale of adven-*
        ture in the Andes. Bellairs & Co., London,
        1895, 312p, Cloth, Novel

BOURNE, JOHN, 1918-

01671   *Computer takes all.* Cassell, London, 1967,
        310p, Cloth, Novel

BOURNE, LAWRENCE R.

01672   *The radium casket.* Oxford University Press,
        London, 1926, 160p, Cloth, Novel

BOUSFIELD, H(enry) T(homas) W(ishart)

01673   *The god with four arms, and other stories.*
        Arthur Barker, London, 1939, 248p, Cloth,
        Coll.

BOUSSENARD, LOUIS, 1847-1910

01674   *10,000 years in a block of ice.* F. Tennyson
        Neely, New York, 1898, 256p, Cloth, Novel

BOUTELL, C(larence) B(urley), 1908-   , with
Sterling North

01675   *Speak of the devil.* Doubleday, Doran, Garden
        City, 1945, 334p, Cloth, Anth.

BOUTELLE, CLARENCE M(iles), d. 1903

01676   *Beyond the end; the story of a ghost's year.*
        F. M. Lupton Publishing Co., New York, 1892,
        208p, Paper, Novel

BOUTON, JOHN BELL, 1830-1902

01677 *The Enchanted; an authentic account of the
         strange origin of the New Psychical Club.*
         Cassell, New York, 1891, 283p, Cloth, Novel

BOUVÉ, EDWARD T(racy)

01678 *Centuries apart.* Little, Brown, Boston, 1894,
         347p, Cloth, Novel

BOVA, BEN(jamin William), 1932-   [*biography
         included*]

01679 *Analog 9.* Doubleday, Garden City, 1973, 249p,
         Cloth, Anth.
01680 *As on a darkling plain.* Walker, New York,
         1972, 193p, Cloth, Novel
01681 *The dueling machine.* Holt, Rinehart & Winston,
         New York, 1969, 247p, Cloth, Novel
01681A retitled: *The duelling machine.* Faber &
         Faber, London, 1971, 249p, Cloth, Novel
01682 *Escape!* Holt, Rinehart & Winston, New York,
         1970, 122p, Cloth, Novel
01683 *Exiled from Earth.* E. P. Dutton, New York,
         1971, 202p, Cloth, Novel [Exiles #1]
01684 *Flight of exiles.* E. P. Dutton, New York,
         1972, 185p, Cloth, Novel [Exiles #2]
01685 *Forward in time; a science fiction story col-
         lection.* Walker, New York, 1973, 234p,
         Cloth, Coll.
01686 *The many worlds of science fiction.* E. P.
         Dutton, New York, 1971, 234p, Cloth, Anth.
01687 *The science fiction Hall of fame, volume 2A.*
         Doubleday, Garden City, 1973, 486p, Cloth,
         Anth.
01687A retitled: *The science fiction Hall of fame,
         volume 2.* Victor Gollancz, London, 1973,
         422p, Cloth, Anth.
01688 *The science fiction Hall of fame, volume 2B.*
         Doubleday, Garden City, 1973, 466p, Cloth,
         Anth.
01688A retitled: *The science fiction Hall of fame,
         volume 3.* Victor Gollancz, London, 1974,
         440p, Cloth, Anth.
01689 *The star conquerors.* John C. Winston, Phila-
         delphia, 1959, 215p, Cloth, Novel
01690 *Star Watchman.* Holt, Rinehart & Winston, New
         York, 1964, 224p, Cloth, Novel
01691 *THX 1138.* Paperback Library, New York, 1971,
         160p, Paper, Movie
01692 *The weathermakers.* Holt, Rinehart & Winston,
         New York, 1967, 249p, Cloth, Novel
01693 *When the sky burned.* Walker, New York, 1973,
         249p, Cloth, Novel
01694 *The winds of Altair.* E. P. Dutton, New York,
         1973, 135p, Cloth, Novel

with Gordon R. Dickson:

04376 *Gremlins, go home!* St. Martin's Press, New
         York, 1974, 150p, Cloth, Novel

BOWDEN, ETTA, with Phil Bowden

01695 *Mercy Island.* Vantage Press, New York, 1965,
         281p, Cloth, Novel

BOWDEN, PHIL, with Etta Bowden

01695 *Mercy Island.* Vantage Press, New York, 1965,
         281p, Cloth, Novel

BOWEN, JOHN (Griffith), 1924-   [*biography in-
         cluded*]

01696 *After the rain.* Faber & Faber, London, 1958,
         203p, Cloth, Novel

BOWEN, MARJORIE, pseud. [Gabrielle Margaret
Vere Campbell Long, 1886-1952]

01697 *The Bishop of Hell, and other stories.* Bodley
         Head, London, 1949, 230p, Cloth, Coll.
01698 *Black magic; a tale of the rise and fall of
         Antichrist.* Alston Rivers, London, 1909,
         390p, Cloth, Novel
01699 *"Five Winds"; a romance.* Hodder & Stoughton,
         London, 1927, 317p, Cloth, Novel
01700 *Great tales of horror, being a collection of
         strange stories of amazement, horror, and
         wonder.* John Lane, The Bodley Head, London,
         1933, 415p, Cloth, Anth.
01701 *The haunted vintage.* Odhams Press, London,
         1921, 320p, Cloth, Novel
01702 *The last bouquet; some twilight tales.* John
         Lane, London, 1933, 348p, Cloth, Coll.
01703 *More great tales of horror, being a collection
         of strange stories of amazement, horror, and
         wonder.* John Lane, The Bodley Head, London,
         1935, 432p, Cloth, Anth.

as Joseph Shearing:

01704 *The fetch.* Hutchinson, London, 1942, 184p,
         Cloth, Novel
01704A retitled: *The spectral bride.* Smith & Durrell,
         New York, 1942, 314p, Cloth, Novel

BOWEN, ROBERT SIDNEY, 1900-1977

01705 *Dusty Ayres; black invaders vs. the Battle
         Birds.* Corinth, San Diego, 1966,   ,
         Paper, Novel [Dusty Ayres #5]
01706 *Dusty Ayres; black lightning.* Corinth, San
         Diego, 1966, 160p, Paper, Novel [Dusty Ayres
         #1]
01707 *Dusty Ayres; crimson doom.* Corinth, San Diego,
         1966, 160p, Paper, Novel [Dusty Ayres #2]
01708 *Dusty Ayres; purple tornado.* Corinth, San
         Diego, 1966,   , Paper, Novel [Dusty Ayres
         #3]
01709 *Dusty Ayres; the Telsa raiders.* Corinth, San
         Diego, 1966, 160p, Paper, Novel [Dusty Ayres
         #4]

BOWEN, WILLIAM (Alvin), 1877-1937

01710 *Philip and the faun.* Little, Brown, Boston,
         1926, 143p, Cloth, Novel
01711 *Solario the tailor; his tales of the magic
         doublet.* Macmillan Co., New York, 1922,
         232p, Cloth, Coll.

BOWER, B. M. [Bertha Muzzy Bower Sinclair,
1874-1940]

01712 *The Adam chasers.* Little, Brown, Boston, 1927,
         275p, Cloth, Novel
01713 *The temple of Demos; a dream.* John Ouseley,
         London, 1912, 282p, Cloth, Novel

BOWER, JOHN GRAHAM
   see: KLAXON

BOWERS, A. HERBERT, with Henry Athey

00611 *With gyves of gold; a novel.* G. W. Dillingham, New York, 1898, 274p, Cloth, Novel

BOWERS, BILL [William L. Bowers], with Bill Mallardi

01714 *The Double:Bill symposium, being 94 replies to 'a questionnaire for professional science fiction writers and editors,' as created by Lloyd Biggle, Jr.* Double:Bill Press, Akron, OH, 1969, 111p, Paper, Nonf.

BOWERS, R. L.

01715 *This second Earth.* Cobra, London, 1957, 158p, Paper, Novel

BOWKER, WILLIAM RUSHTON

01716 *Bizzy-Quizzy the Great; science-detective-fiction adventures.* The Author, Coronado, CA, 1942, 151p, Cloth, Coll.

BOWLES, Colonel JOHN, 1833-1900

01717 *The masked prophet; one's hidden self; a romance in two lives--here and hereafter.* Caxton Co., New York, 1895, 190p, Cloth, Novel

BOWMAN, JOHN S(tewart), 1931- [*biography included*]

01718 *A book of islands.* Doubleday, Garden City, 1971, 345p, Cloth, Anth.

BOYD, HALBERT J(ohnston), 1872-1957

01719 *Strange tales of the borders, old and new.* Moray Press, Edinburgh, 1948, 238p, Cloth, Coll.

BOYD, JOHN, pseud. [Boyd Bradfield Upchurch, 1919-] [*biography included*]

01720 *Andromeda gun.* Berkley Publishing Corp., New York, 1974, 185p, Cloth, Novel
01721 *The doomsday gene.* Weybright & Talley, New York, 1973, 230p, Cloth, Novel
01722 *The Gorgon festival.* Weybright & Talley, New York, 1972, 184p, Cloth, Novel
01723 *The I.Q. merchant.* Weybright & Talley, New York, 1972, 218p, Cloth, Novel
01724 *The last starship from Earth.* Weybright & Talley, New York, 1968, 182p, Cloth, Novel
01725 *The organ bank farm.* Weybright & Talley, New York, 1970, 216p, Cloth, Novel
01726 *The pollinators of Eden.* Weybright & Talley, New York, 1969, 212p, Cloth, Novel

01727 *The rakehells of Heaven.* Weybright & Talley, New York, 1969, 184p, Cloth, Novel
01728 *Sex and the High Command.* Weybright & Talley, New York, 1970, 212p, Cloth, Novel

BOYD, MALCOLM, 1923- [*biography included*]

01729 *The fantasy worlds of Peter Stone, and other fables.* Harper & Row, New York, 1969, 120p, Cloth, Coll.

BOYDEN, POLLY (Chase)

01730 *The pink egg.* Pamet Press, Truro, Mass., 1942, 233p, Cloth, Novel

BOYE, KARIN, 1900-1941

01731 *Kollocain.* University of Wisconsin Press, Madison, 1966, 193p, Cloth, Novel

THE BOYHOOD DAYS OF GUY FAWKES

01732 *The boyhood days of Guy Fawkes; or, The conspirators of Old London.* "Boys of England," London, 1870?, 184p, Paper, Novel

BOYLAND, GRACE DUFFIE, 1861-1935

01733 *The steps to nowhere.* Baker & Taylor, New York, 1910, 230p, Cloth, Novel

BOYLE, [Ms.] JOHN PATRICK

01734 *Teacher's guide; Flowers for Algernon.* Bantam, New York, 1974?, 8p, Paper, Nonf.

BOYLE, VIRGINIA FRAZER, 1863-1938

01735 *Devil tales.* Harper & Bros., New York, 1900, 211p, Cloth, Coll.

BOYS' LIFE

01736 *The Boys' life book of outer space stories.* Random House, New York, 1964, 182p, Cloth, Anth.

BOYS' SPORT AND ADVENTURE STORIES

01737 *Boys' sport and adventure stories.* Goldsmith Publishing Co., Chicago, 1936, 750p, Cloth, Anth. [includes *Big leaguer*, by William Heyliger; *Tahara, boy king of the desert*, by Harold M. Sherman [only SF]; *Herb Kent, West Point cadet*, by Graham M. Dean]

BOZMAN, E(rnest) F(ranklin), 1895-1968

01738 *The traveller's return.* J. M. Dent & Sons, London, 1938, 313p, Cloth, Novel

BRACK, VEKTIS, house pseud. [see also Bruno G. Condray]

01739 *Castaway from space.* Gannet Press, London, 1953, 128p, Paper, Coll.

01740 *Odyssey in space.* Gannet Press, London, 1954, 127p, Paper, Novel [by Leslie Humphreys, alias Bruno G. Condray]

01741 *The "X" People.* Gannet Press, London, 1953, 128p, Paper, Novel

BRACKETT, LEIGH (Douglass),1915-1978 [*biography included*]

01742 *Alpha Centauri--or die!* Ace Double, New York, 1963, 121p, Paper, Novel

01743 *The big jump.* Ace Double, New York, 1955, 131p, Paper, Novel

01744 *The coming of the Terrans.* Ace, New York, 1967, 157p, Paper, Coll. [Mars series]
The galactic breed. [see 01752A]

01745 *The ginger star.* Ballantine, New York, 1974, 186p, Paper, Novel [new Stark series #1]

01746 *The halfling, and other stories.* Ace, New York, 1973, 351p, Paper, Coll. [includes, among others, Mars and Stark stories]

01747 *The long tomorrow.* Doubleday, Garden City, 1955, 222p, Cloth, Novel
The nemesis from Terra. [see 01750A]

01748 *People of the Talisman.* Ace Double, New York, 1964, 128p, Paper, Novel [Mars series; Stark series]

01749 *The secret of Sinharat.* Ace Double, New York, 1964, 95p, Paper, Novel [Mars series; Stark series]

01750 *Shadow over Mars; a new and original novel of Martian adventure.* World Distributors/Sydney Pemberton, Manchester, 1951, 128p, Paper, Novel [Mars series]

01750A retitled: *The nemesis from Terra.* Ace Double, New York, 1961, 120p, Paper, Novel [Mars series]

01751 *Stark #2; the hounds of Skaith.* Ballantine, New York, 1974, 183p, Paper, Novel [new Stark series #2]

01752 *The starmen.* Gnome Press, New York, 1952, 213p, Cloth, Novel

01752A retitled: *The galactic breed.* Ace Double, New York, 1955, 168p, Paper, Novel

01753 *The sword of Rhiannon.* Ace Double, New York, 1953, 131p, Paper, Novel [Mars series]

BRADBURY, EDWARD P., pseud.
see: MOORCOCK, MICHAEL

BRADBURY, RAY (Douglas), 1920- [*biography included*]

01754 *The circus of Dr. Lao, and other improbable stories.* Bantam, New York, 1956, 210p, Paper, Anth.

01755 *Dark carnival.* Arkham House, Sauk City, 1947, 313p, Cloth, Coll.

01756 *The day it rained forever.* Rupert Hart-Davis, London, 1959, 254p, Cloth, Coll. [roughly based on *A medicine for melancholy*]

01757 *Fahrenheit 451.* Ballantine, New York, 1953, 202p, Cloth, Coll.

01758 *Fahrenheit 451.* Rupert Hart-Davis, London, 1954, 158p, Cloth, Novel

01759 *The golden apples of the sun.* Doubleday, Garden City, 1953, 250p, Cloth, Coll.

01760 *The Halloween tree.* Alfred A. Knopf, New York, 1972, 145p, Cloth, Novel

01761 *I sing the Body Electric! stories.* Alfred A. Knopf, New York, 1969, 305p, Cloth, Coll.

01762 *The illustrated man.* Doubleday, Garden City, 1951, 252p, Cloth, Coll.

01763 *The machineries of joy; short stories.* Simon & Schuster, New York, 1964, 255p, Cloth, Coll.

01764 *The Martian chronicles.* Doubleday, Garden City, 1950, 222p, Cloth, Coll.

01765 retitled: *The silver locusts.* Rupert Hart-Davis, London, 1951, 232p, Cloth, Coll. [drops one story, adds one story]

01766 *The Martian chronicles.* Time Inc., New York, 1963, 267p, Cloth, Coll. [adds two stories]

01767 *A medicine for melancholy.* Doubleday, Garden City, 1959, 240p, Cloth, Coll.

01768 *The October country.* Ballantine, New York, 1955, 306p, Cloth, Coll.

01769 *The pedestrian.* Roy Squires, Glendale, 1964, 16p, Paper, Story

01770 *R is for rocket.* Doubleday, Garden City, 1962, 233p, Cloth, Coll.

01771 *S is for space.* Doubleday, Garden City, 1966, 238p, Cloth, Coll.
The silver locusts. [see 01765]

01772 *The small assassin.* Ace, London, 1962, 144p, Paper, Coll.

01773 *Something wicked this way comes; a novel.* Simon & Schuster, New York, 1962, 317p, Cloth, Novel

01774 *Timeless stories for today and tomorrow.* Bantam, New York, 1952, 306p, Paper, Anth.

01775 *Twice twenty-two; The golden apples of the sun; A medicine for melancholy.* Doubleday, Garden City, 1966, 406p, Cloth, Coll.

01776 *The Vintage Bradbury; Ray Bradbury's own selection of his best stories.* Vintage, New York, 1965, 331p, Paper, Coll.

with Lewy Olfson:

01777 *Teacher's guide; science fiction.* Bantam, New York, 1968, 16p, Paper, Nonf.

BRADDON, RUSSELL (Reading), 1921- [*biography included*]

01778 *When the enemy is tired.* Michael Joseph, London, 1968, 270p, Cloth, Novel

01779 *The year of the angry rabbit.* Heinemann, London, 1964, 181p, Cloth, Novel

BRADFORD, COLUMBUS

01780 *Terrania; or, The feminization of the world.* Christopher Publishing House, Boston, 1930, 208p, Cloth, Novel

BRADFORD, J. S.

01781 *Even a worm.* Arthur Barker, London, 1936, 302p, Cloth, Novel

BRADFORD, MATTHEW C.

01782 *Invasion from space.* Atlantic Book Co., London, 195 , 128p, Paper, Novel

BRADFORD, ROARK, 1896-1948

01783 *Ol' King David an' the Philistine boys.* Harper & Bros., New York, 1930, 227p, Cloth, Coll.
01784 *Ol' man Adam an' his chillun, being tales they tell about the time when the Lord walked the Earth like a natural man.* Harper & Bros., New York, 1928, 264p, Cloth, Coll.
01785 *This side of Jordan.* Harper & Bros., New York, 1929, 255p, Cloth, Novel

BRADLEY, GEORGE

01786 *The devil's tool.* Pendulum, Atlanta, 1970, 191p, Paper, Novel

BRADLEY, JACK

01787 *The torch of Ra.* Stellar Publishing Corp., New York, 1930, 24p, Paper, Story

BRADLEY, MARION (Eleanor) ZIMMER, 1930-   [*biography included*]

01788 *The bloody sun.* Ace, New York, 1964, 191p, Paper, Novel [Darkover series]
01789 *The brass dragon.* Ace Double, New York, 1969, 125p, Paper, Novel
01790 *The colors of space.* Monarch, Derby, Conn., 1963, 124p, Paper, Novel
01791 *The dark intruder, and other stories.* Ace Double, New York, 1964, 124p, Paper, Coll.
01792 *Dark satanic.* Berkley Medallion, New York, 1972, 224p, Paper, Novel
01793 *Darkover landfall.* DAW, New York, 1972, 160p, Paper, Novel [Darkover series]
01794 *The door through space.* Ace Double, New York, 1961, 132p, Paper, Novel
01795 *Falcons of Narabedla.* Ace Double, New York, 1964, 127p, Paper, Novel
01796 *Hunters of the Red Moon.* DAW, New York, 1973, 176p, Paper, Novel
01797 *The jewel of Arwen.* T-K Graphics, Baltimore, 1974, 39p, Paper, Story [Arwen #1; adaptation of the Tolkien mythos]
01798 *Men, halflings, & hero worship.* TK Graphics, Baltimore, 1973, 54p, Paper, Nonf.
01799 *The necessity for beauty; Robert W. Chambers and the romantic tradition.* T-K Graphics, Baltimore, 1974, 45p, Paper, Nonf.
01800 *The parting of Arwen.* T-K Graphics, Baltimore, 1974, 10p, Paper, Story [Arwen #2; adaptation of the Tolkien mythos]
01801 *The planet savers.* Ace Double, New York, 1962, 91p, Paper, Novel [Darkover series]
01802 *Seven from the stars.* Ace Double, New York, 1962, 120p, Paper, Novel
01803 *The sixth sense #2; in the steps of the master.* Tempo, New York, 1973, 155p, Paper, Tele. [The Sixth Sense #2]
01804 *The spell sword; a Darkover novel.* DAW, New York, 1974, 158p, Paper, Novel [Darkover series]
01805 *Star of danger.* Ace, New York, 1965, 160p, Paper, Novel [Darkover series]
01806 *The Sword of Aldones.* Ace Double, New York, 1962, 164p, Paper, Novel [Darkover series]
01807 *The winds of Darkover.* Ace Double, New York, 1970, 139p, Paper, Novel [Darkover series]

01808 *The world wreckers; a Darkover novel.* Ace, New York, 1971, 189p, Paper, Novel [Darkover series]

BRADLEY, WILL (H.), 1868-1962

01809 *Launcelot & the ladies.* Harper & Bros., New York, 1927, 327p, Cloth, Novel

BRADSHAW, WILLIAM R(ichard), 1851-1927

01810 *The goddess of Atvatabar, being the history of the discovery of the interior world and conquest of Atvatabar.* J. F. Douthitt, New York 1892, 318p, Cloth, Novel

BRADWELL, JAMES

01811 *Land of the giants; the mean city.* World Distributors, Manchester, 1969, 143p, Paper, Tele. [Land of the Giants series]

BRADY, CYRUS TOWNSEND, 1861-1920

01812 *And thus he came; a Christmas fantasy.* G. P. Putnam's Sons, New York, 1916, 105p, Cloth, Coll.

BRAHMS, CARYL, pseud. [Doris Caroline Abrahams], with S. J. Simon

01813 *No nightingales.* Michael Joseph, London, 1944, 251p, Cloth, Novel
01814 *Titania has a mother.* Michael Joseph, London, 1944, 195p, Cloth, Novel

BRAILSFORD, HENRY NOEL, 1873-1958

01815 *The broom of the war-god; a novel.* D. Appleton New York, 1898, 337p, Cloth, Novel; William Heinemann, London, 1898, 276p, Cloth, Novel

BRAINE, ROBERT D., 1861-

01816 *Messages from Mars, by the aid of the telescope plant.* J. S. Ogilvie, New York, 1892, 259p, Cloth, Novel

BRAINERD, (J.) CHAUNCEY COREY, 1874-1922, with Edith Brainerd as E. J. Rath

01817 *Once again.* G. Howard Watt, New York, 1929, 312p, Cloth, Novel
01818 *The sixth speed.* Moffat, Yard, New York, 1908, 408p, Cloth, Novel

BRAINERD, EDITH RATHBONE, d. 1922, with (J.) Chauncey Corey Brainerd as E. J. Rath

01817 *Once again.* G. Howard Watt, New York, 1929, 312p, Cloth, Novel
01818 *The sixth speed.* Moffat, Yard, New York, 1908, 408p, Cloth, Novel

BRALEY, BERTON, 1882-

01819   *The enchanted flivver.* Century Co., New York, 1925, 255p, Cloth, Novel

BRAMAH, ERNEST, pseud. [Ernest Bramah Smith, 1868-1942]

         The celestial omnibus. [see 01829A]
01820   *Ernest Bramah.* George G. Harrap, London, 1929, 287p, Cloth, Coll.
01821   *Kai Lung beneath the mulberry-tree.* Richards Press, London, 1940, 320p, Cloth, Novel [Kai Lung series]
01822   *The Kai Lung omnibus, containing The wallet of Kai Lung; Kai Lung unrolls his mat; Kai Lung's golden hours.* Philip Allan, London, 1936, 625p, Cloth, Coll. [Kai Lung series]
01823   *Kai Lung: six; uncollected stories from Punch.* Non-Profit Press, Tacoma, Wash., 1974, 58p, Cloth, Coll. [Kai Lung series]
01824   *Kai Lung unrolls his mat.* Richards Press, London, 1928, 343p, Cloth, Coll. [Kai Lung series]
01824A retitled: *Kin Weng and the miraculous tusk, from Kai Lung unrolls his mat.* City of Birmingham School of Printing, Birmingham, 1941, 45p, Cloth?, Story [Kai Lung series; abridged]
01825   *Kai Lung's golden hours.* Grant Richards, London, 1922, 311p, Cloth, Novel [Kai Lung series]
         Kin Weng and the miraculous tusk. [see 01824A]
01826   *The mirror of Kong Ho.* Chapman & Hall, London, 1905, 308p, Cloth, Novel
01827   *The moon of much gladness, related by Kai Lung.* Cassell, London, 1932, 316p, Cloth, Novel [Kai Lung series]
01827A retitled: *The return of Kai Lung.* Sheridan House, New York, 1937, 319p, Cloth, Novel [Kai Lung series]
         The secret of the League. [see 01830A]
01828   *The story of Wan and the remarkable shrub; and, The story of Ching-Kwei and the destinies.* Doubleday, Doran, Garden City, 1927, 98p, Cloth, Coll.
         The transmutation of Ling. [see 01829B]
01829   *The wallet of Kai Lung.* Grant Richards, London, 1900, 337p, Cloth, Coll. [Kai Lung series]
01829A retitled: *The celestial omnibus.* Richards Press, London, 1963, 392p, Cloth, Coll. [Kai Lung series]
01829B retitled: *The transmutation of Ling.* Grant Richards, London, 1911, 80p, Cloth, Novel [Kai Lung series][abridged]

published anonymously:

01830   *What might have been; the story of a social war.* John Murray, London, 1907, 380p, Cloth, Novel
01830A retitled: *The secret of the League; the story of a social war,* by Ernest Bramah. Thomas Nelson & Sons, London, 1909, 287p, Cloth, Novel

BRAMWELL, FRANK

01831   *Voyage to the stars.* Nelson, London, 1968, 162p, Cloth, Novel

BRAMWELL, JAMES (Guy), 1911-   [*biography included*]

01832   *Going west.* Cobden-Sanderson, London, 1935, 263p, Cloth, Novel

BRANAN, JOHN M.

01833   *The future makers.* Vantage Press, New York, 1971, 219p, Cloth, Novel

BRAND, CHRIS

01834   *Trail of the vampire.* Grayling Publishing Co., London,   , 32p, Paper, Story

BRAND, MAX, pseud. [Frederick Faust, 1892-1944]

01835   *The garden of Eden.* Hodder & Stoughton, London, 1927, 320p, Cloth, Novel

BRANDEIS, JULIAN WALTER, 1875-

01836   *The extraordinary exploits and experiences of Munchausen, M.D.* Quip Publishing Co., New York, 1924, 229p, Cloth, Novel [Munchausen series]

BRANDEL, MARC, 1919-   [name originally Marcus Beresford] [*biography included*]

         The Ides of summer. [see 01839A]
01837   *The man who liked women.* Simon & Schuster, New York, 1972, 287p, Cloth, Novel
01838   *The mine of lost days.* J. B. Lippincott, Philadelphia, 1974, 185p, Cloth, Novel
01839   *Rain before seven (a low fantasy).* Harper & Bros., New York, 1945, 230p, Cloth, Novel
01839A retitled: *The Ides of summer; a low fantasy.* Eyre & Spottiswoode, London, 1948, 191p, Cloth, Novel

BRANDON, HENRY

01840   *The afterdeath.* Theosophical Publishing Society, London, 1911, 224p, Cloth, Novel

BRANDON, MICHAEL

01841   *Nonce; a novel.* Coward-McCann, New York, 1944, 181p, Cloth, Novel

BRANLEY, FRANKLYN M(ansfield), 1915-   [*biography included*]

01842   *Lodestar, rocket ship to Mars; the record of the first operation sponsored by the Federal Commission for Interplanetary Exploration, June 1, 1971.* Thomas Y. Crowell, New York, 1951, 248p, Cloth, Novel

BRANT, JOHN IRA, 1872-

01843 *The new regime, A.D. 2202.* Cochrane Publishing
         Co., New York, 1909, 122p, Cloth, Novel

BRASH, MARGARET MAUD
      see: KENDALL, JOHN

BRAUN, WERNHER von
      see: von BRAUN, WERNHER

BRAUTIGAN, RICHARD, 1935-

01844 *The Hawkline Monster; a gothic western.* Simon
         & Schuster, New York, 1974, 216p, Cloth,
         Novel
01845 *In watermelon sugar.* Four Seasons Foundation,
         San Francisco, 1968, 138p, Cloth, Novel
01846 *Trout fishing in America; The pill "versus"
         the Springhill Mill Disaster; and, In water-
         melon sugar.* Delacorte Press, New York,
         1969, 358p, Cloth, Coll.

BRAYTON, GERTRUDE E.
      see: BRYAT, EDITH

BREBNER, PERCY JAMES, 1864-1922

01847 *The ivory disc.* Duffield & Co., New York,
         1920, 254p, Cloth, Novel
       The Knight of the Silver Star. [see 01848A]

as Christian Lys:

01848 *The fortress of Yadasara; a narrative prepared
         from the manuscript of Clinton Verrall, Esq.*
         Frederick Warne, London, 1899, 432p, Cloth,
         Novel
01848A retitled: *The Knight of the Silver Star,* by
         Percy Brebner. R. F. Fenno, New York, 1907,
         411p, Cloth, Novel

BREBNER, WINSTON

01849 *Doubting Thomas.* Rinehart & Co., New York,
         1956, 210p, Cloth, Novel

BRECKENRIDGE, GERALD, 1889?-1964

01850 *The radio boys seek the lost Atlantis.* A. L.
         Burt, New York, 1923, 222p, Cloth, Novel
         [Radio Boys #7]

BREDE, ARNOLD

01851 *Sister Earth.* Scion, London, 1951, 112p, Paper,
         Novel

BREDESON, LENORE

01852 *More from One step beyond; a second volume of
         eerie stories chosen from the television pro-
         gram "Alcoa presents."* Citadel Press, New
         York, 1961, 123p, Paper, Tele. Coll.

01853 *One step beyond; great stories of the psychic
         world selected from the television series
         "Alcoa presents."* Citadel Press, New York,
         1960, 122p, Paper, Tele. Coll.

BREEDLOVE, BILL, pseud.

01854 *Devil sex.* PEC, San Diego, 1967, 184p, Paper,
         Novel

BREEN, WALTER

01855 *The Gemini problem; a study in Darkover.* Wal-
         ter Breen, Berkeley, 1973, 23p, Paper, Nonf.

BREGGIN, PETER ROGER, 1936-   [*biography included*]

01856 *After the good war; a love story.* Stein & Day,
         New York, 1972, 235p, Cloth, Novel

BRENAN, EDWARD FITZ-GERALD
      see: BEATON, GEORGE

BRENHOLTZ, EDWIN ARNOLD, 1859-

01857 *The Recording Angel; a novel.* Charles H. Kerr,
         Chicago, 1905, 287p, Cloth, Novel

BRENNAN, ALICE

01858 *Candace.* Paperback Library, New York, 1970,
         176p, Paper, Novel

BRENNAN, ELIZABETH

01859 *Whispering walls.* Metropolitan Publishing Co.,
         Dublin, 1948, 289p, Cloth, Novel

BRENNAN, Rev. GERALD T(homas), 1898-

01860 *The ghost of kingdom come.* Bruce Publishing
         Co., Milwaukee, 1940, 143p, Cloth, Novel

BRENNAN, JOSEPH PAYNE, 1918-   [*biography included*]

01861 *The casebook of Lucius Leffing.* Macabre House,
         New Haven, Conn., 1973, 191p, Cloth, Coll.
01862 *The dark returners.* Macabre House, New Haven,
         Conn., 1959, 70p, Cloth, Coll.
       H. P. Lovecraft; a bibliography. [see 01867]
01863 *H. P. Lovecraft; an evaluation.* Macabre House,
         New Haven, Conn., 1955, 8p, Paper, Nonf.
01864 *Nine horrors and a dream.* Arkham House, Sauk
         City, 1958, 120p, Cloth, Coll.
01865 *Scream at midnight.* Macabre House, New Haven,
         Conn., 1963, 124p, Cloth, Coll.
01866 *A select bibliography of H. P. Lovecraft.* no
         publisher, New Haven?, 1952, 8p, Paper, Nonf.
01867 retitled: *H. P. Lovecraft; a bibliography.*
         Biblio Press, Washington, 1952, 14p, Paper,
         Nonf. [expanded]

BRENNAN, JOSEPH PAYNE (cont.)

01868 *Stories of darkness and dread.* Arkham House, Sauk City, 1973, 173p, Cloth, Coll.

BRENT, JEREMY

01869 *The plastic man.* New English Library, London, 1974, 127p, Paper, Novel

BRENTWOOD, EVELYN

01870 *Hector Graeme.* John Lane, The Bodley Head, London, 1912, 352p, Cloth, Novel

BRERETON, CLOUDESLEY (Shovell Henry), 1863-1937

01871 *The last days of Olympus; a modern myth.* Kegan Paul, Trench, London, 1889, 153p, Cloth, Novel

BRERETON, Captain F(rederick) S(adleir), 1872-1957

01872 *The great aeroplane; a thrilling tale of adventure.* Blackie & Son, London, 1911, 396p, Cloth, Novel

BRETNALL, GEORGE H(erbert), 1871-1961

01873 *Bulo and Lele.* Comet Press, New York, 1954, 208p, Cloth, Novel

BRETNOR, REGINALD, 1911-   [*biography included*]

01874 *Modern science fiction; its meaning and its future.* Coward-McCann, New York, 1953, 294p, Cloth, Nonf. Anth.
01875 *Science fiction today and tomorrow; a discursive symposium.* Harper & Row, New York, 1974, 342p, Cloth, Nonf. Anth.

as Grendel Briarton:

01876 *Through time and space with Ferdinand Feghoot; the first forty-five Feghoot adventures, with five more never previously heard of.* Paradox Press, Tokyo, 1962, 73p, Paper, Coll.

BRETON, FREDERIC

01877 *The black mass; a contemporary romance.* Hutchinson, London, 1897, 324p, Cloth, Novel

BRETON, THOMAS LE
  see: LE BRETON, THOMAS

BRETT, LEO, pseud.
  see: FANTHORPE, R. LIONEL

BREUER, Dr. MILES J(ohn), 1889-1947, with Jack Williamson

01878 *The girl from Mars.* Stellar Publishing Corp., New York, 1929, 24p, Paper, Story

BREUIL, LINDA DU
  see: DuBREUIL, LINDA

BREWSTER, DENNIS

01879 *I dream of Jeannie.* Pocket Books, New York, 1966, 124p, Paper, Tele.

BREX, J(ohn) TWELLS, 1874-1920

01880 *The Civil War of 1915.* C. Arthur Pearson, London, 1912, 159p, Paper, Novel

BRIARTON, GRENDEL, pseud.
  see: BRETNOR, REGINALD

BRIDGE, ANN, pseud. [Mary Dolling O'Malley, 1891-1974]

01881 *And then you came; a novel.* Chatto & Windus, London, 1948, 319p, Cloth, Novel
01882 *The song in the house; stories.* Chatto & Windus, London, 1936, 283p, Cloth, Coll.

BRIDGE, JAMES HOWARD
  see: BRYDGES, HAROLD

BRIDGES, ROY, 1885-1952

01883 *A mirror of silver.* Hutchinson, London, 1927, 280p, Cloth, Novel

BRIDGES, T(homas) C(harles), 1868-

01884 *The city of no escape.* George Newnes, London, 1925, 255p, Cloth, Novel
01885 *The death star.* Collins, London, 1940, 288p, Cloth, Novel
01886 *The hidden city.* Collins' Clear-Type Press, London, 1923, 320p, Cloth, Novel
01887 *Martin Crusoe; a boy's adventure on Wizard Island.* George G. Harrap, London, 1920, 255p, Cloth, Novel
01888 *Men of the mist.* George G. Harrap, London, 1923, 252p, Cloth, Novel
01889 *The T. C. Bridges adventure book.* George G. Harrap, London, 1933, 756p, Cloth, Coll. [includes *The mystery message; The sky riders; Martin Crusoe*]

as Christopher Beck:

01890 *The people of the chasm.* C. Arthur Pearson, London, 1924, 256p, Cloth, Novel

BRIDGMAN-METCHIM, D.
  see: METCHIM, D. BRIDGMAN-

BRIGGS, PHILIP, pseud. [Phyllis Briggs]

01891   *Escape from gravity.* Lutterworth Press, London, 1955, 192p, Cloth, Novel
01892   *The silent planet.* Lutterworth Press, London, 1957, 189p, Cloth, Novel

BRIGGS, PHYLLIS
   see: BRIGGS, PHILIP

BRIGHT, MARY
   see: EGERTON, GEORGE

BRINEY, ROBERT E(dward), 1933-   [*biography included*]

01893   *Shanadu; a collection of fantasy.* SSR Publications, North Tonawanda, NY, 1953, 101p, Paper, Anth.

with Edward Wood:

01894   *SF bibliographies; an annotated bibliography of bibliographical works on science fiction and fantasy fiction.* Advent: Publishers, Chicago, 1972, 49p, Paper, Nonf.

BRINIG, MYRON, 1900-

01895   *The flutter of an eyelid.* Farrar & Rinehart, New York, 1933, 310p, Cloth, Novel

BRINK, CAROL (Ryrie), 1895-   [*biography included*]

01896   *Andy Buckram's tin men.* Viking Press, New York, 1966, 192p, Cloth, Novel

BRINSMADE, HERMAN HINE

01897   *Utopia achieved; a novel of the future.* Broadway Publishing Co., New York, 1912, 177p, Cloth, Novel

BRINTON, HENRY, 1901-   [*biography included*]

01898   *Purple-6.* Hutchinson, London, 1962, 207p, Cloth, Novel

BRISCO, PAT(ricia) A., 1927-   [*biography included*]

01899   *The other people.* Powell, Reseda, 1970, 204p, Paper, Novel

BRITAIN, DAN, pseud.
   see: PENDLETON, DON

BRIUSOV, VALERII IAKOVLEVICH, 1873-1924

01900   *The fiery angel; a sixteenth century romance,* by Valeri Briussov. Humphrey Toulmin, The Cayme Press, London, 1930, 392p, Cloth, Novel

01901   *The republic of the Southern Cross, and other stories,* by Valery Brussof. Constable, London, 1918, 162p, Cloth, Coll.

BRIUSSOV, VALERI
   see: BRIUSOV, VALERII

BROCK, WALTER S.

01902   *On the crest of the Earth with race.* Carlton Press, New York, 1969, 205p, Cloth, Novel

BROCKIES, ENID FLORENCE
   see: MAGRISKA, HELENE

BROCKLEY, FENTON, pseud. [see also D. Rowland]

01903   *Star quest.* Robert Hale, London, 1974, 189p, Cloth, Novel

BROCKWAY, (Archibald) FENNER, Baron Brockway, 1888-   [*biography included*]

01904   *Purple Plague; a tale of love and revolution.* Sampson Low, Marston, London, 1935, 310p, Cloth, Novel

BRODERICK, DAMIEN

01905   *A man returned.* Horwitz, Sydney, 1965, 130p, Paper, Coll.
01906   *Sorcerer's world.* Signet, New York, 1970, 144p, Paper, Novel

BRODEUR, ARTHUR GILCHRIST, 1888-   , with Farnham Bishop

01336   *The altar of the legion.* Little, Brown, Boston, 1926, 316p, Cloth, Novel

BRODHAY, O(tto) CHESTER, 1875?-1954

01907   *Veiled victory.* Dorrance & Co., Philadelphia, 1941, 357p, Cloth, Novel

BRODIE-INNES, J(ohn) W(illiam), 1848-

01908   *The devil's mistress.* Rebman, London, 1910, 357p, Cloth, Novel
01909   *For the soul of a witch; a romance of Badenoch.* Rebman, London, 1910, 363p, Cloth, Novel
01910   *Morag the Seal.* Rebman, London, 1908, 323p, Cloth, Novel
01911   *Old as the world; a romance of the western islands.* Rebman, London, 1909, 383p, Cloth, Novel

BRODKIN, SYLVIA Z., with Elizabeth J. Pearson

01912   *Science fiction.* McDougal, Littell, Evanston, 1973, 247p, Paper, Anth.

BROMFIELD, LOUIS, 1896-1956

01913 *The strange case of Miss Annie Spragg.* Frederick A. Stokes, New York, 1928, 314p, Cloth, Novel

BRONTË, CHARLOTTE, 1816-1855

01914 *Legends of Angria.* Humphrey Milford, Oxford University Press, London, 1933, 332p, Cloth, Coll. [Angria series]
01915 *The twelve adventurers, and other stories.* Hodder & Stoughton, London, 1925, 214p, Cloth, Coll. [Angria series]

as Ellis Bell:

01916 *Wuthering Heights; a novel.* T. C. Newby, London, 1847, 3vol, Cloth, Novel
01916A *Wuthering Heights; a novel,* by the author of "Jane Eyre." Coolidge & Wiley, Boston, 1848, 112p, Cloth, Novel
01916B *Wuthering Heights,* by Charlotte Brontë. Harper & Bros., New York, 1877, 288p, Cloth, Novel

BRONTE, LOUISA, pseud.
     see: ROBERTS, JANET LOUISE

BROOKE, (Bernard) JOCELYN, 1908-1966

01917 *The scapegoat.* Bodley Head, London, 1948, 128p, Cloth, Novel

BROOKE-ROSE, CHRISTINE, 1923- *[biography included]*

01918 *Out.* Michael Joseph, London, 1964, 196p, Cloth, Novel
01919 *Such.* Michael Joseph, London, 1966, 194p, Cloth, Novel

BROOKFIELD, ARTHUR MONTAGU, 1853-1940

01920 *Simiocracy; a fragment from future history,* by the author of 'Post mortem.' William Blackwood & Sons, Edinburgh, 1884, 186p, Cloth, Novel

BROOKINS, DEWEY C., 1904- *[biography included]*

01921 *Flying high.* Vantage Press, New York, 1965, 91p, Cloth, Novel

BROOKS, BYRON A(lden), 1845-1911

01922 *Earth revisited.* Arena Publishing Co., Boston, 1893, 318p, Cloth, Novel

BROOKS, C. W. ("Ned") Jr.

01923 *Revised Hannes Bok checklist.* T-K Graphics, Baltimore, 1974, 47p, Paper, Nonf.

as Ned Brooks, with Don Martin:

01924 *Hannes Bok illustration index.* Collectors Bureau, National Fantasy Fan Federation, Newport News, VA, 1970, 22p, Paper, Nonf.

BROOKS, (William) COLLIN, 1893-1959

01925 *Mad-Doctor Merciful.* Hutchinson, London, 1932, 255p, Cloth, Novel

BROOKS, EDWY SEARLES
     see: GRAY, BERKELEY

BROOKS, NED
     see: BROOKS, C. W. Jr.

BROOKS, WALTER R(ollin), 1886-1958

01926 *Freddy and Mr. Camphor.* Alfred A. Knopf, New York, 1944, 244p, Cloth, Novel [Freddy #9]
01927 *Freddy and Simon the dictator.* Alfred A. Knopf, New York, 1956, 244p, Cloth, Novel [Freddy #21]
01928 *Freddy and the baseball team from Mars.* Alfred A. Knopf, New York, 1955, 241p, Cloth, Novel [Freddy #20]
01929 *Freddy and the Bean home news.* Alfred A. Knopf, New York, 1943, 230p, Cloth, Novel [Freddy #8]
01930 *Freddy and the dragon.* Alfred A. Knopf, New York, 1958, 239p, Cloth, Novel [Freddy #23]
01931 *Freddy and the flying saucer plans.* Alfred A. Knopf, New York, 1957, 243p, Cloth, Novel [Freddy #22]
01932 *Freddy and the ignoramus.* Alfred A. Knopf, New York, 1941, 286p, Cloth, Novel [Freddy #6]
01933 *Freddy and the men from Mars.* Alfred A. Knopf, New York, 1954, 246p, Cloth, Novel [Freddy #19]
01934 *Freddy and the perilous adventure.* Alfred A. Knopf, New York, 1942, 245p, Cloth, Novel [Freddy #7]
01935 *Freddy and the popinjay.* Alfred A. Knopf, New York, 1945, 244p, Cloth, Novel [Freddy #10]
01936 *Freddy and the space ship.* Alfred A. Knopf, New York, 1953, 262p, Cloth, Novel [Freddy #18]
01937 *Freddy goes camping.* Alfred A. Knopf, New York, 1948, 258p, Cloth, Novel [Freddy #13]
       Freddy goes to Florida. [see 01948A]
       Freddy goes to the North Pole. [see 01946A]
01938 *Freddy plays football.* Alfred A. Knopf, New York, 1949, 265p, Cloth, Novel [Freddy #14]
01939 *Freddy rides again.* Alfred A. Knopf, New York, 1951, 240p, Cloth, Novel [Freddy #16]
01940 *Freddy the cowboy.* Alfred A. Knopf, New York, 1950, 233p, Cloth, Novel [Freddy #15]
01941 *Freddy the detective.* Alfred A. Knopf, New York, 1932, 263p, Cloth, Novel [Freddy #3]
01942 *Freddy the magician.* Alfred A. Knopf, New York, 1947, 258p, Cloth, Novel [Freddy #12]
01943 *Freddy the pied piper.* Alfred A. Knopf, New York, 1946, 253p, Cloth, Novel [Freddy #11]
01944 *Freddy the pilot.* Alfred A. Knopf, New York, 1952, 247p, Cloth, Novel [Freddy #17]
       Freddy the politician. [see 01949A]

BROOKS, WALTER R. (cont.)

01945   *Freddy's cousin Weedly.* Alfred A. Knopf, New
        York, 1940, 283p, Cloth, Novel [Freddy #5]
        Freddy's first adventure. [see 01948B]
01946   *More to and again.* Alfred A. Knopf, New York,
        1930, 306p, Cloth, Novel [Freddy #2]
01946A retitled: *Freddy goes to the North Pole.*
        Alfred A. Knopf, New York, 1951, 306p,
        Cloth, Novel [Freddy #2]
01947   *The original Mr. Ed.* Bantam, New York, 1963,
        118p, Paper, Tele. Coll.
01948   *To and again.* Alfred A. Knopf, New York,
        1927, 197p, Cloth, Novel [Freddy #1]
01948A retitled: *Freddy goes to Florida.* Alfred
        A. Knopf, New York, 1949, 197p, Cloth,
        Novel [Freddy #1]
01948B retitled: *Freddy's first adventure.* Bodley
        Head, London, 1949, 175p, Cloth, Novel
        [Freddy #1]
01949   *Wiggins for president.* Alfred A. Knopf, New
        York, 1939, 252p, Cloth, Novel [Freddy #4]
01949A retitled: *Freddy the politician.* Alfred A.
        Knopf, New York, 1948, 252p, Cloth, Novel
        [Freddy #4]

BROOMHEAD, REGINALD

01950   *A voice from Mars; adventure & romance.* Ar-
        thur H. Stockwell, London, 1923, 176p,
        Cloth, Novel

BROPHY, BRIGID (Antonia), 1929-

01951   *The adventures of God in his search for the
        Black Girl.* Macmillan, London, 1973, 224p,
        Cloth, Coll.

BROPHY, JOHN, 1899-1965 [biography included]

01952   *Thunderclap.* Eric Partridge, The Scholartis
        Press, London, 1931, 198p, Cloth, Novel
01953   *The woman from nowhere; a novel.* Collins,
        London, 1946, 160p, Cloth, Novel

BROSTER, D(orothy) K(athleen), 1877-1950

01954   *Couching at the door.* William Heinemann,
        London, 1942, 130p, Cloth, Coll.
01955   *A fire of driftwood; a collection of short
        stories.* William Heinemann, London, 1932,
        348p, Cloth, Coll.

BROUGHTON, B(ernard) L(ennox)

01956   *The vision of Kwannon Sama; a story of faith
        and love of long ago.* Luzac & Co., London,
        1929, 154p, Cloth, Novel

BROUGHTON, RHODA, 1840-1920

01957   *Tales for Christmas Eve.* Richard Bentley &
        Son, London, 1873, 217p, Cloth, Coll.
01957A retitled: *Twilight stories.* Richard Bentley
        & Son, London, 1879, 181p, Cloth, Coll.

BROUN, HEYWOOD (Campbell), 1888-1939

01958   *Gandle follows his nose.* Boni & Liveright,
        New York, 1926, 191p, Cloth, Novel

BROWN, ALEC (John Charles), 1900-

01959   *Angelo's moon.* Bodley Head, London, 1955, 221p,
        Cloth, Novel

BROWN, ALICE, 1857-1948

01960   *The kingdom in the sky.* Macmillan, New York,
        1932, 357p, Cloth, Novel
01961   *The wind between the worlds.* Macmillan, New
        York, 1920, 258p, Cloth, Novel

BROWN, BETH [biography included]

01962   *Universal Station.* Regent House Publishers,
        New York, 1944, 392p, Cloth, Novel

BROWN, CHARLES R., with Arthur Morgan

01963   *The disintegrator; a romance of modern science.*
        Digby, Long, London, 1891, 220p, Cloth, Novel

BROWN, DOUGLAS (Frank Lambert), 1907-   [bio-
graphy included], with Christopher Serpell

01964   *Loss of Eden; a cautionary tale.* Faber & Faber
        London, 1940, 251p, Cloth, Novel
01964A retitled: *If Hitler comes...* Faber & Faber,
        London, 1941, 251p, Cloth, Novel

BROWN, FRED. H.

01965   *One dollar's worth.* Fred. H. Brown, Chicago,
        1893, 177p, Cloth, Coll. [called *A message
        from the stars* internally]

BROWN, FREDRIC (William), 1906-1972 [biography
included]

01966   *Angels and spaceships.* E. P. Dutton, New York,
        1954, 224p, Cloth, Coll.
01966A retitled: *Star shine.* Bantam, New York, 1956,
        138p, Paper, Coll. [abridged]
01967   *Daymares.* Lancer, New York, 1968, 317p, Paper,
        Coll.
01968   *Honeymoon in Hell.* Bantam, New York, 1958,
        170p, Paper, Coll.
01969   *The lights in the sky are stars.* E. P. Dutton,
        New York, 1953, 254p, Cloth, Novel
01969A retitled: *Project Jupiter.* T. V. Boardman,
        London, 1954, 222p, Cloth, Novel
01970   *Martians, go home.* E. P. Dutton, New York,
        1955, 189p, Cloth, Novel
01971   *The mind thing.* Bantam, New York, 1961, 149p,
        Paper, Novel
01972   *Nightmares and Geezenstacks; 47 stories.* Ban-
        tam, New York, 1961, 137p, Paper, Coll.
01973   *Paradox lost, and twelve other great science
        fiction stories.* Random House, New York,
        1973, 211p, Cloth, Coll.

BROWN, FREDRIC (Cont.)

Project Jupiter. [see 01969A]
01974 *Rogue in space.* E. P. Dutton, New York, 1957,
189p, Cloth, Novel
01975 *Space on my hands.* Shasta Publishers, Chicago,
1951, 224p, Cloth, Coll.
Star shine. [see 01966A]
01976 *What mad universe.* E. P. Dutton, New York,
1949, 255p, Cloth, Novel

with Mack Reynolds:

01977 *Science-fiction carnival; fun in science-
fiction.* Shasta Publishers, Chicago, 1953,
315p, Cloth, Anth.

BROWN, GEORGE SHELDON, pseud.

01978 *Destination Mars.* Edwin Self, London, 1951,
128p, Paper, Novel
01979 *The planetoid peril.* Edwin Self, London,
1952, 128p, Paper, Novel
01980 *The yellow planet,* by George Sheldon Browne.
Edwin Self, London, 1954, 100p, Paper, Novel

BROWN, HARRISON (Scott), 1917-   [*biography
included*], with Chloe Zerwick

01981 *The Cassiopeia affair.* Doubleday, Garden City,
1968, 235p, Cloth, Novel

BROWN, J(ames) G(oldie), 1901-   [*biography
included*]

01982 *From Frankenstein to Andromeda; an anthology
of science fiction.* Macmillan, London,
1966, 150p, Paper, Anth.

BROWN, JAMES COOKE, 1921-   [*biography included*]

01983 *The Troika incident; a tetralogue in two parts.*
Doubleday, Garden City, 1970, 399p, Cloth,
Novel

BROWN, JOHN MACMILLAN
see: SWEVEN, GODFREY

BROWN, JOHN YOUNG, 1858-1921

01984 *To the Moon and back in ninety days; a thrilling narrative of blended science and adventure.* Lunar Publishing Co., Providence, KY,
1922, 214p, Cloth, Novel

BROWN, JOSEPH M(ackey), 1851-1932

01985 *Astyanax; an epic romance of Ilion, Atlantis,
& Amaraca.* Broadway Publishing Co., New
York, 1907, 921p, Cloth, Novel

BROWN, KATE CLARK

01986 *Beauty for ashes.* Arena Publishing Co., Boston, 1895, 120p, Cloth, Novel

BROWN, L. J., pseud.
see: DuBREUIL, LINDA

BROWN, RICHARD BLAKE, 1902-

01987 *A broth of a boy.* Fortune Press, London, 1933,
373p, Cloth, Novel

BROWN, ROBIN

01988 *A forest is a long time growing.* Michael Joseph, London, 1967, 240p, Cloth, Novel

BROWN, ROSEL GEORGE, 1926-1967 [*biography included*]

Galactic Sibyl Sue Blue. [see 01990A]
01989 *A handful of time.* Ballantine, New York, 1963,
160p, Paper, Coll.
01990 *Sibyl Sue Blue.* Doubleday, Garden City, 1966,
183p, Cloth, Novel [Sibyl Sue Blue #1]
01990A retitled: *Galactic Sibyl Sue Blue.* Berkley
Medallion, New York, 1968, 158p, Paper, Novel
[Sibyl Sue Blue #1]
01991 *The waters of Centaurus.* Doubleday, Garden
City, 1970, 181p, Cloth, Novel [Sibyl Sue
Blue #2]

with Keith Laumer:

01992 *Earthblood.* Doubleday, Garden City, 1966, 253p,
Cloth, Novel

BROWN, SENATOR
see: LEIGHTON, FRANCES SPATZ

BROWN, SLATER, 1896-

01993 *Spaceward bound.* Prentice-Hall, New York,
1955, 213p, Cloth, Novel

BROWN, WES, 1921-

01994 *Return.* Dorrance & Co., Philadelphia, 1973,
81p, Cloth, Novel

BROWN, WILLIAM ASHLEY-
see: ASHLEY-BROWN, WILLIAM

BROWNE, BARUM, pseud.

01995 *The devil and X.Y.Z.* Crime Club, Doubleday,
Doran, Garden City, 1931, 310p, Cloth, Novel

BROWNE, GEORGE SHELDON
see: BROWN, GEORGE SHELDON

BROWNE, GERALD A.

01996 *Hazard.* Arbor House, New York, 1973, 319p,
Cloth, Novel

BROWNE, HOWARD, 1908-

01997 *Return of Tharn*. Grandon Company, Publishers,
      Providence, RI, 1956, 253p, Cloth, Novel
      [Tharn #2]
01998 *Warrior of the dawn; the adventures of Tharn*.
      Reilly & Lee, Chicago, 1943, 287p, Cloth,
      Novel [Tharn #1]

BROWNE, REGINALD

01999 *School in space*. Gerald G. Swan, London, 1947,
      189p, Cloth, Novel

BROWNE, WALTER, 1856-1911

02000 *"2894"; or, The fossil man (a mid-winter
      night's dream)*. G. W. Dillingham, New York,
      1894, 298p, Paper, Novel

BROYLES, L(loyd) D(ouglas), 1931-

02001 *Who's who in science fiction fandom, 1961*.
      L. D. Broyles, Waco, TX, 1961, 39p, Paper,
      Nonf.

BRUCE, KENNEDY

02002 *The fakir's curse*. Herbert Jenkins, London,
      1931, 314p, Cloth, Novel

BRUCE, KENNETH
  see: CRAYON, DIEDRICH Jr.

BRUCE, MURIEL

02003 *Mukara; a novel*. Rae D. Henkel, New York,
      1930, 278p, Cloth, Novel

BRUCE, STEWART E.

02004 *The world in 1931*. F. L. Searl, New York,
      1921, 192p, Cloth, Novel

BRUCKBERGER, RAYMOND LÉOPOLD (Jean Joachim),
1907-

02005 *The seven miracles of Gubbio, and the eighth;
      a parable*. Whittlesey House, New York, 1948,
      60p, Cloth, Novel
02005A retitled: *The miracles of the wolf of Gubbio;
      a parable*. Home & Van Thal, London, 1949,
      60p, Cloth, Novel

BRÜCKNER, KARL, 1906-

02006 *The hour of the robots*. Burke, London, 1964,
      187p, Cloth, Novel

BRUÈRE, MARTHA (S.) BENSLEY, 1879-

02007 *Mildred Carver, U.S.A.* Macmillan, New York,
      1919, 289p, Cloth, Novel

LA BRUJA

02008 *La Bruja, the witch; or, A picture of the
      court of Rome, found among the manuscripts
      of a respectable theologian, a great friend
      of that court*. J. Hatchard & Son, London,
      1840, 188p, Cloth, Novel [trans. from the
      Spanish by Markophrates, pseud.]

BRULLER, JEAN
  see: VERCORS

BRUMM, CHARLES [Carl]

02009 *Ahasuerus*. T. Werner Laurie, London, 1916,
      382p, Cloth, Novel

BRUNNER, JOHN (Kilian Houston), 1934-   [bio-
graphy included]

      Age of miracles. [see 02020]
02010 *The altar on Asconel*. Ace Double, New York,
      1965, 143p, Paper, Novel
02011 *The astronauts must not land*. Ace Double,
      New York, 1963, 138p, Paper, Novel
02012 retitled: *More things in Heaven*. Dell, New
      York, 1973, 221p, Paper, Novel [expanded]
02013 *The Atlantic abomination*. Ace Double, New
      York, 1960, 128p, Paper, Novel
      The avengers of Carrig. [see 02053]
02014 *Bedlam planet*. Ace, New York, 1968, 159p,
      Paper, Novel
02015 *Black is the color*. Pyramid, New York, 1969,
      189p, Paper, Novel
02016 *Born under Mars*. Ace, New York, 1967, 127p,
      Paper, Novel
02017 *Castaways' world*. Ace Double, New York, 1963,
      127p, Paper, Novel
02018 retitled: *Polymath*. DAW, New York, 1974, 156p,
      Paper, Novel [expanded]
      Catch a falling star. [see 02043]
02019 *The day of the star cities*. Ace, New York,
      1965, 158p, Paper, Novel
02020 retitled: *Age of miracles*. Ace, New York,
      1973, 300p, Paper, Novel [expanded]
02021 *Double, double*. Ballantine, New York, 1969,
      222p, Paper, Novel
02022 *The dramaturges of Yan*. Ace, New York, 1972,
      157p, Paper, Novel
02023 *The dreaming Earth*. Pyramid, New York, 1963,
      159p, Paper, Novel
02024 *Echo in the skull*. Ace Double, New York, 1959
      94p, Paper, Novel
02025 retitled: *Give warning to the world*. DAW,
      New York, 1974, 158p, Paper, Novel [expanded]
02026 *Endless shadow*. Ace Double, New York, 1964,
      97p, Paper, Novel
02027 *Enigma from Tantalus*. Ace Double, New York,
      1965, 102p, Paper, Novel
02028 *Entry to elsewhen*. DAW, New York, 1972, 172p,
      Paper, Coll.
02029 *The evil that men do*. Belmont Double, New York,
      1969, 92p, Paper, Novel
02030 *Father of lies*. Belmont Double, New York, 1968,
      79p, Paper, Novel
02031 *From this day forward*. Doubleday, Garden City,
      1972, 238p, Cloth, Coll.
02032 *The gaudy shadows*. Constable, London, 1970,
      222p, Cloth, Novel

BRUNNER, JOHN (cont.)

Give warning to the world. [see 02025]
Into the slave nebula. [see 02057]
02033 The jagged orbit. Ace, New York, 1969, 397p,
Paper, Novel
02034 Listen! The stars! Ace Double, New York,
1963, 96p, Paper, Novel
02035 retitled: The stardroppers. DAW, New York,
1972, 144p, Paper, Novel [expanded]
02036 The long result. Faber & Faber, London, 1965,
204p, Cloth, Novel
02037 Meeting at infinity. Ace Double, New York,
1961, 155p, Paper, Novel
More things in Heaven. [see 02012]
02038 No future in it, and other science fiction
stories. Victor Gollancz, London, 1962,
192p, Cloth, Coll.
02039 No other gods but me. Compact, London, 1966,
159p, Paper, Coll.
02040 Not before time; science fiction and fantasy.
New English Library, London, 1968, 128p,
Paper, Coll.
02041 Now then; three stories. Mayflower-Dell, London, 1965, 143p, Paper, Coll.
02042 The 100th millennium. Ace Double, New York,
1959, 110p, Paper, Novel
02043 retitled: Catch a falling star. Ace, New
York, 1968, 158p, Paper, Novel [expanded]
02044 Out of my mind. Ballantine, New York, 1967,
220p, Paper, Coll.
02045 Out of my mind; fantasy and science fiction.
New English Library, London, 1968, 128p,
Paper, Coll. [different contents]
02046 A planet of your own. Ace Double, New York,
1966, 99p, Paper, Novel
Polymath. [see 02018]
02047 The productions of time. Signet, New York,
1967, 139p, Paper, Novel
02048 Quicksand. Doubleday, Garden City, 1967,
240p, Cloth, Novel
02049 The repairmen of Cyclops. Ace Double, New
York, 1965, 150p, Paper, Novel
02050 The rites of Ohe. Ace Double, New York, 1963,
129p, Paper, Novel
02051 Sanctuary in the sky. Ace Double, New York,
1960, 122p, Paper, Novel
02052 Secret agent of Terra. Ace Double, New York,
1962, 127p, Paper, Novel
02053 retitled: The avengers of Carrig. Dell, New
York, 1969, 157p, Paper, Novel
02054 The sheep look up. Harper & Row, New York,
1972, 463p, Cloth, Novel [sequel to Stand
on Zanzibar]
02055 The skynappers. Ace Double, New York, 1960,
117p, Paper, Novel
02056 Slavers of space. Ace Double, New York, 1960,
118p, Paper, Novel
02057 retitled: Into the slave nebula. Lancer,
New York, 1968, 176p, Paper, Novel
02058 The space-time juggler. Ace Double, New York,
1963, 84p, Paper, Novel
02059 The squares of the city. Ballantine, New
York, 1965, 319p, Paper, Novel
02060 Stand on Zanzibar. Doubleday, Garden City,
1968, 507p, Cloth, Novel [sequel is The
sheep look up]
The stardroppers. [see 02035]
02061 The stone that never came down. Doubleday,
Garden City, 1973, 206p, Cloth, Novel
02062 The super barbarians. Ace, New York, 1962,
160p, Paper, Novel
Telepathist. [see 02072A]

02063 Threshold of eternity. Ace Double, New York,
1959, 148p, Paper, Novel
02064 Time-jump. Dell, New York, 1973, 160p, Paper,
Coll.
02065 Times without number. Ace Double, New York,
1962, 139p, Paper, Novel
02066 Times without number. Ace, New York, 1969,
156p, Paper, Novel [expanded]
02067 Timescoop. Dell, New York, 1969, 156p, Paper,
Novel
02068 To conquer chaos. Ace, New York, 1964, 192p,
Paper, Novel
02069 Total eclipse. Doubleday, Garden City, 1974,
187p, Cloth, Novel
02070 The traveler in black. Ace, New York, 1971,
222p, Paper, Coll.
02071 Web of everywhere. Bantam, New York, 1974,
149p, Paper, Novel
02072 The whole man. Ballantine, New York, 1964,
188p, Paper, Novel
02072A retitled: Telepathist; a science fiction novel.
Faber & Faber, London, 1965, 239p, Cloth,
Novel
02073 The world swappers. Ace Double, New York, 1959,
153p, Paper, Novel
02074 The wrong end of time. Doubleday, Garden City,
1971, 204p, Cloth, Novel

as Gill Hunt, house pseud.:

02075 Galactic storm. Curtis Warren, London, 1951,
110p, Paper, Novel

as Keith Woodcott:

02076 I speak for Earth. Ace Double, New York, 1961,
120p, Paper, Novel
02077 The ladder in the sky. Ace Double, New York,
1962, 137p, Paper, Novel
02078 The Martian sphinx. Ace, New York, 1965, 149p,
Paper, Novel
02079 The psionic menace. Ace Double, New York, 1963,
108p, Paper, Novel

BRUNT, Captain SAMUEL, pseud.

02080 A voyage to Cacklogallinia, with a description
of the religion, policy, customs, and manners
of that country. J. Watson, London, 1727,
167p, Cloth, Novel

BRUSSOF(F), VALERY
see: BRIUSOV, VALERII

BRYAN, P(atrick) H(enry) H(amilton)

02081 The Barford cat affair. Abelard-Schuman, London, 1958, 152p, Cloth, Novel

BRYANT, D(orothy) M., 1930-   [biography inclu-
ded]

02082 The comforter; a mystical fantasy. Evan Press,
Berkeley, 1971, 170p, Paper, Novel

BRYANT, EDWARD (Winslow Jr.), 1945-   [biogra-
phy included]

02083 Among the dead, and other events leading up to
the Apocalypse. Macmillan, New York, 1973,
210p, Cloth, Coll.

BRYAT, EDITH, pseud. [Gertrude E. Brayton]

02084 *Tin gods; an adventure of Jonathan Laidlow.*
Vantage Press, New York, 1971, 186p, Cloth,
Novel

BRYDGES, HAROLD, pseud. [James Howard Bridge,
1858-1939]

02085 *A fortnight in Heaven; an unconventional romance.* Sampson Low, Marston, Searle &
Rivington, London, 1886, 177p, Cloth, Novel

BRYHER, (Anna Winifred Ellerman), 1894-

02086 *Visa for Avalon.* Helen & Kurt Wolff, Harcourt,
Brace & World, New York, 1965, 119p, Cloth,
Novel

BUCHAN, BRYAN

/02087 *The forgotten world of Uloc.* Scholastic-TAB
Publications, Richmond Hill, Canada, 1970,
96p, Paper, Novel

BUCHAN, JOHN, Baron Tweedsmuir, 1875-1940

02088 *The blanket of the dark.* Hodder & Stoughton,
London, 1931, 314p, Cloth, Novel
02089 *The Dancing Floor.* Hodder & Stoughton, London,
1926, 311p, Cloth, Novel
02090 *Four tales; The thirty-nine steps; The power-
house; The watcher by the threshold; The
Moon endureth.* William Blackwood & Sons,
Edinburgh, 1936, 632p, Cloth, Coll.
02091 *The gap in the curtain.* Hodder & Stoughton,
London, 1932, 315p, Cloth, Novel
02092 *The Moon endureth; tales and fancies.* William
Blackwood & Sons, Edinburgh, 1912, 324p,
Cloth, Coll.
02093 *The watcher by the threshold, and other tales.*
William Blackwood & Sons, Edinburgh, 1902,
334p, Cloth, Coll.

BUCHANAN, MARIE

02094 *Greenshards; a novel.* Victor Gollancz, London,
1972, 191p, Cloth, Novel
02094A retitled: *Anima.* St. Martin's Press, New
York, 1972, 191p, Cloth, Novel
02095 *An unofficial breath; a novel.* Hodder & Stoughton, London, 1973, 189p, Cloth, Novel

BUCHANAN, ROBERT (Williams), 1841-1901

02096 *The moment after; a tale of the unseen.* Wil-
liam Heinemann, London, 1890, 212p, Cloth,
Novel
02097 *The Rev. Annabel Lee; a tale of to-morrow.*
C. Arthur Pearson, London, 1898, 255p, Cloth,
Novel

BUCHANAN, THOMAS G(ittings), 1919-   [biogra-
phy included]

02098 *The unicorn.* William Sloane Associates, New
York, 1960, 223p, Cloth, Novel

BUCHARD, ROBERT, 1931- [*biography included*]

02099 *Thirty seconds over New York.* Collins, London,
1970, 219p, Cloth, Novel

BUCK, CHARLES W(illiam), 1849-1930

02100 *Under the sun; or, The passing of the Incas;
a story of old Peru.* Sheltman & Co., Louis-
ville, KY, 1902, 413p, Cloth, Novel

BUCK, JAMES S.
see: THE PROPHET JAMES

BUCKLE, (Christopher) RICHARD (Sandford), 191

02101 *John Innocent at Oxford; a phantasy.* Chatto
& Windus, London, 1939, 150p, Cloth, Novel

BUCKMAN, H. H.

02102 *Merope; or, The destruction of Atlantis.* Da
Costa Printing & Publishing House, Jacksonville, FL, 1898, 123p, Cloth, Novel

BUCKMASTER, HENRIETTA, pseud. [Henrietta Hen-
kle Stephens] [*biography included*]

02103 *The lion in the stone; a novel.* Harcourt,
Brace & World, New York, 1968, 464p, Cloth,
Novel

BUCKNER, ROBERT (Henry), 1906-   [biography
included]

02104 *Starfire.* Permabooks, New York, 1960, 139p,
Paper, Novel
02104A retitled: *Moon pilot.* Permabooks, New York,
1962, 139p, Paper, Novel

"BUDGE," pseud.

02105 *The Eastern question solved; a vision of the
future.* W. H. Allen, London, 1881, 82p,
Paper?, Novel

BUDRYS, ALGIS [Algirdas Jonas Budrys, 1931-
[*biography included*]

02106 *The Amsirs and the Iron Thorn.* Fawcett Gold
Medal, Greenwich, 1967, 159p, Paper, Novel
02106A retitled: *The Iron Thorn.* Victor Gollancz,
London, 1968, 189p, Cloth, Novel
02107 *Budrys' inferno.* Berkley Medallion, New York,
1963, 160p, Paper, Coll.
02107A retitled: *The furious future.* Victor Gollancz,
London, 1964, 191p, Cloth, Coll.
02108 *The falling torch.* Pyramid, New York, 1959,
158p, Paper, Novel
02109 *False night.* Lion, New York, 1954, 127p, Paper,
Novel
02110 retitled: *Some will not die; here is a tomorrow.* Regency, Evanston, IL, 1961, 159p,
Paper, Novel [expanded]

BUDRYS, ALGIS (Cont.)

The furious future. [see 02107A]
The Iron Thorn. [see 02106A]
02111 *Man of Earth.* Ballantine, New York, 1958,
144p, Paper, Novel
02112 *Rogue Moon.* Gold Medal, Greenwich, 1960,
176p, Paper, Novel
Some will not die. [see 02110]
02113 *The unexpected dimension.* Ballantine, New
York, 1960, 159p, Paper, Coll.
02114 *Who?* Pyramid, New York, 1958, 157p, Paper,
Novel

BUELL, JOHN (Edward), 1927-

02115 *The pyx; a novel.* Farrar, Straus & Cudahy,
New York, 1959, 174p, Cloth, Novel
02115A retitled: *The chosen girl.* Four Square, London, 1964, 123p, Paper, Novel

BUERGER, GOTTFRIED AUGUST
see: RASPE, RUDOLF ERICH

BULGAKOV, MIKHAIL (Afanas'evich), 1891-1940

02116 *Diaboliad, and other stories.* Indiana University Press, Bloomington, 1972, 236p, Cloth,
Coll.
02117 *Heart of a dog.* Harcourt, Brace & Wolff, New
York, 1968, 146p, Cloth, Novel
02118 *The master and Margarita.* Grove Press, New
York, 1967, 402p, Cloth, Novel; Harper &
Row, New York, 1967, 394p, Cloth, Novel
[different translations released on exactly
the same day]

BULL, ALBERT E.

02119 *The mystery of the hidden city.* Federation
Press, London, 1925, 156p, Cloth, Novel

BULL, LOIS, 1900-

02120 *Captive goddess.* Macaulay Co., New York, 1935,
253p, Cloth, Novel

BULL, RANDOLPH C(ecil)

02121 *Great tales of mystery.* Weidenfeld & Nicolson, London, 1960, 272p, Cloth, Anth.
02121A retitled: *Great tales of terror.* Panther,
London, 1963, 224p, Paper, Anth.
02122 *Perturbed spirits; a book of ghost and terror
stories.* Arthur Barker, London, 1954, 287p,
Cloth, Anth.
02123 *Upon the midnight; an anthology of ghost and
horror stories.* Macdonald, London, 1957,
288p, Cloth, Anth.

BULL, Sergeant TERRY, pseud. [William Samuel
Triplet, 1899-   ]

02124 *Sergeant Terry Bull; his ideas on war and
fighting in general.* Infantry Journal,
Washington, 1943, 174p, Paper, Coll. [in-
cludes some nonf.]

BULLETT, GERALD (William), 1894-1958

02125 *Mr. Godly beside himself.* John Lane, London,
1924, 310p, Cloth, Novel

BULLIVANT, CECIL H(enry)

02126 *The enchantress.* Wright & Brown, London, 1932,
252p, Cloth, Novel

BULMER, (Henry) KENNETH, 1921-   [*biography
included*]

02127 *Behold the stars.* Ace Double, New York, 1965,
120p, Paper, Novel
02128 *Beyond the silver sky.* Ace Double, New York,
1961, 100p, Paper, Novel
Blazon. [see 02156A]
02129 *Challenge,* by H. K. Bulmer. Curtis Books, London, 1954, 160p, Paper, Novel
02130 *The changeling worlds.* Ace Double, New York,
1959, 145p, Paper, Novel
02131 *The Chariots of Ra.* Ace Double, New York,
1972, 130p, Paper, Novel [Keys to the Dimensions #6]
02132 *City under the sea.* Ace Double, New York,
1957, 175p, Paper, Novel
02133 *Cycle of nemesis.* Ace, New York, 1967, 190p,
Paper, Novel
02134 *Defiance.* Digit, London, 1963, 160p, Paper,
Novel
The Demons. [see 02135A]
02135 *Demons' world.* Ace Double, New York, 1964,
139p, Paper, Novel
02135A retitled: *The Demons.* Compact, London, 1965,
190p, Paper, Novel
02136 *The doomsday men.* Doubleday, Garden City,
1968, 207p, Cloth, Novel
02137 *The Earth Gods are coming.* Ace Double, New
York, 1960, 107p, Paper, Novel
Earth's long shadow. [see 02153A]
02138 *The electric sword-swallowers.* Ace Double,
New York, 1971, 121p, Paper, Novel
02139 *Empire of chaos,* by H. K. Bulmer. Panther,
London, 1953, 158p, Cloth, Novel
02140 *Encounter in space,* by H. K. Bulmer. Panther,
London, 1952, 128p, Paper, Novel
02141 *The fatal fire.* Digit, London, 1963, 160p,
Paper, Novel
02142 *Galactic intrigue,* by H. K. Bulmer. Panther,
London, 1953, 160p, Cloth, Novel
02143 *The Hunters of Jundagai.* Ace Double, New York,
1971, 111p, Paper, Novel [Keys to the Dimensions #5]
02144 *The insane city.* Curtis, New York, 1971, 175p,
Paper, Novel
02145 *Kandar.* Paperback Library, New York, 1969,
127p, Paper, Novel
02146 *The key to Irunium.* Ace Double, New York,
1967, 138p, Paper, Novel [Keys to the Dimensions #1]
02147 *The key to Venudine.* Ace Double, New York,
1968, 122p, Paper, Novel [Keys to the Dimensions #2]
02148 *Land beyond the Map.* Ace Double, New York,
1965, 136p, Paper, Novel
02149 *The million year hunt.* Ace Double, New York,
1964, 133p, Paper, Novel
02150 *New writings in SF 22.* Sidgwick & Jackson,
London, 1973, 189p, Cloth, Anth.
02151 *New writings in SF 23.* Sidgwick & Jackson,
London, 1973, 191p, Cloth, Anth.

BULMER, KENNETH (Cont.)

02152 *New writings in SF 24.* Sidgwick & Jackson,
        London, 1974, 190p, Cloth, Anth.
02153 *No man's world.* Ace Double, New York, 1961,
        128p, Paper, Novel
02153A retitled: *Earth's long shadow.* Digit, London,
        1963, 159p, Paper, Novel
02154 *Of Earth foretold; Earthmen run into another
        dominant galactic race.* Digit, London, 1961,
        160p, Paper, Novel
02155 *On the symb-socket circuit.* Ace, New York,
        1972, 174p, Paper, Novel [listed incorrectly
        as "symp" on the title page]
        The patient dark. [see 02158A]
02156 *Quench the burning stars.* Robert Hale, London,
        1970, 191p, Cloth, Novel
02156A retitled: *Blazon.* Curtis, New York, 1970,
        190p, Paper, Novel
02157 *Roller coaster world.* Ace, New York, 1972,
        173p, Paper, Novel
02158 *The secret of ZI.* Ace Double, New York, 1958,
        161p, Paper, Novel
02158A retitled: *The patient dark.* Robert Hale,
        London, 1969, 192p, Cloth, Novel
02159 *The ships of Durostorum.* Ace Double, New York,
        1970, 101p, Paper, Novel [Keys to the Dimen-
        sions #4]
02160 *Space salvage,* by H. K. Bulmer. Panther, Lon-
        don, 1953, 143p, Paper, Novel
02161 *Star trove.* Robert Hale, London, 1970, 192p,
        Cloth, Novel
02162 *The star venturers.* Ace Double, New York,
        1969, 124p, Paper, Novel
02163 *The stars are ours,* by H. K. Bulmer. Panther,
        London, 1953, 158p, Cloth, Novel
02164 *Swords of the barbarians.* New English Library,
        London, 1970, 127p, Paper, Novel
02165 *To outrun doomsday.* Ace, New York, 1967, 159p,
        Paper, Novel
02166 *The ulcer culture.* Macdonald, London, 1969,
        160p, Cloth, Novel
02167 *The wind of liberty; a planet's destiny trem-
        bled in the balance.* Digit, London, 1963,
        159p, Paper, Coll.
02168 *The wizard of Starship Poseidon.* Ace Double,
        New York, 1963, 124p, Paper, Novel
02169 *The Wizards of Senchuria.* Ace Double, New
        York, 1969, 113p, Paper, Novel [Keys to the
        Dimensions #3]
02170 *World aflame,* by H. K. Bulmer. Panther, Lon-
        don, 1954, 144p, Cloth, Novel
02171 *Worlds for the taking.* Ace, New York, 1966,
        159p, Paper, Novel

as Alan Burt Akers:

02172 *Arena of Antares.* DAW, New York, 1974, 207p,
        Paper, Novel [Dray Prescot #7]
02173 *Manhounds of Antares.* DAW, New York, 1974,
        185p, Paper, Novel [Dray Prescot #6]
02174 *Prince of Scorpio.* DAW, New York, 1974, 223p,
        Paper, Novel [Dray Prescot #5]
02175 *The suns of Scorpio.* DAW, New York, 1973,
        192p, Paper, Novel [Dray Prescot #2]
02176 *Swordships of Scorpio.* DAW, New York, 1973,
        191p, Paper, Novel [Dray Prescot #4]
02177 *Transit to Scorpio.* DAW, New York, 1972, 190p,
        Paper, Novel [Dray Prescot #1]
02178 *Warrior of Scorpio.* DAW, New York, 1973, 190p,
        Paper, Novel [Dray Prescot #3]

as Philip Kent:

02179 *Home is the Martian.* Tit-Bits Science Fiction
        Library, London, 1954, 64p, Paper, Novel
02180 *Mission to the stars.* Tit-Bits Science Fiction
        Library, London, 1954, 64p, Paper, Novel
02181 *Slaves of the spectrum.* Tit-Bits Science Fic-
        tion Library, London, 1954, 64p, Paper, Novel
02182 *Vassals of Venus.* Tit-Bits Science Fiction
        Library, London, 1954, 64p, Paper, Novel

as Karl Maras, house pseud.:

02183 *Peril from space.* Comyns (Publishers), London,
        1954, 128p, Paper, Novel
02184 *Zhorani (master of the universe).* Comyns (Pub-
        lishers), London, 1953, 128p, Paper, Novel

as Tully Zetford:

02185 *Hook: the boosted man.* New English Library,
        London, 1974, 110p, Paper, Novel [Hook #2]
02186 *Hook: whirlpool of stars.* New English Library,
        London, 1974, 127p, Paper, Novel [Hook #1]
02187 *Star city.* New English Library, London, 1974,
        127p, Paper, Novel [Hook #3]

as H. K. Bulmer, with A. V. Clarke:

02188 *Cybernetic controller.* Panther, London, 1952,
        112p, Paper, Novel
02189 *Space treason.* Panther, London, 1952, 112p,
        Paper, Novel

BULWER-LYTTON, EDWARD
   see: LYTTON, EDWARD BULWER-

BULWER-LYTTON, ROBERT
   see: LYTTON, ROBERT BULWER-

BUNCE, OLIVER BELL, 1828-1890

02190 *The story of Happinolande, and other legends.*
        D. Appleton, New York, 1889, 188p, Cloth,
        Coll.

BUNCH, DAVID R(oosevelt) [*biography included*]

02191 *Moderan.* Avon, New York, 1971, 240p, Paper,
        Coll.

BUQUE, JEAN de LA
   see: LA BUQUE, JEAN de

BURBANK, LEONE CLARK

02192 *An astral crime.* Mitre Press, London, 1932,
        272p, Cloth, Novel

BURBRIDGE, JUANITA CASSIL

02193 *Cheating the devil.* Nicholas L. Brown, New
        York, 1925, 272p, Cloth, Novel

BURDEKIN, KAY [Katharine]

02194 *The burning ring.* Thornton Butterworth, London,
        1927, 318p, Cloth, Novel

BURDEKIN, KAY (Cont.)

02195 *The rebel passion.* Thornton Butterworth, London, 1929, 316p, Cloth, Novel

BURDETT, CHARLES, 1815-

02196 *Chances and changes; or, Life as it is, illustrated in the history of a straw hat.* D. Appleton, New York, 1846, 158p, Cloth, Novel

BURDICK, EUGENE (Leonard), 1918-1965 [*biography included*], with Harvey Wheeler

02197 *Fail-safe.* McGraw-Hill, New York, 1962, 286p, Cloth, Novel

BURFORD, LOLAH (Mary), 1931- [*biography included*]

02198 *The vision of Stephen; an elegy.* Macmillan, New York, 1972, 192p, Cloth, Novel

BURGER, DIONYS

02199 *Sphereland; a fantasy about curved spaces and an expanding universe.* Thomas Y. Crowell, New York, 1965, 208p, Cloth, Novel [sequel to *Flatland*, by Edwin A. Abbott]

BURGER, JOANNE (Denise), 1938- [*biography included*]

02200 *SF published in 1969.* Joanne Burger, Lake Jackson, TX, 1970, 55p, Paper, Nonf.
02201 *SF published in 1970.* Joanne Burger, Lake Jackson, TX, 1971, 48p, Paper, Nonf.
02202 *SF published in 1971.* Joanne Burger, Lake Jackson, TX, 1972, 48p, Paper, Nonf.
02203 *SF published in 1972.* Joanne Burger, Lake Jackson, TX, 1974, 42p, Paper, Nonf.
02204 *Science fiction books published in 1967.* Joanne Burger, Lake Jackson, TX, 1968, 12p, Paper, Nonf.
02205 *Science fiction books published in 1968.* Joanne Burger, Lake Jackson, TX, 1969, 50p, Paper, Nonf.

BURGESS, ANTHONY, pseud. [John Anthony Burgess Wilson, 1917-] [*biography included*]

02206 *A clockwork orange.* Heinemann, London, 1962, 196p, Cloth, Novel
02207 *The eve of Saint Venus.* Sidgwick & Jackson, London, 1964, 138p, Cloth, Novel
02208 *The wanting seed.* Heinemann, London, 1962, 285p, Cloth, Novel

BURGESS, BRIAN

02209 *Authentic science fiction.* no publisher, England, 1960?, 27p, Paper, Nonf.
02210 *A history and checklist of New worlds.* British Science Fiction Association, London?, 1959, 33p, Paper, Nonf.

BURGESS, ERIC (Alexander), 1912- [*biography included*], with Arthur Friggens

02211 *Anti-Zota.* Robert Hale, London, 1973, 189p, Cloth, Novel
02212 *Mortorio.* Robert Hale, London, 1973, 192p, Cloth, Novel

BURGESS, (Frank) GELETT, 1866-1951

02213 *The maxims of Methuselah, being the advice given by the patriarch in his nine hundred sixty and ninth year to his great grandson at Shem's coming of age, in regard to women.* Frederick A. Stokes, New York, 1907, 108p, Cloth, Coll.
02214 *The maxims of Noah, derived from his experience with women, both before and after the flood, as given in counsel to his son Japhet.* Frederick A. Stokes, New York, 1913, 119p, Cloth, Coll.

with Will Irwin:

02215 *The Picaroons.* McClure, Phillips, New York, 1904, 284p, Cloth, Novel

BURGESS, M. R.
    see: REGINALD, R.

BURGIN, G(eorge) B(rown), 1856-1944

02216 *The woman without a heart.* Alexander-Ouseley, London, 1930, 310p, Cloth, Novel

BURGOYNE, ALAN H(ughes), 1880-1929

02217 *The war inevitable.* Francis Griffiths, London, 1908, 313p, Cloth, Novel

with W. Laird Clowes:

02218 *Trafalgar refought.* Thomas Nelson & Sons, London, 1905, 328p, Cloth, Novel

BURKE, JONATHAN, pseud.
    see: BURKE, JOHN

BURKE, JOHN (Frederick), 1922- [*biography included*]

02219 *Dr. Terror's house of horrors.* Pan, London, 1965, 159p, Paper, Movie
02220 *Expo 80; a novel.* Cassell, London, 1972, 298p, Cloth, Novel
02221 *The Hammer horror omnibus.* Pan, London, 1966, 331p, Paper, Movie Coll.
02222 *Moon Zero Two.* Pan, London, 1969, 141p, Paper, Movie
02223 *More tales of unease.* Pan, London, 1969, 284p, Paper, Anth.
02224 *The second Hammer horror film omnibus.* Pan, London, 1967, 349p, Paper, Movie Coll.
02225 *Tales of unease.* Pan, London, 1966, 271p, Paper, Anth.

as Jonathan Burke:

02226 *Alien landscapes; science fiction stories.* Museum Press, London, 1955, 160p, Cloth, Coll.

BURKE, JOHN (Cont.)

as Jonathan Burke:

02226A retitled: *Exodus from Elysium*. Horwitz, Sydney, 1965, 130p, Paper, Coll.

02227 *The dark gateway*. Panther, London, 1953, 223p, Cloth, Novel

02228 *Deep freeze*. Panther, London, 1955, 144p, Cloth, Novel

02229 *The echoing worlds*. Panther, London, 1954, 159p, Cloth, Novel

02230 *Hotel Cosmos*. Panther, London, 1954, 142p, Cloth, Novel

02231 *Pattern of shadows*. Museum Press, London, 1954, 128p, Cloth, Novel

02232 *Pursuit through time; a modern novel of science and imagination*. Ward, Lock, London, 1956, 187p, Cloth, Novel

02233 *Revolt of the humans*. Panther, London, 1955, 141p, Cloth, Novel

02234 *Twilight of reason*. Panther, London, 1954, 159p, Cloth, Novel

as Robert Miall:

02235 *UFO*. Pan, London, 1970, 127p, Paper, Tele. [UFO #1]

02235A retitled: *UFO-1; flesh hunters*. Warner Paperback Library, New York, 1973, 142p, Paper, Tele. [UFO #1]

02236 *UFO 2*. Pan, London, 1971, 127p, Paper, Tele. [UFO #2]

02236A retitled: *UFO-2; sporting blood*. Warner Paperback Library, New York, 1973, 140p, Paper, Tele. [UFO #2]

BURKE, NORAH (Eileen), 1907-

02237 *The Scarlet Vampire*. Stanley Paul, London, 1936, 288p, Cloth, Novel

BURKE, THOMAS, 1887-1945

02238 *Night-pieces; eighteen tales*. Constable, London, 1935, 311p, Cloth, Coll.

BURKETT, WILLIAM R(ay) Jr., 1943- [biography included]

02239 *Sleeping planet*. Doubleday, Garden City, 1965, 297p, Cloth, Novel

BURKHARDT, EVE, with Robert Burkhardt as Rob Eden

02240 *Golden goddess*. Hopkins, New York, 1935, 253p, Cloth, Novel

BURKHARDT, ROBERT FERDINAND, d. 1947, with Eve Burkhardt as Rob Eden

02240 *Golden goddess*. Hopkins, New York, 1935, 253p, Cloth, Novel

BURKS, ARTHUR J., 1898-1974

02241 *Black medicine*. Arkham House, Sauk City, 1966, 308p, Cloth, Coll.

02242 *The casket*. Tarnhelm Press, Lakemont, GA, 1973, 282p, Paper, Novel

02243 *The great amen*. Egmont Press, New York, 1938, 231p, Cloth, Novel

02244 *The great mirror*. Gerald G. Swan, London, 1952, 128p, Paper, Novel

02245 *Look behind you*. Shroud Publishers, Buffalo, 1954, 73p, Cloth, Coll.

BURLAND, HARRIS
  see: HARRIS-BURLAND, J. B.

BURLAND, J. B. HARRIS-
  see: HARRIS-BURLAND, J. B.

BURMAN, BEN LUCIEN, 1896- [biography included]

02246 *High water at Catfish Bend*. Julian Messner, New York, 1952, 121p, Cloth, Novel [Catfish Bend #1]

02247 *The owl hoots twice at Catfish Bend*. Taplinger, New York, 1961, 115p, Cloth, Novel [Catfish Bend #3]

02248 *Seven stars for Catfish Bend*. Funk & Wagnalls, New York, 1956, 133p, Cloth, Novel [Catfish Bend #2]

02249 *Three from Catfish Bend; High water at Catfish Bend; Seven stars for Catfish Bend; The owl hoots twice at Catfish Bend*. Taplinger, New York, 1967, 377p, Cloth, Coll. [Catfish Bend #s 1-3]

BURMEISTER, Mrs. KATE

02250 *"The Indian maiden's dream"; a novel*. The Author, Kansas City, 1895, 182p, Cloth, Novel

BURNETT, FRANCES (Eliza) HODGSON, 1849-1924

02251 *In the closed room*. McClure, Phillips, New York, 1904, 130p, Cloth, Novel

02252 *The Land of the Blue Flower*. Moffat, Yard, New York, 1909, 67p, Cloth, Novel

02253 *The White People*. Harper & Bros., New York, 1917, 112p, Cloth, Novel

BURNETT, HALLIE (Southgate), 1908- [biography included], with Whit Burnett

02254 *19 tales of terror*. Bantam, New York, 1956, 229p, Paper, Anth.

02255 *Things with claws*. Ballantine, New York, 1961, 159p, Paper, Anth.

BURNETT, WHIT(ney Ewing), 1899-1973

02256 *Two bottles of relish; a book of strange and unusual stories*. Dial Press, New York, 1943, 395p, Cloth, Anth.

with Hallie Burnett:

02254 *19 tales of terror*. Bantam, New York, 1956, 229p, Paper, Anth.

02255 *Things with claws*. Ballantine, New York, 1961, 159p, Paper, Anth.

BURNFORD, SHEILA (Philip Cochrane), 1918-
[biography included]

02257 Mr. Noah and the second flood. Victor Gol-
       lancz, London, 1973, 64p, Cloth, Novel

BURNS, ALAN, 1929-   [biography included]

02258 Babel. Calder & Boyars, London, 1969, 159p,
       Cloth, Novel

BURNS, R. C.

02259 The fantastic battle; the story of an idea.
       Friends' Book Centre, London, 1928, 36p,
       Paper, Story

BURR, FRANK

02260 The genial ghost. Vantage Press, New York,
       1964, 157p, Cloth, Novel

BURR, HANFORD M(ontrose), 1864-1941

02261 Around the fire; stories of beginnings. As-
       sociation Press, New York, 1912, 238p, Cloth,
       Coll.
02262 Cave boys. Association Press, New York, 1923,
       200p, Cloth, Coll.

BURRAGE, A(thol) HARCOURT

02263 Hurtlers through space. Frederick Warne, Lon-
       don, 1951, 255p, Cloth, Novel
02264 Scoundrel of the air; an air story for boys.
       Sampson Low, Marston, London, 1938, 250p,
       Cloth, Novel

BURRAGE, A(lfred) M(cLelland), 1889-1956

02265 Between the minute and the hour. Herbert Jen-
       kins, London, 1967, 221p, Cloth, Coll.
02266 Seeker to the dead. Gerald G. Swan, London,
       1942, 188p, Cloth, Novel
02267 Some ghost stories. Cecil Palmer, London,
       1927, 276p, Cloth, Coll.

as ex-Private X:

02268 Someone in the room. Jarrolds Publishers,
       London, 1931, 285p, Cloth, Coll.

BURROUGHS, EDGAR RICE, 1875-1950 [biography
included]

02269 At the Earth's core. A. C. McClurg, Chicago,
       1922, 277p, Cloth, Novel [Pellucidar #1]
02270 At the Earth's core; Pellucidar; Tanar of
       Pellucidar; three science fiction novels.
       Dover, New York, 1963, 433p, Paper, Coll.
       [Pellucidar #s 1-3]
02271 Back to the stone age. Edgar Rice Burroughs
       Inc., Tarzana, CA, 1937, 318p, Cloth, Novel
       [Pellucidar #5]
02272 The beasts of Tarzan. A. C. McClurg, Chicago,
       1916, 336p, Cloth, Novel [Tarzan #3]

02273 Beyond the farthest star. Ace, New York, 1964,
       125p, Paper, Novel
02274 Beyond Thirty. Lloyd Arthur Eshbach, Reading,
       PA, 1955, 57p, Paper, Novel
02274A retitled: The lost continent. Ace, New York,
       1963, 123p, Paper, Novel
02275 Beyond Thirty; and, The man eater. Science-
       Fiction & Fantasy Publications, South Ozone
       Park, NY, 1957, 229p, Cloth, Coll.
02276 Carson of Venus. Edgar Rice Burroughs Inc.,
       Tarzana, CA, 1939, 312p, Cloth, Novel [Venus
       #3]
02277 The cave girl. A. C. McClurg, Chicago, 1925,
       323p, Cloth, Novel
02278 The chessmen of Mars. A. C. McClurg, Chicago,
       1922, 375p, Cloth, Novel [Mars #5]
02279 Escape on Venus. Edgar Rice Burroughs Inc.,
       Tarzana, CA, 1946, 347p, Cloth, Novel [Venus
       #4]
02280 The eternal lover. A. C. McClurg, Chicago,
       1925, 316p, Cloth, Novel [Tarzan appears as
       a minor character]
02280A retitled: The eternal savage. Ace, New York,
       1963, 192p, Paper, Novel
02281 A fighting man of Mars. Metropolitan Books,
       New York, 1931, 319p, Cloth, Novel [Mars #7]
02282 The gods of Mars. A. C. McClurg, Chicago,
       1918, 348p, Cloth, Novel [Mars #2]
02283 The gods of Mars; and, The Warlord of Mars.
       Nelson Doubleday, Garden City, 1971, 336p,
       Cloth, Coll. [Mars #s 2-3]
02284 John Carter of Mars. Canaveral Press, New York,
       1964, 208p, Cloth, Coll. [Mars #11]
02285 Jungle girl. Edgar Rice Burroughs Inc., Tar-
       zana, CA, 1932, 318p, Cloth, Novel
02285A retitled: The land of hidden men. Ace, New
       York, 1963, 191p, Paper, Novel
02286 Jungle tales of Tarzan. A. C. McClurg, Chicago,
       1919, 319p, Cloth, Coll. [Tarzan #6]
02286A retitled: Tarzan's jungle tales. Four Square,
       London, 1961, 191p, Paper, Coll. [Tarzan #6]
02287 The lad and the lion. Edgar Rice Burroughs Inc.,
       Tarzana, CA, 1938, 317p, Cloth, Novel
       The land of hidden men. [see 02285A]
02288 Land of terror. Edgar Rice Burroughs Inc.,
       Tarzana, CA, 1944, 319p, Cloth, Novel [Pel-
       lucidar #6]
02289 The land that time forgot. A. C. McClurg,
       Chicago, 1924, 422p, Cloth, Coll. [Caspak
       Trilogy; includes The land that time forgot;
       The people that time forgot; Out of time's
       abyss]
02290 The land that time forgot. Ace, New York,
       1963, 126p, Paper, Novel [Caspak #1]
02291 The land that time forgot; and, The Moon maid;
       two science fiction novels. Dover, New York,
       1963, 552p, Paper, Coll.
02292 Llana of Gathol. Edgar Rice Burroughs Inc.,
       Tarzana, CA, 1948, 317p, Cloth, Novel [Mars
       #10]
       The lost continent. [see 02274A]
02293 Lost on Venus. Edgar Rice Burroughs Inc.,
       Tarzana, CA, 1935, 318p, Cloth, Novel [Venus
       #2]
02294 The man-eater. Lloyd Arthur Eshbach, Reading,
       PA, 1955, 50p, Paper, Novel
       The man without a soul. [see 02301A]
02295 The master mind of Mars, being a tale of weird
       and wonderful happenings on the Red Planet.
       A. C. McClurg, Chicago, 1928, 312p, Cloth,
       Novel [Mars #6]

BURROUGHS, EDGAR RICE (Cont.)

02296   *The master mind of Mars; and, A fighting man of Mars.* Nelson Doubleday, Garden City, 1973, 348p, Cloth, Coll. [Mars #s 6-7]

02297   *The monster men.* A. C. McClurg, Chicago, 1929, 304p, Cloth, Novel

02298   *The Moon maid.* A. C. McClurg, Chicago, 1926, 412p, Cloth, Novel

02298A retitled: *The Moon men.* Canaveral Press, New York, 1962, 375p, Cloth, Novel

02299   *The Moon maid.* Ace, New York, 1962, 176p, Paper, Novel [part one of the novel, reprinted from its longer magazine version]

02300   *The Moon men.* Ace, New York, 1962, 222p, Paper, Novel [parts two and three of the novel, reprinted from their longer magazine version]

02301   *The mucker.* A. C. McClurg, Chicago, 1921, 414p, Cloth, Novel

02301A retitled: *The man without a soul.* Methuen, London, 1922, 209p, Cloth, Novel [in Britain, the novel was split into two parts, *The mucker* and *The man without a soul*; this represents the second half of the American version]

02301B retitled: *Return of the mucker.* Ace, New York, 1974, 212p, Paper, Novel [identical with 02301A]

02302   *Out of time's abyss.* Ace, New York, 1963, 125p, Paper, Novel [Caspak #3]

02303   *Pellucidar; a sequel to "At the Earth's core," relating the further adventures of David Innes in the land underneath the Earth's crust.* A. C. McClurg, Chicago, 1923, 322p, Cloth, Novel [Pellucidar #2]

02304   *The people that time forgot.* Ace, New York, 1963, 124p, Paper, Novel [Caspak #2]

02305   *Pirates of Venus.* Edgar Rice Burroughs Inc., Tarzana, CA, 1934, 314p, Cloth, Novel [Venus #1]

02306   *The pirates of Venus; and, Lost on Venus; two Venus novels.* Dover, New York, 1963, 340p, Paper, Coll. [Venus #s 1-2]

02307   *A princess of Mars.* A. C. McClurg, Chicago, 1917, 327p, Cloth, Novel [Mars #1]

02308   *A princess of Mars; and, A fighting man of Mars; two Martian novels.* Dover, New York, 1964, 356p, Paper, Coll. [Mars #s 1, 7]

02309   *The return of Tarzan.* A. C. McClurg, Chicago, 1915, 365p, Cloth, Novel [Tarzan #2]

02310   *Savage Pellucidar.* Canaveral Press, New York, 1963, 274p, Cloth, Novel [Pellucidar #7]

02311   *The son of Tarzan.* A. C. McClurg, Chicago, 1917, 394p, Cloth, Novel [Tarzan #4]

02312   *Swords of Mars.* Edgar Rice Burroughs Inc., Tarzana, CA, 1936, 315p, Cloth, Novel [Mars #8]

02313   *Synthetic men of Mars.* Edgar Rice Burroughs Inc., Tarzana, CA, 1940, 315p, Cloth, Novel [Mars #9]

02314   *Tales of three planets.* Canaveral Press, New York, 1964, 282p, Cloth, Coll.

02315   *Tanar of Pellucidar.* Metropolitan Books, New York, 1930, 312p, Cloth, Novel [Pellucidar #3]

02316   *Tarzan and the ant men.* A. C. McClurg, Chicago, 1924, 350p, Cloth, Novel [Tarzan #10]

02317   *Tarzan and the castaways.* Canaveral Press, New York, 1965, 229p, Cloth, Coll. [Tarzan #24]

02318   *Tarzan and the city of gold.* Edgar Rice Burroughs Inc., Tarzana, CA, 1933, 316p, Cloth, Novel [Tarzan #16]

02319   *Tarzan and the Forbidden City.* Edgar Rice Burroughs Inc., Tarzana, CA, 1938, 315p, Cloth, Novel [Tarzan #20]

02319A retitled: *Tarzan in the Forbidden City.* Bantam Publications, Los Angeles, 1940, 100p, Paper, Novel [Tarzan #20; abridged]

02320   *Tarzan and "The Foreign Legion."* Edgar Rice Burroughs Inc., Tarzana, CA, 1947, 314p, Cloth, Novel [Tarzan #22]

02321   *Tarzan and the golden lion.* A. C. McClurg, Chicago, 1923, 333p, Cloth, Novel [Tarzan #9]

02322   *Tarzan and the jewels of Opar.* A. C. McClurg, Chicago, 1918, 350p, Cloth, Novel [Tarzan #5]

02323   *Tarzan and the Leopard Men.* Edgar Rice Burroughs Inc., Tarzana, CA, 1935, 332p, Cloth, Novel [Tarzan #18]

02324   *Tarzan and the lion man.* Edgar Rice Burroughs Inc., Tarzana, CA, 1934, 318p, Cloth, Novel [Tarzan #17]

02325   *Tarzan and the lost empire.* Metropolitan Books, New York, 1929, 313p, Cloth, Novel [Tarzan #12]

02326   *Tarzan and the madman.* Canaveral Press, New York, 1964, 236p, Cloth, Novel [Tarzan #23]

02327   *Tarzan and the Tarzan twins.* Canaveral Press, New York, 1963, 192p, Cloth, Coll. [Tarzan Twins #s 1-2]

02328   *Tarzan and the Tarzan twins with Jad-Bal-Ja, the golden lion.* Whitman Publishing Co., Racine, 1936, 314p, Cloth, Novel [Tarzan Twins #2]

02329   *Tarzan at the Earth's core.* Metropolitan Books, New York, 1930, 301p, Cloth, Novel [Tarzan #13; Pellucidar #4]

     Tarzan in the forbidden city. [see 02319A]

02330   *Tarzan, Lord of the Jungle.* A. C. McClurg, Chicago, 1928, 377p, Cloth, Novel [Tarzan #11]

02331   *Tarzan of the Apes.* A. C. McClurg, Chicago, 1914, 401p, Cloth, Novel [Tarzan #1]

02332   *Tarzan the invincible.* Edgar Rice Burroughs Inc., Tarzana, CA, 1931, 318p, Cloth, Novel [Tarzan #14]

02333   *Tarzan the magnificent.* Edgar Rice Burroughs Inc., Tarzana, CA, 1939, 318p, Cloth, Novel [Tarzan #21]

02334   *Tarzan the terrible.* A. C. McClurg, Chicago, 1921, 408p, Cloth, Novel [Tarzan #8]

02335   *Tarzan the untamed.* A. C. McClurg, Chicago, 1920, 428p, Cloth, Novel [Tarzan #7]

02336   *Tarzan triumphant.* Edgar Rice Burroughs Inc., Tarzana, CA, 1932, 318p, Cloth, Novel [Tarzan #15]

02337   *The Tarzan twins.* P. F. Volland, Joliet, IL, 1927, 126p, Cloth, Novel [Tarzan Twins #1]

     Tarzan's jungle tales. [see 02286A]

02338   *Tarzan's quest.* Edgar Rice Burroughs Inc., Tarzana, CA, 1936, 318p, Cloth, Novel [Tarzan #19]

02339   *Three Martian novels; Thuvia, maid of Mars; The chessmen of Mars; The master mind of Mars.* Dover, New York, 1962, 499p, Paper, Coll. [Mars #s 4-6]

02340   *Thuvia, maid of Mars.* A. C. McClurg, Chicago, 1920, 256p, Cloth, Novel [Mars #4]

02341   *Thuvia, maid of Mars; and, The chessmen of Mars.* Nelson Doubleday, Garden City, 1972, 341p, Cloth, Coll.

BURROUGHS, EDGAR RICE (Cont.)

02342 *The Warlord of Mars.* A. C. McClurg, Chicago,
       1919, 296p, Cloth, Novel [Mars #3]
02343 *The wizard of Venus.* Ace, New York, 1970,
       158p, Paper, Coll. [Venus #5; includes one
       Venus story and one non-fantasy]

BURROUGHS, JOHN COLEMAN, 1913-   *[biography
included]*

02344 *Treasure of the Black Falcon.* Ballantine,
       New York, 1967, 253p, Paper, Novel

BURROUGHS, JOSEPH BIRKBECK

02345 *Titan, son of Saturn, the coming world emperor;
       a story of the other Christ.* Emeth Publi-
       shers, Oberlin, OH, 1905, 470p, Cloth, Novel

BURROUGHS, WILLIAM S(eward), 1914-   *[biogra-
phy included]*

02346 *The exterminator!* Auerhahn Press, San Fran-
       cisco, 1960, 51p, Cloth?, Novel
02347 *Nova express.* Grove Press, New York, 1964,
       187p, Cloth, Novel [Nova series]
02348 *The soft machine.* Olympia Press, Paris,
       1961, 181p, Paper, Novel
02349 *The ticket that exploded.* Olympia Press,
       Paris, 1962, 182p, Paper, Novel [Nova series]
02350 *The wild boys; a book of the dead.* Grove
       Press, New York, 1971, 184p, Cloth, Novel

BURTIS, THOMSON, 1896-

02351 *Haunted airways.* Doubleday, Doran, Garden
       City, 1930, 250p, Cloth, Novel
02352 *The war of the ghosts; a flying adventure
       story.* Doubleday, Doran, Garden City,
       1932, 262p, Cloth, Novel

BURTON, EDMUND, pseud. [Edmund Burton Childs]

02353 *In quest of the golden orchid.* Lloyd Cole,
       Worthing, UK, 1942, 80p, Cloth, Novel
02354 *Peril of creation.* UTB, London, 1946, 33p,
       Paper, Story
02355 *The radium king.* Lloyd Cole, Worthing, UK,
       1942, 66p, Cloth, Coll.

BURTON, ELIZABETH
    see: KERBY, SUSAN ALICE

BURTON, FRANCIS G(eorge)

02356 *The naval engineer and the command of the sea;
       a story of naval administration.* Technical
       Publishing Co., Manchester, 1896, 231p,
       Cloth, Novel

BURTON, S(amuel) H(olroyd), 1919-   *[biogra-
phy included]*

02357 *Science fiction.* Longmans, Green, London,
       1967, 245p, Cloth, Anth.

as Sam Holroyd:

02358 *Ghosts 3.* Topliners, London, 1974, 128p, Paper,
       Coll.

BURY, F. BLAZE de
    see: DICKBERRY, F.

BUSBY, F. M. (Jr.), 1921-   *[biography inclu-
ded]*

02359 *Cage a man.* Nelson Doubleday, Garden City,
       1973, 151p, Cloth, Novel [Barton #1]

BUSH, GEORGE E(dward), 1938-   , with Jeanne
K. Welcher

02360 *Gulliveriana: I.* Scholars' Facsimiles & Re-
       prints, Gainesville, FL, 1970, 204p, Cloth,
       Anth.
02361 *Gulliveriana: II; The travels of Mr. John Gul-
       liver, son to Lemuel Gulliver (1731), by
       Pierre François Guyot Desfontaines; Modern
       Gulliver's travels: Lilliput (1796), by
       Lemuel Gulliver, Jun. (pseud.); facsimile
       reproductions.* Scholars' Facsimiles & Re-
       prints, Gainesville, FL, 1971, 674p, Cloth,
       Anth.
02362 *Gulliveriana III; Travels into several remote
       nations of the world, vol. III (1727); and,
       Memoirs of the court of Lilliput (1727); fac-
       simile reproductions.* Scholars' Facsimiles
       & Reprints, Delmar, NY, 1972, 465p, Cloth,
       Anth.
02363 *Gulliveriana IV.* Scholars' Facsimiles & Re-
       prints, Delmar, NY, 1973, 384p, Cloth, Anth.
02364 *Gulliveriana V.* Scholars' Facsimiles & Reprints,
       Delmar, NY, 1974, 382p, Cloth, Anth. [in-
       cludes some nonf.]

BUSH, LUCIUS M.

02365 *A peek at Heaven.* Exposition Press, New York,
       1964, 186p, Cloth, Novel

BUSHNELL, ADELYN

02366 *Strange gift.* Coward-McCann, New York, 1951,
       309p, Cloth, Novel

BUSSON, PAUL, 1873-1924

02367 *The man who was born again.* William Heinemann,
       London, 1927, 302p, Cloth, Novel

BUTCHER, MARGARET

02368 *Destiny on demand; a novel.* Skeffington & Son,
       London, 1938, 288p, Cloth, Novel

BUTLER, EWAN

02369 *"Talk of the devil."* Oliver Moxon, London,
       1948, 128p, Cloth, Novel

BUTLER, IVAN, pseud. [Edward Ivan Oakley Beuttler]

02370   *The horror film.* A. Zwemmer, London, 1967, 176p, Paper, Nonf.
02371   retitled: *Horror in the cinema.* A. Zwemmer, London, 1970, 208p, Paper, Nonf. [expanded]

BUTLER, JOAN, pseud. [Robert William Alexander, 1905-]

02372   *Deep freeze.* Stanley Paul, London, 1951, 256p, Cloth, Novel
02373   *Low spirits.* Stanley Paul, London, 1945, 192p, Cloth, Novel

BUTLER, SAMUEL, 1835-1902

02374   *Erewhon; or, Over the range.* Trübner & Co., London, 1872, 246p, Cloth, Novel [published anonymously] [Erewhon #1]
02374A *Erewhon; or, Over the range,* by Samuel Butler. David Bogue, London, 1880, 244p, Cloth, Novel [Erewhon #1]
02375   *Erewhon; and, Erewhon revisited.* Modern Library, New York, 1927, 622p, Cloth, Coll. [Erewhon #s 1-2]
02376   *Erewhon revisited twenty years later, both by the original discoverer of the country and by his son.* Grant Richards, London, 1901, 338p, Cloth, Novel [Erewhon #2]

BUTLER, WILLIAM, 1929-

02377   *The house at Akiya.* Peter Owen, London, 1963, 135p, Cloth, Novel
02378   *Mr. Three.* Peter Owen, London, 1964, 204p, Cloth, Novel

BUTLER, Sir WILLIAM FRANCIS, 1838-1910

02379   *The invasion of England, told twenty years after,* by an old soldier. Sampson Low, Marston, Searle, London, 1882, 190p, Cloth, Novel

BUTTERWORTH, FRANK NESTLE
   see: BLUNDELL, PETER

BUTTERWORTH, OLIVER, 1915-

02380   *The enormous egg.* Little, Brown, Boston, 1956, 187p, Cloth, Novel [Nate Twitchell #1]
02381   *The narrow passage.* Atlantic Monthly Press, Little, Brown, Boston, 1973, 166p, Cloth, Novel [Nate Twitchell #2]

BUTTREY, DOUGLAS NORTON
   see: BARR, DENSIL NEVE

BUZZATI, DINO, 1906-1972

02382   *Larger than life.* Secker & Warburg, London, 1962, 155p, Cloth, Novel

BYATT, HENRY

02383   *The flight of Icarus.* Sisley's, London, 1907, 247p, Cloth, Novel
02384   *Purple and white; a romance.* R. A. Everett, London, 1905, 316p, Cloth, Novel

BYERS, ALBERT F., with Arthur C. Mangels

02385   *The challenge; plan of action for a better tomorrow; a major novel of the near future.* Rolley & Reynolds, Philadelphia, 1961, 416p, Cloth, Novel

BYRD, BOB

02386   *Ka-zar, king of fang and claw.* Wright & Brown London, 1937, 252p, Cloth, Novel

BYRNE, CATHAL O.

02387   *Ashes on the hearth.* At the Sign of the Three Candles, Dublin, 1948, 212p, Cloth, Coll.

BYRNE, STUART J(ames), 1913-   [*biography included*]

02388   *Star man.* Powell Publications, Reseda, CA, 1969, 205p, Paper, Novel

as John Bloodstone:

02389   *Godman.* Powell Publications, Reseda, CA, 1970 207p, Paper, Novel
02390   *Thundar.* Leisure Books, North Hollywood, 1971 192p, Paper, Novel

BYWATER, HECTOR C(harles), 1884-1940

02391   *The great Pacific war; a history of the American-Japanese campaign of 1931-33.* Houghton Mifflin, Boston, 1925, 317p, Cloth, Novel

C., C. M.
   see: CLAY, CHARLES M.

C., S. M.
   see: MARY CATHERINE, Sister

C. J. T.
   see: T., C. J.

C. M. C.
   see: CLAY, CHARLES M.

CABEEN, F(rancis) von A(lbede)

02392   *The Colonel and the Quaker; or, The return of the forefathers.* Goodman's Sons, Philadelphia, 1906, 193p, Cloth, Novel

CABELL, JAMES BRANCH, 1879-1958

02393 *The certain hour (dizain des poëtes)*. Robert M. McBride, New York, 1916, 253p, Cloth, Coll. [Biography of Manuel #12]

02394 *The cream of the jest; a comedy of evasions*. Robert M. McBride, New York, 1917, 280p, Cloth, Novel [Biography of Manuel #18]

02395 *The cream of the jest; The lineage of Lichfield; two comedies of evasion*. Robert M. McBride, New York, 1930, 298p, Cloth, Coll. [Biography of Manuel #s 18-19]

02396 *The devil's own dear son; a comedy of the fatted calf*. Farrar, Straus & Co., New York, 1949, 210p, Cloth, Novel [It Happened in Florida #3]

Domnei. [see 02414A]

02397 *Domnei; The music from behind the Moon; two comedies of woman-worship*. Robert M. McBride, New York, 1928, 291p, Cloth, Coll. [Biography of Manuel #s 4A-5]

02398 *Figures of Earth; a comedy of appearances*. Robert M. McBride, New York, 1921, 356p, Cloth, Novel [Biography of Manuel #2]

02399 *Hamlet had an uncle; a comedy of honor*. Farrar & Rinehart, New York, 1940, 269p, Cloth, Novel

02400 *The high place; a comedy of disenchantment*. Robert M. McBride, New York, 1923, 312p, Cloth, Novel [Biography of Manuel #9]

02401 *The judging of Jurgen*. The Bookfellows, Chicago, 1920, 13p, Cloth, Story

02402 *Jurgen; a comedy of justice*. Robert M. McBride, New York, 1919, 368p, Cloth, Novel [Biography of Manuel #7]

02403 *The line of love; dizain des mariages*. Harper & Bros., New York, 1905, 290p, Cloth, Novel [Biography of Manuel #8]

02404 *The lineage of Lichfield; an essay in eugenics*. Robert M. McBride, New York, 1922, 46p, Cloth, Nonf. [Biography of Manuel #19]

02405 *The music from behind the Moon; an epitome*. John Day, New York, 1926, 54p, Cloth, Novel [Biography of Manuel #4A]

02406 *The nightmare has triplets; an author's note on Smire*. Doubleday, Doran, Garden City, 1937, 14p, Cloth, Nonf.

02407 *The nightmare has triplets; Smirt, Smith, and Smire*. Greenwood Press, Westport, Conn., 1972, 933p, Cloth, Coll. [The Nightmare Has Triplets #s 1-3]

02408 *Preface to the past*. Robert M. McBride, New York, 1936, 309p, Cloth, Nonf. Coll. [the prefaces and notes from the Storisende Edition of the Biography of Manuel]

02409 *The Silver Stallion; a comedy of redemption*. Robert M. McBride, New York, 1926, 358p, Cloth, Novel [Biography of Manuel #2]

02410 *Smire; an acceptance in the third person*. Doubleday, Doran, Garden City, 1937, 311p, Cloth, Novel [The Nightmare Has Triplets #3]

02411 *Smirt; an urbane nightmare*. Robert M. McBride, New York, 1934, 309p, Cloth, Novel [The Nightmare Has Triplets #1]

02412 *Smith; a sylvan interlude*. Robert M. McBride, New York, 1935, 313p, Cloth, Novel [The Nightmare Has Triplets #2]

02413 *Something about Eve; a comedy of fig-leaves*. Robert M. McBride, New York, 1927, 364p, Cloth, Novel [Biography of Manuel #11]

02414 *The soul of Melicent*. Frederick A. Stokes, New York, 1913, 216p, Cloth, Novel [Biography of Manuel #5]

02414A retitled: *Domnei; a comedy of woman-worship*. Robert M. McBride, New York, 1920, 218p, Cloth, Novel [Biography of Manuel #5]

02415 *Taboo; a legend retold from the Dirghis of Saevius Nicanor, with prolegomena, notes, and preliminary memoir*. Robert M. McBride, New York, 1921, 40p, Cloth, Story

02416 *There were two pirates; a comedy of division*. Farrar, Straus & Co., New York, 1946, 121p, Cloth, Novel [It Happened in Florida #2]

02417 *These restless heads; a trilogy of romantics*. Robert M. McBride, New York, 1932, 255p, Cloth, Novel

02418 *Townsend of Lichfield; dizain des adieux*. Robert M. McBride, New York, 1930, 357p, Cloth, Coll. [Biography of Manuel #21] [includes some nonf.]

02419 *The way of Ecben; a comedietta involving a gentleman*. Robert M. McBride, New York, 1929, 209p, Cloth, Novel [Biography of Manuel #4B]

02420 *The white robe; a saint's summary*. Robert M. McBride, New York, 1928, 93p, Cloth, Novel [Biography of Manuel #4C]

02421 *The witch-woman; a trilogy about her*. Farrar, Straus & Co., New York, 1948, 161p, Cloth, Coll. [includes *The music from behind the Moon*; *The way of Ecben*; *The white robe*] [Biography of Manuel #4]

CABOT, CALVIN QUINCY, pseud.
    see: LAWRENCE, JAMES COOPER

CADELL, (Violet) ELIZABETH, 1903- [*biography included*]

02422 *Brimstone in the garden*. William Morrow, New York, 1950, 264p, Cloth, Novel

02423 *Crystal clear*. William Morrow, New York, 1953, 250p, Cloth, Novel

02423A retitled: *Journey's eve*. Hodder & Stoughton, London, 1953, 254p, Cloth, Novel

CAIDIN, MARTIN, 1927- [*biography included*]

02424 *The Cape*. Doubleday, Garden City, 1971, 374p, Cloth, Novel

02425 *Cyborg; a novel*. Arbor House, New York, 1972, 282p, Cloth, Novel [Cyborg (Steve Austin) #1]

Cyborg #2; Operation Nuke. [see 02434A]

02426 *Four came back; a novel*. David McKay, New York, 1968, 275p, Cloth, Novel

02427 *The God Machine*. E. P. Dutton, New York, 1968, 316p, Cloth, Novel

02428 *High crystal*. Arbor House, New York, 1974, 229p, Cloth, Novel [Cyborg (Steve Austin) #3]

02429 *The last fathom*. Meredith Press, New York, 1967, 312p, Cloth, Novel

02430 *The long night*. Dodd, Mead, New York, 1956, 242p, Cloth, Novel

02431 *Marooned; a novel*. E. P. Dutton, New York, 1964, 378p, Cloth, Novel

02432 *The Mendelov conspiracy*. Hawthorn Books, New York, 1969, 274p, Cloth, Novel

02433 *No man's world; a novel*. E. P. Dutton, New York, 1967, 414p, Cloth, Novel

02434 *Operation Nuke*. Arbor House, New York, 1973, 240p, Cloth, Novel [Cyborg (Steve Austin) #2]

02434A retitled: *Cyborg #2; Operation Nuke*. Warner Paperback Library, New York, 1974, 175p, Paper, Novel [Cyborg (Steve Austin) #2]

CAILLOIS, ROGER, 1913-   [*biography included*]

02435   *The dream adventure.* Orion Press, New York,
        1963, 285p, Cloth, Anth.

CAINE, (Sir Thomas Henry) HALL, 1853-1931

02436   *The eternal city.* William Heinemann, London,
        1901, 606p, Cloth, Novel

CAINE, W(illiam) RALPH HALL, 1865-1939

02437   *Annals of the magic isle.* Cecil Palmer, Lon-
        don, 1926, 356p, Cloth, Novel

CAINE, WILLIAM, 1873-1925

02438   *The devil in solution.* Greening & Co., London,
        1911, 320p, Cloth, Novel

with John Fairbairn:

02439   *The confectioners.* J. W. Arrowsmith, Bristol,
        1906, 315p, Cloth, Novel

CAIRD, JANET, 1913-   [*biography included*]

02440   *Perturbing spirit.* Geoffrey Bles, London,
        1966, 255p, Cloth, Novel

CAIRNES, Captain (William Elliot), 1862-1902

02441   *The coming Waterloo.* Archibald Constable,
        Westminster, 1901, 364p, Cloth, Novel

CAIRNES, MAUD, pseud. [Lady Maud Kathleen
  Cairnes Plantagenet Hastings Curzon-Herrick,
  1893-1965]

02442   *Strange journey.* Cobden-Sanderson, London,
        1935, 248p, Cloth, Novel

CALDECOTT, Sir ANDREW, 1884-1951

02443   *Fires burn blue.* Edward Arnold, London, 1948,
        222p, Cloth, Coll.
02444   *Not exactly ghosts.* Edward Arnold, London,
        1947, 213p, Cloth, Coll.

CALDER-MARSHALL, ARTHUR, 1908-   [*biography
included*]

02445   *The Scarlet boy.* Rupert Hart-Davis, London,
        1961, 222p, Cloth, Novel

CALDERON, GEORGE (Leslie), 1868-1915

02446   *Dwala; a romance.* Smith, Elder, London, 1904,
        244p, Cloth, Novel

CALDWELL, (Janet Miriam) TAYLOR (Holland),
  1900-   [*biography included*]

02447   *The devil's advocate.* Crown Publishers, New
        York, 1952, 375p, Cloth, Novel

02448   *Dialogues with the devil.* Doubleday, Garden
        City, 1967, 198p, Cloth, Novel
02449   *The listener.* Doubleday, Garden City, 1960,
        332p, Cloth, Novel [Listener #1]
02450   *No one hears but Him.* Doubleday, Garden City,
        1966, 298p, Cloth, Novel [Listener #2]
02451   *Your sins and mine.* Gold Medal, New York,
        1955, 127p, Paper, Novel

CALHOUN, MARY, 1926-   [*biography included*]

02452   *Magic in the alley.* Atheneum, New York, 1970,
        167p, Cloth, Novel

CALIFORNIA THREE HUNDRED AND FIFTY YEARS AGO
    see: COLE, CORNELIUS

CALISHER, HORTENSE, 1911-   [*biography included*]

02453   *Journal from Ellipsia.* Little, Brown, Boston,
        1965, 375p, Cloth, Novel

CALKINS, ELIZABETH, with Barry McGhan

02454   *Teaching tomorrow; a handbook of science fic-
        tion for teachers.* Pflaum/Standard, Dayton,
        OH, 1972, 103p, Paper, Nonf.

CALLAHAN, WILLIAM, pseud.
    see: GALLUN, RAYMOND Z.

CALLENDER, JULIAN, pseud. [Austin Lee, 1904-
197?] [*biography included*]

02455   *St. Dingan's bones.* Allan Wingate, London,
        1957, 179p, Cloth, Novel

CALSON, ISAAC, pseud. [John Walter Ledoux,
1860-1932]

02456   *The Felicians.* Author, Swarthmore, PA?, 1914,
        116p, Cloth, Novel

CALTHROP, DION (William Palgrave) CLAYTON,
1878-1937

02457   *Hyacinth; an excursion.* Williams & Norgate,
        London, 1927, 176p, Cloth, Novel

CALVANO, TONY, pseud.

02458   *Cult of shame.* Ember Library, San Diego, 1963
        190p, Paper, Novel

CALVERTON, V(ictor) F(rancis), 1900-1940

02459   *The man inside, being the record of the strang
        adventures of Allen Steele among the Xulus.*
        Charles Scribner's Sons, New York, 1936, 313
        Cloth, Novel

CALVINO, ITALO, 1923-   [biography included]

02460 Cosmicomics. Helen & Kurt Wolff, Harcourt,
       Brace & World, New York, 1968, 153p, Cloth,
       Novel [Qfwfq #1]
02461 Invisible cities. Helen & Kurt Wolff, Har-
       court Brace Jovanovich, New York, 1974, 165p,
       Cloth, Novel
02462 The non-existent knight; &, The cloven vis-
       count; two short novels. Random House, New
       York, 1962, 246p, Cloth, Coll.
02463 t zero. Helen & Kurt Wolff, Harcourt, Brace
       & World, New York, 1969, 152p, Cloth,
       Novel [Qfwfq #2]
02463A retitled: Time and the hunter. Jonathan Cape,
       London, 1970, 152p, Cloth, Novel [Qfwfq #2]

CAMERON, ALASTAIR (Graham Walter), 1925-

02464 Fantasy classification system. Canadian Sci-
       ence Fiction Association, St. Vidal, Canada,
       1952, 52p, Paper, Nonf.

CAMERON, BERL, house pseud. [see also John
Glasby, Brian Holloway, Dennis Talbot Hughes,
David O'Brien, and Arthur Roberts]

02465 Black infinity. Curtis Warren, London, 1952,
       127p, Cloth, Novel [by David O'Brien]
02466 Cosmic Echelon. Curtis Warren, London, 1952,
       128p, Cloth, Novel [by John Glasby & Arthur
       Roberts] [Terran Empire series]
02467 Destination Alpha. Curtis Warren, London,
       1952, 127p, Paper, Novel [by Brian Holloway]
02468 Lost aeons. Curtis Warren, London, 1953,
       159p, Cloth, Novel [by Dennis Talbot Hughes]
02469 Photomesis. Curtis Warren, London, 1952,
       127p, Paper, Novel [by David O'Brien]
02470 Solar gravita. Curtis Warren, London, 1953,
       159p, Cloth, Novel [author unknown]
02471 Sphero Nova. Curtis Warren, London, 1952,
       159p, Cloth, Novel [by Arthur Roberts &
       John Glasby]

CAMERON, ELEANOR, 1912-   [biography included]

02472 The court of the stone children. E. P. Dutton,
       New York, 1973, 193p, Cloth, Novel
02473 Mr. Bass's planetoid. Atlantic Monthly Press,
       Little, Brown, Boston, 1958, 227p, Cloth,
       Novel [Tycho Bass #3]
02474 A mystery for Mr. Bass. Little, Brown, Boston,
       1960, 229p, Cloth, Novel [Tycho Bass #4]
02475 Stowaway to the Mushroom Planet. Atlantic
       Monthly Press, Little, Brown, Boston, 1956,
       226p, Cloth, Novel [Tycho Bass #2]
02476 The terrible churnadryne. Little, Brown, Bos-
       ton, 1959, 125p, Cloth, Novel
02477 Time and Mr. Bass; a Mushroom Planet book.
       Atlantic Monthly Press, Little, Brown, Bos-
       ton, 1967, 247p, Cloth, Novel [Tycho Bass #5]
02478 The wonderful flight to the Mushroom Planet.
       Atlantic Monthly Press, Little, Brown, Bos-
       ton, 1954, 214p, Cloth, Novel [Tycho Bass #1]

CAMERON, IAN, pseud.
    see: PAYNE, DONALD GORDON

CAMERON, JOHN, 1927-

02479 The astrologer. Random House, New York, 1972,
       309p, Cloth, Novel

CAMERON, LOU, 1924-   [biography included]

02480 Cybernia. Fawcett Gold Medal, Greenwich, 1972,
       174p, Paper, Novel

as Dagmar:

02481 The spy who came in from the Copa. Lancer, New
       York, 1967, 158p, Paper, Novel [Swinging Spy
       #2]

CAMERON, VERNEY LOVETT, 1844-1894

02482 The Queen's land; or, Ard al Malakat. Swan
       Sonnenschein, London, 1886, 264p, Cloth,
       Novel

CAMMAERTS, ÉMILE, d. 1953

02483 The devil takes the chair. Cresset Press, Lon-
       don, 1949, 157p, Cloth, Novel

CAMP, CATHERINE C. de
    see: de CAMP, CATHERINE C.

CAMP, L. SPRAGUE de
    see: de CAMP, L. SPRAGUE

CAMPBELL, ANGUS, pseud.
    see: CHETWYND-HAYES, R.

CAMPBELL, ARCHIE

02484 The sound of a voice that is still. George
       Redway, London, 1899, 419p, Cloth, Novel

CAMPBELL, AUSTIN, 1884-

02485 The rock of Babylon; adventure in an ancient
       city. Graphic Publishers, Ottawa, Canada,
       1931, 354p, Cloth, Novel

CAMPBELL, COLIN

02486 Out of wild hills; a west highland mystery.
       Hurst & Blackett, London, 1932, 288p, Cloth,
       Novel

CAMPBELL, DONALD

02487 The golden snake. Federation Press, London,
       1924, 155p, Cloth, Coll.

CAMPBELL, DUNCAN

02488 The last millionaire; a tale of the old world
       and the new. Heath Cranton, London, 1923,
       244p, Cloth, Novel

CAMPBELL, FORREST

02489	*Imaginary interviews with the noted and notorious; 101 tales with historical characters about the world of yesterday and today; educational--entertaining.* no publisher, Los Angeles, 1934, 443p, Cloth, Coll.

CAMPBELL, Sir GILBERT (Edward), Bart., 1838-1899

02490	*Dark stories from the sunny south; or, Legends of the Mediterranean.* Ward, Lock, London, 1889, 175p, Paper, Coll.
02491	*Mysteries of the unseen; or, Supernatural stories of English life.* Ward, Lock, London, 1889, 143p, Paper?, Coll.
02492	*Wild and weird; or, Remarkable stories of Russian life.* Ward, Lock, London, 1889, 162p, Paper?, Coll.
02493	*Wild and weird; tales of imagination and mystery, Russian, English, and Italian.* Ward, Lock, London, 1889, 480p, Cloth, Coll. [includes 02490, 02491, 02492]

CAMPBELL, H(ubert) J., 1925-	[variously cited as Herbert J. Campbell]

02494	*Another space--another time.* Panther, London, 1953, 158p, Cloth, Novel
02495	*Authentic book of space.* Hamilton & Co. (Stafford), London, 1954, 102p, Cloth, Anth. [includes some nonf.]
02496	*Beyond the visible.* Hamilton & Co. (Stafford), London, 1952, 189p, Cloth, Novel
02497	*Brain ultimate.* Panther, London, 1953, 157p, Cloth, Novel
02498	*Once upon a space.* Panther, London, 1954, 142p, Cloth, Novel
02499	*The red planet.* Panther, London, 1953, 159p, Cloth, Novel
02500	*Tomorrow's universe; a science fiction anthology.* Panther, London, 1953, 224p, Cloth, Anth.

as Roy Sheldon, house pseud.:

02501	*Atoms in action.* Panther, London, 1953, 159p, Cloth, Novel [Shiny Spear series]
02502	*House of entropy.* Panther, London, 1953, 160p, Cloth, Novel [Shiny Spear series]
02503	*Mammoth man.* Hamilton & Co. (Stafford), 1952, 111p, Paper, Novel [Magdah series]
02504	*The menacing sleep.* Panther, London, 1952, 128p, Paper, Novel
02505	*Two days of terror.* Panther, London, 1952, 112p, Paper, Novel [Magdah series]

CAMPBELL, J(ames) L(awrence), 1889-

02506	*The miracle of Peille.* E. P. Dutton, New York, 1929, 223p, Cloth, Novel

CAMPBELL, JOHN, 1766-1840

02507	*A journey to the Moon, and interesting conversations with the inhabitants respecting the condition of man, by the author of Worlds displayed.* Howard & Evans, London, 1800?, 8p, Paper, Story

CAMPBELL, JOHN W(ood) Jr., 1910-1971 [*biography* included]

02508	*Analog 1.* Doubleday, Garden City, 1963, 219p, Cloth, Anth.
02509	*Analog 2.* Doubleday, Garden City, 1964, 275p, Cloth, Anth.
02510	*Analog 3.* Doubleday, Garden City, 1965, 269p, Cloth, Anth.
02510A	retitled: *A world by the tale.* Curtis, New York, 1970, 191p, Paper, Anth.
02511	*Analog 4.* Doubleday, Garden City, 1966, 224p, Cloth, Anth.
02511A	retitled: *The permanent implosion.* Curtis, New York, 1970, 192p, Paper, Anth.
02512	*Analog 5.* Doubleday, Garden City, 1967, 242p, Cloth, Anth.
02512A	retitled: *Countercommandment, and other stories.* Curtis, New York, 1970, 221p, Paper, Anth.
02513	*Analog 6.* Doubleday, Garden City, 1968, 313p, Cloth, Anth.
02514	*Analog 7.* Doubleday, Garden City, 1969, 352p, Cloth, Anth.
02515	*Analog 8.* Doubleday, Garden City, 1971, 227p, Cloth, Anth.
02516	*Analog anthology.* Dennis Dobson, London, 1965, 797p, Cloth, Anth. [includes *Prologue to Analog; Analog 1; Analog 2*]
02517	*The Astounding science fiction anthology.* Simon & Schuster, New York, 1952, 585p, Cloth, Anth.
02517A	retitled: *The first Astounding science fiction anthology.* Grayson & Grayson, London, 1954, 240p, Cloth, Anth. [abridged]
02517B	retitled: *The second Astounding science fiction anthology.* Grayson & Grayson, London, 1954, 224p, Cloth, Anth. [abridged; 02517A and 02517B together comprise the original volume]
02517C	retitled: *Astounding tales of space and time.* Berkley, New York, 1957, 189p, Paper, Anth. [abridged]
02518	*The best of John W. Campbell.* Sidgwick & Jackson, London, 1973, 278p, Cloth, Coll.
02519	*The black star passes.* Fantasy Press, Reading, PA, 1953, 254p, Cloth, Coll. [Arcot, Wade & Morey series]
02520	*Cloak of Aesir.* Shasta Publishers, Chicago, 1952, 255p, Cloth, Coll.
02521	*Collected editorials from Analog.* Doubleday, Garden City, 1966, 248p, Cloth, Nonf. Coll.
	Countercommandment, and other stories. [see 02512A]
	The first Astounding science fiction anthology. [see 02517A]
02522	*From Unknown worlds.* Street & Smith, New York, 1948, 130p, Paper, Anth.
02523	*The incredible planet.* Fantasy Press, Reading, PA, 1949, 344p, Cloth, Novel [Aarn Munro #2]
02524	*Invaders from the infinite.* Fantasy Press, Reading, PA, 1961, 189p, Cloth, Novel [Arcot, Wade & Morey series]
02525	*Islands of space.* Fantasy Press, Reading, PA, 1956, 224p, Cloth, Novel [Arcot, Wade & Morey series]
02526	*John W. Campbell anthology.* Doubleday, Garden City, 1973, 528p, Cloth, Coll. [includes *The black star passes; Invaders from the infinite; Islands of space*] [Arcot, Wade & Morey series]
02527	*The mightiest machine.* Hadley Publishing Co., Providence, 1947, 228p, Cloth, Novel [Aarn Munro #1]

CAMPBELL, JOHN W. (Cont.)

02528   *The Moon is hell!* Fantasy Press, Reading, PA,
        1951, 256p, Cloth, Coll.
        The permanent implosion. [see 02511A]
02529   *The planeteers.* Ace Double, New York, 1966,
        150p, Paper, Coll.
02530   *Prologue to Analog.* Doubleday, Garden City,
        1962, 308p, Cloth, Anth.
        *The second Astounding science fiction antholo-
        gy.* [see 02517B]
        The thing, and other stories. [see 02534A]
02531   *The thing from another world.* American Sci-
        ence Fiction, Sydney, 1953, 34p, Paper,
        Story
02532   *The ultimate weapon.* Ace Double, New York,
        1966, 106p, Paper, Novel
02533   *Who goes there?* Dell, New York, 1955, 254p,
        Paper, Coll.
02534   *Who goes there? seven tales of science-fiction.*
        Shasta Publishers, Chicago, 1948, 231p,
        Cloth, Coll. [different contents]
02534A retitled: *The thing, and other stories.* Fan-
        tasy Books, London, 1952, 190p, Paper, Coll.
        A world by the tale. [see 02510A]

CAMPBELL, MARION, 1919-

02535   *The dark twin.* Turnstone Press, London, 1973,
        256p, Paper, Novel

CAMPBELL, (John) RAMSEY, 1946-   [*biography
included*]

02536   *Demons by daylight.* Arkham House, Sauk City,
        1973, 153p, Cloth, Coll.
02537   *The inhabitant of the lake, and less welcome
        tenants,* by J. Ramsey Campbell. Arkham
        House, Sauk City, 1964, 207p, Cloth, Coll.

CAMPBELL, REGINALD (Wilfrid), 1894-1950

02538   *The abominable twilight.* Cassell, London,
        1948, 232p, Cloth, Novel
02539   *Brainstorm.* Cassell, London, 1950, 232p,
        Cloth, Novel
02540   *Death by apparition.* Cassell, London, 1949,
        249p, Cloth, Novel

CAMPBELL, SPENCER

02541   *Under the red ensign; a story of England's
        peril.* Andrew Melrose, London, 1912, 128p,
        Cloth, Novel

CAMPERDOWN
   see: GRIFFITH, MARY

CAMPION, SARAH, pseud. [Mary Rose Coulton]

02542   *Thirty million gas masks.* Peter Davies, Lon-
        don, 1937, 313p, Cloth, Novel

CAMRA, ROY, pseud.

02543   *Assault.* Epic Books, Los Angeles, 1962,
        Paper, Novel

02543A retitled: *Space sex,* by Roy Warren. Heart,
        Los Angeles, 196?,   , Paper, Novel
02543B retitled: *Sex machine.* Ram, Los Angeles,
        196?,   , Paper, Novel [published anony-
        mously]

CANDÈZE, ERNEST (Charles Auguste), 1827-1898

02544   *The curious adventures of a field cricket.*
        Sampson Low, Marston, Searle & Rivington,
        London, 1878, 319p, Cloth, Novel
02544A retitled: *The adventures of Grillo; or, The
        cricket who would be king.* Ginn & Co., New
        York, 1912, 226p, Cloth, Novel

CANDLER, EDMUND, 1874-1926

02545   *The dinosaur's egg.* William Blackwood & Sons,
        Edinburgh, 1925, 312p, Cloth, Novel

CANNAN, GILBERT, 1884-1955

02546   *Windmills; a book of fables.* Martin Secker,
        London, 1915, 201p, Cloth, Coll.

CANNING, VICTOR, 1911-

02547   *The finger of Saturn.* Heinemann, London, 1973,
        271p, Cloth, Novel

CANTON, WILLIAM, 1845-1926

02548   *The invisible playmate; a story of the unseen.*
        Isbister & Co., London, 1894, 95p, Cloth,
        Coll.
02549   *The invisible playmate; and, W. V., her book.*
        Isbister & Co., London, 1897, 235p, Cloth,
        Coll. [expanded]

CANTOR, HAL [same person as Hal Kantor?]

02550   *Ghosts and things.* Berkley Medallion, New York,
        1962, 160p, Paper, Anth.

THE CAPACITY AND EXTENT OF THE HUMAN UNDER-
STANDING
   see: KIRKBY, JOHN

CAPE, JUDITH, pseud. [Patricia Kathleen Page,
1916-   ] [*biography included*]

02551   *The Sun and the Moon.* Creative Age Press,
        New York, 1944, 200p, Cloth, Novel

CAPEK, JOSEF, 1887-1945, with Karel Capek

02552   *Fairy tales, with one extra as makeweight by
        Joseph Capek.* George Allen & Unwin, London,
        1933, 288p, Cloth, Coll.

CAPEK, KAREL, 1890-1938

02553   *The absolute at large.* Macmillan, London,
        1927, 293p, Cloth, Novel

CAPEK, KAREL (Cont.)

An atomic phantasy. [see 02554A]
02554 *Krakatit.* Geoffrey Bles, London, 1925, 416p, Cloth, Novel
02554A retitled: *An atomic phantasy; Krakatit, a novel.* George Allen & Unwin, London, 1948, 294p, Cloth, Novel
02555 *The Makropoulos secret.* John W. Luce, Boston, 1925, 165p, Cloth, Novel [also published as a play]
02556 *Meteor.* George Allen & Unwin, London, 1935, 256p, Cloth, Novel
02557 *Three novels: Hordubal; An ordinary life; Meteor.* George Allen & Unwin, London, 1948, 469p, Cloth, Coll.
02558 *War with the Newts.* George Allen & Unwin, London, 1937, 348p, Cloth, Novel

with Josef Capek:

02552 *Fairy tales, with one extra as makeweight by Joseph Capek.* George Allen & Unwin, London, 1933, 288p, Cloth, Coll.

CAPES, BERNARD (Edward Joseph), d. 1918

02559 *At a winter's fire.* C. Arthur Pearson, London, 1899, 303p, Cloth, Coll.

A CAPITALIST, pseud.
    see: VAN DEUSEN, ALONZO

CAPON, (Harry) PAUL, 1911-1969 [*biography included*]

02560 *The cave of Cornelius.* Heinemann, London, 1959, 208p, Cloth, Novel
02560A retitled: *The end of the tunnel.* Bobbs-Merrill, Indianapolis, 1959, 240p, Cloth, Novel
02561 *Down to Earth.* William Heinemann, London, 1954, 196p, Cloth, Novel [Antigeos Trilogy #3]
    The end of the tunnel. [see 02560A]
02562 *Flight of time.* Heinemann, London, 1960, 166p, Cloth, Novel
02563 *Into the tenth millennium.* William Heinemann, London, 1956, 275p, Cloth, Novel
    Lost: a moon. [see 02566A]
02564 *The other half of the planet; a sequel to "The other side of the Sun."* William Heinemann, London, 1952, 255p, Cloth, Novel [Antigeos Trilogy #2]
02565 *The other side of the Sun; a novel.* William Heinemann, London, 1950, 321p, Cloth, Novel [Antigeos Trilogy #1]
02566 *Phobos, the robot planet.* William Heinemann, London, 1955, 178p, Cloth, Novel
02566A retitled: *Lost: a moon.* Bobbs-Merrill, Indianapolis, 1956, 222p, Cloth, Novel
02567 *The wonderbolt.* Ward, Lock, London, 1955, 206p, Cloth, Novel
02568 *The world at bay.* William Heinemann, London, 1953, 199p, Cloth, Novel

CAPPS, CARROLL M.
    see: MacAPP, C. C.

A CAPTAIN OF THE ROYAL NAVY, pseud.

02569 *The battle off Worthing; why the invaders never got to Dorking; a prophecy.* London Literary Society, London, 1887, 96p, Paper?, Novel [Dorking series]

CARAS, ROGER
    see: SARAC, ROGER

CARDINAL, JANE, pseud. [Ethel Williamson]

02570 *The living idol; a romantic melodrama.* Stanley Paul, London, 1933, 288p, Cloth, Novel

CAREW, HENRY

02571 *The secret of the sphinx; a novel.* Hodder & Stoughton, London, 1923, 319p, Cloth, Novel
02572 *The vampires of the Andes.* Jarrolds, London, 1925, 320p, Cloth, Novel

CAREY, ERNESTINE (Moller) GILBRETH, 1908-
[*biography included*]

02573 *Giddy Moment.* Little, Brown, Boston, 1958, 243p, Cloth, Novel

CAREY, Dr. GEORGE W(ashington), 1845-1924

02574 *Road to the Moon; a great occult story.* Chemistry of Life Co., Los Angeles, 1910?, 24p, Paper, Story

CAREY, MARY

02575 *The gnome-mobile.* Whitman, Racine, 1967, 140p, Cloth, Movie [The movie was adapted from the novel of the same name by Upton Sinclair]

CARLIN, GAGE, pseud.

02576 *Psychic swap slave.* Companion Books, San Diego, 1969, 158p, Paper, Novel

CARLISLE, ROBIN

02577 *Blood and roses.* Hillman, New York, 1960, 144p, Paper, Movie

CARLISLE, SAMUEL HANNA

02578 *Nimshi; the adventures of a man to obtain a solution of scriptural geology, to gauge the vast ages of planetary conception, and to open Bab Allah--the gate of God.* H. Cunningham, London, 1845, vol. I-306p, vol. II-268p, Cloth, Novel [published anonymously]

CARLSEN, RUTH CHRISTOFFER, 1918-   [*biography included*]

02579 *Half-past tomorrow*. Houghton Mifflin, Boston, 1973, 164p, Cloth, Novel
02580 *Mr. Pudgins*. Houghton Mifflin, Boston, 1951, 163p, Cloth, Novel
02581 *Ride a wild horse*. Houghton Mifflin, Boston, 1970, 164p, Cloth, Novel

CARLSON, DALE (Bick), 1935-   [*biography included*]

02582 *The human apes*. Atheneum, New York, 1973, 157p, Cloth, Novel
02583 *The mountain of truth*. Atheneum, New York, 1972, 169p, Cloth, Novel

with Mary Wollstonecraft Shelley:

02584 *Frankenstein*. Golden Press, New York, 1968, 158p, Cloth, Novel [an adaptation of Shelley's novel]

CARLTON, MARY SHAFFER

02585 *The golden phoenix*. Vantage Press, New York, 1958, 69p, Cloth, Novel

CARMER, CARL (Lamson),1893-1976 [*biography included*]

02586 *The screaming ghost, and other stories*. Alfred A. Knopf, New York, 1956, 146p, Cloth, Coll.

with Lester del Rey and Cecile Matschat:

02587 *The year after tomorrow; an anthology of science fiction stories*. John C. Winston, Philadelphia, 1954, 339p, Cloth, Anth.

CARNEGIE, JAMES
    see: SOUTHESK, Earl of

CARNELL, (Edward) JOHN, 1912-1972 [*biography included*]

02588 *The best from New worlds science fiction*. T. V. Boardman, London, 1955, 190p, Paper, Anth.
02589 *The best from New writings in SF, first selection*. Dennis Dobson, London, 1971, 253p, Cloth, Anth.
02590 *Gateway to the stars; a science fiction anthology*. Museum Press, London, 1955, 191p, Cloth, Anth.
02591 *Gateway to tomorrow; a science fiction anthology*. Museum Press, London, 1954, 192p, Cloth, Anth.
02592 *Jinn and jitters, and other stories*. Pendulum Publications, London, 1946, 116p, Paper, Anth.
02593 *Lambda I, and other stories*. Berkley Medallion, New York, 1964, 175p, Paper, Anth.
02594 *Lambda 1, and other stories; an anthology*. Penguin, Harmondsworth, 1965, 206p, Paper, Anth. [drops one story, and adds two]
02595 *New writings in S-F 1*. Dennis Dobson, London, 1964, 190p, Cloth, Anth.

02596 *New writings in S-F 2*. Dennis Dobson, London, 1964, 191p, Cloth, Anth.
02597 *New writings in S-F 3*. Dennis Dobson, London, 1965, 189p, Cloth, Anth.
02598 *New writings in S-F 4*. Dennis Dobson, London, 1965, 186p, Cloth, Anth.
02599 *New writings in S-F 5*. Dennis Dobson, London, 1965, 190p, Cloth, Anth.
02600 *New writings in S-F 6*. Dennis Dobson, London, 1965, 190p, Cloth, Anth.
02601 *New writings in S-F 7*. Dennis Dobson, London, 1966, 190p, Cloth, Anth.
02602 *New writings in SF7*. Bantam, New York, 1971, 168p, Paper, Anth. [different contents]
02603 *New writings in S-F 8*. Dennis Dobson, London, 1966, 188p, Cloth, Anth.
02604 *New writings in SF 8*. Bantam, New York, 1971, 184p, Paper, Anth. [different contents]
02605 *New writings in S-F 9*. Dennis Dobson, London, 1966, 187p, Cloth, Anth.
02606 *New writings in SF 9*. Bantam, New York, 1972, 180p, Paper, Anth. [different contents]
02607 *New writings in S-F 10*. Dennis Dobson, London, 1967, 189p, Cloth, Anth.
02608 *New writings in S.F.-11*. Corgi, London, 1967, 190p, Paper, Anth.
02609 *New writings in S.F.-12*. Corgi, London, 1968, 188p, Paper, Anth.
02610 *New writings in S-F 13*. Dennis Dobson, London, 1968, 190p, Cloth, Anth.
02611 *New writings in S-F 14*. Dennis Dobson, London, 1969, 188p, Cloth, Anth.
02612 *New writings in S-F 15*. Dennis Dobson, London, 1969, 189p, Cloth, Anth.
02613 *New writings in S-F 16*. Dennis Dobson, London, 1970, 190p, Cloth, Anth.
02614 *New writings in S-F 17*. Dennis Dobson, London, 1970, 190p, Cloth, Anth.
02615 *New writings in SF-18*. Corgi, London, 1971, 188p, Paper, Anth.
02616 *New writings in S-F 19*. Dennis Dobson, London, 1971, 190p, Cloth, Anth.
02617 *New writings in SF-20*. Corgi, London, 1972, 188p, Paper, Anth.
02618 *New writings in SF (21)*. Sidgwick & Jackson, London, 1972, 189p, Cloth, Anth.
02619 *No place like Earth; a science fiction anthology*. T. V. Boardman, London, 1952, 255p, Cloth, Anth.
02620 *Weird shadows from beyond*. Corgi, London, 1965, 157p, Paper, Anth.

CARNEY, (John) OTIS, 1922-   [*biography included*]

02621 *Good Friday--1963; a journey into the heart of one man--and into the soul of America*. William Morrow, New York, 1961, 123p, Cloth, Novel
02621A retitled: *Good Friday--196?*. Apollo Editions, New York, 1964, 123p, Paper, Novel

CARNSON, MAXWELL

02622 *Monkeys of Hai Tu*. Hutchinson, London, 1927, 288p, Cloth, Novel

CARPENTER, DONALD G.
    see: MERLINO, MERLIN MESMER

CARPENTER, ELMER J.

02623   *Moonspin.* Flagship, New York, 1967, 159p, Paper, Novel

CARPENTER, Rev. W(illiam) B(oyd), 1841-1918

02624   *Twilight dreams.* Macmillan, London, 1893, 225p, Cloth, Coll.

CARPENTIER (y Valmont), ALEJO, 1904-

02625   *The war of time.* Victor Gollancz, London, 1970, 191p, Cloth, Coll.

CARPENTIER, CHARLES

02626   *Flight one.* Simon & Schuster, New York, 1972, 315p, Cloth, Novel

CARR, BARBARA COMYNS-
see: COMYNS-CARR, BARBARA

CARR, CHARLES

02627   *Colonists of space.* Ward, Lock, London, 1954, 192p, Cloth, Novel [Bel #1]
02628   *Salamander war.* Ward, Lock, London, 1955, 190p, Cloth, Novel [Bel #2]

CARR, JOHN DICKSON, 1906-1977 [*biography included*]

02629   *The devil in velvet.* Harper & Bros., New York, 1951, 335p, Cloth, Novel
02630   *Fire, burn!* Harper & Bros., New York, 1957, 265p, Cloth, Novel

as Carter Dickson:

02631   *Fear is the same.* William Morrow, New York, 1956, 284p, Cloth, Novel

CARR, NICK

02632   *America's Secret Service ace; Pulp Classics 7.* Robert E. Weinberg, Oak Lawn, IL, 1974, 64p, Paper, Nonf.

CARR, ROBERT SPENCER, 1909-

02633   *Beyond infinity.* Fantasy Press, Reading, PA, 1951, 236p, Cloth, Coll.
02634   *The room beyond.* Appleton-Century-Crofts, New York, 1948, 427p, Cloth, Novel

CARR, TERRY (Gene), 1937- [*biography included*]

02635   *The best science fiction of the year.* Ballantine, New York, 1972, 340p, Paper, Anth.
02636   *The best science fiction of the year #2.* Ballantine, New York, 1973, 370p, Paper, Anth.
02637   *The best science fiction of the year #3.* Ballantine, New York, 1974, 368p, Paper, Anth.

02638   *An exaltation of stars; transcendental adventures in science fiction.* Simon & Schuster, New York, 1973, 191p, Cloth, Anth.
02639   *Fellowship of the stars; nine science fiction stories.* Simon & Schuster, New York, 1974, 222p, Cloth, Anth.
02640   *Into the unknown; eleven tales of imagination.* Thomas Nelson, Nashville, 1973, 192p, Cloth, Anth.
02641   *New worlds of fantasy.* Ace, New York, 1967, 253p, Paper, Anth.
02641A   retitled: *Step outside your mind.* Dennis Dobson, London, 1969, 253p, Cloth, Anth.
02642   *New worlds of fantasy #2.* Ace, New York, 1970, 254p, Paper, Anth.
02643   *New worlds of fantasy #3.* Ace, New York, 1971, 253p, Paper, Anth.
02644   *On our way to the future.* Ace, New York, 1970, 253p, Paper, Anth.
02645   *The others.* Fawcett Gold Medal, Greenwich, 1969, 192p, Paper, Anth.
02646   *Science fiction for people who hate science fiction.* Doubleday, Garden City, 1966, 190p, Cloth, Anth.
       Step outside your mind. [see 02641A]
02647   *This side of infinity.* Ace, New York, 1972, 237p, Paper, Anth.
02648   *Universe 1.* Ace, New York, 1971, 250p, Paper, Anth.
02649   *Universe 2; an original collection of all-new science fiction.* Ace, New York, 1972, 255p, Paper, Anth.
02650   *Universe 3.* Random House, New York, 1973, 211p, Cloth, Anth.
02651   *Universe 4.* Random House, New York, 1974, 243p, Cloth, Anth.
02652   *Universe 5.* Random House, New York, 1974, 209p, Cloth, Anth.
02653   *Warlord of Kor.* Ace Double, New York, 1963, 97p, Paper, Novel
02654   *Worlds near and far; nine stories of science fiction and fantasy.* Thomas Nelson, Nashville, 1974, 176p, Cloth, Anth.

with Ted White as Norman Edwards:

02655   *Invasion from 2500.* Monarch, Derby, Conn., 1964, 126p, Paper, Novel

with Donald A. Wollheim:

02656   *World's best science fiction: 1965.* Ace, New York, 1965, 288p, Paper, Anth.
02656A   retitled: *World's best science fiction: first series.* Ace, New York, 1970, 288p, Paper, Anth.
02657   *World's best science fiction: 1966.* Ace, New York, 1966, 287p, Paper, Anth.
02657A   retitled: *World's best science fiction: second series.* Ace, New York, 1970, 287p, Paper, Anth.
02658   *World's best science fiction: 1967.* Ace, New York, 1967, 287p, Paper, Anth.
02658A   retitled: *World's best science fiction: third series.* Ace, New York, 1970, 285p, Paper, Anth.
02659   *World's best science fiction: 1968.* Ace, New York, 1968, 319p, Paper, Anth.
02659A   retitled: *World's best S.F. no. 1.* Victor Gollancz, London, 1969, 320p, Cloth, Anth.
02659B   retitled: *World's best science fiction: fourth series.* Ace, New York, 1970, 319p, Paper, Anth.
02660   *World's best science fiction: 1969.* Ace, New York, 1969, 380p, Paper, Anth.

CARR, TERRY, with Donald A. Wollheim (Cont.)

02661 *World's best science fiction: 1970.* Ace, New York, 1970, 349p, Paper, Anth.
02662 *World's best science fiction: 1971.* Ace, New York, 1971, 349p, Paper, Anth.

CARREL, FREDERIC

02663 *2010*, by the author of "The adventures of John Johns." T. Werner Laurie, London, 1914, 249p, Cloth, Novel

CARREL, MARK, pseud.
see: PAINE, LAURAN

CARRELL, CHRISTOPHER

02664 *Beyond this horizon; an anthology of science fact and science fiction.* Ceolfrith Press, Sunderland, UK, 1973, 145p, Paper, Anth.

CARRIGAN, NANCY, with Richard Carrigan

02665 *The siren stars.* Pyramid, New York, 1971, 173p, Paper, Novel

CARRIGAN, RICHARD, with Nancy Carrigan

02665 *The siren stars.* Pyramid, New York, 1971, 173p, Paper, Novel

CARRINGTON, HEREWARD, 1880-d.

02666 *The week-end book of ghost stories.* Ives Washburn, New York, 1953, 280p, Cloth, Anth.

CARROLL, GLADYS (Winifred) HASTY, 1904-
[*biography included*]

02667 *Man on the Mountain.* Little, Brown, Boston, 1969, 223p, Cloth, Novel

CARROLL, JOY

02668 *The moth.* Dell, New York, 1974, 271p, Paper, Novel
02669 *Soul's end.* Dell, New York, 1974, 235p, Paper, Novel

CARROLL, LATROBE, with Ruth Carroll

02670 *The flying house.* Macmillan, New York, 1946, 127p, Cloth, Novel

CARROLL, LESLIE

02671 *You can't hang the dead; a grim story of mystery and romance.* Mitre Press, London, 1944, 31p, Paper, Story

CARROLL, LEWIS, pseud. [Charles Lutwidge Dodgson, 1832-1898]

02672 *Alice's adventures in Wonderland.* Macmillan, London, 1865, 192p, Cloth, Novel [Alice #1]
02672A retitled: *Alice in Wonderland.* P. R. Gawthorn, London, 1944, 104p, Cloth, Novel [Alice #1]
02673 *Alice's adventures in Wonderland; and, Through the looking-glass.* Macmillan, London, 1911, 291p, Cloth, Coll. [Alice #s 1-2]
02674 *Through the looking-glass, and what Alice found there.* Macmillan, London, 1872, 224p, Cloth, Novel [Alice #2]
02674A retitled: *Alice through the looking-glass.* A. Whitman, Chicago, 1930, 221p, Cloth, Novel [Alice #2]

CARROLL, NINA

02675 *Adventure on the Moon.* Hutchinson's Books for Young People, London, 1952, 48p, Cloth, Story

CARROLL, RUTH, 1899-   [*biography included*], with Latrobe Carroll

02670 *The flying house.* Macmillan, New York, 1946, 127p, Cloth, Novel

CARROLL, TED [Thomas Theodore Carroll, Jr., 1925-   ] [*biography included*]

02676 *White pills; a novel.* Crown Publishers, New York, 1964, 191p, Cloth, Novel

CARRUTH, (Fred) HAYDEN, 1862-1932

02677 *The adventures of Jones.* Harper & Bros., New York, 1895, 123p, Cloth, Novel; Chatto & Windus, London, 1895, 123p, Cloth, Novel

CARRYL, CHARLES E(dward), 1841-1920

02678 *Davy and the goblin; or, What followed reading "Alice's adventures in Wonderland."* Houghton Mifflin, Boston, 1885, 160p, Cloth, Novel [Alice series]

CARSON, DeWITT

02679 *"My goodness!" said the Princess; a modern fairy tale for grown-ups.* H. C. Kinsey, New York, 1938, 57p, Cloth, Novel

CARSON, JOHN F., 1920-   [*biography included*]

02680 *The boys who vanished.* Duell, Sloan & Pearce, New York, 1959, 212p, Cloth, Novel

CARSON, ROBIN

02681 *Pawn of time; an extravaganza.* Henry Holt, New York, 1957, 442p, Cloth, Novel

CARTER, ANGELA (Olive), 1940-   [biography included]

02682 Fireworks; nine profane pieces. Quartet, London, 1974, 122p, Cloth, Coll.
02683 Heroes & villains. Heinemann, London, 1969, 214p, Cloth, Novel
02684 The infernal desire machines of Doctor Hoffman. Rupert Hart-Davis, London, 1972, 286p, Cloth, Novel
02684A retitled: The war of dreams. Harcourt Brace Jovanovich, New York, 1974, 286p, Cloth, Novel
02685 The magic toyshop. Heinemann, London, 1967, 200p, Cloth, Novel
       The war of dreams. [see 02684A]

CARTER, BRUCE, pseud. [Richard Alexander Hough, 1922-   ] [biography included]

02686 The perilous descent into a strange lost world. Bodley Head, London, 1952, 179p, Cloth, Novel
02686A retitled: Into a strange lost world. Thomas Y. Crowell, New York, 1953, 196p, Cloth, Novel

CARTER, DEE, pseud.
    see: HUGHES, DENNIS TALBOT

CARTER, DIANA

02687 The ghost writer. Cassell, London, 1974, 218p, Cloth, Novel
02688 Zozu the robot. Sidgwick & Jackson, London, 1974, 95p, Cloth, Novel

CARTER, FREDERICK

02689 Gold like glass; a tale. Twyn Barlwm Press, London, 1932, 16p, Paper, Story

CARTER, GEORGE GOLDSMITH-

02690 Lord of the Chained. Lothrop, Lee & Shepard, New York, 1972, 160p, Cloth, Novel

CARTER, JOHN FRANKLIN
    see: FRANKLIN, JAY

CARTER, JOHN L(ouis Justin), 1880-

02691 Peggy the aeronaut. Everett & Co., London, 1910, 254p, Cloth, Novel

as Compton Irving:

02692 Daughter of Egypt. Philip Allan, London, 1937, 253p, Cloth, Novel

CARTER, LIN(wood Vrooman), 1930-   [biography included]

02693 Beyond the gates of dream. Belmont, New York, 1969, 157p, Paper, Coll.

02694 Black Legion of Callisto. Dell, New York, 1972, 203p, Paper, Novel [Callisto #2]
02695 The Black Star. Dell, New York, 1973, 235p, Paper, Novel [Atlantis #1]
02696 By the light of the Green Star. DAW, New York, 1974, 175p, Paper, Novel [Green Star #3]
02697 Discoveries in fantasy. Ballantine, New York, 1972, 243p, Paper, Anth.
02698 Double phoenix; The firebird; From the world's end. Ballantine, New York, 1971, 210p, Paper, Anth. [published anonymously]
02699 Dragons, elves, and heroes. Ballantine, New York, 1969, 277p, Paper, Anth.
02700 The Flame of Iridar. Belmont Double, New York, 1967, 93p, Paper, Novel
02701 Flashing swords! #1. Nelson Doubleday, Garden City, 1973, 175p, Cloth, Anth.
02702 Flashing swords! #2. Nelson Doubleday, Garden City, 1973, 200p, Cloth, Anth.
02703 Giant of world's end. Belmont, New York, 1969, 141p, Paper, Novel
02704 Golden cities, far. Ballantine, New York, 1970, 299p, Paper, Anth.
02705 Great short novels of adult fantasy. Ballantine, New York, 1972, 278p, Paper, Anth.
02706 Great short novels of adult fantasy, volume II. Ballantine, New York, 1973, 248p, Paper, Anth.
02707 Imaginary worlds; the art of fantasy. Ballantine, New York, 1973, 278p, Paper, Nonf.
02708 Jandar of Callisto. Dell, New York, 1972, 224p, Paper, Novel [Callisto #1]
02709 Lost world of time. Signet, New York, 1969, 128p, Paper, Novel
02710 Lovecraft; a look behind the "Cthulhu Mythos." Ballantine, New York, 1972, 198p, Paper, Nonf.
02711 The magic of Atlantis. Lancer, New York, 1970, 191p, Paper, Anth.
02712 The man who loved Mars. Fawcett Gold Medal, Greenwich, 1973, 157p, Paper, Novel
02713 The man without a planet. Ace Double, New York, 1966, 113p, Paper, Novel [History of the Great Imperium #1]
02714 New worlds for old. Ballantine, New York, 1971, 327p, Paper, Anth.
02715 Outworlder. Lancer, New York, 1971, 175p, Paper, Novel [History of the Great Imperium #3]
02716 The purloined planet. Belmont Double, New York, 1969, 75p, Paper, Novel [Hautley Quicksilver #2]
02717 The quest of Kadji. Belmont, New York, 1971, 188p, Paper, Novel
02718 Sky pirates of Callisto. Dell, New York, 1973, 189p, Paper, Novel [Callisto #3]
02719 The spawn of Cthulhu. Ballantine, New York, 1971, 274p, Paper, Anth.
02720 The star magicians. Ace Double, New York, 1966, 124p, Paper, Novel
02721 Star rogue. Lancer, New York, 1970, 190p, Paper, Novel [History of the Great Imperium #2]
02722 The thief of Thoth. Belmont Double, New York, 1968, 79p, Paper, Novel [Hautley Quicksilver #1]
02723 Thongor against the gods. Paperback Library, New York, 1967, 157p, Paper, Novel [Thongor #3]
       Thongor and the dragon city. [see 02727A]
       Thongor and the Wizard of Lemuria. [see 02736A]
02724 Thongor at the end of time. Paperback Library, New York, 1968, 158p, Paper, Novel [Thongor #5]

CARTER, LIN (Cont.)

02725 *Thongor fights the Pirates of Tarakus.* Berk-
          ley Medallion, New York, 1970, 160p, Paper,
          Novel [Thongor #6]
02726 *Thongor in the City of Magicians.* Paperback
          Library, New York, 1968, 160p, Paper, Novel
          [Thongor #4]
02727 *Thongor of Lemuria.* Ace, New York, 1966, 127p,
          Paper, Novel [Thongor #2]
02727A retitled: *Thongor and the dragon city.* Berk-
          ley Medallion, New York, 1970, 143p, Paper,
          Novel [Thongor #2] [slightly expanded]
02728 *Time war.* Dell, New York, 1974, 160p, Paper,
          Novel
02729 *Tolkien; a look behind "The Lord of the Rings."*
          Ballantine, New York, 1969, 212p, Paper,
          Nonf.
02730 *Tower at the end of time.* Belmont, New York,
          1968, 141p, Paper, Novel
02731 *Tower of the Medusa.* Ace Double, New York,
          1969, 106p, Paper, Novel
02732 *Under the Green Star.* DAW, New York, 1972,
          144p, Paper, Novel [Green Star #1]
02733 *The valley where time stood still.* Doubleday,
          Garden City, 1974, 179p, Cloth, Novel
02734 *The warrior of world's end; the first book of
          the Gondwane epic.* DAW, New York, 1974,
          160p, Paper, Novel [Gondwane #1]
02735 *When the Green Star calls.* DAW, New York,
          1973, 176p, Paper, Novel [Green Star #2]
02736 *The Wizard of Lemuria.* Ace, New York, 1965,
          127p, Paper, Novel [Thongor #1]
02736A retitled: *Thongor and the Wizard of Lemuria.*
          Berkley Medallion, New York, 1969, 143p,
          Paper, Novel [Thongor #1] [slightly expanded]
02737 *The young magicians.* Ballantine, New York,
          1969, 280p, Paper, Anth.

with L. Sprague de Camp:

02738 *Conan of the Isles.* Lancer, New York, 1968,
          189p, Paper, Novel [Conan #12]
02739 *Conan the buccaneer.* Lancer, New York, 1971,
          191p, Paper, Novel [Conan #6]

with David Grinnell:

02740 *Destination: Saturn.* Avalon, New York, 1967,
          192p, Cloth, Novel [Destiny #2]

with Robert E. Howard:

02741 *King Kull.* Lancer, New York, 1967, 223p,
          Paper, Coll.

with Robert E. Howard and L. Sprague de Camp:

02742 *Conan.* Lancer, New York, 1967, 221p, Paper,
          Coll. [Conan #1]
02743 *Conan of Cimmeria.* Lancer, New York, 1969,
          189p, Paper, Coll. [Conan #2]
02744 *Conan the wanderer.* Lancer, New York, 1968,
          222p, Paper, Coll. [Conan #4]

CARTER, M(argaret) L(ouise), 1948-   [*biography included*]

02745 *The curse of the undead.* Fawcett Gold Medal,
          Greenwich, 1970, 223p, Paper, Anth.
02746 *Demon lovers and strange seductions.* Fawcett
          Gold Medal, Greenwich, 1972, 207p, Paper,
          Anth.

CARTER, NICK, house pseud.

02747 *The human time bomb; a Killmaster spy chiller.*
          Award, New York, 1969, 154p, Paper, Novel
          [Nick Carter series]

CARTER, TREMLETT

02748 *The people of the Moon; a novel.* "The Electri-
          cian" Printing & Publishing Co., and Simpkin,
          Marshall, Hamilton, Kent, London, 1895, 402p,
          Cloth, Novel

CARTMELL, ROBERT
    see: TARNACRE, ROBERT

CARUSO, DEE, with Gerald Gardner

02749 *The world's greatest athlete.* Fawcett Gold
          Medal, Greenwich, 1973, 127p, Paper, Movie

CARYL, CHARLES W.

02750 *New Era, presenting the plans for the New Era
          Union, to help develop and utilize the best
          resources of this country; also, to employ
          the best skill there is available to realize
          the highest degree of prosperity that is pos-
          sible for all who will help to attain it;
          based on practical and successful business
          methods.* Office, Denver, 1897, 192p, Cloth,
          Novel [published anonymously]

CASARES, ADOLFO BIOY
    see: BIOY CASARES, ADOLFO

CASE, (Brian) DAVID, 1937-   [*biography included*]

02751 *And now the screaming starts.* Pan, London,
          1973, 124p, Paper, Novel
02752 *The cell, and other tales of horror.* Macdonald,
          London, 1969, 269p, Cloth, Coll.
02753 *Fengriffon, and other stories.* Macdonald, Lon-
          don, 1971, 210p, Cloth, Coll.

THE CASE OF MR. LUCRAFT
    see: BESANT, WALTER and RICE, JAMES

CASELEYR, CAMILLE
    see: DANVERS, JACK

CASEWIT, CURTIS W(erner), 1922-   [*biography
included*]

02754 *The peacemakers.* Avalon, New York, 1960, 224p,
          Cloth, Novel

CASEY, PATRICK, with Terence Casey

02755 *The strange story of William Hyde.* Hearst's
          International Library, New York, 1916, 317p,
          Cloth, Novel

CASEY, TERENCE, with Patrick Casey

02755   *The strange story of William Hyde.* Hearst's International Library, New York, 1916, 317p, Cloth, Novel

CASOLET, JACQUES

02756   *"Theory of flight"; a theoretical science novel.* no publisher, Milwaukee?, 1958, , Paper, Novel

CASSANDRA, pseud.

02757   *The Channel Tunnel; or, England's ruin.* W. Clowes & Sons, London, 1876, 37p, Paper, Story

CASSATT, DAVE

02758   *The birthright of mankind.* Pioneer Press, Tacoma, Wash., 1943, 84p, Paper, Novel

CASSERLY, GORDON, d. 1947

02759   *The elephant god.* Philip Allan, London, 1920, 404p, Cloth, Novel [Badshah #1]
02760   *The jungle girl.* Philip Allan, London, 1921, 328p, Cloth, Novel [Badshah #2]
02761   *The monkey god.* Philip Allan, London, 1933, 319p, Cloth, Novel
02762   *Tiger girl.* Philip Allan, London, 1934, 252p, Cloth, Novel

CASSIDAY, BRUCE
    see: BINGHAM, CARSON

"CASSIUS," pseud. [Michael Mackintosh Foot, 1913-]

02763   *The trial of Mussolini, being a verbatim report of the first great trial for war criminals held in London sometime in 1944 or 1945.* Victor Gollancz, London, 1943, 82p, Cloth, Novel

CASSON, MILES, pseud.

02764   *Time drug.* Curtis Warren, London, 1954, 159p, Paper, Novel

CASTERET, NORBERT, 1897-

02765   *Mission underground.* George G. Harrap, London, 1968, 140p, Cloth, Novel

CASTILLA, CLYDE ANDRE

02766   *Shara-Li.* Clear Thoughts, Hollywood, 1958, 100p, Cloth, Novel

CASTLE, AGNES, d. 1922, with Edgerton Castle

02767   *The star dreamer; a romance.* Frederick A. Stokes, New York, 1903, 375p, Cloth, Novel

CASTLE, EDGERTON, 1858-1920, with Agnes Castle

02767   *The star dreamer; a romance.* Frederick A. Stokes, New York, 1903, 375p, Cloth, Novel

CASTLE, JEFFERY LLOYD [Geoffrey Lloyd Castle, 1898-]

02768   *Satellite E One.* Dodd, Mead, New York, 1954, 223p, Cloth, Novel
02769   *Vanguard to Venus.* Dodd, Mead, New York, 1957, 212p, Cloth, Novel

THE CASTLE OF CAITHNESS
    see: P., F. H.

THE CASTLE OF SAINT DONATS
    see: LUCAS, CHARLES

CASTLETOWN, LORD [Bernard Edward Barnaby Fitz-Patrick, 2nd Baron Castletown, 1849-1937]

02770   *A bundle of lies.* Drane's, London, 1924, 192p, Cloth, Coll.

CASWELL, EDWARD A.

02771   *Toil and self,* by myself and another. Rand, McNally, Chicago, 1900, 154p, Paper, Novel

CAT, CHRISTOPHER, pseud.
    see: CULLEN, COUNTEE

CATTELL, ANN, 1893-

02772   *The mind juggler, and other stories.* Exposition Press, New York, 1966, 172p, Cloth, Coll.

CAUNTER, C(yril) F(rancis), 1899-

02773   *Madness opens the door.* Thornton Butterworth, London, 1932, 319p, Cloth, Novel

CAUSSE, CHARLES, 1862-1904, with Charles Vincent as Peter Maël

02774   *Under the sea to the North Pole.* Sampson Low, Marston, London, 1893, 244p, Cloth, Novel

CAVALIER, Z. L(angrana)

02775   *The soul of the Orient.* Murray & Evenden, London, 1913, 280p, Cloth, Novel

CAVE MAN SEX

02776 *Cave man sex.* Collectors Publications, City of Industry, CA, 1969, 134p, Paper, Novel

CAZEDESSUS, CAMILLE Jr. [published anonymously]

02777 *Ghost stories; stories of ghosts.* Opar Press, Evergreen, Col., 1973, 32p, Paper, Anth.
02778 *The weird menace.* Opar Press, Evergreen, Col., 1972, 68p, Paper, Anth.

CAZOTTE, JACQUES, 1719/20-1792

02779 *The devil in love.* Hookham & Carpenter, London, 1793, 170p, Cloth, Novel

CEBULASH, MEL

02780 *Herbie rides again.* Scholastic Book Services, New York, 1974, 104p, Paper, Movie [Herbie #2]
02781 *The love bug.* Scholastic Book Services, New York, 1969, 128p, Paper, Movie [Herbie #1]

CECIL, ALGERNON, 1879-1953

02782 *Essays in imitation.* John Murray, London, 1910, 153p, Cloth, Coll. [includes some nonf. and a Gulliver parody]

CECIL, Lady GWENDOLEN
    see: THE CURSE OF INTELLECT

THE CELEBRATED "MOON STORY"
    see: LOCKE, RICHARD ADAMS

CENTENNIUS, RALPH, pseud.

02783 *The Dominion in 1983.* Toker & Co., Peterborough, Ontario, Canada, 1883, 30p, Paper?, Story

A CENTURY OF CREEPY STORIES

02784 *A century of creepy stories.* Hutchinson, London, 1934, 1178p, Cloth, Anth.

A CENTURY OF GHOST STORIES

02785 *A century of ghost stories.* Hutchinson, London, 1936, 1013p, Cloth, Anth.
02785A retitled: *Let's talk of graves; tales from 'A century of ghost stories.'* Hutchinson, London, 1970, 318p, Cloth, Anth. [abridged]
02785B retitled: *Walk in dread; tales from 'A century of ghost stories.'* Hutchinson, London, 1970, 319p, Cloth, Anth. [abridged]

CENTURY OF THRILLERS

02786 *Century of thrillers.* President Press, New York, 1937, volume I-367p, II-373p, III-370p, Cloth, Anth. [selections from the two British series, plus additional stories]

A CENTURY OF THRILLERS, FROM POE TO ARLEN

02787 *A century of thrillers, from Poe to Arlen.* Daily Express Publications, London, 1934, 1087p, Cloth, Anth.

A CENTURY OF THRILLERS, SECOND SERIES

02788 *A century of thrillers, second series.* Daily Express Publications, London, 1935, 896p, Cloth, Anth.
02788A retitled: *The world's best mystery stories.* United Press Home Entertainment Library, Melbourne, 1935,   , Cloth, Anth.

CEPTION, JOHN V., pseud.

02789 *Earth sex in the 21st century.* Impact Library, Los Angeles, 1970, 160p, Paper, Coll.

CERF, BENNETT A(lfred), 1898-1971 [*biography included*]

02790 *Famous ghost stories.* Modern Library, New York, 1944, 361p, Cloth, Anth.
02791 *The unexpected.* Bantam, New York, 1948, 273p, Paper, Anth.
02791A retitled: *Stories selected from The unexpected.* Bantam, New York, 1963, 184p, Paper, Anth. [abridged]

CERF, CHRISTOPHER (Bennett), 1941- [*biography included*]

02792 *The Vintage anthology of science fantasy.* Vintage, New York, 1966, 310p, Paper, Anth.

CHADWICK, PHILIP GEORGE

02793 *The Death Guard.* Hutchinson, London, 1939, 431p, Cloth, Novel

CHAIR, SOMERSET DE
    see: DE CHAIR, SOMERSET

CHALKER, JACK L(aurence), 1944- [*biography included*]

02794 *In memoriam: Clark Ashton Smith.* Anthem Fantasy Library, Baltimore, 1963, 97p, Cloth, Nonf.
02795 *An informal biography of Scrooge McDuck.* Mirage Press, Baltimore, 1974, 57p, Paper, Novel
02796 *Mirage on Lovecraft; a literary view.* Jack L. Chalker & Mark Owings, Baltimore, 1965, 46p, Paper, Nonf. Anth.

CHALKER, JACK L. (Cont.)

02797   *The new H. P. Lovecraft bibliography.* Anthem
        Press, Baltimore, 1962, 40p, Paper, Nonf.

with Mark Owings:

02798   *The index to the science-fantasy publishers
        (a bibliography of the science fiction and
        fantasy specialty houses).* Anthem Series,
        Baltimore, 1966, 76p, Paper, Nonf.
02799   *The revised H. P. Lovecraft bibliography.*
        Mirage Press, Baltimore, 1973, 44p, Paper,
        Nonf.

CHAMBERLAIN, H(enry) R(ichardson), 1859-1911

02800   *6,000 tons of gold.* Flood & Vincent, Meadville,
        PA, 1894, 349p, Cloth, Novel

CHAMBERLAIN, (Edwin) WILLIAM, 1903-

02801   *China strike.* Fawcett Gold Medal, Greenwich,
        1967, 191p, Paper, Novel
02802   *Red January.* Paperback Library, New York,
        1964, 158p, Paper, Novel

CHAMBERS, AIDAN, 1934-   [*biography included*]

02803   *Ghosts, no. 2.* Topliners, London, 1972, 127p,
        Paper, Anth.
02804   *The tenth ghost book.* Barrie & Jenkins, Lon-
        don, 1974, 252p, Cloth, Anth.

with Nancy Chambers:

02805   *Ghosts.* Topliners, London, 1969, 125p, Paper,
        Anth.
02806   *In time to come.* Topliners, London, 1973,
        126p, Paper, Anth.
02807   *World zero minus.* Topliners, London, 1971,
        124p, Paper, Anth.

CHAMBERS, DANA, pseud. [Albert Leffingwell,
1895-1946]

02808   *The last secret.* Dial Press, New York, 1943,
        289p, Cloth, Novel

CHAMBERS, DEREK HYDE-
    see: HYDE-CHAMBERS, DEREK

CHAMBERS, I(saiah) MENCH, 1865-1922

02809   *The devil of to-day; his play between the
        false and the good, being a searching alle-
        gory on the subtle intrigues of the devil
        within the church, the home, and modern
        society.* John C. Winston, Philadelphia,
        1903, 456p, Cloth, Novel
02809A retitled: *The modern devil, his play between
        the false and the good, being a searching
        allegory on the subtle intrigues of the de-
        vil within the church, the home, and modern
        society.* International Publishing Co., New
        York, 1903?, 520p, Cloth, Novel

CHAMBERS, (James) JULIUS, 1850-1920

02810   *"In Sargasso"; missing, a romance; narrative
        of Capt. Austin Clark, of the tramp steamer
        "Caribas," who, for two years, was a captive
        among the savage people of the seaweed set.*
        Transatlantic, New York, 1896, 182p, Cloth,
        Novel [title throughout the book is *Missing*]

CHAMBERS, NANCY, with Aidan Chambers

02805   *Ghosts.* Topliners, London, 1969, 125p, Paper,
        Anth.
02806   *In time to come.* Topliners, London, 1973, 126p
        Paper, Anth.
02807   *World zero minus.* Topliners, London, 1971,
        124p, Paper, Anth.

CHAMBERS, ROBERT W(illiam), 1865-1933

02811   *Athalie.* D. Appleton, New York, 1915, 405p,
        Cloth, Novel [Athalie #2]
02812   *The gay rebellion.* D. Appleton, New York,
        1913, 299p, Cloth, Novel
02813   *The Green Mouse.* D. Appleton, New York, 1910,
        281p, Cloth, Novel
02814   *In search of the unknown.* Harper & Bros., New
        York, 1904, 286p, Cloth, Novel
02815   *The King in Yellow.* F. Tennyson Neely, Chicago
        1895, 316p, Cloth, Coll.
02815A retitled: *The mask, and other stories.* Whit-
        man, Racine, 1929, 126p, Cloth, Coll. [abr.]
02816   *The King in Yellow, and other horror stories.*
        Dover, New York, 1970, 287p, Paper, Coll.
        [different contents]
02817   *The maker of moons.* G. P. Putnam's Sons, New
        York, 1896, 401p, Cloth, Coll.
02818   *The maker of moons.* Shroud Publishers, Buffalo
        NY, 1954, 82p, Paper, Novel
        The mask. [see 02815A]
02819   *The mystery of choice.* D. Appleton, New York,
        1897, 288p, Cloth, Coll.
02820   *Police!!!* D. Appleton, New York, 1915, 293p,
        Cloth, Coll.
02821   *Quick action.* D. Appleton, New York, 1914,
        316p, Cloth, Novel [Athalie #1]
02822   *The slayer of souls.* George H. Doran, New
        York, 1920, 301p, Cloth, Novel
02823   *Some ladies in haste.* D. Appleton, New York,
        1908, 242p, Cloth, Novel
02824   *The talkers.* George H. Doran, New York, 1923,
        291p, Cloth, Novel
02825   *The Tracer of Lost Persons.* D. Appleton, New
        York, 1906, 293p, Cloth, Novel
02826   *The tree of Heaven.* D. Appleton, New York,
        1907, 325p, Cloth, Coll.

CHAMBERS, W(allace) JEROME, 1862-

02827   *Altzar the pirate; a tale of reincarnation.*
        Meador Press, Boston, 1944, 239p, Cloth,
        Novel
02828   *In the weaving.* Meador Press, Boston, 1942,
        , Cloth, Novel
02829   *The opal matrix.* Salisbury Hill Press, Wor-
        cester, Mass., 1937, 247p, Cloth, Novel

CHAMBERS, (Elwyn) WHITMAN, 1896-

02830 *Invasion!* E. P. Dutton, New York, 1943, 320p,
Cloth, Novel

CHAMISSO, (Ludwig Carl) ADALBERT von, 1781-
1838

02831 *Peter Schlemihl*, from the German of Lamotte
Fouque [sic]. G. & W. B. Whittaker, London,
1823, 165p, Cloth, Novel [Schlemihl series]
02831A *Peter Schlemihl*, by Adalbert von Chamisso.
Robert Hardwicke, London, 1861, 122p, Cloth,
Novel [Peter Schlemihl series]
02831B retitled: *The wonderful history of Peter
Schlemihl.* Longman, London, 1843, 281p,
Cloth, Novel [Peter Schlemihl series]
02831C retitled: *The shadowless man; or, The wonderful history of Peter Schlemihl.* E. Lumley, London, 1845, 75p, Cloth, Novel [Peter
Schlemihl series]

CHAMPION DE CRESPIGNY, Mrs. PHILIP [Rose],
d. 1935

02832 *The valley of Achor.* Mills & Boon, London,
1910, 331p, Cloth, Novel

THE CHAMPION OF VIRTUE
see: REEVE, CLARA

CHANCE, JOHN NEWTON
see: LYMINGTON, JOHN

CHANCE, JONATHAN, pseud.
see: LYMINGTON, JOHN

CHANCELLOR, J(ohn) W(alter), 1876-

02833 *Through the visograph.* Christopher Publishing
House, Boston, 1928, 202p, Cloth, Novel

CHANDLER, A(rthur) BERTRAM, 1912- [*biography included*]

02834 *The alternate Martians.* Ace Double, New York,
1965, 129p, Paper, Novel
02835 *Alternate orbits.* Ace Double, New York, 1971,
136p, Paper, Coll. [Rim series]
02836 *Beyond the galactic Rim.* Ace Double, New York,
1963, 114p, Paper, Coll. [Rim series]
02837 *The bitter pill.* Wren Publications, Melbourne,
1974, 158p, Cloth, Novel [Rim series]
02838 *Bring back yesterday.* Ace Double, New York,
1961, 173p, Paper, Novel
02839 *Catch the star winds.* Lancer, New York, 1969,
222p, Paper, Coll. [Rim series]
02840 *The coils of time.* Ace Double, New York,
1964, 128p, Paper, Novel
02841 *Contraband from otherspace.* Ace Double, New
York, 1967, 104p, Paper, Novel [Rim series]
02842 *The dark dimensions.* Ace Double, New York,
1971, 117p, Paper, Novel [Rim series; also
includes as a character Dominic Flandry,
from Poul Anderson's future universe]

02843 *The deep reaches of space.* Herbert Jenkins,
London, 1964, 190p, Cloth, Novel [Rim series]
02844 *Empress of outer space.* Ace Double, New York,
1965, 127p, Paper, Novel [Empress #1]
02845 *False fatherland.* Horwitz Publications, North
Sydney, Australia, 1968, 161p, Paper, Novel
[Rim series]
02845A retitled: *Spartan planet.* Dell, New York,
1969, 156p, Paper, Novel [Rim series]
02846 *The gateway to never.* Ace Double, New York,
1972, 138p, Paper, Novel [Rim series]
02847 *Glory planet.* Avalon, New York, 1964, 190p,
Cloth, Novel
02848 *The Hamelin plague.* Monarch, Derby, Conn.,
1963, 126p, Paper, Novel
02849 *The hard way up.* Ace Double, New York, 1972,
162p, Paper, Coll. [Rim series]
02850 *The inheritors.* Ace Double, New York, 1972,
129p, Paper, Novel [Rim series]
02851 *Into the alternate universe.* Ace Double, New
York, 1964, 128p, Paper, Novel [Rim series]
02852 *Nebula alert.* Ace Double, New York, 1967,
121p, Paper, Novel [Rim Series]
02853 *Rendezvous on a lost world.* Ace Double, New
York, 1961, 124p, Paper, Novel [Rim series]
02854 *The Rim gods.* Ace Double, New York, 1969,
142p, Paper, Novel [Rim series]
02855 *The Rim of space.* Avalon, New York, 1961, 220p,
Cloth, Novel [Rim series]
02856 *The road to the Rim.* Ace Double, New York,
1967, 117p, Paper, Novel [Rim series]
02857 *The sea beasts.* Curtis, New York, 1971, 189p,
Paper, Novel
02858 *The ship from outside.* Ace Double, New York,
1963, 108p, Paper, Novel [Rim series]
02859 *Space mercenaries.* Ace Double, New York, 1965,
131p, Paper, Novel [Empress #2]
Spartan planet. [see 02845A]
02860 *To prime the pump.* Curtis, New York, 1971,
157p, Paper, Novel [Rim series]

CHANEY, J(ames) M.

02861 *Poliopolis and Polioland; a trip to the North
Pole.* J. M. Chaney, Jr., Publisher, Kansas
City, 1900, 172p, Cloth, Novel

CHANNING, MARK

02862 *King Cobra.* Hutchinson, London, 1933, 286p,
Cloth, Novel [Colin Gray #1]
02863 *Nine lives.* George G. Harrap, London, 1937,
299p, Cloth, Novel [Colin Gray #4]
02864 *The poisoned mountain.* Hutchinson, London,
1935, 304p, Cloth, Novel [Colin Gray #3]
02865 *White python.* Hutchinson, London, 1934, 285p,
Cloth, Novel [Colin Gray #2]

CHANT, (Eileen) JOY(ce), 1945- [*biography
included*]

02866 *Red Moon and Black Mountain; the end of the
House of Kendreth.* George Allen & Unwin,
London, 1970, 277p, Cloth, Novel

CHANTER, GRATIANA

02867 *The witch of Withyford; a story of Exmoor.* J.
M. Dent & Sons, London, 1896, 187p, Cloth,
Novel

CHAPDELAINE, PERRY A(nthony)

02868 *Swampworld west.* Elmfield Press, Morley, UK, 1974, 156p, Cloth, Novel

CHAPELA, E. SALAZAR
  see: SALAZAR CHAPELA, E.

CHAPIN, MAUD (Louise) HUDNUT, 1872-

02869 *The lost star, and other stories.* Falmouth Publishing House, Portland, Maine, 1948, 79p, Cloth, Coll.

CHAPLIN, W(illiam?) N.

02870 *The pagan city.* John Long, London, 1938, 384p, Cloth, Novel

CHAPMAN, S(amuel) E.

02871 *Doctor Jones' picnic.* Whitaker & Ray, San Francisco, 1898, 177p, Cloth, Novel

CHAPPELL, GEORGE S(hepard), 1877-1946

02872 *Animals arise!!! An animal book to end all animal books.* Frederick A. Stokes, New York, 1935,   , Cloth, Novel
02873 *Through the Alimentary Canal with gun and camera; a fascinating trip to the interior.* Frederick A. Stokes, New York, 1930, 231p, Cloth, Novel

CHARBONNEAU, LOUIS (Henry), 1924-   *[biography included]*

02874 *Antic Earth.* Herbert Jenkins, London, 1967, 221p, Cloth, Novel
02874A retitled: *Down to Earth.* Bantam, New York, 1967, 188p, Paper, Novel
02875 *Barrier world.* Lancer, New York, 1970, 224p, Paper, Novel
02876 *Corpus Earthling.* Zenith, Rockville Centre, NY, 1960, 160p, Paper, Novel
    Down to Earth. [see 02874A]
02877 *No place on Earth.* Doubleday, Garden City, 1958, 184p, Cloth, Novel
02878 *Psychedelic-40.* Bantam, New York, 1965, 184p, Paper, Novel
02878A retitled: *The Specials.* Herbert Jenkins, London, 1965, 191p, Cloth, Novel
02879 *The sensitives; a novel.* Bantam, New York, 1968, 204p, Paper, Movie
02880 *The sentinel stars; a novel of the future.* Bantam, New York, 1963, 156p, Paper, Novel
    The Specials. [see 02878A]

CHARITINA, Sister MARY
  see: MARY CHARITINA, Sister

CHARKIN, PAUL (Samuel), 1907-   *[biography included]*

02881 *Light of Mars.* Badger, London, 1959, 156p, Paper, Novel

02882 *The living gem.* Digit, London, 1963, 160p, Paper, Novel
02883 *The other side of Night.* Badger, London, 1960, 157p, Paper, Novel

CHARLES, JOHN

02884 *The man without a mouth.* Arthur H. Stockwell, London, 1935, 224p, Cloth, Novel

CHARLES, NEIL, house pseud. [see also Brian Holloway, Dennis Talbot Hughes, John W. Jennison]

02885 *Beyond Zoaster.* Curtis Warren, London, 1953, 159p, Cloth, Novel [author unknown]
02886 *The land of Esa.* Curtis Warren, London, 1952, 128p, Cloth, Novel [by Dennis Talbot Hughes]
02887 *Pararobot.* Curtis Warren, London, 1952?, 112p, Paper, Novel [by John W. Jennison]
02888 *Planet Tha.* Curtis Warren, London, 1953, 159p, Cloth, Novel [author unknown]
02889 *Pre-gargantua.* Curtis Warren, London, 1953, 159p, Cloth, Novel [author unknown]
02890 *Research opta.* Curtis Warren, London, 1953, 160p, Cloth, Novel [author unknown]
02891 *Titan's moon.* Curtis Warren, London, 1952, 112p, Paper, Novel [by Brian Holloway]
02892 *Twenty-four hours.* Curtis Warren, London, 1952, 128p, Cloth, Novel [by Dennis Talbot Hughes]
02893 *World of Gol.* Curtis Warren, London, 1953, 159p, Cloth, Novel [author unknown]

CHARLTON, L(ionel) E(velyn) O(swald), 1879-1958

02894 *War over England.* Longmans, Green, London, 1936, 287p, Cloth, Nonf. [includes a large fictional section describing a future war]
02894A retitled: *The next war.* Longmans, Green, London, 1937, 82p, Cloth, Novel [the fictional part of the earlier book excerpted and published separately]

CHARNAS, SUZY McKEE

02895 *Walk to the end of the world.* Ballantine, New York, 1974, 214p, Paper, Novel

CHARQUES, DOROTHY

02896 *The dark stranger.* John Murray, London, 1956, 352p, Cloth, Novel

CHARRINGTON, CHARLES

02897 *Lady Bramber's guest.* Stone & Kimball, New York, 1896, 141p, Cloth, Novel
02898 *A sturdy beggar; and, Lady Bramber's ghost; two stories.* Archibald Constable, London, 1896, 219p, Cloth, Coll.

CHARTERIS, LESLIE, 1907-   [originally Leslie Charles Bowyer Yin] [*biography included*]

02899 *The Saint's choice of impossible crime.* Bond-Charteris, Hollywood, 1945, 125p, Paper, Anth.

CHARTERS, DAVID WILTON, 1900-

02900 *Grotto.* Pageant Press, New York, 1955, 211p, Cloth, Novel

CHASE, ADAM, pseud.
    see: LESSER, MILTON and FAIRMAN, PAUL W.

CHASE, JAMES HADLEY, pseud. [René Raymond, 1906-   ]

02901 *Miss Shumway waves a wand.* Jarrolds Publishers, London, 1944, 169p, Cloth, Novel

CHASE, MARY, 1907-1973

02902 *The wicked pigeon ladies in the garden.* Alfred A. Knopf, New York, 1968, 117p, Cloth, Novel
02902A retitled: *The wicked, wicked ladies in the haunted house.* Scholastic Book Services, New York, 1971, 128p, Paper, Novel

CHATELAIN, Madame [Clara] de, 1807-1876

02903 *The sedan-chair; and, Sir Wilfred's seven flights.* George Routledge & Sons, London, 1866, 300p, Cloth, Coll.
02904 *Sir Wilfred's seven flights.* London, 1874, , Cloth, Novel

CHATRIAN, (Pierre) ALEXANDRE, 1826-1890, with Émile Erckmann as Mm. Erckmann-Chatrian

02905 *The man-wolf, and other tales.* Ward, Lock & Tyler, London, 1876, 252p, Cloth, Coll.
02906 *Stories of the Rhine.* Ward, Lock & Tyler, London, 1875, 217p, Paper, Coll.
02906A retitled: *Fantastic tales of the Rhineland.* John Dicks, London, 1880?, 158p, Paper, Coll.
02907 *The wild huntsman, and other tales.* Ward, Lock, London, 1877, 184p, Cloth, Coll.

CHATTERTON, E(dward) KEBLE

02908 *Through sea and sky.* J. B. Lippincott, Philadelphia, 1929, 259p, Cloth, Novel

CHAVANNES, ALBERT, 1836-1903

02909 *The future commonwealth; or, What Samuel Balcom saw in Socioland.* True Nationalist Publishing Co., New York, 1892, 114p, Cloth, Novel [Socioland #1]
02910 *In brighter climes; or, Life in Socioland; a realistic novel.* Chavannes & Co., Knoxville, Tenn., 1895, 254p, Cloth, Novel [Socioland #2]

CHAYTOR, H(enry) J(ohn), 1871-1954

02911 *The light of the eye; a novel.* Digby, Long, London, 1897, 216p, Cloth, Novel

CHEETHAM, ANTHONY

02912 *Bug-eyed monsters; science fiction.* Sidgwick & Jackson, London, 1972, 280p, Cloth, Anth.
02913 *Science against man.* Avon, New York, 1970, 221p, Paper, Anth.

CHEEVER, GEORGE BARRELL
    see: CHEEVER, HENRY T.

CHEEVER, HENRY T(heodore), 1814-1897 [but actually written by his brother, George Barrell Cheever, 1807-1890, according to most authorities]

02914 *A reel in a bottle for Jack in the Doldrums, being the adventures of two of the King's seamen in a voyage to the celestial country, edited from the manuscripts of an old salt.* Charles Scribner, New York, 1852, 355p, Cloth, Novel

CHENEY, DAVID M(acGregor)

02915 *Son of Minos; a novel.* Robert M. McBride, New York, 1930, 238p, Cloth, Novel

CHENEY, W(alter) T(homas), 1859-

02916 *An apocalypse of life.* Arena Publishing Co., Boston, 1893, 312p, Cloth, Novel

CHENNEVIERE, DANE
    see: RUDHYAR, DANE

CHER, MARIE, pseud. [Marie Scherr]

02917 *The door unlatched.* Gerald Howe, London, 1927, 259p, Cloth, Novel
02918 *The immortal gymnasts.* William Heinemann, London, 1915, 309p, Cloth, Novel

CHESNEY, Sir GEORGE (Tompkyns), 1830-1895

02919 *The Battle of Dorking; reminiscences of a volunteer.* William Blackwood & Sons, Edinburgh, 1871, 64p, Paper, Novel [anonymously issued]
02919A retitled: *The Battle of Dorking and German conquest of England in 1875,* by an eyewitness in 1925. no publisher, Philadelphia, 1871?, 64p, Paper, Novel
02919B retitled: *The fall of England? The Battle of Dorking; reminiscences of a volunteer,* by a contributor to 'Blackwood.' G. P. Putnam's Sons, New York, 1871, 66p, Paper, Novel
02919C retitled: *The German conquest of England in 1875, and Battle of Dorking; or, Reminiscences of a volunteer, describing the arrival of the German armada--destruction of the British fleet--the decisive Battle of Dorking--capture*

CHESNEY, Sir GEORGE (Cont.)

        of London--downfall of the English Empire,
        by an eyewitness in 1925. Porter & Coates,
        Philadelphia, 187?, 62p, Cloth, Novel
02919D   retitled: *The Battle of Dorking; or, Reminis-*
        cences of a volunteer, by an eyewitness in
        1925, by Col. George Chesney. Porter &
        Coates, Philadelphia, 1885, 62p, Paper,
        Story
02920   *The new ordeal,* by the author of 'The Battle
        of Dorking.' William Blackwood & Sons, Edin-
        burgh, 1879, 140p, Cloth, Novel

CHESNEY, WEATHERBY, pseud.
  see: HYNE, C. J. CUTCLIFFE

CHESNOFF, RICHARD Z(eltner), 1937-   [*biogra-*
phy included], with Edward Klein and Robert
Littell

02921   *If Israel lost the war.* Coward-McCann, New
        York, 1969, 253p, Cloth, Novel

CHESTER, ALFRED, 1929?-1971

02922   *The exquisite corpse; a novel.* Simon & Schus-
        ter, New York, 1967, 240p, Cloth, Novel

CHESTER, GEORGE RANDOLPH, 1869-1924

02923   *The cash intrigue; a fantastic melodrama of*
        modern finance. Bobbs-Merrill, Indianapolis,
        1909, 391p, Cloth, Novel
02924   *The jingo.* Bobbs-Merrill, Indianapolis, 1912,
        393p, Cloth, Novel

CHESTER, Lord, pseud. [Cyrus Reed Teed, 1839-
1908]

02925   *The great red dragon; or, The flaming devil*
        of the Orient. Guiding Star Publishing
        House, Estero, FL, 1916, 156p, Cloth, Novel

CHESTER, MICHAEL (Arthur), 1928-   [*biography*
included]

02926   *The mystery of the lost moon.* G. P. Putnam's
        Sons, New York, 1961, 127p, Cloth, Novel

CHESTER, WILLIAM L., 1907-

02927   *Hawk of the wilderness.* Harper & Bros., New
        York, 1936, 308p, Cloth, Novel

CHESTERTON, G(ilbert) K(eith), 1874-1936

02928   *The ball and the cross.* Wells Gardner, Darton,
        London, 1909, 403p, Cloth, Novel
02929   *The flying inn.* Methuen, London, 1914,
        301p, Cloth, Novel
02930   *A G. K. Chesterton omnibus.* Methuen, London,
        1936, 726p, Cloth, Coll. [includes *The*
        Napoleon of Notting Hill; The man who was
        Thursday; The flying inn]

02931   *The man who was Thursday; a nightmare.* J. W.
        Arrowsmith, Bristol; Simpkin, Marshall, Lon-
        don, 1908, 330p, Cloth, Novel
02932   *The Napoleon of Notting Hill.* John Lane, Lon-
        don, 1904, 301p, Cloth, Novel
02933   *The return of Don Quixote.* Chatto & Windus,
        London, 1927, 312p, Cloth, Novel

CHETWODE, R. D.

02934   *The marble city, being the strange adventures*
        of three boys. Sampson Low, Marston, London,
        1895, 312p, Cloth, Novel

CHETWYND, BRIDGET

02935   *Future imperfect.* Hutchinson, London, 1946,
        174p, Cloth, Novel

CHETWYND-HAYES, R(onald Henry Glynn), 1919-
[*biography included*]

02936   *Cold terror.* Tandem, London, 1973, 240p, Paper
        Coll.
02937   *Cornish tales of terror.* Fontana, London,
        1970, 190p, Paper, Anth.
02938   *The dark man.* Sidgwick & Jackson, London,
        1964, 288p, Cloth, Novel
02939   *The elemental.* Fontana, London, 1974, 187p,
        Paper, Coll.
02940   *The man from the bomb.* Badger, London, 1959,
        157p, Paper, Novel
02941   *The ninth Fontana book of great ghost stories.*
        Fontana, London, 1973, 190p, Paper, Anth.
02942   *The tenth Fontana book of great ghost stories.*
        Fontana, London, 1974, 190p, Paper, Anth.
02943   *Terror by night.* Tandem, London, 1974, 186p,
        Paper, Coll.
02944   *The unbidden.* Tandem, London, 1971, 224p,
        Paper, Coll.
02945   *Welsh tales of terror.* Fontana, London, 1973,
        188p, Paper, Anth.

as Angus Campbell:

02946   *Scottish tales of terror.* Fontana, London,
        1972, 190p, Paper, Anth.

CHILDS, EDMUND BURTON
  see: BURTON, EDMUND

CHILDS, EDWARD EARLE

02947   *The wonders of Mouseland.* Abbey Press, New
        York, 1901, 268p, Cloth, Novel

CHILSON, ROBERT, 1945-

02948   *As the curtain falls.* DAW, New York, 1974,
        174p, Paper, Novel

CHILTON, CHARLES (Frederick William), 1917-

02949   *Journey into space.* Herbert Jenkins, London,
        1954, 220p, Cloth, Radio [Jet Morgan #1]
02950   *The Red Planet.* Herbert Jenkins, London, 1956,
        208p, Cloth, Radio [Jet Morgan #2]

CHILTON, CHARLES (Cont.)

    02951   *The world in peril.* Herbert Jenkins, London, 1960, 222p, Cloth, Novel

CHILTON, ELEANOR CARROLL, 1898-1949

    02952   *Shadows waiting; a novel in three parts.* John Day, New York, 1927, 289p, Cloth, Novel

CHILTON, H(enry) HERMAN

    02953   *The lost children.* Hutchinson, London, 1931, 288p, Cloth, Novel
    02954   *Talking totem.* Cornish Bros., Birmingham, 1938, 270p, Cloth, Novel
    02955   *Woman unsexed; a novel.* W. Foulsham, London, 1892, 330p, Cloth, Novel

CHILTON, IRMA, 1930-   [*biography included*]

    02956   *Goldie.* Hamish Hamilton, London, 1969, 92p, Cloth, Novel
          Nightmare. [see 02957A]
    02957   *String of time.* Topliners, London, 1968, 111p, Paper, Novel
    02957A retitled: *Nightmare.* Scholastic Book Services, New York, 1972, 95p, Paper, Novel
    02958   *Take away the flowers; &, Fuller's world.* Heinemann, London, 1967, 90p, Cloth, Coll.
    02959   *The time button.* Hamish Hamilton, London, 1970, 87p, Cloth, Novel

CHIPMAN, C(harles) P(hillips), 1878- , with W. P. Chipman

    02960   *An aërial runaway; the balloon adventures of Rod & Tod in North & South America.* Lothrop Publishing Co., Boston, 1901, 387p, Cloth, Novel

CHIPMAN, W(illiam) P(endleton), 1854-1937, with C. P. Chipman

    02960   *An aërial runaway; the balloon adventures of Rod & Tod in North & South America.* Lothrop Publishing Co., Boston, 1901, 387p, Cloth, Novel

CHISOM, SARAH, pseud. [Tom Filer]

    02961   *The fall of Casa Malvado.* Brandon House, North Hollywood, 1969, 190p, Paper, Novel

CHOATE, PEARSON

    02962   *The king who went on strike.* Eveleigh Nash, London, 1924, 287p, Cloth, Novel

THE CHRIST THAT IS TO BE
    see: COMPTON-RICKETT, JOSEPH

CHRISTIAN, CATHERINE (Mary)

    02963   *The pharaoh's secret.* R. T. S.--Lutterworth Press, London, 1940, 223p, Cloth, Novel

CHRISTIAN, EMELINE FATE

    02964   *The dams can break; a novel.* Storm Publishers, New York, 1951, 216p, Cloth, Novel

CHRISTIE, AGATHA (Mary Clarissa), 1890-1976 [*biography included*]

    02965   *The golden ball, and other stories.* Dodd, Mead, New York, 1971, 280p, Cloth, Coll.
    02966   *The hound of death, and other stories.* Odhams Press, London, 1933, 247p, Cloth, Coll.
    02967   *The mysterious Mr. Quin.* W. Collins Sons, London, 1930, 287p, Cloth, Coll.

CHRISTIE, DOUGLAS

    02968   *The striking force; a story of the North-West frontier.* Rich & Cowan, London, 1934, 311p, Cloth, Novel

CHRISTIE, ROBERT

    02969   *Inherit the night.* Farrar, Straus & Co., New York, 1949, 409p, Cloth, Novel

CHRISTMAS, GRACE V.

    02970   *What Father Cuthbert knew.* Sands & Co., London, 1920, 197p, Cloth, Coll.

"CHRISTMAS EVE" WITH THE SPIRITS

    02971   *"Christmas Eve" with the spirits; or, The canon's wanderings through ways unknown, with some further tidings of the lives of Scrooge and Tiny Tim.* Bull, Simmons, London, 1869, 90p, Cloth, Novel [parody of and sequel to Dickens' *A Christmas carol*]

CHRISTOPHER, JOHN, pseud. [Christopher Samuel Youd, 1922-] [*biography included*]

    02972   *Beyond the Burning Lands.* Hamish Hamilton, London, 1971, 159p, Cloth, Novel [Luke #2]
    02973   *The city of gold and lead.* Hamish Hamilton, London, 1967, 159p, Cloth, Novel [Tripods #2]
          Cloud on silver. [see 02984A]
    02974   *The death of grass.* Michael Joseph, London, 1956, 231p, Cloth, Novel
    02974A retitled: *No blade of grass; a novel.* Simon & Schuster, New York, 1957, 218p, Cloth, Novel
    02975   *Dom and Va.* Macmillan, New York, 1973, 154p, Cloth, Novel
    02976   *The guardians.* Macmillan, New York, 1970, 168p, Cloth, Novel
    02977   *The Little People.* Hodder & Stoughton, London, 1967, 190p, Cloth, Novel

CHRISTOPHER, JOHN (Cont.)

02978 *The long winter.* Simon & Schuster, New York, 1962, 253p, Cloth, Novel
02978A retitled: *The world in winter.* Eyre & Spottiswoode, London, 1962, 253p, Cloth, Novel
02979 *The Lotus Caves.* Hamish Hamilton, London, 1969, 156p, Cloth, Novel
       No blade of grass. [see 02974A]
02980 *Pendulum.* Simon & Schuster, New York, 1968, 254p, Cloth, Novel
       Planet in peril. [see 02990A]
02981 *The pool of fire.* Hamish Hamilton, London, 1968, 156p, Cloth, Novel [Tripods #3]
02982 *The Possessors.* Simon & Schuster, New York, 1964, 252p, Cloth, Novel
02983 *The Prince in Waiting.* Macmillan, New York, 1970, 182p, Cloth, Novel [Luke #1]
       The ragged edge. [see 02989A]
02984 *Sweeney's Island.* Simon & Schuster, New York, 1964, 218p, Cloth, Novel
02984A retitled: *Cloud on silver.* Hodder & Stoughton, London, 1964, 255p, Cloth, Novel
02985 *The sword of the spirits.* Hamish Hamilton, London, 1972, 159p, Cloth, Novel [Luke #3]
02986 *The twenty-second century.* Grayson & Grayson, London, 1954, 239p, Cloth, Coll.
02987 *The White Mountains.* Macmillan, New York, 1967, 184p, Cloth, Novel [Tripods #1]
02988 *Wild Jack.* Macmillan, New York, 1974, 147p, Cloth, Novel
       The world in winter. [see 02978A]
02989 *A wrinkle in the skin.* Hodder & Stoughton, London, 1965, 220p, Cloth, Novel
02989A retitled: *The ragged edge.* Simon & Schuster, New York, 1965, 254p, Cloth, Novel
02990 *The year of the comet.* Michael Joseph, London, 1955, 271p, Cloth, Novel
02990A retitled: *Planet in peril.* Avon, New York, 1959, 159p, Paper, Novel

THE CHRONICLES OF THE LAND OF COLUMBIA
    see: THE PROPHET JAMES

CHURCH, ALFRED J(ohn)

02991 *Stories of the magicians; Thalaba and the magicians of the Domdaniel; Rustem and the genii; Kehama and his sorceries.* Seeley & Co., London, 1887, 309p, Cloth, Coll. [based on Southey's poems, "Thalaba the Destroyer and the Curse of Kehama" and "The Story of Rustem"]

CHURCH, RICHARD (Thomas), 1893-1972

02992 *The French lieutenant; a ghost story.* Heinemann, London, 1971, 153p, Cloth, Novel

CHURCHILL, R(eginald) C(harles), 1916-   [biography included]

02993 *A short history of the future.* Werner Laurie, London, 1955, 192p, Cloth, Nonf. [a history compiled from various SF novels]

CICELLIS, KAY [Catherine-Mathilda Cicellis, 1926-   ]

02994 *The day the fish came out.* Bantam, New York, 1967, 138p, Paper, Movie

CLAIR, MARGARET ST.
    see: ST. CLAIR, MARGARET

CLAIRE, KEITH, pseud.
    see: ANDREWS, CLAIRE and ANDREWS, KEITH

CLAPP, PATRICIA, 1912-   [biography included]

02995 *Jane-Emily.* Lothrop, Lee & Shepard, New York, 1969, 160p, Cloth, Novel

CLAPPERTON, JANE HUME

02996 *A vision of the future, based on the application of ethical principles.* Swan Sonnenschein, London, 1904, 347p, Cloth, Novel

CLARENS, CARLOS (Figueredo y), 1936-   [biography included]

02997 *An illustrated history of the horror films.* G. P. Putnam's Sons, New York, 1967, 256p, Cloth, Nonf.
02997A retitled: *Horror movies--an illustrated survey.* Secker & Warburg, London, 1968, 264p, Cloth, Nonf.

CLARESON, THOMAS D(ean), 1926-   [biography included]

02998 *SF: a dream of other worlds.* Texas A & M University Library, College Station, TX, 1973, 15p, Paper, Nonf.
02999 *SF: the other side of realism; essays on modern fantasy and science fiction.* Bowling Green University Popular Press, Bowling Green, OH, 1971, 356p, Cloth, Nonf. Anth.
03000 *Science fiction criticism; an annotated checklist.* Kent State University Press, Kent, OH, 225p, Cloth, Nonf.
03001 *A spectrum of worlds.* Doubleday, Garden City, 1972, 311p, Cloth, Anth.

CLARK, ALFRED

03002 *The finding of Lot's wife.* Frederick A. Stokes, New York, 1896, 314p, Cloth, Novel; Sampson Low, Marston, London, 1896, 286p, Cloth, Novel

CLARK, CATHERINE ANTHONY, 1892-   [biography included]

03003 *The golden pine cone.* Macmillan, Toronto, 1950, 181p, Cloth, Novel

CLARK, CHARLES

03004 *Skyraft.* Newnes, London, 1937, 248p, Cloth, Novel

CLARK, CHARLES HEBER
    see: ADELER, MAX

CLARK, CHARLOTTE MOORE
    see: CLAY, CHARLES M.

CLARK, CURT, pseud.
    see: WESTLAKE, DONALD E.

CLARK, E. SCOTSON-
    see: SCOTSON-CLARK, E.

CLARK, F(rederick) LE GROS, 1892-

03005 *No stab can kill; a novel.* Boriswood, London, 1935, 286p, Cloth, Novel [spine title: *Between two men*]

CLARK, G. F. SCOTSON-
    see: SCOTSON-CLARK, G. F.

CLARK, GIDEON (Walter)

03006 *Substitute for living.* Ivor Nicholson & Watson, London, 1937, 318p, Cloth, Novel

CLARK, LAURENCE (Walter), 1914-   [*biography included*]

03007 *A father of the nation.* Veracity Ventures, Rickmansworth, UK, 1968, 256p, Cloth, Novel
03008 *More than moon.* Centaur Press, London, 1961, 227p, Cloth, Novel

CLARK, (William) RONALD, 1916-   [*biography included*]

03009 *The bomb that failed.* William Morrow, New York, 1969, 255p, Cloth, Novel
03010 *The last year of the old world; a fiction of history.* Jonathan Cape, London, 1970, 278p, Cloth, Novel
03011 *Queen Victoria's bomb.* Jonathan Cape, London, 1967, 256p, Cloth, Novel

CLARK, SUSIE CHAMPNEY, 1856-

as Cecil StClair:

03012 *To bear witness! a metaphysical sketch.* H. H. Carter, Boston, 1889, 180p, Cloth, Novel

as Susie C. Clark:

03012A *To bear witness! a metaphysical sketch.* Banner of Light Publishing Co., Boston, 1898, 180p, Cloth, Novel

CLARK, THOMAS MARCH, 1812-1903

03013 *John Whopper the newsboy.* Roberts Bros., Boston, 1871, 128p, Cloth, Novel [published anonymously]

CLARK, WILLIAM (Donaldson), 1916-   [*biography included*]

03014 *Number 10.* Heinemann, London, 1966, 215p, Cloth, Novel
03015 *Special relationship.* Heinemann, London, 1968, 223p, Cloth, Novel

CLARK, WILLIAM J.

03016 *An author index to the Doc Savage magazine.* M & B Publishers, Los Angeles, 1971, 21p, Paper, Nonf.

CLARKE, A(lfred) C(harles) G(eorge)

03017 *Into the darkness.* Digit, London, 1961, 160p, Paper, Novel
03018 *The mind master.* Digit, London, 1963, 160p, Paper, Novel

CLARKE, A(ubrey) V(incent), with H. K. Bulmer

02188 *Cybernetic controller.* Panther, London, 1952, 112p, Paper, Novel
02189 *Space treason.* Panther, London, 1952, 112p, Paper, Novel

CLARKE, (Charles) ALLEN, 1863-1935

03019 *Starved into surrender.* C. W. Daniel, London, 1904, 276p, Cloth, Novel
03020 *When the hurly-burly's done.* J. M. Dent & Sons, London, 1919, 242p, Cloth, Coll.

CLARKE, ARTHUR C(harles), 1917-   [*biography included*]

03021 *Across the sea of stars; an omnibus containing the complete novels Childhood's end and Earthlight, and eighteen other short stories.* Harcourt, Brace & Co., New York, 1959, 584p, Cloth, Coll.
03022 *Against the fall of night.* Gnome Press, New York, 1953, 223p, Cloth, Novel
03023 retitled: *The city and the stars.* Harcourt, Brace & Co., New York, 1956, 310p, Cloth, Novel [expanded]
03024 *An Arthur C. Clarke omnibus.* Sidgwick & Jackson, London, 1965, 596p, Cloth, Coll. [includes *Childhood's end*; *Prelude to space*; *Expedition to Earth*]
03025 *An Arthur C. Clarke second omnibus; A fall of moondust; Earthlight; The sands of Mars.* Sidgwick & Jackson, London, 1968, 603p, Cloth, Coll.
03026 *The best of Arthur C. Clarke.* Sidgwick & Jackson, London, 1973, 336p, Cloth, Coll.
03027 *Childhood's end.* Ballantine, New York, 1953, 217p, Cloth, Novel

CLARKE, ARTHUR C. (Cont.)

      The city and the stars. [see 03023]
03028   *The deep range.* Harcourt, Brace & Co., New York, 1957, 238p, Cloth, Novel
03029   *Dolphin Island; a story of the people of the sea.* Holt, Rinehart & Winston, New York, 1963, 186p, Cloth, Novel
03030   *Earthlight.* Ballantine, New York, 1955, 186p, Cloth, Novel
03031   *Expedition to Earth; eleven science-fiction stories.* Ballantine, New York, 1953, 169p, Cloth, Coll.
03032   *A fall of moondust.* Harcourt, Brace & World, New York, 1961, 248p, Cloth, Coll.
03033   *From the ocean, from the stars; an omnibus containing the complete novels The deep range and The city and the stars, and twenty-four short stories.* Harcourt, Brace & World, New York, 1962, 515p, Cloth, Coll.
03034   *Islands in the sky.* Sidgwick & Jackson, London, 1952, 190p, Cloth, Novel
03035   *The lion of Comarre; and, Against the fall of night.* Harcourt, Brace & World, New York, 1968, 213p, Cloth, Coll.
03036   *The lost worlds of 2001.* Signet, New York, 1972, 240p, Paper, Nonf. [includes parts of an early version of *2001: a space odyssey*]
      Master of space. [see 03041A]
03037   *The nine billion names of God; the best short stories of Arthur C. Clarke.* Harcourt, Brace & World, New York, 1967, 277p, Cloth, Coll.
03038   *Of time and stars; the worlds of Arthur C. Clarke.* Victor Gollancz, London, 1972, 208p, Cloth, Coll.
03039   *The other side of the sky.* Harcourt, Brace & Co., New York, 1958, 245p, Cloth, Coll.
03040   *Prelude to Mars; an omnibus containing the complete novels Prelude to space and The sands of Mars, and sixteen short stories.* Harcourt, Brace & World, New York, 1965, 497p, Cloth, Coll.
03041   *Prelude to space; a compelling realistic novel of interplanetary flight.* Galaxy Science Fiction Novel, New York, 1951, 160p, Paper, Novel
03041A retitled: *Master of space.* Lancer, New York, 1961, 158p, Paper, Novel
03041B retitled: *The space dreamers.* Lancer, New York, 1969, 158p, Paper, Novel
03042   *Reach for tomorrow.* Ballantine, New York, 1956, 166p, Cloth, Coll.
03043   *Rendezvous with Rama.* Victor Gollancz, London, 1973, 256p, Cloth, Novel
03044   *The sands of Mars.* Sidgwick & Jackson, London, 1951, 219p, Cloth, Novel
      The space dreamers. [see 03041B]
03045   *Tales from the White Hart.* Ballantine, New York, 1957, 151p, Paper, Coll.
03046   *Tales of ten worlds.* Harcourt, Brace & World, New York, 1962, 245p, Cloth, Coll.
03047   *Time probe; the sciences in science fiction.* Delacorte Press, New York, 1966, 242p, Cloth, Anth.
03048   *2001: a space odyssey.* New American Library, New York, 1968, 221p, Cloth, Movie
03049   *The wind from the Sun; stories of the space age.* Harcourt Brace Jovanovich, New York, 1972, 193p, Cloth, Coll.

CLARKE, COVINGTON, pseud. [Clark Venable, 1892-]

03050   *Desert wings.* Reilly & Lee, Chicago, 1930, 288p, Cloth, Novel
03051   *Mystery flight of the Q2.* Reilly & Lee, Chicago, 1932, 270p, Cloth, Novel

CLARKE, General F. M.

03052   *A maiden of Mars.* Charles H. Sergel, Chicago, 1892, 254p, Paper, Novel

CLARKE, FRANCIS H.

03053   *Morgan Rockefeller's will; a romance of 1991-2.* Clarke-Cree Publishing Co., Portland, OR, 1909, 306p, Cloth, Novel

CLARKE, GEORGE SYDENHAM
    see: SEAFORTH, A. NELSON

CLARKE, I(gnatius) F(rederick), 1918-   [*biography included*]

03054   *The battle of Dorking controversy; a collection of pamphlets.* Cornmarket Reprints, London, 1972, 158p, Cloth, Anth. [published anonymously]
03055   *The tale of the future, from the beginning to the present day; a check-list of those satires, ideal states, imaginary wars and invasions, political warnings and forecasts, interplanetary voyages and scientific romances--all located in an imaginary future period--that have been published in the United Kingdom between 1644 and 1960.* Library Association, London, 1961, 165p, Cloth, Nonf.
03056   *The tale of the future, from the beginning to the present day; an annotated bibliography of those satires, ideal states, imaginary wars and invasions, political warnings and forecasts, interplanetary voyages and scientific romances--all located in an imaginary future period--that have been published in the United Kingdom between 1644 and 1970.* Library Association, London, 1972, 196p, Paper, Nonf. [expanded]
03057   *Voices prophesying war, 1763-1984.* Oxford University Press, London, 1966, 254p, Cloth, Nonf.

CLARKE, ISABEL C(onstance), d. 1951

03058   *Whose name is legion; a novel.* Hutchinson, London, 1915, 347p, Cloth, Novel

CLARKE, JOAN B.

03059   *The happy planet.* Jonathan Cape, London, 1963, 192p, Cloth, Novel

CLARKE, JOSEPH CALVITT
    see: GRANT, RICHARD

CLARKE, MARY (Victoria) COWDEN, 1809-1908

03060 *Kit Bam's adventures; or, The yarns of an old mariner.* Grant & Griffith, London, 1849, 364p, Cloth, Novel

CLARKE, PAULINE, 1921-   [*biography included*]

03061 *The Twelve and the genii.* Faber & Faber, London, 1962, 185p, Cloth, Novel
03061A retitled: *The return of the Twelves.* Coward-McCann, New York, 1963, 253p, Cloth, Novel

CLARKE, T(homas) E(rnest) B(ennett), 1907-

03062 *The world was mine.* Bodley Head, London, 1964, 224p, Cloth, Novel

CLARKSON, HELEN, pseud.

03063 *The last day; a novel of the day after tomorrow.* Torquil, New York, 1959, 183p, Cloth, Novel

CLARO, JOSEPH

03064 *I can predict the future.* Lothrop, Lee & Shepard, New York, 1972, 96p, Cloth, Novel

CLASON, CLYDE B.

03065 *Ark of Venus.* Alfred A. Knopf, New York, 1955, 181p, Cloth, Novel
03066 *I am Lucifer; confessions of the devil.* Muhlenberg Press, Philadelphia, 1960, 254p, Cloth, Novel

CLAUDY, CARL H(arry), 1879-1957

03067 *Adventures in the unknown; a thousand years a minute.* Grosset & Dunlap, New York, 1933, 216p, Cloth, Novel [Adventures in the Unknown #2]
03068 *Adventures in the unknown; the Blue Grotto terror.* Grosset & Dunlap, New York, 1934, 234p, Cloth, Novel [Adventures in the Unknown #4]
03069 *Adventures in the unknown; the Land of No Shadow.* Grosset & Dunlap, New York, 1933, 214p, Cloth, Novel [Adventures in the Unknown #3]
03070 *Adventures in the unknown; the mystery men of Mars.* Grosset & Dunlap, New York, 1933, 216p, Cloth, Novel [Adventures in the Unknown #1]

CLAXTON, JOHN G., pseud. [Donna Brooks Beaumont]

03071 *She of the holy light.* Western Authors' Publishing Association, New York, 1893, 305p, Cloth, Novel

CLAXTON, OLIVER (Hazard Perry)

03072 *Heavens above! a novel.* John Day, New York, 1933, 215p, Cloth, Novel

CLAY, CHARLES M., pseud. [Charlotte Moore Clark, 1829-1895]

03073 *How she came into her kingdom; a romance,* by C. M. C. Jansen, McClurg, Chicago, 1878, 337p, Cloth, Novel
03073A retitled: *A daughter of the gods; or, How she came into her kingdom; a romance,* by Charles M. Clay. White, Stokes & Allen, New York, 1883, 337p, Cloth, Novel

CLAYTON, RICHARD
    see: HAGGARD, WILLIAM

CLEMENS, SAMUEL LANGHORNE
    see: TWAIN, MARK

CLEMENT, HAL, pseud. [Harry Clement Stubbs, 1922-   ] [*biography included*]

03074 *Close to critical.* Ballantine, New York, 1964, 190p, Paper, Novel [Mesklin #2]
03075 *Cycle of fire.* Ballantine, New York, 1957, 185p, Cloth, Novel
03076 *First flights to the Moon.* Doubleday, Garden City, 1970, 217p, Cloth, Anth.
    From outer space. [see 03080A]
03077 *Iceworld.* Gnome Press, New York, 1953, 216p, Cloth, Novel
03078 *Mission of gravity.* Doubleday, Garden City, 1954, 224p, Cloth, Novel [Mesklin #1]
03079 *Natives of space.* Ballantine, New York, 1965, 156p, Paper, Coll.
03080 *Needle.* Doubleday, Garden City, 1950, 222p, Cloth, Novel
03080A retitled: *From outer space.* Avon, New York, 1957, 188p, Paper, Novel
03081 *Ocean on top.* DAW, New York, 1973, 141p, Paper, Novel
03082 *The ranger boys in space.* L. C. Page, Boston, 1956, 257p, Cloth, Novel
03083 *Small changes.* Doubleday, Garden City, 1969, 230p, Cloth, Coll.
03083A retitled: *Space lash.* Dell, New York, 1969, 206p, Paper, Coll.
03084 *Star light.* Ballantine, New York, 1971, 279p, Paper, Novel [Mesklin #3]

CLEMENTS, BRUCE, 1931-   [*biography included*]

03085 *Two against the tide.* Farrar, Straus & Giroux, New York, 1967, 199p, Cloth, Novel

CLERY, WILLIAM EDWARD
    see: FRYERS, AUSTIN

CLEVE, JOHN, pseud.
    see: OFFUTT, ANDREW

CLEWES, HOWARD (Charles Vivian), 1912-

03086 *The mask of wisdom.* Bodley Head, London, 1948, 346p, Cloth, Novel

CLEWES, WINSTON (David Armstrong), 1906-1957

03087 *Sweet river in the morning; a novel.* D. Appleton-Century, New York, 1946, 227p, Cloth, Novel; Michael Joseph, London, 1946, 215p, Cloth, Novel

CLEWETT, G(eoffrey) C(harles)

03088 *Blood dynasty.* New English Library, London, 1973, 142p, Paper, Novel

CLIFFORD, JOHN, pseud.
  see: BAYLISS, J. C.

CLIFFORD, SARAH, 1916- [*biography included*]

03089 *Adam and his women.* Curtis, New York, 1972, 319p, Paper, Novel

CLIFT, DENISON (Halley), 1885-1961

03090 *Guns of Galt.* Edward J. Clode, New York, 1927, 312p, Cloth, Novel

CLIFTON, MARK (Irvin), 1906-1964

03091 *Eight keys to Eden.* Doubleday, Garden City, 1960, 187p, Cloth, Novel
03092 *When they come from space.* Doubleday, Garden City, 1962, 192p, Cloth, Novel

with Frank Riley:

03093 *They'd rather be right.* Gnome Press, New York, 1957, 189p, Cloth, Novel
03093A retitled: *The forever machine.* Galaxy Publishing Corp., New York, 1958, 159p, Paper, Novel

CLIFTON, WALLACE

03094 *Three paths; biography of a man who tried them all; an allegorical romance.* Typosium Publishers, Los Angeles, 1925, 141p, Cloth, Novel

CLINE, LEONARD (Lanson), 1893-1929

03095 *The dark chamber.* Viking Press, New York, 1927, 282p, Cloth, Novel

CLINGERMAN, MILDRED, 1918- [*biography included*]

03096 *A cupful of space.* Ballantine, New York, 1961, 142p, Paper, Coll.

CLINTON, EDWARD M.
  see: MORE, ANTHONY

CLIVE, DENNIS, pseud.
  see: FEARN, JOHN RUSSELL

CLOCK, HERBERT, with Eric Boetzel

01582 *The light in the sky.* Coward-McCann, New York, 1929, 304p, Cloth, Novel

CLOUDESLEY, HUBERT

03097 *Adventures of the remarkable twain.* Digby, Long, London, 1899, 175p, Cloth, Novel

CLOUSTON, J(oseph) STORER, 1870-1944

03098 *Button brains.* Herbert Jenkins, London, 1933, 312p, Cloth, Novel
03099 *The chemical baby.* Herbert Jenkins, London, 1934, 315p, Cloth, Novel
03100 *The man in steel.* Jarrolds Publishers, London, 1939, 256p, Cloth, Novel
03101 *Not since Genesis.* Jarrolds Publishers, London, 1938, 287p, Cloth, Novel

CLOW, MARTHA deMEY, 1932- [*biography included*]

03102 *Starbreed.* Ballantine, New York, 1970, 220p, Paper, Novel

CLOWES, (Sir) W(illiam) LAIRD, 1856-1905

03103 *The captain of the "Mary Rose"; a tale of tomorrow.* Tower Publishing Co., London, 1892, 308p, Cloth, Novel
03104 *The great naval war of 1887.* Hatchards, London, 1887, 58p, Paper, Novel [published anonymously]
03105 *The great peril, and how it was averted.* "Black & White," London, 1893, 133p, Cloth, Novel

with Alan H. Burgoyne:

02218 *Trafalgar refought.* Thomas Nelson & Sons, London, 1905, 328p, Cloth, Novel

COATES, JOHN, 1912-

03106 *Here today; a novel.* Methuen, London, 1949, 264p, Cloth, Novel

COATES, ROBERT M(yron), 1897-1973 [*biography included*]

03107 *The Eater of Darkness.* Contact Editions, Paris, 1926, 179p, Cloth?, Novel

COATSWORTH, ELIZABETH (Jane), 1893- [*biography included*]

03108 *The Enchanted; an incredible tale.* Pantheon, New York, 1951, 158p, Cloth, Novel
03109 *Mountain bride; an incredible tale.* Pantheon, New York, 1954, 154p, Cloth, Novel
03110 *Silky; an incredible tale.* Pantheon, New York, 1953, 144p, Cloth, Novel
03111 *The white room.* Pantheon, New York, 1958, 144p, Cloth, Novel

COBALT, MARTIN

03112 *Pool of swallows.* Thomas Nelson, Nashville, 1974, 139p, Cloth, Novel

COBB, MICHAEL, pseud. [Alfred Daniel Wintle]

03113 *Sir Peter's arm.* Chapman & Hall, London, 1929, 281p, Cloth, Novel

COBB, WELDON J. (Jr.)

03114 *A trip to Mars; or, The spur of adventure.* Round the World Library, Street & Smith, New York, 1928, 320p, Paper, Novel

COBBAN, J(ames) MacLAREN, 1849-1903

03115 *An African treasure; how the doctor and Sandy Peebles outwitted the Basha Misfiwa in his search for the meaning of the strange cryptogram, and how Jim Greathed, by the aid of the lovely Susannah, dispelled the mystery of "Bro'r Sol," together with their adventures in the interior of Morocco.* John Long, London, 1899, 320p, Cloth, Novel
03116 *Master of his fate.* William Blackwood & Sons, Edinburgh, 1890, 247p, Cloth, Novel
03117 *The tyrants of Kool-Sim.* H. Henry, London, 1896, 308p, Cloth, Novel

COBBE, F. P.
 see: NOSTRADAMUS, MERLIN

COBEY, HERBERT T.

03118 *The blonde Corinthian.* Farrar, Straus & Young, New York, 1951, 83p, Cloth, Novel

COBLENTZ, STANTON A(rthur), 1896- [*biography included*]

03119 *After 12,000 years.* Fantasy Publishing Co., Los Angeles, 1950, 295p, Cloth, Novel
 The animal people. [see 03121A]
03120 *The blue barbarians.* Avalon, New York, 1958, 223p, Cloth, Novel
03121 *The crimson capsule.* Avalon, New York, 1967, 190p, Cloth, Novel [Outlanders #2]
03121A retitled: *The animal people.* Belmont, New York, 1970, 156p, Paper, Novel [Outlanders #2]
03122 *The day the world stopped.* Avalon, New York, 1968, 189p, Cloth, Novel

03123 *Hidden world.* Avalon, New York, 1957, 224p, Cloth, Novel
03124 *Into Plutonian depths.* Avon, New York, 1950, 159p, Paper, Novel
03125 *The island people.* Belmont, New York, 1971, 188p, Paper, Novel [Outlanders #3]
03126 *The last of the great race.* Arcadia House, New York, 1964, 192p, Cloth, Novel
03127 *The lizard lords.* Avalon, New York, 1964, 192p, Cloth, Novel
03128 *Lord of Tranerica.* Avalon, New York, 1966, 190p, Cloth, Novel
03129 *The lost Comet.* Arcadia House, New York, 1964, 188p, Cloth, Novel
03130 *The Moon People.* Avalon, New York, 1964, 191p, Cloth, Novel [Outlanders #1]
03131 *Next door to the Sun.* Avalon, New York, 1960, 224p, Cloth, Novel
03132 *The planet of youth.* Fantasy Publishing Co., Los Angeles, 1952, 71p, Cloth, Novel
03133 *The runaway world.* Avalon, New York, 1961, 224p, Cloth, Novel
03134 *The sunken world; a romance of Atlantis.* Fantasy Publishing Co., Los Angeles, 1948, 184p, Cloth, Novel
03135 *Under the triple suns.* Fantasy Press, Reading, PA, 1955, 224p, Cloth, Novel
03136 *When the birds fly south.* Wings Press, Mill Valley, CA, 1945, 223p, Cloth, Novel
03137 *The wonder stick.* Cosmopolitan Book Corp., New York, 1929, 309p, Cloth, Novel

COBURN, PATRICIA, with Mary Kay Becker

01021 *Superspill; an account of the 1978 grounding at Bird Rocks.* Madrona Press, Seattle, 1974, 161p, Paper, Novel

COCKBURN, CLAUD
 see: HELVICK, JAMES

COCKCROFT, T(homas) G. L.

03138 *Index to fiction in Radio news and other magazines.* T. G. L. Cockcroft, Lower Hutt, New Zealand, 1970, 12p, Paper, Nonf.
03139 *Index to the verse in Weird tales.* Thomas G. L. Cockcroft, Lower Hutt, NZ, 1960, 17p, Paper, Nonf.
03140 *Index to the weird fiction magazines.* T. G. L. Cockcroft, Lower Hutt, NZ, 1962/1964, 101p in 2 vol., Paper, Nonf.
03141 *The tales of Clark Ashton Smith; a bibliography.* T. G. L. Cockcroft, Lower Hutt, NZ, 1951, 5p, Paper, Nonf.

COCKCROFT, W. P.

03142 *They came from Mars.* Gerald G. Swan, London, 1945, 16p, Paper, Story

COCKRELL, MARIAN (Brown), 1909-

03143 *Shadow castle.* McGraw-Hill, New York, 1945, 122p, Cloth, Novel

CODY, C. S., pseud. [Leslie Waller, 1923-   ]
[*biography included*]

03144   *The witching night.* World Publishing Co.,
        Cleveland, 1952, 255p, Cloth, Novel

COFFEY, EDWARD HOPE
    see: HOPE, EDWARD

COFFMAN, VIRGINIA (Edith), 1914-   [*biography included*]

03145   *Chalet Diabolique.* Lancer, New York, 1971,
        206p, Paper, Novel [Lucifer Cove #5]
03146   *The devil's mistress.* Lancer, New York,
        1970, 190p, Paper, Novel [Lucifer Cove #1]
03147   *The devil's virgin.* Lancer, New York, 1971,
        189p, Paper, Novel [Lucifer Cove #3]
03148   *From Satan, with love.* Lancer, New York,
        1971, 206p, Paper, Novel [Lucifer Cove #6]
03149   *Masque of Satan.* Lancer, New York, 1971,
        192p, Paper, Novel [Lucifer Cove #4]
03150   *Priestess of the damned.* Lancer, New York,
        1970, 190p, Paper, Novel [Lucifer Cove #2]

COGGS, Dr., pseud. [Ovidio Giberga]

03151   *Teddy in darkest Africa; or, The daring ex-
        ploits of Bwana-Tumbo; an exciting narrative
        of thrilling adventures, and a song to na-
        ture.* no publisher, Chicago?, 1910, 345p,
        Paper, Novel

COGSWELL, THEODORE (Rose), 1918-   [*biography included*]

03152   *The third eye.* Belmont, New York, 1968, 175p,
        Paper, Coll.
03153   *The wall around the world.* Pyramid, New York,
        1962, 160p, Paper, Coll.

COHEN, GENGHIS, pseud.

03154   *The erotic spectacles.* Olympia Press, New
        York, 1971,   , Paper, Novel

COHN, EMIL BERNHARD, 1881-1948

03155   *Stories and fantasies from the Jewish past.*
        Jewish Publication Society of America, Phila-
        delphia, 1951, 262p, Cloth, Coll.

COLBECK, ALFRED

03156   *When the Earth swung over; a strange story of
        the mysterious white people of the Napo.*
        "Boy's Own Paper" Office, London, 1926,
        282p, Cloth, Novel

COLBURN, FRONA EUNICE WAIT, 1859-1946

as Frona Eunice Wait:

03157   *Yermah the Dorado.* W. Doxey, San Francisco,
        1897, 350p, Cloth, Novel

as Frona Eunice Wait Colburn:

03157A *Yermah the Dorado; the story of a lost race.*
        Alice Harriman Co., New York, 1913, 433p,
        Cloth, Novel

COLBY, MARIE W.

03158   *Witch of the sea.* House-Warven Publishers,
        Hollywood, 1954, 236p, Cloth, Novel

COLCORD, LINCOLN, 1883-1947

03159   *The drifting diamond.* Macmillan, New York,
        1912, 279p, Cloth, Novel

COLE, BURT, 1930-

03160   *The Funco file.* Doubleday, Garden City, 1969,
        282p, Cloth, Novel
03161   *Subi, the volcano.* Macmillan, New York, 1957,
        220p, Cloth, Novel

COLE, CHARLES

03162   *Visitors from Mars.* Beattie & Hofmann, Port-
        land, OR, 1901, 99p, Paper, Novel

COLE, (Senator) CORNELIUS, 1822-1924

03163   *California three hundred and fifty years ago;
        Manuelo's narrative, translated from the
        Portuguese, by a pioneer.* Samuel Carson,
        San Francisco, 1888, 333p, Cloth, Novel
        [published anonymously]

COLE, CYRUS

03164   *The auroraphone; a romance.* Charles H. Kerr,
        Chicago, 1890, 249p, Cloth, Novel

COLE, EVERETT B., 1910-

03165   *The Philosophical Corps.* Gnome Press, Hicks-
        ville, NY, 1961, 187p, Cloth, Novel

COLE, IRA A(lbert), 1883-

03166   *Ibe of Atlan.* Johnson Publishing Co., Boulder
        Col., 1947, 358p, Cloth, Novel

COLE, ROBERT WILLIAM

03167   *The death trap.* Greening & Co., London, 1907,
        312p, Cloth, Novel
03168   *The struggle for empire; a story of the year
        2236.* Elliot Stock, London, 1900, 213p,
        Cloth, Novel

COLE, W(alter) R(andall), 1933-   [*biography included*]

03169   *A checklist of science-fiction anthologies.*
        W. R. Cole, Brooklyn, 1964, 374p, Cloth, Nor

COLEMAN, F(rancis) X(avier) J.

03170   *Philip, the draftsman*. J. B. Lippincott,
        Philadelphia, 1970, 158p, Cloth, Novel

COLEMAN, JAMES NELSON

03171   *The null-frequency impulser*. Berkley Medal-
        lion, New York, 1969, 191p, Paper, Novel
03172   *Seeker from the stars*. Berkley Medallion,
        New York, 1967, 159p, Paper, Novel

COLERIDGE, CHRISTABEL (Rose), 1843-1921

03173   *The thought-rope*. Hurst & Blackett, London,
        1898, 235p, Cloth, Novel

COLERIDGE, JOHN, pseud.
    see: BINDER, EARL and BINDER, OTTO

COLERIDGE, SARA, 1802-1852

03174   *Phantasmion*. W. Pickering, London, 1837, 387p,
        Cloth, Novel [published anonymously]
03174A *Phantasmion; a fairy tale*, by Sara Coleridge.
        Henry S. King, London, 1874, 348p, Cloth,
        Novel

COLES, CYRIL HENRY, 1899-1965 [*biography included*], with Adelaide Manning as Manning
Coles

03175   *Brief candles*. Doubleday, Garden City, 1954,
        252p, Cloth, Novel [Latimer #1]
03175A *Brief candles*, by Francis Gaite. Hodder &
        Stoughton, London, 1954, 189p, Cloth, Novel
        [Latimer #1]
03176   *Come and go*. Doubleday, Garden City, 1958,
        236p, Cloth, Novel [Latimer #3]
03176A *Come and go*, by Francis Gaite. Hodder &
        Stoughton, London, 1958, 192p, Cloth, Novel
        [Latimer #3]
03177   *The emperor's bracelet*. University of London
        Press, London, 1947, 234p, Cloth, Novel
03178   *The far traveller*. Doubleday, Garden City,
        1956, 224p, Cloth, Novel
03178A *The far traveller*, by Francis Gaite. Hodder
        & Stoughton, London, 1957, 190p, Cloth,
        Novel
03179   *Great Caesar's ghost*. Doubleday, Doran, Gar-
        den City, 1943, 225p, Cloth, Novel
03180   *Happy returns*. Doubleday, Garden City, 1955,
        224p, Cloth, Novel [Latimer #2]

with Adelaide Manning as Francis Gaite:

        Brief candles. [see 03175A]
        Come and go. [see 03176A]
        The far traveller. [see 03178A]

COLES, MANNING, pseud.
    see: COLES, CYRIL and MANNING, ADELAIDE

COLLADAY, MORRISON (M.)

03181   *When the Moon fell*. Stellar Publishing Corp.,
        New York, 1929, 24p, Paper, Story

COLLIER, DWIGHT A., 1932-

03182   *Kathy's visit to Mars; an adventure story for
        children*. Exposition Press, New York, 1955,
        53p, Cloth, Novel

COLLIER, JOHN (Henry Noyes), 1901-

03183   *The devil and all*. Nonesuch Press, London,
        1934, 124p, Cloth, Coll.
03184   *Fancies and goodnights*. Doubleday, Garden City,
        1951, 364p, Cloth, Coll.
03184A retitled: *Of demons and darkness*. Corgi, Lon-
        don, 1965, 303p, Paper, Coll. [abridged]
        Full circle. [see 03192A]
03185   *Green thoughts*. William Jackson [actually
        Joiner & Steele], London, 1932, 56p, Cloth,
        Novel
03186   *Green thoughts, and other strange tales*. Edi-
        tions for the Armed Services, New York, 1943,
        287p, Paper, Coll.
03187   *His monkey wife; or, Married to a chimp*. Peter
        Davies, London, 1930, 274p, Cloth, Novel
03188   *The John Collier reader*. Alfred A. Knopf, New
        York, 1972, 571p, Cloth, Coll. [includes
        His monkey wife and selected stories]
03189   *No traveller returns*. White Owl Press, London,
        1931, 62p, Cloth, Novel
        Of demons and darkness. [see 03184A]
03190   *Pictures in the fire*. Rupert Hart-Davis, Lon-
        don, 1958, 190p, Cloth, Coll.
03191   *Presenting moonshine; stories*. Macmillan, Lon-
        don, 1941, 351p, Cloth, Coll.
03192   *Tom's a-cold; a tale*. Macmillan, London, 1933,
        320p, Cloth, Novel
03192A retitled: *Full circle; a tale*. D. Appleton,
        New York, 1933, 290p, Cloth, Novel
03193   *The touch of nutmeg, and more unlikely stories*.
        Press of the Readers Club, New York, 1943,
        247p, Cloth, Coll.
03194   *Variation on a theme*. Grayson & Grayson, Lon-
        don, 1935, 48p, Cloth, Story

COLLINGWOOD, HARRY, pseud. [William Joseph
Cosens Lancaster, 1851-1922]

03195   *The cruise of the "Flying Fish," the airship-
        submarine*. Sampson Low, Marston, London,
        1924, 314p, Cloth, Novel [Flying Fish #3]
03196   *Geoffrey Harrington's adventures*. Society for
        Promoting Christian Knowledge, London, 1907,
        511p, Cloth, Novel
03197   *Harry Escombe; a tale of adventure in Peru*.
        Blackie & Son, London, 1910, 303p, Cloth,
        Novel
        In search of El Dorado. [see 03199A]
03198   *The log of the "Flying Fish"; a story of aerial
        and submarine peril and adventure*. Blackie
        & Son, London, 1886, 384p, Cloth, Novel
        [Flying Fish #1]
03199   *A pair of adventurers in search of El Dorado*.
        Sampson Low, Marston, London, 1915, 312p,
        Cloth, Novel
03199A retitled: *In search of El Dorado*. Sampson
        Low, Marston, London, 1925, 280p, Cloth,
        Novel
03200   *With airship and submarine; a tale of adven-
        ture*. Blackie & Son, London, 1907, 376p,
        Cloth, Novel [Flying Fish #2]

COLLINS, BARNABAS, pseud., with Quentin Collins

03201 *The Dark shadows book of vampires and were-wolves.* Paperback Library, New York, 1970, 156p, Paper, Anth.

COLLINS, CHARLES M.

03202 *A feast of blood.* Avon, New York, 1967, 190p, Paper, Anth.
03203 *Fright.* Avon, New York, 1963, 141p, Paper, Anth.
03204 *A walk with the beast.* Avon, New York, 1969, 192p, Paper, Anth.

COLLINS, COLIN

03205 *The Blinding Light; a tale.* Greening & Co., London, 1910, 319p, Cloth, Novel
03206 *Four millions a year.* Greening & Co., London, 1911, 314p, Cloth, Novel
03207 *The human mole.* Greening & Co., London, 1909, 338p, Cloth, Novel

COLLINS, ERROLL

03208 *Mariners of space.* Lutterworth Press, London, 1944, 240p, Cloth, Novel
03209 *Submarine City.* Lutterworth Press, London, 1946, 247p, Cloth, Novel

COLLINS, GILBERT, 1890-

03210 *Flower of Asia; a novel of Nihon.* Duckworth, London, 1922, 320p, Cloth, Novel
03211 *The Starkenden quest.* Duckworth, London, 1925, 316p, Cloth, Novel
03212 *The valley of eyes unseen.* Duckworth, London, 1923, 327p, Cloth, Novel

COLLINS, HUNT, pseud.
   see: HUNTER, EVAN

COLLINS, J. L.
   see: JONQUIL

COLLINS, (Carroll) LEN

03213 *Science fiction collections index.* A. Hayes, South Porcupine, Ont., Canada, 1970/71, 2vol/1, Paper, Nonf.

COLLINS, MABEL [Mabel Collins Cook, 1851-1927]

03214 *The blossom and the fruit; a true story of a black magician.* The author, London, 1888, 332p, Cloth, Novel
03215 *The idyll of the White Lotus,* by M. C., Fellow of the Theosophical Society. Reeves & Turner, London, 1884, 141p, Cloth, Novel
03215A *The idyll of the White Lotus,* by Mabel Collins. John W. Lovell, New York, 1890, 315p, Cloth, Novel

03216 *Morial the Mahatma.* Lovell, Gestefeld, New York, 1892, 270p, Cloth, Novel
03217 *The story of Sensa; an interpretation of The idyll of the White Lotus.* Theosophical Publishing Society, London, 1911, 95p, Paper, Nonf.
03218 *Suggestion.* Lovell, Gestefeld, New York, 1892, 276p, Paper, Novel

COLLINS, MICHAEL, pseud.
   see: LYNDS, DENNIS

COLLINS, (Edward James) MORTIMER, 1827-1876

03219 *Transmigration.* Hurst & Blackett, London, 1874, vol. I-320p, II-264p, III-292p, Cloth, Novel

COLLINS, QUENTIN, pseud., with Barnabas Collins

03201 *The Dark shadows book of vampires and werewolves.* Paperback Library, New York, 1970, 156p, Paper, Anth.

COLLINS, V(ere) H(enry Gratz)

03220 *Ghosts and marvels; a selection of uncanny tales from Daniel Defoe to Algernon Blackwood.* Humphrey Milford, Oxford University Press, London, 1924, 506p, Cloth, Anth.
03221 *More ghosts and marvels; a selection of uncanny tales from Sir Walter Scott to Michael Arlen.* Humphrey Milford, Oxford University Press, London, 1927, 498p, Cloth, Anth.

COLLINS, (William) WILKIE, 1824-1889

03222 *The frozen deep, and other tales.* Richard Bentley & Son, London, 1874, 2vol, Cloth, Coll.
03223 *The ghost's touch; a new story.* John W. Lovell, New York, 1885, 116p, Paper, Coll.
03224 *The ghost's touch, and other stories.* Harper & Bros., New York, 1885, 198p, Cloth, Coll. [different contents]
03225 *The ghost's touch; and, Percy and the prophet.* George Munro's Sons, New York, 1885, Paper, Coll. [different contents]
03226 *The haunted hotel; a mystery of modern Venice.* Chatto & Windus, London, 1878, 341p, Cloth, Novel
03227 *Tales of terror and the supernatural.* Dover, New York, 1972, 294p, Paper, Coll.
03228 *The two destinies; a romance.* Chatto & Windus, London, 1876, 2vol, Cloth, Novel

COLMORE, G.
   see: DUNN, GERTRUDE

COLOMB, Rear-Admiral P(hilip Howard), 1831-1899, with J. F. Maurice, F. N. Maude, Archibald Forbes, Charles Lowe, D. Christie Murray and F. Scudamore

03229 *The Great War of 189-; a forecast.* William Heinemann, London, 1893, 308p, Cloth, Novel

COLTON, ABIGAIL

03230 *The tale of Christopher; a fantasia.* Purdy
        Publishing Co., Chicago, 1917, 144p, Cloth,
        Novel

COLVILLE, W(illiam Wilberforce) J(uvenal),
1862-1917

03231 *Dashed against the rock; a romance of the
        coming age.* Colby & Rich, Boston, 1894,
        310p, Cloth, Novel
03232 *Onesimus Templeton; a psychical romance.*
        Edward Lovell, New York, 1900?, 255p, Cloth,
        Novel
03233 *The throne of Eden; a psychical romance.* Ban-
        ner of Light Publishing Co., Boston, 1902,
        468p, Cloth, Novel

COLVIN, IAN (Goodhope), 1912-

03234 *Domesday village.* Falcon Press, London, 1948,
        126p, Cloth, Novel

COLVIN, JAMES, pseud.
    see: MOORCOCK, MICHAEL

COLWYN, JOHN

03235 *A city without a church.* Arthur H. Stockwell,
        London, 1919, 117p, Cloth, Novel

COMBE, WILLIAM, 1741-1823

03236 *The devil upon two sticks in England, being a
        continuation of Le diable boiteux of Le
        Sage.* Logographic Press, J. Walter, J.
        Richardson, London, 1790, 4vol, Cloth, Novel
        [published anonymously; sequel to Le Sage's
        Devil upon two sticks]

"COME NOT, LUCIFER!"
    see: VERNER, GERALD

COMEAU, ALEXANDER de

03237 *Monk's magic.* Methuen, London, 1931, 250p,
        Cloth, Novel

COMER, RALPH, pseud. [John Sanders]

03238 *The mirror of Dionysos.* Tandem, London, 1969,
        187p, Paper, Novel [Robert Lawson #2]
03238A retitled: *To dream of evil.* Award, New York,
        1973, 186p, Paper, Novel [Robert Lawson #2]
03239 *The witchfinders.* Tandem, London, 1968, 189p,
        Paper, Novel [Robert Lawson #1]

COMFORT, WILL LEVINGTON, 1878-1932, with
Zamin Ki Dost

03240 *Son of power.* Doubleday, Page, Garden City,
        1920, 350p, Cloth, Novel

THE COMING RACE
    see: LYTTON, EDWARD

THE COMMISSIONER
    see: JAMES, G. P. R.

COMMON TIME

03241 *Common time.* American Science Fiction, Sydney,
        1955, 34p, Paper, Anth.

COMP, T. ALLAN, 1942-   [*biography included*],
with Faith K. Pizor

03242 *The man in the Moone, and other Lunar fantasies.*
        Praeger, New York, 1971, 230p, Cloth, Anth.

A COMPLETE ACCOUNT OF THE LATE DISCOVERIES IN
THE MOON
    see: LOCKE, RICHARD ADAMS

COMPTON, D(avid) G(uy), 1930-   [*biography included*]

03243 *Chronocules.* Ace, New York, 1970, 255p, Paper,
        Novel
03243A retitled: *Hot wireless sets, aspirin tablets,
        the sandpaper sides of used matches, and
        something that might have been castor oil.*
        Michael Joseph, London, 1971, 206p, Cloth,
        Novel
        The continuous Katherine Mortenhoe. [see
        03250A]
        The electric crocodile. [see 03248A]
03244 *Farewell, Earth's bliss.* Hodder & Stoughton,
        London, 1966, 191p, Cloth, Novel
        *Hot wireless sets, aspirin tablets, the sand-
        paper sides of used matches, and something
        that might have been castor oil.* [see 03243A]
03245 *The missionaries.* Ace, New York, 1972, 222p,
        Paper, Novel
03246 *The quality of mercy.* Hodder & Stoughton, Lon-
        don, 1965, 157p, Cloth, Novel
03247 *The silent multitude.* Hodder & Stoughton, Lon-
        don, 1967, 190p, Cloth, Novel
03248 *The steel crocodile.* Ace, New York, 1970,
        254p, Paper, Novel
03248A retitled: *The electric crocodile.* Hodder &
        Stoughton, London, 1970, 222p, Cloth, Novel
03249 *Synthajoy.* Hodder & Stoughton, London, 1968,
        190p, Cloth, Novel
03250 *The unsleeping eye.* DAW, New York, 1974, 221p,
        Paper, Novel
03250A retitled: *The continuous Katherine Mortenhoe;
        a novel.* Victor Gollancz, London, 1974,
        256p, Cloth, Novel

COMPTON-RICKETT, Sir JOSEPH, 1847-1919

03251 *The Christ that is to be; a latter-day romance.*
        Chapman & Hall, London, 1891, 279p, Cloth,
        Novel [published anonymously]

COMSTOCK, SARAH, d. 1960

03252　*The Moon is made of green cheese.* Doubleday, Doran, Garden City, 1929, 310p, Cloth, Novel

COMYNS(-Carr), BARBARA (Irene Veronica), 1912-

03253　*The vet's daughter.* Heinemann, London, 1959, 190p, Cloth, Novel

CONAWAY, J. C.

03254　*Angel possessed.* Belmont Tower, New York, 1974, 197p, Paper, Novel

CONDON, RICHARD (Thomas), 1915-　[*biography included*]

03255　*Winter kills.* Dial Press, New York, 1974, 304p, Cloth, Novel

CONDRAY, BRUNO G., pseud. [Leslie George Humphreys]

03256　*The Dissentizens.* Tit-Bits Science-Fiction Library, London, 1954, 64p, Paper, Novel
03257　*Exile from Jupiter.* Tit-Bits Science-Fiction Library, London, 1955, 64p, Paper, Novel

as Vektis Brack, house pseud.:

01740　*Odyssey in space.* Gannet Press, London, 1954, 127p, Paper, Novel

CONEY, MICHAEL G(reatrex), 1932-　[*biography included*]

03258　*Friends come in boxes.* DAW, New York, 1973, 160p, Paper, Novel
03259　*The Hero of Downways.* DAW, New York, 1973, 188p, Paper, Novel
03260　*Mirror image.* DAW, New York, 1972, 174p, Paper, Novel
03261　*Monitor found in orbit.* DAW, New York, 1974, 172p, Paper, Coll.
03262　*Syzygy.* Ballantine, New York, 1973, 216p, Paper, Novel
03263　*Winter's children.* Victor Gollancz, London, 1974, 192p, Cloth, Novel

CONGDON, DON

03264　*Stories for the dead of night.* Dell, New York, 1957, 288p, Paper, Anth.
03265　*Tales of love and horror.* Ballantine, New York, 1961, 144p, Paper, Anth.

with Michael Congdon:

03266　*Alone by night.* Ballantine, New York, 1962, 144p, Paper, Anth.

CONGDON, MICHAEL, with Don Congdon

03266　*Alone by night.* Ballantine, New York, 1962, 144p, Paper, Anth.

CONGDON, RICHARD

03267　*The star spangled crunch.* Bantam, New York, 1974, 131p, Paper, Novel

CONKLIN, (Edward) GROFF, 1904-1968 [*biography included*]

03268　*Another part of the galaxy.* Fawcett Gold Medal, Greenwich, 1966, 224p, Paper, Anth.
03269　*The best of science fiction.* Crown Publishers, New York, 1946, 785p, Cloth, Anth.
03270　*Big book of science fiction.* Crown Publishers, New York, 1950, 545p, Cloth, Anth.
03271　*Br-r-r-! 10 chilling tales.* Avon, New York, 1959, 192p, Paper, Anth.
03272　*Crossroads in time.* Permabooks, Garden City, 1953, 312p, Paper, Anth.
03273　*Dimension 4.* Pyramid, New York, 1964, 159p, Paper, Anth.
03274　*Elsewhere and elsewhen.* Berkley Medallion, New York, 1968, 253p, Paper, Anth.
03274A　retitled: *Science fiction elsewhen.* Rapp & Whiting, London, 1970, 152p, Cloth, Anth. [abridged]
03274B　retitled: *Science fiction elsewhere.* Rapp & Whiting, London, 1970, 166p, Cloth, Anth. [abridged; 03274A and 03274B together comprise the original volume]
　　　　Enemies in space. [see 03283A]
03275　*Five-odd.* Pyramid, New York, 1964, 188p, Paper, Anth.
03275A　retitled: *Possible tomorrows; science fiction.* Sidgwick & Jackson, London, 1972, 188p, Cloth, Anth.
03276　*5 unearthly visions.* Gold Medal, Greenwich, 1965, 175p, Paper, Anth.
03277　*4 for the future; science-fiction short novels.* Pyramid, New York, 1959, 160p, Paper, Anth.
03278　*Giants unleashed.* Grosset & Dunlap, New York, 1965, 248p, Cloth, Anth.
03278A　retitled: *Minds unleashed.* Tempo, New York, 1970, 248p, Paper, Anth.
03279　*The graveyard reader.* Ballantine, 1958, 156p, Paper, Anth.
03280　*Great science fiction by scientists.* Collier, New York, 1962, 313p, Paper, Anth.
03281　*Great stories of space travel.* Tempo, New York, 1963, 256p, Paper, Anth.
03282　*In the grip of terror.* Permabooks, Garden City, 1951, 364p, Paper, Anth.
03283　*Invaders of Earth.* Vanguard Press, New York, 1952, 333p, Cloth, Anth.
03283A　retitled: *Enemies in space.* Digit, London, 1962, 159p, Paper, Anth. [abridged]
　　　　Minds unleashed. [see 03278A]
03284　*Omnibus of science fiction.* Crown Publishers, New York, 1952, 562p, Cloth, Anth.
03284A　retitled: *Science fiction omnibus.* Berkley Medallion, New York, 1956, 187p, Paper, Anth. [abridged]
03284B　retitled: *Strange adventures in science fiction.* Grayson & Grayson, London, 1954, 240p, Cloth, Anth. [abridged]
03284C　retitled: *Strange travels in science fiction.* Grayson & Grayson, London, 1954, 256p, Cloth, Anth. [abridged; 03284B and 03284C together comprise the original volume]
03285　*Operation future.* Permabooks, New York, 1955, 356p, Paper, Anth.

CONKLIN, GROFF (Cont.)

       Possible tomorrows. [see 03275A]
03286 *Possible worlds of science fiction.* Vanguard
      Press, New York, 1951, 372p, Cloth, Anth.
03287 *Science-fiction adventures in dimension.* Van-
      guard Press, New York, 1953, 354p, Cloth,
      Anth.
03288 *Science-fiction adventures in mutation.* Van-
      guard Press, New York, 1955, 316p, Cloth,
      Anth.
03288A retitled: *Selected stories from Science-fic-
      tion adventures in mutation.* Berkley Medal-
      lion, New York, 1965, 174p, Paper, Anth.
      [abridged]
      Science fiction elsewhen. [see 03274A]
      Science fiction elsewhere. [see 03274B]
03289 *The science fiction galaxy.* Permabooks, New
      York, 1950, 242p, Cloth, Anth.
03290 *Science fiction oddities.* Berkley Medallion,
      New York, 1966, 256p, Paper, Anth.
03290A retitled: *Science fiction oddities, second
      series.* Rapp & Whiting, London, 1969, 160p,
      Cloth, Anth. [abridged]
      Science fiction omnibus. [see 03284A]
03291 *Science fiction terror tales.* Gnome Press,
      New York, 1955, 262p, Cloth, Anth.
03292 *Science-fiction thinking machines; robots,
      androids, computers.* Vanguard Press, New
      York, 1954, 370p, Cloth, Anth.
03292A retitled: *Selections from Science-fiction
      thinking machines.* Bantam, New York, 1955,
      183p, Paper, Anth. [abridged]
      *Selected stories from Science-fiction adven-
      tures in mutation.* [see 03288A]
      *Selections from Science-fiction thinking ma-
      chines.* [see 03292A]
03293 *Seven come infinity.* Fawcett Gold Medal, Green-
      wich, 1966, 288p, Paper, Anth.
03294 *Seven trips through time and space.* Fawcett
      Gold Medal, Greenwich, 1968, 256p, Paper,
      Anth.
03295 *17 x infinity.* Dell, New York, 1963, 272p,
      Paper, Anth.
03296 *6 great short novels of science fiction.* Dell,
      New York, 1954, 384p, Paper, Anth.
03297 *Six great short science fiction novels.* Dell,
      New York, 1960, 350p, Paper, Anth.
      Strange adventures in science fiction. [see
      03284B]
      Strange travels in science fiction. [see
      03284C]
03298 *13 above the night.* Dell, New York, 1965,
      286p, Paper, Anth.
03299 *13 great stories of science fiction.* Gold
      Medal, Greenwich, 1960, 192p, Paper, Anth.
03300 *A treasury of science fiction.* Crown Publi-
      shers, New York, 1948, 517p, Cloth, Anth.
03301 *12 great classics of science fiction.* Gold
      Medal, Greenwich, 1963, 192p, Paper, Anth.
03302 *Twisted.* Belmont, New York, 1962, 189p, Paper,
      Anth.
03303 *Worlds of when; five short novels.* Pyramid,
      New York, 1962, 159p, Paper, Anth.

with Isaac Asimov:

00589 *Fifty short science fiction tales.* Collier,
      New York, 1963, 287p, Paper, Anth.

with Lucy Conklin:

03304 *The supernatural reader.* J. B. Lippincott,
      Philadelphia, 1953, 349p, Cloth, Anth.

with Noah D. Fabricant:

03305 *Great science fiction about doctors.* Collier,
      New York, 1963, 412p, Paper, Anth.

CONKLIN, LUCY, d. 1954, with Groff Conklin

03304 *The supernatural reader.* J. B. Lippincott,
      Philadelphia, 1953, 349p, Cloth, Anth.

CONLY, ROBERT L.
    see: O'BRIEN, ROBERT C.

CONNELL, ALAN

03306 *Lords of serpent land.* Currawong Publishing
      Co., Sydney, 1945, 62p, Paper, Novel [Serpent
      Land #1]
03307 *Prisoners in serpent land.* Currawong Publi-
      shing Co., Sydney, 1945, 60p, Paper, Novel
      [cover title: *Prisoners of serpent land*]
      [Serpent Land #2]
03308 *Warriors of serpent land.* Currawong Publishing
      Co., Sydney, 1945, 64p, Paper, Novel [Serpent
      Land #3]

CONNELLY, J(ames) H(enderson), 1840-1903

03309 *Neila Sen; and, My casual death.* United States
      Book Co., New York, 1890, 345p, Cloth, Coll.

CONNINGTON, J. J., pseud. [Alfred Walter Stewart, 1880-1947]

03310 *Nordenholt's million.* Constable, London, 1923,
      303p, Cloth, Novel

CONNOLLY, MYLES, 1898-1964

03311 *The bump on Brannigan's head.* Macmillan, New
      York, 1950, 157p, Cloth, Novel

CONNOLLY, ROY, with Frank McIlraith

03312 *Invasion from the air; a prophetic novel.*
      Grayson & Grayson, London, 1934, 320p, Cloth,
      Novel

CONQUEST, JOAN, 1883?-1941

03313 *Leonie of the jungle.* T. Werner Laurie, London,
      1921, 253p, Cloth, Novel
03314 *The reckoning.* T. Werner Laurie, London, 1931,
      242p, Cloth, Novel

CONQUEST, (George) ROBERT (Acworth), 1917-
[biography included]

03315 *A world of difference; a modern novel of sci-
      ence and imagination.* Ward, Lock, London,
      1955, 192p, Cloth, Novel

CONQUEST, ROBERT (Cont.)

with Kingsley Amis:

00246 *Spectrum; a science fiction anthology.* Victor
          Gollancz, London, 1961, 304p, Cloth, Anth.
00246A retitled: *Spectrum I; a science fiction an-
          thology.* Pan, London, 1964, 316p, Paper,
          Anth.
00247 *Spectrum II; a second science fiction antholo-
          gy.* Victor Gollancz, London, 1962, 271p,
          Cloth, Anth.
00248 *Spectrum III; a third science fiction antholo-
          gy.* Victor Gollancz, London, 1963, 272p,
          Cloth, Anth.
00249 *Spectrum IV; a science fiction anthology.*
          Victor Gollancz, London, 1965, 320p, Cloth,
          Anth.
00250 *Spectrum V; a science fiction anthology.* Vic-
          tor Gollancz, London, 1966, 272p, Cloth,
          Anth.

CONRAD, EARL, 1912-   [*biography included*]

03316 *The da Vinci machine; tales of the population
          explosion.* Fleet Press Corp., New York,
          1969, 189p, Cloth, Coll.
03317 *The premier.* Doubleday, Garden City, 1963,
          295p, Cloth, Novel

CONRAD, JOSEPH [Josef Teodor Konrad Nalecz
Korzeniowski, 1857-1924], with Ford M. Hueffer

03318 *The inheritors; an extravagant story.* William
          Heinemann, London, 1901, 324p, Cloth, Novel

CONRAD, PAUL

03319 *Ex Minus.* Robert Hale, London, 1974, 191p,
          Cloth, Novel

CONROW, HERMAN
    see: ORB, CLAY

CONROY, RICK

03320 *Mission from Mars.* Panther, London, 1952,
          112p, Paper, Novel

THE CONSOLIDATOR
    see: DEFOE, DANIEL

CONSTABLE, FRANK CHALLICE
    see: THE CURSE OF INTELLECT

CONSTANTINE, MURRAY, pseud.

03321 *The devil, poor devil! a novel.* Boriswood,
          London, 1934, 256p, Cloth, Novel
03322 *Proud man.* Boriswood, London, 1934, 318p,
          Cloth, Novel
03323 *Swastika night.* Victor Gollancz, London,
          1937, 288p, Cloth, Novel

CONTINENTAL CLASSICS

03324 *Continental classics, volume XV; modern ghosts.*
          Harper & Bros., New York, 1890, 225p, Cloth,
          Anth.

A CONTRIBUTOR TO 'BLACKWOOD'
    see: CHESNEY, GEORGE T.

CONVERSE, FRANK H.

03325 *Van; or, In search of an unknown race.* United
          States Book Co., New York, 1891, 249p, Paper,
          Novel
03325A retitled: *In search of an unknown race.* Street
          & Smith, New York, 1901, 249p, Paper, Novel

CONWAY, GERARD F., 1952-

03326 *The midnight dancers.* Ace, New York, 1971,
          221p, Paper, Novel
03327 *Mindship.* DAW, New York, 1974, 191p, Paper,
          Novel

CONWAY, HUGH, pseud. [Frederick John Fargus,
1847-1885]

03328 *Bound together; tales.* Remington & Co., London,
          1884, vol. I-268p, II-271p, Cloth, Coll.
03328A retitled: *The secret of the Stradivarius, and
          other stories.* Holerth Press, London, 1924,
          73p, Cloth, Coll. [abridged]

CONWAY, LAURA, pseud. [Dorothy Phoebe Ansle]

03329 *The unforgotten.* Collins, London, 1967, 192p,
          Cloth, Novel

as Hebe Elsna:

03330 *Take heed of loving me.* Collins, London, 1970,
          160p, Cloth, Novel

CONWAY, TROY, house pseud. [see also Michael
Avallone]

03331 *The Coxeman #7; last licks.* Paperback Library,
          New York, 1968, 175p, Paper, Novel [Coxeman
          #7]
03332 *Coxeman #8; keep it up, Rod!* Paperback Library
          New York, 1968, 192p, Paper, Novel [Coxeman
          #8]
03333 *Coxeman #10; the best laid plans.* Paperback
          Library, New York, 1969, 176p, Paper, Novel
          [Coxeman #10]
00664 *Coxeman #12; had any lately?* Paperback Library
          New York, 1969, 160p, Paper, Novel [Coxeman
          #12] [by Michael Avallone]
03334 *Coxeman #13; whatever goes up.* Paperback Lib-
          rary, New York, 1969, 160p, Paper, Novel
          [Coxeman #13]
00665 *Coxeman #17; the big broad jump.* Paperback
          Library, New York, 1968, 158p, Paper, Novel
          [Coxeman #17] [by Michael Avallone]
03335 *Coxeman #18; the sex machine.* Paperback Lib-
          rary, New York, 1970, 156p, Paper, Novel
          [Coxeman #18]

CONWAY, TROY, house pseud. (Cont.)

00666 *Coxeman #19; the blow-your-mind-job; an adult novel.* Paperback Library, New York, 1970, 157p, Paper, Novel [Coxeman #19] [by Michael Avallone]

00667 *Coxeman #20; the cunning linguist; an adult novel.* Paperback Library, New York, 1970, 158p, Paper, Novel [Coxeman #20] [by Michael Avallone]

03336 *Coxeman #25; it's not how long you make it.* Paperback Library, New York, 1970, 174p, Paper, Novel [Coxeman #25]

03337 *Coxeman #26; son of a witch.* Paperback Library, New York, 1971, 175p, Paper, Novel [Coxeman #26]

00668 *Coxeman #28; a stiff proposition.* Paperback Library, New York, 1971, 159p, Paper, Novel [Coxeman #28] [by Michael Avallone]

03338 *Coxeman #31; the cockeyed cuties.* Paperback Library, New York, 1972, 174p, Paper, Novel [Coxeman #31]

03339 *Coxeman 34; a hard man is good to find; an adult novel.* Warner Paperback Library, New York, 1973, 158p, Paper, Novel [Coxeman #34]

03340 *It's getting harder all the time.* Paperback Library, New York, 1968, 174p, Paper, Novel [Coxeman #5]

03341 *The wham! bam! thank you, ma'am affair.* Paperback Library, New York, 1968, 175p, Paper, Novel [Coxeman #4]

CONYERS, BERNARD

03342 *Never forever.* Regency Press, London, 1958, 193p, Cloth, Novel

COOK, FREDERICK S., 1929-

03343 *Fred Cook's index to the Wonder group.* Fred Cook, Grand Haven, 1966, 239p, Paper, Nonf.

COOK, GLEN (Charles), 1944-   [*biography included*]

03344 *The heirs of Babylon.* Signet, New York, 1972, 192p, Paper, Novel

COOK, ROBIN [Robert William Arthur Cook, 1931-   ] [*biography included*]

03345 *A state of Denmark; or, A warning to the incurious; a novel.* Hutchinson, London, 1970, 269p, Cloth, Novel

COOK, S(tanley) **J.**, 1935-   , with Stephen V. Whaley

03346 *Man unwept; visions from the inner eye; an anthology of science and fantasy fiction.* McGraw-Hill, New York, 1974, 350p, Paper, Anth.

COOK, W. PAUL, 1881-1948

03347 *H. P. Lovecraft; a portrait.* Mirage Press, Baltimore, 1968, 66p, Cloth, Nonf.

COOK, WILLIAM WALLACE, 1867-1933

03348 *Adrift in the unknown; or, Queer adventures in a queer realm.* Adventure Library, Street & Smith, New York, 1925, 305p, Paper, Novel

03349 *Around the world in eighty hours; an adventure story.* Chelsea House, New York, 1925, 249p, Cloth, Novel

03350 *Cast away at the Pole.* Adventure Library, Street & Smith, New York, 1926, 311p, Paper, Novel

03351 *The eighth wonder; or, Working for marvels.* Adventure Library, Street & Smith, New York, 1925, 318p, Paper, Novel

03352 *Marooned in 1492; or, Under fortune's flag.* Adventure Library, Street & Smith, New York, 1925, 309p, Paper, Novel

03353 *A round trip to the year 2000; or, A flight through time.* Adventure Library, Street & Smith, New York, 1925, 310p, Paper, Novel

COOKE, CHARLES JAMES
see: THE "RUSSIA'S HOPE"

COOKE, DONALD E(dward), 1916-

03354 *The Firebird.* John C. Winston, Philadelphia, 1939, 144p, Cloth, Novel

COOLIDGE, OLIVIA, 1908-

03355 *The king of men.* Houghton Mifflin, Boston, 1966, 230p, Cloth, Novel

COOMBS, CHARLES (Ira), 1914-   [*biography included*]

03356 *Mystery of satellite 7.* Westminster Press, Philadelphia, 1958, 160p, Cloth, Novel

COON, HORACE, 1897-1961

03357 *43,000 years later.* Signet, New York, 1958, 143p, Paper, Novel

COON, MERLIN J(oseph), 1917-

03358 *The sea horse.* Academy Publishers, Los Angeles, 1952, 135p, Cloth, Novel

COONEY, MICHAEL, 1921-   [*biography included*]

03359 *Doomsday England.* Cassell, London, 1967, 183p, Cloth, Novel [Keys #1]

03360 *Ten days to oblivion.* Cassell, London, 1968, 167p, Cloth, Novel [Keys #2]

COOPER, BRYAN (Robert Wright), 1932-

03361 *Stones of evil; a novel of ancient Britain.* Macdonald & Jane's, London, 1974, 213p, Cloth, Novel

COOPER, COLIN (Symons), 1926-   [*biography included*]

03362   *Outcrop*. Faber & Faber, London, 1969, 231p, Cloth, Novel
03363   *The thunder and lightning man*. Faber & Faber, London, 1968, 182p, Cloth, Novel

COOPER, EDMUND, 1926-   [*biography included*]

03364   *All Fools' Day*. Hodder & Stoughton, London, 1966, 192p, Cloth, Novel
03365   *The Cloud Walker; a novel*. Hodder & Stoughton, London, 1973, 223p, Cloth, Novel
03366   *Deadly image*. Ballantine, New York, 1958, 190p, Paper, Novel
03366A   retitled: *The uncertain midnight*. Hutchinson of London, London, 1958, 224p, Cloth, Novel
03367   *A far sunset*. Hodder & Stoughton, London, 1967, 189p, Cloth, Novel
03368   *Five to twelve*. Hodder & Stoughton, London, 1968, 187p, Cloth, Novel
     Gender genocide. [see 03384A]
     Kronk. [see 03376A]
03369   *The last continent*. Dell, New York, 1969, 156p, Paper, Novel
03370   *News from elsewhere*. Mayflower, New York, 1968, 128p, Paper, Coll.
03371   *The Overman culture*. Hodder & Stoughton, London, 1971, 190p, Cloth, Novel
03372   *Prisoner of fire*. Hodder & Stoughton, London, 1974, 191p, Cloth, Novel
03373   *Sea-horse in the sky*. Hodder & Stoughton, London, 1969, 191p, Cloth, Novel
03374   *Seed of light*. Hutchinson of London, London, 1959, 224p, Cloth, Novel
03375   *The slaves of Heaven*. G. P. Putnam's Sons, New York, 1974, 185p, Cloth, Novel
03376   *Son of Kronk*. Hodder & Stoughton, London, 1970, 189p, Cloth, Novel
03376A   retitled: *Kronk; a science fiction novel*. G. P. Putnam's Sons, New York, 1971, 190p, Cloth, Novel
03377   *The square root of tomorrow*. Robert Hale, London, 1970, 192p, Cloth, Coll.
03378   *The tenth planet; a novel*. G. P. Putnam's Sons, New York, 1973, 214p, Cloth, Novel
03379   *Tomorrow came; twelve stories of many dimensions*. Panther, London, 1963, 123p, Paper, Coll.
03380   *Tomorrow's gift*. Ballantine, New York, 1958, 164p, Paper, Coll.
03381   *Transit; a science fiction novel*. Faber & Faber, London, 1964, 232p, Cloth, Novel
03382   *Unborn tomorrow*. Robert Hale, London, 1971, 223p, Cloth, Coll.
     The uncertain midnight. [see 03366A]
03383   *Voices in the dark; amazing fantasy and science fiction!* Digit, London, 1960, 157p, Paper, Coll.
03384   *Who needs men? a novel*. Hodder & Stoughton, London, 1972, 192p, Cloth, Novel
03384A   retitled: *Gender genocide*. Ace, New York, 1973, 200p, Paper, Novel
03385   *Wish goes to Slumber Land*. Hutchinson, London, 1960, 77p, Cloth, Novel

COOPER, GILES, 1918-1966

03386   *The other man; a novel based on his play for television*. Panther, London, 1964, 207p, Paper, Tele.

COOPER, HUGHES, pseud. [George H. Leonard]

03387   *Sexmax*. Paperback Library, New York, 1969, 176p, Paper, Novel

COOPER, J. C.

03388   *The handwriting on the wall; or, The revolution in 1907, being a revelation of startling facts concerning the terrible influences that are at work destroying the nation, with the sober conclusions drawn from these facts by an ex-Congressman, a man who loves his country and his fellow-man, and would give warning of perils that threaten the very life of our republic*. P. H. Roberts Publishing Co., St. Louis, 1903, 377p, Cloth, Novel [published anonymously]

COOPER, J(ames) FENIMORE, 1789-1851

03389   *The Monikins; a tale*, by the author of "The spy." Carey, Lea & Blanchard, Philadelphia, 1835, 2vol, Cloth, Novel
03389A   *The Monikins; a tale*, by J. Fenimore Cooper. Stringer & Townsend, New York, 1852, 2vol/1, Cloth, Novel

COOPER, JOHN C., pseud. [John Croydon]

03390   *The grip of the strangler--the haunted strangler*. Digit, London, 1958, 188p, Paper, Movie
03390A   retitled: *The haunted strangler*. Ace, New York, 1959, 190p, Paper, Movie

COOPER, LOUISE, 1952-   [*biography included*]

03391   *The Book of Paradox*. Delacorte Press, New York, 1973, 244p, Cloth, Novel

COOPER, MORTON

03392   *The Munsters*. Avon, New York, 1964, 143p, Paper, Tele. [Munsters series]

COOPER, PARLEY J.

03393   *The feminists*. Pinnacle, New York, 1971, 188p, Paper, Novel
03394   *My lady evil; a novel*. Simon & Schuster, New York, 1974, 221p, Cloth, Novel

COOPER, SUSAN (Mary), 1935-   [*biography included*]

03395   *The dark is rising*. Atheneum, New York, 1973, 216p, Cloth, Novel [Dark Is Rising #2]
03396   *Greenwitch*. Atheneum, New York, 1974, 147p, Cloth, Novel [Dark Is Rising #3]
03397   *Mandrake*. Hodder & Stoughton, London, 1964, 253p, Cloth, Novel
03398   *Over sea, under stone*. Jonathan Cape, London, 1965, 252p, Cloth, Novel [Dark Is Rising #1]

COPE, GERTRUDE VENETTA

03399 *The heritage of the quest.* Marshall Jones, Boston, 1936, 154p, Cloth, Novel

COPLEY, FRANK BARKLEY

03400 *The impeachment of President Israels; a novel.* Macmillan, New York, 1913, 124p, Cloth, Novel

COPPARD, A(lfred) E(dgar), 1878-1957

03401 *Adam & Eve & pinch me; tales.* Golden Cockerel Press, Waltham St. Lawrence, UK, 1921, 140p, Cloth, Coll.
03402 *Crotty Shinkwin, a tale of the strange adventure that befell a butcher of County Clare; The beauty spot, a tale concerning the Chilterns.* Golden Cockerel Press, Waltham St. Lawrence, UK, 1932, 67p, Cloth, Coll.
03403 *Fearful pleasures.* Arkham House, Sauk City, 1946, 301p, Cloth, Coll.
03404 *Pink furniture; a tale for lovely children with noble natures.* Jonathan Cape, London, 1929, 251p, Cloth, Novel
03405 *Tapster's tapestry.* Golden Cockerel Press, London, 1938, 58p, Cloth, Novel

COPPARD, AUDREY (Jean), 1931-   [*biography included*]

03406 *Who has poisoned the sea?* Heinemann, London, 1970, 124p, Cloth, Novel

COPPEL, ALFRED [Alfredo José de Araña-Marini y Coppel, 1921-   ] [*biography included*]

03407 *Dark December.* Gold Medal, Greenwich, 1960, 208p, Paper, Novel

as Robert Cham Gilman:

03408 *The navigator of Rhada.* Harcourt, Brace & World, New York, 1969, 223p, Cloth, Novel [Rhada #2]
03409 *The Rebel of Rhada.* Harcourt, Brace & World, New York, 1968, 192p, Cloth, Novel [Rhada #1]
03410 *The Starkahn of Rhada.* Harcourt, Brace & World, New York, 1970, 190p, Cloth, Novel [Rhada #3]

COPPER, BASIL, 1924-   [*biography included*]

03411 *From evil's pillow.* Arkham House, Sauk City, 1973, 177p, Cloth, Coll.
03412 *The great white space.* Robert Hale, London, 1974, 192p, Cloth, Novel
03413 *Not after nightfall; stories of the strange and terrible.* Four Square, London, 1967, 190p, Paper, Coll.

CORBETT, E(lizabeth) B(urgoyne), 1846-

03414 *New Amazonia; a foretaste of the future.* Power Publishing Co., London, 1889, 146p, Cloth, Novel

CORBETT, JAMES

03415 *The air killer.* Herbert Jenkins, London, 1941, 254p, Cloth, Novel
03416 *Devil-man from Mars.* Herbert Jenkins, London, 1935, 312p, Cloth, Novel
03417 *The Ghost Plane.* Herbert Jenkins, London, 1939, 284p, Cloth, Novel
03418 *The monster of Dagenham Hall.* Herbert Jenkins, London, 1935, 288p, Cloth, Novel
03419 *The White Angel.* Herbert Jenkins, London, 1931, 312p, Cloth, Novel

CORBETT, (Sir) JULIAN (Stafford), 1854-1922

03420 *Kophetua the Thirteenth.* Macmillan, London, 1889, 333p, Cloth, Novel

CORBETT, SCOTT, 1913-   [*biography included*]

03421 *The hairy horror trick.* Little, Brown, Boston, 1969, 101p, Cloth, Novel

CORBYN, CLARA A. B.

03422 *La gran Quibira; a musical mystery; opera historique; a romanza in five acts, with overture, prelude, and interlude.* Author's Edition, Los Angeles?, 1904, 533p, Cloth, Novel

CORDELL, ALEXANDER, pseud. [Alexander Graber, 1914-   ] [*biography included*]

03423 *If you believe the soldiers.* Hodder & Stoughton, London, 1973, 224p, Cloth, Novel

CORELLI, MARIE, pseud. [Mary Mackay, 1855-1924]

03424 *'Ardath'; the story of a dead self.* Richard Bentley & Son, London, 1889, 3vol, Cloth, Novel
03425 *Barabbas; a dream of the world's tragedy.* Methuen, London, 1893, 3vol, Cloth, Novel
03426 *The devil's motor; a fantasy.* Hodder & Stoughton, London, 1910, 45p, Cloth, Story
03427 *The life everlasting; a reality of romance.* Methuen, London, 1911, 436p, Cloth, Novel
03428 *The master-Christian.* Methuen, London, 1900, 635p, Cloth, Novel
03429 *A romance of two worlds; a novel.* Richard Bentley & Son, London, 1886, 2vol, Cloth, Novel
03430 *The secret power; a romance of the time.* Methuen, London, 1921, 332p, Cloth, Novel
03431 *The sorrows of Satan; or, The strange experience of one Geoffrey Tempest, millionaire; a romance.* Methuen, London, 1895, 487p, Cloth, Novel
03432 *The soul of Lilith.* Richard Bentley & Son, London, 1892, 3vol, Cloth, Novel
03433 *The strange visitation of Josiah McNason; a Christmas ghost story.* George Newnes, London, 1904, 118p, Paper, Novel
03433A retitled: *The strange visitation.* Hodder & Stoughton, London, 1912, 188p, Cloth, Novel

CORELLI, MARIE (Cont.)

03434   *The young Diana; an experiment of the future.* Hutchinson, London, 1918, 320p, Cloth, Novel

03435   *Ziska; the problem of a wicked soul.* J. W. Arrowsmith, Bristol; Simpkin, Marshall, Hamilton, Kent, London, 1897, 365p, Cloth, Novel

COREY, PAUL (Frederick), 1903-   [*biography included*]

03436   *The planet of the blind.* Robert Hale, London, 1968, 190p, Cloth, Novel

CORIELL, VERNELL, with Ray Lee

03437   *A pictorial history of the Tarzan movies; 50 years of the jungle superman and all-time box office film champion.* Golden State News Co., Los Angeles, 1966, 83p, Paper, Nonf.

CORLEY, DONALD, 1886-1955

03438   *The haunted jester.* Robert M. McBride, New York, 1931, 306p, Cloth, Coll.
03439   *The house of lost identity; tales & drawings.* Robert M. McBride, New York, 1927, 324p, Cloth, Coll.

CORLEY, EDWIN, 1931-   [*biography included*]

03440   *The Jesus factor.* Stein & Day, New York, 1970, 320p, Cloth, Novel
03441   *Siege; a novel.* Stein & Day, New York, 1969, 319p, Cloth, Novel

CORMACK, MARIBELLE, 1902-

03442   *The star-crossed woman.* George G. Harrap, London, 1961, 254p, Cloth, Novel

CORMAN, AVERY

03443   *Oh God! a novel.* Simon & Schuster, New York, 1971, 190p, Cloth, Novel

CORNELIUS, MARY A(nn), 1827-1918

03444   *The white flame.* Stockham Publishing Co., Chicago, 1900, 402p, Cloth, Novel

CORNELL, FRED(erick) C(arruthers)

03445   *A Rip van Winkle of the Kalahari, and other tales of South-West Africa.* T. Fisher Unwin, London, 1915, 320p, Cloth, Coll.

CORNFORD, L(eslie) COPE, 1867-1927

03446   *The fairy man.* J. M. Dent & Sons, London, 1919, 236p, Cloth, Novel

CORNING, WALTER D.

03447   *Out of this world; a story of Heaven and Earth.* Greenwich Book Publishers, New York, 1959, 55p, Cloth, Novel

CORNISH, GERALD WARRE, 1875-1916

03448   *Beneath the surface, and other stories.* Grant Richards, London, 1918, 373p, Cloth, Coll.

CORNWALL, IAN W(olfram)

03449   *Hunter's half-moon.* Baker, London, 1967, 164p, Cloth, Novel

CORNWALLIS-WEST, G(eorge Frederick Myddelton), 1874-1951

03450   *The woman who stopped war; a novel.* Hutchinson, London, 1935, 286p, Cloth, Novel

CORREA da SILVA, JOAQUIM BELFORD
   see: PACO d'ARCOS, J.

CORREY, LEE, pseud. [George Harry Stine, 1928-] [*biography included*]

03451   *Contraband rocket.* Ace Double, New York, 1956, 143p, Paper, Novel
03452   *Rocket man.* Henry Holt, New York, 1955, 224p, Cloth, Novel
03453   *Starship through space.* Henry Holt, New York, 1954, 241p, Cloth, Novel

CORSTON, (Michael) GEORGE, 1932-   [*biography included*]

03454   *Aftermath.* Robert Hale, London, 1968, 206p, Cloth, Novel

CORTÁZAR, JULIO, 1914-   [*biography included*]

03455   *End of the game, and other stories.* Pantheon, New York, 1967, 277p, Cloth, Coll.

CORVO, BARON
   see: ROLFE, FREDERICK WILLIAM

CORWIN, NORMAN (Lewis), 1910-   [*biography included*]

03456   *Dog in the sky; the authentic and unexpurgated odyssey of Runyon Jones.* Simon & Schuster, New York, 1952, 159p, Cloth, Radio [based on Corwin's radio play, "The Odyssey of Runyon Jones"]

CORY, CHARLES B(arney), 1857-1921

03457   *Montezuma's castle, and other weird tales.* Author's Edition, Boston, 1899, 233p, Cloth, Coll.

CORY, DESMOND, pseud. [Shaun Lloyd McCarthy, 1928-]

03458 *High requiem.* Frederick Muller, London, 1955, 224p, Cloth, Novel [Johnny Fedora series]
03459 *Sunburst.* Hodder & Stoughton, London, 1971, 253p, Cloth, Novel [Johnny Fedora series]

CORY, HOWARD L., pseud.
   see: JARDINE, JULIE ANNE and MADDOCK, LARRY

CORY, VIVIAN
   see: CROSS, VICTORIA

COSGRAVE, JOHN O'HARA, 1864-1947

03460 *The academy for souls.* Farrar & Rinehart, New York, 1931, 324p, Cloth, Novel

COSIER, C. H. T.

03461 *The mighty millstone; a scientific-religious novel.* Arthur H. Stockwell, London, 1938, 288p, Cloth, Novel

COSPER, WILBERT LE ROY

03462 *Princess Whoopee, a peppy novelette; making Whoopee on Mars.* Cosmos Publishing House, Oakland, CA, 1929, 134p, Cloth, Novel

COST, MARCH, pseud. [Margaret Mackie Morrison, d. 1973]

03463 *The bespoken mile.* Collins, London, 1950, 448p, Cloth, Novel
03464 *The dark glass.* Collins, London, 1935, 463p, Cloth, Novel
03465 *The dark star.* Collins, London, 1939, 384p, Cloth, Novel
03466 *A man named Luke.* Collins, London, 1932, 290p, Cloth, Novel

COSTAIN, THOMAS B(ertram), 1885-1965 [*biography included*]

03467 *Below the salt; a novel.* Doubleday, Garden City, 1957, 480p, Cloth, Novel

COSTELLO, DUDLEY, 1803-1865

03468 *Holidays with hobgoblins; and, Talk of strange things.* John Camden Hotten, London, 1861, 332p, Cloth, Coll. [includes some nonf.]

COSTELLO, FREDERICK H(ankerson), 1851-1921

03469 *Sure-Dart; a story of strange hunters and stranger game in the days of monsters.* A. C. McClurg, Chicago, 1909, 320p, Cloth, Novel

COSTER, CHARLES de
   see: de COSTER, CHARLES

COTES, MAY, with Grant Allen

00195 *Kalee's shrine.* J. W. Arrowsmith, Bristol, 1886, 196p, Cloth, Novel

COTT, JONATHAN, 1942- [*biography included*]

03470 *Beyond the looking glass; extraordinary works of fantasy and fairy tale,* by Johnathan Cott. Stonehill, New York, 1973, 519p, Cloth, Anth.

COTTON, JOSE MARIO EDMONDSON y
   see: EDMONDSON, G. C.

COUCH, A. T. QUILLER-
   see: QUILLER-COUCH, A. T.

COULDREY, OSWALD (Jennings)

03471 *The mistaken Fury, and other lapses.* B. H. Blackwell, Oxford, 1914, 242p, Cloth, Coll.

COULSON, JUANITA (Ruth), 1933- [*biography included*]

03472 *Crisis on Cheiron.* Ace Double, New York, 1967, 129p, Paper, Novel
03473 *The singing stones.* Ace Double, New York, 1968, 132p, Paper, Novel

COULSON, ROBERT (Stratton), 1928- , with Gene DeWeese as Thomas Stratton

03474 *The man from U.N.C.L.E., number 11; the invisibility affair.* Ace, New York, 1967, 158p, Paper, Tele. [Man from U.N.C.L.E. #11]
03475 *The man from U.N.C.L.E., number 12; the mindtwisters affair.* Ace, New York, 1967, 158p, Paper, Tele. [Man from U.N.C.L.E. #12]

COULTON, MARY ROSE
   see: CAMPION, SARAH

COUNT RODERIC'S CASTLE

03476 *Count Roderic's castle; or, Gothic times; a tale.* William Lane, Minerva-Press, London, 1794, 2vol, Cloth, Novel

COUPPEY, MADELEINE

03477 *The rumour in the forest.* Collins, London, 1947, 144p, Cloth, Novel

COURNOS, JOHN, 1881-1966

03478 *American short stories of the nineteenth century.* J. M. Dent & Sons, London, 1930, 372p, Cloth, Anth.

COURT INTRIGUES IN A COLLECTION OF ORIGINAL LETTERS, FROM THE ISLAND OF THE NEW ATALANTIS
  see: MANLEY, MARY

COURTENAY, T(homas) G.

03479 *The Fayolle formula.* Herbert Jenkins, London, 1934, 311p, Cloth, Novel

COURTENEY, LUKE THEOPHILUS

03480 *Travels in the interior; or, The wonderful adventures of Luke and Belinda.* Ward & Downey, London, 1887, 316p, Cloth, Novel

COURTIER, S(idney) H(obson), 1904-1974 [*biography included*]

03481 *Into the silence.* Robert Hale, London, 1973, 175p, Cloth, Novel

COURY, PHIL

03482 *Anno Domini 2000.* Vantage Press, New York, 1959, 147p, Cloth, Novel

COUSIN de GRAINVILLE, JEAN-BAPTISTE FRANÇOIS XAVIER [published anonymously]

03483 *The last man; or, Omegarus and Syderia; a romance in futurity.* R. Dutton, London, 1806, vol. I-220p, II-204p, Cloth, Novel

COUSINS, E(dmund) G(eorge), 1893-

03484 *I will not cease; a novel.* Denis Archer, London, 1933, 286p, Cloth, Novel

COVE, JOSEPH WALTER
  see: GIBBS, LEWIS

COVERDALE, HENRY STANDISH
  see: THE FALL OF THE GREAT REPUBLIC

COWAN, FRANK, 1844-1905

03485 *Revi-Lona; a romance of love in a marvelous land.* Tribune Press, Greensburg, PA, 188?, 247p, Cloth, Novel

COWAN, JAMES

03486 *Daybreak; a romance of an old world.* George H. Richmond, New York, 1896, 399p, Cloth, Novel

COWIE, DONALD (John)

03487 *The rape of man; or, The zoo let loose.* Tantivy Press, Malvern, UK, 1947, 222p, Cloth, Novel

COWLES, FREDERICK I(gnatius), 1900-

03488 *The horror of Abbot's Grange, and other stories.* Frederick Muller, London, 1936, 256p, Cloth, Coll.
03489 *The night wind howls.* Frederick Muller, London, 1938, 315p, Cloth, Coll.

COWLES, JOHN CLIFFORD

03490 *The whispering Buddha.* Hollyway Publishers, Los Angeles, 1932, 460p, Cloth, Novel

COWPER, GEORGE
  see: FYNE, NEAL

COWPER, RICHARD, pseud. [John Middleton Murry, Jr. (variously Colin Murry), 1926-] [*biography included*]

03491 *Breakthrough; a novel.* Dennis Dobson, London, 1967, 214p, Cloth, Novel
03492 *Clone.* Victor Gollancz, London, 1972, 190p, Cloth, Novel
03493 *Domino; a science fiction novel.* Dennis Dobson, London, 1971, 175p, Cloth, Novel
03494 *Kuldesak.* Victor Gollancz, London, 1972, 187p, Cloth, Novel
03495 *Phoenix; a novel.* Dennis Dobson, London, 1968, 183p, Cloth, Novel
03496 *Time out of mind.* Victor Gollancz, London, 1973, 159p, Cloth, Novel
03497 *The twilight of Briareus.* Victor Gollancz, London, 1974, 255p, Cloth, Novel
03498 *Worlds apart; a science fiction novel.* Victor Gollancz, London, 1974, 159p, Cloth, Novel

COX, A(nthony) B(erkeley), 1893-1970

03499 *The family witch; an essay in absurdity.* Herbert Jenkins, London, 1925, 312p, Cloth, Novel
03500 *The professor on paws.* W. Collins Sons, London, 1926, 306p, Cloth, Novel

COX, ERLE (Harold), 1873-1950

03501 *Fools' harvest.* Robertson & Mullens, Melbourne, 1939, 194p, Paper, Novel
03502 *The missing angel.* Robertson & Mullens, Melbourne, 1947, 298p, Cloth, Novel
03503 *Out of the silence; a romance.* E. A. Vidler, Melbourne, 1925, 318p, Cloth, Novel

COX, LUTHER

03504 *The Earth is mine.* Exposition Press, New York, 1968, 171p, Cloth, Novel

COXE, Mr., pseud.

03505 *The oversexed astronauts.* Bee-Line, New York, 1970, 152p, Paper, Novel

COXE, EDWARD D.

03506 *The fool killer*, by a fugitive. American Publishers' Association, Chicago, 1885, 316p, Cloth, Novel

COZZENS, JAMES GOULD,1903-1978[*biography included*]

03507 *Castaway.* Random House, New York, 1934, 181p, Cloth, Novel
03508 *S.S. San Pedro; and, Castaway.* Modern Library Paperbacks, New York, 1956, 182p, Paper, Coll.

CRABAPPLE, JOHN

03509 *The war of 1908 for the supremacy of the Pacific.* W. H. Smith & Son, London, 1908, 23p, Paper, Story

CRADDOCK, CHARLES EGBERT, pseud. [Mary Noailles Murfree, 1850-1922]

03510 *The phantoms of the foot-bridge, and other stories.* Harper & Bros., New York, 1895, 353p, Cloth, Coll.

CRADOCK, PHYLLIS (Nan Sortain), 1910-

03511 *The eternal echo.* Andrew Dakers, London, 1950, 276p, Cloth, Novel [Amartus #2]
03512 *Gateway to remembrance.* Andrew Dakers, London, 1949, 361p, Cloth, Novel [Amartus #1]

CRAIG, A. E(lsie) R(undall)

03513 *The beloved rajah.* Minton, Balch, New York, 1926, 308p, Cloth, Novel

CRAIG, ALEXANDER

03514 *Ionia; land of wise men and fair women.* E. A. Weeks, Chicago, 1898, 301p, Cloth, Novel

CRAIG, CHARLES THURLOW-
see: THURLOW-CRAIG, CHARLES

CRAIG, COLIN, pseud. [Henry Spencer Booth]

03515 *A suitor from the stars.* Thomas & Evans Printing Co., Baltimore, 1928, 175p, Cloth, Novel

CRAIG, DAVID, pseud. [Allan James Tucker, 1929-   ] [*biography included*]

03516 *The alias man.* Jonathan Cape, London, 1968, 192p, Cloth, Novel [Roy Rickman #1]
03517 *Contact lost.* Jonathan Cape, London, 1970, 209p, Cloth, Novel [Roy Rickman #3]
03518 *Message ends.* Jonathan Cape, London, 1969, 188p, Cloth, Novel [Roy Rickman #2]

CRAIG, HAMILTON

03519 *A hazard at Hansard (the speech from the throne, Ottawa, Fourth August, 2014).* Arthur H. Stockwell, London, 1925, 31p, Paper?, Story

CRAIG, THURLOW
see: THURLOW-CRAIG, CHARLES WILLIAM

CRAIGIE, DAVID, pseud. [Dorothy M. Craigie]

03520 *Dark Atlantis.* William Heinemann, London, 1951, 221p, Cloth, Novel
03521 *The voyage of the Luna I.* Eyre & Spottiswoode, London, 1948, 272p, Cloth, Novel

CRAIK, DINAH MARIA (Mulock), 1826-1887

03522 *Romantic tales*, by the author of "John Halifax, Gentleman." Smith, Elder, London, 1859, 406p, Cloth, Coll.

CRAINE, E(dith) J(anice), 1881-

03523 *Airplane Boys at Belize.* World Syndicate Publishing Co., Cleveland, 1932, 224p, Cloth, Novel [Airplane Boys #8]
03524 *Airplane Boys at Cap Rock.* World Syndicate Publishing Co., Cleveland, 1930, 248p, Cloth, Novel [Airplane Boys #2]
03525 *Airplane Boys at Platinum River.* World Syndicate Publishing Co., Cleveland, 1931, 200p, Cloth, Novel [Airplane Boys #5]
03525A retitled: *At Platinum River.* World Syndicate Publishing Co., Cleveland, 1931?, 200p, Cloth, Novel [Sky Buddies series]
03526 *Airplane Boys discover the secrets of Cuzco.* World Syndicate Publishing Co., Cleveland, 1930, 246p, Cloth, Novel [Airplane Boys #3]
03527 *Airplane Boys flying to Amy-Ran Fastness.* World Syndicate Publishing Co., Cleveland, 1930, 245p, Cloth, Novel [Airplane Boys #4]
03527A retitled: *Flying to Amy-Ran Fastness.* World Syndicate Publishing Co., Cleveland, 1930, 245p, Cloth, Novel [Sky Buddies series]
03528 *Airplane Boys in the Black Woods.* World Syndicate Publishing Co., Cleveland, 1932, 209p, Cloth, Novel [Airplane Boys #7]
03529 *Airplane Boys on the border line.* World Syndicate Publishing Co., Cleveland, 1930, Cloth, Novel [Airplane Boys #1]
03530 *Airplane Boys with the revolutionists in Bolivia.* World Syndicate Publishing Co., Cleveland, 1931, 201p, Cloth, Novel [Airplane Boys #6]
03530A retitled: *With the revolutionists in Bolivia.* World Syndicate Publishing Co., Cleveland, 1931?, 201p, Cloth, Novel [Sky Buddies series]
At Platinum River. [see 03525A]
Flying to Amy-Ran Fastness. [see 03527A]
With the revolutionists in Bolivia. [see 03530A] [Records concerning this series are incomplete, and it is uncertain whether the "Sky Buddies" editions, identical with the "Airplane Boys" books except for title, were actually published first. There probably exist title variations for all eight books similar to the three recorded here.]

CRAM, MILDRED, 1889-   [biography included]

03531 Forever. Alfred A. Knopf, New York, 1935,
       60p, Cloth, Novel
03532 Forever; and, The promise. Bantam, New York,
       1971,   , Paper, Coll.
03533 Kingdom of innocents. Alfred A. Knopf, New
       York, 1940, 296p, Cloth, Novel
03534 The promise. Alfred A. Knopf, New York, 1949,
       68p, Cloth, Novel

CRAM, RALPH ADAMS, 1863-1942

03535 Black spirits & white; a book of ghost stories.
       Stone & Kimball, Chicago, 1895, 151p, Cloth,
       Coll.

CRAMB, JOHN ADAM
    see: REVERMORT, J. A.

CRAMER, MAURICE BROWNING, 1910-

03536 Phoenix at East Hadley. Houghton Mifflin, Bos-
       ton, 1941, 307p, Cloth, Novel [cover title:
       Phoenix in East Hadley]

CRANE, NATHALIA (Clara Ruth), 1913-

03537 An alien from Heaven. Coward-McCann, New York,
       1929, 300p, Cloth, Novel
03538 The sunken garden. Thomas Seltzer, New York,
       1926, 259p, Cloth, Novel

CRANE, ROBERT, pseud. [Bernard Glemser,
  1908-   ]

03539 Hero's walk. Ballantine, New York, 1954, 198p,
       Cloth, Novel

CRANFORD, HOPE

03540 Ida Llymond and her hour of vision. Skeffing-
       ton & Son, London, 1905, 291p, Cloth, Novel

CRANFORD, ROBIN

03541 Leave them their pride. Jarrolds, London,
       1962, 199p, Cloth, Novel

CRAWFORD, F(rancis) MARION, 1854-1909

03542 Cecilia; a story of modern Rome. Macmillan,
       New York, 1902, 421p, Cloth, Novel
03543 A cigarette-maker's romance; and, Khaled, a
       tale of Arabia. Macmillan, London, 1901,
       238p, Cloth, Coll.
03544 Khaled; a tale of Arabia. Macmillan, London,
       1891, 2vol, Cloth, Novel
03545 Man overboard! Macmillan, New York, 1903,
       95p, Cloth, Novel
03546 Uncanny tales. T. Fisher Unwin, London, 1911,
       307p, Cloth, Coll.
03546A retitled: Wandering ghosts. Macmillan, New
       York, 1911, 302p, Cloth, Coll.

03547 The upper berth. G. P. Putnam's Sons, New
       York, 1894, 145p, Cloth, Coll.
       Wandering ghosts. [see 03546A]
03548 The witch of Prague; a fantastic tale. Mac-
       millan, London, 1891, 3vol, Cloth, Novel
03549 With the immortals. Macmillan, London, 1888,
       2vol, Cloth, Novel
03550 Zoroaster. Macmillan, London, 1885, 2vol,
       Cloth, Novel

CRAWFORD, ISABELL C.

03551 The tapestry of time. Christopher Publishing
       House, Boston, 1927, 365p, Cloth, Novel

CRAWFORD, JOSEPH H. Jr., 1932-   , with James
  J. Donahue and Donald M. Grant

03552 "333"; a bibliography of the science-fantasy
       novel. Grandon Co., Providence, 1953, 80p,
       Paper, Nonf.

CRAWFORD, T(heron) C(lark)

03553 The disappearance syndicate; and, Senator Stan-
       ley's story. Charles B. Reed, New York,
       1894, 241p, Cloth, Coll.
03554 A man and his soul; an occult romance of Wash-
       ington life. Charles B. Reed, New York,
       1894, 255p, Cloth, Novel

CRAWFORD, THELMAR (Wyche), 1905-

03555 Terror wears a feathered cloak. Westminster
       Press, Philadelphia, 1969, 160p, Cloth,
       Novel

CRAWFORD, WILLIAM L(evi), 1911-   [biography
  included]

published anonymously:

03556 The garden of fear, by Robert E. Howard, and
       other stories of the bizarre and fantastic.
       Crawford Publications, Los Angeles, 1945,
       79p, Paper, Anth.
03557 Griffin booklet one. Griffin Publishing Co.,
       Los Angeles, 1949, 47p, Paper, Anth.
03558 The machine-god laughs. Griffin Publishing
       Co., Los Angeles, 1949, 134p, Cloth, Anth.

as Garret Ford:

03559 Science and sorcery. Fantasy Publishing Co.,
       Los Angeles, 1953, 327p, Cloth, Anth.

CRAWLEY, RAYBURN

03560 Chattering gods. Harper & Bros., New York,
       1931, 271p, Cloth, Novel [Ned Shackleton #2]
03561 The Valley of Creeping Men. Harper & Bros.,
       New York, 1930, 319p, Cloth, Novel [Ned
       Shackleton #1]

CRAWSHAY-WILLIAMS, ELIOT, 1879-1962

03562 Heaven takes a hand; a fantasy. John Long,
       London, 1949, 256p, Cloth, Novel

CRAWSHAY-WILLIAMS, ELIOT (Cont.)

03563 *The man who met himself, and other stories.*
John Long, London, 1947, 224p, Cloth, Coll.

03564 *Night in no time; a novel.* John Long, London,
1946, 240p, Cloth, Novel

CRAYDER, DOROTHY, 1906-

03565 *The pluperfect of love.* Atheneum, New York,
1971, 185p, Cloth, Novel

CRAYON, DIEDRICK Jr., pseud. [Bruce Kenneth,
1876-1916]

03566 *The return of the Half Moon.* Broadway Publishing Co., New York, 1909, 148p, Cloth,
Novel

CREASEY, JOHN, 1908-1973 [*biography included*]

03567 *The blight; a story of Dr. Palfrey.* Hodder &
Stoughton, London, 1968, 189p, Cloth, Novel
[Dr. Palfrey #27]
The children of despair. [see 03568A]

03568 *The children of hate; the 15th 'Dr. Palfrey'
adventure.* Evans Bros., London, 1952, 264p,
Cloth, Novel [Dr. Palfrey #16]

03568A retitled: *The children of despair.* Jay Books,
London, 1958, 188p, Paper, Novel [Dr. Palfrey #16]

03568B retitled: *The killers of innocence; a Doctor
Palfrey thriller.* Walker, New York, 1971,
191p, Cloth, Novel [Dr. Palfrey #16]

03569 *Dark harvest.* John Long, London, 1947, 304p,
Cloth, Novel [Dr. Palfrey #9]

03570 *The dawn of darkness.* John Long, London,
1949, 319p, Cloth, Novel [Dr. Palfrey #12]

03571 *The depths; a new story of Dr. Palfrey.* Hodder & Stoughton, London, 1963, 190p, Cloth,
Novel [Dr. Palfrey #23]

03572 *The drought; a new Dr. Palfrey story.* Hodder
& Stoughton, London, 1959, 191p, Cloth,
Novel [Dr. Palfrey #21]

03573 *The famine; a new story of 'Dr. Palfrey.'*
Hodder & Stoughton, London, 1967, 188p,
Cloth, Novel [Dr. Palfrey #26]

03574 *The flood.* Hodder & Stoughton, London, 1956,
191p, Cloth, Novel [Dr. Palfrey #19]

03575 *Four of the best; an omnibus volume containing
a complete story from each of the following
series: The Toff, Inspector West, Dr. Palfrey, Department Z.* Hodder & Stoughton,
London, 1955, 767p, Cloth, Coll. [includes
*Hunt the Toff; Inspector West alone; The
prophet of fire; The department of death*]

03576 *The inferno; a Dr. Palfrey story.* Hodder &
Stoughton, London, 1965, 191p, Cloth, Novel
[Dr. Palfrey #25]

03577 *The insulators; the 31st book of Dr. Palfrey.*
Hodder & Stoughton, London, 1972, 191p,
Cloth, Novel [Dr. Palfrey #31]
The killers of innocence. [see 03568B]

03578 *The league of light.* Evans Bros., London,
1949, 309p, Cloth, Novel [Dr. Palfrey #13]

03579 *The man who shook the world; the 13th 'Dr.
Palfrey' adventure.* Evans Bros., London,
1950, 286p, Cloth, Novel [Dr. Palfrey #14]

03580 *The mists of fear; the eighteenth "Dr. Palfrey" adventure.* Hodder & Stoughton, London, 1955, 222p, Cloth, Novel [Dr. Palfrey
#18]

03581 *The oasis; a story of Dr. Palfrey.* Hodder &
Stoughton, London, 1969, 192p, Cloth, Novel
[Dr. Palfrey #28]

03582 *The plague of silence; a "Dr. Palfrey" story.*
Hodder & Stoughton, London, 1958, 188p,
Cloth, Novel [Dr. Palfrey #20]

03583 *The prophet of fire; the 14th 'Dr. Palfrey'
adventure.* Evans Bros., London, 1951, 272p,
Cloth, Novel [Dr. Palfrey #15]

03584 *The sleep.* Hodder & Stoughton, London, 1964,
191p, Cloth, Novel [Dr. Palfrey #24]

03585 *The smog; a story of Dr. Palfrey.* Hodder &
Stoughton, London, 1970, 192p, Cloth, Novel
[Dr. Palfrey #29]

03586 *Sons of Satan.* John Long, London, 1947, 288p,
Cloth, Novel [Dr. Palfrey #10]

03587 *The terror; the return of Dr. Palfrey.* Hodder
& Stoughton, London, 1962, 191p, Cloth, Novel
[Dr. Palfrey #22]

03588 *The touch of death; the seventeenth "Dr. Palfrey" adventure.* Hodder & Stoughton, London,
1954, 224p, Cloth, Novel [Dr. Palfrey #17]

03589 *The unbegotten; the 30th story of Dr. Palfrey.*
Hodder & Stoughton, London, 1971, 189p, Cloth,
Novel [Dr. Palfrey #30]

03590 *The voiceless ones; the 32nd book of Dr. Palfrey.* Hodder & Stoughton, London, 1973, 190p,
Cloth, Novel [Dr. Palfrey #32]

03591 *The wings of peace.* John Long, London, 1948,
288p, Cloth, Novel [Dr. Palfrey #11]

CRÉBILLON, (Claude Prosper Julyot de), le Fils,
1707-1777

03592 *The sopha; a moral tale.* T. Cooper, London,
1742, 2vol, Cloth, Novel

03592A retitled: *The sofa; a moral tale.* George
Routledge & Sons, London, 1927, 293p, Cloth,
Novel

03592B retitled: *The divan (le sofa); a morality
story.* Privately printed for subscribers
only, New York, 1927, 314p, Cloth, Novel

CREEPS

03593 *Creeps; a collection of uneasy tales.* Philip
Allan, London, 1932, 248p, Cloth, Anth.

"CREEPS" OMNIBUS

03594 *The "Creeps" omnibus, containing "Creeps,"
"Shudders," and "Shivers" in one volume.*
Philip Allan, London, 1935, 638p, Cloth,
Anth.

CRELLIN, H. N.
see: ARAWIYAH, al

CRESPIGNY, MRS. PHILIP DE
see: CHAMPION DE CRESPIGNY, ROSE

CRESSWELL, HELEN, 1936- [*biography included*]

03595 *The Bongleweed.* Faber & Faber, London, 1973,
157p, Cloth, Novel

03596 *The night-watchmen.* Faber & Faber, London,
1969, 146p, Cloth, Novel

CRESSWELL, HELEN (cont.)

03597 *Up the pier.* Faber & Faber, London, 1971,
       144p, Cloth, Novel

CRESWICK, PAUL, 1866-1947

03598 *The beaten path; a fantasy.* Hodder & Stoughton,
       London, 1924, 314p, Cloth, Novel
03599 *The turning wheel.* Heath Cranton, London,
       1928, 287p, Cloth, Novel

CRICHTON, (John) MICHAEL, 1942-   [*biography
included*]

03600 *The Andromeda strain.* Alfred A. Knopf, New
       York, 1969, 295p, Cloth, Novel
03601 *The terminal man.* Alfred A. Knopf, New York,
       1972, 247p, Cloth, Novel

as John Lange:

03602 *Drug of choice.* Signet, New York, 1970, 143p,
       Paper, Novel

CRIDGE, ALFRED DENTON

03603 *Utopia; or, The history of an extinct planet.*
       Winchester & Pew, Oakland, CA, 1884, 30p,
       Paper, Story

CRISP, FRANK (Robson), 1915-   [*biography included*]

03604 *The Ape of London.* Hodder & Stoughton, London,
       1959, 192p, Cloth, Novel
03605 *The night callers.* John Long, London, 1960,
       184p, Cloth, Novel

CRISPIN, EDMUND, pseud. [Robert Bruce Montgomery, 1921-1978][*biography included*]

03606 *Best SF; science fiction stories.* Faber &
       Faber, London, 1955, 368p, Cloth, Anth.
03607 *Best SF two; science fiction stories.* Faber
       & Faber, London, 1956, 296p, Cloth, Anth.
03608 *Best SF three; science fiction stories.* Faber
       & Faber, London, 1958, 224p, Cloth, Anth.
03609 *Best SF four; science fiction stories.* Faber
       & Faber, London, 1961, 224p, Cloth, Anth.
03610 *Best SF five; science fiction stories.* Faber
       & Faber, London, 1963, 256p, Cloth, Anth.
03611 *Best SF six; science fiction stories.* Faber
       & Faber, London, 1966, 252p, Cloth, Anth.
03612 *Best SF seven; science fiction stories.* Faber
       & Faber, London, 1970, 212p, Cloth, Anth.
03613 *Best tales of terror.* Faber & Faber, London,
       1962, 255p, Cloth, Anth.
03614 *Best tales of terror two.* Faber & Faber, Lon-
       don, 1965, 224p, Cloth, Anth.
03615 *Outwards from Earth; a selection of science
       fiction.* Faber & Faber, London, 1974, 151p,
       Paper, Anth.
03616 *The stars and under; a selection of science
       fiction.* Faber & Faber, London, 1968, 174p,
       Cloth, Anth.

CRIST, EDA (Szecskay), 1909-   , with Richard
Crist

03617 *The cloud-catcher.* Abelard-Schuman, New York,
       1956, 143p, Cloth, Novel

CRIST, RICHARD (Harrison), with Eda Crist

03617 *The cloud-catcher.* Abelard-Schuman, New York,
       1956, 143p, Cloth, Novel

CRISTABEL, pseud. [Christine Elizabeth Abra-
hamsen, 1916-   ] [*biography included*]

03618 *The Cruachan and the Killane.* Curtis, New
       York, 1970, 287p, Paper, Novel [Veltakin #2]
03619 *The golden olive.* Curtis, New York, 1972,
       239p, Paper, Novel
03620 *Manalacor of Veltákin.* Curtis, New York, 1970,
       222p, Paper, Novel [Veltakin #1]
03621 *The mortal immortals.* Walker, New York, 1971,
       271p, Cloth, Novel

CROCKETT, S(amuel) R(utherford), 1860-1914

03622 *The black Douglas.* Smith, Elder, London, 1899,
       479p, Cloth, Novel
       The light out of the East. [see 03625A]
03623 *Mad Sir Uchtred of the hills,* by the author of
       "The raiders," "The Stickit minister," &c.
       T. Fisher Unwin, London, 1894, 189p, Cloth,
       Novel
03623A *Mad Sir Uchtred of the hills,* by S. R. Crockett
       Macmillan, New York, 1894, 195p, Cloth, Novel
03624 *The playactress; and, Mad Sir Uchtred of the
       hills.* T. Fisher Unwin, London, 1899, 238p,
       Cloth, Coll.
03625 *The white pope, called "the light out of the
       East."* Books Ltd., Liverpool, 1920, 253p,
       Cloth, Novel
03625A retitled: *The light out of the East.* George
       H. Doran, New York, 1920, 254p, Cloth, Novel

CROFFTS, Mrs.

03626 *Ankerwick Castle; a novel.* Minerva-Press, Wil-
       liam Lane, London, 1800, 4vol, Cloth, Novel

CROFT, Sir HERBERT, Bart., 1751-1816 [publishe
anonymously]

03627 *The Abbey of Kilkhampton; or, Monumental record
       for the year 1980, faithfully transcribed
       from the original inscriptions, which are
       still perfect, and appear to be drawn up in
       a stile [sic] devoid of fulsome panegyric or
       unmerited detraction; and compiled with a
       view to ascertain, with precision, the manner
       which prevailed in Great Britain during the
       last fifty years of the eighteenth century.*
       G. Kearsly, London, 1780, 78p, Cloth, Novel
       [Kilkhampton #1]
03628 *The second part of The Abbey of Kilkhampton; or
       Monumental records for the year 1980, faith-
       fully transcribed from the original inscrip-
       tions, which are still perfect, and appear to
       be drawn up in a stile devoid of fulsome pane
       gyric or unmerited detraction.* G. Kearsly,
       London, 1780, 83p-141p, Cloth, Novel [Kilkhamp
       ton #2] [also published with #1 as 2vol/1]

CROFT, Sir HERBERT (Cont.)

03629 *The wreck of Westminster Abbey, alias The year two thousand, alias The ordeal of sepulchral candour, being a selection from the monumental records of the most conspicuous personages who flourished towards the latter end of the eighteenth century, by the author of Kilkhampton Abbey*. Charles Stalker, London, 1788 [dated "2001" in the book], 40p, Cloth, Novel

CROFTON, ALGERNON

03630 *The Queen of Nineveh; a tale of the wickedest city*. Covici-Friede, New York, 1929, 241p, Cloth, Novel

CROFTON, FRANCIS BLAKE, 1841-1912

03631 *Hairbreadth escapes of Major Mendax; a personal narrative*. Hubbard Bros., Philadelphia, 1889, 236p, Cloth, Novel

CROLY, GEORGE, 1780-1860

03632 *Salathiel; a story of the past, the present, and the future*. Henry Colburn, London, 1827, 3vol, Cloth, Novel [published anonymously]
03632A *Salathiel; a story of the past, the present, and the future, by George Croly*. U. P. James, Cincinnati, 1842, 2vol, Cloth, Novel
03632B retitled: *Salathiel the wandering Jew; a story of the past, the present, and the future*. T. B. Peterson, Philadelphia, 1843, 210p, Cloth, Novel
03632C retitled: *Salathiel; or, The wandering Jew; a story of the past, the present, and the future*. T. B. Peterson, Philadelphia, 1850, 210p, Cloth, Novel
03632D retitled: *Salathiel the immortal; a history*. Hurst & Blackett, London, 1855, 468p, Cloth, Novel
03632E retitled: *Tarry thou till I come; or, Salathiel the wandering Jew*. Funk & Wagnalls, New York, 1901, 588p, Cloth, Novel

CROMIE, ROBERT, 1856-1907

03633 *The crack of doom*. Digby, Long, London, 1895, 214p, Cloth, Novel
03634 *For England's sake*. Frederick Warne, London, 1889, 154p, Cloth, Novel
03635 *A new messiah; a novel*. Digby, Long, London, 1902, 320p, Cloth, Novel
03636 *The next crusade*. Hutchinson, London, 1896, 240p, Cloth, Novel
03637 *A plunge into space*. Frederick Warne, London, 1890, 240p, Cloth, Novel

CROMPTON, RICHMAL, pseud. [Richmal Crompton Lamburn, 1890-1969] [*biography included*]

03638 *Dread dwelling*. Boni & Liveright, New York, 1926, 319p, Cloth, Novel
03639 *Mist, and other stories*. Hutchinson, London, 1928, 287p, Cloth, Coll.

03640 *William and the Moon rocket*. George Newnes, London, 1954, 248p, Cloth, Novel [William #29]
03641 *William and the space animal*. George Newnes, London, 1956, 256p, Cloth, Novel [William #30]

CRONIN, BERNARD CHARLES
see: NORTH, ERIC

CROSBY, EDWARD HAROLD, 1859-1934

03642 *Radiana; a novel*. Ivy Press, Boston, 1906, 427p, Cloth, Novel

CROSBY, HARRY C. Jr.
see: ANVIL, CHRISTOPHER

CROSS, GENE

03643 *Nude in orbit*. Nightstand, San Diego, 1968, , Paper, Novel

CROSS, JOHN KEIR, 1914-1967

03644 *The angry planet; an authentic first-hand account of a journey to Mars in the spaceship "Albatross," compiled from notes and records by various members of the expedition, and now assembled and edited for publication by John Keir Cross, from manuscripts made available by Stephen MacFarlane*. Peter Lunn, London, 1945, 200p, Cloth, Novel [Stephen MacFarlane #1]
03645 *Best black magic stories*. Faber & Faber, London, 1960, 269p, Cloth, Anth.
03646 *Best horror stories*. Faber & Faber, London, 1957, 300p, Cloth, Anth.
03647 *Best horror stories two*. Faber & Faber, London, 1965, 270p, Cloth, Anth.
03648 *The Flying Fortunes in an encounter with Rubberface!* Frederick Muller, London, 1952, 219p, Cloth, Novel
03648A retitled: *The stolen sphere; an adventure and a mystery*. E. P. Dutton, New York, 1953, 220p, Cloth, Novel
03649 *The Other Passenger; 18 strange stories*. John Westhouse, London, 1944, 274p, Cloth, Coll.
03649A retitled: *Stories from The Other Passenger*. Ballantine, New York, 1961, 159p, Paper, Coll. [abridged]
The other side of green hills. [see 03650A]
03650 *The owl and the pussycat*. Peter Lunn, London, 1946, 158p, Cloth, Novel
03650A retitled: *The other side of green hills*. Coward-McCann, New York, 1947, 190p, Cloth, Novel
The red journey back. [see 03651A]
03651 *SOS from Mars*. Hutchinson, London, 1954, 216p, Cloth, Novel [Stephen MacFarlane #2]
03651A retitled: *The red journey back; a first-hand account of the second and third Martian expeditions by the space-ships Albatross and Comet, compiled from notes and records by various members of the exploring parties, the whole revised by Stephen MacFarlane, and now fully assembled and edited by John Keir Cross*. Coward-McCann, New York, 1954, 252p, Cloth, Novel [Stephen MacFarlane #2]
The stolen sphere. [see 03648A]
Stories from The Other Passenger. [see 03649A]

CROSS, POLTON, pseud.
    see: FEARN, JOHN RUSSELL

CROSS, (Martha) RUTH, 1887-

    03652   *The unknown goddess; a novel.* Harper & Bros.,
         New York, 1926, 370p, Cloth, Novel

CROSS, THOMPSON

    03653   *The Isle of Forgotten People.* Cassell, London,
         1925, 213p, Cloth, Novel

CROSS, VICTORIA, pseud. [Vivian Cory]

    03654   *Martha Brown, M.P., a girl of to-morrow.*
         T. Werner Laurie, London, 1935, 256p, Cloth,
         Novel

CROSSEN, KENDELL FOSTER, 1910-   [*biography
included*]

    03655   *Adventures in tomorrow.* A Corwin Book, Green-
         berg: Publisher, New York, 1951, 278p, Cloth,
         Anth.
    03656   *Future tense; new and old tales of science
         fiction.* Greenberg: Publisher, New York,
         1952, 364p, Cloth, Anth.
    03657   *Murder out of mind*, by Ken Crossen. Five
         Star Mystery, New York, 1945, 128p, Paper,
         Novel
    03658   *Once upon a star; a novel of the future.* Hen-
         ry Holt, New York, 1953, 237p, Cloth, Novel
    03659   *Year of consent.* Dell, New York, 1954, 224p,
         Paper, Novel

as Richard Foster:

    03660   *The rest must die.* Gold Medal, Greenwich,
         1959, 176p, Paper, Novel

CROSSLAND, JOHN R(edgwick), 1892-   , with
J. M. Parrish

    03661   *The mammoth book of thrillers, ghosts, and
         mysteries.* Odhams Press, London, 1936,
         766p, Cloth, Anth.

CROTTET, ROBERT

    03662   *Stranded in Heaven; a novel.* Richards Press,
         London, 1952, 95p, Cloth, Novel

CROW, MARTHA FOOTE, 1854-1924

    03663   *The world above; a duologue.* Blue Sky Press,
         Chicago, 1905, 37p, Cloth, Story

CROWCROFT, (William) PETER, 1925?-

    03664   *The fallen sky.* Peter Nevill, London, 1954,
         222p, Cloth, Novel

CROYDON, JOHN
    see: COOPER, JOHN C.

CROWLEY, ALEISTER [Edward Alexander Crowley,
1875-1947]

    03665   *Moonchild; a prologue.* Mandrake Press, London,
         1929, 335p, Cloth, Novel
    03666   *The stratagem, and other stories.* Mandrake
         Press, London, 1929, 139p, Cloth, Coll.

CROWN, PETER J.
    see: LEWIS, PETE

CROZETTI, R. WARNER-
    see: WARNER-CROZETTI, R.

CRUIKSHANK, GEORGE
    see: DALTON, JAMES

THE CRUISE OF THE ANTI-TORPEDO

    03667   *The cruise of the anti-torpedo.* Tinsley Bros.,
         London, 1871, 48p, Paper, Story [Dorking
         series]

CRULS, GASTÃO, 1888-

    03668   *The mysterious Amazonia (a Brazilian novel).*
         Livraria-Editora Zelio Valverde, Rio de Janei-
         ro, 1944, 263p, Cloth, Novel

CRUME, VIC

    03669   *Million-dollar duck.* Scholastic Book Services,
         New York, 1971, 111p, Paper, Movie

CRUMLEY, THOMAS W.

    03670   *Star trail.* Vega, Clovis, CA, 1966, 158p,
         Paper, Novel

CRUMP, C(harles) G(eorge), 1862-1935

    03671   *The Red King dreams, 1946-1948.* Faber & Faber,
         London, 1931, 383p, Cloth, Novel

CRUMP, (James) IRVING, 1887-

    03672   *Mog, the Mound Builder.* Dodd, Mead, New York,
         1931, 228p, Cloth, Novel
    03673   *Og--boy of battle.* Dodd, Mead, New York, 1925,
         289p, Cloth, Novel [Og #2]
    03674   *Og of the cave people.* Dodd, Mead, New York,
         1935, 232p, Cloth, Novel [Og #3]
    03675   *Og--son of fire.* Dodd, Mead, New York, 1922,
         198p, Cloth, Novel [Og #1]
    03676   *Og, son of Og.* Dodd, Mead, New York, 1965,
         211p, Cloth, Novel [Og #4]

CRUSO, SOLOMON

    03677   *The last of the Japs and the Jews.* Herman W.
         Lefkowitz, New York, 1933, 334p, Cloth,
         Novel

CRUSO, SOLOMON (Cont.)

03678 *Messiah on the horizon; romance? novel? reve-*
lation? prophecy? reality? Audubon Publishing Co., New York, 1940, 288p, Cloth, Novel

03679 *Two trillion immortals; romance? novel? pro-*
phecy? reality? revelation? Hobson Book
Press, New York, 1946, 291p, Cloth, Novel

CULLEN, COUNTEE, 1903-1946

03680 *My lives and how I lost them*, by Christopher
Cat, in collaboration with Countee Cullen.
Harper & Bros., New York, 1942, 160p, Cloth,
Novel

CULLINGFORD, GUY, pseud. [Constance Lindsay
Taylor, 1907-]

03681 *Post mortem.* J. B. Lippincott, Philadelphia,
1953, 255p, Cloth, Novel; Hammond & Hammond,
London, 1953, 255p, Cloth, Novel

CULLUM, RIDGWELL, 1867-1943

03682 *The vampire of N'Gobi.* Chapman & Hall, London,
1935, 320p, Cloth, Novel

CULVER, TIMOTHY J., pseud.
see: WESTLAKE, DONALD E.

CUMBERLAND, STUART, pseud. [Charles Garner]

03683 *A fatal affinity; a weird story.* Spencer
Blackett, London, 1889, 160p, Cloth, Novel

CUMMINGS, M(onette) A.

03684 *Exile, and other tales of fantasy.* Flagship,
New York, 1968, 160p, Paper, Coll.

CUMMINGS, RAY(mond King), 1887-1957

03685 *Beyond the stars.* Ace, New York, 1963, 160p,
Paper, Novel

03686 *Beyond the vanishing point.* Ace Double, New
York, 1958, 95p, Paper, Novel

03687 *A brand new world.* Ace, New York, 1964, 158p,
Paper, Novel

03688 *Brigands of the Moon.* A. C. McClurg, Chicago,
1931, 386p, Cloth, Novel [Gregg Haljan #1]

03688A *Brigands of the Moon*, by John W. Campbell [an
error]. Duchess Printing Co., Toronto,
1950?,   , Paper, Novel

03689 *The exile of time.* Avalon, New York, 1964,
192p, Cloth, Novel

03690 *Explorers into infinity.* Avalon, New York,
1965, 192p, Cloth, Novel

03691 *The girl in the golden atom.* Methuen, London,
1922, 241p, Cloth, Novel

03692 *The insect invasion.* Avalon, New York, 1967,
191p, Cloth, Novel

03693 *The man who mastered time.* A. C. McClurg,
Chicago, 1929, 351p, Cloth, Novel

03694 *The princess of the atom.* Avon, New York,
1950, 158p, Paper, Novel

03695 *The sea girl.* A. C. McClurg, Chicago, 1930,
302p, Cloth, Novel

03696 *The shadow girl.* Gerald G. Swan, London, 1946,
186p, Cloth, Novel

03697 *Tama of the light country.* Ace, New York,
1965, 124p, Paper, Novel [Tama #1]

03698 *Tama, princess of Mercury.* Ace, New York,
1966, 128p, Paper, Novel [Tama #2]

03699 *Tarrano, the Conqueror.* A. C. McClurg, Chicago,
1930, 345p, Cloth, Novel

03700 *Wandl, the invader.* Ace Double, New York,
1961, 135p, Paper, Novel [Gregg Haljan #2]

CUMMINS, HARLE OREN

03701 *Welsh rarebit tales.* Mutual Book Co., Boston,
1902, 173p, Cloth, Coll.

CUNNINGHAM, BEALL

03702 *Wide white page.* Hutchinson, London, 1936,
288p, Cloth, Novel

CUPPY, WILL(iam Jacob), 1884-1949

03703 *World's great mystery stories; American and*
English masterpieces. World Publishing Co.,
Cleveland, 1943, 299p, Cloth, Anth.

THE CURIOUS BOOK OF CLAMPUS

03704 *The curious book of Clampus; or, Gumshaniana.*
Ancient & Honorable Order of E Clampus Vitus,
Yerba Buena, CA, 1935, 27p, Cloth, Story

CURRAN, RONALD

03705 *Witches, wraiths & warlocks; supernatural tales*
of the American Renaissance. Fawcett Premier,
Greenwich, 1971, 361p, Paper, Anth.

CURRY, JANE LOUISE, 1932-   [biography inclu-
ded]

03706 *Beneath the hill.* Harcourt, Brace & World,
New York, 1967, 255p, Cloth, Novel

03707 *The change-child.* Harcourt, Brace & World,
New York, 1969, 174p, Cloth, Novel

03708 *The daybreakers.* Harcourt, Brace & World,
New York, 1970, 191p, Cloth, Novel [Prince
Lincoas #1]
The housenapper. [see 03710A]

03709 *The lost farm.* Atheneum, New York, 1974, 137p,
Cloth, Novel [Mindy #2]

03710 *Mindy's mysterious miniature.* Harcourt Brace
Jovanovich, New York, 1970, 157p, Cloth,
Novel [Mindy #1]

03710A retitled: *The housenapper.* Longman Young
Books, London, 1971, 141p, Cloth, Novel
[Mindy #1]

03711 *Over the sea's edge.* Longman Young Books, London, 1971, 183p, Cloth, Novel [Prince Lincoas #2]

03712 *The Sleepers.* Harcourt, Brace & World, New
York, 1968, 255p, Cloth, Novel

THE CURSE OF BLOOD

03713 *The curse of blood*. Scientific Thriller, Sydney, 1949, 50p, Paper, Anth.

THE CURSE OF INTELLECT

03714 *The curse of intellect*. Roberts Bros., Boston, 1895, 177p, Cloth, Novel; William Blackwood & Sons, Edinburgh, 1895, 177p, Cloth, Novel [attributed by the National Union Catalog to Lady Gwendolen Cecil, 1860-1933, and by the British Museum Catalogue to Frank Challice Constable]

A CURSORY VIEW OF THE HISTORY OF LILLIPUT

03715 *A cursory view of the history of Lilliput for these last forty three years, containing some remarks upon the origin, nature, and tendency of the religious and political disputes which exist among the subjects*. A. Moore, London, 1727, 24p, Paper, Story [Gulliver series]

CURTIES, Captain HENRY, 1860-

03716 *When England slept*. Everett & Co., London, 1909, 312p, Cloth, Novel

CURTIES, T. J. HORSLEY

03717 *Ancient records; or, The abbey of Saint Oswyth; a romance*. Minerva-Press, William Lane, London, 1801, vol. I-408p, II-396p, III-350p, IV-319p, Cloth, Novel

as T. J. Horsley:

03718 *Ethelwina; or, The house of Fitz-Auburne*. Minerva-Press, William Lane, London, 1799, 3vol, Cloth, Novel

CURTIS, ALBERT CHARLES, 1867-

03719 *A new Trafalgar; a tale of the torpedo fleet*. Smith, Elder, London, 1902, 301p, Cloth, Novel

CURTIS, GEORGE WILLIAM, 1824-1892

03720 *Prue and I*. Dix, Edwards, New York, 1856, 214p, Cloth, Novel
03721 *Prue and I; Lotus eating*. J. M. Dent & Sons, London, 1910, 254p, Cloth, Coll.
03722 *Prue and I; and, The public duty of educated men*. Macmillan, New York, 1919, 224p, Cloth, Coll.

CURTIS, J(ean)-L(ouis), 1917-

03723 *The neon halo; the face of the future*. Secker & Warburg, London, 1958, 239p, Cloth, Novel

CURTIS, MONICA (Mary)

03724 *Landslide*. Victor Gollancz, London, 1934, 286p, Cloth, Novel

CURTIS, RICHARD (Alan), 1937- [*biography included*]

03725 *Future tense*. Dell, New York, 1968, 220p, Paper, Anth.

CURTIS, ROBERT (G.)

03726 *The table; the novel of Edgar Wallace's film story*. Hutchinson, London, 1936, 287p, Cloth, Movie

CURTIS, WARDON ALLAN, 1867-1940

03727 *The strange adventures of Mr. Middleton*. Herbert S. Stone, Chicago, 1903, 311p, Cloth, Novel

CURTISS, F(rank) HOMER, 1875-1946, with Harriette Augusta Curtiss

03728 *The love of Rabiacca; a tragedy in five acts; a tale of a prehistoric race recovered psychically*. Curtiss Philosophic Book Co., Washington, 1934, 67p, Cloth, Novel

CURTISS, HARRIETTE AUGUSTA, 1856?-1932, with F. Homer Curtiss

03728 *The love of Rabiacca; a tragedy in five acts; a tale of a prehistoric race recovered psychically*. Curtiss Philosophic Book Co., Washington, 1934, 67p, Cloth, Novel

CURTOIS, M(argaret) A(nne)

03729 *The romance of a country; a masque*. T. Fisher Unwin, London, 1893, vol. I-272p, II-258p, Cloth, Novel

CURZON-HERRICK, MAUD
see: CAIRNES, MAUD

CUSTOT, PIERRE, 1880-

03730 *Sturly*. Houghton Mifflin, Boston, 1923, 127p, Cloth, Novel

CUTHBERT, ESTELLA Y.
see: YEREX, CUTHBERT

CUTT, W(illiam) TOWRIE, 1898-

03731 *Seven for the sea*. Andre Deutsch, London, 1972, 96p, Cloth, Novel

DABBS, GEORGE H(enry) R(oqué), 1846-1913

03732 *The dream; a phantasy.* Charles William Deacon, London, 1900, 61p, Cloth, Novel
03733 *"Ugly," a hospital dog, told by himself; with, Recitations and readings.* Charles William Deacon, London, 1902, 200p, Cloth, Coll.

DACRE, CHARLOTTE, 1782-

03734 *Zofloya; or, The Moor; a romance of the fifteenth century.* Longman, Hurst, Rees & Orme, London, 1806, 3vol, Cloth, Novel

DAGMAR, pseud.
    see: CAMERON, LOU

DAGMAR, PETER

03735 *Alien skies.* Digit, London, 1962, 160p, Paper, Novel
03736 *Once in time.* Digit, London, 1963, 160p, Paper, Novel
03737 *Sands of time.* Digit, London, 1963, 155p, Paper, Novel
03738 *Spykos 4; strange life-forms on unexplored planets.* Digit, London, 1962, 154p, Paper, Novel

DAHL, ROALD, 1916-   [*biography included*]

03739 *The gremlins.* Random House, New York, 1943, , Cloth, Movie
03740 *Kiss kiss.* Alfred A. Knopf, New York, 1960, 309p, Cloth, Coll.
03741 *Sometime never; a fable for supermen.* Charles Scribner's Sons, New York, 1948, 244p, Cloth, Novel
03742 *Switch bitch.* Alfred A. Knopf, New York, 1974, 210p, Cloth, Coll.
03743 *Twenty-nine kisses from Roald Dahl.* Michael Joseph, London, 1969, 442p, Cloth, Coll. [includes *Kiss kiss* and *Someone like you*]

DAIL, C(harles) C(urtis)

03744 *The stone giant; a story of the Mammoth Cave.* F. Tennyson Neely, New York, 1898, 235p, Paper, Novel
03745 *Willmoth, the wanderer; or, The man from Saturn.* Haskell Printing Co., Atchison, Kans., 1890, 242p, Cloth, Novel

A DAILY EYE-WITNESS, AND FRIEND OF TRUTH
    see: JOURNEYS INTO THE MOON

DAIN, ALEX, pseud. [Alex Lukeman]

03746 *The Bane of Kanthos.* Ace Double, New York, 1969, 124p, Paper, Novel

DAKE, CHARLES ROMYN ["Romeyn" on cover]

03747 *A strange discovery.* H. Ingalls Kimball, New York, 1899, 310p, Cloth, Novel [sequel to Poe's *Arthur Gordon Pym*]

DAKERS, ELAINE
    see: LANE, JANE

DALBY, RICHARD

03748 *Sorceress in stained glass, and other ghost stories.* Tom Stacey, London, 1971, 214p?, Cloth, Anth.
03749 *The spectre spiders, and other ghost stories.* Tom Stacey, London, 1973, , Cloth, Anth.

DALE, ADAM, pseud.
    see: HOLLOWAY, BRIAN

DALE, HARRISON (Clifford), 1885-

03750 *Great ghost stories.* Herbert Jenkins, London, 1930, 399p, Cloth, Anth.
03751 *More great ghost stories.* Herbert Jenkins, London, 1932, 396p, Cloth, Anth.

DALE, J. S. of
    see: STIMSON, FREDERIC JESUP

DALLAS, IAN

03752 *The book of strangers.* Pantheon, New York, 1972, 151p, Cloth, Novel

DALLAS, Captain OSWALD (C. C.)

03753 *The treasures of Asshur.* Jarrolds, London, 1925, 309p, Cloth, Novel
03754 *The valley of mystery.* Thomas Nelson & Sons, London, 1929, 280p, Cloth, Novel

DALLAS, PAUL V.

03755 *The lost planet.* John C. Winston, Philadelphia, 1956, 209p, Cloth, Novel

DALMAINE, JAMES

03756 *The vengeance of science.* Arthur H. Stockwell, London, 1927, 240p, Cloth, Novel

DALMAS, JOHN

03757 *The yngling.* Pyramid, New York, 1971, 224p, Paper, Novel

DALRYMPLE-HAY, JOHN WARWICK
    see: HAY, JOHN

DALSACE, LIONEL
    see: BLECH, AIMEE

DALTON, H(enry) R(obert) S(amuel)

03758 *Lesbia Newman; a novel.* George Redway, London, 1889, 327p, Cloth, Novel

DALTON, JAMES [published anonymously]

03759   *The gentleman in black.* William Kidd, London, 1831, 309p, Cloth, Novel

DALTON, MORAY

03760   *The black death.* Sampson Low, Marston, London, 1934, 316p, Cloth, Novel

DAMNED
   see: DORRANCE, ETHEL SMITH

DAMON, RAY, pseud.
   see: NORDAY, MICHAEL

DAMON, STEVE

03761   *Suck-witch.* Cameo Library, Thousand Oaks, CA, 1973, 192p, Paper, Novel

with Montague Smith:

03762   *The incredible world of Harold Huge.* Pendulum, Los Angeles, 1970, 191p, Paper, Novel

DANA, FRANCIS

03763   *The decoy.* John Lane, The Bodley Head, London, 1902, 314p, Cloth, Novel

DANBY, FRANK, pseud. [Julia Frankau, 1864-1916]

03764   *Twilight.* Dodd, Mead, New York, 1916, 369p, Cloth, Novel; Hutchinson, London, 1916, 332p, Cloth, Novel

DANBY, MARY (Heather), 1941-   [*biography included*]

03765   *The eighth Fontana book of great horror stories.* Fontana, London, 1973, 189p, Paper, Anth.
03766   *The fifth Armada ghost book.* Armada, London, 1973, 125p, Paper, Anth.
03767   *The fifth Fontana book of great horror stories.* Fontana, London, 1970, 189p, Paper, Anth.
03768   *Frighteners.* Fontana, London, 1974, 159p, Paper, Anth.
03769   *The fourth Armada ghost book.* Armada, London, 1972, 128p, Paper, Anth.
03770   *The seventh Fontana book of great horror stories.* Fontana, London, 1972, 190p, Paper, Anth.
03771   *The sixth Armada ghost book.* Armada, London, 1974, 128p, Paper, Anth.
03772   *The sixth Fontana book of great horror stories.* Fontana, London, 1971, 189p, Paper, Anth.
03773   *The third Armada ghost book.* Armada, London, 1970, 128p, Paper, Anth.

DANE, CLEMENCE, pseud. [Winifred Ashton, 1888-1965]

03774   *The arrogant mystery of White Ben.* William Heinemann, London, 1939, 420p, Cloth, Novel

03775   *The Babyons; a family chronicle.* William Heinemann, London, 1927, 380p, Cloth, Novel
03776   *The Moon is feminine.* William Heinemann, London, 1938, 282p, Cloth, Novel

DANFORTH, MILDRED E.

03777   *From outer space.* Digit, London, 1963, 159p, Paper, Novel

DANGERFIELD, PAUL

03778   *Island of the voodoo dolls.* Pompeii Press, El Cajon, CA, 1969, 196p, Paper, Novel

DANIEL, CHARLES (S.)

03779   *Ai; a social vision.* Miller Publication Co., Philadelphia, 1892, 296p, Cloth, Novel

DANIEL, F(erdinand) E(ugene), 1839-1914

03780   *The strange case of Dr. Bruno.* Von Boeckmann-Jones, Austin, TX, 1906, 235p, Cloth, Novel

DANIEL', IUlii (Markovich), 1925-

03781   *This is Moscow speaking, and other stories*, by Yuli Daniel. Collins, Harvill Press, London, 1968, 159p, Cloth, Coll.

DANIEL, JERRY C(layton), 1937-   [*biography included*]

03782   *The space machine.* Lenox Hill Press, New York, 1971, 192p, Cloth, Novel

DANIEL, YULI
   see: DANIEL', IUlii

DANIELS, DOROTHY

03783   *Ghost song.* Pocket, New York, 1974, 222p, Paper, Novel
03784   *The house of many doors.* Warner Paperback Library, 1971, 173p, Paper, Novel
03785   *Lady of the shadows.* Paperback Library, New York, 1968, 159p, Paper, Novel
03786   *Strange paradise.* Paperback Library, New York, 1969, 154p, Paper, Tele. [Strange Paradise #1]
03787   *Strange paradise #2; island of evil.* Paperback Library, New York, 1970, 160p, Paper, Novel [Strange Paradise #2]
03788   *Strange paradise #3; Raxl, voodoo priestess.* Paperback Library, New York, 1970, 159p, Paper, Tele. [Strange Paradise #3]
03789   *The tormented.* Paperback Library, New York, 1969, 160p, Paper, Novel

DANIELS, GIL, pseud.
   see: KULLINGER, J. L.

DANIELS, JONATHAN (Worth), 1902-

03790 *Clash of angels.* Brewer & Warren, New York, 1930, 288p, Cloth, Novel

DANIELS, NORMAN (A.)

03791 *The Avengers; "The magnetic man."* Berkley Medallion, New York, 1968, 128p, Paper, Tele. [Avengers #8]
03792 *Spy ghost.* Pyramid, New York, 1965, 126p, Paper, Novel
03793 *Voodoo slave.* Paperback Library, New York, 1970, 191p, Paper, Novel

as Kenneth Robeson, house pseud.:

03794 *The black spot; a Doc Savage adventure.* Bantam, New York, 1974, 152p, Paper, Novel [Doc Savage #76]
03795 *Cold death; a Doc Savage adventure.* Bantam, New York, 1968, 121p, Paper, Novel [Doc Savage #21]
03796 *Haunted ocean; a Doc Savage adventure.* Bantam, New York, 1970, 140p, Paper, Novel [Doc Savage #51]
03797 *He could stop the world; a Doc Savage adventure.* Bantam, New York, 1970, 140p, Paper, Novel [Doc Savage #54]
03798 *Land of long juju; a Doc Savage adventure.* Bantam, New York, 1970, 140p, Paper, Novel [Doc Savage #47]
03799 *Mad eyes; a Doc Savage adventure.* Bantam, New York, 1969, 120p, Paper, Novel [Doc Savage #34]
03800 *The men who smiled no more; a Doc Savage adventure.* Bantam, New York, 1970, 138p, Paper, Novel [Doc Savage #45]
03801 *Murder melody; a Doc Savage adventure.* Bantam, New York, 1967, 138p, Paper, Novel [Doc Savage #15]
03802 *Murder mirage; a Doc Savage adventure.* Bantam, New York, 1972, 153p, Paper, Novel [Doc Savage #71]

DANN, JACK (Mayo), 1945-   [*biography included*]

03803 *Wandering stars; an anthology of Jewish fantasy and science fiction.* Harper & Row, New York, 1974, 239p, Cloth, Anth. [name on cover: Jack Dunn]

DANNAY, FREDERIC, 1905-   , with Manfred B. Lee as Ellery Queen

03804 *And on the eighth day.* Random House, New York, 1964, 191p, Cloth, Novel

with Manfred B. Lee as Barnaby Ross:

03805 *The scrolls of Lysis.* Simon & Schuster, New York, 1962, 254p, Cloth, Novel

DANVERS, JACK, pseud. [Camille Auguste Marie Caseleyr, 1909-   ] [*biography included*]

03806 *The end of it all.* Heinemann, London, 1962, 231p, Cloth, Novel

DANYERS, GEOFFREY

03807 *Blood is thicker than water; a political dream.* Tower Publishing Co., London, 1894, 159p, Cloth, Novel

DANZIGER, DAVID

03808 *The devil in Miss Jones.* Grove Press, New York, 1973, 158p, Paper, Movie

D'APERY, HELEN
     see: HARPER, OLIVE

DARBY, CHRISTOPHER
     see: OUDEIS

D'ARCOS, J. PACO
     see: PACO de ARCOS, J.

DARD, ROGER

03809 *Fantastic novels; a check list.* Dragon Press, Perth, Australia, 1957, 11p, Paper, Nonf.

DARDENELLE, LOUISE

03810 *World without raiment; a fantasy.* Valiant Press, New York, 1943, 260p, Cloth, Novel

DARDIS, THOMAS A. [published anonymously]

03811 *Beyond.* Berkley Medallion, New York, 1963, 160p, Paper, Anth.

DARE, M(arcus) P(aul), 1902-1962

03812 *Unholy relics, and other uncanny tales.* Edward Arnold, London, 1947, 184p, Cloth, Coll.

DARGON, pseud.

03813 *The nameless order.* John Lane, The Bodley Head, London, 1924, 312p, Cloth, Novel

DARITY, WILLIAM A., 1953-

03814 *The shades of time; a science-fiction novella.* William-Frederick Press, New York, 1969, 67p, Paper, Novel

DARK, JAMES, pseud. [James Workman]

03815 *Horror tales.* Horwitz, Sydney, 1963, 130p, Paper, Coll.
03816 *Operation Octopus.* Signet, New York, 1968, 125p, Paper, Novel [Mark Hood series]
03817 *Operation Scuba.* Signet, New York, 1967, 125p, Paper, Novel [Mark Hood series]
03818 *Terrifying tales.* Horwitz, Sydney, 1963, 130p, Paper, Coll.

THE DARK CITY

03819   *The dark city.* Gerald G. Swan, London, 1944?, 48p, Paper, Anth.

THE DARK DOMINION

03820   *The dark dominion; eight terrifying tales of vampires and werewolves.* Paperback Library, New York, 1970, 158p, Paper, Anth. [includes some nonf.]

DARKNESS AND DAWN

03821   *Darkness and dawn; the peaceful birth of a new age.* Kegan Paul, Trench, London, 1884, 141p, Cloth, Novel

DARLINGTON, W(illiam) A(ubrey Cecil), 1890- [*biography included*]

03822   *Alf's button.* Herbert Jenkins, London, 1919, 320p, Cloth, Novel [Alf Higgins #1]
03823   *Alf's carpet.* Herbert Jenkins, London, 1928, 312p, Cloth, Novel [Alf Higgins #2]
03824   *Alf's new button.* Herbert Jenkins, London, 1940, 284p, Cloth, Novel [Alf Higgins #3]
03825   *Egbert.* Herbert Jenkins, London, 1924, 316p, Cloth, Novel
03826   *Wishes limited.* Herbert Jenkins, London, 1922, 312p, Cloth, Novel

DARRELL, GRATIANA

03827   *The haunted looking-glass.* Digby, Long, London, 1897, 103p, Cloth, Novel

DARRINGTON, HUGH, 1940- [*biography included*]

03828   *Gravitor; science fiction.* Sidgwick & Jackson, London, 1971, 203p, Cloth, Novel

with Tony Halliwell as James Ross:

03829   *The God killers; science fiction.* Sidgwick & Jackson, London, 1970, 190p, Cloth, Novel

DARROW, FRANK M.

03830   *Wife styles and life styles.* Frank M. Darrow, Trona, CA, 1974, 34p, Paper, Story [includes some nonf.; originally published as part of Darrow's *Middle childhood and future life styles*, which is mostly nonf.]

da SILVA, JOAQUIM BELFORD CORREA
   see: PACO d'ARCOS, J.

A DAUGHTER OF INDRA
   see: WARDE, REGINALD

DAUMAL, RENÉ, 1908-1944

03831   *Mount Analogue.* Vincent Stuart, London, 1959, 106p, Cloth, Novel

DAUPHINE, CLAUDE

03832   *Roamin' circus.* Elite Books, no place, 1959, 241p, Cloth, Novel

D'AUREVILLY, J. BARBEY
   see: BARBEY D'AUREVILLY, J.

DAVENPORT, BASIL, 1905-1966

03833   *Deals with the devil; an anthology.* Dodd, Mead, New York, 1958, 349p, Cloth, Anth. [ghost-edited by Albert P. Blaustein]
03833A retitled: *Twelve stories from Deals with the devil; an anthology.* Ballantine, New York, 1959, 160p, Paper, Anth. [abridged; ghost-edited by Albert P. Blaustein]
03834   *Famous monster tales.* Van Nostrand, Princeton, 1967, 201p, Cloth, Anth. [ghost-edited by Albert P. Blaustein]
03835   *Ghostly tales to be told; a collection of stories from the great masters.* Dodd, Mead, New York, 1950, 317p, Cloth, Anth.
     Horror stories from Tales to be told in the dark. [see 03839A]
03836   *Inquiry into science fiction.* Longmans, Green, London, 1955, 87p, Cloth, Nonf.
03837   *An introduction to Islandia; its history, customs, laws, language, and geography, as prepared by Basil Davenport from Islandia: History and Description, by Jean Perrier, first French consul to Islandia, and translated by John Lang, first American consul.* Farrar & Rinehart, New York, 1942, 61p, Cloth, Nonf. [adapted from Austin Tappan Wright's novel, *Islandia*]
03838   *Invisible men.* Ballantine, New York, 1960, 158p, Paper, Anth. [ghost-edited by Albert P. Blaustein]
03839   *Tales to be told in the dark; a selection of stories from the great authors.* Dodd, Mead, New York, 1953, 335p, Cloth, Anth.
03839A retitled: *Horror stories from Tales to be told in the dark; a selection of stories from the great authors.* Ballantine, New York, 1960, 159p, Paper, Anth. [abridged]
     Twelve stories from Deals with the devil. [see 03833A]

DAVENPORT, BENJAMIN RUSH

03840   *Anglo-Saxons onward! a romance of the future.* Hubbell Publishing Co., Cleveland, 1898, 279p, Paper, Novel
03841   *"Uncle Sam's" cabins; a story of American life, looking forward a century.* Mascot Publishing Co., New York, 1895, 271p, Paper, Novel

DAVENPORT, LEONARD (John), 1915- [*biography included*]

03842   *Degree XII.* Robert Hale, London, 1972, 190p, Cloth, Novel
03843   *A man of double deed.* Doubleday, Garden City, 1965, 191p, Cloth, Novel; Victor Gollancz, London, 1965, 176p, Cloth, Novel [released the same day]
03844   *Reflections in a mirage.* Robert Hale, London, 1969, 192p, Cloth, Novel

DAVENTRY, LEONARD (Cont.)

03845 *Reflections in a mirage; and, The ticking is
       in your head.* Doubleday, Garden City, 1969,
       358p, Cloth, Coll.
03846 *Terminus.* Robert Hale, London, 1971, 191p,
       Cloth, Novel
03847 *The ticking is in your head.* Robert Hale,
       London, 1970, 191p, Cloth, Novel
03848 *Twenty-one billionth paradox.* Doubleday, Gar-
       den City, 1971, 204p, Cloth, Novel

DAVEY, (Henry) NORMAN, 1888-

03849 *Judgment day.* Constable, London, 1928, 305p,
       Cloth, Novel
03850 *Pagan parable; an allegory in four acts.*
       Grayson & Grayson, London, 1936, 317p, Cloth,
       Novel
03851 *The penultimate adventure.* Elkin Mathews,
       London, 1924, 62p, Cloth, Novel [Matthew
       Sumner #2]
03852 *Perhaps.* Methuen, London, 1914, 300p, Cloth,
       Novel
03852A retitled: *Yesterday; a Tory fairy-tale.* Chap-
       man & Hall, London, 1924, 240p, Cloth, Novel
03853 *The pilgrim of a smile.* Chapman & Hall, Lon-
       don, 1921, 274p, Cloth, Novel [Matthew Sum-
       ner #1]
03854 *The pilgrim of a smile.* Chapman & Hall, Lon-
       don, 1933, 325p, Cloth, Novel [Matthew Sum-
       ner #s 1-2] [includes *The penultimate adven-
       ture* as a final chapter]
       Yesterday. [see 03852A]

DAVID, JACK
    see: FLANNER, JACK

DAVIDSON, AVRAM, 1923-   [*biography included*]

03855 *The best from Fantasy and science fiction,
       twelfth series.* Doubleday, Garden City,
       1963, 225p, Cloth, Anth.
03856 *The best from Fantasy and science fiction,
       thirteenth series.* Doubleday, Garden City,
       1964, 255p, Cloth, Anth.
03857 *The best from Fantasy and science fiction,
       fourteenth series.* Doubleday, Garden City,
       1965, 251p, Cloth, Anth.
03858 *Clash of star-kings.* Ace Double, New York,
       1966, 105p, Paper, Novel
03859 *The enemy of my enemy.* Berkley Medallion,
       New York, 1966, 160p, Paper, Novel
03860 *The Island under the Earth.* Ace, New York,
       1969, 189p, Paper, Novel
03861 *The Kar-chee reign.* Ace Double, New York,
       1966, 138p, Paper, Novel [Kar-chee #2]
03862 *Masters of the Maze.* Pyramid, New York, 1965,
       158p, Paper, Novel
03863 *Mutiny in space.* Pyramid, New York, 1964,
       159p, Paper, Novel
03864 *Or all the seas with oysters.* Berkley Medal-
       lion, New York, 1962, 176p, Paper, Coll.
03865 *Peregrine: primus.* Walker, New York, 1971,
       174p, Cloth, Novel
03866 *The Phoenix and the mirror.* Doubleday, Garden
       City, 1969, 209p, Cloth, Novel
03867 *Rogue dragon.* Ace, New York, 1965, 142p,
       Paper, Novel [Kar-chee #1]

03868 *Rork!* Berkley Medallion, New York, 1965, 144p,
       Paper, Novel
03869 *Strange seas and shores; a collection of short
       stories.* Doubleday, Garden City, 1971, 219p,
       Cloth, Coll.
03870 *Ursus of Ultima Thule.* Avon, New York, 1973,
       236p, Paper, Novel
03871 *What strange stars and skies.* Ace, New York,
       1965, 188p, Paper, Coll.

with Ward Moore:

03872 *Joyleg; a folly.* Pyramid, New York, 1962,
       160p, Paper, Novel

DAVIDSON, JOHN, 1857-1909

03873 *The pilgrimage of Strongsoul, and other stories.*
       Ward & Downey, London, 1896, 278p, Cloth,
       Coll.

DAVIES, FREDRIC, pseud.
    see: ELLIK, RON and LANGLEY, FREDRIC

DAVIES, HOWELL
    see: MARVELL, ANDREW

DAVIES, HUGH SYKES, 1909-

03874 *The papers of Andrew Melmoth.* Methuen, London,
       1960, 236p, Cloth, Novel

DAVIES, L(eslie) P(urnell), 1914-   [*biography
included*]

03875 *The alien.* Herbert Jenkins, London, 1968, 183p,
       Cloth, Novel
03875A retitled: *The Groundstar conspiracy.* Sphere,
       London, 1972, 157p, Paper, Novel
03876 *The artificial man.* Herbert Jenkins, London,
       1965, 188p, Cloth, Novel
03877 *Dimension A.* Doubleday, Garden City, 1969,
       207p, Cloth, Novel
03878 *Genesis two.* Herbert Jenkins, London, 1969,
       191p, Cloth, Novel
       The Groundstar conspiracy. [see 03875A]
03879 *The Lampton dreamers.* Herbert Jenkins, London,
       1966, 192p, Cloth, Novel
03880 *The paper dolls.* Herbert Jenkins, London, 1964,
       224p, Cloth, Novel
03881 *Psychogeist.* Herbert Jenkins, London, 1966,
       191p, Cloth, Novel
03882 *Twilight journey.* Herbert Jenkins, London,
       1967, 191p, Cloth, Novel

DAVIES, M(ary) CATHERINE

03883 *Adventures with the mermaids.* S. Wood, Sydney,
       1929, 128p, Cloth, Novel

DAVIES, VALENTINE, 1905-1961

03884 *It happens every spring.* Farrar, Straus & Co.,
       New York, 1949, 224p, Cloth, Movie
03885 *Miracle on 34th Street.* Harcourt, Brace & Co.,
       New York, 1947, 120p, Cloth, Movie

d'AVIGDOR, ELIM HENRY
   see: WANDERER

da VINCI, LEONARDO
   see: PAYNE, ROBERT

DAVIS, (G.) BRIAN

   03886   *The old masters.* New English Library, London,
           1970, 128p, Paper, Anth.

DAVIS, ELIZABETH [Lou Ellen Davis, 1936-   ]

   03887   *Along came a spider.* Signet, New York, 1970,
           176p, Paper, Novel
   03888   *Suffer a witch to die.* Signet, New York,
           1969, 205p, Paper, Novel

DAVIS, GERRY

   03889   *Doctor Who and the Cybermen.* Target, London,
           1974, 150p, Paper, Tele. [Doctor Who #11]

with Kit Pedler:

   03890   *Brainrack.* Souvenir Press, London, 1974,
           285p, Cloth, Novel
   03891   *Mutant 59: the plastic-eater.* Souvenir Press,
           London, 1971, 295p, Cloth, Novel

DAVIS, GWEN, 1936-   [*biography included*]

   03892   *Kingdom come.* G. P. Putnam's Sons, New York,
           1973, 160p, Cloth, Novel

DAVIS, GYLE
   see: KULLINGER, J. L.

DAVIS, JAMES
   see: HALL, OWEN

DAVIS, PETER

   03893   *King of the Amazon.* Macaulay Co., New York,
           1933, 310p, Cloth, Novel

DAVIS, RICHARD [*biography included*]

   03894   *Space 1; a collection of science fiction sto-
           ries.* Abelard-Schuman, London, 1973, 155p,
           Cloth, Anth.
   03895   *Space 2; a collection of science fiction sto-
           ries.* Abelard-Schuman, London, 1974, 140p?,
           Cloth, Anth.
   03896   *Spectre 1; a collection of ghost stories.*
           Abelard-Schuman, London, 1973, 176p?, Cloth,
           Anth.
   03897   *Tandem horror 2.* Tandem, London, 1968, 192p,
           Paper, Anth.
   03898   *Tandem horror 3.* Tandem, London, 1969, 190p,
           Paper, Anth.
   03899   *The year's best horror stories, no. 1.* Sphere,
           London, 1971, 189p, Paper, Anth.
   03900   *The year's best horror stories, no. 2.* Sphere,
           London, 1972, 160p, Paper, Anth.

   03901   *The year's best horror stories, no. 3.* Sphere,
           London, 1973, 173p, Paper, Anth.
   03902   *The year's best horror stories, series II.*
           DAW, New York, 1974, 207p, Paper, Anth. [in-
           cludes selections from 03900 and 03901]

DAVIS, RICHARD HARDING, 1864-1916

   03903   *The bar sinister.* Charles Scribner's Sons,
           New York, 1903, 108p, Cloth, Novel

DAVIS, WILLIAM STEARNS, 1877-1930

   03904   *Belshazzar; a tale of the fall of Babylon.*
           Doubleday, Page, New York, 1902, 427p, Cloth,
           Novel; Grant Richards, London, 1902, 427p,
           Cloth, Novel
   03905   *The saint of the Dragon's Dale; a fantastic
           tale.* Macmillan, New York, 1903, 134p, Cloth,
           Novel

DAVY, CATHERINE A.

   03906   *After the clouds.* House of Field-Doubleday,
           New York, 1945, 389p, Cloth, Novel

DAWE, W(illiam) CARLTON (Lanyon), 1865-1935

   03907   *The golden lake; or, The marvellous history of
           a journey through the great lone land of
           Australia.* Trischler, London, 1890, 284p,
           Cloth, Novel
   03908   *A strange destiny.* Ward, Lock, London, 1937,
           320p, Cloth, Novel

THE DAWN OF THE TWENTIETH CENTURY

   03909   *The dawn of the twentieth century; a novel
           social and political.* Remington & Co., Lon-
           don, 1882, 3vol, Cloth, Novel

THE DAWN OF THE TWENTIETH CENTURY, 1ST JANUARY
1901

   03910   *The dawn of the twentieth century, 1st January
           1901.* Field & Tuer, London, 1888, 156p,
           Cloth, Novel

DAWSON, A(lec) J(ohn), 1872-1951

   03911   *His mortal tenement.* Grant Richards, London,
           1924, 176p, Cloth, Novel
   03912   *The message.* Grant Richards, London, 1907,
           386p, Cloth, Novel

DAWSON, BASIL

   03913   *Dan Dare on Mars.* Hulton Press, London, 1956,
           176p, Cloth, Novel [Dan Dare series]

DAWSON, CARLEY

   03914   *Mr. Wicker's window.* Houghton Mifflin, Boston,
           1952, 272p, Cloth, Novel [Mr. Wicker #1]

DAWSON, CARLEY (Cont.)

03915   The Sign of the Seven Seas. Houghton Mifflin,
        Boston, 1954, 287p, Cloth, Novel [Wicker #2]

DAWSON, CONINGSBY (William), 1883-1959

03916   The road to Avalon. George H. Doran, New
        York, 1911, 284p, Cloth, Novel
03917   The unknown country. Hearst's International
        Library, New York, 1915, 62p, Cloth, Novel
03918   The unknown soldier. Butterick Press, London,
        1928, 64p?, Cloth, Novel

DAWSON, EMMA FRANCES, 1851-1926

03919   An itinerant house, and other stories. Wil-
        liam Doxey, San Francisco, 1897, 320p,
        Cloth, Coll.

DAWSON, ERASMUS, pseud. [Paul Devon]

03920   The fountain of youth. Chatto & Windus, Lon-
        don, 1891, 306p, Cloth, Novel

DAWSON, FORBES

03921   A sensational trance. Downey & Co., London,
        1895, 178p, Cloth, Novel

DAWSON, (Francis) WARRINGTON, 1878-1962

03922   The guardian demons. Rider & Co., London,
        1928, 287p, Cloth, Novel
03923   The true dimension. Martin Secker, London,
        1916, 328p, Cloth, Novel

DAWSON, WILLIAM J(ames), 1854-1928

03924   The House of Dreams. Bowden, London, 1897,
        136p, Cloth, Novel
03925   London idylls. Hodder & Stoughton, London,
        1895, 345p, Cloth, Coll.
03926   A soldier of the future. Hodder & Stoughton,
        London, 1908, 312p, Cloth, Novel

DAWSON-SCOTT, C. A.
    see: SCOTT, C. A. DAWSON

DAY, BRADFORD M(arshall), 1916-   [biography
included]

03927   Bibliography of adventure (Mundy, Burroughs,
        Rohmer, Haggard). Science-Fiction & Fantasy
        Publications, Denver, NY, 1964, 126p, Paper,
        Nonf.
03928   The checklist of fantastic literature in paper-
        bound books. Science-Fiction & Fantasy Pub-
        lications, Denver, NY, 1965, 128p, Paper,
        Nonf.
03929   A checklist of fantastic magazines. Bradford
        M. Day, South Ozone Park, NY, 1952, 24p,
        Paper, Nonf.

03930   The complete checklist of science-fiction maga-
        zines. Science-Fiction & Fantasy Publica-
        tions, New York, 1961, 63p, Paper, Nonf.
03931   Edgar Rice Burroughs biblio. Science-Fiction
        & Fantasy Publications, New York, 1956, 29p,
        Paper, Nonf.
03932   retitled: Edgar Rice Burroughs: a bibliogra-
        phy. Science-Fiction & Fantasy Publications,
        Woodhaven, NY, 1962, 45p, Paper, Nonf. [ex-
        panded]
03933   An index on the weird and fantastica in maga-
        zines. Bradford M. Day, South Ozone Park,
        NY, 1953, 162p, Paper, Nonf.
03934   Past and future; and, The last generation.
        Bradford M. Day, New York, 1954, 51p, Paper,
        Anth.
03935   Sax Rohmer: a bibliography. Science-Fiction
        & Fantasy Publications, Denver, NY, 1963,
        34p, Paper, Nonf.
03936   The supplemental checklist of fantastic litera-
        ture. Science-Fiction & Fantasy Publications,
        Denver, NY, 1963, 155p, Paper, Nonf.
03937   Talbot Mundy biblio; materials toward a biblio-
        graphy of the works of Talbot Mundy. Science-
        Fiction & Fantasy Publications, South Ozone
        Park, NY, 1955, 28p, Paper, Nonf.

DAY, DONALD B(yrne), 1909-1978

03938   Index to the science-fiction magazines, 1926-
        1950. Perri Press, Portland, OR, 1952, 184p,
        Cloth, Nonf.

DAY, (Gerald William) LANGSTON, 1894-

03940   The deep blue ice. Cresset Press, London,
        1960, 285p, Cloth, Novel
03941   Magic casements. Rider & Co., London, 1951,
        200p, Cloth, Coll.

DAY, MILLARD F.

03942   Destination Hell--standing room only! a Chris-
        tian allegory of our time. Greenwich Book
        Publishers, New York, 1957, 100p, Cloth,
        Novel

DAY, OSCAR F(ayette) G(aines), 1860-

03943   The Devil's Gold; the story of a forgotten
        race. Morrill Higgins, Chicago, 1892, 309p,
        Paper, Novel

DAY-LEWIS, C.
    see: BLAKE, NICHOLAS

THE DAY THE SUN STOOD STILL

03944   The day the Sun stood still; three original
        novellas of science fiction. Thomas Nelson,
        Nashville, 1972, 240p, Cloth, Anth.

THE DEAD ASTRONAUT
    see: RUSSELL, RAY

DEAD KNOWLEDGE

  03945 *Dead knowledge.* American Science Fiction,
          Sydney, 1953, 34p, Paper, Anth.

A DEAD MAN'S DIARY
    see: KERNAHAN, COULSON

THE DEAD WORLD

  03946 *The dead world.* American Science Fiction, Syd-
          ney, 1953, 34p, Paper, Anth.

de ALARCON, PEDRO A.
    see: ALARCON, PEDRO A. de

DEAMER, DULCIE, 1890-

  03947 *The devil's saint.* T. Fisher Unwin, London,
          1924, 315p, Cloth, Novel
  03948 *Holiday.* Frank Johnson, Sydney, 1940, 326p,
          Cloth, Novel

DEARBORN, LAURA, pseud. [Nina Picton]

  03949 *At the threshold.* Cassell Publishing Co., New
          York, 1893, 144p, Cloth, Novel

DEARMER, GEOFFREY, 1893-

  03950 *Saint on holiday.* William Heinemann, London,
          1933, 337p, Cloth, Novel
  03951 *They chose to be birds.* William Heinemann,
          London, 1935, 280p, Cloth, Novel

DEATH OF THE MOON

  03952 *Death of the Moon.* American Science Fiction,
          Sydney, 1952, 34p, Paper, Anth.

de BALZAC, HONORE
    see: BALZAC, HONORE de

DEBANS, (Jean Baptiste) CAMILLE, 1834-

  03953 *John Bull's downfall; the remarkable history
          of the destruction of England's power on
          land and sea in 1886-'87, the conquest of
          Ireland, and capture of London.* Brookside
          Library, New York, 1884, 46p, Paper, Novel
  03953A retitled: *John Bull's misfortunes; the des-
          truction of the entire English navy--the
          blowing-up of the Woolwich arsenal--the cap-
          ture of London and the downfall of Great
          Britain in the year 1887.* Norman L. Munro,
          New York, 1884, 87p, Paper, Novel

de BANZIE, ERIC, with John Ressich as Gregory
Baxter

  03954 *Blue lightning.* Cassell & Co., London, 1926,
          329p, Cloth, Novel

de BEAUVOIR, SIMONE
    see: BEAUVOIR, SIMONE de

de BERARD, FREDERICK B(righam), 1853-1927

  03955 *Famous occult tales.* Isaac H. Blanchard, New
          York, 1899, 245p, Cloth, Anth.
  03956 *Famous weird tales.* International Book & Pub-
          lishing Co., New York, 1899, 250p, Cloth,
          Anth.

de BIBIENA, JEAN GALLI
    see: GALLI de BIBIENA, JEAN

de BOSSCHERE, JEAN
    see: BOSSCHERE, JEAN de

de BURY, F. BLAZE
    see: DICKBERRY, F.

de CAMP, CATHERINE (Adelaide) CROOK, 1907-
[*biography included*], with L. Sprague de Camp

  03957 *Tales beyond time, from fantasy to science fic-
          tion.* Lothrop, Lee & Shepard, New York,
          1973, 159p, Cloth, Anth.
  03958 *3000 years of fantasy and science fiction.*
          Lothrop, Lee & Shepard, New York, 1972,
          256p, Cloth, Anth.

de CAMP, L(yon) SPRAGUE, 1907-   [*biography
included*]

  03959 *The clocks of Iraz.* Pyramid, New York, 1971,
          190p, Paper, Novel [Jorian #2]
  03960 *The Conan reader.* Mirage Press, Baltimore,
          1968, 150p, Cloth, Nonf. Anth.
  03961 *The continent makers, and other tales of the
          Viagens.* Twayne Publishers, New York, 1953,
          272p, Cloth, Coll. [Viagens (Krishna) series]
  03962 *Cosmic manhunt.* Ace Double, New York, 1954,
          128p, Paper, Novel [Viagens (Krishna) series]
  03962A retitled: *A planet called Krishna.* Compact,
          London, 1966, 158p, Paper, Novel [Viagens
          (Krishna) series]
  03963 *Divide and rule.* Fantasy Press, Reading, PA,
          1948, 231p, Cloth, Coll.
  03964 *The fallible fiend.* Signet, New York, 1973,
          143p, Paper, Novel
  03965 *The fantastic swordsmen.* Pyramid, New York,
          1967, 204p, Paper, Anth.
          The floating continent. [see 03976A]
  03966 *The glory that was.* Avalon, New York, 1960,
          223p, Cloth, Novel
  03967 *The Goblin Tower.* Pyramid, New York, 1968,
          253p, Paper, Novel [Jorian #1]
  03968 *A gun for dinosaur, and other imaginative tales.*
          Doubleday, Garden City, 1963, 359p, Cloth,
          Coll.

de CAMP, L. SPRAGUE (Cont.)

03969 *The hand of Zei.* Avalon, New York, 1963, 222p,
       Cloth, Novel [Viagens (Krishna) series]
03970 *Lest darkness fall.* Henry Holt, New York,
       1941, 379p, Cloth, Novel
03971 *Lost continents; the Atlantis theme in his-
       tory, science, and literature.* Gnome Press,
       New York, 1954, 362p, Cloth, Nonf.
       A planet called Krishna. [see 03962A]
03972 *The reluctant shaman, and other fantastic
       tales.* Pyramid, New York, 1970, 190p,
       Paper, Coll.
03973 *Rogue Queen.* Doubleday, Garden City, 1951,
       222p, Cloth, Novel [Viagens (Krishna) series]
03974 *Science-fiction handbook; the writing of ima-
       ginative fiction.* Hermitage House, New
       York, 1953, 328p, Cloth, Nonf.
03975 *Scribblings.* A Boskone Book, NESFA Press,
       Boston, 1972, 95p, Cloth, Coll. [includes
       some verse and nonf.]
03976 *The search for Zei.* Avalon, New York, 1962,
       224p, Cloth, Novel [Viagens (Krishna) series]
03976A retitled: *The floating continent; the second
       volume in the famous Krishna series.* Com-
       pact, London, 1966, 158p, Paper, Novel
       [Viagens (Krishna) series]
03977 *Solomon's stone.* Avalon, New York, 1957, 224p,
       Cloth, Novel
03978 *The spell of seven; stories of heroic fantasy.*
       Pyramid, New York, 1965, 192p, Paper, Anth.
03979 *Sprague de Camp's new anthology of science
       fiction.* Panther, London, 1953, 159p,
       Cloth, Coll.
03980 *Swords and sorcery; stories of heroic fantasy.*
       Pyramid, New York, 1963, 186p, Paper, Anth.
03981 *The tower of Zanid.* Avalon, New York, 1958,
       220p, Cloth, Novel [Viagens (Krishna) series]
03982 *The Tritonian ring, and other Pusadian tales.*
       Twayne Publishers, New York, 1953, 262p,
       Cloth, Coll.
03983 *The undesired princess.* Fantasy Publishing
       Co., Los Angeles, 1951, 248p, Cloth, Coll.
03984 *Warlocks and warriors.* G. P. Putnam's Sons,
       New York, 1970, 255p, Cloth, Anth.
03985 *The wheels of if, and other science-fiction.*
       Shasta Publishers, Chicago, 1948, 223p,
       Cloth, Coll.

with Lin Carter:

02738 *Conan of the Isles.* Lancer, New York, 1968,
       189p, Paper, Novel [Conan #12]
02739 *Conan the buccaneer.* Lancer, New York, 1971,
       191p, Paper, Novel [Conan #6]

with Catherine Crook de Camp:

03957 *Tales beyond time, from fantasy to science
       fiction.* Lothrop, Lee & Shepard, New York,
       1973, 159p, Cloth, Anth.
03958 *3000 years of fantasy and science fiction.*
       Lothrop, Lee & Shepard, New York, 1972,
       256p, Cloth, Anth.

with Robert E. Howard:

03986 *Conan the adventurer.* Lancer, New York, 1966,
       224p, Paper, Coll. [Conan #5]
03987 *Conan the freebooter.* Lancer, New York, 1968,
       223p, Paper, Coll. [Conan #3]
03988 *Conan the usurper.* Lancer, New York, 1967,
       256p, Paper, Coll. [Conan #8]
03989 *Tales of Conan.* Gnome Press, New York, 1955,
       219p, Cloth, Coll. [Conan series]

with Robert E. Howard and Lin Carter:

02742 *Conan.* Lancer, New York, 1967, 221p, Paper,
       Coll. [Conan #1]
02743 *Conan of Cimmeria.* Lancer, New York, 1969,
       189p, Paper, Coll. [Conan #2]
02744 *Conan the wanderer.* Lancer, New York, 1968,
       222p, Paper, Coll. [Conan #4]

with Robert E. Howard and Björn Nyberg:

03990 *Conan the avenger.* Lancer, New York, 1968,
       192p, Paper, Coll. [Conan #10] [see 03992]

with P. Schuyler Miller:

03991 *Genus Homo.* Fantasy Press, Reading, PA, 1950,
       225p, Cloth, Novel

with Björn Nyberg:

03992 *The return of Conan.* Gnome Press, New York,
       1957, 191p, Cloth, Novel [Conan series] [la-
       ter reprinted (see 03990) as *Conan the
       avenger*, together with an essay by Howard
       explaining his invented world]

with Fletcher Pratt:

03993 *The carnelian cube; a humorous fantasy.* Gnome
       Press, New York, 1948, 230p, Cloth, Novel
03994 *The castle of iron; a science fantasy adventure.*
       Gnome Press, New York, 1950, 224p, Cloth,
       Novel [Harold Shea #2]
03995 *The incomplete enchanter.* Henry Holt, New York,
       1941, 326p, Cloth, Novel [Harold Shea #1]
03996 *Land of unreason.* Henry Holt, New York, 1942,
       260p, Cloth, Novel
03997 *Tales from Gavagan's Bar.* Twayne Publishers,
       New York, 1953, 228p, Cloth, Coll.
03998 *Wall of serpents.* Avalon, New York, 1960,
       223p, Cloth, Novel [Harold Shea #3]

with George H. Scithers:

03999 *The Conan grimoire.* Mirage Press, Baltimore,
       1972, 264p, Cloth, Nonf. Anth.
04000 *The Conan swordbook; 27 examples of heroic
       fiction.* Mirage Press, Baltimore, 1969,
       259p, Cloth, Anth.

DE CHAIR, SOMERSET (Struben), 1911-

04001 *The Teetotalitarian state.* Falcon Press, Lon-
       don, 1947, 175p, Cloth, Novel

de CHATELAIN, Madame
       see: CHATELAIN, CLARA de

THE DECLINE AND FALL OF THE BRITISH EMPIRE
       see: MILLS, ELLIOTT EVANS

THE DECLINE AND FALL OF THE BRITISH EMPIRE; OR, THE WITCH'S CAVERN
       see: WATSON, HENRY CROCKER MARRIOTT

de COMEAU, ALEXANDER
       see: COMEAU, ALEXANDER de

de CREBILLON, CLAUDE
       see: CREBILLON, CLAUDE de

DE CRESPIGNY, MRS. PHILIP
see: CHAMPION DE CRESPIGNY, ROSE

de DIESBACH, GHISLAIN
see: DIESBACH, GHISLAIN de

DEE, ROGER, pseud. [Roger D. Aycock]

04002 *An Earth gone mad.* Ace Double, New York, 1954, 144p, Paper, Novel

DEE, SYLVIA, pseud. [Josephine Moore Proffitt, 1914-]

04003 *Dear guest and ghost.* Macmillan, New York, 1950, 259p, Cloth, Novel

DEEGAN, JON J., pseud.
see: SHARP, R. G.

DEEPING, (George) WARWICK, 1877-1950

04004 *I live again.* Cassell, London, 1942, 228p, Cloth, Novel
04005 *The man who went back.* Cassell, London, 1940, 382p, Cloth, Novel
04006 *Uther & Igraine.* Grant Richards, London, 1903, 354p, Cloth, Novel

DEER, M. J., with George H. Smith as anonymous co-author

04007 *Flames of desire.* France Books, Hollywood, 1963, 160p?, Paper, Novel
04008 *A place named Hell.* France Books, Hollywood, 1963, 160p, Paper, Novel

DEFOE, DANIEL, 1659-1731

04009 *The consolidator; or, Memoirs of sundry transactions from the world in the Moon, translated from the Lunar language,* by the author of The true-born Englishman. Benj. Bragg, London, 1705, 360p, Cloth, Novel
04009A retitled: *A journey to the world in the Moon,* by the author of The true-born Englishman. James Watson, London, 1705, 4p, Paper?, Story [abridged]
04009B retitled: *A journey to the world in the Moon; a dream, containing an historical relation (as receiv'd from a Lunar philosopher) from above an hundred years last past to the present time, of the most material occurrences, as to the religion, politics, &c. of the inhabitants of that globe, and particularly their manner of elections,* by Pythagorolunister. C. Corbett, London, 1705, 84p, Cloth, Novel [abridged]
04009C retitled: *A second, and more strange voyage to the world in the Moon, containing a comican [sic] discription [sic] of that remarkable country, with the characters and humours of the inhabitants,* by the author of The true-born Englishman. London, 1705, 4p, Paper?, Story [abridged]

04009D retitled: *A new journey to the world in the Moon, containing I. a full description of the manner of the author's performing his journey, and his reasons why former Lunarian travellers could not find their way thither, with an exact account of the different roads for their future direction; II. the history of the several sovereigns, religion, politic elections, &c., of the Lunar world, for above an hundred years last past to the present time,* by the author of The true-born Englishman. C. Corbett, London, 1741, 84p, Cloth, Novel [abridged] [second edition of 04009B]
04010 *The earlier life and the chief earlier works of Daniel Defoe.* George Routledge & Sons, London, 1889, 446p, Cloth, Coll. [some nonf.]
04011 *History of the plague in London in 1665; and, The consolidator.* Thomas Tegg, Oxford, 1840 413p, Cloth, Coll. [the former is nonf.]
A journey to the world in the Moon. [see 04009A and 04009B]
A new journey to the world in the Moon. [see 04009D]
A second and more strange voyage to the world in the Moon. [see 04009C]
04012 *Tales of piracy, crime, and ghosts.* Penguin, New York, 1945, 247p, Paper, Coll.

DEFOE, DANIEL
see also: THE HISTORY OF AUTONOUS

de FONTMELL, E. V.
see: FONTMELL, E. V. de

deFORD, MIRIAM ALLEN, 1888-1975 [biography included]

04013 *Elsewhere, elsewhen, elsehow; collected stories.* Walker, New York, 1971, 180p, Cloth, Coll.
04014 *Space, time & crime.* Paperback Library, New York, 1964, 174p, Paper, Anth.
04015 *Xenogenesis.* Ballantine, New York, 1969, 231p Paper, Coll.

DE FOREST, ELEANOR

04016 *Armageddon; a tale of the Antichrist.* Wm. B. Eerdmans Publishing Co., Grand Rapids, Mich. 1938, 219p, Cloth, Novel

DEGEN, VON
see: VON DEGEN

de GLOSSOP, REGINALD
see: GLOSSOP, REGINALD

de GOURMONT, REMY
see: GOURMONT, REMY de

DeGRAEFF, ALLEN, pseud. [Albert Paul Blaustein 1921-] [biography included]

04017 *Human, and other beings.* Collier, New York, 1963, 319p, Paper, Anth.

DeGRAEFF, ALLEN (Cont.)

ghost editor for Basil Davenport:

03833 *Deals with the devil; an anthology.* Dodd,
Mead, New York, 1958, 349p, Cloth, Anth.
03833A retitled: *Twelve stories from Deals with the
devil; an anthology.* Ballantine, New York,
1959, 160p, Paper, Anth.
03834 *Famous monster tales.* Van Nostrand, Princeton,
1967, 201p, Cloth, Anth.
03838 *Invisible men.* Ballantine, New York, 1960,
158p, Paper, Anth.

de GRAINVILLE, JEAN-BAPTISTE COUSIN
see: COUSIN de GRAINVILLE, JEAN-BAPTISTE

de GRANAMOUR, A.
see: THE BEWITCHED

de HAMONG, LEIGH
see: HAMONG, LEIGH de

DEHAN, RICHARD, pseud. [Clotilde Inez Mary
Graves, 1863-1932]

04018 *The just steward.* William Heinemann, London,
1922, 587p, Cloth, Novel; Dodd, Mead, New
York, 1922, 587p, Cloth, Novel
04019 *Under the Hermes, and other stories.* William
Heinemann, London, 1917, 341p, Cloth, Coll.;
Dodd, Mead, New York, 1917, 341p, Cloth, Coll.

de JONG, A. M.
see: JONG, A. M. de

DEKHNEWALLAH, A., pseud.

04020 *The great Russian invasion of India; a sequel
to the Afghanistan campaign of 1878-9.* Harrison, London, 1879, 69p, Paper?, Novel

DEKOBRA, MAURICE, pseud. [Ernst-Maurice Tessier, 1885-1973] [*biography included*]

04021 *Hamydal, the vagabond philosopher.* T. Werner
Laurie, London, 1937, 249p, Cloth, Novel

de KREMER, RAYMOND
see: RAY, JEAN

de LA BUQUE, JEAN
see: LA BUQUE, JEAN de

DELAIRE, JEAN

04022 *Around a distant star.* John Long, London,
1904, 301p, Cloth, Novel
04023 *A pixie's adventures in humanland.* Theosophical Publishing House, London, 1927, 136p,
Cloth, Novel

de la MARE, COLIN

04024 *They walk again; an anthology of ghost stories.*
Faber & Faber, London, 1931, 469p, Cloth,
Anth.
04024A retitled: *The ghost book; or, They walk again;
a collection of the best ghost stories.* Faber & Faber, London, 1932, 469p, Cloth, Anth.

de la MARE, WALTER (John), 1873-1956

04025 *Broomsticks, & other tales.* Constable, London,
1925, 378p, Cloth, Coll.
04026 *The connoisseur, and other stories.* W. Collins
Sons, London, 1926, 357p, Cloth, Coll.
04026A retitled: *The nap, and other stories.* Thomas
Nelson & Sons, London, 1936, 197p, Cloth,
Coll. [abridged]
04027 *Eight tales.* Arkham House, Sauk City, 1971,
108p, Cloth, Coll.
04028 *Ghost stories.* Folio Society, London, 1955,
234p, Cloth, Coll.
04029 *Henry Brocken; his travels and adventures in
the rich, strange, scarce-imaginable regions
of romance.* John Murray, London, 1904, 202p,
Cloth, Novel
04030 *The Lord Fish.* Faber & Faber, London, 1933,
290p, Cloth, Coll.
The nap, and other stories. [see 04026A]
04031 *The old lion, and other stories.* Faber & Faber,
London, 1942, 155p, Cloth, Coll.
04032 *The return.* Edward Arnold, London, 1910, 312p,
Cloth, Novel
04033 *The riddle, and other stories.* Selwyn & Blount,
London, 1923, 303p, Cloth, Coll. [Knopf edition is called *The riddle, and other tales*]
04034 *The scarecrow, and other stories.* Faber &
Faber, London, 1945, 128p, Cloth, Coll.
04035 *The three Mulla-mulgars.* Duckworth, London,
1910, 312p, Cloth, Novel
04035A retitled: *The three royal monkeys; or, The
three Mulla-mulgars.* Faber & Gwyer, London,
1927, 287p, Cloth, Novel
04036 *The Walter de la Mare omnibus; Henry Brocken;
The return; Memoirs of a midget.* W. Collins
Sons, London, 1933, 911p, Cloth, Coll.
04037 *The wind blows over.* Faber & Faber, London,
1936, 326p, Cloth, Coll.

de LA MOTHE FENELON, FRANCOIS
see: FENELON, FRANCOIS

de LA MOTTE-FOUQUE, FREDERIC
see: LA MOTTE-FOUQUE, FREDERIC de

DELANY, SAMUEL R(ay Jr.), 1942-   [*biography
included*]

04038 *Babel-17.* Ace, New York, 1966, 173p, Paper,
Novel
04039 *The Ballad of Beta-2.* Ace Double, New York,
1965, 96p, Paper, Novel
04040 *Captives of the Flame.* Ace Double, New York,
1963, 147p, Paper, Novel [Fall of the Towers
#1]
04040A retitled: *Out of the dead city.* Sphere, London, 1968, 143p, Paper, Novel [Fall of the
Towers #1] [slightly expanded]

DELANY, SAMUEL R. (Cont.)

04041 *City of a thousand suns.* Ace, New York, 1965,
156p, Paper, Novel [Fall of the Towers #3]
04042 *Driftglass; ten tales of speculative fiction.*
Nelson Doubleday, Garden City, 1971, 274p,
Cloth, Coll.
04043 *The Einstein intersection.* Ace, New York,
1967, 142p, Paper, Novel
04044 *Empire Star.* Ace Double, New York, 1966, 102p,
Paper, Novel
04045 *The fall of the towers; a classic science fiction trilogy.* Ace, New York, 1970, 413p,
Paper, Coll. [Fall of the Towers #s 1-3]
04046 *The jewels of Aptor.* Ace Double, New York,
1962, 156p, Paper, Novel
04047 *Nova.* Doubleday, Garden City, 1968, 279p,
Cloth, Novel
Out of the dead city. [see 04040A]
04048 *The towers of Toron.* Ace Double, New York,
1964, 140p, Paper, Novel [Fall of the Towers
#2]

with Marilyn Hacker:

04049 *Quark/1.* Paperback Library, New York, 1970,
240p, Paper, Anth.
04050 *Quark/2.* Paperback Library, New York, 1971,
240p, Paper, Anth.
04051 *Quark/3.* Paperback Library, New York, 1971,
238p, Paper, Anth.
04052 *Quark/4.* Paperback Library, New York, 1971,
240p, Paper, Anth.

de la REE, GERRY

04053 *Fantasy collector's annual--1974.* Gerry de la
Ree, Saddle River, NJ, 1974, 64p, Cloth,
Nonf. Anth.
04054 *An index to novels in the science fiction magazines.* Gerry de la Ree, River Edge, NJ,
1962, 19p, Paper, Nonf.
04055 *The normal Lovecraft.* Gerry de la Ree, Saddle
River, NJ, 1973, 32p, Cloth, Nonf. Anth. [pub-
lished anonymously]

de LA ROCHE, C. F. TIPHAIGNE
see: TIPHAIGNE de la Roche, C. F.

DELATTRE, PIERRE, 1930-

04056 *Tales of a Dalai Lama.* Houghton Mifflin, Boston, 1971, 142p, Cloth, Coll.

DELBLANC, SVEN

04057 *Homunculus; a magic tale.* Prentice-Hall, Englewood Cliffs, NJ, 1969, 188p, Cloth, Novel

de LEFEBVRE-LABOULAYE, EDOUARD
see: LABOULAYE, EDOUARD

de L'ISLE ADAM, JEAN VILLIERS
see: VILLIERS de L'ISLE ADAM, JEAN

DELIUS, ANTHONY (Ronald St. Martin), 1916-
[*biography included*]

04058 *The day Natal took off; a satire.* Insight,
Cape Town, South Africa, 1963, 139p, Paper,
Novel

de LISSER, HERBERT G(eorge), 1878-1944

04059 *The white witch of Rosehall.* Ernest Benn,
London, 1929, 286p, Cloth, Novel [Psyche #1]

DELL, BERENICE V.

04060 *The silent voice.* Four Seas Co., Boston,
1925, 474p, Cloth, Novel

DELL, JEFFREY

04061 *News for Heaven.* Jonathan Cape, London, 1944,
189p, Cloth, Novel

DELLBRIDGE, JOHN, 1887-

04062 *The Moles of Death.* Diamond Press, London,
1927, 303p, Cloth, Novel

DEL MARTIA, ASTRON, house pseud. [see also
John Russell Fearn]

04063 *Dawn of darkness.* Gaywood Press, London, 1951,
98p, Paper, Novel
04064 *Interstellar espionage.* Gaywood Press, London,
1952, 100p, Paper, Novel
04065 *One against time.* Mayflower, London, 1969,
140p, Paper, Novel
04066 *Space pirates.* Gaywood Press, London, 1950?,
112p, Paper, Novel
04067 *The trembling world.* S. D. Frances, London,
1949, 128p, Paper, Novel [by John Russell
Fearn]

DELMONT, JOSEPH

04068 *Mistress of the skies.* Hutchinson, London,
1932, 288p, Cloth, Novel
04069 *The submarine city.* Hutchinson, London, 1930,
288p, Cloth, Novel

DELORME, CHARLES, pseud. [Charles Rumball]

04070 *The marvellous and incredible adventures of
Charles Thunderbolt in the Moon.* T. Gunn,
London, 1851, 391p, Cloth, Novel

DELRAY, CHESTER

04071 *Realm of the alien.* Grafton, Dublin, 1945?,
64p, Paper, Novel

del REY, JUDY-LYNN

04072 *Stellar 1.* Ballantine, New York, 1974, 216p,
Paper, Anth.

del REY, LESTER [Ramon Felipe San Juan Mario
Silvio Enrico Smith Heathcourt-Brace Sierra
y Alvarez-del Rey y de los Verdes, 1915-   ]
[*biography included*]

04073   *"...And some were human"; a dozen.* Prime
        Press, Philadelphia, 1948, 331p, Cloth, Coll.
04073A retitled: *Tales of soaring science fantasy
        from "...And some were human."* Ballantine,
        New York, 1961, 160p, Paper, Coll.
04074   *Attack from Atlantis.* John C. Winston, Phila-
        delphia, 1953, 207p, Cloth, Novel
04075   *Badge of infamy.* Ace Double, New York, 1973,
        121p, Paper, Novel
04076   *Best science fiction stories of the year.* E.
        P. Dutton, New York, 1972, 251p, Cloth, Anth.
04077   *Best science fiction stories of the year, se-
        cond annual collection.* E. P. Dutton, New
        York, 1973, 251p, Cloth, Anth.
04078   *Best science fiction stories of the year,
        third annual collection.* E. P. Dutton, New
        York, 1974, 251p, Cloth, Anth.
04079   *The cave of spears.* Alfred A. Knopf, New York,
        1957, 206p, Cloth, Novel
04080   *Day of the giants.* Avalon, New York, 1959,
        224p, Cloth, Novel
04081   *The eleventh commandment; a novel of a church
        and its world.* Regency, Evanston, IL, 1962,
        159p, Paper, Novel
04082   *Gods and golems; five short novels of science
        fiction.* Ballantine, New York, 1973, 246p,
        Paper, Coll.
04083   *The infinite worlds of maybe.* Holt, Rinehart
        & Winston, New York, 1966, 192p, Cloth,
        Novel [ghost-written by Paul W. Fairman]
        The man without a planet. [see 04096A]
04084   *Marooned on Mars.* John C. Winston, Philadel-
        phia, 1952, 210p, Cloth, Novel
04085   *Mission to the Moon.* John C. Winston, Phila-
        delphia, 1956, 207p, Cloth, Novel [Moon #2]
04086   *Moon of mutiny.* Holt, Rinehart & Winston,
        New York, 1961, 217p, Cloth, Novel [Moon #3]
04087   *Mortals and monsters; twelve science fiction
        stories.* Ballantine, New York, 1965, 188p,
        Paper, Coll.
04088   *Nerves.* Ballantine, New York, 1956, 153p,
        Cloth, Novel
04089   *Outpost of Jupiter.* Holt, Rinehart & Winston,
        1963, 191p, Cloth, Novel
04090   *Prisoners of space.* Westminster Press, Phila-
        delphia, 1968, 142p, Cloth, Novel [ghost-
        written by Paul W. Fairman]
04091   *Pstalemate.* G. P. Putnam's Sons, New York,
        1971, 190p, Cloth, Novel
04092   *Robots and changelings; eleven science fiction
        stories.* Ballantine, New York, 1957, 175p,
        Paper, Coll.
04093   *Rocket from infinity.* Holt, Rinehart & Win-
        ston, New York, 1966, 191p, Cloth, Novel
        [ghost-written by Paul W. Fairman]
04094   *The runaway robot.* Westminster Press, Phila-
        delphia, 1964, 176p, Cloth, Novel [ghost-
        written by Paul W. Fairman]
04095   *The scheme of things.* Belmont, New York,
        1966, 157p, Paper, Novel [ghost-written by
        Paul W. Fairman]
04096   *Siege perilous.* Lancer, New York, 1966, 157p,
        Paper, Novel [ghost-written by Paul W. Fair-
        man]
04096A retitled: *The man without a planet.* Lancer,
        New York, 1969, 157p, Paper, Novel [ghost-
        written by Paul W. Fairman]

04097   *The sky is falling.* Ace Double, New York,
        1973, 124p, Paper, Novel
04098   *Step to the stars; a science fiction novel.*
        John C. Winston, Philadelphia, 1954, 211p,
        Cloth, Novel [Moon #1]
        *Tales of soaring science fantasy from "...And
        some were Human."* [see 04073A]
04099   *Tunnel through time.* Westminster Press, Phila-
        delphia, 1966, 153p, Cloth, Novel [ghost-
        written by Paul W. Fairman]
04100   *Two complete novels; The sky is falling; Badge
        of infamy.* Galaxy Magabook, New York, 1963,
        158p, Paper, Coll.

as Philip St. John:

04101   *Rocket jockey.* John C. Winston, Philadelphia,
        1952, 207p, Cloth, Novel
04101A retitled: *Rocket pilot; a science fiction no-
        vel.* Hutchinson, London, 1955, 216p, Cloth,
        Novel
04102   *Rockets to nowhere.* John C. Winston, Philadel-
        phia, 1954, 214p, Cloth, Novel

as Erik Van Lhin:

04103   *Battle on Mercury.* John C. Winston, Philadel-
        phia, 1953, 207p, Cloth, Novel
04104   *Police your planet.* Avalon, New York, 1956,
        224p, Cloth, Novel

as Kenneth Wright:

04105   *The mysterious planet.* John C. Winston, Phila-
        delphia, 1953, 209p, Cloth, Novel

with Carl Carmer and Cecile Matschat:

02587   *The year after tomorrow; an anthology of sci-
        ence fiction stories.* John C. Winston, Phi-
        ladelphia, 1954, 339p, Cloth, Anth.

with Frederik Pohl as Edson McCann:

04106   *Preferred risk; a science fiction novel.* Simon
        & Schuster, New York, 1955, 248p, Cloth,
        Novel

DE LUBICZ, ISHA SCHWALLER
    see: SCHWALLER DE LUBICZ, ISHA

de MADARIAGA, SALVADOR
    see: MADARIAGA, SALVADOR

de MAISTRE, XAVIER
    see: MAISTRE, XAVIER de

DEMAITRE, EDMUND, 1906-   , with Mark J. Appleman

    00395   *The liberation of Manhattan.* Doubleday, Garden
            City, 1949, 223p, Cloth, Novel

DE MARS, ROBERT, pseud.

    04107   *The Marselite; some helpful observations on
            subjects of interest to the Earth's people.*
            J. F. Ryan, Chicago, 1911, 64p, Cloth, Novel

de MAUPASSANT, GUY
    see: MAUPASSANT, GUY de

DE MENDELSSOHN, PETER, 1908-

04108   *Fortress in the skies; a tale.*   Doubleday, Do-
       ran, Garden City, 1943, 284p, Cloth, Novel

de MEYER, JOHN (Reed), 1909-

04109   *Benjamin Franklin calls on the president.*
       Ives Washburn, New York, 1939, 90p, Cloth,
       Novel

THE DEMIGOD
     see: JACKSON, EDWARD P.

DE MILLE, JAMES, 1837-1880 [published anony-
mously]

04110   *A strange manuscript found in a copper cylin-
       der.*   Harper & Bros., New York, 1888, 291p,
       Cloth, Novel

de MILLE, RICHARD, 1922-   [*biography included*]

04111   *Two qualms & a quirk; The royal banquet; The
       ultimate prosthesis; The transuxors.*   Capra
       Press, Santa Barbara, CA , 1973, 33p, Paper,
       Coll.

de MIOMANDRE, FRANCIS
     see: MIOMANDRE, FRANCIS de

THE DEMI-WANG

04112   *The demi-wang; and, The sex club.*   Collectors
       Publications, City of Industry, CA, 1969,
       160p, Paper, Anth. [the first only is SF,
       and is sometimes attributed to Ben Hecht]

de MONBRON, JEAN-LOUIS FOUGERET
     see: FOUGERET de MONBRON, JEAN-LOUIS

de MONCRIF, AUGUSTIN-PARADIS
     see: MONCRIF, AUGUSTIN-PARADIS de

DEMONICUS, pseud.

04113   *Two gods ride the hydrogen bomb; excursion in
       fantasy.*   J. S. Publishing Co., Schodack
       Landing, NY, 1967?, 63p, Paper, Novel

DE MORGAN, JOHN, 1848-

04114   *In unknown worlds; or, A trip to mystery land.*
       Street & Smith, New York, 1927, 214p, Paper,
       Novel

published anonymously:

04115   *He, a companion to She, being a history of the
       adventures of J. Theodosius Aristophano on
       the island of Rapa Nui in search of his im-
       mortal ancestor.*   Norman L. Munro, New York,
       1887, 213p, Paper, Novel [Aristophano #1;
       a parody of Haggard's novel, *She*]

04116   *"It"; wild, weird history of marvelous, mira-
       culous, phantasmagorical adventures in search
       of He, She, and Jess, and leading to the fin-
       ding of "It"; a Haggard conclusion.*   Norman
       L. Munro, New York, 1887, 242p, Paper, Novel
       [Aristophano #2; a parody of Haggard's novel,
       She]

04117   *King Solomon's treasures,* by the author of
       "He," "It," "Pa," "Ma," etc.   Norman L. Munro,
       New York, 1887, 200p, Paper, Novel [a parody
       of Haggard's novel, *King Solomon's mines*]

04118   *King Solomon's wives,* by the author of "He,"
       "It," "Pa," "Ma," etc.   Norman L. Munro,
       New York, 1887, 239p, Paper, Novel [a parody
       of Haggard's novel, *King Solomon's mines*]

DE MORGAN, WILLIAM (Frend), 1839-1917

04119   *Alice-for-short; a dichronism.*   Henry Holt,
       New York, 1907, 563p, Cloth, Novel

04120   *A likely story.*   Henry Holt, New York, 1911,
       344p, Cloth, Novel

THE DEMURE ONE, pseud.

04121   *The Battle of Boulogne; or, How Calais became
       English again; another version of the Chan-
       nel Tunnel affair.*   C. F. Roworth, London,
       1882, 51p, Paper, Novel

de MUSSET, ALFRED
     see: MUSSET, ALFRED de

DENHAM, ALICE, 1933-   [*biography included*]

04122   *Amo.*   Coward, McCann & Geoghegan, New York,
       1974, 244p, Cloth, Novel

04123   *The ghost and Mrs. Muir.*   Popular Library, New
       York, 1968, 127p, Paper, Tele.

DENISON, THOMAS S(tewart), 1848-1911

04124   *My invisible partner.*   Rand, McNally, Chicago,
       1898, 231p, Cloth, Novel

DENNIS, ALBERT NELSON, with J. Clarence Marple

04125   *Anona of the Mound Builders.*   Progressive Pub-
       lishers, Wheeling, 1920, 210p, Cloth, Novel

DENNIS, CLIFFORD E.

04126   *King Joker.*   Willoughby Books, Hamburg, NJ
       1967, 169p, Cloth, Novel

DENNIS, GEOFFREY (Pomeroy), 1892-1963

04127   *Harvest in Poland.*   William Heinemann, London,
       1925, 299p, Cloth, Novel

DENNIS, ROBERT C.

04128   *Conversations with a corpse.*   Bobbs-Merrill,
       Indianapolis, 1974, 195p, Cloth, Novel [Paul
       Reeder #2]

DENNIS, ROBERT C. (Cont.)

04129 *The sweat of fear.* Bobbs-Merrill, Indianapolis, 1973, 168p, Cloth, Novel [Paul Reeder #1]

DENT, GUY

04130 *Emperor of the if.* William Heinemann, London, 1926, 333p, Cloth, Novel

DENT, JOHN CHARLES, 1841-1888

04131 *The Gerrard Street mystery, and other weird tales.* Rose Publishing Co., Toronto, 1888, 206p, Cloth, Coll.

DENT, LESTER, 1905-1959, as Kenneth Robeson, house pseud. [see also Kenneth Robeson]

04132 *The Annihilist; a Doc Savage adventure.* Bantam, New York, 1968, 138p, Paper, Novel [Doc Savage #31]

04133 *Brand of the werewolf; a Doc Savage adventure.* Bantam, New York, 1965, 138p, Paper, Novel [Doc Savage #5]

04134 *The crimson serpent; a Doc Savage adventure.* Bantam, New York, 1974, 138p, Paper, Novel [Doc Savage #78]

04135 *The czar of fear; a Doc Savage adventure.* Bantam, New York, 1968, 140p, Paper, Novel [Doc Savage #22]

04136 *The dagger in the sky; a Doc Savage adventure.* Bantam, New York, 1969, 120p, Paper, Novel [Doc Savage #40]

04137 *The deadly dwarf; a Doc Savage adventure.* Bantam, New York, 1968, 115p, Paper, Novel [Doc Savage #28]

04138 *Death in silver; a Doc Savage adventure.* Bantam, New York, 1968, 134p, Paper, Novel [Doc Savage #26]

04139 *The derrick devil; a Doc Savage adventure.* Bantam, New York, 1973, 138p, Paper, Novel [Doc Savage #73]

04140 *The devil Genghis.* Bantam, New York, 1974, 149p, Paper, Novel [Doc Savage #79]

04141 *Devil on the Moon; a Doc Savage adventure.* Bantam, New York, 1970, 120p, Paper, Novel [Doc Savage #50]

04142 *Dust of death; a Doc Savage adventure.* Bantam, New York, 1969, 139p, Paper, Novel [Doc Savage #32]

04143 *The fantastic island; a Doc Savage adventure.* Bantam, New York, 1966, 135p, Paper, Novel [Doc Savage #14]

04144 *Fear Cay; a Doc Savage adventure.* Bantam, New York, 1966, 138p, Paper, Novel [Doc Savage #11]

04145 *The Feathered Octopus; a Doc Savage adventure.* Bantam, New York, 1970, 122p, Paper, Novel [Doc Savage #48]

04146 *The flaming falcons; a Doc Savage adventure.* Bantam, New York, 1968, 118p, Paper, Novel [Doc Savage #30]

04147 *Fortress of Solitude; a Doc Savage adventure.* Bantam, New York, 1968, 116p, Paper, Novel [Doc Savage #23]

04148 *The freckled shark; a Doc Savage adventure.* Bantam, New York, 1972, 138p, Paper, Novel [Doc Savage #67]

04149 *The giggling ghosts; a Doc Savage adventure.* Bantam, New York, 1971, 123p, Paper, Novel [Doc Savage #56]

04150 *The gold ogre; a Doc Savage adventure.* Bantam, New York, 1969, 122p, Paper, Novel [Doc Savage #42]

04151 *The golden peril; a Doc Savage adventure.* Bantam, New York, 1970, 138p, Paper, Novel [Doc Savage #55]

04152 *The green death; a Doc Savage adventure.* Bantam, New York, 1971, 138p, Paper, Novel [Doc Savage #65]

04153 *The green eagle; a Doc Savage adventure.* Bantam, New York, 1968, 114p, Paper, Novel [Doc Savage #24]

04154 *Hex; a Doc Savage adventure.* Bantam, New York, 1969, 120p, Paper, Novel [Doc Savage #37]

04155 *Land of always-night; a Doc Savage adventure.* Bantam, New York, 1966, 138p, Paper, Novel [Doc Savage #13]

04156 *The land of fear; a Doc Savage adventure.* Bantam, New York, 1973, 136p, Paper, Novel [Doc Savage #75]

04157 *The land of terror.* Street & Smith, New York, 1933, 252p, Cloth, Novel [Doc Savage #2 (old series), #8 (new series)]

04158 *The living-fire menace; a Doc Savage adventure.* Bantam, New York, 1971, 120p, Paper, Novel [Doc Savage #61]

04159 *The lost oasis; a Doc Savage adventure.* Bantam, New York, 1965, 123p, Paper, Novel [Doc Savage #6]

04160 *Mad Mesa; a Doc Savage adventure.* Bantam, New York, 1972, 122p, Paper, Novel [Doc Savage #66]

04161 *The Majii; a Doc Savage adventure.* Bantam, New York, 1971, 140p, Paper, Novel [Doc Savage #60]

04162 *The man of bronze.* Street & Smith, New York, 1933, 252p, Cloth, Novel [Doc Savage #1]

04163 *The man who shook the Earth; a Doc Savage adventure.* Bantam, New York, 1969, 154p, Paper, Novel [Doc Savage #43]

04164 *The mental wizard; a Doc Savage adventure.* Bantam, New York, 1970, 135p, Paper, Novel [Doc Savage #53]

04165 *Merchants of disaster; a Doc Savage adventure.* Bantam, New York, 1969, 138p, Paper, Novel [Doc Savage #41]

04166 *The Metal Master; a Doc Savage adventure.* Bantam, New York, 1973, 137p, Paper, Novel [Doc Savage #72]

04167 *Meteor menace; a Doc Savage adventure.* Bantam, New York, 1964, 140p, Paper, Novel [Doc Savage #3]

04168 *The Midas man; a Doc Savage adventure.* Bantam, New York, 1970, 121p, Paper, Novel [Doc Savage #46]

04169 *The monsters; a Doc Savage adventure.* Bantam, New York, 1965, 138p, Paper, Novel [Doc Savage #7]

04170 *The motion menace; a Doc Savage adventure.* Bantam, New York, 1971, 123p, Paper, Novel [Doc Savage #64]

04171 *The munitions master; a Doc Savage adventure.* Bantam, New York, 1971, 135p, Paper, Novel [Doc Savage #58]

04172 *The mystery on the snow; a Doc Savage adventure.* Bantam, New York, 1972, 149p, Paper, Novel [Doc Savage #69]

04173 *Mystery under the sea; a Doc Savage adventure.* Bantam, New York, 1968, 120p, Paper, Novel [Doc Savage #27]

DENT, LESTER (Cont.)

04174   *The Mystic Mullah; a Doc Savage adventure.* Bantam, New York, 1965, 137p, Paper, Novel [Doc Savage #9]

04175   *The other world; a Doc Savage adventure.* Bantam, New York, 1968, 119p, Paper, Novel [Doc Savage #29]

04176   *The Phantom City; a Doc Savage adventure.* Bantam, New York, 1966, 137p, Paper, Novel [Doc Savage #10]

04177   *Pirate of the Pacific; a Doc Savage adventure.* Bantam, New York, 1967, 136p, Paper, Novel [Doc Savage #19]

04178   *The pirate's ghost; a Doc Savage adventure.* Bantam, New York, 1971, 135p, Paper, Novel [Doc Savage #62]

04179   *Poison island; a Doc Savage adventure.* Bantam, New York, 1971, 118p, Paper, Novel [Doc Savage #57]

04180   *The polar treasure; a Doc Savage adventure.* Bantam, New York, 1965, 122p, Paper, Novel [Doc Savage #4]

04181   *Quest of Qui; a Doc Savage adventure.* Bantam, New York, 1966, 119p, Paper, Novel [Doc Savage #12]

04182   *Quest of the Spider.* Street & Smith, New York, 1933, 252p, Cloth, Novel [Doc Savage #3 (old series), #68 (new series)]

04183   *The red skull; a Doc Savage adventure.* Bantam, New York, 1967, 124p, Paper, Novel [Doc Savage #17]

04184   *Red snow; a Doc Savage adventure.* Bantam, New York, 1969, 139p, Paper, Novel [Doc Savage #38]

04185   *Resurrection day; a Doc Savage adventure.* Bantam, New York, 1969, 119p, Paper, Novel [Doc Savage #36]

04186   *The Sargasso Ogre; a Doc Savage adventure.* Bantam, New York, 1967, 140p, Paper, Novel [Doc Savage #18]

04187   *The Sea Angel; a Doc Savage adventure.* Bantam, New York, 1970, 120p, Paper, Novel [Doc Savage #49]

04188   *The sea magician; a Doc Savage adventure.* Bantam, New York, 1970, 137p, Paper, Novel [Doc Savage #44]

04189   *The secret in the sky; a Doc Savage adventure.* Bantam, New York, 1967, 119p, Paper, Novel [Doc Savage #20]

04190   *The seven agate devils; a Doc Savage adventure.* Bantam, New York, 1973, 134p, Paper, Novel [Doc Savage #73]

04191   *The South Pole terror; a Doc Savage adventure.* Bantam, New York, 1974, 137p, Paper, Novel [Doc Savage #77]

04192   *Spook Hole; a Doc Savage adventure.* Bantam, New York, 1972, 138p, Paper, Novel [Doc Savage #70]

04193   *The spook legion; a Doc Savage adventure.* Bantam, New York, 1967, 122p, Paper, Novel [Doc Savage #16]

04194   *The Squeaking Goblin; a Doc Savage adventure.* Bantam, New York, 1969, 138p, Paper, Novel [Doc Savage #35]

04195   *The submarine mystery; a Doc Savage adventure.* Bantam, New York, 1971, 121p, Paper, Novel [Doc Savage #63]

04196   *The terror in the Navy; a Doc Savage adventure.* Bantam, New York, 1969, 122p, Paper, Novel [Doc Savage #33]

04197   *The Thousand-headed Man; a Doc Savage adventure.* Bantam, New York, 1964, 150p, Paper, Novel [Doc Savage #2]

04198   *The vanisher; a Doc Savage adventure.* Bantam, New York, 1970, 139p, Paper, Novel [Doc Savage #52]

04199   *World's Fair goblin; a Doc Savage adventure.* Bantam, New York, 1969, 122p, Paper, Novel [Doc Savage #39]

04200   *The yellow cloud; a Doc Savage adventure.* Bantam, New York, 1971, 121p, Paper, Novel [Doc Savage #59]

de PATOT, SIMON TYSSOT
    see: BAYLE, MONSIEUR

de PEREYRA, DIOMEDES
    see: PEREYRA, DIOMEDES de

de QUEIROZ, ECA
    see: ECA de QUEIROZ, JOSE [Addendum]

DERELICT OF SPACE

04201   *Derelict of space.* American Science Fiction, Sydney, 1954, 34p, Paper, Anth.

de REYNA, JORGE, pseud.
    see: DETZER, DIANE

DERLETH, AUGUST (William), 1909-1971 [*biography included*]

04202   *Arkham House: the first 20 years, 1939-1959; a history and bibliography.* Arkham House, Sauk City, 1959, 54p, Paper, Nonf.

04203   *Beachheads in space.* Pellegrini & Cudahy, New York, 1952, 320p, Cloth, Anth.

04203A   retitled: *From other worlds.* Four Square, London, 1964, 186p, Paper, Anth. [abridged]

04204   *The beast in Holger's Woods.* Thomas Y. Crowell, New York, 1968, 194p, Cloth, Novel

04205   *Beyond time & space.* Pellegrini & Cudahy, New York, 1950, 643p, Cloth, Anth.

04206   *The dark brotherhood, and other pieces*, by H. P. Lovecraft & divers hands. Arkham House, Sauk City, 1966, 321p, Cloth, Anth. [includes some nonf.]

04207   *Dark mind, dark heart.* Arkham House, Sauk City, 1962, 249p, Cloth, Anth.

04208   *Dark things.* Arkham House, Sauk City, 1971, 330p, Cloth, Anth.

04209   *Far boundaries; 20 science-fiction stories.* Pellegrini & Cudahy, New York, 1951, 292p, Cloth, Anth.
    From other worlds. [see 04203A]

04210   *H. P. L.; a memoir.* Ben Abramson, New York, 1945, 122p, Cloth, Nonf.

04211   *Lonesome places.* Arkham House, Sauk City, 1962, 198p, Cloth, Coll.

04212   *The mask of Cthulhu.* Arkham House, Sauk City, 1958, 201p, Cloth, Coll.
    Mr. George, and other odd persons. [see 04230]
    New worlds for old. [see 04235A]

04213   *The night side; masterpieces of the strange & terrible.* Rinehart & Co., New York, 1947, 372p, Cloth, Anth.

04214   *Night's yawning peal; a ghostly company.* Arkham House, Sauk City, 1952, 280p, Cloth, Anth.

DERLETH, AUGUST (Cont.)

04215 *Not long for this world*. Arkham House, Sauk City, 1948, 221p, Cloth, Coll.
04215A retitled: *Tales from Not long for this world*. Ballantine, New York, 1961, 159p, Paper, Coll. [abridged]
04216 *100 books by August Derleth*. Arkham House, Sauk City, 1962, 121p, Paper, Nonf.
04217 *The other side of the Moon*. Pellegrini & Cudahy, New York, 1949, 461p, Cloth, Anth.
04218 *The outer reaches; favorite science-fiction tales chosen by their authors*. Pellegrini & Cudahy, New York, 1951, 342p, Cloth, Anth.
04218A retitled: *The time of infinity*. Consul, London, 1963, 205p, Paper, Anth. [abridged]
04219 *Over the edge*. Arkham House, Sauk City, 1964, 297p, Cloth, Anth.
04220 *Portals of tomorrow; the best tales of science fiction and other fantasy*. Rinehart & Co., New York, 1954, 371p, Cloth, Anth.
04221 *The shuttered room, and other pieces*, by H. P. Lovecraft & divers hands. Arkham House, Sauk City, 1959, 313p, Cloth, Anth.
04222 *Sleep no more; twenty masterpieces of horror for the connoisseur*. Farrar & Rinehart, New York, 1944, 374p, Cloth, Anth.
04222A retitled: *Stories from Sleep no more; nine nerve-shattering tales of unrelenting terror!* Bantam, New York, 1967, 149p, Paper, Anth. [abridged]
04223 *The sleeping & the dead; thirty uncanny tales*. Pellegrini & Cudahy, Chicago, 1947, 519p, Cloth, Anth.
04223A retitled: *The unquiet grave; stories*. Four Square, London, 1964, 254p, Paper, Anth. [abridged]
04224 *Some notes on H. P. Lovecraft*. Arkham House, Sauk City, 1959, 42p, Paper, Nonf.
04225 *Someone in the dark*. Arkham House, Sauk City, 1941, 335p, Cloth, Coll.
04226 *Something near*. Arkham House, Sauk City, 1945, 274p, Cloth, Coll.
04227 *Strange ports of call*. Pellegrini & Cudahy, New York, 1948, 393p, Cloth, Anth.
Tales from Not long for this world. [see 04215A]
04228 *Tales of the Cthulhu Mythos*. Arkham House, Sauk City, 1969, 407p, Cloth, Anth.
04228A retitled: *Tales of the Cthulhu Mythos, vol. 2*. Beagle, New York, 1971, 277p, Paper, Anth. [abridged]
04229 *Thirty years of Arkham House, 1939-1969; a history and bibliography*. Arkham House, Sauk City, 1970, 99p, Cloth, Nonf.
The time of infinity. [see 04218A]
04230 *Time to come; science-fiction stories of tomorrow*. Farrar, Straus & Young, New York, 1954, 311p, Cloth, Anth.
04231 *The trail of Cthulhu*. Arkham House, Sauk City, 1962, 248p, Cloth, Coll.
04232 *Travellers by night*. Arkham House, Sauk City, 1967, 261p, Cloth, Anth.
The unquiet grave. [see 04223A]
04233 *When evil wakes; a new anthology of the macabre*. Souvenir Press, London, 1963, 288p, Cloth, Anth.
When graveyards yawn. [see 04236B]
04234 *Who knocks? twenty masterpieces of the spectral for the connoisseur*. Rinehart & Co., New York, 1946, 391p, Cloth, Anth.

04235 *Worlds of tomorrow; science-fiction with a difference*. Pellegrini & Cudahy, New York, 1953, 351p, Cloth, Anth.
04235A retitled: *New worlds for old*. Four Square, London, 1963, 126p, Paper, Anth. [abridged]

as Stephen Grendon:

04236 *Mr. George, and other odd persons*. Arkham House, Sauk City, 1963, 239p, Cloth, Coll.
04236A *Mr. George, and other odd persons*, by August Derleth. Belmont, New York, 1964, 176p, Paper, Coll.
04236B retitled: *When graveyards yawn*, by August Derleth. Tandem, London, 1965, 176p, Paper, Coll.

with H. P. Lovecraft:

04237 *The lurker at the threshold*. Arkham House, Sauk City, 1945, 196p, Cloth, Novel
04238 *The shadow out of time, and other tales of horror*. Victor Gollancz, London, 1968, 384p, Cloth, Coll.
04238A retitled: *The shuttered room, and other tales of horror*. Panther, London, 1970, 205p, Paper, Coll. [abridged]
04239 *The shuttered room, and other tales of horror*. Beagle, New York, 1971, 166p, Paper, Coll. [different contents]
04240 *The survivor, and others*. Arkham House, Sauk City, 1957, 161p, Cloth, Coll.
09266 *The watchers out of time, and others*. Arkham House, Sauk City, 1974, 405p, Cloth, Coll.

with Mark Schorer:

04241 *Colonel Markesan, and less pleasant people*. Arkham House, Sauk City, 1966, 285p, Cloth, Coll.

DERMOTT, VERN, pseud. [Vern D. Frye, 1931-   ]

04242 *Planet finders*. Lenox Hill Press, New York, 1971, 192p, Cloth, Novel

DERN, DOROTHY L(ouise)

04243 *The doctor's secret*. Pageant Press, New York, 1954, 116p, Cloth, Novel

de ROUEN, REED R(andolph), 1917-

04244 *Split image; a novel*. Allan Wingate, London, 1955, 283p, Cloth, Novel

de SACKVILLE, HONORIA

04245 *Alta in the shadows*. Freeway Press, New York, 1974, 220p, Paper, Novel [Trine #1]

de ST.-EXUPERY, ANTOINE
see: ST.-EXUPERY, ANTOINE de

de SALIGNAC de la MOTHE FENELON, FRANCOIS
see: FENELON, FRANCOIS

de SANDISSON, Mr.
see: SANDISSON, Mr. de

DESFONTAINES, PIERRE FRANÇOIS GUYOT, 1685-1745
[published anonymously]

04246 *The travels of Mr. John Gulliver, son to Capt.
        Lemuel Gulliver.* Sam. Harding, London, 1731,
        vol. I-212p, II-198p, Cloth, Novel

d'ESME, JEAN
    see: ESME, JEAN d'

d'ESMENARD, JEAN
    see: ESMENARD, JEAN d'

DESMOND, HUGH

04247 *Fear rides the air.* Wright & Brown, London,
        1953, 160p, Cloth, Novel
04248 *The terrible awakening.* Wright & Brown, Lon-
        don, 1949, 220p, Cloth, Novel

DESMOND, SHAW, 1877-1960

04249 *Black dawn.* Hutchinson, London, 1944, 224p,
        Cloth, Novel
04250 *Chaos.* Hutchinson, London, 1938, 485p, Cloth,
        Novel
04251 *Incarnate Isis.* Hutchinson, London, 1941,
        334p, Cloth, Novel
04252 *Ragnarok.* Duckworth, London, 1926, 351p,
        Cloth, Novel

DESMOND, WILLIAM H.

04253 *The science-fiction magazine checklist, 1961-
        1972.* Archival Press, Cambridge, Mass.,
        1973, 16p, Paper, Nonf.

de SOUCANTON, Baroness ALEXANDRA
    see: SOUCANTON, Baroness ALEXANDRA de

D'ESPERANCE, E.
    see: ESPERANCE, E. d'

A DESPERATE ADVENTURE, AND OTHER STORIES

04254 *A desperate adventure, and other stories.*
        Ward, Lock, London, 1883, 377p, Cloth, Anth.
        [includes *A desperate adventure*, by Max Ade-
        ler, and *Merry utopia*, an anonymous antholo-
        gy]

DESSAR, LEO CHARLES, 1847-1924

04255 *A royal enchantress; the romance of the last
        queen of the Berbers.* Continental Publish-
        ing Co., New York, 1900, 350p, Cloth, Novel

de TARDE, GABRIEL
    see: TARDE, GABRIEL de

de TERAMOND, GUY
    see: TERAMOND, GUY de

DE TIMMS, GRAEME

04256 *Split.* Digit, London, 1963, 160p, Paper, Novel
04257 *Three-quarters.* Digit, London, 1963, 158p,
        Paper, Novel

de TINSEAU, LEON
    see: TINSEAU, LEON de

DETRE, Professor L.

04258 *War of two worlds.* Jarrolds Publishers, Lon-
        don, 1936, 253p, Cloth, Novel

de TREVINO, ELIZABETH BORTON
    see: TREVINO, ELIZABETH BORTON de

DETZER, DIANE, 1930-   [*biography included*]

04259 *Planet of fear.* Avalon, New York, 1968, 190p,
        Cloth, Novel

as Jorge de Reyna:

04260 *The return of the starships.* Avalon, New York,
        1968, 192p, Cloth, Novel

as Adam Lukens:

04261 *Alien world.* Avalon, New York, 1963, 192p,
        Cloth, Novel
04262 *Conquest of life.* Avalon, New York, 1960, 221p
        Cloth, Novel
04263 *Eevalu.* Avalon, New York, 1963, 192p, Cloth,
        Novel
04264 *The glass cage.* Avalon, New York, 1962, 223p,
        Cloth, Novel
04265 *The sea people.* Avalon, New York, 1959, 221p,
        Cloth, Novel
04266 *Sons of the wolf.* Avalon, New York, 1961, 224p
        Cloth, Novel
04267 *The world within.* Avalon, New York, 1962, 222p
        Cloth, Novel

DEUZEN, ALONZO VAN
    see: VAN DEUZEN, ALONZO

DE VALDA, (Frederick W.), 1884-

04268 *Children of the Sun.* Arthur Barker, London,
        1933, 320p, Cloth, Novel

DEVAULX, NOËL

04269 *The tailors' cake.* Allan Wingate, London,
        1946, 107p, Cloth, Coll.

de VEER, WILLEM
    see: VEER, WILLEM de

DE VET, CHARLES V(incent), 1911-   [*biography
included*], with Katherine MacLean

04270 *Cosmic checkmate.* Ace Double, New York, 1962,
        96p, Paper, Novel

THE DEVIL ON TWO STICKS
see: LE SAGE, ALAIN RENE

THE DEVIL UPON CRUTCHES IN ENGLAND

04271 *The devil upon crutches in England; or, Night-scenes in London; a satirical work, written upon the plan of the celebrated Diable Boiteux of Monsieur Le Sage*, by a gentleman of Oxford. P. Hodges, London, 1755, 73p, Cloth, Novel [sequel to Le Sage's *Devil on two sticks*]

THE DEVIL UPON TWO STICKS IN ENGLAND
see: COMBE, WILLIAM

THE DEVIL'S DIAMOND

04272 *The devil's diamond; or, The fortunes of Richard of the Raven's Crest*. Hogarth Press, London, 1875?, 64p, Paper, Novel; Norman L. Munro, New York, 1877, 31p, Paper, Novel

DEVINNE, PAUL

04273 *The day of prosperity; a vision of the century to come*. G. W. Dillingham, New York, 1902, 271p, Cloth, Novel

DEVITO, JOHN A.

04274 *Pawns of destiny; a romance*. Bruce Humphries, Boston, 1931, 252p, Cloth, Novel

de VOISENON, Abbe
see: VOISENON, Abbe de

de VOLNEY, CONSTANTIN
see: VOLNEY, M.

DEVON, PAUL
see: DAWSON, ERASMUS

DeVORE, HOWARD, with Donald Franson

04275 *A history of the Hugo, Nebula, and International Fantasy Award, listing nominees & winners, 1951-1970*. ScienceFiction Sales, Dearborn Heights, Mich., 1969, 45p, Paper, Nonf.

DeWEESE, THOMAS EUGENE, with Robert Coulson as Thomas Stratton

03474 *The man from U.N.C.L.E., number 11; the invisibility affair*. Ace, New York, 1967, 158p, Paper, Tele. [Man from U.N.C.L.E. #11]
03475 *The man from U.N.C.L.E., number 12; the mindtwisters affair*. Ace, New York, 1967, 158p, Paper, Tele. [Man from U.N.C.L.E. #12]

de WITT, DENISE, pseud.
see: SCHOEB, ERIKA

de WOHL, LOUIS, 1903-1961 [name originally: Ludwig von Wohl]

04276 *The second conquest; a novel*. J. B. Lippincott, Philadelphia, 1954, 239p, Cloth, Novel
04277 *Strange daughter*. Lawson & Dunn, London, 1945, 195p, Cloth, Novel

de WREDER, PAUL, pseud.
see: HEMING, J. W.

DEXTER, J. B., pseud.
see: GLASBY, JOHN

DEXTER, JOHN, house pseud.

04278 *Garden of shame*. Ember Library, San Diego, 1966, 159p, Paper, Novel
04279 *The sin veldt*. Leisure Books, San Diego, 1966, 160p, Paper, Novel
04280 *The sinners of HWANG*. Leisure Books, San Diego, 1965, 160p, Paper, Novel

DEXTER, WILLIAM, pseud. [William Thomas Pritchard, 1909-]

04281 *Children of the void; a novel*. Peter Owen, London, 1955, 195p, Cloth, Novel [Denis Grafton #2]
04282 *World in eclipse*. Peter Owen, London, 1954, 195p, Cloth, Novel [Denis Grafton #1]

DEY, FREDERIC VAN RENSSELAER, 1865-1922

04283 *The magic story*. Frank E. Morrison, Publisher, New York, 1900, 63p, Cloth, Novel

LE DIABLE BOITEUX
see: LE SAGE, ALAIN RENE

DIALOGUES OF THE DEAD
see: LYTTLETON, Lord GEORGE

THE DIAMOND LENS

04284 *The diamond lens*. Happy Hour Library, New York, 1900?, 93p, Paper, Anth.

DICK, KAY
see: SCOTT, JEREMY

"DICK, Mr.," pseud.

04285 *James Ingleton; the history of a social state, A.D. 2000*. James Blackwood, London, 1893, 450p, Cloth, Novel

DICK, PHILIP K(indred), 1928-   [biography in-
cluded]

04286 The book of Philip K. Dick. DAW, New York,
          1973, 187p, Paper, Coll.
04287 Clans of the Alphane moon. Ace, New York,
          1964, 192p, Paper, Novel
04288 The cosmic puppets. Ace Double, New York,
          1957, 127p, Paper, Novel
04289 Counter-clock world. Berkley Medallion, New
          York, 1967, 160p, Paper, Novel
04290 The crack in space. Ace, New York, 1966, 190p,
          Paper, Novel
04291 Do androids dream of electric sheep? Double-
          day, Garden City, 1968, 210p, Cloth, Novel
04292 Dr. Bloodmoney; or, How we got along after the
          bomb. Ace, New York, 1965, 222p, Paper,
          Novel
04293 Dr. Futurity. Ace Double, New York, 1960,
          138p, Paper, Novel
04294 Eye in the sky. Ace, New York, 1957, 255p,
          Paper, Novel
04295 Flow my tears, the policeman said. Doubleday,
          Garden City, 1974, 231p, Cloth, Novel
04296 Galactic pot-healer. Berkley Medallion, New
          York, 1969, 144p, Paper, Novel
04297 The Game-players of Titan. Ace, New York,
          1963, 191p, Paper, Novel
04298 A handful of darkness. Rich & Cowan, London,
          1955, 224p, Cloth, Coll.
04299 The man in the high castle; a novel. G. P. Put-
          nam's Sons, New York, 1962, 239p, Cloth, Novel
04300 The man who japed. Ace Double, New York, 1956,
          160p, Paper, Novel
04301 Martian time-slip. Ballantine, New York, 1964,
          220p, Paper, Novel
04302 A maze of death. Doubleday, Garden City, 1970,
          216p, Cloth, Novel
04303 Now wait for last year. Doubleday, Garden
          City, 1966, 214p, Cloth, Novel
04304 Our friends from Frolix 8. Ace, New York,
          1970, 189p, Paper, Novel
04305 The penultimate truth. Belmont, New York,
          1964, 174p, Paper, Novel
04306 A Philip K. Dick omnibus. Sidgwick & Jackson,
          London, 1970, 424p, Cloth, Coll. [includes
          The crack in space; The unteleported man;
          Dr. Futurity]
04307 The Preserving Machine. Ace, New York, 1969,
          317p, Paper, Coll.
04308 The simulacra. Ace, New York, 1964, 192p,
          Paper, Novel
04309 Solar lottery. Ace Double, New York, 1955,
          188p, Paper, Novel
04309A retitled: World of chance. Rich & Cowan, Lon-
          don, 1956, 160p, Cloth, Novel
04310 The three stigmata of Palmer Eldritch. Double-
          day, Garden City, 1965, 278p, Cloth, Novel
04311 Time out of joint. J. B. Lippincott, Philadel-
          phia, 1959, 221p, Cloth, Novel
04312 Ubik. Doubleday, Garden City, 1969, 202p,
          Cloth, Novel
04313 The unteleported man. Ace Double, New York,
          1966, 100p, Paper, Novel
04314 The variable man, and other stories. Ace, New
          York, 1957, 255p, Paper, Coll.
04315 Vulcan's hammer. Ace Double, New York, 1960,
          139p, Paper, Novel
04316 We can build you. DAW, New York, 1972, 206p,
          Paper, Novel
04317 The world Jones made. Ace Double, New York,
          1956, 192p, Paper, Novel
          World of chance. [see 04309A]

04318 The zap gun, being that most excellent account
          of travails and contayning many pretie hys-
          tories by him set foorth in comely colours
          and most delightfully discoursed upon as
          beautified and well furnished divers good
          and commendable in the gesiht of men of that
          most lamentable wepens fasoun designer Lars
          Powderdry and what nearly became of him due
          to certain most dreadful forces. Pyramid,
          New York, 1967, 176p, Paper, Novel

with Ray Nelson:

04319 The Ganymede takeover. Ace, New York, 1967,
          157p, Paper, Novel

DICK, R. A., pseud.
    see: LESLIE, JOSEPHINE

DICK-LAUDER, Sir GEORGE (Andrew), Bart., 1917-
[biography included]

04320 Our man for Ganymede. Dennis Dobson, London,
          1969, 190p, Cloth, Novel
04321 A skull and two crystals. Dennis Dobson, Lon-
          don, 1972, 192p, Cloth, Novel

DICKBERRY, F., pseud. [F. Blaze de Bury]

04322 The storm of London; a social rhapsody. John
          Long, London, 1904, 313p, Cloth, Novel

DICKENS, BRADFORD, pseud.

04323 The fornication formula. Adult Books, San
          Diego, 1970, 157p, Paper, Novel

DICKENS, CHARLES (John Hoffam), 1812-1870

04324 The chimes; a goblin story of some bells that
          rang an old year out and a new year in. Chap
          man & Hall, London, 1845, 175p, Cloth, Novel
04325 Christmas books. Chapman & Hall, London, 1852,
          266p, Cloth, Coll.
04325A retitled: Christmas stories. D. Appleton,
          New York, 1868, 163p, Cloth, Coll.
04326 Christmas books, and sketches by Boz illustra-
          tive of every-day life and every-day people.
          Ticknor & Fields, Boston, 1867, 500p, Cloth,
          Coll. [expanded]
04326A retitled: Charles Dickens's stories from the
          Christmas numbers of "Household words" and
          "All the year round," 1852-1867. Macmillan,
          London, 1896, 662p, Cloth, Coll.
04326B retitled: Christmas stories from "Household
          words" and "All the year round." J. M. Dent
          & Sons, New York, 1910, 708p, Cloth, Coll.
04326C retitled: Christmas tales. George G. Harrap,
          London, 1932, 414p, Cloth, Coll.
04327 A Christmas carol in prose, being a ghost story
          of Christmas. Chapman & Hall, London, 1843,
          166p, Cloth, Novel
04328 A Christmas carol, to which are added The lamp-
          lighter's story, and Sketches of young gentl
          men. Ward, Lock, London, 1885, 238p, Cloth,
          Coll.
04329 The haunted man and the ghost's bargain; a
          fancy for Christmas-time. Bradbury & Evans,
          London, 1848, 188p, Cloth, Novel

DICKESON, ALFRED

04330   *Tychiades; a tale of the Ptolemies, written
        in the third century B.C. by Ornithovius,
        and now faithfully translated out of the
        original.* T. Fisher Unwin, London, 1903,
        299p, Cloth, Novel

DICKIE, E. GORDON

04331   *1976; a novel.* Exposition Press, New York,
        1971, 464p, Cloth, Novel

DICKIE, JAMES, 1934-   [*biography included*]

04332   *The undead.* Neville Spearman, London, 1971,
        222p, Cloth, Anth.

DICKINSON, G(oldsworthy) LOWES, 1862-1932

04333   *The magic flute; a fantasia.* George Allen &
        Unwin, London, 1920, 128p, Cloth, Novel

DICKINSON, PETER (Malcolm), 1927-   [*biography included*]

04334   *The devil's children.* Victor Gollancz, Lon-
        don, 1970, 158p, Cloth, Novel [The Changes
        #1]
04335   *Emma Tupper's diary.* Victor Gollancz, London,
        1971, 191p, Cloth, Novel
04336   *The gift.* Victor Gollancz, London, 1973,
        173p, Cloth, Novel
04337   *The green gene.* Hodder & Stoughton, London,
        1973, 192p, Cloth, Novel
04338   *Heartsease.* Victor Gollancz, London, 1969,
        189p, Cloth, Novel [The Changes #2]
04339   *The weathermonger.* Victor Gollancz, London,
        1968, 160p, Cloth, Novel [The Changes #3]

DICKINSON, SUSAN (Margery), 1931-   [*biography included*]

04340   *The restless ghost, and other encounters and
        experiences.* Collins, London, 1970, 318p,
        Cloth, Anth.
04340A retitled: *The usurping ghost, and other en-
        counters and experiences.* E. P. Dutton,
        New York, 1971, 318p, Cloth, Anth.
04340B retitled: *Ghostly encounters.* Armada Lions,
        London, 1973, 157p, Paper, Anth. [abridged]
04340C retitled: *Ghostly experiences.* Armada Lions,
        London, 1973, 160p?, Paper, Anth. [abridged;
        04340B and 04340C together comprise the
        original volume]

DICKINSON, W(illiam) CROFT, 1897-1963 [*biography included*]

04341   *Borrobil; a tale for children.* Jonathan Cape,
        London, 1944, 189p, Cloth, Novel

DICKS, TERRANCE

04342   *Doctor Who and the abominable snowmen.* Target,
        London, 1974, 142p, Paper, Tele. [Dr. Who
        #10]

04343   *Doctor Who and the Auton invasion.* Target,
        London, 1974, 156p, Paper, Tele. [Dr. Who #4]
04344   *Doctor Who and the day of the Daleks.* Target,
        London, 1974, 140p, Paper, Tele. [Dr. Who #7]

with Malcolm Hulke:

04345   *The making of Doctor Who.* Piccolo, London,
        1972, 115p, Paper, Nonf.

DICKSBERRY, H.
        see: DICKBERRY, F.

DICKSON, CARTER, pseud.
        see: CARR, JOHN DICKSON

DICKSON, GORDON R(upert), 1923-   [*biography
included*]

04346   *Alien art.* E. P. Dutton, New York, 1973, 165p,
        Cloth, Novel
04347   *Alien from Arcturus.* Ace Double, New York,
        1956, 150p, Paper, Novel
04348   *The alien way.* Bantam, New York, 1965, 184p,
        Paper, Novel
04349   *Ancient, my enemy.* Doubleday, Garden City,
        1974, 226p, Cloth, Coll.
        The book of Gordon Dickson. [see 04350A]
04350   *Danger--human.* Doubleday, Garden City, 1970,
        228p, Cloth, Coll.
04350A retitled: *The book of Gordon Dickson.* DAW,
        New York, 1973, 205p, Paper, Coll.
04351   *Delusion world.* Ace Double, New York, 1961,
        100p, Paper, Novel
04352   *The genetic general.* Ace Double, New York,
        1960, 159p, Paper, Novel [Childe Cycle]
04353   *Hour of the Horde.* G. P. Putnam's Sons, New
        York, 1970, 191p, Cloth, Novel
04354   *Mankind on the run.* Ace Double, New York,
        1956, 151p, Paper, Novel
04355   *Mission to universe.* Berkley Medallion, New
        York, 1965, 175p, Paper, Novel
04356   *Mutants; a science fiction adventure.* Macmil-
        lan, New York, 1970, 250p, Cloth, Coll.
04357   *Naked to the stars; a science-fiction novel.*
        Pyramid, New York, 1961, 159p, Paper, Novel
04358   *Necromancer.* Doubleday, Garden City, 1962,
        191p, Cloth, Novel [Childe Cycle]
04358A retitled: *No room for man.* Macfadden-Bartell,
        New York, 1963, 158p, Paper, Novel [Childe
        Cycle]
04359   *None but man.* Doubleday, Garden City, 1969,
        253p, Cloth, Novel
04360   *The Outposter.* J. B. Lippincott, Philadelphia,
        1972, 214p, Cloth, Novel
04361   *The Pritcher Mass.* Doubleday, Garden City,
        1972, 186p, Cloth, Novel
04362   *The R-Master.* J. B. Lippincott, Philadelphia,
        1973, 216p, Cloth, Novel
04363   *Secret under Antarctica.* Holt, Rinehart & Win-
        ston, New York, 1963, 135p, Cloth, Novel
        [Robby Hoenig #2]
04364   *Secret under the Caribbean.* Holt, Rinehart
        & Winston, New York, 1964, 143p, Cloth, Novel
        [Robby Hoenig #3]
04365   *Secret under the sea.* Holt, Rinehart & Winston,
        New York, 1960, 121p, Cloth, Novel [Robby
        Hoenig #1]
04366   *Sleepwalker's world.* J. B. Lippincott, Phila-
        delphia, 1971, 203p, Cloth, Novel

DICKSON, GORDON R. (Cont.)

04367 *Soldier, ask not.* Dell, New York, 1967, 222p,
       Paper, Novel [Childe Cycle]
04368 *The Space Swimmers.* Berkley Medallion, New
       York, 1967, 160p, Paper, Novel
04369 *Space winners.* Holt, Rinehart & Winston, New
       York, 1965, 217p, Cloth, Novel
04370 *Spacepaw.* G. P. Putnam's Sons, New York,
       1969, 222p, Cloth, Novel [Dilbia #2]
04371 *Spacial delivery.* Ace Double, New York, 1961,
       123p, Paper, Novel [Dilbia #1]
04372 *The star road.* Doubleday, Garden City, 1973,
       229p, Cloth, Coll.
04373 *The tactics of mistake.* Doubleday, Garden
       City, 1971, 240p, Cloth, Novel [Childe Cycle]
04374 *Time to teleport.* Ace Double, New York, 1960,
       96p, Paper, Novel
04375 *Wolfling.* Dell, New York, 1969, 157p, Paper,
       Novel

with Poul Anderson:

00319 *Earthman's burden.* Gnome Press, New York,
       1957, 184p, Cloth, Novel

with Ben Bova:

04376 *Gremlins, go home!* St. Martin's Press, New
       York, 1974, 150p, Cloth, Novel

with Keith Laumer:

04377 *Planet run.* Doubleday, Garden City, 1967,
       167p, Cloth, Novel

DIDEROT, DENIS, 1713-1784

04378 *The talking jewels.* Collectors Publications,
       Los Angeles, 1965, 237p, Paper, Novel
04378A retitled: *The talking pussy.* Collectors
       Publications, City of Industry, CA, 1968,
       247p, Paper, Novel

DIEHL, Mrs. A(lice) M(angold), 1844-1912

04379 *Dr. Paull's theory; a romance.* D. Appleton,
       New York, 1893, 276p, Cloth, Novel; J. W.
       Arrowsmith, Bristol, 1893, 300p, Cloth,
       Novel

DIESBACH, GHISLAIN de

04380 *The toys of princes.* Chapman & Hall, London,
       1962, 190p, Cloth, Coll.

DIEUDONNÉ, FLORENCE (Lucinda) CARPENTER, 1850-

04381 *Rondah; or, Thirty-three years in a star.* T.
       B. Peterson & Bros., Philadelphia, 1887,
       230p, Cloth, Novel

DIGBY, LEE

04382 *Come again.* Ophelia Press, New York, 1969,
       159p, Paper, Novel

DIKTY, T(haddeus) E(ugene), 1920-   [*biography
included*]

04383 *The best science-fiction stories and novels,
       1955.* Frederick Fell, New York, 1955, 544p,
       Cloth, Anth.
04383A retitled: *5 tales from tomorrow, selected
       from The best science-fiction stories and
       novels, 1955.* Crest, Greenwich, 1957, 176p,
       Paper, Anth. [abridged]
04384 *The best science-fiction stories and novels,
       1956.* Frederick Fell, New York, 1956, 256p,
       Cloth, Anth.
04384A retitled: *6 from worlds beyond.* Crest, Green-
       wich, 1958, 160p, Paper, Anth. [abridged]
04385 *The best science-fiction stories and novels,
       ninth series.* Advent: Publishers, Chicago,
       1958, 258p, Cloth, Anth.
04386 *Every boy's book of outer space stories.*
       Frederick Fell, New York, 1960, 283p, Cloth,
       Anth.
04387 *Famous fantastic classics #1.* Fax Collector's
       Editions, West Linn, OR, 1974, 128p, Paper,
       Anth. [published anonymously]
       5 tales from tomorrow. [see 04383A]
04388 *Great science fiction stories about Mars.*
       Frederick Fell, New York, 1966, 187p, Cloth,
       Anth.
04389 *Great science-fiction stories about the Moon.*
       Frederick Fell, New York, 1967, 221p, Cloth,
       Anth.
       6 from worlds beyond. [see 04384A]

with Everett F. Bleiler:

01467 *The best science fiction stories, 1949.* Fred-
       erick Fell, New York, 1949, 314p, Cloth, Anth.
01468 *The best science-fiction stories, 1950.* Fred-
       erick Fell, New York, 1950, 347p, Cloth, Anth.
01468A retitled: *The best science fiction stories.*
       Grayson & Grayson, London, 1951, 256p, Cloth,
       Anth. [abridged]
01469 *The best science-fiction stories, 1951.* Fred-
       erick Fell, New York, 1951, 352p, Cloth, Anth.
01469A retitled: *The best science fiction stories,
       second series.* Grayson & Grayson, London,
       1952, 240p, Cloth, Anth. [abridged]
01469B retitled: *The mindworm; a collection of the
       best science fiction stories.* Tandem, Lon-
       don, 1967, 191p, Paper, Anth. [abridged; pub-
       lished anonymously]
01470 *The best science-fiction stories, 1952.* Fred-
       erick Fell, New York, 1952, 288p, Cloth, Anth
01470A retitled: *The best science fiction stories,
       third series.* Grayson & Grayson, London,
       1953, 256p, Cloth, Anth. [abridged]
01471 *The best science-fiction stories, 1953.* Fred-
       erick Fell, New York, 1953, 279p, Cloth, Anth
01471A retitled: *The best science fiction stories,
       fourth series.* Grayson & Grayson, London,
       1955, 239p, Cloth, Anth. [abridged]
01472 *The best science-fiction stories, 1954.* Fred-
       erick Fell, New York, 1954, 316p, Cloth, Anth
01472A retitled: *The best science fiction stories,
       fifth series.* Grayson & Grayson, London,
       1956, 207p, Cloth, Anth. [abridged]
       Category Phoenix. [see 01477A]
01473 *Frontiers in space; selections from The best
       science fiction stories.* Bantam, New York,
       1955, 166p, Paper, Anth. [selections from
       the 1951, 1952, and 1953 series]
01474 *Imagination unlimited; science-fiction and
       science.* Farrar, Straus & Young, New York,
       1952, 430p, Cloth, Anth.

DIKTY, T. E., with Everett F. Bleiler (Cont.)

01474A retitled: *Men of space and time.* Bodley
        Head, London, 1953, 221p, Cloth, Anth.
        [abridged]
        The mindworm. [see 01469B]
01475 *Science fiction omnibus; The best science fic-
        tion stories, 1949, 1950.* Garden City Books,
        Garden City, NY, 1952, 658p, Cloth, Anth.
        [includes 01467 and 01468]
01476 *Year's best science fiction novels, 1952.*
        Frederick Fell, New York, 1952, 352p, Cloth,
        Anth.
01476A retitled: *Year's best science fiction novels.*
        Grayson & Grayson, London, 1953, 263p, Cloth,
        Anth. [abridged]
01477 *Year's best science fiction novels, 1953.*
        Frederick Fell, New York, 1953, 317p, Cloth,
        Anth.
01477A retitled: *Category Phoenix.* Bodley Head,
        London, 1955, 192p, Cloth, Anth. [abridged]
01478 *Year's best science fiction novels, 1954.*
        Frederick Fell, New York, 1954, 318p,
        Cloth, Anth.
01478A retitled: *Year's best science fiction novels,
        second series.* Grayson & Grayson, London,
        1955, 240p, Cloth, Anth. [abridged]

DILKE, Lady (Emilia Francis), 1840-1904

04390 *The shrine of death, and other stories.*
        George Routledge & Sons, London, 1886, 160p,
        Cloth, Coll.
04391 *The shrine of love, and other stories.* George
        Routledge & Sons, London, 1891, 187p, Cloth,
        Coll.

DILNOT, FRANK, 1875-1946

04392 *I warmed both hands.* Lovat Dickson, London,
        1933, 316p, Cloth, Novel

di LUCCA, GAUDENTIO
   see: BERINGTON, SIMON

DIMONDSTEIN, BORIS

04393 *Utopia (the volcano island).* Literarishe
        Heftn Publishing, Tujunga, CA, 1958, 196p,
        Cloth, Novel

DIN, ALI MIRDREKVANDI GUNGA
   see: MIRDREKVANDI, ALI

DINES, (Harry) GLEN, 1925-

04394 *The mysterious machine.* Macmillan, New York,
        1957, 140p, Cloth, Novel

DINESEN, ISAK, pseud. [Baroness Karen Chris-
tentze Dinesen Blixen-Finecke, 1885-1962]
[*biography included*]

04395 *Seven gothic tales.* Putnam, London, 1934,
        522p, Cloth, Coll.

DINESEN, THOMAS, 1892-

04396 *Twilight on the Betzy.* Putnam, London, 1952,
        219p, Cloth, Novel

DINGLE, AYLWARD EDWARD
   see: SINBAD

DIOSCORIDES, Dr., pseud. [Pieter Harting,
1812-1885]

04397 *Anno Domini 2071.* William Tegg, London, 1871,
        132p, Cloth, Novel

A DIPLOMAT, pseud.

04398 *The rise and fall of the United States; a leaf
        from history, A.D. 2060.* F. Tennyson Neely,
        New York, 1898, 205p, Paper, Novel

DIPPER, ALAN, 1922-   [*biography included*]

04399 *The golden virgin.* Michael Joseph, London,
        1972, 224p, Cloth, Novel

DIRAC, HUGH

04400 *The profit of doom; science fiction.* Sidgwick
        & Jackson, London, 1970, 190p, Cloth, Novel

DISCH, THOMAS M(ichael), 1940-   [*biography
included*]

04401 *Bad moon rising.* Harper & Row, New York, 1973,
        302p, Cloth, Anth.
04402 *Camp concentration.* Rupert Hart-Davis, London,
        1968, 177p, Cloth, Novel
04403 *Echo round his bones.* Berkley Medallion, New
        York, 1967, 144p, Paper, Novel
        Fun with your new head. [see 04412A]
04404 *The genocides.* Berkley Medallion, New York,
        1965, 143p, Paper, Novel
04405 *Getting into death; the best short stories of
        Thomas M. Disch.* Hart-Davis MacGibbon, Lon-
        don, 1973, 206p, Cloth, Coll.
04406 *Mankind under the leash, being a true and
        faithful account of the great upheavals of
        2037, with portraits of many of the princi-
        pals involved, as well as reflections by the
        author on the nature of art, revolution, &
        theology.* Ace Double, New York, 1966, 140p,
        Paper, Novel
04407 *One hundred and two H-bombs.* Berkley Medallion,
        New York, 1971, 160p, Paper, Coll.
04408 *One hundred and two H bombs, and other science
        fiction stories.* Compact, London, 1966,
        192p, Paper, Coll. [different contents]
04409 *The prisoner.* Ace, New York, 1969, 188p, Paper,
        Tele. [Prisoner #1]
04410 *The ruins of Earth; an anthology of stories of
        the immediate future.* G. P. Putnam's Sons,
        New York, 1971, 318p, Cloth, Anth.
04411 *334.* MacGibbon & Kee, London, 1972, 201p,
        Cloth, Novel
04412 *Under compulsion.* Rupert Hart-Davis, London,
        1968, 220p, Cloth, Coll.

DISCH, THOMAS M. (Cont.)

04412A retitled: *Fun with your new head.* Doubleday, Garden City, 1971, 207p, Cloth, Coll.
04413 *White Fang goes Dingo, and other funny s.f. stories.* Arrow, London, 1971, 192p, Paper, Coll. [roughly adapted from 04408]

ghost editor with Robert Arthur for Alfred Hitchcock:

00521 *Alfred Hitchcock presents: stories that scared even me.* Random House, New York, 1967, 463p, Cloth, Anth.

DISRAELI, BENJAMIN, Earl of Beaconsfield, 1804-1881

Alroy; a romance. [see 04420A]
04414 *Alroy; Ixion in Heaven; The infernal marriage; Popanilla.* Longmans, Green, London, 1845, 463p, Cloth, Coll.
04415 *Alroy; Popanilla; Count Alarcos; Ixion in Heaven.* John Lane, London, 1906, 691p, Cloth, Coll.
04416 *The infernal marriage.* William Jackson, London, 1929, 85p, Cloth, Novel
04417 *Ixion in Heaven.* Jonathan Cape, London, 1925, 72p, Cloth, Novel
04418 *Popanilla, and other tales.* Peter Davies, London, 1926, 367p, Cloth, Coll.
04419 *The voyage of Captain Popanilla,* by the author of "Vivian Grey." Henry Colburn, London, 1828, 243p, Cloth, Novel
04420 *The wondrous tale of Alroy; the rise of Iskander,* by the author of "Vivian Grey," "Contarini Fleming," &c. Saunders & Otley, London, 1833, 3vol, Cloth, Novel
04420A retitled: *Alroy; a romance.* London, 1846, 286p, Cloth, Novel

DISROBESON, KIN I., pseud. [Mark Stivers]

04421 *The living toilets; a Doc Bandage adventure.* Chast-Katten, Ardmore, 1973, 21p, Paper, Story [The Adventures of Doc Bandage #2 (actually the only one issued); a parody of the Doc Savage series]

DITZEN, RUDOLF
    see: FALLADA, HANS

DIVER, JAMES FRANCIS
    see: DWYER, JAMES FRANCIS

DIVINE, ARTHUR D(urham), 1904-

04422 *Tunnel from Calais.* Collins, London, 1942, 192p, Cloth, Novel

as David Rame:

04422A *Tunnel from Calais.* Macmillan, New York, 1943, 246p, Cloth, Novel

DIX, MAURICE B(uxton)

04423 *The Golden Fluid.* Ward, Lock, London, 1935, 319p, Cloth, Novel

DIXEY, MARMADUKE, pseud. [Geoffrey Howard, 1889-1973]

04424 *Hell's bells; a comedy of the underworld.* Faber & Faber, London, 1936, 304p, Cloth, Novel

DIXIE, Lady FLORENCE (Caroline), 1857-1905

04425 *Gloriana; or, The revolution of 1900.* Henry & Co., London, 1890, 350p, Cloth, Novel

DIXON, CHARLES, 1858-1926

04426 *Fifteen hundred miles an hour.* Bliss, Sands & Foster, London, 1895, 313p, Cloth, Novel

DIXON, MARJORIE, 1887-

04427 *The forbidden island.* Rupert Hart-Davis, London, 1960, 201p, Cloth, Novel

DIXON, RICHARD, pseud. [Clifton Reginald Walker]

04428 *Destination: Amaltheia.* Foreign Languages Publishing House, Moscow, 1962, 420p, Paper, Anth.

DIXON, ROGER, 1930-   [*biography included*]

04429 *Christ on trial.* Pinnacle, New York, 1973, 256p, Paper, Novel
04429A retitled: *"The Christ trial."* Pinnacle, New York, 1974, 256p, Paper, Novel
04430 *Noah II.* Ace, New York, 1970, 288p, Paper, Novel

DIXON, ROYAL (Absalom), 1885-1962

04431 *The ape of Heaven.* Mathis, Van Nort, Dallas, 1936, 332p, Cloth, Novel

DIXON, THOMAS, 1864-1946

04432 *The fall of a nation; a sequel to The birth of a nation.* D. Appleton, New York, 1916, 362p, Cloth, Novel [a sequel to Dixon's novel, *The Clansman,* which was filmed as "The Birth of a Nation"]

DR. CYCLOPS

04433 *Dr. Cyclops.* Popular Library, New York, 1970, 127p, Paper, Anth. [for the novel of the same title, see: KUTTNER, HENRY]

DR. DIOSCORIDES
    see: DIOSCORIDES, Dr.

DOCTOROW, E(dgar) L(aurence), 1931-   [*biography included*]

04434 *Big as life.* Simon & Schuster, New York, 1966, 218p, Cloth, Novel

DODD, ALLEN ROBERT
    see: ALLEN, ROBERT

DODD, ANNA BOWMAN (Blake), 1855-1929

04435 *The republic of the future; or, Socialism a
      reality.* Cassell & Co., London, 1887, 86p,
      Paper, Novel

DODGE, H(oward) L(ewis), 1869-

04436 *Attraction of the compass; a romance of the
      north, based upon facts of a personal ex-
      perience.* Press of Dove & Courtney, Long
      Beach, CA, 1912, 308p, Cloth, Novel

DODGSON, CHARLES LUTWIDGE
    see: CARROLL, LEWIS

DOERR, EDD

04437 *Eden II.* Aquarius Press, Silver Spring, MD,
      1974, 94p, Paper, Coll.

DOGBOLT, BARNABY, pseud. [Herbert Silvette,
1906-]

04438 *Eve's second apple.* E. P. Dutton, New York,
      1946, 318p, Cloth, Novel

DOHERTY, G(eoffrey) D(onald Cosford), 1927-
[biography included]

04439 *Aspects of science fiction.* John Murray, Lon-
      don, 1959, 218p, Cloth, Anth.
04440 *Second orbit; a new science fiction anthology
      for schools.* John Murray, London, 1965,
      218p, Cloth, Anth.
04441 *Stories from science fiction.* Thomas Nelson
      & Sons, London, 1966, 213p, Cloth, Anth.

DOHRMAN, RICHARD

04442 *The gatehouse.* A Seymour Lawrence Book, Dela-
      corte Press, New York, 1971, 353p, Cloth,
      Novel

DOKE, JOSEPH J(ohn), d. 1913

04443 *The queen of the secret city.* Hodder & Stough-.
      ton, London, 1916, 319p, Cloth, Novel [Jus-
      tin Retief #2]
04444 *The secret city; a romance of the Karroo.*
      Hodder & Stoughton, London, 1913, 400p,
      Cloth, Novel [Justin Retief #1]

DOLAN, MIKE (J.)

04445 *Santana morning.* Powell Publications, Reseda,
      CA, 1970, 205p, Paper, Coll.

DOLBIER, MAURICE (Wyman), 1912-

04446 *The half-pint jinni, and other stories.* Ran-
      dom House, New York, 1948, 242p, Cloth, Coll.

DOLINER, ROY, 1932-   [biography included]

04447 *For love or money.* Simon & Schuster, New York,
      1974, 191p, Cloth, Novel

DOLINSKY, MIKE [Meyer Dolinsky, 1923-] [bi-
ography included]

04448 *Mind one.* Dell, New York, 1972, 240p, Paper,
      Novel

DOMBROWSKI, KATRINA [Käthe von Dombrowski zu
Papros und Krusvic, 1881-]

04449 *Abdallah and the donkey; a tale of woe and joy
      for children from eight to eighty years,* by
      K. O. S. Macmillan, New York, 1928, 155p,
      Cloth, Novel [Abdallah #1]
04450 *The fat camel of Bagdad; a new tale of Abdal-
      lah's adventures, for children from eight
      to eighty years,* by K. O. S. Macmillan, New
      York, 1929, 156p, Cloth, Novel [Abdallah #2]

DONAHUE, JAMES J., with Joseph J. Crawford,
Jr. and Donald M. Grant

03552 *"333"; a bibliography of the science-fantasy
      novel.* Grandon Co., Providence, 1953, 80p,
      Cloth, Nonf.

DONALDSON, ELAINE

04451 *"Scrooge."* Cinema Center Films, New York,
      1970, 128p, Cloth, Movie [adapted from the
      motion picture of the same name, which in
      turn was derived from Dickens's story, *A
      Christmas Carol*]

DONALDY, ERNESTINE, with Andre Norton

04452 *Gates to tomorrow; an introduction to science
      fiction.* A Margaret K. McElderry Book, Ath-
      eneum, New York, 1973, 264p, Cloth, Anth.

DONEY, NINA M.

04453 *My life on eight planets; or, A glimpse of
      other worlds.* Doney & Cashill, Auburn, NY,
      1928,   , Cloth, Novel

DONIS, MILES, 1937-   [biography included]

04454 *The fall of New York.* David McKay, New York,
      1971, 216p, Cloth, Novel

DONNE, MAXIM, pseud.
    see: DUKE, MADELAINE

DONNELLY, DESMOND (Louis), 1920-1974

04455 *The nearing storm.* Hutchinson, London, 1968, 216p, Cloth, Novel

DONNELLY, IGNATIUS (Loyola), 1831-1901

04456 *The golden bottle; or, The story of Ephraim Benezet of Kansas.* D. D. Merrill, New York, 1892, 313p, Cloth, Novel

as Edmund Boisgilbert:

04457 *Caesar's column; a story of the twentieth century.* F. J. Schulte, Chicago, 1890, 367p, Cloth, Novel
04457A *Caesar's column; a story of the twentieth century*, by Ignatius Donnelly. Sampson Low, London, 1891, 367p, Cloth, Novel
04458 *Doctor Huguet; a novel.* F. J. Schulte, Chicago, 1891, 309p, Cloth, Novel
04458A *Doctor Huguet; a novel*, by Ignatius Donnelly. Sampson Low, London, 1892, 309p, Cloth, Novel

DONNER, GROVE, pseud. [Florence Harvey]

04459 *The stone of destiny; or, An altar, the cornerstone of the world.* no publisher, Los Angeles, 1938, 244p, Cloth, Novel

DONOVAN, ALEXANDER

04460 *The Irish rebellion of 1898; a chapter in future history.* Hodges, Figgis, Dublin, 1893, 12p, Paper, Story

DONOVAN, DICK
see: MUDDOCK, J. E. PRESTON

DONSON, CYRIL, 1919-   [*biography included*]

04461 *Born in space.* Robert Hale, London, 1968, 191p, Cloth, Novel
04462 *Draco the dragon man.* New English Library, London, 1974, 126p, Paper, Novel
04463 *The perspective process.* Robert Hale, London, 1969, 191p, Cloth, Novel
04464 *Tritonastra--planet of the Gargantua.* Robert Hale, London, 1969, 192p, Cloth, Novel

DOONER, P(ierton) W., 1844-1907?

04465 *Last days of the republic.* Alta California Publishing House, San Francisco, 1880, 258p, Cloth, Novel

DOREN, MARK VAN
see: VAN DOREN, MARK

DORMAN, GEOFFREY, 1894-

04466 *Shattering silence.* Hutchinson, London, 1955, 176p, Cloth, Novel
04467 *Swooping vengeance.* Hutchinson, London, 1954, 176p, Cloth, Novel

DORMER, DANIEL

04468 *The mesmerist's secret.* J. & R. Maxwell, London, 1888, 335p, Cloth, Novel

d'ORMESSON, JEAN
see: ORMESSON, JEAN d'

DORRANCE, ETHEL (Arnold) SMITH, 1880-

04469 *Damned; the intimate story of a girl.* Macaulay, New York, 1923, 352p, Cloth, Novel
04469A *Damned; the intimate story of a girl*, by Anonymous. Stanley Paul, London, 1924, 320p, Cloth, Novel

DORRINGTON, ALBERT, 1871-

04470 *The half-god.* Wright & Brown, London, 1933, 251p, Cloth, Novel
04471 *The radium terrors.* Eveleigh Nash, London, 1912, 316p, Cloth, Novel

DOST, ZAMIN KI
see: KI DOST, ZAMIN

DOSTOEVSKII, FEDOR (Mikhailovich), 1821-1881

04472 *Short stories.* Books Inc., New York, 1940?, 248p, Cloth, Coll. [byline reads: Fiodor Dostoievski]

DOUBLE IDENTITY

04473 *Double identity.* American Science Fiction, Sydney, 1954, 34p, Paper, Anth.

DOUBLE PHOENIX
see: CARTER, LIN

DOUGHTY, FRANCIS WORCESTER, 1850?-1917

04474 *Mirrikh; or, A woman from Mars; a tale of occult adventure.* Burleigh & Johnston Co., New York, 1892, 274p, Cloth, Novel

DOUGLAS, BRYAN

04475 *Great stories of mystery and imagination.* Fontana, London, 1966, 224p, Paper, Anth.

DOUGLAS, DAVID

04476 *The Silver God of the Orang Hutan.* C. Arthur Pearson, London, 1922, 224p, Cloth, Novel

DOUGLAS, DONALD, 1893?-1966

04477 *The Grand Inquisitor.* Boni & Liveright, New York, 1925, 319p, Cloth, Novel

DOUGLAS, DRAKE, pseud. [Werner Zimmermann]

04478 *Horror!* Macmillan, New York, 1966, 309p,
 Cloth, Nonf.
04478A retitled: *Horrors!* John Baker, London, 1967,
 326p, Cloth, Nonf.

DOUGLAS, JEFF, pseud.
 see: OFFUTT, ANDREW J. and BERRY, D. BRUCE

DOUGLAS, (George) NORMAN, 1868-1952

04479 *In the beginning.* Privately Printed, Florence,
 Italy, 1927, 259p, Cloth, Novel
04480 *They went.* Chapman & Hall, London, 1920,
 250p, Cloth, Novel

DOUGLAS, THEO.
 see: EVERETT, Mrs. H. D.

DOUGLASS, ELLSWORTH

04481 *Pharaoh's broker, being the very remarkable
 experiences in another world of Isidor Werner (written by himself).* C. Arthur Pearson, London, 1899, 316p, Cloth, Novel

DOWD, F(reeman) B(enjamin)

04482 *The double man; a novel.* Arena Publishing
 Co., Boston, 1895, 303p, Cloth, Novel

DOWDING, A. L.
 see: RAMSDEN, LEWIS

DOWDING, HENRY WALLACE [Dunraven] [sic]

04483 *The man from Mars; or, Service for service's
 sake.* Cochrane Publishing Co., New York,
 1910, 385p, Cloth, Novel

"DOWN WITH ENGLAND"

04484 *"Down with England!"* Chapman & Hall, London,
 1888, 152p, Cloth, Novel

DOWNEY, EDMUND, 1856-1937

04485 *A house of tears.* John W. Lovell, New York,
 1888, 156p, Paper, Novel

as F. M. Allen:

04486 *Brayhard; the strange adventures of one ass
 and seven champions.* Ward & Downey, London,
 1890, 308p, Cloth, Novel
04487 *London's peril.* Downey & Co., London, 1900,
 96p, Cloth?, Novel
04488 *The voyage of the Ark, as related by Dan Banim.*
 Ward & Downey, London, 1888, 128p, Cloth,
 Novel

DOYLE, Sir A(rthur) CONAN, 1859-1930

04489 *The captain of the Polestar, and other tales.*
 Longmans, Green, London, 1890, 315p, Cloth,
 Coll.
04490 *Danger! and other stories.* John Murray, London,
 1918, 246p, Cloth, Coll.
04491 *The doings of Raffles Haw.* John W. Lovell,
 New York, 1891, 134p, Paper, Novel?
04492 *The doings of Raffles Haw, and other stories.*
 Lovell, Coryell, New York, 1892, 199p, Cloth,
 Coll.
04493 *The great Keinplatz experiment, and other stories.* Rand, McNally, Chicago, 1894, 232p,
 Cloth, Coll.
04494 *The great Keinplatz experiment, and other tales
 of twilight and the unseen.* George H. Doran,
 New York, 1919, 254p, Cloth, Coll. [different
 contents]
04495 *The land of mist.* Hutchinson, London, 1926,
 294p, Cloth, Novel [Professor Challenger #3]
04496 *The lost world, being an account of the recent
 amazing adventures of Professor George E.
 Challenger, Lord John Roxton, Professor Summerlee, and Mr. E. D. Malone of the "Daily
 Gazette."* Hodder & Stoughton, London, 1912,
 319p, Cloth, Novel [Professor Challenger #1]
04497 *The lost world; and, The poison belt.* Eyre &
 Spottiswoode, London, 1950, 290p, Cloth,
 Coll. [Professor Challenger #s 1-2]
04498 *The Maracot Deep.* John Murray, London, 1961,
 153p, Cloth, Novel?
04499 *The Maracot Deep, and other stories.* John
 Murray, London, 1929, 310p, Cloth, Coll. [in-
 cludes several Professor Challenger stories]
04500 *The mystery of Cloomber.* Ward & Downey, London, 1889, 151p, Cloth, Novel
04501 *The parasite.* Acme Library, Archibald Constable, Westminster, 1894, 125p, Cloth, Novel
04502 *The poison belt, being an account of another
 adventure of Prof. George E. Challenger, Lord
 John Roxton, Prof. Summerlee, and Mr. E. D.
 Malone, the discoverers of "The Lost World."*
 Hodder & Stoughton, London, 1913, 199p, Cloth,
 Novel [Professor Challenger #2]
04503 *The Professor Challenger stories; The lost
 world; The poison belt; The land of mist;
 The disintegration machine; When the world
 screamed.* John Murray, London, 1952, 577p,
 Cloth, Coll. [Professor Challenger #s 1-3,
 plus miscellaneous stories]
04504 *The ring of Thoth, and other stories.* John
 Murray, London, 1968, 190p, Paper, Coll.
04505 *Tales of terror and mystery.* John Murray, London, 1922, 310p, Cloth, Coll.
04506 *When the world screamed, and other stories.*
 John Murray, London, 1968, 173p, Cloth, Coll.
 [includes a Professor Challenger story]

DOZOIS, GARDNER R., 1947-

04507 *A day in the life; a science fiction anthology.*
 Harper & Row, New York, 1972, 288p, Cloth,
 Anth.

DRACULA, by Bram Stoker; FRANKENSTEIN, by
Mary Shelley
 see: HORROR OMNIBUS

DRAKE, AUSTIN MANN

04508   *The Vial of Vishnu; the report of a cycle of
        events following the violation of the com-
        mand that the Vial must always remain in the
        possession of its rightful owner.* Percy Ro-
        berts, Chicago, 1915, 400p, Cloth, Novel

DRAKE, H(enry) B(URGESS)

04509   *Cursed by the treasure,* by H. B. Drake. John
        Lane, London, 1926, 310p, Cloth, Novel
04510   *Hush-a-by baby,* by Burgess Drake. Falcon Press,
        London, 1952, 352p, Cloth, Novel
04510A retitled: *Children of the wind,* by Burgess
        Drake. J. B. Lippincott, Philadelphia, 1954,
        352p, Cloth, Novel
04511   *The shadowy thing,* by H. B. Drake. Macy-Mas-
        ius, The Vanguard Press, New York, 1928,
        329p, Cloth, Novel

DRAKE, KATHERINE

04512   *The séance at Radley Manor; a warning.* Mar-
        shall Bros., London, 1926, 88p, Cloth, Novel

DRAKE, MORGAN, pseud.
    see: BERRY, D. BRUCE

DRAPER, BLANCHE A., pseud. [Blanche A. Webb]

04513   *The great awakening.* Vantage Press, New York,
        1953, 177p, Cloth, Novel

DRAYTON, HENRY S(hipman), 1840-1923

04514   *In Oudemon; reminiscences of an unknown people,*
        by an occasional traveler. Grafton Press,
        New York, 1900, 378p, Cloth, Novel

THE DREAM CHINTZ
    see: MACKARNESS, M. A.

DREAM WARNINGS AND MYSTERIES

04515   *Dream warnings and mysteries.* George Redway,
        London, 1930?, 318p, Cloth, Anth.

DREIFUSS, JEROME

04516   *Furlough from Heaven; a novel.* Crown Publi-
        shers, New York, 1946, 254p, Cloth, Novel

DREIFUSS, KURT, 1897-   [biography included]

04517   *The other side of the universe.* Twayne Publi-
        shers, New York, 1961, 224p, Cloth, Novel

DRESSER, MARY
    see: SAVAGE, MARY

DREYER, HANS P.

04518   *The secret of the sphinx.* Burton Publishing
        Co., Kansas City, 1929, 228p, Cloth, Novel

DREYFUSS, ERNST, 1908-

04519   *The unfrozen.* Tower, New York, 1970, 158p,
        Paper, Novel

DRING, NAT, pseud. [R. Curtis McBroom, 1910-   ]
[*biography included*]

04520   *The Earth is your spaceship; the story of man.*
        Space Age Press, Fort Worth, TX, 1967, 113p,
        Cloth, Novel

DRUERY, CHAS. T(homas), 1843-1917

04521   *The new Gulliver; or, Travels in Athomia.* Rox-
        burghe Press, Westminster, 1897, 160p, Cloth,
        Novel

DRUON, MAURICE (Samuel Roger Charles), 1918-
[*biography included*]

04522   *The memoirs of Zeus.* Rupert Hart-Davis, Lon-
        don, 1964, 206p, Cloth, Novel

DRURY, ALLEN (Stuart), 1918-   [*biography included*]

04523   *Advise and consent.* Doubleday, Garden City,
        1959, 616p, Cloth, Novel [Advise & Consent #1]
04524   *Capable of honor; a novel.* Doubleday, Garden
        City, 1966, 531p, Cloth, Novel [Advise & Con-
        sent #3]
04525   *Come Nineveh, come Tyre; the presidency of
        Edward M. Jason.* Doubleday, Garden City,
        1973, 481p, Cloth, Novel [Advise & Consent #5]
04526   *Preserve and protect; a novel.* Doubleday, Gar-
        den City, 1968, 394p, Cloth, Novel [Advise &
        Consent #4]
04527   *A shade of difference; a novel.* Doubleday,
        Garden City, 1962, 603p, Cloth, Novel [Advise
        & Consent #2]
04528   *The throne of Saturn; a novel of space and po-
        litics.* Doubleday, Garden City, 1971, 588p,
        Cloth, Novel

DRURY, W(illiam) P(rice), 1861-1949

04529   *The petrified eye, and other naval stories,
        as originally told to the marines by one of
        themselves.* Charpentier & Co., Printers,
        Portsmouth, UK, 1896, 120p, Cloth, Coll.
04530   *The tadpole of an archangel, and other naval
        stories.* Simpkin, Marshall, Hamilton, Kent,
        London, 1898, 233p, Cloth, Coll.
04531   *The tadpole of an archangel, the petrified eye,
        and other naval stories.* Chapman & Hall,
        London, 1904, 270p, Cloth, Coll. [different
        contents]

DRVOTA, MOJMIR, 1923-

04532 *Solitaire.* Ohio State University Press, Columbus, OH, 1974, 123p, Cloth, Novel

DRYASDUST, pseud.
see: HALIDOM, M. Y.

DUANE, TOBY [W. Paul Ganley?], with Al C. Leverentz

04533 *Blague.* SSR Publications, North Tonawanda, NY, 1952, 99p, Paper, Novel

DuBOIS, GAYLORD, with Oskar Lebeck

04534 *The Hurricane Kids on the lost islands.* Grosset & Dunlap, New York, 1941, 216p, Cloth, Novel [Hurricane Kids series]
04535 *Stratosphere Jim and his flying fortress.* Grosset & Dunlap, New York, 1941, 215p, Cloth, Novel [Stratosphere Jim series]

DU BOIS, SHIRLEY GRAHAM, 1906-1977

04536 *Zulu heart; a novel.* Third Press, New York, 1974, 235p, Cloth, Novel

DuBOIS, THEODORA (McCormick), 1890-

04537 *The devil's spoon.* Frederick A. Stokes, New York, 1930, 312p, Cloth, Novel
04538 *Sara Hall's sea god; a novel.* Doubleday, Garden City, 1952, 250p, Cloth, Novel
04539 *Solution T-25.* Doubleday, Garden City, 1951, 218p, Cloth, Novel

du BOIS, WILLIAM (Sherman) PÈNE, 1916- [*biography included*]

04540 *Peter Graves.* Viking Press, New York, 1950, 168p, Cloth, Novel
04541 *The twenty-one balloons.* Viking Press, New York, 1947, 179p, Cloth, Novel

du BOMB, BONNEE, pseud. [Bone'e on cover]

04542 *Planet of sex and orgies.* Peyote Press, New York, 1969, 154p, Paper, Novel

DuBREUIL, LINDA [Elizabeth Lorinda DuBreuil, 1924-] [*biography included*]

04543 *Doctor Proctor.* Greenleaf Classics, San Diego, 1969, , Paper, Novel [may have appeared under a pseudonym]
04544 *Evil, evil.* Belmont, New York, 1973, 185p, Paper, Novel
04545 *Gettin' it together.* Midwood, New York, 1970, , Paper, Novel
04546 *The hat.* Greenleaf Classics, San Diego, 1971, , Paper, Novel [may have appeared under a pseudonym]
04547 *Nightmare baby.* Belmont, New York, 1970, 185p, Paper, Novel

04548 *Pandora descending.* Midwood, New York, 1970, , Paper, Novel
04549 *Rest in piece.* Midwood, New York, 1970, 203p, Paper, Novel
04550 *Silver bells and cockle shells.* Greenleaf Classics, San Diego, 1967, , Paper, Novel [may have appeared under a pseudonym]

as L. J. Brown:

04551 *A labor of lust.* Nightstand, San Diego, 1968, 160p, Paper, Novel

as D. Barry Linder:

04552 *Libido 23.* Greenleaf Classics, San Diego, 1969, , Paper, Novel

DUCASSE, ISIDORE LUCIEN
see: LAUTREAMONT, Comte de

DUCETTE, VINCE
see: KULLINGER, J. L.

DUCHACEK, IVO
see: DUKA, IVO

THE DUCHESS
see: HUNGERFORD, Mrs.

"DUDBROKE," (M.), pseud.

04553 *The prots; a weird romance.* S. H. Bousfield & Co., London, 1903, 224p, Cloth, Novel

DUDEVANT, AMANDINE
see: SAND, GEORGE

DUDINTSEV, VLADIMIR (Dmitrievich), 1918-

04554 *A New Year's tale.* E. P. Dutton, New York, 1960, 61p, Paper, Novel; Hutchinson, London, 1960, 47p, Cloth, Novel
04554A retitled: *A New Year's fable.* U.S. Joint Publication Research Service, Washington, 1960, 24p, Paper?, Story [true first edition in English unknown]

DUDLEY, EUSTACE, 1883-

04555 *The challenge; a story of conspiracy and the coming crash.* Longmans, Green, London, 1928, 133p, Cloth, Novel

DUDLEY, OWEN FRANCIS, 1882-1952

04556 *The coming of the monster; a tale of the masterful monk; problems of human happiness--V.* Longmans, Green, London, 1936, 275p, Cloth, Novel [Problems of Human Happiness #5]

DUDLEY, ROY C.

04557 *Galactic gambit.* Lenox Hill Press, New York, 1971, 192p, Cloth, Novel

DUDLEY-SMITH, TREVOR
   see: TREVOR, ELLESTON

DUFF, DOUGLAS V(alder), 1901-

04558   *Atomic valley.* Blackie & Son, London, 1947, 224p, Cloth, Novel
04559   *The horned crescent.* Hodder & Stoughton, London, 1936, 316p, Cloth, Novel
04560   *The man from outer space.* Blackie & Son, London, 1953, 222p, Cloth, Novel
04561   *Peril on the Amazon.* Blackie & Son, London, 1946, 207p, Cloth, Novel

DUFF, Sir HECTOR (Livingstone), 1872-1954

04562   *The Ivory Graves; a novel.* Thomas Nelson & Sons, London, 1926, 281p, Cloth, Novel

DUFFUS, R(obert) L(uther), 1888-1972

04563   *Jason Potter's space walk; a novel.* W. W. Norton, New York, 1970, 155p, Cloth, Novel

DUHAMEL, GEORGES, 1884-1966

04564   *America the menace; scenes from the life of the future.* Houghton Mifflin, Boston, 1931, 217p, Cloth, Novel

DUKA, IVO, pseud. [Ivo Maria Rudolf Duchacek, 1913-] [*biography included*], with Helena Kolda

04565   *Martin and his friend from outer space.* Harper & Bros., New York, 1955, 96p, Cloth, Novel

DUKE, MADELAINE (Elizabeth), 1925-   [*biography included*]

      Claret, sandwiches, and sin. [see 04567A]
04566   *This business of Bomfog; a cartoon.* Heinemann, London, 1967, 197p, Cloth, Novel

as Maxim Donne:

04567   *Claret, sandwiches, and sin; a cartoon.* Heinemann, London, 1964, 200p, Cloth, Novel
04567A *Claret, sandwiches, and sin; a cartoon,* by Madelaine Duke. Four Square, London, 1966, 143p, Paper, Novel

DUKE, WINIFRED, 1890?-1962

04568   *The black mirror.* Jarrolds Publishers, London, 1948, 208p, Cloth, Novel
04569   *Dirge for a dead witch.* Jarrolds Publishers, London, 1949, 256p, Cloth, Novel

THE DUKE OF CLARENCE
   see: FOSTER, E. M.

DUMAS, ALEXANDRE, père, 1802-1870

      Edmond Dantès. [see: FLAGG, EDMUND]
04570   *Memoirs of a physician.* George Peirce, London, 1846, 495p, Cloth, Novel [the bibliographical intricacies of this title remain unfathomed and possibly unfathomable; the French original is exceptionally long, and as a result the English translations have often been broken into two or more pieces, each bearing titles similar to fragments published by other firms; only the significant variations are listed here] [Memoirs of a Physician #1; this edition consists of the first section of the original] [co-authored anonymously by Auguste Maquet, 1813-1888]
04570A retitled: *Joseph Balsamo; a novel.* T. B. Peterson & Bros., Philadelphia, 1878, 365p, Cloth, Novel [this edition apparently more or less corresponds with the above; there may have been earlier printings]
04570B retitled: *Balsamo the magician; or, The memoirs of a physician; a historical romance of the great French Revolution.* W. H. Davis, New York, 1892, 206p, Cloth, Novel [this also appears to be a translation of the first part of the French original]
04570C *Memoirs of a physician.* T. B. Peterson, Philadelphia, 1850?, 347p, Cloth, Novel [this seems to be the second half of the French original]
04570D retitled: *Joseph Balsamo; volume II of The memoirs of a physician; an historical romance.* Rand McNally, Chicago, 1895, 525p, Cloth, Novel [apparently more or less the same as 04570C]
04570E retitled: *The elixir of life; the memoirs of a physician.* Collins Clear-Type Press, London, 1928, 476p, Cloth, Novel [chapters 87-139 of the original]
04571   *The queen's necklace; a sequel to "Memoirs of a physician."* Parlour Library, London, 1847, 365p, Cloth, Novel [Memoirs of a Physician #2; anonymously co-authored by Auguste Maquet]
04572   *Tales of the supernatural.* Methuen, London, 1907, 106p, Paper, Coll.
04573   *The wolf-leader.* Methuen, London, 1904, 115p, Cloth, Novel

DUMAS, ALEXANDRE, fils, 1824-1895

04574   *The resuscitated.* Charing Cross Publishing Co. London, 1877, 195p, Cloth, Novel

du MAURIER, DAPHNE, 1907-   [*biography included*]

04575   *The apple tree; a short novel and some stories.* Victor Gollancz, London, 1952, 264p, Cloth, Coll.
04575A retitled: *The birds, and other stories.* Penguin, Harmondsworth, 1963, 239p, Paper, Coll. *The blue lenses, and other stories.* [see 04576A]
04576   *The breaking point; eight stories.* Victor Gollancz, London, 1959, 287p, Cloth, Coll.
04576A retitled: *The blue lenses, and other stories.* Penguin, Harmondsworth, 1970, 288p, Paper, Coll. *Don't look now.* [see 04578A]

du MAURIER, DAPHNE (Cont.)

04577 *The house on the strand.* Victor Gollancz, London, 1969, 351p, Cloth, Novel
04578 *Not after midnight, and other stories.* Victor Gollancz, London, 1971, 285p, Cloth, Coll.
04578A retitled: *Don't look now.* Doubleday, Garden City, 1971, 303p, Cloth, Coll.
04579 *Rule Britannia; a novel.* Victor Gollancz, London, 1972, 318p, Cloth, Novel

du MAURIER, GEORGE (Louis Palmella Busson), 1834-1896

04580 *The Martian; a novel.* George Bell & Sons, London, 1897, 471p, Cloth, Novel
04581 *Peter Ibbetson.* Harper & Bros., New York, 1891, 418p, Cloth, Novel
04582 *Trilby.* Osgood, McIlvaine, London, 1894, 3vol, Cloth, Novel

DUNCAN, BRUCE, pseud.
    see: GREENFIELD, IRVING A.

DUNCAN, DAVID, 1913-   [*biography included*]

        Another tree in Eden. [see 04583A]
04583 *Beyond Eden.* Ballantine, New York, 1955, 169p, Cloth, Novel
04583A retitled: *Another tree in Eden.* William Heinemann, London, 1956, 192p, Cloth, Novel
04584 *Dark dominion.* Ballantine, New York, 1954, 208p, Cloth, Novel
04585 *Occam's razor.* Ballantine, New York, 1957, 165p, Paper, Novel

DUNCAN, LEE

04586 *Fidel Castro assassinated.* Monarch, Derby, Conn., 1961, 140p, Paper, Novel

DUNCAN, LOIS, pseud. [Lois Duncan Arquette, 1934-   ] [*biography included*]

04587 *Down a dark hall.* Little, Brown, Boston, 1974, 181p, Cloth, Novel
04588 *A gift of magic.* Little, Brown, Boston, 1971, 183p, Cloth, Novel

DUNCAN, ROBERT LIPSCOMB
    see: ROBERTS, JAMES HALL

DUNCAN, RONALD (Frederick Henry), 1914-
[*biography included*]

04589 *The last Adam; a story.* Dennis Dobson, London, 1952, 93p, Cloth, Novel

DUNKERLY, WILLIAM ARTHUR
    see: OXENHAM, JOHN

DUNN, ALAN (Cantwell), 1900-1974 [*biography included*]

04590 *Is there intelligent life on Earth? a report to the Congress of Mars, translated into English by the author.* Simon & Schuster, New York, 1960, 118p, Cloth, Novel

DUNN, GERTRUDE, pseud. [Gertrude Renton Weaver]

04591 *And so forever.* Thornton Butterworth, London, 1929, 286p, Cloth, Novel
04592 *The mark of the bat; a tale of vampires living and dead.* Thornton Butterworth, London, 1928, 302p, Cloth, Novel
04593 *Unholy depths.* Thornton Butterworth, London, 1926, 319p, Cloth, Novel

as G. Colmore:

04594 *A Brother of the Shadow.* Noel Douglas, London, 1926, 320p, Cloth, Novel
04595 *The strange story of Hester Wynne, told by herself.* Smith, Elder, London, 1899, 361p, Cloth, Novel

DUNN, J(oseph) ALLAN (Elphinstone), 1872-1941

04596 *The flower of fate.* C. Arthur Pearson, London, 1928, 254p, Cloth, Novel
04597 *The treasure of Atlantis.* Centaur Press, New York, 1970, 126p, Paper, Novel

DUNN, WALDO H(ilary), 1882-1969

04598 *The vanished empire; a tale of the Mound Builders.* Robert Clarke Co., Cincinnati, 1904, 180p, Cloth, Novel

DUNN, WILLIAM B.

04599 *Escape from the planet Karaxe.* Vantage Press, New York, 1970, 158p, Cloth, Novel

DUNNE, J(ohn) W(illiam), 1875-1949

04600 *St. George and the witches.* Henry Holt, New York, 1939, 206p, Cloth, Novel

DUNSANY, Lord [Edward John Moreton Drax Plunkett, 18th Baron Dunsany, 1878-1957]

04601 *At the edge of the world.* Ballantine, New York, 1970, 238p, Paper, Coll.
04602 *Beyond the fields we know.* Ballantine, New York, 1972, 299p, Paper, Coll.
04603 *The blessing of Pan.* G. P. Putnam's Sons, London, 1927, 287p, Cloth, Novel
04604 *The book of wonder.* Boni & Liveright, New York, 1918, 234p, Cloth, Coll. [includes *The book of wonder* and *Time and the gods*]
04605 *The book of wonder; a chronicle of little adventures at the edge of the world.* William Heinemann, London, 1912, 97p, Cloth, Coll.
04606 *Carcassonne.* John W. Luce, Boston, 1916?, 28p, Paper, Story
04607 *The charwoman's shadow.* G. P. Putnam's Sons, London, 1926, 339p, Cloth, Novel

DUNSANY, Lord (Cont.)

04608   *The chronicles of Rodriguez.* G. P. Putnam's
          Sons, London, 1922, 321p, Cloth, Novel
04608A retitled: *Don Rodriguez; chronicles of Shadow
          Valley.* G. P. Putnam's Sons, New York,
          1922, 318p, Cloth, Novel
04609   *The curse of the wise woman.* William Heine-
          mann, London, 1933, 326p, Cloth, Novel
          Don Rodriguez; chronicles of Shadow Valley.
          [see 04608A]
04610   *A dreamer's tales.* George Allen & Sons, Lon-
          don, 1910, 252p, Cloth, Coll.
04611   *A dreamer's tales, and other stories.* Boni &
          Liveright, New York, 1919, 212p, Cloth, Coll.
04612   *Fifty-one tales.* Elkin Mathews, London, 1915,
          111p, Cloth, Coll.
04612A retitled: *The food of death; fifty-one tales.*
          Newcastle Publishing Co., Hollywood, 1974,
          138p, Paper, Coll.
04613   *The fourth book of Jorkens.* Arkham House,
          Sauk City, 1948, 194p, Cloth, Coll. [Jorkens
          #4]
04614   *God, men, and ghosts; the best supernatural
          fiction of Lord Dunsany.* Dover, New York,
          1972, 260p, Paper, Coll.
04615   *The gods of Pegāna.* Elkin Mathews, London,
          1905, 94p, Cloth, Coll.
04616   *If I were dictator; the pronouncements of the
          Grand Macaroni.* Methuen, London, 1934, 107p,
          Cloth, Novel
04617   *Jorkens borrows another whiskey.* Michael Jo-
          seph, London, 1954, 256p, Cloth, Coll. [Jor-
          kens #5]
04618   *Jorkens has a large whiskey.* Putnam, London,
          1940, 323p, Cloth, Coll. [Jorkens #3]
          Jorkens remembers Africa. [see 04622A]
04619   *The king of Elfland's daughter.* G. P. Putnam's
          Sons, London, 1924, 301p, Cloth, Novel
          The last book of wonder. [see 04630A]
04620   *The last revolution; a novel.* Jarrolds Publi-
          shers, London, 1951, 192p, Cloth, Novel
04621   *The man who ate the phoenix.* Jarrolds Publi-
          shers, London, 1949, 223p, Cloth, Coll.
04622   *Mr. Jorkens remembers Africa.* William Heine-
          mann, London, 1934, 299p, Cloth, Coll. [Jor-
          kens #2]
04622A retitled: *Jorkens remembers Africa.* Longmans,
          Green, New York, 1934, 303p, Cloth, Coll.
          [Jorkens #2]
04623   *My talks with Dean Spanley.* William Heine-
          mann, London, 1936, 137p, Cloth, Novel
04624   *Over the hills, and far away.* Ballantine,
          New York, 1974, 234p, Paper, Coll.
04625   *Selections from the writings of Lord Dunsany.*
          Cuala Press, Churchtown, UK, 1912, 99p,
          Cloth, Coll.
04626   *The strange journeys of Colonel Polders.*
          Jarrolds Publishers, London, 1950, 208p,
          Cloth, Novel
04627   *The sword of Welleran, and other stories.*
          George Allen & Sons, London, 1908, 243p,
          Cloth, Coll.
04628   *The sword of Welleran, and other tales of
          enchantment.* Devin-Adair, New York, 1954,
          181p, Cloth, Coll. [different contents]
04629   *Tales of three hemispheres.* John W. Luce,
          Boston, 1919, 147p, Cloth, Coll.
04630   *Tales of wonder.* Elkin Mathews, London, 1916,
          187p, Cloth, Coll.
04630A retitled: *The last book of wonder.* John W.
          Luce, Boston, 1916, 213p, Cloth, Coll.

04631   *Time and the gods.* William Heinemann, London,
          1906, 179p, Cloth, Coll.
04632   *The travel tales of Mr. Joseph Jorkens.* G. P.
          Putnam's Sons, London, 1931, 304p, Cloth,
          Coll. [Jorkens #1]

DUNTON, THEODORE WATTS-
    see: WATTS-DUNTON, THEODORE

DURAND, FRANCOIS
    see: MIOMANDRE, FRANCIS de

DURAND, ROBERT, 1944-   [*biography included*]

04633   *The old man and the monkey-king.* Capricorn
          Press, Santa Barbara, CA, 1972, 94p, Cloth,
          Novel

DURIE, A. J. L.

04634   *An index to the British editions of the 'Maga-
          zine of fantasy and science fiction,' with
          a cross-reference to the original American
          edition.* Fantast (Medway) Ltd., Wisbech,
          UK, 1966, 44p, Paper, Nonf.

DURKIN, DOUGLAS (Leader), 1884-

04635   *Mr. Gumble sits up.* Horace Liveright, New
          York, 1930, 232p, Cloth, Novel

DURRELL, GERALD (Malcolm), 1925-   [*biography
          included*]

04636   *The talking parcel.* Collins, London, 1974,
          190p, Cloth, Novel

DURRELL, LAWRENCE (George), 1912-   [*biogra-
          phy included*]

04637   *Down the Styx.* Capricorn Press, Santa Barbara,
          CA, 1971, 23p, Paper, Story
04638   *Nunquam; a novel.* E. P. Dutton, New York,
          1970, 318p, Cloth, Novel [Felix Charlock #2]
04639   *Tunc; a novel.* E. P. Dutton, New York, 1968,
          359p, Cloth, Novel [Felix Charlock #1]

DUTOURD, JEAN (Hubert), 1920-

04640   *A dog's head.* John Lehmann, London, 1951,
          143p, Cloth, Novel

DUVAR, JOHN HUNTER
    see: HUNTER-DUVAR, JOHN

DWINELL, R(alph) M(ilton), 1894-

04641   *The gutter of creation.* Bruce Humphries, Bos-
          ton, 1934, 270p, Cloth, Novel

DWYER, JAMES FRANCIS, 1874-1952

04642 *"Breath of the jungle."* A. C. McClurg, Chicago, 1915, 356p, Cloth, Coll.
04643 *The city of cobras.* Herbert Jenkins, London, 1938, 284p, Cloth, Novel [Spillane series]
04644 *Evelyn; something more than a story.* Vanguard Press, New York, 1929, 215p, Cloth, Novel
04645 *The Lady with Feet of Gold.* Herbert Jenkins, London, 1937, 311p, Cloth, Novel [Spillane series]
      The Spotted Panther. [see 04646A]

as James Francis Diver:

04646 *The Spotted Panther.* W. R. Caldwell, New York, 1913, 293p, Cloth, Novel
04646A *The Spotted Panther*, by James Francis Dwyer. Doubleday, Page, Garden City, 1913, 293p, Cloth, Novel

DWYER, VERA (G.)

04647 *The stolen ghost.* Quality Press, London, 1943, 254p, Cloth, Novel

DWYER, WINIFRED, pseud. [Winifred Powell Grover]

04648 *The golden star.* Psychic Press, London, 1958, 231p, Cloth, Novel

DYCKE, IGNATZ SAHULA-
    see: SAHULA-DYCKE, IGNATZ

DYE, CHARLES, 1927-1955

04649 *Prisoner in the skull; a science-fiction novel.* Abelard Press, New York, 1952, 256p, Cloth, Novel

DYER, ANNIE RUSSELL

04650 *The touch of a vanished hand.* American Book Exchange, Providence, RI, 1897, 153p, Cloth, Novel

DYKE, HENRY VAN
    see: VAN DYKE, HENRY

DYLLINGTON, ANTHONY

04651 *The unseen thing; a novel.* T. Werner Laurie, London, 1909, 326p, Cloth, Novel

DZIEWICKI, MICHAEL HENRY

04652 *Entombed in flesh.* William Blackwood & Sons, Edinburgh, 1897, 282p, Cloth, Novel

E., A.
    see: RUSSELL, GEORGE WILLIAM

E., T.
    see: ERSKINE, THOMAS

E. M. F.
    see: FOSTER, E. M.

E. W.
    see: W., E.

EADE, CHARLES, 1903-1964, with Ursula Bloom as Lozania Prolé

01555 *Daughter of the devil.* Robert Hale, London, 1963, 192p, Cloth, Novel

EADY, MARY ALINE
    see: WESLEY, MARY

EAGER, EDWARD (McMaken), 1911-1964

04653 *Half magic.* Harcourt, Brace & Co., New York, 1954, 217p, Cloth, Novel [Magic #1]
04654 *Knight's castle.* Harcourt, Brace & Co., New York, 1956, 183p, Cloth, Novel [Magic #2]
04655 *Magic by the lake.* Harcourt, Brace & Co., New York, 1957, 183p, Cloth, Novel [Magic #3]
04656 *Magic or not?* Harcourt, Brace & Co., New York, 1959, 190p, Cloth, Novel
04657 *Seven-day magic.* Harcourt, Brace & World, New York, 1962, 156p, Cloth, Novel
04658 *The time garden.* Harcourt, Brace & Co., New York, 1958, 188p, Cloth, Novel [Magic #4]

EAGLE, ROBIN [published anonymously]

04659 *The sex life of Hercules.* Calga Publishers, Los Angeles, 1971, 191p, Paper, Novel

EARDLEY-WILMOT, (Sir) S(ydney Marow), 1847-1929

04660 *The next naval war.* Edward Stanford, London, 1894, 75p, Cloth?, Novel

as "Searchlight":

04661 *The battle of the North Sea in 1914.* Hugh Rees, London, 1912, 80p, Cloth?, Novel
04661A *The battle of the North Sea in 1914*, by S. Eardley-Wilmot. Hugh Rees, London, 1913, 80p, Cloth?, Novel

EARLE, RICHARD

04662 *Forever Ember.* Bee-Line, New York, 1966, 157p, Paper, Novel

EARLEY, GEORGE W(hiteford), 1927- [*biography included*]

04663 *Encounters with aliens; UFO's and alien beings in science fiction.* Sherbourne Press, Los Angeles, 1968, 244p, Cloth, Anth.

EARNSHAW, ANTHONY, 1924-   [*biography inclu-ded*], with Eric Thacker

04664 *Musrum.* Jonathan Cape, London, 1968, 160p, Cloth, Novel [Wintersol #1]
04665 *Wintersol.* Jonathan Cape, London, 1971, 103p, Cloth, Novel [Wintersol #2]

EARNSHAW, BRIAN, 1929-   [*biography included*]

04666 *Dragonfall 5 and the empty planet.* Pied Piper, Methuen, London, 1973, 125p, Cloth, Novel [Dragonfall 5 #3]
04667 *Dragonfall 5 and the hijackers.* Pied Piper, Methuen, London, 1974, 139p, Cloth, Novel [Dragonfall 5 #4]
04668 *Dragonfall 5 and the Royal Beast.* Pied Piper, Methuen, London, 1972, 104p, Cloth, Novel [Dragonfall 5 #2]
04669 *Dragonfall 5 and the space cowboys.* Pied Piper, Methuen, London, 1972, 104p, Cloth, Novel [Dragonfall 5 #1]
04670 *Planet in the eye of time.* Hodder & Stoughton, London, 1968, 191p, Cloth, Novel

EASSON, ROBERT (Watson), 1941-   [*biography included*]

04671 *The bird; The ghoul; and, In the name of my friend.* Vantage Press, New York, 1968, 66p, Cloth, Coll.

EASTERLEY, ROBERT
   see: POTTER, ROBERT

EASTWOOD, W(ilfred), 1923-

04672 *Science and literature; the literary relations of science and technology; an anthology.* Macmillan, London, 1957, 296p, Cloth, Anth. [includes some nonf.]
04673 *Science and literature; the literary relations of science and technology; an anthology; second series.* Macmillan, London, 1960, 290p, Cloth, Anth. [includes some nonf.]

EATON, EVELYN (Sybil Mary), 1902-   [*biography included*]

04674 *Flight; a novel.* Bobbs-Merrill, Indianapolis, 1954, 246p, Cloth, Novel
04675 *The king is a witch.* Cassell, London, 1965, 262p, Cloth, Novel

EBERS, GEORG (Moritz), 1837-1898

04676 *The elixir, and other tales.* W. S. Gottsber-ger, New York, 1890, 261p, Cloth, Coll.
04677 *The king and queen of Mellebusch; or, The in-dispensables.* Brown & Co., Boston, 1899, 124p, Cloth, Novel

ECCLES, CHARLOTTE O'CONOR
   see: GODFREY, HAL

ECHARD, MARGARET

04678 *The dark fantastic.* Doubleday, Garden City, 1947, 312p, Cloth, Novel

ECKSTROM, JACK DENNIS

04679 *The time of the hedrons.* Avalon, New York, 1968, 190p, Cloth, Novel

EDDISON, E(ric) R(ücker), 1882-1945

04680 *A fish dinner in Memison.* E. P. Dutton, New York, 1941, 349p, Cloth, Novel [Zimiamvia #2]
04681 *The Mezentian gate.* Curwen Press, Plaistow, UK, 1958, 247p, Cloth, Novel [Zimiamvia #3]
04682 *Mistress of mistresses; a vision of Zimiamvia.* Faber & Faber, London, 1935, 463p, Cloth, Novel [Zimiamvia #1]
04683 *Styrbiorn the strong.* Jonathan Cape, London, 1926, 284p, Cloth, Novel.
04684 *The worm Ouroboros; a romance.* Jonathan Cape, London, 1922, 446p, Cloth, Novel [includes a reference to Zimiamvia]

EDDY, C(lifford) M(artin) Jr., 1896-1967

04685 *Exit into eternity; tales of the bizarre and supernatural.* Oxford Press, Providence, RI, 1973, 121p, Cloth, Coll.

EDELSON, EDWARD, 1932-   [*biography included*]

04686 *Great monsters of the movies.* Doubleday, Garden City, 1973, 101p, Cloth, Nonf.

EDEN, ROB, pseud.
   see: BURKHARDT, ROBERT and BURKHARDT, EVE

EDGAR, ALFRED
   see: LYNDON, BARRE

EDGAR, KEN(neth), 1925-   [*biography included*]

04687 *The Starfire.* Boxwood Press, Pittsburgh, 1961, 174p, Paper, Novel

EDGAR, PETER, pseud. [Peter Edgar King King-Scott, 1918-]

04688 *Cities of the dead.* Digit, London, 1963, 160p, Paper, Novel

EDGELL, JOHN

04689 *John Edgell's ghosts; an omnibus of the super-natural, comprising thirty-two original sto-ries by John Edgell, and eleven classic tales.* Wayland (Publishers), London, 1970, 316p, Cloth, Anth.

THE EDITOR OF THE PHOENIX, pseud.
see: REEVE, CLARA

EDMONDS, HARRY (Moreton Southey)

04690 *The North Sea mystery; a story of naval intelligence work*. Ward, Lock, London, 1930,
319p, Cloth, Novel
04691 *The professor's last experiment*. Rich & Cowan, London, 1935, 311p, Cloth, Novel
04691A retitled: *The secret voyage*. Macdonald,
London, 1946, 254p, Cloth, Novel
04692 *The riddle of the Straits*. Ward, Lock, London, 1931, 319p, Cloth, Novel
04693 *The rockets (Operation Manhattan)*. Macdonald,
London, 1951, 286p, Cloth, Novel
The secret voyage. [see 04691A]

EDMONDS, HELEN
see: KAVAN, ANNA

EDMONDSON, G. C. [José Mario Garry Ordoñez
Edmondson y Cotton, 1922-   ] [*biography included*]

Blue face. [see 04694A]
04694 *Chapayeca*. Doubleday, Garden City, 1971,
163p, Cloth, Novel
04694A retitled: *Blue face*. DAW, New York, 1972,
128p, Paper, Novel
04695 *The ship that sailed the time stream*. Ace
Double, New York, 1965, 167p, Paper, Novel
04696 *Stranger than you think*. Ace Double, New
York, 1965, 87p, Paper, Coll.
04697 *T.H.E.M.* Doubleday, Garden City, 1974, 182p,
Cloth, Novel

EDSON, MILAN C.

04698 *Solaris Farm; a story of the twentieth century*. The Author, Washington, DC, 1900,
452p, Cloth, Novel

EDSTROM, O. E.

04699 *Epp's trip to the Moon*. House of Field, New
York, 1945, 117p, Cloth, Novel

EDWARDS, CHARMAN, pseud. [Frederick Anthony
Edwards, 1896-   ]

04700 *Drama of Mr. Dilly*. Robert Hale, London,
1939, 288p, Cloth, Novel

EDWARDS, DAVID, 1945?-

04701 *Next stop--Mars! a novel of the first space-
ship voyage to the Red Planet*. Greenwich
Book Publishers, New York, 1960, 113p,
Cloth, Novel

EDWARDS, FREDERICK ANTHONY
see: EDWARDS, CHARMAN

EDWARDS, GAWAIN, pseud. [George Edward Pendray,
1901-   ]

04702 *The Earth-tube*. D. Appleton, New York, 1929,
309p, Cloth, Novel

EDWARDS, NORMAN, pseud.
see: CARR, TERRY and WHITE, TED

EEDEN, FREDERIK (Willem) van, 1860-1932

04703 *The quest*. John W. Luce, Boston, 1907, 520p,
Cloth, Novel

EENHOORN, MICHAEL

04704 *An omnibus of American mysteries*. Juniper
Press, New York, 1959, 383p, Cloth, Anth.

EFFINGER, GEO(RGE) ALEC, 1947-   [*biography
included*]

04705 *Mixed feelings; short stories*. Harper & Row,
New York, 1974, 208p, Cloth, Coll.
04706 *Planet of the apes; man the fugitive*. Award,
New York, 1974, 172p, Paper, Tele. Coll.
[Planet of the Apes (TV series) #1]
04707 *Relatives; a novel*. Harper & Row, New York,
1974, 212p, Cloth, Novel
04708 *What entropy means to me*. Doubleday, Garden
City, 1972, 191p, Cloth, Novel

EFREMOV, IVAN (Antonovich), 1907-1972 [*biography included*] [spelled Yefremov on his books]

04709 *Andromeda; a space-age tale*. Foreign Languages
Publishing House, Moscow, 1960, 445p, Cloth,
Novel
04710 *A meeting over Tuscarora, and other adventure
stories*. Hutchinson, London, 1946, 124p,
Cloth, Coll.
04711 *Stories*. Foreign Languages Publishing House,
Moscow, 1954, 260p, Cloth, Coll.

EGBERT, H. M., pseud.
see: ROUSSEAU, VICTOR

EGERTON, GEORGE, pseud. [Mary Chavelita Bright]

04712 *Fantasias*. John Lane, The Bodley Head, London,
1897, 156p, Cloth, Coll.

EGGLESTON, K(atherine)

04713 *Red O'Rourke's riches*. Wright & Brown, London,
1937, 288p, Cloth, Novel

EGINARDUS, pseud.
see: MANLEY, MARY

EGLETON, CLIVE (Frederick), 1927- [*biography included*]

04714 *The Judas mandate.* Hodder & Stoughton, London, 1972, 224p, Cloth, Novel [Garnett #3]
04715 *Last post for a partisan.* Hodder & Stoughton, London, 1971, 224p, Cloth, Novel [Garnett #2]
04716 *A piece of resistance.* Hodder & Stoughton, London, 1970, 192p, Cloth, Novel [Garnett #1]

EGREMONT, MICHAEL

04717 *The bride of Frankenstein.* Queensway Press, London, 1935, 252p, Cloth, Movie [Frankenstein series]

EHRLICH, MAX (Simon), 1909- [*biography included*]

04718 *The Big Eye.* Doubleday, Garden City, 1949, 221p, Cloth, Novel
04719 *The Edict; a novel.* Nelson Doubleday, Garden City, 1971, 182p, Cloth, Novel
04720 *The reincarnation of Peter Proud.* Bobbs-Merrill, Indianapolis, 1974, 287p, Cloth, Novel

EHRMANN, MAX, 1872-1945

04721 *A fearsome riddle.* Bowen-Merrill, Indianapolis, 1901, 192p, Cloth, Novel; B. F. Stevens & Brown, London, 1901, 192p, Cloth, Novel

EICHNER, HENRY M., 1909-1971 [*biography included*]

04722 *Atlantean chronicles.* Fantasy Publishing Co., Alhambra, CA, 1971, 230p, Cloth, Nonf.

EIDLITZ, WALTHER, 1892-

04723 *Zodiak.* Harper & Bros., New York, 1931, 328p, Cloth, Novel; Hamish Hamilton, London, 1931, 319p, Cloth, Novel

1895; UNDER HOME RULE

04724 *1895; under home rule.* Hodges, Figgis, Dublin, 1893, 18p, Paper, Story

EINSTEIN, CHARLES, 1926- [*biography included*]

04725 *The day New York went dry.* Gold Medal, Greenwich, 1964, 160p, Paper, Novel

EISEN, ANTHONY FON
    see: FON EISEN, ANTHONY

EISENBERG, LARRY [Lawrence], 1919- [*biography included*]

04726 *The best laid schemes.* Macmillan, New York, 1971, 191p, Cloth, Coll.

EISENBERG, LAWRENCE B.

04727 *The villa of the Ferromonte.* Simon & Schuster, New York, 1974, 191p, Cloth, Novel

EISENBERG, MANUEL

04728 *The University of Intelligence; a pilot-project to fight the mediocrity-crisis.* Mindbuilder Publishers, Hollywood, 1973, 236p, Paper, Novel

EISGRUBER, FRANK Jr.

04729 *Gangland's doom; the Shadow of the pulps.* Robert Weinberg, Oak Lawn, IL, 1974, 64p, Paper, Nonf.

EKBERG, C(arl) WHITWORTH

04730 *The story of Kastán; a novel.* Exposition Press, New York, 1954, 104p, Cloth, Novel

EKLUND, GORDON (Stewart), 1945- [*biography included*]

04731 *All times possible.* DAW, New York, 1974, 191p, Paper, Novel
04732 *Beyond the resurrection.* Doubleday, Garden City, 1973, 202p, Cloth, Novel
04733 *The eclipse of dawn.* Ace, New York, 1971, 221p, Paper, Novel
04734 *A trace of dreams.* Ace, New York, 1972, 256p, Paper, Novel

with Poul Anderson:

00320 *Inheritors of Earth.* Chilton Book Co., Radnor, PA, 1974, 190p, Cloth, Novel

ELAM, RICHARD M(ace), 1920- [*biography included*]

   Science fiction stories. [see 04735A]
   Super science stories. [see 04736A]
04735 *Teen-age science fiction stories.* Lantern Press, New York, 1952, 254p, Cloth, Coll.
04735A retitled: *Science fiction stories.* Lantern Pocket Books, New York, 1964, 212p, Paper, Coll.
04736 *Teen-age super science stories.* Lantern Press, New York, 1957, 253p, Cloth, Coll.
04736A retitled: *Super science stories.* Lantern Press, New York, 1967, 231p, Paper, Coll.
04737 *Young readers' science fiction stories.* Lantern Press, New York, 1957, 191p, Cloth, Coll.
04738 *Young stowaways in space.* Lantern Press, New York, 1960, 191p, Cloth, Novel
04739 *Young visitor to Mars.* Lantern Press, New York, 1953, 256p, Cloth, Novel
04740 *Young visitor to the Moon.* Lantern Press, New York, 1965, 191p, Cloth, Novel

ELDER, ART(hur A.), 1900?-1956

04741 *The Blue Streak and Doctor Medusa.* Whitman, Racine, Wisc., 1946, 248p, Cloth, Novel

ELDER, JOSEPH

04742 *Eros in orbit; a collection of all new science
        fiction stories about sex.* Trident Press,
        New York, 1973, 189p, Cloth, Anth.
04743 *The farthest reaches.* Trident Press, New
        York, 1968, 217p, Cloth, Anth.

ELDER, MICHAEL (Aiken), 1931-   [*biography
included*]

04744 *The alien Earth.* Robert Hale, London, 1971,
        188p, Cloth, Novel
04745 *A different world.* Robert Hale, London,
        1974, 188p, Cloth, Novel
04746 *Down to Earth.* Robert Hale, London, 1973,
        190p, Cloth, Novel [Barclay #3]
04747 *The everlasting man.* Robert Hale, London,
        1972, 174p, Cloth, Novel
        Flight to terror. [see 04750A]
04748 *Nowhere on Earth.* Robert Hale, London, 1972,
        191p, Cloth, Novel [Barclay #1]
04749 *Paradise is not enough.* Robert Hale, London,
        1970, 190p, Cloth, Novel
04750 *The perfumed planet.* Robert Hale, London,
        1973, 192p, Cloth, Novel [Barclay #2]
04750A retitled: *Flight to terror.* Pinnacle, New
        York, 1973, 192p, Paper, Novel [Barclay #2]
04751 *The seeds of frenzy.* Robert Hale, London,
        1974, 188p, Cloth, Novel [Barclay #4]

ELDERSHAW, FLORA SYDNEY PATRICIA, 1897-   ,
with Marjorie Barnard as M. Barnard Eldershaw

00879 *Tomorrow and tomorrow.* Georgian House, Mel-
        bourne, 1947, 466p, Cloth, Novel

ELDERSHAW, M. BARNARD, pseud.
    see: ELDERSHAW, FLORA and BARNARD, MAR-
    JORIE

ELDRIDGE, PAUL, 1888-   [*biography included*],
with George Sylvester Viereck

04752 *The invincible Adam.* Horace Liveright, New
        York, 1932, 451p, Cloth, Novel [The Three
        Immortals #3]
04753 *My first two thousand years; the autobiography
        of the Wandering Jew.* Macauley, New York,
        1928, 501p, Cloth, Novel [The Three Immor-
        tals #1]
04754 *Prince Pax.* Duckworth, London, 1933, 319p,
        Cloth, Novel
04755 *Salome, the Wandering Jewess.* Horace Live-
        right, New York, 1930, 495p, Cloth, Novel
        [The Three Immortals #2]

ELEVE, pseud. [Mrs. H. M. Stowe]

04756 *The elixir of life; or, Robert's pilgrimage;
        an allegory.* Eleve Publishing Co., Chicago,
        1890, 124p, Paper, Novel
04756A retitled: *The progress of the pilgrim.* Eleve
        Publishing Co., Chicago, 1891, 124p, Paper,
        Novel

ELGIN, SUZETTE HADEN, 1936-   [*biography included*]

04757 *At the Seventh Level.* DAW, New York, 1972,
        142p, Paper, Novel [Coyote Jones #3]
04758 *The Communipaths.* Ace Double, New York, 1970,
        110p, Paper, Novel [Coyote Jones #1]
04759 *Furthest.* Ace, New York, 1971, 191p, Paper,
        Novel [Coyote Jones #2]

ELIADE, MIRCEA, 1907-

04760 *Two tales of the occult.* Herder & Herder,
        New York, 1970, 130p, Cloth, Coll.

with Mihai Niculescu:

04761 *Fantastic tales.* Dillon's University Bookshop,
        London, 1969, 100p, Cloth, Coll. [in Rumanian
        and English on facing pages]

ELIADES, DAVID, with Robert Forrest Webb as
David Forrest

04762 *After me, the deluge.* Hodder & Stoughton, Lon-
        don, 1972, 189p, Cloth, Novel
04763 *The undertaker's dozen.* Tandem, London, 1974,
        160p, Paper, Coll.

ELIAT, HÉLÈNE

04764 *Sheba visits Solomon; a novel.* Cassell, London,
        1932, 223p, Cloth, Novel

el-IDDRISSEY, ACHMED
    see: ABDULLAH, ACHMED

ELIMINATION

04765 *Elimination.* American Science Fiction, Sydney,
        1953, 34p, Paper, Anth.

ELIOT, E. C.
    see: ELIOTT, E. C.

ELIOT, Major GEORGE F(ielding), 1894-1971

04766 *The Purple Legion; a G-man thriller.* William
        Caslon, New York, 1936, 255p, Cloth, Novel

ELIOTT, E. C., pseud. [Reginald Alec Martin,
1900-   ]

04767 *Kemlo and the craters of the Moon.* Thomas
        Nelson & Sons, London, 1955, 200p, Cloth,
        Novel [Kemlo #5]
04768 *Kemlo and the Crazy Planet.* Thomas Nelson &
        Sons, London, 1954, 200p, Cloth, Novel [Kem-
        lo #1]
04769 *Kemlo and the end of time.* Thomas Nelson &
        Sons, London, 1957, 196p, Cloth, Novel [Kem-
        lo #10]
04770 *Kemlo and the gravity rays.* Thomas Nelson &
        Sons, London, 1956, 202p, Cloth, Novel [Kem-
        lo #8]

ELIOTT, E. C. (Cont.)

04771   *Kemlo and the Martian ghosts.* Thomas Nelson & Sons, London, 1954, 202p, Cloth, Novel [Kemlo #4]

04772   *Kemlo and the masters of space.* Thomas Nelson & Sons, London, 1963, 194p, Cloth, Novel [Kemlo #15]

04773   *Kemlo and the purple dawn.* Thomas Nelson & Sons, London, 1957, 200p, Cloth, Novel [Kemlo #9]

04774   *Kemlo and the satellite builders.* Thomas Nelson & Sons, London, 1960, 186p, Cloth, Novel [Kemlo #13]

04775   *Kemlo and the sky horse.* Thomas Nelson & Sons, London, 1954, 189p, Cloth, Novel [Kemlo #3]

04776   *Kemlo and the space invaders.* Thomas Nelson & Sons, London, 1961, 214p, Cloth, Novel [Kemlo #14]

04777   *Kemlo and the space lanes.* Thomas Nelson & Sons, London, 1955, 200p, Cloth, Novel [Kemlo #6]

04777A *Kemlo and the space lanes*, by E. C. Eliot. Merlin, Feltham, UK, 1968, 125p, Paper, Novel [Kemlo #6]

04778   *Kemlo and the space men.* Thomas Nelson & Sons, London, 1959, 186p, Cloth, Novel [Kemlo #12]

04779   *Kemlo and the star men.* Thomas Nelson & Sons, London, 1955, 193p, Cloth, Novel [Kemlo #7]

04779A *Kemlo and the star men*, by E. C. Eliot. Merlin, Feltham, UK, 1968, 126p, Paper, Novel [Kemlo #7]

04780   *Kemlo and the zombie men.* Thomas Nelson & Sons, London, 1958, 202p, Cloth, Novel [Kemlo #11]

04781   *Kemlo and the Zones of Silence.* Thomas Nelson & Sons, London, 1954, 201p, Cloth, Novel [Kemlo #2]

04782   *Tas and the postal rocket.* Thomas Nelson & Sons, London, 1955, 119p, Cloth, Novel [Tas series]

04783   *Tas and the space machine.* Thomas Nelson & Sons, London, 1955, 136p, Cloth, Novel [Tas series]

as E. C. Eliot:

    Kemlo and the space lanes. [see 04777A]
    Kemlo and the star men. [see 04779A]

ELISABETH OF ROUMANIA, Queen
    see: SYLVA, CARMEN

ELL, RICHARD G., 1951-

04784   *Eden II.* Vantage Press, New York, 1974, 82p, Cloth, Novel

ELLIK, RON(ald D.), 1938-1968

with Bill Evans:

04785   *The universes of E. E. Smith.* Advent: Publishers, Chicago, 1966, 272p, Cloth, Nonf.

with Fredric Langley as Fredric Davies:

04786   *The man from U.N.C.L.E., number 14; the cross of gold affair.* Ace, New York, 1968, 156p, Paper, Tele. [Man from U.N.C.L.E. #14]

ELLIOT, JOHN (Herbert), 1918- , with Fred Hoyle

04787   *A for Andromeda; a novel of tomorrow.* Souvenir Press, London, 1962, 206p, Cloth, Tele. [Andromeda #1]

04788   *Andromeda breakthrough; a novel of tomorrow's universe.* Souvenir Press, London, 1964, 192p, Cloth, Tele. [Andromeda #2]

ELLIOT, LEE, house pseud. [see also William Henry Bird and Dennis Talbot Hughes]

04789   *Bio-Muton.* Curtis Warren, London, 1952, 128p, Cloth, Novel [by Dennis Talbot Hughes]

04790   *Overlord New York.* Curtis Warren, London, 1953, 159p, Cloth, Novel [author unknown]

01316   *The Third Mutant.* Curtis Warren, London, 1953, 160p, Cloth, Novel [by William Henry Bird]

ELLIOTT, BRUCE (Walter Gardner Lively Stacy), 1914?-1973

04791   *Asylum Earth.* Belmont, New York, 1968, 157p, Paper, Novel

04792   *The rivet in Grandfather's neck.* Curtis, New York, 1970, 157p, Paper, Novel

ELLIOTT, FRANCIS PERRY, 1861-1924

04793   *The gift of Abou Hassan.* Little, Brown, Boston, 1912, 314p, Cloth, Novel

04794   *The haunted pajamas.* Bobbs-Merrill, Indianapolis, 1911, 355p, Cloth, Novel

ELLIOTT, GEORGE

04795   *The case of the missing airmen.* Gerald G. Swan, London, 1944, 36p, Paper, Novel [Martin Speed #1]

ELLIOTT, GEORGE (Paul), 1918- [*biography included*]

04796   *Among the Dangs; ten short stories.* Holt, Rinehart & Winston, New York, 1961, 255p, Cloth, Coll.

ELLIOTT, H(arry) CHANDLER, 1907-

04797   *Reprieve from paradise.* Gnome Press, New York, 1955, 256p, Cloth, Novel

ELLIOTT, HETTIE, with Gordon Harwood Graves

04798   *Fantasies on ancient themes.* Nicolson Printing and Manufacturing Co., Richmond, IN, 1914, 76p, Cloth, Coll.

ELLIOTT, JOHN

04799   *Dragon feast.* Belmont, New York, 1970, 176p, Paper, Novel

ELLIOTT, WILLIAM J(ames), 1886-

04800   *To-morrow's spectacles; a romance.* Gerald G.
        Swan, London, 1946, 188p, Cloth, Novel

ELLIS, AMABEL WILLIAMS-
    see: WILLIAMS-ELLIS, AMABEL

ELLIS, D. E.

04801   *A thousand ages.* Digit, London, 1961, 156p,
        Paper, Novel

ELLIS, EDWARD S(ylvester), 1840-1916

04802   *The dragon of the skies.* Cassell, London,
        1915, 288p, Cloth, Novel

ELLIS, G. A.

04803   *New Britain; a narrative of a journey by Mr.
        Ellis to a country so called by its inhabi-
        tants, discovered in the vast plain of the
        Missouri, in North America, and inhabited
        by a people of British origin who lived un-
        der an equitable system of society produc-
        tive of peculiar independence and happiness;
        also, some account of their constitution,
        customs, and philosophical opinions, to-
        gether with a brief sketch of their history
        from the time of their departure from Great
        Britain.* W. Simpkin & R. Marshall, London,
        1820, 336p, Cloth, Novel

ELLISON, HARLAN (Jay), 1934-   [*biography included*]

04804   *Again, dangerous visions; 46 original stories.*
        Doubleday, Garden City, 1972, 760p, Cloth,
        Anth.
04804A retitled: *Again, dangerous visions I.* Signet,
        New York, 1973, 450p, Paper, Anth. [abridged]
04804B retitled: *Again, dangerous visions II.* Sig-
        net, New York, 1973, 449p, Paper, Anth.
        [abridged; 04804A and 04804B together com-
        prise the original volume]
        All the sounds of fear. [see 04805A]
04805   *Alone against tomorrow; stories of alienation
        in speculative fiction.* Macmillan, New
        York, 1971, 312p, Cloth, Coll.
04805A retitled: *All the sounds of fear.* Panther,
        St. Albans, UK, 1973, 158p, Paper, Coll.
        [abridged]
04805B retitled: *The time of the eye.* Panther, St.
        Albans, UK, 1974, 156p, Paper, Coll.
        [abridged; 04805A and 04805B together com-
        prise the original volume]
04806   *Approaching oblivion; road signs on the tread-
        mill toward tomorrow; eleven uncollected
        stories.* Walker & Co., New York, 1974,
        238p, Cloth, Coll.
04807   *The beast that shouted love at the heart of
        the world.* Avon, New York, 1969, 254p,
        Paper, Coll.
04808   *Dangerous visions; 33 original stories.*
        Doubleday, Garden City, 1967, 520p, Cloth,
        Anth.

04808A retitled: *Dangerous visions #1.* Berkley Me-
        dallion, New York, 1969, 220p, Paper, Anth.
        [abridged]
04808B retitled: *Dangerous visions #2.* Berkley Me-
        dallion, New York, 1969, 224p, Paper, Anth.
        [abridged]
04808C retitled: *Dangerous visions #3.* Berkley Me-
        dallion, New York, 1969, 224p, Paper, Anth.
        [abridged; 04808A, 04808B, and 04808C to-
        gether comprise the original volume]
04808D retitled: *Dangerous visions, vol. 1.* Bruce,
        London, 1967, 359p, Cloth, Anth. [abridged]
04809   *Doomsman.* Belmont Double, New York, 1967,
        68p, Paper, Novel
        Earthman, go home. [see 04810A]
04810   *Ellison wonderland.* Paperback Library, New
        York, 1962, 191p, Paper, Coll.
04810A retitled: *Earthman, go home.* Paperback Lib-
        rary, New York, 1964, 191p, Paper, Coll.
04811   *From the land of fear.* Belmont, New York,
        1967, 176p, Paper, Coll.
04812   *I have no mouth, and I must scream; stories.*
        Pyramid, New York, 1967, 175p, Paper, Coll.
04813   *Love ain't nothing but sex misspelled; twenty-
        two stories.* Trident Press, New York, 1968,
        382p, Cloth, Coll.
04814   *The man with nine lives.* Ace Double, New York,
        1960, 133p, Paper, Novel
04815   *Over the edge; stories from somewhere else.*
        Belmont, New York, 1970, 191p, Paper, Coll.
04816   *Paingod, and other delusions.* Pyramid, New
        York, 1965, 157p, Paper, Coll.
        The time of the eye. [see 04805B]
04817   *A touch of infinity.* Ace Double, New York,
        1960, 123p, Paper, Coll.

with various co-authors:

04818   *Partners in wonder.* Walker & Co., New York,
        1971, 471p, Cloth, Coll. [each story is a
        collaboration between Ellison and another
        author]

ELLWOOD, GRACIA FAY, 1938-   [*biography included*]

04819   *Good news from Tolkien's Middle Earth; two es-
        says on the "applicability" of The Lord of
        the Rings.* William B. Eerdmans Publishing
        Co., Grand Rapids, Mich., 1970, 160p, Cloth,
        Nonf. Coll.

ELMORE, ERNEST

04820   *The Lumpton Gobbelings; a novel.* Putnam, Lon-
        don, 1954, 167p, Cloth, Novel
04821   *The steel grubs; a novel.* Selwyn & Blount, Lon-
        don, 1928, 287p, Cloth, Novel
04822   *This siren song.* W. Collins Sons, London,
        1930, 285p, Cloth, Novel

EL RESHID
    see: HATCH, DAVID

ELSHEMUS, LOUIS M. [Louis Michael Eilshemus,
1864-1941]

04823   *The devil's diary.* Abbey Press, London, 1901,
        271p, Cloth, Novel

ELSNA, HEBE, pseud.
     see: CONWAY, LAURA

ELSON, ROBERT

04824 *"Quack!" the portrait of an experimentalist.*
          Hutchinson, London, 1924, 318p, Cloth, Novel

ELST, VIOLET VAN der
     see: VAN der ELST, VIOLET

ELTON, JAMES

04825 *The quest of the Seeker.* Badger, London, 1958,
          158p, Paper, Novel

ELTON, JOHN, pseud.
     see: MARSH, JOHN

ELWOOD, ROGER (P.), 1943-   [*biography included*]

04826 *Adrift in space, and other stories.* Lerner
          Publications, Minneapolis, 1974, 47p, Cloth,
          Anth. [published anonymously]
04827 *Alien worlds.* Paperback Library, New York,
          1964, 176p, Paper, Anth. [ghost-edited by
          Sam Moskowitz]
04828 *And walk now gently through the fire, and other
          science fiction stories.* Chilton Book Co.,
          Philadelphia, 1972, 187p, Cloth, Anth.
04829 *The berserkers.* Trident Press, New York, 1974,
          217p, Cloth, Anth.
04830 *Children of infinity; original science fiction
          stories for young readers.* Franklin Watts,
          New York, 1973, 178p, Cloth, Anth.
04831 *Chronicles of a comer, and other religious sci-
          ence fiction stories.* John Knox Press, At-
          lanta, 1974, 139p, Paper, Anth.
04832 *Continuum 1.* G. P. Putnam's Sons, New York,
          1974, 246p, Cloth, Anth.
04833 *Continuum 2.* G. P. Putnam's Sons, New York,
          1974, 250p, Cloth, Anth.
04834 *Continuum 3.* Berkley Publishing Corp., New
          York, 1974, 182p, Cloth, Anth.
04835 *Crisis; ten original stories of science fic-
          tion.* Thomas Nelson, Nashville, 1974, 176p,
          Cloth, Anth.
04836 *Demon kind; eleven new stories of children
          with strange and supernatural powers.* Avon,
          New York, 1973, 192p, Paper, Anth.
04837 *The far side of time; thirteen original sto-
          ries; a science fiction anthology.* Dodd,
          Mead, New York, 1974, 235p, Cloth, Anth.
04838 *Flame Tree Planet; an anthology of religious
          science-fantasy.* Concordia Publishing House,
          St. Louis, 1973, 159p, Paper, Anth.
04839 *Frontiers 1; tomorrow's alternatives; original
          science fiction.* Macmillan, New York, 1973,
          198p, Cloth, Anth.
04840 *Frontiers 2; the new mind; original science
          fiction.* Macmillan, New York, 1973, 180p,
          Cloth, Anth.
04841 *Future city.* Trident Press, New York, 1973,
          256p, Cloth, Anth.
04842 *Future kin; eight science fiction stories.*
          Doubleday, Garden City, 1974, 180p, Cloth,
          Anth.
04843 *Future quest.* Avon, New York, 1973, 192p,
          Paper, Anth.
04844 *The graduated robot, and other stories.* Lerner
          Publications, Minneapolis, 1974, 47p, Cloth,
          Anth. [published anonymously]
04845 *Horror tales; spirits, spells, & the unknown.*
          Rand McNally, Chicago, 1974, 123p, Cloth,
          Anth.
04846 *Invasion of the robots.* Paperback Library,
          New York, 1965, 157p, Paper, Anth. [ghost-
          edited by Sam Moskowitz]
04847 *Journey to another star, and other stories.*
          Lerner Publications, Minneapolis, 1974, 47p,
          Cloth, Anth. [published anonymously]
04848 *The killer plants, and other stories.* Lerner
          Publications, Minneapolis, 1974, 47p, Cloth,
          Anth. [published anonymously]
04849 *The learning maze, and other science fiction.*
          Julian Messner, New York, 1974, 191p, Cloth,
          Anth.
04850 *Long night of waiting, and other stories.*
          Aurora Publishers, Nashville, 1974, 212p,
          Cloth, Anth.
04851 *The mind angel, and other stories.* Lerner
          Publications, Minneapolis, 1974, 47p, Cloth,
          Anth. [published anonymously]
04852 *The missing world, and other stories.* Lerner
          Publications, Minneapolis, 1974, 48p, Cloth,
          Anth. [published anonymously]
04853 *Monster tales; vampires, werewolves, & things.*
          Rand McNally, Chicago, 1973, 117p, Cloth,
          Anth.
04854 *More science fiction tales; crystal creatures,
          bird-things, & other weirdies.* Rand McNally
          Chicago, 1974, 124p, Cloth, Anth.
04855 *Night of the sphinx, and other stories.* Lerne
          Publications, Minneapolis, 1974, 48p, Cloth,
          Anth. [published anonymously]
04856 *Omega.* Walker, New York, 1973, 190p, Cloth,
          Anth.
04857 *The other side of tomorrow; original science
          fiction stories about young people of the
          future.* Random House, New York, 1973, 207p,
          Cloth, Anth.
04858 *Science fiction adventures from way out.* Whit
          man, Racine, 1973, 212p, Cloth, Anth.
04859 *Science fiction tales; invaders, creatures,
          and alien worlds.* Rand McNally, Chicago,
          1973, 124p, Cloth, Anth.
04860 *Showcase.* Harper & Row, New York, 1973, 191p,
          Cloth, Anth.
04861 *Signs and wonders.* Fleming H. Revell, Old
          Tappan, NJ, 1972, 157p, Cloth, Anth.
04862 *Strange gods.* Pocket, New York, 1974, 192p,
          Paper, Anth.
04863 *Survival from infinity; original science fic-
          tion stories for young readers.* Franklin
          Watts, New York, 1974, 174p, Cloth, Anth.
04864 *Ten tomorrows.* Fawcett Gold Medal, Greenwich,
          1973, 224p, Paper, Anth.
04865 *The tunnel, and other stories.* Lerner Publi-
          cations, Minneapolis, 1974, 47p, Cloth, Anth
          [published anonymously]
04866 *Vampires, werewolves, and other monsters.*
          Curtis, New York, 1974, 205p, Paper, Anth.

with Vic Ghidalia:

04867 *Androids, time machines, and blue giraffes; a
          panorama of science fiction.* Follett Publi-
          shing Co., Chicago, 1973, 382p, Cloth, Anth.
04868 *Beware the beasts.* Macfadden-Bartell, New
          York, 1970, 160p, Paper, Anth.

ELWOOD, ROGER (Cont.), with Vic Ghidalia

04869 *Horror hunters.* Macfadden-Bartell, New York, 1971, 192p, Paper, Anth.
04870 *The little monsters.* Macfadden-Bartell, New York, 1969, 160p, Paper, Anth.
04871 *More little monsters.* Manor, New York, 1973, 190p, Paper, Anth.
04872 *The Venus factor.* Macfadden-Bartell, New York, 1972, 192p, Paper, Anth.
04873 *Young demons.* Avon, New York, 1972, 160p, Paper, Anth.

with Virginia Kidd:

04874 *Saving worlds; a collection of original science fiction stories.* Doubleday, Garden City, 1973, 237p, Cloth, Anth.
04874A retitled: *The wounded planet.* Bantam, New York, 1974, 236p, Paper, Anth.

with Sam Moskowitz:

04875 *Alien Earth, and other stories.* Macfadden-Bartell, New York, 1969, 208p, Paper, Anth.
04876 *The human zero, and other science-fiction masterpieces.* Tower, New York, 1967, 224p, Paper, Anth.
04877 *Other worlds, other times.* Macfadden-Bartell, New York, 1969, 192p, Paper, Anth.
04878 *Strange signposts; an anthology of the fantastic.* Holt, Rinehart & Winston, New York, 1966, 319p, Cloth, Anth.
04879 *The time curve.* Tower, New York, 1968, 189p, Paper, Anth.

ELY, GEORGE HERBERT, 1880?-1958, with C. J. L'Estrange as Herbert Strang

04880 *The cruise of the gyro-car.* Henry Frowde, Hodder & Stoughton, London, 1910, 244p, Cloth, Novel
04881 *The flying boat; a story of adventure and misadventure.* Henry Frowde, Hodder & Stoughton, London, 1912, 272p, Cloth, Novel
04882 *King of the air; or, To Morocco on an airship.* Henry Frowde, Hodder & Stoughton, London, 1908, 272p, Cloth, Novel
04883 *The Old Man of the Mountain.* Henry Frowde, Hodder & Stoughton, London, 1916, 322p, Cloth, Novel
04884 *A thousand miles an hour.* Humphrey Milford, Oxford University Press, London, 1924, 160p, Cloth, Novel

EMANUEL, VICTOR ROUSSEAU
    see: ROUSSEAU, VICTOR

EMANUEL, WALTER (Lewis), 1869-1915

04885 *One hundred years hence, being some extracts from "The hourly mail."* Eveleigh Nash, London, 1911, 76p, Cloth, Novel

EMBREE, CHARLES FLEMING, 1874-1905

04886 *A dream of a throne; the story of a Mexican revolt.* Little, Brown, Boston, 1900, 464p, Cloth, Novel

EMERSIE, JOHN

04887 *Allisto; a romance.* John D. Williams, New York, 1884, 327p, Cloth, Novel

EMERSON, CAROLINE D(wight), 1891-1973

04888 *The magic tunnel; a story of old New York.* Frederick A. Stokes, New York, 1940, 120p, Cloth, Novel

EMERSON, WILLIS GEORGE, 1856-1918

04889 *The Smoky God; or, A voyage to the inner world.* Forbes & Co., Chicago, 1908, 186p, Cloth, Novel

ENCK, JOHN EDWARD

04890 *A better sunset.* Exposition Press, Jericho, NY, 1973, 127p, Cloth, Novel

ENDORE, (Samuel) GUY, 1900-1970 [*biography included*]

04891 *The werewolf of Paris.* Farrar & Rinehart, New York, 1933, 325p, Cloth, Novel

ENDREY, EUGENE, 1891-1967

04892 *Dance of the golden calf.* New Men Publishing Co., New York, 1935, 190p, Cloth, Novel

ENEY, DICK [Richard Harris Eney, 1937-   ] [*biography included*]

04893 *Fancyclopedia II*, by R. H. Eney. Operation Crifanac, Alexandria, VA, 1959, 226p, Paper, Nonf.
04894 *The proceedings; Discon.* Advent: Publishers, Chicago, 1965, 191p, Paper, Nonf.

ENFIELD, HUGH, pseud. [Gwilym Fielden Hughes, 1920?-   ] [*biography included*]

04895 *Kronos.* Fontana, London, 1972, 125p, Paper, Movie

ENGDAHL, SYLVIA LOUISE, 1933-   [*biography included*]

04896 *Beyond the Tomorrow Mountains.* Atheneum, New York, 1973, 258p, Cloth, Novel [Noren #2]
04897 *Enchantress from the stars.* Atheneum, New York, 1970, 275p, Cloth, Novel [Elana #1]
04898 *The far side of evil.* Atheneum, New York, 1971, 292p, Cloth, Novel [Elana #2]
       Heritage of the star. [see 04900A]
04899 *Journey between worlds.* Atheneum, New York, 1970, 235p, Cloth, Novel
04900 *This star shall abide.* Atheneum, New York, 1972, 247p, Cloth, Novel [Noren #1]
04900A retitled: *Heritage of the star.* Victor Gollancz, London, 1973, 246p, Cloth, Novel [Noren #1]

ENGEL, LEONARD, 1916-1964, with Emanuel S. Piller

04901   *World aflame; the Russian-American War of 1950.* Dial Press, New York, 1947, 126p, Cloth, Novel

ENGLAND, GEORGE ALLAN, 1877-1936

      The afterglow. [see 04904E]
04902   *The Air Trust.* Phil Wagner, St. Louis, 1915, 333p, Cloth, Novel
      Beyond the great oblivion. [see 04904B]
04903   *Cursed.* Small, Maynard, Boston, 1919, 349p, Cloth, Novel
04904   *Darkness and dawn.* Small, Maynard, Boston, 1914, 672p, Cloth, Novel
04904A *Darkness and dawn.* Avalon, New York, 1964, 191p, Cloth, Novel [Darkness & Dawn #1]
04904B retitled: *Beyond the great oblivion.* Avalon, New York, 1965, 190p, Cloth, Novel [Darkness & Dawn #2]
04904C retitled: *The people of the abyss.* Avalon, New York, 1966, 192p, Cloth, Novel [Darkness & Dawn #3]
04904D retitled: *Out of the abyss.* Avalon, New York, 1967, 189p, Cloth, Novel [Darkness & Dawn #4]
04904E retitled: *The afterglow.* Avalon, New York, 1967, 191p, Cloth, Novel [Darkness & Dawn #5; 04905A, 04905B, 04905C, 04905D, 04905E together comprise the original volume]
04905   *The Flying Legion.* A. C. McClurg, Chicago, 1920, 394p, Cloth, Novel
04906   *The golden blight.* H. K. Fly, New York, 1916, 350p, Cloth, Novel
04907   *Keep off the grass.* Small, Maynard, Boston, 1919, 140p, Cloth, Novel
      Out of the abyss. [see 04904D]
      The people of the abyss. [see 04904C]

ENGLAND IN 1910

04908   *England in 1910.* Willing & Co., London, 1884, 16p, Paper, Story
04908A retitled: *Glasgow in 1910.* Macrone & Co., Glasgow, 1884, 16p, Paper, Story

ENGLAND'S DOWNFALL
    see: EX-REVOLUTIONIST

ENGLE, ELOISE, 1923-   [*biography included*]

04909   *Countdown for Cindy.* C. S. Hammond, Maplewood, NJ, 1962, 191p, Cloth, Novel

ENGLE, MADELEINE L'
    see: L'ENGLE, MADELEINE

ENGLISH, CHARLES, pseud.
    see: NUETZEL, CHARLES

EPERNAY, MARK, pseud.
    see: GALBRAITH, JOHN KENNETH

EQUALITY

04910   *Equality; or, A history of Lithconia.* Liberal Union, Philadelphia, 1837, 119p, Cloth, Novel

ERCHOMENON
    see: WATSON, HENRY CROCKER MARRIOTT

ERCKMANN, ÉMILE, 1822-1899, with Alexandre Chatrian as Mm. Erckmann-Chatrian

02905   *The man-wolf, and other tales.* Ward, Lock & Tyler, London, 1876, 252p, Cloth, Coll.
02906   *Stories of the Rhine.* Ward, Lock & Tyler, London, 1875, 217p, Paper, Coll.
02906A retitled: *Fantastic tales of the Rhineland.* John Dicks, London, 1880?, 158p, Paper, Coll.
02907   *The wild huntsman, and other tales.* Ward, Lock, London, 1877, 184p, Cloth, Coll.

ERCKMANN-CHATRIAN, Mm.
    see: ERCKMANN, EMILE and CHATRIAN, ALEXANDRE

ERDAHL, SIVERT

04911   *The devil's altar boys.* Capitol Hill Press, Washington, 1945, 39p, Paper, Story

ERLANGER, MICHAEL, 1915-

04912   *Silence in Heaven.* Atheneum, New York, 1961, 171p, Cloth, Novel

ERNSBERGER, GEORGE, with Donald A. Wollheim

04913   *The Avon fantasy reader.* Avon, New York, 1969, 173p, Paper, Anth.
04914   *The 2nd Avon fantasy reader.* Avon, New York, 1969, 173p, Paper, Anth.

ERNST, PAUL, 1886-   , as Kenneth Robeson, house pseud.

04915   *The Avenger; death in slow motion.* Warner Paperback Library, New York, 1973, 158p, Paper, Novel [Avenger #18]
04916   *The Avenger; Nevlo.* Warner Paperback Library, New York, 1973, 159p, Paper, Novel [Avenger #17]
04917   *The Avenger; river of ice.* Warner Paperback Library, New York, 1973, 157p, Paper, Novel [Avenger #11]
04918   *The Avenger; the black death.* Warner Paperback Library, New York, 1974, 158p, Paper, Novel [Avenger #22]
04919   *The Avenger; the flame breathers.* Warner Paperback Library, New York, 1973, 157p, Paper, Novel [Avenger #12]
04920   *The Avenger; the frosted death.* Warner Paperback Library, New York, 1972, 157p, Paper, Novel [Avenger #5]
04921   *The Avenger; the green killer.* Warner Paperback Library, New York, 1974, 158p, Paper, Novel [Avenger #20]

ERNST, PAUL, as Kenneth Robeson (Cont.)

04922 *The Avenger; the hate master.* Warner Paperback Library, New York, 1973, 158p, Paper,
Novel [Avenger #16]
04923 *The Avenger; the sky walker.* Warner Paperback
Library, New York, 1972, 156p, Paper, Novel
[Avenger #3]
04924 *The Avenger; tuned for murder.* Warner Paperback Library, New York, 1973, 158p, Paper,
Novel [Avenger #9]

EROS, JOHN, pseud.

04925 *The Hippocratic oath.* Exposition Press, Jericho, NY, 1974, 142p, Cloth, Novel

ERSKINE, DOUGLAS

04926 *A bit of Atlantis.* A. T. Chapman, Montreal,
1900, 197p, Cloth, Novel

ERSKINE, JOHN, 1879-1951

04927 *Adam and Eve, though he knew better.* Bobbs-
Merrill, Indianapolis, 1927, 338p, Cloth,
Novel
04928 *Cinderella's daughter, and other sequels and
consequences.* Bobbs-Merrill, Indianapolis,
1930, 305p, Cloth, Coll.
04929 *Penelope's man; the homing instinct.* Bobbs-
Merrill, Indianapolis, 1928, 275p, Cloth,
Novel
04930 *Uncle Sam in the eyes of his family.* Bobbs-
Merrill, Indianapolis, 1930, 351p, Cloth,
Novel
04931 *Unfinished business.* Bobbs-Merrill, Indianapolis, 1931, 347p, Cloth, Novel
04932 *Venus, the lonely goddess.* William Morrow,
New York, 1949, 155p, Cloth, Novel

ERSKINE, THOMAS, Baron Erksine, 1750-1823
[published anonymously]

04933 *Armata; a fragment.* John Murray, London,
1817, 210p, Cloth, Novel [Armata #1]
04934 *Armata; a fragment.* John Murray, London,
1817, 419p, Cloth, Coll. [includes *Armata*
and *The second part of Armata*; Armata # 1-2]
04935 *The second part of Armata.* John Murray, London, 1817, 209p, Cloth, Novel [Armata #2]

ERTZ, SUSAN, 1894?-   [*biography included*]

04936 *Woman alive.* Hodder & Stoughton, London,
1935, 206p, Cloth, Novel

ERVINE, ST. JOHN (Greer), 1883-1971

04937 *Sophia.* Macmillan, New York, 1941, 351p,
Cloth, Novel [name spelled "Irvine" on
cover]

ERWIN, BETTY K.

04938 *Who is Victoria?* Little, Brown, Boston, 1973,
134p, Cloth, Novel

ESCOTT, T(homas) H(ay) S(weet), 1844-1924

04939 *A trip to Paradoxia, and other humours of the
hour, being contemporary pictures of social
fact and political fiction.* Greening & Co.,
London, 1899, 283p, Cloth, Coll.

ESCOTT-INMAN, H.
see: INMAN, HERBERT ESCOTT

ESENWEIN, J(oseph) BERG, 1867-1946

04940 *Adventures to come.* McLoughlin Bros., Springfield, Mass., 1937, 187p, Cloth, Anth.

ESHBACH, LLOYD ARTHUR, 1910-

04941 *Of worlds beyond; the science of science fiction writing; a symposium.* Fantasy Press,
Reading, PA, 1947, 96p, Cloth, Nonf. Anth.
04942 *Tyrant of time.* Fantasy Press, Reading, PA,
1955, 253p, Cloth, Novel

ESMÉ, JEAN d', pseud. [Jean d'Esménard, Vicomte, 1893-1966]

04943 *The Red Gods (Les Dieux Rouges); a romance.*
E. P. Dutton, New York, 1924, 365p, Cloth,
Novel

ESMENARD, JEAN d'
see: ESME, JEAN d'

ESMOND, SIDNEY

04944 *Sacrament of death.* Alvin Redman, London,
1950, 289p, Cloth, Novel

ESPÉRANCE, E. d'

04945 *Northern lights, and other psychic stories.*
George Redway, London, 1899, 288p, Cloth,
Coll.

ESSEX, ROSAMUND (Sibyl), 1900-

04946 *Into the forest.* Brockhampton Press, Leicester,
UK, 1963, 128p, Cloth, Novel

ESSOE, GABE [Gabor Attila Essoe, 1944-   ]
[*biography included*]

04947 *Tarzan of the movies; a pictorial history of
more than fifty years of Edgar Rice Burrough's
legendary hero.* Citadel Press, New York,
1968, 208p, Cloth, Nonf.

ESTABROOKS, G(eorge) H(oben), 1895-   , with
Richard Lockridge

04948 *Death in the mind.* E. P. Dutton, New York,
1945, 251p, Cloth, Novel

ESTES, ELEANOR (Ruth), 1906-   [biography in-
cluded]

04949   The witch family. Harcourt, Brace & Co., New
        York, 1960, 186p, Cloth, Novel

ESTIVAL, (Ivan Leon)

04950   Mandragora. Staples Press, London, 1952,
        239p, Cloth, Novel

ESTRANGE, C. J. L'
    see: L'ESTRANGE, C. J.

ESTRANGE, HENRY L'
    see: L'ESTRANGE, HENRY

ESTRANGE, MILES L'
    see: L'ESTRANGE, MILES

ESTRIDGE, ROBIN
    see: LORAINE, PHILIP

ETERNAL REDIFFUSION
    see: HARBOTTLE, PHILIP

EUREKA
    see: WILLIAMS, ROBERT FOLKESTONE

EVAIN, ELAINE, 1931-   [biography included]

04951   Return trip. Pyramid, New York, 1974, 215p,
        Paper, Novel

EVANS, BILL [William Harrington Evans,
1921-   ] [biography included]

04952   The index of science fiction. Robert Peter-
        son, Denver, 1950?, 148p, Paper, Nonf.

with Ron Ellik:

04785   The universes of E. E. Smith. Advent: Publi-
        shers, Chicago, 1966, 272p, Cloth, Nonf.

EVANS, CHRISTOPHER (Riche), 1931-   [biogra-
phy included]

04953   Mind at bay; eleven horror stories. Panther,
        London, 1969, 186p, Paper, Anth.
04954   Mind in chains; fourteen horror stories.
        Panther, London, 1970, 223p, Paper, Anth.

EVANS, CICELY LOUISE, pseud.

04955   Nemesis wife. Doubleday, Garden City, 1970,
        253p, Cloth, Novel

EVANS, DEREK

04956   Who put the devil in Miss Jones? Orpheus Clas-
        sic, New York, 1974, 251p, Paper, Novel

EVANS, E(dward) EVERETT, 1893-1958

04957   Alien minds. Fantasy Press, Reading, PA, 1955
        223p, Cloth, Novel [George Hanlon #2]
04958   Food for demons. Kenneth J. Krueger, Shroud
        Publishers, San Diego, 1971, 154p, Paper,
        Coll.
04959   Man of many minds. Fantasy Press, Reading, PA
        1953, 222p, Cloth, Novel [George Hanlon #1]
04960   The planet mappers. Dodd, Mead, New York,
        1955, 242p, Cloth, Novel

EVANS, GRANT

04961   Swapping with Satan. Companion, San Diego,
        1970, 157p, Paper, Novel

EVANS, GWYN

04962   Satan, Ltd. Wright & Brown, London, 1935,
        285p, Cloth, Novel

EVANS, I(drisyn) O(liver), 1894-1977 [biograp

04963   The coming of a king; a story of the Stone Age
        Frederick Warne, London, 1950, 256p, Cloth,
        Novel
04964   Jules Verne and his work. Arco Publications,
        London, 1965, 188p, Cloth, Nonf.
04965   Science fiction through the ages 1. Panther,
        London, 1966, 156p, Paper, Anth.
04966   Science fiction through the ages 2. Panther,
        London, 1966, 173p, Paper, Anth.

EVANS, ROBLEY (J.), 1933-   [biography inclu-
ded]

04967   J. R. R. Tolkien. Warner, New York, 1972, 206
        Paper, Nonf.

EVARTS, R(ichard) C(onover), 1890-

04968   Alice's adventures in Cambridge. Harvard Lam-
        poon, Cambridge, Mass., 1913, 67p, Cloth,
        Novel [parody of Alice in Wonderland]

EVENING STANDARD

04969   The Evening standard book of strange stories.
        Hutchinson, London, 1934, 1024p, Cloth, Anth
04970   The Evening standard second book of strange
        stories. Hutchinson, London, 1937, 1021p,
        Cloth, Anth.

EVERETT, FRANCES

04971   John Bull, Socialist. Swan Sonnenschein, Lon-
        don, 1909, 188p, Cloth, Novel

EVERETT, Mrs. H. D.

04972   The death-mask, and other ghosts. Philip Alla
        London, 1920, 321p, Cloth, Coll.

EVERETT, Mrs. H. D. (Cont.)

as Theo. Douglas:

04973 *Iras; a mystery*. William Blackwood & Sons, Edinburgh, 1896, 281p, Cloth, Novel

EVERSON, WILLIAM K(eith), 1929- [*biography included*]

04974 *Classics of the horror film*. Citadel Press, Secaucus, NJ, 1974, 247p, Cloth, Nonf.

EVERYTHING BUT LOVE
    see: SHKAROVSKY-RAFFE, ARTHUR

EWALD, CARL, 1856-1908

04975 *Two-Legs*. Charles Scribner's Sons, New York, 1906, 148p, Cloth, Novel
04976 *Two-Legs, and other stories*. Methuen, London, 1907, 213p, Cloth, Coll.

EWERS, HANNS HEINZ, 1871-1943

04977 *Alraune*. John Day, New York, 1929, 342p, Cloth, Novel [Frank Braun series]
04978 *The sorcerer's apprentice*. John Day, New York, 1927, 337p, Cloth, Novel [Frank Braun series]

AN EX-M.P., pseud.

04979 *A radical nightmare; or, England forty years hence*. Field & Tuer, London, 1885, 62p, Paper, Novel

AN EX-REVOLUTIONIST, pseud.

04980 *"England's downfall"; or, The last great revolution*. Digby, Long, London, 1893, 175p, Cloth, Novel

AN EYEWITNESS, pseud.
    see: CHESNEY, GEORGE T.

AN EYE-WITNESS, pseud.

04981 *The socialist revolution of 1888*. Harrison & Sons, London, 1884, 35p, Paper, Story

AN EYEWITNESS 1N 1925, pseud.
    see: CHESNEY, GEORGE T.

EYLES, ALLEN, with Robert Adkinson and Nicholas Fry

00062 *The house of horror; the story of Hammer Films*. Lorrimer Publishing, London, 1973, 127p, Paper, Nonf.

EYLES, (Margaret) LEONORA, 1889-1960

04982 *Strength of the spirit*. Constable, London, 1930, 350p, Cloth, Novel

EYRE, KATHERINE WIGMORE, 1901-1970

04983 *The lute and the glove*. Appleton-Century-Crofts, New York, 1955, 313p, Cloth, Novel

EYTON, JOHN (Seymour), 1890-

04984 *Jungle-born; a romance*. Arrowsmith, London, 1924, 288p, Cloth, Novel

ezra, pseud.

04985 *Skyjak*. Ramhorn, Tempe, AZ, 1972, 72p, Paper, Novel

EZRA, I. B.

04986 *Twice they lived*. A. S. Barnes, New York, 1965, 319p, Cloth, Novel

F., E. M.
    see: FOSTER, E. M.

F. H. P.
    see: P., F. H.

FABER, ARTHUR

04987 *Outerspace sex orgy*. Barnaby Press, no place, 1970, 192p, Paper, Novel

FABER, (Sir) GEOFFREY (Cust), 1889-1961

04988 *Elnovia; an entertainment for novel-readers*. Faber & Gwyer, London, 1925, 304p, Cloth, Novel

FABRE-LUCE, (André Edmond) ALFRED, 1899-

04989 *The trial of Charles de Gaulle*. Praeger, New York, 1963, 270p, Cloth, Novel

FABRICANT, NOAH D(aniel), 1904-1964, with Groff Conklin

03305 *Great science fiction about doctors*. Collier, New York, 1963, 412p, Paper, Anth.

FADIMAN, CLIFTON (Paul), 1904- [*biography included*]

04990 *Fantasia mathematica, being a set of stories together with a group of oddments and diversions, all drawn from the universe of mathematics*. Simon & Schuster, New York, 1958, 298p, Cloth, Anth. [includes some nonf.]

FADIMAN, CLIFTON (Cont.)

04991   *The mathematical magpie, being more stories,
        mainly transcendental, plus subsets of es-
        says, rhymes, anecdotes, epigrams, and other
        prime oddments and diversions, rational or
        irrational, all derived from the infinite
        domain of mathematics.* Simon & Schuster,
        New York, 1962, 300p, Cloth, Anth. [includes
        nonf. and verse]

FAGAN, HENRY A(llan), 1889-1963

04992   *Ninya; a fantasy of a strange little world.*
        Jonathan Cape, London, 1956, 221p, Cloth,
        Novel

FAGNAN, MARIE ANTOINETTE [published anony-
mously]

04993   *Kanor; a tale, translated from the savage.*
        R. Griffiths, London, 1750, 151p; Cloth,
        Novel

FAIRBAIRN, JOHN, with William Caine

02439   *The confectioners.* J. W. Arrowsmith, Bristol,
        1906, 315p, Cloth, Novel

FAIRBURN, EDWIN
   see: MOHOAO

FAIRCLOUGH, PETER

04994   *Three gothic novels.* Penguin, Harmondsworth,
        1968, 505p, Paper, Anth. [includes *The Castle
        of Otranto*, by Horace Walpole; *Vathek*, by
        William Beckford; *Frankenstein*, by Mary
        Shelley]

FAIRMAN, HENRY CLAY

04995   *The third world; a tale of love and strange
        adventure.* Third World Publishing Co., At-
        lanta, 1895, 313p, Cloth, Novel

FAIRMAN, PAUL W(arren?), 1916-1977

04996   *City under the sea.* Pyramid, New York, 1965,
        141p, Paper, Tele. [Voyage to the Bottom
        of the Sea #2]
        The diabolist. [see 05004A]
04997   *The doomsday exhibit.* Lancer, New York, 1971,
        160p, Paper, Coll.
04998   *The forgetful robot.* Holt, Rinehart & Winston,
        New York, 1968, 163p, Paper, Novel
04999   *The Frankenstein wheel.* Popular Library, New
        York, 1972, 190p, Paper, Novel [Frankenstein
        series]
05000   *I, the Machine.* Lancer, New York, 1968,
        205p, Paper, Novel
05001   *Nine worlds west.* American Science Fiction,
        Sydney, 1955, 34p, Paper, Story
        Rest in agony. [see 05004]
05002   *The world grabbers; a dramatic novel inspired
        by the popular TV program, One step beyond.*
        Monarch, Derby, 1964, 126p, Paper, Tele.

as IVAR JORGENSEN:

05003   *Rest in agony.* Monarch, Derby, Conn., 1963,
        125p, Paper, Novel
05004   *Rest in agony,* by Paul W. Fairman. Lancer,
        New York, 1967, 223p, Paper, Novel [expanded
05004A retitled: *The diabolist,* by Paul W. Fairman.
        Lancer, New York, 1972, 223p, Paper, Novel
05005   *Ten from infinity.* Monarch, Derby, Conn.,
        1963, 139p, Paper, Novel
05005A retitled: *The deadly sky.* Pinnacle, New
        York, 1971, 188p, Paper, Novel
05006   *Whom the gods would slay.* Belmont, New York,
        1968, 140p, Paper, Novel

as F. W. Paul:

05007   *The man from S.T.U.D. in Rape is a no-no.*
        Lancer, New York, 1969, 159p, Paper, Novel
        [Man from S.T.U.D. #6]
05008   *The man from S.T.U.D. in Sock it to me, zom-
        bie!* Lancer, New York, 1968, 189p, Paper,
        Novel [Man from S.T.U.D. #3]
05009   *The man from S.T.U.D. in The lay of the land.*
        Lancer, New York, 1969, 160p, Paper, Novel
        [Man from S.T.U.D. #8]
05010   *The man from S.T.U.D. in The orgy at Madame
        Dracula's.* Lancer, New York, 1968, 157p,
        Paper, Novel [Man from S.T.U.D. #2]
05011   *The man from S.T.U.D. vs. the mafia.* Lancer,
        New York, 1972, 506p, Paper, Coll. [Man from
        S.T.U.D. #s 2, 3, 8; includes *The orgy at
        Madame Dracula's*; *Sock it to me, zombie!*;
        The lay of the land]
05012   *The planned planethood caper.* Lancer, New
        York, 1969, 189p, Paper, Novel [Man from
        S.T.U.D. #7]

ghost writer for Lester del Rey:

04083   *The infinite worlds of maybe.* Holt, Rinehart
        & Winston, New York, 1966, 192p, Cloth, Nov
04090   *Prisoners of space.* Westminster Press, Phila
        delphia, 1968, 142p, Cloth, Novel
04093   *Rocket from infinity.* Holt, Rinehart & Win-
        ston, New York, 1966, 191p, Cloth, Novel
04094   *The runaway robot.* Westminster Press, Phila-
        delphia, 1964, 176p, Cloth, Novel
04095   *The scheme of things.* Belmont, New York,
        1966, 157p, Paper, Novel
04096   *Siege perilous.* Lancer, New York, 1966, 157p
        Paper, Novel
04096A retitled: *The man without a planet.* Lancer,
        New York, 1969, 157p, Paper, Novel
04099   *Tunnel through time.* Westminster Press, Phil
        delphia, 1966, 153p, Cloth, Novel

with Milton Lesser as Adam Chase:

05013   *The golden ape.* Avalon, New York, 1959, 221p
        Cloth, Novel

FAIRWEATHER, MARY

05014   *The passion stroke; a tale of ancient masonry*
        Richard G. Badger, Boston, 1906, 255p,
        Cloth, Novel

FAIRY TALES FOR COMPUTERS

05015   *Fairy tales for computers.* Eakins Press, New
        York, 1969, 163p, Paper, Anth. [includes
        some nonf.]

FALCONER, LANOE, pseud. [Mary Elizabeth Hawker, 1848-1908]

05016 *Cecilia de Noël*. Macmillan, London, 1891, 197p, Cloth, Novel

FALKNER, J(ohn) MEADE, 1858-1932

05017 *The lost Stradivarius*. William Blackwood & Sons, Edinburgh, 1895, 296p, Cloth, Novel

FALKNER, JOHN, pseud. [E. F. Gale]

05018 *Overlords of Andromeda*. Panther, London, 1955, 144p, Paper, Novel
05019 *Untrodden streets of time*. Panther, London, 1955, 144p, Paper, Novel

FALKON, FELIX LANCE

05020 *Hung in space*. Pleasure Reader, San Diego, 1969, 191p, Paper, Novel

THE FALL OF ENGLAND?
    see: CHESNEY, GEORGE T.

THE FALL OF THE GREAT REPUBLIC

05021 *The fall of the great republic*. Roberts Bros., Boston, 1885, 226p, Cloth, Novel [book has second (false) title page which reads: *The fall of the great republic (1886-88)*, by Sir Henry Standish Coverdale]

FALLADA, HANS, pseud. [Rudolf Wilhelm Friedrich Ditzen, 1893-1947]

05022 *Sparrow farm; the tale of the city clerk who flew into the country for a holiday*. Putnam, London, 1937, 239p, Cloth, Novel

FALLAW, L. M.

05023 *The Ugglians*. Philosophical Library, New York, 1957, 90p, Cloth, Novel [Ugglians #1]
05024 *The Ugglians at large; second book of Ugg*. Philosophical Library, New York, 1959, 117p, Cloth, Novel [Ugglians #2]

FAMOUS FANTASTIC CLASSICS #1
    see: DIKTY, T. E.

FANE, BRON, pseud.
    see: FANTHORPE, R. LIONEL

A FANTASTICAL EXCURSION INTO THE PLANETS

05025 *A fantastical excursion into the planets*. Saunders & Otley, London, 1839, 194p, Cloth, Novel

FANTASY TWIN

05026 *Fantasy twin*. Fantasy Publishing Co., Los Angeles, 1953, 503p, Cloth, Anth. [includes *The undesired princess*, by L. Sprague de Camp; *The dark other*, by Stanley G. Weinbaum]

FANTHORPE, R(obert) L(IONEL), 1935-   [*biography included*]

05027 *Alien from the stars*. Badger, London, 1959, 156p, Paper, Novel
05028 *Asteroid man*. Badger, London, 1960, 142p, Paper, Novel
05029 *Doomed world*. Badger, London, 1960, 157p, Paper, Novel
05030 *Fiends*. Badger, London, 1959, 157p, Paper, Novel
05031 *Flame Mass*. Badger, London, 1961, 158p, Paper, Novel
05032 *The golden Chalice*. Badger, London, 1961, 158p, Paper, Novel
05033 *Hand of doom*. Badger, London, 1960, 158p, Paper, Novel
05034 *Hyperspace*. Badger, London, 1959, 157p, Paper, Novel
05035 *Negative minus*. Badger, London, 1963, 158p, Paper, Novel
05036 *Neuron world*. Badger, London, 1965, 159p, Paper, Novel
05037 *Out of the darkness*. Badger, London, 1960, 142p, Paper, Novel
05038 *Satellite*. Badger, London, 1960, 157p, Paper, Novel
05039 *Space-borne*. Badger, London, 1959, 156p, Paper, Novel [includes a short story, "Destination--Infinity," by Rod Patterson]
05040 *Space fury*. Badger, London, 1962, 159p, Paper, Novel
05041 *The triple man*. Badger, London, 1965, 158p, Paper, Novel
05042 *The unconfined*. Badger, London, 1966, 158p, Paper, Novel
05043 *The Waiting World*. Badger, London, 1958, 158p, Paper, Novel
05044 *The watching world*. Badger, London, 1966, 142p, Paper, Novel

as Erle Barton:

05045 *The planet seekers*. Badger, London, 1964, 158p, Paper, Novel

as Lee Barton:

05046 *The shadow man*. Badger, London, 1966, 158p, Paper, Novel
05047 *The unseen*. Badger, London, 1963, 158p, Paper, Novel

as Thornton Bell:

05048 *Chaos*. Badger, London, 1964, 158p, Paper, Novel
05049 *Space trap*. Badger, London, 1964, 158p, Paper, Novel

as Leo Brett:

05050 *The alien ones*. Badger, London, 1963, 158p, Paper, Novel
05051 *Black infinity*. Badger, London, 1961, 158p, Paper, Novel
05052 *Exit humanity*. Badger, London, 1960, 142p, Paper, Novel
05053 *Face in the night*. Badger, London, 1962, 158p, Paper, Novel

FANTHORPE, R. LIONEL, as Leo Brett (Cont.)

05054 *Faceless planet*. Badger, London, 1960, 158p,
          Paper, Novel
05055 *The forbidden*. Badger, London, 1963, 158p,
          Paper, Novel
05056 *From realms beyond*. Badger, London, 1963,
          158p, Paper, Novel
05057 *The immortals*. Badger, London, 1962, 158p,
          Paper, Novel
05058 *March of the robots*. Badger, London, 1961,
          158p, Paper, Novel
05059 *The microscopic ones*. Badger, London, 1960,
          158p, Paper, Novel
05060 *Mind force*. Badger, London, 1961, 158p, Paper,
          Novel
05061 *Nightmare*. Badger, London, 1962, 158p, Paper,
          Novel
05062 *Power sphere*. Badger, London, 1963, 158p,
          Paper, Novel
05063 *They never come back*. Badger, London, 1963,
          158p, Paper, Novel

as Bron Fane:

       Blue juggernaut. [see 05065A]
05064 *The intruders*. Badger, London, 1963, 158p,
          Paper, Novel [La Noire #1]
05065 *Juggernaut*. Badger, London, 1960, 142p, Paper,
          Novel
05065A retitled: *Blue juggernaut*. Arcadia House,
          New York, 1965, 190p, Cloth, Novel
05066 *Last man on Earth*. Badger, London, 1960,
          158p, Paper, Novel
05067 *The macabre ones*. Badger, London, 1964, 160p,
          Paper, Novel [La Noire #7]
05068 *Nemesis*. Badger, London, 1964, 158p, Paper,
          Novel [La Noire #5]
05069 *Rodent mutation*. Badger, London, 1961, 158p,
          Paper, Novel
05070 *Softly by moonlight*. Badger, London, 1963,
          158p, Paper, Novel [La Noire #3]
05071 *Somewhere out there*. Badger, London, 1963,
          158p, Paper, Novel [La Noire #2]
05072 *Suspension*. Badger, London, 1964, 160p, Paper,
          Novel [La Noire #6]
05073 *U.F.O. 517*. Badger, London, 1966?, 158p,
          Paper, Novel [La Noire #8]
05074 *Unknown destiny*. Badger, London, 1964, 158p,
          Paper, Novel [La Noire #4]

as Mel Jay:

       Orbit one. [see 05091A]

as Marston Johns:

       Beyond time. [see 05077A]
       The Venus venture. [see 05105A]

as Victor La Salle, house pseud.:

05075 *Menace from Mercury*. John Spencer, London,
          1954, 128p, Paper, Novel [includes a short
          story, "More Than Mortal," by T. W. Wade]

as Robert Lionel:

       The face of X. [see 05109A]
       Time echo. [see 05114A]

as John E. Muller, house pseud.:

05076 *Beyond the void*. Badger, London, 1965, 158p,
          Paper, Novel
05077 *Beyond time*. Badger, London, 1962, 158p,
          Paper, Novel
05077A *Beyond time*, by Marston Johns. Arcadia House,
          New York, 1966, 188p, Cloth, Novel

05078 *Crimson planet*. Badger, London, 1961, 158p,
          Paper, Novel
05079 *Dark continuum*. Badger, London, 1964, 160p,
          Paper, Novel
05080 *The day the world died*. Badger, London, 1962,
          159p, Paper, Novel
05081 *The exorcists*. Badger, London, 1965, 158p,
          Paper, Novel
05082 *The Eye of Karnak*. Badger, London, 1962, 158p,
          Paper, Novel
05083 *Forbidden planet*. Badger, London, 1961, 158p,
          Paper, Novel
05084 *Infinity machine*. Badger, London, 1962, 158p,
          Paper, Novel
05085 *The man from beyond*. Badger, London, 1965,
          158p, Paper, Novel
05086 *The man who conquered time*. Badger, London,
          1962, 156p, Paper, Novel
05087 *Mark of the beast*. Badger, London, 1964, 160p,
          Paper, Novel
05088 *Micro infinity*. Badger, London, 1962, 158p,
          Paper, Novel
05089 *The mind makers*. Badger, London, 1961, 158p,
          Paper, Novel
05090 *The negative ones*. Badger, London, 1965, 158p,
          Paper, Novel
05091 *Orbit one*. Badger, London, 1962, 158p, Paper,
          Novel
05091A *Orbit one*, by Mel Jay. Arcadia House, New
          York, 1966, 189p, Cloth, Novel
05092 *Out of the night*. Badger, London, 1965?, 159p,
          Paper, Novel
05093 *Perilous galaxy*. Badger, London, 1962, 160p,
          Paper, Novel
05094 *Phenomena X*. Badger, London, 1966, 143p, Paper,
          Novel
05095 *Reactor XK9*. Badger, London, 1963, 158p, Paper,
          Novel
05096 *Return of Zeus*. Badger, London, 1962, 160p,
          Paper, Novel
05097 *Special mission*. Badger, London, 1963, 158p,
          Paper, Novel
05098 *Spectre of darkness*. Badger, London, 1965,
          158p, Paper, Novel
05099 *Survival project*. Badger, London, 1966, 143p,
          Paper, Novel
05100 *A 1,000 years on*. Badger, London, 1961, 160p,
          Paper, Novel
05101 *The ultimate man*. Badger, London, 1961, 158p,
          Paper, Novel
05102 *The uninvited*. Badger, London, 1961, 158p,
          Paper, Novel
05103 *Uranium 235*. Badger, London, 1962, 158p, Paper,
          Novel
05104 *Vengeance of Siva*. Badger, London, 1962, 160p,
          Paper, Novel
05105 *The Venus venture*. Badger, London, 1961, 158p,
          Paper, Novel
05105A *The Venus venture*, by Marston Johns. Arcadia
          House, New York, 1965, 191p, Cloth, Novel
05106 *The X-machine*. Badger, London, 1962, 157p,
          Paper, Novel

as Lionel Roberts:

05107 *Cyclops in the sky*. Badger, London, 1960,
          156p, Paper, Novel
05108 *Dawn of the Mutants*. Badger, London, 1959,
          156p, Paper, Novel
05109 *The face of X*. Badger, London, 1960, 141p,
          Paper, Novel
05109A *The face of X*, by Robert Lionel. Arcadia
          House, New York, 1965, 192p, Cloth, Novel

FANTHORPE, R. LIONEL, as Lionel Roberts (Cont.)

05110 *Flame Goddess.* Badger, London, 1961, 158p, Paper, Novel
05111 *The in-world.* Badger, London, 1960, 142p, Paper, Novel
05112 *The last Valkyrie.* Badger, London, 1961, 158p, Paper, Novel
05113 *The synthetic ones.* Badger, London, 1961, 158p, Paper, Novel
05114 *Time echo.* Badger, London, 1959, 157p, Paper, Novel
05114A *Time echo,* by Robert Lionel. Arcadia House, New York, 1964, 192p, Cloth, Novel

as Neil Thanet:

05115 *Beyond the veil.* Badger, London, 1964, 160p, Paper, Novel
05116 *The man who came back.* Badger, London, 1964, 158p, Paper, Novel

as Trebor Thorpe:

05117 *Five faces of fear.* Badger, London, 1960, 156p, Paper, Novel
05118 *Lightning world.* Badger, London, 1960, 142p, Paper, Novel

as Pel Torro:

Beyond the barrier of space. [see 05121A]
Exiled in space. [see 05127A]
05119 *The face of fear.* Badger, London, 1963, 158p, Paper, Novel
05120 *Force 97X.* Badger, London, 1965, 158p, Paper, Novel
05121 *Formula 29X.* Badger, London, 1963, 158p, Paper, Novel
05121A retitled: *Beyond the barrier of space.* Tower, New York, 1969, 154p, Paper, Novel
05122 *Frozen planet.* Badger, London, 1960, 142p, Paper, Novel
05123 *Galaxy 666.* Badger, London, 1963, 158p, Paper, Novel
05124 *The last astronaut.* Badger, London, 1963, 158p, Paper, Novel
05125 *Legion of the lost.* Badger, London, 1962, 158p, Paper, Novel
Man of metal. [see 05128A]
05126 *The phantom ones.* Badger, London, 1961, 158p, Paper, Novel
05127 *The return.* Badger, London, 1964, 158p, Paper, Novel
05127A retitled: *Exiled in space.* Arcadia House, New York, 1969, 192p, Cloth, Novel
05128 *Space no barrier.* Badger, London, 1964, 160p, Paper, Novel
05128A retitled: *Man of metal.* Lenox Hill Press, New York, 1970, 192p, Cloth, Novel
05129 *The strange ones.* Badger, London, 1963, 158p, Paper, Novel
05130 *Through the barrier.* Badger, London, 1963, 158p, Paper, Novel
05131 *The timeless ones.* Badger, London, 1963, 158p, Paper, Novel
05132 *World of the gods.* Badger, London, 1960, 158p, Paper, Novel

as Karl Zeigfreid:

05133 *Android.* Badger, London, 1962, 158p, Paper, Novel
05134 *Atomic nemesis.* Badger, London, 1962, 158p, Paper, Novel
05135 *Barrier 346.* Badger, London, 1965, 158p, Paper, Novel

05136 *Escape to infinity.* Badger, London, 1963, 158p, Paper, Novel
05137 *The girl from tomorrow.* Badger, London, 1965?, 158p, Paper, Novel
05138 *Gods of darkness.* Badger, London, 1962, 158p, Paper, Novel
05139 *No way back.* Badger, London, 1964, 160p, Paper, Novel
05140 *Projection infinity.* Badger, London, 1964, 158p, Paper, Novel
05141 *Radar alert.* Badger, London, 1963, 157p, Paper, Novel
05142 *Walk through to-morrow.* Badger, London, 1962, 158p, Paper, Novel
World of the future. [see 05143A]
05143 *World of tomorrow.* Badger, London, 1963, 158p, Paper, Novel
05143A retitled: *World of the future.* Arcadia House, New York, 1964, 189p, Cloth, Novel
05144 *The world that never was.* Badger, London, 1963, 158p, Paper, Novel
05145 *Zero minus X.* Badger, London, 1962, 160p, Paper, Novel

FANU, J. SHERIDAN LE
see: LE FANU, J. SHERIDAN

FARADAY, ROBERT

05146 *The anytime rings.* Dell, New York, 1963, 119p, Paper, Novel [Adventures in the Time Machine #1]
05147 *Samax, the gladiator.* Dell, New York, 1964, 119p, Paper, Novel [Adventures in the Time Machine #2]

FARADAY, W(ilfred) BARNARD, 1874-1953

05148 *The milk in the cocoanut.* Denis Archer, London, 1933, 261p, Cloth, Novel

FARALLA, DANA, 1909- [*biography included*]

05149 *Dream in the stone.* Julian Messner, New York, 1948, 234p, Cloth, Novel

FARCA, MARIE C., 1935- [*biography included*]

05150 *Complex man.* Doubleday, Garden City, 1973, 247p, Cloth, Novel [Andrew Ames #2]
05151 *Earth.* Doubleday, Garden City, 1972, 183p, Cloth, Novel [Andrew Ames #1]

FARGUS, FREDERICK J.
see: CONWAY, HUGH

FARJEON, B(enjamin) L(eopold), 1833-1903

05152 *The clairvoyante.* Hutchinson, London, 1905, 277p, Cloth, Novel
05153 *Devlin the barber.* Ward & Downey, London, 1888, 191p, Cloth, Novel
05154 *The last tenant.* Hutchinson, London, 1893, 320p, Cloth, Novel
05155 *Something occurred.* George Routledge & Sons, London, 1893, 328p, Cloth, Novel

FARJEON, ELEANOR, 1881-1965 [*biography inclu-ded*]

05156 *Ariadne and the bull.* Michael Joseph, London, 1945, 208p, Cloth, Novel
05157 *The Fair of St. James; a fantasia.* Faber & Faber, London, 1932, 352p, Cloth, Novel
05158 *Humming bird.* Michael Joseph, London, 1936, 320p, Cloth, Novel
05159 *Kaleidoscope.* W. Collins Sons, London, 1928, 239p, Cloth, Novel
05160 *Martin Pippin in the apple-orchard.* W. Collins Sons, London, 1921, 369p, Cloth, Novel [Martin Pippin series]
05161 *Martin Pippin in the daisy-field.* Michael Joseph, London, 1937, 330p, Cloth, Novel [Martin Pippin series]
05162 *The soul of Kol Nikon.* W. Collins Sons, London, 1923, 260p, Cloth, Novel

FARJEON, J(oseph) JEFFERSON, 1883-1955

05163 *Death of a world.* Collins, London, 1948, 192p, Cloth, Novel
05164 *The invisible companion, and other stories.* Polybooks, London, 1946, 62p, Paper, Coll.

FARLEY, RALPH MILNE, pseud. [Roger Sherman Hoar, 1887-1963]

05165 *Dangerous love; complete romantic novel.* Utopian Publications, London, 1946, 63p, Paper, Novel
An Earth man on Venus. [see 05170A]
05166 *The hidden universe.* Fantasy Publishing Co., Los Angeles, 1950, 134p, Cloth, Coll.
05167 *The Immortals.* Popular Publications, Toronto, 1947, 96p, Paper, Novel
05168 *The omnibus of time.* Fantasy Publishing Co., Los Angeles, 1950, 315p, Cloth, Coll.
05169 *The radio beasts.* Ace, New York, 1964, 191p, Paper, Novel [Miles Cabot #2]
05170 *The radio man.* Fantasy Publishing Co., Los Angeles, 1948, 177p, Cloth, Novel [Miles Cabot #1]
05170A retitled: *An Earth man on Venus.* Avon, New York, 1950, 125p, Paper, Novel [Miles Cabot #1]
05171 *The radio planet.* Ace, New York, 1964, 224p, Paper, Novel [Miles Cabot #3]
05172 *Strange worlds.* Fantasy Publishing Co., Los Angeles, 1953, 311p, Cloth, Coll. [includes *The radio man* and *The hidden universe*]

FARLEY, WALTER, 1915-   [*biography included*]

05173 *The black stallion's ghost.* Random House, New York, 1969, 187p, Cloth, Novel [Black Stallion #18]
05174 *The island stallion races.* Random House, New York, 1955, 256p, Cloth, Novel [Black Stallion #11]

FARMER, ARTHUR, pseud.
    see: MADDOCK, LARRY

FARMER, PENELOPE (Jane), 1939-   [*biography included*]

05175 *A castle of bone.* A Margaret K. McElderry Book, Atheneum, New York, 1972, 152p, Cloth, Novel
05176 *Charlotte sometimes.* Harcourt, Brace & World, New York, 1969, 192p, Cloth, Novel [Emma #3]
05177 *Emma in winter.* Harcourt, Brace & World, New York, 1966, 160p, Cloth, Novel [Emma #2]
05178 *The magic stone.* Harcourt, Brace & World, New York, 1964, 224p, Cloth, Novel
05179 *The summer birds.* Harcourt, Brace & World, New York, 1962, 155p, Cloth, Novel [Emma #1]
05180 *William and Mary; a story.* A Margaret K. McElderry Book, Atheneum, New York, 1974, 160p, Cloth, Novel

FARMER, PHILIP JOSÉ, 1918-   [*biography inclu-ded*]

05181 *The adventure of the peerless peer,* by John H. Watson, M.D. Aspen Press, Boulder, Col., 1974, 112p, Cloth, Novel [Tarzan series; Sherlock Holmes series]
05182 *The alley god.* Ballantine, New York, 1962, 176p, Paper, Coll.
05183 *Behind the walls of Terra.* Ace, New York, 1970, 188p, Paper, Novel [World of Tiers #4]
05184 *Blown; or, Sketches among the ruins of my mind (an exorcism: ritual 2).* Essex House, North Hollywood, 1969, 208p, Paper, Novel [Herald Childe #2]
05185 *The book of Philip José Farmer; or, The wares of Simple Simon's custard pie and space man.* DAW, New York, 1973, 239p, Paper, Coll.
05186 *Cache from outer space.* Ace Double, New York, 1962, 139p, Paper, Novel
05187 *The celestial blueprint, and other stories.* Ace Double, New York, 1962, 114p, Paper, Coll.
05188 *Dare.* Ballantine, New York, 1965, 159p, Paper, Novel
The day of timestop. [see 05218A]
05189 *Doc Savage: his apocalyptic life, as the arch-angel of Technopolis and exotica, as the gol-den-eyed hero of 181 super-sagas, as the bronze knight of the running board, including his final battle against the forces of Hell itself.* Doubleday, Garden City, 1973, 226p, Cloth, Nonf.
05190 *Down in the black gang, and others; a story collection.* Nelson Doubleday, Garden City, 1971, 215p, Cloth, Coll.
05191 *The fabulous Riverboat; a science fiction novel in the Riverworld series.* G. P. Putnam's Sons, New York, 1971, 253p, Cloth, Novel [Riverworld #2]
05192 *A feast unknown; volume IX of the memoirs of Lord Grandith.* Essex House, North Hollywood, 1969, 286p, Paper, Novel [Lord Grandith #1; Doc Caliban #1]
05193 *Flesh.* Galaxy Magazine Prize Selection for Beacon Books, New York, 1960, 160p, Paper, Novel
05194 *Flesh.* Doubleday, Garden City, 1968, 212p, Cloth, Novel [expanded]
05195 *The gate of time.* Belmont, New York, 1966, 176p, Paper, Novel
05196 *The gates of creation.* Ace, New York, 1966, 159p, Paper, Novel [World of Tiers #2]
05197 *The Green odyssey.* Ballantine, New York, 195?, 152p, Cloth, Novel

FARMER, PHILIP JOSÉ (Cont.)

05198 *Hadon of ancient Opar*. DAW, New York, 1974, 224p, Paper, Novel [a prequel to Edgar Rice Burroughs's *Tarzan and the Jewels of Opar*, set in the Opar of prehistoric times; Hadon #1]

05199 *The image of the beast [an exorcism, ritual 1]*. Essex House, North Hollywood, 1968, 255p, Paper, Novel [Herald Childe #1]

05200 *Inside outside*. Ballantine, New York, 1964, 156p, Paper, Novel

05201 *Lord of the trees*. Ace Double, New York, 1970, 122p, Paper, Novel [Lord Grandith #2]

05202 *Lord Tyger*. Doubleday, Garden City, 1970, 335p, Cloth, Novel

05203 *The lovers*. Ballantine, New York, 1961, 160p, Paper, Novel

05204 *The mad goblin*. Ace Double, New York, 1970, 130p, Paper, Novel [Doc Caliban #2]

05205 *The maker of universes*. Ace, New York, 1965, 191p, Paper, Novel [World of Tiers #1]

05206 *Mother was a lovely beast; a feral man anthology; fiction and fact about humans raised by animals*. Chilton, Radnor, PA, 1974, 246p, Cloth, Anth. [includes some nonf.]

05207 *Night of Light*. Berkley Medallion, New York, 1966, 160p, Paper, Novel

05208 *The other log of Phileas Fogg*. DAW, New York, 1973, 191p, Paper, Novel [complements Jules Verne's novel, *Around the world in eighty days*]

05209 *A private cosmos*. Ace, New York, 1968, 192p, Paper, Novel [World of Tiers #3]

05210 *The stone god awakens*. Ace, New York, 1970, 190p, Paper, Novel

05211 *Strange relations*. Ballantine, New York, 1960, 190p, Paper, Coll.

05212 *Tarzan alive; a definitive biography of Lord Greystoke*. Doubleday, Garden City, 1972, 312p, Cloth, Nonf.

05213 *Time's last gift*. Ballantine, New York, 1972, 201p, Paper, Novel
       Timestop! [see 05218B]

05214 *To your scattered bodies go; a science fiction novel*. G. P. Putnam's Sons, New York, 1971, 223p, Cloth, Novel [Riverworld #1]

05215 *Tongues of the Moon*. Pyramid, New York, 1964, 143p, Paper, Novel

05216 *Traitor to the living*. Ballantine, New York, 1973, 220p, Paper, Novel [Herald Childe #3]

05217 *The wind whales of Ishmael*. Ace, New York, 1971, 157p, Paper, Novel [sequel to Herman Melville's novel, *Moby Dick*]

05218 *A woman a day*. Galaxy Magazine Prize Selection for Beacon Books, New York, 1960, 160p, Paper, Novel

05218A retitled: *The day of timestop*. Lancer, New York, 1968, 192p, Paper, Novel

05218B retitled: *Timestop!* Lancer, New York, 1970, 192p, Paper, Novel

FARNCOMBE, FRANK E., with R. L. Hadfield

05219 *Red radio*. Herbert Jenkins, London, 1927, 256p, Cloth, Novel

05220 *Ruled by radio*. Herbert Jenkins, London, 1925, 256p, Cloth, Novel

FARNINGHAM, MARIANNE, pseud. [Mary Ann Hearn, 1834-1909]

05221 *Nineteen hundred? a forecast and a story*. James Clarke, London, 1892, 318p, Cloth, Novel

FARNOL, (John) JEFFERY, 1878-1952

05222 *Beltane the smith; a romance*. Sampson Low, Marston, London, 1915, 504p, Cloth, Novel

05223 *The geste of Duke Jocelyn; a romance in prose and verse*. Sampson Low, Marston, London, 1919, 333p, Cloth, Novel [includes some verse]

FARRAR, STEWART

05224 *The twelve maidens; a novel of witchcraft*. Michael Joseph, London, 1974, 222p, Cloth, Novel

FARREN, MICK

05225 *The texts of Festival*. Hart-Davis MacGibbon, London, 1973, 206p, Cloth, Novel

FARRÈRE, CLAUDE, pseud. [Frédéric Charles Pierre Édouard Bargone, 1876-1957]

05226 *Black opium (Fumée d'opium)*. Nicholas L. Brown, New York, 1929, 263p, Cloth, Novel

05227 *The house of the secret (La maison des hommes vivants)*. E. P. Dutton, New York, 1923, 234p, Cloth, Novel; J. M. Dent & Sons, London, 1923, 234p, Cloth, Novel

05228 *Useless hands*. E. P. Dutton, New York, 1926, 300p, Cloth, Novel

FAST, HOWARD (Melvin), 1914-   [*biography included*]

05229 *The edge of tomorrow*. Bantam, New York, 1961, 120p, Paper, Coll.

05230 *The general zapped an angel; new stories of fantasy and science fiction*. William Morrow, New York, 1970, 159p, Cloth, Coll.

05231 *The hunter; and, The trap*. Dial Press, New York, 1967, 216p, Cloth, Coll.

05232 *Tony and the wonderful door*. Alfred A. Knopf, New York, 1968, 80p, Cloth, Novel

05233 *A touch of infinity; thirteen new stories of fantasy and science fiction*. William Morrow, New York, 1973, 182p, Cloth, Coll.

FAST, JULIUS, 1919-   [*biography included*]

05234 *The league of grey-eyed women*. J. B. Lippincott, Philadelphia, 1970, 219p, Cloth, Novel

05235 *Out of this world; an anthology*. Penguin, New York, 1944, 245p, Paper, Anth.

FATAL REVENGE
       see: MATURIN, CHARLES ROBERT

FAUCETTE, JOHN M(atthew Jr.), 1943-   [biography included]

05236   *The Age of Ruin.* Ace Double, New York, 1968, 114p, Paper, Novel
05237   *Crown of infinity.* Ace Double, New York, 1968, 129p, Paper, Novel
05238   *Siege of Earth.* Belmont, New York, 1971, 158p, Paper, Novel [Peacemakers #2]
05239   *The warriors of Terra.* Belmont, New York, 1970, 175p, Paper, Novel [Peacemakers #1]

FAULCONBRIDGE, PHILIP, pseud.

05240   *Commissars over Britain.* Beaufort Press Book Dept., London, 1947, 84p, Cloth, Novel

FAULEY, WILBUR
    see: FAWLEY, WILBUR

FAURE, RAOUL C(ohen), 1909-

05241   *The cave and the rock.* William Morrow, New York, 1953, 276p, Cloth, Novel
05242   *Mister St. John; a novel.* Harper & Bros., New York, 1947, 279p, Cloth, Novel

FAUST, FREDERICK
    see: BRAND, MAX

FAVENC, ERNEST, 1846-1908

05243   *Marooned on Australia, being the narration by Diedrich Buys of his discoveries and exploits in Terra Australis Incognita, about the year 1630.* Blackie & Son, London, 1896, 224p, Cloth, Novel
05244   *The secret of the Australian desert.* Blackie & Son, London, 1896, 223p, Cloth, Novel

FAWCETT, E(dward) DOUGLAS, 1866-1960

05245   *Hartmann the anarchist; or, The doom of the great city.* Edward Arnold, London, 1893, 214p, Cloth, Novel
05246   *The secret of the desert; or, How we crossed Arabia in the "Antelope."* Edward Arnold, London, 1895, 246p, Cloth, Novel
05247   *Swallowed by an earthquake.* Edward Arnold, London, 1894, 235p, Cloth, Novel

FAWCETT, EDGAR, 1847-1904

05248   *The ghost of Guy Thyrle.* Ward, Lock & Bowden, London, 1895, 282p, Cloth, Novel

FAWCETT, F(rank) DUBREZ, 1891-1968

05249   *Hole in Heaven.* Sidgwick & Jackson, London, 1954, 244p, Cloth, Novel

as Simpson Stokes:

05250   *Air-gods' parade.* Arthur Barron, London, 1935, 180p, Cloth, Novel

FAWKES, FRANK ATTFIELD

05251   *Marmaduke, Emperor of Europe, being a record of some strange adventures in the remarkable career of a political and social reformer who was famous at the commencement of the twentieth century,* by X. E. Durrant, Chelmsford, UK, 1895, 271p, Cloth, Novel

FAWLEY, WILBUR, pseud. [Wilbur Finley Fauley, 1872-1942]

05252   *Shuddering castle.* Green Circle Books, New York, 1936, 320p, Cloth, Novel

FAYETTE, JOHN B. [published anonymously]

05253   *Voices from many hill tops, echoes from many valleys; or, The experiences of spirits Eon and Eoná, in Earth life and spirit spheres, given through the sun angels' order of light.* Press Springfield Printing Co., Springfield, 1886, 650p, Cloth, Novel

FEAR, W(illiam) H(enry Charles)

05254   *Lunar flight.* Badger, London, 1958, 158p, Paper, Novel
05255   *Operation Satellite.* Badger, London, 1958, 158p, Paper, Novel
05256   *Return to space.* Badger, London, 1958, 158p, Paper, Novel
05257   *The ultimate.* Badger, London, 1958, 158p, Paper, Novel

FEARING, KENNETH (Flexner), 1902-1961

05258   *Clark Gifford's body.* Random House, New York, 1942, 286p, Cloth, Novel
05259   *Loneliest girl in the world; a novel.* Harcourt Brace & Co., New York, 1951, 238p, Cloth, Novel

FEARN, JOHN (Francis) RUSSELL, 1908-1960 [biography included]

05260   *The Amazon strikes again.* World's Work, Kingswood, UK, 1954, 175p, Cloth, Novel [Golden Amazon #5]
05261   *The Amazon's diamond quest.* World's Work, Kingswood, UK, 1953, 175p, Cloth, Novel [Golden Amazon #4]
05262   *Conquest of the Amazon.* Cosmos Science Fiction Series, Wallsend, UK, 1973, 34p, Paper, Story [Golden Amazon #7]
        The deathless Amazon. [see 05266A]
05263   *Emperor of Mars.* Hamilton & Co. (Stafford), London, 1950, 127p, Paper, Novel [Clayton Drew #1]
05264   *Goddess of Mars.* Hamilton & Co. (Stafford), London, 1950, 126p, Paper, Novel [Clayton Drew #4]
05265   *The Golden Amazon; a master thriller science fiction novel.* World's Work, Kingswood, UK, 1944, 117p, Cloth, Novel [Golden Amazon #1]
05266   *The Golden Amazon returns.* World's Work, Kingswood, UK, 1948, 133p, Cloth, Novel [Golden Amazon #2]

FEARN, JOHN RUSSELL (Cont.)

05266A retitled: *The deathless Amazon*. Harlequin, Winnipeg, 1955, 160p, Paper, Novel [Golden Amazon #2]

05267 *The Golden Amazon's triumph*. World's Work, Kingswood, UK, 1953, 192p, Cloth, Novel [Golden Amazon #3]

05268 *The intelligence gigantic*. World's Work, Kingswood, UK, 1943, 100p, Cloth, Novel

05269 *Liners of time*. World's Work, Kingswood, UK, 1947, 156p, Cloth, Novel

05270 *Operation Venus!* Scion, London, 1950, 128p, Paper, Novel

05271 *Red men of Mars*. Hamilton & Co. (Stafford), London, 1950, 127p, Paper, Novel [Clayton Drew #3]

05272 *Slaves of Ijax; a complete mystery romance*. Kaner Publishing Co., Llandudno, Wales, 1947, 80p, Paper, Novel

05273 *Twin of the Amazon*. World's Work, Kingswood, UK, 1954, 159p, Cloth, Novel [Golden Amazon #6]

05274 *Warrior of Mars*. Hamilton & Co. (Stafford), London, 1950, 127p, Paper, Novel [Clayton Drew #2]

05275 *Wings across the cosmos*. Fantasy Booklet, Wallsend, UK, 1972, 12p, Paper, Story

as Hugo Blayn:

05276 *What happened to Hammond?* Stanley Paul, London, 1951, 204p, Cloth, Novel

as Dennis Clive:

05277 *Valley of pretenders*. Columbia Publications, New York, 1942?, 24p, Paper, Story

05278 *The Voice commands*. Columbia Publications, New York, 1942?, 24p, Paper, Story

as Polton Cross:

05279 *Other eyes watching*. Pendulum Publications, London, 1946, 120p, Paper, Novel

as Astron del Martia, house pseud.:

04067 *The trembling world*. S. D. Frances, London, 1949, 128p, Paper, Novel

as Volsted Gridban, house pseud.:

05280 *The dyno-depressant*. Scion, London, 1953, 128p, Paper, Novel

05281 *Exit life*. Scion, London, 1953, 128p, Paper, Novel

05282 *The frozen limit*. Scion, London, 1954, 128p, Paper, Novel

05283 *The genial dinosaur*. Scion, London, 1954, 128p, Paper, Novel [Herbert #2]

05284 *I came--I saw--I wondered*. Scion, London, 1954, 126p, Paper, Novel

05285 *The lonely astronomer; an Adam Quirke adventure*. Scion, London, 1954, 128p, Paper, Novel [Adam Quirke #2]

05286 *The magnetic brain*. Scion, London, 1953, 128p, Paper, Novel

05287 *The Master must die*. Scion, London, 1953, 128p, Paper, Novel [Adam Quirke #1]

05288 *Moons for sale*. Scion, London, 1953, 128p, Paper, Novel

05289 *The purple wizard*. Scion, London, 1953, 128p, Paper, Novel

05290 *Scourge of the atom*. Scion, London, 1953, 128p, Paper, Novel

05291 *A thing of the past*. Scion, London, 1953, 128p, Paper, Novel [Herbert #1]

as "Griff," house pseud.:

05292 *Liquid death*. Modern Fiction, London, 1953, 126p, Paper, Novel

as Conrad G. Holt:

05293 *Cosmic exodus*. Tit-Bits Science Fiction Library, London, 1953, 64p, Paper, Novel

as Paul Lorraine, house pseud.:

05294 *Dark Boundaries*. Curtis Warren, London, 1953, 159p, Cloth, Novel

as Lawrence F. Rose:

05295 *The hell fruit*. Tit-Bits Science Fiction Library, London, 1953, 64p, Paper, Novel

as John Russell:

05296 *Account settled*. Paget Publications, London, 1949?, 128p, Paper, Novel

as Brian Shaw, house pseud.

05297 *Z formations*. Curtis Warren, London, 1953, 159p, Cloth, Novel [name given as "Bryan" on title page]

as Vargo Statten:

05298 *Across the ages*. Scion, London, 1952, 96p, Paper, Novel

05299 *Annihilation*. Scion, London, 1950, 128p, Paper, Novel

05300 *The avenging Martian*. Scion, London, 1951, 128p, Paper, Novel

05301 *The Black Avengers*. Scion, London, 1953, 128p, Paper, Novel

05302 *Black bargain*. Scion, London, 1953, 128p, Paper, Novel

05303 *Black-wing of Mars*. Scion, London, 1953, 128p, Paper, Novel

05304 *Born of Luna*. Scion, London, 1951, 128p, Paper, Novel

05305 *Cataclysm!* Scion, London, 1951, 128p, Paper, Novel

05306 *The catalyst*. Scion, London, 1951, 112p, Paper, Novel

05307 *The cosmic flame*. Scion, London, 1950, 128p, Paper, Novel

05308 *Creature from the black lagoon*. Dragon Publications, London, 1954, 176p, Cloth, Movie

05309 *Deadline to Pluto*. Scion, London, 1951, 128p, Paper, Novel

05310 *De-creation*. Scion, London, 1952, 96p, Paper, Novel

05311 *The Devouring Fire*. Scion, London, 1951, 112p, Paper, Novel

05312 *The dust destroyer*. Scion, London, 1953, 127p, Paper, Novel [*Destroyers* on cover]

05313 *Earth 2*. Dragon Publications, Luton, UK, 1955, 128p, Paper, Novel

05314 *The eclipse express*. Scion, London, 1952, 112p, Paper, Novel

05315 *The G-bomb*. Scion, London, 1952, 112p, Paper, Novel

05316 *The grand illusion*. Scion, London, 1954, 128p, Paper, Novel [author's pseudonym reads "Volsted Gridban" on spine]

05317 *I spy...* Scion, London, 1954, 128p, Paper, Novel

05318 *Inferno!* Scion, London, 1950, 128p, Paper, Novel

05319 *Inner cosmos*. Scion, London, 1952, 112p, Paper, Novel

05320 *The interloper*. Scion, London, 1953, 128p, Paper, Novel

FEARN, JOHN RUSSELL (Cont.), as Vargo Statten

05321 *The last Martian.* Scion, London, 1952, 96p, Paper, Novel

05322 *Laughter in space.* Scion, London, 1952, 112p, Paper, Novel

05323 *The lie destroyer.* Scion, London, 1953, 127p, Paper, Novel

05324 *The man from to-morrow.* Scion, London, 1952, 112p, Paper, Novel

05325 *Man in duplicate.* Scion, London, 1953, 128p, Paper, Novel

05326 *Man of two worlds.* Scion, London, 1953, 128p, Paper, Novel

05327 *The micro man.* Scion, London, 1950, 128p, Paper, Novel

05328 *The multi-man.* Dragon, London, 1954, 128p, Paper, Novel

05329 *Nebula X.* Scion, London, 1950, 128p, Paper, Novel

05330 *The new satellite.* Scion, London, 1951, 112p, Paper, Novel

05331 *The odyssey of 9.* Scion, London, 1953, 128p, Paper, Novel

05332 *"1,000-year voyage."* Dragon Publications, Luton, UK, 1954, 128p, Paper, Novel

05333 *Petrified planet.* Scion, London, 1951, 112p, Paper, Novel

05334 *Pioneer 1990.* Scion, London, 1953, 128p, Paper, Novel

05335 *The red insects.* Scion, London, 1951, 128p, Paper, Novel

05336 *Renegade star.* Scion, London, 1951, 112p, Paper, Novel

05337 *Science metropolis.* Scion, London, 1952, 128p, Paper, Novel

05338 *Space warp.* Scion, London, 1952, 112p, Paper, Novel

05339 *The sunmakers.* Scion, London, 1950, 128p, Paper, Novel

05340 *A time appointed.* Scion, London, 1954, 126p, Paper, Novel

05341 *The time bridge.* Scion, London, 1952, 112p, Paper, Novel

05342 *The time trap.* Scion, London, 1952, 96p, Paper, Novel

05343 *To the ultimate.* Scion, London, 1952, 128p, Paper, Novel

05344 *2,000 years on.* Scion, London, 1950, 128p, Paper, Novel

05345 *Ultra spectrum.* Scion, London, 1953, 128p, Paper, Novel

05346 *Wanderer of space.* Scion, London, 1950, 128p, Paper, Novel

05347 *Wealth of the void.* Scion, London, 1954, 128p, Paper, Novel

05348 *Worlds to conquer.* Scion, London, 1952, 96p, Paper, Novel

05349 *Zero hour.* Scion, London, 1953, 128p, Paper, Novel

as Earl Titan:

05350 *Anjani the mighty.* Scion, London, 1951, 128p, Paper, Novel [Anjani #2]

05351 *The gold of Akada.* Scion, London, 1951, 128p, Paper, Novel [Anjani #1]

with Eando Binder, Jack Williamson, Edmond Hamilton, and Raymond Z. Gallun:

01304 *The great illusion.* Fantasy Booklet, Wallsend, UK, 1973, 12p, Paper, Story

FEDAKH, FATIMA, pseud.

05352 *The sexorcist.* Windsor Library Press, San Diego, 1974, 188p, Paper, Novel

FEDER, ROBERT ARTHUR
    see: ARTHUR, ROBERT

FEDERBUSH, ARNOLD

05353 *The man who lived in inner space.* Houghton Mifflin, Boston, 1973, 180p, Cloth, Novel

FEDUCHA, BERTHA

05354 *Two legends.* Clear Thoughts, Hollywood, 1961, 45p, Paper, Coll.

FEGAN, CAMILLA, 1939-   [*biography included*]

05355 *Late for Hallowe'en.* Methuen, London, 1966, 109p, Cloth, Novel

FEILING, C. A., with John Oxenham

05356 *Tales from the German, comprising specimens from the most celebrated authors.* Chapman & Hall, London, 1844, 446p, Cloth, Anth.

FELLOWES, EDWARD COLTON, 1864-1928

05357 *Stories of the stone age; a boy's life in 16,000 B.C.* Small, Maynard, Boston, 1925, 170p, Cloth, Novel

FELSEN, HENRY GREGOR, 1916-   [*biography included*]

05358 *The boy who discovered the Earth.* Charles Scribner's Sons, New York, 1955, 140p, Cloth, Novel

FENN, G(eorge) MANVILLE, 1831-1909

05359 *The man with a shadow.* Ward & Downey, London, 1881, 3vol, Cloth, Novel

FENN, W(illiam) W(ilthew), 1827?-

05360 *Woven in darkness; a medley of stories, essays, and dreamwork.* Kelly & Co., London, 1885, vol. I-451p, II-434p, Cloth, Coll.

FENNER, PHYLLIS R(eid), 1899-   [*biography included*]

05361 *Ghosts, ghosts, ghosts; stories of spooks and spirits, haunts and hobgoblins, werewolves and will-o'-the-wisps.* Franklin Watts, New York, 1952, 281p, Cloth, Anth.

FENNERTON, WILLIAM

05362 *The Lucifer cell*. Atheneum, New York, 1968, 306p, Cloth, Novel

FENNESSY, J. C.

05363 *The sonnet in the bottle*. Herbert Jenkins, London, 1951, 270p, Cloth, Novel

FENTON, EDWARD, 1917-

05364 *Once upon a Saturday*. Doubleday, Garden City, 1958, 232p, Cloth, Novel

FENTON, ROBERT W.

05365 *The big swingers*. Prentice-Hall, Englewood Cliffs, NJ, 1967, 258p, Cloth, Nonf.

FERENCZY, ÁRPÁD, 1877-

05366 *The ants of Timothy Thümmel*. Jonathan Cape, London, 1924, 320p, Cloth, Novel
05367 *Kunala; an Indian fantasy*. Jonathan Cape, London, 1925, 255p, Cloth, Novel

FERM, BETTY, 1926-   [*biography included*]

05368 *False idols*. G. P. Putnam's Sons, New York, 1974, 218p, Cloth, Novel

FERMAN, EDWARD L(ewis), 1937-   [*biography included*]

05369 *The best from Fantasy and science fiction, a special 25th anniversary anthology*. Doubleday, Garden City, 1974, 326p, Cloth, Anth. [actually the 21st series]
05370 *The best from Fantasy and science fiction, fifteenth series*. Doubleday, Garden City, 1966, 248p, Cloth, Anth.
05371 *The best from Fantasy and science fiction, sixteenth series*. Doubleday, Garden City, 1967, 264p, Cloth, Anth.
05372 *The best from Fantasy and science fiction, seventeenth series*. Doubleday, Garden City, 1968, 260p, Cloth, Anth.
05373 *The best from Fantasy and science fiction, eighteenth series*. Doubleday, Garden City, 1969, 285p, Cloth, Anth.
05374 *The best from Fantasy and science fiction, nineteenth series*. Doubleday, Garden City, 1971, 286p, Cloth, Anth.
05375 *The best of Fantasy and science fiction, 20th series*. Doubleday, Garden City, 1973, 296p, Cloth, Anth. [cover title reads: *The best from...*]
05376 *Once and future tales from The magazine of fantasy and science fiction*. Delphi Press, Jacksonville, IL, 1968, 366p, Cloth, Anth.

with Barry N. Malzberg:

05377 *Final stage; the ultimate science fiction anthology*. Charterhouse, New York, 1974, 309p, Cloth, Anth.

with Robert P. Mills:

05378 *Twenty years of The magazine of fantasy and science fiction*. G. P. Putnam's Sons, New York, 1970, 264p, Cloth, Anth.

FERMAN, JOSEPH W(olfe), 1906-1974 [*biography included*]

05379 *No limits*. Ballantine, New York, 1964, 192p, Paper, Anth.

FERNÁNDEZ FLÓREZ, WENCESLAO, 1888-

05380 *Laugh, and the ghosts laugh with you.....* British Technical & General Press, London, 1951, 176p, Cloth, Coll.
05381 *The seven pillars*. Macmillan, London, 1934, 289p, Cloth, Novel

FERRAR, WILLIAM M(oore)

05382 *Artabanzanus, the demon of the great lake; an allegorical romance of Tasmania arranged from the diary of the late Oliver Ubertus*. Elliot Stock, London, 1896, 314p, Cloth, Novel

FERRIS, PAUL (Frederick), 1929-   [*biography included*]

05383 *The cure; a novel*. Weidenfeld & Nicolson, London, 1974, 232p, Cloth, Novel

FESSENDEN, LAURA (Canfield Spencer) DAYTON, d. 1924

05384 *"2002"; childlife one hundred years from now*. Jamieson-Higgins Co., Chicago, 1902, 184p, Cloth, Novel

FESSIER, MICHAEL, 1907-

05385 *Clovis*. Dial Press, New York, 1948, 189p, Cloth, Novel
05386 *Fully dressed and in his right mind; a novel*. Alfred A. Knopf, New York, 1935, 216p, Cloth, Novel

FEVER DREAM, AND OTHER FANTASIES
    see: SINGER, KURT

FEZANDIÉ, CLEMENT

05387 *Through the Earth*. Century Co., New York, 1898, 238p, Cloth, Novel

FIALKO, NATHAN (Moiseevich), 1881-

05388 *The new city*. Margent Press, New York, 1937, 153p, Cloth, Novel

FIDLER, KATHLEEN, pseud. [Kathleen Annie Gol-
die]

05389 *The boy with the bronze axe.* Oliver & Boyd,
       Edinburgh, 1968, 192p, Cloth, Novel

FIEDLER, LESLIE A(aron), 1917-   [*biography
included*]

05390 *The messengers will come no more.* Stein & Day,
       New York, 1974, 216p, Cloth, Novel

FIELD, BEN, 1901-

05391 *Ramola twice born.* House of Field, New York,
       1944, 427p, Cloth, Novel

FIELD, EUGENE, 1850-1895

05392 *The first Christmas tree.* Sterling Press, no
       place, no date, 22p, Cloth, Story
05393 *The holy cross, and other tales.* Stone & Kim-
       ball, Chicago, 1893, 191p, Cloth, Coll.
05394 *A little book of profitable tales.* J. Wilson
       & Son, Printers, Chicago, 1889, 286p, Cloth,
       Coll.
05395 *Second book of tales.* Charles Scribner's Sons,
       New York, 1896, 314p, Cloth, Coll.
05396 *The temptation of Friar Gonsol; a story of the
       devil, two saints, and a booke* [sic]. Wood-
       ward & Lothrop, Washington, 1900, 40p, Cloth,
       Story

FIELD, GANS T., pseud.
     see: WELLMAN, MANLY WADE

FIELD, JULIAN OSGOOD

05397 *Aut diabolus aut nihil, and other tales,* by
       X. L. Methuen, London, 1894, 303p, Cloth,
       Coll.

FIELD, MARLO

05398 *Astro bubbles.* Four Seas Co., Boston, 1928,
       297p, Cloth, Novel

FIELD, RACHEL (Lyman), 1894-1942

05399 *Hitty; her first hundred years.* Macmillan,
       New York, 1929, 207p, Cloth, Novel

FIELDING, HENRY, 1707-1754

05400 *A journey from this world to the next.* Harri-
       son & Co., London, 1783, 67p, Cloth, Novel

THE FIEND
     see: RUSSELL, RAY

FIFIELD, Mrs. JAMES C., pseud. [Effie Merriman, 1857-   ]

05401 *Rejuvenated.* Midwest Co., Minneapolis, 1928,
       294p, Cloth, Novel

FIFIELD, WILLIAM, 1916-   [*biography included*]

05402 *The sign of Taurus; a novel.* Weidenfeld &
       Nicolson, London, 1959, 367p, Cloth, Novel

FIFTY MASTERPIECES OF MYSTERY
     see: MURRAY, V. T.

FIFTY YEARS HENCE

05403 *Fifty years hence; an old soldier's tale of
       England's downfall.* G. W. Bacon & Co.,
       London, 1877, 32p, Paper, Story

50 YEARS OF GHOST STORIES

05404 *50 years of ghost stories.* Hutchinson, London,
       1935, 702p, Cloth, Anth.

FIGGIS, (M.) DARRELL

as Michael Ireland:

05405 *The return of the hero.* Chapman & Dodd,
       London, 1923, 256p, Cloth, Novel

as Darrell Figgis:

05405A *The return of the hero.* Charles Boni, New
       York, 1930, 221p, Paper, Novel

FIGUEREDO y CLARENS, CARLOS
     see: CLARENS, CARLOS

FIGUEROA (Ramirez), MEDARDO, 1887-

05406 *The Valley of Josaphat; a message to America.*
       The Banner, Sonora, 1927, 142p, Cloth, Nove

FILANOVSKY, ALEXANDER
     see: FINDLAY, ALEXANDER

FILER, TOM
     see: CHISOM, SARAH

FILKIN, ROLAND

05407 *Agar Halfi the mystic.* William Rider & Son,
       London, 1915, 317p, Cloth, Novel

FINDLAY, ALEXANDER (Tobias) [Alexander Fila-
novsky], 1873-

05408 *Adoniram.* Adoniram Publishing Co., San Fran-
       cisco, 1927, 195p, Cloth, Novel

FINE, PETER
    see: HEATH, PETER

FINE, RALPH ADAM, 1941- [biography included]

    05409 *Mary Jane versus Pennsylvania; the day the Supreme Court heard the arguments for and against the legalization of marijuana.* Mc-Call Publishing Co., New York, 1970, 154p, Cloth, Novel

FINGER, CHARLES J(oseph), 1869-1941

    05410 *The spreading stain; a tale for boys and men with boys' hearts.* Doubleday, Page, Garden City, 1927, 245p, Cloth, Novel

FINLAY, VIRGIL (Warden), 1914-1971, with Clark Ashton Smith

    05411 *Klarkash-Ton and Monstro Ligriv; previously unpublished poems and art.* Gerry de la Ree, Saddle River, NJ, 1974, 28p, Paper, Nonf.

FINLEY, HARRY T. [Henry Taylor Finley, 1866-1940]

    05412 *Where the needle points.* Abbey Press, New York, 1902, 300p, Cloth, Novel

FINN, RALPH L(eslie), 1912- [biography included]

    05413 *Captive on the flying saucers.* Gaywood Press, London, 1951?, 123p, Paper, Novel
    05414 *Freaks against supermen.* Gaywood Press, London, 1951, 123p, Paper, Novel
    05415 *Time marches sideways.* Hutchinson, London, 1950, 224p, Cloth, Novel

FINNEY, CHARLES G(randison), 1905- [biography included]

    05416 *The circus of Dr. Lao.* Viking Press, New York, 1935, 154p, Cloth, Novel
    05417 *The ghosts of Manacle.* Pyramid, New York, 1964, 159p, Paper, Coll.
    05418 *The unholy city.* Vanguard Press, New York, 1937, 168p, Cloth, Novel
    05419 *The unholy city.* Pyramid, New York, 1968, 221p, Paper, Coll.

FINNEY, JACK [Walter Braden Finney, 1911-]

    05420 *The body snatchers.* Dell First Editions, New York, 1955, 191p, Paper, Novel
    05420A retitled: *The invasion of the body snatchers.* Award, New York, 1973, 187p, Paper, Novel
    The clock of time. [see 05423A]
    05421 *I love Galesburg in the springtime.* Simon & Schuster, New York, 1963, 224p, Cloth, Coll.
    The invasion of the body snatchers. [see 05420A]
    05422 *Marion's wall; a novel.* Simon & Schuster, New York, 1973, 187p, Cloth, Novel
    05423 *The third level.* Rinehart, New York, 1957, 188p, Cloth, Coll.

    05423A retitled: *The clock of time.* Eyre & Spottiswoode, London, 1958, 189p, Cloth, Coll.
    05424 *Time and again.* Simon & Schuster, New York, 1970, 399p, Cloth, Novel
    05425 *The Woodrow Wilson dime.* Simon & Schuster, New York, 1968, 190p, Cloth, Novel

FINNEY, LEWIS E(rwin)

    05426 *Calno, the super-man; a fictional study of the anti-Christ.* Ozark Publishing Co., Dallas, TX, 1918,   , Cloth, Novel

FINNEY, WALTER B.
    see: FINNEY, JACK

FIRBANK, (Arthur Annesley) RONALD, 1886-1926

    05427 *Two early stories.* Albondocani Press, New York, 1971, 54p, Paper, Coll.

FIRES OF FOREVER

    05428 *Fires of forever.* American Science Fiction, Sydney, 1953, 34p, Paper, Anth.

FIRTH, N. WESLEY

    05429 *Terror strikes.* Hamilton & Co. (Stafford), London, 1948?, 80p, Paper, Novel

FIRTH, VIOLET MARY
    see: FORTUNE, DION

FISCHER, LEONARD

    05430 *Let out the beast.* News Stand Library, Toronto, Canada, 1950, 159p, Paper, Novel

FISCHER, MARJORIE, 1903-1961, with Rolfe Humphries

    05431 *Pause to wonder; stories of the marvelous, mysterious, and strange.* Julian Messner, New York, 1944, 572p, Cloth, Anth.
    05432 *Strange to tell; stories of the marvelous and mysterious.* Julian Messner, New York, 1946, 532p, Cloth, Anth.

FISHER, GENE
    see: LANCOUR, GENE

FISHER, HOWARD S.

    05433 *Lightning in the East.* Golden Coast, Goleta, CA, 1972, 240p, Paper, Novel

FISHER, JAMES P.

    05434 *The great brain robbery.* Belmont, New York, 1970, 154p, Paper, Novel

FISHER, MARY A(nn), 1839-

05435 *Among the immortals in the land of desire; a glimpse of the beyond.* Shakespeare Press, New York, 1916, 276p, Cloth, Novel

FISHER, STEVE [Stephen Gould Fisher, 1912-]

05436 *Destroyer.* D. Appleton-Century, New York, 1941, 236p, Cloth, Novel
05437 *Saxon's ghost.* Sherbourne Press, Los Angeles, 1969, 211p, Cloth, Novel

FISHER, VARDIS (Alvero), 1895-1968 [*biography included*]

05438 *Adam and the serpent.* Vanguard Press, New York, 1947, 335p, Cloth, Novel [Testament of Man #4]
05439 *Darkness and the deep.* Vanguard Press, New York, 1943, 296p, Cloth, Novel [Testament of Man #1]
05440 *The divine passion.* Vanguard Press, New York, 1948, 373p, Cloth, Novel [Testament of Man #5]
05441 *The golden rooms.* Vanguard Press, New York, 1944, 324p, Cloth, Novel [Testament of Man #2]
05442 *Intimations of Eve.* Vanguard Press, New York, 1946, 331p, Cloth, Novel [Testament of Man #3]

FISK, NICHOLAS, pseud.?, 1923- [*biography included*]

05443 *Grinny.* Heinemann, London, 1973, 96p, Cloth, Novel
05444 *Space hostages.* Hamish Hamilton, London, 1967, 160p, Cloth, Novel
05445 *Trillions.* Hamish Hamilton, London, 1971, 158p, Cloth, Novel

FISKE, AMOS K(idder), 1842-1921

05446 *Beyond the bourn; reports of a traveller returned from "the undiscovered country."* Fords, Howard & Hulbert, New York, 1891, 222p, Cloth, Novel

FITCH, ANNA M(ariska), with Thomas Fitch

05447 *Better days; or, A millionaire of to-morrow.* Better Days Publishing Co., San Francisco, 1891, 373p, Cloth, Novel

FITCH, THOMAS, with Anna M. Fitch

05447 *Better days; or, A millionaire of to-morrow.* Better Days Publishing Co., San Francisco, 1891, 373p, Cloth, Novel

FITZGERALD, ENA

05448 *The witch queen of Khem; a tale of a wrong made right.* Greening & Co., London, 1909, 316p, Cloth, Novel

FITZ GERALD, GREGORY, 1923- [*biography included*], with Jack C. Wolf

05449 *Past, present, and future perfect; a text anthology of speculative and science fiction.* Fawcett Premier, Greenwich, 1973, 544p, Paper, Anth.

FITZ GIBBON, (Robert Louis) CONSTANTINE (Dillon), 1919- [*biography included*]

05450 *The iron hoop.* Alfred A. Knopf, New York, 1949, 268p, Cloth, Novel
05451 *When the kissing had to stop.* Cassell, London, 1960, 248p, Cloth, Novel

FITZ-GIBBON, RALPH EDGERTON

05452 *The man with two bodies.* Vantage Press, New York, 1952, 137p, Cloth, Novel

FITZHARDINGE, JOAN MARGARET
   see: PHIPSON, JOAN

FITZPATRICK, ERNEST HUGH

05453 *The coming conflict of nations; or, The Japanese-American War; a narrative.* H. W. Rokker, Springfield, IL, 1909, 306p, Cloth, Novel

as Hugo Barnaby:

05454 *The marshal duke of Denver; or, The labor revolution of 1920; a novel.* Donohue & Henneberry, Chicago, 1895, 208p, Cloth, Novel

FITZPORTER, J(ohn) L.

05455 *My vacation; or, The millennium; a novel.* no publisher, St. Louis, 1891, 154p, Paper, Novel

"FIVE MEN AND A WOMAN," pseud.

05456 *The adventures of the Adventurers' Club; a shocker in six shocks.* Gardner & Co., London, 1890, 124p, Cloth, Coll.

FLACK, ISAAC HARVEY
   see: GRAHAM, HARVEY

FLACKES, B.

05457 *Duel in nightmare worlds.* Hamilton & Co. (Stafford), London, 1952, 112p, Paper, Novel

FLAGG, FRANCIS, pseud. [Henry George Weiss, 1898-1946]

05458 *The night people.* Fantasy Publishing Co., Los Angeles, 1947, 32p, Paper, Story

FLAMMARION, (Nicolas) CAMILLE, 1842-1925

      Lumen. [see 05460A]
05459 *Omega; the last days of the world.* Cosmopoli-
      tan Publishing Co., New York, 1894, 287p,
      Cloth, Novel
05460 *Stories of infinity; Lumen--the history of a*
      comet in infinity. Roberts Bros., Boston,
      1873, 287p, Cloth, Novel
05460A retitled: *Lumen; experiences in the infinite.*
      Cassell, New York, 1892, 275p, Cloth, Novel
05461 *Urania; a romance.* Estes & Lauriat, Boston,
      1890, 314p, Cloth, Novel
05461A retitled: *Uranie.* Cassell, New York, 1890,
      252p, Paper?, Novel

FLAMMENBERG, LAWRENCE, pseud. [Karl Friedrich
Kahlert, 1765-1813]

05462 *The necromancer; or, The tale of the Black*
      Forest, founded on facts. William Lane,
      The Minerva-Press, London, 1794, 2vol, Cloth,
      Novel

FLANAGAN, RICHARD

05463 *The hunting variety.* G. P. Putnam's Sons,
      New York, 1973, 183p, Cloth, Novel

FLANIGAN, MICHAEL C(letus), 1936- , with
Lawana Trout

05464 *Unknown worlds.* Holt, Rinehart & Winston,
      New York, 1969, 157p, Paper, Anth.

FLANNER, JACK

05465 *Come slo, Devlin* [sic]. Echelon, Los Angeles,
      1967, 160p, Paper, Novel [Cover title: *Come*
      slow, Devlin! by Jack David]

FLATAU, DOROTA

05466 *Seven journeys.* Hutchinson, London, 1920,
      288p, Cloth, Novel

FLATLAND
  see: ABBOTT, EDWIN A.

FLAUBERT, GUSTAVE, 1821-1880

05467 *The temptation of Saint Antony.* H. S. Nichols,
      London, 1895, 360p, Cloth, Novel
05467A retitled: *The first temptation of Saint An-*
      thony. Duckworth, London, 1910, 296p, Cloth,
      Novel

FLECKENSTEIN, ALFRED C.

05468 *The Prince of Gravas; a story of the past.*
      G. W. Jacobs, Philadelphia, 1898, 270p,
      Cloth, Novel

FLECKER, JAMES ELROY, 1884-1915

05469 *The King of Alsander.* Max Goschen, London,
      1914, 304p, Cloth, Novel
05470 *The last generation; a story of the future.*
      New Age Press, London, 1908, 56p, Paper,
      Novel

FLEISCHER, MAX, 1888-

05471 *Noah's shoes.* S. J. Bloch Publishing Co.,
      Detroit, 1944, 160p, Cloth, Novel

FLEISCHMAN, THÉO, 1893-

05472 *Double exposure; a novel.* Vanguard Press,
      New York, 1956, 249p, Cloth, Novel

FLEMING, A(ndrew) M(agnus), 1868-

05473 *Captain Kiddle; a fantastic romance.* J. B.
      Alden, New York, 1889, 306p, Cloth, Novel
05474 *The gold diggers.* Meador Publishing Co., Bos-
      ton, 1930, 256p, Cloth, Novel

FLEMING, (Jiles) BERRY, 1899- [*biography*
included]

05475 *The square root of Valentine.* W. W. Norton,
      New York, 1932, 282p, Cloth, Novel

FLEMING, HARRY, pseud.
  see: BIRD, WILLIAM HENRY

FLEMING, JOAN (Margaret)

05476 *The chill and the kill.* Collins, London, 1964,
      256p, Cloth, Novel

FLEMING, KEITH

05477 *"Can such things be?"; or, The weird of the*
      Beresfords; a study in occult will-power.
      George Routledge & Sons, London, 1889, 250p,
      Cloth, Novel

FLEMING, MAY AGNES, 1840-1880

05478 *The midnight queen; a novel.* G. W. Dilling-
      ham, New York, 1888, 396p, Cloth, Novel

FLEMING, (Robert) PETER, 1907-1971

05479 *The flying visit.* Jonathan Cape, London,
      1940, 128p, Cloth, Novel
05480 *The sixth column; a singular tale of our times.*
      Rupert Hart-Davis, London, 1951, 224p, Cloth,
      Novel

FLES, BARTHOLD, 1902- [*biography included*]

05481 *The Saturday evening post fantasy stories.*
      Avon, New York, 1951, 126p, Paper, Anth.

FLETCHER, GEORGE U., pseud.
    see: PRATT, FLETCHER

FLETCHER, J(oseph) S(mith), 1863-1935

05482 *The air-ship, and other stories.* Digby, Long,
        London, 1903, 303p, Cloth, Coll.
05483 *The Matheson formula.* Alfred A. Knopf, New
        York, 1929, 276p, Cloth, Novel
05484 *The ransom for London.* John Long, London,
        1914, 295p, Cloth, Novel
05485 *The three days' terror.* John Long, London,
        1901, 307p, Cloth, Novel
05486 *The wonderful city.* Thomas Nelson & Sons,
        London, 1894, 185p, Cloth, Novel

FLETCHER, LAWRENCE

05487 *Into the unknown; a romance of South Africa.*
        Cassell, London, 1892, 215p, Cloth, Novel
        [Dick Grenville #1]
05488 *Zero the slaver; a romance of equatorial Afri-
        ca.* Cassell, London, 1892, 213p, Cloth,
        Novel [Dick Grenville #2]

FLIGHT ON TITAN
    see: HARBOTTLE, PHILIP

FLIGHT OUT OF FANCY

05489 *Flight out of fancy; an account of a brief
        detachment, or capriole, from the charted
        courses of the world, containing the writer's
        explanation of the hazards of his departure,
        of the puzzling rigours of his detention,
        and of the fortunate circumstances of his
        return.* Bodley Head, London, 1948, 116p,
        Cloth, Novel

FLINDERS, KARL, pseud. [Saul Milton]

05490 *The love machinery.* Olympia Press, New York,
        1971,   , Paper, Novel

FLINT, HOMER EON, d. 1924 [originally Homer
Eon Flindt]

05491 *The devolutionist; and, The emancipatrix.*
        Ace, New York, 1965, 191p, Paper, Coll.
05492 *The lord of death; and, The queen of life.*
        Ace, New York, 1965, 143p, Paper, Coll.

with Austin Hall:

05493 *The Blind Spot.* Prime Press, Philadelphia,
        1951, 293p, Cloth, Novel [Blind Spot #1]

FLOOD, CHARLES BRACELEN, 1929-   [*biography
included*]

05494 *Trouble at the top.* McGraw-Hill, New York,
        1972, 272p, Cloth, Novel

FLOOD, JNO. H. Jr. [John Heber Flood, 1863-   ]

05495 *The great seven--the greater nine; a story for
        the people.* W. B. Conkey, Chicago, 1897,
        162p, Cloth, Novel

FLORES, ANGEL, 1900-

05496 *Nineteenth century German tales.* Anchor, New
        York, 1959, 390p, Paper, Anth.

FLOREZ, WENCESLAO FERNANDEZ
    see: FERNANDEZ FLOREZ, WENCESLAO

FLOWERS, T. J.

05497 *Moonglow.* Midwood, New York, 1974, 215p,
        Paper, Novel

FOGG, LAWRENCE DANIEL, 1879-1914

05498 *The asbestos society of sinners, detailing the
        diversions of Dives and others on the play-
        ground of Pluto, with some broken threads
        of dropstitch history, picked up by a news-
        paper man in Hades, and woven into a Stygian
        nights' entertainment.* Mayhew Publishing
        Co., Boston, 1906, 163p, Cloth, Novel

FOLEŸ, CHARLES, 1861-

05499 *Kowa the mysterious.* Everett & Co., London,
        1909, 320p, Cloth, Novel

FOLEY, DAVE
    see: HATCH, GERALD

FOLINGSBY, KENNETH

05500 *Meda: a tale of the future.* Aird & Coghill,
        Dublin, 1891, 325p, Cloth, Novel

FON EISEN, ANTHONY (T.), 1911-   [*biography
included*]

05501 *Bond of the fire.* World Publishing Co., Cleve-
        land, 1965, 188p, Cloth, Novel

FONTANA, D(orothy) C.

05502 *The Questor tapes.* Ballantine, New York, 1974,
        156p, Paper, Tele.

FONTENAY, CHARLES L(ouis), 1917-   [*biography
included*]

05503 *The day the oceans overflowed.* Monarch, Derby,
        Conn., 1964, 128p, Paper, Novel
05504 *Rebels of the red planet.* Ace Double, New
        York, 1961, 143p, Paper, Novel
05505 *Twice upon a time.* Ace Double, New York,
        1958, 152p, Paper, Novel

FONTMELL, E. V. de, pseud.

  05506 *Forbidden marches.* Scholartis Press, London, 1929, 241p, Cloth, Novel

FOOT, MICHAEL MACKINTOSH
  see: CASSIUS

FOOTMAN, DAVID J(ohn), 1895–

  05507 *The mine in the desert.* John Long, London, 1929, 287p, Cloth, Novel

FORBES, ALEXANDER, 1882–

  05508 *The radio gunner.* Houghton Mifflin, Boston, 1924, 318p, Cloth, Novel [published anonymously]

FORBES, ARCHIBALD, 1838–1900, with P. Colomb, J. F. Maurice, F. N. Maude, Charles Lowe, D. Christie Murray, and F. Scudamore

  03229 *The Great War of 189–; a forecast.* William Heinemann, London, 1893, 308p, Cloth, Novel

FORBES, ESTHER, 1891–1967 [*biography included*]

  05509 *A mirror for witches, in which is reflected the life, machinations, and death of famous Doll Bilby, who, with a more than feminine perversity, preferred a demon to a mortal lover; here is also told how and why a righteous and most awfull judgement befell her, destroying both corporeal body and immortal soul.* Houghton Mifflin, Boston, 1928, 214p, Cloth, Novel

FORD, CHARLES HENRI, 1913–   [*biography included*]

  05510 *A night with Jupiter, and other fantastic stories.* View Editions, New York, 1945, 128p, Cloth, Anth.

FORD, CONSUELO URISARRI
  see: URN, ALTHEA

FORD, DOUGLAS MORET [published anonymously]

  05511 *The raid of Dover; a romance of the reign of woman, A.D. 1940.* King, Sell & Olding, London, 1910, 188p, Cloth, Novel
  05512 *A time of terror; the story of a great revenge (A.D. 1910).* Greening & Co., London, 1906, 340p, Cloth, Novel
  05512A retitled: *A time of terror, the story of a great revenge (A.D. 1912).* Hurst & Blackett, London, 1908, 174p, Cloth, Novel

FORD, FORD MADOX, pseud.
  see: HUEFFER, FORD MADOX

FORD, GARRET, pseud.
  see: CRAWFORD, WILLIAM L.

FORD, KEN, pseud.

  05513 *Prototype PZ-642.* Curtis Warren, London, 1952?, 111p, Paper, Novel

FORD, MIRIAM ALLEN de
  see: deFORD, MIRIAM ALLEN

FORD, T. MURRAY
  see: LE BRETON, THOMAS

FORD, WILLISTON MERRICK
  see: MERRICK, WILLISTON

FOREST, ELEANOR DE
  see: DE FOREST, ELEANOR

FOREST, SALAMBO, pseud. [Tina Bellini]

  05514 *Night of the wolf.* Ophelia Press, New York, 1969, 187p, Paper, Novel
  05515 *On my throbbing engine.* Ophelia Press, New York, 1970, 190p, Paper, Novel
  05516 *Pan on a rampage.* Ophelia Press, New York, 1970, 188p, Paper, Novel
  05517 *Witch power.* Olympia Press, New York, 1971, 215p, Paper, Novel

FORESTER, C(ecil) S(cott), 1899–1966

  05518 *The Peacemaker.* Little, Brown, Boston, 1934, 310p, Cloth, Novel

FORESTER, E(lspeth) LASCELLES

  05519 *'Ware wolf!* Cassell, London, 1928, 314p, Cloth, Novel

A FORMER RESIDENT OF "THE HUB," pseud.
  see: BACHELDER, JOHN

FORREST, ASTON

  05520 *The extraordinary islanders, being an authentic account of the cruise of the "Asphodel," as related by her owner.* R. A. Everett, London, 1903, 312p, Cloth, Novel

FORREST, DAVID, pseud.
  see: ELIADES, DAVID and FORREST-WEBB, ROBERT

FORREST, MARYANN

  05521 *Here (away from it all).* Michael Joseph, London, 1969, 210p, Cloth, Novel
  05521A retitled: *Here.* Coward-McCann, New York, 1970, 210p, Cloth, Novel

FORREST-WEBB, ROBERT, 1929-   [biography included], with David Eliades as David Forrest

04762   *After me, the deluge.* Hodder & Stoughton, London, 1972, 189p, Cloth, Novel
04763   *The undertaker's dozen.* Tandem, London, 1974, 160p, Paper, Coll.

FORRESTER, MARY

05522   *The seer.* Hutchinson, London, 1935, 288p, Cloth, Novel

FORSTER, E(dward) M(organ), 1879-1970

05523   *The celestial omnibus, and other stories.* Sidgwick & Jackson, London, 1911, 164p, Cloth, Coll.
05524   *Collected short stories of E. M. Forster.* Sidgwick & Jackson, London, 1947, 246p, Cloth, Coll. [includes 05523 and 05525]
05524A retitled: *The collected tales of E. M. Forster.* Alfred A. Knopf, New York, 1974, 308p, Cloth, Coll.
05525   *The eternal moment, and other stories.* Sidgwick & Jackson, London, 1928, 188p, Cloth, Coll.

FORTH, C.

05526   *The surprise of the Channel Tunnel (a sensational story of the future).* Wightman & Co., Liverpool, 1883, 22p, Paper, Story

FORTUNE, DION, pseud. [Violet Mary Firth, 1890-1946]

05527   *The demon lover.* Noel Douglas, London, 1927, 286p, Cloth, Novel
05528   *The goat-foot god.* Williams & Norgate, London, 1936, 383p, Cloth, Novel
05529   *Moon magic.* Aquarian Press, London, 1956, 241p, Cloth, Novel
05530   *The sea priestess.* The Author, London, 1938, 316p, Cloth, Novel
05531   *The secrets of Dr. Taverner.* Noel Douglas, London, 1926, 253p, Cloth, Novel
05532   *The winged bull; a romance of modern magic.* Williams & Norgate, London, 1935, 323p, Cloth, Novel

FOSTER, ALAN DEAN, 1946-   [biography included]

05533   *Bloodhype.* Ballantine, New York, 1973, 249p, Paper, Novel [AAnn #2]
05534   *Dark star.* Ballantine, New York, 1974, 183p, Paper, Movie
05535   *Icerigger.* Ballantine, New York, 1974, 313p, Paper, Novel
05536   *Luana.* Ballantine, New York, 1974, 182p, Paper, Movie
05537   *Star trek, log one.* Ballantine, New York, 1974, 184p, Paper, Tele. Coll. [Star Trek series]
05538   *Star trek, log two.* Ballantine, New York, 1974, 177p, Paper, Tele. Coll. [Star Trek series]

05539   *The Tar-Aiym Krang.* Ballantine, New York, 1972 252p, Paper, Novel [AAnn #1]

FOSTER, C(larence) E., 1919-

05540   *Journey to the future; a novel.* Exposition Press, New York, 1966, 204p, Cloth, Novel

FOSTER, DAVID SKAATS, 1852-1920

05541   *Prince Timoteo.* F. Tennyson Neely, London, 1899, 254p, Cloth, Novel

FOSTER, E. M.

05542   *The Duke of Clarence; an historical novel,* by E. M. F. William Lane, The Minerva-Press, London, 1795, 4vol, Cloth, Novel

FOSTER, GEORGE C(ecil), 1893-

05543   *Awakening.* Chapman & Hall, London, 1932, 308p, Cloth, Novel
05544   *The change.* Digit, London, 1963, 160p, Paper, Novel
05545   *Full fathom five.* Herbert Jenkins, London, 1930, 320p, Cloth, Novel
05546   *The lost garden.* Chapman & Hall, London, 1930, 267p, Cloth, Novel

as "Seaforth," pseud.:

05547   *Cats in the coffee.* Herbert Jenkins, London, 1938, 285p, Cloth, Novel
05548   *We band of brothers.* Herbert Jenkins, London, 1939, 288p, Cloth, Novel

FOSTER, L(ionel) B(rist)

05549   *The hocus root.* Hogbin, Poole, Sydney, 1944, 155p, Paper, Novel

FOSTER, R(eginald) FRANCIS, 1896-1975

05550   *Murder from beyond.* Eveleigh Nash & Grayson, London, 1930, 317p, Cloth, Novel

FOSTER, RICHARD, pseud.
   see: CROSSEN, KENDELL FOSTER

FOSTER, ROBERT, 1949-

05551   *A guide to Middle-Earth.* Mirage Press, Baltimore, 1971, 283p, Cloth, Nonf.

FOUGERET de MONBRON, (Louis-Charles), 1704-1761

05552   *The amorous adventures of Margot; and, The scarlet sofa.* Brandon House, North Hollywood, 1967, 174p, Paper, Coll.

FOUQUE, FRIEDRICH de LA MOTTE-
   see: LA MOTTE-FOUQUE, FRIEDRICH de

FOUR FUTURES

05553 *Four futures; four original novellas of science fiction.* Hawthorn, New York, 1971, 195p, Cloth, Anth.

FOUR-IN-ONE WEIRD AND OCCULT SHORTS

05554 *Four-in-one weird and occult shorts.* Gerald G. Swan, London, 1949, 144p, Paper, Anth.

FOUR THRILLING ADVENTURE NOVELS

05555 *Four thrilling adventure novels; Hearts of three, by Jack London; The crystal skull, by Jack McLaren; The master of Merripit, by Eden Phillpotts; Shadows by the sea, by J. Jefferson Farjeon.* Odhams Press, London, 1938, 704p, Cloth, Anth.

FOWLER, GEO(rge)

05556 *A flight to the Moon; or, The vision of Randalthus.* A. Miltenberger, Baltimore, 1813, 185p, Cloth, Novel

FOWLER, SYDNEY, pseud.
see: WRIGHT, S. FOWLER

FOX, DAVID, pseud. [Isabel Egenton Ostrander, 1883-1924]

05557 *The man who convicted himself.* Robert M. McBride, New York, 1920, 308p, Cloth, Novel

FOX, GARDNER F(rancis), 1911- [*biography included*]

05558 *The arsenal of miracles.* Ace Double, New York, 1964, 156p, Paper, Novel
05559 *Conehead.* Ace, New York, 1973, 224p, Paper, Novel
05560 *Escape across the cosmos.* Paperback Library, New York, 1964, 160p, Paper, Novel
05561 *The hunter out of time.* Ace, New York, 1965, 126p, Paper, Novel
05562 *Kothar and the conjurer's curse.* Belmont, New York, 1970, 156p, Paper, Novel [Kothar #4]
05563 *Kothar and the demon queen.* Tower, New York, 1969, 155p, Paper, Novel [Kothar #3]
05564 *Kothar and the wizard slayer.* Belmont, New York, 1970, 156p, Paper, Novel [Kothar #5]
05565 *Kothar, barbarian swordsman.* Belmont, New York, 1969, 153p, Paper, Novel [Kothar #1]
05566 *Kothar of the magic sword!* Belmont, New York, 1969, 154p, Paper, Novel [Kothar #2]
05567 *Thief of Llarn.* Ace, New York, 1966, 158p, Paper, Novel [Alan Morgan #2]
05568 *Warrior of Llarn.* Ace, New York, 1964, 160p, Paper, Novel [Alan Morgan #1]

as Simon Majors:

05569 *The druid stone.* Paperback Library, New York, 1967, 157p, Paper, Novel

as Bart Somers:

05570 *Abandon galaxy!* Paperback Library, New York, 1967, 160p, Paper, Novel [Commander Craig Galactic Adventure #2]
05571 *Beyond the black Enigma.* Paperback Library, New York, 1965, 156p, Paper, Novel [Commander Craig Galactic Adventure #1]

FOX, GEORGE (Richard), 1934- [*biography included*]

05572 *Earthquake; the story of a movie.* Signet, New York, 1974, 128p, Paper, Movie [includes some nonf.]

FOX, LESLIE H.

05573 *The vampire, and sixteen other stories.* Alliance Press, London, 1945, 32p, Paper, Coll.

FOX, Lady MARY

05574 *Account of an expedition to the interior of New Holland.* Richard Bentley, London, 1837, 243p, Cloth, Novel
05574A retitled: *The Southlanders; an account of an expedition to the interior of New Holland.* J. W. Parker & Son, London, 1860, 216p, Cloth, Novel

FOX, NETTIE PEASE

05575 *Mysteries of the border land; or, The conscious side of unconscious life.* D. M. & N. P. Fox, Ottumwa, Iowa, 1883, 536p, Cloth, Coll.

FOX, RICHARD A.

05576 *The people on other planets.* Walter Southworth, Benton Harbor, Mich., 1925, 118p, Cloth, Novel

FOX, SAMUEL MIDDLETON, 1856- [published anonymously]

05577 *Our own Pompeii; a romance of to-morrow.* William Blackwood & Sons, Edinburgh, 1887, 2vol, Cloth, Novel

FOX-DAVIES, A(rthur) C(harles), 1871-1928

05578 *The sex triumphant.* George Routledge & Sons, London, 1909, 166p, Cloth, Novel

FRAME, JANET (Paterson), 1924- [*biography included*]

05579 *Intensive care; a novel.* George Braziller, New York, 1970, 342p, Cloth, Novel

FRANCE, ANATOLE, pseud. [Jacques Anatole Thibault, 1844-1924]

05580	*Golden tales of Anatole France.* Dodd, Mead, New York, 1926, 352p, Cloth, Coll. *Mother of pearl.* [see 05584A]
05581	*Penguin Island.* John Lane, The Bodley Head, London, 1909, 345p, Cloth, Novel
05582	*The revolt of the angels.* John Lane, The Bodley Head, 1914, 348p, Cloth, Novel
05583	*The six greatest novels of Anatole France: Penguin Island; The crime of Sylvestre Bonnard; The revolt of the angels; The gods are athirst; Thaïs; The red lily.* Garden City Publishing Co., Garden City, 1936?, 966p, Cloth, Coll.
05584	*Tales from a mother-of-pearl casket.* G. H. Richmond, New York, 1896, 247p, Cloth, Coll.
05584A	retitled: *Mother of pearl.* John Lane, The Bodley Head, London, 1908, 291p, Cloth, Coll.
05585	*Thaïs.* N. C. Smith Publishing Co., Chicago, 1891, 205p, Cloth, Novel
05586	*The well of St. Clare.* John Lane, The Bodley Head, London, 1909, 302p, Cloth, Novel

FRANCIS, FRANCIS, d. 1941

05587	*Mother of gold.* Wright & Brown, London, 1931, 284p, Cloth, Novel

FRANCIS, MARIANNE

05588	*Egyptian light.* Regency Press, London, 1957, 160p, Cloth, Novel

FRANCIS-WILLIAMS, BARON
see: WILLIAMS, FRANCIS

FRANK, ALAN G.

05589	*The movie treasury: horror movies; tales of terror in the cinema.* Octopus Books, London, 1974, 160p, Cloth, Nonf.

FRANK, JOSEPH, 1916-	[*biography included*]

05590	*The doomed astronaut.* Winthrop Publishers, Cambridge, Mass., 1972, 158p, Cloth, Anth.

FRANK, PAT (Harry Hart), 1907-1964 [*biography included*]

05591	*Alas Babylon; a novel.* J. B. Lippincott, Philadelphia, 1959, 253p, Cloth, Novel
05592	*Forbidden area.* J. B. Lippincott, Philadelphia, 1956, 252p, Cloth, Novel
05592A	retitled: *Seven days to never.* Constable, London, 1957, 252p, Cloth, Novel
05593	*Mr. Adam; a novel.* J. B. Lippincott, Philadelphia, 1946, 252p, Cloth, Novel
Seven days to never. [see 05592A]

FRANK, ROBERT, 1893-

05594	*Social integration; a brief fictional history of the United States during the period 1935-1945.* Christopher Publishing House, Boston, 1935, 199p, Cloth, Novel

FRANK, WALDO (David), 1889-1967

05595	*Chalk face.* Boni & Liveright, New York, 1924, 252p, Cloth, Novel
05596	*The invaders; a novel.* Duell, Sloan & Pearce, New York, 1948, 239p, Cloth, Novel

FRANKAU, GILBERT, 1884-1952

05597	*The seeds of enchantment, being some attempt to narrate the curious discoveries of Doctor Cyprian Beamish, M.D., Glasgow; Commandant René De Gys, Annamite Army; and the Honourable Richard Assheton Smith, in the golden land of Indo-China.* Hutchinson, London, 1921, 327p, Cloth, Novel
05598	*Son of the morning.* Macdonald, London, 1949, 432p, Cloth, Novel
05599	*Unborn tomorrow; a last story.* Macdonald, London, 1953, 302p, Cloth, Novel

FRANKAU, JULIA
see: DANBY, FRANK

FRANKAU, (Sydney) PAMELA, 1908-1967

05600	*The bridge.* Heinemann, London, 1957, 299p, Cloth, Novel
05601	*Sing for your supper; a novel.* Heinemann, London, 1963, 293p, Cloth, Novel [Clothes of a King's Son #1]
05602	*Slaves of the lamp.* Heinemann, London, 1965, 421p, Cloth, Novel [Clothes of a King's Son #2]

FRANKE, HERBERT W(erner), 1927-

05603	*The mind net.* DAW, New York, 1974, 173p, Paper, Novel
05604	*The orchid cage.* DAW, New York, 1973, 174p, Paper, Novel
05605	*Zone null.* A Continuum Book, Seabury Press, New York, 1974, 214p, Cloth, Novel

FRANKENSTEIN
see: SHELLEY, MARY WOLLSTONECRAFT

FRANKISH, H.

05606	*Dr Cunliffe, investigator.* [sic] Heath, Cranton & Ouseley, London, 1913, 317p, Cloth, Coll.

FRANKLIN, EDGAR, pseud. [Edgar Franklin Stearns, 1879-]

05607	*Mr. Hawkins' humorous adventure.* Dodge Publishing Co., New York, 1904, 323p, Cloth, Coll.

FRANKLIN, H(oward) BRUCE, 1934- [*biography included*]

05608	*Future perfect; American science fiction of the nineteenth century.* Oxford University Press, New York, 1966, 402p, Cloth, Anth. [includes some nonf.]

FRANKLIN, JAY, pseud. [John Franklin Carter, 1897-1967]

05609   *Champagne Charlie.* Duell, Sloan & Pearce, New York, 1950, 190p, Cloth, Novel
05610   *The rat race.* Fantasy Publishing Co., Los Angeles, 1950, 371p, Cloth, Novel

FRANSON, DONALD (Lewis), 1916-   [*biography included*]

05611   *Fandbook no. 1; a key to the terminology of science-fiction fandom.* National Fantasy Fan Federation, Heiskell, 1962, 17p, Paper, Nonf.

with Howard DeVore:

04275   *A history of the Hugo, Nebula, and International Fantasy Award, listing nominees & winners, 1951-1970.* Sciencefiction Sales, Dearborn Heights, Mich., 1969, 45p, Paper, Nonf.

with Michael Viggiano:

05612   *Science fiction title changes; a guide to the changing titles of science fiction and fantasy stories published in magazines and books.* National Fantasy Fan Federation, Heiskell, 1965, 47p, Paper, Nonf.

FRASER, ANTHEA, 1930-

05613   *Laura possessed.* Milton House Books, London, 1974, 239p, Cloth, Novel

FRASER, PHYLLIS (Maurine), 1915-   , with Herbert A. Wise

05614   *Great tales of terror and the supernatural.* Random House, New York, 1944, 1080p, Cloth, Anth.

FRASER, (Sir Arthur) RONALD, 1888-1974

05615   *Beetle's career.* Jonathan Cape, London, 1951, 160p, Cloth, Novel
05616   *The fiery gate.* Jonathan Cape, London, 1943, 183p, Cloth, Novel
05617   *The flying draper.* T. Fisher Unwin, London, 1924, 315p, Cloth, Novel
05618   *Jupiter in the chair.* Jonathan Cape, London, 1958, 190p, Cloth, Novel [Venus #2]
05619   *Landscape with figures.* T. Fisher Unwin, London, 1925, 285p, Cloth, Novel
05620   *Miss Lucifer.* Jonathan Cape, London, 1939, 316p, Cloth, Novel
05621   *Sun in Scorpio.* Jonathan Cape, London, 1949, 351p, Cloth, Novel
05622   *Trout's testament.* Jonathan Cape, London, 1960, 191p, Cloth, Novel [Venus #3]
05623   *A visit from Venus.* Jonathan Cape, London, 1958, 188p, Cloth, Novel [Venus #1]

FRASER, W(illiam) A(lexander), 1859-1933

05624   *The outcasts.* William Briggs, Toronto, 1901, 138p, Cloth, Novel

FRATER VIII°, pseud.

05625   *Outwitting tomorrow.* Golden Dawn Press, Los Angeles, 1948, 64p, Paper, Novel

FRAYN, MICHAEL (J.), 1933-   [*biography included*]

05626   *Sweet dreams.* Collins, London, 1973, 223p, Cloth, Novel
05627   *The tin men.* Collins, London, 1965, 191p, Cloth, Novel
05628   *A very private life.* Collins, London, 1968, 192p, Cloth, Novel

FRAZAR, DOUGLAS, 1836-1896

05629   *Perserverance Island; or, The Robinson Crusoe of the nineteenth century.* Lee & Shepard, Boston, 1884, 373p, Cloth, Novel

FRAZEE, STEVE [Charles Stephen Frazee, 1909-] [*biography included*]

05630   *The sky block.* Rinehart & Co., New York, 1953, 247p, Cloth, Novel

FRAZER, SHAMUS [James Ian Arbuthnot Frazer, 1912-   ]

05631   *Blow, blow your trumpets; a novel.* Chapman & Hall, London, 1945, 291p, Cloth, Novel

FREDRICK, OTTO

05632   *Count Dracula's Canadian affair.* Pageant Press, New York, 1960, 118p, Cloth, Novel [Dracula series]

FREE, COLIN, 1925-

05633   *The soft kill.* Berkley Medallion, New York, 1973, 159p, Paper, Novel

FREEDMAN, NANCY, 1920-   [*biography included*]

05634   *Joshua, son of none.* Delacorte Press, New York, 1973, 291p, Cloth, Novel

FREEDMAN, RUSSELL (Bruce), 1929-   [*biography included*]

05635   *2000 years of space travel.* Holiday House, New York, 1963, 256p, Cloth, Nonf. [includes many excerpts from SF works]

FREEMAN, KATHLEEN, 1897-1959

05636   *Adventure from the grave.* Peter Davies, London, 1936, 284p, Cloth, Novel

FREEMAN, MARY E. WILKINS
   see: WILKINS, MARY E.

FREEMAN, R(obert) M(assie), 1866-

05637   *The new Boswell.* John Lane, The Bodley Head,
        London, 1922, 242p, Cloth, Novel

FREER, A. GOODRICH-
    see: GOODRICH-FREER, A.

FREMLIN, CELIA (Margaret Goller), 1914-
[*biography included*]

05638   *By horror haunted; stories.* Victor Gollancz,
        London, 1974, 160p, Cloth, Coll.

FRENCH, JOSEPH LEWIS, 1858-1936

05639   *The best ghost stories.* Boni & Liveright,
        New York, 1919, 217p, Cloth, Anth. [published
        anonymously; includes some nonf.]
05640   *The best psychic stories.* Boni & Liveright,
        New York, 1920, 299p, Cloth, Anth.
05641   *The ghost story omnibus.* Dodd, Mead, New
        York, 1933, 672p, Cloth, Anth. [includes
        05642 and 05643]
05642   *Ghosts, grim and gentle; a collection of moving
        ghost stories.* Dodd, Mead, New York, 1926,
        292p, Cloth, Anth.
05643   *Great ghost stories.* Dodd, Mead, New York,
        1918, 365p, Cloth, Anth.
05644   *Masterpieces of mystery in four volumes; ghost
        stories.* Doubleday, Page, Garden City, 1920,
        241p, Cloth, Anth.
05645   *Masterpieces of mystery in four volumes; mys-
        tic-humorous stories.* Doubleday, Page, Gar-
        den City, 1920, 265p, Cloth, Anth.
05646   *Masterpieces of mystery in four volumes; riddle
        stories.* Doubleday, Page, Garden City, 1920,
        258p, Cloth, Anth.
05647   *Tales of terror.* Small, Maynard, Boston, 1925,
        224p, Cloth, Anth.

A FRENCH AUTHOR
    see: N., N.

A FRENCH STAFF OFFICER, pseud.

05648   *The English invasion of Germany.* David Nutt,
        London, 1910, 70p, Paper, Novel

FRETLAND, D(onald) JOHN

05649   *The Persimmon Sequence; part I of the Oleandre
        Trilogy, a science fiction epic.* Apollo,
        Woodbridge, Conn., 1971, 252p, Paper, Novel
        [Oleandre Trilogy #1]
05650   *Winds of the Heliopolis; part II of the Ole-
        andre Trilogy, a science fiction epic.*
        Apollo, Woodbridge, Conn., 1972, 198p, Paper,
        Novel [Oleandre Trilogy #2] [section 3 never
        issued]

FREUDENTHAL, ELISABETH

05651   *Fantastic reality.* Vantage Press, New York,
        1969, 95p, Cloth, Novel

FREWER, GLYN (Mervyn Louis), 1931-   [*biography included*]

05652   *Adventure in forgotten valley.* Faber & Faber,
        London, 1962, 195p, Cloth, Novel

FREWIN, ANTHONY, 1947-

05653   *One hundred years of science fiction illustra-
        tion, 1840-1940.* Jupiter Books, London,
        1974, 128p, Cloth, Nonf.

FREYER, DERMOT J.

05654   *Night on the river, a queer story; together
        with Two stories of childhood; &, The cloud,
        a love episode.* W. Hefner & Sons, Cambridge,
        UK, 1923, 85p, Cloth, Coll.

FRIEDBERG, GERTRUDE, 1908-   [*biography included*]

05655   *The revolving boy.* Doubleday, Garden City,
        1966, 191p, Cloth, Novel

FRIEDELL, EGON, 1878-1938

05656   *The return of the Time Machine.* DAW, New York,
        1972, 127p, Paper, Novel [sequel to H. G.
        Wells's *The time machine*]

FRIEDLI, EMILIE IDA
    see: VAN ITH, LILY

FRIEDMAN, FAVIUS (Louis)

05657   *Great horror movies.* Scholastic Book Services,
        New York, 1974, 160p, Paper, Nonf.

FRIEDMAN, JERROLD DAVID
    see: GERROLD, DAVID

FRIEL, ARTHUR O(lney), 1885-1959

05658   *The King of No Man's Land.* Harper & Bros.,
        New York, 1924, 347p, Cloth, Novel [McKay,
        Knowlton & Ryan series]
05659   *Mountains of mystery.* Harper & Bros., New
        York, 1925, 399p, Cloth, Novel [McKay, Knowl-
        ton & Ryan series]
05660   *The pathless trail.* Harper & Bros., New York,
        1922, 337p, Cloth, Novel [McKay, Knowlton &
        Ryan series]
05661   *Tiger River.* Harper & Bros., New York, 1923,
        352p, Cloth, Novel [McKay, Knowlton & Ryan
        series]

FRIEND, BEVERLY

05662   *Science fiction: the classroom in orbit.* Edu-
        cational Impact, Glassboro, NJ, 1974, 92p,
        Paper, Nonf.
05663   *Science fiction: the classroom in orbit; a
        supplement.* Educational Impact, Glassboro,
        NJ, 1974, 15p, Paper, Nonf.

FRIEND, ED, pseud.
    see: WORMSER, RICHARD

FRIEND, OSCAR J(erome), 1898-1963 [*biography included*]

05664 *The Kid from Mars*. Frederick Fell, New York,
           1949, 270p, Cloth, Novel
05665 *Roar of the rocket*. Fantasy Fiction, Sydney,
           1950, 32p, Paper, Story
05666 *The star men*. Avalon, New York, 1963, 221p,
           Cloth, Novel

as Owen Fox Jerome:

05667 *The hand of horror*. Edward J. Clode, New York,
           1927, 309p, Cloth, Novel

with Leo Margulies:

05668 *From off this world; gems of science fiction*.
           Merlin Press, New York, 1949, 430p, Cloth,
           Anth.
05669 *The giant anthology of science fiction; 10
           complete short novels*. Merlin Press, New
           York, 1954, 580p, Cloth, Anth.
05669A retitled: *Race to the stars*. Crest, Green-
           wich, 1958, 224p, Paper, Anth. [abridged]
05670 *My best science fiction story, as selected by
           25 outstanding authors*. Merlin Press, New
           York, 1949, 556p, Cloth, Anth.
           Race to the stars. [see 05669A]

THE FRIEND OF DEATH
    see: ALARCON, PEDRO de

FRIERSON, MEADE (III), 1940-   [*biography included*]

05671 *Science fiction on radio*. Meade Frierson,
           Birmingham, Ala., 1973, 54p, Paper, Nonf.

with Penny Frierson:

05672 *HPL*. Meade & Penny Frierson, Birmingham,
           1972, 143p, Cloth, Nonf. Anth.

FRIERSON, PENNY, with Meade Frierson

05672 *HPL*. Meade & Penny Frierson, Birmingham,
           1972, 143p, Cloth, Nonf. Anth.

FRIGGENS, ARTHUR (Henry), 1920-   [*biography included*], with Eric Burgess

02211 *Anti-Zota*. Robert Hale, London, 1973, 189p,
           Cloth, Novel
02212 *Mortorio*. Robert Hale, London, 1973, 192p,
           Cloth, Novel

FRINGS, KETTI

05673 *God's front porch; a novel*. William Morrow,
           New York, 1944, 121p, Cloth, Novel

FRITCH, CHARLES E.

05674 *Crazy mixed up planet*. Powell Publications,
           Reseda, CA, 1969, 203p, Paper, Coll.

05675 *Horses' asteroid*. Powell Publications, Reseda,
           CA, 1970, 206p, Paper, Coll.

FROM THE "S" FILE
    see: RUSSELL, RAY

FROST, BRIAN J.

05676 *Book of the werewolf*. Sphere, London, 1973,
           325p, Paper, Anth.

FROST, FRANCES (Mary), 1905-1959

05677 *Village of glass*. Farrar & Rinehart, New
           York, 1942, 273p, Cloth, Novel

FROST, KELMAN (Dalgety)

05678 *The riddle of the Caid's jewels*. Abelard-
           Schuman, London, 1969, 160p, Cloth, Novel
05678A retitled: *Men of the Mirage*. Lothrop, Lee &
           Shepard, New York, 1969, 160p, Cloth, Novel

THE FROZEN PLANET

05679 *The frozen planet, and other stories*. Macfad-
           den-Bartell, New York, 1966, 160p, Paper,
           Anth.

FRUEH, A(lfred) J(oseph), with I. L. Gordon

05680 *The log of the Ark, by Noah; hieroglyphics by
           Ham*. E. P. Dutton, New York, 1915, 147p,
           Cloth, Novel

FRY, H. R.

05681 *Amateur ghost stories*. Barclay & Fry, London,
           1932, 62p, Cloth, Coll.

FRY, NICHOLAS, with Allen Eyles and Robert
Adkinson

00062 *The house of horror; the story of Hammer Films*.
           Lorrimer Publishing, London, 1973, 127p,
           Paper, Nonf.

FRYE, VERN D.
    see: DERMOTT, VERN

FRYERS, AUSTIN, pseud. [William Edward Clery]

05682 *The devil and the inventor*. C. Arthur Pearson,
           London, 1900, 272p, Cloth, Novel

FUENTES, ROBERTO, 1934-   , with Piers Anthony

00379 *The bamboo bloodbath*. Berkley Medallion, New
           York, 1974, 188p, Paper, Novel [Jason Striker
           #3]
00380 *Kiai!* Berkley Medallion, New York, 1974, 191p,
           Paper, Novel [Jason Striker #1]

FUENTES, ROBERTO, with Piers Anthony (cont.)

00381 *Mistress of death.* Berkley Medallion, New
           York, 1974, 192p, Paper, Novel [Jason Stri-
           ker #2]

A FUGITIVE, pseud.
    see: COXE, EDWARD D.

FULLER, Miss (Anne), d. 1790

05683 *Alan Fitz-Osborne; an historical tale.* P.
           Byrne, Dublin, 1786, 2vol, Cloth, Novel

FULLER, Lieut. ALVARADO M(ortimer), 1851-

05684 *A.D. 2000.* Laird & Lee, Chicago, 1890, 415p,
           Cloth, Novel
05684A retitled: *Back to life (A.D. 2000); a thril-
           ling novel.* Laird & Lee, Chicago, 1911,
           415p, Paper, Novel

FULLER, FREDERICK T.

05685 *Beyond the Selvas; a vision of a republic that
           might have been--and still might be.* Author,
           Boston, 1929, 95p, Cloth, Novel

FULLER, IRA C.

05686 *Mysteries of Earth, continents, and man re-
           vealed.* Charles Wells Moulton, Buffalo, NY,
           1899,   , Cloth, Novel

FULLER, LOIS HAMILTON, 1915-   [*biography included*]

05687 *Keo, the cave boy.* Abingdon Press, New York,
           1961, 128p, Cloth, Novel

FULLER, ROGER, pseud.
    see: TRACY, DON

FULLER, SAM(uel Michael), 1911-

05688 *Test tube baby.* Godwin Publishers, New York,
           1936, 292p, Cloth, Novel

FULLERTON, (John) CHARLES (Mark), 1924-

05689 *The man who spoke dog.* Harvill Press, London,
           1959, 159p, Cloth, Novel

THE FULLY AUTOMATED LOVE LIFE OF HENRY KEAN-
RIDGE
    see: RUSSELL, RAY

FUNARO, SERGIO (F.), 1922-

05690 *How it all ended; the decline and demise of
           the West as reconstructed by Johann Sebas-
           tian Barberini in the year of our Lord 4776.*
           A. M. Aronowitz, New York, 1973, 152p, Cloth,
           Novel

FUREY, MICHAEL, pseud.
    see: ROHMER, SAX

FURMAN, A(braham) L(oew), 1902-

           Outer space stories. [see 05691A]
05691 *Teen-age outer space stories.* Lantern Press,
           New York, 1962, 190p, Cloth, Anth.
05691A retitled: *Outer space stories.* Lantern Pocket
           Books, New York, 1965, 173p, Paper, Anth.
05692 *Teenage space adventures.* Lantern Press, New
           York, 1972, 192p, Cloth, Anth.

FURNAS, J(oseph) C(hamberlain), 1905-

05693 *Lightfoot Island.* Atheneum, New York, 1968,
           271p, Cloth, Novel

FURNELL, JOHN, pseud.

05694 *The dark portal.* Skeffington & Son, London,
           1950, 288p, Cloth, Novel

FURNILL, JOHN

05695 *Culmination.* Elkin Mathews & Marriot, London,
           1932, 534p, Cloth, Novel

FUSEE, CLAUDE HENRI
    see: VOISENON, Abbe de

FUTRELLE, JACQUES, 1875-1912

05696 *The diamond master.* Bobbs-Merrill, Indiana-
           polis, 1909, 212p, Cloth, Coll.

FUTURE, STEVE, pseud.

05697 *Doomed nation of the skies!* Tit-Bits Science
           Fiction Library, London, 1953, 64p, Paper,
           Novel
05698 *Slave traders of the sky.* Tit-Bits Science
           Fiction Library, London, 1954, 64p, Paper,
           Novel

FUTURISTIC STORIES

05699 *Futuristic stories.* Hamilton & Co. (Stafford
           London, 1946, 48p, Paper, Anth.

FYFE, H(orace) B(owne Jr.), 1918-   [*biography included*]

05700 *D-99; a science-fiction novel.* Pyramid, New
           York, 1962, 144p, Paper, Novel

FYNE, NEAL, pseud.

05701 *The land of the living dead; a narration of
           the perilous sojourn therein of George Cow-
           per, mariner, in the year 1835.* Henry J.
           Drane, London, 1897, 251p, Cloth, Novel

FYSH, pseud.

05702 *Planet war.* Archer Press, London, 1952, 96p, Paper, Novel

G., T. S.
see: GUEULLETTE, THOMAS SIMON

GABRIEL OVER THE WHITE HOUSE
see: TWEED, THOMAS F.

GAIL, WILLI OTTO, 1896-1956

05703 *By rocket to the Moon; the story of Hans Hardt's miraculous flight.* Sears Publishing Co., New York, 1931, 303p, Cloth, Novel

GAILLARD, STEPHEN

05704 *The pirates of the sky; a tale of modern adventure.* Rand McNally, Chicago, 1915, 351p, Cloth, Novel

GAINES, AUDREY

05705 *The voodoo goat.* Thomas Y. Crowell, New York, 1942, 255p, Cloth, Novel

GAINESS, ARTHUR A.

05706 *The woman marches; a novel.* Parker, Stone & Baird, Los Angeles, 1936, 225p, Paper, Novel

GALAXY CHECKLIST

05707 *Galaxy checklist.* British Science Fiction Association, England, 195?, 60p, Paper, Nonf.

GALBRAITH, ALEXANDER
see: WILSON, SANDY

GALBRAITH, JOHN KENNETH, 1908-   [*biography included*]

05708 *The McLandress dimension,* by Mark Epernay. Houghton Mifflin, Boston, 1963, 126p, Cloth, Novel
05708A *The McLandress dimension,* by John Kenneth Galbraith. Signet, New York, 1968, 126p, Paper, Novel [slightly revised]

GALE, E. F.
see: FALKNER, JOHN

GALE, OLIVER MARBLE, 1877-

05709 *Carnack, the life-bringer; the story of a dawn man told by himself.* Wm. H. Wise & Co., New York, 1928, 378p, Cloth, Novel

GALE, ZONA, 1874-1938

05710 *Romance island.* Bobbs-Merrill, Indianapolis, 1906, 394p, Cloth, Novel

GALL, EDWARD R. HOME-
see: HOME-GALL, EDWARD R.

GALL, W. B. HOME-
see: WRAY, REGINALD

GALLANT, JOSEPH, 1907-1957

05711 *Stories of scientific imagination.* Oxford Book Co., New York, 1954, 152p, Paper, Anth.

GALLEGO, S. G.
see: GONZALES GALLEGO, S.

GALLERY, DANIEL V(incent), 1901-

05712 *The brink.* Doubleday, Garden City, 1968, 317p, Cloth, Novel

GALLI de BIBIENA, JEAN, 1710?-1780?

05713 *The fairy doll (la poupée).* Chapman & Hall, London, 1925, 153p, Cloth, Novel
05713A retitled: *Amorous Philandre.* Avon, New York, 1948, 124p, Paper, Novel

GALLICO, PAUL (William), 1897-1976 [*biography included*]

05714 *The abandoned.* Alfred A. Knopf, New York, 1950, 307p, Cloth, Novel
05715 *The foolish immortals.* Doubleday, Garden City, 1953, 224p, Cloth, Novel
05716 *Ludmila; a story of Liechtenstein.* Quick, Vaduz, Liech., 1954, 53p, Cloth, Novel
05717 *The man who was magic; a tale of innocence.* Doubleday, Garden City, 1966, 203p, Cloth, Novel
05718 *The silent miaow; a manual for kittens, strays, and homeless cats.* Crown Publishers, New York, 1964, 159p, Cloth, Novel
05719 *Thomasina; the cat who thought she was God.* Doubleday, Garden City, 1957, 288p, Cloth, Novel
Three legends. [see 05720A]
05720 *Three stories.* Michael Joseph, London, 1964, 118p, Cloth, Coll.
05720A retitled: *Three legends: The snow goose; The small miracle; Ludmila.* Doubleday, Garden City, 1966, 126p, Cloth, Coll.
05721 *Too many ghosts.* Doubleday, Garden City, 1959, 288p, Cloth, Novel

GALLION, JANE

05722 *Biker.* Essex House, North Hollywood, 1969, 159p, Paper, Novel

GALLIZIER, NATHAN, 1866-1927

05723   *The court of Lucifer; a tale of the Renaissance.*
        L. C. Page, Boston, 1910, 464p, Cloth, Novel
        [third in trilogy]
05724   *The sorceress of Rome.* The Page Co., Boston,
        1907, 463p, Cloth, Novel [second in trilogy]
        [the first in this series is *Castel del Mon-
        te; a romance of the fall of the Hohenstaufen
        Dynasty in Italy* (1905)]
05725   *Under the witches' moon; a romantic tale of
        medieval Rome.* The Page Co., Boston, 1917,
        455p, Cloth, Novel

GALLON, TOM, 1866-1914

05726   *The charity ghost; a tale of Christmas.* Hut-
        chinson, London, 1902, 311p, Cloth, Novel

GALLOWAY, JAMES M.

05727   *John Harvey; a tale of the twentieth century,*
        by Anon Moore. Charles H. Kerr, Chicago,
        1897, 407p, Cloth, Novel
05727A retitled: *Lock and key,* by James M. Galloway.
        G. W. Dillingham, New York, 1899, 407p,
        Cloth, Novel

GALLUN, RAYMOND Z(inke), 1910-   [*biography
included*]

05728   *The Eden cycle.* Ballantine, New York, 1974,
        232p, Paper, Novel
05729   *People minus X; a science-fiction novel.* Simon
        & Schuster, New York, 1957, 186p, Cloth,
        Novel
05730   *The planet strappers.* Pyramid, New York, 1961,
        157p, Paper, Novel

as William Callahan:

05731   *The machine that thought.* Columbia Publica-
        tions, New York, 1942?, 24p, Paper, Story

with Eando Binder, Jack Williamson, Edmond
Hamilton, and John Russell Fearn:

01304   *The great illusion.* Fantasy Booklet, Wallsend,
        UK, 1973, 12p, Paper, Story

GALOUYE, DANIEL F(rancis), 1920-1976 [*biography included*]

05732   *Counterfeit world.* Victor Gollancz, London,
        1964, 159p, Cloth, Novel
05732A retitled: *Simulacron-3.* Bantam, New York,
        1964, 152p, Paper, Novel
05733   *Dark universe.* Bantam, New York, 1961, 154p,
        Paper, Novel
05734   *The infinite man.* Bantam, New York, 1973,
        202p, Paper, Novel
05735   *The last leap, and other stories of the super
        mind.* Corgi, London, 1964, 172p, Paper,
        Coll.
05736   *Lords of the Psychon.* Bantam, New York, 1963,
        153p, Paper, Novel
05737   *The lost perception.* Victor Gollancz, London,
        1966, 190p, Cloth, Novel
05737A retitled: *A scourge of screamers.* Bantam,
        New York, 1968, 172p, Paper, Novel

05738   *Project barrier.* Victor Gollancz, London,
        1968, 208p, Cloth, Coll.
        A scourge of screamers. [see 05737A]
        Simulacron-3. [see 05732A]

GALT, JOHN, 1779-1839

05739   *The Spaewife; a tale of the Scottish chronicl*
        by the author of "Annals of the parish,"
        "A Ringan Gilhaize," &c. Oliver & Boyd,
        Edinburgh, 1823, vol. I-312p, II-318p, III-
        315p, Cloth, Novel

GAMMON, DAVID (J.)

05740   *The secret of the sacred lake.* Lutterworth
        Press, Redhill, UK, 1947, 240p, Cloth, Nove

GAMON, RICHARD B.

05741   *The strange thirteen.* Drane's, London, 1925,
        365p, Cloth, Coll.

GAMOW, GEORGE (Antony), 1904-1968

05742   *Mr. Tompkins explores the atom.* Cambridge
        University Press, Cambridge, UK, 1944, 97p,
        Cloth, Novel [Mr. Tompkins #2]
05743   *Mr. Tompkins in paperback.* Cambridge Univer-
        sity Press, Cambridge, UK, 1965, 185p, Pape
        Coll. [includes 05742 and 05744; Mr. Tompki
        #s 1-2]
05744   *Mr. Tompkins in Wonderland; or, Stories of
        c, G, & h.* Cambridge University Press, Cam
        bridge, 1939, 91p, Cloth, Novel [Mr. Tompki
        #1]
05745   *Mr. Tompkins learns the facts of life.* Cam-
        bridge University Press, Cambridge, UK, 195
        87p, Cloth, Novel [Mr. Tompkins #3]

with Martynas Ycas:

05746   *Mr. Tompkins inside himself; adventures in th
        new biology.* Viking Press, New York, 1967,
        274p, Cloth, Novel [Mr. Tompkins #4]

GANDON, YVES, 1899-

05747   *The last white man; a novel.* Cassell, London
        1948, 254p, Cloth, Novel

GANN, W(illiam) D., 1878-1955

05748   *The tunnel thru the air; or, Looking back fro
        1940.* Financial Guardian Publishing Co.,
        New York, 1927, 418p, Cloth, Novel

"GANPAT," pseud. [Martin Louis Alan Gompertz,
1886-1951]

05749   *Fairy silver; a traveller's tale.* Hodder &
        Stoughton, London, 1932, 320p, Cloth, Novel
05750   *Harilek; a romance of modern central Asia.*
        William Blackwood & Sons, Edinburgh, 1923,
        342p, Cloth, Novel [Sakaeland #1]
05751   *Mirror of dreams; a tale of Oriental mystery.*
        Hodder & Stoughton, London, 1928, 319p, Clo
        Novel

"GANPAT," pseud. (cont.)

05752 *The voice of Dashin; a romance of wild moun-
       tains.* Hodder & Stoughton, London, 1926,
       319p, Cloth, Novel
05753 *The war breakers.* Hodder & Stoughton, London,
       1939, 296p, Cloth, Novel
05754 *Wrexham's romance, being a continuation of
       "Harilek."* Hodder & Stoughton, London,
       1935, 316p, Cloth, Novel [Sakaeland #2]

GANTHONY, RICHARD, with Lester Lurgan

05755 *A message from Mars.* Greening & Co., London,
       1912, 288p, Cloth, Novel [an adaptation of
       the play of the same title by Ganthony]

GANTZ, KENNETH F(ranklin), 1905-

05756 *Not in solitude.* Doubleday, Garden City,
       1959, 240p, Cloth, Novel

GARBO, NORMAN, 1919- [*biography included*]

05757 *The Movement.* William Morrow, New York, 1969,
       408p, Cloth, Novel

GARBY, Mrs. LEE HAWKINS, 1890-   , with Edward
E. Smith

05758 *The Skylark of space; the tale of the first
       inter-stellar cruise.* Buffalo Book Co.,
       Providence, RI, 1946, 303p, Cloth, Novel
       [Skylark #1]

GARCÍA MÁRQUEZ, GABRIEL, 1928- [*biography
       included*]

05759 *One hundred years of solitude.* Harper & Row,
       New York, 1970, 422p, Cloth, Novel

GARD, JOYCE

05760 *The mermaid's daughter.* Holt, Rinehart & Win-
       ston, New York, 1969, 320p, Cloth, Novel;
       Victor Gollancz, London, 1969, 320p, Cloth,
       Novel
05761 *Talargain, the seal's whelp.* Victor Gollancz,
       London, 1964, 160p, Cloth, Novel
05761A retitled: *Talargain.* Holt, Rinehart & Win-
       ston, New York, 1965, 253p, Cloth, Novel

THE GARDEN OF FEAR
     see: CRAWFORD, WILLIAM L.

GARDNER, CELIA E(mmeline), 1844-

05762 *Seraph--or mortal? a romance.* G. W. Dilling-
       ham, New York, 1890, 430p, Cloth, Novel
05762A retitled: *Her last lover.* G. W. Dillingham,
       New York, 1898, 430p, Cloth, Novel

GARDNER, G. B.
     see: SCRIRE. O.T.O. 4=7

GARDNER, GERALD (C.), with Dee Caruso

02749 *The world's greatest athlete.* Fawcett Gold
       Medal, Greenwich, 1973, 127p, Paper, Movie

GARDNER, JOHN (Champlin), 1933-

05763 *Grendel.* Alfred A. Knopf, New York, 1971,
       174p, Cloth, Novel

GARDNER, MATT

05764 *The curse of Quintana Roo.* Popular Library,
       New York, 1972, 206p, Paper, Novel

GARDNER, MAURICE B(enjamin), 1905-   [*biography included*]

05765 *Bantan and the mermaids.* Theos Gaus' Sons,
       Brooklyn, 1970, 316p, Cloth, Novel [Bantan
       #9]
05766 *Bantan fearless.* Forum Publishing Co., Boston,
       1963, 349p, Cloth, Novel [Bantan #8]
05767 *Bantan incredible.* Forum Publishing Co., Bos-
       ton, 1960, 366p, Cloth, Novel [Bantan #6]
05768 *Bantan primeval.* Forum Publishing Co., Boston,
       1961, 373p, Cloth, Novel [Bantan #7]

GARFIELD, LEON, 1921- [*biography included*]

05769 *The ghost downstairs.* Longman, London, 1972,
       93p, Cloth, Novel
05770 *Mister Corbett's ghost.* Pantheon, New York,
       1968, 87p, Cloth, Novel
05771 *Mr. Corbett's ghost, & other stories.* Long-
       man's Young Books, London, 1969, 159p, Cloth,
       Coll.
05772 *The restless ghost; three stories.* Pantheon,
       New York, 1969, 132p, Cloth, Coll. [similar
       to 05771, but drops the title story of the
       other collection, and adds another]

with Edward Blishen:

01525 *The god beneath the sea.* Longman, London,
       1970, 168p, Cloth, Novel
01526 *The golden shadow.* Longman Young Books, Har-
       mondsworth, 1973, 159p, Cloth, Novel

GARFORTH, JOHN

05773 *Heil Harris!* Panther, London, 1967, 124p,
       Paper, Tele. [Avengers #4]
05774 *The laugh was on Lazarus.* Panther, London,
       1967, 144p, Paper, Tele. [Avengers #2]

GARGILIS, STEPHEN

05775 *The path of the great.* Athena Publishers,
       Boston, 1945, 480p, Cloth, Novel [adapted
       from the poem "Erotokritos," by Vitzentzos
       Kornaros (supposed author)]

GARIS, HOWARD R(oger), 1873-1962

05776 *Rocket Riders across the ice; or, Racing
       against time.* A. L. Burt, New York, 1933,
       251p, Cloth, Novel [Rocket Riders #1]

GARIS, HOWARD R. (cont.)

05777   *Rocket Riders in stormy seas; or, Trailing the treasure divers.* A. L. Burt, New York, 1933, 246p, Cloth, Novel [Rocket Riders #3]

05778   *Rocket Riders in the air; or, A chase in the clouds.* A. L. Burt, New York, 1934, 251p, Cloth, Novel [Rocket Riders #4]

05779   *Rocket Riders over the desert; or, Seeking the lost city.* A. L. Burt, New York, 1933, 250p, Cloth, Novel [Rocket Riders #2]

05780   *Tam of the fire cave.* D. Appleton, New York, 1927, 257p, Cloth, Novel

as Victor Appleton, house pseud.:

00397   *Tom Swift among the diamond makers; or, The secret of Phantom Mountain.* Grosset & Dunlap, New York, 1911, 216p, Cloth, Novel [Tom Swift #7]

00398   *Tom Swift among the fire fighters; or, Battling with flames from the air.* Grosset & Dunlap, New York, 1921, 214p, Cloth, Novel [Tom Swift #24]

00399   *Tom Swift and his aerial warship; or, The naval terror of the seas.* Grosset & Dunlap, New York, 1915, 218p, Cloth, Novel [Tom Swift #18]

00400   *Tom Swift and his air glider; or, Seeking the platinum treasure.* Grosset & Dunlap, New York, 1912, 209p, Cloth, Novel [Tom Swift #12]

00401   *Tom Swift and his air scout; or, Uncle Sam's mastery of the sky.* Grosset & Dunlap, New York, 1919, 218p, Cloth, Novel [Tom Swift #22]

00402   *Tom Swift and his airline express; or, From ocean to ocean by daylight.* Grosset & Dunlap, New York, 1926, 218p, Cloth, Novel [Tom Swift #29]

00403   *Tom Swift and his airship; or, The stirring cruise of the Red Cloud.* Grosset & Dunlap, New York, 1910, 216p, Cloth, Novel [Tom Swift #3]

00404   *Tom Swift and his big dirigible; or, Adventures over the forest of fire.* Grosset & Dunlap, New York, 1930, 214p, Cloth, Novel [Tom Swift #33]

00405   *Tom Swift and his big tunnel; or, The hidden city of the Andes.* Grosset & Dunlap, New York, 1916, 218p, Cloth, Novel [Tom Swift #19]

00406   *Tom Swift and his chest of secrets; or, Tracing the stolen inventions.* Grosset & Dunlap, New York, 1925, 216p, Cloth, Novel [Tom Swift #28]

00407   *Tom Swift and his electric locomotive; or, Two miles a minute on the rails.* Grosset & Dunlap, New York, 1922, 212p, Cloth, Novel [Tom Swift #25]

00408   *Tom Swift and his electric rifle; or, Daring adventures in elephant land.* Grosset & Dunlap, New York, 1911, 212p, Cloth, Novel [Tom Swift #10]

00409   *Tom Swift and his electric runabout; or, The speediest car on the road.* Grosset & Dunlap, New York, 1910, 216p, Cloth, Novel [Tom Swift #5]

00410   *Tom Swift and his flying boat; or, The castaways of the giant iceberg.* Grosset & Dunlap, New York, 1923, 212p, Cloth, Novel [Tom Swift #26]

00411   *Tom Swift and his giant cannon; or, The longest shots on record.* Grosset & Dunlap, New York, 1913, 216p, Cloth, Novel [Tom Swift #16]

00412   *Tom Swift and his giant magnet; or, Bringing up the lost submarine.* Grosset & Dunlap, New York, 1932, 216p, Cloth, Novel [Tom Swift #35]

00413   *Tom Swift and his giant oil gusher; or, The treasure of Goby Farm.* Grosset & Dunlap, New York, 1924, 210p, Cloth, Novel [Tom Swift #27]

00414   *Tom Swift and his great searchlight; or, On the border for Uncle Sam.* Grosset & Dunlap, New York, 1912, 214p, Cloth, Novel [Tom Swift #15]

00415   *Tom Swift and his house on wheels; or, A trip to the mountain of mystery.* Grosset & Dunlap, New York, 1929, 216p, Cloth, Novel [Tom Swift #32]

00416   *Tom Swift and his motor-boat; or, The rivals of Lake Carlopa.* Grosset & Dunlap, New York, 1910, 212p, Cloth, Novel [Tom Swift #2]

00417   *Tom Swift and his motor-cycle; or, Fun and adventure on the road.* Grosset & Dunlap, New York, 1910, 206p, Cloth, Novel [Tom Swift #1]

00419   *Tom Swift and his photo telephone; or, The picture that saved a fortune.* Grosset & Dunlap, New York, 1914, 216p, Cloth, Novel [Tom Swift #17]

00421   *Tom Swift and his sky racer; or, The quickest flight on record.* Grosset & Dunlap, New York, 1911, 207p, Cloth, Novel [Tom Swift #9]

00422   *Tom Swift and his sky train; or, Overland through the clouds.* Grosset & Dunlap, New York, 1931, 218p, Cloth, Novel [Tom Swift #34]

00423   *Tom Swift and his submarine boat; or, Under the ocean for sunken treasure.* Grosset & Dunlap, New York, 1910, 216p, Cloth, Novel [Tom Swift #4]

00424   *Tom Swift and his talking pictures; or, The greatest invention on record.* Grosset & Dunlap, New York, 1928, 216p, Cloth, Novel [Tom Swift #31]

00426   *Tom Swift and his undersea search; or, The treasure on the floor of the Atlantic.* Grosset & Dunlap, New York, 1920, 218p, Cloth, Novel [Tom Swift #23]

00427   *Tom Swift and his war tank; or, Doing his best for Uncle Sam.* Grosset & Dunlap, New York, 1918, 218p, Cloth, Novel [Tom Swift #21]

00428   *Tom Swift and his wireless message; or, The castaways of Earthquake Island.* Grosset & Dunlap, New York, 1911, 211p, Cloth, Novel [Tom Swift #6]

00429   *Tom Swift and his wizard camera; or, Thrilling adventures while taking moving pictures.* Grosset & Dunlap, New York, 1912, 210p, Cloth, Novel [Tom Swift #14]

00430   *Tom Swift circling the globe; or, The daring cruise of the Air Monarch.* Grosset & Dunlap, New York, 1927, 216p, Cloth, Novel [Tom Swift #30]

00431   *Tom Swift in captivity; or, A daring escape by airship.* Grosset & Dunlap, New York, 1912, 218p, Cloth, Novel [Tom Swift #13]

00432   *Tom Swift in the caves of ice; or, The wreck of the airship.* Grosset & Dunlap, New York, 1911, 214p, Cloth, Novel [Tom Swift #8]

00433   *Tom Swift in the city of gold; or, Marvelous adventures underground.* Grosset & Dunlap, New York, 1912, 216p, Cloth, Novel [Tom Swift #11]

00434   *Tom Swift in the land of wonders; or, The search for the idol of gold.* Grosset & Dunlap, New York, 1917, 218p, Cloth, Novel [Tom Swift #20]

GARLAND, HAMLIN, 1860-1940

05781 *The tyranny of the dark.* Harper & Bros., London, 1905, 439p, Cloth, Novel

GARLAND, RUFUS CUMMINS

05782 *Zaléa; a psychological episode and tale of love.* Neale Co., Washington, 1900, 146p, Cloth, Novel

GARNER, ALAN, 1934-

05783 *Elidor.* Collins, London, 1965, 160p, Cloth, Novel
05784 *The moon of Gomrath.* Collins, London, 1963, 160p, Cloth, Novel [Colin & Susan #2]
05785 *The owl service.* Collins, London, 1967, 157p, Cloth, Novel
05786 *Red shift.* Collins, London, 1973, 158p, Cloth, Novel
       The weirdstone. [see 05787A]
05787 *The weirdstone of Brisingamen; a tale of Alderley.* Collins, London, 1960, 224p, Cloth, Novel [Colin & Susan #1]
05787A retitled: *The weirdstone; a tale of Alderley.* Franklin Watts, New York, 1961, 224p, Cloth, Novel [Colin & Susan #1]

GARNER, CHARLES
    see: CUMBERLAND, STUART

GARNER, GRAHAM

05788 *Space probe.* Robert Hale, London, 1974, 182p, Cloth, Novel

GARNER, ROLF, pseud.
    see: BERRY, BRYAN

GARNER, WILLIAM, 1920- [*biography included*]

05789 *Overkill.* New American Library, New York, 1966, 185p, Cloth, Novel

GARNETT, BILL

05790 *Down-bound train.* Doubleday, Garden City, 1973, 189p, Cloth, Novel

GARNETT, DAV
    see: GARNETT, DAVID S.

GARNETT, DAVID, 1892- [*biography included*]

05791 *Lady into fox.* Chatto & Windus, London, 1922, 91p, Cloth, Novel
05792 *Lady into fox; and, A man in the zoo.* Chatto & Windus, London, 1928, 190p, Cloth, Coll.
05793 *Two by two; a story of survival.* Longmans, London, 1963, 144p, Cloth, Novel
05794 *Ulterior motives.* Longmans, London, 1966, 188p, Cloth, Novel

GARNETT, DAVID S., 1947- [*biography included*]

05795 *Mirror in the sky*, by Dav Garnett. Berkley Medallion, New York, 1969, 160p, Paper, Novel
05796 *The starseekers*, by Dav Garnett. Berkley Medallion, New York, 1971, 192p, Paper, Novel
05797 *Time in eclipse.* Robert Hale, London, 1974, 176p, Cloth, Novel

GARNETT, EDWARD (William), 1868-1937

05798 *Papa's war, and other satires.* The Office of the Herald, at the Pelican Press, London, 1918, 120p, Cloth, Coll.

GARNETT, RICHARD, 1835-1906

05799 *The twilight of the gods, and other tales.* T. Fisher Unwin, London, 1888, 346p, Cloth, Coll.

GARRATT, EVELYN R.

05800 *The cry.* Smiths, Ipswich; C. J. Thynne, London; 1919, 467p, Cloth, Novel

GARRETT, CHARLES W(alter), 1873-

05801 *Aurilly, the virgin isle.* Christopher Publishing House, Boston, 1923, 152p, Cloth, Novel

GARRETT, GARET [Edward Peter Garrett, 1878-1954]

05802 *The blue wound.* G. P. Putnam's Sons, New York, 1921, 184p, Cloth, Novel

GARRETT, GEORGE (Palmer), 1929-

05803 *The magic striptease.* Doubleday, Garden City, 1973, 272p, Cloth, Coll.

GARRETT, (Gordon) RANDALL (Philip David)

       Anything you can do... [see 05806A]
05804 *Too many magicians.* Doubleday, Garden City, 1967, 260p, Cloth, Novel
05805 *Unwise child.* Doubleday, Garden City, 1962, 215p, Cloth, Novel

as Darrel T. Langart:

05806 *Anything you can do...* Doubleday, Garden City, 1963, 192p, Cloth, Novel
05806A *Anything you can do...*, by Randall Garrett. Lancer, New York, 1969, 192p, Paper, Novel

with Larry M. Harris:

05807 *Pagan passions.* Galaxy Publishing Corp., New York, 1959, 158p, Paper, Novel

with Laurence M. Janifer as Mark Phillips:

05808 *Brain twister; a science-fiction novel.* Pyramid, New York, 1962, 144p, Paper, Novel [Ken Malone #1]

GARRETT, RANDALL (cont.), with Laurence M.
Janifer as Mark Phillips

05809   *The impossibles*. Pyramid, New York, 1963,
          157p, Paper, Novel [Ken Malone #2]
05810   *Supermind*. Pyramid, New York, 1963, 192p,
          Paper, Novel [Ken Malone #3]

with Robert Silverberg as Robert Randall:

05811   *The dawning light*. Gnome Press, New York,
          1959, 191p, Cloth, Novel [Nidor #2]
05812   *The shrouded planet*. Gnome Press, New York,
          1957, 188p, Cloth, Novel [Nidor #1]

GARRETT, WILLIAM (A.), 1890-1967

05813   *The man in the mirror; a biographical reflec-
          tion*. John Lane, The Bodley Head, London,
          1931, 310p, Cloth, Novel

GARRISON, CHARLES M.
     see: MacDANIEL, CHARLES

GARRISON, WENDELL PHILLIPS, 1840-1907

05814   *The new Gulliver*. Marion Press, Jamaica, NY,
          1898, 51p, Cloth, Novel [Gulliver series]

GARRON, MARCO, pseud.

05815   *Jungle fever*. Curtis Warren, London, 1950?,
          128p, Paper, Novel [Azan #3]
05816   *King hunters*. Curtis Warren, London, 1951?,
          112p, Paper, Novel [Azan #6]
05817   *The lost city*, by Marco Garon. Curtis Warren,
          London, 1950, 128p, Paper, Novel [Azan #2]
05818   *The missing safari*, by Marco Garon. Curtis
          Warren, London, 1950, 128p, Paper, Novel
          [Azan #1]
05819   *Tribal war*. Curtis Warren, London, 1951?,
          112p, Paper, Novel [Azan #5]
05820   *White fangs*. Curtis Warren, London, 1951?,
          112p, Paper, Novel [Azan #4]

GARSON, (Gary) PAUL, 1946-   [biography in-
cluded]

05821   *The Great Quill*. Doubleday, Garden City,
          1973, 216p, Cloth, Novel

GARSON, VASELEOS [William J. Garson]

05822   *Brother Earth*. Imagination Plus, Rockford,
          IL, 1974, 189p, Cloth, Novel

GARSON, WILLIAM J.
     see: GARSON, VASELEOS

GARTH, WILL, pseud.
     see: KUTTNER, HENRY

GARVER, RONALD G.

05823   *The saucer people*. Meador Publishing Co., Bo
          ton, 1957, 132p, Cloth, Novel

GARVER, WILL(iam) L(incoln), 1867-

05824   *Brother of the third degree*. Arena Publishin
          Co., Boston, 1894, 377p, Cloth, Novel

GARVIN, RICHARD M(cClellan), 1934-   [biogra-
phy included], with Edmond G. Addeo

00055   *The FORTEC conspiracy*. Sherbourne Press, Los
          Angeles, 1968, 181p, Cloth, Novel
00056   *The Talbott Agreement*. Sherbourne Press, Los
          Angeles, 1968, 255p, Cloth, Novel

GARY, ROMAIN, pseud. [Romain Kassev, 1914-

05825   *The dance of Genghis Cohn*. World Publishing
          Co., New York, 1968, 244p, Cloth, Novel
          [Genghis Cohn #1]
05826   *The gasp; a novel*. G. P. Putnam's Sons, New
          York, 1973, 253p, Cloth, Novel
05827   *The guilty head*. World Publishing Co., New
          York, 1969, 255p, Cloth, Novel [Genghis
          Cohn #2]
05828   *The talent scout*. Harper & Bros., New York,
          1961, 212p, Cloth, Novel

GASK, ARTHUR

05829   *The fall of a dictator*. Herbert Jenkins, Lon
          don, 1939, 284p, Cloth, Novel

GASKELL, JANE, pseud. [Jane Gaskell Lynch,
1941-   ] [biography included]

05830   *Atlan*. Hodder & Stoughton, London, 1965,
          286p, Cloth, Novel [Cija #2]
05831   *The City*. Hodder & Stoughton, London, 1966,
          190p, Cloth, Novel [Cija #3]
05832   *King's daughter*. Hutchinson, London, 1958,
          280p, Cloth, Novel
05833   *The serpent*. Hodder & Stoughton, London,
          1963, 445p, Cloth, Novel [Cija #1]
05834   *The shiny narrow grin*. Hodder & Stoughton,
          London, 1964, 128p, Cloth, Novel
05835   *Strange evil*. Hutchinson, London, 1957, 256p
          Cloth, Novel
05836   *A sweet, sweet summer*. Hodder & Stoughton,
          London, 1969, 223p, Cloth, Novel

GASTINE, LOUIS (Jules), 1858-1935

05837   *War in space; or, An air-craft war between
          France and Germany*. Walter Scott Publishi
          Co., London, 1913, 339p, Cloth, Novel

GASTON, HENRY A.

05838   *Mars revealed; or, Seven days in the spirit
          world, containing an account of the spirit
          trip to Mars, and his return to Earth*, by
          a spirit yet in the flesh. A. L. Bancroft
          San Francisco, 1880, 208p, Cloth, Novel

GAT, DIMITRI V(sevolod), 1936-   [*biography included*]

05839 *The Shepherd is my Lord.* Doubleday, Garden City, 1971, 208p, Cloth, Novel

GATCH, TOM Jr., 1926-

05840 *King Julian; a novel.* Vantage Press, New York, 1954, 187p, Cloth, Novel

GATES, H(enry) L(eyford), 1880-1937

05841 *The laughing peril.* Macaulay, New York, 1933, 247p, Cloth, Novel

GATOS, ROBERT L., pseud.

05842 *Erection to eternal lust.* Pendulum, Los Angeles, 1970, 190p, Paper, Novel

GAUNT, JEFFREY
    see: ROCHESTER, GEORGE ERNEST

GAUTIER, THÉOPHILE, 1811-1872

05843 *Avatar; or, The double transformation.* Vizetelly & Co., London, 1887, 220p, Cloth, Novel
05844 *Avatar; Jettatura; The water pavilion.* C. T. Brainard, Boston, 1902, 372p, Cloth, Coll.
        The beautiful vampire. [see 05846B]
05846 *Clarimonde.* Brentano's, New York, 1899, 81p, Cloth, Novel
05846A retitled: *Clarimonde, vampire and harlot.* Haldeman-Julius Co., Girard, Kans., 1922?, 64p?, Paper, Novel
05846B retitled: *The beautiful vampire (La morte amoureuse).* A. M. Philpot, London, 1926, 110p, Cloth, Novel
05847 *Clarimonde, and other stories.* T. C. & E. C. Jack, London, 1908, 150p, Cloth, Coll.
        Clarimonde, vampire and harlot. [see 05846A]
05848 *Cleopatra.* H. S. Nichols, London, 1899, 113p, Cloth, Novel
05849 *Jettatura.* Percival & Co., London, 1891, 135p, Cloth, Novel
05850 *Mademoiselle de Maupin.* Hamish Hamilton, London, 1937, 332p, Cloth, Coll. [includes *One of Cleopatra's nights*]
05850A retitled: *Mademoiselle de Maupin; and, One of Cleopatra's nights.* Random House, New York, 1948, 332p, Cloth, Coll.
05851 *The mummy's romance.* Greening & Co., London, 1902, 254p, Cloth, Coll.
05852 *One of Cleopatra's nights, and other fantastic romances.* R. Worthington, New York, 1882, 220p, Cloth, Coll.
05853 *The romance of a mummy.* J. Bradburn, New York, 1863, 254p, Cloth, Novel
05854 *Spirite; a fantasy.* D. Appleton, New York, 1877, 214p, Cloth, Novel
05854A retitled: *Stronger than death; or, Spirite.* Rand, McNally, Chicago, 1898, 293p, Cloth, Novel
05855 *Spirite; The vampire; Arria Marcella.* C. T. Brainard, Boston, 1901, 367p, Cloth, Coll.
05856 *Stories.* T. C. & E. C. Jack, London, 1908, 150p, Cloth, Coll.
        Stronger than death. [see 05854A]

05857 *Tales.* Brentano's, New York, 1909, 146p, Cloth, Coll.
05858 *Tales and romances.* Gibbings, London, 1909, 388p, Cloth, Coll.
05859 *Tales from Gautier.* Eveleigh Nash & Grayson, London, 1927, 265p, Cloth, Coll.
05860 *Théophile Gautier.* G. P. Putnam's Sons, New York, 1909, 288p, Cloth, Coll.
05861 *Three romances.* Brentano's, New York, 1888, 255p, Cloth, Coll.
05862 *The works of Théophile Gautier.* W. J. Black, New York, 1928, 649p, Cloth, Coll. [not a true "collected works"]

GAWRON, JEAN MARK

05863 *An apology for rain.* Doubleday, Garden City, 1974, 176p, Cloth, Novel

GAWSWORTH, JOHN, pseud.
    see: ARMSTRONG, FYTTON

GAY, J. DREW, pseud.
    see: WELCH, EDGAR L.

GAY, WILLIAM S., 1881-

05864 *Syra; the story of an extraordinary experience.* Comet Press, New York, 1958, 60p, Cloth, Novel

GAYLE, HAROLD, 1910-

05865 *Spawn of the vortex.* Comet Press, New York, 1957, 138p, Cloth, Novel

GAYTON, BERTRAM

05866 *The gland stealers.* Herbert Jenkins, London, 1922, 312p, Cloth, Novel

GAZDANOV, GAITO [Georgii Gazdanov, 1903-   ]

05867 *Buddha's return.* E. P. Dutton, New York, 1951, 224p, Cloth, Novel

GEBHART, FRED J.
    see: WISE, ROBERT A.

GED, CAER, pseud.
    see: WYATT, LEE

GEDDES, GEORGE T(homas)

05868 *Miracles of rare device; an introductory selection of science fiction.* Jordanhill College Library, Glasgow, 1972, 48p, Paper, Nonf.

GEDULD, CAROLYN

05869 *Filmguide to 2001: a space odyssey.* Indiana University Press, Bloomington, IN, 1973, 87p, Cloth, Nonf.

GEIGLEY, VANCE A(cton), 1907-

05870 *Will it end this way?* Vantage Press, New York,
       1968, 295p, Cloth, Novel

GEIS, RICHARD E(rwin), 1927-   [*biography included*]

05871 *The arena women.* Brandon Books, Chatsworth,
       CA, 1972, 222p, Paper, Novel
05872 *The endless orgy.* Brandon House, North Holly-
       wood, 1968, 190p, Paper, Novel [Roi Kunzer
       #2]
05873 *Raw meat.* Essex House, North Hollywood, 1969,
       224p, Paper, Novel
05874 *The sex machine.* Brandon House, North Holly-
       wood, 1967, 190p, Paper, Novel [Roi Kunzer
       #1]

as Peggy Swenson:

05875 *A girl possessed.* Brandon Books, Chatsworth,
       CA, 1973, 190p, Paper, Novel

GEISSLER, L(udwig) A.

05876 *Looking beyond; a sequel to "Looking Backward"
       by Edward Bellamy and an answer to "Looking
       Further Forward" by Richard Michaelis.* W. M.
       Reeves, London, 1891?, 102p, Paper, Novel;
       L. Graham & Son, New Orleans, 1891, 134p,
       Cloth, Novel [sequel to Bellamy]

'GENERAL STAFF,' pseud.

05877 *The writing on the wall.* William Heinemann,
       London, 1906, 228p, Cloth, Novel

GENONE, HUDOR, pseud. [William James Roe,
1843-1915]

05878 *Bellona's husband; a romance.* J. B. Lippin-
       cott, Philadelphia, 1887, 332p, Cloth, Novel
05879 *Inquirendo Island.* G. P. Putnam's Sons, New
       York, 1886, 347p, Cloth, Novel

GENTIL, SPIRITO, pseud. [George W. Hanna]

05880 *Earth-born! a novel of the misty past--the
       story of a strange search--a tale of the
       beginning--a romance of the end.* The Press
       Bureau, New York, 1889, 263p, Paper, Novel

"GENTLE JOSEPH," pseud.

05881 *A peaceful revolution.* E. J. Adams, Bath, UK,
       1916, 104p, Cloth, Novel

GENTLEMAN, FRANCIS
    see: LUNATIC, Sir HUMPHREY

A GENTLEMAN OF THE UNIVERSITY, pseud.
    see: SHELLEY, PERCY BYSSHE

GENTRY, CURT, 1931-   [*biography included*]

05882 *The last days of the late, great state of Cal-
       fornia.* G. P. Putnam's Sons, New York, 196
       384p, Cloth, Novel

GEORGE, EDWARD, pseud.

05883 *Pleasure planet.* Orpheus Series, New York,
       1974, 187p, Paper, Novel

GEORGE, PETER (Bryan), 1924-1966

05884 *Commander-1.* Heinemann, London, 1965, 253p,
       Cloth, Novel
05885 *Dr. Strangelove; or, How I learned to stop
       worrying and love the bomb.* Corgi, London,
       1963, 145p, Paper, Movie

GEORGE, Flight Lieut. S(idney) C(harles),
1898-   [*biography included*]

05886 *The blue ray.* Frederick Warne, London, 1938,
       256p, Cloth, Novel

GEORGE, VERNON, pseud. [George Shirra Gibb
Vernon, 1885-   ]

05887 *The crown of Asia.* Stanley Paul, London, 193
       286p, Cloth, Novel

GEORGE, W(alter) L(ionel), 1882-1926

05888 *Children of the morning.* Chapman & Hall, Lon-
       don, 1926, 246p, Cloth, Novel

GERALD, GREGORY FITZ
    see: FITZ GERALD, GREGORY

GÉRARD, FRANCIS, 1905-

05889 *Secret sceptre.* Rich & Cowan, London, 1937,
       286p, Cloth, Novel

GERARD, MORICE, pseud. [John Jessop Teague,
1856-1929]

05890 *The new order.* Hodder & Stoughton, London,
       1917, 269p, Cloth, Novel

GERBER, RICHARD (Ernst Hans)

05891 *Utopian fantasy; a study of English utopian
       fiction since the end of the nineteenth cen-
       tury.* Routledge & Kegan Paul, London, 1955
       162p, Cloth, Nonf.

GERBERG, MORT

05892 *The high society; what happened when the coun-
       try finally went to pot; an informal chron-
       icle.* Warner Paperback Library, New York,
       1973, 158p, Paper, Novel

GERHARDI(e), WILLIAM (Alexander),1895-1977 [bi-
ography included]

05893 Jazz and jasper; the story of Adams and Eva.
       Duckworth, London, 1928, 312p, Cloth, Novel
05893A retitled: Eva's apples; a story of jazz and
       jasper. Duffield & Co., New York, 1928,
       393p, Cloth, Novel
05893B retitled: My sinful Earth. Macdonald, London,
       1947, 272p, Cloth, Novel
05893C retitled: Doom. Macdonald, London, 1974,
       275p, Cloth, Novel
05894 Resurrection. Cassell, London, 1934, 374p,
       Cloth, Novel

with Brian Lunn:

05895 The memoirs of Satan. Cassell, London, 1932,
       382p, Cloth, Novel

GERMAIN, MARIE ST.
    see: ST. GERMAIN, MARIE

GERMAINE, VICTOR WALLACE

05896 Colonel to princess. Methuen, London, 1936,
       327p, Cloth, Novel
05897 Crusoe Warburton. Coward-McCann, New York,
       1954, 250p, Cloth, Novel

THE GERMAN CONQUEST OF ENGLAND IN 1875
    see: CHESNEY, GEORGE T.

GERMANO, PETER B., as Jack Bertin, house pseud.

01208 The interplanetary adventurers. Lenox Hill
       Press, New York, 1970, 192p, Cloth, Novel
01209 The pyramids from space. Lenox Hill Press,
       New York, 1970, 192p, Cloth, Novel

THE GERMANS IN CORK
    see: von KARTOFFEL, BARON

GERMESHAUSEN, ANNA LOUISE, 1906-1968

05898 Cats in crime...and others. Luther Norris,
       Culver City, CA, 1970, 30p, Paper, Coll.

GERNSBACK, HUGO, 1884-1967

05899 Evolution of modern science fiction. Hugo
       Gernsback, New York, 1952, 12p, Paper, Nonf.
05900 Ralph 124C 41+; a romance of the year 2660.
       Stratford Co., Boston, 1925, 293p, Cloth,
       Novel
05901 Ultimate world. Walker & Co., New York, 1972,
       187p, Cloth, Novel

GERRARE, WIRT, pseud. [William Oliver Greener,
1862-   ]

05902 Phantasms; original stories illustrating post-
       humous personality and character. Roxburghe
       Press, London, 1895, 234p, Cloth, Coll.
05903 The Warstock; a tale of to-morrow. W. W. Gree-
       ner, London, 1898, 218p, Cloth, Novel

GERROLD, DAVID, pseud. [Jerrold David Friedman, 1944-   ] [biography included]

05904 Battle for the planet of the apes. Award,
       New York, 1973, 158p, Paper, Movie [Planet
       of the Apes #5]
05905 The man who folded himself. Random House,
       New York, 1973, 148p, Cloth, Novel
05906 Space skimmer. Ballantine, New York, 1972,
       218p, Paper, Novel
05907 The trouble with tribbles. Ballantine, New
       York, 1973, 275p, Paper, Nonf.
05908 When Harlie was one; a novel. Nelson Double-
       day, New York, 1972, 247p, Cloth, Novel
05909 With a finger in my I. Ballantine, New York,
       1972, 245p, Paper, Coll.
05910 The world of Star trek. Ballantine, New York,
       1973, 278p, Paper, Nonf.
05911 Yesterday's children. Dell, New York, 1972,
       251p, Paper, Novel

with Stephen Goldin:

05912 Alternities. Dell, New York, 1974, 175p,
       Paper, Anth.
05913 Generation; an anthology of speculative fic-
       tion. Dell, New York, 1972, 236p, Paper,
       Anth.
05914 Protostars. Ballantine, New York, 1971, 271p,
       Paper, Anth.
05915 Science fiction emphasis I; an anthology of
       original science fiction. Ballantine, New
       York, 1974, 211p, Paper, Anth.

with Larry Niven:

05916 The flying sorcerers. Ballantine, New York,
       1971, 316p, Paper, Novel

GERSON, NOEL B(ertram), 1914-

05917 Double vision. Doubleday, Garden City, 1972,
       234p, Cloth, Novel

GERSTÄCKER, FRIEDRICH (Wilhelm Christian),
1816-1872

05918 Germelshausen. C. W. Sever, Cambridge, Mass.,
       1888, 31p, Cloth, Story

GERVAIS, ALBERT, 1892-

05919 The ghosts of Sin-chang. Hamish Hamilton, Lon-
       don, 1936, 319p, Cloth, Novel

GESTON, MARK S(ymington), 1946-   [biography
included]

05920 The day star. DAW, New York, 1972, 126p,
       Paper, Novel
05921 Lords of the starship. Ace, New York, 1967,
       156p, Paper, Novel [Havengore #1]
05922 Out of the mouth of the dragon. Ace, New York,
       1969, 156p, Paper, Novel [Havengore #2]

GHIDALIA, VIC(tor Simon), 1926-   [biography
included]

05923 The devil's generation. Lancer, New York,
       1973, 175p, Paper, Anth.

GHIDALIA, VIC (Cont.)

05924   *Dracula's guest, and other stories.* Xerox Education Publications, Middletown, Conn., 1972, 125p, Paper, Anth.
05925   *Eight strange tales.* Fawcett Gold Medal, Greenwich, 1972, 160p, Paper, Anth.
05926   *Gooseflesh!* Berkley Medallion, New York, 1974, 152p, Paper, Anth.
05927   *The mummy walks among us.* Xerox Education Publications, Middletown, Conn., 1971, 151p, Paper, Anth.
05928   *The oddballs.* Manor, New York, 1973, 192p, Paper, Anth.
05929   *Satan's pets.* Manor, New York, 1972, 224p, Paper, Anth.
05930   *Wizards and warlocks.* Manor, New York, 1972, 224p, Paper, Anth.

with Roger Elwood:

04867   *Androids, time machines, and blue giraffes; a panorama of science fiction.* Follett Publishing Co., Chicago, 1973, 382p, Cloth, Anth.
04868   *Beware the beasts.* Macfadden-Bartell, New York, 1970, 160p, Paper, Anth.
04869   *Horror hunters.* Macfadden-Bartell, New York, 1971, 192p, Paper, Anth.
04870   *The little monsters.* Macfadden-Bartell, New York, 1969, 160p, Paper, Anth.
04871   *More little monsters.* Manor, New York, 1973, 190p, Paper, Anth.
04872   *The Venus factor.* Macfadden-Bartell, New York, 1972, 192p, Paper, Anth.
04873   *Young demons.* Avon, New York, 1972, 160p, Paper, Anth.

GHOSH, SARATH KUMAR, 1883-   [cited in various sources as A. Saratkumara Ghosha]

05931   *The verdict of the gods.* Dodd, Mead, New York, 1905, 307p, Cloth, Novel

GHOST STORIES, AND OTHER QUEER TALES

05932   *Ghost stories, and other queer tales.* C. Arthur Pearson, London, 1931, 256p, Cloth, Anth.

GHOST STORIES AND PRESENTIMENTS

05933   *Ghost stories and presentiments.* George Redway, London, 1888, 308p, Cloth, Coll.

GHOST STORIES AND TALES OF MYSTERY
   see: LE FANU, J. SHERIDAN

GHOST STORIES (SELECTED)

05934   *Ghost stories (selected).* Happy Hour Library, New York, 1947?, 94p, Paper, Anth.

GHOST STORIES; STORIES OF GHOSTS
   see: CAZEDESSUS, CAMILLE

GIBBARD, T. S. J.

05935   *Vandals of eternity.* Robert Hale, London, 1974, 191p, Cloth, Novel

GIBBON, CONSTANTINE FITZ
   see: FITZ GIBBON, CONSTANTINE

GIBBON, RALPH FITZ-
   see: FITZ-GIBBON, RALPH

GIBBONS, CHARLES HARRISON, 1869-

05936   *The marbled catskin.* Stanley Paul, London, 1928, 288p, Cloth, Novel

GIBBONS, CROMWELL, 1893-

05937   *The bat woman.* World Press, New York, 1938, 224p, Cloth, Novel

GIBBONS, (Raphael) FLOYD (Phillips), 1886-19?

05938   *The red Napoleon.* Jonathan Cape & Harrison Smith, New York, 1929, 475p, Cloth, Novel

GIBBONS, GAVIN, 1922-

05939   *By space ship to the Moon; a tale of adventur in outer space for boys.* Basil Blackwell, Oxford, 1958, 128p, Cloth, Novel

GIBBONS, ROBERT

05940   *The EM discoveries; an account of the 3 technological wonders that opened the EM Age.* Exposition Press, Hicksville, NY, 1974, 175 Cloth, Novel

GIBBS, ANTHONY, 1902-   [*biography included*]

05941   *The New Crusade.* Hutchinson, London, 1931, 287p, Cloth, Novel

GIBBS, GEORGE (Fort), 1870-1942

05942   *The Silver Death.* D. Appleton-Century, New York, 1939, 270p, Cloth, Novel

GIBBS, HENRY (St. John Clair) [*biography included*]

05943   *Pawns in ice.* Jarrolds Publishers, London, 1948, 222p, Cloth, Novel

GIBBS, LEWIS, pseud. [Joseph Walter Cove, 1891-   ]

05944   *Late final.* J. M. Dent & Sons, London, 1951, 216p, Cloth, Novel

GIBBS, Sir PHILIP (Hamilton), 1877-1962

05945 *Darkened rooms; a novel.* Hutchinson, London, 1929, 286p, Cloth, Novel
05946 *The key of life.* Hennel Locke, London, 1948, 123p, Cloth, Novel

GIBERGA, OVIDIO
   see: COGGS, Dr.

GIBRAN, KAHLIL, 1883-1931 [variously cited as Khalil Gibrán Gibrán or Jabrān Khalīl Jabrān]

05947 *Nymphs of the valley.* Alfred A. Knopf, New York, 1948, 77p, Cloth, Coll.

GIBSON, EDMUND H.

05948 *A.D. 2018; recollections of the chaplain of a space ship.* Greenwich Book Publishers, New York, 1958, 62p, Cloth, Novel
05949 *It may be so; a fantasy of the afterlife.* Greenwich Book Publishers, New York, 1958, 66p, Cloth, Novel

GIBSON, FLOYD

05950 *A slip in time.* Robert Hale, London, 1974, 191p, Cloth, Novel

GIBSON, W(illiam) C(urtis), 1857-   , with Bert Leston Taylor

05951 *Extra dry, being further adventures of the Water Wagon.* G. W. Dillingham, New York, 1906, 120p, Cloth, Novel [Water Wagon #2]
05952 *The log of the Water Wagon; or, The cruise of the good ship "Lithia."* H. M. Caldwell, Boston, 1905, 128p, Cloth, Novel

GIBSON, WALTER B(rown), 1897-

05953 *Return of the Shadow.* Belmont, New York, 1963, 141p, Paper, Novel [New Shadow #1]
05954 *Rod Serling's The twilight zone.* Grosset & Dunlap, New York, 1963, 207p, Cloth, Tele. Coll.
05954A retitled: *Chilling stories from Rod Serling's The twilight zone.* Tempo, New York, 1965, 190p, Paper, Tele. Coll. [abridged]
05955 *Twilight zone revisited.* Grosset & Dunlap, New York, 1964, 208p, Cloth, Tele. Coll.
05956 *The weird adventures of the Shadow.* Grosset & Dunlap, New York, 1966, 216p, Cloth, Coll.

as Maxwell Grant, house pseud.:

05957 *The black master.* Pyramid, New York, 1974, 174p, Paper, Novel [Pyramid Shadow #2]
05958 *The death tower.* Bantam, New York, 1969, 138p, Paper, Novel [Bantam Shadow #4]
05959 *The eyes of the Shadow.* Bantam, New York, 1969, 171p, Paper, Novel [Bantam Shadow #2]
05960 *Gangdom's doom.* Bantam, New York, 1970, 166p, Paper, Novel [Bantam Shadow #7]
05961 *The ghost makers.* Bantam, New York, 1970, 120p, Paper, Novel [Bantam Shadow #5]

05962 *Hidden death.* Bantam, New York, 1970, 138p, Paper, Novel [Bantam Shadow #6]
05963 *The living Shadow.* Street & Smith, New York, 1933,   , Cloth, Novel [Shadow #1]
05964 *The mobsmen on the spot.* Pyramid, New York, 1974, 190p, Paper, Novel [Pyramid Shadow #3]
05965 *The Shadow and the voice of murder.* Bantam Publications, Los Angeles, 1940, 100p, Paper, Novel [Shadow series]
05966 *The Shadow laughs!* Bantam, New York, 1969, 156p, Paper, Novel [Bantam Shadow #3]
05967 *The weird adventures of the Shadow; grove of doom.* Tempo, New York, 1969, 154p, Paper, Novel [Shadow series]

GIDE, ANDRÉ (Paul Guillaume), 1869-1951

05968 *Marshlands; and, Prometheus misbound; two satires.* New Directions, New York, 1953, 192p, Cloth, Coll.; Secker & Warburg, London, 1953, 192p, Cloth, Coll.
05969 *Urien's voyage.* Philosophical Library, New York, 1964, 94p, Cloth, Novel; Peter Owen, London, 1964, 94p, Cloth, Novel

GIESKE, HERMAN EVERETT, 1892?-1954

05970 *Utopia, Inc.* Fortuny's Publishers, New York, 1940, 223p, Cloth, Novel

GIESY, J(ohn) U(lrich), 1877-1947

05971 *All for his country.* Macaulay Co., New York, 1915, 320p, Cloth, Novel
05972 *Jason, son of Jason.* Avalon, New York, 1966, 192p, Cloth, Novel [Jason Croft #3]
05973 *The Mouthpiece of Zitu.* Avalon, New York, 1965, 192p, Cloth, Novel [Jason Croft #2]
05974 *Palos of the Dog Star Pack.* Avalon, New York, 1965, 192p, Cloth, Novel [Jason Croft #1]

GIFFORD, DENIS, 1927-   [*biography included*]

05975 *Karloff: the man, the monster, the movies.* Curtis, New York, 1973, 350p, Paper, Nonf.
05976 *Movie monsters.* Studio Vista, London, 1969, 159p, Cloth, Nonf.
05977 *A pictorial history of horror films.* Hamlyn, Feltham, UK, 1973, 216p, Cloth, Nonf.
05978 *Science fiction film.* Studio Vista, London, 1971, 160p, Cloth, Nonf.

GIFFORD, HARDINGE GOULBURN
   see: HALSBURY, Earl of

THE GIFT OF THE GODS

05979 *The gift of the gods.* American Science Fiction, Sydney, 1955, 34p, Paper, Anth.

GILBERT, (William) STEPHEN, 1912-   [*biography included*]

05980 *The landslide.* Faber & Faber, London, 1943, 224p, Cloth, Novel

GILBERT, STEPHEN (cont.)

05981 *Monkeyface.* Faber & Faber, London, 1948,
    252p, Cloth, Novel
05982 *Ratman's notebooks.* Michael Joseph, London,
    1968, 189p, Cloth, Novel [Ben #1]
05982A retitled: *Willard.* Lancer, New York, 1971,
    191p, Paper, Novel [Ben #1]

GILBERT, WILLIAM, 1804-1890

05983 *The magic mirror; a round of tales for old and
    young.* Alexander Strahan, London, 1866,
    290p, Cloth, Coll.
05984 *Modern wonders of the world; or, The new Sin-
    bad.* Strahan & Co., London, 1881, 306p,
    Cloth, Novel
05985 *The wizard of the mountain.* Strahan & Co.,
    London, 1867, 2vol, Cloth, Coll.

GILCHRIST, (Robert) MURRAY, 1868-1917

05986 *The stone dragon, and other tragic romances.*
    Methuen, London, 1894, 208p, Cloth, Coll.

GILCHRIST, ROSETTA

05987 *Tibby; a novel dealing with psychic forces
    and telepathy.* Neale Publishing Co., New
    York, 1904, 332p, Cloth, Novel

GILES, ELIZABETH, pseud.
    see: GILES, RAYMOND

GILES, RAYMOND, pseud. [John Robert Holt,
    1926-   ] [*biography included*]

    Night of the griffin. [see 05990A]
05988 *Night of the vampire.* Avon, New York, 1969,
    176p, Paper, Novel
05989 *Night of the warlock.* Paperback Library, New
    York, 1968, 160p, Paper, Novel

as Elizabeth Giles:

05990 *Children of the griffin.* Lancer, New York,
    1971,   , Paper, Novel
05990A retitled: *Night of the griffin,* by Raymond
    Giles. New English Library, London, 1971,
    142p, Paper, Novel

GILFORD, C(harles) B(ernard), 1920-   [*bio-
    graphy included*]

05991 *The liquid man.* Lancer, New York, 1969, 222p,
    Paper, Novel

GILHOOLEY, Lord, pseud. [Frederick Henri Sey-
    mour, 1850-1913]

05992 *Maugis, ye sorcerer, from ye ancient French;
    a wonderful tale from ye writings of ye mad
    savant of ye Maison Maugis, in ye olde cite
    of Mouzin, France.* F. Tennyson Neely, Lon-
    don, 1898, 252p, Cloth, Novel

05993 *Ye wisdom of Confucius; or, Ye mummyfyed fyn-
    ger; ye strange relation of a vysyt of ye
    spiryt of Yen Hûi ye dyscyple of Confucius
    to Sir Patryck Gylhoolye, Bart., at his
    chambers at ye inner temple, London, and ye
    strange circumstances connected therewyth,
    A.D. 1604.* Frederick A. Stokes, New York,
    1900, 319p, Cloth, Novel

GILLET, A(lexis) F(rancois), 1861-

05994 *Titan and Volcan; a story woven into the lives
    of two young men; the fate of Peter Shaw,
    depicting Volcan Island and the unsolved mys-
    teries of its people.* Meador Publishing Co.,
    Boston, 1933, 170p, Cloth, Novel

GILLIATT, PENELOPE (Ann Douglass), 1932-
    [*biography included*]

05995 *One by one; a novel.* Secker & Warburg, London,
    1965, 190p, Cloth, Novel

GILLIES, ROBERT PEARSE, 1788-1858 [published
anonymously]

05996 *Tales of a voyager to the Arctic Ocean.* Henry
    Colburn, London, 1826, vol. I-347p, II-336p,
    III-350p, Cloth, Novel
05997 *Tales of a voyager to the Arctic Ocean, second
    series.* Henry Colburn, London, 1829, 3vol,
    Cloth, Novel

GILLMORE, INEZ HAYNES
    see: IRWIN, INEZ HAYNES

GILLMORE, PARKER

05999 *The Amphibion's voyage.* W. H. Allen, London,
    1885, 366p, Cloth, Novel

GILLON, DIANA (Pleasance), 1915-   [*biography
included*], with Meir Gillon

06000 *The unsleep.* Barrie & Rockliff, London, 1961,
    246p, Cloth, Novel

GILLON, MEIR (Selig), 1907-   [*biography included*], with Diana Gillon

06000 *The unsleep.* Barrie & Rockliff, London, 1961,
    246p, Cloth, Novel

GILMAN, ROBERT CHAM, pseud.
    see: COPPEL, ALFRED

GILMORE, ANTHONY, pseud. [Harry Bates, 1900-

06001 *Space Hawk; the greatest of interplanetary ad-
    venturers.* A Corwin Book, Greenberg: Pub-
    lisher, New York, 1952, 274p, Cloth, Novel

GILSON, CHARLES (James Louis), 1878-1943

06002 *The cat and the curate; a phenomenal experience.* Frederick A. Stokes, New York, 1934, 314p, Cloth, Novel
06003 *The city of the sorcerer.* Hutchinson, London, 1934, 219p, Cloth, Novel
06004 *The lost city.* "The Boys' Own Paper" Office, London, 1923, 378p, Cloth, Novel
06005 *The pirate aeroplane.* Henry Frowde, Hodder & Stoughton, London, 1913, 327p, Cloth, Novel
06006 *The realm of the wizard king; a romance of central Africa.* "The Boys' Own Paper" Office, London, 1922, 380p, Cloth, Novel

GINSBURG, MIRRA [*biography included*]

06007 *Last door to Aiya; a selection of the best new science fiction from the Soviet Union.* S. G. Phillips, New York, 1968, 192p, Cloth, Anth.
06008 *The ultimate threshold; a collection of the finest in Soviet science fiction.* Holt, Rinehart & Winston, New York, 1970, 244p, Cloth, Anth.

GIPHANTIA
   see: TIPHAIGNE de LA ROCHE, C. F.

GIRAUDOUX, JEAN, 1882-1944

06009 *Elpénor.* Noonday Press, New York, 1958, 117p, Paper, Novel

GIRONELLA, JOSÉ MARÍA, 1917-

06010 *Phantoms and fugitives; journeys to the improbable.* Sheed & Ward, New York, 1964, 177p, Cloth, Coll.

GIVINS, ROBERT C(artwright), 1845-1915

06011 *A thousand miles an hour.* Maclear & Marcus, Chicago, 1913, 103p, Cloth, Novel

GJELLERUP, KARL (Adolph), 1857-1919

06012 *The pilgrim Kamanita; a legendary romance.* William Heinemann, London, 1911, 305p, Cloth, Novel

GLANVILLE, ERNEST, 1856-1925

06013 *Tyopa; a bush romance.* Methuen, London, 1920, 247p, Cloth, Novel

GLASBY, JOHN (Stephen), 1928-   [*biography included*]

06013 *Project Jove.* Ace Double, New York, 1971, 140p, Paper, Novel

as J. B. Dexter:

06014 *The Time Kings.* Badger, London, 1958, 158p, Paper, Novel

as Victor La Salle, house pseud.:

06015 *Dawn of the half-gods.* John Spencer, London, 1953, 128p, Paper, Novel

as A. J. Merak:

06016 *Barrier unknown.* Badger, London, 1960, 142p, Paper, Novel
06017 *Dark Andromeda.* Panther, London, 1954, 159p, Cloth, Novel
06018 *Dark conflict.* Badger, London, 1959, 157p, Paper, Novel
06019 *The dark millennium.* Badger, London, 1959, 157p, Paper, Novel
      The frozen planet. [see 06021A]
06020 *Hydrosphere.* Badger, London, 1960, 142p, Paper, Novel
06021 *No dawn and no horizon.* Badger, London, 1959, 158p, Paper, Novel
06021A retitled: *The frozen planet.* Belmont, New York, 1969, 142p, Paper, Novel

as J. L. Powers:

06022 *Black abyss.* Badger, London, 1960, 142p, Paper, Novel

with Arthur Roberts as Berl Cameron, house pseud:

02466 *Cosmic Echelon.* Curtis Warren, London, 1952, 128p, Cloth, Novel [Terran Empire series]
02471 *Sphero Nova.* Curtis Warren, London, 1952, 159p, Cloth, Novel

with Arthur Roberts as Rand Le Page, house pseud:

06023 *Satellite B.C.* Curtis Warren, London, 1952, 127p, Paper, Novel
06024 *Time and space.* Curtis Warren, London, 1952, 128p, Cloth, Novel [Terran Empire series]
06025 *Zero Point.* Curtis Warren, London, 1952, 128p, Cloth, Novel

with Arthur Roberts as Paul Lorraine, house pseud:

06026 *Zenith-D.* Curtis Warren, London, 1952, 159p, Cloth, Novel

GLASGOW, ELLEN (Anderson Gholson), 1874-1945

06027 *The shadowy third.* Jenkins, Richmond, 192?, 42p, Cloth?, Story
06028 *The shadowy third, and other stories.* Doubleday, Page, Garden City, 1923, 291p, Cloth, Coll.

GLASGOW IN 1910
   see: ENGLAND IN 1910

GLASKIN, GERALD M(arcus), 1923-   [*biography included*]

06029 *A change of mind.* Barrie & Rockliff, London, 1959, 232p, Cloth, Novel

GLASS, Reverend Mrs. CHARLES WILDER [Kate Elizabeth Glass, 1874-]

06030 *Her invisible spirit mate; a scientific novel; and psychological lessons on how to make the world more beautiful.* J. F. McElheney, Los Angeles, 1917, 116p, Paper, Novel

GLASS, Rev. Mrs. CHARLES WILDER (cont.)

06031   *Romance in starland; a scientific novel.* J.
        F. McElheney Printing Co., Los Angeles,
        1915, 83p, Paper, Novel
06032   *Romance in starland, and other stories.* Los
        Angeles, 192?, 272p, Paper?, Coll. [includes
        06030, 06031, 06033]
06033   *Ruth's marriage in Mars; a scientific novel.*
        J. F. McElheney, Los Angeles, 1912, 56p,
        Paper, Novel

GLASS, THEODORE
    see: THEODAMUS

GLEIG, CHARLES, 1862-

06034   *When all men starve, showing how England ha-
        zarded her naval supremacy, and the horrors
        which followed the interruption of her food
        supply.* John Lane, The Bodley Head, London,
        1898, 192p, Cloth, Novel

GLEMSER, BERNARD
    see: CRANE, ROBERT

GLENDON, GEORGE

06035   *The Emperor of the air.* Methuen, London,
        1910, 311p, Cloth, Novel

GLENNING, RAYMOND

06036   *The corpse sat up.* Scientific Thriller, Syd-
        ney, 1951, 30p, Paper, Story [cover byline
        reads "Paul Valdez"]
06037   *Seven for murder.* Scientific Thriller, Syd-
        ney, 1951, 30p, Paper, Story

GLICKSOHN, SUSAN WOOD

06038   *The poison maiden and the great bitch; female
        stereotypes in Marvel superhero comics.*
        T-K Graphics, Baltimore, 1974, 36p, Paper,
        Nonf.

GLOAG, JOHN (Edwards), 1896-

06039   *First one and twenty; an omnibus volumes in-
        cluding To-morrow's yesterday and twenty
        short stories.* George Allen & Unwin, Lon-
        don, 1946, 240p, Cloth, Coll.
06040   *Manna.* Cassell, London, 1940, 280p, Cloth,
        Novel
06041   *The new pleasure.* George Allen & Unwin, Lon-
        don, 1933, 304p, Cloth, Novel
06042   *99%.* Cassell, London, 1944, 186p, Cloth, Novel
06043   *To-morrow's yesterday.* George Allen & Unwin,
        London, 1932, 184p, Cloth, Novel
06044   *Winter's youth.* George Allen & Unwin, London,
        1934, 312p, Cloth, Novel

GLOSSOP, REGINALD

06045   *Burning sands.* "Studies" Publications, Mar-
        seille, France, 1928, 328p, Cloth, Novel
06046   *The Crystal Globe.* Odhams Press, London,
        1922, 288p, Cloth, Novel
06047   *The Egyptian Venus; a romance.* Regency Press,
        London, 1946, 202p, Cloth, Novel
06048   *The ghastly few.* Reginald Glossop, London
        [but actually published in France], 1932,
        227p, Paper, Novel
06049   *The magic mirror; a romance.* Odhams Press,
        London, 1923, 288p, Cloth, Novel
06050   *The orphan of space; a tale of downfall.* G.
        MacDonald & Co., London, 1926, 310p, Cloth,
        Novel

GLOVATSKI, ALEXANDER [Aleksander Glowacki,
1847-1912]

as Boleslaus Prus:

06051   *Pharaoh; an historical romance of ancient
        Egypt.* Abbey Press, New York, 1901, 187p,
        Cloth, Novel [abridged?]

as Alexander Glovatski:

06051A retitled: *The pharaoh and the priest; an his-
        torical novel of ancient Egypt.* Little,
        Brown, Boston, 1902, 696p, Cloth, Novel

GLOWACKI, ALEKSANDER
    see: GLOVATSKI, ALEXANDER

GLUCK, SINCLAIR, 1887-

06052   *The house of the missing.* Dodd, Mead, New
        York, 1924, 303p, Cloth, Novel

GLUT, DONALD F(rank), 1944-   [*biography included*]

06053   *Bugged!* Manor, New York, 1974, 192p, Paper,
        Novel
06054   *The Frankenstein legend; a tribute to Mary
        Shelley and Boris Karloff.* Scarecrow Press
        Metuchen, NJ, 1973, 372p, Cloth, Nonf.

GLUYAS, CONSTANCE, 1920-

06055   *Vantage Hall.* Leisure, North Hollywood, 1971
        190p, Paper, Novel

GLYN, (Alice) CORALIE, 186?-1928

06056   *A woman of to-morrow; a tale of the 20th cen-
        tury.* Women's Printing Society, London,
        1896, 172p, Cloth, Novel

GLYNN, A(nthony) A(rthur), 1929-

06057   *Plan for conquest.* Badger, London, 1963, 15?
        Paper, Novel

as John E. Muller, house pseud:

06058   *Search the dark stars.* Badger, London, 1961
        158p, Paper, Novel

GNOLI, DOMENICO, 1933-

06059 *Orestes; or, The art of smiling.* Simon & Schuster, New York, 1961, 71p, Cloth, Novel

GOBLE, (Lloyd) NEIL, 1933-   [*biography included*]

06060 *Asimov analyzed.* Mirage Press, Baltimore, 1972, 174p, Cloth, Nonf.
06061 *Condition green: Tokyo.* Charles E. Tuttle, Rutland, Vermont, 1967, 215p, Cloth, Novel

GOBSCH, HANNS, 1883-

06062 *Death rattle.* Faber & Faber, London, 1932, 322p, Cloth, Novel

GODBER, NOËL (Lambert), 1881-

06063 *Amazing spectacles!* John Long, London, 1931, 288p, Cloth, Novel

GODDARD, RICHARD E.

06064 *The Whistling Ancestors.* Stanley Smith, London, 1936, 256p, Cloth, Novel

GODDEN, (Margaret) RUMER, 1907-   [*biography included*]

06065 *Chinese puzzle.* Peter Davies, London, 1936, 149p, Cloth, Novel

GODFREY, HAL, pseud. [Charlotte O'Conor Eccles]

06066 *The rejuvenation of Miss Semaphore; a farcical novel.* Jarrold & Sons, London, 1897, 239p, Cloth, Novel

GODFREY, HOLLIS, 1874-1936

06067 *The man who ended war.* Little, Brown, Boston, 1908, 301p, Cloth, Novel

GODOLPHIN
    see: LYTTON, EDWARD

GODWIN, GEORGE (Stanley), 1889-

06068 *Empty victory.* John Long, London, 1932, 288p, Cloth, Novel

GODWIN, TOM, 1915-

06069 *Beyond another sun.* Curtis, New York, 1971, 190p, Paper, Novel
06070 *The space barbarians.* Pyramid, New York, 1964, 169p, Paper, Novel [Ragnarok #2]
    Space prison. [see 06071A]
06071 *The survivors.* Gnome Press, Hicksville, NY, 1958, 190p, Cloth, Novel [Ragnarok #1]

06071A retitled: *Space prison.* Pyramid, New York, 1960, 158p, Paper, Novel [Ragnarok #1]

GODWIN, WILLIAM, 1756-1836

06072 *St. Leon; a tale of the thirteenth century.* G.G. & J. Robinson, London, 1799, 4vol, Cloth, Novel; Richard Bentley, London, 1799, 3vol, Cloth, Novel

GOETHE, JOHANN WOLFGANG von, 1749-1832

06073 *The tale.* James R. Osgood, Boston, 1877, 86p, Cloth, Novel
06073A retitled: *The parable.* Harcourt, Brace & World, New York, 1963, 73p, Cloth, Novel

GOFF, GEORGENA

06074 *The black dog.* Belmont, New York, 1971, 156p, Paper, Novel

GOLD, H(orace) L(eonard), 1914-   [*biography included*]

06075 *Bodyguard, and four other short novels from Galaxy.* Doubleday, Garden City, 1960, 312p, Cloth, Anth.
06076 *The fifth Galaxy reader.* Doubleday, Garden City, 1961, 260p, Cloth, Anth.
06077 *Five Galaxy short novels.* Doubleday, Garden City, 1958, 287p, Cloth, Anth.
06078 *The fourth Galaxy reader.* Doubleday, Garden City, 1959, 264p, Cloth, Anth.
06079 *Galaxy reader of science fiction.* Crown Publishers, New York, 1952, 566p, Cloth, Anth.
06080 *Mind partner, and 8 other novelets from Galaxy.* Doubleday, Garden City, 1961, 263p, Cloth, Anth.
06081 *The old die rich, and other science fiction stories, with working notes and an analysis of each story.* Crown Publishers, New York, 1955, 250p, Cloth, Coll.
06082 *The second Galaxy reader of science fiction.* Crown Publishers, New York, 1954, 504p, Cloth, Anth.
06082A retitled: *Galaxy science fiction omnibus.* Grayson & Grayson, London, 1955, 350p, Cloth, Anth. [abridged]
06083 *The sixth Galaxy reader.* Doubleday, Garden City, 1962, 240p, Cloth, Anth.
06084 *The third Galaxy reader.* Doubleday, Garden City, 1958, 262p, Cloth, Anth.
06085 *The world that couldn't be, and 8 other novelets from Galaxy.* Doubleday, Garden City, 1959, 288p, Cloth, Anth.

GOLDBLATT, BURT, with Chris Steinbrunner

06086 *Cinema of the fantastic.* Saturday Review Press, New York, 1972, 282p, Cloth, Nonf.

GOLDFRAP, JOHN HENRY
    see: LAWTON, Capt. WILBUR

GOLDIE, Mrs. BARRÉ [Bertha], d. 1938

06087   *The piper of Arristoun.* Ward, Lock, London,
        1935, 318p, Cloth, Novel

GOLDIN, STEPHEN (Charles), 1947-   [*biography
included*]

06088   *The alien condition.* Ballantine, New York,
        1973, 206p, Paper, Anth.

with David Gerrold:

05912   *Alternities.* Dell, New York, 1974, 175p,
        Paper, Anth.
05913   *Generation; an anthology of speculative fic-
        tion.* Dell, New York, 1972, 236p, Paper,
        Anth.
05914   *Protostars.* Ballantine, New York, 1971, 271p,
        Paper, Anth.
05915   *Science fiction emphasis I; an anthology of
        original science fiction.* Ballantine, New
        York, 1974, 211p, Paper, Anth.

GOLDING, LOUIS, 1895-1958

        The call of the hand, and other stories. [see
        06089A]
06089   *The Doomington wanderer; a book of tales.*
        Victor Gollancz, London, 1934, 286p, Cloth,
        Coll.
06089A retitled: *The call of the hand, and other
        stories.* Poynings Press, Wineham, UK, 1944,
        32p, Paper, Coll. [abridged]
06090   *The frightening talent.* W. H. Allen, London,
        1973, 189p, Cloth, Novel
06091   *Honey for the ghost.* Hutchinson, London,
        1949, 412p, Cloth, Novel
06092   *The Miracle Boy.* Alfred A. Knopf, London,
        1927, 315p, Cloth, Novel

GOLDING, MORTON J(ay), 1925-   [*biography included*]

06093   *Night mare.* Dell, New York, 1970, 174p,
        Paper, Novel

as Jay Martin:

06094   *Digging the love goddess.* Berkley Medallion,
        New York, 1972, 192p, Paper, Novel
06095   *Laying the ghost.* Berkley Medallion, New
        York, 1970, 222p, Paper, Novel
06096   *Make love, not waves.* Lancer, New York,
        1967, 159p, Paper, Novel

GOLDING, WILLIAM (Gerald), 1911-   [*biography
included*]

06097   *The inheritors.* Faber & Faber, London, 1955,
        233p, Cloth, Novel
06098   *Lord of the flies; a novel.* Faber & Faber,
        London, 1954, 248p, Cloth, Novel
06099   *The scorpion god; three short novels.* Faber
        & Faber, London, 1971, 178p, Cloth, Coll.

GOLDMAN, LAWRENCE LOUIS

06100   *Takeover.* Curtis, New York, 1973, 221p, Paper,
        Novel

GOLDMAN, WILLIAM (W.), 1931-   [*biography included*]

06101   *The princess bride; S. Morgenstern's classic
        tale of true love and high adventure; the
        'good parts' version, abridged.* Harcourt
        Brace Jovanovich, New York, 1973, 308p,
        Cloth, Novel

GOLDRING, DOUGLAS, 1887-1960

06102   *The merchant of souls.* Jarrolds Publishers,
        London, 1926, 253p, Cloth, Novel

with Hubert Nepean:

06103   *The solvent.* C. W. Daniel, London, 1920,
        256p, Cloth, Novel

GOLDSMITH, JOHN FRANCIS

06104   *President Randolph as I knew him; an account
        of the historic events of the 1950's and
        1960's, written from the personal experi-
        ences of the secretary to the President.*
        Dorrance & Co., Philadelphia, 1935, 448p,
        Cloth, Novel

GOLDSMITH-CARTER, GEORGE
    see: CARTER, GEORGE GOLDSMITH-

GOLDSTEIN, WILLIAM (Isaac), 1932-

06105   *Dr. Phibes.* Award, New York, 1971, 152p,
        Paper, Movie [Dr. Phibes #1]
06106   *Dr. Phibes rises again.* Award, New York,
        1973, 187p, Paper, Movie [Dr. Phibes #2]

GOLDSTON, ROBERT C(onroy), 1927-   [*biography included*]

06107   *The eighth day.* Rinehart & Co., New York,
        1956, 345p, Cloth, Novel
06108   *The last of Lazarus.* Random House, New York,
        1966, 245p, Cloth, Novel

GOLL, REINHOLD W(eimar), 1897-   [*biography
included*]

06109   *Spaceship to Planet Veta.* Westminster Press,
        Philadelphia, 1962, 160p, Cloth, Novel [Veta
        #2]
06110   *Through space to Planet T.* Westminster Press,
        Philadelphia, 1963, 156p, Cloth, Novel
06111   *The visitors from Planet Veta.* Westminster
        Press, Philadelphia, 1961, 116p, Cloth,
        Novel [Veta #1]

GOLON, ANNE, with Serge Golon as Sergeanne
Golon

06112   *Angélique and the demon.* Heinemann, London,
        1973, 482p, Cloth, Novel [Angelique #8]

GOLON, SERGE, 1903-1972, with Anne Golon as
Sergeanne Golon

06112 *Angélique and the demon.* Heinemann, London,
1973, 482p, Cloth, Novel [Angelique #8]

GOLON, SERGEANNE, pseud.
see: GOLON, ANNE and GOLON, SERGE

GOMPERTZ, MARTIN L. A.
see: GANPAT

G(onzalez) GALLEGO, S(erapio), 1883-1944

06113 *John Smith, Emperor.* Guild Press, St. Paul,
Minn., 1944, 160p, Cloth, Novel

GOOD, CHARLES H.
see: GOODRICH, CHARLES

GOODCHILD, GEORGE, 1888-1969

06114 *Doctor Zils' experiment.* Ward, Lock, London,
1953, 206p, Cloth, Novel
06115 *A message from space.* Jarrolds, London, 1931,
354p, Cloth, Novel

GOODE, ARTHUR RUSSELL
see: RUSSELL, ARTHUR

GOODRICH, CHARLES (H.)

06116 *The Genesis of Nam; a new Earth with its own
blue heaven.* Dorrance & Co., Philadelphia,
1956, 136p, Cloth, Novel

as Charles H. Good:

06117 *The wheel comes a turn; a novel based on scientific study of war of the sexes.* Vantage
Press, New York, 1963, 224p, Cloth, Novel

GOODRICH-FREER, A(dela M.) [Miss X], d. 1931

06118 *The professional, and other psychic stories.*
Hurst & Blackett, London, 1900, 288p, Cloth,
Anth.

GOODRIDGE ROBERTS, G. E. T.
see: ROBERTS, THEODORE

GOODWIN, HAROLD LELAND
see: BLAINE, JOHN

GOODWIN, JOHN C(uthbert), 1891-

06119 *The Rainbox.* Hutchinson, London, 1935, 286p,
Cloth, Novel

GOPČEVIĆ, SPIRIDION, 1855-

06120 *The conquest of Britain in 1888, and the sea
fights and battles that led to it.* R. N.
Griffith, Portsmouth, UK, 1887, 54p, Paper?,
Novel

GORDON, CAROLINE, 1895-

06121 *The glory of Hera.* Doubleday, Garden City,
1972, 398p, Cloth, Novel

GORDON, CHARLES PIRIE-
see: PIRIE-GORDON, CHARLES

GORDON, D. M.

06122 *Disciples of darkness.* Orpheus Series, New
York, 1968, 187p, Paper, Novel

GORDON, DAVID

06123 *The five stories of man.* Christopher Publishing House, Boston, 1948, 76p, Cloth, Coll.

GORDON, DONALD, pseud.
see: PAYNE, DONALD GORDON

GORDON, FRITZ, pseud.
see: JARVIS, FRED G. and VAN BEEVER, ROBERT

GORDON, Lord GRANVILLE (Armyne), 1856-1907

06124 *Notes from another world.* Remington & Co.,
London, 1886, 267p, Cloth, Novel

GORDON, HELEN
see: VAN ANDERSON, HELEN

GORDON, I(rwin) L(eslie), 1888-1954, with
A. J. Frueh

05680 *The log of the Ark, by Noah; hieroglyphics by
Ham.* E. P. Dutton, New York, 1915, 147p,
Cloth, Novel

GORDON, JOHN, 1925-   [*biography included*]

06125 *The giant under the snow.* Hutchinson Junior
Books, London, 1968, 184p, Cloth, Novel
06126 *The house on the brink.* Hutchinson, London,
1970, 184p, Cloth, Novel

GORDON, NANCY McKAY

06127 *Her bungalow; an Atlantian memory.* Hermetic
Publishing Co., Chicago, 1898, 238p, Cloth,
Novel

GORDON, NEIL, pseud. [Archibald Gordon Macdonell, 1895-1941]

06128   *The professor's poison.* Harcourt, Brace, New York, 1928, 280p, Cloth, Novel; Longmans, Green, London, 1928, 302p, Cloth, Novel

GORDON, REX, pseud. [Stanley Bennett Hough, 1917-   ] [*biography included*]

        First on Mars. [see 06131A]
06129   *First through time.* Ace, New York, 1962, 160p, Paper, Novel
06129A retitled: *The time factor.* Anthony Gibbs & Phillips, London, 1964, 125p, Cloth, Novel
06130   *First to the stars.* Ace, New York, 1959, 190p, Paper, Novel
06130A retitled: *The worlds of Eclos.* Consul, London, 1961, 160p, Paper, Novel
06131   *No man Friday.* William Heinemann, London, 1956, 201p, Cloth, Novel
06131A retitled: *First on Mars.* Ace, New York, 1957, 192p, Paper, Novel
        The paw of God. [see 06132A]
        The time factor. [see 06129A]
06132   *Utopia minus X.* Ace, New York, 1966, 190p, Paper, Novel
06132A retitled: *The paw of God.* Library 33, London, 1967, 189p, Cloth, Novel
06133   *Utopia 239.* William Heinemann, London, 1955, 208p, Cloth, Novel
        The worlds of Eclos. [see 06130A]
06134   *The Yellow fraction.* Ace, New York, 1969, 160p, Paper, Novel

as S. B. Hough:

06135   *Beyond the eleventh hour.* Hodder & Stoughton, London, 1961, 190p, Cloth, Novel
06136   *Extinction bomber.* Bodley Head, London, 1956, 192p, Cloth, Novel
06137   *Mission in Guemo; a novel.* Hodder & Stoughton, London, 1953, 195p, Cloth, Novel

GORDON, (Richard) STUART

06138   *One-Eye.* DAW, New York, 1973, 224p, Paper, Novel [Eyes Trilogy #1]
06139   *Time story.* New English Library, London, 1972, 144p, Paper, Novel
06140   *Two-Eyes.* DAW, New York, 1974, 240p, Paper, Novel [Eyes Trilogy #2]

GORDON, THEODORE J., 1930-   [*biography included*], with Harry Harrison

06141   *Ahead of time.* Doubleday, Garden City, 1972, 201p, Cloth, Nonf. Anth.

GORER, GEOFFREY (Edgar Solomon), 1905-

06142   *Nobody talks politics; a satire.* Michael Joseph, London, 1936, 224p, Cloth, Novel

GOREY, EDWARD (St. John), 1925-   [*biography included*]

06143   *The haunted looking glass; ghost stories.* Looking Glass Library, New York, 1959, 314p, Cloth, Anth.

GORMAN, Major J(ames) T(homas), 1869-

06144   *Gorilla gold.* Blackie & Son, London, 1937, 224p, Cloth, Novel

GORST, H(arold) E(dward), 1868-1950

06145   *Farthest south; an account of the startling discovery made by the Wise Antarctic Expedition.* Greening & Co., London, 1900, 181p, Cloth, Novel
06146   *Without bloodshed; a probability of the twentieth century.* Roxburghe Press, Westminster, 1897, 109p, Cloth, Novel

GORTSCHAKOFF AND BISMARCK

06147   *Gortschakoff and Bismarck; or, Europe in 1940; a dream.* J. Parker & Co., Oxford, 1878, 14p, Paper, Story

GOSS, GARY (L.), 1934-

06148   *Hitler's daughter.* Lyle Stuart, Secaucus, NJ, 1973, 274p, Cloth, Novel

GOSSE, JEANNE

06149   *The stone of Lauzières.* Falcon Press, London, 1947, 221p, Cloth, Novel

GOTLIEB, PHYLLIS (Fay), 1926-   [*biography included*]

06150   *Sunburst.* Gold Medal, Greenwich, 1964, 160p, Paper, Novel

GOTTHELF, EZRA GERSON, 1907-

06151   *The island of Not-me; a true chronicle of the life of Geoghan Willbe on the island of Not-me, preceded by an account of his person before his arrival upon that famous isle.* Galleon Press, New York, 1935, 156p, Cloth, Novel

GOTTHELF, JEREMIAS, pseud. [Albert Bitzius, 1797-1854]

06152   *The black spider.* John Calder, London, 1958, 135p, Cloth, Novel

GOTTLIEB, HINKO

06153   *The key to the great gate.* Simon & Schuster, New York, 1947, 179p, Cloth, Novel

GOTTLIEB, SEYMOUR

06154   *Pattern of a man.* Exposition Press, New York, 1952, 246p, Cloth, Novel

GOUDGE, ELIZABETH (de Beauchamp), 1900-   [biography included]

06155 Linnets and Valerians. Brockhampton Press, Leicester, UK, 1964, 232p, Cloth, Novel
06156 The little white horse. University of London Press, London, 1946, 286p, Cloth, Novel
06157 The lost angel; stories. Hodder & Stoughton, London, 1971, 95p, Cloth, Coll.
06158 The middle window. Duckworth, London, 1935, 344p, Cloth, Novel

GOULART, RON (ald Joseph), 1933-   [biography included]

06159 After things fell apart. Ace, New York, 1970, 189p, Paper, Novel
06160 Broke down engine, and other troubles with machines. Macmillan, New York, 1971, 192p, Cloth, Coll.
06161 The Chameleon Corps, & other shape changers. Macmillan, New York, 1972, 216p, Cloth, Coll. [Ben Jolson #2]
06162 Cheap thrills; an informal history of the pulp magazines. Arlington House, New Rochelle, NY, 1972, 192p, Cloth, Nonf.
06162A retitled: An informal history of the pulp magazines. Ace, New York, 1973, 192p, Paper, Nonf.
06163 Clockwork's pirates. Ace Double, New York, 1971, 111p, Paper, Novel
06164 Death Cell. Beagle, New York, 1971, 153p, Paper, Novel [Barnum System series; Jack Sumner #1]
06165 The fire-eater. Ace, New York, 1970, 159p, Paper, Novel [Barnum System series]
06166 Flux. DAW, New York, 1974, 159p, Paper, Novel [Ben Jolson #3]
06167 Gadget Man. Doubleday, Garden City, 1971, 161p, Cloth, Novel
06168 Ghost breaker. Ace Double, New York, 1971, 142p, Paper, Coll.
06169 Hawkshaw. Doubleday, Garden City, 1972, 162p, Cloth, Novel
       An informal history of the pulp magazines. [see 06162A]
06170 Odd job #101, and other future crimes and intrigues. Charles Scribner's Sons, New York, 1974, 166p, Cloth, Coll.
06171 Plunder. Beagle, New York, 1972, 156p, Paper, Novel [Barnum System series; Jack Sumner #2]
06172 Shaggy planet. Lancer, New York, 1972, 175p, Paper, Novel [Barnum System series]
06173 Spacehawk, Inc. DAW, New York, 1974, 160p, Paper, Novel [Barnum System series]
06174 The sword swallower. Doubleday, Garden City, 1968, 181p, Cloth, Novel [Ben Jolson #1]
06175 A talent for the invisible. DAW, New York, 1973, 144p, Paper, Novel
06176 The tin angel. DAW, New York, 1973, 144p, Paper, Novel
06177 What's become of Screwloose? and other inquiries. Charles Scribner's Sons, New York, 1971, 184p, Cloth, Coll.
06178 Wildsmith. Ace, New York, 1972, 128p, Paper, Novel

as Kenneth Robeson, house pseud.:

06179 The Avenger; black chariots. Warner Paperback Library, New York, 1974, 142p, Paper, Novel [Avenger #30]

06180 The Avenger; red moon. Warner Paperback Library, New York, 1974, 158p, Paper, Novel [Avenger #26]
06181 The Avenger; the purple zombie. Warner Paperback Library, New York, 1974, 141p, Paper, Novel [Avenger #27]

as Con Steffanson, house pseud.:

06182 Flash Gordon; the lion men of Mongo. Avon, New York, 1974, 159p, Paper, Novel [Flash Gordon #1]
06183 Flash Gordon; the plague of sound. Avon, New York, 1974, 158p, Paper, Novel [Flash Gordon #2]
06184 Flash Gordon; the space circus. Avon, New York, 1974, 157p, Paper, Novel [Flash Gordon #3]

GOULD, ARTHUR LEE, pseud. [Arthur Stanley Gould Lee, 1894-1975]

06185 An airplane in the Arabian nights. T. Werner Laurie, London, 1947, 240p, Cloth, Novel

GOULD, (Sir) F(rancis) C(arruthers), 1844-1925

06186 Explorations in the Sit-tee Desert, being a comic account of the supposed discovery of the ruins of the London Stock Exchange some 2000 years hence. Unwin Bros., London, 1880?, 15p, Cloth, Story

GOULD, MAGGY

06187 The dowry; a novel. William Morrow, New York, 1949, 244p, Cloth, Novel

GOULD, S. BARING-
    see: BARING-GOULD, S.

GOURMONT, RÉMY de, 1858-1915

06188 Mr. Antiphilos, satyr. Lieber & Lewis, New York, 1922, 272p, Cloth, Novel
06189 A night in the Luxembourg. J. W. Luce, Boston, 1912, 223p, Cloth, Novel; Stephen Swift, London, 1912, 221p, Cloth, Novel

GOUVRIEUX, MARC, pseud.

06190 With wings outspread; a romance of the War of 1920. William Heinemann, London, 1916, 243p, Cloth, Novel

GOUVY, GERTRUDE

06191 Moonflight; a science-fiction fantasy for young readers and readers who will be young in heart forever. Greenwich Book Publishers, New York, 1956, 88p, Cloth, Novel

GOVE, PHILIP BABCOCK, 1902-1972 [*biography included*]

06192   *The imaginary voyage in prose fiction; a history of its criticism and a guide for its study, with an annotated check list of 215 imaginary voyages from 1700 to 1800...* Columbia University Press, New York, 1941, 445p, Cloth, Nonf.

GOWANS, ADAM L(uke)

06193   *Famous ghost-stories by English authors.* Gowans & Gray, London, 1910, 128p, Cloth, Anth.

GOWING, Mrs. (Emilia) AYLMER

06194   *By Thames and Tiber.* John Long, London, 1903, 315p, Cloth, Novel

GOWLAND, JOHN STAFFORD, 1898-

06195   *Beyond Mars.* Gryphon, London, 1956, 191p, Cloth, Novel

GOYNE, RICHARD

06196   *The kiss of Pharaoh; the love story of Tutankhamen.* Frederick A. Stokes, New York, 1923, 307p, Cloth, Novel

GOZLAN, LÉON, 1806-1866

06197   *The man among the monkeys; or, Ninety days in apeland.* Ward, Lock, London, 1873, 312p, Cloth, Novel [published anonymously]
06197A retitled: *The emotions of Polydore Marasquin.* Vizetelly & Co., London, 1888, 257p, Cloth, Novel
06197B retitled: *Monkey Island; or, The emotions of Polydore Marasquin.* Frederick Warne, London, 1888, 156p, Cloth, Novel

GRAAT, HEINRICH, pseud. [George Wolk]

06198   *The devil and Ben Camden.* Belmont, New York, 1970, 151p, Paper, Novel [Ben Camden #2]
06199   *A place of demons.* Belmont, New York, 1972, 147p, Paper, Novel [Ben Camden #3]
06200   *The revenge of Increase Sewell.* Belmont, New York, 1969, 157p, Paper, Novel [Ben Camden #1]

GRABER, ALEXANDER
   see: CORDELL, ALEXANDER

THE GRADUATED ROBOT, AND OTHER STORIES
   see: ELWOOD, ROGER

GRAEME, BRUCE, pseud. [Graham Montague Jeffries, 1900-   ], with Anthony Armstrong

00497   *When the bells rang; a tale of what might have been.* George G. Harrap, London, 1943, 240p, Cloth, Novel

GRAHAM, HARVEY, pseud. [Isaac Harvey Flack, 1912-1966]

06201   *A crab was crushed; a novel.* Rich & Cowan, London, 1937, 281p, Cloth, Novel

GRAHAM, J(ohn) M(ichael)

06202   *Voice from Earth.* Robert Hale, London, 1972, 191p, Cloth, Novel

GRAHAM, P(eter) ANDERSON, d. 1925

06203   *The collapse of Homo sapiens.* G. P. Putnam's Sons, London, 1923, 276p, Cloth, Novel

GRAHAM, ROGER PHILLIPS
   see: PHILLIPS, ROG

GRAHAM, VICTORIA

06204   *The Witchstone.* Pyramid, New York, 1974, 254, Paper, Novel

GRAHAM, (Matilda) WINIFRED (Muriel), d. 1950

06205   *Angels and devils and man.* Cassell, London, 1904, 344p, Cloth, Novel
06206   *The frozen death.* Hutchinson, London, 1938, 287p, Cloth, Novel
06207   *Ghostly strength.* Hutchinson, London, 1936, 288p, Cloth, Novel
06208   *Glenvirgin's ghost.* Hutchinson, London, 1938, 295p, Cloth, Novel
06209   *The gods of the dead.* William Rider & Son, London, 1912, 316p, Cloth, Novel
06210   *Hallowmas Abbey.* Hutchinson, London, 1935, 304p, Cloth, Novel
06211   *"Ninety and nine just persons."* Hutchinson, London, 1924, 288p, Cloth, Novel

GRAHAME, EDITH

06212   *Terrenia.* Presbyterian Board of Publication, Philadelphia, 1866, 120p, Cloth, Novel

GRAHAME-WHITE, CLAUDE, 1879-1959, with Harry Harper

06213   *The invisible war-plane; a tale of air adventure in the great campaign.* Blackie & Son, London, 1915, 272p, Cloth, Novel

GRAINGER, BOYNE, pseud., 1882-

06214   *The Jester's Reign.* Carrick & Evans, New York, 1938, 318p, Cloth, Novel

GRAINGER, F. E.
    see: HILL, HEADON

GRAINVILLE, JEAN-BAPTISTE COUSIN de
    see: COUSIN de GRAINVILLE, JEAN-BAPTISTE

GRANAMOUR, A. de
    see: THE BEWITCHED

GRANT, DONALD M(etcalf), 1927-

06215 *Swordsmen and supermen.* Centaur Press, New
       York, 1972, 120p, Paper, Anth. [published
       anonymously]

with Joseph H. Crawford Jr. and James J.
Donahue:

03552 *"333"; a bibliography of the science-fantasy
       novel.* Grandon Co., Providence, RI, 1953,
       80p, Cloth, Nonf.

with Thomas G. Hadley:

06216 *Rhode Island on Lovecraft.* (Donald M. Grant),
       Providence, RI, 1945, 26p, Paper, Nonf. Anth.

GRANT, GARY

06217 *Supernatural tales I.* Quartet, London, 1974,
       62p, Paper, Anth.
06218 *Supernatural tales II.* Quartet, London, 1974,
       59p, Paper, Anth.

GRANT, JOAN, pseud. [Joan Marshall Kelsey,
1907-   ] [*biography included*]

       Castle Cloud. [see 06220A]
06219 *Eyes of Horus.* Methuen, London, 1942, 404p,
       Cloth, Novel [Ra-Ab Hotep #1]
06220 *The laird and the lady.* Methuen, London, 1949,
       281p, Cloth, Novel
06220A retitled: *Castle Cloud.* Ace, New York, 1971,
       253p, Paper, Novel
06221 *Life as Carola.* Methuen, London, 1939, 396p,
       Cloth, Novel
06222 *Lord of the horizon.* Methuen, London, 1943,
       291p, Cloth, Novel [Ra-Ab Hotep #2]
06223 *Redskin morning, and other stories.* Methuen,
       London, 1944, 115p, Cloth, Coll.
06224 *Return to Elysium.* Methuen, London, 1947,
       317p, Cloth, Novel
06225 *Scarlet feather.* Methuen, London, 1945, 264p,
       Cloth, Novel
06226 *So Moses was born.* Methuen, London, 1952,
       247p, Cloth, Novel
06227 *Winged pharaoh.* Arthur Barker, London, 1937,
       382p, Cloth, Novel

GRANT, JOE [Joseph Clarence Grant, 1908-   ],
with Dick Huemer

06228 *Baby Weems.* Doubleday, Doran, Garden City,
       1941, 66p, Cloth, Movie

GRANT, MARCUS

06229 *Horror.* Heinemann Educational, London, 1974,
       92p, Paper, Nonf.

GRANT, MATTHEW

06230 *Hyper-drive.* Digit, London, 1962, 160p, Paper,
       Novel

GRANT, MAXWELL, house pseud. [see also Walter
B. Gibson and Dennis Lynds]

05957 *The black master.* Pyramid, New York, 1974,
       174p, Paper, Novel [Pyramid Shadow #2] [by
       Walter B. Gibson]
06231 *Cry shadow!* Belmont, New York, 1965, 157p,
       Paper, Novel [New Shadow #4] [by Dennis
       Lynds]
05958 *The death tower.* Bantam, New York, 1969, 138p,
       Paper, Novel [Bantam Shadow #4] [by Walter
       B. Gibson]
05959 *The eyes of the Shadow.* Bantam, New York,
       1969, 171p, Paper, Novel [Bantam Shadow #2]
       [by Walter B. Gibson]
05960 *Gangdom's doom.* Bantam, New York, 1970, 166p,
       Paper, Novel [Bantam Shadow #7] [by Walter
       B. Gibson]
05961 *The ghost makers.* Bantam, New York, 1970,
       120p, Paper, Novel [Bantam Shadow #5] [by
       Walter B. Gibson]
05962 *Hidden death.* Bantam, New York, 1970, 138p,
       Paper, Novel [Bantam Shadow #6] [by Walter
       B. Gibson]
05963 *The living Shadow.* Street & Smith, New York,
       1933,   , Cloth, Novel [Shadow #1] [by
       Walter B. Gibson]
06232 *Mark of the Shadow.* Belmont, New York, 1966,
       157p, Paper, Novel [New Shadow #6] [by Den-
       nis Lynds]
05964 *The mobsmen on the spot.* Pyramid, New York,
       1974, 190p, Paper, Novel [Pyramid Shadow #3]
       [by Walter B. Gibson]
06233 *The night of the Shadow.* Belmont, New York,
       1966, 156p, Paper, Novel [New Shadow #8]
       [by Dennis Lynds]
05965 *The Shadow and the voice of murder.* Bantam
       Publications, Los Angeles, 1940, 100p, Paper,
       Novel [Shadow series] [by Walter B. Gibson]
06234 *Shadow beware.* Belmont, New York, 1965, 157p,
       Paper, Novel [New Shadow #3] [by Dennis
       Lynds]
06235 *The Shadow; destination: Moon.* Belmont, New
       York, 1967, 156p, Paper, Novel [New Shadow
       #9] [by Dennis Lynds]
06236 *Shadow--go mad!* Belmont, New York, 1966, 160p,
       Paper, Novel [New Shadow #7] [by Dennis
       Lynds]
05966 *The Shadow laughs!* Bantam, New York, 1969,
       156p, Paper, Novel [Bantam Shadow #3] [by
       Walter B. Gibson]
06237 *The Shadow strikes.* Belmont, New York, 1964,
       157p, Paper, Novel [New Shadow #2] [by Den-
       nis Lynds]
06238 *The Shadow's revenge.* Belmont, New York, 1965,
       156p, Paper, Novel [New Shadow #5] [by Den-
       nis Lynds]
05967 *The weird adventures of the Shadow; grove of
       doom.* Tempo, New York, 1969, 154p, Paper,
       Novel [Shadow series] [by Walter B. Gibson]

GRANT, RICHARD, pseud. [Joseph Calvitt Clarke, 1888-]

06239   *Lives in a box.* Stanley Paul, London, 1951, 224p, Cloth, Novel

GRANT, ROBERT, 1852-1940, with John Boyle O'Reilly, J. S. of Dale, and John T. Wheelright

06240   *The King's men; a tale of to-morrow.* Charles Scribner's Sons, New York, 1884, 270p, Cloth, Novel

GRANT, SEBASTIAN

06241   *Camille 2,000.* Award, New York, 1969, 155p, Paper, Movie

GRANT WATSON, E(lliot) L(ovegood), 1885-

06242   *Moonlight in Ur; a romance.* Noel Douglas, London, 1932, 286p, Cloth, Novel

GRANVILLE, AUSTYN (W.)

06243   *The fallen race.* F. Tennyson Neely, New York, 1892, 352p, Cloth, Novel

with W. Wilson Knott:

06244   *If the devil came to Chicago.* Bow-Knot Publishing Co., Chicago, 1894, 353p, Paper, Novel

GRANVILLE BARKER, (Harley Granville), 1877-1946

06245   *Souls on Fifth.* Little, Brown, Boston, 1917, 61p, Cloth, Novel

GRATACAP, L(ouis) P(ope), 1851-1917

06246   *The certainty of a future life in Mars, being the posthumous papers of Bradford Torrey Dodd.* Irving Press, New York, 1903, 266p, Cloth, Novel
06247   *The end; how the Great War was stopped; a novelistic vagary.* Thomas Benton, New York, 1917, 274p, Cloth, Novel
06248   *The evacuation of England; the twist in the Gulf Stream.* Brentano's, New York, 1908, 321p, Cloth, Novel
06249   *The mayor of New York; a romance of days to come.* G. W. Dillingham, New York, 1910, 471p, Cloth, Novel
06250   *The new northland.* Thomas Benton, New York, 1915, 391p, Cloth, Novel [book has false title page reading: *Crocker Land; a romance of discovery,* by Alfred Erickson, Prof. Hlmath Bjornsen, Antoine Goritz, Spruce Hopkins]
06251   *A woman of the ice age.* Brentano's, New York, 1906, 230p, Cloth, Novel

GRATTAN-SMITH, T(homas) E(dward)

06252   *The cave of a thousand columns.* Hutchinson, London, 1938, 288p, Cloth, Novel

GRAU, WERNHER von, pseud.
   see: SCHOEB, ERIKA

GRAUTOFF, FERDINAND (Heinrich), 1871-1935

as Parabellum:

06253   *Banzai!* Musson Book Co., Toronto, 1908, 320p, Cloth, Novel

as Seestern:

06254   *Armageddon 190-.* Kegan Paul, Trench, Trübner, London, 1907, 402p, Cloth, Novel

GRAVES, C(harles) L(arcom), 1856-1944, with E. V. Lucas

06255   *The war of the Wenuses.* J. W. Arrowsmith, Bristol, 1898, 140p, Paper, Novel [a parody of H. G. Wells' *The war of the worlds*]

GRAVES, CLOTILDE
   see: DEHAN, RICHARD

GRAVES, GORDON HARWOOD, 1884- , with Hettie Elliott

04798   *Fantasies on ancient themes.* Nicholson Printing & Manufacturing Co., Richmond, IN, 1914, 76p, Cloth, Coll.

GRAVES, ROBERT (von Ranke), 1895- [biography included]

06256   *The golden fleece.* Cassell, London, 1944, 371p, Cloth, Novel
06256A   retitled: *Hercules, my shipmate; a novel.* Creative Age Press, New York, 1945, 464p, Cloth, Novel
06257   *Seven days in New Crete; a novel.* Cassell, London, 1949, 281p, Cloth, Novel
06257A   retitled: *Watch the northwind rise.* Creative Age Press, New York, 1949, 290p, Cloth, Novel

GRAY, ARTHUR
   see: INGULPHUS

GRAY, BERKELEY, pseud. [Edwy Searles Brooks, 1889-1965]

06258   *The lost world of Everest.* Collins, London, 1941, 256p, Cloth, Novel

GRAY, CURME

06259   *Murder in Millennium VI.* Shasta Publishers, Chicago, 1951, 249p, Cloth, Novel

GRAY, FRANCES

06260 *B.U.N.C.; a novel.* Constable, London, 1938,
       414p, Cloth, Novel

GRAY, JOHN, 1866-1934

06261 *Park; a fantastic story.* Sheed & Ward, London,
       1932, 128p, Cloth, Novel

GRAY, MARY, 1886-1952

06262 *The temple of Amon Ra.* Margent Press, New
       York, 1945, 249p, Cloth, Novel

GRAY, NICHOLAS STUART, 1922-   [*biography in-cluded*]

06263 *The apple-stone.* Dennis Dobson, London, 1965,
       191p, Cloth, Novel
06264 *Down in the cellar.* Dennis Dobson, London,
       1961, 203p, Cloth, Novel
06265 *Grimbold's other world.* Faber & Faber, London,
       1963, 158p, Cloth, Novel
06266 *Mainly in moonlight; ten stories of sorcery
       and the supernatural.* Faber & Faber, London,
       1965, 159p, Cloth, Coll.
06267 *Over the hills to Fabylon.* Oxford University
       Press, London, 1954, 206p, Cloth, Novel
06268 *The seventh swan; an adventure story.* Dennis
       Dobson, London, 1962, 252p, Cloth, Novel
06269 *The stone cage.* Dennis Dobson, London, 1963,
       246p, Cloth, Novel

GRAY, ROD, house pseud.

06270 *Blow my mind.* Tower, New York, 1970, 153p,
       Paper, Novel [Lady from L.U.S.T. #12]
06271 *The copulation explosion.* Tower, New York,
       1970, 159p, Paper, Novel [Lady from L.U.S.T.
       #14]
06272 *Laid in the future.* Tower, New York, 1969,
       157p, Paper, Novel [Lady from L.U.S.T. #13]
06273 *The poisoned pussy.* Tower, New York, 1969,
       154p, Paper, Novel [Lady from L.U.S.T. #9]

GRAYDON, WILLIAM MURRAY

06274 *The river of darkness; or, Under Africa.*
       Thompson & Thomas, Chicago, 1902, 296p,
       Cloth, Novel
06274A retitled: *Guy in the jungle.* M. A. Donohue,
       Chicago, 1903?, 296p?, Cloth, Novel

GRAZIER, JAMES

06275 *Runts of 61 Cygni C.* Belmont, New York, 1970,
       156p, Paper, Novel

GREAT ASTRONOMICAL DISCOVERIES LATELY MADE BY
SIR JOHN HERSCHEL AT THE CAPE OF GOOD HOPE
   see: LOCKE, RICHARD ADAMS

GREAT BRITAIN IN 1841

06276 *Great Britain in 1841; or, The results of the
       Reform Bill.* Roake & Varty, London, 1831,
       21p, Paper, Story

THE GREAT NAVAL WAR OF 1887
   see: CLOWES, WILLIAM LAIRD

GREAT TALES OF HORROR AND SUSPENSE

06277 *Great tales of horror and suspense; weird tales
       of Edgar Allan Poe; The ghost ship, and other
       ghostly stories; Dracula.* Galahad Books,
       New York, 1974, 268p, Cloth, Anth.

GREAT WAS THE FALL
   see: M., A. H.

GREEN, A. LINCOLN

06278 *The end of an epoch, being the personal nar-
       rative of Adam Godwin, the survivor.* Wil-
       liam Blackwood & Son, Edinburgh, 1901, 391p,
       Cloth, Novel

GREEN, EDITH PIÑERO

06279 *The mark of Lucifer.* Dell, New York, 1974,
       221p, Paper, Novel

GREEN, EDWIN

06280 *Air monster.* Goldsmith Publishing Co., Chica-
       go, 1932, 245p, Cloth, Novel

GREEN, F(rederick) L(awrence), 1902-1953

06281 *A fragment of glass.* Michael Joseph, London,
       1947, 263p, Cloth, Novel
06282 *The magician.* Michael Joseph, London, 1951,
       255p, Cloth, Novel

GREEN, FITZHUGH, 1888-1947

06283 *ZR wins.* D. Appleton, New York, 1924, 271p,
       Cloth, Novel

GREEN, HENRY, pseud. [Henry Vincent Yorke,
1905-   ]

06284 *Concluding; a novel.* Hogarth Press, London,
       1948, 254p, Cloth, Novel

GREEN, I. G., pseud. [Ira Greenblatt]

06285 *Time beyond time.* Belmont, New York, 1971,
       155p, Paper, Novel

GREEN, JOSEPH (Lee), 1931- [*biography inclu-ded*]

06286 *An affair with genius.* Victor Gollancz, London, 1969, 190p, Cloth, Coll.
06287 *Conscience interplanetary.* Victor Gollancz, London, 1972, 221p, Cloth, Novel
06288 *Gold the man.* Victor Gollancz, London, 1971, 221p, Cloth, Novel
06288A retitled: *The mind behind the eye.* DAW, New York, 1972, 191p, Paper, Novel
06289 *The Loafers of Refuge.* Victor Gollancz, London, 1965, 176p, Cloth, Novel
       The mind behind the eye. [see 06288A]

GREEN, JULIEN [originally Julian] (Hartridge), 1900- [*biography included*]

06290 *If I were you*, by Julian Green. Harper & Bros., New York, 1949, 247p, Cloth, Novel

GREEN, ROBERT

06291 *The great leap backward.* Robert Hale, London, 1968, 190p, Cloth, Novel

GREEN, ROBERT JAMES

06292 *Kor and the wolf dogs.* Lothrop, Lee & Shepard, Boston, 1956, 220p, Cloth, Novel

GREEN, ROGER (Gilbert) LANCELYN, 1918- [*biography included*]

06293 *From the world's end; a fantasy.* Edmund Ward, Leicester, 1948, 127p, Cloth, Novel
06294 *Into other worlds; space-flight in fiction, from Lucian to Lewis.* Abelard-Schuman, London, 1958, 190p, Cloth, Nonf.
06295 *Strange adventures in time.* J. M. Dent & Sons, London, 1974, 147p, Cloth, Anth.
06296 *Thirteen uncanny tales.* J. M. Dent & Sons, London, 1970, 201p, Cloth, Anth.

GREEN, ROLAND (James), 1944- [*biography included*]

06297 *Wandor's ride.* Avon, New York, 1973, 190p, Paper, Novel [Wandor #1]

as Jeffrey Lord, house pseud.:

06298 *Dimension of dreams.* Pinnacle, New York, 1974, 181p, Paper, Novel [Richard Blade #11]
06299 *Ice dragon; the Richard Blade series.* Pinnacle, New York, 1974, 183p, Paper, Novel [Richard Blade #10]
06300 *Kingdom of Royth; the Richard Blade series.* Pinnacle, New York, 1974, 188p, Paper, Novel [Richard Blade #9]

GREEN, WILLIAM CHILD

06301 *Abbot of Montserrat; or, The pool of blood; a romance.* A. K. Newman, London, 1826, vol. I-229p, II-256p, Cloth, Novel
06302 *Alibeg the tempter; a tale, wild and wonderful.* A. K. Newman, London, 1831, 4vol, Cloth, Novel

GREENAWAY, PETER VAN
    see: VAN GREENAWAY, PETER

GREENBERG, MARTIN, 1918-

06303 *All about the future.* Gnome Press, New York, 1955, 374p, Cloth, Anth. [includes some nonf
06304 *Coming attractions.* Gnome Press, New York, 1957, 254p, Cloth, Nonf. Anth.
       The crucible of power. [see 06305A]
06305 *Five science fiction novels.* Gnome Press, New York, 1952, 382p, Cloth, Anth.
06305A retitled: *The crucible of power; three scienc fiction novels.* Bodley Head, London, 1953, 236p, Cloth, Anth. [abridged]
06306 *Journey to infinity.* Gnome Press, New York, 1951, 381p, Cloth, Anth.
06307 *Men against the stars.* Gnome Press, New York, 1950, 351p, Cloth, Anth.
06307A retitled: *9 stories from Men against the star* Pyramid, New York, 1963, 191p, Paper, Anth. [abridged]
06308 *The robot and the man.* Gnome Press, New York, 1953, 251p, Cloth, Anth.
06309 *Travelers of space.* Gnome Press, New York, 1951, 400p, Cloth, Anth.

GREENBERG, MARTIN HARRY, 1941- [*biography included*]

with Harvey A. Katz and Patricia S. Warrick:

06310 *Introductory psychology through science fiction.* Rand McNally College Publishing Co., Chicago, 1974, 510p, Paper, Anth.

with Carol Mason and Patricia S. Warrick:

06311 *Anthropology through science fiction.* St. Martin's Press, New York, 1974, 387p, Cloth, Anth.

with John D. Milstead, Patricia S. Warrick, and Joseph D. Olander:

06312 *Sociology through science fiction.* St. Martin's Press, New York, 1974, 412p, Cloth, Anth.

with Joseph D. Olander and Patricia S. Warrick:

06313 *American government through science fiction.* Rand McNally College Publishing Co., Chicago 1974, 360p, Paper, Anth.
06314 *School and society through science fiction.* Rand McNally College Publishing Co., Chicago 1974, 396p, Paper, Anth.

with Patricia S. Warrick:

06315 *Political science fiction; an introductory reader.* Prentice-Hall, Englewood Cliffs, NJ, 1974, 415p, Cloth, Anth.

GREENBLATT, IRA
    see: GREEN, I. G.

GREENE, (Henry) GRAHAM, 1904- [*biography included*]

06316 *A sense of reality.* Bodley Head, London, 196? 140p, Cloth, Coll.

GREENE, JAY E(lihu), 1914-   [*biography inclu-*
ded]

06317   *Modern mystery and adventure novels.* Globe
        Book Co., New York, 1951, 554p, Cloth, Anth.

GREENE, JOHN O.

06318   *The Ke Whonkus people.* Vincent Publishing Co.,
        Indianapolis, 1893, 426p, Cloth, Novel

GREENE, JOSEPH (Ingham), 1897-1953

06319   *Captives in space.* Golden Press, New York,
        1960, 188p, Cloth, Novel [Dig Allen #2]
06320   *The forgotten star; a science fiction adven-
        ture.* Golden Press, New York, 1959, 188p,
        Cloth, Novel [Dig Allen #1]
06321   *Journey to Jupiter.* Golden Press, New York,
        1961, 186p, Cloth, Novel [Dig Allen #3]
06322   *Lost city of Uranus.* Golden Press, New York,
        1962, 187p, Cloth, Novel [Dig Allen #6]
06323   *Robots of Saturn.* Golden Press, New York,
        1962, 187p, Cloth, Novel [Dig Allen #5]
06324   *Trappers of Venus.* Golden Press, New York,
        1961, 186p, Cloth, Novel [Dig Allen #4]

GREENER, LESLIE, 1900-1974 [*biography included*]

06325   *Moon ahead.* Viking Press, New York, 1951,
        256p, Cloth, Novel

GREENER, WILLIAM OLIVER
        see: GERRARE, WIRT

GREENFIELD, IRVING A., 1928-   [*biography included*]

06326   *The ancient of days.* Avon, New York, 1973,
        317p, Paper, Novel
06327   *The others.* Lancer, New York, 1969, 190p,
        Paper, Novel
06328   *A play of darkness.* Avon, New York, 1974,
        319p, Paper, Novel
06329   *The stars will judge.* Dell, New York, 1974,
        160p, Paper, Novel
06330   *Succubus.* Dell, New York, 1970, 205p, Paper,
        Novel
06331   *The waters of death.* Lancer, New York, 1967,
        157p, Paper, Novel

as Bruce Duncan:

06332   *Mirror image.* Belmont Double, New York, 1968,
        90p, Paper, Novel

GREENING, FRANK

06333   *Tales of the supernatural.* Arthur H. Stock-
        well, Ilfracombe, UK, 1954, 15p, Paper, Coll.

GREENLEAF, SUE

06334   *Liquid from the Sun's rays.* Abbey Press, New
        York, 1901, 305p, Cloth. Novel
06334A retitled: *Don Miguel Lehumada, discoverer of
        liquid from the Sun's rays; an occult ro-
        mance of Mexico and the United States.* B.

W. Dodge, New York, 1906, 305p, Cloth, Novel

GREENLEE, SAM, 1930-

06335   *The spook who sat by the door; a novel.*
        Richard W. Baron, New York, 1969, 248p,
        Cloth, Novel

GREENOUGH, Mrs. RICHARD S. [Sarah Dana],
1827-1885

06336   *Arabesques; Monarè, Apollyona, Domitia, Ombra.*
        Roberts Bros., Boston, 1872, 213p, Cloth,
        Coll.

GREENWOOD, EDWIN

06337   *Miracle in the drawing-room; a daring and
        cynical novel of the modern world's reaction
        to an old-fashioned miracle.* Skeffington
        & Son, London, 1935, 320p, Cloth, Novel

GREENWOOD, JAMES

06338   *The Bear king; a narrative confided to the
        marines.* Griffith & Farran, London, 1868,
        98p, Cloth, Novel
06339   *The purgatory of Peter the Cruel.* George Rout-
        ledge & Sons, London, 1868, 164p, Cloth,
        Novel

GREENWOOD, JULIA
        see: ASKHAM, FRANCIS

GREER, TOM

06340   *A modern Daedalus.* Griffith, Farran, Okeden
        & Welsh, London, 1887, 261p, Cloth, Novel

GREG, PERCY, 1836-1889

06341   *Across the Zodiac; the story of a wrecked re-
        cord.* Trübner & Co., Edinburgh, 1880, vol.
        I-296p, II-288p, Cloth, Novel

GREGG, HILDA CAROLINE
        see: GRIER, SYDNEY C.

GREGORY, FRANKLIN (Long), 1905-

06342   *The white wolf.* Random House, New York, 1941,
        271p, Cloth, Novel

GREGORY, H. B.

06343   *Dark sanctuary.* Rider & Co., London, 1940,
        288p, Cloth, Novel

GREGORY, JACKSON, 1882-1943

06344   *Daughter of the sun; a tale of adventure,* by
        Quién Sabe. Charles Scribner's Sons, New
        York, 1921, 271p, Cloth, Novel

GREGORY, JACKSON (cont.)

06344A *Daughter of the sun; a tale of adventure*, by
Gregory Jackson. Charles Scribner's Sons,
New York, 1926, 271p, Cloth, Novel
06345 *Ru, the conqueror.* Charles Scribner's Sons,
New York, 1933, 289p, Cloth, Novel

GREGORY, JULIAN R., pseud. [Leo Knowles), with
Roger Price

06346 *The Tomorrow People in The visitor.* Piccolo/
TV Times, London, 1973, 118p, Paper, Tele.
[Tomorrow People #1]

GREGORY, OWEN

06347 *Meccania, the super-state.* Methuen, London,
1918, 298p, Cloth, Novel

GRENDON, STEPHEN, pseud.
see: DERLETH, AUGUST W.

GRESSWELL, ELISE KAY

06348 *When Yvonne was dictator.* John Heritage, London, 1935, 306p, Cloth, Novel

GREVE, TORA

06349 *Night on Eros; a tale from Sirius solar system.*
Vantage Press, New York, 1973, 158p, Cloth,
Novel

GREY, CHARLES, pseud.
see: TUBB, E. C.

GREY, EDWARD, pseud.

06350 *Concealed for thirty years, being the narrative
of one E. Grey.* Remington & Co., London,
1890, 315p, Cloth, Novel

GREY, LYNN

06351 *The return of Karl Marx.* Chancery Press, London, 1942, 117p, Paper, Novel

GREY, ROBERT MUNSON

06352 *I, Yahweh; a novel in the form of an autobiography.* Willett, Clark, Chicago, 1937,
352p, Cloth, Novel

GRIDBAN, VOLSTED, house pseud. [see also E.
C. Tubb and John Russell Fearn]

06353 *Alien universe.* Scion, London, 1952, 96p,
Paper, Novel [by E. C. Tubb]
06354 *De Bracy's drug.* Scion, London, 1953, 127p,
Paper, Novel [by E. C. Tubb]
05280 *The dyno-depressant.* Scion, London, 1953,
128p, Paper, Novel [by John Russell Fearn]

05281 *Exit life.* Scion, London, 1953, 128p, Paper,
Novel [by John Russell Fearn]
05282 *The frozen limit.* Scion, London, 1954, 128p,
Paper, Novel [by John Russell Fearn]
06355 *Fugitive of time.* Milestone, London, 1953,
112p, Paper, Novel [by E. C. Tubb]
05283 *The genial dinosaur.* Scion, London, 1954,
128p, Paper, Novel [Herbert #2] [by John
Russell Fearn]
05284 *I came--I saw--I wondered.* Scion, London,
1954, 126p, Paper, Novel [by John Russell
Fearn]
05285 *The lonely astronomer; an Adam Quirke adventure.* Scion, London, 1954, 128p, Paper,
Novel [Adam Quirke #2] [by John Russell
Fearn]
05286 *The magnetic brain.* Scion, London, 1953, 128p
Paper, Novel [by John Russell Fearn]
05287 *The Master must die.* Scion, London, 1953,
128p, Paper, Novel [Adam Quirke #1] [by
John Russell Fearn]
05288 *Moons for sale.* Scion, London, 1953, 128p,
Paper, Novel [by John Russell Fearn]
06356 *Planetoid Disposals Ltd.* Milestone, London,
1953, 112p, Paper, Novel [by E. C. Tubb]
05289 *The purple wizard.* Scion, London, 1953, 128p,
Paper, Novel [by John Russell Fearn]
06357 *Reverse universe.* Scion, London, 1952, 128p,
Paper, Novel [by E. C. Tubb]
05290 *Scourge of the atom.* Scion, London, 1953,
128p, Paper, Novel [by John Russell Fearn]
05291 *A thing of the past.* Scion, London, 1953,
128p, Paper, Novel [Herbert #1] [by John
Russell Fearn]

GRIER, SYDNEY C., pseud. [Hilda Caroline Greg
1868-1933]

06358 *A crowned queen; the romance of a minister of
state.* William Blackwood & Sons, Edinburgh,
1898, 590p, Cloth, Novel
06359 *The Kings of the East; a romance of the near
future.* William Blackwood & Sons, Edinburgh,
1900, 363p, Cloth, Novel
06360 *The power of the keys.* William Blackwood &
Sons, Edinburgh, 1907, 360p, Cloth, Novel

GRIERSON, FRANCIS D(urham), 1888-

06361 *Heart of the Moon.* Alston Rivers, London,
1928, 287p, Cloth, Novel

GRIFF, house pseud.
see: FEARN, JOHN RUSSELL

GRIFF, ALAN, pseud.
see: SUDDABY, DONALD

GRIFFEN, ELIZABETH L.

06362 *The shaggy dog.* Scholastic Book Services,
New York, 1967, 96p, Paper, Movie

GRIFFIN, SERCOMBE

06363 *The crimson caterpillar.* Sampson Low, Marston
London, 1935, 250p, Cloth, Novel

GRIFFIN BOOKLET ONE
    see: CRAWFORD, WILLIAM L.

GRIFFITH(-Jones), GEORGE (Chetwynd), 1857-1906

06364 *The angel of the revolution; a tale of the
        coming terror.* Tower Publishing Co., Lon-
        don, 1893, 393p, Cloth, Novel [Romanoff #1]
06365 *Briton or Boer? a tale of the fight for Africa.*
        F. V. White, London, 1897, 296p, Cloth, Novel
06366 *Captain Ishmael; a saga of the South Seas.*
        Hutchinson, London, 1901, 344p, Cloth, Novel
06367 *A criminal Croesus.* John Long, London, 1904,
        319p, Cloth, Novel
06368 *Denver's double; a story of inverted identity.*
        F. V. White, London, 1901, 310p, Cloth, Novel
06369 *The destined maid.* F. V. White, London, 1898,
        314p, Cloth, Novel
06370 *Gambles with destiny.* F. V. White, London,
        1899, 232p, Cloth, Coll.
06371 *The gold-finder.* F. V. White, London, 1898,
        312p, Cloth, Novel
06372 *The great pirate syndicate.* F. V. White, Lon-
        don, 1899, 302p, Cloth, Novel
06373 *The Great Weather Syndicate.* F. V. White, Lon-
        don, 1906, 312p, Cloth, Novel
06374 *A honeymoon in space.* C. Arthur Pearson, Lon-
        don, 1901, 302p, Cloth, Novel
06375 *The justice of revenge.* F. V. White, London,
        1901, 303p, Cloth, Novel
06376 *The lake of gold; a narrative of the Anglo-
        American conquest of Europe.* F. V. White,
        London, 1903, 319p, Cloth, Novel
06377 *The lord of labour.* F. V. White, London, 1911,
        310p, Cloth, Novel
06378 *A Mayfair magician; a romance of criminal sci-
        ence.* F. V. White, London, 1905, 306p,
        Cloth, Novel
06379 *The mummy and Miss Nitocris; a phantasy of the
        fourth dimension.* T. Werner Laurie, London,
        1906, 312p, Cloth, Novel
06380 *Novels.* F. V. White, London, 1906, 639p,
        Cloth, Coll. [includes *A Mayfair magician*;
        The world peril of 1910; *The lake of gold*;
        The missionary]
06381 *Olga Romanoff; or, The syren of the skies; a
        sequel to "The angel of the revolution."*
        Tower Publishing Co., London, 1894, 377p,
        Cloth, Novel [Romanoff #2]
06382 *The outlaws of the air.* Tower Publishing Co.,
        London, 1895, 376p, Cloth, Novel
06383 *The raid of 'Le Vengeur,' and other stories.*
        Ferret Fantasy, London, 1974, 144p, Paper,
        Coll.
06384 *The romance of Golden Star.* F. V. White, Lon-
        don, 1897, 284p, Cloth, Novel
06385 *The Sacred Skull.* Everett & Co., London,
        1908, 308p, Cloth, Novel
06386 *The stolen submarine; a tale of the Russo-
        Japanese War.* F. V. White, London, 1904,
        320p, Cloth, Novel
06387 *Valdar the oft-born; a saga of seven ages.*
        C. Arthur Pearson, London, 1895, 416p, Cloth,
        Novel
06388 *The White Witch of Mayfair.* F. V. White, Lon-
        don, 1902, 312p, Cloth, Novel
06389 *A woman against the world.* F. V. White, Lon-
        don, 1903, 320p, Cloth, Novel
06390 *The World Masters.* John Long, London, 1903,
        303p, Cloth, Novel
06391 *The world peril of 1910.* F. V. White, London,
        1907, 312p, Cloth, Novel

GRIFFITH, MARY, d. 1877

06392 *Camperdown; or, News from our neighborhood*, by
        an author of our neighborhood. Carey, Lea
        & Blanchard, Philadelphia, 1836, 300p, Cloth,
        Coll. [includes *Three hundred years hence*]
06393 *Three hundred years hence.* Prime Press, Phila-
        delphia, 1950, 131p, Cloth, Novel

GRIFFITHS, ALAN

       Authors in paradise. [see 06395A]
06394 *The passionate astrologer.* Arthur Barker,
        London, 1936, 284p, Cloth, Novel
06395 *Spirits under proof.* T. Werner Laurie, Lon-
        don, 1935, 252p, Cloth, Novel
06395A retitled: *Authors in paradise.* Frederick A.
        Stokes, New York, 1939, 336p, Cloth, Novel
06396 *Strange news from Heaven.* Lovat Dickson, Lon-
        don, 1934, 311p, Cloth, Novel

GRIFFITHS, DAVID ARTHUR

   as Gill Hunt, house pseud:

06397 *Fission.* Curtis Warren, London, 1952?, 111p,
        Paper, Novel
06398 *Vega.* Curtis Warren, London, 1951, 111p,
        Paper, Novel

   as King Lang, house pseud:

06399 *Astro-race.* Curtis Warren, London, 1951, 112p,
        Paper, Novel
06400 *Gyrator control.* Curtis Warren, London, 1951,
        112p, Paper, Novel
06401 *Rocket invasion.* Curtis Warren, London, 1951,
        111p, Paper, Novel
06402 *Task flight.* Curtis Warren, London, 1951,
        112p, Paper, Novel

   as Brian Shaw, house pseud.:

06403 *"Argentis."* Curtis Warren, London, 1952?,
        112p, Paper, Novel [actually by E. C. Tubb]

   as David Shaw:

06404 *Laboratory "X."* Curtis Warren, London, 1950?,
        128p, Paper, Novel
06405 *Planet federation.* Curtis Warren, London,
        1950, 128p, Paper, Novel
06406 *Space men.* Curtis Warren, London, 1951?,
        128p, Paper, Novel

GRIFFITHS, ISABEL

06407 *Three worlds.* Arthur H. Stockwell, London,
        1922, 198p, Cloth, Novel

GRIFFITHS, JOHN, 1934-

06408 *The survivors.* Collins, London, 1965, 159p,
        Cloth, Novel

GRIGGS, WILLIAM N.
    see: LOCKE, RICHARD ADAMS

GRIGSBY, ALCANOAN O.
    see: ADAMS, JACK

GRILLET, ALAIN ROBBE-
    see: ROBBE-GRILLET, ALAIN

GRIMM, BENJAMIN

06409 *Nightland spell*. Olympia Press, New York,
    1969,   , Paper, Novel

GRIMSHAW, BEATRICE (Ethel), 1871?-1953

06410 *The sorcerer's stone*. John C. Winston, Phila-
    delphia, 1914, 306p, Cloth, Novel

GRIMSHAW, ROBERT, 1850-1941

06411 *Fifty years hence; or, What may be in 1943; a
    prophecy supposed to be based on scientific
    deductions by an improved graphical method*.
    Practical Publishing Co., New York, 1892,
    89p, Cloth, Novel

GRINDON, MAURICE

06412 *Kathleen O'Leavon; a fantasy*. Simpkin, Mar-
    shall, Hamilton, Kent, London, 1896, 107p,
    Cloth, Novel

GRINNELL, DAVID, pseud.
    see: WOLLHEIM, DONALD A.

GRINSTEAD, GORDON

06413 *Angela darling*. Rylee Ltd., London, 1948,
    125p, Paper, Novel

GRIP, pseud.
    see: WELCH, EDGAR L.

GRIPE, MARIA (Kristina), 1923-

06414 *The land beyond*. A Merloyd Lawrence Book,
    Delacorte Press, New York, 1974, 215p,
    Cloth, Novel

GRISEWOOD, HARMAN (Joseph Gerard), 1906-
[*biography included*]

06415 *The recess*. Macdonald, London, 1963, 192p,
    Cloth, Novel

GRISEWOOD, R(obert) NORMAN, 1876-

06416 *The venture; a story of the shadow world*.
    R. F. Fenno, New York, 1911, 228p, Cloth,
    Novel
06417 *Zarlah, the Martian*. R. F. Fenno, New York,
    1909, 194p, Cloth, Novel

GROC, LÉON, 1882-

06418 *The bus that vanished*. Macaulay, New York,
    1928, 282p, Cloth, Novel

GROGAN, GERALD, 1884-1918

06419 *A drop in infinity*. John Lane, The Bodley Head,
    London, 1915, 325p, Cloth, Novel

GROH, IRWIN (William)

06420 *The lady likes blue white, and other stories*.
    Christopher Publishing House, Boston, 1948,
    70p, Cloth, Coll.

GRONER, AUGUSTE, 1850-

06421 *Mene tekel; a tale of strange happenings*.
    Duffield & Co., New York, 1912, 243p, Cloth,
    Novel

GROOM, ARTHUR (William), 1898-1964 [*biography
included*]

06422 *The ghost of Gordon Gregory*. Peter Lunn, Lon-
    don, 1946, 236p, Cloth, Novel

GROOM, (Arthur John) PELHAM

06423 *The fourth seal*. Jarrolds Publishers, London,
    1948, 208p, Cloth, Novel
06424 *The purple twilight*. T. Werner Laurie, London,
    1948, 282p, Cloth, Novel

GROSS, ANNA GOLDMARK

06425 *The gnomes of the Saline Mountains; a fantas-
    tic narrative*. Shakespeare Press, New York,
    1912, 181p, Cloth, Coll.

GROSSER, MORTON

06426 *The snake horn*. Atheneum, New York, 1973,
    131p, Cloth, Novel

GROSSINGER, RICHARD (Selig), 1944-   [*biography included*]

06427 *Mars; a science fiction vision*. Io Books,
    Cape Elizabeth, NY, 1971, 223p, Paper, Coll.
    [includes some verse]

GROULING, THOMAS E(dward), 1940-   [*biography
included*]

06428 *Project 12*. Vantage Press, New York, 1962,
    109p, Cloth, Novel

GROUSSET, PASCHAL
    see: LAURIE, ANDRE

GROVE, W.

06429 *A Mexican mystery*. Digby & Long, London,
    1889, 144p, Paper, Novel
06430 *The wreck of a world*. Digby & Long, London,
    1890, 151p, Paper, Novel

GROVER, WINIFRED POWELL
   see: DWYER, WINIFRED

GROVES, J(ohn) W(illiam), 1910-   [*biography included*]

06431 *The heels of Achilles*. Robert Hale, London, 1969, 192p, Cloth, Novel
06432 *Shellbreak*. Robert Hale, London, 1968, 190p, Cloth, Novel

GROVES, JAY (Voelker), 1922-   [*biography included*]

06433 *Fireball at the lake; a story of encounter with another world*. Exposition Press, New York, 1967, 65p, Cloth, Novel

GRUBB, DAVIS (Alexander), 1919-   [*biography included*]

       One foot in the grave. [see 06434A]
06434 *Twelve tales of suspense and the supernatural*. Charles Scribner's Sons, New York, 1964, 175p, Cloth, Coll.
06434A retitled: *One foot in the grave*. Arrow, London, 1966, 186p, Paper, Coll.
06435 *The voices of glory*. Charles Scribner's Sons, New York, 1962, 469p, Cloth, Novel

GRUEN, VON, pseud.

06436 *The mortals of Reni*. Curtis Warren, London, 1953, 159p, Cloth, Novel

GRUHN, CARRIE E. (Myers), 1907-   [*biography included*]

06437 *A trumpet in Zion*. Moody Press, Chicago, 1951, 285p, Cloth, Novel
06437A retitled: *Lost city*. Moody Press, Chicago, 1969, 285p, Paper, Novel

GUARESCHI, GIOVANNI, 1908-1968

06438 *Comrade Don Camillo*. Farrar, Straus & Co., New York, 1964, 212p, Cloth, Novel [Don Camillo #5]
06439 *Don Camillo and his flock*. Pellegrini & Cudahy, New York, 1952, 250p, Cloth, Novel [Don Camillo #2]
06439A retitled: *Don Camillo and the prodigal son*. Victor Gollancz, London, 1952, 221p, Cloth, Novel [Don Camillo #2]
       Don Camillo and the devil. [see 06442A]
       Don Camillo and the prodigal son. [see 06439A]
06440 *Don Camillo; his little world and his dilemma*. Farrar, Straus & Young, New York, 1954, 460p, Cloth, Coll. [includes 06443 and 06444; Don Camillo #s 1, 3]
       Don Camillo meets Hell's Angels. [see 06441A]
06441 *Don Camillo meets the flower children*. Farrar, Straus & Giroux, New York, 1969, 247p, Cloth, Novel [Don Camillo #6]
06441A retitled: *Don Camillo meets Hell's Angels*. Victor Gollancz, London, 1970, 190p, Cloth, Novel [Don Camillo #6]
06442 *Don Camillo takes the devil by the tail*. Farrar, Straus & Cudahy, New York, 1957, 218p, Cloth, Novel [Don Camillo #4]
06442A retitled: *Don Camillo and the devil*. Victor Gollancz, London, 1957, 223p, Cloth, Novel [Don Camillo #4]
06443 *Don Camillo's dilemma*. Farrar, Straus & Young, New York, 1954, 255p, Cloth, Novel [Don Camillo #3]
06444 *The little world of Don Camillo*. Pellegrini & Cudahy, New York, 1950, 205p, Cloth, Novel [Don Camillo #1]

GUBBINS, HERBERT

06445 *The elixir of life; or, 2905 A.D.; a novel of the far future*. Henry J. Drane, London, 1914, 254p, Cloth, Novel

GUELLETEE, Mr.
   see: GUEULLETTE, THOMAS SIMON

GUENTHER, JOHANNES von, 1886-

06446 *Cagliostro; a novel*. William Heinemann, London, 1928, 615p, Cloth, Novel

GUERARD, ALBERT JOSEPH, 1914-   [*biography included*]

06447 *Night journey*. Alfred A. Knopf, New York, 1950, 357p, Cloth, Novel

GUEST, ERNEST

06448 *At the end of the world; a vision*. Elkin Mathews & Marrot, London, 1929, 112p, Cloth, Novel

GUEULETTE, THOMAS SIMON, 1683-1766

06449 *Chinese tales; or, The wonderful adventures of the Mandarin Fum-Hoam, related by himself to divert the Sultana, upon the celebration of her nuptials*. J. Brotherton, London, 1725, 2vol, Cloth, Coll. [published anonymously]
06449A *Chinese tales; or, The wonderful adventures of the Mandarin Fum-Hoam, related by himself to divert the Sultana, upon the celebration of her nuptials, by Mr. Guelletee*. J. Hodges, London, 1740, 236p, Cloth, Coll.
06449B retitled: *The transmigrations of the Mandarin Fum-Hoam (Chinese Tales)*. H. S. Nichols, London, 1894, 252p, Cloth, Coll. [published anonymously]
06450 *Mogul tales; or, The dreams of man awake, by Mr. Guelletee*. J. Brindley, London, 1736, 2vol, Cloth, Coll.
       Tartarian tales. [see 06451A]
06451 *A thousand and one quarters of hours, being Tartarian tales, by T. S. G.* Jacob Tonson, London, 1716, 254p, Cloth, Coll.
06451A retitled: *Tartarian tales; or, A thousand and one quarters of hours, by Mr. Guelletee*. J. & R. Tonson, London, 1759, 369p, Cloth, Coll.
       The transmigrations of the Mandarin Fum-Hoam. [see 06449B]

GUILD, LEO
    see: SCRAM, ARTHUR N.

GUILLOT, RENÉ, 1900-1969 [*biography included*]

06452 *The king of the cats.* Collins, London, 1962,
       159p, Cloth, Novel

GUIN, URSULA K. LE
    see: LE GUIN, URSULA K.

GUIN, WYMAN (Woods), 1915- [*biography included*]

       Beyond bedlam. [see 06453A]
06453 *Living way out.* Avon, New York, 1967, 208p,
       Paper, Coll.
06453A retitled: *Beyond bedlam.* Sphere, London,
       1973, 206p, Paper, Coll.
06454 *The standing joy.* Avon, New York, 1969, 224p,
       Paper, Novel

GUINN, JACK

06455 *The caperberry bush; a novel.* Little, Brown,
       Boston, 1954, 273p, Cloth, Novel

GUIRDHAM, ARTHUR

06456 *The lights were going out.* Quality Press,
       London, 1944, 192p, Cloth, Novel

GULL, (Cyril Arthur Edward) RANGER, 1876-1923

06457 *The air pirate.* Hurst & Blackett, London,
       1919, 287p, Cloth, Novel
06458 *Cinema city.* Hurst & Blackett, London, 1922,
       287p, Cloth, Novel
06459 *The City in the Clouds.* Hurst & Blackett,
       London, 1921, 288p, Cloth, Novel
06460 *The enemies of England.* T. Werner Laurie,
       London, 1914, 292p, Cloth, Novel
       The Ravenscroft affair. [see 06461A]
06461 *The Ravenscroft horror.* T. Werner Laurie,
       London, 1917, 266p, Cloth, Novel
06461A retitled: *The Ravenscroft affair.* Edward J.
       Clode, New York, 1924, 315p, Cloth, Novel
06462 *The soul stealer.* F. V. White, London, 1906,
       312p, Cloth, Novel

as Guy Thorne:

06463 *The angel.* Ward, Lock, London, 1908, 328p,
       Cloth, Novel
06464 *The cruiser on wheels.* T. C. & E. C. Jack,
       London, 1915, 192p, Cloth, Novel
06465 *Harder than steel.* T. Werner Laurie, London,
       1919, 217p, Cloth, Novel
06466 *Lucky Mr. Loder.* Ward, Lock, London, 1918,
       319p, Cloth, Novel
06467 *Made in his image.* Hutchinson, London, 1906,
       360p, Cloth, Novel
06468 *The secret sea-plane.* Hodder & Stoughton,
       London, 1915, 243p, Cloth, Novel
06469 *When the world reeled.* Ward, Lock, London,
       1924, 313p, Cloth, Novel

GULLIVER, Captain, pseud.

06470 *Memoirs of the court of Lilliput, containing
       an account of the intrigues, and some other
       particular transactions of that nation,
       omitted in the two volumes of his travels.*
       J. Roberts, London, 1727, 159p, Cloth, Novel
       [Gulliver series]

GULLIVER, JOHN, pseud.
    see: DESFONTAINES, PIERRE

GULLIVER, LEMUEL, pseud.
    see: SWIFT, JONATHAN

GULLIVER, LEMUEL, pseud. [A new voyage to the
country of the Houyhnhnms]
    see: HODGART, MATTHEW

GULLIVER, Capt. LEMUEL, pseud.

06471 *Travels into several remote nations of the
       world, vol. III.* no publisher, London, 1727,
       118p, Cloth, Novel [Gulliver series]
06472 *Travels into several remote nations of the
       world, vol. III, part II; a voyage to
       Severambia, &c.* no publisher, London, 1727,
       159p, Cloth, Novel [Gulliver series] [both
       of these volumes, billed as part of Swift's
       *Travels into several remote nations of the
       world* (i.e., *Gulliver's Travels*), were ac-
       tually written by some other anonymous
       author, and released by a different publisher
       to take advantage of the original's popu-
       larity]

GULLIVER, LEMUEL Jun., pseud.

06473 *Lilliput, being a new journey to that celebra-
       ted island, containing a faithful account
       of the manners, character, customs, religion,
       laws, politics, revenue, taxes, learning,
       general progress in arts and sciences, dress,
       amusements, and gallantry of those famous
       little people, from the year 1702 (when they
       were first discovered and visited by Captain
       Lemuel Gulliver, the father of the compiler
       of this work), to the present aera, 1796.*
       T. Chapman, London, 1796, 226p, Cloth, Novel
       [Gulliver series]

GULLIVER REVIVED
    see: RASPE, RUDOLPH ERICH

GUNDRAN, OLIVE, 1912-

06474 *The mysterious stranger.* A Milestone Book,
       Comet Press, New York, 1958, 56p, Cloth,
       Novel

GUNGA DIN, ALI MIRDREKVANDI
    see: MIRDREKVANDI, ALI

GUNN, EDMUND S.

06475 *The romance of paradise.* Sampson Low, Marston, London, 1895, 123p, Cloth, Novel

GUNN, JAMES E(dwin), 1923-   [*biography included*]

06476 *Breaking point.* Walker, New York, 1972, 182p, Cloth, Coll.
06477 *The burning.* Dell, New York, 1972, 154p, Paper, Novel
06478 *Future imperfect.* Bantam, New York, 1964, 137p, Paper, Coll.
06479 *The immortal; a novel.* Bantam, New York, 1970, 136p, Paper, Tele.
06480 *The Immortals.* Bantam, New York, 1962, 154p, Paper, Novel
06481 *The joy makers.* Bantam, New York, 1961, 160p, Paper, Novel
06482 *The listeners.* Charles Scribner's Sons, New York, 1972, 275p, Cloth, Novel
06483 *Some dreams are nightmares.* Charles Scribner's Sons, New York, 1974, 220p, Cloth, Coll.
06484 *Station in space.* Bantam, New York, 1958, 156p, Paper, Coll.
06485 *This fortress world.* Gnome Press, New York, 1955, 216p, Cloth, Novel
06486 *The witching hour.* Dell, New York, 1970, 188p, Paper, Coll.

with Jack Williamson:

06487 *Star bridge.* Gnome Press, New York, 1955, 221p, Cloth, Novel

GUNN, NEIL M(iller), 1891-1973

06488 *The Green Isle of the Great Deep.* Faber & Faber, London, 1944, 256p, Cloth, Novel
06489 *The other landscape.* Faber & Faber, London, 1954, 318p, Cloth, Novel
06490 *The well at the world's end.* Faber & Faber, London, 1951, 295p, Cloth, Novel

GUNTER, ARCHIBALD CLAVERING, 1847-1907

06491 *The city of mystery (taken from the archives of ancient Paris, as found in the secret Prison of the Exempt, Pomerou, in the Rue de la Tixeranderie, when the buildings were torn down in 1851).* Home Publishing Co., New York, 1902, 276p, Cloth, Coll.

with Fergus Redmond:

06492 *A Florida enchantment; a novel.* Home Publishing Co., New York, 1892, 260p, Paper, Novel

GUNTHER, JOHN, 1901-1970 [*biography included*]

06493 *Eden for one; an amusement.* Harper & Bros., New York, 1927, 224p, Cloth, Novel

GURDJIEFF, G(eorges Ivanovitch), 1872-1949

06494 *An objectively impartial criticism of the life of man; or, Beelzebub's tales to his grandson.* Harcourt, Brace & Co., New York, 1950, 1238p, Cloth, Novel

06494A retitled: *All and everything; ten books, in three series, of which this is the first series; Beelzebub's tales to his grandson.* E. P. Dutton, New York, 1963, 1238p, Cloth, Novel

GURDON, J(ohn) E(verard)

06495 *The secret of the south.* Frederick Warne, London, 1950, 256p, Cloth, Novel

GURNEY, A(lbert) R(amsdell) Jr., 1930-

06496 *The gospel according to Joe; a novel.* Harper & Row, New York, 1974, 100p, Cloth, Novel

GURNEY, DAVID, pseud. [Patrick Bair]

06497 *The conjurers.* New English Library, London, 1972, 285p, Cloth, Novel
06498 *The "F" certificate; a novel.* Bernard Geis, London, 1968, 251p, Cloth, Novel

GUSTAVE, OLGA, pseud.

06499 *Amazon lunch.* Pendulum, Atlanta, 1970, 156p, Paper, Novel
06500 *The devil you lay.* Pendulum, Los Angeles, 1970, 159p, Paper, Novel

GUTHRIE, ELLEN JANE (Emma)

06501 *Tales, legends, and historical reminiscences of the Scottish Covenanters.* M'Phun, Glasgow, 1862, 303p, Cloth, Coll.
06501A retitled: *Tales of the Covenanters.* Hamilton, Adams, London, 1880, 303p, Cloth, Coll.

GUTHRIE, KENNETH SYLVAN (Launfal), 1871-1940

06502 *A romance of two centuries; a tale of the year 2025.* Platonist Press, Alpine, NJ, 1919, 365p, Cloth, Novel

GUTHRIE, THOMAS ANSTEY
   see: ANSTEY, F.

THE GUTHRIE METHOD

06503 *The Guthrie method.* American Science Fiction, Sydney, 1955, 34p, Paper, Anth.

GUTTENBERG, VIOLET

06504 *A modern exodus; a novel.* Greening & Co., London, 1904, 328p, Cloth, Novel

GUTTERIDGE, LINDSAY, 1923-   [*biography included*]

06505 *Cold war in a country garden.* Jonathan Cape, London, 1971, 189p, Cloth, Novel [Matthew Dilke #1]

GUTTERIDGE, LINDSAY (cont.)

06506 *Killer pine*. Jonathan Cape, London, 1973,
205p, Cloth, Novel [Matthew Dilke #2]

GWATKIN, FRANK ASHTON-
see: PARIS, JOHN

GWINN, D. HOWARD

06507 *The gold of Ophir*. F. Tennyson Neely, London,
1898, 335p, Cloth, Novel

GWYNNE, PAUL, pseud. [Ernest Slater, d. 1942]

06508 *Nightshade*. Constable, London, 1910, 431p,
Cloth, Novel

GYGAX, (E.) GARY, with Terry Stafford

06509 *Victorious German arms; an alternate military
history of World War Two*. TK Graphics,
Baltimore, 1973, 76p, Paper, Novel

H., A. K.
see: HOPKINS, ALICE K.

H. M. P.
see: P., H. M.

H. W.
see: WILLIAMS, HERBERT

HAAS, BEN
see: MEADE, RICHARD

HAAS, CHARLES

06510 *Adel Hitro*. Vantage Press, New York, 1962,
93p, Cloth, Novel

HACKER, MARILYN (Terry), 1942-   , with Samuel
R. Delany

04049 *Quark/1*. Paperback Library, New York, 1970,
240p, Paper, Anth.
04050 *Quark/2*. Paperback Library, New York, 1971,
240p, Paper, Anth.
04051 *Quark/3*. Paperback Library, New York, 1971,
238p, Paper, Anth.
04052 *Quark/4*. Paperback Library, New York, 1971,
240p, Paper, Anth.

HADER, BERTA (Hoerner), with Elmer Hader

06511 *The skyrocket*. Macmillan, New York, 1946,
146p, Cloth, Novel

HADER, ELMER (Stanley), 1889-   , with Berta
Hader

06511 *The skyrocket*. Macmillan, New York, 1946,
146p, Cloth, Novel

HADFIELD, JOHN (Charles Heywood), 1907-

06512 *A chamber of horrors; an anthology of the
macabre in words and pictures*. Studio Vista,
London, 1965, 320p, Cloth, Anth.

HADFIELD, R(obert) L., with Frank E. Farncomb

05219 *Red radio*. Herbert Jenkins, London, 1927,
256p, Cloth, Novel
05220 *Ruled by radio*. Herbert Jenkins, London, 1925,
256p, Cloth, Novel

HADLEY, ARTHUR T(wining), 1924-

06513 *The joy wagon*. Viking Press, New York, 1958,
223p, Cloth, Novel

HADLEY, FRANKLIN, pseud.
see: WINTERBOTHAM, RUSS

HADLEY, GEORGE, d. 1798

06514 *Argal; or, The silver devil, being the adventures of an evil spirit, comprising a series
of interesting anecdotes in public and private life, with which the demon became ac-
quainted in various parts of the world during
his confinement in the metalline substance
to which he was condemned; related by himself*. T. Vernon, London, 1793, vol. I--216p,
II-205p, Cloth, Novel

HADLEY, THOMAS G., with Donald M. Grant

06216 *Rhode Island on Lovecraft*. (Donald M. Grant),
Providence, RI, 1945, 26p, Paper, Nonf. Anth.

HAGGARD, Capt. ANDREW (Charles Parker), 1854-
1923

06515 *Leslie's fate; and, Hilda, or, The ghost of
Erminstein*. J. W. Arrowsmith, Bristol,
1892, 214p, Cloth, Coll.
06516 *Two worlds (a man's career)*. Stanley Paul,
London, 1911, 302p, Cloth, Novel

HAGGARD, Captain (Edward) ARTHUR [Arthur Am-
yand], 1860-1925

06517 *The kiss of Isis; and, The mystery of Castlebourne*. Hurst & Blackett, London, 1900,
306p, Cloth, Coll.

HAGGARD, AUDREY

06518 *The Double Axe; a romance of ancient Crete*.
J. M. Dent & Sons, London, 1929, 289p, Cloth,
Novel

HAGGARD, (Sir) H(enry) RIDER, 1856-1925

Allan and the Holy Flower. [see 06541A]

06519 *Allan and the ice-gods; a tale of beginnings.* Hutchinson, London, 1927, 287p, Cloth, Novel; Doubleday, Page, Garden City, 1927, 316p, Cloth, Novel [issued the same day; Allan #17]

06520 *Allan Quatermain, being an account of his further adventures and discoveries in company with Sir Henry Curtis, Bart., Commander John Good, R.N., and one Umslopogaas.* Longmans, Green, London, 1887, 278p, Cloth, Novel; Harper & Bros., New York, 1887, 310p, Paper, Novel [issued the same day; Allan #18]

06521 *Allan the hunter; A tale of three lions.* Lothrop Publishing Co., Boston, 1898, 111p, Cloth, Coll. [Allan #s 6, 4]

06522 *Allan's wife.* George Munro's Sons, New York, 1887, 177p, Paper, Novel [Allan #2]

06523 *Allan's wife, and other tales.* Spencer Blackett, London, 1889, 331p, Cloth, Coll. [includes "Allan's Wife" (Allan #2), "Hunter Quatermain's Story" (Allan #6), "A Tale of Three Lions" (Allan #4), and "Long Odds" (Allan #7)]

06524 *The ancient Allan.* Cassell, London, 1920, 310p, Cloth, Novel [Allan #16]

06525 *Ayesha; the return of She.* Ward, Lock, London, 1905, 384p, Cloth, Novel; Doubleday, Page, New York, 1905, 359p, Cloth, Novel [issued the same day; She #4]

06525A retitled: *The return of She: Ayesha.* Lancer, New York, 1967, 350p, Paper, Novel [She #4]

06526 *Beatrice; a novel.* Longmans, Green, London, 1890, 312p, Cloth, Novel

06527 *Belshazzar.* Stanley Paul, London, 1930, 285p, Cloth, Novel

06528 *Benita; an African romance.* Cassell, London, 1906, 344p, Cloth, Novel

06528A retitled: *The spirit of Bambatse; a romance.* Longmans, Green, New York, 1906, 329p, Cloth, Novel [issued the same day as 06528]

Black Heart and White Heart; and, Elissa. [see 06534A]

06529 *Black Heart and White Heart, and other stories.* Longmans, Green, London, 1900, 414p, Cloth, Coll. [includes *Black Heart and White Heart; Elissa; The wizard*]

Black Heart and White Heart; and, The wizard. [see 06579A]

06530 *The brethren.* Cassell, London, 1904, 342p, Cloth, Novel

06531 *Child of storm.* Cassell, London, 1913, 348p, Cloth, Novel [Allan #3; Zulu Nation #3]

06532 *Cleopatra, being an account of the fall and vengeance of Harmachis, the royal Egyptian, as set forth by his own hand.* George Munro, New York, 1889, 227p, Paper, Novel

06533 *Elissa; or, The doom of Zimbabwe.* Hodder & Stoughton, London, 1917, 244p, Cloth, Novel

06534 *Elissa, the doom of Zimbabwe; Black Heart & White Heart, a Zulu idyll.* Longmans, Green, New York, 1900, 351p, Cloth, Coll.

06534A retitled: *Black Heart and White Heart; and, Elissa.* Bernhard Tauchnitz, Leipzig, 1900, 277p, Cloth, Coll.

06535 *Eric Brighteyes.* Longmans, Green, London, 1891, 319p, Cloth, Novel

The favorite novels of H. Rider Haggard. [see 06580A]

06536 *Finished.* Paget Literary Agency, New York, 1916, 145p, Paper, Novel [Allan #13; Zulu Nation #4]

06537 *Five adventure novels of H. Rider Haggard.* Dover, New York, 1951, 821p, Cloth, Coll. [includes *She; Maiwa's revenge; Allan Quatermain; Allan's wife; King Solomon's mines*]

06538 *The ghost kings.* Cassell, London, 1908, 376p, Cloth, Novel

06538A retitled: *The lady of the heavens.* Authors & Newspapers Association, New York, 1908, 342p, Paper, Novel

06539 *Heart of the world.* Longmans, Green, New York, 1895, 347p, Cloth, Novel

06540 *Heu-Heu; or, The monster.* Hutchinson, London, 1924, 286p, Cloth, Novel [Allan #9]

06541 *The Holy Flower.* Ward, Lock, London, 1915, 368p, Cloth, Novel [Allan #8]

06541A retitled: *Allan and the Holy Flower.* Longmans, Green, New York, 1915, 384p, Cloth, Novel [Allan #8]

06542 *The ivory child.* Cassell, London, 1916, 344p, Cloth, Novel [Allan #12]

06543 *King Solomon's mines.* Cassell, London, 1885, 320p, Cloth, Novel [Allan #15]

06544 *King Solomon's mines; Allan Quatermain.* Royal Books, New York, 1953?, 319p, Paper, Coll. [Allan #s 15, 18]

06545 *The lady of Blossholme.* Hodder & Stoughton, London, 1909, 316p, Cloth, Novel

The lady of the heavens. [see 06538A]

06546 *Lost civilizations; three adventure novels.* Dover, New York, 1953, 769p, Cloth, Coll. [includes *Eric Brighteyes; Montezuma's daughter; Cleopatra*]

06547 *Love eternal.* Cassell, London, 1918, 344p, Cloth, Novel

06548 *Lysbeth; a tale of the Dutch.* Longmans, Green, New York, 1901, 496p, Cloth, Novel

06549 *The Mahatma and the Hare; a dream story.* Longmans, Green, London, 1911, 165p, Cloth, Novel; Henry Holt, New York, 1911, 165p, Cloth, Novel [issued the same day]

06550 *Maiwa's revenge; a novel.* Harper & Bros., New York, 1888, 157p, Paper, Novel [Allan #5]

06551 *Marie.* Cassell, London, 1912, 346p, Cloth, Novel [Allan #1; Zulu Nation #2]

Marion Isle. [see 06552A]

06552 *Mary of Marion Isle.* Hutchinson, London, 1929, 286p, Cloth, Novel

06552A retitled: *Marion Isle.* Doubleday, Doran, Garden City, 1929, 323p, Cloth, Novel

06553 *"The missionary and the witch doctor."* Paget Literary Agency, New York, 1920, 64p, Paper, Novel

06554 *Montezuma's daughter.* Longmans, Green, London, 1893, 325p, Cloth, Novel

06555 *Moon of Israel; a tale of the Exodus.* John Murray, London, 1918, 328p, Cloth, Novel

06556 *Morning Star.* Cassell, London, 1910, 308p, Cloth, Novel

06557 *Nada the Lily.* Longmans, Green, New York, 1892, 295p, Cloth, Novel [Zulu Nation #1]

06558 *Pearl-Maiden; a tale of the fall of Jerusalem.* Longmans, Green, London, 1903, 463p, Cloth, Novel

06559 *The people of the mist.* Longmans, Green, London, 1894, 343p, Cloth, Novel

06560 *Queen of the dawn; a love tale of old Egypt.* Doubleday, Page, Garden City, 1925, 307p, Cloth, Novel

06561 *Queen Sheba's ring.* Eveleigh Nash, London, 1910, 319p, Cloth, Novel

06562 *Red Eve.* Hodder & Stoughton, London, 1911, 296p, Cloth, Novel

The return of She: Ayesha. [see 06525A]

HAGGARD, H. RIDER (cont.)

06563   *She; a history of adventure.* Harper & Bros.,
        New York, 1886, 64p, Paper, Novel [She #3]
06564   *She and Allan.* Longmans, Green, New York,
        1921, 392p, Cloth, Novel [She #2; Allan #10]
06565   *She; and, King Solomon's mines.* Modern Lib-
        rary, New York, 1957, 266p, Cloth, Coll.
        [She #3; Allan #15]
06566   *She; and, The return of She.* Lancer, New
        York, 1972, 606p, Paper, Coll. [She #s 3-4]
06567   *Smith and the pharaohs, and other tales.* J.
        W. Arrowsmith, Bristol; Simpkin, Marshall,
        Hamilton, Kent, London, 1920, 320p, Cloth,
        Coll. [includes the story "Magepa the Buck"
        (Allan #14)]
        The spirit of Bambatse. [see 06528A]
06568   *Stella Fregelius; a tale of three destinies.*
        Longmans, Green, New York, 1903, 361p,
        Cloth, Novel
06569   *Swallow; a tale of the Great Trek.* Longmans,
        Green, New York, 1899, 348p, Cloth, Novel
06570   *A tale of three lions.* John W. Lovell, New
        York, 1887, 58p, Paper, Novel [Allan #4]
06571   *Three adventure novels of H. Rider Haggard:
        She; King Solomon's mines; Allan Quatermain.*
        Dover, New York, 1960, 636p, Paper, Coll.
06572   *Treasure of the lake.* Doubleday, Page, Garden
        City, 1926, 312p, Cloth, Novel [Allan #11]
06573   *The virgin of the Sun.* Cassell, London, 1922,
        308p, Cloth, Novel
06574   *The wanderer's necklace.* Cassell, London,
        1914, 328p, Cloth, Novel
06575   *When the world shook, being an account of the
        great adventure of Bastin, Bickley, and Ar-
        buthnot.* Cassell, London, 1919, 347p, Cloth,
        Novel
06576   *Wisdom's daughter; the life and love story of
        She-Who-Must-Be-Obeyed.* Hutchinson, London,
        1923, 288p, Cloth, Novel; Doubleday, Page,
        Garden City, 1923, 383p, Cloth, Novel [issued
        the same day; She #1]
06577   *The witch's head, a novel; Allan's wife.* P.
        F. Collier & Son, New York, 1895?, 474p,
        Cloth, Coll. [*The witch's head* is not SF]
06578   *The wizard.* J. W. Arrowsmith, Bristol; Simp-
        kin, Marshall, Hamilton, Kent, London, 1896,
        208p, Paper, Novel
06579   *The wizard; and, Black Heart and White Heart.*
        George Newnes, London, 1907, 158p, Cloth,
        Coll.
06579A retitled: *Black Heart and White Heart; and,
        The wizard.* Hodder & Stoughton, London,
        1924, 318p, Cloth, Coll.
06580   *The works of H. Rider Haggard.* W. J. Black,
        New York, 1928, 728p, Cloth, Coll. [includes
        *She; Cleopatra; King Solomon's mines; Allan
        Quatermain; Maiwa's revenge*]
06580A retitled: *The favorite novels of H. Rider
        Haggard.* Blue Ribbon, New York, 1928?,
        728p, Cloth, Coll.
06581   *The Yellow God; an idol of Africa.* Cupples &
        Leon, New York, 1908, 320p, Cloth, Novel

with Andrew Lang:

06582   *The world's desire; a novel.* Longmans, Green,
        London, 1890, 316p, Cloth, Novel

with Don Ward:

06583   *She; the story retold.* Dell, New York, 1949,
        192p, Paper, Movie [rewritten]

with Jean Francis Webb:

06584   *King Solomon's mines.* Dell, New York, 1950,
        192p, Paper, Movie [rewritten]

HAGGARD, WILLIAM, pseud. [Richard Henry Michael Clayton, 1907-   ] [*biography included*]

06585   *The doubtful disciple.* Cassell, London, 1969,
        188p, Cloth, Novel
06586   *The Haggard omnibus; three complete novels;
        Slow Burner; Venetian blind; Closed circuit.*
        Cassell, London, 1967, 580p, Cloth,
        Coll.
06587   *Slow Burner.* Cassell, London, 1958, 192p,
        Cloth, Novel

HAHN, CHARLES CURTZ

06588   *The wreck of the South Pole; or, The Great
        Dissembler, and other strange tales.* Street
        & Smith, New York, 1899, 222p, Cloth, Coll.

HAIBLUM, ISIDORE, 1935-   [*biography included*]

06589   *The return.* Dell, New York, 1973, 188p, Paper,
        Novel
06590   *Transfer to yesterday.* Ballantine, New York,
        1972, 210p, Paper, Novel
06591   *The Tsaddik of the seven wonders.* Ballantine,
        New York, 1971, 185p, Paper, Novel

HAILE, TERENCE

06592   *Galaxies ahead.* Digit, London, 1963, 160p,
        Paper, Novel
06593   *Space train.* Digit, London, 1962, 159p, Paper,
        Novel

HAINES, DONAL HAMILTON, 1886-1951

06594   *Clearing the seas; or, The last of the war-
        ships.* Harper & Bros., New York, 1915,
        282p, Cloth, Novel
06595   *The last invasion.* Harper & Bros, New York,
        1914, 340p, Cloth, Novel

HAINING, PETER (Alexander), 1940-   [*biography
included*]

06596   *Beyond the curtain of dark.* Four Square, Lon-
        don, 1966, 320p, Paper, Anth.
06597   *Christopher Lee's new chamber of horrors.*
        Souvenir Press, London, 1974, 316p, Cloth,
        Anth.
06598   *A circle of witches; an anthology of Victorian
        witchcraft stories.* Robert Hale, London,
        1971, 235p, Cloth, Anth. [includes some non-
06599   *The clans of darkness; Scottish stories of
        fantasy and horror.* Victor Gollancz, London,
        1971, 272p, Cloth, Anth.
06600   *The craft of terror; extracts from the rare
        and famous gothic 'horror' novels.* Four
        Square, London, 1966, 188p, Paper, Anth.
        Detours into the macabre. [see 06613A]
06601   *Dr. Caligari's black book; an excursion into
        the macabre, in thirteen acts.* W. H. Allen,
        London, 1968, 190p, Cloth, Anth.

HAINING, PETER (cont.)

06602 *The evil people, being thirteen strange and terrible accounts of witchcraft, black magic, and voodoo.* Leslie Frewin, London, 1968, 252p, Cloth, Anth.

06603 *The freak show; tales of fantasy and horror.* Rapp & Whiting, London, 1970, 256p, Cloth, Anth.

06604 *The future makers; a selection of science fiction.* Sidgwick & Jackson, London, 1968, 191p, Cloth, Anth.

06605 *The gentlewomen of evil; an anthology of rare supernatural stories from the pens of Victorian ladies.* Robert Hale, London, 1967, 254p, Cloth, Anth.

06606 *The ghouls.* W. H. Allen, London, 1971, 383p, Cloth, Anth.

06606A retitled: *The ghouls, book one.* Orbit, London, 1974, 198p, Paper, Anth. [abridged]

06606B retitled: *The ghouls, book two.* Orbit, London, 1974, 201p, Paper, Anth. [abridged; 06606A and 06606B together comprise the original volume]

06607 *Gothic tales of terror; classic horror stories from Great Britain, Europe, and the United States, 1765-1840.* Taplinger, New York, 1972, 928p, Cloth, Anth. [comprises 06608 and 06609 together]
Gothic tales of terror, volume one. [see 06608A]
Gothic tales of terror, volume two. [see 06609A]

06608 *Great British tales of terror; gothic stories of horror and romance, 1765-1840.* Victor Gollancz, London, 1972, 487p, Cloth, Anth.

06608A retitled: *Gothic tales of terror, volume one; classic horror stories from Great Britain.* Penguin, Baltimore, 1973, 543p, Paper, Anth.

06609 *Great tales of terror from Europe and America; gothic stories of horror and romance, 1765-1840.* Victor Gollancz, London, 1972, 440p, Cloth, Anth.

06609A retitled: *Gothic tales of terror, volume two; classic horror stories from Europe and the United States.* Penguin, Baltimore, 1973, 506p, Paper, Anth.

06610 *The hell of mirrors.* Four Square, London, 1965, 189p, Paper, Anth.

06611 *The Hollywood nightmare; tales of fantasy and horror from the film world.* Macdonald, London, 1970, 276p, Cloth, Anth.

06612 *Legends for the dark; tales of fantasy and horror.* New English Library, London, 1968, 127p, Paper, Anth.

06613 *The Lucifer society.* W. H. Allen, London, 1972, 256p, Cloth, Anth.

06613A retitled: *Detours into the macabre.* Pan, London, 1974, 264p, Paper, Anth.

06614 *The magic valley travellers; Welsh stories of fantasy and horror.* Victor Gollancz, London, 1974, 256p, Cloth, Anth.

06615 *The magicians; occult stories.* Peter Owen, London, 1972, 220p, Cloth, Anth. [includes some nonf.]

06616 *The midnight people, being eighteen terrifying and bizarre tales of vampires.* Leslie Frewin, London, 1968, 255p, Cloth, Anth.

06616A retitled: *Vampires at midnight; seventeen brilliant and chilling tales of the ghastly bloodsucking undead.* Grosset & Dunlap, New York, 1970, 255p, Cloth, Anth.

06617 *The monster makers.* Victor Gollancz, London, 1974, 288p, Cloth, Anth.

06618 *Nightfrights; an anthology of macabre tales that have terrified three generations.* Victor Gollancz, London, 1972, 254p, Cloth, Anth.

06619 *The nightmare reader.* Victor Gollancz, London, 1973, 340p, Cloth, Anth.

06620 *The Satanists.* Neville Spearman, London, 1969, 249p, Cloth, Anth.

06621 *Summoned from the tomb; great tales of horror.* Brown, Watson, London, 1966, 160p, Paper, Anth.

06622 *Summoned from the tomb; great tales of horror.* Sidgwick & Jackson, London, 1973, 213p, Cloth, Anth. [includes *Summoned from the tomb* and *Legends for the dark*]

06623 *The unspeakable people, being twenty of the world's most horrible horror stories.* Leslie Frewin, London, 1969, 246p, Cloth, Anth.
Vampires at midnight. [see 06616A]

06624 *Where nightmares are.* Mayflower-Dell, London, 1966, 174p, Paper, Anth.

06625 *The wild night company; Irish stories of fantasy and horror.* Victor Gollancz, London, 1970, 287p, Cloth, Anth.

06626 *The witchcraft reader.* Dennis Dobson, London, 1969, 223p, Cloth, Anth.

HALACY, D(aniel) S(tephen) Jr., 1919- [biography included]

06627 *Return from Luna.* Grosset & Dunlap, New York, 1969, 181p, Cloth, Novel

06628 *Rocket rescue.* W. W. Norton, New York, 1968, 191p, Cloth, Novel

HALDANE, CHARLOTTE (Franken), 1894-1969

06629 *Man's world.* Chatto & Windus, London, 1926, 299p, Cloth, Novel

06630 *Melusine; or, Devil take her! a romantic novel.* Arthur Barker, London, 1936, 317p, Cloth, Novel

06631 *The shadow of a dream.* George Weidenfeld & Nicholson, London, 1952, 287p, Cloth, Novel

HALDANE, J(ohn) B(urdon) S(anderson), 1892-1964

06632 *My friend Mr. Leakey.* Cresset Press, London, 1937, 179p, Cloth, Coll.

HALDEMAN, JOE W(illiam), 1943- [biography included]

06633 *Cosmic laughter; science fiction for the fun of it.* Holt, Rinehart & Winston, New York, 1974, 189p, Cloth, Anth.

HALE, EDWARD EVERETT, 1822-1909

06634 *The brick moon, from the papers of Captain Frederic Ingham.* Spiral Press, Imprint Society, Barre, Mass., 1971, 80p, Cloth, Novel [the collection, *The brick moon, and other stories*, is not SF]

HALE, EDWARD EVERETT (cont.)

06635   *His level best, and other stories.* Roberts
        Bros., Boston, 1872, 293p, Cloth, Coll.
06636   *Sybaris, and other homes.* Field, Osgood, Bos-
        ton, 1869, 206p, Cloth, Coll. [includes some
        nonf.]

as Col. Frederic Ingham:

06637   *Ten times one is ten; the possible reformation;
        a story in nine chapters.* Roberts Bros.,
        Boston, 1871, 148p, Cloth, Coll.

HALE, JOHN, 1926-

06638   *The Paradise man; a black and white farce.*
        Bobbs-Merrill, Indianapolis, 1969, 221p,
        Cloth, Novel; Rapp & Whiting, London, 1969,
        221p, Cloth, Novel

HALE, MARICE RUTLEDGE
    see: RUTLEDGE, MARYSE

HALE, MARTIN

06639   *The Fourth Reich; a fantasy of the United
        Nations.* Jonathan Cape, London, 1965, 189p,
        Cloth, Novel

HALE, ROBERT BEVERLY, 1901-

06640   *Snowland.* Doubleday, Garden City, 1971,
        174p, Cloth, Novel

HALES, C. L.

06641   *The wooden heads.* Wells Gardner, Darton,
        London, 1926, 279p, Cloth, Novel

HALEY, CLAUDE

06642   *Beyond the solar system.* Arc Press, London,
        1953?, 141p, Paper, Novel [name reads "Claud
        Haley" on cover]

HALEY, HARRY F(ranklin), 1883-

06643   *Immortal Athalia.* Dorrance, Philadelphia,
        1922, 310p, Cloth, Novel

HALFORD, JOHN

06644   *Hidden Saria.* J. Heritage, London, 1934,
        301p, Cloth, Novel

HALIDOM, M. Y., pseud.

        The last of the Wonder Club. [see 06649B]
06645   *The poet's curse; a tale.* Greening & Co.,
        London, 1911, 320p, Cloth, Novel
        Tales of the Wonder Club. [see 06648A]
        Tales of the Wonder Club, second series.
        [see 06649A]

06646   *A weird transformation.* Thomas Burleigh, Lon-
        don, 1904, 296p, Cloth, Novel
06647   *Zoe's revenge.* Greening & Co., London, 1908,
        336p, Cloth, Novel

as Dryasdust:

06648   *Tales of the Wonder Club.* Harrison & Sons,
        London, 1899, 401p, Cloth, Coll.
06648A *Tales of the Wonder Club,* by M. Y. Halidom.
        Thomas Burleigh, London, 1903, 316p, Cloth,
        Coll.
06649   *Tales of the Wonder Club, vol. II-vol. III.*
        Harrison & Sons, London, 1900, 662p, Cloth,
        Coll.
06649A retitled: *Tales of the Wonder Club, second
        series,* by M. Y. Halidom. Thomas Burleigh,
        London, 1904, 318p, Cloth, Coll. [abridged]
06649B retitled: *The last of the Wonder Club; The
        Gipsy queen, a romantic play.* Thomas Bur-
        leigh, London, 1905, 302p, Cloth, Coll.
        [abridged; 06649A and 06649B together com-
        prise the original volume] [by M. Y. Halidom]
06650   *The wizard's mantle.* no publisher, London?,
        1902, 289p, Cloth, Novel
06650A *The wizard's mantle,* by M. Y. Halidom. Thomas
        Burleigh, London, 1903, 311p, Cloth, Novel

HALL, ANGUS, 1932-   [*biography included*]

06651   *Devilday.* Sphere, London, 1969, 157p, Paper,
        Novel [Devilday #1]
06651A retitled: *Madhouse.* Award, New York, 1974,
        157p, Paper, Novel
06652   *The scars of Dracula.* Sphere, London, 1971,
        140p, Paper, Movie [Dracula series]
06653   *To play the devil.* Sphere, London, 1971, 140p,
        Paper, Novel [Devilday #2]

HALL, AUSTIN, d. 1933

06654   *People of the comet.* Griffin Publishing Co.,
        Los Angeles, 1948, 131p, Cloth, Novel
06655   *The Spot of Life.* Ace, New York, 1965, 187p,
        Paper, Novel [Blind Spot #2]

with Homer Eon Flint:

05493   *The Blind Spot.* Prime Press, Philadelphia,
        1951, 293p, Cloth, Novel [Blind Spot #1]

HALL, BRIAN P(atrick), 1935-   , with Joseph
Osburn

06656   *Nog's vision.* Paulist Press, New York, 1973,
        141p, Paper, Novel

HALL, D. W.
    see: GILMORE, ANTHONY

HALL, G(eorge) ROME

06657   *The black fortnight; or, The invasion of 1915.*
        Swan Sonnenschein, London, 1904, 128p, Paper,
        Novel

HALL, G(ranville) STANLEY, 1844-1924

06658 *Recreations of a psychologist.* D. Appleton, New York, 1920, 336p, Cloth, Coll.

HALL, (Anna) GERTRUDE, 1863-1961

06659 *Foam of the sea, and other tales.* Roberts Bros., Boston, 1895, 299p, Cloth, Coll.

HALL, GRAHAM M.

06660 *Robert Bloch bibliography.* Graham M. Hall, Tewksbury, UK, 1965, 32p, Paper, Nonf.

HALL, H(albert) W(eldon), 1941- [*biography included*]

06661 *SFBRI; science fiction book review index, 1970.* H. W. Hall, Bryan, TX, 1971, 36p, Paper, Nonf.
06662 *SFBRI; science fiction book review index, 1971 (volume 2).* H. W. Hall, Bryan, TX, 1972, 33p, Paper, Nonf.
06663 *SFBRI; science fiction book review index, 1972, volume 3.* H. W. Hall, Bryan, TX, 1973, 35p, Paper, Nonf.
06664 *SFBRI; science fiction book review index, volume 4, 1973.* H. W. Hall, Bryan, TX, 1974, 31p, Paper, Nonf.

HALL, HAL, 1911-

06665 *The great conflict.* Haynes Corp., Los Angeles, 1942, 150p, Cloth, Novel

HALL, LELAND (Boylston), 1883-1957

06666 *Sinister house.* Houghton Mifflin, Boston, 1919, 226p, Cloth, Novel

HALL, LOU KING-
    see: KING-HALL, LOU

HALL, MAGDALEN KING-
    see: KING-HALL, MAGDALEN

HALL, MANLY P(almer), 1901-

06667 *Lady of dreams; a fable in the manner of the Chinese.* Philosophical Research Society, Los Angeles, 1943, 47p, Cloth, Story
06668 *Shadow forms; a collection of occult stories.* Hall Publishing Co., Los Angeles, 1925, 165p, Cloth, Coll.
06669 *The way of Heaven, and other fantasies told in the manner of the Chinese.* Philosophical Research Society, Los Angeles, 1946, 185p, Cloth, Coll.
06670 *The ways of the lonely ones, when the sons of compassion speak.* The Author, Santa Monica, CA, 1923, 64p, Cloth, Coll.

HALL, OWEN, pseud. [James Davis, 1853-1907]

06671 *Eureka.* Chatto & Windus, London, 1899, 299p, Cloth, Novel

HALL, RONALD, 1929-

06672 *The open cage.* Collins, London, 1970, 286p, Cloth, Novel

HALL, STEPHEN KING-
    see: KING-HALL, STEPHEN

HALLAHAN, WILLIAM H.

06673 *The search for Joseph Tully; a novel.* Bobbs-Merrill, Indianapolis, 1974, 271p, Cloth, Novel

HALLAM, (Samuel Benoni) ATLANTIS, 1915-
[*biography included*]

06674 *Star ship on Saddle Mountain.* Macmillan, New York, 1955, 182p, Cloth, Novel

HALLE, LOUIS J(oseph Jr.), 1910- [*biography included*]

06675 *Sedge.* Frederick A. Praeger, Publisher, New York, 1963, 118p, Cloth, Novel

HALLEN, A. L.

06676 *Angilin, a Venite king.* Digby, Long, London, 1907, 314p, Cloth, Novel

HALLINAN, TIM

06677 *Teenage ghost stories, volume 1.* Tiger Beat, New York, 1973, 127p, Paper, Coll. [volume 2 never issued]

HALLIWELL, TONY, with Hugh Darrington as James Ross

03829 *The God killers; science fiction.* Sidgwick & Jackson, London, 1970, 190p, Cloth, Novel

HALLUMS, JAMES R.

06678 *They came, they saw.* Brown, Watson, London, 1965, 159p, Paper, Novel

HALSBURY, (Hardinge Goulburn Gifford, 2nd) Earl of, 1880-1943

06679 *1944.* Thornton Butterworth, London, 1926, 302p, Cloth, Novel

HAMBROOK, EMERSON C.

06680   *The red to-morrow.* Proletarian Press, London, 1920, 325p, Cloth, Novel

HAMILTON, ALEX (John) [*biography included*]

06681   *Beam of malice; fifteen short, dark stories.* Hutchinson, London, 1966, 222p, Cloth, Coll.

06682   *Best horror stories three.* Faber & Faber, London, 1972, 236p, Cloth, Anth.

06683   *The cold embrace, and other stories.* Corgi, London, 1966, 188p, Paper, Anth.

06684   *Flies on the wall.* Hutchinson of London, London, 1972, 224p, Cloth, Coll.

06685   *Splinters; a new anthology of modern macabre fiction.* Hutchinson, London, 1968, 237p, Cloth, Anth.

HAMILTON, Count ANTHONY, 1645?-1719

06686   *Fairy tales and romances.* Henry G. Bohn, London, 1846, 562p, Cloth, Coll. [includes Hamilton's version of *The four Facardins*]

with M. G. Lewis and M. de Levis:

06687   *The four Facardins; a fairy tale.* Lutetian Society, London, 1899, 286p, Paper, Novel [includes Hamilton's original story with two sequels by Lewis and de Levis]

HAMILTON, BERNARD

06688   *The light? a romance.* Hurst & Blackett, London, 1898, 523p, Cloth, Novel

HAMILTON, CICELY (Mary), 1872-1952

06689   *Theodore Savage; a story of the past or the future.* Leonard Parsons, London, 1922, 320p, Cloth, Novel

06689A retitled: *Lest ye die.* Jonathan Cape, London, 1928, 285p, Cloth, Novel [somewhat abridged and rewritten]

HAMILTON, EDMOND (Moore), 1904-1977 [*biography included*]

06690   *Battle for the stars.* Torquil, New York, 1961, 206p, Cloth, Novel
        Beyond the Moon. [see 06713A]

06691   *Calling Captain Future.* Popular Library, New York, 1969, 144p, Paper, Novel [Captain Future #8]

06692   *Captain Future and the Space Emperor.* Popular Library, New York, 1969, 128p, Paper, Novel [Captain Future #13]

06693   *Captain Future's challenge.* Popular Library, New York, 1969, 128p, Paper, Novel [Captain Future #9]

06694   *City at world's end.* Frederick Fell, New York, 1951, 239p, Cloth, Novel

06695   *The Closed Worlds; Starwolf #2.* Ace, New York, 1968, 157p, Paper, Novel [Starwolf #2]

06696   *The comet kings.* Popular Library, New York, 1969, 127p, Paper, Novel [Captain Future #6]

06697   *Crashing suns.* Ace, New York, 1965, 192p, Paper, Coll. [Interstellar Patrol series]

06698   *Doomstar.* Belmont, New York, 1966, 158p, Paper, Novel

06699   *Fugitive of the stars.* Ace Double, New York, 1965, 116p, Paper, Novel

06700   *Galaxy mission.* Popular Library, New York, 1969, 128p, Paper, Novel [Captain Future #1]

06701   *The haunted stars.* Torquil, New York, 1960, 192p, Cloth, Novel

06702   *The horror on the asteroid, and other tales o. planetary horror.* Philip Allan, London, 1936, 256p, Cloth, Coll.

06703   *The Magician of Mars.* Popular Library, New York, 1969, 128p, Paper, Novel [Captain Future #11]

06704   *The metal giants.* Swanson Book Co., Washburn ND, 1935?, 35p, Paper, Story

06705   *The monsters of Juntonheim; a complete book-length novel of amazing adventure.* World Distributors/Sydney Pemberton, Manchester, 1950, 160p, Paper, Novel

06705A retitled: *A yank at Valhalla.* Ace Double, New York, 1973, 128p, Paper, Novel

06706   *Murder in the clinic.* Utopian Publications, London, 1946, 36p, Paper, Coll.

06707   *Outlaw World.* Popular Library, New York, 196. 126p, Paper, Novel [Captain Future #3]

06708   *Outlaws of the Moon.* Popular Library, New Yo. 1969, 128p, Paper, Novel [Captain Future #5]

06709   *Outside the universe.* Ace, New York, 1964, 173p, Paper, Novel [Interstellar Patrol series]

06710   *Planets in peril.* Popular Library, New York, 1969, 128p, Paper, Novel [Captain Future #7]

06711   *Quest beyond the stars.* Popular Library, New York, 1969, 142p, Paper, Novel [Captain Future #4]

06712   *Return to the stars.* Lancer, New York, 1970, 207p, Paper, Novel [Star Kings #2]

06713   *The star kings.* Frederick Fell, New York, 1949, 262p, Cloth, Novel [Star Kings #1]

06713A retitled: *Beyond the Moon (The star kings).* Signet, New York, 1950, 167p, Paper, Novel [Star Kings #1]

06714   *The star of life.* Torquil, New York, 1959, 192p, Cloth, Novel

06715   *The sun smasher.* Ace Double, New York, 1959, 110p, Paper, Novel

06716   *Tharkol, lord of the unknown; a novel.* World Distributors/Sydney Pemberton, Manchester, 1950, 160p, Paper, Novel

06717   *The valley of creation.* Lancer, New York, 1964, 159p, Paper, Novel

06718   *The weapon from beyond; Starwolf #1.* Ace, New York, 1967, 158p, Paper, Novel [Starwolf #1]

06719   *What's it like out there? and other stories.* Ace, New York, 1974, 320p, Paper, Coll.

06720   *World of the Starwolves; Starwolf #3.* Ace, New York, 1968, 158p, Paper, Novel [Starwolf #3]
        A yank at Valhalla. [see 06705A]

as Brett Sterling, house pseud:

06721   *Danger planet.* Popular Library, New York, 1968, 128p, Paper, Novel [Captain Future #1.]

with Eando Binder, Jack Williamson, Raymond Z. Gallun, and John Russell Fearn:

01304   *The great illusion.* Fantasy Booklet, Wallsen. UK, 1973, 12p, Paper, Story

HAMILTON, EUGENE LEE-
see: LEE-HAMILTON, EUGENE

HAMILTON, M(arianne) LYNN [Hamilton Lewis]

06722 *The hidden kingdom.* N. Wentworth-Evans, Melbourne, 1932, 141p, Cloth, Novel

HAMILTON, (Anthony Walter) PATRICK, 1904-1962

06723 *Impromptu in Moribundia.* Constable, London, 1939, 289p, Cloth, Novel

HAMMETT, (Samuel) DASHIELL, 1894-1961

06724 *Creeps by night; chills and thrills.* John Day, New York, 1931, 525p, Cloth, Anth.
06724A retitled: *Modern tales of horror.* Victor Gollancz, London, 1932, 448p, Cloth, Anth. [abridged]
06724B retitled: *The Red Brain, and other thrillers.* Belmont, New York, 1961, 141p, Paper, Anth. [abridged]
06724C retitled: *Breakdown, and other thrillers.* Four Square, London, 1968, 128p, Paper, Anth. [abridged]

HAMON, LOUIS
see: HAMONG, Count LEIGH de

HAMONG, Count LEIGH de, pseud. [Louis de Hamon, 1866-1936]

06725 *A study of destiny.* Saxon & Co., London, 1898, 156p, Cloth, Novel

HAMPDEN, JOHN, 1898-1974

06726 *Ghost stories.* J. M. Dent & Sons, London, 1939, 366p, Cloth, Anth.

HAMPTON, LOU

06727 *Ghosts of my study; a book of short stories.* Authors & Publishers Corp., New York, 1927, 284p, Cloth, Coll.

HANARANDA, MULLA, 1882-

06728 *Cabriba, the garden of the gods.* American Library Service, New York, 1925, 421p, Cloth, Novel

HANCOCK, H(arrie) IRVING, 1868-1922

06729 *At the defense of Pittsburgh; or, The struggle to save America's "fighting steel" supply.* Henry Altemus, Philadelphia, 1916, 255p, Cloth, Novel [Conquest of the U.S. #3]
06730 *In the battle for New York; or, Uncle Sam's boys in the desperate struggle for the metropolis.* Henry Altemus, Philadelphia, 1916, 256p, Cloth, Novel [Conquest of the U.S. #2]

06731 *The invasion of the United States; or, Uncle Sam's boys at the capture of Boston.* Henry Altemus, Philadelphia, 1916, 256p, Cloth, Novel [Conquest of the U.S. #1]
06732 *Making the stand for Old Glory; or, Uncle Sam's boys in the last frantic drive.* Henry Altemus, Philadelphia, 1916, 256p, Cloth, Novel [Conquest of the U.S. #4]

THE HANDWRITING ON THE WALL
see: COOPER, J. C.

HANIFIN, JOHN M.
see: PHINEAS

HANKINSON, CHARLES JAMES
see: HOLLAND, CLIVE

HANKS, KEITH, 1940-

06733 *Falk; a novel.* Cassell, London, 1972, 285p, Cloth, Novel

HANLEY, JAMES, 1901-

06734 *What Farrar saw.* Ivor Nicholson & Watson, London, 1946, 202p, Cloth, Novel

HANLON, JON

06735 *Death's loving arms, and other terror tales.* Corinth, San Diego, 1966, 159p, Paper, Anth.
06736 *The house of living death, and other terror tales.* Corinth, San Diego, 1966, 160p, Paper, Anth.
06737 *Stories from Doctor Death, and other terror tales.* Corinth, San Diego, 1966, 160p, Paper, Anth.

HANNA, GEORGE W.
see: GENTIL, SPIRITO

HANNA, W. C.

06738 *The Tandar saga.* Arcadia House, New York, 1964, 190p, Cloth, Novel

HANNAN, CHARLES

06739 *The betrothal of James.* Bliss, Sands, London, 1898, 243p, Cloth, Novel
06740 *Thuka of the Moon.* Digby, Long, London, 1906, 280p, Cloth, Novel

HANNAY, J(ames) F(rederick) W(ynne), 1906-

06741 *Rebels' triumph.* Methuen, London, 1933, 279p, Cloth, Novel

HANSEN, VERN

06742   *Claws of the night.* Digit, London, 1963, 158p,
        Paper, Novel
06743   *Creatures of the mist.* Digit, London, 1963,
        160p, Paper, Novel
06744   *The grip of fear.* Digit, London, 1964, 158p,
        Paper, Novel
06745   *The twisters.* Digit, London, 1963, 157p,
        Paper, Novel

HANSMAN, WILLIAM (Donald), 1913-   [*biography
included*]

06746   *The A.G. man.* Vantage Press, New York, 1968,
        193p, Cloth, Novel

HANSOM, MARK

06747   *The beasts of Brahm.* Wright & Brown, London,
        1937, 248p, Cloth, Novel
06748   *The ghost of Gaston Revere.* Wright & Brown,
        London, 1935, 253p, Cloth, Novel
06749   *Master of souls.* Wright & Brown, London,
        1937, 256p, Cloth, Novel
06750   *Sorcerer's chessmen.* Wright & Brown, London,
        1939, 252p, Cloth, Novel
06751   *The wizard of Berner's Abbey.* Wright & Brown,
        London, 1935, 255p, Cloth, Novel

HANSON, RITA MOHLER

06752   *The desert road to Shani Lun; a romance of
        Mongolia.* Binfords & Mort, Publishers,
        Portland, OR, 1939, 288p, Cloth, Novel

HANVEY, ROBERT E.

06753   *Myora; or, The land of eternal sunshine, in
        three parts.* Gimlin Press, Chicago, 1903,
        92p, Paper, Novel [parts 2-3 never issued]

HAPPY, the King's dog, pseud.

06754   *If I were King George.* Hodder & Stoughton,
        London, 1911, 54p, Cloth, Novel

HARBEN, WILL(iam) N(athaniel), 1858-1919

06755   *The land of the changing sun.* Merriam Co.,
        New York, 1894, 233p, Cloth, Novel

HARBOTTLE, PHILIP (James), 1941-   [*biography
included*]

06756   *John Russell Fearn--an evaluation.* Coulson
        Publications, Wabash, IN, 1963, 10p, Paper,
        Nonf.
06757   retitled: *John Russell Fearn: the ultimate
        analysis.* Philip Harbottle, Wallsend-on-
        Tyne, UK, 1965, 94p, Paper, Nonf. [expanded]
06758   retitled: *The multi-man; a biographic and
        bibliographic study of John Russell Fearn
        (1908-60).* Philip James Harbottle, Wallsend,
        UK, 1968, 69p, Paper, Nonf. [expanded]

published anonymously:

06759   *Eternal rediffusion.* Fantasy Booklet, Wall-
        send, UK, 1973, 12p, Paper, Anth.
06760   *Flight on Titan.* Cosmos Science Fiction Seri
        Wallsend-on-Tyne, UK, 1973, 28p, Paper,
        Anth.
06761   *Passage to Saturn.* Fantasy Booklet, Wallsend
        1973, 12p, Paper, Anth.

HARBOU, THEA von
    see: von HARBOU, THEA

HARDIE, JOHN L(ipp)

06762   *Another 7 strange stories.* Art & Educational
        Publishers, Glasgow, 1944, 80p, Paper, Anth.
06763   *Seven more strange stories.* Art & Educationa
        Publishers, Glasgow, 1945, 80p, Paper, Anth
06764   *7 strange stories.* Art & Educational Publi-
        shers, Glasgow, 1943, 80p, Paper, Anth.
06765   *Strange stories--the last seven.* Art & Educa
        tional Publishers, Glasgow, 1946, 80p, Pape
        Anth.
06766   *Twenty-two strange stories.* Art & Educationa
        Publishers, Glasgow, 1945, 280p, Cloth, Ant

HARDIN, GARRETT (James), 1915-   [*biography
included*]

06767   *Exploring new ethics for survival; the voyage
        of the spaceship Beagle.* Viking Press, New
        York, 1972, 273p, Cloth, Novel [the novel
        alternates with nonfiction text]

HARDING, ELLISON

06768   *The Demetrian.* Brentano's, New York, 1907,
        315p, Cloth, Novel
06768A retitled: *The woman who vowed.* T. Fisher
        Unwin, London, 1908, 315p, Cloth, Novel

HARDING, JOHN WILLIAM, 1864-

06769   *A conjuror of phantoms.* F. Tennyson Neely,
        London, 1898, 177p, Cloth, Novel

HARDING, RONALD S. L.

06770   *"One dreadful night..." a tale of the unknown
        Modern Publishing Co., London, 1935, 254p,
        Cloth, Novel

HARDY, PHILIP

06771   *The buried country.* Schoolboys' Pocket Lib-
        rary, London, 1945?, 32p, Paper, Story
        [Smith Minor #1]
06772   *Smith minor on the Moon.* Schoolboys' Pocket
        Library, London, 1945?, 32p, Paper, Story
        [Smith Minor #2]

HARDY, W(illiam) G(eorge), 1895-

06773 *All the trumpets sounded; a novel based on the life of Moses.* Coward-McCann, New York, 1942, 501p, Cloth, Novel

HARFORD, SCOTT

06774 *Lustopia.* Pendulum, Los Angeles, 1970, 191p, Paper, Novel

HARGER, CATHARINE, with Leon Pritcher

06775 *Disturbers of the peace.* Bruce Humphries, Boston, 1945, 231p, Cloth, Novel

HARGRAVE, JOHN (Gordon), 1894-

06776 *The imitation man.* Victor Gollancz, London, 1931, 288p, Cloth, Novel

HARINGTON, DONALD, 1935- [*biography included*]

06777 *Some other place. The right place; a novel.* Little, Brown, Boston, 1972, 462p, Cloth, Novel

HARKER, KENNETH, 1927- [*biography included*]

06778 *The flowers of February.* Robert Hale, London, 1970, 191p, Cloth, Novel
06779 *The Symmetrians.* Compact, London, 1966, 160p, Paper, Novel

HARKINS, PHILIP, 1912- [*biography included*], with Harold Goodwin as John Blaine

01437 *Danger below!* Grosset & Dunlap, New York, 1968, 178p, Cloth, Novel [Rick Brant #23]

HARKON, FRANZ, pseud.

06780 *Spawn of space.* Scion, London, 1951, 112p, Paper, Novel

HARLAN, ETHEL ANDREWS

06781 *The adventures of little man Coco.* Branden Press, Boston, 1966, 133p, Cloth, Novel

HARLAND, HENRY
   see: LUSKA, SIDNEY

HARMON, JIM [James Judson Harmon, 1933-] [*biography included*]

06782 *Sex burns like fire.* PEC, El Cajon, CA, 1964, 160p, Paper, Novel

HARNESS, CHARLES L(eonard), 1915- [*biography included*]

06783 *Flight into yesterday.* Bouregy & Curl, New York, 1953, 256p, Cloth, Novel
06783A retitled: *The paradox men.* Ace Double, New York, 1955, 187p, Paper, Novel
06784 *The Ring of Ritornel.* Victor Gollancz, London, 1968, 221p, Cloth, Novel
06785 *The Rose.* Compact, London, 1966, 189p, Paper, Coll.

HARNISHFEGER, LLOYD

06786 *Prisoner of the Mound Builders.* Lerner Publishing Co., Minneapolis, 1973, 141p, Cloth, Novel

HARPER, C. ARMITAGE

06787 *American ghost stories.* Houghton Mifflin, Boston, 1928, 287p, Cloth, Anth.

HARPER, CHARLES G(eorge), 1863-1943

06788 *Mr. Pickwick's second time on Earth.* Cecil Palmer, London, 1927, 88p, Cloth, Novel

HARPER, HARRY, 1880-1960

06789 *Winged world; the coming of the air age.* John Gifford, London, 1946, 159p, Cloth, Novel

with Claude Grahame-White:

06213 *The invisible war-plane; a tale of air adventure in the great campaign.* Blackie & Son, London, 1915, 272p, Cloth, Novel

HARPER, OLIVE, pseud. [Helen Burnell D'Apery, 1842-1915]

06790 *The sociable ghost, being the adventures of a reporter who was invited by the sociable ghost to a grand banquet, ball, and convention under the ground of old Trinity churchyard; a true tale of the things he saw and did not see while he was not there.* J. S. Ogilvie, New York, 1903, 235p, Cloth, Novel

HARPER, VINCENT

06791 *The mortgage on the brain, being the confessions of the late Ethelbert Croft, M.D.* Doubleday, Page, New York, 1905, 293p, Cloth, Novel

HARRÉ, T(homas) EVERETT, 1884-1948

06792 *Behold the woman! a tale of redemption.* J. B. Lippincott, Philadelphia, 1916, 400p, Cloth, Novel
06793 *Beware after dark! the world's most stupendous tales of mystery, horror, thrills, and terror.* Macaulay Co., New York, 1929, 461p, Cloth, Anth.

HARRINGTON, LEN

06794 *Satan's stud*. Trojan Classic, Chatsworth, CA,
        1972?, 185p, Paper, Novel

HARRINGTON, RICHARD

06795 *Hellfire today*. New English Library, London,
        1972, 127p, Paper, Novel

HARRIS, ALFRED, 1928- [*biography included*],
with Arthur Moore as Harris Moore

06796 *The marrow eaters*. Popular Library, New York,
        1972, 189p, Paper, Novel
06797 *Slater's planet*. Pinnacle, New York, 1971,
        188p, Paper, Novel

HARRIS, BARBARA S., 1927- [*biography included*]

06798 *Who is Julia?* David McKay, New York, 1972,
        309p, Cloth, Novel

HARRIS, CHRISTIE (Lucy), 1907- [*biography
included*]

06799 *Secret in the Stlalakum Wild*. Atheneum, New
        York, 1972, 186p, Cloth, Novel

HARRIS, CLARE WINGER, 1891-

06800 *Away from the here and now; stories in pseudo-
        science*. Dorrance, Philadelphia, 1947, 365p,
        Cloth, Coll.

HARRIS, FRANK [James Thomas Harris, 1856-1931]

06801 *Pantopia*. Panurge Press, New York, 1930,
        229p, Cloth, Novel
06802 *Unpath'd waters*. Mitchell Kennerley, New York,
        1913, 279p, Cloth, Novel

HARRIS, J. HENRY

06803 *A romance in radium*. Greening & Co., London,
        1906, 235p, Cloth, Novel

HARRIS, JOHN, 1916-

06804 *Right of reply*. Hutchinson of London, London,
        1968, 232p, Cloth, Novel

HARRIS, JOHN BEYNON
    see: WYNDHAM, JOHN

HARRIS, JOHNSON, pseud.
    see: WYNDHAM, JOHN

HARRIS, LARRY M.
    see: JANIFER, LAURENCE M.

HARRIS, MARILYN, 1931- [*biography included*]

06805 *The conjurers*. Random House, New York, 1974,
        305p, Cloth, Novel

HARRIS, ROSEMARY (Jeanne)

06806 *The bright and morning star*. Faber & Faber,
        London, 1972, 239p, Cloth, Novel [Reuben #3]
06807 *The moon in the cloud*. Faber & Faber, London
        1968, 176p, Cloth, Novel [Reuben #1]
06808 *The seal-singing*. Faber & Faber, London,
        1971, 224p, Cloth, Novel
06809 *The shadow on the sun*. Faber & Faber, London
        1970, 189p, Cloth, Novel [Reuben #2]

HARRIS, Rev. W(illiam) S(huler), 1865-

06810 *Life in a thousand worlds*. G. Holzapfel,
        Cleona, PA, 1905, 344p, Cloth, Novel
06811 *Sermons by the devil*. Minter Co., Harrisburg
        PA, 1904, 304p, Cloth, Coll.

HARRIS, WALTER, 1925-

06812 *The mistress of Downing Street*. Michael
        Joseph, London, 1972, 191p, Cloth, Novel

HARRIS-BURLAND, J(ohn) B(urland), 1870-1926

       Dr. Silex. [see 06816A]
06813 *The gold worshippers*. G. W. Dillingham, New
        York, 1906, 310p, Cloth, Novel
06814 *Workers in darkness*. Greening & Co., London,
        1908, 323p, Cloth, Novel

as Harris Burland:

06815 *Dacobra; or, The white priests of Ahriman*.
        R. A. Everett, London, 1903, 315p, Cloth,
        Novel
06816 *The Princess Thora*. Little, Brown, Boston,
        1904, 360p, Cloth, Novel
06816A retitled: *Dr. Silex*, by J. B. Harris-Burland
        Ward, Lock, London, 1905, 344p, Cloth, Nove

HARRISON, G(eorge) B(agshawe), 1894- [*biography included*]

06817 *The fires of Arcadia*. Harcourt, Brace & Worl
        New York, 1965, 153p, Cloth, Novel

HARRISON, HARRY (Maxwell), 19?5- [*biography
included*]

06818 *Astounding; John W. Campbell memorial antholo
        gy*. Random House, New York, 1973, 333p,
        Cloth, Anth.
06818A retitled: *The John W. Campbell memorial anth
        logy*. Sidgwick & Jackson, London, 1974,
        297p, Cloth, Anth.
06819 *Backdrop of stars*. Dennis Dobson, London,
        1968, 222p, Cloth, Anth.
06819A retitled: *SF: authors' choice*. Berkley Meda
        lion, New York, 1968, 224p, Paper, Anth.
06820 *Bill, the galactic hero*. Doubleday, Garden
        City, 1965, 185p, Cloth, Novel

HARRISON, HARRY (cont.)

06821   *Blast off; S.F. for boys.* Faber & Faber, London, 1969, 237p, Cloth, Anth.
06821A retitled: *Worlds of wonder; sixteen tales of science fiction.* Doubleday, Garden City, 1969, 287p, Cloth, Anth.
06822   *Captive universe.* G. P. Putnam's Sons, New York, 1969, 185p, Cloth, Novel
06823   *The Daleth effect; a science fiction novel.* G. P. Putnam's Sons, New York, 1970, 217p, Cloth, Novel
06823A retitled: *In our hands, the stars.* Faber & Faber, London, 1970, 217p, Cloth, Novel
06824   *Deathworld.* Bantam, New York, 1960, 154p, Paper, Novel [Deathworld #1]
06824A retitled: *Deathworld 1.* Sphere, London, 1973, 157p, Paper, Novel [Deathworld #1]
06825   *Deathworld 2; a sequel to Deathworld.* Bantam, New York, 1964, 151p, Paper, Novel [Deathworld #2]
06825A retitled: *The ethical engineer.* Victor Gollancz, London, 1964, 176p, Cloth, Novel [Deathworld #2]
06826   *Deathworld 3.* Dell, New York, 1968, 188p, Paper, Novel [Deathworld #3]
06827   *The Deathworld trilogy; three novels.* Nelson Doubleday, Garden City, 1974, 440p, Cloth, Coll. [Deathworld #s 1-3]
    The ethical engineer. [see 06825A]
06828   *Four for the future; an anthology on the themes of sacrifice and redemption.* Macdonald, London, 1969, 188p, Cloth, Anth.
    In our hands, the stars. [see 06823A]
    The John W. Campbell memorial anthology. [see 06818A]
    The Jupiter legacy. [see 06838A]
06829   *The light fantastic; science fiction classics from the mainstream.* Charles Scribner's Sons, New York, 1971, 216p, Cloth, Anth.
06830   *Make room! Make room!* Doubleday, Garden City, 1966, 216p, Cloth, Novel
06831   *The man from P.I.G.* Camelot, New York, 1968, 120p, Paper, Novel
06832   *The men from PIG and ROBOT.* Faber & Faber, London, 1974, 141p, Cloth, Coll.
06833   *Nova 1; an anthology of original science fiction stories.* Delacorte Press, New York, 1970, 222p, Cloth, Anth.
06834   *Nova 2.* Walker, New York, 1972, 209p, Cloth, Anth.
06835   *Nova 3.* Walker, New York, 1973, 243p, Cloth, Anth.
06836   *Nova 4.* Walker, New York, 1974, 216p, Cloth, Anth.
06837   *One step from Earth.* Macmillan, New York, 1970, 210p, Cloth, Coll.
06838   *Plague from space.* Doubleday, Garden City, 1965, 207p, Cloth, Novel
06838A retitled: *The Jupiter legacy.* Bantam, New York, 1970, 218p, Paper, Novel
06839   *Planet of the damned.* Bantam, New York, 1962, 135p, Paper, Novel
06839A retitled: *Sense of obligation.* Dennis Dobson, London, 1967, 135p, Cloth, Novel
06840   *Prime number.* Berkley Medallion, New York, 1970, 191p, Paper, Coll.
    SF: authors' choice. [see 06819A]
06841   *SF: authors' choice 2.* Berkley Medallion, New York, 1970, 286p, Paper, Anth.
06842   *SF: authors' choice 3.* G. P. Putnam's Sons, New York, 1971, 222p, Cloth, Anth.

06843   *SF: authors' choice 4.* G. P. Putnam's Sons, New York, 1974, 248p, Cloth, Anth.
    Sense of obligation. [see 06839A]
06844   *Spaceship medic.* Faber & Faber, London, 1970, 126p, Cloth, Novel
06845   *The Stainless Steel Rat; a science-fiction novel.* Pyramid, New York, 1961, 158p, Paper, Novel [Slippery Jim DiGriz #1]
06846   *The Stainless Steel Rat saves the world.* G. P. Putnam's Sons, New York, 1972, 191p, Cloth, Novel [Slippery Jim DiGriz #3]
06847   *The Stainless Steel Rat's revenge.* Walker, New York, 1970, 185p, Cloth, Novel [Slippery Jim DiGriz #2]
06848   *Star smashers of the galaxy rangers.* G. P. Putnam's Sons, New York, 1973, 212p, Cloth, Novel
06849   *The Technicolor® time machine.* Doubleday, Garden City, 1967, 190p, Cloth, Novel
    A transatlantic tunnel, hurrah! [see 06850A]
06850   *Tunnel through the deeps.* G. P. Putnam's Sons, New York, 1972, 192p, Cloth, Novel
06850A retitled: *A transatlantic tunnel, hurrah!* Faber & Faber, London, 1972, 192p, Cloth, Novel
06851   *Two tales and 8 tomorrows.* Victor Gollancz, London, 1965, 191p, Cloth, Coll.
06852   *War with the robots; science-fiction stories.* Pyramid, New York, 1962, 158p, Paper, Coll.
    Worlds of wonder. [see 06821A]
06853   *The year 2000; an anthology.* Doubleday, Garden City, 1970, 288p, Cloth, Anth.

with Brian W. Aldiss:

    All about Venus. [see 00165A]
00156   *The Astounding-Analog reader, volume one.* Doubleday, Garden City, 1972, 530p, Cloth, Anth.
00156A retitled: *The Astounding-Analog reader, book 1.* Sphere, London, 1973, 291p, Paper, Anth. [abridged]
00156B retitled: *The Astounding-Analog reader, book 2.* Sphere, London, 1973, 320p, Paper, Anth. [abridged; 00156A and 00156B together comprise the original volume]
00157   *The Astounding-Analog reader, volume two.* Doubleday, Garden City, 1973, 458p, Cloth, Anth.
00158   *Best SF: 1967.* Berkley Medallion, New York, 1968, 256p, Paper, Anth.
00158A retitled: *The year's best science fiction no. 1.* Sphere, London, 1968, 207p, Paper, Anth.
00159   *The year's best science fiction no. 2.* Sphere, London, 1969, 207p, Paper, Anth.
00159A retitled: *Best SF: 1968.* G. P. Putnam's Sons, New York, 1969, 245p, Cloth, Anth.
00160   *The year's best science fiction 3.* Sphere, London, 1970, 206p, Paper, Anth.
00160A retitled: *Best SF 1969.* G. P. Putnam's Sons, New York, 1970, 243p, Cloth, Anth.
00161   *The year's best science fiction no. 4.* Sphere, London, 1971, 221p, Paper, Anth.
00161A retitled: *Best SF: 1970.* G. P. Putnam's Sons, New York, 1971, 224p, Cloth, Anth.
00162   *The year's best science fiction no. 5.* Sphere, London, 1972, 239p, Paper, Anth.
00162A retitled: *Best SF: 1971.* G. P. Putnam's Sons, New York, 1972, 253p, Cloth, Anth.
00163   *Best SF: 1972.* G. P. Putnam's Sons, New York, 1973, 254p, Cloth, Anth.
00163A retitled: *The year's best science fiction no. 6.* Sphere, London, 1973, 236p, Paper, Anth.

HARRISON, HARRY, with Brian W. Aldiss (cont.)

00164 *Best SF: 1973*. G. P. Putnam's Sons, New York, 1974, 238p, Cloth, Anth.
00165 *Farewell, fantastic Venus! a history of the planet Venus in fact and fiction*. Macdonald, London, 1968, 293p, Cloth, Anth.
00165A retitled: *All about Venus; a revelation of the planet Venus in fact and fiction*. Dell, New York, 1968, 221p, Paper, Anth. [abridged]
00166 *Nebula award stories two*. Doubleday, Garden City, 1967, 252p, Cloth, Anth.

with Theodore J. Gordon:

06141 *Ahead of time*. Doubleday, Garden City, 1972, 201p, Cloth, Nonf. Anth.

with Carol Pugner:

06854 *A science fiction reader*. Charles Scribner's Sons, New York, 1973, 272p, Paper, Anth.

with Leon E. Stover:

06855 *Apeman, spaceman; anthropological science fiction*. Doubleday, Garden City, 1968, 355p, Cloth, Anth.
06856 *Stonehenge*. Charles Scribner's Sons, New York, 1972, 254p, Cloth, Novel

HARRISON, HELGA (Susan Barbara), 1924-

06857 *The catacombs; a novel*. Chatto & Windus, London, 1962, 223p, Cloth, Novel

HARRISON, M(ichael) JOHN, 1945-   [*biography included*]

06858 *The Centauri device*. Doubleday, Garden City, 1974, 185p, Cloth, Novel
06859 *The committed men*. New Authors, London, 1971, 184p, Cloth, Novel
06860 *The Pastel City*. New English Library, London, 1971, 144p, Paper, Novel

HARRISON, MARY ST. LEGER
   see: MALET, LUCAS

HARRISON, MICHAEL, 1907-

06861 *The brain*. Cassell, London, 1953, 286p, Cloth, Novel
06862 *Higher things*. Macdonald, London, 1945, 187p, Cloth, Novel
06863 *Transit of Venus*. Fortune Press, London, 1936, 231p, Cloth, Coll.

HARRISON, T(homas) MILNER, 1865-

06864 *Modern arms and a feudal throne; the romantic story of an unexplored sea*. R. F. Fenno, New York, 1904, 376p, Cloth, Novel

HARRISON, WILLIAM, 1933-   [*biography included*]

06865 *Roller Ball Murder*. William Morrow, New York, 1974, 189p, Cloth, Coll.

HARSHMAN, TOM, with Geoffrey Holder

06866 *Black gods, green islands*. Doubleday, Garden City, 1959, 235p, Cloth, Coll.

HART, STEVE

06867 *The golden voyage of Sinbad*. Warner Paperback Library, New York, 1974, 110p, Paper, Movie

HARTING, PIETER
   see: DIOSCORIDES, Dr.

HARTL, HAROLD W.

06868 *Things...and other things; tales of the diabolic*. Exposition Press, Jericho, NY, 1973, 107p, Cloth, Coll.

HARTLEY, L(eslie) P(oles), 1895-1972 [*biography included*]

06869 *Facial justice*. Hamish Hamilton, London, 1960, 256p, Cloth, Novel
06870 *The killing bottle*. Putnam, London, 1932, 303p, Cloth, Coll.
06871 *The travelling grave, and other stories*. Arkham House, Sauk City, 1948, 235p, Cloth, Coll.

HARTLEY, (Harry) LIVINGSTON, 1900-   [*biography included*]

06872 *Yankee viking; a saga of love and reincarnation*. Exposition Press, New York, 1951, 155p, Cloth, Novel

HARTMAN, DARLENE
   see: LANG, SIMON

HARTMAN, EMERSON B., 1890-

06873 *The giant of the Sierras*. Chapman & Grimes, Boston, 1945, 158p, Cloth, Novel
06874 *Lunarchia, that strange world beneath the Moon's crust*. Daniel Ryerson, Chicago, 1937, 256p, Cloth, Novel

HARTMAN, LOU(is E.)

06875 *The monstrous leathern man*. Atheneum, New York, 1970, 185p, Cloth, Novel

HARTMANN, FRANZ, 1838-1912

06876 *An adventure among the Rosicrucians*, by a student of occultism. Occult Publishing Co., Boston, 1887, 181p, Cloth, Novel
06876A *An adventure among the Rosicrucians*, by Franz Hartmann. Occult Publishing Co., Boston, 1890, 188p, Cloth, Novel
06877 *Among the gnomes; an occult tale of adventure in the Untersberg*. T. Fisher Unwin, London, 1895, 272p, Cloth, Novel

HARTMANN, FRANZ (cont.)

06878 *The talking image of Urur.* John W. Lovell, New York, 1890, 307p, Cloth, Novel

HARTMANN, HELMUT
    see: SEYMOUR, HENRY

HARTRIDGE, JON

06879 *Binary divine.* Macdonald, London, 1969, 172p, Cloth, Novel
06880 *Earthjacket.* Macdonald, London, 1970, 182p, Cloth, Novel

HARVEY, ALEXANDER, 1868-1949

06881 *The toe, and other tales.* Mitchell Kennerley, New York, 1913, 251p, Cloth, Coll.

HARVEY, FLORENCE
    see: DONNER, GROVE

HARVEY, FRANK (Laird), 1913-   *[biography included]*

06882 *Air Force! stories.* Ballantine, New York, 1959, 142p, Paper, Coll.

HARVEY, JAMES CLARENCE, 1859-1917, with Clara Lanza

06883 *Scarabaeus; the story of an African beetle.* Lovell & Coryell, New York, 1892, 283p, Cloth, Novel

HARVEY, WALTER

06884 *Strange conquest.* Lincoln Williams, London, 1934, 255p, Cloth, Novel

HARVEY, WILLIAM FRYER, 1885-1937

06885 *The beast with five fingers, and other tales.* J. M. Dent & Sons, London, 1928, 228p, Cloth, Coll.
The beast with five fingers; twenty tales of the uncanny. [see 06887A]
06886 *Midnight house, and other tales.* J. M. Dent & Sons, London, 1910, 243p, Cloth, Coll.
06887 *Midnight tales.* J. M. Dent & Sons, London, 1946, 200p, Cloth, Coll.
06887A retitled: *The beast with five fingers; twenty tales of the uncanny.* E. P. Dutton, New York, 1947, 219p, Cloth, Coll.
06888 *Moods and tenses.* Basil Blackwell, Oxford, 1933, 224p, Cloth, Coll.

HARVEY, WILLIAM W(irt), 1866-

06889 *Lige Golden, the man who twinkled.* B. J. Brimmer, Boston, 1924, 207p, Cloth, Novel

HARWOOD, H(enry) **C**(ecil), 1893-1964

06890 *Judgment eve; stories.* Constable, London, 1924, 299p, Cloth, Coll.

HARWOOD, JOHN

06891 *The literature of Burroughsiana; a listing of magazine articles, book commentaries, news items, book reviews, movie reviews, fanzines, amateur publications, and related items concerning the life and/or works of Edgar Rice Burroughs.* Camille Cazedessus Jr., Baton Rouge, LA, 1963, 104p, Paper, Nonf.

HASSE, HENRY L., d. 1977

06892 *The stars will wait.* Avalon, New York, 1968, 191p, Cloth, Novel

HASSLER, KENNETH W(ayne), 1932-   *[biography included]*

06893 *Destination: Terra.* Lenox Hill Press, New York, 1970, 192p, Cloth, Novel
06894 *The dream squad.* Lenox Hill Press, New York, 1970, 192p, Cloth, Novel
06895 *The glass cage.* Lenox Hill Press, New York, 1969, 192p, Cloth, Novel
06896 *Intergalac agent.* Lenox Hill Press, New York, 1971, 192p, Cloth, Novel
06897 *A message from Earth.* Lenox Hill Press, New York, 1970, 192p, Cloth, Novel
06898 *The multiple man.* Lenox Hill Press, New York, 1972, 192p, Cloth, Novel

HASTINGS, GEORGE GORDON

06899 *The first American king.* Smart Set Publishing Co., London. 1904, 354p, Cloth, Novel

HASTINGS, MACDONALD, 1909-   *[biography included]*

06900 *A glimpse of Arcadia.* Michael Joseph, London, 1960, 216p, Cloth, Novel

HASTINGS, MICHAEL (Gerald Tailor), 1938-

06901 *The nightcomers; a speculation.* Delacorte Press, New York, 1972, 170p, Cloth, Novel [a prequel to Henry James's *The turn of the screw*]

HASTINGS, MILO (Milton), 1884-1957

06902 *City of endless night.* Dodd, Mead, New York, 1920, 346p, Cloth, Novel

HATCH, DAVID PATTERSON, 1846-1912

as Anonymous:

06903 *El Reshid; a novel.* B. R. Baumgardt, Los Angeles, 1899, 438p, Cloth, Novel

HATCH, DAVID PATTERSON (cont.)

as Paul Karishka:

06903A *El Reshid.* Rand McNally, Chicago, 1900, 438p, Cloth, Novel

HATCH, ERIC (Stowe), 1901-1973

06904 *The beautiful bequest.* Little, Brown, Boston, 1950, 243p, Cloth, Novel
06905 *Two and two is six.* Crown Publishers, New York, 1969, 126p, Cloth, Novel

HATCH, GERALD, pseud. [Dave Foley]

06906 *The day the Earth froze.* Monarch, Derby, Conn., 1963, 125p, Paper, Novel

HATCH, MARY R. P(latt), 1848-1935

06907 *The missing man.* Lee & Shepard, Boston, 1893, 308p, Cloth, Novel

HATCH, RICHARD W(arren), 1898-

06908 *The curious lobster.* Harcourt, Brace & Co., New York, 1937, 248p, Cloth, Novel [Curious Lobster #1]
06909 *The curious lobster's island.* Dodd, Mead, New York, 1939, 264p, Cloth, Novel [Curious Lobster #2]
06910 *The lobster books: The curious lobster; and, The curious lobster's island.* Houghton Mifflin, Boston, 1951, 347p, Cloth, Coll. [Curious Lobster #s 1-2]

HATFIELD, FRANK, pseud. [John Stevens]

06911 *The Realm of Light.* Reid Publishing Co., Boston, 1908, 430p, Cloth, Novel

HATFIELD, RICHARD, 1853-

06912 *Geyserland; empiricisms in social reform, being data and observations recorded by the late Mark Stubble, M.D., Ph.D.* Richard Hatfield, Washington, 1908, 451p, Cloth, Novel

HATHAWAY, ALAN, as Kenneth Robeson, house pseud.

06913 *The devil's playground; a Doc Savage adventure.* Bantam, New York, 1968, 119p, Paper, Novel [Doc Savage #25]

HATHAWAY, LOUISE, pseud. [Maria Metlova]

06914 *The enchanted hour.* John J. Newbegin, San Francisco, 1940, 129p, Cloth, Coll.

HATTON, JOSEPH, 1841-1907

06915 *The white king of Manoa.* R. F. Fenno, New York, 1890, 338p, Cloth, Novel

HAUFF, WILHELM, 1802-1827

06916 *Arabian days' entertainments.* Phillips, Sampson, Boston, 1858, 438p, Cloth, Coll.
06917 *The caravan, and other tales.* J. Burns, London, 184?, 120p, Cloth, Coll.
06918 *The caravan; The sheik of Alexandria.* George Bell & Sons, London, 1889, 190p, Cloth, Coll.
06919 *Fairy tales.* David McKay, Philadelphia, 1895, 303p, Cloth, Coll.
06920 *Hauff's tales.* James Finch, London, 1905, 430p, Cloth, Coll.
06921 *Tales.* George Bell & Sons, London, 1886, 342p, Cloth, Coll.
06922 *Tales of the caravan, inn, and palace.* Jansen, McClure, Chicago, 1881, 397p, Cloth, Coll.
06923 *Three tales; The beggar girl of the Pont des Arts; The emperor's picture; The cold hat.* Bernhard Tauchnitz, Leipzig, 1869, 326p, Cloth, Coll.
06924 *The wine-ghosts of Bremen.* Basil Blackwell, Oxford, 1889, 64p, Cloth, Novel

HAUN, BLAIR A.

06925 *Slanting Earth; a novel of modern science and primitive human passions.* Greenwich Book Publishers, New York, 1960, 139p, Cloth, Novel

THE HAUNTED HOTEL

06926 *The haunted hotel, and twenty-five other ghost stories.* Avon, New York, 1941, 492p, Paper, Anth. [includes *The haunted hotel*, by Wilkie Collins, and the anthology *Twenty-five ghost stories*, edited anonymously by W. Bob Holland]

THE HAUNTERS AND THE HAUNTED

06927 *The haunters and the haunted, and other ghost stories.* Corgi, London, 1963, 158p, Paper, Anth.

HAUPTMANN, GERHART (Johann Robert), 1862-1946

06928 *The Island of the Great Mother; or, The miracl of Île des Dames; a story from the Utopian archipelago.* Martin Secker, London, 1925, 256p, Cloth, Novel; B. W. Huebsch and The Viking Press, New York, 1925, 328p, Cloth, Novel

HAWEIS, STEPHEN

06929 *Egyptian love.* Doubleday, Page, Garden City, 1924, 255p, Cloth, Novel

HAWKE, NAPIER

06930 *The invasion that did not come off.* Henry J.
Drane, London, 1909, 128p, Cloth, Novel

HAWKER, CALEB

06931 *The great peril.* Blackie & Son, London, 1937,
255p, Cloth, Novel

HAWKER, MARY ELIZABETH
see: FALCONER, LANOE

HAWKES, (Jessie) JACQUETTA, 1910-

06932 *Fables.* Cresset Press, London, 1953, 164p,
Cloth, Coll.
06932A retitled: *A woman as great as the world, and
other fables.* Random House, New York, 1953,
184p, Cloth, Coll.
06933 *Providence Island; an archaeological tale.*
Chatto & Windus, London, 1959, 251p, Cloth,
Novel

HAWKESWORTH, JOHN, 1715?-1773

06934 *Almoran and Hamet; an Oriental tale.* H. Payne,
London, 1761, 2vol/1, Cloth, Novel [pub-
lished anonymously]
06934A *Almoran and Hamet; an Oriental tale,* by Dr.
Hawkesworth. H. & R. Joy, Belfast, 1779,
2vol, Cloth, Novel

HAWKEY, RAYMOND, with Roger Bingham

01309 *Wild Card; a novel.* Stein & Day, New York,
1974, 248p, Cloth, Novel

HAWKIN, MARTIN, pseud. [Martin Hawkins]

06935 *When Adolf came; a novel.* Jarrold's, London,
1943, 176p, Cloth, Novel

HAWKINS, BRUCE A.

06936 *Jupiter's passion.* Presse de L'Amour, San
Rafael, CA, 1970, 188p, Paper, Novel

HAWKINS, MARTIN
see: HAWKIN, MARTIN

HAWKINS, PETER, as Karl Maras, house pseud.

06937 *The plant from infinity.* Paladin Press, London, 1954, 128p, Paper, Novel

HAWKS, CHESTER, pseud.

06938 *Python Men of Lost City; pulp classics 2.*
Robert E. Weinberg, Oak Lawn, IL, 1974, 64p,
Paper, Novel

HAWKWOOD, ALLAN, pseud.
see: BEDFORD JONES, H.

HAWTHORNE, JULIAN, 1846-1934

06939 *David Poindexter's disappearance, and other
tales.* D. Appleton, New York, 1888, 210p,
Paper, Coll.
06940 *Ellice Quentin, and other stories.* Chatto &
Windus, London, 1880, 2vol, Cloth, Coll.
06941 *Kildhurm's oak.* A. L. Burt, New York, 1888,
219p, Cloth, Coll.
06942 *The Laughing Mill, and other stories.* Macmillan, London, 1879, 326p, Cloth, Coll.
06943 *Library of the world's best mystery and detective stories; American.* Review of Reviews
Co., New York, 1908, 304p, Cloth, Anth.
06944 *The Lock and Key Library; classic mystery and
detective stories; American.* Review of
Reviews Co., New York, 1909, 370p, Cloth,
Anth.
06945 *The Lock and Key Library; classic mystery and
detective stories; modern French.* Review
of Reviews Co., New York, 1909, 366p, Cloth,
Anth.
06946 *The Lock and Key Library; classic mystery and
detective stories; old time English.* Review
of Reviews Co., New York, 1915, 370p, Cloth,
Anth.
06947 *The professor's sister; a romance.* Belford,
Clarke, New York, 1888, 180p, Cloth, Novel
06947A retitled: *The spectre of the camera; or, The
professor's sister; a romance.* Chatto &
Windus, London, 1888, 246p, Cloth, Novel
06948 *The trial of Gideon; and, Countess Almara's
murder.* Funk & Wagnalls, New York, 1886,
96p, Cloth, Coll.

HAWTHORNE, NATHANIEL, 1804-1864

06949 *Allegories of the heart.* Henry Altemus, Phila-
delphia, 1905?, 238p, Cloth, Coll.
06950 *The birthmark, and other stories.* Scholastic
Book Services, New York, 1968, 240p, Paper,
Coll.
06951 *The celestial railroad, and other stories.*
Signet Classic, New York, 1963, 301p, Paper,
Coll.
06952 *Doctor Grimshawe's secret; a romance.* James
R. Osgood, Boston, 1883, 368p, Cloth, Novel
06953 *The Dolliver romance, and kindred tales.*
Houghton Mifflin, Boston, 1900, 433p, Cloth,
Coll.
06954 *The Dolliver romance, and other pieces.* James
R. Osgood, Boston, 1876, 213p, Cloth, Coll.
06955 *Hawthorne.* Doubleday, Page, Garden City, 1922,
152p, Cloth, Coll.
06956 *Hawthorne's short stories.* Dodd, Mead, New
York, 1962, 422p, Cloth, Coll.
06957 *Little masterpieces.* Doubleday & McClure,
New York, 1898, 192p, Cloth, Coll.
06958 *Mosses from an Old Manse.* Wiley & Putnam,
New York, 1846, 2vol/1, Cloth, Coll.
06959 *Selected tales and sketches.* Rinehart & Co.,
New York, 1950, 410p, Paper, Coll.
06960 *The snow-image, and other tales.* Henry G.
Bohn, London, 1851, 176p, Cloth, Coll.
06961 *Twice-told tales.* American Stationers Co.,
Boston, 1837, 334p, Cloth, Coll.
06962 *Twice-told tales.* J. Munroe, Boston, 1842,
2vol, Cloth, Coll. [the second volume is new]

HAWTON, HECTOR, 1901-   [biography included]

06963   *The lost valley.* Hodder & Stoughton, London,
        1953, 192p, Cloth, Novel [Col. Max Master-
        son #4]
06964   *Operation superman.* Ward, Lock, London, 1951,
        224p, Cloth, Novel

HAY, GEORGE (Albert)

06965   *Flight of the "Hesper."* Hamilton & Co. (Staf-
        ford), London, 1952, 112p, Paper, Novel
06966   *This planet for sale.* Hamilton & Co. (Staf-
        ford), London, 1951, 111p, Paper, Novel

as King Lang, house pseud:

06967   *Terra!* Curtis Warren, London, 1952?, 111p,
        Paper, Novel

as Roy Sheldon, house pseud.:

06968   *Moment out of time.* Hamilton & Co. (Stafford),
        London, 1952, 111p, Paper, Novel

HAY, GEORGE [Oswyn Robert Tregonwell Hay,
1922-   ]

06969   *The disappearing future; a symposium of specu-
        lation.* Panther, London, 1970, 158p, Paper,
        Anth. [includes some nonf.]
06970   *Hell hath fury; an 'Unknown' anthology.*
        Neville Spearman, London, 1963, 240p, Cloth,
        Anth.
06971   *Stopwatch; a collection of international SF
        stories.* New English Library, London, 1974,
        224p, Cloth, Anth.

HAY, IAN, pseud. [John Hay Beith, 1876-1952]

06972   *Half a sovereign; an improbable romance.* Hod-
        der & Stoughton, London, 1926, 304p, Cloth,
        Novel; Houghton Mifflin, Boston, 1926, 307p,
        Cloth, Novel

HAY, JACOB, 1920-   [biography included],
with John M. Keshishian

06973   *Autopsy for a cosmonaut; a novel.* Little,
        Brown, Boston, 1969, 242p, Cloth, Novel
06973A retitled: *Death of a cosmonaut; a novel.*
        J. M. Dent & Sons, London, 1970, 242p,
        Cloth, Novel

HAY, JOHN (Warwick Dalrymple-), 1928-   [bio-
graphy included]

06974   *The invasion.* Hodder & Stoughton, London,
        1968, 192p, Cloth, Novel

HAY, OSWYN
    see: HAY, GEORGE

HAY, WILLIAM DELISLE

06975   *The doom of the great city, being the narra-
        tive of a survivor, written A.D. 1942.* New-
        man & Co., London, 1880, 52p, Paper, Novel

06976   *Three hundred years hence; or, A voice from
        posterity.* Newman & Co., London, 1881,
        356p, Cloth, Novel

HAYDEN, J. J.

06977   *A letter to Mars.* Baxter Printing Co., Denver,
        1892, 128p, Paper, Novel

HAYES, FREDERICK W(illiam), 1848-1918

06978   *The great revolution of 1905; or, The story
        of the Phalanx, with an introductory account
        of civilisation in Great Britain at the clo
        of the nineteenth century.* R. Forder, Lon-
        don, 1893, 316p, Cloth, Novel
06978A retitled: *State industrialism; the story of
        the Phalanx, with an account of civilizatio
        in Great Britain at the close of the nine-
        teenth century.* William Reeves, London,
        1901, 316p, Cloth, Novel

HAYES, HIRAM W(allace), 1858-1939

06979   *The man of clay (a tale of life).* Davis &
        Bond, Boston, 1911, 376p, Cloth, Novel
06980   *The peacemakers (a tale of love).* Reid Pub-
        lishing Co., Boston, 1909, 420p, Cloth,
        Novel

HAYES, JEFF W., 1853-1917

        Paradise on Earth. [see 06982A]
06981   *Pleiades Club; life on planet Mars.* Multnoma
        Printing Co., Portland, OR, 1917, 80p, Pape
        Novel
06982   *Portland, Oregon A.D. 1999, and other sketche
        F. W. Baltes, Portland, OR, 1913, 112p,
        Paper, Coll.
06982A retitled: *Paradise on Earth.* F. W. Baltes,
        Portland, OR, 1913, 112p, Paper, Coll.

HAYES, LILIAN

06983   *The thirtieth piece of silver.* Macmillan,
        New York, 1924, 326p, Cloth, Novel

HAYES, R. CHETWYND-
    see: CHETWYND-HAYES, R.

HAYES, RALPH (Eugene), 1927-   [biography
included]

06984   *The visiting moon.* Lenox Hill Press, New
        York, 1971, 192p, Cloth, Novel

HAYES, WILLIAM D.

06985   *Mr. Boyton--merchant, millionaire, and king.*
        Simpkin, Marshall, Hamilton, Kent, London,
        1899, 266p, Cloth, Novel

HAYLES, BRIAN, 1931-

06986   *Doctor Who and the curse of Peladon*. Target,
        London, 1974, 142p, Paper, Tele. [Doctor
        Who #12]

HAYMAN, ART

06987   *Murder gives notice*. Scientific Thriller,
        Sydney, 1951, 34p, Paper, Story [cover says
        "Paul Valdez"]

HAYNES, DOROTHY K(ate), 1918-

06988   *Robin Ritchie*. Methuen, London, 1949, 198p,
        Cloth, Novel

HAYNES, JOHN ROBERT, pseud.
    see: WILDING, PHILIP

HAYWARD, ABRAHAM, 1801-1884

06989   *The second Armada; a chapter of future history,
        being a reply to The German conquest of Eng-
        land in 1875, and Battle of Dorking*. Porter
        & Coates, Philadelphia, 1871, 16p, Paper,
        Story [published anonymously; Dorking series]

HAYWARD, WILLIAM S(tephens)

06990   *The cloud king; or, Up in the air and down in
        the sea*. Darton & Stodge, London, 1865,
        356p, Cloth, Novel

HAYWOOD, ELIZA (Fowler), 1693?-1756

06991   *The adventures of Eovaai, Princess of Ijaveo;
        a pre-Adamitical history, interspersed with
        a great number of remarkable occurrences,
        by the son of a mandarin*. S. Baker, London,
        1736, 224p, Cloth, Novel
06991A retitled: *The unfortunate princess; or, The
        life and surprizing [sic] adventures of the
        Princess of Ijaveo, interspersed with seve-
        ral curious and entertaining novels*. James
        Hodges, London, 1741, 224p, Cloth, Novel
        [published anonymously]
06992   *Memoirs of a certain island adjacent to the
        Kingdom of Utopia, written by a celebrated
        author of that country, now translated into
        English*. The Booksellers of London & West-
        minster, London, 1725, 294p, Cloth, Novel
06993   *Memoirs of a certain island adjacent to the
        Kingdom of Utopia, written by a celebrated
        author of that country, now translated into
        English, vol. II*. The Booksellers of London
        & Westminster, London, 1726, 282p, Cloth,
        Novel

HAZARD, R. H.

06994   *The House on Stilts; a novel*. G. W. Dilling-
        ham, New York, 1910, 346p, Cloth, Novel

HAZLITT, HENRY, 1894-   [*biography included*]

06995   *The great idea*. Appleton-Century-Crofts, New
        York, 1951, 374p, Cloth, Novel
06995A retitled: *Time will run back*. Ernest Benn,
        London, 1952, 256p, Cloth, Novel

HE
    see: LANG, ANDREW and POLLOCK, WALTER

HE, A COMPANION TO SHE
    see: DE MORGAN, JOHN

HEALY, DOMINIC

06996   *Voyage to Venus; a novel*. Currawong Publi-
        shing Co., Sydney, 1943, 165p, Paper, Novel

HEALY, RAYMOND J(ohn), 1907-

06997   *New tales of space and time*. Henry Holt, New
        York, 1951, 294p, Cloth, Anth.
06998   *9 tales of space and time*. Henry Holt, New
        York, 1954, 307p, Cloth, Anth.

with J. Francis McComas:

06999   *Adventures in time and space; an anthology of
        modern science-fiction stories*. Random
        House, New York, 1946, 997p, Cloth, Anth.
06999A retitled: *Selections from Adventures in time
        and space*. Pennant, New York, 1954, 200p,
        Paper, Anth. [abridged]
06999B retitled: *More adventures in time and space;
        selections from Adventures in time and space*.
        Bantam, New York, 1955, 142p, Paper, Anth.
        [abridged]
06999C retitled: *Famous science-fiction stories;
        adventures in time and space*. Modern Lib-
        rary, New York, 1957, 997p, Cloth, Anth.

HEARD, H(enry) F(itzGerald), 1889-1971 [vari-
ously Gerald Heard] [*biography included*]

07000   *The black fox; a novel of the 'Seventies*, by
        Gerald Heard. Cassell, London, 1950, 234p,
        Cloth, Novel
07001   *Doppelgangers; an episode of the fourth, the
        psychological, revolution, 1997*. Vanguard
        Press, New York, 1947, 281p, Cloth, Novel
07002   *Gabriel and the creatures*, by Gerald Heard.
        Harper & Bros., New York, 1952, 244p, Cloth,
        Novel
07003   *The great fog, and other weird tales*. Van-
        guard Press, New York, 1944, 238p, Cloth,
        Coll.
07003A retitled: *The great fog; weird tales of
        terror and detection*. Sun Dial Press,
        Garden City, 1946, 238p, Cloth, Coll.
07004   *The great fog, and other weird tales*. Cassell,
        London, 1947, 234p, Cloth, Coll. [adds two
        stories to 07003, drops one]
07005   *The lost cavern, and other tales of the fan-
        tastic*. Vanguard Press, New York, 1948,
        262p, Cloth, Coll.
07006   *Reply paid; a mystery*. Vanguard Press, New
        York, 1942, 274p, Cloth, Novel [Mr. Mycroft
        #2]

HEARD, H. F. (cont.)

07007   *A taste for honey.* Vanguard Press, New York, 1941, 234p, Cloth, Novel [Mr. Mycroft #1]
07007A   retitled: *A taste for murder.* Avon, New York, 1955, 127p, Paper, Novel [Mr. Mycroft #1]

HEARN, (Patricio) LAFCADIO (Tessima Carlos), 1850-1904

07008   *Fantastics, and other fancies.* Houghton Mifflin, Boston, 1914, 242p, Cloth, Coll.
07009   *In ghostly Japan.* Little, Brown, Boston, 1899, 241p, Cloth, Coll. [includes some nonf.]
07010   *A Japanese miscellany.* Little, Brown, Boston, 1901, 305p, Cloth, Coll.
07011   *Karma.* Boni & Liveright, New York, 1918, 163p, Cloth, Coll. [includes some nonf.]
07012   *Karma, and other stories and essays.* George G. Harrap, London, 1921, 205p, Cloth, Coll. [includes four more stories than 07011]
07013   *Kwaidan; stories and studies of strange things.* Houghton Mifflin, Boston, 1904, 240p, Cloth, Coll.
07014   *Shadowings.* Little, Brown, Boston, 1900, 268p, Cloth, Coll.
07015   *Some Chinese ghosts.* Roberts Bros., Boston, 1887, 185p, Cloth, Coll.
07016   *Tales out of the East.* Story Classics, Emmaus, PA, 1952, 253p, Cloth, Coll. [includes *Some Chinese ghosts* and *Some Japanese glimpses*]

HEARN, MARY ANN
    see: FARNINGHAM, MARIANNE

THE HEART OF THE SERPENT

07017   *The heart of the serpent.* Foreign Languages Publishing House, Moscow, 1961, 267p, Paper, Anth.
07017A   retitled: *More Soviet science fiction.* Collier, New York, 1962, 190p, Paper, Anth.

HEATH, PETER, pseud. [Peter Fine]

07018   *Assassins from tomorrow.* Lancer, New York, 1967, 160p, Paper, Novel [Mind Brothers #2]
07019   *Men who die twice.* Lancer, New York, 1968, 160p, Paper, Novel [Mind Brothers #3]
07020   *The Mind Brothers.* Lancer, New York, 1967, 159p, Paper, Novel [Mind Brothers #1]

HEATH, THOMAS EDWARD

07021   *Tales in prose and verse, and dramas.* King, Sell & Olding, London, 1906, 259p, Cloth, Coll.

HECHT, BEN, 1893-1964

07022   *A book of miracles.* Viking Press, New York, 1939, 465p, Cloth, Coll.
07023   *Fantazius Mallare; a mysterious oath.* Covici-McGee, Chicago, 1922, 174p, Cloth, Novel [Fantazius Mallare #1]

07024   *The Kingdom of Evil; a continuation of the journal of Fantazius Mallare.* Pascal Covici, Chicago, 1924, 211p, Cloth, Novel [Fantazius Mallare #2]
07025   *Miracle in the rain.* Alfred A. Knopf, New York, 1943, 52p, Cloth, Novel

as Peter Long:

07026   *The demi-wang.* privately printed, New York, 1931, 50p, Cloth, Novel [attributed to Hecht]

HECKEL, FREDERICK C.

07027   *A tale of ancient Egypt.* Philosophical Library, New York, 1963, 126p, Cloth, Novel

HEDGES, DORIS

07028   *Dumb spirit; a novel of Montreal.* Arthur Barker, London, 1952, 224p, Cloth, Novel

HEDGES, F. A. MITCHELL-
    see: MITCHELL-HEDGES, F. A.

HEDGES, SID(ney George), 1897-1974

07029   *Plague panic.* Herbert Jenkins, London, 1934, 311p, Cloth, Novel

HEELEY, MAUREEN

07030   *The secret warrior.* Mills & Boon, London, 1934, 253p, Cloth, Novel

HEIM, MICHAEL

07031   *Aswan! a novel.* Alfred A. Knopf, New York, 1972, 225p, Cloth, Novel
07031A   retitled: *The waters of Aswan; preconstruction of a disaster.* Collins, London, 1972, 255p, Cloth, Novel

HEINE, IRVING, pseud.

07032   *Dimension of Illion.* Tit-Bits Science Fiction Library, London, 1955, 64p, Paper, Novel

HEINE, WILLIAM C., 1919-

07033   *The last Canadian.* Simon & Schuster of Canada, Markham, Ontario, 1974,   , Paper, Novel

HEINLEIN, ROBERT A(nson), 1907-   [*biography included*]

07034   *Assignment in eternity; four long science fiction stories.* Fantasy Press, Reading, PA, 1953, 256p, Cloth, Coll.
07034A   retitled: *Lost legacy.* Digit, London, 1960, 156p, Paper, Coll. [abridged]
07035   *The best of Robert Heinlein.* Sidgwick & Jackson, London, 1973, 348p, Cloth, Coll.

HEINLEIN, ROBERT A. (cont.)

07036 *Between planets.* Charles Scribner's Sons, New York, 1951, 222p, Cloth, Novel

07037 *Beyond this horizon.* Fantasy Press, Reading, PA, 1948, 242p, Cloth, Novel

07038 *Citizen of the Galaxy.* Charles Scribner's Sons, New York, 1957, 302p, Cloth, Novel

The day after tomorrow. [see 07061A]

07039 *The door into summer.* Doubleday, Garden City, 1957, 188p, Cloth, Novel

07040 *Double star.* Doubleday, Garden City, 1956, 186p, Cloth, Novel

07041 *Farmer in the sky.* Charles Scribner's Sons, New York, 1950, 216p, Cloth, Novel

07042 *Farnham's Freehold; a novel.* G. P. Putnam's Sons, New York, 1964, 315p, Cloth, Novel

07043 *Glory Road; a novel.* G. P. Putnam's Sons, New York, 1963, 288p, Cloth, Novel

07044 *The green hills of Earth; Rhysling and the adventure of the entire Solar System!* Shasta Publishers, Chicago, 1951, 256p, Cloth, Coll. [Future History series]

07045 *Have space suit--will travel.* Charles Scribner's Sons, New York, 1958, 276p, Cloth, Novel

A Heinlein triad. [see 07067A]

07046 *I will fear no evil.* G. P. Putnam's Sons, New York, 1970, 401p, Cloth, Novel

Lost legacy. [see 07034A]

07047 *The man who sold the Moon.* American Science Fiction, Sydney, 1952, 32p, Paper, Story

07048 *The man who sold the Moon; Harriman and the escape from Earth to the Moon!* Shasta Publishers, Chicago, 1950, 288p, Cloth, Coll. [Future History series]

07049 *The menace from Earth.* Gnome Press, Hicksville, NY, 1959, 255p, Cloth, Coll.

07050 *Methuselah's children.* Gnome Press, Hicksville, NY, 1958, 188p, Cloth, Novel [Future History series; Lazarus Long #1]

07051 *The Moon is a harsh mistress.* G. P. Putnam's Sons, New York, 1966, 383p, Cloth, Novel

Orphans of the sky. [see 07073]

07052 *The past through tomorrow; 'future history' stories.* G. P. Putnam's Sons, New York, 1967, 667p, Cloth, Coll. [Future History series]

07053 *Podkayne of Mars, her life and times.* G. P. Putnam's Sons, New York, 1963, 191p, Cloth, Novel

07054 *The puppet masters.* Doubleday, Garden City, 1951, 219p, Cloth, Novel

07055 *Red planet; a colonial boy on Mars.* Charles Scribner's Sons, New York, 1949, 211p, Cloth, Novel

07056 *Revolt in 2100; the prophets and the triumph of reason over superstition!* Shasta Publishers, Chicago, 1953, 317p, Cloth, Coll.

07057 *Robert Heinlein omnibus.* Science Fiction Book Club, London, 1958, 480p?, Cloth, Coll. [includes *The man who sold the Moon* and *The green hills of Earth*]

07058 *A Robert Heinlein omnibus; Beyond this horizon; The man who sold the Moon; The green hills of Earth.* Sidgwick & Jackson, London, 1966, 644p, Cloth, Coll.

07059 *Rocket ship Galileo.* Charles Scribner's Sons, New York, 1947, 212p, Cloth, Novel

07060 *The Rolling Stones.* Charles Scribner's Sons, New York, 1952, 276p, Cloth, Novel

07060A retitled: *Space family Stone.* Victor Gollancz, London, 1969, 267p, Cloth, Novel

6 x H. [see 07074A]

07061 *Sixth column; a science fiction novel of a strange intrigue.* Gnome Press, New York, 1949, 256p, Cloth, Novel

07061A retitled: *The day after tomorrow.* Signet, New York, 1951, 160p, Paper, Novel

07062 *Space cadet.* Charles Scribner's Sons, New York, 1948, 242p, Cloth, Novel

Space family Stone. [see 07060A]

07063 *The star beast.* Charles Scribner's Sons, New York, 1954, 282p, Cloth, Novel

07064 *Starman Jones.* Charles Scribner's Sons, New York, 1953, 305p, Cloth, Novel

07065 *Starship troopers.* G. P. Putnam's Sons, New York, 1959, 309p, Cloth, Novel

07066 *Stranger in a strange land.* G. P. Putnam's Sons, New York, 1961, 408p, Cloth, Novel

07067 *Three by Heinlein; The puppet masters; Waldo; Magic, Inc.* Doubleday, Garden City, 1965, 426p, Cloth, Coll.

07067A retitled: *A Heinlein triad; The puppet masters; Waldo; Magic, Inc.* Victor Gollancz, London, 1966, 426p, Cloth, Coll.

07068 *Time enough for love; the lives of Lazarus Long; a novel.* G. P. Putnam's Sons, New York, 1973, 605p, Cloth, Novel [Future History series; Lazarus Long #2]

07069 *Time for the stars.* Charles Scribner's Sons, New York, 1956, 244p, Cloth, Novel

07070 *Tomorrow, the stars; a science fiction anthology.* Doubleday, Garden City, 1952, 249p, Cloth, Anth.

07071 *Tunnel in the sky.* Charles Scribner's Sons, New York, 1955, 273p, Cloth, Novel

07072 *Universe.* Dell, New York, 1951, 64p, Paper, Novel [Future History series]

07073 retitled: *Orphans of the sky.* Victor Gollancz, London, 1963, 160p, Cloth, Novel [Future History series] [expanded]

07074 *The unpleasant profession of Jonathan Hoag.* Gnome Press, Hicksville, NY, 1959, 256p, Cloth, Coll.

07074A retitled: *6 x H; six stories.* Pyramid, New York, 1961, 191p, Paper, Coll.

07075 *Waldo; and, Magic, Inc.* Doubleday, Garden City, 1950, 219p, Cloth, Coll.

07075A retitled: *Waldo: genius in orbit.* Avon, New York, 1958, 191p, Paper, Coll.

07076 *The worlds of Robert A. Heinlein.* Ace, New York, 1966, 189p, Paper, Coll.

HEINRICH, CARL, 1880-1955

07077 *Orphan of eternity; or, The katabasis of the Lord Lucifer Satan.* Louis Carrier, New York, 1929, 303p, Cloth, Novel

HEINS, HENRY HARDY, 1923-

07078 *A golden anniversary bibliography of Edgar Rice Burroughs.* Henry Hardy Heins, Albany, NY, 1962, 122p, Paper, Nonf.

07079 *A golden anniversary bibliography of Edgar Rice Burroughs, complete edition, revised.* Donald M. Grant, West Kingston, RI, 1964, 418p, Cloth, Nonf.

HEKKING, AVIS

07080 *A king of Mars.* John Long, London, 1908,
318p, Cloth, Novel

HELD, JOHN Jr., 1889-1958

07081 *The gods were promiscuous.* Vanguard Press,
New York, 1937, 248p, Cloth, Novel

HELDERS, Major, pseud. [Robert Knauss, 1892-
1955]

07082 *The war in the air, 1936.* John Hamilton, London, 1932, 254p, Cloth, Novel
07082A retitled: *War in the air.* John Hamilton, London, 1935, 223p, Cloth, Novel

HELFENSTEIN, ERNEST
see: SMITH, E. OAKES

HELIONDE
see: WHITING, SYDNEY

HELMS, RANDEL, 1942-   [*biography included*]

07083 *Tolkien's world.* Houghton Mifflin, Boston,
1974, 167p, Cloth, Nonf.

HELPS, Sir ARTHUR, 1813-1875

07084 *Realmah,* by the author of "Friends in Council."
Macmillan, London, 1868, 2vol, Cloth, Novel

HELVICK, JAMES, pseud. [Francis Claud Cockburn, 1904-   ]

07085 *Overdraft on glory.* J. P. Lippincott, Philadelphia, 1955, 320p, Cloth, Novel

HEMING, J(ohn) W(inton), 1900-1953

07086 *From Earth to Mars.* Currawong Publishing Co.,
Sydney, 1943, 64p, Paper, Novel
07087 *King of the underseas.* Currawong Publishing
Co., Sydney, 1942, 64p, Paper, Novel
07088 *The living dead.* Currawong Publishing Co.,
Sydney, 1942, 80p, Paper, Novel
07089 *Other worlds.* Currawong Publishing Co.,
Sydney, 1942, 80p, Paper, Novel
07090 *Subterranean city.* Currawong Publishing Co.,
Sydney, 1942, 80p, Paper, Novel

as Paul de Wreder:

07091 *Time marches off.* Currawong Publishing Co.,
Sydney, 1942, 80p, Paper, Novel

HEMING, JACK

07092 *The lost world of the Colorado.* Frederick
Warne, London, 1940, 256p, Cloth, Novel

HEMYNG, BRACEBRIDGE, 1841-1901

07093 *The commune in London; or, Thirty years hence;
a chapter of anticipated history.* C. H.
Clarke, London, 1871, 45p, Paper, Story

HENDERSON, BILL
see: WALTON, LUKE

HENDERSON, PHILIP (Prichard), 1906-1977 [*biography included*]

07094 *Shorter novels, eighteenth century.* J. M.
Dent & Sons, London, 1930, 306p, Cloth, Anth.
[includes: *Rasselas, Prince of Abissinia,*
by Samuel Johnson; *The Castle of Otranto,* by
Horace Walpole; *Vathek,* by William Beckford]

HENDERSON, ZENNA, 1917-   [*biography included*]

07095 *The Anything Box.* Doubleday, Garden City,
1965, 205p, Cloth, Coll.
07096 *Holding wonder.* Doubleday, Garden City, 1971,
302p, Cloth, Coll.
07097 *The People: no different flesh.* Victor Gollancz, London, 1966, 223p, Cloth, Coll.
[The People #2]
07098 *Pilgrimage: the book of the People.* Doubleday, Garden City, 1961, 239p, Cloth, Novel
[The People #1]

HENDOW, Z. S.

07099 *The future power; or, The great revolution of
190-.* Roxburghe Press, Westminster, 1897,
79p, Paper?, Novel

HENHAM, ERNEST G(eorge), 1870-

07100 *Bonanza; a story of the outside.* Hutchinson,
London, 1901, 320p, Cloth, Novel

as John Trevena:

07101 *Furze the cruel.* Alston Rivers, London, 1907,
391p, Cloth, Novel
07102 *The reign of the saints.* Alston Rivers, London, 1911, 376p, Cloth, Novel

HENLEY, CARRA DUPUY

07103 *The man from Mars.* B. R. Baumgardt Publishing
Co., Los Angeles, 1901, 66p, Cloth, Novel

HENNINGS, JOS(eph) P.

07104 *Astron Imago; a book of wish dreams grown out
of intense longings for science blended with
mystic insight, for astronomy blended with
faith in the great analogy, for astrology
lifted from the mire of fortune telling and
superstition, and provided with a basis of
demonstrable facts, results of unprejudiced
research.* The Author, St. Louis, 1931,
184p, Cloth, Novel

HENNINGSEN, CHARLES FREDERICK, 1815-1877

07105 *Sixty years hence; a novel*, by the author of "The white slave," "Revelations of Russia," "Eastern Europe and the Emperor Nicholas." Thomas Cautley Newby, London, 1847, 3vol, Cloth, Novel

HENOT, GEORGES
  see: OHNET, GEORGES

HENRICKSEN, HENRY C(hristian), 1869-

07106 *Planet problems; science fiction that could happen*. William-Frederick Press, New York, 1957, 56p, Paper, Novel

HENRY, EDGAR, pseud. [Albion Winegar Tourgée, 1838-1905]

07107 *"89*. Cassell, London, 1891, 498p, Cloth, Novel

HENRY, PAUL-MARC

07108 *Poodlestan; a poodle's eye view of history*, by Bête Noire, as told to Paul-Marc Henry. Reynal & Co., New York, 1965, 114p, Cloth, Novel

THE HENS WHO TRIED TO CROW

07109 *The hens who tried to crow; an apologue*. Robert Hardwicke, London, 1871, 48p, Paper, Story [Dorking series]

HEPWORTH, GEORGE H(ughes), 1833-1902

07110 *!!!* Harper & Bros., New York, 1881, 196p, Cloth, Novel
07111 *Brown studies; or, Camp fires and morals*. E. P. Dutton, New York, 1895, 332p, Cloth, Novel
07112 *The queerest man alive, and other stories*. R. F. Fenno, New York, 1897, 256p, Cloth, Coll.

HERBERT, A(lan) P(atrick), 1890-1971

07113 *Number Nine; or, The mind-sweepers*. Methuen, London, 1951, 244p, Cloth, Novel

HERBERT, BENSON, 1912-

07114 *Crisis! 1992; a novel*. Richards, London, 1936, 286p, Cloth, Novel
07115 *Hand of Glory; strange adventures in the Pennines*. Lloyd Cole, London, 1943?, 31p, Paper, Story
07116 *The red-haired girl*. Lloyd Cole, London, 1944, 36p, Paper, Story
07117 *Strange romance*. Lloyd Cole, London, 1943, 95p, Paper, Novel

with Festus Pragnall:

07118 *Thieves of the air*. Lloyd Cole, London, 1943?, 27p, Paper, Story

HERBERT, FRANK (Patrick), 1920- [*biography included*]

07119 *The book of Frank Herbert*. DAW, New York, 1973, 189p, Paper, Coll.
07120 *Destination: void*. Berkley Medallion, New York, 1966, 190p, Paper, Novel
07121 *The dragon in the sea*. Doubleday, Garden City, 1956, 192p, Cloth, Novel
07121A retitled: *21st century sub*. Avon, New York, 1956, 190p, Paper, Novel
07121B retitled: *Under pressure*. Ballantine, New York, 1974, 220p, Paper, Novel
07122 *Dune*. Chilton, Philadelphia, 1965, 412p, Cloth, Novel [Dune #1]
07123 *Dune messiah*. G. P. Putnam's Sons, New York, 1969, 256p, Cloth, Novel [Dune #2]
07124 *The eyes of Heisenberg*. Berkley Medallion, New York, 1966, 158p, Paper, Novel
07125 *The god makers*. G. P. Putnam's Sons, New York, 1972, 190p, Cloth, Novel
07126 *The Green Brain*. Ace, New York, 1966, 160p, Paper, Novel
07127 *The Heaven makers*. Avon, New York, 1968, 159p, Paper, Novel
07128 *Hellstrom's hive*. Nelson Doubleday, Garden City, 1973, 278p, Cloth, Novel
07129 *The Santaroga Barrier*. Berkley Medallion, New York, 1968, 255p, Paper, Novel
  21st century sub. [see 07121A]
  Under pressure. [see 07121B]
07130 *Whipping star; a science fiction novel*. G. P. Putnam's Sons, New York, 1970, 186p, Cloth, Novel
07131 *The worlds of Frank Herbert*. New English Library, London, 1970, 142p, Paper, Coll.

HERBERT, FREDERICK WILLIAM von

07132 *The shunned vicar of the Gilliflowers; a fantasy*. Andrew Melrose, London, 1914, 320p, Cloth, Novel

HERBERT, JAMES

07133 *The rats*. New English Library, London, 1974, 175p, Cloth, Novel

HERBERT, WILLIAM, pseud.

07134 *The world grown young, being a brief record of reforms carried out from 1894-1914 by the late Mr. Philip Adams, millionaire and philanthropist*. W. H. Allen, London, 1892, 304p, Cloth, Novel

HERCK, PAUL VAN
  see: VAN HERCK, PAUL

HERING, HENRY A(ugustus), 1864-

07135 *Adventures and fantasy*. Wright & Brown, London, 1930, 288p, Cloth, Coll.

HERMES, pseud.
    see: LUMLEY, BENJAMIN

HERNAMAN-JOHNSON, F(rancis), 1879-1949

07136   *The Polyphemes; a story of strange adventures
          among strange beings.* Ward, Lock, London,
          1906, 318p, Cloth, Novel

HERON, E., pseud.
    see: PRICHARD, KATE O'BRIEN

HERON, H., pseud.
    see: PRICHARD, HESKETH VERNON

HERON-ALLEN, EDWARD, 1861-1943

with Selina Delaro:

07137   *The princess Daphne; a novel.* Henry J. Drane,
          London, 1885, 264p, Cloth, Novel

as Christopher Blayre:

07138   *The cheetah girl.* privately printed, London,
          1923, 100p, Cloth, Novel [University of
          Cosmopoli series; the pages are numbered from
          209-308pp]
07139   *The Purple Sapphire, and other posthumous
          papers, selected from the unofficial records
          of the University of Cosmopoli.* Philip
          Allan, London, 1921, 211p, Cloth, Coll.
07140   retitled: *The strange papers of Dr Blayre.*
          Philip Allan, London, 1932, 271p, Cloth,
          Coll. [University of Cosmopoli series; in-
          cludes several additional stories]
07141   *Some women of the university, being a last
          selection from the strange papers of Chris-
          topher Blayre.* R. Stockwell, London, 1934,
          171p, Cloth, Coll. [University of Cosmopoli
          series]
          The strange papers of Dr Blayre. [see 07140]

HERR, DAN(iel J.), 1917-   [biography inclu-
ded], with Joel Wells

07142   *Bodies and souls.* Crime Club, Doubleday, Gar-
          den City, 1961, 261p, Cloth, Anth.
07143   *Bodies and spirits.* Crime Club, Doubleday,
          Garden City, 1964, 192p, Cloth, Anth.

HERRICK, MAUD CURZON
    see: CAIRNES, MAUD

HERRICK, ROBERT, 1868-1938

07144   *Sometime.* Farrar & Rinehart, New York, 1933,
          338p, Cloth, Novel

HERRMAN, LOUIS

07145   *In the sealed cave, being a modern commentary
          on a strange discovery made by Captain Lem-
          uel Gulliver in the year 1721, and now pub-
          lished from manuscript notes recently come
          to light; a scientific fantasy.* Williams &
          Norgate, London, 1935, 226p, Cloth, Novel
          [Gulliver series]

HERSCHEL, Sir JOHN
    see: LOCKE, RICHARD ADAMS

HERSCHOLT, WOLFE

07146   *Magnetic peril.* Scientific Thriller, Sydney,
          1949, 50p, Paper, Novel
07147   *X-ray menace.* Scientific Thriller, Sydney,
          1949, 50p, Paper, Novel

HERSEY, JOHN (Richard), 1914-   [biography
included]

07148   *The child buyer; a novel in the form of hear-
          ings before the Standing Committee on Educa-
          tion, Welfare, & Public Morality of a cer-
          tain state senate, investigating the conspi-
          racy of Mr. Wissey Jones, with others, to
          purchase a male child.* Alfred A. Knopf, New
          York, 1960, 258p, Cloth, Novel
07149   *My petition for more space.* Alfred A. Knopf,
          New York, 1974, 182p, Cloth, Novel
07150   *White Lotus.* Alfred A. Knopf, New York, 1965,
          683p, Cloth, Novel

HERSHMAN, MORRIS, 1920-   [biography included]

07151   *Shareworld.* Walker, New York, 1972, 186p,
          Cloth, Novel

HERTZKA, Dr. THEODOR, 1845-1924

07152   *Freeland; a social anticipation.* Chatto &
          Windus, London, 1891, 443p, Cloth, Novel
07152A   retitled: *A visit to Freeland; or, The new
          paradise regained.* William Reeves, London,
          1894, 155p, Cloth, Novel

HERVEY, HARRY (Clay), 1900-1951

07153   *Caravans by night; a romance of India.* Cen-
          tury Co., New York, 1922, 400p, Cloth, Novel

HERVEY, MICHAEL, 1920-   [biography included]

07154   *Creeps medley.* Hampton Press, Prittlewell, UK,
          1946, 64p, Paper, Coll.
07155   *Horror medley.* Hampton Press, Prittlewell, UK,
          1945, 32p, Paper, Coll.
07156   *Murder medley.* Hampton Press, Prittlewell, UK,
          1945, 32p, Paper, Coll.
07157   *Strange hunger.* Hamilton & Co. (Stafford),
          London, 1946, 128p, Paper, Novel

HERWER, CHRIS

07158   *Dwellers in the Temple of Mondama.* DeVorss,
          Los Angeles, 1949, 257p, Cloth, Novel

HERZOG, ARTHUR (III), 1927-   [biography in-
cluded]

07159   *The swarm.* Simon & Schuster, New York, 1974,
          256p, Cloth, Novel

HESKY, OLGA L., d. 1974 [biography included]

07160   *The purple armchair.* Anthony Blond, London,
        1961, 232p, Cloth, Novel

HESLOP, VAL

07161   *The lost civilization; a story of adventure in
        central Australia.* St. George Publishing
        Co., Sydney, 1936, 283p, Cloth, Novel

HESSE, HERMANN, 1877-1962

07162   *Magister Ludi; the Nobel prize novel "Das Glas-
        perlenspiel."* Henry Holt, New York, 1949,
        502p, Cloth, Novel
07162A retitled: *The glass bead game (Magister Ludi).*
        Holt, Rinehart & Winston, New York, 1969,
        558p, Cloth, Novel
07163   *Strange news from another star, and other
        tales.* Farrar, Straus & Giroux, New York,
        1972, 145p, Cloth, Coll.

HESSENSTEIN, Countess GABRIELLE

07164   *Monkey paradise; a tale of the jungle.* Methu-
        en, London, 1945, 146p, Cloth, Novel

HETTINGER, JOHN
        see: JOHNHETT

HEWLETT, MAURICE (Henry), 1861-1923

07165   *Lore of Proserpine.* Charles Scribner's Sons,
        New York, 1913, 245p, Cloth, Novel; Macmil-
        lan, London, 1913, 287p, Cloth, Novel

HEWSON, IRENE DALE
        see: ROSS, JEAN

HEXT, HARRINGTON, pseud.
        see: PHILLPOTTS, EDEN

HEYNE, WILLIAM P., 1910-

07166   *Tale of two futures; a novel of life on Earth
        and the planet Paliades in 1975.* Exposition
        Press, New York, 1958, 160p, Cloth, Novel

HEYSE, PAUL (Johann Ludwig von), 1830-1914

07167   *At the ghost hour; the house of the Unbeliev-
        ing Thomas.* Dodd, Mead, New York, 1894,
        96p, Cloth, Novel

HEYWARD, DuBOSE, 1885-1940

07168   *The half pint flask.* Farrar & Rinehart, New
        York, 1929, 55p, Cloth, Novel

HEYWOOD, VICTOR D.

07169   *Prison planet.* Papillon, San Diego, 1974,
        192p, Paper, Novel

HICHENS, ROBERT S(mythe), 1864-1950

07170   *Bye-ways.* Dodd, Mead, New York, 1897, 356p,
        Cloth, Coll.
07171   *Dr. Artz.* Hutchinson, London, 1929, 432p,
        Cloth, Novel
07172   *The dweller on the threshold.* Methuen, Lon-
        don, 1911, 313p, Cloth, Novel
07173   *Flames; a London phantasy.* William Heinemann,
        London, 1897, 414p, Cloth, Novel
07174   *Harps in the wind.* Cassell, London, 1945,
        191p, Cloth, Novel
07174A retitled: *The woman in the house; a novel.*
        Macrae-Smith, Philadelphia, 1945, 224p,
        Cloth, Novel
07175   *Snake-bite, and other stories.* Cassell, Lon-
        don, 1919, 351p, Cloth, Coll.
07176   *Tongues of conscience.* Methuen, London, 1900,
        368p, Cloth, Coll.
        The woman in the house. [see 07174A]

HICKEY, T. EARL

07177   *The time chariot.* Avalon, New York, 1966,
        191p, Cloth, Novel

HICKLING, (Reginald) HUGH, 1920-

07178   *The furious evangelist, being the memoirs of
        Richard Civet during a time of moral break-
        down, and now at last set forth and edited.*
        Alvin Redman, London, 1950, 384p, Cloth,
        Novel

HICKS, CLIFFORD B., 1920-   [biography inclu-
ded]

07179   *First boy on the Moon; a junior science fiction
        novel.* John C. Winston, Philadelphia, 1959,
        120p, Cloth, Novel

HICKS, GRANVILLE, 1901-   [biography included],
with Richard M. Bennett

01113   *The first to awaken.* Modern Age Books, New
        York, 1940, 347p, Cloth, Novel

HIGDON, HAL, 1931-   [biography included]

07180   *The horse that played center field.* Holt,
        Rinehart & Winston, New York, 1968, 118p,
        Cloth, Novel

HIGGINBOTTOM, W(illiam) HUGH, 1881-

07181   *King of Kulturia.* Walter Scott Publishing
        Co., London, 1915, 160p, Paper, Novel

HIGGINS, CHARLES ELI
   see: MULIER

HIGGINS, MARGARET

07182   *The changeling*. Ace, New York, 1973, 222p, Paper, Novel

HIGGINSON, H. W.

07183   *The elixir*. Stellar Publishing Corp., New York, 1930, 24p, Paper, Story

HIGH, PHILIP E(mpson), 1914-   [*biography included*]

07184   *Butterfly planet*. Robert Hale, London, 1971, 160p, Cloth, Novel
07185   *Come, hunt an Earthman*. Robert Hale, London, 1973, 176p, Cloth, Novel
     Double illusion. [see 07187A]
07186   *Invader on my back*. Robert Hale, London, 1968, 176p, Cloth, Novel
07187   *The mad metropolis*. Ace Double, New York, 1966, 142p, Paper, Novel
07187A retitled: *Double illusion*. Dennis Dobson, London, 1970, 142p, Cloth, Novel
07188   *No truce with Terra*. Ace Double, New York, 1964, 110p, Paper, Novel
07189   *The prodigal sun*. Ace, New York, 1964, 192p, Paper, Novel
07190   *Reality forbidden*. Ace Double, New York, 1967, 151p, Paper, Novel
07191   *Sold--for a spaceship*. Robert Hale, London, 1973, 175p, Cloth, Novel
07192   *Speaking of dinosaurs*. Robert Hale, London, 1974, 192p, Cloth, Novel
07193   *These savage futurians*. Ace Double, New York, 1967, 134p, Paper, Novel
07194   *The time mercenaries*. Ace Double, New York, 1968, 118p, Paper, Novel
07195   *Twin planets*. Paperback Library, New York, 1967, 159p, Paper, Novel

HIGHAM, CHARLES, 1931-   [*biography included*]

07196   *The curse of Dracula, and other terrifying tales*. Horwitz, Sydney, 1962, 130p, Paper, Anth.
07197   *Nightmare stories*. Horwitz, Sydney, 1962, 130p, Paper, Anth.
07198   *Spine-tingling tales*. Horwitz, Sydney, 1962, 162p, Paper, Anth.
07199   *Tales of horror*. Horwitz, Sydney, 1962, 160p, Paper, Anth.
07200   *Tales of terror*. Horwitz, Sydney, 1961, 194p, Paper, Anth.
07201   *Weird stories*. Horwitz, Sydney, 1961, 127p, Paper, Anth.

HILDRETH, CHARLES LOTIN, 1858?-1896

07202   *The mysterious city of Oo; adventures in Orbello Land*. W. B. Conkey, Chicago, 1889, 316p, Cloth, Novel
07202A retitled: *Oo; adventures in Orbello Land*. Belford, New York, 1889, 316p, Cloth, Novel

HILL, DOROTHY

07203   *The Little Blue Man*. Skeffington & Son, London, 1948, 200p, Cloth, Novel

HILL, DOUGLAS (Arthur), 1935-   [*biography included*]

07204   *The devil his due; science fantasy stories*. Rupert Hart-Davis, London, 1967, 156p, Cloth, Anth.
07205   *Warlocks and warriors; a fantasy anthology*. Mayflower, London, 1971, 159p, Paper, Anth.
07206   *Way of the werewolf; an anthology of horror stories*. Panther, London, 1966, 143p, Paper, Anth.
07207   *Window on the future; science fiction stories*. Rupert Hart-Davis, London, 1966, 159p, Cloth, Anth.

HILL, ELIZABETH STARR, 1925-   [*biography included*]

07208   *Master Mike and the miracle maid*. Holt, Rinehart & Winston, New York, 1967, 110p, Cloth, Novel
07209   *Pardon my fangs*. Holt, Rinehart & Winston, New York, 1968, 81p, Cloth, Novel

HILL, ERNEST, 1914-   [*biography included*]

07210   *The G.C. radiation*. Robert Hale, London, 1971, 159p, Cloth, Novel
07211   *Pity about Earth*. Ace Double, New York, 1968, 132p, Paper, Novel

HILL, HEADON, pseud. [Francis Edward Grainger, 1857-1927]

07212   *Seaward for the foe*. Ward, Lock, London, 1903, 378p, Cloth, Coll.

HILL, MERTON A.

07213   *The life and habits of city bred earthworms, including their sex life*. Merton A. Hill, Olympia, Wash., 1974, 22p, Paper, Story [includes some nonf.]

HILL, ROBERT, with Albert Zugsmith

07214   *The private lives of Adam and Eve*. Bantam, New York, 1960, 153p, Paper, Movie

HILL, WILLIAM BOYLE

07215   *A new Earth and a new Heaven*. Watts & Co., London, 1936, 312p, Cloth, Novel

HILLAM, S. A.

07216   *Sheykh Hassan, the spiritualist; a view of the supernatural*. W. H. Allen, London, 1888, 223p, Cloth, Novel

HILLEGAS, MARK (Robert), 1926-   [*biography included*]

07217 *The future as nightmare; H. G. Wells and the anti-utopians.* Oxford University Press, New York, 1967, 200p, Cloth, Nonf.

07218 *Shadows of imagination; the fantasies of C. S. Lewis, J. R. R. Tolkien, and Charles Williams.* Southern Illinois University Press, Carbondale, IL, 1969, 170p, Cloth, Nonf.

HILLIARD, MAURICE, 1931-

07219 *The witchfinder.* Heinemann, London, 1974, 182p, Cloth, Novel

HILLIERS, ASHTON, pseud. [Henry Marriage Wallace]

07220 *The Master-Girl; a romance.* G. P. Putnam's Sons, New York, 1910, 245p, Cloth, Novel; Methuen, London, 1910, 296p, Cloth, Novel

HILLS, BALDWIN, pseud. [Burton Wohl]

07221 *Simon, king of the witches.* Dell, New York, 1971, 234p, Paper, Movie

HILTON, JAMES, 1900-1954

07222 *Lost horizon.* William Morrow, New York, 1933, 277p, Cloth, Novel

HILTON, MARGERY

07223 *The flower of eternity.* Mills & Boon, London, 1970, 189p, Cloth, Novel

HILZINGER, J(ohn) GEO(rge)

07224 *The Skystone; a romance of prehistoric Arizona, being vol. I of the chronicles of Mázacl.* F. Tennyson Neely, London, 1899, 281p, Cloth, Novel

HIMMEL, ERNST von
       see: PETERSILEA, CARLYLE

HIND, C(harles) LEWIS, 1862-1927

07225 *The enchanted stone; a romance.* Adam & Charles Black, London, 1898, 343p, Cloth, Novel

07226 *The invisible guide.* Headley Bros., London, 1917, 181p, Cloth, Novel

HINDENBURG'S MARCH INTO LONDON
       see: MUNCH, P. G.

HINE, AL(fred Blakelee), 1915-   [*biography included*]

07227 *Bewitched.* Dell, New York, 1965, 157p, Paper, Tele.

07228 *Signs and portents.* Avon, New York, 1973, 304p, Paper, Novel

HINGLEY, RONALD (Francis), 1920-   [*biography included*]

07229 *Up Jenkins!* Longmans, Green, London, 1956, 226p, Cloth, Novel

HINTON, C(harles) H(oward), 1853-1907

07230 *An episode of Flatland; or, How a plane folk discovered the third dimension, to which is added an outline of the history of Unaea.* Swan Sonnenschein, London, 1907, 181p, Cloth, Novel [a sequel to Abbott's *Flatland*]

07231 *Scientific romances, first series.* Swan Sonnenschein, London, 1884, 2vol, Cloth, Coll.

07232 *Scientific romances, second series.* Swan Sonnenschein, London, 1896, 177p, Cloth, Coll.

HINTZE, NAOMI (A.), 1909-   [*biography included*]

07233 *Listen, please listen.* Random House, New York, 1973, 219p, Cloth, Novel

07234 *The stone carnation.* Random House, New York, 1971, 247p, Cloth, Novel

HIPOLITO, JANE, with Willis E. McNelly

07235 *Mars, we love you; tales of Mars, men, and Martians.* Doubleday, Garden City, 1971, 332p, Cloth, Anth.

HIRAI TARO
       see: RAMPO, EDOGAWA

HIRSCHFELD, BURT, 1923-

07236 *Gas! or, It became necessary to destroy the world in order to save it.* Curtis, New York, 1970, 126p, Paper, Movie

HISCOCK, LESLIE
       see: MARSH, PATRICK

THE HISTORY OF A VOYAGE TO THE MOON

07237 *The history of a voyage to the Moon, with an account of the adventurers' subsequent discoveries; an exhumed narrative supposed to have been ejected from a Lunar volcano.* Lockwood & Co., London, 1864, 204p, Cloth, Novel

THE HISTORY OF AUTONOUS

07238 *The history of Autonous, containing a relation how that young nobleman was accidentally left alone, in his infancy, upon a desolate island, where he lived nineteen years, remote from all human society, 'till taken up by his father; with an account of his life, reflections, and improvements in knowledge during*

THE HISTORY OF AUTONOUS (cont.)

> *his continuance in that solitary state; the whole, as taken from his own mouth.* J. Roberts, London, 1736, 117p, Cloth, Novel [sometimes attributed to Daniel Defoe]

THE HISTORY OF ISRAEL JOBSON
    see: WILSON, MILES

THE HISTORY OF THE CALIPH VATHEK, etc.

07239 *The history of the Caliph Vathek; also, Rasselas, Prince of Abyssinia.* Nimmo & Bain, London, 1883, 405p, Cloth, Anth. [by William Beckford and Samuel Johnson respectively]

THE HISTORY OF THE SUDDEN AND TERRIBLE INVASION OF ENGLISH

07240 *The history of the sudden and terrible invasion of English by the French in the month of May, 1852.* T. Bosworth, London, 1851, 23p, Paper, Story

HITCHCOCK, ALFRED (Joseph), 1899-

> *Alfred Hitchcock presents: 14 of my favorites in suspense.* [see 07241A]
> *Alfred Hitchcock presents: More of my favorites in suspense.* [see 07241B]
> *Alfred Hitchcock presents: More stories for late at night.* [see 07242B]
> *Alfred Hitchcock presents: More stories my mother never told me.* [see 07243A]
> *Alfred Hitchcock presents: More stories not for the nervous.* [see 00520A]

07241 *Alfred Hitchcock presents: My favorites in suspense.* Random House, New York, 1959, 502p, Cloth, Anth.
07241A retitled: *Alfred Hitchcock presents: 14 of my favorites in suspense.* Dell, New York, 1963, 286p, Paper, Anth. [abridged]
07241B retitled: *Alfred Hitchcock presents: More of my favorites in suspense.* Dell, New York, 1964, 287p, Paper, Anth. [abridged; 07241A and 07241B together comprise the original volume]
> *Alfred Hitchcock presents: Scream along with me.* [see 00521A]
07242 *Alfred Hitchcock presents: Stories for late at night.* Random House, New York, 1961, 469p, Cloth, Anth.
07242A retitled: *Alfred Hitchcock presents: 12 stories for late at night.* Dell, New York, 1962, 223p, Paper, Anth. [abridged]
07242B retitled: *Alfred Hitchcock presents: More stories for late at night.* Dell, New York, 1962, 207p, Paper, Anth. [abridged; 07242A and 07242B together comprise the original volume]
07243 *Alfred Hitchcock presents: Stories my mother never told me.* Random House, New York, 1963, 401p, Cloth, Anth.
07243A retitled: *Alfred Hitchcock presents: More stories my mother never told me.* Dell, New York, 1965, 190p, Paper, Anth. [abridged]

07244 *Alfred Hitchcock presents: Stories they wouldn't let me do on TV.* Simon & Schuster, New York, 1957, 372p, Cloth, Anth.
07244A retitled: *Alfred Hitchcock presents: 12 stories they wouldn't let me do on TV.* Dell, New York, 1958, 224p, Paper, Anth. [abridged]
07244B retitled: *Alfred Hitchcock presents: 13 more stories they wouldn't let me do on TV.* Dell, New York, 1959, 224p, Paper, Anth. [abridged; 07244A and 07244B together comprise the original volume]
> *Alfred Hitchcock presents: 12 stories for late at night.* [see 07242A]
> *Alfred Hitchcock presents: 12 stories they wouldn't let me do on TV.* [see 07244A]
07245 *Alfred Hitchcock's Monster museum.* Random House, New York, 1965, 207p, Cloth, Anth.
07246 *Alfred Hitchcock's Supernatural tales of terror and suspense.* Random House, New York, 1973, 172p, Cloth, Anth.
07247 *Bar the doors; terror tales.* Dell, New York, 1946, 192p, Paper, Anth.
07248 *Fear and trembling; shivery stories.* Dell, New York, 1948, 192p, Paper, Anth.
07249 *Ghostly gallery.* Random House, New York, 1962, 206p, Cloth, Anth.
07250 *Haunted houseful.* Random House, New York, 1961, 208p, Cloth, Anth.

HITCHCOCK, RAYMOND (John), 1922- [*biography included*]

07251 *Percy.* W. H. Allen, London, 1969, 192p, Cloth, Novel [Percy #1]
07252 *Percy's progress.* Sphere, London, 1972, 123p, Paper, Movie [Percy #2]
07253 *Venus 13; a cautionery space tale.* W. H. Allen, London, 1972, 160p, Cloth, Novel

HJORTSBERG, WILLIAM (Reinhold), 1941- [*biography included*]

07254 *Gray matters; a novel.* Simon & Schuster, New York, 1971, 160p, Cloth, Novel

HOAR, ROGER SHERMAN
    see: FARLEY, RALPH MILNE

HOBAN, RUSSELL (Conwell), 1925- [*biography included*]

07255 *Kleinzeit.* Jonathan Cape, London, 1974, 191p, Cloth, Novel
07256 *The lion of Boaz-Jachin and Jachin-Boaz.* Jonathan Cape, London, 1973, 192p, Cloth, Novel

HOBSON, (Sir) HAROLD, 1904-

07257   The devil in Woodford Wells; a fantastic novel.
         Longmans, Green, London, 1946, 244p, Cloth,
         Novel

HOCH, EDWARD D(entinger), 1930-   [biography included]

07258   City of Brass. Leisure Books, North Hollywood,
         CA, 1971, 190p, Paper, Coll. [Simon Ark #2]
07259   The fellowship of the HAND. Walker & Co., New
         York, 1973, 198p, Cloth, Novel
07260   The judges of Hades, and other Simon Ark sto-
         ries. Leisure Books, North Hollywood, CA,
         1971, 174p, Paper, Coll. [Simon Ark #1]
07261   The transvection machine. Walker & Co., New
         York, 1971, 220p, Cloth, Novel

HOCHSTEIN, PETER
    see: SHORT, JACKSON

HOCKING, JOSEPH, 1860-1937

07262   The tenant of Cromlech Cottage. Ward, Lock,
         London, 1927, 318p, Cloth, Novel
07263   The weapons of mystery. George Routledge &
         Sons, London, 1890, 192p, Cloth, Novel

HOCKING, SILAS K(itto), 1850-1935

07264   The strange adventures of Israel Pendray.
         Frederick Warne, London, 1899, 429p, Cloth,
         Novel

HODDER, WILLIAM REGINALD

07265   The daughter of the dawn; a realistic story of
         Maori magic. Jarrold & Sons, London, 1902,
         333p, Cloth, Novel
07266   Ultus, the man from the dead. Hodder & Stough-
         ton, London, 1916, 184p, Cloth, Movie

HODDER-WILLIAMS, (John) CHRISTOPHER (Glaze-
brook), 1926-   [biography included]

07267   Chain reaction. Hodder & Stoughton, London,
         1959, 224p, Cloth, Novel
07268   The egg-shaped thing. Hodder & Stoughton,
         London, 1967, 249p, Cloth, Novel
07269   Fistful of digits. Hodder & Stoughton, London,
         1968, 288p, Cloth, Novel
07270   The main experiment. Hodder & Stoughton, Lon-
         don, 1964, 224p, Cloth, Novel
07271   98.4; a novel. Hodder & Stoughton, London,
         1969, 221p, Cloth, Novel
07272   Panic o'clock. United Writers Publications,
         St. Ives, UK, 1973, 327p, Cloth, Novel

HODGART, MATTHEW (John Caldwell), 1916-   [bi-
ography included]

07273   A new voyage to the country of the Houyhnhnms,
         being the fifth part of the Travels into
         several remote parts of the world, by Lemuel
         Gulliver, first a surgeon and then a captain
         of several ships; wherein the author returns
         and finds a new state of liberal horses and
         revolting Yahoos. Duckworth, London, 1969,
         91p, Cloth, Novel [Gulliver series]

HODGE, T. SHIRBY, pseud. [Roger Sherman Tracy,
1841-1926]

07274   The white man's burden; a satirical forecast.
         R. Badger, The Gorham Press, Boston, 1915,
         225p, Cloth, Novel

HODGSON, JOHN (Lawrence)

07275   The time-journey of Dr. Barton; an engineering
         and sociological forecast based on present
         possibilities. John Hodgson, Eggington, UK,
         1929, 89p, Paper, Novel

HODGSON, W(illiam) EARL, d. 1910

07276   Haunted by posterity. Adam & Charles Black,
         London, 1895, 464p, Cloth, Novel

HODGSON, WILLIAM HOPE, 1877-1918

07277   The boats of the 'Glen Carrig,' being an ac-
         count of their adventures in the strange
         places of the Earth, after the foundering
         of the good ship Glen Carrig through strik-
         ing upon a hidden rock in the unknown seas
         to the southward, as told by John Winter-
         straw, Gent., to his son James Wintershaw,
         in the year 1757, and by him commited very
         properly and legibly to manuscript. Chapman
         & Hall, London, 1907, 312p, Cloth, Novel
07278   Carnacki, the ghost-finder. Eveleigh Nash,
         London, 1913, 287p, Cloth, Coll.
07279   Carnacki, the ghost-finder. Mycroft & Moran,
         Sauk City, Wisc., 1947, 241p, Cloth, Coll.
         [includes three additional stories]
07280   Carnacki, the ghost-finder; and, A poem.
         no publisher, London, 1910, 14p, Cloth, Coll.;
         Paul R. Reynolds, New York, 1910, 14p, Cloth,
         Coll.
07281   Deep waters. Arkham House, Sauk City, 1967,
         300p, Cloth, Coll.
07282   The ghost pirates. Stanley Paul, London,
         1909, 276p, Cloth, Novel
07283   The ghost pirates, a chaunty, and another
         story. Paul R. Reynolds, New York, 1909,
         68p, Cloth, Coll. [The ghost pirates is
         abridged]
07284   The house on the borderland, from the manu-
         script discovered in 1877 by Messrs. Tonni-
         son and Berreggnog, in the ruins that lie
         to the south of the village of Kraighten,
         in the west of Ireland. Chapman & Hall,
         London, 1908, 300p, Cloth, Novel
07285   The house on the borderland, and other novels.
         Arkham House, Sauk City, 1946, 639p, Cloth,
         Coll. [includes The house on the borderland;
         The boats of the 'Glen Carrig'; The ghost
         pirates; The Night Land]
07286   Men of the deep waters. Eveleigh Nash, London,
         1914, 303p, Cloth, Coll.
07287   The Night Land; a love tale. Eveleigh Nash,
         London, 1912, 583p, Cloth, Novel

HODGSON, WILLIAM HOPE (cont.)

07288   *"Poems"; and, "A dream of X."* A. P. Watt & Son, London, 1912, 84p, Cloth, Coll. ["A Dream of X" is an abridged version of *The Night Land*]

HOFFMAN, DAVID, 1784-1854

07289   *Chronicles selected from the originals of Cartaphilus, the wandering Jew, embracing a period of nearly XIX centuries; series the first.* Thomas Bosworth, London, 1853/54, 3vol, Cloth, Novel [second series never published]

HOFFMAN, EVERETT, 1921-

07290   *The coming up of Mr. Rattus; a fable.* Adams Press, Chicago, 1968, 104p, Paper, Novel

HOFFMAN, KURT

07291   *Blackmarket brains.* Scientific Thriller, Sydney, 1949, 50p, Paper, Story

HOFFMAN, LEE [Shirley Bell Hoffman, 1932-] [*biography included*]

07292   *Always the black knight.* Avon, New York, 1970, 160p, Paper, Novel
07293   *The caves of Karst.* Ballantine, New York, 1969, 224p, Paper, Novel
07294   *Change song.* Doubleday, Garden City, 1972, 203p, Cloth, Novel
07295   *Telepower.* Belmont Double, New York, 1967, 83p, Paper, Novel

HOFFMAN, STUART [published anonymously]

07296   *An index to Unknown and Unknown worlds, by author and by title.* Sirius Press, Black Earth, Wisc., 1955, 34p, Paper, Nonf.

HOFFMANN, E(rnst) T(heodor) A(madeus), 1776-1822 [originally Ernst Theodor Wilhelm Hoffmann]

07297   *The best tales of Hoffmann.* Dover, New York, 1967, 419p, Paper, Coll.
07298   *The devil's elixir.* William Blackwood, Edinburgh, 1824, vol. I-379p, II-339p, Cloth, Novel
07298A   retitled: *The devil's elixirs.* John Calder, London, 1963, 324p, Cloth, Novel
07299   *Eight tales of Hoffmann.* Pan, London, 1952, 223p, Paper, Coll.
07300   *The fairy tales of Hoffmann.* George G. Harrap, London, 1960, 94p, Cloth, Coll.
07301   *Four tales.* Four Square, London, 1962, 216p, Paper, Coll.
07302   *Hoffmann's fairy tales.* Burnham Bros., Boston, 1857, 274p, Cloth, Coll.
07303   *Hoffmann's strange stories.* Burnham Bros, Boston, 1855, 444p, Cloth, Coll.
07304   *The king's bride.* John Calder, London, 1959, 89p, Paper, Novel

07305   *Selected writings of E. T. A. Hoffmann.* University of Chicago Press, Chicago, 1969, 2vol, Cloth, Coll.
07305A   retitled: *Tales of E. T. A. Hoffmann.* University of Chicago Press, Chicago, 1972, 279p, Paper, Coll. [originally volume one of the hardcover edition]
07306   *The Serapion Brethren.* George Bell & Sons, London, 1886/92, volume I-552p, II-528p, Cloth, Coll.
07307   *Stories by Ernst Theodor Wilhelm Hoffmann.* T. C. & E. C. Jack, London, 1908, 151p, Cloth, Coll.
07308   *Tales from Hoffmann.* Bodley Head, London, 1951, 314p, Cloth, Novel
       Tales of E. T. A. Hoffmann. [see 07305A]
07309   *Tales of Hoffmann.* Chatto & Windus, London, 1913, 206p, Cloth, Coll.
07310   *Tales of Hoffmann.* A. A. Wyn, New York, 1946, 509p, Cloth, Coll. [different contents]
07311   *The tales of Hoffmann.* Frederick Ungar, New York, 1963, 248p, Paper, Coll. [different contents]
07312   *Tales of Hoffmann.* Blackie & Son, London, 1966, 105p, Cloth, Coll. [different contents]
07313   *The tales of Hoffmann; stories.* Limited Editions Club, New York, 1943, 336p, Cloth, Coll. [different contents]
07314   *Three märchen of E. T. A. Hoffmann.* University of South Carolina Press, Columbia, SC, 1971, 402p, Cloth, Coll.
07315   *Weird tales.* J. C. Nimmo, London, 1885, 2vol, Cloth, Coll.

HOGAN, ROBERT J., 1897-1963

07316   *Ace of the white death; G-8 and his Battle Aces.* Berkley Medallion, New York, 1970, 128p, Paper, Novel [G-8 #3]
07317   *G-8 and his Battle Aces #1; The bat staffel.* Berkley Medallion, New York, 1969, 142p, Paper, Novel [G-8 #1]
07318   *G-8 and his Battle Aces #4; Bombs from the murder wolves.* Berkley Medallion, New York, 1971, 128p, Paper, Novel [G-8 #4]
07319   *G-8 and his Battle Aces #5; Vultures of the white death.* Berkley Medallion, New York, 1971, 127p, Paper, Novel [G-8 #5]
07320   *G-8 and his Battle Aces #6; Flight from the grave.* Berkley Medallion, New York, 1971, 126p, Paper, Novel [G-8 #6]
07321   *G-8 and his Battle Aces #7; Fangs of the sky leopard.* Berkley Medallion, New York, 1971, 128p, Paper, Novel [G-8 #7]
07322   *G-8 and his Battle Aces #8; The mark of the vulture.* Berkley Medallion, New York, 1971, 128p, Paper, Novel [G-8 #8]
07323   *Purple Aces; G-8 and his Battle Aces.* Berkley Medallion, New York, 1970, 157p, Paper, Novel [G-8 #2]

HOGG, JAMES, 1770-1835

       The confessions of a justified sinner. [see 07324B]
07324   *The private memoirs and confessions of a justified sinner, written by himself, with a detail of curious traditionary facts and other evidence.* Longman, Hurst, Rees, Orme, Brown & Green, London, 1824, 390p, Cloth, Novel

HOGG, JAMES (cont.)

07324A retitled: *The suicide's grave; or, Memoirs and confessions of a sinner.* Longman, Hurst, Rees, Orme, Brown & Green, London, 1828, 390p, Cloth, Novel

07324B retitled: *The confessions of a justified sinner.* J. Shiells, London, 1898, 266p, Cloth, Novel

07325 *Winter evening tales, collected among the cottagers in the south of Scotland.* Oliver & Boyd, Edinburgh; G & W. B. Whittaker, London, 1820, vol. I-340p, II-335p, Cloth, Coll.

HOKE, HELEN, 1903-

07326 *Weirdies; a horrifying concatenation of the super-sur-real or almost or not-quite real.* Franklin Watts, London, 1973, 242p, Cloth, Anth.

HOLBERG, LUDVIG, Baron af, 1684-1754

07327 *A journey to the world under-ground,* by Nicholas Klimius. T. Astley & B. Collins, London, 1742, 324p, Cloth, Novel

07327A retitled: *Journey to the world under ground, being the subterraneous travels of Niels Klim,* from the Latin of Lewis Holberg. T. North, London, 1828, 420p, Cloth, Novel

07327B retitled: *Niels Klim's journey under the ground, being a narrative of his wonderful descent to the subterranean lands, together with an account of the sensible animals and trees inhabiting the planet Nazar of the firmament,* by Louis Holberg. Saxton, Peirce, Boston, 1845, 190p, Cloth, Novel

07327C retitled: *Niels Klim, being an incomplete translation by Thomas De Quincy.* Auckland University College, Auckland, NZ, 1953, 37p, Paper?, Story [published anonymously; an abridged version]

07327D retitled: *The journey of Niels Klim to the world underground.* University of Nebraska Press, Lincoln, Neb., 1960, 236p, Paper, Novel

HOLDEN, Lord [Angus William Eden Holden, Baron Holden, 1898-1951]

07328 *Purgatory revisited; a Victorian parody.* Skeffington & Son, London, 1949, 216p, Cloth, Novel

HOLDEN, RICHARD (Cort)

07329 *Snow fury.* Dodd, Mead, New York, 1955, 248p, Cloth, Novel

HOLDER, C(harles) F(rederick), 1851-1915

07330 *The treasure divers; a boy's adventures in the depths of the sea.* Dodd, Mead, New York, 1898, 207p, Cloth, Novel

HOLDER, GEOFFREY, 1930-   , with Tom Harshman

06866 *Black gods, green islands.* Doubleday, Garden City, 1959, 235p, Cloth, Coll.

HOLDING, ELISABETH SANXAY, 1889-1955

07331 *Miss Kelly.* William Morrow, New York, 1947, 125p, Cloth, Novel

HOLDRIDGE, HERBERT C(harles), 1892-

07332 *The fables of Moronia.* Holdridge Foundation for the Advancement of Social Sciences, Sherman Oaks, CA, 1953, 173p, Cloth, Coll.

HOLENIA, ALEXANDER LERNET-
     see: LERNET-HOLENIA, ALEXANDER

HOLFORD, CASTELLO N.

07333 *Aristopia; a romance-history of the new world.* Arena Publishing Co., Boston, 1895, 234p, Cloth, Novel

HOLGATE, JEROME B(onaparte)

07334 *Noachidae; or, Noah and his descendants.* Breed, Butler & Co., Buffalo, NY, 1860, 354p, Cloth, Novel [cover title: *Noah and his descendants*]

HOLLAND, CLIVE, pseud. [Charles James Hankinson, 1866-1959]

07335 *An Egyptian coquette.* C. Arthur Pearson, London, 1898, 232p, Cloth, Novel

07335A retitled: *The spell of Isis; a romance of Egypt.* Lynwood & Co., London, 1913, 214p, Cloth, Novel

07336 *Raymi; or, The children of the Sun.* Henry & Co., London, 1889, 318p, Cloth, Novel

HOLLAND, W(est) BOB, 1868-1932

07337 *Twenty-five ghost stories.* J. S. Ogilvie Publishing Co., New York, 1904, 255p, Cloth, Anth. [includes some nonf.]

07337A retitled: *The Perma book of ghost stories.* Permabooks, Garden City, NY, 1950, 188p, Cloth, Anth.

07337B retitled: *Twenty-five great ghost stories.* Avon, New York, 1943, 190p, Paper, Anth. [published anonymously]

07337C retitled: *20 great ghost stories.* Avon, New York, 1955, 127p, Paper, Anth. [published anonymously; abridged]

HOLLISTER, BERNARD C(laiborne), 1938-   [*biography included*]

07338 *Another tomorrow; a science fiction anthology.* Pflaum Publishing, Dayton, OH, 1974, 121p, Paper, Anth.

HOLLISTER, BERNARD C. (cont.), with Deane C. Thompson

07339 *Grokking the future; science fiction in the classroom.* Pflaum/Standard, Dayton, OH, 1973, 168p, Paper, Nonf.

HOLLISTER, (C.) WARREN, 1930-   , with Judith Pike

07340 *The moons of Meer.* Henry Z. Walck, New York, 1969, 208p, Cloth, Novel

HOLLOWAY, BRIAN

as Berl Cameron, house pseud.:

02467 *Destination Alpha.* Curtis Warren, London, 1952, 127p, Paper, Novel

as Neil Charles, house pseud.:

02891 *Titan's moon.* Curtis Warren, London, 1952, 112p, Paper, Novel

as Adam Dale:

07341 *Southern exploration.* Curtis Warren, London, 1953, 160p, Cloth, Novel

as King Lang, house pseud.:

07342 *Trans-Mercurian.* Curtis Warren, London, 1952, 112p, Paper, Novel

as Rand Le Page, house pseud.:

07343 *"A" men.* Curtis Warren, London, 1952, 127p, Paper, Novel

as Brian Storm:

07344 *Red storm.* Curtis Warren, London, 1952, 112p, Paper, Novel

HÖLLRIEGEL, ARNOLD, pseud. [Richard Arnold Bermann, 1883-1939]

07345 *The forest ship; a book of the Amazon.* Putnam, London, 1930, 254p, Cloth, Novel

HOLLY, J(oan Carol) HUNTER, 1932-   [*biography included*]

07346 *The dark enemy.* Avalon, New York, 1965, 190p, Cloth, Novel
07347 *The dark planet.* Avalon, New York, 1962, 224p, Cloth, Novel
07348 *Encounter.* Avalon, New York, 1959, 224p, Cloth, Novel
07349 *The Flying Eyes.* Monarch, Derby, Conn., 1962, 140p, Paper, Novel
07350 *The gray aliens.* Avalon, New York, 1963, 192p, Cloth, Novel
07350A retitled: *The grey aliens.* Mayflower-Dell, London, 1964, 125p, Paper, Novel
07351 *The green planet.* Avalon, New York, 1960, 222p, Cloth, Novel
       The grey aliens. [see 07350A]
07352 *The man from U.N.C.L.E., number 10; The assassination affair.* Ace, New York, 1967, 158p, Paper, Tele. [Man from U.N.C.L.E. #10]
07353 *The mind traders.* Avalon, New York, 1966, 192p, Cloth, Novel

07354 *The Running Man.* Monarch, Derby, Conn., 1963, 142p, Paper, Novel
07355 *The time twisters.* Avon, New York, 1964, 160p, Paper, Novel

HOLM, JOHN CECIL, 1904-

07356 *McGarrity & the pigeons.* Rinehart & Co., New York, 1947, 239p, Cloth, Novel

HOLM, SVEN, 1940-   [*biography included*]

07357 *Termush.* Faber & Faber, London, 1969, 110p, Cloth, Novel

HOLMAN, FELICE, 1919-

07358 *The future of Hooper Toote.* Charles Scribner's Sons, New York, 1972, 138p, Cloth, Novel

HOLMAN, JEAN PARKE
   see: PARKE, JEAN

HOLMES, CLARA H.

07359 *Floating fancies among the weird and the occult.* F. Tennyson Neely, London, 1898, 248p, Cloth, Coll.

HOLMES, F. RATCLIFFE

07360 *The secret people; adventure in Africa.* Doubleday, Doran, Garden City, 1928, 258p, Cloth, Novel

HOLMES, H. H., pseud.
   see: BOUCHER, ANTHONY

HOLMES, LARRY W.

07361 *Evil seed.* Orpheus Series, New York, 1968, 187p, Paper, Novel

HOLMES, LAWRANCE

07362 *A very short walk; a novel.* Macmillan, New York, 1970, 184p, Cloth, Novel

HOLMES, OLIVER WENDELL, 1809-1894

07363 *Elsie Venner; a romance of destiny.* Ticknor & Fields, Boston, 1861, 2vol, Cloth, Novel

HOLROYD, SAM, pseud.
   see: BURTON, S. H.

HOLST, SPENCER

07364 *The language of cats, and other stories.* McCall Publishing Co., New York, 1971, 86p, Cloth, Coll.

HOLT, CONRAD G., pseud.
        see: FEARN, JOHN RUSSELL

HOLT, JOHN ROBERT
        see: GILES, RAYMOND

HOLT-WHITE, W(illiam Edward Bradden), 1878-

07365   *The earthquake; a romance of London in 1907.*
        E. Grant Richards, London, 1906, 334p, Cloth,
        Novel
07366   *Helen of all time.* T. Fisher Unwin, London,
        1910, 331p, Cloth, Novel
07367   *The man who dreamed right.* Everett & Co.,
        London, 1910, 319p, Cloth, Novel
07368   *The man who stole the Earth.* T. Fisher Unwin,
        London, 1909, 382p, Cloth, Novel
07369   *The woman who saved the world.* Everett & Co.,
        London, 1914, 222p, Cloth, Novel
07370   *The world stood still.* Everett & Co., London,
        1912, 312p, Cloth, Novel

HOLTBY, WINIFRED, 1898-1935

07371   *Mandoa, Mandoa! a comedy of irrelevance.* Col-
        lins, London, 1933, 382p, Cloth, Novel

HOLZER, HANS, 1920-   [*biography included*]

07372   *The alchemy deception.* Award, New York, 1973,
        184p, Paper, Novel [Randy Knowles #2]
07373   *The Red Chindvit conspiracy.* Award, New York,
        1970, 154p, Paper, Novel [Randy Knowles #1]

HOME-GALL, EDWARD R(eginald)

07374   *The Human Bat; no. 1 in the series, "Caught
        in the spider's web."* Mark Goulden, London,
        1950, 127p, Paper, Novel [Human Bat #1]
07375   *The Human Bat v. the robot gangster.* Mark
        Goulden, London, 1950, 128p, Paper, Novel
        [Human Bat #2]

HOME-GALL, W. B.
        see: WRAY, REGINALD

HOMER AND ASSOCIATES
        see: WILLIAMS, GERALD

HOMUNCULUS, pseud.

07376   *John Bull and his wonderful lamp; a new read-
        ing of an old tale.* J. Petheram, London,
        1849, 59p, Cloth, Novel [sometimes attributed
        to William Makepeace Thackeray]

HONEYCOMBE, GORDON, 1936-

07377   *Dragon under the hill.* Hutchinson, London,
        1972, 335p, Cloth, Novel

HOOD, ARCHER LESLIE, 1869?-1944, with Violet
Lilian Perkins as Lilian Leslie

07378   *The melody from Mars.* Authors' International
        Publishing Co., New York, 1924, 206p, Cloth,
        Novel

HOOD, THOMAS, 1799-1845

07379   *Whims and oddities in prose and verse.* Lupton
        Relfe, London, 1826, 146p, Cloth, Coll.
07380   *Whims and oddities in prose and verse, vol. II.*
        Charles Tilt, London, 1827, 150p, Cloth, Coll.

HOOD, THOMAS, 1835-1874

07381   *Vere Vereker's vengeance; a sensation in seve-
        ral paroxysms.* John Camden Hotten, London,
        1865, 146p, Cloth, Novel

HOOKER, LE ROY, 1840?-1906

07382   *Enoch, the Philistine; a traditional romance
        of Philistia, Egypt, and the great pyramid.*
        Rand, McNally, Chicago, 1898, 250p, Cloth,
        Novel

HOOKHAM, ALBERT E.

07383   *Amid the strife; or, The lust of Mars.* Andrew
        Prickett, London, 1909, 323p, Cloth, Novel

HOOPES, NED E(dward), 1932-   [*biography included*]

07384   *Speak of the devil; 17 diabolic tales.* Dell,
        New York, 1967, 205p, Paper, Anth.

HOOVER, H. M.

07385   *Children of Morrow.* Four Winds Press, New
        York, 1973, 229p, Cloth, Novel

HOPE, CORAL

07386   *Listening hands.* Macdonald, London, 1944,
        191p, Cloth, Novel

HOPE, EDWARD, pseud. [Edward Hope Coffey, Jr.,
1896-1958]

07387   *Alice in the Delighted States.* Lincoln Mac-
        Veagh, The Dial Press, New York, 1928, 303p,
        Cloth, Novel

HOPKINS, ALICE K(imball), 1839-

07388   *A daughter of the Druids*, by A. K. H. Alfred
        Mudge & Son, Boston, 1892, 297p, Cloth,
        Novel
07389   *Mona the Druidess; or, The astral science of
        old Britain.* Eastern Publishing Co., Boston,
        1904, 345p, Cloth, Novel

HOPKINS, JEUNE [Squire D. Hopkins]

07390 *The mysterious hunter; or, The last of the Aztecs*, by Vic St. L. (Jeune Hopkins). Jeune Hopkins Co., Chicago, 1892, 293p, Cloth, Novel

HOPKINS, KENNETH
    see: MANNON, WARWICK

HOPKINS, R(obert) THURSTON, 1884-1958

07391 *Cavalcade of ghosts*. World's Work, Kingswood, UK, 1956, 246p, Cloth, Coll. [includes some nonf.]
07392 *Horror parade; a selection of the best uncanny stories written by that master of this type of story*. Mitre Press, London, 1945, 63p, Paper, Coll.
07393 *Uncanny tales*. Mitre Press, London, 1945, 32p, Paper, Coll.
07394 *Weird and uncanny stories*. Mitre Press, London, 1945, 32p, Paper, Coll.

with Forbes Phillips:

07395 *War and the weird*. Simpkin, Marshall, Hamilton, Kent, London, 1916, 182p, Cloth, Coll. [includes some nonf.]

HOPKINS, SQUIRE D.
    see: HOPKINS, JEUNE

HOPLEY, GEORGE, pseud.
    see: WOOLRICH, CORNELL

HOPLEY-WOOLRICH, CORNELL GEORGE
    see: WOOLRICH, CORNELL

HOPPER, NORA, 1871-1906

07396 *Ballads in prose*. Roberts Bros., Boston, 1894, 186p, Cloth, Coll.; John Lane, London, 1894, 186p, Cloth, Coll.

HORAN, KEITH

07397 *The squid*. Barnardo Amalgamated Industries, London, 1946, 64p, Paper, Novel

HORGAN, PAUL (George Vincent O'Shaughnessy), 1903-   [biography included]

07398 *The saintmaker's Christmas Eve*. Farrar, Straus & Cudahy, New York, 1955, 112p, Cloth, Novel

HORLER, SYDNEY, 1888-1954

07399 *The formula; a novel of Harley Street*. John Long, London, 1933, 286p, Cloth, Novel
07400 *The house of the uneasy dead*. Arthur Barker, London, 1950, 208p, Cloth, Novel
07401 *Lord of Terror; a Paul Vivanti story*. Collins, London, 1935, 252p, Cloth, Novel [Paul Vivanti series]

07402 *The man who shook the Earth*. Hutchinson, London, 1933, 288p, Cloth, Coll.
07403 *The order of the octopus*. George H. Doran, New York, 1926, 310p, Cloth, Novel
07404 *The screaming skull, and other stories*. Hodder & Stoughton, London, 1930, 318p, Cloth, Coll.
07405 *The vampire*. Hutchinson, London, 1935, 288p, Cloth, Novel
07406 *Virus X; a Paul Vivanti story*. Quality Press, London, 1945, 159p, Cloth, Novel [Paul Vivanti series]

HORN, EDWARD NEWMAN, 1903-

07407 *Faster faster*. Coward-McCann, New York, 1946, 215p, Cloth, Novel

HORNER, DONALD W(illiam)

07408 *By aeroplane to the Sun, being the adventures of a daring aviator and his friends*. Century Press, London, 1910, 268p, Cloth, Novel
07409 *Their winged destiny, being a tale of two planets*. Simpkin, Marshall, Hamilton, Kent, London, 1912, 240p, Cloth, Novel
07409A retitled: *The world's double, being a tale of two planets*. Simpkin, Marshall, Hamilton, Kent, London, 1913, 243p, Cloth, Novel

HORNIMAN, ROY, 1874-1930

07410 *The living Buddha*. T. Fisher Unwin, London, 1903, 312p, Cloth, Novel
07411 *The sin of Atlantis*. John Macqueen, London, 1900, 328p, Cloth, Novel

HORROR OMNIBUS

07412 *Horror omnibus, containing two complete novels: Dracula, by Bram Stoker; Frankenstein, by Mary W. Shelley*. Grosset & Dunlap, New York, 1939, 594p, Cloth, Anth.
07412A retitled: *Dracula, by Bram Stoker; Frankenstein (or, The modern Prometheus), by Mary Shelley*. Nelson Doubleday, Garden City, 1973, 655p, Cloth, Anth.

HORROR STORIES

07413 *Horror stories; short stories*. Bestseller Library, London, 1961, 256p, Paper, Anth.
07413A retitled: *The Arrow book of horror stories*. Arrow, London, 1965, 256p, Paper, Anth.

HORRORS

07414 *Horrors; a collection of uneasy tales*. Philip Allan, London, 1933, 252p, Cloth, Anth.

HORSEMAN, ELAINE, 1925-   [biography included]

07415 *The Hubbles and the robot*. Chatto & Windus, London, 1968, 176p, Cloth, Novel [Hubbles #3]
07416 *Hubble's bubble*. Chatto & Windus, London, 196 220p, Cloth, Novel [Hubbles #1]

HORSLEY, T. J., pseud.
see: CURTIES, T. J. HORSLEY

HORSNELL, HORACE, 1882-1949

07417 *Castle Cottage.* Hamish Hamilton, London,
1940, 260p, Cloth, Novel
07418 *The cool of the evening.* Hamish Hamilton,
London, 1942, 142p, Cloth, Novel
07419 *Man alone.* Hamish Hamilton, London, 1940,
160p, Cloth, Novel

HORT, Lieut.-Colonel (Richard), 1803/4-1857

07420 *The embroidered banner, and other marvels.*
John & Daniel A. Darling, London, 1850,
288p, Cloth, Novel

HOSKINS, ROBERT (P.), 1933-   [*biography included*]

07421 *The edge of never; classic and contemporary
tales of the supernatural.* Fawcett Premier,
Greenwich, 1973, 287p, Paper, Anth.
07422 *The far-out people; a science fiction anthology.* Signet, New York, 1971, 191p, Paper,
Anth.
07423 *First step outward.* Dell, New York, 1969,
224p, Paper, Anth.
07424 *Infinity one; a magazine of speculative fiction in book form.* Lancer, New York, 1970,
253p, Paper, Anth.
07425 *Infinity two.* Lancer, New York, 1971, 237p,
Paper, Anth.
07426 *Infinity three.* Lancer, New York, 1972, 224p,
Paper, Anth.
07427 *Infinity four.* Lancer, New York, 1972, 270p,
Paper, Anth.
07428 *Infinity five.* Lancer, New York, 1973, 208p,
Paper, Anth.
07429 *The liberated future.* Fawcett Crest, Greenwich, 1974, 304p, Paper, Anth.
07430 *The stars around us; a science fiction anthology.* Signet, New York, 1970, 191p, Paper,
Anth.
07431 *Strange tomorrows.* Lancer, New York, 1972,
352p, Paper, Anth.
07432 *Swords against tomorrow.* Signet, New York,
1970, 176p, Paper, Anth.
07433 *Tomorrow I; a science fiction anthology.* Signet, New York, 1971, 192p, Paper, Anth.
07434 *Wondermakers; an anthology of classic science
fiction.* Fawcett Premier, Greenwich, 1972,
351p, Paper, Anth.
07435 *Wondermakers 2.* Fawcett Premier, Greenwich,
1974, 320p, Paper, Anth.

HOTCHIN, F. E., with A. A. Allinson

00207 *SF.* Cheshire, Melbourne, 1968, 31p, Paper,
Nonf.

HOTSON, CORNELIA HINKLEY

07436 *The shining east; a story of life after death.*
Vantage Press, New York, 1965, 107p, Cloth,
Novel

HOUBLON, GRAHAME

07437 *The crack in the wall.* Arthur H. Stockwell,
London, 1924, 107p, Cloth, Coll.

HOUGH, EMERSON, 1857-1923

07438 *Mother of gold.* D. Appleton, New York, 1924,
327p, Cloth, Novel
07439 *The singing mouse stories.* Forest & Stream
Publishing Co., New York, 1895, 176p, Cloth,
Coll.

HOUGH, RICHARD ALEXANDER
see: CARTER, BRUCE

HOUGH, S. B.
see: GORDON, REX

HOUGHTON, CLAUDE, pseud. [Claude Houghton Oldfield, 1889-1961]

07440 *The beast.* Quota Press, Belfast, 1936, 44p,
Cloth, Story
07441 *Julian Grant loses his way.* William Heinemann,
London, 1933, 332p, Cloth, Novel
07442 *The man who could still laugh.* Bantam Books
(Todd Publishing Co.), London, 1943, 16p,
Paper, Story
07443 *The passing of the third floor back.* Queens-
bury Press, London, 1935, 316p, Cloth, Novel
[based upon the short story and play of the
same title by Jerome K. Jerome]
07444 *This was Ivor Trent.* William Heinemann, London, 1935, 323p, Cloth, Novel
07445 *Three fantastic tales.* F. C. Joiner, London,
1934, 83p, Cloth, Coll.

HOUGHTON, J. A.

07446 *The supreme rulers.* Henry J. Drane, London,
1908, 240p, Cloth, Novel

HOUSE, EDWARD MANDELL, 1858-1938 [published
anonymously]

07447 *Philip Dru, Administrator; a story of tomorrow,
1920-1935.* B. W. Huebsch, New York, 1912,
312p, Cloth, Novel

HOUSEHOLD, GEOFFREY (Edward West), 1900-

07448 *Dance of the dwarfs.* Michael Joseph, London,
1968, 209p, Cloth, Novel
07449 *The terror of Villadonga.* Hutchinson, London,
1936, 160p, Cloth, Novel
07449A retitled: *The Spanish cave.* Little, Brown,
Boston, 1936, 202p, Cloth, Novel

HOUSER, LIONEL (Louis)

07450 *Caress and farewell.* Julian Messner, New York,
1934, 287p, Cloth, Novel

HOUSMAN, CLEMENCE (Annie), 1861-1955

07451   *The were-wolf.* John Lane, The Bodley Head,
        London, 1896, 123p, Cloth, Novel

HOUSMAN, LAURENCE, 1865-1959

07452   *All-Fellows; and, The cloak of friendship.*
        Jonathan Cape, London, 1923, 192p, Cloth,
        Coll.
07453   *All-Fellows; seven legends of lower redemption,*
        with insets in verse. Kegan Paul, Trench,
        Trübner, London, 1896, 138p, Cloth, Coll.
07454   *The field of clover.* Kegan Paul, Trench, Trüb-
        ner, London, 1898, 148p, Cloth, Coll.
07455   *Gods and their makers.* John Lane, The Bodley
        Head, London, 1897, 213p, Cloth, Novel
07456   *Gods and their makers, and other stories.*
        George Allen & Unwin, London, 1920, 221p,
        Cloth, Coll.
07457   *Ironical tales.* Jonathan Cape, London, 1926,
        224p, Cloth, Coll.
07458   *Strange ends and discoveries; tales of this*
        world and the next. Jonathan Cape, London,
        1948, 189p, Cloth, Coll.
07459   *Trimblerigg; a book of revelation.* Jonathan
        Cape, London, 1924, 320p, Cloth, Novel
07460   *What next? provocative tales of faith and*
        morals. Jonathan Cape, London, 1937, 336p,
        Cloth, Coll.

HOUSTON, JAMES D., 1933-

07461   *The adventures of Charlie Bates.* Capra Press,
        Santa Barbara, CA, 1973, 123p, Cloth, Coll.
07462   *An occurrence at Norman's Burger Castle, from*
        The adventures of Charlie Bates. Capra Press,
        Santa Barbara, CA, 1972, 34p, Cloth, Story

HOVORRÈ, M. AUBERRÉ, pseud. [Albert Waldo
Howard]

07463   *The milltillionaire.* The Author, Boston,
        1895?, 30p, Paper, Story

HOW SHE CAME INTO HER KINGDOM
    see: CLAY, CHARLES M.

HOWARD, ALBERT WALDO
    see: HOVORRE, M. AUBERRE

HOWARD, CHARLES F.

07464   *Olympus.* Simpkin, Marshall & Co., London,
        1855, 321p, Cloth, Novel

HOWARD, (Richard) CHRISTOPHER

07465   *Paris prelude.* J. Bale & Co., London, 1932,
        229p, Cloth, Novel

HOWARD, DANA

07466   *Vesta, the Earth born Venusian.* Essene Press,
        Corpus Christi, TX, 1959, 287p, Cloth, Novel

HOWARD, ELIZABETH JANE, 1923-   [*biography*
included], with Robert Aickman

00087   *We are for the dark; six ghost stories.* Jona-
        than Cape, London, 1951, 285p, Cloth, Coll.

HOWARD, GEOFFREY
    see: DIXEY, MARMADUKE

HOWARD, (John) HAYDEN

07467   *The Eskimo invasion.* Ballantine, New York,
        1967, 380p, Paper, Novel

HOWARD, IVAN

07468   *Escape to Earth.* Belmont, New York, 1963,
        173p, Paper, Anth.
07469   *Novelets of science fiction.* Belmont, New Yor
        1963, 173p, Paper, Anth.
07470   *Rare science fiction.* Belmont, New York, 1963
        173p, Paper, Anth.
07471   *6 and the silent scream.* Belmont, New York,
        1963, 173p, Paper, Anth.
07472   *Things.* Belmont, New York, 1964, 157p, Paper,
        Anth.
07473   *Way out.* Belmont, New York, 1963, 173p, Paper
        Anth.
07474   *The weird ones.* Belmont, New York, 1962, 173p
        Paper, Anth. [published anonymously]

HOWARD, KATHARINE, 1858-

07475   *The book of the serpent.* Sherman, French &
        Co., Boston, 1912, 53p, Cloth, Novel

HOWARD, KEBLE, pseud. [John Keble Bell, 1875-
1928]

07476   *The peculiar Major; an almost incredible story*
        Hutchinson, London, 1919, 246p, Cloth, Novel

HOWARD, MAUDE LESSEUR

07477   *Myriam and the mystic brotherhood.* John Wur-
        tele Lovell, New York, 1912, 370p, Cloth,
        Novel

HOWARD, ROBERT E(rvin), 1906-1936

07478   *Almuric.* Ace, New York, 1964, 157p, Paper,
        Novel
07479   *Bran Mak Morn.* Dell, New York, 1969, 192p,
        Paper, Coll.
07480   *The coming of Conan.* Gnome Press, New York,
        1953, 224p, Cloth, Coll. [Conan series]
07481   *Conan the barbarian.* Gnome Press, New York,
        1954, 224p, Cloth, Coll. [Conan series]
07482   *Conan the Conqueror; the Hyborean Age.* Gnome
        Press, New York, 1950, 255p, Cloth, Novel
        [Conan #9]
07483   *Conan the warrior.* Lancer, New York, 1967,
        222p, Paper, Coll. [Conan #7]
07484   *The Dark Man, and others.* Arkham House, Sauk
        City, 1963, 284p, Cloth, Coll.

HOWARD, ROBERT E. (cont.)

07485 *Etchings in ivory; poems in prose.* Glenn Lord, Pasadena, TX, 1968, 26p, Paper, Coll.
The hand of Kane. [see 07489B]

07486 *King Conan; the Hyborean Age.* Gnome Press, New York, 1953, 255p, Cloth, Coll. [Conan series]

07487 *Marchers of Valhalla.* Donald M. Grant, Publisher, West Kingston, RI, 1972, 121p, Cloth, Coll.
The moon of skulls. [see 07489A]

07488 *The people of the black circle.* Donald M. Grant, Publisher, West Kingston, RI, 1974, 149p, Cloth, Coll. [Conan series]

07489 *Red shadows.* Donald M. Grant, West Kingston, RI, 1968, 381p, Cloth, Coll.

07489A retitled: *The moon of skulls.* Centaur, New York, 1969, 127p, Paper, Coll. [Solomon Kane #1] [abridged]

07489B retitled: *The hand of Kane.* Centaur, New York, 1970, 127p, Paper, Coll. [Solomon Kane #2] [abridged]

07489C retitled: *Solomon Kane.* Centaur, New York, 1971, 126p, Paper, Coll. [Solomon Kane #3] [abridged; 07489A, 07489B, and 07489C together comprise the original volume]

07490 *Skull-face, and others.* Arkham House, Sauk City, 1946, 475p, Cloth, Coll.

07490A retitled: *Skull face omnibus.* Neville Spearman, Jersey, Channel Islands, 1974, 475p, Cloth, Coll.

07491 *The sword of Conan; the Hyborean Age.* Gnome Press, New York, 1952, 251p, Cloth, Coll. [Conan series]

07492 *Tigers of the sea.* Donald M. Grant, Publisher, West Kingston, RI, 1974, 212p, Cloth, Coll.

07493 *Wolfshead.* Lancer, New York, 1968, 190p, Paper, Coll.

07494 *Worms of the Earth.* Donald M. Grant, Publisher, West Kingston, RI, 1974, 233p, Cloth, Coll.

with Lin Carter:

02741 *King Kull.* Lancer, New York, 1967, 223p, Paper, Coll.

with L. Sprague de Camp:

03986 *Conan the adventurer.* Lancer, New York, 1966, 224p, Paper, Coll. [Conan #5]

03987 *Conan the freebooter.* Lancer, New York, 1968, 223p, Paper, Coll. [Conan #3]

03988 *Conan the usurper.* Lancer, New York, 1967, 256p, Paper, Coll. [Conan #8]

03989 *Tales of Conan.* Gnome Press, New York, 1955, 219p, Cloth, Coll. [Conan series]

with L. Sprague de Camp and Lin Carter:

02742 *Conan.* Lancer, New York, 1967, 221p, Paper, Coll. [Conan #1]

02743 *Conan of Cimmeria.* Lancer, New York, 1969, 189p, Paper, Coll. [Conan #2]

02744 *Conan the wanderer.* Lancer, New York, 1968, 222p, Paper, Coll. [Conan #4]

with L. Sprague de Camp and Björn Nyberg:

03990 *Conan the avenger.* Lancer, New York, 1968, 192p, Paper, Coll. [see also 03992]

HOWARD, TROY, pseud.
see: PAINE, LAURAN

HOWDEN SMITH, ARTHUR D.
see: SMITH, ARTHUR D. HOWDEN

HOWATCH, SUSAN, 1940- [*biography included*]

07495 *The devil on Lammas Night.* Ace, New York, 1970, 190p, Paper, Novel

07496 *The waiting sands; and, The devil on Lammas Night.* Stein & Day, New York, 1974?, 402p, Cloth, Coll. [*The waiting sands* is not SF]

HOWE, BEA, 1898-

07497 *A fairy leapt upon my knee.* Chatto & Windus, London, 1927, 191p, Cloth, Novel

HOWELL, GEORGE ROGERS, 1833-1899

07498 *Noah's log book; how two Americans blasted the ice on Mt. Ararat and found Noah's Ark and some curious relics.* F. Tennyson Neely, New York, 1898, 345p, Cloth, Coll.

HOWELL, SCOTT

07499 *Menace from Magor.* Robert Hale, London, 1974, 190p, Cloth, Novel

HOWELLS, W(illiam) D(ean), 1837-1920

07500 *Between the dark and the daylight; romances.* Harper & Bros., New York, 1907, 185p, Cloth, Coll.

07501 *Questionable shapes.* Harper & Bros., New York, 1903, 219p, Cloth, Coll.

07502 *The seen and unseen at Stratford-on-Avon; a fantasy.* Harper & Bros., New York, 1914, 112p, Cloth, Novel

with Henry Mills Alden:

00116 *Shapes that haunt the dusk; Harper's novelettes.* Harper & Bros., New York, 1907, 301p, Cloth, Anth.

HOWORTH, MURIEL K. [*biography included*]

07503 *This is armageddon.* Arthur H. Stockwell, London, 1939, 288p, Cloth, Novel

HOYLE, (Sir) FRED, 1915- [*biography included*]

07504 *The Black Cloud.* Heinemann, London, 1957, 250p, Cloth, Novel

07505 *Element 79.* New American Library, New York, 1967, 180p, Cloth, Coll.

07506 *October the First is too late.* Heinemann, London, 1966, 200p, Cloth, Novel

07507 *Ossian's ride.* Heinemann, London, 1959, 252p, Cloth, Novel

with John Elliot:

04787 *A for Andromeda; a novel of tomorrow.* Souvenir Press, London, 1962, 206p, Cloth, Tele. [Andromeda #1]

04788 *Andromeda breakthrough; a novel of tomorrow's universe.* Souvenir Press, London, 1964, 192p, Cloth, Tele. [Andromeda #2]

HOYLE, FRED (cont.), with Geoffrey Hoyle

07508   *Fifth planet*. Heinemann, London, 1963, 218p, Cloth, Novel

07509   *The inferno*. Heinemann, London, 1973, 210p, Cloth, Novel

07510   *Into deepest space*. Harper & Row, New York, 1974, 215p, Cloth, Novel

07511   *The molecule men; and, The monster of Loch Ness*. Heinemann, London, 1971, 255p, Cloth, Coll.

07511A   retitled: *The molecule men*. Harper & Row, New York, 1972, 254p, Cloth, Coll.

07512   *Rockets in Ursa Major; a novel*. Heinemann, London, 1969, 169p, Cloth, Novel

07513   *Seven steps to the Sun*. Heinemann, London, 1970, 247p, Cloth, Novel

HOYLE, GEOFFREY, 1941-   [*biography included*], with Fred Hoyle

07508   *Fifth planet*. Heinemann, London, 1963, 218p, Cloth, Novel

07509   *The inferno*. Heinemann, London, 1973, 210p, Cloth, Novel

07510   *Into deepest space*. Harper & Row, New York, 1974, 215p, Cloth, Novel

07511   *The molecule men; and, The monster of Loch Ness*. Heinemann, London, 1971, 255p, Cloth, Coll.

07511A   retitled: *The molecule men*. Harper & Row, New York, 1972, 254p, Cloth, Coll.

07512   *Rockets in Ursa Major; a novel*. Heinemann, London, 1969, 169p, Cloth, Novel

07513   *Seven steps to the Sun*. Heinemann, London, 1970, 247p, Cloth, Novel

HOYNE, THOMAS TEMPLE, 1875-1946

07514   *Intrigue on the Upper Level; a story of crime, love, adventure, and revolt in 2050 A.D.* Reilly & Lee, Chicago, 1934, 292p, Cloth, Novel

HUBBARD, L(aFayette) RON(ald), 1911-

07515   *Death's deputy*. Fantasy Publishing Co., Los Angeles, 1948, 167p, Cloth, Novel

07516   *Fear; an outstanding psychological science fiction novel*. Galaxy SF Novel, New York, 1957, 125p, Paper, Novel

07517   *Fear; and, The ultimate adventure*. Berkley Medallion, New York, 1970, 221p, Paper, Coll.

07518   *Final blackout*. Hadley Publishing Co., Providence, RI, 1948, 154p, Cloth, Novel

07519   *From death to the stars*. Fantasy Publishing Co., Los Angeles, 1952, 375p, Cloth, Coll. [includes *Death's deputy* and *The kingslayer*]

07520   *The kingslayer*. Fantasy Publishing Co., Los Angeles, 1949, 208p, Cloth, Coll.

07521   *Ole Doc Methuselah*. Theta Press, Austin, TX, 1970, 176p, Cloth, Coll.

07522   *Return to tomorrow*. Ace, New York, 1954, 157p, Paper, Novel

07523   *Slaves of sleep*. Shasta Publishers, Chicago, 1948, 207p, Cloth, Novel

07524   *Triton; and, Battle of wizards*. Fantasy Publishing Co., Los Angeles, 1949, 172p, Cloth, Coll.

07525   *Two science fantasy novels by L. Ron Hubbard; Typewriter in the sky; Fear*. Gnome Press, New York, 1951, 256p, Cloth, Coll.

HUBBARD, RICHARD
    see: STRATTON, CHRIS

HUBBARD, T(homas) O'B(rien), 1882-

07526   *To-morrow is a new day; a fantasy*. privately printed, Kyrenia?, 1933, 109p, Cloth?, Novel

HUBBARD, WYNANT DAVIS, 1900-1961

07527   *The thousandth frog; a scientific fantasy*. Blackie & Son, London, 1935, 233p, Cloth, Novel

HUDDLESTON, GEORGE, 1862-1944

07528   *The white fakir; a tale of the mystical east*. Ocean Publishing Co., London, 1932, 244p, Cloth, Novel

HUDSON, ROBERT

07529   *Beyond the dragon temple*. Thomas Nelson & Sons, London, 1913, 364p, Cloth, Novel

HUDSON, W(illiam) H(enry), 1841-1922

07530   *A crystal age*. T. Fisher Unwin, London, 1887, 287p, Cloth, Novel [published anonymously]

07530A   *A crystal age*, by W. H. Hudson. T. Fisher Unwin, London, 1906, 316p, Cloth, Novel

07531   *Green mansions; a romance of the tropical forest*. Duckworth, London, 1904, 315p, Cloth, Novel

HUEFFER, (Joseph Leopold) FORD (Hermann) MADO, 1873-1939

07532   *The 'Half Moon'; a romance of the old world and the new*. Eveleigh Nash, London, 1909, 346p, Cloth, Novel

07533   *Ladies whose bright eyes; a romance*. Constable, London, 1911, 363p, Cloth, Novel

as Ford Madox Ford:

07534   *Vive le roy; a novel*. J. B. Lippincott, Philadelphia, 1936, 342p, Cloth, Novel

as Ford Madox Ford, with Joseph Conrad:

03318   *The inheritors; an extravagant story*. William Heinemann, London, 1901, 324p, Cloth, Novel

HUEMER, DICK [Richard Martin Huemer, 1898- with Joe Grant

06228   *Baby Weems*. Doubleday, Doran, Garden City, 1941, 66p, Cloth, Movie

HUGHART, SARAH

07535   *The girl from yesterday.* Avon, New York, 1970,
          190p, Paper, Novel

HUGHES, (John) CLEDWYN, 1920-   [*biography
included*]

07536   *He dared not look behind.* A. A. Wyn, New
          York, 1947, 159p, Cloth, Novel

HUGHES, DEN(n)IS (Talbot)

07537   *The Earth invasion battalion.* Curtis Warren,
          London, 1950, 128p, Paper, Novel
07538   *Formula 695.* Curtis Warren, London, 1950?,
          128p, Paper, Novel
07539   *Moon war.* Curtis Warren, London, 1951, 128p,
          Paper, Novel
07540   *Murder by Telecopter.* Curtis Warren, London,
          1950, 127p, Paper, Novel
07541   *War lords of space.* Curtis Warren, London,
          1950, 128p, Paper, Novel

as Ray Barry:

07542   *Blue Peril.* Curtis Warren, London, 1952,
          128p, Paper, Novel
07543   *Death dimension.* Curtis Warren, London,
          1952?, 112p, Paper, Novel
07544   *Gamma product.* Curtis Warren, London, 1952,
          127p, Paper, Novel
07545   *Humanoid puppets.* Curtis Warren, London, 1952,
          127p, Paper, Novel
07546   *Ominous folly.* Curtis Warren, London, 1952,
          112p, Paper, Novel

as Berl Cameron, house pseud.:

02468   *Lost aeons.* Curtis Warren, London, 1953,
          159p, Cloth, Novel

as Dee Carter:

07547   *Blue Cordon.* Curtis Warren, London, 1952,
          128p, Cloth, Novel
07548   *Chloroplasm.* Curtis Warren, London, 1952,
          159p, Cloth, Novel
07549   *Purple islands.* Curtis Warren, London, 1953,
          159p, Cloth, Novel

as Neil Charles, house pseud.:

02886   *The Land of Esa.* Curtis Warren, London, 1952,
          128p, Cloth, Novel
02892   *Twenty-four hours.* Curtis Warren, London,
          1952, 128p, Cloth, Novel

as Lee Elliot, house pseud.:

04789   *Bio-Muton.* Curtis Warren, London, 1952, 128p,
          Cloth, Novel

as Gill Hunt, house pseud.:

07550   *Elektron Union.* Curtis Warren, London,
          1951, 112p, Paper, Novel
07551   *Hostile worlds.* Curtis Warren, London, 1951,
          112p, Paper, Novel
07552   *Planet X.* Curtis Warren, London, 1951, 112p,
          Paper, Novel
07553   *Space flight.* Curtis Warren, London, 1951,
          111p, Paper, Novel
07554   *Spatial ray.* Curtis Warren, London, 1951,
          111p, Paper, Novel

as Brad Kent, house pseud.:

07555   *Biology "A."* Curtis Warren, London, 1952,
          128p, Paper, Novel
07556   *Catalyst.* Curtis Warren, London, 1952?, 112p,
          Paper, Novel
07557   *The fatal law.* Curtis Warren, London, 1952,
          112p, Paper, Novel

as John Lane, house pseud.:

07558   *Maid of Thuro.* Curtis Warren, London, 1952,
          128p, Cloth, Novel

as Van Reed, house pseud.:

07559   *House of many changes.* Curtis Warren, London,
          1952, 128p, Cloth, Novel

as Russell Rey, house pseud.:

07560   *The queen people.* Curtis Warren, London, 1952,
          127p, Cloth, Novel

HUGHES, DOROTHY B(elle), 1904-

07561   *The delicate ape.* Duell, Sloan & Pearce, New
          York, 1944, 252p, Cloth, Novel

HUGHES, FIELDEN
     see: ENFIELD, HUGH

HUGHES, JAMES, 1937-

07562   *Ends.* Alfred A. Knopf, New York, 1971, 227p,
          Cloth, Novel

HUGHES, PETER TUESDAY, pseud.

07563   *Alien.* Pleasure Reader, San Diego, 1972, 155p,
          Paper, Novel
07564   *Remake.* Greenleaf Classics, San Diego, 1971,
          188p, Paper, Novel

HUGHES, RICHARD (Arthur Warren), 1900-1976
[*biography included*]

07565   *A moment of time.* Chatto & Windus, London,
          1926, 243p, Cloth, Coll.

HUGHES, RILEY

07566   *The hills were liars; a novel.* Bruce Publi-
          shing Co., Milwaukee, 1955, 250p, Cloth,
          Novel

HUGHES, RODNEY

07567   *The dragon keepers.* Popular Library, New York,
          1974, 207p, Paper, Novel

HUGHES, RUPERT, 1872-1956

07568   *Destiny.* Harper & Bros., New York, 1925, 385p,
          Cloth, Novel

HUGHES, WALTER LLEWELLYN
     see: WALTERS, HUGH

HUGHES, WILLIAM

07569   *Lust for a vampire.* Spher. ondon, 1971,
159p, Paper, Movie

HUGHES, ZACH, pseud. [Hugh Zachary, 1928-   ]
[*biography included*]

07570   *The book of Rack the Healer.* Award, New York,
1973, 184p, Paper, Novel
07571   *The legend of Miaree.* Ballantine, New York,
1974, 187p, Paper, Novel
07572   *Seed of the gods.* Berkley Medallion, New
York, 1974, 157p, Paper, Novel
07573   *Tide.* Berkley Publishing Corp., New York,
1974, 192p, Cloth, Novel

as Pablo Kane:

07574   *A Dick for all seasons.* Ophelia Press, New
York, 1970, 190p, Paper, Novel

as Peter Kanto:

07575   *Rosy cheeks.* Bee-Line, New York, 1969, 184p,
Paper, Novel
07576   *The world where sex was born.* Ophelia Press,
New York, 1968, 164p, Paper, Novel

as Hugh Zachary:

07577   *Gwen, in green.* Fawcett Gold Medal, Greenwich,
1974, 191p, Paper, Novel

HUGI, MAURICE GASPARD, as Brad Kent, house
pseud.

07578   *Out of the silent places.* Curtis Warren,
London, 1952, 127p, Paper, Novel

HUGO, VICTOR (Marie, Comte), 1802-1885

07579   *The story of the bold Pécopin; a legend of the
Rhine.* Smith, Elder, London, 1902, 92p,
Cloth, Novel

HUIDOBRO (Fernández), VICENTE (García), 1893-
1948

07580   *Mirror of a mage.* Houghton Mifflin, Boston,
1931, 185p, Cloth, Novel

HULKE, MALCOLM, 1924-   [*biography included*]

07581   *Doctor Who and the cave-monsters.* Target,
London, 1974, 158p, Paper, Tele. [Doctor
Who #5]
07582   *Doctor Who and the doomsday weapon.* Target,
London, 1974, 166p, Paper, Tele. [Doctor
Who #6]
07583   *Doctor Who and the Sea-Devils.* Target, London,
1974, 139p, Paper, Tele. [Doctor Who #9]

with Terrance Dicks:

04345   *The making of Doctor Who.* Piccolo, London,
1972, 115p, Paper, Nonf.

HULL, E(dna) MAYNE, 1905-1975 [*biography included*], with A. E. van Vogt

07584   *Out of the unknown.* Fantasy Publishing Co.,
Los Angeles, 1948, 141p, Cloth, Coll.
07585   *Out of the unknown.* Powell Publications, Res
da, CA, 1969, 222p, Paper, Coll. [includes
one additional story]
07585A   retitled: *The sea thing, and other stories;
science fiction.* Sidgwick & Jackson, Londo
1970, 222p, Cloth, Coll.
07586   *Planets for sale*, by E. Mayne Hull. Frederic
Fell, New York, 1954, 192p, Cloth, Novel
07586A   *Planets for sale*, by E. Mayne Hull and A. E.
van Vogt. Book Company of America, Beverly
Hills, CA, 1965, 171p, Paper, Novel
     The sea thing, and other stories. [see 07585
07587   *A van Vogt omnibus; 'Planets for sale' (with
Mayne Hull); 'The beast'; 'The book of Ptat
Sidgwick & Jackson, London, 1967, 498p, Clo
Coll.
07588   *van Vogt omnibus (2).* Sidgwick & Jackson, Lo
don, 1971, 512p, Cloth, Coll. [includes *Sla
The mind cage; The winged man*]
07589   *The winged man.* Doubleday, Garden City, 1966
190p, Cloth, Novel

HULME-BEAMAN, EMERIC

07590   *The experiment of Doctor Nevill; a novel.* Jo
Long, London, 1900, 317p, Cloth, Novel
07591   *Ozmar the mystic; a novel.* Bliss, Sands, Lon
don, 1896, 378p, Cloth, Novel

HUME, CYRIL, 1900-1966

07592   *The golden dancer.* George H. Doran, New York
1926, 261p, Cloth, Novel
07593   *Myself and the young bowman, and other fantasies.* Doubleday, Doran, Garden City, 1932,
166p, Cloth, Coll. [includes some verse]

HUME, FERGUS(on Wright), 1859-1932

07594   *Aladdin in London; a romance.* Adam & Charles
Black, London, 1892, 432p, Cloth, Novel
07595   *The Blue Talisman; a detective story.* T. Wer
ner Laurie, London, 1912, 323p, Cloth, Nove
07596   *The dwarf's chamber, and other stories.* Ward
Lock & Bowden, London, 1896, 386p, Cloth,
Coll.
07597   *The expedition of Captain Flick; a story of
adventure.* Jarrold & Sons, London, 1896,
363p, Cloth, Novel
07598   *For the defense.* Rand, McNally, Chicago, 189
254p, Cloth, Novel
07599   *The gentleman who vanished; a psychological
phantasy.* F. V. White, London, 1890, 102p,
Cloth, Novel
07599A   retitled: *The man who vanished; a psychologi
phantasy.* Liberty Book Co., New York, 1892
170p, Cloth, Novel
07599B   retitled: *The man that vanished.* George Mun
New York, 1892, 116p, Paper, Novel
07600   *The harlequin opal; a romance.* W. H. Allen,
London, 1893, 3vol, Cloth, Novel
     The man that vanished. [see 07599B]
     The man who vanished. [see 07599A]
07601   *The mother of emeralds.* Hurst & Blackett, Lo
don, 1901, 337p, Cloth, Novel

HUME, FERGUS (cont.)

07602 *The sacred herb*. John Long, London, 1908,
         319p, Cloth, Novel
07603 *A son of perdition; an occult romance*. Wil-
         liam Rider & Son, London, 1912, 403p, Cloth,
         Novel
07604 *The year of miracle; a tale of the year one
         thousand nine hundred*. George Routledge &
         Sons, London, 1891, 148p, Cloth, Novel

HUMPHREYS, LESLIE GEORGE
     see: CONDRAY, BRUNO G.

HUMPHRIES, (George) ROLFE, 1894-1969 [*biography included*], with Marjorie Fischer

05431 *Pause to wonder; stories of the marvelous, mys-
         terious, and strange*. Julian Messner, New
         York, 1944, 572p, Cloth, Anth.
05432 *Strange to tell; stories of the marvelous and
         mysterious*. Julian Messner, New York, 1946,
         532p, Cloth, Anth.

HUNEKER, JAMES (Gibbons), 1857-1921

07605 *Visionaries*. T. Werner Laurie, London, 1905,
         342p, Cloth, Coll.

HUNGER, ANNA, with R. DeWitt Miller

07606 *The man who lived forever*. Ace Double, New
         York, 1956, 137p, Paper, Novel
07606A retitled: *Year 3097*. Satellite, London,
         1958, 128p, Paper, Novel

HUNGERFORD, Mrs. (Margaret Wolfe) [The Duch-
ess], 1855?-1897

07607 *The professor's experiment; a novel*. Chatto
         & Windus, London, 1895, 3vol, Cloth, Novel

HUNT, BARBARA, 1907-   [*biography included*]

07608 *Sea change*. Rinehart & Co., New York, 1946,
         270p, Cloth, Novel

as Barbara H. Watters:

07608A *Sea change; the evolution of a witch*. Val-
         halla Paperbacks, Washington, 1970, 270p,
         Paper, Novel

HUNT, E. HOWARD
     see: ST. JOHN, DAVID

HUNT, GILL, house pseud. [see also: John Brunner, David Arthur Griffiths, Dennis Talbot
Hughes, John William Jennison, E. C. Tubb]

07550 *Elektron Union*. Curtis Warren, London, 1951,
         112p, Paper, Novel [by Dennis Hughes]
06397 *Fission*. Curtis Warren, London, 1952?, 111p,
         Paper, Novel [by David Griffiths]
02075 *Galactic storm*. Curtis Warren, London, 1951,
         110p, Paper, Novel [by John Brunner]

07551 *Hostile worlds*. Curtis Warren, London, 1951,
         112p, Paper, Novel [by Dennis Hughes]
07552 *Planet X*. Curtis Warren, London, 1951, 112p,
         Paper, Novel [by Dennis Hughes]
07609 *Planetfall*. Curtis Warren, London, 1951, 111p,
         Paper, Novel [by E. C. Tubb]
07553 *Space flight*. Curtis Warren, London, 1951,
         111p, Paper, Novel [by Dennis Hughes]
07554 *Spatial ray*. Curtis Warren, London, 1951, 111p,
         Paper, Novel [by Dennis Hughes]
07610 *Station 7*. Curtis Warren, London, 1952, 112p,
         Paper, Novel [by John Jennison]
06398 *Vega*. Curtis Warren, London, 1951, 111p,
         Paper, Novel [by David Griffiths]
07611 *Zero field*. Curtis Warren, London, 1952?,
         112p, Paper, Novel [by John Jennison]

HUNT, LAURA SHELLABARGER

07612 *Ultra; a story of pre-natal influence*. Times-
         Mirror Press, Los Angeles, 1923, 365p, Cloth,
         Novel

HUNT, (James Henry) LEIGH, 1784-1859

07613 *Tales by Leigh Hunt*. W. Paterson, London,
         1891, 388p, Cloth, Coll.

as James Sprat:

07614 *The rebellion of the beasts; or, The ass is
         dead, long live the ass!!!* J. & H. L. Hunt,
         London, 1825, 166p, Cloth, Novel

HUNT, (Isobel) VIOLET, 1866-1942

07615 *More tales of the uneasy*. William Heinemann,
         London, 1925, 287p, Cloth, Coll.
07616 *Tales of the uneasy*. William Heinemann, Lon-
         don, 1911, 319p, Cloth, Coll.

HUNTER, EVAN, 1926-   [*biography included*]
[name legally changed from Salvatore A. Lom-
bino]

07617 *Find the feathered serpent*. John C. Winston,
         Philadelphia, 1952, 207p, Cloth, Novel
07618 *Nobody knew they were there*. Doubleday, Gar-
         den City, 1971, 249p, Cloth, Novel

as Hunt Collins:

07619 *Tomorrow's world*. Avalon, New York, 1956,
         223p, Cloth, Novel
07619A retitled: *Tomorrow and tomorrow*. Pyramid,
         New York, 1956, 190p, Paper, Novel

as Richard Marsten:

07620 *Danger: dinosaurs!* John C. Winston, Philadel-
         phia, 1953, 210p, Cloth, Novel
07621 *Rocket to Luna*. John C. Winston, Philadelphia,
         1953, 211p, Cloth, Novel

HUNTER, HELEN

07622 *Magnificent white men*. Vantage Press, New
         York, 1964, 153p, Cloth, Novel

HUNTER, JIM, 1939-   [*biography included*]

07623   *The flame.* Faber & Faber, London, 1966, 279p, Cloth, Novel

HUNTER, MOLLIE, pseud. [Maureen Mollie McIlwraith, 1922-   ] [*biography included*]

07624   *The ferlie.* Blackie & Son, London, 1968, 122p, Cloth, Novel
07625   *The haunted mountain.* Hamish Hamilton, London, 1972, 127p, Cloth, Novel
07626   *The kelpie's pearls.* Blackie & Son, London, 1964, 107p, Cloth, Novel
07627   *A sound of chariots.* Harper & Row, New York, 1972, 242p, Cloth, Novel
07628   *The stronghold.* Hamish Hamilton, London, 1974, 205p, Cloth, Novel
07629   *Thomas and the warlock.* Blackie & Son, London, 1967, 108p, Cloth, Novel
07630   *The walking stones; a story of suspense.* Harper & Row, New York, 1970, 143p, Cloth, Novel

HUNTER, N(orman) C(harles), 1908-1971

07631   *The ascension of Mr. Judson; a novel.* Robert Hale, London, 1950, 237p, Cloth, Novel

HUNTER-BLAIR, JOHN

07632   *War of the Xromatids; the MHT alternative.* Vantage Press, New York, 1974, 218p, Cloth, Novel

HUNTER-DUVAR, JOHN, 1830-1899

07633   *Annals of the court of Oberon, extracted from the records.* Digby, Long, London, 1895, 246p, Cloth, Novel

HUNTING, (Henry) GARDNER, 1872-1958

07634   *The Vicarion.* Unity School of Christianity, Kansas City, MO, 1926, 397p, Cloth, Novel

HUNTINGTON, CHARLES, pseud.?

07635   *Nightmare on Vega 3.* Award, New York, 1973, 155p, Paper, Novel [Space Probe 6 #2]
07636   *The soul stealers.* Award, New York, 1973, 156p, Paper, Novel [Space Probe 6 #1]

HUNTINGTON, EDWARD STANTON
    see: STANTON, EDWARD

HUNTLEY, FLORENCE, d. 1912

07637   *The dream child.* Arena Publishing Co., Boston, 1892, 227p, Cloth, Novel
07638   *The gay Gnani of Gingalee; or, Discords of devolution; a tragical entanglement of modern mysticism and modern science.* Indo-American Book Co., Chicago, 1908, 206p, Cloth, Novel

HURD, DOUGLAS (Richard), 1930-   [*biography included*]

07639   *Truth game.* Collins, London, 1972, 254p, Cloth, Novel

with Andrew Osmond:

07640   *Scotch on the rocks.* Collins, London, 1971, 255p, Cloth, Novel
07641   *Send him victorious.* Collins, London, 1975, 287p, Cloth, Novel
07642   *The smile on the face of the tiger.* Collins, London, 1969, 286p, Cloth, Novel

HURLEY, RICHARD J(ames), 1906-

07643   *Beyond belief.* Scholastic Book Services, New York, 1966, 188p, Paper, Anth.

HURRELL, F(rancis) G(ordon), 1885-

07644   *John Lillibud.* Rich & Cowan, London, 1934, 286p, Cloth, Novel

HURST, FANNIE, 1889-1968 [*biography included*]

07645   *The hands of Veronica; a novel.* Harper & Bro, New York, 1947, 278p, Cloth, Novel

HURT, FREDA (Mary Elizabeth), 1911-

07646   *Benny and the dolphin.* Epworth Press, London, 1968, 128p, Cloth, Novel [Crab Island series]
07647   *Benny and the space boy.* Epworth Press, London, 1970, 134p, Cloth, Novel [Crab Island series]

HURWOOD, BERNHARDT J(ackson), 1926-   [*biography included*]

07648   *Eerie tales of terror and dread.* Scholastic Book Services, New York, 1973, 111p, Paper, Coll.
07649   *The invisibles.* Fawcett Gold Medal, Greenwich, 1971, 192p, Paper, Novel [Invisibles #1]
07650   *The mind master.* Fawcett Gold Medal, Greenwich, 1973, 160p, Paper, Novel [Invisibles #2]
07651   *Monsters galore.* Gold Medal, Greenwich, 1965, 224p, Paper, Anth.
07652   *Passport to the supernatural; an occult compendium from all ages and many lands.* Taplinger Publishing Co., New York, 1972, 319p, Cloth, Anth. [includes some nonf.]

as Mallory T. Knight:

07653   *The bra-burner's brigade.* Award, New York, 1971, 156p, Paper, Novel [Man from T.O.M.C.A.T. #9]
07654   *Dracutwig.* Award, New York, 1969, 156p, Paper, Novel [Dracula series]
07655   *The man from T.O.M.C.A.T.; The dirty rotten depriving ray.* Award, New York, 1967, 191p, Paper, Novel [Man from T.O.M.C.A.T. #4]
07656   *The man from T.O.M.C.A.T.; The dozen deadly dragons of joy.* Award, New York, 1967, 175p, Paper, Novel [Man from T.O.M.C.A.T. #1]

HURWOOD, BERNHARDT J., as Mallory T. Knight (cont.)

07657 *The man from T.O.M.C.A.T.; The malignant metaphysical menace.* Award, New York, 1968, 156p, Paper, Novel [Man from T.O.M.C.A.T. #6]

07658 *The man from T.O.M.C.A.T.; The million missing maidens.* Award, New York, 1967, 192p, Paper, Novel [Man from T.O.M.C.A.T. #2]

07659 *The man from T.O.M.C.A.T.; The ominous orgy.* Award, New York, 1969, , Paper, Novel [Man from T.O.M.C.A.T. #7]

07660 *The man from T.O.M.C.A.T.; The Peking pornographer.* Award, New York, 1969, 152p, Paper, Novel [Man from T.O.M.C.A.T. #8]

07661 *The man from T.O.M.C.A.T.; The terrible ten.* Award, New York, 1967, 190p, Paper, Novel [Man from T.O.M.C.A.T. #3]

07662 *The man from T.O.M.C.A.T.; Tsimmis in Tangier.* Award, New York, 1968, 156p, Paper, Novel [Man from T.O.M.C.A.T. #5]

HUSS, ROY (Gerard), 1927- [*biography included*], with T. J. Ross

07663 *Focus on the horror film.* Spectrum Books, Englewood Cliffs, NJ, 1972, 186p, Cloth, Nonf. Anth.

HUSSINGTREE, MARTIN, pseud. [Oliver Ridsdale Baldwin, 1899-]

07664 *Konyetz.* Hodder & Stoughton, London, 1924, 320p, Cloth, Novel

HUTCHINSON, LORING, 1912-

07665 *The secret of Hidden Valley.* Random House, New York, 1956, 240p, Cloth, Novel

HUTCHINSON, R(ay) C(oryton), 1907-1975 [*biography included*]

07666 *Thou hast a devil; a fable.* Ernest Benn, London, 1930, 320p, Cloth, Novel

HUTCHINSON, TOM, 1930-

07667 *Horror & fantasy in the cinema.* Studio Vista, London, 1974, 159p, Cloth, Nonf.

HUXLEY, ALDOUS (Leonard), 1894-1963

07668 *After many a summer dies the swan.* Harper & Bros., New York, 1939, 356p, Cloth, Novel

07668A retitled: *After many a summer.* Chatto & Windus, London, 1939, 314p, Cloth, Novel

07669 *Ape and essence.* Harper & Bros., New York, 1948, 205p, Cloth, Novel

07670 *Brave new world; a novel.* Doubleday, Doran, Garden City, 1932, 311p, Cloth, Novel

07671 *Brave new world; and, Brave new world revisited.* Harper & Bros., New York, 1960, 457p, Cloth, Coll. [*Brave new world revisited* is nonf.]

07672 *Island; a novel.* Harper & Row, New York, 1962, 335p, Cloth, Novel

07673 *Time must have a stop.* Harper & Bros., New York, 1944, 311p, Cloth, Novel

HUYSMANS, JORIS KARL, 1848-1907

07674 *Down there (Là-bas).* Albert & Charles Boni, New York, 1924, 317p, Cloth, Novel

07674A retitled: *Là-bas; a novel.* Fortune Press, London, 1946, 216p, Cloth, Novel

HYAMS, EDWARD (Solomon), 1910-1975 [*biography included*]

07675 *The astrologer; a satirical novel.* Longmans, Green, London, 1950, 244p, Cloth, Novel

07676 *Not in our stars.* Longmans, Green, London, 1949, 287p, Cloth, Novel

HYDE, CHRISTOPHER

07677 *Temple of the Winds.* World Publishing Co., Cleveland, 1965, 254p, Cloth, Novel

HYDE, MARK POWELL

07678 *The strange inventor; a curious adventure story.* Doubleday, Page, Garden City, 1927, 224p, Cloth, Novel

HYDE-CHAMBERS, DEREK

07679 *The orgy of Bubastis.* New English Library, London, 1974, 125p, Paper, Novel

HYDER, ALAN

07680 *Vampires overhead.* Philip Allan, London, 1935, 248p, Cloth, Novel

HYLAND, M. E. F.
see: WYLWYNNE, KYTHE

HYNAM, JOHN CHARLES
see: KIPPAX, JOHN

HYNE, C(harles) J(ohn) CUTCLIFFE (Wright), 1866-1944

07681 *Abbs; his story through many ages.* Hutchinson, London, 1929, 288p, Cloth, Novel

07682 *Beneath your very boots, being a few striking episodes from the life of Anthony Merlwood Haltoun, Esq.* Digby & Long, London, 1889, 388p, Cloth, Novel
Emperor of the world. [see 07683A]

07683 *Empire of the world.* Everett & Co., London, 1910, 314p, Cloth, Novel

07683A retitled: *Emperor of the world; a tale of an Anglo-German war.* George Newnes, London, 1915, 254p, Cloth, Novel

07684 *Ivory valley; an adventure of Captain Kettle.* Ward, Lock, London, 1938, 315p, Cloth, Novel [Capt. Kettle series]

HYNE, C. J. CUTCLIFFE (cont.)

07685   *The lost continent.* Hutchinson, London, 1900,
          368p, Cloth, Novel
07686   *Man's understanding; a volume of short stories.*
          Ward, Lock, London, 1933, 287p, Cloth, Coll.
07687   *The new Eden.* Longmans, Green, London, 1892,
          258p, Cloth, Novel
07688   *The recipe for diamonds.* William Heinemann,
          London, 1893, 241p, Cloth, Novel
07689   *Wishing Smith.* Robert Hale, London, 1939,
          282p, Cloth, Novel

as Weatherby Chesney:

07690   *The adventures of a solicitor.* James Bowden,
          London, 1898, 268p, Cloth, Coll.

HYTES, JASON

07691   *Her magic spell.* Midwood, New York, 1974,
          217p, Paper, Novel

IBANEZ, FELIX MARTI-
     see: MARTI-IBANEZ, FELIX

THE ICE WITCH

07691   *The ice witch; or, The frozen hand.* no publi-
          sher, London?, 1830?, 16p, Paper?, Story

IDDRISSYEH, ACHMED ABDULLAH el-
     see: ABDULLAH, ACHMED

IF I WERE KING GEORGE
     see: HAPPY, THE KING'S DOG

IF; OR, HISTORY REWRITTEN
     see: SQUIRE, J. C.

IGGULDEN, JOHN M(anners), 1917-   [*biography
included*]

07692   *Breakthrough.* Chapman & Hall, London, 1960,
          240p, Cloth, Novel

IGNOTUS, AUCTOR, pseud.
     see: AUCTOR IGNOTUS

ILIOWIZI, HENRY, 1850-1911

07693   *In the pale; stories and legends of the Rus-
          sian Jews.* Jewish Publication Society of
          America, Philadelphia, 1897, 267p, Cloth,
          Coll.
07694   *The weird orient; nine mystic tales.* Henry
          T. Coates, Philadelphia, 1900, 360p, Cloth,
          Coll.

ILTON, PAUL, 1901-1958

07695   *The last days of Sodom and Gomorrah.* Signet,
          New York, 1957, 160p, Paper, Movie

IMBERT, ENRIQUE ANDERSON
     see: ANDERSON IMBERT, ENRIQUE

AN IMPENITENT POLITICIAN
     see: MUIR, RAMSAY

IMPERIAL OVERTURE

07696   *Imperial overture, and other stories.* Pictor-
          al Art, London, 1946, 32p, Paper, Anth.

IN THE FUTURE

07697   *In the future; a sketch in ten chapters.* "Ex-
          press" Office, Hampstead, UK, 1875, 104p,
          Cloth, Novel

INCA-PABLO-OZOLLO, pseud. [Alfred Francis
Sears]

07698   *The lost Inca; the discovery in the vale of
          Inti-Mayu.* Cassell, New York, 1889, 287p,
          Paper, Novel

INCE, R(ichard) B(asil), 1881-

07699   *At the sign of Sagittarius.* Faber & Gwyer,
          London, 1926, 255p, Cloth, Coll.

INDEX TO BRITISH SCIENCE FICTION MAGAZINES

07700   *Index to British science fiction magazines,
          1934-1953.* Australian Science Fiction Assoc-
          ation, Canberra City, 1968/71, 176p in five
          parts, Paper, Nonf.

INDEX TO PERRY RHODAN

07701   *Index to Perry Rhodan, U.S. edition, 1-25.*
          NESFA Press, Cambridge, Mass., 1973, 12p,
          Paper, Nonf.

AN INDEX TO UNKNOWN AND UNKNOWN WORLDS
     see: HOFFMAN, STUART

INGALESE, ISABELLA, 1855-

07702   *Linked lives; a tale of yesterday and to-day.*
          Occult Book Concern, New York, 1903, 232p,
          Cloth, Novel
07703   *Mata the magician; a romance of the new era.*
          Abbey Press, New York, 1901, 183p, Cloth,
          Novel

INGHAM, FREDERIC, pseud.
     see: HALE, EDWARD EVERETT

INGLEFIELD, ELEANOR

07704   *The gates of Paradise; short stories with un-
          canny endings.* Regency Press, London, 1970,
          142p, Cloth, Coll.

INGRAHAM, Rev. J(oseph) H(olt), 1809-1860

07705   *The pillar of fire; or, Israel in bondage.*
      Pudney & Russell, New York, 1859, 600p,
      Cloth, Novel

INGRAM, ANNE (Whitten) BOWER, 1937-   [*biography included*]

07706   *Shudders and shakes; ghostly tales from Aus-
      tralia.* Collins, Sydney, 1972, 176p, Cloth,
      Anth.

INGRAM, ELEANOR M(arie), 1886-1921

07707   *The Thing from the lake.* J. B. Lippincott,
      Philadelphia, 1921, 315p, Cloth, Novel

INGRAM, (Archibald) KENNETH, 1882-1965 [*biography included*]

07708   *Midsummer sanity.* Philip Allan, London, 1933,
      296p, Cloth, Novel
07709   *The premier tells the truth.* Quality Press,
      London, 1944, 164p, Cloth, Novel

INGRAM, TOM [Thomas Henry Ingram, 1924-   ]

07710   *The hungry cloud.* Collins, London, 1971,
      192p, Cloth, Novel
07710A retitled: *Garranane.* Bradbury Press, Scars-
      dale, NY, 1972, 191p, Cloth, Novel

INGREY, DEREK

07711   *Pig on a lead.* Faber & Faber, London, 1963,
      252p, Cloth, Novel

"INGULPHUS," pseud. [Arthur Gray, 1852-1940]

07712   *Tedious brief tales of Granta and Gramarye.*
      W. Heffer & Sons, Cambridge; Simpkin, Mar-
      shall, Hamilton, Kent, London, 1919, 93p,
      Cloth, Coll.

INMAN, H(erbert) ESCOTT-

07713   *Wulnoth the Wanderer; a story of King Alfred
      of England.* Ward, Lock, London, 1908, 336p,
      Cloth, Novel

THE INNER LANDSCAPE

07714   *The inner landscape.* Allison & Busby, London,
      1969, 151p, Cloth, Anth.

INNES, J. W. BRODIE-
    see: BRODIE-INNES, J. W.

THE INTELLIGENCE OFFICER, pseud.
    see: JAMES, LIONEL

INTO THE FOURTH DIMENSION

07715   *Into the fourth dimension, and other stories.*
      Gerald G. Swan, London, 1943, 128p, Paper,
      Anth.

THE INVADERS

07716   *The invaders.* American Science Fiction, Syd-
      ney, 1953, 34p, Paper, Anth.

THE INVASION OF 1883

07717   *The invasion of 1883.* J. Maclehose, Glasgow,
      1876, 62p, Paper?, Novel

THE INVASION OF ENGLAND, TOLD TWENTY YEARS
AFTER
    see: BUTLER, W. F.

INVESTIGATIONS AND EXPERIENCE OF M. SHAWTIN-
BACH, AT SAAR SOONG, SUMATRA
    see: SMILIE, ELTON R.

IONEL, pseud. [Yuval Ronn]

07718   *Godd; a novel.* Macmillan, New York, 1972, 262p,
      Cloth, Novel

IONESCO, EUGÈNE, 1912-   [*biography included*]

07719   *The colonel's photograph.* Faber & Faber, Lon-
      don, 1967, 178p, Cloth, Coll.

IPCAR, DAHLOV, 1917-   [*biography included*]

07720   *The Queen of Spells.* Viking Press, New York,
      1973, 155p, Cloth, Novel
07721   *The Warlock of Night.* Viking Press, New York,
      1969, 160p, Cloth, Novel

IRELAND, MICHAEL
    see: FIGGIS, DARRELL

IRELAND, (Samuel) W(illiam) H(enry), 1777-1835

07722   *Gondez the monk; a romance of the thirteenth
      century.* Longman, Hurst, Rees & Orme, London,
      1805, 4vol in two, Cloth, Novel

IRESON, BARBARA, 1927-   [*biography included*]

07723   *Haunting tales.* Faber & Faber, London, 1973,
      279p, Cloth, Anth.

THE IRRATIONALS

07724   *The irrationals.* American Science Fiction,
      Sydney, 1955, 34p, Paper, Anth.

IRVINE, A(ndrew) A(lexander), 1871-1939

07725   *The devil's finger.* John Murray, London, 1937,
        320p, Cloth, Novel

IRVINE, A(my) M(ary), 1866-

07726   *The dreams of Orlow.* George Allen & Unwin,
        London, 1916, 256p, Cloth, Novel

IRVINE, G(ilbert) M(arshall)

07727   *In the valley of vision.* Simpkin, Marshall,
        Hamilton, Kent, London, 1911, 155p, Cloth,
        Novel

IRVING, COMPTON
    see: CARTER, JOHN LOUIS JUSTIN

IRVING, WASHINGTON, 1783-1859

07728   *The bold dragon, and other ghostly tales.*
        Alfred A. Knopf, New Amsterdam [i.e., New
        York], 1930, 240p, Cloth, Coll.
07729   *Rip Van Winkle; a posthumous writing of Died-
        rich Knickerbocker.* J. Cundall, London,
        1850, 31p, Cloth, Story

IRWIN, BERNICE PIILANI

07730   *In Menehune land.* Printshop Co., Honolulu,
        1936, 136p, Cloth, Coll.

IRWIN, H. C.
    see: TIME, MARK

IRWIN, INEZ HAYNES, 1873-1970

07731   *Out of the air.* Harcourt, Brace & Co., New
        York, 1921, 269p, Cloth, Novel

as Inez Haynes Gillmore:

05998   *Angel Island.* Henry Holt, New York, 1914,
        351p, Cloth, Novel

IRWIN, MARGARET (Emma Faith), d. 1967

07732   *Bloodstock, and other stories.* Chatto & Win-
        dus, London, 1953, 206p, Cloth, Coll.
07733   *Madame fears the dark; seven stories and a
        play.* Chatto & Windus, London, 1935, 276p,
        Cloth, Coll.
07734   *Still she wished for company.* William Heine-
        mann, London, 1924, 307p, Cloth, Novel
07734A retitled: *Who will remember?* Thomas Seltzer,
        New York, 1924, 293p, Cloth, Novel
07735   *These mortals.* William Heinemann, London,
        1925, 279p, Cloth, Novel
        Who will remember? [see 07734A]

IRWIN, WILL(iam Henry), 1873-1948, with Gelett
Burgess

02215   *The Picaroons.* McClure, Phillips, New York,
        1904, 284p, Cloth, Novel

ISAACS, NEIL D(avid), 1931-   [*biography included*], with Rose A. Zimbardo

07736   *Tolkien and the critics; essays on J. R. R.
        Tolkien's The Lord of the Rings.* University
        of Notre Dame Press, Notre Dame, IN, 1968,
        296p, Cloth, Nonf. Anth.

ISBERT, MARGOT BENARY-
    see: BENARY-ISBERT, MARGOT

ISH-KISHOR, SULAMITH, 1896-1977

07737   *The master of miracle; a new novel of the
        golem.* Harper & Row, New York, 1971, 111p,
        Cloth, Novel

THE ISLAND OF ANARCHY
    see: W., E.

THE ISLAND OF ATLANTIS
    see: THE AUTHOR OF 'ATLANTIS'

IT
    see: DE MORGAN, JOHN

ITH, LILY VAN
    see: VAN ITH, LILY

J., J. J., pseud.

07738   *The blue shirts.* Simpkin, Marshall, Hamilton,
        Kent, London, 1926, 280p, Cloth, Novel

J. A. C. K.
    see: K., J. A. C.

J. M.
    see: MACGREGOR, JOHN

J. S. OF DALE
    see: STIMSON, FREDERIC JESUP

J. W. M.
    see: M., J. W.

JABRAN KHALIL JABRAN
    see: GIBRAN, KAHLIL

JACKS, L(awrence) P(earsall), 1860-1955

07739   *The heroes of Smokeover.* Hodder & Stoughton,
        London, 1926, 318p, Cloth, Novel [Smokeover
        series]

JACKS, L. P. (cont.)

07740 *The last legend of Smokeover.* Hodder & Stoughton, London, 1939, 249p, Cloth, Novel [Smokeover series]

JACKSON, AMBROSE LESTER

07741 *When Shiloh came.* J. S. Ogilvie Publishing Co., New York, 1899, 295p, Cloth, Novel

JACKSON, CHARLES LORING, 1847-1935

07742 *The Gold Point, and other strange stories.* Stratford Co., Boston, 1926, 275p, Cloth, Coll.

JACKSON, EDWARD PAYSON, 1840-1905 [published anonymously]

07743 *A demigod; a novel.* Harper & Bros., New York, 1887, 337p, Cloth, Novel

JACKSON, G(eorge) GIBBARD, 1877-

07744 *Arctic air terror.* Sampson Low, Marston, London, 1937, 250p, Cloth, Novel

JACKSON, GEO(rge) RUSSELL

07745 *Ambergris Island; or, The new El Dorado; a tale of love and adventure in the southern seas.* W. A. Evans & Bro., Boston, 1882, 236p, Cloth, Novel

JACKSON, JAMES W.

07746 *A queen of Amazonia.* Henry Walker, London, 1928, 290p, Cloth, Novel

JACKSON, JOHN WILLIAM, Jr.
see: SILENT, WILLIAM T.

JACKSON, NOEL, 1917-

07747 *The test-tube babies.* Exposition Press, New York, 1974, 318p, Cloth, Novel

JACKSON, SHIRLEY, 1919-1965 [biography included]

07748 *The haunting of Hill House.* Viking Press, New York, 1959, 246p, Cloth, Novel
07749 *The lottery; or, The adventures of James Hardis.* Farrar, Straus & Co., New York, 1949, 306p, Cloth, Coll.

JACKSON, STEPHEN, pseud. [John Stevenson, 1853-]

07750 *The Magic Mantle, and other stories.* M. S. Greene & Co., New York, 1903, 333p, Cloth, Coll.

JACKSON, (Sir) THOMAS GRAHAM, (Bart.), 1835-1924

07751 *Six ghost stories.* John Murray, London, 1919, 243p, Cloth, Coll.

JACOB, PIERS ANTHONY
see: ANTHONY, PIERS

JACOBI, CARL (Richard), 1908- [biography included]

07752 *Disclosures in scarlet.* Arkham House, Sauk City, 1972, 181p, Cloth, Coll.
07753 *Portraits in moonlight.* Arkham House, Sauk City, 1964, 213p, Cloth, Coll.
07754 *Revelations in black.* Arkham House, Sauk City, 1947, 272p, Cloth, Coll.

THE JACOBITE DOCTORS
see: A MEMBER OF THE LEGITIMIST CLUB

JACOBS, HARVEY (Jay), 1930- [biography included]

07755 *The egg of the Glak, and other stories.* Harper & Row, New York, 1969, 276p, Cloth, Coll.

JACOBS, T. C. H., pseud. [Jacques Pendower, 1899-] [biography included]

07756 *The curse of Khatra.* Stanley Paul, London, 1947, 224p, Cloth, Novel
07757 *The Kestrel House mystery.* Stanley Paul, London, 1932, 288p, Cloth, Novel

JACOBSON, DAN, 1929- [biography included]

07758 *The rape of Tamar; a novel.* Weidenfeld & Nicolson, London, 1970, 183p, Cloth, Novel

JACOBSON, SID

07759 *Dirty son of a witch.* Lancer, New York, 1969, 157p, Paper, Novel

JACOMB, C(harles) E(rnest)

07760 *And a new Earth; a romance.* George Routledge & Sons, London, 1926, 239p, Cloth, Novel

JACQUEMARD, SIMONNE, 1922-

07761 *The night watchman.* Holt, Rinehart & Winston, New York, 1964, 142p, Cloth, Novel

JACQUES, NORBERT, 1880-1954

07762 *Dr. Mabuse, master of mystery; a novel.* George Allen & Unwin, London, 1923, 324p, Cloth, Novel

JAEGER, C(yril) K(arel Stuart) [*biography included*]

07763   *The man in the top hat.* Grey Walls Press, London, 1949, 264p, Cloth, Novel

JAEGER, M(URIEL)

07764   *Hermes speaks.* Duckworth, London, 1933, 288p, Cloth, Novel
07765   *The man with six senses*, by M. Jaeger. Leonard & Virginia Woolf, The Hogarth Press, London, 1927, 272p, Cloth, Novel
07766   *The question mark*, by M. Jaeger. Leonard & Virginia Woolf, The Hogarth Press, London, 1926, 252p, Cloth, Novel
07767   *Retreat from armageddon.* Duckworth, London, 1936, 224p, Cloth, Novel

JAFFEE, IRVING (Lincoln), with Mary Jaffee

07768   *Beyond Baker Street.* Luther Norris, Publisher, The Pontine Press, Culver City, CA, 1973, 48p, Paper, Coll.

JAFFEE, MARY (Flora) [*biography included*], with Irving Jaffee

07768   *Beyond Baker Street.* Luther Norris, Publisher, The Pontine Press, Culver City, CA, 1973, 48p, Paper, Coll.

JAKES, JOHN (William), 1932-   [*biography included*]

07769   *The asylum world.* Paperback Library, New York, 1969, 171p, Paper, Novel
07770   *Black in time.* Paperback Library, New York, 1970, 171p, Paper, Novel
07771   *Brak the barbarian.* Avon, New York, 1968, 173p, Paper, Novel [Brak #1]
      Brak the barbarian--The mark of the demons. [see 07772A]
      Brak the barbarian--The sorceress. [see 07773A]
07772   *Brak the barbarian versus the mark of the demons.* Paperback Library, New York, 1969, 159p, Paper, Novel [Brak #3]
07772A retitled: *Brak the barbarian--The mark of the demons.* Tandem, London, 1970, 159p, Paper, Novel [Brak #3]
07773   *Brak the barbarian versus the sorceress.* Paperback Library, New York, 1969, 160p, Paper, Novel [Brak #2]
07773A retitled: *Brak the barbarian--The sorceress.* Tandem, London, 1970, 156p, Paper, Novel [Brak #2]
07774   *Conquest of the planet of the apes.* Award, New York, 1974, 187p, Paper, Movie [Planet of the Apes #4]
07775   *The hybrid.* Paperback Library, New York, 1969, 160p, Paper, Novel
07776   *The last magicians.* Signet, New York, 1969, 190p, Paper, Novel
07777   *Mask of chaos.* Ace, New York, 1970, 134p, Paper, Novel
07778   *Master of the dark gate.* Lancer, New York, 1970, 219p, Paper, Novel [Gavin Black #1]

07779   *Mention my name in Atlantis--being, at last, the true account of the calamitous destruction of the great island kingdom, together with a narrative of its wondrous intercourses with a superior race of other-worldlings, as transcribed from the manuscript of a survivor, Hoptor the vintner, for the enlightenment of a dubious posterity.* DAW, New York, 1972, 142p, Paper, Novel
07780   *Monte Cristo #99.* Curtis, New York, 1970, 176p, Paper, Novel
07781   *On wheels.* Warner Paperback Library, New York, 1973, 174p, Paper, Novel
07782   *The planet wizard.* Ace, New York, 1969, 159p, Paper, Novel [II Galaxy #2]
07783   *Secrets of Stardeep.* Westminster Press, Philadelphia, 1969, 192p, Cloth, Novel
07784   *Six-gun planet.* Paperback Library, New York, 1970, 174p, Paper, Novel
07785   *Time gate.* Westminster Press, Philadelphia, 1972, 174p, Cloth, Novel
07786   *Tonight we steal the Stars.* Ace Double, New York, 1969, 173p, Paper, Novel [II Galaxy #3]
07787   *When the star kings die.* Ace, New York, 1967, 160p, Paper, Novel [II Galaxy #1]
07788   *Witch of the dark gate.* Lancer, New York, 1972, 175p, Paper, Novel [Gavin Black #2]

JAKUBOWSKI, MAXIM

07789   *Nebula; an index.* British Science Fiction Association, London?, 1963, 18p, Paper, Nonf.

JAMES, DOLAN

07790   *Space swappers.* Scorpio, North Hollywood, 1970, 190p, Paper, Novel

JAMES, EDWARD (Frank Willis), 1907-

07791   *The gardener who saw God.* Duckworth, London, 1937, 380p, Cloth, Novel

JAMES, G. de S. WENTWORTH-
   see: WENTWORTH-JAMES, G. de S.

JAMES, G(eorge) P(ayne) R(ainsforth), 1801?-1860

07792   *The Castle of Ehrenstein; its lords, spiritual and temporal; its inhabitants, earthly and unearthly.* Smith, Elder, London, 1847, vol. I-303p, II-301p, III-306p, Cloth, Novel
07793   *The commissioner; or, de Lunatico enquirendo.* William Curry Jr., Dublin, 1843, 440p, Cloth Novel [published anonymously]
07794   *The string of pearls*, by the author of "Darnley." Richard Bentley, London, 1832, vol. I-283p, II-282p, Cloth, Coll.

JAMES, GEORGE WHARTON, 1858-1923

07795   *The story of Scraggles.* Little, Brown, Boston 1906, 88p, Cloth, Novel

JAMES, GUNTHAR

07796 *The witch's spell.* Rear Window Series, Sausalito, CA, 1969, 207p, Paper, Novel

JAMES, HENRY, 1843-1916

07797 *The ghostly tales of Henry James.* Rutgers University Press, New Brunswick, NJ, 1948, 766p, Cloth, Coll.
07797A retitled: *Stories of the supernatural.* Taplinger Publishing Co., New York, 1970, 762p, Cloth, Coll.
07798 *The sense of the past.* W. Collins Sons, London, 1917, 350p, Cloth, Novel
Stories of the supernatural. [see 07797A]
07799 *The turn of the screw.* William Heinemann, London, 1898, 169p, Cloth, Novel
07800 *The turn of the screw; and, Daisy Miller.* Dell, New York, 1954, 191p, Paper, Coll.
07801 *The turn of the screw, and other short novels.* Signet Classic, New York, 1962, 452p, Paper, Coll.
07802 *The turn of the screw, and other stories.* Scholastic Book Services, New York, 1966, 316p, Paper, Coll.
07803 *The turn of the screw, and other stories.* Penguin, Harmondsworth, 1969, 204p, Paper, Coll.
07804 *The turn of the screw; The Aspern papers.* J. M. Dent & Sons, London, 1935, 299p, Cloth, Coll.
07805 *The turn of the screw, The Aspern papers, and other stories.* Collins, London, 1956, 480p, Cloth, Coll.
07806 *The turn of the screw; The lesson of the master.* Modern Library, New York, 1930, 211p, Cloth, Coll.
07807 *The two magics; The turn of the screw; The covering end.* Macmillan, New York, 1898, 393p, Cloth, Coll.
07808 *Two short novels.* Prentice-Hall, Englewood Cliffs, NJ, 1963, 110p, Cloth, Coll.

JAMES, (David) JOHN [*biography included*]

07809 *Votan.* Cassell, London, 1966, 233p, Cloth, Novel

JAMES, LAURENCE

07810 *Earth lies sleeping.* Zebra, New York, 1974, 180p, Paper, Novel [Simon Rack #1]
07810A retitled: *Simon Rack; Earth lies sleeping.* Sphere, London, 1974, 159p, Paper, Novel [Simon Rack #1]
07811 *War on Aleph.* Zebra, New York, 1974, 178p, Paper, Novel [Simon Rack #2]
07811A retitled: *Simon Rack; Starcross.* Sphere, London, 1974, 155p, Paper, Novel [Rack #2]

JAMES, LEIGH, pseud.

07812 *The push-button spy.* Prentice-Hall, Englewood Cliffs, NJ, 1970, 314p, Cloth, Novel

JAMES, LIONEL, 1871-1955

07813 *The boy galloper*, by the intelligence officer. William Blackwood & Sons, Edinburgh, 1903, 332p, Cloth, Novel

JAMES, M(ontague) R(hodes), 1862-1936

07814 *Best ghost stories of M. R. James.* World Publishing Co., Cleveland, 1944, 319p, Cloth, Coll.
07815 *The collected ghost stories of M. R. James.* Edward Arnold, London, 1931, 647p, Cloth, Coll.
07815A retitled: *The ghost stories of M. R. James, second edition.* Edward Arnold, London, 1974, 647p, Cloth, Coll.
07816 *The five jars.* Edward Arnold, London, 1922, 172p, Cloth, Novel
07817 *Ghost-stories of an antiquary.* Edward Arnold, London, 1904, 270p, Cloth, Coll.
07818 *Ghost stories of an antiquary.* Penguin, Harmondsworth, 1974, 304p, Paper, Coll. [includes *Ghost stories of an antiquary* and *More ghost stories*]
07819 *Ghost stories of M. R. James.* Folio Society, London, 1973, 208p, Cloth, Coll.
The ghost stories of M. R. James. [see 07815A]
07820 *More ghost stories of an antiquary.* Edward Arnold, London, 1911, 274p, Cloth, Coll.
07820A retitled: *More ghost stories.* Penguin, Harmondsworth, 1959, 152p, Paper, Coll.
07821 *Selected ghost stories of M. R. James.* Editions for the Armed Services, New York, 1944, 352p, Paper, Coll.
07822 *A thin ghost, and others.* Edward Arnold, London, 1919, 152p, Cloth, Coll.
07823 *A warning to the curious, and other ghost stories.* Edward Arnold, London, 1925, 200p, Cloth, Coll.

JAMES, ROWLAND, 1885-

07824 *While England slept; a novel.* John Bale & Sons, London, 1932, 249p, Cloth, Novel

JAMES, WILLIAM

07825 *Dark wisdom, and other tales.* Misfit Press, Farmington, Mich., 1949, 39p, Paper, Coll.

JAMESON, MALCOLM, 1891-1945

07826 *Atomic bomb.* Bond-Charteris, Hollywood, 1945, 128p, Paper, Novel
07827 *Bullard of the Space Patrol.* World Publishing Co., Cleveland, 1951, 255p, Cloth, Coll.
07828 *Tarnished utopia.* Galaxy SF Novel, New York, 1956, 126p, Paper, Novel

JAMESON, (Margaret) STORM, 1891-

07829 *In the second year.* Cassell, London, 1936, 300p, Cloth, Novel
07830 *The moment of truth.* Macmillan, London, 1949, 176p, Cloth, Novel
07831 *Then we shall hear singing; a fantasy in C major.* Cassell, London, 1942, 232p, Cloth, Novel

as William Lamb:

08548 *The world ends.* J. M. Dent & Sons, London, 1937, 204p, Cloth, Novel

JAMESON, TWIGGS, pseud. [James Twiggs, 1933-]

07832 *Billy and Betty; a novel.* Grove Press, New
       York, 1968, 224p, Cloth, Novel

JANE, (John) FRED(erick) T(homas), 1865-1916

07833 *Blake of the "Rattlesnake"; or, The man who
       saved England; a story of torpedo warfare
       in 189-.* Tower Publishing Co., London,
       1895, 269p, Cloth, Novel
07834 *The incubated girl.* Tower Publishing Co.,
       London, 1896, 347p, Cloth, Novel
07835 *To Venus in five seconds, being an account of
       the strange disappearance of Thomas Plummer,
       pill-maker.* A. D. Innes & Co., London,
       1897, 130p, Cloth, Novel
07836 *The violet flame; a story of armageddon and
       after.* Ward, Lock, London, 1899, 245p,
       Cloth, Novel

JANES, H(enry) HURFORD

07837 *The revenge of Frankenstein.* Panther, London,
       1958, 158p, Paper, Movie [Frankenstein
       series]

JANES, HENRY P., with Frederic Arnold Kummer

07838 *The second coming; a vision.* Dodd, Mead,
       New York, 1916, 96p, Cloth, Novel

JANIFER, LAURENCE M., pseud. [Larry Mark Harris, 1933-   ] [*biography included*]

       Bloodworld. [see 07845A]
       18 greatest science fiction stories. [see
          07840C]
07839 *Impossible?* Belmont, New York, 1968, 159p,
       Paper, Coll.
07840 *Masters' choice; the best science-fiction
       stories of all time, chosen by the masters
       of science fiction.* Simon & Schuster, New
       York, 1966, 350p, Cloth, Anth.
07840A retitled: *Masters' choice 1.* Tandem, London,
       1969, 175p, Paper, Anth. [abridged]
07840B retitled: *Masters' choice 2.* Tandem, London,
       1969, 160p, Paper, Anth. [abridged; 07840A
       and 07840B together comprise the original
       volume]
07840C retitled: *18 greatest science fiction stories.*
       Tempo, New York, 1971, 310p, Paper, Anth.
07841 *A piece of Martin Cann.* Belmont, New York,
       1968, 141p, Paper, Novel
07842 *Power.* Dell, New York, 1974, 219p, Paper,
       Novel
07843 *Slave planet; a science fiction novel.* Pyra-
       mid, New York, 1963, 142p, Paper, Novel
07844 *The wonder war.* Pyramid, New York, 1964,
       128p, Paper, Novel [Michael Kurland provided
       some uncredited assistance]
07845 *You sane men.* Lancer, New York, 1965, 159p,
       Paper, Novel
07845A retitled: *Bloodworld.* Lancer, New York,
       1968, 159p, Paper, Novel

as Larry M. Harris, with Randall Garrett:

05807 *Pagan passions.* Galaxy Publishing Corp.,
       New York, 1959, 158p, Paper, Novel

with Randall Garrett as Mark Phillips:

05808 *Brain twister; a science-fiction novel.* Pyra-
       mid, New York, 1962, 144p, Paper, Novel [Ken
       Malone #1]
05809 *The impossibles.* Pyramid, New York, 1963,
       157p, Paper, Novel [Ken Malone #2]
05810 *Supermind.* Pyramid, New York, 1963, 192p,
       Paper, Novel [Ken Malone #3]

with S. J. Treibich:

07846 *The high hex.* Ace Double, New York, 1969, 112p,
       Paper, Novel [Angelo DiStefano #2]
07847 *Target: Terra.* Ace Double, New York, 1968,
       104p, Paper, Novel [Angelo DiStefano #1]
07848 *The wagered world.* Ace Double, New York,
       1969, 79p, Paper, Novel [Angelo DiStefano #3]

JANNEY, RUSSELL, 1884-1963

07849 *The miracle of the bells.* Prentice-Hall, New
       York, 1946, 497p, Cloth, Novel

JANSON, HANK, house pseud.

07850 *Tomorrow and a day.* Alexander Moring, London,
       1955, 160p, Paper, Novel [by Stephen Francis?]
07851 *The unseen assassin.* Alexander Moring, London,
       1956, 159p, Paper, Novel [attributed to
       Reginald Herbert Carter]

JANVIER, THOMAS A(llibone), 1849-1913

07852 *The Aztec treasure-house; a romance of contem-
       poraneous antiquity.* Harper & Bros., New
       York, 1890, 446p, Cloth, Novel
07853 *In the Sargasso Sea; a novel.* Harper & Bros.,
       New York, 1898, 293p, Cloth, Novel

JARDINE, JACK
   see: MADDOCK, LARRY

JARDINE, JULIE ANNE, 1926-   [*biography included*], with Jack Jardine as Howard L. Cory

07854 *The mind monsters.* Ace Double, New York, 1966,
       156p, Paper, Novel
07855 *The sword of Lankor.* Ace, New York, 1966,
       158p, Paper, Novel

JARMON, MARY DELORES, with Marjorie B. Smiley
and Domenica Paterno

07856 *Something strange.* Macmillan, New York, 1969,
       246p, Paper, Anth.

JARRELL, RANDALL, 1914-1965 [*biography included*]

07857 *The animal family.* Pantheon, New York, 1965,
       180p, Cloth, Novel

JARRETT, CORA (Hardy), 1877-

07858 *Strange houses; a tale.* Farrar & Rinehart,
       New York, 1936, 369p, Cloth, Novel

JARVIS, FRED(erick) G(ordon) Jr., 1930- [bi-
ography included], with Robert F. Van Beever
as Fritz Gordon

07859 *The flight of the bamboo saucer.* Award, New
York, 1967, 176p, Paper, Novel

JAVOR, F(rank) A.

07860 *The rim-world legacy.* Signet, New York,
1967, 144p, Paper, Novel

JAY, ERIC

07861 *The mating.* Midwood, New York, 1970, 200p,
Paper, Novel

JAY, MEL, pseud.
see: FANTHORPE, R. LIONEL

JAY, VICTOR

07862 *Devil soul.* Belmont, New York, 1970, 156p,
Paper, Novel
07863 *The gay haunt.* Other Traveller, New York,
1970, 185p, Paper, Novel

JAYNE, MITCHELL F.

07864 *The forest in the wind.* Bobbs-Merrill, Indianapolis, 1966, 150p, Cloth, Novel

JEAN, (Marie Joseph) ALBERT, 1892-   , with
Maurice Renard

07865 *Blind circle.* E. P. Dutton, New York, 1928,
324p, Cloth, Novel

JEEVES, B(yron) T(erry)

07866 *A checklist of Astounding.* ERG Publication,
Sheffield, UK, 1963/1965/1970, 3vol, Paper,
Nonf.

JEFFERIES, (John) RICHARD, 1848-1887

07867 *After London; or, Wild England, in two parts:
part I, the relapse into barbarism; part II,
wild England.* Cassell, London, 1885, 442p,
Cloth, Novel
07868 *Wood magic; a fable.* Cassell, London, 1881,
2vol, Cloth, Novel

JEFFRIES, GRAHAM MONTAGUE
see: GRAEME, BRUCE

JENKIN, LEONARD, with Leonard Allison and
Robert Perrault

00229 *Survival printout.* Vintage, New York, 1973,
335p, Paper, Anth.

JENKINS, ALAN C(harles), 1914-

07869 *Ghosts! an anthology of spectral stories.*
Blackie & Son, London, 1971, 383p, Cloth,
Anth.
07870 *Thin air; an anthology of ghost stories.*
Blackie & Son, London, 1966, 412p, Cloth,
Anth.

JENKINS, ESTHER BIGGER, 1894-

07871 *The golden age.* Vantage Press, New York,
1970, 231p, Cloth, Novel

JENKINS, GEOFFREY, 1920-   [biography included]

07872 *Hunter--killer.* Collins, London, 1966, 288p,
Cloth, Novel
07873 *A twist of sand.* Collins, London, 1959, 320p,
Cloth, Novel

JENKINS, WILL F.
see: LEINSTER, MURRAY

JENKS, ALMET, 1892-1966

07874 *The huntsman at the gate.* J. B. Lippincott,
Philadelphia, 1952, 116p, Cloth, Novel

JENKS, ANTON SHREWSBURY

07875 *A dead president makes answer to The president's
daughter.* Golden Hind Press, New York, 1929,
94p, Cloth, Novel

JENKS, TUDOR, 1857-1922

07876 *Imaginotions; truthless tales.* Century Co.,
New York, 1894, 230p, Cloth, Coll.
07877 *Young folks' library, vol. IV; Tales of fantasy.*
Hall & Locke, Boston, 1902, 395p, Cloth, Anth.

JENNISON, JOHN W(illiam)

07878 *Lost world.* World Distributors, Manchester,
1966, 205p, Cloth, Novel [Thunderbirds series]

as Neil Charles, house pseud.:

02887 *Pararobot.* Curtis Warren, London, 1952?, 112p,
Paper, Novel

as Gill Hunt, house pseud.:

07610 *Station 7.* Curtis Warren, London, 1952, 112p,
Paper, Novel
07611 *Zero field.* Curtis Warren, London, 1952?,
112p, Paper, Novel

as King Lang, house pseud.:

07879 *Space line.* Curtis Warren, London, 1952?,
112p, Paper, Novel

JENSEN, AXEL, 1932-

07880 *Epp.* Chatto & Windus, London, 1967, 116p,
Cloth, Novel

JENSEN, JOHANNES V(ilhelm), 1873-1950

07881 *The long journey.* Alfred A. Knopf, New York, 1933, 919p, Cloth, Coll. [includes 07882, 07883, 07884]
07882 *The long journey; Christopher Columbus.* Gyldendal, London, 1924, 313p, Cloth, Novel [Long Journey #3]
07882A retitled: *Christopher Columbus.* Alfred A. Knopf, New York, 1924, 253p, Cloth, Novel [Long Journey #3]
07883 *The long journey; The Cimbrians.* Gyldendal, London, 1923, 319p, Cloth, Novel [Long Journey #2]
07883A retitled: *The Cimbrians.* Alfred A. Knopf, New York, 1923, 340p, Cloth, Novel [Long Journey #2]
07884 *The long journey; Fire and ice.* Gyldendal, London, 1922, 313p, Cloth, Novel [Long Journey #1]
07884A retitled: *Fire and ice.* Alfred A. Knopf, New York, 1923, 294p, Cloth, Novel [Long Journey #1]

JENSEN, NORMAN

07885 *The galactic colonizers.* Robert Hale, London, 1971, 192p, Cloth, Novel

JEPPSON, J(anet) O(pal), 1926-   [*biography included*]

07886 *The second experiment.* Houghton Mifflin, Boston, 1974, 240p, Cloth, Novel

JEPSON, EDGAR (Alfred), 1863-1938

       The garden at 19. [see 07890A]
07887 *The horned shepherd.* Sons of the Vine, Wembley, UK, 1904, 103p, Cloth?, Novel
07888 *The keepers of the people.* C. Arthur Pearson, London, 1898, 358p, Cloth, Novel
07889 *The Moon gods.* Herbert Jenkins, London, 1930, 312p, Cloth, Novel
07890 *No. 19.* Mills & Boon, London, 1910, 309p, Cloth, Novel
07890A retitled: *The garden at 19.* Wessels & Bissell, New York, 1910, 299p, Cloth, Novel

JEPSON, R(owland) W(alter), 1888-1954

07891 *Strange stories.* Longmans, Green, London, 1938, 191p, Cloth, Anth.

JEPSON, SELWYN, 1899-

07892 *The death gong.* George G. Harrap, London, 1927, 317p, Cloth, Novel

JEROME, JEROME K(lapka), 1859-1927

07893 *The passing of the third floor back, and other stories.* Hurst & Blackett, London, 1907, 160p, Cloth, Coll.
07893A retitled: *The passing of the third floor back.* Dodd, Mead, New York, 1908, 186p, Cloth, Coll.

JEROME, OWEN FOX, pseud.
    see: FRIEND, OSCAR J.

JERROLD, DOUGLAS (William), 1803-1857

07894 *The chronicles of Clovernook, with some account of the hermit of Bellyfulle.* Punch Office, London, 1846, 183p, Cloth, Coll.
07895 *A man made of money.* Punch Office, London, 1849, 283p, Cloth, Novel
07896 *A man made of money; and, The chronicles of Clovernook.* Bradbury & Evans, London, 1853, 344p, Cloth, Coll.
07897 *The story of a feather.* Punch Office, London, 1844, 255p, Cloth, Novel

JESSE, F(ryniwind Marsh) TENNYSON, 1889-1958

07898 *The Solange stories.* William Heinemann, London, 1931, 285p, Cloth, Coll.

JEWEL SOWERS
    see: ALLONBY, EDITH

JOAD, C(yril) E(dwin) M(itchinson), 1891-1953

07899 *The adventures of a young soldier in search of the better world.* Faber & Faber, London, 1943, 124p, Cloth, Novel

JOBSON, ISRAEL
    see: WILSON, MILES

JOHANNESSON, OLOF, pseud. [Hannes Olof Goesta Alfvén, 1908-   ] [*biography included*]

07900 *The great computer; a vision.* Victor Gollancz, London, 1968, 126p, Cloth, Novel
07900A retitled: *The tale of the big computer; a vision.* Coward-McCann, New York, 1968, 126p, Cloth, Novel
07900B retitled: *The end of man?* Award, New York, 1969, 128p, Paper, Novel

JOHN, J. ALLEN ST.
    see: ST. JOHN, J. ALLEN

JOHN, JASPER, pseud. [Rosalie Muspratt]

07901 *Sinister stories.* Henry Walker, London, 1930, 171p, Cloth, Coll.

as Rosalie Muspratt:

07902 *Tales of terror*, by Rosalie Muspratt (Jasper John). Henry Walker, London, 1931, 167p, Cloth, Coll.

JOHN, OWEN, 1918-

07903 *The shadow in the sea.* E. P. Dutton, New York, 1972p, 188p, Cloth, Novel

JOHN, PHILIP ST.
    see: del REY, LESTER

JOHN-LOE, GLADYS ST.
see: ST. JOHN-LOE, GLADYS

JOHN-MARTIN, pseud. [Morgan Shepard, 1865-1947], with William Morris

07904 *The wolf's-head and the queen.* Charles Scribner's Sons, New York, 1931, 244p, Cloth, Novel [adapted from Morris's novel, *Child Christopher and Goldilind the fair*]

THE JOHN FRANKLIN LETTERS

07905 *The John Franklin letters.* The Bookmailer, New York, 1959, 178p, Paper, Novel

JOHN WHOPPER THE NEWSBOY
see: CLARK, THOMAS MARCH

JOHNHETT, pseud. [John Hettinger, 1880-   ]

07906 *Our glorious future; a novel in two parts: the miracle child; the battle of the spirits.* C. W. Daniel, London, 1931, 308p, Cloth, Novel

JOHNS, MARSTON, house pseud.
see: FANTHORPE, R. LIONEL and MULLER, JOHN E.

JOHNS, W(illiam) E(arl), 1893-1968

07907 *Biggles--charter pilot; the adventures of Biggles & Co. on a world-wide cruise of scientific investigation.* Oxford University Press, Humphrey Milford, London, 1943, 157p, Cloth, Coll. [Biggles series]
07908 *The death rays of Ardilla; a story of interplanetary exploration.* Hodder & Stoughton, London, 1959, 192p, Cloth, Novel [Rex Clinton #6]
07909 *The edge of beyond; a story of interplanetary exploration.* Hodder & Stoughton, London, 1958, 192p, Cloth, Novel [Rex Clinton #5]
07910 *Kings of space; a story of interplanetary exploration.* Hodder & Stoughton, London, 1954, 192p, Cloth, Novel [Rex Clinton #1]
07911 *The man who vanished into space; another adventure of the spacecraft 'Tavona' in the great unknown.* Hodder & Stoughton, London, 1963, 160p, Cloth, Novel [Rex Clinton #10]
07912 *Now to the stars; a story of interplanetary exploration.* Hodder & Stoughton, London, 1956, 190p, Cloth, Novel [Rex Clinton #3]
07913 *The quest for the perfect planet; a story of space exploration.* Hodder & Stoughton, London, 1961, 157p, Cloth, Novel [Rex Clinton #8]
07914 *Return to Mars; a story of interplanetary flight; a sequel to Kings of space.* Hodder & Stoughton, London, 1955, 160p, Cloth, Novel [Rex Clinton #2]
07915 *To outer space.* Hodder & Stoughton, London, 1957, 184p, Cloth, Novel [Rex Clinton #4]
07916 *To worlds unknown; a story of interplanetary exploration.* Hodder & Stoughton, London, 1960, 157p, Cloth, Novel [Rex Clinton #7]

07917 *Worlds of wonder; more adventures in space.* Hodder & Stoughton, London, 1962, 160p, Cloth, Novel [Rex Clinton #9]

JOHNS, WILLY, pseud.

07918 *The fabulous journey of Hieronymous Meeker.* Little, Brown, Boston, 1954, 370p, Cloth, Novel

JOHNSON, DAVID

07919 *Jungle nymph.* Scorpion Books, no place, 1964, 155p, Paper, Novel

JOHNSON, DOROTHY

07920 *To meet Mr. Stanley.* Longmans, Green, London, 1926, 312p, Cloth, Novel

JOHNSON, DOROTHY

07921 *Witch princess.* Houghton Mifflin, Boston, 1967, 216p, Cloth, Novel

JOHNSON, EDGAR, 1901-1972 [*biography included*]

07922 *Unweave a rainbow; a sentimental fantasy.* Doubleday, Doran, Garden City, 1931, 308p, Cloth, Novel

JOHNSON, F. HERNAMAN-
see: HERNAMAN-JOHNSON, F.

JOHNSON, FORREST B.
see: JOHNSON, FROSTY

JOHNSON, FROSTY [Forrest B. Johnson, 1935-   ]

07923 *The strange case of Big Harry.* Exposition Press, Jericho, NY, 1972, 168p, Cloth, Novel

JOHNSON, GEORGE CLAYTON, with William F. Nolan

07924 *Logan's run; a novel.* Dial Press, New York, 1967, 133p, Cloth, Novel

JOHNSON, GEORGE LINDSAY, 1853-1943

07925 *The weird adventures of Professor Delapine of the Sorbonne.* George Routledge & Sons, London, 1916, 344p, Cloth, Novel

JOHNSON, HENRY T.

07926 *The ape man.* Modern Publishing Co., London, 1930?, 220p, Cloth, Novel

JOHNSON, L(eRoy) P(eter) V(ernon), 1905-

07927 *In the time of the Thetans.* P. R. Macmillan, London, 1961, 274p, Cloth, Novel

JOHNSON, MAUD LALITA
   see: LALITA

JOHNSON, OWEN (McMahon), 1878-1952

07928 *The coming of the Amazons; a satiristic speculation on the scientific future of civilization.* Longmans, Green, New York, 1931,
251p, Cloth, Novel

JOHNSON, Dr. RAY W., 1900-

07929 *Astera, the planet that committed suicide.*
Exposition Press, New York, 1959, 27p,
Cloth, Story

JOHNSON, ROSSITER, 1840-1931

07930 *Little classics; intellect.* James R. Osgood,
Boston, 1876, 207p, Cloth, Anth.
07931 *Little classics; mystery.* James R. Osgood,
Boston, 1876, 231p, Cloth, Anth.

JOHNSON, STANLEY (Patrick), 1940-　[*biography included*]

07932 *The presidential plot.* Simon & Schuster, New
York, 1968, 216p, Cloth, Novel
07932A retitled: *Panther Jones for president.* Heinemann, London, 1968, 183p, Cloth, Novel

JOHNSON, THOMAS M(arvin), 1889-　, with
Judson P. Philips

07933 *Red war.* Doubleday, Doran, Garden City, 1936,
306p, Cloth, Novel

JOHNSON, W. CAIRNES

07934 *Beyond the ether.* The Author, Andover, Maine,
1896, 86p, Paper, Novel

JOHNSON, WILLIAM, 1927-

07935 *Focus on the science fiction film.* Spectrum,
Englewood Cliffs, NJ, 1972, 182p, Cloth,
Nonf. Anth.

JOHNSTON, GUNNAR

07936 *Soria Moria Castle; the manuscript of Donald
Gayforth Forbes.* Rider & Co., London,
1937, 282p, Cloth, Novel

JOHNSTON, MARY, 1870-1936

07937 *The exile.* Little, Brown, Boston, 1927, 276p,
Cloth, Novel
07938 *Sweet Rocket.* Harper & Bros., New York, 1920,
194p, Cloth, Novel
07939 *The wanderers.* Houghton Mifflin, Boston,
1917, 426p, Cloth, Coll.

JOHNSTON, THOMAS

07940 *The fight for Arkenvald.* Collins, London,
1970, 159p, Cloth, Novel

JOHNSTON, WILLIAM, 1924-

07941 *And loving it!* Tempo, New York, 1967, 153p,
Paper, Tele. [Get Smart #6]
07942 *Asylum.* Bantam, New York, 1972, 139p, Paper,
Movie
07943 *Bewitched; The opposite uncle.* Whitman, Racine
Wisc., 1970, 212p, Cloth, Tele. [Bewitched
series]
07944 *Captain Nice.* Tempo, New York, 1967, 155p,
Paper, Tele.
07945 *Dick Tracy.* Tempo, New York, 1970, 158p,
Paper, Novel [based on the cartoon character
of the same name]
07946 *The flying nun; Miracle at San Tanco.* Ace,
New York, 1968, 175p, Paper, Tele. [Flying
Nun #1]
07947 *Get Smart!* Tempo, New York, 1965, 159p, Paper
Tele. [Get Smart #1]
07948 *Get Smart once again!* Tempo, New York, 1966,
154p, Paper, Tele. [Get Smart #3]
07949 *The little green men.* Ace, New York, 1969,
175p, Paper, Tele. [Flying Nun #4]
07950 *The littlest rebels.* Ace, New York, 1968,
175p, Paper, Tele. [Flying Nun #2]
07951 *Max Smart and the ghastly ghost affair.* Tempo
New York, 1969, 154p, Paper, Tele. [Get
Smart #9]
07952 *Max Smart and the perilous pellets.* Tempo,
New York, 1966, 154p, Paper, Tele. [Get
Smart #4]
07953 *Max Smart loses control.* Tempo, New York,
1968, 148p, Paper, Tele. [Get Smart #8]
07954 *Max Smart--the spy who went out to the cold.*
Tempo, New York, 1968, 152p, Paper, Tele.
[Get Smart #7]
07955 *Missed it by that much!* Tempo, New York, 1967
151p, Paper, Tele. [Get Smart #5]
07956 *Mother of invention.* Ace, New York, 1969,
175p, Paper, Tele. [Flying Nun #3]
07957 *The Munsters and the great camera caper.* Whit
man, Racine, Wisc., 1965, 212p, Cloth, Tele.
[Munsters series]
07958 *The Munsters; The last resort.* Whitman, Racin
Wisc., 1966, 214p, Cloth, Tele. [Munsters
series]
07959 *Sam Weskit on the planet Framingham.* Tempo,
New York, 1970, 154p, Paper, Novel
07960 *Sorry, Chief...* Tempo, New York, 1966, 154p,
Paper, Tele. [Get Smart #2]
07961 *The underground picnic.* Ace, New York, 1970,
157p, Paper, Tele. [Flying Nun #5]

JOHNSTONE, CHARLES, 1719?-1800?

07962 *Chrysal; or, The adventures of a guinea, where
in are exhibited views of several striking
scenes, with curious and interesting anecdotes of the most noted persons in every ran
of life, whose hands it passed through, in
America, England, Holland, Germany, and Por-
tugal.* T. Becket, London, 1760, vol. I-264p
II-300p, Cloth, Novel

JOHNSTONE, D(avid) LAWSON

07963 *The mountain kingdom; a narrative of adven-
      ture.* Sampson Low, Marston, Searle & Riving-
      ton, London, 1888, 322p, Cloth, Novel
07964 *The paradise of the north; a story of disco-
      very and adventure around the Pole.* Reming-
      ton & Co., London, 1890, 298p, Cloth, Novel
07965 *The white princess of the hidden city, being
      the record of Leslie Rutherford's strange
      adventures in central Africa.* W. & R. Cham-
      bers, London, 1898, 289p, Cloth, Novel

JÓKAI, MAURUS [Mór Jókai, 1825-1904]

07966 *Tales from Jókai.* Jarrold & Sons, London,
      1904, 275p, Cloth, Coll.
07967 *Told by the death's head; a romantic tale.*
      Saafield Publishing Co., Chicago, 1902,
      348p, Cloth, Novel

JOLAS, EUGÈNE, 1894-1952

07968 *I have seen monsters and angels.* Transition
      Press, Paris, 1938, 224p, Cloth, Coll. [in-
      cludes some verse]

JONES, ADRIENNE, 1915-   [*biography included*]

07969 *The mural master.* Houghton Mifflin, Boston,
      1974, 249p, Cloth, Novel

JONES, ALICE ILGENFRITZ, d. 1906, with Ella
Marchant

07970 *Unveiling a parallel*, by two women of the west.
      Arena Publishing Co., Boston, 1893, 269p,
      Cloth, Novel

JONES, ARTHUR KEPPEL-
    see: KEPPEL-JONES, ARTHUR

JONES, CONSTANCE BRIDGES, with Guy Pearce
Jones

07971 *Peabody's mermaid.* Random House, New York,
      1946, 242p, Cloth, Novel
07972 *There was a little man.* Random House, New
      York, 1948, 245p, Cloth, Novel

JONES, D(ennis) F(eltham)

07973 *Colossus.* Rupert Hart-Davis, London, 1966,
      246p, Cloth, Novel [Colossus #1]
07974 *Denver is missing.* Walker, New York, 1971,
      224p, Cloth, Novel
07974A retitled: *Don't pick the flowers.* Panther,
      London, 1971, 237p, Paper, Novel
07975 *The fall of Colossus.* G. P. Putnam's Sons,
      New York, 1974, 186p, Cloth, Novel [Colos-
      sus #2]
07976 *Implosion.* Rupert Hart-Davis, London, 1967,
      264p, Cloth, Novel

JONES, DIANA WYNNE, 1934-

07977 *Wilkin's tooth.* Macmillan, London, 1973, 172p,
      Cloth, Novel
07977A retitled: *Witch's business.* E. P. Dutton, New
      York, 1974, 168p, Cloth, Novel

JONES, DOROTHY

07978 *Star trek concordance of people, places, &
      things.* Mathom House Publishers, Los Angeles,
      1969, 84p, Paper, Nonf.

with Bjo Trimble:

07979 *The third season supplement to the Star trek
      concordance.* Mathom House Publishers, Los
      Angeles, 1973, 70p, Paper, Nonf.

JONES, DuPRE (Anderson), 1937-

07980 *The adventures of Gremlin.* J. B. Lippincott,
      Philadelphia, 1966, 112p, Cloth, Novel

JONES, EWART C(harles)

07981 *Head in the sand.* Arthur Barker, London, 1958,
      222p, Cloth, Novel

JONES, GEORGE GRIFFITH-
    see: GRIFFITH, GEORGE

JONES, (Thomas Frederick) GONNER

07982 *The dome.* Faber & Faber, London, 1968, 239p,
      Cloth, Novel

JONES, GUY PEARCE, with Constance Bridges Jones

07971 *Peabody's mermaid.* Random House, New York,
      1946, 242p, Cloth, Novel
07972 *There was a little man.* Random House, New York,
      1948, 245p, Cloth, Novel

JONES, H. BEDFORD-
    see: BEDFORD-JONES, H.

JONES, IRA L.

07983 *Beoni, the Sphinx; a novel.* no publisher,
      Chicago?, 1898, 160p, Cloth, Novel

JONES, J(ohn) B(eauchamp), 1810-1866

07984 *Border war; a tale of disunion.* Rudd & Carle-
      ton, New York, 1859, 502p, Cloth, Novel
07984A retitled: *Wild Southern scenes; a tale of dis-
      union! and border war!* T. B. Peterson &
      Bros., Philadelphia, 1859, 502p, Cloth, Novel
07984B retitled: *Secession, coercion, and civil war;
      the story of 1861.* T. B. Peterson & Bros.,
      Philadelphia, 1861, 502p, Cloth, Novel [pub-
      lished anonymously]

JONES, JACK R(ay), 1934-

07985 *Fantasy films and their fiends.* Collector's
       Edition, Oklahoma City, 1964, 131p, Cloth?,
       Nonf.

JONES, L. Q.

07986 *The Brotherhood of Satan.* Award, New York,
       1971, 155p, Paper, Movie

JONES, LANGDON, 1942-

07987 *The eye of the lens.* Macmillan, New York,
       1972, 173p, Cloth, Coll.
07988 *The new S.F.; an original anthology of modern
       speculative fiction.* Hutchinson of London,
       London, 1969, 223p, Cloth, Anth.

with Michael Moorcock:

07989 *The nature of the catastrophe.* Hutchinson,
       London, 1971, 213p, Cloth, Anth.

JONES, MARGARET

07990 *The day they put Humpty together again.* Col-
       lins, London, 1968, 224p, Cloth, Novel
07990A retitled: *Transplant.* Stein & Day, New York,
       1968, 224p, Cloth, Novel

JONES, MERVYN, 1922-   [*biography included*]

07991 *On the last day.* Jonathan Cape, London, 1958,
       266p, Cloth, Novel

JONES, NEIL R(onald), 1909-   [*biography included*]

07992 *Doomsday on Ajiat.* Ace, New York, 1968, 159p,
       Paper, Coll. [Professor Jameson #5]
07993 *The planet of the double sun.* Ace, New York,
       1967, 123p, Paper, Coll. [Professor Jameson
       #1]
07994 *Space war.* Ace, New York, 1967, 158p, Paper,
       Coll. [Professor Jameson #2]
07995 *The sunless world.* Ace, New York, 1967, 189p,
       Paper, Coll. [Professor Jameson #3]
07996 *Twin worlds.* Ace, New York, 1967, 157p, Paper,
       Coll. [Professor Jameson #4]

JONES, Prof. P.

07997 *The probatim; a Slav novel.* H. S. Nichols,
       London, 1895, 398p, Cloth, Novel

JONES, RAYMOND F., 1915-

07998 *The alien; a gripping novel of discovery and
       conquest in interstellar space.* Galaxy SF
       Novel, New York, 1951, 160p, Paper, Novel
07999 *The cybernetic brains.* Avalon, New York,
       1962, 223p, Cloth, Novel
       The Deviates. [see 08004A]
       Man of two worlds. [see 08003A]
08000 *Moonbase One.* Abelard-Schuman, New York,
       1971, 144p, Cloth, Novel

08001 *The non-statistical man.* Belmont, New York,
       1964, 158p, Paper, Coll.
08002 *Planet of light.* John C. Winston, Philadelphia,
       1953, 211p, Cloth, Novel [Ron Barron #2]
08003 *Renaissance; a science fiction novel of two
       human worlds.* Gnome Press, New York, 1951,
       255p, Cloth, Novel
08003A retitled: *Man of two worlds; a science-fiction
       novel.* Pyramid, New York, 1963, 268p, Paper,
       Novel
08004 *The secret people.* Avalon, New York, 1956,
       224p, Cloth, Novel
08004A retitled: *The Deviates.* Galaxy Publishing
       Corp., New York, 1959, 160p, Paper, Novel
08005 *Son of the stars.* John C. Winston, Philadel-
       phia, 1952, 210p, Cloth, Novel [Ron Barron #1]
08006 *Syn.* Belmont, New York, 1969, 141p, Paper,
       Novel
08007 *This island Earth.* Shasta Publishers, Chicago,
       1952, 220p, Cloth, Novel
08008 *The toymaker.* Fantasy Publishing Co., Los An-
       geles, 1951, 287p, Cloth, Coll.
08009 *Voyage to the bottom of the sea.* Whitman,
       Racine, Wisc., 1965, 212p, Cloth, Tele. [Vo-
       yage to the Bottom of the Sea series]
08010 *The year when stardust fell; a science fiction
       novel.* John C. Winston, Philadelphia, 1958,
       203p, Cloth, Novel

JONES, RICH(ard L.), 1948-   , with Richard L.
Roe

08011 *Valence and vision; a reader in psychology.*
       Rinehart Press, San Francisco, 1974, 482p,
       Paper, Anth.

JONES, ROBERT F(rancis), 1934-   [*biography
included*]

08012 *Blood sport; a journey up the Hassayampa.*
       Simon & Schuster, New York, 1974, 255p,
       Cloth, Novel

JONES, ROBERT WEBSTER

08013 *Light interviews with shades.* Dorrance Publi-
       shers, Philadelphia, 1922, 151p, Cloth, Novel

JONG, A(drianus) M(ichael) de, 1888-1943

08014 *The platter, being a dramatic tale filled with
       wicked passions, weird complications, and
       the triumph of pleasure in the misfortune of
       others.* Querido, New York, 1946, 160p, Cloth,
       Novel

"JONQUIL," pseud. [J. L. Collins]

08015 *Queen Krinaleen's plagues; or, How a simple
       people were destroyed; a discourse in the
       twenty-second century,* by "Jonquil," author
       of "Was she engaged?" American News Co.,
       New York, 1874, 151p, Cloth, Novel

JORDAN, ELIZABETH (Garver), 1867-1947

08016 *First port of call.* ·D. Appleton-Century, New York, 1940, 265p, Cloth, Novel; John Long, London, 1940, 223p, Cloth, Novel

JORDAN, F. DORMER

08017 *Heirs of the ages.* James Nisbet, London, 1914, 320p, Cloth, Novel

JORDAN-SMITH, PAUL
see: SMITH, PAUL JORDAN-

JORGENSEN, IVAR, pseud.
see: FAIRMAN, PAUL W.

JORGENSON, ALF. A.
see: ARNE, AARON

JORGENSON, IVAR, pseud.
see: SILVERBERG, ROBERT

JOSCELYNE, CYRIL

08018 *When Gubbins ruled.* Fortune & Merriman, London, 1923, 96p, Cloth, Novel

JOSEPH, M(ichael) K(ennedy), 1914- [*biography included*]

08019 *The hole in the zero; a novel.* Victor Gollancz, London, 1967, 192p, Cloth, Novel

JOURNEY ACROSS THREE WORLDS

08020 *Journey across three worlds; science-fiction stories.* Mir Publishers, Moscow, 1973, 397p, Cloth, Anth.

JOURNEY TO ANOTHER STAR, AND OTHER STORIES
see: ELWOOD, ROGER

A JOURNEY TO THE MOON
see: CAMPBELL, JOHN

A JOURNEY TO THE WORLD UNDER-GROUND
see: HOLBERG, LUDVIG

JOURNEYS INTO THE MOON

08021 *Journeys into the Moon, several planets, and the Sun; history of a female somnambulist, of Weilheim on the Teck, in the Kingdom of Wuertemberg, in the years 1832 and 1833; a book in which all persons will find important disclosures, concerning their fate hereafter; translated from the original, in German, which was published by a daily eyewitness and friend of truth.* Vollmer & Haggenmacher, Philadelphia, 1837, 203p, Cloth, Novel

JUDD, CYRIL, pseud.
see: KORNBLUTH, C. M. and MERRIL, JUDITH

JUDE, CHRISTOPHER

08022 *The terror of the Shape.* Sampson Low, Marston, London, 1937, 250p, Cloth, Novel

JUDGE, W(illiam) Q(uan), 1851-1896, with H. P. Blavatsky

01460 *The tell-tale picture gallery; occult stories.* International Book House, Bombay, 194?, 218p, Cloth, Coll.

JUDSON, JEANNE (Margaret Antonia), 1890-

08023 *The stars incline.* Dodd, Mead, New York, 1920, 286p, Cloth, Novel

JUENGER, ERNST, 1895-

08024 *The glass bees.* Noonday Press, New York, 1961, 149p, Cloth, Novel
08025 *On the Marble Cliffs; a novel.* New Directions, Norfolk, Conn., 1947, 120p, Cloth, Novel

JUFFE, MEL

08026 *Flash.* Viking Press, New York, 1974, 265p, Cloth, Novel

"JULIUS," pseud.

08027 *The sorrows of Jupiter.* Greening & Co., London, 1904, 222p, Cloth, Novel

JUNIUS Junior, pseud.

08028 *Pope Pacificus.* Society for Promoting Christian Knowledge, London, 1908, 64p, Paper?, Novel

JUSTER, NORTON, 1929- [*biography included*]

08029 *Alberic the wise, and other journeys.* Pantheon, New York, 1965, 67p, Cloth, Coll.
08030 *The phantom tollbooth.* Epstein & Carroll, New York, 1961, 255p, Cloth, Novel

K., J. A. C.

08031 *Golf in the year 2000; or, What we are coming to.* T. Fisher Unwin, London, 1892, 159p, Cloth, Novel

K. B.
see: B., K.

K. O. S.
see: DOMBROWSKI, KATRINA

KAFKA, FRANZ, 1883-1924

08032   *The Great Wall of China, and other pieces.*
     Martin Secker, London, 1933, 285p, Cloth,
     Coll.
08033   *The metamorphosis.* Parton Press, London,
     1937, 74p, Cloth, Novel
08034   *The metamorphosis.* Bantam, New York, 1972,
     202p, Paper, Coll. [includes letters, essays
     about the book]
08035   *Metamorphosis, and other other stories.* Pen-
     guin, Harmondsworth, 1961, 218p, Paper, Coll.
08036   *The penal colony; stories and short pieces.*
     Schocken Books, New York, 1948, 317p, Cloth,
     Coll. [includes some nonf.]
08036A   retitled: *In the penal settlement; tales and
     short prose works.* Secker & Warburg, Lon-
     don, 1949, 298p, Cloth, Coll.
08037   *Selected short stories of Franz Kafka.* Mo-
     dern Library, New York, 1952, 328p, Cloth,
     Coll.

KAHLERT, KARL FRIEDRICH
     see: FLAMMENBERG, LAWRENCE

KAHN, JOAN

08038   *Some things dark and dangerous.* Harper &
     Row, New York, 1970, 294p, Cloth, Anth.
     [includes some nonf.]
08039   *Some things strange and sinister.* Harper &
     Row, New York, 1973, 245p, Cloth, Anth.

KAINEN, RAY, pseud. [Ray Kainulainen]

08040   *The cosmic gash.* Traveller's Companion Series,
     New York, 1969, 180p, Paper, Novel
08041   *Earth station sex.* Traveller's Companion
     Series, New York, 1969, 192p, Paper, Novel
08042   *Satyr trek.* Olympia Press, New York, 1970,
     219p, Paper, Novel
08043   *A sea of thighs.* Traveller's Companion Series,
     New York, 1968, 181p, Paper, Novel

as Ray Kalnen:

08044   *The day the universe came.* Nightstand, San
     Diego, 1968, 160p, Paper, Novel
08045   *The love box; a tale of character development
     in man and machine.* Greenleaf Classic, San
     Diego, 1967, 160p, Paper, Novel

KAINULAINEN, RAY
     see: KAINEN, RAY

KALER, OTIS J.
     see: OTIS, JAMES

KALLAS, AINO (Julia Maria), 1878-1956

08046   *The wolf's bride; a tale from Estonia.* Jona-
     than Cape, London, 1930, 115p, Cloth, Novel

KALNEN, RAY, pseud.
     see: KAINEN, RAY

KAMIN, NICK, pseud. [Robert J. Antonick,
1939-] [*biography included*]

08047   *Earthrim.* Ace Double, New York, 1969, 147p,
     Paper, Novel
08048   *The HEROD men.* Ace Double, New York, 1971,
     149p, Paper, Novel

KAMPF, HAROLD (Bertram), 1916-

08049   *My brother, o my brother!* Chapman & Hall,
     London, 1953, 190p, Cloth, Novel
08049A   retitled: *When He shall appear.* Little, Brown
     Boston, 1954, 177p, Cloth, Novel

KANE, JAS. J. [James Johnson Kane, 1837-1921]

08050   *Miriam vs. Milton; or, The mystery of Everdale
     Lake.* Charles Birchall, London, 1894, 378p,
     Cloth, Novel; American News Co., New York,
     1894, 477p, Cloth, Novel

KANE, PABLO, pseud.
     see: HUGHES, ZACH

KANER, H(yman)

08051   *Ape-man's offering.* Kaner Publishing Co., Llan-
     dudno, Wales, 1946, 64p, Paper, Coll.
08052   *The Cynic's desperate mission.* Kaner Publi-
     shing Co., Llandudno, Wales, 1946, 64p,
     Paper, Coll.
08053   *Fire watchers night.* Kaner Publishing Co.,
     Llandudno, Wales, 1944, 56p, Paper, Coll.
08054   *People of the twilight.* Kaner Publishing Co.,
     Llandudno, Wales, 1946, 188p, Cloth, Novel
08055   *The sun queen.* Kaner Publishing Co., Llandudno
     Wales, 1946, 204p, Cloth, Novel
08056   *The terror catches up.* Kaner Publishing Co.,
     Llandudno, Wales, 1946, 65p, Paper, Coll.

KANOR
     see: FAGNAN, MARIE ANTOINETTE

KANTO, PETER, pseud.
     see: HUGHES, ZACH

KANTOR, HAL [same as Hal Cantor?]

08057   *The adult version of Dracula.* Calga Publishers
     Los Angeles, 1970, 190p, Paper, Novel [pub-
     lished anonymously] [Dracula series]
08058   *The adult version of Frankenstein.* Calga Pub-
     lishers, Los Angeles, 1970, 191p, Paper,
     Novel [Frankenstein series]
08059   *The sex life of Ulysses.* Calga Publishers,
     Los Angeles, 1971, 190p, Paper, Novel [pub-
     lished anonymously]

KANTOR, MacKINLAY, 1904-1977 [*biography included*]

08060   *If the South had won the Civil War.* Bantam,
     New York, 1961, 113p, Paper, Novel

KAPLAN, BARRY
see: KINGSLEY, BETTINA

KAPP, COLIN

08061 *The patterns of chaos.* Victor Gollancz, London, 1972, 222p, Cloth, Novel
08062 *Transfinite man.* Berkley Medallion, New York, 1964, 160p, Paper, Novel
08062A retitled: *The dark mind.* Corgi, London, 1965, 158p, Paper, Novel
08063 *The wizard of Anharitte.* Award, New York, 1973, 190p, Paper, Novel

KARIG, WALTER, 1898-1956

08064 *Zotz!* Rinehart & Co., New York, 1947, 268p, Cloth, Novel

KARINTHY, FRIGYES, 1887-1938

08065 *Voyage to Faremido; Capillaria.* Corvina Books, Budapest, 1965, 127p, Cloth, Coll. [Gulliver series]

KARISHKA, PAUL, pseud.
see: HATCH, DAVID PATTERSON

KARLINS, MARVIN, 1941-   [*biography included*]

08066 *The last man is out.* Prentice-Hall, Englewood Cliffs, NJ, 1969, 217p, Cloth, Novel

with Lewis M. Andrews:

00339 *Gomorrah.* Doubleday, Garden City, 1974, 163p, Cloth, Novel

KARLOFF, BORIS, pseud. [William Henry Pratt, 1887-1969]

08067 *And the darkness falls.* World Publishing Co., Cleveland, 1946, 631p, Cloth, Anth.
08068 *Boris Karloff's favorite horror stories.* Avon, New York, 1965, 176p, Paper, Anth.
08068A retitled: *The Boris Karloff horror anthology.* Souvenir Press, London, 1965, 190p, Cloth, Anth.
08069 *Tales of terror.* World Publisning Co., Cleveland, 1943, 317p, Cloth, Anth.

KARLOVA, IRINA

08070 *Broomstick; a spine-chiller.* Hurst & Blackett, London, 1946, 190p, Cloth, Novel
08071 *Dreadful hollow (a spine-chiller).* Hurst & Blackett, London, 1942, 160p, Cloth, Novel
08072 *The empty house; a spine-chiller.* Hurst & Blackett, London, 1944, 168p, Cloth, Novel

KARLSON, HANS, pseud.

08073 *Atomic death.* Scientific Thriller, Sydney, 1948, 50p, Paper, Story

KARMATH
see: UPHAM, EDWARD

KARP, DAVID, 1922-   [*biography included*]

08074 *One; a novel.* Vanguard Press, New York, 1953, 311p, Cloth, Novel
08074A retitled: *Escape to nowhere.* Lion, New York, 1955, 222p, Paper, Novel

KARP, MARVIN ALLEN

08075 *The unhumans.* Popular Library, New York, 1965, 141p, Paper, Anth.

KARTOFFEL, Baron von
see: von KARTOFFEL, Baron

KASACK, HERMANN, 1896-1966

08076 *The city beyond the river.* Longmans, Green, London, 1953, 356p, Cloth, Novel

KASSEF, ROMAIN
see: GARY, ROMAIN

KASSIL, LEO [Lev Abramovich Kassil', 1905-   ]

08077 *The land of Shvambrania; a novel with maps, a coat of arms, and a flag.* Viking Press, New York, 1935, 289p, Cloth, Novel

KASTLE, HERBERT D(avid), 1924-   [*biography included*]

08078 *The reassembled man.* Gold Medal, Greenwich, Conn., 1964, 192p, Paper, Novel

KATZ, HARVEY A., with Martin Harry Greenberg & Patricia S. Warrick

06310 *Introductory psychology through science fiction.* Rand McNally College Publishing Co., Chicago, 1974, 510p, Paper, Anth.

KATZ, STEVE(n), 1935-   [*biography included*]

08079 *Saw.* Alfred A. Knopf, New York, 1972, 170p, Cloth, Novel

KAUL, FEDOR

08080 *Contagion to this world.* Geoffrey Bles, London, 1933, 317p, Cloth, Novel
08081 *Maniu.* Geoffrey Bles, London, 1935, 314p, Cloth, Novel

KAVAN, ANNA, pseud. [Helen Edmonds, 1904-1968]

08082 *Eagles' Nest.* Peter Owen, London, 1957, 179p, Cloth, Novel

KAVAN, ANNA (cont.)

08083 *Ice; a novel.* Peter Owen, London, 1967, 158p, Cloth, Novel

KAYE, H. R., pseud.
  see: KNOX, HUGH

KAYE, PAMELA

08084 *Confessions of a captive sibyl.* Midwood, New York, 1970,   , Paper, Novel

KAYE-SMITH, SHEILA, 1887-1956

08085 *Ember Lane; a winter's tale.* Cassell, London, 1940, 312p, Cloth, Novel

KAYSER, MARTHA

08086 *The aerial flight to the realm of peace.* Lincoln Press & Publishing Co., St. Louis, 1922, 54p, Cloth, Novel

KEALING, ETHEL BLACK

08087 *Desra of the Egyptians; a romance of the earlier centuries.* Wheeler & Kalb, Indianapolis, 1910, 213p, Cloth, Novel

KEARNEY, C. B.

08088 *The great calamity (an atom-bomb story of the Midlands and Birmingham).* The Author, Birmingham, 1948, 23p, Paper, Story

KEARNEY, (Elfric Wells) CHALMERS, 1881-1966

08089 *Erōne.* Biddles Ltd., Guildford, UK, 1943, 253p, Cloth, Novel

KEATING, ELIZA H.

08090 *Raymond Bury; a tale.* Arthur Hall, Virtue, London, 1853, 319p, Cloth, Novel [based on Thomas Hood's poem, "The Haunted House"]

KECK, MAUD, with Olive Orbison

08091 *Behind the Devil Screen.* Ives Washburn, New York, 1928, 325p, Cloth, Novel

KEE, ROBERT, 1919-

08092 *A sign of the times.* Eyre & Spottiswoode, London, 1955, 256p, Cloth, Novel

KEEFER, LOWELL B.

08093 *Visitors from outer space.* Carlton Press, New York, 1969, 149p, Cloth, Novel

KEEL, JOHN A., pseud. [John Alva Kiehle]

08094 *The fickle finger of fate.* Fawcett Gold Medal, Greenwich, Conn., 1966, 160p, Paper, Novel

KEELER, H(arry) S(tephen), 1890-1967

08095 *The box from Japan.* E. P. Dutton, New York, 1932, 765p, Cloth, Novel
08096 *The man with the magic eardrums; a mystery novel.* E. P. Dutton, New York, 1939, 305p, Cloth, Novel
08096A retitled: *The magic eardrums.* Ward, Lock, London, 1939, 285p, Cloth, Novel

KEENE, DAY, with Leonard Pruyn

08097 *World without women.* Gold Medal, Greenwich, Conn., 1960, 176p, Paper, Novel

KEIGHTLEY, DAVID NOEL
  see: KEYES, NOEL

KEITH, BRANDON

08098 *The Green Hornet; The case of the disappearing doctor.* Whitman, Racine, Wisc., 1966, 212p, Cloth, Tele. [Green Hornet series]
08099 *The man from U.N.C.L.E. and the affair of the gentle saboteur.* Whitman, Racine, Wisc., 1966, 210p, Cloth, Tele. [Man from U.N.C.L.E. series]

KEITH, DONALD, pseud.
  see: MONROE, DONALD and MONROE, KEITH

KEITH, SAMUEL JAMES

08100 *"The day the angels cried."* Hartford House, Las Vegas, 1972, 240p, Cloth, Novel

KELLAM, IAN

08101 *The first summer year.* Oxford University Press, London, 1972, 274p, Cloth, Novel

KELLAND, CLARENCE B(udington), 1881-1964

08102 *Thirty pieces of silver.* Harper & Bros., New York, 1913, 32p, Cloth, Story

KELLAR, VON, house pseud.

08103 *Ionic barrier.* Curtis Warren, London, 1953, 159p, Cloth, Novel
08104 *Tri-planet.* Curtis Warren, London, 1953, 159p, Cloth, Novel

KELLEAM, JOSEPH E(veridge), 1913-   [*biography included*]

08105 *Hunters of space.* Avalon, New York, 1960, 223p, Cloth, Novel [Jack Odin #2]

KELLEAM, JOSEPH E. (cont.)

08106   *The little men.* Avalon, New York, 1960, 226p,
        Cloth, Novel [Jack Odin #1]
08107   *Overlords from space.* Ace Double, New York,
        1956, 146p, Paper, Novel
08108   *When the Red King awoke.* Avalon, New York,
        1966, 192p, Cloth, Novel

KELLER, DAVID H(enry), 1880-1966

08109   *The devil and the doctor.* Simon & Schuster,
        New York, 1940, 308p, Cloth, Novel
08110   *The eternal conflict.* Prime Press, Philadel-
        phia, 1949, 191p, Cloth, Novel
08111   *A figment of a dream.* Mirage Press, Baltimore,
        1962, 39p, Paper, Story
08112   *The final war.* Perri Press, Portland, OR,
        1949, 10p, Paper, Story
08113   *The Folsom flint, and other curious tales.*
        Arkham House, Sauk City, 1969, 213p, Cloth,
        Coll.
08114   *The homunculus.* Prime Press, Philadelphia,
        1949, 160p, Cloth, Novel
08115   *The lady decides.* Prime Press, Philadelphia,
        1950, 133p, Cloth, Novel
08116   *Life everlasting, and other tales of science,
        fantasy, and horror.* Avalon Co., Newark,
        NJ, 1947, 382p, Cloth, Coll. [includes a
        separately printed bibliography of 12 pages
        that was inserted into most copies]
08117   *The sign of the burning hart; a tale of Arca-
        dia.* Imprimerie de la Manche, Saint Lo,
        France, 1938, 163p, Paper, Coll.
08118   *The solitary hunters; and, The abyss; two fan-
        tastic novels.* New Era Publishers, Phila-
        delphia, 1948, 265p, Cloth, Coll.
08119   *Tales from Underwood.* Published for Arkham
        House by Pellegrini & Cudahy, New York,
        1952, 322p, Cloth, Coll.
08120   *The television detective.* LASFL, Los Angeles,
        1938, 15p, Paper, Story
08121   *The thing in the cellar.* Bizarre Series, Mill-
        heim, PA, 1940, 32p, Paper, Story
08122   *The thought projector.* Stellar Publishing
        Corp., New York, 1929, 24p, Paper, Story
08123   *Waters of Lethe.* Kirby, Great Barrington,
        Mass., 1937,   , Paper, Story

KELLER, MARC F., with A. H. Barzevi

00928   *Migrants of the stars, being an account of
        the discovery of the marvelous land of Nia-
        mes, and of the secret of its inhabitants.*
        Classic Press, New York, 1931, 406p, Cloth,
        Novel

KELLERMAN, BERNARD [Bernhard Kellermann,
1879-1951]

08124   *The Tunnel.* Hodder & Stoughton, London,
        1915, 319p, Cloth, Novel

KELLETT, E(rnest) E(dward), 1864-1950

08125   *A corner in sleep, and other impossibilities.*
        Jarrold & Sons, London, 1900, 259p, Cloth,
        Coll.

KELLEY, FRANCIS CLEMENT, 1870-1948

08126   *Pack Rat; a metaphoric phantasy.* Bruce Publi-
        shing Co., Milwaukee, 1942, 146p, Cloth,
        Novel

KELLEY, LEO P(atrick), 1928-   [*biography included*]

08127   *The accidental Earth.* Belmont, New York, 1970,
        173p, Paper, Novel
08128   *Brother John.* Avon, New York, 1971, 160p,
        Paper, Movie
08129   *The Coins of Murph.* Berkley Medallion, New
        York, 1971, 191p, Paper, Novel
08130   *The Counterfeits; a startling science fiction
        novel,* by Leo F. Kelley. Belmont, New York,
        1967, 157p, Paper, Novel
08131   *The Earth tripper.* Fawcett Gold Medal, Green-
        wich, Conn., 1973, 159p, Paper, Novel
08132   *Fantasy; the literature of the marvelous.*
        McGraw-Hill, New York, 1973, 305p, Paper,
        Anth.
        The man from maybe. [see 08138A]
08133   *Mindmix.* Fawcett Gold Medal, Greenwich, Conn.,
        1972, 176p, Paper, Novel
08134   *Mythmaster.* Dell, New York, 1973, 224p, Paper,
        Novel
08135   *Odyssey to Earthdeath.* Belmont, New York,
        1968, 174p, Paper, Novel
08136   *The supernatural in fiction.* McGraw-Hill, New
        York, 1973, 313p, Paper, Anth.
08137   *Themes in science fiction; a journey into won-
        der.* McGraw-Hill, New York, 1972, 428p,
        Paper, Anth.
08138   *Time: 110100.* Walker, New York, 1972, 202p,
        Cloth, Novel
08138A retitled: *The man from maybe.* Coronet, Lon-
        don, 1974, 175p, Paper, Novel
08139   *Time rogue.* Lancer, New York, 1970, 190p,
        Paper, Novel

KELLEY, THOMAS P.

08140   *The face that launched a thousand ships; a com-
        plete novel of the weird.* Handy Library,
        Toronto, 1941, 125p, Paper, Novel
08141   *I found Cleopatra.* Export Publishing, Toronto,
        1946, 126p, Paper, Novel

KELLINO, PAMELA, pseud. [Pamela Ostrer Mason]

08142   *A lady possessed.* Robert Hale, London, 1943,
        269p, Cloth, Novel
08142A retitled: *Del Palma; a novel.* E. P. Dutton,
        New York, 1948, 254p, Cloth, Novel

KELLY, JAMES PAUL

08143   *Prince Izon; a romance of the Grand Canyon.*
        A. C. McClurg, Chicago, 1910, 399p, Cloth,
        Novel

KELLY, ROBERT, 1935-   [*biography included*]

08144   *Cities.* Frontier Press, West Newbury, Mass.,
        1971, 65p, Paper, Novel

KELLY, ROBERT (cont.)

08145   *The Scorpions*. Doubleday, Garden City, 1967, 188p, Cloth, Novel

KELLY, T(eague) M.

08146   *Mucca Scob; or, Threads of prehistoric and present history, concatenated*. The Author, Oakland, CA, 1885, 144p, Paper, Novel

KELLY, WILLIAM PATRICK, 1848-

08147   *Doctor Baxter's invention; a story*. Greening & Co., London, 1912, 317p, Cloth, Novel

KELSEY, FRANKLYN

08148   *The children of the Sun*. George G. Harrap, London, 1939, 286p, Cloth, Radio [James Armitage #2]
08149   *The island in the mist*. George G. Harrap, London, 1937, 319p, Cloth, Radio [James Armitage #1]
08150   *The prowlers of the deep*. George G. Harrap, London, 1942, 240p, Cloth, Novel [James Armitage #3]

KELTON, ARYAN [Aryon Lewis Kelton, 1892-]

08151   *The great Haddon*. Hart Publishing Co., Los Angeles, 1933, 203p, Cloth, Novel

KEMP, EARL, 1929-   [*biography included*]

08152   *Proceedings of the 20th World Science Fiction Convention--Chicon III*. Advent: Publishers, Chicago, 1963, 208p, Paper, Nonf.
08153   *Who killed science fiction?* SaFari, Chicago, 1960, 108p, Paper, Nonf.

KEMPER, W(illia)m. E. Jr.

08154   *Another man's hell*. Chicago Paperback House, Chicago, 1962, 191p, Paper, Novel

KEMPSTER, (James) AQUILA, 1864-

08155   *The mark*. Doubleday, Page, New York, 1903, 374p, Cloth, Novel

KENDALL, CAROL, 1917-   [*biography included*]

08156   *The Gammage cup*. Harcourt, Brace & Co., New York, 1959, 221p, Cloth, Novel [Minnipins #1]
08156A retitled: *The Minnipins*. J. M. Dent & Sons, London, 1960, 221p, Cloth, Novel [Minnipins #1]
08157   *The whisper of Glocken*. Harcourt, Brace & World, New York, 1965, 256p, Cloth, Novel [Minnipins #2]

KENDALL, JOHN, pseud. [Margaret Maud Brash, 1880-]

08158   *Unborn to-morrow*. W. Collins Sons, London, 1933, 319p, Cloth, Novel

KENDALL, MAY

08159   *"That very Mab."* Longmans, Green, London, 1885, 215p, Cloth, Novel

KENEALLY, THOMAS (Michael), 1935-

08160   *Blood red, Sister Rose*. Collins, London, 1974, 384p, Cloth, Novel

KENNEDY, BART, 1861-1930

08161   *Darab's wine-cup, and other tales*. Sidney L. Ollif, London, 1897, 262p, Cloth, Coll.
08162   *The voice in the light; tales of life and imagination*. Simpkin, Marshall, Hamilton, Kent London, 1917, 308p, Cloth, Coll.

KENNEDY, EDGAR REES, pseud.

08163   *Conquerors of Venus*. Edwin Self, London, 1951 128p, Paper, Novel
08164   *The mystery planet*. Edwin Self, London, 1952, 128p, Paper, Novel

KENNEDY, R. A.

08165   *The triuneverse; a scientific romance*, by the author of "Space and spirit." Charles Knight, London, 1912, 221p, Cloth, Novel

KENNEY, DOUGLAS C., with Henry N. Beard

00982   *Bored of the Rings; a parody of J. R. R. Tolkien's The Lord of the Rings*. Signet, New York, 1969, 160p, Paper, Novel

KENSCH, OTTO, pseud.

08166   *Death is a habit*. Scientific Thriller, Sydney 1949, 50p, Paper, Story
08167   *Image of death*. Scientific Thriller, Sydney, 1950, 50p, Paper, Story
08168   *Murder has wings*. Scientific Thriller, Sydney 1949, 50p, Paper, Story
08169   *Sleep is death*. Scientific Thriller, Sydney, 1950, 50p, Paper, Story
08170   *Time has a door*. Scientific Thriller, Sydney 1949, 50p, Paper, Story

KENSETT, PERCY F.

08171   *The amulet of Tarv; a romance of the South Downs, 1,000 years B.C.* Ed. J. Burrow, London, 1925, 268p, Cloth, Novel

KENT, BRAD, house pseud. [see also Dennis Talbot Hughes and Maurice Hugi]

07555 *Biology "A."* Curtis Warren, London, 1952,
         128p, Paper, Novel [by Dennis Hughes]
07556 *Catalyst.* Curtis Warren, London, 1952?, 112p,
         Paper, Novel [by Dennis Hughes]
07557 *The fatal law.* Curtis Warren, London, 1952,
         112p, Paper, Novel [by Dennis Hughes]
07578 *Out of the silent places.* Curtis Warren, London, 1952, 127p, Paper, Novel [by Maurice
         Hugi]

KENT, JIM

08172 *Women of Landau.* Scripts, Sydney, 1970,
         124p, Paper, Novel

KENT, PHILIP, pseud.
       see: BULMER, KENNETH

KENT, RYLAND

08173 *After this; a novel.* Harper & Bros., New York,
         1939, 245p, Cloth, Novel

KENT, SAUL

08174 *Future sex.* Warner Paperback Library, New
         York, 1974, 190p, Paper, Nonf. [includes
         numerous SF vignettes throughout the text]

KENTON, L. P.

08175 *Destination Moon.* Badger, London, 1959, 157p,
         Paper, Novel

KENWARD, JAMES (Macara), 1908-   [*biography
included*]

08176 *Summervale; a fantasy.* Constable, London,
         1935, 249p, Cloth, Novel

KENYON, C(harles) **R**(ichard)

08177 *The Argonauts of the Amazon.* W. & R. Chambers,
         London, 1901, 305p, Cloth, Novel
08178 *A Polar Eden; or, The goal of the "Dauntless."*
         S. W. Partridge, London, 1897, 288p, Cloth,
         Novel

KENYON, PAUL

08179 *Death is a ruby light.* Pocket Books, New
         York, 1974, 207p, Paper, Novel [Baroness #3]
08180 *Diamonds are for dying.* Pocket Books, New
         York, 1974, 173p, Paper, Novel [Baroness #2]
08181 *The ecstasy connection.* Pocket Books, New
         York, 1974, 223p, Paper, Novel [Baroness #1]
08182 *Flicker of doom.* Pocket Books, New York,
         1974, 222p, Paper, Novel [Baroness #7]
08183 *Hard-core murder.* Pocket Books, New York,
         1974, 223p, Paper, Novel [Baroness #4]
08184 *Operation Doomsday.* Pocket Books, New York,
         1974, 218p, Paper, Novel [Baroness #5]

08185 *Sonic slave.* Pocket Books, New York, 1974,
         216p, Paper, Novel [Baroness #6]

KEON, MILES GERALD, 1821-1875

08186 *Dion and the Sibyls; a romance of the first
         century.* Bentley Bros., London, 1866, 2vol,
         Cloth, Novel

KEOWN, ANNA GORDON, 1902-1957

08187 *The cat who saw God.* Peter Davies, London,
         1932, 296p, Cloth, Novel
08188 *Mr. Theobald's devil.* Macmillan, London,
         1935, 342p, Cloth, Novel

KEPPEL-JONES, ARTHUR (Mervyn), 1909-

08189 *When Smuts goes; a history of South Africa
         from 1952 to 2010, first published in 2015.*
         African Bookman, Cape Town, 1947, 203p, Cloth,
         Novel

KER, DAVID, 1842-1914

08190 *Lost among white Africans; a boy's adventures
         on the upper Congo.* Cassell, London, 1886,
         228p, Cloth, Novel

KERBY, SUSAN ALICE, pseud. [Alice Elizabeth
Burton, 1908-   ]

08191 *Miss Carter and the ifrit.* Hutchinson, London, 1945, 160p, Cloth, Novel
08192 *Mr. Kronion; a novel.* Werner Laurie, London,
         1949, 223p, Cloth, Novel
08193 *The roaring dove.* Dodd, Mead, New York, 1948,
         260p, Cloth, Novel

KERN, GREGORY, pseud.
       see: TUBB, E. C.

KERNAHAN, (John) **COULSON**, 1858-1943

08194 *The apples of sin (the garden of God).* Ward,
         Lock, London, 1898, 47p, Cloth, Coll.
08195 *A book of strange sins.* Ward, Lock & Bowden,
         London, 1893, 195p, Cloth, Coll.
08196 *A dead man's diary, written after his decease.*
         Ward, Lock, London, 1890, 218p, Cloth, Novel
         [published anonymously]
08196A *A dead man's diary, written after his decease,*
         by Coulson Kernahan. Ward, Lock & Bowden,
         London, 1892, 218p, Cloth, Novel
08197 *The face beyond the door.* Hodder & Stoughton,
         London, 1904, 86p, Paper, Novel
08198 *The red peril.* Hurst & Blackett, London, 1908,
         329p, Cloth, Novel
08199 *Visions.* Hodder & Stoughton, London, 1905,
         300p, Cloth, Coll.
08200 *Visions old and new.* Hodder & Stoughton,
         London, 1921, 240p, Cloth, Coll.

KERR, A(rtemus) P.

08201   *The lost tribes and the land of Nod; an origi-
        nal natural gas story.* Indiana Newspaper
        Union, Indianapolis, 1897, 73p, Cloth, Novel

KERR, A(ndrew) W(illiam), 1848-

08202   *Space; a mirage.* R. Grant & Son, Edinburgh,
        1913, 484p, Cloth, Novel

KERR, ALVAH MILTON, 1858-1924

08203   *Two young inventors; the story of a flying
        boat.* Lee & Shepard, Boston, 1904, 312p,
        Cloth, Novel

KERR, GEOFFREY (Kemble Grinham), 1895-

08204   *Under the influence.* Michael Joseph, London,
        1953, 238p, Cloth, Novel

KERR, SOPHIE, 1880-1965

08205   *The man who knew the date.* Rinehart & Co.,
        New York, 1951, 248p, Cloth, Novel

KERR, STEPHEN T.

08206   *A bibliographical guide to Soviet fantasy and
        science fiction, 1957-1968.* Stephen T. Kerr,
        New York, 1969, 184p, Paper?, Nonf.

KERRUISH, JESSIE DOUGLAS

08207   *Babylonian nights' entertainments; a selection
        of narratives from the texts of certain un-
        discovered cuneiform tablets.* Denis Archer,
        London, 1934, 288p, Cloth, Novel
08208   *The Raksha Rajah; or, The king of the ogres;
        a wonderful story from our empire in the
        east; also, The story of the princess who
        went out and begged.* "Books for the Bairns,"
        London, 1911?, 61p, Paper, Coll.
08209   *The undying monster; a tale of the fifth di-
        mension.* Heath Cranton, London, 1922, 280p,
        Cloth, Novel

KERSH, GERALD, 1911-1968

08210   *The Brighton monster, and others.* William
        Heinemann, London, 1953, 197p, Cloth, Coll.
08211   *The great wash.* William Heinemann, London,
        1953, 246p, Cloth, Novel
08211A retitled: *The secret masters.* Ballantine,
        New York, 1953, 228p, Cloth, Novel
08212   *Men without bones.* Paperback Library, New
        York, 1962, 223p, Paper, Coll.
08213   *Men without bones, and other stories.* Wil-
        liam Heinemann, London, 1955, 194p, Cloth,
        Coll.
08214   *Nightshade & damnations.* Fawcett Gold Medal,
        Greenwich, Conn., 1968, 192p, Paper, Coll.
08215   *On an odd note; science fiction stories.*
        Ballantine, New York, 1958, 154p, Paper,
        Coll.
        The secret masters. [see 08211A]

KESHISHIAN, JOHN M., 1923-   [*biography included*], with Jacob Hay

06973   *Autopsy for a cosmonaut; a novel.* Little,
        Brown, Boston, 1969, 242p, Cloth, Novel
06973A retitled: *Death of a cosmonaut; a novel.*
        J. M. Dent & Sons, London, 1970, 242p,
        Cloth, Novel

KETTERER, DAVID (Anthony Theodor), 1942-
[*biography included*]

08216   *New worlds for old; the apocalyptic imaginatio,
        science fiction, and American literature.*
        Anchor Press, Garden City, 1974, 347p, Paper,
        Nonf.

KETTLE, PAMELA

08217   *The day of the women.* Leslie Frewin, London,
        1969, 208p, Cloth, Novel

KEY, ALEXANDER (Hill), 1904-   [*biography included*]

08218   *Bolts, a robot dog.* Westminster Press, Phila-
        delphia, 1966, 172p, Cloth, Novel [Sprockets
        #3]
08219   *Escape to Witch Mountain.* Westminster Press,
        Philadelphia, 1968, 172p, Cloth, Novel
08220   *Flight to the lonesome place.* Westminster
        Press, Philadelphia, 1971, 192p, Cloth, Novel
08221   *The forgotten door.* Westminster Press, Phila-
        delphia, 1965, 126p, Cloth, Novel
08222   *The golden enemy.* Westminster Press, Philadel-
        phia, 1969, 176p, Cloth, Novel
08223   *The incredible tide.* Westminster Press, Phila-
        delphia, 1970, 159p, Cloth, Novel
08224   *The preposterous adventures of Swimmer.* West-
        minster Press, Philadelphia, 1973, 128p,
        Cloth, Novel
08225   *Rivets and Sprockets.* Westminster Press, Phil-
        adelphia, 1964, 160p, Cloth, Novel [Sprockets
        #2]
08226   *Sprockets, a little robot.* Westminster Press,
        Philadelphia, 1963, 144p, Cloth, Novel [Sproc-
        kets #1]

KEY, DAVID

08227   *The S.E.X. machine.* Bee-Line, New York, 1968,
        155p, Paper, Novel

KEY, EUGENE GEORGE

08228   *Mars mountain.* Fantasy Publications, Everett,
        PA, 1934?, 142p, Cloth, Coll.

KEY, (Sam)UEL (Whittell), 1874-

08229   *The broken fang, and other experiences of a
        specialist in spooks.* Hodder & Stoughton,
        London, 1920, 303p, Cloth, Coll. [Prof. Rhy-
        mer #1]
08230   *Yellow death (a tale of occult mysteries),
        recording a further experience of Professor
        Rhymer, the "spook" specialist.* Books Ltd.,
        London, 1921, 299p, Cloth, Novel [Rhymer #2]

KEYES, DANIEL, 1927-   [*biography included*]

08231 *Flowers for Algernon*. Harcourt, Brace &
       World, New York, 1966, 274p, Cloth, Novel

KEYES, NOEL, pseud. [David Noel Keightley,
1932-   ] [*biography included*]

08232 *Contact*. Paperback Library, New York, 1963,
       176p, Paper, Anth. [ghost edited by Sam
       Moskowitz]

KHARAFRA, RAMON

08233 *A queen of the east*. no publisher, no place,
       1915?, 191p, Cloth, Novel

KHOSROFIAN, HARRY, 1924-

08234 *The fallen star*. A Milestone Book, Comet
       Press, New York, 1959, 71p, Cloth, Novel

KIDD, (Mildred) VIRGINIA, 1921-   [*biography
included*], with Roger Elwood

04874 *Saving worlds; a collection of original sci-
       ence fiction stories*. Doubleday, Garden
       City, 1973, 237p, Cloth, Anth.
04874A retitled: *The wounded planet*. Bantam, New
       York, 1974, 236p, Paper, Anth.

KI DOST, ZAMIN, pseud. [Willimina Leonora
Armstrong, 1866-   ], with Will Levington
Comfort

03240 *Son of power*. Doubleday, Page, Garden City,
       1920, 350p, Cloth, Novel

KIEHLE, JOHN A.
     see: KEEL, JOHN A.

THE KILLER PLANTS, AND OTHER STORIES
     see: ELWOOD, ROGER

KINDER, STEPHEN

08235 *The sabertooth; a romance of Put-in-Bay*.
       Laird & Lee, Chicago, 1902, 270p, Cloth,
       Novel

KINDLER, ASTA, pseud. [Una Hicken]

08236 *Sun children of Ra*. Regency Press, London,
       1967, 377p, Cloth, Novel

KING, ALBERT

08237 *Stage two*. Robert Hale, London, 1974, 190p,
       Cloth, Novel

KING, (William Benjamin) BASIL, 1859-1928

08238 *Abraham's bosom*. Harper & Bros., New York,
       1918, 54p, Cloth, Novel
08239 *Going west*. Harper & Bros., New York, 1919,
       49p, Cloth, Story
08240 *The spreading dawn; stories of the great tran-
       sition*. Harper & Bros., New York, 1927,
       316p, Cloth, Coll. [includes 08238 and 08239,
       with other stories]

KING, CHRISTOPHER

08241 *Operation Mora*. Robert Hale, London, 1974,
       191p, Cloth, Novel

KING, (Frank) HARVEY

08242 *The inaugurator*. Holsum Publishing Co, South-
       port, UK, 1962, 11p, Paper, Story

KING, JOHN, pseud. [Ernest Lionel McKeag,
1896-   ] [*biography included*]

08243 *Shuna and the lost tribe*. Harborough Publish-
       ing Co., Stoke-on-Trent, UK, 1951, 128p,
       Paper, Novel [Shuna #2]
08244 *Shuna, white queen of the jungle*. Harborough
       Publishing Co., Stoke-on-Trent, UK, 1951,
       128p, Paper, Novel [Shuna #1]

KING, RUFUS (Frederick), 1893-

08245 *The fatal kiss mystery*. Crime Club, Doubleday,
       Doran, Garden City, 1928, 264p, Cloth, Novel

KING, STEPHEN, 1947-   [*biography included*]

08246 *Carrie*. Doubleday, Garden City, 1974, 199p,
       Cloth, Novel

KING, VINCENT, pseud. [Rex Thomas Vinson,
1935-   ] [*biography included*]

08246 *Another end*. Ballantine, New York, 1971, 185p,
       Paper, Novel
08247 *Candy Man*. Ballantine, New York, 1971, 250p,
       Paper, Novel
08248 *Light a last candle*. Ballantine, New York,
       1969, 217p, Paper, Novel

KING-HALL, LOU(ise Olga Elizabeth), 1897-

08249 *Fly envious time*. Peter Davies, London, 1944,
       176p, Cloth, Novel

KING-HALL, MAGDALEN, 1904-1971 [*biography included*]

08250 *Tea at Crumbo Castle; a novel*. Peter Davies,
       London, 1949, 221p, Cloth, Novel

KING-HALL, (William) STEPHEN (Richard), Baron King-Hall, 1893-1966 [*biography included*]

08251 *Men of destiny; or, The moment of no return.* K-H Services, London, 1960, 207p, Cloth, Novel
08251A retitled: *Moment of no return.* Ballantine, New York, 1961, 192p, Paper, Novel
08252 *Post-war pirate.* Methuen, London, 1931, 252p, Cloth, Novel

KING-SCOTT, PETER
    see: EDGAR, PETER

KING BERTIE

08253 *King Bertie, A.D. 1900.* Crown Publishing Co., London, 1883,   , Cloth, Novel

KING RAT

08254 *King rat.* Scientific Thriller, Sydney, 1950, 50p, Paper, Anth.

KING SOLOMON'S TREASURES
    see: DE MORGAN, JOHN

KING SOLOMON'S WIVES
    see: DE MORGAN, JOHN

KINGMAN, LEE, pseud. [Mary Lee Natti, 1919-]

08255 *Escape from the evil prophecy.* Houghton Mifflin, Boston, 1973, 188p, Cloth, Novel

KINGSBURY, R. H.

08256 *Science fiction reader.* Collier-Macmillan, London, 1970, 64p, Paper, Anth.

KINGSFORD, ANNA BONUS, 1846-1888

08257 *Dreams and dream-stories.* George Redway, London, 1888, 281p, Cloth, Coll.

KINGSLAND, WILLIAM, 1855-1936

08258 *A child's story of Atlantis.* Theosophical Publishing Society, London, 1908, 84p, Cloth, Novel
08259 *The mystic quest; a tale of two incarnations.* George Allen, London, 1891, 215p, Cloth, Novel

KINGSLEY, BETTINA, pseud. [Barry Kaplan]

08260 *The captive.* Dell, New York, 1974, 222p, Paper, Novel

KINGSMILL, HUGH, pseud. [Hugh Kingsmill Lunn, 1889-1949]

08261 *The dawn's delay.* Elkin Mathews, London, 1924, 203p, Cloth, Coll.
08262 *The dawn's delay, comprising The end of the world, disintegration of a politician and "W.J."; and, The return of William Shakespeare.* Eyre & Spottiswoode, London, 1948, 348p, Cloth, Coll.
08263 *The return of William Shakespeare.* Duckworth, London, 1929, 254p, Cloth, Novel

with Malcolm Muggeridge:

08264 *Brave old world; a mirror for the times.* Eyre & Spottiswoode, London, 1936, 187p, Cloth, Novel
08265 *1938; a pre-view of next year's news.* Eyre & Spottiswoode, London, 1937, 160p, Paper, Coll.

KINLEY, GEORGE, pseud.

08266 *Ferry Rocket.* Curtis Warren, London, 1954, 159p, Cloth, Novel

KINROSS, ALBERT, 1870-1929

08267 *The fearsome island, being a modern rendering of the narrative of one Silas Fordred, master mariner of Hythe, whose shipwreck and subsequent adventures are herein set forth; also an appendix accounting in a rational manner for the seeming marvels that Silas Fordred encountered during his sojourn on the fearsome island of Don Diego Rodriguez.* J. W. Arrowsmith, Bristol, 1896, 199p, Cloth, Novel

KIP, LEONARD, 1826-1906

08268 *Hannibal's man, and other tales; the Argus Christmas stories.* Argus Company, Printers, Albany, NY, 1878, 371p, Cloth, Coll.

KIPLING, ARTHUR WELLESLEY

08269 *The new dominion; a tale of to-morrow's wars.* Francis Griffiths, London, 1908, 292p, Cloth, Novel
08270 *The shadow of glory, being a history of the great war of 1910-1911.* Alston Rivers, London, 1910, 440p, Cloth, Novel

KIPLING, (Joseph) RUDYARD, 1865-1936

08271 *Actions and reactions.* Macmillan, London, 1909, 301p, Cloth, Coll.
08272 *The jungle book.* Macmillan, London, 1894, 212p, Cloth, Coll.
       The jungle book; The second jungle book. [see 08281A]
       The jungle books. [see 08281B]
08273 *The phantom 'rickshaw, and other tales.* A. H. Wheeler, Allahabad, India, 1888, 114p, Cloth Coll.
08274 *The phantom 'rickshaw, City of dreadful night, and other tales.* Lovell, New York, 189?, 224p, Cloth, Coll.

KIPLING, RUDYARD (cont.)

08275 *Puck of Pook's Hill.* Macmillan, London, 1906,
       306p, Cloth, Coll. [Puck #1]
08276 *Puck of Pook's Hill.* Doubleday, Page, New
       York, 1906, 277p, Cloth, Coll. [includes
       several more stories than the British edi-
       tion; Puck #1]
08277 *Rewards and fairies.* Macmillan, London, 1910,
       338p, Cloth, Coll. [Puck #2]
08278 *The second jungle book.* Macmillan, London,
       1895, 238p, Cloth, Coll.
08279 *They.* Charles Scribner's Sons, New York,
       1904, 76p, Cloth?, Novel
08280 *'They'; and, The brushwood boy.* Macmillan,
       London, 1925, 160p, Cloth, Coll.
08281 *The two jungle books.* Macmillan, London,
       1924, 576p, Cloth, Coll.
08281A retitled: *The jungle book; The second jungle
       book.* Doubleday, Page, Garden City, 1927,
       438p, Cloth, Coll.
08281B retitled: *The jungle books.* Doubleday, Gar-
       den City, 1948, 2vol, Cloth, Coll.
08282 *With the night mail; a story of 2000 A.D. (to-
       gether with extracts from the contemporary
       magazine in which it appeared).* Macmillan,
       London, 1909, 77p, Paper, Novel

KIPPAX, JOHN, pseud. [John Charles Hynam,
1915-1974 [*biography included*], with Dan Morgan

08283 *The neutral stars.* Ballantine, New York, 1973,
       215p, Paper, Novel [Venturer Twelve #3]
08284 *Seed of stars.* Ballantine, New York, 1972,
       213p, Paper, Novel [Venturer Twelve #2]
08285 *Thunder of stars.* Macdonald, London, 1968,
       159p, Cloth, Novel [Venturer Twelve #1]

KIRBAN, SALEM

08286 *666.* Tyndale House Publishers, Wheaton, PA,
       1970, 285p, Paper, Novel

KIRK, ELEANOR, pseud. [Eleanor Maria Ames,
1831-1905]

08287 *Libra; an astrological romance.* Eleanor Kirk,
       Brooklyn, 1896, 270p, Cloth, Novel

KIRK, ELMER R.

08288 *Four days with the dead.* Elmer Kirk, Buffalo,
       MO, 1953, 39p, Paper, Coll.

KIRK, HYLAND C(lare), 1846-1917

08289 *The revolt of the brutes; a fantasy of the
       Chicago Fair.* Charles T. Dillingham, New
       York, 1893, 123p, Paper, Novel
08290 *When age grows young; a romance.* Charles T.
       Dillingham, New York, 1888, 281p, Paper,
       Novel

KIRK, LAURENCE, pseud. [Eric Andrew Simson,
1895-   ]

08291 *The gale of the world.* Cassell, London, 1948,
       187p, Cloth, Novel

KIRK, RUSSELL (Amos), 1918-   [*biography included*]

08292 *A creature of the twilight; his memorials,
       being some account of episodes in the career
       of His Excellency Manfred Arcane, minister
       without portfolio to the hereditary president
       of the Commonwealth of Hamnegri, and de facto
       field commander of the armies of that august
       prince.* Fleet Publishing Corp., New York,
       1966, 320p, Cloth, Novel
       Lost Lake. [see 08294A]
08293 *Old House of Fear.* Fleet Publishing Corp.,
       New York, 1961, 256p, Cloth, Novel
08294 *The surly sullen bell; ten stories and sketches,
       uncanny or uncomfortable.* Fleet Publishing
       Corp., New York, 1962, 240p, Cloth, Coll.
08294A retitled: *Lost Lake.* Paperback Library, New
       York, 1964, 159p, Paper, Coll.

KIRKBY, JOHN, 1705-1754 [published anonymously]

08295 *The capacity and extent of the human understan-
       ding, as exemplified in the extraordinary
       case of Automathes, a young nobleman, who
       was accidentally left in his infancy upon a
       desolate island, and continued nineteen years
       in that solitary state, separate from all
       human society; a narrative abounding with
       many surprizing occurrences, both useful and
       entertaining to the reader.* R. Manby & H.
       Shute Cox, London, 1745, 284p, Cloth, Novel
       [adapted from *The history of Autonous*]

KIRKHAM, NELLIE

08296 *Unrest of their time.* Cresset Press, London,
       1935, 263p, Cloth, Novel

KIRMESS, C. H.

08297 *The Australian crisis.* Walter Scott Publishing
       Co., London, 1909, 335p, Cloth, Novel

KIRST, HANS HELLMUT, 1914-

08298 *No one will escape; a novel.* Weidenfeld & Ni-
       colson, London, 1959, 412p, Cloth, Novel
08298A retitled: *The seventh day.* Doubleday, Garden
       City, 1959, 424p, Cloth, Novel

KISHOR, SULAMITH ISH-
    see: ISH-KISHOR, SULAMITH

KISSLING, DOROTHY HIGHT
    see: LANGLEY, DOROTHY

KITCHELL, JOSEPH GRAY, 1862-1947

08299   *The Earl of Hell.* Century Co., New York, 1924, 325p, Cloth, Novel

KITMAN, MARVIN, 1929-   , with Jack Newfield, Victor S. Navasky, Richard R. Lingeman, and Karla Kuskin

08300   *Animal ranch; the great American fable.* Parallax Publishing Co., New York, 1966, 63p, Paper, Novel

KJELGAARD, JIM [James Arthur Kjelgaard, 1910-1959]

08301   *Fire-hunter.* Holiday House, New York, 1951, 217p, Cloth, Novel

KLAINER, ALBERT S., with Jo-Ann Klainer as L. T. Peters

08302   *The eleventh plague.* Simon & Schuster, New York, 1973, 192p, Cloth, Novel

KLAINER, JO-ANN, with Albert S. Klainer as L. T. Peters

08302   *The eleventh plague.* Simon & Schuster, New York, 1973, 192p, Cloth, Novel

KLARMANN, ANDREW (Francis), 1866-1931

08303   *The fool of God; a historical novel.* Frederick Pustet, New York, 1912, 533p, Cloth, Novel

KLASS, PHILIP
    see: TENN, WILLIAM

"KLAXON," pseud. [John Graham Bower, 1886-1940]

08304   *H.M.S.____.* William Blackwood & Sons, Edinburgh, 1918, 327p, Cloth, Coll.

KLEIN, EDWARD, with Richard Z. Chesnoff and Robert Littell

02921   *If Israel lost the war.* Coward-McCann, New York, 1969, 253p, Cloth, Novel

KLEIN, GÉRARD, 1937-   [*biography included*]

08305   *The day before tomorrow.* DAW, New York, 1972, 128p, Paper, Novel
08306   *The overlords of war.* Doubleday, Garden City, 1973, 186p, Cloth, Novel
08307   *Starmasters' gambit.* DAW, New York, 1973, 172p, Paper, Novel

KLEIN, JAY KAY, 1931-   [*biography included*]

08308   *Convention annual no. 1; Pittcon edition.* Jay Kay Klein, New York, 1961, 50p, Paper, Nonf.
08309   *Convention annual no. 2; Chicon III edition.* Jay Kay Klein, New York, 1963, 74p, Paper, Nonf.
08310   *Convention annual no. 3; Discon edition.* Jay Kay Klein, New York, 1964, 104p, Paper, Nonf.
08311   *Convention annual no. 4; Tricon edition.* Jay Kay Klein, New York, 1968, 100p, Paper, Nonf.

KLETTE, C(harles) H(erman) B(runo), 1861-

08312   *The lost mine of the Mono; a tale of the Sierra Nevada.* Cochrane Publishing Co., New York, 1909, 215p, Cloth, Novel

KLEVEN, ARTHUR

08313   *Memoirs of a smoking jacket.* Associated Booksellers, Westport, Conn., 1962, 126p, Cloth, Novel

KLIM, NIELS
    see: HOLBERG, LUDVIG

KLIMIUS, NICHOLAS
    see: HOLBERG, LUDVIG

KLINE, OTIS A(DELBERT), 1891-1946

08314   *Call of the savage.* Edward J. Clode, New York, 1937, 256p, Cloth, Novel [Jan #1]
08314A retitled: *Jan of the jungle.* Ace, New York, 1966, 172p, Paper, Novel [Jan #1]
08315   *Jan in India.* Fictioneer Books, Lakemont, GA, 1974, 191p, Paper, Novel [Jan #2]
       Jan of the jungle. [see 08314A]
08316   *Maza of the Moon.* A. C. McClurg, Chicago, 1930, 341p, Cloth, Novel
08317   *The outlaws of Mars.* Avalon, New York, 1960, 224p, Cloth, Novel [Mars #2]
08318   *The planet of peril.* A. C. McClurg, Chicago, 1929, 358p, Cloth, Novel [Grandon #1]
08319   *The port of peril.* Grandon Co., Providence, RI, 1949, 218p, Cloth, Novel [Grandon #3]
08320   *The prince of peril; the weird adventures of Zinlo, man of three worlds, upon the mysterious planet of Venus.* A. C. McClurg, Chicago, 1930, 322p, Cloth, Novel [Grandon #2]
08321   *The swordsman of Mars.* Avalon, New York, 1960, 218p, Cloth, Novel [Mars #1]
08322   *Tam, son of the tiger.* Avalon, New York, 1962, 222p, Cloth, Novel

KLISE, ROBERT S., 1928-1978

08323   *The last western.* Argus Communications, New York, 1974, 559p, Cloth, Novel

KLOOR, MARY CONWAY

08324   *My beloved Troshanus.* Vantage Press, New York, 1963, 169p, Cloth, Novel

KNAPP, ADELINE, 1860-1909

08325 *One thousand dollars a day; studies in practical economics.* Arena Publishing Co., Boston, 1894, 132p, Cloth, Coll.

KNAPP, GEORGE L(eonard), 1872-

08326 *The face of air.* John Lane, New York, 1912, 170p, Cloth, Novel

KNAPP, MARY CLAY

08327 *Whose soul have I now? a novel.* Arena Publishing Co., Boston, 1896, 242p, Cloth, Novel

KNAUSS, ROBERT
    see: HELDERS, Major

KNEBEL, FLETCHER, 1911-   [*biography included*]

08328 *Trespass.* Doubleday, Garden City, 1969, 371p, Cloth, Novel

with Charles W. Bailey II:

00708 *Seven days in May.* Harper & Row, New York, 1962, 342p, Cloth, Novel

KNERR, MICHAEL (E.)

08329 *Autosex,* by Mike Knerr. France Books, Hollywood, 1963, 159p, Paper, Novel
08330 *Sex life of the gods.* Uptown, Los Angeles, 1962, 160p, Paper, Novel

KNIGHT, DAMON (Francis), 1922-   [*biography included*]

    A for anything. [see 08368A]
    Analogue men. [see 08343A]
08331 *Beyond the barrier.* Doubleday, Garden City, 1964, 188p, Cloth, Novel
08332 *Beyond tomorrow; ten science fiction adventures.* Harper & Row, New York, 1965, 332p, Cloth, Anth.
08333 *A century of great short science fiction novels.* Delacorte Press, New York, 1964, 379p, Cloth, Anth.
08334 *A century of science fiction.* Simon & Schuster, New York, 1962, 352p, Cloth, Anth.
08335 *Cities of wonder.* Doubleday, Garden City, 1966, 252p, Cloth, Anth.
08336 *The dark side.* Doubleday, Garden City, 1965, 241p, Cloth, Anth.
08337 *Dimension X; five science fiction novellas.* Simon & Schuster, New York, 1970, 351p, Cloth, Anth.
08337A retitled: *Elsewhere x 3; three novellas.* Coronet, London, 1974, 192p, Paper, Anth. [abridged]
08338 *Far out; 13 science fiction stories.* Simon & Schuster, New York, 1961, 282p, Cloth, Coll.
08339 *First contact.* Pinnacle, New York, 1971, 219p, Paper, Anth.
08340 *First flight.* Lancer, New York, 1963, 160p, Paper, Anth.

08340A retitled: *Now begins tomorrow.* Lancer, New York, 1969, 160p, Paper, Anth.
08341 *The golden road; great tales of fantasy and the supernatural.* Simon & Schuster, New York, 1974, 447p, Cloth, Anth.
08342 *Happy endings; 15 stories by the masters of the macabre.* Bobbs-Merrill, Indianapolis, 1974, 205p, Cloth, Anth.
08343 *Hell's pavement.* Lion, New York, 1955, 192p, Paper, Novel
08343A retitled: *Analogue men.* Berkley Medallion, New York, 1962, 160p, Paper, Novel
08344 *In deep.* Berkley Medallion, New York, 1963, 158p, Paper, Coll.
08345 *In search of wonder; essays on modern science fiction.* Advent: Publishers, Chicago, 1956, 180p, Cloth, Nonf. Coll.
08346 *In search of wonder; essays on modern science fiction, revised and enlarged.* Advent: Publishers, Chicago, 1967, 306p, Cloth, Nonf. Coll.
08347 *Masters of evolution.* Ace Double, New York, 1959, 96p, Paper, Novel
08348 *The metal smile.* Belmont, New York, 1968, 158p, Paper, Anth.
08349 *Mind switch.* Berkley Medallion, New York, 1965, 144p, Paper, Novel
08349A retitled: *The other foot.* Rapp Whiting & Wheaton, London, 1966, 159p, Cloth, Novel
08350 *Nebula Award stories 1965.* Doubleday, Garden City, 1966, 301p, Cloth, Anth.
    Now begins tomorrow. [see 08340A]
08351 *Off center; a scintillating science-fiction collection.* Ace Double, New York, 1965, 141p, Paper, Coll.
08351A retitled: *Off centre.* Victor Gollancz, London, 1969, 192p, Cloth, Coll.
08352 *One hundred years of science fiction.* Simon & Schuster, New York, 1968, 384p, Cloth, Anth.
08352A retitled: *One hundred years of science fiction, book one.* Pan, London, 1972, 226p, Paper, Anth. [abridged]
08352B retitled: *One hundred years of science fiction, book two.* Pan, London, 1972, 179p, Paper, Anth. [abridged; 08352A and 08352B together comprise the original volume]
08353 *Orbit 1; a science fiction anthology.* G. P. Putnam's Sons, New York, 1966, 192p, Cloth, Anth.
08354 *Orbit 2; the best new science fiction of the year.* G. P. Putnam's Sons, New York, 1967, 255p, Cloth, Anth.
08355 *Orbit 3; the best new science fiction of the year.* G. P. Putnam's Sons, New York, 1968, 224p, Cloth, Anth.
08356 *Orbit 4; the best new science fiction of the year.* G. P. Putnam's Sons, New York, 1968, 254p, Cloth, Anth.
08357 *Orbit 5; the best all-new science fiction of the year.* G. P. Putnam's Sons, New York, 1969, 222p, Cloth, Anth.
08358 *Orbit 6; an anthology of new science fiction stories.* G. P. Putnam's Sons, New York, 1970, 245p, Cloth, Anth.
08359 *Orbit 7; an anthology of new science fiction stories.* G. P. Putnam's Sons, New York, 1970, 217p, Cloth, Anth.
08360 *Orbit 8; an anthology of new science fiction stories.* G. P. Putnam's Sons, New York, 1970, 219p, Cloth, Anth.
08361 *Orbit 9; an anthology of new science fiction stories.* G. P. Putnam's Sons, New York, 1971, 255p, Cloth, Anth.

KNIGHT, DAMON (cont.)

08362   *Orbit 10; an anthology of new science fiction
         stories*. G. P. Putnam's Sons, New York,
         1972, 254p, Cloth, Anth.
08363   *Orbit 11; an anthology of new stories*. G. P.
         Putnam's Sons, New York, 1972, 255p, Cloth,
         Anth.
08364   *Orbit 12; an anthology of new science fiction
         stories*. G. P. Putnam's Sons, New York,
         1973, 254p, Cloth, Anth.
08365   *Orbit 13; an anthology of new science fiction
         stories*. Berkley Publishing Corp., New
         York, 1974, 250p, Cloth, Anth.
08366   *Orbit 14*. Harper & Row, New York, 1974, 210p,
         Cloth, Anth.
08367   *Orbit 15*. Harper & Row, New York, 1974, 207p,
         Cloth, Anth.
         The other foot. [see 08349A]
08368   *The people maker*. Zenith, Rockville Centre,
         NY, 1959, 159p, Paper, Novel
08368A   retitled: *A for anything*. Four Square, Lon-
         don, 1961, 160p, Paper, Novel
08369   *Perchance to dream*. Doubleday, Garden City,
         1972, 208p, Cloth, Anth.
08370   *A pocketful of stars*. Doubleday, Garden City,
         1971, 294p, Cloth, Anth.
08371   *The Rithian Terror*. Ace Double, New York,
         1965, 111p, Paper, Novel
08372   *A science fiction argosy*. Simon & Schuster,
         New York, 1972, 828p, Cloth, Anth.
08373   *Science fiction inventions*. Lancer, New York,
         1967, 256p, Paper, Anth.
08374   *The shape of things*. Popular Library, New
         York, 1965, 206p, Paper, Anth.
08375   *A shocking thing*. Pocket Books, New York,
         1974, 245p, Paper, Anth.
08376   *The sun saboteurs*. Ace Double, New York,
         1961, 101p, Paper, Novel
08377   *Thirteen French science-fiction stories*.
         Bantam, New York, 1965, 167p, Paper, Anth.
08378   *Three novels: Rule golden; Natural state;
         The dying man*. Doubleday, Garden City,
         1967, 189p, Cloth, Coll.
08379   *Tomorrow and tomorrow; ten tales of the fu-
         ture*. Simon & Schuster, New York, 1973,
         253p, Cloth, Anth.
08380   *Tomorrow x 4*. Gold Medal, Greenwich, Conn.,
         1964, 176p, Paper, Anth.
08381   *Toward infinity; 9 science fiction tales*.
         Simon & Schuster, New York, 1968, 319p,
         Cloth, Anth.
08381A   retitled: *Towards infinity; nine science fic-
         tion adventures*. Victor Gollancz, London,
         1970, 319p, Cloth, Anth.
08382   *Turning on; thirteen stories*. Doubleday,
         Garden City, 1966, 180p, Cloth, Coll.
08383   *Turning on; fourteen stories*. Victor Gol-
         lancz, London, 1967, 159p, Cloth, Coll.
         [slightly different contents]
08384   *Two novels*. Victor Gollancz, London, 1974,
         223p, Cloth, Coll.
08385   *World without children; and, The Earth Quar-
         ter; two science fiction novels*. Lancer,
         New York, 1970, 192p, Paper, Coll. [*The
         Earth Quarter* is a retitled version of *The
         sun saboteurs*]
08386   *Worlds to come; nine science fiction adven-
         tures*. Harper & Row, New York, 1967, 337p,
         Cloth, Anth.

KNIGHT, ERIC (Mowbray), 1897-1943

08387   *The flying Yorkshireman*. C. Bush, Toronto,
         1940, 47p, Cloth, Story [Sam Small series]
08388   *Sam Small flies again; the amazing adventures
         of the flying Yorkshireman*. Harper & Bros.
         New York, 1942, 285p, Cloth, Coll. [Sam
         Small series]
08388A   retitled: *Sam Small, the flying Yorkshireman*
         Neville Spearman, London, 1957, 235p, Cloth
         Coll. [Sam Small series; abridged]

KNIGHT, L(eonard) A(lfred), 1895-

08389   *The astounding Doctor Yell*. Sampson Low, Mar-
         ston, London, 1950, 186p, Cloth, Novel

KNIGHT, MALLORY T., pseud.
    see: HURWOOD, BERNHARDT J.

KNIGHT, NORMAN L(ouis), 1895-1970? [*biography
included*], with James Blish

01523   *A torrent of faces*. Doubleday, Garden City,
         1967, 270p, Cloth, Novel

KNIGHT, RANDY

08390   *Tomorrow has arrived*. Saber, Los Angeles?,
         1970, 153p, Paper, Novel

KNITTEL, JOHN (Herman Emanuel), 1891-1970

08391   *Nile gold; a legend of modern Egypt*. Double-
         day, Doran, Garden City, 1929, 322p, Cloth,
         Novel

KNOBLOCK, EDWARD [Edward Knoblauch, 1874-1945]

08392   *The ant heap; a novel*. Chapman & Hall, London
         1929, 327p, Cloth, Novel

KNOLES, WILLIAM
    see: ALLISON, CLYDE

KNOTT, WILLIAM C(ecil), 1927-   [*biography included*]

08393   *Journey across the third planet*. Chilton Book
         Co., Philadelphia, 1969, 160p, Cloth, Novel

KNOTT, WILLIAM WILSON, with Austyn Granville

06244   *If the devil came to Chicago*. Bow-Knot Publi-
         shing Co., Chicago, 1894, 353p, Paper, Novel

KNOWLES, LEO
    see: GREGORY, JULIAN R.

KNOWLES, MABEL WINIFRED
    see: LURGAN, LESTER

KNOWLES, VERNON, 1899-1968

08394 *Eternity in an hour; a study in childhood.* Collins, London, 1932, 141p, Cloth, Novel

08395 *Here and otherwise.* Robert Holden, London, 1926, 257p, Cloth, Coll.

08396 *The ladder.* Mandrake Press, London, 1929, 98p, Cloth, Novel

08397 *Silver nutmegs.* Robert Holden, London, 1927, 202p, Cloth, Coll. [includes *The ladder*]

08398 *The street of queer houses, and other stories.* Boullion-Biggs, New York, 1924, 156p, Cloth, Coll.

08399 *Two and two make five.* George Newnes, London, 1935, 256p, Cloth, Coll.

KNOWLES, W(illiam) P(lenderleith)

08400 *Jim McWhirter.* C. W. Daniel, London, 1933, 282p, Cloth, Novel

KNOWLTON, J(ames) A(lbert)

08401 *Origin.* Eastern Publishing Co., Boston, 1900, 339p, Cloth, Novel

KNOX, CALVIN M., pseud.
see: SILVERBERG, ROBERT

KNOX, G(ordon) D(aniell), with T. C. Wignall

08402 *Atoms.* Mills & Boon, London, 1923, 288p, Cloth, Novel

KNOX, HUGH (Randolph), 1942- [*biography included*]

08403 *The satyr.* Holloway House, Los Angeles, 1970, 286p, Paper, Novel

as H. R. Kaye:

08404 *Eros 2000 A.D.* Brandon House, North Hollywood, CA, 1970, 174p, Paper, Novel

KNOX, RONALD A(rbuthnott), 1888-1957

08405 *Memoirs of the future, being memoirs of the years 1915-1972, written in the year of grace 1988, by Opal, Lady Porstock.* Methuen, London, 1923, 244p, Cloth, Novel

KOCH, ERIC, 1919-

08406 *The leisure riots; a comic novel.* Tundra Books, Plattsburgh, NY, 1973, 219p, Cloth, Novel

KOCHER, PAUL H(arold), 1907-

08407 *Master of Middle-Earth; the fiction of J. R. R. Tolkien.* Houghton Mifflin, Boston, 1972, 247p, Cloth, Nonf.

KOENIGSMARK THE ROBBER
see: RASPE, RUDOLF ERICH

KOESTER, FRANK, 1876-1927

08408 *Under the desert stars; a novel.* Washington Square Publishing Co., New York, 1923, 317p, Cloth, Novel

KOESTLER, ARTHUR, 1905-

08409 *The age of longing.* Collins, London, 1951, 448p, Cloth, Novel

KOLDA, HELENA, 1928- , with Ivo Duka

04565 *Martin and his friend from outer space.* Harper & Bros., New York, 1955, 96p, Cloth, Novel

KOMROFF, MANUEL, 1890-1974 [*biography included*]

08410 *I, the tiger.* Coward-McCann, New York, 1933, 249p, Cloth, Novel

KONIGSBURG, E(laine) L(obl), 1930-

08411 *A proud taste for scarlet and miniver.* Atheneum, New York, 1973, 201p, Cloth, Novel

KONVITZ, JEFFREY, 1944- [*biography included*]

08412 *The sentinel.* Simon & Schuster, New York, 1974, 315p, Cloth, Novel

KOOMOTER, ZENO, pseud. [Joseph Marnell]

08413 *Visitor from planet Phlox.* Vantage Press, New York, 1964, 56p, Cloth, Novel

KOONTZ, DEAN R(ay), 1945- [*biography included*]

08414 *Anti-man.* Paperback Library, New York, 1970, 142p, Paper, Novel

08415 *Beastchild.* Lancer, New York, 1970, 189p, Paper, Novel

08416 *The Crimson Witch.* Curtis, New York, 1971, 176p, Paper, Novel

08417 *Dark of the woods.* Ace Double, New York, 1970, 108p, Paper, Novel

08418 *The dark symphony.* Lancer, New York, 1970, 205p, Paper, Novel

08419 *A darkness in my soul.* DAW, New York, 1972, 124p, Paper, Novel

08420 *Demon seed.* Bantam, New York, 1973, 182p, Paper, Novel

08421 *The fall of the dream machine.* Ace Double, New York, 1969, 129p, Paper, Novel

08422 *Fear that man.* Ace Double, New York, 1969, 131p, Paper, Novel

08423 *The flesh in the Furnace.* Bantam, New York, 1972, 132p, Paper, Novel

08424 *The haunted Earth.* Lancer, New York, 1973, 192p, Paper, Novel

KOONTZ, DEAN R. (cont.)

08425 *Hell's gate*. Lancer, New York, 1970, 190p, Paper, Novel
08426 *Soft come the dragons*. Ace Double, New York, 1970, 143p, Paper, Coll.
08427 *Star quest*. Ace Double, New York, 1968, 127p, Paper, Novel
08428 *Starblood*. Lancer, New York, 1972, 157p, Paper, Novel
08429 *Time thieves*. Ace Double, New York, 1972, 109p, Paper, Novel
08430 *Warlock*. Lancer, New York, 1972, 221p, Paper, Novel
08431 *A werewolf among us*. Ballantine, New York, 1973, 211p, Paper, Novel

KOONTZ, GERDA
   see: AMBER, GRACIE

KOPF, SEYMOUR O.

08432 *Land of the Moobs*. South China, Hong Kong, 1968, 57p, Paper, Coll.

KORNBLUTH, C(yril) M., 1923-1958

08433 *Best SF stories of C. M. Kornbluth*. Faber & Faber, London, 1968, 277p, Cloth, Coll. *Christmas Eve*. [see 08438A]
08434 *The explorers; short stories*. Ballantine, New York, 1954, 147p, Paper, Coll.
08435 *The marching morons, and other famous science fiction stories*. Ballantine, New York, 1959, 158p, Paper, Coll.
08436 *A mile beyond the Moon*. Doubleday, Garden City, 1958, 239p, Cloth, Coll.
08437 *The mindworm*. Michael Joseph, London, 1955, 256p, Cloth, Coll.
08438 *Not this August*. Doubleday, Garden City, 1955, 190p, Cloth, Novel
08438A retitled: *Christmas Eve*. Michael Joseph, London, 1956, 207p, Cloth, Novel
08439 *The Syndic*. Doubleday, Garden City, 1953, 223p, Cloth, Novel
08440 *Takeoff*. Doubleday, Garden City, 1952, 218p, Cloth, Novel
08441 *Thirteen o'clock, and other zero hours*. Dell, New York, 1970, 155p, Paper, Coll.

with Judith Merril as Cyril Judd:

08442 *Gunner Cade*. Simon & Schuster, New York, 1952, 218p, Cloth, Novel
08442A *Gunner Cade*, by C. M. Kornbluth and Judith Merril. Dell, New York, 1969, 160p, Paper, Novel
08443 *Outpost Mars; a science-fiction novel*. Abelard Press, New York, 1952, 268p, Cloth, Novel
08443A retitled: *Sin in space; an expose of the scarlet planet*. Galaxy Publishing Corp., New York, 1961, 190p, Paper, Novel

with Frederik Pohl:

08444 *Gladiator-at-law*. Ballantine, New York, 1955, 171p, Cloth, Novel
08445 *Search the sky*. Ballantine, New York, 1954, 166p, Cloth, Novel
08446 *The space merchants*. Ballantine, New York, 1953, 181p, Cloth, Novel

08447 *Wolfbane*. Ballantine, New York, 1959, 140p, Paper, Novel
08448 *The wonder effect*. Ballantine, New York, 196[?], 159p, Paper, Coll.

KORNBLUTH, MARY, 1920-

08449 *Science fiction showcase; an anthology*. Doubleday, Garden City, 1959, 264p, Cloth, Anth[?]

KORZENIOWSKI, JOSEF
   see: CONRAD, JOSEPH

KRAMER, NORA

08450 *Arrow book of ghost stories*. Scholastic Book Services, New York, 1960, 116p, Paper, Anth[?]

KRANZ, E(dwin) KIRKER, 1949- [*biography included*]

08451 *The clouded mirror*. Lenox Hill Press, New York, 1971, 192p, Cloth, Novel

KRASSNOFF, PETER N. [Petr Nikolaevich Krasno[?] 1869-1947]

08452 *The black mass*. Duffield & Green, New York, 1931, 130p, Cloth, Novel
08453 *The white coat*. Duffield & Co., New York, 1929, 439p, Cloth, Coll. [includes *The black mass*]

KREISHEIMER, H. C.

08454 *The Whooping Crane*. Pageant Press, New York, 1955, 89p, Cloth, Novel

KREMER, RAYMOND de
   see: RAY, JEAN

KREUDER, ERNST, 1903-

08455 *The attic pretenders*. Putnam & Co., London, 1948, 186p, Cloth, Novel

KREUPP, W.

08456 *The extraordinary professor*. Colt Press, Paterson, NJ, 1944, 263p, Cloth, Novel

KREYMBORG, ALFRED, 1883-1966

08457 *Funnybone Alley*. Macaulay, New York, 1927, 268p, Cloth, Novel

KROPP, LLOYD (Edward), 1936?- [*biography included*]

08458 *The drift*. Doubleday, Garden City, 1969, 263p, Cloth, Novel

KROPP, LLOYD (cont.)

08459 *Who is Mary Stark?* Doubleday, Garden City,
        1974, 348p, Cloth, Novel

KUBIN, ALFRED, 1877-1959

08460 *The other side; a fantastic novel.* Crown
        Publishers, New York, 1967, 350p, Cloth,
        Novel [includes the author's 78-page auto-
        biography]

KUDLAY, ROBERT R., with Joan Leiby

08461 *Burroughs' science fiction, with an analytical
        subject and name index.* School of Library
        and Information Science, State University
        College of Arts & Sciences, Geneseo, NY,
        1973, 236p, Paper, Nonf.

KUEBLER, HAROLD W.

08462 *The treasury of science fiction classics.*
        Hanover House, Garden City, NY, 1954, 694p,
        Cloth, Anth.

KUEHNELT-LEDDIHN, (Marie) CHRISTIANE von, with
Erik von Kuehnelt-Leddihn

08463 *Moscow 1979.* Sheed & Ward, New York, 1940,
        337p, Cloth, Novel

KUEHNELT-LEDDIHN, ERIK (Maria), Ritter von,
1909- [*biography included*], with Christiane von Kuehnelt-Leddihn

08463 *Moscow 1979.* Sheed & Ward, New York, 1940,
        337p, Cloth, Novel

KULLINGER, J. L., pseud. [Vince Ducette]

08464 *Sex 99.* Classic Publications, Los Angeles,
        1968, 190p, Paper, Novel [name on cover is
        Gyle Davis]
08464A retitled: *1999 sex erotics*, by Gil Daniels.
        Classic Publications, Los Angeles, 1970,
        190p, Paper, Novel

KUMMER, FREDERIC ARNOLD, 1873-1943

08465 *The first days of man, as narrated quite simp-
        ly for young readers.* George H. Doran, New
        York, 1922, 293p, Cloth, Novel
08466 *Gentlemen in Hades; the story of a damned
        débutante.* Sears Publishing Co., New York,
        1930, 269p, Cloth, Novel [Hades #2]
08467 *Ladies in Hades; a story of Hell's smart set.*
        J. H. Sears, New York, 1928, 272p, Cloth,
        Novel [Hades #1]
08468 *Maypoles and morals.* J. H. Sears, New York,
        1929, 279p, Cloth, Novel

with Henry P. Janes:

07838 *The second coming; a vision.* Dodd, Mead, New
        York, 1916, 96p, Cloth, Novel

KUNST, EARLE

08469 *The mystery of Evangeline Fairfax.* Metropoli-
        tan Press, New York, 1910, 242p, Cloth, Novel

KUPPORD, SKELTON, pseud. [J. Adams]

08470 *A fortune from the sky.* Thomas Nelson & Sons,
        London, 1902, 230p, Cloth, Novel

KURLAND, MICHAEL (Joseph), 1938- [*biography
included*]

08471 *Transmission error.* Pyramid, New York, 1970,
        159p, Paper, Novel
08472 *The Unicorn Girl.* Pyramid, New York, 1969,
        159p, Paper, Novel [Greenwich Village #2]

with Chester Anderson:

00257 *Ten years to doomsday; a science fiction novel.*
        Pyramid, New York, 1964, 158p, Paper, Novel

KURTZ, KATHERINE (Irene), 1944- [*biography
included*]

08473 *Deryni checkmate; volume II in the Chronicles
        of the Deryni.* Ballantine, New York, 1972,
        303p, Paper, Novel [Deryni #2]
08474 *Deryni rising.* Ballantine, New York, 1970,
        271p, Paper, Novel [Deryni #1]
08475 *High Deryni; volume III of the Deryni Chroni-
        cles.* Ballantine, New York, 1973, 369p,
        Paper, Novel [Deryni #3]

KUSKIN, KARLA, 1932- [*biography included*],
with Jack Newfield, Victor S. Navasky, Richard
R. Lingeman, & Marvin Kitman

08300 *Animal ranch; the great American fable.* Para-
        llax Publishing Co., New York, 1966, 63p,
        Paper, Novel

KUTTNER, HENRY, 1915-1958 [*biography included*]
[everything written by Kuttner from 1940-1958
was to some degree a collaboration with his
wife, C. L. Moore, and is so indicated here]

08476 *Ahead of time; ten stories of science fiction
        and fantasy.* Ballantine, New York, 1953,
        179p, Cloth, Coll. [with C. L. Moore]
08477 *As you were.* American Science Fiction, Sydney,
        1955, 34p, Paper, Story
08478 *The best of Kuttner, volume 1.* Mayflower-Dell,
        London, 1965, 286p, Paper, Coll. [with C. L.
        Moore]
08479 *The best of Kuttner, volume 2.* Mayflower-Dell,
        London, 1966, 288p, Paper, Coll. [with C. L.
        Moore]
08480 *Bypass to otherness.* Ballantine, New York,
        1961, 144p, Paper, Coll. [with C. L. Moore]
08481 *The creature from beyond infinity.* Popular
        Library, New York, 1968, 125p, Paper, Novel
08482 *The Dark World.* Ace, New York, 1965, 126p,
        Paper, Novel [with C. L. Moore]
        Destination infinity. [see 08483A]
08483 *Fury.* Grosset & Dunlap, New York, 1950, 186p,
        Cloth, Novel [with C. L. Moore]

KUTTNER, HENRY (cont.)

08483A retitled: *Destination infinity.* Avon, New
         York, 1958, 192p, Paper, Novel [with Moore]
08484 *The Mask of Circe.* Ace, New York, 1971, 158p,
         Paper, Novel [with C. L. Moore]
       Mutant. [see 08499A]
08485 *Remember tomorrow.* American Science Fiction,
         Sydney, 1954, 34p, Paper, Story [with C. L.
         Moore]
08486 *Return to otherness.* Ballantine, New York,
         1962, 240p, Paper, Coll. [with C. L. Moore]
       Robots have no tails. [see 08500A]
08487 *Sword of tomorrow.* American Science Fiction,
         Sydney, 1955, 34p, Paper, Story [with C. L.
         Moore]
08488 *The time axis.* Ace, New York, 1965, 142p,
         Paper, Novel [with C. L. Moore]
08489 *Valley of the Flame.* Ace, New York, 1964,
         156p, Paper, Novel [with C. L. Moore]
08490 *Way of the gods.* American Science Fiction,
         Sydney, 1954, 34p, Paper, Story [with C. L.
         Moore]
       The Well of the Worlds. [see 08503A]

as Will Garth:

08491 *Dr. Cyclops.* Phoenix Press, New York, 1940,
         255p, Cloth, Movie

with C. L. Moore:

08492 *Earth's last citadel.* Ace, New York, 1964,
         128p, Paper, Novel
08493 *No boundaries.* Ballantine, New York, 1955,
         151p, Cloth, Coll.

with C. L. Moore as Lawrence O'Donnell:

08494 *Clash by night.* American Science Fiction,
         Sydney, 1952, 34p, Paper, Story

as Lewis Padgett, with C. L. Moore:

08495 *Beyond Earth's gates.* Ace Double, New York,
         1954, 138p, Paper, Novel

with C. L. Moore as Lewis Padgett:

08496 *Chessboard planet.* Galaxy SF Novel, New York,
         1956, 124p, Paper, Novel
08496A retitled: *The far reality.* Consul, London,
         1963, 155p, Paper, Novel
08497 *A gnome there was, and other tales of science
         fiction and fantasy.* Simon & Schuster, New
         York, 1950, 276p, Cloth, Coll.
08498 *Line to tomorrow.* Bantam, New York, 1954,
         184p, Paper, Coll.
08499 *Mutant.* Gnome Press, New York, 1953, 210p,
         Cloth, Novel
08499A *Mutant,* by Henry Kuttner. Weidenfeld & Nicol-
         son, London, 1954, 224p, Cloth, Novel
08500 *Robots have no tails.* Gnome Press, New York,
         1952, 224p, Cloth, Coll.
08500A *Robots have no tails,* by Henry Kuttner. Lan-
         cer, New York, 1973, 221p, Paper, Coll.
08501 *Tomorrow and tomorrow.* Consul, London, 1963,
         106p, Paper, Novel
08502 *Tomorrow and tomorrow; and, The fairy chess-
         men; two science fiction novels.* Gnome
         Press, New York, 1951, 254p, Cloth, Coll.
08503 *Well of the Worlds.* Galaxy SF Novel, New
         York, 1953, 127p, Paper, Novel
08503A *The Well of the Worlds,* by Henry Kuttner.
         Ace, New York, 1965, 142p, Paper, Novel

books by C. L. Moore with anonymous contributions by Kuttner:

08504 *Doomsday morning.* Doubleday, Garden City,
         1957, 216p, Cloth, Novel
08505 *Judgment night; a selection of science fictio*
         Gnome Press, New York, 1952, 344p, Cloth,
         Coll.
08506 *There shall be darkness.* American Science
         Fiction, Sydney, 1954, 34p, Paper, Story

KUYUMJIAN, DIKRAN
    see: ARLEN, MICHAEL

KYFFIN-TAYLOR, BESSIE, 1880?-1922

08507 *From out of the silence; seven strange storie*
         Books Ltd., London, 1920, 284p, Cloth, Coll

L., VIC ST.
    see: HOPKINS, JEUNE

L., X.
    see: FIELD, JULIAN OSGOOD

L W J S, pseud.
    see: ROWEL, M.

LABOULAYE, ÉDOUARD RENÉ LEFEBVRE- (de), 1811-
1883

08508 *Abdallah; or, The four-leaved shamrock.* Samp
         son Low, Son & Marston, London, 1868, 181p,
         Cloth, Novel
08508A retitled: *The quest of the four-leaved clove
         a story of Arabia.* Ginn & Co., Boston, 191
         211p, Cloth, Novel

LA BRUJA
    see: BRUJA, LA

LABRY, MICHEL

08509 *The sextuplets of Loqmaria.* George Allen &
         Unwin, London, 1964, 158p, Cloth, Novel

LA BUQUE, JEAN de

08510 *Slave island.* Bell House, New York?, 1969,
         179p, Paper, Novel

LACH-SZYRMA, W(ladislaw) S(omerville), 1841-
1915

08511 *A voice from another world,* by W. S. L. S.
         James Parker, Oxford, 1874, 68p, Cloth,
         Novel [Venus #1]
08512 retitled: *Aleriel; or, A voyage to other worl
         a tale.* Wyman & Sons, London, 1883, 220p,
         Cloth, Novel [expanded; Venus #1]
08513 *Under other conditions; a tale.* Adam & Charl
         Black, London, 1892, 229p, Cloth, Novel
         [Venus #2]

LADY IN DANGER

08514 *Lady in danger.* Utopian Publications, London, 1945, 36p, Paper, Anth.

LAFARGUE, PAUL, 1842-1911

08515 *The sale of an appetite.* Charles H. Kerr, Chicago, 1904, 57p, Cloth, Novel

LAFARGUE, PHILIP, pseud. [Joseph Henry Philpot, 1850-1939]

08516 *The forsaken way; a romance.* Hurst & Blackett, London, 1900, 287p, Cloth, Novel

LAFFERTY, R(aphael) A(loysius), 1914- [biography included]

08517 *Arrive at Easterwine; the autobiography of a ktistec machine.* Charles Scribner's Sons, New York, 1971, 216p, Cloth, Novel
08518 *The devil is dead.* Avon, New York, 1971, 224p, Paper, Novel
08519 *Does anyone else have something further to add? stories about secret places and mean men.* Charles Scribner's Sons, New York, 1974, 273p, Cloth, Coll.
08520 *The flame is green.* Walker, New York, 1971, 245p, Cloth, Novel
08521 *Fourth Mansions.* Ace, New York, 1969, 252p, Paper, Novel
08522 *Nine hundred grandmothers.* Ace, New York, 1970, 318p, Paper, Coll.
08523 *Past master.* Ace, New York, 1968, 191p, Paper, Novel
08524 *The reefs of Earth.* Berkley Medallion, New York, 1968, 144p, Paper, Novel
08525 *Space chantey.* Ace Double, New York, 1968, 123p, Paper, Novel
08526 *Strange doings; stories.* Charles Scribner's Sons, New York, 1972, 276p, Cloth, Coll.

LAFOND, pseud.

08527 *Diane.* Utopian Publications, London, 1945?, 32p, Paper, Story

LAFORGUE, JULES, 1860-1887

08528 *Six moral tales from Jules Laforgue.* Horace Liveright, New York, 1928, 292p, Cloth, Coll.

LAGERKVIST, PÄR (Fabian), 1891-1974

08529 *The eternal smile, and other stories.* Random House, New York, 1954, 389p, Cloth, Coll.
08530 *The eternal smile, and other stories.* Chatto & Windus, London, 1971, 206p, Cloth, Coll. [different contents]
08530A retitled: *The eternal smile; three stories.* Hill & Wang, New York, 1971, 206p, Cloth, Coll.
08531 *The sibyl.* Chatto & Windus, London, 1958, 152p, Cloth, Novel

LAGERLÖF, SELMA (Ottiliana Lovisa), 1858-1940

08532 *The general's ring.* Doubleday, Doran, Garden City, 1928, 212p, Cloth, Novel
08533 *The ring of the Löwenskölds, including The general's ring, Charlotte Löwensköld, Anna Svärd.* Doubleday, Doran, Garden City, 1931, 827p, Cloth, Coll.
08534 *The story of Gösta Berling.* Little, Brown, Boston, 1898, 473p, Cloth, Novel

LAHMAN, DAMON

08535 *Stories in fantasia.* Exposition Press, New York, 1967, 99p, Cloth, Coll.

LAING, ALEXANDER (Kinnan), 1903- [biography included]

08536 *The cadaver of Gideon Wyck, by a medical student*, edited by Alexander Laing. Farrar & Rinehart, New York, 1934, 376p, Cloth, Novel
08537 *Dr. Scarlett; a narrative of his mysterious behavior in the east.* Farrar & Rinehart, New York, 1936, 338p, Cloth, Novel
Great ghost stories of the world. [see 08538A]
08538 *The haunted omnibus.* Farrar & Rinehart, New York, 1937, 848p, Cloth, Anth.
08538A retitled: *Great ghost stories of the world; The haunted omnibus.* Garden City Publishing Co., Garden City, NY, 1939, 848p, Cloth, Anth.

with Thomas Painter:

08539 *The motives of Nicholas Holtz, being the weird tale of the Ironville virus.* Farrar & Rinehart, New York, 1936, 309p, Cloth, Novel
08539A retitled: *The glass centipede, retold from the original sources.* Thornton Butterworth, London, 1936, 285p, Cloth, Novel

LALITA, pseud. [Maud Lalita Johnson, 1875-]

08540 *Square.* Order of Loving Service, Laguna Beach, CA, 1934, 145p, Cloth, Novel

LA MARE, COLIN de
see: DE LA MARE, COLIN

LA MARE, WALTER de
see: DE LA MARE, WALTER

LaMASTER, SLATER, 1890-

08541 *Cupid Napoleon.* Bruce Humphries, Boston, 1934, 359p, Cloth, Novel
08542 *The phantom in the rainbow.* A. C. McClurg, Chicago, 1929, 376p, Cloth, Novel

LAMB, HAROLD (Albert), 1892-1962

08543 *A garden to the eastward.* Doubleday, Garden City, 1947, 374p, Cloth, Novel
08544 *Marching sands.* D. Appleton, New York, 1920, 308p, Cloth, Novel

LAMB, HUGH, 1946- [biography included]

08545 A tide of terror. W. H. Allen, London, 1972,
      243p, Cloth, Anth.
08546 Victorian tales of terror. W. H. Allen, Lon-
      don, 1974, 287p, Cloth, Anth.
08547 A wave of fear. W. H. Allen, London, 1973,
      253p, Cloth, Anth.

LAMB, WILLIAM, pseud.
   see: JAMESON, STORM

LAMBERT, S. H., pseud.
   see: BELL, NEIL

LAMBERT, WILLIAM J. III

08549 Adonis. Pleasure Reader, San Diego, 1969,
      156p, Paper, Novel [Adonis #1]
08550 Adonis at Actum. Pleasure Reader, San Diego,
      1970, 155p, Paper, Novel [Adonis #2]
08551 Adonis at Bomasa. Pleasure Reader, San Diego,
      1970, 156p, Paper, Novel [Adonis #3]
08552 Demon's coronation. Pleasure Reader, San
      Diego, 1971, 159p, Paper, Novel [Demon #2]
08553 Demon's stalk. Pleasure Reader, San Diego,
      1970, 195p, Paper, Novel [Demon #1]
08554 Five roads to Tlen. Greenleaf Classic, San
      Diego, 1970, 195p, Paper, Novel [Tlen #1]
08555 The gods of Tlen. Greenleaf Classic, San
      Diego, 1970, 195p, Paper, Novel [Tlen #2]
08556 Male sex idol. Parisian Press, San Francisco,
      1972, 147p, Paper, Novel
08557 Valley of the damned. Greenleaf Classic, San
      Diego, 1971, 156p, Paper, Novel

LAMBOURNE, JOHN [John Battersby Crompton
Lamburn, 1893-   ] [biography included]

08558 The kingdom that was. John Murray, London,
      1931, 302p, Cloth, Novel [Prof. Ellis #1]
08559 The second leopard. John Murray, London,
      1932, 316p, Cloth, Novel [Prof. Ellis #2]
08560 The unmeasured place. John Murray, London,
      1933, 364p, Cloth, Novel

LAMBURN, JOHN
   see: LAMBOURNE, JOHN

LAMBURN, RICHMAL CROMPTON
   see: CROMPTON, RICHMAL

LAMONT, GIL(van Derwent), 1947-   [biography
included]

08561 Pecker's bad boy. Eros Goldstripe, Wilming-
      ton, Dela., 1974, 184p, Paper, Novel
08562 Roach. Essex House, North Hollywood, 1969,
      172p, Paper, Novel

LA MOTHE FENELON, FRANCOIS de SALIGNAC de
   see: FENELON, FRANCOIS

LA MOTTE-FOUQUÉ, FRIEDRICH (Heinrich Karl),
Freiherr de, 1777-1843

08563 Sintram and his companions; a romance. C. &
      J. Ollier, London; William Blackwood, Edin-
      burgh, 1820, 267p, Cloth, Novel
08563A retitled: The story of Sintram and his compa-
      nions. Wells Gardner, Darton, London, 1911
      129p, Cloth, Novel
      Sintram and his companions; and, Undine. [see
      08568A]
08564 Sintram and his companions; Aslauga's knight.
      Cassell, London, 1887, 192p, Cloth, Coll.
08565 Undine; a romance. W. Simpkin & R. Marshall,
      London, 1818, 205p, Cloth, Novel [published
      anonymously]
08565A Undine; or, The spirit of the waters, by La
      Motte-Fouque. J. Cunningham, London, 1840,
      32p, Cloth, Novel [abridged]
08565B retitled: The story of Undine. Wells Gardne
      Darton, London, 1912, 133p, Cloth, Novel
08566 Undine; and, Aslauga's knight. George Newnes
      London, 1901, 192p, Cloth, Coll.
08567 Undine, and other tales. Houghton Mifflin,
      Boston, 1867, 416p, Cloth, Coll.
08568 Undine; and, Sintram and his companions. Wil
      & Putnam, New York, 1845, 238p, Cloth, Coll
08568A retitled: Sintram and his companions; and,
      Undine. Wells Gardner, Darton, London, 189
      279p, Cloth, Coll.
08569 Undine; and, The two captains. Sampson Low,
      Marston, London, 1875, 162p, Cloth, Coll.

LAMPEN, C(harles) DUDLEY, 1859-1943

08570 Barcali the mutineer; a tale of the great Pac
      fic. R. A. Everett, London, 1900, 408p,
      Cloth, Novel
08571 Mirango the man eater; a tale of central Afri
      being the narrative of George Pryce, travel
      ler and exile, first writ down Anno Domini
      1706, and now retold. Society for Promotin
      Christian Knowledge, London, 1899, 248p,
      Cloth, Novel
08572 The queen of the extinct volcano; a story of
      adventure. Society for Promoting Christian
      Knowledge, London, 1898, 224p, Cloth, Novel

LAMPLUGH, LOIS, pseud. [Lois Carlile Davis,
1921-   ] [biography included]

08573 Mandog. British Broadcasting Corp., London,
      1972, 126p, Cloth, Tele.

LAMPMAN, BEN HUR, 1886-1954

08574 Here comes somebody. Metropolitan Press, Por
      land, OR, 1935, 275p, Cloth, Novel

LAMPMAN, EVELYN (Sibley), 1907-   [biography
included]

08575 Rusty's space ship. Doubleday, Garden City,
      1957, 240p, Cloth, Novel
08576 The shy stegosaurus of Cricket Creek. Double
      day, Garden City, 1955, 218p, Cloth, Novel

LAMPORT, RICHARD FIFIELD

08577 *Veeni the Master; "the story of a dream"; a
        romance.* Stanley Paul, London, 1912, 305p,
        Cloth, Novel

LAMSZUS, WILHELM, 1881-

08578 *The human slaughter-house (scenes from the
        war that is sure to come).* Hutchinson,
        London, 1913, 126p, Cloth, Novel

LANCASTER, ALBERT EDMUND

08579 *"All's dross but love"; a strange record of
        two reincarnated souls.* John W. Lovell,
        New York, 1889, 64p, Cloth, Novel

LANCASTER, WILLIAM
    see: COLLINGWOOD, HARRY

LANCOUR, GENE, pseud. [Gene Fisher]

08580 *The Lerios mecca.* Doubleday, Garden City,
        1973, 180p, Cloth, Novel

THE LAND OF DARKNESS
    see: OLIPHANT, Mrs.

THE LAND OF THE UNSEEN
    see: LOCKE, GEORGE

LANDIS, S(imon) M(ohler)

08581 *An entirely new feature of a thrilling novel!
        entitled, The social war of the year 1900;
        or, The conspirators and lovers! a lesson
        for saints and sinners!* "Landis Publishing
        Society," Philadelphia, 1872, 401p, Cloth,
        Novel

LANDOLFI, TOMMASO, 1908-

08582 *Cancerqueen, and other stories.* Dial Press,
        New York, 1971, 276p, Cloth, Coll.

LANDON, MELVILLE D.
    see: PERKINS, ELI

LANE, JANE, pseud. [Elaine Dakers, 1905-   ]

08583 *A state of mind.* Frederick Muller, London,
        1964, 203p, Cloth, Novel

LANE, JOHN, house pseud. [see also Dennis
Talbot Hughes]

07558 *Maid of Thuro.* Curtis Warren, London, 1952,
        128p, Cloth, Novel [by Dennis T. Hughes]
08584 *Mammalia.* Curtis Warren, London, 1953, 159p,
        Cloth, Novel

LANE, MARY E.
    see: ZAROVITCH, VERA

LANE, TEMPLE, pseud. [Mary Isabel Leslie]

08585 *The bands of Orion.* Jarrolds Publishers, Lon-
        don, 1928, 344p, Cloth, Novel

LANG, ALLEN KIM, 1928-   [*biography included*]

08586 *Wild and outside.* Chilton, Philadelphia, 1966,
        139p, Cloth, Novel

LANG, ANDREW, 1844-1912

08587 *The Disentanglers.* Longmans, Green, New York,
        1901, 67p, Paper?, Novel
08588 *The Disentanglers.* Longmans, Green, London,
        1902, 418p, Cloth, Novel [expanded]
08589 *In the wrong paradise, and other stories.*
        Kegan Paul, Trench, London, 1886, 316p,
        Cloth, Coll.
08590 *The mark of Cain.* J. W. Arrowsmith, Bristol,
        1886, 198p, Cloth, Novel
08591 *A monk of Fife; a romance of the days of Jeanne
        d'Arc.* Longmans, Green, New York, 1895,
        335p, Cloth, Novel
08592 *My own fairy book; namely, certain chronicles
        of Pantouflia, as notably the adventures of
        Prigio, Prince of that country, and of his
        son, Ricardo, with an excerpt from the Annals
        of Scotland, as touching Ker of Fairnilee,
        his sojourn with the Queen of Faery.* J. W.
        Arrowsmith, Bristol, 1895, 312p, Cloth, Coll.
        [includes 08593 and 08594; Pantouflia #s 1-2]
08593 *Prince Prigio.* J. W. Arrowsmith, Bristol,
        1889, 144p, Cloth, Novel [Pantouflia #1]
08594 *Prince Ricardo of Pantouflia, being the adven-
        tures of Prince Prigio's son.* J. W. Arrow-
        smith, Bristol, 1893, 204p, Cloth, Novel
        [Pantouflia #2]
08595 *When it was light; a reply to "When it was
        dark," by a well-known author.* John Long,
        London, 1906, 208p, Cloth, Novel [a sequel
        to Guy Thorne's *When it was dark*]

with H. Rider Haggard:

06582 *The world's desire; a novel.* Longmans, Green,
        London, 1890, 316p, Cloth, Novel

with Walter Herries Pollock:

08596 *He, by the author of 'It,' 'King Solomon's
        wives,' 'Bess,' 'Much darker days,' 'Mr.
        Morton's subtler,' and other romances.* Long-
        mans, Green, London, 1887, 119p, Paper, Novel

LANG, GREGOR, pseud. [Faber Birren, 1900-   ]
[*biography included*]

08597 *Terra; an allegory.* Philosophical Library,
        New York, 1953, 338p, Cloth, Novel

LANG, HERRMANN

08598 *The air battle; a vision of the future.* Wil-
        liam Penny, London, 1859, 112p, Cloth, Novel

LANG, KING, house pseud. [see also David Griffiths, George A. Hay, Brian Holloway, John Jennison, E. C. Tubb]

06399 *Astro-race.* Curtis Warren, London, 1951, 112p, Paper, Novel [by David Griffiths]
06400 *Gyrator control.* Curtis Warren, London, 1951, 112p, Paper, Novel [by David Griffiths]
08599 *Projectile war.* Curtis Warren, London, 1951, 111p, Paper, Novel
06401 *Rocket invasion.* Curtis Warren, London, 1951, 111p, Paper, Novel [by David Griffiths]
08600 *Saturn Patrol.* Curtis Warren, London, 1951, 111p, Paper, Novel [by E. C. Tubb]
07879 *Space line.* Curtis Warren, London, 1952?, 112p, Paper, Novel [by John Jennison]
06402 *Task flight.* Curtis Warren, London, 1951, 128p, Paper, Novel [by David Griffiths]
06967 *Terra!* Curtis Warren, London, 1952?, 111p, Paper, Novel [by George A. Hay]
07342 *Trans-Mercurian.* Curtis Warren, London, 1952, 112p, Paper, Novel [by Brian Holloway]

LANG, SIMON, pseud. [Darlene Hartman, 1934-] [*biography included*]

08601 *All the gods of Eisernon.* Avon, New York, 1973, 302p, Paper, Novel

LANGART, DARREL T., pseud.
    see: GARRETT, RANDALL

LANGDON, NORMAN E(arle), 1888-

08602 *Your story, Zalea; the record of a spirit's 8 reincarnations.* Exposition Press, New York, 1962, 131p, Cloth, Novel

LANGE, JOHN, pseud.
    see: CRICHTON, MICHAEL

LANGE, JOHN FREDERICK
    see: NORMAN, JOHN

LANGE, OLIVER

08603 *Vandenberg; a novel.* Stein & Day, New York, 1971, 333p, Cloth, Novel

LANGELAAN, GEORGE, 1908-

08604 *Out of time.* Four Square, London, 1964, 190p, Paper, Coll.

LANGFORD, GEORGE, 1876-1964

08605 *Kutnar, son of Pic.* Boni & Liveright, New York, 1921, 221p, Cloth, Novel [Pic #2]
08606 *Pic, the weapon-maker.* Boni & Liveright, New York, 1920, 270p, Cloth, Novel [Pic #1]
08607 *Senrac, the lion man; adventures of a boy in the stone age.* Liveright Publishing Corp., New York, 1954, 216p, Cloth, Novel

LANGGUTH, A(rthur) J(ohn), 1933-   [*biography included*]

08608 *Jesus Christs.* Harper & Row, New York, 1968, 227p, Cloth, Novel

LANGLEY, DOROTHY, pseud. [Dorothy Hight Kissling, 1904-]

08609 *Mr. Bremble's buttons; a novel.* Simon & Schuster, New York, 1947, 187p, Cloth, Novel

LANGLEY, FREDRIC, with Ron Ellik as Fredric Davies

04786 *The man from U.N.C.L.E., number 14; The cross of gold affair.* Ace, New York, 1968, 156p, Paper, Tele. [Man from U.N.C.L.E. #14]

LANGLEY, KENLIS

08610 *The mountain of mystery; a tale of the Arabian desert.* Thomas Nelson & Sons, London, 1929, 347p, Cloth, Novel

LANGLEY, NOEL (A.), 1911-

08611 *The rift in the lute.* Arthur Barker, London, 1952, 192p, Cloth, Novel
08612 *The tale of the land of green ginger.* Arthur Barker, London, 1937, 143p, Cloth, Novel
08612A retitled: *The land of green ginger.* Arthur Barker, London, 1947, 122p, Cloth, Novel
08613 *Tales of mystery and revenge.* Arthur Barker, London, 1950, 189p, Cloth, Coll.

LANGLOIS, DORA

08614 *In the shadow of Pa-Menkh.* Sampson Low, Marston, London, 1908, 328p, Cloth, Novel

LANGTON, JOY

08615 *Broken circle.* Hutchinson, London, 1946, 192p, Cloth, Novel

LANG-TUNG, pseud.

08616 *The decline and fall of the British Empire, being a history of England between the years 1840-1981.* F. V. White, London, 1881, 32p, Paper?, Story

LANIER, STERLING E(dmund), 1927-   [*biography included*]

08617 *Hiero's journey; a romance of the future.* Chilton Book Co., Radnor, PA, 1973, 280p, Cloth, Novel
08618 *The peculiar exploits of Brigadier Ffellowes.* Walker, New York, 1972, 159p, Cloth, Coll.
08619 *The war for the Lot; a tale of fantasy and terror.* Follett Publishing Co., Chicago, 1969, 256p, Cloth, Novel

LANNING, GEORGE (William Jr.), 1925- [bio-graphy included]

08620 *Green corn moon*. Viking Press, New York, 1968, 250p, Cloth, Novel
08621 *The pedestal*. Harper & Row, New York, 1966, 198p, Cloth, Novel

LANZA, CLARA (Hammond), 1859-1939, with James Clarence Harvey

06883 *Scarabaeus; the story of an African beetle*. Lovell & Coryell, New York, 1892, 283p, Cloth, Novel

LA PRADE, ERNEST, 1889-

08622 *Alice in Orchestralia*. Doubleday, Page, Garden City, 1925, 171p, Cloth, Novel [Alice series]
08622A retitled: *Alice in Orchestra Land*. Cobden-Sanderson, London, 1934, 170p, Cloth, Novel [Alice series]
08622B retitled: *Alice in Music Land; adventures in the land of harmony*. Bodley Head, London, 1952, 136p, Cloth, Novel [believed to be a retitling of 08622, but not verified]
08623 *Marching notes*. Doubleday, Doran, Garden City, 1929, 190p, Cloth, Novel [Alice series; a sequel to *Alice in Orchestralia*]

LAPUTA

08624 *Laputa, revisited by Gulliver Redivivus in 1905*. Hirschfeld Bros., London, 1905, 120p, Cloth, Novel [Gulliver series]

LA REE, GERRY de
    see: DE LA REE, GERRY

LARGE, E(rnest) C(harles)

08625 *Asleep in the afternoon*. Jonathan Cape, London, 1938, 413p, Cloth, Novel [Charles Pry #1]
08626 *Dawn in Andromeda*. Jonathan Cape, London, 1956, 282p, Cloth, Novel
08627 *Sugar in the air; a romance*. Jonathan Cape, London, 1937, 447p, Cloth, Novel [Charles Pry #2]

LARNACH, S. L.

08628 *A checklist of Australian fantasy*. Futurian Press, Sydney, 1950, 22p, Paper, Nonf.

LA ROCHE, C. F. TIPHAIGNE de
    see: TIPHAIGNE de la ROCHE, C. F.

LARSEN, EGON, pseud. [Egon Lehrburger, 1904-] [biography included]

08629 *You'll see; report from the future*. Rider, London, 1957, 176p, Cloth, Novel

LARSEN, J. ANKER
    see: ANKER LARSEN, J.

LARSSON, GÖSTA, 1898-

08630 *Revolt in Arcadia*. American Publishers, New York, 1942, 159p, Cloth, Novel

LA SALLE, VICTOR, house pseud. [see also John Glasby and R. Lionel Fanthorpe]

08631 *After the atom*. John Spencer, London, 1953, 108p, Paper, Novel
08632 *Assault from infinity*. John Spencer, London, 1953, 108p, Paper, Novel
08633 *The black sphere*. John Spencer, London, 1952, 108p, Paper, Novel
06015 *Dawn of the half-gods*. John Spencer, London, 1953, 128p, Paper, Novel [by John Glasby]
05075 *Menace from Mercury*. John Spencer, London, 1954, 128p, Paper, Novel [by R. Lionel Fanthorpe; includes a short story, "More than Mortal," by T. W. Wade]
08634 *The seventh dimension*. John Spencer, London, 1953, 124p, Paper, Novel
08635 *Suns in duo*. John Spencer, London, 1953, 108p, Paper, Novel
08636 *Twilight Zone*. John Spencer, London, 1954, 130p, Paper, Novel
08637 *Twilight Zone*. Badger, London, 1959, 158p, Paper, Coll. [includes a short story, "Point of No Return," by Max Chartair, pseud. of John Glasby]

LASKI, MARGHANITA, 1915-

08638 *Tory heaven; or, Thunder on the right*. Cresset Press, London, 1948, 172p, Cloth, Novel
08639 *The tower*. Lanthorne Press, Tacoma, Wash., 1974, 12p, Paper, Story
08640 *The Victorian chaise-longue*. Cresset Press, London, 1953, 159p, Cloth, Novel

LA SPINA, (Fanny) GREYE, 1880-1969 [biography included]

08641 *Invaders from the dark*. Arkham House, Sauk City, 1960, 168p, Cloth, Novel
08641A retitled: *Shadow of evil*. Paperback Library, New York, 1966, 160p, Paper, Novel

LASSWITZ, KURD, 1848-1910

08642 *Two planets; Auf zwei planeten*. Southern Illinois University Press, Carbondale, IL, 1971, 405p, Cloth, Novel

THE LAST EGYPTIAN
    see: BAUM, L. FRANK

THE LAST MAN
    see: SHELLEY, MARY WOLLSTONECRAFT

THE LAST MAN; OR, OMEGARUS AND SYDERIA
    see: COUSIN de GRAINVILLE, JEAN-BAPTISTE

THE LAST PEER

08643   *The last peer; a novel.* T. Cautley Newby,
          London, 1851, 3vol, Cloth, Novel

LAST TRAIN TO LIMBO
      see: RUSSELL, RAY

A LATE ASSOCIATE OF THE SOCIETY FOR PSYCHICAL
RESEARCH, pseud.

08644   *The twice=born.* Philip Wellby, London, 1906,
          173p, Cloth, Novel

A LATE FELLOW OF ST. JOHN'S COLLEGE, CAMBRIDGE
      see: SPRAT, JOHN

LATH, J. A., pseud.

08645   *The lost city of the Aztecs; or, The mystery
          of the hidden crater.* Cupples & Leon, New
          York, 1934, 203p, Cloth, Novel

LATHAM, PHILIP, pseud.
      see: RICHARDSON, ROBERT S.

LATHOM, FRANCIS, 1777-1832

08646   *Mystic events; or, The vision of the tapestry;
          a romantic legend of the days of Anne Boleyn.*
          A. K. Newman, London, 1830, 4vol, Cloth,
          Novel

LATIMER, JOHN, 1937-

08647   *Border of darkness.* Crime Club, Doubleday,
          Garden City, 1972, 184p, Cloth, Novel
08648   *The last Pharaoh; a novel.* Thomas Nelson,
          New York, 1970, 128p, Cloth, Novel

LA TOURRETTE, JACQUELINE, 1926-   [*biography
included*]

08649   *The Joseph Stone.* Leisure Books, North Holly-
          wood, 1971, 190p, Paper, Novel

LATTER, SIMON

08650   *The global globules affair.* Four Square,
          London, 1967, 126p, Paper, Tele. [Girl from
          U.N.C.L.E. #1]
08651   *The golden boats of Taradata affair.* Four
          Square, London, 1967, 128p, Paper, Tele.
          [Girl from U.N.C.L.E. #3]

LAUBENTHAL, SANDERS ANNE, 1943-   [*biography
included*]

08652   *Excalibur.* Ballantine, New York, 1973, 236p,
          Paper, Novel

LAUDER, GEORGE DICK-
      see: DICK-LAUDER, GEORGE

LAUMER, (John) KEITH, 1925-   [*biography included*]

08653   *Assignment in nowhere.* Berkley Medallion, New
          York, 1968, 143p, Paper, Novel [Imperium #3]
08654   *The Avengers #6; "The drowned Queen."* Berkley
          Medallion, New York, 1968, 127p, Paper,
          Tele. [Avengers #6]
08655   *The big show.* Ace, New York, 1972, 153p, Paper
          Coll.
08656   *Catastrophe planet.* Berkley Medallion, New
          York, 1966, 158p, Paper, Novel
08657   *The day before forever; and, Thunderhead.*
          Doubleday, Garden City, 1968, 164p, Cloth,
          Coll.
08658   *Dinosaur Beach.* Charles Scribner's Sons, New
          York, 1971, 186p, Cloth, Novel
08659   *Enemies from beyond; an Invaders adventure.*
          Pyramid, New York, 1967, 159p, Paper, Tele.
          Coll. [Invaders #2]
08660   *Envoy to new worlds.* Ace Double, New York,
          1963, 134p, Paper, Coll. [Retief #1]
08661   *Five fates.* Doubleday, Garden City, 1970,
          256p, Cloth, Anth. [published anonymously]
08662   *Galactic diplomat; nine incidents of the Corps
          Diplomatique Terrestrienne.* Doubleday, Gar-
          den City, 1965, 227p, Cloth, Coll. [Retief
08663   *Galactic odyssey.* Berkley Medallion, New York
          1967, 160p, Paper, Novel
08664   *The glory game.* Doubleday, Garden City, 1973
          186p, Cloth, Novel
08665   *The great time machine hoax.* Simon & Schuster
          New York, 1964, 190p, Cloth, Novel
08666   *Greylorn.* Berkley Medallion, New York, 1968,
          192p, Paper, Coll.
08666A retitled: *The other sky.* Dennis Dobson, Lon-
          don, 1968, 192p, Cloth, Coll.
08667   *The house in November; a science fiction nove*
          G. P. Putnam's Sons, New York, 1970, 192p,
          Cloth, Novel
08668   *The infinite cage.* G. P. Putnam's Sons, New
          York, 1972, 221p, Cloth, Novel
08669   *The Invaders.* Pyramid, New York, 1967, 142p,
          Paper, Tele. Coll. [Invaders #1]
08669A retitled: *The meteor men,* by Anthony LeBaron
          Corgi, London, 1968, 127p, Paper, Tele. Col
          [Invaders #2 (UK edition)]
08670   *It's a mad, mad, mad galaxy.* Berkley Medalli
          New York, 1968, 160p, Paper, Coll.
08671   *The long twilight.* G. P. Putnam's Sons, New
          York, 1969, 222p, Cloth, Novel
08672   *The Monitors.* Berkley Medallion, New York,
          1966, 160p, Paper, Novel
08673   *Night of delusions.* G. P. Putnam's Sons, New
          York, 1972, 190p, Cloth, Novel
08674   *Nine by Laumer.* Doubleday, Garden City, 1967
          222p, Cloth, Coll.
08675   *Once there was a giant.* Doubleday, Garden
          City, 1971, 252p, Cloth, Coll.
08676   *The other side of time.* Berkley Medallion,
          New York, 1965, 160p, Paper, Novel [Imperiu
          #2]
        The other sky. [see 08666A]
08677   *A plague of demons.* Berkley Medallion, New
          York, 1965, 159p, Paper, Novel
08678   *Retief: ambassador to space; seven incidents
          of the Corps Diplomatique Terrestrienne.*
          Doubleday, Garden City, 1969, 216p, Cloth,
          Coll. [Retief #5]

LAUMER, KEITH (cont.)

08679 *Retief and the warlords*. Doubleday, Garden
        City, 1968, 188p, Cloth, Novel [Retief #4]
08680 *Retief of the CDT*. Doubleday, Garden City,
        1971, 172p, Cloth, Coll. [Retief #7]
08681 *Retief's ransom; a science fiction novel*.
        G. P. Putnam's Sons, New York, 1971, 189p,
        Cloth, Novel [Retief #6]
08682 *Retief's war*. Doubleday, Garden City, 1966,
        208p, Cloth, Novel [Retief #3]
08683 *The shape changer; a science fiction novel*.
        G. P. Putnam's Sons, New York, 1972, 189p,
        Cloth, Novel [Lafayette O'Leary #3]
08684 *The star treasure; a science fiction novel*.
        G. P. Putnam's Sons, New York, 1971, 188p,
        Cloth, Novel
08685 *The time bender*. Berkley Medallion, New York,
        1966, 160p, Paper, Novel [Lafayette O'Leary
        #1]
08686 *Time trap; a science fiction novel*. G. P.
        Putnam's Sons, New York, 1970, 150p, Cloth,
        Novel
08687 *Timetracks*. Ballantine, New York, 1972, 216p,
        Paper, Coll.
08688 *A trace of memory*. Berkley Medallion, New
        York, 1963, 174p, Paper, Novel
08689 *The undefeated*. Dell, New York, 1974, 207p,
        Paper, Coll.
08690 *The world shuffler*. G. P. Putnam's Sons, New
        York, 1970, 185p, Cloth, Novel [Lafayette
        O'Leary #2]
08691 *Worlds of the Imperium*. Ace Double, New York,
        1962, 133p, Paper, Novel [Imperium #1]

as Anthony LeBaron:

      The meteor men. [see 08669A]

with Rosel George Brown:

01992 *Earthblood*. Doubleday, Garden City, 1966,
        253p, Cloth, Novel

with Gordon R. Dickson:

04377 *Planet run*. Doubleday, Garden City, 1967,
        167p, Cloth, Novel

LAUMER, MARCH

08692 *Aillinn o' my dreams; a fantasia on Irish
        themes*. Opium Books, Hong Kong, 1969, 166p,
        Paper, Novel

as Felix Severance:

08693 *Green dusk for dreams; a romance*. Opium Books,
        Hong Kong, 1969, 199p, Paper, Novel
08694 *The time machine that never got past first
        base; a laugh--at the future?* Opium Books,
        Hong Kong, 1968, 152p, Paper, Novel

as Xavier Xanthus:

08695 *The tides in the Bay of Fundy; a vazzle*.
        Opium Books, Hong Kong, 1969, 187p, Paper,
        Novel

LAUN, H. van
      see: van LAUN, H.

LAURENCE, JOHN, pseud. [John Laurence Pritchard, 1885-1968]

08696 *Murder in the stratosphere*. Sampson Low, Mar-
        ston, London, 1938, 314p, Cloth, Novel

LAURENS, MARSHALL

08697 *The Z effect*. Pocket Books, New York, 1974,
        192p, Paper, Novel

LAURENTZ, TOWNSEND

08698 *Black mass maiden*. Greenleaf Classic, San
        Diego, 1971, 159p, Paper, Novel

LAURIA, FRANK (Jonathan), 1935-   [*biography
included*]

08699 *Baron Orgaz*. Bantam, New York, 1974, 344p,
        Paper, Novel [Dr. Orient #4]
08700 *Doctor Orient*. Bantam, New York, 1970, 214p,
        Paper, Novel [Dr. Orient #1]
08701 *Lady Sativa*. Curtis, New York, 1973, 238p,
        Paper, Novel [Dr. Orient #3]
08702 *Raga Six*. Bantam, New York, 1972, 278p, Paper,
        Novel [Dr. Orient #2]

LAURIE, A(NDRÉ), pseud. [Paschal Grousset,
1844-1909]

08703 *Axel Ebersen, the graduate of Upsala*. Sampson
        Low, Marston, Searle & Rivington, London,
        1892, 286p, Cloth, Novel
08704 *The conquest of the Moon; a story of the Bayou-
        da*. Sampson Low, Marston, Searle & Riving-
        ton, London, 1889, 354p, Cloth, Novel
08705 *The crystal city under the sea*. Sampson Low,
        Marston, Searle & Rivington, London, 1896,
        293p, Cloth, Novel
08705A retitled: *The crystal city*. Estes & Lauriat,
        Boston, 1896, 293p, Cloth, Novel
08706 *New York to Brest in seven hours*. Sampson Low,
        Marston, Searle & Rivington, London, 1890,
        302p, Cloth, Novel
08707 *The secret of the Magian; or, The mystery of
        Ecbatana*. Sampson Low, Marston, Searle &
        Rivington, London, 1891, 314p, Cloth, Novel

LAURIE'S SPACE ANNUAL

08708 *Laurie's space annual*. Werner Laurie, London,
        1953, 96p, Paper, Anth. [includes some nonf.]

LAUTRÉAMONT, Comte de, pseud. [Isidore Lucien
Ducasse, 1846-1870]

08709 *The lay of Maldoror*. Casanova Society, London,
        1924, 319p, Cloth, Novel
08709A retitled: *Maldoror (Les chants de Maldoror)*.
        Peter Owen, London, 1943, 303p, Cloth, Novel

LAVER, JAMES, 1899-1975 [*biography included*]

08710 *Panic among Puritans*. William Heinemann, Lon-
        don, 1936, 317p, Cloth, Novel

LAW, WINIFRED

08711   *Rangers of the universe.* New Century Press, Sydney, 1945, 176p, Cloth, Novel [Ralph Hannon #2]
08712   *Through space to the planets.* New Century Press, Sydney, 1944, 174p, Cloth, Novel [Ralph Hannon #1]

A LAW-ABIDING REVOLUTIONIST
    see: WELLMAN, BERT J.

LAWRENCE, CHARLES EDWARD, 1870-1940 [published anonymously]

08713   *The trial of man; an allegorical romance.* John Murray, London, 1902, 319p, Cloth, Novel

LAWRENCE, D(avid) H(erbert), 1885-1930

08714   *The escaped cock.* Black Sun Press, Paris, 1929, 95p, Cloth, Novel
08714A   retitled: *The man who died.* Martin Secker, London, 1931, 97p, Cloth, Novel
08715   *The man who died; The ladybird; The captain's doll.* Bernhard Tauchnitz, Leipzig, 1932, 286p, Cloth, Coll.
08716   *St. Mawr; and, The man who died.* Vintage, New York, 1953, 211p, Paper, Coll.

LAWRENCE, HARRIET

08717   *H. Philip Birdsong's ESP.* W. R. Scott, New York, 1969, 303p, Cloth, Novel

LAWRENCE, H(enry) L(ionel), 1908-   [biography included]

08718   *The children of light.* Macdonald, London, 1960, 191p, Cloth, Novel

LAWRENCE, JAMES COOPER, 1890-1932

08719   *The year of regeneration; an improbable fiction.* Harper & Bros., New York, 1932, 220p, Cloth, Novel

LAWRENCE, JOSEPHINE

08720   *Not a cloud in the sky.* Harcourt, Brace & World, New York, 1964, 250p, Cloth, Novel

LAWRENCE, LOUISE, pseud. [Elizabeth Rhoda Wintle, 1943-   ] [biography included]

08721   *Andra.* Collins, London, 1971, 191p, Cloth, Novel
08722   *The power of stars.* Collins, London, 1972, 159p, Cloth, Novel
08723   *The Wyndcliffe.* Collins, London, 1974, 158p, Cloth, Novel

LAWRENCE, MARGERY, d. 1969

08724   *Bride of darkness.* Robert Hale, London, 1967, 189p, Cloth, Novel
08725   *The bridge of wonder.* Robert Hale, London, 1939, 479p, Cloth, Novel
08726   *The floating café, and other stories.* Jarrolds Publishers, London, 1936, 303p, Cloth, Coll.
08727   *Nights of the Round Table; a book of strange tales.* Hutchinson, London, 1926, 283p, Cloth, Coll. [Club of the Round Table #1]
08728   *Number seven Queer Street, being some stories from the private casebook of Doctor Miles Pennoyer, recorded by his friend and occasional assistant, Jerome Latimer.* Robert Hale, London, 1945, 350p, Cloth, Coll.
08729   *The rent in the veil.* Robert Hale, London, 1951, 391p, Cloth, Novel
08730   *Strange caravan.* Robert Hale, London, 1941, 304p, Cloth, Coll.
08731   *The terraces of night, being further chronicles of the "Club of the Round Table."* Hurst & Blackett, London, 1932, 287p, Cloth, Coll. [Club of the Round Table #2]
08732   *The tomorrow of yesterday.* Robert Hale, London, 1966, 190p, Cloth, Novel

THE LAWS OF LEFLO
    see: AUTHOR OF "MISS MOLLY"

LAWSON, ALFRED WILLIAM, 1869-1954

08733   *Born again; a novel.* Wox, Conrad, New York, 1904, 297p, Cloth, Novel

LAWSON, JOHN (Shults)

08734   *The Spring Rider.* Thomas Y. Crowell, New York, 1968, 147p, Cloth, Novel

LAWSON, ROBERT, 1892-1957

08735   *The fabulous flight.* Little, Brown, Boston, 1949, 152p, Cloth, Novel
08736   *Mr. Wilmer.* Little, Brown, Boston, 1945, 218p, Cloth, Novel

LAWSON, ROBERT N(eale), 1873-1945

08737   *Beloved shipmates.* Grant Richards, London, 1924, 336p, Cloth, Novel

LAWTON, Capt. WILBUR, pseud. [John Henry Goldfrap, 1879-1917]

08738   *The boy aviators in Nicaragua; or, In league with the insurgents.* Hurst & Co., New York, 1910, 336p, Cloth, Novel [Boy Aviators series]

LAYLAND BARRATT, F(rances), Lady, d. 1953

08739   *Lycanthia.* Herbert Jenkins, London, 1935, 312p, Cloth, Novel

LAZARUS, HENRY

08740 *The English revolution of the twentieth cen-
        tury; a prospective history.* T. Fisher Un-
        win, London, 1894, 463p, Cloth, Novel

LAZARUS, KEO FELKER, 1913-   [*biography included*]

08741 *The gismo.* Follett Publishing Co., Chicago,
        1970, 126p, Cloth, Novel
08741A retitled: *The gismo from outer space.* Scho-
        lastic Book Services, New York, 1974, 92p,
        Paper, Novel
08742 *The shark in the window.* William Morrow, New
        York, 1972, 159p, Cloth, Novel

LAZENBY, NORMAN (Austin)

08743 *The coming of the beetle-men.* Shenstone Press,
        Mansfield, UK, 1950, 78p, Paper, Coll [co-
        ver title: *Terror-trap!*]

LAZLO, GUSTAVE

08744 *Spires, bells, and dreams! a story of the
        second coming.* Cassell, London, 1928, 306p,
        Cloth, Novel

LAZO, HECTOR, 1899-1965 [*biography included*]

08745 *On the trail of Inca gold.* Prentice-Hall,
        Englewood Cliffs, NJ, 1956, 212p, Cloth,
        Novel

LEA, DAVE

08746 *His psychic daughter.* Greenleaf Classic, San
        Diego, 1972, 156p, Paper, Novel

LEA, (Alec) RICHARD

08747 *The outward urge; a novel.* Rich & Cowan, Lon-
        don, 1944, 216p, Cloth, Novel

LEA, TERREA
     see: STACY, TERRY

LEACH, BAILEY KAY

08748 *Soulless saints; a strange revelation.* Ameri-
        can Publishing Co., Chicago, 1892, 253p,
        Cloth, Novel

LEACH, DECIMA

08749 *The Garthians.* Arthur H. Stockwell, Ilfra-
        combe, UK, 1962, 168p, Cloth, Novel

LEACOCK, STEPHEN (Butler), 1869-1944

08750 *Afternoons in utopia; tales of the new time.*
        Dodd, Mead, New York, 1932, 221p, Cloth,
        Coll.

08751 *The iron man & the tin woman, with other such
        futurities; a book of little sketches of to-
        day and to-morrow.* Dodd, Mead, New York,
        1929, 309p, Cloth, Coll.

LEADER, MARY

08752 *Triad.* Coward, McCann & Geoghegan, New York,
        1973, 223p, Cloth, Novel

A LEAF FROM THE FUTURE HISTORY OF ENGLAND

08753 *A leaf from the future history of England, on
        the subject of reform in Parliament.* W.
        Clowes, London, 1831, 6p, Paper, Story

LEAHY, JOHN MARTIN, 1886-

08754 *Drome.* Fantasy Publishing Co., Los Angeles,
        1952, 295p, Cloth, Novel

LEATHERWOOD, HANK, pseud.

08755 *Startail.* Pleasure Reader, San Diego, 1969,
        156p, Paper, Novel

LEBAR, JOHN, pseud. [Gilbert Munger Wright,
1901-   ], with Harold Bell Wright

08756 *The devil's highway.* D. Appleton, New York,
        1932, 335p, Cloth, Novel

LeBARON, ANTHONY, pseud.
     see: LAUMER, KEITH

LEBECK, OSKAR, with Gaylord DuBois

04534 *The Hurricane Kids on the lost islands.* Gros-
        set & Dunlap, New York, 1941, 216p, Cloth,
        Novel [Hurricane Kids series]
04535 *Stratosphere Jim and his flying fortress.*
        Grosset & Dunlap, New York, 1941, 215p, Cloth,
        Novel [Stratosphere Jim series]

LeBLANC, MAURICE (Marie Émile), 1864-1941

08757 *The three eyes.* Macaulay, New York, 1921,
        315p, Cloth, Novel
08758 *The tremendous event.* Macaulay, New York,
        1922, 316p, Cloth, Novel

LE BRETON, THOMAS, pseud. [T. Murray Ford]

08759 *Mr. Teedles, the gland old man.* T. Werner
        Laurie, London, 1927, 188p, Cloth, Novel

LECALE, ERROL

08760 *Castledoom.* New English Library, London, 1974,
        128p, Paper, Novel [Specialist #2]
08761 *The death box.* New English Library, London,
        1974, 124p, Paper, Novel [Specialist #4]

LECALE, ERROL (cont.)

08762 *The severed hand.* New English Library, London,
        1974, 127p, Paper, Novel [Specialist #3]
08763 *The tigerman of Terrahpur.* New English Library,
        London, 1973, 128p, Paper, Novel [Specialist
        #1]

LECKIE, PETER MARTIN
        see: MARTIN, PETER

LEDDIHN, CHRISTIANE von KUEHNELT-
        see: KUEHNELT-LEDDIHN, CHRISTIANE von

LEDDIHN, ERIK von KUEHNELT-
        see: KUEHNELT-LEDDIHN, ERIK von

LEDERMAN, FRANK

08764 *Tremor.* Kaye Publications, London, 1953,
        112p, Paper, Novel

LEDOUX, J. W.
        see: CALSON, ISAAC

LEE, ARTHUR STANLEY GOULD
        see: GOULD, ARTHUR LEE

LEE, AUSTIN
        see: CALLENDER, JULIAN

LEE, DAVID

08765 *Destiny past.* Robert Hale, London, 1974,
        157p, Cloth, Novel

LEE, ELIZABETH

08766 *More horror stories; short stories.* Best-
        seller Library, London, 1962, 222p, Paper,
        Anth.
08766A retitled: *The second Arrow book of horror
        stories.* Arrow, London, 1965, 222p, Paper,
        Anth. [published anonymously]
08767 *Spine chillers; an anthology of mystery and
        horror.* Elek, London, 1961, 528p, Cloth,
        Anth.

LEE, ELSIE

08768 *Masque of the Red Death.* Lancer, New York,
        1964, 142p, Paper, Movie [the movie was
        loosely adapted from Poe's story of the
        same name]

LEE, HENRY BOYLE
        see: McCRIB, THEOPHILUS

LEE, JENNETTE (Barbour), 1860-1951

08769 *Uncle Bijah's ghost.* Charles Scribner's Sons,
        New York, 1922, 187p, Cloth, Novel

LEE, MANFRED B(ennington), 1905-1971, with
Frederic Dannay as Ellery Queen

03804 *And on the eighth day.* Random House, New York,
        1964, 191p, Cloth, Novel

with Frederic Dannay as Barnaby Ross:

03805 *The scrolls of Lysis.* Simon & Schuster, New
        York, 1962, 254p, Cloth, Novel

LEE, Mrs. NORMAN

08771 *A woman--or what?* Alston Rivers, London, 1931,
        283p, Cloth, Novel

LEE, RAY(mond), with Vernell Coriell

03437 *A pictorial history of the Tarzan movies; 50
        years of the jungle superman and all-time
        box office champion.* Golden State News Co.,
        Los Angeles, 1966, 83p, Paper, Nonf.

LEE, ROBERT C(orwin Jr.), 1931-   [*biography
included*]

08772 *The day it rained forever.* Little, Brown,
        Boston, 1968, 178p, Cloth, Novel [Mike Glenn
        #2]
08773 *The iron arm of Michael Glenn.* Little, Brown,
        Boston, 1965, 153p, Cloth, Novel [Mike Glenn
        #1]

LEE, THOMAS

08774 *Falsivir's travels; the remarkable adventures
        of John Falsivir, seaman, at the North Pole
        and in the interior of the Earth, with a
        description of the wonderful people and the
        things he discovered there.* The Proprietor,
        London, 1886, 122p, Cloth, Novel

LEE, TUNG

08775 *The wind obeys Lama Toru.* Kutub-Popular, Bom-
        bay, 1967, 191p, Cloth, Novel

LEE, VERNON, pseud. [Violet Paget, 1856-1935]

08776 *The ballet of the nations; a present-day mora-
        lity.* G. P. Putnam's Sons, New York, 1915,
        23p, Cloth, Story
08777 *For Maurice; five unlikely stories.* John Lane
        The Bodley Head, London, 1927, 223p, Cloth,
        Coll.
08778 *Hauntings; fantastic stories.* William Heine-
        mann, London, 1890, 237p, Cloth, Coll.
08779 *A phantom lover; a fantastic story.* W. Black-
        wood & Sons, Edinburgh, 1886, 116p, Cloth,
        Novel

LEE, VERNON (cont.)

08780 *Pope Jacynth, and more supernatural tales; excursions into fantasy.* Peter Owen, London, 1956, 208p, Cloth, Coll.

08780A retitled: *Ravenna and her ghosts.* Corgi, London, 1962, 126p, Paper, Coll. [abridged]

08781 *Pope Jacynth, and other fantastic tales.* Grant Richards, London, 1904, 200p, Cloth, Coll.

08782 *Pope Jacynth, to which are added Ariadne in Mantua, and other romantic inventions.* Bernhard Tauchnitz, Leipzig, 1906, 278p, Paper, Coll.

Ravenna and her ghosts. [see 08780A]

08783 *The Snake Lady, and other stories.* Grove Press, New York, 1954, 288p, Cloth, Coll.

08783A retitled: *Supernatural tales; excursions into fantasy.* Peter Owen, London, 1955, 222p, Cloth, Coll.

08783B retitled: *The virgin of the seven daggers.* Corgi, London, 1962, 158p, Paper, Coll.

LEE, WALT(er William), 1931-   [*biography included*], with Bill Warren

08784 *Reference guide to fantastic films; science fiction, fantasy, and horror.* Chelsea-Lee, Los Angeles, 1972/74, 3vol, Paper, Nonf.

LEE, WAYNE C.
    see: SHELDON, LEE

LEE-HAMILTON, EUGENE, 1845-1907

08785 *The lord of the dark red star, being the story of the supernatural influences in the life of an Italian despot of the thirteenth century.* Walter Scott Publishing Co., London, 1903, 295p, Cloth, Novel

LEECH, JOSEPH

08786 *Ghosts and glamour.* J. W. Arrowsmith, Bristol, 1886, 187p, Cloth, Coll. [includes some nonf.]

LEEK, SYBIL, 1923-   [*biography included*]

08787 *The tree that conquered the world.* Prentice-Hall, Englewood Cliffs, NJ, 1969, 135p, Cloth, Novel

LEEMING, JOHN F(ishwick), 1900-   [*biography included*]

08788 *Claudius the bee.* George G. Harrap, London, 1936, 160p, Cloth, Novel [Claudius #1]

08789 *Thanks to Claudius.* George G. Harrap, London, 1937, 157p, Cloth, Novel [Claudius #2]

LE FANU, J(oseph) SHERIDAN, 1814-1873

08790 *Best ghost stories of J. S. Le Fanu.* Dover, New York, 1964, 467p, Paper, Coll.

08791 *The best horror stories.* Sphere, London, 1970, 158p, Paper, Coll.

08792 *Carmilla.* Scholastic Book Services, New York, 1971, 112p, Paper, Novel

08793 *Carmilla; &, The haunted baronet.* Paperback Library, New York, 1970, 221p, Paper, Coll.

08794 *Ghost stories and tales of mystery.* James McGlashan, Dublin; William S. Orr, London, 1851, 304p, Cloth, Cloth, Coll. [published anonymously]

08795 *Green tea.* Polybooks, London, 1943, 16p, Paper, Story

Green tea. [see 08797A]

08796 *Green tea, and other ghost stories.* Arkham House, Sauk City, 1945, 357p, Cloth, Coll.

08797 *In a glass darkly.* Richard Bentley & Son, London, 1872, 3vol, Cloth, Coll.

08797A retitled: *Green tea.* George Newnes, London, 1907, 152p, Cloth, Coll. [abridged]

08798 *Madam Crowl's ghost, and other tales of mystery.* G. Bell & Sons, London, 1923, 277p, Cloth, Coll.

08799 *The Purcell papers.* Richard Bentley & Son, London, 1880, 3vol, Cloth, Coll.

08800 *Sheridan La Fanu: the diabolic genius.* [sic] Juniper Press, New York, 1959, 384p, Paper, Coll.

08801 *Vampire lovers, and other stories.* Fontana, London, 1970, 190p, Paper, Coll.

08802 *The watcher, and other weird stories.* Downey & Co., London, 1894, 271p, Cloth, Coll.

LEFEBVRE-LABOULAYE, EDOUARD RENE
    see: LABOULAYE, EDOUARD RENE LEFEBVRE de

LEFFINGWELL, ALBERT
    see: CHAMBERS, DANA

THE LEGAL REVOLUTION OF 1902
    see: WELLMAN, BERT J.

LEGER, RAYMOND ALFRED, 1883-   , with Edward McDonald as Raymond McDonald

08803 *The mad scientist; a tale of the future, with which is incorporated a secret cipher, for the best solution of which the publishers offer $1,000.* Cochrane Publishing Co., New York, 1909, 242p, Cloth, Novel

LEGGE, J(ames) G(ranville), 1861-1940

08804 *The Millennium.* Basil Blackwell, Oxford, 1927, 164p, Cloth, Novel

LEGGE, RONALD

08805 *The hawk; a story of aerial war.* J. McBride, New York, 1909, 310p, Cloth, Novel

LEGGETT, M(ortimer) D(ormer), 1821-1896

08806 *A dream of a modest prophet.* J. B. Lippincott, Philadelphia, 1890, 207p, Cloth, Novel

LE GUIN, URSULA K(roeber), 1929-   [*biography included*]

08807 *City of illusions.* Ace, New York, 1967, 160p, Paper, Novel [Future History #6]

08808 *The dispossessed; an ambiguous utopia.* Harper & Row, New York, 1974, 341p, Cloth, Novel [Future History #2]

08809 *The farthest shore.* Atheneum, New York, 1972, 223p, Cloth, Novel [Earthsea Trilogy #3]

08810 *From Elfland to Poughkeepsie.* Pendragon Press, Portland, OR, 1973, 33p, Paper, Nonf.

08811 *The lathe of heaven.* Charles Scribner's Sons, New York, 1971, 185p, Cloth, Novel [Future History #1]

08812 *The left hand of darkness.* Ace, New York, 1969, 286p, Paper, Novel [Future History #7]

08813 *Planet of exile.* Ace Double, New York, 1966, 113p, Paper, Novel [Future History #5]

08814 *Rocannon's World.* Ace Double, New York, 1966, 117p, Paper, Novel [Future History #4]

08815 *The tombs of Atuan.* Atheneum, New York, 1971, 163p, Cloth, Novel [Earthsea Trilogy #2]

08816 *A wizard of Earthsea.* Parnassus Press, Berkeley, CA, 1968, 205p, Cloth, Novel [Earthsea Trilogy #1]

LEHRBURGER, EGON
  see: LARSEN, EGON

LEIBER, FRITZ (Reuter Jr.), 1910-   [*biography included*]

08817 *The best of Fritz Leiber.* Sphere, London, 1974, 368p, Paper, Coll.

08818 *The Big Time.* Ace Double, New York, 1961, 129p, Paper, Novel

08819 *The book of Fritz Leiber.* DAW, New York, 1974, 173p, Paper, Coll.

08820 *Conjure wife.* Twayne Publishers, New York, 1953, 154p, Cloth, Novel

08821 *Destiny times three.* Galaxy SF Novel, New York, 1956, 126p, Paper, Novel

08822 *Gather, darkness!* Pellegrini & Cudahy, New York, 1950, 240p, Cloth, Novel

08823 *The green millennium.* Abelard Press, New York, 1953, 256p, Cloth, Novel

08824 *The Mind Spider, and other stories.* Ace Double, New York, 1961, 127p, Paper, Coll.

08825 *Night monsters.* Ace Double, New York, 1969, 80p, Paper, Coll.

08826 *Night monsters.* Victor Gollancz, London, 1974, 190p, Cloth, Coll. [different contents]

08827 *The night of the wolf.* Ballantine, New York, 1966, 221p, Paper, Coll.

08828 *Night's black agents.* Arkham House, Sauk City, 1947, 237p, Cloth, Coll.

08828A retitled: *Tales from Nights black agents.* Ballantine, New York, 1961, 143p, Paper, Coll. [abridged; author's name is given as "Lieber" on cover]

08829 *A pail of air.* Ballantine, New York, 1964, 191p, Paper, Coll.

08830 *The secret songs.* Rupert Hart-Davis, London, 1968, 229p, Cloth, Coll.

08831 *Shadows with eyes.* Ballantine, New York, 1962, 128p, Paper, Coll.

08832 *Ships to the stars.* Ace Double, New York, 1964, 122p, Paper, Coll.

08833 *The silver eggheads.* Ballantine, New York, 1962, 192p, Paper, Novel

08834 *The sinful ones.* Universal Giant, New York, 1953, 319p for entire book, Paper, Novel [bound with *Bulls, blood, and passion*, by David Williams (not SF)]

08834A retitled: *You're all alone.* Ace, New York, 1972, 191p, Paper, Novel

08835 *A specter is haunting Texas.* Walker, New York, 1969, 250p, Cloth, Novel

08836 *Swords against death.* Ace, New York, 1970, 251p, Paper, Coll. [Fafhrd & Gray Mouser #2]

08837 *Swords against wizardry.* Ace, New York, 1968, 188p, Paper, Novel [Fafhrd & Gray Mouser #4]

08838 *Swords and deviltry.* Ace, New York, 1970, 254p, Paper, Coll. [Fafhrd & Gray Mouser #1]

08839 *Swords in the mist.* Ace, New York, 1968, 190p, Paper, Novel [Fafhrd & Gray Mouser #3]

08840 *The swords of Lankhmar.* Ace, New York, 1968, 224p, Paper, Novel [Fafhrd & Gray Mouser #5]

08841 *Tarzan and the valley of gold.* Ballantine, New York, 1966, 317p, Paper, Novel [Tarzan #25]

08842 *Two sought adventure; exploits of Fafhrd and the Gray Mouser.* Gnome Press, New York, 1957, 186p, Cloth, Coll. [Fafhrd & Gray Mouser series]

08843 *The Wanderer.* Ballantine, New York, 1964, 318p, Paper, Novel
You're all alone. [see 08834A]

LEIBY, JOAN, with Robert R. Kudlay

08461 *Burroughs' science fiction, with an analytical subject and name index.* School of Library & Information Science, State University College of Arts & Sciences, Geneseo, NY, 1973, 236p, Paper, Nonf.

LEIGH, EDMUND

08844 *Our ghosts.* Digby, Long, London, 1893, 244p, Cloth, Coll. [includes some verse]

LEIGHTON, FRANCES SPATZ

08845 *The memoirs of Senator Brown, a Capitol cat, as told to Frances Spatz Leighton.* Fleet Publishing Corp., New York, 1965, 154p, Cloth, Novel

LEIGHTON, PETER

08846 *Moon travellers; a dream that is becoming a reality.* Oldbourne Book Co., London, 1960, 240p, Cloth, Nonf. [includes many excerpts from SF works]

LEIGHTON, ROBERT, 1859-1934

08847 *The thirsty sword; a story of the Norse invasion of Scotland (1262-1263).* Blackie & Son, London, 1892, 352p, Cloth, Novel

LEINSTER, MURRAY, pseud. [William Fitzgerald Jenkins, 1896-1975] [*biography included*]

08848 *The aliens.* Berkley Medallion, New York, 1960, 144p, Paper, Coll.

LEINSTER, MURRAY (cont.)

08849   *The black galaxy.* Galaxy SF Novel, New York,
        1954, 127p, Paper, Novel

08850   *The brain-stealers.* Ace Double, New York,
        1954, 139p, Paper, Novel

08851   *Checkpoint Lambda.* Berkley Medallion, New
        York, 1966, 143p, Paper, Novel

08852   *City on the Moon.* Avalon, New York, 1957,
        224p, Cloth, Novel [Joe Kenmore #3]

08853   *Colonial survey.* Gnome Press, New York, 1957,
        185p, Cloth, Novel

08853A retitled: *Planet explorer.* Avon, New York,
        1957, 171p, Paper, Novel

08854   *Conquest of the stars.* American Science Fic-
        tion, Sydney, 1952, 34p, Paper, Story

08855   *Creatures of the abyss.* Berkley Medallion,
        New York, 1961, 143p, Paper, Novel

08855A retitled: *The listeners; science fiction.*
        Sidgwick & Jackson, London, 1969, 192p,
        Cloth, Novel

08856   *Doctor to the stars; three novelettes of the
        Interstellar Medical Service.* Pyramid, New
        York, 1964, 176p, Paper, Coll. [Med Service
        #3]

08857   *The duplicators.* Ace Double, New York, 1964,
        143p, Paper, Novel

08858   *Fight for life; a complete novel of the atomic
        age.* Crestwood Publishing Co., New York,
        1949?, 118p, Paper, Novel

08859   *The forgotten planet.* Gnome Press, New York,
        1954, 177p, Cloth, Novel

08860   *Four from Planet 5.* Gold Medal, Greenwich,
        Conn., 1959, 160p, Paper, Novel

08861   *Gateway to elsewhere.* Ace Double, New York,
        1954, 139p, Paper, Novel

08862   *Get off my world!* Belmont, New York, 1966,
        157p, Paper, Coll.

08863   *Great stories of science fiction.* Random
        House, New York, 1951, 321p, Cloth, Anth.

08864   *The Greks bring gifts.* Macfadden-Bartell,
        New York, 1964, 143p, Paper, Novel

08865   *Invaders of space.* Berkley Medallion, New
        York, 1964, 144p, Paper, Novel

08866   *Land of the giants.* Pyramid, New York, 1968,
        156p, Paper, Tele. [Land of the Giants #1]

08867   *Land of the giants #2; The hot spot.* Pyramid,
        New York, 1969, 158p, Paper, Tele. [Land of
        the Giants #2]

08868   *Land of the giants #3; Unknown danger.* Pyra-
        mid, New York, 1969, 160p, Paper, Tele.
        [Land of the Giants #3]

08869   *The last space ship.* Frederick Fell, New York,
        1949, 239p, Cloth, Novel
        The listeners. [see 08855A]

08870   *Men into space.* Berkley Medallion, New York,
        1960, 142p, Paper, Tele.

08871   *Miners in the sky.* Avon, New York, 1967,
        127p, Paper, Novel

08872   *The monster from Earth's end.* Gold Medal,
        Greenwich, Conn., 1959, 176p, Paper, Novel

08873   *Monsters and such.* Avon, New York, 1959,
        174p, Paper, Coll.

08874   *Murder madness.* Brewer & Warren, New York,
        1931, 298p, Cloth, Novel

08875   *A Murray Leinster omnibus.* Sidgwick & Jack-
        son, London, 1968, 444p, Cloth, Coll. [in-
        cludes *Operation terror; Invaders of space;
        Checkpoint Lambda*]

08876   *The mutant weapon.* Ace Double, New York,
        1959, 93p, Paper, Novel [Med Service #1]

08877   *Operation: Outer Space.* Fantasy Press, Read-
        ing, PA, 1954, 208p, Cloth, Novel

08878   *Operation terror.* Berkley Medallion, New York,
        1962, 160p, Paper, Novel

08879   *The other side of here.* Ace Double, New York,
        1955, 134p, Paper, Novel

08880   *The Other Side of Nowhere.* Berkley Medallion,
        New York, 1964, 142p, Paper, Novel

08881   *Out of this world.* Avalon, New York, 1958,
        221p, Cloth, Novel

08882   *The pirates of Zan.* Ace Double, New York,
        1959, 163p, Paper, Novel
        Planet explorer. [see 08853A]

08883   *S.O.S. from three worlds.* Ace, New York, 1967,
        140p, Paper, Coll. [Med Service #4]

08884   *Sidewise in time, and other scientific adven-
        tures.* Shasta Publishers, Chicago, 1950,
        213p, Cloth, Coll.

08885   *Space captain.* Ace Double, New York, 1966,
        112p, Paper, Novel

08886   *Space gypsies.* Avon, New York, 1967, 128p,
        Paper, Novel

08887   *Space Platform; a Shasta junior.* Shasta Pub-
        lishers, Chicago, 1953, 223p, Cloth, Novel
        [Joe Kenmore #1]

08888   *Space Tug; a Shasta junior.* Shasta Publishers,
        Chicago, 1953, 223p, Cloth, Novel [Joe Ken-
        more #2]

08889   *Talents, Incorporated.* Avon, New York, 1962,
        159p, Paper, Novel

08890   *This world is taboo.* Ace, New York, 1961,
        127p, Paper, Novel [Med Service #2]

08891   *Time tunnel.* Pyramid, New York, 1964, 140p,
        Paper, Novel

08892   *The Time Tunnel.* Pyramid, New York, 1967,
        143p, Paper, Tele. [Time Tunnel #1]

08893   *Timeslip! a Time Tunnel adventure.* Pyramid,
        New York, 1967, 140p, Paper, Tele. [Time
        Tunnel #2]

08894   *Twists in time.* Avon, New York, 1960, 160p,
        Paper, Coll.

08895   *The unknown.* American Science Fiction, Sydney,
        1952, 34p, Paper, Story

08896   *The wailing asteroid.* Avon, New York, 1960,
        143p, Paper, Novel

08897   *War with the Gizmos.* Gold Medal, Greenwich,
        Conn., 1958, 156p, Paper, Novel

as Will F. Jenkins:

08898   *The murder of the U.S.A.* Crown Publishers,
        New York, 1946, 172p, Cloth, Novel

08898A retitled: *Destroy the U.S.A.* News Stand
        Library, Toronto, 1950, 157p, Paper, Novel

LEITCH, LAVINIA, pseud. [Lavinia Leitch Hynd]

08899   *A vampire, and other stories.* Christopher
        Publishing House, Boston, 1927, 231p, Cloth,
        Coll.

LELAND, CHARLES GODFREY, 1824-1903

08900   *Flaxius; leaves from the life of an immortal.*
        Philip Wellby, London, 1902, 320p, Cloth,
        Novel

ŁEM, STANISŁAW, 1921-

08901   *The cyberiad; fables for the cybernetic age.*
        Continuum Book, Seabury Press, New York,
        1974, 295p, Cloth, Coll.

LEM, STANISLAW (cont.)

08902 *The Futurological Congress (from the memoirs*
       of Ijon Tichy). Continuum Book, Seabury
       Press, New York, 1974, 149p, Cloth, Novel
08903 *The investigation*. Continuum Book, Seabury
       Press, New York, 1974, 216p, Cloth, Novel
08904 *The invincible*. Continuum Book, Seabury
       Press, New York, 1973, 183p, Cloth, Novel
08905 *Memoirs found in a bathtub*. Continuum Book,
       Seabury Press, New York, 1973, 188p, Cloth,
       Novel
08906 *Solaris*. Walker, New York, 1970, 216p, Cloth,
       Novel

LeMAÎTRE, (François Élie) JULES, 1853-1914

08907 *On the margins of old books*. Coward-McCann,
       New York, 1929, 322p, Cloth, Coll.
08908 *Serenvs, & other stories of the past & pre-*
       sent. Selwyn & Blount, London, 1920,
       286p, Cloth, Coll.

LEMAN, BOB, with Gerald Bishop

01340 *Venture science fiction magazine; a checklist*
       of the first American series, and the first
       British series, with an index to both of
       these by author and title; also, an index
       of the first three issues of the second
       American series. Aardvark House, Exeter,
       UK, 1970, 28p, Paper, Nonf.

L'ENGLE, MADELEINE, 1918-   [*biography inclu-*
ded]

08909 *The arm of the starfish*. Ariel, New York,
       1965, 243p, Cloth, Novel [Canon Tellis #1]
08910 *A wind in the door*. Farrar, Straus & Giroux,
       New York, 1973, 211p, Cloth, Novel [Meg
       Murry #2]
08911 *A wrinkle in time*. Ariel, New York, 1962,
       211p, Cloth, Novel [Meg Murry #1]
08912 *The young unicorns*. Ariel Books, Farrar,
       Straus & Giroux, New York, 1968, 245p,
       Cloth, Novel [Canon Tellis #2]

LEO, BESSIE [Leslie Murray] (sic)

08913 *The romance of the stars, being a series of*
       astrological stories. "Modern Astrology"
       Office, London, 1914, 201p, Cloth, Coll.

LEONARD, GEORGE H.
    see: COOPER, HUGHES

LEONARD, JOHN, 1939-   [*biography included*]

08914 *Crybaby of the western world; a novel of pe-*
       tit guignol in Long Beach, California.
       Macdonald, London, 1968, 308p, Cloth, Novel

LEONARDO, da Vinci
    see: PAYNE, ROBERT

LÉOURIER, CHRISTIAN, 1948-

08915 *The mountains of the Sun*. Berkley Medallion,
       New York, 1974, 176p, Paper, Novel

LE PAGE, RAND, house pseud. [see also: William Henry Bird, John Glasby, Brian Holloway,
David O'Brien, Cyril Protheroe, Arthur Ro-
berts]

07343 *"A" men*. Curtis Warren, London, 1952, 127p,
       Paper, Novel [by Brian Holloway]
08916 *Asteroid forma*. Curtis Warren, London, 1953,
       159p, Cloth, Novel
08917 *Beyond these suns*. Curtis Warren, London,
       1952, 128p, Cloth, Novel [by Cyril Protheroe]
08918 *Blue Asp*. Curtis Warren, London, 1952, 128p,
       Cloth, Novel [by David O'Brien]
06023 *Satellite B.C.* Curtis Warren, London, 1952,
       127p, Paper, Novel [by Arthur Roberts &
       John Glasby]
06024 *Time and space*. Curtis Warren, London, 1952,
       128p, Cloth, Novel [by Arthur Roberts &
       John Glasby; Terran Empire series]
01318 *War of Argos*. Curtis Warren, London, 1952,
       127p, Paper, Novel [by William Henry Bird]
06025 *Zero Point*. Curtis Warren, London, 1952,
       128p, Cloth, Novel [by Arthur Roberts &
       John Glasby]

LePIRE, JOE H.

08919 *I was alone; a novel of life on Earth and*
       elsewhere. Exposition Press, New York,
       1963, 192p, Cloth, Novel

LE PRÊTRE, W(illia)m.

08920 *The Bolshevik*. Henry Walker, London, 1931,
       291p, Cloth, Novel

LE QUEUX, WILLIAM (Tufnell), 1864-1927

08921 *The Eye of Istar; a romance of the land of the*
       no return. F. V. White, London, 1897, 298p,
       Cloth, Novel
08922 *The great war in England in 1897*. Tower Pub-
       lishing Co., London, 1894, 330p, Cloth, Novel
08923 *The great white queen; a tale of treasure and*
       treason... F. V. White, London, 1896, 312p,
       Cloth, Novel
       The invasion. [see 08924A]
08924 *The invasion of 1910, with a full account of*
       the siege of London. Eveleigh Nash, London,
       1906, 550p, Cloth, Novel
08924A retitled: *The invasion*. George Newnes, Lon-
       don, 1910, 158p, Cloth, Novel [abridged]
08925 *A madonna of the music halls*. F. V. White,
       London, 1897, 118p, Cloth, Novel
08925A retitled: *A secret sin; or, A madonna of the*
       music halls. A. M. Gardner, London, 1913,
       200p, Cloth, Novel
08926 *The mystery of the green ray*. Hodder & Stough-
       ton, London, 1915, 244p, Cloth, Novel
       A secret sin. [see 08925A]
08927 *The Terror of the Air*. Lloyd's, London, 1920,
       278p, Cloth, Novel
08928 *The unknown to-morrow; how the rich fared at*
       the hands of the poor, together with a full
       account of the social revolution in England.
       F. V. White, London, 1910, 305p, Cloth, Novel

LE QUEUX, WILLIAM (cont.)

08929 *The Zeppelin destroyer, being some chapters of secret history.* Hodder & Stoughton, London, 1916, 251p, Cloth, Novel
08930 *Zoraida; a romance of the harem and the great Sahara.* Tower Publishing Co., London, 1895, 444p, Cloth, Novel

LERMAN, RHODA, 1936- [*biography included*]

08931 *Call me Ishtar.* Doubleday, Garden City, 1973, 247p, Cloth, Novel

LERNER, FRED

08932 *An annotated checklist of science fiction bibliographical works.* Fred Lerner, East Paterson, NJ, 1969, 6p, Paper, Nonf.

LERNET-HOLENIA, ALEXANDER (Maria), 1897-

08933 *Count Luna; two tales of the real and the unreal: Baron Bagge; and, Count Luna.* Criterion, New York, 1956, 252p, Cloth, Coll.
08933A retitled: *Count Luna; and, Baron Bagge.* Anthony Blond, London, 1960, 252p, Cloth, Coll.

LEROND, DENNIS

08934 *An Arthurian concordance.* T-K Graphics, Baltimore, 1974, 51p, Paper, Nonf.

LEROUX, GASTON, 1868-1927

08935 *The bride of the Sun.* McBride, Nast, New York, 1915, 303p, Cloth, Novel
08936 *The burgled heart.* John Long, London, 1925, 254p, Cloth, Coll.
08936A retitled: *The new terror.* Macaulay, New York, 1926, 256p, Cloth, Coll.
08937 *The double life.* John E. Kearney, New York, 1909, 299p, Cloth, Novel
08938 *The haunted chair.* E. P. Dutton, New York, 1931, 235p, Cloth, Novel
08939 *The kiss that killed.* Macaulay, New York, 1934, 264p, Cloth, Novel
08940 *The machine to kill.* Macaulay, New York, 1935, 254p, Cloth, Novel
08941 *The man with the black feather.* Hurst & Blackett, London, 1912, 314p, Cloth, Novel
The new terror. [see 08936A]

LE SAGE, ALAIN RENÉ, 1668-1747

08942 *Le diable boiteux; or, The devil upon two sticks.* Jacob Tonson, London, 1708, 278p, Cloth, Novel
08942A retitled: *The devil upon crutches.* J. Osborn, London, 1750, 2vol, Cloth, Novel
08942B retitled: *The devil upon two sticks.* J. & R. Tonson, London, 1757, 338p, Cloth, Novel
08942C retitled: *The devil on two sticks.* Walker, London, 1815, 265p, Cloth, Novel
08942D retitled: *Asmodeus; or, The devil on two sticks.* J. Thomas, London, 1841, 401p, Cloth, Novel

08942E retitled: *The lame devil.* C. Tucker, London, 1870, 152p, Cloth, Novel [abridged]

LESLIE, DESMOND (Peter Arthur), 1921- [*biography included*]

08943 *The amazing Mr. Lutterworth.* Allan Wingate, London, 1958, 215p, Cloth, Novel
08944 *Angels weep.* T. Werner Laurie, London, 1948, 269p, Cloth, Novel

LESLIE, JOSEPHINE (Aimee Campbell), 1898-

08945 *The devil and Mrs. Devine.* Pocket Books, New York, 1974, 282p, Paper, Novel
The ghost and Mrs. Muir. [see 08946A]

as R. A. Dick:

08946 *The ghost and Mrs. Muir.* Ziff-Davis Publishing Co., Chicago, 1945, 174p, Cloth, Novel
08946A *The ghost and Mrs. Muir,* by Josephine Leslie. Pocket Books, New York, 1974, 143p, Paper, Novel

LESLIE, LILIAN, pseud.
see: PERKINS, VIOLET and HOOD, ARCHER

LESLIE, MARY ISABEL
see: LANE, TEMPLE

LESLIE, PETER, 1922- [*biography included*]

08947 *The autumn accelerator.* Corgi, London, 1969, 128p, Paper, Tele. [Invaders #4]
08948 *The Cornish pixie affair.* Four Square, London, 1967, 117p, Paper, Tele. [Girl from U.N.C.L.E. #4]
08949 *The man from U.N.C.L.E., number 5; The finger in the sky affair.* Four Square, London, 1966, 117p, Paper, Tele. [Man from U.N.C.L.E. #5 (U.K. edition); Man from U.N.C.L.E. #23 (U.S. Edition)]
08950 *The man from U.N.C.L.E., number 7; The radioactive camel affair.* Four Square, London, 1966, 141p, Paper, Tele. [Man from U.N.C.L.E. #7 (U.K. edition); Man from U.N.C.L.E. #7 (U.S. edition)]
08951 *The man from U.N.C.L.E., number 10; The diving dames affair.* Four Square, London, 1967, 140p, Paper, Tele. [Man from U.N.C.L.E. #10 (U.K. edition); Man from U.N.C.L.E. #9 (U.S. edition)]
08952 *The man from U.N.C.L.E., number 14; The splintered sunglasses affair.* Four Square, London, 1968, 124p, Paper, Tele. [Man from U.N.C.L.E. #14 (U.K. edition); Man from U.N.C.L.E. #16 (U.S. edition)]
08953 *The man from U.N.C.L.E., number 16; The unfair fare affair.* Four Square, London, 1968, 127p, Paper, Tele. [Man from U.N.C.L.E. #16 (U.K. edition); Man from U.N.C.L.E. #18 (U.S. edition)]
08954 *The night of the trilobites.* Corgi, London, 1968, 128p, Paper, Tele. [Invaders #3 (U.K. edition)]

LESLIE, (Sir John Randolph) SHANE, Bart., 1885-1971

08955   *Fifteen odd stories.* Hutchinson, London, 1935, 288p, Cloth, Coll.
08956   *A ghost in the Isle of Wight.* Elkin Mathews & Marrot, London, 1929, 31p, Cloth, Story
08957   *Masquerades; studies in the morbid.* John Long, London, 1924, 318p, Cloth, Coll.

LESSER, MILTON, 1928-   [biography included]

08958   *Earthbound.* John C. Winston, Philadelphia, 1952, 208p, Cloth, Novel
08959   *Looking forward; an anthology of science fiction.* Beechhurst Press, New York, 1953, 400p, Cloth, Anth.
08960   *Recruit for Andromeda.* Ace Double, New York, 1959, 117p, Paper, Novel
08961   *Secret of the black planet.* Belmont, New York, 1965, 157p, Paper, Coll.
08962   *Spacemen, go home.* Holt, Rinehart & Winston, New York, 1961, 221p, Cloth, Novel
08963   *Stadium beyond the stars.* John C. Winston, Philadelphia, 1960, 206p, Cloth, Novel
08964   *The star seekers.* John C. Winston, Philadelphia, 1953, 212p, Cloth, Novel

with Paul W. Fairman as Adam Chase:

05013   *The golden ape.* Avalon, New York, 1959, 221p, Cloth, Novel

LESSING, DORIS (May), 1919-   [biography included]

08965   *The four-gated city.* Alfred A. Knopf, New York, 1969, 613p, Cloth, Novel [Children of Violence #5]
08966   *The memoirs of a survivor.* Octagon Press, London, 1974, 182p, Cloth, Novel

LESSNER, ERWIN (Christian), 1898-1959

08967   *Phantom victory; the Fourth Reich, 1945-1960.* G. P. Putnam's Sons, New York, 1944, 227p, Cloth, Novel

LESTER, EDWARD

08968   *The siege of Bodike; a prophecy of Ireland's future.* J. Heywood, Manchester, 1886, 140p, Cloth, Novel

LESTER, H(orace) F(rank), 1853-

08969   *The taking of Dover.* J. W. Arrowsmith, Bristol, 1888, 44p, Paper, Story

LESTER, TERI

08970   *The ouija board.* Signet, New York, 1969, 159p, Paper, Novel

L'ESTRANGE, C. J(ames), 1880?-1947, with George Herbert Ely as Herbert Strang

04880   *The cruise of the gyro-car.* Henry Frowde, Hodder & Stoughton, London, 1910, 244p, Cloth, Novel
04881   *The flying boat; a story of adventure and mis-adventure.* Henry Frowde, Hodder & Stoughton, London, 1912, 272p, Cloth, Novel
04882   *King of the air; or, To Morocco on an airship.* Henry Frowde, Hodder & Stoughton, London, 1908, 272p, Cloth, Novel
04883   *The Old Man of the Mountain.* Henry Frowde, Hodder & Stoughton, London, 1916, 322p, Cloth, Novel
04884   *A thousand miles an hour.* Humphrey Milford, Oxford University Press, London, 1924, 160p, Cloth, Novel

L'ESTRANGE, HENRY

08971   *Platonia; a tale of other worlds.* J. W. Arrowsmith, Bristol, 1893, 190p, Cloth, Novel

L'ESTRANGE, MILES

08972   *What we are coming to.* David Douglas, Edinburgh, 1892, 124p, Cloth, Novel

LET'S TALK OF GHOSTS
      see: A CENTURY OF GHOST STORIES

LETTERS FROM HELL
      see: ROWEL, M.

LETTS, BARRY

08973   *Doctor Who and the Daemons.* Target, London, 1974, 172p, Paper, Tele. [Doctor Who #8]

LEVENE, MALCOLM, 1937-   [biography included]

08974   *Carder's paradise.* Rupert Hart-Davis, London, 1968, 184p, Cloth, Novel

LEVERENTZ, AL(lan) C., with Toby Duane

04533   *Blague.* SSR Publications, North Tonawanda, NY, 1952, 99p, Paper, Novel

LEVETT, ARTHUR

08975   *A Martian examines Christianity.* Watts & Co., London, 1934, 118p, Paper, Novel

LEVI, ARISTOTLE
      see: SCHOEB, ERIKA

LEVIE, REX DEAN

08976   *The insect warriors.* Ace, New York, 1965, 143p, Paper, Novel

LEVIN, BETTY

08977 *The sword of Culann.* Macmillan, New York, 1973, 280p, Cloth, Novel

LEVIN, IRA, 1929- *[biography included]*

08978 *Rosemary's baby; a novel.* Random House, New York, 1967, 245p, Cloth, Novel
08979 *The Stepford wives; a novel.* Random House, New York, 1972, 145p, Cloth, Novel
08980 *This perfect day; a novel.* Random House, New York, 1970, 309p, Cloth, Novel

LEVIN, MEYER, 1905- *[biography included]*

08981 *The spell of time; a tale of love in Jerusalem.* Praeger Publishers, New York, 1974, 127p, Cloth, Novel

LEVIS, M. de
    see: de LEVIS, M.

LEVY, DAVID, 1913- *[biography included]*

08982 *The gods of Foxcroft.* Arbor House, New York, 1970, 277p, Cloth, Novel

LEWIN, ALBERT, 1894-1968

08983 *The unaltered cat.* Charles Scribner's Sons, New York, 1967, 192p, Cloth, Novel

LEWIN, LEONARD C(ase), 1916-

08984 *Triage.* Dial Press, New York, 1972, 215p, Cloth, Novel

LEWIS, AL

08985 *Index to the science fiction and fantasy magazines, 1963.* Al Lewis, Los Angeles, 1964, 62p, Paper, Nonf.
08986 *Index to the science fiction magazines, 1961.* Al Lewis, Los Angeles, 1962, 41p, Paper, Nonf.
08987 *Index to the science fiction magazines, 1962.* Al Lewis, Los Angeles, 1963, 54p, Paper, Nonf.

LEWIS, ANTHONY R.

08988 *Index to the science fiction magazines, 1966.* New England Science Fiction Association, Cambridge, Mass., 1969, 17p, Paper, Nonf.
08989 *Index to the science fiction magazines, 1966-1970.* New England Science Fiction Association, Cambridge, Mass., 1971, 82p, Cloth, Nonf.
08990 *Index to the science fiction magazines, 1967.* New England Science Fiction Association, Cambridge, Mass., 1968, 16p, Paper, Nonf.
08991 *Index to the science fiction magazines, 1968.* New England Science Fiction Association, Cambridge, Mass., 1969, 17p, Paper, Nonf.

08992 *Index to the science fiction magazines, 1969.* New England Science Fiction Association, Cambridge, Mass., 1970, 20p, Paper, Nonf.

with Andrew A. Whyte:

08993 *The N.E.S.F.A. index; science fiction magazines, 1971-1972, and original anthologies, 1971-1972.* NESFA Press, Cambridge, Mass., 1973, 42p, Paper, Nonf.
08994 *The N.E.S.F.A. index to the science fiction magazines and original anthologies, 1973.* NESFA Press, Cambridge, Mass., 1974, 30p, Paper, Nonf.

LEWIS, ARTHUR O(rcutt), Jr., 1920- *[biography included]*

08995 *American utopias; selected short fiction.* Arno Press, New York, 1971, 339p, Cloth, Anth.
08996 *Of men and machines.* E. P. Dutton, New York, 1963, 349p, Paper, Anth.

LEWIS, BENN E.

08997 *I, John, the reincarnated apostle.* Exposition Press, Jericho, NY, 1970, 310p, Cloth, Novel

LEWIS, C(live) S(taples), 1898-1963

08998 *The chronicles of Narnia; with, The lion of Judah in never-never land.* Religious Book Club, New York, 1973, 2vol, Cloth, Coll. [Narnia Chronicles #s 1-7]
08999 *The horse and his boy.* Geoffrey Bles, London, 1954, 199p, Cloth, Novel [Narnia Chronicles #5]
09000 *The last battle; a story for children.* Bodley Head, London, 1956, 184p, Cloth, Novel [Narnia Chronicles #7]
09001 *The lion, the witch, and the wardrobe; a story for children.* Geoffrey Bles, London, 1950, 172p, Cloth, Novel [Narnia Chronicles #1]
09002 *The magician's nephew.* Bodley Head, London, 1955, 183p, Cloth, Novel [Narnia Chronicles #6]
09003 *Of other worlds; essays and stories.* Geoffrey Bles, London, 1966, 148p, Cloth, Coll. [includes some nonf.]
09004 *Out of the silent planet.* John Lane, London, 1938, 264p, Cloth, Novel [Ransom #1]
09005 *Perelandra; a novel.* John Lane, London, 1943, 256p, Cloth, Novel [Ransom #2]
09005A retitled: *Voyage to Venus (Perelandra).* Pan, London, 1953, 188p, Paper, Novel [Ransom #2]
09006 *Prince Caspian; the return to Narnia.* Geoffrey Bles, London, 1951, 195p, Cloth, Novel [Narnia Chronicles #2]
09007 *The Screwtape letters.* Geoffrey Bles, London, 1942, 160p, Cloth, Novel [Screwtape #1]
09008 *The Screwtape letters; and, Screwtape proposes a toast.* Geoffrey Bles, London, 1961, 157p, Cloth, Coll. [Screwtape #s 1-2]
09009 *Screwtape proposes a toast, and other pieces.* Fontana, London, 1965, 126p, Paper, Coll.
09010 *The silver chair.* Geoffrey Bles, London, 1953, 217p, Cloth, Novel [Narnia Chronicles #4]
09011 *That hideous strength; a modern fairy-tale for grown-ups.* John Lane, The Bodley Head, London, 1945, 476p, Cloth, Novel [Ransom #3]

LEWIS, C. S. (cont.)

09011A retitled: *The tortured planet*. Avon, New York, 1958, 254p, Paper, Novel [abridged]

09012 *Till we have faces; a myth retold*. Geoffrey Bles, London, 1956, 320p, Cloth, Novel
The tortured planet. [see 09011A]

09013 *The voyage of the Dawn Treader*. Geoffrey Bles, London, 1952, 223p, Cloth, Novel [Narnia Chronicles #3]
Voyage to Venus. [see 09005A]

LEWIS, CAROLINE, pseud.
see: BEGBIE, HAROLD and RANSOME, J. STAFFORD, and TEMPLE, M. H.

LEWIS, CECIL DAY-
see: BLAKE, NICHOLAS

LEWIS, CHARLES BERTRAND
see: QUAD, M.

LEWIS, GOGO, with Seon Manley

09014 *Baleful beasts; great supernatural stories of the animal kingdom*. Lothrop, Lee & Shepard, New York, 1974, 222p, Cloth, Anth.

09015 *Bewitched beings; phantoms, familiars, and the possessed in stories from two centuries*. Lothrop, Lee & Shepard, New York, 1974, 224p, Cloth, Anth.

09016 *A gathering of ghosts; a treasury*. Funk & Wagnalls, New York, 1970, 217p, Cloth, Anth.

09017 *Ladies of horror; two centuries of supernatural stories by the gentle sex*. Lothrop, Lee & Shepard, New York, 1971, 288p, Cloth, Anth.

09018 *Magic; a treasury for young readers*. Funk & Wagnalls, New York, 1967, 238p, Cloth, Anth.

09019 *Mistresses of mystery; two centuries of suspense stories by the gentle sex*. Lothrop, Lee & Shepard, New York, 1973, 221p, Cloth, Anth.

09020 *Shapes of the supernatural*. Doubleday, Garden City, 1969, 370p, Cloth, Anth.

LEWIS, H. MILO

09021 *The castle of mystery*. Carlton Press, New York, 1964, 227p, Cloth, Novel

LEWIS, H(arve) SPENCER, 1883-1939

09022 *A thousand years of yesterdays; a strange story of mystic revelations*. College Press, San Francisco, 1920, 80p, Cloth, Novel

LEWIS, HAMILTON
see: HAMILTON, M. LYNN

LEWIS, HENRY

09023 *The way out; the social revolution in retrospect, viewed from A.D. 2050*. Elliot Stock, London, 1933, 60p, Cloth?, Novel

LEWIS, HILDA (Winifred), 1896-1974

09024 *The witch and the priest*. Jarrolds Publishers, London, 1956, 304p, Cloth, Novel

LEWIS, IRWIN, 1916- [*biography included*]

09025 *The day New York trembled*. Avon, New York, 1967, 144p, Paper, Novel [Horace Clarke #2]

09026 *The day they invaded New York*. Avon, New York, 1964, 160p, Paper, Novel [Horace Clarke #1]

LEWIS, JACK

09027 *Blood money*. Headline Books, Los Angeles, 1960, 160p, Paper, Novel

LEWIS, L. A.

09028 *Tales of the grotesque; a collection of uneasy tales*. Philip Allan, London, 1934, 244p, Cloth, Coll.

LEWIS, LEON, 1833-1920

09029 *Andrée at the North Pole, with details of his fate*. G. W. Dillingham, New York, 1899, 279p, Paper, Novel

LEWIS, M(atthew) G(regory), 1775-1818

09030 *The monk; a romance*. J. Bell, London, 1796, 2vol, Cloth, Novel

09030A retitled: *Ambrosio; or, The monk*. J. Bell, London, 1798, 3vol, Cloth, Novel

with Anthony Hamilton and M. de Levis:

06687 *The four Facardins; a fairy tale*. Lutetian Society, London, 1899, 286p, Paper, Novel

LEWIS, OSCAR, 1893- [*biography included*]

09031 *The lost years; a biographical fantasy*. Alfred A. Knopf, New York, 1951, 121p, Cloth, Novel

LEWIS, PETE, pseud. [Peter J. Crown]

09032 *Father of the Amazons*. Kozy Books, Manhasset, NY, 1961, 158p, Paper, Novel

LEWIS, PHILIP C.

09033 *Horan; the story of the world's first cure for sex*. Harper & Row, New York, 1974, 200p, Cloth, Novel

LEWIS, R. M.

09034 *The divine gift*. Lumley & Co., London, 1906, 264p, Cloth, Novel

LEWIS, (Ernest Michael) ROY, 1913- [biography included]

09035 *What we did to father.* Hutchinson, London, 1960, 166p, Cloth, Novel
09035A retitled: *The evolution man.* Penguin, Harmondsworth, 1963, 123p, Paper, Novel

LEWIS, (Harry) SINCLAIR, 1885-1951

09036 *It can't happen here; a novel.* Doubleday, Doran, Garden City, 1935, 458p, Cloth, Novel

LEWIS, (Percy) WYNDHAM, 1882-1957

09037 *The Childermass, section I.* Chatto & Windus, London, 1928, 322p, Cloth, Novel [Human Age #1]
09037A retitled: *The human age, book 1; The Childermass.* Methuen, London, 1956, 401p, Cloth, Novel [Human Age #1]
09038 *The human age: book two, Monstre Gai; book three, Malign fiesta.* Methuen, London, 1955, 566p, Cloth, Coll. [Human Age #s 2-3]
09039 *Malign fiesta.* Jupiter, London, 1966, 240p, Paper, Novel [Human Age #3]
09040 *Monstre Gai.* Jupiter, London, 1965, 254p, Paper, Novel [Human Age #2]

LEWISOHN, LUDWIG, 1882-1955

09041 *Trumpet of jubilee; a novel.* Harper & Bros., New York, 1937, 345p, Cloth, Novel

LEY, ARTHUR GORDON
    see: SELLINGS, ARTHUR

LEY-PISCATOR, MARIA, 1905-

09042 *Lot's wife; a novel.* Bobbs-Merrill, Indianapolis, 1954, 506p, Cloth, Novel

LHIN, ERIK VAN, pseud.
    see: del REY, LESTER

LICATA, TONY

09043 *Great science-fiction.* Three Star Books, Chicago, 1965, 128p, Paper, Anth.

LICHTENBERG, JACQUELINE, 1942-

09044 *House of Zeor.* Doubleday, Garden City, 1974, 206p, Cloth, Novel

LIEBER, MAXIM, 1897-

09045 *Ghosts, ghouls, and other nuisances.* Seven Seas Publishers, Berlin, 1959, 272p, Paper, Anth.

LIEBERMAN, ROSALIE [biography included]

09046 *The man who captivated New York; the further adventures of Brother Angelo.* Doubleday, Garden City, 1960, 190p, Cloth, Novel [Brother Angelo #2]
09047 *The man who sold Christmas.* Longmans, Green, New York, 1951, 128p, Cloth, Novel [Brother Angelo #1]

LIEBSCHER, WALT

09048 *Alien carnival; a fantastic extravaganza.* Fantasy House, North Hollywood, 1974, 71p, Paper, Coll.

THE LIFE AND ADVENTURES OF PETER WILKINS
    see: PALTOCK, ROBERT

THE LIFE VAPOR

09049 *The life vapor.* Stellar Publishing Corp., New York, 1930, 24p, Paper, Anth. [includes "The Life Vapor," by Clyde Farrar; "Thirty Miles Down," by D. D. Sharp]

LIGHTNER, A(lice) M(artha), 1904- [biography included]

09050 *The day of the drones.* W. W. Norton, New York, 1969, 256p, Cloth, Novel
09051 *Doctor to the galaxy.* W. W. Norton, New York, 1965, 175p, Cloth, Novel
09052 *The galactic troubadours.* W. W. Norton, New York, 1965, 240p, Cloth, Novel
09053 *Gods or demons?* Four Winds Press, New York, 1973, 208p, Cloth, Novel
09054 *The planet poachers.* G. P. Putnam's Sons, New York, 1965, 184p, Cloth, Novel [Rock #2]
09055 *The rock of three planets.* G. P. Putnam's Sons, New York, 1963, 157p, Cloth, Novel [Rock #1]
09056 *The space ark.* G. P. Putnam's Sons, New York, 1968, 190p, Cloth, Novel [Rock #3]
09057 *The space gypsies.* McGraw-Hill, New York, 1974, 216p, Cloth, Novel
09058 *The Space Olympics.* W. W. Norton, New York, 1967, 211p, Cloth, Novel
09059 *The space plague.* W. W. Norton, New York, 1966, 156p, Cloth, Novel
09060 *Star dog.* McGraw-Hill, New York, 1973, 179p, Cloth, Novel
09061 *The Thursday toads.* McGraw-Hill, New York, 1971, 189p, Cloth, Novel

LILJENCRANTZ, OTTILIE A(delina), 1876-1910

09062 *The thrall of Leif the Lucky; a story of Viking days.* A. C. McClurg, Chicago, 1902, 354p, Cloth, Novel

"LIMBO," pseud.

09063 *My own death.* Henry J. Drane, London, 1902, 272p, Cloth, Novel

LIN, YUTANG [Lin Yü-t'ang, 1895-1976] [*bio-graphy included*]

09064   *The unexpected island.* William Heinemann, London, 1955, 351p, Cloth, Novel
09064A   retitled: *Looking beyond.* Prentice-Hall, New York, 1955, 387p, Cloth, Novel

LINCOLN, MAURICE, pseud.

09065   *The man from up there.* John Hamilton, London, 1928, 255p, Cloth, Novel
09066   *Nothing ever happens.* John Hamilton, London, 1927, 319p, Cloth, Novel

LINDELOF, O(tto) J(ulius) S(wenson), 1852-

09067   *A trip to the North Pole; or, The discovery of the Ten Tribes, as found in the Arctic Ocean.* Tribune Printing Co., Salt Lake City, Utah, 1903, 200p, Paper, Novel

LINDEN, MARGARET

09068   *Pasha the Persian.* Claude Kendall, New York, 1936, 108p, Cloth, Novel

LINDER, D. BARRY, pseud.
   see: DuBREUIL, LINDA

LINDSAY, C(harles) McD(onald)

09069   *Betrayed!! or, What might come to pass.* Henry J. Drane, London, 1928, 299p, Cloth, Novel

LINDSAY, DAVID, 1876-1945

09070   *Adventures of Monsieur de Mailly.* Andrew Melrose, London, 1926, 319p, Cloth, Novel
09070A   retitled: *A blade for sale; the adventures of Monsieur de Mailly.* Robert M. McBride, New York, 1927, 319p, Cloth, Novel
09071   *Devil's Tor.* G. P. Putnam's Sons, London, 1932, 487p, Cloth, Novel
09072   *The haunted woman.* Methuen, London, 1922, 197p, Cloth, Novel
09073   *Sphinx.* John Long, London, 1923, 318p, Cloth, Novel
09074   *A voyage to Arcturus.* Methuen, London, 1920, 303p, Cloth, Novel

LINDSAY, DAVID T.

09075   *The green ray.* John Hamilton, London, 1937, 223p, Cloth, Novel
09076   *The ninth plague.* John Hamilton, London, 1936, 317p, Cloth, Novel

LINDSAY, DOUGLAS

09077   *Blue moon; an anthology of science fiction stories.* Mayflower, London, 1970, 176p, Paper, Anth.

LINDSAY, KATHLEEN, 1903-

09078   *Unbroken barriers.* Herbert Jenkins, London, 1940, 255p, Cloth, Novel

LINDSAY, NORMAN (Alfred William), 1879-1969

09079   *The magic pudding, being the adventures of Bunyip Bluegum and his friends Bill Barnacle and Sam Sawnoff.* Angus & Robertson, Sydney, 1918, 171p, Cloth, Novel

LINDSAY, (Nicholas) VACHELL, 1879-1931

09080   *The Golden Book of Springfield, being the review of a book that will appear in the autumn of the year 2018, and an extended description of Springfield, Illinois, in that year.* Macmillan, New York, 1920, 329p, Cloth, Novel

LINDSKOOG, KATHRYN ANN

09081   *The lion of Judah in never-never land; the theology of C. S. Lewis expressed in his fantasies for children.* William B. Eerdmans Publishing Co., Grand Rapids, Mich., 1973, 141p, Paper, Nonf.

LINEBARGER, PAUL
   see: SMITH, CORDWAINER

LINES, KATHLEEN (Mary)

09082   *The house of the nightmare, & other eerie tales.* Bodley Head, London, 1967, 208p, Cloth, Anth. [includes some nonf.]

LINGEMAN, RICHARD R(oberts), 1931- [*biography included*], with Jack Newfield, Victor Navasky, Karla Kuskin, and Marvin Kitman

08300   *Animal ranch; the great American fable.* Parallax Publishing Co., New York, 1966, 63p, Paper, Novel

LINKLATER, ERIC (Robert Russell), 1899-1974

09083   *The impregnable women.* Jonathan Cape, London, 1938, 348p, Cloth, Novel
09084   *Sealskin trousers, and other stories.* Rupert Hart-Davis, London, 1947, 127p, Cloth, Coll.
09085   *A spell for old bones.* Jonathan Cape, London, 1949, 223p, Cloth, Novel
09086   *The wind on the Moon; a story for children.* Macmillan, London, 1944, 363p, Cloth, Novel

LINKROUM, RICHARD

09087   *One before bedtime; a novel.* J. B. Lippincott, Philadelphia, 1968, 201p, Cloth, Novel

LINTON, Dr. C(harles) E(llsworth), 1865?-1930

  09088 *The Earthomotor, and other stories.* Press of Statesman Publishing Co., Salem, OR, 1920?, 231p, Cloth, Coll. [cover title: *The Earth motor*]

LINTON, Mrs. (Elizabeth) LYNN, 1822-1898

  09089 *The second youth of Theodora Desanges.* Hutchinson, London, 1900, 335p, Cloth, Novel

LIONEL, ROBERT, pseud.
    see: FANTHORPE, R. LIONEL

LIPPARD, GEORGE, 1822-1854

  09090 *The ladye Annabel; or, The doom of the poisoner; a romance,* by an unknown author. R. G. Berford, Publisher, Philadelphia, 1844, 133p, Cloth, Novel [published anonymously]
  09090A retitled: *The mysteries of Florence.* T. B. Peterson & Bros., Philadelphia, 1864, 258p, Cloth, Novel

LIPPINCOTT, DAVID (McCord), 1925-   [*biography included*]

  09091 *E pluribus bang!* Viking Press, New York, 1970, 212p, Cloth, Novel

LIPTON, ROBERT
    see: STERLING, BARRY

LISLE, CHARLES WENTWORTH

  09092 *The ring of Gyges; some passages in the life of Francis Neville.* Richard Bentley & Son, London, 1886, 308p, Cloth, Novel

L'ISLE ADAM, JEAN VILLIERS de
    see: VILLIERS de L'ISLE ADAM, JEAN

LISSENDEN, GEORGE B.

  09093 *The seeress; a novel.* Heath Cranton, London, 1927, 286p, Cloth, Novel

LISSER, HERBERT G. de
    see: de LISSER, HERBERT G.

LISTER, STEPHEN, pseud.

  09094 *Hail Bolonia!* Peter Davies, London, 1948, 171p, Cloth, Novel

LISTON, EDWARD (J.), 1900-

  09095 *The bowl of night.* Coward-McCann, New York, 1948, 246p, Cloth, Novel

LITTELL, PHILIP, 1868-1943

  09096 *This way out.* Coward-McCann, New York, 1928, 314p, Cloth, Novel

LITTELL, ROBERT, with Richard Z. Chesnoff and Edward Klein

  02921 *If Israel lost the war.* Coward-McCann, New York, 1969, 253p, Cloth, Novel

LITTLE, JANE

  09097 *The philosopher's stone.* Atheneum, New York, 1971, 123p, Cloth, Novel
  09098 *Sneaker Hill.* Atheneum, New York, 1967, 183p, Cloth, Novel

LITTLE, PAUL H.
    see: PAUL, HUGO

LITTLE, W(illiam) J(ohn) KNOX, 1839-1918

  09099 *The broken vow; a story of here and hereafter.* Chapman & Hall, London, 1887, 263p, Cloth, Novel

A LITTLE PILGRIM
    see: OLIPHANT, Mrs.

A LITTLE PILGRIM IN THE UNSEEN
    see: OLIPHANT, Mrs.

LITTLEDALE, FREYA (Lota), 1929-   [*biography included*]

  09100 *13 ghostly tales.* Scholastic Book Services, New York, 1966, 92p, Paper, Anth.

LIVELY, PENELOPE, 1933-   [*biography included*]

  09101 *The Driftway.* Heinemann, London, 1972, 140p, Cloth, Novel
  09102 *The ghost of Thomas Kempe.* Heinemann, London, 1973, 153p, Cloth, Novel
  09103 *The whispering knights.* Heinemann, London, 1971, 160p, Cloth, Novel
  09104 *The wild hunt of Hagworthy.* Heinemann, London, 1971, 149p, Cloth, Novel
  09104A retitled: *The wild hunt of the ghost hounds.* E. P. Dutton, New York, 1972, 141p, Cloth, Novel

LIVESEY, ERIC M.

  09105 *The desolate land.* Digit, London, 1964, 158p, Paper, Novel

LIVINGSTON, ARMSTRONG, 1885-

  09106 *Magic for murder.* Skeffington & Son, London, 1936, 254p, Cloth, Novel

LIVINGSTON, BERKELEY

09107 *Meteor of death.* American Science Fiction, Sydney, 1954, 34p, Paper, Coll.

LIVINGSTON, HAROLD, 1924- [*biography included*]

09108 *The Climacticon.* Ballantine, New York, 1960, 191p, Paper, Novel

LIVINGSTON, MARJORIE (Prout), 1893-

09109 *Delphic echo.* Andrew Dakers, London, 1948, 432p, Cloth, Novel [Karmic Destiny #3]
09110 *The future of Mr. Purdew; a novel.* Wright & Brown, London, 1936, 320p, Cloth, Novel
09111 *Island sonata.* Andrew Dakers, London, 1944, 331p, Cloth, Novel [Karmic Destiny #1]
09112 *Moloch.* Andrew Dakers, London, 1942, 295p, Cloth, Novel
09113 *Muted strings.* Andrew Dakers, London, 1946, 446p, Cloth, Novel [Karmic Destiny #2]

LJOKA, DAN(iel John), 1935- [*biography included*]

09114 *Shelter.* Manor, New York, 1973, 224p, Paper, Novel

LLEWELLYN, (David William) ALUN, 1903-

09115 *The strange invaders.* G. Bell & Sons, London, 1934, 309p, Cloth, Novel

LLOYD, J(ohn) W(illia)m., 1857-

09116 *The dwellers in Vale Sunrise; how they got together, and lived happy ever after; a sequel to "The natural man," being an account of the tribes of him.* Ariel Press, Westwood, Mass., 1904, 195p, Cloth, Novel [Natural Man #2]
09117 *The natural man; a romance of the golden age.* Benedict Prieth, Publisher, Newark, NJ, 1902, 140p, Cloth, Novel [Natural Man #1]

LLOYD, JEREMY

09118 *The further adventures of Captain Gregory Dangerfield, as told to Jeremy Lloyd by the late P. W. Arnold.* Michael Joseph, London, 1973, 222p, Cloth, Novel

LLOYD, JOHN (Seaton)

09119 *Tales from the beyond.* Tandem, London, 1966, 200p, Paper, Coll.

LLOYD, JOHN URI, 1849-1936

09120 *Etidorpha; or, The end of Earth; the strange history of a mysterious being and the account of a remarkable journey, as communicated in manuscript to Llewellyn Drury, who promised to print the same, but finally evaded the responsibility, which was assumed by J. U. Lloyd.* John Uri Lloyd, Cincinnati, 1895, 376p, Cloth, Novel

LLOYD, ROGER (Bradshaigh), 1901-

09121 *The troubling of the city.* George Allen & Unwin, London, 1962, 214p, Cloth, Novel

LOBO, GEORGE OLIVER
see: SHERRY, OLIVER

LOCH, J. M.

09122 *The hopping ha'penny.* Methuen, London, 1935, 241p, Cloth, Novel

LOCKE, GEORGE (Walter), 1936- [*biography included*]

09123 *At the mountains of murkiness, and other parodies.* Ferret Fantasy, London, 1973, 111p, Paper, Anth. [published anonymously]
09124 *Ferret Fantasy's Christmas annual for 1972.* Ferret Fantasy, London, 1972, 76p, Paper, Nonf.
09125 *Ferret Fantasy's Christmas annual for 1973.* Ferret Fantasy, London, 1974, 54p, Paper, Nonf.
09126 *From an ultimate dim Thule; a review of the early works of Sidney H. Sime.* Ferret Fantasy, London, 1973, 64p, Paper, Nonf.
09127 *The land of the unseen; lost supernatural stories, 1828-1902.* Ferret Fantasy, London, 1973, 110p, Paper, Anth. [published anonymously]
09128 *Worlds apart; an anthology in facsimile.* Cornmarket Reprints, London, 1972, 180p, Cloth, Anth.

LOCKE, RICHARD ADAMS, 1800-1871

09129 *Great astronomical discoveries lately made by Sir John Herschel at the Cape of Good Hope.* no publisher, New York, 1835, 28p, Paper, Story
09129A retitled: *A complete account of the late discoveries in the Moon.* no publisher, New York, 1835?, 11p, Paper, Story
09129B retitled: *The celebrated "Moon story," its origin and incidents, with a memoir of the author, and an appendix, containing I. An authentic description of the Moon; II. A new theory of the Lunar surface in relation to that of the Earth, by William N. Griggs.* Bunnell & Price, New York, 1852, 143p, Paper, Coll.
09129C retitled: *The Moon hoax; or, A discovery that the Moon has a vast population of human beings.* William Gowans, New York, 1859, 63p, Paper, Story
09129D retitled: *The great Moon hoax of Richard Adams Locke.* W. W. Osgoodby, Rochester, NY, 1886, 67p, Paper, Story

LOCKE, WILLIAM J(ohn), 1863-1930

09130 *A Christmas mystery; the story of three wise men.* John Lane, New York, 1910, 54p, Cloth, Novel

LOCKHART-ROSS, H. S.

09131 *Hamtura; a tale of an unknown land.* Digby, Long, London, 1892, 388p, Cloth, Novel

LOCKLEY, RONALD (Mathias), 1903- [*biography included*]

09132 *Seal woman.* Rex Collings, London, 1974, 154p, Cloth, Novel

LOCKRIDGE, RICHARD (Orson), 1898- , with G. H. Estabrooks

04948 *Death in the mind.* E. P. Dutton, New York, 1945, 251p, Cloth, Novel

LOCKWOOD, INGERSOLL, 1841-1918

09133 *Baron Trump's marvellous underground journey.* Lee & Shepard, Boston, 1893, 235p, Cloth, Novel [Baron Trump #2]
09134 *1900; or, The last president.* American News Co., New York, 1896, 48p, Paper, Story
09135 *Travels and adventures of little Baron Trump and his wonderful dog Bulger.* Lee & Shepard, Boston, 1890, 287p, Cloth, Novel [Baron Trump #1]

LODEN, ERLE van
    see: van LODEN, ERLE

LOE, GLADYS ST. JOHN-
    see: ST. JOHN-LOE, GLADYS

LOFTS, NORAH (Ethel), 1904- [*biography included*]

09136 *Afternoon of an autocrat.* Michael Joseph, London, 1956, 351p, Cloth, Novel
09137 *Is there anybody there?* Corgi, London, 1974, 174p, Paper, Coll.

LOGAN, A FAMILY HISTORY
    see: NEAL, JOHN

LOMBARD, LOUIS, 1861-1927

09138 *The vicious virtuoso.* F. Tennyson Neely, London, 1898, 232p, Cloth, Novel

LOMBARDI, CYNTHIA, d. 1942

09139 *Lighting seven candles.* D. Appleton, New York, 1926, 291p, Cloth, Novel

LOMBINO, S. A.
    see: HUNTER, EVAN

LONDON, JACK [John Griffith London, 1876-1916]

09140 *Before Adam.* Macmillan, New York, 1906, 215p, Cloth, Novel
09141 *Before Adam; and, The game.* Macmillan, New York, 1936, 228p, Cloth, Coll.
09142 *The call of the wild; The scarlet plague; Tales of the fish patrol.* Leslie-Judge, New York, 1925, 622p, Cloth, Coll. [*The scarlet plague* is the only SF part of this three-in-one volume]
09143 *The call of the wild; White Fang; The scarlet plague.* Collins, London, 1952, 381p, Cloth, Coll.
09144 *The dream of Debs; a story of industrial revolt.* Charles H. Kerr, London, 1912?, 32p, Paper, Story
09145 *Goliah; a utopian essay.* Thorp Springs Press, Berkeley, 1973, 25p, Paper, Story
09146 *Hearts of three.* Mills & Boon, London, 1918, 292p, Cloth, Movie
09147 *The Iron Heel.* Macmillan, New York, 1907, 354p, Cloth, Novel
       The jacket. [see 09153A]
09148 *Moon-face, and other stories; The strength of the strong.* Macmillan, New York, 1929, 530p, Cloth, Coll. [*The strength of the strong* is the only SF part of this two-in-one volume]
09149 *The red one.* Macmillan, New York, 1918, 193p, Cloth, Coll.
09150 *The scarlet plague.* Macmillan, New York, 1915, 181p, Cloth, Novel
09151 *The scarlet plague; and, Before Adam.* Arco, London, 1968, 173p, Cloth, Coll.
09152 *The scarlet plague; Love of life; The unexpected; three stories by Jack London.* Staples Press, London, 1946, 100p, Cloth, Coll.
09153 *The star rover.* Macmillan, New York, 1915, 329p, Cloth, Novel
09153A retitled: *The jacket.* Mills & Boon, London, 1915, 334p, Cloth, Novel
09154 *The strength of the strong.* Macmillan, New York, 1914, 257p, Cloth, Coll.

THE LONELY PLANET

09155 *The lonely planet.* American Science Fiction, Sydney, 1954, 34p, Paper, Anth.

LONG, CHARLES R(ussell), 1904- [*biography included*]

09156 *The eternal man.* Avalon, New York, 1964, 191p, Cloth, Novel
09157 *The infinite brain.* Avalon, New York, 1957, 224p, Cloth, Novel

LONG, FRANK BELKNAP, 1903- [*biography included*]

09158 *...And others shall be born.* Belmont Double, New York, 1968, 86p, Paper, Novel
       The androids. [see 09165A]
       The dark beasts. [see 09161A]
09159 *The horror expert.* Belmont, New York, 1961, 141p, Paper, Novel

LONG, FRANK BELKNAP (cont.)

09160   *The horror from the hills.* Arkham House,
        Sauk City, 1963, 110p, Cloth, Novel
        The horror from the hills. [see 09172A]
09161   *The Hounds of Tindalos.* Arkham House, Sauk
        City, 1946, 316p, Cloth, Coll.
09161A retitled: *The dark beasts, and eight other
        stories from The Hounds of Tindalos.* Bel-
        mont, New York, 1964, 141p, Paper, Coll.
        [abridged]
09162   *It was the day of the robot.* Belmont, New
        York, 1963, 141p, Paper, Novel
09163   *John Carstairs, space detective.* Frederick
        Fell, New York, 1949, 265p, Cloth, Coll.
09164   *Journey into darkness.* Belmont, New York,
        1967, 156p, Paper, Novel
09165   *Lest Earth be conquered.* Belmont, New York,
        1966, 144p, Paper, Novel
09165A retitled: *The androids.* Tower, New York,
        1969, 144p, Paper, Novel
09166   *Mars is my destination; a science-fiction
        adventure.* Pyramid, New York, 1962, 158p,
        Paper, Novel
09167   *The Martian visitors.* Avalon, New York, 1964,
        192p, Cloth, Novel
09168   *The mating center.* Chariot, New York, 1961,
        160p, Paper, Novel
09169   *Mission to a star.* Avalon, New York, 1964,
        192p, Cloth, Novel
09170   *Monster from out of time.* Popular Library,
        New York, 1970, 127p, Paper, Novel
09171   *The night of the wolf.* Popular Library, New
        York, 1972, 175p, Paper, Novel
09172   *Odd science fiction.* Belmont, New York, 1964,
        141p, Paper, Coll.
09172A retitled: *The horror from the hills.* Brown,
        Watson, London, 1965, 159p, Paper, Coll.
09173   *The rim of the unknown.* Arkham House, Sauk
        City, 1972, 291p, Cloth, Coll.
09174   *Space Station 1.* Ace Double, New York, 1957,
        157p, Paper, Novel
09175   *Survival world.* Lancer, New York, 1971, 157p,
        Paper, Novel
09176   *This strange tomorrow.* Belmont, New York,
        1966, 158p, Paper, Novel
09177   *The three faces of time.* Tower, New York,
        1969, 156p, Paper, Novel
09178   *Three steps spaceward.* Avalon, New York,
        1963, 192p, Cloth, Novel
09179   *Woman from another planet.* Chariot, New York,
        1960, 190p, Paper, Novel

as Lyda Belknap Long:

09180   *Crucible of evil.* Avon, New York, 1974, 158p,
        Paper, Novel

LONG, GABRIELLE MARGARET
    see: BOWEN, MARJORIE

LONG, GEORGE

09181   *Two lives in parenthesis.* Henry J. Drane,
        London, 1906, 286p, Cloth, Novel
09182   *Valhalla; a novel.* Henry J. Drane, London,
        1906, 280p, Cloth, Novel

LONG, HANIEL (Clark), 1888-1956

09183   *Notes for a new mythology.* The Bookfellows,
        Chicago, 1926, 167p, Cloth, Coll.

LONG, LYDA BELKNAP, pseud.
    see: LONG, FRANK BELKNAP

LONG, PAUL, with Alan Wye

09184   *The remnants of 1927.* Long's Publications,
        London, 1925, 191p, Cloth, Novel

LONG, PETER, pseud.
    see: HECHT, BEN

LONGLEY, MARY T(heresa), 1853-

09185   *Nameless.* Progressive Thinker Publishing
        House, Chicago, 1912, 181p, Cloth, Novel

LONGMATE, NORMAN (Richard), 1925-   [*biography included*]

09186   *If Britain had fallen.* British Broadcasting
        Corp., Hutchinson, London, 1972, 276p, Cloth,
        Tele.

LONGO, CHRIS

09187   *Succubus up.* Pendulum, Atlanta, GA, 1970,
        191p, Paper, Novel

LONGSTRETH, T(homas) MORRIS, 1886-   [*biography included*]

09188   *Time flight.* Macmillan, New York, 1954, 216p,
        Cloth, Novel

LONGWORTH, NICHOLAS, 1844-1890

09189   *The marquis and the Moon; a story.* Robert
        Clarke, Cincinnati, 1889, 39p, Cloth, Story

LONSDALE, H. M.

09190   *D'Abra the Buddhist.* Ward, Lock, London, 1903
        312p, Cloth, Novel

LOOKING AHEAD
    see: MORRIS, ALFRED

LOOMIS, NOEL (Miller), 1905-1969 [*biography
included*]

09191   *City of glass; a complete science fiction no-
        vel.* Double-Action Pocketbook, New York,
        1955, 128p, Paper, Novel

as Silas Water:

09192   *The man with absolute motion.* Rich & Cowan,
        London, 1955, 206p, Cloth, Novel

LOON, HENDRIK WILLEM van
    see: van LOON, HENDRIK WILLEM

LOPEZ, HANK [Enrique Lopez]

  09193 *Afro-6.* Dell, New York, 1969, 237p, Paper, Novel

LORAINE, PHILIP, pseud. [Robin Estridge]

  09194 *Day of the arrow.* Collins, London, 1964, 192p, Cloth, Novel
  09194A retitled: *13.* Lancer, New York, 1966, 158p, Paper, Novel
  09195 *Voices in an empty room.* Crime Club, Collins, London, 1973, 192p, Cloth, Novel

LORCA, FEDERICO GARCIA
    see: GARCIA LORCA, FEDERICO

LORD, BEMAN, 1924- [*biography included*]

  09196 *The day the spaceship landed.* Henry Z. Walck, New York, 1967, 63p, Cloth, Novel [Spaceship #1]
  09197 *The spaceship returns.* Henry Z. Walck, New York, 1970, 62p, Cloth, Novel [Spaceship #2]

LORD, JEFFREY, house pseud. [see also Roland Green]

  09198 *The bronze axe.* Macfadden-Bartell, New York, 1969, 191p, Paper, Novel [Richard Blade #1]
  06298 *Dimension of dreams.* Pinnacle, New York, 1974, 181p, Paper, Novel [Richard Blade #11] [by Roland Green]
  06299 *Ice dragon; the Richard Blade series.* Pinnacle, New York, 1974, 183p, Paper, Novel [Richard Blade #10] [by Roland Green]
  09199 *The jade warrior.* Macfadden-Bartell, New York, 1969, 192p, Paper, Novel [Richard Blade #2]
  09200 *Jewel of Tharn.* Macfadden-Bartell, New York, 1969, 160p, Paper, Novel [Richard Blade #3]
  06300 *Kingdom of Royth; the Richard Blade series.* Pinnacle, New York, 1974, 188p, Paper, Novel [Richard Blade #9] [by Roland Green]
  09201 *Liberator of Jedd.* Macfadden-Bartell, New York, 1971, 224p, Paper, Novel [Richard Blade #5]
  09202 *Monster of the maze.* Macfadden-Bartell, New York, 1972, 192p, Paper, Novel [Richard Blade #6]
  09203 *Pearl of Patmos; the Richard Blade series.* Pinnacle, New York, 1973, 190p, Paper, Novel [Richard Blade #7]
  09204 *Slave of Sarma.* Macfadden-Bartell, New York, 1970, 192p, Paper, Novel [Richard Blade #4]
  09205 *Undying world.* Pinnacle, New York, 1973, 189p, Paper, Novel [Richard Blade #8]

THE LORD COMMISSIONER, pseud.
    see: McCOY, JOHN

LORENSEN, CHARLES (E.)

  09206 *Courtships in the air; or, The strange adventures of Hurry Harry, being a romance in two parts, written by himself.* Broadway Publishing Co., New York, 1914, 325p, Cloth, Novel

LORENZEN, JAN A.

  09207 *"20 years of Analog/Astounding science fiction* science fact, 1952-1971."* Locomotive Workshop, Avon Lake, OH, 1971, 40p, Paper, Nonf.

LORIMER, NORMA (Octavia), 1864-1948

  09208 *There was a king in Egypt.* Stanley Paul, London, 1918, 404p, Cloth, Novel

LORING, ANN

  09209 *The mark of Satan.* Award, New York, 1969, 155p, Paper, Novel

LORRAINE, LILITH, pseud. [Mary M. Wright, 1894-]

  09210 *The brain of the planet.* Stellar Publishing Corp., New York, 1929, 24p, Paper, Story

LORRAINE, PAUL, house pseud. [see also: John Russell Fearn, William Henry Bird, John Glasby, and Arthur Roberts]

  05294 *Dark Boundaries.* Curtis Warren, London, 1953, 159p, Cloth, Novel [by John Russell Fearn]
  01319 *Two worlds.* Curtis Warren, London, 1952, 128p, Cloth, Novel [by William Henry Bird]
  06026 *Zenith-D.* Curtis Warren, London, 1952, 159p, Cloth, Novel [by Arthur Roberts & John Glasby]

LORY, ROBERT (Edward), 1936- [*biography included*]

  09211 *Dracula returns.* Pinnacle, New York, 1973, 189p, Paper, Novel [Dracula Horror #1]
  09212 *Dracula's brother.* Pinnacle, New York, 1973, 186p, Paper, Novel [Dracula Horror #3; cover title: *Dracula's brothers*]
  09213 *Dracula's gold.* Pinnacle, New York, 1973, 182p, Paper, Novel [Dracula Horror #4]
  09214 *Dracula's lost world.* Pinnacle, New York, 1974, 181p, Paper, Novel [Dracula Horror #7]
  09215 *Drums of Dracula.* Pinnacle, New York, 1974, 189p, Paper, Novel [Dracula Horror #5]
  09216 *The eyes of Bolsk.* Ace Double, New York, 1969, 90p, Paper, Novel [Trovo #1]
  09217 *The hand of Dracula.* Pinnacle, New York, 1973, 224p, Paper, Novel [Dracula Horror #2]
  09218 *A harvest of hoodwinks.* Ace Double, New York, 1970, 117p, Paper, Coll.
  09219 *Horrorscope; The curse of Leo.* Pinnacle, New York, 1974, 176p, Paper, Novel [Horrorscope #3]
  09220 *Horrorscope; The revenge of Taurus.* Pinnacle, New York, 1974, 178p, Paper, Novel [Horrorscope #2]

LORY, ROBERT (cont.)

09221 *Horrorscopes; The green flames of Aries.*
        Pinnacle, New York, 1974, 158p, Paper,
        Novel [Horrorscope #1]
09222 *Identity Seven.* DAW, New York, 1974, 155p,
        Paper, Novel
09223 *Master of the Etrax.* Dell, New York, 1970,
        156p, Paper, Novel [Trovo #2]
09224 *Masters of the lamp.* Ace Double, New York,
        1970, 136p, Paper, Novel [Shamryke Odell #1]
09225 *The thirteen bracelets.* Ace, New York, 1974,
        188p, Paper, Novel
09226 *The veiled world.* Ace Double, New York,
        1972, 116p, Paper, Novel [Shamryke Odell #2]
09227 *The witching of Dracula.* Pinnacle, New York,
        1974, 177p, Paper, Novel [Dracula Horror #6]

LOTHAR, ERNST, pseud.

09228 *The clairvoyant.* Martin Secker, London,
        1931, 327p, Cloth, Novel

LOTT, S. MAKEPEACE
    see: MAKEPEACE LOTT, S.

LOTUS
    see: AUTHOR OF "A NEW MARGUERITE"

LOUDON, Mrs. (Jane), 1807-1858

09229 *The mummy! a tale of the twenty-second cen-
        tury.* Henry Colburn, London, 1827, 3vol,
        Cloth, Novel

LOUGHLIN, RICHARD L(awrence), 1907- [bio-
    graphy included], with Lilian M. Popp

09230 *Journeys in science fiction.* Globe Book Co.,
        New York, 1961, 656p, Cloth, Anth.

LOUNSBERRY, Lieut. LIONEL

09231 *The treasure of the golden crater.* Street &
        Smith, New York, 1928, 248p, Paper, Novel

LOVE, EDMUND G(eorge), 1912- [biography in-
    cluded]

09232 *An end to bugling.* Harper & Row, New York,
        1963, 150p, Cloth, Novel

LOVECRAFT, H(oward) P(hillips), 1890-1937

09233 *At the mountains of madness, and other novels.*
        Arkham House, Sauk City, 1964, 432p, Cloth,
        Coll.
09234 *Autobiography; some notes on a nonentity.*
        Arkham House, Sauk City, 1963, 17p, Paper,
        Nonf.
09235 *Best supernatural stories of H. P. Lovecraft.*
        World Publishing Co., Cleveland, 1945, 307p,
        Cloth, Coll.
09236 *Beyond the wall of sleep.* Arkham House, Sauk
        City, 1943, 458p, Cloth, Coll.

09237 *The case of Charles Dexter Ward; a novel.* Vic-
        tor Gollancz, London, 1951, 160p, Cloth,
        Novel
09238 *The cats of Ulthar.* Dragon-Fly Press, Cassia,
        FL, 1935, 10p, Paper, Story
        The colour out of space, and others. [see
        09245A]
        Cry horror! [see 09250A]
09239 *Dagon, and other macabre tales.* Arkham House,
        Sauk City, 1965, 413p, Cloth, Coll.
09239A retitled: *The tomb, and other tales.* Panther,
        London, 1969, 190p, Paper, Coll. [abridged]
09240 *The doom that came to Sarnath.* Ballantine,
        New York, 1971, 208p, Paper, Coll.
09241 *The dream-quest of unknown Kadath.* Shroud,
        Buffalo, 1955, 107p, Cloth, Novel
09242 *The dream-quest of unknown Kadath.* Ballantine,
        New York, 1970, 242p, Paper, Coll.
09243 *Dreams and fancies.* Arkham House, Sauk City,
        1962, 174p, Cloth, Coll.
        The Dunwich horror. [see 09255A]
09244 *The Dunwich horror, and other weird tales.*
        Editions for the Armed Services, New York,
        1945, 383p, Paper, Coll.
09245 *The Dunwich horror, and others; the best super-
        natural stories of H. P. Lovecraft.* Arkham
        House, Sauk City, 1963, 431p, Cloth, Coll.
09245A retitled: *The colour out of space, and others.*
        Lancer, New York, 1964, 222p, Paper, Coll.
        [abridged]
09246 *Ec'H-Pi-el speaks.* Gerry de la Ree, Saddle
        River, NJ, 1972, 12p, Paper, Nonf.
09247 *Hail, Klarkash-Ton! being nine missives in-
        scribed upon postcards by H. P. Lovecraft
        to Clark Ashton Smith.* no publisher, no
        place, 1971, 16p, Paper, Nonf.
09248 *The haunter of the dark, and other tales of
        horror.* Victor Gollancz, London, 1951, 303p,
        Cloth, Coll.
09249 *The Lovecraft collector's library.* SSR Publi-
        cations, North Tonawanda, NY, 1952/55, 7vol,
        Paper, Coll. [includes verse and nonf.]
09250 *The lurking fear, and other stories.* Avon,
        New York, 1947, 223p, Paper, Coll.
09250A retitled: *Cry horror!* Avon, New York, 1958,
        191p, Paper, Coll.
09251 *The lurking fear, and other stories.* Panther,
        London, 1964, 208p, Paper, Coll. [different
        contents]
09252 *The lurking fear, and other stories.* Beagle,
        New York, 1971, 182p, Paper, Coll. [different
        contents]
09253 *Marginalia.* Arkham House, Sauk City, 1944,
        377p, Cloth, Coll.
09254 *The notes & commonplace book employed by the
        late H. P. Lovecraft, including his sugges-
        tions for story-writing, analyses of the
        weird story, and a list of certain basic
        underlying horrors, &c., &c., designed to
        stimulate the imagination.* Futile Press,
        Lakeport, CA, 1938, 45p, Paper?, Nonf.
09255 *The outsider, and others.* Arkham House, Sauk
        City, 1939, 553p, Cloth, Coll.
09255A retitled: *The Dunwich horror.* Bart House,
        New York, 1945, 186p, Paper, Coll. [abridged]
09256 *Selected letters, 1911-1924.* Arkham House,
        Sauk City, 1965, 362p, Cloth, Nonf.
09257 *Selected letters, 1925-1929.* Arkham House,
        Sauk City, 1968, 359p, Cloth, Nonf.
09258 *Selected letters, 1929-1931.* Arkham House,
        Sauk City, 1971, 451p, Cloth, Nonf.
09259 *The shadow over Innsmouth.* Visionary Press,
        Everett, PA, 1936, 158p, Cloth, Novel

LOVECRAFT, H. P. (cont.)

09260 *The shadow over Innsmouth, and other stories
of horror.* Scholastic Book Services, New
York, 1971, 255p, Paper, Coll.
09261 *The shunned house.* Recluse Press, Athol,
Mass., 1928, 59p, Cloth, Novel [printed in
1928, but no copies were bound until 1936;
the majority of the run was stored and later
bound up by Arkham House in 1962]
09262 *Something about cats, and other pieces.* Arkham House, Sauk City, 1949, 306p, Cloth,
Coll.
09263 *Supernatural horror in literature.* Ben Abramson, New York, 1945, 111p, Cloth, Nonf.
09264 *3 tales of horror.* Arkham House, Sauk City,
1967, 134p, Cloth, Coll.
The tomb, and other tales. [see 09239A]
09265 *The weird shadow over Innsmouth, and other
stories of the supernatural.* Bart House,
New York, 1944, 190p, Paper, Coll.

with August Derleth:

04237 *The lurker at the threshold.* Arkham House,
Sauk City, 1945, 196p, Cloth, Novel
04238 *The shadow out of time, and other tales of
horror.* Victor Gollancz, London, 1968,
384p, Cloth, Coll.
04238A retitled: *The shuttered room, and other
tales of horror.* Panther, London, 1970,
205p, Paper, Coll. [abridged]
04239 *The shuttered room, and other tales of horror.*
Beagle, New York, 1971, 166p, Paper, Coll.
[different contents]
04240 *The survivor, and others.* Arkham House, Sauk
City, 1957, 161p, Cloth, Coll.
09266 *The watchers out of time, and others.* Arkham
House, Sauk City, 1974, 405p, Cloth, Coll.

with various co-authors:

09267 *The horror in the museum, and other revisions.*
Arkham House, Sauk City, 1970, 383p, Cloth,
Coll.
09267A retitled: *Nine stories from The horror in
the museum, and other revisions.* Beagle,
New York, 1971, 245p, Paper, Coll. [abridged]

LOVELACE, DELOS W(heeler), 1894-1967 [*biography included*]

09268 *King Kong.* Grosset & Dunlap, New York, 1932,
249p, Cloth, Movie

LOVELL, MARC, pseud. [Mark McShane, 1930-   ]
[*biography included*]

09269 *An enquiry into the existence of vampires.*
Doubleday, Garden City, 1974, 181p, Cloth,
Novel

A LOVER OF THE MARVELLOUS AND THE TRUE
see: RIDLEY, JAMES

LOVETT, MARGARET (Rose), 1915-

09270 *The great and terrible quest.* Faber & Faber,
London, 1967, 170p, Cloth, Novel

LOW, A(rchibald) M(ontgomery), 1888-1956

09271 *Adrift in the stratosphere.* Blackie & Son,
London, 1937, 224p, Cloth, Novel
09272 *Mars breaks through; or, The great Murchison
mystery.* Herbert Joseph, London, 1937, 251p,
Cloth, Novel
09273 *Peter down the well; a tale of adventure in
thought.* Grayson & Grayson, London, 1933,
192p, Cloth, Novel
09274 *Satellite in space.* Herbert Jenkins, London,
1956, 191p, Cloth, Novel

LOWE, ARTHUR

09275 *Death of the last taxpayer.* Forward Publishing
Co., Toronto, 1944, 23p, Paper, Story

LOWE, CHARLES, 1948-1931, with P. Colomb, J.
F. Maurice, F. N. Maude, Archibald Forbes,
D. Christie Murray, and F. Scudamore

03229 *The Great War of 189-; a forecast.* William
Heinemann, London, 1893, 308p, Cloth, Novel

LOWELL, J. R., pseud.
see: LOWELL, JAN and LOWELL, ROBERT

LOWELL, JAN, with Robert Lowell as J. R. Lowell

09276 *Daughter of darkness; a novel.* Delacorte
Press, New York, 1972, 238p, Cloth, Novel

LOWELL, ROBERT, with Jan Lowell as J. R. Lowell

09276 *Daughter of darkness; a novel.* Delacorte
Press, New York, 1972, 238p, Cloth, Novel

LÖWENELL, JOHANN WILHELM von BRANDENBURG-HO-
HENZOLLERN

09277 *Forebodings and forbearance; what the fatherland would do if drawn into an European conflict.* C. Schwappacher, Detroit, 1915, 264p,
Cloth, Novel

LOWNDES, Mrs. (Marie Adelaide) BELLOC, 1868-
1947

09278 *From out the vasty deep.* Hutchinson, London,
1920, 288p, Cloth, Novel
09279 *What Timmy did.* Hutchinson, London, 1921,
288p, Cloth, Novel

LOWNDES, ROBERT (Augustine) W(ard), 1916-
[*biography included*]

09280 *Believers' world.* Avalon, New York, 1961,
224p, Cloth, Novel
09281 *Mystery of the third mine.* John C. Winston,
Philadelphia, 1953, 201p, Cloth, Novel
09282 *The puzzle planet.* Ace Double, New York,
1961, 119p, Paper, Novel
09283 *Three faces of science fiction.* A Boskone Book,
NESFA Press, Boston, 1973, 96p, Cloth, Nonf.
Coll.

LOWNDES, ROBERT W. (cont.), with James Blish

01524   *The duplicated man.* Avalon, New York, 1959, 222p, Cloth, Novel

LOWTHER, GEORGE (Francis), 1913-1975

09284   *Superman.* Random House, New York, 1942, 215p, Cloth, Novel [adapted from the comic book character of the same name]

LUBAN, MILTON, 1909-1956

09285   *The spirit was willing.* Greenberg, Publisher, New York, 1951, 188p, Cloth, Novel

LUBICZ, ISHA SCHALLER DE
    see: SCHWALLER DE LUBICZ, ISHA

LUCAS, Rev. CHARLES, 1769-1854

09286   *The Castle of Saint Donats; or, The history of Jack Smith.* William Lane, Minerva-Press, London, 1798, 3vol, Cloth, Novel [published anonymously]
09286A retitled: *The history of Jack Smith; or, The Castle of Saint Donats.* Thomas, Andrews & Butler, Baltimore, 1800?, 291p, Cloth, Novel

LUCAS, E(dward) V(errall), 1868-1938, with C. L. Graves

06255   *The war of the Wenuses.* J. W. Arrowsmith, Bristol, 1898, 140p, Paper, Novel [a parody of H. G. Wells's *The war of the worlds*]

LUCAS, REGINALD (Jaffray), 1865-1914

09287   *A clear case of supernatural.* Simpkin & Marshall, London, 1895, 86p, Paper, Novel

LUCCA, GAUDENTIO di
    see: BERINGTON, SIMON

LUCE, ALFRED FABRE-
    see: FABRE-LUCE, ALFRED

LUCIAN, pseud.

09288   *1920; dips into the near future.* Headley Bros., London, 1918, 98p, Cloth, Coll.

LUCKY, ROBERT MONTFORT

09289   *Devil worshippers; or, The "bitru" of fact.* F. Tennyson Neely, New York, 1897, 281p, Paper, Novel

LUDLAM, HARRY

09290   *The coming of Jonathan Smith.* John Long, London, 1964, 184p, Cloth, Novel

09291   *Witch's curse.* Award, New York, 1969, 154p, Paper, Novel

LUDLOW, EDMUND, 1898-

09292   *The coming of the unselves.* Exposition Press, New York, 1965, 194p, Cloth, Novel

LUDLOW, PHILL

09293   *Three men and a maid; a tale of the mysteries of Manoa.* Henry J. Drane, London, 1903, 279p, Cloth, Novel

LUDWIG, BORIS, pseud.

09294   *Jaws of doom.* Scientific Thriller, Sydney, 1948, 50p, Paper, Novel
09295   *The whistle of doom.* Scientific Thriller, Sydney, 1949, 50p, Paper, Novel

LUDWIG, EDWARD W(illiam), 1920-   [*biography included*]

09296   *The mask of Jon Culon.* Lenox Hill Press, New York, 1970, 192p, Cloth, Novel

LUIGI, BELLI, pseud.

09297   *Cosmic calamity.* Scientific Thriller, Sydney, 1949, 50p, Paper, Novel
09298   *Crime flies.* Scientific Thriller, Sydney, 1950, 50p, Paper, Novel
09299   *Curse of the mummy.* Scientific Thriller, Sydney, 1950, 50p, Paper, Novel
09300   *Death has no weight.* Scientific Thriller, Sydney, 1949, 50p, Paper, Novel
09301   *Depths of death.* Scientific Thriller, Sydney, 1950, 50p, Paper, Novel
09302   *The freezing peril strikes.* Scientific Thriller, Sydney, 1951, 34p, Paper, Story
09303   *The glowing globe.* Scientific Thriller, Sydney, 1950, 50p, Paper, Novel
09304   *Lightning crime.* Scientific Thriller, Sydney, 1949, 50p, Paper, Novel
09305   *The lost underworld.* Scientific Thriller, Sydney, 1950, 50p, Paper, Novel
09306   *Master-mind menace.* World Distributors/Sydney Pemberton, London, 1950, 128p, Paper, Novel
09307   *The metal monster; a complete book-length novel of amazing adventure.* World Distributors/Sydney Pemberton, London, 1950, 128p, Paper, Novel
09308   *The mummy walks.* Scientific Thriller, Sydney, 1950, 50p, Paper, Novel
09309   *Toppling terror.* Scientific Thriller, Sydney, 1950, 50p, Paper, Novel

LUKEMAN, ALEC
    see: DAIN, ALEX

LUKENS, ADAM, pseud.
    see: DETZER, DIANE

LUKODIANOV, ISAI (Borisovich), 1913-   [*biography included*], with Evgenii Voiskunskii

09310 *The crew of the Mekong, being an account of the latest fantastic discoveries, happenings of the eighteenth century, mysteries of matter, and adventures on land and sea*, by I. Lukodyanov and E. Voiskunsky. Mir Publishers, Moscow, 1974, 422p, Paper, Novel

LUKODYANOV, I.
      see: LUKODIANOV, ISAI

LULL, Rev. D.

09311 *Celestia.* Press of the Reliance Trading Co., New York, 1907, 238p, Cloth, Novel [a response to Bellamy's *Looking backward*]

LUMLEY, BENJAMIN, 1812-1875

09312 *Sirenia; or, Recollections of a past existence.* Richard Bentley, London, 1862, 388p, Cloth, Novel [published anonymously]

as Hermes:

09313 *Another world; or, Fragments from the star city of Montalluyah.* Samuel Tinsley, London, 1873, 306p, Cloth, Novel

LUMLEY, BRIAN, 1937-

09314 *Beneath the moors.* Arkham House, Sauk City, 1974, 145p, Cloth, Novel
09315 *The burrowers beneath.* DAW, New York, 1974, 160p, Paper, Novel
09316 *The caller of the black.* Arkham House, Sauk City, 1971, 235p, Cloth, Coll.

LUNA, KRIS, house pseud. [see also: William Henry Bird and David O'Brien]

01320 *Operation orbit.* Curtis Warren, London, 1953, 159p, Cloth, Novel [by William Bird]
09317 *Stella radium discharge.* Curtis Warren, London, 1952, 128p, Cloth, Novel [by David O'Brien]

LUNATIC, Sir HUMPHREY, Bart., pseud. [Francis Gentleman, 1728-1784]

09318 *A trip to the Moon, containing an account of the island of Noibla, its inhabitants, religious and political customs, &c.* A. Ward, York, UK, 1764, 205p, Cloth, Novel [Noibla #1]
09319 *A trip to the Moon, containing an account of the island of Noibla, its inhabitants, religious and political customs, &c., volume II.* S. Crowder, W. Nicoll, W. Bristow, C. Therington, London, 1765, 212p, Cloth, Novel [Noibla #2] [since the first volume is unnumbered, it appears that the second book should be regarded as a sequel, and not the second half of a novel, although there is close connection between the two]

LUNATIC, NICHOLAS, pseud.

09320 *Satiric tales, consisting of A voyage to the Moon; The tailors, or, The old cloak; and, The fat witch of London.* George Hughes & H. D. Symons, London, 1808, 212p, Cloth, Coll.

LUND, IVAR

09321 *The end of Lucifer's tail.* Simco Press, New York, 1943, 436p, Cloth, Novel

LUNDBERG, KNUD, 1920-

09322 *The Olympic hope; a story from the Olympic Games, 1996.* Stanley Paul, London, 1958, 171p, Cloth, Novel

LUNDWALL, SAM J(errie), 1941-   [*biography included*]

09323 *Alice's world.* Ace Double, New York, 1971, 122p, Paper, Novel [uses the same theme as *No time for heroes*, with a different slant]
09324 *Bernhard the conqueror.* DAW, New York, 1973, 159p, Paper, Novel
09325 *No time for heroes.* Ace Double, New York, 1971, 131p, Paper, Novel [uses the same theme as *Alice's world*, with a different slant]
09326 *Science fiction; what it's all about.* Ace, New York, 1971, 256p, Paper, Nonf.

LUNN, BRIAN (Holdsworth), 1893-   , with William Gerhardi

05895 *The memoirs of Satan.* Cassell, London, 1932, 382p, Cloth, Novel

LUNN, HUGH KINGSMILL
      see: KINGSMILL, HUGH

LUNN, JANET (Louise Swoboda), 1928-

09327 *Double spell.* Peter Martin Associates, Toronto, 1968, 134p, Cloth, Novel
09327A retitled: *Twin spell.* Harper & Row, New York, 1969, 158p, Cloth, Novel

LUPOFF, RICHARD A(llen), 1935-   [*biography included*]

09328 *Edgar Rice Burroughs: master of adventure.* Canaveral Press, New York, 1965, 297p, Cloth, Nonf.
09329 *Into the aether.* Dell, New York, 1974, 220p, Paper, Novel
09330 *One million centuries.* Lancer, New York, 1967, 352p, Paper, Novel
09331 *Sacred Locomotive flies; a science fiction novel.* Beagle, New York, 1971, 209p, Paper, Novel

LURGAN, LESTER, pseud. [Mabel Winifred Knowles, 1875-1949], with Richard Ganthony

05755   *A message from Mars.* Greening & Co., London, 1912, 288p, Cloth, Novel [adapted from the play of the same name by Ganthony]

LUSKA, SIDNEY, pseud. [Henry Harland, 1861-1905]

09332   *As it was written; a Jewish musician's story.* Cassell, New York, 1885, 253p, Cloth, Novel

LUSTY, G. H.

09333   *Into the unseen.* William Rider & Son, London, 1913, 330p, Cloth, Novel

LUTHER, RAY, pseud.
    see: SELLINGS, ARTHUR

LUZ, BERTHE ST.
    see: ST. LUZ, BERTHE

LYALL, EDNA, pseud. [Ada Ellen Bayly, 1857-1903]

09334   *The autobiography of a slander.* Longmans, Green, London, 1887, 119p, Paper, Novel

LYMINGTON, JOHN, pseud. [John Newton Chance, 1911-   ] [*biography included*]

09335   *The coming of the strangers.* Hodder & Stoughton, London, 1961, 190p, Cloth, Novel
09336   *Froomb!* Hodder & Stoughton, London, 1964, 224p, Cloth, Novel
09337   *The giant stumbles.* Hodder & Stoughton, London, 1960, 158p, Cloth, Novel
09338   *Give daddy the knife, darling.* Hodder & Stoughton, London, 1969, 191p, Cloth, Novel
09339   *The green drift.* Hodder & Stoughton, London, 1965, 191p, Cloth, Novel
09340   *The grey ones.* Hodder & Stoughton, London, 1960, 160p, Cloth, Novel
09341   *The hole in the world.* Hodder & Stoughton, London, 1974, 224p, Cloth, Novel
09342   *Night of the big heat.* Hodder & Stoughton, London, 1959, 160p, Cloth, Novel
09343   *The night spiders.* Corgi, London, 1964, 159p, Paper, Coll.
09344   *The nowhere place.* Hodder & Stoughton, London, 1969, 192p, Cloth, Novel
09345   *The screaming face.* Hodder & Stoughton, London, 1963, 160p, Cloth, Novel
09346   *The Sleep Eaters.* Hodder & Stoughton, London, 1963, 221p, Cloth, Novel
09347   *The star witches.* Hodder & Stoughton, London, 1965, 128p, Paper, Novel
09348   *A sword above the night.* Hodder & Stoughton, London, 1962, 158p, Cloth, Novel
09349   *Ten million years to Friday.* Hodder & Stoughton, London, 1967, 191p, Cloth, Novel
09350   *The year dot.* Hodder & Stoughton, London, 1972, 192p, Cloth, Novel

as Jonathan Chance:

09351   *The light benders.* Robert Hale, London, 1968, 159p, Cloth, Novel

LYNCH, Colonel ARTHUR (Alfred), 1861-1934

09352   *Seraph wings.* John Long, London, 1923, 318p, Cloth, Novel

LYNCH, (John Gilbert) BOHUN, 1884-1928

09353   *A muster of ghosts (ghost-stories).* Cecil Palmer, London, 1924, 353p, Cloth, Anth.
09353A   retitled: *The best ghost stories.* Small, Maynard, Boston, 1924, 326p, Cloth, Anth.
09354   *Menace from the Moon.* Jarrolds Publishers, London, 1925, 306p, Cloth, Novel

LYNCH, JANE GASKELL
    see: GASKELL, JANE

LYNCH, MIRIAM

09355   *The mark of the rope.* Avon, New York, 1972, 157p, Paper, Novel

LYNDON, BARRE, pseud. [Alfred Edgar], with Jimmy Sangster as John Sansom

09356   *The man who could cheat death.* Ace, London, 1959, 188p, Paper, Movie
09356A   *The man who could cheat death,* by Barre Lyndon & Jimmy Sangster. Avon, New York, 1959, 160p, Paper, Movie

LYNDS, DENNIS, 1924-   [*biography included*]

as Michael Collins:

09357   *Lukan war.* Belmont, New York, 1969, 157p, Paper, Novel
09358   *The planets of death.* Berkley Medallion, New York, 1970, 159p, Paper, Novel

as Maxwell Grant, house pseud.:

06231   *Cry Shadow!* Belmont, New York, 1965, 157p, Paper, Novel [New Shadow #4]
06232   *Mark of the Shadow.* Belmont, New York, 1966, 157p, Paper, Novel [New Shadow #6]
06233   *The night of the Shadow.* Belmont, New York, 1966, 156p, Paper, Novel [New Shadow #8]
06234   *Shadow beware.* Belmont, New York, 1965, 157p, Paper, Novel [New Shadow #3]
06235   *The Shadow; destination: Moon.* Belmont, New York, 1967, 156p, Paper, Novel [New Shadow #...]
06236   *Shadow--go mad!* Belmont, New York, 1966, 160p, Paper, Novel [New Shadow #7]
06237   *The Shadow strikes.* Belmont, New York, 1964, 157p, Paper, Novel [New Shadow #2]
06238   *The Shadow's revenge.* Belmont, New York, 196., 156p, Paper, Novel [New Shadow #5]

LYNES, (Joseph) RUSSELL (Jr.), 1910-

09359   *Cadwallader; a diversion.* Harper & Bros., New York, 1959, 124p, Cloth, Novel

LYNN, DAVID

09360 *Cybro sex.* Nightstand, San Diego, 1968, 160p,
       Paper, Novel

LYONS, DELPHINE C., pseud.
     see: SMITH, EVELYN

LYON, Capt. E(dmund) D(avid)

09361 *Ireland's dream; a romance of the future.*
       Swan Sonnenschein, Lowrey, London, 1888,
       2vol, Cloth, Novel

LYONS, EDGAR ALBION

09362 *The chosen race.* Cavalier Publishing Co.,
       St. Petersburg, FL, 1936, 442p, Cloth, Novel

LYONS, VICTOR S(am)

09363 *The unconquerable survivor of 2055 A.D.; a
       novel.* Exposition Press, New York, 1973,
       201p, Cloth, Novel

LYS, CHRISTIAN, pseud.
     see: BREBNER, PERCY

LYTLE, ANDREW (Nelson), 1902-   [*biography
included*]

09364 *A name for evil; a novel.* Bobbs-Merrill,
       Indianapolis, 1947, 215p, Cloth, Novel
09365 *A novel, a novella, and four short stories.*
       McDowell, Obolensky, New York, 1958, 327p,
       Cloth, Coll. [includes *A name for evil* and
       selected stories]

LYTTLETON, GEORGE, 1st Baron, 1709-1773 [pub-
lished anonymously]

09366 *An additional dialogue of the dead, between
       Pericles and Aristides, being a sequel to
       the dialogue between Pericles and Cosmo.*
       W. Sandby, London, 1760,   , Cloth, Story
09367 *Dialogues of the dead.* W. Sandby, London,
       1760, 320p, Cloth, Coll.
09368 *Dialogues of the dead.* W. Sandby, London,
       1765, 406p, Cloth, Coll. [includes four
       new dialogues]
09369 *Four new dialogues of the dead.* W. Sandby,
       London, 1765, 56p, Cloth, Coll.

LYTTON, EDWARD (George Earle Lytton Bulwer-
Lytton), 1st Baron, 1803-1873

09370 *The coming race.* William Blackwood & Sons,
       Edinburgh, 1871, 292p, Cloth, Novel [pub-
       lished anonymously]
09370A *The coming race,* by Edward Bulwer-Lytton.
       George Routledge & Sons, London, 1874, 248p,
       Cloth, Novel
09370B retitled: *Vril; the power of the coming race.*
       Rudolf Steiner Publications, Blauvelt, NY,
       1972, 248p, Paper, Novel

09371 *The coming race; and, The haunted and the haun-
       ters.* Humphrey Milford, Oxford University
       Press, London, 1928, 229p, Cloth, Coll.
09372 *The coming race; Falkland; Zicci; and, Pausani-
       as the Spartan.* George Routledge & Sons,
       London, 1878, 523p, Cloth, Coll.
09373 *The coming race; Pausanias the Spartan; and,
       The haunted and the haunters.* George Rout-
       ledge & Sons, London, 1892, 157p, Cloth, Coll.
09374 *Falkland; and, Zicci.* George Routledge & Sons,
       London, 1874, 245p, Cloth, Coll. [only *Zicci*
       is SF]
09375 *Godolphin; a novel.* Richard Bentley, London,
       1833, 3vol, Cloth, Novel [published anony-
       mously]
09375A *Godolphin; a novel,* by Edward Bulwer-Lytton.
       Harper & Bros., New York, 1840, 2vol, Cloth,
       Novel
09376 *Godolphin; and, Falkland.* Bernhard Tauchnitz,
       Leipzig, 1842, 414p, Cloth, Coll.
09377 *The haunted and the haunters; or, The house and
       the brain.* Gowan's International Library,
       London, 1905, 57p, Cloth, Novel
09378 *The haunted house; and, Calderon the courtier.*
       John W. Lovell, New York, 1882, 78p, Paper?,
       Coll.
09379 *The pilgrims of the Rhine; The coming race.*
       Dana Estes, Boston, 191?, 392p, Cloth, Coll.
09380 *The pilgrims of the Rhine, to which is prefixed
       The ideal world; and, Zicci, a tale.* Little,
       Brown, Boston, 1893, 432p, Cloth, Coll.
09381 *The pilgrims of the Rhine, to which is prefixed
       The ideal world; The coming race.* George
       Routledge & Sons, London, 1891, 392p, Cloth,
       Coll.
09382 *A strange story,* by the author of "Rienzi,"
       "My novel," etc., etc. Sampson Low, London,
       1862, 2vol, Cloth, Novel
09382A *A strange story,* by Edward Bulwer-Lytton. Har-
       per & Bros., New York, 1862, 199p, Cloth,
       Novel
09383 *A strange story; and, Eugene Aram.* United
       States Book Co., New York, 1895?, 984p,
       Cloth, Coll.
09384 *A strange story; and, The haunted and the haun-
       ters,* by the author of "Rienzi." George
       Routledge & Sons, London, 1865, 365p, Cloth,
       Coll.
       Vril. [see 09370B]
09385 *Zanoni,* by the author of "Night and morning,"
       "Rienzi," etc. Saunders & Otley, London,
       1842, 3vol, Cloth, Novel
09385A *Zanoni,* by Edward Bulwer-Lytton. Wilson & Co.,
       New York, 1842, 80p, Paper, Novel
09386 *Zanoni; Zicci.* Little, Brown, Boston, 1912,
       666p, Cloth, Coll.

LYTTON, (Edward) ROBERT BULWER-(Lytton), 1st
Earl of, 1831-1891

as Owen Meredith:

09387 *The ring of Amasis, from the papers of a German
       physician.* Chapman & Hall, London, 1863,
       2vol, Cloth, Novel
09387A *The ring of Amasis; a romance,* by Robert Bul-
       wer Lytton. Harper & Bros., New York, 1863,
       301p, Cloth, Novel

M., A. H., pseud.

09388   *Great was the fall*, by a naval officer. John Long, London, 1912, 320p, Cloth, Novel [the introduction is signed A. H. M.]

M., J.
    see: MACGREGOR, JOHN

M., J. W., pseud.

09389   *The coming Cromwell*. British and Colonial Publishing Co., London, 1871, 48p, Paper?, Story

M., J. W., pseud.

09390   *The siege of London*. Robert Hardwicke, London, 1871, 64p, Paper?, Novel

M. W.
    see: WILSON, MILES

MABIE, HAMILTON WRIGHT, 1846-1916

09391   *In Arcady*. Dodd, Mead, New York, 1903, 127p, Cloth, Coll.
09392   *In the forest of Arden*. Dodd, Mead, New York, 1898, 124p, Cloth, Novel

MABY, J(oseph) **CECIL**

09393   *By Stygian waters*. Houghton Publishing Co., London, 1933, 158p, Cloth, Coll.

MACAO, MARSHALL

09394   *K'ing Kung Fu #1; Son of the flying tiger*. Venus Freeway Press, New York, 1973, 188p, Paper, Novel [K'ing Kung Fu #1]
09395   *K'ing Kung Fu #2; Return of the opium wars*. Venus Freeway Press, New York, 1973, 189p, Paper, Novel [K'ing Kung Fu #2]
09396   *K'ing Kung Fu #3; The rape of Sun Lee Fong*. Venus Freeway Press, New York, 1973, 187p, Paper, Novel [K'ing Kung Fu #3]
09397   *K'ing Kung Fu #4; The Kak-Abdullah conspiracy*. Freeway Press, New York, 1973, 197p, Paper, Novel [K'ing Kung Fu #4]
09398   *K'ing Kung Fu #5; Red plague in Bolivia*. Freeway Press, New York, 1974, 178p, Paper, Novel [K'ing Kung Fu #5]
09399   *K'ing Kung Fu #6; New York necromancy*. Freeway Press, New York, 1974, 180p, Paper, Novel [K'ing Kung Fu #6]
09400   *K'ing Kung Fu #7; Mark of the vulture*. Freeway Press, New York, 1974, 186p, Paper, Novel [K'ing Kung Fu #7]

MacAPP, C. C., pseud. [Carroll M. Capps, 1917?-1971]

09401   *Bumsider*. Lancer, New York, 1972, 223p, Paper, Novel

09402   *Omha abides*. Paperback Library, New York, 1968, 160p, Paper, Novel
09403   *Prisoners of the sky*. Lancer, New York, 1969 224p, Paper, Novel
09404   *Recall not Earth*. Dell, New York, 1970, 192p Paper, Novel
09405   *Secret of the sunless world*. Dell, New York, 1969, 204p, Paper, Novel [cover byline read Carroll M. Capps]
09406   *Subb*. Paperback Library, New York, 1971, 187p, Paper, Novel
09407   *Worlds of the Wall*. Avon, New York, 1969, 222p, Paper, Novel

MACARDLE, DOROTHY (Margaret Callan), 1889-

09408   *Fantastic summer*. Peter Davies, London, 1946 277p, Cloth, Novel
09408A retitled: *The unforeseen*. Doubleday, Garden City, 1946, 278p, Cloth, Novel
09409   *Uneasy freehold*. Peter Davies, London, 1941, 304p, Cloth, Novel
09409A retitled: *The uninvited*. Doubleday, Doran, Garden City, 1942, 342p, Cloth, Novel

MacARTHUR, ARTHUR, 1896-

09410   *After the afternoon*. D. Appleton-Century, New York, 1941, 290p, Cloth, Novel
09410A retitled: *Aphrodite's lover*. Universal Gian, New York, 1953, 287p, Paper, Novel

MACARTNEY, CLEM

09411   *Dark side of Venus*. Hamilton & Co. (Stafford London, 1951, 111p, Paper, Novel

MACAULAY, CLARENDON, pseud. [Walter Marsham Adams, 1838-]

09412   *The carving of Turkey; a chapter of European history, from sources hitherto unpublished* Mead & Co., London, 1874, 80p, Paper?, Nove

MACAULAY, L.

09413   *The decadence; an excerpt from "A history of the triumph and decay of England," dateable 1949*. Watts & Co., London, 1929, 108p, Cloth, Novel

MACAULAY, ROSE, 1881-1958

09414   *Orphan island*. W. Collins Sons, London, 1924 322p, Cloth, Novel
09415   *What not; a prophetic comedy*. Constable, London, 1919, 236p, Cloth, Novel

MACAULEY, CHARLES RAYMOND, 1871-1934

09416   *Fantasma Land*. Bobbs-Merrill, Indianapolis, 1904, 204p, Cloth, Novel

MacCARTHY, JOHN LLOYD
    see: CORY, DESMOND

MacCLURE, VICTOR (Thom MacWalter), 1887-1963

09417 *Ultimatum; a romance of the air.* George G. Harrap, London, 1924, 327p, Cloth, Novel
09417A retitled: *The Ark of the Covenant; a romance of the air and of science.* Harper & Bros., New York, 1924, 414p, Cloth, Novel

MACCOLL, HUGH

09418 *Mr. Stranger's sealed packet.* Chatto & Windus, London, 1889, 338p, Cloth, Novel

MacCREIGH, JAMES, pseud.
    see: POHL, FREDERIK

MacDONALD, BERNARD
    see: MACDONNAILL, BRIAN

MacDANIEL, CHARLES, pseud. [Charles M. Garrison]

09419 *Murder on the Moon.* Vantage Press, New York, 1968, 224p, Cloth, Novel

MacDONALD, DONALD K., with Alaric J. Roberts

09420 *You do take it with you.* Vantage Press, New York, 1953, 161p, Cloth, Novel

MacDONALD, FRANCIS CHARLES, 1874-1952

09421 *Sorcery.* Century Co., New York, 1919, 215p, Cloth, Novel

MACDONALD, GEORGE, 1824-1905

09422 *Evenor.* Ballantine, New York, 1972, 210p, Paper, Coll.
09423 *Lilith; a romance.* Chatto & Windus, London, 1895, 351p, Cloth, Novel
09424 *Phantastes; a faerie romance for men and women.* Smith, Elder, London, 1858, 323p, Cloth, Novel
    Phantastes; and, Lilith. [see 09427A]
09425 *The portent; a story of the inner vision of the Highlanders, commonly called the second sight.* Smith, Elder, London, 1864, 290p, Cloth, Novel
09426 *The portent, and other stories.* T. Fisher Unwin, London, 1909, 275p, Cloth, Coll.
09427 *Visionary novels: Lilith; Phantastes.* Noonday Press, New York, 1954, 434p, Cloth, Coll.
09427A retitled: *Phantastes; and, Lilith.* Victor Gollancz, London, 1962, 420p, Cloth, Coll.

MacDONALD, JOHN D(ann), 1916-   [*biography included*]

09428 *Ballroom of the skies.* Greenberg: Publisher, New York, 1952, 206p, Cloth, Novel
09429 *The girl, the gold watch, & everything.* Gold Medal, Greenwich, Conn., 1962, 207p, Paper, Novel

09430 *Wine of the Dreamers.* Greenberg: Publisher, New York, 1951, 219p, Cloth, Novel
09430A retitled: *Planet of the Dreamers.* Pocket Books, New York, 1953, 164p, Paper, Novel

MACDONALD, ROBERT M(aclaughlan), 1874-

09431 *The secret of the Sargasso.* Brentano's, New York, 1909, 368p, Cloth, Novel; T. Fisher Unwin, London, 1909, 368p, Cloth, Novel

MACDONELL, ARCHIBALD GORDON
    see: GORDON, NEIL

MACDONNAILL, BRIAN, pseud. [Bernard McDonald, 1923-   ]

09432 *Mañanaland.* Vantage Press, New York, 1963, 86p, Cloth, Novel

MACDOUGALL, MARGARET
    see: ARMOUR, MARGARET

MacEWEN, GWENDOLYN (Margaret), 1941-   [*biography included*]

09433 *Julian the magician; a novel.* Corinth Books, New York, 1963, 151p, Cloth, Novel

MacEWEN, MARY E.

09434 *Stories of suspense.* Scholastic Book Services, New York, 1963, 220p, Paper, Anth.

MACEY, PETER

09435 *Stationary orbit.* Dennis Dobson, London, 1974, 184p, Cloth, Novel

MacFADYEN, VIRGINIA

09436 *At the sign of the Sun; a novel.* Albert & Charles Boni, New York, 1925, 248p, Cloth, Novel

MACFALL, (Chambers) HALDANE (Cooke), 1860-1928

09437 *The wooings of Jezebel Pettyfer, being the personal history of Jehu Sennacherib Dyle, commonly called Masheen Dyle, together with an account of certain things that chanced in the house of the sorcerer.* Grant Richards, London, 1898, 403p, Cloth, Novel
09437A retitled: *The house of the sorcerer, being an account of certain events that chanced therein.* Richard G. Badger, Boston, 1900, 233p, Cloth, Novel

MACFARLANE, CLAIRE, 1906-

09438 *Winged victory.* Mann Publishers, Jersey City, NJ, 1954, 341p, Cloth, Novel

MacGREGOR, ELLEN, 1906-1954

09439   *Miss Pickerell and the geiger counter.* Whittlesey House, New York, 1953, 123p, Cloth, Novel [Miss Pickerell #2]

09440   *Miss Pickerell goes to Mars.* Whittlesey House, New York, 1951, 128p, Cloth, Novel [Miss Pickerell #1]

09441   *Miss Pickerell goes to the Arctic.* Whittlesey House, New York, 1954, 126p, Cloth, Novel [Miss Pickerell #4]

09442   *Miss Pickerell goes undersea.* Whittlesey House, New York, 1953, 128p, Cloth, Novel [Miss Pickerell #3]

with Dora Pantell:

09443   *Miss Pickerell and the weather satellite.* McGraw-Hill, New York, 1971, 157p, Cloth, Novel [Miss Pickerell #8]

09444   *Miss Pickerell goes on a dig.* McGraw-Hill, New York, 1966, 128p, Cloth, Novel [Miss Pickerell #6]

09445   *Miss Pickerell harvests the sea.* McGraw-Hill, New York, 1968, 144p, Cloth, Novel [Miss Pickerell #7]

09446   *Miss Pickerell meets Mr. H.U.M.* McGraw-Hill, New York, 1974, 160p, Cloth, Novel [Miss Pickerell #9]

09447   *Miss Pickerell on the Moon.* McGraw-Hill, New York, 1965, 142p, Cloth, Novel [Miss Pickerell #5]

MacGREGOR, (John) GEDDES, 1909-   [*biography included*]

09448   *From a Christian ghetto; letters of ghostly wit, written A.D. 2453.* Longmans, Green, London, 1954, 140p, Cloth, Novel

MACGREGOR, JAMES MURDOCH
see: McINTOSH, J. T.

MACGREGOR, JOHN

09449   *Popery in A.D. 1900*, by one J. M. Seeleys, London, 1852, 16p, Paper, Story

MacGREGOR, RICHARD

09450   *The creeping plague.* Digit, London, 1963, 160p, Paper, Novel

09451   *The day a village died.* Digit, London, 1963, 158p, Paper, Novel

09452   *The deadly sun.* Digit, London, 1964, 158p, Paper, Novel

09453   *Horror in the night.* Digit, London, 1963, 158p, Paper, Novel

MacHARG, WILLIAM (Briggs), 1872-1951, with Edwin Balmer

00800   *The achievements of Luther Trant.* Small, Maynard, Boston, 1910, 365p, Cloth, Novel

MACHEN, ARTHUR (Llewellyn Jones), 1863-1947

09454   *The angels of Mons; the bowmen, and other legends of the war.* Simpkin, Marshall, Hamilton, Kent, London, 1915, 86p, Paper, Coll. *Black crusade.* [see 09474A]

09455   *The Children of the Pool, and other stories.* Hutchinson, London, 1936, 255p, Cloth, Coll.

09456   *The chronicle of Clemendy; or, The history of the IX. joyous journeys, in which are contained the amorous inventions and facetious tales of Master Gervase Perrot, Gent.; now for the first time done into English.* Society of Pantagruelists, Carbonnek, 1888, 314, Cloth, Coll.

09457   *The great god Pan.* Simpkin, Marshall, Hamilton, Kent, London, 1916, 115p, Cloth, Novel

09458   *The great god Pan.* Martin Secker, London, 1926, 177p, Cloth, Coll.

09459   *The great god Pan; and other weird tales.* Editions for the Armed Services, New York, 1943, 223p, Paper, Coll.

09460   *The great god Pan; and, The inmost light.* John Lane, London, 1894, 168p, Cloth, Coll.

09461   *The green round.* Ernest Benn, London, 1933, 218p, Cloth, Novel

09462   *The hill of dreams.* E. Grant Richards, London, 1907, 309p, Cloth, Novel

09463   *Holy terrors; short stories.* Penguin, Harmonsworth, 1946, 140p, Paper, Coll.

09464   *The house of souls.* E. Grant Richards, London, 1906, 514p, Cloth, Coll.

09465   *The novel of the black seal, and other stories.* Corgi, London, 1965, 158p, Paper, Coll.

09466   *The novel of the white powder, and other stories.* Corgi, London, 1965, 158p, Paper, Coll.

09467   *The Secret Glory.* Martin Secker, London, 19, 309p, Cloth, Novel

09468   *The shining pyramid.* Martin Secker, London, 1925, 189p, Cloth, Coll. [the Covici-McGee edition of 1923 has different contents, and is not SF]

09469   *The strange world of Arthur Machen.* Juniper Press, New York, 1960, 381p, Paper, Coll.

09470   *Tales of horror and the supernatural.* Alfred A. Knopf, New York, 1948, 427p, Cloth, Coll.

09470A   retitled: *Tales of horror and the supernatural volume one.* Pinnacle, New York, 1971, 219, Paper, Coll. [abridged]

09470B   retitled: *Tales of horror and the supernatural volume two.* Pinnacle, New York, 1973, 284, Paper, Coll. [abridged; 09470A and 09470B together comprise the original volume]

09471   *Tales of the strange and supernatural.* Haldeman-Julius, Girard, Kans., 1926?, 64p, Paper, Coll.

09472   *The Terror; a fantasy.* Duckworth, London, 1917, 190p, Cloth, Novel

09473   *The three impostors.* Alfred A. Knopf, New York, 1923, 287p, Cloth, Coll. [includes an extra story]

09474   *The three impostors; or, The transmutations.* John Lane, London, 1895, 290p, Cloth, Coll.

09474A   retitled: *Black crusade.* Corgi, London, 19, 158p, Paper, Coll.

THE MACHINE-GOD LAUGHS
see: CRAWFORD, WILLIAM L.

MacISAAC, FRED(erick John), 1886-1940

09475 *The hothouse world.* Avalon, New York, 1965, 191p, Cloth, Novel
09476 *The vanishing professor.* Henry Waterson, New York, 1927, 266p, Cloth, Novel

MACKARNESS, MATILDA ANNE, 1826-1881

09477 *The dream Chintz*, by the author of "A trap to catch a sunbeam," "Old Jolliffe," &c. W. N. Wright, London, 1851, 118p, Cloth, Novel

MACKAY, (James Alexander) KENNETH, 1859-1935

09478 *The yellow wave; a romance of the Asiatic invasion of Australia.* Richard Bentley & Son, London, 1895, 435p, Cloth, Novel

MACKAY, LEWIS HUGH
    see: MATHESON, HUGH

MACKAY, MARY
    see: CORELLI, MARIE

MACKAYE, HAROLD STEELE, 1866-1928

09479 *The Panchronicon.* Charles Scribner's Sons, New York, 1904, 350p, Cloth, Novel

MacKELLAR, WILLIAM, 1914-

09480 *Alfie and me and the ghost of Peter Stuyvesant.* Dodd, Mead, New York, 1974, 151p, Cloth, Novel

MACKELWORTH, R(onald) W(alter), 1930-   [*biography included*]

09481 *Firemantle.* Robert Hale, London, 1968, 188p, Cloth, Novel
09481A retitled: *The Diabols.* Paperback Library, New York, 1969, 144p, Paper, Novel
09482 *Starflight 3000.* Ballantine, New York, 1972, 184p, Paper, Novel
09483 *Tiltangle.* Ballantine, New York, 1970, 184p, Paper, Novel

MACKENZIE, (Sir Edward Montague) COMPTON, 1883-1972 [*biography included*]

09484 *The Lunatic Republic.* Chatto & Windus, London, 1959, 223p, Cloth, Novel

MacKENZIE, DAVID GLENN
    see: McMASTERS, WILLIAM H.

MACKENZIE, NIGEL

09485 *Adventure in space.* Wright & Brown, London, 1967, 174p, Cloth, Novel
09486 *Day of judgment.* Wright & Brown, London, 1956, 191p, Cloth, Novel

09487 *Invasion from space.* Wright & Brown, London, 1954, 158p, Cloth, Novel
09488 *The Moon is ours.* Wright & Brown, London, 1958, 192p, Cloth, Novel
09489 *A storm is rising.* Wright & Brown, London, 1958, 189p, Cloth, Novel
09490 *The terror in the sky.* Wright & Brown, London, 1955, 188p, Cloth, Novel
09491 *World without end.* Wright & Brown, London, 1955, 159p, Cloth, Novel
09492 *The wrath to come.* Wright & Brown, London, 1957, 188p, Cloth, Novel

MacKINNON, ALLAN

09493 *Summons from Baghdad.* Crime Club, Doubleday, Garden City, 1958, 191p, Cloth, Novel

MACKWORTH, JOHN D(olben), 1887-1939

09494 *The menace of the Terribore; a modern adventure story.* George G. Harrap, London, 1936, 319p, Cloth, Novel
09494A retitled: *The raid of the Terribore; a modern adventure story.* J. B. Lippincott, Philadelphia, 1937, 308p, Cloth, Novel

MACLAGAN, DAVID (T.), 1932-

09495 *Adventures into unknowns; five stories for young readers.* Charles E. Tuttle, Rutland, VT, 1972, 111p, Cloth, Coll.

MacLANE, MARY, 1881-1929

09496 *The devil's letters to Mary MacLane, by Himself.* Inter-State Book Co., Chicago, 1903, 217p, Cloth, Novel

MacLAREN, BERNARD

09497 *Day of misjudgment.* Victor Gollancz, London, 1956, 272p, Cloth, Novel

MacLEAN, KATHERINE (Anne), 1925-   [*biography included*]

09498 *The diploids.* Avon, New York, 1962, 192p, Paper, Coll.

with Charles V. De Vet:

04270 *Cosmic checkmate.* Ace Double, New York, 1962, 96p, Paper, Novel

MacLENNAN, PHYLLIS

09499 *Turned loose on Irdra.* Doubleday, Garden City, 1970, 182p, Cloth, Novel

MacLEOD, ANGUS (M.), 1906-   [*biography included*]

09500 *The body's guest.* Dennis Dobson, London, 1958, 192p, Cloth, Novel

MacLEOD, ANGUS (cont.)

09501   *The eighth seal.* Dennis Dobson, London, 1962, 190p, Cloth, Novel

MACLEOD, FIONA, pseud. [William Sharp, 1855-1905]

09502   *The dominion of dreams.* Archibald Constable, Westminster, 1899, 327p, Cloth, Coll.
09503   *The dominion of dreams; Under the dark star.* William Heinemann, London, 1910, 428p, Cloth, Coll.
09504   *The hills of Ruel, and other stories.* William Heinemann, London, 1921, 92p, Cloth, Coll.
09505   *Pharais; a romance of tne isles.* Harpur & Murray, Derby, UK, 1894, 171p, Cloth, Novel
09506   *Pharais; and, The mountain lovers.* Duffield, New York, 1909, 401p, Cloth, Coll.
09507   *The sin-eater, and other tales.* Patrick Geddes & Colleagues, Edinburgh, 1895, 294p, Cloth, Coll.
09508   *The sin-eater; The washer of the ford, and other legendary moralities.* William Heinemann, London, 1910, 449p, Cloth, Coll.
09509   *The sunset of old tales.* Bernhard Tauchnitz, Leipzig, 1905, 288p, Paper, Coll.
09510   *The washer of the ford, and other legendary moralities.* Patrick Geddes & Colleagues, Edinburgh, 1896, 320p, Cloth, Coll.

MACLEOD, JOSEPH (Todd) GORDON, 1903-

09511   *Overture to Cambridge; a satirical story.* George Allen & Unwin, London, 1936, 264p, Cloth, Novel

MacLEOD, SHEILA

09512   *The Snow-White soliloquies.* Viking Press, New York, 1970, 142p, Cloth, Novel

MACMILLAN, (John) ARMOUR

09513   *This incredible adventure.* Hodder & Stoughton, London, 1928, 312p, Cloth, Novel

MACNIE, JOHN
   see: THIUSEN, ISMAR

MACPHERSON, DONALD

09514   *Go home, unicorn.* Faber & Faber, London, 1935, 271p, Cloth, Novel [Reggie Brooks #1]
09515   *Men are like animals.* Faber & Faber, London, 1937, 322p, Cloth, Novel [Reggie Brooks #2]

MACPHERSON, IAN [John Cook Macpherson]

09516   *Wild harbour.* Methuen, London, 1936, 252p, Cloth, Novel

MACPHERSON, JOHN F.

09517   *A Yankee Napoleon; a novel.* John Long, London, 1907, 318p, Cloth, Novel

MACROW, BRENDA G(race Joan), 1916-

09518   *The amazing Mr. Whisper.* Blackie & Son, London, 1958, 175p, Cloth, Novel

MacTYRE, PAUL, pseud. [Robert James Adam, 1924-]

09519   *Midge.* Hodder & Stoughton, London, 1962, 159p, Cloth, Novel [the last page of the book is erroneously numbered "195"]
09519A   retitled: *Doomsday, 1999.* Ace, New York, 1963, 158p, Paper, Novel

MacVICAR, ANGUS, 1908-   [biography included]

09520   *The lost planet.* Burke, London, 1953, 183p, Cloth, Novel [Jeremy Grant #1]
09521   *Peril on the lost planet.* Burke, London, 1960, 144p, Cloth, Novel [Jeremy Grant #5]
09522   *Red fire on the lost planet.* Burke, London, 1959, 158p, Cloth, Novel [Jeremy Grant #4]
09523   *Return to the lost planet.* Burke, London, 1954, 158p, Cloth, Novel [Jeremy Grant #2]
09524   *Satellite 7.* Burke, London, 1958, 160p, Cloth, Novel
09525   *Secret of the lost planet.* Burke, London, 1955, 158p, Cloth, Novel [Jeremy Grant #3]
09526   *Space agent and the ancient peril.* Burke, London, 1964, 151p, Cloth, Novel [Jeremy Grant #8]
09527   *Space agent and the Isles of Fire.* Burke, London, 1962, 152p, Cloth, Novel [Jeremy Grant #7]
09528   *Space agent from the lost planet.* Burke, London, 1961, 158p, Cloth, Novel [Jeremy Grant #6]
09529   *'Super Nova' and the frozen man.* Brockhampton Press, Leicester, UK, 1970, 160p, Cloth, Novel [Super Nova #2]
09530   *'Super Nova' and the rogue satellite.* Black Knight, Leicester, UK, 1969, 160p, Paper, Novel [Super Nova #1]
09531   *Tiger Mountain.* Burke, London, 1952, 192p, Cloth, Novel

MADARIAGA (y Rojo), SALVADOR, 1886-   [biography included]

09532   *The sacred giraffe, being the second volume of the posthumous works of Julio Arceval.* M. Hopkinson, London, 1925, 269p, Cloth, Novel

MADDEN, SAMUEL, 1686-1765 [published anonymously]

09533   *Memoirs of the twentieth century, being original letters of state under George the Sixth relating to the most important events in Great-Britain and Europe, as to church and state, arts and sciences, trade, taxes and treaties, peace and war, and characters of the greatest persons of those times, from*

MADDEN, SAMUEL (cont.)

> the middle of the eighteenth to the end of
> the twentieth century; and the world; re-
> ceived and revealed in the year 1728, and
> now published for the instruction of all
> eminent statesmen, churchmen, patriots,
> politicians, projectors, papists, and pro-
> testants; vol. I. Osborn & Longman, London,
> 1733, 527p, Cloth, Novel [volume 2 never
> issued]

MADDOCK, LARRY, pseud. [Jack Owen Jardine,
1931-   ] [biography included]

09534 Agent of T.E.R.R.A., no. 1; The flying saucer
       gambit. Ace, New York, 1966, 159p, Paper,
       Novel [Agent of T.E.R.R.A. #1]
09535 Agent of T.E.R.R.A. #2; The Golden Goddess
       gambit. Ace, New York, 1967, 158p, Paper,
       Novel [Agent of T.E.R.R.A. #2]
09536 Agent of T.E.R.R.A. #3; The emerald elephant
       gambit. Ace, New York, 1967, 158p, Paper,
       Novel [Agent of T.E.R.R.A. #3]
09537 The time trap gambit. Ace, New York, 1969,
       255p, Paper, Novel [Agent of T.E.R.R.A. #4]

as Arthur Farmer:

09538 The nymph and the satyr. All Star Books,
       Hollywood, 1962, 154p, Paper, Novel

with Julie Jardine as Howard L. Cory:

07854 The mind monsters. Ace Double, New York,
       1966, 156p, Paper, Novel
07855 The sword of Lankor. Ace, New York, 1966,
       158p, Paper, Novel

MADDOCK, REGINALD (Bertram), 1912-

09539 The time maze. Thomas Nelson & Sons, London,
       1960, 185p, Cloth, Novel

MADDOX, CARL, pseud.
    see: TUBB, E. C.

MADDUX, RACHEL, 1912-   [biography included]

09540 The Green Kingdom; a novel. Simon & Schuster,
       New York, 1957, 563p, Cloth, Novel

MADER, FRIEDRICH (Wilhelm), 1866-

09541 Distant worlds; the story of a voyage to the
       planets. Charles Scribner's Sons, New York,
       1932, 343p, Cloth, Novel

MADISON, J. J.

09542 The body shop. Cameo Editions, New York,
       1970, 198p, Paper, Novel
09543 Ohhhhh, it feels like dying. Peacock Series,
       New York, 1971, 196p, Paper, Novel
09543A retitled: The thing. Belmont, New York,
       1972, 186p, Paper, Novel

MADSEN, ALAN L.

09544 A collection of prose and poetry on the theme
       of tomorrow; science fiction and the future.
       Scholastic Book Services, New York, 1973,
       192p, Paper, Anth. [includes some verse]

MAEL, PETER, pseud.
    see: CAUSSE, CHARLES and VINCENT, CHARLES

MAGIDOFF, ROBERT, 1905-1970 [biography inclu-
ded]

09545 Russian science fiction; an anthology. George
       Allen & Unwin, London, 1963, 272p, Cloth,
       Anth.
09546 Russian science fiction, 1968; an anthology.
       New York University Press, New York, 1968,
       211p, Cloth, Anth.
09547 Russian science fiction, 1969; an anthology.
       New York University Press, New York, 1969,
       210p, Cloth, Anth.

MAGINN, WILLIAM, 1793-1842

09548 Ten tales. Eric Partridge, London, 1933,
       192p, Cloth, Coll.

MAGNUS, LEONARD A(rthur), 1879-1924

09549 A Japanese utopia. George Routledge & Sons,
       London, 1905, 131p, Paper, Novel

MAGOG, ALDER MARTIN-
    see: MARTIN-MAGOG, ALDER

MAGOR, NANCY, with Margaret Murray Woods

09550 Life marches on. Skeffington & Son, London,
       1946, 216p, Cloth, Novel

MAGRISKA, HÉLÈNE, pseud. [Enid Florence Brockies, 1911-   ]

09551 Ten poplars. Constable, London, 1937, 321p,
       Cloth, Novel

MAGROON, VECTOR, pseud.

09552 Burning void. Scion Ltd., London, 1952, 128p,
       Paper, Novel

MAGUIRE, DON

09553 The American adventurer. Trow's Printing &
       Bookbinding Co., New York, 1879, 307p, Cloth,
       Novel

MAGUIRE, JOHN FRANCIS, 1815-1872

09554 The next generation. Hurst & Blackett, London,
       1871, 3vol, Cloth, Novel

THE MAHATMA

09555   *The mahatma; a tale of modern theosophy.* Downey & Co., London, 1895, 284p, Cloth, Novel

MAHER, RICHARD AUMERLE

09556   *The works of Satan.* Macmillan, New York 1921, 370p, Cloth, Novel

MAHNER-MONS, HANS
    see: POSSENDORF, HANS

MAINE, CHARLES ERIC, pseud. [David McIlwain, 1921-   ] [*biography included*]

09557   *Alph.* Nelson Doubleday, Garden City, 1972, 218p, Cloth, Novel [World Without Men #2]
09558   *B.E.A.S.T.; biological evolutionary animal simulation test.* Hodder & Stoughton, London, 1966, 190p, Cloth, Novel
09559   *Calculated risk.* Hodder & Stoughton, London, 1960, 191p, Cloth, Novel
09560   *Count-down.* Hodder & Stoughton, London, 1959, 191p, Cloth, Novel
09560A   retitled: *Fire past the future.* Ballantine, New York, 1959, 160p, Paper, Novel
09561   *Crisis 2000.* Hodder & Stoughton, London, 1955, 191p, Cloth, Novel
09562   *The darkest of nights.* Hodder & Stoughton, London, 1962, 254p, Cloth, Novel
09562A   retitled: *Survival margin.* Fawcett Gold Medal, Greenwich, Conn., 1968, 192p, Paper, Novel
09563   *Escapement.* Hodder & Stoughton, London, 1956, 224p, Cloth, Novel
09563A   retitled: *The man who couldn't sleep.* J. B. Lippincott, Philadelphia, 1958, 224p, Cloth, Novel
         Fire past the future. [see 09560A]
09564   *He owned the world.* Avalon, New York, 1960, 224p, Cloth, Novel
09564A   retitled: *The man who owned the world.* Hodder & Stoughton, London, 1961, 190p, Cloth, Novel
09565   *High vacuum.* Hodder & Stoughton, London, 1957, 192p, Cloth, Novel
09566   *The isotope man.* Hodder & Stoughton, London, 1957, 189p, Cloth, Novel [Mike Delaney #1]
         The man who couldn't sleep. [see 09563A]
         The man who owned the world. [see 09564A]
09567   *The mind of Mr. Soames.* Hodder & Stoughton, London, 1961, 252p, Cloth, Novel
09568   *Never let up.* Hodder & Stoughton, London, 1964, 191p, Cloth, Novel [Mike Delaney #3]
09569   *The random factor.* Hodder & Stoughton, London, 1971, 187p, Cloth, Novel
09570   *Spaceways; a story of the very near future.* Hodder & Stoughton, London, 1953, 191p, Cloth, Radio
09570A   retitled: *Spaceways satellite.* Avalon, New York, 1958, 224p, Cloth, Radio
09571   *Subterfuge.* Hodder & Stoughton, London, 1959, 192p, Cloth, Novel [Mike Delaney #2]
         Survival margin. [see 09562A]
09572   *The tide went out.* Hodder & Stoughton, London, 1958, 190p, Cloth, Novel
09573   *Timeliner; a story of time and space.* Hodder & Stoughton, London, 1955, 192p, Cloth, Radio

09574   *World without men.* Ace, New York, 1958, 191p, Paper, Novel [World Without Men #1]

MAIR, GEORGE B(rown), 1914-

09575   *The day Khrushchev panicked.* Cassell, London, 1961, 172p, Cloth, Novel

MAISTRE, (François) XAVIER de, Comte, 1763-1852

09576   *A journey round my chamber.* J. McCreery, London, 1818, 151p, Cloth, Novel [anonymous]
09576A   retitled: *A journey round my room.* London, 1840,   , Cloth, Novel
09576B   retitled: *A nocturnal expedition round my room.* Privately printed, Edinburgh, 1886, 70p, Paper, Novel

MAITLAND, EDWARD, 1824-1897

09577   *By and by; an historical romance of the future.* Richard Bentley & Son, London, 1873, 948p, Cloth, Novel

MAITRE, JULES LE
    see: LeMAITRE, JULES

MAJORS, SIMON, pseud.
    see: FOX, GARDNER F.

MAKEPEACE LOTT, S(tanley)

09578   *Escape to Venus.* Rich & Cowan, London, 1956, 221p, Cloth, Novel

MALAQUAIS, JEAN, 1908-

09579   *The joker; a novel.* Doubleday, Garden City, 1954, 319p, Cloth, Novel; Victor Gollancz, London, 1954, 320p, Cloth, Novel

MALCOLM, ED

09580   *Tele-sex.* Greenleaf Classic, San Diego, 1968 224p, Paper, Novel

MALCOLM, MARY, 1918-

09581   *Chaucer the flying saucer; a fantasy for grown ups and other children.* Exposition Press, New York, 1954, 39p, Cloth, Story

MALCOLM, SIBBALD, with Richard Valentine

09582   *Archibald the Great; a fable.* Collins, London 1937, 72p, Cloth, Novel

MALCOLM-SMITH, GEORGE, 1901-

09583   *The grass is always greener.* Doubleday, Garden City, 1947, 217p, Cloth, Novel

MALCOLM-SMITH, GEORGE (cont.)

09584   *Professor Peckam's adventures in a drop of
        water*. Rand McNally, New York, 1931, 144p,
        Cloth, Novel

MALCOM, GRANT

09585   *Ray Ellis in The Green Mandarin mystery*.
        Curtis Warren, London, 1952?, 127p, Paper,
        Novel

MALDEN, R(ichard) H(enry), 1879-1951

09586   *Nine ghosts*. Edward Arnold, London, 1943,
        132p, Cloth, Coll.

MALEC, ALEXANDER

09587   *Extrapolasis; stories*. Doubleday, Garden
        City, 1967, 192p, Cloth, Coll.

MALET, LUCAS, pseud. [Mary St. Leger Harrison,
1852-1931]

09588   *The carissima; a modern grotesque*. Herbert
        S. Stone, Chicago, 1896, 335p, Cloth, Novel
09589   *The gateless barrier*. Dodd, Mead, New York,
        1900, 354p, Cloth, Novel
09590   *The tall villa*. George H. Doran, New York,
        1919, 256p, Cloth, Novel

MALET, ORIEL, pseud. [Lady Auriel Rosemary
Malet Vaughan, 1923-   ]

09591   *My bird sings*. Faber & Faber, London, 1945,
        185p, Cloth, Novel

MALKUS, ALIDA SIMS, 1895-

09592   *The dark star of Itza; the story of a pagan
        princess*. Harcourt, Brace & Co., New York,
        1930, 217p, Cloth, Novel

MALLARDI, BILL [William C. Mallardi], with
Bill Bowers

01714   *The Double:Bill symposium, being 94 replies
        to 'a questionnaire for professional sci-
        ence fiction writers and editors,' as cre-
        ated by Lloyd Biggle, Jr*. Double:Bill
        Press, Akron, OH, 1969, 111p, Paper, Nonf.

MALLORY, ARTHUR

09593   *The fiery serpent; a detective story*. Chel-
        sea House, New York, 1929, 248p, Cloth,
        Novel

MALYN, THOMAS

09594   *The romance of a demon; a story of the occult
        and superhuman*. Digby, Long, London, 1892,
        122p, Cloth, Novel

MALZBERG, BARRY N(orman), 1939-   [*biography
included*]

09595   *Beyond Apollo*. Random House, New York, 1972,
        138p, Cloth, Novel
09596   *The day of the burning*. Ace, New York, 1974,
        166p, Paper, Novel
09597   *The destruction of the temple*. Pocket Books,
        New York, 1974, 159p, Paper, Novel
09598   *The falling astronauts*. Ace, New York, 1971,
        191p, Paper, Novel
09599   *Guernica night; a science fiction masterwork*.
        Bobbs-Merrill, Indianapolis, 1974, 140p,
        Cloth, Novel
09600   *Herovit's world*. Random House, New York,
        1973, 209p, Cloth, Novel
09601   *In the enclosure*. Avon, New York, 1973, 190p,
        Paper, Novel
09602   *The men inside*. Lancer, New York, 1973, 175p,
        Paper, Novel
09603   *On a planet alien*. Pocket Books, New York,
        1974, 144p, Paper, Novel
09604   *Out from Ganymede*. Warner, New York, 1974,
        188p, Paper, Coll.
09605   *Overlay*. Lancer, New York, 1972, 189p, Paper,
        Novel
09606   *Phase IV*. Pan, London, 1973, 127p, Paper,
        Movie
09607   *Revelations; a paranoid novel of suspense*.
        Warner, New York, 1972, 141p, Paper, Novel
09608   *The Sodom and Gomorrah business*. Pocket Books,
        New York, 1974, 126p, Paper, Novel
09609   *Tactics of conquest*. Pyramid, New York, 1974,
        173p, Paper, Novel

as K. M. O'Donnell:

09610   *Dwellers of the deep*. Ace Double, New York,
        1970, 113p, Paper, Novel
09611   *The empty people*. Lancer, New York, 1969,
        159p, Paper, Novel
09612   *Final war, and other fantasies*. Ace Double,
        New York, 1969, 118p, Paper, Coll.
09613   *Gather in the Hall of the Planets*. Ace Double,
        New York, 1971, 121p, Paper, Novel
09614   *In the pocket, and other S-F stories*. Ace
        Double, New York, 1971, 132p, Paper, Coll.
09615   *Universe day*. Avon, New York, 1971, 160p,
        Paper, Novel

with Edward L. Ferman:

05377   *Final stage; the ultimate science fiction an-
        thology*. Charterhouse, New York, 1974, 309p,
        Cloth, Anth.

MAMMUTH
    see: THOMSON, WILLIAM

MAN ABROAD

09616   *Man abroad; a yarn of some other century*.
        G. W. Dillingham, New York, 1886, 114p,
        Paper, Novel

THE MAN AMONG THE MONKEYS
    see: GOZLAN, LEON

A MAN IN THE MOON, pseud.
    see: THOMSON, WILLIAM

THE MAN IN THE MOON; OR, TRAVELS IN THE LUNAR REGION
see: THOMSON, WILLIAM

A MAN MADE OF MONEY

09617 *A man made of money.* John Dicks, London, 1870?, 192p, Paper, Anth.

THE MAN OF THE PEOPLE, pseud.
see: THOMSON, WILLIAM

THE MAN OF TWO LIVES
see: BOADEN, JAMES

THE MAN WHO WAS WARNED
see: BEGBIE, HAROLD

MANCHEL, FRANK, 1935-   [*biography included*]

09618 *Terrors of the screen.* Prentice-Hall, Englewood Cliffs, NJ, 1970, 122p, Cloth, Nonf.

MANGELS, ARTHUR C., with Albert F. Byers

02385 *The challenge; plan of action for a better tomorrow; a major novel of the near future.* Rolley & Reynolds, Philadelphia, 1961, 416p, Cloth, Novel

MANKOWITZ, (Cyril) WOLF, 1924-

09619 *The biggest pig in Barbados; a fable.* Longmans, Green, London, 1965, 91p, Cloth, Novel

MANLEY, DAVID L.

09620 *Aros of Atlantis.* Dorrance, Philadelphia, 1972, 139p, Cloth, Novel

MANLEY, MARY (de la Rivière), 1663-1724

09621 *Court intrigues in a collection of original letters, from the island of the New Atalantis, &c.* John Morphew & James Woodward, London, 1711, 120p, Cloth, Novel [New Atalantis series] [published anonymously]
09622 *The modern Atalantis; or, The devil in an air balloon, containing the characters and secret memoirs of the most conspicuous persons of high quality of both sexes in the island of Libertusia.* G. Kearsley, London, 1784, 125p, Cloth, Novel [New Atalantis series]
09623 *Secret memoirs and manners of several persons of quality, of both sexes, from the New Atalantis, an island in the Mediterranean.* John Morphew & James Woodward, London, 1709, 246p, Cloth, Novel [New Atalantis series]
09624 *Secret memoirs and manners of several persons of quality, of both sexes, from the New Atalantis, an island in the Mediterranean, the second volume.* John Morphew & James Woodward, London, 1709, 272p, Cloth, Novel [New Atalantis series]

09625 *Secret memoirs and manners of several persons of quality, of both sexes, from the New Atalantis, an island in the Mediterranean.* John Morphew, London, 1716, 2vol, Cloth, Novel [includes 09623 and 09624 in the first volume, and 09626 and 09627 in the second]

as Eginardus:

09626 *Memoirs of Europe, towards the close of the eighth century.* John Morphew, London, 1710, 380p, Cloth, Novel [New Atalantis series]
09627 *Memoirs of Europe, towards the close of the eighth century, vol. II.* John Morphew, London, 1710, 336p, Cloth, Novel [New Atalantis series]

MANLEY, R. M.

09628 *The queen of Ecuador; a novel.* H. W. Hagemann, New York, 1894, 331p, Paper, Novel

MANLEY, SEON, with Gogo Lewis

09014 *Baleful beasts; great supernatural stories of the animal kingdom.* Lothrop, Lee & Shepard, New York, 1974, 222p, Cloth, Anth.
09015 *Bewitched beings; phantoms, familiars, and the possessed in stories from two centuries.* Lothrop, Lee & Shepard, New York, 1974, 224p, Cloth, Anth.
09016 *A gathering of ghosts; a treasury.* Funk & Wagnalls, New York, 1970, 217p, Cloth, Anth.
09017 *Ladies of horror; two centuries of supernatural stories by the gentle sex.* Lothrop, Lee & Shepard, New York, 1971, 288p, Cloth, Anth.
09018 *Magic; a treasury for young readers.* Funk & Wagnalls, New York, 1967, 238p, Cloth, Anth.
09019 *Mistresses of mystery; two centuries of suspense stories by the gentle sex.* Lothrop, Lee & Shepard, New York, 1973, 221p, Cloth, Anth.
09020 *Shapes of the supernatural.* Doubleday, Garden City, 1969, 370p, Cloth, Anth.

MANN, A. PHILO, pseud.

09629 *The kingdom of Fukkian.* Belmont, New York, 1969, 173p, Paper, Novel

MANN, EDWARD ANDREW

09630 *The portals.* Simon & Schuster, New York, 1974, 252p, Cloth, Novel

MANN, FRANCIS OSCAR

09631 *The devil in a nunnery, and other mediaeval tales.* E. P. Dutton, New York, 1914, 212p, Cloth, Coll.; Constable, London, 1914, 212p, Cloth, Coll.

MANN, JACK, pseud.
see: VIVIAN, E. CHARLES

MANN, JOHN (Harvey)

09632 *Students of the light; an educational odyssey.* Grossman Publishers, New York, 1972, 246p, Cloth, Novel

MANN, KLAUS (Heinrich Thomas), 1906-1949

09633 *Alexander; a novel of utopia.* Brewer & Warren, New York, 1930, 322p, Cloth, Novel

MANN, THOMAS, 1875-1955

09634 *The holy sinner.* Alfred A. Knopf, New York, 1951, 336p, Cloth, Novel
09635 *Mario and the magician.* Martin Secker, London, 1930, 137p, Cloth, Novel
09636 *The transposed heads; a legend of India.* Secker & Warburg, London, 1941, 158p, Cloth, Novel

MANNERS, ALEXANDRA, pseud. [Anne Rundle] [*biography included*]

09637 *The stone maiden.* G. P. Putnam's Sons, New York, 1973, 285p, Cloth, Novel

MANNES, MARYA, 1904- [*biography included*]

09638 *Message from a stranger; a novel.* Viking Press, New York, 1948, 246p, Cloth, Novel
09639 *They; a novel.* Doubleday, Garden City, 1968, 215p, Cloth, Novel

MANNHEIM, KARL, pseud.

09640 *Vampires of Venus.* World Distributors/Sydney Pemberton, Manchester, 1950, 128p, Paper, Novel
09641 *When the Earth died; a complete book-length novel of amazing adventure.* World Distributors/Sydney Pemberton, Manchester, 1950, 128p, Paper, Novel

MANNIN, ETHEL (Edith), 1900- [*biography included*]

09642 *Lucifer and the child.* Jarrolds Publishers, London, 1946, 187p, Cloth, Novel

MANNING, ADELAIDE FRANCES, d. 1959, with Cyril Henry Coles as Manning Coles

03175 *Brief candles.* Doubleday, Garden City, 1954, 252p, Cloth, Novel [Latimer #1]
03175A *Brief candles*, by Francis Gaite. Hodder & Stoughton, London, 1954, 189p, Cloth, Novel [Latimer #1]
03176 *Come and go.* Doubleday, Garden City, 1958, 236p, Cloth, Novel [Latimer #3]
03176A *Come and go*, by Francis Gaite. Hodder & Stoughton, London, 1958, 192p, Cloth, Novel [Latimer #3]
03177 *The emperor's bracelet.* University of London Press, London, 1947, 234p, Cloth, Novel

03178 *The far traveller.* Doubleday, Garden City, 1956, 224p, Cloth, Novel
03178A *The far traveller*, by Francis Gaite. Hodder & Stoughton, London, 1957, 190p, Cloth, Novel
03179 *Great Caesar's ghost.* Doubleday, Doran, Garden City, 1943, 225p, Cloth, Novel
03180 *Happy returns.* Doubleday, Garden City, 1955, 224p, Cloth, Novel [Latimer #2]

with Cyril Coles as Francis Gaite:

Brief candles. [see 03175A]
Come and go. [see 03176A]
The far traveller. [see 03178A]

MANNING, P. L.

09643 *The destroyers.* Badger, London, 1958, 158p, Paper, Novel

MANNON, WARWICK, pseud. [Kenneth Hopkins, 1914-] [*biography included*]

09644 *Miranda.* World Film Publications, London, 1948, 78p, Paper, Movie
09645 *Vice versa.* World Film Publications, London, 1947, 78p, Paper, Movie [based on Anstey's novel of the same name]

MANO, D. KEITH, 1942- [*biography included*]

09646 *The bridge.* Doubleday, Garden City, 1973, 240p, Cloth, Novel
09647 *Horn.* Houghton Mifflin, Boston, 1969, 337p, Cloth, Novel

MANSFIELD, CHARLOTTE, 1881-

09648 *Trample the lilies ("lilia destrue pedibus"); a modern romance of England and Spain.* Stanley Paul, London, 1926, 316p, Cloth, Novel

MANSFIELD, ROGER (Ernest), 1939- [*biography included*]

09649 *The starlit corridor; modern science fiction short stories and poems.* Pergamon Press, Oxford, 1967, 145p, Cloth, Anth. [includes some verse]

MANSFORD, CHARLES J(odrell)

09650 *The great green serpent.* Heath Cranton, London, 1926, 256p, Cloth, Novel

MANSON, MARGARET
  see: ALDISS, MARGARET

MANSON, MARSDEN, 1850-1931

09651 *The yellow peril in action; a possible chapter in history, dedicated to the men who train and direct the men behind the guns.* Britton & Rey, Printers, San Francisco, 1907, 28p, Paper, Story

MANTLEY, JOHN (Truman), 1920-

09652   *The twenty-seventh day.* Michael Joseph, London, 1956, 272p, Cloth, Novel

MANVELL, (Arnold) ROGER, 1909-   [*biography included*]

09653   *The dreamers; a novel.* Victor Gollancz, London, 1958, 206p, Cloth, Novel

MAPPLE, NELSON

09654   *The haunted suit.* Hurst & Blackett, London, 1939, 320p, Cloth, Novel

MARAS, KARL, house pseud. [see also: Kenneth Bulmer and Peter Hawkins]

02183   *Peril from space.* Comyns (Publishers), London, 1954, 128p, Paper, Novel [by Kenneth Bulmer]
06937   *The plant from infinity.* Paladin Press, London, 1954, 128p, Paper, Novel [by Peter Hawkins]
02184   *Zhorani (master of the universe).* Comyns (Publishers), London, 1953, 128p, Paper, Novel [by Kenneth Bulmer]

MARASCO, ROBERT

09655   *Burnt offerings.* Delacorte Press, New York, 1973, 260p, Cloth, Novel

MARCELIN, PHILIPPE THOBY-
    see: THOBY-MARCELIN, PHILIPPE

MARCELIN, (Léonce Perceval) PIERRE, 1908- with Philippe Thoby-Marcelin

09656   *All men are mad.* Farrar, Straus & Giroux, New York, 1970, 179p, Cloth, Novel
09657   *The beast of the Haitian hills.* Rinehart & Co., New York, 1946, 210p, Cloth, Novel
09658   *Canapé-Vert.* Farrar & Rinehart, New York, 1944, 225p, Cloth, Novel
09659   *The pencil of God.* Houghton Mifflin, Boston, 1951, 204p, Cloth, Novel

MARCHANT, ELLA, with Alice Ilgenfritz Jones

07970   *Unveiling a parallel*, by two women of the west. Arena Publishing Co., Boston, 1893, 269p, Cloth, Novel

MARCUS, CARL VAN
    see: VAN MARCUS, CARL

MARDEN, WILLIAM (Edward), 1947-   [*biography included*]

09660   *The exile of Ellendon.* Doubleday, Garden City, 1974, 186p, Cloth, Novel

MARDRUS, J(oseph) C(harles Victor), 1868-1949

09661   *The Queen of Sheba.* Casanova Society, London, 1924, 103p, Cloth, Novel

MARE, COLIN de la
    see: de la MARE, COLIN

MARE, WALTER de la
    see: de la MARE, WALTER

MARFAX, CLYDE

09662   *Planets of peril.* Baker, Brighton, 1953, 62p, Paper, Novel

MARGOLIES, JOSEPH A(aron), 1889-

09663   *Strange and fantastic stories; fifty tales of terror, horror, and fantasy.* Whittlesey House, New York, 1946, 762p, Cloth, Anth.

MARGRIE, WILLIAM, 1877-

09664   *The story of a great experiment; how England produced the first superman.* Watts & Co., London, 1927, 119p, Cloth, Novel

MARGROFF, ROBERT (Ervien), 1930-   [*biography included*], with Piers Anthony

00382   *The E.S.P. worm.* Paperback Library, New York, 1970, 159p, Paper, Novel
00383   *The ring.* Ace, New York, 1968, 254p, Paper, Novel

MARGULIES, LEO, 1900-1975 [*biography included*]

09665   *Get out of my sky; three short novels of science fiction.* Crest, Greenwich, Conn., 1960, 176p, Paper, Anth.
09666   *The ghoul keepers; nine fantastic stories.* Pyramid, New York, 1961, 157p, Paper, Anth.
09667   *3 from out there.* Crest, Greenwich, Conn., 1959, 192p, Paper, Anth.
09668   *Three in one; novels.* Pyramid, New York, 1963, 144p, Paper, Anth. [ghost-edited by Sam Moskowitz]
09669   *Three times infinity.* Gold Medal, Greenwich, Conn., 1958, 176p, Paper, Anth. [ghost-edited by Sam Moskowitz]
09670   *The unexpected; 11 strange stories.* Pyramid, New York, 1961, 160p, Paper, Anth.
09671   *Weird tales; stories of fantasy.* Pyramid, New York, 1964, 155p, Paper, Anth. [ghost-edited by Sam Moskowitz]
09672   *Worlds of weird.* Pyramid, New York, 1965, 158p, Paper, Anth. [ghost-edited by Moskowitz]

with Oscar J. Friend:

05668   *From off this world; gems of science fiction.* Merlin Press, New York, 1949, 430p, Cloth, Anth.
05669   *The giant anthology of science fiction; 10 complete short novels.* Merlin Press, New York, 1954, 580p, Cloth, Anth.

MARGULIES, LEO (cont.), with Oscar J. Friend

05669A retitled: *Race to the stars.* Crest, Green-
        wich, 1958, 224p, Paper, Anth. [abridged]
05670 *My best science fiction story, as selected by
        25 outstanding authors.* Merlin Press, New
        York, 1949, 556p, Cloth, Anth.

MARIE, Queen of Roumania, 1875-1938

09673 *The stealers of light; a legend.* Hodder &
        Stoughton, London, 1916, 190p, Cloth, Novel

MARIE, ANNE

09674 *Naughty positions.* Bee-Line, New York, 1972?,
        , Paper, Novel

MARIGOLD
    see: ALLONBY, EDITH

MARINER, DAVID, pseud. [David McLeod Smith,
    1920-   ] [*biography included*]

09675 *A Shackleton called Sheila.* Robert Hale, Lon-
        don, 1970, 221p, Cloth, Novel
09675A retitled: *Countdown 1000.* Pinnacle, New York,
        1974, 221p, Paper, Novel

MARINI y COPPEL, ALFREDO
    see: COPPEL, ALFRED

MARKOPHRATES
    see: LA BRUJA

MARKS, PERCY L(eman), 1867-

09676 *The merging of Ronald Letheredge.* Robert
        Scott, London, 1928, 156p, Cloth, Novel

MARKS, W(illiam) DENNIS, 1849-1914

09677 *An equal opportunity; a plea for individual-
        ism.* Patterson & White, Philadelphia,
        1905, 354p, Cloth, Novel

MARKWICK, EDWARD

09678 *The City of Gold; a tale of sport, travel,
        and adventure in the heart of the dark con-
        tinent.* Tower Publishing Co., London, 1896,
        324p, Cloth, Novel

MARLOW, LOUIS, pseud. [Louis Umfreville Wil-
    kinson, 1881-1966]

09679 *The devil in crystal.* Faber & Faber, London,
        1944, 113p, Cloth, Novel

MARNELL, JOSEPH
    see: KOOMOTER, ZENO

MARPLE, J. CLARENCE, with Albert Nelson Dennis

04125 *Anona of the Mound Builders; a story of many
        thousands of years ago.* Progressive Publi-
        shers, Wheeling, WV, 1920, 210p, Cloth, Novel

MARQUEZ, GABRIEL GARCIA
    see: GARCIA MARQUEZ, GABRIEL

MARQUIS, DON (Robert Perry), 1878-1937

09680 *Chapters for the orthodox.* Doubleday, Doran,
        Garden City, 1934, 314p, Cloth, Coll.
09681 *The revolt of the oyster.* Doubleday, Page,
        Garden City, 1922, 229p, Cloth, Coll.

MARQUIS, ROY

09682 *The Moon monsters.* Barrington Gray, Leigh-on-
        Sea, UK, 1953, 128p, Paper, Novel

MARRIOTT, CRITTENDEN, 1867-1932

09683 *The Isle of Dead Ships.* J. B. Lippincott, Phi-
        ladelphia, 1909, 265p, Cloth, Novel
09683A retitled: *The isle of lost ships.* Readers
        Library Publishing Co., London, 1930, 252p,
        Cloth, Novel

MARRIOTT, JAMES WILLIAM
    see: WRAY, ROGER

MARRIOTT, RONALD, with Hazel Adair

00037 *Stranger from space.* Weidenfeld & Nicolson,
        London, 1953, 191p, Cloth, Tele.

MARRYAT, FLORENCE (Church), 1837-1899

09684 *The blood of the vampire.* Hutchinson, London,
        1897, 345p, Cloth, Novel
09685 *The dead man's message; an occult romance.*
        Charles B. Reed, Publisher, New York, 1894,
        178p, Cloth, Novel
09685A retitled: *A soul on fire.* Bliss, Sands, Lon-
        don, 1898, 275p, Cloth, Novel
09686 *The ghost of Charlotte Cray, and other stories.*
        George Munro's Sons, New York, 1884, 93p,
        Paper, Coll.
09687 *The strange transfiguration of Hannah Stubbs.*
        Hutchinson, London, 1896, 339p, Cloth, Novel

MARRYAT, Capt. FREDERICK, 1792-1848

09688 *The phantom ship*, by Capt. Marryat. Henry
        Colburn, London, 1839, 3vol, Cloth, Novel

MARS, ALASTAIR (Campbell Gillespie), 1915-

09689 *Arctic submarine.* Elek, London, 1955, 191p,
        Cloth, Novel
09690 *Atomic submarine; a story of tomorrow.* Elek,
        London, 1957, 192p, Cloth, Novel

MARS, ALASTAIR (cont.)

09690A retitled: *Fire in anger; a novel.* M. S. Mill
& William Morrow, New York, 1958, 222p,
Cloth, Novel

MARS, ROBERT DE
    see: DE MARS, ROBERT

MARS REVEALED
    see: GASTON, HENRY A.

MARSH, CARL (David)

09691 *And wars shall cease.* Broadway Publishing
Co., New York, 1939, 351p, Cloth, Novel

MARSH, JOHN, 1907-   [*biography included*]

09692 *Body made alive; a study in the macabre.*
Stanley Smith, London, 1936, 232p, Cloth,
Novel

as John Elton:

09693 *The green plantations.* Ward, Lock, London,
1955, 192p, Cloth, Novel

MARSH, PATRICK, pseud. [Leslie Hiscock,
1902-   ]

09694 *Breakdown.* Longmans, Green, London, 1952,
212p, Cloth, Novel

MARSH, RICHARD, 1867-1915

09695 *The ape and the diamond; or, A brother's legacy.* Adventure Library, Street & Smith,
New York, 1928, 320p, Paper, Novel
09696 *The beetle; a mystery.* Skeffington & Son,
London, 1897, 351p, Cloth, Novel
09696A retitled: *The mystery of the beetle; or, The
house with the open window.* Westlake,
Cleveland, OH, 1912, 310p, Paper, Novel
09697 *Both sides of the veil.* Methuen, London,
1901, 306p, Cloth, Coll.
09698 *The mahatma's pupil.* H. Henry, London, 1893,
217p, Cloth, Novel
The mystery of the beetle. [see 09696A]
09699 *A second coming.* John Lane, The Bodley Head,
London, 1900, 305p, Cloth, Novel
09700 *The seen and the unseen.* Methuen, London,
1900, 320p, Cloth, Coll.
09701 *A spoiler of men.* Chatto & Windus, London,
1905, 306p, Cloth, Novel
09702 *Tom Ossington's ghost.* James Bowden, London,
1898, 315p, Cloth, Novel

MARSHALL, ARCHIBALD [Arthur Hammond Marshall,
1866-1934]

09703 *Upsidonia.* Stanley Paul, London, 1915, 286p,
Cloth, Novel

MARSHALL, ARTHUR CALDER-
    see: CALDER-MARSHALL, ARTHUR

MARSHALL, ARTHUR HAMMOND
    see: MARSHALL, ARCHIBALD

MARSHALL, BRUCE, 1899-   [*biography included*]

09704 *Father Malachy's miracle; a heavenly story with
an earthly meaning.* William Heinemann, London, 1931, 325p, Cloth, Novel
09705 *Urban the Ninth.* Constable, London, 1973,
192p, Cloth, Novel

MARSHALL, EDISON (Telsa), 1894-1967 [*biography
included*]

09706 *Dian of the lost land.* H. C. Kinsey, New York,
1935, 269p, Cloth, Novel
09706A retitled: *The lost land.* Curtis, New York,
1972, 189p, Paper, Novel
09707 *Ogden's strange story.* H. C. Kinsey, New York,
1934, 283p, Cloth, Novel

MARSHALL, JAMES S(cott), with Margaret Marshall

09708 *1960 (a retrospect).* J. F. Rowny Press, Los
Angeles, 1919, 96p, Cloth, Novel [includes
some nonf.]
09709 retitled: *World of tomorrow.* James Scott
Marshall, Chico, CA, 1954, 112p, Paper, Novel
[expanded]

MARSHALL, LUTHER

09710 *Thomas Boobig; a complete enough account of
his life and singular disappearance; narration of his scribe.* Lee & Shepard, Boston,
1895, 349p, Cloth, Novel

MARSHALL, MARGARET SCOTT, with James Marshall

09708 *1960 (a retrospect).* J. F. Rowny Press, Los
Angeles, 1919, 96p, Cloth, Novel [includes
some nonf.]
09709 retitled: *World of tomorrow.* James Scott
Marshall, Chico, CA, 1954, 112p, Paper,
Novel [expanded]

MARSHALL, ROBERT, 1863-1910

09711 *The haunted major.* Moray Press, Edinburgh,
1902, 192p, Cloth, Novel
09711A retitled: *The enchanted golf clubs.* Frederick A. Stokes, New York, 1920, 152p, Cloth,
Novel

MARSHALL, SIDNEY J(ohn), 1866-

09712 *The king of Kor; or, She's promise kept; a continuation of the great story of "She" by H.
Rider Haggard.* S. J. Marshall, Washington,
1903, 258p, Cloth, Novel [a sequel to Haggard's novel; She series]

MARSON, G(erald) F(rancis)

09713   *Ghosts, ghouls, and gallows.* Rider & Co.,
          London, 1946, 176p, Cloth, Coll. [includes
          some nonf.]

MARSTEN, RICHARD, pseud.
     see: HUNTER, EVAN

MARTEL, SUZANNE (Chouinard)

09714   *The city under ground.* Viking Press, New
          York, 1964, 157p, Cloth, Novel

MARTENS, PAUL, pseud.
     see: BELL, NEIL

MARTÍ-IBÁÑEZ, FÉLIX, d. 1972

09715   *All the wonders we seek; thirteen tales of
          surprise and prodigy.* Clarkson N. Potter,
          New York, 1963, 450p, Cloth, Coll.

MARTIA, ASTRON DEL
     see: DEL MARTIA, ASTRON

MARTIN, AL(bert Harry), 1897-

09716   *Dog gone Hollywood.* Martin Publishing Co.,
          Hollywood, 1930, 47p, Cloth, Story

MARTIN, DAVID S(tephen), 1913-   [*biography
included*]

09717   *No lack of space.* Arthur H. Stockwell, Ilfra-
          combe, UK, 1967, 182p, Cloth, Coll.

MARTIN, DON, with Ned Brooks

01924   *Hannes Bok illustration index.* Collectors
          Bureau, National Fantasy Fan Federation,
          Newport News, VA, 1970, 22p, Paper, Nonf.

MARTIN, ED(gar A.)

09718   *Busy bodies.* Traveller's Companion, Paris,
          1963, 246p, Paper, Novel
09719   *Frankenstein '69.* Traveller's Companion, New
          York, 1969, 176p, Paper, Novel [Frankenstein
          series]

MARTIN, EDWARD
     see: SIRIUS

MARTIN, EVA M.

09720   *The secret of a star.* Theosophical Publishing
          House, Adyar, India, 1913, 139p, Cloth,
          Novel

MARTIN, HARRISON (Pillsbury), 1911-

09721   *Spook and Bones.* Privately printed, New York,
          1924, 67p, Cloth, Novel

MARTIN, JAY, pseud.
     see: GOLDING, MORTON J.

MARTIN, JOHN-
     see: JOHN-MARTIN

MARTIN, JOHN S(tuart), 1900-   [*biography included*]

09722   *General Manpower.* Simon & Schuster, New York,
          1938, 307p, Cloth, Novel

MARTIN, KAY

09723   *Vanessa; a novel.* G. P. Putnam's Sons, New
          York, 1974, 256p, Cloth, Novel

MARTIN, (Henry) LASTER, 1917-

09724   *Noah's stowaway.* no publisher, Long Beach, CA,
          1954, 154p, Cloth, Novel

MARTIN, NETTIE PARRISH

09725   *A pilgrim's progress in other worlds, recoun-
          ting the wonderful adventures of Ulysum Stor-
          ries and his discovery of the lost star
          "Eden."* Mayhew Publishing Co., Boston, 1908,
          482p, Cloth, Novel

MARTIN, PETER, pseud. [Peter Martin Leckie,
  1890-   ]

09726   *Summer in three thousand.* Quality Press, Lon-
          don, 1946, 184p, Cloth, Novel

MARTIN, RALPH

09727   *The man who haunted himself.* Tandem, London,
          1970, 125p, Paper, Movie

MARTIN, RAY

09728   *Island in a strange sea.* F.E.B.S., Helsinki,
          1970, 318p, Cloth, Novel

MARTIN, REED

09729   *Beginner's lust.* Late-Hour Library, San Diego,
          1969, 152p, Paper, Novel

MARTIN, REGINALD ALEC
     see: ELIOTT, E. C.

MARTIN, THOMAS HECTOR
     see: THOMAS, MARTIN

MARTIN-MAGOG, ALDER

09730   *Man or ape?* George Newnes, London, 1933, 256p, Cloth, Novel

MARTINDALE, C(yril) C(harles), 1879-1963

09731   *The goddess of ghosts.* Burns & Oates, London, 1915, 219p, Cloth, Coll.

MARTINEZ, DIANA, with Doris M. Paine

09732   *Guide to science fiction; exploring possibilities and alternatives.* Bantam, New York, 1974, 72p, Paper, Nonf.

MARTINI, VIRGILIO, 1903-   [*biography included*]

09733   *The world without women.* Dial Press, New York, 1971, 125p, Cloth, Novel

MARTYN, WYNDHAM, 1875-

09734   *Stones of enchantment.* Herbert Jenkins, London, 1948, 253p, Cloth, Novel [Anthony Trent series]

MARVELL, ANDREW, pseud. [Howell Davies]

09735   *Congratulate the devil.* Victor Gollancz, London, 1939, 285p, Cloth, Novel
09736   *Minimum Man; or, Time to be gone.* Victor Gollancz, London, 1938, 350p, Cloth, Novel
09737   *Three men make a world.* Victor Gollancz, London, 1939, 286p, Cloth, Novel

MARY CATHERINE, Sister [the religious name of Kathleen Agness Cicely Anderson], as S. M. C.

09738   *Brother Petroc's return; a story.* Chatto & Windus, London, 1937, 201p, Cloth, Novel
09739   *The dark wheel.* Sands & Co., London, 1939, 218p, Cloth, Novel

MARY CHARITINA, Sister

09740   *The adventures of the Redcrosse Knight.* Sheed & Ward, London, 1945, 110p, Cloth, Novel [a somewhat embellished retelling of Spenser's "Faerie Queen"]

MARYE, BEATRISSIA

09741   *The circle.* Austin Publishing Co., Los Angeles, 1927, 105p, Cloth, Novel

MASEFIELD, JOHN (Edward), 1878-1967

09742   *The box of delights; or, When the wolves were running.* William Heinemann, London, 1935, 418p, Cloth, Novel [Kay Harker #2]

09743   *The midnight folk; a novel.* William Heinemann, London, 1927, 327p, Cloth, Novel [Kay Harker #1]

MASEFIELD, LEWIS (Crommelin)

09744   *Cross double cross.* Putnam, London, 1936, 331p, Cloth, Novel

MASKS
    see: RUSSELL, RAY

MASON, A(lfred) E(dward) W(oodley), 1865-1948

09745   *The four corners of the world.* Hodder & Stoughton, London, 1917, 319p, Cloth, Coll.

MASON, ARTHUR, 1876-

09746   *The flying bo'sun; a mystery of the sea.* Henry Holt, New York, 1920, 241p, Cloth, Novel

MASON, CAROL, with Martin Harry Greenberg and Patricia S. Warrick

06311   *Anthropology through science fiction.* St. Martin's Press, New York, 1974, 387p, Cloth, Anth.

MASON, COLIN, 1926-

09747   *Hostage.* Macmillan, London, 1973, 221p, Cloth, Novel

MASON, DAVID, d. 1974

09748   *The deep gods.* Lancer, New York, 1973, 192p, Paper, Novel
09749   *Devil's food.* Ophelia Press, New York, 1969, 192p, Paper, Novel
09750   *Kavin's world.* Lancer, New York, 1969, 221p, Paper, Novel [Kavin #1]
09751   *The return of Kavin.* Lancer, New York, 1972, 286p, Paper, Novel [Kavin #2]
09752   *The shores of tomorrow.* Lancer, New York, 1971, 240p, Paper, Novel
09753   *The sorcerer's skull.* Lancer, New York, 1970, 192p, Paper, Novel

MASON, DOUGLAS R(ankine), 1918-   [*biography included*]

09754   *Dilation effect.* Ballantine, New York, 1971, 185p, Paper, Novel
       Eight against utopia. [see 09756A]
09755   *The end bringers.* Ballantine, New York, 1973, 208p, Paper, Novel
09756   *From Carthage then I came.* Doubleday, Garden City, 1966, 190p, Cloth, Novel
09756A   retitled: *Eight against utopia.* Paperback Library, New York, 1967, 158p, Paper, Novel
09757   *Horizon Alpha.* Ballantine, New York, 1971, 168p, Paper, Novel
09758   *The Janus syndrome.* Robert Hale, London, 1969, 190p, Cloth, Novel

MASON, DOUGLAS R. (cont.)

09759 *Landfall is a state of mind.* Robert Hale,
London, 1968, 192p, Cloth, Novel
09760 *Matrix.* Ballantine, New York, 1970, 202p,
Paper, Novel
09761 *The Phaeton condition.* G. P. Putnam's Sons,
New York, 1973, 192p, Cloth, Novel
09762 *The resurrection of Roger Diment.* Ballantine,
New York, 1972, 186p, Paper, Novel
09763 *Ring of violence.* Robert Hale, London, 1968,
190p, Cloth, Novel
09764 *Satellite 54-Zero.* Ballantine, New York,
1971, 185p, Paper, Novel
09765 *The Tower of Rizwan.* Robert Hale, London,
1968, 189p, Cloth, Novel

as John Rankine:

09766 *Binary Z.* Dennis Dobson, London, 1969, 190p,
Cloth, Novel
09767 *The blockade of Sinitron; four adventures of
Dag Fletcher.* Thomas Nelson & Sons, London,
1966, 122p, Cloth, Coll. [Dag Fletcher
series]
09768 *The Bromius phenomenon.* Ace, New York, 1973,
207p, Paper, Novel [Dag Fletcher #4]
09769 *The Fingalnan conspiracy; science fiction.*
Sidgwick & Jackson, London, 1973, 190p,
Cloth, Novel
09770 *Interstellar Two-Five.* Dennis Dobson, London,
1966, 183p, Cloth, Novel [Dag Fletcher #2]
09771 *Moons of Triopus.* Dennis Dobson, London,
1968, 176p, Cloth, Novel [Space Corporation
#2]
09772 *Never the same door.* Dennis Dobson, London,
1968, 173p, Cloth, Novel [Space Corporation
#1]
09773 *One is one.* Dennis Dobson, London, 1968,
176p, Cloth, Novel [Dag Fletcher #5]
09774 *Operation Umanaq.* Ace, New York, 1973, 188p,
Paper, Novel
09775 *The Plantos affair.* Dennis Dobson, London,
1971, 173p, Cloth, Novel [Dag Fletcher #3]
09776 *The Ring of Garamas.* Dennis Dobson, London,
1972, 186p, Cloth, Novel [Dag Fletcher #1]
09777 *The Weisman experiment.* Dennis Dobson, London, 1969, 184p, Cloth, Novel

MASON, E(veleen) L(aura), 1838-

09778 *Hiero-salem: the vision of peace; a fiction
founded on ideals which are grounded in the
real that is greater than the greatest of
all human great ideals.* J. G. Cupples,
Boston, 1889, 508p, Cloth, Novel
09778A retitled: *An episode in the doings of the
dualized.* Evaleen Laura Mason, Brookline,
Mass., 1898, 117p, Cloth, Novel [adapted
from *Hiero-salem*]

MASON, GREGORY, 1889-1968

09779 *The golden Archer; a satirical novel of 1975.*
Twayne Publishers, New York, 1956, 296p,
Cloth, Novel

MASON, Capt. H. A.

09780 *He conquered the Kaiser.* Macaulay, New York,
1915, 311p, Cloth, Novel

MASON, H(ugh) C(hurchill)

09781 *The devil's Christmas box.* Heath Cranton,
London, 1921, 339p, Cloth, Novel

MASON, J(ohn) EDWARD, 1892-

09782 *Witches, warlocks, and ghosts; tales of the
supernatural.* Oliver & Boyd, Edinburgh,
1938, 127p, Cloth, Anth.

MASON, LOWELL B(lake), 1893-

09783 *The bull on the bench.* Arcturus Publishing
Co., Oak Park, IL, 1967, 234p, Cloth, Novel

MASON, PAMELA
see: KELLINO, PAMELA

MASON, (Francis) VAN WYCK, 1901-1978

09784 *Two tickets for Tangier; a Colonel North story.*
Doubleday, Garden City, 1955, 285p, Cloth,
Novel [Colonel North series]

MASSENET, PIERRE BESSAND-
see: BESSAND-MASSENET, PIERRE

MASSIE, CHRIS, pseud.

09785 *Death goes hunting.* Faber & Faber, London,
1953, 188p, Cloth, Novel

MASSIE, DOUGLAS

09786 *Mr. Ciggers goes to Heaven; a satire.* Sampson
Low, Marston, London, 1931, 314p, Cloth,
Novel

MASSON, DAVID I(rvine), 1915- [*biography
included*]

09787 *The caltraps of time.* Faber & Faber, London,
1968, 192p, Cloth, Coll.

MASTER OF DREAMS

09788 *Master of dreams.* Utopian Publications, London, 1946, 36p, Paper, Anth.

MASTERMAN, WALTER S(idney), 1876-

09789 *The border line.* E. P. Dutton, New York, 1937,
287p, Cloth, Novel
09790 *The Flying Beast.* E. P. Dutton, New York,
1932, 288p, Cloth, Novel
09791 *The yellow mistletoe.* E. P. Dutton, New York,
1930, 288p, Cloth, Novel

MASTERPIECE OF THRILLS

09792   *Masterpiece of thrills.* Daily Express Publication, London, 1936, 735p, Cloth, Anth.

MASTERS, JOHN, 1914-

09793   *The breaking strain.* Michael Joseph, London, 1967, 288p, Cloth, Novel
09794   *The Rock; an epic.* Michael Joseph, London, 1970, 396p, Cloth, Novel

MASTERS OF SCIENCE FICTION

09795   *Masters of science fiction.* Belmont, New York, 1964, 157p, Paper, Anth.

MASTIN, JOHN, 1865-1932

09796   *The autobiography of a picture.* F. V. White, London, 1910, 303p, Cloth, Novel
09797   *The immortal light.* Cassell, London, 1907, 307p, Cloth, Novel
09798   *The stolen planet; a scientific romance.* Philip Wellby, London, 1906, 282p, Cloth, Novel [Regina #1]
09799   *Through the Sun in an airship.* Charles Griffin, London, 1909, 317p, Cloth, Novel [Regina #2]

MATHERS, HELEN (Buckingham), 1853-1920

09800   *The juggler and the soul.* Skeffington & Son, London, 1896, 220p, Cloth, Novel

MATHESON, HUGH, pseud. [Lewis Hugh Mackay]

09801   *The third force.* Allan Wingate, London, 1959, 248p, Cloth, Novel

MATHESON, JEAN

09802   *The cistern and the fountain.* Charles Scribner's Sons, New York, 1951, 256p, Cloth, Novel; Collins, London, 1951, 256p, Cloth, Novel

MATHESON, JOAN
   see: TRANSUE, JACOB

MATHESON, RICHARD (Burton), 1926-   [*biography included*]

09803   *Born of man and woman; tales of science fiction and fantasy.* Chamberlain Press, Philadelphia, 1954, 252p, Cloth, Coll.
09803A   retitled: *Third from the Sun.* Bantam, New York, 1955, 180p, Paper, Coll. [abridged]
09804   *Hell House.* Viking Press, New York, 1971, 279p, Cloth, Novel
09805   *I am legend.* Gold Medal, New York, 1954, 160p, Paper, Novel
09805A   retitled: *The omega man; I am legend.* Berkley Medallion, New York, 1971, 174p, Paper, Novel

09806   *Shock!* Dell, New York, 1961, 191p, Paper, Coll.
09807   *Shock II.* Dell, New York, 1964, 192p, Paper, Coll.
09808   *Shock III.* Dell, New York, 1966, 192p, Paper, Coll.
09809   *Shock waves.* Dell, New York, 1970, 190p, Paper, Coll.
09810   *The shores of space.* Bantam, New York, 1957, 184p, Paper, Coll.
09811   *The shrinking man.* Gold Medal, New York, 1956, 192p, Paper, Novel
09812   *A stir of echoes.* J. B. Lippincott, Philadelphia, 1958, 220p, Cloth, Novel
     Third from the Sun. [see 09803A]

MATHEWS, FRANCES (H.), with Vere Shortt

09813   *The Rod of the Snake.* John Lane, The Bodley Head, London, 1917, 310p, Cloth, Novel

MATHIEWS, FRANKLIN K., 1873?-1950

09814   *The boy scout's year book of ghost and mystery stories.* D. Appleton-Century, New York, 1933, 286p, Cloth, Anth.

MATSCHAT, CECILE (Hulse), with Carl Carmer and Lester del Rey

02587   *The year after tomorrow; an anthology of science fiction stories.* John C. Winston, Philadelphia, 1954, 339p, Cloth, Anth.

MATSON, NORMAN (Häghejm), 1893-1965

09815   *Bats in the belfry; sequel to Thorne Smith's last novel, The passionate witch, which was finished by Norman Matson.* Doubleday, Doran, Garden City, 1943, 242p, Cloth, Novel [Jennifer #2]
09816   *Doctor Fogg.* Macmillan, New York, 1929, 165p, Cloth, Novel
09817   *Flecker's magic.* Boni & Liveright, New York, 1926, 243p, Cloth, Novel
09817A   retitled: *Enchanted beggar.* J. B. Lippincott, Philadelphia, 1959, 187p, Cloth, Novel

with Thorne Smith:

09818   *The passionate witch.* Doubleday, Doran, Garden City, 1941, 267p, Cloth, Novel [Jennifer #1]

MATTES, ARTHUR S., 1901-   [*biography included*]

09819   *Soul mates.* Regency Press, London, 1963, 94p, Cloth, Novel

MATTHEWS, (James) BRANDER, 1852-1929

09820   *Tales of fantasy and fact.* Harper & Bros., New York, 1896, 216p, Cloth, Coll.

with various co-authors:

09821   *With my friends; tales told in partnership.* Longmans, Green, New York, 1891, 284p, Cloth, Coll.

MATTHEWS, E. PAUL

09822 *Beyond this day.* Vantage Press, New York, 1958, 276p, Cloth, Novel

MATTHEWS, RONALD (de Couves), 1903-1967

09823 *Red sky at night.* Hollis & Carter, London, 1951, 219p, Cloth, Novel

MATTINGLY, SIDNEY

09824 *The terror by night.* C. Arthur Pearson, London, 1913, 158p, Cloth, Novel

MATURIN, CHARLES ROBERT, 1780-1824

09825 *The Albigenses; a romance*, by the author of "Bertram, a tragedy," "Woman; or, Pour et contre," &c. Hurst, Robinson & Co., & A. Constable, London, 1824, 4vol, Cloth, Novel
Fatal revenge; or, The family of Montorio; a romance. [see 09827B]
09826 *Melmoth, the wanderer; a tale*, by the author of "Bertram." Hurst, Robinson & Co., & A. Constable, London, 1820, 4vol, Cloth, Novel

as Dennis Jasper Murphy:

09827 *Fatal revenge; or, The family of Montorio; a romance.* Longman, Hurst, Rees & Orme, London, 1807, 3vol, Cloth, Novel
09827A *Fatal revenge; or, The family of Montorio; a romance*, by the author of The wild Irish boy. A. K. Newman, London, 1824, 4vol, Cloth, Novel
09827B *Fatal revenge; or, The family of Montorio; a romance*, by Rev. R. Maturin. J. Clements, London, 1840, 255p, Cloth, Novel

MAUDE, F(rederic) N(atusch), 1854-1933

09828 *The new Battle of Dorking*, by ******. Grant Richards, London, 1900, 255p, Cloth, Novel [Dorking series]

with P. Colomb, J. F. Maurice, Archibald Forbes, Charles Lowe, D. Christie Murray, and F. Scudamore:

03229 *The Great War of 189-; a forecast.* William Heinemann, London, 1893, 308p, Cloth, Novel

MAUGHAM, ROBIN [Robert Cecil Romer Maugham, 2nd Viscount Maugham, 1916-   ] [*biography included*]

09829 *The 1946 ms.* War Facts Press, London, 1943, 44p, Paper, Story

MAUGHAM, W(illiam) SOMERSET, 1874-1965 [*biography included*]

09830 *Catalina; a romance.* Doubleday, Garden City, 1948, 275p, Cloth, Novel
09831 *The magician.* William Heinemann, London, 1908, 310p, Cloth, Novel

MAUPASSANT, (Henri René Albert) GUY de, 1850-1893

09832 *Tales of supernatural horror.* Pan, London, 1972, 160p, Paper, Coll.

MAURICE, J(ohn) F(rederick), 1841-1912, with P. Colomb, F. N. Maude, Archibald Forbes, Charles Lowe, D. Christie Murray, F. Scudamore

03229 *The Great War of 189-; a forecast.* William Heinemann, London, 1893, 308p, Cloth, Novel

MAURICE, MICHAEL, pseud. [Conrad Arthur Skinner, 1889-   ]

09833 *Not in our stars.* T. Fisher Unwin, London, 1923, 288p, Cloth, Novel

MAURIER, DAPHNE du
see: du MAURIER, DAPHNE

MAURIER, GEORGE du
see: du MAURIER, GEORGE

MAURO, JOHN F(rancis), 1911-

09834 *Rhapsody in death.* Fortuny's, New York, 1940, 190p, Cloth, Novel

MAUROIS, ANDRÉ, 1885-1967 [original name: Émile Salomon Wilhelm Herzog] [*biography included*]

09835 *The next chapter; the war against the Moon.* Kegan Paul, Trench, Trubner, London, 1927, 74p, Cloth, Novel
09836 *The thought-reading machine.* Jonathan Cape, London, 1938, 191p, Cloth, Novel
09837 *A voyage to the island of the Articoles.* Jonathan Cape, London, 1928, 63p, Cloth, Novel
09838 *The weigher of souls.* Cassell, London, 1931, 125p, Cloth, Novel
09839 *The weigher of souls; &, The Earth dwellers.* Macmillan, New York, 1963, 189p, Cloth, Coll.

MAWSON, L. A.

09840 *Methods from Mars.* Arthur H. Stockwell, London, 1913, 208p, Cloth, Novel

MAX, NICHOLAS, pseud. [Bernard Asbell, 1923-   ] [*biography included*]

09841 *President McGovern's first term.* Doubleday, Garden City, 1973, 158p, Cloth, Novel

MAXON, P. B.

09842 *The waltz of death.* Mystery House, New York, 1941, 252p, Cloth, Novel

MAXWELL, EDWARD, pseud.

09843 *Quest for Pajaro.* Heinemann, London, 1957,
       116p, Cloth, Novel

MAXWELL, JOHN C.

09844 *"The world makers."* Badger, London, 1958,
       160p, Paper, Novel

MAXWELL, MAY

09845 *"The city of the golden gates."* Goodmount
       Press, London, 1937, 145p, Paper, Novel

MAXWELL, PERRITON, 1868-1947

09846 *A third of life.* Small, Maynard, Boston,
       1921, 304p, Cloth, Novel

MAY, ERNEST R.

09847 *Private war with Russia; a novel; place:
       Washington, D.C.; time: tomorrow.* Dorrance,
       Philadelphia, 1963, 143p, Cloth, Novel

MAYNE, JOHN D(awson), 1828-1917

09848 *The triumph of socialism, and how it succeed-
       ed.* Swan Sonnenschein, London, 1908, 139p,
       Cloth, Novel

MAYNE, WILLIAM (James Carter), 1928-   [*biography included*]

09849 *Earthfasts.* Hamish Hamilton, London, 1966,
       154p, Cloth, Novel
09850 *A game of dark.* E. P. Dutton, New York, 1971,
       143p, Cloth, Novel
09851 *Ghosts; an anthology.* Hamish Hamilton, Lon-
       don, 1971, 188p, Cloth, Anth. [includes
       some nonf.]
09852 *Over the hills and far away.* Hamish Hamilton,
       London, 1968, 144p, Cloth, Novel
09852A retitled: *The hill road.* E. P. Dutton, New
       York, 1969, 144p, Cloth, Novel
09853 *Skiffy.* Hamish Hamilton, London, 1972, 120p,
       Cloth, Novel

MAYO, W(illiam) S(tarbuck), 1812-1895

09854 *Kaloolah; or, Journeyings to the Djébel Kumri;
       an autobiography of Jonathan Romer.* George
       P. Putnam, New York, 1849, 514p, Cloth,
       Novel

MAYOE, FRANKLIN
    see: ROSEWATER, FRANK

MAYOE, MARIAN
    see: ROSEWATER, FRANK

MAYOR, F(lora) M(acdonald), 1872-

09855 *The room opposite, and other tales of mystery
       and imagination.* Longmans, Green, London,
       1935, 322p, Cloth, Coll.

MAYS, JULIA WEBB

09856 *Luda, the occult girl; a romance.* Broadway
       Publishing Co., New York, 1912, 280p, Cloth,
       Novel

MAZZEO, HENRY (J. Jr.)

09857 *Hauntings; tales of the supernatural.* Double-
       day, Garden City, 1968, 318p, Cloth, Anth.

McALLISTER, BRUCE (Hugh), 1946-   [*biography
included*]

09858 *Humanity Prime.* Ace, New York, 1971, 285p,
       Paper, Novel

McAULEY, JACQUELIN ROLLIT, 1925-

09859 *The cloud.* Exposition Press, New York, 1964,
       119p, Cloth, Novel

McBROOM, R. CURTIS
    see: DRING, NAT

McCAFFREY, ANNE (Inez), 1926-   [*biography
included*]

09860 *Alchemy and academe; a collection of original
       stories concerning themselves with trans-
       mutations, mental and elemental, alchemical
       and academic.* Doubleday, Garden City, 1970,
       239p, Cloth, Anth.
09861 *Cooking out of this world.* Ballantine, New
       York, 1973, 213p, Paper, Nonf. Anth.
09862 *Decision at Doona.* Ballantine, New York, 1969,
       246p, Paper, Novel
09863 *Dragonflight.* Ballantine, New York, 1968,
       310p, Paper, Novel [Dragonriders #1]
09864 *Dragonquest, being the further adventures of
       the dragonriders of Pern.* Ballantine, New
       York, 1971, 333p, Paper, Novel [Dragonriders
       #2]
09865 *Restoree.* Ballantine, New York, 1967, 252p,
       Paper, Novel
09866 *The ship who sang.* Walker, New York, 1969,
       248p, Cloth, Coll.
09867 *To ride Pegasus.* Ballantine, New York, 1973,
       243p, Paper, Coll.

McCANN, EDSON, pseud.
    see: del REY, LESTER and POHL, FREDERIK

McCARTHY, JUSTIN HUNTLY, 1860-1936

09868 *The Dryad; a novel.* Harper & Bros., New York,
       1905, 314p, Cloth, Novel

McCAULEY, MOTLY RANKE, pseud.

09869   *Chapters from future history; the Battle of*
        Berlin (Die schlacht von Königsberg). Tins-
        ley Bros., London, 1871, 54p, Paper?, Novel
        [cover title: *The Battle of Britain*]

McCLARY, THOMAS CALVERT

09870   *Rebirth; when everyone forgot.* Bart House,
        New York, 1944, 187p, Paper, Novel
09871   *Three thousand years.* Fantasy Press, Reading,
        PA, 1954, 224p, Cloth, Novel

McCLELLAND, M(ary) G(reenaway), 1853-1895

09872   *Madame Silva.* Cassell, New York, 1888, 320p,
        Cloth, Coll.

McCOMAS, J(esse) FRANCIS, 1910-1978

09873   *Special wonder; the Anthony Boucher memorial*
        anthology of fantasy and science fiction.
        Random House, New York, 1970, 410p, Cloth,
        Anth.
09873A retitled: *Special wonder, volume 1; the An-*
        thony Boucher memorial anthology of fantasy
        and science fiction. Beagle, New York,
        1971, 235p, Paper, Anth. [abridged]
09873B retitled: *Special wonder, volume 2; the An-*
        thony Boucher memorial anthology of fantasy
        and science fiction. Beagle, New York,
        1971, 256p, Paper, Anth. [abridged; 09873A
        and 09873B together comprise the original
        volume]

with Anthony Boucher:

01654   *The best from Fantasy and science fiction.*
        Little, Brown, Boston, 1952, 214p, Cloth,
        Anth.
01655   *The best from Fantasy and science fiction,*
        second series. Little, Brown, Boston,
        1953, 270p, Cloth, Anth.
01656   *The best from Fantasy and science fiction,*
        third series. Doubleday, Garden City,
        1954, 252p, Cloth, Anth.

with Raymond J. Healy:

06999   *Adventures in time and space; an anthology*
        of modern science-fiction stories. Random
        House, New York, 1946, 997p, Cloth, Anth.
06999A retitled: *Selections from Adventures in time*
        and space. Pennant, New York, 1954, 200p,
        Paper, Anth. [abridged]
06999B retitled: *More adventures in time and space;*
        selections from Adventures in time and space.
        Bantam, New York, 1955, 142p, Paper, Anth.
        [abridged]
06999C retitled: *Famous science-fiction stories;*
        adventures in time and space. Modern Lib-
        rary, New York, 1957, 997p, Cloth, Anth.

McCORD, P(eter) B., d. 1908

09874   *Wolf; the memoirs of a cave-dweller.* B. W.
        Dodge, New York, 1906, 133p, Cloth, Novel

McCOWAN, ARCHIBALD

09875   *The billionaire; a peep into the future.* Jen-
        kins & McCowan, New York, 1900, 79p, Paper,
        Novel

McCOY, JOHN

09876   *A prophetic romance; Mars to Earth*, by the
        Lord Commissioner. Arena Publishing Co.,
        Boston, 1896, 283p, Cloth, Novel

McCUTCHAN, PHILIP (Donald), 1920-   [biography
included]

09877   *The all-purpose bodies; a 'Commander Shaw'*
        novel. George G. Harrap, London, 1969, 205p,
        Cloth, Novel [Commander Shaw #11]
09878   *Bowering's breakwater.* George G. Harrap, Lon-
        don, 1964, 248p, Cloth, Novel
09879   *The bright red businessmen; a 'Commander Shaw'*
        novel. George G. Harrap, London, 1969, 224p,
        Cloth, Novel [Commander Shaw #10]
09880   *The day of the Coastwatch.* George G. Harrap,
        London, 1968, 207p, Cloth, Novel
09881   *Hartinger's mouse; a Commander Shaw novel.*
        George G. Harrap, London, 1970, 222p, Cloth,
        Novel [Commander Shaw #12]
09882   *REDCAP; a Commander Shaw novel.* George G. Har-
        rap, London, 1961, 283p, Cloth, Novel [Com-
        mander Shaw #2]
09883   *The screaming dead balloons; a 'Commander Shaw'*
        novel. George G. Harrap, London, 1968, 224p,
        Cloth, Novel [Commander Shaw #9]
09884   *Skyprobe; a "Commander Shaw" novel.* George
        G. Harrap, London, 1966, 208p, Cloth, Novel
        [Commander Shaw #8]
09885   *A time for survival.* George G. Harrap, London,
        1966, 207p, Cloth, Novel

McCUTCHEON, GEORGE BARR, 1866-1928

09886   *West wind drift.* Dodd, Mead, New York, 1920,
        368p, Cloth, Novel

McDANIEL, DAVID (Edward), 1939-1977 [biogra-
phy included]

09887   *The arsenal out of time.* Ace, New York, 1967,
        156p, Paper, Novel
09888   *The man from U.N.C.L.E., number 4; The Dagger*
        affair. Ace, New York, 1965, 159p, Paper,
        Tele. [Man from U.N.C.L.E. #4 (U.S. edition);
        Man from U.N.C.L.E. #6 (U.K. edition)]
09889   *The man from U.N.C.L.E., number 6; The vampire*
        affair. Ace, New York, 1966, 159p, Paper,
        Tele. [Man from U.N.C.L.E. #6 (U.S. edition);
        Man from U.N.C.L.E. #9 (U.K. edition)]
09890   *The man from U.N.C.L.E., number 8; The monster*
        wheel affair. Ace, New York, 1967, 159p,
        Paper, Tele. [Man from U.N.C.L.E. #8 (U.S.
        edition); Man from U.N.C.L.E. #12 (U.K. edi-
        tion)]
09891   *The man from U.N.C.L.E., number 13; The Rain-*
        bow affair. Ace, New York, 1967, 157p,
        Paper, Tele. [Man from U.N.C.L.E. #13]
09892   *The man from U.N.C.L.E., number 15; The utopia*
        affair. Ace, New York, 1968, 157p, Paper,
        Tele. [Man from U.N.C.L.E. #15]

McDANIEL, DAVID (cont.)

09893   *The man from U.N.C.L.E., number 17; The hollow crown affair.* Ace, New York, 1969, 156p, Paper, Tele. [Man from U.N.C.L.E. #17]

09894   *The prisoner #2; Number Two.* Ace, New York, 1969, 158p, Paper, Tele. [Prisoner #2]

McDERMOT, MURTAGH, pseud.

09895   *A trip to the Moon by Mr. Murtagh McDermot, containing some observations and reflections made by him during his stay in that planet upon the manners of the inhabitants.* J. Roberts, Dublin, 1728, 96p, Cloth, Novel

McDONALD, BERNARD
    see: MACDONNAILL, BRIAN

McDONALD, EDWARD RICHARD, 1873-   , with Raymond Leger as Raymond McDonald

08803   *The mad scientist; a tale of the future, with which is incorporated a secret cipher, for the best solution of which the publishers offer $1,000.* Cochrane Publishing Co., New York, 1908, 242p, Cloth, Novel

McDONALD, RAYMOND, pseud.
    see: McDONALD, EDWARD and LEGER, RAYMOND

McDOUGALL, WALTER H(ugh), 1858-1938

09896   *The hidden city; or, The strange adventure of Eric Gilbert.* Cassell Publishing Co., New York, 1891, 321p, Cloth, Novel

McELHINEY, GAILE CHURCHILL

09897   *Into the dawn.* DeVorss, Los Angeles, 1945, 177p, Cloth, Novel

McGARRY, JIM

09898   *Irish tales of terror.* Fontana, London, 1971, 158p, Paper, Anth.

McGAUGHY, DUDLEY DEAN
    see: OWEN, DEAN

McGHAN, BARRY (Robert), 1939-   [*biography included*]

09899   *An index to science fiction book reviews in Astounding/Analog, 1949-1969; Fantasy and science fiction, 1949-1969; Galaxy, 1950-1969.* SFRA Miscellaneous Publication, College Station, TX, 1973, 88p, Paper, Nonf.

09900   *Science fiction and fantasy pseudonyms.* Howard DeVore, Dearborn, Mich., 1971, 34p, Paper, Nonf.

09901   *Science fiction and fantasy pseudonyms, with 1973 supplement.* Misfit Press, Dearborn, Mich., 1973, 65p, Paper, Nonf.

with Elizabeth Calkins:

02454   *Teaching tomorrow; a handbook of science fiction for teachers.* Pflaum/Standard, Dayton, OH, 1972, 103p, Paper, Nonf.

McGOWEN, TOM [Thomas McGowen, 1927-   ] [*biography included*]

09902   *Sir MacHinery.* Follett Publishing Co., Chicago, 1970, 157p, Cloth, Novel

McGRADY, T(homas), 1863-

09903   *Beyond the black ocean.* Charles H. Kerr, Chicago, 1901, 304p, Cloth, Novel

McGREGOR, R(eginald) J(ames)

09904   *The monkey-god's secret; a story of adventure.* Hutchinson, London, 1924, 254p, Cloth, Novel

McGUIRE, JOHN J(oseph), 1917-   , with H. Beam Piper

09905   *Crisis in 2140.* Ace Double, New York, 1957, 120p, Paper, Novel

09906   *A planet for Texans.* Ace Double, New York, 1958, 101p, Paper, Novel

McHARGUE, GEORGESS [*biography included*]

09907   *Hot and cold running cities; an anthology of science fiction.* Holt, Rinehart & Winston, New York, 1974, 245p, Cloth, Anth.

McHUGH, VINCENT, 1904-

09908   *Caleb Catlum's America; the enlivening wonders of his adventures, voyages, discoveries, loves, hoaxes, bombast, and rigmaroles in all parts of America, from his birth in 1798 almost to the present year, told by himself; together with a surprising account of his family, from Eric the Red Catlum's discovery of America to their vanishment in the country of the Great Cave, including the tale of the man sawed up for firewood, the rape of the temperate zone, and a thousand tricks of lovemaking.* Stackpole Sons, New York, 1936, 340p, Cloth, Novel

09909   *I am thinking of my darling; an adventure story.* Simon & Schuster, New York, 1943, 294p, Cloth, Novel

McILRAITH, FRANK, with Roy Connolly

03312   *Invasion from the air; a prophetic novel.* Grayson & Grayson, London, 1934, 320p, Cloth, Novel

McILWAIN, DAVID
    see: MAINE, CHARLES ERIC

McILWRAITH, MAUREEN MOLLIE
see: HUNTER, MOLLIE

McINNES, GRAHAM (Campbell), 1912- [biography included]

09910 Lost island; an adventure. Macmillan, London, 1954, 230p, Cloth, Novel

McINTOSH, J. T., pseud. [James Murdoch Macgregor, 1925-] [biography included]

09911 Born leader. Doubleday, Garden City, 1954, 221p, Cloth, Novel
09911A retitled: Worlds apart. Avon, New York, 1958, 189p, Paper, Novel
09912 The cosmic spies. Robert Hale, London, 1972, 192p, Cloth, Novel
09913 The fittest. Doubleday, Garden City, 1955, 192p, Cloth, Novel
09913A retitled: The rule of the pagbeasts. Crest, Greenwich, Conn., 1956, 192p, Paper, Novel
09914 Flight from rebirth. Avon, New York, 1971, 160p, Paper, Novel
09915 Galactic takeover bid. Robert Hale, London, 1973, 190p, Cloth, Novel
09916 The Million Cities. Pyramid, New York, 1963, 141p, Paper, Novel
09917 The Noman way. Digit, London, 1964, 158p, Paper, Novel
09918 One in three hundred. Doubleday, Garden City, 1954, 223p, Cloth, Novel
09919 Out of chaos. Digit, London, 1965, 159p, Paper, Novel
       The rule of the pagbeasts. [see 09913A]
09920 Six gates from Limbo. Michael Joseph, London, 1968, 175p, Cloth, Novel
       Snow White and the giants. [see 09922A]
09921 The space sorcerers. Robert Hale, London, 1972, 183p, Cloth, Novel
09921A retitled: The suiciders. Avon, New York, 1973, 159p, Paper, Novel
09922 Time for a change. Michael Joseph, London, 1967, 183p, Cloth, Novel
09922A retitled: Snow White and the giants. Avon, New York, 1968, 159p, Paper, Novel
09923 Transmigration. Avon, New York, 1970, 176p, Paper, Novel
09924 200 years to Christmas. Ace Double, New York, 1961, 81p, Paper, Novel
09925 World out of mind. Doubleday, Garden City, 1953, 222p, Cloth, Novel
       Worlds apart. [see 09911A]

McINTYRE, MARGARET A.

09926 The cave boy of the age of stone. D. Appleton, New York, 1907, 131p, Cloth, Novel

McIVER, G. (M.)

09927 Neuroomia; a new continent. G. Robertson, London, 1894, 307p, Cloth, Novel

McIVOR, ALLAN, pseud.

09928 The overlord; the story of the peons of Canada. William Ritchie, New York, 1904, 423p, Cloth, Novel

McKEAG, ERNEST LIONEL
see: KING, JOHN

McKECHNIE, N(eil) K(enneth), 1873-

09929 Heir of all the ages; the family tree of Mr. Smith. Bobbs-Merrill, Indianapolis, 1926, 300p, Cloth, Novel

McKENNA, RICHARD (Milton), 1913-1964 [biography included]

09930 Casey Agonistes, and other science fiction and fantasy stories. Harper & Row, New York, 1973, 150p, Cloth, Coll.

McKENNA, STEPHEN, 1888-1967 [biography included]

09931 Beyond Hell; a novel. Chapman & Hall, London, 1931, 353p, Cloth, Novel
09932 The oldest god; a novel. Thornton Butterworth, London, 1926, 350p, Cloth, Novel
09933 The sixth sense; a novel. Chapman & Hall, London, 1915, 307p, Cloth, Novel
09934 Superstition; a novel. Hutchinson, London, 1932, 288p, Cloth, Novel

McKENZIE, ELLEN KINDT

09935 Drujienna's harp. E. P. Dutton, New York, 1971, 307p, Cloth, Novel
09936 Taash and the jesters. Holt, Rinehart & Winston, New York, 1968, 234p, Cloth, Novel

McKESSON, CHARLES L.

09937 Under Pike's Peak; or, Mahalma, child of the fire father. F. Tennyson Neely, New York, 1898, 302p, Cloth, Novel

McKILLIP, PATRICIA A(nne), 1948- [biography included]

09938 The forgotten beasts of Eld. Atheneum, New York, 1974, 217p, Cloth, Novel
09939 The house on Parchment Street. Atheneum, New York, 1973, 190p, Cloth, Novel

McKINSTRY, LOHR, with Robert Weinberg

09940 The hero-pulp index. Robert Weinberg, Hillside, NJ, 1970, 54p, Paper, Nonf.

McLANDBURGH, FLORENCE, 1850-

09941 The automaton ear, and other sketches. Jansen, McClurg, Chicago, 1876, 282p, Cloth, Coll.

McLAREN, F. V.

09942 I told you so! a romance of to-day, in three parts: aspiration--concentration--realisation. C. W. Daniel, London, 1937, 304p, Cloth, Novel

McLAREN, JACK, 1887-1954

09943   *The devil of the depths; a strange story of
          the south seas.* Philip Allan, London, 1935,
          256p, Cloth, Novel
09944   *Stories of fear.* Pendulum Publications, Lon-
          don, 1947, 64p, Cloth, Coll.

McLAREN, Mrs. JACK [Ada Moore McLaren]

09945   *Which hath been; a novel of reincarnation.*
          Cecil Palmer, London, 1926, 318p, Cloth,
          Novel

McLAUGHLIN, DEAN (Benjamin Jr.), 1931-   [*biography included*]

09946   *Dome world; a science-fiction novel.* Pyramid,
          New York, 1962, 159p, Paper, Novel
09947   *The fury from Earth.* Pyramid, New York, 1963,
          192p, Paper, Novel
09948   *The man who wanted stars.* Lancer, New York,
          1965, 222p, Paper, Novel

McLAUGHLIN, N(athan) MONROE

09949   *The last man; a novel.* Neale Co., Washington,
          1900, 221p, Cloth, Novel

McMAHON, JEREMIAH

09950   *Devil's channel.* Pyramid, New York, 1972,
          174p, Paper, Novel

McMAHON, THOMAS PATRICK

09951   *The Hubschmann effect.* Simon & Schuster, New
          York, 1973, 167p, Cloth, Novel

McMASTERS, WILLIAM H(enry)

09952   *Blind; the story of the world tragedy, by
          David Glenn MacKenzie, as seen through the
          eyes of William H. McMasters.* Stratford
          Co., Boston, 1934, 218p, Cloth, Novel
09953   *Revolt; an American novel.* David D. Nicker-
          son, Boston, 1919, 281p, Cloth, Novel

McMICHAEL, R. DANIEL, 1925-

09954   *The journal of David Q. Little.* Arlington
          House, New Rochelle, NY, 1967, 527p, Cloth,
          Novel

McMURDIE, ANNIE LAURIE

09955   *Nightmare hall.* Lancer, New York, 1973, 303p,
          Paper, Novel

McNALLY, RAYMOND T., 1931-   [*biography included*]

09956   *A clutch of vampires, these being among the
          best from history and literature.* New York

Graphic Society, Greenwich, Conn., 1974,
255p, Cloth, Anth. [includes some nonf.]

McNAUGHTON, CHARLES Jr.

09957   *Mindblower.* Essex House, North Hollywood,
          1969, 272p, Paper, Novel

McNAUGHTON, MILDRED

09958   *Four great oaks.* Creative Age Press, New York,
          1946, 327p, Cloth, Novel

McNEER, MAY (Yonge), 1902-   [*biography included*], with Lynd Ward

09959   *Prince Bantam, being the adventures of Yoshit-
          sune the Brave, and his faithful henchman
          great Benkei of the western pagoda.* Macmil-
          lan, New York, 1929, 231p, Cloth, Novel

McNEIL, (Henry) EVERETT, 1862-1929

09960   *The lost nation.* E. P. Dutton, New York,
          1918, 335p, Cloth, Novel [Dick Orson #3]

McNEILE, H(erman) C(yril), 1888-1937

09961   *Guardians of the treasure.* Crime Club, Double-
          day, Doran, Garden City, 1931, 320p, Cloth,
          Novel

as Sapper:

09962   *The island of terror.* Musson Book Co., Toronto
          1931, 320p, Cloth, Novel

McNEILLIE, JOHN
      see: NIALL, IAN

McNEILLY, WILFRED GLASSFORD
      see: BAKER, W. HOWARD

McNELLY, WILLIS E(verett), 1920-   [*biography
included*]

09963   *Science fiction: the academic awakening.* CEA
          Chap Book, Shreveport, LA, 1974, 59p, Paper,
          Nonf. Anth.

with Jane Hipolito:

07235   *Mars, we love you; tales of Mars, men, and
          Martians.* Doubleday, Garden City, 1971,
          332p, Cloth, Anth.

with Leon E. Stover:

09964   *Above the human landscape; a social science
          fiction anthology.* Goodyear Publishing Co.,
          Pacific Palisades, CA, 1972, 387p, Cloth,
          Anth.

M'CRIB, THEOPHILUS, pseud. [Henry Boyle Lee]

09965   *Kennaquhair; a narrative of utopian travel.*
          Chapman & Hall, London, 1872, 335p, Cloth,
          Novel

McSHANE, MARK
    see: LOVELL, MARC

McSPADDEN, J(oseph) WALTER, 1874-1960

09966 *Famous ghost stories.* Thomas Y. Crowell, New
       York, 1918, 302p, Cloth, Anth.
09967 *Famous mystery and detective stories.* Blue
       Ribbon, New York, 1938, 639p, Cloth, Anth.
       [includes *Famous mystery stories* and *Famous
       detective stories* (not SF)]
09968 *Famous mystery stories.* Thomas Y. Crowell,
       New York, 1922, 292p, Cloth, Anth.
09969 *Famous psychic and ghost stories.* Blue Rib-
       bon, New York, 1938, 628p, Cloth, Anth.
       [includes *Famous psychic stories* and *Famous
       ghost stories*]
09970 *Famous psychic stories.* Thomas Y. Crowell,
       New York, 1920, 305p, Cloth, Anth.

McWILLIAMS, J(ames) A(loysius), 1882-

09971 *Starman, the stranger from outer space.* Ex-
       position Press, New York, 1958, 143p, Cloth,
       Novel

MEAD, HAROLD (Charles Hugh), 1910-   [*biography included*]

09972 *The bright phoenix.* Michael Joseph, London,
       1955, 303p, Cloth, Novel
09973 *Mary's country.* Michael Joseph, London, 1957,
       288p, Cloth, Novel

MEAD, (Edward) SHEPHERD, 1914-   [*biography
included*]

09974 *The big ball of wax; a story of tomorrow's
       happy world.* Simon & Schuster, New York,
       1954, 246p, Cloth, Novel
09975 *The carefully considered rape of the world;
       a novel about the unspeakable.* Simon &
       Schuster, New York, 1965, 245p, Cloth, Novel
09976 *The magnificent MacInnes.* Farrar, Straus &
       Co., New York, 1949, 255p, Cloth, Novel
09976A retitled: *The sex machine (The magnificent
       MacInnes).* Popular Library, New York,
       1950, 160p, Paper, Novel

MEADE, L. T., pseud. [Elizabeth Thomasina
Smith, 1854-1914]

09977 *The desire of men; an impossibility.* Digby,
       Long, London, 1899, 314p, Cloth, Novel

MEADE, RICHARD, pseud. [Benjamin Leopold Haas,
1926-1977][*biography included*]

09978 *Exile's quest.* Signet, New York, 1970, 190p,
       Paper, Novel [Gray Lands #2]
09979 *The sword of Morning Star.* Signet, New York,
       1969, 144p, Paper, Novel [Gray Lands #1]

MEAGHER, GEORGE E(dward), 1895-

09980 *Tomorrow's horizon; a novel of the world of
       tomorrow.* Dorrance, Philadelphia, 1947,
       136p, Cloth, Novel

MEAGHER, MAUDE

09981 *The green Scamander.* Houghton Mifflin, Boston,
       1933, 298p, Cloth, Novel

MEARS, A(melia) GARLAND

09982 *Mercia, the astronomer royal; a romance.* Simp-
       kin, Marshall, Hamilton, Kent, London, 1895,
       349p, Cloth, Novel

MEARSON, LYON, 1888-1966

09983 *Phantom fingers.* Macaulay, New York, 1927,
       256p, Cloth, Novel

THE MECHANICAL MAN

09984 *The mechanical man.* Stellar Publishing Corp.,
       New York, 1930, 24p, Paper, Anth. [includes
       "The Mechanical Man," by Amelia Reynolds
       Long, and "The Thought Stealer," by Frank
       Bourne]

MECKAUER, WALTER, 1889-

09985 *The Books of the Emperor Wu Ti.* Martin Secker,
       London, 1930, 214p, Cloth, Novel

MEEK, S(terner St.) P(aul), 1894-1972 [*biography included*]

09986 *Arctic bride.* Utopian Publications, London,
       1944, 36p, Paper, Coll.
09987 *The Drums of Tapajos.* Avalon, New York, 1961,
       224p, Cloth, Novel [Troyana #1]
09988 *The monkeys have no tails in Zamboanga.* Wil-
       liam Morrow, New York, 1935, 288p, Cloth,
       Coll.
09989 *Troyana.* Avalon, New York, 1961, 224p, Cloth,
       Novel [Troyana #2]

MEIK, VIVIAN (Bernard), 1895-

09990 *Devils' drums.* Philip Allan, London, 1933,
       252p, Cloth, Coll. [Geoffrey Aylett #1]
09991 *Veils of fear.* Philip Allan, London, 1934,
       228p, Cloth, Novel [Geoffrey Aylett #2]

MEINHOLD, (Johann) WILHELM, 1797-1851

09992 *Sidonia the sorceress, the supposed destroyer
       of the whole reigning ducal House of Pomera-
       nia.* Wiley & Putnam, New York, 1845, 180p,
       Cloth, Novel

MELDE, G. R., pseud.

09993 *Pacific advance.* Curtis Books, London, 1954,
         159p, Cloth, Novel

MELLING, LEONARD, 1913-

09994 *First man on Mars.* Torch Publishing, Manches-
         ter, 1971, 151p, Cloth, Novel

MELLOWS, SUZANNE

09995 *The sex-ray.* Liverpool Library, Sausalito,
         CA, 1973, 181p, Paper, Novel

MELTZER, DAVID, 1937-   [*biography included*]

09996 *The Agency.* Essex House, North Hollywood,
         1968, 160p, Paper, Novel [Agency #1]
09997 *The agent.* Essex House, North Hollywood,
         1968, 160p, Paper, Novel [Agency #2]
09998 *Brain-plant book 1; Lovely.* Essex House,
         North Hollywood, 1969, 159p, Paper, Novel
         [Brain-Plant #1]
09999 *Brain-plant book 2; Healer.* Essex House,
         North Hollywood, 1969, 176p, Paper, Novel
         [Brain-Plant #2]
10000 *Brain-plant book 3; Out.* Essex House, North
         Hollywood, 1969, 192p, Paper, Novel [Brain-
         Plant #3]
10001 *Brain-plant book 4; Glue factory.* Essex House,
         North Hollywood, 1969, 192p, Paper, Novel
         [Brain-Plant #4]
10002 *How many blocks in the pile?* Essex House,
         North Hollywood, 1968, 160p, Paper, Novel
         [Agency #3]

MELVILLE, G. J. WHYTE-
      see: WHYTE-MELVILLE, G. J.

A MEMBER OF THE LEGITIMIST CLUB, pseud.

10003 *The Jacobite doctors; a story of the second
         restoration.* Box & Gillham, Egham, UK,
         1896, 16p, Paper, Story

MEMOIRS OF A CERTAIN ISLAND ADJACENT TO THE
KINGDOM OF UTOPIA
      see: HAYWOOD, ELIZA F.

MEMOIRS OF EUROPE
      see: MANLEY, MARY

THE MEMOIRS OF SIGR. GAUDENTIO di LUCCA
      see: BERINGTON, SIMON

MEMOIRS OF THE TWENTIETH CENTURY
      see: MADDEN, SAMUEL

MEMOIRS OF THE YEAR TWO THOUSAND FIVE HUNDRED
      see: MERCIER, LOUIS-SEBASTIEN

MEN AGAINST THE STARS

10004 *Men against the stars.* American Science Fic-
         tion, Sydney, 1954, 34p, Paper, Anth.

MENDELSOHN, FELIX Jr., 1906-   [*biography included*]

10005 *Club Tycoon sends man to Moon.* Book Company
         of America, Beverly Hills, CA , 1965, 122p,
         Paper, Novel
10006 *Superbaby.* Nash Publishing, Los Angeles,
         1969, 211p, Cloth, Novel

MENDELSSOHN, PETER DE
      see: DE MENDELSSOHN, PETER

MENDÈS, CATULLE (Abraham), 1841-1909

10007 *Number 56, and other stories.* T. Werner Laurie
         London, 1928, 240p, Cloth, Coll.

MENDES, H(enry) PEREIRA, 1852-1937

10008 *Looking ahead; twentieth century happenings.*
         F. Tennyson Neely, London, 1899, 381p, Cloth,
         Novel

MENDHAM, CLEMENT A.

10009 *The buried mystery.* Digby, Long, London, 1898,
         308p, Cloth, Novel

MENEN, (Salvator) AUBREY (Clarence), 1912-
[*biography included*]

10010 *The fig tree.* Chatto & Windus, London, 1959,
         220p, Cloth, Novel
10011 *The prevalence of witches; a novel.* Chatto &
         Windus, London, 1947, 271p, Cloth, Novel
10012 *Rama retold.* Chatto & Windus, London, 1954,
         246p, Cloth, Novel
10012A retitled: *Ramayana.* Charles Scribner's Sons,
         New York, 1954, 276p, Cloth, Novel
10013 *SheLa; a satire.* Random House, New York, 1962
         173p, Cloth, Novel

MENTOR, LILLIAN FRANCES

10014 *The day of Resis.* G. W. Dillingham, New York,
         1897, 398p, Cloth, Novel

MERAK, A. J., pseud.
      see: GLASBY, JOHN

MERCER, ARCHIE [Archibald Henry Mercer]

10015 *The meadows of fantasy (the story of a golden
         age).* Mercatorial Publication, Bristol,
         1965, 138p, Paper, Novel

MERCER, CECIL WILLIAM
      see: YATES, DORNFORD

MERCER, HENRY C(hapman), 1856-1930

10016 *November night tales; a book of short stories.*
Walter Neale, New York, 1928, 244p, Cloth,
Coll.

MERCIER, LOUIS-SÉBASTIEN, 1740-1814

10017 *Memoirs of the year two thousand five hundred.*
G. Robinson, London, 1772, 2vol, Cloth,
Novel [published anonymously]
10017A retitled: *Astraea's return; or, The halcyon
days of France in the year 2440; a dream.*
Harriot Augusta Freeman, London, 1797, 308p,
Cloth, Novel

MERCIER, MARIO

10018 *Jeanne's journal.* Heinrich Hanau Publications,
London, 1972, 148p, Cloth, Novel

MEREDITH, EDGAR

10019 *Our stranger; a kinemato-romance.* Grayson &
Grayson, London, 1936, 407p, Cloth, Novel

MEREDITH, ELLIS, 1865-

10020 *The master-knot of human fate.* Little, Brown,
Boston, 1901, 309p, Cloth, Novel

MEREDITH, GEOFFREY

10021 *The Radium Rebels.* Thomas Nelson & Sons,
London, 1946, 252p, Cloth, Novel

MEREDITH, GEORGE, 1828-1909

10022 *The shaving of Shagpat; an Arabian entertainment.* Chapman & Hall, London, 1856, 384p,
Cloth, Novel
10022A retitled: *The story of Bhanavar the beautiful.* Archibald Constable, London, 1900,
135p, Cloth, Novel [abridged]

MEREDITH, JAMES CREED (Jr.), d. 1942

10023 *The rainbow in the valley.* Browne & Nolan,
Dublin, 1939, 258p, Cloth, Novel

MEREDITH, OWEN, pseud.
see: LYTTON, ROBERT BULWER

MEREDITH, RICHARD C., 1937-

10024 *At the narrow passage.* G. P. Putnam's Sons,
New York, 1973, 256p, Cloth, Novel
10025 *The sky is filled with ships.* Ballantine,
New York, 1969, 184p, Paper, Novel
10026 *We all died at Breakaway Station.* Ballantine,
New York, 1969, 244p, Paper, Novel

MERLE, ROBERT (Jean Georges), 1908-

10027 *The day of the dolphin.* Simon & Schuster, New
York, 1969, 320p, Cloth, Novel
10028 *Malevil.* Simon & Schuster, New York, 1974,
575p, Cloth, Novel

MERLINO, MERLIN MESMER, pseud. [Donald G. Car-
penter]

10029 *The treacherous time machine.* Vantage Press,
New York, 1973, 170p, Cloth, Novel

MERRICK, WILLISTON, pseud. [Williston Merrick
Ford, 1886-   ]

10030 *Quest; an agelong romance.* Exposition Press,
New York, 1953, 223p, Cloth, Novel

MERRIL, (Josephine) JUDITH, 1923-   [*biography included*]

The best of sci-fi. [see 10051B]
The best of sci-fi--two. [see 10048B]
The best of sci-fi, no. 4. [see 10034B]
The best of sci-fi 5. [see 10037B]
The best of sci-fi 12. [see 10047A]
The best of science fiction 9. [see 10040C]
The best of science fiction 10. [see 10053B]
10031 *Beyond human ken; twenty-one startling stories
of science fiction and fantasy.* Random House,
New York, 1952, 334p, Cloth, Anth.
10031A retitled: *Selections from Beyond human ken.*
Pennant, New York, 1954, 248p, Paper, Anth.
[abridged]
10032 *Beyond the barriers of space and time.* Random
House, New York, 1954, 295p, Cloth, Anth.
10033 *Daughters of Earth.* Victor Gollancz, London,
1968, 256p, Cloth, Coll.
8th annual edition, the year's best S-F. [see
10034A]
10034 *The 8th annual of the year's best SF.* Simon &
Schuster, New York, 1963, 382p, Cloth, Anth.
10034A retitled: *8th annual edition, the year's best
S-F.* Dell, New York, 1964, 382p, Paper,
Anth.
10034B retitled: *The best of sci-fi, no. 4.* Mayflower-Dell, London, 1965, 382p, Paper, Anth.
10035 *11th annual edition, the year's best S-F.* Delacorte Press, New York, 1966, 384p, Cloth,
Anth.
10036 *England swings SF; stories of speculative fiction.* Doubleday, Garden City, 1968, 406p,
Cloth, Anth.
10036A retitled: *The space-time journal.* Panther,
London, 1972, 206p, Paper, Anth. [abridged]
10037 *The 5th annual of the year's best S-F.* Simon
& Schuster, New York, 1960, 320p, Cloth,
Anth.
10037A retitled: *The year's best S-F, 5th annual edition.* Dell, New York, 1961, 320p, Paper,
Anth.
10037B retitled: *The best of sci-fi 5.* Mayflower-
Dell, London, 1966, 317p, Paper, Anth.
10038 *Galaxy of ghouls.* Lion, New York, 1955, 192p,
Paper, Anth.
10038A retitled: *Off the beaten orbit.* Pyramid, New
York, 1959, 192p, Paper, Anth.
10039 *Human??????* Lion, New York, 1954, 190p, Paper,
Anth.

MERRIL, JUDITH (cont.)

9th annual edition, the year's best S-F. [see 10040A]

10040   *The 9th annual of the year's best SF.* Simon & Schuster, New York, 1964, 384p, Cloth, Anth.

10040A retitled: *9th annual edition, the year's best S-F.* Dell, New York, 1965, 384p, Paper, Anth.

10040B retitled: *9th annual S-F.* Mayflower-Dell, London, 1967, 381p, Paper, Anth.

10040C retitled: *The best of science fiction 9.* Mayflower, London, 1970, 381p, Paper, Anth.

Off the beaten orbit. [see 10038A]

10041   *Out of bounds; seven stories.* Pyramid, New York, 1960, 160p, Paper, Coll.

10042   *SF: the best of the best.* Delacorte Press, New York, 1967, 438p, Cloth, Anth.

10042A retitled: *SF: the best of the best, part one.* Mayflower, London, 1970, 203p, Paper, Anth. [abridged]

10042B retitled: *SF: the best of the best, part two.* Mayflower, London, 1970, 221p, Paper, Anth. [abridged; 10042A and 10042B together comprise the original volume]

SF: '57; the year's greatest science-fiction and fantasy. [see 10045A]

SF: '58; the year's greatest science fiction and fantasy. [see 10046A]

10043   *SF: '59; the year's greatest science-fiction and fantasy.* Gnome Press, Hicksville, NY, 1959, 256p, Cloth, Anth.

10043A retitled: *SF; the year's greatest science-fiction and fantasy, fourth annual volume.* Dell, New York, 1959, 256p, Paper, Anth.

10044   *S-F; the year's greatest science-fiction and fantasy stories and novelettes.* Dell, New York, 1956, 352p, Paper, Anth.

10045   *SF; the year's greatest science-fiction and fantasy, second annual volume.* Dell, New York, 1957, 320p, Paper, Anth.

10045A retitled: *SF: '57; the year's greatest science-fiction and fantasy.* Gnome Press, New York, 1957, 320p, Cloth, Anth.

10046   *SF; the year's greatest science-fiction and fantasy, third annual volume.* Dell, New York, 1958, 255p, Paper, Anth.

10046A retitled: *SF: '58; the year's greatest science fiction and fantasy.* Gnome Press, Hicksville, NY, 1958, 255p, Cloth, Anth.

SF; the year's greatest science-fiction and fantasy, fourth annual volume. [see 10043A]

10047   *SF12.* Delacorte Press, New York, 1968, 384p, Cloth, Anth.

10047A retitled: *The best of sci-fi 12.* Mayflower, London, 1970, 364p, Paper, Anth.

Selections from Beyond human ken. [see 10031A]

7th annual edition, the year's best S-F. [see 10048A]

10048   *The 7th annual of the year's best S-F.* Simon & Schuster, New York, 1962, 399p, Cloth, Anth.

10048A retitled: *7th annual edition, the year's best S-F.* Dell, New York, 1963, 399p, Paper, Anth.

10048B retitled: *The best of sci-fi--two.* Mayflower-Dell, London, 1964, 399p, Paper, Anth.

10049   *Shadow on the hearth.* Doubleday, Garden City, 1950, 277p, Cloth, Novel

10050   *Shot in the dark.* Bantam, New York, 1950, 310p, Paper, Anth.

6th annual edition, the year's best S-F. [see 10051A]

10051   *The 6th annual of the year's best S-F.* Simon & Schuster, New York, 1961, 384p, Cloth, Anth.

10051A retitled: *6th annual edition, the year's best S-F.* Dell, New York, 1962, 384p, Paper, Anth.

10051B retitled: *The best of sci-fi.* Mayflower-Dell, London, 1963, 384p, Paper, Anth.

The space-time journal. [see 10036A]

10052   *Survival ship, and other stories.* Kakabeka Publishing Co., Toronto, 1973, 229p, Paper, Coll.

10053   *10th annual edition, the year's best SF.* Delacorte Press, New York, 1965, 400p, Cloth, Anth.

10053A retitled: *10th annual S-F.* Mayflower-Dell, London, 1967, 382p, Paper, Anth.

10053B retitled: *The best of science fiction 10.* Mayflower, London, 1970, 382p, Paper, Anth.

10054   *The tomorrow people; a science-fiction novel.* Pyramid, New York, 1960, 192p, Paper, Novel

The year's best S-F, 5th annual edition. [see 10037A]

with C. M. Kornbluth as Cyril Judd:

08442   *Gunner Cade.* Simon & Schuster, New York, 1952, 218p, Cloth, Novel

08442A *Gunner Cade*, by C. M. Kornbluth and Judith Merril. Dell, New York, 1969, 160p, Paper, Novel

08443   *Outpost Mars; a science-fiction novel.* Abelard Press, New York, 1952, 268p, Cloth, Novel

08443A retitled: *Sin in space; an expose of the scarlet planet.* Galaxy Publishing Corp., New York, 1961, 190p, Paper, Novel

MERRILL, ALBERT ADAMS

10055   *The great awakening; the story of the twenty-second century.* George Book Publishing Co., Boston, 1899, 345p, Cloth, Novel

MERRILL, JEAN (Fairbanks), 1923-   [*biography included*]

10056   *The pushcart war.* W. R. Scott, New York, 1964, 222p, Cloth, Novel

MERRILL, STUART, 1863-1915

10057   *Pastels in prose.* Harper & Bros., New York, 1890, 268p, Cloth, Anth.

MERRIMAN, EFFIE
see: FIFIELD, Mrs. JAMES

MERRITT, A(braham), 1882-1943

10058   *Burn witch burn!* Liveright Publishers, New York, 1933, 301p, Cloth, Novel [Dr. Lowell #1]

10059   *Creep, shadow!* Crime Club, Doubleday, Doran, Garden City, 1934, 301p, Cloth, Novel [Dr. Lowell #2]

10059A retitled: *Creep, shadow, creep!* Methuen, London, 1935, 287p, Cloth, Novel [Dr. Lowell #2]

MERRITT, A. (cont.)

10060   *The drone man.* no publisher, no place, no
        date, 13p, Paper, Story
10061   *Dwellers in the mirage.* Liveright Publishers,
        New York, 1932, 295p, Cloth, Novel
10062   *Dwellers in the mirage; and, The face in the
        abyss.* Liveright Publishing Corp., New
        York, 1953, 635p, Cloth, Coll.
10063   *The face in the abyss.* Horace Liveright, New
        York, 1931, 343p, Cloth, Novel
10064   *The fox woman, & other stories.* Avon, New
        York, 1949, 157p, Paper, Coll.
10065   *The Metal Monster.* Avon, New York, 1946,
        203p, Paper, Novel [Dr. Goodwin #2]
10066   *The Moon Pool.* G. P. Putnam's Sons, New York,
        1919, 433p, Cloth, Novel [Dr. Goodwin #1]
10067   *Rhythm of the spheres.* no publisher, no place,
        no date, 23p, Paper, Story
10068   *7 footprints to Satan.* Boni & Liveright, New
        York, 1928, 310p, Cloth, Novel
10069   *Seven footprints to Satan; and, Burn witch
        burn!* Liveright Publishing Corp., New York,
        1952, 533p, Cloth, Coll.
10070   *The Ship of Ishtar.* G. P. Putnam's Sons, New
        York, 1926, 326p, Cloth, Novel
10071   *Three lines of old French.* Bizarre Series,
        Millheim, PA, 1936,   , Paper, Story
10072   *Thru the dragon glass.* ARRA Printers, Jamai-
        ca, NY, 1933, 24p, Paper, Story

with Hannes Bok:

01588   *The black wheel.* New Collector's Group, New
        York, 1947, 115p, Cloth, Novel
01589   *The fox woman; and, The blue pagoda.* New Col-
        lector's Group, Denver, 1946, 109p, Cloth,
        Coll. [includes Merritt's story, *The fox
        woman*, with Bok's sequel, *The blue pagoda*]

MERTENS, KARL R. [published anonymously]

10073   *The woodnymph's song; a rhapsody in words.*
        no publisher, Glendale, CA, 1912, 18p,
        Cloth, Story

MERTINS, GUSTAVE FREDERICK, 1872-

10074   *A watcher of the skies.* Thomas Y. Crowell,
        New York, 1911, 376p, Cloth, Novel

MERTZ, BARBARA
        see: MICHAELS, BARBARA

MERWIN, SAM(uel Kimball) Jr., 1910-

10075   *The house of many worlds.* Doubleday, Garden
        City, 1951, 216p, Cloth, Novel [Elspeth
        Marriner #1]
10076   *Killer to come.* Abelard Press, New York,
        1953, 251p, Cloth, Novel
10077   *Three faces of time.* Ace Double, New York,
        1955, 135p, Paper, Novel [Elspeth Marriner
        #2]
10078   *The time shifters.* Lancer, New York, 1971,
        173p, Paper, Novel
10079   *The White Widows.* Doubleday, Garden City,
        1953, 224p, Cloth, Novel
10079A retitled: *The sex war.* Galaxy Magazine &
        Beacon Books, New York, 1960, 160p, Paper,
        Novel

A MESSAGE FROM A LOST SOUL
        see: ROWEL, M.

MESSMANN, JOHN
        see: NICOLE, CLAUDETTE

METCALF, NORM(an), 1937-

10080   *The index of science fiction magazines, 1951-
        1965.* J. Ben Stark, El Cerrito, CA, 1968,
        253p, Paper, Nonf.

METCALFE, JOHN, 1891-1965

10081   *The feasting dead.* Arkham House, Sauk City,
        1954, 123p, Cloth, Novel
10082   *Judas, and other stories.* Constable, London,
        1931, 303p, Cloth, Coll.
10083   *The smoking leg, and other stories.* Jarrolds,
        London, 1925, 347p, Cloth, Coll.

METCHIM, D. BRIDGMAN-

10084   *Atlantis; the book of the angels.* Swan Sonnen-
        schein, London, 1900, 461p, Cloth, Novel

METLOVA, MARIA
        see: HATHAWAY, LOUISE

MEYER, J(oseph) A., with Alan E. Nourse

10085   *The invaders are coming!* Ace, New York, 1959,
        223p, Paper, Novel

MEYER, JOHN de
        see: de MEYER, JOHN

MEYER, JOHN J(oseph), 1873-1948

10086   *The deer-smellers of Haunted Mountain; the al-
        most unbelieveable experiences of a cerebroic
        hunter in the hills of this world and the
        lowlands of the universe with a gypsy-eyed
        spirit adventurer, humorously tattle-taled.*
        Cerebroscope Co., New York, 1921, 247p,
        Cloth, Novel
10087   *13 seconds that rocked the world; or, The Men-
        tator; a romance of a mankind director in an
        age of certified reason.* Rae D. Henkle,
        New York, 1935, 205p, Cloth, Novel
10088   *Try another world; a saga coursing its way
        through the six adventures of Joe Shaun which
        thrilled the village of Caryldale.* Business
        Bourse, New York, 1942, 256p, Cloth, Novel
10088A retitled: *The immortal tales of Joe Shaun; an
        enchanting artist makes the five immortal
        hopes and dreams of mankind come true; de-
        lightful catnip for the mind.* Caryldale Lib-
        rary, New York, 1944, 256p, Cloth, Novel
10089   *20,000 trails under the universe with the cere-
        broscope; a tale of wonderful adventures.*
        Privately printed, New York, 1917, 144p,
        Cloth, Novel

MEYERS, ROY (Lethbridge), 1910-1974 [*biography included*]

10090 *Daughters of the dolphin*. Ballantine, New York, 1968, 224p, Paper, Novel [Dolphin #2]
10091 *Destiny and the dolphins*. Ballantine, New York, 1969, 210p, Paper, Novel [Dolphin #3]
10092 *Dolphin boy*. Ballantine, New York, 1967, 224p, Paper, Novel [Dolphin #1]
10092A retitled: *The dolphin rider*. Rapp & Whiting, London, 1968, 189p, Cloth, Novel [Dolphin #1]

MEYNELL, ESTHER (Hallam), d. 1955

10093 *Time's door*. Chapman & Hall, London, 1935, 368p, Cloth, Novel; Macmillan, New York 1935, 337p, Cloth, Novel

MEYNELL, LAURENCE (Walter), 1899-

10094 *Storm against the wall*. Hutchinson, London, 1931, 288p, Cloth, Novel

MEYRINK, GUSTAV, 1868-1932

10095 *The Golem*. Victor Gollancz, London, 1928, 288p, Cloth, Novel

M'GUIRE, SEAN

10096 *Beast or man?* Cecil Palmer, London, 1930, 285p, Cloth, Novel
10097 *Spider Island*. Selwyn & Blount, London, 1928, 286p, Cloth, Novel

MIALL, ROBERT, pseud.
    see: BURKE, JOHN

MIAN, MARY (Lawrence)

10098 *The merry miracle*. Houghton Mifflin, Boston, 1949, 132p, Cloth, Novel
10099 *Take three witches*. Houghton Mifflin, Boston, 1971, 279p, Cloth, Novel

MICHAEL, CECIL, 1909-

10100 *Round trip to Hell in a flying saucer*. Vantage Press, New York, 1955, 61p, Cloth, Novel

MICHAELIS, RICHARD (C.), 1839-1909

10101 *Looking further forward; an answer to Looking backward, by Edward Bellamy*. Rand, McNally, Chicago, 1890, 123p, Paper, Novel [a sequel to Bellamy's novel]
10101A retitled: *A sequel to Looking backward; or, "Looking further forward."* William Reeves, London, 1891, 110p, Paper, Novel [a sequel to Bellamy's novel]

MICHAELS, BARBARA, pseud. [Barbara Mertz, 1927-   ] [*biography included*]

10102 *Ammie, come home*. Meredith Press, New York, 1968, 252p, Cloth, Novel
10103 *The crying child*. Dodd, Mead, New York, 1971 273p, Cloth, Novel
10104 *The dark on the other side*. Dodd, Mead, New York, 1970, 250p, Cloth, Novel
10105 *House of many shadows*. Dodd, Mead, New York, 1974, 244p, Cloth, Novel
10106 *Prince of darkness*. Meredith Press, New York 1969, 230p, Cloth, Novel
10107 *Witch*. Dodd, Mead, New York, 1973, 274p, Cloth, Novel

MICHAUD, A(lfred) C(harles), 1876-

10108 *Our coming world*. World Publications Press, Philadelphia, 1951, 162p, Cloth, Novel

MICHEL, (Milton) SCOTT, 1916-   [*biography included*]

10109 *Journey into limbo; a novel of intimate adventure*. Liveright Publishing Corp., New York 1962, 303p, Cloth, Novel

MICHELMORE, REG

10110 *An adventure in Venus*. Stellar Publishing Corp., New York, 1929, 24p, Paper, Story

MICHELSON, MIRIAM, 1870-1942

10111 *The awakening of Zojas*. Doubleday, Page, New York, 1910, 268p, Cloth, Coll.

MIDDLETON, A. SAFRONI-
    see: SAFRONI-MIDDLETON, A.

MIDDLETON, JOHN B.

10112 *The God of this world; a story for the times*. Kegan Paul, Trench, Trubner, London, 1905, 205p, Cloth, Novel

MIDDLETON, RICHARD (Barham), 1882-1911

10113 *The ghost ship, from The ghost ship and other stories*. Aries Press, Village of Eden, NY, 1926, 22p, Cloth, Story [the collection of stories of the same title is not SF]

MIDNIGHT HORRORS
    see: AUTHOR OF MIDNIGHT HORRORS, FEMALE PILGRIM, &C.

MIERLO, H. A. VAN
    see: VAN MIERLO, H. A.

MIESEL, SANDRA (Louise), 1941- [*biography included*]

10114 *Myth, symbol, & religion in The Lord of the Rings*. TK Graphics, Baltimore, 1973, 73p, Paper, Nonf.

MIGHELS, ELLA STERLING, 1853-1934

10115 *Fairy tale of the white man, told from the gates of sunset*. Pacific Publication Co., San Francisco, 1915, 72p, Paper, Novel

MIGHELS, PHILIP VERRILL, 1869-1911

10116 *The crystal sceptre; a story of adventure*. R. F. Fenno, New York, 1901, 389p, Cloth, Novel
10116A retitled: *The king of the missing links; or, The crystal sceptre*. R. F. Fenno, New York, 1904, 389p, Cloth, Novel

MIKALOWITCH, NICOLAI, pseud. [Nicholas Aloysius Michels]

10117 *The godhood of man; his religious, political, and economic development and the sources of social inequality*. The Author, Chicago, 1899, 150p, Cloth, Novel
10118 *Numa's vision; an allegory*. Nicholas Michels, Publisher, Chicago, 1899, 173p, Cloth, Novel

MIKES, GEORGE [György Mikes, 1912-   ]

10119 *Down with everybody! a cautionary tale for children over twenty-one, and other stories*. Allan Wingate, London, 1951, 142p, Cloth, Coll. [includes some nonf.]

MIKSCH, WILLIAM (F.)

10120 *The Addams family strikes back*. Pyramid, New York, 1965,   , Paper, Tele. [Addams Family #2]

MILDRED, E. W.

10121 *The ghost-house; or, The story of Rose Lichen*. A. D. Randolph, New York, 1893, 65p, Cloth, Novel

MILES, pseud.
    see: BELL, NEIL

MILES, CHARLES A.

10122 *Argosy; the imaginary memoirs of an astronaut*. Vantage Press, New York, 1961, 123p, Cloth, Novel

MILES, KEITH, pseud.
    see: TRALINS, ROBERT

MILES, ROBERT

10123 *Safespace*. Optimum Press, Los Angeles, 1972, 104p, Paper, Novel

MILKOMANE, GEORGE
    see: BORODIN, GEORGE

MILL, GARRETT, pseud. [Margaret Miller]

10124 *In the hands of the Czar*. William Blackwood & Sons, Edinburgh, 1905, 362p, Cloth, Novel

MILLARD, JOSEPH (John), 1908- [*biography included*]

10125 *The gods hate Kansas*. Monarch, Derby, Conn., 1964, 126p, Paper, Novel

MILLE, JAMES DE
    see: DE MILLE, JAMES

MILLE, RICHARD de
    see: de MILLE, RICHARD

MILLER, ALAN

10126 *The king of men*. Nash & Grayson, London, 1931, 320p, Cloth, Novel
10127 *The phantoms of a physician*. Grayson & Grayson, London, 1934, 288p, Cloth, Novel

MILLER, ELIZABETH (Jane), 1878-

10128 *The yoke; a romance of the days when the Lord redeemed the children of Israel from the bondage of Egypt*. Bobbs-Merrill, Indianapolis, 1904, 616p, Cloth, Novel

MILLER, EUGENIA, 1916-

10129 *The sign of the salamander*. Holt, Rinehart & Winston, New York, 1967, 223p, Cloth, Novel

MILLER, IRENE

10130 *Sekhet*. John Lane, The Bodley Head, London, 1912, 368p, Cloth, Novel

MILLER, JIMMY

10131 *The Big Win*. Alfred A. Knopf, New York, 1969, 241p, Cloth, Novel

MILLER, JOAQUIN [Cincinnatus Hiner Miller, 1841-1913]

10132 *The building of the city beautiful*. Stone & Kimball, Chicago, 1893, 196p, Cloth, Novel
10133 *The destruction of Gotham*. Funk & Wagnalls, New York, 1886, 214p, Cloth, Novel

MILLER, LEO E(dward), 1887-1952

10134 *The hidden people; the story of a search for Incan treasure.* Charles Scribner's Sons, New York, 1920, 321p, Cloth, Novel [Hidden People #1]
10135 *In the tiger's lair.* Charles Scribner's Sons, New York, 1921, 252p, Cloth, Novel [Hidden People #2]

MILLER, MARGARET
see: MILL, GARRETT

MILLER, MARJORIE M., 1922- [*biography included*]

10136 *Isaac Asimov; a checklist of works published in the United States, March 1939-May 1972.* Kent State University Press, Kent, OH, 1972, 98p, Cloth, Nonf.

MILLER, P(eter) SCHUYLER, 1912-1974 [*biography included*]

10137 *The titan.* Fantasy Press, Reading, PA, 1952, 252p, Cloth, Coll.

with L. Sprague de Camp:

03991 *Genus Homo.* Fantasy Press, Reading, PA, 1950, 225p, Cloth, Novel

MILLER, R(ichard) DeWITT, 1910-1958

10138 *The loose board in the floor.* Vantage Press, New York, 1951, 111p, Cloth, Novel

with Anna Hunger:

07606 *The man who lived forever.* Ace Double, New York, 1956, 137p, Paper, Novel
07606A retitled: *Year 3097.* Satellite, London, 1958, 128p, Paper, Novel

MILLER, RUSS

10139 *The impossible transplant.* Greenleaf Classic, San Diego, 1972, 190p, Paper, Novel

MILLER, STEPHEN O.

10140 *Mithrandir.* T-K Graphics, Baltimore, 1974, 47p, Paper, Nonf.

MILLER, SUTRO

10141 *Ghost stories.* Sentinel Publications, London, 1947, 80p, Paper, Coll. [cover title: *"H" for horrific*]

MILLER, WALTER M(ichael) Jr., 1923- [*biography included*]

10142 *A canticle for Leibowitz; a novel.* J. B. Lippincott, Philadelphia, 1960, 320p, Cloth, Novel
10143 *Conditionally human.* Ballantine, New York, 1962, 191p, Paper, Coll.
10144 *The view from the stars.* Ballantine, New York, 1965, 192p, Paper, Coll.

MILLER, WARREN, 1921-1966

10145 *Looking for the general.* McGraw-Hill, New York, 1964, 203p, Cloth, Novel
10146 *The siege of Harlem.* McGraw-Hill, New York, 1964, 166p, Cloth, Novel

MILLER, WILLIAM AMOS

10147 *The sovereign guide; a tale of Eden.* Geo. Rice & Sons, Los Angeles, 1898, 130p, Cloth, Novel

MILLERS, REINHOLD (R.)

10148 *Time exile.* Echo Publishers, New York, 1972, 159p, Cloth, Novel

MILLET, F(rancis) D(avis), 1846-1912

10149 *A capillary crime, and other stories.* Harper & Bros., New York, 1892, 284p, Cloth, Coll.

MILLHISER, MARLYS (Joy), 1938- [*biography included*]

10150 *Nella waits.* G. P. Putnam's Sons, New York, 1974, 294p, Cloth, Novel

MILLIGAN, ALFRED L(ee), 1893- [*biography included*]

10151 *The strange flight of Frank Shapar.* Pan Pres Tahlequah, OK, 1965, 225p, Cloth, Novel

MILLS, Lady DOROTHY (Rachel Melissa), 1889-1959

10152 *The Arms of the Sun.* Duckworth, London, 1924 284p, Cloth, Novel
10153 *The dark gods.* Duckworth, London, 1925, 284p Cloth, Novel

MILLS, ELLIOTT EVANS [published anonymously]

10154 *The decline and fall of the British Empire; a brief account of those causes which resulte in the destruction of our late ally, togeth with a comparison between the British and Roman Empires; appointed for use in the national schools of Japan, Tokio, 2005.* Alde & Co., Oxford, 1905, 50p, Paper, Novel

MILLS, G. H. SAXON
see: SAXON MILLS, G. H.

MILLS, J(anet) M(elanie) A(ilsa), 1894-

10155 *Lords of the Earth.* Andrew Dakers, London, 1940, 302p, Cloth, Novel
10156 *The tomb of the dark ones.* Rider & Co., London, 1937, 285p, Cloth, Novel

MILLS, ROBERT P(ark), 1920-   [biography included]

10157   The best from Fantasy and science fiction,
           ninth series. Doubleday, Garden City, 1960,
           264p, Cloth, Anth.
10158   The best from Fantasy and science fiction,
           tenth series. Doubleday, Garden City, 1961,
           262p, Cloth, Anth.
10159   The best from Fantasy and science fiction,
           eleventh series. Doubleday, Garden City,
           1962, 258p, Cloth, Anth.
10160   A decade of Fantasy and science fiction.
           Doubleday, Garden City, 1960, 406p, Cloth,
           Anth.
10161   The worlds of science fiction. Dial Press,
           New York, 1963, 349p, Cloth, Anth.

with Edward L. Ferman:

05378   Twenty years of The magazine of fantasy and
           science fiction. G. P. Putnam's Sons, New
           York, 1970, 264p, Cloth, Anth.

MILLS, SAXON
     see: SAXON MILLS, G. H.

MILLS, WEYMER JAY, 1880-1938

10162   The ghosts of their ancestors. Fox, Duffield,
           New York, 1906, 143p, Cloth, Novel

MILNE, A(lan) A(lexander), 1882-1956

10163   Once on a time. Hodder & Stoughton, London,
           1917, 316p, Cloth, Novel

MILSTEAD, JOHN W., with Martin Harry Greenberg, Patricia S. Warrick, and Joseph D.
Olander

06312   Sociology through science fiction. St. Mar-
           tin's Press, New York, 1974, 412p, Cloth,
           Anth.

MILTON, SAUL
     see: FLINDERS, KARL

MILWARD, VIRGINIA

10164   The door ajar, and other stories. William
           Rider & Son, London, 1912, 128p, Cloth,
           Coll.

THE MIND ANGEL, AND OTHER STORIES
     see: ELWOOD, ROGER

THE MINDWORM
     see: BLEILER, EVERETT F. and DIKTY, T. E.

MINES, SAMUEL, 1909-   [biography included]

10165   The best from Startling stories. Henry Holt,
           New York, 1953, 301p, Cloth, Anth.

10165A retitled: Startling stories. Cassell, London,
           1954, 301p, Cloth, Anth.
10165B retitled: Moment without time. Science Fic-
           tion Book Club, London, 1956,   , Cloth,
           Anth.

MINGSTON, R. GRESHAM, pseud. [Roger Stamp]

10166   Ten days to the Moon; an engineer's essay into
           space. William MacLellan, Glasgow, 1955,
           217p, Cloth, Novel

MINIATURE ROMANCES FROM THE GERMAN
     see: TRACY, THOMAS

MINNETT, CORA

10167   The day after to-morrow. F. V. White, London,
           1911, 310p, Cloth, Novel
10168   The girdle of Kaf. W. J. Ham-Smith, London,
           1912, 284p, Cloth, Novel

MINOR, JOHN W., pseud.

10169   "Bietigheim." Funk & Wagnalls, New York,
           1886, 172p, Paper, Novel

MINOR, THOMAS C(halmers), 1846-1912

10170   Athothis; a satire on modern medicine. Robert
           Clarke, Cincinnati, 1887, 194p, Cloth, Novel

MINOT, STEPHEN, 1927-   [biography included]

10171   Chill of dusk. Doubleday, Garden City, 1964,
           327p, Cloth, Novel

MIOMANDRE, FRANCIS de, pseud. [François Durand,
1880-1959]

10172   The love life of Venus (La vie amoureuse de
           Venus). Brentano's, New York, 1930, 228p,
           Cloth, Novel

MIRDREKVANDI, ALI, GUNGA DIN

10173   No heaven for Gunga Din, consisting of the
           British and American officers' book. E. P.
           Dutton, New York, 1965, 128p, Cloth, Novel

MIRRLEES, (Helen) HOPE, 1889?-1978

10174   Lud-in-the-Mist. W. Collins Sons, London,
           1926, 319p, Cloth, Novel

THE MISSING WORLD, AND OTHER STORIES
     see: ELWOOD, ROGER

Mr. DICK
     see: DICK, Mr.

MISTRAL, BENGO, house pseud.

10175   *The Brains of Helle*. Gannet Press, London, 1953, 127p, Paper, Novel

10176   *Pirates of Cerebus*. Gannet Press, London, 1953, 128p, Paper, Novel

10177   *Space flight 139*. Gannet Press, London, 1954, 128p, Paper, Novel

MITCHELL, ADRIAN, 1932-   [*biography inclu- ded*]

10178   *The Bodyguard*. Jonathan Cape, London, 1970, 188p, Cloth, Novel

MITCHELL, EDMUND, 1861-1917

10179   *Tales of destiny*. Constable, London, 1913, 190p, Cloth, Novel

MITCHELL, EDWARD PAGE, 1852-1927

10180   *The crystal man; landmark science fiction*. Doubleday, Garden City, 1973, 358p, Cloth, Coll.

MITCHELL, J(ohn) A(mes), 1845-1918

10181   *Amos Judd*. Charles Scribner's Sons, New York, 1895, 199p, Cloth, Novel

10182   *Drowsy*. Frederick A. Stokes, New York, 1917, 301p, Cloth, Novel

10183   *Gloria Victis*. Charles Scribner's Sons, New York, 1897, 269p, Cloth, Novel

10183A retitled: *Dr Thorne's idea, originally pub- lished as "Gloria Victis."* Life Publishing Co., New York, 1910, 244p, Cloth, Novel

10184   *The last American; a fragment from the journal of Khan-Li, Prince of Dimph-Yoo-Chur, and Admiral in the Persian Navy*. Frederick A. Stokes & Brother, New York, 1889, 78p, Cloth, Novel

10185   *Life's fairy tales*. Frederick A. Stokes, New York, 1892, 117p, Cloth, Coll.

10186   *That first affair, and other sketches*. Charles Scribner's Sons, New York, 1902, 177p, Cloth, Coll.

10187   *The Villa Claudia*. Life Publishing Co., New York, 1904, 306p, Cloth, Novel

MITCHELL, J(ames) LESLIE, 1901-1935

10188   *The calends of Cairo*. Jarrolds, London, 1931, 283p, Cloth, Coll.

10188A retitled: *Cairo dawns; a story cycle with a proem*. Bobbs-Merrill, Indianapolis, 1931, 314p, Cloth, Coll.

10189   *Gay Hunter*. William Heinemann, London, 1934, 286p, Cloth, Novel

10190   *The lost trumpet*. Jarrolds, London, 1932, 286p, Cloth, Novel

10191   *Three go back*. Jarrolds, London, 1932, 254p, Cloth, Novel

MITCHELL, LINDA

10192   *A witch's mouth*. Copenhagen Compacts, Copenha 1974, 128p, Paper, Novel

MITCHELL, M. E.

10193   *'Yet in my flesh--'* J. M. Dent & Sons, Londo 1933, 316p, Cloth, Novel

MITCHELL, RONALD (Elwy), 1905-

10194   *Dan Owen and the angel Joe; a novel*. Harper & Bros., New York, 1948, 250p, Cloth, Novel

MITCHELL, S(ilas) WEIR, 1829-1914

10195   *Little stories*. Century Co., New York, 1903, 110p, Cloth, Coll.

MITCHELL, Professor W(illis)

10196   *The inhabitants of Mars, their manners and advancements in civilization and their opin on of us*. C. E. Spofford, Malden, Mass., 1895, 178p, Paper, Novel

MITCHELL-HEDGES, F(rederick) A(lbert), 1882- 1959

10197   *The White Tiger*. Duckworth, London, 1931, 286p, Cloth, Novel

MITCHISON, G(ilbert) R(ichard), Baron, 1890- 1970

10198   *Banking (being a chapter from The history of the 1935 socialist government, written in 1970)*. Socialist League, London, 1935, 29p Paper, Story

10199   *The first workers' government; or, New times for Henry Dubb*. Victor Gollancz, London, 1934, 528p, Cloth, Novel

MITCHISON, NAOMI (Mary Margaret), 1897-   [*bi graphy included*]

10200   *Barbarian stories*. Jonathan Cape, London, 1929, 290p, Cloth, Coll.

10201   *The fourth pig*. Constable, London, 1936, 289 Cloth, Coll. [includes some verse]

10202   *Memoirs of a spacewoman*. Victor Gollancz, London, 1962, 176p, Cloth, Novel

10203   *The powers of light*. Pharos, London, 1932, 63p, Cloth, Novel

10204   *To the chapel perilous*. George Allen & Unwi London, 1955, 172p, Cloth, Novel

MITFORD, BERTRAM, 1855-1914

10205   *The King's Assegai; a Matabili story*. Chatt & Windus, London, 1894, 248p, Cloth, Novel [Untuswa #1]

10206   *A legacy of the granite hills*. John Long, Lo don, 1909, 318p, Cloth, Novel

MITFORD, BERTRAM (cont.)

10207 *The sign of the spider; an episode.* Methuen, London, 1896, 312p, Cloth, Novel

10208 *The white shield.* Cassell, London, 1895, 364p, Cloth, Novel [Untuswa #2]

10209 *The word of the sorceress.* Hutchinson, London, 1902, 309p, Cloth, Novel [Untuswa #3]

MITGANG, HERBERT, 1920-   [*biography included*]

10210 *Get these men out of the hot sun.* Arbor House, New York, 1972, 203p, Cloth, Novel

MOANING CANYON
    see: UNKNOWN AUTHOR

MODAD, AL-
    see: MOORE, M. LOUISE

MODERN GHOSTS

10211 *Modern ghosts.* Harper & Bros., New York, 1890, 225p, Cloth, Anth.

MOFFAT, W. GRAHAM, with John White

10212 *What's the world coming to? a novel of the twenty-first century.* Elliot Stock, London, 1893, 172p, Cloth, Novel

MOFFATT, ADAH TERRELL

10213 *The queen's gift; a fantasy.* Roxburgh Publishing Co., Boston, 1923, 73p, Cloth, Novel

MOFFATT, JAMES

10214 *The sleeping bomb.* New English Library, London, 1970, 125p, Paper, Novel
10214A retitled: *The Cambri plot.* Belmont Tower, New York, 1973, 125p, Paper, Novel

MOFFETT, CLEVELAND (Langston), 1863-1926

10215 *The conquest of America; a romance of disaster and victory: U.S.A., 1921 A.D.; based on extracts from the diary of James E. Langston, war correspondent of the "London Times."* George H. Doran, New York, 1916, 310p, Cloth, Novel
10216 *The mysterious card.* Small, Maynard, Boston, 1912, 103p, Cloth, Coll.
10217 *Possessed.* James A. McCann, New York, 1920, 254p, Cloth, Novel

MOGRIDGE, STEPHEN

10218 *Peter and the atomic valley.* Hutchinson, London, 1955, 216p, Cloth, Novel [Peter #2]
10219 *Peter and the flying saucers.* Hutchinson, London, 1954, 192p, Cloth, Novel [Peter #1]
10220 *Peter and the Moon bomb.* Hutchinson, London, 1956, 202p, Cloth, Novel [Peter #3]

MOHOAO, pseud. [Edwin Fairburn]

10221 *The ships of Tarshish, being a sequel to the "Wandering Jew."* Hall & Co., London, 1867, 104p, Cloth, Novel [a sequel to Sue's novel, *The wandering Jew*]

MOHS, MAYO

10222 *Other worlds, other gods; adventures in religious science fiction.* Doubleday, Garden City, 1971, 264p, Cloth, Anth.

THE MOLECULAR CAFE

10223 *The Molecular Cafe; science-fiction stories.* Mir Publishers, Moscow, 1968, 279p, Paper, Anth.

THE MOLECULE MONSTERS

10224 *The molecule monsters.* Fantasy Fiction, Sydney, 1951, 32p, Paper, Anth.

MOLESWORTH, Mrs. (Mary Louisa), 1842-1921

10225 *Fairies--of sorts.* Macmillan, London, 1908, 249p, Cloth, Coll.
10226 *Four ghost stories.* Macmillan, London, 1888, 255p, Cloth, Coll.
10227 *Uncanny tales.* Hutchinson, London, 1896, 228p, Cloth, Coll.

MOLESWORTH, VOL(taire), 1924-1965

10228 *Ape of God.* Currawong Publishing Co., Sydney, 1943, 64p, Paper, Novel
10229 *Blinded they fly; a fantasy.* Futurian Press, Sydney, 1951, 31p, Paper, Story
10230 *Let there be monsters; a fantasy.* Futurian Press, Sydney, 1952, 23p, Paper, Story
10231 *Monster at large.* Currawong Publishing Co., Sydney, 1943, 63p, Paper, Story

MOLIN, CHARLES

10232 *Ghosts, spooks, and spectres.* Hamish Hamilton, London, 1967, 237p, Cloth, Anth.

MOLLOY, HERCULES, pseud.

10233 *Oedipus in Disneyland; Queen Victoria's reincarnation as Superman.* Paranoid Press, San Francisco, 1972, 304p, Paper, Novel

MOLLY X.
    see: X., MOLLY

MOLNAR, E(ugene) F(rank), 1891-

10234 *The slave of Ea; a Sumerian legend.* Dorrance, Philadelphia, 1934, 299p, Cloth, Novel

MOLTRUHN, MAXIMILIAN, pseud.

10235   *The other side at the Battle of Dorking; or,*
The reminiscences of an invader, translated
from the German by an "Autumn campaigner,"
August 1921. Whittaker, London, 1871, 84p,
Paper, Novel [Dorking series]

MON ANONYM
     see: ANONYM, MON

MONBRON, JEAN-LOUIS FOUGERET de
     see: FOUGERET de MONBRON, JEAN-LOUIS

MONCRIEFF, D. SCOTT
     see: SCOTT MONCRIEFF, D.

MONCRIF, (François) AUGUSTIN-PARADIS de, 1687-
1770

10236   *The adventures of Zeloide and Amanzarifdine.*
George Routledge & Sons, London, 1929,
205p, Cloth, Coll.

MONGELARD, JOSEPH CYRIL

10237   *Society of the new generation in the year 2001.*
Vantage Press, New York, 1971, 125p, Cloth,
Novel

MONROE, DONALD, 1888-   , with Keith Monroe
as Donald Keith

10238   *Mutiny in the time machine.* Random House,
New York, 1963, 181p, Cloth, Novel [Time
Machine #1]
10239   *Time machine to the rescue.* Random House,
New York, 1967, 157p, Cloth, Novel [Time
Machine #2]

MONROE, KEITH, 1917-   , with Donald Monroe
as Donald Keith

10238   *Mutiny in the time machine.* Random House,
New York, 1963, 181p, Cloth, Novel [Time
Machine #1]
10239   *Time machine to the rescue.* Random House,
New York, 1967, 157p, Cloth, Novel [Time
Machine #2]

MONS, HANS MAHNER-
     see: POSSENDORF, HANS

MONSARRAT, NICHOLAS (John Turney), 1910-

10240   *The time before this.* Cassell, London, 1962,
127p, Cloth, Novel

MONSTERS

10241   *Monsters; a collection of uneasy tales.* Philip Allan, London, 1934, 249p, Cloth, Anth.

MONTAGUE, EDWARD

10242   *The demon of Sicily; a romance.* J. F. Hughes,
London, 1807, 4vol, Cloth, Novel

MONTERROSO, AUGUSTO

10243   *The black sheep, and other fables.* Doubleday,
Garden City, 1971, 112p, Cloth, Coll.

MONTGOMERY, FRANCES TREGO, 1858?-1925

10244   *On a lark to the planets; a sequel to "The*
wonderful electric elephant." Saalfield Publishing Co., Akron, OH, 1904, 180p, Cloth,
Novel [Electric Elephant #2]
10245   *The wonderful electric elephant.* Saalfield
Publishing Co., Akron, OH, 1903, 253p, Cloth,
Novel [Electric Elephant #1]

MONTGOMERY, RICHARD R.

10246   *Two boys' trip to an unknown planet.* F. Tou-
sey, Pluck & Luck, New York, 1901, 21p,
Paper, Story

MONTGOMERY, ROBERT BRUCE
     see: CRISPIN, EDMUND

MONTGOMERY, RUTHERFORD GEORGE, 1894-   [*bio-*
graphy included]

10247   *Kent Barstow: space man.* Duell, Sloan & Pearce,
New York, 1961, 148p, Cloth, Novel [Kent
Barstow #4]

MONTOREL
     see: N., N.

MOODY, Dr. H. A.

10248   *The city without a name.* F. Tennyson Neely,
London, 1898, 290p, Cloth, Novel

MOON, SHEILA (Elizabeth), 1910-   [*biography*
included]

10249   *Hunt down the prize.* Atheneum, New York, 1971,
244p, Cloth, Novel [Maris #2]
10250   *Knee-deep in thunder.* Atheneum, New York,
1967, 309p, Cloth, Novel [Maris #1]

MOON-BLIND

10251   *Moon-blind.* American Science Fiction, Sydney,
1953, 34p, Paper, Anth.

THE MOON CONQUERORS

10252   *The Moon conquerors.* Gerald G. Swan, London,
1943, 176p, Paper, Anth.

THE MOON ERA
     see: MOSKOWITZ, SAM

THE MOON GODDESS

10253 *The Moon goddess; and, The new girl at Lady Griselda's; two stories.* A. Soloway, London, 1946, 64p, Paper, Anth.

THE MOON TERROR

10254 *The Moon terror.* Popular Fiction Publishing Co., Indianapolis, 1927, 192p, Cloth, Anth.

MOONEY, LEO F.

10255 *Under the sign of pain.* Star, New York, 1971, 192p, Paper, Novel

MOONWALK

10256 *Moonwalk.* American Science Fiction, Sydney, 1953, 34p, Paper, Anth.

MOORCOCK, MICHAEL (John), 1939- [*biography included*]

10257 *An alien heat; volume one of a trilogy, 'The dancers at the end of time.'* MacGibbon & Kee, London, 1972, 158p, Cloth, Novel [Dancers at the End of Time #1]

10258 *Behold the man; a novel.* Allison & Busby, London, 1969, 144p, Cloth, Novel [Karl Glogauer #1]

10259 *The best of New worlds.* Compact, London, 1965, 318p, Paper, Anth.

10260 *Best S.F. stories from New worlds.* Panther, London, 1967, 141p, Paper, Anth.

10261 *Best S.F. stories from New worlds 2.* Panther, London, 1968, 157p, Paper, Anth.

10262 *Best S.F. stories from New worlds 3.* Panther, London, 1968, 157p, Paper, Anth.

10263 *Best SF stories from New worlds 4.* Panther, London, 1969, 158p, Paper, Anth.

10264 *Best S.F. stories from New worlds 5.* Panther, London, 1969, 157p, Paper, Anth.

10265 *Best S.F. stories from New worlds 6.* Panther, London, 1970, 176p, Paper, Anth.

10266 *Best S.F. stories from New worlds 7.* Panther, London, 1971, 175p, Paper, Anth.

10267 *Best S.F. stories from New worlds 8.* Panther, St. Albans, UK, 1974, 204p, Paper, Anth.

10268 *The black corridor.* Ace, New York, 1969, 187p, Paper, Novel
The Blood Red Game. [see 10302A]

10269 *Breakfast in the ruins; a novel of inhumanity.* New English Library, London, 1972, 175p, Cloth, Novel [Karl Glogauer #2]

10270 *The bull and the spear; the chronicle of Prince Corum and the silver hand, volume one.* Allison & Busby, London, 1973, 168p, Cloth, Novel [Corum #4]

10271 *The Champion of Garathorm; the chronicles of Castle Brass, being a sequel to The high history of the Runestaff, of which this is the second volume.* Mayflower, St. Albans, UK, 1973, 127p, Paper, Novel [Castle Brass #2; Eternal Champion #2-A]
The city of the beast. [see 10313A]

10272 *Count Brass; the chronicles of Castle Brass, being a sequel to The high history of the Runestaff, of which this is the first volume.* Mayflower, St. Albans, UK, 1973, 140p, Paper, Novel [Castle Brass #1]

10273 *A cure for cancer.* Allison & Busby, London, 1972, 256p, Cloth, Novel [Jerry Cornelius #2]
The dreaming city. [see 10274A]

10274 *Elric of Melniboné.* Hutchinson, London, 1972, 191p, Cloth, Novel [Elric #1]

10274A retitled: *The dreaming city.* Lancer, New York, 1972, 189p, Paper, Novel [Elric #1]

10275 *The English assassin; a romance of entropy.* Allison & Busby, London, 1972, 254p, Cloth, Novel [Jerry Cornelius #3]

10276 *The Eternal Champion.* Dell, New York, 1970, 188p, Paper, Novel [Eternal Champion #1]

10277 *The final programme.* Avon, New York, 1968, 191p, Paper, Novel [Jerry Cornelius #1]

10278 *The Fireclown.* Compact, London, 1965, 189p, Paper, Novel

10278A retitled: *The winds of Limbo.* Paperback Library, New York, 1969, 158p, Paper, Novel

10279 *The hollow lands; volume two of a trilogy, The dancers at the end of time.* Harper & Row, New York, 1974, 182p, Cloth, Novel [Dancers at the End of Time #2]

10280 *The ice schooner.* Sphere, London, 1969, 158p, Paper, Novel

10281 *The Jade Man's eyes.* Unicorn Bookshop, Brighton, UK, 1973, 75p, Paper, Novel [Elric series]

10282 *The jewel in the skull; the history of the Runestaff, volume one.* Lancer, New York, 1967, 175p, Paper, Novel [Runestaff #1]

10283 *The King of the Swords.* Berkley, New York, 1971, 158p, Paper, Novel [Corum #3]

10284 *The Knight of the Swords; volume the first of the books of Corum.* Mayflower, London, 1971, 143p, Paper, Novel [Corum #1]

10285 *The Land Leviathan; a new scientific romance.* Quartet, London, 1974, 161p, Cloth, Novel [Oswald Bastable #2]
The lord of the spiders. [see 10312A]
The Mad God's amulet. [see 10299A]
The masters of the pit. [see 10311A]

10286 *New worlds quarterly.* Sphere, London, 1971, 175p, Paper, Anth. [cover title: *New worlds 1*]

10286A retitled: *New worlds quarterly #1.* Berkley Medallion, New York, 1971, 192p, Paper, Anth.

10287 *New worlds quarterly 2.* Sphere, London, 1971, 187p, Paper, Anth.

10287A retitled: *New worlds quarterly #2.* Berkley Medallion, New York, 1971, 192p, Paper, Anth.

10288 *New worlds quarterly 3.* Sphere, London, 1972, 208p, Paper, Anth.

10288A retitled: *New worlds quarterly #3.* Berkley Medallion, New York, 1972, 223p, Paper, Anth.

10289 *New worlds quarterly 4.* Sphere, London, 1972, 224p, Paper, Anth.

10289A retitled: *New worlds quarterly #4.* Berkley Medallion, New York, 1972, 223p, Paper, Anth.

10290 *New worlds quarterly 5.* Sphere, London, 1973, 275p, Paper, Anth.

10291 *The oak and the ram; volume the second of the chronicle of Prince Corum and the silver hand.* Allison & Busby, London, 1973, 168p, Cloth, Novel [Corum #5]

10292 *Phoenix in obsidian, being the second book of the Eternal Champion.* Mayflower, London, 1970, 127p, Paper, Novel [Eternal Champion #2]

10292A retitled: *The Silver Warriors.* Dell, New York, 1973, 220p, Paper, Novel [Eternal Champion #2]

MOORCOCK, MICHAEL (cont.)

10293 *The Queen of the Swords*. Berkley Medallion, New York, 1971, 160p, Paper, Novel [Corum #2]
The rituals of infinity. [see 10310]
The Runestaff. [see 10296A]

10294 *SF reprise 1; first-rate science fiction originally published in New worlds magazine*. Compact, London, 1966, 236p, Paper, Anth.

10295 *SF reprise 2; first-rate science fiction originally published in New worlds magazine*. Compact, London, 1966, 216p, Paper, Anth.

10296 *The secret of the Runestaff; the history of the Runestaff, volume four*. Lancer, New York, 1969, 192p, Paper, Novel [Runestaff #4]

10296A retitled: *The Runestaff; the history of the Runestaff, volume four*. Mayflower, London, 1969, 143p, Paper, Novel [Runestaff #4]
The shores of death. [see 10307A]
The Silver Warriors. [see 10292A]

10297 *The singing citadel; four tales of heroic fantasy*. Mayflower, London, 1970, 125p, Paper, Coll. [Elric #5]

10298 *The sleeping sorceress; an Elric novel*. New English Library, London, 1971, 140p, Cloth, Novel [Elric #3]

10299 *Sorcerer's amulet; the history of the Runestaff, volume two*. Lancer, New York, 1968, 190p, Paper, Novel [Runestaff #2]

10299A retitled: *The Mad God's amulet; the history of the Runestaff, volume two*. Mayflower, London, 1969, 142p, Paper, Novel [Runestaff #2]

10300 *The stealer of souls, and other stories*. Neville Spearman, London, 1963, 215p, Cloth, Coll. [Elric #2]

10301 *Stormbringer*. Herbert Jenkins, London, 1965, 192p, Cloth, Novel [Elric #4]

10302 *The sundered worlds*. Compact, London, 1965, 190p, Paper, Novel

10302A retitled: *The Blood Red Game*. Sphere, London, 1970, 154p, Paper, Novel

10303 *The sword and the stallion*. Berkley Medallion, New York, 1974, 160p, Paper, Novel [Corum #6]

10304 *Sword of the dawn; the history of the Runestaff, volume three*. Lancer, New York, 1968, 191p, Paper, Novel [Runestaff #3]

10305 *The Time Dweller*. Rupert Hart-Davis, London, 1969, 176p, Cloth, Coll.

10306 *The traps of time*. Rapp & Whiting, London, 1968, 207p, Cloth, Anth.

10307 *The twilight man*. Compact, London, 1966, 190p, Paper, Novel

10307A retitled: *The shores of death*. Sphere, London, 1970, 156p, Paper, Novel

10308 *The Warlord of the air; a scientific romance*. Ace, New York, 1971, 187p, Paper, Novel [Oswald Bastable #1]
The winds of Limbo. [see 10278A]

10309 *The wrecks of time*. Ace Double, New York, 1967, 135p, Paper, Novel

10310 retitled: *The rituals of infinity; or, The new adventures of Doctor Faustus*. Arrow, London, 1971, 192p, Paper, Novel [expanded]

as Edward P. Bradbury:

10311 *Barbarians of Mars*. Compact, London, 1965, 158p, Paper, Novel [Michael Kane #3]

10311A retitled: *The masters of the pit*, by Michael Moorcock. Lancer, New York, 1971, 158p, Paper, Novel [Michael Kane #3]

10312 *Blades of Mars*. Compact, London, 1965, 158p, Paper, Novel [Michael Kane #2]

10312A retitled: *The lord of the spiders*, by Michael Moorcock. Lancer, New York, 1971, 159p, Paper, Novel [Michael Kane #2]

10313 *Warriors of Mars*. Compact, London, 1965, 157p, Paper, Novel [Michael Kane #1]

10313A retitled: *The city of the beast*, by Michael Moorcock. Lancer, New York, 1970, 159p, Paper, Novel [Michael Kane #1]

as James Colvin:

10314 *The deep fix*. Compact, London, 1966, 159p, Paper, Coll. [one story in this collection is a collaboration with Barrington Bayley]

with Langdon Jones:

07989 *The nature of the catastrophe*. Hutchinson, London, 1971, 213p, Cloth, Anth. [some stories belong in the Jerry Cornelius series]

with Charles Platt:

10315 *New worlds 6; the science fiction quarterly*. Sphere, London, 1973, 263p, Paper, Anth.

10315A retitled: *New worlds #5*. Avon, New York, 1974, 267p, Paper, Anth.

MOORE, ANON, pseud.
see: GALLOWAY, JAMES M.

MOORE, ARTHUR
see: ORIEL, ANTRIM

MOORE, ARTHUR, with Alf Harris as Harris Moore

06796 *The marrow eaters*. Popular Library, New York, 1972, 189p, Paper, Novel

06797 *Slater's Planet*. Pinnacle, New York, 1971, 188p, Paper, Novel

MOORE, BIDWELL, 1917-

10316 *As long as tomorrow*. R. B. Luce, Washington, 1971, 318p, Cloth, Novel

MOORE, BRIAN, 1921- [*biography included*]

10317 *Catholics*. Jonathan Cape, London, 1972, 102p, Cloth, Novel

MOORE, C(atherine) L(ucile), 1911- [*biography included*] [everything written by Moore between 1940-1958 was to some degree a collaboration with her husband, Henry Kuttner, and is so indicated here]

08504 *Doomsday morning*. Doubleday, Garden City, 1957, 216p, Cloth, Novel [with Henry Kuttner]

10318 *Jirel of Joiry*. Paperback Library, New York, 1969, 175p, Paper, Coll.

08505 *Judgment night; a selection of science fiction*. Gnome Press, New York, 1952, 344p, Cloth, Coll. [with Henry Kuttner]

10319 *Northwest of Earth*. Gnome Press, New York, 1954, 212p, Cloth, Coll.

10320 *Shambleau, and others*. Gnome Press, New York, 1953, 224p, Cloth, Coll.

MOORE, C. L. (cont.)

08506 *There shall be darkness.* American Science
       Fiction Sydney, 1954, 34p, Paper, Story
       [with Henry Kuttner]

with Henry Kuttner:

08492 *Earth's last citadel.* Ace, New York, 1964,
       128p, Paper, Novel
08493 *No boundaries.* Ballantine, New York, 1955,
       151p, Cloth, Coll.

with Henry Kuttner as Lawrence O'Donnell:

08494 *Clash by night.* American Science Fiction,
       Sydney, 1952, 34p, Paper, Story

with Lewis Padgett (Henry Kuttner):

08495 *Beyond Earth's gates.* Ace Double, New York,
       1954, 138p, Paper, Novel

with Henry Kuttner as Lewis Padgett:

08496 *Chessboard planet.* Galaxy SF Novel, New York,
       1956, 124p, Paper, Novel
08496A retitled: *The far reality.* Consul, London,
       1963, 155p, Paper, Novel
08497 *A gnome there was, and other tales of science
       fiction and fantasy.* Simon & Schuster, New
       York, 1950, 276p, Cloth, Coll.
08498 *Line to tomorrow.* Bantam, New York, 1954,
       184p, Paper, Coll.
08499 *Mutant.* Gnome Press, New York, 1953, 210p,
       Cloth, Novel
08499A *Mutant,* by Henry Kuttner. Weidenfeld & Nicol-
       son, London, 1954, 224p, Cloth, Novel
08500 *Robots have no tails.* Gnome Press, New York,
       1952, 224p, Cloth, Coll.
08500A *Robots have no tails,* by Henry Kuttner. Lan-
       cer, New York, 1973, 221p, Paper, Coll.
08501 *Tomorrow and tomorrow.* Consul, London, 1963,
       106p, Paper, Novel
08502 *Tomorrow and tomorrow; and, The fairy chess-
       men; two science fiction novels.* Gnome
       Press, New York, 1951, 254p, Cloth, Coll.
08503 *Well of the worlds.* Galaxy SF Novel, New
       York, 1953, 127p, Paper, Novel
08503A *The Well of the Worlds,* by Henry Kuttner.
       Ace, New York, 1965, 142p, Paper, Novel

books by Henry Kuttner with anonymous contributions by C. L. Moore:

08476 *Ahead of time; ten stories of science fiction
       and fantasy.* Ballantine, New York, 1953,
       179p, Cloth, Coll.
08478 *The best of Kuttner, volume 1.* Mayflower-
       Dell, London, 1965, 286p, Paper, Coll.
08479 *The best of Kuttner, volume 2.* Mayflower-
       Dell, London, 1966, 288p, Paper, Coll.
08480 *Bypass to otherness.* Ballantine, New York,
       1961, 144p, Paper, Coll.
08482 *The Dark World.* Ace, New York, 1965, 126p,
       Paper, Novel
08483 *Fury.* Grosset & Dunlap, New York, 1950, 186p,
       Cloth, Novel
08483A retitled: *Destination infinity.* Avon, New
       York, 1958, 192p, Paper, Novel
08484 *The Mask of Circe.* Ace, New York, 1971, 158p,
       Paper, Novel
08485 *Remember tomorrow.* American Science Fiction,
       Sydney, 1954, 34p, Paper, Story
08486 *Return to otherness.* Ballantine, New York,
       1962, 240p, Paper, Coll.

08487 *Sword of tomorrow.* American Science Fiction,
       Sydney, 1955, 34p, Paper, Story
08488 *The time axis.* Ace, New York, 1965, 142p,
       Paper, Novel
08489 *Valley of the Flame.* Ace, New York, 1964,
       156p, Paper, Novel
08490 *Way of the gods.* American Science Fiction,
       Sydney, 1954, 34p, Paper, Story

MOORE, DAVID A(lbert), 1814-

10321 *The age of progress; or, A panorama of time,
       in four visions.* Sheldon, Blakeman, New
       York, 1856, 321p, Cloth, Novel

MOORE, ERICA
     see: AKIRA

MOORE, FRANK FRANKFORT, 1855-1931

10322 *The other world.* Eveleigh Nash, London, 1904,
       274p, Cloth, Coll.
10323 *The secret of the court; a romance of life and
       death.* Hutchinson, London, 1895, 277p,
       Cloth, Novel

MOORE, GEORGE, 1852-1933

10324 *The Brook Kerith; a Syrian story.* T. Werner
       Laurie, London, 1916, 471p, Cloth, Novel

MOORE, HARRIS, pseud.
     see: MOORE, ARTHUR and HARRIS, ALFRED

MOORE, ISABEL

10325 *The day the Communists took over America.* Wis-
       dom House, New York, 1961, 158p, Paper, Novel

MOORE, M. LOUISE

10326 *Al-Modad; or, Life scenes byeond the polar cir-
       cumflex; a religio-scientific solution of
       problems of present and future life,* by an
       untrammeled free-thinker. M. Louise Moore &
       M. Beauchamp, Shell Bank, LA, 1892, 220p,
       Paper, Novel

MOORE, PATRICK (Alfred), 1923-   [*biography
included*]

10327 *Captives of the Moon.* Burke, London, 1960,
       160p, Cloth, Novel
10328 *Caverns of the Moon.* Burke, London, 1964,
       149p, Cloth, Novel [Robin North #4]
10329 *Crater of fear.* Burke, London, 1962, 156p,
       Cloth, Novel [Robin North #2]
10330 *Destination Luna.* Lutterworth Press, London,
       1955, 192p, Cloth, Novel
10331 *The domes of Mars.* Burke, London, 1956, 160p,
       Cloth, Novel [Maurice Gray #2]
10332 *The frozen planet.* Museum Press, London, 1954,
       184p, Cloth, Novel
10333 *Invader from space.* Burke, London, 1963, 152p,
       Cloth, Novel [Robin North #3]

MOORE, PATRICK (cont.)

10334   *The island of fear.* Museum Press, London,
        1954, 192p, Cloth, Novel [Grenfell & Wright
        #2]
10335   *The master of the Moon; an enthralling science-
        fiction story.* Museum Press, London, 1952,
        223p, Cloth, Novel [Grenfell & Wright #1]
10336   *Mission to Mars.* Burke, London, 1955, 158p,
        Cloth, Novel [Maurice Gray #1]
10337   *Peril on Mars.* Burke, London, 1958, 158p,
        Cloth, Novel [Maurice Gray #4]
10338   *Planet of fire.* World's Work, Tadsworth, UK,
        1969, 157p, Cloth, Novel
10339   *Quest of the spaceways.* Frederick Muller, Lon-
        don, 1955, 119p, Cloth, Novel [Gregory Quest
        #1]
10340   *Raiders of Mars.* Burke, London, 1959, 159p,
        Cloth, Novel [Maurice Gray #5]
10341   *Science and fiction.* George G. Harrap, London,
        1957, 192p, Cloth, Nonf.
10342   *The voices of Mars.* Burke, London, 1957, 160p,
        Cloth, Novel [Maurice Gray #3]
10343   *Wanderer in space.* Burke, London, 1961, 158p,
        Cloth, Novel [Robin North #1]
10344   *Wheel in space.* Lutterworth Press, London,
        1956, 152p, Cloth, Novel
10345   *World of mists.* Frederick Muller, London,
        1956, 160p, Cloth, Novel [Gregory Quest #2]

MOORE, SILAS (L. Jr.)

10346   *Scarlet arena 30303.* Oddo Publishing, Fayette-
        ville, GA, 1972, 197p, Cloth, Novel

MOORE, THOMAS, 1779-1852

10347   *The Epicurean; a tale.* Longman, Rees, Orme,
        Brown & Green, London, 1827, 332p, Cloth,
        Novel
10348   *The Epicurean, a tale; and, Alciphron, a poem.*
        Chatto & Windus, London, 1890, 302p, Cloth,
        Coll.

MOORE, THOMAS EMMET, 1861?-1950

10349   *The haunted king.* C. M. Clark, Boston, 1910,
        348p, Cloth, Novel

MOORE, (Joseph) WARD, 1903-1978 [*biography included*]

10350   *Bring the jubilee.* Farrar, Straus & Young,
        New York, 1953, 196p, Cloth, Novel
10351   *Greener than you think.* William Sloane Associ-
        ates, New York, 1947, 358p, Cloth, Novel

with Avram Davidson:

03872   *Joyleg; a folly.* Pyramid, New York, 1962,
        160p, Paper, Novel

MOOSDORF, JOHANNA

10352   *Flight to Africa.* Harcourt, Brace & Co., New
        York, 1954, 256p, Cloth, Novel

MORAND, PAUL, 1888-1976

10353   *East India and Company.* Albert & Charles Boni,
        New York, 1927, 237p, Cloth, Coll.
10354   *The living Buddha.* Alfred A. Knopf, New York,
        1927, 247p, Cloth, Novel

MORAVIA, ALBERTO, pseud. [Alberto Pincherle,
1907-   ]

10355   *A ghost at noon.* Farrar, Straus & Young, New
        York, 1955, 247p, Cloth, Novel

MORE, ANTHONY, pseud. [Edwin M. Clinton,
1926-   ]

10356   *Puzzle box.* Trover Hall, San Francisco, 1946,
        111p, Cloth, Coll.

MORE, E(noch) ANSON Jr., 1854-1932

10357   *Out of the past.* Arena Publishing Co., Boston,
        1895, 249p, Cloth, Novel

MORE HORROR STORIES
    see: LEE, ELIZABETH

MORE SOVIET SCIENCE FICTION
    see: THE HEART OF THE SERPENT

MORE TALES OF TERROR AND SURPRISE

10358   *More tales of terror and surprise.* Mitre Press,
        London, 1943, 127p, Paper, Anth.

MORE UNCANNY TALES SELECTED FROM THE NOVEL
MAGAZINE

10359   *More uncanny tales selected from The novel
        magazine.* C. Arthur Pearson, London, 1918,
        110p, Cloth, Anth.

MOREHOUSE, WILLIAM RUSSELL, 1879-1937

10360   *Mystica Algooat; an Indian legend and story of
        Southern California.* Editor Publishing Co.,
        Franklin, OH, 1903, 200p, Cloth, Novel

MOREL, DIGHTON, pseud. [Kenneth Lewis Warner,
1915-   ] [*biography included*]

10361   *Moonlight red.* Secker & Warburg, London, 196?,
        287p, Cloth, Novel

MORELL, Sir CHARLES, pseud.
    see: RIDLEY, JAMES

MORESBY, Lord CHARLES, pseud.

10362   *A hundred years hence; or, The memoirs of
        Charles, Lord Moresby, written by himself.*
        Longman, Rees, Orme, Brown & Green, London,
        1828, 210p, Cloth, Novel

MORESBY, LOUIS, pseud.
    see: BECK, L. ADAMS

MORGAN, AL(bert Edward), 1920-   *[biography included]*

  10363 *Minor miracle.* Dodd, Mead, New York, 1961,
        212p, Cloth, Novel

MORGAN, ARTHUR, with Charles R. Brown

  01963 *The disintegrator; a romance of modern sci-*
        ence. Digby, Long, London, 1891, 220p,
        Cloth, Novel

MORGAN, DAN, 1925-   *[biography included]*

  10364 *Cee-Tee man.* Panther, London, 1955, 144p,
        Cloth, Novel
  10365 *The high destiny.* Berkley Medallion, New
        York, 1973, 192p, Paper, Novel
  10366 *Inside.* Corgi, London, 1971, 158p, Paper,
        Novel
  10367 *Mind trap.* Avon, New York, 1970, 189p, Paper,
        Novel [Sixth Perception #3]
  10368 *The new minds.* Corgi, London, 1967, 158p,
        Paper, Novel [Sixth Perception #1]
  10369 *The richest corpse in show business.* Compact,
        London, 1966, 190p, Paper, Novel
  10370 *The several minds.* Corgi, London, 1969, 190p,
        Paper, Novel [Sixth Perception #2]
  10371 *The uninhibited.* Digit, London, 1961, 160p,
        Paper, Novel

with John Kippax:

  08283 *The neutral stars.* Ballantine, New York,
        1973, 215p, Paper, Novel [Venturer Twelve
        #3]
  08284 *Seed of stars.* Ballantine, New York, 1972,
        213p, Paper, Novel [Venturer Twelve #2]
  08285 *Thunder of stars.* Macdonald, London, 1968,
        159p, Cloth, Novel [Venturer Twelve #1]

MORGAN, HELENE

  10372 *Seed of the beast.* Exotik, San Diego, 1965,
        160p, Paper, Novel

MORGAN, JOHN DE
    see: DE MORGAN, JOHN

MORGAN, JOHN MINTER, 1782-1854 [published anonymously]

  10373 *The revolt of the bees.* Longman, Rees, Orme,
        Brown & Green, London, 1826, 272p, Cloth,
        Novel

MORGAN, LOUISA

  10374 *Baron Bruno; or, The unbelieving philosopher,*
        and other fairy stories. Macmillan, London,
        1875, 259p, Cloth, Coll.

MORGAN, WILLIAM DE
    see: DE MORGAN, WILLIAM

MORICE, CHARLES, 1861-1919

  10375 *The re-appearing (Il est ressuscité!); a vision*
        of Christ in Paris. George H. Doran, New
        York, 1911, 211p, Cloth, Novel
  10375A retitled: *He is risen again; a vision.* Eve-
        leigh Nash, London, 1911, 230p, Cloth, Novel

MORISON, FRANK, pseud. [Albert Henry Ross, 1891-]

  10376 *Sunset.* Century Co., New York, 1932, 281p,
        Cloth, Novel; Faber & Faber, London, 1932,
        286p, Cloth, Novel

MORLAND, DICK, pseud. [Reginald Charles Hill, 1936-]

  10377 *Albion! Albion!* Faber & Faber, London, 1974,
        213p, Cloth, Novel
  10378 *Heart clock.* Faber & Faber, London, 1973,
        213p, Cloth, Novel

MORLAND, NIGEL, 1905-   *[biography included]*

  10379 *The street of the leopard.* Cassell, London,
        1936, 296p, Cloth, Novel [Mrs. Pym series]

MORLEY, CHRISTOPHER (Darlington), 1890-1957

  10380 *The arrow.* William Heinemann, London, 1927,
        85p, Cloth, Novel
  10381 *The arrow, and two other stories.* William
        Heinemann, London, 1927, 252p, Cloth, Coll.
  10382 *Thunder on the left.* William Heinemann, Lon-
        don, 1925, 273p, Cloth, Novel
  10383 *Where the blue begins.* Doubleday, Page, Gar-
        den City, 1922, 215p, Cloth, Novel

MORLEY, FELIX (Muskett), 1894-

  10384 *Gumption Island; a fantasy of coexistence.*
        Caxton Printers, Caldwell, Idaho, 1956, 306p,
        Cloth, Novel

MORRESSY, JOHN, 1930-   *[biography included]*

  10385 *The humans of Ziax II.* Walker, New York,
        1974, 62p, Cloth, Novel
  10386 *Nail down the stars.* Walker, New York, 1973,
        244p, Cloth, Novel [Del Whitby #2]
  10387 *Starbrat.* Walker, New York, 1972, 239p, Cloth,
        Novel [Del Whitby #1]

MORRILL, FRED B(rown), 1858-

  10388 *Beyond the horizon; a novel.* Neale Publishing
        Co., New York, 1918, 296p, Cloth, Novel

MORRIS, ALFRED [published anonymously]

10389   *Looking ahead; a tale of adventure (not by the author of "Looking backward")*. Henry & Co., London, 1892, 264p, Cloth, Novel [a reply to Bellamy's *Looking backward*]

MORRIS, ANTHONY P.

10390   *Electro Pete, the man of fire; or, The wharf rats of Locust Point; a Baltimore detective tale*. Arthur Westbrook, Cleveland, 1884?, 246p, Paper, Novel

MORRIS, GOUVERNEUR, 1876-1953

10391   *The pagan's progress*. A. S. Barnes, New York, 1904, 258p, Cloth, Novel

MORRIS, GWENDOLEN SUTHERLAND
    see: SUTHERLAND, MORRIS

MORRIS, HENRY O.

10392   *Waiting for the signal; a novel*. Schulte Publishing Co., Chicago, 1897, 407p, Cloth, Novel

MORRIS, J(ohn)

10393   *What will Japan do? a forecast*. Lawrence & Bullen, London, 1898, 190p, Cloth, Novel

MORRIS, JOE ALEX, 1904-

10394   *The bird watcher*. David McKay, New York, 1966, 247p, Cloth, Novel

MORRIS, KENNETH, 1879-1937

10395   *Book of the three dragons*. Longmans, Green, New York, 1930, 206p, Cloth, Novel
10396   *The secret mountain, and other tales*. Faber & Gwyer, London, 1926, 199p, Cloth, Coll.

as Cenydd Morus:

10397   *The fates of the princes of Dyfed*. Aryan Theosophical Press, Point Loma, CA, 1914, 365p, Cloth, Novel

MORRIS, M(artha Anne) MARLOW, 1867-   , with Laura B. Speer

10398   *No borderland; a novel*. Mathis, Van Nort, Dallas, 1938, 269p, Cloth, Novel

MORRIS, RALPH

10399   *A narrative of the life and astonishing adventures of John Daniel, a smith at Royston in Hertfordshire for a course of seventy years; containing the melancholy occasion of his travels; his shipwreck with one companion on a desolate island; their way of life; his accidental discovery of a woman for his companion; their peopling the island; also, a description of a most surprising engine invented by his son Jacob, on which he flew to the Moon, with some account of its inhabitants, his return and accidental fall into the habitation of a sea monster, with whom he lived two years; his further excursions in search of England; his residence in Lapland and travels to Norway, from whence he arrived at Aldborough; and further transactions till his death in 1711, aged 97*. M. Cooper, London, 1751, 319p, Cloth, Novel
10399A   retitled: *The life and astonishing adventures of John Daniel, a smith at Royston in Hertfordshire for a course of seventy years*. T. Parker, London, 1770, 319p, Cloth, Novel
10399B   retitled: *The life and astonishing transactions of John Daniel, who experienced the most surprising adventures that any man in the universe ever met with*. T. Hurst, London, 1801, 84p, Cloth, Novel
10399C   retitled: *Flying and no failure! or, Aerial transit accomplished more than a century ago being a minute descriptive account of "a most surprising engine" invented, constructed and used by Jacob Daniel*. Charles Clark, Totham, UK, 1848, 18p, Cloth, Story [abridged]

MORRIS, ROSAMUND

10400   *Great detective stories*. Hart Publishing Co., New York, 1965, 191p, Paper, Anth.
10401   *Great horror stories*. Hart Publishing Co., New York, 1965, 191p, Paper, Anth.
10402   *Masterpieces of horror*. Hart Publishing Co., New York, 1966, 255p, Paper, Anth.

MORRIS, WILLIAM, 1834-1896

10403   *Child Christopher and Goldilind the Fair*. Kelmscott Press, Hammersmith, UK, 1895, Vol. I-256p, II-239p, Cloth, Novel
10404   *A dream of John Ball*. Little Leather Library, New York, 1915?, 128p, Paper, Novel
10405   *A dream of John Ball; and, A king's lesson*. Reeves & Turner, London, 1888, 143p, Cloth, Coll.
10406   *Early romances*. Collins, London, 1924, 112p, Cloth, Coll.
10407   *The early romances of William Morris in prose and verse*. J. M. Dent & Sons, London, 1907, 303p, Cloth, Coll.
10408   *Gertha's lovers; a tale*. Thomas B. Mosher, Portland, Maine, 1905, 123p, Cloth, Novel
10409   *Golden wings; a prose romance and a poem*. H. M. Caldwell, Boston, 1904, 66p, Cloth, Novel
10410   *Golden wings; Svend and his brethren*. Thomas B. Mosher, Portland, Maine, 1909, 76p, Paper, Coll.
10411   *The hollow land; a tale*. Thomas B. Mosher, Portland, Maine, 1897, 78p, Paper, Novel
10412   *The hollow land, and other contributions to the Oxford and Cambridge magazine (1856)*. Longmans, Green, London, 1903, 332p, Cloth, Coll.
10413   *News from nowhere; or, An epoch of rest, being some chapters from a utopian romance*. Roberts Bros., Boston, 1890, 278p, Cloth, Novel

MORRIS, WILLIAM (cont.)

10414 *Prose and poetry (1856-1870)*. Humphrey Mil-
       ford, Oxford University Press, London, 1913,
       656p, Cloth, Coll. [includes some verse]
10415 *The roots of the mountains, wherein is told
       somewhat of the lives of the men of Burg-
       dale, their friends, their neighbours, their
       foemen, and their fellows in arms*. Reeves
       & Turner, London, 1889, 424p, Cloth, Novel
10416 *Selections from the prose works of William
       Morris*. Cambridge University Press, Cam-
       bridge, UK, 1931, 224p, Cloth, Coll.
10417 *Stories in Prose, stories in verse, shorter
       poems, lectures, and essays*. Nonesuch Press,
       London, 1934, 671p, Cloth, Coll.
10418 *The story of the Glittering Plain, which has
       been called the Land of Living Men, or the
       Acre of the Undying*. Kelmscott Press, Ham-
       mersmith, UK, 1891, 188p, Cloth, Novel
10419 *The story of the unknown church; and, Linden-
       borg Pool*. Avon Booklet, Warwick, UK, 1904,
       39p, Paper?, Coll.
10420 *The story of the unknown church, and other
       tales*. Thomas B. Mosher, Portland, Maine,
       1902, 96p, Paper, Coll.
10421 *The Sundering Flood*. Kelmscott Press, Hammer-
       smith, UK, 1897, 507p, Cloth, Novel
10422 *Svend & his brethren; a tale*. Palmetto Press,
       Aiken, SC, 1901, 50p, Paper?, Story
10423 *A tale of the House of the Wolfings, and all
       the kindreds of the Mark, written in prose
       and verse*. Reeves & Turner, London, 1888,
       199p, Cloth, Novel
10424 *Three works by William Morris: A dream of
       John Ball; The pilgrims of hope; News from
       nowhere*. International Publishers, New
       York, 1968, 404p, Paper, Coll.
10425 *The water of the Wondrous Isles*. Kelmscott
       Press, Hammersmith, UK, 1897, 340p, Cloth,
       Novel
10426 *The Well at the world's end*. Kelmscott Press,
       Hammersmith, UK, 1896, 496p, Cloth, Novel
10427 *William Morris*. Thomas Nelson & Sons, London,
       1923, 420p, Cloth, Coll.
10428 *William Morris: selected writings and designs*.
       Pelican, Harmondsworth, 1962, 309p, Paper,
       Coll.
10429 *The wood beyond the world*. Kelmscott Press,
       Hammersmith, UK, 1894, 261p, Cloth, Novel

with John-Martin:

07904 *The wolf's-head and the queen*. Charles Scrib-
       ner's Sons, New York, 1931, 244p, Cloth,
       Novel [adapted from *Child Christopher*]

MORRISH, (Leslie) FURZE

10430 *Bridge over dark gods; an occult novel*. Ri-
       der & Co., London, 1946, 160p, Cloth, Novel

MORRISON, EMMELINE

10431 *The glittering serpent*. Robert Hale, London,
       1950, 352p, Cloth, Novel

MORRISON, PEGGY
    see: COST, MARCH

MORRISON, WILLIAM, pseud.
    see: SAMACHSON, JOSEPH

MORRISSEY, J(oseph) L(awrence), 1905-

10432 *City of the hidden eyes*. World Distributors,
       Manchester, 1960, 160p, Paper, Radio

as Henry Richards:

       The hour of the Phoenix. [see 10435A]

as Richard Saxon:

10433 *Cosmic crusade*. Consul, London, 1964, 160p,
       Paper, Novel
10434 *Future for sale*. Consul, London, 1964, 151p,
       Paper, Novel
10435 *The hour of the Phoenix*. Consul, London,
       1964, 140p, Paper, Novel
10435A *The hour of the Phoenix*, by Henry Richards.
       Arcadia House, New York, 1965, 191p, Cloth,
       Novel
10436 *The stars came down*. Consul, London, 1964,
       167p, Paper, Novel

MORROUGH, E. R. [Abu Nadaar] (sic)

10437 *The temple serpent, and other stories*. Long-
       mans, Green, London, 1930, 307p, Cloth, Coll.

MORROW, LOWELL HOWARD

10438 *Atalantis; a novel*. Eastern Publishing Co.,
       Boston, 1902, 285p, Cloth, Novel

MORROW, W(illiam) C(hambers), 1853-1923

10439 *Lentala of the south seas; the romantic tale
       of a lost colony*. Frederick A. Stokes, New
       York, 1908, 278p, Cloth, Novel

MORSE, A(lbert) REYNOLDS, 1914-   [*biography
included*]

10440 *The works of M. P. Shiel; a study in biblio-
       graphy*. Fantasy Publishing Co., Los Angeles,
       1948, 170p, Cloth, Nonf.

MORTON, A. S.

10441 *Beyond the palaeocrystic sea; or, The legend
       of Halfjord*. R. R. Donnelley & Sons, Chica-
       go, 1895, 264p, Cloth, Novel

MORTON, FRANK, 1869-1923

10442 *The angel of the earthquake*. Atlas Press,
       Melbourne, 1909, 99p, Paper, Coll.

MORTON, HENRY C(anova) V(ollam), 1892-

10443 *I, James Blunt*. Methuen, London, 1942, 56p,
       Cloth, Novel

MORUS, CENYDD, pseud.
see: MORRIS, KENNETH

MOSELEY, MABOTH, 1906-

10444 *War upon women; a topical drama.* Hutchinson,
       London, 1934, 286p, Cloth, Novel

MOSKOWITZ, SAM, 1920-   [*biography included*]

10445 *The coming of the robots.* Collier, New York,
       1963, 254p, Paper, Anth.
       Doorway into time. [see 10456A]
10446 *Editor's choice in science fiction.* McBride
       Co., New York, 1954, 285p, Cloth, Anth.
10447 *Explorers of the infinite; shapers of science
       fiction.* World Publishing Co., Cleveland,
       1963, 354p, Cloth, Nonf.
10448 *Exploring other worlds.* Collier, New York,
       1963, 256p, Paper, Anth.
10449 *Futures to infinity.* Pyramid, New York,
       1970, 222p, Paper, Anth.
10450 *Horrors unknown; newly discovered masterpieces
       by great names in fantastic terror.* Walker,
       New York, 1971, 214p, Cloth, Anth.
10451 *Horrors unseen.* Berkley Medallion, New York,
       1974, 208p, Paper, Anth.
10452 *Hugo Gernsback: father of science fiction.*
       Criterion Linotyping & Printing Co., New
       York, 1959, 32p, Paper, Nonf.
10453 *The immortal storm; a history of science fic-
       tion fandom.* Atlanta Science Fiction Organ-
       ization Press, Atlanta, 1954, 269p, Cloth,
       Nonf.
       A man called Poe. [see 10454A]
10454 *The man who called himself Poe.* Doubleday,
       Garden City, 1969, 244p, Cloth, Anth.
10454A retitled: *A man called Poe.* Sphere, London,
       1972, 223p, Paper, Anth.
10455 *Masterpieces of science fiction.* World Publi-
       shing Co., Cleveland, 1967, 552p, Cloth,
       Anth.
       Microcosmic God. [see 10456B]
10456 *Modern masterpieces of science fiction.* World
       Publishing Co., Cleveland, 1965, 518p,
       Cloth, Anth.
10456A retitled: *Doorway into time, and other sto-
       ries from Modern masterpieces of science
       fiction.* Macfadden-Bartell, New York, 1966,
       144p, Paper, Anth. [abridged]
10456B retitled: *Microcosmic God, and other stories
       from Modern masterpieces of science fiction.*
       Macfadden-Bartell, New York, 1968, 142p,
       Paper, Anth. [abridged]
10456C retitled: *The vortex blasters, and other
       stories from Modern masterpieces of science
       fiction.* Macfadden-Bartell, New York, 1968,
       144p, Paper, Anth. [abridged; 10456A,
       10456B, and 10456C together comprise the
       original volume]
       The Moon era. [see 10459B]
10457 *Science fiction by gaslight; a history and
       anthology of science fiction in the popular
       magazines, 1891-1911.* World Publishing Co.,
       Cleveland, 1968, 364p, Cloth, Anth.
10458 *Seekers of tomorrow; masters of science fic-
       tion.* World Publishing Co., Cleveland,
       1966, 441p, Cloth, Nonf.
       A sense of wonder. [see 10459A]
10459 *Three stories.* Doubleday, Garden City, 1967,
       184p, Cloth, Anth. [published anonymously]

10459A retitled: *A sense of wonder; three science
       fiction stories.* Sidgwick & Jackson, London
       1967, 197p, Cloth, Anth.
10459B retitled: *The Moon era; three stories.* Curti
       New York, 1969, 192p, Paper, Anth. [publishe
       anonymously]
10460 *Under the moons of Mars; a history and antholo
       gy of "the scientific romance" in the Munsey
       magazines, 1912-1920.* Holt, Rinehart & Win-
       ston, New York, 1970, 433p, Cloth, Anth.
       The vortex blasters. [see 10456C]
10461 *When women rule.* Walker, New York, 1972, 221p
       Cloth, Anth.

with Roger Elwood:

04875 *Alien Earth, and other stories.* Macfadden-
       Bartell, New York, 1969, 208p, Paper, Anth.
04827 *Alien worlds.* Paperback Library, New York,
       1964, 176p, Paper, Anth. [ghost-edited by
       Moskowitz]
04876 *The human zero, and other science fiction mas-
       terpieces.* Tower, New York, 1967, 224p,
       Paper, Anth.
04846 *Invasion of the robots.* Paperback Library,
       New York, 1965, 157p, Paper, Anth. [ghost-
       edited by Moskowitz]
04877 *Other worlds, other times.* Macfadden-Bartell,
       New York, 1969, 192p, Paper, Anth.
04878 *Strange signposts; an anthology of the fantas-
       tic.* Holt, Rinehart & Winston, New York,
       1966, 319p, Cloth, Anth.
04879 *The time curve.* Tower, New York, 1968, 189p,
       Paper, Anth.

with Noel Keyes:

08232 *Contact.* Paperback Library, New York, 1963,
       176p, Paper, Anth. [ghost-edited by Mosko-
       witz]

with Leo Margulies:

09668 *Three in one; novels.* Pyramid, New York, 1963
       144p, Paper, Anth. [ghost-edited by Mosko-
       witz]
09669 *Three times infinity.* Gold Medal, Greenwich,
       Conn., 1958, 176p, Paper, Anth. [ghost-edite
       by Moskowitz]
09671 *Weird tales; stories of fantasy.* Pyramid, New
       York, 1964, 155p, Paper, Anth. [ghost-edite
       by Moskowitz]
09672 *Worlds of weird.* Pyramid, New York, 1965,
       158p, Paper, Anth. [ghost-edited by Mosko-
       witz]

with Alden H. Norton:

10462 *The Award science fiction reader.* Award, New
       York, 1966, 188p, Paper, Anth. [ghost-edite
       by Moskowitz]
10463 *Ghostly by gaslight; fearful tales of a lost
       era.* Pyramid, New York, 1971, 223p, Paper,
       Anth.
10464 *Great untold stories of fantasy and horror.*
       Pyramid, New York, 1969, 222p, Paper, Anth.
10465 *Hauntings and horrors; ten grisly tales.* Berk
       ley Medallion, New York, 1969, 171p, Paper,
       Anth. [ghost-edited by Moskowitz]
10466 *Horror times ten.* Berkley Medallion, New York
       1967, 176p, Paper, Anth. [ghost-edited by
       Moskowitz]
10467 *Horrors in hiding.* Berkley Medallion, New
       York, 1973, 192p, Paper, Anth.
10468 *Masters of horror.* Berkley Medallion, New
       York, 1968, 192p, Paper, Anth. [ghost-edite
       by Moskowitz]

MOSKOWITZ, SAM, with Alden H. Norton (cont.)

10469 *The space magicians*. Pyramid, New York, 1971, 206p, Paper, Anth.

MOSS, ROBERT F.

10470 *Karloff and company: the horror film*. Pyramid, New York, 1974, 159p, Paper, Nonf.

MOSZKOWSKI, ALEXANDER, 1851-1934

10471 *The Isles of Wisdom*. George Routledge & Sons, London, 1924, 322p, Cloth, Novel

MOTHE FENELON, FRANCOIS de SALIGNAC de la
    see: FENELON, FRANCOIS

MOTTA, LUIGI, 1881-

10472 *The Princess of the Roses*. Stanley Paul, London, 1919, 288p, Cloth, Novel

MOTTE-FOUQUE, FRIEDRICH de la
    see: LA MOTTE-FOUQUE, FRIEDRICH de

MOTTRAM, R(alph) H(ale), 1883-1971

10473 *The gentleman of leisure; a romance*. Hutchinson, London, 1948, 208p, Cloth, Novel
10474 *The ghost and the maiden*. Hutchinson, London, 1940, 223p, Cloth, Novel
10475 *Visit of the princess; a romance of the nineteen-sixties*. Hutchinson, London, 1946, 174p, Cloth, Novel

MOUDY, WALTER (Frank), 1929-1973 [*biography included*]

10476 *No man on Earth*. Berkley Medallion, New York, 1964, 176p, Paper, Novel

THE MOVING FINGER

10477 *The moving finger*. American Science Fiction, Sydney, 1954, 34p, Paper, Anth.

MOXLEY, F(rank) WRIGHT, 1889-1937

10478 *Red snow*. Simon & Schuster, New York, 1930, 411p, Cloth, Novel

MROZEK, SŁAWOMIR, 1930-   [*biography included*]

10479 *The ugupu bird*. Macdonald, London, 1968, 170p, Cloth, Coll.

MUDDOCK, J(oyce) E(mmerson) PRESTON, 1843-1934

10480 *Stories weird and wonderful*. Chatto & Windus, London, 1889, 316p, Cloth, Coll.

10481 *The sunless city, with an authentic account of Hoi-Pithēkoeideis-Mesēs-Tēs-Gaiēs-Oiketai*. F. V. White, London, 1905, 308p, Cloth, Novel

as Dick Donovan:

10482 *Tales of terror*. Chatto & Windus, London, 1899, 325p, Cloth, Coll.

MUGGERIDGE, MALCOLM, 1903-   , with Hugh Kingsmill

08264 *Brave old world; a mirror for the times*. Eyre & Spottiswoode, London, 1936, 187p, Cloth, Novel
08265 *1938; a pre-view of next year's news*. Eyre & Spottiswoode, London, 1937, 160p, Paper, Coll.

MÜHLBACH, L(OUISA), pseud. [Klara Mundt, 1814-1873]

10483 *Old Fritz and the new era; an historical romance*. Chesterfield Society, London, 1868, 407p, Cloth, Novel; D. Appleton, New York, 1868, 271p, Cloth, Novel

MUIR, (John) RAMSAY (Bryce), 1872-1941

10484 *Robinson the Great; a political fantasia on the problems of to-day and the solutions of to-morrow, extracted from the works of Professor Solomon Slack, LL.D., by an impenitent politician* [Ramsay Muir]. Christophers, London, 1929, 149p, Cloth, Novel

MUIR, WARD, 1878-1927

10485 *"Further east than Asia"; a romantic adventure*. Simpkin, Marshall, Hamilton, Kent, London, 1919, 252p, Cloth, Novel

MUIRDEN, JAMES

10486 *The Moon-winners*. Hamish Hamilton, London, 1965, 192p, Cloth, Novel
10487 *Space intruder*. Hamish Hamilton, London, 1965, 160p, Cloth, Novel

MÜLIËR, pseud. [Charles Eli Higgins]

10488 *Signor; a segment from the eternal circle*. Gnostic Press, San Diego, 1917, 219p, Cloth, Novel
10489 *Sojourners by the wayside; travellers on the long road*. Gnostic Press, San Diego, 1917, 203p, Cloth, Novel

MULLEN, STANLEY, 1911-1973?

10490 *Kinsmen of the dragon*. Shasta Publishers, Chicago, 1951, 336p, Cloth, Novel
10491 *Moonfoam and sorceries*. Gorgon Press, Denver, 1948, 264p, Cloth, Coll. [includes some verse]
10492 *The sphinx child*. New Collector's, New York, 1948, 23p, Paper, Story

MULLER, ERNST
    see: WEST, JULIAN

MULLER, FREDERIK PALUDAN-
    see: PALUDAN-MULLER, FREDERIK

MULLER, JOHN E., house pseud. [see also: R. Lionel Fanthorpe and A. A. Glynn]

10493   *Alien.* Badger, London, 1961, 158p, Paper, Novel

05076   *Beyond the void.* Badger, London, 1965, 158p, Paper, Novel [by R. Lionel Fanthorpe]

05077   *Beyond time.* Badger, London, 1962, 158p, Paper, Novel [by R. Lionel Fanthorpe]

05077A *Beyond time*, by Marston Johns. Arcadia House, New York, 1966, 188p, Cloth, Novel [by R. Lionel Fanthorpe]

05078   *Crimson planet.* Badger, London, 1961, 158p, Paper, Novel [by R. Lionel Fanthorpe]

05079   *Dark continuum.* Badger, London, 1964, 160p, Paper, Novel [by R. Lionel Fanthorpe]

10494   *Day of the beasts.* Badger, London, 1961, 158p, Paper, Novel

05080   *The day the world died.* Badger, London, 1962, 159p, Paper, Novel [by R. L. Fanthorpe]

10495   *The edge of eternity.* Badger, London, 1962, 158p, Paper, Novel

05081   *The exorcists.* Badger, London, 1965, 158p, Paper, Novel [by R. Lionel Fanthorpe]

05082   *The Eye of Karnak.* Badger, London, 1962, 158p, Paper, Novel [by R. L. Fanthorpe]

05083   *Forbidden planet.* Badger, London, 1961, 158p, Paper, Novel [by R. Lionel Fanthorpe]

10496   *In the beginning.* Badger, London, 1962, 159p, Paper, Novel

05084   *Infinity machine.* Badger, London, 1962, 158p, Paper, Novel [by R. Lionel Fanthorpe]

05085   *The man from beyond.* Badger, London, 1965, 158p, Paper, Novel [by R. L. Fanthorpe]

05086   *The man who conquered time.* Badger, London, 1962, 156p, Paper, Novel [by R. L. Fanthorpe]

05087   *Mark of the beast.* Badger, London, 1964, 160p, Paper, Novel [by R. L. Fanthorpe]

05088   *Micro infinity.* Badger, London, 1962, 158p, Paper, Novel [by R. Lionel Fanthorpe]

05089   *The mind makers.* Badger, London, 1961, 158p, Paper, Novel [by R. Lionel Fanthorpe]

       Moon rocket. [see 10497A]

05090   *The negative ones.* Badger, London, 1965, 158p, Paper, Novel [by R. Lionel Fanthorpe]

10497   *Night of the big fire.* Badger, London, 1962, 159p, Paper, Novel

10497A retitled: *Moon rocket.* Arcadia House, New York, 1967, 189p, Cloth, Novel

05091   *Orbit one.* Badger, London, 1962, 158p, Paper, Novel [by R. Lionel Fanthorpe]

05091A *Orbit one*, by Mel Jay. Arcadia House, New York, 1966, 189p, Cloth, Novel [by Fanthorpe]

05092   *Out of the night.* Badger, London, 1965?, 159p, Paper, Novel [by R. L. Fanthorpe]

05093   *Perilous galaxy.* Badger, London, 1962, 160p, Paper, Novel [by R. Lionel Fanthorpe]

05094   *Phenomena X.* Badger, London, 1966, 143p, Paper, Novel [by R. Lionel Fanthorpe]

05095   *Reactor XK9.* Badger, London, 1963, 158p, Paper, Novel [by R. Lionel Fanthorpe]

05096   *Return of Zeus.* Badger, London, 1962, 160p, Paper, Novel [by R. Lionel Fanthorpe]

06058   *Search the dark stars.* Badger, London, 1961, 158p, Paper, Novel [by A. A. Glynn]

10498   *Space void.* Badger, London, 1960, 141p, Paper, Novel

10498A *Space void*, by Marston Johns. Arcadia House, New York, 1965, 192p, Cloth, Novel

05097   *Special mission.* Badger, London, 1963, 158p, Paper, Novel [by R. Lionel Fanthorpe]

05098   *Spectre of darkness.* Badger, London, 1965, 158p, Paper, Novel [by R. Lionel Fanthorpe]

05099   *Survival project.* Badger, London, 1966, 143p, Paper, Novel [by R. Lionel Fanthorpe]

05100   *A 1,000 years on.* Badger, London, 1961, 160p, Paper, Novel [by R. Lionel Fanthorpe]

05101   *The ultimate man.* Badger, London, 1961, 158p, Paper, Novel [by R. Lionel Fanthorpe]

05102   *The uninvited.* Badger, London, 1961, 158p, Paper, Novel [by R. Lionel Fanthorpe]

10499   *The unpossessed.* Badger, London, 1961, 158p, Paper, Novel

05103   *Uranium 235.* Badger, London, 1962, 158p, Paper, Novel [by R. Lionel Fanthorpe]

05104   *Vengeance of Siva.* Badger, London, 1962, 160p, Paper, Novel [by R. Lionel Fanthorpe]

05105   *The Venus venture.* Badger, London, 1961, 158p, Paper, Novel [by R. Lionel Fanthorpe]

05105A *The Venus venture*, by Marston Johns. Arcadia House, New York, 1965, 191p, Cloth, Novel [by R. Lionel Fanthorpe]

05106   *The X-machine.* Badger, London, 1962, 157p, Paper, Novel [by R. Lionel Fanthorpe]

as Mel Jay:

    Orbit one. [see 05091A]

as Marston Johns:

    Beyond time. [see 05077A]
    Space void. [see 10498A]
    The Venus venture. [see 05105A]

MULLER, JULIUS W(ashington), 1867-

10500   *The invasion of America; a fact story based on the inexorable mathematics of war.* E. P. Dutton, New York, 1916, 352p, Cloth, Novel

MULLER, PAUL, 1924-

10501   *The man from Ger.* Robert Hale, London, 1974, 191p, Cloth, Novel

MULLER, ROBERT, 1925-

10502   *The lost diaries of Albert Smith.* Jonathan Cape, London, 1965, 352p, Cloth, Novel

MUMFORD, E(dwin) E(mbree), 1932-

10503   *The five flights of the Starfire; collected space fantasies.* Exposition Press, New York, 1974, 261p, Paper, Coll. [Starfire #s 1-5]

10504   *Flight of the Starfire; a fantasy.* Exposition Press, New York, 1972, 61p, Paper, Novel [Starfire #1]

10505   *The fourth flight of the Starfire; a fantasy.* Exposition Press, New York, 1972, 48p, Paper, Story [Starfire #4]

10506   *The second flight of the Starfire; a fantasy.* Exposition Press, New York, 1972, 57p, Paper, Novel [Starfire #2]

MUMFORD, E. E. (cont.)

10507 *The third flight of the Starfire; a fantasy.*
Exposition Press, New York, 1972, 48p,
Paper, Story [Starfire #3]

10508 *The voyage of the Starfire to Atlantis; a
fantasy.* Exposition Press, New York, 1973,
47p, Paper, Story [Starfire #5]

THE MUMMY
see: WEBB, JANE

MUNBY, A(lan) N(oel) L(atimer), 1913-1974
[*biography included*]

10509 *The alabaster hand, and other ghost stories.*
Dennis Dobson, London, 1949, 192p, Cloth,
Coll.

MÜNCH, PAUL GEORGE, 1877-   [published anony-
mously]

10510 *Hindenburg's march into London.* John Long,
London, 1916, 254p, Cloth, Novel

MUNCHAUSEN, Baron
see: RASPE, RUDOLPH ERICH

MUNCHAUSEN, Capt.
see: RASPE, RUDOLPH ERICH

MUNCHAUSEN AT WALCHERON
see: RASPE, RUDOLPH ERICH

MUNCHAUSEN XX
see: WORFEL, W. G.

MUNDAY, JOHN WILLIAM
see: SEELEY, CHARLES SUMNER

MUNDO, OTO, pseud.

10511 *The recovered continent; a tale of the Chinese
invasion.* Harper-Osgood Co., Columbus, OH,
1898, 331p, Paper, Novel

MUNDT, KLARA
see: MUHLBACH, LOUISA

MUNDY, TALBOT, pseud. [William Lancaster Grib-
bon, 1879-1940]

10512 *All four winds, being four novels of India,
containing King--of the Khyber Rifles; Jimgrim; Black light; Om.* Hutchinson, London,
1933, 1232p, Cloth, Coll.

10513 *Black light.* Bobbs-Merrill, Indianapolis,
1930, 315p, Cloth, Novel

10514 *The Devil's Guard.* Bobbs-Merrill, Indianapolis, 1926, 334p, Cloth, Novel [Jimgrim
series]

10514A retitled: *Ramsden.* Hutchinson, London, 1926,
287p, Cloth, Novel [Jimgrim series]

10515 *Full Moon.* D. Appleton-Century, New York,
1935, 312p, Cloth, Novel

10515A retitled: *There was a door.* Hutchinson, Lon-
don, 1935, 287p, Cloth, Novel
Helene. [see 10524D]
Helma. [see 10524B]

10516 *Jimgrim.* Century Co., New York, 1931, 385p,
Cloth, Novel [Jimgrim series]

10516A retitled: *Jimgrim sahib.* Royal, New York,
1953, 319p, Paper, Novel [Jimgrim series]

10517 *King--of the Khyber Rifles; a romance of adventure.* Bobbs-Merrill, Indianapolis, 1916,
395p, Cloth, Novel [King series]

10518 *The Nine Unknown.* Bobbs-Merrill, Indianapolis,
1924, 353p, Cloth, Novel [Jimgrim series;
King series]

10519 *Old Ugly-Face.* Hutchinson, London, 1939, 608p,
Cloth, Novel

10520 *Om; the secret of Ahbor Valley.* Bobbs-Merrill,
Indianapolis, 1924, 392p, Cloth, Novel

10521 *The purple pirate.* D. Appleton-Century, New
York, 1935, 367p, Cloth, Novel [Tros #3]

10522 *Queen Cleopatra; a novel.* Bobbs-Merrill, In-
dianapolis, 1929, 426p, Cloth, Novel [Tros #2]
Ramsden. [see 10514A]
There was a door. [see 10515A]

10523 *The Thunder Dragon Gate.* D. Appleton-Century,
New York, 1937, 335p, Cloth, Novel

10524 *Tros of Samothrace.* D. Appleton-Century, New
York, 1934, 949p, Cloth, Novel [Tros #1]

10524A retitled: *The first book of Tros of Samothrace;
Tros.* Avon, New York, 1967, 239p, Paper,
Novel [abridged]

10524B retitled: *The second book of Tros of Samothrace; Helma.* Avon, New York, 1967, 240p,
Paper, Novel [abridged]

10524C retitled: *The third book of Tros of Samothrace;
Liafail.* Avon, New York, 1967, 255p, Paper,
Novel [abridged]

10524D retitled: *The fourth book of Tros of Samothrace; Helene.* Avon, New York, 1967, 157p,
Paper, Novel [abridged; 10525A, 10525B,
10525C, and 10525D together comprise the
original book]

MUNN, BERTRAM

10525 *The skeleton man; a story of A.D. 1950.* Angold's, London, 1919, 118p, Cloth, Novel

MUNN, H(arold) WARNER, 1903-   [*biography included*]

10526 *King of the world's edge.* Ace, New York,
1966, 191p, Paper, Novel [Gwalchmai #1]

10527 *Merlin's ring.* Ballantine, New York, 1974,
366p, Paper, Novel [Gwalchmai #3]

10528 *The ship from Atlantis.* Ace Double, New York,
1967, 117p, Paper, Novel [Gwalchmai #2]

10529 *The werewolf of Ponkert.* Grandon Co., Providence, RI, 1958, 138p, Cloth, Coll.

MUNRO, H(ector) H(ugh), 1870-1916

10530 *When William came; a story of London under the
Hohenzollerns.* John Lane, London, 1914,
322p, Cloth, Novel

MUNRO, JOHN

    10531 *A trip to Venus; a novel.* Jarrold & Sons, London, 1897, 254p, Cloth, Novel

MUNSON, DONALD, with Monroe Rosenthal

    10532 *President Kissinger; a political fiction.* Freeway Press, New York, 1974, 273p, Paper, Novel

MURFREE, MARY NOAILLES
    see: CRADDOCK, CHARLES

MURPHY, DENNIS JASPER, pseud.
    see: MATURIN, CHARLES ROBERT

MURPHY, G(eorge) READ

    10533 *Beyond the ice, being a story of the newly discovered region round the North Pole, edited from Dr. Frank Farleigh's diary.* Sampson Low, Marston, London, 1894, 326p, Cloth, Novel

MURPHY, ROBERT (William), 1902-1971 [*biography included*]

    10534 *The phantom setter, and other stories.* E. P. Dutton, New York, 1966, 256p, Cloth, Coll.

MURPHY, WARREN, with Richard Sapir

    10535 *The Destroyer; Dr. Quake.* Pinnacle, New York, 1972, 187p, Paper, Novel [Destroyer #5]

MURRAY, ALFRED

    10536 *The old French professor; or, The tragedy of the Café Bertin; a new yarn of New York.* Hurst & Blackett, London, 1907, 220p, Cloth, Novel

MURRAY, (Sir) CHARLES A(ugustus), 1806-1895

    10537 *Nour-ed-Dyn; or, The light of the faith; an Eastern fairy tale.* Society for Promoting Christian Knowledge, London, 1883, 128p, Cloth, Novel

MURRAY, D(avid) CHRISTIE, 1847-1907, with P. Colomb, J. F. Maurice, F. N. Maude, Archibald Forbes, Charles Lowe, and F. Scudamore

    03229 *The Great War of 189-; a forecast.* William Heinemann, London, 1893, 308p, Cloth, Novel

MURRAY, D(avid) L(eslie), 1888-1962

    10538 *Come like shadows; a romance in three ages.* Hodder & Stoughton, London, 1955, 413p, Cloth, Novel

    10539 *Commander of the mists.* Hodder & Stoughton, London, 1938, 477p, Cloth, Novel

MURRAY, G(eorge) G(ilbert) A(imé), 1866-1957

    10540 *Gobi or Shamo; a story of three songs.* Longmans, Green, London, 1889, 376p, Cloth, Novel

MURRAY, JACQUELINE

    10541 *Daughter of Atlantis; a novel.* Regency Press, London, 1958, 167p, Cloth, Novel

MURRAY, LESLIE
    see: LEO, BESSIE

MURRAY, PATRICIA HAGAN, with Florence Stevenson

    10542 *Bianca.* Signet, New York, 1973, 144p, Paper, Novel

MURRAY, V(iolet) T(orlesse), 1874-

    10543 *Fifty masterpieces of mystery.* Odhams Press, London, 1937, 768p, Cloth, Anth. [published anonymously]
    10544 *The rule of the beasts.* Stanley Paul, London, 1925, 191p, Cloth, Novel

MURRY, JOHN MIDDLETON
    see: COWPER, RICHARD

MUSPRATT, ROSALIE (Helen), 1906-1976

    07902 *Tales of terror.* Henry Walker, London, 1931, 167p, Cloth, Coll.

as Jasper John:

    07901 *Sinister stories.* Henry Walker, London, 1930, 171p, Cloth, Coll.

MUSSER, JOE [Joseph L. Musser, 1936-] [*biography included*]

    10545 *Behold a pale horse; a novel.* Zondervan Publishing House, Grand Rapids, Mich., 1970, 140p, Paper, Novel

MUSSET, (Louis Charles) ALFRED de, 1810-1857

    10546 *The white blackbird.* Rodale Press, London, 1955, 56p, Cloth, Novel

MY GREAT-GRANDSON, pseud.

    10547 *1975; a tradition.* E. West, Simpkin, Marshall, London, 1876, 163p, Cloth, Novel

MY GRIMMEST NIGHTMARE

10548 *My grimmest nightmare*. George Allen & Unwin, London, 1935, 210p, Cloth, Anth.
10548A retitled: *Not long for this world*. Telegraph Press, New York, 1936, 224p, Cloth, Anth.

MYERS, HENRY, 1893-

10549 *O king, live for ever; a novel*. Crown Publishers, New York, 1953, 214p, Cloth, Novel
10550 *The utmost island*. Crown Publishers, New York, 1951, 216p, Cloth, Novel

MYERS, JOHN MYERS, 1906- [*biography included*]

10551 *Silverlock*. E. P. Dutton, New York, 1949, 349p, Cloth, Novel

MYERS, WILLIAM WILSHIRE

10552 *Hotep; a dream of the Nile*. Robert Clarke, Cincinnati, 1905, 356p, Cloth, Novel

MYRA, H(arold) L(awrence), 1939-

10553 *No man in Eden*. Word Inc., Waco, TX, 1969, 217p, Cloth, Novel

MYSELF AND ANOTHER, pseud.
see: CASWELL, EDWARD A.

MYSTERY

10554 *Mystery; an anthology of the mysterious in fact and fiction*. Hulton Press, London, 1952, 439p, Cloth, Anth.

MYSTERY TALES OF GHOSTS AND VILLAINS

10555 *Mystery tales of ghosts and villains*. Haldeman-Julius, Girard, KS, 192?, 63p, Paper, Anth.

MYTH, ALLEGORY, AND GOSPEL

10556 *Myth, allegory, and gospel; an interpretation of J. R. R. Tolkien, C. S. Lewis, G. K. Chesterton, Charles Williams*. Bethany Fellowship, Minneapolis, 1974, 159p, Cloth, Nonf. Anth.

N., N.

10557 *Montorel; the story of a coincidence*, by a French author (N. N.). Iris Publishing Co., London, 1915, 277p, Cloth, Novel

NABOKOV, VLADIMIR (Vladimirovich), 1899-1977 [*biography included*]

10558 *Ada; or, Ardor; a family chronicle*. McGraw-Hill, New York, 1969, 589p, Cloth, Novel
10559 *Bend sinister*. Henry Holt, New York, 1947, 242p, Cloth, Novel

NADAAR, ABU
see: MORROUGH, E. R.

NAGPAL, VEENA

10560 *Adventure in space; and, The time travellers*. Echo, Bombay, India, 1967, 104p, Cloth, Coll.

NAILLEN, A. van der
see: van der NAILLEN, A.

NAPIER, MELISSA

10561 *The possession of Elizabeth Calder*. Pocket Books, New York, 1973, 174p, Paper, Novel

NARCEJAC, THOMAS, pseud. [Pierre Ayraud, 1908-], with Pierre Boileau

01590 *Choice cuts*. Arthur Barker, London, 1966, 207p, Cloth, Novel

THE NARRATIVE OF ARTHUR GORDON PYM
see: POE, EDGAR ALLAN

NASH, MARY, 1925- [*biography included*]

10562 *Mrs. Coverlet's magicians*. Little, Brown, Boston, 1961, 189p, Cloth, Novel [Mrs. Coverlet #2]

NATAS, ETH, pseud.

10563 *Exorcism*. Lexington House, Jamaica, NY, 1972, 190p, Paper, Novel

NATHAN, RICHARD

10564 *Sex slaves of the black mass*. Bee-Line, New York, 1971, 156p, Paper, Coll.

NATHAN, ROBERT (Gruntal), 1894- [*biography included*]

10565 *The adventures of Tapiola*. Alfred A. Knopf, New York, 1950, 258p, Cloth, Coll. [includes *Journey of Tapiola* and *Tapiola's brave regiment*; Tapiola #s 1-2]
10566 *The barly fields; a collection of five novels*. Alfred A. Knopf, New York, 1938, 524p, Cloth, Coll. [includes: *The fiddler in barly; The woodcutter's house; The bishop's wife; The orchid; There is another Heaven*]
10567 *The bishop's wife*. Bobbs-Merrill, Indianapolis, 1928, 208p, Cloth, Novel

NATHAN, ROBERT (cont.)

10568 *But gently day.* Alfred A. Knopf, New York,
      1943, 161p, Cloth, Novel
10569 *The devil with love.* Alfred A. Knopf, New
      York, 1963, 203p, Cloth, Novel
10570 *The elixir.* Alfred A. Knopf, New York, 1971,
      176p, Cloth, Novel
10571 *The fair.* Alfred A. Knopf, New York, 1964,
      208p, Cloth, Novel
10572 *The fiddler in barly.* Robert M. McBride, New
      York, 1926, 194p, Cloth, Novel
10573 *The innocent Eve.* Alfred A. Knopf, New York,
      1951, 184p, Cloth, Novel
10574 *Jonah.* Robert M. McBride, New York, 1925,
      212p, Cloth, Novel
10574A retitled: *Son of Amittai.* William Heinemann,
      London, 1925, 166p, Cloth, Novel
10575 *Journey of Tapiola.* Alfred A. Knopf, New
      York, 1938, 121p, Cloth, Novel [Tapiola #1]
10576 *The Mallot diaries.* Alfred A. Knopf, New
      York, 1965, 179p, Cloth, Novel
10577 *The married look.* Alfred A. Knopf, New York,
      1950, 195p, Cloth, Novel
10578 *Mia.* Alfred A. Knopf, New York, 1970, 179p,
      Cloth, Novel
10579 *Mr. Whittle and the morning star.* Alfred A.
      Knopf, New York, 1947, 175p, Cloth, Novel
10580 *Nathan 3; The sea-gull cry; The innocent Eve;
      The river journey; three complete novels.*
      Staples Press, London, 1952, 247p, Cloth,
      Coll.
10581 *Portrait of Jennie.* Alfred A. Knopf, New
      York, 1940, 212p, Cloth, Novel
10582 *The puppet master.* Robert M. McBride, New
      York, 1923, 221p, Cloth, Novel
10583 *The river journey.* Alfred A. Knopf, New York,
      1949, 196p, Cloth, Novel
10584 *Road of ages.* Alfred A. Knopf, New York,
      1935, 232p, Cloth, Novel
10585 *Sir Henry.* Alfred A. Knopf, New York, 1955,
      187p, Cloth, Novel
10586 *So love returns.* Alfred A. Knopf, New York,
      1958, 214p, Cloth, Novel
      Son of Amittai. [see 10574A]
10587 *Stonecliff.* Alfred A. Knopf, New York, 1967,
      176p, Cloth, Novel
10588 *The summer meadows.* Delacorte Press, New York,
      1973, 117p, Cloth, Novel
10589 *Tapiola's brave regiment.* Alfred A. Knopf,
      New York, 1941, 137p, Cloth, Novel [Tapiola
      #2]
10590 *There is another Heaven.* Bobbs-Merrill, In-
      dianapolis, 1929, 190p, Cloth, Novel
10591 *They went on together.* Alfred A. Knopf, New
      York, 1941, 191p, Cloth, Novel
10592 *The train in the meadow.* Alfred A. Knopf,
      New York, 1953, 178p, Cloth, Novel
10593 *The Weans.* Alfred A. Knopf, New York, 1960,
      56p, Cloth, Novel
10594 *The wilderness-stone.* Alfred A. Knopf, New
      York, 1961, 204p, Cloth, Novel
10595 *The woodcutter's house.* Bobbs-Merrill, Indi-
      anapolis, 1927, 205p, Cloth, Novel

NATSUME, SŌSEKI, pseud. [Natsume, Kin'nosuke,
1867-1916]

10596 *I am a cat.* H. Shoten, Tokyo, 1906, 133p,
      Cloth, Novel

NATTI, MARY LEE
      see: KINGMAN, LEE

A NAVAL OFFICER
      see: M., A. H.

NAVARCHUS, pseud.
      see: VAUX, PATRICK and YEXLEY, LIONEL

NAVASKY, VICTOR, 1932-   [*biography included*],
with Jack Newfield, Richard Lingeman, Karla
Kuskin, and Marvin Kitman

08300 *Animal ranch; the great American fable.* Paral-
      lax Publishing Co., New York, 1966, 63p,
      Paper, Novel

NEAL, JOHN, 1793-1876

10597 *Logan; a family history.* H. C. Carey & I. Lea,
      Philadelphia, 1822, vol. I-317p, II-341p,
      Cloth, Novel [published anonymously]
10598 *Rachel Dyer; a North American story.* Shirley
      & Hyde, Portland, Maine, 1828, 276p, Cloth,
      Novel

NEALE, ARTHUR

10599 *The great weird stories.* Duffield & Co., New
      York, 1929, 409p, Cloth, Anth.

NEARING, H(omer) Jr., 1915-

10600 *The sinister researches of C. P. Ransom.* Doub-
      leday, Garden City, 1954, 217p, Cloth, Coll.

NECKER, CLAIRE (Kral), 1917-   [*biography included*]

10601 *Supernatural cats; an anthology.* Doubleday,
      Garden City, 1972, 439p, Cloth, Anth.

"NEDRAM," pseud.

10602 *John Sagur.* Heath Cranton, London, 1921, 272p,
      Cloth, Novel

NEESAM, MALCOLM

10603 *Into space.* Library Association, Youth Lib-
      raries Group, Birmingham, UK, 1972, 16p,
      Paper, Nonf.

NEGLEY, GLENN (Robert), 1907-   [*biography included*], with J. Max Patrick

10604 *The quest for utopia; an anthology of imaginary
      societies.* Henry Schuman, New York, 1952,
      599p, Cloth, Anth.

NEILL, A(lexander) S(utherland), 1883-1973

10605 *The last man alive; a story for children from the age of seven to seventy.* Herbert Jenkins, London, 1938, 255p, Cloth, Novel

NEILL, PETER, 1941-

10606 *A time piece.* Grossman Publishers, New York, 1970, 151p, Cloth, Novel

NEILL, ROBERT

10607 *So fair a house.* Hutchinson, London, 1960, 255p, Cloth, Novel

NELSON, ALBERT D.

10608 *America betrayed; save the nation.* Suttonhouse Publishers, Los Angeles, 1936, 299p, Cloth, Novel

NELSON, ARTHUR A.

10609 *Wings of danger; a novel.* Robert M. McBride, New York, 1915, 448p, Cloth, Novel

NELSON, RAY [Radell Faraday Nelson, 1931-] [*biography included*], with Philip K. Dick

04319 *The Ganymede takeover.* Ace, New York, 1967, 157p, Paper, Novel

NEMBHARD, MABEL

10610 *Fantasies.* George Allen, London, 1896, 198p, Cloth, Coll.

NEPEAN, HUBERT, with Douglas Goldring

06103 *The solvent.* C. W. Daniel, London, 1920, 256p, Cloth, Novel

NESBIT, E(dith), 1858-1924

10611 *The book of dragons.* Harper & Bros., New York, 1901, 290p, Cloth, Coll.
10612 retitled: *The complete book of dragons.* Hamish Hamilton, London, 1972, 198p, Cloth, Coll. [includes one extra story]
10613 *The enchanted castle.* T. Fisher Unwin, London, 1907, 352p, Cloth, Novel
10614 *Fear.* Stanley Paul, London, 1910, 318p, Cloth, Coll.
10615 *Five children and it.* T. Fisher Unwin, London, 1902, 301p, Cloth, Novel [Psammaed #1]
10616 *The five children, containing Five children and it, The phoenix and the carpet, The story of the amulet.* Coward-McCann, New York, 1930, 808p, Cloth, Coll. [Psammaed #s 1-3]
10617 *Grim tales.* A. D. Innes, London, 1893, 167p, Cloth, Coll.
10618 *The magic city.* Macmillan, London, 1910, 333p, Cloth, Novel

10619 *The phoenix and the carpet.* George Newnes, London, 1904, 236p, Cloth, Novel [Psammaed #2]
10620 *The story of the amulet.* T. Fisher Unwin, London, 1906, 374p, Cloth, Novel [Psammaed #3]

NESVADBA, JOSEF, 1926- [*biography included*]

10621 *In the footsteps of the abominable snowman; stories of science and fantasy.* Victor Gollancz, London, 1970, 215p, Cloth, Coll.
10621A retitled: *The lost face; best science fiction from Czechoslovakia.* Taplinger Publishing Co., New York, 1971, 215p, Cloth, Coll.
10622 *Vampires Ltd.; stories of science and fantasy.* Artia, Prague, 1964, 225p, Paper, Coll.

NETHERCLIFT, BERYL

10623 *The snowstorm.* Hutchinson, London, 1967, 183p, Cloth, Novel

NETHERWOOD, BRYAN A(rthur)

10624 *Medley macabre; an anthology of stories of the supernatural, being ghosts, psychical phenomena, uncanny mysteries.* Hammond & Co., London, 1966, 544p, Cloth, Anth.
10625 *Terror! an anthology of blood-curdling stories.* Blackie & Son, London, 1970, 392p, Cloth, Anth.
10626 *Uncanny; tales of the spectral and supernatural.* Blackie & Son, London, 1974, 306p, Cloth, Anth.

NETTERVILLE, LUKE, pseud. [Standish James O'Grady, 1846-1928]

10627 *The queen of the world; or, Under the tyranny.* Lawrence & Bullen, London, 1900, 293p, Cloth, Novel

NEUFELD, JOHN (Arthur), 1938- [*biography included*]

10628 *Sleep, two, three, four! a political thriller.* Harper & Row, New York, 1971, 201p, Cloth, Novel

NEVER TRUST A MARTIAN

10629 *Never trust a Martian.* American Science Fiction, Sydney, 1954, 34p, Paper, Anth.

NEVILLE, DEREK

10630 *Bright morrow.* John Crowther, London, 1947, 157p, Cloth, Novel

NEVILLE, KRIS (Ottman), 1925- [*biography included*]

10631 *Bettyann.* Tower, New York, 1970, 170p, Paper, Novel

NEVILLE, KRIS (cont.)

10632   *Invaders on the Moon*. Belmont, New York, 1970, 173p, Paper, Novel

10633   *Mission: manstop*. Leisure, North Hollywood, 1971, 173p, Paper, Coll.

10634   *The mutants*. Belmont, New York, 1966, 158p, Paper, Novel

10635   *Peril of the starmen*. Belmont Double, New York, 1967, 72p, Paper, Novel

10636   *Special delivery*. Belmont Double, New York, 1967, 78p, Paper, Novel

10637   *The unearth people*. Belmont, New York, 1964, 157p, Paper, Novel

NEVINSON, C(hristopher) R(ichard) W(ynne), 1889-1946, with Princess Paul Troubetzkoy

10638   *Exodus A.D.; a warning to civilians*. Hutchinson, London, 1934, 288p, Cloth, Novel

NEW ATALANTIS
    see: MANLEY, MARY

THE NEW BATTLE OF DORKING
    see: MAUDE, F. N.

NEW ERA
    see: CARYL, CHAS. W.

NEW LIVES FOR OLD
    see: SNOW, CHARLES P.

THE NEW ORDEAL
    see: CHESNEY, GEORGE T.

NEW TALES OF HORROR BY EMINENT AUTHORS

10639   *New tales of horror by eminent authors*. Hutchinson, London, 1934, 256p, Cloth, Anth.

NEW WAGGINGS OF OLD TALES
    see: BANGS, JOHN KENDRICK and SHERMAN, FRANK DEMPSTER

NEWBOLT, (Sir) HENRY (John), 1862-1938

10640   *Aladore*. William Blackwood & Sons, Edinburgh, 1914, 363p, Cloth, Novel

NEWBY, P(ercy) H(oward), 1918-   [*biography included*]

10641   *The spirit of Jem*. John Lehmann, London, 1947, 205p, Cloth, Novel

NEWCOMB, CYRUS F(lint), 1831-1905 [published anonymously]

10642   *The book of Algoonah, being a concise account of the history of the early people of the continent of America, known as the Mound*

Builders. Little & Becker, Printers, St. Louis, 1884, 353p, Cloth, Novel

NEWCOMB, SIMON, 1835-1909

10643   *His Wisdom, the Defender; a story*. Harper & Bros., New York, 1900, 329p, Cloth, Novel

NEWELL, C(harles) M(artin), 1821-1900

10644   *The isle of palms; adventures while wrecking for gold, encounter with a mad whale, battle with a devil-fish, and capture of a mermaid*. DeWolfe, Fiske & Co., Boston, 1888, 460p, Cloth, Novel

10645   *Kalani of Oahu; an historical romance of Hawaii* The Author, Boston, 1881, 415p, Cloth, Novel

NEWFIELD, JACK, 1939-   [*biography included*], with Victor S. Navasky, Richard R. Lingeman, Karla Kuskin, and Marvin Kitman

08300   *Animal ranch; the great American fable*. Parallax Publishing Co., New York, 1966, 63p, Paper, Novel

NEWMAN, BERNARD (Charles), 1897-1968

10646   *Armoured doves; a peace book*. Jarrolds Publishers, London, 1931, 288p, Cloth, Novel

10647   *The blue ants; the first authentic account of the Russian-Chinese war of 1970*. Robert Hale, London, 1962, 192p, Cloth, Novel

10648   *The flying saucer*. Victor Gollancz, London, 1948, 250p, Cloth, Novel

10649   *Hosanna! the remarkable novel*. Denis Archer, London, 1933, 287p, Cloth, Novel

10650   *Secret weapon*. Victor Gollancz, London, 1941, 189p, Cloth, Novel

10651   *Shoot!* Victor Gollancz, London, 1949, 241p, Cloth, Novel

10652   *The wishful think*. Robert Hale, London, 1954, 192p, Cloth, Novel

NEWMAN, HOWARD, 1911-   [*biography included*]

10653   *The exorcist; the strange story behind the film*. Pinnacle, New York, 1974, 169p, Paper, Nonf.

NEWMAN, ROBERT (Howard), 1909-   [*biography included*]

10654   *The boy who could fly*. Atheneum, New York, 1967, 121p, Cloth, Novel

10655   *Corbie*. Harcourt, Brace & World, New York, 1966, 314p, Cloth, Novel

10656   *Merlin's mistake*. Atheneum, New York, 1970, 237p, Cloth, Novel [Tertius #1]

10657   *The testing of Tertius*. Atheneum, New York, 1973, 186p, Cloth, Novel [Tertius #2]

NEWQUIST, ROY
    see: STERLAND, CARL

NEWRY BRIDGE

10658 *Newry Bridge; or, Ireland in 1887.* William
         Blackwood & Sons, Edinburgh, 1886, 72p,
         Paper?, Novel

NEWTE, HORACE W(ykeham) C(an), 1870-1949

10659 *The Ealing miracle; a realistic story.* Mills
         & Boon, London, 1911, 414p, Cloth, Novel
10660 *The master beast, being a true account of the
         ruthless tyranny inflicted on the British
         people by socialism, A.D. 1888-2020.* Reb-
         man Ltd., London, 1907, 249p, Cloth, Novel
10660A retitled: *The red fury; Britain under Bolshe-
         vism.* Holden & Hardingham, London, 1919,
         249p, Cloth, Novel

NEWTON, BERTHA

10661 *My life in time.* C. W. Daniel, London, 1938,
         236p, Cloth, Novel

NEWTON, (Wilfrid) DOUGLAS, 1884-1951

10662 *The beggar, and other stories.* Washbourne &
         Bogan, London, 1933, 286p, Cloth, Coll.
10663 *Dr. Odin.* Cassell, London, 1933, 280p, Cloth,
         Novel
10664 *The North afire; a picture of what may be.*
         Methuen, London, 1914, 200p, Cloth, Novel
10665 *Savaran and the Great Sand.* Cassell, London,
         1939, 282p, Cloth, Novel

NEWTON, J(ohn) H.

10666 *The Aztec treasure.* Thomas Nelson & Sons,
         London, 1936, 288p, Cloth, Novel

NEWTON, JOSEPH EMERSON

10667 *White kimono.* Pageant Press, New York, 1957,
         202p, Cloth, Novel

NEWTON, JULIUS P.

10668 *The forgotten race.* Digit, London, 1963,
         158p, Paper, Novel

NIALL, IAN, pseud. [John McNeillie]

10669 *The boy who saw tomorrow.* William Heinemann,
         London, 1952, 259p, Cloth, Novel

NICHOL, C. A. SCRYMSOUR

10670 *The mystery of the North Pole.* Francis Grif-
         fiths, London, 1908, 238p, Cloth, Novel

NICHOLS, ROBERT (Malise Bowyer), 1893-1944

10671 *Fantastica, being The smile of the sphinx,
         and other tales of imagination.* Chatto &
         Windus, London, 1923, 515p, Cloth, Coll.

NICHOLS, (Joanna) RUTH, 1948-   [*biography included*]

10672 *The marrow of the world.* A Margaret K. McEl-
         derry Book, Atheneum, New York, 1972, 168p,
         Cloth, Novel
10673 *A walk out of the world.* Harcourt, Brace &
         World, New York, 1969, 192p, Cloth, Novel

NICHOLSON, C(elia) A(nna)

10674 *Wrath of the shades.* Methuen, London, 1933,
         279p, Cloth, Novel

NICHOLSON, JOHN, pseud. [Norman Howe Parcell]

10675 *Costello, psychic investigator.* Arthur H.
         Stockwell, Ilfracombe, UK, 1954, 238p, Cloth,
         Coll.
10676 *Space ship to Venus, being an account of an
         amazing journey undertaken by Docter Laviers,
         scientist, Jeremy Cousins, Jack Carruthers,
         Donald Trew, and Job Winch, with a record of
         some of their strange adventures on the sil-
         ver planet.* Venturebooks, Bath, UK, 1948,
         233p, Cloth, Novel

NICHOLSON, JOHN H(enry), 1838-1923

10677 *The adventures of Halek; an autobiographical
         fragment.* Griffith & Farran, London, 1882,
         373p, Cloth, Novel
10677A retitled: *Halek; a romance.* A. J. Ross, Bris-
         bane, 1896, 390p, Cloth, Novel

NICHOLSON, JOSEPH SHIELD, 1850-1927 [published
anonymously]

10678 *A dreamer of dreams; a modern romance,* by the
         author of "Thoth." William Blackwood & Sons,
         Edinburgh, 1889, 250p, Cloth, Novel
10679 *Thoth; a romance.* William Blackwood & Sons,
         Edinburgh, 1888, 209p, Cloth, Novel
10680 *Toxar; a romance,* by the author of "Thoth."
         Longmans, Green, London, 1890, 289p, Cloth,
         Novel

NICHOLSON, MALCOLM WHEELER-
   see: WHEELER-NICHOLSON, MALCOLM

NICOLE, CLAUDETTE, pseud. [John Messmann]

10681 *The haunting of Drumroe.* Fawcett Gold Medal,
         Greenwich, Conn., 1971, 144p, Paper, Novel

NICOLL, MAURICE
   see: SWAYNE, MARTIN

NICOLSON, HAROLD (George), 1886-1968 [*biography included*]

10682 *Public faces; a novel.* Constable, London,
         1932, 350p, Cloth, Novel

NICOLSON, J(ohn) U(rban), 1885-

10683 *Fingers of fear.* Covici-Friede Publishers, New York, 1937, 309p, Cloth, Novel

NICOLSON, MARJORIE (Hope), 1894- [*biography included*]

10684 *Voyages to the Moon.* Macmillan, New York, 1948, 297p, Cloth, Nonf.

NICULESCU, MIHAI, 1909- , with Mircea Eliade

04761 *Fantastic tales.* Dillon's University Book-shop, London, 1969, 100p, Cloth, Coll. [in Rumanian and English]

NIELS KLIM
    see: HOLBERG, LUDVIG

NIELSEN, HELGA

10685 *Deep in the sky; a science fiction novel.* Exposition Press, New York, 1955, 161p, Cloth, Novel

NIEMANN, (Wilhelm Otto) AUGUST, 1839-1919

10686 *The coming conquest of England.* George Routledge & Sons, London, 1904, 384p, Cloth, Novel

NIGHT OF THE SPHINX, AND OTHER STORIES
    see: ELWOOD, ROGER

NIGHTMARES

10687 *Nightmares; a collection of uneasy tales.* Philip Allan, London, 1933, 255p, Cloth, Anth.

NIMSHI
    see: CARLISLE, SAMUEL

NIN, ANAÏS, 1903-1977

10688 *House of incest.* Siana Éditions, Paris, 1936, 89p, Cloth, Novel

1945

10689 *1945; a vision.* F. & J. Rivington, London, 1845, 39p, Paper, Story

NISBET, HUME, 1849-1921?

10690 *A crafty foe; romance of the sea.* F. V. White, London, 1901, 318p, Cloth, Novel
10691 *The empire builders; a romance of adventure and war in South Africa.* F. V. White, London, 1900, 312p, Cloth, Novel

10692 *The great secret; a tale of to-morrow.* F. V. White, London, 1895, 304p, Cloth, Novel
10693 *The haunted station, and other stories.* F. V. White, London, 1893, 314p, Cloth, Coll.
10694 *The "Jolly Roger"; a story of sea heroes and pirates.* Digby, Long, London, 1892, 308p, Cloth, Novel
10695 *Stories weird and wonderful.* F. V. White, London, 1900, 127p, Paper, Coll.
10696 *Valdmer the Viking; a romance of the eleventh century by sea and land.* Hutchinson, London, 1893, 306p, Cloth, Novel

NISOT, MAVIS ELIZABETH
    see: PENMARE, WILLIAM

NISWONGER, CHARLES ELLIOT

10697 *The Isle of Feminine.* Brown Printing Co., Little Rock, Ark., 1893, 160p, Cloth, Novel

NIVEN, LARRY [Laurence Van Cott Niven, 1938-] [*biography included*]

10698 *All the myriad ways.* Ballantine, New York, 1971, 181p, Paper, Coll.
10699 *The flight of the horse.* Ballantine, New York, 1973, 212p, Paper, Coll.
10700 *A gift from Earth.* Ballantine, New York, 1968, 254p, Paper, Novel
10701 *A hole in space.* Ballantine, New York, 1974, 196p, Paper, Coll.
10702 *Inconstant moon.* Victor Gollancz, London, 1973, 251p, Cloth, Coll.
10703 *Neutron star.* Ballantine, New York, 1968, 285p, Paper, Coll.
10704 *Protector.* Ballantine, New York, 1973, 218p, Paper, Novel
10705 *Ringworld.* Ballantine, New York, 1970, 342p, Paper, Novel
10706 *The shape of space.* Ballantine, New York, 1969, 244p, Paper, Coll.
10707 *World of Ptavvs.* Ballantine, New York, 1966, 188p, Paper, Novel

with David Gerrold:

05916 *The flying sorcerers.* Ballantine, New York, 1971, 316p, Paper, Novel

with Jerry Pournelle:

10708 *The mote in God's eye.* Simon & Schuster, New York, 1974, 537p, Cloth, Novel

NIZZI, GUIDO "SKIPPER," 1900- [*biography included*]

10709 *The daring trip to the Moon.* Carlton Press, New York, 1968, , Cloth, Novel [Paralyzing Ray series]
10710 *The paralyzing ray vs. the nuclears; a novel.* Vantage Press, New York, 1964, 185p, Cloth, Novel [Paralyzing Ray series]
10711 *The victor; a novel.* Exposition Press, New York, 1946, 147p, Cloth, Novel [Paralyzing Ray series]

NO MIND OF MAN

10712   *No mind of man; three original novellas of
        science fiction.* Hawthorn, New York, 1973,
        182p, Cloth, Anth.

NOBES, PATRICK, with John Wyndham

10713   *The triffids.* Bulls-Eye Book, Hutchinson,
        London, 1973, 124p, Paper, Novel [adapted
        from Wyndham's novel, *The day of the trif-
        fids*]

NOBLE, EDWARD, 1857-1941

10714   *Fisherman's gat; a story of the Thames estu-
        ary.* William Blackwood & Sons, Edinburgh,
        1906, 355p, Cloth, Novel
10714A retitled: *The issue; a story of the river
        Thames.* Doubleday, Page, New York, 1907,
        407p, Cloth, Novel

NOBLE, WILLIAM

10715   *Consternation in Mars; dispatches of Faynt
        Dams, ex mock M.P.* Noble Bros., London,
        1932, 149p, Cloth, Novel

NOEL, L., pseud. [Leonard Noel Barker]

10716   *The golden star; a love story of to-morrow.*
        Stanley Paul, London, 1935, 288p, Cloth,
        Novel

NOEL, STERLING, 1903-   [*biography included*]

10717   *I killed Stalin.* Farrar, Straus & Young, New
        York, 1951, 281p, Cloth, Novel
10718   *We who survived.* Avon, New York, 1959, 160p,
        Paper, Novel

NOLAN, BRIAN O'
    see: O'BRIEN, FLANN

NOLAN, WILLIAM F(rancis), 1928-   [*biography
included*]

10719   *Alien horizons.* Pocket Books, New York,
        1974, 191p, Paper, Coll.
        Almost human. [see 10724A]
10720   *The future is now; all-new all-star science
        fiction stories.* Sherbourne Press, Los An-
        geles, 1970, 248p, Cloth, Anth.
10721   *The human equation; 4 science fiction novels
        of tomorrow.* Sherbourne Press, Los Angeles,
        1972, 254p, Cloth, Anth.
10722   *Impact 20.* Paperback Library, New York, 1963,
        158p, Paper, Anth.
10723   *Man against tomorrow.* Avon, New York, 1965,
        191p, Paper, Anth.
10724   *The pseudo-people; androids in science fic-
        tion.* Sherbourne Press, Los Angeles, 1965,
        238p, Cloth, Anth.
10724A retitled: *Almost human; androids in science
        fiction.* Souvenir Press, London, 1966,
        227p, Cloth, Anth.

10725   *Ray Bradbury review.* William F. Nolan, San
        Diego, 1952, 63p, Paper, Nonf. Anth.
10726   *A sea of space.* Bantam, New York, 1970, 195p,
        Paper, Anth.
10727   *Space for hire.* Lancer, New York, 1971, 174p,
        Paper, Novel
10728   *3 to the highest power.* Avon, New York, 1968,
        160p, Paper, Anth.
10729   *A wilderness of stars; stories of man in con-
        flict with space.* Sherbourne Press, Los
        Angeles, 1969, 277p, Cloth, Anth.

with George Clayton Johnson:

07924   *Logan's run; a novel.* Dial Press, New York,
        1967, 133p, Cloth, Novel

NOONE, EDWINA, pseud.
    see: AVALLONE, MICHAEL

NORDAY, MICHAEL, pseud.

10730   *Dark magic.* Vixen Press, New York, 1954, 182p,
        Cloth, Novel
10730A retitled: *The thrill seeker*, by Ray Damon.
        Chariot, New York, 1960, 188p, Paper, Novel

as Ray Damon:

        The thrill seeker. [see 10730A]

NORDEN, ERIC

10731   *The ultimate solution.* Warner, New York, 1973,
        142p, Paper, Novel

THE NORMAL LOVECRAFT
    see: de la REE, GERRY

NORMAN, DOREEN

10732   *To vanishing point.* Carousel, London, 1971,
        93p, Paper, Novel

NORMAN, (Sir) HENRY, Bart., 1858-1939

10733   *The broken shaft; tales in mid-ocean.* T. Fi-
        sher Unwin, London, 1886, 108p, Cloth, Anth.
10734   *The witching time; tales for the year's end.*
        D. Appleton, New York, 1887, 315p, Cloth,
        Anth.

NORMAN, JAMES, pseud. [James Norman Schmidt,
1912-   ]

10735   *A little north of everywhere.* Pellegrini &
        Cudahy, New York, 1951, 192p, Cloth, Novel

NORMAN, JOHN, pseud. [John Frederick Lange,
Jr., 1931-   ] [*biography included*]

10736   *Assassin of Gor.* Ballantine, New York, 1970,
        409p, Paper, Novel [Tarl Cabot #5]
10737   *Captive of Gor.* Ballantine, New York, 1972,
        370p, Paper, Novel [Tarl Cabot #7]
10738   *Gor omnibus; the chronicles of Counter Earth.*
        Sidgwick & Jackson, London, 1972, 789p,

NORMAN, JOHN (cont.)

       Cloth, Coll. [includes *Tarnsman of Gor*, *Outlaw of Gor*, and *Priest-Kings of Gor*]

10739   *Hunters of Gor*. DAW, New York, 1974, 320p, Paper, Novel [Tarl Cabot #8]

10740   *Imaginative sex*. DAW, New York, 1974, 269p, Paper, Nonf.

10741   *Nomads of Gor*. Ballantine, New York, 1969, 344p, Paper, Novel [Tarl Cabot #4]

10742   *Outlaw of Gor*. Ballantine, New York, 1967, 255p, Paper, Novel [Tarl Cabot #2]

10743   *Priest-Kings of Gor*. Ballantine, New York, 1968, 317p, Paper, Novel [Tarl Cabot #3]

10744   *Raiders of Gor*. Ballantine, New York, 1971, 312p, Paper, Novel [Tarl Cabot #6]

10745   *Tarnsman of Gor*. Ballantine, New York, 1966, 219p, Paper, Novel [Tarl Cabot #1]

NORRIS, (Benjamin) FRANK(lin), 1870-1902

10746   *The joyous miracle*. Doubleday, Page, New York, 1906, 27p, Cloth, Story

NORRIS, FRANK (Callan), 1907-1967

10747   *Nutro 29; a romance*. Rinehart & Co., New York, 1950, 307p, Cloth, Novel

NORRIS, KATHLEEN, 1880-1966

10748   *Through a glass darkly*. Doubleday, Garden City, 1957, 287p, Cloth, Novel

NORRIS, MARY HARRIOTT, 1848-1919

10749   *The veil; a fantasy*. Richard G. Badger, Boston, 1907, 309p, Cloth, Novel

NORTH, ANDREW, pseud.
   see: NORTON, ANDRE

NORTH, ERIC, pseud. [Bernard Charles Cronin, 1884-]

10750   *The ant men; a science fantasy novel*. John C. Winston, Philadelphia, 1955, 216p, Cloth, Novel

as Bernard Cronin:

10751   *Toad*. Hodder & Stoughton, London, 1929, 320p, Cloth, Novel

NORTH, FRANKLIN H.

10752   *The awakening of Noahville*. New York Publishing Co., New York, 1898, 383p, Cloth, Novel

NORTH, JOAN (Marian), 1920- [*biography included*]

10753   *The Cloud Forest*. Rupert Hart-Davis, London, 1965, 192p, Cloth, Novel

10754   *Emperor of the Moon*. Geoffrey Bles, London, 1956, 127p, Cloth, Novel

10755   *The Light Maze*. An Ariel Book, Farrar, Straus & Giroux, New York, 1971, 186p, Cloth, Novel

10756   *The Whirling Shapes*. An Ariel Book, Farrar, Straus & Giroux, New York, 1967, 183p, Cloth, Novel

NORTH, STERLING, 1906-1974 [*biography included*], with C. B. Boutell

01675   *Speak of the devil*. Doubleday, Doran, Garden City, 1945, 334p, Cloth, Anth.

THE NORTH POLE, AND CHARLIE WILSON'S ADVENTURES IN SEARCH OF IT
   see: The author of "The realm of the ice king"

NORTHCOTE, AMYAS

10757   *In ghostly company*. John Lane, The Bodley Head, London, 1921, 287p, Cloth, Coll.

NORTHRUP, EDWIN FITCH
   see: PSEUDOMAN, AKKAD

NORTHUMBERLAND, (Alan Ian Percy, eighth) Duke of, 1880-1930

10758   *The shadow of the moor*. William Blackwood & Sons, Edinburgh, 1930, 69p, Cloth, Novel

NORTON, ALDEN H(olmes), 1903- [*biography included*]

10462   *The Award science fiction reader*. Award, New York, 1966, 188p, Paper, Anth. [ghost-edited by Sam Moskowitz]

10759   *Futures unlimited*. Pyramid, New York, 1969, 239p, Paper, Anth.

10465   *Hauntings and horrors; ten grisly tales*. Berkley Medallion, New York, 1969, 171p, Paper, Anth. [ghost-edited by Sam Moskowitz]

10466   *Horror times ten*. Berkley Medallion, New York, 1967, 176p, Paper, Anth. [ghost-edited by Sam Moskowitz]

10468   *Masters of horror*. Berkley Medallion, New York, 1968, 192p, Paper, Anth. [ghost-edited by Sam Moskowitz]

with Sam Moskowitz:

10463   *Ghostly by gaslight; fearful tales of a lost era*. Pyramid, New York, 1971, 223p, Paper, Anth.

10464   *Great untold stories of fantasy and horror*. Pyramid, New York, 1969, 222p, Paper, Anth.

10467   *Horrors in hiding*. Berkley Medallion, New York, 1973, 192p, Paper, Anth.

10469   *The space magicians*. Pyramid, New York, 1971, 206p, Paper, Anth.

NORTON, ANDRE (Alice), 1912- [*biography included*] [originally Alice Mary Norton]

10760 *Android at arms.* Harcourt Brace Jovanovich, New York, 1971, 253p, Cloth, Novel

10761 *The Beast Master.* Harcourt, Brace & Co., New York, 1959, 192p, Cloth, Novel [Hosteen Storm #1]

10762 *Breed to come.* Viking Press, New York, 1972, 285p, Cloth, Novel

10763 *Catseye.* Harcourt, Brace & World, New York, 1961, 192p, Cloth, Novel [Dipple #1]

10764 *The crossroads of time.* Ace Double, New York, 1956, 169p, Paper, Novel [Blake Walker #1]

10765 *The crystal gryphon.* A Margaret K. McElderry Book, Atheneum, New York, 1972, 234p, Cloth, Novel [Witch World--High Hallack #1]

10766 *Dark piper.* Harcourt, Brace & World, New York, 1968, 249p, Cloth, Novel
Daybreak...2250 A.D. [see 10810A]

10767 *The defiant agents.* World Publishing Co., Cleveland, 1962, 224p, Cloth, Novel [Time Agents #3]

10768 *Dragon magic.* Thomas Y. Crowell, New York, 1972, 213p, Cloth, Novel

10769 *Dread companion.* Harcourt Brace Jovanovich, New York, 1970, 234p, Cloth, Novel

10770 *Exiles of the stars.* Viking Press, New York, 1971, 255p, Cloth, Novel [Lydis #2]

10771 *Eye of the monster.* Ace Double, New York, 1962, 80p, Paper, Novel

10772 *Forerunner foray.* Viking Press, New York, 1973, 286p, Cloth, Novel

10773 *Fur magic.* World Publishing Co., Cleveland, 1968, 174p, Cloth, Novel

10774 *Galactic derelict.* World Publishing Co., Cleveland, 1959, 224p, Cloth, Novel [Time Agents #2]

10775 *Garan the eternal.* Fantasy Publishing Co., Alhambra, CA, 1972, 199p, Cloth, Coll.
Gray magic. [see 10813A]

10776 *Here abide monsters.* A Margaret K. McElderry Book, Atheneum, New York, 1973, 215p, Cloth, Novel

10777 *High sorcery.* Ace, New York, 1970, 156p, Paper, Coll.

10778 *Huon of the horn, being a tale of that Duke of Bordeaux who came to sorrow at the hands of Charlemagne, and yet who won the favor of Oberon, the elf king, to his lasting fame and great glory.* Harcourt, Brace & Co., New York, 1951, 208p, Cloth, Novel

10779 *Ice crown.* Viking Press, New York, 1970, 256p, Cloth, Novel

10780 *Iron cage.* Viking Press, New York, 1974, 288p, Cloth, Novel

10781 *The jargoon pard.* A Margaret K. McElderry Book, Atheneum, New York, 1974, 194p, Cloth, Novel [Witch World--High Hallack #4]

10782 *Judgment on Janus.* Harcourt, Brace & World, New York, 1963, 220p, Cloth, Novel [Naill Renfro #1; Dipple #2]

10783 *Key out of time.* World Publishing Co., Cleveland, 1963, 224p, Cloth, Novel [Time Agents #4]
The last planet. [see 10811A]

10784 *Lavender-green magic.* Thomas Y. Crowell, New York, 1974, 241p, Cloth, Novel

10785 *Lord of Thunder.* Harcourt, Brace & World, New York, 1962, 192p, Cloth, Novel [Hosteen Storm #2]

10786 *The many worlds of Andre Norton.* Chilton Book Co., Radnor, PA, 1974, 208p, Cloth, Coll.

10787 *Moon of three rings.* Viking Press, New York, 1966, 316p, Cloth, Novel [Lydis #1]

10788 *Night of masks.* Harcourt, Brace & World, New York, 1964, 191p, Cloth, Novel [Dipple #3]

10789 *Octagon magic.* World Publishing Co., Cleveland, 1967, 189p, Cloth, Novel

10790 *Operation time search.* Harcourt, Brace & World, New York, 1967, 224p, Cloth, Novel

10791 *Ordeal in otherwhere.* World Publishing Co., Cleveland, 1964, 221p, Cloth, Novel [Warlock #2]

10792 *Outside.* Walker, New York, 1974, 126p, Cloth, Novel

10793 *Postmarked the stars.* Harcourt, Brace & World, New York, 1969, 223p, Cloth, Novel [Solar Queen #4]

10794 *Quest crosstime.* Viking Press, New York, 1965, 253p, Cloth, Novel [Blake Walker #2]

10795 *Rogue Reynard, being a tale of the fortunes and misfortunes and divers misdeeds of that great villain, Baron Reynard, the fox, and how he was served with King Lion's justice; based upon the beast saga.* Houghton Mifflin, Boston, 1947, 96p, Cloth, Novel
Sargasso of space. [see 10826A]

10796 *Sea siege.* Harcourt, Brace & Co., New York, 1957, 216p, Cloth, Novel

10797 *Secret of the lost race.* Ace Double, New York, 1959, 132p, Paper, Novel

10798 *The Sioux Spaceman.* Ace Double, New York, 1960, 133p, Paper, Novel

10799 *Small shadows creep.* E. P. Dutton, New York, 1974, 195p, Cloth, Anth.

10800 *Sorceress of the witch world.* Ace, New York, 1968, 221p, Paper, Novel [Witch World--Estcarp #5]

10801 *Space pioneers.* World Publishing Co., Cleveland, 1954, 294p, Cloth, Anth.

10802 *Space police.* World Publishing Co., Cleveland, 1956, 255p, Cloth, Anth.

10803 *Space service; stories.* World Publishing Co., Cleveland, 1953, 277p, Cloth, Anth.

10804 *Spell of the witch world.* DAW, New York, 1972, 159p, Paper, Coll. [Witch World--High Hallack #2]

10805 *Star born.* World Publishing Co., Cleveland, 1957, 212p, Cloth, Novel [Astra #2]

10806 *Star Gate.* Harcourt, Brace & Co., New York, 1958, 192p, Cloth, Novel

10807 *Star guard.* Harcourt, Brace & Co., New York, 1955, 247p, Cloth, Novel

10808 *Star hunter.* Ace Double, New York, 1961, 96p, Paper, Novel

10809 *Star hunter; &, Voodoo planet.* Ace, New York, 1968, 159p, Paper, Coll.

10810 *Star Man's son, 2250 A.D.* Harcourt, Brace & Co., New York, 1952, 248p, Cloth, Novel

10810A retitled: *Daybreak...2250 A.D.* Ace Double, New York, 1954, 182p, Paper, Novel

10811 *Star rangers.* Harcourt, Brace & Co., New York, 1953, 280p, Cloth, Novel

10811A retitled: *The last planet.* Ace Double, New York, 1955, 192p, Paper, Novel

10812 *The stars are ours!* World Publishing Co., Cleveland, 1954, 239p, Cloth, Novel [Astra #1]

10813 *Steel magic.* World Publishing Co., Cleveland, 1965, 155p, Cloth, Novel

10813A retitled: *Gray magic.* Scholastic Book Services, New York, 1967, 159p, Paper, Novel

10814 *Storm over Warlock.* World Publishing Co., Cleveland, 1960, 251p, Cloth, Novel [Warlock #1]

NORTON, ANDRE (cont.)

10815   *Three against the witch world.* Ace, New York, 1965, 189p, Paper, Novel [Witch World--Estcarp #3]

10816   *The time traders.* World Publishing Co., Cleveland, 1958, 219p, Cloth, Novel [Time Agents #1]

10817   *Uncharted stars.* Viking Press, New York, 1969, 253p, Cloth, Novel [Murdoc Jern #2]

10818   *Victory on Janus.* Harcourt, Brace & World, New York, 1966, 224p, Cloth, Novel [Naill Renfro #2]

10819   *Warlock of the witch world.* Ace, New York, 1967, 222p, Paper, Novel [Witch World--Estcarp #4]

10820   *Web of the witch world.* Ace, New York, 1964, 192p, Paper, Novel [Witch World--Estcarp #2]

10821   *Witch world.* Ace, New York, 1963, 222p, Paper, Novel [Witch World--Estcarp #1]

10822   *The X factor.* Harcourt, Brace & World, New York, 1965, 191p, Cloth, Novel

10823   *Year of the unicorn.* Ace, New York, 1965, 224p, Paper, Novel [Witch World--High Hallack #3]

10824   *The zero stone.* Viking Press, New York, 1968, 286p, Cloth, Novel [Murdoc Jern #1]

as Andrew North:

10825   *Plague ship; a Dane Thorson-Solar Queen adventure.* Gnome Press, New York, 1956, 192p, Cloth, Novel [Solar Queen #2]

10826   *Sargasso of space.* Gnome Press, New York, 1955, 185p, Cloth, Novel [Solar Queen #1]

10826A   *Sargasso of space,* by Andre Norton. Victor Gollancz, London, 1970, 191p, Cloth, Novel [Solar Queen #1]

10827   *Voodoo planet.* Ace Double, New York, 1959, 78p, Paper, Novel [Solar Queen #3]

with Ernestine Donaldy:

04452   *Gates to tomorrow; an introduction to science fiction.* A Margaret K. McElderry Book, Atheneum, New York, 1973, 264p, Cloth, Anth.

NORTON, MARY, 1903-

10828   *Bed-knob and broomstick.* J. M. Dent & Sons, London, 1957, 192p, Cloth, Coll. [includes *The magic bed-knob* and *Bonfire and broomsticks*]

10829   *Bonfires and broomsticks.* J. M. Dent & Sons, London, 1947, 119p, Cloth, Novel [a sequel to *The magic bed-knob*]

10830   *The Borrowers.* J. M. Dent & Sons, London, 1952, 159p, Cloth, Novel [Borrowers #1]

10831   *The Borrowers afield.* J. M. Dent & Sons, London, 1955, 194p, Cloth, Novel [Borrowers #2]

10832   *The Borrowers afloat.* J. M. Dent & Sons, London, 1959, 191p, Cloth, Novel [Borrowers #3]

10833   *The Borrowers aloft.* J. M. Dent & Sons, London, 1961, 154p, Cloth, Novel [Borrowers #4]

10834   *The Borrowers omnibus.* J. M. Dent & Sons, London, 1966, 699p, Cloth, Coll. [includes all four Borrowers books]

10834A   retitled: *The complete adventures of the Borrowers.* Harcourt, Brace & World, New York, 1967, 778p, Cloth, Coll. [Borrowers #s 1-4]

10835   *The magic bed-knob; or, How to become a witch in ten easy lessons.* Hyperion Press, New York, 1943, 50p, Cloth, Novel

NORTON, PHILIP
    see: SMITH, ARTEGALL

NORTON, ROY, 1869-1942

10836   *The flame; a story of what might have been.* Mills & Boon, London, 1916, 307p, Cloth, Novel

10837   *The toll of the sea.* D. Appleton, New York, 1909, 377p, Cloth, Novel

10837A   retitled: *The land of the lost.* Hodder & Stoughton, London, 1925, 318p, Cloth, Novel [abridged]

10838   *The vanishing fleets.* D. Appleton, New York, 1908, 350p, Cloth, Novel

NORWAY, NEVIL SHUTE
    see: SHUTE, NEVIL

NORWOOD, VICTOR (George Charles), 1920-
[*biography included*]

10839   *Caves of death (a jungle story featuring Jacare the untamed).* Scion, London, 1951, 112p, Paper, Novel [Jacare #2]

10840   *Cry of the beast.* Scion, London, 1953, 128p, Paper, Novel [Jacare series]

10841   *Drums along the Amazon.* Scion, London, 1953, , Paper, Novel [Jacare series]

10842   *The island of creeping death.* Scion, London, 1952, 112p, Paper, Novel [Jacare #5]

10843   *Night of the black horror.* Badger, London, 1962, 158p, Paper, Novel

10844   *The skull of Kanaima.* Scion, London, 1951, 112p, Paper, Novel [Jacare #4]

10845   *The temple of the dead.* Scion, London, 1951, 112p, Paper, Novel [Jacare #3]

10846   *The untamed.* Scion, London, 1951, 112p, Paper, Novel [Jacare #1]

NOSTRADAMUS, MERLIN, pseud. [Frances Power Cobbe, 1822-1904]

10847   *The age of science; a newspaper of the twentieth century.* Ward, Lock & Tyler, London, 1877, 50p, Cloth, Story

NOT BY THE AUTHOR OF "LOOKING BACKWARD"
    see: MORRIS, ALFRED

NOT LONG FOR THIS WORLD
    see: MY GRIMMEST NIGHTMARE

NOTO, COSIMO

10848   *The ideal city.* no publisher, New York, 1903, 377p, Cloth, Novel

NOURSE, ALAN E(dward), 1928-   [biography included]

Beyond infinity. [see 10859A]

10849 The bladerunner. David McKay, New York, 1974, 245p, Cloth, Novel

10850 The counterfeit man. David McKay, New York, 1963, 185p, Cloth, Coll.

10851 A man obsessed. Ace Double, New York, 1955, 127p, Paper, Novel

10852 retitled: The Mercy Men. David McKay, New York, 1968, 180p, Cloth, Novel [expanded]

10853 Psi high, and others. David McKay, New York, 1967, 180p, Cloth, Coll.

10854 Rx for tomorrow; tales of science fiction, fantasy, and medicine. David McKay, New York, 1971, 216p, Cloth, Coll.

10855 Raiders from the Rings. David McKay, New York, 1962, 211p, Cloth, Novel

10856 Rocket to Limbo. David McKay, New York, 1957, 184p, Cloth, Novel

10857 Scavengers in space. David McKay, New York, 1959, 180p, Cloth, Novel

10858 Star surgeon. David McKay, New York, 1960, 182p, Cloth, Novel

10859 Tiger by the tail, and other science fiction stories. David McKay, New York, 1961, 184p, Cloth, Coll.

10859A retitled: Beyond infinity; nine science fiction stories. Corgi, London, 1964, 174p, Paper, Coll.

10860 Trouble on Titan. John C. Winston, Philadelphia, 1954, 208p, Cloth, Novel

10861 The universe between. David McKay, New York, 1965, 208p, Cloth, Novel

with J. A. Meyer:

10085 The invaders are coming! Ace, New York, 1959, 223p, Paper, Novel

NOW AND BEYOND

10862 Now and beyond; eight great science fiction adventures. Belmont, New York, 1965, 157p, Paper, Anth.

NOWLAN, PHILIP FRANCIS, 1887?-1940

10863 Armageddon 2419 A.D. Avalon, New York, 1962, 224p, Cloth, Novel

NOY, JOHN, 1892-

10864 The Vulture. John Hamilton, London, 1927, 285p, Cloth, Novel

NOYES, ALFRED, 1880-1958

10865 Beyond the desert; a tale of Death Valley. Frederick A. Stokes, New York, 1920, 85p, Cloth, Novel

10866 The devil takes a holiday. John Murray, London, 1955, 184p, Cloth, Novel

10867 The last man. John Murray, London, 1940, 272p, Cloth, Novel

10867A retitled: No other man. Frederick A. Stokes, New York, 1940, 320p, Cloth, Novel

NOYES, PIERREPONT B(urt), 1870-1959

10868 The pallid giant; a tale of yesterday and tomorrow. Fleming H. Revell, New York, 1927, 300p, Cloth, Novel

10868A retitled: Gentlemen: you are mad! Baxter Frères, New York, 1946, 245p, Cloth, Novel

NOYES, SHERMAN A.

10869 Robinson Christopher. Dorrance & Co., Philadelphia, 1970, 172p, Cloth, Novel

NUETZEL, CHARLES (Alexander), 1934-   [biography included]

10870 If this goes on. Book Company of America, Beverly Hills, CA, 1965, 256p, Paper, Anth.

10871 Images of tomorrow. Powell Publications, Reseda, CA, 1969, 224p, Paper, Coll.

10872 Jungle jungle. Powell Publications, Reseda, CA, 1969, 203p, Paper, Coll. [part one is an abridged version of Lost city of the damned]

10873 Last call for the stars. Lenox Hill Press, New York, 1971, 192p, Cloth, Novel

10874 Queen of blood. Greenleaf Classics, San Diego, 1966, 160p, Paper, Movie

10875 Raiders of Noomas. Powell Publications, Reseda, CA, 1969, 208p, Paper, Novel [Noomas #2]

10876 Swordmen of Vistar. Powell Publications, Reseda, CA, 1969, 223p, Paper, Novel

10877 Warriors of Noomas. Powell Publications, Reseda, CA, 1969, 211p, Paper, Novel [Noomas #1]

as Albert Augustus, Jr.:

10878 The slaves of Lomooro. Powell Publications, Reseda, CA, 1969, 203p, Paper, Novel

as Charles English:

10879 Lovers: 2075. Scorpion, Los Angeles?, 1964, 160p, Paper, Novel

as Alec Rivere:

10880 Lost city of the damned. Pike, Van Nuys, CA, 1961, 160p, Paper, Novel

NUNES, CLAUDE, 1924-   [biography included]

10881 Inherit the Earth. Ace Double, New York, 1966, 127p, Paper, Novel

with Rhoda Nunes:

10882 Recoil. Ace Double, New York, 1971, 136p, Paper, Novel

NUNES, RHODA (Gwylleth), 1938-   [biography included], with Claude Nunes

10882 Recoil. Ace Double, New York, 1971, 136p, Paper, Novel

NUTT, CHARLES
    see: BEAUMONT, CHARLES

NUTT, LILY CLIVE
    see: ARDEN, CLIVE

NYBERG, BJÖRN (Emil Oscar), 1929-   [*biography included*]

with L. Sprague de Camp:

03992   *The return of Conan.* Gnome Press, New York, 1957, 191p, Cloth, Novel [Conan series]

with L. Sprague de Camp and Robert E. Howard:

03990   *Conan the avenger.* Lancer, New York, 1968, 192p, Paper, Coll. [Conan #10] [a reprint of 03992, with an essay by Howard explaining his invented world]

NYLAND, THEO

10883   *The Aquarian pioneers; adventure and romance on the high sea.* A. Wagner Publishing Co., Manzanar, CA, 1927, 395p, Cloth, Novel

O., A. J.
    see: OGILVY, ARTHUR JAMES

OAKES, PHILIP (Barlow), 1928-   [*biography included*]

10884   *Experiment at Proto; a novel.* Andre Deutsch, London, 1973, 239p, Cloth, Novel
10884A retitled: *The Proto papers; a novel.* Quartet, London, 1974, 218p, Paper, Novel

OAKHURST, WILLIAM

10885   *The universal strike of 1899.* William Reeves, London, 1891, 90p, Cloth?, Novel
10885A retitled: *The universal strike.* Odhams Press, London, 1911, 89p, Cloth?, Novel

OBER, FREDERICK A(lbion), 1849-1913

10886   *The silver city; a story of adventure in Mexico.* D. Lothrop, Boston, 1893, 95p, Cloth, Novel

OBOLER, ARCH, 1907-

10887   *House on fire; a novel.* Bartholomew House, New York, 1969, 249p, Cloth, Novel

O'BRIEN, CLIFFORD
    see: O'BRIEN, LARRY

O'BRIEN, DAVID

as Berl Cameron, house pseud.:

02465   *Black infinity.* Curtis Warren, London, 1952, 127p, Cloth, Novel
02469   *Photomesis.* Curtis Warren, London, 1952, 127p, Paper, Novel

as Rand Le Page, house pseud.:

08918   *Blue asp.* Curtis Warren, London, 1952, 128p, Cloth, Novel

as Kris Luna, house pseud.:

09317   *Stella radium discharge.* Curtis Warren, London, 1952, 128p, Cloth, Novel

as Brian Shaw, house pseud.:

10888   *Ships of Vero.* Curtis Warren, London, 1952, 128p, Cloth, Novel

O'BRIEN, (Michael) FITZ-JAMES, 1828-1862

10889   *Collected stories.* Albert & Charles Boni, New York, 1925, 240p, Cloth, Coll.
10890   *The diamond lens.* Henry Altemus, Philadelphia, 1909, 88p, Cloth, Novel
10891   *The diamond lens, with other stories.* Charles Scribner's Sons, New York, 1885, 337p, Cloth, Coll.
10892   *The poems and stories of Fitz-James O'Brien.* James R. Osgood, Boston, 1881, 485p, Cloth, Coll.
10893   *What was it? and other stories.* Ward, Downey, London, 1889, 177p, Cloth, Coll.
10894   *Two great mystery stories.* Haldeman-Julius, Girard, Kans., 192?, 64p, Paper, Coll.

O'BRIEN, FLANN, pseud. [Brian O Nuallain, variously spelled Brian O'Nolan, 1911-1966] [*biography included*]

10895   *The Dalkey archive.* MacGibbon & Kee, London, 1964, 222p, Cloth, Novel
10896   *The third policeman.* MacGibbon & Kee, London, 1967, 200p, Cloth, Novel

O'BRIEN, JOSEPH

10897   *The devil; a tragedy of the heart and conscience.* J. S. Ogilvie Publishing Co., New York, 1908, 189p, Cloth, Novel [an adaptation of the play of the same name by Ference Molnar]

O'BRIEN, LARRY CLINTON, pseud. [Clifford Edward O'Brien]

10898   *Earth waits for dawn.* Vantage Press, New York, 1956, 284p, Cloth, Novel

O'BRIEN, ROBERT C., pseud. [Robert Lesley Conly, 1918?-1973]

10899   *Mrs. Frisby and the rats of NIMH.* Atheneum, New York, 1971, 233p, Cloth, Novel
10900   *A report from Group 17.* Atheneum, New York, 1972, 210p, Cloth, Novel
10901   *The silver crown.* Atheneum, New York, 1968, 274p, Cloth, Novel

O'BRIEN, SEUMAS, 1880-

10902   *The whale and the grasshopper, and other fables.* Little, Brown, Boston, 1916, 302p, Cloth, Co

OBRUCHEV, VLADIMIR (Afanas'evich), 1863-1956

10903 *Plutonia*. Foreign Languages Publishing House, Moscow, 1956, 327p, Cloth, Novel
10904 *Sannikov Land*. Foreign Languages Publishing House, Moscow, 1955, 372p, Cloth, Novel

OBUKHOVA, LYDIA [Lidiia Alekseevna Obukhova]

10905 *Daughter of night; a tale of three worlds*. Macmillan, New York, 1974, 161p, Cloth, Novel

OCCULT

10906 *Occult; a collection of stories of the supernatural*. Gerald G. Swan, London, 1945, 36p, Paper, Anth.

OCCULT SHORTS, 2ND COLLECTION

10907 *Occult shorts, 2nd collection*. Gerald G. Swan, London, 1945, 36p, Paper, Anth.

THE OCCULTS IN COUNCIL
    see: WILLIAM, Sir

O'CLUNY, THOMAS

10908 *The merry multifleet and the mounting multicorps*. J. M. Dent & Sons, London, 1904, 206p, Cloth, Novel

O'CONNELL, CHARLES C(hristopher)

10909 *The vanishing island*. Talbot Press, Dublin, 1957, 187p, Cloth, Novel

O'CONNOR, WILLIAM DOUGLAS, 1832-1889

10910 *The ghost*. G. P. Putnam & Son, New York, 1867, 93p, Cloth, Novel
10911 *Three tales: The ghost; The brazen android; The carpenter*. Houghton, Mifflin, Boston, 1892, 320p, Cloth, Coll.

AN OCTOGENARIAN, pseud.

10912 *The British Federal Empire: how it was founded; a speech delivered in a certain year of the twentieth century, in a certain city of the Empire*. C. H. Clarke, London, 1872, 32p, Paper, Story

ODELL, SAMUEL W., 1864-1948

10913 *Atlanteans; Adam Lore's choice; stories for young men*. Hunt & Eaton, New York, 1889, 310p, Cloth, Coll.
10914 *The last war; or, The triumph of the English tongue; a story of the twenty-sixth century, compiled from the offical notes of Newman, reporter to the President of United States*. Charles H. Kerr, Chicago, 1898, 162p, Cloth, Novel

10915 *The princess Athura; a romance of Iran*. Thomas Y. Crowell, New York, 1913, 312p, Cloth, Novel

ODELL, WILLIAM. with Henry Bamman and Robert Whitehead

00818 *Bone people*. Benefic Press, Westchester, 1970, 72p, Cloth, Novel
00819 *Ice men of Rime*. Benefic Press, Westchester, 1970, 72p, Cloth, Novel
00820 *Inviso man*. Benefic Press, Westchester, 1970, 72p, Cloth, Novel
00821 *Milky Way*. Benefic Press, Westchester, 1970, 71p, Cloth, Novel
00822 *Planet of the whistlers*. Benefic Press, Westchester, 1970, 72p, Cloth, Novel
00823 *Space pirate*. Benefic Press, Westchester, 1970, 72p, Cloth, Novel

ODLE, E. V.

10916 *The Clockwork man*. William Heinemann, London, 1923, 213p, Cloth, Novel

O'DONNELL, ELLIOTT, 1872-1965 [*biography included*]

10917 *The dead riders*. Rider & Co., London, 1952, 208p, Cloth, Novel
10918 *The devil in the pulpit*. Denis Archer, London, 1932, 286p, Cloth, Novel
10919 *Dread of night; five short ghost stories*. Pillar Publishing Co., Dublin, 1945, 32p, Paper, Coll.
10920 *For Satan's sake*. Greening & Co., London, 1904, 322p, Cloth, Novel
10921 *Haunted highways and byways*. Eveleigh Nash, London, 1914, 219p, Cloth, Coll. [includes some nonf.]
10922 *The sorcery club*. William Rider & Son, London, 1912, 342p, Cloth, Novel
10923 *The unknown depths; a tale*. Greening & Co., London, 1905, 315p, Cloth, Novel

O'DONNELL, K. M., pseud.
    see: MALZBERG, BARRY N.

O'DONNELL, LAWRENCE, pseud.
    see: KUTTNER, HENRY and MOORE, C. L.

O'DONNELL, PETER

10924 *I, Lucifer*. Doubleday, Garden City, 1967, 305p, Cloth, Novel [Modesty Blaise series]

O'DUFFY, EIMAR (Ultan), 1893-1935

10925 *Asses in clover*. Putnam, London, 1933, 331p, Cloth, Novel [King Goshawk #2; Aloysius O'Kennedy #2]
10926 *King Goshawk and the birds*. Macmillan, New York, 1926, 319p, Cloth, Novel [King Goshawk #1]
10927 *The spacious adventures of the man in the street*. Macmillan, London, 1928, 407p, Cloth, Novel [Aloysius O'Kennedy #1]

OF SUCH AS THESE

10928   *Of such as these.* American Science Fiction, Sydney, 1955, 34p, Paper, Anth.

O'FARRELL, EDDY

10929   *The ghost came twice.* Orpheus Series, New York, 1970, 212p, Paper, Novel

O'FARRELL, WILLIAM, 1904-

10930   *Repeat performance.* Houghton Mifflin, Boston, 1942, 298p, Cloth, Novel

THE OFFICIAL DESPATCHES AND CORRESPONDENCE RELATIVE TO THE BATTLE OF DORKING

10931   *The official despatches and correspondence relative to the Battle of Dorking as moved for in the House of Commons, 21st July, 1920.* W. H. Elliott, London, 1871, 8p, Paper, Story [Dorking series]

OFFIN, T(homas) W(illiam) Jun.

10932   *How the Germans took London; forewarned, forearmed.* E. Durrant, Chelmsford, UK, 1900, 64p, Cloth?, Novel

OFFUTT, ANDREW J(efferson V), 1934-   [*biography included*]

10933   *Ardor on Aros.* Dell, New York, 1973, 192p, Paper, Novel
10934   *The castle keeps.* Berkley Medallion, New York, 1972, 191p, Paper, Novel
10935   *Evil is live spelled backwards.* Paperback Library, New York, 1970, 158p, Paper, Novel
10936   *The galactic rejects.* Lothrop, Lee & Shepard, New York, 1973, 191p, Cloth, Novel
10937   *The great 24-hour thing.* Orpheus Series, New York, 1971, 187p, Paper, Novel
10938   *Messenger of Zhuvastou.* Berkley Medallion, New York, 1973, 286p, Paper, Novel

as John Cleve:

10939   *Barbarana.* Brandon House, North Hollywood, 1970, 192p, Paper, Novel
10940   *Jodinareh.* Brandon House, North Hollywood, 1970, 176p, Paper, Novel
10941   *Manlib.* Orpheus Series, New York, 1974, 187p, Paper, Novel
10942   *The sexorcist.* Orpheus Series, New York, 1974, 251p, Paper, Novel

as J. X. Williams, house pseud.

10943   *The sex pill.* Pleasure Reader, San Diego, 1968, 160p, Paper, Novel

with D. Bruce Berry as Jeff Douglas:

01203   *The balling machine.* Orpheus Series, New York, 1971, 192p, Paper, Novel

O'FLANNAGAN, PHINEAS, pseud.

10944   *Ireland a nation! the diary of an Irish cabinet minister, being the history of the first and only Irish National Administration, 1894.* Olley & Co., Belfast, 1893, 37p, Paper, Story

OGDEN, ANTOINETTE

10945   *Christmas stories from French and Spanish writers.* A. C. McClurg, Chicago, 1892, 265p, Cloth, Anth.

OGDEN, GEORGE W(ashington), 1871-1966

10946   *Custodian of ghosts.* Robert Hale, London, 1951, 254p, Cloth, Novel

O(gilvy), A(rthur) J(ames)

10947   *The ape man.* Daily Post, Hobart, Tasmania, 1913, 58p, Paper, Novel

O'GRADY, ROHAN, pseud. [June Margaret O'Grady Skinner, 1922-]

10948   *Pippin's journal; or, Rosemary is for remembrance.* Macmillan, New York, 1962, 230p, Cloth, Novel

O'GRADY, STANDISH JAMES
see: NETTERVILLE, LUKE

OHLE, DAVID

10949   *Motorman.* Alfred A. Knopf, New York, 1972, 117p, Cloth, Novel

OHLSON, HEREWARD

10950   *Thunderbolt and the rebel planet.* Lutterworth Press, London, 1954, 190p, Cloth, Novel [Thunderbolt #2]
10951   *Thunderbolt of the spaceways.* Lutterworth Press, London, 1954, 190p, Cloth, Novel [Thunderbolt #1]

OHNET, GEORGES, pseud. [Georges Hénot, 1848-1918]

10952   *A weird gift.* Chatto & Windus, London, 1890, 280p, Cloth, Novel

O'KELLY, SEUMAS, 1881-1918

10953   *The leprechaun of Killmeen.* Martin Lester, Dublin, 1920, 120p, Cloth, Novel

OLANDER, JOSEPH D., with Martin Harry Greenberg and Patricia S. Warrick

06313   *American government through science fiction.* Rand McNally College Publishing Co., Chicago, 1974, 360p, Paper, Anth.

OLANDER, JOSEPH D. (cont.), with Martin Harry
Greenberg and Patricia S. Warrick

06314 *School and society through science fiction.*
Rand McNally College Publishing Co., Chicago, 1974, 396p, Paper, Anth.

with Martin Harry Greenberg, Patricia S. Warrick, and John D. Milstead:

06312 *Sociology through science fiction.* St. Martin's Press, New York, 1974, 412p, Cloth,
Anth.

AN OLD SOLDIER, pseud.
see: BUTLER, WILLIAM FRANCIS

OLDFIELD, CLAUDE HOUGHTON
see: HOUGHTON, CLAUDE

OLDMEADOW, ERNEST (James), 1867-1949

10954 *The North Sea bubble; a fantasia.* E. Grant
Richards, London, 1906, 353p, Cloth, Novel

OLDREY, JOHN

10955 *The devil's henchmen.* Methuen, London, 1926,
250p, Cloth, Novel

OLDS, C(harles) BURNELL

10956 *The Quas of Quasar, by Mr. Wood, narrator.*
Vantage Press, New York, 1970, 105p, Cloth,
Novel

O'LEARY, CON

10957 *This delicate creature.* Constable, London,
1928, 281p, Cloth, Novel

OLECK, JACK, 1914-   [*biography included*]

10958 *Tales from the crypt; a novel.* Bantam, New
York, 1972, 121p, Paper, Movie
10959 *Tales from the House of mystery.* Warner, New
York, 1973, 159p, Paper, Coll.
10960 *Tales from the House of mystery, volume 2.*
Warner, New York, 1973, 158p, Paper, Coll.
10961 *The vault of horror.* Bantam, New York, 1973,
122p, Paper, Movie

OLEMY, P. T., pseud. [George Baker]

10962 *The Clones.* Flagship, New York, 1968, 160p,
Paper, Novel

OLERICH, HENRY, 1851-

10963 *A cityless and countryless world; an outline
of practical co-operative individualism.*
Gilmore & Olerich, Holstein, Iowa, 1893,
447p, Cloth, Novel

OLFSON, LEWY, with Ray Bradbury

01777 *Teacher's guide; science fiction.* Bantam,
New York, 1968, 16p, Paper, Nonf.

OLIN, ROSS
see: ROSS, OLIN

OLIPHANT, Mrs. (Margaret Oliphant), 1828-1897

10964 *A beleaguered city, being a narrative of certain recent events in the city of Semur, in
the department of the Haute Bourgogne; a
story of the seen and the unseen.* Macmillan,
London, 1880, 267p, Cloth, Novel
10965 *The land of darkness, with some further chapters in the experiences of the little pilgrim.* Macmillan, London, 1888, 238p, Cloth,
Coll. [published anonymously]
10966 *A little pilgrim in the unseen.* Macmillan,
London, 1882, 147p, Cloth, Novel [published
anonymously]
10966A retitled: *A little pilgrim, by Mrs. Oliphant.*
George Munro, New York, 1883, 75p, Paper,
Novel
10966B retitled: *A little pilgrim in the seen and
the unseen, by Mrs. Oliphant.* Progressive
Thinker Publishing House, Chicago, 1913,
117p, Cloth, Novel
10967 *A little pilgrim: further experiences.* Roberts
Bros., Boston, 1889, 190p, Cloth, Novel
10968 *The open door; The portrait; two stories of
the seen and the unseen,* by the author of
"A little pilgrim" and "Old Lady Mary."
Roberts Bros., Boston, 1885, 164p, Cloth,
Coll.
10969 *Stories of the seen and unseen.* Roberts Bros.,
Boston, 1889, 61lp, Cloth, Coll.
10970 *Two stories of the seen and unseen; The open
door; Old Lady Mary.* William Blackwood &
Sons, Edinburgh, 1885, 212p, Cloth, Coll.

OLIVER, (Symmes) CHAD(wick), 1928-   [*biography included*]

10971 *Another kind; science-fiction stories.* Ballantine, New York, 1955, 170p, Cloth, Coll.
10972 *The edge of forever; classic anthropological
science fiction.* Sherbourne Press, Los Angeles, 1971, 305p, Cloth, Coll.
10973 *Mists of dawn.* John C. Winston, Philadelphia,
1952, 208p, Cloth, Novel
10974 *Shadows in the Sun.* Ballantine, New York,
1954, 152p, Cloth, Novel
10975 *The shores of another sea.* Signet, New York,
1971, 159p, Paper, Novel
10976 *Unearthly neighbors.* Ballantine, New York,
1960, 144p, Paper, Novel
10977 *The winds of time.* Doubleday, Garden City,
1957, 192p, Cloth, Novel

OLIVER, FREDERICK SPENCER
see: PHYLOS THE THIBETAN

OLIVER, GEORGE
see: ONIONS, OLIVER

OLIVER, JANE, pseud. [Helen Christina Easson Rees, 1903-   ] [biography included]

10978 The hour of the angel. Collins, London, 1942, 256p, Cloth, Novel
10979 In no strange land. Collins, London, 1944, 256p, Cloth, Novel
10980 Morning for Mr. Prothero; a novel. Hammond, Hammond, London, 1950, 255p, Cloth, Novel

OLIVER, JEROME, 1886-

10981 Khan, phantom emperor of 1940. J. C. Reklar, New York, 1934, 337p, Cloth, Novel

OLIVER, JOHN RATHBONE, 1872-1943

10982 Priest or pagan. Alfred A. Knopf, New York, 1933, 461p, Cloth, Novel

OLIVIER, EDITH (Maud), d. 1948

10983 The love-child. Martin Secker, London, 1927, 173p, Cloth, Novel

OLLIVANT, ALFRED, 1874-1927

10984 To-morrow; a romance of the future. Alston Rivers, London, 1927, 320p, Cloth, Novel

OLNEY, ROSS R(obert), 1929-   [biography included]

10985 Tales of time and space. Whitman Publishing Co., Racine, Wisc., 1969, 212p, Cloth, Anth.
10986 Ten tales calculated to give you shudders. Whitman Publishing Co., Racine, Wisc., 1972, 212p, Cloth, Anth.

OLSEN, BOB [Alfred John Olsen Jr., 1884-1956]

10987 Rhythm rides the rocket. Columbia Publications, New York, 1942?, 23p, Paper, Story

OLSON, EUGENE E.
   see: STEIGER, BRAD

O'MALLEY, FRANK
   see: O'ROURKE, FRANK

O'MALLEY, MARY
   see: BRIDGE, ANN

O'MEARA, WALTER (Andrew), 1897-   [biography included]

10988 Tales of the two borders. Bobbs-Merrill, Indianapolis, 1952, 197p, Cloth, Coll.

OMEN, EDWARD

10989 Nutopia; or, Nineteen twenty-one. Henry J. Drane, London, 1908, 181p, Cloth, Novel

AN OMNIBUS THRILLER OF MURDER AND MYSTERY

10990 An omnibus thriller of murder and mystery; four novels by Ranger Gull, Fergus Hume, Florence Warden, Guy Thorne. T. Werner Laurie, London, 1931, 1009p, Cloth, Anth.
10991 An omnibus thriller of murder and mystery; three long complete novels. T. Werner Laurie, London, 1931, 703p, Cloth, Anth.

ONE OF THE UNEMPLOYED, pseud.

10992 The brain-box. Hurst & Blackett, London, 192 287p, Cloth, Novel

ONE THOUSAND EIGHT HUNDRED AND TWENTY NINE

10993 One thousand eight hundred and twenty nine; c "Shall it be so?" J. J. Stockdale, London, 1819, 36p, Paper?, Story

ONE WHO SAW IT, pseud.
   see: THE SACK OF LONDON IN THE GREAT FRENCH WAR OF 1901

O'NEIL, DENNIS (Joseph), 1939-   [biography included]

10994 The bite of monsters. Belmont, New York, 197 156p, Paper, Novel

O'NEIL, HENRY (Nelson), 1817-1880

10995 Two thousand years hence. Chapman & Hall, London, 1868, 351p, Cloth, Novel

O'NEIL, RUSSELL

10996 Jonathan. Appleton-Century-Crofts, New York, 1959, 214p, Cloth, Novel ["based on an idea by Ann Noyes Guettel"]

O'NEILL, JOHN, 1869-

10997 Souls in Hell; a mystery of the unseen. Nicholas L. Brown, New York, 1924, 383p, Cloth, Novel
10997A retitled: As we sow; a mystery of the unseen Methuen, London, 1926, 282p, Cloth, Novel

O'NEILL, JOSEPH, 1886-1953

10998 Day of wrath. Victor Gollancz, London, 1936, 288p, Cloth, Novel
10999 Land under England. Victor Gollancz, London, 1935, 334p, Cloth, Novel
11000 Wind from the north. Jonathan Cape, London, 1934, 341p, Cloth, Novel

O'NEILL, SCOTT, pseud.
    see: SCOTT, PEG O'NEILL

ONIONS, (George) OLIVER, 1873-1961 [later changed his name legally to George Oliver]

        Bells rung backward. [see 11002A]
11001 A certain man. William Heinemann, London,
         1931, 360p, Cloth, Novel
11002 The collected ghost stories of Oliver Onions.
         Ivor Nicholson & Watson, London, 1935, 689p,
         Cloth, Coll.
11002A retitled: Bells rung backward. Staples Press,
         London, 1953, 285p, Cloth, Coll. [abridged]
11003 Ghosts in daylight. Chapman & Hall, London,
         1924, 236p, Cloth, Coll.
11004 The new moon; a romance in reconstruction.
         Hodder & Stoughton, London, 1918, 312p,
         Cloth, Novel
11005 The painted face. William Heinemann, London,
         1929, 294p, Cloth, Coll.
11006 The tower of oblivion. Hodder & Stoughton,
         London, 1921, 423p, Cloth, Novel
11007 Widdershins. Martin Secker, London, 1911,
         315p, Cloth, Coll.

O'NOLAN, BRIAN
    see: O'BRIAN, FLANN

O NUALLAIN, BRIAN
    see: O'BRIEN, FLANN

THE OPEN DOOR; THE PORTRAIT
    see: OLIPHANT, Mrs.

OPPENHEIM, E(dward) PHILLIPS, 1866-1946

11008 The black box. Grosset & Dunlap, New York,
         1915, 334p, Cloth, Movie
11009 A daughter of Astrea. J. W. Arrowsmith, Bris-
         tol, 1898, 191p, Cloth, Novel
11010 The double life of Mr. Alfred Burton. Little,
         Brown, Boston, 1913, 322p, Cloth, Novel
11011 The dumb gods speak. Little, Brown, Boston,
         1937, 304p, Cloth, Novel
11012 Exit a dictator. Little, Brown, Boston, 1939,
         315p, Cloth, Novel
         Gabriel Samara. [see 11013A]
11013 Gabriel Samara, peacemaker. Little, Brown,
         Boston, 1925, 323p, Cloth, Novel
11013A retitled: Gabriel Samara. Hodder & Stough-
         ton, London, 1925, 319p, Cloth, Novel
11014 The golden beast. Little, Brown, Boston,
         1926, 298p, Cloth, Novel
11015 The great awakening. Ward, Lock, London,
         1902, 320p, Cloth, Novel
11015A retitled: A sleeping memory. G. W. Dilling-
         ham, New York, 1902, 311p, Cloth, Novel
11016 The great Prince Shan. Little, Brown, Boston,
         1922, 303p, Cloth, Novel
11017 Havoc. Little, Brown, Boston, 1911, 323p,
         Cloth, Novel
11018 Matorni's vineyard. Little, Brown, Boston,
         1928, 308p, Cloth, Novel
11019 Mr. Mirakel. Little, Brown, Boston, 1943,
         279p, Cloth, Novel
         A sleeping memory. [see 11015A]

11020 The traitors. Ward, Lock, London, 1902, 304p,
         Cloth, Novel
11021 Up the ladder of gold. Little, Brown, Boston,
         1931, 312p, Cloth, Novel
11022 The wrath to come. Little, Brown, Boston,
         1924, 355p, Cloth, Novel

ORAM, JOHN, pseud. [Jack Thomas]

11023 The man from U.N.C.L.E., number 3; The Copen-
         hagen affair. Ace, New York, 1965, 144p,
         Paper, Tele. [Man from U.N.C.L.E. #3 (U.S.
         series); #3 (U.K. series)]
11024 The man from U.N.C.L.E., no. 4; The stone-cold
         dead in the market affair. Four Square,
         London, 1966, 126p, Paper, Tele. [Man from
         U.N.C.L.E. #4 (U.K. series); #22 (U.S. ser-
         ies)]

ORB, CLAY, pseud. [Herbert Conrow, 1874-   ]

11025 The man in the Moon is talking. Warwick Book
         Press, New York, 1946, 133p, Cloth, Novel

ORBISON, OLIVE, with Maud Keck

08091 Behind the Devil Screen. Ives Washburn, New
         York, 1928, 325p, Cloth, Novel

ORCUTT, EMMA LOUISE

11026 The divine seal. C. M. Clark Publishing Co.,
         Boston, 1909, 315p, Cloth, Novel

ORCUTT, H(arriet) E.

11027 The empire of the invisibles. Metaphysical
         Publishing Co., New York, 1899, 80p, Cloth,
         Novel

ORCZY, Baroness (Emma Magdalena Rosalia Maria Josefa Barbara), 1865-1947

11028 By the gods beloved; a romance. Greening &
         Co., London, 1905, 310p, Cloth, Novel
11028A retitled: The gates of Kamt. Dodd, Mead,
         New York, 1907, 326p, Cloth, Novel

O'REILLY, JOHN, 1906-

11029 The Glob. Viking Press, New York, 1952, 63p,
         Cloth, Novel

O'REILLY, JOHN BOYLE, 1844-1890, with Robert Grant, J. S. of Dale, and John T. Wheelright

06240 The King's men; a tale of to-morrow. Charles
         Scribner's Sons, New York, 1884, 270p, Cloth,
         Novel

ORFORD, Earl of
    see: WALPOLE, HORACE

THE ORGY PUPPETS

    11030   *The orgy puppets.* Collectors, City of Indus-
         try, CA, 1968, 226p, Paper, Novel

ORIEL, ANTRIM, pseud. [Arthur Moore]

    11031   *The miracle.* Archibald Constable, London,
         1908, 271p, Cloth, Novel

ORKOW, BEN (Harrison), 1896-   *[biography
included]*

    11032   *When time stood still.* Signet, New York,
         1962, 174p, Paper, Novel

ORMESSON, JEAN (Bruno Waldemar François-de-
Paule Lefevre d', Comte), 1925-

    11033   *The glory of the Empire; a novel, a history.*
         Alfred A. Knopf, New York, 1974, 395p,
         Cloth, Novel

ORMONDROYD, EDWARD

    11034   *Castaways on Long Ago.* Parnassus Press,
         Berkeley, CA, 1973, 182p, Cloth, Novel
    11035   *Time at the top.* Parnassus Press, Berkeley,
         CA, 1963, 176p, Cloth, Novel

ORNA, ADOLPHE (O.)

    11036   *The reincarnations of Lupus Andronicus.* Jona-
         than Cape, London, 1923, 223p, Cloth, Novel

ORNDORFF, FRANK

    11037   *Kongo--the gorilla-man.* House of Field-Doub-
         leday, New York, 1945, 206p, Cloth, Novel

O'ROURKE, FRANK, pseud. [Frank O'Malley,
1916-]

    11038   *Instant gold.* William Morrow, New York,
         1964, 156p, Cloth, Novel

ORR, PAUL (Wright), 1904-   *[biography inclu-
ded]*, with Violet Orr

    11039   *1993: the world of tomorrow.* Pacific Progress
         Publishers, Altadena, CA, 1968, 273p,
         Paper, Novel

ORR, VIOLET (May), 1904-   *[biography inclu-
ded]*, with Paul Orr

    11039   *1993: the world of tomorrow.* Pacific Progress
         Publishers, Altadena, CA, 1968, 273p,
         Paper, Novel

ORWELL, GEORGE, pseud. [Eric Arthur Blair,
1903-1950]

    11040   *Animal farm; a fairy story.* Secker & Warburg
         London, 1945, 92p, Cloth, Novel
    11041   *Nineteen eighty-four; a novel.* Secker & War-
         burg, London, 1949, 312p, Cloth, Novel

OSBORN, E(dward) B(olland), 1867-1938

    11042   *The maid with wings, and other fantasies grav*
         to gay. John Lane, The Bodley Head, London
         1917, 263p, Cloth, Coll.

OSBORN, LAUGHTON, 1809-1878

    11043   *Travels by sea and land of Alethitheras.* Moo
         head, Simpson & Bond, New York, 1868, 381p,
         Cloth, Novel

OSBORNE, CHESTER G(orham), 1915-

    11044   *The wind and the fire.* Prentice-Hall, Engle-
         wood Cliffs, NJ, 1959, 148p, Cloth, Novel

OSBORNE, DAVID, pseud.
    see: SILVERBERG, ROBERT

OSBORNE, (Samuel) DUFFIELD, 1858-1917

    11045   *The secret of the crater (a mountain Moloch).*
         G. P. Putnam's Sons, New York, 1900, 312p,
         Cloth, Novel
    11046   *The spell of Ashtaroth.* Charles Scribner's
         Sons, New York, 1888, 234p, Cloth, Novel

OSBOURNE, LLOYD, 1868-1947

    11047   *The adventurer.* D. Appleton, New York, 1907,
         396p, Cloth, Novel

OSBURN, JOSEPH, with Brian P. Hall

    06656   *Nog's vision.* Paulist Press, New York, 1973,
         140p, Paper, Novel

O'SHEA, SEAN, pseud.
    see: TRALINS, ROBERT

O'SHEEL, SHAEMAS, 1886-1954

    11048   *It never could happen; or, The second America*
         Revolution. Coventry House, New York, 1932
         191p, Cloth, Novel

OSLER, WILLIAM, 1921-

    11049   *Premature angel.* Dorrance & Co., Philadelphi
         1954, 282p, Cloth, Novel

OSMOND, ANDREW, 1938- [*biography included*],
with Douglas Hurd

07640 *Scotch on the rocks.* Collins, London, 1971,
       255p, Cloth, Novel
07641 *Send him victorious.* Collins, London, 1975,
       287p, Cloth, Novel
07642 *The smile on the face of the tiger.* Collins,
       London, 1969, 286p, Cloth, Novel

OSTRANDER, ISABEL
    see: FOX, DAVID

O'SULLIVAN, JAMES BRENDAN, 1919-

11050 *I die possessed.* M. S. Mill & William Morrow,
       New York, 1953, 249p, Cloth, Novel

O'SULLIVAN, VINCENT, 1872-1940

11051 *A book of bargains.* Leonard Smithers, Lon-
       don, 1896, 185p, Cloth, Coll.
11052 *Human affairs.* David Nutt, London, 1907,
       274p, Cloth, Coll.

OSWALD, DAVE

11053 *The only way to go.* Parisian Press, San Fran-
       cisco?, 1972, 147p, Paper, Novel

OSWALD, E(lizabeth) J(ane)

11054 *The dragon of the north; a tale of the Normans
       in Italy.* Seeley & Co., London, 1887, 350p,
       Cloth, Novel

THE OTHER SIDE

11055 *The other side.* American Science Fiction,
       Sydney, 1954, 34p, Paper, Anth.

OTIS, JAMES, pseud. [James Otis Kaler, 1848-
1912]

11056 *The search for the silver city; a tale of ad-
       venture in Yucatan.* A. L. Burt, New York,
       1893, 323p, Cloth, Novel

O'TOOLE, GEORGE

11057 *An agent on the other side.* David McKay, New
       York, 1973, 249p, Cloth, Novel

OTTERBOURG, EDWIN M(ax), 1885-1967

11058 *Alice in Rankbustland (with apologies to Lewis
       Carroll).* W. W. Williams, New York, 1923,
       84p, Paper, Novel [Alice series]

OTTOLENGUI, RODRIGUES, 1861-1937

11059 *A modern wizard.* G. P. Putnam's Sons, New
       York, 1894, 434p, Cloth, Novel

OTTUM, BOB [Robert K. Ottum, Jr.]

11060 *All right, everybody off the planet! a novel.*
       Random House, New York, 1972, 241p, Cloth,
       Novel

OUDEIS, pseud. [Christopher Lovett Darby]

11061 *Hell.* Roxburghe Press, Westminster, UK, 1897,
       125p, Cloth, Novel

OUR HERO

11062 *Our hero; or, Who wrote "The Battle of Dorking."*
       Bradbury, Evans, London, 1871, 48p, Paper,
       Story [Dorking series]

OUR OWN POMPEII
    see: FOX, S. MIDDLETON

OURSLER, (Charles) FULTON, 1893-1952

11063 *The house at Fernwood; and, The wager; two
       thrilling mystery novels exploring strange
       bypaths of twisted marriage relationships.*
       Pony Books, Stamford, Conn., 1946, 154p,
       Paper, Coll.

with Achmed Abdullah:

00008 *The Flower of the Gods.* Green Circle, New
       York, 1936, 254p, Cloth, Novel

OUSDAL, ASBJØRN P(ederson), 1879-

11064 *Our revolting society (evolution in reverse);
       a satire.* Schauer Printing Studio, Santa
       Barbara, CA, 1945, 84p, Cloth, Novel

OUSELEY, G. J. R.
    see: THEOSOPHO & ELLORA, pseud.

OUSPENSKY, P. D.
    see: USPENSKII, PETR

OVERTON, GRANT (Martin), 1887-1930

11065 *The world's one hundred best short stories,
       volume nine, ghosts.* Funk & Wagnalls, New
       York, 1927, 212p, Cloth, Anth.

OWEN, BETTY M.

11066 *11 great horror stories, including The oblong
       box and The Dunwich horror.* Scholastic Book
       Services, New York, 1969, 239p, Paper, Anth.
11067 *Nine strange stories.* Scholastic Book Services,
       New York, 1974, 155p, Paper, Anth.
11068 *Stories of the supernatural.* Scholastic Book
       Services, New York, 1967, 224p, Paper, Anth.

OWEN, DEAN, pseud. [Dudley Dean McGaughy]

11069 *The brides of Dracula*. Monarch, Derby, Conn.,
       1960, 141p, Paper, Movie [Dracula series]
11070 *End of the world*. Ace, New York, 1962, 127p,
       Paper, Movie
11071 *Konga*. Monarch, Derby, Conn., 1960, 144p,
       Paper, Movie
11072 *Reptilicus*. Monarch, Derby, Conn., 1961, 143p,
       Paper, Movie

OWEN, FRANK, 1893-1968

11073 *Della-Wu, Chinese courtesan, and other orien-
       tal love tales*. Lantern Press, New York,
       1931, 313p, Cloth, Coll.
11074 *The House Mother*. Lantern Press, New York,
       1929, 300p, Cloth, Novel [Scobee Trent #2]
11075 *A husband for Kutani*. Lee Furman, New York,
       1938, 199p, Cloth, Coll.
11076 *The porcelain magician; a collection of orien-
       tal fantasies*. Gnome Press, New York, 1948,
       256p, Cloth, Coll.
11077 *The purple sea; more splashes of Chinese color*.
       Lantern Press, New York, 1930, 153p, Cloth,
       Coll.
11078 *Rare earth*. Lantern Press, New York, 1931,
       292p, Cloth, Novel [Scobee Trent #1]
11079 *The scarlet hill*. Carlyle House, New York,
       1941, 368p, Cloth, Novel
11080 *The wind that tramps the world; splashes of
       Chinese color*. Lantern Press, New York,
       1929, 118p, Cloth, Coll.

as Roswell Williams:

11081 *Loves of Lo-Foh*. Claude Kendall, New York,
       1936, 287p, Cloth, Novel

OWEN, GEORGE W(ashington), d. 1916

11082 *The Leech Club; or, The mysteries of the Cat-
       skills*. Lee & Shepard, Boston, 1874, 298p,
       Cloth, Novel

OWEN, GEORGE W.

11083 *BEEP*. Vantage Press, New York, 1973, 312p,
       Cloth, Novel

OWEN, HARRY COLLINSON
     see: ADDISON, HUGH

OWEN, MABLY (Ceredig), 1912-1969 [*biography
included*], with Amabel Williams-Ellis

11084 *Out of this world; an anthology of science
       fiction*. Blackie & Son, London, 1971, 357p,
       Cloth, Anth. [includes *Out of this world 3*
       and *Out of this world 4*]
11085 *Out of this world 1; an anthology of science
       fiction*. Blackie & Son, London, 1960, 197p,
       Cloth, Anth.
11086 *Out of this world 2; an anthology of science
       fiction*. Blackie & Son, London, 1961, 188p,
       Cloth, Anth.
11087 *Out of this world 3; an anthology of science
       fiction*. Blackie & Son, London, 1962, 175p,
       Cloth, Anth.

11088 *Out of this world 4; an anthology of science
       fiction*. Blackie & Son, London, 1964, 187p,
       Cloth, Anth.
11089 *Out of this world 5; an anthology of science
       fiction*. Blackie & Son, London, 1965, 188p,
       Cloth, Anth.
11090 *Out of this world 6; an anthology of science
       fiction*. Blackie & Son, London, 1967, 196p,
       Cloth, Anth.
11091 *Out of this world 7; an anthology of science
       fiction*. Blackie & Son, London, 1968, 214p,
       Cloth, Anth.
11092 *Out of this world 8; an anthology of science
       fiction*. Blackie & Son, London, 1970, 187p,
       Cloth, Anth.
11093 *Out of this world choice; an anthology of
       science fiction*. Blackie & Son, London,
       1972, 370p, Cloth, Anth. [includes *Out of
       this world 2* and *Out of this world 5*]
11094 *Worlds apart; an anthology of science fiction*.
       Blackie & Son, London, 1966, 416p, Cloth,
       Anth.

OWEN, MAURICE (Leslie Lloyd), 1925-   [*biogra
phy included*]

11095 *The white mantle*. Robert Hale, London, 1967,
       192p, Cloth, Novel

OWEN, OLIN MARVIN, 1847-1918

11096 *The great celestial railroad from the city of
       sin to the city of God, the only direct and
       through line, with a description of persons,
       places, and scenes on the route*. no publi-
       sher, Utica, NY, 1889,   , Cloth, Novel

OWEN, RYE

11097 *Red-headed Gill*. Henry Holt, New York, 1903,
       347p, Cloth, Novel; J. W. Arrowsmith, Bristo
       1903, 416p, Cloth, Novel

OWEN, WALTER, 1884-

11098 *The cross of Carl, an allegory; the story of
       one who went down into the depths and was
       buried; who, doubting much, yet at last lif
       ted up his eyes until the hills and rose
       again and was transfigured*. Grant Richards
       London, 1931, 120p, Cloth, Novel
11099 *'More things in Heaven...'* Andrew Dakers,
       London, 1947, 332p, Cloth, Novel

OWINGS, MARK (Samuel), 1945-   [*biography in
cluded*]

11100 *The electric bibliograph, part I; Clifford D.
       Simak*. Alice & Jay Haldeman, Baltimore,
       1971, 13p, Paper, Nonf.
11101 *James H. Schmitz: a bibliography*. Croatan
       House, Baltimore, 1973, 33p, Paper, Nonf.
11102 *The Necronomicon: a study*. Anthem Series,
       Baltimore, 1967, 31p, Paper, Nonf.
11103 *Robert A. Heinlein: a bibliography*. Croatan
       House, Baltimore, 1973, 23p, Paper, Nonf.

OWINGS, MARK (cont.), with Jack L. Chalker

02798 *An index to the science-fantasy publishers (a bibliography of the science fiction and fantasy specialty houses).* Anthem Series, Baltimore, 1966, 76p, Paper, Nonf.
02799 *The revised H. P. Lovecraft bibliography.* Mirage Press, Baltimore, 1973, 44p, Paper, Nonf.

OXENFORD, JOHN, 1812-1877, with C. A. Feiling

05356 *Tales from the German, comprising specimens from the most celebrated authors.* Chapman & Hall, London, 1844, 446p, Cloth, Anth.

OXENHAM, JOHN, pseud. [William Arthur Dunkerley, 1852-1941]

11104 *The cedar box.* Longmans, Green, London, 1924, 44p, Cloth, Story
11105 *The man who would save the world.* Longmans, Green, London, 1927, 210p, Cloth, Novel

P., F. H.

11106 *The castle of Caithness; a romance of the thirteenth century.* Minerva Press, Lane & Newman, London, 1802, 2vol, Cloth, Novel

P., H. M.

11107 *A vampire of souls.* Alexander Gardner, Paisley, UK, 1904, 94p, Paper, Novel

PABLO-OZOLLO, INCA-
see: INCA-PABLO-OZOLLO

PAÇO d'ARCOS, J., pseud. [Joaquim Belford Corrêa da Silva, 1908-]

11108 *Memoirs of a banknote.* Henry Regnery, Chicago, 1968, 180p, Cloth, Novel

PADGETT, LEWIS, pseud.
see: KUTTNER, HENRY and MOORE, C. L.

PAGE, FRANCIS

11109 *Confucius comes to Broadway.* Wisdom House, New York, 1940, 64p, Cloth, Novel

PAGE, NORVELL W., 1904?-1961

11110 *Flame Winds.* Berkley Medallion, New York, 1969, 144p, Paper, Novel [Prester John #1]
11111 *Sons of the Bear-God.* Berkley Medallion, New York, 1969, 143p, Paper, Novel [Prester John #2]

PAGE, PATRICIA KATHLEEN
see: CAPE, JUDITH

PAGE, RAND LE
see: LE PAGE, RAND

PAGE, THOMAS (Walker IV), 1942- [*biography included*]

11112 *The Hephaestus plague.* G. P. Putnam's Sons, New York, 1973, 191p, Cloth, Novel

PAGET, JOHN, pseud.
see: AIKEN, JOHN

PAGET, VIOLET
see: LEE, VERNON

PAIN, BARRY (Eric Odell), 1865-1928

11113 *Collected tales, volume one.* Martin Secker, London, 1916, 306p, Cloth, Coll. [volume two never published]
11114 *The diary of a baby, being a free record of the unconscious thought of Rosalys Ysolde Smith, aged one year.* Eveleigh Nash, London, 1907, 175p, Cloth, Novel
11115 *An exchange of souls.* Eveleigh Nash, London, 1911, 256p, Cloth, Novel
11116 *Going home, being the fantastic romance of the girl with angel eyes and the man who had wings.* T. Werner Laurie, London, 1921, 186p, Cloth, Novel
11117 *In a Canadian canoe, The nine muses minus one, and other stories.* Henry & Co., London, 1891, 210p, Cloth, Coll.
11118 *More stories.* T. Werner Laurie, London, 1930, 784p, Cloth, Coll. [includes *In a Canadian canoe; The octave of Claudius; The memoirs of Constantine Dix; The exiles of Faloo; An exchange of souls*]
11119 *The new Gulliver, and other stories.* T. Werner Laurie, London, 1912, 261p, Cloth, Coll.
11120 *The One Before.* Grant Richards, London, 1902, 231p, Cloth, Novel
The return of Robinson Crusoe. [see 11121A]
11121 *Robinson Crusoe's return.* Hodder & Stoughton, London, 1906, 168p, Paper, Novel
11121A retitled: *The return of Robinson Crusoe.* T. Werner Laurie, London, 1921, 96p, Cloth, Novel
11122 *Stories and interludes.* Henry & Co., London, 1892, 215p, Cloth, Coll.
11123 *Stories in the dark.* Grant Richards, London, 1901, 192p, Paper, Coll.

with James Blyth:

01574 *The shadow of the unseen.* Chapman & Hall, London, 1907, 295p, Cloth, Novel

PAINE, ALBERT BIGELOW, 1861-1937

11124 *The great white way; a record of an unusual voyage of discovery, and some romantic love affairs amid strange surroundings, the whole recounted by one Nicholas Chase, promoter of the expedition, whose reports have been arranged for publication by Albert Bigelow Paine.* J. F. Taylor, New York, 1901, 327p, Cloth, Novel

PAINE, DORIS M., with Diana Martinez

09732   *Guide to science fiction; exploring possibili-*
        ties and alternatives. Bantam, New York,
        1974, 72p, Paper, Nonf.

PAINE, LAURAN (Bosworth), 1916-   [*biography
included*]

11125   *This time tomorrow.* Consul, London, 1963,
        154p, Paper, Novel

as Mark Carrel:

11126   *Another view.* Robert Hale, London, 1972,
        189p, Cloth, Novel
11127   *Bannister's Z-matter.* Robert Hale, London,
        1973, 159p, Cloth, Novel
11128   *A crack in time.* Robert Hale, London, 1971,
        192p, Cloth, Novel
11129   *The undine.* Robert Hale, London, 1972, 192p,
        Cloth, Novel

as Troy Howard:

11130   *Kernel of death.* Robert Hale, London, 1973,
        192p, Cloth, Novel
11131   *The misplaced psyche.* Robert Hale, London,
        1973, 192p, Cloth, Novel

PAINTER, THOMAS, with Alexander Laing

08539   *The motives of Nicholas Holtz, being the*
        weird tale of the Ironville virus. Farrar
        & Rinehart, New York, 1936, 309p, Cloth,
        Novel
08539A retitled: *The glass centipede, retold from*
        the original sources. Thornton Butterworth,
        London, 1936, 285p, Cloth, Novel

A PAIR FROM SPACE

11132   *A pair from space: Giants in the Earth,*
        James Blish; We, the marauders, Robert
        Silverberg. Belmont, New York, 1965, 159p,
        Paper, Anth.

PAIRAULT, PIERRE
    see: WUL, STEFAN

PAKENHAM, IVO

11133   *Fanfaronade.* Rich & Cowan, London, 1934,
        318p, Cloth, Novel

PALLANDER, EDWIN

11134   *Across the Zodiac; a story of adventure.*
        Digby, Long, London, 1896, 306p, Cloth,
        Novel
11135   *The adventures of a micro-man.* Digby, Long,
        London, 1902, 304p, Cloth, Novel

PALLEN, CONDÉ B(énoist), 1858-1929

11136   *Crucible island; a romance, an adventure, and*
        an experiment. Manhattanville Press, New
        York, 1919, 215p, Cloth, Novel

11137   *Ghost house.* Manhattanville Press, New York,
        1928, 239p, Cloth, Novel

PALM, GENE, pseud. [Luigi Palmisano]

11138   *The illusion and the reality.* Pageant Press
        International Corp., New York, 1969, 337p,
        Cloth, Novel

PALMER, BERNARD (Alvin), 1914-   [*biography
included*]

11139   *Jim Dunlap and the long lunar walk.* Moody
        Press, Chicago, 1974, 127p, Paper, Novel
        [Jim Dunlap series]
        Jim Dunlap and the mysterious orbiting rocket.
        [see 11143A]
11140   *Jim Dunlap and the mysterious spy.* Moody Press
        Chicago, 1974, 125p, Paper, Novel [Jim Dun-
        lap series]
        Jim Dunlap and the secret rocket formula. [see
        11145A]
        Jim Dunlap and the strange Dr. Brockton. [see
        11144A]
        Jim Dunlap and the wingless plane. [see 11146
11141   *Pat Collins and the captive scientist.* Moody
        Press, Chicago, 1958,   , Cloth, Novel
        [Pat Collins #6]
11142   *Pat Collins and the hidden treasure.* Moody
        Press, Chicago, 1957, 63p, Cloth, Novel
        [Pat Collins #3]
11143   *Pat Collins and the mysterious orbiting rocket*
        Moody Press, Chicago, 1958, 60p, Cloth, Nove
        [Pat Collins #5]
11143A retitled: *Jim Dunlap and the mysterious orbi-*
        ting rocket. Moody Press, Chicago, 1968,
        128p, Paper, Novel [Jim Dunlap series; sligh
        ly revised]
11144   *Pat Collins and the peculiar Dr. Brockton.*
        Moody Press, Chicago, 1957, 61p, Cloth, Nove
        [Pat Collins #1]
11144A retitled: *Jim Dunlap and the strange Dr.*
        Brockton. Moody Press, Chicago, 1967, 127p
        Paper, Novel [Jim Dunlap series; revised]
11145   *Pat Collins and the secret engine.* Moody Pre
        Chicago, 1957, 63p, Cloth, Novel [Pat Colli
        #2]
11145A retitled: *Jim Dunlap and the secret rocket*
        formula. Moody Press, Chicago, 1967,   ,
        Paper, Novel [Jim Dunlap series; revised]
11146   *Pat Collins and the wingless plane.* Moody
        Press, Chicago, 1957, 60p, Cloth, Novel [Pat
        Collins #4]
11146A retitled: *Jim Dunlap and the wingless plane.*
        Moody Press, Chicago, 1968, 128p, Paper,
        Novel [Jim Dunlap series; revised]

PALMER, CUTHBERT A.

11147   *The man without a navel.* Dragon Press, Ithac
        NY, 1932, 70p, Cloth, Novel

PALMER, FREDERICK, 1873-1958

11148   *So a leader came.* Ray Long & Richard R. Smit
        New York, 1932, 367p, Cloth, Novel

PALMER, J(ohn) H(enry)

11149 *The invasion of New York; or, How Hawaii was annexed*. F. Tennyson Neely, New York, 1897, 248p, Cloth, Novel

PALMER, JOHN (Leslie), 1885-1944

11150 *The Hesperides; a looking-glass fugue*. Martin Secker & Warburg, London, 1936, 319p, Cloth, Novel

with Hilary Saunders as Francis Beeding:

11151 *The One Sane Man*. Little, Brown, Boston, 1934, 314p, Cloth, Novel
11152 *The seven sleepers*. Little, Brown, Boston, 1925, 317p, Cloth, Novel

PALMER, LUCILE

11153 *Cat-eye*. Sargent House Publishers, Los Angeles, 1949, 244p, Cloth, Novel
11154 *Lovers in Mars*. Sargent House Publishers, Los Angeles, 1954, 123p, Paper, Novel

PALMER, P. K.
 see: PARNELL, KEITH

PALMER, WILLIAM

11155 *Under home rule; a novel*. Baines & Scarsbrook, London, 1912, 170p, Cloth, Novel

PALMER, WILLIAM J., 1890- [*biography included*]

11156 *The curious culture of the planet Loretta*. Vantage Press, New York, 1968, 126p, Cloth, Novel

PALMISANO, LUIGI
 see: PALM, GENE

PALTOCK, ROBERT, 1697-1767

11157 *The life and adventures of Peter Wilkins, a Cornish man, relating particularly his shipwreck near the South Pole...his extraordinary conveyance to the country of Glums and Gawrys, or men and women that fly; likewise a description of this strange country, with the laws...of its inhabitants, and the author's remarkable transactions among them; taken from his own mouth, in his passage to England...in the ship Hector, by R. S.* J. Robinson & R. Dodsley, London, 1751, 2vol, Cloth, Novel
11157A retitled: *The unrivalled adventures of that great aeronaut and Glum, Peter Wilkins, taken from the original ms. of the author, containing his shipwreck...near the South Pole, his precipitation into a new country...his marriage there...also, the extraordinary manner of his being taken on board the Hector, by T. Trueman, F.R.S., Peter's amanuensis on board the Hector*. T. Tegg, London, 1802, 39p, Cloth, Novel [abridged]

11157B retitled: *Peter Wilkins and the flying Indians*. no publisher, Newcastle, UK, 18??, 10p, Paper?, Story [abridged; published anonymously]
11157C retitled: *Peter Wilkins*. E. P. Dutton, New York, 1914, 352p, Cloth, Novel

PALUDAN-MÜLLER, FREDERIK, 1809-1876

11158 *The fountain of youth*. Macmillan, London, 1866, 147p, Cloth, Novel

PAN, pseud.
 see: BERESFORD, LESLIE

PANGBORN, EDGAR, 1909-1976 [*biography included*]

11159 *Davy*. St. Martin's Press, New York, 1964, 308p, Cloth, Novel
11160 *Good neighbors, and other strangers*. Macmillan, New York, 1972, 195p, Cloth, Coll.
11161 *The judgment of Eve; a novel of human inquiry*. Simon & Schuster, New York, 1966, 224p, Cloth, Novel
11162 *A mirror for observers*. Doubleday, Garden City, 1954, 222p, Cloth, Novel
11163 *West of the Sun*. Doubleday, Garden City, 1953, 219p, Cloth, Novel

PANICS

11164 *Panics; a collection of uneasy tales*. Philip Allan, London, 1934, 241p, Cloth, Anth.

PANSHIN, ALEXEI [Alexis A. Panshin, 1940-]
[*biography included*]

11165 *An Anthony Villiers adventure; Star Well*. Ace, New York, 1968, 157p, Paper, Novel [Anthony Villiers #1]
11166 *An Anthony Villiers adventure; The Thurb revolution*. Ace, New York, 1968, 159p, Paper, Novel [Anthony Villiers #2]
11167 *Heinlein in dimension; a critical analysis*. Advent: Publishers, Chicago, 1968, 204p, Cloth, Nonf.
11168 *Masque world*. Ace, New York, 1969, 157p, Paper, Novel [Anthony Villiers #3]
11169 *Rite of passage*. Ace, New York, 1968, 254p, Paper, Novel

PANTELL, DORA (F.), with Ellen MacGregor

09443 *Miss Pickerell and the weather satellite*. McGraw-Hill, New York, 1971, 157p, Cloth, Novel [Miss Pickerell #8]
09444 *Miss Pickerell goes on a dig*. McGraw-Hill, New York, 1966, 128p, Cloth, Novel [Miss Pickerell #6]
09445 *Miss Pickerell harvests the sea*. McGraw-Hill, New York, 1968, 144p, Cloth, Novel [Miss Pickerell #7]
09446 *Miss Pickerell meets Mr. H.U.M.* McGraw-Hill, New York, 1974, 160p, Cloth, Novel [Miss Pickerell #9]

PANTELL, DORA (cont.), with Ellen MacGregor

09447   *Miss Pickerell on the Moon.* McGraw-Hill, New
         York, 1965, 142p, Cloth, Novel [Miss Pick-
         erell #5]

PAPE, RICHARD (Bernard), 1916-   [*biography
included*]

11170   *And so ends the world.* Elek, London, 1961,
         222p, Cloth, Novel

PAPPAS, ANGELOS
     see: PAPPAZISIS, EVANGELOS

PAPPAZISIS, EVANGELOS, pseud. [Angelos Pappas, 1883-   ]

11171   *In the path of the beast.* no publisher,
         Cleveland, 1952, 238p, Cloth, Novel

PARABELLUM, pseud.
     see: GRAUTOFF, FERDINAND

A PARALLEL CASE

11172   *A parallel case; or, The Straits of Dover
         question, A.D. 2345.* Bell, Darlington,
         London, 1876, 11p, Paper, Story

PARASITE PLANET

11173   *Parasite planet, by Stanley Weinbaum; and,
         Life-line, by Robert A. Heinlein.* Fantasy
         Fiction, Sydney, 1950, 48p, Paper, Anth.

PARCELL, NORMAN HOWE
     see: NICHOLSON, JOHN

PARDOE, MARGOT (Mary), 1902-

11174   *Argle's mist.* Routledge & Kegan Paul, London,
         1956, 258p, Cloth, Novel
11174A retitled: *Curtain of mist.* Funk & Wagnalls,
         New York, 1957, 246p, Cloth, Novel

PARGETER, EDITH (Mary), 1913-   [*biography
included*]

11175   *The city lies four-square; a novel.* William
         Heinemann, London, 1939, 290p, Cloth, Novel

PARIS, JOHN, pseud. [Frank Trelawny Arthur
Ashton-Gwatkin]

11176   *The island beyond Japan.* W. Collins Sons,
         London, 1929, 276p, Cloth, Novel

PARKE, JEAN

11177   *The fountain of heart's desire; legendary
         theme and variations.* Servire, The Hague,
         1927, 54p, Paper, Novel

PARKER, E. FRANK

11178   *Girl in trouble.* Utopian Publications, London,
         1944, 36p, Paper, Story

PARKER, JOSEPH D.

11179   *Zeus Bentley; or, A love that conquered death.*
         Meador Publishing Co., Boston, 1934, 190p,
         Cloth, Novel

PARKER, NORTON (S.)

11180   *The strange bedfellows of Montague Ames.*
         Hermitage House, New York, 1953, 288p, Cloth,
         Novel

PARKER, RICHARD, 1915-

11181   *The Hendon fungus.* Victor Gollancz, London,
         1967, 157p, Cloth, Novel
11182   *The old powder line.* Victor Gollancz, London,
         1971, 144p, Cloth, Novel
11183   *Spell seven.* Longman Young Books, London,
         1971, 123p, Cloth, Novel
11184   *A time to choose.* Hutchinson, London, 1973,
         128p, Cloth, Novel

PARKES, LUCAS, pseud.
     see: WYNDHAM, JOHN

PARKHIRST, DOUGLAS

11185   *I, Scheherazade; memoirs of a Siamese cat.*
         Bonanza, New York, 1963, 112p, Cloth, Novel

PARKINSON, ETHELYN M(inerva), 1906-

11186   *Rupert Piper and Megan, the valuable girl.*
         Abingdon, New York, 1972, 160p, Cloth, Novel

PARKINSON, H(arold) F(rederick)

11187   *They shall not die.* Constable, London, 1939,
         277p, Cloth, Novel [title throughout the
         book: *Immune*]

PARKMAN, SYDNEY (Müller), 1895-

11188   *Life begins tomorrow.* Hodder & Stoughton,
         London, 1948, 319p, Cloth, Novel
11189   *Ship ashore.* Hodder & Stoughton, London,
         1936, 314p, Cloth, Novel

PARMELE, MARY PLATT, 1843-1911

11190   *Ariel; or, The author's world.* Alliance, New
         York, 1898, 79p, Paper, Novel

PARNELL, JOHN

11191   *Cromwell the Third; or, The jubilee of liberty;
         a letter written by Julius Boanerges to his
         son.* J. Parnell, London, 1886, 11p, Paper,
         Story

PARNELL, KEITH, pseud. [P. K. Palmer, d. 1973?]

11192 *Dementia.* Zebra, New York, 1974, 247p, Paper, Novel

PARRISH, ANNE, 1888-1957, with Dillwyn Parrish

11193 *Lustres.* George H. Doran, New York, 1924, 215p, Cloth, Coll.

PARRISH, (George) DILLWYN, 1894- , with Anne Parrish

11193 *Lustres.* George H. Doran, New York, 1924, 215p, Cloth, Coll.

PARRISH, J(ohn) M(axey), with John R. Crossland

03661 *The mammoth book of thrillers, ghosts, and mysteries.* Odhams Press, London, 1936, 766p, Cloth, Anth.

PARRISH, RANDALL, 1858-1923

11194 *Prisoners of chance; the story of what befell Geoffrey Benteen, borderman, through his love for a lady of France.* A. C. McClurg, Chicago, 1908, 423p, Cloth, Novel

PARRY, DAVID M(aclean), 1852-1915

11195 *The scarlet empire.* Bobbs-Merrill, Indianapolis, 1906, 400p, Cloth, Novel

PARRY, DENNIS (Arthur), 1912-

11196 *The survivor.* Robert Hale, London, 1940, 298p, Cloth, Novel

PARRY, MICHEL (Patrick), 1947- [*biography included*]

11197 *Beware of the cat; weird tales about cats.* Victor Gollancz, London, 1972, 191p, Cloth, Anth.
11198 *Countess Dracula.* Sphere, London, 1971, 140p, Paper, Movie [Dracula series]
11199 *The devil's children; tales of demons and exorcists.* Orbit, London, 1974, 213p, Paper, Anth.
11200 *Dream trips; stories of weird and unearthly drugs.* Panther, St. Albans, UK, 1974, 160p, Paper, Anth.
11201 *The first Mayflower book of black magic stories.* Mayflower, St. Albans, UK, 1974, 222p, Paper, Anth.
11202 *The hounds of Hell; weird tales about dogs.* Victor Gollancz, London, 1974, 192p, Cloth, Anth.
11203 *The second Mayflower book of black magic stories.* Mayflower, St. Albans, UK, 1974, 205p, Paper, Anth.

11204 *Strange ecstasies; stories about strange and unearthly drugs.* Panther, St. Albans, UK, 1973, 157p, Paper, Anth.

with Garry Rusoff:

11205 *Chariots of fire.* Orbit, London, 1974, 192p, Paper, Novel

PARTRIDGE, BELLAMY
see: BAILEY, THOMAS

PASSAGE TO SATURN
see: HARBOTTLE, PHILIP

PATCHETT, M(ary Osborne) E(lwyn), 1897- [*biography included*]

11206 *Adam Troy, astroman; the exciting story of how a great space-pilot saved the world from radiation beasts.* Lutterworth Press, London, 1954, 189p, Cloth, Novel
11207 *Farm beneath the sea.* George G. Harrap, London, 1969, 173p, Cloth, Novel
Flight to the misty planet. [see 11209A]
11208 *Kidnappers of space; the story of two boys in a spaceship abducted by the golden men of Mars.* Lutterworth Press, London, 1953, 208p, Cloth, Novel
11208A retitled: *Space captives of the golden men.* Bobbs-Merrill, Indianapolis, 1955, 222p, Cloth, Novel
11209 *Lost on Venus.* Lutterworth Press, London, 1954, 192p, Cloth, Novel
11209A retitled: *Flight to the misty planet.* Bobbs-Merrill, Indianapolis, 1956, 236p, Cloth, Novel
11210 *Send for Johnny Danger; the amazing adventures of the ace pilot, Captain Danger, and his crew on the Moon.* Lutterworth Press, London, 1956, 174p, Cloth, Novel
Space captives of the golden men. [See 11208A]
11211 *The Venus project.* Brockhampton Press, Leicester, UK, 1963, 160p, Cloth, Novel

PATERNO, DOMENICA, with Marjorie Smiley and Mary Delores Jarmon

07856 *Something strange.* Macmillan, New York, 1969, 246p, Paper, Anth.

PATERNOSTER, G(eorge) SIDNEY, 1866-

11212 *The cruise of the Conqueror, being the further adventures of the motor pirate.* L. C. Page, Boston, 1906, 317p, Cloth, Novel [Motor Pirate #2]
11213 *The motor pirate.* Chatto & Windus, London, 1903, 248p, Cloth, Novel [Motor Pirate #1]

PATERSON, ARTHUR ELLIOTT

11214 *Venus: one world nearer paradise?* Traversity Press, Penobscot, Maine, 1961, 132p, Cloth, Novel

PATH INTO THE UNKNOWN

   11215 *Path into the unknown; the best Soviet SF.*
       MacGibbon & Kee, London, 1966, 191p, Cloth,
       Anth.

PATON, A(ndrew) A(rchibald), 1811-1874

   11216 *Melusina; a new Arabian night's entertainment.*
       Longman, Green, Longman & Roberts, London,
       1860, 272p, Cloth, Novel

PATON, RAYMOND

   11217 *The tale of Lal; a fantasy.* Chapman & Hall,
       London, 1914, 298p, Cloth, Novel

PATOT, SIMON TYSSOT de
    see: BAYLE, Monsieur

PATRICK, J(ohn) MAX, 1911-   [*biography included*], with Glenn Negley

   10604 *The quest for utopia; an anthology of imagi-
       nary societies.* Henry Schuman, London,
       1952, 599p, Cloth, Anth.

PATROUCH, JOSEPH F(rancis), Jr., 1935-
[*biography included*]

   11218 *Isaac Asimov's I, robot; a study guide.* Faw-
       cett Publications, Greenwich, Conn., 1972,
       10p, Paper, Nonf.
   11219 *The science fiction of Isaac Asimov.* Double-
       day, Garden City, 1974, 283p, Cloth, Nonf.
   11220 *The short fiction of Isaac Asimov; a study
       guide.* Fawcett Publications, Greenwich,
       Conn., 1972, 10p, Paper, Nonf.

PATTEN, WILLIAM, 1868-1936

   11221 *Great short stories; a new collection of fa-
       mous examples from the literatures of France,
       England, and America; volume II, ghost sto-
       ries.* P. F. Collier, New York, 1906, 428p,
       Cloth, Anth.

PATTERSON, JAMES ERNEST WILLIAM

   11222 *The call of the planets.* A. J. Chapple, Bala,
       UK, 1968, 90p, Cloth, Novel

PATTISON, EMILIA
    see: DILKE, Lady

PAUL, AUREN, pseud. [Auren Uris, 1913-   ]

   11223 *The love machine.* Merit, Chicago, 1960,
       160p, Paper, Novel

PAUL, F. W., pseud.
    see: FAIRMAN, PAUL W.

PAUL, HUGO, pseud. [Paul H. Little, 1915-   ]
[*biography included*]

   11224 *Master of the undead.* Lancer, New York, 1968,
       221p, Paper, Novel

PAUL, PHYLLIS

   11225 *Rox Hall illuminated.* William Heinemann, Lon-
       don, 1956, 277p, Cloth, Novel

PAULS, THEODORE

   11226 *Just under Heaven.* Chapman & Grimes, Boston,
       1945, 177p, Cloth, Novel

PAULTON, EDWARD A(ntonio), 1868-1939

   11227 *The American Faust.* Belford Co., Publishers,
       New York, 1890, 256p, Paper, Novel

PAVLENKO, PIOTR [Pëtr Andreevich Pavlenko,
1899-1951]

   11228 *Red planes fly east.* George Routledge & Sons,
       London, 1938, 523p, Cloth, Novel
   11228A retitled: *Red wings over Tokio; excerpt from
       Soviet novel, "In the east."* New South Wales
       Bookstall Co., Sydney, 1942, 64p, Paper,
       Novel [abridged]

PAWLE, HANBURY, 1886-1972

   11229 *Before dawn.* Hutchinson, London, 1955, 248p,
       Cloth, Novel

PAYES, RACHEL COSGROVE
    see: ARCH, E. L.

PAYNE, CHARLES

   11230 *The secret of Josiah Black; a novel.* Arthur H.
       Stockwell, London, 1935, 240p, Cloth, Novel

PAYNE, DONALD GORDON, 1924-   [*biography included*]

as Ian Cameron:

   11231 *The lost ones.* Hutchinson, London, 1961, 320p,
       Cloth, Novel
   11231A retitled: *Island at the top of the world.*
       Avon, New York, 1974, 190p, Paper, Novel
   11232 *The mountains at the bottom of the world; a
       novel of adventure.* William Morrow, New
       York, 1972, 212p, Cloth, Novel

as Donald Gordon:

   11233 *Star-Raker.* Hodder & Stoughton, London, 1962,
       256p, Cloth, Novel; William Morrow, New York,
       1962, 288p, Cloth, Novel

PAYNE, (Pierre Stephen) ROBERT, 1911-   [biography included]

11234 *The deluge; a novel.* Twayne Publishers, New York, 1954, 99p, Cloth, Novel [based on notes left by Leonardo da Vinci]

as Robert Young:

11235 *The war in the marshes.* Faber & Faber, London, 1938, 353p, Cloth, Novel

PEABODY, JOEL R.

11236 *A world of wonders; or, Divers developments, showing the thorough triumph of animal magnetism in New England.* Robert S. Davis, Boston, 1838, 158p, Cloth, Novel

PEACEY, HOWARD (Marriott), 1880-

11237 *Magic hours.* Humphrey Toulmin, London, 1930, 282p, Cloth, Novel

PEACOCK, LUCY

11238 *The adventures of the six princesses of Babylon in their travels to the Temple of Virtue; an allegory.* T. Bensley, London, 1785, 131p, Cloth, Novel

PEACOCK, THOMAS LOVE, 1785-1866

11239 *Headlong Hall; and, Nightmare Abbey.* Ward & Lock, London, 1856, 171p, Cloth, Coll.
11240 *Nightmare Abbey,* by the author of Headlong Hall. T. Hookham, Junior, London, 1818, 218p, Cloth, Novel [published anonymously]
11240A *Nightmare Abbey,* by T. Love Peacock. J. M. Dent & Sons, London, 1891, 134p, Cloth, Novel
11241 *Nightmare Abbey; and, Crotchet Castle.* Hamish Hamilton, London, 1947, 228p, Cloth, Coll.
11242 *The novels of Thomas Love Peacock.* George Newnes, London, 1903, 958p, Cloth, Coll.
11243 *Three novels: Headlong Hall; Nightmare Abbey; Crotchet Castle.* Thomas Nelson & Sons, London, 1940, 320p, Cloth, Coll.

PEAKE, MERVYN (Laurence), 1911-1968 [biography included]

11244 *Gormenghast.* Eyre & Spottiswoode, London, 1950, 454p, Cloth, Novel [Gormenghast Trilogy #2]
11245 *Mr. Pye.* William Heinemann, London, 1953, 278p, Cloth, Novel
11246 *Titus alone.* Eyre & Spottiswoode, London, 1959, 223p, Cloth, Novel [Gormenghast Trilogy #3]
11247 *Titus alone, new ed.* Eyre & Spottiswoode, London, 1970, 263p, Cloth, Novel [Gormenghast Trilogy #3; restores the author's original text]
11248 *Titus Groan.* Eyre & Spottiswoode, London, 1946, 438p, Cloth, Novel [Gormenghast Trilogy #1]

PEARCE, A(nn) PHILIPPA [biography included]

11249 *Tom's midnight garden.* Oxford University Press, London, 1958, 229p, Cloth, Novel

PEARCE, J(oseph) H(enry)

11250 *Drolls from shadowland.* Lawrence & Bullen, London, 1893, 166p, Cloth, Coll.
11251 *Tales of the masque.* Lawrence & Bullen, London, 1894, 207p, Cloth, Coll.

PEARL, JACK [Jacques Bain Pearl, 1923-   ] [biography included]

11252 *The invaders; dam of death.* Whitman Publishing Co., Racine, Wisc., 1967, 212p, Cloth, Tele. [Invaders series]
11253 *Our man Flint.* Pocket Books, New York, 1965, 158p, Paper, Movie
11254 *Space Eagle; operation doomsday.* Whitman Publishing Co., Racine, Wisc., 1967, 215p, Cloth, Novel [Space Eagle #1]
11255 *The Space Eagle; operation star voyage.* Whitman Publishing Co., Racine, Wisc., 1970, 211p, Cloth, Novel [Space Eagle #2]

PEARLMAN, GILBERT

11256 *Young Frankenstein.* Ballantine, New York, 1974, 152p, Paper, Movie

PEARSON, (An)DREW (Russell), 1897-1969 [biography included]

11257 *The president.* Doubleday, Garden City, 1970, 470p, Cloth, Novel

PEARSON, EDWARD (Max), 1908-   [biography included]

11258 *Chamiel.* Quartet, London, 1973, 119p, Paper, Novel

PEARSON, ELIZABETH J., with Sylvia Z. Brodkin

01912 *Science fiction.* McDougal, Littell, Evanston, IL, 1973, 247p, Paper, Anth.

PEARSON, MICHAEL (Edward), 1941-   [biography included], with Amabel Williams-Ellis

11259 *Out of this world 9; an anthology of science fiction.* Blackie & Son, London, 1972, 191p, Cloth, Anth.
11260 *Out of this world 10; an anthology of science fiction.* Blackie & Son, London, 1973, 190p, Cloth, Anth.
11261 *Strange universe; an anthology of science fiction.* Blackie & Son, London, 1974, 192p, Cloth, Anth.
11262 *Tales from the galaxies.* Piccolo, London, 1973, 126p, Paper, Anth.

PEASE, HARLAN T(rask)

11263 *Leonard.* Exposition Press, New York, 1967, 92p, Cloth, Novel

PEASE, HOWARD, 1863-

11264 *Border ghost stories.* Erskine Macdonald, London, 1919, 303p, Cloth, Coll.
11265 *The mark o' the deil, and other Northumbrian tales.* T. Fisher Unwin, London, 1894, 166p, Cloth, Coll.

PEATTIE, Mrs. ELIA W(ilkinson), 1862-1935

11266 *The shape of fear, and other ghostly tales.* Macmillan, New York, 1898, 175p, Cloth, Coll.

PECK, BRADFORD

11267 *The world a department store; a story of life under a coöperative system.* Bradford Peck, Lewiston, Maine, 1900, 311p, Cloth, Novel

PECK, GEORGE WASHINGTON
see: BIGLY, CANTELL A.

PECK, IRA

11268 *A treasury of great ghost stories.* Popular Library, New York, 1965, 256p, Paper, Anth.

PECK, RICHARD E.

11269 *Final solution.* Doubleday, Garden City, 1973, 189p, Cloth, Novel

PECK, VERNON

11270 *Super sex captain.* Pigalle Press, 1969,   , Paper, Novel

PEDDIE, JAMES (Anderson)

11271 *Capture of London.* General Publishing Co., London, 1887, 15p, Paper, Story

PEDLER, KIT [Christopher Magnus Howard Pedler, 1927-   ] [*biography included*], with Gerry Davis

03890 *Brainrack.* Souvenir Press, London, 1974, 285p, Cloth, Novel
03891 *Mutant 59: the plastic-eater.* Souvenir Press, London, 1971, 295p, Cloth, Novel

PEDLEY, HUGH

11272 *Looking forward; the strange experience of the Rev. Fergus McCheyne.* William Briggs, Toronto, 1913, 294p, Cloth, Novel

PEDROE-SAVIDGE, E. VAN
see: VAN PEDROE-SAVIDGE, E.

PEEK, HEDLEY

11273 *The chariot of the flesh.* Lawrence & Bullen, London, 1897, 296p, Cloth, Novel
11274 *Nema, and other stories.* Chapman & Hall, London, 1895, 207p, Cloth, Coll.

PEEKE, MARGARET B(loodgood), 1838-1908

11275 *Born of flame; a Rosicrucian story.* J. B. Lippincott, Philadelphia, 1892, 299p, Cloth, Novel
11276 *Zenia, the Vestal; or, The problem of vibrations.* Arena Publishing Co., Boston, 1893, 356p, Cloth, Novel

PEEPLES, EDWIN A(ugustus Jr.), 1915-

11277 *Blue boy.* Houghton Mifflin, Boston, 1964, 176p, Cloth, Novel

PEI, MARIO (Andrew),1901-1978 [*biography included*]

11278 *The sparrows of Paris.* Philosophical Library, New York, 1958, 121p, Cloth, Novel
11279 *Tales of the natural and supernatural.* Devin-Adair, Old Greenwich, Conn., 1971, 310p, Cloth, Coll.

PELTON, GUY CATHCART

11280 *An atomic visitor.* Hobson Book Press, New York, 1946, 50p, Paper, Novel

PEMBERTON, (Sir) MAX, 1863-1950

11281 *Captain Black; a sequel to "The iron pirate."* Cassell, London, 1911, 338p, Cloth, Novel [Capt. Black #2]
11282 *The house under the sea; a romance.* George Newnes, London, 1902, 318p, Cloth, Novel
11283 *The impregnable city; a romance.* Cassell, London, 1895, 416p, Cloth, Novel
11284 *The iron pirate; a plain tale of strange happenings on the sea.* Cassell, London, 1893, 298p, Cloth, Novel [Capt. Black #1]
11284A retitled: *The shadow on the sea; a tale of strange happenings.* Arthur Westbrook, Cleveland, 1907, 298p, Cloth, Novel [Capt. Black #1]
11285 *Pro patriâ.* Ward, Lock, London, 1901, 316p, Cloth, Novel
The shadow on the sea. [see 11284A]

PENDERED, MARY L(ucy), 1858-1940

11286 *The secret of the Dragon; a romance ancient and modern.* Harper & Bros., London, 1911, 347p, Cloth, Novel
11287 *The uncanny house.* Hutchinson, London, 1927, 285p, Cloth, Novel

PENDLETON, DON(ald Eugene), 1927-   [biography included]

11288 *Cataclysm: the day the world died.* Pinnacle, New York, 1969, 256p, Paper, Novel
       The Godmakers. [see 11294A]
11289 *The guns of Terra 10.* Pinnacle, New York, 1970, 189p, Paper, Novel
11290 *1989: population doomsday.* Pinnacle, New York, 1970, 192p, Paper, Novel
11290A retitled: *Population doomsday.* Pinnacle, New York, 1974, 192p, Paper, Novel
11291 *The Olympians.* Greenleaf Classics, San Diego, 1969, 207p, Paper, Novel
       Population doomsday. [see 11290A]
11292 *Revolt!* Bee-Line Special, New York, 1968, 247p, Paper, Novel

as Dan Britain:

11293 *Civil War II: the day it finally happened!* Pinnacle, New York, 1971, 251p, Paper, Novel [adapted from *Revolt!*]
11294 *The Godmakers.* Pinnacle, New York, 1970, 188p, Paper, Novel
11294A *The Godmakers*, by Don Pendleton. Pinnacle, New York, 1974, 188p, Paper, Novel

PENDLETON, JOHN

11295 *The ivory queen; a story of strange adventure.* Osgood, McIlvaine, London, 1897, 263p, Cloth, Novel

PENDLETON, LOUIS (Beauregard), 1861-1939

11296 *In Assyrian tents; the story of the strange adventures of Uriel.* Jewish Publication Society of America, Philadelphia, 1904, 248p, Cloth, Novel
11297 *The invisible police; a novel.* New-Church Press, New York, 1932, 223p, Cloth, Novel
11298 *The wedding garment; a tale of the life to come.* Roberts Bros., Boston, 1894, 246p, Cloth, Novel

PENDOWER, JACQUES
    see: JACOBS, T. C. H.

PENDRAY, EDWARD
    see: EDWARDS, GAWAIN

PENGREEP, WILLIAM

11299 *The temple of Sähr.* Cecil Palmer, London, 1932, 328p, Cloth, Novel

PENMARE, WILLIAM, pseud. [Mavis Elizabeth Nisot, 1893-   ]

11300 *The man who could stop war.* Hodder & Stoughton, London, 1929, 308p, Cloth, Novel

PENNY, F(anny) E(mily Farr), 1857?-1939

11301 *Magic in the air.* Hodder & Stoughton, London, 1933, 318p, Cloth, Novel

11302 *The Malabar magician.* Chatto & Windus, London, 1912, 344p, Cloth, Novel
11303 *The Sanyasi.* Chatto & Windus, London, 1904, 328p, Cloth, Novel
11304 *The swami's curse.* Hodder & Stoughton, London, 1922, 319p, Cloth, Novel
11305 *The wishing stone.* Hodder & Stoughton, London, 1930, 320p, Cloth, Novel

PENRICE, ARTHUR, pseud.

11306 *Skyward and Earthward.* Samuel Tinsley, London, 1875, 279p, Cloth, Novel

PENZOLDT, PETER

11307 *The supernatural in fiction.* Peter Nevill, London, 1952, 271p, Cloth, Nonf.

PEPLE, EDWARD (Henry), 1869-1924

11308 *A night out.* Moffat, Yard, New York, 1909, 44p, Cloth, Story
11309 *Semiramis; a tale of battle and of love.* Moffat, Yard, New York, 1907, 375p, Cloth, Novel

PERCE, ELBERT, 1831-1869

11310 *Gulliver Joi: his three voyages, being an account of his marvelous adventures in Kailoo, Hydrogenia, and Ejario.* Charles Scribner, New York, 1851, 272p, Cloth, Novel [Gulliver series]

PERCIVAL, Dr. (C.)

11311 *The Flaming Sword, being an account of the extraordinary adventures and discoveries of Dr. Percival in the wilds of Africa, written by himself.* Digby, Long, London, 1894, 309p, Cloth, Novel

PERCY, ALAN IAN
    see: NORTHUMBERLAND, Duke of

PERCY, WALKER, 1916-   [biography included]

11312 *Love in the ruins; the adventures of a bad Catholic at a time near the end of the world.* Farrar, Straus & Giroux, New York, 1971, 403p, Cloth, Novel

PEREIRA, W(ilfred) D(ennis), 1921-   [biography included]

11313 *Aftermath 15.* Robert Hale, London, 1973, 183p, Cloth, Novel

PEREIRA MENDES, H.
    see: MENDES, H. PEREIRA

PEREYRA, DIOMEDES de

11314 *The land of the golden scarabs.* Bobbs-Merrill,
       Indianapolis, 1928, 309p, Cloth, Novel

PERIL, BRUCE

11315 *Rocket to the Moon; a story for boys.* Faber
       & Faber, London, 1946, 220p, Cloth, Novel

PERKINS, D. M.

11316 *Deep throat; a novel.* Dell/Quicksilver, New
       York, 1973, 190p, Paper, Movie [Linda Love-
       lace #1]
11317 *Deep throat, part II; a novel.* Dell/Quick-
       silver, New York, 1974, 190p, Paper, Movie
       [Linda Lovelace #2]

PERKINS, ELI, pseud. [Melville De Lancey Landon, 1839-1910]

11318 *Saratoga in 1901; fun, love, society, & satire.*
       Sheldon & Co., New York, 1872, 249p, Cloth,
       Novel

PERKINS, FREDERICK B(eecher), 1828-1899 [real
name is actually Frederic Beecher Perkins]

11319 *Devil-puzzlers, and other studies.* G. P.
       Putnam's Sons, New York, 1877, 215p, Cloth,
       Coll.

PERKINS, MICHAEL, 1942-   [*biography included*]

11320 *Terminus.* Essex House, North Hollywood, 1969,
       160p, Paper, Novel

PERKINS, VIOLET LILIAN, with Arthur Leslie
Hood as Lilian Leslie

07378 *The melody from Mars.* Authors' International
       Publishing Co., New York, 1924, 206p, Cloth,
       Novel

PERRAULT, ROBERT, with Leonard Allison and
Leonard Jenkin

00229 *Survival printout.* Vintage, New York, 1973,
       335p, Paper, Anth.

PERRET, JACQUES (Louis Alfred Marie), 1901-

11321 *The wind in the sails.* Rupert Hart-Davis,
       London, 1954, 243p, Cloth, Novel
11321A retitled: *The honor of Gaston Le Torch; a
       novel.* W. W. Norton, New York, 1955, 276p,
       Cloth, Novel

PERRIN, A(lice), 1867-1934

11322 *East of Suez.* Anthony Treherne, London, 1901,
       311p, Cloth, Coll.

11323 *Rough passages.* Cassell, London, 1926, 279p,
       Cloth, Coll.

PERRY, DICK
    see: WINFIELD, DICK

PERRY, RICHARD, 1944-

11324 *Changes.* Bobbs-Merrill, Indianapolis, 1974,
       176p, Cloth, Novel

PERRY, TED, 1931-

11325 *The final amendment.* Little, Brown, Boston,
       1969, 310p, Cloth, Novel

PERRY, WALTER COPLAND, 1814-1911

11326 *The revolt of the horses.* Grant Richards,
       London, 1898, 229p, Cloth, Novel [Gulliver
       series]

PERRY RHODAN

11327 #1 *Enterprise Stardust.* Ace, New York, 1969,
       189p, Paper, Anth.
11328 #2 *The radiant dome.* Ace, New York, 1969,
       188p, Paper, Anth.
11329 #3 *Galactic alarm.* Ace, New York, 1969, 187p,
       Paper, Anth.
11330 #4 *Invasion from space.* Ace, New York, 1970,
       187p, Paper, Anth.
11331 #5 *The Vega sector.* Ace, New York, 1970,
       189p, Paper, Anth.
11332 #6 *The secret of the time vault.* Ace, New
       York, 1971, 126p, Paper, Anth.
11333 #7 *Fortress of the six moons.* Ace, New York,
       1971, 124p, Paper, Anth.
11334 #8 *The galactic riddle.* Ace, New York, 1971,
       127p, Paper, Anth.
11335 #9 *Quest through space and time.* Ace, New
       York, 1971, 125p, Paper, Anth.
11336 #10 *The ghosts of Gol.* Ace, New York, 1971,
       124p, Paper, Anth.
11337 #11 *The planet of the dying sun.* Ace, New
       York, 1972, 125p, Paper, Anth.
11338 #12 *The rebels of Tuglan.* Ace, New York,
       1972, 126p, Paper, Anth.
11339 #13 *The immortal unknown.* Ace, New York,
       1972, 120p, Paper, Anth.
11340 14 *Venus in danger.* Ace, New York, 1972,
       122p, Paper, Anth.
11341 15 *Escape to Venus.* Ace, New York, 1972,
       128p, Paper, Anth.
11342 16 *Secret barrier X.* Ace, New York, 1972,
       128p, Paper, Anth.
11343 17 *The Venus trap.* Ace, New York, 1972, 158p,
       Paper, Anth.
11344 18 *Menace of the mutant master.* Ace, New York,
       1972, 158p, Paper, Anth.
11345 19 *Mutants vs. mutants.* Ace, New York, 1972,
       160p, Paper, Anth.
11346 20 *The thrall of hypno.* Ace, New York, 1972,
       159p, Paper, Anth.
11347 21 *The cosmic decoy.* Ace, New York, 1973,
       173p, Paper, Anth.
11348 22 *The fleet of the Springers.* Ace, New York,
       1973, 158p, Paper, Anth.

PERRY RHODAN (cont.)

11349 23 *Peril on ice planet.* Ace, New York, 1973, 158p, Paper, Anth.

11350 24 *Infinity flight.* Ace, New York, 1973, 160p, Paper, Anth.

11351 25 *Snowman in flames.* Ace, New York, 1973, 173p, Paper, Anth.

11352 26 *Cosmic traitor.* Ace, New York, 1973, 159p, Paper, Anth.

11353 27 *Planet of the Gods.* Ace, New York, 1973, 155p, Paper, Anth.

11354 28 *The plague of oblivion.* Ace, New York, 1973, 157p, Paper, Anth.

11355 29 *A world gone mad.* Ace, New York, 1973, 160p, Paper, Anth.

11356 30 *To Arkon!* Ace, New York, 1973, 155p, Paper, Anth.

11357 31 *Realm of the tri-planets.* Ace, New York, 1973, 160p, Paper, Anth.

11358 32 *Challenge of the unknown.* Ace, New York, 1973, 160p, Paper, Anth.

11359 33 *The giant's partner.* Ace, New York, 1973, 155p, Paper, Anth.

11360 34 *SOS: spaceship Titan!* Ace, New York, 1973, 144p, Paper, Anth.

11361 35 *Beware the microrobots.* Ace, New York, 1973, 155p, Paper, Anth.

11362 36 *Man and monster.* Ace, New York, 1973, 156p, Paper, Anth.

11363 37 *Epidemic center: Aralon.* Ace, New York, 1974, 160p, Paper, Anth.

11364 38 *Project: Earthsave.* Ace, New York, 1974, 160p, Paper, Anth.

11365 39 *The silence of Gom.* Ace, New York, 1974, 144p, Paper, Anth.

11366 40 *Red eye of Betelgeuse.* Ace, New York, 1974, 153p, Paper, Anth.

11367 41 *The Earth dies.* Ace, New York, 1974, 158p, Paper, Anth.

11368 42 *Time's lonely one.* Ace, New York, 1974, 154p, Paper, Anth.

11369 43 *Life hunt.* Ace, New York, 1974, 155p, Paper, Anth.

11370 44 *The pseudo one.* Ace, New York, 1974, 158p, Paper, Anth.

11371 45 *Unknown sector: Milky Way.* Ace, New York, 1974, 144p, Paper, Anth.

11372 46 *Again: Atlan!* Ace, New York, 1974, 159p, Paper, Anth.

11373 47 *Shadow of the mutant master.* Ace, New York, 1974, 152p, Paper, Anth.

11374 48 *The dead live.* Ace, New York, 1974, 157p, Paper, Anth.

11375 49 *Solar assassins.* Ace, New York, 1974, 153p, Paper, Anth.

11376 50 *Attack from the unseen.* Ace, New York, 1974, 159p, Paper, Anth.

11377 51 *Return from the void.* Ace, New York, 1974, 156p, Paper, Anth.

11378 52 *Fortress Atlantis.* Ace, New York, 1974, 157p, Paper, Anth.

11379 53 *Spybot!* Ace, New York, 1974, 155p, Paper, Anth.

11380 54 *The blue dwarfs.* Ace, New York, 1974, 155p, Paper, Anth.

11381 55 *The micro-techs.* Ace, New York, 1974, 156p, Paper, Anth.

11382 56 *Prisoner of time.* Ace, New York, 1974, 157p, Paper, Anth.

11383 57 *A touch of eternity.* Ace, New York, 1974, 159p, Paper, Anth.

11384 58 *The guardians.* Ace, New York, 1974, 152p, Paper, Anth.

11385 59 *Interlude on Siliko 5.* Ace, New York, 1974, 160p, Paper, Anth.

11385 60 *Dimension search.* Ace, New York, 1974, 157p, Paper, Anth.

PERTWEE, ROLAND, 1885-1963

11386 *MW-XX.3.* William Heinemann, London, 1929, 335p, Cloth, Novel

11386A retitled: *Hell's loose.* Houghton Mifflin, Boston, 1929, 301p, Cloth, Novel

11386B retitled: *The million pound cypher; or, MW-XX.3.* William Heinemann, London, 1931, 336p, Cloth, Novel

PERUTZ, LEO, 1884-1957

11387 *The Marquis de Bolibar.* John Lane, London, 1926, 306p, Cloth, Novel

11388 *The master of the day of judgment.* Elkin Mathews & Marrot, London, 1929, 256p, Cloth, Novel

PESEK, LUDEK, 1919-   [*biography included*]

11389 *The Earth is near.* Longman Young Books, London, 1973, 206p, Cloth, Novel

11390 *The log of a Moon expedition.* Collins, London, 1969, 96p, Cloth, Novel

PESIN, HARRY, 1919-   [*biography included*]

11391 *Welcome, Stranger & Partners; the story of God and the man who succeeded him; a novel.* Perspective Publications, New York, 1974, 150p, Cloth, Novel

PETAJA, EMIL (Theodore), 1915-   [*biography included*]

11392 *Alpha yes, Terra no!* Ace Double, New York, 1965, 156p, Paper, Novel

11393 *And flights of angels; the life and legend of Hannes Bok.* Bokanalia Memorial Foundation, San Francisco, 1968, 156p, Paper, Nonf. Anth.

11394 *The caves of Mars.* Ace Double, New York, 1965, 125p, Paper, Novel

11395 *Doom of the Green Planet.* Ace Double, New York, 1968, 127p, Paper, Novel [Green Planet #2]

11396 *The Hannes Bok memorial showcase of fantasy art.* SISU Publishers, San Francisco, 1974, 166p, Paper, Nonf. Anth.

11397 *Lord of the Green Planet.* Ace Double, New York, 1967, 118p, Paper, Novel [Green Planet #1]

11398 *The nets of space.* Berkley Medallion, New York, 1969, 128p, Paper, Novel

11399 *The path beyond the stars.* Dell, New York, 1969, 188p, Paper, Novel

11400 *The Prism.* Ace Double, New York, 1968, 126p, Paper, Novel

11401 *Saga of lost Earths.* Ace, New York, 1966, 124p, Paper, Novel [Kalevala #1]

11402 *Seed of the dreamers.* Ace Double, New York, 1970, 103p, Paper, Novel

PETAJA, EMIL (cont.)

11403   *The star mill.* Ace, New York, 1966, 128p,
            Paper, Novel [Kalevala #2]
11404   *Stardrift, and other fantastic flotsam.* Fan-
            tasy Publishing Co., Alhambra, CA, 1971,
            220p, Cloth, Coll.
11405   *The stolen sun.* Ace Double, New York, 1967,
            136p, Paper, Novel [Kalevala #3]
11406   *The time twister.* Dell, New York, 1968, 158p,
            Paper, Novel
11407   *Tramontane.* Ace Double, New York, 1967, 119p,
            Paper, Novel [Kalevala #4]

PETER SCHLEMIHL IN AMERICA
      see: WOOD, GEORGE

PETER WILKINS
      see: PALTOCK, ROBERT

PETERKIEWICZ, JERZY [Jerzy Michal Pietrkiewicz, 1916-   ] [*biography included*]

11408   *Inner circle.* Macmillan, London, 1966, 186p,
            Cloth, Coll.
11409   *The quick and the dead; a novel.* Macmillan,
            London, 1961, 247p, Cloth, Novel

PETERS, ALAN

11410   *The secret formula.* Heath Cranton, London,
            1932, 296p, Cloth, Novel

PETERS, L. T., pseud.
      see: KLAINER, JO-ANN and KLAINER, ALBERT

PETERS, LUDOVIC, pseud. [Peter Brent, 1931-   ]

11411   *Riot '71.* Hodder & Stoughton, London, 1967,
            190p, Cloth, Novel

PETERSILEA, CARLYLE, 1844-1903

            The discovered country. [see 11413A]
11412   *Mary Anne Carew: wife, mother, spirit, angel.*
            Colby & Rich, Boston, 1893, 250p, Cloth,
            Novel
            Oceanides. [see 11414A]

as Ernst von Himmel:

11413   *The discovered country.* Ernst von Himmel Pub-
            lishing Co., Boston, 1889, 234p, Cloth,
            Novel
11413A *The discovered country,* by Carlyle Petersilea.
            Colby & Rich, Boston, 1892, 234p, Cloth,
            Novel
11414   *Oceanides; a psychical novel.* Ernst von Him-
            mel Publishing Co., Boston, 1890, 418p,
            Cloth, Novel
11414A *Oceanides; a psychical novel,* by Carlyle
            Petersilea. Colby & Rich, Boston, 1892,
            418p, Cloth, Novel

PETERSON, JOHN VICTOR

11415   *Rock the big rock.* Curtis, New York, 1970,
            221p, Paper, Novel

PETERSON, MARGARET (Ann), 1883-1933

11416   *Moonflowers.* Hutchinson, London, 1926, 252p,
            Cloth, Novel
11417   *The yellow people; or, Queen of Sheba's tomb;
            a story of adventure in central Africa.*
            John F. Shaw, London, 1930, 320p, Cloth,
            Novel

PETERSON, ROBERT C. [published anonymously]

11418   *The science-fictional Sherlock Holmes.* Coun-
            cil of Four, Denver, 1960, 137p, Cloth, Anth.

PETERSON, RUSSELL C., 1943-

11419   *Tales of love, fantasy, and horror; a taste of
            Poe in the Spanish-American short story.*
            Exposition Press, New York, 1971, 108p,
            Cloth, Anth.

PETERSON, SIDNEY, 1912-

11420   *A fly in the pigment.* Contact Editions, Sausa-
            lito, CA, 1961, 159p, Paper, Novel

THE PETRIFIED PLANET

11421   *The petrified planet; a Twayne science fiction
            triplet.* Twayne Publishers, New York, 1952,
            263p, Cloth, Anth.

PETTEN, ALBERT VAN
      see: VAN PETTEN, ALBERT

PETTERSEN, RENA OLDFIELD

11422   *Venus.* Dorrance, Philadelphia, 1924, 248p,
            Cloth, Novel

PETTY, JOHN, 1919-

11423   *The last refuge.* Whiting & Wheaton, London,
            1966, 204p, Cloth, Novel

PEYTON, ROGER G.

11424   *A checklist of Poul Anderson.* Roger G. Peyton,
            Birmingham, 1965, 26p, Paper, Nonf.
11425   *A checklist of Science fiction adventures (Bri-
            tish edition).* no publisher, Birmingham,
            1963, 13p, Paper, Nonf.

PEZET, A(lfonso) WASHINGTON, 1889-

11426   *Aristokia.* Century Co., New York, 1919, 214p,
            Cloth, Novel

PFEIFFER, JOHN R.

11427 *Fantasy and science fiction: a critical guide.*
Filter Press, Palmer Lake, Col., 1971, 64p,
Paper, Nonf.

PHELON, MIRA M., with William P. Phelon as
The Phelons

11428 *Three sevens; a story of ancient initiations.*
Hermetic Publishing Co., Chicago, 1889, 271p,
Cloth, Novel

PHELON, W(illiam) P.

11429 *A witch of the nineteenth century.* Hermetic
Publishing Co., Chicago, 1893, 149p, Cloth,
Novel

with Mira M. Phelon as The Phelons:

11428 *Three sevens; a story of ancient initiations.*
Hermetic Publishing Co., Chicago, 1889, 271p,
Cloth, Novel

THE PHELONS
see: PHELON, MIRA M. and PHELON, W. P.

PHELPS, ELIZABETH STUART, 1844-1911

11430 *Beyond the gates.* Houghton, Mifflin, Boston,
1883, 196p, Cloth, Novel
11431 *The gates between.* Houghton, Mifflin, Boston,
1887, 223p, Cloth, Novel
11432 *Men, women, and ghosts.* Fields, Osgood, Boston, 1869, 334p, Cloth, Coll.

with Herbert D. Ward:

11433 *The master of the magicians.* Houghton Mifflin,
Boston, 1890, 324p, Cloth, Novel

PHELPS, GILBERT (Henry Jr.), 1915- [*biography included*]

11434 *The centenarians; a fable.* Heinemann, London,
1958, 218p, Cloth, Novel
11435 *The Winter People; a novel.* Bodley Head,
London, 1963, 219p, Cloth, Novel

PHELPS, WILLIAM LYON, 1865-1943

11436 *A dash at the Pole.* Ball Publishing Co., Boston, 1909, 72p, Cloth, Novel

PHILBROOK, ROSE (Miriam), 1911-

11437 *The winds of Dr. Smidge.* Caxton Printers,
Caldwell, Idaho, 1954, 158p, Cloth, Novel

PHILIP, ALEX(ander) J(ohn), 1879-

11438 *Rabbits; a novel of realism.* Mariner Press,
Gravesend, UK, 1946, 208p, Cloth, Novel

PHILIP DRU, ADMINISTRATOR
see: HOUSE, EDWARD M.

PHILIPS, JUDSON P(entecost), 1903-   , with
Thomas M. Johnson

07933 *Red war.* Doubleday, Doran, Garden City, 1936,
306p, Cloth, Novel

PHILIPS, MARY ALICE

11439 *The beast in the cave.* Franklin Watts, New
York, 1959, 182p, Cloth, Novel

PHILLIFENT, JOHN T(homas), 1916-1976 [*biography included*]

11440 *Genius unlimited.* DAW, New York, 1972, 141p,
Paper, Novel
11441 *Hierarchies.* Ace Double, New York, 1973, 141p,
Paper, Novel
11442 *King of Argent.* DAW, New York, 1973, 191p,
Paper, Novel
11443 *Life with Lancelot.* Ace Double, New York,
1973, 132p, Paper, Coll.
11444 *The man from U.N.C.L.E., number 5; The mad
scientist affair.* Ace, New York, 1966, 159p,
Paper, Tele. [Man from U.N.C.L.E. #5 (U.S.
edition); Man from U.N.C.L.E. #8 (U.K. edition)]
11445 *The man from U.N.C.L.E., no. 13; The Corfu
affair.* Four Square, London, 1967, 125p,
Paper, Tele. [Man from U.N.C.L.E. #13 (U.K.
edition); Man from U.N.C.L.E. #20 (U.S. edition)]
11446 *The man from U.N.C.L.E., no. 15; The power cube
affair.* Four Square, London, 1968, 127p,
Paper, Tele. [Man from U.N.C.L.E. #15 (U.K.
edition); Man from U.N.C.L.E. #19 (U.S. edition)]

as John Rackham:

11447 *Alien sea.* Ace Double, New York, 1968, 154p,
Paper, Novel
11448 *Alien virus.* Tit-Bits Science-Fiction Library,
London, 1955, 63p, Paper, Novel [Space Puppet
#4]
11449 *The anything Tree.* Ace Double, New York, 1970,
114p, Paper, Novel
11450 *Beanstalk.* DAW, New York, 1973, 158p, Paper,
Novel
11451 *The beasts of Kohl.* Ace Double, New York,
1966, 154p, Paper, Novel
11452 *Beyond Capella.* Ace Double, New York, 1971,
132p, Paper, Novel
11453 *Danger from Vega.* Ace Double, New York, 1966,
149p, Paper, Novel
11454 *Dark planet.* Ace Double, New York, 1971, 103p,
Paper, Novel
11455 *The double invaders.* Ace Double, New York,
1967, 120p, Paper, Novel
11456 *Earthstrings.* Ace Double, New York, 1972, 141p,
Paper, Novel
11457 *Flower of Doradil.* Ace Double, New York, 1970,
126p, Paper, Novel
11458 *Ipomoea.* Ace Double, New York, 1969, 128p,
Paper, Novel
11459 *Jupiter equilateral.* Tit-Bits Science-Fiction
Library, London, 1954, 64p, Paper, Novel
[Space Puppet #3]

PHILLIFENT, JOHN T. (cont.), as John Rackham

11460　*The master weed (another adventure of the Space Puppet)*. Tit-Bits Science-Fiction Library, London, 1954, 64p, Paper, Novel [Space Puppet #2]

11461　*The Proxima project*. Ace Double, New York, 1968, 149p, Paper, Novel

11462　*Space puppet*. Tit-Bits Science-Fiction Library, London, 1954, 64p, Paper, Novel [Space Puppet #1]

11463　*Time to live*. Ace Double, New York, 1966, 141p, Paper, Novel

11464　*The touch of evil*. Digit, London, 1963, 157p, Paper, Novel

11465　*Treasure of Tau Ceti*. Ace Double, New York, 1969, 134p, Paper, Novel

11466　*Watch on Peter*. Jonathan Cape, London, 1964, 184p, Cloth, Novel

11467　*We, the Venusians*. Ace Double, New York, 1965, 138p, Paper, Novel

PHILLIPS, ALEXANDER M(oore), 1907-

11468　*The mislaid charm*. Prime Press, Philadelphia, 1947, 92p, Cloth, Novel

PHILLIPS, FORBES, with R. Thurston Hopkins

07395　*War and the weird*. Simpkin, Marshall, Hamilton, Kent, London, 1916, 182p, Cloth, Coll. [includes some nonf.]

PHILLIPS, L(undern) M.

11469　*The mind reader*. F. Tennyson Neely, London, 1898, 312p, Cloth, Novel

PHILLIPS, MARK, pseud.
　　see: GARRETT, RANDALL and JANIFER, LAURENCE M.

PHILLIPS, MICKEY [Alan Meyrick Kerr Phillips, 1916-　] [*biography included*]

11470　*Meat*. Michael Joseph, London, 1963, 156p, Cloth, Novel

11470A retitled: *Blood rare*. Coward-McCann, New York, 1963, 156p, Cloth, Novel

PHILLIPS, ROG, pseud. [Roger Phillips Graham, 1909-1965] [*biography included*]

11471　*The involuntary immortals*. Avalon, New York, 1959, 223p, Cloth, Novel

11472　*Time trap*. Century, Chicago, 1949, 158p, Paper, Novel

11473　*World of if*. Merit, Chicago, 1951, 126p, Paper, Novel

11474　*Worlds within*. Century, Chicago, 1950, 159p, Paper, Novel

PHILLIPS, ROLAND ASHFORD

11475　*Golden isle; an adventure story*. Chelsea House, New York, 1925, 249p, Cloth, Novel

PHILLPOTTS, EDEN, 1862-1960

11476　*Address unknown*. Hutchinson, London, 1949, 219p, Cloth, Novel

11477　*Alcyone (a fairy story)*. Ernest Benn, London, 1930, 189p, Cloth, Novel

11478　*The apes*. Faber & Faber, London, 1929, 182p, Cloth, Novel

11479　*Arachne*. Faber & Gwyer, London, 1927, 223p, Cloth, Novel

11480　*Circé's island; and, The girl & the faun*. Grant Richards, London, 1925, 238p, Cloth, Coll.

11481　*A deal with the devil*. Bliss, Sands & Foster, London, 1895, 190p, Cloth, Novel

11482　*Evander*. Grant Richards, London, 1919, 199p, Cloth, Novel

11483　*Fancy free*. Methuen, London, 1901, 302p, Cloth, Coll.

11484　*The flint heart; a fairy story*. Smith, Elder, London, 1910, 310p, Cloth, Novel

11485　*The lavender dragon*. Grant Richards, London, 1923, 199p, Cloth, Novel

11486　*The miniature*. Watts & Co., London, 1926, 125p, Cloth, Novel

11487　*The owl of Athene*. Hutchinson, London, 1936, 199p, Cloth, Novel

11488　*Pan and the twins*. Grant Richards, London, 1922, 239p, Cloth, Novel

11489　*Saurus*. John Murray, London, 1938, 281p, Cloth, Novel

11490　*Tabletop*. Macmillan. New York, 1939, 236p, Cloth, Novel

11491　*The treasures of Typhon*. Grant Richards, London, 1924, 249p, Cloth, Novel

as Harrington Hext:

11492　*The monster*. Macmillan, New York, 1925, 328p, Cloth, Novel

11493　*Number 87*. Thornton Butterworth, London, 1922, 287p, Cloth, Novel

PHILMUS, LOIS C.

11494　*A funny thing happened on the way to the Moon*. A Spartan Book, Books Inc., New York, 1966, 188p, Cloth, Novel

PHILMUS, ROBERT M(ichael), 1943-　[*biography included*]

11495　*Into the unknown; the evolution of science fiction from Francis Godwin to H. G. Wells*. University of California Press, Berkeley, CA, 1970, 174p, Cloth, Nonf.

PHILPOT, JOSEPH HENRY
　　see: LAFARGUE, PHILIP

PHINEAS, pseud. [John M. Hanifin, d. 1898/99]

11496　*The blind men and the devil*. Lee & Shepard, Boston, 1891, 219p, Cloth, Novel

PHIPSON, JOAN, pseud. [Joan Margaret Fitzhardinge, 1912-　] [*biography included*]

11497　*The way home*. A Margaret K. McElderry Book, Atheneum, New York, 1973, 184p, Cloth, Novel

PHYLOS the Thibetan, pseud. [Frederick Spencer Oliver, 1866-1899]

11498 *A dweller on two planets; or, The dividing of the way.* Baumgardt Publishing Co., Los Angeles, 1905, 423p, Cloth, Novel [Zailm #1]
11499 *An Earth dweller's return.* Lemurian Press, Milwaukee, 1940, 509p, Cloth, Novel [Zailm #2]

PHYSICK, EDWARD HAROLD
   see: VISIAK, E. H.

PICK, J(ohn) B(arclay), 1921- , with Colin Wilson and E. H. Visiak

11500 *The strange genius of David Lindsay; an appreciation.* John Baker, London, 1970, 183p, Cloth, Nonf.

PICKERSGILL, FREDERICK

11501 *And graves give up their dead.* Corgi, London, 1964, 174p, Paper, Anth.
11502 *Horror-7, and other stories.* Corgi, London, 1965, 157p, Paper, Anth.
11503 *No such thing as a vampire.* Corgi, London, 1964, 126p, Paper, Anth.

PICKERSGILL, JOSHUA Junior

11504 *The three brothers; a romance.* John Stockdale, Piccadilly, UK, 1803, 4vol, Cloth, Novel

PICTON, NINA
   see: DEARBORN, LAURA

PIER, ARTHUR STANWOOD, 1874-1966

11505 *God's secret.* Charles Scribner's Sons, New York, 1935, 327p, Cloth, Novel

PIER, GARRETT CHATFIELD, 1875-1943

11506 *Hanit the enchantress.* E. P. Dutton, New York, 1921, 283p, Cloth, Novel
11507 *Hidden valley.* Stratford Co., Boston, 1925, 236p, Cloth, Novel

PIERCY, MARGE, 1936- [*biography included*]

11508 *Dance the eagle to sleep.* Doubleday, Garden City, 1970, 232p, Cloth, Novel

PIERSON, ERNEST de LANCEY

11509 *A bargain in souls; an impossible story.* Laird & Lee, Chicago, 1892, 264p, Cloth, Novel
11509A retitled: *An uncle from India (A bargain in souls); an impossible story.* Laird & Lee, Chicago, 1897, 264p, Paper, Novel

PIETRKIEWICZ, JERZY
   see: PETERKIEWICZ, JERZY

PIGGOTT, WILLIAM
   see: WALES, HUBERT

PIGOTT, PERCY

11510 *Kondora; a romance of the magic of Egypt.* Anglo-American Publications, London, 1930, 258p, Cloth, Novel

PIKE, JUDITH, with Warren Hollister

07340 *The moons of Meer.* Henry Z. Walck, New York, 1969, 208p, Cloth, Novel

PILIBÍN, AN, pseud. [John Hackett Pollock, 1887-]

11511 *Mount Kestrel.* M. H. Gill & Son, Dublin, 1945, 130p, Cloth, Novel

PILKINGTON, MARY, 1766-1839

11512 *The accusing spirit; or, De Courcy and Eglantine; a romance*, by the author of Delia, Rosina, and The subterranean cavern. Minerva-Press, Lane & Newman, London, 1802, 4vol, Cloth, Novel

PILKINGTON, (Thomas) ROGER (Edward)

11513 *Stringer's folly.* Dennis Yates, London, 1951, 256p, Cloth, Novel

PILLER, EMANUEL (A.), 1907- , with Leonard Engel

04901 *World aflame; the Russian-American war of 1950.* Dial Press, New York, 1947, 126p, Cloth, Novel

PINCHER, (Henry) CHAPMAN, 1914- [*biography included*]

11514 *The giantkiller.* Weidenfeld & Nicolson, London, 1967, 293p, Cloth, Novel
11515 *Not with a bang.* Weidenfeld & Nicolson, London, 1965, 302p, Cloth, Novel

PINCHERLE, ALBERTO
   see: MORAVIA, ALBERTO

PINCHIN, FRANK J.

11516 *Mars 314.* Allan Wingate-Baker, London, 1970, 144p, Cloth, Novel

PINCKNEY, JOSEPHINE (Lyons Scott), 1895-1957

11517 *Great mischief*. Viking Press, New York, 1948,
       247p, Cloth, Novel

PINKERTON, THOMAS A.

11518 *No rates and taxes; a romance of five worlds*.
       J. W. Arrowsmith, Bristol, 1902, 125p, Cloth,
       Novel

A PIONEER
    see: COLE, CORNELIUS

PIPER, H(enry) BEAM, 1904-1964

       The cosmic computer. [see 11520A]
11519 *Four-day planet*. G. P. Putnam's Sons, New
       York, 1961, 221p, Cloth, Novel
11520 *Junkyard planet*. G. P. Putnam's Sons, New
       York, 1963, 224p, Cloth, Novel
11520A retitled: *The cosmic computer*. Ace, New
       York, 1964, 190p, Paper, Novel
11521 *Little Fuzzy*. Avon, New York, 1962, 160p,
       Paper, Novel [Fuzzy #1]
11522 *Lord Kalvan of otherwhen*. Ace, New York,
       1965, 192p, Paper, Novel
11523 *The other human race*. Avon, New York, 1964,
       190p, Paper, Novel [Fuzzy #2]
11524 *Space Viking*. Ace, New York, 1963, 191p,
       Paper, Novel

with John J. McGuire:

09905 *Crisis in 2140*. Ace Double, New York, 1957,
       120p, Paper, Novel
09906 *A planet for Texans*. Ace Double, New York,
       1958, 101p, Paper, Novel

PIPER, WALTER

11525 *Space swap, 1984-8612*. Narcissus, San Diego,
       1970, 208p, Paper, Novel

PIRE, JOE H. LE
    see: LePIRE, JOE H.

PIRIE, DAVID (Tarbat), 1946-   [*biography
included*]

11526 *A heritage of horror; the English gothic cine-
       ma, 1946-1972*. Gordon Fraser Gallery, Lon-
       don, 1973, 192p, Cloth, Nonf.

PIRIE-GORDON, (Charles) HARRY (Clinton),
1883-1969, with Frederick Rolfe [Baron Cor-
vo] as Prospero & Caliban

11527 *Hubert's Arthur, being certain curious docu-
       ments found among the literary remains of
       Mr. N. C., here produced by Prospero & Cali-
       ban*. Cassell, London, 1935, 353p, Cloth,
       Novel
11528 *The weird of the wanderer, being the papyrus
       records of some incidents in one of the
       previous lives of Mr. Nicholas Crabbe, here
       produced by Prospero & Caliban*. William
       Rider & Son, London, 1912, 299p, Cloth, Novel

PIRULI, MADIGAN

11529 *The devil and Juan Pistolas*. Trucha Publica-
       tions, Lubbock, TX, 1973, 18p, Paper, Story

PISCATOR, MARIA LEY-
    see: LEY-PISCATOR, MARIA

PISERCHIA, DORIS (Elaine), 1928-   [*biography
included*]

11530 *Mister Justice*. Ace Double, New York, 1973,
       176p, Paper, Novel
11531 *Star rider*. Bantam, New York, 1974, 220p,
       Paper, Novel

PITCHFORD, DENYS WATKINS-
    see: B. B.

PITTARD, HELENE
    see: ROGER, NOELLE

PIZER, LAURETTE NAOMI

11532 *More stories strange and sinister*. Panther,
       London, 1967, 127p, Paper, Anth.
11533 *Stories strange and sinister*. Panther, London,
       1965, 173p, Paper, Anth.

PIZOR, FAITH K., with T. Allan Comp

03242 *The man in the Moone, and other Lunar fantasies*.
       Praeger, New York, 1971, 230p, Cloth, Anth.

PLACE, MARIAN T(empleton), 1910-

11534 *Brad's flying saucer*. Ives Washburn, New York,
       1969, 148p, Cloth, Novel

PLANET OF DOOM

11535 *Planet of doom, and other stories*. Satellite,
       London, 1958, 113p, Paper, Anth.

PLATT, CHARLES (Nathaniel), 1943?-   [*biography included*]

11536 *The city dwellers; science fiction*. Sidgwick
       & Jackson, London, 1970, 189p, Cloth, Novel
11537 *Garbage world*. Berkley Medallion, New York,
       1967, 144p, Paper, Novel
11538 *The gas*. Ophelia Press, New York, 1970, 216p,
       Paper, Novel
11539 *Planet of the Voles; a science fiction novel*.
       G. P. Putnam's Sons, New York, 1971, 192p,
       Cloth, Novel

with Hilary Bailey:

00709 *New worlds 7*. Sphere, London, 1974, 213p,
       Paper, Anth.

with Michael Moorcock:

10315 *New worlds 6; the science fiction quarterly*.
       Sphere, London, 1973, 263p, Paper, Anth.

PLATT, CHARLES (cont.), with Michael Moorcock

10315A retitled: *New worlds #5.* Avon, New York, 1974, 267p, Paper, Anth.

PLATT, JAMES Junior

11540 *Tales of the supernatural; six romantic stories.* Simpkin, Marshall, Hamilton, Kent, London, 1894, 173p, Paper, Coll.

PLATT, KIN, 1911-

11541 *The Blue Man.* Harper & Bros., New York, 1961, 185p, Cloth, Novel
11542 *Mystery of the witch, who wouldn't.* Chilton Book Co., Philadelphia, 1969, 266p, Cloth, Novel

as Wesley Simon York:

11543 *Lovers & exorcists.* Brandon, Chatsworth, CA, 1974, 190p, Paper, Novel

THE PLAYBOY BOOK OF HORROR AND THE SUPERNATURAL
see: RUSSELL, RAY

THE PLAYBOY BOOK OF SCIENCE FICTION AND FANTASY
see: RUSSELL, RAY

PLAYBOY'S STORIES OF THE SINISTER AND STRANGE
see: RUSSELL, RAY

PLUNKETT, EDWARD
see: DUNSANY, Lord

PLUS ENCORE d'ANGLETERRE
see: B., A. G. F.

PLYM, DON, with Thea Plym

11544 *The prophetess; Rana Ten.* D. & T. Plym, Tempe, AZ, 1972, 44p, Paper, Story
11545 *2150: "the macro love story."* Macro Development Center, Grosse Pointe, 1971, 281p, Paper, Novel

PLYM, THEA, with Don Plym

11544 *The prophetess; Rana Ten.* D. & T. Plym, Tempe, AZ, 1972, 44p, Paper, Story
11545 *2150: "the macro love story."* Macro Development Center, Grosse Pointe, 1971, 281p, Paper, Novel

POCOCK, BYRANT WALKER

11546 *The mists of Zwillingzeit.* Vantage Press, New York, 1972, 234p, Cloth, Novel

POCOCK, ROGER (S.), 1865-1941

11547 *The chariot of the Sun; a fantasy.* Chapman & Hall, London, 1910, 305p, Cloth, Novel
11548 *The wolf trail; a novel.* Basil Blackwell, Oxford, 1923, 309p, Cloth, Novel

POE, EDGAR ALLAN, 1809-1849

Arthur Gordon Pym. [see 11610A]
11549 *The assignation, and other tales.* John W. Lovell, New York, 1884, 192p, Cloth, Coll.
11550 *The best known works of Edgar Allan Poe: poems, tales, essays, criticisms.* Blue Ribbon, New York, 1931, 918p, Cloth, Coll.
11551 *The best of Edgar Allan Poe.* Royce Publishers, Chicago, 1945, 128p, Cloth, Coll.
11552 *The best tales of Edgar Allan Poe.* A. C. McClurg, Chicago, 1903, 476p, Cloth, Coll.
11553 *Bizarre and arabesque; a new anthology of tales, poems, and prose.* Panther, London, 1967, 202p, Paper, Coll.
11554 *The black cat.* Winthrop Press, New York, 1914, 31p, Cloth, Story
11555 *The black cat, and other short stories.* Todd Publishing Co., London, 1943, 16p, Paper, Coll.
11556 *The black cat, and other stories.* Vallancey Press, London, 1945, 16p, Paper, Coll.
11557 *The black cat, and other tales.* Holerth Library, London, 1924, 84p, Cloth?, Coll.
11558 *The book of Poe: tales, criticisms, poems.* Doubleday, Doran, Garden City, 1929, 519p, Cloth, Coll.
11559 *The centenary Poe: tales, poems, criticism, marginalia, and Eureka.* Bodley Head, London, 1949, 559p, Cloth, Coll.
11560 *The choice works of Edgar Allan Poe: poems, stories, essays.* Chatto & Windus, London, 1899, 676p, Cloth, Coll.
11561 *Comic tales of Edgar Allan Poe.* Canongate Publishing, Edinburgh, 1973, 125p, Cloth, Coll.
The complete short stories of Edgar Allan Poe. [see 11621A]
11562 *Complete stories and poems.* Doubleday, Garden City, 1966, 819p, Cloth, Coll.
11563 *The complete tales and poems of Edgar Allan Poe.* Modern Library, New York, 1938, 1027p, Cloth, Coll.
11564 *Descent into the Maelström.* Digit, London, 1961, 160p, Paper, Coll.
11565 *Descent into the Maelström; a tale.* Devambez, Paris, 1920, 51p, Cloth?, Story
11566 *A descent into the Maelström, and other stories; tales of mystery and imagination.* Ivon Nicholson & Watson, London, 1948, 128p, Paper, Coll.
11567 *Edgar Allan Poe.* Doubleday & McClure, New York, 1901, 207p, Cloth, Coll.
11568 *Edgar Allan Poe and the Philadelphia Saturday courier; facsimile reproductions of the first texts of Poe's earliest tales, and "Raising the wind."* University of Virginia, Charlottesville, VA, 1933, 85p, Cloth, Coll.
11569 *Edgar Allan Poe's tales; a selection.* Cassell, London, 1904, 190p, Cloth, Coll.
11570 *Eight tales of terror.* Scholastic Book Services, New York, 1961, 197p, Paper, Coll.
11571 *18 best stories by Edgar Allan Poe.* Dell, New York, 1965, 287p, Paper, Coll.

POE, EDGAR ALLAN (cont.)

11572   *Essays and stories.* George Bell & Sons, London, 1914, 360p, Cloth, Coll.
       The facts in the case of M. Valdemar. [see 11605A]

11573   *The fall of the house of Usher.* Blue Sky Press, Chicago, 1903, 57p, Cloth, Story

11574   *The fall of the house of Usher.* Merrill, Columbus, OH, 1971, 138p, Cloth, Coll. [includes Poe's story, and essays about it]

11575   *The fall of the house of Usher, and four other tales: The black cat, Ms. found in a bottle, Three Sundays in a week, The oval portrait.* Franklin Watts, New York, 1967, 82p, Cloth, Coll.

11576   *The fall of the house of Usher, and other stories.* Digit, London, 1961, 156p, Paper, Coll.

11577   *The fall of the house of Usher, and other tales.* Signet Classic, New York, 1960, 383p, Paper, Coll.

11578   *The fall of the house of Usher, and other tales and prose writings.* W. Scott, London, 1889, 312p, Cloth, Coll.

11579   *The fall of the house of Usher, and other tales of imagination.* Ward, Lock, London, 189?, 138p, Cloth, Coll.

11580   *The fall of the house of Usher; Ligeia; The cask of Amontillado; The assignation; Ms. found in a bottle; The black cat; The gold bug.* Doubleday & McClure, New York, 1897, 207p, Cloth, Coll.

11581   *Fantastic tales.* Bernhard Tauchnitz, Leipzig, 1915, 285p, Cloth, Coll.

11582   *Fantastic tales.* New English Library, London, 1969, 111p, Paper, Coll.

11583   *The gold bug.* Digit, London, 1960, 160p, Paper, Coll.

11584   *The gold bug, and other selections from the works of Edgar Allan Poe.* B. F. Johnson Publishing Co., Atlanta, 1912, 128p, Cloth, Coll.

11585   *The gold bug, and other stories.* World Publishing Co., Cleveland, 1940, 248p, Cloth, Coll.

11586   *The gold bug, and other stories.* Gilbertson Co., New York, 1951, 50p, Paper?, Coll.

11587   *The gold-bug, and other tales.* Downey & Co., London, 1898, 316p, Cloth, Coll.

11588   *The gold bug, and other tales.* A. L. Burt, New York, 1902?, 398p, Cloth, Coll.

11589   *The gold-bug, and other tales.* International Pocket Library, Boston, 1919, 91p, Paper, Coll.

11590   *The gold bug, & other tales.* Grosset & Dunlap, New York, 1936, 248p, Cloth, Coll.

11591   *The gold bug, and other tales and poems.* Macmillan, New York, 1930, 199p, Cloth, Coll.

11592   *The gold bug; and, The black cat.* R. F. Fenno, New York, 1899, 135p, Cloth, Coll.

11593   *The gold bug, The purloined letter, and other tales.* Houghton Mifflin, Boston, 1898, 95p, Cloth, Coll.

11594   *Great short works of Edgar Allan Poe.* Perennial Classic, New York, 1970, 564p, Paper, Coll.

11595   *The great tales and poems of Edgar Allan Poe.* Pocket Books, New York, 1940, 360p, Paper, Coll.

11596   *Great tales of horror.* Bantam Pathfinder, New York, 1964, 151p, Paper, Coll.

       The indispensable Edgar Allan Poe. [see 11626A]

11597   *Introduction to Poe; a thematic reader.* Scott, Foresman, Glenview, IL, 1967, 601p, Cloth, Coll.

11598   *King Pest, and other tales.* Holerth Library, London, 1924, 80p, Cloth?, Coll.

11599   *Ligeia.* Gulliver Book Co., Lower Chelston, UK, 1943, 31p, Paper, Story
       The mask of the red death. [see 11600A]

11600   *The masque of the red death.* Byway Studio Press, Cincinnati, OH, 1923, 17p, Paper?, Story

11600A retitled: *The mask of the red death; a fantasy.* Aquarius Press, Baltimore, 1969, 65p, Cloth?, Story

11601   *The masque of the red death, and other stories.* Holerth Library, London, 1924, 101p, Cloth, Coll.

11602   *The masque of the red death, and other tales.* Phonographic Institute, Cincinnati, 1892, 12p, Paper?, Coll.

11603   *The masque of the red death, and other tales.* Halcyon Press, Maastricht, 1932, 170p, Cloth, Coll.

11604   *The masque of the red death, and other tales.* Panther, London, 1964, 191p, Paper, Coll.

11605   *Mesmerism "in articulo mortis"; an astounding and horrifying narrative.* Short & Co., London, 1846, 16p, Cloth, Story

11605A retitled: *The facts in the case of M. Valdemar.* Vallencey Press, London, 1944, 16p, Paper, Coll.

11606   *The murders in the Rue Morgue; and, A tale of the Ragged Mountains.* R. F. Fenno, New York, 1899, 134p, Cloth, Coll.

11607   *The murders in the Rue Morgue, and other stories.* J. H. Sears, New York, 1920?, 246p, Cloth, Coll.

11608   *Murders in the Rue Morgue, and other stories.* Walter Edwards, London, 1948, 304p, Cloth, Coll.

11609   *The murders in the Rue Morgue, and other tales.* Porter & Coates, Philadelphia, 1880?, 379p, Cloth, Coll.

11610   *The narrative of Arthur Gordon Pym of Nantucket, comprising the details of a mutiny and atrocious butchery on board the American brig Grampus, on her way to the South Seas, in the month of June, 1827, with an account of the recapture of the vessel by the survivors, their shipwreck and subsequent horrible sufferings from famine, their deliverance by means of the British schooner Jane Guy, the brief cruise of this latter vessel in the Antarctic Ocean; her capture, and the massacre of her crew among a group of islands in the eighty-fourth parallel of southern latitude, together with the incredible adventures and discoveries still further south to which that distressing calamity gave rise.* Harper & Bros., New York, 1838, 201p, Cloth, Novel

11610A retitled: *Arthur Gordon Pym; or, Shipwreck, mutiny, and famine, being the extraordinary adventures of Arthur Gordon Pym, mariner, of Nantucket, North America, during a voyage to the South Seas, and his various discoveries in the eighty-fourth parallel of southern latitude.* J. Cunningham, London, 1841, 80p, Cloth, Novel

11610B retitled: *The wonderful adventures of Arthur Gordon Pym.* W. Kent, London, 1861, 219p, Cloth, Novel

POE, EDGAR ALLAN (cont.)

Phantasy-pieces. [see 11733A]

11611 *The pit and the pendulum.* Digit, London, 1962, 158p, Paper, Coll.

11612 *The pit and the pendulum, and five other tales.* Franklin Watts, New York, 1967, 87p, Cloth, Coll.

11613 *The pit and the pendulum, and other stories; tales of mystery and imagination.* Ivor Nicholson & Watson, London, 1948, 128p, Paper, Coll.

11614 *Poe.* Doubleday, Page, Garden City, 1922, 143p, Cloth, Coll.

11615 *Poems and tales.* D. C. Heath, Boston, 1918, 216p, Cloth, Coll.

11616 *Poems and tales by Edgar Allan Poe.* University Publishing Co., Lincoln, Neb., 1924, 229p, Cloth, Coll.

11617 *Poems and tales from the writings of Edgar Allan Poe.* Houghton Mifflin, Boston, 1897, , Cloth, Coll.

11618 *Poems and tales of Edgar Allan Poe.* Scott, Foresman, Chicago, 1898, 323p, Cloth, Coll.

11619 *Poems and tales of Edgar Allan Poe.* B. F. Johnson Publishing Co., Atlanta, 1911, 249p, Cloth, Coll.

11620 *Poems; and, The story of Arthur Gordon Pym.* Charles Scribner's Sons, New York, 1909, 234p, Cloth, Coll.

11621 *Poe's short stories.* Harcourt, Brace & Co., New York, 1927, 460p, Cloth, Coll.

11621A retitled: *The complete short stories of Edgar Allan Poe.* Sun Dial Press, New York, 1943, 460p, Cloth, Coll.

11622 *Poe's tales.* "The Morning Herald," London, 1899, 322p, Cloth, Coll.

11623 *Poe's tales.* Education Publishing Co., Boston, 1906, 220p, Cloth, Coll.

11624 *Poe's tales, and other prose writings.* F. M. Lupton Publishing Co., New York, 1893?, 236p, Cloth, Coll.

11625 *The popular tales of Edgar Allan Poe.* Wood & Clarke, New York, 1891?, 548p, Cloth, Coll.

11626 *The portable Edgar Allan Poe.* Viking Press, New York, 1945, 665p, Cloth, Coll.

11626A retitled: *The indispensable Edgar Allan Poe.* Book Society, New York, 1950, 665p, Cloth, Coll.

11627 *The prose tales.* Thomas Y. Crowell, New York, 1897, 354p, Cloth, Coll.

11628 *Prose tales.* Kenyusha, Tokyo, 1922, 313p, Cloth, Coll.

11629 *The prose tales of Edgar Allan Poe, first series.* W. J. Widdleton, New York, 1877, 571p, Cloth, Coll.

11630 *The prose tales of Edgar Allan Poe, second series.* W. J. Widdleton, New York, 1877, 370p, Cloth, Coll.

11631 *The prose tales of Edgar Allan Poe, third series.* A. C. Armstrong, New York, 1889, 446p, Cloth, Coll.

11632 *Prose tales of mystery and imagination.* Grosset & Dunlap, New York, 1903, 496p, Cloth, Coll.

11633 *The purloined letter, and other stories.* Happy Hour Library, New York, 1920?, 93p, Cloth, Coll.

11634 *The purloined letter, and other tales.* Holerth Library, London, 1924, 67p, Cloth?, Coll.

11635 *The raven, The fall of the house of Usher, and other poems and tales.* Houghton Mifflin, Boston, 1897, 95p, Cloth, Coll.

11636 *Representative selections.* American Book Co., New York, 1935, 563p, Cloth, Coll.

11637 *Select tales.* Internationale Bibliothek, Berlin, 1922, 261p, Cloth, Coll.

11638 *The select works of Edgar Allan Poe.* A. Dürr, Leipzig, 1856, 2vol/1, Cloth, Coll.

11639 *Select works of Edgar Allan Poe, poetical and prose.* W. J. Widdleton, New York, 1880, 676p, Cloth, Coll.

11640 *Selected poems and tales of Edgar Allan Poe.* Silver Burdett, New York, 1906, 158p, Cloth, Coll.

11641 *Selected poems and tales of Edgar Allan Poe.* American Book Co., New York, 1914, 172p, Cloth, Coll.

11642 *Selected poetry and prose of Edgar Allan Poe.* Modern Library, New York, 1951, 428p, Cloth, Coll.

11643 *Selected prose and poetry.* Rinehart & Co., New York, 1950, 528p, Cloth, Coll.

11644 *Selected prose, poetry, and Eureka.* Holt, Rinehart & Winston, New York, 1968?, 590p, Cloth, Coll. [an expanded edition of 11643]

11645 *Selected short stories.* Fine Editions Press, Cleveland, 1952, 257p, Cloth, Coll.

11646 *Selected stories.* Editions for the Armed Services, New York, 1944?, 349p, Paper, Coll.

11647 *Selected stories and poems.* Airmont, New York, 1962, 192p, Paper, Coll.

11648 *Selected stories and poems.* Franklin Watts, New York, 1967, 363p, Cloth, Coll.

11649 *Selected tales.* Penguin, Harmondsworth, 1956, 405p, Paper, Coll.

11650 *Selected tales.* Oxford University Press, London, 1967, 378p, Cloth, Coll.

11651 *Selected tales.* Heron, London, 1969, 393p, Cloth, Coll.

11652 *Selected tales and poems.* W. J. Black, New York, 1943, 286p, Cloth, Coll.

11653 *Selected tales of mystery.* J. B. Lippincott, Philadelphia, 1909, 335p, Cloth, Coll.

11654 *Selected writings.* Houghton Mifflin, Boston, 1956, 508p, Cloth, Coll.

11655 *Selected writings of Edgar Allan Poe: poems, tales, essays, and reviews.* Penguin, Harmondsworth, 1967, 540p, Paper, Coll.

11656 *Selections from Edgar Allan Poe.* Stanwix House, Pittsburgh, 1968, 301p, Cloth, Coll.

11657 *Selections from Edgar Allan Poe, prose and poetry.* Cassell, London, 1886, 382p, Cloth, Coll.

11658 *Selections from Poe.* Ginn & Co., Boston, 1907, 200p, Cloth, Coll.

11659 *Selections from the prose tales of Edgar Allan Poe.* Macmillan, New York, 1901, 343p, Cloth, Coll.

11660 *Seven select stories from Edgar Allan Poe.* Hokuseido Press, Tokyo, 1935, 130p, Cloth, Coll.

11661 *Seven tales, with a French translation and prefatory essays by Charles Baudelaire.* Schocken, New York, 1971, 245p, Cloth, Coll.

11662 *Short stories.* D. M. MacLellan Book Co., New York, 1908, 328p, Cloth, Coll.

11663 *Silence.* Jonathan Vickers, London, 1963, 18p, Paper?, Story

11664 *Six stories by Edgar Allan Poe.* Ballantine, New York, 1961, 128p, Paper, Coll.

11665 *Some tales of mystery and imagination.* Penguin, Harmondsworth, 1938, 248p, Paper, Coll.

11666 *Stories.* E. P. Dutton, New York, 1908, 164p, Cloth, Coll.

11667 *Stories.* Prentice-Hall, Englewood Cliffs, NJ, 1962, 116p, Paper?, Coll.

POE, EDGAR ALLAN (cont.)

11668 *Stories.* McGraw-Hill, New York, 1968, 85p, Cloth, Coll.

11669 *Stories and poems.* University Publishing Co., New York, 1904, 124p, Cloth, Coll.

11670 *Stories and poems.* Globe Book Co., New York, 1951, 257p, Cloth, Coll.

11671 *Stories; twenty-eight thrilling tales by the master of suspense.* Pratt & Munk, New York, 1961, 510p, Cloth, Coll.

11672 *The tales.* Wiley & Putnam, New York, 1845, 228p, Cloth, Coll.

11673 *Tales.* Bernhard Tauchnitz, Leipzig, 1884, 328p, Cloth, Coll.

11674 *Tales.* Hurst, New York, 1888?, 379p, Cloth, Coll.

11675 *Tales.* Century Co., New York, 1901, 499p, Cloth, Coll.

11676 *Tales.* Duffield & Co., New York, 1909, 218p, Cloth, Coll.

11677 *Tales.* Roycrofters, East Aurora, NY, 1922, 136p, Cloth, Coll.

11678 *Tales.* Oxford University Press, Humphrey Milford, 1927, 688p, Cloth, Coll.

11679 *Tales.* Macmillan, New York, 1928, 520p, Cloth, Coll.

11680 *Tales.* Lakeside Press, Chicago, 1930, 495p, Cloth, Coll.

11681 *Tales.* Dodd, Mead, New York, 1952, 666p, Cloth, Coll.

11682 *Tales.* West Virginia Pulp & Paper Co., New York, 1964, , Cloth, Coll.

11683 *Tales and poems.* Charles E. Merrill, New York, 1914, 323p, Cloth, Coll.

11684 *Tales and poems of Edgar Allan Poe.* Macmillan, New York, 1963, 388p, Cloth, Coll.

11685 *Tales and sketches, to which is added The raven, a poem.* London, 1852, , Cloth, Coll.

11686 *Tales; and, The raven and other poems.* Charles E. Merrill, Columbus, OH, 1969, 91p, Cloth, Coll.

11687 *Tales, criticisms, poems.* Doubleday, Doran, Garden City, 1929, 519p, Cloth, Coll.

11688 *Tales grotesque.* Collins, London, 1931, 382p, Cloth, Coll.

11689 *Tales grotesque and weird.* Haldeman-Julius, Girard, Kans., 1926?, 64p, Paper, Coll.

11690 *Tales of adventure, mystery, and imagination.* Ward, Lock, London, 1890, 557p, Cloth, Coll.

11691 *Tales of Edgar Allan Poe.* Charles Scribner's Sons, New York, 1927, 525p, Cloth, Coll.

11692 *Tales of Edgar Allan Poe.* Random House, New York, 1944, 572p, Cloth, Coll.

11693 *Tales of Edgar Allan Poe.* Whitman Publishing Co., Racine, Wisc., 1963, 282p, Cloth, Coll.

11694 *Tales of Edgar Allan Poe.* Parent's Magazine Cultural Institute, New York, 1964, 420p, Cloth, Coll.

11695 *The tales of Edgar Allan Poe; The gold beetle, The Maelström, The pit and the pendulum.* Langham Booklets, London?, 1906, 202p, Cloth, Coll.

11696 *Tales of effect; a selection of the best short stories of Edgar Allan Poe.* Art & Educational Publishers, London, 1948, 232p, Cloth, Coll.

11697 *Tales of hypnotism and revenge.* Haldeman-Julius, Girard, Kans., 1927?, 64p, Paper, Coll.

11698 *Tales of imaginative science.* Haldeman-Julius, Girard, Kans., 1926?, 64p, Paper, Coll.

11699 *Tales of mystery.* H. W. Bell, New York, 1903, 507p, Cloth, Coll.

11700 *Tales of mystery.* Haldeman-Julius, Girard, Kans., 1919, 61p, Paper, Coll.

11701 *Tales of mystery.* T. C. & E. J. Jack, London, 1940, 164p, Cloth, Coll.

11702 *Tales of mystery.* Pan, London, 1949, 223p, Paper, Coll.

11703 *Tales of mystery.* Award, New York, 1965?, 143p, Paper, Coll.

11704 *Tales of mystery and imagination.* Milner & Sowerby, Halifax, NS, 1855, 424p, Cloth, Coll.

11705 *Tales of mystery and imagination.* George Routledge & Sons, London, 1882, 160p, Cloth, Coll.

11706 *Tales of mystery and imagination.* Grant Richards, London, 1902, 367p, Cloth, Coll.

11707 *Tales of mystery and imagination.* C. Arthur Pearson, London, 1905, 416p, Cloth, Coll.

11708 *Tales of mystery and imagination.* John Long, London, 1905, 158p, Cloth, Coll.

11709 *Tales of mystery and imagination.* J. M. Dent & Sons, London, 1908, 527p, Cloth, Coll.

11710 *Tales of mystery and imagination.* Thomas Nelson & Sons, London, 1910, 374p, Cloth, Coll.

11711 *Tales of mystery and imagination.* George G. Harrap, London, 1919, 381p, Cloth, Coll.

11712 *Tales of mystery and imagination.* Brentano's, New York, 1923, 412p, Cloth, Coll.

11713 *Tales of mystery and imagination.* Eibungakusha, Tokyo, 1929, 699p, Cloth, Coll.

11714 *Tales of mystery and imagination.* J B. Lippincott, Philadelphia, 1935, 317p, Cloth, Coll.

11715 *Tales of mystery and imagination.* Spencer Press, New York?, 1936, 404p, Cloth, Coll.

11716 *Tales of mystery and imagination.* Limited Editions Club, New York, 1941, 476p, Cloth, Coll

11717 *Tales of mystery and imagination.* Heritage Press, New York, 1941, 366p, Cloth, Coll.

11718 *Tales of mystery and imagination.* Burgess & Bowes, London, 1948, 128p, Cloth, Coll.

11719 *Tales of mystery and imagination.* Fountain Press, Chicago, 1949, 337p, Cloth, Coll.

11720 *Tales of mystery and imagination.* Bruce Publishing Co., London, 1953, 256p, Cloth, Coll.

11721 *Tales of mystery and imagination.* Geoffrey Cumberlege, Oxford University Press, London, 1956, 419p, Cloth, Coll.

11722 *Tales of mystery and imagination.* Folio Society, London, 1957, 302p, Cloth, Coll.

11723 *Tales of mystery and imagination.* Pan, London, 1960, 223p, Paper, Coll.

11724 *Tales of mystery and imagination.* Longmans, Green, London, 1964, 118p, Cloth, Coll.

11725 *Tales of mystery and imagination.* Thomas Nelson & Sons, London, 1966, 96p, Cloth, Coll.

11726 *Tales of mystery and imagination, and poems.* Clarke, Beeton, London, 1855?, 517p, Cloth, Coll.

11727 *Tales of mystery and terror.* Lancer, New York, 1967, 319p, Paper, Coll.

11728 *Tales of mystery, imagination, and humour.* Ward, Lock, London, 1878, 395p, Cloth, Coll.

11729 *Tales of mystery, imagination, and humour, second series.* Clarke, Beeton, London, 1856?, 252p, Cloth, Coll.

11730 *Tales of mystery, imagination, and humour, and poems.* H. Vizetelly, London, 1852, 256p, Cloth, Coll.

11731 *Tales of terror and fantasy; ten stories from "Tales of mystery and imagination."* J. M. Dent & Sons, London, 1971, 150p, Cloth, Coll.

POE, EDGAR ALLAN (cont.)

11732 *Tales of terror and of fantasy.* John Dicks, London, 1870?, 140p, Paper, Coll.

11733 *Tales of the grotesque and arabesque.* Lea & Blanchard, Philadelphia, 1840, 2vol, Cloth, Coll.

11733A retitled: *Phantasy-pieces.* Paris, 1927?, 2vol, Cloth, Coll.

11734 *Tales of the grotesque and arabesque, with other stories.* Charles Scribner's Sons, New York, 1902, 787p, Cloth, Coll.

11735 *Tales of the grotesque and arabesque.* Dolphin, Garden City, 1960, 320p, Paper, Coll.

11736 *Tales, poems, essays.* W. W. Norton, New York, 1952, 576p, Cloth, Coll.

11737 *Tales psychological and gruesome.* Haldeman-Julius, Girard, Kans., 1926?, 64p, Paper, Coll.

11738 *The tell-tale heart.* J. H. Eggers, New York, 1916, 31p, Cloth?, Story

11739 *The tell-tale heart, and other stories.* John Lehmann, London, 1948, 272p, Cloth, Coll.

11740 *Ten great mysteries by Edgar Allan Poe.* Scholastic Book Services, New York, 1960, 218p, Paper, Coll.

11741 *Three tales: The masque of the red death; The cask of Amontillado; The oval portrait.* S. Wellwood, London, 1907, 41p, Cloth, Coll.

11742 *Two fantastic tales: The mystery of Marie Roget; The oval portrait.* A. Juncker, Berlin, 1946, 112p, Cloth, Coll.

11743 *Uncanny tales.* Little Blue Book Co., London, 1925?, 64p, Paper, Coll.

11744 *Visions of darkness; masterpieces of Edgar Allan Poe.* Hallmark Cards, Kansas City, MO, 1971, 62p, Cloth, Coll.

11745 *Weird tales.* Henry Altemus, Philadelphia, 1895, 258p, Cloth, Coll.

11746 *Weirdest of weird tales; The murders in the Rue Morgue, and other thrilling mystery stories.* Foulsham, London, 1930, 192p, Cloth, Coll.

The wonderful adventure of Arthur Gordon Pym. [see 11610B]

11747 *The works of Edgar Allan Poe.* Walter J. Black, New York, 1927, 1296p, Cloth, Coll. [the first collected works in one volume]

with Eunice Sudak:

11748 *Tales of terror.* Lancer, New York, 1962, 126p, Paper, Movie Coll. [adapted by Sudak from the film and the Poe stories]

with Jules Verne:

11749 *The mystery of Arthur Gordon Pym.* Arco Publications, London, 1960, 191p, Cloth, Coll. [includes *The narrative of Arthur Gordon Pym* with Verne's sequel]

POHL, CAROL, with Frederik Pohl

11750 *Jupiter.* Ballantine, New York, 1973, 265p, Paper, Anth.

11751 *Science fiction: the great years.* Ace, New York, 1973, 349p, Paper, Anth.

POHL, FREDERIK, 1919-   [*biography included*]

11752 *The abominable Earthman.* Ballantine, New York, 1963, 159p, Paper, Coll

11753 *The age of the pussyfoot.* Trident Press, New York, 1969, 191p, Cloth, Novel

11754 *Alternating currents.* Ballantine, New York, 1956, 154p, Cloth, Coll.

11755 *Assignment in tomorrow; an anthology.* Hanover House, Garden City, 1954, 317p, Cloth, Anth.

11756 *Best science fiction for 1972.* Ace, New York, 1972, 315p, Paper, Anth.

11757 *The best science fiction from Worlds of if magazine.* Galaxy Publishing Corp., New York, 1964, 162p, Paper, Anth.

11758 *Beyond the end of time.* Permabooks, Garden City, 1952, 407p, Paper, Anth.

11759 *The case against tomorrow; science-fiction stories.* Ballantine, New York, 1957, 152p, Paper, Coll.

11760 *Day Million.* Ballantine, New York, 1970, 213p, Paper, Coll.

11761 *Digits and dastards.* Ballantine, New York, 1966, 192p, Paper, Coll. [includes some nonf.]

Door to anywhere. [see 11785A]

11762 *Drunkard's walk.* Gnome Press, Hicksville, NY, 1960, 160p, Cloth, Novel

11763 *The eighth Galaxy reader.* Doubleday, Garden City, 1965, 248p, Cloth, Anth.

11763A retitled: *Final encounter.* Curtis, New York, 1970, 223p, Paper, Anth.

11764 *The eleventh Galaxy reader.* Doubleday, Garden City, 1969, 254p, Cloth, Anth.

11765 *The expert dreamers.* Doubleday, Garden City, 1962, 248p, Cloth, Anth.

Final encounter. [see 11763A]

11766 *The Frederik Pohl omnibus.* Victor Gollancz, London, 1966, 318p, Cloth, Coll.

11767 *The gold at the starbow's end.* Ballantine, New York, 1972, 215p, Paper, Coll.

11768 *The If reader of science fiction.* Doubleday, Garden City, 1966, 252p, Cloth, Anth.

11769 *The man who ate the world.* Ballantine, New York, 1960, 144p, Paper, Coll.

11770 *Nightmare age.* Ballantine, New York, 1970, 312p, Paper, Anth.

11771 *The ninth Galaxy reader.* Doubleday, Garden City, 1966, 203p, Cloth, Anth.

11772 *A plague of pythons.* Ballantine, New York, 1965, 158p, Paper, Novel

11773 *The second If reader of science fiction.* Doubleday, Garden City, 1968, 239p, Cloth, Anth.

11774 *The seventh Galaxy reader.* Doubleday, Garden City, 1964, 247p, Cloth, Anth.

11775 *Shadow of tomorrow; 17 great science fiction stories.* Permabooks, Garden City, 1953, 379p, Paper, Anth.

11776 *Slave ship.* Ballantine, New York, 1957, 148p, Cloth, Novel

Star fourteen. [see 11777A]

11777 *Star of stars.* Doubleday, Garden City, 1960, 240p, Cloth, Anth.

11777A retitled: *Star fourteen.* Whiting & Wheaton, London, 1966, 240p, Cloth, Anth.

11778 *Star science fiction, no. 6.* Ballantine, New York, 1959, 156p, Paper, Anth.

11778A retitled: *Star science fiction stories, no. 6.* Ballantine, New York, 1972, 156p, Paper, Anth.

11779 *Star science fiction stories.* Ballantine, New York, 1953, 203p, Cloth, Anth.

11779A retitled: *Star science fiction stories, no. 1.* Ballantine, New York, 1972, 196p, Paper, Anth.

11780 *Star science fiction stories, no. 2.* Ballantine, New York, 1954, 197p, Cloth, Anth.

11781 *Star science fiction stories, no. 3.* Ballantine, New York, 1954, 186p, Cloth, Anth.

POHL, FREDERIK (cont.)

11782 *Star science fiction stories, no. 4.* Ballantine, New York, 1958, 157p, Paper, Anth.
11783 *Star science fiction stories, no. 5.* Ballantine, New York, 1959, 159p, Paper, Anth.
Star science fiction stories, no. 6. [see 11778A]
11784 *Star short novels.* Ballantine, New York, 1954, 168p, Cloth, Anth.
11785 *The tenth Galaxy reader.* Doubleday, Garden City, 1967, 232p, Cloth, Anth.
11785A retitled: *Door to anywhere.* Curtis, New York, 1970, 224p, Paper, Anth.
11786 *Time waits for Winthrop, and four other short novels from Galaxy.* Doubleday, Garden City, 1962, 336p, Cloth, Anth.
11787 *Tomorrow times seven; science fiction stories.* Ballantine, New York, 1959, 160p, Paper, Coll.
11788 *Turn left at Thursday; 3 novelettes and 3 stories.* Ballantine, New York, 1961, 159p, Paper, Coll.

as James MacCreigh:

11789 *Danger Moon.* American Science Fiction, Sydney, 1953, 34p, Paper, Story [cover byline reads James MaCreigh]

with Lester del Rey as Edson McCann:

04106 *Preferred risk; a science fiction novel.* Simon & Schuster, New York, 1955, 248p, Cloth, Novel

with C. M. Kornbluth:

08444 *Gladiator-at-law.* Ballantine, New York, 1955, 171p, Cloth, Novel
08445 *Search the sky.* Ballantine, New York, 1954, 166p, Cloth, Novel
08446 *The space merchants.* Ballantine, New York, 1953, 181p, Cloth, Novel
08447 *Wolfbane.* Ballantine, New York, 1959, 140p, Paper, Novel
08448 *The wonder effect.* Ballantine, New York, 1962, 159p, Paper, Coll.

with Carol Pohl:

11750 *Jupiter.* Ballantine, New York, 1973, 265p, Paper, Anth.
11751 *Science fiction: the great years.* Ace, New York, 1973, 349p, Paper, Anth.

with Jack Williamson:

11790 *The Reefs of Space.* Ballantine, New York, 1964, 188p, Paper, Novel [Starchild #1]
11791 *Rogue star.* Ballantine, New York, 1969, 213p, Paper, Novel [Starchild #3]
11792 *Starchild.* Ballantine, New York, 1965, 191p, Paper, Novel [Starchild #2]
11793 *Undersea city.* Gnome Press, Hicksville, NY, 1958, 188p, Cloth, Novel [Eden #3]
11794 *Undersea fleet.* Gnome Press, New York, 1956, 187p, Cloth, Novel [Eden #2]
11795 *Undersea quest.* Gnome Press, New York, 1954, 189p, Cloth, Novel [Eden #1]

POHLMAN, EDWARD (Wendell), 1933- [*biography included*]

11796 *The god of Planet 607.* Westminster Press, Philadelphia, 1972, 123p, Cloth, Novel

POLIDORI, JOHN WILLIAM, 1795-1821

11797 *Ernestus Berchtold; or, The modern Oedipus; a tale.* Longman, Hurst, Rees, Orme & Brown, London, 1819, 275p, Cloth, Novel
11798 *The vampyre; a tale,* by the Right Honourable Lord Byron. Sherwood, Neely & Jones, London, 1819, 84p, Cloth, Novel [misattributed by the publisher to Byron]

POLITICS AND LIFE IN MARS

11799 *Politics and life in Mars; a story of a neighboring planet.* Sampson Low, Marston, Searle & Rivington, London, 1883, 201p, Cloth, Novel

POLLARD, Capt. A(lfred) O(liver), 1893-

11800 *Air reprisal.* Hutchinson, London, 1938, 272p, Cloth, Novel
11801 *The cipher five.* Hutchinson, London, 1932, 288p, Cloth, Novel
11802 *The murder germ.* Hutchinson, London, 1937, 288p, Cloth, Novel
11803 *The secret formula.* Hutchinson, London, 1939, 256p, Cloth, Novel

POLLARD, LESLIE

11804 *Menace; a novel of the near future.* T. Werner Laurie, London, 1935, 256p, Cloth, Novel

POLLEXFEN, MURIEL A.

11805 *Grey Ghost.* George Newnes, London, 1910, 186p, Cloth, Coll.

POLLOCK, Lieut.-Colonel A(rthur) W(illiamson) A(lsager), 1853-1923

11806 *In the cockpit of Europe.* Smith, Elder, London, 1913, 340p, Cloth, Novel
11807 *Lord Roastem's campaign in north-eastern Europe.* Hugh Rees, London, 1911, 63p, Cloth?, Novel

POLLOCK, JOHN H.
see: PILIBIN, AN

POLLOCK, WALTER HERRIES, 1850-1926, with Andrew Lang [published anonymously]

08596 *He,* by the author of 'It,' 'King Solomon's wives,' 'Bess,' 'Much darker days,' 'Mr. Morton's subtler,' and other romances. Longmans Green, London, 1887, 119p, Paper, Novel [a parody of Haggard's novel, *She*]

POMEROY, WILLIAM C.

11808 *The lords of misrule; a tale of gods and of men.* Laird & Lee, Chicago, 1894, 316p, Paper, Novel

PONDER, ZITA INEZ

11809 *The bandaged face.* Selwyn & Blount, London, 1927, 288p, Cloth, Novel

PONS, MAURICE, 1927- [*biography included*]

11810 *Rosa.* Dial Press, New York, 1972, 141p, Cloth, Novel
11810A retitled: *A faithful chronicle of the events which occurred during the last century in the Principality of Waskelham, including revelations as to the strange power of one Rosa, who unknown to herself made happy the most miserable of men.* New English Library, London, 1973, 139p, Paper, Novel

PONSOT, GEORGES

11811 *The romance of the river.* Dodd, Mead, New York, 1924, 290p, Cloth, Novel; Hodder & Stoughton, London, 1924, 290p, Cloth, Novel

POODLESTAN
    see: HENRY, PAUL-MARC

POOLE, JOSEPHINE, 1933- [*biography included*]

11812 *Moon eyes.* Hutchinson, London, 1965, 159p, Cloth, Novel

POOR, KATHARINE HILLWOOD

11813 *The lodge in the wilderness; a novel of reincarnation and karma.* Hobson Book Press, New York, 1945, 238p, Cloth, Novel

POPE, GUSTAVUS W.

11814 *Journey to Mars, the wonderful world, its beauty and splendor, its mighty races and kingdoms, its final doom.* G. W. Dillingham, New York, 1894, 543p, Cloth, Novel
11815 *A journey to Venus, the primeval world, its wonderful creations and gigantic monsters.* Arena Publishing Co., Boston, 1895, 499p, Cloth, Novel

POPE, MARION MANVILLE, 1859-

11816 *Up the Matterhorn in a boat.* Century Co., New York, 1897, 199p, Cloth, Novel

POPE BOOTH

11817 *Pope Booth; the Salvation Army, A.D. 1950.* W. Lucas, London, 1890, 16p, Paper, Story

POPERY IN A.D. 1900
    see: MACGREGOR, JOHN

POPHAM, MELINDA, 1944- [*biography included*]

11818 *A blank book.* Bobbs-Merrill, Indianapolis, 1974, 161p, Cloth, Novel

POPP, LILIAN M., with Richard L. Loughlin

09230 *Journeys in science fiction.* Globe Book Co., New York, 1961, 656p, Cloth, Anth.

POPULAR TALES AND ROMANCES OF THE NORTHERN NATIONS

11819 *Popular tales and romances of the Northern nations.* W. Simpkin, R. Marshall & H. H. Bohte, London, 1823, vol. I-332p, II-316p, III-349p, Cloth, Anth.

PORTAL, ELLIS, pseud.
    see: POWE, BRUCE

PORTER, Admiral (David Dixon), 1813-1891

11820 *The adventures of Harry Marline; or, Notes from an American midshipman's lucky bag.* D. Appleton, New York, 1885, 378p, Cloth, Novel

PORTWIN(e), E. T.

11821 *Death swamp, and other adventure stories.* Vawser & Wiles, London, 1946, 135p, Cloth, Coll.
11822 *The zero ray terrors.* Vawser & Wiles, London, 1946, 122p, Cloth, Novel

POSSENDORF, HANS, pseud. [Hans Mahner-Mons]

11823 *Dambala calls; a love story of Haiti.* Hutchinson, London, 1936, 287p, Cloth, Novel

POST, J(erry) B(enjamin), 1937- [*biography included*]

11824 *An atlas of fantasy.* Mirage Press, Baltimore, 1973, 284p, Cloth, Nonf.

POST, JOYCE, 1939- [*biography included*]

11825 *Let's drink to that, being a compendium of events, real & imaginary, of interest to the reader of science, fiction, & science fiction.* Terminus, Owlswick & Ft. Mudge Electrick Street Railway Gazette, Philadelphia, 1970, 58p, Paper, Nonf.

POST, MELVILLE DAVISSON, 1871-1930

11826 *The revolt of the birds.* D. Appleton, New York, 1927, 144p, Cloth, Novel

THE POST READER OF FANTASY AND SCIENCE FICTION

11827 *The Post reader of fantasy and science fiction.*
       Doubleday, Garden City, 1964, 311p, Cloth,
       Anth.
11827A retitled: *The Saturday evening post reader
       of fantasy and science fiction.* Souvenir
       Press, London, 1964, 311p, Cloth, Anth.

POSTERITAS, pseud.

11828 *The siege of London.* Wyman & Sons, Lincoln's-
       Inn Fields, UK, 1884, 68p, Paper, Novel

POSTERITY

11829 *Posterity, its verdicts and its methods; or,
       Democracy, A.D. 2100.* Williams & Norgate,
       London, 1897, 171p, Cloth, Novel

POTOCKI, JAN, Hrabia [Count], 1761-1815

11830 *The new Decameron; further tales from the
       Saragossa Manuscript.* Orion Press, New
       York, 1967, 433p, Cloth, Coll. [Saragossa
       Manuscript #2]
11831 *The Saragossa Manuscript; a collection of
       weird tales.* Orion Press, New York, 1960,
       233p, Cloth, Coll. [Saragossa Manuscript #1]

POTTER, MARGARET HORTON, 1881-1911

11832 *The flame-gatherers.* Macmillan, New York,
       1904, 417p, Cloth, Novel
11833 *Istar of Babylon; a phantasy.* Harper & Bros.,
       New York, 1902, 494p, Cloth, Novel

POTTER, MARTIN H.

11834 *Life--the jade.* Everett & Co., London, 1912,
       319p, Cloth, Novel
11835 *The sea surrenders.* Everett & Co., London,
       1911, 319p, Cloth, Novel

POTTER, ROBERT

       The germ growers. [see 11836A]

as Robert Easterley & John Wilbraham:

11836 *The germ growers; an Australian story of
       adventure and mystery.* Melville, Mullen &
       Slade, Melbourne, 1892, 274p, Cloth, Novel
11836A *The germ growers; the strange adventures of
       Robert Easterley and John Wilbraham,* by
       Robert Potter. Hutchinson, London, 1892,
       274p, Cloth, Novel

POULSON, THEODORE FREDERICK

11837 *The flying wig; a horrifying tale, being the
       first time in the history of the great art
       of story writing that the reader will meet
       the ghost of an hallucination.* Abel Skiff,
       Honolulu, 1948, 45p, Cloth, Story

POURNELLE, JERRY (Eugene), 1933- [*biography included*]

11838 *Escape from the planet of the apes.* Award,
       New York, 1974, 156p, Paper, Movie [Planet
       of the Apes #3]
11839 *A spaceship for the king.* DAW, New York, 1973,
       157p, Paper, Novel
11840 *2020 vision.* Avon, New York, 1974, 192p, Paper,
       Anth.

with Larry Niven:

10708 *The mote in God's eye.* Simon & Schuster, New
       York, 1974, 537p, Cloth, Novel

POWE, BRUCE, 1925- [*biography included*]

11841 *The last days of the American empire.* Macmil-
       lan of Canada, Toronto, 1974, 326p, Cloth,
       Novel

as Ellis Portal:

11842 *Killing ground; the Canadian civil war.* Peter
       Martin Associates, Toronto, 1968, 269p,
       Cloth, Novel

POWELL, F. INGLIS

11843 *The snake.* John Lane, The Bodley Head, London,
       1912, 304p, Cloth, Novel

POWELL, FRANK

11844 *The wolf-men; a tale of amazing adventures in
       the under-world.* Cassell, London, 1906,
       264p, Cloth, Novel

POWELL, TALMAGE, 1920- [*biography included*]

11845 *The thing in B-3; a tale of the supernatural.*
       Whitman Publishing Co., Racine, Wisc., 1969,
       210p, Cloth, Novel

POWELL, VAN

11846 *The mystery boys and the Inca gold.* A. L. Burt,
       New York, 1931, 283p, Cloth, Novel [Mystery
       Boys #1]
11847 *The mystery boys and the Inca gold; and, The
       mystery boys and Captain Kidd's message.*
       World Publishing Co., Cleveland, 193?,
       564p, Cloth, Coll. [only the first book is
       SF]

POWERS, J. L., pseud.
   see: GLASBY, JOHN

POWERS OF DARKNESS

11848 *Powers of darkness; a collection of uneasy
       tales.* Philip Allan, London, 1934, 243p,
       Cloth, Anth.

POWYS, JOHN COWPER, 1872-1963

11849 *All or nothing.* Macdonald, London, 1960, 219p, Cloth, Novel
11850 *Atlantis.* Macdonald, London, 1954, 462p, Cloth, Novel
11851 *Morwyn; or, The vengeance of God.* Cassell, London, 1937, 322p, Cloth, Novel
11852 *Up and out.* Macdonald, London, 1957, 224p, Cloth, Coll.

POWYS, T(heodore) F(rancis), 1875-1953

11853 *Fables.* Chatto & Windus, London, 1929, 275p, Cloth, Coll.
11854 *Mr. Weston's good wine.* Chatto & Windus, London, 1927, 315p, Cloth, Novel
11855 *Unclay.* Chatto & Windus, London, 1931, 343p, Cloth, Novel

POYER, JOE [Joseph John Power, 1939-   ] [*biography included*]

11856 *North Cape.* Doubleday, Garden City, 1969, 231p, Cloth, Novel
11857 *Operation Malacca.* Doubleday, Garden City, 1968, 208p, Cloth, Novel
11858 *The shooting of the green.* Doubleday, Garden City, 1973, 227p, Cloth, Novel

POYNET, QUINTIN

11859 *The wizard priest and the witch; a romance.* A. K. Newman, London, 1822, 3vol, Cloth, Novel

PRADE, ERNEST LA
     see: LA PRADE, ERNEST

PRAED, Mrs. CAMPBELL [Rosa Caroline Praed, 1851-1935]

11860 *'As a watch in the night'; a drama of waking and dreaming in five acts.* Chatto & Windus, London, 1900, 468p, Cloth, Novel
11861 *The body of his desire; a romance of the soul.* Cassell, London, 1912, 344p, Cloth, Novel
11862 *The Brother of the Shadow; a mystery of to-day.* George Routledge & Sons, London, 1886, 158p, Cloth, Novel
11863 *Fugitive Anne; a romance of the unexplored bush.* John Long, London, 1902, 428p, Cloth, Novel
11864 *The insane root; a romance of a strange country.* T. Fisher Unwin, London, 1902, 380p, Cloth, Novel
11865 *The mystery woman.* Cassell, London, 1913, 348p, Cloth, Novel
11866 *The soul of Countess Adrian; a romance.* Trischler & Co., London, 1891, 192p, Cloth, Novel

PRAGNELL, FESTUS, 1905-

11867 *The green man of Kilsona.* Philip Allan, London, 1936, 240p, Cloth, Novel

11867A retitled: *The green man of Graypec.* Greenberg: Publisher, New York, 1950, 189p, Cloth, Novel [revised]
11868 *The terror from Timorkal.* Bear, Hudson, London, 1946, 192p, Paper, Novel

with Benson Herbert:

07118 *Thieves of the air.* Lloyd Cole, London, 1943?, 27p, Paper, Story

PRATHER, HUGH, 1938-   [*biography included*]

11869 *Wipe your face, you just swallowed my soul.* Doubleday, Garden City, 1974, 89p, Cloth, Novel

PRATT, AMBROSE, 1874-1944

11870 *The living mummy.* Frederick A. Stokes, New York, 1910, 313p, Cloth, Novel

PRATT, CORNELIA ATWOOD, d. 1929, with Richard Slee

11871 *Dr. Berkeley's discovery.* G. P. Putnam's Sons, New York, 1899, 219p, Cloth, Novel

PRATT, (Murray) FLETCHER, 1897-1956 [*biography included*]

11872 *Alien planet.* Avalon, New York, 1962, 224p, Cloth, Novel
11873 *The Blue Star.* Ballantine, New York, 1969, 240p, Paper, Novel
11874 *Double in space; two novels.* Doubleday, Garden City, 1951, 217p, Cloth, Coll.
11875 *Double in space; two science-fiction novels.* T. V. Boardman, London, 1954, 222p, Cloth, Coll. [different contents; includes *The undying fire*]
11876 *Double jeopardy.* Doubleday, Garden City, 1952, 214p, Cloth, Novel
11877 *Invaders from Rigel.* Avalon, New York, 1960, 224p, Cloth, Novel
11878 *The undying fire.* Ballantine, New York, 1953, 149p, Cloth, Novel
     The well of the unicorn. [see 11880A]
11879 *World of wonder; an introduction to imaginative literature.* Twayne Publishers, New York, 1951, 445p, Cloth, Anth.

as George U. Fletcher:

11880 *The well of the unicorn.* William Sloane Associates, New York, 1948, 338p, Cloth, Novel
11880A *The well of the unicorn,* by Fletcher Pratt. Lancer, New York, 1967, 384p, Paper, Novel

with L. Sprague de Camp:

03993 *The carnelian cube; a humorous fantasy.* Gnome Press, New York, 1948, 230p, Cloth, Novel
03994 *The castle of iron; a science fantasy adventure.* Gnome Press, New York, 1950, 224p, Cloth, Novel [Harold Shea #2]
03995 *The incomplete enchanter.* Henry Holt, New York, 1941, 326p, Cloth, Novel [Harold Shea #1]
03996 *Land of unreason.* Henry Holt, New York, 1942, 260p, Cloth, Novel
03997 *Tales from Gavagan's Bar.* Twayne Publishers, New York, 1953, 228p, Cloth, Coll.

PRATT, FLETCHER (cont.), with L. Sprague de Camp

03998   *Wall of serpents.* Avalon, New York, 1960, 223p, Cloth, Novel

PRATT, THEODORE, 1901-1969 [*biography included*]

11881   *Mr. Atom.* Wake-Brook House, Fort Lauderdale, FL, 1969, 197p, Cloth, Novel
11882   *Mr. Limpet.* Alfred A. Knopf, New York, 1942, 144p, Cloth, Novel
11883   *Mr. Thurtle's trolley; a novel.* Duell, Sloan & Pearce, New York, 1947, 214p, Cloth, Novel

PRATT, WILLIAM HENRY
    see: KARLOFF, BORIS

THE PREMATURE BURIAL

11884   *The premature burial, and other tales of horror.* Corgi, London, 1966, 157p, Paper, Anth.

PRENTICE, HARRY

11885   *The King of Apeland; the wonderful adventures of a young animal-trainer.* A. L. Burt, New York, 1888, 286p, Cloth, Novel
11885A   retitled: *Captured by apes; or, How Philip Garland became King of Apeland.* A. L. Burt, New York, 1892, 286p, Cloth, Novel

PRESCOTT, HARRIET ELIZABETH, 1835-1921 [published anonymously]

11886   *Sir Rohan's ghost; a romance.* J. E. Tilton, Boston, 1860, 352p, Cloth, Novel

THE PRESIDENT VANISHES
    see: STOUT, REX

PRESLAND, JOHN, pseud. [Gladys Skelton, 1889-1975]

11887   *Escape me--never!* Philip Allan, London, 1928, 296p, Cloth, Novel

PREST, (Thomas) PECKETT, 1810?-1879?

11888   *Schamyl; or, The wild woman of Circassia; an original historical romance.* Henry Lea, London, 1856, 420p, Cloth, Novel
       Varney the vampyre. [see: VARNEY THE VAMPYRE]

PRESTON, EDNA MITCHELL

11889   *Arrow book of spooky stories.* Scholastic Book Services, New York, 1962, 90p, Paper, Anth.

PRETRE, WM. LE
    see: LE PRETRE, WM.

PREUSSLER, OTFRIED

11890   *The Satanic mill.* Abelard-Schuman, London, 1972, 185p, Cloth, Novel

PREVOT, FRANCIS C(lare)

11891   *Ghosties and ghoulies.* Chelsea Publishing House, London, 1923, 88p, Cloth, Coll.

PRICE, E(dgar) HOFFMANN, 1898- [*biography included*]

11892   *Strange gateways.* Arkham House, Sauk City, 1967, 208p, Cloth, Coll.

PRICE, ROGER (Damon Mainwaring), 1941- [*biography included*]

11893   *The Tomorrow People in Three in three.* Piccolo/TV Times, London, 1974, 136p, Paper, Tele. Coll. [Tomorrow People #2]

with Julian R. Gregory:

06346   *The Tomorrow People in The visitor.* Piccolo/TV Times, London, 1973, 118p, Paper, Tele. [Tomorrow People #1]

PRICE, ROGER (Taylor), 1921- [*biography included*]

11894   *J. G., the upright ape, being a novel about the way things are, as discovered in the adventures of an innocent hero, and illuminated by his forthright reaction to women, men, progress, and other contemporary phenomena.* Lyle Stuart, New York, 1960, 239p, Cloth, Novel

PRICE, THEO(dore)

11895   *God in the sand; an Australian mythical roman.* P. R. Stephensen & Co., Sydney, 1934, 288p, Cloth, Novel

PRICHARD, HESKETH (Vernon Hesketh-), 1876-192 with K. Prichard

11896   *Ghosts, being the experiences of Flaxman Low.* C. Arthur Pearson, London, 1899, 300p, Cloth, Coll.

with K. Prichard as H. & E. Heron:

11897   *Ghost stories.* C. Arthur Pearson, London, 1916, 117p, Cloth, Coll.

PRICHARD, K(ate O'Brien Hesketh-), with Hesketh Prichard

11896   *Ghosts, being the experiences of Flaxman Low.* C. Arthur Pearson, London, 1899, 300p, Cloth, Coll.

with Hesketh Prichard as E. & H. Heron:

11897   *Ghost stories.* C. Arthur Pearson, London, 1916, 117p, Cloth, Coll.

PRICKETT, MARMADUKE A.

11898 *The Brain City; a fantasy.* Museum Arts &
Letters Association, London, 1913, 206p,
Cloth, Novel

PRIEST, CHRISTOPHER (McKenzie), 1943- [*bio-graphy included*]

Darkening island. [see 11899A]
11899 *Fugue for a darkening island.* Faber & Faber,
London, 1972, 147p, Cloth, Novel
11899A retitled: *Darkening island.* Harper & Row,
New York, 1972, 147p, Cloth, Novel
11900 *Indoctrinaire.* Faber & Faber, London, 1970,
227p, Cloth, Novel
11901 *Inverted world.* Faber & Faber, London, 1974,
256p, Cloth, Novel
11902 *Real-time world.* New English Library, London,
1974, 158p, Cloth, Coll.

A PRIEST, pseud.

11903 *The open secret.* Arena Publishing Co., Boston, 1893, 62p, Cloth, Novel

PRIESTLEY, J(ohn) B(oynton), 1894- [*biogra-phy included*]

11904 *Adam in moonshine.* William Heinemann, London,
1927, 293p, Cloth, Novel
11905 *Benighted; and, Adam in moonshine.* William
Heinemann, London, 1932, 638p, Cloth, Coll.
[only the second book is SF]
11906 *The doomsday men; an adventure.* William Heinemann, London, 1938, 312p, Cloth, Novel
11907 *Jenny Villiers; a story of the theatre.* William Heinemann, London, 1947, 190p, Cloth,
Novel
11908 *The Magicians.* William Heinemann, London,
1954, 256p, Cloth, Novel
11909 *The other place, and other stories of the
same sort.* William Heinemann, London,
1953, 265p, Cloth, Coll.
11910 *Saturn over water; an account of his adventures in London, South America, and Australia, by Tim Belford, painter; edited,
with some preliminary and concluding remarks, by Henry Sulgrave, and here presented to the reading public.* Heinemann, London, 1961, 296p, Cloth, Novel
11911 *Snoggle; a story for anybody between 9 and
90.* Heinemann, London, 1971, 138p, Cloth,
Novel
11912 *The thirty-first of June; a tale of true love,
enterprise, and progress, in the Arthurian
and ad-Atomic ages.* Heinemann, London,
1961, 168p, Cloth, Novel

PRIME, Lord, pseud. [Walter Doty Reynolds,
1860-]

11913 *Mr. Jonnemacher's machine; the port to which
we drifted.* Knickerbocker Book Co., Philadelphia, 1898, 255p, Paper, Novel

PRINCE, DON

11914 *S-w-o-o-p.* Julian Messner, New York, 1941,
256p, Cloth, Novel
11915 *Tom; a novel.* Julian Messner, New York, 1940,
272p, Cloth, Novel

PRINCE, EDWARD

11916 *Wake up, England! being the amazing story of
John Bull--Socialist.* St. Stephen's Press,
Westminster, UK, 1910, 188p, Cloth, Novel

THE PRINCE OF ARGOLIS

11917 *The Prince of Argolis; a story of old Greek
fairy time.* Chatto & Windus, London, 1877,
127p, Cloth, Novel

PRINCE OF DARKNESS
see: VERNER, GERALD

PRIOR, ANN, 1949- [*biography included*]

11918 *The sky cage.* Chatto & Windus, London, 1967,
210p, Cloth, Novel

PRITCHARD, JOHN LAURENCE
see: LAURENCE, JOHN

PRITCHARD, JOHN WALLACE
see: WALLACE, IAN

PRITCHARD, WILLIAM THOMAS
see: DEXTER, WILLIAM

PRITCHER, LEON, with Catharine Harger

06775 *Disturbers of the peace; a novel.* Bruce Humphries, Boston, 1945, 231p, Cloth, Novel

PRITCHETT, E. BLANCHE

11919 *Japhalein, mother ship of this galaxy.* Marcap
Council, Arlington, Wash., 1968, 169p, Paper,
Novel

THE PRIVATE MEMOIRS OF A JUSTIFIED SINNER
see: HOGG, JAMES

PROBY, WILLIAM C.

11920 *The spirit of the castle; a romance.* Warner
& Hanna, Philadelphia, 1801, 294p, Cloth,
Novel

PROCTOR, HENRY

11921 *Perpetual youth; an occult and historical
romance.* L. N. Fowler, London, 1913, 123p,
Cloth, Novel

PROFFITT, JOSEPHINE
   see: DEE, SYLVIA

PROLE, LOZANIA, pseud.
   see: BLOOM, URSULA and EADE, CHARLES

THE PROPHET JAMES, pseud. [James Smith Buck, 1812-1892]

11922 *The chronicles of the land of Columbia, commonly called America, from the landing of the Pilgrim fathers, to the second reign of Ulysses the I., a period of two hundred and fifty-two years, book I.* F. W. Stearns, Milwaukee, 1876, 112p, Cloth, Novel [book II never published]

PROSPERO and CALIBAN, pseud.
   see: ROLFE, FREDERICK and PIRIE-GORDON, HARRY

PROSSER, H(arold) L(ee II)

11923 *The capricorn, and other fantasy stories.* Mafdet Press, Springfield, MO, 1974, 16p, Paper, Coll.

PROTHEROE, CYRIL, as Rand Le Page, house pseud.

08917 *Beyond these suns.* Curtis Warren, London, 1952, 128p, Cloth, Novel

PROTTER, ERIC, 1927-

11924 *Monster festival.* Vanguard Press, New York, 1965, 286p, Cloth, Anth.

PRUD'HOMMEAUX, RENÉ

11925 *The mystery of Marr's Hill.* Macrae Smith, Philadelphia, 1958, 190p, Cloth, Novel

PRUNING KNIFE, pseud.
   see: ALLEN, HENRY FRANCIS

PRUS, BOLESLAUS
   see: GLOVATSKI, ALEXANDER

PRUYN, LEONARD, with Day Keene

08097 *World without women.* Gold Medal, Greenwich, Conn., 1960, 176p, Paper, Novel

PRYCE, DEVEREUX

11926 *Out of the ages.* Leonard Parson, London, 1923, 320p, Cloth, Novel

PRYCE, GEORGE
   see: LAMPEN, C. DUDLEY

PSEUDOMAN, AKKAD, pseud. [Edwin Fitch Northrup, 1866-1940]

11927 *Zero to eighty, being my lifetime doings, reflections, and inventions, also my journey around the Moon.* Scientific Publishing Co., Princeton, NJ, 1937, 283p, Cloth, Novel

PUCCETTI, ROLAND (Peter), 1924- [*biography included*]

11928 *The death of the Führer.* St. Martin's Press, New York, 1972, 223p, Cloth, Novel
11929 *The trial of John and Henry Norton; a novel.* Hutchinson, London, 1973, 156p, Cloth, Novel

PUGNER, (Wanda) CAROL, 1943- [*biography included*], with Harry Harrison

06854 *A science fiction reader.* Charles Scribner's Sons, New York, 1973, 272p, Paper, Anth.

PULLAR, A. L.

11930 *Celestalia; a fantasy, A.D. 1975.* Canberra Press, Sydney, 1933, 279p, Cloth, Novel

PULLEN, HENRY WILLIAM, 1836-1903 [published anonymously]

11931 *Venus and Cupid; a trip from Mount Olympus to London, by the personal conductor of the party; a new fantastic romance*, by the author of "The fight at Dame Europa's school." J. B. Lippincott, Philadelphia, 1896, 296p, Cloth, Novel; J. M. Dent & Sons, London, 1896, 307p, Cloth, Novel

PURDOM, TOM [Thomas Edward Purdom, 1936-] [*biography included*]

11932 *The barons of behavior.* Ace, New York, 1972, 189p, Paper, Novel
11933 *Five against Arlane.* Ace Double, New York, 1967, 136p, Paper, Novel
11934 *I want the stars.* Ace Double, New York, 1964, 115p, Paper, Novel
11935 *Reduction in arms.* Berkley Medallion, New York, 1971, 176p, Paper, Novel
11936 *The tree lord of Imeten.* Ace Double, New York, 1966, 152p, Paper, Novel

PURTILL, RICHARD (L.), 1931- [*biography included*]

11937 *Lord of the elves and eldils; fantasy and philosophy in C. S. Lewis and J. R. R. Tolkien.* Zondervan Publishing House, Grand Rapids, Mich., 1974, 216p, Paper, Nonf.

PUTNEY, SUSAN K.

11938 *Against Arcturus.* Ace Double, New York, 1972, 144p, Paper, Novel

PYGASTER, CAL I.

11939 *Zero gravity swap.* Candid Reader, San Diego,
       1970, 160p, Paper, Novel

PYLE, HOWARD, 1853-1911

11940 *A modern Aladdin; or, The wonderful adventures
       of Oliver Munier; an extravaganza in four
       acts.* Harper & Bros., New York, 1892,
       205p, Cloth, Novel
11941 *Stolen treasure.* Harper & Bros., New York,
       1907, 254p, Cloth, Coll.

PYM, HERBERT

11942 *The man with thirty lives; a romance.* Everett
       & Co., London, 1909, 304p, Cloth, Novel

PYTHAGOROLUNISTER, pseud.
   see: DEFOE, DANIEL

"Q," pseud.
   see: QUILLER-COUCH, A. T.

QUACKENBOS, JOHN D(uncan), 1848-1926

11943 *Magnhild; a tale of psychic love.* Richard G.
       Badger, The Gorham Press, Boston, 1918,
       335p, Cloth, Novel

QUAD, M., pseud. [Charles Bertrand Lewis,
1842-1924]

11944 *Under five lakes; or, The cruise of the "Des-
       troyer."* George Munro, New York, 1886,
       171p, Paper, Novel

QUADRATIC

11945 *Quadratic.* Fantasy Publishing Co., Los Ange-
       les, 1953, 580p, Cloth, Anth. [includes
       Murray Leinster's *Murder madness* and Olaf
       Stapledon's *Worlds of wonder*]

QUAKES

11946 *Quakes; a collection of uneasy tales.* Philip
       Allan, London, 1933, 252p, Cloth, Anth.

QUEEN, ELLERY, pseud.
   see: DANNAY, FREDERIC and LEE, MANFRED B.

QUEEN FLORA'S RECOLLECTIONS

11947 *Queen Flora's recollections, being a true
       synthetic record of the events immediately
       preceding the glorious restoration of the
       monarchy in the year of Our Lord 1998.*
       Elliott Stock, London, 1911, 235p, Cloth,
       Novel

THE QUEEN NORLATIADEK REGIME OF ORDER 32, pseud.

11948 *The planet of the cross.* Little Elmo Publica-
       tions, Tri-Cities, Wash., 1972, 55p, Paper,
       Novel

QUEIROZ, ECA de
   see: ECA de QUEIROZ [Addendum]

QUEST, RODNEY, 1897-   [*biography included*]

11949 *Countdown to doomsday.* George G. Harrap, Lon-
       don, 1966, 293p, Cloth, Novel

QUEUX, WILLIAM LE
   see: LE QUEUX, WILLIAM

QUICK, DOROTHY, 1900-1962

11950 *Strange awakening.* House of Field, New York,
       1938, 266p, Cloth, Novel

QUICK, (John) HERBERT, 1861-1925

11951 *Virginia of the air lanes.* Bobbs-Merrill, In-
       dianapolis, 1909, 424p, Cloth, Novel

QUIEN SABE, pseud.
   see: GREGORY, JACKSON

QUILLER-COUCH, (Sir) A(rthur) T(homas), 1863-
1944

11952 *Old fires and profitable ghosts; a book of
       stories.* Cassell, London, 1900, 341p, Cloth,
       Coll.

as "Q":

11953 *Selected stories.* J. M. Dent & Sons, London,
       1921, 240p, Cloth, Coll.
11954 *Wandering heath; stories, studies, and sketches.*
       Cassell, London, 1895, 293p, Cloth, Coll.

QUILP, JOCELYN

11955 *Baron Verdigris; a romance of the reversed
       direction.* Henry & Co., London, 1894,
       214p, Cloth, Novel

QUILTY, RAFE

11956 *The tenth session.* Jonathan Cape, London,
       1972, 188p, Cloth, Novel

QUINCY, J(osiah) P(hillips), 1829-1910

11957 *The Peckster professorship; an episode in the
       history of psychical research.* Houghton,
       Mifflin, Boston, 1888, 310p, Cloth, Coll.

QUINN, JAMES L(ouis), with Eve Wulff

11958　*The first world of If.* Quinn Publishing Co.,
Kingston, NY, 1957, 160p, Paper, Anth.
11959　*The second world of If.* Quinn Publishing Co.,
Kingston, NY, 1958, 159p, Paper, Anth.

QUINN, SEABURY (Grandin), 1889-1969

11960　*Is the devil a gentleman? the best fiction of
Seabury Quinn.* Mirage Press, The Voyager
Series, Baltimore, 1970, 258p, Cloth, Coll.
11961　*The phantom-fighter; ten memoirs of Jules de
Grandin, sometime member of La Sûreté Général, La Faculté de Medicine Legal de Paris,
etc., etc.* Mycroft & Moran, Sauk City, 1966,
263p, Cloth, Coll.
11962　*Roads.* Conrad H. Ruppert, New York, 1938, 47p,
Paper, Story

QUINTERO, JORGE

11963　*Radio Rocketeers.* Pied-Piper Press, Los Angeles, 1938, 308p, Cloth, Novel

QUOIN, pseud.

11964　*E pluribus unum; a story of today and of today's tomorrow.* Patriot Publishing Co.,
Los Angeles, 1936, 182p, Paper, Novel

"QUONDAM," pseud. [Charles McClellan Stevens,
1861-   ]

11965　*The Egyptian harp girl; a mystery of the peristyle.* Laird & Lee, Chicago, 1894, 272p,
Cloth, Novel

R., A. M.
see: RICHARDS, ANNA MATLOCK

R. S.
see: PALTOCK, ROBERT

RAABE, Capt. H. E.

11966　*Krakatoa, hand of the gods.* Brewer & Warren,
New York, 1930, 352p, Cloth, Novel

RABE, Baroness ANN von
see: VON DEGEN

RACKHAM, JOHN, pseud.
see: PHILLIFENT, JOHN T.

RADCLIFFE, ANNE, 1764-1823

11967　*Gaston de Blondeville; or, The court of Henry
III; Keeping festival in Ardennne, a romance;
St. Alban's Abbey, a metrical tale; with some
poetical pieces.* Henry Colburn, London,
1826, Vol. I-460p, II-399p, III-375p, IV-
331p, Cloth, Coll.

RADCLIFFE, (Henry) GARNETT, 1899-

11968　*The lady from Venus.* Macdonald, London, 1947,
255p, Cloth, Novel
11969　*The return of the ceteosaurus, and other tales*
Drane's, London, 1926, 310p, Cloth, Coll.

A RADICAL NIGHTMARE
see: AN EX-M.P.

RADIN, MAX, 1880-1950

11970　*The day of reckoning.* Alfred A. Knopf, New
York, 1943, 144p, Cloth, Novel

THE RADIO GUNNER
see: FORBES, ALEXANDER

RAFCAM, NAL, pseud.

11971　*The Troglodytes; or, Dwellers of the deep.*
Arthur H. Stockwell, Ilfracombe, UK, 1961,
296p, Cloth, Novel

RAFFALOVICH, GEORGE, 1880-

11972　*Planetary journeys and earthly sketches.* Arnold Fairbairns, London, 1908, 163p, Cloth,
Coll.
11972A retitled: *On the loose; planetary journeys
and earthly sketches.* Office of the Equinox
London, 1910, 163p, Cloth, Coll.

RAFFE, ARTHUR SHKAROVSKY-
see: SHKAROVSKY-RAFFE, ARTHUR

RAFFIN, ALAIN

11973　*Zoe & Zaida; a romantic reconstruction.* C. W
Daniel, London, 1927, 64p, Cloth, Coll.

RAGGED, HYDER, pseud. [Sir Henry Chartres
Biron, 1863-1940]

11974　*King Solomon's wives; or, The phantom mines.*
Vizetelly & Co., London, 1887, 125p, Paper,
Novel [a parody of Haggard's *King Solomon's
mines*]

THE RAID OF DOVER
see: FORD, D. M.

RAIDEN, EDWARD

11975　*The Gogglers; a political satire.* Saturn Boo
Los Angeles, 1967, 142p, Cloth, Novel

RAIFE, RAIMOND

11976　*The sheik's white slave, being an account of
the unravelling of the mysteries of the tem
ple of Djaramos, the city of the desert.*
Lovell, Coryell, New York, 1895, 320p, Clot
Novel

RALEIGH, H(ilary) M(ason), 1893-

11977   *The machinations of Dr. Grue.* Geoffrey Bles,
        London, 1938, 287p, Cloth, Novel

RALLI, CONSTANTINE (Scaramanga)

11978   *Vanessa; a romance of the new century and the
        new world.* Cassell, London, 1904, 344p,
        Cloth, Novel

RALSTON, GILBERT A(lexander), 1912-   [*biography included*]

11979   *Ben.* Bantam, New York, 1972, 154p, Paper,
        Movie [Ben #2]

RAMDAGGER, GEOFFREY, pseud.

11980   *Sexualis 1984.* Midwood, New York, 1973, 188p,
        Paper, Novel [cover byline reads Goeffrey
        Ramdagger]

RAME, DAVID, pseud.
   see: DIVINE, ARTHUR D.

RAMIREZ, ALICE LOUISE

11981   *The geek.* Essex House, North Hollywood,
        1969, 190p, Paper, Novel

as Tiny Alice:

11982   *Naked in her coffin.* Brandon House, North
        Hollywood, 1970, 160p, Paper, Novel

RAMIREZ, MEDARDO FIGUEROA
   see: FIGUEROA, MEDARDO

RAMPO, EDOGAWA, pseud. [Tarō Hirai, 1894-   ]

11983   *Japanese tales of mystery and imagination.*
        Charles E. Tuttle, Rutland, Vt., 1956,
        222p, Cloth, Coll.

RAMPTON, ANTHONY

11984   *The first Panther book of horror.* Panther,
        London, 1965, 268p, Paper, Anth.
11984A retitled: *The Panther book of horror.* Pan-
        ther, London, 1968, 268p, Paper, Anth.

RAMSDEN, LEWIS, pseud. [A. L. Dowding]

11985   *The temple of fire.* Collins Clear-Type Press,
        London, 1905, 360p, Cloth, Novel

RAMSEY, MILTON W(orth), 1848?-1906

11986   *The austral globe.* M. W. Ramsey, Minneapolis,
        1892, 219p, Paper, Novel
11987   *Future dark ages; a story of a trip through a
        dark continent.* Milton W. Ramsey, Minnea-
        polis, 1900, 223p, Cloth, Novel

11988   *Six thousand years hence.* A. Roper, Minneapo-
        lis, 1891, 239p, Cloth, Novel
11989   *Two billions of miles; or, The story of a trip
        through the Solar System.* Milton W. Ramsey,
        Minneapolis, 1900, 248p, Cloth, Novel

RAMSEYER, EDWIN, 1896-

11990   *Airmen over the suburb.* Victor Gollancz, Lon-
        don, 1939, 287p, Cloth, Novel

RAMUZ, C(harles) F(erdinand), 1878-1947

11991   *The end of all men.* Pantheon, New York, 1944,
        223p, Cloth, Novel
11991A retitled: *The triumph of death.* Routledge,
        London, 1946, 155p, Cloth, Novel
11992   *The reign of the evil one.* Harcourt, Brace &
        Co., New York, 1922, 195p, Cloth, Novel

RAND, AYN, 1905-   [*biography included*]

11993   *Anthem.* Cassell, London, 1938, 147p, Cloth,
        Novel
11994   *Atlas shrugged.* Random House, New York, 1957,
        1168p, Cloth, Novel

RANDALL, FLORENCE ENGEL, 1917-   [*biography
included*]

11995   *The almost year.* Atheneum, New York, 1971,
        239p, Cloth, Novel
11996   *Haldane Station.* Harcourt Brace Jovanovich,
        New York, 1973, 243p, Cloth, Novel
11997   *A place of sapphires.* Harcourt, Brace & World,
        New York, 1969, 248p, Cloth, Novel

RANDALL, ROBERT, pseud.
   see: GARRETT, RANDALL and SILVERBERG,
   ROBERT

RANDERSON, W., with D. A. Spencer

11998   *North Sea monster; a novel.* Houghton & Scott-
        Snell, London, 1934, 246p, Cloth, Novel

RANDOLPH, P(aschal) B(everly), 1825-1874

11999   *The Rosicrucian's story; the wonderful things
        that happened to Mr. Thomas W. and his wife.*
        M. J. Randolph, Utica, NY, 1863, 106p, Cloth,
        Novel
12000   *The wonderful story of Ravelette; also, Tom
        Clark and his wife, and the curious things
        that befell them, being the Rosicrucian's
        story.* Sinclair Tousey, New York, 1863,
        146p, Cloth, Coll.
12000A retitled: *Ravalette: the Rosicrucian's story.*
        Philosophical Publishing Co., Quakerstown,
        PA, 1939, 283p, Cloth, Coll.

RANDOM, ALEX, pseud. [see also Donald Rowland]

12001   *Star Cluster Seven.* Robert Hale, London, 1974,
        192p, Cloth, Novel

RANGER-GULL, C.
    see: GULL, C. RANGER

RANKINE, JOHN, pseud.
    see: MASON, DOUGLAS R.

RANSOME, ARTHUR (Michell), 1884-1967

12002 *The Elixir of life.* Methuen, London, 1915,
          312p, Cloth, Novel
12003 *The hoofmarks of the faun.* Martin Secker,
          London, 1911, 168p, Cloth, Coll.

RANSOME, (James) STAFFORD, 1860-1931, with
M. H. Temple and Harold Begbie as Caroline
Lewis

01038 *Clara in Blunderland.* William Heinemann, Lon-
          don, 1902, 150p, Cloth, Novel [Clara #1;
          a parody of *Alice in Wonderland*]
01039 *Lost in Blunderland; the further adventures
          of Clara.* William Heinemann, London, 1903,
          145p, Cloth, Novel [Clara #2]

RANZETTA, LUAN

12004 *The Maru invasion; turmoil and destruction on
          Earth.* Digit, London, 1962, 159p, Paper,
          Novel
12005 *The night of the death rain.* Digit, London,
          1963, 157p, Paper, Novel
12006 *The world in reverse.* Digit, London, 1962,
          154p, Paper, Novel
12007 *The yellow inferno.* Digit, London, 1964,
          158p, Paper, Novel

RANZETTA, V.

12008 *The uncharted planet.* Digit, London, 1962,
          155p, Paper, Novel

RAPHAEL, JOHN N(athan), 1868-1917

12009 *Up above, being the record of the doings of
          the "shadow people" in the year of grace
          1915.* Hutchinson, London, 1913, 271p,
          Cloth, Novel

RAPHAEL, RICK, 1919-   [*biography included*]

12010 *Code Three; a science fiction novel.* Simon &
          Schuster, New York, 1966, 252p, Cloth, Novel
12011 *The thirst quenchers.* Victor Gollancz, Lon-
          don, 1965, 175p, Cloth, Coll.

RAPPORT, SAMUEL (Berder), with Hamilton
Wright and Helen Wright

12012 *To the Moon!* Meredith Press, New York, 1968,
          300p, Cloth, Anth. [includes some nonf.]

RASPE, RUDOLF [variously spelled Rudolph]
ERICH, 1737-1794

12013 *Koenigsmark the robber; or, The terror of
          Bohemia, in which is introduced Stella; or,
          The maniac of the wood, a pathetick tale,*
          by H. J. Sarratt [actually the translator].
          Tegg & Castleman, London, 1803, 80p, Paper,
          Novel [published anonymously]

RASPE, RUDOLF ERICH, 1737-1794, and others
unknown [It has clearly been established that
Raspe wrote the first short Munchausen story;
however, the second and subsequent editions
all contained additional episodes by other
unidentified hands, and are listed here alphabetically by title. Munchausen stories by
other, identified authors are listed under
those authors' names.]

12014 *The adventures of Baron Munchausen.* Cassell,
          Petter & Galpin, London, 1865, 216p, Cloth,
          Novel
12015 *Baron Munchausen's miraculous adventures on
          land.* United States Library Association,
          Los Angeles, 1933, 63p, Cloth?, Novel
12016 *Baron Munchausen's narrative of his marvellous
          travels and campaigns in Russia, humbly dedi-
          cated and recommended to country gentlemen;
          and, if they please, to be repeated as their
          own, after a hunt, at horse races, in water-
          ing places, and other such polite assemblies
          round the bottle and fireside.* M. Smith,
          London, 1786 [actually 1785], 49p, Paper,
          Story [the first edition]
12017 *"Complete original edition" of the surprising
          travels and adventures of Baron Munchausen,
          in Russia, the Caspian Sea, Iceland, Turkey
          also, an account of a voyage into the Moon
          and Dog Star...to which is added, a sequel,
          containing his expedition into Africa.* R.
          Kirby, London, 1819, 179p, Cloth, Novel
12018 *The curious and entertaining adventures and
          travels by sea and land of the renowned Baron
          Munchausen, including a tour through the
          United States in the year MDCCCIII.* Farmer
          & Daggers, New York, 1845, 56p, Cloth, Novel
12019 *Gulliver redivious; or, The celebrated & enter-
          taining travels and adventures by sea and
          land of the renowned Baron Munchausen, inclu-
          ding a tour to the United States of America
          in the year 1803.* The Editor, Dublin, 1805,
          116p, Cloth, Novel
12020 *Gulliver revived; or, The curious and enter-
          taining travels and adventures by sea and
          land of the renowned Baron Munchausen, inclu-
          ding a tour to the United States of America
          in 1803, and the first two chapters of a
          second tour in 1810.* Editor, New York, 1810,
          190p, Cloth, Novel
12021 *Gulliver revived, containing singular travels,
          campaigns, voyages, and adventures in Russia,
          Iceland, Turkey, Egypt, Gibraltar, up the
          Mediterranean, and on the Atlantic Ocean;
          also, an account of a voyage into the Moon,
          with many extraordinary particulars relative
          to the cooking animal in that planet, which
          are here called the human species.* G. Kear-
          ley, London, 1786, 172p, Cloth, Novel [the
          fourth edition]

RASPE, RUDOLF ERICH, with others (cont.)

12022 *Gulliver revived, containing singular travels, campaigns, voyages, and adventures in Russia, the Caspian Sea, Iceland, Turkey, Egypt, Gibraltar, up the Mediterranean, on the Atlantic Ocean and through the centre of Mount Etna into the South Sea; also, an account of a voyage to the Moon and Dog Star, with many extraordinary particulars relative to the cooking animal in those planets, which are here called the human species.* G. Kearsley, London, 1787, 208p, Cloth, Novel [the fifth edition]

12023 *Gulliver revived; or, The singular travels, campaigns, voyages, and adventures of Baron Munikhouson, commonly called Munchausen.* G. Kearsley, London, 1786, 156p, Cloth, Novel [the third edition]

12024 *Gulliver revived; or, The vice of lying properly exposed, containing singular travels, campaigns, voyages, and adventures in Russia, the Caspian Sea, Iceland, Turkey, Egypt, Gibraltar, up the Mediterranean, on the Atlantic Ocean and through the centre of Mount Etna into the South Sea; also, an account of a voyage into the Moon and Dog-Star, with many extraordinary particulars relative to the cooking animal in those planets, which are there called the human species.* G. Kearsley, London, 1789, 252p, Cloth, Novel [the sixth edition]

12025 *Munchausen at the Pole; or, The surprising and wonderful adventures of a voyage of discovery, consisting of some of the most marvellous exploits ever performed by man, together with a correct list of the curiosities brought home and deposited in the museum and Tower of London,* by Capt. Munchausen. J. Johnston, London, 1819, 164p, Cloth, Novel

12026 *Munchausen at Walcheron; or, A continuation of the renowned Baron's surprising travels, adventures, expeditions, and exploits at Walcheron, the Dardanelles, Talavera, Cintra, &c., &c.* J. Johnston, London, 1811, 180p, Cloth, Novel

12027 *Original travels and surprising adventures of Baron Munchausen.* Trübner & Co., London, 1889, 253p, Cloth, Novel

12028 *The original travels of Baron Munchausen.* Rand McNally, Chicago, 1900, 283p, Cloth, Novel

12029 *The real Munchausen.* Devin-Adair, New York, 1960, 138p, Cloth, Novel

12030 *A sequel to the adventures of Baron Munchausen, humbly dedicated to Mr Bruce the Abyssinian traveller, as the Baron conceives that it may be of some service to him making another expedition into Abyssinia; but if this does not delight Mr Bruce, the Baron is willing to fight him on any terms he pleases.* H. D. Symonds, London, 1792, 240p, Cloth, Novel

12031 *The singular adventures of Baron Munchausen.* Max Parrish, London, 1950, 119p, Cloth, Novel

12032 *Singular travels, campaigns, and adventures of Baron Munchausen.* Cresset Press, London, 1948, 178p, Cloth, Novel

12033 *Singular travels, campaigns, voyages, and sporting adventures of Baron Munnikhouson, commonly pronounced Munchausen, as he relates them over a bottle when surrounded by his friends.* M. Smith, London, 1786, 87p, Cloth?, Novel [the second edition]

12034 *The surprising adventures of Baron Munchausen.* C. & G. Kearsley, London, 1793, , Cloth, Novel

12035 *The surprising adventures of the renowned Baron Munchausen abridged, containing singular travels, campaigns, voyages, and adventures; also, an account of a voyage into the Moon and Dog Star.* Cameron & Co., Glasgow, 1804, 87p, Cloth, Novel

12036 *The surprising adventures, singular travels, miraculous escapes, and wonderful voyages and campaigns of the renowned Baron Munchausen, in Russia, the Caspian Sea, Iceland, Egypt, up the Mediterranean, through the centre of Mount Etna into the South Sea; also, an account of a voyage into the Moon, with many extraordinary particulars relative to the inhabitants & in the Moon.* Thomas Richardson, Derby, UK, 1830?, 24p, Paper, Story

12037 *The surprising travels and adventures of Baron Munchausen, in Russia, the Caspian Sea, Iceland, Turkey, Egypt...* The Booksellers, London, 1792, 162p, Cloth, Novel

12038 *Tales from the travels of Baron Munchausen.* D. C. Heath, New York, 1900, 78p, Cloth, Novel

12039 *The travels and adventures by sea and land of Baron Munchausen.* G. V. Nickerson, Baltimore, 1834, 90p, Cloth, Novel

12040 *The travels and surprising adventures of Baron Munchausen.* Trübner & Co., London, 1859, 159p, Cloth, Novel

12041 *The travels by sea and land of the renowned Baron Munchausen, including a tour through the United States in the year 1803.* Nafis & Cornish, New York, 1800, 108p, Cloth, Novel

12042 *The travels of Baron Münchausen.* George Vickers, London, 1862, 31p, Cloth, Story

12043 *12 adventures of the celebrated Baron Munchausen.* Peter Lunn, London, 1947, 104p, Cloth, Novel

RATH, E. J., pseud.
   see: BRAINERD, CHAUNCEY and BRAINERD, EDITH

RATHBONE, BASIL, 1892-1967

12044 *Basil Rathbone selects strange tales.* Belmont, New York, 1965, 157p, Paper, Anth. [probably ghost-edited by Lyle Kenyon Engel]

RATHJEN, CARL HENRY, 1909- [*biography included*]

12045 *Land of the giants; flight of fear.* Whitman Publishing Co., Racine, Wisc., 1969, 212p, Cloth, Tele. [Land of the Giants series]

RAUCHER, HERMAN, 1928- [*biography included*]

12046 *Watermelon man.* Ace, New York, 1970, 160p, Paper, Movie

RAVEN, ANTHONY

12047 *The ruby toad; a tale of fantasy.* Bob Lynn, Waldwick, NJ, 1973, 16p, Paper, Story

RAVEN, SIMON (Arthur Noel), 1927-   [*biography included*]

12048   *Doctors wear scarlet; a romantic tale.* Anthony Blond, London, 1960, 240p, Cloth, Novel

RAVN, CLARA IZA von
    see: von RAVN, CLARA IZA

RAY, JAMES

12049   *The scene is changed.* John Heritage, London, 1932, 294p, Cloth, Novel

RAY, JEAN, pseud. [Raymond Jean Marie de Kremer, 1887-1964]

12050   *Ghouls in my grave.* Berkley Medallion, New York, 1965, 143p, Paper, Coll.

RAY, RENE

12051   *The strange world of Planet X.* Herbert Jenkins, London, 1957, 190p, Cloth, Novel
12052   *Wraxton Marne.* John Green, London, 1946, 214p, Cloth, Novel

RAY, ROBERT

12053   *No stars for us.* Digit, London, 1964, 158p, Paper, Novel
12054   *The seedy.* Panther, London, 1969, 159p, Paper, Novel

RAYER, FRANCIS G(eorge), 1921-   [*biography included*]

12055   *Cardinal of the stars.* Digit, London, 1964, 158p, Paper, Novel
12055A retitled: *Journey to the stars.* Arcadia House, New York, 1964, 190p, Cloth, Novel
12056   *The iron and the anger.* Digit, London, 1964, 158p, Paper, Novel
        Journey to the stars. [see 12055A]
12057   *The star seekers.* Tit-Bits Science-Fiction Library, London, 1953, 64p, Paper, Novel
12058   *Tomorrow sometimes comes.* Home & Van Thal, London, 1951, 256p, Cloth, Novel

RAYMOND, ALEX, 1909-1956

12059   *Flash Gordon in the caverns of Mongo.* Grosset & Dunlap, New York, 1937, 219p, Cloth, Novel

RAYMOND, BEN

12060   *The miracle of the foomtra.* E. L. Publishing Co., New York, 1968, 149p, Paper, Novel

RAYMOND, JAMES F., 1826-

12061   *The lost colony.* T. B. Peterson & Bros., Philadelphia, 1891, 413p, Cloth, Novel
12062   *The old mountain hermit.* Broadway Publishing Co., New York, 1904, 304p, Cloth, Novel

RAYMOND, RENE
    see: CHASE, JAMES HADLEY

RAYNER, A(ugustus) A(lfred), 1894-

12063   *The Curry experiment.* R. & L. Locker, Stoke-on-Trent, UK, 1947, 192p, Cloth, Novel

RAYNER, CLAIRE (Berenice), 1931-   [*biography included*]

12064   *The meddlers.* Simon & Schuster, New York, 1970, 314p, Cloth, Novel
12064A retitled: *The baby factory.* Lancer, New York, 1971, 352p, Paper, Novel

RAYNER, WILLIAM

12065   *Stag boy.* Collins, London, 1972, 160p, Cloth, Novel

READ, HERBERT (Edward), 1893-1968

12066   *The Green Child; a romance.* William Heinemann, London, 1935, 256p, Cloth, Novel

READ, OPIE (Percival), 1852-1939

12067   *The son of the swordmaker; a romance.* Laird & Lee, Chicago, 1905, 333p, Paper, Novel

READE, QUINN

12068   *Quest of the Dark Lady.* Belmont, New York, 1969, 140p, Paper, Novel

READER, EMILY E.

12069   *Priestess and queen; a tale of the white race of Mexico, being the adventures of Ignigene and her twenty-six fair maidens.* Longmans, Green, London, 1899, 308p, Cloth, Novel

READY, WILLIAM B(ernard), 1914-   [*biography included*]

12070   *The great disciple, and other stories.* Bruce Publishing Co., Milwaukee, 1951, 158p, Cloth, Coll.
12071   *The Tolkien relation; a personal inquiry.* Henry Regnery, Chicago, 1968, 184p, Cloth, Nonf.
12071A retitled: *Understanding Tolkien and The Lord of the Rings.* Paperback Library, New York, 1969, 96p, Paper, Nonf.

REALMAH
    see: HELPS, ARTHUR

RED DEATH OF MARS

    12072 *Red death of Mars.* American Science Fiction,
           Sydney, 1952, 34p, Paper, Anth.

RED ENGLAND

    12073 *Red England; a tale of the Socialist terror.*
           John Milne, London, 1909, 223p, Cloth, Novel

REE, GERRY de la
    see: de la REE, GERRY

REED, CLIFFORD C(ecil), 1911-   [*biography
included*]

    12074 *Martian enterprise.* Digit, London, 1963,
           160p, Paper, Novel

REED, DAVID V., pseud. [David Vern, 1924-   ]

    12075 *Murder in space; a complete science fiction
           novel.* Galaxy SF Novel, New York, 1954,
           127p, Paper, Novel
    12076 *The thing that made love.* Universal, New
           York, 1952?, 160p, Paper, Novel
    12077 *The whispering gorilla; a novel.* World Dis-
           tributors/Sydney Pemberton, Manchester,
           1950, 160p, Paper, Novel [Tuck states that
           Don Wilcox was an anonymous co-author for
           this book only]

REED, IVY KELLERMAN, 1877-

    12078 *A messenger to the gods.* Vantage Press, New
           York, 1955, 166p, Cloth, Novel

REED, KIT [Lillian Craig Reed, 1932-   ] [*biography included*]

    12079 *Armed camps.* Faber & Faber, London, 1969,
           176p, Cloth, Novel
    12080 *Mr. da V., and other stories.* Faber & Faber,
           London, 1967, 222p, Cloth, Coll.

REED, (Herbert) LANGFORD, 1889-1954, with
Hetty Spiers

    12081 *The mantle of Methuselah; a farcical novel.*
           Rich & Cowan, London, 1939, 288p, Cloth,
           Novel

REED, MYRTLE, 1874-1911

    12082 *The book of clever beasts; studies in unnatu-
           ral history.* G. P. Putnam's Sons, New York,
           1904, 231p, Cloth, Coll.

REED, P(eter) FISHE, 1819-

    12083 *Beyond the snow, being a history of Trim's ad-
           ventures in Nordlichtschein.* Lakeside Press,
           Chicago, 1873, 326p, Cloth, Novel

REED, VAN, house pseud. [see also Dennis Talbot Hughes]

    12084 *Dwellers in space.* Curtis Warren, London,
           1953, 159p, Cloth, Novel
    07559 *House of many changes.* Curtis Warren, London,
           1952, 128p, Cloth, Novel [by Dennis Hughes]

REES, ARTHUR J(ohn), 1872-1942

    12085 *The threshold of fear; a sober fantasy.* Hut-
           chinson, London, 1925, 284p, Cloth, Novel

REES, HELEN
    see: OLIVER, JANE

REEVE, ARTHUR B(enjamin), 1880-1936

    12086 *The adventuress; a Craig Kennedy detective
           story.* Harper & Bros., New York, 1917, 342p,
           Cloth, Novel [Craig Kennedy #12]
    12087 *Atavar; a Craig Kennedy novel.* Harper & Bros.,
           New York, 1924, 360p, Cloth, Novel [Craig
           Kennedy #17]
           The black hand. [see 12104A]
    12088 *The Boy Scouts' Craig Kennedy.* Harper & Bros.,
           New York, 1925, 237p, Cloth, Coll. [Craig
           Kennedy #19]
    12089 *The Clutching Hand; a Craig Kennedy novel.*
           Reilly & Lee, Chicago, 1934, 311p, Cloth,
           Novel [Craig Kennedy #24]
            Craig Kennedy, detective. [see 12110A]
    12090 *Craig Kennedy listens in; adventures of Craig
           Kennedy, scientific detective.* Harper &
           Bros., New York, 1923, 391p, Cloth, Coll.
           [Craig Kennedy #16]
    12091 *Craig Kennedy on the farm.* Harper & Bros.,
           New York, 1925, 359p, Cloth, Coll. [Craig
           Kennedy #20]
            The diamond queen. [see 12105A]
    12092 *The dream doctor; the new adventures of Craig
           Kennedy, scientific detective.* Hearst's In-
           ternational Library, New York, 1914, 379p,
           Cloth, Coll. [Craig Kennedy #3]
    12093 *The ear in the wall.* Hearst's International
           Library, New York, 1916, 341p, Cloth, Novel
           [Craig Kennedy #8]
    12094 *The exploits of Elaine; a detective novel.*
           Hearst's International Library, New York,
           1915, 303p, Cloth, Novel [Elaine #1; Craig
           Kennedy #6]
    12095 *The film mystery.* Harper & Bros., New York,
           1921, 379p, Cloth, Novel [Craig Kennedy #15]
    12096 *The fourteen points; tales of Craig Kennedy,
           master of mystery.* Harper & Bros., New
           York, 1925, 456p, Cloth, Coll. [Craig Ken-
           nedy #18]
    12097 *The gold of the gods; the mystery of the Incas
           solved by Craig Kennedy--scientific detec-
           tive.* Hearst's International Library, New
           York, 1915, 291p, Cloth, Novel [Craig Ken-
           nedy #5]

REEVE, ARTHUR B. (cont.)

12098   *The kidnap club.* Macaulay Co., New York,
        1932, 238p, Cloth, Novel [Craig Kennedy #23]
12099   *The Panama plot; Pan-American adventures of
        Craig Kennedy, scientific detective.* Har-
        per & Bros., New York, 1918, 326p, Cloth,
        Coll. [Craig Kennedy #13]
12100   *Pandora.* Harper & Bros., New York, 1926,
        261p, Cloth, Novel [Craig Kennedy #22]
12101   *The poisoned pen; further adventures of Craig
        Kennedy.* Dodd, Mead, New York, 1913, 399p,
        Cloth, Coll. [Craig Kennedy #2]
12102   *The radio detective.* Grosset & Dunlap, New
        York, 1926, 251p, Cloth, Movie [Craig Ken-
        nedy #21]
12103   *The romance of Elaine; sequel to "Exploits of
        Elaine."* Hearst's International Library,
        New York, 1916, 352p, Cloth, Movie [Elaine
        #2; Craig Kennedy #9]
12104   *The silent bullet; the adventures of Craig
        Kennedy, scientific detective.* Dodd, Mead,
        New York, 1912, 390p, Cloth, Coll. [Craig
        Kennedy #1]
12104A retitled: *The black hand; the adventures of
        Craig Kennedy, scientific detective.* Eve-
        leigh Nash, London, 1912, 339p, Cloth, Coll.
        [Craig Kennedy #1]
12105   *The social gangster; adventures of Craig Ken-
        nedy, scientific detective.* Hearst's Inter-
        national Library, New York, 1916, 342p,
        Cloth, Coll. [Craig Kennedy #7]
12105A retitled: *The diamond queen.* Hodder & Stough-
        ton, London, 1917, 281p, Cloth, Coll. [Craig
        Kennedy #7]
12106   *The soul scar; a Craig Kennedy scientific
        mystery novel.* Harper & Bros., New York,
        1919, 299p, Cloth, Novel [Craig Kennedy #14]
12107   *The stars scream murder; a Craig Kennedy
        Novel.* D. Appleton-Century, New York,
        1936, 307p, Cloth, Novel [Craig Kennedy #26]
12108   *The treasure-train; adventures of Craig Ken-
        nedy, scientific detective, which ultimately
        take him abroad.* Harper & Bros., New York,
        1917, 335p, Cloth, Coll. [Craig Kennedy #11]
12109   *The triumph of Elaine.* Hodder & Stoughton,
        London, 1916, 186p, Cloth, Novel [Elaine #3;
        Craig Kennedy #10]
12110   *The war terror; further adventures with Craig
        Kennedy, scientific detective.* Hearst's
        International Library, New York, 1915, 376p,
        Cloth, Coll. [Craig Kennedy #4]
12110A retitled: *Craig Kennedy, detective.* Simpkin,
        Marshall, Hamilton, Kent, London, 1916, 376p,
        Cloth, Coll. [Craig Kennedy #4]

with Ashley Locke:

12111   *Enter Craig Kennedy.* Macaulay Co., New York,
        1935, 256p, Cloth, Novel [Craig Kennedy
        #25]

REEVE, CLARA, 1729-1807

12112   *The champion of virtue; gothic story,* by the
        editor of The phoenix. W. Keymer, Colches-
        ter, UK, 1777, 190p, Cloth, Novel
12112A retitled: *The old English baron; a gothic
        story.* Edward & Charles Dilly, London,
        1778, 232p, Cloth, Novel

REEVES, JAMES

12113   *Sex teacher, 2000 A.D.* Pad Adult Library,
        , 1972,   , Paper, Novel

REEVES, JAMES [John Morris Reeves, 1909-   ]
[*biography included*]

12114   *The cold flame.* Hamish Hamilton, London, 1967,
        121p, Cloth, Novel
12115   *The strange light.* Heinemann, London, 1964,
        121p, Cloth, Novel

REEVES, JOHN MORRIS
    see: REEVES, JAMES, 1909-

REEVES, WILLIAM

12116   *Satan's Drome.* Robert Hale, London, 1937,
        288p, Cloth, Novel

REFUGE FOR TONIGHT

12117   *Refuge for tonight.* American Science Fiction,
        Sydney, 1953, 34p, Paper, Anth.

REGBERG, S. L.

12118   *Sweet illusions.* Malter Co., Los Angeles,
        1972, 63p, Cloth, Novel

REGINALD, R(obert), pseud. [M. R. Burgess,
1948-   ] [*biography included*]

12119   *Stella nova: the contemporary science fiction
        authors.* Unicorn & Son, Los Angeles, 1970,
        358p, Paper, Nonf. [published anonymously]

REGNAS, C.

12120   *The land of Nison; a novel.* C. W. Daniel,
        London, 1906, 319p, Cloth, Novel

REICH, EMIL, 1854-1910

12121   *Nights with the gods.* T. Werner Laurie, Lon-
        don, 1908, 225p, Cloth, Novel

REID, C. LESTOCK

12122   *Dark destiny.* Philip Allan, London, 1936,
        256p, Cloth, Novel
12123   *Sons of Solomon.* John Long, London, 1931,
        288p, Cloth, Novel
12124   *The trail of Pharaoh's treasure; a romance of
        Africa.* T. Fisher Unwin, London, 1924, 319p
        Cloth, Novel

REID, FORREST, 1876-1947

12125   *Demophon; a traveller's tale.* W. Collins Sons
        London, 1927, 270p, Cloth, Novel

REID, FORREST (cont.)

12126 *Pender among the residents.* W. Collins Sons, London, 1922, 278p, Cloth, Novel

REID, LESLIE (Hartley), 1895-

12127 *Cauldron bubble.* Victor Gollancz, London, 1934, 448p, Cloth, Novel

REID, MAYNE
see: REACH, CHARLES A.

REID, VERA W.

12128 *The silver unicorn.* Aquarian Press, London, 1951, 16p, Paper, Story

REID, WALTER

12129 *Off land's end, homeward bound; or, Christmas Eve on board the "Oberon."* Chas. Griffin, London, 1867, 202p, Cloth, Coll.

REIDA, ALVAH

12130 *Fault lines.* World Publishing Co., New York, 1972, 278p, Cloth, Novel

REIFF, STEPHANIE, with Peter Travers

12131 *The story behind The exorcist.* Crown Publishers, New York, 1974, 245p, Cloth, Nonf.

REIFSNIDER, Mrs. CALVIN K. [Anna Cyrene Reifsnider, 1850-1932]

12132 *Between two worlds.* A. C. Reifsnider Book Co., St. Louis, 1897, 292p, Cloth, Novel

THE REIGN OF GEORGE VI

12133 *The reign of George VI, 1900-1925.* W. Nicoll, London, 1763, 192p, Cloth, Novel

REIN, HAROLD

12134 *Few were left; a novel.* Methuen, London, 1955, 219p, Cloth, Novel; John Day, New York, 1955, 248p, Cloth, Novel

REINEKE, L. THOMAS

12135 *The hormone holocaust; a novel.* Exposition Press, Jericho, NY, 1974, 276p, Cloth, Novel

REISEN, MARX, pseud.

12136 *Before the beginning.* Tit-Bits Science Fiction Library, London, 1954, 64p, Paper, Novel

REITMEISTER, LOUIS AARON, 1903-1975 [*biography included*]

12137 *If tomorrow comes; a tale of two worlds.* Walden Press, New York, 1934, 348p, Cloth, Novel

REIZENSTEIN, ELMER L.
see: RICE, ELMER L.

REMENHAM, JOHN, pseud. [John Alexander Vlasto, 1877-1958]

12138 *The peacemaker.* Macdonald, London, 1947, 256p, Cloth, Novel

RENARD, MAURICE, 1875-1939

12139 *The flight of the Aerofix.* Stellar Publishing Corp., New York, 1932, 24p, Paper, Story
12140 *The hands of Orlac.* E. P. Dutton, New York, 1929, 337p, Cloth, Novel
12141 *New bodies for old.* Macaulay Co., New York, 1923, 308p, Cloth, Novel

with Albert Jean:

07865 *Blind circle.* E. P. Dutton, New York, 1928, 324p, Cloth, Novel

RENN, THOMAS EDWARD
see: STRIKE, JEREMY

RENNIE, J(ames) ALAN, 1899-1969 [*biography included*]

12142 *The footstool of the Moon.* Hurst & Blackett, London, 1938, 254p, Cloth, Novel

REPP, ED(ward) EARL, 1900- [*biography included*]

12143 *The radium pool.* Fantasy Publishing Co., Los Angeles, 1949, 188p, Cloth, Coll.
12144 *The stellar missiles.* Fantasy Publishing Corp., Los Angeles, 1949, 192p, Cloth, Coll.

RESNICK, MICHAEL D(iamond), 1942- [*biography included*]

12145 *The forgotten sea of Mars.* Camille E. Cazedessus, Jr., Baton Rouge, LA, 1965, 26p, Paper, Story [a sequel to Burroughs's Mars series]
12146 *The Goddess of Ganymede.* Donald M. Grant, West Kingston, RI, 1967, 246p, Cloth, Novel [Ganymede #1]
12147 *Pursuit on Ganymede.* Paperback Library, New York, 1968, 144p, Paper, Novel [Ganymede #2]
12148 *Redbeard.* Lancer, New York, 1969, 192p, Paper, Novel

RESSICH, JOHN (Sellar Matheson), with Eric de Banzie as Gregory Baxter

03954 *Blue lightning.* Cassell, London, 1926, 329p, Cloth, Novel

RETTIG, HELEN, with Gourgen Yanikian

12149 *Mirror in the darkness; a novel.* Exposition
       Press, New York, 1966, 197p, Cloth, Novel

REVELATIONS OF THE DEAD-ALIVE
    see: BANIM, JOHN

REVERMORT, J. A., pseud. [John Adam Cramb,
1862-1913]

12150 *Lucius Scarfield; a philosophical romance of
       the twentieth century.* Archibald Constable,
       London, 1908, 574p, Cloth, Novel

THE REVOLT OF MAN
    see: BESANT, WALTER

THE REVOLT OF THE BEES
    see: MORGAN, JOHN M.

REVOLUTIONIST, EX-
    see: EX-REVOLUTIONIST

REY, JUDY-LYNN del
    see: del REY, JUDY-LYNN

REY, LESTER del
    see: del REY, LESTER

REY, RUSSELL, house pseud. [see also Dennis
Talbot Hughes]

07560 *The Queen People.* Curtis Warren, London,
       1952, 127p, Cloth, Novel [by Dennis Talbot
       Hughes]
12151 *Valley of terror.* Curtis Warren, London,
       1953, 159p, Cloth, Novel

REYNA, JORGE de, pseud.
    see: DETZER, DIANE

REYNARD, ELIZABETH, 1898?-1962

12152 *The mutinous wind.* Houghton Mifflin, Boston,
       1951, 210p, Cloth, Novel

REYNOLDS, BONNIE JONES

12153 *The truth about unicorns.* Stein & Day, New
       York, 1972, 369p, Cloth, Novel

REYNOLDS, DALLAS McCORD
    see: REYNOLDS, MACK

REYNOLDS, GEORGE W(illiam) M(acArthur), 1814-
1879

12154 *The coral island; or, The hereditary curse.*
       John Dicks, London, 1849, 308p, Cloth, Novel

12155 *Faust; a romance of the secret tribunals.* G.
       Vickers, London, 1847, 218p, Cloth, Novel
12156 *The necromancer; a romance.* John Dicks, Lon-
       don, 1857, 264p, Cloth, Novel
12157 *The pixy; or, The unbaptized child; a story
       for Christmas.* John Dicks, London, 1860?,
       26p, Paper, Story
12158 *Wagner, the wehr-wolf.* John Dicks, London,
       1848, 186p, Cloth, Novel

REYNOLDS, JOHN MURRAY, 1901-

12159 *The private life of Henry Perkins.* Thomas Y.
       Crowell, New York, 1947, 181p, Cloth, Novel

REYNOLDS, JOSEPH

12160 *Operation: sextrip.* Orpheus Series, New York,
       1970, 188p, Paper, Novel

REYNOLDS, MACK [Dallas McCord Reynolds,
1917-   ] [*biography included*]

12161 *After some tomorrow.* Belmont, New York, 1967,
       158p, Paper, Novel
12162 *Blackman's burden.* Ace Double, New York, 1972,
       137p, Paper, Novel [Homer Crawford series]
12163 *Border, breed, nor birth.* Ace Double, New
       York, 1972, 150p, Paper, Novel [Homer Craw-
       ford series]
12164 *The case of the little green men.* Phoenix
       Press, New York, 1951, 224p, Cloth, Novel
       [a mystery set among SF fans]
12165 *Code duello.* Ace Double, New York, 1968, 141p,
       Paper, Novel [Planetary Agent #4]
12166 *Commune 2000 A.D.* Bantam, New York, 1974,
       183p, Paper, Novel
12167 *Computer war.* Ace Double, New York, 1967,
       111p, Paper, Novel
12168 *Computer world.* Curtis, New York, 1970, 190p,
       Paper, Novel
12169 *The cosmic eye.* Belmont, New York, 1969,
       157p, Paper, Novel
12170 *Dawnman planet.* Ace Double, New York, 1966,
       123p, Paper, Novel [Planetary Agent #2]
12171 *Depression or bust; and, Dawnman planet.* Ace,
       New York, 1974, 313p, Paper, Coll.
       Earth unaware. [see 12175A]
12172 *The Earth war.* Pyramid, New York, 1963, 141p,
       Paper, Novel [Joe Mauser #2]
12173 *Looking backward, from the year 2000.* Ace,
       New York, 1973, 237p, Paper, Novel [a res-
       ponse to Bellamy's novel]
12174 *Mercenary from tomorrow.* Ace Double, New
       York, 1968, 131p, Paper, Novel [Joe Mauser
       #1]
12175 *Of godlike power.* Belmont, New York, 1966,
       174p, Paper, Novel
12175A retitled: *Earth unaware.* Belmont, New York,
       1968, 174p, Paper, Novel
12176 *Once departed.* Curtis, New York, 1970, 128p,
       Paper, Novel
12177 *Planetary Agent X.* Ace Double, New York, 1965,
       133p, Paper, Novel [Planetary Agent #1]
12178 *The rival Rigelians.* Ace Double, New York,
       1967, 132p, Paper, Novel [Planetary Agent #3]
12179 *The rival Rigelians; Planetary Agent X.* Ace,
       New York, 1974, 265p, Paper, Coll. [Plane-
       tary Agent #s 1 & 3]

REYNOLDS, MACK (cont.)

12180 *The space barbarians.* Ace Double, New York,
       1969, 162p, Paper, Novel
12181 *Space pioneer.* Four Square, London, 1966,
       160p, Paper, Novel
12182 *Star trek; mission to Horatius.* Whitman Pub-
       lishing Co., Racine, Wisc., 1968, 210p,
       Cloth, Tele. [Star Trek series]
12183 *Time gladiator.* Four Square, London, 1966,
       157p, Paper, Novel [Joe Mauser #3]

with Fredric Brown:

01977 *Science-fiction carnival; fun in science-fic-*
       tion. Shasta Publishers, Chicago, 1953,
       315p, Cloth, Anth.

REYNOLDS, PAMELA, 1923-   [biography included]

12184 *Earth times two.* Lothrop, Lee & Shepard, New
       York, 1970, 160p, Cloth, Novel

REYNOLDS, PHILIP, pseud., 1916-

12185 *When and if; a novel.* William Sloane Associ-
       ates, New York, 1952, 246p, Cloth, Novel
12185A retitled: *It happened like this.* Eyre &
       Spottiswoode, London, 1953, 191p, Cloth,
       Novel

REYNOLDS, STEPHEN (Sydney), 1881-1919

12186 *The holy mountain; a satire on tendencies.*
       John Lane, The Bodley Head, London, 1909,
       309p, Cloth, Novel

REYNOLDS, WALTER DOTY
    see: PRIME, Lord

RHEINGOLD, HOWARD

12187 *Jack Anderson against Dr. Tek!* Freeway Press,
       New York, 1974, 215p, Paper, Novel [Savage
       Report #1]
12188 *Mama Liz drinks deep.* Venus Freeway Press,
       New York, 1973, 186p, Paper, Novel [Sister-
       hood Trilogy #1]
12189 *Mama Liz tastes flesh.* Venus Freeway Press,
       New York, 1973, 180p, Paper, Novel [Sister-
       hood Trilogy #2]
12190 *Secret sisterhood.* Venus Freeway Press, New
       York, 1973,   , Paper, Novel [Sisterhood
       Trilogy #3]
12191 *War of the gurus.* Freeway Press, New York,
       1974, 210p, Paper, Novel [Savage Report #2]

RHODES, H. HENRY

12192 *Where men have walked; a story of the Lucayos.*
       C. M. Clark Publishing Co., Boston, 1909,
       294p, Cloth, Novel

RHODES, W(illiam) H(enry), 1822-1876

12193 *The case of Summerfield.* Paul Elder, San
       Francisco, 1907, 54p, Cloth, Novel

12194 *Caxton's book; a collection of essays, poems,*
       tales, and sketches. A. L. Bancroft, San
       Francisco, 1876, 300p, Cloth, Coll.

RHYS, ERNEST, 1859-1946

12195 *The garden of romance; romantic tales of all*
       times. New Amsterdam Book Co., New York,
       1897, 238p, Cloth, Anth.
12196 *The haunters & the haunted; ghost stories*
       and tales of the supernatural. Daniel O'Con-
       nor, London, 1921, 395p, Cloth, Anth.

with C. A. Dawson-Scott:

12197 *Tales of mystery; startling stories of the*
       supernatural. Hutchinson, London, 1927,
       287p, Cloth, Anth.
12198 *26 mystery stories old and new, by twenty and*
       six authors. D. Appleton, New York, 1927,
       310p, Cloth, Anth.

RICCI, BARBARA GUIGNON

12199 *The year of the rats.* Walker, New York, 1973,
       275p, Cloth, Novel

RICE, ELMER (Leopold), 1892-1967 [name originally Elmer Leopold Reizenstein] [biography
included]

12200 *A voyage to Purilia.* Cosmopolitan Book Corp.,
       New York, 1930, 298p, Cloth, Novel

RICE, HARRY E.

12201 *Eve and the evangelist; a romance of A.D. 2108.*
       Roxburgh Publishing Co., Boston, 1908, 224p,
       Cloth, Novel

RICE, JAMES, 1843-1882, with Walter Besant

01214 *The case of Mr. Lucraft, and other tales,* by
       the authors of "Ready-money Mortiboy." Samp-
       son Low, Marston, Searle & Rivington, London,
       1876, 2vol, Cloth, Coll.
01214A *The case of Mr. Lucraft, and other tales,* by
       Walter Besant and James Rice. Chatto & Win-
       dus, London, 1877, 341p, Cloth, Coll.

RICE, JEFF

12202 *The night stalker.* Pocket Books, New York,
       1973, 192p, Paper, Tele. [Kolchak #1]
12203 *The night strangler.* Pocket Books, New York,
       1974, 160p, Paper, Tele. [Kolchak #2]

RICHARDS, ANNA M(atlock) Jr.

12204 *A new Alice in the old Wonderland.* J. B. Lip-
       pincott, Philadelphia, 1895, 309p, Cloth,
       Novel [Alice series]

RICHARDS, CHARLES NAPIER

12205 *Atalanta; or, Twelve months in the Evening Star.* H. & C. Treacher, Brighton, UK, 1909, 271p, Cloth, Novel

RICHARDS, DICK
    see: WELLS, BARRY

RICHARDS, GUY, 1905-   [*biography included*]

12206 *Two rubles to Times Square.* Duell, Sloan & Pearce, New York, 1956, 249p, Cloth, Novel
12206A retitled: *Brother Bear.* Michael Joseph, London, 1957, 206p, Cloth, Novel

RICHARDS, HARVEY D.

12207 *Sorak and the clouded tiger; or, How the terrible ruler of the north is hunted and destroyed.* Cupples & Leon, New York, 1934, 201p, Cloth, Novel [Sorak #2]
12208 *Sorak and the Sultan's ankus; or, How a perilous journey leads to a kingdom of giants.* Cupples & Leon, New York, 1934, 206p, Cloth, Novel [Sorak #3]
12209 *Sorak and the tree-men; or, How Sorak and his friend escape from their captives.* Cupples & Leon, New York, 1936, 208p, Cloth, Novel [Sorak #4]
12210 *Sorak of the Malay jungle; or, How two young Americans face death and win a friend.* Cupples & Leon, New York, 1934, 206p, Cloth, Novel [Sorak #1]

RICHARDS, HENRY, pseud.
    see: MORRISSEY, J. L.

RICHARDS, LAURA E(lizabeth), 1850-1943

12211 *The silver crown; another book of fables.* Little, Brown, Boston, 1906, 105p, Cloth, Coll.

RICHARDS, LYSANDER SALMON, 1835-1926

12212 *Breaking up; or, The birth, development, and death of the Earth and its satellite in story.* J. E. Farwell, Boston, 1896, 247p, Cloth, Novel

RICHARDS, R. P. J.

12213 *The blonde goddess.* Ken-Pax Publishing Co., London, 1948, 237p, Cloth, Novel

RICHARDS, TAD

12214 *Blazing saddles.* Warner Paperback Library, New York, 1974, 175p, Paper, Movie

RICHARDSON, (Sir) BENJAMIN WARD, 1828-1896

12215 *The son of a star; a romance of the second century.* Longmans, Green, London, 1888, 3vol, Cloth, Novel

RICHARDSON, DALE

12216 *Starfire.* Vantage Press, New York, 1958, 105p, Cloth, Novel

RICHARDSON, E.

12217 *Neutopia.* Simpkin, Marshall, Hamilton, Kent, London, 1925, 304p, Cloth, Novel

RICHARDSON, FRANK (Collins), 1870-1917

12218 *The secret kingdom.* Duckworth, London, 1905, 340p, Cloth, Novel

RICHARDSON, MAURICE (Lane), 1907-

12219 *Novels of mystery from the Victorian age; four complete unabridged novels.* Pilot Press, London, 1945, 678p, Cloth, Anth.
12220 *A strong man needed.* W. Collins Sons, London, 1931, 252p, Cloth, Novel

RICHARDSON, ROBERT S(hirley), 1902-   [*biography included*]

12221 *Second satellite.* Whittlesey House, New York, 1956, 192p, Cloth, Novel

as Philip Latham:

12222 *Five against Venus.* John C. Winston, Philadelphia, 1952, 214p, Cloth, Novel
12223 *Missing men of Saturn.* John C. Winston, Philadelphia, 1953, 215p, Cloth, Novel

RICHARDSON, WARREN

12224 *Dr. Zell and the Princess Charlotte; an autobiographical relation of adventures in the life of a distinguished modern necromancer, seer, and theosophist.* L. Kabis, New York, 1892, 342p, Cloth, Novel

RICHER, CLÉMENT

12225 *Son of Ti-Coyo.* Rupert Hart-Davis, London, 1954, 143p, Cloth, Novel [Ti-Coyo #2]
12226 *Ti-Coyo and his shark; an immoral fable.* Rupert Hart-Davis, London, 1951, 184p, Cloth, Novel [Ti-Coyo #1]

RICHMOND, LEIGH [*biography included*], with Walt Richmond

12227 *Gallagher's glacier.* Ace Double, New York, 1970, 106p, Paper, Novel
12228 *The lost millennium.* Ace Double, New York, 1967, 137p, Paper, Novel

RICHMOND, LEIGH (cont.), with Walt Richmond

12229 *Phoenix ship.* Ace Double, New York, 1969,
106p, Paper, Novel
12230 *Positive charge.* Ace Double, New York, 1970,
148p, Paper, Coll.
12231 *Shock wave.* Ace Double, New York, 1967, 127p,
Paper, Novel

RICHMOND, MARY

12232 *The grim tomorrow.* Wright & Brown, London,
1953, 224p, Cloth, Novel
12233 *The valley of doom.* Wright & Brown, London,
1947, 190p, Cloth, Novel

RICHMOND, WALT(er F.), 1922-1977 [*biography
included*], with Leigh Richmond

12227 *Gallagher's glacier.* Ace Double, New York,
1970, 106p, Paper, Novel
12228 *The lost millennium.* Ace Double, New York,
1967, 137p, Paper, Novel
12229 *Phoenix ship.* Ace Double, New York, 1969,
106p, Paper, Novel
12230 *Positive charge.* Ace Double, New York, 1970,
148p, Paper, Coll.
12231 *Shock wave.* Ace Double, New York, 1967, 127p,
Paper, Novel

RICHTER, CONRAD (Michael), 1890-1968

12234 *The waters of Kronos.* Alfred A. Knopf, New
York, 1960, 176p, Cloth, Novel

RICHTER, EUGENE [Eugen Richter, 1838-1906]

12235 *Pictures of the Socialist future (freely adapted from Bebel).* Swan Sonnenschein, London,
1893, 134p, Cloth, Novel
12235A retitled: *Pictures of the future; an experiment in a modern social world, and what
came of it.* Optimus Printing Co., New York,
1894, 190p, Paper, Novel

RICKETT, JOSEPH COMPTON-
see: COMPTON-RICKETT, JOSEPH

RICO, DON

12236 *Lorelei.* Belmont, New York, 1966, 157p,
Paper, Novel

RIDDELL, Mrs. J. H. [Charlotte Eliza Lawson
Riddell, 1832-1906]

12237 *The uninhabited house.* George Routledge &
Sons, London, 1876, 96p, Paper, Novel
12238 *The uninhabited house; and, The haunted river.*
George Routledge & Sons, London, 1883, 364p,
Cloth, Coll.
12239 *Weird stories.* J. Hogg, London, 1884, 314p,
Cloth, Coll.

RIDLER, ANNE (Barbara), 1912- [*biography included*]

12240 *Best ghost stories.* Faber & Faber, London,
1945, 360p, Cloth, Anth.

RIDLEY, F(rancis) A(mbrose)

12241 *The green machine,* by F. H. Ridley. Noel Douglas, London, 1926, 255p, Cloth, Novel

RIDLEY, JAMES, 1736-1765
as Sir Charles Morell:

12242 *The tales of the genii; or, The delightful lessons of Horam, the son of Asmar, faithfully
translated from the Persian manuscript, and
compared with the French and Spanish editions
published at Paris and Madrid.* J. Wilkie,
London, 1764, 2vol, Cloth, Coll.

published anonymously:

12242A retitled: *Selected tales of the genii, re-
vised, purified, and in part re-modeled.*
Parker, Son & Bourn, London, 1861, 352p,
Cloth, Coll. [abridged]

RIEFE, ALAN, 1925- [*biography included*]

12243 *Tales of horror.* Pocket Books, New York, 1965,
63p, Paper, Coll.

RIENOW, LEONA TRAIN

12244 *The bewitched caverns.* Charles Scribner's
Sons, New York, 1948, 151p, Cloth, Novel
12245 *The dark pool.* Charles Scribner's Sons, New
York, 1949, 149p, Cloth, Novel [a sequel to
12244]

with Robert Rienow:

12246 *The year of the last eagle.* Ballantine, New
York, 1970, 246p, Paper, Novel

RIENOW, ROBERT, 1909- [*biography included*],
with Leona Train Rienow

12246 *The year of the last eagle.* Ballantine, New
York, 1970, 246p, Paper, Novel

RILEY, FRANK, with Mark Clifton

03093 *They'd rather be right.* Gnome Press, New York,
1957, 189p, Cloth, Novel
03093A retitled: *The forever machine.* Galaxy Publishing Corp., New York, 1958, 159p, Paper,
Novel

RIMEL, DUANE
see: WELDON, REX

RIMMER, ROBERT H(enry), 1917- [*biography included*]

12247 *The Zolotov affair; a novel.* Sherbourne Press,
Los Angeles, 1967, 191p, Cloth, Novel

RINKOFF, BARBARA, d. 1975

12248 *Elbert, the mind reader.* Lothrop, Lee & Shepard, New York, 1967, 112p, Cloth, Novel

RIOS, (Marie) TERE(sa), 1917-   [*biography included*]

12249 *The fifteenth pelican.* Doubleday, Garden City, 1965, 118p, Cloth, Novel [Flying Nun series]
12249A retitled: *The flying nun.* Doubleday, Garden City, 1968?, 120p, Cloth, Novel [Flying Nun series]

RIPLEY, B. K.

12250 *Who's that lady in the president's bed?* Dodd, Mead, New York, 1972, 282p, Cloth, Novel

RISSE, HEINZ, 1898-

12251 *The earthquake.* Farrar, Straus & Young, New York, 1953, 254p, Cloth, Novel; Secker & Warburg, London, 1953, 254p, Cloth, Novel

RITTENBERG, MAX, 1880-

12252 *The mind-reader, being some pages from the strange life of Dr. Xavier Wycherley.* D. Appleton, New York, 1913, 325p, Cloth, Novel

RIVA, VALERIA, with Ornella Volta

12253 *The vampire; an anthology.* Neville Spearman, London, 1963, 286p, Cloth, Anth. [this book should not be confused with *The vampire* (Tandem Books, London, 1965), by the same authors, which is nonfiction]

RIVERE, ALEC, pseud.
  see: NUETZEL, CHARLES

RIVES, AMÉLIE, 1863-1945

12254 *The ghost garden; a novel.* Frederick A. Stokes, New York, 1918, 299p, Cloth, Novel

ROBB, JOHN, pseud. [Norman Robson]

12255 *Space beam.* Hamilton & Co. (Stafford), London, 1951, 111p, Paper, Novel

ROBBE-GRILLET, ALAIN, 1922-   [*biography included*]

12256 *Project for a revolution in New York; a novel.* Grove Press, New York, 1972, 183p, Cloth, Novel

ROBBINS, TOD [Clarence Aaron Robbins, 1888-1949]

12257 *Silent, white, and beautiful, and other stories.* Boni & Liveright, New York, 1920, 256p, Cloth, Coll.

12258 *Who wants a green bottle? and other uneasy tales.* Philip Allan, London, 1926, 280p, Cloth, Coll.

ROBBINS, TOM [Thomas E. Robbins]

12259 *Another roadside attraction.* Doubleday, Garden City, 1971, 400p, Cloth, Novel

ROBERTS, ALARIC J.

12260 *New trade winds for the seven seas.* J. F. Rowny Press, Santa Barbara, CA, 1942, 411p, Cloth, Novel

with Donald M. MacDonald:

09420 *You do take it with you.* Vantage Press, New York, 1953, 161p, Cloth, Novel

ROBERTS, ARTHUR, with John Glasby

as Berl Cameron, house pseud.:

02466 *Cosmic Echelon.* Curtis Warren, London, 1952, 128p, Cloth, Novel [Terran Empire series]
02471 *Sphero Nova.* Curtis Warren, London, 1952, 159p, Cloth, Novel

as Rand Le Page, house pseud.:

06023 *Satellite B.C.* Curtis Warren, London, 1952, 127p, Paper, Novel
06024 *Time and space.* Curtis Warren, London, 1952, 128p, Cloth, Novel [Terran Empire series]
06025 *Zero Point.* Curtis Warren, London, 1952, 128p, Cloth, Novel

as Paul Lorraine, house pseud.:

06026 *Zenith-D.* Curtis Warren, London, 1952, 159p, Cloth, Novel

ROBERTS, C(harles) B(lanton), 1874-

12261 *The second man.* Fleming H. Revell, New York, 1939, 285p, Cloth, Novel

ROBERTS, CECIL (Edric Mornington), 1892-1976 [*biography included*]

12262 *Eight for eternity.* Hodder & Stoughton, London, 1947, 318p, Cloth, Novel

ROBERTS, CHARLES G(eorge) D(ouglas), 1860-1943

12263 *In the morning of time.* Hutchinson, London, 1919, 319p, Cloth, Novel

ROBERTS, COLIN

12264 *Nuclear subtraction.* Digit, London, 1963, 159p, Paper, Novel

ROBERTS, ELEANOR, with Jeanne A'Dair

00038 *Once upon a summertime; a story with lyrics for children.* Exposition Press, New York, 1951, 139p, Cloth, Novel

ROBERTS, J. W.

12265 *Looking within; the misleading tendencies of "Looking backward" made manifest.* A. S. Barnes, New York, 1893, 279p, Cloth, Novel [a response to Bellamy's novel]

ROBERTS, JAMES HALL, pseud. [Robert Lipscomb Duncan, 1927-]

12266 *The burning sky.* William Morrow, New York, 1966, 318p, Cloth, Novel

ROBERTS, JANE, 1929- [*biography included*]

12267 *The education of Oversoul Seven.* Prentice-Hall, Englewood Cliffs, NJ, 1973, 226p, Cloth, Novel
12268 *The rebellers.* Ace Double, New York, 1963, 155p, Paper, Novel

ROBERTS, JANET LOUISE, 1925-

12269 *Isle of the dolphins.* Avon, New York, 1973, 190p, Paper, Novel

as Louisa Bronte:

12270 *Her demon lover.* Avon, New York, 1973, 156p, Paper, Novel
12271 *Lord Satan.* Avon, New York, 1972, 159p, Paper, Novel

ROBERTS, KEITH (John Kingston), 1935- [*biography included*]

12272 *Anita.* Ace, New York, 1970, 221p, Paper, Coll.
12273 *The chalk giants.* Hutchinson, London, 1974, 271p, Cloth, Novel
12274 *The Furies.* Berkley Medallion, New York, 1966, 192p, Paper, Novel
12275 *The inner wheel.* Rupert Hart-Davis, London, 1970, 203p, Cloth, Novel
12276 *Machines and men; science fiction stories.* Hutchinson, London, 1973, 288p, Cloth, Coll.
12277 *Pavane.* Doubleday, Garden City, 1968, 279p, Cloth, Coll.
12278 *Pavane.* Ace, New York, 1969, 285p, Paper, Coll. [expanded]

ROBERTS, LIONEL, pseud.
 see: FANTHORPE, R. LIONEL

ROBERTS, MORLEY, 1857-1942

12279 *Midsummer madness.* Eveleigh Nash, London, 1909, 255p, Cloth, Coll.

ROBERTS, PAUL K.

12280 *To bring the judgment.* Vantage Press, New York, 1969, 279p, Cloth, Novel

ROBERTS, TERENCE, pseud. [Ivan Terence Sanderson, 1911-1973] [*biography included*]

12281 *Report on the status quo.* Merlin Press, New York, 1955, 63p, Cloth, Novel

ROBERTS, (George Edward) THEODORE, 1877-1953 [later changed name to George Edward Theodore Goodridge Roberts]

12282 *The red feathers; a story of remarkable adventures when the Earth was young.* L. C. Page, Boston, 1907, 325p, Cloth, Novel

ROBERTS, W(alter) ADOLPHE, 1886-1962

12283 *The mind reader; a mystery.* Macaulay Co., New York, 1929, 277p, Cloth, Novel

ROBERTSON, ALICE ABERTHE
 see: ST. LUZ, BERTHE

ROBERTSON, FRANCES FORBES

12284 *The devil's pronoun, and other phantasies.* Reeves & Turner, London, 1894, 122p, Cloth, Coll.

ROBERTSON, MORGAN (Andrew), 1861-1915

12285 *Over the border.* McClure's Magazine & Metropolitan Magazine, New York, 1914?, 263p, Cloth, Coll.

ROBERTSON, W. C., with H. Bedford-Jones

01030 *The Temple of the Ten.* Donald M. Grant, Publisher, West Kingston, RI, 1973, 159p, Cloth, Novel

ROBESON, ANNA WEBER

12286 *Fleshpots.* Margent Press, New York, 1937, 121p, Cloth, Novel

ROBESON, KENNETH, house pseud. [see also: Lester Dent, Norman Daniels, Paul Ernst, Ron Goulart, and Alan Hathaway]

04132 *The Annihilist; a Doc Savage adventure.* Bantam, New York, 1968, 138p, Paper, Novel [Doc Savage #31] [by Lester Dent]
06179 *The Avenger; black chariots.* Warner Paperback Library, New York, 1974, 142p, Paper, Novel [Avenger #30] [by Ron Goulart]
04915 *The Avenger; death in slow motion.* Warner Paperback Library, New York, 1973, 158p, Paper, Novel [Avenger #18] [by Paul Ernst]
04916 *The Avenger; Nevlo.* Warner Paperback Library, New York, 1973, 159p, Paper, Novel [Avenger #17] [by Paul Ernst]
06180 *The Avenger; red moon.* Warner Paperback Library, New York, 1974, 158p, Paper, Novel [Avenger #26] [by Ron Goulart]

ROBESON, KENNETH (cont.)

04917 *The Avenger; river of ice.* Warner Paperback Library, New York, 1973, 157p, Paper, Novel [Avenger #11] [by Paul Ernst]

04918 *The Avenger; tuned for murder.* Warner Paperback Library, New York, 1973, 158p, Paper, Novel [Avenger #9] [by Paul Ernst]

04919 *The Avenger; the black death.* Warner Paperback Library, New York, 1974, 158p, Paper, Novel [Avenger #22] [by Paul Ernst]

04920 *The Avenger; the flame breathers.* Warner Paperback Library, New York, 1973, 157p, Paper, Novel [Avenger #12] [by Paul Ernst]

04921 *The Avenger; the frosted death.* Warner Paperback Library, New York, 1972, 157p, Paper, Novel [Avenger #5] [by Paul Ernst]

04922 *The Avenger; the green killer.* Warner Paperback Library, New York, 1974, 158p, Paper, Novel [Avenger #20] [by Paul Ernst]

04923 *The Avenger; the hate master.* Warner Paperback Library, New York, 1973, 158p, Paper, Novel [Avenger #16] [by Paul Ernst]

06181 *The Avenger; the purple zombie.* Warner Paperback Library, New York, 1974, 141p, Paper, Novel [Avenger #27] [by Ron Goulart]

04924 *The Avenger; the sky walker.* Warner Paperback Library, New York, 1972, 156p, Paper, Novel [Avenger #3] [by Paul Ernst]

03794 *The black spot; a Doc Savage adventure.* Bantam, New York, 1974, 152p, Paper, Novel [Doc Savage #76] [by Norman Daniels]

04133 *Brand of the werewolf; a Doc Savage adventure.* Bantam, New York, 1965, 138p, Paper, Novel [Doc Savage #5] [by Lester Dent]

03795 *Cold death; a Doc Savage adventure.* Bantam, New York, 1968, 121p, Paper, Novel [Doc Savage #21] [by Norman Daniels]

04134 *The crimson serpent; a Doc Savage adventure.* Bantam, New York, 1974, 138p, Paper, Novel [Doc Savage #78] [by Lester Dent]

04135 *The czar of fear; a Doc Savage adventure.* Bantam, New York, 1968, 140p, Paper, Novel [Doc Savage #22] [by Lester Dent]

04136 *The dagger in the sky; a Doc Savage adventure.* Bantam, New York, 1969, 120p, Paper, Novel [Doc Savage #40] [by Lester Dent]

04137 *The deadly dwarf; a Doc Savage adventure.* Bantam, New York, 1968, 115p, Paper, Novel [Doc Savage #28] [by Lester Dent]

04138 *Death in silver; a Doc Savage adventure.* Bantam, New York, 1968, 134p, Paper, Novel [Doc Savage #26] [by Lester Dent]

04139 *The derrick devil; a Doc Savage adventure.* Bantam, New York, 1973, 138p, Paper, Novel [Doc Savage #74] [by Lester Dent]

04140 *The devil Genghis.* Bantam, New York, 1974, 149p, Paper, Novel [Doc Savage #79] [by Lester Dent]

04141 *Devil on the Moon; a Doc Savage adventure.* Bantam, New York, 1970, 120p, Paper, Novel [Doc Savage #50] [by Lester Dent]

06913 *The devil's playground; a Doc Savage adventure.* Bantam, New York, 1968, 119p, Paper, Novel [Doc Savage #25] [by Alan Hathaway]

04142 *Dust of death; a Doc Savage adventure.* Bantam, New York, 1969, 139p, Paper, Novel [Doc Savage #32] [by Lester Dent]

04143 *The fantastic island; a Doc Savage adventure.* Bantam, New York, 1966, 135p, Paper, Novel [Doc Savage #14] [by Lester Dent]

04144 *Fear Cay; a Doc Savage adventure.* Bantam, New York, 1966, 138p, Paper, Novel [Doc Savage #11] [by Lester Dent]

04145 *The Feathered Octopus; a Doc Savage adventure.* Bantam, New York, 1970, 122p, Paper, Novel [Doc Savage #48] [by Lester Dent]

04146 *The flaming falcons; a Doc Savage adventure.* Bantam, New York, 1968, 118p, Paper, Novel [Doc Savage #30] [by Lester Dent]

04147 *Fortress of Solitude; a Doc Savage adventure.* Bantam, New York, 1968, 116p, Paper, Novel [Doc Savage #23] [by Lester Dent]

04148 *The freckled shark; a Doc Savage adventure.* Bantam, New York, 1972, 138p, Paper, Novel [Doc Savage #67] [by Lester Dent]

04149 *The giggling ghosts; a Doc Savage adventure.* Bantam, New York, 1971, 123p, Paper, Novel [Doc Savage #56] [by Lester Dent]

04150 *The gold ogre; a Doc Savage adventure.* Bantam, New York, 1969, 122p, Paper, Novel [Doc Savage #42] [by Lester Dent]

04151 *The golden peril; a Doc Savage adventure.* Bantam, New York, 1970, 138p, Paper, Novel [Doc Savage #55] [by Lester Dent]

04152 *The green death; a Doc Savage adventure.* Bantam, New York, 1971, 138p, Paper, Novel [Doc Savage #65] [by Lester Dent]

04153 *The green eagle; a Doc Savage adventure.* Bantam, New York, 1968, 114p, Paper, Novel [Doc Savage #24] [by Lester Dent]

03796 *Haunted ocean; a Doc Savage adventure.* Bantam, New York, 1970, 140p, Paper, Novel [Doc Savage #51] [by Norman Daniels]

03797 *He could stop the world; a Doc Savage adventure.* Bantam, New York, 1970, 140p, Paper, Novel [Doc Savage #54] [by Norman Daniels]

04154 *Hex; a Doc Savage adventure.* Bantam, New York, 1969, 120p, Paper, Novel [Doc Savage #37] [by Lester Dent]

04155 *Land of always-night; a Doc Savage adventure.* Bantam, New York, 1966, 138p, Paper, Novel [Doc Savage #13] [by Lester Dent]

04156 *The land of fear; a Doc Savage adventure.* Bantam, New York, 1973, 136p, Paper, Novel [Doc Savage #75] [by Lester Dent]

03798 *Land of long juju; a Doc Savage adventure.* Bantam, New York, 1970, 140p, Paper, Novel [Doc Savage #47] [by Norman Daniels]

04157 *The land of terror; Doc Savage and his pals in a novel of unusual adventure.* Street & Smith, New York, 1933, 252p, Cloth, Novel [Doc Savage #2 (old series), #8 (new series)] [by Lester Dent]

04158 *The living fire menace; a Doc Savage adventure.* Bantam, New York, 1971, 120p, Paper, Novel [Doc Savage #61] [by Lester Dent]

04159 *The lost oasis; a Doc Savage adventure.* Bantam, New York, 1965, 123p, Paper, Novel [Doc Savage #6] [by Lester Dent]

03799 *Mad eyes; a Doc Savage adventure.* Bantam, New York, 1969, 120p, Paper, Novel [Doc Savage #34] [by Norman Daniels]

04160 *Mad Mesa; a Doc Savage adventure.* Bantam, New York, 1972, 122p, Paper, Novel [Doc Savage #66] [by Lester Dent]

04161 *The Majii; a Doc Savage adventure.* Bantam, New York, 1971, 140p, Paper, Novel [Doc Savage #60] [by Lester Dent]

04162 *The man of bronze; Doc Savage and his pals in a novel of unusual adventure.* Street & Smith, New York, 1933, 252p, Cloth, Novel [Doc Savage #1] [by Lester Dent]

ROBESON, KENNETH (cont.)

04163 *The man who shook the Earth; a Doc Savage adventure.* Bantam, New York, 1969, 154p, Paper, Novel [Doc Savage #43] [by Lester Dent]

03800 *The men who smiled no more; a Doc Savage adventure.* Bantam, New York, 1970, 138p, Paper, Novel [Doc Savage #45] [by Norman Daniels]

04164 *The mental wizard; a Doc Savage adventure.* Bantam, New York, 1970, 135p, Paper, Novel [Doc Savage #53] [by Lester Dent]

04165 *Merchants of disaster; a Doc Savage adventure.* Bantam, New York, 1969, 138p, Paper, Novel [Doc Savage #41] [by Lester Dent]

04166 *The Metal Master; a Doc Savage adventure.* Bantam, New York, 1973, 137p, Paper, Novel [Doc Savage #72] [by Lester Dent]

04167 *Meteor menace; a Doc Savage adventure.* Bantam, New York, 1964, 140p, Paper, Novel [Doc Savage #3] [by Lester Dent]

04168 *The Midas man; a Doc Savage adventure.* Bantam, New York, 1970, 121p, Paper, Novel [Doc Savage #46] [by Lester Dent]

04169 *The monsters; a Doc Savage adventure.* Bantam, New York, 1965, 138p, Paper, Novel [Doc Savage #7] [by Lester Dent]

04170 *The motion menace; a Doc Savage adventure.* Bantam, New York, 1971, 123p, Paper, Novel [Doc Savage #64] [by Lester Dent]

04171 *The munitions master; a Doc Savage adventure.* Bantam, New York, 1971, 135p, Paper, Novel [Doc Savage #58] [by Lester Dent]

03801 *Murder melody; a Doc Savage adventure.* Bantam, New York, 1967, 138p, Paper, Novel [Doc Savage #15] [by Norman Daniels]

03802 *Murder mirage; a Doc Savage adventure.* Bantam, New York, 1972, 153p, Paper, Novel [Doc Savage #71] [by Norman Daniels]

04172 *The mystery on the snow; a Doc Savage adventure.* Bantam, New York, 1972, 149p, Paper, Novel [Doc Savage #69] [by Lester Dent]

04173 *Mystery under the sea; a Doc Savage adventure.* Bantam, New York, 1968, 120p, Paper, Novel [Doc Savage #27] [by Lester Dent]

04174 *The Mystic Mullah; a Doc Savage adventure.* Bantam, New York, 1965, 137p, Paper, Novel [Doc Savage #9] [by Lester Dent]

04175 *The other world; a Doc Savage adventure.* Bantam, New York, 1968, 119p, Paper, Novel [Doc Savage #29] [by Lester Dent]

04176 *The Phantom City; a Doc Savage adventure.* Bantam, New York, 1966, 137p, Paper, Novel [Doc Savage #10] [by Lester Dent]

04177 *Pirate of the Pacific; a Doc Savage adventure.* Bantam, New York, 1967, 136p, Paper, Novel [Doc Savage #19] [by Lester Dent]

04178 *The pirate's ghost; a Doc Savage adventure.* Bantam, New York, 1971, 135p, Paper, Novel [Doc Savage #62] [by Lester Dent]

04179 *Poison island; a Doc Savage adventure.* Bantam, New York, 1971, 118p, Paper, Novel [Doc Savage #57] [by Lester Dent]

04180 *The polar treasure; a Doc Savage adventure.* Bantam, New York, 1965, 122p, Paper, Novel [Doc Savage #4] [by Lester Dent]

04181 *Quest of Qui; a Doc Savage adventure.* Bantam, New York, 1966, 119p, Paper, Novel [Doc Savage #12] [by Lester Dent]

04182 *Quest of the Spider.* Street & Smith, New York, 1933, 252p, Cloth, Novel [Doc Savage #3 (old series), #68 (new series)] [by Lester Dent]

04183 *The red skull; a Doc Savage adventure.* Bantam, New York, 1967, 124p, Paper, Novel [Doc Savage #17] [by Lester Dent]

04184 *Red snow; a Doc Savage adventure.* Bantam, New York, 1969, 139p, Paper, Novel [Doc Savage #38] [by Lester Dent]

04185 *Resurrection day; a Doc Savage adventure.* Bantam, New York, 1969, 119p, Paper, Novel [Doc Savage #36] [by Lester Dent]

04186 *The Sargasso ogre; a Doc Savage adventure.* Bantam, New York, 1967, 140p, Paper, Novel [Doc Savage #18] [by Lester Dent]

04187 *The Sea Angel; a Doc Savage adventure.* Bantam, New York, 1970, 120p, Paper, Novel [Doc Savage #49] [by Lester Dent]

04188 *The sea magician; a Doc Savage adventure.* Bantam, New York, 1970, 137p, Paper, Novel [Doc Savage #44] [by Lester Dent]

04189 *The secret in the sky; a Doc Savage adventure.* Bantam, New York, 1967, 119p, Paper, Novel [Doc Savage #20] [by Lester Dent]

04190 *The seven agate devils; a Doc Savage adventure.* Bantam, New York, 1973, 134p, Paper, Novel [Doc Savage #73] [by Lester Dent]

04191 *The South Pole terror; a Doc Savage adventure.* Bantam, New York, 1974, 137p, Paper, Novel [Doc Savage #77] [by Lester Dent]

04192 *Spook Hole; a Doc Savage adventure.* Bantam, New York, 1972, 138p, Paper, Novel [Doc Savage #70] [by Lester Dent]

04193 *The spook legion; a Doc Savage adventure.* Bantam, New York, 1967, 122p, Paper, Novel [Doc Savage #16] [by Lester Dent]

04194 *The Squeaking Goblin; a Doc Savage adventure.* Bantam, New York, 1969, 138p, Paper, Novel [Doc Savage #35] [by Lester Dent]

04195 *The submarine mystery; a Doc Savage adventure.* Bantam, New York, 1971, 121p, Paper, Novel [Doc Savage #63] [by Lester Dent]

04196 *The terror in the Navy; a Doc Savage adventure.* Bantam, New York, 1969, 122p, Paper, Novel [Doc Savage #33] [by Lester Dent]

04197 *The Thousand-headed Man; a Doc Savage adventure.* Bantam, New York, 1964, 150p, Paper, Novel [Doc Savage #2] [by Lester Dent]

04198 *The vanisher; a Doc Savage adventure.* Bantam, New York, 1970, 139p, Paper, Novel [Doc Savage #52] [by Lester Dent]

04199 *World's Fair goblin; a Doc Savage adventure.* Bantam, New York, 1969, 122p, Paper, Novel [Doc Savage #39] [by Lester Dent]

04200 *The yellow cloud; a Doc Savage adventure.* Bantam, New York, 1971, 121p, Paper, Novel [Doc Savage #59] [by Lester Dent]

ROBINETT, RALPH F., with Paul W. Bell

01059 *English: target 1, the space visitors.* Harcourt, Brace & World, New York, 1968, 168p, Cloth, Novel

ROBINSON, C(harles) H(enry), 1843-1930

12287 *Longhead; the story of the first fire.* L. C. Page, Boston, 1913, 127p, Cloth, Novel

ROBINSON, E(dward) A., with G. A. Wall

12288 *The disk; a prophetic reflection.* Griffith, Farran, Okeden & Welsh, London, 1884, 182p, Paper, Novel

ROBINSON, E(dward) KAY, 1857-1928, with Phil
Robinson and H. Perry Robinson

12289   *Tales by three brothers*. Isbister & Co., Lon-
        don, 1902, 310p, Cloth, Coll.

ROBINSON, FRANK M(alcolm), 1926-   [*biography
included*]

12290   *The Power*. J. B. Lippincott, Philadelphia,
        1956, 218p, Cloth, Novel

ROBINSON, FREDERICK

12291   *The war of the world; a tale of the year 2,000
        A.D.* no publisher, Chicago, 1914, 111p,
        Paper, Novel

ROBINSON, G(eorge) P(latt), 1893-

12292   *The debt*. Duckworth, London, 1921, 320p,
        Cloth, Novel

ROBINSON, (Sir) H(arry) PERRY, 1859-1930

12293   *The gift of fernseed*. The Author, London,
        1902, 77p, Cloth, Novel

with Phil Robinson & E. Kay Robinson:

12289   *Tales by three brothers*. Isbister & Co., Lon-
        don, 1902, 310p, Cloth, Coll.

ROBINSON, Sir J(ohn) C(harles), 1824-1913

12294   *The dead sailor, and other stories*. Kegan
        Paul, Trench, London, 1889, 149p, Cloth,
        Coll.

ROBINSON, PHIL(ip Stewart), 1847-1902, with
E. Kay Robinson and H. Perry Robinson

12289   *Tales by three brothers*. Isbister & Co., Lon-
        don, 1902, 310p, Cloth, Coll.

ROBINSON, PHILIP BEDFORD, 1926-   [*biography
included*]

12295   *Masque of a Savage Mandarin*. Macdonald, Lon-
        don, 1969, 199p, Cloth, Novel

ROBINSON, WILL(iam) H(enry), 1867-1938

12296   *The witchery of Rita; and, Waiting for Tonti*.
        Berryhill Co., Phoenix, 1919, 71p, Cloth,
        Coll.

ROBINSON THE GREAT
    see: MUIR, RAMSAY

ROBLES SOLER, ANTONIO
    see: ANTONIORROBLES

ROBSON, JAMES, 1944/45-

12297   *Budgie Bill; a novel*. Constable, London, 1968,
        128p, Cloth, Novel
12297A retitled: *Backward to the front of the day*.
        Doubleday, Garden City, 1969, 144p, Cloth,
        Novel

ROBSON, NORMAN
    see: ROBB, JOHN

ROCHA, ADOLFO
    see: TORGE, MIGUEL

ROCHE, C. F. TIPHAIGNE de la
    see: TIPHAIGNE de la ROCHE, C. F.

ROCHE, JAMES JEFFREY, 1847-1908

12298   *The sorrows of Sap'ed ; a problem story of the
        East*. Harper & Bros., New York, 1904, 195p,
        Cloth, Novel

ROCHESTER, GEORGE E(rnest), 1905?-

12299   *The moth men*. Hutchinson, London, 1950, 183p,
        Cloth, Novel

as Jeffrey Gaunt:

12300   *The haunted man*. Eldon Press, London, 1951,
        247p, Cloth, Novel

ROCK, JAMES

12301   *Thro' space*. New England Druggist Publishing
        Co., Boston, 1909, 188p, Cloth, Novel

ROCK, PHILLIP, 1927-

12302   *The extraordinary seaman*. Meredith Press, New
        York, 1967, 250p, Cloth, Novel

ROCK, WYNDAN

12303   *Blackaton's Boy; a fantasy*. Home & Van Thal,
        London, 1948, 124p, Cloth, Novel

ROCKER, RUDOLF, 1873-1958

12304   *The six*. Rocker Publications Committee, Los
        Angeles, 1938, 255p, Cloth, Novel

ROCKLIN, ROSS L.
    see: ROCKLYNNE, ROSS

ROCKLYNNE, ROSS, pseud. [Ross Louis Rocklin,
    1913-   ] [*biography included*]

12305   *The men and the mirror*. Ace, New York, 1973,
        208p, Paper, Coll.
12306   *The Sun Destroyers*. Ace Double, New York,
        1973, 156p, Paper, Novel

ROCKOW, KAREN, 1949-

12307 *Funeral customs in Tolkien's trilogy.* TK Graphics, Baltimore, 1973, 30p, Paper, Nonf.

ROCKWELL, CAREY, pseud.

12308 *Danger in deep space.* Grosset & Dunlap, New York, 1953, 209p, Cloth, Novel [Tom Corbett #2]

12309 *On the trail of space pirates.* Grosset & Dunlap, New York, 1953, 211p, Cloth, Novel [Tom Corbett #3]

12310 *The revolt on Venus.* Grosset & Dunlap, New York, 1954, 213p, Cloth, Novel [Tom Corbett #5]

12311 *The robot rocket.* Grosset & Dunlap, New York, 1956, 181p, Cloth, Novel [Tom Corbett #8]

12312 *Sabotage in space.* Grosset & Dunlap, New York, 1955, 212p, Cloth, Novel [Tom Corbett #7]

12313 *The space pioneers.* Grosset & Dunlap, New York, 1953, 210p, Cloth, Novel [Tom Corbett #4]

12314 *Stand by for Mars!* Grosset & Dunlap, New York, 1952, 216p, Cloth, Novel [Tom Corbett #1]

12315 *Treachery in outer space.* Grosset & Dunlap, New York, 1954, 210p, Cloth, Novel [Tom Corbett #6]

ROCKWOOD, ROY, pseud.

12316 *Bomba the jungle boy among the pygmies; or, Battling with stealthy foes.* Cupples & Leon, New York, 1931, 212p, Cloth, Novel [Bomba #12]

12317 *Bomba the jungle boy among the slaves; or, Daring adventures in the Valley of Skulls.* Cupples & Leon, New York, 1929, 210p, Cloth, Novel [Bomba #8]

12318 *Bomba the jungle boy and the cannibals; or, Winning against native dangers.* Cupples & Leon, New York, 1932, 207p, Cloth, Novel [Bomba #13]

12319 *Bomba the jungle boy and the hostile chieftain; or, A hazardous trek to the sea.* Cupples & Leon, New York, 1934, 212p, Cloth, Novel [Bomba #16]

12320 *Bomba the jungle boy and the lost explorers; or, A wonderful revelation.* Cupples & Leon, New York, 1930, 210p, Cloth, Novel [Bomba #10]

12321 *Bomba the jungle boy and the painted hunters; or, A long search rewarded.* Cupples & Leon, New York, 1932, 206p, Cloth, Novel [Bomba #14]

12322 *Bomba the jungle boy and the river demons; or, Outwitting the savage medicine man.* Cupples & Leon, New York, 1933, 209p, Cloth, Novel [Bomba #15]

12323 *Bomba the jungle boy at the giant cataract; or, Chief Nascanora and his captives.* Cupples & Leon, New York, 1926, 204p, Cloth, Novel [Bomba #3]

12324 *Bomba the jungle boy at the moving mountain; or, The mystery of the caverns of fire.* Cupples & Leon, New York, 1926, 204p, Cloth, Novel [Bomba #2]

12325 *Bomba the jungle boy in a strange land; or, Facing the unknown.* Cupples & Leon, New York, 1931, 209p, Cloth, Novel [Bomba #11]

12326 *Bomba the jungle boy in the abandoned city; or, A treasure ten thousand years old.* Cupples & Leon, New York, 1927, 208p, Cloth, Novel [Bomba #5]

12327 *Bomba the jungle boy in the land of burning lava; or, Outwitting superstitious natives.* Cupples & Leon, New York, 1936, 206p, Cloth, Novel [Bomba #18]

12328 *Bomba the jungle boy in the perilous kingdom; or, Braving strange hazards.* Cupples & Leon, New York, 1937, 208p, Cloth, Novel [Bomba #19]

12329 *Bomba the jungle boy in the steaming grotto; or, Victorious through flame and fury.* Cupples & Leon, New York, 1938, 209p, Cloth, Novel [Bomba #20]

12330 *Bomba the jungle boy in the swamp of death; or, The sacred alligators of Abarago.* Cupples & Leon, New York, 1929, 210p, Cloth, Novel [Bomba #7]

12331 *Bomba the jungle boy on Jaguar Island; or, Adrift on the river of mystery.* Cupples & Leon, New York, 1927, 209p, Cloth, Novel [Bomba #4]

12332 *Bomba the jungle boy on terror trail; or, The mysterious men from the sky.* Cupples & Leon, New York, 1928, 208p, Cloth, Novel [Bomba #6]

12333 *Bomba the jungle boy on the underground river; or, The cave of bottomless pits.* Cupples & Leon, New York, 1930, 204p, Cloth, Novel [Bomba #9]

12334 *Bomba the jungle boy; or, The old naturalist's secret.* Cupples & Leon, New York, 1926, 204p, Cloth, Novel [Bomba #1]

12335 *Bomba the jungle boy trapped by the cyclone; or, Shipwrecked on the swirling seas.* Cupples & Leon, New York, 1935, 210p, Cloth, Novel [Bomba #17]

12336 *By air express to Venus; or, Captives of a strange people.* Cupples & Leon, New York, 1929, 248p, Cloth, Novel [Great Marvel Series #8]

12337 *By space ship to Saturn; or, Exploring the ringed planet.* Cupples & Leon, New York, 1935, 203p, Cloth, Novel [Great Marvel Series #9]

12338 *The city beyond the clouds; or, Captured by the red dwarfs.* Cupples & Leon, New York, 1925, 244p, Cloth, Novel [Great Marvel Series #7]

12339 *Five thousand miles underground; or, The mystery of the center of the Earth.* Cupples & Leon, New York, 1908, 242p, Cloth, Novel [Great Marvel Series #3]

12340 *Lost on the Moon; or, In quest of the field of diamonds.* Cupples & Leon, New York, 1911, 248p, Cloth, Novel [Great Marvel Series #5]

12341 *On a torn-away world; or, The captives of the great earthquake.* Cupples & Leon, New York, 1913, 246p, Cloth, Novel [Great Marvel Series #6]

12342 *Through space to Mars; or, The longest journey on record.* Cupples & Leon, New York, 1910, 248p, Cloth, Novel [Great Marvel Series #4]

12343 *Through the air to the North Pole; or, The wonderful cruise of the Electric Monarch.* Cupples & Leon, New York, 1906, 240p, Cloth, Novel [Great Marvel Series #1]

12344 *Under the ocean to the South Pole; or, The strange cruise of the submarine wonder.* Cupples & Leon, New York, 1907, 248p, Cloth, Novel [Great Marvel Series #2]

ROCKWOOD, ROY (cont.)

12345   *The wizard of the sea; or, A trip under the
        ocean.* Mershon Co., New York, 1901, 188p,
        Cloth, Novel

RODDA, (Percival) CHARLES, 1891-   [*biography
included*]

12346   *The house upstairs.* James Barrie, London,
        1949, 146p, Cloth, Novel

RODDENBERRY, (Eu)GENE (Wesley), 1921-   [*biography included*], with Stephen E. Whitfield

12347   *The making of Star trek.* Ballantine, New York,
        1968, 414p, Paper, Nonf.

RODGERS, MARY, 1931-   [*biography included*]

12348   *A billion for Boris.* Harper & Row, New York,
        1974, 211p, Cloth, Novel [Annabel Andrews
        #2]
12349   *Freaky Friday.* Harper & Row, New York, 1972,
        145p, Cloth, Novel [Annabel Andrews #1]

RODGERS, SEARN LEONARD

12350   *Final payment; a novel.* Hicks Publishing Co.,
        Los Angeles, 1933, 127p, Cloth, Novel

RODNEY, GEORGE B(rydges), 1872-

12351   *Beyond the range.* Edward J. Clode, New York,
        1934, 256p, Cloth, Novel
12352   *Edge of the world.* Duffield & Green, New York,
        1931, 235p, Cloth, Novel

ROE, IVAN
     see: SAVAGE, RICHARD

ROE, RICHARD L., with Rich Jones

08011   *Valence and vision; a reader in psychology.*
        Rinehart Press, San Francisco, 1974, 482p,
        Paper, Anth.

ROE, WILLIAM JAMES
     see: GENONE, HUDOR

ROGER, NOËLLE, pseud. [Hélène Pittard, 1874-
1953]

12353   *He who sees.* George G. Harrap, London, 1935,
        296p, Cloth, Novel
12354   *The new Adam.* Stanley Paul, London, 1926,
        256p, Cloth, Novel

ROGERS, ALVA (C.), 1923-   [*biography included*]

12355   *A requiem for Astounding.* Advent: Publishers,
        Chicago, 1964, 224p, Cloth, Nonf.

ROGERS, EVA C.

12356   *Dartmoor legends.* Pilgrim Press, London, 1900?,
        295p, Cloth, Novel

ROGERS, LEBBEUS HARDING, 1847-1932

12357   *The Kite Trust (a romance of wealth).* Kite
        Trust Publishing Co., New York, 1900, 475p,
        Cloth, Novel

ROGERS, LEW, 1923-

12358   *The eternity kick; a novel.* Exposition Press,
        New York, 1973, 95p, Cloth, Novel

ROGERS, MELBOURNE A.

12359   *A brain outlives its body.* Vantage Press, New
        York, 1969, 236p, Cloth, Novel

ROGERS, MICHAEL, 1950-   [*biography included*]

12360   *Mindfogger.* Alfred A. Knopf, New York, 1973,
        199p, Cloth, Novel

ROGERSOHN, WILLIAM

12361   *Amiro.* Brown Watson, London, 1952?, 111p,
        Paper, Novel
12362   *North dimension.* Brown Watson, London, 1952?,
        111p, Paper, Novel

ROHMER, ELIZABETH SAX, pseud. [Rose Elizabeth
Ward, 1886-   ], with Cay Van Ash

12363   *Master of villainy; a biography of Sax Rohmer.*
        Bowling Green University Popular Press, Bow-
        ling Green, OH, 1972, 312p, Cloth, Nonf.

ROHMER, RICHARD H.

12364   *Ultimatum.* Clarke, Irwin & Co., Toronto, 1973,
        227p, Cloth, Novel

ROHMER, SAX, pseud. [Arthur Sarsfield Ward,
1883-1959] [name originally Arthur Henry Ward]

12365   *The bat flies low; in the Book of Thoth, and
        behind the golden curtain, lay one of Egypt's
        most dangerous secrets.* Crime Club, Double-
        day, Doran, Garden City, 1935, 314p, Cloth,
        Novel
12366   *The book of Fu Manchu, being a complete and
        detailed account of the amazing career in
        crime of the sinister Chinaman.* Robert M.
        McBride, New York, 1929, 1331p, Cloth, Coll.
        [includes *The insidious Dr. Fu-Manchu, The
        return of Dr. Fu-Manchu, The hand of Fu-Man-
        chu, The golden scorpion*] [Fu Manchu #s 1-4]
        The bride of Fu Manchu. [see 12377A]
12367   *Brood of the Witch-Queen.* C. Arthur Pearson,
        London, 1918, 212p, Cloth, Novel
12368   *Daughter of Fu Manchu.* Doubleday, Garden City,
        1931, 316p, Cloth, Novel [Fu Manchu #5]

ROHMER, SAX (cont.)

12369 *The day the world ended; he had three days-- in which to save the world!* Crime Club, Doubleday, Doran, Garden City, 1930, 306p, Cloth, Novel

12370 *The devil doctor; hitherto unpublished adventures in the career of the mysterious Dr. Fu-Manchu.* Methuen, London, 1916, 306p, Cloth, Novel [Fu Manchu #2]

12370A retitled: *The return of Dr. Fu-Manchu.* Robert M. McBride, New York, 1916, 332p, Cloth, Novel [Fu Manchu #2]

12371 *The dream-detective, being some account of the methods of Moris Klaw.* Jarrolds, London, 1920, 256p, Cloth, Coll.

12372 *The dream-detective, being some account of the methods of Moris Klaw.* Doubleday, Page, Garden City, 1925, 309p, Cloth, Coll. [expanded]

12373 *The drums of Fu Manchu.* Crime Club, Doubleday, Doran, Garden City, 1939, 308p, Cloth, Novel [Fu Manchu #10]

12374 *Emperor Fu Manchu.* Herbert Jenkins, London, 1959, 221p, Cloth, Novel [Fu Manchu #14]

12375 *The emperor of America.* Crime Club, Doubleday, Doran, Garden City, 1929, 310p, Cloth, Novel

The fire goddess. [see 12403A]

12376 *Fire-Tongue.* Cassell, London, 1921, 314p, Cloth, Novel

12377 *Fu Manchu's bride; Fu Manchu brings terror to a quiet corner of France--until Sir Denis Nayland Smith smashes his world-shaking plans, and reveals the eerie secret of the girl whose frightful fate was to be Fu Manchu's bride.* Crime Club, Doubleday, Doran, Garden City, 1933, 319p, Cloth, Novel [Fu Manchu #7]

12377A retitled: *The bride of Fu Manchu.* Cassell, London, 1933, 312p, Cloth, Novel [Fu Manchu #7]

12378 *The golden scorpion.* Methuen, London, 1919, 250p, Cloth, Novel [Fu Manchu #4]

12379 *The golden scorpion omnibus.* Grosset & Dunlap, New York, 1938, 693p, Cloth, Coll. [includes *The golden scorpion* and *Dope* (not SF)]

12380 *The green eyes of Bâst.* Cassell, London, 1920, 314p, Cloth, Novel

12381 *Grey face.* Cassell, London, 1924, 297p, Cloth, Novel

The hand of Fu-Manchu. [see 12395A]

12382 *The haunting of Low Fennel.* C. Arthur Pearson, London, 1920, 252p, Cloth, Coll.

The insidious Dr. Fu-Manchu. [see 12386A]

12383 *The island of Fu Manchu.* Crime Club, Doubleday, Doran, Garden City, 1941, 299p, Cloth, Novel [Fu Manchu #11]

12384 *The mask of Fu Manchu.* Crime Club, Doubleday, Doran, Garden City, 1932, 330p, Cloth, Novel [Fu Manchu #6]

12385 *The Moon is red.* Herbert Jenkins, London, 1954, 188p, Cloth, Novel

12386 *The mystery of Dr. Fu-Manchu.* Methuen, London, 1913, 314p, Cloth, Novel [Fu Manchu #1]

12386A retitled: *The insidious Dr. Fu-Manchu, being a somewhat detailed account of the amazing adventures of Nayland Smith in his trailing of the sinister Chinaman.* McBride, Nast, New York, 1913, 383p, Cloth, Novel [Fu Manchu #1]

12387 *Nude in mink.* Gold Medal, New York, 1950, 174p, Paper, Novel [Sumuru #1]

12387A retitled: *Sins of Sumuru.* Herbert Jenkins, London, 1950, 224p, Cloth, Novel [Sumuru #1]

12388 *President Fu Manchu.* Crime Club, Doubleday, Doran, Garden City, 1936, 342p, Cloth, Novel [Fu Manchu #9]

12389 *Re-enter Fu Manchu.* Gold Medal, Greenwich, Conn., 1957, 144p, Paper, Novel [Fu Manchu #13]

The return of Dr. Fu-Manchu. [see 12370A]

12390 *Return of Sumuru.* Gold Medal, New York, 1954, 172p, Paper, Novel [Sumuru #4]

12390A retitled: *Sand and satin.* Herbert Jenkins, London, 1955, 192p, Cloth, Novel [Sumuru #4]

12391 *Sax Rohmer omnibus.* Grosset & Dunlap, New York, 1938, 740p, Cloth, Coll. [includes *The yellow claw* (not SF) and *Tales of secret Egypt*]

12392 *The secret of Holm Peel, and other strange stories.* Ace, New York, 1970, 191p, Paper, Coll. [includes several Fu Manchu stories]

12393 *Seven sins.* Robert M. McBride, New York, 1943, 328p, Cloth, Novel

12394 *Shadow of Fu Manchu.* Crime Club, Doubleday, Garden City, 1948, 190p, Cloth, Novel [Fu Manchu #12]

12395 *The Si-Fan mysteries.* Methuen, London, 1917, 306p, Cloth, Novel [Fu Manchu #3]

12395A retitled: *The hand of Fu-Manchu, being a new phase in the activities of Fu-Manchu, the evil doctor.* Robert M. McBride, New York, 1917, 308p, Cloth, Novel [Fu Manchu #3]

12396 *Sinister madonna.* Herbert Jenkins, London, 1956, 187p, Cloth, Novel [Sumuru #5]

12397 *Sins of Séverac Bablon.* Cassell, London, 1914, 342p, Cloth, Novel

Sins of Sumuru. [see 12387A]

Slaves of Sumuru. [see 12398A]

12398 *Sumuru.* Gold Medal, New York, 1951, 179p, Paper, Novel [Sumuru #2]

12398A retitled: *Slaves of Sumuru.* Herbert Jenkins, London, 1952, 190p, Cloth, Novel [Sumuru #2]

12399 *Tales of Chinatown.* Doubleday, Page, Garden City, 1922, 376p, Cloth, Coll.

12400 *Tales of east and west; thirteen little masterpieces of death and fear and terror.* Crime Club, Doubleday, Doran, Garden City, 1933, 345p, Cloth, Coll.

12401 *Tales of secret Egypt.* Methuen, London, 1918, 312p, Cloth, Coll.

12402 *The trail of Fu Manchu.* Crime Club, Doubleday, Doran, Garden City, 1934, 329p, Cloth, Novel [Fu Manchu #8]

12403 *Virgin in flames.* Herbert Jenkins, London, 1953, 204p, Cloth, Novel [Sumuru #3]

12403A retitled: *The fire goddess.* Gold Medal, New York, 1953, 204p, Paper, Novel [Sumuru #3]

12404 *The wrath of Fu Manchu, and other stories.* Tom Stacey, London, 1973, 244p, Cloth, Coll. [includes several Fu Manchu stories]

12405 *Yu'an Hee See laughs.* Crime Club, Doubleday, Doran, Garden City, 1932, 312p, Cloth, Novel

as Michael Furey:

12406 *Wulfheim.* Jarrolds Publishers, London, 1950, 208p, Cloth, Novel

ROLAND, NICHOLAS, pseud. [Arnold Robert Walmsley, 1912-] [*biography included*]

12407 *The Great One; a novel.* Harvill Press, London, 1967, 254p, Cloth, Novel

ROLFE, FR(ederick William Serafino Austin Lewis Mary, "Baron Corvo"), 1860-1913

12408 *Hadrian the Seventh; a romance.* Chatto & Windus, London, 1904, 413p, Cloth, Novel

with Harry Pirie-Gordon as Prospero & Caliban:

11527 *Hubert's Arthur, being certain curious documents found among the literary remains of Mr. N. C., here produced by Prospero & Caliban.* Cassell, London, 1935, 353p, Cloth, Novel
11528 *The weird of the wanderer, being the papyrus records of some incidents in one of the previous lives of Mr. Nicholas Crabbe, here produced by Prospero & Caliban.* William Rider & Son, London, 1912, 299p, Cloth, Novel

ROLLS, BRIAN

12409 *Something in mind.* Robert Hale, London, 1973, 190p, Cloth, Novel

ROLT-WHEELER, FRANCIS (William), 1876-1960

12410 *The finder of fire.* D. Appleton, New York, 1927, 273p, Cloth, Novel
12411 *The tamer of herds.* D. Appleton, New York, 1928, 241p, Cloth, Novel

ROMAN, CHET, pseud.

12412 *The gay ghouls.* Greenleaf Classics, San Diego, 1970, 195p, Paper, Novel

ROMANO, DEANE (Louis), 1927-   [*biography included*]

12413 *Flight from Time One.* Walker, New York, 1972, 259p, Cloth, Novel

ROMANTIC TALES
    see: CRAIK, D. M.

ROMILLY, ERIC, 1886-1953

12414 *Bleeding from the Roman.* Chapman & Hall, London, 1949, 255p, Cloth, Novel

ROMILUS, ARN, house pseud.

12415 *Beyond geo.* Curtis Warren, London, 1953, 159p, Cloth, Novel
12416 *Brain palaeo.* Curtis Warren, London, 1953, 159p, Cloth, Novel
12417 *Organic destiny.* Curtis Warren, London, 1953, 159p, Cloth, Novel

RONALD, BRUCE W(alton), 1931-   [*biography included*]

12418 *Our man in space.* Ace Double, New York, 1965, 131p, Paper, Novel

RONN, YUVAL
    see: IONEL

ROOF, KATHARINE METCALF

12419 *The great demonstration.* D. Appleton, New York, 1920, 335p, Cloth, Novel

ROOSBROECK, G. L. VAN
    see: VAN ROOSBROECK, G. L.

ROOT, ALBERT (Waldo), 1891-   [*biography included*]

12420 *Tomorrow's harvest; or, Death takes a holiday.* Vantage Press, New York, 1967, 176p, Cloth, Novel

ROPES, ARTHUR REED
    see: ROSS, ADRIAN

ROSCOE, THEODORE

12421 *I'll grind their bones.* Dodge Publishing Co., New York, 1936, 323p, Cloth, Novel

ROSE, CHRISTINE BROOK-
    see: BROOK-ROSE, CHRISTINE

ROSE, F(rederick) HORACE (Vincent), 1876-

12422 *Bride of the Kalahari; a romance.* Duckworth, London, 1940, 272p, Cloth, Novel
12423 *The maniac's dream; a novel of the atomic bomb.* Duckworth, London, 1946, 237p, Cloth, Novel
12424 *The night of the world.* Duckworth, London, 1944, 254p, Cloth, Novel
12425 *Pharoah's crown; a romance.* Duckworth, London, 1943, 224p, Cloth, Novel

ROSE, GEORGE
    see: SKETCHLEY, ARTHUR

ROSE, HOWARD

12426 *Twelve ravens; a novel.* Macmillan, New York, 1969, 405p, Cloth, Novel

ROSE, LAWRENCE F., pseud.
    see: FEARN, JOHN RUSSELL

ROSE, LOIS, with Stephen Rose

12427 *The shattered ring; science fiction and the quest for meaning.* John Knox Press, Richmond, VA, 1970, 127p, Cloth, Nonf.

ROSE, STEPHEN (C.), with Lois Rose

12427 *The shattered ring; science fiction and the quest for meaning.* John Knox Press, Richmond, VA, 1970, 127p, Cloth, Nonf.

ROSELLE, DANIEL, 1920-   [biography included]

12428 Transformations; understanding world history
       through science fiction. Fawcett Premier,
       Greenwich, Conn., 1973, 176p, Paper, Anth.
12429 Transformations II; understanding American
       history through science fiction. Fawcett
       Crest, Greenwich, Conn., 1974, 143p, Paper,
       Anth.

ROSENBERG, ETHEL, 1915-   [biography inclu-
ded]

12430 Uncle Julius and the angel with heartburn.
       Simon & Schuster, New York, 1951, 239p,
       Cloth, Novel

ROSENBERGER, JOSEPH (R.)

12431 Death merchant; Laser war. Pinnacle, New
       York, 1974, 187p, Paper, Novel [Death
       Merchant #9]

ROSENFIELD, JOE Jr.

12432 Decameron, 1965. Citadel Press, New York,
       1963, 130p, Cloth, Novel

ROSENTHAL, MUNROE, with Donald Munson

10532 President Kissinger; a political fiction.
       Freeway Press, New York, 1974, 273p, Paper,
       Novel

ROSEWATER, FRANK, 1856-

12433 '96; a romance of utopia, presenting a solu-
       tion of the labour problem, a new God, and
       a new religion. Utopia Co., Omaha, Neb.,
       1894, 268p, Cloth, Novel
12433A retitled: Utopia; a romance of today, presen-
       ting a solution of the labor problem, a new
       God, & a new religion. F. Tennyson Neely,
       London, 1897, 268p, Paper, Novel

as Franklin & Marian Mayoe:

12434 Doomed; a startling message to the people of
       our day, interwoven in an antidiluvian ro-
       mance of two old worlds and two young lovers,
       by Queen Metel and Prince Loab of Atlo, re-
       incarnated in its editors, Marian and Frank-
       lin Mayoe, by the Atlon calendar the year
       14,009, by our calendar the year 1920.
       Frank Rosewater, Publisher, New York, 1920,
       282p, Cloth, Novel

ROSHWALD, MORDECAI (Marceli), 1921-   [bio-
graphy included]

12435 Level 7. McGraw-Hill, New York, 1959, 186p,
       Cloth, Novel
12436 A small armageddon. Heinemann, London, 1962,
       211p, Cloth, Novel

ROSITZKE, HARRY (August), 1911-   [biography
included]

12437 Left on! the glorious bourgeois cultural revo-
       lution. Quadrangle, New York, 1973, 200p,
       Cloth, Novel

ROSKOLENKO, HARRY, 1907-   [biography inclu-
ded]

12438 Black is a man. Padell, New York, 1954, 191p,
       Cloth, Novel

ROSMANITH, OLGA (L.)

12439 Unholy flame. Gold Medal, New York, 1952,
       184p, Paper, Novel

ROSNER, SARA

12440 The other dimension; nine stories of the super-
       natural. Scholastic Book Services, New York,
       1972, 304p, Paper, Anth.

ROSNY, J. H., aîné, pseud. [Joseph Henri Honoré Boëx-Borel, 1856-1940]

12441 The giant cat; or, The quest of Aoun and Zouhr.
       Robert M. McBride, New York, 1924, 242p,
       Cloth, Novel
12441A retitled: Quest of the dawn man. Ace, New
       York, 1964, 156p, Paper, Novel
12442 The quest for fire; a novel of prehistoric
       times. Pantheon, New York, 1967, 193p,
       Cloth, Novel

ROSS, ADRIAN, pseud. [Arthur Reed Ropes, 1859-
1933]

12443 The hole of the pit. Edward Arnold, London,
       1914, 300p, Cloth, Novel

ROSS, ALBERT HENRY
    see: MORISON, FRANK

ROSS, BARNABY, pseud.
    see: LEE, MANFRED B. and DANNAY, FREDERIC

ROSS, Major-General CHARLES, 1864-1930

12444 When the devil was sick. John Murray, London,
       1924, 320p, Cloth, Novel

ROSS, CLARISSA, pseud.
    see: ROSS, MARILYN

ROSS, H. S. LOCKHART-
    see: LOCKHART-ROSS, H. S.

ROSS, JAMES, pseud.
    see: DARRINGTON, HUGH and HALLIWELL, TONY

ROSS, JEAN, pseud. [Irene Dale Hewson]

12445 *A view of the island; a post-atomic fairy tale.* Hutchinson, London, 1965, 200p, Cloth, Novel

ROSS, JOSEPH, pseud. [Joseph Henry Wrzos, 1929-] [*biography included*]

12446 *The best of Amazing.* Doubleday, Garden City, 1967, 222p, Cloth, Anth.

ROSS, MALCOLM (Harrison), 1895-1965

12447 *The man who lived backward.* Farrar, Straus & Co., New York, 1950, 461p, Cloth, Novel

ROSS, MARILYN, pseud. [William Edward Daniel Ross]

12448 *Barnabas Collins.* Paperback Library, New York, 1968, 157p, Paper, Tele. [Dark Shadows #6]
12449 *Barnabas Collins and Quentin's demon.* Paperback Library, New York, 1970, 157p, Paper, Tele. [Dark Shadows #14]
12450 *Barnabas Collins and the gypsy witch.* Paperback Library, New York, 1970, 160p, Paper, Tele. [Dark Shadows #15]
12451 *Barnabas Collins and the mysterious ghost.* Paperback Library, New York, 1970, 160p, Paper, Tele. [Dark Shadows #13]
12452 *Barnabas Collins versus the warlock.* Paperback Library, New York, 1969, 156p, Paper, Tele. [Dark Shadows #11]
12453 *Barnabas, Quentin, and Dr. Jekyll's son.* Paperback Library, New York, 1971, 157p, Paper, Tele. [Dark Shadows #27]
12454 *Barnabas, Quentin, and the avenging ghost.* Paperback Library, New York, 1970, 159p, Paper, Tele. [Dark Shadows #17]
12455 *Barnabas, Quentin, and the body snatchers.* Paperback Library, New York, 1971, 156p, Paper, Tele. [Dark Shadows #26]
12456 *Barnabas, Quentin, and the crystal coffin.* Paperback Library, New York, 1970, 157p, Paper, Tele. [Dark Shadows #19]
12457 *Barnabas, Quentin, and the frightened bride.* Paperback Library, New York, 1970, 159p, Paper, Tele. [Dark Shadows #22]
12458 *Barnabas, Quentin, and the grave robbers.* Paperback Library, New York, 1971, 159p, Paper, Tele. [Dark Shadows #28]
12459 *Barnabas, Quentin, and the haunted cave.* Paperback Library, New York, 1970, 158p, Paper, Tele. [Dark Shadows #21]
12460 *Barnabas, Quentin, and the hidden tomb.* Paperback Library, New York, 1971, 158p, Paper, Tele. [Dark Shadows #31]
12461 *Barnabas, Quentin, and the mad magician.* Paperback Library, New York, 1971, 158p, Paper, Tele. [Dark Shadows #30]
12462 *Barnabas, Quentin, and the magic potion.* Paperback Library, New York, 1971, 158p, Paper, Tele. [Dark Shadows #25]
12463 *Barnabas, Quentin, and the mummy's curse.* Paperback Library, New York, 1970, 159p, Paper, Tele. [Dark Shadows #16]
12464 *Barnabas, Quentin, and the nightmare assassin.* Paperback Library, New York, 1970, 159p, Paper, Tele. [Dark Shadows #18]

12465 *Barnabas, Quentin, and the Scorpio curse.* Paperback Library, New York, 1970, 157p, Paper, Novel [Dark Shadows #23]
12466 *Barnabas, Quentin, and the sea ghost.* Paperback Library, New York, 1971, 158p, Paper, Tele. [Dark Shadows #29]
12467 *Barnabas, Quentin, and the serpent.* Paperback Library, New York, 1970, 155p, Paper, Tele. [Dark Shadows #24]
12468 *Barnabas, Quentin, and the vampire beauty.* Paperback Library, New York, 1972, 158p, Paper, Tele. [Dark Shadows #32]
12469 *Barnabas, Quentin, and the witch's curse.* Paperback Library, New York, 1970, 158p, Paper, Tele. [Dark Shadows #20]
12470 *The curse of Collinwood.* Paperback Library, New York, 1968, 158p, Paper, Tele. [Dark Shadows #5]
12471 *Dark shadows.* Paperback Library, New York, 1966, 159p, Paper, Tele. [Dark Shadows #1]
12472 *The demon of Barnabas Collins.* Paperback Library, New York, 1969, 159p, Paper, Tele. [Dark Shadows #8]
12473 *The foe of Barnabas Collins.* Paperback Library, New York, 1969, 158p, Paper, Tele. [Dark Shadows #9]
12474 *House of dark shadows.* Paperback Library, New York, 1970, 157p, Paper, Movie [Dark Shadows series]
12475 *The mystery of Collinwood.* Paperback Library, New York, 1968, 159p, Paper, Tele. [Dark Shadows #4]
12476 *The peril of Barnabas Collins.* Paperback Library, New York, 1969, 158p, Paper, Tele. [Dark Shadows #12]
12477 *The phantom and Barnabas Collins.* Paperback Library, New York, 1969, 158p, Paper, Tele. [Dark Shadows #10]
12478 *The secret of Barnabas Collins.* Paperback Library, New York, 1969, 159p, Paper, Tele. [Dark Shadows #7]
12479 *Strangers at Collins House.* Paperback Library, New York, 1967, 159p, Paper, Tele. [Dark Shadows #3]
12480 *The vampire contessa, from the journal of Jeremy Quentain.* Pinnacle, New York, 1974, 181p, Paper, Novel
12481 *Victoria Winters.* Paperback Library, New York, 1967, 160p, Paper, Tele. [Dark Shadows #2]

as Clarissa Ross:

12482 *Gemini in darkness.* Lancer, New York, 1969, 224p, Paper, Novel

ROSS, OLIN

12483 *Lust planet.* France Books, Hollywood, 1962, 160p, Paper, Novel [byline on spine reads Ross Olin]

ROSS, OLIN J(ones), 1858-

12484 *The sky blue; a tale of the iron horse and of the coming civilization.* Olin J. Ross, Columbus, OH, 1904, 280p, Cloth, Novel

ROSS, RAYMOND GEORGE

12485 *Beyond the chains of bondage.* Vantage Press, New York, 1964, 143p, Cloth, Novel

ROSS, (Sir) RONALD, 1857-1932

12486 *The revels of Orsera; a mediaeval romance.*
John Murray, London, 1920, 393p, Cloth,
Novel

ROSS, SAMUEL ALBERT

12487 *The coming terror; or, The Australian revolu-*
tion; a romance of the twentieth century.
Samuel Ross, Sydney, 1894, 306p, Cloth,
Novel

ROSS, T(heodore) J(ohn), 1924-   [*biography*
included], with Roy Huss

07663 *Focus on the horror film.* Spectrum Books,
Englewood Cliffs, NJ, 1972, 186p, Cloth,
Nonf. Anth.

ROSS, W. E. D.
  see: ROSS, MARILYN

ROSSETTO, LOUIS, Jr.

12488 *Take-over; a speculative and otherwise utterly*
fictional account of how Richard Milhous
Nixon will usurp the power to his office,
take over the country, and commit other
heinous and nasty acts. Lyle Stuart, Secaucus, NJ, 1974, 262p, Cloth, Novel

ROSSI, MARCIANUS F(ilomeno), 1869-

12489 *A trip to Mars.* Smith McKay, San Jose, CA,
1920, 92p, Paper, Novel

ROSSITER, OSCAR

12490 *Tetrasomy two.* Doubleday, Garden City, 1974,
186p, Cloth, Novel

ROSSMANN, HERMANN, 1902-

12491 *Claus the fish.* Peter Davies, London, 1930,
128p, Cloth, Novel

ROSSMANN, JOHN F.

12492 *The mind masters.* Signet, New York, 1974,
236p, Paper, Novel [Britt St. Vincent #1]

ROTH, ARTHUR (J.), 1925-

12493 *The iceburg hermit.* Four Winds Press, New
York, 1974, 201p, Cloth, Novel

ROTH, PHILIP (Milton), 1933-   [*biography in-*
cluded]

12494 *The breast.* Holt, Rinehart & Winston, New
York, 1972, 78p, Cloth, Novel

12495 *Our gang (starring Tricky and his friends).*
Random House, New York, 1971, 200p, Cloth,
Novel

ROTHBERG, ABRAHAM, 1922-   [*biography inclu-*
ded]

12496 *The sword of the Golem.* McCall Publishing Co.,
New York, 1971, 232p, Cloth, Novel

ROTHENBERG, ALAN B(aer), 1907-

12497 *The mind reader.* Greenberg: Publisher, New
York, 1956, 223p, Cloth, Novel

ROTHERY, AGNES (Edwards), 1888-1954

12498 *Balm of Gilead.* Dodd, Mead, New York, 1946,
244p, Cloth, Novel

ROTSLER, WILLIAM, 1926-   [*biography included*]

12499 *Patron of the arts.* Ballantine, New York,
1974, 210p, Paper, Novel

ROTTENSTEINER, FRANZ, 1942-   [*biography in-*
cluded]

12500 *View from another shore; European science fic-*
tion. Continuum Book, Seabury Press, New
York, 1973, 234p, Cloth, Anth.

ROUECHÉ, BERTON, 1911-   [*biography included*]

12501 *Feral.* Harper & Row, New York, 1974, 137p,
Cloth, Novel

ROUEN, REED de
  see: de ROUEN, REED

ROUSSEAU, VICTOR, pseud. [Victor Rousseau
Emanuel, 1879-1960]

12502 *The messiah of the cylinder.* A. C. McClurg,
Chicago, 1917, 319p, Cloth, Novel
12502A retitled: *The apostle of the cylinder.* Hodder
& Stoughton, London, 1918, 312p, Cloth, Novel

as H. M. Egbert:

12503 *Draught of eternity.* John Long, London, 1924,
254p, Cloth, Novel
12504 *Eric of the strong heart.* John Long, London,
1925, 254p, Cloth, Novel
12505 *Mrs. Aladdin.* John Long, London, 1925, 254p,
Cloth, Novel
12506 *My lady of the Nile.* Hodder & Stoughton, London, 1923, 286p, Cloth, Novel
12507 *The sea demons.* John Long, London, 1924, 254p,
Cloth, Novel

ROUSSEL, RAYMOND, 1877-1933

12508 *Locus Solus.* University of California Press,
Berkeley, CA, 1970, 254p, Cloth, Novel

ROW, ARTHUR

12509 *Researches into the unknown, being the experiences and adventures of a psychologist on the subject of ghosts and other obscure problems.* Arthur H. Stockwell, London, 1936, 143p, Cloth, Coll.

ROWCROFT, CHARLES, d. 1856

12510 *The triumph of woman; a Christmas story.* Parry, London, 1848, 271p, Cloth, Novel

ROWE, JOHN G(abriel), 1874-

12511 *The death flash.* Modern Publishing Co., London, 1936, 254p, Cloth, Novel
12512 *The lost city of Manoa; or, The sacred talisman.* Modern Publishing Co., London, 1936, 253p, Cloth, Novel

ROWEL, M., pseud. [Valdemar Adolph Thisted, 1815-1887]

12513 *Letters from Hell.* Richard Bentley, London, 1866, vol. I-336p, II-329p, Cloth, Novel
12513A *Letters from Hell, given in English,* by L W J S. Richard Bentley & Son, London, 1884, 348p, Cloth, Novel
12513B *Letters from Hell.* Hunter, Robinson, New York, 1889, 239p, Cloth, Novel [published anonymously]
12513C retitled: *A message from a lost soul; or, Letters from Hell, with an introductory chapter on Hell as God has revealed it in his world,* by Rev. R. A. Torrey, *and a concluding chapter on Heaven, the home of the redeemed,* by Rev. Wm. H. Lindemuth. P. W. Ziegler, Philadelphia, 1906, 382p, Cloth, Novel

ROWLAND, DONALD S(ydney), 1928- [*biography included*][see also A. Random & F. Brockley]

12514 *Despot in space.* John Gresham (Robert Hale), London, 1973, 190p, Cloth, Novel
12515 *Master of space.* Robert Hale, London, 1974, 178p, Cloth, Novel

as Roland Starr:

12516 *Omina uncharted.* Robert Hale, London, 1974, 189p, Cloth, Novel [Omina #2]
12517 *Operation Omina.* Lenox Hill Press, New York, 1970, 192p, Cloth, Novel [Omina #1]

ROWLAND, FLORENCE WIGHTMAN, 1900- [*biography included*]

12518 *Eo of the caves.* Henry Z. Walck, New York, 1959, 160p, Cloth, Novel

ROWLAND, HENRY C(ottrell), 1874-1933

12519 *Many mansions.* Ray Long & Richard R. Smith, New York, 1932, 364p, Cloth, Novel

ROWLEY, RICHARD, pseud. [Richard Valentine Williams]

12520 *Tales of Mourne.* Duckworth, London, 1937, 240p, Cloth, Coll.

ROXBURY, KYLE

12521 *Cry wolf!* Darkroom Reader, San Diego, 1970, 159p, Paper, Novel
12522 *The golden girl of Hockeinbeck.* Greenleaf Classics, San Diego, 1969, 224p, Paper, Novel

ROY, KATHARINE (Morris), 1907- [*biography included*]

12523 *The gentle fraud.* Peter Davies, London, 1959, 183p, Cloth, Novel

ROY, LILLIAN ELIZABETH, 1868-1932

12524 *The prince of Atlantis.* Educational Press, New York, 1929, 351p, Cloth, Novel

ROYAL, MATTHEW J.

12525 *The Isle of the Virgins; a romance.* Wenborne-Sumner Co., Buffalo, 1899, 329p, Cloth, Novel
12525A retitled: *The unknown island; or, The Isle of the Virgins.* Medal Library, Street & Smith, New York, 1925?, 329p, Paper, Novel

ROYCE, E. R.

12526 *Experiment in telepathy.* Curtis Books, London, 1954, 159p, Paper, Novel

ROYS, WILLIS E.

12527 *Flame eternal; and, Maharajah's son.* Frederick C. Osberg, New York, 1936, 403p, Cloth, Coll.

RUBEN, WILLIAM S.
see: SHANNON, FRED

RUCK, (Amy Ro)BERTA, 1878- [*biography included*]

12528 *The immortal girl; a novel.* Hodder & Stoughton, London, 1925, 314p, Cloth, Novel
12529 *Sherry and ghosts.* Hurst & Blackett, London, 1961, 192p, Cloth, Novel
12530 *A wish a day.* Hutchinson, London, 1956, 225p, Cloth, Novel

RUDHYAR, DANE, pseud. [Daniel Chenneviere, 1895-] [*biography included*]

12531 *Rania; an epic narrative.* Unity Press, San Francisco, 1973, 202p, Paper, Novel
12532 *Return from no-return; a paraphysical novel.* The Seed Center, Palo Alto, CA, 1973, 167p, Paper, Novel

RUDORFF, RAYMOND

12533 *The Dracula archives.* David Bruce & Watson, London, 1971, 207p, Cloth, Novel [Dracula series]

12534 *The house of the Brandersons; a novel of possession.* Arbor House, New York, 1973, 307p, Cloth, Novel

RUDWIN, MAXIMILIAN J(osef), 1885-

12535 *Devil stories; an anthology.* Alfred A. Knopf, New York, 1921, 332p, Cloth, Anth.

RUMBALL, CHARLES
see: DELORME, CHARLES

RUNDLE, ANNE
see: MANNERS, ALEXANDRA

RUNYON, CHARLES W(est), 1928- [*biography included*]

12536 *Ames Holbrook, deity.* Curtis, New York, 1972, 160p, Paper, Novel

12537 *I, weapon.* Doubleday, Garden City, 1974, 206p, Cloth, Novel

12538 *Pig world.* Doubleday, Garden City, 1971, 215p, Cloth, Novel

12539 *Soulmate.* Avon, New York, 1974, 159p, Paper, Novel

RUSOFF, GARRY, with Michel Parry

11205 *Chariots of fire.* Orbit, London, 1974, 192p, Paper, Novel

RUSS, JOANNA, 1937- [*biography included*]

12540 *And chaos died.* Ace, New York, 1970, 189p, Paper, Novel

12541 *Picnic on Paradise.* Ace, New York, 1968, 157p, Paper, Novel

RUSSELL, A(rthur) J(ames)

12542 *Christ comes to town.* Cassell, London, 1935, 374p, Cloth, Novel

RUSSELL, ARTHUR, pseud. [Arthur Russell Goode, 1889-]

12543 *Dr. Hades.* Wilke & Co., Sydney, 1942, 64p, Paper, Novel

RUSSELL, AUSTIN

12544 *Mr. Arrow.* Beechhurst Press, New York, 1947, 352p, Cloth, Novel

RUSSELL, BERTRAND (Arthur William), 3rd Earl Russell, 1872-1970 [*biography included*]

12545 *The collected stories of Bertrand Russell.* George Allen & Unwin, London, 1972, 349p, Cloth, Coll.

12546 *History of the world in epitome, for use in Martian infant schools.* Gaberbocchus Press, London, 1962, 11p, Paper, Story

12547 *Nightmares of eminent persons, and other stories.* Bodley Head, London, 1954, 150p, Cloth, Coll.

12548 *Satan in the suburbs, and other stories.* Bodley Head, London, 1953, 138p, Cloth, Coll.

RUSSELL, ERIC FRANK, 1905-1978 [*biography included*]

12549 *Dark tides.* Dennis Dobson, London, 1962, 184p, Cloth, Coll.

12550 *Deep space.* Fantasy Press, Reading, PA, 1954, 249p, Cloth, Coll.

12550A retitled: *Selections from Deep space.* Bantam, New York, 1955, 165p, Paper, Coll. [abridged]

12551 *Dreadful sanctuary.* Fantasy Press, Reading, PA, 1951, 276p, Cloth, Novel

12552 *Far stars.* Dennis Dobson, London, 1961, 191p, Cloth, Coll.

12553 *The Great Explosion.* Dennis Dobson, London, 1962, 203p, Cloth, Novel

12554 *Men, Martians, and machines.* Dennis Dobson, London, 1955, 191p, Cloth, Coll.
The mindwarpers. [see 12562A]
Next of kin. [see 12559A]
Selections from Deep space. [see 12550A]

12555 *Sentinels from space.* Bouregy & Curl, New York, 1953, 256p, Cloth, Novel

12556 *Sinister barrier.* World's Work, Kingswood, UK, 1943, 135p, Cloth, Novel

12557 *Six worlds yonder.* Ace Double, New York, 1958, 125p, Paper, Coll.

12558 *Somewhere a voice.* Dennis Dobson, London, 1965, 184p, Cloth, Coll.

12559 *The space willies.* Ace Double, New York, 1958, 131p, Paper, Novel

12559A retitled: *Next of kin.* Dennis Dobson, London, 1959, 187p, Cloth, Novel

12560 *Three to conquer.* Avalon, New York, 1956, 224p, Cloth, Novel

12561 *Wasp.* Avalon, New York, 1957, 223p, Cloth, Novel

12562 *With a strange device.* Dennis Dobson, London, 1964, 183p, Cloth, Novel

12562A retitled: *The mindwarpers.* Lancer, New York, 1965, 158p, Paper, Novel

RUSSELL, G(eorge) WARREN, 1854-1937

12563 *A new Heaven.* Methuen, London, 1919, 248p, Cloth, Novel

RUSSELL, GEORGE WILLIAM, 1867-1935, as A. E.

12564 *The Avatars; a futurist fantasy.* Macmillan, London, 1933, 188p, Cloth, Novel

12565 *The mask of Apollo, and other stories.* Whaley & Co., Dublin, 1904, 53p, Cloth, Coll.

RUSSELL, JOHN, pseud.
see: FEARN, JOHN RUSSELL

RUSSELL, JOHN ROBERT

12566 *Cabu.* Pocket Books, New York, 1974, 159p, Paper, Novel
12567 *Sar.* Pocket Books, New York, 1974, 157p, Paper, Novel

RUSSELL, JOHN RUSSELL, 1st Earl, 1792-1878, supposed author

12568 *Adventures in the Moon, and other worlds.* Longman, Rees, Orme, Brown, Green & Longman, London, 1836, 447p, Cloth, Coll.

RUSSELL, RAY (Robert), 1924- [*biography included*]

12569 *The case against Satan; a melodramatic novel.* Ivan Obolensky, New York, 1962, 179p, Cloth, Novel
12570 *Prince of darkness.* Sphere, London, 1971, 157p, Paper, Coll.
12571 *Sagittarius.* Playboy Press, Chicago, 1971, 184p, Paper, Coll.
12572 *Sardonicus, and other stories.* Ballantine, New York, 1961, 143p, Paper, Coll.
12573 *Unholy trinity; three short novels of gothic terror.* Bantam, New York, 1967, 115p, Paper, Coll.

published anonymously:

12574 *The dead astronaut.* Playboy Press, Chicago, 1971, 186p, Paper, Anth.
12575 *The fiend.* Playboy Press, Chicago, 1971, 192p, Paper, Anth.
12576 *From the "S" file.* Playboy Press, Chicago, 1971, 192p, Paper, Anth.
12577 *The fully automated love life of Henry Kean-ridge.* Playboy Press, Chicago, 1971, 186p, Paper, Anth.
12578 *Last train to Limbo.* Playboy Press, Chicago, 1971, 187p, Paper, Anth.
12579 *Masks.* Playboy Press, Chicago, 1971, 187p, Paper, Anth.
12580 *The Playboy book of horror and the supernatu-ral.* Playboy Press, Chicago, 1967, 390p, Cloth, Anth.
12581 *The Playboy book of science fiction and fan-tasy.* Playboy Press, Chicago, 1966, 403p, Cloth, Anth.
12582 *Playboy's stories of the sinister & strange.* Playboy Press, Chicago, 1969, 217p, Paper, Anth.
12583 *Transit of Earth.* Playboy Press, Chicago, 1971, 188p, Paper, Anth.
12584 *Weird show.* Playboy Press, Chicago, 1971, 192p, Paper, Anth.

RUSSELL, W(illiam) CLARK, 1844-1911

12585 *The death ship, a strange story; an account of a cruise in "The Flying Dutchman," collected from the papers of the late Mr. Geoffrey Fenton, of Poplar, master mariner.* Hurst & Blackett, London, 1888, vol. I-289p, II-279p, III-271p, Cloth, Novel

12585A retitled: *The Flying Dutchman; or, The death ship.* John W. Lovell, New York, 1888, 257p, Cloth, Novel
12586 *The frozen pirate.* Sampson Low, Marston, Searle & Rivington, London, 1887, vol. I-318p, II-277p, Cloth, Novel

RUSSEN, DAVID

12587 *Iter Lunare; or, A voyage to the Moon, contain-ing some considerations on the nature of that planet, the possibility of getting thi-ther, with other pleasant conceits about the inhabitants, their manners and customs.* J. Nutt, London, 1703, 147p, Cloth, Novel

THE "RUSSIA'S HOPE"

12588 *The "Russia's Hope"; or, Britannia no longer rules the waves, showing how the Muscovite bear got at the British whale.* Chapman & Hall, London, 1888, 175p, Cloth, Novel

RUSSO, JOHN

12589 *Night of the living dead.* Warner, New York, 1974, 191p, Paper, Movie

RUTLEDGE, LYMAN V.

12590 *Adam's crusade; an autumn fantasy, as revealed in the love letters and dialogues of the late Adam and Eve, discovered and transcribed by a direct descendant.* Exposition Press, New York, 1971, 180p, Cloth, Novel

RUTLEDGE, MARYSE, pseud. [Marice Louise Gibson 1884-]

12591 *The Silver Peril.* Fiction League, New York, 1931, 320p, Cloth, Novel

RUTLEY, C(ecil) BERNARD

12592 *The cave of winds.* Frederick Warne, London, 1947, 256p, Cloth, Novel
12593 *The exploding ray.* Blackie & Son, London, 1945, 222p, Cloth, Novel
12594 *The khan's carpet.* Blackie & Son, London, 1940, 224p, Cloth, Novel
12595 *The quest of Honor.* George Newnes, London, 1945, 208p, Cloth, Novel [Honor Lang #2]
12596 *Valley of doom.* George Newnes, London, 1947, 231p, Cloth, Novel

RUTLEY, OWEN, 1889-1944

12597 *Lucky star.* Hutchinson, London, 1929, 288p, Cloth, Novel
12597A retitled: *Once in a new Moon.* Hutchinson, London, 1934, 288p, Cloth, Novel
12598 *The monster of Mu.* Ernest Benn, London, 1932, 159p, Cloth, Novel

RYAN, MARAH ELLIS (Martin), 1866-1934

12599   *The Druid path.* A. C. McClurg, Chicago, 1917,
          321p, Cloth, Coll.

RYAN, R. H.

12600   *Fifteen months in the Moon.* G. H. Ryan, Lon-
          don, 1880, 96p, Paper, Novel

RYAN, R(achel) R.

12601   *Echo of a curse.* Herbert Jenkins, London,
          1939, 284p, Cloth, Novel
12602   *Freak Museum.* Herbert Jenkins, London, 1938,
          282p, Cloth, Novel
12603   *The subjugated beast.* Herbert Jenkins, Lon-
          don, 1938, 312p, Cloth, Novel

RYAN, THOMAS

12604   *Men in chains.* Peter Davies, London, 1939,
          328p, Cloth, Coll.

RYARK, FELIX

12605   *A strange land.* Hutchinson, London, 1908,
          316p, Cloth, Novel

RYDBERG, (Abraham) VIKTOR, 1828-1895

12606   *Singoalla; a romance.* Grafton Press, New York,
          1903, 209p, Cloth, Novel

RYDER, JAMES

12607   *Kark.* Robert Hale, London, 1969, 190p, Cloth,
          Novel

RYMER, JAMES MALCOLM [published anonymously]

12608   *The black monk; or, The secret of the grey
          turret,* by the author of "Ada, the betrayed,"
          "Jane Brightwell," etc. E. Lloyd, London,
          1844, 412p, Cloth, Novel
          Varney the vampyre. [see: VARNEY THE VAMPYRE]

RYUNOSUKE AKUTAGAWA
     see: AKUTAGAWA, RYUNOSUKE

RYVES, T(homas) E(van), 1895-

12609   *Bandersnatch.* Grey Walls Press, London,
          1950, 299p, Cloth, Novel

S., A. F.
     see: SILVANI, ANITA

S., DAVY

12610   *Gay vampire.* 101 Books, New York?, 1969,
          , Paper, Novel

S., J., of Dale
     see: STIMSON, FREDERIC JESUP

S., K. O.
     see: DOMBROWSKI, KATRINA

S., L. W. J.
     see: ROWEL, M.

S., R.
     see: PALTOCK, ROBERT

S., W. S. L.
     see: LACH-SZYRMA, W. S.

S. M. C.
     see: MARY CATHERINE, Sister

SABERHAGEN, FRED (Thomas), 1930-   [*biography
included*]

12611   *Berserker.* Ballantine, New York, 1967, 190p,
          Paper, Coll. [Berserker #1]
12612   *The Black Mountains.* Ace, New York, 1971,
          159p, Paper, Novel [Earth's End #2]
12613   *The Broken Lands.* Ace, New York, 1968, 191p,
          Paper, Novel [Earth's End #1]
12614   *Brother assassin.* Ballantine, New York, 1969,
          222p, Paper, Novel [Berserker #2]
12614A retitled: *Brother Berserker.* Macdonald, Lon-
          don, 1969, 167p, Cloth, Novel [Berserker #2]
12615   *Changeling Earth.* DAW, New York, 1973, 176p,
          Paper, Novel [Earth's End #3]
12616   *The Golden people.* Ace Double, New York,
          1964, 118p, Paper, Novel
12617   *The water of thought.* Ace Double, New York,
          1965, 117p, Paper, Novel

SABIN, EDWIN L(egrand), 1870-

12618   *The City of the Sun.* George W. Jacobs, Phila-
          delphia, 1924, 316p, Cloth, Novel

THE SACK OF LONDON IN THE GREAT FRENCH WAR OF
1901

12619   *The sack of London in the great French war of
          1901, being a drama of the twentieth century,
          as related by one who saw it.* F. V. White,
          London, 1901, 119p, Cloth, Novel

SACKERMAN, HENRY (Claude), 1940-   [*biography
included*]

12620   *The love bomb.* Bantam, New York, 1972, 215p,
          Paper, Novel

SACKVILLE, HONORIA de
     see: de SACKVILLE, HONORIA

SACKVILLE, ORME

12621 *The jungle goddess.* Modern Publishing Co.,
London, 1935?, 254p, Cloth, Novel

SACKVILLE-WEST, EDWARD (Charles), 5th Baron
Sackville, 1901-1965

12622 *The ruin; a gothic novel.* William Heinemann,
London, 1926, 363p, Cloth, Novel

SACKVILLE-WEST, V(ictoria Mary), 1892-1962

12623 *Grand Canyon; a novel.* Michael Joseph, London, 1942, 206p, Cloth, Novel

SADLER, ADAM

12624 *Red ending.* Ward, Lock, London, 1928, 314p,
Cloth, Novel

SAFRONI-MIDDLETON, A(rnold)

12625 *The dreaming skull (the terrors of a triple
personality).* World Wide Press, London,
1948, 246p, Paper, Novel

SAGE, ALAIN RENE LE
see: LE SAGE, ALAIN RENE

SAHA, ARTHUR W(illiam), 1923- *[biography
included]*, with Donald A. Wollheim

12626 *The 1972 annual world's best SF.* DAW, New
York, 1972, 302p, Paper, Anth.
12627 *The 1973 annual world's best SF.* DAW, New
York, 1973, 253p, Paper, Anth.
12628 *The 1974 annual world's best SF.* DAW, New
York, 1974, 280p, Paper, Anth.

SAHULA-DYCKE, IGNATZ, 1900-

12629 *Alias Kinson; or, The ghost of Billy the Kid.*
Pageant Press, New York, 1963, 198p, Cloth,
Novel

StCLAIR, CECIL, pseud.
see: CLARK, SUSIE CHAMPNEY

ST. CLAIR, MARGARET, 1911- *[biography in-
cluded]*

12630 *Agent of the unknown.* Ace Double, New York,
1956, 128p, Paper, Novel
12631 *Change the sky, and other stories.* Ace, New
York, 1974, 300p, Paper, Coll.
12632 *The Dancers of Noyo.* Ace, New York, 1973,
224p, Paper, Novel
12633 *The dolphins of Altair.* Dell, New York,
1967, 188p, Paper, Novel
12634 *The games of Neith.* Ace Double, New York,
1960, 149p, Paper, Novel
12635 *The Green Queen.* Ace Double, New York, 1956,
128p, Paper, Novel

12636 *Message from the Eocene.* Ace Double, New York,
1964, 114p, Paper, Novel
12637 *The shadow people.* Dell, New York, 1969, 189p,
Paper, Novel
12638 *Sign of the Labrys.* Bantam, New York, 1963,
139p, Paper, Novel
12639 *Three worlds of futurity.* Ace Double, New York,
1964, 142p, Paper, Coll.

ST. EXUPÉRY, ANTOINE (Jean Baptiste Marie
Roger) de, 1900-1944

12640 *The little prince.* Reynal & Hitchcock, New
York, 1943, 91p, Cloth, Novel

ST. GERMAIN, MARIE

12641 *Tales of the weird and the west countree.* William Brendon & Son, Plymouth, UK, 1924, 142p,
Paper, Coll.

ST. IRVYNE
see: SHELLEY, PERCY BYSSHE

ST. JOHN, DAVID, pseud. [Everette Howard Hunt
Jr., 1918-]

12642 *The coven.* Weybright & Talley, New York, 1972,
159p, Cloth, Novel

ST. JOHN, J(ames) ALLEN, 1872-1957

12643 *The face in the pool; a faerie tale.* A. C.
McClurg, Chicago, 1905, 155p, Cloth, Novel

ST. JOHN, PHILIP, pseud.
see: del REY, LESTER

ST. JOHN-LOE, GLADYS

12644 *The door of beyond.* Duckworth, London, 1926,
223p, Cloth, Novel

ST. L., VIC
see: HOPKINS, JEUNE

ST. LUZ, BERTHE, pseud. [Alice Alberthe Robertson, 1871-]

12645 *Tamar Curze.* R. F. Fenno, New York, 1908,
206p, Cloth, Novel

SAINTSBURY, GEORGE (Edward Bateman), 1845-1933

12646 *Tales of mystery.* Percival & Co., London,
1891, 319p, Cloth, Anth.

SALAZAR (y) CHAPELA, E(steban), 1902-

12647 *Naked in Piccadilly.* Abelard-Schuman, London,
1961, 285p, Cloth, Novel

SALE, RICHARD (Bernard), 1911-   [*biography included*]

12648 *Not too narrow...not too deep; a novel*. Simon & Schuster, New York, 1936, 240p, Cloth, Novel

SALIGNAC de la MOTHE FENELON, FRANCOIS de
    see: FENELON, FRANCOIS

SALINGER, PIERRE (Emil George), 1925-

12649 *On instructions of my government*. Doubleday, Garden City, 1971, 408p, Cloth, Novel

SALISBURY, H(enry) B(arnard)

12650 *Miss Worden's hero; a novel*. G. W. Dillingham, New York, 1890, 149p, Cloth, Novel
12650A retitled: *The birth of freedom; a socialist novel*. Humboldt Publishing Co., New York, 1894, 149p, Cloth, Novel

SALISBURY, WILLIAM, 1875-

12651 *The American Emperor; a novel*. Tabard Inn Press, New York, 1913, 398p, Cloth, Novel
12652 *The Squareheads; the story of a socialized state; a futuristic novel*. Independent Publishing Co., New Rochelle, NY, 1929, 168p, Paper, Novel

SALLASKA, GEORGIA (Myrle), 1933-   [*biography included*]

12653 *Priam's daughter*. Doubleday, Garden City, 1970, 353p, Cloth, Novel
12654 *Three ships and three kings*. Doubleday, Garden City, 1969, 383p, Cloth, Novel

SALLIS, JAMES, 1944-   [*biography included*]

12655 *The shores beneath; novellas*. Avon, New York, 1971, 192p, Paper, Anth.
12656 *The war book*. Rupert Hart-Davis, London, 1969, 188p, Cloth, Anth.

SALMON, ARTHUR L(eslie), 1865-

12657 *The ferry of souls; a book of fantasies and sketches*. Foulis Publishers, London, 1927, 94p, Cloth, Coll.

SALTEN, FELIX, pseud. [Sigmund Salzmann, 1869-1945]

12658 *The hound of Florence; a novel*. Simon & Schuster, New York, 1930, 237p, Cloth, Novel

SALTOUN, M(ary Helena), 1863?-1940

12659 *After*. Duckworth, London, 1930, 192p, Cloth, Novel

SALZMANN, SIGMUND
    see: SALTEN, FELIX

SAMACHSON, JOSEPH, 1906-   [*biography included*]
  as William Morrison:

12660 *Mel Oliver and Space Rover on Mars*. Gnome Press, New York, 1954, 191p, Cloth, Novel

  as Brett Sterling, house pseud.:

12661 *The tenth planet*. Popular Library, New York, 1969, 128p, Paper, Novel [Captain Future #12]

SAMBROT, WILLIAM (Anthony), 1920-   [*biography included*]

12662 *Island of fear, and other science fiction stories*. Permabooks, New York, 1963, 166p, Paper, Coll.

SAMPSON, ASHLEY, 1900-

12663 *The ghost of Mr. Brown*. Fortune Press, London, 1941, 100p, Cloth, Novel

SAMUEL, (Herbert Louis), Viscount, 1870-1963

12664 *An unknown land*. George Allen & Unwin, London, 1942, 221p, Cloth, Novel

SAMUEL, HORACE B(arnett), 1883-

12665 *The Quisto-box*. A. M. Philpot, London, 1925, 284p, Cloth, Novel

SAMUEL, MAURICE, 1895-1972

12666 *The devil that failed*. Alfred A. Knopf, New York, 1952, 271p, Cloth, Novel

SAMUELS, VICTOR, pseud.
    see: BANIS, VICTOR

SANBORN, ROBERT ALDEN

12667 *Mr. Mudge cuts across; a fantasy on friendship*. Suttonhouse, Los Angeles, 1937, 263p, Cloth, Novel

SANBORN, ROBIN

12668 *The Book of Stier*. Berkley Medallion, New York, 1971, 191p, Paper, Novel

SAND, GEORGE, pseud. [Amandine Aurore Lucie Dudevant, 1804-1876]

12669 *The naiad; a ghost story*. William R. Jenkins, New York, 1892, 116p, Cloth, Novel

SANDERS, JOHN
    see: COMER, RALPH

SANDERS, LEONARD M. Jr.
   see: THOMAS, DAN

SANDERS, THOMAS E(dward Nippawanock), 1926-
[biography included]

12670   Speculations; an introduction to literature
       through fantasy and science fiction. Glen-
       coe Press, Beverly Hills, CA, 1973, 621p,
       Paper, Anth.

SANDERSON, IVAN T.
   see: ROBERTS, TERENCE

SANDISSON, Mr. de, pseud. [Jean Paul Bignon,
1662-1743]

12671   The adventures of Abdalla, son of Hanif, sent
       by the Sultan of the Indies to make a dis-
       covery of the Island of Borico, where the
       fountain which restores past youth is sup-
       posed to be found; also, an account of the
       travels of Rouschen, a Persian lady, to the
       Topsy-Turvy island, undiscover'd to this
       day; the whole intermix'd with several curi-
       ous and instructive histories. T. Worrall,
       London, 1729, 169p, Cloth, Novel

SANDOZ, MAURICE (Yves), 1892-1958

12672   The maze. Doubleday, Doran, Garden City,
       1945, 110p, Cloth, Novel

SANDRUS, MARY YOST

12673   Famous mysteries. Scott, Foresman, Chicago,
       1955, 298p, Cloth, Anth.

THE SANDS OF MARS

12674   The sands of Mars, and other stories. Satel-
       lite, London, 1958, 113p, Paper, Anth.

SANGSTER, JIMMY, 1927-   [biography included],
with Barre Lyndon as John Sansom

09356   The man who could cheat death. Ace, London,
       1959, 188p, Paper, Movie
09356A The man who could cheat death, by Jimmy Sang-
       ster and Barre Lyndon. Avon, New York,
       1959, 160p, Paper, Movie

SANSOM, JOHN, pseud.
   see: SANGSTER, JIMMY and LYNDON, BARRE

SANSOM, WILLIAM, 1912-1976 [biography inclu-
ded]

12675   Fireman flower, and other stories. Hogarth
       Press, London, 1944, 163p, Cloth, Coll.

SANTESSON, HANS STEFAN, 1914-1975 [biography
included]

12676   Crime prevention in the 30th century. Walker,
       New York, 1969, 175p, Cloth, Anth.
12677   The days after tomorrow; science fiction sto-
       ries. Little, Brown, Boston, 1971, 261p,
       Cloth, Anth.
12678   The Fantastic universe omnibus. Prentice-Hall,
       Englewood Cliffs, NJ, 1960, 270p, Cloth,
       Anth.
12679   Flying saucers in fact and fiction. Lancer,
       New York, 1968, 224p, Paper, Anth. [includes
       some nonf.]
12680   Gentle invaders. Belmont, New York, 1969,
       176p, Paper, Anth.
12681   Gods for tomorrow. Award, New York, 1967,
       208p, Paper, Anth.
12682   The mighty barbarians; great sword and sorcery
       heroes. Lancer, New York, 1969, 221p, Paper,
       Anth.
12683   The mighty swordsmen. Lancer, New York, 1970,
       256p, Paper, Anth.
12684   Rulers of men. Pyramid, New York, 1965, 173p,
       Paper, Anth.

SANTUCCI, LUIGI

12685   Orfeo in paradise. Alfred A. Knopf, New York,
       1969, 210p, Cloth, Novel

SANZ, JOSÉ

12686   SF symposium; FC simpósio. Instituto Nacional
       do Cinema, Rio de Janeiro, 1970, 188p, Paper,
       Nonf. Anth. [in English and Portuguese]

SAPIR, RICHARD, with Warren Murphy

10535   The Destroyer; Dr. Quake. Pinnacle, New York,
       1972, 187p, Paper, Novel [Destroyer #5]

SAPPER, pseud.
   see: McNEILE, HERMAN C.

SAPTE, W(illiam) Jr.

12687   Hosts of ghosts. Family Reader Office, London,
       1906, 130p, Paper, Coll.

SARAC, ROGER, pseud. [Roger Andrew Caras,
1928-] [biography included]

12688   The throwbacks. Belmont, New York, 1965, 140p,
       Paper, Novel

SARATKUMARA GHOSHA, A.
   see: GHOSH, SARATH KUMAR

SARBAN, pseud. [John William Wall, 1910-]

12689   The doll maker. Ballantine, New York, 1960,
       144p, Paper, Novel
12690   The doll maker, and other tales of the uncanny.
       Peter Davies, London, 1953, 247p, Cloth, Coll.

SARBAN (cont.)

12691 *Ringstones.* Ballantine, New York, 1961, 139p, Paper, Novel
12692 *Ringstones, and other curious tales.* Peter Davies, London, 1951, 283p, Cloth, Coll.
12693 *The sound of his horn.* Peter Davies, London, 1952, 154p, Cloth, Novel

SARBROW, CÈPRE, pseud. [P. S. Barrows]

12694 *More about Scheherazade.* Exposition Press, New York, 1964, 406p, Cloth, Novel

SARRATT, H. J.
  see: RASPE, RUDOLF ERICH

SARTON, (Eleanor) MAY, 1912-

12695 *The Fur Person.* Rinehart, New York, 1957, 106p, Cloth, Novel

SARTRE, JEAN-PAUL, 1905- [*biography inclu-ded*]

12696 *The chips are down (Les jeux sont faits).* Lear, New York, 1948, 187p, Cloth, Novel

SATCHELL, WILLIAM

12697 *The elixir of life.* Chapman & Hall, London, 1907, 320p, Cloth, Novel

THE SATURDAY EVENING POST READER OF FANTASY AND SCIENCE FICTION
  see: THE POST READER OF FANTASY AND SCI-ENCE FICTION

SAUER, JULIA L(ina), 1891-

12698 *Fog magic.* Viking Press, New York, 1943, 107p, Cloth, Novel

SAUER, ROB(ert C.)

12699 *Voyages; scenarios for a ship called Earth.* Ballantine, New York, 1971, 316p, Paper, Anth.

SAUL, GEORGE BRANDON, 1901- [*biography in-cluded*]

12700 *Carved in findruine; tales out of Irish tra-dition.* Walton Press, Philadelphia, 1969, 70p, Cloth, Coll.
12701 *Liadain and Curithir; a medieval Irish love story, and four tales from the elf-mounds.* Walton Press, Philadelphia, 1970, 73p, Cloth, Coll.
12702 *A little book of strange tales.* Walton Press, Philadelphia, 1969, 70p, Cloth, Coll.
12703 *Owls' watch.* Crest, Greenwich, Conn., 1965, 238p, Paper, Anth.

SAUNDERS, EDITH (Alice)

12704 *Fanny Penquite.* Humphrey Milford, Oxford University Press, London, 1932, 43p, Cloth, Story

SAUNDERS, HILARY (Aidan St. George), 1898-1951, with John Palmer as Francis Beeding

11151 *The One Sane Man.* Little, Brown, Boston, 1934, 314p, Cloth, Novel
11152 *The seven sleepers.* Little, Brown, Boston, 1925, 317p, Cloth, Novel

SAUNDERS, JAKE, with Howard Waldrop

12705 *The Texas-Israeli War: 1999.* Ballantine, New York, 1974, 209p, Paper, Novel

SAUNDERS, MARGARET BAILLIE-
  see: BAILLIE-SAUNDERS, MARGARET

SAUNDERS, W. J.

12706 *Kalomera; the story of a remarkable community.* Elliot Stock, London, 1911, 301p, Cloth, Novel

SAURAT, DENIS

12707 *Angels and beasts; new short stories from France.* Westhouse, London, 1947, 285p, Cloth, Anth.

SAVA, GEORGE
  see: BORODIN, GEORGE

SAVAGE, BLAKE, pseud.
  see: BLAINE, JOHN

SAVAGE, HARDLEY, pseud.

12708 *Jetman meets the mad madam.* Bee-Line, New York, 1966,   , Paper, Novel

SAVAGE, JOSEPH W(eber), 1861-

12709 *Greed's grip broken; or, The right to live.* Avondale Press, New York, 1928, 225p, Cloth, Novel

SAVAGE, JUANITA

12710 *The city of desire.* Geoffrey Bles, London, 1926, 319p, Cloth, Novel

SAVAGE, MARY, pseud. [Mary Dresser]

12711 *A likeness to voices.* Torquil, New York, 1963, 214p, Cloth, Novel

SAVAGE, RICHARD, pseud. [Ivan Roe, 1917-   ]

12712 *When the Moon died; a modern novel of science
          and imagination.* Ward, Lock, London, 1955,
          189p, Cloth, Novel

SAVAGE, TIMOTHY

12713 *The Amazonian Republic, recently discovered in
          the interior of Peru.* Samuel Colman, New
          York, 1842, 177p, Cloth, Novel

SAVAGE PASSIONS

12714 *Savage passions.* no publisher, Oxford, NJ,
          1950?, 48p, Paper, Anth.

SAVARIN, JULIAN JAY

12715 *Waiters on the dance.* Arlington Books, London,
          1972, 221p, Cloth, Novel [Lemmus #1]

SAVIDGE, E. VAN PEDROE-
    see: VAN PEDROE-SAVIDGE, E.

SAVILE, FRANK (Mackenzie)

12716 *Beyond the great south wall; the secret of the
          Antarctic.* Sampson Low, Marston, Searle &
          Rivington, London, 1899, 302p, Cloth, Novel

SAVILL, MERVYN

12717 *Snapdragon; a collection of queer stories.*
          Arthur Barker, London, 1955, 235p, Cloth,
          Anth.

SAVILLE, (Leonard) MALCOLM, 1901-

12718 *Saucers over the moor; a Lone Pine story.*
          George Newnes, London, 1955, 244p, Cloth,
          Novel [Lone Pine #8]

SAXON, PETER, house pseud. [see also Martin
Thomas and W. Howard Baker]

12719 *Black Honey.* Mayflower, London, 1968, 157p,
          Paper, Novel
12720 *Corruption.* Sphere, London, 1968, 144p, Paper,
          Novel
12721 *The curse of Rathlaw.* Lancer, New York, 1968,
          190p, Paper, Novel [Guardians series] [by
          Martin Thomas]
12722 *Dark ways to death.* Howard Baker, London,
          1968, 176p, Cloth, Novel [Guardians series]
12722A retitled: *The Guardians #2; Dark ways to
          death.* Berkley Medallion, New York, 1969,
          143p, Paper, Novel [Guardians #2]
00753 *The darkest night.* Mayflower, London, 1966,
          157p, Paper, Novel [by W. Howard Baker]
12723 *The disorientated man.* Mayflower, London,
          1966, 126p, Paper, Novel
12723A retitled: *Scream and scream again.* Paperback
          Library, New York, 1967, 158p, Paper, Novel

12724 *The Guardians #1; The killing bone.* Berkley
          Medallion, New York, 1969, 159p, Paper, Novel
          [Guardians #1]
       The Guardians #2; Dark ways to death. [see
          12722]
12725 *The Guardians #3; The haunting of Alan Mais.*
          Berkley Medallion, New York, 1969, 143p,
          Paper, Novel [Guardians #3]
12726 *The Guardians #4; The vampires of Finistère.*
          Berkley Medallion, New York, 1970, 190p,
          Paper, Novel [Guardians #4]
12726A retitled: *The vampires of Finistère.* Howard
          Baker, London, 1970, 190p, Cloth, Novel
          [Guardians series]
00754 *Satan's child.* Mayflower, London, 1967, 127p,
          Paper, Novel [by W. Howard Baker]
       Scream and scream again. [see 12723A]
12727 *Through the dark curtain.* Lancer, New York,
          1968, 190p, Paper, Novel [Guardians series]
00755 *The Torturer.* Mayflower, London, 1966, 159p,
          Paper, Novel [by W. Howard Baker]
       The vampires of Finistère. [see 12726A]
12728 *Vampire's moon.* Belmont, New York, 1970,
          176p, Paper, Novel

SAXON, RICHARD, pseud.
    see: MORRISSEY, J. L.

SAXON MILLS, G(odfrey) H(ope)

12729 *Interruption.* William Heinemann, London,
          1932, 333p, Cloth, Novel

SAXTON, JOSEPHINE (Mary), 1935-   [*biography
included*]

12730 *Group feast.* Doubleday, Garden City, 1971,
          184p, Cloth, Novel
12731 *The hieros gamos of Sam and An Smith.* Double-
          day, Garden City, 1969, 138p, Cloth, Novel
12732 *Vector for seven; the weltanschaung of Mrs.
          Amelia Mortimer and friends.* Doubleday,
          Garden City, 1970, 238p, Cloth, Novel

SAXTON, MARK

12733 *The Islar; a narrative of Lang III.* Houghton
          Mifflin, Boston, 1969, 308p, Cloth, Novel
          [Islandia #2]

SAYERS, DOROTHY L(eigh), 1898-1957

12734 *Great short stories of detection, mystery, and
          horror.* Victor Gollancz, London, 1928,
          1231p, Cloth, Anth.
12734A retitled: *Great stories of detection, mystery
          and horror, part II: mystery and horror.*
          Victor Gollancz, London, 1939, 619p, Cloth,
          Anth. [abridged; part I is not in itself SF]
12735 *Great short stories of detection, mystery, and
          horror, second series.* Victor Gollancz, Lon-
          don, 1931, 1147p, Cloth, Anth.
12736 *Great short stories of detection, mystery, and
          horror, third series.* Victor Gollancz, Lon-
          don, 1934, 1069p, Cloth, Anth.
12737 *The omnibus of crime.* Payson & Clarke, New
          York, 1929, 1177p, Cloth, Anth. [based rough-
          ly on 12734]

SAYERS, DOROTHY L. (cont.)

12737A retitled: *Human and inhuman stories.* Macfadden-Bartell, New York, 1963, 176p, Paper, Anth. [abridged]

12737B retitled: *Stories of the supernatural.* Macfadden-Bartell, New York, 1963, 144p, Paper, Anth. [abridged]

12738 *The second omnibus of crime.* Coward-McCann, New York, 1932, 855p, Cloth, Anth. [roughly based on 12735]

12738A retitled: *The world's great crime stories.* Blue Ribbon, New York, 1932?, 855p, Cloth, Anth.

12739 *The third omnibus of crime.* Coward-McCann, New York, 1935, 808p, Cloth, Anth. [roughly based on 12736]

SAYLER, H(arry) L(incoln), 1863-1913

12740 *The Airship Boys adrift; or, Saved by an aeroplane.* Reilly & Britton, Chicago, 1909, 312p, Cloth, Novel [Airship Boys #2]

12741 *The Airship Boys due north; or, By balloon to the Pole.* Reilly & Britton, Chicago, 1910, 335p, Cloth, Novel [Airship Boys #3]

12742 *The Airship Boys in finance; or, The flight of the flying cow.* Reilly & Britton, Chicago, 1911, 295p, Cloth, Novel [Airship Boys #5]

12743 *The Airship Boys in the barren lands; or, The secret of the white Eskimos.* Reilly & Britton, Chicago, 1910, 326p, Cloth, Novel [Airship Boys #4]

12744 *The Airship Boys' ocean flyer; or, New York to London in twelve hours.* Reilly & Britton, Chicago, 1911, 327p, Cloth, Novel [Airship Boys #6]

12745 *The Airship Boys; or, The quest of the Aztec treasure.* Reilly & Britton, Chicago, 1909, 315p, Cloth, Novel [Airship Boys #1]

SCAEVOLA, PETER

12746 *'68; a novel of presidential politics.* W. W. Norton, New York, 1964, 287p, Cloth, Novel

SCARBOROUGH, DOROTHY, 1878-1935

12747 *Famous modern ghost stories.* G. P. Putnam's Sons, New York, 1921, 419p, Cloth, Anth.

12748 *Humorous ghost stories.* G. P. Putnam's Sons, New York, 1921, 431p, Cloth, Anth.

12749 *The supernatural in modern English fiction.* G. P. Putnam's Sons, New York, 1917, 329p, Cloth, Nonf.

SCARBOROUGH, HAROLD E(llicott), 1897-

12750 *The immortals.* T. Fisher Unwin, London, 1924, 266p, Cloth, Novel

SCARM, ARTHUR N.
see: SCRAM, ARTHUR N.

SCHACHNER, NAT(han), 1895-1955

12751 *Space lawyer.* Gnome Press, New York, 1953, 222p, Cloth, Novel

SCHAEFER, JACK (Warner), 1907-

12752 *The canyon.* Houghton Mifflin, Boston, 1953, 132p, Cloth, Novel

12753 *The canyon, and other stories.* Andre Deutsch, London, 1955, 160p, Cloth, Coll.

SCHAPER, EDZARD (Hellmuth), 1908-

12754 *Star over the frontier.* Helicon Press, Baltimore, 1960, 64p, Cloth, Novel

SCHARY, JILL, 1936-

12755 *Thanks for the rubies, now please pass the Moon.* Dial Press, New York, 1972, 367p, Cloth, Novel

SCHEALER, JOHN M(ilton), 1920- [biography included]

12756 *Zip-Zip and his flying saucer.* E. P. Dutton, New York, 1956, 118p, Cloth, Novel [Zip-Zip #1]

12757 *Zip-Zip and the red planet.* E. P. Dutton, New York, 1961, 128p, Cloth, Novel [Zip-Zip #3]

12758 *Zip-Zip goes to Venus.* E. P. Dutton, New York, 1958, 125p, Cloth, Novel [Zip-Zip #2]

SCHERR, MARIE
see: CHER, MARIE

SCHINDLER, SOLOMON, 1842-1915

12759 *Young West; a sequel to Edward Bellamy's celebrated novel, Looking backward.* Arena Publishing Co., Boston, 1894, 283p, Cloth, Novel [a sequel to Bellamy's novel]

SCHLEPPEY, BLANCHE BLOOR

12760 *The soul of a mummy, and other stories.* no publisher, Indianapolis, 1908, 260p, Cloth, Coll.

SCHMELTZER, KARL

12761 *The axe of bronze; a story of Stonehenge.* Sterling Publishing Co., New York, 1958, 142p, Cloth, Novel

SCHMIDT, JAMES NORMAN
see: NORMAN, JAMES

SCHMITZ, JAMES H(enry), 1911-   [*biography included*]

12762   *Agent of Vega.* Gnome Press, Hicksville, NY, 1960, 191p, Cloth, Coll.
12763   *The demon breed.* Ace, New York, 1968, 157p, Paper, Novel [Hub series]
12764   *The eternal frontiers.* G. P. Putnam's Sons, New York, 1973, 190p, Cloth, Novel
12765   *The Lion Game.* DAW, New York, 1973, 157p, Paper, Novel [Telzey #2; Hub series]
12766   *A nice day for screaming, and other tales of the Hub.* Chilton, Philadelphia, 1965, 159p, Cloth, Coll. [Hub series]
12767   *A pride of monsters.* Macmillan, New York, 1970, 248p, Cloth, Coll. [Hub series]
12768   *A tale of two clocks.* Torquil, New York, 1962, 206p, Cloth, Novel [Hub series]
12769   *The Telzey toy.* DAW, New York, 1973, 175p, Paper, Coll. [Telzey #3; Hub series]
12770   *The universe against her.* Ace, New York, 1964, 160p, Paper, Novel [Telzey #1; Hub series]
12771   *The witches of Karres.* Chilton, Philadephia, 1966, 202p, Cloth, Novel

SCHNABEL, ERNST (Georg), 1913-

12772   *Story for Icarus; projects, incidents, and conclusions from the life of D., engineer.* Harcourt, Brace & Co., New York, 1961, 313p, Cloth, Novel

SCHNEIDER, JOHN G., 1908?-1964

12773   *The golden kazoo.* Rinehart, New York, 1956, 246p, Cloth, Novel

SCHOEB, ERIKA

as Denise de Witt:

12774   *The daughters of Pan.* Svea, Copenhagen, 1970, 148p, Paper, Novel

as Aristotle Levi:

12775   *Spawn of the devil.* Svea, Copenhagen, 1969, 175p, Paper, Novel

as Wernher von Grau:

12776   *A sex odyssey (8001: a sex odyssey).* Svea, Copenhagen, 1969, 173p, Paper, Novel

SCHOEPFLIN, HAROLD VINCENT
    see: VINCENT, HARL

SCHOONOVER, LAWRENCE (Lovell), 1906-   [*biography included*]

12777   *Central passage.* William Sloane Associates, New York, 1962, 246p, Cloth, Novel

SCHOPFER, JEAN
    see: ANET, CLAUDE

SCHORER, MARK (R.), 1908-1977 [*biography included*], with August Derleth

04241   *Colonel Markesan, and less pleasant people.* Arkham House, Sauk City, 1966, 285p, Cloth, Coll.

SCHRAM, IRENE, 1941-

12778   *Ashes, ashes, we all fall down; a novel.* Simon & Schuster, New York, 1972, 192p, Cloth, Novel

SCHRAMM, WILBUR (Lang), 1907-

12779   *Windwagon Smith, and other yarns.* Harcourt, Brace & Co., New York, 1947, 208p, Cloth, Coll.

SCHREINER, OLIVE (Emilie Albertina), 1855-192?

12780   *So here then are dreams.* Roycrofter Shop, East Aurora, NY, 1901, 82p, Cloth, Coll.
12781   *Stories, dreams, and allegories.* T. Fisher Unwin, London, 1923, 156p, Cloth, Coll.

SCHUCK, FRED(erick) H(ugo) P(aul), 1916-   [*biography included*]

12782   *The phantom caravan.* Vantage Press, New York 1964, 212p, Cloth, Novel

SCHUETTE, H. GEORGE, 1850-

12783   *Athonia; or, The original Four Hundred.* The Author, Manitowoc, Wisc., 1910, 483p, Cloth Novel

SCHULMAN, L(ester) M(artin), 1934-   [*biography included*]

12784   *The cracked looking glass; stories of other realities.* Macmillan, New York, 1971, 254p Cloth, Anth.

SCHURÉ, ÉDOUARD, 1841-1929

12785   *The priestess of Isis.* William Rider & Son, London, 1910, 318p, Cloth, Novel

SCHÜTZ, HEINRICH

12786   *When mammoths ruled the frozen Earth.* Jonathan Cape & Harrison Smith, New York, 1929, 197p, Cloth, Novel

SCHUYLER, GEORGE S(amuel), 1895-

12787   *Black no more, being an account of the strange and wonderful workings of science in the land of the free, A.D. 1933-1940.* Macaulay Co., New York, 1931, 250p, Cloth, Novel

SCHWAB, GÜNTHER, 1904-

12788 *Dance with the devil; a dramatic encounter.*
Geoffrey Bles, London, 1963, 271p, Cloth,
Novel

SCHWALLER DE LUBICZ, ISHA, 1885-

12789 *Her-Bak, "Chick-Pea"; the living face of ancient Egypt.* Hodder & Stoughton, London,
1954, 344p, Cloth, Novel [Her-Bak #1]
12790 *Her-Bak, Egyptian initiate.* Hodder & Stoughton, London, 1967, 220p, Cloth, Novel [Her-
Bak #2]

SCHWARTZ, ALAN

12791 *The wandering Tellurian.* Ace Double, New
York, 1967, 116p, Paper, Novel

SCIENCE FANTASY QUINTETTE

12792 *Science fantasy quintette.* Fantasy Publishing
Co., Los Angeles, 1953, 364p, Cloth, Anth.
[includes L. Ron Hubbard's *Triton* and Ed
Earl Repp's *The radium pool*]

SCIENCE FICTION: A BIBLIOGRAPHY

12793 *Science fiction: a bibliography.* Provincial
Library, Regina, Sask., 1973, 33p, Paper,
Nonf.

SCIENCE-FICTION LIBRARY

12794 *Science-fiction library, no. 1.* Gerald G.
Swan, London, 1950?, 64p, Paper, Anth.
12795 *Science-fiction library, no. 2.* Gerald G.
Swan, London, 1950?, 64p, Paper, Anth.

THE SCIENCE FICTION NOVEL

12796 *The science fiction novel; imagination and
social criticism.* Advent: Publishers, Chicago, 1959, 160p, Cloth, Nonf. Anth.

A SCIENCE FICTION OMNIBUS ON POLLUTION

12797 *A science fiction omnibus on pollution.* Sidgwick & Jackson, London, 1971, 511p, Cloth,
Anth. [includes *Make room! Make room!* by
Harry Harrison; *City*, by Clifford Simak;
and a short story]

SCIENCE FICTION SPECIAL

12798 *Science fiction special (1).* Sidgwick & Jackson, London, 1970, 546p, Cloth, Anth. [in-
cludes *The world Jones made*, by Philip K.
Dick; *The space swimmers*, by Gordon R. Dickson; *Waters of death*, by Irving Greenfield]
12799 *Science fiction special (2).* Sidgwick & Jackson, London, 1970, 572p, Cloth, Anth. [in-
cludes *The listeners*, by Murray Leinster;
Bright new universe, by Jack Williamson;
Escape into space, by E. C. Tubb]

12800 *Science fiction special (3).* Sidgwick & Jackson, London, 1971, 656p, Cloth, Anth. [in-
cludes: *Caviar*, by Theodore Sturgeon; *The
time-hoppers*, by Robert Silverberg; *Overmind*,
by Phyllis Marie Wadsworth]
12801 *Science fiction special (4).* Sidgwick & Jackson, London, 1971, 573p, Cloth, Anth. [in-
cludes: *The man in the maze*, by Robert Silverberg; *The winged man*, by E. Mayne Hull &
A. E. van Vogt; *The rose*, by Charles L. Har-
ness]
12802 *Science fiction special (5).* Sidgwick & Jackson, London, 1971, 635p, Cloth, Anth. [in-
cludes: *Rite of passage*, by Alexei Panshin;
Cradle of the Sun, by Brian M. Stableford;
The future makers, by Peter Haining]
12803 *Science fiction special (6).* Sidgwick & Jackson, London, 1973, 414p, Cloth, Anth. [in-
cludes: *Children of tomorrow*, by A. E. van
Vogt; *Now comes tomorrow*, by Robert Moore
Williams]
12804 *Science fiction special (7).* Sidgwick & Jackson, London, 1973, 868p, Cloth, Anth. [in-
cludes: *A Murray Leinster omnibus*; *A Philip
K. Dick omnibus*]
12805 *Science fiction special (8).* Sidgwick & Jackson, London, 1973, 599p, Cloth, Anth. [in-
cludes: *Timescoop*, by John Brunner; *Quest
for the future*, by A. E. van Vogt; *The profit
of doom*, by Hugh Dirac]
12806 *Science fiction special (9).* Sidgwick & Jackson, London, 1974, 439p, Cloth, Anth. [in-
cludes: *Possible tomorrows*, by Groff Conklin; *Trilogy of the future*, by Donald A.
Wollheim]
12807 *Science fiction special (10).* Sidgwick & Jackson, London, 1974, 538p, Cloth, Anth. [in-
cludes: *Nightwings*, by Robert Silverberg;
Destiny doll, by Clifford Simak; *The dreaming
Earth*, by John Brunner]
12808 *Science fiction special (11).* Sidgwick & Jackson, London, 1974, 611p, Cloth, Anth. [in-
cludes: *Time tunnel*, by Murray Leinster;
The battle of forever, by A. E. van Vogt;
Bug-eyed monsters, by Anthony Cheetham]

THE SCIENCE-FICTIONAL SHERLOCK HOLMES
see: PETERSON, ROBERT C.

SCITHERS, GEORGE H(arry), 1929- [*biography
included*], with L. Sprague de Camp

03999 *The Conan grimoire.* Mirage Press, Baltimore,
1972, 264p, Cloth, Nonf. Anth.
04000 *The Conan swordbook; 27 examples of heroic
fiction.* Mirage Press, Baltimore, 1969,
260p, Cloth, Anth.

SCOGGINS, C(harles) E(lbert), 1888-1955

12809 *The house of darkness.* Bobbs-Merrill, Indianapolis, 1931, 319p, Cloth, Novel
12810 *The house of dawn.* Skeffington & Son, London,
1935, 288p, Cloth, Novel [Colin O'Leary ser-
ies]
12811 *Lost road.* Doubleday, Doran, Garden City,
1941, 302p, Cloth, Novel [Colin O'Leary ser-
ies]
12812 *The red gods call.* Bobbs-Merrill, Indianapolis,
1926, 364p, Cloth, Novel

SCORTIA, THOMAS N(icholas), 1926-   [biography included]

12813   *Artery of Fire*. Doubleday, Garden City, 1972, 181p, Cloth, Novel
12814   *Earthwreck!* Fawcett Gold Medal, Greenwich, Conn., 1974, 224p, Paper, Novel
12815   *Strange bedfellows; sex and science fiction*. Random House, New York, 1972, 274p, Cloth, Anth.

with Chelsea Quinn Yarbro:

12816   *Two views of wonder*. Ballantine, New York, 1973, 274p, Paper, Anth.

SCOT, HEW

12817   *The way of war*. John Long, London, 1907, 318p, Cloth, Novel

SCOTSON-CLARK, E(thel), with G. F. Scotson-Clark

12818   *An amazing ancestor*. T. Fisher Unwin, London, 1924, 287p, Cloth, Novel

SCOTSON-CLARK, G(eorge) F(rederick), 1872-1927, with E. Scotson-Clark

12818   *An amazing ancestor*. T. Fisher Unwin, London, 1924, 287p, Cloth, Novel

SCOTT, ALAN, 1947-

12819   *Project Dracula*. Sphere, London, 1971, 319p, Paper, Novel

SCOTT, BILLY

12820   *The King of America*. Traveller's Companion Series, New York, 1969, 198p, Paper, Novel

SCOTT, C(atherine) A(my) DAWSON-, 1868?-1934

12821   *The haunting*. William Heinemann, London, 1921, 310p, Cloth, Novel

with Ernest Rhys:

12197   *Tales of mystery; startling stories of the supernatural*. Hutchinson, London, 1927, 287p, Cloth, Anth.
12198   *26 mystery stories old and new, by twenty and six authors*. D. Appleton, New York, 1927, 310p, Cloth, Anth.

SCOTT, EDWARD

12822   *The marvellous experience of John Rydal*. S. C. Brown, Langham, London, 1904, 312p, Cloth, Novel

SCOTT, G(eorge) FIRTH

12823   *The last Lemurian; a Westralian romance*. James Bowden, London, 1898, 339p, Cloth, Novel

12824   *Possessed*. William Rider & Son, London, 1912, 303p, Cloth, Novel

SCOTT, GABRIEL, 1874-1958

12825   *The golden gospel; a legend*. Macy-Massius, The Vanguard Press, New York, 1928, 313p, Cloth, Novel

SCOTT, J(ames) M(aurice), 1906-

12826   *Dingo*. Heinemann, London, 1966, 181p, Cloth, Novel

SCOTT, J(ean) M., with Robert Theobald

12827   *Teg's 1994; an anticipation of the near future*. Swallow Press, Chicago, 1972, 211p, Cloth, Novel

SCOTT, JEREMY, pseud. [Kay Dick]

12828   *At close of eve; an anthology of new curious stories*. Jarrolds Publishers, London, 1947, 224p, Cloth, Anth.
12829   *The mandrake root; an anthology of fantastic tales*. Jarrolds Publishers, London, 1946, 224p, Cloth, Anth.
12830   *The uncertain element; an anthology of fantastic conceptions*, by Kay Dick (Jeremy Scott). Jarrolds Publishers, London, 1950, 280p, Cloth, Anth.

SCOTT, JOHN REED, 1869-

12831   *The duke of oblivion*. J. B. Lippincott, Philadelphia, 1914, 351p, Cloth, Novel

SCOTT, PEG O'NEILL

as Scott O'Neill:

12832   *Martian sexpot*. Jade, Hollywood, 1963, 159p, Paper, Novel

as Barton Werper, house pseud.:

12833   *Tarzan and the snake people*. Gold Star, Derby, Conn., 1964, 126p, Paper, Novel [New Tarzan series #3]

SCOTT, PETER KING-
    see: EDGAR, PETER

SCOTT, PETER T., as Barton Werper, house pseud

12834   *Tarzan and the Abominable Snowmen*. Gold Star, Derby, Conn., 1965, 126p, Paper, Novel [New Tarzan series #4]
12835   *Tarzan and the cave city*. Gold Star, Derby, Conn., 1964, 126p, Paper, Novel [New Tarzan series #2]
12836   *Tarzan and the Silver Globe*. Gold Star, Derby, Conn., 1964, 126p, Paper, Novel [New Tarzan series #1]
12837   *Tarzan and the winged invaders*. Gold Star, Derby, Conn., 1965, 125p, Paper, Novel [New Tarzan series #5]

SCOTT, R(eginald) T(homas) M(aitland), 1882-

12838   *The mad monk.* Claude Kendall, New York, 1931, 288p, Cloth, Novel

SCOTT, ROBERT
   see: BLUE WOLF

SCOTT, T(homas) H(enry), 1878-

12839   *The treasure trail; a tale of adventure on the Amazon.* Frederick Warne, London, 1931, 154p, Cloth, Novel

SCOTT MONCRIEFF, D(avid William Hardy), 1907-

12840   *Not for the squeamish.* Background Books, London, 1948, 108p, Paper, Coll.
12841   *The Vaivaisukko's bride.* Scots Digest, Glasgow, 1949, 63p, Paper, Coll. [cover title reads: *The horror club*]

SCRAM, ARTHUR N., pseud. [Leo Guild]

12842   *The werewolf vs the vampire woman.* Guild-Hartford Publishing Co., Beverly Hills, CA, 1972, 190p, Paper, Movie [cover byline reads: Arthur N. Scarm]

SCRIRE. O.T.O. 4=7, pseud. [Gerald Brosseau Gardner, 1884-]

12843   *High magic's aid.* Michael Houghton, London, 1949, 352p, Cloth, Novel

SCRIVEN, GERARD F., 1920-1949

12844   *The ghost shop.* Samuel Walker, London, 1948, 104p, Cloth, Coll.

SCRYMSOUR, ELLA (M.)

12845   *The bridge of distances.* Philip Allan, London, 1924, 310p, Cloth, Novel
12846   *The perfect world; a romance of strange people and strange places.* Eveleigh Nash & Grayson, London, 1922, 320p, Cloth, Novel

SCUDAMORE, F(rancis), with P. Colomb, J. F. Maurice, F. N. Maude, Archibald Forbes, D. Christie Murray, and Charles Lowe

03229   *The Great War of 189-; a forecast.* William Heinemann, London, 1893, 308p, Cloth, Novel

SCUDDER, ANTOINETTE (Quinby), 1898-1958

12847   *The grey studio.* Ruth Hill, Publisher, Boston, 1934, 127p, Cloth, Novel

SCYOC, SYDNEY VAN
   see: VAN SCYOC, SYDNEY

SEA KISSED

12848   *Sea kissed.* Utopian Publications, London, 1946?, 36p, Paper, Anth. [a variant on the collection of the same name by Robert Bloch, with an extra story by Benson Herbert]

SEABORN, Captain ADAM, pseud. [attributed to John Cleves Symmes, 1780-1829]

12849   *Symzonia; voyage of discovery.* J. Seymour, New York, 1820, 248p, Cloth, Novel

SEAFORTH, pseud.
   see: FOSTER, GEORGE C.

SEAFORTH, A. NELSON, pseud. [George Sydenham Clarke, 1st Baron Sydenham of Combe, 1848-1933]

12850   *The last great naval war; an historical retrospect.* Cassell, London, 1891, 120p, Paper, Novel

'SEA-LION,' pseud. [Geoffrey Martin Bennett, 1909-] [*biography included*]

12851   *The invisible ships.* Hutchinson, London, 1950, 208p, Cloth, Novel
12852   *This creeping evil.* Hutchinson, London, 1950, 176p, Cloth, Novel

SEAMARK, pseud.
   see: SMALL, AUSTIN J.

SEARCH, (Marion) PAMELA

12853   *The supernatural in the English short story.* Bernard Hanison, London, 1959, 480p, Cloth, Anth.

SEARCHLIGHT, pseud.
   see: EARDLEY-WILMOT, SYDNEY

SEARLS, HANK [Henry Hunt Searls Jr., 1922-] [*biography included*]

12854   *The Pilgrim project; a novel.* McGraw-Hill, New York, 1964, 274p, Cloth, Novel

SEARS, ALFRED F.
   see: INCA-PABLO-OZOLLO

SECESSION, COERCION, AND CIVIL WAR
   see: JONES, J. B.

SECHRIST, (Anne) ELIZABETH HOUGH, 1903-
[*biography included*]

12855   *Thirteen ghostly yarns.* Roland Swain, Philadelphia, 1932, 299p, Cloth, Anth.

SECHRIST, ELIZABETH HOUGH (cont.)

12856   *Thirteen ghostly yarns.* Macrae-Smith, Philadelphia, 1942, 240p, Cloth, Anth. [different contents]

with Janette Woolsey:

12857   *Terribly strange tales.* Macrae Smith Co., Philadelphia, 1967, 253p, Cloth, Anth.

THE SECOND ARMADA
    see: HAYWARD, ABRAHAM

THE SECOND ARROW BOOK OF HORROR STORIES
    see: LEE, ELIZABETH

A SECOND FRANCO-GERMAN WAR

12858   *A second Franco-German war and its consequences for England; I. The invasion of Belgium, by a Belgian officer; II. Belgian neutrality and British Naval supremacy, by Civis Britannicus.* Alden & Co., Oxford, 1907, 146p, Cloth?, Anth.?

THE SECOND PART OF ARMATA
    see: ERSKINE, THOMAS

THE SECOND PART OF THE ABBEY OF KILKHAMPTON
    see: CROFT, HERBERT

SECRET MEMOIRS AND MANNERS OF SEVERAL PERSONS OF QUALITY, OF BOTH SEXES, FROM THE NEW ATALANTIS
    see: MANLEY, MARY

THE SECRET OF MANKIND

12859   *The secret of mankind, with some singular hints gathered in the elsewhere or afterlife, from certain eminent personages.* G. P. Putnam's Sons, New York, 1895, 417p, Cloth, Novel

THE SECRET OF THE LAMAS

12860   *The secret of the lamas; a tale of Thibet.* Cassell, London, 1889, 235p, Cloth, Novel

SEDBERRY, J(ames) HAMILTON, 1863-

12861   *Under the flag of the cross.* C. M. Clark Publishing Co., Boston, 1908, 472p, Cloth, Novel

SEDGWICK, ANNE DOUGLAS, 1873-1935

12862   *The third window.* Houghton Mifflin, Boston, 1920, 155p, Cloth, Novel; Martin Secker, London, 1920, 181p, Cloth, Novel

SEDGWICK, S(idney) N(ewman), 1872-1941

12863   *The last persecution.* Grant Richards, London, 1909, 314p, Cloth, Novel

SEELEY, CHARLES SUMNER, pseud. [John William Munday, 1844-]

12864   *The lost canyon of the Toltecs; an account of strange adventures in Central America.* A. C McClurg, Chicago, 1893, 275p, Cloth, Novel

SEESTERN, pseud.
    see: GRAUTOFF, FERDINAND

SEFTON, CATHERINE

12865   *The back house ghosts.* Faber & Faber, London, 1974, 141p, Cloth, Novel
12866   *In a blue velvet dress...almost a ghost story.* Faber & Faber, London, 1972, 135p, Cloth, Novel

SEGAL, LESLEY KEEN

12867   *Many enchantments.* Peter Davies, London, 1936 287p, Cloth, Novel

SEGALL, DON
    see: AUGUST, LEO

SEIBEL, GEORGE, 1872-1958

12868   *The fall, being a true account of what happene in Paradise, for the benefit of all scandalmongers, with a new interpretation of sacred history, vindicating snakes and apples.* Lessing Co., Pittsburgh, 1918, 62p, Paper, Novel

SELDEN, GEORGE, pseud. [George Selden Thompson, 1929-] [*biography included*]

12869   *The cricket in Times Square.* Ariel Books, Farrar, Straus & Co., New York, 1960, 151p, Cloth, Novel
12870   *The genie of Sutton Place.* Farrar, Straus & Giroux, New York, 1973, 175p, Cloth, Tele.
12871   *Oscar Lobster's fair exchange.* Harper & Bros. New York, 1966, 172p, Cloth, Novel

SELECTED TALES OF THE GENII
    see: RIDLEY, JAMES

SELLERS, CON(nie L., Jr.), 1922- [*biography included*]

12872   *F.S.C.* Novel Books, Chicago, 1963, 182p, Paper, Novel
12873   *The pleasure mongers.* Novel Books, Chicago, 1964, 128p, Paper, Novel
12873A   retitled: *Mr. Tomorrow.* Papillon, San Diego, 1974, 160p, Paper, Novel

SELLERS, CON (cont.)

12874 *Red rape*, by Connie Sellers. Headline Books, Los Angeles, 1960, 188p, Paper, Novel

SELLINGS, ARTHUR, pseud. [Arthur Gordon Ley, 1911-1968] [*biography included*]

Intermind. [see 12882A]
12875 *Junk day*. Dennis Dobson, London, 1970, 188p, Cloth, Novel
12876 *The long eureka; a collection of short stories*. Dennis Dobson, London, 1968, 184p, Cloth, Coll.
12877 *The power of X*. Dennis Dobson, London, 1968, 156p, Cloth, Novel
12878 *The Quy Effect*. Dennis Dobson, London, 1966, 141p, Cloth, Novel
The silent speakers. [see 12879A]
12879 *Telepath*. Ballantine, New York, 1962, 160p, Paper, Novel
12879A retitled: *The silent speakers*. Dennis Dobson, London, 1963, 184p, Cloth, Novel
12880 *Time transfer, and other stories*. Michael Joseph, London, 1956, 240p, Cloth, Coll.
12881 *The uncensored man*. Dennis Dobson, London, 1964, 183p, Cloth, Novel

as Ray Luther:

12882 *Intermind*. Banner, New York, 1967, 144p, Paper, Novel
12882A *Intermind*, by Arthur Sellings. Dennis Dobson, London, 1969, 144p, Cloth, Novel

SELTZER, RICHARD (Warren Jr.), 1946- [*biography included*]

12883 *The Lizard of Oz; an adult fable*. B&R Samizdat Express, West Roxbury, Mass., 1974, 126p, Paper, Novel

SEOLA
    see: SMITH, Mrs. J. GREGORY

A SEQUEL TO THE ADVENTURES OF BARON MUNCHAUSEN
    see: RASPE, RUDOLF ERICH

SERJEANT, CONSTANCIA

12884 *When the saints are gone*. John Long, London, 1908, 221p, Cloth, Novel

SERLING, ROD(man), 1924-1975

12885 *From The twilight zone*. Nelson Doubleday, Garden City, 1970?, 314p, Cloth, Coll. [selections from 12886, 12887, 12893]
12886 *More stories from The twilight zone*. Bantam, New York, 1961, 149p, Paper, Tele. Coll.
12887 *New stories from The twilight zone*. Bantam, New York, 1962, 122p, Paper, Tele. Coll.
12888 *Night gallery*. Bantam, New York, 1971, 147p, Paper, Tele. Coll.
12889 *Night gallery 2*. Bantam, New York, 1972, 152p, Paper, Tele. Coll.
12890 *Rod Serling's devils and demons; a collection*. Bantam, New York, 1967, 213p, Paper, Anth.

12891 *Rod Serling's triple W: witches, warlocks, and werewolves; a collection*. Bantam, New York, 1963, 181p, Paper, Anth.
12892 *The season to be wary*. Little, Brown, Boston, 1967, 276p, Cloth, Coll.
12893 *Stories from The twilight zone*. Bantam, New York, 1960, 151p, Paper, Tele. Coll.

SERNICOLI, DAVIDE

12894 *The land which loveth silence*. Sampson Low, Marston, London, 1948, 216p, Cloth, Novel

SERPELL, CHRISTOPHER, with Douglas Brown

01964 *Loss of Eden; a cautionary tale*. Faber & Faber, London, 1940, 251p, Cloth, Novel
01964A retitled: *If Hitler comes...* Faber & Faber, London, 1941, 251p, Cloth, Novel

SERRANO, MARY J.
    see: ALARCON, PEDRO de and WAR UNDER WATER

SERRANO, MIGUEL, 1917-

12895 *El/ella; book of magic love*. Harper & Row, New York, 1972, 75p, Cloth, Coll.
12896 *The ultimate flower*. Routledge & Kegan Paul, London, 1969, 101p, Cloth, Novel
12897 *The visits of the Queen of Sheba*. P. S. Jayasinghe, Asia Publishing House, Bombay, 1960, 72p, Cloth, Novel

SERVICE, ROBERT W(illiam), 1876-1958

12898 *The house of fear; a novel*. T. Fisher Unwin, London, 1927, 336p, Cloth, Novel
12899 *The master of the microbe; a fantastic romance*. T. Fisher Unwin, London, 1926, 415p, Cloth, Novel

SERVISS, GARRETT P(utnam), 1851-1929

12900 *A Columbus of space*. D. Appleton, New York, 1911, 298p, Cloth, Novel
12901 *Edison's conquest of Mars*. Carcosa House, Los Angeles, 1947, 193p, Cloth, Novel [a sequel to Wells' novel, *The war of the worlds*]
12901A retitled: *Forrest J Ackerman presents Invasion of Mars*. Powell Publications, Reseda, CA, 1969, 201p, Paper, Novel [abridged]
12902 *The Moon metal*. Harper & Bros., New York, 1900, 164p, Cloth, Novel
12903 *The second deluge*. McBride, Nast, New York, 1912, 399p, Cloth, Novel

SETON, ANYA, 1916?- [*biography included*]

12904 *Green darkness*. Hodder & Stoughton, London, 1972, 573p, Cloth, Novel
12905 *The turquoise*. Hodder & Stoughton, London, 1946, 352p, Cloth, Novel

SETTEL, IRVING, 1916-   [*biography included*], with Marvin Allen Karp

08075   *Suddenly*. Popular Library, New York, 1965, 144p, Paper, Anth.

SEVERANCE, FELIX, pseud.
    see: LAUMER, MARCH

SÉVERIN, JEAN, 1911-

12906   *The star of Les Baux*. Harcourt Brace Jovanovich, New York, 1970, 160p, Cloth, Novel

SEVERN, DAVID, pseud. [David Storr Unwin, 1918-] [*biography included*]

12907   *Foxy-boy*. Bodley Head, London, 1959, 165p, Cloth, Novel
12907A retitled: *The wild valley*. E. P. Dutton, New York, 1963, 165p, Cloth, Novel
12908   *The future took us*. Bodley Head, London, 1957, 173p, Cloth, Novel
12909   *The girl in the grove*. George Allen & Unwin, London, 1974, 238p, Cloth, Novel

SEVERY, MELVIN L(inwood), 1863-

12910   *The awakening; a novel*. Foster Hope Co., Los Angeles, 1940, 472p, Cloth, Novel
12911   *Fleur-de-Lis, and other stories*. Esoteric Publishing Co., Boston, 1889, 150p, Cloth, Coll.

SEWELL, (Margaret) ELIZABETH, 1919-   [*biography included*]

12912   *The dividing of time*. Chatto & Windus, London, 1951, 213p, Cloth, Novel; Doubleday, Garden City, 1951, 249p, Cloth, Novel

SEWELL, ELIZABETH M(issing)

12913   *Uncle Peter's fairy tale for the nineteenth century*. Longmans, Green, London, 1867, 478p, Cloth, Novel

THE SEX LIFE OF HERCULES
    see: EAGLE, ROBIN

THE SEX LIFE OF ULYSSES
    see: KANTOR, HAL

SEX MACHINE
    see: CAMRA, ROY

THE SEX SERUM

12914   *The sex serum*. Utopian Publications, London, 1945, 36p, Paper, Anth.

THE SEXORCIST

12915   *The sexorcist*. Bleep Publications, New York, 1974, 48p, Paper, Story

SEYMOUR, ALAN, 1927-   [*biography included*]

12916   *The coming self-destruction of the United States of America*. Souvenir Press, London, 1969, 314p, Cloth, Novel

SEYMOUR, FREDERICK HENRI
    see: GILHOOLEY, Lord

SEYMOUR, HENRY, pseud. [Helmut Henry Hartmann, 1931-]

12917   *Infernal idol*. John Gifford, London, 1967, 188p, Cloth, Novel

SHADEGG, STEPHEN C., 1909-   [*biography included*]

12918   *The remnant*. Arlington House, New Rochelle, NY, 1968, 336p, Cloth, Novel

SHAFER, ROBERT (Jones), 1915-

12919   *The conquered place*. G. P. Putnam's Sons, New York, 1954, 313p, Cloth, Novel
12919A retitled: *The naked and the damned (The conquered place)*. Popular Library, New York, 1955, 207p, Paper, Novel

SHAFFER, EUGENE CARL

12920   *The last breath*. Papillon, San Diego, 1974, 192p, Paper, Novel

SHANKLIN, IMELDA OCTAVIA

12921   *Treasure box*. Unity Tract Society, Kansas City, 1925, 36p, Paper, Story

SHANKS, EDWARD (Richard Buxton), 1892-1953

12922   *The people of the ruins; a story of the English revolution and after*. Frederick A. Stokes, New York, 1920, 314p, Cloth, Novel; W. Collins Sons, London, 1920, 290p, Cloth, Novel

SHANNON, DORIS, 1924-   [*biography included*]

12923   *22 Hallowfield*. Fawcett Gold Medal, Greenwich, Conn., 1974, 175p, Paper, Novel

SHANNON, FRANK, pseud. [Dennis Francis Joseph Shine, 1908-]

12924   *Once around the park*. William Morrow, New York, 1953, 186p, Cloth, Novel

SHANNON, FRED, pseud. [William S. Ruben]

12925 *Weightless in Gaza*. Tower, New York, 1970, 138p, Paper, Novel

SHANNON, JOHN C.

12926 *Who shall condemn? and other stories*. W. Henry Robinson, Walsall, UK, 1894, 154p, Cloth, Coll.

12927 *Zylgrahof, and other stories*. Simpkin, Marshall, Hamilton, Kent, London, 1901, 163p, Cloth, Coll.

THE SHAPE OF THE WAR TO COME
    see: ANTHEIL, GEORGE

SHARKEY, JACK [John Michael Sharkey, 1931-]
[*biography included*]

12928 *The Addams family*. Pyramid, New York, 1965, 175p, Paper, Tele. [Addams Family #1]

12929 *The secret Martians*. Ace Double, New York, 1960, 132p, Paper, Novel

12930 *Ultimatum in 2050 A.D.* Ace Double, New York, 1965, 120p, Paper, Novel

SHARP, DOLPH, 1914- [*biography included*]

12931 *Ludwig von Wolfgang Vulture*. Price/Sloan/ Stern Publishers, Los Angeles, 1973, 63p, Paper, Novel [a parody of Richard Bach's *Jonathan Livingston Seagull*]

SHARP, EVELYN, 1869-1955

12932 *Somewhere in Christendom*. George Allen & Unwin, London, 1919, 256p, Cloth, Novel

SHARP, MARGERY, 1905- [*biography included*]

12933 *Miss Bianca*. Little, Brown, New York, 1962, 152p, Cloth, Novel [Miss Bianca #2]

12934 *Miss Bianca and the bridesmaid*. Little, Brown, Boston, 1972, 123p, Cloth, Novel [Miss Bianca #7]

12935 *Miss Bianca in the Antarctic*. Little, Brown, Boston, 1971, 134p, Cloth, Novel [Miss Bianca #6]

12936 *Miss Bianca in the Orient*. Little, Brown, Boston, 1970, 144p, Cloth, Novel [Miss Bianca #5]

12937 *Miss Bianca in the salt mines*. Little, Brown, Boston, 1966, 148p, Cloth, Novel [Miss Bianca #4]

12938 *The rescuers*. Little, Brown, Boston, 1959, 149p, Cloth, Novel [Miss Bianca #1]

12939 *The stone of chastity*. Little, Brown, Boston, 1940, 280p, Cloth, Novel

12940 *The turret*. Little, Brown, Boston, 1963, 138p, Cloth, Novel [Miss Bianca #3]

SHARP, ROBERT (George)

12941 *Horror castle*. Arthur Gray, London, 1936, 256p, Cloth, Novel

as Jon J. Deegan:

12942 *Amateurs in alchemy*. Panther, London, 1952, 128p, Paper, Novel [Old Growler series]

12943 *Antro, the life-giver*. Panther, London, 1953, 144p, Cloth, Novel [Old Growler series]

12944 *Beyond the fourth door*. Panther, London, 1954, 159p, Cloth, Novel [Dysart #2]

12945 *Corridors of time*. Panther, London, 1953, 159p, Cloth, Novel [Dysart #1]

12946 *Exiles in time*. Panther, London, 1954, 159p, Paper, Novel [Dysart #3]

12947 *The Great Ones*. Panther, London, 1953, 158p, Cloth, Novel [Old Growler series]

12948 *Underworld of Zello*. Panther, London, 1952, 128p, Paper, Novel

SHARP, WILLIAM
    see: MACLEOD, FIONA

SHATTUCK, WILLIAM, 1864-1946

12949 *The keeper of the salamander's order; tale of strange adventure in unknown climes*. Roberts Bros., Boston, 1895, 326p, Cloth, Novel

SHAVER, RICHARD S(harpe), 1907-1975

12950 *I remember Lemuria; and, The return of Sathanas*. Venture Books, Evanston, IL, 1948, 215p, Cloth, Coll.

SHAW, ARNOLD

12951 *The greatest adventure stories ever told*. J. P. Feiner, Long Island, NY, 1945, 129p, Paper, Anth.

12952 *30 tales of romance and adventure*. Dorene Publishing Co., New York, 1945, 126p, Paper, Anth.

SHAW, BOB [Robert Shaw, 1931-] [*biography included*]

12953 *Ground zero man*. Avon, New York, 1971, 160p, Paper, Novel

12954 *Night walk*. Banner, New York, 1967, 160p, Paper, Novel

12955 *One million tomorrows*. Ace, New York, 1970, 191p, Paper, Novel

12956 *Other days, other eyes*. Victor Gollancz, London, 1972, 160p, Cloth, Novel

12957 *The palace of Eternity*. Ace, New York, 1969, 222p, Paper, Novel

12958 *Shadow of Heaven*. Avon, New York, 1969, 175p, Paper, Novel

12959 *Tomorrow lies in ambush*. Victor Gollancz, London, 1973, 204p, Cloth, Coll.

12960 *The two-timers*. Ace, New York, 1968, 191p, Paper, Novel

SHAW, BRIAN, house pseud. [see also John Russell Fearn, David Griffiths, David O'Brien, and E. C. Tubb]

06403 *"Argentis."* Curtis Warren, London, 1952?, 112p, Paper, Novel [by E. C. Tubb]

SHAW, BRIAN (cont.)

12962 *Lost world*. Curtis Warren, London, 1953,
         159p, Cloth, Novel
10889 *Ships of Vero*. Curtis Warren, London, 1952,
         128p, Cloth, Novel [by David O'Brien]
05297 *Z formations*. Curtis Warren, London, 1953,
         159p, Cloth, Novel [by John Russell Fearn]
         [name cited as "Bryan Shaw" on title page]

SHAW, DAVID, pseud.
   see: GRIFFITHS, DAVID

SHAW, Captain FRANK H(ubert), 1878-

12963 *Outlaws of the air*. Cassell, London, 1927,
         216p, Cloth, Novel

SHAW, FREDERICK L(incoln) Jr., 1928-   [*biography included*]

12964 *Envoy to the Dog Star*. Ace Double, New York,
         1967, 127p, Paper, Novel

SHAW, GEORGE

12965 *Astrosex*. Midwood, New York, 1970, 203p,
         Paper, Novel

SHAW, GEORGE BERNARD, 1856-1950

12966 *The adventures of the black girl in her search
         for God*. Constable, London, 1932, 74p,
         Cloth, Novel
12967 *The black girl in search of God, and some les-
         ser tales*. Penguin, Harmondsworth, 1946,
         285p, Paper, Coll.

SHAW, LARRY T. [Lawrence Taylor Shaw, 1924-   ]
[*biography included*]

12968 *Great science fiction adventures*. Lancer, New
         York, 1963, 174p, Paper, Anth.
12969 *Terror!* Lancer, New York, 1966, 192p, Paper,
         Anth.

SHAW, (Frederick) STANLEY, 1870-

12970 *The locust horde*. Hodder & Stoughton, London,
         1925, 319p, Cloth, Novel

SHAW, W(illiam) J(enkins)

12971 *Under the Auroras; a marvelous tale of the
         interior world*. Excelsior Publishing House,
         New York, 1888, 376p, Cloth, Novel
12971A retitled: *Cresten, Queen of the Toltus; or,
         Under the Auroras*. Excelsior Publishing
         House, New York, 1892, 376p, Paper, Novel

SHEA, MICHAEL

12972 *A quest for Simbilis*. DAW, New York, 1974,
         159p, Paper, Novel [Dying Earth #3]

SHEAR, DAVID

12973 *Cloning*. Walker, New York, 1972, 162p, Cloth,
         Novel

SHEARING, JOSEPH, pseud.
   see: BOWEN, MARJORIE

SHECKLEY, ROBERT, 1928-   [*biography included*]

12974 *Can you feel anything when I do this?* Double-
         day, Garden City, 1971, 191p, Cloth, Coll.
12974A retitled: *The same to you doubled, and other
         stories*. Pan, London, 1974, 172p, Paper,
         Coll.
12975 *Citizen in space*. Ballantine, New York, 1955,
         200p, Cloth, Coll.
12976 *Dimension of miracles*. Dell, New York, 1968,
         190p, Paper, Novel
12977 *Immortality delivered*. Avalon, New York, 1958,
         221p, Cloth, Novel
12977A retitled: *Immortality, Inc*. Bantam, New York,
         1959, 152p, Paper, Novel
12978 *Journey beyond tomorrow*. Signet, New York,
         1962, 144p, Paper, Novel
12979 *Mindswap; a novel*. Delacorte Press, New York,
         1966, 216p, Cloth, Novel
12980 *Notions: unlimited*. Bantam, New York, 1960,
         170p, Paper, Coll.
12981 *The people trap, and other pitfalls, snares,
         devices, and delusions, as well as two snig-
         gles and a contrivance*. Dell, New York,
         1968, 204p, Paper, Coll.
12982 *Pilgrimage to Earth*. Bantam, New York, 1957,
         167p, Paper, Coll.
12983 *The Robert Sheckley omnibus*. Victor Gollancz,
         London, 1973, 320p, Cloth, Coll.
         The same to you doubled, and other stories.
         [see 12974A]
12984 *Shards of space*. Bantam, New York, 1962, 152p,
         Paper, Coll.
12985 *The status civilization*. Signet, New York,
         1960, 127p, Paper, Novel
12986 *Store of infinity*. Bantam, New York, 1960,
         151p, Paper, Coll.
12987 *The 10th victim*. Ballantine, New York, 1965,
         158p, Paper, Movie
12988 *Untouched by human hands; thirteen stories*.
         Ballantine, New York, 1954, 170p, Cloth, Coll.

SHECTER, BEN

12989 *The whistling whirligig*. Harper & Row, New
         York, 1974, 143p, Cloth, Novel

SHEEAN, (James) VINCENT, 1899-1975 [*biography
included*]

12990 *The tide; a novel*. Doubleday, Doran, Garden
         City, 1933, 308p, Cloth, Novel

SHEEHAN, CAROLYN, with Edmund Sheehan

12991 *Magnifi-Cat*. Doubleday, Garden City, 1972,
         229p, Cloth, Novel

SHEEHAN, EDMUND, with Carolyn Sheehan

12991 *Magnifi-Cat.* Doubleday, Garden City, 1972, 229p, Cloth, Novel

SHEEHAN, MURRAY

12992 *Eden.* E. P. Dutton, New York, 1928, 304p, Cloth, Novel
12993 *Half-gods.* E. P. Dutton, New York, 1927, 467p, Cloth, Novel

SHEEHAN, PERLEY POORE, 1875-1943

12994 *The abyss of wonders.* Polaris Press, Reading, PA, 1953, 190p, Cloth, Novel
12995 *The one gift.* Fantasy House, North Hollywood, CA, 1974, 48p, Paper, Story

SHEEHAN, RICHARD G., with Lee Wright

12996 *These will chill you; twelve terrifying tales of malignant evil.* Bantam, New York, 1967, 169p, Paper, Anth.
12997 *Wake up screaming; sixteen chilling tales of the macabre.* Bantam, New York, 1967, 214p, Paper, Anth.

SHELDON, ALICE
see: TIPTREE, JAMES Jr.

SHELDON, LEE, pseud. [Wayne Cyril Lee, 1917-] [*biography included*]

12998 *Doomed planet.* Avalon, New York, 1967, 190p, Cloth, Novel

SHELDON, ROY, house pseud. [see also: H. J. Campbell, George Hay, and E. C. Tubb]

02501 *Atoms in action.* Panther, London, 1953, 159p, Cloth, Novel [Shiny Spear series] [by H. J. Campbell]
02502 *House of entropy.* Panther, London, 1953, 160p, Cloth, Novel [Shiny Spear series] [by H. J. Campbell]
02503 *Mammoth man.* Hamilton & Co. (Stafford), London, 1952, 111p, Paper, Novel [Magdah series] [by H. J. Campbell]
02504 *The menacing sleep.* Panther, London, 1952, 128p, Paper, Novel [by H. J. Campbell]
12999 *The metal eater.* Panther, London, 1954, 159p, Cloth, Novel [by E. C. Tubb]
06968 *Moment out of time.* Hamilton & Co. (Stafford), London, 1952, 111p, Paper, Novel [by George Hay]
02505 *Two days of terror.* Panther, London, 1952, 112p, Paper, Novel [Magdah series] [by H. J. Campbell]

SHELDON, WILLIAM D., with Warren H. Wheelock

13000 *Over the edge.* Allyn & Bacon, Boston, 1972, 97p, Paper, Anth.

SHELDON-WILLIAMS, MILES

13001 *The power of Ula.* Ward, Lock, London, 1906, 320p, Cloth, Novel [byline on cover: J. Sheldon Williams]

SHELLEY, MARY WOLLSTONECRAFT, 1797-1851

13002 *Frankenstein; or, The modern Prometheus.* Lackington, Hughes, Harding, Mavor & Jones, London, 1818, 3vol, Cloth, Novel [published anonymously]
13002A *Frankenstein; or, The modern Prometheus*, by Mary W. Shelley. G. & W. B. Whittaker, London, 1823, 2vol, Cloth, Novel
13002B *Frankenstein; or, The modern Prometheus*, by the author of The last man, Perkin Warbeck, &c., &c. H. Colburn & R. Bentley, London, 1831, 202p, Cloth, Novel
13003 *The last man*, by the author of Frankenstein. Henry Colburn, London, 1826, 3vol, Cloth, Novel
13003A *The last man*, by Mary W. Shelley. Carey, Lea & Blanchard, Philadelphia, 1833, 2vol, Cloth, Novel
13004 *The mortal immortal.* Mossant, Vallon, New York, 1910?, 26p, Cloth, Story

with Dale Carlson:

02584 *Frankenstein.* Golden Press, New York, 1968, 158p, Cloth, Novel [an adaptation of Shelley's novel]

SHELLEY, PERCY BYSSHE, 1792-1822 [published anonymously]

13005 *St. Irvyne; or, The Rosicrucian; a romance*, by a gentleman of the University of Oxford. J. J. Stockdale, London, 1811, 236p, Cloth, Novel

SHELTON, FREDERIC(k) WILLIAM, 1814-1881

13006 *Salander and the dragon; a romance of the Hartz Prison.* S. Hueston, G. P. Putnam, New York, 1850, 184p, Cloth, Novel

SHELTON, WILLIAM R(oy), 1919- [*biography included*]

13007 *Stowaway to the Moon; the Camelot odyssey.* Doubleday, Garden City, 1973, 343p, Cloth, Novel

SHEPARD, JANE

13008 *Coolman.* Belmont, New York, 1966, 142p, Paper, Novel

SHEPARD, MORGAN
see: JOHN-MARTIN

SHEPPARD, ALFRED TRESIDDER, 1871-1947

13009 *Here comes an old sailor.* Hodder & Stoughton, London, 1927, 415p, Cloth, Novel

SHERBURNE, ZOA (L.), 1912-   [*biography inclu-ded*]

13010　*The girl who knew tomorrow.* William Morrow, New York, 1970, 190p, Cloth, Novel
13011　*Why have the birds stopped singing?* William Morrow, New York, 1974, 189p, Cloth, Novel

SHERIDAN, Mrs. (Frances), 1724-1766

13012　*The history of Nourjahad,* by the editor of "Sidney Bidulph." J. Dodsley, London, 1767, 240p, Cloth, Novel
13012A　*The history of Nourjahad, the Persian,* by Mrs. Sheridan. C. Cooke, London, 1798?, 72p, Cloth, Novel
13012B　retitled: *Nourjahad.* Whittingham & Arliss, London, 1816, 92p, Cloth, Novel [published anonymously]

SHERMAN, FRANK DEMPSTER, 1860-1916, with John Kendrick Bangs as Two Wags

00840　*New waggings of old tales.* Ticknor & Co., Boston, 1888, 165p, Cloth, Coll.

SHERMAN, HAROLD M(orrow), 1898-

13013　*The green man; a visitor from space.* Century Publications, Chicago, 1946, 128p, Paper, Novel
13014　*Tahara among African tribes.* Goldsmith Publishing Co., Chicago, 1933, 246p, Cloth, Novel [Tahara #2]
13015　*Tahara, boy king of the desert.* Goldsmith Publishing Co., Chicago, 1933, 250p, Cloth, Novel [Tahara #1]
13016　*Tahara, boy mystic of India.* Goldsmith Publishing Co., Chicago, 1933, 252p, Cloth, Novel [Tahara #3]
13017　*Tahara in the land of Yucatan.* Goldsmith Publishing Co., Chicago, 1933, 246p, Cloth, Novel [Tahara #4]

SHERMAN, JORY
　　see: ANVIC, FRANK

SHERRED, T. L., 1915-

13018　*Alien island.* Ballantine, New York, 1970, 217p, Paper, Novel
13019　*First person, peculiar.* Ballantine, New York, 1972, 214p, Paper, Coll.

SHERRIFF, R(obert) C(edric), 1896-1975

13020　*The Hopkins manuscript.* Victor Gollancz, London, 1939, 352p, Cloth, Novel
13020A　retitled: *The cataclysm.* Pan, London, 1958, 253p, Paper, Novel

SHERRY, OLIVER, pseud. [George Oliver Lobo]

13021　*Mandrake.* Jarrolds Publishers, London, 1929, 287p, Cloth, Novel

SHERWOOD, MARY MARTHA, 1775-1851

13022　*The traditions; a legendary tale,* by a young lady. William Lane, The Minerva Press, London, 1795, 2vol/1, Cloth, Novel

SHIEL, M(atthew) P(hipps), 1865-1947

　　　　Above all else. [see 13033A]
13023　*The best short stories of M. P. Shiel.* Victor Gollancz, London, 1948, 310p, Cloth, Coll.
13024　*The dragon.* Grant Richards, London, 1913, 356p, Cloth, Novel
13024A　retitled: *The yellow peril.* Victor Gollancz, London, 1929, 367p, Cloth, Novel [slightly revised]
13025　*The isle of lies.* T. Werner Laurie, London, 1908, 250p, Cloth, Novel
13026　*The last miracle.* T. Werner Laurie, London, 1906, 320p, Cloth, Novel
13027　*The lord of the sea.* Grant Richards, London, 1901, 496p, Cloth, Novel
13028　*The pale ape, and other pulses.* T. Werner Laurie, London, 1911, 339p, Cloth, Coll.
13029　*Prince Zaleski.* John Lane, The Bodley Head, London, 1895, 183p, Cloth, Novel
13030　*The purple cloud.* Chatto & Windus, London, 1901, 463p, Cloth, Novel
13031　*The rajah's sapphire.* Ward, Lock & Bowden, London, 1896, 119p, Cloth, Novel
13032　*Shapes in the fire, being a mid-winter-night's entertainment in two parts and an interlude.* John Lane, The Bodley Head, London, 1896, 324p, Cloth, Novel
13033　*This above all.* Vanguard Press, London, 1933, 304p, Cloth, Novel
13033A　retitled: *Above all else.* Lloyd Cole, London, 1943, 127p, Cloth, Novel
13034　*The yellow danger; the story of the world's greatest war.* Grant Richards, London, 1898, 348p, Cloth, Novel
　　　　The yellow peril. [see 13024A]
13035　*The Young Men are coming!* George Allen & Unwin, London, 1937, 375p, Cloth, Novel

SHINE, DENNIS
　　see: SHANNON, FRANK

THE SHIP FROM NOWHERE

13036　*The ship from nowhere,* by Sidney Patzer; and, *The Moon mirage,* by Raymond Gallun. Stellar Publishing Corp., New York, 1932, 24p, Paper, Anth.

SHIPWAY, GEORGE, 1908-

13037　*The Chilian Club (a diversion).* Peter Davies, London, 1971, 246p, Cloth, Novel
13037A　retitled: *The Yellow Room.* Doubleday, Garden City, 1971, 278p, Cloth, Novel

SHIRAS, WILMAR H(ouse), 1908-

13038　*Children of the atom.* Gnome Press, New York, 1953, 216p, Cloth, Coll.

SHIRLEY, GEORGE E(rnest), 1898- [*biography included*]

13039 *The robot rulers.* Vantage Press, New York, 1967, 77p, Cloth, Novel
13040 *A world beyond.* Vantage Press, New York, 1967, 80p, Cloth, Novel
13041 *A world of their own.* Vantage Press, New York, 1965, 67p, Cloth, Novel

SHIRLEY, ROBERT

13042 *Teenocracy.* Ace, New York, 1969, 318p, Paper, Novel

SHIVERS

13043 *Shivers; a collection of uneasy tales.* Philip Allan, London, 1932, 254p, Cloth, Anth.

SHKAROVSKY-RAFFÉ, ARTHUR [published anonymously]

13044 *Everything but love; science-fiction stories.* Mir Publishers, Moscow, 1973, 172p, Paper, Anth.

SHORES, LOUIS, 1904- [*biography included*]

13045 *Looking forward to 1999.* South Pass Press, Tallahassee, FL, 1972, 262p, Cloth, Novel

SHORT, JACKSON, pseud. [Peter Hochstein, 1939-] [*biography included*]

13046 *Blue Alice.* Dell, New York, 1972, 252p, Paper, Novel [a parody of Carroll's *Alice in Wonderland*]
13047 *The secret sex curse of Bertha T.* Dell, New York, 1973, 255p, Paper, Novel

SHORT, RICHARD, 1841-1916

13048 *Saronia; a romance of ancient Ephesus.* Elliot Stock, London, 1900, 258p, Cloth, Novel

SHORTT, VERE (Dawson), 1872-1915, with Frances Mathews

09813 *The Rod of the Snake.* John Lane, The Bodley Head, London, 1917, 310p, Cloth, Novel

SHUDDERS

13049 *Shudders; a collection of uneasy tales.* Philip Allan, London, 1932, 254p, Cloth, Anth.

SHULMAN, SANDRA (Dawn), 1944- [*biography included*]

13050 *The daughters of Astaroth.* Paperback Library, New York, 1968, 159p, Paper, Novel
13050A retitled: *The daughters of Satan.* New English Library, London, 1969, 128p, Paper, Novel

SHUMWAY, HARRY IRVING, 1883-

13051 *The wonderful voyages of Cap'n Penn.* Little, Brown, Boston, 1929, 275p, Cloth, Novel

SHUTE, NEVIL, pseud. [Nevil Shute Norway, 1899-1960]

13052 *In the wet.* William Heinemann, London, 1953, 355p, Cloth, Novel
13053 *A Nevil Shute omnibus.* Heinemann, London, 1973, 711p, Cloth, Coll. [includes *No highway*; *A town like Alice*; *On the beach*]
13054 *An old captivity.* William Heinemann, London, 1940, 312p, Cloth, Novel
13055 *On the beach.* Heinemann, London, 1957, 312p, Cloth, Novel
       Ordeal. [see 13056A]
13056 *What happened to the Corbetts.* William Heinemann, London, 1939, 267p, Cloth, Novel
13056A retitled: *Ordeal.* Lancer, New York, 1965, 222p, Paper, Novel

SIBOL, FRANK

13057 *Heaven and Earth.* Vantage Press, New York, 1961, 194p, Cloth, Novel

SIBSON, FRANCIS H.

13058 *The stolen continent.* Andrew Melrose, London, 1934, 288p, Cloth, Novel [Survivors #2]
13059 *The survivors.* William Heinemann, London, 1932, 293p, Cloth, Novel [Survivors #1]
13060 *Unthinkable.* Methuen, London, 1933, 272p, Cloth, Novel

SICARD, CLARA

13061 *The ghost; a legend.* Chas. H. Clark, London, 1866?, 267p, Cloth, Novel

SIDNEY, EDWARD WILLIAM, pseud.
       see: TUCKER, BEVERLY

SIEGEL, MARTIN, 1940?-1972

13062 *Agent of entropy.* Lancer, New York, 1969, 189p, Paper, Novel
13063 *The unreal people.* Lancer, New York, 1973, 158p, Paper, Novel

SIEGELE, H(erman) H(ugo), 1883-

13064 *Pushing buttons.* Chapman & Grimes, Boston, 1946, 34p, Cloth, Story

SIEMON, FREDERICK

13065 *Ghost story index; an author-title index to more than 2,200 stories of ghosts, horrors, and the macabre, appearing in 190 books and anthologies.* Library Research Associates, San Jose, CA, 1967, 141p, Paper, Nonf.

SIEMON, FREDERICK (cont.)

13066   *Science fiction story index, 1950-1968.* American Library Association, Chicago, 1971, 274p, Paper, Nonf.

SIEVEKING, L(ancelot) de GIBERNE, 1896-1972

13067   *A private volcano; a modern novel of science and imagination*, by Lance Sieveking. Ward, Lock, London, 1955, 255p, Cloth, Novel
13068   *Stampede!* Cayme Press, Kensington, UK, 1924, 306p, Cloth, Novel
13069   *The Ultimate Island; a strange adventure.* George Routledge & Sons, London, 1925, 340p, Cloth, Novel

SIGERSON, DORA (Mary), d. 1918

13070   *The story and song of Black Roderick.* Alexander Moring, London, 1906, 82p, Cloth, Novel

SILBERSTANG, EDWIN, 1930-   [*biography included*]

13071   *Sweet land of liberty; a novel.* G. P. Putnam's Sons, New York, 1972, 319p, Cloth, Novel

SILENT, WILLIAM T., pseud. [John William Jackson, Jr., 1945-] [*biography included*]

13072   *Lord of the red sun.* Walker, New York, 1972, 181p, Cloth, Novel

SILLITOE, ALAN, 1928-   [*biography included*]

13073   *The General; a novel.* W. H. Allen, London, 1960, 189p, Cloth, Novel
13074   *Travels in Nihilon.* W. H. Allen, London, 1971, 254p, Cloth, Novel

SILVANI, ANITA

13075   *The strange story of Ahrinziman*, by A. F. S. R. R. Donnelley & Sons, Chicago, 1906, 284p, Cloth, Novel
13075A *The strange story of Ahrinziman*, by Anita Silvani. Progressive Thinker Publishing Co., Chicago, 1908, 284p, Cloth, Novel

SILVERBERG, BARBARA

13076   *Kitten kaboodle; a collection of feline fiction.* Holt, Rinehart & Winston, New York, 1969, 204p, Cloth, Anth.
13077   *Phoenix feathers; a collection of mythical monsters.* E. P. Dutton, New York, 1973, 206p, Cloth, Anth. [includes some folklore]

SILVERBERG, ROBERT, 1935-   [*biography included*]

13078   *Across a billion years.* Dial Press, New York, 1969, 249p, Cloth, Novel

13079   *Alpha one.* Ballantine, New York, 1970, 278p, Paper, Anth.
13080   *Alpha two.* Ballantine, New York, 1971, 310p, Paper, Anth.
13081   *Alpha three.* Ballantine, New York, 1972, 277p, Paper, Anth.
13082   *Alpha 4.* Ballantine, New York, 1973, 281p, Paper, Anth.
13083   *Alpha 5.* Ballantine, New York, 1974, 267p, Paper, Anth.
       The anvil of time. [see 13103A]
13084   *Beyond control; seven stories of science fiction.* Thomas Nelson, Nashville, 1972, 219p, Cloth, Anth.
13085   *The Book of Skulls.* Charles Scribner's Sons, New York, 1972, 222p, Cloth, Novel
13086   *Born with the dead; three novellas.* Random House, New York, 1974, 269p, Cloth, Coll.
13087   *The calibrated alligator, and other science fiction stories.* Holt, Rinehart & Winston, New York, 1969, 227p, Cloth, Coll.
13088   *Chains of the sea; three original novellas of science fiction.* Thomas Nelson, Nashville, 1973, 221p, Cloth, Anth.
13089   *Collision course.* Avalon, New York, 1961, 224p, Cloth, Novel
13090   *Conquerors from the darkness.* Holt, Rinehart & Winston, New York, 1965, 191p, Cloth, Novel
13091   *The cube root of uncertainty.* Macmillan, New York, 1970, 239p, Cloth, Coll.
13092   *Dark stars.* Ballantine, New York, 1969, 309p, Paper, Anth.
13093   *Deep space; eight stories of science fiction.* Thomas Nelson, Nashville, 1973, 223p, Cloth, Anth.
13094   *Dimension thirteen.* Ballantine, New York, 1969, 215p, Paper, Coll.
13095   *Downward to the Earth.* Doubleday, Garden City, 1970, 180p, Cloth, Novel
13096   *Dying inside.* Charles Scribner's Sons, New York, 1972, 245p, Cloth, Novel
13097   *Earthmen and strangers; nine stories of science fiction.* Duell, Sloan & Pearce, New York, 1966, 240p, Cloth, Anth.
13098   *Earth's other shadow; nine science fiction stories.* Signet, New York, 1973, 207p, Paper, Coll.
13099   *The ends of time; eight stories of science fiction.* Hawthorn, New York, 1970, 225p, Cloth, Anth.
13100   *The gate of worlds.* Holt, Rinehart & Winston, New York, 1967, 244p, Cloth, Novel
13101   *Godling, go home!* Belmont, New York, 1964, 157p, Paper, Coll.
13102   *Great short novels of science fiction.* Ballantine, New York, 1970, 373p, Paper, Anth.
13103   *Hawksbill Station.* Doubleday, Garden City, 1968, 166p, Cloth, Novel
13103A retitled: *The anvil of time; science fiction.* Sidgwick & Jackson, London, 1969, 192p, Cloth, Novel
13104   *Infinite jests; the lighter side of science fiction.* Chilton Book Co., Radnor, PA, 1974, 231p, Cloth, Anth.
13105   *Invaders from Earth.* Ace Double, New York, 1958, 169p, Paper, Novel
13106   *Invaders from space; ten stories of science fiction.* Hawthorn, New York, 1972, 241p, Cloth, Anth.
13107   *Lost race of Mars.* John C. Winston, Philadelphia, 1960, 120p, Cloth, Novel
13108   *The man in the maze.* Avon, New York, 1969, 192p, Paper, Novel

SILVERBERG, ROBERT (cont.)

13109 *The masks of time.* Ballantine, New York, 1968, 252p, Paper, Novel

13109A retitled: *Vornan-19; science fiction.* Sidgwick & Jackson, London, 1970, 252p, Cloth, Novel

13110 *Master of life and death.* Ace Double, New York, 1957, 163p, Paper, Novel

13111 *Men and machines; ten stories of science fiction.* Meredith Press, New York, 1968, 240p, Cloth, Anth.

13112 *Mind to mind; nine stories of science fiction.* Thomas Nelson, Nashville, 1971, 270p, Cloth, Anth.

13113 *The mirror of infinity; a critics' anthology of science fiction.* Harper & Row, New York, 1970, 324p, Cloth, Anth.

13114 *Moonferns and starsongs.* Ballantine, New York, 1971, 245p, Paper, Coll.

13115 *Mutants; eleven stories of science fiction.* Thomas Nelson, Nashville, 1974, 224p, Cloth, Anth.

13116 *Needle in a timestack.* Ballantine, New York, 1966, 190p, Paper, Coll.

13117 *New dimensions I; fourteen original science fiction stories.* Doubleday, Garden City, 1971, 246p, Cloth, Anth.

13118 *New dimensions II.* Doubleday, Garden City, 1972, 229p, Cloth, Anth.

13119 *New dimensions 3.* Nelson Doubleday, Garden City, 1973, 212p, Cloth, Anth.

13120 *New dimensions IV.* Signet, New York, 1974, 237p, Paper, Anth.

13121 *Next stop the stars.* Ace Double, New York, 1962, 114p, Paper, Coll.

13122 *Nightwings.* Avon, New York, 1969, 190p, Paper, Novel

13123 *Other dimensions; ten stories of science fiction.* Hawthorn, New York, 1973, 178p, Cloth, Anth.

13124 *Parsecs and parables; ten science fiction stories.* Doubleday, Garden City, 1970, 203p, Cloth, Coll.

13125 *The planet killers.* Ace Double, New York, 1959, 131p, Paper, Novel

13126 *Planet of death.* Holt, Rinehart & Winston, New York, 1967, 125p, Cloth, Novel

13127 *The Reality Trip, and other implausibilities.* Ballantine, New York, 1972, 211p, Paper, Coll.

13128 *Recalled to life.* Lancer, New York, 1962, 144p, Paper, Novel

13129 *Recalled to life.* Doubleday, Garden City, 1972, 184p, Cloth, Novel [rewritten]

13130 *Regan's Planet; a science-fiction novel.* Pyramid, New York, 1964, 141p, Paper, Novel

13131 retitled: *World's Fair, 1992.* Follett Publishing Co., Chicago, 1970, 248p, Cloth, Novel [extensively rewritten]

13132 *Revolt on Alpha C.* Thomas Y. Crowell, New York, 1955, 148p, Cloth, Novel

13133 *A Robert Silverberg omnibus.* Sidgwick & Jackson, London, 1970, 468p, Cloth, Coll. [includes: *Master of life and death*; *Invaders from Earth*; *The time-hoppers*]

13134 *The science fiction bestiary; nine stories of science fiction.* Thomas Nelson, New York, 1971, 256p, Cloth, Anth.

13135 *The science fiction hall of fame, volume one.* Doubleday, Garden City, 1970, 558p, Cloth, Anth.

13135A retitled: *Science fiction hall of fame, volume one.* Sphere, London, 1972, 349p, Paper, Anth. [abridged]

13135B retitled: *Science fiction hall of fame, volume two.* Sphere, London, 1972, 352p, Paper, Anth. [abridged; 13135A and 13135B together comprise the original volume]

13136 *The second trip.* Nelson Doubleday, Garden City, 1972, 185p, Cloth, Novel

13137 *The seed of Earth.* Ace Double, New York, 1962, 139p, Paper, Novel

13138 *The silent invaders.* Ace Double, New York, 1963, 117p, Paper, Novel

13139 *Son of man.* Ballantine, New York, 1971, 215p, Paper, Novel

13140 *Starman's quest.* Gnome Press, Hicksville, NY, 1958, 185p, Cloth, Novel

13141 *Stepsons of Terra.* Ace Double, New York, 1958, 128p, Paper, Novel

13142 *Sundance, and other science fiction stories.* Thomas Nelson, Nashville, 1974, 192p, Cloth, Coll.

13143 *The 13th immortal.* Ace Double, New York, 1957, 129p, Paper, Novel

13144 *Thorns.* Ballantine, New York, 1967, 222p, Paper, Novel

13145 *Those who watch.* Signet, New York, 1967, 143p, Paper, Novel

13146 *Threads of time; three original novellas of science fiction.* Thomas Nelson, Nashville, 1974, 219p, Cloth, Anth.

13147 *Three survived.* Holt, Rinehart & Winston, New York, 1969, 117p, Cloth, Novel

13148 *The time-hoppers.* Doubleday, Garden City, 1967, 182p, Cloth, Novel

13149 *A time of changes.* Nelson Doubleday, Garden City, 1971, 183p, Cloth, Novel

13150 *Time of the great freeze.* Holt, Rinehart & Winston, New York, 1964, 192p, Cloth, Novel

13151 *To live again.* Doubleday, Garden City, 1969, 231p, Cloth, Novel

13152 *To open the sky.* Ballantine, New York, 1967, 222p, Paper, Novel

13153 *To the stars; eight stories of science fiction.* Hawthorn, New York, 1971, 255p, Cloth, Anth.

13154 *To worlds beyond; stories of science fiction.* Chilton, Philadelphia, 1965, 170p, Cloth, Coll.

13155 *Tomorrow's worlds; ten stories of science fiction.* Meredith Press, New York, 1969, 234p, Cloth, Anth.

13156 *Tower of glass.* Charles Scribner's Sons, New York, 1970, 247p, Cloth, Novel

13157 *Unfamiliar territory.* Charles Scribner's Sons, New York, 1973, 212p, Cloth, Coll.

13158 *Up the line.* Ballantine, New York, 1969, 250p, Paper, Novel

13159 *Valley beyond time.* Dell, New York, 1973, 223p, Paper, Coll.

Vornan-19. [see 13109A]

13160 *Voyagers in time; twelve stories of science fiction.* Meredith Press, New York, 1967, 243p, Cloth, Anth.

13161 *Windows into tomorrow; nine stories of science fiction.* Hawthorn, New York, 1974, 197p, Cloth, Anth.

13162 *The world inside.* Doubleday, Garden City, 1971, 201p, Cloth, Novel

World's Fair, 1992. [see 13131]

13163 *Worlds of maybe; seven stories of science fiction.* Thomas Nelson, Camden, NJ, 1970, 256p, Cloth, Anth.

SILVERBERG, ROBERT (cont.)

as Ivar Jorgenson:

13164 *Starhaven.* Avalon, New York, 1958, 220p, Cloth, Novel

as Calvin M. Knox:

13165 *Lest we forget thee, Earth.* Ace Double, New York, 1958, 126p, Paper, Novel

13166 *One of our asteroids is missing.* Ace Double, New York, 1964, 124p, Paper, Novel

13167 *The plot against Earth.* Ace Double, New York, 1959, 138p, Paper, Novel

as David Osborne:

13168 *Aliens from space.* Avalon, New York, 1958, 223p, Cloth, Novel

13169 *Invisible barriers.* Avalon, New York, 1958, 223p, Cloth, Novel

with Randall Garrett as Robert Randall:

05811 *The dawning light.* Gnome Press, New York, 1959, 191p, Cloth, Novel [Nidor #2]

05812 *The shrouded planet.* Gnome Press, New York, 1957, 188p, Cloth, Novel [Nidor #1]

SILVETTE, HERBERT
  see: DOGBOLT, BARNABY

SIMAK, CLIFFORD D(onald), 1904-   [biography included]

     Aliens for neighbours. [see 13195A]

13170 *All flesh is grass.* Doubleday, Garden City, 1965, 260p, Cloth, Novel

13171 *All the traps of Earth, and other stories.* Doubleday, Garden City, 1962, 287p, Cloth, Coll.

13172 *Best science fiction stories of Clifford Simak.* Faber & Faber, London, 1967, 251p, Cloth, Coll.

13173 *Cemetery world.* G. P. Putnam's Sons, New York, 1973, 191p, Cloth, Novel

13174 *A choice of gods.* G. P. Putnam's Sons, New York, 1971, 190p, Cloth, Novel

13175 *City.* Gnome Press, New York, 1952, 224p, Cloth, Novel

13176 *Cosmic Engineers; an interplanetary novel.* Gnome Press, New York, 1950, 224p, Cloth, Novel

13177 *The Creator.* Crawford Publications, Los Angeles, 1946, 48p, Paper, Story

13178 *Destiny doll; a science fiction novel.* G. P. Putnam's Sons, New York, 1971, 189p, Cloth, Novel

13179 *Empire; a powerful novel of intrigue and action in the not-so-distant future.* Galaxy SF Novel, New York, 1951, 160p, Paper, Novel

     First he died. [see 13189A]

13180 *The goblin reservation.* G. P. Putnam's Sons, New York, 1968, 192p, Cloth, Novel

13181 *Nebula award stories six.* Doubleday, Garden City, 1971, 204p, Cloth, Anth.

13182 *The night of the puudly.* Four Square, London, 1964, 143p, Paper, Coll. [loosely adapted from 13171]

     Other worlds of Clifford Simak. [see 13195B]

13183 *Our children's children.* G. P. Putnam's Sons, New York, 1974, 186p, Cloth, Novel

13184 *Out of their minds.* G. P. Putnam's Sons, New York, 1970, 186p, Cloth, Novel

13185 *Ring around the Sun; a story of tomorrow.* Simon & Schuster, New York, 1953, 242p, Cloth, Novel

13186 *So bright the vision.* Ace Double, New York, 1968, 141p, Paper, Coll.

13187 *Strangers in the universe; science-fiction stories.* Simon & Schuster, New York, 1956, 371p, Cloth, Coll.

13188 *They walked like men.* Doubleday, Garden City, 1962, 234p, Cloth, Novel

13189 *Time and again.* Simon & Schuster, New York, 1951, 235p, Cloth, Novel

13189A retitled: *First he died (Time and again).* Dell, New York, 1953, 222p, Paper, Novel

13190 *Time is the simplest thing.* Doubleday, Garden City, 1961, 263p, Cloth, Novel

13191 *The trouble with Tycho.* Ace Double, New York, 1961, 82p, Paper, Novel

13192 *Way Station.* Doubleday, Garden City, 1963, 210p, Cloth, Novel

13193 *The Werewolf Principle.* G. P. Putnam's Sons, New York, 1967, 216p, Cloth, Novel

13194 *Why call them back from Heaven?* Doubleday, Garden City, 1967, 190p, Cloth, Novel

13195 *The worlds of Clifford Simak.* Simon & Schuster, New York, 1960, 378p, Cloth, Coll.

13195A retitled: *Aliens for neighbours; science fiction stories.* Faber & Faber, London, 1961, 255p, Cloth, Coll. [abridged]

13195B retitled: *Other worlds of Clifford Simak.* Avon, New York, 1962, 143p, Paper, Coll. [abridged]

13196 *Worlds without end.* Belmont, New York, 1964, 140p, Paper, Coll.

SIMIOCRACY
  see: BROOKFIELD, A. M.

SIMON, EDITH, 1917-   [biography included]

13197 *The twelve pictures; a novel.* G. P. Putnam's Sons, New York, 1955, 367p, Cloth, Novel

SIMON, S. J., pseud. [Simon Jasha Skidelsky], with Caryl Brahms

01813 *No nightingales.* Michael Joseph, London, 1944, 251p, Cloth, Novel

01814 *Titania has a mother.* Michael Joseph, London, 1944, 194p, Cloth, Novel

SIMONEAU, ARTHUR G., d. 1955

13198 *Stolen from the Earth.* Vantage Press, New York, 1965, 67p, Cloth, Novel

SIMPSON, HELEN (De Guerry), 1897-1940

13199 *The woman on the beast, viewed from three angles.* William Heinemann, London, 1933, 492p, Cloth, Novel; Doubleday, Doran, Garden City, 1933, 438p, Cloth, Novel

SIMPSON, HOWARD

13200 *West of the Moon.* Vantage Press, New York, 1968, 101p, Cloth, Novel

SIMPSON, WILLIAM
    see: BLOT, THOMAS

SIMS, ALAN

    13201 *Anna Perenna*. Chatto & Windus, London, 1930,
           316p, Cloth, Novel
    13202 *Phoinix*. Chatto & Windus, London, 1928,
           338p, Cloth, Novel

SIMS, D(enise) N(atalie), 1940-   [*biography
included*]

    13203 *A plenteous seed*. Robert Hale, London, 1973,
           160p, Cloth, Novel

SIMS, GEO(rge) R(obert), 1847-1922

    13204 *The devil in London*. Stanley Paul, London,
           1908, 158p, Cloth, Novel

SIMSON, ERIC ANDREW
    see: KIRK, LAURENCE

"SINBAD," pseud. [Aylward Edward Dingle, 1874-
1947]

    13205 *The age-old kingdom*. Hutchinson, London,
           1947, 176p, Cloth, Novel

SINCLAIR, ANDREW (Annandale), 1935-   [*biography included*]

    13206 *The Project*. Faber & Faber, London, 1960,
           190p, Cloth, Novel

SINCLAIR, BERTHA MUZZY
    see: BOWER, B. M.

SINCLAIR, DAVID

    13207 *The Gilead bomb*. Dell, New York, 1963, 120p,
           Paper, Novel

SINCLAIR, MAY [Mary Amelia St. Clair Sinclair,
1863-1946]

    13208 *The flaw in the crystal*. E. P. Dutton, New
           York, 1912, 198p, Cloth, Novel
    13209 *The intercessor, and other stories*. Hutchin-
           son, London, 1931, 222p, Cloth, Coll.
    13210 *The tree of Heaven*. Cassell, London, 1917,
           358p, Cloth, Novel
    13211 *Uncanny stories*. Hutchinson, London, 1923,
           247p, Cloth, Coll.

SINCLAIR, UPTON (Beall), 1878-1968 [*biography
included*]

    13212 *The gnomobile; a gnice gnew gnarrative with
           gnonsense, but gnothing gnaughty*. The
           Author, Pasadena, CA, 1936, 181p, Cloth,
           Novel

    13213 *I, Governor of California, and how I ended po-
           verty; a true story of the future*. Upton
           Sinclair, Los Angeles, 1933, 64p, Paper,
           Novel
    13214 *The millennium; a comedy of the year 2000*.
           Haldeman-Julius, Girard, Kans., 1924, vol.
           I-64p, II-64p, III-60p, Paper, Novel [based
           on the play of the same name]
    13215 *Our Lady*. The Author, New York, 1938, 162p,
           Cloth, Novel
    13216 *The overman*. Doubleday, Page, New York, 1907,
           90p, Cloth, Novel
    13217 *Prince Hagen; a phantasy*. L. C. Page, Boston,
           1903, 249p, Cloth, Novel
    13218 *Roman holiday*. Farrar & Rinehart, New York,
           1931, 288p, Cloth, Novel
    13219 *We, people of America, and how we ended poverty*.
           National EPIC League, Pasadena, CA, 1935,
           64p, Paper, Novel
    13220 *What Didymus did*. Allan Wingate, London, 1954,
           151p, Cloth, Novel
    13220A retitled: *It happened to Didymus*. Sagamore
           Press, New York, 1958, 151p, Cloth, Novel

SINDERBY, DONALD, pseud. [Donald Ryder Step-
phens, 1898-   ]

    13221 *Mother-in-law India*. Albert E. Marriott, Lon-
           don, 1930, 319p, Cloth, Novel

SINGER, ISAAC BASHEVIS, 1904-   [*biography included*]

    13222 *Gimpel the fool, and other stories*. Noonday
           Press, New York, 1957, 205p, Cloth, Coll.
    13223 *An Isaac Bashevis Singer reader*. Farrar,
           Straus & Giroux, New York, 1971, 560p, Cloth,
           Coll.
    13224 *Satan in Goray*. Noonday Press, New York, 1955,
           239p, Cloth, Novel
    13225 *The séance, and other stories*. Farrar, Straus
           & Giroux, New York, 1968, 276p, Cloth, Coll.
    13226 *Short Friday, and other stories*. Farrar,
           Straus & Giroux, New York, 1964, 243p, Cloth,
           Coll.
    13227 *The Spinoza of Market Street*. Farrar, Straus
           & Cudahy, New York, 1961, 214p, Cloth, Coll.

SINGER, KURT (Deutsch), 1911-   [*biography included*]

    13228 *Bloch and Bradbury; ten masterpieces of science
           fiction*. Tower, New York, 1969, 155p, Paper,
           Anth.
    13228A retitled: *Fever dream, and other fantasies*.
           Sphere, London, 1970, 157p, Paper, Anth.
           The day of the dragon. [see 13236A]
           Fever dream, and other fantasies. [see 13228A]
    13229 *Ghouls and ghosts*. W. H. Allen, London, 1972,
           320p, Cloth, Anth.
    13230 *The gothic reader*. Ace, New York, 1966, 253p,
           Paper, Anth.
    13231 *Horror omnibus*. W. H. Allen, London, 1965,
           317p, Cloth, Anth.
           The house in the valley. [see 13236B]
    13232 *I can't sleep at night; 13 weird tales*. Whit-
           ing & Wheaton, London, 1966, 238p, Cloth,
           Anth.
    13233 *Kurt Singer's ghost omnibus*. W. H. Allen, Lon-
           don, 1965, 287p, Cloth, Anth.

SINGER, KURT (cont.)

13233A retitled: *Kurt Singer's second ghost omnibus.*
Four Square, London, 1967, 125p, Paper, Anth.
[abridged]
13234 *Kurt Singer's gothic horror book.* W. H. Allen,
London, 1974, 305p, Cloth, Anth.
The oblong box. [see 13238A]
The plague of the living dead. [see 13238B]
13235 *Satanic omnibus.* W. H. Allen, London, 1973,
293p, Cloth, Anth.
13236 *Tales of terror.* W. H. Allen, London, 1967,
255p, Cloth, Anth.
13236A retitled: *The day of the dragon, and other
tales of terror.* Sphere, London, 1971,
160p, Paper, Anth. [abridged]
13236B retitled: *The house in the valley, and other
tales of terror.* Sphere, London, 1970,
142p, Paper, Anth. [abridged; 13236A and
13236B together comprise the original book]
13237 *Tales of the macabre.* New English Library,
London, 1969, 125p, Paper, Anth.
13238 *Tales of the uncanny.* W. H. Allen, London,
1968, 286p, Cloth, Anth.
13238A retitled: *The oblong box, and other tales of
the uncanny.* Sphere, London, 1970, 160p?,
Paper, Anth. [abridged]
13238B retitled: *The plague of the living dead, and
more tales of the uncanny.* Sphere, London,
1970, 159p, Paper, Anth. [abridged; 13238A
and 13238B together comprise the original
volume]
13239 *Weird tales of the supernatural.* W. H. Allen,
London, 1966, 352p, Cloth, Anth.

SINGER, NORMAN, 1925–

13240 *The man who raped San Francisco.* Ophelia
Press, New York, 1968, 219p, Paper, Novel

SINGLETON, ESTHER, 1865-1930

13241 *Shakespearian fantasias; adventures in the
fourth dimension.* privately printed, Norwood, Mass., 1929, 269p, Cloth, Coll.

SINGULAR TRAVELS, CAMPAIGNS, VOYAGES, AND
SPORTING ADVENTURES OF BARON MUNNIKHOUSON
    see: RASPE, RUDOLF ERICH

SINIAVSKII, ANDREI
    see: TERTZ, ABRAM

SINYAVSKY, ANDREI
    see: TERTZ, ABRAM

SIODMAK, CURT [originally Kurt], 1902–
[biography included]

13242 *City in the sky.* G. P. Putnam's Sons, New
York, 1974, 218p, Cloth, Novel
13243 *Donovan's brain.* Alfred A. Knopf, New York,
1943, 234p, Cloth, Novel [Cory #1]
13244 *F.P.1 does not reply,* by Kurt Siodmak. Little, Brown, Boston, 1933, 290p, Cloth, Novel
13244A retitled: *F.P.1 fails to reply.* Collins,
London, 1933, 252p, Cloth, Novel

13245 *Hauser's memory.* G. P. Putnam's Sons, New
York, 1968, 184p, Cloth, Novel [Cory #2]
13246 *Skyport.* Crown Publishers, New York, 1959,
223p, Cloth, Novel
13247 *The third ear.* G. P. Putnam's Sons, New York,
1971, 254p, Cloth, Novel

SIR ROHAN'S GHOST
    see: PRESCOTT, HARRIET ELIZABETH

SIRENIA
    see: LUMLEY, BENJAMIN

SIRIUS, pseud. [Edward Martyn, 1859-1923]

13248 *Morgante the Lesser, his notorious life and
wonderful deeds.* Swan Sonnenschein, London,
1890, 329p, Cloth, Novel

SISSON, MARJORIE

13249 *The cave.* Vine Press, Hemingford Grey, UK,
1957, 20p, Cloth, Story

SISSONS, (Thomas) MICHAEL (Beswick)

13250 *Asleep in armageddon; an anthology of science-
fiction stories.* Panther, London, 1962,
189p, Paper, Anth.
13251 *In the dead of night; an anthology of horror
stories.* Anthony Gibbs & Phillips, London,
1961, 191p, Cloth, Anth.
13252 *The masque of the Red Death, and other tales
of horror.* Panther, London, 1964, 192p,
Paper, Anth.

SITWELL, (Sir Francis) OSBERT (Sacheverell,
Bart.), 1892-1969 [biography included]

13253 *The man who lost himself.* Duckworth, London,
1929, 288p, Cloth, Novel
13254 *Miracle on Sinai; a satirical novel.* Duckworth,
London, 1933, 382p, Cloth, Novel
13255 *A place of one's own.* Macmillan, London, 1941,
71p, Cloth, Novel

THE 6 FINGERS OF TIME

13256 *The 6 fingers of time, and other stories.* Macfadden-Bartell, New York, 1965, 128p, Paper,
Anth.

SIXTY YEARS HENCE
    see: HENNINGSEN, C.

SIZEMORE, JULIUS C., with Wilkie G. Sizemore

13257 *The sea people; a fantasy.* Exposition Press,
New York, 1957, 263p, Cloth, Novel

SIZEMORE, WILKIE G., with Julius C. Sizemore

13257 *The sea people; a fantasy.* Exposition Press,
New York, 1957, 263p, Cloth, Novel

SKAIFE, S(ydney) H(arold), 1889-

13258 *The strange old man.* Longmans, Green, London, 1930, 283p, Cloth, Novel

SKELTON, GLADYS
see: PRESLAND, JOHN

SKELTON, RED [Richard Bernard Skelton, 1913-]

13259 *A Red Skelton in your closet; ghost stories gay and grim.* Grosset & Dunlap, New York, 1965, 224p, Cloth, Anth.
13259A retitled: *Red Skelton's favorite ghost stories.* Tempo, New York, 1968, 187p, Paper, Anth.

SKETCHLEY, ARTHUR, pseud. [George Rose, 1817-1882]

13260 *Mrs. Brown on the Battle of Dorking.* George Routledge & Sons, London, 1871, 58p, Paper, Story [Dorking series]

SKIDELSKY, SIMON JASHA
see: SIMON, S. J.

SKINKLE, DOROTHY E.

13261 *Star giant.* Tower, New York, 1969, 154p, Paper, Novel

SKINNER, CLAUDE M., 1916-

13262 *Time of the great death.* Vantage Press, New York, 1971, 193p, Cloth, Novel

SKINNER, CONRAD
see: MAURICE, MICHAEL

SKINNER, JUNE
see: O'GRADY, ROHAN

SKIPPER, MERVYN

13263 *The white man's garden; a tale of Borneo.* Elkin Mathews & Marrot, London, 1930, 118p, Cloth, Novel

SKORPIOS, ANTARES, pseud.
see: BARLOW, JAMES WILLIAM

SKUNKS, Major, pseud.

13264 *The great battle of Patchumup, fought off Cape Keckumover, June 1st, in the year of the three naughts; the only official report.* Ward, Lock & Tyler, London, 1865, 130p, Cloth, Novel

SLACK, SOLOMON, pseud.
see: MUIR, RAMSAY

SLADEK, JOHN (Thomas), 1937- [biography included]

13265 *The Müller-Fokker effect.* Hutchinson, London, 1970, 247p, Cloth, Novel
13266 *The Reproductive System; a science fiction novel.* Victor Gollancz, London, 1968, 192p, Cloth, Novel
13266A retitled: *Mechasm.* Ace, New York, 1969, 222p, Paper, Novel
13267 *The steam-driven boy, and other strangers.* Panther, St. Albans, UK, 1973, 189p, Paper, Coll.

SLADEN, DOUGLAS (Brooke Wheelton), 1856-1947

13268 *The crystal and the sphinx; a romance of crystal-gazing in Egypt.* Stanley Paul, London, 1924, 344p, Cloth, Novel
13269 *Fair Inez; a romance of Australia.* Hutchinson, London, 1918, 283p, Cloth, Novel
13270 *The tragedy of the pyramids; a romance of army life in Egypt.* Hurst & Blackett, London, 1909, 428p, Cloth, Novel

SLATER, ERNEST
see: GWYNNE, PAUL

SLATER, HENRY J.

13271 *Ship of destiny.* Jarrolds Publishers, London, 1951, 200p, Cloth, Novel
13272 *The smashed world.* Jarrolds Publishers, London, 1952, 221p, Cloth, Novel

SLATER, W. H.

13273 *The golden load.* T. Fisher Unwin, London, 1926, 252p, Cloth, Novel

SLAUGHTER, CHARLES E.

13274 *Hahtibee, the elephant.* Alfred A. Knopf, New York, 1930, 161p, Cloth, Novel

SLAUGHTER, FRANK G(ill), 1908- [biography included]

13275 *Epidemic!* Doubleday, Garden City, 1961, 286p, Cloth, Novel

SLAVITT, DAVID
see: SUTTON, HENRY

SLEATOR, WILLIAM (Warner III), 1945- [biography included]

13276 *Blackbriar.* E. P. Dutton, New York, 1972, 212p, Cloth, Novel
13277 *House of stairs.* E. P. Dutton, New York, 1974, 166p, Cloth, Novel

SLEE, RICHARD, with Cornelia Atwood Pratt

11871 *Dr. Berkeley's discovery.* G. P. Putnam's Sons, New York, 1899, 219p, Cloth, Novel

SLEIGH, BARBARA, 1906- [*biography included*]

13278 *Carbonel.* Max Parrish, London, 1955, 188p, Cloth, Novel [Carbonel #1]
13278A retitled: *Carbonel, the king of the cats.* Bobbs-Merrill, Indianapolis, 1957, 253p, Cloth, Novel [Carbonel #1]
13279 *Jessamy.* Bobbs-Merrill, Indianapolis, 1967, 246p, Cloth, Novel
13280 *The kingdom of Carbonel.* Max Parrish, London, 1959, 254p, Cloth, Novel [Carbonel #2]

SLEIGH, BERNARD, 1872-

13281 *Witchcraft.* Oriole Press, Berkeley Heights, NJ, 1934, 90p, Cloth, Novel

SLOANE, WILLIAM (Milligan III), 1906-1974

13282 *The edge of running water.* Farrar & Rinehart, New York, 1939, 295p, Cloth, Novel
13282A retitled: *The unquiet corpse.* Dell, New York, 1956, 223p, Paper, Novel
13283 *The rim of morning, including The edge of running water; To walk the night.* Dodd, Mead, New York, 1964, 602p, Cloth, Coll.
13284 *Space space space; stories about the time when men will be adventuring to the stars.* Franklin Watts, New York, 1953, 288p, Cloth, Anth.
13285 *Stories for tomorrow; an anthology of modern science fiction.* Funk & Wagnalls, New York, 1954, 628p, Cloth, Anth.
13286 *To walk the night; a novel.* Farrar & Rinehart, New York, 1937, 307p, Cloth, Novel

SLOBODKIN, LOUIS, 1903-1975 [*biography included*]

13287 *Round trip space ship.* Macmillan, New York, 1968, 167p, Cloth, Novel [Space Ship #4]
13288 *The space ship in the park.* Macmillan, New York, 1972, 167p, Cloth, Novel [Space Ship #5]
13289 *The space ship returns to the apple tree.* Macmillan, New York, 1958, 127p, Cloth, Novel [Space Ship #2]
13290 *The space ship under the apple tree.* Macmillan, New York, 1952, 114p, Cloth, Novel [Space Ship #1]
13291 *The three-seated space ship, the latest model of the space ship under the apple tree.* Macmillan, New York, 1962, 126p, Cloth, Novel [Space Ship #3]

SLOCOMBE, GEORGE (Edward), 1894-1963

13292 *Escape into the past; a novel.* George G. Harrap, London, 1943, 335p, Cloth, Novel

SŁOWACKI, JULIUSZ, 1809-1849

13293 *Anhelli.* George Allen & Unwin, London, 1930, 118p, Cloth, Novel

SMALL, AUSTIN J.

       The avenging ray. [see 13296A]
13294 *The death maker.* George H. Doran, New York, 1926, 309p, Cloth, Novel
13295 *The man they couldn't arrest.* Hodder & Stoughton, London, 1927, 320p, Cloth, Novel

as Seamark:

13296 *The avenging ray.* Hodder & Stoughton, London, 1930, 314p, Cloth, Novel
13296A *The avenging ray,* by Austin J. Small. Crime Club, Doubleday, Doran, Garden City, 1930, 287p, Cloth, Novel

SMEATON, (William Henry) OLIPHANT, 1856-1914

13297 *A mystery of the Pacific.* Blackie & Son, London, 1899, 335p, Cloth, Novel

SMILE, R. ELTON, pseud.
  see: SMILIE, ELTON R.

SMILEY, MARJORIE B., with Domenica Paterno and Mary Delores Jarmon

07856 *Something strange.* Macmillan, New York, 1969, 246p, Paper, Anth.

SMILIE, ELTON R.

13298 *Investigations and experience of M. Shawtinbach, at Saar Soong, Sumatra; a ret or sequel to "The Manatitlans."* Joseph Winterburn, San Francisco, 1879, 263p, Cloth, Novel [published anonymously; Manatitlans #2]

as R. Elton Smile:

13299 *The Manatitlans; or, A record of recent scientific explorations in the Andean La Plata, S.A.* Riverside Press, Cambridge, Mass., 1877, 478p, Cloth, Novel [Manatitlans #1]

SMITH, AGNES, 1906-

13300 *An edge of the forest.* Viking Press, New York, 1959, 192p, Cloth, Novel

SMITH, ANN ELIZA
  see: SMITH, Mrs. J. GREGORY

SMITH, ARTEGALL, pseud. [Philip Norton]

13301 *Sub sole; or, Under the Sun; missionary adventures in the great Sahara.* James Nisbet, London, 1890, 256p, Cloth, Novel

SMITH, ARTHUR D(ouglas) HOWDEN, 1887-1945

13302 *Grey Maiden; the story of a sword through the ages*. Longmans, Green, New York, 1929, 306p, Cloth, Novel

SMITH, CLARK ASHTON, 1893-1961

13303 *The abominations of Yondo*. Arkham House, Sauk City, 1960, 227p, Cloth, Coll.

13304 *The double shadow, and other fantasies*. Auburn Journal Print, Auburn, CA, 1933, 30p, Paper, Coll.

13305 *Ebony and crystal; poems in verse and prose*. Auburn Journal, Auburn, CA, 1922, 152p, Cloth, Coll. [includes some verse]

13306 *Genius loci, and other tales*. Arkham House, Sauk City, 1948, 228p, Cloth, Coll.

13307 *Hyperborea*. Ballantine, New York, 1971, 205p, Paper, Coll.

13308 *The immortals of Mercury*. Stellar Publishing Corp., New York, 1932, 24p, Paper, Story

13309 *Lost worlds*. Arkham House, Sauk City, 1944, 419p, Cloth, Coll.

13309A retitled: *Lost worlds, volume 1; Zothique, Averoigne, and others*. Panther, St. Albans, UK, 1974, 205p, Paper, Coll. [abridged]

13309B retitled: *Lost worlds, volume 2; Atlantis, Hyperborea, Xiccarph, and others*. Panther, St. Albans, UK, 1974, 188p, Paper, Coll. [abridged; 13309A and 13309B together comprise the original volume]

13310 *The mortuary*. Roy Squires, Glendale, CA, 1971, 8p, Paper, Story

13311 *Other dimensions*. Arkham House, Sauk City, 1970, 329p, Cloth, Coll.

13312 *Out of space and time*. Arkham House, Sauk City, 1942, 370p, Cloth, Coll.

13312A retitled: *Out of space and time, volume I*. Panther, St. Albans, UK, 1974, 204p, Paper, Coll. [abridged]

13312B retitled: *Out of space and time, volume II*. Panther, St. Albans, UK, 1974, 192p, Paper, Coll. [abridged; 13312A and 13312B together comprise the original volume]

13313 *Planets and dimensions; collected essays of Clark Ashton Smith*. Mirage Press, Baltimore, 1973, 87p, Cloth, Nonf. Coll.

13314 *Poems in prose*. Arkham House, Sauk City, 1965, 54p, Cloth, Coll.

13315 *Poseidonis*. Ballantine, New York, 1973, 210p, Paper, Coll.

13316 *Sadastor*. Roy Squires, Glendale, CA, 1972, 12p, Paper, Story

13317 *Tales of science and sorcery*. Arkham House, Sauk City, 1964, 256p, Cloth, Coll.

13318 *Xiccarph*. Ballantine, New York, 1972, 247p, Paper, Coll.

13319 *Zothique*. Ballantine, New York, 1970, 273p, Paper, Coll.

with Virgil Finlay:

05411 *Klarkash-Ton and Monstro Ligriv; previously unpublished poems and art*. Gerry de la Ree, Saddle River, NJ, 1974, 28p, Paper, Nonf.

SMITH, CORDELIA (Meda) TITCOMB, 1902- [*biography included*]

13320 *Great science fiction stories*. Dell, New York, 1964, 288p, Paper, Anth.

13320A retitled: *The best of sci-fi (three)*. Mayflower-Dell, London, 1964, 288p, Paper, Anth.

SMITH, CORDWAINER, pseud. [Paul Myron Anthony Linebarger, 1913-1966]

13321 *The planet buyer; a science-fiction novel*. Pyramid, New York, 1964, 156p, Paper, Novel [Instrumentality series]

13322 *Quest of the three worlds*. Ace, New York, 1966, 174p, Paper, Novel [Instrumentality series]

13323 *Space lords*. Pyramid, New York, 1965, 206p, Paper, Coll. [Instrumentality series]

13324 *Stardreamer*. Beagle, New York, 1971, 185p, Paper, Coll. [Instrumentality series]

13325 *Under old Earth, and other explorations*. Panther, London, 1970, 188p, Paper, Coll. [Instrumentality series]

13326 *The underpeople*. Pyramid, New York, 1968, 159p, Paper, Novel [Instrumentality series]

13327 *You will never be the same*. Regency, Evanston, IL, 1963, 156p, Paper, Coll. [Instrumentality series]

SMITH, DAVID McLEOD
 see: MARINER, DAVID

SMITH, DODIE [Dorothy Gladys Smith, 1896-] [*biography included*]

13328 *The hundred and one dalmatians*. Heinemann, Melbourne, 1956, 190p, Cloth, Novel [101 Dalmatians #1]

13329 *The starlight barking; more about the hundred and one dalmatians*. Heinemann, London, 1967, 145p, Cloth, Novel [101 Dalmatians #2]

SMITH, E(dward) E(lmer), 1890-1965 [*biography included*]

13330 *Children of the lens*. Fantasy Press, Reading, PA, 1954, 293p, Cloth, Novel [Lensmen #6]

13331 *First Lensman*. Fantasy Press, Reading, PA, 1950, 306p, Cloth, Novel [Lensmen #2]

13332 *Galactic Patrol*. Fantasy Press, Reading, PA, 1950, 273p, Cloth, Novel [Lensmen #3]

13333 *The Galaxy Primes*. Ace, New York, 1965, 192p, Paper, Novel

13334 *Gray Lensman*. Fantasy Press, Reading, PA, 1951, 306p, Cloth, Novel [Lensmen #4]
 Masters of the vortex. [see 13342A]

13335 *Second stage Lensmen*. Fantasy Press, Reading, PA, 1953, 308p, Cloth, Novel [Lensmen #5]

13336 *Skylark DuQuesne*. Pyramid, New York, 1966, 238p, Paper, Novel [Skylark #4]

13337 *Skylark of Valeron*. Fantasy Press, Reading, PA, 1949, 252p, Cloth, Novel [Skylark #3]

13338 *Skylark Three*. Fantasy Press, Reading, PA, 1948, 247p, Cloth, Novel [Skylark #2]

13339 *Spacehounds of IPC; a tale of the Inter-Planetary Corporation*. Fantasy Press, Reading, PA, 1947, 257p, Cloth, Novel

13340 *Subspace explorers*. Canaveral Press, New York, 1965, 278p, Cloth, Novel

13341 *Triplanetary; a tale of cosmic adventure*. Fantasy Press, Reading, PA, 1948, 287p, Cloth, Novel [Lensmen #1]

SMITH, E. E. (cont.)

13342   *The Vortex Blaster.* Gnome Press, Hicksville,
        NY, 1960, 191p, Cloth, Novel [Lensmen #7]
13342A retitled: *Masters of the vortex.* Pyramid,
        New York, 1968, 191p, Paper, Novel [Lensmen
        #7]

with Lee Hawkins Garby:

05758   *The Skylark of space; the tale of the first
        inter-stellar cruise.* Buffalo Book Co.,
        Providence, RI, 1946, 303p, Cloth, Novel
        [Skylark #1]

SMITH, E(lizabeth) OAKES, 1806-1893

13343   *The Salamander; a legend for Christmas, found
        amongst the papers of the late Ernest Helfen-
        stein.* George P. Putnam, New York, 1848,
        149p, Cloth, Novel

SMITH, Lady ELEANOR FURNEAUX, 1902-1945

13344   *Lovers' meeting.* Hutchinson, London, 1940,
        384p, Cloth, Novel
13345   *Satan's circus, and other stories.* Victor
        Gollancz, London, 1931, 287p, Cloth, Coll.
13345A retitled: *Satan's circus.* Bobbs-Merrill, In-
        dianapolis, 1934, 329p, Cloth, Coll.

SMITH, ELIZABETH THOMASINA
    see: MEADE, L. T.

SMITH, ERNEST BRAMAH
    see: BRAMAH, ERNEST

SMITH, EVELYN E., 1927-

13346   *The perfect planet.* Avalon, New York, 1962,
        224p, Cloth, Novel

as Delphine C. Lyons:

13347   *Valley of shadows.* Lancer, New York, 1968,
        413p, Paper, Novel

SMITH, G(eorge) LAWSON

13348   *Transfer.* Vantage Press, New York, 1970, 95p,
        Cloth, Novel

SMITH, GARRET, 1876?-1954

13349   *Between worlds.* Stellar Publishing Corp., New
        York, 1930, 93p, Paper, Novel

SMITH, GEORGE H(ENRY), 1922-   [*biography included*]

13350   *The coming of the rats.* Pike, Van Nuys, CA,
        1961, 158p, Paper, Novel
13351   *Doomsday Wing.* Monarch, Derby, Conn., 1963,
        124p, Paper, Novel
13352   *Druids' world*, by George Henry Smith. Avalon,
        New York, 1967, 192p, Cloth, Novel

13353   *The forgotten planet*, by George Henry Smith.
        Avalon, New York, 1965, 189p, Cloth, Novel
13354   *The four day weekend*, by George Henry Smith.
        Belmont, New York, 1966, 157p, Paper, Novel
13355   *Kar Kaballa.* Ace Double, New York, 1969, 145p,
        Paper, Novel [Annwn series]
13356   *1976...the year of terror.* Epic, Los Angeles,
        1961, 154p, Paper, Novel
13356A retitled: *The year for love.* Moonlight Rea-
        der, Los Angeles, 1965?, 154p, Paper, Novel
        [published anonymously]
13357   *Scourge of the blood cult.* Epic, Los Angeles,
        1961, 158p, Paper, Novel [Annwn series]
13358   *The unending night.* Monarch, Derby, Conn.,
        1964, 128p, Paper, Novel
13359   *Witch Queen of Lochlann.* Signet, New York,
        1969, 159p, Paper, Novel [Annwn series]

anonymously, with M. J. Deer:

04007   *Flames of desire.* France, Hollywood, 1963,
        160p?, Paper, Novel
04008   *A place named Hell.* France, Hollywood, 1963,
        160p, Paper, Novel

SMITH, GEORGE MALCOLM-
    see: MALCOLM-SMITH, GEORGE

SMITH, GEORGE O(liver), 1911-   [*biography included*]

        The brain machine. [see 13361A]
13360   *Fire in the heavens.* Avalon, New York, 1958,
        224p, Cloth, Novel
13361   *The fourth "R."* Ballantine, New York, 1959,
        160p, Paper, Novel
13361A retitled: *The brain machine.* Lancer, New
        York, 1968, 221p, Paper, Novel
13362   *Hellflower; a science-fiction novel.* Abelard
        Press, New York, 1953, 264p, Cloth, Novel
13363   *Highways in hiding.* Gnome Press, New York,
        1956, 223p, Cloth, Novel
13363A retitled: *The space plague.* Avon, New York,
        1957, 191p, Paper, Novel
13364   *Lost in space.* Avalon, New York, 1959, 224p,
        Cloth, Novel
13365   *Nomad.* Prime Press, Philadelphia, 1950, 286p,
        Cloth, Novel
13366   *Operation interstellar.* Merit, Chicago, 1950,
        127p, Paper, Novel
13367   *The path of unreason.* Gnome Press, Hicksville,
        NY, 1958, 187p, Cloth, Novel
13368   *Pattern for conquest; an interplanetary adven-
        ture.* Gnome Press, New York, 1949, 252p,
        Cloth, Novel
        The space plague. [see 13363A]
13369   *Troubled star.* Avalon, New York, 1957, 220p,
        Cloth, Novel
13370   *Venus Equilateral.* Prime Press, Philadelphia,
        1947, 455p, Cloth, Coll.

SMITH, GUY N(ewman), 1939-

13371   *Werewolf by moonlight.* New English Library,
        London, 1974, 110p, Paper, Novel

SMITH, H(arry) ALLEN, 1907-1976 [*biography
included*]

13372   *The age of the tail.* Little, Brown, Boston,
        1955, 159p, Cloth, Novel

SMITH, H. ALLEN (cont.)

13373 *Mr. Klein's kampf; or, His life as Hitler's double.* Stackpole Sons, New York, 1939, 202p, Cloth, Novel

SMITH, Mrs. J. GREGORY [Ann Eliza Smith, 1818-1905]

13374 *Atla; the story of the lost island.* Harper & Bros., New York, 1886, 284p, Cloth, Novel
13375 *Seola.* Lee & Shepard, Boston, 1878, 251p, Cloth, Novel [published anonymously]
13376 retitled: *Angels and women; a revision of the unique novel, Seola.* A. B. Abac Co., New York, 1924, 268p, Cloth, Novel [revised]

SMITH, JAMES, with John Wren Sutton

13377 *The secret of the sphinx; or, The ring of Moses.* Philip Wellby, London, 1906, 288p, Cloth, Novel

SMITH, L. H.
see: WILLIAMS, SPEEDY

SMITH, MARTIN (Cruz), 1942- [*biography included*]

13378 *The analog bullet.* Belmont, New York, 1972, 189p, Paper, Novel
13379 *The Indians won.* Belmont, New York, 1970, 219p, Paper, Novel

SMITH, MONTAGUE, with Steve Damon

03762 *The incredible world of Harold Huge.* Pendulum, Los Angeles, 1970, 191p, Paper, Novel

SMITH, PAUL JORDAN-, 1885-1971

13380 *Nomad.* Minton, Balch, New York, 1925, 253p, Cloth, Novel

SMITH, PERRY MICHAEL, 1937-

13381 *Last rites.* Charles Scribner's Sons, New York, 1971, 389p, Cloth, Novel

SMITH, REGINALD

13382 *Weird tales in the thirties.* Reg Smith, Santa Ana, CA, 1966, 41p, Paper, Nonf.

SMITH, ROBERT (Eugene), 1920-

13383 *Riders to the stars.* Ballantine, New York, 1954, 166p, Paper, Movie

SMITH, SHEILA KAYE-
see: KAYE-SMITH, SHEILA

SMITH, SURREY, pseud.

13384 *The village that wandered.* T. V. Boardman, London, 1960, 223p, Cloth, Novel

SMITH, T. E. GRATTAN-
see: GRATTAN-SMITH, T. E.

SMITH, TEVIS CLYDE

13385 *The cardboard god.* Tevis Clyde Smith, Brownwood, TX, 1970, 54p, Cloth, Coll.

SMITH, (James) THORNE (Jr.), 1893-1934

13386 *The glorious pool.* Doubleday, Doran, Garden City, 1934, 292p, Cloth, Novel
       The jovial ghosts. [see 11395A]
13387 *Lazy Bear Lane.* Doubleday, Doran, Garden City, 1931, 240p, Cloth, Novel
13388 *The night life of the gods.* Doubleday, Doran, Garden City, 1931, 311p, Cloth, Novel
13389 *Rain in the doorway.* Doubleday, Doran, Garden City, 1933, 304p, Cloth, Novel
13390 *Skin and bones.* Doubleday, Doran, Garden City, 1933, 306p, Cloth, Novel
13391 *The stray lamb.* Cosmopolitan Book Corp., New York, 1929, 303p, Cloth, Novel
13392 *The Thorne Smith three-bagger: The glorious pool; Skin and bones; Topper.* Doubleday, Doran, Garden City, 1943, 685p, Cloth, Coll.
13393 *The Thorne Smith 3-decker.* Doubleday, Doran, Garden City, 1936, 698p, Cloth, Coll. [includes: *The stray lamb; Turnabout; Rain in the doorway*]
13394 *The Thorne Smith triplets.* Doubleday, Doran, Garden City, 1938, 758p, Cloth, Coll. [includes: *Topper takes a trip; The night life of the gods; The Bishop's jaegers*]
13395 *Topper; an improbable adventure.* Robert M. McBride, New York, 1926, 292p, Cloth, Novel [Topper #1]
13395A retitled: *The jovial ghosts; the misadventures of Topper.* Arthur Barker, London, 1933, 320p, Cloth, Novel [Topper #1]
13396 *Topper takes a trip.* Doubleday, Doran, Garden City, 1932, 325p, Cloth, Novel [Topper #2]
13397 *Turnabout.* Doubleday, Doran, Garden City, 1931, 312p, Cloth, Novel

with Norman Matson:

09818 *The passionate witch.* Doubleday, Doran, Garden City, 1941, 267p, Cloth, Novel [Jennifer #1]

SMITH, TITUS K(eiper), 1859-

13398 *Altruria.* Altruria Publishing Co., New York, 1895, 120p, Paper, Novel

SMITH, TREVOR DUDLEY-
see: DUDLEY-SMITH, TREVOR

SMITH, W(alter) J(ames), 1917- [*biography included*]

13399 *The grand voyage.* Robert Hale, London, 1973, 175p, Cloth, Novel

SMITH, WAYLAND, pseud.

13400 *The machine stops.* Robert Hale, London, 1936, 284p, Cloth, Novel

SMITH, WILBUR (Addison), 1933- [*biography included*]

13401 *The Sunbird.* Heinemann, London, 1972, 486p, Cloth, Novel

SMITH, WILLIAM AUGUSTUS

13402 *His Pseudoic Majesty; or, The Knights of the Fleece.* Liberty Publishing Co., New York, 1903, 397p, Cloth, Novel; Watts & Co., London, 1903, 397p, Cloth, Novel

SMITHSON, ANNIE M(ary) P(atricia), 1883-

13403 *The white owl.* Talbot Press, Dublin, 1937, 300p, Cloth, Novel

SMOLLETT, Dr. (Tobias George), 1721-1777

13404 *The history and adventures of an atom.* Robinson & Roberts, London, 1749, 2vol, Cloth, Novel

SMYTH, CLIFFORD, 1866-1943

13405 *The Gilded Man; a romance of the Andes.* Boni & Liveright, New York, 1918, 356p, Cloth, Novel

SMYTHE, ALFRED

13406 *Van Hoff; or, The new Faust.* American Publishers Corp., New York, 1897, 322p, Cloth, Novel

SMYTHE, R. JOHN, pseud.

13407 *The coming of Morikand; a sequel to The conception.* Darkroom, San Diego, 1970, 159p, Paper, Novel [Conception #2]
13408 *The conception.* Late-Hour Library, San Diego, 1969, 175p, Paper, Novel [Conception #1]
13409 *Doctor Swapus.* Companion, San Diego, 1970, 156p, Paper, Novel
13410 *The naked Phantom.* Nightstand, San Diego, 1970, 158p, Paper, Novel
13411 *Switch-off.* Adult, San Diego, 1970, 158p, Paper, Novel

SNAITH, J(ohn) C(ollis), 1876-1936

13412 *Thus far.* Hodder & Stoughton, London, 1925, 318p, Cloth, Novel

SNELL, EDMUND

13413 *Blue murder.* T. Fisher Unwin, London, 1927, 288p, Cloth, Novel

13414 *Kontrol.* Ernest Benn, London, 1928, 288p, Cloth, Novel
13415 *The Sound-Machine.* Skeffington & Son, London, 1932, 288p, Cloth, Novel
13416 *The White Owl.* Hodder & Stoughton, London, 1930, 312p, Cloth, Novel
13417 *The Yu-Chi Stone.* T. Fisher Unwin, London, 1925, 286p, Cloth, Novel
13418 *The "Z" ray.* Skeffington & Son, London, 1932, 287p, Cloth, Novel

SNELL, ROY J(udson), 1878-

13419 *The Flying Sub.* Reilly & Lee, Chicago, 1925, 282p, Cloth, Novel [Radio-Phone Boys #5]
13420 *The seagoing tank.* Reilly & Lee, Chicago, 1924, 264p, Cloth, Novel [Radio-Phone Boys #4]

SNEVE, VIRGINIA DRIVING HAWK, 1933- [*biography included*]

13421 *When Thunders spoke.* Holiday House, New York, 1974, 93p, Cloth, Novel

SNOW, C(harles) P(ercy), Baron Snow, 1905- [*biography included*]

13422 *New lives for old.* Victor Gollancz, London, 1933, 399p, Cloth, Novel [published anonymously]

SNOW, HELEN
  see: WALES, NYM

SNOW, JACK, 1907-

13423 *Dark music, and other spectral tales.* Herald Publishing Co., New York, 1947, 208p, Cloth, Coll.

SNYDER, CECIL III

13424 *The hawks of Arcturus.* DAW, New York, 1974, 159p, Paper, Novel

SNYDER, E(ugene) V(incent), 1943- [*biography included*], with William Jon Watkins

13425 *Ecodeath.* Doubleday, Garden City, 1972, 180p, Cloth, Novel

SNYDER, GUY (Eugene Jr.), 1951- [*biography included*]

13426 *Testament XXI.* DAW, New York, 1973, 144p, Paper, Novel

SNYDER, ZILPHA KEATLEY, 1927- [*biography included*]

13427 *Black and blue magic.* Atheneum, New York, 1966, 186p, Cloth, Novel

SNYDER, ZILPHA KEATLEY (cont.)

13428 *Eyes in the fishbowl.* Atheneum, New York,
        1968, 168p, Cloth, Novel
13429 *The headless cupid.* Atheneum, New York, 1971,
        203p, Cloth, Novel
13430 *The truth about Stone Hollow.* Atheneum, New
        York, 1974, 211p, Cloth, Novel

SOBEL, ROBERT, 1931- [*biography included*]

13431 *For want of a nail...; if Burgoyne had won at
        Saratoga.* Macmillan, New York, 1973, 441p,
        Cloth, Novel

SOHL, JERRY [Gerald Allan Sohl, Sr., 1913-   ]
[*biography included*]

13432 *The altered ego.* Rinehart, New York, 1954,
        248p, Cloth, Novel
13433 *The anomaly.* Curtis, New York, 1971, 160p,
        Paper, Novel
13434 *Costigan's Needle.* Rinehart, New York, 1953,
        250p, Cloth, Novel
13435 *The haploids.* Rinehart, New York, 1952,
        248p, Cloth, Novel
13436 *The Mars monopoly.* Ace Double, New York,
        1956, 183p, Paper, Novel
13437 *Night slaves.* Gold Medal, Greenwich, Conn.,
        1965, 174p, Paper, Novel
13438 *The odious ones.* Rinehart, New York, 1959,
        245p, Cloth, Novel
13439 *One against Herculum.* Ace Double, New York,
        1959, 124p, Paper, Novel
13440 *Point Ultimate.* Rinehart, New York, 1955,
        244p, Cloth, Novel
13441 *The time dissolver.* Avon, New York, 1957,
        158p, Paper, Novel
13442 *The transcendent man.* Rinehart, New York,
        1953, 244p, Cloth, Novel

SOHN, DAVID A., 1929- [*biography included*]

13443 *Ten top stories.* Bantam Pathfinder, New York,
        1964, 168p, Paper, Anth.

THE SOLDADO ANT

13444 *The Soldado ant.* American Science Fiction,
        Sydney, 1952, 34p, Paper, Anth.

SOLER, ANTONIO ROBLES
    see: ANTONIORROBLES

SOLO, GABRIELLO

13445 *Pleasures of Xanada.* Cad, New York, 1969,
        185p, Paper, Novel

SOLOVIEV, MIKHAIL, 1908-

13446 *The smiling Kouros; a novel of ancient and
        modern Greece.* David McKay, Philadelphia,
        1962, 271p, Cloth, Novel

SOMERS, BART, pseud.
    see: FOX, GARDNER F.

SOMETIME, NEVER

13447 *Sometime, never; three tales of imagination.*
        Eyre & Spottiswoode, London, 1956, 224p,
        Cloth, Anth.

SOMMERFELD, ADOLF, 1870-

13448 *"How Germany crushed France" (the story of the
        greatest conspiracy in history).* Everett &
        Co., London, 1914, 159p, Cloth, Novel

THE SON OF A MANDARIN, pseud.
    see: HAYWOOD, ELIZA

SØRENSEN, VILLY, 1929-

13449 *Strange stories.* Secker & Warburg, London,
        1956, 204p, Cloth, Coll.
13449A retitled: *Tiger in the kitchen, and other
        strange stories.* Abelard-Schuman, New York,
        1957, 204p, Cloth, Coll.

SOUCANTON, Baroness ALEXANDRA de

13450 *The beloved of Sennacherib; a novel.* Heath
        Cranton, London, 1922, 234p, Cloth, Novel

SOUTAR, ANDREW, 1879-1941

13451 *The perverted village.* Hutchinson, London,
        1936, 476p, Cloth, Novel

SOUTHALL, IVAN (Francis), 1921- [*biography
included*]

13452 *Meet Simon Black.* Angus & Robertson, Sydney,
        1950, 210p, Cloth, Novel [Simon Black #1]
13453 *Simon Black and the spacemen.* Angus & Robert-
        son, Sydney, 1955, 228p, Cloth, Novel [Simon
        Black #6]
13454 *Simon Black in peril.* Angus & Robertson, Syd-
        ney, 1951, 224p, Cloth, Novel [Simon Black
        #2]
13455 *Simon Black in space.* Angus & Robertson, Syd-
        ney, 1952, 223p, Cloth, Novel [Simon Black
        #4]

SOUTHESK, (James Carnegie, 9th) Earl of, 1827-
1905

13456 *Suomiria; a fantasy.* David Douglas, Edinburgh,
        1899, 322p, Cloth, Novel

SOUTHWELL, SAMUEL B(eall), 1922-

13457 *If all the rebels die.* Doubleday, Garden City,
        1966, 400p, Cloth, Novel

SOUTHWOLD, STEPHEN
    see: BELL, NEIL

SOUZA, STEVEN M(ichael), 1953-   [biography included]

    13458   The espers. Lenox Hill Press, New York, 1972, 192p, Cloth, Novel

SOVIET SCIENCE FICTION
    see: A VISITOR FROM OUTER SPACE

SOWDEN, LEWIS, 1903-1974 [biography included]

    13459   Tomorrow's comet; a tale of our own times. Robert Hale, London, 1951, 302p, Cloth, Novel

SPACE STATION 42, AND OTHER STORIES

    13460   Space Station 42, and other stories. Satellite, London, 1958, 113p, Paper, Anth.

THE SPACE STORY OMNIBUS

    13461   The space story omnibus. Collins, London, 1955, 128p, Cloth, Anth.

THE SPAEWIFE
    see: GALT, JOHN

SPALDING, HELEN

    13462   The white witnesses. Charles Scribner's Sons, New York, 1948, 271p, Cloth, Novel; Methuen, London, 1948, 289p, Cloth, Novel

SPANNER, E(dward) F(rank), 1888-

    13463   The broken trident. Williams & Norgate, London, 1926, 309p, Cloth, Novel
    13464   The harbour of death. Williams & Norgate, London, 1927, 311p, Cloth, Novel
    13465   The naviators. Williams & Norgate, London, 1926, 303p, Cloth, Novel

SPARK, MURIEL (Sarah), 1918-

    13466   The hothouse by the East River. Macmillan, London, 1973, 168p, Cloth, Novel

SPAWN OF THE VAMPIRE

    13467   Spawn of the vampire. Bear, Hudson, London, 1946, 80p, Paper, Anth.

SPEAIGHT, ROBERT (William), 1904-1976 [biography included]

    13468   The angel in the mist. Cassell, London, 1936, 324p, Cloth, Novel
    13468A retitled: Legend of Helena Vaughan. G. P. Putnam's Sons, New York, 1936, 306p, Cloth, Novel

SPEARS, JOHN R(andolph), 1850-1936

    13469   The port of missing ships, and other stories of the sea. Macmillan, New York, 1897, 183p, Cloth, Coll.

SPECTOR, ROBERT D(onald), 1922-   [biography included]

    13470   The candle and the tower. Warner, New York, 1974, 272p, Paper, Anth.
    13471   Seven masterpieces of gothic horror. Bantam, New York, 1963, 467p, Paper, Anth.

SPECTORSKY, A(uguste) C(omte), 1910-1972

    13472   Man into beast; strange tales of transformation. Doubleday, Garden City, 1947, 368p, Cloth, Anth.

THE SPECTRE, pseud.

    13473   Ye vampyres; a legend of the National Betting-Ring, showing what became of it. Samuel Tinsley, London, 1875, 344p, Cloth, Novel

THE SPECTRE BULLET

    13474   The spectre bullet. Stellar Publishing Corp., New York, 1932, 24p, Paper, Anth. [includes "The Spectre Bullet," by Thomas Mack; "The Avenging Note," by Alfred Sprissler]

THE SPECTRE MOTHER
    see: THE AUTHOR OF MIDNIGHT HORRORS

SPEED, DONALD

    13475   My blood ran cold. Corgi, London, 1966, 188p, Paper, Anth.

SPEER, LAURA B(elle), 1883-   , with M. Marlow Morris

    10398   No borderland; a novel. Mathis, Van Nort, Dallas, 1938, 269p, Cloth, Novel

SPEIGHT, E(rnest) E(dwin)

    13476   The galleon of Torbay; a romance, telling how some western men and women, Virginia bound, were lost for three hundred years; how a Devon boy found their old city beyond the lagoons, and led the folk from havoc; how a brown maiden fell in love with him in the heart of danger, and followed him through the unknown mountains; and how a Yorkshire cricketer harboured them in Mexico; with many another adventure, into which is woven a span of the wild girlhood of the Moon-wind Chatto & Windus, London, 1908, 400p, Cloth, Novel

SPEIGHT, T(homas) W(ilkinson), 1830-1915

13477 *The strange experiences of Mr. Verschoyle.*
Gentleman's Annual, London, 1900, 126p,
Paper, Novel

SPELLER, JANE, with Robert Speller

13478 *Adam's first wife.* Macaulay Co., New York,
1929, 243p, Cloth, Novel

SPELLER, ROBERT, with Jane Speller

13478 *Adam's first wife.* Macaulay Co., New York,
1929, 243p, Cloth, Novel

SPENCE, (James) LEWIS (Thomas Chalmers), 1874-
1955

13479 *The archer in the arras, and other tales of
mystery.* Grant & Murray, Edinburgh, 1932,
256p, Cloth, Coll.

SPENCER, D. A., with W. Randerson

11998 *North Sea monster; a novel.* Houghton & Scott-
Snell, London, 1934, 246p, Cloth, Novel

SPENCER, G. F.

13480 *Heavens for all; a romance of the space age.*
Mitre Press, London, 1955, 191p, Cloth,
Novel

SPENCER, R(obin) E(dgerton), 1896-1956

13481 *Felicita.* Bobbs-Merrill, Indianapolis, 1937,
159p, Cloth, Novel
13482 *The lady who came to stay.* Alfred A. Knopf,
New York, 1931, 284p, Cloth, Novel

SPENCER, SCOTT

13483 *Last night at the brain thieves ball; a novel.*
Houghton Mifflin, Boston, 1973, 178p, Cloth,
Novel

SPERRY, J(ane) E., 1920- [*biography included*]

13484 *The challenge of Aab.* Harper & Bros, New York,
1962, 216p, Cloth, Novel

SPICER, PAUL R.

13485 *The outlander.* Burton, Kansas City, 1930,
Cloth, Novel

SPIEGEL, CHARLES A.

13486 *Math on Mars; a new path to math.* Exposition
Press, New York, 1969, 85p, Cloth, Novel

SPIEGELMAN, J(oseph) MARVIN, 1926-

13487 *The tree; tales in psycho-mythology.* Phoenix
House, Los Angeles, 1974, 464p, Cloth, Coll.

SPIERS, HETTY, with Langford Reed

12081 *The mantle of Methuselah; a farcical novel.*
Rich & Cowan, London, 1939, 288p, Cloth,
Novel

SPIKE, PAUL, 1947-

13488 *Bad news.* Holt, Rinehart & Winston, New York,
1971, 152p, Cloth, Coll.

SPINA, GREYE LA
see: LA SPINA, GREYE

SPINRAD, NORMAN (Richard), 1940-   [*biography
included*]

13489 *Agent of Chaos.* Belmont, New York, 1967, 157p,
Paper, Novel
13490 *Bug Jack Barron.* Walker, New York, 1969, 327p,
Cloth, Novel
13491 *The iron dream.* Avon, New York, 1972, 255p,
Paper, Novel [includes a false title page
listing author and title as: *Lord of the
swastika*, by Adolf Hitler]
13492 *The last hurrah of the Golden Horde.* Nelson
Doubleday, Garden City, 1970, 215p, Cloth,
Coll.
13493 *The men in the jungle.* Doubleday, Garden City,
1967, 240p, Cloth, Novel
13494 *Modern science fiction.* Anchor Press, New York,
1974, 540p, Paper, Anth.
13495 *The new tomorrows.* Belmont, New York, 1971,
235p, Paper, Anth.
13496 *The Solarians.* Paperback Library, New York,
1966, 160p, Paper, Novel

"SPINSTER," pseud.
see: AUTHOR OF "THE TRUTH ABOUT MAN"

THE SPIRIT OF TURRETVILLE

13497 *The spirit of Turretville; or, The mysterious
resemblance; a romance of the 12th century.*
R. Dutton, London, 1800, vol. I-200p, II-
223p, Cloth, Novel

A SPIRIT YET IN THE FLESH, pseud.
see: GASTON, HENRY A.

SPITTELER, CARL, 1845-1924

13498 *Prometheus and Epimetheus; a prose epic.* Jarrolds Publishers, London, 1931, 318p, Cloth,
Novel

SPITZ, JACQUES, 1896-1963

 13499 *Sever the Earth.* John Lane, The Bodley Head,
     London, 1936, 167p, Cloth, Novel

SPIVEY, THOMAS SAWYER, 1856-1938

 13500 *The seven sons of Ballyhack.* Cosmopolitan
     Press, New York, 1911, 317p, Cloth, Novel

SPOOKS IN YOUR CUPBOARD

 13501 *Spooks in your cupboard; 19th century British
     ghost stories.* Seven Seas Publishers, Ber-
     lin, 1966, 260p, Paper, Anth.

SPOTSWOOD, CHRISTOPHER

 13502 *The voyage of Will Rogers to the South Pole.*
     "Examiner" and "Tasmanian," Launceston,
     Aust., 1888, 372p, Cloth, Novel

SPOTSWOOD, CLAIRE MYERS

 13503 *The unpredictable adventure; a comedy of wo-
     man's independence.* Doubleday, Doran,
     Garden City, 1935, 456p, Cloth, Novel

SPRAT, JOHN, pseud.
  see: HUNT, LEIGH

SPRIGG, C(hristopher) ST. JOHN, 1907-1937

 13504 *Uncanny stories.* Thomas Nelson & Sons, Lon-
     don, 1936, 397p, Cloth, Anth.

SPRINGER, NORMAN

 13505 *The dark river.* G. Howard Watt, New York,
     1928, 318p, Cloth, Novel

SPURRELL, H(erbert) G(eorge) F(laxman), 1877-
1918

 13506 *Out of the past.* Greening & Co., London,
     1903, 300p, Cloth, Coll.

A SQUARE, pseud.
  see: ABBOTT, EDWIN A.

SQUIRE, (Sir) J(ohn) C(ollings), 1884-1958

 13507 *If it had happened otherwise; lapses into
     imaginary history.* Longmans, Green, London,
     1931, 289p, Cloth, Anth.
 13508 retitled: *If; or, History rewritten.* Viking
     Press, New York, 1931, 379p, Cloth, Anth.
     [published anonymously; adds one story and
     drops one story from 13507]

SQUIRES, PATRICIA, pseud. [Patricia Sylvia
Ball, 1936-] [*biography included*]

 13509 *The ghost in the mirror, and other ghost sto-
     ries.* Frederick Muller, London, 1972, 180p,
     Cloth, Coll.

A STABLE FOR NIGHTMARES

 13510 *A stable for nightmares; or, Weird tales.* New
     Amsterdam Book Co., New York, 1896, 256p,
     Cloth, Anth.

STABLEFORD, BRIAN M(ichael), 1948- [*biography included*]

 13511 *The Blind Worm.* Ace Double, New York, 1970,
     149p, Paper, Novel
 13512 *Cradle of the Sun.* Ace Double, New York, 1969,
     140p, Paper, Novel
 13513 *Day of wrath; Dies Irae III.* Ace, New York,
     1971, 174p, Paper, Novel [Dies Irae #3]
 13514 *The days of glory; Dies Irae 1.* Ace, New York,
     1971, 158p, Paper, Novel [Dies Irae #1]
 13515 *The Fenris device.* DAW, New York, 1974, 156p,
     Paper, Novel [Star-Pilot Grainger #5]
 13516 *The Halcyon Drift.* DAW, New York, 1972, 175p,
     Paper, Novel [Star-Pilot Grainger #1]
 13517 *In the kingdom of the Beasts; Dies Irae II.*
     Ace, New York, 1971, 188p, Paper, Novel [Dies
     Irae #2]
 13518 *The paradise game.* DAW, New York, 1974, 158p,
     Paper, Novel [Star-Pilot Grainger #4]
 13519 *Promised land.* DAW, New York, 1974, 160p,
     Paper, Novel [Star-Pilot Grainger #3]
 13520 *Rhapsody in black.* DAW, New York, 1973, 157p,
     Paper, Novel [Star-Pilot Grainger #2]
 13521 *To challenge Chaos.* DAW, New York, 1972, 160p,
     Paper, Novel

STABLES, (William) GORDON, 1840-1910

 13522 *The city at the Pole.* James Nisbet, London,
     1906, 352p, Cloth, Novel
 13523 *The cruise of the Crystal Boat; the wild, the
     weird, the wonderful.* Hutchinson, London,
     1891, 343p, Cloth, Novel
 13524 *The cruise of the Snowbird; a story of Arctic
     adventure.* Hodder & Stoughton, London,
     1882, 366p, Cloth, Novel [Snowbird #1]
 13525 *The cruise of the "Vengeful"; a story of the
     Royal Navy.* John F. Shaw, London, 1902,
     268p, Cloth, Novel
 13526 *From Pole to Pole; a tale of the sea.* Hodder
     & Stoughton, London, 1886, 388p, Cloth, Novel
 13527 *In quest of the giant sloth; a tale of adven-
     ture in South America.* Blackie & Son, Lon-
     don, 1901, 288p, Cloth, Novel
13527A retitled: *The strange quest; a tale of adven-
     ture in South America.* Blackie & Son, Lon-
     don, 1937, 288p, Cloth, Novel
 13528 *In the great white land; a tale of the Antarc-
     tic Ocean.* Blackie & Son, London, 1902, 288p,
     Cloth, Novel
 13529 *Wild adventures round the Pole; or, The cruise
     of the 'Snowbird' crew in the 'Arrandoon.'*
     Henry Frowde, Hodder & Stoughton, London,
     1883, 333p, Cloth, Novel [Snowbird #2]

STACPOOLE, H(enry) de VERE, 1863-1951

13530 *The city in the sea.* George H. Doran, New
         York, 1925, 307p, Cloth, Novel
13531 *Death, the knight, and the lady; a ghost story.*
         John Lane, The Bodley Head, London, 1897,
         164p, Cloth, Novel
13532 *The story of my village.* Hutchinson, London,
         1947, 124p, Cloth, Novel

STACTON, DAVID (Derek), 1925-1968 [*biography
included*]

13533 *Segaki.* Faber & Faber, London, 1958, 198p,
         Cloth, Novel

STACY, TERRY, pseud. [Terrea Lea]

13534 *The adult version of Dr. Jekyll and Mr. Hyde.*
         Calga, Los Angeles, 1970, 192p, Paper, Novel

STADLER, JOHN

13535 *Eco-fiction.* Washington Square Press, New
         York, 1971, 211p, Paper, Anth.

STAFFORD, PETER, pseud.
    see: TABORI, PAUL

STAFFORD, TERRY, with E. Gary Gygax

06509 *Victorious German arms; an alternate military
         history of World War Two.* TK Graphics,
         Baltimore, 1973, 76p, Paper, Novel

STAHL, BEN(jamin), 1910-   [*biography included*]

13536 *Blackbeard's ghost.* Houghton Mifflin, Boston,
         1965, 184p, Cloth, Novel [Blackbeard #1]
13537 *The secret of Red Skull.* Houghton Mifflin,
         Boston, 1971, 243p, Cloth, Novel [Black-
         beard #2]

STAIR, BILL, with John Boorman

01620 *Zardoz.* Signet, New York, 1974, 127p, Paper,
         Movie

STAIRS, GORDON, pseud.
    see: AUSTIN, MARY

STALLARD, Mrs. ARTHUR [Constance Louisa Stal-
lard]

13538 *The uttermost.* John Murray, London, 1926,
         382p, Cloth, Novel

STAMM, RUSSELL

13539 *Invisible Scarlet O'Neil; a new story based
         on the famous newspaper strip.* Whitman Pub-
         lishing Co., Racine, Wisc., 1943, 248p,
         Cloth, Novel

STAMP, ROGER
    see: MINGSTON, R. GRESHAM

STAMPER, JOSEPH

13540 *"The bote upon the watter."* Hutchinson, Lon-
         don, 1933, 288p, Cloth, Novel

STANFORD, J(ohn) K(eith), 1892-1971 [*biography included*]

13541 *Full Moon at Sweatenham; a nightmare.* Faber
         & Faber, London, 1953, 238p, Cloth, Novel
13542 *The twelfth.* Faber & Faber, London, 1944, 85p,
         Cloth, Novel

STANILAND, MEABURN

13543 *Back to the future.* Nicholas Vane, London,
         1947, 264p, Cloth, Novel

STANLEY, A(lfred) M(ortimer), 1888-

13544 *Tomorrow's yesterday.* Dorrance, Philadelphia,
         1949, 174p, Cloth, Novel

STANLEY, DOROTHY, d. 1926

13545 *Miss Pim's camouflage.* Hutchinson, London,
         1918, 256p, Cloth, Novel

STANLEY, WILLIAM (Ford Robinson), 1829-1909

13546 *The case of Mr. Fox, being his prophecies under
         hypnotism of the period ending A.D. 1950;
         a political utopia.* Truslove & Hanson, Lon-
         don, 1903, 199p, Cloth, Novel

STANTON, EDWARD, pseud. [Edward Stanton Hun-
tington]

13547 *Dreams of the dead.* Lee & Shepard, Boston,
         1892, 268p, Cloth, Novel

STANTON, KEN, pseud.?

13548 *The Aquanauts #10; Operation sea monster.*
         Manor, New York, 1974, 190p, Paper, Novel
         [Aquanauts #10]
13549 *The Aquanauts #11; Operation mermaid.* Manor,
         New York, 1974, 192p, Paper, Novel [Aquanauts
         #11]

STAPLEDON, (William) OLAF, 1886-1950 [*biography included*]

13550 *Darkness and the light.* Methuen, London, 1942,
         181p, Cloth, Novel
13551 *Death into life.* Methuen, London, 1946, 159p,
         Cloth, Novel
13552 *The flames; a fantasy.* Secker & Warburg, Lon-
         don, 1947, 84p, Cloth, Novel
13553 *Last and first men; a story of the near and far
         future.* Methuen, London, 1930, 355p, Cloth,
         Novel [Last Men #1]

STAPLEDON, OLAF (cont.)

13554   *Last and first men; and, Last men in London.*
        Penguin, Harmondsworth, 1972, 605p, Paper,
        Coll. [Last Men #s 1-2]
13555   *Last and first men; &, Star maker; two science-
        fiction novels.* Dover, New York, 1968,
        438p, Paper, Coll.
13556   *Last men in London.* Methuen, London, 1932,
        312p, Cloth, Novel [Last Men #2]
13557   *A man divided.* Methuen, London, 1950, 187p,
        Cloth, Novel
13558   *Odd John; a story between jest and earnest.*
        Methuen, London, 1935, 282p, Cloth, Novel
13559   *Odd John; &, Sirius; two science-fiction no-
        vels.* Dover, New York, 1972, 309p, Paper,
        Coll.
13560   *Old man in new world.* George Allen & Unwin,
        London, 1944, 36p, Cloth, Story
13561   *Sirius; a fantasy of love and discord.* Secker
        & Warburg, London, 1944, 200p, Cloth, Novel
13562   *Star Maker.* Methuen, London, 1937, 339p,
        Cloth, Novel
13563   *To the end of time; the best of Olaf Staple-
        don.* Funk & Wagnalls, New York, 1953, 775p,
        Cloth, Coll. [includes: *Last and first men;
        Star maker; Odd John; Sirius; The flames*]
13564   *Worlds of wonder; three tales of fantasy.*
        Fantasy Publishing Co., Los Angeles, 1949,
        282p, Cloth, Coll. [includes: *The flames;
        Death into life; Old man in new world*]

STAPP, ARTHUR D(onald), 1906-1972 [*biography
included*]

13565   *5 who disappeared; a science adventure mystery.*
        Sterling Publishing Co., New York, 1958,
        224p, Cloth, Novel

STAPP, ROBERT

13566   *A more perfect union; a novel.* Harper's Maga-
        zine Press, New York, 1970, 375p, Cloth,
        Novel

STAR OF THE MORNING
    see: AUTHOR OF "THE TRUTH ABOUT MAN"

STARK, BEN

13567   *Come, come, come!* Pendulum, Los Angeles,
        1970, 160p, Paper, Novel

STARK, HARRIET

13568   *The bacillus of beauty; a romance of to-day.*
        Frederick A. Stokes, New York, 1900, 340p,
        Cloth, Novel

STARK, (Delbert) RAYMOND, 1919-

13569   *Crossroads to nowhere.* Ward, Lock, London,
        1956, 208p, Cloth, Novel

STARR, ROLAND, pseud.
    see: ROWLAND, DONALD S.

STARRETT, (Charles) VINCENT (Emerson), 1886-
1974

13570   *The quick and the dead.* Arkham House, Sauk
        City, 1965, 145p, Cloth, Coll.
13571   *Seaports in the Moon; a fantasia on romantic
        themes.* Doubleday, Doran, Garden City,
        1928, 289p, Cloth, Novel

STASHEFF, CHRISTOPHER

13572   *King Kobold.* Ace, New York, 1971, 254p, Paper
        Novel [Gallowglass #2]
13573   *The warlock in spite of himself.* Ace, New Yor
        1969, 285p, Paper, Novel [Gallowglass #1]

STATTEN, VARGO, pseud.
    see: FEARN, JOHN RUSSELL

STAUFFER, DONALD A(lfred), 1902-1952

13574   *The saint and the hunchback.* Simon & Schuster
        New York, 1946, 248p, Cloth, Novel

STAUFFER, MACK, 1857-1941

13575   *Humanity and the mysterious knight.* Roxburgh
        Publishing Co., Boston, 1915, 295p, Cloth,
        Novel

STAUGHTON, SIMON

13576   *Prince Lucifer; a biography of the devil.*
        Eynesbury Press, London, 1950, 270p, Cloth,
        Novel

STEAD, CHRISTINA (Ellen), 1902-   [*biography
included*]

13577   *The Salzburg tales.* D. Appleton-Century, New
        York, 1934, 415p, Cloth, Novel; Peter Davie
        London, 1934, 498p, Cloth, Novel

STEAD, F(rancis) HERBERT, 1857-1928

13578   *No more war! "truth embodied in a tale."*
        Simpkin, Marshall, Hamilton, Kent, London,
        1917, 424p, Cloth, Novel

STEAD, ROBERT J(ames) C(ampbell), 1880-1959

13579   *The copper disc.* Crime Club, Doubleday, Dora
        Garden City, 1931, 312p, Cloth, Novel

STEARNS, ALBERT

13580   *Chris and the wonderful lamp.* Century Co.,
        New York, 1895, 253p, Cloth, Novel
13581   *Sindbad, Smith & Co.* Century Co., New York,
        1896, 271p, Cloth, Novel

STEARNS, EDGAR FRANKLIN
    see: FRANKLIN, EDGAR

STEBBING, W(illiam)

13582 *Probable tales.* Longmans, Green, London,
       1899, 240p, Cloth, Coll.

STEEGMULLER, FRANCIS
     see: STEEL, BYRON

STEEL, BYRON, pseud. [Francis Steegmüller,
1906-] [*biography included*]

13583 *Java-Java.* Alfred A. Knopf, New York, 1928,
       275p, Cloth, Novel

STEEL, F(lora) A(nnie), 1847-1929

13584 *The law of the threshold.* William Heinemann,
       London, 1924, 310p, Cloth, Novel

STEEL, MARK, pseud.

13585 *Trouble planet.* Gannet Press, London, 1954,
       127p, Paper, Novel

STEELE, ALEX

13586 *The new people; They came from the sea.* Tem-
       po, New York, 1969, 150p, Paper, Tele.

STEELE, CURTIS, pseud. [Emile Tepperman]

13587 *Operator 5; Blood reign of the dictator.*
       Corinth, San Diego, 1966, 160p, Paper,
       Novel [Operator 5 #6]
13588 *Operator 5; Hosts of the flaming death.*
       Corinth, San Diego, 1966, 159p, Paper,
       Novel [Operator 5 #5]
13589 *Operator 5; Invasion of the yellow warlords.*
       Corinth, San Diego, 1966, 160p, Paper,
       Novel [Operator 5 #8]
13590 *Operator 5; Legions of the death master.*
       Corinth, San Diego, 1966, 160p, Paper,
       Novel [Operator 5 #1]
13591 *Operator 5; March of the flame marauders.*
       Corinth, San Diego, 1966, 159p, Paper,
       Novel [Operator 5 #7]
13592 *Operator 5; Master of broken men.* Corinth,
       San Diego, 1966, 158p, Paper, Novel [Opera-
       tor 5 #4]
13594 *Operator 5 #3; The yellow scourge.* Freeway
       Press, New York, 1974, 182p, Paper, Novel
       [Operator 5 (new series) #3]
13595 *Operator 5; The army of the dead.* Corinth,
       San Diego, 1966, 160p, Paper, Novel [Opera-
       tor 5 #2]
13596 *Operator 5; The invisible empire.* Corinth,
       San Diego, 1966, 159p, Paper, Novel [Opera-
       tor 5 #3; new series #2]
13597 *Operator 5; The masked invasion.* Freeway
       Press, New York, 1974, 188p, Paper, Novel
       [Operator 5 (new series) #1]

STEELE, MARY Q(uintard), 1922- [*biography
included*]

13598 *The first of the penguins.* Macmillan, New
       York, 1973, 154p, Cloth, Novel
13599 *Journey outside.* Viking Press, New York, 1969,
       143p, Cloth, Novel

STEELE, ROBERT D.

13600 *The Sun rises.* Lemurian Fellowship, Ramona,
       CA, 1952, 442p, Cloth, Novel

STEEN, MARGUERITE, 1894-1975

13601 *The unquiet spirit; a tale.* Collins, London,
       1955, 254p, Cloth, Novel

STEEVES, HARRISON R(oss), 1881-

13602 *Three eighteenth century romances: The Castle
       of Otranto; Vathek; The romance of the forest.*
       Charles Scribner's Sons, New York, 1931,
       585p, Cloth, Anth.

STEFFANSON, CON, house pseud. [see also: Ron
Goulart and Carson Bingham]

06182 *Flash Gordon; The lion men of Mongo.* Avon,
       New York, 1974, 159p, Paper, Novel [Flash
       Gordon #1] [by Ron Goulart]
06183 *Flash Gordon; The plague of sound.* Avon, New
       York, 1974, 158p, Paper, Novel [Flash Gordon
       #2] [by Ron Goulart]
06184 *Flash Gordon; The space circus.* Avon, New
       York, 1974, 157p, Paper, Novel [Flash Gordon
       #3] [by Ron Goulart]
01308 *Flash Gordon; The time trap of Ming XIII.* Avon,
       New York, 1974, 160p, Paper, Novel [Flash
       Gordon #4] [by Carson Bingham]

STEIGER, ANDREW JACOB, 1900- [*biography included*]

13603 *The Moon man.* Philosophical Library, New York,
       1961, 318p, Cloth, Novel

STEIGER, BRAD, pseud. [Eugene E. Olson,
1936-] [*biography included*]

13604 *Bizarre honeymoon.* Merit, Chicago, 1964, 128p,
       Paper, Novel

STEINBECK, JOHN (Ernst), 1902-1968 [*biography
included*

13605 *The short reign of Pippin IV; a fabrication.*
       Viking Press, New York, 1957, 188p, Cloth,
       Novel

STEINBRUNNER, (Peter) CHRIS(tian), 1933-
[*biography included*], with Burt Goldblatt

06086 *Cinema of the fantastic.* Saturday Review Press,
       New York, 1972, 282p, Cloth, Nonf.

STEINER, GEROLF
    see: STUMPKE, HARALD

STELLA NOVA
    see: REGINALD, R.

STENBOCK, S(tanislaus) E(ric), 1860-1895

13606 *Studies of death; romantic tales.* David Nutt,
        Edinburgh, 1894, 168p, Cloth, Coll.

STEPHAN, PETER

13607 *Sex trek.* Carlyle Collection, New York, 1974,
        220p, Paper, Novel

STEPHENS, D(aniel) OWEN, 1893-1937

13608 *Flow of horizons.* John Day Co., New York,
        1936, 190p, Cloth, Novel

STEPHENS, DONALD RYDER
    see: SINDERBY, DONALD

STEPHENS, HENRIETTA
    see: BUCKMASTER, HENRIETTA

STEPHENS, JAMES, 1882-1950

13609 *The crock of gold.* Macmillan, London, 1912,
        311p, Cloth, Novel
13610 *Deirdre.* Macmillan, London, 1923, 286p, Cloth,
        Novel
13611 *The demi-gods.* Macmillan, London, 1914, 279p,
        Cloth, Novel
13612 *Etched in moonlight.* Macmillan, London, 1928,
        199p, Cloth, Coll.
13613 *In the land of youth.* Macmillan, London,
        1924, 303p, Cloth, Novel

STERLAND, CARL, pseud. [Roy Newquist, 1925-]

13614 *Chuck.* Doubleday, Garden City, 1969, 181p,
        Cloth, Novel

STERLING, BARRY, pseud. [Robert Lipton]

13615 *The terrible sexy secret of Castle McNab.*
        Warner, New York, 1974, 174p, Paper, Novel

STERLING, BRETT, house pseud. [see also:
Edmond Hamilton and Joseph Samachson]

06721 *Danger planet.* Popular Library, New York,
        1968, 128p, Paper, Novel [Captain Future #1]
        [by Edmond Hamilton]
12661 *The tenth planet.* Popular Library, New York,
        1969, 128p, Paper, Novel [Captain Future
        #12] [by Joseph Samachson]

STERLING, JOHN, 1806-1844

13616 *The onyx ring.* Whittemore, Niles & Hall, Bos-
        ton, 1856, 263p, Cloth, Novel

STERLING, PETER, pseud.
    see: STERN, DAVID

STERN, DANIEL, 1928-   [*biography included*]

13617 *The rose rabbi.* McGraw-Hill, New York, 1971,
        135p, Cloth, Novel

STERN, DAVID (III), 1909-

13618 *Francis.* Farrar, Straus & Co., New York,
        1946, 216p, Cloth, Novel [Francis #2]
13619 *Francis goes to Washington.* Farrar, Straus &
        Co., New York, 1948, 243p, Cloth, Novel
        [Francis #3]

as Peter Sterling:

13620 *Francis...the Army mule.* Commercial Printing
        Division, Advertiser Publishing Co., Hono-
        lulu, 1945, 37p, Paper?, Coll. [Francis #1]

STERN, G(ladys) B(ronwyn), 1890-1973

13621 *A duck to water.* Cassell, London, 1949, 118p,
        Cloth, Novel
13622 *The ugly dachshund.* Cassell, London, 1938,
        147p, Cloth, Novel

STERN, J(ulius) DAVID, 1886-1971

13623 *Eidolon; a philosophical phantasy built on a
        syllogism.* Julian Messner, New York, 1952,
        246p, Cloth, Novel

STERN, PHILIP VAN DOREN, 1900-

13624 *The midnight reader; great stories of haunting
        and horror.* Henry Holt, New York, 1942,
        564p, Cloth, Anth.
13624A retitled: *The Pocket book of ghost stories;
        great stories of haunting and horror.* Pocket
        Books, New York, 1947, 405p, Paper, Anth.
13624B retitled: *Great ghost stories.* Washington
        Square Press, New York, 1962, 326p, Paper,
        Anth. [abridged]
13625 *The moonlight traveler; great tales of fantasy
        and imagination.* Doubleday, Doran, Garden
        City, 1943, 488p, Cloth, Anth.
13625A retitled: *Great tales of fantasy and imagina-
        tion.* Pocket Books, New York, 1954, 485p,
        Paper, Anth.
13626 *The other side of the clock; stories out of
        time.* Van Nostrand Reinhold, New York,
        1969, 192p, Cloth, Anth.
13627 *Strange beasts and unnatural monsters.* Faw-
        cett Crest, Greenwich, Conn., 1968, 224p,
        Paper, Anth.
13628 *Travelers in time; strange tales of man's jour-
        neyings into the past and the future.* Doub-
        leday, Garden City, 1947, 483p, Cloth, Anth.

STERNBERG, JACQUES, 1923-

13629   *Future without future.* Continuum Book, Sea-
        bury Press, New York, 1974, 210p, Cloth,
        Coll.
13630   *Sexualis '95.* Berkley Medallion, New York,
        1967, 160p, Paper, Novel

STERNE, JULIAN

13631   *The secret of the Zodiac.* Boswell Publishing
        Co., London, 1933, 320p, Cloth, Novel

STERNE, RICHARD E.

13632   *The peace of 1975; a sort of novel.* Dorrance,
        Philadelphia, 1972, 162p, Cloth, Novel

STERNS, JUSTIN

13633   *Osru; a tale of many incarnations; the history
        of a soul.* Lenox Publishing Co., New York,
        1910, 197p, Cloth, Novel

STEVENS, CHARLES McCLELLAN
    see: "QUONDAM"

STEVENS, CLIFFORD (J.), 1926-   [*biography
included*]

13634   *Flame out of Dorset.* Doubleday, Garden City,
        1964, 192p, Cloth, Novel

STEVENS, FRANCIS, pseud. [Gertrude Barrows
Bennett, 1884-1940?]

13635   *The citadel of fear.* Paperback Library, New
        York, 1970, 270p, Paper, Novel
13636   *Claimed.* Avalon, New York, 1966, 192p, Cloth,
        Novel
13637   *The heads of Cerberus.* Polaris Press, Reading,
        PA, 1952, 190p, Cloth, Novel

STEVENS, ISAAC N(ewton), 1858-1920

13638   *The liberators; a story of future American
        politics.* B. W. Dodge, New York, 1908,
        352p, Cloth, Novel

STEVENS, JOHN
    see: HATFIELD, FRANK

STEVENSON, BURTON E(gbert), 1872-1962

13639   *The destroyer; a tale of international in-
        intrigue.* Dodd, Mead, New York, 1913,
        434p, Cloth, Novel
13640   *A King in Babylon.* Small, Maynard, Boston,
        1917, 391p, Cloth, Novel

STEVENSON, D(orothy) E(mily), 1892-1973 [*biography included*]

13641   *The empty world (a romance of the future).*
        Herbert Jenkins, London, 1936, 312p, Cloth,
        Novel
13641A retitled: *A world in spell.* Farrar & Rine-
        hart, New York, 1939, 298p, Cloth, Novel

STEVENSON, FLORENCE

13642   *Altar of evil.* Award, New York, 1973, 154p,
        Paper, Novel [Kitty Telfair #3]
13643   *The curse of the Concullens.* World Publishing
        Co., New York, 1970, 143p, Cloth, Novel
13644   *Dark odyssey.* Signet, New York, 1974, 159p,
        Paper, Novel
13645   *Kilmeny in the dark wood.* Signet, New York,
        1973, 157p, Paper, Novel
13646   *Mistress of Devil's Manor.* Award, New York,
        1973, 156p, Paper, Novel [Kitty Telfair #4]
13647   *Ophelia.* New American Library, New York, 1968,
        179p, Cloth, Novel
13648   *The sorcerer of the castle.* Award, New York,
        1974, 155p, Paper, Novel [Kitty Telfair #5]
13649   *Where Satan dwells.* Award, New York, 1971,
        155p, Paper, Novel [Kitty Telfair #2]
13650   *The witching hour.* Award, New York, 1971,
        155p, Paper, Novel [Kitty Telfair #1]

with Patricia Hagan Murray:

10542   *Bianca.* Signet, New York, 1973, 144p, Paper,
        Novel

STEVENSON, JOHN
    see: JACKSON, STEPHEN

STEVENSON, ROBERT LOUIS, 1850-1894

13651   *The bottle imp.* George Munro's Sons, New York,
        1896, 70p, Paper, Novel
13651A retitled: *Kaëwe's bottle.* Kegan Paul, Trench,
        Trubner, London, 1935, 73p, Cloth, Novel
13652   *The bottle imp; and, The isle of voices.* Kair-
        yud, Tokyo, 1920?, 107p, Cloth?, Coll.
        Dr. Jekyll and Mr. Hyde. [see 13663A]
13653   *Dr. Jekyll and Mr. Hyde.* Digit, London, 1962,
        156p, Paper, Coll.
13654   *Dr. Jekyll and Mr. Hyde; and, An inland voyage.*
        Bernhard Tauchnitz, Leipzig, 1886, 287p,
        Cloth, Coll.
13655   *Dr. Jekyll and Mr. Hyde, and other stories of
        the supernatural.* Scholastic Book Services,
        New York, 1963, 216p, Paper, Coll.
13656   *Dr. Jekyll and Mr. Hyde; and, The suicide club.*
        Arco Publishing Co., New York, 1964, 191p,
        Cloth, Coll.
13657   *Great short stories of Robert Louis Stevenson.*
        Pocket Books, New York, 1951, 370p, Paper,
        Coll.
13658   *Island nights' entertainments, consisting of
        The beach of Falesá, The bottle imp, The
        isle of voices.* Cassell, London, 1893, 277p,
        Cloth, Coll.
        Kaewe's bottle. [see 13651A]
13659   *Markheim.* Holerth Library, London, 1925, 55p,
        Cloth, Coll.
13660   *Markheim; and, Will o' the mill.* Kenkyusha,
        Tokyo, 1936, 143p, Cloth, Coll.

STEVENSON, ROBERT LOUIS (cont.)

13661   *The merry men, and other tales and fables;
         Strange case of Dr. Jekyll and Mr. Hyde.*
         Charles Scribner's Sons, New York, 1895,
         372p, Cloth, Coll.
13662   *The short stories of Robert Louis Stevenson.*
         Charles Scribner's Sons, New York, 1923,
         540p, Cloth, Coll.
13663   *Strange case of Dr. Jekyll and Mr. Hyde.*
         Longmans, Green, London, 1886, 141p, Cloth,
         Novel
13663A   retitled: *Dr. Jekyll and Mr. Hyde.* W. Col-
         lins Sons, London, 1929, 254p, Cloth, Novel
13664   *Strange case of Dr. Jekyll and Mr. Hyde.* Lo-
         vell Brothers & Co., New York, 1900?, 278p,
         Cloth, Coll.
13665   *The strange case of Dr. Jekyll and Mr. Hyde,
         and other fables.* Longmans, Green, London,
         1896, 247p, Cloth, Coll.
13666   *The strange case of Dr. Jekyll and Mr. Hyde,
         and other famous tales.* Dodd, Mead, New
         York, 1961, 339p, Cloth, Coll.
13667   *The strange case of Dr. Jekyll and Mr. Hyde,
         and other stories.* J. M. Dent & Sons, Lon-
         don, 1930, 256p, Cloth, Coll.
13668   *The strange case of Dr. Jekyll and Mr. Hyde,
         and other stories.* Pocket Books, New York,
         1941, 375p, Paper, Coll.
13669   *The strange case of Dr. Jekyll and Mr. Hyde,
         and other stories.* Coward-McCann, New York,
         1950, 525p, Cloth, Coll.
13670   *Strange case of Dr. Jekyll and Mr. Hyde, and
         other stories.* G. P. Putnam's Sons, New
         York, 1963, 504p, Cloth, Coll.
13671   *The strange case of Dr. Jekyll and Mr. Hyde,
         and other stories.* Dell, New York, 1966,
         192p, Paper, Coll.
13672   *The strange case of Dr. Jekyll and Mr. Hyde;
         and, The story of a lie.* Thomas Nelson &
         Sons, London, 1928, 282p, Cloth, Coll.
13673   *The strange case of Dr. Jekyll and Mr. Hyde,
         fables, other stories and fragments.* Heine-
         mann, London, 1924, 216p, Cloth, Coll.
13674   *The suicide club, and other stories.* Perga-
         mon Press, Oxford, 1970, 199p, Cloth, Coll.
13675   *Tales and fantasies.* Chatto & Windus, London,
         1905, 237p, Cloth, Coll.
13676   *The tales of Tusitala; a selection of the
         best short stories of Robert Louis Stevenson.*
         Art & Educational Publishers, London, 1946,
         445p, Cloth, Coll.
13677   *Thrawn Janet; Markheim; two tales.* Mosher
         Press, Portland, Maine, 1906, 74p, Cloth,
         Coll.
13678   *Two mediaeval tales.* Limited Editions Club,
         New York, 1930, 67p, Cloth, Coll.
13679   *The waif woman.* Chatto & Windus, London,
         1916, 44p, Cloth, Story
13680   *Will o' the mill; Markheim.* Haldeman-Julius,
         Girard, Kans., 1922?, 60p, Paper, Coll.

STEWART, ALFRED WALTER
    see: CONNINGTON, J. J.

STEWART, BRUCE, 1927-   [*biography included*]

13681   *Timeslip.* Pan, London, 1970, 188p, Paper,
         Tele.

STEWART, FRED MUSTARD, 1936-   [*biography included*]

13682   *The Mephisto Waltz; a novel.* Coward-McCann,
         New York, 1969, 256p, Cloth, Novel
13683   *The Methuselah enzyme; a novel.* Arbor House,
         New York, 1970, 244p, Cloth, Novel
13684   *Star child; a novel.* Arbor House, New York,
         1974, 224p, Cloth, Novel

STEWART, GEORGE R(ippey), 1895-   [*biography
included*]

13685   *Earth abides.* Random House, New York, 1949,
         373p, Cloth, Novel

STEWART, MARY (Florence Elinor), 1916-   [*bio
graphy included*]

13686   *The crystal cave.* Hodder & Stoughton, London,
         1970, 464p, Cloth, Novel [Merlin #1]
13687   *The hollow hills.* Hodder & Stoughton, London,
         1973, 446p, Cloth, Novel [Merlin #2]
13688   *Ludo and the star horse.* Brockhampton Press,
         Leicester, UK, 1974, 128p, Cloth, Novel

STEWART, RAMONA, 1922-   [*biography included*]

13689   *The apparition.* Little, Brown, Boston, 1973,
         216p, Cloth, Novel
13690   *The possession of Joel Delaney; a novel.*
         Little, Brown, Boston, 1970, 246p, Cloth,
         Novel

STEWART, RITSON, with Stanley Stewart

13691   *The professor's last experiment.* Swan Sonnen-
         schein, London, 1888, 129p, Paper, Novel

STEWART, STANLEY, with Ritson Stewart

13691   *The professor's last experiment.* Swan Sonnen-
         schein, London, 1888, 129p, Paper, Novel

STEWART, WILL, pseud.
    see: WILLIAMSON, JACK

STILGEBAUER, EDWARD, 1868-

13692   *The ship of death; a novel of the war.* Bren-
         tano's, New York, 1918, 232p, Cloth, Novel;
         Cassell, London, 1918, 279p, Cloth, Novel

STILSON, CHARLES B(illings)

13693   *Minos of Sardanes.* Avalon, New York, 1966,
         190p, Cloth, Novel [Polaris #2]
13694   *Polaris and the immortals.* Avalon, New York,
         1968, 190p, Cloth, Novel [Polaris #3]
13695   *Polaris--of the Snows.* Avalon, New York, 196?
         192p, Cloth, Novel [Polaris #1]

STIMPSON, CATHARINE R(oslyn), 1936-   [bio-
graphy included]

13696 *J. R. R. Tolkien.* Columbia University Press,
New York, 1969, 48p, Paper, Nonf.

STIMSON, F(rederic) J(essup) [J. S. of Dale],
1855-1943

13697 *In the three zones.* Charles Scribner's Sons,
New York, 1893, 204p, Cloth, Coll.

as J. S. of Dale, with Robert Grant, John
Boyle O'Reilly, and John T. Wheelright:

06240 *The King's men; a tale of to-morrow.* Charles
Scribner's Sons, New York, 1884, 270p, Cloth,
Novel

STINE, G. HARRY
see: CORREY, LEE

STINE, HANK [Henry Eugene Stine, 1945-   ]
[biography included]

13698 *The Prisoner #3; A day in the life.* Ace, New
York, 1970, 158p, Paper, Tele. [Prisoner #3]
13699 *Season of the witch.* Essex House, North Hollywood, 1968, 224p, Paper, Novel
13700 *Thrill city.* Essex House, North Hollywood,
1969, 159p, Paper, Novel

STINE, WILBUR MORRIS, 1863-1934

13701 *Amos Meakin's ghost.* Acorn Press, Philadelphia, 1924, 327p, Cloth, Novel

STITZER, DAN(iel) A(hrens), 1869-

13702 *Stories of the occult.* Richard G. Badger,
Boston, 1917, 216p, Cloth, Coll.

STIVENS, DAL(las George), 1911-

13703 *The gambling ghost, and other tales.* Angus &
Robertson, Sydney, 1953, 113p, Cloth, Coll.
[Ironbark Bill #1]
13704 *Ironbark Bill.* Angus & Robertson, Sydney,
1955, 66p, Cloth, Coll. [Ironbark Bill #2]

STIVERS, MARK
see: DISROBESON, KIN I.

STOCK, E. ELLIOT

13705 *The ring of Ug, and other weird tales.* John
Ouseley, London, 1911, 172p, Cloth, Coll.

STOCK, RALPH, 1882-1962

13706 *The recipe for rubber; a Fijian romance.* Lynwood & Co., London, 1912, 264p, Cloth, Novel

STOCKING, CHARLES FRANCIS, 1873-

13707 *The diary of Jean Evarts.* Standard Publishing
Co., Freeport, IL, 1912, 352p, Cloth, Novel

STOCKTON, FRANK R(ichard), 1834-1902

13708 *The bee-man of Orn, and other fanciful tales.*
Charles Scribner's Sons, New York, 1887,
193p, Cloth, Coll.
13709 *A borrowed month, and other stories.* David
Douglas, Edinburgh, 1887, 276p, Paper, Coll.
13710 *A chosen few; short stories.* Charles Scribner's
Sons, New York, 1895, 240p, Cloth, Coll.
13711 *The clocks of Rondaine, and other stories.*
Charles Scribner's Sons, New York, 1892,
174p, Cloth, Coll.
13712 *Fanciful tales.* Charles Scribner's Sons, New
York, 1894, 135p, Cloth, Coll.
13713 *The great stone of Sardis; a novel.* Harper &
Bros., New York, 1898, 230p, Cloth, Novel
13714 *The great stone of Sardis; The water-devil.*
Charles Scribner's Sons, New York, 1900,
269p, Cloth, Coll.
13715 *The Great War Syndicate.* P. F. Collier, New
York, 1889, 191p, Cloth, Novel
13716 *John Gayther's garden, and the stories told
therein.* Charles Scribner's Sons, New York,
1902, 365p, Cloth, Coll.
13717 *The lost Dryad.* Eastern Branch of the United
Workers of Greenwich, Riverside, Conn., 1912,
28p, Cloth, Story
13718 *The Queen's mvsevm, and other fanciful tales.*
Charles Scribner's Sons, New York, 1906,
219p, Cloth, Coll.
13719 *Ting-a-ling.* Hurd & Houghton, Boston, 1870,
187p, Cloth, Coll.
13719A retitled: *Ting-a-ling tales.* Charles Scribner's Sons, New York, 1955, 161p, Cloth, Coll.
13720 *The vizier of the Two-horned Alexander.* Century Co., New York, 1899, 235p, Cloth, Novel

STODDARD, CHARLES, pseud. [Charles Stanley
Strong, 1906-1962]

13721 *North of the stars.* Dodge Publishing Co., New
York, 1937, 256p, Cloth, Novel

STODDARD, Dr. THOMAS A.

13722 *"The quest."* Cochrane Publishing Co., New
York, 1909, 167p, Cloth, Novel

STODDARD, WILLIAM O(sborn), 1835-1925

13723 *Ned, the son of Webb; what he did.* Dana Estes,
Boston, 1900, 333p, Cloth, Novel
13724 *Ulric the jarl; a story of the penitent thief.*
Eaton & Mains, New York, 1899, 459p, Cloth,
Novel

STOKER, BRAM [Abraham Stoker, 1847-1912]

13725 *The Bram Stoker bedside companion; stories of
fantasy and horror.* Victor Gollancz, London,
1973, 244p, Cloth, Coll.
13726 *Dracula.* Archibald Constable, Westminster, UK,
1897, 390p, Cloth, Novel

STOKER, BRAM (cont.)

13727　*Dracula's curse; and, The Jewel of Seven Stars.*
Tower, New York, 1968, 218p, Paper, Coll.
13728　*Dracula's guest, and other weird stories.*
George Routledge & Sons, London, 1914,
200p, Cloth, Coll.
13728A　retitled: *Dracula's guest.* Hillman-Curl,
New York, 1937, 284p, Cloth, Coll.
The garden of evil. [see 13731A]
13729　*The Jewel of Seven Stars.* William Heinemann,
London, 1903, 337p, Cloth, Novel
13730　*The lady of the shroud.* William Heinemann,
London, 1909, 367p, Cloth, Novel
13731　*The lair of the White Worm.* William Rider &
Son, London, 1911, 324p, Cloth, Novel
13731A　retitled: *The garden of evil.* Paperback
Library, New York, 1966, 220p, Paper,
Novel
13732　*The mystery of the sea; a novel.* William
Heinemann, London, 1902, 454p, Cloth, Novel
13733　*Under the sunset.* Sampson Low, Marston,
Searle & Rivington, London, 1881, 190p,
Cloth, Coll.

STOKES, H. A. C.

13734　*Harold in Heavenland.* Vantage Press, New
York, 1972, 199p, Cloth, Novel

STOKES, PEG [*biography included*]

13735　*I am Anthony.* Prentice-Hall, Englewood Cliffs,
NJ, 1961, 317p, Cloth, Novel

STOKES, SIMPSON, pseud.
see: FAWCETT, F. DUBREZ

STONE, ALMA

13736　*The banishment, and three stories: The portrait; The traveler; Oh pity the dwarf's
butt.* Doubleday, Garden City, 1973, 279p,
Cloth, Coll.

STONE, Mrs. C. H.

13737　*One of "Berrian's" novels.* Welch, Fracker Co.,
New York, 1890, 210p, Cloth, Novel [a sequel
to Bellamy's *Looking backward*]

STONE, GRAHAM BRICE, 1926-　[*biography included*]

13738　*Australian science fiction index, 1939-1962.*
Futurian Society of Sydney, Sydney, 1964,
113p, Paper, Nonf.
13739　*Australian science fiction index, 1925-1967.*
Australian Science Fiction Association,
Canberra, 1968, 158p, Paper, Nonf.

STONE, IDELLA PURNELL, 1901-　[*biography included*]

13740　*14 great tales of ESP.* Fawcett Gold Medal,
Greenwich, Conn., 1969, 303p, Paper, Anth.

13741　*Never in this world.* Fawcett Gold Medal,
Greenwich, Conn., 1971, 253p, Paper, Anth.

STONE, ISOBEL

13742　*The city of a hundred gates.* Bruce Humphries,
Boston, 1942, 203p, Cloth, Novel

STONE, LESLIE F(rances), 1905-　[*biography
included*]

13743　*Out of the void.* Avalon, New York, 1967, 191p,
Cloth, Novel
13744　*When the Sun went out.* Stellar Publishing
Corp., New York, 1929, 24p, Paper, Story

STONE, WELDON

13745　*Devil take a whittler.* Rinehart & Co., New
York, 1948, 252p, Cloth, Novel [adapted from
the play of the same name]

STONE, WILLIAM S(tandish), 1907-

13746　*The ship of flame; a saga of the South Seas.*
Alfred A. Knopf, New York, 1945, 165p, Cloth,
Novel

STONEHAM, C(harles) T(hurley), 1895-

13747　*Kaspa, the lion man; a romance.* Methuen, London, 1933, 254p, Cloth, Novel [Kaspa #2]
13748　*The lion's way; a story of men and lions.* Hutchinson, London, 1931, 287p, Cloth, Novel
[Kaspa #1]
13748A　retitled: *King of the jungle.* Grosset & Dunlap, New York, 1932, 325p, Cloth, Novel [Kas-
pa #1]

STONG, PHIL(lip Duffield), 1899-1957

13749　*The other worlds.* Wilfred Funk, New York,
1941, 466p, Cloth, Anth.

STONIER, G(eorge) W(alter), 1903-

13750　*The memoirs of a ghost.* Grey Walls Press,
London, 1947, 109p, Cloth, Novel

STONOR, OLIVER
see: BISHOP, MORCHARD

STOPECK, PHILIP

13751　*Promiscuous Philbert.* Nite-Time, Hollywood,
1964, 159p, Paper, Novel

STOPWATCH ON THE WORLD

13752　*Stopwatch on the world.* American Science Fiction, Sydney, 1955, 34p, Paper, Anth.

STOREY, (Elizabeth) MARGARET (Carlton), 1926-

13753 *The dragon's sister; and, Timothy travels.*
Faber & Faber, London, 1967, 139p, Cloth,
Coll.

STORIES BY AMERICAN AUTHORS, V

13754 *Stories by American authors, V.* Charles
Scribner's Sons, New York, 1891, 191p,
Cloth, Anth.

STORIES BY ENGLISH AUTHORS; IRELAND

13755 *Stories by English authors; Ireland.* Charles
Scribner's Sons, New York, 1896, 180p, Cloth,
Anth.

STORKE, FRANCIS EUGENE

13757 *Mr. De Lacy's double.* Continental Publishing
Co., New York, 1898, 306p, Cloth, Novel

STORM, BRIAN, pseud.
see: HOLLOWAY, BRIAN

STORY, JACK TREVOR, 1917- [*biography included*]

13758 *Little dog's day; a novel.* Allison & Busby,
London, 1971, 174p, Cloth, Novel

STOUT, REX (Todhunter), 1886-1975 [*biography
included*], as Anonymous

13759 *The president vanishes.* Farrar & Rinehart,
New York, 1934, 296p, Cloth, Novel

STOUTENBURG, ADRIEN (Pearl), 1916- [*biography included*]

13760 *Out there.* Viking Press, New York, 1971,
222p, Cloth, Novel
13761 *Rain boat.* Coward-McCann, New York, 1965,
159p, Cloth, Novel

STOVER, LEON E(ugene), 1929- [*biography included*]

with Harry Harrison:

06855 *Apeman, spaceman; anthropological science fiction.* Doubleday, Garden City, 1968, 355p,
Cloth, Anth.
06856 *Stonehenge.* Charles Scribner's Sons, New
York, 1972, 254p, Cloth, Novel

with Willis E. McNelly:

09964 *Above the human landscape; a social science
fiction anthology.* Goodyear Publishing Co.,
Pacific Palisades, CA, 1972, 387p, Cloth,
Anth.

STOW, (Julian) RANDOLPH, 1935- [*biography
included*]

13762 *Midnite; the story of a wild colonial boy.*
F. W. Cheshire, Melbourne, 1967, 140p,
Cloth, Novel

STOWE, Mrs. H. M.
see: ELEVE

STRACHEY, J(ohn) ST. LOE, 1860-1927

13763 *How England became a republic; a romance of
the Constitution.* J. W. Arrowsmith, Bristol,
1891, 71p, Paper?, Novel

STRANG, HERBERT, pseud.
see: ELY, GEORGE and L'ESTRANGE, C. J.

THE STRANGE CASE OF DR. JEKYLL AND MR. HYDE

13764 *The strange case of Dr. Jekyll and Mr. Hyde,
and other macabre stories; an anthology.*
Corgi, London, 1964, 141p, Paper, Anth.

STRANGE HAPPENINGS

13765 *Strange happenings.* Methuen, London, 1901,
309p, Cloth, Anth.

STRANGE LOVE STORIES

13766 *Strange love stories.* Utopian Publications,
London, 1946, 74p, Paper, Anth.

STRANGE LUST

13767 *Strange lust.* Private Edition, Hollywood,
1963, 160p, Paper, Novel

A STRANGE MANUSCRIPT FOUND IN A COPPER CYLIN-
DER
see: DE MILLE, JAMES

STRANGE OFFSPRING

13768 *Strange offspring.* Utopian Publications,
London, 1944/45, 36p, Paper, Anth.

STRANGE SECRETS

13769 *Strange secrets, told by A. Conan Doyle and
others.* R. F. Fenno, New York, 1895, 287p,
Cloth, Anth.

STRANGE STORIES OF COINCIDENCE AND GHOSTLY
ADVENTURE

13770 *Strange stories of coincidence and ghostly
adventure.* George Redway, London, 1891,
320p, Cloth, Anth. [includes some nonf.]

THE STRANGE STORY OF AHRINZIMAN
    see: SILVANI, ANITA

STRANGE TALES

13771   *Strange tales; weird & fantastic fiction.*
       Utopian Publications, London, 1945?, 67p,
       Paper, Anth.

STRANGE TALES FROM "BLACKWOOD"

13772   *Strange tales from "Blackwood."* William
       Blackwood & Sons, Edinburgh, 1950, 521p,
       Cloth, Anth.

STRANGE TALES OF THE MYSTERIOUS AND SUPER-
NATURAL

13773   *Strange tales of the mysterious and superna-*
       tural, second selection. Utopian Publica-
       tions, London, 1946, 68p, Paper, Anth.

STRATING, J(ozeph) J(acob)

13774   *European tales of terror.* Fontana, London,
       1968, 222p, Paper, Anth.
13775   *Oriental tales of terror.* Fontana, London,
       1971, 191p, Paper, Anth.
13776   *Sea tales of terror.* Fontana, London, 1974,
       188p, Paper, Anth.

STRATTON, CHRIS, pseud. [Richard Hubbard]

13777   *The Bugaloos and the vile Vibes.* Curtis, New
       York, 1971, 128p, Paper, Tele. [Bugaloos #1]
13778   *The Bugaloos #2; Rock City rebels.* Curtis,
       New York, 1971, 126p, Paper, Tele. [Buga-
       loos #2]
13779   *The Bugaloos #3; Benita's platter pollution.*
       Curtis, New York, 1971, 125p, Paper, Tele.
       [Bugaloos #3]
13780   *Change of mind.* Pyramid, New York, 1969,
       159p, Paper, Movie

STRATTON, THOMAS, pseud.
    see: COULSON, ROBERT and DeWEESE, GENE

STRAUS, RALPH, 1882-1950

13781   *The dust which is God; an undimensional adven-*
       ture. Samurai Press, Norwich, UK, 1907,
       62p, Cloth, Novel

STRAUSS, ERWIN S.

13782   *The MIT Science Fiction Society's index to*
       the S-F magazines, 1951-1965. MIT Science
       Fiction Society, Cambridge, Mass., 1966,
       207p, Cloth, Nonf.

STREET, A(rthur) G(eorge), 1892-1966 [biogra-
phy included]

13783   *Already walks to-morrow.* Faber & Faber, Lon-
       don, 1938, 431p, Cloth, Novel

STRETZER, THOMAS, d. 1738

13784   *A new description of Merryland, containing a*
       topographical, geographical, and natural
       history of that country, by Robert Pheuque-
       well. J. Leake & W. Curll, Bath, UK, 1741,
       31p, Paper?, Story
13784A retitled: *Merryland.* Robin Hood House, New
       York, 1932, 136p, Cloth, Story

STRICKLAND, W(illiam) P(eter), 1809-1884

13785   *The astrologer of Chaldea; or, The life of*
       faith. Jacob Ernst, Cincinnati, 1855, 268p,
       Cloth, Novel

STRICKLAND, (Sir) W(alter) W(illiam), Bart.,
1851-1938

13786   *Vishnu; or, The planet of the sevenfold unity;*
       an autobiographical, scientific, and mystical
       romance. B. Westermann, New York, 1928,
       411p, Cloth, Novel

STRIKE, JEREMY, pseud. [Thomas Edward Renn,
1939-] [biography included]

13787   *A promising planet.* Ace Double, New York,
       1970, 125p, Paper, Novel

THE STRING OF PEARLS
    see: JAMES, G. P. R.

STRINGER, ARTHUR (John Arbuthnott), 1874-1950

13788   *The woman who couldn't die.* Bobbs-Merrill,
       Indianapolis, 1929, 315p, Cloth, Novel

STRODE, WILLIAM

13789   *Three ghosts.* Sampson Low, London, 1947, 48p,
       Cloth, Anth.

STRONG, CHARLES STANLEY
    see: STODDARD, CHARLES

STRONG, L(eonard) A(lfred) G(eorge), 1896-195

13790   *The doll.* Salamander Press, Leeds, UK, 1946,
       20p, Cloth, Story
13791   *The jealous ghost; a novel.* Victor Gollancz,
       London, 1930, 288p, Cloth, Novel
13792   *The last enemy; a study of youth.* Victor Gol-
       lancz, London, 1936, 384p, Cloth, Novel

STRONG, ROD, pseud.

13793   *Orgy twins.* Orpheus Series, New York, 1974,
       187p, Paper, Novel

STRUGATSKII, ARKADII (Natanovich), 1925-
[*biography included*], with Boris Strugatskii

13794 *Far Rainbow*, by A. and B. Strugatsky. Mir
      Publishers, Moscow, 1967, 148p, Paper, Novel
13795 *Hard to be a god*, by Arkady and Boris Strugat-
      sky. Continuum Book, Seabury Press, New
      York, 1973, 219p, Cloth, Novel

STRUGATSKII, BORIS (Natanovich), 1933-
[*biography included*], with Arkadii Strugatskii

13794 *Far Rainbow*, by A. & B. Strugatsky. Mir Pub-
      lishers, Moscow, 1967, 148p, Paper, Novel
13795 *Hard to be a god*, by Arkady and Boris Strugat-
      sky. Continuum Book, Seabury Press, New
      York, 1973, 219p, Cloth, Novel

STRUGATSKY, ARKADY
    see: STRUGATSKII, ARKADII

STRUGATSKY, BORIS
    see: STRUGATSKII, BORIS

STRUNKSY, SIMEON, 1879-1948

13796 *Two came to town*. E. P. Dutton, New York,
      1947, 219p, Cloth, Novel

STRUTTON, BILL [William Harold Strutton,
1918-]

13797 *Doctor Who and the Zarbi*. Frederick Muller,
      London, 1965, 174p, Cloth, Tele. [Doctor
      Who #2]

STUART, (Henry) FRANCIS (Montgomery), 1902-
[*biography included*]

13798 *Glory*. Victor Gollancz, London, 1933, 287p,
      Cloth, Novel

STUART, Mrs. G.

13799 *On the shores of the infinite*. Simpkin, Mar-
      shall, London, 1931, 312p, Cloth, Novel

STUART, RUTH McENERY, 1856-1917

13800 *The haunted photograph; Whence and whither;
      A case in diplomacy; The afterglow*. Cen-
      tury Co., New York, 1911, 170p, Cloth, Coll.

STUART, SIDNEY, pseud.
    see: AVALLONE, MICHAEL

STUART, W. J.

13801 *Forbidden planet*. Farrar, Straus & Cudahy,
      New York, 1956, 184p, Cloth, Movie

STUBBS, HARRY CLEMENT
    see: CLEMENT, HAL

STUBBS, JAMES BAGNALL-
    see: BAGNALL-STUBBS, JAMES

A STUDENT OF OCCULTISM
    see: HARTMANN, FRANZ

A STUDENT OF THE ROSICRUCIAN FELLOWSHIP TEACH-
INGS, pseud.

13802 *Aquarian age stories for children, volume I*.
      Rosicrucian Fellowship, Oceanside, CA, 1951,
      95p, Paper, Anth.
13803 *Aquarian age stories for children, volume II*.
      Rosicrucian Fellowship, Oceanside, CA, 1953,
      96p, Paper, Anth.
13804 *Aquarian age stories for children, volume III*.
      Rosicrucian Fellowship, Oceanside, CA, 1958,
      96p, Paper, Anth.
13805 *Aquarian age stories for children, volume IV*.
      Rosicrucian Fellowship, Oceanside, CA, 1969,
      96p, Paper, Anth.

STUDER, PAUL

13806 *In the shadow of gold*. Greenberg: Publisher,
      New York, 1935, 232p, Cloth, Novel

STUMP, D(avid) L(eroy)

13807 *From world to world; a novel*. World to World
      Publishing Co., Asbury, MO, 1896, 125p,
      Cloth, Novel
13808 *The love of Meltha Laone; or, Beyond the Sun;
      a novel*. Roxburgh Publishing Co., Boston,
      1913, 262p, Cloth, Novel

STÜMPKE, HARALD, pseud. [Gerolf Steiner,
1908-] [*biography included*]

13809 *The snouters; form and life of the Rhinogrades*.
      Natural History Press, Garden City, 1967,
      92p, Cloth, Fiction

STURGE, ERNEST ADOLPHUS, 1856-1934

13810 *Living in two worlds*. Sturge Zenshu Kankokai,
      Tokyo, 1930?, 391p, Cloth, Novel [in English
      and Japanese]

STURGEON, THEODORE (Hamilton), 1918- [*biography included*] [name originally Edward Hamilton Waldo]

13811 *Aliens 4*. Avon, New York, 1959, 224p, Paper,
      Coll.
13812 *Beyond*. Avon, New York, 1960, 157p, Paper,
      Coll.
13813 *Case and the Dreamer, and other stories*. Nel-
      son Doubleday, Garden City, 1974, 152p, Cloth,
      Coll.
13814 *Caviar*. Ballantine, New York, 1955, 168p,
      Cloth, Coll.

STURGEON, THEODORE (cont.)

13815   *The cosmic rape; an original novel.* Dell, New
        York, 1958, 160p, Paper, Novel
13816   *The dreaming jewels.* Corwin Book, Greenberg,
        New York, 1950, 217p, Cloth, Novel
13816A retitled: *The synthetic man (The dreaming
        jewels).* Pyramid, New York, 1957, 174p,
        Paper, Novel
13817   *E pluribus unicorn; a collection of short
        stories of Theodore Sturgeon.* Abelard Press,
        New York, 1953, 276p, Cloth, Coll.
13818   *It.* Prime Press, Philadelphia, 1948, 28p,
        Paper, Story
13819   *The joyous invasions.* Victor Gollancz, Lon-
        don, 1965, 208p, Cloth, Coll.
13820   *More than human.* Farrar, Straus & Young, New
        York, 1953, 234p, Cloth, Novel
        Not without sorcery. [see 13830A]
13821   *Starshine.* Pyramid, New York, 1966, 174p,
        Paper, Coll.
13822   *Sturgeon in orbit.* Pyramid, New York, 1964,
        159p, Paper, Coll.
13823   *Sturgeon is alive and well...a collection of
        short stories.* G. P. Putnam's Sons, New
        York, 1971, 221p, Cloth, Coll.
        The synthetic man. [see 13816A]
        Thunder and roses. [see 13829A]
13824   *To here and the easel.* Victor Gollancz, Lon-
        don, 1973, 255p, Cloth, Coll.
13825   *A touch of strange.* Doubleday, Garden City,
        1958, 262p, Cloth, Coll.
13826   *Two complete novels; ...And my fear is great;
        Baby is three.* Galaxy Magabook, New York,
        1965, 127p, Paper, Coll.
13827   *Venus plus X.* Pyramid, New York, 1960, 160p,
        Paper, Novel
13828   *Voyage to the bottom of the sea.* Pyramid,
        New York, 1961, 159p, Paper, Movie [Voyage
        to the Bottom of the Sea #1]
13829   *A way home; stories of science fiction and
        fantasy.* Funk & Wagnalls, New York, 1955,
        335p, Cloth, Coll.
13829A retitled: *Thunder and roses; stories of sci-
        ence-fiction and fantasy.* Michael Joseph,
        London, 1957, 255p, Cloth, Coll. [abridged]
13830   *Without sorcery; thirteen tales.* Prime Press,
        Philadelphia, 1948, 355p, Cloth, Coll.
13830A retitled: *Not without sorcery.* Ballantine,
        New York, 1961, 160p, Paper, Coll. [abridged]
13831   *The worlds of Theodore Sturgeon.* Ace, New
        York, 1972, 286p, Paper, Coll.

STUTFIELD, HUGH E(dward) M(illington), 1858-
1929

13832   *The brethren of Mount Atlas, being the first
        part of an African theosophical story.*
        Longmans, Green, London, 1891, 313p, Cloth,
        Novel

SUDAK, EUNICE

13833   *The raven.* Lancer, New York, 1963, 127p,
        Paper, Movie
13834   *X.* Lancer, New York, 1963, 126p, Paper, Movie

with Edgar Allan Poe:

11748   *Tales of terror.* Lancer, New York, 1962, 126p,
        Paper, Movie [adapted by Sunak from the
        movie and the Poe stories]

SUDBERY, RODIE, 1943-

13835   *The house in the wood.* Andre Deutsch, London,
        1968, 140p, Cloth, Novel
13835A retitled: *A sound of crying.* McCall Publish-
        ing Co., New York, 1970, 149p, Cloth, Novel

SUDDABY, (William) DONALD, 1900-1964

13836   *The death of metal.* Geoffrey Cumberlege, Ox-
        ford University Press, London, 1952, 192p,
        Cloth, Novel
13837   *Masterless swords; variations on a theme.* T.
        Werner Laurie, London, 1947, 251p, Cloth,
        Coll.
13838   *Prisoners of Saturn.* Bodley Head, London,
        1957, 190p, Cloth, Novel
13839   *The star raiders.* Geoffrey Cumberlege, Oxford
        University Press, London, 1950, 232p, Cloth,
        Novel
13840   *Village fanfare; or, The man from the future.*
        Oxford University Press, London, 1954,
        195p, Cloth, Novel

as Alan Griff:

13841   *Lost men in the grass.* Oxford University Press
        London, 1940, 192p, Cloth, Novel

SUE, (Marie Joseph) EUGÈNE, 1804-1857

13842   *The wandering Jew.* Chapman & Hall, London,
        1844/45, 3vol, Cloth, Novel

SUFFLING, ERNEST R(ichard)

13843   *The story hunter; or, Tales of the weird and
        wild.* Jarrold & Sons, London, 1895, 226p,
        Cloth, Coll.

SUGAR, ANDREW

13844   *The Enforcer.* Lancer, New York, 1973, 222p,
        Paper, Novel [Enforcer #1]
13845   *The Enforcer; Calling Doctor Kill!* Lancer,
        New York, 1973, 221p, Paper, Novel [Enforcer
        #2]
13846   *The Enforcer #3; Kill city.* Lancer, New York,
        1973, 221p, Paper, Novel [Enforcer #3]
13847   *The Enforcer #4; Kill deadline.* Lancer, New
        York, 1973, 221p, Paper, Novel [Enforcer #4]

SULLIVAN, (Edward) ALAN, 1868-1947

13848   *"...And from that day."* Ryerson Press, Toronto
        1944, 195p, Cloth, Novel
13849   *The days of their youth.* Hurst & Blackett,
        London, 1926, 320p, Cloth, Novel
13850   *In the beginning.* Hurst & Blackett, London,
        1927, 280p, Cloth, Novel
13851   *The jade god.* Geoffrey Bles, London, 1924,
        316p, Cloth, Novel
13852   *A little way ahead.* John Murray, London, 1929
        316p, Cloth, Novel
13853   *Mr. Absalom.* John Murray, London, 1930, 316p,
        Cloth, Novel

SULLIVAN, CHARLES W(illia)M. III, 1944-

13854 *As tomorrow becomes today.* Prentice-Hall,
       Englewood Cliffs, NJ, 1974, 456p, Cloth,
       Anth.

SULLIVER, JA(me)S. F(rank), d. 1936

13855 *The flame-flower, and other stories.* J. M.
       Dent, London, 1896, 285p, Cloth, Coll.
13856 *Queer side stories.* Downey & Co., London,
       1900, 302p, Cloth, Coll.

SULLIVAN, PHILIP A(loysius), 1882-

13857 *Man finds the way.* Margent Press, New York,
       1939, 217p, Cloth, Novel

SULLIVAN, T(homas) R(ussell), 1849-1916

13858 *Day and night stories.* Charles Scribner's
       Sons, New York, 1890, 253p, Cloth, Coll.
13859 *Day and night stories, second series.* Charles
       Scribner's Sons, New York, 1893, 249p,
       Cloth, Coll.

SULLY, KATHLEEN (M.), 1910-   [*biography included*]

13860 *Skrine.* Peter Davies, London, 1960, 156p,
       Cloth, Novel

SULZBERGER, C(yrus) L(eo II), 1912-   [*biography included*]

13861 *The tooth merchant; a novel.* Quadrangle,
       New York, 1973, 275p, Cloth, Novel

SUMMERS, EDWARD G.

13862 *Venus bound.* Webster Division, McGraw-Hill,
       St. Louis, 1968, 252p, Cloth, Anth.

SUMMERS, (Alphonsus Joseph-Mary Augustus)
MONTAGUE, 1880-1948

13863 *A gothic bibliography.* Fortune Press, London,
       1941, 621p, Cloth, Nonf.
13864 *The gothic quest; a history of the gothic
       novel.* Fortune Press, London, 1938, 443p,
       Cloth, Nonf.
13865 *The grimoire, and other supernatural stories.*
       Fortune Press, London, 1936, 295p, Cloth,
       Anth.
13866 *The supernatural omnibus, being a collection
       of stories of apparitions, witchcraft,
       werewolves, diabolism, necromancy, Satanism,
       divination, sorcery, goetry, voodoo, pos-
       session, occult doom, and destiny.* Victor
       Gollancz, London, 1931, 622p, Cloth, Anth.
13866A retitled: *The supernatural omnibus II.* Pan-
       ther, London, 1967, 250p, Paper, Anth. [ab-
       ridged]
13867 *Victorian ghost stories.* Fortune Press, Lon-
       don, 1933, 366p, Cloth, Anth.

SUPERNATURAL STORIES FOR BOYS

13868 *Supernatural stories for boys.* Paul Hamlyn,
       Feltham, UK, 1968, 359p, Cloth, Anth.

SUPERVIELLE, JULES, 1884-1960

13869 *Along the road to Bethlehem.* E. P. Dutton,
       New York, 1933, 65p, Cloth, Coll.
13869A retitled: *Souls of the soulless.* Methuen,
       London, 1933, 65p, Cloth, Coll.

THE SURPRISING ADVENTURES OF BARON MUNCHAUSEN
    see: RASPE, RUDOLF ERICH

SURREY, LIONEL

13870 *Polar peril.* Thomas Nelson & Sons, London,
       1939, 285p, Cloth, Novel

SUTCLIFF, ROSEMARY, 1920-   [*biography included*]

13871 *Warrior Scarlet.* Oxford University Press,
       London, 1958, 207p, Cloth, Novel

SUTHERLAND, G(eorge), 1855-1905

13872 *The capture of Adelaide; a possibility of 1894.*
       The Author, Adelaide, 1893,   , Paper,
       Novel

SUTHERLAND, JAMES (Edward), 1948-   [*biography
included*]

13873 *Stormtrack.* Pyramid, New York, 1974, 188p,
       Paper, Novel

SUTHERLAND, JAMES (Runcieman), 1900-

13874 *The narrative of Jasper Weeple.* Eric Partridge,
       London, 1930, 260p, Cloth, Novel

SUTHERLAND, MORRIS, pseud. [Gwendolen Sutherland Morris]

13875 *Second storm.* Thornton Butterworth, London,
       1930, 319p, Cloth, Novel

SUTPHEN, (William Gilbert) van TASSEL, 1861-
1945

13876 *The Doomsman.* Harper & Bros., New York, 1906,
       295p, Cloth, Novel
13877 *In jeopardy.* Harper & Bros., New York, 1922,
       300p, Cloth, Novel

SUTTER, A. OLIVER

13878 *The super-woman.* Arthur H. Stockwell, London,
       1937, 235p, Cloth, Novel

SUTTNER, BERTHA (Felice Sophie, Freifrau) von, 1843-1914

13879   *When thoughts will soar; a romance of the immediate future.* Houghton Mifflin, Boston, 1914, 449p, Cloth, Novel

SUTTON, DAVID (Ambrose), 1947-   [*biography included*]

13880   *New writings in horror and the supernatural.* Sphere, London, 1971, 155p, Paper, Anth.
13881   *New writings in horror and the supernatural, vol. 2.* Sphere, London, 1972, 159p, Paper, Anth.

SUTTON, (Eric) GRAHAM, 1892-

13882   *Damnation of Mr. Zinkler.* Jonathan Cape, London, 1935, 347p, Cloth, Novel

SUTTON, HENRY, pseud. [David Rytman Slavitt, 1935-   ] [*biography included*]

13883   *Vector.* Bernard Geis Associates, New York, 1970, 354p, Cloth, Novel

SUTTON, JEAN [Eugenia Geneva Sutton, 1917-   ] [*biography included*], with Jeff Sutton

13884   *Alien from the stars.* G. P. Putnam's Sons, New York, 1970, 223p, Cloth, Novel
13885   *The beyond.* G. P. Putnam's Sons, New York, 1968, 223p, Cloth, Novel
13886   *The boy who had the power.* G. P. Putnam's Sons, New York, 1971, 189p, Cloth, Novel
13887   *Lord of the stars.* G. P. Putnam's Sons, New York, 1969, 220p, Cloth, Novel
13888   *The programmed man.* G. P. Putnam's Sons, New York, 1968, 192p, Cloth, Novel

SUTTON, JEFF(erson Howard), 1913-   [*biography included*]

13889   *Alton's unguessable.* Ace Double, New York, 1970, 151p, Paper, Novel
13890   *Apollo at go.* G. P. Putnam's Sons, New York, 1963, 183p, Cloth, Novel
13891   *The atom conspiracy.* Avalon, New York, 1963, 192p, Cloth, Novel
13892   *Beyond Apollo.* G. P. Putnam's Sons, New York, 1966, 223p, Cloth, Novel
13893   *Bombs in orbit.* Ace, New York, 1959, 192p, Paper, Novel
13894   *First on the Moon.* Ace, New York, 1958, 192p, Paper, Novel
13895   *H-bomb over America.* Ace, New York, 1967, 190p, Paper, Novel
13896   *The man who saw tomorrow.* Ace Double, New York, 1968, 115p, Paper, Novel
13897   *The mindblocked man.* DAW, New York, 1972, 159p, Paper, Novel
13898   *Spacehive.* Ace, New York, 1960, 192p, Paper, Novel
13899   *Whisper from the stars.* Dell, New York, 1970, 157p, Paper, Novel

with Jean Sutton:

13884   *Alien from the stars.* G. P. Putnam's Sons, New York, 1970, 223p, Cloth, Novel
13885   *The beyond.* G. P. Putnam's Sons, New York, 1968, 223p, Cloth, Novel
13886   *The boy who had the power.* G. P. Putnam's Sons, New York, 1971, 189p, Cloth, Novel
13887   *Lord of the stars.* G. P. Putnam's Sons, New York, 1969, 220p, Cloth, Novel
13888   *The programmed man.* G. P. Putnam's Sons, New York, 1968, 192p, Cloth, Novel

SUTTON, JOHN WREN, with James Smith

13377   *The secret of the sphinx; or, The ring of Moses.* Philip Wellby, London, 1906, 288p, Cloth, Novel

SUTTON, (Homer) LEE, 1916-   [*biography included*]

13900   *Venus boy.* Lothrop, Lee & Shepard, New York, 1955, 182p, Cloth, Novel

SUTTON, PARALEE SWEETEN

13901   *White city; a novel.* Palopress, Palo Alto, CA, 1949, 140p, Cloth, Novel

SUTTON, STEPHEN P.

13902   *More tales to tremble by; a second collection of great stories of haunting and suspense.* Whitman Publishing Co., Racine, Wisc., 1968, 210p, Cloth, Anth.
13903   *Tales to tremble by; a collection of famous stories of haunting and suspense.* Whitman Publishing Co., Racine, Wisc., 1966, 214p, Cloth, Anth.

SUVIN, DARKO (R.), 1930-   [*biography included*]

13904   *Other worlds, other seas; science-fiction stories from Socialist countries.* Random House, New York, 1970, 219p, Cloth, Anth.
13905   *Russian science fiction and criticism, 1956-1970; a bibliography.* "Secondary Universe 4" Conference, Toronto, 1971, 35p, Paper, Nonf.

SWAFFER, HANNAN, 1879-1962

13906   *When men talk truth, and other stories.* Rich & Cowan, London, 1934, 159p, Cloth, Coll.

SWAIN, DWIGHT V(reeland), 1915-   [*biography included*]

13907   *The transposed man.* Ace Double, New York, 1955, 97p, Paper, Novel

SWAIN, E(dmund) G(ill), 1861-1938

13908   *The Stoneground ghost tales, compiled from
        the recollections of the Reverend Roland
        Batchel, vicar of the parish.* W. Heffer &
        Sons, Cambridge, UK, 1912, 187p, Cloth,
        Coll.

SWAIN, VIRGINIA, 1899-

13909   *The hollow skin.* Farrar & Rinehart, New York,
        1938, 275p, Cloth, Novel

SWAN, THOR

13910   *Furfooze; a tale fantastique.* Murray & Gee,
        Hollywood, 1939, 170p, Cloth, Novel

SWANN, THOMAS BURNETT (Jr.), 1928-1976 [*biography included*]

13911   *Day of the Minotaur.* Ace, New York, 1966,
        159p, Paper, Novel [Eunostos #1]
13912   *The dolphin and the deep.* Ace, New York,
        1968, 160p, Paper, Coll.
13913   *The forest of forever.* Ace, New York, 1971,
        158p, Paper, Novel [Eunostos #2]
13914   *The goat without horns.* Ballantine, New York,
        1971, 175p, Paper, Novel
13915   *Green Phoenix.* DAW, New York, 1972, 141p,
        Paper, Novel
13916   *How are the mighty fallen.* DAW, New York,
        1974, 160p, Paper, Novel
13917   *Moondust.* Ace, New York, 1968, 160p, Paper,
        Novel
13918   *The Weirwoods.* Ace, New York, 1967, 125p,
        Paper, Novel
13919   *Where is the bird of fire?* Ace, New York,
        1970, 155p, Paper, Coll.
13920   *Wolfwinter.* Ballantine, New York, 1972,
        205p, Paper, Novel

SWAYNE, MARTIN, pseud. [(Henry) Maurice (Dunlop) Nicoll, 1884-1953]

13921   *The blue germ.* Hodder & Stoughton, London,
        1918, 279p, Cloth, Novel

SWENSON, PEGGY, pseud.
    see: GEIS, RICHARD E.

SWEVEN, GODFREY, pseud. [John Macmillan Brown,
1846-1935]

13922   *Limanora, the island of progress.* G. P. Put-
        nam's Sons, New York, 1903, 711p, Cloth,
        Novel
13923   *Riallaro, the archipelago of exiles.* G. P.
        Putnam's Sons, New York, 1901, 420p, Cloth,
        Novel

SWIFT, JONATHAN, 1667-1745

13924   *Travels into several remote nations of the
        world, in four parts*, by Lemuel Gulliver.
        Benj. Motte, London, 1726, vol. I-312p, II-
        354p, Cloth, Novel [the first edition; other
        variations are listed below in alphabetical
        order]
13924A retitled: *The adventures of Captain Gulliver
        in a voyage to Lilliput*, by Lemuel Gulliver.
        J. Lumsden & Son, Glasgow, 1815, 47p, Cloth,
        Story [abridged]
13924B retitled: *The adventures of Captain Gulliver
        in a voyage to the islands of Lilliput and
        Brobdingnag.* S. Hall, Boston, 1794, 119p,
        Cloth, Novel [abridged]
13924C retitled: *The adventures of Gulliver.* Blackie
        & Son, London, 1954, 63p, Cloth, Novel [ab-
        ridged]
13924D retitled: *The children's Gulliver.* George G.
        Harrap, London, 1935, 63p, Cloth, Novel [ab-
        ridged]
13924E retitled: *Dwarfs and giants, being selections
        from Gulliver's Travels.* Thomas Nelson &
        Sons, London, 1930, 127p, Cloth, Novel [ab-
        ridged]
13924F retitled: *Gulliver in Lilliput.* Kegan Paul,
        Trench, Trubner, London, 1934, 111p, Cloth,
        Novel [abridged; see 13924A]
13924G retitled: *Gulliver's Travels.* John Ballan-
        tyne, London, 1821,   , Cloth, Novel
13924H retitled: *Gulliver's travels among the little
        people of Lilliput.* Penn Publishing Co.,
        Philadelphia, 1908, 60p, Cloth, Novel [ab-
        ridged; see also 13924A, 13924F]
13924I retitled: *Gulliver's travels among the little
        people of Lilliput and the giants of Brob-
        dingnag.* Jonathan Cape, London, 1928, 167p,
        Cloth, Novel [abridged; see also 13924B]
13924J retitled: *Gulliver's travels in Lilliput.*
        Max Parrish, London, 1949, 95p, Cloth, Novel
        [abridged; see also 13924A, 13924F, 13924H]
13924K retitled: *Gulliver's travels in Lilliput and
        Brobdingnag*, by Lemuel Gulliver. G. Vickers,
        London, 1861, 36p, Cloth, Story [abridged;
        see also 13924B, 13924I]
13924L retitled: *Gulliver's Travels into several
        remote nations of the world.* J. Walker, Lon-
        don, 1808, 322p, Cloth, Novel
13924M retitled: *Gulliver's Travels: I. A voyage to
        Lilliput; II. A voyage to Brobdingnag.* Long-
        mans, Green, London, 1884, 184p, Cloth, Novel
        [abridged; see also 13924B, 13924I, 13924K]
13924N retitled: *Gulliver's Travels; The voyage to
        Lilliput.* Clark & Maynard, New York, 1886,
        54p, Cloth, Novel [see also 13924A, 13924F,
        13924H, 13924J]
13924O retitled: *Gulliver's voyage to Lilliput.* F.
        Pitman, London, 1883, 92p, Cloth, Novel [ab-
        ridged; see also 13924A, 13924F, 13924H,
        13924J, 13924N]
13924P retitled: *Gulliver's voyages to Lilliput and
        Brobdingnag.* Sidgwick & Jackson, London,
        1912, 235p, Cloth, Novel [abridged; see also
        13924B, 13924I, 13924K, 13924M]
13924Q retitled: *The story of Gulliver's Travels.*
        Birn Bros., London, 1939, 32p, Cloth, Story
        [Lilliput only; see also 13924A, 13924F,
        13924H, 13924J, 13924O]
13924R retitled: *The surprising adventures of Cap-
        tain Gulliver in a voyage to the Kingdom of
        Lilliput*, by Lemuel Gulliver. Lumsden & Son,
        Glasgow, 1800?, 52p, Cloth, Novel [abridged;
        see also 13924A, 13924F, 13924H, 13924J,
        13924N, 13924Q]
13924S retitled: *Tales from Gulliver's Travels.* Ox-
        ford University Press, London, 1937, 57p,
        Cloth, Novel [abridged]

SWIFT, JONATHAN (cont.)

13924T retitled: *Travels of Lemuel Gulliver into
        several remote regions of the world*, by
        Lemuel Gulliver. A. Jardine, Edinburgh,
        1803, 2vol, Cloth, Novel
13924U retitled: *Two voyages of Gulliver*. Collins,
        London, 1940, 253p, Cloth, Novel [abridged]
13924V retitled: *The voyage of Lemuel Gulliver to
        Lilliput and Brobdingnag*. Folio Society,
        London, 1948, 153p, Cloth, Novel [abridged;
        see also 13924B, 13924I, 13924K, 13924M,
        13924P]
13924W retitled: *A voyage to Brobdingnag, made by
        Lemuel Gulliver in the year MDCCII*. Limi-
        ted Editions Club, New York, 1950, 2vol,
        Cloth, Novel [abridged]
13924X retitled: *The voyage to Laputa*. Christopher
        Johnson, London, 1948, 80p, Cloth, Novel
        [abridged]
13924Y retitled: *The voyage to Lilliput*. Adam &
        Charles Black, Edinburgh, 1858, 122p,
        Cloth, Novel [abridged; see also 13924A,
        13924F, 13924H, 13924J, 13924N, 13924O,
        13924Q, 13924R]
13924Z retitled: *The wonderful voyages of Gulliver*.
        George G. Harrap, London, 1909, 160p, Cloth,
        Novel
13925   *Gulliver's Travels, and other works*. George
        Routledge & Sons, London, 1906, 445p, Cloth,
        Coll.
13926   *Gulliver's Travels, and other writings*. Mo-
        dern Library, New York, 1958, 550p, Cloth,
        Coll.
13927   *Gulliver's Travels, and other writings*. Hough-
        ton Mifflin, Boston, 1960, 564p, Cloth,
        Coll.
13928   *Gulliver's Travels, and other writings*. Ban-
        tam, New York, 1962, 535p, Paper, Coll.
13929   *Gulliver's Travels, The tale of a tub, and
        The battle of the books*. Humphrey Milford,
        Oxford University Press, London, 1919, 599p,
        Cloth, Coll.

SWIGART, LESLIE KAY, 1948-   [*biography included*]

13930   *Harlan Ellison: a bibliographical checklist*.
        Williams Publishing Co., Dallas, TX, 1973,
        118p, Paper, Nonf.

SWITZER, ROBERT

13931   *The living idol*. Signet, New York, 1956,
        128p, Paper, Movie

SWORDSMEN AND SUPERMEN
    see: GRANT, DONALD M.

SYDENHAM, Baron
    see: SEAFORTH, A. NELSON

SYKES, PAMELA

13932   *Come back, Lucy*. Hamish Hamilton, London,
        1973, 183p, Cloth, Novel
13932A retitled: *Mirror of danger*. Thomas Nelson,
        Nashville, 1974, 175p, Cloth, Novel

SYKES, W(illiam) STANLEY, 1894-1961

13933   *The ray of doom; a detective novel*. Hodder &
        Stoughton, London, 1935, 312p, Cloth, Novel

SYLVA, CARMEN, Queen ELISABETH of Roumania
[Paulina Elisabeth Ottilia Louisa, Queen Con-
sort of Carol I, King of Romania, 1843-1916]

13934   *Pilgrim sorrow; a cycle of tales*. T. Fisher
        Unwin, London, 1883, 262p, Cloth, Coll.

SYLVESTER, JOHN

13935   *The flying saucer*. Ward, Lock, London, 1952,
        191p, Cloth, Novel
13936   *Master of the world*. Ward, Lock, London, 1949,
        224p, Cloth, Novel

SYMMES, JOHN CLEVES
    see: SEABORN, ADAM

SYMONS, J(ohn) H(enry), 1873-

13937   *A splendid angel*. C. W. Daniel, London, 1925,
        283p, Cloth, Novel
13938   *The supreme mystery*. Methuen, London, 1917,
        310p, Cloth, Novel

SYRETT, NETTA, d. 1943

13939   *The farm on the downs*. Geoffrey Bles, London,
        1936, 159p, Cloth, Novel
13940   *The house that was*. Rich & Cowan, London,
        1933, 254p, Cloth, Novel

SZERB, ANTAL, 1901-1945

13941   *The Pendragon legend*. Corvina Press, Budapest,
        1963, 231p, Cloth, Novel

SZILARD, LEO, 1898-1964

13942   *The Voice of the Dolphins, and other stories*.
        Simon & Schuster, New York, 1961, 122p,
        Cloth, Coll.

SZYRMA, W. S. LACH-
    see: LACH-SZYRMA, W. S.

T., C. J.

13943   *Terrible tales; French*. W. W. Gibbings, Lon-
        don, 1891, 180p, Cloth, Anth.
13943A retitled: *The best terrible tales from the
        French*. William Reeves, London, 1912, 180p,
        Cloth, Anth.
13944   *Terrible tales; German*. W. W. Gibbings, London
        1890, 193p, Cloth, Anth.
13944A retitled: *The best terrible tales from the
        German*. William Reeves, London, 1912, 193p,
        Cloth, Anth.
13945   *Terrible tales; Italian*. W. W. Gibbings, Lon-
        don, 1891, 181p, Cloth, Anth.

T., C. J. (cont.)

13945A retitled: *The best terrible tales from the Italian*. William Reeves, London, 1912, 181p, Cloth, Anth.
13946 *Terrible tales; Spanish*. W. W. Gibbings, London, 1890, 178p, Cloth, Anth.
13946A retitled: *The best terrible tales from the Spanish*. William Reeves, London, 1912, 178p, Cloth, Anth.

T. E.
see: ERSKINE, THOMAS

T. S. G.
see: GUEULLETTE, THOMAS SIMON

TABOO

13947 *Taboo*. Collectors Publications, City of Industry, CA, 1969,   , Paper, Novel

TABORI, PAUL, 1908-1974 [*biography included*]
[name originally Pál Tábori]

13948 *The Cleft*. Pyramid, New York, 1969, 174p, Paper, Novel
13949 *The demons of Sandorra*. Award, New York, 1970, 154p, Paper, Novel
13950 *The doomsday brain*. Pyramid, New York, 1967, 188p, Paper, Novel [Hunters #1]
13951 *The Green Rain*. Pyramid, New York, 1961, 192p, Paper, Novel
13952 *The invisible eye*. Pyramid, New York, 1967, 173p, Paper, Novel [Hunters #2]
13953 *Lily Dale*. New English Library, London, 1972, 254p, Cloth, Novel
13954 *Solo; a novel*. Sampson Low, Marston, London, 1948, 232p, Cloth, Novel
13955 *The survivors*. Consul, London, 1964, 170p, Paper, Novel
13956 *The torture machine*. Pyramid, New York, 1969, 160p, Paper, Novel [Hunters #3]

as Peter Stafford:

13957 *The wild white witch*. New English Library, London, 1973, 127p, Paper, Novel

TAINE, JOHN, pseud. [Eric Temple Bell, 1883-1960]

13958 *Before the dawn*. Williams & Wilkins Co., Baltimore, 1934, 247p, Cloth, Novel
13959 *The cosmic geoide, and one other*. Fantasy Publishing Co., Los Angeles, 1949, 179p, Cloth, Coll.
13960 *The crystal horde*. Fantasy Press, Reading, PA, 1952, 254p, Cloth, Novel
13961 *The forbidden garden*. Fantasy Press, Reading, PA, 1947, 278p, Cloth, Novel
13962 *G.O.G. 666*. Fantasy Press, Reading, PA, 1954, 251p, Cloth, Novel
13963 *The gold tooth*. E. P. Dutton, New York, 1927, 436p, Cloth, Novel
13964 *The greatest adventure*. E. P. Dutton, New York, 1929, 258p, Cloth, Novel

13965 *Green fire; the story of the terrible days in the summer of 1990, now told in full for the first time*. E. P. Dutton, New York, 1928, 313p, Cloth, Novel
13966 *The iron star*. E. P. Dutton, New York, 1930, 357p, Cloth, Novel
13967 *The purple sapphire*. E. P. Dutton, New York, 1924, 325p, Cloth, Novel
13968 *Quayle's invention*. E. P. Dutton, New York, 1927, 451p, Cloth, Novel
13969 *Seeds of life*. Fantasy Press, Reading, PA, 1951, 255p, Cloth, Novel
13970 *Seeds of life; and, White Lily; two science fiction novels*. Dover, New York, 1966, 367p, Paper, Coll. [*White Lily* was originally published as *The crystal horde*]
13971 *The time stream*. Buffalo Book Co. & G. H. E., Providence, RI, 1946, 251p, Cloth, Novel
13972 *Time stream, and other stories*. Remploy, Newcastle-under-Lyme, UK, 1971, 532p?, Cloth, Coll.
13973 *The time stream; The greatest adventure; The purple sapphire; three great science-fiction novels*. Dover, New York, 1964, 532p, Paper, Coll.

TAIT, GEORGE B.
see: BARCLAY, ALAN

TAIT, STEPHEN, with Kenneth Allott

00233 *The rhubarb tree*. Cresset Press, London, 1937, 293p, Cloth, Novel

TALBOT, GEORGE E., 1901-

13974 *Glory to Ajeba!* Vantage Press, New York, 1972, 297p, Cloth, Novel

TALES FOR A STORMY NIGHT

13975 *Tales for a stormy night; translations from the French*. Robert Clarke, Cincinnati, 1891, 279p, Cloth, Anth.

TALES OF A VOYAGER TO THE ARCTIC OCEAN
see: GILLIES, ROBERT PEARSE

TALES OF DEATH

13976 *Tales of death; a collection of uneasy tales*. Philip Allan, London, 1936, 254p, Cloth, Anth.

TALES OF DREAD

13977 *Tales of dread; a collection of uneasy tales*. Philip Allan, London, 1936, 248p, Cloth, Anth.

TALES OF FEAR

13978 *Tales of fear; a collection of uneasy tales*. Philip Allan, London, 1935, 243p, Cloth, Anth.

TALES OF MYSTERY AND SURPRISE

13979 *Tales of mystery and surprise.* Everybody's
Books, London, 1943, 32p, Paper, Anth.

TALES OF TERROR AND THE UNKNOWN

13980 *Tales of terror and the unknown.* Everybody's
Books, London, 1944, 96p, Paper, Anth.

TALES OF TERROR AND SURPRISE

13981 *Tales of terror and surprise.* Mitre Press,
London, 1942, 127p, Paper, Anth.

TALES OF THE DEAD
see: UTTERSON, SARAH

THE TALES OF THE GENII
see: RIDLEY, JAMES

TALES OF THE SUPERNATURAL

13982 *Tales of the supernatural.* Pan, London,
1947, 183p, Paper, Anth.

TALES OF THE SUPERNATURAL

13983 *Tales of the supernatural.* Panther, London,
1962, 124p, Paper, Anth. [different contents]

TALES OF THE UNCANNY

13984 *Tales of the uncanny.* Panther, London, 1962,
128p, Paper, Anth.

TALLANT, ROBERT, 1909-1957

13985 *Mrs. Candy and Saturday night.* Doubleday,
Garden City, 1947, 269p, Cloth, Novel [Mrs.
Candy #1]

TANDRUP, HARALD (Konrad Niels Viggo), 1874-

13986 *Jonah and the voice; a novel.* Peter Davies,
London, 1937, 336p, Cloth, Novel
13986A retitled: *Reluctant prophet.* Alfred A. Knopf,
New York, 1939, 311p, Cloth, Novel

TANTON, ERNEST C(oveney)

13987 *If twelve today.* Chapman & Hall, London,
1937, 261p, Cloth, Novel

TARDE, (Jean) GABRIEL (de), 1843-1904

13988 *Underground man.* Duckworth, London, 1905,
198p, Cloth, Novel

TARN, (Sir) W(illiam) W(oodthorpe), 1869-1957

13989 *The treasure of the Isle of Mist.* Philip Allan, London, 1919, 163p, Cloth, Novel

TARNACRE, ROBERT, pseud. [Robert Cartmell,
1877-   ]

13990 *Beyond the swamps.* John Lane, London, 1929,
324p, Cloth, Novel

TARZAN AND THE LOST SAFARI

13991 *Tarzan and the lost safari.* Whitman Publishing
Co., Racine, Wisc., 1966, 282p, Cloth, Movie
[Tarzan series]

TATE, PETER

13992 *Country love and poison rain.* Doubleday, Garden City, 1973, 178p, Cloth, Novel
13993 *Gardens One to Five.* Doubleday, Garden City,
1971, 181p, Cloth, Novel
13993A retitled: *Gardens 1, 2, 3, 4, 5.* Faber &
Faber, London, 1971, 207p, Cloth, Novel
13994 *Moon on an iron meadow.* Doubleday, Garden
City, 1974, 210p, Cloth, Novel
13995 *The thinking seat.* Doubleday, Garden City,
1969, 225p, Cloth, Novel

TATHAM, H(erbert) F(rancis) W(illiam), d. 1909

13996 *The footprints in the snow.* Macmillan, London,
1910, 187p, Cloth, Coll.

TAUNTON, H(arold) R(oby)

13997 *It prowls at dark.* Hurst & Blackett, London,
1937, 287p, Cloth, Novel

TAYLOR, ANN

13998 *Door of desire.* PEC, El Cajon, CA, 1964,
160p, Paper, Novel

TAYLOR, ANNA, 1944-

13999 *Drustan the wanderer; a historical novel based
on the legend of Tristan and Yseult.* Longman, Harlow, UK, 1971, 168p, Cloth, Novel

TAYLOR, BERT LESTON, 1866-1921, with W. C.
Gibson

05951 *Extra dry, being further adventures of the
Water Wagon.* G. W. Dillingham, New York,
1906, 120p, Cloth, Novel [Water Wagon #2]
05952 *The log of the Water Wagon; or, The cruise of
the good ship "Lithia."* H. M. Caldwell,
Boston, 1905, 128p, Cloth, Novel

TAYLOR, BESSIE KYFFIN-
see: KYFFIN-TAYLOR, BESSIE

TAYLOR, C. BRYSON, 1880-

14000 *In the dwellings of the wilderness.* Henry
Holt, New York, 1904, 184p, Cloth, Novel

TAYLOR, CONSTANCE LINDSAY
see: CULLINGFORD, GUY

TAYLOR, FRANK

14001 *House of the hunter.* Chicago Paperback House,
Chicago, 1962, 255p, Paper, Novel

TAYLOR, GEOFF(rey)

14002 *Day of the republic.* Peter Davies, London,
1968, 183p, Cloth, Novel

TAYLOR, MALCOLM

14003 *PX.* Houghton Mifflin, Boston, 1943, 231p,
Cloth, Novel
14004 *Wings over Eldorado.* Basil Blackwell, Oxford,
1936, 256p, Cloth, Novel

TAYLOR, RAY WARD, 1908-

14005 *Doomsday square; a novel.* E. P. Dutton, New
York, 1966, 254p, Cloth, Novel

TAYLOR, ROBERT LEWIS, 1912- [*biography included*]

14006 *Adrift in a boneyard.* Doubleday, Garden City,
1947, 255p, Cloth, Novel

TAYLOR, WILLIAM ALEXANDER, 1837-1912

14007 *Intermere.* XX. Century Publishing Co., Columbus, OH, 1901, 148p, Cloth, Novel

TCHI, XONGO-TEE-FOH-
see: XONGO-TEE-FOH-TCHI

TEAGUE, JOHN JESSOP
see: GERARD, MORICE

TEBBETTS, LEON (Harold)

14008 *O big Earth!* Falmouth Book House, Portland,
Maine, 1938, 210p, Cloth, Novel

TEED, CYRUS
see: CHESTER, Lord

TEMPLE, M. H., with J. Stafford Ransome and
Harold Begbie as Caroline Lewis

01038 *Clara in Blunderland.* William Heinemann, London, 1902, 150p, Cloth, Novel [Clara #1;
a parody of Carroll's *Alice in Wonderland*]

01039 *Lost in Blunderland; the further adventures of
Clara.* William Heinemann, London, 1903,
145p, Cloth, Novel [Clara #2]

TEMPLE, WILLIAM F(rederick), 1914- [*biography included*]

14009 *The automated Goliath.* Ace Double, New York,
1962, 143p, Paper, Novel
14010 *Battle on Venus.* Ace Double, New York, 1963,
104p, Paper, Novel
14011 *The fleshpots of Sansato.* Macdonald, London,
1968, 188p, Cloth, Novel
14012 *Four-sided triangle; a romance.* John Long,
London, 1949, 240p, Cloth, Novel
14013 *Martin Magnus on Mars.* Frederick Muller, London, 1956, 191p, Cloth, Novel [Martin Magnus
#3]
14014 *Martin Magnus on Venus.* Frederick Muller, London, 1955, 176p, Cloth, Novel [Martin Magnus
#2]
14015 *Martin Magnus, planet rover.* Frederick Muller,
London, 1955, 167p, Cloth, Novel [Martin Magnus #1]
14016 *Shoot at the Moon.* Whiting & Wheaton, London,
1966, 192p, Cloth, Novel
14017 *The three suns of Amara.* Ace Double, New York,
1962, 80p, Paper, Novel

TEMPLETON, HERMINIE

14018 *Darby O'Gill and the good people.* McClure,
Phillips, New York, 1903, 294p, Cloth, Novel

TEMS DYVIRTA
see: DYVIRTA, TEMS

TENN, WILLIAM, pseud. [Philip Klass, 1920-   ]

14019 *Children of wonder; 21 remarkable and fantastic
tales.* Simon & Schuster, New York, 1953,
337p, Cloth, Anth.
14019A retitled: *Outsiders: children of wonder; 21
remarkable and fantastic tales.* Permabooks,
Garden City, 1954, 356p, Paper, Anth.
14020 *The human angle.* Ballantine, New York, 1956,
153p, Cloth, Coll.
14021 *A lamp for Medusa.* Belmont Double, New York,
1968, 72p, Paper, Novel
14022 *Of all possible worlds; stories.* Ballantine,
New York, 1955, 161p, Cloth, Coll.
14023 *Of men and monsters.* Ballantine, New York,
1968, 253p, Paper, Novel
Outsiders: children of wonder. [see 14019A]
14024 *The seven sexes.* Ballantine, New York, 1968,
238p, Paper, Coll.
14025 *The square root of man.* Ballantine, New York,
1968, 221p, Paper, Coll.
14026 *Time in advance.* Bantam, New York, 1958, 153p,
Paper, Coll.
14027 *The wooden star.* Ballantine, New York, 1968,
253p, Paper, Coll.

TENNANT, EMMA

14028 *The time of the crack.* Jonathan Cape, London,
1973, 142p, Cloth, Novel

TEPPER, MATTHEW BRUCE, 1953- [*biography included*]

14029 *The Asimov science fiction bibliography.* Chinese Ducked Press, Santa Monica, CA, 1970, 89p, Paper, Nonf. [text on one side of the page only]

TEPPERMAN, EMILE
see: STEELE, CURTIS

TÉRAMOND, GUY de [Edmond Gautier de Téramond, 1869-1957]

14030 *The mystery of Lucien Delorme.* D. Appleton, New York, 1915, 314p, Cloth, Novel

TERHUNE, EVERIT BOGERT, 1877?-1956

14031 *Michel Gulpe.* G. W. Dillingham, New York, 1902, 182p, Cloth, Novel

TERRIBLE TALES; FRENCH
see: T., C. J.

TERRIBLE TALES; GERMAN
see: T., C. J.

TERRIBLE TALES; ITALIAN
see: T., C. J.

TERRIBLE TALES; SPANISH
see: T., C. J.

TERRORS

14032 *Terrors; a collection of uneasy tales.* Philip Allan, London, 1933, 252p, Cloth, Anth.

TERROT, CHARLES (Hugh), 1917-

14033 *The angel who pawned her harp.* Collins, London, 1953, 189p, Cloth, Novel

TERTZ, ABRAM, pseud. [Andrei Donat'evich Siniavskii, 1925-]

14034 *The icicle, and other stories.* Collins & Harvill Press, London, 1963, 191p, Cloth, Coll.
14034A retitled: *Fantastic stories.* Pantheon, New York, 1963, 213p, Cloth, Coll.
14035 *The Makepeace experiment.* Collins & Harvill Press, London, 1965, 192p, Cloth, Novel

TESSIER, ERNEST MAURICE
see: DEKOBRA, MAURICE

TEVIS, WALTER (Stone Jr.)

14036 *The man who fell to Earth.* Gold Medal, Greenwich, Conn., 1963, 144p, Paper, Novel

THACKER, ERIC (Lee), 1923- [*biography included*], with Anthony Earnshaw

04664 *Musrum.* Jonathan Cape, London, 1968, 160p, Cloth, Novel [Wintersol #1]
04665 *Wintersol.* Jonathan Cape, London, 1971, 103p, Cloth, Novel [Wintersol #2]

THACKERAY, WILLIAM MAKEPEACE
see: HOMUNCULUS

THAL, HERBERT van
see: van THAL, HERBERT

THANE, ELSWYTH, 1900-

14037 *Remember today; leaves from a guardian angel's notebook.* Duell, Sloan & Pearce, New York, 1941, 266p, Cloth, Novel
14038 *Tryst.* Harcourt, Brace & Co., New York, 1939, 256p, Cloth, Novel

THANET, NEIL, pseud.
see: FANTHORPE, R. LIONEL

THAT VERY MAB
see: KENDALL, MAY and LANG, ANDREW

THAYER, TIFFANY (Ellsworth), 1902-1959

14039 *Doctor Arnoldi.* Julian Messner, New York, 1934, 334p, Cloth, Novel
14040 *The Greek.* Albert & Charles Boni, New York, 1931, 338p, Cloth, Novel
14041 *One-man show.* Julian Messner, New York, 1937, 314p, Cloth, Novel

THEMERSON, STEFAN, 1910-

14042 *Professor Mmaa's lecture.* Gaberbocchus, London, 1953, 251p, Cloth, Novel

THEOBALD, ROBERT, 1929- [*biography included*], with J. M. Scott

12827 *Teg's 1994; an anticipation of the near future.* Swallow Press, Chicago, 1972, 211p, Cloth, Novel

THEODAMUS, pseud. [Theodore Glass, 1896-]

14043 *Tales of cosmic wisdom.* House-Warven, Los Angeles, 1949, 92p, Cloth, Coll.

THEOSOPHO & ELLORA, pseud. [Gideon Jasper Richard Ouseley, 1835-1906]

14044 *Palingenesia; or, The Earth's new birth.* Hay Nisbet, Glasgow, 1884, 359p, Cloth, Novel

THEYDON, JOHN

14045 *The Angels and the creeping enemy*. Armada, London, 1968, 125p, Paper, Tele.

14046 *Calling Thunderbirds*. Armada, London, 1966, 125p, Paper, Tele. [Thunderbirds #2]

14047 *Captain Scarlet and the Mysterons*. Armada, London, 1967, 128p, Paper, Tele. [Captain Scarlet #1]

14048 *Captain Scarlet and the silent saboteur*. Armada, London, 1967, 128p, Paper, Tele. [Captain Scarlet #2]

14049 *Lady Penelope; The Albanian affair*. Armada, London, 1967, 128p, Paper, Tele. [Thunderbirds #5]

14050 *Stingray*. Armada, London, 1965, 157p, Paper, Tele. [Stingray #1]

14051 *Stingray and the monster*. Armada, London, 1966, 125p, Paper, Tele. [Stingray #2]

14052 *Thunderbirds*. Armada, London, 1966, 126p, Paper, Tele. [Thunderbirds #1]

14053 *Thunderbirds ring of fire*. Armada, London, 1966, 125p, Paper, Tele. [Thunderbirds #3]

THIBAULT, JACQUES ANATOLE
see: FRANCE, ANATOLE

THISTED, VALDEMAR
see: ROWEL, M.

THIUSEN, ISMAR, pseud. [John Macnie, 1835-1909]

14054 *The Diothas; or, A far look ahead*. G. P. Putnam's Sons, New York, 1883, 358p, Cloth, Novel

14054A retitled: *Looking forward; or, The Diothas*. G. P. Putnam's Sons, London, 1890, 358p, Cloth, Novel

14054B retitled: *A far look ahead; or, The Diothas*. G. P. Putnam's Sons, New York, 1890, 358p, Paper, Novel

THOBY-MARCELIN, (Émile) PHILIPPE, 1904-1975, with Pierre Marcelin

09656 *All men are mad*. Farrar, Straus & Giroux, New York, 1970, 179p, Cloth, Novel

09657 *The beast of the Haitian hills*. Rinehart & Co., New York, 1946, 210p, Cloth, Novel

09658 *Canapé-Vert*. Farrar & Rinehart, New York, 1944, 225p, Cloth, Novel

09659 *The pencil of God*. Houghton Mifflin, Boston, 1951, 204p, Cloth, Novel

THOM, ROBERT, 1929- [biography included]

14055 *Wild in the streets; a novel*. Pyramid, New York, 1968, 128p, Paper, Movie

THOMA, pseud.

14056 *Tragedy in blue*. Obelisk Press, Paris, 1936, 86p, Paper, Novel

THOMAS, AUGUSTUS, 1857-1934

14057 *The witching hour*. Harper & Bros., New York, 1908, 249p, Cloth, Novel [based on the play]

THOMAS, CHAUNCEY, 1822-1898

14058 *The crystal button; or, Adventures of Paul Prognosis in the forty-ninth century*. Houghton Mifflin, Boston, 1891, 302p, Cloth, Novel

THOMAS, DAN, pseud. [Leonard M. Sanders, Jr., 1929-] [biography included]

14059 *The seed*. Ballantine, New York, 1968, 252p, Paper, Novel

THOMAS, DONALD (Serrell)

14060 *Prince Charlie's bluff*. Macmillan, London, 1974, 280p, Cloth, Novel

THOMAS, DOROTHY (Ada), 1903-

14061 *The call of the Phoenix; a story of a man who, like the phoenix, arose out of his ashes*. New Age Publishing Co., Los Angeles, 1945, 287p, Cloth, Novel ["based on an unpublished manuscript, 'I Am the Way,' by Charles E. Sleator"]

THOMAS, EUGENE E., 1893-

14062 *Brotherhood of Mt. Shasta*. DeVorss & Co., Los Angeles, 1946, 307p, Cloth, Novel

14063 *The dancing dead*. Sears Publishing Co., New York, 1933, 298p, Cloth, Novel [Chu-Sheng series]

14064 *Fragments from the past*. E. E. Thomas, Los Angeles?, 1930, 379p, Cloth, Novel

14065 *Yellow magic*. Sears Publishing Co., New York, 1934, 266p, Cloth, Novel [Chu-Sheng series]

THOMAS, EVAN

14066 *Dead hard*. Eros Goldstripe, Wilmington, Del., 1973, 182p, Paper, Novel

THOMAS, JACK
see: ORAM, JOHN

THOMAS, MARTIN, pseud. [Thomas Hector Martin, 1913-] [biography included]

14067 *Beyond the spectrum*. Digit, London, 1964, 158p, Paper, Novel

14068 *The hands of Cain*. Mayflower-Dell, London, 1966, 156p, Paper, Novel

14068A retitled: *The hand of Cain*. Lancer, New York, 1967, 159p, Paper, Novel

14069 *Sorcerers of Set*. Mayflower-Dell, London, 1966, 141p, Paper, Novel [Sexton Blake series]

THOMAS, MARTIN (cont.), as Peter Saxon, house pseud.

12721   *The curse of Rathlaw.* Lancer, New York, 1968, 190p, Paper, Novel [Guardians series]

THOMAS, ROWLAND

14070   *Fatima; or, Always pick a fool for your husband, being the strange adventures of a woman who was the most beautiful creature, and quite, quite the cleverest creature ever was, and knew it.* Little, Brown, Boston, 1913, 353p, Cloth, Novel

THOMAS, THEODORE L., 1920-   [*biography included*], with Kate Wilhelm

14071   *The clone.* Berkley Medallion, New York, 1965, 143p, Paper, Novel
14072   *The year of the cloud.* Doubleday, Garden City, 1970, 216p, Cloth, Novel

THOMAS, UNTRUTHFUL
    see: UNTRUTHFUL THOMAS

THOMPSON, ANTONY A.
    see: ALBAN, ANTONY

THOMPSON, ARNOLD

14073   *Science fictions; an anthology.* University Tutorial Press, London, 1971, 168p, Cloth, Anth.

THOMPSON, CRESWICK J. [Charles John Samuel Thompson, 1862-1943]

14074   *Zorastro; a romance.* Greening & Co., London, 1899, 275p, Cloth, Novel

THOMPSON, DEANE C., with Bernard C. Hollister

07339   *Grokking the future; science fiction in the classroom.* Pflaum/Standard, Dayton, OH, 1973, 168p, Paper, Nonf.

THOMPSON, GEORGE SELDEN
    see: SELDEN, GEORGE

THOMPSON, HARLAN (Howard), 1894-   [*biography included*]

14075   *Silent running.* Scholastic Book Services, New York, 1972, 116p, Paper, Movie

THOMPSON, VANCE, 1863-1925

14076   *The carnival of destiny.* Moffat, Yard, New York, 1916, 314p, Cloth, Novel

THOMSON, CHRISTINE CAMPBELL

14077   *At dead of night.* Selwyn & Blount, London, 1931, 251p, Cloth, Anth.
14078   *By daylight only.* Selwyn & Blount, London, 1929, 288p, Cloth, Anth.
14079   *Grim death.* Selwyn & Blount, London, 1932, 254p, Cloth, Anth.
14080   *Gruesome cargoes.* Selwyn & Blount, London, 1928, 245p, Cloth, Anth.
14081   *Keep on the light; tales of thrill and horror.* Selwyn & Blount, London, 1933, 254p, Cloth, Anth.
14082   *More not at night.* Selwyn & Blount, London, 1926, 256p, Cloth, Anth.
14083   *More not at night.* Arrow, London, 1961, 192p, Paper, Anth. [different contents]
14083A   retitled: *Never at night; horror stories.* Arrow, London, 1972, 191p, Paper, Anth.
14084   *Nightmare by daylight.* Selwyn & Blount, London, 1936, 251p, Cloth, Anth.
14085   *Not at night.* Selwyn & Blount, London, 1925, 240p, Cloth, Anth.
14086   *Not at night.* Arrow, London, 1960, 192p, Paper, Anth. [different contents]
14087   *The "Not at night" omnibus.* Selwyn & Blount, London, 1937, 511p, Cloth, Anth.
        Only by daylight. [see 14088A]
14088   *Still not at night.* Arrow, London, 1962, 192p, Paper, Anth.
14088A   retitled: *Only by daylight; horror stories.* Arrow, London, 1972, 191p, Paper, Anth.
14089   *Switch on the light.* Selwyn & Blount, London, 1931, 256p, Cloth, Anth.
14090   *Terror by night.* Selwyn & Blount, London, 1934, 252p, Cloth, Anth.
14091   *You'll need a night light.* Selwyn & Blount, London, 1927, 254p, Cloth, Anth.

THOMSON, H(enry) DOUGLAS

14092   *The great book of thrillers.* Odhams Press, London, 1935, 768p, Cloth, Anth.
14093   *The mystery book.* Odhams Press, London, 1934, 1086p, Cloth, Anth.

THOMSON, K(enneth) GRAHAM

14094   *People of the South Pole.* Lutterworth Press, London, 1941, 187p, Cloth, Novel

THOMSON, WILLIAM, 1746-1817 [published anonymously]

14095   *Mammuth; or, Human nature displayed on a grand scale, in a tour with the tinkers into the inland parts of Africa, by a man in the Moon.* J. Murray, London, 1789, vol. I-285p, II-320p, Cloth, Novel
14096   *The man in the Moon; or, Travels in the Lunar region, by a man of the people.* J. Murray, London, 1783, vol. I-178p, II-214p, Cloth, Novel

THORBURN, S(eptimus) S(met), 1844-1924

14097   *His Majesty's greatest subject.* Archibald Constable, Westminster, 1897, 324p, Cloth, Novel

THORN, JOE

14098 *Oic-? science fiction.* McClain Printing Co., Parsons, WV, 1971, 106p, Cloth, Novel

THORNDIKE, (Arthur) RUSSELL, 1885-1972

14099 *The Master of the Macabre.* Rich & Cowan, London, 1947, 192p, Cloth, Novel
14100 *The Vandekkers.* Thornton Butterworth, London, 1929, 318p, Cloth, Novel

THORNE, GUY, pseud.
    see: GULL, C. RANGER

THORNER, WILLIAM E.

14101 *The cat of Bast, and other stories of mystery.* Regency Press, London, 1958, 109p, Cloth, Coll.

THORPE, FRED

14102 *The Silent City; or, Queer adventures among queer people.* Round the World Library, Street & Smith, New York, 1925?, 314p, Paper, Novel

THORPE, TREBOR, pseud.
    see: FANTHORPE, R. LIONEL

THOTH
    see: NICHOLSON, JOSEPH SHIELD

THE THOUGHT TRANSLATOR

14103 *The thought translator.* Stellar Publishing Corp., New York, 1930, 24p, Paper, Anth. [includes "The Thought Translator," by Merab Eberle; "The Creation," by Milton Mitchell]

A THOUSAND AND ONE QUARTERS OF HOURS
    see: GUEULLETTE, THOMAS SIMON

THREE FOR TOMORROW

14104 *Three for tomorrow; three original novellas of science fiction.* Meredith Press, New York, 1969, 204p, Cloth, Anth.

3 GREAT CLASSICS

14105 *3 great classics.* Arc Books, New York, 1964, 255p, Paper, Anth.

THREE STORIES
    see: MOSKOWITZ, SAM

THREE TRIPS IN TIME AND SPACE

14106 *Three trips in time and space; original novellas of science fiction.* Hawthorn, New York, 1973, 193p, Cloth, Anth.

THRILLERS

14107 *Thrillers; startling tales.* Edward J. Clode, New York, 1929, 313p, Cloth, Anth.

THRILLING STORIES

14108 *Thrilling stories.* Utopian Publications, London, 1946, 36p, Paper, Anth.

THRILLING TALES OF UNUSUAL INTEREST

14109 *Thrilling tales of unusual interest.* Gulliver Books, Lower Chelston, UK, 1943?, 47p, Paper, Anth.

THRILLS

14110 *Thrills; a collection of uneasy tales.* Philip Allan, London, 1935, 249p, Cloth, Anth.

THRILLS, CRIMES, AND MYSTERIES

14111 *Thrills, crimes, and mysteries; a specially selected collection of sixty-three complete stories by well-known authors.* Associated Newspapers, London, 1932?, 864p, Cloth, Anth.

THRUSH, ARTHUR, 1894-

14112 *The capture of Nina Carroll; an extravagance.* Cecil Palmer, London, 1924, 278p, Cloth, Novel

THURBER, ALWYN M.

14113 *The hidden faith; an occult story of the period.* F. M. Harley Publishing Co., Chicago, 1895, 294p, Cloth, Novel
14114 *Zelma, the mystic; or, White magic versus black.* Authors Publishing Co., Chicago, 1897, 380p, Cloth, Novel

THURBER, JAMES (Grover), 1894-1961

14115 *Fables for our times, and famous poems.* Harper & Bros., New York, 1940, 124p, Cloth, Coll. [includes some verse by other authors]
14116 *Further fables for our times.* Simon & Schuster, New York, 1956, 174p, Cloth, Coll.
14117 *The great Quillow.* Harcourt, Brace & Co., New York, 1944, 54p, Cloth, Novel
14118 *The 13 clocks.* Simon & Schuster, New York, 1950, 124p, Cloth, Novel
14119 *The 13 clocks; and, The wonderful O.* Puffin, Harmondsworth, 1962, 158p, Paper, Coll.
14120 *The white deer.* Harcourt, Brace & Co., New York, 1945, 115p, Cloth, Novel

THURBER, JAMES (cont.)

14121   *The wonderful O.* Simon & Schuster, New York,
        1957, 72p, Cloth, Novel

THURLOW CRAIG, (Charles William), 1901-

14122   *Plague over London.* Hutchinson, London, 1939,
        256p, Cloth, Novel

THURSTAN, FREDERIC

14123   *The romances of Amosis Ra: I. The coming of
        Amosis Ra; II. The testing of Amosis Ra.*
        Francis Griffiths, London, 1914, 388p,
        Cloth, Coll.

THURSTON, EMILY (Frances) TEMPLE

14124   *The wandering Jew.* Putnam, London, 1934,
        396p, Cloth, Novel [adapted from the play
        of the same name by Temple Thurston]

THURSTON, (Ernest) TEMPLE, 1879-1933

14125   *Man in a black hat.* Cassell, London, 1930,
        312p, Cloth, Novel
14126   *The Rosicrucian.* G. P. Putnam's Sons, London,
        1930, 284p, Cloth, Coll.

TIGER GIRL

14127   *Tiger girl.* Utopian Publications, London,
        1945, 36p, Paper, Anth.

TILLYARD, AELFRIDA (Catherine Wetenhall)

14128   *The approaching storm.* Hutchinson, London,
        1932, 287p, Cloth, Novel
14129   *Concrete; a story of two hundred years hence.*
        Hutchinson, London, 1930, 288p, Cloth, Novel

TIME, MARK, pseud. [H. C. Irwin]

14130   *A derelict empire.* William Blackwood & Sons,
        Edinburgh, 1912, 303p, Cloth, Novel

THE TIME OF TERROR
    see: FORD, D. M.

TIME UNTAMED

14131   *Time untamed.* Belmont, New York, 1967, 175p,
        Paper, Anth.

TIMLETT, PETER VALENTINE, 1933-

14132   *The seedbearers.* Quartet, London, 1974,
        247p, Cloth, Novel

TIMLIN, WILLIAM M.

14133   *The ship that sailed to Mars; a fantasy.*
        George G. Harrap, London, 1923, 96p, Cloth,
        Novel

TIMMERMANS, FELIX (Leopoldus Maximilianus
Maria), 1886-1947

14134   *The triptych of the three kings.* McFarlane,
        Warde, McFarlane, New York, 1936, 39p, Cloth,
        Story

TIMMS, E(dward) V(ivian), 1895-1960

14135   *The cities under the sea.* Angus & Robertson,
        Sydney, 1948, 242p, Cloth, Novel

TIMMS, GRAEME DE
    see: DE TIMMS, GRAEME

TIMPERLEY, ROSEMARY (Kenyon), 1920-   [*biography included*]

        Child in the dark. [see 14138A]
14136   *The eighth ghost book.* Barrie & Jenkins, Lon-
        don, 1972, 268p, Cloth, Anth.
14137   *The fifth ghost book.* Barrie & Rockliff, The
        Cresset Press, London, 1969, 256p, Cloth,
        Anth.
14138   *The listening child; three short novels.* James
        Barrie, London, 1956, 256p, Cloth, Coll.
14138A retitled: *Child in the dark; three novelettes.*
        Thomas Y. Crowell, New York, 1956, 256p,
        Cloth, Coll.
14139   *The long black dress.* Robert Hale, London,
        1972, 192p, Cloth, Novel
14140   *The ninth ghost book.* Barrie & Jenkins, London
        1973, 284p, Cloth, Anth.
14141   *The seventh ghost book.* Barrie & Jenkins, Lon-
        don, 1971, 303p, Cloth, Anth.
14142   *The sixth ghost book.* Barrie & Jenkins, Lon-
        don, 1970, 320p, Cloth, Anth.
14142A retitled: *The sixth ghost book, book one;
        The blood goes round, and other stories.*
        Pan, London, 1972, 128p, Paper, Anth. [ab-
        ridged]
14142B retitled: *The sixth ghost book, book two;
        The Judas joke, and other stories.* Pan,
        London, 1972, 148p, Paper, Anth. [abridged;
        14142A and 14142B together comprise the
        original volume]

TINCKER, MARY AGNES, 1831-1907

14143   *San Salvador.* Houghton Mifflin, Boston, 1892,
        335p, Cloth, Novel

TINSEAU, LÉON de, Comte, 1844-1921

14144   *Duc Rollon.* Harper & Bros., New York, 1913,
        302p, Cloth, Novel

TINY ALICE, pseud.
    see: RAMIREZ, ALICE

TIPHAIGNE de la ROCHE, C(harles) F(rançois), 1729-1774 [published anonymously]

14145 *Giphantia; or, A view of what has passed, what is now passing, and, during the present century, what will pass in the world.* R. Horsfield, London, 1760/61, 2vol, Cloth, Novel [volume II was issued first]

TIPTREE, JAMES Jr., pseud. [Alice Hastings Sheldon, 1915-] [*biography included*]

14146 *Ten thousand light-years from home.* Ace, New York, 1973, 319p, Paper, Coll.

TITAN, EARL, pseud.
see: FEARN, JOHN RUSSELL

TITTERTON, W(illiam) R(ichard)

14147 *The death ray dictator, and other stories.* Douglas Organ, London, 1946, 127p, Paper, Coll.

TO JUPITER VIA HELL

14148 *To Jupiter via Hell.* Juno Society, New York, 1908, 318p, Cloth, Novel

TO THE LAND OF FAIR DELIGHT

14149 *To the land of fair delight; three Victorian tales of the imagination.* Franklin Watts, New York, 1960, 583p, Cloth, Anth.

TOBIER, ARTHUR

14150 *How McGovern won the presidency, & why the polls were wrong.* Outerbridge & Lazard/ Ballantine, New York, 1972, 96p, Paper, Novel

TODD, RUTHVEN, 1914-

14151 *The lost traveller.* Grey Walls Press, London, 1943, 160p, Cloth, Novel
14152 *Over the mountain.* George G. Harrap, London, 1939, 280p, Cloth, Novel
14153 *Space cat.* Charles Scribner's Sons, New York, 1952, 69p, Cloth, Novel [Space Cat #1]
14154 *Space cat and the kittens.* Charles Scribner's Sons, New York, 1958, 94p, Cloth, Novel [Space Cat #4]
14155 *Space cat meets Mars.* Charles Scribner's Sons, New York, 1957, 72p, Cloth, Novel [Space Cat #3]
14156 *Space cat visits Venus.* Charles Scribner's Sons, New York, 1955, 87p, Cloth, Novel [Space Cat #2]

TODD, W.

14157 *The City Moated and Walled.* Hodder & Stoughton, London, 1930, 319p, Cloth, Novel

TODOROV, TZVETAN

14158 *The fantastic; a structural approach to a literary genre.* Press of Case Western Reserve University, Cleveland, OH, 1973, 179p, Cloth, Nonf.

THE TOKEN

14159 *The token; a gift for all seasons.* D. Appleton, New York, 1856, 288p, Cloth, Anth.

TOKSVIG, SIGNE (Kirstine), 1891-

14160 *The last devil.* John Day Co., New York, 1927, 306p, Cloth, Novel; Faber & Gwyer, London, 1927, 316p, Cloth, Novel

TOLKIEN, J(ohn) R(onald) R(euel), 1892-1973 [*biography included*]

14161 *Farmer Giles of Ham; Aegidii Ahenobarbi Julii Agricole de Hammo, Domini de Domito, Aule Comitis, Regni Minimi Regis et mirabilis exortus; or, in the vulgar tongue, The rise and wonderful adventures of Farmer Giles, Lord of Tame, Count of Worminghall, and King of the Little Kingdom.* George Allen & Unwin, London, 1949, 79p, Cloth, Novel
14162 *The Fellowship of the Ring.* George Allen & Unwin, London, 1954, 423p, Cloth, Novel [Lord of the Rings #1]
14163 *The hobbit; or, There and back again.* George Allen & Unwin, London, 1937, 310p, Cloth, Novel [a prequel to *The Lord of the Rings*]
14164 *The Lord of the Rings.* George Allen & Unwin, London, 1968, 1077p, Paper, Novel [Lord of the Rings #s 1-3]
14165 *The return of the King.* George Allen & Unwin, London, 1955, 416p, Cloth, Novel [Lord of the Rings #3]
14166 *The road goes ever on; a song cycle.* George Allen & Unwin, London, 1967, 62p, Cloth, Nonf. [includes some verse; music by Donald Swann]
14167 *Smith of Wootton Major.* George Allen & Unwin, London, 1967, 62p, Cloth, Novel
14168 *Smith of Wootton Major; and, Farmer Giles of Ham.* Ballantine, New York, 1970, 156p, Paper, Coll.
14169 *The Tolkien reader.* Ballantine, New York, 1966, 288p, Paper, Coll.
14170 *Tree and leaf.* George Allen & Unwin, London, 1964, 92p, Paper, Coll. [includes some nonf.]
14171 *The two towers.* George Allen & Unwin, London, 1954, 352p, Cloth, Novel [Lord of the Rings #2]

THE TOLKIEN PAPERS

14172 *The Tolkien papers; Mankato studies in English, no. 2.* Mankato State College, Mankato, Minn., 1967, 100p, Paper, Nonf. Anth.

TOLSTOI, ALEKSEI (Konstantinovich), 1817-1875

14173 *Vampires; stories of the supernatural.* Hawthorn, New York, 1969, 183p, Cloth, Coll.

TOLSTOI, ALEKSEI (Nikolaevich), Graf, 1882-
1945

14174 *Aelita*. Foreign Languages Publishing House,
         Moscow, 1957, 275p, Cloth, Novel
14175 *The death box*. Methuen, London, 1936, 375p,
         Cloth, Novel
14175A retitled: *The Garin death ray*. Foreign Lan-
         guages Publishing House, Moscow, 1955, 342p,
         Cloth, Novel

TOLSTOY, ALEXIS
    see: TOLSTOI, ALEKSEI

TOMBLESON, J(ames) B(ennett)

14176 *Under the label*. John Heritage, London, 1934,
         288p, Cloth, Novel

TOMLINSON, DOROTHY

14177 *Walk in dread; twelve classic eerie tales*.
         Taplinger Publishing Co., New York, 1972,
         287p, Cloth, Anth.

TOMPKINS, WALKER A(llison), 1909-   [biogra-
phy included]

14178 *Ozar, the Aztec*. Gramol Publications, London,
         1935, 128p, Paper, Novel

TONKS, ANGELA

14179 *Mind out of time; a novel*. Victor Gollancz,
         London, 1958, 240p, Cloth, Novel

TOOKER, RICHARD, 1902-

14180 *The dawn boy*. Penn Publishing Co., Philadel-
         phia, 1932, 284p, Cloth, Novel
14181 *The day of the brown horde*. Payson & Clarke,
         New York, 1929, 309p, Cloth, Novel
14182 *Inland deep*. Penn Publishing Co., Philadel-
         phia, 1936, 267p, Cloth, Novel

TOOMBS, ALFRED (Gerald), 1912-

14183 *Good as gold*. Thomas Y. Crowell, New York,
         1955, 281p, Cloth, Novel

TOOMEY, ROBERT E(mmett), Jr., 1945-   [bio-
graphy included]

14184 *A world of trouble*. Ballantine, New York,
         1973, 209p, Paper, Novel

TORDAY, URSULA
    see: BLACKSTOCK, CHARITY

TORGE, MIGUEL, pseud. [Adolfo Rocha, 1907-   ]

14185 *Farrusco the blackbird, and other stories
         from the Portuguese*. George Allen & Unwin,
         London, 1950, 93p, Cloth, Coll.

TORRO, PEL, pseud.
    see: FANTHORPE, R. LIONEL

TOURGEE, ALBION
    see: HENRY, EDGAR

TOURNEUR, NIGEL

14186 *Hidden witchery*. Leonard Smithers, London,
         1898, 244p, Cloth, Coll.

TOURRETTE, JACQUELINE LA
    see: LA TOURRETTE, JACQUELINE

TOWER, WASHINGTON L.

14187 *Interior world; a romance illustrating a new
         hypothesis of terrestrial organization*.
         Milton H. Tower, Publisher, Oakland, CA,
         1885,   , Cloth, Novel [includes some nonf.

TOWNE, ANTHONY, 1928-   [biography included]

14188 *Excerpts from the diary of the late God*. Har-
         per & Row, New York, 1968, 108p, Paper,
         Novel

TOWNSEND, ALEXANDER

14189 *The wooden woman*. Doubleday, Doran, Garden
         City, 1930, 320p, Cloth, Novel; William Heine-
         mann, London, 1930, 335p, Cloth, Novel

TOWNSEND, JOHN (Howard)

14190 *A warning to Earth*. Chatto & Windus, London,
         1960, 186p, Cloth, Novel

TOWNSEND, LARRY

14191 *Beware the god who smiles*. Pleasure Reader,
         San Diego, 1971, 159p, Paper, Novel
14192 *Jovencachoteca*. Pleasure Reader, San Diego,
         1970, 158p, Paper, Novel
14193 *The Scorpius equation*. Other Traveller, New
         York, 1971, 247p, Paper, Novel
14194 *2069*. Pleasure Reader, San Diego, 1969, 206p,
         Paper, Novel [2069 #1]
14195 *2069+1*. Pleasure Reader, San Diego, 1970, 173p
         Paper, Novel [2069 #2]
14196 *2069+2*. Pleasure Reader, San Diego, 1970, 158p
         Paper, Novel [2069 #3]

TOXAR
    see: NICHOLSON, JOSEPH SHIELD

TOYNBEE, POLLY (Mary Louisa), 1946-   [biogra-
phy included]

14197 *Leftovers; a novel*. Weidenfeld & Nicolson,
         London, 1966, 189p, Cloth, Novel

TRACY, DON(ald Fiske), 1905- [biography included]

14198 *The black amulet.* Pocket Books, New York, 1968, 188p, Paper, Novel

as Roger Fuller:

14199 *Son of Flubber.* Permabooks, New York, 1963, 135p, Paper, Movie

TRACY, LOUIS, 1863-1928

14200 *An American emperor; the story of the Fourth Empire of France.* C. Arthur Pearson, London, 1897, 336p, Cloth, Novel [Vansittart #1]

14201 *The final war; a story of the great betrayal.* C. Arthur Pearson, London, 1896, 372p, Cloth, Novel

14202 *The invaders; a story of Britain's peril.* C. Arthur Pearson, London, 1901, 428p, Cloth, Novel

14203 *Karl Grier; the strange story of a man with a sixth sense.* Hodder & Stoughton, London, 1906, 277p, Cloth, Novel

14203A retitled: *The man with the sixth sense.* Odhams Press, London, 1921, 80p, Cloth, Novel

14204 *The lost provinces; a sequel to "An American Emperor."* C. Arthur Pearson, London, 1898, 380p, Cloth, Novel [Vansittart #2]

TRACY, ROGER S.
    see: HODGE, T. SHIRBY

TRACY, THOMAS, 1781-1872 [published anonymously]

14205 *Miniature romances from the German, with other prolusions of light literature.* C. C. Little & J. Brown, Boston, 1841, 324p, Cloth, Anth.

THE TRADITIONS
    see: SHERWOOD, MARY

TRAILL, H(enry) D(uff), 1842-1900

14206 *The barbarous Britishers; a tip-top novel.* John Lane, The Bodley Head, London, 1896, 95p, Paper, Novel [a parody of Grant Allen's *The British barbarians*]

14207 *The new Lucian, being a series of dialogues of the dead.* Chapman & Hall, London, 1884, 312p, Cloth, Coll.

14208 *Number twenty; fables and fantasies.* Henry & Co., London, 1892, 207p, Cloth, Coll.

TRAIN, ARTHUR (Chesney), 1875-1945

14209 *Mortmain.* D. Appleton, New York, 1907, 314p, Cloth, Coll.

with Robert Williams Wood:

14210 *The man who rocked the Earth.* Doubleday, Page, Garden City, 1915, 228p, Cloth, Novel [Benjamin Hooker #1]

14211 *The Moon maker.* Krueger, Hamburg, NY, 1958, 84p, Cloth, Novel [Benjamin Hooker #2]

TRALINS, (Sandor) ROBERT, 1926- [biography included]

14212 *Android armageddon.* Pinnacle, New York, 1974, 180p, Paper, Novel

14213 *The Cosmozoids.* Belmont, New York, 1966, 143p, Paper, Novel

14214 *Ghoul lover.* Popular Library, New York, 1972, 208p, Paper, Novel

as Keith Miles:

14215 *Dragon's teeth.* Popular Library, New York, 1973, 207p, Paper, Novel

as Sean O'Shea:

14216 *The nymph island affair.* Belmont, New York, 1967, 141p, Paper, Novel [Valentine Flynn #4]

14217 *Operation Boudoir.* Belmont, New York, 1967, 157p, Paper, Novel [Valentine Flynn #2]

14218 *What a way to go! a Valentine Flynn adventure.* Belmont, New York, 1966, 156p, Paper, Novel [Valentine Flynn #1]

THE TRANSFIGURATION OF THE MANDARIN FUM-HOAM
    see: GUEULLETTE, THOMAS SIMON

TRANSIT OF EARTH
    see: RUSSELL, RAY

THE TRANSPOSED MAN

14219 *The transposed man.* Panther, London, 1957, 143p, Paper, Anth. [includes "The Transposed Man," by Dwight V. Swain and "The Predators" by E. C. Tubb]

TRANSUE, JACOB, pseud. [Joan Matheson, 1924-] [biography included]

14220 *Twilight of the basilisks.* Berkley Medallion, New York, 1973, 175p, Paper, Novel

TRASK, MARGARET

14221 *Fantasy, science fiction, science materials; papers presented at the course offered by the School of Librarianship through the Division of Postgraduate Extension Studies, University of New South Wales, 16th-19th May, 1972.* University of New South Wales School of Librarianship, Kensington, Aust., 1972, 204p, Paper?, Nonf. Anth.

TRAVELS BY SEA AND LAND OF ALETHITHERAS
    see: OSBORN, LAUGHTON

THE TRAVELS OF MR. JOHN GULLIVER
    see: DESFONTAINES, PIERRE

TRAVEN, B., pseud. [Traven Torsvan, 1890?-1969]

14222 *The bridge in the jungle.* Alfred A. Knopf, New York, 1938, 286p, Cloth, Novel

TRAVERS, P(amela) L(yndon), 1906-

14223 *Mary Poppins.* Gerald Howe, London, 1934, 206p, Cloth, Novel [Mary Poppins #1]
14224 *Mary Poppins; and, Mary Poppins comes back.* Reynal & Hitchcock, New York, 1937, 349p, Cloth, Coll. [Mary Poppins #s 1-2]
14224A retitled: *Mary Poppins.* Peter Davies, London, 1940, 503p, Cloth, Coll. [Mary Poppins #s 1-2]
14225 *Mary Poppins comes back.* L. Dickson & Thompson, London, 1935, 303p, Cloth, Novel [Mary Poppins #2]
14226 *Mary Poppins in the park.* Peter Davies, London, 1952, 212p, Cloth, Coll. [Mary Poppins #4]
14227 *Mary Poppins opens the door.* Reynal & Hitchcock, New York, 1943, 239p, Cloth, Novel [Mary Poppins #3]

TRAVERS, PETER, with Stephanie Reiff

12131 *The story behind The exorcist.* Crown Publishers, New York, 1974, 245p, Cloth, Nonf.

TRAVERS, S.
see: RADCLIFFE, GARNETT

TREECE, HENRY, 1911-1966 [biography included]

14228 *The dream-time.* Brockhampton Press, London, 1967, 96p, Cloth, Novel
14229 *The golden strangers.* The Bodley Head, London, 1956, 224p, Cloth, Novel
14230 *Men of the hills.* The Bodley Head, London, 1957, 170p, Cloth, Novel

TREGARRON, YATE, pseud.

14231 *Murderers' island.* Methuen, London, 1925, 250p, Cloth, Novel

TREHUNE, MORGAN

14232 *Erotica Satanica.* Cameo Editions, New York, 1970, 262p, Paper, Novel [cover byline reads Morgana Trehune]

TREIBICH, S(tephen) J(ohn), 1936-1972 [biography included], with Laurence M. Janifer

07846 *The high hex.* Ace Double, New York, 1969, 112p, Paper, Novel [Angelo DiStefano #2]
07847 *Target: Terra.* Ace Double, New York, 1968, 104p, Paper, Novel [Angelo DiStefano #1]
07848 *The wagered world.* Ace Double, New York, 1969, 79p, Paper, Novel [Angelo DiStefano #3]

TRELL, MAX, 1900- [biography included]

14233 *The small gods & Mr. Barnum.* McCall Publishing Co., New York, 1971, 230p, Cloth, Novel

TREVARTHEN, HAL P. [Harold Philip Trevarthen]

14234 *World D, being a brief account of the founding of Helioxenon.* Sheed & Ward, New York, 1935, 320p, Cloth, Novel

TREVELYAN, G(ertrude) E(ileen)

14235 *Appius and Virginia.* Martin Secker, London, 1932, 291p, Cloth, Novel
14236 *Trance by appointment.* George G. Harrap, London, 1939, 268p, Cloth, Novel

TREVENA, JOHN
see: HENHAM, ERNEST GEORGE

TREVIÑO, ELIZABETH BORTON de, 1904- [biography included]

14237 *Beyond the Gates of Hercules; a tale of the lost Atlantis.* Victor Gollancz, London, 1971, 247p, Cloth, Novel; Farrar, Straus & Giroux, New York, 1971, 246p, Cloth, Novel

TREVOR, ELLESTON, pseud. [Trevor Dudley-Smith, 1920-] [biography included]

14238 *The immortal error.* Gerald G. Swan, London, 1946, 189p, Cloth, Novel
14239 *The mind of Max Duvine.* Gerald G. Swan, London, 1960, 252p, Cloth, Novel

TREVOR, (Lucy) MERIOL, 1919- [biography included]

14240 *Hunt the king, hide the fox.* Faber & Faber, London, 1950, 228p, Cloth, Novel
14241 *The other side of the Moon.* Collins, London, 1956, 192p, Cloth, Novel

TREW, ANTONY (Francis), 1906- [biography included]

14242 *Two hours to darkness.* no publisher, South Africa?, 1962, 312p, Cloth, Novel

THE TRIAL OF MAN
see: LAWRENCE, C. E.

TRIMBLE, BJO, with Dorothy Jones

07979 *The third season supplement to the Star trek concordance.* Mathom House Publishers, Los Angeles, 1973, 70p, Paper, Nonf.

TRIMBLE, JACQUELYN, 1927- [biography included], with Louis Trimble

14243 *Guardians of the Gate.* Ace, New York, 1972, 157p, Paper, Novel

TRIMBLE, LOUIS (Preston), 1917-   [*biography included*]

14244 *Anthropol.* Ace Double, New York, 1968, 136p, Paper, Novel [Anthropol #1]
14245 *The Bodelan way.* DAW, New York, 1974, 158p, Paper, Novel
14246 *The City machine.* DAW, New York, 1972, 143p, Paper, Novel
14247 *The noblest experiment in the galaxy.* Ace Double, New York, 1970, 143p, Paper, Novel [Anthropol #2]
14248 *The wandering variables.* DAW, New York, 1972, 158p, Paper, Novel

with Jacquelyn Trimble:

14243 *Guardians of the Gate.* Ace, New York, 1972, 157p, Paper, Novel

TRIPLET, WILLIAM SAMUEL
     see: BULL, TERRY

THE TRIUNEVERSE
     see: KENNEDY, R. A.

TROLLOPE, ANTHONY, 1815-1882

14249 *The Fixed Period; a novel.* William Blackwood & Sons, Edinburgh, 1882, vol. I-200p, II-203p, Cloth, Novel

TROLLOPE, FRANCES ELEANOR, d. 1913

14250 *Black spirits and white; a novel.* Richard Bentley & Son, London, 1877, 3vol, Cloth, Novel

TROUBETZKOY, Princess PAUL [Mariia Trubetskaia], with C. R. W. Nevinson

10638 *Exodus A.D.; a warning to civilians.* Hutchinson, London, 1934, 288p, Cloth, Novel

TROUT, LAWANA, with Michael C. Flanigan

05464 *Unknown worlds.* Holt, Rinehart & Winston, New York, 1969, 157p, Paper, Anth.

TROWBRIDGE, JOHN, 1843-1923

14251 *The electrical boy; or, The career of Greatman and Greatthings.* Roberts Bros., Boston, 1891, 390p, Cloth, Novel

TRUE, JOHN PRESTON, 1859-1933

14252 *The iron star, and what it saw on its journey through the ages, from myth to history.* Little, Brown, Boston, 1899, 146p, Cloth, Novel

TRUEMAN, T.
     see: PALTOCK, ROBERT

TRUMAN, OLIVIA M.

14253 *The spirit juggler.* F. V. White, London, 1907, 315p, Cloth, Novel

TRUMBO, DALTON, 1905-1976 [*biography included*]

14254 *The remarkable Andrew, being the chronicle of a literal man.* J. B. Lippincott, Philadelphia, 1941, 350p, Cloth, Novel

TRYON, THOMAS, 1926-   [*biography included*]

14255 *The Other.* Alfred A. Knopf, New York, 1971, 280p, Cloth, Novel

TSIOLKOVSKII, KONSTANTIN (Eduardovich), 1857-1935

14256 *Beyond the planet Earth.* Pergamon Press, Oxford, 1960, 190p, Cloth, Novel
14257 *The call of the cosmos.* Foreign Languages Publishing House, Moscow, 1961, 472p, Cloth, Coll. [includes some nonf.]

TSIOLKOVSKY, KONSTANTIN
     see: TSIOLKOVSKII, KONSTANTIN

TUBB, E(dwin) C(harles), 1919-   [*biography included*]

14258 *Alien dust.* T. V. Boardman, London, 1955, 224p, Cloth, Novel
14259 *Alien life.* Paladin Press, London, 1954, 128p, Paper, Novel
14260 *Atom-war on Mars.* Panther, London, 1952, 112p, Paper, Novel
14261 *C.O.D. Mars.* Ace Double, New York, 1968, 99p, Paper, Novel
14262 *Century of the manikin.* DAW, New York, 1972, 142p, Paper, Novel
14263 *City of no return.* Scion, London, 1954, 144p, Paper, Novel
14264 *Death is a dream.* Rupert Hart-Davis, London, 1967, 170p, Cloth, Novel
14265 *Derai.* Ace Double, New York, 1968, 121p, Paper, Novel [Dumarest #2]
14266 *Escape into space; science fiction.* Sidgwick & Jackson, London, 1969, 188p, Cloth, Novel
       Gath. [see 14287A]
14267 *The hell planet.* Scion, London, 1954, 144p, Paper, Novel
14268 *The jester at Scar.* Ace Double, New York, 1970, 126p, Paper, Novel [Dumarest #5]
14269 *Jondelle.* DAW, New York, 1973, 159p, Paper, Novel [Dumarest #10]
14270 *Journey to Mars.* Scion, London, 1954, 144p, Paper, Novel
14271 *Kalin.* Ace Double, New York, 1969, 131p, Paper, Novel [Dumarest #4]
14272 *Lallia.* Ace Double, New York, 1971, 116p, Paper, Novel [Dumarest #6]
14273 *Mayenne.* DAW, New York, 1973, 159p, Paper, Novel [Dumarest #8]
       The mechanical monarch. [see 14191A]
14274 *Moon base.* Herbert Jenkins, London, 1964, 175p, Cloth, Novel

TUBB, E. C. (cont.)

14275 *The mutants rebel.* Panther, London, 1953, 144p, Paper, Novel

14276 *The resurrected man.* Dragon, London, 1954, 120p, Paper, Novel

14277 *S.T.A.R. flight.* Paperback Library, New York, 1969, 144p, Paper, Novel

14278 *A scatter of stardust.* Ace Double, New York, 1972, 119p, Paper, Coll.

14279 *The space-born.* Ace Double, New York, 1956, 158p, Paper, Novel

14280 *The Stellar Legion.* Scion, London, 1954, 144p, Paper, Novel

14281 *Sword in the snow.* Fantasy Booklet, Wallsend, UK, 1973, 12p, Paper, Story

14282 *Technos.* Ace Double, New York, 1972, 136p, Paper, Novel [Dumarest #7]

14283 *Ten from tomorrow.* Rupert Hart-Davis, London, 1966, 187p, Cloth, Coll.

14284 *Toyman.* Ace Double, New York, 1969, 124p, Paper, Novel [Dumarest #3]

14285 *Venusian adventure.* Comyns (Publishers), London, 1953, 128p, Paper, Novel

14286 *Veruchia.* Ace, New York, 1973, 190p, Paper, Novel [Dumarest #9]

14287 *The winds of Gath.* Ace Double, New York, 1967, 126p, Paper, Novel [Dumarest #1]

14287A retitled: *Gath.* Rupert Hart-Davis, London, 1968, 143p, Cloth, Novel [Dumarest #1]

14288 *World at bay.* Panther, London, 1954, 159p, Cloth, Novel

14289 *Zenya.* DAW, New York, 1974, 157p, Paper, Novel [Dumarest #11]

as Charles Grey:

14290 *Dynasty of doom.* Milestone, London, 1953, 126p, Paper, Novel

14291 *Enterprise 2115.* Merit, London, 1954, 160p, Cloth, Novel

14291A retitled: *The mechanical monarch*, by E. C. Tubb. Ace Double, New York, 1958, 167p, Paper, Novel

14292 *The extra man.* Milestone, London, 1954, 128p, Paper, Novel

14293 *The hand of havoc.* Merit, London, 1954, 128p, Paper, Novel

14294 *I fight for Mars.* Milestone, London, 1953, 128p, Paper, Novel

14295 *Space hunger.* Milestone, London, 1953, 128p, Paper, Novel

14296 *The tormented city.* Milestone, London, 1953, 126p, Paper, Novel

14297 *The Wall.* Milestone, London, 1953, 128p, Paper, Novel

as Volsted Gridban, house pseud.:

06353 *Alien universe.* Scion, London, 1952, 96p, Paper, Novel

06354 *De Bracy's drug.* Scion, London, 1953, 127p, Paper, Novel

06355 *Fugitive of time.* Milestone, London, 1953, 112p, Paper, Novel

06356 *Planetoid Disposals Ltd.* Milestone, London, 1953, 112p, Paper, Novel

06357 *Reverse universe.* Scion, London, 1952, 128p, Paper, Novel

as Gill Hunt, house pseud.:

07609 *Planetfall.* Curtis Warren, London, 1951, 111p, Paper, Novel

as Gregory Kern:

14298 *Earth enslaved; a "Cap Kennedy" novel.* DAW, New York, 1974, 128p, Paper, Novel [Cap Kennedy #9]

14299 *The eater of worlds; a "Cap Kennedy" novel.* DAW, New York, 1974, 126p, Paper, Novel [Cap Kennedy #8]

14300 *Enemy within the skull; a "Cap Kennedy" novel.* DAW, New York, 1974, 127p, Paper, Novel [Cap Kennedy #4]

14301 *Galaxy of the lost; a "Cap Kennedy" novel.* DAW, New York, 1973, 125p, Paper, Novel [Cap Kennedy #1]

14302 *The genetic buccaneer; a "Cap Kennedy" novel.* DAW, New York, 1974, 125p, Paper, Novel [Cap Kennedy #12]

14303 *The Gholan Gate; a "Cap Kennedy" novel.* DAW, New York, 1974, 124p, Paper, Novel [Cap Kennedy #7]

14304 *Jewel of Jarhen; a "Cap Kennedy" novel.* DAW, New York, 1974, 143p, Paper, Novel [Cap Kennedy #5]

14305 *Monster of Metelaze; a "Cap Kennedy" novel.* DAW, New York, 1973, 125p, Paper, Novel [Cap Kennedy #3]

14306 *Planet of dread; a "Cap Kennedy" novel.* DAW, New York, 1974, 126p, Paper, Novel [Cap Kennedy #10]

14307 *Seetee alert! a "Cap Kennedy" novel.* DAW, New York, 1974, 126p, Paper, Novel [Cap Kennedy #6]

14308 *Slave ship from Sergan; a "Cap Kennedy" novel.* DAW, New York, 1973, 127p, Paper, Novel [Cap Kennedy #2]

14309 *Spawn of Laban; a "Cap Kennedy" novel.* DAW, New York, 1974, 127p, Paper, Novel [Cap Kennedy #11]

14310 *A world aflame.* DAW, New York, 1974, 128p, Paper, Novel [Cap Kennedy #13]

as King Lang, house pseud.:

08600 *Saturn Patrol.* Curtis Warren, London, 1951, 111p, Paper, Novel

as Carl Maddox:

14311 *The living world.* Tit-Bits Science Fiction Library, London, 1954, 64p, Paper, Novel

14312 *Menace from the past.* Tit-Bits Science Fiction Library, London, 1954, 64p, Paper, Novel

as Brian Shaw, house pseud.:

06403 *"Argentis."* Curtis Warren, London, 1952, 112p, Paper, Novel [copyrighted by David Griffiths, but actually written by Tubb]

as Roy Sheldon, house pseud.:

12999 *The metal eater.* Panther, London, 1954, 159p, Cloth, Novel

TUCK, DONALD H(enry), 1922-   [*biography included*]

14313 *The encyclopedia of science fiction and fantasy through 1968; a bibliographic survey of the fields of science fiction, fantasy, and weird fiction through 1968; volume 1, Who's who, A-L.* Advent: Publishers, Chicago, 1974, 286p, Cloth, Nonf. [the third edition of 14314]

14314 *A handbook of science fiction and fantasy.* Donald H. Tuck, Hobart, Tasmania, 1954, 151p, Paper, Nonf.

TUCK, DONALD H. (cont.)

14315 *A handbook of science fiction and fantasy;
a collection of material acting as a bibliographic survey to the fields of science fiction and fantasy (including weird), covering
the magazines, books, pocket books, person-
alities, etc., of these fields up to December, 1957; second edition, revised and enlarged.* Donald H. Tuck, Hobart, Tasmania,
1959, 2vol, Paper, Nonf.

TUCKER, ALLAN JAMES
 see: CRAIG, DAVID

TUCKER, (Nathaniel) BEVERLY, 1784-1851

as Edward William Sidney:

14316 *The partisan leader; a tale of the future.*
James Caxton, Washington, 1856 [actually
published by D. Green, Washington, 1836],
vol. I-195p, II-196p, Cloth, Novel
14316A *The partisan leader; a tale of the future,*
by Beverly Tucker. Rudd & Carleton, New
York, 1861, 392p, Cloth, Novel

TUCKER, GEORGE
 see: ATTERLEY, JOSEPH

TUCKER, JAMES B(enjamin)

14317 *Not an earthly chance.* Robert Hale, London,
1970, 160p, Cloth, Novel

TUCKER, PRENTISS

14318 *In the land of the living dead; an occult
story.* Rosicrucian Fellowship, Oceanside,
CA, 1921, 168p, Cloth, Novel

TUCKER, (Arthur) WILSON, 1914-   [*biography
included*]

14319 *The Chinese doll.* Rinehart & Co., New York,
1946, 236p, Cloth, Novel [a mystery set
among SF fans]
14320 *The city in the sea.* Rinehart & Co., New
York, 1951, 250p, Cloth, Novel
14321 *Ice and iron.* Doubleday, Garden City, 1974,
181p, Cloth, Novel
14322 *The Lincoln hunters.* Rinehart & Co., New
York, 1958, 221p, Cloth, Novel
14323 *The long loud silence.* Rinehart & Co., New
York, 1952, 217p, Cloth, Novel
The man from tomorrow. [see 14329A]
14324 *The science-fiction subtreasury.* Rinehart &
Co., New York, 1954, 240p, Cloth, Coll.
14324A retitled: *Time: X.* Bantam, New York, 1955,
140p, Paper, Coll. [abridged]
14325 *This witch.* Crime Club, Doubleday, Garden
City, 1971, 179p, Cloth, Novel
14326 *Time bomb.* Rinehart & Co., New York, 1955,
246p, Cloth, Novel [Gilbert Nash #2]
14326A retitled: *Tomorrow plus X.* Avon, New York,
1957, 158p, Paper, Novel [Gilbert Nash #2]
Time: X. [see 14324A]

14327 *The time masters.* Rinehart & Co., New York,
1953, 249p, Cloth, Novel [Gilbert Nash #1]
14328 *To the Tombaugh Station.* Ace Double, New York,
1960, 145p, Paper, Novel
Tomorrow plus X. [see 14326A]
14329 *Wild talent.* Rinehart & Co., New York, 1954,
250p, Cloth, Novel
14329A retitled: *The man from tomorrow.* Bantam, New
York, 1955, 148p, Paper, Novel
14330 *The year of the quiet sun.* Ace, New York,
1970, 252p, Paper, Novel

TUCKWELL, Rev. W(illiam), 1829-1919

14331 *The new utopia; or, England in 1985; a lecture.*
Birmingham Sunday Lecture Society, Birmingham, 1885, 16p, Paper, Story

TÜGEL, LUDWIG (Carl), 1889-

14332 *The visitant.* Martin Secker, London, 1931,
351p, Cloth, Novel

TUNG, LANG-
 see: LANG-TUNG

TUNG, LEE
 see: LEE TUNG

THE TUNNEL, AND OTHER STORIES
 see: ELWOOD, ROGER

TUNSTALL, (William Cuthbert) BRIAN, 1900-1970

14333 *Eagles restrained.* George Allen & Unwin, London, 1936, 320p, Cloth, Novel

TURENNE, RAYMOND AUZIAS-
 see: AUZIAS-TURENNE, RAYMOND

TURGENEV, IVAN (Sergeevich), 1818-1883

14334 *Dream tales and prose poems.* William Heinemann, London, 1897, 323p, Cloth, Coll.

TURNER, C(harles) C(yril), 1870-1952

14335 *Dusk and dawn.* Hurst & Blackett, London,
1924, 286p, Cloth, Novel
14336 *The secret of the desert.* Hurst & Blackett,
London, 1923, 286p, Cloth, Novel
14337 *Unlawful.* Stanley Paul, London, 1927, 256p,
Cloth, Novel

TURNER, DAVID G.

14338 *The first editions of Andre Norton.* David G.
Turner--Bookman, Menlo Park, CA, 1974, 12p,
Paper, Nonf.

TURNER, EDGAR

14339   *The submarine girl.* Stanley Paul, London,
        1909, 336p, Cloth, Novel

TURNER, GEORGE KIBBE, 1869-1952

14340   *Red Friday.* Little, Brown, Boston, 1919,
        253p, Cloth, Novel

TURNER, GERRY

14341   *Stranger from the depths.* Doubleday, Garden
        City, 1967, 205p, Cloth, Novel

TURNER, JAMES (Ernest), 1909-

14342   *The fourth ghost book.* Barrie & Rockliff,
        London, 1965, 303p, Cloth, Anth.
14343   *The unlikely ghosts; a collection of twelve
        ghost stories.* Cassell, London, 1967, 218p,
        Cloth, Anth.

TURNER, W(alter) J(ames), 1889-1946

14344   *The Duchess of Popocatapetl.* J. M. Dent &
        Sons, London, 1939, 316p, Cloth, Novel
        [Henry Airbubble #3]

TURNERELLI, (Edward) TRACY

14345   *A Russian princess; and, A Russian ghost sto-
        ry; two historical and personal narratives
        depictive of Russian aristocratic society
        at the close of the last, and at the com-
        mencement and middle, of the present century.*
        Hansom Cab Publishing Co., London, 1888,
        190p, Paper, Coll.

TURNEY, CATHERINE, 1906-   [*biography included*]

14346   *The other one.* Henry Holt, New York, 1952,
        248p, Cloth, Novel
14346A retitled: *Possessed.* Paperback Library, New
        York, 1968, 206p, Paper, Novel

TURTON, GODFREY (Edmund), 1901-

14347   *The festival of Flora; a story of ancient and
        modern times.* Doubleday, Garden City, 1972,
        360p, Cloth, Novel
14348   *There was once a city.* Methuen, London, 1927,
        152p, Cloth, Novel

TUSIANI, JOSEPH, 1924-   [*biography included*]

14349   *Envoy from Heaven; a novel.* Ivan Obolensky,
        New York, 1965, 310p, Cloth, Novel

TUTTLE, HUDSON, 1836-1910

14350   *Life in two spheres; or, Scenes in the spirit-
        world.* Partridge & Brittan, New York, 1855,
        143p, Cloth, Novel

14350A retitled: *Scenes in the spirit world; or, Life
        in the spheres.* Partridge & Brittan, New
        York, 1855, 143p, Cloth, Novel [There appear
        to be two variations of this book, under re-
        versed titles; the true first edition has
        not been determined]
14350B retitled: *Life in the spheres; or, Scenes in
        the spirit world.* Carter Publishing Co.,
        Philadelphia, 1892, 242p, Cloth, Novel

TUTUOLA, AMOS, 1920-   [*biography included*]

14351   *Ajaiyi and his inherited poverty.* Faber &
        Faber, London, 1967, 235p, Cloth, Novel
14352   *The brave African huntress.* Faber & Faber,
        London, 1958, 150p, Cloth, Novel
14353   *Feather woman of the jungle.* Faber & Faber,
        London, 1962, 132p, Cloth, Novel
14354   *My life in the bush of ghosts.* Faber & Faber,
        London, 1954, 174p, Cloth, Novel
14355   *The palm-wine drinkard, and his dead palm-wine
        tapster in the Deads' Town.* Faber & Faber,
        London, 1952, 125p, Cloth, Novel
14356   *Simbi and the satyr of the dark jungle.* Faber
        & Faber, London, 1955, 136p, Cloth, Novel

TUYL, ZAARA VAN
   see: VAN TUYL, ZAARA

TWAIN, MARK, pseud. [Samuel Langhorne Clemens,
1835-1910]

14357   *A Connecticut Yankee in King Arthur's court.*
        C. L. Webster, New York, 1889, 575p, Cloth,
        Novel
14357A retitled: *A Yankee at the court of King Arthur.*
        Chatto & Windus, London, 1889, 525p, Cloth,
        Novel
14358   *Eve's diary.* Harper & Bros., New York, 1906,
        109p, Cloth, Novel
14359   *Extract from Captain Stormfield's visit to
        Heaven.* Harper & Bros., New York, 1909,
        121p, Cloth, Novel
14360   *Extracts from Adam's diary.* Harper & Bros.,
        New York, 1904, 89p, Cloth, Novel
14361   *The mysterious stranger; a romance.* Harper
        & Bros., New York, 1916, 151p, Cloth, Novel
14362   *The mysterious stranger, and other stories.*
        Harper & Bros., New York, 1922, 323p, Cloth,
        Coll.
14363   *The private life of Adam and Eve, being ex-
        tracts from their diaries, translated from
        the original mss.* Harper & Bros., New York,
        1931, 196p, Cloth, Coll. [includes 14358 and
        14360]
14364   *Report from Paradise.* Harper & Bros., New York,
        1952, 93p, Cloth, Coll. [includes 14359 and
        "Letter from the Recording Angel"]

TWEED, THOMAS F(rederic), 1890-1940

14365   *Blind mouths; a novel.* Arthur Barker, London,
        1934, 386p, Cloth, Novel
14366   *Rinehard; a melodrama of the nineteen-thirties.*
        Arthur Barker, London, 1933, 311p, Cloth,
        Novel
14366A retitled: *Gabriel over the White House; a novel
        of the presidency.* Farrar & Rinehart, New
        York, 1933, 306p, Cloth, Novel [published
        anonymously]

TWEED, THOMAS F. (cont.)

14366B retitled: *Gabriel over the White House*, by
Thomas F. Tweed. Cherry Tree, London, 1952,
190p, Paper, Novel

TWEEDALE, VIOLET (Chambers), d. 1936

14367 *The green lady.* Herbert Jenkins, London,
1920, 312p, Cloth, Novel
14368 *The house of the other world.* John Long, London, 1913, 320p, Cloth, Novel
14369 *An unholy alliance.* John Long, London, 1914,
320p, Cloth, Novel

TWEEDSMUIR, Baron
see: BUCHAN, JOHN

TWENTY-FIVE GREAT GHOST STORIES
see: HOLLAND, W. BOB

20 GREAT GHOST STORIES
see: HOLLAND, W. BOB

2010
see: CARREL, FREDERIC

TWIFORD, WILLIAM RICHARD

14370 *Sown in the darkness, A.D. 2000.* Orlin Tre-
maine Co., New York, 1941, 371p, Cloth,
Novel

TWIGGS, JAMES
see: JAMESON, TWIGGS

TWO STORIES OF THE SEEN AND UNSEEN
see: OLIPHANT, Mrs.

TWO TRAVELLERS
see: BEYOND THE SUNRISE

TWO WAGS, pseud.
see: BANGS, JOHN KENDRICK and SHERMAN,
FRANK DEMPSTER

TWO WOMEN OF THE WEST, pseud.
see: JONES, ALICE and MARCHANT, ELLA

TYLER, THEODORE, pseud. [Edward William Ziegler, 1932-   ] [*biography included*]

14371 *The man whose name wouldn't fit; or, The case
of Cartwright-Chickering.* Doubleday, Garden City, 1968, 262p, Cloth, Novel

TYMN, MARSHALL (Benton)

14372 *A directory of science fiction and fantasy
publishing houses and book dealers.* Marshall Tymn, Ypsilanti, Mich., 1974,
Paper, Nonf.

TYNER, PAUL

14373 *Through the invisible; a love story.* Continental Publishing Co., New York, 1897, 196p,
Cloth, Novel

TYRWHITT-WILSON, GERALD
see: BERNERS, Lord

TYSON, ESME WYNNE-
see: WYNNE-TYSON, ESME

TYSON, J(ohn) AUBREY, 1870-

14374 *The Barge of Haunted Lives.* Macmillan, New
York, 1923, 333p, Cloth, Novel
14375 *The Scarlet Tanager.* Macmillan, New York,
1922, 340p, Cloth, Novel

TYSSOT de PATOT, SIMON
see: BAYLE, Monsieur

UBERTUS, OLIVER
see: FERRAR, WILLIAM M.

UEDA AKINARI
see: UYEDA AKINARI

ULIDIA, pseud.

14376 *The Battle of Newry; or, The result of thirty
years' Liberal legislation.* Hodges, Figgis,
Dublin, 1883, 42p, Paper, Story

ULLMAN, JAMES RAMSEY, 1907-1971 [*biography included*]

14377 *The sands of Karakorum.* J. B. Lippincott, Philadelphia, 1953, 254p, Cloth, Novel

UNCANNY STORIES

14378 *Uncanny stories.* C. Arthur Pearson, London,
1916, 125p, Cloth, Anth.

UNDERHILL, EVELYN, 1875-1941

14379 *The grey world.* William Heinemann, London,
1904, 320p, Cloth, Novel
14379A retitled: *The gray world.* Century Co., New
York, 1904, 351p, Cloth, Novel
14380 *The lost word.* William Heinemann, London,
1907, 316p, Cloth, Novel

UNDERWOOD, LEON, 1890-

14381 *The Siamese cat.* Brentano's, New York, 1928,
269p, Cloth, Novel

UNDINE
see: LA MOTTE-FOUQUE, FRIEDRICH

THE UNFORTUNATE PRINCESS
    see: HAYWOOD, ELIZA

UNIACKE, T. I.

14382   *The living wheel; a drama in five acts.* Philip Wellby, London, 1903, 235p, Cloth, Novel [not a play]

AN UNKNOWN AUTHOR, pseud.
    see: LIPPARD, GEORGE

UNKNOWN AUTHOR, pseud.

14383   *Moaning Canyon; a novel.* Stratford Co., Boston, 1931, 403p, Cloth, Novel

AN UNLAID GHOST

14384   *An unlaid ghost; a study in metempsychosis.* D. Appleton, New York, 1888, 178p, Cloth, Novel

UNTERMEYER, LOUIS, 1885-1977 [*biography included*]

14385   *The donkey of God.* Lederer, Street & Zeus, Berkeley, CA, 1951, 31p, Cloth, Story

AN UNTRAMMELED FREE-THINKER, pseud.
    see: MOORE, M. LOUISE

UNTRUTHFUL THOMAS, pseud.

14386   *Bombardment of Scarbro' by the Russian fleet in 1891, and terrr-ific Battle of Scalby Beck, and other stories.* Crown Printing Co., London, 1889, 36p, Paper, Coll.

UNWIN, DAVID STORR
    see: SEVERN, DAVID

UPCHURCH, BOYD
    see: BOYD, JOHN

UPDIKE, JOHN (Hoyer), 1932-   [*biography included*]

14387   *The poorhouse fair.* Alfred A. Knopf, New York, 1959, 185p, Cloth, Novel

UPHAM, EDWARD, 1776-1834 [published anonymously]

14388   *Karmath; an Arabian tale,* by the author of "Rameses." Charles Frederick Cock, London, 1827, 341p, Cloth, Novel

UPTON, SMYTH

14389   *The last of the vampires; a tale.* J. Whereat, The Columbian Press, Weston-super-Mare, UK, 1845, 76p, Cloth, Novel

UPWARD, ALLEN, 1863-1926

14390   *The discovery of the dead.* A. C. Fifield, London, 1910, 190p, Cloth, Novel
14391   *Romance of politics; the fourth conquest of England; a sequel to "Treason."* Tyndale Press, London, 1904, 72p, Paper?, Novel
14392   *The yellow hand.* Digby, Long, London, 1904, 320p, Cloth, Novel

URANG, GUNNAR

14393   *Shadows of Heaven; religion and fantasy in the writing of C. S. Lewis, Charles Williams, and J. R. R. Tolkien.* Pilgrim Press, Philadelphia, 1971, 186p, Cloth, Nonf.

URBANEK, MAE (Bobb), 1903-   [*biography included*]

14394   *The second man.* Sage, Denver, 1962, 183p, Cloth, Novel

URIS, AUREN
    see: PAUL, AUREN

URISARRI FORD, CONSUELO
    see: URN, ALTHEA

URN, ALTHEA, pseud. [Consuelo Urisarri Ford, 1903-]

14395   *Five miles from Candia.* Henry Holt, New York, 1959, 188p, Cloth, Novel

USHER, WILFRED

14396   *The great hold-up mystery.* Stanley Paul, London, 1928, 288p, Cloth, Novel

USPENSKII, PËTR (Dem'ianovich), 1878-1947, as P. D. Ouspensky

14397   *Strange life of Ivan Osokin; a novel.* Holme Press, New York, 1947, 166p, Cloth, Novel; Stourton Press, London, 1947, 179p, Cloth, Novel
14398   *Talks with a devil.* Turnstone Press, London, 1972, 158p, Cloth, Coll.

UTLEY, BRIAN R.

14399   *Martyr.* Curtis, New York, 1971, 160p, Paper, Novel

UTTERSON, SARAH E(lizabeth) B(rown), 1782?-
1851 [published anonymously]

14400 *Tales of the dead.* White, Cochrane & Co.,
London, 1813, 248p, Cloth, Anth.

UTTLEY, ALISON [Alice Jane Uttley, 1884-1976]

14401 *A traveller in time.* Faber & Faber, London,
1939, 331p, Cloth, Novel
14401A retitled: *A traveler in time.* G. P. Putnam's
Sons, New York, 1940, 306p, Cloth, Novel

UYEDA, AKINARI, 1734-1809

14402 *Tales of moonlight and rain; Japanese gothic
tales.* University of Tokyo Press, Tokyo,
1972, 150p, Cloth, Coll.

VACHELL, HORACE ANNESLEY, 1861-1955

14403 *The other side; the record of certain passages
in the life of a genius.* George H. Doran,
New York, 1910, 359p, Cloth, Novel

VADER, JOHN

14404 *Battle of Sydney; a novel.* New English Library, London, 1971, 144p, Cloth, Novel

VALDA, DE
see: DE VALDA, FREDERICK W.

VALDEZ, PAUL, pseud.

14405 *Celluloid suicide.* Scientific Thriller, Sydney, 1951, 34p, Paper, Story
14406 *The crook who wasn't there!* Scientific Thriller, Sydney, 1952, 34p, Paper, Story [cover
title: *The killer who wasn't there*]
14407 *The fatal focus.* Scientific Thriller, Sydney,
1950, 50p, Paper, Novel
14408 *Feline frame-up.* Scientific Thriller, Sydney,
1952, 34p, Paper, Story
14409 *Flight into horror.* Scientific Thriller, Sydney, 1951, 34p, Paper, Story
14410 *Ghosts don't kill.* Scientific Thriller, Sydney, 1951, 34p, Paper, Story
14411 *Hypnotic death.* Scientific Thriller, Sydney,
1949, 50p, Paper, Novel
14412 *Kill him gently.* Scientific Thriller, Sydney,
1951, 34p, Paper, Story
14413 *Killer by night.* Scientific Thriller, Sydney,
1951, 30p, Paper, Story
14414 *The maniac murders.* Scientific Thriller, Sydney, 1952, 34p, Paper, Story
14415 *The murder I don't remember.* Scientific Thriller, Sydney, 1952, 34p, Paper, Story
14416 *No future in murder.* Scientific Thriller,
Sydney, 1952, 34p, Paper, Story [cover title
reads: *There's no future in murder*]
14417 *Satan's sabbath.* Scientific Thriller, Sydney,
1951, 34p, Paper, Story
14418 *The time thief.* Scientific Thriller, Sydney,
1951, 34p, Paper, Story
14419 *You can't keep murder out.* Scientific Thriller, Sydney, 1951, 34p, Paper, Story

VALE, RENA (Marie), 1898-

14420 *Beyond the sealed world.* Paperback Library,
New York, 1965, 192p, Paper, Novel
14421 *The day after doomsday; a fantasy of time travel.* Paperback Library, New York, 1970,
159p, Paper, Novel
14422 *The Red Court, last seat of national government of the United States of America; the
story of the revolution to come through
communism.* Nelson Publishing Co., Detroit,
1952, 148p, Paper, Novel
14423 *Taurus Four.* Paperback Library, New York,
1970, 156p, Paper, Novel

VALE, ROBERT B.

14424 *Efficiency in Hades; the romantic adventures
of an enterprising expert in the lower world.*
Frederick A. Stokes, New York, 1923, 148p,
Cloth, Novel

VALENTINE, RICHARD, with Sibbald Malcolm

09582 *Archibald the Great; a fable.* Collins, London,
1937, 72p, Cloth, Novel

VALENTINE, VICTOR

14425 *Cure for death.* Sidgwick & Jackson, London,
1960, 238p, Cloth, Novel

VALENTINER, BRIGITTA

14426 *The maidens of Osiris, and other stories.*
Vantage Press, New York, 1970, 212p, Cloth,
Coll.

VALLANCE, KARL, pseud.

14427 *Global blackout.* Gannet Press, London, 1954,
126p, Paper, Novel

A VAMPIRE OF SOULS
see: P., H. M.

THE VAMPYRE
see: POLIDORI, JOHN W.

VAN-ANDERSON, HELEN, 1859-

14428 *It is possible; a story of life.* New Era Publishing Co., Chicago, 1891, 342p, Cloth,
Novel

VAN ARNAM, DAVE [David G. Van Arnam]

14429 *Greyland.* Belmont, New York, 1972, 214p,
Paper, Novel
14430 *Lord of blood.* Lancer, New York, 1970, 192p,
Paper, Novel [Jamnar #2]
14431 *The players of Hell.* Belmont Double, New York,
1968, 95p, Paper, Novel [Konarr #1]

VAN ARNAM, DAVE (cont.)

14432 *Star barbarian*. Lancer, New York, 1969, 223p, Paper, Novel [Jamnar #1]
14433 *Star gladiator*. Belmont Double, New York, 1967, 89p, Paper, Novel
14434 *Starmind*. Ballantine, New York, 1969, 216p, Paper, Novel
14435 *Wizard of storms*. Belmont, New York, 1970, 125p, Paper, Novel [Konarr #2]

with Ron Archer:

14436 *Lost in space*. Pyramid, New York, 1967, 157p, Paper, Tele. [Lost in Space series]

with Ted White:

14437 *Sideslip*. Pyramid, New York, 1968, 188p, Paper, Novel

VAN ASH, CAY, with Elizabeth Sax Rohmer

12363 *Master of villainy; a biography of Sax Rohmer*. Bowling Green University Popular Press, Bowling Green, OH, 1972, 312p, Cloth, Nonf.

VAN BEEVER, ROBERT F., with Fred G. Jarvis as Fritz Gordon

07859 *The flight of the bamboo saucer*. Award, New York, 1967, 176p, Paper, Novel

VANCE, JACK [John Holbrook Vance, 1916-   ] [*biography included*]

14438 *The Anome; Durdane, Book I*. Dell, New York, 1973, 224p, Paper, Novel [Durdane #1]
14439 *The Asutra*. Dell, New York, 1974, 204p, Paper, Novel [Durdane #3]
14440 *Big Planet*. Avalon, New York, 1957, 223p, Cloth, Novel
14441 *The blue world*. Ballantine, New York, 1966, 190p, Paper, Novel
14442 *The brains of Earth*. Ace Double, New York, 1966, 108p, Paper, Novel
14443 *The Brave Free Men; Durdane, Book II*. Dell, New York, 1973, 251p, Paper, Novel [Durdane #2]
14444 *The Dirdir; planet of adventure #3*. Ace, New York, 1969, 188p, Paper, Novel [Tschai #3]
14445 *The dragon masters*. Ace Double, New York, 1963, 102p, Paper, Novel
14446 *The dying Earth*. Hillman Periodicals, New York, 1950, 175p, Paper, Coll. [Dying Earth #1]
14447 *Eight fantasms and magics; a science fiction adventure*. Macmillan, New York, 1969, 288p, Cloth, Coll.
14448 *Emphyrio*. Doubleday, Garden City, 1969, 261p, Cloth, Novel
14449 *The Eyes of the Overworld*. Ace, New York, 1966, 189p, Paper, Novel [Dying Earth #2]
The five gold bands. [see 14465A]
14450 *Future tense*. Ballantine, New York, 1964, 160p, Paper, Coll.
14451 *The gray prince; a science fiction novel*. Bobbs-Merrill, Indianapolis, 1974, 191p, Cloth, Novel
14452 *The houses of Iszm*. Ace Double, New York, 1964, 112p, Paper, Novel

14453 *The Killing Machine*. Berkley Medallion, New York, 1964, 158p, Paper, Novel [Demon Prince #2]
14454 *The languages of Pao*. Avalon, New York, 1958, 223p, Cloth, Novel
14455 *The last castle*. Ace Double, New York, 1967, 72p, Paper, Novel
14456 *The many worlds of Magnus Ridolph*. Ace Double, New York, 1966, 146p, Paper, Coll.
14457 *Monsters in orbit*. Ace Double, New York, 1965, 119p, Paper, Novel
14458 *The Palace of Love*. Berkley Medallion, New York, 1967, 189p, Paper, Novel [Demon Prince #3]
14459 *Planet of adventure #1; City of the Chasch*. Ace, New York, 1968, 157p, Paper, Novel [Tschai #1]
14460 *The Pnume; planet of adventure #4*. Ace, New York, 1970, 156p, Paper, Novel [Tschai #4]
14461 *Servants of the Wankh; planet of adventure #2*. Ace, New York, 1969, 158p, Paper, Novel [Tschai #2]
14462 *Slaves of the Klau*. Ace Double, New York, 1958, 129p, Paper, Novel
14463 *Son of the Tree*. Ace Double, New York, 1964, 111p, Paper, Novel
14464 *Space opera*. Pyramid, New York, 1965, 143p, Paper, Novel
14465 *The space pirate; a science fiction novel*. Toby Press, New York, 1953, 128p, Paper, Novel
14465A retitled: *The five gold bands*. Ace Double, New York, 1963, 122p, Paper, Novel
14466 *The Star King*. Berkley Medallion, New York, 1964, 158p, Paper, Novel [Demon Prince #1]
14467 *To live forever*. Ballantine, New York, 1956, 185p, Cloth, Novel
14468 *Trullion: Alastor 2262*. Ballantine, New York, 1973, 247p, Paper, Novel [Alastor #1]
14469 *Vandals of the void*. John C. Winston, Philadelphia, 1953, 213p, Cloth, Novel
14470 *The world between, and other stories*. Ace Double, New York, 1965, 134p, Paper, Coll.
14471 *The worlds of Jack Vance*. Ace, New York, 1973, 302p, Paper, Coll.

VANCE, LOUIS JOSEPH, 1879-1933

14472 *The dark mirror*. Doubleday, Page, Garden City, 1920, 368p, Cloth, Novel

VANDEL, JEAN GASTON

14473 *Enemy beyond Pluto*. Hector Kelly, London, 1954, 192p, Cloth, Novel

VANDEN, DIRK

14474 *Twin orbs*. Greenleaf Classics, San Diego, 1969, 195p, Paper, Novel

VAN der ELST, VIOLET, 1882-1966

14475 *The brain master*. Van der Elst Press, London, 1946, 80p, Paper, Coll.
14476 *Death of the vampire baroness*. Van der Elst Press, London, 1945, 80p, Paper, Coll.
14477 *The mummy comes to life*. Van der Elst Press, London, 1946, 79p, Paper, Coll.

VAN der ELST, VIOLET (cont.)

14478   *The Satanic power.* Van der Elst Press, London, 1946, 81p, Paper, Coll.
14479   *The secret power; short stories.* Van der Elst Press, London, 1946, 80p, Paper, Coll.
14480   *The strange doctor, and other mystic stories.* Van der Elst Press, London, 1946, 81p, Paper, Coll.
14481   *The torture chamber, and other stories, with some personal reminiscences.* Doge Press, London, 1937, 237p, Cloth, Coll. [includes some nonf.]

VAN der NAILLEN, A(lbert), 1830-1928

14482   *Balthazar the Magus.* R. F. Fenno, New York, 1904, 270p, Cloth, Novel [Magi #3]
14483   *In the sanctuary; sequel to On the heights of Himalay.* W. Doxey, San Francisco, 1896, 250p, Cloth, Novel [Magi #2]
14484   *On the heights of Himalay.* American Book Co., New York, 1890, 272p, Cloth, Novel [Magi #1]

VAN DEUSEN, ALONZO [published anonymously]

14485   *Rational communism; the present and future Republic of North America*, by a capitalist. Social Science Publishing Co., New York, 1885, 498p, Cloth, Novel

VAN DOREN, MARK (Albert), 1894-1972 [*biography included*]

14486   *The transients.* William Morrow, New York, 1935, 266p, Cloth, Novel

VAN DYKE, HENRY (Jackson), 1852-1933

14487   *The blue flower.* Charles Scribner's Sons, New York, 1902, 298p, Cloth, Coll.
14488   *The broken soldier and the Maid of France.* Harper & Bros., New York, 1919, 69p, Cloth, Novel
14489   *Great short works of Henry Van Dyke.* Perennial Library, New York, 1966, 209p, Paper, Coll.
14490   *The mansion.* Harper & Bros., New York, 1911, 44p, Cloth, Story
14491   *The story of the other wise man.* Harper & Bros., New York, 1896, 82p, Cloth, Novel
14491A retitled: *The other wise man.* Sheldon Press, London, 1945, 15p, Cloth?, Story [abridged]

VANE, (Vane Hunt) SUTTON, 1888-

14492   *Outward bound.* Chatto & Windus, London, 1929, 311p, Cloth, Novel [based on the play of the same name]

van EEDEN, FREDERIK
    see: EEDEN, FREDERIK van

VANEWORDS, JOHN PRE

14493   *The great miracle; or, The man who could not be killed, being a personal statement by Mr. Roderick Faiburn, who, though now a fugitive from justice, nevertheless, during the short period described by him, subdued a nation and perplexed mankind.* Stanley Paul, London, 1914, 316p, Cloth, Novel

VAN GREENAWAY, PETER, 1929-

14494   *The crucified city.* New Authors, London, 1962, 221p, Cloth, Novel
14495   *Judas!* Victor Gollancz, London, 1972, 240p, Cloth, Novel
14495A retitled: *The Judas gospel.* Atheneum, New York, 1972, 239p, Cloth, Novel
14496   *The man who held The Queen to ransom and sent Parliament packing; a novel.* Weidenfeld & Nicolson, London, 1968, 256p, Cloth, Novel
14497   *The Medusa touch.* Victor Gollancz, London, 1973, 256p, Cloth, Novel

VAN HERCK, PAUL, 1938-

14498   *Where were you last Pluterday?* DAW, New York, 1973, 159p, Paper, Novel

VAN ITH, LILY, pseud. [Emilie Ida Friedli, 1889-   ]

14499   *The light beyond the zodiac.* Wetzel Publishing Co., Los Angeles, 1947, 186p, Cloth, Novel

van LAUN, H(enri), 1820-1896

14500   *The gates of Afree, A.D. 1928; a romance of the new Empire.* F. V. White, London, 1903, 109p, Cloth, Novel

VAN LHIN, ERIK, pseud.
    see: del REY, LESTER

van LODEN, ERLE, pseud.

14501   *Curse of planet Kuz.* Edwin Self, London, 1952, 128p, Paper, Novel
14502   *Voyage into space.* Edwin Self, London, 1954, 100p, Paper, Novel

van LOON, HENDRIK WILLEM, 1882-1944

14503   *Invasion, being the personal recollections of what happened to our own family and to some of our friends during the first hours of that terrible incident in our history which is now known as the great invasion, and how we escaped with our lives, and the strange adventures which befell us before the Nazis were driven from our territories; written down at the time and now for the first time presented to the public at large.* Harcourt, Brace & Co., New York, 1940, 203p, Cloth, Novel

VAN MARCUS, CARL

14504   *A jungle orgy*. Tiburon, Sausalito, CA, 1973,
        191p, Paper, Novel

VAN MIERLO, H. A.

14505   *By then mankind ceased to exist*. Arthur H.
        Stockwell, Ilfracombe, UK, 1960, 112p, Cloth,
        Novel

VAN PEDROE-SAVIDGE, E.

14506   *The flying submarine*. Arthur Stockwell, Lon-
        don, 1922, 255p, Cloth, Novel

VAN PETTEN, ALBERT ARCHER, 1925-

14507   *The great man's life, 1925 to 2000 A.C.* Uto-
        pian Publishers, New York, 1959, 319p,
        Cloth, Novel

VAN ROOSBROECK, G(ustave) L(eopold), 1888-
1936

14508   *Grotesques*. Living Art, New York, 1929,
        104p, Paper, Coll.

VAN SCYOC, SYDNEY (Joyce), 1939-   [*biography
included*]

14509   *Assignment Nor'Dyren*. Avon, New York, 1973,
        222p, Paper, Novel
14510   *Saltflower*. Avon, New York, 1971, 176p,
        Paper, Novel

van THAL, HERBERT (Maurice), 1904-   [*biography included*]

14511   *The bedside book of horror*. Arthur Barker,
        London, 1973, 271p, Cloth, Anth.
14512   *The bedside book of strange stories*. Arthur
        Barker, London, 1974, 232p, Cloth, Anth.
14513   *A book of strange stories*. Pan, London, 1954,
        190p, Paper, Anth.
14514   *The eighth Pan book of horror stories*. Pan,
        London, 1967, 236p, Paper, Anth.
14515   *The eleventh Pan book of horror stories*. Pan,
        London, 1970, 220p, Paper, Anth.
14516   *Famous tales of the fantastic*. Arthur Barker,
        London, 1965, 207p, Cloth, Anth.
14517   *The 15th Pan book of horror stories*. Pan,
        London, 1974, 223p, Paper, Anth.
14518   *The fifth Pan book of horror stories*. Pan,
        London, 1964, 267p, Paper, Anth.
14518A retitled: *Selections from The Pan book of
        horror stories #5*. Berkley Medallion, New
        York, 1970, 189p, Paper, Anth. [abridged]
        The first Pan book of horror stories. [see
        14524A]
14519   *The 14th Pan book of horror stories*. Pan,
        London, 1973, 189p, Paper, Anth.
14520   *The fourth Pan book of horror stories*. Pan,
        London, 1963, 271p, Paper, Anth.
14520A retitled: *Selections from The Pan book of
        horror stories #4*. Berkley Medallion, New
        York, 1970, 160p, Paper, Anth. [abridged]

14521   *Great ghost stories*. Weidenfeld & Nicolson,
        London, 1960, 239p, Cloth, Anth.
14522   *Lie ten nights awake; ten tales of horror*.
        Hodder & Stoughton, London, 1967, 190p,
        Paper, Anth.
14523   *The ninth Pan book of horror stories*. Pan,
        London, 1968, 252p, Paper, Anth.
14524   *The Pan book of horror stories*. Pan, London,
        1959, 317p, Paper, Anth.
14524A retitled: *The first Pan book of horror stories*.
        Pan, London, 1969?, 317p, Paper, Anth.
14525   *The second Pan book of horror stories*. Pan,
        London, 1960, 319p, Paper, Anth.
        *Selections from The Pan book of horror stories
        #3*. [see 14530A]
        *Selections from The Pan book of horror stories
        #4*. [see 14520A]
        *Selections from The Pan book of horror stories
        #5*. [see 14518A]
14526   *The seventh Pan book of horror stories*. Pan,
        London, 1966, 239p, Paper, Anth.
14527   *The sixth Pan book of horror stories*. Pan,
        London, 1965, 222p, Paper, Anth.
14528   *Striking terror! a selection of great horror
        stories*. Arthur Barker, London, 1963, 204p,
        Cloth, Anth.
14529   *The tenth Pan book of horror stories*. Pan,
        London, 1969, 236p, Paper, Anth.
14530   *The third Pan book of horror stories*. Pan,
        London, 1962, 268p, Paper, Anth.
14530A retitled: *Selections from The Pan book of
        horror stories #3*. Berkley Medallion, New
        York, 1970, 192p, Paper, Anth. [abridged]
14531   *The 13th Pan book of horror stories*. Pan,
        London, 1972, 220p, Paper, Anth.
14532   *Told in the dark*. Pan, London, 1950, 256p,
        Paper, Anth.
14533   *The twelfth Pan book of horror stories*. Pan,
        London, 1971, 190p, Paper, Anth.

VAN TUYL, ZAARA [Rosealtha Van Tuyl, 1901-
[*biography included*]

14534   *Skyways for Doorian*. C. Beaconsfield, Las
        Vegas, Nevada, 1967, 144p, Paper, Novel

van VOGT, A(lfred) E(lton), 1912-   [*biography
included*]

14535   *Away and beyond*. Pellegrini & Cudahy, New
        York, 1952, 309p, Cloth, Coll.
14536   *The battle of forever*. Ace, New York, 1971,
        191p, Paper, Novel
14537   *The beast*. Doubleday, Garden City, 1963, 207p,
        Cloth, Novel
14537A retitled: *Moonbeast*. Panther, London, 1969,
        187p, Paper, Novel
14538   *The best of A. E. van Vogt*. Sphere, London,
        1974, 437p, Paper, Coll.
14539   *The book of Ptath*. Fantasy Press, Reading, PA,
        1947, 227p, Cloth, Novel
14539A retitled: *Two hundred million A.D.* Paperback
        Library, New York, 1964, 159p, Paper, Novel
14540   *The book of van Vogt*. DAW, New York, 1972,
        191p, Paper, Coll.
14541   *The changeling*. Macfadden-Bartell, New York,
        1967, 96p, Paper, Novel
14542   *Children of tomorrow*. Ace, New York, 1970,
        254p, Paper, Novel
14543   *The darkness on Diamondia*. Ace, New York,
        1972, 254p, Paper, Novel

van VOGT, A. E. (cont.)

14544 *Destination: universe!* Pellegrini & Cudahy, New York, 1952, 295p, Cloth, Coll.

14545 *Earth's last fortress.* Ace Double, New York, 1960, 114p, Paper, Novel

14545A retitled: *Masters of time.* Macfadden-Bartell, New York, 1967, 128p, Paper, Novel

14546 *Empire of the atom.* Shasta Publishers, Chicago, 1956, 192p, Cloth, Novel [Linn #1]

14547 *The far-out worlds of A. E. van Vogt.* Ace, New York, 1968, 223p, Paper, Coll.

14548 *Future glitter.* Ace, New York, 1973, 216p, Paper, Novel

14549 *The house that stood still.* Corwin Book, Greenberg: Publisher, New York, 1950, 210p, Cloth, Novel

14549A retitled: *The mating cry; a prize science fiction novel selected by Galaxy magazine for Beacon Books.* Beacon Books, New York, 1960, 160p, Paper, Novel

14550 *M33 in Andromeda.* Paperback Library, New York, 1971, 252p, Paper, Coll.

14551 *The man with a thousand names.* DAW, New York, 1974, 159p, Paper, Novel

14552 *Masters of time.* Fantasy Press, Reading, PA, 1950, 227p, Cloth, Coll. [includes *Masters of time* and *The changeling*]

Masters of time. [see 14545A]

The mating cry. [see 14549A]

14553 *The mind cage; a science fiction novel.* Simon & Schuster, New York, 1957, 220p, Cloth, Novel

Mission: interplanetary. [see 14569A]

Mission to the stars. [see 14554A]

14554 *The mixed men.* Gnome Press, New York, 1952, 223p, Cloth, Novel

14554A retitled: *Mission to the stars.* Berkley, New York, 1955, 126p, Paper, Novel

14555 *Monsters.* Paperback Library, New York, 1965, 154p, Paper, Coll.

Moonbeast. [see 14537A]

14556 *More than superhuman.* Dell, New York, 1971, 215p, Paper, Coll. [includes two stories written in collaboration with other authors]

One against eternity. [see 14571A]

14557 *The pawns of null-A.* Ace, New York, 1956, 254p, Paper, Novel [Null-A #2]

14557A retitled: *The players of null-A.* Berkley Medallion, New York, 1966, 192p, Paper, Novel [Null-A #2]

14558 *The proxy intelligence, and other mind benders.* Paperback Library, New York, 1971, 206p, Paper, Coll.

14559 *Quest for the future.* Ace, New York, 1970, 253p, Paper, Novel

14560 *Rogue ship.* Doubleday, Garden City, 1965, 213p, Cloth, Novel

14561 *The secret galactics.* Reward, Englewood Cliffs, NJ, 1974, 215p, Paper, Novel

14562 *Siege of the unseen.* Ace Double, New York, 1959, 103p, Paper, Novel

14563 *The Silkie.* Ace, New York, 1969, 191p, Paper, Novel

14564 *Slan.* Arkham House, Sauk City, 1946, 216p, Cloth, Novel

14565 *The three eyes of evil; and, Earth's last fortress; two science fiction novels.* Sidgwick & Jackson, London, 1973, 218p, Cloth, Coll. [*The three eyes of evil* was originally published as *Siege of the unseen*]

14566 *Triad; three complete science fiction novels: The world of Ā; The voyage of the Space Beagle; Slan.* Simon & Schuster, New York, 1959, 528p, Cloth, Coll.

14567 *The twisted men.* Ace Double, New York, 1964, 130p, Paper, Coll.

Two hundred million A.D. [see 14539A]

14568 *The universe maker.* Ace Double, New York, 1953, 138p, Paper, Novel

14569 *The voyage of the Space Beagle.* Simon & Schuster, New York, 1950, 241p, Cloth, Novel

14569A retitled: *Mission: interplanetary.* Signet, New York, 1952, 174p, Paper, Novel

14570 *The war against the Rull.* Simon & Schuster, New York, 1959, 244p, Cloth, Novel

14571 *The weapon makers.* Hadley Publishing Co., Providence, RI, 1947, 224p, Cloth, Novel [Isher #1]

14571A retitled: *One against eternity.* Ace Double, New York, 1955, 186p, Paper, Novel [Isher #1]

14572 *The weapon shops of Isher.* Corwin Book, Greenberg: Publisher, New York, 1951, 231p, Cloth, Novel [Isher #2]

14573 *The wizard of Linn.* Ace, New York, 1962, 190p, Paper, Novel [Linn #2]

14574 *The world of Ā.* Simon & Schuster, New York, 1948, 247p, Cloth, Novel [Null-A #1]

14574A retitled: *The world of null-A.* Ace Double, New York, 1953, 182p, Paper, Novel [Null-A #1]

14575 *The worlds of A. E. van Vogt.* Ace, New York, 1974, 330p, Paper, Coll. [an expanded version of *The far-out worlds of A. E. van Vogt*]

with E. Mayne Hull:

07584 *Out of the unknown.* Fantasy Publishing Co., Los Angeles, 1948, 141p, Cloth, Coll.

07585 *Out of the unknown.* Powell Publications, Reseda, CA, 1969, 222p, Paper, Coll. [includes an additional story]

07585A retitled: *The sea thing, and other stories; science fiction.* Sidgwick & Jackson, London, 1970, 222p, Cloth, Coll.

07586 *Planets for sale,* by E. Mayne Hull. Frederick Fell, New York, 1954, 192p, Cloth, Novel

07586A *Planets for sale,* by E. Mayne Hull and A. E. van Vogt. Book Company of America, Beverly Hills, CA, 1965, 171p, Paper, Novel

The sea thing, and other stories. [see 07585A]

07587 *A van Vogt omnibus; 'Planets for sale' (with E. Mayne Hull); 'The beast'; 'The book of Ptath.'* Sidgwick & Jackson, London, 1967, 498p, Cloth, Coll.

07588 *van Vogt omnibus (2).* Sidgwick & Jackson, London, 1971, 512p, Cloth, Coll. [includes: *Slan; The mind cage; The winged man*]

07589 *The winged man.* Doubleday, Garden City, 1966, 190p, Cloth, Novel

VAN WINKLE, MONICA F.

14576 *Whirlwind harvest; a phantasy.* Academy Library Guild, Fresno, CA, 1952, 143p, Cloth, Novel

VAN ZELLER, CLAUDE HUBERT

see: VENNING, HUGH

VAN ZILE, EDWARD S(ims), 1863-1931

14577 *A magnetic man, and other stories.* Frank F.
       Lovell, New York, 1890, 211p, Paper, Coll.
14578 *Perkins, the fakeer; a travesty on reincarna-
       tion.* Smart Set Publishing Co., New York,
       1903, 377p, Cloth, Coll.

VARÈ, DANIELE, 1880-1956

14579 *The doge's ring.* Methuen, London, 1949, 212p,
       Cloth, Novel

VARNEY THE VAMPYRE [variously attributed to
James Malcolm Rymer or Thomas Peckett Prest]

14580 *Varney the vampyre; or, The feast of blood;
       a romance,* by the author of "Grace Rivers;
       or, The merchant's daughter." E. Lloyd,
       London, 1847, 868p, Cloth, Novel

VASSEUR, JOHN

14581 *Typhon's beard.* George H. Doran, New York,
       1927, 261p, Cloth, Novel

VASSILIKOS, VASSILIS, 1933-

14582 *The plant, The well, The angel; a trilogy.*
       Alfred A. Knopf, New York, 1964, 273p,
       Cloth, Coll.

VASSOS, JOHN, with Ruth Vassos

14583 *Ultimo; an imaginative narration of life under
       the Earth.* E. P. Dutton, New York, 1930,
       92p, Cloth, Novel

VASSOS, RUTH, 1896-1965, with John Vassos

14583 *Ultimo; an imaginative narration of life under
       the Earth.* E. P. Dutton, New York, 1930,
       92p, Cloth, Novel

VATHEK
    see: BECKFORD, WILLIAM

VATHEK, AN ARABIAN TALE; THE AMBER WITCH

14584 *Vathek, an Arabian tale; The amber witch.*
       H. G. Bohn, London, 1852, 2vol/1, Cloth,
       Anth. [by William Beckford and W. Meinhold
       respectively]

VATHEK; THE CASTLE OF OTRANTO; THE BRAVO OF
VENICE

14585 *Vathek; The Castle of Otranto; The bravo of
       Venice.* Richard Bentley, London, 1834,
       589p, Cloth, Anth. [by William Beckford,
       Horace Walpole, and M. G. Lewis respective-
       ly]

VAUGHAN, Lady AURIEL
    see: MALET, ORIEL

VAUGHAN, H(erbert) M(illingchamp), 1870-1948

14586 *The dial of Ahaz.* Martin Secker, London, 1917,
       359p, Cloth, Novel
14587 *Meleager; a fantasy.* Martin Secker, London,
       1916, 324p, Cloth, Novel

VAUGHAN, THOMAS HUNTER

14588 *The gates of the past.* John Long, London,
       1911, 384p, Cloth, Novel

VAUX, PATRICK

14589 *The shock of battle.* G. P. Putnam's Sons, New
       York, 1906, 379p, Cloth, Novel

with Lionel Yexley as Navarchus:

14590 *The world's awakening.* Hodder & Stoughton,
       London, 1908, 463p, Cloth, Novel
14590A retitled: *When the great war came.* Hodder &
       Stoughton, London, 1909, 312p, Paper, Novel

VEER, WILLEM de, 1865-

14591 *An emperor in the dock.* John Lane, The Bodley
       Head, London, 1915, 320p, Cloth, Novel

VEILED KNOWLEDGE

14592 *Veiled knowledge.* American Science Fiction,
       Sydney, 1953, 34p, Paper, Anth.

VELÁSQUEZ, PEDRO, pseud.

14593 *Memoir of an eventful expedition in Central
       America, resulting in the discovery of the
       idolatrous city of Iximaya, in an unexplored
       region, and the possession of two remarkable
       Aztec children, descendants and specimens
       of the sacerdotal caste (now nearly extinct)
       of the ancient Aztec founders of the ruined
       temples of that country, described by John
       L. Stevens, Esq., and other travellers.*
       E. F. Applegate, Printer, New York, 1850,
       35p, Paper, Story
14593A retitled: *Illustrated memoir of an eventful
       expedition into Central America, resulting
       in the discovery of the idolatrous city of
       Iximaya, in an unexplored region, and the
       possession of two remarkable Aztec children,
       Maximo (the man), and Bartola (the girl),
       descendants and specimens of the sacerdotal
       cast* [sic] *(now nearly extinct) of the an-
       cient Aztec founders of the ruined temples
       of that country, described by John L. Step-
       hens, Esq., and other travellers.* no pub-
       lisher, London?, 1856?, 38p, Paper, Story

VELOZ, NARD, pseud.

14594 *Fire flesh.* Masterpiece Classics, Los Angeles,
       1972, 187p, Paper, Novel

VENABLE, CLARKE
   see: CLARKE, COVINGTON

VENNING, HUGH, pseud. [Claude van Zeller (religious name: Hubert van Zeller), 1905-] [*biography included*]

  14595 *The end; a projection, not a prophecy.* Douglas Organ, London, 1947, 298p, Cloth, Novel

VENUS AND CUPID
   see: PULLEN, HENRY W.

VERCORS, pseud. [Jean Marcel Bruller, 1902-]

  14596 *Sylva; a novel.* G. P. Putnam's Sons, New York, 1962, 256p, Cloth, Novel
  14597 *You shall know them.* Little, Brown, Boston, 1953, 249p, Cloth, Novel
  14597A retitled: *Borderline.* Macmillan, London, 1954, 231p, Cloth, Novel
  14597B retitled: *The murder of the missing link.* Pocket Books, New York, 1958, 196p, Paper, Novel

VERN, DAVID
   see: REED, DAVID V.

VERNE, JULES (Gabriel), 1828-1905 [Note: the bibliography of Jules Verne is exceedingly complex, with many of his longer novels having been issued in several volumes under different titles in two or three competing editions. It has been assumed here (perhaps falsely) that the Sampson Low editions are the true firsts; the Ward, Lock and American editions are listed secondly, unless earlier publication dates are evident. Further elucidation of Verne's editions must await the publication of the "V" entries in the <u>National Union Catalog</u> pre-1956 imprints.]

  14598 *Abandoned.* Sampson Low, Marston, Searle & Rivington, London, 1875, 304p, Cloth, Novel [Mysterious Island #1; Capt. Nemo #2A]
  14599 *The adventures of a Chinaman in China.* Lee & Shepard, Boston, 1889, 271p, Cloth, Novel
  14600 *The adventures of Captain Hatteras: The English at the North Pole; The field of ice.* George Routledge & Sons, London, 1876, 583p, Cloth, Coll. [Captain Hatteras #s 1-2]
  14600A retitled: *The voyages and adventures of Captain Hatteras; The English at the North Pole.* Ward, Lock & Tyler, London, 1876, 471p, Cloth, Coll. [Captain Hatteras #s 1-2]
  All around the Moon. [see 14626C]
  The American Gun Club. [see 14626A]
  Anomalous phenomena. [see 14647A]
  14601 *An Antarctic mystery.* Sampson Low, Marston, Searle & Rivington, London, 1898, 336p, Cloth, Novel [a sequel to Edgar Allan Poe's *The narrative of Arthur Gordon Pym*; see also 11749]
  Around the Moon. [see 14640A]
  Around the world in eighty days. [see 14648A]
  Astounding adventures among the comets. [see 14628A]
  At the North Pole. [see 14615B]

  The Baltimore Gun Club. [see 14626B]
  14602 *The begum's fortune.* Sampson Low, Marston, Searle & Rivington, London, 1879, 272p, Cloth, Novel
  14602A retitled: *The 500 millions of the begum.* George Munro, New York, 1879, 23p, Paper, Novel [abridged?]
  14603 *The blockade runners.* Sampson Low, Marston, Searle & Rivington, London, 1876, 120p, Cloth, Novel [Floating City #2]
  Carpathian castle. [see 14604A]
  14604 *The castle of the Carpathians.* Sampson Low, Marston, Searle & Rivington, London, 1893, 211p, Cloth, Novel
  14604A retitled: *Carpathian castle.* Arco Publications, London, 1963, 189p, Cloth, Novel
  14605 *The chase of the golden meteor.* Grant Richards, London, 1909, 292p, Cloth, Novel
  14605A retitled: *The hunt for the meteor.* Arco Publications, London, 1965, 191p, Cloth, Novel
  14606 *The city in the Sahara; part two of the Barsac Mission.* Arco Publications, London, 1960, 190p, Cloth, Novel [Barsac Mission #2]
  14607 *The clipper of the clouds.* Sampson Low, Marston, Searle & Rivington, London, 1887, 234p, Cloth, Novel [Robur #1]
  14607A retitled: *Robur the conqueror; or, A trip round the world in a flying machine.* George Munro, New York, 1887, 181p, Paper, Novel [Robur #1]
  14607B retitled: *A trip around the world in a flying machine.* Donohue & Henneberry, Chicago, 1887, 181p, Cloth, Novel
  14608 *The demon of Cawnpore.* Sampson Low, Marston, Searle & Rivington, London, 1881, 262p, Cloth, Novel [Steam House #1]
  The desert of ice. [see 14617A]
  14609 *Dr Ox, and other stories.* Arco Publications, London, 1964, 191p, Cloth, Coll.
  14610 *Doctor Ox, and other stories.* James R. Osgood, Boston, 1874, 292p, Cloth, Coll. [different contents]
  14611 *Dr. Ox's experiment.* George Munro, New York, 1879, 29p, Paper, Story
  Dr. Ox's experiment. [see 14624A]
  14612 *Dr. Ox's experiment; and, A field of ice.* Donnelley, Loyd, Chicago, 1877,   , Paper, Coll.
  14613 *Doctor Ox's experiment; and, Master Zacharius.* Sampson Low, Marston, Searle & Rivington, London, 1876,   , Cloth, Coll.
  14614 *Dr. Ox's experiment, and other stories.* James R. Osgood, Boston, 1875, 332p, Cloth, Coll. [different from any others]
  Dropped from the clouds. [see 14643A]
  14615 *The English at the North Pole.* George Routledge & Sons, London, 1874, 314p, Cloth, Novel [Capt. Hatteras #1]
  14615A retitled: *A journey to the North Pole.* George Routledge & Sons, London, 1874, 315p, Cloth, Novel [Capt. Hatteras #1]
  14615B retitled: *At the North Pole; or, The adventures of Capt. Hatteras.* Porter & Coates, Philadelphia, 1874, 231p, Cloth, Novel [Capt. Hatteras #1]
  Facing the flag. [see 14623A]
  14616 *The fancy of Dr. Ox; and, The tour of the world in eighty days.* Office of the Evening Telegraph, Philadelphia, 1874, 124p, Cloth, Coll.
  14617 *The field of ice.* George Routledge & Sons, London, 1876, 269p, Cloth, Novel [Capt. Hatteras #2]

VERNE, JULES (cont.)

14617A retitled: *The desert of ice.* Porter & Coates, Philadelphia, 1876,   , Cloth, Novel [Capt. Hatteras #2]

14617B retitled: *The ice desert.* Ward, Lock, London, 1937, 251p, Cloth, Novel [Capt. Hatteras #2]

14617C retitled: *The wilderness of ice; part two of The adventures of Captain Hatteras.* Arco Publications, London, 1961, 192p, Cloth, Novel [Capt. Hatteras #2]

The 500 millions of the begum. [see 14602A]

14618 *Five weeks in a balloon; or, Journeys and discoveries in Africa.* D. Appleton, New York, 1869, 345p, Cloth, Novel

14619 *Five weeks in a balloon; and, Around the world in eighty days.* J. M. Dent & Sons, London, 1926, 374p, Cloth, Coll.

14620 *A floating city.* Sampson Low, Marston, Searle & Rivington, London, 1876, 208p, Cloth, Novel [Floating City #1]

14621 *A floating city; and, The blockade runners.* Sampson Low, Marston, Searle & Rivington, London, 1874, 286p, Cloth, Coll. [Floating City #s 1-2]

14622 *The floating island; or, The pearl of the Pacific.* Sampson Low, Marston, Searle & Rivington, London, 1896, 382p, Cloth, Novel

14622A retitled: *Propeller Island.* Arco Publications, London, 1961, 192p, Cloth, Novel

14623 *For the flag.* Sampson Low, Marston, Searle & Rivington, London, 1897, 312p, Cloth, Novel

14623A retitled: *Facing the flag.* F. Tennyson Neely, New York, 1897, 217p, Cloth, Novel

From Earth to Moon. [see 14626F]

14624 *From the clouds to the mountains, comprising narratives of strange adventures by air, land, and water.* W. F. Gill & Co., Boston, 1874, 284p, Cloth, Coll.

14624A retitled: *Dr. Ox's experiment.* H. M. Caldwell, New York, 1890?, 292p, Cloth, Coll.

14625 *From the Earth to the Moon, passage direct in 97 hours and 20 minutes.* Newark Printing & Publishing Co., Newark, NJ, 1869, 84p, Cloth?, Novel [Gun Club #1A]

14626 *From the Earth to the Moon in 97 hours 20 minutes; and, A trip round it.* Sampson Low, Marston, Searle & Rivington, London, 1873, 323p, Cloth, Coll. [Gun Club #1]

14626A retitled: *The American Gun Club.* Charles Scribner's Sons, New York, 1874,   , Cloth, Coll. [Gun Club #1]

14626B retitled: *The Baltimore Gun Club.* King & Baird, Philadelphia, 1874, 442p, Cloth, Coll. [Gun Club #1]

14626C retitled: *All around the Moon.* Catholic Publication Society, New York, 1876, 484p, Cloth, Coll. [Gun Club #1]

14626D retitled: *The Moon-voyage.* Ward, Lock & Tyler, London, 1877, 279p, Cloth, Coll. [Gun Club #1]

14626E retitled: *A voyage to the Moon.* Haldeman-Julius, Girard, Kans., 1923, 64p, Paper, Coll. [Gun Club #1; abridged]

14626F retitled: *From Earth to Moon.* J. M. Dent & Sons, London, 1930, 256p, Cloth, Coll. [Gun Club #1]

14626G retitled: *From the Earth to the Moon; and, A tour of the Moon.* Didier, New York, 1949, 256p, Cloth, Coll. [Gun Club #1]

14626H retitled: *From the Earth to the Moon; All around the Moon; space novels.* Dover, New York, 1960, 470p, Paper, Coll. [Gun Club #1]

14627 *Hector Servadac; travels and adventures through the Solar System.* George Munro, New York, 1877, 39p, Paper, Story [This appears to be an abridged version of both sections put together]

14628 *Hector Servadac; or, The career of a comet.* Sampson Low, Marston, Searle & Rivington, London, 1878, 370p, Cloth, Coll. [Hector Servadac #s 1-2]

14628A retitled: *Astounding adventures among the comets.* Hurst & Co., New York, 1910?, Cloth, Coll.?

14628B retitled: *Off on a comet.* Ace, New York, 1957, 318p, Paper, Coll. [Hector Servadac #s 1-2; abridged]

14628C retitled: *Space novels by Jules Verne: To the Sun? Off on a comet!* Dover, New York, 1960, 462p, Paper, Coll. [Hector Servadac #s 1-2]

Homeward bound. [see 14636A]

The hunt for the meteor. [see 14605A]

The ice desert. [see 14617B]

14629 *Into the Niger Bend; part one of the Barsac Mission.* Arco Publications, London, 1960, 192p, Cloth, Novel [Barsac Mission #1]

A journey into the interior of the Earth. [see 14630A]

14630 *A journey to the centre of the Earth.* Griffith & Farran, London, 1871, 384p, Cloth, Novel

14630A retitled: *A journey into the interior of the Earth.* Ward, Lock & Tyler, London, 1875?, 267p, Cloth, Novel

14630B retitled: *A journey to the interior of the Earth.* Ward, Lock & Tyler, London, 1876, 276p, Cloth, Novel

14630C retitled: *A trip to the center of the Earth.* Didier, New York, 1950, 210p, Cloth, Novel

A journey to the North Pole. [see 14615A]

14631 *Jules Verne, master of science fiction.* Sidgwick & Jackson, London, 1956, 236p, Cloth, Coll. [excerpts from ten Verne novels]

14632 *The lottery ticket; and, The begum's fortune.* Sampson Low, Marston, London, 1919, Cloth, Coll.

14633 *The master of the world; a tale of mystery and marvel.* Sampson Low, Marston, London, 1914, 317p, Cloth, Novel [Robur #2]

Master of the world, including Robur the conqueror. [see 14639A]

The Moon-voyage. [see 14626D]

14634 *The mysterious island.* Sampson Low, Marston, Searle & Rivington, London, 1875, 3vol, Cloth, Coll. [Capt. Nemo #2]

14635 *Novels: Twenty thousand leagues under the sea; Around the world in eighty days; Floating island; The blockade runners; Hector Servadac.* Victor Gollancz, London, 1929, 1168p, Cloth, Coll.

Off on a comet. [see 14628B]

14636 *Off on a comet! a journey through planetary space.* Claxton, Remsen & Haffelfinger, Philadelphia, 1878, 472p, Cloth, Novel [Hector Servadac #2]

14636A retitled: *Homeward bound; part two of Hector Servadac.* Arco Publications, London, 1965, 192p, Cloth, Novel [Hector Servadac #2]

14637 *The omnibus Jules Verne.* J. B. Lippincott, Philadelphia, 1931, 822p, Cloth, Coll. [includes: *Twenty thousand leagues under the sea; The blockade runners; Around the world*

VERNE, JULES (cont.)

in eighty days; From the Earth to the Moon;
A trip round it]

14638 The purchase of the North Pole; a sequel to
From the Earth to the Moon. Sampson Low,
Marston, Searle & Rivington, London, 1890,
182p, Cloth, Novel [Gun Club #2]

14639 Robur the conqueror; and, Master of the world.
Didier, New York, 1951, 261p, Cloth, Coll.
[Robur #s 1-2]

14639A retitled: Master of the world, including
Robur the conqueror. Ace, New York, 1961,
254p, Paper, Coll. [Robur #s 1-2]

Robur the conqueror; or, A trip round the
world in a flying machine. [see 14607A]

14640 Round the Moon; a sequel to "From the Earth
to the Moon." Sampson Low, Marston, Searle
& Rivington, London, 1876, 192p, Cloth,
Novel [Gun Club #1B]

14640A retitled: Around the Moon. John W. Lovell,
New York, 1888, 151p, Cloth, Novel [Gun
Club #1B]

Round the world in eighty days. [see 14648B]

14641 The secret of the island. Sampson Low, Mars-
ton, Searle & Rivington, London, 1875, 299p,
Cloth, Novel [Mysterious Island #3; Capt.
Nemo #2C]

14642 The secret of Wilhelm Storitz. Arco Publications, London, 1963, 190p, Cloth, Novel

14643 Shipwrecked in the air. Henry L. Shepard,
Boston, 1874,   , Cloth, Novel [Mysterious
Island #2; Capt. Nemo #2B]

14643A retitled: Dropped from the clouds. Sampson
Low, Marston, Searle & Rivington, London,
1875, 310p, Cloth, Novel [Mysterious Island
#2; Capt. Nemo #2B]

Space novels by Jules Verne; To the Sun? Off
on a comet! [see 14628C]

14644 The steam house. Sampson Low, Marston, Searle
& Rivington, London, 1881, 508p, Cloth,
Coll. [Steam House #s 1-2]

14645 Stories of adventures. Scribner, Armstrong,
New York, 1874, 2vol/1, Cloth, Coll. [in-
cludes Meridiana and Around the world in
eighty days]

14646 Tigers and traitors. Sampson Low, Marston,
Searle & Rivington, London, 1881, 246p,
Cloth, Novel [Steam House #2]

14647 To the Sun? a journey through planetary space.
Claxton, Remsen & Haffelfinger, Philadelphia,
1878, 401p, Cloth, Novel [Hector Servadac
#1]

14647A retitled: Anomalous phenomena; part one of
Hector Servadac. Arco Publications, London,
1965, 192p, Cloth, Novel [Hector Servadac
#1]

14648 A tour of the world in eighty days. James R.
Osgood, Boston, 1873, 291p, Cloth, Novel

14648A retitled: Around the world in eighty days.
Sampson Low, Marston, Searle & Rivington,
London, 1874,   , Cloth, Novel

14648B retitled: Round the world in eighty days.
George Routledge & Sons, London, 1878,
254p, Cloth, Novel

A trip around the world in a flying machine.
[see 14607B]

A trip to the center of the Earth. [see
14630C]

14649 Twenty thousand leagues under the sea. Sampson Low, Marston, Searle & Rivington, London, 1872, 303p, Cloth, Novel [Capt. Nemo
#1]

14650 The village in the treetops. Arco Publications,
London, 1964, 191p, Cloth, Novel

A voyage to the Moon. [see 14626E]

The voyages and adventures of Captain Hatteras.
[see 14600A]

The wilderness of ice. [see 14617C]

14651 A winter amid the ice, and other stories. London, 1890,   , Cloth, Coll.

14652 The wonderful travellers. Ward, Lock, London,
1877,   , Cloth, Coll. [includes Journey to
the centre of the Earth and Five weeks in a
balloon]

14653 Yesterday and tomorrow. Arco Publications,
London, 1965, 188p, Cloth, Coll.

with Edgar Allan Poe:

11749 The mystery of Arthur Gordon Pym. Arco Publications, London, 1960, 191p, Cloth, Coll.
[includes Poe's The narrative of Arthur Gordon Pym and Verne's sequel, An Antarctic
mystery]

VERNER, GERALD

14654 "Come not, Lucifer!" a romantic anthology.
John Westhouse, London, 1945, 267p, Cloth,
Anth. [published anonymously]

14655 Prince of darkness. John Westhouse, London,
1946, 250p, Cloth, Anth. [published anonymously; includes some nonf.]

14655A Prince of darkness, by Gerald Verner. Rider &
Co., London, 1951, 250p, Cloth, Anth.

VERNON, GEORGE
see: GEORGE, VERNON

VERNON, ROGER LEE, 1924-

14656 Robot hunt. Avalon, New York, 1959, 224p,
Cloth, Novel

14657 The space frontiers. Signet, New York, 1955,
152p, Paper, Coll.

VERRILL, A(lpheus) HYATT, 1871-1954

14658 The boy adventurers in the land of the monkey
men. G. P. Putnam's Sons, New York, 1923,
284p, Cloth, Novel [Boy Adventurers #3]

14659 The Bridge of Light. Fantasy Press, Reading,
PA, 1950, 248p, Cloth, Novel

14660 The golden city; a tale of adventure in unknown
Guiana. Duffield & Co., New York, 1916,
272p, Cloth, Novel

14661 The trail of the white Indians; sequel to The
trail of the cloven foot. E. P. Dutton, New
York, 1920, 197p, Cloth, Novel

as Ray Ainsbury:

14662 When the Moon ran wild. Consul, London, 1962,
158p, Paper, Novel

VERRON, ROBERT

14663 The day of the dust. Wright & Brown, London,
1964, 190p, Cloth, Novel

14664 The point of no return. Wright & Brown, London,
1955, 190p, Cloth, Novel

VERSCHOYLE, CATHERINE M(ildred)

14665 *Oldham; a novel.* Longmans, Green, London,
       1927, 278p, Cloth, Novel

VÉRY, PIERRE, 1900-1960

14666 *In what strange land.* Allan Wingate, London,
       1949, 215p, Cloth, Novel

VET, CHARLES V. DE
    see: DE VET, CHARLES V.

VETCH, THOMAS

14667 *The amber city, being some account of the ad-
       ventures of a steam crocodile in central
       Africa.* Biggs & Debenham, London, 1888,
       291p, Cloth, Novel

VIAN, BORIS, 1920-1959

14668 *Froth on the daydream.* Rapp & Carroll, London,
       1967, 221p, Cloth, Novel
14668A retitled: *Mood indigo.* Grove Press, New York,
       1968, 191p, Cloth, Novel

VIARD, HENRI
    see: WARD, HENRY

VIDAL, GORE [Eugene Luther Vidal, Jr., 1925-]
    [*biography included*]

14669 *Messiah.* E. P. Dutton, New York, 1954, 254p,
       Cloth, Novel
14670 *Myron; a novel.* Random House, New York, 1974,
       244p, Cloth, Novel
14671 *A search for the king; a twelfth century le-
       gend.* E. P. Dutton, New York, 1950, 255p,
       Cloth, Novel

VIELLE, E(ugene) E(mile), 1913-

14672 *No subway.* Collins, London, 1968, 191p, Cloth,
       Novel

VIERECK, GEORGE SYLVESTER, 1884-1962

14673 *The house of the vampire.* Moffat, Yard, New
       York, 1907, 190p, Cloth, Novel
14674 *The nude in the mirror.* Woodford Press, New
       York, 1953, 253p, Cloth, Novel

with Paul Eldridge:

04752 *The invincible Adam.* Horace Liveright, New
       York, 1932, 451p, Cloth, Novel [The Three
       Immortals #3]
04753 *My first two thousand years; the autobiography
       of the wandering Jew.* Macaulay Co., New
       York, 1928, 501p, Cloth, Novel [The Three
       Immortals #1]
04754 *Prince Pax.* Duckworth, London, 1933, 319p,
       Cloth, Novel
04755 *Salome, the wandering Jewess.* Horace Liveright,
       New York, 1930, 495p, Cloth, Novel [The
       Three Immortals #2]

VIGERS, DAPHNE

14675 *Atlantis rising.* Andrew Dakers, London, 1944,
       179p, Cloth, Novel

VIGGIANO, MICHAEL, with Donald Franson

05612 *Science fiction title changes; a guide to the
       changing titles of science fiction and fan-
       tasy stories published in magazines and
       books.* National Fantasy Fan Federation,
       Heiskell, 1965, 47p, Paper, Nonf.

VIKING, OTTO, 1883-

14676 *A world intervenes.* Exposition Press, New
       York, 1964, 227p, Cloth, Novel

VILLA, SILVIO

14677 *Ultra-violet tales.* Macmillan, New York,
       1927, 154p, Cloth, Coll.

VILLARD, ALEXANDER

14678 *New world of pain-masters.* Star Distributors,
       New York, 1972, 190p, Paper, Novel

VILLIERS de L'ISLE-ADAM, (Jean Marie Mathias
Philippe Auguste, Comte de), 1838-1889

14679 *Claire Lenoir.* Albert & Charles Boni, New
       York, 1925, 222p, Cloth, Novel

VINCENT, CHARLES, 1851-1920, with Charles
Causse as Peter Maël

02774 *Under the sea to the North Pole.* Sampson Low,
       Marston, London , 1893, 244p, Cloth, Novel

VINCENT, FLORENCE SMITH

14680 *Peter's adventures in Birdland.* Frederick A.
       Stokes, New York, 1922, 331p, Cloth, Novel

VINCENT, HARL, pseud. [Harold Vincent Schoepflin, 1893-1968] [*biography included*]

14681 *The doomsday planet.* Tower, New York, 1966,
       141p, Paper, Novel

VINCENT, JOYCE

14682 *The celestial hand; a sensational story.* J. C
       MacCartie, Sydney, 1903, 137p, Cloth, Novel

VINCI, LEONARDO da
    see: PAYNE, ROBERT

VINDEX, pseud.

14683 *England crushed; the secret of the Channel Tunnel revealed.* P. S. King, London, 1882, 16p, Paper, Story

VINES, (Walter) SHERARD, 1890-

14684 *Return, Belphegor!* Wishart, London, 1932, 310p, Cloth, Novel

VINGE, VERNOR (Steffen), 1944- [*biography included*]

14685 *Grimm's world.* Berkley Medallion, New York, 1969, 176p, Paper, Novel

VINSON, REX THOMAS
see: KING, VINCENT

VINTON, ARTHUR DUDLEY, 1852-1906

14686 *Looking further backward, being a series of lectures delivered to the freshman class at Shawmut College by Professor Won Lung Li (successor of Prof. Julian West).* Albany Book Co., Albany, NY, 1890, 236p, Cloth, Novel [a sequel to Bellamy's *Looking backward*]

VISIAK, E. H., pseud. [Edward Harold Physick, 1878-1972]

14687 *The haunted island; a pirate romance.* Elkin Mathews, London, 1910, 194p, Cloth, Novel
14688 *Medusa; a story of mystery and ecstasy & strange horror.* Victor Gollancz, London, 1929, 286p, Cloth, Novel

with J. B. Pick and Colin Wilson:

11500 *The strange genius of David Lindsay; an appreciation.* John Baker, London, 1970, 183p, Cloth, Nonf.

VISICK, JACQUELYN

14689 *London tales of terror.* Fontana, London, 1972, 187p, Paper, Anth.

A VISITOR AND HIS OPINION

14690 *A visitor and his opinion.* no publisher, Boston, 1902, 70p, Cloth, Novel

A VISITOR FROM OUTER SPACE

14691 *A visitor from outer space.* Foreign Languages Publishing House, Moscow, 1961, 202p, Paper, Anth.
14691A retitled: *Soviet science fiction.* Collier, New York, 1962, 189p, Paper, Anth.

VITARELLI, ROBERT (Francis), 1940- [*biography included*]

14692 *The haunted spacesuit, and other science fiction stories.* American Education Publications, Middletown, Conn., 1970, 94p, Paper, Anth.
14693 *Strange happenings; weird tales of science fiction and the supernatural.* American Education Publications, Middletown, Conn., 1972, 93p, Paper, Anth.
14694 *The weird witch's spell; eight strange haunted tales.* Xerox Education Publications, Middletown, Conn., 1972, 95p, Paper, Anth.

VITO, JOHN A. de
see: DE VITO, JOHN A.

VIVIAN, E(velyn) CHARLES (H.)

14695 *City of wonder.* Hutchinson, London, 1922, 287p, Cloth, Novel
14696 *Fields of sleep.* Hutchinson, London, 1923, 288p, Cloth, Novel [Aia #1]
14697 *A king there was--.* Hodder & Stoughton, London, 1926, 320p, Cloth, Novel
14698 *The lady of the terraces.* Hodder & Stoughton, London, 1925, 319p, Cloth, Novel
14699 *Passion-fruit.* William Heinemann, London, 1912, 312p, Cloth, Novel
14700 *People of the darkness.* Hutchinson, London, 1924, 288p, Cloth, Novel [Aia #2]
14701 *Star dust.* Hutchinson, London, 1925, 287p, Cloth, Novel
14702 *Woman dominant.* Ward, Lock, London, 1929, 311p, Cloth, Novel

as Jack Mann:

14703 *Coulson goes south.* Wright & Brown, London, 1933, 288p, Cloth, Novel [Coulson series]
14704 *The glass too many.* Wright & Brown, London, 1940, 284p, Cloth, Novel [Gees series]
14705 *Grey shapes.* Wright & Brown, London, 1937, 286p, Cloth, Novel [Gees series]
14706 *Her ways are death.* Wright & Brown, London, 1941, 284p, Cloth, Novel [Gees series]
14707 *Maker of shadows.* Wright & Brown, London, 1938, 288p, Cloth, Novel [Gees series]
14708 *Nightmare farm.* Wright & Brown, London, 1937, 288p, Cloth, Novel [Gees series]
14709 *The ninth life.* Wright & Brown, London, 1939, 282p, Cloth, Novel [Gees series]

VIVIAN, FRANCIS, pseud. [Arthur Ernest Ashley, 1906-] [*biography included*]

14710 *Dark Moon.* Herbert Jenkins, London, 1939, 284p, Cloth, Novel

VLASTO, JOHN ALEXANDER
see: REMENHAM, JOHN

VOGEL, (Sir) JULIUS, 1835-1899

14711 *Anno Domini 2000; or, Woman's destiny.* Hutchinson, London, 1889, 331p, Cloth, Novel

VOGEL, KLAUS

14712 *Virgin witch*. Corgi, London, 1971, 160p,
       Paper, Movie

VOGT, A. E. van
    see: van VOGT, A. E.

A VOICE FROM ANOTHER WORLD
    see: LACH-SZYRMA, W. S.

VOICES FROM MANY HILL TOPS
    see: FAYETTE, JOHN B.

VOISENON, Abbé de [Claude Henri de Fusée,
Abbé de Voisenon, 1708-1775]

14713 *Fairy tales*. Erotika Biblion Society, Athens,
       1895, 165p, Cloth, Coll.
14713A retitled: *Erotic fairy tales*. Panurge Press,
       New York, 1932,   , Cloth, Coll.

VOISKUNSKII, E(vgenii Lvovich), 1922-   [*biography included*], with I. Lukodianov

09310 *The crew of the Mekong, being an account of
       the latest fantastic discoveries, happenings
       of the eighteenth century, mysteries of mat-
       ter, and adventures on land and at sea*, by
       E. Voiskunsky and I. Lukodyanov. Mir Publi-
       shers, Moscow, 1974, 422p, Paper, Novel

VOISKUNSKY, E.
    see: VOISKUNSKII, E.

VOLTA, ORNELLA, with Valeria Riva

12253 *The vampire; an anthology*. Neville Spearman,
       London, 1963, 286p, Cloth, Anth. [not the
       same as *The vampire* (Tandem Books, 1965), by
       the same authors, which is nonf.]

VOLTAIRE, (François Marie Arouët de), 1694-1778

14714 *The best known works of Voltaire; the complete
       romances, including Candide, The philosophy
       of history, The ignorant philosopher, Dia-
       logues, and Philosophic criticism*. Blue
       Ribbon, New York, 1931, 504p, Cloth, Coll.
       [includes some nonf.]
14715 *Candide, and other tales*. J. M. Dent & Sons,
       London, 1937, 352p, Cloth, Coll. [*Candide*
       itself is not SF]
14716 *Candide; &, Zadig*. Washington Square Press,
       New York, 1962, 217p, Paper, Coll.
14717 *Candide, Zadig, and selected stories*. Indiana
       University Press, Bloomington, Ind., 1961,
       351p, Cloth, Coll.
14718 *The famous romances of Voltaire*. Laird & Lee,
       Chicago, 1893, 498p, Cloth, Coll.
       The hermit. [see 14729A]
       The history of Zadig. [see 14729B]
14719 *Micromegas; a comic romance, being a severe
       satire upon the philosophy, ignorance, and
       self-conceit of mankind; together with a*

       *detail of the Crusades, and a new plan for
       the history of the human mind*. D. Wilson &
       T. Durham, London, 1753, 252p, Cloth, Novel
14720 *Miscellanies by M. de Voltaire, containing I.
       The pupil of nature; II. The princess of
       Babylon; III. Zadig; or, The book of fate,
       an Oriental history*. Robert Bell, Philadel-
       phia, 1778, 3vol/1, Cloth, Coll.
14721 *The princess of Babylon; a romance*. Bladon,
       London, 1768, 348p, Cloth, Novel
14722 *The romances of Voltaire*. Lincoln MacVeagh,
       The Dial Press, New York, 1928, 350p, Cloth,
       Coll.
14723 *Romances, tales, and smaller pieces of M. de
       Voltaire*. P. Dodsley, London, 1794, 2vol,
       Cloth, Coll.
       Le taureau blanc. [see 14726A]
14724 *Voltaire; a Laurel reader*. Dell, New York,
       1959, 383p, Paper, Coll.
14725 *Voltaire's romances*. P. Eckler, New York,
       1885, 430p, Cloth, Coll.
14726 *The white bull; an Oriental history, from an
       ancient Syrian manuscript communicated by
       Mr. Voltaire*. J. Bew, London, 1774, 2vol,
       Cloth, Novel
14726A retitled: *Le taureau blanc; or, The white
       bull*. John Murray, London, 1774, 75p, Cloth
       Novel
14727 *The white bull, with Saul and various short
       pieces*. Scholartis Press, London, 1729,
       207p, Cloth, Coll.
14728 *Zadig, and other romances*. E. P. Dutton, New
       York, 1923, 320p, Cloth, Coll.
14729 *Zadig; or, The book of fate; an Oriental his-
       tory*. J. Brindley, London, 1749, 238p,
       Cloth, Novel
14729A retitled: *The hermit; an Oriental tale*. P.
       Middleton, London, 1779, 43p, Cloth, Story
14729B retitled: *The history of Zadig; or, Destiny;
       an Oriental tale*. Limited Editions Club,
       Paris, 1952, 171p, Cloth, Novel

A VOLUNTEER
    see: CHESNEY, GEORGE T.

von BRAUN, WERNHER, 1912-1977 [*biography included*]

14730 *First men to the Moon*. Holt, Rinehart & Win-
       ston, New York, 1960, 96p, Cloth, Novel

von CHAMISSO, ADALBERT
    see: CHAMISSO, ADALBERT von

VON DEGEN, pseud. [Baroness Ann von Rabe]

14731 *A mystery of the Campagna; and, A shadow on a
       wave*. T. Fisher Unwin, London, 1891, 203p,
       Cloth, Coll.

von GOETHE, JOHANN WOLFGANG
    see: GOETHE, JOHANN WOLFGANG von

VON GRUEN
    see: GRUEN, VON

von GUENTHER, JOHANNES
    see: GUENTHER, JOHANNES von

von GRAU, WERNHER, pseud.
    see: SCHOEB, ERIKA

von HARBOU, THEA, 1888-1953

  14732 *The girl in the Moon.* Readers Library Publishing Co., London, 1930, 250p, Cloth, Movie
  14732A retitled: *The rocket to the Moon, from the novel "The girl in the Moon."* World Wide Publishing Co., New York, 1930, 187p, Cloth, Movie
  14733 *Metropolis.* Readers Library Publishing Co., London, 1927, 250p, Cloth, Movie

von HERBERT, FREDERICK WILLIAM
    see: HERBERT, FREDERICK WILLIAM von

von HEYSE, PAUL
    see: HEYSE, PAUL von

von HIMMEL, ERNST, pseud.
    see: PETERSILEA, CARLYLE

von KARTOFFEL, Baron, pseud.

  14734 *The Germans in Cork, being the letters of his excellency the Baron von Kartoffel (military governor of Cork in 1918), and others.* Talbot Press, Dublin, 1917, 112p, Paper, Novel

VON KELLAR
    see: KELLAR, VON

von KUEHNELT-LEDDIHN, CHRISTIANE
    see: KUEHNELT-LEDDIHN, CHRISTIANE von

von KUEHNELT-LEDDIHN, ERIK
    see: KUEHNELT-LEDDIHN, ERIK von

von LOWENELL, JOHANN
    see: LOWENELL, JOHANN von

VONNEGUT, KURT, Jr., 1922- [*biography included*]

  14735 *Breakfast of champions; or, Goodbye, blue Monday!* Delacorte Press, New York, 1973, 297p, Cloth, Novel
  14736 *Canary in a cat house.* Gold`Medal, Greenwich, Conn., 1961, 160p, Paper, Coll.
  14737 *Cat's cradle.* Holt, Rinehart & Winston, New York, 1963, 231p, Cloth, Novel
  14738 *Player piano.* Charles Scribner's Sons, New York, 1952, 295p, Cloth, Novel
  14738A retitled: *Utopia 14.* Bantam, New York, 1954, 312p, Paper, Novel

  14739 *The sirens of Titan; an original novel.* Dell, New York, 1959, 319p, Paper, Novel
  14740 *Slaughterhouse-five; or, The children's crusade; a duty-dance with death.* Seymour Lawrence, Delacorte Press, New York, 1969, 186p, Cloth, Novel
      Utopia 14. [see 14738A]
  14741 *Welcome to the monkey house; a collection of short works.* Seymour Lawrence, Delacorte Press, 1968, 298p, Cloth, Coll.

von RABE, ANN
    see: VON DEGEN

von RAVN, CLARA IZA, 1870-

  14742 *Selestor's men of Atlantis.* Christopher Publishing House, Boston, 1937, 173p, Cloth, Novel

von SUTTNER, BERTHA
    see: SUTTNER, BERTHA von

VORHIES, JOHN ROYAL (Harris), 1920- [*biography included*]

  14743 *Pre-empt; a novel.* Henry Regnery, Chicago, 1967, 220p, Cloth, Novel
  14743A retitled: *The 'Nathan Hale.'* Neville Spearman, London, 1968, 220p, Cloth, Novel

VOSS, RICHARD, 1851-1918

  14744 *Amata.* Neale Publishing Co., Washington, DC, 1901, 116p, Cloth, Novel

VOSS-BARK, C(onrad Lyddon)

  14745 *Sealed entrance; a novel.* Chapman & Hall, London, 1947, 224p, Cloth, Novel

A VOYAGE TO THE MOON
    see: ARATUS

A VOYAGE TO THE WORLD IN THE CENTRE OF THE EARTH

  14746 *A voyage to the world in the centre of the Earth, giving an account of the manners, customs, laws, government, and religion of the inhabitants...in which is introduced The history of the air, written by himself; with some account of the planetary worlds.* S. Crowder & H. Woodgate, London, 1755, 275p, Cloth, Novel

VOYAGER, KRYSTOFALUS, pseud.

  14747 *The sons of Priapus.* Greenleaf Classics, San Diego, 1970, 195p, Paper, Novel

W., E.

14748   *The island of anarchy; a fragment of history in the 20th century.* Miss Langley Lovejoy's Library, Reading, UK, 1888, 105p, Cloth, Novel

W., H.
see: WILLIAMS, HERBERT

W., M.
see: WILSON, MILES

W., W.
see: BLOOM, WILLIAM

W. S. L. S.
see: LACH-SZYRMA, W. S.

WADE, TOM

14749   *The voice from Baru.* Digit, London, 1962, 157p, Paper, Novel
14750   *The world of Theda.* Digit, London, 1962, 154p, Paper, Novel

WADELTON, MAGGIE-OWEN [Maggie Jeanne Wadelton, 1896-]

14751   *Sarah Mandrake.* Bobbs-Merrill, Indianapolis, 1946, 319p, Cloth, Novel

WADEY, VICTOR

14752   *A planet named Terra.* Digit, London, 1962, 160p, Paper, Novel
14753   *The united planets.* Digit, London, 1962, 160p, Paper, Novel

WADSWORTH, PHYLLIS MARIE

14754   *Overmind.* Sidgwick & Jackson, London, 1967, 284p, Cloth, Novel

WAGENKNECHT, EDWARD (Charles), 1900-   [*biography included*]

14755   *The fireside book of ghost stories.* Bobbs-Merrill, Indianapolis, 1947, 593p, Cloth, Anth.
14756   *Six novels of the supernatural.* Viking Press, New York, 1944, 883p, Cloth, Anth.

WAGNER, BELLE M.

14757   *Within the Temple of Isis.* Astro-Philosophical Publishing Co., Denver, 1899, 156p, Cloth, Novel

WAGNER, GEOFFREY (Atheling), 1927-

14758   *Axel.* Greenleaf Classics, San Diego, 1968, 352p, Paper, Novel

WAGNER, KARL EDWARD, 1945-   [*biography included*]

14759   *Darkness weaves with many shades...* Powell Publications, Reseda, CA, 1970, 205p, Paper, Novel [Kane #1]
14760   *Death Angel's Shadow.* Warner, New York, 1973, 205p, Paper, Coll. [Kane #2]

WAGNER, SHARON (Blythe), 1936-   [*biography included*]

14761   *Maridu.* Lancer, New York, 1970, 239p, Paper, Novel

WAIT, FRONA EUNICE
see: COLBURN, FRONA

WAITE, ARTHUR EDWARD, 1857-1942

14762   *The quest of the golden stairs; a mystery of kinghood in Faërie.* Theosophical Publishing House, London, 1927, 176p, Cloth, Novel

WAKEFIELD, H(erbert) **RUSSELL**, 1888-1965 [*biography included*]

14763   *The clock strikes twelve; tales of the supernatural.* Herbert Jenkins, London, 1939, 271p, Cloth, Coll.
14763A   retitled: *Stories from The clock strikes twelve.* Ballantine, New York, 1961, 159p, Paper, Coll.
14764   *Ghost stories.* Jonathan Cape, London, 1932, 288p, Cloth, Coll.
14765   *A ghostly company.* Jonathan Cape, London, 1935, 256p, Cloth, Coll.
14766   *Imagine a man in a box.* Philip Allan, London, 1931, 317p, Cloth, Coll.
14767   *Old man's beard; fifteen disturbing tales.* Geoffrey Bles, London, 1929, 278p, Cloth, Coll.
14767A   retitled: *Others who returned; fifteen disturbing tales.* D. Appleton, New York, 1929, 275p, CLoth, Coll.
    Stories from The clock strikes twelve. [see 14763A]
14768   *Strayers from Sheol.* Arkham House, Sauk City, 1961, 186p, Cloth, Coll.
14769   *They return at evening; a book of ghost stories.* Philip Allan, London, 1928, 313p, Cloth, Coll.

WALDO, CEDRIC DANE, pseud. [Cecil Drummond Wolff]

14770   *The ban of the Gubbe.* William Blackwood & Sons, Edinburgh, 1896, 195p, Cloth, Novel

WALDO, EDWARD HAMILTON
see: STURGEON, THEODORE

WALDROP, HOWARD, with Jake Saunders

12705 *The Texas-Israeli War: 1999*. Ballantine, New
York, 1974, 209p, Paper, Novel

WALES, HUBERT, pseud. [William Piggott, 1870-
1943]

14771 *The Brocklebank riddle*. Century Co., New
York, 1914, 329p, Cloth, Novel
14771A retitled: *The thirty days*. Cassell, London,
1915, 311p, Cloth, Novel

WALES, NYM, pseud. [Helen Foster Snow, 1907-]

14772 *Fables and parables for the mid-century*.
Philosophical Library, New York, 1952,
339p, Cloth, Coll.

WALFORD, FRANK, 1882-

14773 *The ghost and Albert, and other stories*.
T. Werner Laurie, London, 1945, 189p, Cloth,
Coll.

WALK IN DREAD
see: A CENTURY OF GHOST STORIES

WALKER, CLIFTON
see: DIXON, RICHARD

WALKER, DALE L(ee), 1935-   [*biography included*]

14774 *The alien worlds of Jack London*. Wolf House
Books, Grand Rapids, Mich., 1973, 47p,
Paper, Nonf.

WALKER, DAVID (Harry), 1911-   [*biography included*]

14775 *The Lord's pink ocean*. Houghton Mifflin, Boston, 1972, 185p, Cloth, Novel
14776 *Winter of madness; a novel*. Houghton Mifflin,
Boston, 1964, 272p, Cloth, Novel

WALKER, EARL

14777 *Pasquinade*. Futura Press, Philadelphia, 1931,
160p, Cloth, Novel

WALKER, GWEN

14778 *The golden stile*. John Day Co., New York,
1958, 188p, Cloth, Novel

WALKER, J(ohn) BERNARD, 1858-

14779 *American fallen! the sequel to the European
War*. Dodd, Mead, New York, 1915, 203p,
Cloth, Novel

WALKER, JERRY

14780 *A date with destiny*. Cosmos Publishing Co.,
New York, 1949, 225p, Cloth, Novel [Lawrence
Marley #2]
14781 *Mission accomplished; a novel of 1950*. Cosmos
Publications, New York, 1947, 246p, Cloth,
Novel [Lawrence Marley #1]

WALKER, KENNETH M(acfarlane), 1882-1966, with
Geoffrey M. Boumphrey

01664 *The log of the Ark*. Constable, London, 1923,
214p, Cloth, Novel
01664A retitled: *What happened in the Ark*. E. P.
Dutton, New York, 1926, 275p, Cloth, Novel

WALKER, NORMAN, 1897-

14782 *Loona; a strange tail*. Longmans, Green, London, 1931, 307p, Cloth, Novel

WALKER, ROWLAND, 1876-

14783 *By airship to the tropics; the amazing adventures of two schoolboys*. Ward, Lock, London, 1923, 256p, Cloth, Novel
14784 *The lost expedition*. Sampson Low, Marston,
London, 1923, 256p, Cloth, Novel

WALKER, VICTORIA, 1947-

14785 *The winter of enchantment*. Rupert Hart-Davis,
London, 1969, 150p, Cloth, Novel

WALKER, W. H.

14786 *The invasion*. Turner & Henderson, Sydney,
1877,   , Paper, Novel

WALKEY, SAMUEL

14787 *In quest of Sheba's treasure*. Frederick Warne,
London, 1897, 320p, Cloth, Novel

WALL, A(lfred H.), with A. A. Anderson

00253 *A romance of N'Shabé, being a record of start-
ling adventures in south central Africa*.
Chapman & Hall, London, 1891, 366p, Cloth,
Novel

WALL, G(eorge) A., with E. A. Robinson

12288 *The disk; a prophetic reflection*. Griffith,
Farran, Okeden & Welsh, London, 1884, 182p,
Paper, Novel

WALL, JOHN W.
see: SARBAN

WALL, MERVYN, 1908-

14788   *The return of Fursey*. Pilot Press, London,
        1948, 234p, Cloth, Novel [Fursey #2]
14789   *The unfortunate Fursey*. Pilot Press, London,
        1946, 241p, Cloth, Novel [Fursey #1]

WALLACE, B(ryan) E(dgar), 1904-

14790   *The device*. Hodder & Stoughton, London, 1962,
        255p, Cloth, Novel

WALLACE, DOREEN [Dora Eileen Agnew Wallace,
1897-   ] [*biography included*]

14791   *Forty years on*. Collins, London, 1958, 255p,
        Cloth, Novel

WALLACE, (Richard Horatio) EDGAR, 1875-1932

14792   *Captains of souls*. Small, Maynard, Boston,
        1922, 362p, Cloth, Novel
14793   *The Council of Justice*. Ward, Lock, London,
        1908, 319p, Cloth, Novel
14794   *The green rust*. Ward, Lock, London, 1919,
        319p, Cloth, Novel
14795   *"1925"; the story of a fatal peace*. George
        Newnes, London, 1915, 128p, Paper, Novel
14796   *Planetoid 127; and, The Sweizer pump*. Readers
        Library Publishing Co., London, 1929, 252p,
        Cloth, Coll.
14797   *Private Selby*. Ward, Lock, London, 1912,
        319p, Cloth, Novel

WALLACE, F(loyd) L.

14798   *Address: Centauri*. Gnome Press, New York,
        1955, 220p, Cloth, Novel
14799   *Worlds in balance*. Atlas, Melbourne, 1955,
        112p, Paper, Coll.

WALLACE, IAN, pseud. [John Wallace Pritchard,
1912-   ] [*biography included*]

14800   *Croyd; a downtime fantasy*. G. P. Putnam's
        Sons, New York, 1967, 184p, Cloth, Novel
        [Croyd #1]
14801   *Deathstar voyage; a downtime mystery cruise*.
        G. P. Putnam's Sons, New York, 1969, 191p,
        Cloth, Novel [Croyd #2; Pan Sagittarius #1]
14802   *Dr. Orpheus; a downtime myth*. G. P. Putnam's
        Sons, New York, 1968, 205p, Cloth, Novel
        [Claudine St. Cyr #1]
14803   *Pan Sagittarius*. G. P. Putnam's Sons, New
        York, 1973, 223p, Cloth, Novel [Pan Sagit-
        tarius #2]
14804   *The purloined prince*. McCall Books, New York,
        1971, 207p, Cloth, Novel [Claudine St. Cyr
        #2]
14805   *A voyage to Dari*. DAW, New York, 1974, 239p,
        Paper, Novel [Croyd #3; Pan Sagittarius #3]

WALLACE, HENRY MARRIAGE
    see: HILLIERS, ASHTON

WALLACE, KING

14806   *The next war*. Martyn Publishing House, Washing-
        ton, 1892, 130p, Paper, Novel

WALLACE, MAY NICKERSON

14807   *The ghost of Dibble Hollow*. Scholastic Book
        Services, New York, 1965, 155p, Paper, Novel

WALLER, LESLIE
    see: CODY, C. S.

WALLER, ROBERT (Ferns), 1913-

14808   *Shadow of authority*. Jonathan Cape, London,
        1956, 224p, Cloth, Novel

WALLERSTEIN, JAMES S., 1910-

14809   *The demon's mirror*. Harbinger House, New York,
        1951, 326p, Cloth, Novel

WALLING, WILLIAM (Herbert), 1926-   [*biography
included*]

14810   *No one goes there now*. Doubleday, Garden City,
        1971, 248p, Cloth, Novel

WALLIS, DAVE [David Wallis, 1917-   ]

14811   *Only lovers left alive*. Anthony Blond, London,
        1964, 256p, Cloth, Novel

WALLIS, G(eraldine June) McDONALD, 1925-
[*biography included*]

14812   *Legend of lost Earth*. Ace Double, New York,
        1963, 133p, Paper, Novel
14813   *The light of Lilith*. Ace Double, New York,
        1961, 123p, Paper, Novel

WALLIS, GEORGE C.

14814   *The call of Peter Gaskell; a master thriller
        science fiction novel*. World's Work, Kings-
        wood, UK, 1948, 130p, Cloth, Novel
14815   *The children of the sphinx; a romance of the
        old Orient*. Cosmopolitan Printing, Publi-
        shing & Advertising Co., Bristol, 1901, 344p,
        Cloth, Novel

WALLOP, (John) DOUGLASS (III), 1920-

14816   *The mermaid in the swimming pool*. W. W. Norton,
        New York, 1968, 219p, Cloth, Novel
14817   *What has four wheels and flies? a tale*. W. W.
        Norton, New York, 1959, 192p, Cloth, Novel
14818   *The year the Yankees lost the pennant; a novel*.
        W. W. Norton, New York, 1954, 250p, Cloth,
        Novel

WALMSLEY, ARNOLD ROBERT
    see: ROLAND, NICHOLAS

WALPOLE, HORACE, Earl of Orford, 1717-1797

14819   *The castle of Otranto; a story, from the ori-*
       ginal Italian of Onophurio Muralto. T.
       Lownds, London, 1765, 200p, Cloth, Novel
14819A *The castle of Otranto; a story,* by H. W.
       William Bathoe & Thomas Lownds, London,
       1765, 200p, Cloth, Novel
14819B *The castle of Otranto; a story,* by Horace
       Walpole. London, 1809, 196p, Cloth, Novel
14820   *Hieroglyphic tales.* Strawberry Hill Press,
       London?, 1785, mixed pagination, Cloth?,
       Coll. [published anonymously in an edition
       of seven copies]
14820A *Hieroglyphic tales,* by Horace Walpole. Elkin
       Mathews, London, 1926, 85p, Cloth, Coll.

WALPOLE, (Sir) HUGH (Seymour), 1884-1941

14821   *All souls' night; a book of stories.* Double-
       day, Doran, Garden City, 1933, 316p, Cloth,
       Coll.
14822   *The killer and the slain; a strange story.*
       Doubleday, Doran, Garden City, 1942, 300p,
       Cloth, Novel
14823   *A second century of creepy stories.* Hutchin-
       son, London, 1937, 1023p, Cloth, Anth.

WALSH, CHAD, 1914-   [*biography included*]

14824   *From utopia to nightmare.* Geoffrey Bles, Lon-
       don, 1962, 191p, Cloth, Nonf.

WALSH, GOODWIN

14825   *The voice of the murderer.* G. P. Putnam's
       Sons, New York, 1926, 309p, Cloth, Novel

WALSH, J(ames) M(organ), 1897-1952

14826   *Secret weapons.* Collins, London, 1940, 252p,
       Cloth, Novel
14827   *Vandals of the void.* John Hamilton, London,
       1931, 288p, Cloth, Novel
14828   *Vanguard to Neptune.* Cherry Tree, London,
       1952?, 190p, Paper, Novel

WALSH, MAURICE, 1879-1964

14829   *Son of apple; an old Irish folk-story.* Fred-
       erick A. Stokes, New York, 1940, 211p, Cloth,
       Novel

WALSH, RUPERT

14830   *The fate of the Triple Alliance; a jeu d'es-*
       prit. Simpkin, Marshall, Hamilton, Kent,
       London, 1890, 64p, Paper?, Novel

WALSH, W(illiam) E(mmet), 1868-

14831   *The doom of Conaire Mōr (Conary the Great).*
       Louis Carrier, New York, 1929, 346p, Cloth,
       Novel

WALTARI, MIKA (Toimi), 1908-

14832   *A nail merchant at nightfall; a novel.* Putnam,
       London, 1954, 176p, Cloth, Novel

WALTER, ELIZABETH [*biography included*]

14833   *Come and get me, and other uncanny invitations.*
       Harvill Press, London, 1973, 191p, Cloth,
       Coll.
14834   *Davy Jones's tale, and other supernatural sto-*
       ries. Harvill Press, London, 1971, 189p,
       Cloth, Coll.
14835   *The sin-eater, and other scientific impossibi-*
       lities. Harvill Press, London, 1967, 192p,
       Cloth, Coll.
14836   *Snowfall, and other chilling events.* Harvill
       Press, London, 1965, 191p, Cloth, Coll.

WALTER, WILLIAM GREY, 1910-1977 [*biography included*]

14837   *Further outlook.* Gerald Duckworth, London,
       1956, 224p, Cloth, Novel
14837A retitled: *The curve of the Snowflake.* W. W.
       Norton, New York, 1956, 282p, Cloth, Novel

WALTERMIRE, BEECHER W(esley), 1858-1932

14838   *The adventures of a skeleton; a tale of natural*
       gas. J. S. Ogilvie Publishing Co., New York,
       1890, 281p, Paper, Novel

WALTERS, EUGENE

14839   *Love witch.* Bee-Line, New York, 1968, 187p,
       Paper, Novel

WALTERS, HUGH, pseud. [Walter Llewellyn Hughes,
1910-   ] [*biography included*]

       Blast-off at 0300. [see 14840A]
14840   *Blast off at Woomera.* Faber & Faber, London,
       1957, 202p, Cloth, Novel [Chris Godfrey (U.N.
       Exploration Agency) #1]
14840A retitled: *Blast-off at 0300.* Criterion, New
       York, 1958, 187p, Cloth, Novel [Chris Godfrey
       #1; the U.S. editions of this series have
       all been modified for the American reader]
14841   *Destination Mars.* Faber & Faber, London,
       1963, 160p, Cloth, Novel [Chris Godfrey #6]
14842   *The domes of Pico.* Faber & Faber, London,
       1958, 196p, Cloth, Novel [Chris Godfrey #2]
14842A retitled: *Menace from the Moon.* Criterion,
       New York, 1959, 191p, Cloth, Novel [Chris
       Godfrey #2]
14843   *Expedition Venus.* Faber & Faber, London,
       1962, 160p, Cloth, Novel [Chris Godfrey #5]
14844   *First contact?* Faber & Faber, London, 1971,
       172p, Cloth, Novel [Chris Godfrey #13]

WALTERS, HUGH (cont.)

　　　　First on the Moon. [see 14850A]
14845　*Journey to Jupiter.* Faber & Faber, London,
　　　　1965, 159p, Cloth, Novel [Chris Godfrey #8]
　　　　Menace from the Moon. [see 14842A]
14846　*Mission to Mercury.* Faber & Faber, London,
　　　　1965, 158p, Cloth, Novel [Chris Godfrey #9]
　　　　The Mohole menace. [see 14847A]
14847　*The Mohole mystery.* Faber & Faber, London,
　　　　1968, 185p, Cloth, Novel [Chris Godfrey #11]
14847A　retitled: *The Mohole menace.* Criterion, New
　　　　York, 1969, 192p, Cloth, Novel [Chris God-
　　　　frey #11]
14848　*Moon Base One.* Faber & Faber, London, 1961,
　　　　189p, Cloth, Novel [Chris Godfrey #4]
14848A　retitled: *Outpost on the Moon.* Criterion,
　　　　New York, 1962, 191p, Cloth, Novel [Chris
　　　　Godrey #4]
14849　*Nearly Neptune.* Faber & Faber, London, 1969,
　　　　165p, Cloth, Novel [Chris Godfrey #12]
14849A　retitled: *Neptune One is missing.* Ives Wash-
　　　　burn, New York, 1970, 184p, Cloth, Novel
　　　　[Chris Godfrey #12]
14850　*Operation Columbus.* Faber & Faber, London,
　　　　1960, 191p, Cloth, Novel [Chris Godfrey #3]
14850A　retitled: *First on the Moon.* Criterion,
　　　　New York, 1960, 192p, Cloth, Novel [Chris
　　　　Godfrey #3]
　　　　Outpost on the Moon. [see 14848A]
14851　*Passage to Pluto.* Faber & Faber, London,
　　　　1973, 148p, Cloth, Novel [Chris Godfrey #14]
14852　*Spaceship to Saturn.* Faber & Faber, London,
　　　　1967, 160p, Cloth, Novel [Chris Godfrey #10]
14853　*Terror by satellite.* Faber & Faber, London,
　　　　1964, 159p, Cloth, Novel [Chris Godfrey #7]
14854　*Tony Hale, space detective.* Faber & Faber,
　　　　London, 1973, 154p, Cloth, Novel [Chris
　　　　Godfrey #15]

WALTON, BRYCE, 1918-   [*biography included*]

14855　*Sons of the ocean deeps.* John C. Winston,
　　　　Philadelphia, 1952, 216p, Cloth, Novel

WALTON, EVANGELINE

14856　*The children of Llyr.* Ballantine, New York,
　　　　1971, 223p, Paper, Novel [Mabinogion #2]
14857　*Prince of Annwn; the first branch of the
　　　　Mabinogion.* Ballantine, New York, 1974,
　　　　179p, Paper, Novel [Mabinogion #1]
14858　*The song of Rhiannon; the third branch of the
　　　　Mabinogion.* Ballantine, New York, 1972,
　　　　208p, Paper, Novel [Mabinogion #3]
14859　*The virgin and the swine; the fourth branch
　　　　of the Mabinogi.* Willett, Clark, Chicago,
　　　　1936, 313p, Cloth, Novel [Mabinogion #4]
14859A　retitled: *The island of the mighty; the
　　　　fourth branch of the Mabinogi.* Ballantine,
　　　　New York, 1970, 368p, Paper, Novel [Mabi-
　　　　nogion #4]
14860　*Witch House.* Arkham House, Sauk City, 1945,
　　　　200p, Cloth, Novel

WALTON, LUKE, pseud. [Bill Henderson, 1941-   ]
　　[*biography included*]

14861　*The Galápagos Kid; or, The spirit of 1976; a
　　　　novel.* Nautilus, North Plainfield, NJ,
　　　　1971, 168p, Cloth, Novel

WALTON, STEPHEN, 1945-

14862　*No transfer.* Vanguard Press, New York, 1967,
　　　　236p, Cloth, Novel

WALTON, SU, 1944-   [*biography included*]

14863　*Here before Kilroy.* Peter Davies, London,
　　　　1968, 252p, Cloth, Novel
14864　*Horace Sippog and the sirens' song.* Peter
　　　　Davies, London, 1967, 232p, Cloth, Novel

WANDERER, pseud. [Elim Henry d'Avigdor, 1841-
1895]

14865　*Whims.* Gilbert & Rivington, London, 1889, 305p,
　　　　Cloth, Coll.

WANDREI, DONALD, 1908-

14866　*The eye and the finger.* Arkham House, Sauk
　　　　City, 1944, 344p, Cloth, Coll.
14867　*Strange harvest.* Arkham House, Sauk City,
　　　　1965, 289p, Cloth, Coll.
14868　*The web of Easter Island.* Arkham House, Sauk
　　　　City, 1948, 191p, Cloth, Novel

WAR UNDER WATER

14869　*War under water.* Cassell Publishing Co., New
　　　　York, 1892, 373p, Paper, Novel [translated
　　　　from the French by Mary J. Serrano]

WARBURG, SANDOL STODDARD, 1927-   [*biography
included*]

14870　*On the way home.* Houghton Mifflin, Boston,
　　　　1973, 137p, Cloth, Novel

WARD, ARTHUR SARSFIELD
　　see: ROHMER, SAX

WARD, CHRISTOPHER (Longstreth), 1868-1943

14871　*Gentleman into goose, being the exact and true
　　　　account of Mr. Timothy Teapot, Gent., of
　　　　Puddleditch in Dorset, that was changed into
　　　　a great grey gander at the wish of his wife;
　　　　how, though a gander, he did wear breeches
　　　　and smoke a pipe; how he near lost his life
　　　　to his dog Tyger; you have also an account
　　　　of his gallantries with a goose, very diver-
　　　　ting to read, with many other surprizing
　　　　adventures, full of wonder and merriment,
　　　　and a full relation of the manner of his sad
　　　　dismal end; worthy to be had in all families
　　　　for a warning to wives and by all batchelors
　　　　intending marriage.* T. Werner Laurie, London,
　　　　1924, 78p, Cloth, Novel

WARD, DON(ald G.), 1911-

14872　*Black magic; thirteen chilling tales.* Dell,
　　　　New York, 1967, 252p, Paper, Anth.

WARD, DON (cont.)

14873　*The dark of the soul.*　Tower, New York, 1970,
　　　157p, Paper, Anth.
14874　*Favorite stories of hypnotism.*　Dodd, Mead,
　　　New York, 1965, 265p, Cloth, Anth.

with H. Rider Haggard:

06583　*She; the story retold.*　Dell, New York, 1949,
　　　192p, Paper, Movie [rewritten from the
　　　Haggard novel]

WARD, E. D., pseud.

14875　*Sir Pulteney; a fantasy.*　Methuen, London,
　　　1910, 95p, Cloth, Novel

WARD, GEORGE WHITELEY

14876　*Drelma; a tale of the great Sahara.*　Greening
　　　& Co., London, 1908, 312p, Cloth, Novel

WARD, HAROLD
　　see: ZORRO

WARD, HENRY, pseud. [Henri Louis Luc Viard,
　1921-　]

14877　*The Green Suns.*　Sidgwick & Jackson, London,
　　　1961, 206p, Cloth, Novel
14878　*Hell's above us.*　Sidgwick & Jackson, London,
　　　1960, 319p, Cloth, Novel

WARD, HERBERT D(ickinson), 1861-1932

14879　*A dash to the Pole; a tale of adventure in the
　　　ice-bound North.*　Lovell, Coryell, New York,
　　　1895, 270p, Cloth, Novel
14880　*A republic without a president, and other sto-
　　　ries.*　Tait, Sons & Co., New York, 1891,
　　　271p, Cloth, Coll.

with Elizabeth Stuart Phelps:

11433　*The master of the magicians.*　Houghton Miff-
　　　lin, Boston, 1890, 324p, Cloth, Novel

WARD, LYND (Kendall), 1905-　[*biography in-
　cluded*], with May McNeer

09959　*Prince Bantam, being the adventures of Yoshi-
　　　tsune the Brave, and his faithful henchman
　　　great Benkei of the western pagoda.*　Mac-
　　　millan, New York, 1929, 231p, Cloth, Novel

WARD, MARGARETE

14881　*Born to the purple; the karma of Princess
　　　Minerva.*　Kellaway-Ide Co., Los Angeles,
　　　1938, 323p, Cloth, Novel

WARD, RICHARD HERON

14882　*The Sun shall rise.*　Ivor Nicholson & Watson,
　　　London, 1935, 364p, Cloth, Novel

WARD, WILL(iam) J.

14883　*Shanghaied socialists; a romance.*　Maritime
　　　Review, Cardiff, Wales, 1911, 374p, Cloth,
　　　Novel

WARDE, BEATRICE
　　see: BEAUJON, PAUL

WARDE, REGINALD, 1878-　[published anonymous-
ly]

14884　*A daughter of Indra.*　Essene Publishing Co.,
　　　San Francisco, 1925, 255p, Cloth, Novel

WARMAN, (William) ERIC, 1904-　[*biography included*]

14885　*A matter of life and death; the book of the
　　　film.*　World Film Publications, London,
　　　1946, 124p, Cloth, Movie

WARNER, ANNE, 1869-1913

14886　*The panther; a tale of temptation.*　Small, May-
　　　nard, Boston, 1908, 91p, Cloth, Novel

WARNER, DOUGLAS

14887　*Death on a warm wind.*　Rapp & Whiting, London,
　　　1968, 158p, Cloth, Novel

WARNER, HARRY (Backer) Jr., 1922-　[*biography included*]

14888　*All our yesterdays; an informal history of
　　　science fiction fandom in the forties.*
　　　Advent: Publishers, Chicago, 1969, 336p,
　　　Cloth, Nonf.

WARNER, KENNETH LEWIS
　　see: MOREL, DIGHTON

WARNER, REX [Reginald Ernest Warner, 1905-　]

14889　*Why was I killed? a dramatic dialogue.*　John
　　　Lane, London, 1943, 191p, Cloth, Novel
14889A　retitled: *Return of the traveller.*　J. B.
　　　Lippincott, Philadelphia, 1944, 208p, Cloth,
　　　Novel
14890　*The Wild Goose Chase; a novel.*　Boriswood,
　　　London, 1937, 442p, Cloth, Novel

WARNER, SYLVIA TOWNSEND, 1893-1978 [*biography
included*]

14891　*The cat's cradle-book.*　Viking Press, New York,
　　　1940, 180p, Cloth, Coll.
14892　*Some world far from ours; and, 'Stay, Corydon,
　　　thou swain.'*　Elkin Mathews & Marrot, Lon-
　　　don, 1929, 31p, Cloth, Coll.

WARNER, WILLIAM HENRY

14893   *The bridge of time.*   Scott & Seltzer, New York, 1919, 372p, Cloth, Novel
14894   *Sacrilegious hands.*   Greenberg Publisher, New York, 1925, 305p, Cloth, Novel

WARNER-CROZETTI, R. [Ruth G. "Lora" Warner Crozetti, 1913-] [*biography included*]

14895   *The Widderburn horror.*   Leisure Books, North Hollywood, 1971, 191p, Paper, Novel

WARR, (Sir) CHARLES L(aing), 1892-1969

14896   *The call of the island.*   Robert Grant & Son, Edinburgh, 1929, 310p, Cloth, Coll.

WARREN, B(enjamin) C(lark), 1859?-1952

14897   *Arsareth; a tale of the Luray Caverns.*   A. Lovell, New York, 1893, 273p, Cloth, Novel

WARREN, BILL, with Walt Lee

08784   *Reference guide to fantastic films; science fiction, fantasy, and horror.*   Chelsea-Lee, Los Angeles, 1972/74, 3vol, Paper, Nonf.

WARREN, C. DELVES

14898   *Some cases of Sherwood Lang, detective.*   Drane's, London, 1923, 161p, Cloth, Coll.

WARREN, J(ohn) RUSSELL, 1886-

14899   *This mortal coil.*   Andrew Melrose, London, 1947, 272p, Cloth, Novel
14899A   retitled: *This inward light.*   E. P. Dutton, New York, 1948, 256p, Cloth, Novel

WARRICK, PATRICIA S(cott), 1925- [*biography included*]

with Martin Harry Greenberg:

06315   *Political science fiction; an introductory reader.*   Prentice-Hall, Englewood Cliffs, NJ, 1974, 415p, Cloth, Anth.

with Martin Harry Greenberg & Harvey A. Katz:

06310   *Introductory psychology through science fiction.*   Rand McNally College Publishing Co., Chicago, 1974, 510p, Paper, Anth.

with Martin Harry Greenberg & Carol Mason:

06311   *Anthropology through science fiction.*   St. Martin's Press, New York, 1974, 387p, Cloth, Anth.

with Martin Harry Greenberg, John D. Milstead, and Joseph D. Olander:

06312   *Sociology through science fiction.*   St. Martin's Press, New York, 1974, 412p, Cloth, Anth.

with Martin Harry Greenberg & Joseph Olander:

06313   *American government through science fiction.*   Rand McNally College Publishing Co., Chicago, 1974, 360p, Paper, Anth.
06314   *School and society through science fiction.*   Rand McNally College Publishing Co., Chicago, 1974, 396p, Paper, Anth.

WARREN, ROY
   see: CAMRA, ROY

WARRINGTON, MARIS
   see: BILLINGS, MARIS HERRINGTON

WARTOFSKY, (William) VICTOR, 1931-

14900   *Year of the yahoo; a novel.*   John Day, New York, 1972, 223p, Cloth, Novel

WASON, SANDYS

14901   *Palafox.*   Cope & Fenwick, London, 1927, 274p, Cloth, Novel

WATER, SILAS, pseud.
   see: LOOMIS, NOEL M.

WATERLOO, STANLEY, 1846-1913

14902   *Armageddon; a tale of love, war, and invention.*   Rand, McNally, Chicago, 1898, 259p, Cloth, Novel
14903   *A son of the ages; the reincarnations and adventures of Scar, the Link; a story of man from the beginning.*   Doubleday, Page, Garden City, 1914, 334p, Cloth, Novel
14904   *The story of Ab; a tale of the time of the cave man.*   Way & Williams, Chicago, 1897, 351p, Cloth, Novel

WATERS, T(homas) A(llen)

14905   *CenterForce.*   Dell, New York, 1974, 175p, Paper, Novel
14906   *The probability pad.*   Pyramid, New York, 1970, 144p, Paper, Novel [Greenwich Village Trilogy #3]

WATKIN, LAWRENCE EDWARD, 1901-

14907   *Darby O'Gill and the Little People.*   Dell, New York, 1959, 159p, Paper, Movie
14908   *On borrowed time.*   Alfred A. Knopf, New York, 1937, 269p, Cloth, Novel

WATKINS, PETER

14909   *The war game.*   Sphere Books, Deutsch, London, 1967, 126p, Paper, Movie

WATKINS, WILLIAM JON, 1942-   [*biography included*]

14910 *Clickwhistle*. Doubleday, Garden City, 1973, 179p, Cloth, Novel
14911 *The God Machine*. Doubleday, Garden City, 1973, 208p, Cloth, Novel

with E. V. Snyder:

13425 *Ecodeath*. Doubleday, Garden City, 1972, 180p, Cloth, Novel

WATKINS-PITCHFORD, DENYS JAMES
    see: B. B.

WATLOCK, W. A.

14912 *The next Ninety-Three; or, Crown, commune, and colony, told in a citizen's diary*. Field & Tuer, London, 1886, 36p, Paper, Story

WATSON, AARON, 1850-1926

14913 *For lust of gold; a romance*. Walter Scott, London, 1892, 312p, Cloth, Novel

WATSON, E. L. GRANT
    see: GRANT WATSON, E. L.

WATSON, FREDERICK, 1885-1935

14914 *Credulity Island*. Herbert Jenkins, London, 1916, 243p, Cloth, Novel

WATSON, GILBERT, 1864-1941

14915 *The amazing guest*. Houghton Mifflin, Boston, 1924, 377p, Cloth, Novel

WATSON, H(enry) B(rereton) MARRIOTT, 1863-1921

14916 *Marahuna; a romance*. Longmans, Green, London, 1888, 298p, Cloth, Novel

WATSON, HENRY CROCKER MARRIOTT [published anonymously]

14917 *The decline and fall of the British Empire; or, The witch's cavern*. Trischler & Co., London, 1890, 291p, Cloth, Novel
14918 *Erchomenon; or, The republic of materialism*, by * * * *. Sampson Low, Marston, Searle & Rivington, London, 1879, 226p, Cloth, Novel

WATSON, IAN, 1943-   [*biography included*]

14919 *The embedding*. Victor Gollancz, London, 1973, 254p, Cloth, Novel

WATSON, SYDNEY

14920 *"In the twinkling of an eye."* W. Nicholson & Sons, London, 1916, 266p, Cloth, Novel
14921 *"The mark of the beast."* W. Nicholson & Sons, London, 1915, 276p, Cloth, Novel

WATTERS, BARBARA H.
    see: HUNT, BARBARA

WATTS, NEWMAN, 1895-

14922 *The man who could not sin*. Fleming H. Revell, New York, 1938, 223p, Cloth, Novel
14922A retitled: *The man who did not sin*. H. E. Walter, London, 1939, 216p, Cloth, Novel

WATTS-DUNTON, (Walter) THEODORE, 1832-1914

14923 *Aylwin*. Dodd, Mead, New York, 1898, 460p, Cloth, Novel

WAUGH, EVELYN (Arthur St. John), 1903-1966

14924 *Love among the ruins; a romance of the near future*. Chapman & Hall, London, 1953, 51p, Cloth, Novel
14925 *Vile bodies*. Chapman & Hall, London, 1930, 253p, Cloth, Novel
14926 *Vile bodies; and, Black mischief*. Dell, New York, 1960, 381p, Paper, Coll.

WAUGH, MICHAEL

14927 *The abominable snowman*. Cleveland Publishing Co., Sydney?, 1954, 34p, Paper, Story [cover title: *The mystery of the abominable snowman*]
14928 *Back from the dead*. Vampire Mystery, Sydney, 1955, 34p, Paper, Story
14929 *The living dead*. Vampire Mystery, Sydney, 1955, 34p, Paper, Story

WAY, PETER

14930 *The Kretzmer Syndrome*. Herbert Jenkins, London, 1968, 186p, Cloth, Novel

WAYMAN, TONY RUSSELL, 1929-   [*biography included*]

14931 *Ads infinitum (being a second tale from the Dream House)*. Curtis, New York, 1971, 240p, Paper, Novel [Dreamhouse #2]
14932 *Dunes of Pradai*. Curtis, New York, 1971, 319p, Paper, Novel
14933 *World of the sleeper*. Ace Double, New York, 1967, 184p, Paper, Novel [Dreamhouse #1]

WEAVER, HENRIETTA

14934 *Flame and the shadow-eater*. Henry Holt, New York, 1917, 330p, Cloth, Coll.

WEBB, A(ugustus) C(aesar), 1894-   [biography included]

14935 *Farewell to the bomb.* Vantage Press, New York, 1967, 93p, Cloth, Novel

WEBB, BLANCHE A.
    see: DRAPER, BLANCHE A.

WEBB, CHRISTOPHER, pseud.
    see: WIBBERLEY, LEONARD

WEBB, JANE
    see: LOUDON, JANE

WEBB, JEAN FRANCIS (III), 1910-   [biography included], with H. Rider Haggard

06584 *King Solomon's Mines.* Dell, New York, 1950, 192p, Paper, Movie [rewritten]

WEBB, ROBERT FORREST-
    see: FORREST-WEBB, ROBERT

WEBER, HENRY (William), 1783-1816

14936 *Popular romances, consisting of imaginary voyages and travels.* John Ballantyne, Edinburgh, 1812, 638p, Cloth, Anth.

WEBSTER, ELIZABETH CHARLOTTE

14937 *Ceremony of innocence.* Jonathan Cape, London, 1949, 221p, Cloth, Novel

WEBSTER, F(rederick) A(nnesley) M(ichael), 1886-

14938 *The curse of the lion.* United Press Ltd., London, 1922, 282p, Cloth, Novel
14939 *The land of forgotten women.* Skeffington & Son, London, 1950, 256p, Cloth, Novel
14940 *Lord of the leopards; a novel.* Hutchinson, London, 1935, 256p, Cloth, Novel
14941 *Lost City of Light.* Frederick Warne, London, 1934, 288p, Cloth, Novel
14942 *The man who knew.* Selwyn & Blount, London, 1927, 318p, Cloth, Novel
14943 *Mubendi girl.* Hutchinson, London, 1935, 304p, Cloth, Novel
14944 *The odyssey of Husky Hillier.* Chapman & Hall, London, 1924, 243p, Cloth, Novel
14944A retitled: *Husky Hillier.* Readers Library Publishing Co., London, 1938, 252p, Cloth, Novel
14945 *Star lady.* Hutchinson, London, 1935, 288p, Cloth, Novel
14946 *The trail of the skull; a story of African adventure.* Juvenile Productions, London, 1937, 256p, Cloth, Novel
14947 *When strange drums sound; an African story.* Frederick Warne, London, 1935, 288p, Cloth, Novel

WEBSTER, HENRY KITCHELL, 1875-1932

14948 *The sky-man.* Century Co., New York, 1910, 344p, Cloth, Novel

WEBSTER, J. PROVAND

14949 *The oracle of Baal; a narrative of some curious events in the life of Horatio Carmichael, M.A.* J. B. Lippincott, Philadelphia, 1896, 374p, Cloth, Novel; Hutchinson, London, 1896, 374p, Cloth, Novel

WECHTER, NELL WISE, 1913-   [biography included]

14950 *Teach's light.* J. F. Blair, Winston-Salem, NC, 1974, 144p, Cloth, Novel

WEDLAKE, G(eorge) E. C.

14951 *The wrecking ray.* Herbert Jenkins, London, 1935, 312p, Cloth, Novel

WEEKLEY, IAN (George), 1933-

14952 *The moving snow.* John Murray, London, 1974, 182p, Cloth, Novel

WEESE, GENE DE
    see: DeWEESE, GENE

WEINBAUM, STANLEY G(rauman), 1902-1935

14953 *The best of Stanley G. Weinbaum.* Ballantine, New York, 1974, 306p, Paper, Coll.
14954 *The Black Flame.* Fantasy Press, Reading, PA, 1948, 240p, Cloth, Novel
14955 *The dark other.* Fantasy Publishing Co., Los Angeles, 1950, 256p, Cloth, Novel
14956 *Dawn of flame, and other stories.* Milwaukee Fictioneers, Milwaukee, 1936, 313p, Cloth, Coll.
14957 *A Martian odyssey.* Lancer, New York, 1962, 159p, Paper, Coll.
14958 *A Martian odyssey, and other science fiction tales.* Hyperion Press, Westport, Conn., 1974, 555p, Cloth, Coll.
14959 *A Martian odyssey, and others.* Fantasy Press, Reading, PA, 1949, 289p, Cloth, Coll.
14960 *The new Adam.* Ziff-Davis Publishing Co., Chicago, 1939, 262p, Cloth, Novel
14961 *The Red Peri.* Fantasy Press, Reading, PA, 1952, 270p, Cloth, Coll.

WEINBERG, ROBERT E(dward), 1946-   [biography included]

14962 *Dr. Satan; pulp classics 6.* Robert Weinberg, Oak Lawn, IL, 1974, 95p, Paper, Anth.
14963 *Far below, and other horrors.* Fax Collector's Editions, West Linn, OR, 1974, 151p, Cloth, Anth.
14964 *An index to Analog (January 1960 to June 1965).* Robert Weinberg, no place, 1965?, 10p, Paper, Nonf.

WEINBERG, ROBERT E. (cont.)

14965 *Revelry in Hell; pulp classics 3.* Robert Weinberg, Oak Lawn, IL, 1974, 64p, Paper, Anth.
14966 *The Robert E. Howard fantasy biblio.* Robert Weinberg & Mike Deckinger, Newark, NJ, 1969, 7p, Paper, Nonf.
14967 *WT50; a tribute to Weird tales.* Robert Weinberg, Oak Lawn, IL, 1974, 135p, Paper, Nonf. Anth.

with E. P. Berglund:

01169 *Reader's guide to the Cthulhu Mythos, second revised edition.* Silver Scarab Press, Albuquerque, NM, 1973, 88p, Paper, Nonf.

with Lohr McKinstry:

09940 *The hero-pulp index.* Robert Weinberg, Hillside, NJ, 1970, 54p, Paper, Nonf.

WEINSTEIN, NATHAN
see: WEST, NATHANAEL

WEINSTEIN, SOL, 1928- *[biography included]*

14968 *Loxfinger; a thrilling adventure of Hebrew agent Oy-Oy-7, Israel Bond.* Pocket Books, New York, 1965, 127p, Paper, Novel [Israel Bond #1]
14969 *Matzohball; a new adventure of Hebrew secret agent Oy-Oy-7, Israel Bond.* Pocket Books, New York, 1966, 126p, Paper, Novel [Israel Bond #2]

with Howard Albrecht:

00114 *The Exerciser.* Ballantine, New York, 1974, 147p, Paper, Novel [a parody of Blatty's *The exorcist*]
00115 *Jonathan Segal Chicken.* Pinnacle, New York, 1973, 122p, Paper, Novel [a parody of Bach's *Jonathan Livingston Seagull*]

THE WEIRD MENACE
see: CAZEDESSUS, CAMILLE

THE WEIRD ONES
see: HOWARD, IVAN

WEIRD SHORTS

14970 *Weird shorts, first selection.* Gerald G. Swan, London, 1944, 35p, Paper, Anth.

WEIRD SHOW
see: RUSSELL, RAY

WEIRD TALES

14971 *Weird tales.* Gerald G. Swan, London, 1942, 63p, Paper, Anth.

WEIRD TALES; AMERICAN

14972 *Weird tales; American.* William Paterson, London, 1888, 256p, Cloth, Anth.
14972A retitled: *Weird tit-bits; American.* White & Allen, New York, 1895?, 256p, Cloth, Anth.

WEIRD TALES; ENGLISH

14973 *Weird tales; English.* William Paterson, London, 1888, 256p, Cloth, Anth.
14973A retitled: *Weird tit-bits; English.* White & Allen, New York, 1895?, 256p, Cloth, Anth.

WEIRD TALES; GERMAN

14974 *Weird tales; German.* William Paterson, London, 1888, 256p, Cloth, Anth.
14974A retitled: *Weird tit-bits; German.* White & Allen, New York, 1895?, 256p, Cloth, Anth.

WEIRD TALES; IRISH

14975 *Weird tales; Irish.* William Paterson, London, 1888, 256p, Cloth, Anth.
14975A retitled: *Weird tit-bits; Irish.* White & Allen, New York, 1895?, 256p, Cloth, Anth.

WEIRD TALES; SCOTTISH

14976 *Weird tales; Scottish.* William Paterson, London, 1888, 256p, Cloth, Anth.
14976A retitled: *Weird tit-bits; Scottish.* White & Allen, New York, 1895?, 256p, Cloth, Anth.

WEIRD TIT-BITS; AMERICAN
see: WEIRD TALES; AMERICAN

WEIRD TIT-BITS; ENGLISH
see: WEIRD TALES; ENGLISH

WEIRD TIT-BITS; GERMAN
see: WEIRD TALES; GERMAN

WEIRD TIT-BITS; IRISH
see: WEIRD TALES; IRISH

WEIRD TIT-BITS; SCOTTISH
see: WEIRD TALES; SCOTTISH

WEISS, HENRY GEORGE
see: FLAGG, FRANCIS

WEISS, JIRI, 1913-

14977 *The lost government; or, Do you really like it? a fairy tale for grown-ups.* Nicholson & Watson, London, 1945, 269p, Cloth, Novel

WEISSNER, CARL

14978 *The Braille film.* Nova Broadcast Press, San Francisco, 1970, 105p, Paper, Novel

WELBORE, M(ina) W(alker)

14979 *Some fantasies of fate.* Digby, Long, London, 1899, 280p, Cloth, Coll.

WELCH, EDGAR L(uderne), 1855-

as J. Drew Gay:

14980 *The mystery of the shroud; a tale of socialism.* J. W. Arrowsmith, Bristol, 1887, 134p, Paper, Novel

as "Grip":

14981 *How John Bull lost London; or, The capture of the Channel Tunnel.* Sampson Low, Marston, Searle & Rivington, London, 1882, 127p, Paper, Novel
14982 *The monster municipality; or, Gog and Magog reformed; a dream.* Sampson Low, Marston, Searle & Rivington, London, 1882, 128p, Paper?, Novel

WELCHER, JEANNE K., with George E. Bush, Jr.

02360 *Gulliveriana: I.* Scholars' Facsimiles & Reprints, Gainesville, FL, 1970, 204p, Cloth, Anth.
02361 *Gulliveriana: II; The travels of Mr. John Gulliver, son to Lemuel Gulliver (1731), by Pierre François Guyot Desfontaines; Modern Gulliver's travels: Lilliput (1796), by Lemuel Gulliver, Jun. (pseud.); fascimile reproductions.* Scholars' Facsimiles & Reprints, Gainesville, FL, 1971, 674p, Cloth, Anth.
02362 *Gulliveriana III; Travels into several remote nations of the world, vol. III (1727); and, Memoirs of the court of Lilliput (1727); facsimile reproductions.* Scholars' Facsimiles & Reprints, Delmar, NY, 1972, 465p, Cloth, Anth.
02363 *Gulliveriana IV.* Scholars' Facsimiles & Reprints, Delmar, NY, 1973, 384p, Cloth, Anth.
02364 *Gulliveriana V.* Scholars' Facsimiles & Reprints, Delmar, NY, 1974, 382p, Cloth, Anth. [includes some nonf.]

WELCOME, S. BYRON

14983 *From Earth's center; a Polar gateway message.* Charles H. Kerr, Chicago, 1894, 274p, Paper, Novel

WELDON, REX, pseud. [Duane Weldon Rimel, 1915-] [biography included]

14984 *Time swap.* PEC, El Cajon, CA, 1969, 148p, Paper, Novel

A WELL-KNOWN AUTHOR, pseud.
see: LANG, ANDREW

A WELL-KNOWN MEMBER OF PARLIAMENT, pseud.

14985 *When woman rules; a tale of the first women's government.* John Long, London, 1923, 252p, Cloth, Novel

WELLARD, JAMES (Howard), 1909- [biography included]

14986 *Night in Babylon; a novel.* Macmillan, London, 1953, 298p, Cloth, Novel

WELLEN, EDWARD (Paul), 1919- [biography included]

14987 *Hijack.* Beagle, New York, 1971, 140p, Paper, Novel

WELLES, (George) ORSON, 1915-

14988 *Invasion from Mars; interplanetary stories; thrilling adventures in space.* Dell, New York, 1949, 191p, Paper, Anth.

WELLMAN, BERT J. [published anonymously]

14989 *The legal revolution of 1902,* by a law-abiding revolutionist. Charles H. Kerr, Chicago, 1898, 334p, Cloth, Novel

WELLMAN, MANLY WADE, 1903- [biography included]

14990 *The beasts from beyond; a complete book-length novel of amazing adventure.* World Distributors/Sydney Pemberton, Manchester, 1950, 160p, Paper, Novel [author's byline reads: Manley Wade Wellman]
14991 *The dark destroyers.* Avalon, New York, 1959, 224p, Cloth, Novel
14992 *Devil's planet; a new and original novel of Martian adventure.* World Distributors/Sydney Pemberton, Manchester, 1951, 128p, Paper, Novel [author's byline reads: Manley Wade Wellman]
14993 *Giants from eternity.* Avalon, New York, 1959, 223p, Cloth, Novel
14994 *The invading asteroid.* Stellar Publishing Corp., New York, 1932, 24p, Paper, Story
14995 *Island in the sky.* Avalon, New York, 1961, 223p, Cloth, Novel
14996 *Sojarr of Titan; a complete scientifiction novel.* Crestwood Publishing Co., New York, 1949?, 120p, Paper, Novel
14997 *The Solar invasion.* Popular Library, New York, 1968, 126p, Paper, Novel [Captain Future #2]
14998 *Twice in time.* Avalon, New York, 1957, 222p, Cloth, Novel
14999 *Who fears the devil?* Arkham House, New York, 1963, 213p, Cloth, Coll.
15000 *Worse things waiting.* Carcosa, Chapel Hill, NC, 1973, 354p, Cloth, Coll.

as Gans T. Field:

15001 *Romance in black; a thrilling novel.* Utopian Publications, London, 1946, 64p, Paper, Novel

WELLS, BARRY, pseud. [Dick Richards]

15002 *The day the Earth caught fire.* Four Square, London, 1961, 160p, Paper, Movie

WELLS, BASIL (Eugene), 1912- *[biography included]*

15003 *Doorways to space.* Fantasy Publishing Co., Los Angeles, 1951, 206p, Cloth, Coll.
15004 *Planets of adventure.* Fantasy Publishing Co., Los Angeles, 1949, 280p, Cloth, Coll.

WELLS, CAROLYN, 1872?-1942

15005 *American mystery stories.* Oxford University Press, New York, 1927, 232p, Cloth, Anth.

WELLS, GEORGE

15006 *The Danecourt romance; a novel.* Arthur H. Stockwell, London, 1923, 267p, Cloth, Novel

WELLS, H(erbert) G(eorge), 1866-1946

15007 *All aboard for Ararat.* Secker & Warburg, London, 1940, 105p, Cloth, Novel
15008 *The autocracy of Mr. Parham; his remarkable adventures in this changing world.* William Heinemann, London, 1930, 370p, Cloth, Novel
15009 *Best science fiction stories of H. G. Wells.* Dover, New York, 1966, 303p, Paper, Coll.
15010 *Best stories of H. G. Wells.* Ballantine, New York, 1960, 320p, Paper, Coll.
15011 *The brothers; a story.* Chatto & Windus, London, 1938, 140p, Cloth, Novel
15012 *The Camford Visitation.* Methuen, London, 1937, 76p, Cloth, Novel
The complete short stories. [see 15067B]
15013 *The cone; another collection of horror stories.* Fontana, London, 1965, 160p, Cloth, Coll.
15014 *The country of the blind.* Privately Printed, New York, 1915, 47p, Paper?, Story
15015 *The country of the blind.* Golden Cockerell Press, London, 1939, 67p, Cloth, Novel [expanded]
15016 *The country of the blind.* Haldeman-Julius, Girard, Kans., 1921?, 63p, Paper, Coll.
15017 *The country of the blind, and other stories.* Thomas Nelson & Sons, London, 1911, 574p, Cloth, Coll.
15018 *The country of the blind, and other stories.* Bernhard Tauchnitz, Leipzig, 1926, 267p, Cloth, Coll. [different contents]
15019 *The country of the blind, and other stories.* Longmans, Green, London, 1947, 82p, Cloth, Coll. [different contents]
15020 *The croquet player; a story.* Chatto & Windus, London, 1936, 81p, Cloth, Novel
15021 *The door in the wall, and other stories.* Grant Richards, London, 1911, 153p, Cloth, Coll.
15022 *The dream; a novel.* Jonathan Cape, London, 1924, 320p, Cloth, Novel
15023 *The empire of the ants.* Bantam Books, Todd Publishing Co., London, 1943, 16p, Paper, Story
15024 *The empire of the ants, and other stories.* Haldeman-Julius, Girard, Kans., 1925?, 60p, Paper, Coll.

The famous short stories of H. G. Wells. [see 15067A]
15025 *The favorite short stories of H. G. Wells.* Doubleday, Doran, Garden City, 1937, 347p, Cloth, Coll.
15026 *The first men in the Moon.* George Newnes, London, 1901, 342p, Cloth, Novel
15027 *The first men in the Moon, and more human stories.* T. Fisher Unwin, London, 1925, 448p, Cloth, Coll.
15028 *The first men in the Moon, The world set free, and short stories.* Odhams Press, London, 1930?, 376p, Cloth, Coll.
The food of the gods. [see 15029A]
15029 *The food of the gods, and how it came to Earth.* Macmillan, London, 1904, 317p, Cloth, Novel
15029A retitled: *The food of the gods.* W. Collins Sons, London, 1932, 311p, Cloth, Novel
15030 *The food of the gods; The sea lady.* T. Fisher Unwin, London, 1925, 479p, Cloth, Coll.
15031 *The history of Mr. Polly; and, The war in the air.* Odhams Press, London, 1930?, 375p, Cloth, Coll. [*The history of Mr. Polly* is not SF]
15032 *The history of Mr. Polly; The wonderful visit.* Heron, London, 1969?, 441p, Cloth, Coll.
15033 *The holy terror.* Michael Joseph, London, 1939, 447p, Cloth, Novel
15034 *In the days of the comet.* Macmillan, London, 1906, 305p, Cloth, Novel
15035 *In the days of the comet, and seventeen short stories.* T. Fisher Unwin, London, 1925, 652p, Cloth, Coll.
15036 *The inexperienced ghost.* Bantam Books, Todd Publishing Co., London, 1943, 15p, Paper, Story
15037 *The inexperienced ghost, and nine other stories.* Bantam, New York, 1965, 167p, Paper, Coll.
15038 *The inexperienced ghost; and, The new accelerator.* Vallancey Press, London, 1944, 16p, Paper, Coll.
15039 *The invisible man; a grotesque romance.* C. Arthur Pearson, London, 1897, 245p, Cloth, Novel
15040 *The invisible man; and, The war of the worlds.* Washington Square Press, New York, 1962, 329p, Paper, Coll.
15041 *The invisible man; Secret places of the heart; God the invisible king.* Odhams Press, London, 1930?, 375p, Cloth, Coll. [includes some nonf.]
15042 *The invisible man; The war of the worlds; A dream of armageddon.* T. Fisher Unwin, London, 1924, 492p, Cloth, Coll.
15043 *The island of Doctor Moreau.* William Heinemann, London, 1896, 219p, Cloth, Novel
15044 *The island of Doctor Moreau; The invisible man.* Heron, London, 1969?, 381p, Cloth, Coll.
15045 *The island of Doctor Moreau; The sleeper awakes.* T. Fisher Unwin, London, 1924, 480p, Cloth, Coll.
15046 *The land ironclads.* Bantam Books, Todd Publishing Co., London, 1943, 16p, Paper, Story
15047 *The man who could work miracles.* Haldeman-Julius, Girard, Kans., 1931, 64p, Paper, Coll.
15048 *The man who could work miracles; The Hammerpond Park burglary; and, The apple.* Polybooks, London, 1943, 16p, Paper, Coll.
15049 *Men like gods.* Cassell, London, 1923, 304p, Cloth, Novel
15050 *Men like gods; and, The dream.* T. Fisher Unwin, London, 1927, 658p, Cloth, Coll.
15051 *Mr. Blettsworthy on Rampole Island.* Ernest Benn, London, 1928, 287p, Cloth, Novel

WELLS, H. G. (cont.)

15052 *Mr. Britling sees it through; and, In the days of the comet.* Odhams Press, London, 1930?, 502p, Cloth, Coll. [*Mr. Britling* is not SF]

15053 *The new accelerator.* Bantam Books, Todd Publishing Co., London, 1943, 15p, Paper, Story

15054 *The new Machiavelli; and, The food of the gods.* Odhams Press, London, 1930?, 503p, Cloth, Coll. [*The new Machiavelli* is not SF]

15055 *The obliterated man, and other stories.* Haldeman-Julius, Girard, Kans., 1925?, 64p, Paper, Coll.

15056 *The Plattner story, and others.* Methuen, London, 1897, 301p, Cloth, Coll.

15057 *The scientific romances of H. G. Wells.* Victor Gollancz, London, 1933, 1222p, Cloth, Coll. [includes: *The time machine; The island of Doctor Moreau; The invisible man; The war of the worlds; The first men in the Moon; The food of the gods; In the days of the comet; Men like gods*]

15058 *The sea lady; a tissue of moonshine.* Methuen, London, 1902, 301p, Cloth, Novel

15059 *Selected short stories.* Penguin, Harmondsworth, 1958, 352p, Paper, Coll.

15060 *Selections from the early prose works of H. G. Wells.* University of London Press, London, 1931, 160p, Paper, Coll.

15061 *Seven famous novels.* Alfred A. Knopf, New York, 1934, 860p, Cloth, Coll. [includes: *The time machine; The island of Doctor Moreau; The invisible man; The war of the worlds; The first men in the Moon; The food of the gods; In the days of the comet*]

15061A retitled: *Seven science fiction novels.* Dover, New York, 1950, 1015p, Cloth, Coll.

15062 *Seven stories.* Oxford University Press, London, 1953, 148p, Cloth, Coll.

15063 *The shape of things to come; the ultimate revolution.* Hutchinson, London, 1933, 431p, Cloth, Novel

15064 *The short stories.* Odhams Press, London, 1930?, 375p, Cloth, Coll.

15065 *Short stories by H. G. Wells, first series.* Thomas Nelson & Sons, London, 1940, 218p, Cloth, Coll.

15066 *Short stories by H. G. Wells, second series.* Thomas Nelson & Sons, London, 1940, 215p, Cloth, Coll.

15067 *The short stories of H. G. Wells.* Ernest Benn, London, 1927, 1148p, Cloth, Coll.

15067A retitled: *The famous short stories of H. G. Wells.* Garden City Publishing Co., Garden City, 1938, 1015p, Cloth, Coll.

15067B retitled: *The complete short stories of H. G. Wells.* Ernest Benn, London, 1965, 1038p, Cloth, Coll.

The sleeper awakes. [see 15114A]

15068 *The sleeper awakes; and, Men like gods.* Odhams Press, London, 1930?, 376p, Cloth, Coll.

15069 *The sleeper awakes; Tales of the unexpected.* Heron, London, 1969, 453p, Cloth, Coll.

15070 *A slip under the microscope.* Haldeman-Julius, Girard, Kans., 1931, 63p, Paper, Coll.

15071 *The soul of a bishop, and three short stories.* Waterlow & Sons, London, 1933, 255p, Cloth, Coll.

15072 *The star.* Simplified Speling Sosieti, London, 1912?, 28p, Paper, Story

15073 *Star-begotten; a biological fantasia.* Chatto & Windus, London, 1937, 198p, Cloth, Novel

15074 *The stolen bacillus, and other incidents.* Methuen, London, 1895, 275p, Cloth, Coll.

15075 *The stolen bacillus, and other stories.* Haldeman-Julius, Girard, Kans., 1925?, 63p, Paper, Coll.

15076 *The stolen body, and other tales of the unexpected.* London Book Co., London, 1931, 254p, Cloth, Coll.

15077 *Tales of life and adventure.* W. Collins Sons, London, 1923, 279p, Cloth, Coll.

15078 *Tales of life and adventure; Tales of wonder.* Heron, London, 1969?, 473p, Cloth, Coll.

15079 *Tales of space and time.* Harper & Bros., London, 1899, 358p, Cloth, Coll.

15080 *Tales of the unexpected.* W. Collins Sons, London, 1922, 280p, Cloth, Coll.

15081 *Tales of wonder.* W. Collins Sons, London, 1923, 249p, Cloth, Coll.

15082 *Thirty strange stories.* Edward Arnold, London, 1897, 504p, Cloth, Coll.

15083 *Three novels: The time machine; The war of the worlds; The island of Doctor Moreau.* Heinemann, London, 1963, 322p, Cloth, Coll.

15084 *Three prophetic novels of H. G. Wells.* Dover, New York, 1960, 335p, Paper, Coll. [includes: *The time machine; A story of the days to come; When the sleeper wakes*]

15085 *The time machine; an invention.* William Heinemann, London, 1895, 152p, Cloth, Novel

15086 *The time machine, an invention, and other stories.* Penguin, Harmondsworth, 1946, 284p, Paper, Coll.

15087 *The time machine, and other stories.* Ernest Benn, London, 1927, 215p, Cloth, Coll.

15088 *The time machine, and other stories.* Scholastic Book Services, New York, 1963, 217p, Paper, Coll. [different contents]

15089 *The time machine; and, The first men in the Moon.* Heron, London, 1969?, 387p, Cloth, Coll.

15090 *The time machine; and, The invisible man.* Children's Press, Chicago, 1969, 256p, Cloth, Coll.

15091 *The time machine; and, The man who could work miracles.* Pan, London, 1953, 157p, Paper, Coll.

The time machine; and, The war of the worlds. [see 15110A]

15092 *The time machine, The wonderful visit, and other stories.* T. Fisher Unwin, London, 1924, 467p, Cloth, Coll.

15093 *The treasure in the forest.* London Book Co., London, 1929, 244p, Cloth, Coll.

15094 *The treasure in the forest, and other stories.* Haldeman-Julius, Girard, Kans., 1931, 63p, Paper, Coll.

15095 *The truth about Pyecraft, and other short stories.* Polybooks, London, 1943, 16p, Paper, Coll.

15096 *The truth about Pyecraft, and other stories.* Vallancey Press, London, 1944, 16p, Paper, Coll.

15097 *Twelve stories and a dream.* Macmillan, London, 1903, 377p, Cloth, Coll.

15098 *28 science fiction stories.* Dover, New York, 1952, 915p, Cloth, Coll.

15099 *Two tales.* Signorelli, Rome, 1956, 55p, Paper, Coll.

15100 *The undying fire; a contemporary novel.* Cassell, London, 1919, 253p, Cloth, Novel

15101 *The undying fire, and philosophical and theological speculations.* T. Fisher Unwin, London, 1925, 511p, Cloth, Coll. [includes nonf.

WELLS, H. G. (cont.)

15102   *The valley of spiders*. London Book Co., London, 1930, 252p, Cloth, Coll.

15103   *The valley of spiders; a new collection of short stories*. Fontana, London, 1964, 191p, Paper, Coll.

15104   *The valley of spiders, and other stories*. Haldeman-Julius, Girard, Kans., 1931, 59p, Paper, Coll.

15105   *The war in the air, and other war forebodings*. T. Fisher Unwin, London, 1926, 484p, Cloth, Coll. [includes some nonf.]

15106   *The war in the air, and particularly how Mr. Bert Smallways fared while it lasted*. George Bell & Sons, London, 1908, 389p, Cloth, Novel

15107   *The war in the air; In the days of the comet; The food of the gods: three science fiction novels*. Dover, New York, 1963, 645p, Paper, Coll.

15108   *The war of the worlds*. William Heinemann, London, 1898, 303p, Cloth, Novel

15109   *The war of the worlds; A dream of armageddon; The land ironclads*. Heron, London, 1968, 319p, Cloth, Coll.

15110   *The war of the worlds; and, The time machine*. Globe Book Co., New York, 1956, 404p, Cloth, Coll.

15110A retitled: *The time machine; and, The war of the worlds*. Dolphin, Garden City, 1961, 276p, Paper, Coll.

15111   *The war of the worlds, The time machine, and selected short stories*. Platt & Munk, New York, 1963, 514p, Cloth, Coll.

15112   *The wheels of chance; The time machine*. J. M. Dent & Sons, London, 1935, 303p, Cloth, Coll. [*The wheels of chance* is not SF]

15113   *The wheels of chance; The world set free*. Heron, London, 1969, 487p, Cloth, Coll.

15114   *When the Sleeper wakes*. Harper & Bros., London, 1899, 329p, Cloth, Novel

15114A retitled: *The Sleeper awakes*. Thomas Nelson & Sons, London, 1910, 288p, Cloth, Novel

15115   *A woman's heart, and other stories*. Haldeman-Julius, Girard, Kans., 1931, 64p, Paper, Coll.

15116   *The wonderful visit*. J. M. Dent & Sons, London, 1895, 251p, Cloth, Novel

15117   *The world set free; a story of mankind*. Macmillan, London, 1914, 286p, Cloth, Novel

15118   *The world set free, and other war papers*. T. Fisher Unwin, London, 1926, 431p, Cloth, Coll. [includes some nonf.]

with Bernard Bergonzi:

01170   *The early H. G. Wells; a study of the scientific romances*. University Press, Manchester, 1961, 226p, Cloth, Anth. [includes several stories by Wells, and extensive commentary by Bergonzi]

WELLS, JOEL (Freeman), 1930-   [*biography included*], with Dan Herr

07142   *Bodies and souls*. Crime Club, Doubleday, Garden City, 1961, 261p, Cloth, Anth.

07143   *Bodies and spirits*. Crime Club, Doubleday, Garden City, 1964, 192p, Cloth, Anth.

WELLS, O. R., pseud.

15119   *All-stud*. Greenleaf Classics, San Diego, 1969, 195p, Paper, Novel

WELLS, (Frank Charles) ROBERT, 1929-   [*biography included*]

15120   *Candle in the Sun*. Berkley Medallion, New York, 1971, 158p, Paper, Novel

15121   *The parasaurians*. Berkley Medallion, New York, 1969, 190p, Paper, Novel

15122   *Right-handed wilderness*. Ballantine, New York, 1973, 184p, Paper, Novel

WENTWORTH-JAMES, G(ertie) de S.

15123   *Girl everlasting*. Hurst & Blackett, London, 1927, 300p, Cloth, Novel

15124   *Magic mating; an emotional alphabet*. Alston Rivers, London, 1929, 256p, Cloth, Novel

15125   *Mr. Lynke*. C. W. Daniel, London, 1925, 284p, Cloth, Novel

15126   *The soul that came back*. T. Werner Laurie, London, 1922, 240p, Cloth, Novel

15127   *The television girl; a novel*. Hurst & Blackett, London, 1928, 288p, Cloth, Novel

WENTZ, W(alter) JA(me)S.

15128   *A. Merritt; a bibliography of fantastic writings*. George A. Bibbly, Roseville, CA, 1965, 33p, Paper, Nonf.

WERFEL, FRANZ (V.), 1890-1945

15129   *The song of Bernadette*. Hamish Hamilton, London, 1942, 397p, Cloth, Novel

15130   *Star of the unborn*. Viking Press, New York, 1946, 645p, Cloth, Novel

WERPER, BARTON, house pseud. [see also: Peter T. Scott and Peg O'Neill Scott]

12834   *Tarzan and the Abominable Snowmen*. Gold Star, Derby, Conn., 1965, 126p, Paper, Novel [New Tarzan #4] [by Peter T. Scott]

12835   *Tarzan and the cave city*. Gold Star, Derby, Conn., 1964, 126p, Paper, Novel [New Tarzan #2] [by Peter T. Scott]

12836   *Tarzan and the Silver Globe*. Gold Star, Derby, Conn., 1964, 126p, Paper, Novel [New Tarzan #1] [by Peter T. Scott]

12833   *Tarzan and the snake people*. Gold Star, Derby, Conn., 1964, 126p, Paper, Novel [New Tarzan #3] [by Peg O'Neill Scott]

12837   *Tarzan and the winged invaders*. Gold Star, Derby, Conn., 1965, 125p, Paper, Novel [New Tarzan #5] [by Peter T. Scott]

WERTHAM, FREDRIC, 1895-   [*biography included*] [name originally Frederick Ignace Wertheimer]

15131   *The world of fanzines; a special form of communication*. Southern Illinois University Press, Carbondale, IL, 1973, 144p, Cloth, Nonf.

WERTHEIMER, FREDERICK
see: WERTHAM, FREDRIC

WESLEY, MARY, pseud. [Mary Aline Eady,
1912-   ] [biography included]

15132 The sixth seal. Macdonald, London, 1969,
       252p, Cloth, Novel

WESSEX, MARTYN

15133 The slowing down process. Robert Hale, Lon-
       don, 1974, 183p, Cloth, Novel

WEST, ALROY

15134 Stratosphere express. Wright & Brown, London,
       1936, 251p, Cloth, Novel

WEST, ANTHONY (Panther), 1914-   [biography
included]

15135 Another kind. Eyre & Spottiswoode, London,
       1951, 351p, Cloth, Novel
15136 On a dark night. Eyre & Spottiswoode, London,
       1949, 324p, Cloth, Novel
15136A retitled: The vintage. Houghton Mifflin,
       Boston, 1950, 310p, Cloth, Novel

WEST, EDWARD SACKVILLE-
see: SACKVILLE-WEST, EDWARD

WEST, G. CORNWALLIS-
see: CORNWALLIS-WEST, G.

WEST, (Mary) JESSAMYN, 1907-   [biography
included]

15137 The Chilekings. Ballantine, New York, 1967,
       123p, Paper, Novel

WEST, JULIAN, pseud. [Ernst Müller]

15138 My afterdream; a sequel to the late Mr. Ed-
       ward Bellamy's Looking backward. T. Fisher
       Unwin, London, 1900, 247p, Cloth, Novel
       [a response to Bellamy's novel]

WEST, NATHANAEL, pseud. [Nathan Wallenstein
Weinstein, 1903-1940]

15139 The complete works of Nathanael West. Farrar,
       Straus & Cudahy, New York, 1957, 421p,
       Cloth, Coll.
15140 A cool million; the dismantling of Lemuel Pit-
       kin. Covici, Friede, New York, 1934, 229p,
       Cloth, Novel
15141 The dream life of Balso Snell; A cool million;
       two novels. Noonday Press, New York, 1963,
       174p, Paper, Coll. [Balso Snell is not SF]
15141A retitled: A cool million; The dream life of
       Balso Snell. Bard, New York, 1965, 158p,
       Paper, Coll.

15142 Miss Lonelyhearts; and, A cool million. Pen-
       guin, Harmondsworth, 1961, 176p, Paper, Coll.
       [Miss Lonelyhearts is not SF]

WEST, PAUL, 1930-   [biography included]

15143 Colonel Mint; a novel. E. P. Dutton, New York,
       1972, 189p, Cloth, Novel

WEST, REBECCA, pseud. [Cecily Isobel Andrews,
1892-   ] [biography included]

15144 Harriet Hume; a London fantasy. Doubleday,
       Doran, Garden City, 1929, 277p, Cloth, Novel

WEST, RICHARD C.

15145 Tolkien criticism; an annotated checklist.
       Kent State University Press, Kent, OH, 1970,
       73p, Cloth, Nonf.

WEST, V. SACKVILLE-
see: SACKVILLE-WEST, V.

WEST, (George) WALLACE, 1900-   [biography
included]

15146 The bird of time. Gnome Press, Hicksville,
       NY, 1959, 256p, Cloth, Novel
15147 The everlasting exiles. Avalon, New York,
       1967, 190p, Cloth, Novel
15148 Lords of Atlantis. Avalon, New York, 1960,
       220p, Cloth, Novel
15149 The Memory Bank. Avalon, New York, 1961, 221p,
       Cloth, Novel
15150 Outposts in space. Avalon, New York, 1962,
       224p, Cloth, Novel
15151 River of time. Avalon, New York, 1963, 221p,
       Cloth, Novel
15152 The time-lockers. Avalon, New York, 1964,
       190p, Cloth, Novel

WESTALL, WILLIAM (Bury), 1835-1903

15153 The Phantom City; a volcanic romance. Harper
       & Bros., New York, 1886, 158p, Cloth, Novel
15154 A queer race; the story of a strange people.
       Cassell, London, 1887, 303p, Cloth, Novel

WESTERMAN, JOHN F(rancis) C(yril)

15155 The looted gold. Ward, Lock, London, 1932,
       256p, Cloth, Novel
15156 The power projector. Oxford University Press,
       Humphrey Milford, London, 1933, 224p, Cloth,
       Novel
15157 The Soten monoplane. Oxford University Press,
       Humphrey Milford, London, 1936, 255p, Cloth,
       Novel

WESTERMAN, PERCY F(rancis), 1876-1959

15158 The dreadnought of the air. S. W. Partridge,
       London, 1914, 382p, Cloth, Novel

WESTERMAN, PERCY F. (cont.)

15159 *The flying submarine.* James Nisbet, London, 1912, 312p, Cloth, Novel
15160 *On the wings of the wind.* Blackie & Son, London, 1928, 207p, Cloth, Novel
15161 *The sea monarch.* Adam & Charles Black, London, 1912, 247p, Cloth, Novel
15162 *The secret battleplane.* S. W. Partridge, London, 1916, 254p, Cloth, Novel
15163 *The secret of the plateau.* Blackie & Son, London, 1931, 224p, Cloth, Novel
15164 *Unconquered wings.* Blackie & Son, London, 1924, 320p, Cloth, Novel
15165 *The war of the wireless waves.* Humphrey Milford, Oxford University Press, London, 1923, 287p, Cloth, Novel

WESTERMAYR, ARTHUR J(oseph), 1864-

15166 *Rudra; a romance of ancient India.* G. W. Dillingham, New York, 1912, 447p, Cloth, Novel

WESTERN, ERNEST

15167 *Ninety North; a romance.* Thomas Burleigh, London, 1899, 289p, Cloth, Novel

WESTHEIMER, DAVID, 1917- [*biography included*]

15168 *Lighter than a feather; a novel.* Little, Brown, Boston, 1971, 431p, Cloth, Novel
15168A retitled: *Downfall; a novel.* Bantam, New York, 1972, 468p, Paper, Novel

WESTLAKE, DONALD E(dwin), 1933-

as Curt Clark:

15169 *Anarchaos.* Ace, New York, 1967, 143p, Paper, Novel

as Timothy J. Culver:

15170 *Ex officio.* M. Evans, New York, 1970, 498p, Cloth, Novel

WESTON, GEORGE, 1880-1965

15171 *His first million women.* Farrar & Rinehart, New York, 1934, 312p, Cloth, Novel
15171A retitled: *Comet 'Z.'* Methuen, London, 1934, 280p, Cloth, Novel
15172 *Queen of the world.* Dodd, Mead, New York, 1923, 254p, Cloth, Novel

WESTON, KIM

15173 *The Schwartz index.* Anthem Series, Baltimore, 1965, 30p, Paper, Nonf.

WESTREICH, ALICE, with Budd Westreich

15174 *Uncle Morgan's ghost.* David McKay, New York, 1970, 148p, Cloth, Novel

WESTREICH, BUDD, with Alice Westreich

15174 *Uncle Morgan's ghost.* David McKay, New York, 1970, 148p, Cloth, Novel

WESTWARD, ELTON

15175 *Return to Mars.* Brown, Watson, London, 1952?, 111p, Paper, Novel

WESTWOOD, ALVIN

15176 *Sinister forces.* Brown, Watson, London, 1952?, 111p, Paper, Novel

WETHERELL, JUNE (Pat), 1909-

15177 *Blueprint for yesterday.* Walker, New York, 1971, 179p, Cloth, Novel
15178 *A touch of the witch.* Lancer, New York, 1969, 189p, Paper, Novel

WETJEN, ALBERT RICHARD, 1900-1948

15179 *Fiddlers' Green; or, The strange adventure of Tommy Lawn; a tale of the great divide of the sailormen.* Little, Brown, Boston, 1931, 261p, Cloth, Novel

WETMORE, CLAUDE H(azeltine), 1863-

15180 *Sweepers of the sea; the story of a strange navy.* Bowen-Merrill, Indianapolis, 1900, 349p, Cloth, Novel

WETZEL, GEORGE (T.)

15181 *Howard Phillips Lovecraft: memoirs, critiques, & bibliographies.* SSR Publications, North Tonawanda, NY, 1955, 83p, Paper, Nonf.

WEVERKA, ROBERT, 1926- [*biography included*]

15182 *Moonrock; a novel.* Bantam, New York, 1973, 151p, Paper, Tele. [Search #2]
15183 *Search.* Bantam, New York, 1973, 152p, Paper, Tele. [Search #1]

WHALEY, STEPHEN V., with S. J. Cook

03346 *Man unwept; visions from the inner eye; an anthology of science and fantasy fiction.* McGraw-Hill, New York, 1974, 350p, Paper, Anth.

WHARTON, EDITH (Newbold), 1862-1937

15184 *The ghost stories of Edith Wharton.* Charles Scribner's Sons, New York, 1973, 276p, Cloth, Coll.
15185 *Ghosts.* D. Appleton-Century, New York, 1937, 406p, Cloth, Coll.
15186 *Here and beyond.* D. Appleton, New York, 1926, 325p, Cloth, Coll.

WHAT HAPPENED AFTER THE BATTLE OF DORKING

15187 *What happened after the Battle of Dorking; or, The victory of Tunbridge Wells.* George Routledge & Sons, London, 1871, 60p, Paper, Novel [Dorking series]

WHAT MAY HAPPEN IN THE NEXT 90 DAYS

15188 *What may happen in the next 90 days; the disruption of the United States, or the origin of the second Civil War.* no publisher, New York, 1877, 33p, Paper, Story

WHEAT, SUSANNE CHAMBERS

15189 *Something new under the sun.* Exposition Press, New York, 1972, 62p, Cloth, Novel

WHEATLEY, DENNIS (Yeats), 1897-1977 [*biography included*]

15190 *Black August; a novel.* Hutchinson, London, 1934, 349p, Cloth, Novel [Gregory Sallust series]
15191 *The black magic omnibus, comprising The devil rides out, Strange conflict, To the devil--a daughter.* Hutchinson, London, 1956, 992p, Cloth, Coll.
15192 *A century of horror stories.* Hutchinson, London, 1935, 1024p, Cloth, Anth.
15192A retitled: *Quiver of horror; tales of strange happenings.* Arrow, London, 1965, 288p, Paper, Anth. [abridged]
15192B retitled: *Dennis Wheatley's second book of horror stories; tales of strange happenings.* Hutchinson, London, 1968, 288p, Cloth, Anth. [abridged; identical to 15192A]
15192C retitled: *Shafts of fear; tales of strange doings.* Arrow, London, 1965, 288p, Paper, Anth. [abridged]
15192D retitled: *Dennis Wheatley's first book of horror stories; tales of 'strange doings.'* Hutchinson, London, 1968, 288p, Cloth, Anth. [abridged; identical to 15192C]
        Dennis Wheatley's first book of horror stories. [see 15192D]
        Dennis Wheatley's second book of horror stories. [see 15192B]
15193 *The devil rides out.* Hutchinson, London, 1935, 328p, Cloth, Novel [Duc de Richleau series]
15194 *Gateway to Hell.* Hutchinson, London, 1970, 319p, Cloth, Novel
15195 *Gunmen, gallants, and ghosts.* Hutchinson, London, 1943, 222p, Cloth, Coll.
15196 *The haunting of Toby Jugg.* Hutchinson, London, 1948, 292p, Cloth, Novel
15197 *Into the unknown, comprising 'Sixty days to live,' 'Star of ill-omen,' 'Curtain of fear.'* Hutchinson, London, 1960, 1105p, Cloth, Coll.
15198 *The Irish witch.* Hutchinson, London, 1973, 446p, Cloth, Novel [Roger Brook series]
15199 *The island where time stands still; a Gregory Sallust story.* Hutchinson, London, 1954, 336p, Cloth, Novel [Gregory Sallust series]
15200 *The ka of Gifford Hillary.* Hutchinson, London, 1956, 407p, Cloth, Novel

15201 *The man who missed the war; a novel.* Hutchinson, London, 1945, 288p, Cloth, Novel
15202 *Plot and counterplot; three adventures of Gregory Sallust.* Hutchinson, London, 1959, 848p, Cloth, Coll. [includes: *Black August; Contraband; The island where time stands still*]
        Quiver of horror. [see 15192A]
15203 *The Satanist.* Hutchinson, London, 1960, 448p, Cloth, Novel
        Shafts of fear. [see 15192C]
15204 *Sixty days to live; a novel.* Hutchinson, London, 1939, 391p, Cloth, Novel
15205 *Star of ill-omen.* Hutchinson, London, 1952, 320p, Cloth, Novel
15206 *Strange conflict.* Hutchinson, London, 1941, 291p, Cloth, Novel [Duc de Richleau series]
15207 *They found Atlantis; a novel.* Hutchinson, London, 1936, 344p, Cloth, Novel
15208 *They used dark forces.* Hutchinson, London, 1964, 511p, Cloth, Novel
15209 *To the devil--a daughter.* Hutchinson, London, 1953, 384p, Cloth, Novel
15210 *Uncanny tales 1.* Sphere, London, 1974, 223p, Paper, Anth.
15211 *Uncanny tales 2.* Sphere, London, 1974, 172p, Paper, Anth.
15212 *Uncharted seas; a novel.* Hutchinson, London, 1938, 408p, Cloth, Novel
15213 *Unholy crusade.* Hutchinson, London, 1967, 379p, Cloth, Novel
15214 *Worlds far from here.* Hutchinson, London, 1952, 1120p, Cloth, Coll. [includes: *Uncharted seas; The man who missed the war; They found Atlantis*]

WHEELER, FRANCIS ROLT-
    see: ROLT-WHEELER, FRANCIS

WHEELER, (John) HARVEY, Jr., 1918- [*biography included*], with Eugene Burdick

02197 *Fail-safe.* McGraw-Hill, New York, 1962, 286p, Cloth, Novel

WHEELER, IDA WORDEN

15215 *Siegfried the mystic; a novel.* Arena Publishing Co., Boston, 1896, 295p, Cloth, Novel

WHEELER, PAUL, 1934- [*biography included*]

15216 *The friendly persuaders.* Hutchinson, London, 1968, 208p, Cloth, Novel

WHEELER, POST, 1869-1956

15217 *Hathoo of the elephants.* Viking Press, New York, 1943, 333p, Cloth, Novel

WHEELER, THOMAS GERALD

15218 *Loose Chippings; a novel.* S. G. Phillips, New York, 1969, 190p, Cloth, Novel
15219 *Lost threshold; a novel.* S. G. Phillips, New York, 1968, 189p, Cloth, Novel

WHEELER, WILLIAM W(allace), 1853-1916

15220 *Life; a novel*. Case, Lockwood & Brainard, Printers, Meriden, Conn., 1890, 287p, Cloth, Novel
15221 *Rest*. Arena Publishing Co., Boston, 1894, 280p, Cloth, Novel

WHEELER-NICHOLSON, MALCOLM, 1890-

15222 *Death over London*. Gateway, New York, 1940, 256p, Cloth, Novel

WHEELOCK, WARREN H., with William D. Sheldon

13000 *Over the edge*. Allyn & Bacon, Boston, 1972, 97p, Paper, Anth.

WHEELRIGHT, JOHN T(yler), 1856-1925, with Robert Grant, J. S. of Dale, and John Boyle O'Reilly

06240 *The King's men; a tale of to-morrow*. Charles Scribner's Sons, New York, 1884, 270p, Cloth, Novel

WHEN IT WAS LIGHT
     see: LANG, ANDREW

WHITAKER, DAVID, 1930-   [*biography included*]

15223 *Doctor Who and the crusaders*. Frederick Muller, London, 1965, 160p, Cloth, Tele. [Dr. Who #3]
15224 *Doctor Who, in an exciting adventure with the Daleks*. Frederick Muller, London, 1964, 157p, Cloth, Tele. [Dr. Who #1]

WHITE, A(rnold Henry), 1848-1925, with H. W. Wilson

15225 *When war breaks out, being a selection from the letters of Andrew D. Jones, the London correspondent of "Calner's weekly," during the war between Great Britain and the allied powers of France and Russia, September 21st, 1900, to January 1st, 1901*. Harper & Bros., New York, 1898, 94p, Cloth, Novel

WHITE, ARED

15226 *Attack on America*. Houghton Mifflin, Boston, 1939, 302p, Cloth, Novel

WHITE, CLAUDE GRAHAME-
     see: GRAHAME-WHITE, CLAUDE

WHITE, EDWARD LUCAS, 1866-1934

15227 *Lukundoo, and other stories*. George H. Doran, New York, 1927, 328p, Cloth, Coll.
15228 *The song of the Sirens, and other stories*. E. P. Dutton, New York, 1919, 348p, Cloth, Coll.

WHITE, F(rederick) M(errick)

15229 *The white battalions*. C. Arthur Pearson, London, 1900, 341p, Cloth, Novel

WHITE, H. RAY

15230 *Virgins of mystery*. The Author, Phoenix?, 1959, 181p, Cloth, Novel

WHITE, JAMES, 1928-   [*biography included*]

15231 *The aliens among us*. Ballantine, New York, 1969, 217p, Paper, Coll.
15232 *All judgement fled*. Rapp & Whiting, London, 1968, 190p, Cloth, Novel
     Dark inferno. [see 15237A]
15233 *Deadly litter*. Ballantine, New York, 1964, 175p, Paper, Coll.
15234 *The dream millennium*. Michael Joseph, London, 1974, 222p, Cloth, Novel
15235 *The escape orbit*. Ace, New York, 1965, 188p, Paper, Novel
15235A retitled: *Open prison*. Four Square, London, 1965, 158p, Paper, Novel
15236 *Hospital station*. Ballantine, New York, 1962, 191p, Paper, Novel [Sector General #1]
15237 *Lifeboat*. Ballantine, New York, 1972, 186p, Paper, Novel
15237A retitled: *Dark inferno*. Michael Joseph, London, 1972, 158p, Cloth, Novel
15238 *Major operation*. Ballantine, New York, 1971, 183p, Paper, Coll. [Sector General #3]
     Open prison. [see 15235A]
15239 *Second ending*. Ace Double, New York, 1962, 100p, Paper, Novel
15240 *The secret visitors*. Ace Double, New York, 1957, 155p, Paper, Novel
15241 *Star surgeon*. Ballantine, New York, 1963, 159p, Paper, Novel [Sector General #2]
15242 *Tomorrow is too far*. Ballantine, New York, 1971, 183p, Paper, Novel
15243 *The watch below*. Ballantine, New York, 1966, 189p, Paper, Novel

WHITE, JAY C., 1925-

15244 *A cup of life*. Vantage Press, New York, 1962, 292p, Cloth, Novel

WHITE, JOHN, with W. Graham Moffat

10212 *What's the world coming to? a novel of the twenty-first century*. Elliot Stock, London, 1893, 172p, Cloth, Novel

WHITE, PERCY, 1852-1938, with E. G. Boulenger

01658 *The centaur passes*. Duckworth, London, 1933, 303p, Cloth, Novel

WHITE, STEWART EDWARD, 1873-1946

15245 *On tiptoe; a romance of the redwoods*. George H. Doran, New York, 1922, 264p, Cloth, Novel
15246 *The sign at six*. Bobbs-Merrill, Indianapolis, 1912, 265p, Cloth, Novel [Percy Darrow #2]

WHITE, STEWART EDWARD (cont.), with Samuel Hopkins Adams

00053　*The mystery.* McClure, Phillips, New York, 1907, 286p, Cloth, Novel [Percy Darrow #1]

WHITE, T(erence) H(anbury), 1906-1964

15247　*Earth stopped; or, Mr. Marx's sporting tour.* Collins, London, 1934, 252p, Cloth, Novel
15248　*The elephant and the kangaroo.* G. P. Putnam's Sons, New York, 1947, 254p, Cloth, Novel
15249　*Gone to ground; a novel.* Collins, London, 1935, 267p, Cloth, Novel
15250　*The ill-made knight.* G. P. Putnam's Sons, New York, 1940, 291p, Cloth, Novel [King Arthur #3]
15251　*The Master; an adventure story.* Jonathan Cape, London, 1957, 256p, Cloth, Novel
15252　*Mistress Masham's repose.* G. P. Putnam's Sons, New York, 1946, 255p, Cloth, Novel [Gulliver series]
15253　*The once and future king.* Collins, London, 1958, 677p, Cloth, Coll. [King Arthur #s 1-4]
15254　*The sword in the stone.* Collins, London, 1938, 338p, Cloth, Novel [King Arthur #1]
15255　*The witch in the wood.* G. P. Putnam's Sons, New York, 1939, 270p, Cloth, Novel [King Arthur #2]

WHITE, TED [Theodore Edwin White, 1938-   ] [*biography included*]

15256　*Android avenger.* Ace Double, New York, 1965, 113p, Paper, Novel
15257　*The best from Amazing stories.* Manor, New York, 1973, 192p, Paper, Anth.
15258　*The best from Fantastic.* Manor, New York, 1973, 192p, Paper, Anth.
15259　*By furies possessed; a novel of tomorrow.* Signet, New York, 1970, 192p, Paper, Novel
15260　*Captain America; The great gold steal.* Bantam, New York, 1968, 118p, Paper, Novel [Captain America #2]
15261　*The Jewels of elsewhen.* Belmont, New York, 1967, 172p, Paper, Novel
15262　*No time like tomorrow.* Crown Publishers, New York, 1969, 152p, Cloth, Novel
15263　*Phoenix prime.* Lancer, New York, 1966, 189p, Paper, Novel [Qanar #1]
15264　*Secret of the marauder satellite.* Westminster Press, Philadelphia, 1967, 171p, Cloth, Novel
15265　*The Sorceress of Qar.* Lancer, New York, 1966, 191p, Paper, Novel [Qanar #2]
15266　*The spawn of the death machine.* Paperback Library, New York, 1968, 175p, Paper, Novel
15267　*Star wolf!* Lancer, New York, 1971, 190p, Paper, Novel [Qanar #3]
15268　*Trouble on Project Ceres.* Westminster Press, Philadelphia, 1971, 157p, Cloth, Novel

with Terry Carr as Norman Edwards:

02655　*Invasion from 2500.* Monarch, Derby, Conn., 1964, 126p, Paper, Novel

as Ron Archer, with Dave Van Arnam:

14436　*Lost in space.* Pyramid, New York, 1967, 157p, Paper, Tele. [Lost in Space series]

with Dave Van Arnam:

14437　*Sideslip.* Pyramid, New York, 1968, 188p, Paper, Novel

WHITE, W. HOLT
　　see: HOLT WHITE, W.

WHITE, WILLIAM ANTHONY PARKER
　　see: BOUCHER, ANTHONY

WHITE, WILLIAM CHAPMAN, 1903-1955

15269　*The pale blonde of Sands Street.* Viking Press, New York, 1946, 224p, Cloth, Novel

THE WHITE SYBIL

15270　*The white sybil,* by Clark Ashton Smith; *Men of Avalon,* by David H. Keller, M.D. Fantasy Publishing Co., Everett, PA, 1935?, 38p, Paper, Anth.

WHITEHEAD, HENRY S(t. Clair), 1882-1932

15271　*Jumbee, and other uncanny tales.* Arkham House, Sauk City, 1944, 394p, Cloth, Coll.
15272　*West India lights.* Arkham House, Sauk City, 1946, 367p, Cloth, Coll.

WHITEHEAD, ROBERT (John), 1928-   [*biography included*], with Henry Bamman and William Odell

00818　*Bone people.* Benefic Press, Westchester, 197?, 72p, Cloth, Novel
00819　*Ice men of Rime.* Benefic Press, Westchester, 1970, 72p, Cloth, Novel
00820　*Inviso man.* Benefic Press, Westchester, 1970, 72p, Cloth, Novel
00821　*Milky Way.* Benefic Press, Westchester, 1970, 71p, Cloth, Novel
00822　*Planet of the whistlers.* Benefic Press, Westchester, 1970, 72p, Cloth, Novel
00823　*Space pirate.* Benefic Press, Westchester, 1970, 72p, Cloth, Novel

WHITELEY, ELIZABETH

15273　*The devil's throne.* Digby, Long, London, 190?, 275p, Cloth, Novel

WHITELEY, JOHN

15274　*Kidnapped in space.* Tiger, London, 1969, 89p, Paper, Novel

WHITELL, EVELYN

15275　*Shekinah.* DeVorss, Los Angeles, 1937, 342p, Cloth, Novel

WHITENIGHT, CYNTHIA S.

15276 *Prophecies and possibilities; the science fiction novel.* Independent Study, Division of Continuing Education, University of Kansas, Lawrence, Kans., 1973, 91p, Paper, Nonf.

WHITESIDE, EDWARD

15277 *A warning from Mars.* Inter-Planetary Publications, New York, 1948, 79p, Cloth, Novel

WHITFIELD, STEPHEN (Edward), with Gene Roddenberry

12347 *The making of Star trek.* Ballantine, New York, 1968, 414p, Paper, Nonf.

WHITHAM, JOHN W.

15278 *Interworld; a novel.* Film Row Press, Seattle, 1932, 278p, Cloth, Novel

WHITING, SYDNEY, d. 1875

15279 *Heliondé; or, Adventures in the Sun.* Chapman & Hall, London, 1854, 424p, Cloth, Novel [published anonymously]
15279A *Heliondé; or, Adventures in the Sun,* by Sydney Whiting. Chapman & Hall, London, 1855, 424p, Cloth, Novel

WHITNALL, HAROLD O(rville), **1877-1945**

15280 *Hunter of the caverns.* Thomas Y. Crowell, New York, 1939, 119p, Cloth, Novel

WHITNEY, VERNER MEURICE

15281 *Immortal hero.* C. P. Hoagland, Somerville, NJ, 1951, 226p, Cloth, Novel
15282 *The unearthly kingdom.* Grafton Press, New York, 1930, 130p, Cloth, Novel

WHITTEN, LESLIE H(unter), **1928-** [*biography included*]

15283 *Moon of the wolf.* Crime Club, Doubleday, Garden City, 1967, 215p, Cloth, Novel
15283A retitled: *Death of a nurse.* Robert Hale, London, 1969, 175p, Cloth, Novel
15284 *Progeny of the adder.* Crime Club, Doubleday, Garden City, 1965, 191p, Cloth, Novel

WHITTINGTON, HARRY

15285 *The man from U.N.C.L.E., #2; The doomsday affair.* Ace, New York, 1965, 159p, Paper, Tele. [Man from U.N.C.L.E. #2 (both U.S. & U.K. series)]

WHYTE, ANDREW ADAMS

15286 *The new SF bulletin index to SF books, 1974.* Spike MacPhee, Publisher, Paratime Press Publications, Boston, 1974, 42p, Paper, Nonf.

with Anthony Lewis:

08993 *The N.E.S.F.A. index; science fiction magazines, 1971-1972, and original anthologies, 1971-1972.* NESFA Press, Cambridge, Mass., 1973, 42p, Paper, Nonf.
08994 *The N.E.S.F.A. index to the science fiction magazines and original anthologies, 1973.* NESFA Press, Cambridge, Mass., 1974, 30p, Paper, Nonf.

WHYTE-MELVILLE, G(eorge) **J**(ohn), **1821-1878**

15287 *"Bones and I"; or, The skeleton at home.* Chapman & Hall, London, 1868, 287p, Cloth, Novel
15288 *Sarchedon; a legend of the great queen.* Longmans, Green, London, 1899, 435p, Cloth, Novel
15288A retitled: *A knight of the east, from the novel entitled "Sarchedon."* Thomas Nelson & Sons, London, 1928, 126p, Cloth, Novel [abridged; "arranged by Susan Cunnington"]

WIBBERLEY, LEONARD (Patrick O'Connor), **1915-** [*biography included*]

15289 *Attar of the ice valley.* Ariel Book, Farrar, Straus & Giroux, New York, 1968, 166p, Cloth, Novel
15290 *Beware of the mouse.* G. P. Putnam's Sons, New York, 1958, 189p, Cloth, Novel [Grand Fenwick #1]
15291 *Encounter near Venus.* Ariel Book, Farrar, Straus & Giroux, New York, 1967, 214p, Cloth, Novel [Uncle Bill #1]
15292 *A feast of freedom.* William Morrow, New York, 1964, 186p, Cloth, Novel
15293 *Journey to Untor.* Ariel Book, Farrar, Straus & Giroux, New York, 1970, 188p, Cloth, Novel [Uncle Bill #2]
15294 *McGillicuddy McGotham.* Little, Brown, Boston, 1956, 111p, Cloth, Novel
15295 *The mouse on the Moon.* William Morrow, New York, 1962, 191p, Cloth, Novel [Grand Fenwick #3]
15296 *The mouse on Wall Street.* William Morrow, New York, 1969, 159p, Cloth, Novel [Grand Fenwick #4]
15297 *The mouse that roared.* Little, Brown, Boston, 1955, 280p, Cloth, Novel [Grand Fenwick #2]
15297A retitled: *The wrath of grapes.* Robert Hale, London, 1955, 191p, Cloth, Novel [Grand Fenwick #2]
15298 *Mrs. Searwood's secret weapon.* Little, Brown, Boston, 1954, 294p, Cloth, Novel
15299 *The quest of Excalibur.* G. P. Putnam's Sons, New York, 1959, 190p, Cloth, Novel
15300 *Stranger at Killknock.* G. P. Putnam's Sons, New York, 1961, 192p, Cloth, Novel
15301 *Take me to your president.* G. P. Putnam's Sons, New York, 1957, 186p, Cloth, Novel
The wrath of grapes. [see 15297A]

as Christopher Webb:

15302 *Eusebius, the Phoenician.* Funk & Wagnalls, New York, 1969, 188p, Cloth, Novel

WICKERSHAM, JAMES A(lexander), 1851-

15303 *Enoch Willoughby; a novel.* Charles Scribner's
       Sons, New York, 1900, 356p, Cloth, Novel

WICKHAM, HARVEY, 1872-1930

15304 *Jungle terror.* Doubleday, Page, Garden City,
       1920, 244p, Cloth, Novel

WICKS, MARK

15305 *To Mars via the Moon; an astronomical story.*
       Seeley & Co., London, 1911, 328p, Cloth,
       Novel

WIDENER, DON(ald), 1930-   [*biography included*]

15306 *N.U.K.E.; a novel.* Hawthorn, New York,
       1974, 218p, Cloth, Novel

WIDNALL, SAMUEL PAGE

15307 *A mystery of sixty centuries; or, A modern
       St. George and the dragon.* S. P. Widnall,
       Grantchester, UK, 1889, 195p, Cloth, Novel

WIDNEY, STANLEY A.

15308 *Elevator to the Moon.* Follett Publishing Co.,
       Chicago, 1955, 128p, Cloth, Novel

WIGGINS, WALTER Jr.

15309 *Dreams in reality of the undersea craft.* Pa-
       geant Press, New York, 1954, 206p, Cloth,
       Novel

WIGNALL, T(revor) C., 1883-   , with G. D.
Knox

08402 *Atoms.* Mills & Boon, London, 1923, 288p,
       Cloth, Novel

WILBRAHAM, JOHN
     see: POTTER, ROBERT

WILBRANDT, ADOLF (von), 1837-1911

15310 *A new humanity; or, The Easter Island.* J. B.
       Lippincott, Philadelphia, 1905, 360p, Cloth,
       Novel; Maclaren & Co., London, 1905, 360p,
       Cloth, Novel

WILBRANDT, CONRAD

15311 *Mr. East's experiences in Mr. Bellamy's world;
       records of the years 2001 and 2002.* Harper
       & Bros., New York, 1891, 255p, Cloth, Novel
       [a sequel to Bellamy's *Looking backward*]

WILCOX, COLLIN, 1924-

15312 *The black door.* Dodd, Mead, New York, 1967,
       181p, Cloth, Novel

WILCOX, DON, with David Vern as David V. Reed

12077 *The whispering gorilla; a novel.* World Distri-
       butors/Sydney Pemberton, London, 1950, 160p,
       Paper, Novel

WILDE, OSCAR (Fingal O'Flahertie Wills), 1854-
1900

15313 *The Canterville ghost.* J. W. Luce, Boston,
       1906, 123p, Cloth, Novel
15314 *Fairy tales.* G. P. Putnam's Sons, New York,
       1913, 256p, Cloth, Coll.
15315 *Fairy tales.* Peter Pauper Press, Mt. Vernon,
       NY, 1950, 87p, Cloth, Coll. [different book]
15316 *Fairy tales.* Bodley Head, London, 1960, 189p,
       Cloth, Coll. [different contents]
15317 *The fisherman and his soul, and other fairy
       tales.* Farrar & Rinehart, New York, 1929,
       212p, Cloth, Coll.
15318 *The happy prince, and other tales.* David Nutt
       London, 1888, 116p, Cloth, Coll.
15318A retitled: *The happy prince, and other fairy
       tales.* G. P. Putnam's Sons, New York, 1908,
       124p, Cloth, Coll.
15318B retitled: *The happy prince, and other stories*
       Frederick A. Stokes, New York, 1913, 204p,
       Cloth, Coll.
15319 *The happy prince, and other tales.* Haldeman-
       Julius, Girard, Kans., 1922?, 56p, Paper,
       Coll.
15320 *Lord Arthur Savile's crime, and other stories.*
       James R. Osgood, McIlvaine, London, 1891,
       168p, Cloth, Coll.
15321 *The picture of Dorian Gray.* Ward, Lock, Lon-
       don, 1891, 334p, Cloth, Novel
15322 *The picture of Dorian Gray, and selected sto-
       ries.* Signet Classic, New York, 1962, 304p,
       Paper, Coll.
15323 *The sphinx without a secret; The Canterville
       ghost; The model millionaire.* Privately
       printed, London, 1904, 64p, Cloth?, Coll.

WILDING, PHILIP

15324 *Shadow over the Earth.* Hennel Locke, London,
       1956, 160p, Cloth, Novel
15325 *Spaceflight Venus.* Hennel Locke, London,
       1954, 190p, Cloth, Novel

as John Robert Haynes:

15326 *Scream from outer space.* Rich & Cowan, London
       1955, 176p, Cloth, Novel

WILEY, RAY H., 1909-

15327 *On the trail of 1960; a utopian novel.* Expo-
       sition Press, New York, 1950, 156p, Cloth,
       Novel

WILHELM, KAT(i)E, 1928- [biography inclu-
ded]

15328 Abyss; two novellas. Doubleday, Garden City,
       1971, 158p, Cloth, Coll.
15329 The downstairs room, and other speculative
       fiction. Doubleday, Garden City, 1968,
       215p, Cloth, Coll.
15330 The killer thing. Doubleday, Garden City,
       1967, 190p, Cloth, Novel
15330A retitled: The killing thing. Herbert Jenkins,
       London, 1967, 174p, Cloth, Novel
15331 Let the fire fall. Doubleday, Garden City,
       1969, 228p, Cloth, Novel
15332 Margaret and I; a novel. Little, Brown, Bos-
       ton, 1971, 247p, Cloth, Novel
15333 The mile-long spaceship. Berkley Medallion,
       New York, 1963, 160p, Paper, Coll.
15333A retitled: Andover and the android. Dennis
       Dobson, London, 1966, 160p, Cloth, Coll.
15334 Nebula award stories nine. Harper & Row,
       New York, 1974, 241p, Cloth, Anth.
15335 The nevermore affair. Doubleday, Garden City,
       1966, 236p, Cloth, Novel

with Theodore L. Thomas:

14071 The clone. Berkley Medallion, New York, 1965,
       143p, Paper, Novel
14072 The year of the cloud, by Kate Wilhelm & Ted
       Thomas. Doubleday, Garden City, 1970, 216p,
       Cloth, Novel

WILHELM, LAMBERT, pseud.

15336 Starship Intercourse. Companion, San Diego,
       1971, 155p, Paper, Novel

WILIS, pseud.

15337 The tales of the rat; Mary, part 1 (being the
       first of the tales). no publisher, Nassau-
       in-the-Bahamas, 1972, 208p, Paper, Novel

WILKINS, MARY E(leanor), 1852-1930

15338 The green door. Moffat, Yard, New York,
       1910, 62p, Cloth, Novel
15339 The wind in the rose-bush, and other stories
       of the supernatural. Doubleday, Page, New
       York, 1903, 237p, Cloth, Coll.

as Mary E. Wilkins Freeman:

15340 Collected ghost stories. Arkham House, Sauk
       City, 1974, 189p, Cloth, Coll.

WILKINS, PETER
  see: PALTOCK, ROBERT

WILKINS, (William) VAUGHAN, 1890-1959

15341 The City of Frozen Fire. Jonathan Cape, Lon-
       don, 1950, 281p, Cloth, Novel
15342 Fanfare for a witch. Jonathan Cape, London,
       1954, 286p, Cloth, Novel
15343 Valley beyond time. Jonathan Cape, London,
       1955, 304p, Cloth, Novel

WILKINSON, LOUIS UMFREVILLE
  see: MARLOW, LOUIS

WILKINSON, SARAH SCUDGELL

15344 The priory of St. Clair; or, Spectre of the
       murdered nun; a gothic tale. R. Harrild,
       London, 1811, 35p, Paper, Story

WILL, JOHN N.

15345 My blond princess of space. Carlton Press,
       New York, 1968, 51p, Cloth, Novel

WILLARD, CHARLES DWIGHT, 1860-1914

15346 The fall of Ulysses; an elephant story. George
       H. Doran, New York, 1912, 77p, Cloth, Novel

WILLARD, MILDRED WILDS, 1911- [biography in-
cluded]

15347 The cloud crasher. Transition Press, San Di-
       ego, 1969, 192p, Paper, Novel

WILLARD, T(heodore) A(rthur), 1862-1943

15348 The wizard of Zacna, a lost city of the Mayas;
       remarkable adventures of an ahmen, wizard
       and mystic of Yucatan, in an unknown coun-
       try to which the ancient Mayans had fled,
       leaving their great stone cities silent and
       desolate to be overgrown with forest and
       jungle. Stratford Co., Boston, 1929, 319p,
       Cloth, Novel

WILLEFORD, CHARLES (Ray III), 1919- [bio-
graphy included]

15349 The machine in Ward Eleven. Belmont, New York,
       1963, 141p, Paper, Coll.

WILLER, JIM

15350 Paramind; a novel. McClelland & Stewart, To-
       ronto, 1973, 206p, Cloth, Novel

WILLIAM, Sir, pseud.

15351 The occults in council; or, The great learning.
       Smith-Brooks Printing Co., Denver, 1901,
       , Cloth, Novel

WILLIAMS, ALFRED ROWBERRY, 1888-

15352 Dreams from the past. Arthur H. Stockwell,
       London, 1923, 191p, Cloth, Coll.

WILLIAMS, CHARLES (Walter Stansby), 1886-1945

15353 All Hallow's Eve. Faber & Faber, London,
       1945, 206p, Cloth, Novel

WILLIAMS, CHARLES (cont.)

15354 *Descent into Hell.* Faber & Faber, London, 1937, 305p, Cloth, Novel

15355 *The greater trumps.* Victor Gollancz, London, 1932, 287p, Cloth, Novel

15356 *Many dimensions.* Victor Gollancz, London, 1931, 317p, Cloth, Novel

15357 *The place of the lion; a new novel.* Victor Gollancz, London, 1931, 288p, Cloth, Novel

15358 *Shadows of ecstasy.* Victor Gollancz, London, 1933, 287p, Cloth, Novel

15359 *War in Heaven.* Victor Gollancz, London, 1930, 288p, Cloth, Novel

WILLIAMS, CHRISTOPHER HODDER-
   see: HODDER-WILLIAMS, CHRISTOPHER

WILLIAMS, EARL (Willoughby), 1885-

15360 *The court of Belshazzar; a romance of the great captivity.* Bobbs-Merrill, Indianapolis, 1918, 352p, Cloth, Novel

WILLIAMS, ELIOT CRAWSHAY-
   see: CRAWSHAY-WILLIAMS, ELIOT

WILLIAMS, ERIC C(yril), 1918-   [*biography included*]

15361 *The call of utopia.* Robert Hale, London, 1971, 192p, Cloth, Novel

15362 *Flash.* Robert Hale, London, 1972, 158p, Cloth, Novel

15363 *Monkman comes down.* Robert Hale, London, 1969, 190p, Cloth, Novel

15364 *Project--Renaissance.* Robert Hale, London, 1973, 176p, Cloth, Novel

15365 *The time injection.* Robert Hale, London, 1968, 191p, Cloth, Novel

15366 *To end all telescopes.* Robert Hale, London, 1969, 190p, Cloth, Novel

WILLIAMS, F(rank) CHENHALLS, 1880-

15367 *The inner number.* Longmans, Green, London, 1927, 274p, Cloth, Novel

WILLIAMS, FRANCES FENWICK

15368 *A soul on fire.* John Lane, New York, 1915, 316p, Cloth, Novel

15368A retitled: *Theodora; a soul on fire.* John Lane, The Bodley Head, London, 1915, 316p, Cloth, Novel

WILLIAMS, (Edward) FRANCIS, Baron Francis-Williams, 1903-1970

15369 *The Richardson story; a novel.* William Heinemann, London, 1951, 209p, Cloth, Novel

15369A retitled: *It happened tomorrow; a novel.* Abelard Press, New York, 1952, 217p, Cloth, Novel

WILLIAMS, FRANCIS HOWARD, 1844-1922

15370 *Âtman; the documents in a strange case.* Cassell, New York, 1891, 303p, Cloth, Novel

WILLIAMS, (Frank) GARFIELD HODDER, 1881-1960

15371 *What if He came?* Hodder & Stoughton, London, 1930, 219p, Cloth, Novel

WILLIAMS, GEOFFREY

15372 *The magicians of Charno.* John Murray, London, 1913, 304p, Cloth, Novel

WILLIAMS, GERALD

15373 *A bedside odyssey*, by Homer and associates. Traveller's Companion, New York, 1967, 192p, Paper, Novel

WILLIAMS, HARPER

15374 *The thing in the woods.* Robert McBride, New York, 1924, 291p, Cloth, Novel

WILLIAMS, HERBERT, 1914-

15375 *Avon ghost reader.* Avon, New York, 1946, 258p, Paper, Anth. [published anonymously; introduction signed "H. W."]

15376 *Terror at night; 13 tales of mystery and imagination.* Avon, New York, 1947, 194p, Paper, Anth.

WILLIAMS, ISLWYN

15377 *Dangerous waters.* Gryphon, London, 1952, 224p, Cloth, Novel

15378 *Newbury in Orm.* Gryphon, London, 1952, 191p, Cloth, Novel

WILLIAMS, J. SHELDON
   see: SHELDON-WILLIAMS, MILES

WILLIAMS, J. X., house pseud. [see also Andrew Offutt]

15379 *Devil's degradation.* Evening Reader, San Diego, 1966, 190p, Paper, Novel

15380 *ESP orgy.* Adult Books, San Diego, 1968, 159p, Paper, Novel

15381 *Her.* Leisure Books, San Diego, 1967, 160p, Paper, Novel [Tarzan series; a parody of Haggard's *She*]

10943 *The sex pill.* Pleasure Reader, San Diego, 1968, 160p, Paper, Novel [by Andrew Offutt]

WILLIAMS, JAMES

15382 *"Objective Venus."* Badger, London, 1958, 158p, Paper, Novel

WILLIAMS, JAY, 1914-1978 [*biography included*]

15383 *The hawkstone.* Henry Z. Walck, New York, 1971, 142p, Cloth, Novel
15384 *The hero from otherwhere.* Henry Z. Walck, New York, 1972, 175p, Cloth, Novel
15385 *The people of the ax.* Henry Z. Walck, New York, 1974, 145p, Cloth, Novel
15386 *UNIAD.* Charles Scribner's Sons, New York, 1968, 246p, Cloth, Novel

with Raymond Abrashkin:

00017 *Danny Dunn and the anti-gravity paint.* Whittlesey House, New York, 1956, 154p, Cloth, Novel [Danny Dunn #1]
00018 *Danny Dunn and the automatic house.* Whittlesey House, New York, 1965, 139p, Cloth, Novel [Danny Dunn #9]
00019 *Danny Dunn and the fossil cave.* Whittlesey House, New York, 1961, 146p, Cloth, Novel [Danny Dunn #6]
00020 *Danny Dunn and the heat ray.* Whittlesey House, New York, 1962, 144p, Cloth, Novel [Danny Dunn #7]
00021 *Danny Dunn and the homework machine.* Whittlesey House, New York, 1958, 141p, Cloth, Novel [Danny Dunn #3]
00021A retitled: *The homework machine.* Brockhampton Press, Leicester, UK, 1960, 120p, Cloth, Novel [Danny Dunn #3]
00022 *Danny Dunn and the smallifying machine.* McGraw-Hill, New York, 1969, 139p, Cloth, Novel [Danny Dunn #11]
00023 *Danny Dunn and the swamp monster.* McGraw-Hill, New York, 1971, 142p, Cloth, Novel [Danny Dunn #12]
00024 *Danny Dunn and the voice from space.* McGraw-Hill, New York, 1967, 157p, Cloth, Novel [Danny Dunn #10]
00025 *Danny Dunn and the weather machine.* Whittlesey House, New York, 1959, 144p, Cloth, Novel [Danny Dunn #4]
00026 *Danny Dunn, invisible boy.* McGraw-Hill, New York, 1974, 154p, Cloth, Novel [Danny Dunn #13]
00027 *Danny Dunn on a desert island.* Whittlesey House, New York, 1957, 159p, Cloth, Novel [Danny Dunn #2]
00028 *Danny Dunn on the ocean floor.* Whittlesey House, New York, 1960, 156p, Cloth, Novel [Danny Dunn #5]
00029 *Danny Dunn, time traveller.* Whittlesey House, New York, 1963, 138p, Cloth, Novel [Danny Dunn #8]

WILLIAMS, JOHN A(lfred), 1925- [*biography included*]

15387 *Sons of darkness, sons of light; a novel of some probability.* Little, Brown, Boston, 1969, 279p, Cloth, Novel

WILLIAMS, MILES SHELDON-
see: SHELDON-WILLIAMS, MILES

WILLIAMS, NEIL WYNN

15388 *The electric theft; a story.* Small, Maynard, Boston, 1906, 311p, Cloth, Novel; Greening & Co., London, 1906, 311p, Cloth, Novel

WILLIAMS, NICK BODDIE, 1906- [*biography included*]

15389 *The atom curtain.* Ace Double, New York, 1956, 168p, Paper, Novel

WILLIAMS, RICHARD VALENTINE
see: ROWLEY, RICHARD

WILLIAMS, ROBERT FOLKESTONE, 1805-1872 [published anonymously]

15390 *Eureka; a prophecy of the future,* by the author of "Mephistopheles in London." Longman, Rees, Orme, Brown, Green & Longman, London, 1837, 3vol, Cloth, Novel

WILLIAMS, ROBERT MOORE, 1907-1977 [*biography included*]

15391 *Beachhead planet.* Dell, New York, 1970, 190p, Paper, Novel
15392 *The bell from infinity.* Lancer, New York, 1968, 189p, Paper, Novel
15393 *The Blue Atom.* Ace Double, New York, 1958, 124p, Paper, Novel
15394 *The chaos fighters.* Ace, New York, 1955, 160p, Paper, Novel
15395 *Conquest of the space sea.* Ace Double, New York, 1955, 151p, Paper, Novel
15396 *The darkness before tomorrow.* Ace Double, New York, 1962, 118p, Paper, Novel
15397 *The day they H-bombed Los Angeles.* Ace, New York, 1961, 128p, Paper, Novel
15398 *Doomsday eve.* Ace Double, New York, 1957, 138p, Paper, Novel
15399 *Flight from yesterday.* Ace Double, New York, 1963, 120p, Paper, Novel
15400 *Jongor fights back.* Popular Library, New York, 1970, 128p, Paper, Novel [Jongor #3]
15401 *Jongor of Lost Land.* Popular Library, New York, 1970, 126p, Paper, Novel [Jongor #1]
15402 *King of the fourth planet.* Ace Double, New York, 1962, 128p, Paper, Novel
15403 *Love is forever--we are for tonight.* Curtis, New York, 1970, 141p, Paper, Novel
15404 *The Lunar eye.* Ace Double, New York, 1964, 115p, Paper, Novel
15405 *Now comes tomorrow.* Curtis, New York, 1971, 160p, Paper, Novel
15406 *The return of Jongor.* Popular Library, New York, 1970, 127p, Paper, Novel [Jongor #2]
15407 *The second Atlantis.* Ace, New York, 1965, 123p, Paper, Novel
15408 *Seven tickets to Hell.* Popular Library, New York, 1972, 190p, Paper, Novel
15409 *The star wasps.* Ace Double, New York, 1963, 126p, Paper, Novel
15410 *To the end of time, and other stories.* Ace Double, New York, 1960, 108p, Paper, Coll.
15411 *Vigilante, 21st century.* Lancer, New York, 1967, 189p, Paper, Novel
15412 *The void beyond, and other stories.* Ace Double, New York, 1958, 130p, Paper, Coll.
15413 *Walk up the sky.* Avalon, New York, 1962, 221p, Cloth, Novel
15414 *When two worlds meet; stories of men on Mars.* Curtis, New York, 1970, 222p, Paper, Coll.
15415 *World of the masterminds.* Ace Double, New York, 1960, 148p, Paper, Novel

WILLIAMS, ROBERT MOORE (cont.)

15416 *Zanthar at Moon's madness.* Lancer, New York, 1968, 189p, Paper, Novel [Zanthar #3]
15417 *Zanthar at the edge of never.* Lancer, New York, 1968, 285p, Paper, Novel [Zanthar #2]
15418 *Zanthar at trip's end.* Lancer, New York, 1969, 191p, Paper, Novel [Zanthar #4]
15419 *Zanthar of the many worlds.* Lancer, New York, 1967, 192p, Paper, Novel [Zanthar #1]

WILLIAMS, ROSWELL, pseud.
  see: OWEN, FRANK

WILLIAMS, SPEEDY, pseud. [L. H. Smith, 1916-]

15420 *Journey through space; to a Martian satellite and back.* Exposition Press, New York, 1958, 108p, Cloth, Novel

WILLIAMS, T. OWEN

15421 *A month for mankind.* Robert Hale, London, 1970, 191p, Cloth, Novel

WILLIAMS, TENNESSEE [Thomas Lanier Williams, 1914-] [*biography included*]

15422 *The knightly quest; a novella and four stories.* J. Laughlin, New Directions Publishing Corp., New York, 1966, 183p, Cloth, Coll.

WILLIAMS, THAD(deus) W(arsaw)

15423 *In quest of life; or, The revelation of the Wiyatatao of Xipantl, the last high priest of the Aztecs.* F. Tennyson Neely, London, 1898, 363p, Cloth, Novel

WILLIAMS, THOMAS LANIER
  see: WILLIAMS, TENNESSEE

WILLIAMS, URSULA MORAY, 1911- [*biography included*]

15424 *Castle Merlin.* George Allen & Unwin, London, 1972, 112p, Cloth, Novel
15425 *The moonball.* Hamish Hamilton, London, 1958, 141p, Cloth, Novel

WILLIAMS-ELLIS, (Mary) AMABEL (Nassau), 1894- [*biography included*]

with Mably Owen:

11084 *Out of this world; an anthology of science fiction.* Blackie & Son, London, 1971, 357p, Cloth, Anth. [includes *Out of this world 3* and *Out of this world 4*]
11085 *Out of this world 1; an anthology of science fiction.* Blackie & Son, London, 1960, 197p, Cloth, Anth.
11086 *Out of this world 2; an anthology of science fiction.* Blackie & Son, London, 1961, 188p, Cloth, Anth.

11087 *Out of this world 3; an anthology of science fiction.* Blackie & Son, London, 1962, 175p, Cloth, Anth.
11088 *Out of this world 4; an anthology of science fiction.* Blackie & Son, London, 1964, 187p, Cloth, Anth.
11089 *Out of this world 5; an anthology of science fiction.* Blackie & Son, London, 1965, 188p, Cloth, Anth.
11090 *Out of this world 6; an anthology of science fiction.* Blackie & Son, London, 1967, 196p, Cloth, Anth.
11091 *Out of this world 7; an anthology of science fiction.* Blackie & Son, London, 1968, 214p, Cloth, Anth.
11092 *Out of this world 8; an anthology of science fiction.* Blackie & Son, London, 1970, 187p, Cloth, Anth.
11093 *Out of this world choice; an anthology of science fiction.* Blackie & Son, London, 1972, 370p, Cloth, Anth. [includes *Out of this world 2* and *Out of this world 5*]
11094 *Worlds apart; an anthology of science fiction.* Blackie & Son, London, 1966, 416p, Cloth, Anth.

with Michael Pearson:

11259 *Out of this world 9; an anthology of science fiction.* Blackie & Son, London, 1972, 191p, Cloth, Anth.
11260 *Out of this world 10; an anthology of science fiction.* Blackie & Son, London, 1973, 190p, Cloth, Anth.
11261 *Strange universe; an anthology of science fiction.* Blackie & Son, London, 1974, 192p, Cloth, Anth.
11262 *Tales from the galaxies.* Piccolo, London, 1973, 126p, Paper, Anth.

WILLIAMSON, ETHEL
  see: CARDINAL, JANE

WILLIAMSON, JACK [John Stewart Williamson, 1908-] [*biography included*]

15426 *After world's end; an amazing science-fiction story.* Digit, London, 1961, 156p, Paper, Novel [Legion of Time #2]
15427 *Bright new universe.* Ace, New York, 1967, 158p, Paper, Novel
15428 *The Cometeers.* Fantasy Press, Reading, PA, 1950, 310p, Cloth, Coll. [Legion of Space #s 2-3; includes *The Cometeers* and *One against the Legion*]
15429 *The Cometeers.* Pyramid, New York, 1967, 157p, Paper, Novel [Legion of Space #2]
15430 *Darker than you think.* Fantasy Press, Reading, PA, 1948, 310p, Cloth, Novel
15431 *Dome around America.* Ace Double, New York, 1955, 133p, Paper, Novel
15432 *Dragon's island.* Simon & Schuster, New York, 1951, 246p, Cloth, Novel
15432A retitled: *The not-men; a science-fiction adventure.* Tower, New York, 1968, 222p, Paper, Novel
15433 *Golden blood.* Lancer, New York, 1964, 157p, Paper, Novel
15434 *The Green Girl.* Avon, New York, 1950, 125p, Paper, Novel
15435 *H. G. Wells: critic of progress.* Mirage Press, Baltimore, 1973, 162p, Cloth, Nonf.

WILLIAMSON, JACK (cont.)

15436 *The humanoids*. Simon & Schuster, New York, 1949, 240p, Cloth, Novel

15437 *The Legion of Space*. Fantasy Press, Reading, PA, 1947, 259p, Cloth, Novel [Legion of Space #1]

15438 *The legion of time*. Fantasy Press, Reading, PA, 1952, 252p, Cloth, Coll. [Legion of Time #s 1-2; includes *The legion of time* and *After world's end*]

15438A retitled: *Two complete novels: After world's end; The legion of time*. Galaxy Magabook, New York, 1963, 160p, Paper, Coll. [Legion of Time #s 1-2]

15439 *The legion of time*. Digit, London, 1961, 156p, Paper, Novel [Legion of Time #1]

15440 *The Moon children*. G. P. Putnam's Sons, New York, 1972, 190p, Cloth, Novel
The not-men. [see 15432A]

15441 *One against the Legion*. Pyramid, New York, 1967, 220p, Paper, Coll. [Legion of Space #s 3-4; includes *One against the Legion* and *Nowhere near*]

15442 *The Pandora Effect*. Ace, New York, 1969, 189p, Paper, Coll.

15443 *People machines*. Ace, New York, 1971, 189p, Paper, Coll.

15444 *The reign of wizardry*. Lancer, New York, 1964, 142p, Paper, Novel

15445 *Science fiction comes to college; a preliminary survey of courses offered*. Jack Williamson, Portales, NM, 1971, 17p, Paper, Nonf.

15446 *Science fiction comes to college; a preliminary survey of courses offered*. Jack Williamson, Portales, NM, 1971, 22p, Paper, Nonf. [expanded]

15447 *Science fiction in college; a survey of courses offered*. Jack Williamson, Portales, NM, 1971, 39p, Paper, Nonf.

15448 *Science fiction in college; a survey of courses offered*. Jack Williamson, Portales, NM, 1972, 46p, Paper, Nonf. [expanded]
Seetee ship. [see 15456A]
Seetee shock. [see 15457A]

15449 *Seetee ship/Seetee shock*. Lancer, New York, 1972, 445p, Paper, Coll. [Seetee #s 1-2]

15450 *Teaching SF*. Jack Williamson, Portales, NM, 1972, 39p, Paper, Nonf.

15451 *Teaching SF*. Jack Williamson, Portales, NM, 1973, 55p, Paper, Nonf. [expanded]

15452 *Teaching SF*. Jack Williamson, Portales, NM, 1973, 61p, Paper, Nonf. [expanded]

15453 *Teaching SF*. Jack Williamson, Portales, NM, 1974, 69p, Paper, Nonf. [expanded]

15454 *Trapped in space*. Doubleday, Garden City, 1968, 144p, Cloth, Novel

15455 *The trial of Terra*. Ace, New York, 1962, 159p, Paper, Novel
Two complete novels. [see 15438A]

as Will Stewart:

15456 *Seetee ship*. Gnome Press, New York, 1951, 255p, Cloth, Novel [Seetee #1]

15456A *Seetee ship*, by Jack Williamson. Lancer, New York, 1968, 222p, Paper, Novel [Seetee #1]

15457 *Seetee shock*. Simon & Schuster, New York, 1950, 238p, Cloth, Novel [Seetee #2]

15457A *Seetee shock*, by Jack Williamson. Lancer, New York, 1968, 223p, Paper, Novel [Seetee #2]

with Eando Binder, Edmond Hamilton, Raymond Z. Gallun and John Russell Fearn:

01304 *The great illusion*. Fantasy Booklet, Wallsend, UK, 1973, 12p, Paper, Story

with Miles J. Breuer:

01878 *The girl from Mars*. Stellar Publishing Corp., New York, 1929, 24p, Paper, Story

with James E. Gunn:

06487 *Star bridge*. Gnome Press, New York, 1955, 221p, Cloth, Novel

with Frederik Pohl:

11790 *The Reefs of Space*. Ballantine, New York, 1964, 188p, Paper, Novel [Starchild #1]

11791 *Rogue star*. Ballantine, New York, 1969, 213p, Paper, Novel [Starchild #3]

11792 *Starchild*. Ballantine, New York, 1965, 191p, Paper, Novel [Starchild #2]

11793 *Undersea city*. Gnome Press, Hicksville, NY, 1958, 188p, Cloth, Novel [Eden #3]

11794 *Undersea fleet*. Gnome Press, New York, 1956, 187p, Cloth, Novel [Eden #2]

11795 *Undersea quest*. Gnome Press, New York, 1954, 189p, Cloth, Novel [Eden #1]

WILLIAMSON, THAMES (Ross), 1894-

15458 *Beginning at dusk; an interlude*. Doubleday, Doran, Garden City, 1935, 301p, Cloth, Novel

15459 *The man who cannot die*. Small, Maynard, Boston, 1926, 406p, Cloth, Novel

WILLIS, DONALD C(halmers), 1947-   [*biography included*]

15460 *Horror and science fiction films; a checklist*. Scarecrow Press, Metuchen, NJ, 1972, 612p, Cloth, Nonf.

WILLIS, GEORGE ANTHONY ARMSTRONG
see: ARMSTRONG, ANTHONY

WILMOT, EILEEN

15461 *Voodoo drums*. Fiction House, London, 1947, 96p, Paper, Novel

WILMOT, S. EARDLEY-
see: EARDLEY-WILMOT, S.

WILSON, ANGUS (Frank Johnstone), 1913-   [*biography included*]

15462 *The old men at the Zoo*. Secker & Warburg, London, 1961, 352p, Cloth, Novel

WILSON, COLIN (Henry), 1931-   [*biography included*]

15463 *The god of the labyrinth*. Rupert Hart-Davis, London, 1970, 305p, Cloth, Novel [Gerard Sorme #3]

15463A retitled: *The hedonists*. Signet, New York, 1971, 253p, Paper, Novel [Gerard Sorme #3]

WILSON, COLIN (cont.)

15464 *Man without a shadow; the diary of an existentialist.* Arthur Barker, London, 1963, 266p, Cloth, Novel [Gerard Sorme #2]
15464A retitled: *The sex diary of Gerard Sorme.* Dial Press, New York, 1963, 256p, Cloth, Novel [Gerard Sorme #2]
15465 *The mind parasites.* Arthur Barker, London, 1967, 222p, Cloth, Novel
15466 *The philosopher's stone.* Arthur Barker, London, 1969, 315p, Cloth, Novel
15467 *The return of the Lloigor.* Village Press, London, 1974, 60p, Paper, Novel
 The sex diary of Gerard Sorme. [see 15464A]
15468 *Tree by Tolkien.* Covent Garden Press, INCA Books, London, 1973, 20p, Cloth?, Nonf.

with J. B. Pick and E. H. Visiak:

11500 *The strange genius of David Lindsay; an appreciation.* John Baker, London, 1970, 183p, Cloth, Nonf.

WILSON, DAVID ALEC, 1864-1933

15469 *Modern Lilliput; a history of the recent rediscovery of the Lilliput Archipelago, and what has been happening there.* C. W. Daniel, London, 1924, 320p, Cloth, Novel [Gulliver series]

WILSON, EDMUND, 1895-1972 [*biography included*]

15470 *The memoirs of Hecate County.* Doubleday, Garden City, 1946, 338p, Cloth, Coll.

WILSON, ELLSWORTH

15471 *The devil's own (a bizarre adventure of intrigue and comedy).* Christopher Publishing House, Boston, 1947, 256p, Cloth, Novel

WILSON, GERALD HUGH TYRWHITT
 see: BERNERS, Lord

WILSON, (John) GROSVENOR, 1866-

15472 *The monarch of millions; or, The rise and fall of the American Empire.* F. Tennyson Neely, New York, 1900, 204p, Paper, Novel

WILSON, H(erbert) W(rigley), 1866-1940, with Arnold White

15225 *When war breaks out, being a selection from the letters of Andrew D. Jones, the London correspondent of "Calner's weekly," during the war between Great Britain and the allied powers of France and Russia, September 21st, 1900, to January 1st, 1901.* Harper & Bros., New York, 1898, 94p, Cloth, Novel

WILSON, HAZEL (Emma), 1898- [*biography included*]

15473 *Herbert.* Alfred A. Knopf, New York, 1950, 184p, Cloth, Novel [Herbert series]
15474 *Herbert's space trip.* Alfred A. Knopf, New York, 1965, 160p, Cloth, Novel [Herbert series]

WILSON, HENRY LOVEJOY, 1908-1958

15475 *Of Lunar kingdoms.* Caxton Printers, Caldwell, Idaho, 1937, 120p, Cloth, Coll.

WILSON, J(esse)

15476 *When the women reign, 1930.* Arthur H. Stockwell, London, 1909, 159p, Cloth, Novel

WILSON, JOHN BURGESS
 see: BURGESS, ANTHONY

WILSON, JOHN ROWAN, 1919-

15477 *Hall of mirrors; a novel.* Doubleday, Garden City, 1966, 417p, Cloth, Novel; Collins, London, 1966, 384p, Cloth, Novel

WILSON, MARY BADGER

15478 *Stolen light.* Hurst & Blackett, London, 1949, 208p, Cloth, Novel

WILSON, MILES, as M. W.

15479 *The history of Israel Jobson, the wandering Jew,* by M. W. J. Nicholson, London, 1757, 95p, Cloth, Novel

WILSON, RATHMELL

15480 *Re-birth; a romantic novel.* Greening & Co., London, 1909, 318p, Cloth, Novel

WILSON, RAYMOND, with Alan Frank Barter

00919 *Untravelled worlds; an anthology of science fiction.* Macmillan, London, 1966, 168p, Paper, Anth.

WILSON, RICHARD, 1920- [*biography included*]

15481 *And then the town took off.* Ace Double, New York, 1960, 123p, Paper, Novel
15482 *The girls from Planet 5.* Ballantine, New York, 1955, 184p, Cloth, Novel
15483 *30-day wonder.* Ballantine, New York, 1960, 158p, Paper, Novel
15484 *Those idiots from Earth; ten science-fiction stories.* Ballantine, New York, 1957, 160p, Paper, Coll.
15485 *Time out for tomorrow.* Ballantine, New York, 1962, 159p, Paper, Coll.

WILSON, ROBERT ANTON, 1932-

15486 *The sex magicians.* Sheffield House, Chatsworth, CA, 1973, 185p, Paper, Novel

WILSON, ROBIN SCOTT, 1928-   [*biography included*]

15487 *Clarion; an anthology of speculative fiction and criticism from the Clarion Writers' Workshop.* Signet, New York, 1971, 239p, Paper, Anth.
15488 *Clarion II; an anthology of speculative fiction and criticism.* Signet, New York, 1972, 256p, Paper, Anth.
15489 *Clarion III; an anthology of speculative fiction and criticism.* Signet, New York, 1973, 224p, Paper, Anth.
15490 *Those who can; a science fiction reader.* Mentor, New York, 1973, 333p, Paper, Anth.

WILSON, SANDY [Alexander Galbraith Wilson, 1924-   ]

15491 *This is Sylvia, her lives and loves.* Max Parrish, London, 1954, 116p, Cloth, Novel

WILSON, THEODORA WILSON, d. 1941

15492 *The last weapon; a vision.* C. W. Daniel, London, 1916, 184p, Paper, Novel

WILSON, WILFRED, 1869-   with Algernon Blackwood

01412 *The wolves of God, and other fey stories.* Cassell, London, 1921, 328p, Cloth, Coll.

WILSON, WILLIAM

15493 *Candleleer; a modern myth.* Exposition Press, New York, 1973, 96p, Cloth, Novel

WILSON, WILLIAM HUNTINGTON, 1870-

15494 *Rafnaland; the strange story of John Heath Howard.* Harper & Bros., New York, 1900, 352p, Cloth, Novel

WILSON, YATES

15495 *More 'Alice.'* T. V. Boardman, London, 1959, 125p, Cloth, Novel [Alice series]

WINCH, E(dgar)

15496 *The Mountain of Gold.* Hurst & Blackett, London, 1928, 288p, Cloth, Novel

WINDSOR, WILLIAM, 1857-

15497 *Loma, a citizen of Venus.* Windsor & Lewis Publishing Co., St. Paul, Minn., 1897, 429p, Cloth, Novel

WINFIELD, DICK, pseud. [Dick Perry, 1922-   ]

15498 *Doolie's private goddess.* Paperback Library, New York, 1964, 176p, Paper, Novel
15498A retitled: *Up-tight.* Paperback Library, New York, 1967, 176p, Paper, Novel

WINGRAVE, ANTHONY, pseud.
see: WRIGHT, S. FOWLER

WINKLE, M. F. VAN
see: VAN WINKLE, M. F.

WINSHIP, GLEN B(rion), 1887?-1966

15499 *Volonor.* Thomas Seltzer, New York, 1925, 313p, Cloth, Novel

WINSLOW, DORIAN, pseud. [Daoma Winston, 1922-]

15500 *The sorcerers.* Avon, New York, 1973, 160p, Paper, Novel

WINSOR, G(eorge) McLEOD

15501 *Station X.* Herbert Jenkins, London, 1919, 317p, Cloth, Novel
15502 *Vanishing men.* William Morrow, New York, 1927, 309p, Cloth, Novel

WINSTON, DAOMA
see: WINSLOW, DORIAN

WINTERBOTHAM, RUSS(ell Robert), 1904-1971 [*biography included*]

15503 *The lord of Nardos.* Avalon, New York, 1966, 192p, Cloth, Novel
15504 *The men from Arcturus.* Avalon, New York, 1963, 192p, Cloth, Novel
15505 *The puppet planet.* Avalon, New York, 1964, 189p, Cloth, Novel
15506 *The red planet; a science fiction novel.* Monarch, Derby, Conn., 1962, 140p, Paper, Novel
15507 *The space egg.* Avalon, New York, 1958, 224p, Cloth, Novel

as J. Harvey Bond:

15508 *The other world.* Avalon, New York, 1963, 191p, Cloth, Novel

as Franklin Hadley:

15509 *Planet Big Zero.* Monarch, Derby, Conn., 1964, 126p, Paper, Novel

WINTERFELD, HENRY

15510 *Castaways in Lilliput.* Harcourt, Brace & Co., New York, 1960, 188p, Cloth, Novel [Gulliver series]
15511 *Star girl.* Harcourt, Brace & Co., New York, 1957, 191p, Cloth, Novel

WINTLE, ALFRED DAVID
    see: COBB, MICHAEL

WINTLE, ELIZABETH RHODA
    see: LAWRENCE, LOUISE

WINTLE, HAROLD

  15512 *The cleansing of the "Lords."* John Lane, The
        Bodley Head, London, 1906, 296p, Cloth,
        Novel

WINTLE, HECTOR

  15513 *The Hodsall wizard; a grim thought.* Methuen,
        London, 1938, 282p, Cloth, Novel

WINTLE, W(illiam) JAMES

  15514 *Ghost gleams; tales of the uncanny.* Heath
        Cranton, London, 1921, 287p, Cloth, Coll.

WISE, ARTHUR, 1923-   [*biography included*]

  15515 *The day the Queen flew to Scotland for the
        grouse shooting; a document.* Cavalier Pub-
        lishing, Dublin, 1968, 189p, Cloth, Novel
  15516 *Who killed Enoch Powell? a thriller.* Weiden-
        feld & Nicolson, London, 1970, 197p, Cloth,
        Novel

WISE, HERBERT A(lvin), 1893?-1961, with Phyllis Fraser

  05614 *Great tales of terror and the supernatural.*
        Random House, New York, 1944, 1080p, Cloth,
        Anth.

WISE, ROBERT A., pseud. [Fred J. Gebhart]

  15517 *12 to the Moon.* Badger, London, 1961, 158p,
        Paper, Movie

WISTER, OWEN, 1860-1938

  15518 *The dragon of Wantley, his rise, his voracity,
        & his downfall; a romance.* J. B. Lippin-
        cott, Philadelphia, 1892, 149p, Cloth, Novel

WITCHES THREE

  15519 *Witches three: Conjure wife, by Fritz Leiber;
        There shall be no darkness, by James Blish;
        The blue star, by Fletcher Pratt.* Twayne
        Publishers, New York, 1952, 423p, Cloth,
        Anth.

WITH MY FRIENDS
    see: MATTHEWS, BRANDER

WITHERS, JULIA

  15520 *The shuttered room.* Dell, New York, 1966,
        156p, Paper, Movie [adapted from the film of
        the same name, which was in turn based on
        the Lovecraft story]

WITT, CURRIE B., with Lavinia Lee Witt

  08770 *The cat can yield but its skin.* American Pat-
        riots Society, Tampa, FL, 1962, 46p, Cloth,
        Story

WITT, DENISE de
    see: de WITT, DENISE

WITT, LAVINIA LEE, with Currie B. Witt

  08770 *The cat can yield but its skin.* American Pat-
        riots Society, Tampa, FL, 1962, 46p, Cloth,
        Story

WITTIG, MONIQUE

  15521 *Les Guérillères.* Viking Press, New York, 1971,
        144p, Cloth, Novel

WOBIG, ELLEN, 1911-   [*biography included*]

  15522 *The youth monopoly.* Ace Double, New York,
        1968, 114p, Paper, Novel

WODEHOUSE, (Sir) P(elham) G(renville), 1881-
1975 [*biography included*]

  15523 *Laughing gas.* Herbert Jenkins, London, 1936,
        311p, Cloth, Novel
  15524 *The swoop! or, How Clarence saved English; a
        tale of the great invasion.* Alston Rivers,
        London, 1909, 122p, Paper, Novel

WODHAMS, JACK

  15525 *The authentic touch.* Curtis, New York, 1971,
        189p, Paper, Novel

WOHL, BURTON
    see: HILLS, BALDWIN

WOHL, LOUIS de
    see: de WOHL, LOUIS

WOLF, BARBARA H(errman), 1932-   [*biography
included*], with Jack C. Wolf

  15526 *Ghosts, castles, and victims; studies in gothic
        terror.* Fawcett Crest, Greenwich, Conn.,
        1974, 576p, Cloth, Anth.

WOLF, BLUE
    see: BLUE WOLF

WOLF, JACK C(lifford), 1922-   [*biography included*]

with Gregory Fitz Gerald:

05449 *Past, present, and future perfect; a text anthology of speculative and science fiction.* Fawcett Premier, Greenwich, Conn., 1973, 544p, Paper, Anth.

with Barbara H. Wolf:

15526 *Ghosts, castles, and victims; studies in gothic terror.* Fawcett Crest, Greenwich, Conn., 1974, 576p, Paper, Anth.

WOLF, VICTORIA (Trude), 1903-

15527 *Spell of Egypt; a novel.* L. B. Fischer, New York, 1943, 310p, Cloth, Novel

WOLFE, BERNARD, 1915-   [*biography included*]

15528 *Limbo.* Random House, New York, 1952, 438p, Cloth, Novel
15528A retitled: *Limbo '90.* Secker & Warburg, London, 1953, 438p, Cloth, Novel

WOLFE, GENE (Rodman), 1931-   [*biography included*]

15529 *The fifth head of Cerberus; three novellas.* Charles Scribner's Sons, New York, 1972, 244p, Cloth, Coll.
15530 *Operation ARES.* Berkley Medallion, New York, 1970, 208p, Paper, Novel

WOLFE, LOUIS, 1905-   [*biography included*]

15531 *Journey of the Oceanauts; across the bottom of the Atlantic Ocean on foot.* W. W. Norton, New York, 1968, 263p, Cloth, Novel

WOLFF, CECIL DRUMMOND
    see: WALDO, CEDRIC DANE

WOLK, GEORGE
    see: GRAAT, HEINRICH

WOLLHEIM, DONALD A(llen), 1914-   [*biography included*]

15532 *Ace science fiction reader.* Ace, New York, 1971, 251p, Paper, Anth.
15532A retitled: *Trilogy of the future: The trouble with Tycho, Clifford D. Simak; The last castle, Jack Vance; Empire star, Samuel R. Delany.* Sidgwick & Jackson, London, 1972, 251p, Cloth, Anth.
15533 *Adventures in the far future.* Ace Double, New York, 1954, 177p, Paper, Anth.
15534 *Adventures on other planets.* Ace, New York, 1955, 160p, Paper, Anth.
15535 *Avon fantasy reader, no. 1.* Avon, New York, 1947, 130p, Paper, Anth.
15536 *Avon fantasy reader, no. 2.* Avon, New York, 1947, 130p, Paper, Anth.

15537 *Avon fantasy reader, no. 3.* Avon, New York, 1947, 128p, Paper, Anth.
15538 *Avon fantasy reader, no. 4.* Avon, New York, 1947, 130p, Paper, Anth.
15539 *Avon fantasy reader, no. 5.* Avon, New York, 1947, 126p, Paper, Anth.
15540 *Avon fantasy reader, no. 6.* Avon, New York, 1948, 121p, Paper, Anth.
15541 *Avon fantasy reader, no. 7.* Avon, New York, 1948, 126p, Paper, Anth.
15542 *Avon fantasy reader, no. 8.* Avon, New York, 1948, 126p, Paper, Anth.
15543 *Avon fantasy reader, no. 9.* Avon, New York, 1949, 127p, Paper, Anth.
15544 *Avon fantasy reader, no. 10.* Avon, New York, 1949, 127p, Paper, Anth.
15545 *Avon fantasy reader, no. 11.* Avon, New York, 1949, 126p, Paper, Anth.
15546 *Avon fantasy reader, no. 12.* Avon, New York, 1950, 125p, Paper, Anth.
15547 *Avon fantasy reader, no. 13.* Avon, New York, 1950, 126p, Paper, Anth.
15548 *Avon fantasy reader, no. 14.* Avon, New York, 1950, 124p, Paper, Anth.
15549 *Avon fantasy reader, no. 15.* Avon, New York, 1951, 125p, Paper, Anth.
15550 *Avon fantasy reader, no. 16.* Avon, New York, 1951, 128p, Paper, Anth.
15551 *Avon fantasy reader, no. 17.* Avon, New York, 1951, 128p, Paper, Anth.
15552 *Avon fantasy reader, no. 18.* Avon, New York, 1952, 128p, Paper, Anth.
15553 *Avon science-fiction reader, no. 1.* Avon, New York, 1951, 124p, Paper, Anth.
15554 *Avon science-fiction reader, no. 2.* Avon, New York, 1951, 127p, Paper, Anth.
15555 *Avon science-fiction reader, no. 3.* Avon, New York, 1952, 128p, Paper, Anth.
15556 *The Earth in peril.* Ace Double, New York, 1957, 158p, Paper, Anth.
15557 *The end of the world.* Ace, New York, 1956, 160p, Paper, Anth.
15558 *Every boy's book of science-fiction.* Frederick Fell, New York, 1951, 254p, Cloth, Anth.
15559 *Flight into space; great science-fiction stories of interplanetary travel.* Frederick Fell, New York, 1950, 251p, Cloth, Anth.
15560 *The girl with the hungry eyes, and other stories.* Avon, New York, 1949, 127p, Paper, Anth. [published anonymously]
15561 *The hidden planet; science-fiction adventures on Venus.* Ace, New York, 1959, 190p, Paper, Anth.
15562 *The macabre reader.* Ace, New York, 1959, 223p, Paper, Anth.
15563 *Men on the Moon.* Ace Double, New York, 1958, 137p, Paper, Anth.
15564 *Mike Mars and the mystery satellite.* Doubleday, Garden City, 1963, 190p, Cloth, Novel [Mike Mars #7]
15565 *Mike Mars around the Moon.* Doubleday, Garden City, 1964, 192p, Cloth, Novel [Mike Mars #8]
15566 *Mike Mars, astronaut.* Doubleday, Garden City, 1961, 188p, Cloth, Novel [Mike Mars #1]
15567 *Mike Mars at Cape Canaveral.* Doubleday, Garden City, 1961, 186p, Cloth, Novel [Mike Mars #3]
15567A retitled: *Mike Mars at Cape Kennedy.* Paperback Library, New York, 1966, 128p, Paper, Novel [Mike Mars #3]
15568 *Mike Mars flies the Dyna-Soar.* Doubleday, Garden City, 1962, 188p, Cloth, Novel [Mike Mars #5]

WOLLHEIM, DONALD A. (cont.)

15569 *Mike Mars flies the X-15.* Doubleday, Garden City, 1961, 187p, Cloth, Novel [Mike Mars #2]
15570 *Mike Mars in orbit.* Doubleday, Garden City, 1961, 188p, Cloth, Novel [Mike Mars #4]
15571 *Mike Mars, South Pole spaceman.* Doubleday, Garden City, 1962, 190p, Cloth, Novel [Mike Mars #6]
15572 *More adventures on other planets.* Ace, New York, 1963, 190p, Paper, Anth.
15573 *More macabre.* Ace, New York, 1961, 192p, Paper, Anth.
 More terror in the modern vein. [see 15584A]
15574 *One against the Moon.* World Publishing Co., Cleveland, 1956, 220p, Cloth, Novel
15575 *Operation phantasy; the best from the Phantagraph.* Phantagraph Press, Rego Park, NY, 1967, 59p, Cloth, Anth.
15576 *The Pocket book of science-fiction.* Pocket Books, New York, 1943, 310p, Paper, Anth.
15577 *The portable novels of science.* Viking Press, New York, 1945, 737p, Cloth, Anth.
15578 *Prize science fiction.* McBride Co., New York, 1953, 230p, Cloth, Anth.
15578A retitled: *Prize stories of space and time.* Weidenfeld & Nicolson, London, 1953, 248p, Cloth, Anth.
15579 *The secret of Saturn's rings.* John C. Winston, Philadelphia, 1954, 207p, Cloth, Novel
15580 *The secret of the Martian moons.* John C. Winston, Philadelphia, 1955, 206p, Cloth, Novel
15581 *The secret of the ninth planet.* John C. Winston, Philadelphia, 1959, 203p, Cloth, Novel
15582 *Swordsmen in the sky.* Ace, New York, 1964, 192p, Paper, Anth.
15583 *Tales of outer space.* Ace Double, New York, 1954, 140p, Paper, Anth.
15584 *Terror in the modern vein; an anthology.* Hanover House, Garden City, 1955, 315p, Cloth, Anth.
15584A retitled: *More terror in the modern vein.* Digit, London, 1961, 156p, Paper, Anth. [abridged]
 Trilogy of the future. [see 15532A]
15585 *Two dozen dragon eggs.* Powell Publications, Reseda, CA, 1969, 207p, Paper, Coll.
15586 *The ultimate invader, and other science-fiction; stories from the four corners of time.* Ace Double, New York, 1954, 139p, Paper, Anth.
15587 *The universe makers; science fiction today.* Harper & Row, New York, 1971, 122p, Cloth, Nonf.

as David Grinnell:

15588 *Across time.* Avalon, New York, 1957, 223p, Cloth, Novel
15589 *Destiny's orbit.* Avalon, New York, 1961, 224p, Cloth, Novel [Destiny #1]
15590 *Edge of time.* Avalon, New York, 1958, 221p, Cloth, Novel
15591 *The Martian missile.* Avalon, New York, 1959, 224p, Cloth, Novel
15592 *To Venus! To Venus!* Ace Double, New York, 1970, 128p, Paper, Novel

as David Grinnell, with Lin Carter:

02740 *Destination: Saturn.* Avalon, New York, 1967, 192p, Cloth, Novel [Destiny #2]

with Terry Carr:

02656 *World's best science fiction: 1965.* Ace, New York, 1965, 288p, Paper, Anth.
02656A retitled: *World's best science fiction: first series.* Ace, New York, 1970, 288p, Paper, Anth.
02657 *World's best science fiction: 1966.* Ace, New York, 1966, 287p, Paper, Anth.
02657A retitled: *World's best science fiction: second series.* Ace, New York, 1970, 287p, Paper, Anth.
02658 *World's best science fiction: 1967.* Ace, New York, 1967, 285p, Paper, Anth.
02658A retitled: *World's best science fiction: third series.* Ace, New York, 1970, 285p, Paper, Anth.
02659 *World's best science fiction: 1968.* Ace, New York, 1968, 319p, Paper, Anth.
02659A retitled: *World's best science fiction: fourth series.* Ace, New York, 1970, 319p, Paper, Anth.
02659B retitled: *World's best S.F., no. 1.* Victor Gollancz, London, 1969, 320p, Cloth, Anth.
02660 *World's best science fiction: 1969.* Ace, New York, 1969, 380p, Paper, Anth.
02661 *World's best science fiction: 1970.* Ace, New York, 1970, 349p, Paper, Anth.
02662 *World's best science fiction: 1971.* Ace, New York, 1971, 349p, Paper, Anth.

with George Ernsberger:

04913 *The Avon fantasy reader.* Avon, New York, 1969, 173p, Paper, Anth.
04914 *The 2nd Avon fantasy reader.* Avon, New York, 1969, 173p, Paper, Anth.

with Arthur W. Saha:

12626 *The 1972 annual world's best SF.* DAW, New York, 1972, 302p, Paper, Anth.
12627 *The 1973 annual world's best SF.* DAW, New York, 1973, 253p, Paper, Anth.
12628 *The 1974 annual world's best SF.* DAW, New York, 1974, 280p, Paper, Anth.

THE WONDERFUL HISTORY OF THE SHADOWLESS MAN

15593 *The wonderful history of the shadowless man, by A. von Chamisso; and, The cold heart, by Wilhelm Hauff.* Holden & Hardingham, London, 1913, 166p, Cloth, Anth.

WOOD, CHARLES ERSKINE SCOTT, 1852-1944

15594 *Heavenly discourse.* Vanguard Press, New York, 1927, 325p, Cloth, Novel

WOOD, EDWARD, with Robert E. Briney

01894 *SF bibliographies; an annotated bibliography of bibliographical works on science fiction and fantasy fiction.* Advent: Publishers, Chicago, 1972, 49p, Paper, Nonf.

WOOD, EDWARD D., Jr.

15595 *Orgy of the dead.* Greenleaf Classics, San Diego, 1966, 160p, Paper, Movie

WOOD, GEORGE, 1799-1870

15596 *Future life; or, Scenes in another world.*
Derby & Jackson, New York, 1858, 359p,
Cloth, Novel [Peter Schlemihl series]
15596A retitled: *The gates wide open; or, Scenes
in another world.* Lee & Shepard, Boston,
1869, 354p, Cloth, Novel [Peter Schlemihl
series]
15597 *Peter Schlemihl in America.* Carey & Hart,
Philadelphia, 1848, 495p, Cloth, Novel [pub-
lished anonymously; Peter Schlemihl series]

WOOD, JAMES PLAYSTED, 1905-

15598 *The mammoth parade.* Pantheon, New York, 1969,
148p, Cloth, Novel

WOOD, MICHAEL

15599 *The white island.* J. M. Dent & Sons, London,
1918, 206p, Cloth, Novel

WOOD, Mr.
see: OLDS, C. BURNELL

WOOD, ROBERT WILLIAMS, 1868-1955 [*biography
included*], with Arthur Train

14210 *The man who rocked the Earth.* Doubleday,
Page, Garden City, 1915, 228p, Cloth, Novel
[Benjamin Hooker #1]
14211 *The Moon maker.* Krueger, Hamburg, NY, 1958,
84p, Cloth, Novel [Benjamin Hooker #2]

WOOD, S(amuel) ANDREW, 1890-

15600 *I'll blackmail the world.* Hodder & Stoughton,
London, 1935, 312p, Cloth, Novel
15601 *Winged heels.* Herbert Jenkins, London, 1927,
256p, Cloth, Novel

WOOD, WALLACE

15602 *The world of the wizard king.* Real Free Press,
Amsterdam, 1974, 20p, Paper, Story

WOOD, WALTER, 1866-1961

15603 *The enemy in our midst; the story of a raid
on England.* John Long, London, 1906, 320p,
Cloth, Novel

WOOD, WILLIAM (Parker Jr.), 1931-

15604 *The news from Karachi; a novel.* Macmillan,
New York, 1962, 124p, Cloth, Novel

WOODARD, GEORGE C.

15605 *New day, big world, few people; a novel of
the past and future.* Book Sales, Ft. Worth,
TX, 1969, 324p, Cloth, Novel

WOODBRIDGE, W(illiam) W(itherspoon), 1883-

15606 *That something.* Smith-Digby Co., Tacoma, Wash.,
1914, 49p, Cloth, Story

WOODBURY, DAVID O(akes), 1896-

15607 *Mr. Faraday's formula; a Dean Riam suspense
story.* Devin-Adair Co., New York, 1965,
274p, Cloth, Novel [Dean Riam #2]

WOODCOTT, KEITH, pseud.
see: BRUNNER, JOHN

WOODFORDE, CHRISTOPHER, 1907-1962

15608 *A pad in the straw; stories.* J. M. Dent &
Sons, London, 1952, 235p, Cloth, Coll.

WOODHOUSE, MARTIN, 1932-

15609 *Blue bone.* Heinemann, London, 1973, 222p,
Cloth, Novel
15610 *Mama doll.* Heinemann, London, 1972, 201p,
Cloth, Novel

WOODIWISS, JOHN (Cecil)

15611 *Smugglers' ride; a tale of witchcraft in old
Dorset.* Quality Press, London, 1946, 246p,
Cloth, Novel

WOODMAN, GEORGE (David)

15612 *The heretic.* Shipyard Press, Whitstable, UK,
1963, 11p, Paper, Story

WOODMAN, T. E.

15613 *Britain in the ice grip.* Boys' Ace Library,
London, 1937, 64p, Paper, Novel

THE WOODNYMPH'S SONG
see: MERTENS, KARL R.

WOODS, MARGARET L(ouisa), 1856-1945

15614 *The invader.* William Heinemann, London, 1907,
311p, Cloth, Novel

WOODS, MARGARET MURRAY, with Nancy Magor

09550 *Life marches on.* Skeffington & Son, London,
1946, 216p, Cloth, Novel

WOOLDRIDGE, C(harles) W(illiam), 1847-1908

15615 *Perfecting the Earth; a piece of possible history.* Utopia Publishing Co., Cleveland,
1902, 326p, Cloth, Novel

WOOLF, (Adeline) VIRGINIA, 1882-1941

15616   *Orlando; a biography.* Leonard & Virginia
        Woolf, London, 1928, 299p, Cloth, Novel

WOOLRICH, CORNELL, pseud. [Cornell George
Hopley-Woolrich, 1903-1968]

15617   *The doom stone.* Avon, New York, 1960, 159p,
        Paper, Novel
15618   *Beyond the night.* Avon, New York, 1959,
        160p, Paper, Coll.

as George Hopley:

15619   *Night has a thousand eyes.* Farrar & Rinehart,
        New York, 1945, 301p, Cloth, Novel
15619A *Night has a thousand eyes*, by William Irish.
        Dell, New York, 1953,   , Paper, Novel

as William Irish:

        Night has a thousand eyes. [see 15619A]

WOOLSEY, JANETTE, 1904-   [*biography included*], with Elizabeth Hough Sechrist

12857   *Terribly strange tales.* Macrae Smith Co.,
        Philadelphia, 1967, 253p, Cloth, Anth.

WOOTTON, BARBARA (Frances), Baroness Wootton
of Abinger, 1897-

15620   *London's burning; a novel for the decline and
        fall of the liberal age.* George Allen &
        Unwin, London, 1936, 284p, Cloth, Novel

WORFEL, W. G., as The Baron

15621   *Munchausen XX, by The Baron, being wondrous
        but veracious happenings which befell my an-
        cestors, here translated and for the first
        time printed from manuscripts found most
        miraculously by myself, containing as well
        not alone my adventures in securing these
        remarkable documents, but a very entrancing
        and entertaining series of thrilling inci-
        dents that took place in my life prior to
        and while searching for the glorious crea-
        ture whose husband I became as a fitting
        climax to a career so unceasingly fraught
        with danger.* Rand, McNally, Chicago, 1904,
        205p, Cloth, Novel [Munchausen series]

WORKMAN, JAMES
    see: DARK, JAMES

WORLDS AT WAR

15622   *Worlds at war.* Tempest Publishing Co., Bol-
        ton, UK, 1950, 128p, Paper, Anth.

THE WORLD'S BEST MYSTERY STORIES
    see: A CENTURY OF THRILLERS, SECOND
    SERIES

WORLEY, FREDERICK U.
    see: BENEFICE

WORMSER, G(wendolyn) RANGER, 1893-

15623   *The scarecrow, and other stories.* E. P. Dut-
        ton, New York, 1918, 243p, Cloth, Coll.

WORMSER, RICHARD (Edward), 1908-

15624   *The last days of Sodom and Gomorrah.* Gold
        Medal, Greenwich, Conn., 1962, 160p, Paper,
        Movie
15625   *Pan Satyrus.* Avon, New York, 1963, 144p,
        Paper, Novel
15626   *Thief of Baghdad.* Dell, New York, 1961, 191p,
        Paper, Movie

as Ed Friend:

15627   *The Green Hornet in The infernal light.* Dell,
        New York, 1966, 127p, Paper, Tele. [Green
        Hornet series]

WORTH, MARGARET, pseud. [Helen Arvonen]

15628   *Red wine of rapture.* Avon, New York, 1973,
        187p, Paper, Novel

WORTH, NIGEL, pseud. [Noel Wright, 1890-1975]

15629   *The arms of Phaedra; a tale of wonder and ad-
        venture.* Mills & Boon, London, 1924, 284p,
        Cloth, Novel

WORTS, GEORGE (Frank), 1892-

15630   *The monster of the lagoon.* Popular Publica-
        tions, Toronto, 1947, 96p, Paper, Novel
15631   *The phantom president.* Jonathan Cape & Robert
        Ballou, New York, 1932, 363p, Cloth, Novel

WOUK, HERMAN, 1915-

15632   *The "Lomokome" papers.* Pocket Books, New York,
        1968, 113p, Paper, Novel

WRAY, REGINALD, pseud. [W. B. Home-Gall]

15633   *Beyond the northern lights; tale of strange
        adventure in unknown seas.* Thomas Burleigh,
        London, 1903, 336p, Cloth, Novel

WRAY, ROGER, pseud. [James William Marriott,
1884-1953]

15634   *The dweller in the half-light.* Odhams Press,
        London, 1920, 320p, Cloth, Novel

THE WRECK OF WESTMINSTER ABBEY
    see: CROFT, HERBERT

WREDER, PAUL de
    see: HEMING, J. W.

WREN, PERCIVAL CHRISTOPHER, 1885-1941

15635 *Beggars' horses.* John Murray, London, 1934,
       444p, Cloth, Novel
15636 *Rough shooting; true tales & strange stories.*
       John Murray, London, 1938, 320p, Cloth, Coll.

WRIGHT, A(lbert) J(ay), 1858-1940

15637 *The Red Demon; a dramatic novel.* G. P. Put-
       nam's Sons, New York, 1933, 254p, Cloth,
       Novel

WRIGHT, ALLEN KENDRICK

15638 *Dalleszona and the seventh treasure.* Roxburgh
       Publishing Co., Boston, 1922, 234p, Cloth,
       Novel
15639 *To the poles by airship; or, Around the world
       endways.* Baumgardt Publishing Co., Los
       Angeles, 1909, 109p, Cloth, Novel

WRIGHT, AUSTIN TAPPAN, 1883-1931

15640 *Islandia.* Farrar & Rinehart, New York, 1942,
       1014p, Cloth, Novel [Islandia #1]

WRIGHT, GILBERT
   see: LEBAR, JOHN

WRIGHT, GRAHAME, 1947-

15641 *Jog Rummage.* Heinemann, London, 1974, 202p,
       Cloth, Novel

WRIGHT, HAMILTON, 1912-   with Helen Wright
and Samuel Rapport

12012 *To the Moon!* Meredith Press, New York, 1968,
       300p, Cloth, Anth. [includes some nonf.]

WRIGHT, HAROLD BELL, 1872-1944

15642 *The uncrowned king.* Book Supply Co., Chicago,
       1910, 118p, Cloth, Novel

with John Lebar:

08756 *The devil's highway.* D. Appleton, New York,
       1932, 335p, Cloth, Novel

WRIGHT, (Mary) HELEN, 1914-   [*biography included*], with Hamilton Wright & Samuel Rapport

12012 *To the Moon!* Meredith Press, New York, 1968,
       300p, Cloth, Anth. [includes some nonf.]

WRIGHT, KENNETH, pseud.
   see: del REY, LESTER

WRIGHT, LAN [Lionel Percy Wright, 1923-   ]
[*biography included*]

15643 *Assignment Luther.* Digit, London, 1963, 158p,
       Paper, Novel
       The creeping shroud. [see 15645A]
15644 *Exile from Xanadu.* Ace Double, New York, 1964,
       137p, Paper, Novel
15644A retitled: *Space born.* Herbert Jenkins, Lon-
       don, 1964, 173p, Cloth, Novel
15645 *The last hope of Earth.* Ace, New York, 1965,
       159p, Paper, Novel
15645A retitled: *The creeping shroud.* Compact, Lon-
       don, 1966, 190p, Paper, Novel
15646 *A man called Destiny.* Ace Double, New York,
       1958, 128p, Paper, Novel
15647 *The Pictures of Pavanne.* Ace Double, New York,
       1968, 139p, Paper, Novel
15647A retitled: *A planet called Pavanne.* Herbert
       Jenkins, London, 1968, 186p, Cloth, Novel
       Space born. [see 15644A]
15648 *Who speaks of conquest?* Ace Double, New York,
       1957, 160p, Paper, Novel

WRIGHT, LAURA JANE, 1954-

15649 *To whom it may concern, and other short stories.*
       Exposition Press, New York, 1972, 85p, Cloth,
       Coll.

WRIGHT, LEE

15650 *The Pocket book of mystery stories.* Pocket
       Books, New York, 1941, 439p, Paper, Anth.

with Richard G. Sheehan:

12996 *These will chill you; twelve terrifying tales
       of malignant evil.* Bantam, New York, 1967,
       169p, Paper, Anth.
12997 *Wake up screaming; sixteen chilling tales of
       the macabre.* Bantam, New York, 1967, 214p,
       Paper, Anth.

WRIGHT, MARY M.
   see: LORRAINE, LILITH

WRIGHT, NOEL
   see: WORTH, NIGEL

WRIGHT, R. H.

15651 *The outer darkness.* Greening & Co., London,
       1906, 312p, Cloth, Novel

WRIGHT, S(ydney) FOWLER, 1874-1965

15652 *The adventure of Wyndham Smith.* Herbert Jen-
       kins, London, 1938, 284p, Cloth, Novel
15653 *The amphibians; a romance of 500,000 years
       hence.* Merton Press, London, 1925, 279p,
       Cloth, Novel [Amphibians #1]
15653A retitled: *The world below.* Panther, London,
       1953, 160p, Paper, Novel [Amphibians #1]
15654 *The Bell Street murders.* George G. Harrap,
       London, 1931, 255p, Cloth, Novel
15655 *Beyond the rim.* Jarrolds Publishers, London,
       1932, 319p, Cloth, Novel

WRIGHT, S. FOWLER (cont.)

15656   *Dawn.* Cosmopolitan Book Corp., New York, 1929,
        349p, Cloth, Novel [Martin Webster #2]
15657   *Deluge; a romance.* Fowler Wright, London,
        1927, 320p, Cloth, Novel [Martin Webster #1]
15658   *Dream; or, The simian maid.* George G. Harrap,
        London, 1931, 251p, Cloth, Novel [Marguerite
        Cranleigh #1]
        The dwellers. [see 15671A]
15659   *Four days war.* Robert Hale, London, 1936,
        288p, Cloth, Novel [War of 1938 #2]
15660   *The hidden tribe.* Robert Hale, London, 1938,
        284p, Cloth, Novel
15661   *The island of Captain Sparrow.* Victor Gollancz,
        London, 1928, 254p, Cloth, Novel
15662   *Justice; and, The rat (two famous stories).*
        Books of Today, London, 1945, 36p, Paper,
        Coll.
15663   *Meggido's Ridge.* Robert Hale, London, 1937,
        284p, Cloth, Novel [War of 1938 #3]
15664   *The new gods lead.* Jarrolds Publishers, Lon-
        don, 1932, 288p, Cloth, Coll.
15665   *Power.* Jarrolds Publishers, London, 1933,
        381p, Cloth, Novel
15666   *Prelude in Prague; a story of the War of 1938.*
        George Newnes, London, 1935, 317p, Cloth,
        Novel [War of 1938 #1]
15666A retitled: *The War of 1938.* G. P. Putnam's
        Sons, New York, 1936, 308p, Cloth, Novel
        [War of 1938 #1]
15667   *The screaming lake.* Robert Hale, London, 1937,
        288p, Cloth, Novel
15668   *Spiders' war; a fantasy novel.* Abelard Press,
        New York, 1954, 256p, Cloth, Novel [Margue-
        rite Cranleigh #2]
15669   *The throne of Saturn.* Arkham House, Sauk City,
        1949, 186p, Cloth, Coll.
        Vengeance of Gwa. [see 15673A]
        The war of 1938. [see 15666A]
15670   *The world below.* W. Collins Sons, London,
        1929, 314p, Cloth, Coll. [Amphibians #s 1-2]
15671   *The world below.* Galaxy SF Novel, New York,
        1951, 121p, Paper, Novel [Amphibians #2]
15671A retitled: *The dwellers.* Panther, London,
        1954, 127p, Paper, Novel [Amphibians #2]
        The world below. [see 15653A]

as Sydney Fowler:

15672   *The adventure of the blue room.* Rich & Cowan,
        London, 1945, 168p, Cloth, Novel

as Anthony Wingrave:

15673   *Vengeance of Gwa.* Thornton Butterworth, Lon-
        don, 1935, 280p, Cloth, Novel
15673A *Vengeance of Gwa,* by S. Fowler Wright. Books
        of To-day, London, 1945, 204p, Cloth, Novel

WRIGHT, THOMAS, 1859-1936

15674   *The Blue Firedrake; or, The wonderful and
        strange relation of the life and adventures
        of Nathan Souldrop, showing how he was for-
        spoken by that terrible sorceress Elinor
        Shaw, the which for her various and abomina-
        ble crimes was brought to tryal at Northamp-
        ton in the year 1705; together with particu-
        lars of her amazing pranks and remarkable
        actions, both before and after her apprehen-
        sion, the like never before heard of; written
        by himselfe, and now set forth.* Simpkin,
        Marshall, Hamilton, Kent, London, 1892, 293p,
        Cloth, Novel

WRIGHT, VINCENT

15675   *An ancient Englishman, A.D. 1599-1906, being
        the strange narrative of one Geoffrey Gren-
        ville, Elizabethan, written by himself.*
        Henry J. Drane, London, 1907, 256p, Cloth,
        Novel

WRIGHT, W(illiam) H(enry)

15676   *The Great Bread Trust.* Abbey Press, New York,
        1900, 54p, Cloth, Novel

WRIGHTSON, PATRICIA, 1921-   [*biography included*]

15677   *Down to Earth.* Hutchinson, London, 1965, 192p,
        Cloth, Novel
15678   *The Nargun and the stars.* Hutchinson, London,
        1973, 158p, Cloth, Novel
15679   *An older kind of magic.* Hutchinson, London,
        1972, 152p, Cloth, Novel

WRZOS, JOSEPH
   see: ROSS, JOSEPH

WUL, STEFAN, pseud. [Pierre Pairault, 1922-
[*biography included*]

15680   *The temple of the past.* Continuum Book, Sea-
        bury Press, New York, 1973, 137p, Cloth,
        Novel

WULFF, EVE, with James L. Quinn

11958   *The first world of If.* Quinn Publishing Co.,
        Kingston, NY, 1957, 160p, Paper, Anth.
11959   *The second world of If.* Quinn Publishing Co.,
        Kingston, NY, 1958, 159p, Paper, Anth.

WURLITZER, RUDOLPH

15681   *Flats; a novel.* E. P. Dutton, New York, 1970,
        160p, Cloth, Novel
15682   *Quake; a novel.* E. P. Dutton, New York, 1972,
        158p, Cloth, Novel

WYATT, HORACE (Matthew), 1876-1954

15683   *Malice in Kulturland.* The Car Illustrated,
        London, 1914, 80p, Cloth, Novel [a parody
        of Carroll's *Alice in Wonderland*]

WYATT, LEE, pseud.

15684   *The flesh hunters.* Orpheus Series, New York,
        1974, 187p, Paper, Novel

as Caer Ged:

15685   *The coming of Cormac.* Orpheus Series, New
        York, 1974, 184p, Paper, Novel

WYCKOFF, NICHOLAS E(lston), 1906-

15686   *The Braintree mission; a fictional narrative
         of London and Boston, 1770-1771.* Victor
         Gollancz, London, 1957, 208p, Cloth, Novel

WYE, ALAN, with Paul Long

09184   *The remnants of 1927.* Long's Publications,
         London, 1925, 191p, Cloth, Novel

WYLIE, ELINOR (Hoyt), 1885-1928

15687   *The Venetian glass nephew.* George H. Doran,
         New York, 1925, 182p, Cloth, Novel

WYLIE, PHILIP (Gordon), 1902-1971 [*biography
included*]

15688   *The answer.* Rinehart & Co., New York, 1956,
         63p, Cloth, Novel
15689   *The disappearance.* Rinehart & Co., New York,
         1951, 405p, Cloth, Novel
15690   *The end of the dream.* Doubleday, Garden City,
         1972, 264p, Cloth, Novel
15691   *Gladiator.* Alfred A. Knopf, New York, 1930,
         332p, Cloth, Novel
15692   *Los Angeles: A.D. 2017.* Popular Library, New
         York, 1971, 221p, Paper, Tele.
15693   *The murderer invisible.* Farrar & Rinehart,
         New York, 1931, 314p, Cloth, Novel
15694   *Night unto night.* Farrar & Rinehart, New
         York, 1944, 372p, Cloth, Novel
15695   *Tomorrow!* Rinehart & Co., New York, 1954,
         372p, Cloth, Novel
15696   *Triumph.* Doubleday, Garden City, 1963, 277p,
         Cloth, Novel

with Edwin Balmer:

00801   *After worlds collide.* Frederick A. Stokes,
         New York, 1934, 341p, Cloth, Novel [Bronson
         Beta #2]
00802   *When worlds collide.* Frederick A. Stokes,
         New York, 1933, 344p, Cloth, Novel [Bronson
         Beta #1]

WYLWYNNE, KYTHE, pseud. [M. E. F. Hyland]

15697   *The Dream-Woman.* T. Fisher Unwin, London,
         1901, 343p, Cloth, Novel

WYNDHAM, ERIC

15698   *Revelation; a romance.* Digby, Long, London,
         1897, 267p, Cloth, Novel

WYNDHAM, JOHN, pseud. [John Wyndham Parkes
Lucas Beynon Harris, 1903-1969] [*biography
included*]

15699   *The best of John Wyndham.* Sphere, London,
         1973, 318p, Paper, Coll.
15700   *Chocky.* Michael Joseph, London, 1968, 184p,
         Cloth, Novel
         The chrysalids. [see 15708A]
15701   *Consider her ways, and others.* Michael Joseph,
         London, 1961, 223p, Cloth, Coll.

15702   *The day of the triffids.* Michael Joseph,
         London, 1951, 302p, Cloth, Novel
15702A   retitled: *Revolt of the triffids (The day of
         the triffids).* Popular Library, New York,
         1952, 224p, Paper, Novel
15703   *The infinite moment.* Ballantine, New York,
         1961, 159p, Paper, Coll. [loosely adapted
         from *Consider her ways, and others*]
15704   *Jizzle.* Dennis Dobson, London, 1954, 251p,
         Cloth, Coll.
15705   *The John Wyndham omnibus.* Michael Joseph, Lon-
         don, 1964, 532p, Cloth, Coll. [includes:
         *The day of the triffids; The Kraken wakes;
         The chrysalids*]
15706   *The Kraken wakes.* Michael Joseph, London,
         1953, 288p, Cloth, Novel
15706A   retitled: *Out of the deeps.* Ballantine, New
         York, 1953, 182p, Cloth, Novel
15707   *The Midwich cuckoos.* Michael Joseph, London,
         1957, 239p, Cloth, Novel
15707A   retitled: *Village of the damned.* Ballantine,
         New York, 1960, 189p, Paper, Novel
         Out of the deeps. [see 15706A]
15708   *Re-birth.* Ballantine, New York, 1955, 187p,
         Cloth, Novel
15708A   retitled: *The chrysalids.* Michael Joseph,
         London, 1955, 239p, Cloth, Novel
         Revolt of the triffids. [see 15702A]
         The secret people. [see 15716B]
15709   *The seeds of time.* Michael Joseph, London,
         1956, 253p, Cloth, Coll.
15710   *Sleepers of Mars.* Coronet, London, 1973, 155p,
         Paper, Coll.
15711   *Tales of gooseflesh and laughter.* Ballantine,
         New York, 1956, 151p, Paper, Coll. [loosely
         adapted from *Jizzle*]
15712   *Trouble with lichen.* Michael Joseph, London,
         1960, 190p, Cloth, Novel
         Village of the damned. [see 15707A]
15713   *Wanderers of time.* Coronet, London, 1973,
         158p, Paper, Coll.

as John Wyndham and Lucas Parkes:

15714   *The outward urge.* Michael Joseph, London,
         1959, 192p, Cloth, Novel

as John Beynon:

15715   *Planet plane.* George Newnes, London, 1936,
         248p, Cloth, Novel
15715A   retitled: *Stowaway to Mars; an outstanding
         adventure novel of the first interplanetary
         flight to Mars.* Nova Publications, London,
         1953, 128p, Paper, Novel
15716   *The secret people.* George Newnes, London,
         1935, 256p, Cloth, Novel
15716A   *The secret people,* by John Beynon Harris. Lan-
         cer, New York, 1964, 175p, Paper, Novel
15716B   *The secret people,* by John Wyndham. Fawcett
         Gold Medal, Greenwich, Conn., 1973, 206p,
         Paper, Novel

as John Beynon Harris:

         The secret people. [see 15716A]

as Johnson Harris:

15717   *Love in time.* Utopian Publications, London,
         1945, 36p, Paper, Story

with Patrick Nobes:

10713   *The triffids.* Hutchinson, London, 1973, 124p,
         Paper, Novel [adapted from *The day of the
         triffids*]

WYNNE-TYSON, (Dorothy Estelle) ESMÉ, 1898-
[biography included], with J. D. Beresford

01162   The riddle of the tower. Hutchinson, London,
            1944, 152p, Cloth, Novel

X., pseud.
    see: FAWKES, FRANK ATTFIELD

"X," pseud.

15718   The setting Sun; an ante-dated picture for a
            people. Skeffington & Son, London, 1904,
            167p, Cloth, Novel

X, ex-Private, pseud.
    see: BURRAGE, A. M.

X, Miss
    see: GOODRICH-FREER, A.

X, MOLLY, pseud.

15719   My wicked pleasures; the memoirs of Molly X.
            Midwood, New York, 1969,   , Paper, Novel

X. L.
    see: FIELD, JULIAN OSGOOD

XANTHUS, XAVIER, pseud.
    see: LAUMER, MARCH

XONGO-TEE-FOH-TCHI, Mandarin of the Third
Class, pseud.

15720   Napoleon in the other world; a narrative writ-
            ten by himself, and found near his tomb in
            the island of St. Helena. Henry Colburn,
            London, 1827, 406p, Cloth, Novel

YANIKIAN, GOURGEN, 1895-   , with Helen Rettig

12149   Mirror in the darkness; a novel. Exposition
            Press, New York, 1966, 197p, Cloth, Novel

YARBRO, CHELSEA QUINN, 1942-   [biography in-
cluded], with Thomas N. Scortia

12816   Two views of wonder. Ballantine, New York,
            1973, 274p, Paper, Anth.

YATES, DORNFORD, pseud. [Cecil William Mercer,
1885-1960]

15721   The stolen march. Ward, Lock, London, 1926,
            319p, Cloth, Novel

YCAS, MARTYNAS, 1917-   , with George Gamow

05746   Mr. Tompkins inside himself; adventures in the
            new biology. Viking Press, New York, 1967,
            274p, Cloth, Novel [Mr. Tompkins #4]

THE YEAR FOR LOVE
    see: SMITH, GEORGE H.

YEFREMOV, IVAN
    see: EFREMOV, IVAN

YELNICK, CLAUDE

15722   The trembling tower. Museum Press, London,
            1956, 160p, Cloth, Novel

YELVERTON, CHRISTOPHER

15723   Oneiros; or, Some questions of the day. Kegan
            Paul, Trench, London, 1889, 246p, Cloth,
            Novel

YENTER, CHARLES E.

15724   William F. Nolan; a checklist. Charles E. Yen-
            ter, Tacoma, Wash., 1974, 57p, Paper, Nonf.

YEP, LAURENCE (Michael), 1948-   [biography
included]

15725   Sweetwater. Harper & Row, New York, 1973,
            201p, Cloth, Novel

YEREX, CUTHBERT, pseud. [Estella Y. Cuthbert]

15726   Christopher Brand; looking forward. Wetzel
            Publishing Co., Los Angeles, 1934, 219p,
            Cloth, Novel [a response to Bellamy's Look-
            ing backward]

YERSHOV, PETER, 1895-

15727   Science fiction and utopian fantasy in Soviet
            literature. Research Program on the U.S.S.R.,
            New York, 1954, 66p, Paper, Nonf.

YEXLEY, LIONEL, 1861-1933, with Patrick Vaux
as Navarchus

14590   The world's awakening. Hodder & Stoughton,
            London, 1908, 463p, Cloth, Novel
14590A retitled: When the great war came. Hodder &
            Stoughton, London, 1909, 312p, Paper, Novel

YIN, LESLIE
    see: CHARTERIS, LESLIE

YOLEN, JANE (Hyatt), 1939-   [biography in-
cluded]

15728   The magic three of Solatia. Thomas Y. Crowell,
            New York, 1974, 172p, Cloth, Novel
15729   Zoo 2000; twelve stories of science fiction
            and fantasy beasts. Seabury Press, New York,
            1973, 224p, Cloth, Anth.

YORK, WESLEY SIMON, pseud.
    see: PLATT, KIN

YORKE, HENRY VINCENT
    see: GREEN, HENRY

YORKE, JACQUELINE

15730 *Brides of the devil.* Comyns (Publishers),
       London, 1946, 192p, Cloth, Novel

YORKE, PRESTON

15731 *The gamma ray murders.* Everybody's Books,
       London, 1943, 128p, Paper, Novel
15732 *Space-time task force.* Hector Kelly, London,
       1953, 192p, Cloth, Novel

YOUD, SAM
    see: CHRISTOPHER, JOHN

YOUNG, ALFRED MICHAEL

15733 *The Aster disaster; a tale of two planets.*
       Arthur H. Stockwell, Ilfracombe, UK, 1958,
       250p, Cloth, Novel

YOUNG, BERTRAM ALFRED, 1912-

15734 *Cabinet pudding.* Hamish Hamilton, London,
       1967, 209p, Cloth, Novel

YOUNG, CHARLES V(an) P(atten), 1876-1960

15735 *Across the borderline.* Richard R. Smith,
       New York, 1946, 127p, Cloth, Novel

YOUNG, F(lorence) E(thel Mills), 1875-1945

15736 *The war of the sexes.* John Long, London,
       1905, 298p, Cloth, Novel

YOUNG, FRANCIS BRETT, 1884-1954

15737 *Cold Harbour.* W. Collins Sons, London, 1924,
       286p, Cloth, Novel

YOUNG, LAURENCE DITTO

15738 *The Climbing Doom.* G. W. Dillingham, New
       York, 1909, 326p, Cloth, Novel

YOUNG, MICHAEL (Dunlop), 1915-

15739 *The rise of the meritocracy, 1870-2033; an
       essay on education and quality.* Thames &
       Hudson, London, 1958, 160p, Cloth, Novel

YOUNG, MIRIAM, 1913-1974 [*biography included*]

15740 *A witch's garden.* A Margaret K. McElderry
       Book, Atheneum, New York, 1973, 156p, Cloth,
       Novel

YOUNG, PETER (William), 1920-

15741 *Zag the Great and Zig the Big.* Schonfield &
       Sims, Huddersfield, UK, 1966, 71p, Paper,
       Novel [Zig & Zag #2]
15742 *Zig and Zag from planet ZV7.* Schonfield & Sims,
       Huddersfield, UK, 1966, 57p, Paper, Novel
       [Zig & Zag #1]

YOUNG, PHYLLIS BRETT

15743 *Undine.* G. P. Putnam's Sons, New York, 1964,
       256p, Cloth, Novel

YOUNG, RED

15744 *Sex life of the immortals.* Classic Publica-
       tions, Los Angeles, 1969, 190p, Paper, Novel

YOUNG, ROBERT, pseud.
    see: PAYNE, ROBERT

YOUNG, ROBERT F(ranklin), 1915- [*biography
included*]

15745 *A glass of stars.* Harris-Wolfe, Jacksonville,
       IL, 1968, 356p, Cloth, Coll.
15746 *The worlds of Robert F. Young; sixteen stories
       of science fiction and fantasy.* Simon &
       Schuster, New York, 1965, 224p, Cloth, Coll.

A YOUNG LADY, pseud.
    see: SHERWOOD, MARY

YOUTH MADNESS

15747 *Youth madness.* Utopian Publications, London,
       1945?, 36p, Paper, Anth.

YOXALL, (Sir) J(ames) H(enry), 1857-1925

15748 *The lonely pyramid; a tale of adventures, being
       the strange experiences of Roy Lefevre in
       the desert during the year 1884.* Blackie &
       Son, London, 1892, 192p, Cloth, Novel

YULEE, C(harles) WICKLIFFE, 1849-

15749 *Overshadowed.* William Rider & Son, London,
       1920, 384p, Cloth, Novel

YUMA, GARY

15750 *Flesh probe.* Eros Goldstripe, Wilmington, Del.,
       1973, 182p, Paper, Novel

YUTANG, LIN
    see: LIN, YU-TANG

ZACHARY, HUGH
    see: HUGHES, ZACH

ZACHERLEY, pseud. [John C. Zacherle, 1919-   ]

15751   *Zacherleys midnight snacks.* Ballantine, New
      York, 1960, 157p, Paper, Anth.
15752   *Zacherley's vulture stew.* Ballantine, New
      York, 1960, 160p, Paper, Anth.

ZAGAT, ARTHUR LEO, 1895-1949

15753   *Seven out of time.* Fantasy Press, Reading,
      PA, 1949, 240p, Cloth, Novel

ZAMIATIN, EVGENII (Ivanovich), 1884-1937

15754   *We,* by Eugene Zamyatin. E. P. Dutton, New
      York, 1924, 286p, Cloth, Novel

ZAMYATIN, EUGENE
    see: ZAMIATIN, EVGENII

ZAREM, LEWIS

15755   *The green man from space.* E. P. Dutton, New
      York, 1955, 160p, Cloth, Novel

ZAROVITCH, Princess VERA, pseud. [Mary E.
Lane]

15756   *Mizora; a prophecy; a mss. found among the
      private papers of the Princess Vera Zaro-
      vitch, being a true and faithful account of
      her journey to the interior of the Earth,
      with a careful description of the country
      and its inhabitants, their customs, manners,
      and government, written by herself.* G. W.
      Dillingham, New York, 1890, 312p, Paper,
      Novel

ZEBROWSKI, GEORGE (T.), 1945-   [*biography
included*]

15757   *The Omega point.* Ace, New York, 1972, 169p,
      Paper, Novel

ZEIGFREID, KARL, pseud.
    see: FANTHORPE, R. LIONEL

ZEIGFRIED, KARL, house pseud.

15758   *Beyond the galaxy.* John Spencer, London,
      1953, 112p, Paper, Novel
15759   *Chaos in Arcturus.* John Spencer, London,
      1953, 124p, Paper, Novel
15760   *Chariot into time.* John Spencer, London,
      1953, 128p, Paper, Novel
15761   *"Dark Centauri."* John Spencer, London, 1954,
      130p, Paper, Novel

15762   *The uranium seekers.* John Spencer, London,
      1953, 128p, Paper, Novel

ZEITLIN, IDA

15763   *Gessar Khan; a legend of Tibet.* George H.
      Doran, New York, 1927, 203p, Cloth, Novel

ZELAZNY, ROGER (Joseph), 1937-   [*biography
included*]

15764   *Creatures of light and darkness.* Doubleday,
      Garden City, 1969, 187p, Cloth, Novel
15765   *Damnation Alley.* G. P. Putnam's Sons, New
      York, 1969, 157p, Cloth, Novel
15766   *The doors of his face, the lamps of his mouth,
      and other stories.* Doubleday, Garden City,
      1971, 229p, Cloth, Coll.
15767   *The dream master.* Ace, New York, 1966, 155p,
      Paper, Novel
15768   *Four for tomorrow.* Ace, New York, 1967, 191p,
      Paper, Coll.
15768A retitled: *A rose for Ecclesiastes.* Rupert
      Hart-Davis, London, 1969, 207p, Cloth, Coll.
15769   *The guns of Avalon.* Doubleday, Garden City,
      1972, 180p, Cloth, Novel [Amber #2]
15770   *Isle of the Dead.* Ace, New York, 1969, 190p,
      Paper, Novel
15771   *Jack of Shadows.* Walker, New York, 1971, 207p,
      Cloth, Novel
15772   *Lord of Light.* Doubleday, Garden City, 1967,
      257p, Cloth, Novel
15773   *Nebula award stories three.* Doubleday, Garden
      City, 1968, 272p, Cloth, Anth.
15774   *Nine princes in Amber.* Doubleday, Garden City,
      1970, 188p, Cloth, Novel [Amber #1]
      A rose for Ecclesiastes. [see 15768A]
15775   *This immortal.* Ace, New York, 1966, 174p,
      Paper, Novel
15776   *To die in Italbar.* Doubleday, Garden City,
      1973, 182p, Cloth, Novel
15777   *Today we choose faces.* Signet, New York, 1973,
      174p, Paper, Novel

ZELLER, CLAUDE HUBERT VAN
    see: VENNING, HUGH

ZERWICK, CHLOE, 1923-   [*biography included*],
with Harrison Brown

01981   *The Cassiopeia affair.* Doubleday, Garden
      City, 1968, 235p, Cloth, Novel

ZETFORD, TULLY, pseud.
    see: BULMER, KENNETH

ZIEGLER, EDWARD WILLIAM
    see: TYLER, THEODORE

ZIEROLD, NORMAN (J.), 1927-

15778   *The skyscraper doom.* Lenox Hill Press, New
      York, 1972, 192p, Cloth, Novel

ZILE, EDWARD S. VAN
    see: VAN ZILE, EDWARD S.

ZIMBARDO, ROSE A(bdelnour), 1932-   [*biogra-*
phy included], with Neil D. Isaacs

07736 *Tolkien and the critics; essays on J. R. R.*
        Tolkien's The Lord of the Rings. Univer-
        sity of Notre Dame Press, Notre Dame, 1968,
        296p, Cloth, Nonf. Anth.

ZIMMERMANN, WERNER
    see: DOUGLAS, DRAKE

ZIMPEL, LLOYD, 1929-   [*biography included*]

15779 *Meeting the bear; journal of the black wars.*
        Macmillan, New York, 1971, 238p, Cloth,
        Novel

ZORRO, pseud. [Harold Ward]

15780 *Doctor Death; The gray creatures.* Corinth,
        San Diego, 1966, 159p, Paper, Novel [Doctor
        Death #2]
15781 *Doctor Death; The shriveling murders.* Cor-
        inth, San Diego, 1966, 159p, Paper, Novel
        [Doctor Death #3]
15782 *Doctor Death; 12 must die.* Corinth, San Di-
        ego, 1966, 159p, Paper, Novel [Doctor Death
        #1]

ZUBER, STANLEY

15783 *The golden promise; a novel of the coming era.*
        Pageant Press, New York, 1955, 127p, Cloth,
        Novel

ZUGSMITH, ALBERT, with Robert Hill

07214 *The private lives of Adam and Eve.* Bantam,
        New York, 1960, 153p, Paper, Movie

Addendum to Author Index

ADDENDUM TO AUTHOR INDEX

ADDINGTON, SARAH, 1891-1940

03939 *Hound of Heaven*. D. Appleton-Century, New York, 1935, 50p, Cloth, Novel

AIKEN, JOAN [see also main entry]

12961 *Black hearts in Battersea*. Doubleday, Garden City, 1964, 240p, Cloth, Novel [Willoughby Chase #2]
13593 *The cuckoo tree*. Doubleday, Garden City, 1971, 314p, Cloth, Novel [Willoughby Chase #5]
13756 *Nightbirds on Nantucket*. Doubleday, Garden City, 1966, 216p, Cloth, Novel [Willoughby Chase #3]
15784 *The wolves of Willoughby Chase*. Jonathan Cape, London, 1962, 159p, Cloth, Novel [Willoughby Chase #1]

ANDERSON, KAREN

15785 *Henry Kuttner; a memorial symposium*. Sevagram Enterprises, Berkeley, CA, 1958, 34p, Paper, Nonf. Anth.

APPLETON, VICTOR, house pseud. [see also main entry]

15786 *Don Sturdy in the port of lost ships; or, Adrift in the Sargasso Sea*. Grosset & Dunlap, New York, 1926, 214p, Cloth, Novel [Don Sturdy #6]

ARTHUR, RUTH M. [see also main entry]

15787 *Requiem for a princess*. Atheneum, New York, 1967, 182p, Cloth, Novel

BAILEY, ALBERT EDWARD, 1871-1951

15788 *The wise man's story; a Christmas tale for dreamers*. Pilgrim Press, Boston, 1916, 54p, Cloth, Novel

BAKER, NINA BROWN, 1888-1957

15789 *Inca gold*. W. A. Wilde Co., Boston, 1938, 320p, Cloth, Novel

BALZAC, HONORÉ de [see also main entry]

15790 *The quest of the absolute; Séraphita*. McKinlay, Stone & MacKenzie, New York, 1915, 341p, Cloth, Coll.

BENCHLEY, NATHANIEL (Goddard), 1915-

15791 *The visitors*. McGraw-Hill, New York, 1964, 248p, Cloth, Novel

BERNANOS, GEORGES, 1888-1948

15792 *The star of Satan*. John Lane, The Bodley Head, London, 1927, 339p, Cloth, Novel
15792A retitled: *Under the sun of Satan; a novel*. Pantheon, New York, 1949, 253p, Cloth, Novel

CHASE, MARY [see also main entry]

15793 *Loretta Mason Potts*. J. B. Lippincott, Philadelphia, 1958, 221p, Cloth, Novel

CLARKE, PAULINE [see also main entry]

15794 *The two faces of Silenus*. Faber & Faber, London, 1972, 162p, Cloth, Novel

CORON, HANNAH

15795 *Ten years hence?* J. M. Ouseley & Son, London, 1924, 255p, Cloth, Novel

CREASEY, JOHN [see also main entry]

15796 *The island of peril*. John Long, London, 1940, 224p, Cloth, Novel [Dept. Z series]

DARK, JAMES [see also main entry]

15797 *The invisibles*. Signet, New York, 1969, 127p, Paper, Novel [Mark Hood series]

DELARO, SELINA, with Edward Heron-Allen

07137 *The princess Daphne; a novel*. Henry J. Drane, London, 1885, 264p, Cloth, Novel

DOGBOLT, BARNABY [see also main entry]

15798 *The goose's tale*. E. P. Dutton, New York, 1947, 317p, Cloth, Novel

DRUON, MAURICE [see also main entry]

15799 *Tistou of the green fingers*. Rupert Hart-Davis, London, 1958, 141p, Cloth, Novel
15799A retitled: *Tistou of the green thumbs*. Charles Scribner's Sons, New York, 1958, 178p, Cloth, Novel

EÇA de QUEIROZ, (Jose Maria de), 1845-1900

15800 *The mandarin, and other stories*. Ohio University Press, Athens, OH, 1965, 176p, Cloth, Coll.

EDMONDS, WALTER D(umaux), 1903-

15801 *Hound dog Moses and the promised land*. Dodd, Mead, New York, 1954, 81p, Cloth, Novel

ELIOT, ETHEL COOK, 1890-

15802 *The Wind Boy.* Doubleday, Page, Garden City,
       1923, 238p, Cloth, Novel

FARJEON, ELEANOR [see also main entry]

15803 *The silver curlew.* Oxford University Press,
       London, 1953, 182p, Cloth, Novel

FENTON, EDWARD [see also main entry]

15804 *The nine questions.* Doubleday, Garden City,
       1959, 235p, Cloth, Novel

FEYDY, ANNE LINDBERGH

15805 *Osprey Island.* Houghton Mifflin, Boston,
       1974, 164p, Cloth, Novel

FLAGG, EDMUND, 1815-1890 [published anony-
mously]

15806 *Edmond Dantès; a sequel to The Count of Monte-
       Cristo.* T. B. Peterson & Bros., Philadel-
       phia, 1878, 203p, Cloth, Novel [The Count
       of Monte Cristo #2]
15807 *Edmond Dantès; the sequel to Alexandre Dumas'
       celebrated novel, The Count of Monte-Cristo;
       an entire new and enlarged edition.* T. B.
       Peterson & Bros., Philadelphia, 1884, 378p,
       Cloth, Novel [The Count of Monte Cristo #2;
       expanded]

FRITZ, JEAN (Guttery), 1915-

15808 *Magic to burn.* Coward-McCann, New York, 1964,
       255p, Cloth, Novel

GALLICO, PAUL [see also main entry]

15809 *Manxmouse.* Heinemann, London, 1968, 191p,
       Cloth, Novel

GOUDGE, ELIZABETH [see also main entry]

15810 *Smoky-House.* Duckworth, London, 1940, 208p,
       Cloth, Novel
15811 *The Valley of Song.* University of London
       Press, London, 1951, 255p, Cloth, Novel

GRAHAME, KENNETH, 1859-1932

15812 *The wind in the willows.* Methuen, London,
       1908, 302p, Cloth, Novel

HALDEMAN-JULIUS, E(manuel), 1889-1951

15813 *Five great ghost stories.* Haldeman-Julius,
       Girard, Kans., 1920?, 127p, Paper, Anth.

HAMLEY, DENNIS, 1935-

15814 *Pageants of despair.* S. G. Phillips, New York,
       1974, 175p, Cloth, Novel; Andre Deutsch,
       London, 1974, 175p, Cloth, Novel

HARBOTTLE, PHILIP [see also main entry]

15815 *E. C. Tubb; an evaluation.* Philip Harbottle,
       Wallsend-on-Tyne, UK, 1964, 20p, Paper, Nonf.

HOBAN, RUSSELL [see also main entry]

15816 *The mouse and his child.* Harper & Row, New
       York, 1967, 181p, Cloth, Novel

HOLLIDAY, DON, pseud.

15817 *Beast of shame.* Pillar Books, San Diego,
       1964, 189p, Paper, Novel

HOLM, (Else) ANNE (Lise), 1922-

15818 *Peter.* Harcourt, Brace & World, New York,
       1968, 224p, Cloth, Novel

HOWARD, MILFORD W(riarson), 1862-

15819 *The bishop of the Ozarks.* Times-Mirror Press,
       Los Angeles, 1923, 232p, Cloth, Movie

HUDSON, W. H. [see also main entry]

15820 *A little boy lost.* Duckworth, London, 1905,
       201p, Cloth, Novel

HYERS, (M.) CONRAD, 1933-

15821 *The chickadees; a contemporary fable.* West-
       minster Press, Philadelphia, 1974, 64p,
       Cloth, Novel

JONES, FRANK EARL

15822 *The Big-Ball; a novel.* Jones Publication,
       Bloomington, IL, 1958, 156p, Paper, Novel

KING, CYNTHIA, 1925-

15823 *In the morning of time; the story of the Norse
       god Balder.* Four Winds Press, New York,
       1970, 237p, Cloth, Novel

LAMPMAN, EVELYN SIBLEY [see also main entry]

15824 *The shy stegosaurus of Indian Springs.* Double-
       day, Garden City, 1962, 232p, Cloth, Novel
       [Stegosaurus #2]

LANGTON, JANE (Gillson), 1922-

15825 *The astonishing stereoscope*. Harper & Row, New York, 1971, 240p, Cloth, Novel [Eleanor #3]

15826 *The diamond in the window*. Harper & Row, New York, 1962, 242p, Cloth, Novel [Eleanor #1]

15827 *The swing in the summerhouse*. Harper & Row, New York, 1967, 185p, Cloth, Novel [Eleanor #2]

LAWRENCE, ANN, 1942-

15828 *The half-brothers*. Henry Z. Walck, New York, 1973, 172p, Cloth, Novel

LAWSON, ROBERT [see also main entry]

15829 *Mr. Twigg's mistake*. Little, Brown, Boston, 1947, 141p, Cloth, Novel

LEE, TANITH, 1947-

15830 *The dragon hoard*. Macmillan, London, 1971, 169p, Cloth, Novel

LEITCH, PATRICIA, 1933-

15831 *The black loch*. Collins, London, 1963, 192p, Cloth, Novel

LEWIS, HILDA [see also main entry]

15832 *The ship that flew*. Oxford University Press, London, 1939, 320p, Cloth, Novel

LIVELY, PENELOPE [see also main entry]

15833 *The house in Norham Gardens*. Heinemann, London, 1974, 154p, Cloth, Novel

LOBSANG RAMPA, T(uesday), pseud. [C. H. Hoskin]

15834 *Living with the lama, by Mrs. Fifi Greywhiskers, P.S.C., translated from the Siamese Cat language* by T. Lobsang Rampa. Corgi, London, 1964, 190p, Paper, Novel

LOCKE, ASHLEY, with Arthur B. Reeve

12111 *Enter Craig Kennedy*. Macaulay Co., New York, 1935, 256p, Cloth, Novel [Craig Kennedy #25]

LOFTING, HUGH (John), 1886-1947

15835 *The twilight of magic*. Jonathan Cape, London, 1930, 285p, Cloth, Novel

MacDONALD, GEORGE [see also main entry]

15836 *At the back of the north wind*. Strahan & Co., London, 1870, 378p, Cloth, Novel

15837 *The princess and Curdie*. Chatto & Windus, London, 1883, 255p, Cloth, Novel [Curdie #2]

15838 *The princess and the goblin*. Strahan & Co., London, 1871, 313p, Cloth, Novel [Curdie #1]

MACVEY, JOHN W(ishart), 1923-

15839 *Journey to Alpha Centauri*. Macmillan, New York, 1965, 256p, Cloth, Coll. [largely nonfiction, but includes a novella-length account of a trip to Alpha Centauri]

MASTERS, DEXTER

15840 *The cloud chamber*. Little, Brown, Boston, 1971, 302p, Cloth, Novel

MAUROIS, ANDRÉ [see also main entry]

15841 *Fatapouts & Thinifers*. Henry Holt, New York, 1940, 92p, Cloth, Novel

15841A retitled: *Fattypuffs and Thinifers*. John Lane, London, 1941, 92p, Cloth, Novel

McHARGUE, GEORGESS [see also main entry]

15842 *The best of both worlds; an anthology of stories for all ages*. Doubleday, Garden City, 1968, 722p, Cloth, Anth.

McNEILL, JANET, 1907-

15843 *Tom's tower*. Faber & Faber, London, 1965, 141p, Cloth, Novel

MEYER, BILL

15844 *Ultimatum*. Signet, New York, 1966, 189p, Paper, Novel

MICHAELS, BARBARA [see also main entry]

15845 *Sons of the wolf*. Meredith Press, New York, 1967, 265p, Cloth, Novel

NESBIT, E. [see also main entry]

15846 *Harding's luck*. Hodder & Stoughton, London, 1909, 281p, Cloth, Novel [Arden #2]

15847 *The house of Arden; a story for children*. T. Fisher Unwin, London, 1908, 349p, Cloth, Novel [Arden #1]

15848 *Wet magic*. T. Werner Laurie, London, 1913, 274p, Cloth, Novel

ORMONDROYD, EDWARD [see also main entry]

15849 *David and the Phoenix*. Follett Publishing Co., Chicago, 1957, 173p, Cloth, Novel

PARGETER, EDITH [see also main entry]

15850 *By firelight.* William Heinemann, London, 1948, 324p, Cloth, Novel
15850A retitled: *By this strange fire.* Reynal & Hitchcock, New York, 1948, 310p, Cloth, Novel

PEEPLES, EDWIN A., Jr. [see also main entry]

15851 *A hole in the hill.* Thomas Nelson, Camden, NJ, 1969, 189p, Cloth, Novel

POOLE, JOSEPHINE [see also main entry]

15852 *The visitor; a story of suspense.* Harper & Row, New York, 1972, 148p, Cloth, Novel

POPE, ELIZABETH MARIE, 1917-

15853 *The Sherwood ring.* Houghton Mifflin, Boston, 1958, 266p, Cloth, Novel

PRINCE, DON [see also main entry]

11915A retitled: *Tom's temptations.* Diversey, Chicago, 1949, 123p, Paper, Novel

REEVE, ARTHUR B. [see also main entry]

15854 *Constance Dunlap, woman detective.* Hearst's International Library, New York, 1916, 342p, Cloth, Novel
15855 *Guy Garrick; an adventure with a scientific gunman.* Hearst's International Library, New York, 1914, 326p, Cloth, Novel

ROBERTSON, OLIVIA (Melian), 1917-

15856 *Miranda speaks.* Peter Davies, London, 1950, 220p, Cloth, Novel

ROMAINS, JULES, pseud. [Louis Farigoule, 1885-1972]

15857 *Tussles with time.* Sidgwick & Jackson, London, 1952, 243p, Cloth, Coll.

ST. CLAIR, HENRY

15858 *Tales of terror; or, The mysteries of magic; a selection of wonderful and supernatural stories.* C. Gaylord, Boston, 1835, 277p, Cloth, Anth.
15858A retitled: *Evening tales for the winter, being a selection of wonderful & supernatural stories.* R. Marsh, New York, 1856, 370p, Cloth, Anth.

SELDEN, GEORGE [see also main entry]

15859 *Harry Cat's pet puppy.* Farrar, Straus & Giroux, New York; 1974, 167p, Cloth, Novel [Tucker & Harry #3]

15860 *Tucker's countryside.* Ariel Book, Farrar, Straus & Giroux, New York, 1969, 166p, Cloth, Novel [Tucker & Harry #2]

SMITH, GEORGE H. [see also main entry]

as Jerry Jason:

15861 *Sexodus.* Boudoir Limited Editions, Hollywood, 1963, 160p, Paper, Novel

SMITH, KEITH

15862 *OGF, being the private papers of George Cockburn, bus conductor, a resident of Hurstfield, a suburb of Sydney, Australia.* Ure Smith, Sydney, 1965, 259p, Cloth, Novel

SNYDER, ZILPHA KEATLEY [see also main entry]

15863 *Season of ponies.* Atheneum, New York, 1964, 133p, Cloth, Novel

SOMERLOTT, ROBERT

15864 *The inquisitor's house.* Viking Press, New York, 1968, 377p, Cloth, Novel

STEVENSON, ROBERT LOUIS [see also main entry]

15865 *The body-snatcher.* Merriam Co., New York, 1895, 61p, Cloth, Novel

SWAN, MARK E(lbert), 1871-

15866 *Top o' the world; a once upon a time tale.* E. P. Dutton, New York, 1908, 194p, Cloth, Novel [adapted from the musical of the same name]

TABORI, PAUL [see also main entry]

15867 *The talking tree.* Sampson Low, Marston, London, 1950, 246p, Cloth, Novel

TALES OF MYSTERY AND HORROR

15868 *Tales of mystery and horror.* World Society Editions,   , 1966, 210p, Paper, Anth.

THACKERAY, WILLIAM MAKEPEACE, 1811-1863

15869 *The rose and the ring; or, The history of Prince Giglio and Prince Bulbo; a fire-side pantomime for great and small children,* by M. A. Titmarsh. Smith, Elder, London, 1855, 128p, Cloth, Novel
15869A *The rose and the ring; or, The history of Prince Giglio and Prince Bulbo,* by W. M. Thackeray. Estes & Lauriat, Boston, 1883, 148p, Cloth, Novel

TOWER, HARKER, pseud.

15870 *Two weird tails*. Neptune Readers, no place, 1971, 160p, Paper, Coll.

TWITCHELL, PAUL, 1908-1971

15871 *Talons of Time*. Illuminated Way Press, San Diego, 1974, 188p, Paper, Novel

VARMA, DEVENDRA P., 1923-

15872 *Gothic flame, being a history of the gothic novel in England, its origins, efflorescence, and residuary influences*. Arthur Barker, London, 1957, 246p, Cloth, Nonf.

VAUGHAN, HILDA, 1892-

15873 *Iron and gold*. Macmillan, London, 1948, 233p, Cloth, Novel

VIRG, LEO, pseud.

15874 *Twenty trillion light-years through space*. Vantage Press, New York, 1958, 126p, Cloth, Novel

WALLER, LESLIE [see also main entry under C. S. Cody], with Louise Waller

15875 *Take me to your leader*. G. P. Putnam's Sons, New York, 1961,   , Paper, Fiction

WALLER, LOUISE, with Leslie Waller

15875 *Take me to your leader*. G. P. Putnam's Sons, New York, 1961,   , Paper, Fiction

WAYNE, CHARLES M., pseud.

15876 *The duke of sin*. Vantage Press, New York, 1954, 74p, Cloth, Novel

WESTERMAN, PERCY F. [see also main entry]

15877 *The rival submarines*. S. W. Partridge, London, 1913, 432p, Cloth, Novel

WILLIAMS, URSULA MORAY [see also main entry]

15878 *The Line*. Puffin, Harmondsworth, 1974, 127p, Paper, Coll.
15879 *Malkin's mountain*. George G. Harrap, London, 1948, 140p, Cloth, Novel [Rudi #2]
15880 *The three toymakers*. George G. Harrap, London, 1945, 142p, Cloth, Novel [Rudi #1]

WINN, ROWLAND (Denis Guy), 4th Baron St. Oswald, 1916-

15881 *My dear, it's Heaven*. Cassell, London, 1950, 224p, Cloth, Novel

WOOLRICH, CORNELL [see also main entry]

15882 *Savage bride*. Gold Medal, New York, 1950, 178p, Paper, Novel

WRIGHT, MABEL OSGOOD, 1859-1934

15883 *Wabeno, the magician; the sequel to "Tommy-Anne and the three hearts."* Macmillan, New York, 1899, 346p, Cloth, Novel

YOUNG, ELLA, 1867-1956

15884 *The unicorn with silver shoes*. Longmans, Green, New York, 1932, 215p, Cloth, Novel

Title Index

!!!. + Hepworth, George H.
An ABC of science fiction. + Boardman, Tom
A.D. 2018. + Gibson, Edmund H.
A.D. 2050. + Bachelder, John
A.D. 2500. + none
A.D. 2000. + Fuller, Alvarado M.
AE, the open persuader. + Auctor ignotus
A for Andromeda. + Elliot, John & Hoyle, Fred
A for anything. + Knight, Damon
The A.G. man. + Hansman, William
"A" men. + Le Page, Rand
A. Merritt. + Wentz, W. Jas.
Abandon galaxy! + Somers, Bart
The abandoned. + Gallico, Paul
Abandoned. + Verne, Jules
The Abbey of Kilkhampton. + (Croft, Herbert)
Abbot of Montserrat. + Green, William Child
Abbs. + Hyne, C. J. Cutcliffe
Abdallah. + Laboulaye, Edouard Rene Lefebvre-
Abdallah and the donkey. + Kos
Abishag. + Arnoux, Alexandre
The abominable Earthman. + Pohl, Frederik
The abominable snowman. + Waugh, Michael
The abominable snowman, and other stories. + Baughman, Grace
The abominable twilight. + Campbell, Reginald
The abominations of Yondo. + Smith, Clark Ashton
Above all else. + Shiel, M. P.
Above the human landscape. + McNelly, Willis E. & Stover, Leon E.
Abraham's bosom. + King, Basil
The absolute at large. + Capek, Karel
Abyss. + Wilhelm, Kate
The abyss of wonders. + Sheehan, Perley Poore
The academy for souls. + Cosgrave, John O'Hara
The accidental Earth. + Kelley, Leo P.
Account of an expedition to the interior of New Holland. + Fox, Lady Mary
An account of the state of learning in the Empire of Lilliput. + (Arbuthnot, John)
Account settled. + Russell, John
The accusing spirit. + (Pilkington, Mary)
Ace of the white death. + Hogan, Robert J.
Ace science fiction reader. + Wollheim, Donald A.
The achievements of Luther Trant. + Balmer, Edwin & MacHarg, William
The Acolhuans. + Beatty, John
Across a billion years. + Silverberg, Robert
Across Paris, and other stories. + Ayme, Marcel
Across the ages. + Statten, Vargo
Across the borderline. + Young, Charles V. P.
Across the sea of stars. + Clarke, Arthur C.
Across the stream. + Benson, E. F.
Across the Zodiac. + Greg, Percy
Across the Zodiac. + Pallander, Edwin
Across time. + Grinnell, David
Act of God. + Ashby, Richard
Actions and reactions. + Kipling, Rudyard
Ada. + Nabokov, Vladimir
Adam. + Bolt, David
Adam and Eve and Newbury. + Bennett, Diana
Adam & Eve & pinch me. + Coppard, A. E.
Adam and Eve, though he knew better. + Erskine, John
Adam and Eve, 2020 A.D. + Blackden, Paul
Adam and his women. + Clifford, Sarah
Adam and the serpent. + Fisher, Vardis
The Adam chasers. + Bower, B. M.
Adam in moonshine. + Priestley, J. B.
Adam Link in the past. + Binder, Eando
Adam Link--robot. + Binder, Eando
Adam M-1. + Anderson, William C.
Adam Troy, astroman. + Patchett, M. E.

Adam's crusade. + Rutledge, Lyman V.
Adam's first wife. + Speller, Jane & Speller, Robert
The Addams family. + Sharkey, Jack
The Addams family strikes back. + Miksch, William
An additional dialogue of the dead. + Lyttleton, Lord
Address: Centauri. + Wallace, F. L.
Address unknown. + Phillpotts, Eden
Adel Hitro. + Haas, Charles
Adoniram. + Findlay, Alexander
Adonis. + Lambert, William J. III
Adonis at Actum. + Lambert, William J. III
Adonis at Bomasa. + Lambert, William J. III
Adrift in a boneyard. + Taylor, Robert Lewis
Adrift in space, and other stories. + (Elwood, Roger)
Adrift in the stratosphere. + Low, A. M.
Adrift in the unknown. + Cook, William Wallace
Ads infinitum. + Wayman, Tony Russell
The adult version of Dr. Jekyll and Mr. Hyde. + Stacy, Terry
The adult version of Dracula. + (Kantor, Hal)
The adult version of Frankenstein. + Kantor, Hal
An adventure among the Rosicrucians. + Hartmann, Franz
Adventure from the grave. + Freeman, Kathleen
Adventure in forgotten valley. + Frewer, Glyn
Adventure in space. + none
Adventure in space. + Mackenzie, Nigel
Adventure in space; and, The time travellers. + Nagpal, Veena
Adventure in time. + none
An adventure in Venus. + Michelmore, Reg
The adventure of the blue room. + Fowler, Sydney
The adventure of the peerless peer. + Farmer, Philip Jose
The adventure of Wyndham Smith. + Wright, S. Fowler
Adventure on the Moon. + Carroll, Nina
The adventurer. + Osbourne, Lloyd
Adventures and fantasy. + Hering, Henry A.
Adventures in Heaven. + Angoff, Charles
Adventures in the far future. + Wollheim, Donald A.
Adventures in the Moon, and other worlds. + (Russell, John)
Adventures in the unknown; A thousand miles a minute. + Claudy, Carl H.
Adventures in the unknown; The Blue Grotto terror. + Claudy, Carl H.
Adventures in the unknown; The Land of No Shadow. + Claudy, Carl H.
Adventures in the unknown; The mystery men of Mars. + Claudy, Carl H.
Adventures in time and space. + Healy, Raymond J. & McComas, J. Francis
Adventures in tomorrow. + Crossen, Kendell Foster
Adventures into unknowns. + Maclagan, David
The adventures of a Chinaman in China. + Verne, Jules
The adventures of a micro-man. + Pallander, Edwin
The adventures of a skeleton. + Waltermire, Beecher W.
The adventures of a solicitor. + Chesney, Weatherby
The adventures of Abdalla, son of Hanif. + Sandisson, Mr.
The adventures of an atom. + (Angelo)
The adventures of Baron Munchausen. + (Raspe, Rudolf)
The adventures of Captain Gulliver in a voyage to Lilliput. + Swift, Jonathan
The adventures of Captain Gulliver in a voyage to the islands of Lilliput and Brobdingnag. + Swift, Jonathan
The adventures of Captain Hatteras. + Verne, Jules
The adventures of Charlie Bates. + Houston, James D.
The adventures of Eovaai, Princess of Ijaveo. + (Haywood, Eliza)
The adventures of God in his search for the Black Girl. + Brophy, Brigid

The adventures of Gremlin. + Jones, DuPre
The adventures of Grillo. + Candeze, Ernest
The adventures of Gulliver. + Swift, Jonathan
The adventures of Halek. + Nicholson, John H.
The adventures of Harry Marline. + Porter, Admiral
The adventures of Jones. + Carruth, Hayden
The adventures of little man Coco. + Harlan, Ethel
   Andrews
Adventures of Monsieur de Mailly. + Lindsay, David
The adventures of Sigr. Gaudentio di Lucca. + (Bering-
   ton, Simon)
The adventures of Tapiola. + Nathan, Robert
The adventures of the Adventurers' Club. + "Five Men
   and a Woman"
The adventures of the black girl in her search for God.
   + Shaw, George Bernard
The adventures of the Redcrosse Knight. + Mary Chari-
   tina, Sister
Adventures of the remarkable twain. + Cloudesley,
   Hubert
The adventures of the six princesses of Babylon in
   their travels to the Temple of Virtue. + Peacock,
   Lucy
The adventures of the young soldier in search of the
   better world. + Joad, C. E. M.
The adventures of Zeloide and Amanzarifdine. + Mon-
   crif, Augustin-Paradis de
Adventures on other planets. + Wollheim, Donald A.
Adventures to come. + Esenwein, J. Berg
Adventures with the mermaids. + Davies, M. Catherine
The adventuress. + Reeve, Arthur B.
Advise and consent. + Drury, Allen
Aelita. + Tolstoi, Alexei
The aerial burglars. + Blyth, James
The aerial flight to the realm of peace. + Kayser,
   Martha
An aerial runaway. + Chipman, C. P. & Chipman, W. P.
The aerobus. + none
An affair with genius. + Green, Joseph
An African treasure. + Cobban, J. MacLaren
Afro-6. + Lopez, Hank
After. + Saltoun, M.
After doomsday. + Anderson, Poul
After London. + Jefferies, Richard
After many a summer. + Huxley, Aldous
After many a summer dies the swan. + Huxley, Aldous
After me, the deluge. + Forrest, David
After some tomorrow. + Reynolds, Mack
After the afternoon. + MacArthur, Arthur
After the atom. + La Salle, Victor
After the Battle of Dorking. + none
After the Cataclysm. + Blanchard, H. Percy
After the clouds. + Davy, Catherine A.
After the good war. + Breggin, Peter Roger
After the rain. + Bowen, John
After things fell apart. + Goulart, Ron
After this. + Kent, Ryland
After 12,000 years. + Coblentz, Stanton
After worlds collide. + Balmer, Edwin & Wylie, Philip
After world's end. + Williamson, Jack
The afterdeath. + Brandon, Henry
The afterglow. + England, George Allan
Aftermath. + Corston, George
Aftermath 15. + Pereira, W. D.
Afternoon of an autocrat. + Lofts, Norah
Afternoons in utopia. + Leacock, Stephen
Again: Atlan! + Perry Rhodan 46
Again, dangerous visions. + Ellison, Harlan
Again, dangerous visions I. + Ellison, Harlan
Again, dangerous visions II. + Ellison, Harlan
Against Arcturus. + Putney, Susan K.
Against the fall of night. + Clarke, Arthur C.

Against the red sky. + Barbor, H. R.
Agar Halfi, the mystic. + Filkin, Roland
An age. + Aldiss, Brian W.
The age of longing. + Koestler, Arthur
Age of miracles. + Brunner, John
The age of progress. + Moore, David A.
The Age of Ruin. + Faucette, John M.
The age of science. + Nostradamus, Merlin
The age of the pussyfoot. + Pohl, Frederik
The age of the tail. + Smith, H. Allen
The age-old kingdom. + "Sinbad"
The Agency. + Meltzer, David
The agent. + Meltzer, David
Agent of chaos. + Spinrad, Norman
Agent of entropy. + Siegel, Martin
Agent of T.E.R.R.A., no. 1; The flying saucer gambit.
   + Maddock, Larry
Agent of T.E.R.R.A., no. 2; The Golden Goddess gambit.
   + Maddock, Larry
Agent of T.E.R.R.A., no. 3; The emerald elephant gambit.
   + Maddock, Larry
Agent of the Terran Empire. + Anderson, Poul
Agent of the unknown. + St. Clair, Margaret
Agent of Vega. + Schmitz, James H.
An agent on the other side. + O'Toole, George
Ahasuerus. + Brumm, Charles
Ahead of time. + Gordon, Theodore J. & Harrison, Harry
Ahead of time. + Kuttner, Henry
Ai. + Daniel, Charles.
Aillinn o' my dreams. + Laumer, March
The air battle. + Lang, Herrmann
Air Force. + Harvey, Frank
Air-gods' parade. + Stokes, Simpson
The air killer. + Corbett, James
Air monster. + Green, Edwin
The air pirate. + Gull, Ranger
Air reprisal. + Pollard, A. O.
The Air Trust. + England, George Allan
Airmen over the suburb. + Ramseyer, Edwin
Airplane Boys at Belize. + Craine, E. J.
Airplane Boys at Cap Rock. + Craine, E. J.
Airplane Boys at Platinum River. + Craine, E. J.
Airplane Boys discover the secrets of Cuzco. + Craine,
   E. J.
Airplane Boys flying to Amy-Ran Fastness. + Craine,
   E. J.
Airplane Boys in the Black Woods. + Craine, E. J.
Airplane Boys on the border line. + Craine, E. J.
Airplane Boys with the revolutionists in Bolivia. +
   Craine, E. J.
An airplane in the Arabian nights. + Gould, Arthur Lee
The airs of Earth. + Aldiss, Brian W.
The air-ship, and other stories. + Fletcher, J. S.
The Airship Boys. + Sayler, H. L.
The Airship Boys adrift. + Sayler, H. L.
The Airship Boys due north. + Sayler, H. L.
The Airship Boys in finance. + Sayler, H. L.
The Airship Boys in the barren lands. + Sayler, H. L.
The Airship Boys' ocean flyer. + Sayler, H. L.
Ajaiyi and his inherited poverty. + Tutuola, Amos
Al-Modad. + (Moore, M. Louise)
The alabaster hand, and other ghost stories. + Munby,
   A. N. L.
Aladdin in London. + Hume, Fergus W.
Aladore. + Newbolt, Henry
Alan Fitz-Osborne. + Fuller, Miss
Alaric, galactic diplomat. + Andre, Lee
Alas, Babylon. + Frank, Pat
Alas, that great city. + Ashton, Francis
The Albanian affair. + Theydon, John
Alberic the wise, and other journeys. + Juster, Norton
The Albigenses. + (Maturin, Charles R.)

Albion! Albion! + Morland, Dick

The alchemist. + Balzac, Honore de

Alchemy and academe. + McCaffrey, Anne

The alchemy deception. + Holzer, Hans

Alcyone. + Phillpotts, Eden

Aleriel. + Lach-Szyrma, W. S.

Alexander. + Mann, Klaus

Alfie and me and the ghost of Peter Stuyvesant. + MacKellar, William

An Alfred Bester omnibus. + Bester, Alfred

Alfred Hitchcock presents: 14 of my favorites in suspense. + Hitchcock, Alfred

Alfred Hitchcock presents: more of my favorites in suspense. + Hitchcock, Alfred

Alfred Hitchcock presents: more stories for late at night. + Hitchcock, Alfred

Alfred Hitchcock presents: more stories my mother never told me. + Hitchcock, Alfred

Alfred Hitchcock presents: more stories not for the nervous. + Hitchcock, Alfred

Alfred Hitchcock presents: my favorites in suspense. + Hitchcock, Alfred

Alfred Hitchcock presents: scream along with me. + Hitchcock, Alfred

Alfred Hitchcock presents: stories for late at night. + Hitchcock, Alfred

Alfred Hitchcock presents: stories my mother never told me. + Hitchcock, Alfred

Alfred Hitchcock presents: stories not for the nervous. + Hitchcock, Alfred

Alfred Hitchcock presents: stories that scared even me. + Hitchcock, Alfred

Alfred Hitchcock presents: stories they wouldn't let me do on TV. + Hitchcock, Alfred

Alfred Hitchcock presents: 13 more stories they wouldn't let me do on TV. + Hitchcock, Alfred

Alfred Hitchcock presents: 12 stories for late at night. + Hitchcock, Alfred

Alfred Hitchcock presents: 12 stories they wouldn't let me do on TV. + Hitchcock, Alfred

Alfred Hitchcock's monster museum. + Hitchcock, Alfred

Alfred Hitchcock's supernatural tales of terror and suspense. + Hitchcock, Alfred

Alf's button. + Darlington, W. A.

Alf's carpet. + Darlington, W. A.

Alf's new button. + Darlington, W. A.

Alias Kinson. + Sahula-Dycke, Ignatz

The alias man. + Craig, David

Alibeg the tempter. + Green, William Child

Alice-for-short. + De Morgan, William

Alice in Blunderland. + Bangs, John Kendrick

Alice in Music Land. + La Prade, Ernest

Alice in Orchestra Land. + La Prade, Ernest

Alice in Orchestralia. + La Prade, Ernest

Alice in Rankbustland. + Otterbourg, Edwin M.

Alice in the Delighted States. + Hope, Edward

Alice in Wonderland. + Carroll, Lewis

Alice through the looking-glass. + Carroll, Lewis

Alice's adventures in Cambridge. + Evarts, R. C.

Alice's adventures in Wonderland. + Carroll, Lewis

Alice's adventures in Wonderland; and, Through the looking-glass. + Carroll, Lewis

Alice's world. + Lundwall, Sam J.

The alien. + Davies, L. P.

Alien. + Hughes, Peter Tuesday

The alien. + Jones, Raymond F.

Alien. + Muller, John E.

The alien abductors. + Bevis, H. U.

Alien art. + Dickson, Gordon R.

Alien carnival. + Liebscher, Walt

The alien condition. + Goldin, Stephen

Alien dust. + Tubb, E. C.

The alien Earth. + Elder, Michael

Alien Earth, and other stories. + Elwood, Roger & Moskowitz, Sam

Alien from Arcturus. + Dickson, Gordon R.

An alien from Heaven. + Crane, Nathalia

Alien from the stars. + Fanthorpe, R. L.

Alien from the stars. + Sutton, Jean & Sutton, Jeff

An alien heat. + Moorcock, Michael

Alien horizons. + Nolan, William F.

Alien island. + Sherred, T. L.

Alien landscapes. + Burke, Jonathan

Alien life. + Tubb, E. C.

Alien minds. + Evans, E. Everett

The alien ones. + Brett, Leo

Alien planet. + Pratt, Fletcher

Alien sea. + Rackham, John

Alien skies. + Dagmar, Peter

Alien universe. + Gridban, Volsted

Alien virus. + Rackham, John

The alien way. + Dickson, Gordon R.

Alien world. + Lukens, Adam

Alien worlds. + Elwood, Roger

The alien worlds of Jack London. + Walker, Dale L.

The aliens. + Leinster, Murray

The aliens among us. + White, James

Aliens for neighbours. + Simak, Clifford D.

Aliens 4. + Sturgeon, Theodore

Aliens from space. + Osborne, David

The alkahest. + Balzac, Honore de

All aboard for Ararat. + Wells, H. G.

All about the future. + Greenberg, Martin

All about Venus. + Aldiss, Brian W. & Harrison, Harry

All and everything. + Gurdjieff, G.

All around the Moon. + Verne, Jules

All-Fellows. + Housman, Laurence

All-Fellows; and, The cloak of friendship. + Housman, Laurence

All flesh is grass. + Simak, Clifford D.

All Fools' day. + Cooper, Edmund

All for his country. + Giesy, J. U.

All four winds. + Mundy, Talbot

All Hallow's Eve. + Williams, Charles

All judgement fled. + White, James

All men are mad. + Marcelin, Pierre & Thoby-Marcelin, Philippe

All men are mortal. + Beauvoir, Simone de

All or nothing. + Powys, John Cowper

All our yesterdays. + Warner, Harry Jr.

The all-purpose bodies. + McCutchan, Philip

All right, everybody off the planet! + Ottum, Bob

All souls' night. + Walpole, Hugh

All-stud. + Wells, O. R.

All the colors of darkness. + Biggle, Lloyd Jr.

All the gods of Eisernon. + Lang, Simon

All the myriad ways. + Niven, Larry

All the sounds of fear. + Ellison, Harlan

All the traps of Earth, and other stories. + Simak, Clifford D.

All the trumpets sounded. + Hardy, W. G.

All the wonders we seek. + Marti-Ibanez, Felix

All times possible. + Eklund, Gordon

Allan and the Holy Flower. + Haggard, H. Rider

Allan and the ice-gods. + Haggard, H. Rider

Allan Quatermain. + Haggard, H. Rider

Allan the hunter. + Haggard, H. Rider

Allan's wife. + Haggard, H. Rider

Allan's wife, and other tales. + Haggard, H. Rider

Allegories of the heart. + Hawthorne, Nathaniel

The alley god. + Farmer, Philip Jose

Allisto. + Emersie, John

"All's dross but love." + Lancaster, Albert Edmund

Almoran and Hamet. + Hawkesworth, John
Almost human. + Nolan, William F.
The almost year. + Randall, Florence Engel
Almuric. + Howard, Robert E.
Alone against tomorrow. + Ellison, Harlan
Alone by night. + Congdon, Don & Congdon, Michael
Along came a spider. + Davis, Elizabeth
Along the road to Bethlehem. + Supervielle, Jules
Alph. + Maine, Charles Eric
Alpha Centauri--or die! + Brackett, Leigh
Alpha 5. + Silverberg, Robert
Alpha 4. + Silverberg, Robert
Alpha one. + Silverberg, Robert
Alpha three. + Silverberg, Robert
Alpha two. + Silverberg, Robert
Alpha yes, Terra no! + Petaja, Emil
Alraune. + Ewers, Hanns Heinz
Already walks to-morrow. + Street, A. G.
Alroy. + Disraeli, Benjamin
Alroy; Ixion in Heaven; The infernal marriage; Popa-
    nilla. + Disraeli, Benjamin
Alroy; Popanilla; Count Alarcos; Ixion in Heaven. +
    Disraeli, Benjamin
Alta in the shadows. + de Sackville, Honoria
Altar of evil. + Stevenson, Florence
The altar of the legion. + Bishop, Farnham & Brodeur,
    Arthur Gilchrist
The altar on Asconel. + Brunner, John
The altered ego. + Sohl, Jerry
The alternate Martians. + Chandler, A. Bertram
Alternate orbits. + Chandler, A. Bertram
Alternating currents. + Pohl, Frederik
Alternities. + Gerrold, David
Alton's unguessable. + Sutton, Jeff
Altruria. + Smith, Titus K.
Altzar the pirate. + Chambers, W. Jerome
Always hard! + Amber, Gracie
Always the black knight. + Hoffman, Lee
Amata. + Voss, Richard
Amateur ghost stories. + Fry, H. R.
Amateurs in alchemy. + Deegan, Jon J.
An amazing ancestor. + Scotson-Clark, E. & Scotson-
    Clark, G. F.
The amazing guest. + Watson, Gilbert
The amazing Mr. Blunden. + Barber, Antonia
The amazing Mr. Lutterworth. + Leslie, Desmond
The amazing Mr. Whisper. + Macrow, Brenda G.
An amazing revolution and after. + none
Amazing spectacles! + Godber, Noel
Amazon lunch. + Gustave, Olga
The Amazon strikes again. + Fearn, John Russell
The Amazonian republic. + Savage, Timothy
The Amazons. + Bannet, Ivor
The Amazon's diamond quest. + Fearn, John Russell
The amber city. + Vetch, Thomas
The amber necklace. + Akira
Ambergris Island. + Jackson, Geo. Russell
Ambrosio. + Lewis, M. G.
America betrayed. + Nelson, Albert D.
America fallen! + Walker, J. Bernard
America the menace. + Duhamel, Georges
The American adventurer. + Maguire, Don
The American Emperor. + Salisbury, William
An American emperor. + Tracy, Louis
The American Faust. + Paulton, Edward A.
American ghost stories. + Harper, C. Armitage
American government through science fiction. + Green-
    berg, Martin Harry & Olander, Joseph D. & Warrick,
    Patricia S.
The American Gun Club. + Verne, Jules
American mystery stories. + Wells, Carolyn
American short stories of the nineteenth century. +
    Cournos, John

American utopias. + Lewis, Arthur O. Jr.
America's Secret Service agent. + Carr, Nick
Ames Holbrook, deity. + Runyon, Charles W.
Amid the strife. + Hookham, Albert E.
Amiro. + Rogersohn, William
Ammie, come home. + Michaels, Barbara
Amo. + Denham, Alice
Among the Dangs. + Elliott, George
Among the dead, and other events leading up to the
    Apocalypse. + Bryant, Edward
Among the gnomes. + Hartmann, Franz
Among the immortals in the land of desire. + Fisher,
    Mary A.
The amorous adventures of Margot; and, The scarlet sofa.
    + Fougeret de Monbron
Amorous ghost. + Bessand-Massenet, Pierre
Amorous Philandre. + Galli de Bibiena, Jean
Amos Judd. + Mitchell, J. A.
Amos Meakin's ghost. + Stine, Wilbur Morris
The amphibian. + Belyaev, Alexander
The amphibians. + Wright, S. Fowler
The Amphibion's voyage. + Gillmore, Parker
The Amsirs and the Iron Thorn. + Budrys, Algis
The Amulet. + Blackledge, Katharine Treat
The amulet of Tarv. + Kensett, Percy F.
Analog anthology. + Campbell, John W.
The analog bullet. + Smith, Martin
Analog 8. + Campbell, John W.
Analog 5. + Campbell, John W.
Analog 4. + Campbell, John W.
Analog 9. + Bova, Ben
Analog 1. + Campbell, John W.
Analog 7. + Campbell, John W.
Analog 6. + Campbell, John W.
Analog 3. + Campbell, John W.
Analog 2. + Campbell, John W.
Analogue men. + Knight, Damon
Anarchaos. + Clark, Curt
The ancient Allan. + Haggard, H. Rider
An ancient Englishman. + Wright, Vincent
Ancient, my enemy. + Dickson, Gordon R.
The ancient of days. + Greenfield, Irving A.
Ancient records. + Curties, T. J. Horsley
Ancient sorceries, and other stories. + Blackwood,
    Algernon
Ancient sorceries, and other tales. + Blackwood,
    Algernon
And a new Earth. + Jacomb, C. E.
...And all the stars a stage. + Blish, James
And chaos died. + Russ, Joanna
And flights of angels. + Petaja, Emil
..."And from that day." + Sullivan, Alan
And graves give up their dead. + Pickersgill, Fred-
    erick
And loving it! + Johnston, William
And now the screaming starts. + Case, David
And on the eighth day. + Queen, Ellery
...And others shall be born. + Long, Frank Belknap
And so ends the world. + Pape, Richard
And so forever. + Dunn, Gertrude
"...And some were human." + del Rey, Lester
And the darkness falls. + Karloff, Boris
"And the dead spake--"; and, The horror-horn. + Ben-
    son, E. F.
And the stars remain. + Berry, Bryan
And the waters prevailed. + Barringer, D. Moreau
And then the town took off. + Wilson, Richard
And then you came. + Bridge, Ann
And thus he came. + Brady, Cyrus Townsend
And walk now gently through the fire, and other science
    fiction stories. + Elwood, Roger
And wars shall cease. + Marsh, Carl
Andover and the android. + Wilhelm, Kate

The archer in the arras, and other tales of mystery. + Spence, Lewis
Archibald the Great. + Malcolm, Sibbald & Valentine, Richard
Arctic air terror. + Jackson, G. Gibbard
Arctic bride. + Meek, S. P.
Arctic submarine. + Mars, Alastair
'Ardath.' + Corelli, Marie
Ardor on Aros. + Offutt, Andrew J.
Arena of Antares. + Akers, Alan Burt
The arena women. + Geis, Richard E.
Argal. + (Hadley, George)
"Argentis." + Shaw, Brian
Argle's mist. + Pardoe, Margot
The Argonauts of the Amazon. + Kenyon, Charles R.
Argosy. + Miles, Charles A.
Ariadne and the bull. + Farjeon, Eleanor
Ariel. + Parmele, Mary Platt
Aristokia. + Pezet, A. Washington
Aristopia. + Holford, Castello N.
The ark of Mars. + none
The Ark of the Covenant. + MacClure, Victor
Ark of Venus. + Clason, Clyde B.
Arkham House: the first twenty years. + Derleth, August
The arm of the starfish. + L'Engle, Madeleine
The Armada ghost book. + Bernard, Christine
Armada of the air. + Bentley, Norman
Armageddon. + De Forest, Eleanor
Armageddon. + Waterloo, Stanley
Armageddon 190-. + Seestern
Armageddon 2419 A.D. + Nowlan, Philip Francis
Armata. + (Erskine, Thomas)
Armed camps. + Reed, Kit
Armitage, Armitage, fly away home. + Aiken, Joan
Armoured doves. + Newman, Bernard
The armourer's son. + none
The arms of Phaedra. + Worth, Nigel
The Arms of the Sun. + Mills, Lady Dorothy
The army of the dead. + Steele, Curtis
Army of the undead. + Bernard, Rafe
Aros of Atlantis. + Manley, David L.
Around a distant star. + Delaire, Jean
Around the fire. + Burr, Hanford M.
Around the Moon. + Verne, Jules
Around the world in eighty days. + Verne, Jules
Around the world in eighty hours. + Cook, William Wallace
Arrive at Easterwine. + Lafferty, R. A.
The arrogant mystery of White Ben. + Dane, Clemence
The arrow. + Morley, Christopher
The arrow, and two other stories. + Morley, Christopher
Arrow book of ghost stories. + Kramer, Nora
The Arrow book of horror stories. + none
Arrow book of spooky stories. + Preston, Edna Mitchell
Arsareth. + Warren, B. C.
The arsenal of miracles. + Fox, Gardner F.
The arsenal out of time. + McDaniel, David
Artabanzanus. + Ferrar, William M.
Artery of Fire. + Scortia, Thomas N.
An Arthur C. Clarke omnibus. + Clarke, Arthur C.
An Arthur C. Clarke second omnibus. + Clarke, Arthur C.
Arthur Gordon Pym. + Poe, Edgar Allan
An Arthurian concordance. + Lerond, Dennis
The artificial man. + Davies, L. P.
'As a watch in the night.' + Praed, Mrs. Campbell
As it was written. + Luska, Sidney
As long as tomorrow. + Moore, Bidwell
As on a darkling plain. + Bova, Ben
As the curtain falls. + Chilson, Robert

As tomorrow becomes today. + Sullivan, Charles Wm. III
As we sow. + O'Neill, John
As you were. + Kuttner, Henry
The asbestos society of sinners. + Fogg, Lawrence Daniel
The ascension of Mr. Judson. + Hunter, N. C.
Ashes, ashes. + Barjavel, Rene
Ashes, ashes, we all fall down. + Schram, Irene
The ashes of a god. + Bain, F. W.
The ashes of my heart. + Blinn, Edith
Ashes on the hearth. + Byrne, Cathal O.
Asimov analyzed. + Goble, Neil
The Asimov science fiction bibliography. + Tepper, M. B.
Asimov's mysteries. + Asimov, Isaac
Asleep in armageddon. + Sissons, Michael
Asleep in the afternoon. + Large, E. C.
Asmodeus. + Le Sage, Alain Rene
Aspects of science fiction. + Doherty, G. D.
Assassin of Gor. + Norman, John
The assassination affair. + Holly, J. Hunter
Assassins from tomorrow. + Heath, Peter
Assault. + Camra, Roy
Assault from infinity. + La Salle, Victor
Asses in clover. + O'Duffy, Eimar
The assignation, and other tales. + Poe, Edgar Allan
Assignment in eternity. + Heinlein, Robert A.
Assignment in nowhere. + Laumer, Keith
Assignment in space with Rip Foster. + Savage, Blake
Assignment in tomorrow. + Pohl, Frederik
Assignment Luther. + Wright, Lan
Assignment Nor'Dyren. + Van Scyoc, Sydney
Assignment to disaster. + Aarons, Edward S.
The assimilator. + Bannon, Mark
The Aster disaster. + Young, Alfred Michael
Astera. + Johnson, Ray W.
Asteroid forma. + Le Page, Rand
Asteroid man. + Fanthorpe, R. Lionel
The astonishing adventures of Sig. Gaudentio di Lucca. + (Berington, Simon)
The astonishing stereoscope. + Langton, Jane [see Addendum]
Astounding. + Harrison, Harry
Astounding adventures among the comets. + Verne, Jule
The Astounding-Analog reader, book 1. + Aldiss, Brian W. & Harrison, Harry
The Astounding-Analog reader, book 2. + Aldiss, Brian W. & Harrison, Harry
The Astounding-Analog reader, volume one. + Aldiss, Brian W. & Harrison, Harry
The Astounding-Analog reader, volume two. + Aldiss, Brian W. & Harrison, Harry
The astounding Doctor Yell. + Knight, L. A.
The Astounding science fiction anthology. + Campbell, John W.
Astounding story-key, 1920-1951. + Boggs, D. W.
Astounding tales of space and time. + Campbell, John W.
Astraea's return. + Mercier, Louis-Sebastien
An astral crime. + Burbank, Leone Clark
Astro bubbles. + Field, Marlo
Astro-race. + Lang, King
The astrologer. + Cameron, John
The astrologer. + Hyams, Edward
The astrologer of Chaldea. + Strickland, W. P.
Astron Imago. + Hennings, Jos. P.
The astronauts must not land. + Brunner, John
Astrosex. + Shaw, George
Astyanax. + Brown, Joseph M.
The Asutra. + Vance, Jack
Aswan! + Heim, Michael
Asylum. + Johnston, William

Asylum Earth. + Elliott, Bruce
The asylum world. + Jakes, John
At a winter's fire. + Capes, Bernard
At close of eve. + Scott, Jeremy
At dead of night. + Thomson, Christine Campbell
At Platinum River. + Craine, E. J.
At the back of the north wind. + MacDonald, George
At the defense of Pittsburgh. + Hancock, H. Irving
At the Earth's core. + Burroughs, Edgar Rice
At the Earth's core; Pellucidar; Tanar of Pellucidar.
  + Burroughs, Edgar Rice
At the edge of the world. + Dunsany, Lord
At the end of the world. + Guest, Ernest
At the ghost hour. + Heyse, Paul
At the mountains of madness, and other novels. +
  Lovecraft, H. P.
At the mountains of murkiness, and other parodies. +
  (Locke, George)
At the narrow passage. + Meredith, Richard C.
At the North Pole. + Verne, Jules
At the queen's mercy. + Blodgett, Mabel Fuller
At the Seventh Level. + Elgin, Suzette Haden
At the sign of Sagittarius. + Ince, R. B.
At the sign of the sun. + MacFadyen, Virginia
At the threshold. + Dearborn, Laura
Atalanta. + Richards, Charles Napier
Atalantis. + Morrow, Lowell
Atavar. + Reeve, Arthur B.
Athalie. + Chambers, Robert W.
Athonia. + Schuette, H. George
Athothis. + Minor, Thomas C.
Atla. + Smith, Mrs. J. Gregory
Atlan. + Gaskell, Jane
Atlantean chronicles. + Eichner, Henry M.
Atlanteans. + Odell, Samuel W.
The Atlantic abomination. + Brunner, John
Atlantida. + Benoit, Pierre
Atlantis. + Metchim, D. Bridgman-
Atlantis. + Powys, John Cowper
Atlantis adventure. + Clifford, John
Atlantis rising. + Vigers, Daphne
An atlas of fantasy. + Post, J. B.
Atlas shrugged. + Rand, Ayn
Atman. + Williams, Francis Howard
The atom conspiracy. + Sutton, Jeff
The atom curtain. + Williams, Nick Boddie
Atom-war on Mars. + Tubb, E. C.
Atomic bomb. + Jameson, Malcolm
Atomic death. + Karlson, Hans
Atomic nemesis. + Zeigfreid, Karl
An atomic phantasy. + Capek, Karel
Atomic submarine. + Mars, Alastair
Atomic valley. + Duff, Douglas
An atomic visitor. + Pelton, Guy Cathcart
Atoms. + Knox, G. D. & Wignall, T. C.
Atoms and evil. + Bloch, Robert
Atoms in action. + Sheldon, Roy
The atrocity exhibition. + Ballard, J. G.
Atta. + Bellamy, Francis Rufus
Attack from Atlantis. + del Rey, Lester
Attack from the unseen. + Perry Rhodan 50
Attack on America. + White, Ared
Attar of the ice valley. + Wibberley, Leonard
The attic pretenders. + Kreuder, Ernst
Attraction of the compass. + Dodge, H. L.
Auburn. + Blackstone, Valerius D.
Aurifodina. + Bigly, Cantell A.
Aurilly, the virgin isle. + Garrett, Charles W.
Auriol. + Ainsworth, W. Harrison
The auroraphone. + Cole, Cyrus
The austral globe. + Ramsey, Milton W.
The Australian crisis. + Kirmess, C. H.

Australian science fiction index, 1939-1962. + Stone,
  Graham Brice
Australian science fiction index, 1925-1967. + Stone,
  Graham Brice
Aut diabolus aut nihil, and other tales. + (Field,
  Julian Osgood)
Authentic book of space. + Campbell, H. J.
Authentic science fiction. + Burgess, Brian
The authentic touch. + Wodhams, Jack
An author index to the Doc Savage magazine. + Clark,
  William J.
Authors' choice 2. + none
Authors in paradise. + Griffiths, Alan
Autobiography. + Lovecraft, H. P.
The autobiography of a flea. + none
Autobiography of a flea, book two. + none
Autobiography of a louse. + none
Autobiography of a louse, vol. III. + none
The autobiography of a picture. + Mastin, John
The autobiography of a slander. + Lyall, Edna
The autobiography of Methuselah. + Bangs, John Ken-
  drick
The autobiography of Satan. + Beard, John R.
The autocracy of Mr. Parham. + Wells, H. G.
The automated Goliath. + Temple, William F.
The automaton ear, and other sketches. + McLandburgh,
  Florence
Autopsy for a cosmonaut. + Hay, Jacob & Keshishian,
  John M.
Autosex. + Knerr, Mike
The autumn accelerator. + Leslie, Peter
The Autumn People. + Arthur, Ruth
Avatar. + Gautier, Theophile
Avatar; Jettatura; The water pavilion. + Gautier,
  Theophile
The Avatars. + (Russell, George William)
The Avenger; Black chariots. + Robeson, Kenneth
The Avenger; Death in slow motion. + Robeson, Kenneth
The Avenger; Nevlo. + Robeson, Kenneth
The Avenger; Red moon. + Robeson, Kenneth
The Avenger; River of ice. + Robeson, Kenneth
The Avenger; The black death. + Robeson, Kenneth
The Avenger; The flame breathers. + Robeson, Kenneth
The Avenger; The frosted death. + Robeson, Kenneth
The Avenger; The green killer. + Robeson, Kenneth
The Avenger; The hate master. + Robeson, Kenneth
The Avenger; The purple zombie. + Robeson, Kenneth
The Avenger; The sky walker. + Robeson, Kenneth
The Avenger; Tuned for murder. + Robeson, Kenneth
The Avengers battle the Earth-wrecker. + Binder, Otto
The Avengers #6; "The drowned Queen." + Laumer, Keith
The avengers of Carrig. + Brunner, John
The Avengers; "The magnetic man." + Daniels, Norman
The avenging Martian. + Statten, Vargo
The avenging ray. + Seamark
The avenging ray. + Small, Austin J.
Avernus. + Bond, Mary Bligh
The Avon fantasy reader. + Ernsberger, George &
  Wollheim, Donald A.
Avon fantasy reader, no. 1. + Wollheim, Donald A.
Avon fantasy reader, no. 2. + Wollheim, Donald A.
Avon fantasy reader, no. 3. + Wollheim, Donald A.
Avon fantasy reader, no. 4. + Wollheim, Donald A.
Avon fantasy reader, no. 5. + Wollheim, Donald A.
Avon fantasy reader, no. 6. + Wollheim, Donald A.
Avon fantasy reader, no. 7. + Wollheim, Donald A.
Avon fantasy reader, no. 8. + Wollheim, Donald A.
Avon fantasy reader, no. 9. + Wollheim, Donald A.
Avon fantasy reader, no. 10. + Wollheim, Donald A.
Avon fantasy reader, no. 11. + Wollheim, Donald A.
Avon fantasy reader, no. 12. + Wollheim, Donald A.
Avon fantasy reader, no. 13. + Wollheim, Donald A.

Avon fantasy reader, no. 14. + Wollheim, Donald A.
Avon fantasy reader, no. 15. + Wollheim, Donald A.
Avon fantasy reader, no. 16. + Wollheim, Donald A.
Avon fantasy reader, no. 17. + Wollheim, Donald A.
Avon fantasy reader, no. 18. + Wollheim, Donald A.
Avon ghost reader. + (Williams, Herbert)
Avon science-fiction reader, no. 1. + Wollheim, Donald A.
Avon science-fiction reader, no. 2. + Wollheim, Donald A.
Avon science-fiction reader, no. 3. + Wollheim, Donald A.
The awakening. + Benson, Stella
Awakening. + Foster, George C.
The awakening. + Severy, Melvin L.
The awakening of Noahville. + North, Franklin H.
The awakening of Zojas. + Michelson, Miriam
The Award science fiction reader. + Norton, Alden H.
Away and beyond. + van Vogt, A. E.
Away from the here and now. + Harris, Clare Winger
Awkward magic. + Beresford, Elisabeth
The axe of bronze. + Schmeltzer, Karl
Axel. + Wagner, Geoffrey
Axel Ebersen. + Laurie, A.
Ayesha. + Haggard, H. Rider
Aylwin. + Watts-Dunton, Theodore
The Aztec treasure. + Newton, J. H.
The Aztec treasure-house. + Janvier, Thomas A.

B.E.A.S.T. + Maine, Charles Eric
BEEP. + Owen, George W.
B.U.N.C. + Gray, Frances
Babel. + Burns, Alan
Babel-17. + Delany, Samuel R.
The baby factory. + Rayner, Claire
Baby Weems. + Grant, Joe & Huemer, Dick
Babylon electrified. + Bleunard, A.
Babylonian nights' entertainments. + Kerruish, Jessie Douglas
The Babyons. + Dane, Clemence
The bacillus of beauty. + Stark, Harriet
Back again. + none
Back from the dead. + Waugh, Michael
The back house ghosts. + Sefton, Catherine
Back to life (A.D. 2000). + Fuller, Alvarado M.
Back to the future. + Staniland, Meaburn
Back to the Stone Age. + Burroughs, Edgar Rice
Backdrop of stars. + Harrison, Harry
Backward to the front of the day. + Robson, James
Bad Moon rising. + Disch, Thomas M.
Bad news. + Spike, Paul
Badge of infamy. + del Rey, Lester
Baleful beasts. + Lewis, Gogo & Manley, Seon
The ball and the cross. + Chesterton, G. K.
The Ballad of Beta-2. + Delany, Samuel R.
Ballads in prose. + Hopper, Nora
The ballet of the nations. + Lee, Vernon
The balling machine. + Douglas, Jeff
Ballroom of the skies. + MacDonald, John D.
Balm of Gilead. + Rothery, Agnes
Balzamo the magician. + Dumas, Alexandre
Balthazar. + Balzac, Honore de
Balthazar the Magus. + van der Naillen, A.
The Baltimore Gun Club. + Verne, Jules
The bamboo bloodbath. + Anthony, Piers & Fuentes, Roberto
The ban of the Gubbe. + Waldo, Cedric Dane
The bandaged face. + Ponder, Zita Inez
Bandersnatch. + Ryves, T. E.
The bands of Orion. + Lane, Temple
The Bane of Kanthos. + Dain, Alex
Bang the doll slowly. + Ames, Clyde

The banishment, and three stories. + Stone, Alma
Banking. + Mitchison, G. R.
Bannister's Z-matter. + Carrel, Mark
Bantan and the mermaids. + Gardner, Maurice B.
Bantan fearless. + Gardner, Maurice B.
Bantan incredible. + Gardner, Maurice B.
Bantan primeval. + Gardner, Maurice B.
Banzai! + Parabellum
Baphomet's meteor. + Barbet, Pierre
The bar sinister. + Davis, Richard Harding
Bar the doors. + Hitchcock, Alfred
Barabbas. + Corelli, Marie
Barbarana. + Cleve, John
Barbarian stories. + Mitchison, Naomi
Barbarians of Mars. + Bradbury, Edward P.
The barbarous Britishers. + Traill, H. D.
Barcali the mutineer. + Lampen, C. Dudley
Barefoot in the head. + Aldiss, Brian W.
The Barford cat affair. + Bryan, P. H. H.
A bargain in souls. + Pierson, Ernest de Lancey
The Barge of Haunted Lives. + Tyson, J. Aubrey
The barly fields. + Nathan, Robert
Barnabas Collins. + Ross, Marilyn
Barnabas Collins and Quentin's demon. + Ross, Marilyn
Barnabas Collins and the gypsy witch. + Ross, Marilyn
Barnabas Collins and the mysterious ghost. + Ross, Marilyn
Barnabas Collins versus the warlock. + Ross, Marilyn
Barnabas, Quentin, and Dr. Jekyll's son. + Ross, Marilyn
Barnabas, Quentin, and the avenging ghost. + Ross, Marilyn
Barnabas, Quentin, and the body snatchers. + Ross, Marilyn
Barnabas, Quentin, and the crystal coffin. + Ross, Marilyn
Barnabas, Quentin, and the frightened bride. + Ross, Marilyn
Barnabas, Quentin, and the grave robbers. + Ross, Marilyn
Barnabas, Quentin, and the haunted cave. + Ross, Marilyn
Barnabas, Quentin, and the hidden tomb. + Ross, Marilyn
Barnabas, Quentin, and the mad magician. + Ross, Marilyn
Barnabas, Quentin, and the magic potion. + Ross, Marilyn
Barnabas, Quentin, and the mummy's curse. + Ross, Marilyn
Barnabas, Quentin, and the nightmare assassin. + Ross, Marilyn
Barnabas, Quentin, and the Scorpio curse. + Ross, Marilyn
Barnabas, Quentin, and the sea ghost. + Ross, Marilyn
Barnabas, Quentin, and the serpent. + Ross, Marilyn
Barnabas, Quentin, and the vampire beauty. + Ross, Marilyn
Barnabas, Quentin, and the witch's curse. + Ross, Marilyn
Baron Bruno. + Morgan, Louisa
Baron Munchausen's miraculous adventures on land. + (Raspe, Rudolf)
Baron Munchausen's narrative of his marvellous travels and campaigns in Russia. + (Raspe, Rudolf)
Baron Orgaz. + Lauria, Frank
Baron Trump's marvellous underground journey. + Lockwood, Ingersoll
Baron Verdigris. + Quilp, Jocelyn
The barons of behavior. + Purdom, Tom
Barrier 346. + Zeigfreid, Karl
Barrier unknown. + Merak, A. J.

The best from Fantasy and science fiction, eighth series. + Boucher, Anthony

The best from Fantasy and science fiction, eleventh series. + Mills, Robert P.

The best from Fantasy and science fiction, fifteenth series. + Ferman, Edward L.

The best from Fantasy and science fiction, fifth series. + Boucher, Anthony

The best from Fantasy and science fiction, fourteenth series. + Davidson, Avram

The best from Fantasy and science fiction, fourth series. + Boucher, Anthony

The best from Fantasy and science fiction, nineteenth series. + Ferman, Edward L.

The best from Fantasy and science fiction, ninth series. + Mills, Robert P.

The best from Fantasy and science fiction, second series. + Boucher, Anthony & McComas, J. Francis

The best from Fantasy and science fiction, seventeenth series. + Ferman, Edward L.

The best from Fantasy and science fiction, seventh series. + Boucher, Anthony

The best from Fantasy and science fiction, sixteenth series. + Ferman, Edward L.

The best from Fantasy and science fiction, sixth series. + Boucher, Anthony

The best from Fantasy and science fiction, tenth series. + Mills, Robert P.

The best from Fantasy and science fiction, third series. + Boucher, Anthony & McComas, J. Francis

The best from Fantasy and science fiction, thirteenth series. + Davidson, Avram

The best from Fantasy and science fiction, twelfth series. + Davidson, Avram

The best from Fantasy and science fiction, twentieth series. + Ferman, Edward L.

The best from Galaxy. + none

The best from Galaxy, volume II. + none

The best from If. + none

The best from If, vol. 2. + none

The best from New worlds science fiction. + Carnell, John

The best from New writings in SF, first selection. + Carnell, John

The best from Startling stories. + Mines, Samuel

The best ghost stories. + (French, Joseph Lewis)

The best ghost stories. + Lynch, Bohun

Best ghost stories. + Ridler, Anne

Best ghost stories of Algernon Blackwood. + Blackwood, Algernon

Best ghost stories of J. S. Le Fanu. + Le Fanu, J. Sheridan

Best ghost stories of M. R. James. + James, M. R.

Best horror stories. + Cross, John Keir

The best horror stories. + Le Fanu, Sheridan

Best horror stories three. + Hamilton, Alex

Best horror stories 2. + Cross, John Keir

The best known works of Edgar Allan Poe. + Poe, Edgar Allan

The best known works of Voltaire. + Voltaire

The best laid plans. + Conway, Troy

The best laid schemes. + Eisenberg, Larry

The best of A. E. van Vogt. + van Vogt, A. E.

The best of Amazing. + Ross, Joseph

The best of Arthur C. Clarke. + Clarke, Arthur C.

The best of both worlds. + McHargue, Georgess [see Addendum]

The best of Edgar Allan Poe. + Poe, Edgar Allan

The best of Fantasy and science fiction, twentieth series. + Ferman, Edward L.

The best of Fritz Leiber. + Leiber, Fritz

The best of Isaac Asimov. + Asimov, Isaac

The best of John W. Campbell. + Campbell, John W.

The best of John Wyndham. + Wyndham, John

The best of Kuttner, volume 1. + Kuttner, Henry

The best of Kuttner, volume 2. + Kuttner, Henry

The best of New worlds. + Moorcock, Michael

The best of Robert Heinlein. + Heinlein, Robert A.

The best of SF. + none

The best of sci-fi. + Merril, Judith

The best of sci-fi 5. + Merril, Judith

The best of sci-fi, no. 4. + Merril, Judith

The best of sci-fi (three). + Smith, Cordelia Titcomb

The best of sci-fi 12. + Merril, Judith

The best of sci-fi--two. + Merril, Judith

The best of science fiction. + Conklin, Groff

The best of science fiction 9. + Merril, Judith

The best of science fiction 10. + Merril, Judith

The best of Stanley G. Weinbaum. + Weinbaum, Stanley G.

The best psychic stories. + French, Joseph Lewis

Best SF. + Crispin, Edmund

Best SF five. + Crispin, Edmund

Best SF four. + Crispin, Edmund

Best SF: 1967. + Aldiss, Brian W. & Harrison, Harry

Best SF: 1968. + Aldiss, Brian W. & Harrison, Harry

Best SF: 1969. + Aldiss, Brian W. & Harrison, Harry

Best SF: 1970. + Aldiss, Brian W. & Harrison, Harry

Best SF: 1971. + Aldiss, Brian W. & Harrison, Harry

Best SF: 1972. + Aldiss, Brian W. & Harrison, Harry

Best SF: 1973. + Aldiss, Brian W. & Harrison, Harry

Best SF seven. + Crispin, Edmund

Best SF six. + Crispin, Edmund

Best S.F. stories from New worlds. + Moorcock, Michael

Best S.F. stories from New worlds 8. + Moorcock, Michael

Best S.F. stories from New worlds 5. + Moorcock, Michael

Best S.F. stories from New worlds 4. + Moorcock, Michael

Best S.F. stories from New worlds 7. + Moorcock, Michael

Best S.F. stories from New worlds 6. + Moorcock, Michael

Best S.F. stories from New worlds 3. + Moorcock, Michael

Best S.F. stories from New worlds 2. + Moorcock, Michael

Best SF stories of C. M. Kornbluth. + Kornbluth, C. M.

Best SF three. + Crispin, Edmund

Best SF two. + Crispin, Edmund

Best science fiction for 1972. + Pohl, Frederik

Best science fiction for 1973. + Ackerman, Forrest J.

The best science fiction from Worlds of if magazine. + Pohl, Frederik

The best science fiction of the year. + Carr, Terry

The best science fiction of the year #3. + Carr, Terry

The best science fiction of the year #2. + Carr, Terry

The best science fiction stories. + Bleiler, Everett F. & Dikty, T. E.

The best science fiction stories, fifth series. + Bleiler, Everett F. & Dikty, T. E.

The best science fiction stories, fourth series. + Bleiler, Everett F. & Dikty, T. E.

The best science fiction stories: 1949. + Bleiler, Everett F. & Dikty, T. E.

The best science-fiction stories: 1950. + Bleiler, Everett F. & Dikty, T. E.

The best science-fiction stories: 1951. + Bleiler, Everett F. & Dikty, T. E.

The best science-fiction stories: 1952. + Bleiler,
Everett F. & Dikty, T. E.
The best science-fiction stories: 1953. + Bleiler,
Everett F. & Dikty, T. E.
The best science-fiction stories: 1954. + Bleiler,
Everett F. & Dikty, T. E.
The best science fiction stories, second series. +
Bleiler, Everett F. & Dikty, T. E.
The best science fiction stories, third series. +
Bleiler, Everett F. & Dikty, T. E.
The best science fiction stories and novels: 1955. +
Dikty, T. E.
The best science-fiction stories and novels: 1956. +
Dikty, T. E.
The best science-fiction stories and novels, ninth
series. + Dikty, T. E.
Best science fiction stories of Brian W. Aldiss. +
Aldiss, Brian W.
Best science fiction stories of Brian W. Aldiss (re-
vised edition). + Aldiss, Brian W.
Best science fiction stories of Clifford Simak. +
Simak, Clifford D.
Best science fiction stories of H. G. Wells. + Wells,
H. G.
Best science fiction stories of James Blish. + Blish,
James
Best science fiction stories of James Blish, revised
edition. + Blish, James
Best science fiction stories of the year. + del Rey,
Lester
Best science fiction stories of the year, second annual
collection. + del Rey, Lester
Best science fiction stories of the year, third annual
collection. + del Rey, Lester
The best short stories of M. P. Shiel. + Shiel, M. P.
Best stories of H. G. Wells. + Wells, H. G.
Best supernatural stories of H. P. Lovecraft. + Love-
craft, H. P.
The best supernatural tales of Algernon Blackwood. +
Blackwood, Algernon
The best tales of Edgar Allan Poe. + Poe, Edgar Allan
The best tales of Hoffmann. + Hoffmann, E. T. A.
Best tales of terror. + Crispin, Edmund
Best tales of terror 2. + Crispin, Edmund
The best terrible tales from the French. + T., C. J.
The best terrible tales from the German. + T., C. J.
The best terrible tales from the Italian. + T., C. J.
The best terrible tales from the Spanish. + T., C. J.
Betrayed! + Lindsay, C. McD.
The betrothal of James. + Hannan, Charles
Better days. + Fitch, Anna M. & Fitch, Thomas
A better sunset. + Enck, John Edward
Bettyann. + Neville, Kris
Between planets. + Heinlein, Robert A.
Between the dark and the daylight. + Howells, W. D.
Between the minute and the hour. + Burrage, A. M.
Between two men. + Clark, F. Le Gros
Between two worlds. + Reifsnider, Mrs. Calvin K.
Between worlds. + Smith, Garret
Beware after dark! + Harre, T. Everett
Beware of the cat. + Parry, Michel
Beware of the mouse. + Wibberley, Leonard
Beware the beasts. + Elwood, Roger & Ghidalia, Vic
Beware the god who smiles. + Townsend, Larry
Beware the microrobots. + Perry Rhodan 35
The bewitched. + none
Bewitched. + Barbey D'Aurevilly, J.
Bewitched. + Hine, Al
Bewitched beings. + Lewis, Gogo & Manley, Seon
The bewitched caverns. + Rienow, Leona Train
Bewitched; The opposite uncle. + Johnston, William
Beyond. + (Dardis, Thomas A.)

Beyond. + Sturgeon, Theodore
The beyond. + Sutton, Jean & Sutton, Jeff
Beyond another sun. + Godwin, Tom
Beyond Apollo. + Malzberg, Barry N.
Beyond Apollo. + Sutton, Jeff
Beyond Baker Street. + Jaffee, Irving & Jaffee, Mary
Beyond bedlam. + Guin, Wyman
Beyond belief. + Hurley, Richard J.
Beyond Capella. + Rackham, John
Beyond control. + Silverberg, Robert
Beyond Earth's gates. + Padgett, Lewis & Moore, C. L.
Beyond Eden. + Duncan, David
Beyond geo. + Romilus, Arn
Beyond Hell. + McKenna, Stephen
Beyond human ken. + Merril, Judith
Beyond infinity. + Carr, Robert Spencer
Beyond infinity. + Nourse, Alan E.
Beyond Mars. + Gowland, John Stafford
Beyond the barrier. + Knight, Damon
Beyond the barrier of space. + Torro, Pel
Beyond the barriers of space and time. + Merril,
Judith
Beyond the beyond. + Anderson, Poul
Beyond the black Enigma. + Somers, Bart
Beyond the black ocean. + McGrady, T.
Beyond the blue. + Blake, Stacey
Beyond the bourn. + Fiske, Amos K.
Beyond the Burning Lands. + Christopher, John
Beyond the chains of bondage. + Ross, Raymond George
Beyond the curtain of dark. + Haining, Peter
Beyond the desert. + Noyes, Alfred
Beyond the dragon temple. + Hudson, Robert
Beyond the eleventh hour. + Hough, S. B.
Beyond the end. + Boutelle, Clarence M.
Beyond the end of time. + Pohl, Frederik
Beyond the ether. + Johnson, W. Cairnes
Beyond the farthest star. + Burroughs, Edgar Rice
Beyond the fields we know. + Dunsany, Lord
Beyond the fourth door. + Deegan, Jon J.
Beyond the galactic Rim. + Chandler, A. Bertram
Beyond the galaxy. + Zeigfried, Karl
Beyond the gates. + Phelps, Elizabeth Stuart
Beyond the gates of dream. + Carter, Lin
Beyond the Gates of Hercules. + Trevino, Elizabeth
Borton de
Beyond the golden stair. + Bok, Hannes
Beyond the great oblivion. + England, George Allan
Beyond the great south wall. + Savile, Frank
Beyond the horizon. + Morrill, Fred B.
Beyond the ice. + Murphy, G. Read
Beyond the looking glass. + Cott, Jonathan
Beyond the Moon. + Hamilton, Edmond
Beyond the night. + Woolrich, Cornell
Beyond the Northern Lights. + Wray, Reginald
Beyond the palaeocrystic sea. + Morton, A. S.
Beyond the planet Earth. + Tsiolkovskii, Konstantin
Beyond the range. + Rodney, George B.
Beyond the resurrection. + Eklund, Gordon
Beyond the rim. + Wright, S. Fowler
Beyond the sealed world. + Vale, Rena
Beyond the Selvas. + Fuller, Frederick T.
Beyond the silver sky. + Bulmer, Kenneth
Beyond the snow. + Reed, P. Fishe
Beyond the solar system. + Haley, Claude
Beyond the spectrum. + Thomas, Martin
Beyond the stars. + Cummings, Ray
Beyond the stars, and other stories. + none
Beyond the sunrise. + none
Beyond the swamps. + Tarnacre, Robert
Beyond the Tomorrow Mountains. + Engdahl, Sylvia
Louise
Beyond the vanishing point. + Cummings, Ray

Beyond the veil. + Thanet, Neil
Beyond the visible. + Campbell, H. J.
Beyond the void. + Muller, John E.
Beyond the wall of sleep. + Lovecraft, H. P.
Beyond these suns. + Le Page, Rand
Beyond Thirty. + Burroughs, Edgar Rice
Beyond Thirty; and, The man eater. + Burroughs, Edgar Rice
Beyond this day. + Matthews, E. Paul
Beyond this horizon. + Carrell, Christopher
Beyond this horizon. + Heinlein, Robert A.
Beyond this life. + Borgia, Anthony
Beyond time. + Johns, Marston
Beyond time. + Muller, John E.
Beyond time & space. + Derleth, August
Beyond tomorrow. + Knight, Damon
Beyond Zoaster. + Charles, Neil
Bianca. + Murray, Patricia Hagan & Stevenson, Florence
A bibliographical guide to Soviet fantasy and science fiction, 1957-1968. + Kerr, Stephen T.
Bibliography of adventure. + Day, Bradford M.
A bid for fortune. + Boothby, Guy
"Bietigheim." + Minor, John W.
Big as life. + Doctorow, E. L.
The Big-Ball. + Jones, Frank Earl [see Addendum]
The big ball of wax. + Mead, Shepherd
The big book of mystery stories. + none
Big book of science fiction. + Conklin, Groff
The big broad jump. + Conway, Troy
The Big Eye. + Ehrlich, Max
The big jump. + Brackett, Leigh
Big Planet. + Vance, Jack
The big show. + Laumer, Keith
The big sun of Mercury. + Asimov, Isaac
The big swingers. + Fenton, Robert W.
The Big Time. + Leiber, Fritz
The Big Win. + Miller, Jimmy
The biggest pig in Barbados. + Mankowitz, Wolf
Biggles--charter pilot. + Johns, W. E.
Biker. + Gallion, Jane
Bikey the skicycle, and other tales of Jimmieboy. + Bangs, John Kendrick
Bill, the galactic hero. + Harrison, Harry
Billenium. + Ballard, J. G.
A billion for Boris. + Rodgers, Mary
Billion year spree. + Aldiss, Brian W.
The billionaire. + McCowan, Archibald
Billy and Betty. + Jameson, Twiggs
Binary divine. + Hartridge, Jon
Binary Z. + Rankine, John
Bio-Muton. + Elliot, Lee
Biology "A." + Kent, Brad
The bird of time. + West, Wallace
The bird, The ghoul, and In the name of my friend. + Easson, Robert
The bird watcher. + Morris, Joe Alex
The birds. + Baker, Frank
The birds, and other stories. + du Maurier, Daphne
The birds-of-a-feather affair. + Avallone, Michael
The birth of freedom. + Salisbury, H. B.
The birthmark, and other stories. + Hawthorne, Nathaniel
The birthright of mankind. + Cassatt, Dave
The Bishop of Hell, and other stories. + Bowen, Marjorie
The bishop of the Ozarks. + Howard, Milford W. [see Addendum]
The bishop's wife. + Nathan, Robert
Bison of clay. + Begouen, Max
A bit of Atlantis. + Erskine, Douglas
The bite of monsters. + O'Neil, Dennis
The bitter pill. + Chandler, A. Bertram

Bizarre and arabesque. + Poe, Edgar Allan
Bizarre honeymoon. + Steiger, Brad
Bizzy-Quizzy the Great. + Bowker, William Rushton
Black abyss. + Powers, J. L.
The black amulet. + Tracy, Don
Black and blue magic. + Snyder, Zilpha Keatley
Black August. + Wheatley, Dennis
The Black Avengers. + Statten, Vargo
Black bargain. + Statten, Vargo
The black box. + Oppenheim, E. Phillips
The black cap. + Asquith, Cynthia
The black cat. + Poe, Edgar Allan
The black cat, and other short stories. + Poe, Edgar Allan
The black cat, and other stories. + Poe, Edgar Allan
The black cat, and other tales. + Poe, Edgar Allan
The Black Cauldron. + Alexander, Lloyd
Black chariots. + Robeson, Kenneth
The black circle. + Baines, Cuthbert Edward
The Black Cloud. + Hoyle, Fred
The black corridor. + Moorcock, Michael
Black crusade. + Machen, Arthur
Black dawn. + Desmond, Shaw
The black death. + Dalton, Moray
The black death. + Robeson, Kenneth
The black dog. + Goff, Georgena
The black door. + Wilcox, Collin
The black Douglas. + Crockett, S. R.
Black Easter. + Blish, James
The Black Flame. + Weinbaum, Stanley G.
The black fortnight. + Hall, G. Rome
The black fox. + Heard, Gerald
The black galaxy. + Leinster, Murray
The black girl in search of God, and other lesser tales. + Shaw, George Bernard
Black gods, green islands. + Harshman, Tom & Holder, Geoffrey
The black hand. + Reeve, Arthur B.
Black Heart and White Heart; and, Elissa. + Haggard, H. Rider
Black Heart and White Heart, and other stories. + Haggard, H. Rider
Black Heart and White Heart; and, The wizard. + Haggard, H. Rider
Black hearts in Battersea. + Aiken, Joan [see Addendum]
Black Honey. + Saxon, Peter
Black in time. + Jakes, John
Black infinity. + Brett, Leo
Black infinity. + Cameron, Berl
Black invaders vs. the Battle Birds. + Bowen, Robert Sidney
Black is a man. + Roskolenko, Harry
Black is the color. + Brunner, John
Black Legion of Callisto. + Carter, Lin
Black light. + Mundy, Talbot
Black lightning. + Bowen, Robert Sidney
The black loch. + Leitch, Patricia [see Addendum]
Black magic. + Bowen, Marjorie
Black magic. + Ward, Don
The black magic omnibus. + Wheatley, Dennis
The black mass. + Breton, Frederic
The black mass. + Krassnoff, Peter N.
Black mass maiden. + Laurentz, Townsend
The black master. + Grant, Maxwell
Black medicine. + Burks, Arthur J.
The black mirror. + Duke, Winifred
The black monk. + (Rymer, James Malcolm)
The Black Mountains. + Saberhagen, Fred
Black no more. + Schuyler, George S.
The black opal. + Ash, Fenton
Black opium. + Farrere, Claude

Bomba the jungle boy at the giant cataract. + Rockwood, Roy

Bomba the jungle boy at the moving mountain. + Rockwood, Roy

Bomba the jungle boy in a strange land. + Rockwood, Roy

Bomba the jungle boy in the abandoned city. + Rockwood, Roy

Bomba the jungle boy in the land of burning lava. + Rockwood, Roy

Bomba the jungle boy in the perilous kingdom. + Rockwood, Roy

Bomba the jungle boy in the steaming grotto. + Rockwood, Roy

Bomba the jungle boy in the swamp of death. + Rockwood, Roy

Bomba the jungle boy on Jaguar Island. + Rockwood, Roy

Bomba the jungle boy on terror trail. + Rockwood, Roy

Bomba the jungle boy on the underground river. + Rockwood, Roy

Bomba the jungle boy trapped by the cyclone. + Rockwood, Roy

Bombardment of Scarbro' by the Russian fleet in 1891. + Untruthful Thomas

Bombs from the murder wolves. + Hogan, Robert J.

Bombs in orbit. + Sutton, Jeff

Bonanza. + Henham, Ernest G.

Bond of the fire. + Fon Eisen, Anthony

Bone people. + Bamman, Henry & Odell, William & Whitehead, Robert

"Bones and I." + Whyte-Melville, G. J.

Bonfires and broomsticks. + Norton, Mary

The Bongleweed. + Cresswell, Helen

The book of Algoonah. + (Newcomb, Cyrus)

A book of bargains. + O'Sullivan, Vincent

The book of Brian Aldiss. + Aldiss, Brian W.

The book of clever beasts. + Reed, Myrtle

The book of dragons. + Nesbit, E.

The book of Frank Herbert. + Herbert, Frank

The book of Fritz Leiber. + Leiber, Fritz

The book of Fu Manchu. + Rohmer, Sax

A book of ghosts. + Baring-Gould, S.

The book of Gordon Dickson. + Dickson, Gordon R.

A book of islands. + Bowman, John S.

A book of miracles. + Hecht, Ben

A book of modern ghosts. + Asquith, Cynthia

The Book of Paradox. + Cooper, Louise

The book of Philip Jose Farmer. + Farmer, Philip Jose

The book of Philip K. Dick. + Dick, Philip K.

The book of Poe. + Poe, Edgar Allan

The book of Ptath. + van Vogt, A. E.

A book of queer stories. + none

The book of Rack the Healer. + Hughes, Zach

The Book of Skulls. + Silverberg, Robert

The Book of Stier. + Sanborn, Robin

The book of strange loves. + Bloch, Regina Miriam

A book of strange sins. + Kernahan, Coulson

A book of strange stories. + van Thal, Herbert

The book of strangers. + Dallas, Ian

The book of the serpent. + Howard, Katharine

Book of the three dragons. + Morris, Kenneth

Book of the werewolf. + Frost, Brian J.

The Book of Three. + Alexander, Lloyd

The book of van Vogt. + van Vogt, A. E.

The book of wonder. + Dunsany, Lord

The Books of the Emperor Wu Ti. + Meckauer, Walter

The boosted man. + Zetford, Tully

Border, breed, nor birth. + Reynolds, Mack

Border ghost stories. + Pease, Howard

The border line. + Masterman, Walter S.

Border of darkness. + Latimer, John

Border war. + Jones, J. B.

Borderline. + Vercors

Bored of the rings. + Beard, Henry N. & Kenney, Douglas C.

The Boris Karloff horror anthology. + Karloff, Boris

Boris Karloff presents Tales of the frightened. + Avallone, Michael

Boris Karloff's favorite horror stories. + Karloff, Boris

Born again. + Lawson, Alfred William

Born in captivity. + Berry, Bryan

Born in space. + Donson, Cyril

Born leader. + McIntosh, J. T.

Born of flame. + Peeke, Margaret B.

Born of Luna. + Statten, Vargo

Born of man and woman. + Matheson, Richard

Born to the purple. + Ward, Margarete

Born under Mars. + Brunner, John

Born with the dead. + Silverberg, Robert

Borrobil. + Dickinson, W. Croft

A borrowed month, and other stories. + Stockton, Frank R.

The Borrowers. + Norton, Mary

The Borrowers afield. + Norton, Mary

The Borrowers afloat. + Norton, Mary

The Borrowers aloft. + Norton, Mary

The Borrowers omnibus. + Norton, Mary

"The bote upon the watter." + Stamper, Joseph

Both sides of the veil. + Marsh, Richard

The bottle imp. + Stevenson, Robert Louis

The bottle imp; and, The isle of voices. + Stevenson, Robert Louis

Bound for Mars. + Ballou, Arthur W.

The bound man, and other stories. + Aichinger, Ilse

Bound together. + Conway, Hugh

Bow down to nul. + Aldiss, Brian W.

Bowering's breakwater. + McCutchan, Philip

The bowl of night. + Liston, Edward

The box from Japan. + Keeler, H. S.

The Box of delights. + Masefield, John

The boy adventurers in the land of the monkey men. + Verrill, A. Hyatt

The boy aviators in Nicaragua. + Lawton, Wilbur

Boy beyond the Moon. + Allum, Tom

The boy galloper. + (James, Lionel)

The boy inventors and the vanishing gun. + Bonner, Richard

The boy inventors' diving torpedo boat. + Bonner, Richard

The boy inventors' electric hydroaeroplane. + Bonner, Richard

The boy inventors' flying ship. + Bonner, Richard

The boy inventors' radio-telephone. + Bonner, Richard

The boy inventors' wireless triumph. + Bonner, Richard

The Boy Scouts' Craig Kennedy. + Reeve, Arthur B.

The Boy Scout's year book of ghost and mystery stories. + Mathiews, Franklin K.

The boy who could fly. + Newman, Robert

The boy who discovered the truth. + Felsen, Henry Gregor

The boy who had the power. + Sutton, Jean & Sutton, Jeff

The boy who saw tomorrow. + Niall, Ian

The boy with the bronze axe. + Fidler, Kathleen

The boyhood days of Guy Fawkes. + none

The Boys' life book of outer space stories. + none

Boys' sport and adventure stories. + none

The boys who vanished. + Carson, John F.

The bra-burner's brigade. + Knight, Mallory T.

Brad's flying saucer. + Place, Marian T.

The Braille film. + Weissner, Carl

The brain. + Harrison, Michael

The building of the city beautiful. + Miller, Joaquin
The building of Thelema. + Ashbee, C. R.
The bull and the spear. + Moorcock, Michael
The bull on the bench. + Mason, Lowell B.
Bullard of the Space Patrol. + Jameson, Malcolm
Bulo and Lele. + Bretnall, George H.
The bump on Brannigan's head. + Connolly, Myles
Bumsider. + MacApp, C. C.
A bundle of lies. + Castletown, Lord
Bungay Castle. + Bonhote, Mrs.
The burgled heart. + Leroux, Gaston
The buried country. + Hardy, Philip
The buried mystery. + Mendham, Clement A.
Burn witch burn! + Merritt, A.
The burning. + Gunn, James E.
The burning ring. + Burdekin, Kay
Burning sands. + Glossop, Reginald
The burning sky. + Roberts, James Hall
Burning void. + Magroon, Vector
The burning world. + Ballard, J. G.
Burnt offerings. + Marasco, Robert
Burroughs' science fiction. + Kudlay, Robert R. &
  Leiby, Joan
The burrowers beneath. + Lumley, Brian
Bury him darkly. + Blackburn, John
The bus that vanished. + Groc, Leon
Busy bodies. + Martin, Ed
But gently day. + Nathan, Robert
But soft--we are observed! + Belloc, Hilaire
The Butterfly Kid. + Anderson, Chester
Butterfly planet. + High, Philip E.
Button brains. + Clouston, J. Storer
By aeroplane to the Sun. + Horner, Donald W.
By air express to Venus. + Rockwood, Roy
By airship to Ophir. + Ash, Fenton
By airship to the tropics. + Walker, Rowland
By and by. + Maitland, Edward
By daylight only. + Thomson, Christine Campbell
By firelight. + Pargeter, Edith [see Addendum]
By furies possessed. + White, Ted
By horror haunted. + Fremlin, Celia
By rocket to the Moon. + Gail, Otto Willi
By space ship to Saturn. + Rockwood, Roy
By space ship to the Moon. + Gibbons, Gavin
By Stygian waters. + Maby, J. Cecil
By Thames and Tiber. + Gowing, Mrs. Aylmer
By the gods beloved. + Orczy, Baroness
By the light of the Green Star. + Carter, Lin
By then mankind ceased to exist. + Van Mierlo, H. A.
By this strange fire. + Pargeter, Edith [see Adden-
  dum]
Bye-ways. + Hichens, Robert S.
Bypass to otherness. + Kuttner, Henry
The byworlder. + Anderson, Poul

C.O.D. Mars. + Tubb, E. C.
Cabinet pudding. + Young, Bertram Alfred
Cabriba. + Hanaranda, Mulla
Cabu. + Russell, John Robert
Cache from outer space. + Farmer, Philip Jose
The cadaver of Gideon Wyck. + Laing, Alexander
Cadwallader. + Lynes, Russell
Caesar's column. + Boisgilbert, Edmund
Caesar's column. + Donnelly, Ignatius
Cage a man. + Busby, F. M.
Cagliostro. + Guenther, Johannes von
Cairo dawns. + Mitchell, J. Leslie
Calculated risk. + Maine, Charles Eric
Caleb Catlum's America. + McHugh, Vincent
The calends of Cairo. + Mitchell, J. Leslie
The calibrated alligator, and other science fiction
  stories. + Silverberg, Robert

California three hundred and fifty years ago. + (Cole,
  Cornelius)
Call for an exorcist. + Bixby, Jerome
Call me Ishtar. + Lerman, Rhoda
The call of Peter Gaskell. + Wallis, George C.
The call of the cosmos. + Tsiolkovsky, K.
The call of the hand, and other stories. + Golding,
  Louis
The call of the island. + Warr, Charles L.
The call of the Phoenix. + Thomas, Dorothy
The call of the planets. + Patterson, James Ernest
  William
Call of the savage. + Kline, Otis A.
The call of the wild; The scarlet plague; Tales of the
  fish patrol. + London, Jack
The call of the wild; White fang; The scarlet plague.
  + London, Jack
The call of utopia. + Williams, Eric C.
The caller of the black. + Lumley, Brian
Calling Captain Future. + Hamilton, Edmond
Calling Doctor Kill! + Sugar, Andrew
Calling Thunderbirds. + Theydon, John
Calno, the super-man. + Finney, Lewis E.
The caltraps of time. + Masson, David I.
The Camberwell miracle. + Beresford, J. D.
The Cambri plot. + Moffatt, James
The Camford Visitation. + Wells, H. G.
Camille 2,000. + Grant, Sebastian
Camp concentration. + Disch, Thomas M.
Camperdown. + (Griffith, Mary)
Can such things be? + Bierce, Ambrose
"Can such things be?" + Fleming, Keith
Can you feel anything when I do this? + Sheckley,
  Robert
Canape-Vert. + Marcelin, Pierre & Thoby-Marcelin,
  Philippe
Canary in a cat house. + Vonnegut, Kurt
The cancer machine. + Binder, Eando
Cancerqueen, and other stories. + Landolfi, Tommaso
Candace. + Brennan, Alice
Candide, and other tales. + Voltaire
Candide; and, Zadig. + Voltaire
Candide, Zadig, and selected stories. + Voltaire
The candle and the tower. + Spector, Robert D.
A candle in her room. + Arthur, Ruth M.
Candle in the sun. + Wells, Robert
The candle virgins. + Baillie-Saunders, Margaret
Candleleer. + Wilson, William
Candles in the dark. + Black, Dorothy
Candy Man. + King, Vincent
The canopy of time. + Aldiss, Brian W.
The Canterville ghost. + Wilde, Oscar
A canticle for Leibowitz. + Miller, Walter M. Jr.
The canyon. + Schaefer, Jack
The canyon, and other stories. + Schaefer, Jack
Capable of honor. + Drury, Allen
The capacity and extent of the human understanding. +
  (Kirkby, John)
The Cape. + Caidin, Martin
The caperberry bush. + Guinn, Jack
A capillary crime, and other stories. + Millet, F. D.
The capricorn, and other fantasy stories. + Prosser,
  H. L.
Captain American; The great gold steal. + White, Ted
Captain Black. + Pemberton, Max
Captain Future and the Space Emperor. + Hamilton,
  Edmond
Captain Future's challenge. + Hamilton, Edmond
Captain Gardiner of the International Police. + Allen,
  Robert
Captain Ishmael. + Griffith, George
Captain Kiddle. + Fleming, A. M.

Caxton's book. + Rhodes, W. H.
Cecilia. + Crawford, F. Marion
Cecilia de Noel. + Falconer, Lanoe
The cedar box. + Oxenham, John
Cee-Tee man. + Morgan, Dan
The celebrated "Moon story." + (Locke, Richard Adams)
Celestalia. + Pullar, A. L.
Celestia. + Lull, D.
The celestial blueprint, and other stories. + Farmer, Philip Jose
The celestial hand. + Vincent, Joyce
The celestial omnibus. + Bramah, Ernest
The celestial omnibus, and other stories. + Forster, E. M.
The celestial railroad, and other stories. + Hawthorne, Nathaniel
The cell, and other tales of horror. + Case, David
Celluloid suicide. + Valdez, Paul
Cemetery world. + Simak, Clifford D.
The centaur. + Blackwood, Algernon
The centaur passes. + Boulenger, E. G. & White, Percy
The Centauri device. + Harrison, M. John
The Centaurians. + Biagi, L. D.
The centenarians. + Phelps, Gilbert
The centenary Poe. + Poe, Edgar Allan
CenterForce. + Waters, T. A.
Central passage. + Schoonover, Lawrence
Centuries apart. + Bouve, Edward T.
A century of creepy stories. + none
A century of ghost stories. + none
A century of great short science fiction novels. + Knight, Damon
A century of horror stories. + Wheatley, Dennis
A century of science fiction. + Knight, Damon
Century of the manikin. + Tubb, E. C.
Century of thrillers. + none
A century of thrillers, from Poe to Arlen. + none
A century of thrillers, second series. + none
Ceremony of innocence. + Webster, Elizabeth Charlotte
The certain hour. + Cabell, James Branch
A certain man. + Onions, Oliver
The certainty of a future life in Mars. + Gratacap, L. P.
Chain reaction. + Hodder-Williams, Christopher
Chains. + Barbusse, Henri
Chains of the sea. + Silverberg, Robert
Chalet Diabolique. + Coffman, Virginia
Chalk face. + Frank, Waldo
The chalk giants. + Roberts, Keith
Challenge. + Bulmer, H. K.
The challenge. + Byers, Albert F. & Mangels, Arthur C.
The challenge. + Dudley, Eustace
The challenge of Aab. + Sperry, J. E.
Challenge of the unknown. + Perry Rhodan 32
Chamber of horrors. + Bloch, Robert
A chamber of horrors. + Hadfield, John
The Chameleon Corps, & other shape changers. + Goulart, Ron
Chamiel. + Pearson, Edward
Champagne Charlie. + Franklin, Jay
The Champion of Garathorm. + Moorcock, Michael
The champion of virtue. + (Reeve, Clara)
Chances and changes. + Burdett, Charles
The change. + Foster, George C.
The change-child. + Curry, Jane Louise
A change in the cabinet. + Belloc, H.
Change of heart. + Allan, Mea
A change of mind. + Glaskin, Gerald M.
Change of mind. + Stratton, Chris
Change song. + Hoffman, Lee
Change the sky, and other stories. + St. Clair, Margaret

The changeling. + Higgins, Margaret
The changeling. + van Vogt, A. E.
Changeling Earth. + Saberhagen, Fred
The changeling worlds. + Bulmer, Kenneth
Changes. + Perry, Richard
The Channel Tunnel. + Cassandra
Chaos. + Bell, Thornton
Chaos. + Desmond, Shaw
The chaos fighters. + Williams, Robert Moore
Chaos in Arcturus. + Zeigfried, Karl
The chaos spawn. + Adams, Fred C.
Chapayeca. + Edmondson, G. C.
Chapters for the orthodox. + Marquis, Don
Chapters from future history. + McCauley, Motly Ranke
Chariot into time. + Zeigfried, Karl
The chariot of the flesh. + Peek, Hedley
The chariot of the Sun. + Pocock, Roger
Chariots of fire. + Parry, Michel & Rusoff, Garry
The Chariots of Ra. + Bulmer, Kenneth
The charity ghost. + Gallon, Tom
Charles Dickens's stories from the Christmas numbers of "Household words" and "All the year round," 1852-1867. + Dickens, Charles
Charlotte sometimes. + Farmer, Penelope
The charwoman's shadow. + Dunsany, Lord
The chase of the golden meteor. + Verne, Jules
Chattering gods. + Crawley, Rayburn
Chaucer, the flying saucer. + Malcolm, Mary
Cheap thrills. + Goulart, Ron
Cheating the devil. + Burbridge, Juanita Cassil
A checklist of Astounding. + Jeeves, B. T.
A checklist of Australian fantasy. + Larnach, S. L.
The checklist of fantastic literature. + Bleiler, Everett F.
The checklist of fantastic literature in paperbound books. + Day, Bradford M.
A checklist of fantastic magazines. + Day, Bradford M.
A checklist of Poul Anderson. + Peyton, Roger G.
A checklist of Science fiction adventures (British edition). + Peyton, Roger G.
A checklist of science-fiction anthologies. + Cole, W. R.
Checkpoint Lambda. + Leinster, Murray
The cheetah girl. + Blayre, Christopher
The chemical baby. + Clouston, J. Storer
Chessboard planet. + Padgett, Lewis
The chessmen of Mars. + Burroughs, Edgar Rice
Chetwynd Calverley. + Ainsworth, W. Harrison
The chickadees. + Hyers, Conrad [see Addendum]
The child buyer. + Hersey, John
Child Christopher and Goldilind the Fair. + Morris, William
Child in the dark. + Timperley, Rosemary
Child of storm. + Haggard, H. Rider
The child of the dawn. + Benson, Arthur Christopher
The Childermass, section I. + Lewis, Wyndham
Childhood's end. + Clarke, Arthur C.
The children of despair. + Creasey, John
The children of Green Knowe. + Boston, L. M.
The children of hate. + Creasey, John
Children of infinity. + Elwood, Roger
The children of light. + Lawrence, H. L.
The children of Llyr. + Walton, Evangeline
Children of Morrow. + Hoover, H. M.
Children of the atom. + Shiras, Wilmar H.
Children of the griffin. + Giles, Elizabeth
Children of the lens. + Smith, E. E.
Children of the morning. + George, W. L.
Children of the night. + Blackburn, John
The Children of the Pool, and other stories. + Machen, Arthur

The city without a name. + Moody, H. A.
The city without Jews. + Bettauer, Hugo
A cityless and countryless world. + Olerich, Henry
The Civil War of 1915. + Brex, J. Twells
Civil War II. + Britain, Dan
Claimed. + Stevens, Francis
Claire Lenoir. + Villiers de L'Isle-Adam
The clairvoyant. + Lothar, Ernst
The clairvoyante. + Farjeon, B. L.
The clans of darkness. + Haining, Peter
Clans of the Alphane moon. + Dick, Philip K.
Clara in Blunderland. + Lewis, Caroline
Claret, sandwiches, and sin. + Donne, Maxim
Claret, sandwiches, and sin. + Duke, Madeleine
Clarimonde. + Gautier, Theophile
Clarimonde, and other stories. + Gautier, Theophile
Clarimonde, vampire and harlot. + Gautier, Theophile
Clarion. + Wilson, Robin Scott
Clarion III. + Wilson, Robin Scott
Clarion II. + Wilson, Robin Scott
Clark Clifford's body. + Fearing, Kenneth
Clash by night. + O'Donnell, Lawrence
Clash of angels. + Daniels, Jonathan
A clash of cymbals. + Blish, James
Clash of star-kings. + Davidson, Avram
Classics of the horror film. + Everson, William K.
Claudius the bee. + Leeming, John F.
Claus the fish. + Rossmann, Hermann
Claws of the night. + Hansen, Vern
The cleansing of the "Lords." + Wintle, Harold
A clear case of the supernatural. + Lucas, Reginald
Clearing the seas. + Haines, Donal Hamilton
The Cleft. + Tabori, Paul
Cleomenes. + Warrington, Maris
Cleopatra. + Gautier, Theophile
Cleopatra. + Haggard, H. Rider
Clickwhistle. + Watkins, William Jon
The Climacticon. + Livingston, Harold
The Climbing Doom. + Young, Laurence Ditto
The clipper of the clouds. + Verne, Jules
Cloak of Aesir. + Campbell, John W.
The clock of time. + Finney, Jack
The clock strikes twelve. + Wakefield, H. Russell
The clocks of Iraz. + de Camp, L. Sprague
The clocks of Rondaine, and other stories. + Stock-
ton, Frank R.
The Clockwork man. + Odle, E. V.
A clockwork orange. + Burgess, Anthony
Clockwork's pirates. + Goulart, Ron
Clone. + Cowper, Richard
The clone. + Thomas, Theodore L. & Wilhelm, Kate
The Clones. + Olemy, P. T.
Cloning. + Shear, David
Close to critical. + Clement, Hal
The Closed Worlds. + Hamilton, Edmond
The cloud. + McAuley, Jacquelin Rollit
The cloud-catcher. + Crist, Eda & Crist, Richard
The cloud chamber. + Masters, Dexter [see Addendum]
The cloud crasher. + Willard, Mildred Wilds
The Cloud Forest. + North, Joan
The cloud king. + Hayward, William S.
Cloud on silver. + Christopher, John
The Cloud Walker. + Cooper, Edmund
The clouded mirror. + Kranz, E. Kirker
Clovis. + Fessier, Michael
Club Tycoon sends man to Moon. + Mendelsohn, Felix Jr.
A clutch of vampires. + McNally, Raymond T.
The Clutching Hand. + Reeve, Arthur B.
The cocked connection. + Blake, Kevin
The cockeyed cuties. + Conway, Troy
Code duello. + Reynolds, Mack
Code Three. + Raphael, Rick

The coils of time. + Chandler, A. Bertram
The Coins of Murph. + Kelley, Leo P.
Cold death. + Robeson, Kenneth
The cold embrace, and other stories. + Hamilton, Alex
The cold flame. + Reeves, James
Cold Harbour. + Young, Francis Brett
Cold terror. + Chetwynd-Hayes, R.
Cold war in a country garden. + Gutteridge, Lindsay
Cold war in Hell. + Blamires, Harry
Colin. + Benson, E. F.
Colin II. + Benson, E. F.
The collapse of Homo sapiens. + Graham, P. Anderson
Collected editorials from Analog. + Campbell, John W.
Collected ghost stories. + Freeman, Mary E.
The collected ghost stories of M. R. James. + James,
M. R.
The collected ghost stories of Oliver Onions. + Onions
Oliver
Collected short stories. + Benson, Stella
Collected short stories of E. M. Forster. + Forster,
E. M.
Collected stories. + O'Brien, Fitz-James
The collected stories of Bertrand Russell. + Russell,
Bertrand
The collected tales of E. M. Forster. + Forster, E. M.
Collected tales, volume one. + Pain, Barry
The collected writings of Ambrose Bierce. + Bierce,
Ambrose
A collection of ghosts. + Bevan, C. Elnith
A collection of prose and poetry on the theme of to-
morrow. + Madsen, Alan L.
A college mystery. + Baker, A. P.
Collision course. + Bayley, Barrington J.
Collision course. + Silverberg, Robert
The Colonel and the Quaker. + Cabeen, F. von A.
Colonel Markesan, and less pleasant people. + Derleth,
August & Schorer, Mark
Colonel Mint. + West, Paul
Colonel to princess. + Germains, Victor Wallace
The colonel's photograph. + Ionesco, Eugene
Colonial survey. + Leinster, Murray
Colonists of space. + Carr, Charles
The colors of space. + Bradley, Marion Zimmer
Colossus. + Jones, D. F.
The colour out of space, and others. + Lovecraft, H.
P.
A Columbus of space. + Serviss, Garrett P.
Come again. + Digby, Lee
Come and get me, and other uncanny invitations. +
Walter, Elizabeth
Come and go. + Coles, Manning
Come back, Lucy. + Sykes, Pamela
Come, come, come! + Stark, Ben
Come, hunt an Earthman. + High, Philip E.
Come like shadows. + Murray, D. L.
Come Nineveh, come Tyre. + Drury, Allen
"Come not, Lucifer!" + (Verner, Gerald)
Come slo, Devlin. + Flanner, Jack
The comet kings. + Hamilton, Edmond
Comet 'Z.' + Weston, George
The Cometeers. + Williamson, Jack
The comforter. + Bryant, D. M.
The comic inferno. + Aldiss, Brian W.
Comic tales of Edgar Allan Poe. + Poe, Edgar Allan
Coming attractions. + Greenberg, Martin
The coming conflict of nations. + Fitzpatrick, Ernest
Hugh
The coming conquest of England. + Niemann, August
The coming Cromwell. + M., J. W.
The coming hour. + Blakemore, F. J.
The coming of a king. + Evans, I. O.
The coming of Conan. + Howard, Robert E.

Contraband rocket. + Correy, Lee
Convention annual, no. 1; Pittcon edition. + Klein,
    Jay Kay
Convention annual, no. 2; Chicon III edition. + Klein,
    Jay Kay
Convention annual, no. 3; Discon edition. + Klein,
    Jay Kay
Convention annual, no. 4; Tricon edition. + Klein,
    Jay Kay
Conversations with a corpse. + Dennis, Robert C.
Cooking out of this world. + McCaffrey, Anne
A cool million. + West, Nathanael
A cool million; The dream life of Balso Snell. + West,
    Nathanael
The cool of the evening. + Horsnell, Horace
Coolman. + Shepard, Jane
The Copenhagen affair. + Oram, John
The copper disc. + Stead, Robert J. C.
The copulation explosion. + Gray, Rod
The coral island. + Reynolds, George W. M.
Corbie. + Newman, Robert
The Corfu affair. + Phillifent, John T.
A corner in sleep, and other impossibilities. + Kel-
    lett, E. E.
The Cornish pixie affair. + Leslie, Peter
Cornish tales of terror. + Chetwynd-Hayes, R.
The corpse sat up. + Glenning, Raymond
Corpus Earthling. + Charbonneau, Louis
The corridors of time. + Anderson, Poul
Corridors of time. + Deegan, Jon J.
Corruption. + Saxon, Peter
Cosmic calamity. + Luigi, Belli
Cosmic checkmate. + De Vet, Charles V. & MacLean,
    Katherine
The cosmic computer. + Piper, H. Beam
Cosmic conquest. + Blair, Adrian
Cosmic crusade. + Saxon, Richard
The cosmic decoy. + Perry Rhodan 21
Cosmic Echelon. + Cameron, Berl
Cosmic Engineers. + Simak, Clifford D.
Cosmic exodus. + Holt, Conrad G.
The cosmic eye. + Reynolds, Mack
The cosmic flame. + Statten, Vargo
The cosmic gash. + Kainen, Ray
The cosmic geoide, and one other. + Taine, John
Cosmic laughter. + Haldeman, Joe W.
Cosmic manhunt. + de Camp, L. Sprague
The cosmic puppets. + Dick, Philip K.
Cosmic rape. + Bennett, Jeff
The cosmic rape. + Sturgeon, Theodore
The cosmic spies. + McIntosh, J. T.
Cosmic traitor. + Perry Rhodan 26
Cosmicomics. + Calvino, Italo
The Cosmozoids. + Tralins, Robert
Costello, psychic investigator. + Nicholson, John
Costigan's Needle. + Sohl, Jerry
Couching at the door. + Broster, D. K.
Coulson goes south. + Mann, Jack
The Council of Justice. + Wallace, Edgar
Count Brass. + Moorcock, Michael
Count-down. + Maine, Charles Eric
Count Dracula's Canadian affair. + Fredrick, Otto
Count Luna. + Lernet-Holenia, Alexander
Count Luna; and, Baron Bagge. + Lernet-Holenia,
    Alexander
Count Omega. + Berners, Lord
Count Roderic's castle. + none
Countdown. + Becker, Kurt
Countdown for Cindy. + Engle, Eloise
Countdown 1000. + Mariner, David
Countdown to doomsday. + Quest, Rodney
Counter-clock world. + Dick, Philip K.

Countercommandment, and other stories. + Campbell,
    John W.
The counterfeit man. + Nourse, Alan E.
Counterfeit world. + Galouye, Daniel F.
The Counterfeits. + Kelley, Leo P.
Counterparts. + Baum, Tom
Countess Dracula. + Parry, Michel
Country love and poison rain. + Tate, Peter
The country of the blind. + Wells, H. G.
The country of the blind, and other stories. + Wells,
    H. G.
Court intrigues in a collection of original letters
    from the island of the New Atalantis. + (Manley,
    Mary)
The court of Belshazzar. + Williams, Earl
The court of Lucifer. + Gallizier, Nathan
The court of the stone children. + Cameron, Eleanor
Courtships in the air. + Lorensen, Charles
The coven. + 7 St. John, David
The Coxeman #7; Last licks. + Conway, Troy
Coxeman #8; Keep it up, Rod! + Conway, Troy
Coxeman #10; The best laid plans. + Conway, Troy
Coxeman #12; Had any lately? + Conway, Troy
Coxeman #13; Whatever goes up. + Conway, Troy
Coxeman #17; The big broad jump. + Conway, Troy
Coxeman #18; The sex machine. + Conway, Troy
Coxeman #19; The blow-your-mind job. + Conway, Troy
Coxeman #20; The cunning linguist. + Conway, Troy
Coxeman #25; It's not how long you make it. + Conway,
    Troy
Coxeman #26; Son of a witch. + Conway, Troy
Coxeman #28; A stiff proposition. + Conway, Troy
Coxeman #31; The cockeyed cuties. + Conway, Troy
Coxeman 34; A hard man is good to find. + Conway, Troy
A crab was crushed. + Graham, Harvey
The crack in space. + Dick, Philip K.
The crack in the wall. + Houblon, Grahame
A crack in time. + Carrel, Mark
The crack of doom. + Cromie, Robert
The cracked looking glass. + Schulman, L. M.
Cradle of the Sun. + Stableford, Brian M.
The craft of terror. + Haining, Peter
A crafty foe. + Nisbet, Hume
The Craghold creatures. + Noone, Edwina
The Craghold crypt. + Noone, Edwina
The Craghold curse. + Noone, Edwina
The Craghold legacy. + Noone, Edwina
Craig Kennedy, detective. + Reeve, Arthur B.
Craig Kennedy listens in. + Reeve, Arthur B.
Craig Kennedy on the farm. + Reeve, Arthur B.
Crashing suns. + Hamilton, Edmond
Crater of fear. + Moore, Patrick
Crazy mixed-up planet. + Fritch, Charles E.
The cream of the jest. + Cabell, James Branch
The cream of the jest; The lineage of Lichfield. +
    Cabell, James Branch
The Creator. + Simak, Clifford D.
The creature from beyond infinity. + Kuttner, Henry
Creature from the black lagoon. + Statten, Vargo
A creature of the twilight. + Kirk, Russell
Creature reader. + Arneson, D. J.
Creatures of light and darkness. + Zelazny, Roger
Creatures of the abyss. + Leinster, Murray
Creatures of the mist. + Hansen, Vern
Credulity Island. + Watson, Frederick
Creep, shadow! + Merritt, A.
Creep, shadow, creep! + Merritt, A.
The creeping plague. + MacGregor, Richard
The creeping shroud. + Wright, Lan
Creeps. + none
Creeps by night. + Hammett, Dashiell
Creeps medley. + Hervey, Michael

The "Creeps" omnibus. + none
Cresten, Queen of the Toltus. + Shaw, W. J.
The crew of the Mekong. + Ludodyanov, I. & Voiskunsky, E.
The cricket in Times Square. + Selden, George
Crime flies. + Luigi, Belli
Crime prevention in the 30th century. + Santesson, Hans Stefan
A criminal Croesus. + Griffith, George
The crimson capsule. + Coblentz, Stanton A.
The crimson caterpillar. + Griffin, Sercombe
Crimson doom. + Bowen, Robert Sidney
Crimson planet. + Muller, John E.
The crimson rope. + Asbury, Herbert
The crimson serpent. + Robeson, Kenneth
The Crimson Witch. + Koontz, Dean R.
Crisis. + Elwood, Roger
Crisis in 2140. + McGuire, John J. & Piper, H. Beam
Crisis! 1992. + Herbert, Benson
Crisis on Cheiron. + Coulson, Juanita
Crisis 2000. + Maine, Charles Eric
The crock of gold. + Stephens, James
Cromwell the Third. + Parnell, John
The crook who wasn't there! + Valdez, Paul
The croquet player. + Wells, H. G.
Cross double cross. + Masefield, Lewis
The cross of Carl. + Owen, Walter
The cross of gold affair. + Davies, Fredric
Crossroads in time. + Conklin, Groff
The crossroads of time. + Norton, Andre
Crossroads to nowhere. + Stark, Raymond
Crotty Shinkwin. + Coppard, A. E.
The crown of Asia. + George, Vernon
Crown of infinity. + Faucette, John M.
A crowned queen. + Grier, Sydney C.
Croyd. + Wallace, Ian
The Cruachan and the Killane. + Cristabel
Crucible Island. + Pallen, Conde B.
Crucible of evil. + Long, Lyda Belknap
The crucible of power. + Greenberg, Martin
The crucified city. + Van Greenaway, Peter
The cruise of the anti-torpedo. + none
The cruise of the Conqueror. + Paternoster, G. Sidney
The cruise of the Crystal Boat. + Stables, Gordon
The cruise of the "Flying Fish." + Collingwood, Harry
The cruise of the gyro-car. + Strang, Herbert
The cruise of the Snowbird. + Stables, Gordon
The cruise of the "Vengeful." + Stables, Gordon
The cruiser on wheels. + Thorne, Guy
Crusoe Warburton. + Germains, Victor Wallace
The cry. + Garratt, Evelyn R.
Cry horror! + Lovecraft, H. P.
Cry of the beast. + Norwood, Victor
Cry Shadow! + Grant, Maxwell
Cry wolf! + Roxbury, Kyle
Crybaby of the western world. + Leonard, John
The crying child. + Michaels, Barbara
Cryptozoic! + Aldiss, Brian W.
A crystal age. + Hudson, W. H.
The crystal and the sphinx. + Sladen, Douglas
The crystal button. + Thomas, Chauncey
The crystal cave. + Stewart, Mary
The crystal city. + Laurie, Andre
The crystal city under the sea. + Laurie, Andre
Crystal clear. + Cadell, Elizabeth
The Crystal Globe. + Glossop, Reginald
The crystal gryphon. + Norton, Andre
The crystal horde. + Taine, John
The crystal man. + Mitchell, Edward Page
The crystal sceptre. + Mighels, Philip Verrill
The crystal world. + Ballard, J. G.
The cube root of uncertainty. + Silverberg, Robert

The cuckoo tree. + Aiken, Joan [see Addendum]
Culmination. + Furnill, John
Cult of shame. + Calvano, Tony
The cunning linguist. + Conway, Troy
A cup of life. + White, Jay C.
A cupful of space. + Clingerman, Mildred
Cupid Napoleon. + LaMaster, Slater
The cure. + Ferris, Paul
A cure for cancer. + Moorcock, Michael
Cure for death. + Valentine, Victor
The curious adventures of a field cricket. + Candeze, Ernest
The curious and entertaining adventures and travels by sea and land of the renowned Baron Munchausen. + (Raspe, Rudolf)
The curious book of Clampus. + none
The curious culture of the planet Loretta. + Palmer, William J.
The curious lobster. + Hatch, Richard W.
The curious lobster's island. + Hatch, Richard W.
The currents of space. + Asimov, Isaac
The Curry experiment. + Rayner, A. A.
The curse of blood. + none
The curse of Collinwood. + Ross, Marilyn
The curse of Dracula, and other terrifying tales. + Higham, Charles
The curse of intellect. + none
The curse of Khatra. + Jacobs, T. C. H.
The curse of Leo. + Lory, Robert
Curse of planet Kuz. + van Loden, Erle
The curse of Quintana Roo. + Gardner, Matt
The curse of Rathlaw. + Saxon, Peter
The curse of the Concullens. + Stevenson, Florence
The curse of the lion. + Webster, F. A. M.
Curse of the mummy. + Luigi, Belli
The curse of the snake. + Boothby, Guy
The curse of the undead. + Carter, M. L.
The curse of the wise woman. + Dunsany, Lord
The curse of Yig. + Bishop, Zealia Brown
Cursed. + England, George Allan
Cursed be the treasure. + Drake, H. B.
A cursory view of the history of Lilliput for these last forty three years. + none
Curtain of mist. + Pardoe, M.
The curve of the snowflake. + Walter, W. Grey
Custodian of ghosts. + Ogden, George W.
The cyberiad. + Lem, Stanislaw
The cybernetic brains. + Jones, Raymond F.
Cybernetic controller. + Bulmer, H. K. & Clarke, A. V.
Cybernia. + Cameron, Lou
Cyborg. + Caidin, Martin
Cyborg #2; Operation Nuke. + Caidin, Martin
Cybro sex. + Lynn, David
Cycle of fire. + Clement, Hal
Cycle of nemesis. + Bulmer, Kenneth
Cyclops in the sky. + Roberts, Lionel
The Cynic's desperate mission. + Kaner, H.
The czar of fear. + Robeson, Kenneth

D-99. + Fyfe, H. B.
D'Abra the Buddhist. + Lonsdale, H. M.
Dacobra. + Burland, Harris
The Dagger affair. + McDaniel, David
The dagger in the sky. + Robeson, Kenneth
Dagon, and other macabre tales. + Lovecraft, H. P.
The Dakota Project. + Beeching, Jack
The Daleth effect. + Harrison, Harry
The Dalkey archive. + O'Brien, Flann
Dalleszona and the seventh treasure. + Wright, Allen Kendrick
Dam of death. + Pearl, Jack

Dambala calls. + Possendorf, Hans
Dame Fortune smiled. + Barnes, Willis
Damnation Alley. + Zelazny, Roger
Damnation of Mr. Zinkler. + Sutton, Graham
Damned. + (Dorrance, Ethel)
The dams can break. + Christian, Emeline Fate
Dan Dare on Mars. + Dawson, Basil
Dan Owen and the angel Joe. + Mitchell, Ronald
Dan Yeo. + Binns, Ottwell
The dance of death, and other tales. + Blackwood, Algernon
The dance of Genghis Cohn. + Gary, Romain
Dance of the dwarfs. + Household, Geoffrey
Dance of the golden calf. + Endrey, Eugene
Dance the eagle to sleep. + Piercy, Marge
Dance with the devil. + Schwab, Gunther
The dancer from Atlantis. + Anderson, Poul
The Dancers of Noyo. + St. Clair, Margaret
The dancing dead. + Thomas, Eugene
The Dancing Floor. + Buchan, John
The Danecourt romance. + Wells, George
Danger! and other stories. + Doyle, A. Conan
Danger below! + Blaine, John
Danger: dinosaurs! + Marsten, Richard
Danger from Vega. + Rackham, John
Danger--human. + Dickson, Gordon R.
Danger in deep space. + Rockwell, Carey
Danger Moon. + MacCreigh, James
Danger planet. + Sterling, Brett
Dangerous love. + Farley, Ralph Milne
Dangerous visions. + Ellison, Harlan
Dangerous visions #1. + Ellison, Harlan
Dangerous visions #3. + Ellison, Harlan
Dangerous visions #2. + Ellison, Harlan
Dangerous visions, vol. 1. + Ellison, Harlan
Dangerous waters. + Williams, Islwyn
Danny Dunn and the anti-gravity paint. + Abrashkin, Raymond & Williams, Jay
Danny Dunn and the automatic house. + Abrashkin, Raymond & Williams, Jay
Danny Dunn and the fossil cave. + Abrashkin, Raymond & Williams, Jay
Danny Dunn and the heat ray. + Abrashkin, Raymond & Williams, Jay
Danny Dunn and the homework machine. + Abrashkin, Raymond & Williams, Jay
Danny Dunn and the smallifying machine. + Abrashkin, Raymond & Williams, Jay
Danny Dunn and the swamp monster. + Abrashkin, Raymond & Williams, Jay
Danny Dunn and the voice from space. + Abrashkin, Raymond & Williams, Jay
Danny Dunn and the weather machine. + Abrashkin, Raymond & Williams, Jay
Danny Dunn, invisible boy. + Abrashkin, Raymond & Williams, Jay
Danny Dunn on a desert island. + Abrashkin, Raymond & Williams, Jay
Danny Dunn on the ocean floor. + Abrashkin, Raymond & Williams, Jay
Danny Dunn, time traveller. + Abrashkin, Raymond & Williams, Jay
Dar Tellum. + Berry, James R.
Darab's wine-cup, and other tales. + Kennedy, Bart
Darby O'Gill and the good people. + Templeton, Herminie
Darby O'Gill and the Little People. + Watkin, Lawrence Edward
Dare. + Farmer, Philip Jose
The daring trip to the Moon. + Nizzi, Guido "Skipper"
Dark Andromeda. + Merak, A. J.
Dark Atlantis. + Craigie, David

The dark beasts. + Long, Frank Belknap
Dark Boundaries. + Lorraine, Paul
The dark brotherhood, and other pieces. + (Derleth, August)
Dark carnival. + Bradbury, Ray
"Dark Centauri." + Zeigfried, Karl
The dark chamber. + Cline, Leonard
The dark city. + none
Dark conflict. + Merak, A. J.
Dark continuum. + Muller, John E.
Dark December. + Coppel, Alfred
Dark destiny. + Reid, C. Lestock
The dark destroyers. + Wellman, Manly Wade
The dark dimensions. + Chandler, A. Bertram
The dark dominion. + none
Dark dominion. + Duncan, David
The dark enemy. + Holly, J. Hunter
Dark entries. + Aickman, Robert
The dark fantastic. + Echard, Margaret
The dark frontier. + Ambler, Eric
The dark gateway. + Burke, Jonathan
The dark glass. + Cost, March
The dark gods. + Mills, Dorothy
Dark harvest. + Creasey, John
Dark inferno. + White, James
The dark intruder, and other stories. + Bradley, Marion Zimmer
The dark is rising. + Cooper, Susan
The dark light years. + Aldiss, Brian W.
Dark magic. + Norday, Michael
The dark man. + Chetwynd-Hayes, R.
The Dark Man, and others. + Howard, Robert E.
Dark menace. + Birkin, Charles
The dark millennium. + Merak, A. J.
The dark mind. + Kapp, Colin
Dark mind, dark heart. + Derleth, August
The dark mirror. + Vance, Louis Joseph
Dark moon. + Vivian, Francis
Dark music, and other spectral tales. + Snow, Jack
Dark odyssey. + Stevenson, Florence
The dark of the soul. + Ward, Don
Dark of the woods. + Koontz, Dean R.
The dark on the other side. + Michaels, Barbara
The dark other. + Weinbaum, Stanley G.
Dark piper. + Norton, Andre
The dark planet. + Holly, J. Hunter
Dark planet. + Rackham, John
The dark pool. + Rienow, Leona Train
The dark portal. + Furnell, John
The dark returners. + Brennan, Joseph Payne
The dark river. + Springer, Norman
Dark sanctuary. + Gregory, H. B.
Dark Satanic. + Bradley, Marion Zimmer
Dark shadows. + Ross, Marilyn
The Dark shadows book of vampires and werewolves. + Collins, Barnabas & Collins, Quentin
The dark side. + Knight, Damon
The dark side of Earth. + Bester, Alfred
Dark side of Venus. + Macartney, Clem
The dark star. + Cost, March
Dark star. + Foster, Alan Dean
The dark star of Itza. + Malkus, Alida Sims
Dark stars. + Silverberg, Robert
Dark stories from the sunny south. + Campbell, Gilbert
The dark stranger. + Charques, Dorothy
The dark symphony. + Koontz, Dean R.
Dark things. + Derleth, August
Dark tides. + Russell, Eric Frank
The dark twin. + Campbell, Marion
Dark universe. + Galouye, Daniel F.
Dark ways to death. + Saxon, Peter

Daybreak. + Cowan, James
Daybreak...2250 A.D. + Norton, Andre
The daybreakers. + Curry, Jane Louise
Daymares. + Brown, Fredric
The days after tomorrow. + Santesson, Hans Stefan
The days of glory. + Stableford, Brian M.
The days of their youth. + Sullivan, Alan
Daze, the magician. + Baerlein, Anthony
The dead astronaut. + (Russell, Ray)
Dead hard. + Thomas, Evan
Dead knowledge. + none
The dead live. + Perry Rhodan 48
A dead man's diary. + Kernahan, Coulson
The dead man's message. + Marryat, Florence
A dead president makes answer to The President's daughter. + Jenks, Anton Shrewsbury
The dead riders. + O'Donnell, Elliott
The dead sailor, and other stories. + Robinson, J. C.
The dead world. + none
Deadline to Pluto. + Statten, Vargo
The deadly Dutchman. + Blaine, John
The deadly dwarf. + Robeson, Kenneth
Deadly image. + Cooper, Edmund
Deadly litter. + White, James
The deadly sky. + Jorgensen, Ivar
The deadly sun. + MacGregor, Richard
A deal with the devil. + Phillpotts, Eden
Deals with the devil. + Davenport, Basil
Dear guest and ghost. + Dee, Sylvia
Death Angel's Shadow. + Wagner, Karl Edward
The death box. + Lecale, Errol
The death box. + Tolstoi, Alexei
Death by apparition. + Campbell, Reginald
Death Cell. + Goulart, Ron
Death dimension. + Barry, Ray
The death flash. + Rowe, John G.
Death goes hunting. + Massie, Chris
The death gong. + Jepson, Selwyn
The Death Guard. + Chadwick, Philip George
Death has no weight. + Luigi, Belli
Death in silver. + Robeson, Kenneth
Death in slow motion. + Robeson, Kenneth
Death in the mind. + Estabrooks, G. H. & Lockridge, Richard
Death into life. + Stapledon, Olaf
Death is a dream. + Tubb, E. C.
Death is a habit. + Kensch, Otto
Death is a ruby light. + Kenyon, Paul
The death maker. + Small, Austin J.
The death-mask, and other ghosts. + Everett, Mrs. H. D.
The death master. + Appel, Benjamin
Death Merchant; Laser war. + Rosenberger, Joseph
Death of a cosmonaut. + Hay, Jacob & Keshishian, John M.
Death of a nurse. + Whitten, Leslie H.
Death of a world. + Farjeon, J. Jefferson
The death of grass. + Christopher, John
The death of metal. + Suddaby, Donald
The death of the Fuhrer. + Puccetti, Roland
Death of the last taxpayer. + Lowe, Arthur
Death of the Moon. + none
Death of the vampire baroness. + Van der Elst, Violet
Death on a warm wind. + Warner, Douglas
Death over London. + Wheeler-Nicholson, Malcolm
Death rattle. + Gobsch, Hanns
The death ray dictator, and other stories. + Titterton, W. R.
The death rays of Ardilla. + Johns, W. E.
Death rocks the cradle. + Martens, Paul
The death ship. + Russell, W. Clark
The death star. + Bridges, T. C.

Death swamp, and other adventure stories. + Portwin, E. T.
Death, the knight, and the lady. + Stacpoole, H. de Vere
The death tower. + Grant, Maxwell
The death trap. + Cole, Robert William
The deathless Amazon. + Fearn, John Russell
Death's deputy. + Hubbard, L. Ron
Death's loving arms, and other terror tales. + Hanlon, Jon
Deathstar voyage. + Wallace, Ian
The deathstones. + Arch, E. L.
Deathworld. + Harrison, Harry
Deathworld 1. + Harrison, Harry
Deathworld 3. + Harrison, Harry
The Deathworld trilogy. + Harrison, Harry
Deathworld 2. + Harrison, Harry
De Bracy's drug. + Gridban, Volsted
The debt. + Robinson, G. P.
A decade of Fantasy and science fiction. + Mills, Robert P.
The decadence. + Macaulay, L.
Decameron, 1965. + Rosenfield, Joe Jr.
Decision at Doona. + McCaffrey, Anne
The decline and fall of the British Empire. + Lang-Tung
The decline and fall of the British Empire. + (Mills, Elliott E.)
The decline and fall of the British Empire. + (Watson, H. C. M.)
The decoy. + Dana, Francis
De-creation. + Statten, Vargo
The deep blue ice. + Day, Langston
The deep fix. + Colvin, James
Deep freeze. + Burke, Jonathan
Deep freeze. + Butler, Joan
The deep gods. + Mason, David
Deep in the sky. + Nielsen, Helga
The deep range. + Clarke, Arthur C.
The deep reaches of space. + Chandler, A. Bertram
Deep space. + Russell, Eric Frank
Deep space. + Silverberg, Robert
Deep throat. + Perkins, D. M.
Deep throat, part II. + Perkins, D. M.
Deep waters. + Hodgson, William Hope
Deeper than the darkness. + Benford, Greg
The deer-smellers of Haunted Mountain. + Meyer, John J.
Defiance. + Bulmer, Kenneth
The defiant agents. + Norton, Andre
Degree XII. + Daventry, Leonard
Deirdre. + Stephens, James
Del Palma. + Kellino, Pamela
The delicate ape. + Hughes, Dorothy B.
Deliver me from Eva. + Bailey, Paul
Della-Wu, Chinese courtesan. + Owen, Frank
Delphic echo. + Livingston, Marjorie
The deluge. + Payne, Robert
Deluge. + Wright, S. Fowler
Delusion world. + Dickson, Gordon R.
Dementia. + Parnell, Keith
The Demetrian. + Harding, Ellison
A demigod. + (Jackson, Edward Payson)
The demigods. + Bennett, Alfred Gordon
Demigods. + Biggs, John Jr.
The demi-gods. + Stephens, James
The demi-wang. + Long, Peter
The demi-wang; and, The sex club. + none
The demolished man. + Bester, Alfred
The demon breed. + Schmitz, James H.
Demon kind. + Elwood, Roger
The demon lover. + Fortune, Dion

The devil's diamond. + none
The devil's diary. + Elshemus, Louis M.
Devils' drums. + Meik, Vivian
The devil's elixir. + Hoffmann, E. T. A.
The devil's elixirs. + Hoffmann, E. T. A.
The devil's finger. + Irvine, A. A.
Devil's food. + Mason, David
The devil's generation. + Ghidalia, Vic
The Devil's Gold. + Day, Oscar F. G.
The Devil's Guard. + Mundy, Talbot
The devil's henchmen. + Oldrey, John
The devil's highway. + Lebar, John & Wright, Harold
  Bell
The devil's hunting-ground. + Blamires, Harry
The devil's letters to Mary MacLane. + MacLane, Mary
The devil's mistress. + Brodie-Innes, J. W.
The devil's mistress. + Coffman, Virginia
The devil's motor. + Corelli, Marie
The devil's note book. + Bainbridge, Oliver
The devil's own. + Wilson, Ellsworth
The devil's own dear son. + Cabell, James Branch
Devil's peak. + Ball, Brian
Devil's planet. + Wellman, Manly Wade
The devil's playground. + Robeson, Kenneth
The devil's pronoun, and other phantasies. + Robert-
  son, Frances Forbes
The devil's saint. + Deamer, Dulcie
Devil's scrapbook. + Bixby, Jerome
The devil's spoon. + DuBois, Theodora
The devil's throne. + Whiteley, Elizabeth
The devil's tool. + Bradley, George
Devil's Tor. + Lindsay, David
The devil's virgin. + Coffman, Virginia
Devlin the barber. + Farjeon, B. L.
The devolutionist; and, The emancipatrix. + Flint,
  Homer Eon
The Devouring Fire. + Statten, Vargo
Le diable boiteux. + (Le Sage, Alain Rene)
Diaboliad, and other stories. + Bulgakov, Mikhail
The diabolist. + Fairman, Paul W.
The diabolists. + Arthur, Wallace
The Diabols. + Mackelworth, R. W.
The dial of Ahaz. + Vaughan, H. M.
Dialogues of the dead. + (Lyttleton, Lord)
Dialogues with the devil. + Caldwell, Taylor
The diamond in the window. + Langton, Jane [see
  Addendum]
The diamond lens. + none
The diamond lens. + O'Brien, Fitz-James
The diamond lens, with other stories. + O'Brien,
  Fitz-James
The diamond master. + Futrelle, Jacques
The diamond queen. + Reeve, Arthur B.
Diamonds are for dying. + Kenyon, Paul
Dian of the lost land. + Marshall, Edison
Diane. + Lafond
The diary of a baby. + Pain, Barry
The diary of Jean Evarts. + Stocking, Charles Francis
Diary of the War of the Pig. + Bioy Casares, Adolfo
A Dick for all seasons. + Kane, Pablo
Dick Tracy. + Johnston, William
Dido, Queen of Hearts. + Atherton, Gertrude
A different world. + Elder, Michael
Digging the love goddess. + Martin, Jay
A digit of the Moon. + Bain, F. W.
A digit of the Moon, and other love stories from the
  Hindoo. + Bain, F. W.
Digits and dastards. + Pohl, Frederik
Dilation effect. + Mason, Douglas R.
Dimension A. + Davies, L. P.
Dimension 4. + Conklin, Groff
Dimension of dreams. + Lord, Jeffrey

Dimension of horror. + Bounds, S. J.
Dimension of Illion. + Heine, Irving
Dimension of miracles. + Sheckley, Robert
Dimension search. + Perry Rhodan 60
Dimension thirteen. + Silverberg, Robert
Dimension X. + Knight, Damon
Dingo. + Scott, J. M.
Dinosaur Beach. + Laumer, Keith
The dinosaur's egg. + Candler, Edmund
Dion and the Sibyls. + Keon, Miles Gerald
The Diothas. + Thiusen, Ismar
The diploids. + MacLean, Katherine
The Dirdir. + Vance, Jack
A directory of science fiction and fantasy publishing
  houses and book dealers. + Tymn, Marshall
Dirge for a dead witch. + Duke, Winifred
The dirty rotten depriving ray. + Knight, Mallory T.
Dirty son of a witch. + Jacobson, Sid
The disappearance. + Wylie, Philip
The disappearance of the 7 teenage Aquarians. + Baugh-
  man, Grace A.
The disappearance syndicate; and, Senator Stanley's
  story. + Crawford, T. C.
The disappearing future. + Hay, George
The disaster area. + Ballard, J. G.
Disciples of darkness. + Gordon, D. M.
Disclosures in scarlet. + Jacobi, Carl
The discovered country. + Petersilea, Carlyle
The discovered country. + von Himmel, Ernst
Discoveries in fantasy. + Carter, Lin
The discovery of the dead. + Upward, Allen
The Disentanglers. + Lang, Andrew
The disintegrator. + Brown, Charles R. & Morgan,
  Arthur
The disk. + Robinson, E. A. & Wall, G. A.
The disorientated man. + Saxon, Peter
The dispossessed. + Le Guin, Ursula K.
The Dissentizens. + Condray, Bruno G.
The distant lurs. + Behn, Harry
Distant worlds. + Mader, Friedrich
Disturbers of the peace. + Harger, Catharine &
  Pritcher, Leon
The disturbing affair of Noel Blake. + Bell, Neil
The divan. + Crebillon le Fils
Divide and rule. + de Camp, L. Sprague
The dividing of time. + Sewell, Elizabeth
The divine gift. + Lewis, R. M.
The divine passion. + Fisher, Vardis
The divine seal. + Orcutt, Emma Louise
The diving dames affair. + Leslie, Peter
D'Mars affinity. + Bloomer, J. M.
Do androids dream of electric sheep? + Dick, Philip K.
Doc Savage: his apocalyptic life. + Farmer, Philip
  Jose
Doctor Arnoldi. + Thayer, Tiffany
Dr. Artz. + Hichens, Robert
Doctor Baxter's invention. + Kelly, William Patrick
Dr. Berkeley's discovery. + Pratt, Cornelia Atwood
  & Slee, Richard
Dr. Bloodmoney. + Dick, Philip K.
Dr. Caligari's black book. + Haining, Peter
Dr Cunliffe, investigator. + Frankish, H.
Dr. Cyclops. + none
Dr. Cyclops. + Garth, Will
Doctor Death; The gray creatures. + Zorro
Doctor Death; The shriveling murders. + Zorro
Doctor Death; 12 must die. + Zorro
Doctor Fogg. + Matson, Norman
Dr. Futurity. + Dick, Philip K.
Doctor Grimshaw's secret. + Hawthorne, Nathaniel
Dr. Hades. + Russell, Arthur
Dr. Heidenhoff's process. + Bellamy, Edward

Doomsday, 1999. + MacTyre, Paul
Doomsday on Ajiat. + Jones, Neil R.
The doomsday planet. + Vincent, Harl
Doomsday square. + Taylor, Ray Ward
Doomsday Wing. + Smith, George H.
Doomsman. + Ellison, Harlan
The Doomsman. + Sutphen, Van Tassel
Doomstar. + Hamilton, Edmond
The door ajar, and other stories. + Milward, Virginia
The door in the wall, and other stories. + Wells,
   H. G.
The door into summer. + Heinlein, Robert A.
The door of beyond. + St. John-Loe, Gladys
The door of darkness. + Annesley, Maude
Door of desire. + Taylor, Ann
The door of the unreal. + Biss, Gerald
The door through space. + Bradley, Marion Zimmer
Door to anywhere. + Pohl, Frederik
The door unlatched. + Cher, Marie
The doors of his face, the lamps of his mouth, and
   other stories. + Zelazny, Roger
Doorway into time, and other stories. + Moskowitz,
   Sam
Doorways to space. + Wells, Basil
Doppelgangers. + Heard, H. F.
The Double Axe. + Haggard, Audrey
A double bed on Olympus. + Ames, Delano
The Double:Bill symposium. + Bowers, Bill & Mallardi,
   Bill
Double, double. + Brunner, John
Double exposure. + Fleischman, Theo
Double identity. + none
Double illusion. + High, Philip E.
Double in space. + Pratt, Fletcher
The double invaders. + Rackham, John
Double jeopardy. + Pratt, Fletcher
The double life. + Leroux, Gaston
The double life of Mr. Alfred Burton. + Oppenheim,
   E. Phillips
The double man. + Binder, Eando
The double man. + Dowd, F. B.
The double-minded man. + Arch, E. L.
Double phoenix. + (Carter, Lin)
The double shadow, and other fantasies. + Smith,
   Clark Ashton
Double spell. + Lunn, Janet
Double star. + Heinlein, Robert A.
Double vision. + Gerson, Noel B.
The doubtful disciple. + Haggard, William
Doubting Thomas. + Brebner, Winston
The doubts of Dives. + Besant, Walter
Down a dark hall. + Duncan, Lois
Down-bound train. + Garnett, Bill
Down in the black gang, and others. + Farmer, Philip
   Jose
Down in the cellar. + Gray, Nicholas Stuart
Down the Styx. + Durrell, Lawrence
Down there. + Huysmans, Joris Karl
Down to Earth. + Capon, Paul
Down to Earth. + Charbonneau, Louis
Down to Earth. + Elder, Michael
Down to Earth. + Wrightson, Patricia
"Down with England!" + none
Down with everybody! + Mikes, George
Downfall. + Westheimer, David
The downstairs room, and other speculative fiction.
   + Wilhelm, Kate
Downward to the Earth. + Silverberg, Robert
The dowry. + Gould, Maggy
The dozen deadly dragons of joy. + Knight, Mallory T.
Dr.--For titles beginning with this word see: Doctor.
Draco the dragon man. + Donson, Cyril

Dracula. + Stoker, Bram
Dracula and the virgins of the undead. + Aubin, Eti-
   enne
The Dracula archives. + Rudorff, Raymond
Dracula, by Bram Stoker; Frankenstein, by Mary Shelley.
   + none
Dracula returns. + Lory, Robert
Dracula's brother. + Lory, Robert
Dracula's curse; and, The Jewel of Seven Stars. +
   Stoker, Bram
Dracula's gold. + Lory, Robert
Dracula's guest. + Stoker, Bram
Dracula's guest, and other stories. + Ghidalia, Vic
Dracula's guest, and other weird stories. + Stoker,
   Bram
Dracula's lost world. + Lory, Robert
Dracutwig. + Knight, Mallory T.
The dragon. + Shiel, M. P.
Dragon feast. + Elliott, John
The dragon hoard. + Lee, Tanith [see Addendum]
The dragon in the sea. + Herbert, Frank
The dragon keepers. + Hughes, Rodney
Dragon magic. + Norton, Andre
The dragon masters. + Vance, Jack
The dragon of the north. + Oswald, E. J.
The dragon of the skies. + Ellis, Edward S.
The dragon of Wantley. + Wister, Owen
Dragon summer. + Arthur, Ruth M.
Dragon under the hill. + Honeycombe, Gordon
Dragonfall 5 and the empty planet. + Earnshaw, Brian
Dragonfall 5 and the hijackers. + Earnshaw, Brian
Dragonfall 5 and the Royal Beast. + Earnshaw, Brian
Dragonfall 5 and the space cowboys. + Earnshaw, Brian
Dragonflight. + McCaffrey, Anne
Dragonquest. + McCaffrey, Anne
Dragons and nightmares. + Bloch, Robert
Dragons, elves, and heroes. + Carter, Lin
Dragon's island. + Williamson, Jack
The dragon's sister; and, Timothy travels. + Storey,
   Margaret
Dragon's teeth. + Miles, Keith
Drama of Mr. Dilly. + Edwards, Charman
The dramaturges of Yan. + Brunner, John
Draught of eternity. + Egbert, H. M.
A draught of the blue. + Bain, F. W.
A draught of the blue, together with An essence of the
   dusk. + Bain, F. W.
Dread companion. + Norton, Andre
Dread dwelling. + Crompton, Richmal
Dread of night. + O'Donnell, Elliott
Dread visitor. + Berry, Bryan
The dreadful dragon of Hay Hill. + Beerbohm, Max
Dreadful hollow. + Karlova, Irina
Dreadful sanctuary. + Russell, Eric Frank
The dreadnought of the air. + Westerman, Percy F.
The dream. + Dabbs, George H. R.
The dream. + Wells, H. G.
Dream. + Wright, S. Fowler
The dream adventure. + Caillois, Roger
The dream child. + Huntley, Florence
The dream Chintz. + (Mackarness, M. A.)
The dream-detective. + Rohmer, Sax
The dream doctor. + Reeve, Arthur B.
Dream in the stone. + Faralla, Dana
The dream life of Balso Snell; A cool million. +
   West, Nathanael
The dream master. + Zelazny, Roger
The dream millennium. + White, James
A dream of a modest prophet. + Leggett, M. D.
A dream of a throne. + Embree, Charles Fleming
The dream of a Warringtonian. + Bennett, Arthur
The dream of an Englishman. + Bennett, Arthur

The dream of Debs. + London, Jack
A dream of John Ball. + Morris, William
A dream of John Ball; and, A king's lesson. + Morris, William
The dream-quest of unknown Kadath. + Lovecraft, H. P.
The dream squad. + Hassler, Kenneth W.
Dream tales and prose poems. + Turgenev, Ivan
The dream-time. + Treece, Henry
Dream trips. + Parry, Michel
Dream warnings and mysteries. + none
The Dream-Woman. + Wylwynne, Kythe
A dreamer of dreams. + (Nicholson, Joseph Shield)
The dreamers. + Manvell, Roger
A dreamer's tales. + Dunsany, Lord
A dreamer's tales, and other stories. + Dunsany, Lord
The dreaming city. + Moorcock, Michael
The dreaming Earth. + Brunner, John
The dreaming jewels. + Sturgeon, Theodore
The dreaming skull. + Safroni-Middleton, A.
Dreams and delights. + Beck, L. Adams
Dreams and dream-stories. + Kingsford, Anna Bonus
Dreams and fancies. + Lovecraft, H. P.
Dreams from the past. + Williams, Alfred Rowberry
Dreams in reality of the undersea craft. + Wiggins, Walter Jr.
The dreams of Orlow. + Irvine, A. M.
Dreams of the dead. + Stanton, Edward
Drelma. + Ward, George Whiteley
The drift. + Kropp, Lloyd
Driftglass. + Delany, Samuel R.
The drifting diamond. + Colcord, Lincoln
The Driftway. + Lively, Penelope
Drolls from shadowland. + Pearce, J. H.
Drome. + Leahy, John Martin
The drone man. + Merritt, A.
A drop in infinity. + Grogan, Gerald
Dropped from the clouds. + Verne, Jules
The drought. + Ballard, J. G.
The drought. + Creasey, John
"The drowned Queen." + Laumer, Keith
The drowned world. + Ballard, J. G.
The drowned world; and, The wind from nowhere. + Ballard, J. G.
Drowsy. + Mitchell, J. A.
Drug of choice. + Lange, John
The Druid path. + Ryan, Marah Ellis
The druid stone. + Majors, Simon
Druids' world. + Smith, George Henry
Drujienna's harp. + McKenzie, Ellen Kindt
Drums along the Amazon. + Norwood, Victor
Drums of Dracula. + Lory, Robert
The drums of Fu Manchu. + Rohmer, Sax
The Drums of Tapajos. + Meek, S. P.
Drums of the dark gods. + Ballinger, W. A.
Drunkard's walk. + Pohl, Frederik
Drustan the wanderer. + Taylor, Anna
The Dryad. + McCarthy, Justin Huntly
Duc Rollon. + Tinseau, Leon de
The Duchess of Popocatapetl. + Turner, W. J.
A duck to water. + Stern, G. B.
Dudley & Gilderoy. + Blackwood, Algernon
Duel in nightmare worlds. + Flackes, B.
The dueling machine. + Bova, Ben
The duelling machine. + Bova, Ben
The Duke of Clarence. + (Foster, E. M.)
The duke of oblivion. + Scott, John Reed
The duke of sin. + Wayne, Charles M.
The dumb gods speak. + Oppenheim, E. Phillips
Dumb spirit. + Hedges, Doris
Dune. + Herbert, Frank
Dune messiah. + Herbert, Frank
Dunes of Pradai. + Wayman, Tony Russell

The Dunwich horror. + Lovecraft, H. P.
The Dunwich horror, and other weird tales. + Lovecraft, H. P.
The Dunwich horror, and others. + Lovecraft, H. P.
The duplicated man. + Blish, James & Lowndes, Robert W.
The duplicators. + Leinster, Murray
Duringwitch. + Claire, Keith
Dusk and dawn. + Turner, Charles Cyril
The dust destroyer. + Statten, Vargo
Dust of death. + Robeson, Kenneth
The dust which is God. + Straus, Ralph
Dusty Ayres; Black invaders vs. the Battle Birds. + Bowen, Robert Sidney
Dusty Ayres; Black lightning. + Bowen, Robert Sidney
Dusty Ayres; Crimson doom. + Bowen, Robert Sidney
Dusty Ayres; Purple tornado. + Bowen, Robert Sidney
Dusty Ayres; The Telsa raiders. + Bowen, Robert Sidney
Dwala. + Calderon, George
Dwarfs and giants. + Swift, Jonathan
The dwarf's chamber, and other stories. + Hume, Fergus
The dweller in the half-light. + Wray, Roger
The dweller on the threshold. + Hichens, Robert
A dweller on two planets + Phylos the Thibetan
The dwellers. + Wright, S. Fowler
Dwellers in space. + Reed, Van
Dwellers in the mirage. + Merritt, A.
Dwellers in the mirage; and, The face in the abyss. + Merritt, A.
Dwellers in the Temple of Mondama. + Herwer, Chris
The dwellers in Vale Sunrise. + Lloyd, J. Wm.
Dwellers of the deep. + O'Donnell, K. M.
Dwifa's curse. + Blue Wolf
The dying Earth. + Vance, Jack
Dying inside. + Silverberg, Robert
Dynasty of doom. + Grey, Charles
The dyno-depressant. + Gridban, Volsted

E. C. Tubb. + Harbottle, Philip [see Addendum]
The EM discoveries. + Gibbons, Robert
E pluribus bang! + Lippincott, David
E pluribus unicorn. + Sturgeon, Theodore
E pluribus unum. + Quoin
ESP orgy. + Williams, J. X.
The E.S.P. worm. + Anthony, Piers & Margroff, Robert
ESPer. + Blish, James
Eagles' Nest. + Kavan, Anna
Eagles restrained. + Tunstall, Brian
The Ealing miracle. + Newte, Horace W. C.
The ear in the wall. + Reeve, Arthur B.
The Earl of Hell. + Kitchell, Joseph Gray
The earlier life and the chief earlier works of Daniel Defoe. + Defoe, Daniel
The early Asimov. + Asimov, Isaac
The early Asimov, book one. + Asimov, Isaac
The early Asimov, book two. + Asimov, Isaac
The early Asimov, volume 1. + Asimov, Isaac
The early Asimov, volume 3. + Asimov, Isaac
The early Asimov, volume 2. + Asimov, Isaac
The early H. G. Wells. + Bergonzi, Bernard & Wells, H. G.
Early romances. + Morris, William
The early romances of William Morris in prose and verse. + Morris, William
Earth. + Farca, Marie C.
Earth abides. + Stewart, George R.
Earth-born! + Gentil, Spirito
The Earth dies. + Perry Rhodan 41
An Earth dweller's return. + Phylos the Thibetan
Earth eagles. + Bayliss, Marguerite

Earth enslaved. + Kern, Gregory
The Earth Gods are coming. + Bulmer, Kenneth
An Earth gone mad. + Dee, Roger
The Earth in peril. + Wollheim, Donald A.
The Earth invasion battalion. + Hughes, Denis
The Earth is mine. + Cox, Luther
The Earth is near. + Pesek, Ludek
Earth is room enough. + Asimov, Isaac
The Earth is your spaceship. + Dring, Nat
Earth lies sleeping. + James, Laurence
An Earth man on Venus. + Farley, Ralph Milne
Earth revisited. + Brooks, Byron A.
Earth sex in the 21st century. + Ception, John V.
Earth station sex. + Kainen, Ray
Earth stopped. + White, T. H.
Earth times two. + Reynolds, Pamela
The Earth tripper. + Kelley, Leo P.
The Earth-tube. + Edwards, Gawain
Earth 2. + Statten, Vargo
Earth unaware. + Reynolds, Mack
Earth waits for dawn. + O'Brien, Larry Clinton
The Earth war. + Reynolds, Mack
Earthblood. + Brown, Rosel George & Laumer, Keith
Earthbound. + Lesser, Milton
Earthfasts. + Mayne, William
Earthjacket. + Hartridge, Jon
Earthlight. + Clarke, Arthur C.
Earthman, come home. + Blish, James
Earthman, go home! + Anderson, Poul
Earthman, go home. + Ellison, Harlan
Earthman's burden. + Anderson, Poul & Dickson, Gordon
Earthmen and strangers. + Silverberg, Robert
The Earthomotor, and other stories. + Linton, C. E.
Earthquake. + Fox, George
The earthquake. + Holt White, W.
The earthquake. + Risse, Heinz
Earthrim. + Kamin, Nick
Earth's last citadel. + Kuttner, Henry & Moore, C. L.
Earth's last fortress. + van Vogt, A. E.
Earth's long shadow. + Bulmer, Kenneth
Earth's other shadow. + Silverberg, Robert
Earthstrings. + Rackham, John
Earthworks. + Aldiss, Brian W.
Earthwreck! + Scortia, Thomas N.
East India and Company. + Morand, Paul
East of Suez. + Perrin, A.
The Eastern question solved. + "Budge"
The Eater of Darkness. + Coates, Robert M.
The eater of worlds. + Kern, Gregory
Ebony and crystal. + Smith, Clark Ashton
Ec'H-Pi-el speaks. + Lovecraft, H. P.
Echo. + Desmond, Shaw
Echo in the skull. + Brunner, John
Echo of a curse. + Ryan, R. R.
Echo round his bones. + Disch, Thomas M.
Echo X. + Barzman, Ben
The echoing worlds. + Burke, Jonathan
The eclipse express. + Statten, Vargo
The eclipse of dawn. + Eklund, Gordon
Ecodeath. + Snyder, E. V. & Watkins, William Jon
Eco-fiction. + Stadler, John
The ecstasy connection. + Kenyon, Paul
Eddie and the archangel Mike. + Benefield, Barry
Eden. + Sheehan, Murray
The Eden cycle. + Gallun, Raymond Z.
Eden for one. + Gunther, John
Eden II. + Doerr, Edd
Eden II. + Ell, Richard G.
Edgar Allan Poe. + Poe, Edgar Allan
Edgar Allan Poe and the Philadelphia Saturday courier. + Poe, Edgar Allan
Edgar Allan Poe's tales. + Poe, Edgar Allan

Edgar Rice Burroughs; a bibliography. + Day, Bradford M.
Edgar Rice Burroughs biblio. + Day, Bradford M.
Edgar Rice Burroughs bibliography and price guide. + Adkins, P. H.
Edgar Rice Burroughs: master of adventure. + Lupoff, Richard A.
The edge. + Beaumont, Charles
The edge of beyond. + Johns, W. E.
The edge of eternity. + Muller, John E.
The edge of forever. + Oliver, Chad
The edge of never. + Hoskins, Robert
The edge of running water. + Sloane, William
An edge of the forest. + Smith, Agnes
The edge of the universe. + Allen, Harold W. G.
Edge of the world. + Rodney, George Brydges
The edge of things. + Barrett, William E.
Edge of time. + Grinnell, David
The edge of tomorrow. + Fast, Howard
The Edict. + Ehrlich, Max
Edison's conquest of Mars. + Serviss, Garrett P.
Editor's choice in science fiction. + Moskowitz, Sam
Edmond Dantes. + (Flagg, Edmund)
The education of Oversoul Seven. + Roberts, Jane
The education of Uncle Paul. + Blackwood, Algernon
Eegoboo. + Banister, Manly
The eerie book. + Armour, Margaret
Eerie tales of terror and dread. + Hurwood, Bernhardt J.
Eevalu. + Lukens, Adam
Efficiency in Hades. + Vale, Robert B.
Egbert. + Darlington, W. A.
The egg of the Glak, and other stories. + Jacobs, Harvey
The egg-shaped thing. + Hodder-Williams, Christopher
The Egyptian cat mystery. + Blaine, John
An Egyptian coquette. + Holland, Clive
The Egyptian harp girl. + "Quondam"
Egyptian light. + Francis, Marianne
Egyptian love. + Haweis, Stephen
An Egyptian love spell. + Billings, Maris Herrington
The Egyptian Venus. + Glossop, Reginald
Eidolon. + Stern, J. David
Eight against utopia. + Mason, Douglas R.
Eight fantasms and magics. + Vance, Jack
Eight for eternity. + Roberts, Cecil
Eight keys to Eden. + Clifton, Mark
Eight stories from The rest of the robots. + Asimov, Isaac
Eight strange tales. + Ghidalia, Vic
Eight tales. + de la Mare, Walter
Eight tales of Hoffmann. + Hoffmann, E. T. A.
Eight tales of terror. + Poe, Edgar Allan
18 best stories by Edgar Allan Poe. + Poe, Edgar Allan
18 greatest science fiction stories. + Janifer, Laurence M.
1895. + none
8th annual edition, the year's best S-F. + Merril, Judith
The 8th annual of the year's best SF. + Merril, Judith
The eighth day. + Goldston, Robert C.
The eighth Fontana book of great ghost stories. + Aickman, Robert
The eighth Fontana book of great horror stories. + Danby, Mary
The eighth Galaxy reader. + Pohl, Frederik
The eighth ghost book. + Timperley, Rosemary
The eighth Pan book of horror stories. + van Thal, Herbert
The eighth seal. + MacLeod, Angus
The eighth stage of fandom. + Bloch, Robert
The eighth wonder. + Cook, William Wallace

England crushed. + Vindex
England in 1910. + none
England swings SF. + Merril, Judith
"England's downfall." + Ex-Revolutionist
The English assassin. + Moorcock, Michael
The English at the North Pole. + Verne, Jules
The English invasion of Germany. + A French Staff Officer
The English revolution of the twentieth century. + Lazarus, Henry
English, target 1; The space visitors. + Bell, Paul W. & Robinett, Ralph F.
Enigma from Tantalus. + Brunner, John
Enoch, the Philistine. + Hooker, Le Roy
Enoch Willoughby. + Wickersham, James A.
The enormous egg. + Butterworth, Oliver
An enquiry into the existence of vampires. + Lovell, Marc
Ensign Flandry. + Anderson, Poul
Enslaved brains. + Binder, Eando
Enter Craig Kennedy. + Reever, Arthur B.
Enterprise Stardust. + Perry Rhodan #1
Enterprise 2115. + Grey, Charles
An entirely new feature of a thrilling novel! entitled, The social war of the year 1900. + Landis, S. M.
Entombed in flesh. + Dziewicki, Michael Henry
Entry to elsewhen. + Brunner, John
Envoy from Heaven. + Tusiani, Joseph
Envoy to new worlds. + Laumer, Keith
Envoy to the Dog Star. + Shaw, Frederick L. Jr.
Eo of the caves. + Rowland, Florence Wightman
The Epicurean. + Moore, Thomas
The Epicurean; and, Alciphron. + Moore, Thomas
Epidemic! + Slaughter, Frank G.
Epidemic center: Aralon. + Perry Rhodan 37
An episode in the doings of the dualized. + Mason, Eveleen L.
An episode of Flatland. + Hinton, C. H.
The episodes of Vathek. + Beckford, William
Epp. + Jensen, Axel
Epp's trip to the Moon. + Edstrom, O. E.
An equal opportunity. + Marks, W. Dennis
Equality. + none
Equality. + Bellamy, Edward
Equator. + Aldiss, Brian W.
Erchomenon. + (Watson, Henry Crocker Marriott)
Erection to eternal lust. + Gatos, Robert L.
Erewhon. + Butler, Samuel
Erewhon; and, Erewhon revisited. + Butler, Samuel
Erewhon revisited. + Butler, Samuel
Eric Brighteyes. + Haggard, H. Rider
Eric of the strong heart. + Egbert, H. M.
Ernest Bramah. + Bramah, Ernest
Ernestus Berchtold. + Polidori, John William
Erone. + Kearney, Chalmers
Eros in orbit. + Elder, Joseph
Eros 2000 A.D. + Kaye, H. R.
Erotic fairy tales. + Voisenon, Abbe de
The erotic spectacles. + Cohen, Genghis
Erotica Satanica. + Trehune, Morgan
Escape! + Bova, Ben
Escape across the cosmos. + Fox, Gardner F.
Escape from gravity. + Briggs, Philip
Escape from the Crater. + Biemiller, Carl
Escape from the evil prophecy. + Kingman, Lee
Escape from the planet Karaxe. + Dunn, William B.
Escape from the planet of the apes. + Pournelle, Jerry
Escape into space. + Tubb, E. C.
Escape into the past. + Slocombe, George
Escape me--never! + Presland, John
Escape on Venus. + Burroughs, Edgar Rice

The escape orbit. + White, James
Escape to Berkshire. + Asterley, H. C.
Escape to Earth. + Howard, Ivan
Escape to infinity. + Zeigfreid, Karl
Escape to nowhere. + Karp, David
Escape to Venus. + Makepeace Lott, S.
Escape to Venus. + Perry Rhodan 15
Escape to Witch Mountain. + Key, Alexander
The escaped cock. + Lawrence, D. H.
Escapement. + Maine, Charles Eric
The escapes of Mr. Honey. + Atkey, Bertram
The Eskimo invasion. + Howard, Hayden
The espers. + Souza, Steven M.
Essays and stories. + Poe, Edgar Allan
Essays in imitation. + Cecil, Algernon
An essence of the dusk. + Bain, F. W.
Etched in moonlight. + Stephens, James
Etchings in ivory. + Howard, Robert E.
The Eternal Champion. + Moorcock, Michael
The eternal city. + Caine, Hall
The eternal conflict. + Keller, David H.
The eternal echo. + Cradock, Phyllis
The eternal frontiers. + Schmitz, James H.
The eternal lover. + Burroughs, Edgar Rice
The eternal man. + Long, Charles R.
The eternal moment, and other stories. + Forster, E. M.
Eternal rediffusion. + (Harbottle, Philip)
The eternal savage. + Burroughs, Edgar Rice
The eternal smile, and other stories. + Lagerkvist, Par
Eternity in an hour. + Knowles, Vernon
The eternity kick. + Rogers, Lew
Ethel Barrett's Holy war. + Barrett, Ethel
Ethelwina. + Horsley, T. J.
The ethical engineer. + Harrison, Harry
Etidorpha. + Lloyd, John Uri
Eureka. + Hall, Owen
Eureka. + (Williams, Robert Folkestone)
European tales of terror. + Strating, J. J.
Eusebius, the Phoenician. + Webb, Christopher
The evacuation of England. + Gratacap, L. P.
Evander. + Phillpotts, Eden
Evangel Ahvallah. + Barton, C. Josephine
Eva's apples. + Gerhardi, William
Eve and the evangelist. + Rice, Harry E.
The eve of Saint Venus. + Burgess, Anthony
Evelyn. + Dwyer, James Francis
Even a worm. + Bradford, J. S.
The Evening standard book of strange stories. + none
The Evening standard second book of strange stories. + none
Evening tales for the winter. + St. Clair, Henry [see Addendum]
Evenor. + MacDonald, George
The everlasting exiles. + West, Wallace
The everlasting man. + Elder, Michael
Every boy's book of outer space stories. + Dikty, T. E.
Every boy's book of science-fiction. + Wollheim, Donald A.
Everything but love. + (Shkarovsky-Raffe, Arthur)
Eve's diary. + Twain, Mark
Eve's second apple. + Dogbolt, Barnaby
Evil, evil. + DuBreuil, Linda
Evil is live spelled backwards. + Offutt, Andrew J.
The evil people. + Haining, Peter
Evil seed. + Holmes, Larry W.
The evil that men do. + Brunner, John
The evolution man. + Lewis, Roy
Evolution of modern science fiction. + Gernsback, Hug
Ex Minus. + Conrad, Paul

Ex officio. + Culver, Timothy J.
An exaltation of stars. + Carr, Terry
Excalibur. + Laubenthal, Sanders Anne
Excerpts from the diaries of the late God. + Towne, Anthony
An exchange of souls. + Pain, Barry
The Exerciser. + Albrecht, Howard & Weinstein, Sol
The exile. + Johnston, Mary
Exile, and other tales of fantasy. + Cummings, M. A.
Exile from Jupiter. + Condray, Bruno G.
Exile from Xanadu. + Wright, Lan
The exile of Ellendon. + Marden, William
The exile of time. + Cummings, Ray
Exiled from Earth. + Bova, Ben
Exiled in space. + Torro, Pel
Exiles in time. + Deegan, Jon J.
Exiles of the stars. + Norton, Andre
Exiles of time. + Bond, Nelson
Exile's quest. + Meade, Richard
Exit a dictator. + Oppenheim, E. Phillips
Exit humanity. + Brett, Leo
Exit into eternity. + Eddy, C. M. Jr.
Exit life. + Gridban, Volsted
Exodus A.D. + Nevinson, C. R. W. & Troubetzkoy, Princess Paul
Exodus from Elysium. + Burke, Jonathan
Exorcism. + Natas, Eth
The exorcist. + Blatty, William Peter
The Exorcist. + Newman, Howard
The exorcists. + Muller, John E.
The exotic swamp plant, and other stories. + Baughman, Grace
The expedition of Captain Flick. + Hume, Fergus
Expedition to Earth. + Clarke, Arthur C.
Expedition Venus. + Walters, Hugh
Experiment at Proto. + Oakes, Philip
Experiment in telepathy. + Royce, E. R.
The experiment of Doctor Nevill. + Hulme-Beaman, Emeric
The expert dreamers. + Pohl, Frederik
The exploding ray. + Rutley, C. Bernard
The exploits of Elaine. + Reeve, Arthur B.
Explorations in the Sit-tee Desert. + Gould, F. C.
The explorers. + Kornbluth, C. M.
Explorers into infinity. + Cummings, Ray
Explorers of the infinite. + Moskowitz, Sam
Exploring new ethics for survival. + Hardin, Garrett
Exploring other worlds. + Moskowitz, Sam
Expo 80. + Burke, John
The exquisite corpse. + Chester, Alfred
The exterminator! + Burroughs, William
Extinction bomber. + Hough, S. B.
The extra day. + Blackwood, Algernon
Extra dry. + Gibson, W. C. & Taylor, Bert Leston
The extra man. + Grey, Charles
Extract from Captain Stormfield's visit to Heaven. + Twain, Mark
Extracts from Adam's diary. + Twain, Mark
The extraordinary exploits and experiences of Munchausen, M.D. + Brandeis, Julian Walter
The extraordinary islanders. + Forrest, Aston
The extraordinary professor. + Kreupp, W.
The extraordinary seaman. + Rock, Phillip
Extrapolasis. + Malec, Alexander
The eye and the finger. + Wandrei, Donald
Eye in the sky. + Dick, Philip K.
The Eye of Istar. + Le Queux, William
The Eye of Karnak. + Muller, John E.
The eye of the god. + Aston, B. G.
The eye of the lens. + Jones, Langdon
Eye of the monster. + Norton, Andre
Eyes in the fishbowl. + Snyder, Zilpha Keatley
The eyes of Bolsk. + Lory, Robert

The eyes of Heisenberg. + Herbert, Frank
Eyes of Horus. + Grant, Joan
The Eyes of the Overworld. + Vance, Jack
Eyes of the panther. + Bierce, Ambrose
The eyes of the Shadow. + Grant, Maxwell

The "F" certificate. + Gurney, David
The FORTEC conspiracy. + Addeo, Edmund G. & Garvin, Richard M.
F.P.1 does not reply. + Siodmak, Kurt
F.P.1 fails to reply. + Siodmak, Kurt
F.S.C. + Sellers, Con
The fable and the flesh. + Ayme, Marcel
Fables. + Hawkes, Jacquetta
Fables. + Powys, T. F.
Fables and parables for the mid-century. + Wales, Nym
Fables for our times. + Thurber, James
The fables of Moronia. + Holdridge, Herbert C.
The fabulous flight. + Lawson, Robert
The fabulous journey of Hieronymus Meeker. + Johns, Willy
The fabulous Riverboat. + Farmer, Philip Jose
The fabulous wink. + Bennett, Kem
The face beyond the door. + Kernahan, Coulson
The face in the abyss. + Merritt, A.
The face in the frost. + Bellairs, John
The face in the mirror. + Baker, Denys Val
Face in the night. + Brett, Leo
The face in the pool. + St. John, J. Allen
The face of air. + Knapp, George L.
The face of fear. + Torro, Pel
The face of X. + Lionel, Robert
The face of X. + Roberts, Lionel
The face that launched a thousand ships. + Kelley, Thomas P.
Faceless planet. + Brett, Leo
Facial justice. + Hartley, L. P.
Facing the flag. + Verne, Jules
The facts in the case of M. Valdemar. + Poe, Edgar Allan
Fahrenheit 451. + Bradbury, Ray
Fail-safe. + Burdick, Eugene & Wheeler, Harvey
The fair. + Nathan, Robert
Fair Inez. + Sladen, Douglas
The Fair of St. James. + Farjeon, Eleanor
Fairies--of sorts. + Molesworth, Mrs.
The fairy doll. + Galli de Bibiena, Jean
A fairy leapt upon my knee. + Howe, Bea
The fairy man. + Cornford, L. Cope
Fairy silver. + "Ganpat"
Fairy tale of the white man. + Mighels, Ella Sterling
Fairy tales. + Hauff, Wilhelm
Fairy tales. + Voisenon, Abbe de
Fairy tales. + Wilde, Oscar
Fairy tales and romances. + Hamilton, Anthony
Fairy tales for computers. + none
The fairy tales of Hoffmann. + Hoffmann, E. T. A.
Fairy tales, with one extra as a makeweight. + Capek, Karel & Capek, Josef
A faithful chronicle of the events which occurred during the last century in the Principality of Waskelham. + Pons, Maurice
The fakir's curse. + Bruce, Kennedy
Falcons of Narabedla. + Bradley, Marion Zimmer
Falk. + Hanks, Keith
Falkland; and, Zicci. + Lytton, Edward
The fall. + Seibel, George
The fall of a dictator. + Gask, Arthur
The fall of a nation. + Dixon, Thomas
The fall of Casa Malvado. + Chisom, Sarah
The fall of Chronopolis. + Bayley, Barrington J.
The fall of Colossus. + Jones, D. F.

The fall of England? + (Chesney, George T.)
A fall of moondust. + Clarke, Arthur C.
The fall of New York. + Donis, Miles
The fall of the dream machine. + Koontz, Dean R.
The fall of the great republic. + none
The fall of the House of Usher. + Poe, Edgar Allan
The fall of the House of Usher, and four other tales.
    + Poe, Edgar Allan
The fall of the House of Usher, and other stories. +
    Poe, Edgar Allan
The fall of the House of Usher, and other tales. +
    Poe, Edgar Allan
The fall of the House of Usher, and other tales and
    prose writings. + Poe, Edgar Allan
The fall of the House of Usher, and other tales of
    imagination. + Poe, Edgar Allan
The fall of the House of Usher; Ligeia; The cask of
    Amontillado; The assignation; Ms. found in a bottle;
    The black cat; The gold bug. + Poe, Edgar Allan
The fall of the towers. + Delany, Samuel R.
The fall of Ulysses. + Willard, Charles Dwight
The fall of utopia. + Bayne, Charles J.
A fallen idol. + Anstey, F.
The fallen race. + Granville, Austyn
The fallen sky. + Crowcroft, Peter
Fallen star. + Blish, James
The fallen star. + Khosrofian, Harry
The fallible fiend. + de Camp, L. Sprague
The falling astronauts. + Malzberg, Barry N.
The falling torch. + Budrys, Algis
False fatherland. + Chandler, A. Bertram
False idols. + Ferm, Betty
False night. + Budrys, Algis
Falsivir's travels. + Lee, Thomas
A family affair. + Benedict, Lynn
The family witch. + Cox, A. B.
The famine. + Creasey, John
Famous fantastic classics #1. + (Dikty, T. E.)
Famous ghost stories. + Cerf, Bennett
Famous ghost stories. + McSpadden, J. Walker
Famous ghost-stories by English authors. + Gowans,
    Adam L.
Famous modern ghost stories. + Scarborough, Dorothy
Famous monster tales. + Davenport, Basil
Famous monsters of filmland strike back! + Ackerman,
    Forrest J.
Famous mysteries. + Sandrus, Mary Yost
Famous mystery and detective stories. + McSpadden,
    J. Walker
Famous mystery stories. + McSpadden, J. Walker
Famous occult tales. + de Berard, Frederick B.
Famous psychic and ghost stories. + McSpadden, J.
    Walker
Famous psychic stories. + McSpadden, J. Walker
The famous romances of Voltaire. + Voltaire
Famous science-fiction stories. + Healy, Raymond J.
    & McComas, J. Francis
The famous short stories of H. G. Wells. + Wells,
    H. G.
Famous tales of the fantastic. + van Thal, Herbert
Famous weird tales. + De Berard, Frederick B.
Fancies and goodnights. + Collier, John
Fanciful tales. + Stockton, Frank R.
Fancy free. + Phillpotts, Eden
The fancy of Dr. Ox; and, The tour of the world in
    eighty days. + Verne, Jules
Fancyclopedia II. + Eney, R. H.
Fandbook no. 1. + Franson, Donald
Fanfare for a witch. + Wilkins, Vaughan
Fanfaronade. + Pakenham, Ivo
Fangs of the sky leopard. + Hogan, Robert J.
Fanny Penquite. + Saunders, Edith

Fantastica mathematica. + Fadiman, Clifton
Fantasias. + Egerton, George
Fantasies. + Nembhard, Mabel
Fantasies on ancient themes. + Elliott, Hettie &
    Graves, Gordon Harwood
Fantasma Land. + Macauley, Charles Raymond
The fantastic. + Todorov, Tzvetan
The fantastic battle. + Burns, R. C.
Fantastic debunking fables. + Bierce, Ambrose
Fantastic fables. + Bierce, Ambrose
The fantastic history of the celebrated Pierrot. +
    Assollant, Alfred
The fantastic island. + Robeson, Kenneth
The fantastic mirror. + Appel, Benjamin
Fantastic novels. + Dard, Roger
Fantastic reality. + Freudenthal, Elisabeth
Fantastic stories. + Tertz, Abram
Fantastic summer. + Macardle, Dorothy
The fantastic swordsmen. + de Camp, L. Sprague
Fantastic tales. + Eliade, Mircea & Niculescu, Mihai
Fantastic tales. + Poe, Edgar Allan
Fantastic tales of Rhineland. + Erckmann-Chatrian
The Fantastic universe omnibus. + Santesson, Hans
    Stefan
Fantastic voyage. + Asimov, Isaac
Fantastica. + Nichols, Robert
A fantastical excursion into the planets. + none
Fantastics, and other fancies. + Hearn, Lafcadio
Fantasy. + Kelley, Leo P.
Fantasy and science fiction. + Pfeiffer, John R.
Fantasy classification system. + Cameron, Alastair
Fantasy collector's annual--1974. + de la Ree, Gerry
Fantasy films and their fiends. + Jones, Jack R.
Fantasy, science fiction, science materials. + Trask
    Margaret
Fantasy twin. + none
The fantasy worlds of Peter Stone, and other fables.
    + Boyd, Malcolm
Fantazius Mallare. + Hecht, Ben
Far and away. + Boucher, Anthony
Far below, and other horrors. + Weinberg, Robert E.
Far beyond the blue. + Amper, Drax
Far boundaries. + Derleth, August
A far look ahead. + Thiusen, Ismar
Far out. + Knight, Damon
The far-out people. + Hoskins, Robert
The far-out worlds of A. E. van Vogt. + van Vogt,
    A. E.
Far Rainbow. + Strugatsky, A. & Strugatsky, B.
The far reality. + Padgett, Lewis
The far side of evil. + Engdahl, Sylvia Louise
The far side of time. + Elwood, Roger
Far stars. + Russell, Eric Frank
A far sunset. + Cooper, Edmund
The far traveller. + Coles, Manning
The faraway lurs. + Behn, Harry
Farewell, Earth's bliss. + Compton, D. G.
Farewell, fantastic Venus! + Aldiss, Brian W. &
    Harrison, Harry
"Farewell, Nikola!" + Boothby, Guy
Farewell to the bomb. + Webb, A. C.
Farm beneath the sea. + Patchett, Mary
The farm on the downs. + Syrett, Netta
Farmer Giles of Ham. + Tolkien, J. R. R.
Farmer in the sky. + Heinlein, Robert A.
Farnham's Freehold. + Heinlein, Robert A.
Farrusco the blackbird, and other stories from the
    Portuguese. + Torge, Miguel
The farthest reaches. + Elder, Joseph
The farthest shore. + Le Guin, Ursula K.
Farthest south. + Gorst, H. E.
Faster faster. + Horn, Edward Newman

A fire of driftwood. + Broster, D. K.
Fire past the future. + Maine, Charles Eric
Fire Time. + Anderson, Poul
Fire-Tongue. + Rohmer, Sax
Fire watcher's night. + Kaner, H.
Fireball at the lake. + Groves, Jay
The Firebird. + Cooke, Donald E.
The Fireclown. + Moorcock, Michael
Fireman flower, and other stories. + Sansom, William
Firemantle. + Mackelworth, R. W.
Fires burn blue. + Caldecott, Andrew
The fires of Arcadia. + Harrison, G. B.
Fires of forever. + none
The fireside book of ghost stories. + Wagenknecht, Edward
Fireworks. + Carter, Angela
The first American king. + Hastings, George Gordon
The first Astounding science fiction anthology. + Campbell, John W.
First book of horror stories. + Wheatley, Dennis
The first book of Tros of Samothrace; Tros. + Mundy, Talbot
First boy on the Moon. + Hicks, Clifford B.
The first Christmas tree. + Field, Eugene
First contact. + Knight, Damon
First contact? + Walters, Hugh
The first days of man. + Kummer, Frederic Arnold
The first editions of Andre Norton. + Turner, David G.
First flight. + Knight, Damon
First flights to the Moon. + Clement, Hal
First he died. + Simak, Clifford D.
The first immortals. + Arch, E. L.
First Lensman. + Smith, E. E.
First man on Mars. + Melling, Leonard
The first Mayflower book of black magic stories. + Parry, Michel
The first men in the Moon. + Wells, H. G.
The first men in the Moon, and more human stories. + Wells, H. G.
The first men in the Moon, The world set free, and short stories. + Wells, H. G.
First men to the Moon. + von Braun, Wernher
The first of the penguins. + Steele, Mary Q.
First on Mars. + Gordon, Rex
First on the Moon. + Sutton, Jeff
First on the Moon. + Walters, Hugh
First one and twenty. + Gloag, John
The first Pan book of horror stories. + van Thal, Herbert
The first Panther book of horror. + Rampton, Anthony
First person, peculiar. + Sherred, T. L.
First port of call. + Jordan, Elizabeth
First step outward. + Hoskins, Robert
The first summer year. + Kellam, Ian
The first team. + Ball, John
The first temptation of Saint Anthony. + Flaubert, Gustave
First through time. + Gordon, Rex
The first to awaken. + Bennett, Richard M. & Hicks, Granville
First to the stars. + Gordon, Rex
The first workers' government. + Mitchison, G. R.
The first world of If. + Quinn, James L. & Wulff, Eve
A fish dinner in Memison. + Eddison, E. R.
The fisherman and his soul, and other fairy tales. + Wilde, Oscar
Fisherman's gat. + Noble, Edward
Fission. + Hunt, Gill
Fistful of digits. + Hodder-Williams, Christopher
The fittest. + McIntosh, J. T.
Five adventure novels of H. Rider Haggard. + Haggard, H. Rider

Five against Arlane. + Purdom, Tom
Five against Venus. + Latham, Philip
The five children. + Nesbit, E.
Five children and it. + Nesbit, E.
Five faces of fear. + Thorpe, Trebor
Five fates. + (Laumer, Keith)
The five flights of the Starfire. + Mumford, E. E.
Five Galaxy short novels. + Gold, H. L.
The five gold bands. + Vance, Jack
Five great ghost stories. + Haldeman-Julius, E. [see Addendum]
The 500 millions of the begum. + Verne, Jules
The five jars. + James, M. R.
Five miles from Candia. + Urn, Althea
Five-odd. + Conklin, Groff
Five roads to Tlen. + Lambert, William J. III
Five science fiction novels. + Greenberg, Martin
Five steps to tomorrow. + Binder, Eando
The five stories of man. + Gordon, David
5 tales from tomorrow. + Dikty, T. E.
Five thousand miles underground. + Rockwood, Roy
Five to twelve. + Cooper, Edmund
5 unearthly visions. + Conklin, Groff
Five Victorian ghost novels. + Bleiler, E. F.
Five weeks in a balloon. + Verne, Jules
Five weeks in a balloon; and, Around the world in eighty days. + Verne, Jules
5 who disappeared. + Stapp, Arthur D.
"Five Winds." + Bowen, Marjorie
The Fixed Period. + Trollope, Anthony
The flame. + Hunter, Jim
The flame. + Norton, Roy
Flame and the shadow-eater. + Weaver, Henrietta
The flame breathers. + Robeson, Kenneth
Flame eternal; and, Maharajah's son. + Roys, Willis E.
The flame-flower, and other stories. + Sullivan, Jas. F.
The flame-gatherers. + Potter, Margaret Horton
Flame Goddess. + Roberts, Lionel
The flame is green. + Lafferty, R. A.
Flame Mass. + Fanthorpe, R. Lionel
The Flame of Iridar. + Carter, Lin
Flame out of Dorset. + Stevens, Clifford
Flame Tree Planet. + Elwood, Roger
Flame Winds. + Page, Norvell W.
Flames. + Hichens, Robert
The flames. + Stapledon, Olaf
Flames of desire. + Deer, M. J.
The flaming falcons. + Robeson, Kenneth
The flaming mountain. + Blaine, John
The Flaming Sword. + Percival, Dr.
Flandry of Terra. + Anderson, Poul
Flash. + Juffe, Mel
Flash. + Williams, Eric C.
Flash Gordon in the caverns of Mongo. + Raymond, Alex
Flash Gordon; The lion men of Mongo. + Steffanson, Con
Flash Gordon; The plague of sound. + Steffanson, Con
Flash Gordon; The space circus. + Steffanson, Con
Flash Gordon; The time trap of Ming XIII. + Steffanson, Con
Flash Gordon; The witch queen of Mongo. + Bingham, Carson
Flashing swords! #1. + Carter, Lin
Flashing swords! #2. + Carter, Lin
Flatland. + Abbott, Edwin A.
Flats. + Wurlitzer, Rudolph
The flaw in the crystal. + Sinclair, May
Flaxius. + Leland, Charles Godfrey
Flecker's magic. + Matson, Norman H.
The fleet of the Springers. + Perry Rhodan 22

Forbidden planet. + Stuart, W. J.
Force 97X. + Torro, Pel
Forebodings and forbearance. + Lowenell, Johann W. von
Forerunner foray. + Norton, Andre
The forest in the wind. + Jayne, Mitchell F.
A forest is a long time growing. + Brown, Robin
The forest of fear. + Bennett, Alfred Gordon
The forest of forever. + Swann, Thomas Burnett
The forest ship. + Hollriegel, Arnold
Forever. + Cram, Mildred
Forever; and, The promise. + Cram, Mildred
Forever Ember. + Earle, Richard
The forever machine. + Clifton, Mark & Riley, Frank
The forgetful robot. + Fairman, Paul W.
The forgotten beasts of Eld. + McKillip, Patricia A.
The forgotten door. + Key, Alexander
The forgotten planet. + Leinster, Murray
The forgotten planet. + Smith, George Henry
The forgotten race. + Newton, Julius P.
The forgotten sea of Mars. + Resnick, Michael D.
The forgotten star. + Greene, Joseph
The forgotten world of Uloc. + Buchan, Bryan
The formula. + Horler, Sydney
Formula for power. + Batt, Leon
Formula 695. + Hughes, Denis
Formula 29X. + Torro, Pel
The fornication formula. + Dickens, Bradford
Forrest J Ackerman presents Invasion of Mars. + Serviss, Garrett P.
The forsaken way. + Lafargue, Philip
A fortnight in Heaven. + Brydges, Harold
Fortress Atlantis. + Perry Rhodan 52
Fortress in the skies. + De Mendelssohn, Peter
Fortress of Solitude. + Robeson, Kenneth
Fortress of the six moons. + Perry Rhodan #7
The fortress of Yadasara. + Lys, Christian
A fortune from the sky. + Kuppord, Skelton
The 49 days of death. + Ballinger, Bill S.
43,000 years later. + Coon, Horace
Forty years on. + Wallace, Doreen
Forty years with the damned. + Aikin, Charles
Forward in time. + Bova, Ben
Foundation. + Asimov, Isaac
Foundation and empire. + Asimov, Isaac
The Foundation Trilogy. + Asimov, Isaac
The foundling, and other tales of Prydain. + Alexander, Lloyd
The fountain of heart's desire. + Parke, Jean
The fountain of youth. + Dawson, Erasmus
The fountain of youth. + Paludan-Muller, Frederik
Four came back. + Caidin, Martin
The four corners of the world. + Mason, A. E. W.
Four-day planet. + Piper, H. Beam
The four day weekend. + Smith, George Henry
Four days war. + Wright, S. Fowler
Four days with the dead. + Kirk, Elmer R.
The four-dimensional nightmare. + Ballard, J. G.
The four Facardins. + Hamilton, Anthony & Lewis, M. G. & Levis, M. de
4 for the future. + Conklin, Groff
Four for the future. + Harrison, Harry
Four for tomorrow. + Zelazny, Roger
Four from Planet 5. + Leinster, Murray
Four futures. + none
The four-gated city. + Lessing, Doris
Four ghost stories. + Molesworth, Mrs.
Four great oaks. + McNaughton, Mildred
Four-in-one weird and occult shorts. + none
Four millions a year. + Collins, Colin
Four new dialogues of the dead. + Lyttleton, Lord
Four of the best. + Creasey, John
Four-sided triangle. + Temple, William F.

Four tales. + Buchan, John
Four tales. + Hoffmann, E. T. A.
Four thrilling adventure novels. + none
14 great tales of ESP. + Stone, Idella Purnell
14 of my favorites in suspense. + Hitchcock, Alfred
The fourteen points. + Reeve, Arthur B.
The 14th Pan book of horror stories. + van Thal, Herbert
The fourth Armada ghost book. + Danby, Mary
The fourth book of Jorkens. + Dunsany, Lord
The fourth book of Tros of Samothrace; Helene. + Mundy, Talbot
The fourth flight of the Starfire. + Mumford, Edwin
The fourth Fontana book of great ghost stories. + Aickman, Robert
The fourth Fontana book of great horror stories. + Bernard, Christine
The fourth Galaxy reader. + Gold, H. L.
The fourth ghost book. + Turner, James
Fourth Mansions. + Lafferty, R. A.
The fourth Napoleon. + Benham, Charles
The fourth Pan book of horror stories. + van Thal, Herbert
The fourth pig. + Mitchison, Naomi
The fourth programme. + Adams, W. S.
The fourth "R." + Smith, George O.
The Fourth Reich. + Hale, Martin
The fourth seal. + Groom, Pelham
The fox woman, and other stories. + Merritt, A.
The fox woman; The blue pagoda. + Merritt, A. & Bok, Hannes
Foxy-boy. + Severn, David
A fragment of glass. + Green, F. L.
Fragments from the past. + Thomas, Eugene E.
Francis. + Stern, David
Francis goes to Washington. + Stern, David
Francis...the army mule. + Stern, David
The Frankenscience monster. + Ackerman, Forrest J.
Frankenstein. + Shelley, Mary Wollstonecraft
Frankenstein. + Shelley, Mary & Carlson, Dale
The Frankenstein legend. + Glut, Donald F.
The Frankenstein reader. + Beck, Calvin
Frankenstein '69. + Martin, Ed
Frankenstein unbound. + Aldiss, Brian W.
The Frankenstein Wheel. + Fairman, Paul W.
Freak Museum. + Ryan, R. R.
The freak show. + Haining, Peter
Freaks against supermen. + Finn, Ralph L.
Freaky Friday. + Rodgers, Mary
The freckled shark. + Robeson, Kenneth
Fred Cook's index to the Wonder group. + Cook, Fred
Freddy and Mr. Camphor. + Brooks, Walter R.
Freddy and Simon the dictator. + Brooks, Walter R.
Freddy and the baseball team from Mars. + Brooks, Walter R.
Freddy and the Bean home news. + Brooks, Walter R.
Freddy and the dragon. + Brooks, Walter R.
Freddy and the flying saucer plans. + Brooks, Walter R.
Freddy and the ignoramus. + Brooks, Walter R.
Freddy and the men from Mars. + Brooks, Walter R.
Freddy and the perilous adventure. + Brooks, Walter R.
Freddy and the popinjay. + Brooks, Walter R.
Freddy and the space ship. + Brooks, Walter R.
Freddy goes camping. + Brooks, Walter R.
Freddy goes to Florida. + Brooks, Walter R.
Freddy goes to the North Pole. + Brooks, Walter R.
Freddy plays football. + Brooks, Walter R.
Freddy rides again. + Brooks, Walter R.
Freddy the cowboy. + Brooks, Walter R.
Freddy the detective. + Brooks, Walter R.
Freddy the magician. + Brooks, Walter R.

Futures unlimited. + Norton, Alden H.
Futuristic stories. + none
The Futurological Congress. + Lem, Stanislaw

The G-bomb. + Statten, Vargo
The G.C. radiation. + Hill, Ernest
G-8 and his battle aces #1; The bat staffel. + Hogan, Robert J.
G-8 and his battle aces #4; Bombs from the murder wolves. + Hogan, Robert J.
G-8 and his battle aces #5; Vultures of the white death. + Hogan, Robert J.
G-8 and his battle aces #6; Flight from the grave. + Hogan, Robert J.
G-8 and his battle aces #7; Fangs of the sky leopard. + Hogan, Robert J.
G-8 and his battle aces #8; The mark of the vulture. + Hogan, Robert J.
A G. K. Chesterton omnibus. + Chesterton, G. K.
G.O.G. 666. + Taine, John
Gabriel and the creatures. + Heard, Gerald
Gabriel over the White House. + Tweed, Thomas F.
Gabriel Samara. + Oppenheim, E. Phillips
Gabriel Samara, peacemaker. + Oppenheim, E. Phillips
Gadget Man. + Goulart, Ron
Galactic alarm. + Perry Rhodan #3
The galactic breed. + Brackett, Leigh
Galactic cluster. + Blish, James
The galactic colonizers. + Jensen, Norman
Galactic derelict. + Norton, Andre
Galactic diplomat. + Laumer, Keith
Galactic gambit. + Dudley, Roy C.
Galactic intrigue. + Bulmer, H. K.
Galactic odyssey. + Laumer, Keith
Galactic Patrol. + Smith, E. E.
Galactic pot-healer. + Dick, Philip K.
The galactic rejects. + Offutt, Andrew J.
The galactic riddle. + Perry Rhodan #8
Galactic Sibyl Sue Blue. + Brown, Rosel George
Galactic storm. + Hunt, Gill
Galactic takeover bid. + McIntosh, J. T.
The galactic troubadours. + Lightner, A. M.
The Galapagos kid. + Walton, Luke
Galaxies ahead. + Haile, Terence
Galaxies like grains of sand. + Aldiss, Brian W.
Galaxy checklist. + none
Galaxy mission. + Hamilton, Edmond
Galaxy of ghouls. + Merril, Judith
Galaxy of the lost. + Kern, Gregory
The Galaxy Primes. + Smith, Edward E.
Galaxy reader of science fiction. + Gold, H. L.
Galaxy science fiction omnibus. + Gold, H. L.
Galaxy 666. + Torro, Pel
The gale of the world. + Kirk, Laurence
Gallagher's glacier. + Richmond, Leigh & Richmond, Walt
The galleon of Torbay. + Speight, E. E.
Gambles with destiny. + Griffith, George
The gambling ghost, and other tales. + Stivens, Dal
A game of dark. + Mayne, William
The Game-players of Titan. + Dick, Philip K.
Gamefinger. + Allison, Clyde
The games of Neith. + St. Clair, Margaret
Games psyborgs play. + Barbet, Pierre
Gamma product. + Barry, Ray
The gamma ray murders. + Yorke, Preston
The Gammage cup. + Kendall, Carol
Gandle follows his nose. + Broun, Heywood
Gangdom's doom. + Grant, Maxwell
Gangland's doom. + Eisgruber, Frank Jr.
The Ganymede takeover. + Dick, Philip K. & Nelson, Ray

The gap in the curtain. + Buchan, John
Garan the eternal. + Norton, Andre
Garbage world. + Platt, Charles
The garden at 19. + Jepson, Edgar
The garden of Eden. + Brand, Max
The garden of Eden, U.S.A. + Bishop, W. H.
The garden of evil. + Stoker, Bram
The garden of fear. + (Crawford, William L.)
The garden of romance. + Rhys, Ernest
Garden of shame. + Dexter, John
The garden of survival. + Blackwood, Algernon
The Garden of Vision. + Beck, L. Adams
Garden on the Moon. + Boulle, Pierre
A garden to the eastward. + Lamb, Harold
The gardener who saw God. + James, Edward
Gardens One to Five. + Tate, Peter
Gardens 1, 2, 3, 4, 5. + Tate, Peter
The Garin death ray. + Tolstoi, A.
Garranane. + Ingram, Tom
The Garthians. + Leach, Decima
Gas! + Hirschfeld, Burt
The gas. + Platt, Charles
The gas war of 1940. + Bell, Neil
The gasp. + Gary, Romain
Gaston de Blondeville. + Radcliffe, Anne
The gate of time. + Farmer, Philip Jose
The gate of worlds. + Silverberg, Robert
The gatehouse. + Dohrman, Richard
The gateless barrier. + Malet, Lucas
The gates between. + Phelps, Elizabeth Stuart
The gates of Afree, A.D. 1928. + van Laun, Henri
The gates of creation. + Farmer, Philip Jose
The gates of Kamt. + Orczy, Baroness
The gates of paradise. + Inglefield, Eleanor
The gates of the past. + Vaughan, Thomas Hunter
The gates of time. + Barrett, Neal Jr.
Gates to tomorrow. + Donaldy, Ernestine & Norton, Andre
The gates wide open. + Wood, George
Gateway to elsewhere. + Leinster, Murray
Gateway to Hell. + Wheatley, Dennis
The gateway to never. + Chandler, A. Bertram
Gateway to remembrance. + Cradock, Phyllis
Gateway to the stars. + Carnell, John
Gateway to tomorrow. + Carnell, John
Gath. + Tubb, E. C.
Gather, darkness! + Leiber, Fritz
Gather in the Hall of the Planets. + O'Donnell, K. M.
A gathering of ghosts. + Lewis, Gogo & Manley, Seon
The gaudy shadows. + Brunner, John
The gay ghouls. + Roman, Chet
The gay Gnani of Gingalee. + Huntley, Florence
The gay haunt. + Jay, Victor
Gay Hunter. + Mitchell, J. Leslie
The gay rebellion. + Chambers, Robert W.
Gay vampire. + S., Davy
The geek. + Ramirez, Alice Louise
Gemini in darkness. + Ross, Clarissa
The Gemini problem. + Breen, Walter
Gender genocide. + Cooper, Edmund
The General. + Sillitoe, Alan
General Manpower. + Martin, John S.
The general zapped an angel. + Fast, Howard
The general's ring. + Lagerlof, Selma
Generation. + Gerrold, David
Genesis Five. + Allen, Henry Wilson
The Genesis of Nam. + Goodrich, Charles
Genesis two. + Davies, L. P.
The genetic buccaneer. + Kern, Gregory
The genetic general. + Dickson, Gordon R.
The genial dinosaur. + Gridban, Volsted
The genial ghost. + Burr, Frank

The ghost's touch; and, Percy and the prophet. + Collins, Wilkie

The ghoul keepers. + Margulies, Leo

Ghoul lover. + Tralins, Robert

The ghouls. + Haining, Peter

Ghouls and ghosts. + Singer, Kurt

The ghouls, book one. + Haining, Peter

The ghouls, book two. + Haining, Peter

Ghouls in my grave. + Ray, Jean

The giant anthology of science fiction. + Friend, Oscar J. & Margulies, Leo

The giant cat. + Rosny, J. H.

The giant of the north. + Ballantyne, R. M.

The giant of the Sierras. + Hartman, Emerson

Giant of world's end. + Carter, Lin

The giant stumbles. + Lymington, John

The giant under the snow. + Gordon, John

The giantkiller. + Pincher, Chapman

Giants from eternity. + Wellman, Manly Wade

The giant's partner. + Perry Rhodan 33

Giants unleashed. + Conklin, Groff

Giddy Moment. + Carey, Ernestine Gilbreth

The gift. + Dickinson, Peter

A gift from Earth. + Niven, Larry

The gift of Abou Hassan. + Elliott, Francis Perry

The gift of fernseed. + Robinson, H. Perry

A gift of magic. + Duncan, Lois

The gift of the gods. + none.

The giggling ghosts. + Robeson, Kenneth

The Gilded Man. + Smyth, Clifford

The Gilead bomb. + Sinclair, David

Giles Goat-Boy. + Barth, John

Gimpel the fool, and other stories. + Singer, Isaac Bashevis

The ginger star. + Brackett, Leigh

Giphantia. + (Tiphaigne de la Roche, C. F.)

The girdle of Kaf. + Minnett, Cora

Girl everlasting. + Wentworth-James, G. de S.

The girl from Mars. + Breuer, Miles J. & Williamson, Jack

The girl from tomorrow. + Zeigfreid, Karl

The girl from U.N.C.L.E.; The birds-of-a-feather affair. + Avallone, Michael

The girl from U.N.C.L.E.; The blazing affair. + Avallone, Michael

The girl from yesterday. + Hughart, Sarah

The girl in the golden atom. + Cummings, Ray

The girl in the grove. + Severn, David

The girl in the Moon. + von Harbou, Thea

Girl in trouble. + Parker, E. Frank

A girl possessed. + Swenson, Peggy

The girl, the gold watch, & everything. + MacDonald, John D.

The girl who knew tomorrow. + Sherburne, Zoa

The girl with the hungry eyes, and other stories. + (Wollheim, Donald A.)

The girls from Planet 5. + Wilson, Richard

The gismo. + Lazarus, Keo Felker

The gismo from outer space. + Lazarus, Keo Felker

Give daddy the knife, darling. + Lymington, John

Give warning to the world. + Brunner, John

Gladiator. + Wylie, Philip

Gladiator-at-law. + Kornbluth, C. M. & Pohl, Frederik

The gland stealers. + Gayton, Bertram

Glasgow in 1910. + none

The glass bead game. + Hesse, Hermann

The glass bees. + Juenger, Ernst

The glass cage. + Hassler, Kenneth W.

The glass cage. + Lukens, Adam

The glass centipede. + Laing, Alexander & Painter, Thomas

The glass mender, and other stories. + Baring, Maurice

A glass of stars. + Young, Robert F.

The glass too many. + Mann, Jack

Glenvirgin's ghost. + Graham, Winifred

The glimpse. + Bennett, Arnold

A glimpse of Arcadia. + Hastings, Macdonald

The glittering serpent. + Morrison, Emmeline

The Glob. + O'Reilly, John

Global blackout. + Vallance, Karl

The global globules affair. + Latter, Simon

Gloria Victis. + Mitchell, J. A.

Gloriana. + Dixie, Lady Florence

The glorious pool. + Smith, Thorne

Glory. + Stuart, Francis

The glory game. + Laumer, Keith

The glory of Egypt. + Moresby, Louis

The glory of Hera. + Gordon, Caroline

The glory of the Empire. + Ormesson, Jean d'

Glory planet. + Chandler, A. Bertram

Glory Road. + Heinlein, Robert A.

The glory that was. + de Camp, L. Sprague

Glory to Ajeba! + Talbot, George E.

The glowing globe. + Luigi, Belli

Glue factory. + Meltzer, David

A gnome there was, and other tales of science fiction and fantasy. + Padgett, Lewis

The gnome-mobile. + Carey, Mary

The gnomes of the Saline Mountains. + Gross, Anna Goldmark

The gnomobile. + Sinclair, Upton

Go-go SADISTO. + Allison, Clyde

Go home, unicorn. + Macpherson, Donald

The goat-foot god. + Fortune, Dion

The goat without horns. + Swann, Thomas Burnett

Gobi or Shamo. + Murray, G. G. A.

The goblin reservation. + Simak, Clifford D.

The Goblin Tower. + de Camp, L. Sprague

The god beneath the sea. + Blishen, Edward & Garfield, Leon

God in the sand. + Price, Theo

The God killers. + Baxter, John

The God killers. + Ross, James

The God Machine. + Caidin, Martin

The God Machine. + Watkins, William Jon

The god makers. + Herbert, Frank

The god of Planet 607. + Pohlman, Edward

The god of the labyrinth. + Wilson, Colin

The god of this world. + Middleton, John B.

The god with four arms, and other stories. + Bousfield, H. T. W.

Godd. + Ionel

The goddess of Atvatabar. + Bradshaw, William R.

The Goddess of Ganymede. + Resnick, Michael D.

The goddess of ghosts. + Martindale, C. C.

Goddess of Mars. + Fearn, John Russell

The godhood of man. + Mikalowitch, Nicolai

Godling, go home! + Silverberg, Robert

The Godmakers. + Britain, Dan

The Godmakers. + Pendleton, Don

Godman. + Bloodstone, John

Godolphin. + Lytton, Edward Bulwer-

Godolphin; and, Falkland. + Lytton, Edward

Gods and golems. + del Rey, Lester

Gods and their makers. + Housman, Laurence

Gods and their makers, and other stories. + Housman, Laurence

God's children. + Allman, James

Gods for tomorrow. + Santesson, Hans Stefan

God's front porch. + Frings, Ketti

The gods hate Kansas. + Millard, Joseph

Gods, men, and ghosts. + Dunsany, Lord

Gods of darkness. + Zeigfreid, Karl

The gods of Foxcroft. + Levy, David

The gods of Mars. + Burroughs, Edgar Rice
The gods of Mars; and, The Warlord of Mars. + Burroughs, Edgar Rice
The gods of Pegana. + Dunsany, Lord
The gods of the dead. + Graham, Winifred
The gods of Tlen. + Lambert, William J. III
Gods or demons? + Lightner, A. M.
God's secret. + Pier, Arthur Stanwood
The gods themselves. + Asimov, Isaac
The gods were promiscuous. + Held, John Jr.
The Godwhale. + Bass, T. J.
The Gogglers. + Raiden, Edward
Going home. + Pain, Barry
Going west. + Bramwell, James
Going west. + King, Basil
The gold at the starbow's end. + Pohl, Frederik
The gold bug. + Poe, Edgar Allan
The gold bug, and other selections from the works of Edgar Allan Poe. + Poe, Edgar Allan
The gold bug, and other stories. + Poe, Edgar Allan
The gold-bug, and other tales. + Poe, Edgar Allan
The gold bug, and other tales and poems. + Poe, Edgar Allan
The gold bug; and, The black cat. + Poe, Edgar Allan
The gold bug, The purloined letter, and other tales. + Poe, Edgar Allan
The gold diggers. + Fleming, A. M.
The gold-finder. + Griffith, George
Gold like glass. + Carter, Frederick
The gold of Akada. + Titan, Earl
The gold of Ophir. + Gwinn, D. Howard
The gold of the gods. + Reeve, Arthur B.
The gold ogre. + Robeson, Kenneth
The Gold Point, and other strange stories. + Jackson, Charles Loring
Gold the man. + Green, Joseph
The gold tooth. + Taine, John
The gold worshippers. + Harris-Burland, J. B.
The golden age. + Jenkins, Esther Bigger
The Golden Amazon. + Fearn, John Russell
The Golden Amazon returns. + Fearn, John Russell
The Golden Amazon's triumph. + Fearn, John Russell
A golden anniversary bibliography of Edgar Rice Burroughs. + Heins, Henry Hardy
The golden ape. + Chase, Adam
The golden apples of the Sun. + Bradbury, Ray
The golden Archer. + Mason, Gregory
The golden ball, and other stories. + Christie, Agatha
The golden beast. + Oppenheim, E. Phillips
The golden blight. + England, George Allan
Golden blood. + Williamson, Jack
The golden boats of Taradata affair. + Latter, Simon
The Golden Book of Springfield. + Lindsay, Vachel
The golden bottle. + Donnelly, Ignatius
The golden Chalice. + Fanthorpe, R. L.
Golden cities, far. + Carter, Lin
The golden city. + Verrill, A. Hyatt
The golden dancer. + Hume, Cyril
The golden enemy. + Key, Alexander
The golden fleece. + Graves, Robert
The Golden Fluid. + Dix, Maurice B.
The golden girl of Hockeinbeck. + Roxbury, Kyle
Golden goddess. + Eden, Rob
The Golden Goddess gambit. + Maddock, Larry
The golden gospel. + Scott, Gabriel
Golden isle. + Phillips, Roland Ashford
The golden kazoo. + Schneider, John G.
The golden lake. + Dawe, W. Carlton
The golden load. + Slater, W. H.
The golden olive. + Cristabel
The Golden people. + Saberhagen, Fred
The golden peril. + Robeson, Kenneth

The golden phoenix. + Carlton, Mary Shaffer
The golden pine cone. + Clark, Catherine Anthony
The golden promise. + Zuber, Stanley
The golden road. + Knight, Damon
The golden rooms. + Fisher, Vardis
The golden scarab. + Adye, John
The golden scorpion. + Rohmer, Sax
The golden scorpion omnibus. + Rohmer, Sax
The golden shadow. + Blishen, Edward & Garfield, Leon
The golden skull. + Blaine, John
The golden snake. + Campbell, Donald
The golden star. + Dwyer, Winifred
The golden star. + Noel, L.
The golden stile. + Walker, Gwen
The golden strangers. + Treece, Henry
Golden tales of Anatole France. + France, Anatole
The golden virgin. + Dipper, Alan
The golden voyage of Sinbad. + Hart, Steve
Golden wings. + Morris, William
Golden wings; Svend and his brethren. + Morris, William
Goldie. + Chilton, Irma
The golem. + Bloch, Chayim
The Golem. + Meyrink, Gustav
Golf in the year 2000. + K., J. A. C.
Goliah. + London, Jack
Gomorrah. + Andrews, Lewis M. & Karlins, Marvin
Gondez the monk. + Ireland, W. H.
Gone to be snakes now. + Bell, Neal
Gone to ground. + White, T. H.
Good as gold. + Toombs, Alfred
Good Friday--1963. + Carney, Otis
Good neighbors, and other strangers. + Pangborn, Edgar
Good news from Tolkien's Middle Earth. + Ellwood, Gracia Fay
Goodbye Charlie. + Albert, Marvin H.
Good-bye, white man. + Bouic, Frederic Vernon
Goods and chattels. + Benet, Laura
Gooseflesh! + Ghidalia, Vic
The goose's tale. + Dogbolt, Barnaby [see Addendum]
Gor omnibus. + Norman, John
Gorgo. + Bingham, Carson
The Gorgon festival. + Boyd, John
The Gorgon's head. + Black, Ladbroke
Gorgonzola, won't you please come home? + Ames, Clyde
Gorilla gold. + Gorman, J. T.
Gormenghast. + Peake, Mervyn
Gortschakoff and Bismarck. + none
Goslings. + Beresford, J. D.
The gospel according to Joe. + Gurney, A. R. Jr.
A gothic bibliography. + Summers, Montague
Gothic flame. + Varma, Devendra P. [see Addendum]
Gothic horror book. + Singer, Kurt
The gothic quest. + Summers, Montague
The gothic reader. + Singer, Kurt
Gothic tales of terror. + Haining, Peter
Gothic tales of terror, volume one. + Haining, Peter
Gothic tales of terror, volume two. + Haining, Peter
Governor Hardy. + Blair, Hamish
The graduated robot, and other stories. + (Elwood, Roger)
La gran Quibira. + Corbyn, Clara A. B.
Grand Canyon. + Sackville-West, V.
The grand illusion. + Statten, Vargo
The Grand Inquisitor. + Douglas, Donald
The grand voyage. + Smith, W. J.
The grass is always greener. + Malcolm-Smith, George
The graveyard reader. + Conklin, Groff
Gravitor. + Darrington, Hugh
Gray--For titles beginning with this word see also: Grey
The gray aliens. + Holly, J. Hunter

The gray creatures. + Zorro
Gray Lensman. + Smith, E. E.
Gray magic. + Norton, Andre
Gray matters. + Hjortsberg, William
The gray prince. + Vance, Jack
The gray world. + Underhill, Evelyn
The great aeroplane. + Brereton, F. S.
The great amen. + Burks, Arthur J.
The great and terrible quest. + Lovett, Margaret
The great Anglo-American War of 1900. + Anson, Capt.
Great astronomical discoveries lately made by Sir John Herschel at the Cape of Good Hope. + (Locke, Richard Adams)
The great awakening. + Draper, Blanche A.
The great awakening. + Merrill, Albert Adams
The great awakening. + Oppenheim, E. Phillips
The great battle of Patchumup. + Skunks, Major
The great book of thrillers. + Thomson, H. Douglas
The great brain robbery. + Fisher, James P.
The Great Bread Trust. + Wright, W. H.
Great Britain in 1841. + none
Great British tales of terror. + Haining, Peter
Great Caesar's ghost. + Coles, Manning
The great calamity. + Kearney, C. B.
The great celestial railroad from the city of sin to the city of God. + Owen, Olin Marvin
The great computer. + Johannesson, Olof
The great conflict. + Hall, Hal
The great demonstration. + Roof, Katharine Metcalf
Great detective stories. + Morris, Rosamund
The great disciple, and other stories. + Ready, W. B.
The Great Explosion. + Russell, Eric Frank
The great fog. + Heard, H. F.
The great fog, and other weird tales. + Heard, H. F.
The great gesture. + Blair, Hamish
Great ghost stories. + Dale, Harrison
Great ghost stories. + French, Joseph Lewis
Great ghost stories. + Stern, Philip Van Doren
Great ghost stories. + van Thal, Herbert
Great ghost stories of the old west. + Baker, Betty
Great ghost stories of the world. + Laing, Alexander
The great god Pan. + Machen, Arthur
The great god Pan, and other weird stories. + Machen, Arthur
The great god Pan; and, The inmost light. + Machen, Arthur
The great gold steal. + White, Ted
The great green serpent. + Mansford, Charles J.
The great Haddon. + Kelton, Aryan
The great hold-up mystery. + Usher, Wilfred
Great horror movies. + Friedman, Favius
Great horror stories. + Morris, Rosamund
The great idea. + Hazlitt, Henry
The great illusion. + Binder, Eando & Williamson, Jack & Hamilton, Edmond & Gallun, Raymond Z. & Fearn, John Russell
The great image. + "Pan"
The great Keinplatz experiment, and other stories. + Doyle, A. Conan
The great Keinplatz experiment, and other tales of twilight and the unseen. + Doyle, A. Conan
The great leap backward. + Green, Robert
The great man's life, 1925 to 2000 A.C. + Van Petten, Albert Archer
The great miracle. + Vanewords, John Pre
The great mirror. + Burks, Arthur J.
Great mischief. + Pinckney, Josephine
Great monsters of the movies. + Edelson, Edward
The great Moon hoax of Richard Adams Locke. + Locke, Richard Adams
The great naval war of 1887. + (Clowes, W. Laird)
The Great One. + Roland, Nicholas

The Great Ones. + Deegan, Jon J.
The great Pacific war. + Bywater, Hector C.
The great peril. + Hawker, Caleb
The great peril, and how it was averted. + Clowes, W. Laird
The great pirate syndicate. + Griffith, George
The great Prince Shan. + Oppenheim, E. Phillips
The Great Quill. + Garson, Paul
The great Quillow. + Thurber, James
The great red dragon. + Chester, Lord
The great revolution of 1905. + Hayes, Frederick W.
The great Russian invasion of India. + Dekhnewallah, A.
Great science-fiction. + Licata, Tony
Great science fiction about doctors. + Conklin, Groff & Fabricant, Noah D.
Great science fiction adventures. + Shaw, Larry T.
Great science fiction by scientists. + Conklin, Groff
Great science fiction stories. + Smith, Cordelia Titcomb
Great science fiction stories about Mars. + Dikty, T. E.
Great science-fiction stories about the Moon. + Dikty, T. E.
The great secret. + Nisbet, Hume
The great seven. + Flood, Jno. H. Jr.
Great short novels of adult fantasy. + Carter, Lin
Great short novels of adult fantasy, volume II. + Carter, Lin
Great short novels of science fiction. + Silverberg, Robert
Great short stories. + Patten, William
Great short stories of detection, mystery, and horror. + Sayers, Dorothy L.
Great short stories of detection, mystery, and horror, second series. + Sayers, Dorothy L.
Great short stories of detection, mystery, and horror, third series. + Sayers, Dorothy L.
Great short stories of Robert Louis Stevenson. + Stevenson, Robert Louis
Great short works of Edgar Allan Poe. + Poe, Edgar Allan
Great short works of Henry Van Dyke. + Van Dyke, Henry
The great stone of Sardis. + Stockton, Frank R.
The great stone of Sardis; The water-devil. + Stockton, Frank R.
Great stories of detection, mystery, and horror, part II. + Sayers, Dorothy L.
Great stories of mystery and imagination. + Douglas, Bryan
Great stories of science fiction. + Leinster, Murray
Great stories of space travel. + Conklin, Groff
The great tales and poems of Edgar Allan Poe. + Poe, Edgar Allan
Great tales of fantasy and imagination. + Stern, Philip Van Doren
Great tales of horror. + Bowen, Marjorie
Great tales of horror. + Poe, Edgar Allan
Great tales of horror and suspense. + none
Great tales of mystery. + Bull, Randolph C.
Great tales of terror. + Bull, Randolph C.
Great tales of terror and the supernatural. + Fraser, Phyllis & Wise, Herbert A.
Great tales of terror from Europe and America. + Haining, Peter
The great time machine hoax. + Laumer, Keith
The great 24-hour thing. + Offutt, Andrew J.
Great untold stories of fantasy and horror. + Moskowitz, Sam & Norton, Alden H.
The Great Wall of China, and other pieces. + Kafka, Franz

The great war in England in 1897. + Le Queux, William
The Great War of 189-. + Colomb, P. & Maurice, J. F.
  & Maude, F. N. & Forbes, Archibald & Lowe, Charles
  & Murray, D. Christie & Scudamore, F.
The Great War Syndicate. + Stockton, Frank R.
Great was the fall. + (M., A. H.)
The great wash. + Kersh, Gerald
The Great Weather Syndicate. + Griffith, George
The great weird stories. + Neale, Arthur
The great white queen. + Le Queux, William
The great white space. + Copper, Basil
The great white way. + Paine, Albert Bigelow
The greater trumps. + Williams, Charles
The greatest adventure. + Taine, John
The greatest adventure stories ever told. + Shaw,
  Arnold
The greatest lover in the world. + Austin, Alex
Greed's grip broken. + Savage, Joseph W.
The Greek. + Thayer, Tiffany
The Green Brain. + Herbert, Frank
The Green Child. + Read, Herbert
Green corn moon. + Lanning, George
Green darkness. + Seton, Anya
The green death. + Robeson, Kenneth
The green door. + Wilkins, Mary E.
The green drift. + Lymington, John
Green dusk for dreams. + Severance, Felix
The green eagle. + Robeson, Kenneth
The green eyes of Bast. + Rohmer, Sax
Green fire. + Taine, John
The green flames of Aries. + Lory, Robert
The green flash, and other stories of horror, suspense,
  and fantasy. + Aiken, Joan
The green gene. + Dickinson, Peter
The Green Girl. + Williamson, Jack
The green hill of Nendrum. + Andrews, J. S.
The green hills of Earth. + Heinlein, Robert A.
The Green Hornet in The infernal light. + Friend, Ed
The Green Hornet; The case of the disappearing doctor.
  + Keith, Brandon
The Green Isle of the Great Deep. + Gunn, Neil M.
The green killer. + Robeson, Kenneth
The Green Kingdom. + Maddux, Rachel
The green lacquer pavilion. + Beauclerk, Helen
The green lady. + Tweedale, Violet
The green machine. + Ridley, F. H.
The green man. + Amis, Kingsley
The green man. + Sherman, Harold M.
The green man from space. + Zarem, Lewis
The green man of Graypec. + Pragnell, Festus
The green man of Kilsona. + Pragnell, Festus
The green Mandarin mystery. + Malcom, Grant
Green mansions. + Hudson, W. H.
The green mare. + Ayme, Marcel
The green millennium. + Leiber, Fritz
The Green Mouse. + Chambers, Robert W.
The Green odyssey. + Farmer, Philip Jose
Green Phoenix. + Swann, Thomas Burnett
The green planet. + Holly, J. Hunter
The green plantations. + Elton, John
The Green Queen. + St. Clair, Margaret
The Green Rain. + Tabori, Paul
The green ray. + Lindsay, David T.
The green round. + Machen, Arthur
The green rust. + Wallace, Edgar
The green Scamander. + Meagher, Maude
The Green Suns. + Ward, Henry
Green tea. + Le Fanu, J. Sheridan
Green tea,and other ghost stories. + Le Fanu, J.
  Sheridan
Green thoughts. + Collier, John
Green thoughts, and other strange tales. + Collier,
  John

Greener than you think. + Moore, Ward
Greenshards. + Buchanan, Marie
Greenwitch. + Cooper, Susan
The Greks bring gifts. + Leinster, Murray
The gremlins. + Dahl, Roald
Gremlins, go home! + Dickson, Gordon R. & Bova, Ben
Grendel. + Gardner, John
Grey--For titles beginning with this word see also:
  Gray
The grey aliens. + Holly, J. Hunter
The grey beast. + Atholl, Justin
Grey face. + Rohmer, Sax
Grey Ghost. + Pollexfen, Muriel A.
Grey Maiden. + Smith, Arthur D. Howden
The grey ones. + Lymington, John
Grey shapes. + Mann, Jack
The grey studio. + Scudder, Antoinette
The grey world. + Underhill, Evelyn
Greybeard. + Aldiss, Brian W.
Greyland. + Van Arnam, Dave
Greylorn. + Laumer, Keith
Griffin booklet one. + (Crawford, William L.)
The grim caretaker. + Ascher, Eugene
Grim death. + Thomson, Christine Campbell
Grim tales. + Nesbit, E.
The grim tomorrow. + Richmond, Mary
Grimbold's other world. + Gray, Nicholas Stuart
Grimm's world. + Vinge, Vernor
The grimoire, and other supernatural stories. + Sum-
  mers, Montague
Grinny. + Fisk, Nicholas
The grip of fear. + Hansen, Vern
The grip of the strangler. + Cooper, John C.
Grokking the future. + Hollister, Bernard C. &
  Thompson, Deane C.
Grotesques. + Van Roosbroeck, G. L.
Grotto. + Charters, David Wilton
Ground zero man. + Shaw, Bob
The Groundstar conspiracy. + Davies, L. P.
Group feast. + Saxton, Josephine
Grove of doom. + Grant, Maxwell
Gruesome cargoes. + Thomson, Christine Campbell
Grugan's god. + Andrews, F. Emerson
The guardian demons. + Dawson, Warrington
The Guardians. + Baker, W. Howard
The guardians. + Christopher, John
The guardians. + Perry Rhodan 58
The Guardians #1; The killing bone. + Saxon, Peter
The Guardians #2; Dark ways to death. + Saxon, Peter
The Guardians #3; The haunting of Alan Mais. + Saxon,
  Peter
The Guardians #4; The vampires of Finistere. + Saxon,
  Peter
Guardians of the Gate. + Trimble, Jacquelyn & Trimble,
  Louis
Guardians of the treasure. + McNeile, H. C.
Guardians of time. + Anderson, Poul
Les Guerilleres. + Wittig, Monique
Guernica night. + Malzberg, Barry N.
A guide to Middle-Earth. + Foster, Robert
Guide to science fiction. + Martinez, Diana & Paine,
  Doris M.
The guilty head. + Gary, Romain
Gulliver in Lilliput. + Swift, Jonathan
Gulliver Joi. + Perce, Elbert
Gulliver of Mars. + Arnold, Edwin L.
Gulliver redivious. + (Raspe, Rudolf)
Gulliver revived. + (Raspe, Rudolf)
Gulliveriana V. + Bush, George E. Jr. & Welcher,
  Jeanne K.
Gulliveriana IV. + Bush, George E. Jr. & Welcher,
  Jeanne K.

Gulliveriana: I. + Bush, George E. Jr. & Welcher, Jeanne K.

Gulliveriana III. + Bush, George E. Jr. & Welcher, Jeanne K.

Gulliveriana: II. + Bush, George E. Jr. & Welcher, Jeanne K.

Gulliver's travels. + Gulliver, Lemuel

Gulliver's travels. + Swift, Jonathan

Gulliver's travels among the little people of Lilliput. + Swift, Jonathan

Gulliver's travels among the little people of Lilliput and the giants of Brobdingnag. + Swift, Jonathan

Gulliver's travels, and other works. + Swift, Jonathan

Gulliver's travels, and other writings. + Swift, Jonathan

Gulliver's travels in Lilliput. + Swift, Jonathan

Gulliver's travels in Lilliput and Brobdingnag. + Swift, Jonathan

Gulliver's travels into several remote nations of the World. + Swift, Jonathan

Gulliver's travels, The tale of a tub, and The battle of the books. + Swift, Jonathan

Gulliver's voyage to Lilliput. + Swift, Jonathan

Gulliver's voyages to Lilliput and Brobdingnag. + Swift, Jonathan

Gumption Island. + Morley, Felix

A gun for dinosaur, and other imaginative tales. + de Camp, L. Sprague

Gunmen, gallants, and ghosts. + Wheatley, Dennis

Gunner Cade. + Judd, Cyril

Gunner Cade. + Kornbluth, C. M. & Merril, Judith

The guns of Avalon. + Zelazny, Roger

Guns of Galt. + Clift, Denison

The guns of Terra 10. + Pendleton, Don

The Guthrie method. + none

The gutter of creation. + Dwinell, R. M.

Guy Garrick. + Reeve, Arthur B. [see Addendum]

Guy in the jungle. + Graydon, William Murray

Gwen, in green. + Zachary, Hugh

Gyrator control. + Lang, King

HAL in the classroom. + Amelio, Ralph J.

H-bomb over America. + Sutton, Jeff

The HEROD men. + Kamin, Nick

H. G. Wells: critic of progress. + Williamson, Jack

H.M.S. ____. + "Klaxon"

HPL. + Frierson, Maude & Frierson, Penny

H.P.L.: a memoir. + Derleth, August

H. P. Lovecraft: a bibliography. + Brennan, Joseph Payne

H. P. Lovecraft: a portrait. + Cook, W. Paul

H. P. Lovecraft: an evaluation. + Brennan, Joseph Payne

H. Philip Birdsong's ESP. + Lawrence, Harriet

Had any lately? + Conway, Troy

Hadon of ancient Opar. + Farmer, Philip Jose

Hadrian the Seventh. + Rolfe, Fr.

The Haggard omnibus. + Haggard, William

Hahtibee, the elephant. + Slaughter, Charles E.

Hail Bolonia! + Lister, Stephen

Hail, Klarkash-Ton! + Lovecraft, H. P.

Hairbreadth escapes of Major Mendax. + Crofton, Francis Blake

The hairy horror trick. + Corbett, Scott

The Halcyon Drift. + Stableford, Brian M.

Haldane Station. + Randall, Florence Engel

Halek. + Nicholson, John H.

Half a minute's silence, and other stories. + Baring, Maurice

Half a sovereign. + Hay, Ian

The half-brothers. + Lawrence, Ann [see Addendum]

The half-god. + Dorrington, Albert

Half-gods. + Sheehan, Murray

Half magic. + Eager, Edward

The 'Half Moon.' + Hueffer, Ford Madox

Half past human. + Bass, T. J.

Half-past tomorrow. + Carlsen, Ruth Christoffer

The half pint flash. + Heyward, DuBose

The half-pint jinni, and other stories. + Dolbier, Maurice

The halfling, and other stories. + Brackett, Leigh

Hall of mirrors. + Wilson, John Rowan

Hallowmas Abbey. + Graham, Winifred

The Halloween tree. + Bradbury, Ray

The halo highway. + Bernard, Rafe

The Hamelin plague. + Chandler, A. Bertram

Hamlet had an uncle. + Cabell, Branch

The Hammer horror omnibus. + Burke, John

The Hampdenshire Wonder. + Beresford, J. D.

Hamtura. + Lockhart-Ross, H. S.

Hamydal, the vagabond philosopher. + Dekobra, Maurice

The hand of Cain. + Thomas, Martin

Hand of doom. + Fanthorpe, R. Lionel

The hand of Dracula. + Lory, Robert

The hand of Fu-Manchu. + Rohmer, Sax

Hand of Glory. + Herbert, Benson

The hand of havoc. + Grey, Charles

The hand of horror. + Jerome, Owen Fox

The hand of Kane. + Howard, Robert E.

The hand of Zei. + de Camp, L. Sprague

A handbook of science fiction and fantasy. + Tuck, Donald H.

A handful of darkness. + Dick, Philip K.

A handful of time. + Brown, Rosel George

Hands across the water. + Arnold, Ralph

The hands of Cain. + Thomas, Martin

The hands of Orlac. + Bateman, Robert

The hands of Orlac. + Renard, Maurice

The hands of Veronica. + Hurst, Fannie

The handwriting on the wall. + (Cooper, J. C.)

Hanit the enchantress. + Pier, Garrett Chatfield

Hannes Bok illustration index. + Brooks, Ned & Martin, Don

The Hannes Bok memorial showcase of fantasy art. + Petaja, Emil

Hannibal's man, and other tales. + Kip, Leonard

The haploids. + Sohl, Jerry

Happy endings. + Knight, Damon

The happy planet. + Clarke, Joan B.

The happy prince, and other fairy tales. + Wilde, Oscar

The happy prince, and other stories. + Wilde, Oscar

The happy prince, and other tales. + Wilde, Oscar

Happy returns. + Coles, Manning

The harbour of death. + Spanner, E. F.

Hard-core murder. + Kenyon, Paul

A hard man is good to find. + Conway, Troy

Hard to be a god. + Strugatsky, Arkady & Strugatsky, Boris

The hard way up. + Chandler, A. Bertram

Harder than steel. + Thorne, Guy

Harding's luck. + Nesbit, E. [see Addendum]

Harilek. + "Ganpat"

Harlan Ellison: a bibliographical checklist. + Swigart, Leslie Kay

The harlequin opal. + Hume, Fergus

Harold in Heavenland. + Stokes, H. A. C.

Harps in the wind. + Hichens, Robert

Harriet Hume. + West, Rebecca

Harry Cat's pet puppy. + Selden, George [see Addendum]

Harry Escombe. + Collingwood, Harry

Harry Harrison bibliographia (1951-1965). + Biamonti, Francesco

Her demon lover. + Bronte, Louisa
Her invisible spirit mate. + Glass, Mrs. Charles Wilder
Her last lover. + Gardner, Celia E.
Her magic spell. + Hytes, Jason
Her ways are death. + Mann, Jack
Herbert. + Wilson, Hazel
Herbert's space ship. + Wilson, Hazel
Herbie rides again. + Cebulash, Mel
Hercules, my shipmate. + Graves, Robert
Hercules--sportsman. + Graves, Robert
Here. + Forrest, Maryann
Here abide monsters. + Norton, Andre
Here and beyond. + Wharton, Edith
Here and otherwise. + Knowles, Vernon
Here (away from it all). + Forrest, Maryann
Here before Kilroy. + Walton, Su
Here comes an old sailor. + Sheppard, Alfred Tresidder
Here comes somebody. + Lampman, Ben Hur
Here is thy victory. + Barry, Iris
Here today. + Coates, John
The heretic. + Woodman, George
A heritage of horror. + Pirie, David
The heritage of the quest. + Cope, Gertrude Venetta
Heritage of the star. + Engdahl, Sylvia Louise
Hermes speaks. + Jaeger, Muriel
The hermit. + Voltaire
Herne the hunter. + Ainsworth, W. Harrison
The hero from otherwhere. + Williams, Jay
The Hero of Downways. + Coney, Michael G.
The hero-pulp index. + McKinstry, Lohr & Weinberg, Robert
Heroes & villains. + Carter, Angela
The heroes of Smokeover. + Jacks, L. P.
The heroine. + Barrett, Eaton Stannard
Heroneous in 69. + Arthur, William
Hero's walk. + Crane, Robert
Herovit's world. + Malzberg, Barry N.
The Hesperides. + Palmer, John
Heu-Heu. + Haggard, H. Rider
Hex. + Robeson, Kenneth
The hidden city. + Bridges, T. C.
The hidden city. + McDougall, Walter H.
Hidden death. + Grant, Maxwell
The hidden faith. + Thurber, Alwyn M.
The hidden kingdom. + Hamilton, M. Lynn
The hidden people. + Miller, Leo E.
The hidden planet. + Wollheim, Donald A.
Hidden Saria. + Halford, John
The hidden tribe. + Wright, S. Fowler
The hidden universe. + Farley, Ralph Milne
Hidden valley. + Pier, Garritt Chatfield
Hidden witchery. + Tourneur, Nigel
Hidden world. + Coblentz, Stanton A.
Hierarchies. + Phillifent, John T.
Hieroglyphic tales. + Walpole, Horace
The hieros gamos of Sam and An Smith. + Saxton, Josephine
Hiero's journey. + Lanier, Sterling E.
Hiero-salem. + Mason, E. L.
The high crusade. + Anderson, Poul
High crystal. + Caidin, Martin
High Deryni. + Kurtz, Katherine
The high destiny. + Morgan, Dan
The high hex. + Janifer, Laurence M. & Treibich, S. J.
The High King. + Alexander, Lloyd
High magic's aid. + Scrire. O.T.O. 4=7
The high place. + Cabell, James Branch
High requiem. + Cory, Desmond
The high society. + Gerberg, Mort
High sorcery. + Norton, Andre

High thrust. + Auden, Renee
High vacuum. + Maine, Charles Eric
High water at Catfish Bend. + Burman, Ben Lucien
Higher things. + Harrison, Michael
Highways in hiding. + Smith, George O.
Highwood. + Barrett, Neal Jr.
Hijack. + Wellen, Edward
The hill of dreams. + Machen, Arthur
The hill of trouble. + Benson, Arthur Christopher
The hill road. + Mayne, William
The hills of Ruel, and other stories. + Macleod, Fiona
The hills were liars. + Hughes, Riley
Hindenburg's march into London. + (Munch, P. G.)
The Hippocratic oath. + Eros, John
His first million women. + Weston, George
His level best, and other stories. + Hale, Edward Everett
His Majesty's greatest subject. + Thorburn, S. S.
His monkey wife. + Collier, John
His mortal tenement. + Dawson, A. J.
His Pseudoic Majesty. + Smith, William Augustus
His psychic daughter. + Lea, Dave
His Wisdom, the Defender. + Newcomb, Simon
The history and adventures of an atom. + Smollett, Dr.
A history and checklist of New worlds. + Burgess, Brian
The history of a voyage to the Moon. + none
History of a world of immortals without a god. + Skorpios, Antares
The history of Autonous. + none
The history of Israel Jobson, the wandering Jew. + (Wilson, Miles)
The history of Jack Smith. + Lucas, Charles
The history of Mr. Polly; and, The war in the air. + Wells, H. G.
The history of Mr. Polly; The wonderful visit. + Wells, H. G.
The history of Nourjahad. + Sheridan, Mrs.
The history of the Caliph Vathek. + Beckford, William
The history of the Caliph Vathek; also, Rasselas, Prince of Abyssinia. + none
A history of the Hugo, Nebula, and International Fantasy Award. + DeVore, Howard & Franson, Donald
History of the plague in London in 1665; and, The consolidator. + Defoe, Daniel
The history of the science fiction magazine, part 1. Ashley, Michael
A history of the sudden and terrible invasion of English by the French in the month of May, 1852. + none
History of the world in epitome. + Russell, Bertrand
The history of Zadig. + Voltaire
Hitler's daughter. + Goss, Gary
Hitty. + Field, Rachel
The hobbit. + Tolkien, J. R. R.
The hocus root. + Foster, L. B.
The Hodsall wizard. + Wintle, Hector
Hoffmann's fairy tales. + Hoffmann, E. T. A.
Hoffmann's strange stories. + Hoffmann, E. T. A.
Holding wonder. + Henderson, Zenna
Hole in Heaven. + Fawcett, F. Dubrez
A hole in space. + Niven, Larry
A hole in the hill. + Peeples, Edwin A. Jr.
The hole in the world. + Lymington, John
The hole in the zero. + Joseph, M. K.
The hole of the pit. + Ross, Adrian
Holiday. + Deamer, Dulcie
Holidays with hobgoblins; and, Talk of strange things. + Costello, Dudley
The hollow crown affair. + McDaniel, David
The hollow hills. + Stewart, Mary

The hollow land. + Morris, William
The hollow land, and other contributions to the Oxford and Cambridge magazine (1856). + Morris, William
The hollow lands. + Moorcock, Michael
The hollow skin. + Swain, Virginia
The Hollywood nightmare. + Haining, Peter
Holocaust. + Boland, John
The holy cross, and other tales. + Field, Eugene
The Holy Flower. + Haggard, H. Rider
The holy mountain. + Reynolds, Stephen
The holy sinner. + Mann, Thomas
The holy terror. + Wells, H. G.
Holy terrors. + Machen, Arthur
Home is the Martian. + Kent, Philip
The homecoming. + Angus, John
Homeward bound. + Verne, Jules
The homework machine. + Abrashkin, Raymond & Williams, Jay
Homunculus. + Delblanc, Sven
The homunculus. + Keller, David H.
Honey for the ghost. + Golding, Louis
Honeymoon in Hell. + Brown, Fredric
A honeymoon in space. + Griffith, George
The honor of Gaston Le Torch. + Perret, Jacques
The hoofmarks of the faun. + Ransome, Arthur
Hook; The boosted man. + Zetford, Tully
Hook; Whirlpool of stars. + Zetford, Tully
The Hopkins manuscript. + Sherriff, R. C.
The hopping ha'penny. + Loch, J. M.
Horace Sippog and the sirens' song. + Walton, Su
Horan. + Lewis, Philip C.
Horizon Alpha. + Mason, Douglas R.
The hormone holocaust. + Heineke, L. Thomas
Horn. + Mano, D. Keith
The horn of time. + Anderson, Poul
The horned crescent. + Duff, Douglas V.
The horned shepherd. + Jepson, Edgar
The horrific world of monsters. + Barber, Dulan
Horror! + Douglas, Drake
Horror. + Grant, Marcus
Horror & fantasy in the cinema. + Hutchinson, Tom
Horror and science fiction films. + Willis, Donald C.
Horror anthology. + Bentlif, Syd
Horror castle. + Sharp, Robert
The horror expert. + Long, Frank Belknap
The horror film. + Butler, Ivan
The horror from the hills. + Long, Frank Belknap
The horror horn, and other stories. + Benson, E. F.
Horror hunters. + Elwood, Roger & Ghidalia, Vic
Horror in the cinema. + Butler, Ivan
The horror in the museum, and other revisions. + Lovecraft, H. P.
Horror in the night. + MacGregor, Richard
Horror medley. + Hervey, Michael
Horror movies. + Clarens, Carlos
The horror of Abbot's Grange, and other stories. + Cowles, Frederick I.
Horror omnibus. + none
Horror omnibus. + Singer, Kurt
The horror on the asteroid, and other tales of planetary horror. + Hamilton, Edmond
Horror parade. + Hopkins, R. Thurston
Horror-7. + Bloch, Robert
Horror-7, and other stories. + Pickersgill, Frederick
Horror stories. + none
Horror stories from Tales to be told in the dark. + Davenport, Basil
Horror tales. + Dark, James
Horror tales. + Elwood, Roger
Horror times ten. + Norton, Alden H.
Horrors. + none
Horrors! + Douglas, Drake

Horrors in hiding. + Moskowitz, Sam & Norton, Alden H.
Horrors unknown. + Moskowitz, Sam
Horrors unseen. + Moskowitz, Sam
Horrorscope; The curse of Leo. + Lory, Robert
Horrorscope; The revenge of Taurus. + Lory, Robert
Horrorscopes; The green flames of Aries. + Lory, Robert
The horse and his boy. + Lewis, C. S.
The horse that played center field. + Higdon, Hal
Horsemen from nowhere. + Abramov, Aleksandr & Abramov, Sergei
Horses' asteroid. + Fritch, Charles E.
Hosanna! + Newman, Bernard
The hospital horror. + Binder, Otto
Hospital station. + White, James
Hostage. + Mason, Colin
Hostile worlds. + Hunt, Gill
Hosts of ghosts. + Sapte, W. Jr.
Hosts of the flaming death. + Steele, Curtis
Hot and cold running cities. + McHargue, Georgess
The hot spot. + Leinster, Murray
Hot wireless sets, aspirin tablets, the sandpaper sides of used matches, and something that might have been castor oil. + Compton, D. G.
Hotel Cosmos. + Burke, Jonathan
Hotep. + Myers, William Wilshire
Hothouse. + Aldiss, Brian W.
The hothouse by the East River. + Spark, Muriel
The hothouse world. + MacIsaac, Fred
Hound dog Moses and the promised land. + Edmonds, Walter D. [see Addendum]
The hound of death, and other stories. + Christie, Agatha
The hound of Florence. + Salten, Felix
Hound of Heaven. + Addington, Sarah [see Addendum]
The hounds of Hell. + Parry, Michel
The hounds of Skaith. + Brackett, Leigh
The Hounds of Tindalos. + Long, Frank Belknap
The hour of the angel. + Oliver, Jane
Hour of the Horde. + Dickson, Gordon R.
The hour of the Phoenix. + Richards, Henry
The hour of the Phoenix. + Saxon, Richard
The hour of the robots. + Bruckner, Karl
The house at Akiya. + Butler, William
The house at Fernwood; and, The wager. + Oursler, Fulton
A house-boat on the Styx. + Bangs, John Kendrick
The house in Half Moon Street, and other stories. + Bolitho, Hector
The house in Norham Gardens. + Lively, Penelope [see Addendum]
The house in November. + Laumer, Keith
The house in the valley, and other tales of terror. + Singer, Kurt
The house in the wood. + Sudbery, Rodie
The house mother. + Owen, Frank
The house of Arden. + Nesbit, E.
House of dark shadows. + Ross, Marilyn
The house of darkness. + Scoggins, C. E.
The house of dawn. + Scoggins, C. E.
The house of defence. + Benson, E. F.
The house of dreams. + Dawson, William J.
House of entropy. + Sheldon, Roy
The house of fear. + Service, Robert W.
The house of fulfillment. + Beck, L. Adams
The house of horror. + Adkinson, Robert & Eyles, Allen & Fry, Nicholas
House of incest. + Nin, Anais
The house of living death. + Blore, Trevor
The house of lost identity. + Corley, Donald
House of many changes. + Reed, Van
The house of many doors. + Daniels, Dorothy

House of many shadows. + Michaels, Barbara
The house of many worlds. + Merwin, Sam Jr.
The house of souls. + Machen, Arthur
House of stairs. + Sleator, William
A house of tears. + Downey, Edmund
The house of the Brandersons. + Rudorff, Raymond
The house of the hatchet, and other tales of horror.
    + Bloch, Robert
House of the hunter. + Taylor, Frank
The house of the living dead, and other terror tales.
    + Hanlon, Jon
The house of the missing. + Gluck, Sinclair
The house of the nightmare, & other eerie tales. +
    Lines, Kathleen
The house of the other world. + Tweedale, Violet
The house of the secret. + Farrere, Claude
The house of the sorcerer. + Macfall, Haldane
The house of the unbelieving Thomas. + Heyse, Paul
The house of the uneasy dead. + Horler, Sydney
The house of the vampire. + Viereck, George Sylvester
House of Zeor. + Lichtenberg, Jacqueline
House on fire. + Oboler, Arch
The house on Parchment Street. + McKillip, Patricia
The House on Stilts. + Hazard, R. H.
The house on the borderland. + Hodgson, William Hope
The house on the borderland, and other novels. + Hodg-
    son, William Hope
The house on the brink. + Gordon, John
The house on the strand. + du Maurier, Daphne
The house that stood still. + van Vogt, A. E.
The house that was. + Syrett, Netta
The house under the sea. + Pemberton, Max
The house upstairs. + Rodda, Charles
The house with a clock in its walls. + Bellairs, John
The housenapper. + Curry, Jane Louise
The houses of Iszm. + Vance, Jack
How are the mighty fallen. + Swann, Thomas Burnett
How England became a republic. + Strachey, J. St. Loe
How England was saved. + Agricola
"How Germany crushed France." + Sommerfeld, Adolf
How it all ended. + Funaro, Sergio
How John Bull lost London. + "Grip"
How many blocks in the pile? + Meltzer, David
How McGovern won the presidency, & why the polls were
    wrong. + Tobier, Arthur
How she came into her kingdom. + (Clay, Charles M.)
How the Germans took London. + Offin, T. W.
Howard Phillips Lovecraft. + Wetzel, George
Hrolf Kraki's saga. + Anderson, Poul
Hubert's Arthur. + Prospero & Caliban
The Hubbles and the robot. + Horseman, Elaine
Hubble's bubble. + Horseman, Elaine
The Hubschmann effect. + McMahon, Thomas Patrick
Hugo Gernsback: father of science fiction. + Mosko-
    witz, Sam
The Hugo winners. + Asimov, Isaac
The Hugo winners, volume one. + Asimov, Isaac
The Hugo winners, volume 2. + Asimov, Isaac
The Hugo winners, volume two, 1968-1970. + Asimov,
    Isaac
The Hugo winners, volumes one and two. + Asimov,
    Isaac
Human?????? + Merril, Judith
Human affairs. + O'Sullivan, Vincent
The human age, book l. + Lewis, Wyndham
The human age, book two [and] book three. + Lewis,
    Wyndham
Human and inhuman stories. + Sayers, Dorothy L.
Human, and other beings. + DeGraeff, Allen
The human angle. + Tenn, William
The human apes. + Carlson, Dale
The Human Bat. + Home-Gall, Edward R.

The Human Bat v. the robot gangster. + Home-Gall,
    Edward R.
The human chord. + Blackwood, Algernon
The human equation. + Nolan, William F.
The human mole. + Collins, Colin
The human slaughter-house. + Lamszus, Wilhelm
The human time bomb. + Carter, Nick
The human zero, and other science-fiction masterpieces.
    Elwood, Roger & Moskowitz, Sam
Humanity and the mysterious knight. + Stauffer, Mack
Humanity Prime. + McAllister, Bruce
Humanoid puppets. + Barry, Ray
The humanoids. + Williamson, Jack
The humans of Ziax II. + Morressy, John
Humming bird. + Farjeon, Eleanor
Humorous ghost stories. + Scarborough, Dorothy
Humour and fantasy. + Anstey, F.
The hundred and one dalmatians. + Smith, Dodie
A hundred years hence. + Moresby, Charles
Hung in space. + Falkon, Felix Lance
The hunger, and other stories. + Beaumont, Charles
The hungry cloud. + Ingram, Tom
Hunt down the prize. + Moon, Sheila
The hunt for the meteor. + Verne, Jules
Hunt the king, hide the fox. + Trevor, Meriol
The hunter; and, The trap. + Fast, Howard
Hunter--killer. + Jenkins, Geoffrey
Hunter of the caverns. + Whitnall, Harold O.
The hunter out of time. + Fox, Gardner F.
Hunter's half-moon. + Cornwall, Ian W.
Hunters of Gor. + Norman, John
The Hunters of Jundagai. + Bulmer, Kenneth
Hunters of space. + Kelleam, Joseph E.
Hunters of the Red Moon. + Bradley, Marion Zimmer
Hunting on Kunderer. + Barton, William
The hunting variety. + Flanagan, Richard
The huntsmen at the gate. + Jenks, Almet
Huon of the horn. + Norton, Andre
The Hurricane Kids on the lost islands. + DuBois,
    Gaylord & Lebeck, Oskar
Hurtlers through space. + Burrage, A. Harcourt
A husband for Kutani. + Owen, Frank
Hush-a-by baby. + Drake, Burgess
Husky Hillier. + Webster, F. A. M.
Hyacinth. + Calthrop, Dion Clayton
The hybrid. + Jakes, John
The hydronauts. + Biemiller, Carl
Hydrosphere. + Merak, A. J.
Hyperborea. + Smith, Clark Ashton
Hyper-drive. + Grant, Matthew
Hyperspace. + Fanthorpe, R. Lionel
Hypnotic death. + Valdez, Paul

I am a cat. + Natsume, Soseki
I am Anthony. + Stokes, Peg
I am legend. + Matheson, Richard
I am Lucifer. + Clason, Clyde B.
I am thinking of my darling. + McHugh, Vincent
I, Billy Shakespeare. + Blatty, William Peter
I came--I saw--I wondered. + Gridban, Volsted
I can predict the future. + Claro, Joseph
I can't sleep at night. + Singer, Kurt
I die possessed. + O'Sullivan, James Brendan
I dream of Jeannie. + Brewster, Dennis
I fight for Mars. + Grey, Charles
I found Cleopatra. + Kelley, Thomas P.
I, Governor of California, and how I ended poverty. +
    Sinclair, Upton
I have no mouth, and I must scream. + Ellison, Harlan
I have seen monsters and angels. + Jolas, Eugene
I, James Blunt. + Morton, Henry C. V.
I, John, the reincarnated apostle. + Lewis, Benn E.

I killed Stalin. + Noel, Sterling
I live again. + Deeping, Warwick
I love Galesburg in the springtime. + Finney, Jack
I, Lucifer. + O'Donnell, Peter
The I.Q. merchant. + Boyd, John
I remember Lemuria; and, The return of Sathanas. +
   Shaver, Richard S.
I, Robot. + Asimov, Isaac
I, Scheherazade. + Parkhirst, Douglass
I sing the Body Electric! + Bradbury, Ray
I speak for Earth. + Woodcott, Keith
I spy... + Statten, Vargo
I, the Machine. + Fairman, Paul W.
I, the tiger. + Komroff, Manuel
I told you so! + McLaren, F. V.
I want the stars. + Purdom, Tom
I warmed both hands. + Dilnot, Frank
I was alone. + LePire, Joe H.
I, weapon. + Runyon, Charles W.
I will fear no evil. + Heinlein, Robert A.
I will not cease--. + Cousins, E. G.
I, Yahweh. + Grey, Robert Munson
Ibe of Atlan. + Cole, Ira A.
Ice. + Kavan, Anna
Ice and iron. + Tucker, Wilson
Ice crown. + Norton, Andre
The ice desert. + Verne, Jules
Ice dragon. + Lord, Jeffrey
The ice maiden. + Allison, Clyde
Ice men of Rime. + Bamman, Henry & Odell, William &
   Whitehead, Robert
The ice people. + Barjavel, Rene
The ice schooner. + Moorcock, Michael
The ice witch. + none
The iceburg hermit. + Roth, Arthur
Icerigger. + Foster, Alan Dean
Iceworld. + Clement, Hal
Ichabod. + Blyth, James
The icicle, and other stories. + Tertz, Abram
Ida Llymond and her hour of vision. + Cranford, Hope
The ideal city. + Noto, Cosimo
The Identity Exchange. + Andom, R.
Identity Seven. + Lory, Robert
The Ides of summer. + Brandel, Marc
The idyll of the White Lotus. + Collins, Mabel
If. + (Squire, J. C.)
If all the rebels die. + Southwell, Samuel B.
If Britain had fallen. + Longmate, Norman
If Hitler comes... + Brown, Douglas & Serpell, Chris-
   topher
If I were dictator. + Dunsany, Lord
If I were King George. + Happy, the King's dog
If I were you. + Green, Julien
If Israel lost the war. + Chesnoff, Richard Z. &
   Klein, Edward & Littell, Robert
If it had happened otherwise. + Squire, J. C.
The If reader of science fiction. + Pohl, Frederik
If the devil came to Chicago. + Granville, Austyn &
   Knott, W. Wilson
If the South had won the Civil War. + Kantor, Mac-
   Kinlay
If this goes on. + Nuetzel, Charles
If tomorrow comes. + Reitmeister, Louis Aaron
If twelve today. + Tanton, Ernest C.
If you believe the soldiers. + Cordell, Alexander
The ikon. + Barbeau, Clayton C.
I'll blackmail the world. + Wood, S. Andrew
I'll grind their bones. + Roscoe, Theodore
The ill-made knight. + White, T. H.
The illusion and the reality. + Palm, Gene
An illustrated history of the horror films. + Clarens,
   Carlos

The illustrated man. + Bradbury, Ray
Illustrated memoir of an eventful expedition into Cen-
   tral America. + Velasquez, Pedro
The image in the sand. + Benson, E. F.
Image of death. + Kensch, Otto
The image of the beast. + Farmer, Philip Jose
Images of tomorrow. + Nuetzel, Charles
Imaginary interviews with the noted and notorious. +
   Campbell, Forrest
The imaginary voyage in prose fiction. + Gove, Philip
   Babcock
Imaginary worlds. + Bloomfield, Paul
Imaginary worlds. + Carter, Lin
Imagination unlimited. + Bleiler, Everett F. & Dikty,
   T. E.
Imaginative sex. + Norman, John
Imagine a man in a box. + Wakefield, H. Russell
Imaginotions. + Jenks, Tudor
The imitation man. + Hargrave, John
The immortal. + Gunn, James E.
Immortal Athalia. + Haley, Harry F.
The immortal error. + Trevor, Elleston
The immortal girl. + Ruck, Berta
The immortal gymnasts. + Cher, Marie
Immortal hero. + Whitney, Verner Meurice
The immortal light. + Mastin, John
The immortal storm. + Moskowitz, Sam
The immortal tales of Joe Shaun. + Meyer, John J.
The immortal unknown. + Perry Rhodan #13
Immortality delivered. + Sheckley, Robert
Immortality, Inc. + Sheckley, Robert
The immortals. + Barjavel, Rene
The immortals. + Brett, Leo
The Immortals. + Farley, Ralph Milne
The Immortals. + Garner, Rolf
The Immortals. + Gunn, James E.
The immortals. + Scarborough, Harold E.
The Immortals' great quest. + Barlow, James William
The immortals of Mercury. + Smith, Clark Ashton
Impact 20. + Nolan, William F.
The impeachment of President Israels. + Copley, Frank
   Barkley
Imperial overture, and other stories. + none
Implosion. + Jones, D. F.
Impossible? + Janifer, Laurence M.
The impossible man, and other stories. + Ballard,
   J. G.
The impossible transplant. + Miller, Russ
The impossible world. + Binder, Eando
The impossibles. + Phillips, Mark
The impregnable city. + Pemberton, Max
The impregnable women. + Linklater, Eric
Impromptu in Moribundia. + Hamilton, Patrick
In a blue velvet dress... + Sefton, Catherine
In a Canadian canoe. + Pain, Barry
In a glass darkly. + Le Fanu, J. Sheridan
In Arcady. + Mabie, Hamilton Wright
In Assyrian tents. + Pendleton, Louis
In brief authority. + Anstey, F.
In brighter climes. + Chavannes, Albert
In deep. + Knight, Damon
In ghostly company. + Northcote, Amyas
In ghostly Japan. + Hearn, Lafcadio
In jeopardy. + Sutphen, Van Tassel
In memoriam: Clark Ashton Smith. + Chalker, Jack L.
In Menehune land. + Irwin, Bernice Piilani
In no strange land. + Oliver, Jane
In Oudemon. + Drayton, Henry S.
In our hands, the stars. + Harrison, Harry
In quest of life. + Williams, Thad. W.
In quest of Sheba's treasure. + Walkey, Samuel
In quest of the giant sloth. + Stables, Gordon

In quest of the golden orchid. + Burton, Edmund
In realms unknown. + Bell, Robert
"In Sargasso." + Chambers, Julius
In search of an unknown race. + Converse, Frank H.
In search of El Dorado. + Collingwood, Harry
In search of the unknown. + Chambers, Robert W.
In search of wonder. + Knight, Damon
In the battle for New York. + Hancock, H. Irving
In the beginning. + Douglas, Norman
In the beginning. + Muller, John E.
In the beginning. + Sullivan, Alan
In the closed room. + Burnett, Frances Hodgson
In the cockpit of Europe. + Pollock, A. W.
In the days of the comet. + Wells, H. G.
In the days of the comet, and seventeen short stories. + Wells, H. G.
In the dead of night. + Sissons, Michael
In the dwellings of the wilderness. + Taylor, C. Bryson
In the enclosure. + Malzberg, Barry N.
In the footsteps of the abominable snowman. + Nesvadba, Josef
In the forest of Arden. + Mabie, Hamilton Wright
In the future. + none
In the great god's hair. + Bain, F. W.
In the great white land. + Stables, W. Gordon
In the grip of terror. + Conklin, Groff
In the hands of the Czar. + Mill, Garrett
In the heart of the silent sea. + Bolton, F. H.
In the kingdom of the Beasts. + Stableford, Brian M.
In the land of the living dead. + Tucker, Prentiss
In the land of youth. + Stephens, James
In the midst of life. + Bierce, Ambrose
In the midst of life, and other tales. + Bierce, Ambrose
In the morning of time. + King, Cynthia [see Addendum]
In the morning of time. + Roberts, Charles G. D.
In the pale. + Iliowizi, Henry
In the path of the beast. + Pappazisis, Evangelos
In the penal settlement. + Kafka, Franz
In the pocket, and other S-F stories. + O'Donnell, K. M.
In the realm of terror. + Blackwood, Algernon
In the sanctuary. + van der Naillen, A.
In the Sargasso Sea. + Janvier, Thomas A.
In the Sealed Cave. + Herrman, Louis
In the second year. + Jameson, Storm
In the shadow of gold. + Studer, Paul
In the shadow of Pa-Menkh. + Langlois, Dora
In the steps of the Master. + Bradley, Marion Zimmer
In the three zones. + Stimson, F. J.
In the tiger's lair. + Miller, Leo E.
In the time of the Thetans. + Johnson, L. P. V.
"In the twinkling of an eye." + Watson, Sydney
In the valley of vision. + Irvine, G. M.
In the wet. + Shute, Nevil
"In the world celestial." + Bland, T. A.
In the wrong paradise, and other stories. + Lang, Andrew
In time to come. + Chambers, Aidan & Chambers, Nancy
In unknown worlds. + De Morgan, John
In watermelon sugar. + Brautigan, Richard
In what strange land...? + Very, Pierre
The in-world. + Roberts, Lionel
The inaugurator. + King, Harvey
Inca gold. + Baker, Nina Brown [see Addendum]
Incarnate Isis. + Desmond, Shaw
An incarnation of the snow. + Bain, F. W.
The incomplete enchanter. + de Camp, L. Sprague & Pratt, Fletcher
Inconstant Moon. + Niven, Larry
Incredible adventures. + Blackwood, Algernon

The incredible planet. + Campbell, John W. Jr.
The incredible tide. + Key, Alexander
The incredible world of Harold Huge. + Damon, Steve & Smith, Montague
The incubated girl. + Jane, Fred T.
Independence. + Bland, C. A.
The indestructible. + Garner, Rolf
An index finger. + Abrojal, Tulis
The index of science fiction. + Evans, Bill
The index of science fiction magazines, 1951-1965. + Metcalf, Norm
An index on the weird and fantastica in magazines. + Day, Bradford M.
An index to Analog. + Weinberg, Robert
Index to British science fiction magazines, 1934-1953. + none
Index to fiction in Radio news and other magazines. + Cockcroft, T. G. L.
An index to novels in the science fiction magazines. + de la Ree, Gerry
Index to Perry Rhodan. + none
An index to science fiction book reviews in Astounding/Analog, 1949-1969. + McGhan, Barry
An index to the British editions of the 'Magazine of fantasy and science fiction.' + Durie, A. J. L.
The index to the science-fantasy publishers. + Chalker, Jack L. & Owings, Mark
Index to the science fiction and fantasy magazines, 1963. + Lewis, Al
Index to the science-fiction magazines, 1926-1950. + Day, Donald B.
Index to the science fiction magazines, 1961. + Lewis, Al
Index to the science fiction magazines, 1962. + Lewis, Al
Index to the science fiction magazines, 1966. + Lewis, Anthony R.
Index to the science fiction magazines, 1966-1970 + Lewis, Anthony R.
Index to the science fiction magazines, 1967. + Lewis, Anthony R.
Index to the science fiction magazines, 1968. + Lewis, Anthony R.
Index to the science fiction magazines, 1969. + Lewis, Anthony R.
Index to the verse in Weird tales. + Cockcroft, T. G. L.
Index to the weird fiction magazines. + Cockcroft, T. G. L.
An index to Unknown and Unknown worlds. + (Hoffman, Stuart)
"The Indian maiden's dream." + Burmeister, Mrs. Kate
The Indians won. + Smith, Martin
The indispensable Poe. + Poe, Edgar Allan
Indoctrinaire. + Priest, Christopher
The inevitable hour. + Boggon, Martyn
The inexperienced ghost. + Wells, H. G.
The inexperienced ghost, and nine other stories. + Wells, H. G.
The inexperienced ghost; and, The new accelerator. + Wells, H. G.
The infernal desire machines of Doctor Hoffman. + Carter, Angela
Infernal idol. + Seymour, Henry
The infernal light. + Friend, Ed
The infernal marriage. + Disraeli, Benjamin
The inferno. + Creasey, John
The inferno. + Hoyle, Fred & Hoyle, Geoffrey
Inferno! + Statten, Vargo
The infinite brain. + Long, Charles R.
The infinite cage. + Laumer, Keith
Infinite jests. + Silverberg, Robert

The infinite man. + Galouye, Daniel F.
The infinite moment. + Wyndham, John
The infinite worlds of maybe. + del Rey, Lester
Infinity five. + Hoskins, Robert
Infinity flight. + Perry Rhodan 24
Infinity four. + Hoskins, Robert
Infinity machine. + Muller, John E.
Infinity one. + Hoskins, Robert
Infinity three. + Hoskins, Robert
Infinity two. + Hoskins, Robert
An informal biography of Scrooge McDuck. + Chalker, Jack L.
An informal history of the pulp magazines. + Goulart, Ron
The inhabitant of the lake, and less welcome tenants. Campbell, J. Ramsey
The inhabitants of Mars. + Mitchell, W.
Inherit the Earth. + Nunes, Claude
Inherit the night. + Christie, Robert
The inheritor. + Benson, E. F.
The inheritors. + Chandler, A. Bertram
The inheritors. + Conrad, Joseph & Hueffer, Ford M.
The inheritors. + Golding, William
Inheritors of Earth. + Anderson, Poul & Eklund, Gordon
Inland deep. + Tooker, Richard
Inner circle. + Peterkiewicz, Jerzy
Inner cosmos. + Statten, Vargo
The inner house. + Besant, Walter
The inner landscape. + none
The inner number. + Williams, F. Chenhalls
The inner wheel. + Roberts, Keith
The innocence of Pastor Muller. + Beuf, Carlo
The innocent Eve. + Nathan, Robert
Inquirendo Island. + Genone, Hudor
Inquiry into science fiction. + Davenport, Basil
The inquisitor's house. + Somerlott, Robert [see Addendum]
The insane city. + Bulmer, Kenneth
The insane root. + Praed, Mrs. Campbell
The insanity of Jones, and other tales. + Blackwood, Algernon
The insect invasion. + Cummings, Ray
The insect warriors. + Levie, Rex Dean
Inside. + Morgan, Dan
Inside outside. + Farmer, Philip Jose
The insidious Dr. Fu-Manchu. + Rohmer, Sax
Instant gold. + O'Rourke, Frank
The insulators. + Creasey, John
Intangibles, Inc., and other stories. + Aldiss, Brian W.
The intelligence gigantic. + Fearn, John Russell
Intensive care. + Frame, Janet
Inter ice age 4. + Abe, Kobo
The intercessor, and other stories. + Sinclair, May
Interface. + Adlard, Mark
Intergalac agent. + Hassler, Kenneth W.
Interior world. + Tower, Washington L.
The interloper. + Statten, Vargo
Interlude on Siliko 5. + Perry Rhodan 59
Intermere. + Taylor, William Alexander
Intermind. + Luther, Ray
Intermind. + Sellings, Arthur
The interplanetary adventurers. + Bertin, Jack
Interplanetary hunter. + Barnes, Arthur K.
The interpreter. + Aldiss, Brian W.
Interruption. + Saxon Mills, G. H.
Interstellar espionage. + Del Martia, Astron
Interstellar Two-Five. + Rankine, John
Interworld. + Whitham, John W.
Intimations of Eve. + Fisher, Vardis
Into a strange lost world. + Carter, Bruce
Into deepest space. + Hoyle, Fred & Hoyle, Geoffrey

Into other worlds. + Green, Roger Lancelyn
Into Plutonian depths. + Coblentz, Stanton A.
Into space. + Neesam, Malcolm
Into the aether. + Lupoff, Richard A.
Into the alternate universe. + Chandler, A. Bertram
Into the darkness. + Clarke, A. C. G.
Into the dawn. + McElhiney, Gaile
Into the forest. + Essex, Rosamund
Into the fourth dimension, and other stories. + none
Into the Niger Bend. + Verne, Jules
Into the silence. + Courtier, S. H.
Into the slave nebula. + Brunner, John
Into the tenth millennium. + Capon, Paul
Into the unknown. + Carr, Terry
Into the unknown. + Fletcher, Lawrence
Into the unknown. + Philmus, Robert M.
Into the unknown. + Wheatley, Dennis
Into the unseen. + Lusty, G. H.
The intoxicated ghost, and other stories. + Bates, Arlo
Intrigue on the Upper Level. + Hoyne, Thomas Temple
Introducing SF. + Aldiss, Brian W.
An introduction to Islandia. + Davenport, Basil
Introduction to Poe. + Poe, Edgar Allan
Introductory psychology through science fiction. + Greenberg, Martin Harry & Warrick, Patricia S. & Katz, Harvey A.
The intruders. + Fane, Bron
The invader. + Woods, Margaret L.
Invader from space. + Moore, Patrick
Invader on my back. + High, Philip E.
The invaders. + none
The invaders. + Frank, Waldo
The Invaders. + Laumer, Keith
The invaders. + Tracy, Louis
The invaders are coming! + Meyer, J. A. & Nourse, Alan E.
The Invaders; Dam of death. + Pearl, Jack
Invaders from Earth. + Silverberg, Robert
Invaders from Rigel. + Pratt, Fletcher
Invaders from space. + Silverberg, Robert
Invaders from the dark. + La Spina, Greye
Invaders from the infinite. + Campbell, John W. Jr.
Invaders of Earth. + Conklin, Groff
Invaders of space. + Leinster, Murray
Invaders on the Moon. + Neville, Kris
The invading asteroid. + Wellman, Manly Wade
Invasion! + Chambers, Whitman
The invasion. + Hay, John
The invasion. + Le Queux, William
Invasion. + van Loon, Hendrik Willem
The invasion. + Walker, W. H.
Invasion from Mars. + Welles, Orson
Invasion from space. + Bradford, Matthew C.
Invasion from space. + Mackenzie, Nigel
Invasion from space. + Perry Rhodan #4
Invasion from the air. + Connolly, Roy & McIlraith, Frank
Invasion from 2500. + Edwards, Norman
The invasion of America. + Muller, Julius W.
The invasion of 1883. + none
The invasion of England. + (Butler, William Francis)
Invasion of Mars. + Serviss, Garrett P.
The invasion of New York. + Palmer, J. H.
The invasion of 1910. + Le Queux, William
The invasion of the body snatchers. + Finney, Jack
Invasion of the robots. + Elwood, Roger
The invasion of the United States. + Hancock, H. Irving
Invasion of the yellow warlords. + Steele, Curtis
The invasion that did not come off. + Hawke, Napier
The invention of Morel, and other stories. + Bioy Casares, Adolfo

Inverted world. + Priest, Christopher
The investigation. + Lem, Stanislaw
Investigations and experience of M. Shawtinbach. +
  (Smilie, Elton R.)
The invincible. + Lem, Stanislaw
The invincible Adam. + Eldridge, Paul & Viereck,
  George Sylvester
The invisibility affair. + Stratton, Thomas
Invisible barriers. + Osborne, David
Invisible cities. + Calvino, Italo
The invisible companion, and other stories. + Farjeon,
  J. Jefferson
The invisible empire. + Steele, Curtis
The invisible eye. + Tabori, Paul
The invisible guide. + Hind, C. Lewis
The invisible man. + Wells, H. G.
The invisible man; and, The war of the worlds. +
  Wells, H. G.
The invisible man; Secret places of the heart; God the
  invisible king. + Wells, H. G.
The invisible man; The war of the worlds; A dream of
  armageddon. + Wells, H. G.
Invisible men. + Davenport, Basil
The invisible playmate. + Canton, William
The invisible playmate; and, W. V., her book. + Can-
  ton, William
The invisible police. + Pendleton, Louis
Invisible Scarlet O'Neil. + Stamm, Russell
The invisible ships. + 'Sea-Lion'
The invisible war-plane. + Grahame-White, Claude &
  Harper, Harry
The invisibles. + Dark, James [see Addendum]
The invisibles. + Hurwood, Bernhardt J.
Inviso man. + Bamman, Henry & Odell, William & White-
  head, Robert
The involuntary immortals. + Phillips, Rog
Ionia. + Craig, Alexander
Ionic barrier. + Kellar, Von
Ipomoea. + Rackham, John
Iras. + Douglas, Theo.
Ireland a nation! + O'Flannagan, Phineas
Ireland's dream. + Lyon, E. D.
The Irish Rebellion of 1898. + Donovan, Alexander
Irish tales of terror. + McGarry, Jim
The Irish witch. + Wheatley, Dennis
Iron and gold. + Vaughan, Hilda
The iron and the anger. + Rayer, Francis G.
The iron arm of Michael Glenn. + Lee, Robert C.
Iron cage. + Norton, Andre
The iron dream. + Spinrad, Norman
The Iron Heel. + London, Jack
The iron hoop. + FitzGibbon, Constantine
The iron man and the tin woman, and other futurities.
  + Leacock, Stephen
The iron pirate. + Pemberton, Max
The iron star. + Taine, John
The iron star, and what it saw on its journey through
  the ages. + True, John Preston
The Iron Thorn. + Budrys, Algis
Ironbark Bill. + Stivens, Dal
Ironical tales. + Housman, Laurence
The irrationals. + none
Is the devil a gentleman? + Quinn, Seabury
Is there anybody there? + Lofts, Norah
Is there intelligent life on Earth? + Dunn, Alan
Isaac Asimov. + Miller, Marjorie M.
An Isaac Asimov double. + Asimov, Isaac
Isaac Asimov: first visit to Britain, 1974. + Bishop,
  Gerald
An Isaac Asimov omnibus. + Asimov, Isaac
An Isaac Asimov second omnibus. + Asimov, Isaac
Isaac Asimov's I, Robot. + Patrouch, Joseph F. Jr.

An Isaac Bashevis Singer reader. + Singer, Isaac
  Bashevis
Island. + Huxley, Aldous
Island at the top of the world. + Cameron, Ian
The island beyond Japan. + Paris, John
Island in a strange sea. + Martin, Ray
The island in the mist. + Kelsey, Franklyn
Island in the sky. + Wellman, Manly Wade
Island nights' entertainments. + Stevenson, Robert
  Louis
The island of anarchy. + W., E.
The Island of Atlantis. + (The Author of 'Atlantis')
The island of Captain Sparrow. + Wright, S. Fowler
The island of creeping death. + Norwood, Victor
The island of Doctor Moreau. + Wells, H. G.
The island of Doctor Moreau; The invisible man. +
  Wells, H. G.
The island of Doctor Moreau; The sleeper awakes. +
  Wells, H. G.
Island of evil. + Daniels, Dorothy
The island of fear. + Moore, Patrick
Island of fear, and other science fiction stories. +
  Sambrot, William
The island of Fu Manchu. + Rohmer, Sax
The island of Not-me. + Gotthelf, Ezra Gerson
The island of peril. + Creasey, John
The island of terror. + Sapper
The Island of the Great Mother. + Hauptmann, Gerhart
The island of the mighty. + Walton, Evangeline
Island of the voodoo dolls. + Dangerfield, Paul
The island people. + Coblentz, Stanton A.
Island sonata. + Livingston, Marjorie
The island stallion races. + Farley, Walter
The Island under the Earth. + Davidson, Avram
The island where time stands still. + Wheatley, Dennis
Islandia. + Wright, Austin Tappan
Islands in the sky. + Clarke, Arthur C.
Islands of space. + Campbell, John W. Jr.
The Islar. + Saxton, Mark
The Isle of Dead Ships. + Marriott, Crittenden
The Isle of Feminine. + Niswonger, Charles Elliot
The Isle of Forgotten People. + Cross, Thompson
The isle of lies. + Shiel, M. P.
The isle of lost ships. + Marriott, Crittenden
The isle of palms. + Newell, C. M.
Isle of the Dead. + Zelazny, Roger
Isle of the dolphins. + Roberts, Janet Louise
The isle of the virgins. + Royal, Matthew J.
The Isles of Sunset. + Benson, Arthur Christopher
The Isles of Wisdom. + Moszkowski, Alexander
The isotope man. + Maine, Charles Eric
The issue. + Noble, Edward
The issue at hand. + Atheling, William Jr.
Istar of Babylon. + Potter, Margaret Horton
"It." + (De Morgan, John)
It. + Sturgeon, Theodore
It can't happen here. + Lewis, Sinclair
It happened like this. + Reynolds, Philip
It happened to Didymus. + Sinclair, Upton
It happened tomorrow. + Williams, Francis
It happens every spring. + Davies, Valentine
It is possible. + Van-Anderson, Helen
It may be so. + Gibson, Edmund H.
It never could happen. + O'Sheel, Shaemas
It prowls at dark. + Taunton, H. R.
It was the day of the robot. + Long, Frank Belknap
Item eighty-three. + Aldiss, Margaret
Item forty-three. + Manson, Margaret
Iter Lunare. + Russen, David
An itinerant house, and other stories. + Dawson,
  Emma Frances
It's a mad, mad, mad galaxy. + Laumer, Keith

It's all in your mind. + Bloch, Robert
It's getting harder all the time. + Conway, Troy
It's not how long you make it. + Conway, Troy
The ivory child. + Haggard, H. Rider
The ivory disc. + Brebner, Percy James
The Ivory Graves. + Duff, Hector
The ivory queen. + Pendleton, John
Ivory valley. + Hyne, C. J. Cutcliffe
Ixion in Heaven. + Disraeli, Benjamin

J.G., the upright ape. + Price, Roger
J. R. R. Tolkien. + Evans, Robley
J. R. R. Tolkien. + Stimpson, Catharine R.
Jack and the check book. + Bangs, John Kendrick
Jack Anderson against Dr. Tek! + Rheingold, Howard
Jack of eagles. + Blish, James
Jack of Shadows. + Zelazny, Roger
The jacket. + London, Jack
The Jacobite doctors. + A Member of the Legitimist
   Club
The jade god. + Sullivan, Alan
The Jade Man's eyes. + Moorcock, Michael
The jade warrior. + Lord, Jeffrey
The jagged orbit. + Brunner, John
James H. Schmitz: a bibliography. + Owings, Mark
James Ingleton. + "Dick, Mr."
James Warren presents Famous monsters of filmland
   strike back! + Ackerman, Forrest J.
James Warren presents Son of Famous monsters of film-
   land. + Ackerman, Forrest J.
James Warren presents The best from Famous monsters of
   filmland. + Ackerman, Forrest J.
Jan in India. + Kline, Otis Adelbert
Jan of the jungle. + Kline, Otis Adelbert
Jandar of Callisto. + Carter, Lin
Jane-Emily. + Clapp, Patricia
The Janus syndrome. + Mason, Douglas R.
A Japanese miscellany. + Hearn, Lafcadio
Japanese tales of mystery and imagination. + Rampo,
   Edogawa
A Japanese utopia. + Magnus, Leonard A.
Japhalein, mother ship of this galaxy. + Pritchett,
   E. Blanche
The jargoon pard. + Norton, Andre
Jason Potter's space walk. + Duffus, R. L.
Jason, son of Jason. + Giesy, J. U.
Java-Java. + Steel, Byron
Jaws of doom. + Ludwig, Boris
Jazz and jasper. + Gerhardi, William
The jealous ghost. + Strong, L. A. G.
Jeanne's journal. + Mercier, Mario
Jehovah's day. + Borden, Mary
Jenny Villiers. + Priestley, J. B.
Jessamy. + Sleigh, Barbara
The jester at Scar. + Tubb, E. C.
The Jester's Reign. + Grainger, Boyne
Jesus Christs. + Langguth, A. J.
The Jesus Factor. + Corley, Edwin
Jetman meets the mad madam. + Savage, Hardley
Jettatura. + Gautier, Theophile
The jewel in the skull. + Moorcock, Michael
The jewel of Arwen. + Bradley, Marion Zimmer
Jewel of Jarhen. + Kern, Gregory
The Jewel of Seven Stars. + Stoker, Bram
Jewel of Tharn. + Lord, Jeffrey
Jewel sowers. + (Allonby, Edith)
The jeweled serpent. + Blackledge, Katharine Treat
The jewels of Aptor. + Delany, Samuel R.
The Jewels of elsewhen. + White, Ted
Jim Dunlap and the long Lunar walk. + Palmer, Bernard
Jim Dunlap and the mysterious orbiting rocket. +
   Palmer, Bernard

Jim Dunlap and the mysterious spy. + Palmer, Bernard
Jim Dunlap and the secret rocket formula. + Palmer,
   Bernard
Jim Dunlap and the strange Dr. Brockton. + Palmer,
   Bernard
Jim Dunlap and the wingless plane. + Palmer, Bernard
Jim McWhirter. + Knowles, W. P.
Jimbo. + Blackwood, Algernon
Jimgrim. + Mundy, Talbot
Jimgrim sahib. + Mundy, Talbot
The jingo. + Chester, George Randolph
Jinn and jitters, and other stories. + Carnell, John
Jirel of Joiry. + Moore, C. L.
Jizzle. + Wyndham, John
Jodinareh. + Cleve, John
Jog Rummage. + Wright, Grahame
John Brown's body. + Boshell, Gordon
John Bull and his wonderful lamp. + Homunculus
John Bull: socialist. + Everett, Frances
John Bull's downfall. + Debans, Camille
John Bull's misfortunes. + Debans, Camille
John Carstairs: space detective. + Long, Frank Bel-
   knap
John Carter of Mars. + Burroughs, Edgar Rice
The John Collier reader. + Collier, John
John Edgell's ghosts. + Edgell, John
The John Franklin letters. + none
John Gayther's garden, and the stories told therein.
   + Stockton, Frank R.
John Harvey. + Moore, Anon
John Innocent at Oxford. + Buckle, Richard
John Lillibud. + Hurrell, F. G.
John Russell Fearn. + Harbottle, Philip
John Sagur. + "Nedram"
John Silence, physician extraordinary. + Blackwood,
   Algernon
John Smith, Emperor. + Gallego, S. G.
John W. Campbell; an Australian tribute. + Bangsund,
   John
John W. Campbell anthology. + Campbell, John W.
The John W. Campbell memorial anthology. + Harrison,
   Harry
John Whopper the newsboy. + (Clark, Thomas)
The John Wyndham omnibus. + Wyndham, John
Johnny Pye & the Fool-Killer. + Benet, Stephen Vin-
   cent
The joker. + Malaquais, Jean
The "Jolly Roger." + Nisbet, Hume
Jonah. + Nathan, Robert
Jonah and the voice. + Tandrup, Harald
Jonathan. + O'Neil, Russell
Jonathan Livingston Fliegle. + Bermont, Hubert
Jonathan Livingston Seagull. + Bach, Richard
Jonathan Segal Chicken. + Albrecht, Howard & Wein-
   stein, Sol
Jondelle. + Tubb, E. C.
Jongor fights back. + Williams, Robert Moore
Jongor of Lost Land. + Williams, Robert Moore
Joris of the Rock. + Barringer, Leslie
Jorkens borrows another whiskey. + Dunsany, Lord
Jorkens has a large whiskey. + Dunsany, Lord
Jorkens remembers Africa. + Dunsany, Lord
Joseph Balsamo. + Dumas, Alexandre
The Joseph Stone. + La Tourrette, Jacqueline
Joshua, son of none. + Freedman, Nancy
Journal from Ellipsia. + Calisher, Hortense
The journal of David Q. Little. + McMichael, R.
   Daniel
Journey across the third planet. + Knott, William C.
Journey across three worlds. + none
Journey between worlds. + Engdahl, Sylvia Louise
Journey beyond tomorrow. + Sheckley, Robert

A journey from this world to the next. + Fielding, Henry

A journey in other worlds. + Aston, John Jacob

Journey into darkness. + Long, Frank Belknap

Journey into limbo. + Michel, Scott

Journey into space. + Chilton, Charles

A journey into the interior of the Earth. + Verne, Jules

The journey of Niels Klim to the world underground. + Holberg, Ludvig

Journey of Tapiola. + Nathan, Robert

Journey of the Oceanauts. + Wolfe, Louis

Journey outside. + Steele, Mary Q.

A journey round my chamber. + (Maistre, Xavier de)

A journey round my room. + Maistre, Xavier de

Journey through space. + Williams, Speedy

Journey to Alpha Centauri. + Macvey, John W. [see Addendum]

Journey to another star, and other stories. + (Elwood, Roger)

Journey to infinity. + Greenberg, Martin

Journey to Jupiter. + Greene, Joseph

Journey to Jupiter. + Walters, Hugh

Journey to Mars. + Tubb, E. C.

Journey to Mars, the wonderful world. + Pope, Gustavus W.

A journey to the centre of the Earth. + Verne, Jules

Journey to the future. + Foster, C. E.

A journey to the interior of the Earth. + Verne, Jules

A journey to the Moon. + (Campbell, John)

A journey to the North Pole. + Verne, Jules

Journey to the stars. + Rayer, Francis G.

A journey to the world in the Moon. + (Defoe, Daniel)

A journey to the world in the Moon. + Pythagorolunister

A journey to the world under ground. + Holberg, Ludvig

A journey to the world under-ground. + Klimius, Nicholas

Journey to Untor. + Wibberley, Leonard

A journey to Venus, the primeval world. + Pope, Gustavus W.

Journey's eve. + Cadell, Elizabeth

Journeys in science fiction. + Loughlin, Richard L. & Popp, Lilian M.

Journeys into the Moon. + none

Jovencachoteca. + Townsend, Larry

The jovial ghosts. + Smith, Thorne

The joy makers. + Gunn, James E.

The joy wagon. + Hadley, Arthur T.

Joyleg. + Davidson, Avram & Moore, Ward

The joyous invasions. + Sturgeon, Theodore

The joyous miracle. + Norris, Frank

Judas! + Van Greenaway, Peter

Judas, and other stories. + Metcalfe, John

The Judas gospel. + Van Greenaway, Peter

The Judas joke, and other stories. + Timperley, Rosemary

The Judas mandate. + Egleton, Clive

The judge of Jerusalem. + Bloom, Ursula

The judges of Hades, and other Simon Ark stories. + Hoch, Edward D.

The judging of Jurgen. + Cabell, James Branch

Judgment day. + Davey, Norman

Judgment eve. + Harwood, H. C.

The judgment of Eve. + Pangborn, Edgar

Judgment on Janus. + Norton, Andre

Juggernaut. + Fane, Bron

The juggler and the soul. + Mathers, Helen

Jules Verne and his work. + Evans, I. O.

Jules Verne, master of science fiction. + Verne, Jules

Julian Grant loses his way. + Houghton, Claude

Julian the magician. + MacEwen, Gwendolyn

Julius LeVallon. + Blackwood, Algernon

Jumbee, and other uncanny tales. + Whitehead, Henry S.

The jungle book. + Kipling, Rudyard

The jungle book; The second jungle book. + Kipling, Rudyard

The jungle books. + Kipling, Rudyard

Jungle-born. + Eyton, John

Jungle fever. + Garron, Marco

Jungle girl. + Burroughs, Edgar Rice

The jungle girl. + Casserly, Gordon

The jungle goddess. + Sackville, Orme

Jungle jungle. + Nuetzel, Charles

Jungle nymph. + Johnson, David

A jungle orgy. + Van Marcus, Carl

Jungle tales of Tarzan. + Burroughs, Edgar Rice

Jungle terror. + Wickham, Harvey

Junk day. + Sellings, Arthur

Junkyard planet. + Piper, H. Beam

Jupiter. + Pohl, Carol & Pohl, Frederik

Jupiter equilateral. + Rackham, John

Jupiter in the chair. + Fraser, Ronald

The Jupiter legacy. + Harrison, Harry

Jupiter's passion. + Hawkins, Bruce A.

Jurgen. + Cabell, James Branch

The just steward. + Dehan, Richard

Just under Heaven. + Pauls, Theodore

Justice; and, The rat. + Wright, S. Fowler

The justice of revenge. + Griffith, George

The justification of Andrew Lebrun. + Barrett, Frank

The ka of Gifford Hillary. + Wheatley, Dennis

Kaewe's bottle. + Stevenson, Robert Louis

Kai Lung beneath the mulberry-tree. + Bramah, Ernest

The Kai Lung omnibus. + Bramah, Ernest

Kai Lung: six. + Bramah, Ernest

Kai Lung unrolls his mat. + Bramah, Ernest

Kai Lung's golden hours. + Bramah, Ernest

The Kak-Abdullah conspiracy. + Macao, Marshall

Kalani of Oahu. + Newell, C. M.

Kalee's shrine. + Allen, Grant & Cotes, May

Kaleidoscope. + Farjeon, Eleanor

Kalin. + Tubb, E. C.

Kalomera. + Saunders, W. J.

Kaloolah. + Mayo, W. S.

Kandar. + Bulmer, Kenneth

Kanor. + (Fagnan, Marie Antoinette)

Kappa. + Akutagawa, Ryunosuke

The Kar-chee reign. + Davidson, Avram

Kar Kaballa. + Smith, George H.

Kark. + Ryder, James

Karl Grier. + Tracy, Louis

Karloff. + Gifford, Denis

Karloff and company. + Moss, Robert F.

Karma. + Hearn, Lafcadio

Karma, and other stories and essays. + Hearn, Lafcadio

Karmath. + (Upham, Edward)

Kaspa, the lion man. + Stoneham, C. T.

Kathleen O'Leovan. + Grindon, Maurice

Kathy's visit to Mars. + Collier, Dwight A.

Kavin's world. + Mason, David

Ka-zar, king of fang and claw. + Byrd, Bob

The Ke Whonkus people. + Greene, John O.

Keep it up, Rod! + Conway, Troy

Keep off the grass. + England, George Allan

Keep on the light. + Thomson, Christine Campbell

The keeper of the salamander's order. + Shattuck, William

The keepers of the people. + Jepson, Edgar

The kelpie's pearls. + Hunter, Mollie

Kelwin. + Barrett, Neal

Kemlo and the craters of the Moon. + Eliott, E. C.

Kemlo and the Crazy Planet. + Eliott, E. C.
Kemlo and the end of time. + Eliott, E. C.
Kemlo and the gravity rays. + Eliott, E. C.
Kemlo and the Martian ghosts. + Eliott, E. C.
Kemlo and the masters of space. + Eliott, E. C.
Kemlo and the purple dawn. + Eliott, E. C.
Kemlo and the satellite builders. + Eliott, E. C.
Kemlo and the sky horse. + Eliott, E. C.
Kemlo and the space invaders. + Eliott, E. C.
Kemlo and the space lanes. + Eliott, E. C.
Kemlo and the space men. + Eliott, E. C.
Kemlo and the star men. + Eliott, E. C.
Kemlo and the zombie men. + Eliott, E. C.
Kemlo and the Zones of Silence. + Eliott, E. C.
Kennaquhair. + M'Crib, Theophilus
Kent Barstow: space man. + Montgomery, Rutherford
  George
Keo, the cave boy. + Fuller, Lois Hamilton
Kernel of death. + Howard, Troy
The Kestrel House mystery. + Jacobs, T. C. H.
The key of dreams. + Beck, L. Adams
The key of industrial co-operative government. +
  Pruning Knife
The key of life. + Gibbs, Philip
Key out of time. + Norton, Andre
The key to Irunium. + Bulmer, Kenneth
The key to the great gate. + Gottlieb, Hinko
The key to Venudine. + Bulmer, Kenneth
Khaled. + Crawford, F. Marion
Khan, phantom emperor of 1940. + Oliver, Jerome
The khan's carpet. + Rutley, C. Bernard
Kiai! + Anthony, Piers & Fuentes, Roberto
The Kid from Mars. + Friend, Oscar J.
The kidnap club. + Reeve, Arthur B.
Kidnapped in space. + Whiteley, John
Kidnappers of space. + Patchett, M. E.
Kildhurm's oak. + Hawthorne, Julian
Kill city. + Sugar, Andrew
Kill deadline. + Sugar, Andrew
Kill him gently. + Valdez, Paul
The killer and the slain. + Walpole, Hugh
Killer by night. + Valdez, Paul
Killer pine. + Gutteridge, Lindsay
The killer plants, and other stories. + (Elwood,
  Roger)
The killer thing. + Wilhelm, Kate
Killer to come. + Merwin, Sam Jr.
The killers of innocence. + Creasey, John
The killing bone. + Saxon, Peter
The killing bottle. + Hartley, L. P.
The killing ground. + Portal, Ellis
The Killing Machine. + Vance, Jack
The killing thing. + Wilhelm, Kate
Kilmeny in the dark wood. + Stevenson, Florence
Kin Weng and the miraculous tusk. + Bramah, Ernest
The King and Queen of Mollebusch. + Ebers, Georg
King Bertie, A.D. 1900. + none
King Cobra. + Channing, Mark
King Conan. + Howard, Robert E.
King Goshawk and the birds. + O'Duffy, Eimar
King hunters. + Garron, Marco
A King in Babylon. + Stevenson, Burton E.
The King in Yellow. + Chambers, Robert W.
The King in Yellow, and other horror stories. + Cham-
  bers, Robert W.
The king is a witch. + Eaton, Evelyn
King Joker. + Dennis, Clifford E.
King Julian. + Gatch, Tom Jr.
King Kobold. + Stasheff, Christopher
King Kong. + Lovelace, Delos W.
King Kull. + Carter, Lin & Howard, Robert E.
K'ing Kung Fu #1; Son of the flying tiger. + Macao,
  Marshall

K'ing Kung Fu #2; Return of the opium wars. + Macao,
  Marshall
K'ing Kung Fu #3; The rape of Sun Lee Fong. + Macao,
  Marshall
K'ing Kung Fu #4; The Kak-Abdullah conspiracy. +
  Macao, Marshall
K'ing Kung Fu #5; Red plague in Bolivia. + Macao,
  Marshall
K'ing Kung Fu #6; New York necromancy. + Macao, Mar-
  shall
K'ing Kung Fu #7; Mark of the vulture. + Macao, Mar-
  shall
The King of Alsander. + Flecker, James Elroy
The King of America. + Scott, Billy
The King of Apeland. + Prentice, Harry
King of Argent. + Phillifent, John T.
The king of Elfland's daughter. + Dunsany, Lord
The king of Kor. + Marshall, Sidney J.
King of Kulturia. + Higginbottom, W.H.
A king of Mars. + Hekking, Avis
The king of men. + Coolidge, Olivia
The king of men. + Miller, Alan
The King of No Man's Land. + Friel, Arthur O.
King of the air. + Strang, Herbert
King of the Amazon. + Davis, Peter
The king of the cats. + Guillot, Rene
King of the dead. + Aubrey, Frank
King of the fourth planet. + Williams, Robert Moore
King of the jungle. + Stoneham, C. T.
King--of the Khyber Rifles. + Mundy, Talbot
The king of the missing links. + Mighels, Philip
  Verrill
The King of the Swords. + Moorcock, Michael
King of the underseas. + Heming, J. W.
King of the world's edge. + Munn, H. Warner
King Pest, and other tales. + Poe, Edgar Allan
King rat. + none
King Solomon's mines. + Haggard, H. Rider
King Solomon's mines. + Haggard, H. Rider & Webb,
  Jean Francis
King Solomon's mines; Allan Quatermain. + Haggard,
  H. Rider
King Solomon's treasures. + (De Morgan, John)
King Solomon's wives. + (De Morgan, John)
King Solomon's wives. + Ragged, Hyder
A king there was--. + Vivian, E. Charles
The king who went on strike. + Choate, Pearson
The kingdom and the cave. + Aiken, Joan
Kingdom come. + Davis, Gwen
The kingdom in the sky. + Brown, Alice
The kingdom of Carbonel. + Sleigh, Barbara
The kingdom of content. + Pan
The Kingdom of Evil. + Hecht, Ben
The kingdom of Fukkian. + Mann, A. Philo
Kingdom of innocents. + Cram, Mildred
Kingdom of Royth. + Lord, Jeffrey
The kingdom that was. + Lambourne, John
The King's Assegai. + Mitford, Bertram
The king's bride. + Hoffmann, E. T. A.
King's daughter. + Gaskell, Jane
The King's men. + Grant, Robert & O'Reilly, John
  Boyle & J. S. of Dale & Wheelright, John T.
The king's missal. + Beamish, Noel De Vic
Kings of infinite space. + Balchin, Nigel
Kings of space. + Johns, W. E.
The Kings of the East. + Grier, Sydney C.
The kingslayer. + Hubbard, L. Ron
Kinsmen of the dragon. + Mullen, Stanley
Kiss kiss. + Dahl, Roald
The kiss of death, and other horror stories. + Bir-
  kin, Charles
The kiss of Isis; and, The mystery of Castlebourne.
  + Haggard, Arthur

The kiss of Pharaoh. + Goyne, Richard
The kiss that killed. + Leroux, Gaston
Kit Bam's adventures. + Clarke, Mary Cowden
The Kite Trust. + Rogers, Lebbeus Harding
Kitten kaboodle. + Silverberg, Barbara
Klarkash-Ton and Monstro Ligriv. + Finlay, Virgil & Smith, Clark Ashton
Kleinzeit. + Hoban, Russell
Knee-deep in thunder. + Moon, Sheila
A knight of ghosts and shadows. + Anderson, Poul
A knight of the east. + Whyte-Melville, G. J.
The Knight of the Silver Star. + Brebner, Percy
The Knight of the Swords. + Moorcock, Michael
The knightly quest. + Williams, Tennessee
Knight's castle. + Eager, Edward
Koenigsmark, the robber. + (Raspe, Rudolf)
Kollocain. + Boye, Karin
Kondora. + Pigott, Percy
Konga. + Owen, Dean
Kongo--the gorilla-man. + Orndorff, Frank
Kontrol. + Snell, Edmund
Konyetz. + Hussingtree, Martin
Kophetua the Thirteenth. + Corbett, Julian
Kor and the wolf dogs. + Green, Robert James
Kothar and the conjurer's curse. + Fox, Gardner F.
Kothar and the demon queen. + Fox, Gardner F.
Kothar and the wizard slayer. + Fox, Gardner F.
Kothar, barbarian swordsman. + Fox, Gardner F.
Kothar of the magic sword! + Fox, Gardner F.
Kowa the mysterious. + Foley, Charles
Krakatit. + Capek, Karel
Krakatoa, hand of the gods. + Raabe, H. E.
The Kraken wakes. + Wyndham, John
The Kretzmer Syndrome. + Way, Peter
Krishna fluting. + Berry, John
Kronk. + Cooper, Edmund
Kronos. + Enfield, Hugh
Kuldesak. + Cowper, Richard
Kunala. + Ferenczy, Arpad
Kurt Singer's Ghost omnibus. + Singer, Kurt
Kurt Singer's Gothic horror book. + Singer, Kurt
Kurt Singer's Second ghost omnibus. + Singer, Kurt
Kutnar, son of Pic. + Langford, George
Kwaidan. + Hearn, Lafcadio

L.P.M. + Barney, J. Stewart
La-bas. + Huysmans, Joris Karl
A labor of lust. + Brown, L. J.
Laboratory "X." + Shaw, David
The lad and the lion. + Burroughs, Edgar Rice
The ladder. + Knowles, Vernon
The ladder in the sky. + Woodcott, Keith
Ladies' day; and, This crowded Earth. + Bloch, Robert
Ladies in Hades. + Kummer, Frederic Arnold
Ladies of horror. + Lewis, Gogo & Manley, Seon
Ladies whose bright eyes. + Heuffer, Ford Madox
Lady Bramber's guest. + Charrington, Charles
The lady decides. + Keller, David H.
Lady Eve. + Blaydes, R. O.
The lady from Venus. + Radcliffe, Garnett
Lady in danger. + none
Lady into fox. + Garnett, David
Lady into fox; and, A man in the zoo. + Garnett, David
The lady likes blue white, and other stories. + Groh, Irwin
The lady of Blossholme. + Haggard, H. Rider
Lady of dreams. + Hall, Manly P.
The lady of the fjords. + Balogh, Barnard
The lady of the heavens. + Haggard, H. Rider
Lady of the shadows. + Daniels, Dorothy
The lady of the shroud. + Stoker, Bram
The lady of the terraces. + Vivian, E. Charles

Lady Penelope; The Albanian affair. + Theydon, John
A lady possessed. + Kellino, Pamela
Lady Sativa. + Lauria, Frank
The lady who came to stay. + Spencer, R. E.
The lady who kept her promise. + Bendix, Hans
The Lady with Feet of Gold. + Dwyer, James Francis
The ladye Amabel. + Lippard, George
Laid in the future. + Gray, Rod
The lair of the White Worm. + Stoker, Bram
The laird and the lady. + Grant, Joan
The lake of gold. + Griffith, George
Lallia. + Tubb, E. C.
Lambda I, and other stories. + Carnell, John
The lame devil. + Le Sage, Alain Rene
A lamp for Medusa. + Tenn, William
The Lampton dreamers. + Davies, L. P.
The Lancashire witches. + Ainsworth, William Harrison
The land beyond. + Gripe, Maria
Land beyond the Map. + Bulmer, Kenneth
The land ironclads. + Wells, H. G.
The Land Leviathan. + Moorcock, Michael
The land of a million elephants. + Baber, Asa
Land of always-night. + Robeson, Kenneth
The land of darkness. + (Oliphant, Mrs.)
The Land of Esa. + Charles, Neil
The land of fear. + Robeson, Kenneth
The land of forgotten women. + Webster, F. A. M.
The land of green ginger. + Langley, Noel
Land of hidden death. + Atholl, Justin
The land of hidden men. + Burroughs, Edgar Rice
Land of long juju. + Robeson, Kenneth
The land of mist. + Doyle, A. Conan
The land of Nison. + Regnas, C.
The Land of No Shadow. + Claudy, Carl H.
The land of Shvambrania. + Kassil, Leo
Land of terror. + Burroughs, Edgar Rice
The land of terror. + Robeson, Kenneth
The Land of the Blue Flower. + Burnett, Frances Hodgson
The land of the changing sun. + Harben, Will N.
Land of the giants. + Leinster, Murray
Land of the giants; Flight of fear. + Rathjen, Carl Henry
Land of the giants #2; The hot spot. + Leinster, Murray
Land of the giants #3; Unknown danger. + Leinster, Murray
Land of the giants; The mean city. + Bradwell, James
The land of the golden scarabs. + Pereyra, Diomedes
The land of the living dead. + Fyne, Neal
The land of the lost. + Norton, Roy
Land of the Moobs. + Kopf, Seymour O.
The land of the unseen. + (Locke, George)
Land of unreason. + de Camp, L. Sprague & Pratt, Fletcher
The land that time forgot. + Burroughs, Edgar Rice
The land that time forgot; and, The Moon maid. + Burroughs, Edgar Rice
Land under England. + O'Neill, Joseph
The land which loveth silence. + Sernicoli, Davide
Landfall is a state of mind. + Mason, Douglas R.
Landscape with figures. + Fraser, Ronald
Landslide. + Curtis, Monica
The landslide. + Gilbert, Stephen
The language of cats, and other stories. + Holst, Spencer
The languages of Pao. + Vance, Jack
The Lani people. + Bone, J. F.
Laputa. + none
Larger than life. + Buzzati, Dino
Laser war. + Rosenberger, Joseph
The last Adam. + Duncan, Ronald

Let out the beast. + Fischer, Leonard
Let the fire fall. + Wilhelm, Kate
Let the spacemen beware! + Anderson, Poul
Let there be monsters! + Molesworth, Vol
Let's drink to that. + Post, Joyce
Let's talk of graves. + none
A letter to Mars. + Hayden, J. J.
Letters from Hell. + L W J S
Letters from Hell. + Rowel, M.
Level Seven. + Roshwald, Mordecai
Liadain and Curithir. + Saul, George Brandon
Liafail. + Mundy, Talbot
The liberated future. + Hoskins, Robert
The liberation of Manhattan. + Appleman, Mark J. &
   Demaitre, Edmund
Liberator of Jedd. + Lord, Jeffrey
The liberators. + Stevens, Isaac N.
Libido 23. + Linder, D. Barry
Libra. + Kirk, Eleanor
Library of the world's best mystery and detective sto-
   ries; American. + Hawthorne, Julian
The lid comes off. + Best, Harry
The lie destroyer. + Statten, Vargo
Lie ten nights awake. + van Thal, Herbert
Lieut. Gullivar Jones. + Arnold, Edwin L.
Life. + Wheeler, William W.
The life and adventures of Peter Wilkins. + Paltock,
   Robert
The life and adventures of Sig. Gaudentio di Lucca.
   + (Berington, Simon)
Life and Andrew Otway. + Bell, Neil
The life and astonishing adventures of John Daniel.
   + Morris, Ralph
The life and astonishing transactions of John Daniel.
   + Morris, Ralph
The life and habits of city bred earthworms. + Hill,
   Merton A.
Life as Carola. + Grant, Joan
Life begins tomorrow. + Parkman, Sydney
Life comes to Seathorpe. + Bell, Neil
The life everlasting. + Corelli, Marie
Life everlasting, and other tales of science, fantasy,
   and horror. + Keller, David H.
A life for the stars. + Blish, James
Life hunt. + Perry Rhodan 43
Life in a thousand worlds. + Harris, W. S.
Life in the spheres. + Tuttle, Hudson
Life in two spheres. + Tuttle, Hudson
Life marches on. + Magor, Nancy & Woods, Margaret
   Murray
Life--the jade. + Potter, Martin H.
The life vapor. + none
Life with Lancelot. + Phillifent, John T.
Lifeboat. + White, James
Life's fairy tales. + Mitchell, J. A.
Lige Golden, the man who twinkled. + Harvey, William
Ligeia. + Poe, Edgar Allan
The light? + Hamilton, Bernard
Light a last candle. + King, Vincent
The light benders. + Chance, Jonathan
The light beyond the zodiac. + Van Ith, Lily
The light fantastic. + Harrison, Harry
The light from Sealonia. + Barker, Arthur W.
The light in the sky. + Boetzel, Eric & Clock, Herbert
Light interviews with the shades. + Jones, Robert
   Webster
The light invisible. + Benson, R. H.
The Light Maze. + North, Joan
The light of Lilith. + Wallis, G. McDonald
Light of Mars. + Charkin, Paul
The light of the eye. + Chaytor, H. J.
The light out of the East. + Crockett, S. R.

The light that never was. + Biggle, Lloyd Jr.
Lighter than a feather. + Westheimer, David
Lightfoot Island. + Furnas, J. C.
Lighting seven candles. + Lombardi, Cynthia
Lightning crime. + Luigi, Belli
Lightning in the East. + Fisher, Howard S.
Lightning world. + Thorpe, Trebor
Lights and shadows. + Blech, Aimee
The lights in the sky are stars. + Brown, Fredric
The lights were going out. + Guirdham, Arthur
A likely story. + De Morgan, William
A likeness to voices. + Savage, Mary
Lila the werewolf. + Beagle, Peter S.
Lilith. + MacDonald, George
Lilliput. + Gulliver, Lemuel Jun.
Lily Dale. + Tabori, Paul
Limanora, the island of progress. + Sweven, Godfrey
Limbo. + Wolfe, Bernard
Limbo '90. + Wolfe, Bernard
The Lincoln hunters. + Tucker, Wilson
The Line. + Williams, Ursula Moray [see Addendum]
The line of love. + Cabell, James Branch
Line to tomorrow. + Padgett, Lewis
The lineage of Lichfield. + Cabell, James Branch
Liners of time. + Fearn, John Russell
Linked lives. + Ingalese, Isabella
Linnets and Valerians. + Goudge, Elizabeth
The Lion Game. + Schmitz, James H.
The lion in the stone. + Buckmaster, Henrietta
The lion men of Mongo. + Steffanson, Con
The lion of Boaz-Jachin and Jachin-Boaz. + Hoban,
   Russell
The lion of Comarre; and, Against the fall of night.
   + Clarke, Arthur C.
The lion of Judah in never-never land. + Lindskoog,
   Kathryn Ann
The lion, the witch, and the wardrobe. + Lewis, C. S.
The lion's way. + Stoneham, C. T.
Liquid death. + "Griff"
Liquid from the Sun's rays. + Greenleaf, Sue
The liquid man. + Gilford, C. B.
Listen, please listen. + Hintze, Naomi
Listen! The stars! + Brunner, John
The listener. + Caldwell, Taylor
The listener, and other stories. + Blackwood, Alger-
   non
The listeners. + Gunn, James E.
The listeners. + Leinster, Murray
The listening child. + Timperley, Rosemary
Listening hands. + Hope, Coral
The literature of Burroughsiana. + Harwood, John
Literature of the supernatural. + Beck, Robert E.
The Little Blue Man. + Hill, Dorothy
A little book of humor, horror, and the supernatural.
   + Bierce, Ambrose
A little book of profitable tales. + Field, Eugene
A little book of strange tales. + Saul, George Bran-
   don
A little boy lost. + Hudson, W. H. [see Addendum]
Little classics; intellect. + Johnson, Rossiter
Little classics; mystery. + Johnson, Rossiter
Little dog's day. + Story, Jack Trevor
Little Fuzzy. + Piper, H. Beam
The little green men. + Johnston, William
The little grey men. + B. B.
The little laundress and the fearful knight. + Bloch
   Bertram
Little masterpieces. + Hawthorne, Nathaniel
The little men. + Kelleam, Joseph E.
The little monsters. + Elwood, Roger & Ghidalia, Vic
A little night reading. + Allen, Dave
A little north of everywhere. + Norman, James

Lord Tyger. + Farmer, Philip Jose
Lords of Atlantis. + West, Wallace
Lords of creation. + Binder, Eando
The lords of misrule. + Pomeroy, William C.
Lords of serpent land. + Connell, Alan
Lords of the Earth. + Mills, J. M. A.
Lords of the Psychon. + Galouye, Daniel F.
Lords of the starship. + Geston, Mark S.
The Lord's pink ocean. + Walker, David
Lore of Proserpine. + Hewlett, Maurice
Lorelei. + Rico, Don
Loretta Mason Potts. + Chase, Mary [see Addendum]
Los Angeles: A.D. 2017. + Wylie, Philip
Loss of Eden. + Brown, Douglas & Serpell, Christopher
Lost: a moon. + Capon, Paul
Lost aeons. + Cameron, Berl
Lost among white Africans. + Ker, David
The lost angel. + Goudge, Elizabeth
The lost bomb. + Allison, Clyde
The lost canyon of the Toltecs. + Seeley, Charles
   Sumner
The lost cavern, and other tales of the fantastic. +
   Heard, H. F.
The lost children. + Chilton, H. Herman
The Lost City. + Badger, Joseph E. Jr.
The lost city. + Blaine, John
The lost city. + Garon, Marco
The lost city. + Gilson, Charles
Lost city. + Gruhn, Carrie E.
Lost City of Light. + Webster, F. A. M.
The lost city of Manoa. + Rowe, John G.
The lost city of the Aztecs. + Lath, J. A.
Lost city of the damned. + Rivere, Alec
Lost city of Uranus. + Greene, Joseph
The lost civilization. + Heslop, Val
Lost civilizations. + Haggard, H. Rider
The lost colony. + Raymond, James F.
The lost comet. + Coblentz, Stanton A.
The lost continent. + Burroughs, Edgar Rice
The lost continent. + Hyne, Cutcliffe
Lost continents. + de Camp, L. Sprague
The lost diaries of Albert Smith. + Muller, Robert
The lost Dryad. + Stockton, Frank R.
The lost expedition. + Walker, Rowland
The lost face. + Nesvadba, Josef
The lost farm. + Curry, Jane Louise
The lost fleet of Astranides. + Barrett, G. J.
The lost garden. + Foster, Geo. C.
The lost government. + Weiss, Jiri
Lost horizon. + Hilton, James
Lost in Blunderland. + Lewis, Caroline
Lost in space. + Smith, George O.
Lost in space. + Van Arnam, Dave & Archer, Ron
The lost Inca. + Inca-Pablo-Ozollo
Lost island. + McInnes, Graham
Lost Lake. + Kirk, Russell
The lost land. + Marshall, Edison
Lost legacy. + Heinlein, Robert A.
Lost men in the grass. + Griff, Alan
The lost millennium. + Richmond, Leigh & Richmond,
   Walt
The lost mine of the Mono. + Klette, C. H. B.
The lost nation. + Aronstam, Noah E.
The lost nation. + McNeil, Everett
The lost oasis. + Robeson, Kenneth
Lost on the Moon. + Rockwood, Roy
Lost on Venus. + Burroughs, Edgar Rice
Lost on Venus. + Patchett, M. E.
The lost ones. + Cameron, Ian
The lost perception. + Galouye, Daniel F.
The lost planet. + Dallas, Paul V.
The lost planet. + MacVicar, Angus

The lost provinces. + Tracy, Louis
Lost race of Mars. + Silverberg, Robert
Lost road. + Scoggins, C. E.
The lost star, and other stories. + Chapin, Maud
   Hudnut
The lost Stradivarius. + Falkner, J. Meade
Lost threshold. + Wheeler, Thomas Gerald
The lost traveller. + Todd, Ruthven
The lost tribe. + Aronin, Ben
The lost tribes and the land of Nod. + Kerr, A. P.
The lost trumpet. + Mitchell, J. Leslie
The lost underworld. + Luigi, Belli
The lost valley. + Hawton, Hector
The lost valley, and other stories. + Blackwood,
   Algernon
The lost Vikings. + Bechdolt, Jack
The lost word. + Underhill, Evelyn
The lost world. + Doyle, A. Conan
Lost world. + Jennison, John W.
Lost world. + Shaw, Brian
The lost world; and, The poison belt. + Doyle, A.
   Conan
The lost world of Everest. + Gray, Berkeley
The lost world of the Colorado. + Heming, Jack
Lost world of time. + Carter, Lin
Lost worlds. + Smith, Clark Ashton
Lost worlds, volume 1. + Smith, Clark Ashton
Lost worlds, volume 2. + Smith, Clark Ashton
The lost worlds of 2001. + Clarke, Arthur C.
The lost years. + Lewis, Oscar
Lot's wife. + Ley-Piscator, Maria
The lottery. + Jackson, Shirley
The lottery ticket; and, The Begum's fortune. + Verne
   Jules
Lotus. + Author of "A new Marguerite"
The Lotus Caves. + Christopher, John
Love ain't nothing but sex misspelled. + Ellison,
   Harlan
Love among the ruins. + Waugh, Evelyn
The love bomb. + Sackerman, Henry
The love box. + Kalnen, Ray
The love bug. + Cebulash, Mel
The love-child. + Olivier, Edith
Love eternal. + Haggard, H. Rider
Love in the ruins. + Percy, Walker
Love in time. + Harris, Johnson
Love is forever--we are for tonight. + Williams,
   Robert Moore
The love life of Venus. + Miomandre, Francis de
The love machine. + Paul, Auren
The love machinery. + Flinders, Karl
The love of Meltha Laone. + Stump, David Leroy
The love of Prince Raameses. + Armstrong, Anthony
The love of Rabiacca. + Curtiss, F. Homer & Curtiss,
   Harriette Augusta
The love of the foolish angel. + Beauclerk, Helen
Love witch. + Walters, Eugene
Lovecraft. + Carter, Lin
The Lovecraft collector's library. + Lovecraft, H. P.
Lovely. + Meltzer, David
The lovers. + Farmer, Philip Jose
Lovers & exorcists. + York, Wesley Simon
Lovers in Mars. + Palmer, Lucile
Lovers' meeting. + Smith, Eleanor Furneaux
Lovers: 2075. + English, Charles
Loves of Lo-Foh. + Williams, Roswell
Low spirits. + Butler, Joan
Loxfinger. + Weinstein, Sol
Luana. + Foster, Alan Dean
Lucifer and the child. + Mannin, Ethel
The Lucifer cell. + Fennerton, William
The Lucifer society. + Haining, Peter

The maidens of Osiris, and other stories. + Valenti-
ner, Brigitta
The main experiment. + Hodder-Williams, Christopher
Mainly in moonlight. + Gray, Nicholas Stuart
Maiwa's revenge. + Haggard, H. Rider
The Majii. + Robeson, Kenneth
Major operation. + White, James
Make love, not waves. + Martin, Jay
Make room! Make room! + Harrison, Harry
The Makepeace experiment. + Tertz, Abram
The maker of moons. + Chambers, Robert W.
Maker of shadows. + Mann, Jack
The maker of universes. + Farmer, Philip Jose
The makeshift rocket. + Anderson, Poul
The making of Doctor Who. + Dicks, Terrance & Hulke,
Malcolm
The making of Kubrick's 2001. + Agel, Jerome
The making of Star trek. + Roddenberry, Gene &
Whitfield, Stephen E.
Making the stand for Old Glory. + Hancock, H. Irving
The Makropoulos secret. + Capek, Karel
The Malabar magician. + Penny, F. E.
The malachite casket. + Bazhov, P.
Maldoror. + Lautreamont, Comte de
The male response. + Aldiss, Brian W.
Male sex idol. + Lambert, William J. III
Malevil. + Merle, Robert
Malice in Kulturland. + Wyatt, Horace
Malign fiesta. + Lewis, Wyndham
The malignant metaphysical menace. + Knight, Mallory
T.
Malkin's mountain. + Williams, Ursula Moray
The Mallot diaries. + Nathan, Robert
Mama doll. + Woodhouse, Martin
Mama Liz drinks deep. + Rheingold, Howard
Mama Liz tastes flesh. + Rheingold, Howard
Mammalia. + Lane, John
The mammoth book of thrillers, ghosts, and mysteries.
+ Crossland, John R. & Parrish, J. M.
Mammoth man. + Sheldon, Roy
The mammoth parade. + Wood, James Playsted
Mammuth. + (Thomson, William)
Man abroad. + none
Man against tomorrow. + Nolan, William F.
Man alone. + Horsnell, Horace
The man among the monkeys. + Gozlan, Leon
A man and his soul. + Crawford, T. C.
Man and monster. + Perry Rhodan 36
A man called Destiny. + Wright, Lan
A man called Poe. + Moskowitz, Sam
A man divided. + Stapledon, Olaf
The man eater. + Burroughs, Edgar Rice
Man finds the way. + Sullivan, Philip A.
The man from Avon. + Avallone, Michael
The man from beyond. + Muller, John E.
The man from Ger. + Muller, Paul
The man from Mars. + Blot, Thomas
The man from Mars. + Dowding, Henry Wallace
The man from Mars. + Henley, Carra Dupuy
The man from maybe. + Kelley, Leo P.
The man from outer space. + Duff, Douglas V.
The man from P.I.G. + Harrison, Harry
The man from S.T.U.D. in, Rape is a no-no. + Paul,
F. W.
The man from S.T.U.D. in, Sock it to me, zombie! +
Paul, F. W.
The man from S.T.U.D. in, The lay of the land. +
Paul, F. W.
The man from S.T.U.D. in, The orgy at Madame Dracula's.
Paul, F. W.
The man from S.T.U.D. vs. the mafia. + Paul, F. W.
The man from T.O.M.C.A.T.; The dirty rotten depriving
ray. + Knight, Mallory T.

The man from T.O.M.C.A.T.; The dozen deadly dragons of
joy. + Knight, Mallory T.
The man from T.O.M.C.A.T.; The malignant metaphysical
menace. + Knight, Mallory T.
The man from T.O.M.C.A.T.; The million missing maidens.
+ Knight, Mallory T.
The man from T.O.M.C.A.T.; The ominous orgy. + Knight,
Mallory T.
The man from T.O.M.C.A.T.; The Peking pornographer. +
Knight, Mallory T.
The man from T.O.M.C.A.T.; The terrible ten. + Knight,
Mallory T.
The man from T.O.M.C.A.T.; Tsimmis in Tangier. +
Knight, Mallory T.
The man from the bomb. + Chetwynd-Hayes, R.
The man from the sea. + Andrews, J. S.
The man from to-morrow. + Statten, Vargo
The man from tomorrow. + Tucker, Wilson
The man from U.N.C.L.E. + Avallone, Michael
The man from U.N.C.L.E. and the affair of the gentle
saboteur. + Keith, Brandon
The man from U.N.C.L.E. #2; The doomsday affair. +
Whittington, Harry
The man from U.N.C.L.E., no. 3; The Copenhagen affair.
+ Oram, John
The man from U.N.C.L.E., number 4; The Dagger affair.
+ McDaniel, David
The man from U.N.C.L.E., no. 4; The stone-cold dead in
the market affair. + Oram, John
The man from U.N.C.L.E., no. 5; The finger in the sky
affair. + Leslie, Peter
The man from U.N.C.L.E., number 5; The mad scientist
affair. + Phillifent, John T.
The man from U.N.C.L.E., number 6; The vampire affair.
+ McDaniel, David
The man from U.N.C.L.E., no. 7; The radioactive camel
affair. + Leslie, Peter
The man from U.N.C.L.E., number 8; The monster wheel
affair. + McDaniel, David
The man from U.N.C.L.E., number 10; The assassination
affair. + Holly, J. Hunter
The man from U.N.C.L.E., no. 10; The diving dames af-
fair. + Leslie, Peter
The man from U.N.C.L.E., number 11; The invisibility
affair. + Stratton, Thomas
The man from U.N.C.L.E., no. 11; The thinking machine
affair. + Bernard, Joel
The man from U.N.C.L.E., number 12; The mind-twisters
affair. + Stratton, Thomas
The man from U.N.C.L.E., no. 13; The Corfu affair.
+ Phillifent, John T.
The man from U.N.C.L.E., number 13; The Rainbow affair.
+ McDaniel, David
The man from U.N.C.L.E., number 14; The cross of gold
affair. + Davies, Fredric
The man from U.N.C.L.E., no. 14; The splintered sun-
glasses affair. + Leslie, Peter
The man from U.N.C.L.E., no. 15; The power cube affair.
+ Phillifent, John T.
The man from U.N.C.L.E., number 15; The utopia affair.
+ McDaniel, David
The man from U.N.C.L.E., no. 16; The unfair fare affair.
+ Leslie, Peter
The man from U.N.C.L.E., number 17; The hollow crown
affair. + McDaniel, David
The man from up there. + Lincoln, Maurice
Man in a black hat. + Thurston, Temple
Man in duplicate. + Statten, Vargo
The man in steel. + Clouston, J. Storer
The man in the high castle. + Dick, Philip K.
The man in the maze. + Silverberg, Robert
The man in the mirror. + Garrett, William
The man in the Moon. + (Thomson, William)

Many mansions. + Rowland, Henry C.
The many worlds of Andre Norton. + Norton, Andre
The many worlds of Magnus Ridolph. + Vance, Jack
The many worlds of Poul Anderson. + Anderson, Poul
The many worlds of science fiction. + Bova, Ben
The Maracot Deep. + Doyle, A. Conan
The Maracot Deep, and other stories. + Doyle, A. Conan
Marahuna. + Watson, H. B. Marriott
The marble city. + Chetwode, R. D.
The marbled catskin. + Gibbons, Charles Harrison
March of the flame marauders. + Steele, Curtis
March of the robots. + Brett, Leo
Marchers of Valhalla. + Howard, Robert E.
The marching morons, and other famous science fiction
    stories. + Kornbluth, C. M.
Marching notes. + La Prade, Ernest
Marching sands. + Lamb, Harold
Margaret and I. + Wilhelm, Kate
Marginalia. + Lovecraft, H. P.
Maridu. + Wagner, Sharon
Marie. + Haggard, H. Rider
Marigold. + (Allonby, Edith)
Mariners of space. + Collins, Erroll
Mario and the magician. + Mann, Thomas
Marion Isle. + Haggard, H. Rider
Marion's wall. + Finney, Jack
The mark. + Kempster, Aquila
The mark of Cain. + Lang, Andrew
The mark of Lucifer. + Green, Edith Pinero
The mark of Satan. + Lorig, Ann
The mark of the bat. + Dunn, Gertrude C.
Mark of the beast. + Muller, John E.
"The mark of the beast."   Watson, Sydney
The mark o' the deil   other Northumbrian tales. +
    Pease, Howard
The mark of the demons. + Jakes, John
The mark of the rope. + Lynch, Miriam
Mark of the Shadow. + Grant, Maxwell
The mark of the vulture. + Hogan, Robert J.
Mark of the vulture. + Macao, Marshall
Markheim. + Stevenson, Robert Louis
Markheim; and, Will o' the mill. + Stevenson, Robert
    Louis
Marmaduke, Emperor of Europe. + X.
Marooned. + Caidin, Martin
Marooned in 1492. + Cook, William Wallace
Marooned in orbit. + Ballou, Arthur W.
Marooned on Australia. + Favenc, Ernest
Marooned on Mars. + del Rey, Lester
The marquis and the Moon. + Longworth, Nicholas
The Marquis de Bolibar. + Perutz, Leo
The married look. + Nathan, Robert
The marrow eaters. + Moore, Harris
The marrow of the world. + Nichols, Ruth
Mars. + Grossinger, Richard
Mars breaks through. + Low, A. M.
Mars is my destination. + Long, Frank Belknap
The Mars monopoly. + Sohl, Jerry
Mars mountain. + Key, Eugene George
Mars revealed. + (Gaston, Henry A.)
Mars 314. + Pinchin, Frank J.
Mars, we love you. + Hipolito, Jane & McNelly, Willis
The Marselite. + De Mars, Robert
The marshal duke of Denver. + Barnaby, Hugo
Marshlands; and, Prometheus misbound. + Gide, Andre
Martha Brown, M.P. + Cross, Victoria
The Martian. + du Maurier, George
The Martian chronicles. + Bradbury, Ray
The Martian Emperor-President. + Bailey, Andrew J.
Martian enterprise. + Reed, Clifford C.
A Martian examines Christianity. + Levett, Arthur
Martian martyrs. + Coleridge, John

The Martian missile. + Grinnell, David
A Martian odyssey. + Weinbaum, Stanley G.
A Martian odyssey, and other science fiction tales. +
    Weinbaum, Stanley G.
A Martian odyssey, and others. + Weinbaum, Stanley
    G.
Martian sexpot. + O'Neill, Scott
The Martian sphinx. + Woodcott, Keith
Martian time-slip. + Dick, Philip K.
The Martian visitors. + Long, Frank Belknap
The Martian way, and other stories. + Asimov, Isaac
Martians, go home. + Brown, Fredric
Martin and his friend from outer space. + Duka, Ivo
    & Kolda, Helena
Martin Crusoe. + Bridges, T. C.
Martin Magnus on Mars. + Temple, William F.
Martin Magnus on Venus. + Temple, William F.
Martin Magnus, planet rover. + Temple, William F.
Martin Pippin in the apple-orchard. + Farjeon, Eleanor
Martin Pippin in the daisy-field. + Farjeon, Eleanor
Martyr. + Utley, Brian R.
The Maru invasion. + Ranzetta, Luan
The marvellous adventures of me. + Andom, R.
The marvellous and incredible adventures of Charles
    Thunderbolt in the Moon. + Delorme, Charles
The marvellous experience of John Rydal. + Scott,
    Edward
The marvellous misadventures of Sebastian. + Alexan-
    der, Lloyd
Mary Anne Carew. + Petersilea, Carlyle
Mary Jane versus Pennsylvania. + Fine, Ralph Adam
Mary of Marion Isle. + Haggard, H. Rider
Mary, part 1. + Wilis
Mary Poppins. + Travers, P. L.
Mary Poppins; and, Mary Poppins comes back. + Travers,
    P. L.
Mary Poppins comes back. + Travers, P. L.
Mary Poppins in the park. + Travers, P. L.
Mary Poppins opens the door. + Travers, P. L.
Mary's country. + Mead, Harold
The mask, and other stories. + Chambers, Robert W.
The mask of Apollo, and other stories. + (Russell,
    George William)
Mask of chaos. + Jakes, John
The Mask of Circe. + Kuttner, Henry
The mask of Cthulhu. + Derleth, August
The mask of Fu Manchu. + Rohmer, Sax
The mask of Jon Culon. + Ludwig, Edward W.
The mask of the red death. + Poe, Edgar Allan
The mask of wisdom. + Clewes, Howard
The masked invasion. + Steele, Curtis
The masked prophet. + Bowles, John
Masks. + (Russell, Ray)
The masks of time. + Silverberg, Robert
Masque of a Savage Mandarin. + Robinson, Philip Bed-
    ford
Masque of Satan. + Coffman, Virginia
Masque of the Red Death. + Lee, Elsie
The Masque of the Red Death. + Poe, Edgar Allan
The Masque of the Red Death, and other stories. +
    Poe, Edgar Allan
The Masque of the Red Death, and other tales. + Poe,
    Edgar Allan
The Masque of the Red Death, and other tales of horror.
    + Sissons, Michael
Masque world. + Panshin, Alexei
Masquerades. + Leslie, Shane
The Master. + White, T. H.
The master and Margarita. + Bulgakov, Mikhail
The master beast. + Newte, Horace W. C.
The master-Christian. + Corelli, Marie
The Master-Girl. + Hilliers, Ashton

The master key. + Baum, L. Frank
The master-knot of human fate. + Meredith, Ellis
Master Mike and the miracle maid. + Hill, Elizabeth Starr
Master-mind menace. + Luigi, Belli
The master mind of Mars. + Burroughs, Edgar Rice
The master mind of Mars; and, A fighting man of Mars. + Burroughs, Edgar Rice
The Master must die. + Gridban, Volsted
Master of broken men. + Steele, Curtis
Master of dreams. + none
Master of his fate. + Cobban, J. MacLaren
Master of life and death. + Silverberg, Robert
Master of Middle-Earth. + Kocher, Paul H.
The master of miracle. + Ish-Kishor, Sulamith
The master of silence. + Bacheller, Irving
Master of souls. + Hansom, Mark
Master of space. + Clarke, Arthur C.
Master of space. + Rowland, Donald S.
Master of the dark gate. + Jakes, John
The master of the day of judgment. + Perutz, Leo
Master of the Etrax. + Lory, Robert
The Master of the Macabre. + Thorndike, Russell
The master of the magicians. + Phelps, Elizabeth Stuart & Ward, Herbert D.
The master of the microbe. + Service, Robert W.
The master of the Moon. + Moore, Patrick
Master of the undead. + Paul, Hugo
Master of the world. + Sylvester, John
The master of the world. + Verne, Jules
Master of the world, including Robur the Conqueror. + Verne, Jules
Master of villainy. + Rohmer, Elizabeth Sax & Van Ash, Cay
The master weed. + Rackham, John
Masterless swords. + Suddaby, Donald
Masterpiece of thrills. + none
Masterpieces of horror. + Morris, Rosamund
Masterpieces of mystery in four volumes; ghost stories. + French, Joseph Lewis
Masterpieces of mystery in four volumes; mystic-humorous stories. + French, Joseph Lewis
Masterpieces of mystery in four volumes; riddle stories. + French, Joseph Lewis
Masterpieces of science fiction. + Moskowitz, Sam
Masters' choice. + Janifer, Laurence M.
Masters' choice 1. + Janifer, Laurence M.
Masters' choice 2. + Janifer, Laurence M.
Masters of evolution. + Knight, Damon
Masters of horror. + Norton, Alden H.
Masters of science fiction. + none
Masters of the lamp. + Lory, Robert
Masters of the Maze. + Davidson, Avram
The masters of the pit. + Moorcock, Michael
Masters of the vortex. + Smith, E. E.
Masters of time. + van Vogt, A. E.
Mata the magician. + Ingalese, Isabella
Math on Mars. + Spiegel, Charles A.
The mathematical magpie. + Fadiman, Clifton
The Matheson formula. + Fletcher, J. S.
The mating. + Jay, Eric
The mating center. + Long, Frank Belknap
The mating cry. + van Vogt, A. E.
The mating of the blades. + Abdullah, Achmed
Matorni's vineyard. + Oppenheim, E. Phillips
Matrix. + Mason, Douglas R.
A matter of life and death. + Warman, Eric
Matthew Looney and the space pirates. + Beatty, Jerome Jr.
Matthew Looney in the outback. + Beatty, Jerome Jr.
Matthew Looney's invasion of the Earth. + Beatty, Jerome Jr.

Matthew Looney's voyage to the Earth. + Beatty, Jerome Jr.
Matzohball. + Weinstein, Sol
Maugis, ye sorcerer. + Gilhooley, Lord
Max Smart and the ghastly ghost affair. + Johnston, William
Max Smart and the perilous pellets. + Johnston, William
Max Smart loses Control. + Johnston, William
Max Smart--the spy who went out to the cold. + Johnston, William
The maxims of Methuselah. + Burgess, Gelett
The maxims of Noah. + Burgess, Gelett
Mayday orbit. + Anderson, Poul
Mayenne. + Tubb, E. C.
A Mayfair magician. + Griffith, George
The mayor of New York. + Barrett, Laurence
The mayor of New York. + Gratacap, L. P.
Maypoles and morals. + Kummer, Frederic Arnold
Maza of the Moon. + Kline, Otis Adelbert
The maze. + Sandoz, Maurice
The Maze Maker. + Ayrton, Michael
A maze of death. + Dick, Philip K.
McGarrity & the pigeons. + Holm, John Cecil
McGillicuddy McGotham. + Wibberley, Leonard
The McLandress dimension. + Epernay, Mark
The McLandress dimension. + Galbraith, John Kenneth
The meadows of fantasy. + Mercer, Archie
The mean city. + Bradwell, James
Meat. + Phillips, Mickey
Meccania, the super-state. + Gregory, Owen
The mechanical men. + none.
The mechanical monarch. + Tubb, E. C.
Mechasm. + Sladek, John T.
Meda. + Folingsby, Kenneth
The meddlers. + Rayner, Claire
A medicine for melancholy. + Bradbury, Ray
Medley macabre. + Netherwood, Bryan
Medusa. + Visiak, E. H.
The medusa touch. + Van Greenaway, Peter
Medusa's head. + Bacon, Josephine Daskam
Meet Simon Black. + Southall, Ivan
Meeting at infinity. + Brunner, John
A meeting over Tuscarora, and other adventure stories. + Yefremov, Ivan
Meeting the bear. + Zimpel, Lloyd
Meggido's Ridge. + Wright, S. Fowler
Mel Oliver and Space Rover on Mars. + Morrison, William
Meleager. + Vaughan, H. M.
Melmoth, the wanderer. + Maturin, Charles Robert
The melody from Mars. + Leslie, Lilian
Melusina. + Paton, A. A.
Melusine. + Haldane, Charlotte
Memoir of an eventful expedition in Central America. + Velasquez, Pedro
Memoirs found in a bathtub. + Lem, Stanislaw
Memoirs of a banknote. + Paco d'Arcos, J.
Memoirs of a certain island adjacent to the Kingdom of Utopia. + (Haywood, Eliza F.)
The memoirs of a ghost. + Stonier, G. W.
Memoirs of a physician. + Dumas, Alexandre
Memoirs of a smoking jacket. + Kleven, Arthur
Memoirs of a spacewoman. + Mitchison, Naomi
The memoirs of a survivor. + Lessing, Doris
Memoirs of Europe. + Eginardus
The memoirs of Hecate County. + Wilson, Edmund
The memoirs of Satan. + Gerhardi, William & Lunn, Brian
The memoirs of Senator Brown, a Capitol cat. + Leighton, Frances Spatz
The memoirs of Sigr. Gaudentio di Lucca. + Berington, Simon

Memoirs of the court of Lilliput. + Gulliver, Captain

Memoirs of the twentieth century. + (Madden, Samuel)

Memoirs of the year two thousand five hundred. + (Mercier, Louis-Sebastien)

The memoirs of Zeus. + Druon, Maurice

Memories of the future. + Knox, Ronald A.

The Memory Bank. + West, Wallace

Men against the stars. + none

Men against the stars. + Greenberg, Martin

Men and machines. + Silverberg, Robert

The men and the mirror. + Rocklynne, Ross

Men are like animals. + Macpherson, Donald

The men from Arcturus. + Winterbotham, Russ

The men from PIG and ROBOT. + Harrison, Harry

The men from the meteor. + Black, Pansy E.

Men, halflings & hero worship. + Bradley, Marion Zimmer

Men in chains. + Ryan, Thomas

The men in the jungle. + Spinrad, Norman

The men inside. + Malzberg, Barry N.

Men into space. + Leinster, Murray

Men like gods. + Wells, H. G.

Men like gods; and, The dream. + Wells, H. G.

Men, Martians, and machines. + Russell, Eric Frank

Men of destiny. + King-Hall, Stephen

Men of space and time. + Bleiler, Everett F. & Dikty, T. E.

Men of the deep waters. + Hodgson, William Hope

Men of the hills. + Treece, Henry

Men of the Mirage. + Frost, Kelman

Men of the mist. + Bridges, T. C.

Men on the Moon. + Wollheim, Donald A.

Men who die twice. + Heath, Peter

The men who smiled no more. + Robeson, Kenneth

Men without bones. + Kersh, Gerald

Men without bones, and other stories. + Kersh, Gerald

Men, women, and ghosts. + Phelps, Elizabeth Stuart

Menace. + Pollard, Leslie

The menace from Earth. + Heinlein, Robert A.

Menace from Magor. + Howell, Scott

Menace from Mercury. + La Salle, Victor

Menace from the Moon. + Lynch, Bohun

Menace from the Moon. + Walters, Hugh

Menace from the past. + Maddox, Carl

Menace of the mutant master. + Perry Rhodan 18

Menace of the saucers. + Binder, Eando

The menace of the Terribore. + Mackworth, John D.

The menacing sleep. + Sheldon, Roy

The Mendelov conspiracy. + Caidin, Martin

Mene tekel. + Groner, Auguste

The mental wizard. + Robeson, Kenneth

Mention my name in Atlantis. + Jakes, John

The Mephisto Waltz. + Stewart, Fred Mustard

Mercenary from tomorrow. + Reynolds, Mack

The merchant of souls. + Goldring, Douglas

Merchants of disaster. + Robeson, Kenneth

Mercia, the astronomer royal. + Mears, A. Garland

Merciless mermaids. + Allison, Clyde

Mercy Island. + Bowden, Etta & Bowden, Phil

The Mercy Men. + Nourse, Alan E.

The merging of Ronald Letheredge. + Marks, Percy L.

Merlin's mistake. + Newman, Robert

Merlin's ring. + Munn, H. Warner

The mermaid in the swimming pool. + Wallop, Douglass

The mermaid's daughter. + Gard, Joyce

Merope. + Buckman, H. H.

The merry men and other tales and fables; Strange case of Dr. Jekyll and Mr. Hyde. + Stevenson, Robert Louis

The merry miracle. + Mian, Mary

The merry multifleet and the mounting multicorps. + O'Cluny, Thomas

Merryland. + Stretzer, Thomas

Mesmerism "in articulo mortis." + Poe, Edgar Allan

The Mesmerist's secret. + Dormer, Daniel

The message. + Dawson, A. J.

Message ends. + Craig, David

A message from a lost soul. + (Rowel, M.)

Message from a stranger. + Mannes, Marya

A message from Earth. + Hassler, Kenneth W.

A message from Mars. + Ganthony, Richard & Lurgan, Lester

A message from space. + Goodchild, George

Message from the Eocene. + St. Clair, Margaret

Messages from Mars. + Braine, Robert D.

Messenger of Zhuvastou. + Offutt, Andrew J.

A messenger to the gods. + Reed, Ivy Kellerman

The messengers will come no more. + Fiedler, Leslie A.

Messiah. + Vidal, Gore

The messiah of the cylinder. + Rousseau, Victor

Messiah on the horizon. + Cruso, Solomon

The metal eater. + Sheldon, Roy

The metal giants. + Hamilton, Edmond

The Metal Master. + Robeson, Kenneth

The metal monster. + Luigi, Belli

The Metal Monster. + Merritt, A.

The metal smile. + Knight, Damon

The metallic muse. + Biggle, Lloyd

The metamorphosis. + Kafka, Franz

Metamorphosis, and other stories. + Kafka, Franz

Metatopia. + Ball, F. N.

Meteor. + Capek, Karel

The meteor men. + LeBaron, Anthony

Meteor menace. + Robeson, Kenneth

Meteor of death. + Livingston, Berkeley

Methods from Mars. + Mawson, L. A.

The Methuselah enzyme. + Stewart, Fred Mustard

Methuselah's children. + Heinlein, Robert A.

Metropolis. + von Harbou, Thea

A Mexican mystery. + Grove, W.

The Mezentian gate. + Eddison, E. R.

Mia. + Nathan, Robert

Michel Gulpe. + Terhune, Everit Bogert

Micro infinity. + Muller, John E.

The micro men. + Statten, Vargo

The micro-techs. + Perry Rhodan 55

Microcosmic God, and other stories. + Moskowitz, Sam

Micromegas. + Voltaire

The microscopic ones. + Brett, Leo

The Midas man. + Robeson, Kenneth

The middle of midnight (12:20 A.M.). + Beymer, William Gilmore

The middle window. + Goudge, Elizabeth

Midge. + MacTyre, Paul

The midnight dancers. + Conway, Gerard F.

The midnight folk. + Masefield, John

Midnight horrors. + The Author of Midnight Horrors

Midnight house, and other tales. + Harvey, William Fryer

The midnight people. + Haining, Peter

The midnight queen. + Fleming, May Agnes

The midnight reader. + Stern, Philip Van Doren

Midnight snacks. + Zacherley

Midnight tales. + Harvey, William Fryer

Midnite. + Stow, Randolph

Midsummer century. + Blish, James

Midsummer madness. + Roberts, Morley

Midsummer sanity. + Ingram, Kenneth

A midsummer tempest. + Anderson, Poul

The Midwich cuckoos. + Wyndham, John

The mightiest machine. + Campbell, John W.

The mighty barbarians. + Santesson, Hans Stefan

A mighty empire. + Barlow, J. Swindells

The mighty millstone. + Cosier, C. H. T.

Miss Pickerell harvests the sea. + MacGregor, Ellen & Pantell, Dora
Miss Pickerell meets Mr. H.U.M. + MacGregor, Ellen & Pantell, Dora
Miss Pickerell on the Moon. + MacGregor, Ellen & Pantell, Dora
Miss Pim's camouflage. + Stanley, Dorothy
Miss Shumway waves a wand. + Chase, James Hadley
Miss Worden's hero. + Salisbury, H. B.
Missed it by that much! + Johnston, William
Missing! + Avallone, Michael
Missing. + Chambers, Julius
The missing angel. + Cox, Erle
The missing man. + Hatch, Mary R. P.
Missing men of Saturn. + Latham, Philip
The missing safari. + Garon, Marco
The missing world, and other stories. + (Elwood, Roger)
Mission accomplished. + Walker, Jerry
Mission from Mars. + Conroy, Rick
Mission in Guemo. + Hough, S. B.
Mission: interplanetary. + van Vogt, A. E.
Mission: manstop. + Neville, Kris
Mission of gravity. + Clement, Hal
Mission to a star. + Long, Frank Belknap
Mission to Horatius. + Reynolds, Mack
Mission to Mars. + Moore, Patrick
Mission to Mercury. + Walters, Hugh
Mission to the heart stars. + Blish, James
Mission to the Moon. + del Rey, Lester
Mission to the stars. + Kent, Philip
Mission to the stars. + van Vogt, A. E.
Mission to universe. + Dickson, Gordon R.
Mission underground. + Casteret, Norbert
The missionaries. + Compton, D. G.
"The missionary and the witch doctor." + Haggard, H. Rider
Mist, and other stories. + Crompton, Richmal
The mistaken Fury, and other lapses. + Couldrey, Oswald
Mr. Absalom. + Sullivan, Alan
Mr. Adam. + Frank, Pat
Mr. Allenby loses the way. + Baker, Frank
Mr. Antiphilos, satyr. + Gourmont, Remy de
Mr. Arrow. + Russell, Austin
Mr. Atom. + Pratt, Theodore
Mr. Bass's planetoid. + Cameron, Eleanor
Mr. Blettsworthy on Rampole Island. + Wells, H. G.
Mr. Bonaparte of Corsica. + (Bangs, John Kendrick)
Mr. Boyton. + Hayes, William D.
Mr. Bremble's buttons. + Langley, Dorothy
Mr. Britling sees it through; and, In the days of the comet. + Wells, H. G.
Mr. Chang's crime ray. + Apple, A. E.
Mr. Ciggers goes to Heaven. + Massie, Douglas
Mr. Clutterbuck's election. + Belloc, H.
Mister Corbett's ghost. + Garfield, Leon
Mister Corbett's ghost, and other stories. + Garfield, Leon
Mr. da V., and other stories. + Reed, Kit
Mr. De Lacy's double. + Storke, Francis Eugene
Mr. East's experiences in Mr. Bellamy's world. + Wilbrandt, Conrad
Mr. Faraday's formula. + Woodbury, David O.
Mr. George, and other odd persons. + Derleth, August
Mr. George, and other odd persons. + Grendon, Stephen
Mr. Godly beside himself. + Bullett, Gerald
Mr. Gumble sits up. + Durkin, Douglas
Mr. Hawkins' humorous adventure. + Franklin, Edgar
Mr. Jonnemacher's machine. + Prime, Lord
Mr. Jorkens remembers Africa. + Dunsany, Lord
Mister Justice. + Piserchia, Doris

Mr. Klein's kampf. + Smith, H. Allen
Mr. Kronion. + Kerby, Susan Alice
Mr. Limpet. + Pratt, Theodore
Mr. Lynke. + Wentworth-James, Gertie de S.
Mr. Mergenthwirker's lobblies, and other fantastic tales. + Bond, Nelson
Mr. Mirakel. + Oppenheim, E. Phillips
Mr. Mudge cuts across. + Sanborn, Robert Alden
Mr. Munchausen. + Bangs, John Kendrick
Mr. Noah and the second flood. + Burnford, Sheila
Mr. Oseba's last discovery. + Bell, Geo. W.
Mr. Petre. + Belloc, Hilaire
Mr. Pickwick's second time on Earth. + Harper, Charles
Mr. Pudgins. + Carlsen, Ruth Christoffer
Mr. Pye. + Peake, Mervyn
Mister St. John. + Faure, Raoul C.
Mr. Stranger's sealed packet. + Maccoll, Hugh
Mr. Teedles, the gland old man. + Le Breton, Thomas
Mr. Theobald's devil. + Keown, Anna Gordon
Mr. Three. + Butler, William
Mr. Thurtle's trolley. + Pratt, Theodore
Mr. Tomorrow. + Sellers, Con
Mr. Tompkins explores the atom. + Gamow, George
Mr. Tompkins in paperback. + Gamow, George
Mr. Tompkins in Wonderland. + Gamow, G.
Mr. Tompkins inside himself. + Gamow, George & Ycas, Martynas
Mr. Tompkins learns the facts of life. + Gamow, George
Mr. Twigg's mistake. + Lawson, Robert [see Addendum]
Mr. Weston's good wine. + Powys, T. F.
Mr. Whittle and the morning star. + Nathan, Robert
Mr. Wicker's window. + Dawson, Carley
Mr. Wilmer. + Lawson, Robert
Mistress Masham's repose. + White, T. H.
Mistress of death. + Anthony, Piers & Fuentes, Roberto
Mistress of Devil's Manor. + Stevenson, Florence
The mistress of Downing Street. + Harris, Walter
Mistress of mistresses. + Eddison, E. R.
Mistress of the skies. + Delmont, Joseph
Mistresses of mystery. + Lewis, Gogo & Manley, Seon
Mists of dawn. + Oliver, Chad
The mists of fear. + Creasey, John
The mists of Zwillingzeit. + Pocock, Bryant Walker
Mithrandir. + Miller, Stephen O.
Mixed feelings. + Effinger, George Alec
The mixed men. + van Vogt, A. E.
Mizora. + Zarovitch, Princess Vera
Moaning Canyon. + Unknown Author
The mobsmen on the spot. + Grant, Maxwell
Moderan. + Bunch, David R.
A modern Aladdin. + Pyle, Howard
Modern arms and a feudal throne. + Harrison, T. Milner
The modern Atalantis. + Manley, Mary
A modern Daedalus. + Greer, Tom
The modern devil. + Chambers, I. Mench
A modern exodus. + Guttenberg, Violet
Modern ghosts. + none
Modern Lilliput. + Wilson, David Alec
Modern masterpieces of science fiction. + Moskowitz, Sam
Modern mystery and adventure novels. + Greene, Jay E.
Modern science fiction. + Bretnor, Reginald
Modern science fiction. + Spinrad, Norman
Modern tales of horror. + Hammett, Dashiell
A modern wizard. + Ottolengui, Rodrigues
Modern wonders of the world. + Gilbert, William
Mog, the Mound Builder. + Crump, Irving
Mogul tales. + Gueullette, Thomas
The Mohole menace. + Walters, Hugh
The Mohole mystery. + Walters, Hugh
The Molecular Cafe. + none

More adventures on other planets. + Wollheim, Donald A.
More 'Alice.' + Wilson, Yates
More from One step beyond. + Bredeson, Lenore
More ghost stories. + James, M. R.
More ghost stories of an antiquary. + James, M. R.
More ghosts and marvels. + Collins, V. H.
More great ghost stories. + Dale, Harrison
More great tales of horror. + Bowen, Marjorie
More horror stories. + Lee, Elisabeth
More issues at hand. + Atheling, William Jr.
More little monsters. + Elwood, Roger & Ghidalia, Vic
More macabre. + Wollheim, Donald A.
More nightmares. + Bloch, Robert
More not at night. + Thomson, Christine Campbell
More of my favorites in suspense. + Hitchcock, Alfred
More Penguin science fiction. + Aldiss, Brian W.
A more perfect union. + Stapp, Robert
More science fiction tales. + Elwood, Roger
More Soviet science fiction. + none
More spook stories. + Benson, E. F.
More stories. + Pain, Barry
More stories for late at night. + Hitchcock, Alfred
More stories from The Hugo winners, volume II. + Asimov, Isaac
More stories from The twilight zone. + Serling, Rod
More stories my mother never told me. + Hitchcock, Alfred
More stories not for the nervous. + Hitchcock, Alfred
More stories strange and sinister. + Pizer, Laurette Naomi
More tales of terror and surprise. + none
More tales of the uneasy. + Hunt, Violet
More tales of unease. + Burke, John
More tales to tremble by. + Sutton, Stephen P.
More terror in the modern vein. + Wollheim, Donald A.
More than human. + Sturgeon, Theodore
More than moon. + Clark, Laurence
More than superhuman. + van Vogt, A. E.
More things in Heaven. + Brunner, John
'More things in Heaven...' + Owen, Walter
More to and again. + Brooks, Walter R.
More uncanny stories selected from The novel magazine. + none
Morgan Rockefeller's will. + Clarke, Francis H.
Morgante the Lesser. + Sirius
Morial the Mahatma. + Collins, Mabel
Morning for Mr. Prothero. + Oliver, Jane
Morning Star. + Haggard, H. Rider
The mortal immortal. + Shelley, Mary Wollstonecraft
The mortal immortals. + Cristabel
Mortals and monsters. + del Rey, Lester
The mortals of Reni. + Gruen, Von
The mortgage on the brain. + Harper, Vincent
Mortmain. + Train, Arthur
Mortorio. + Burgess, Eric & Friggens, Arthur
The mortuary. + Smith, Clark Ashton
Morwyn. + Powys, John Cowper
Moscow 1979. + Kuehnelt-Leddihn, Christiane von & Kuehnelt-Leddihn, Erik
Mosses from an Old Manse. + Hawthorne, Nathaniel
The mote in God's eye. + Niven, Larry & Pournelle, Jerry
The moth. + Carroll, Joy
The moth men. + Rochester, George E.
Mother-in-law India. + Sinderby, Donald
The mother of emeralds. + Hume, Fergus W.
Mother of gold. + Francis, Francis
Mother of gold. + Hough, Emerson
Mother of invention. + Johnston, William
Mother of pearl. + France, Anatole
Mother was a lovely beast. + Farmer, Philip Jose

The motion menace. + Robeson, Kenneth
The motives of Nicholas Holtz. + Laing, Alexander & Painter, Thomas
The motor pirate. + Paternoster, G. Sidney
Motorman. + Ohle, David
Mount Analogue. + Daumal, Rene
Mount Horeb. + Birdwell, Russell
Mount Kestrel. + Piliban, An
The Mountain and the Summer Stars. + Baker, Michael
The mountain and the tree. + Beauclerk, Helen
Mountain bride. + Coatsworth, Elizabeth
The mountain kingdom. + Johnstone, D. Lawson
The Mountain of Gold. + Winch, E.
The mountain of mystery. + Langley, Kenlis
The mountain of truth. + Carlson, Dale
The mountains at the bottom of the world. + Cameron, Ian
Mountains of mystery. + Friel, Arthur O.
The mountains of the sun. + Leourier, Christian
The mouse and his child. + Hoban, Russell [see Addendum]
The mouse on the Moon. + Wibberley, Leonard
The mouse on Wall Street. + Wibberley, Leonard
The mouse that roared. + Wibberley, Leonard
The Mouthpiece of Zitu. + Giesy, J. U.
The Movement. + Garbo, Norman
Movie monsters. + Gifford, Denis
The movie treasury; horror movies. + Frank, Alan G.
The moving finger. + none
The moving snow. + Weekley, Ian
Mr.--For titles beginning with this word see: Mister.
Mrs. Aladdin. + Egbert, H. M.
Mrs. Brown on the Battle of Dorking. + Sketchley, Arthur
Mrs. Candy and Saturday night. + Tallant, Robert
Mrs. Coverlet's magicians. + Nash, Mary
Mrs. Frisby and the rats of NIMH. + O'Brien, Robert C.
Mrs. Hephaestus, and other short stories. + Baker, George A.
Mrs. Searwood's secret weapon. + Wibberley, Leonard
Mubendi girl. + Webster, F. A. M.
Mucca Scob. + Kelly, T. M.
The mucker. + Burroughs, Edgar Rice
Mukara. + Bruce, Muriel
Mulata. + Asturias, Miguel Angel
The mulatta and Mr. Fly. + Asturias, Miguel Angel
The Muller-Fokker effect. + Sladek, John
The multi-man. + Harbottle, Philip
The multi-man. + Statten, Vargo
The multiple man. + Hassler, Kenneth W.
The mummy. + Loudon, Mrs. Jane
The mummy and Miss Nitocris. + Griffith, George
The mummy comes to life. + Van der Elst, Violet
The mummy walks. + Luigi, Belli
The mummy walks among us. + Ghidalia, Vic
The mummy's romance. + Gautier, Theophile
Munchausen at the Pole. + (Raspe, Rudolf)
Munchausen at Walcheron. + (Raspe, Rudolf)
Munchausen XX. + The Baron
The munitions master. + Robeson, Kenneth
The Munsters. + Cooper, Morton
The Munsters and the great camera caper. + Johnston, William
The Munsters; The last resort. + Johnston, William
The mural master. + Jones, Adrienne
Murder by Telecopter. + Hughes, Denis
Murder from beyond. + Foster, R. Francis
The murder germ. + Pollard, A. O.
Murder gives notice. + Hayman, Art
Murder in millennium VI. + Gray, Curme
Murder has wings. + Kensch, Otto
The murder I don't remember. + Valdez, Paul

Murder in space. + Reed, David V.
Murder in the clinic. + Hamilton, Edmond
Murder in the stratosphere. + Laurence, John
Murder madness. + Leinster, Murray
Murder medley. + Hervey, Michael
Murder melody. + Robeson, Kenneth
Murder mirage. + Robeson, Kenneth
The murder of the missing link. + Vercors
The murder of the U.S.A. + Jenkins, Will F.
Murder on the Moon. + MacDaniel, Charles
Murder out of mind. + Crossen, Ken
The murderer invisible. + Wylie, Philip
Murderers' island. + Tregarron, Yate
The murders in the Rue Morgue; and, A tale of the Rag-
    ged Mountains. + Poe, Edgar Allan
The murders in the Rue Morgue, and other stories. +
    Poe, Edgar Allan
The murders in the Rue Morgue, and other tales. +
    Poe, Edgar Allan
A Murray Leinster omnibus. + Leinster, Murray
The music from behind the Moon. + Cabell, James Branch
Musrum. + Earnshaw, Anthony & Thacker, Eric
A muster of ghosts. + Lynch, Bohun
Mutant. + Kuttner, Henry
Mutant. + Padgett, Lewis
Mutant 59: the plastic-eater. + Davis, Gerry & Pedler,
    Kit
The mutant weapon. + Leinster, Murray
Mutants. + Dickson, Gordon R.
The mutants. + Neville, Kris
Mutants. + Silverberg, Robert
The mutants rebel. + Tubb, E. C.
Mutants vs. mutants. + Perry Rhodan 19
Muted strings. + Livingston, Marjorie
The mutinous wind. + Reynard, Elizabeth
Mutiny in space. + Davidson, Avram
Mutiny in the time machine. + Keith, Donald
My afterdream. + West, Julian
My beloved Troshanus. + Kloor, Mary Conway
My best science fiction story. + Friend, Oscar J. &
    Margulies, Leo
My bird sings. + Malet, Oriel
My blond princess of space. + Will, John N.
My blood ran cold. + Speed, Donald
My brother, o my brother! + Kampf, Harold
My dear, it's Heaven. + Winn, Rowland [see Addendum]
My favorites in suspense. + Hitchcock, Alfred
My first two thousand years. + Eldridge, Paul &
    Viereck, George Sylvester
My friend Mr. Leakey. + Haldane, J. B. S.
"My goodness!" said the Princess. + Carson, De Witt
My grimmest nightmare. + none
My invisible partner. + Denison, Thomas S.
My journeys with Astargo. + Barnhouse, Perl T.
My lady evil. + Cooper, Parley J.
My lady of the Nile. + Egbert, H. M.
My life in the bush of ghosts. + Tutuola, Amos
My life in time. + Newton, Bertha
My life on eight planets. + Doney, Nina M.
My lives and how I lost them. + Cullen, Countee
My name is death, and other new tales of horror. +
    Birkin, Charles
My name is Vladimir Sloifoiski. + Alper, Gerald A.
My own death. + "Limbo"
My own fairy book. + Lang, Andrew
My petition for more space. + Hersey, John
My sinful Earth. + Gerhardi, William
My talks with Dean Spanley. + Dunsany, Lord
My vacation. + Fitzporter, J. L.
My wicked pleasures. + X., Molly
Myora. + Hanvey, Robert E.
Myriam and the mystic brotherhood. + Howard, Maude
    Lesseur

Myron. + Vidal, Gore
Myself and the young bowman, and other fantasies. +
    Hume, Cyril
Mysteries of Asia. + Abdullah, A.
Mysteries of Earth, continents, and man revealed. +
    Fuller, Ira C.
The mysteries of Florence. + Lippard, George
Mysteries of the border land. + Fox, Nettie Pease
Mysteries of the unseen. + Campbell, Gilbert E.
The mysterious Amazonia. + Cruls, Gastao
The mysterious card. + Moffett, Cleveland
The mysterious city of Oo. + Hildreth, Charles Lotin
The mysterious hunter. + St. L., Vic
The mysterious island. + Verne, Jules
The mysterious machine. + Dines, Glen
The mysterious Mr. Quin. + Christie, Agatha
The mysterious planet. + Wright, Kenneth
The mysterious stranger. + Gundran, Olive
The mysterious stranger. + Twain, Mark
The mysterious stranger, and other stories. + Twain,
    Mark
Mystery. + none
The mystery. + Adams, Samuel Hopkins & White, Stewart
    Edward
The mystery book. + Thomson, H. Douglas
The mystery boys and the Inca gold. + Powell, Van
The mystery boys and the Inca gold; and, The mystery
    boys and Captain Kidd's message. + Powell, Van
Mystery flight of the Q2. + Clarke, Covington
A mystery for Mr. Bass. + Cameron, Eleanor
The mystery men of Mars. + Claudy, Carl H.
The mystery of Arthur Gordon Pym. + Poe, Edgar Allan
    & Verne, Jules
The mystery of choice. + Chambers, Robert W.
The mystery of Cloomber. + Doyle, A. Conan
The mystery of Collinwood. + Ross, Marilyn
The mystery of Dr. Fu-Manchu. + Rohmer, Sax
The mystery of Evangeline Fairfax. + Kunst, Earle
The mystery of Lucien Delorme. + Teramond, Guy de
The mystery of Marr's Hill. + Prud'hommeaux, Rene
Mystery of satellite 7. + Coombs, Charles
A mystery of sixty centuries. + Widnall, Samuel Page
The mystery of the beetle. + Marsh, Richard
A mystery of the Campagna; and, A shadow on a wave. +
    Von Degen
A mystery of the Cordillera. + Bourne, Arthur M.
The mystery of the green ray. + Le Queux, William
The mystery of the hidden city. + Bull, Albert E.
The mystery of the lost moon. + Chester, Michael
The mystery of the North Pole. + Nichol, C. A. Scrym-
    sour
A mystery of the Pacific. + Smeaton, Oliphant
The mystery of the sea. + Stoker, Bram
The mystery of the shroud. + Gay, J. Drew
Mystery of the third mine. + Lowndes, Robert W.
Mystery of the witch who wouldn't + Platt, Kin
The mystery on the snow. + Robeson, Kenneth
The mystery planet. + Kennedy, Edgar Rees
Mystery tales of ghosts and villains. + none
Mystery under the sea. + Robeson, Kenneth
The mystery woman. + Praed, Mrs. Campbell
Mystic events. + Lathom, Francis
Mystic-humorous stories. + French, Joseph Lewis
The Mystic Mullah. + Robeson, Kenneth
The mystic quest. + Kingsland, William
Mystica Algooat. + Morehouse, William Russell
Myth, allegory, and gospel. + none
Myth, symbol, & religion in The Lord of the Rings. +
    Miesel, Sandra
Mythmaster. + Kelley, Leo P.

The N.E.S.F.A. index, 1971-1972. + Lewis, Anthony &
    Whyte, Andrew A.

The N.E.S.F.A. index to the science fiction magazines and original anthologies, 1973. + Lewis, Anthony & Whyte, Andrew A.
N.U.K.E.E. + Widener, Don
Nada the Lily. + Haggard, H. Rider
The naiad. + Sand, George
Nail down the stars. + Morressy, John
A nail merchant at nightfall. + Waltari, Mika
The naked and the damned. + Shafer, Robert
A naked girl. + Athanassiades, Nikos
Naked in her coffin. + Alice, Tiny
Naked in Piccadilly. + Salazar Chapela, E.
The naked Phantom. + Smythe, R. John
The naked sun. + Asimov, Isaac
Naked to the stars. + Dickson, Gordon R.
A name for evil. + Lytle, Andrew
Nameless. + Longley, Mary T.
The nameless order. + Dargon
Naomi, daughter of Ruth. + Bone, Leon
The nap, and other stories. + de la Mare, Walter
Napoleon in the other world. + Xongo-Tee-Foh-Tchi
The Napoleon of Notting Hill. + Chesterton, G. K.
The Nargun and the stars. + Wrightson, Patricia
The narrative of Arthur Gordon Pym of Nantucket. + Poe, Edgar Allan
The narrative of Jasper Wheeple. + Sutherland, James
A narrative of the life and astonishing adventures of John Daniel. + Morris, Ralph
The narrow passage. + Butterworth, Oliver
The Nathan Hale. + Vorhies, John R.
Nathan 3. + Nathan, Robert
Natives of space. + Clement, Hal
The natural man. + Lloyd, J. William
The nature of the catastrophe. + Jones, Langdon & Moorcock, Michael
Naughty positions. + Marie, Anne
The naughty princess. + Armstrong, Anthony
Nautipuss. + Allison, Clyde
The Naval engineer and the command of the sea. + Burton, Francis G.
The naviators. + Spanner, E. F.
The navigator of Rhada. + Gilman, Robert Cham
Neanderthal planet. + Aldiss, Brian W.
The nearing storm. + Donnelly, Desmond
Nearly Neptune. + Walters, Hugh
Nebula. + Jakubowski, Maxim
Nebula alert. + Chandler, A. Bertram
Nebula award stories eight. + Asimov, Isaac
Nebula award stories five. + Blish, James
Nebula award stories four. + Anderson, Poul
Nebula award stories nine. + Wilhelm, Kate
Nebula award stories 1965. + Knight, Damon
Nebula award stories seven. + Biggle, Lloyd
Nebula award stories six. + Simak, Clifford D.
Nebula award stories three. + Zelazny, Roger
Nebula award stories two. + Aldiss, Brian W. & Harrison, Harry
Nebula X. + Statten, Vargo
The necessity for beauty. + Bradley, Marion Zimmer
Necromancer. + Dickson, Gordon R.
The necromancer. + Flammenberg, Lawrence
The necromancer. + Reynolds, George W. M.
The necromancers. + Benson, Robert Hugh
The Necronomicon. + Owings, Mark
Ned, the son of Webb. + Stoddard, William O.
Nedoure, priestess of the Magi. + Betiero, T. J.
Needle. + Clement, Hal
Needle in a timestack. + Silverberg, Robert
Negative minus. + Fanthorpe, R. L.
The negative ones. + Muller, John E.
Neila Sen; and, My casual death. + Connelly, J. H.
Nella waits. + Millhiser, Marlys

Nema, and other stories. + Peek, Hedley
Nemesis. + Fane, Bron
The nemesis from Terra. + Brackett, Leigh
Nemesis wife. + Evans, Cicely Louise
The neon halo. + Curtis, J-L
Nephele. + Bourdillon, Francis William
Neptune One is missing. + Walters, Hugh
Nequa. + Adams, Jack
Nerves. + del Rey, Lester
The nets of space. + Petaja, Emil
Neuron world. + Fanthorpe, R. L.
Neuroomia. + McIver, G.
Neutopia. + Richardson, E.
The neutral stars. + Kippax, John & Morgan, Dan
Neutron star. + Niven, Larry
Never at night. + Thomson, Christine Campbell
Never forever. + Conyers, Bernard
Never in this world. + Stone, Idella Purnell
Never let up. + Maine, Charles Eric
Never the same door. + Rankine, John
Never trust a Martian. + none
The nevermore affair. + Wilhelm, Kate
A Nevil Shute omnibus. + Shute, Nevil
Nevlo. + Robeson, Kenneth
The new accelerator. + Wells, H. G.
The new Adam. + Roger, Noelle
The new Adam. + Weinbaum, Stanley G.
A new Alice in the old Wonderland. + Richards, Anna M.
New Amazonia. + Corbett, E. B.
New anthology of science fiction. + de Camp, L. Sprague
The new Battle of Dorking. + (Maude, F. N.)
New bodies for old. + Renard, Maurice
The new Boswell. + Freeman, R. M.
New Britain. + Ellis, G. A.
New British science fiction and fantasy books published during 1970 & 1971. + Bishop, Gerald
The new city. + Fialko, Nathan
The New Crusade. + Gibbs, Anthony
New day, big world, few people. + Woodard, George C.
A new day dawns. + Blanchard, Charles Elton
The new Decameron. + Potocki, Jan
A new description of Merryland. + (Stretzer, Thomas)
New dimensions IV. + Silverberg, Robert
New dimensions I. + Silverberg, Robert
New dimensions 3. + Silverberg, Robert
New dimensions II. + Silverberg, Robert
The new dominion. + Kipling, Arthur Wellesley
New dreams this morning. + Blish, James
A new Earth and a new Heaven. + Hill, William Boyle
The new Eden. + Hyne, C. J. Cutcliffe
New Era. + (Caryl, Chas. W.)
The new gods lead. + Wright, S. Fowler
The new Gulliver. + Druery, Chas. T.
The new Gulliver. + Garrison, Wendell Phillips
The new Gulliver, and other stories. + Pain, Barry
The new H. P. Lovecraft bibliography. + Chalker, Jack L.
A new Heaven. + Russell, G. Warren
A new humanity. + Wilbrandt, Adolf
A new journey to the world in the Moon. + (Defoe, Daniel)
A new lease of life; and, Saving a daughter's dowry. + About, Edmond
The new life. + Coleridge, John
New lives for old. + (Snow, C. P.)
The new Lucian. + Traill, H. D.
The new Macchiavelli; and, The food of the gods. + Wells, H. G.
New maps of Hell. + Amis, Kingsley
A new messiah. + Cromie, Robert
The new mind. + Elwood, Roger

The new minds. + Morgan, Dan
The new Moon. + Onions, Oliver
The new northland. + Gratacap, L. P.
The new ordeal. + (Chesney, George T.)
The new order. + Gerard, Morice
The new people; They came from the sea. + Steele,
    Alex
The new pleasure. + Gloag, John
The new race of devils. + Bernard, John
The new regime, A.D. 2202. + Brant, John Ira
The new S.F. + Jones, Langdon
The new SF bulletin index to SF books, 1974. + Whyte,
    Andrew Adams
The new satellite. + Statten, Vargo
New science fiction books published in Great Britain,
    1968, 1969. + Bishop, Gerald
New stories from The twilight zone. + Serling, Rod
New tales of horror by eminent authors. + none
New tales of space and time. + Healy, Raymond J.
The new terror. + Leroux, Gaston
The new tomorrows. + Spinrad, Norman
New trade winds for the seven seas. + Roberts, Alaric
A new Trafalgar. + Curtis, Albert Charles
The new utopia. + Tuckwell, Rev. W.
A new voyage to the country of the Houyhnhnms. + Hod-
    gart, Matthew
New waggings of old tales. + (Bangs, John Kendrick &
    Sherman, Frank Dempster)
New world of pain-masters. + Villard, Alexander
New worlds for old. + Carter, Lin
New worlds for old. + Derleth, August
New worlds for old. + Ketterer, David
New worlds #5. + Moorcock, Michael & Platt, Charles
New worlds of fantasy. + Carr, Terry
New worlds of fantasy #3. + Carr, Terry
New worlds of fantasy #2. + Carr, Terry
New worlds quarterly. + Moorcock, Michael
New worlds quarterly 5. + Moorcock, Michael
New worlds quarterly 4. + Moorcock, Michael
New worlds quarterly #4. + Moorcock, Michael
New worlds quarterly #1. + Moorcock, Michael
New worlds quarterly #3. + Moorcock, Michael
New worlds quarterly #2. + Moorcock, Michael
New worlds quarterly 3. + Moorcock, Michael
New worlds quarterly 2. + Moorcock, Michael
New worlds 7. + Bailey, Hilary & Platt, Charles
New worlds 6. + Moorcock, Michael & Platt, Charles
New writings in horror and the supernatural. + Sutton,
    David
New writings in horror and the supernatural, vol. 2.
    + Sutton, David
New writings in S-F 8. + Carnell, John
New writings in SF-18. + Carnell, John
New writings in S.F.-11. + Carnell, John
New writings in S-F 15. + Carnell, John
New writings in S-F 5. + Carnell, John
New writings in S-F 4. + Carnell, John
New writings in S-F 14. + Carnell, John
New writings in S-F 9. + Carnell, John
New writings in S-F 19. + Carnell, John
New writings in S-F 1. + Carnell, John
New writings in S-F 7. + Carnell, John
New writings in S-F 17. + Carnell, John
New writings in S-F 6. + Carnell, John
New writings in S-F 16. + Carnell, John
New writings in S-F 10. + Carnell, John
New writings in S-F 13. + Carnell, John
New writings in S-F 3. + Carnell, John
New writings in S.F.-12. + Carnell, John
New writings in SF-20. + Carnell, John
New writings in SF (24). + Bulmer, Kenneth
New writings in SF (21). + Carnell, John

New writings in SF (23). + Bulmer, Kenneth
New writings in SF (22). + Bulmer, Kenneth
New writings in S-F 2. + Carnell, John
A New Year's fable. + Dudintsev, Vladimir
A New Year's tale. + Dudintsev, Vladimir
New York necromancy. + Macao, Marshall
New York to Brest in seven hours. + Laurie, Andre
Newbury in Orm. + Williams, Islwyn
Newry Bridge. + none
News for Heaven. + Dell, Jeffrey
News from elsewhere. + Cooper, Edmund
The news from Karachi. + Wood, William
News from nowhere. + Morris, William
The next chapter. + Maurois, Andre
The next crusade. + Cromie, Robert
Next door to the Sun. + Coblentz, Stanton A.
The next generation. + Maguire, John Francis
The next naval war. + Eardley-Wilmot, Capt. S.
The next Ninety-Three. + Watlock, W. A.
Next of kin. + Russell, Eric Frank
Next stop--Mars! + Edwards, David
Next stop the stars. + Silverberg, Robert
The next war. + Charlton, L. E. O.
The next war. + Wallace, King
A nice day for screaming, and other tales of the Hub.
    + Schmitz, James H.
Niels Klim. + (Holberg, Ludvig)
Niels Klim's journey under the ground. + Holberg,
    Ludvig
The night callers. + Crisp, Frank
The night creature. + Ball, Brian
Night gallery. + Serling, Rod
Night gallery 2. + Serling, Rod
Night has a thousand eyes. + Hopley, George
Night has a thousand eyes. + Irish, William
Night in Babylon. + Wellard, James
Night in no time. + Crawshay-Williams, Eliot
A night in the Luxembourg. + Gourmont, Remy de
Night journey. + Guerard, Albert Joseph
The Night Land. + Hodgson, William Hope
The night life of the gods. + Smith, Thorne
Night mare. + Golding, Morton J.
Night monsters. + Leiber, Fritz
Night of delusions. + Laumer, Keith
Night of Light. + Farmer, Philip Jose
Night of masks. + Norton, Andre
Night of the big fire. + Muller, John E.
Night of the big heat. + Lymington, John
Night of the black horror. + Norwood, Victor
The night of the death rain. + Ranzetta, Luan
Night of the griffin. + Giles, Raymond
Night of the living dead. + Russo, John
The night of the puudly. + Simak, Clifford D.
Night of the robots. + Ball, Brian N.
Night of the saucers. + Binder, Eando
The night of the Shadow. + Grant, Maxwell
Night of the sphinx, and other stories. + (Elwood,
    Roger)
The night of the Trilobites. + Leslie, Peter
Night of the vampire. + Giles, Raymond
Night of the warlock. + Giles, Raymond
Night of the wolf. + Forest, Salambo
The night of the wolf. + Leiber, Fritz
The night of the wolf. + Long, Frank Belknap
The night of the world. + Rose, F. Horace
Night on Eros. + Greve, Tora
Night on the river. + Freyer, Dermot
A night out. + Peple, Edward
The night people. + Flagg, Francis
Night-pieces. + Burke, Thomas
Night ride, and other journeys. + Beaumont, Charles
The night shapes. + Blish, James

The night side. + Derleth, August
Night slaves. + Sohl, Jerry
The night spiders. + Lymington, John
The night stalker. + Rice, Jeff
The night strangler. + Rice, Jeff
Night unto night. + Wylie, Philip
Night walk. + Shaw, Bob
The night walker. + Stuart, Sidney
The night watchman. + Jacquemard, Simonne
The night-watchmen. + Cresswell, Helen
The night wind howls. + Cowles, Frederick I.
A night with Jupiter, and other fantastic stories. +
   Ford, Charles Henri
Nightbirds on Nantucket. + Aiken, Joan [see Addendum]
The nightcomers. + Hastings, Michael
Nightfall, and other stories. + Asimov, Isaac
Nightfall one. + Asimov, Isaac
Nightfall two. + Asimov, Isaac
Nightfrights. + Haining, Peter
Nightland spell. + Grimm, Benjamin
Nightmare. + Brett, Leo
Nightmare. + Chilton, I. M.
Nightmare Abbey. + (Peacock, Thomas Love)
Nightmare Abbey; and, Crotchet Castle. + Peacock,
   Thomas Love
Nightmare age. + Pohl, Frederik
Nightmare baby. + DuBreuil, Linda
Nightmare by daylight. + Thomson, Christine Campbell
Nightmare farm. + Mann, Jack
Nightmare hall. + McMurdie, Annie Laurie
The nightmare has triplets. + Cabell, James Branch
Nightmare on Vega 3. + Huntington, Charles
The nightmare reader. + Haining, Peter
Nightmare stories. + Higham, Charles
Nightmare tales. + Blavatsky, H. P.
Nightmares. + none
Nightmares. + Bloch, Robert
Nightmares and daydreams. + Bond, Nelson
Nightmares and Geezenstacks. + Brown, Fredric
Nightmares of eminent persons. + Russell, Bertrand
Night's black agents. + Leiber, Fritz Jr.
Nights of the Round Table. + Lawrence, Margery
Nights with the gods. + Reich, Emil
Night's yawning peal. + Derleth, August
Nightshade. + Gwynne, Paul
Nightshade & damnations. + Kersh, Gerald
Nightwings. + Silverberg, Robert
Nile gold. + Knittel, John
Nimshi. + (Carlisle, Samuel Hanna)
The nine billion names of God. + Clarke, Arthur C.
Nine by Laumer. + Laumer, Keith
Nine ghosts. + Malden, R. H.
Nine horrors and a dream. + Brennan, Joseph Payne
Nine hundred grandmothers. + Lafferty, R. A.
Nine lives. + Channing, Mark
Nine princes in Amber. + Zelazny, Roger
The nine questions. + Fenton, Edward
9 stories from Men against the stars. + Greenberg,
   Martin
Nine stories from The horror in the museum, and other
   revisions. + Derleth, August
Nine strange stories. + Owen, Betty M.
9 tales of space and time. + Healy, Raymond J.
Nine tomorrows. + Asimov, Isaac
The Nine Unknown. + Mundy, Talbot
Nine worlds west. + Fairman, Paul W.
Nineteen eighty-four. + Orwell, George
1989. + Pendleton, Don
1957. + Blair, Hamish
1945. + none
1944. + Halsbury, Earl of
The 1946 ms. + Maugham, Robin

Nineteen hundred? + Farningham, Marianne
1900. + Lockwood, Ingersoll
Nineteen impressions. + Beresford, J. D.
1999 sex erotics. + Daniels, Gil
1993. + Orr, Paul & Orr, Violet
1975. + My Great-Grandson
The 1974 annual world's best SF. + Saha, Arthur W. &
   Wollheim, Donald A.
1976. + Dickie, E. Gordon
1976...the year of terror. + Smith, George H.
The 1973 annual world's best SF. + Saha, Arthur W. &
   Wollheim, Donald A.
The 1972 annual world's best SF. + Saha, Arthur W. &
   Wollheim, Donald A.
1960. + Marshall, James & Marshall, Margaret Scott
19 tales of terror. + Burnett, Whit & Burnett, Hallie
1938. + Kingsmill, Hugh & Muggeridge, Malcolm
1920. + Lucian
"1925." + Wallace, Edgar
Nineteenth century German tales. + Flores, Angel
"Ninety and nine just persons." + Graham, Winifred
98.4 + Hodder-Williams, Christopher
99%. + Gloag, John
Ninety North. + Western, Ernest
'96. + Rosewater, Frank
9th annual edition, the year's best S-F. + Merril,
   Judith
The 9th annual of the year's best SF. + Merril, Judith
9th annual S-F. + Merril, Judith
The ninth Fontana book of great ghost stories. +
   Chetwynd-Hayes, R.
The ninth Galaxy reader. + Pohl, Frederik
The ninth ghost book. + Timperley, Rosemary
The ninth life. + Mann, Jack
The ninth Pan book of horror stories. + van Thal,
   Herbert
The ninth plague. + Lindsay, David T.
The Ninth Vibration, and other stories. + Beck, L.
   Adams
Ninya. + Fagan, Henry A.
No blade of grass. + Christopher, John
No borderland. + Morris, M. Marlow & Speer, Laura B.
No boundaries. + Kuttner, Henry & Moore, C. L.
No dawn and no horizon. + Merak, A. J.
No future in it. + Brunner, John
No future in murder. + Valdez, Paul
No heaven for Gunga Din. + Mirdrekvandi, Ali, Gunga
   Din
No lack of space. + Martin, David S.
No limits. + Ferman, Joseph W.
No man Friday. + Gordon, Rex
No man in Eden. + Myra, H. L.
No man on Earth. + Moudy, Walter
No man's world. + Bulmer, Kenneth
No man's world. + Caidin, Martin
No mind of man. + none
No more war! + Stead, F. Herbert
No nightingales. + Brahms, Caryl & Simon, S. J.
No one goes there now. + Walling, William
No one hears but Him. + Caldwell, Taylor
No one will escape. + Kirst, Hans Hellmut
No other gods but me. + Brunner, John
No other man. + Noyes, Alfred
No place like Earth. + Carnell, John
No place on Earth. + Charbonneau, Louis
No rates and taxes. + Pinkerton, Thomas A.
No refuge. + Boland, John
No room for man. + Dickson, Gordon R.
No stab can kill. + Clark, F. Le Gros
No stars for us. + Ray, Robert
No subway. + Vielle, E. E.
No such thing as a vampire. + Pickersgill, Frederick

Occam's razor. + Duncan, David
Occult. + none
Occult shorts, 2nd collection. + none
The occults in council. + William, Sir
An occurrence at Norman's Burger Castle. + Houston, James D.
Ocean on top. + Clement, Hal
Oceanides. + Petersilea, Carlyle
Oceanides. + von Himmel, Ernst
The oceans of Venus. + Asimov, Isaac
Octagon magic. + Norton, Andre
The October country. + Bradbury, Ray
October the First is too late. + Hoyle, Fred
Odd job #101, and other future crimes and intrigues. + Goulart, Ron
Odd John. + Stapledon, Olaf
Odd John; &, Sirius. + Stapledon, Olaf
Odd science fiction. + Long, Frank Belknap
The oddballs. + Ghidalia, Vic
The odious ones. + Sohl, Jerry
Odyssey in space. + Brack, Vektis
The odyssey of Husky Hillier. + Webster, F. A. M.
The odyssey of 9. + Statten, Vargo
Odyssey to Earthdeath. + Kelley, Leo P.
Oedipus in Disneyland. + Molloy, Hercules
Of all possible worlds. + Tenn, William
Of demons and darkness. + Collier, John
Of Earth and fire. + Barclay, Alan
Of Earth foretold. + Bulmer, Kenneth
Of godlike power. + Reynolds, Mack
Of Lunar kingdoms. + Wilson, Henry Lovejoy
Of men and machines. + Lewis, Arthur O. Jr.
Of men and monsters. + Tenn, William
Of other worlds. + Lewis, C. S.
Of such as these. + none
Of time and stars. + Clarke, Arthur C.
Of worlds beyond. + Eshbach, Lloyd Arthur
Off center. + Knight, Damon
Off land's end. + Reid, Walter
Off on a comet. + Verne, Jules
Off the beaten orbit. + Merril, Judith
The off-worlders. + Baxter, John
The official despatches and correspondence relative to the Battle of Dorking. + none
Og--boy of battle. + Crump, Irving
Og of the cave people. + Crump, Irving
Og--son of fire. + Crump, Irving
Og, son of Og. + Crump, Irving
Ogden's strange story. + Marshall, Edison
Oh, God! + Corman, Avery
Ohhhhh, it feels like dying. + Madison, J. J.
Oic-? + Thorn, Joe
Ol' King David an' the Philistine boys. + Bradford, Roark
Ol' man Adam an' his chillun. + Bradford, Roark
Old as the world. + Brodie Innes, J. W.
An old captivity. + Shute, Nevil
The old die rich, and other science fiction stories. + Gold, H. L.
The old English baron. + Reeve, Clara
Old fires and profitable ghosts. + Quiller-Couch, A. T.
The old French professor. + Murray, Alfred
Old Fritz and the new era. + Muhlbach, Louisa
Old House of Fear. + Kirk, Russell
The old lion, and other stories. + de la Mare, Walter
The old man and the monkey-king. + Durand, Robert
Old man in new world. + Stapledon, Olaf
The Old Man of the Mountain. + Strang, Herbert
Old man's beard. + Wakefield, H. R.
The old masters. + Davis, Brian
The old men at the Zoo. + Wilson, Angus

The old mountain hermit. + Raymond, James F.
The old powder line. + Parker, Richard
Old Ugly-Face. + Mundy, Talbot
An older kind of magic. + Wrightson, Patricia
The oldest god. + McKenna, Stephen
Oldham. + Verschoyle, Catherine M.
Ole Doc Methuselah. + Hubbard, L. Ron
Olga Romanoff. + Griffith, George
Olympian nights. + Bangs, John Kendrick
The Olympians. + Pendleton, Don
The Olympic hope. + Lundberg, Knud
Olympus. + Howard, Charles F.
Om. + Mundy, Talbot
Omar. + Blunt, Wilfrid
Omega. + Elwood, Roger
Omega. + Flammarion, Camille
The omega man. + Matheson, Richard
The Omega point. + Zebrowski, George
Omha abides. + MacApp, C. C.
Omina uncharted. + Starr, Roland
Ominous folly. + Barry, Ray
The ominous orgy. + Knight, Mallory T.
The omnibus Jules Verne. + Verne, Jules
An omnibus of American mysteries. + Eenhoorn, Michael
An omnibus of continental mysteries, part I. + Bisserov, George
The omnibus of crime. + Sayers, Dorothy L.
Omnibus of science fiction. + Conklin, Groff
The omnibus of time. + Farley, Ralph Milne
An omnibus thriller of murder and mystery. + none
Omnivore. + Anthony, Piers
On a dark night. + West, Anthony
On a lark to the planets. + Montgomery, Frances Trego
On a planet alien. + Malzberg, Barry N.
On a torn-away world. + Rockwood, Roy
On an odd note. + Kersh, Gerald
On borrowed time. + Watkin, Lawrence Edward
On instructions of my government. + Salinger, Pierre
On my throbbing engine. + Forest, Salambo
On our way to the future. + Carr, Terry
On the beach. + Shute, Nevil
On the borderland. + Austin, F. Britten
On the crest of Earth with race. + Brock, Walter S.
On the heights of Himalay. + van der Naillen, A.
On the last day. + Jones, Mervyn
On the loose. + Raffalovich, George
On the Marble Cliffs. + Juenger, Ernst
On the margins of old books. + LeMaitre, Jules
On the shores of the infinite. + Stuart, Mrs. G.
On the symb-socket circuit. + Bulmer, Kenneth
On the trail of Inca gold. + Lazo, Hector
On the trail of 1960. + Wiley, Ray H.
On the trail of the space pirates. + Rockwell, Carey
On the way home. + Warburg, Sandol Stoddard
On the wings of the wind. + Westerman, Percy F.
On tiptoe. + White, Stewart Edward
On wheels. + Jakes, John
Once again. + Rath, E. J.
The once and future king. + White, T. H.
Once and future tales from The magazine of fantasy and science fiction. + Ferman, Edward L.
Once around the park. + Shannon, Frank
Once departed. + Reynolds, Mack
Once in a new moon. + Rutter, Owen
Once in time. + Dagmar, Peter
Once on a time. + Milne, A. A.
Once there was a giant. + Laumer, Keith
Once upon a Saturday. + Fenton, Edward
Once upon a space. + Campbell, H. J.
Once upon a star. + Crossen, Kendell Foster
Once upon a summertime. + A'Dair, Jeanne & Roberts, Eleanor

One. + Karp, David
One against eternity. + van Vogt, A. E.
One against Herculum. + Sohl, Jerry
One against the Legion. + Williamson, Jack
One against the Moon. + Wollheim, Donald A.
One against time. + del Martia, Astron
The One Before. + Pain, Barry
One before bedtime. + Linkroum, Richard
One by one. + Gilliatt, Penelope
One came back. + Bell, Neil
One dollar's worth. + Brown, Fred. H.
"One dreadful night..." + Harding, Ronald S. L.
One-Eye. + Gordon, Stuart
One foot in the grave. + Grubb, Davis
The one gift. + Sheehan, Perley Poore
One half of the world. + Barlow, James
One hundred and two H-bombs. + Disch, Thomas M.
One hundred and two H bombs, and other science fiction stories. + Disch, Thomas M.
100 books by August Derleth. + Derleth, August
100 fathoms under. + Blaine, John
One hundred years hence. + Emanuel, Walter
One hundred years of science fiction. + Knight, Damon
One hundred years of science fiction, book one. + Knight, Damon
One hundred years of science fiction, book two. + Knight, Damon
One hundred years of science fiction illustration. + Frewin, Anthony
One hundred years of solitude. + Garcia Marquez, Gabriel
The 100th millennium. + Brunner, John
One in three hundred. + McIntosh, J. T.
One is one. + Rankine, John
One-man show. + Thayer, Tiffany
One million centuries. + Lupoff, Richard A.
One million tomorrows. + Shaw, Bob
One of "Berrian's" novels. + Stone, Mrs. C. H.
One of Cleopatra's nights, and other fantastic romances. + Gautier, Theophile
One of our asteroids is missing. + Knox, Calvin M.
The One Sane Man. + Beeding, Francis
One step beyond. + Bredeson, Lenore
One step from Earth. + Harrison, Harry
One thousand dollars a day. + Knapp, Adeline
One thousand eight hundred and twenty nine. + none
The 1,000 year plan. + Asimov, Isaac
"1,000-year voyage." + Statten, Vargo
The One who is legion. + Barney, Natalie Clifford
Oneiros. + Yelverton, Christopher
Onesimus Templeton. + Colville, W. J.
Only by daylight. + Thomson, Christine Campbell
Only lovers left alive. + Wallis, Dave
Only toys! + Anstey, F.
The only way to go. + Oswald, Dave
The onyx ring. + Sterling, John
Oo. + Hildreth, Charles Lotin
The opal matrix. + Chambers, W. Jerome
The open cage. + Hall, Ronald
The open door. + (Oliphant, Mrs.)
Open prison. + White, James
The open secret. + A Priest
The opener of the way. + Bloch, Robert
The openers of the gate. + Beck, L. Adams
Operation ARES. + Wolfe, Gene
Operation Boudoir. + O'Shea, Sean
Operation Chaos. + Anderson, Poul
Operation Columbus. + Walters, Hugh
Operation Doomsday. + Kenyon, Paul
Operation doomsday. + Pearl, Jack
Operation future. + Conklin, Groff
Operation interstellar. + Smith, George O.

Operation Malacca. + Poyer, Joe
Operation mermaid. + Stanton, Ken
Operation Mora. + King, Christopher
Operation Nuke. + Caidin, Martin
Operation Octopus. + Dark, James
Operation Omina. + Starr, Roland
Operation orbit. + Luna, Kris
Operation: outer space. + Leinster, Murray
Operation phantasy. + Wollheim, Donald A.
Operation Satellite. + Fear, W. H.
Operation Scuba. + Dark, James
Operation sea monster. + Stanton, Ken
Operation: sextrip. + Reynolds, Joseph
Operation space. + Ball, John
Operation Springboard. + Ball, John
Operation star voyage. + Pearl, Jack
Operation superman. + Hawton, Hector
Operation terror. + Leinster, Murray
Operation time search. + Norton, Andre
Operation Umanaq. + Rankine, John
Operation Venus! + Fearn, John Russell
Operator 5; Blood reign of the dictator. + Steele, Curtis
Operator 5; Hosts of the flaming death. + Steele, Curtis
Operator 5; Invasion of the yellow warlords. + Steele, Curtis
Operator 5; Legions of the death master. + Steele, Curtis
Operator 5; March of the flame marauders. + Steele, Curtis
Operator 5; Master of broken men. + Steele, Curtis
Operator 5 #3; The yellow scourge. + Steele, Curtis
Operator 5 #2; The invisible empire. + Steele, Curtis
Operator 5; The army of the dead. + Steele, Curtis
Operator 5; The invisible empire. + Steele, Curtis
Operator 5; The masked invasion. + Steele, Curtis
Ophelia. + Stevenson, Florence
The opposite uncle. + Johnston, William
Opus 100. + Asimov, Isaac
Or all the seas with oysters. + Davidson, Avram
The oracle of Baal. + Webster, J. Provand
Orbit 8. + Knight, Damon
Orbit 11. + Knight, Damon
Orbit 15. + Knight, Damon
Orbit 5. + Knight, Damon
Orbit 4. + Knight, Damon
Orbit 14. + Knight, Damon
Orbit 9. + Knight, Damon
Orbit one. + Jay, Mel
Orbit 1. + Knight, Damon
Orbit one. + Muller, John E.
Orbit 7. + Knight, Damon
Orbit 6. + Knight, Damon
Orbit 10. + Knight, Damon
Orbit 13. + Knight, Damon
Orbit 3. + Knight, Damon
Orbit 12. + Knight, Damon
Orbit 2. + Knight, Damon
Orbit unlimited. + Anderson, Poul
The orchid cage. + Franke, Herbert W.
Ordeal. + Shute, Nevil
Ordeal in otherwhere. + Norton, Andre
The order of Isis. + Bagnall-Stubbs, James
The order of the octopus. + Horler, Sydney
An ordinary man. + Arrighi, Mel
Orestes. + Gnoli, Domenico
Orfeo in paradise. + Santucci, Luigi
The organ bank farm. + Boyd, John
Organic destiny. + Romilus, Arn
The orgy at Madame Dracula's. + Paul, F. W.
The orgy of Bubastis. + Hyde-Chambers, Derek

Orgy of the dead. + Wood, Edward D. Jr.
The orgy puppets. + none
Orgy twins. + Strong, Rod
Oriental tales of terror. + Strating, J. J.
Origin. + Knowlton, J. A.
The original Mr. Ed. + Brooks, Walter
Original travels and surprising adventures of Baron
    Munchausen. + (Raspe, Rudolf)
The original travels of Baron Munchausen. + (Raspe,
    Rudolf)
Orlando. + Woolf, Virginia
Orn. + Anthony, Piers
Orphan island. + Macaulay, Rose
Orphan of eternity. + Heinrich, Carl
The orphan of space. + Glossop, Reginald
Orphans of the sky. + Heinlein, Robert A.
Oscar Lobster's fair exchange. + Selden, George
Osprey Island. + Feydy, Anne Lindbergh
Osru. + Sterns, Justin
Ossian's ride. + Hoyle, Fred
The Other. + Tryon, Thomas
Other days, other eyes. + Shaw, Bob
The other dimension. + Rosner, Sara
Other dimensions. + Silverberg, Robert
Other dimensions. + Smith, Clark Ashton
Other eyes watching. + Cross, Polton
The other foot. + Knight, Damon
The other half of the planet. + Capon, Paul
The other human race. + Piper, H. Beam
The other landscape. + Gunn, Neil M.
The other log of Phileas Fogg. + Farmer, Philip Jose
The other man. + Cooper, Giles
The other one. + Turney, Catherine
The other passenger. + Cross, John Keir
The other people. + Brisco, Pat A.
The other place, and other stories of the same sort.
    + Priestley, J. B.
The other side. + none
The other side. + Kubin, Alfred
The other side. + Vachell, Horace Annesley
The other side at the Battle of Dorking. + Moltruhn,
    Maximilian
The other side of green hills. + Cross, John Keir
The other side of here. + Leinster, Murray
The other side of Night. + Charkin, Paul
The Other Side of Nowhere. + Leinster, Murray
The other side of the clock. + Stern, Philip Van
    Doren
The other side of the mirror. + Anderson Imbert,
    Enrique
The other side of the Moon. + Derleth, August
The other side of the Moon. + Trevor, Meriol
The other side of the mountain. + Bernanos, Michel
The other side of the sky. + Clarke, Arthur C.
The other side of the Sun. + Capon, Paul
The other side of the universe. + Dreifuss, Kurt
The other side of time. + Laumer, Keith
The other side of tomorrow. + Elwood, Roger
The other sky. + Laumer, Keith
The other wise man. + Van Dyke, Henry
The other world. + Bond, J. Harvey
The other world. + Moore, Frank Frankfort
The other world. + Robeson, Kenneth
Other worlds. + Heming, J. W.
The other worlds. + Stong, Phil
Other worlds of Clifford Simak. + Simak, Clifford D.
Other worlds, other gods. + Mohs, Mayo
Other worlds, other seas. + Suvin, Darko
Other worlds, other times. + Elwood, Roger & Mosko-
    witz, Sam
The others. + Carr, Terry
The others. + Greenfield, Irving A.

Others who returned. + Wakefield, H. R.
The ouija board. + Lester, Teri
Our children's children. + Simak, Clifford D.
Our coming world. + Michaud, A. C.
Our friends from Frolix 8. + Dick, Philip K.
Our gang. + Roth, Philip
Our ghosts. + Leigh, Edmund
Our girl from MEPHISTO. + Allison, Clyde
Our glorious future. + Johnhett
Our hero. + none
Our Lady. + Sinclair, Upton
Our man Flint. + Pearl, Jack
Our man for Ganymede. + Dick-Lauder, Sir George
Our man from SADISTO. + Allison, Clyde
Our man in space. + Ronald, Bruce W.
Our next president. + Baker, Russell
Our own Pompeii. + (Fox, S. Middleton)
Our revolting society. + Ousdal, Asbjorn P.
Our stranger. + Meredith, Edgar
Out. + Brooke-Rose, Christine
Out. + Meltzer, David
Out from Ganymede. + Malzberg, Barry N.
Out of bounds. + Merril, Judith
Out of chaos. + McIntosh, J. T.
Out of my mind. + Brunner, John
Out of space and time. + Smith, Clark Ashton
Out of space and time, volume I. + Smith, Clark Ash-
    ton
Out of space and time, volume II. + Smith, Clark Ash-
    ton
Out of the abyss. + England, George Allan
Out of the ages. + Pryce, Devereux
Out of the air. + Irwin, Inez Haynes
Out of the darkness. + Fanthorpe, R. Lionel
Out of the dead city. + Delany, Samuel R.
Out of the deeps. + Wyndham, John
Out of the mouth of the dragon. + Geston, Mark S.
Out of the night. + Muller, John E.
Out of the past. + More, E. Anson Jr.
Out of the past. + Spurrell, H. G. F.
Out of the silence. + Cox, Erle
Out of the silent places. + Kent, Brad
Out of the silent planet. + Lewis, C. S.
Out of the unknown. + Hull, E. Mayne & van Vogt, A. E.
Out of the void. + Stone, Leslie F.
Out of their minds. + Simak, Clifford D.
Out of this world. + Bova, Ben
Out of this world. + Corning, Walter D.
Out of this world. + Fast, Julius
Out of this world. + Leinster, Murray
Out of this world. + Owen, Mably & Williams-Ellis,
    Amabel
Out of this world choice. + Owen, Mably & Williams-
    Ellis, Amabel
Out of this world 8. + Owen, Mably & Williams-Ellis,
    Amabel
Out of this world 5. + Owen, Mably & Williams-Ellis,
    Amabel
Out of this world 4. + Owen, Mably & Williams-Ellis,
    Amabel
Out of this world 9. + Pearson, Michael & Williams-
    Ellis, Amabel
Out of this world 1. + Owen, Mably & Williams-Ellis,
    Amabel
Out of this world 7. + Owen, Mably & Williams-Ellis,
    Amabel
Out of this world 6. + Owen, Mably & Williams-Ellis,
    Amabel
Out of this world 10. + Pearson, Michael & Williams-
    Ellis, Amabel
Out of this world 3. + Owen, Mably & Williams-Ellis,
    Amabel

Out of this world 2. + Owen, Mably & Williams-Ellis, Amabel
Out of time. + Langelaan, George
Out of time's abyss. + Burroughs, Edgar Rice
Out of wild hills. + Campbell, Colin
Out there. + Stoutenberg, Adrien
Out went the taper. + Ashby, R. C.
The outcasts. + Fraser, W. A.
Outcrop. + Cooper, Colin
The outer darkness. + Wright, R. H.
The outer reaches. + Derleth, August
Outer space stories. + Furman, A. L.
Outerspace sex orgy. + Faber, Arthur
Outland. + Austin, Mary
Outland. + Stairs, Gordon
The outlander. + Spicer, Paul R.
Outlaw of Gor. + Norman, John
Outlaw World. + Hamilton, Edmond
The outlaws of Mars. + Kline, Otis Adelbert
The outlaws of the air. + Griffith, George
Outlaws of the air. + Shaw, Frank H.
Outlaws of the Moon. + Hamilton, Edmond
Outpost Mars. + Judd, Cyril
Outpost of Jupiter. + del Rey, Lester
Outpost on the Moon. + Walters, Hugh
The Outposter. + Dickson, Gordon R.
Outposts in space. + West, Wallace
Outside. + Norton, Andre
Outside the universe. + Hamilton, Edmond
The outsider, and others. + Lovecraft, H. P.
Outsiders: children of wonder. + Tenn, William
Outward bound. + Vane, Sutton
The outward urge. + Lea, Richard
The outward urge. + Wyndham, John & Parkes, Lucas
Outwards from Earth. + Crispin, Edmund
Outwitting tomorrow. + Frater VIII°
Outworlder. + Carter, Lin
Over sea, under stone. + Cooper, Susan
Over the border. + Robertson, Morgan
Over the edge. + Derleth, August
Over the edge. + Ellison, Harlan
Over the edge. + Sheldon, William D. & Wheelock, Warren H.
Over the hills, and far away. + Dunsany, Lord
Over the hills, and far away. + Mayne, William
Over the hills to Fabylon. + Gray, Nicholas Stuart
Over the mountain. + Todd, Ruthven
Over the plum-pudding. + Bangs, J. K.
Over the sea's edge. + Curry, Jane Louise
Overdraft on glory. + Helvick, James
Overkill. + Garner, William
Overlay. + Malzberg, Barry N.
The overloaded man. + Ballard, J. G.
The overlord. + McIvor, Allan
Overlord New York. + Elliot, Lee
Overlords from space. + Kelleam, Joseph E.
Overlords of Andromeda. + Falkner, John
The overlords of war. + Klein, Gerard
The overman. + Sinclair, Upton
The Overman culture. + Cooper, Edmund
Overmind. + Wadsworth, Phyllis Marie
The oversexed astronauts. + Coxe, Mr.
Overshadowed. + Yulee, C. Wickliffe
Overture to Cambridge. + Macleod, Joseph Gordon
The owl and the pussycat. + Cross, John Keir
The owl hoots twice at Catfish Bend. + Burman, Ben Lucien
The owl of Athene. + Phillpotts, Eden
The owl service. + Garner, Alan
Owls' watch. + Saul, George Brandon
Ozar, the Aztec. + Tompkins, Walker A.
Ozmar the mystic. + Hulme-Beaman, Emeric

PX. + Taylor, Malcolm
Pacific advance. + Melde, G. R.
The Pacific book of Australian SF. + Baxter, John
The pack of pieces. + Armstrong, Anthony
Pack Rat. + Kelley, Francis Clement
A pad in the straw. + Woodforde, Christopher
The pagan city. + Chaplin, W. N.
Pagan parable. + Davey, Norman
Pagan passions. + Garrett, Randall & Harris, Larry M.
The pagan's progress. + Morris, Gouverneur
Pageants of despair. + Hamley, Dennis
A pail of air. + Leiber, Fritz
Paingod, and other delusions. + Ellison, Harlan
The painted face. + Onions, Oliver
A pair from space. + none
A pair of adventurers in search of El Dorado. + Collingwood, Harry
The palace of Eternity. + Shaw, Bob
The Palace of Love. + Vance, Jack
Palafox. + Wason, Sandys
The pale ape, and other pulses. + Shiel, M. P.
The pale blonde of Sands Street. + White, William Chapman
Paleface and redskin, and other stories for boys and girls. + Anstey, F.
Palingenesia. + Theosopho & Ellora
The pallid giant. + Noyes, Pierrepont B.
The palm-wine drinkard, and his dead palm-wine tapster in the Deads' town. + Tutuola, Amos
Palos of the Dog Star Pack. + Giesy, J. U.
Pan and the twins. + Phillpotts, Eden
The Pan book of horror stories. + van Thal, Herbert
Pan on a rampage. + Forest, Salambo
Pan Sagittarius. + Wallace, Ian
Pan Satyrus. + Wormser, Richard
The Panama plot. + Reeve, Arthur B.
The Panchronicon. + Mackaye, Harold Steele
Pandemonium on the Potomac. + Anderson, William C.
Pandora. + Reeve, Arthur B.
Pandora descending. + DuBreuil, Linda
The Pandora Effect. + Williamson, Jack
Pandora's planet. + Anvil, Christopher
Panic among Puritans. + Laver, James
Panic o'clock. + Hodder-Williams, Christopher
Panics. + none
Pan's garden. + Blackwood, Algernon
The panther. + Warner, Anne
The Panther book of horror. + Rampton, Anthony
Panther Jones for president. + Johnson, Stanley
Pantopia. + Harris, Frank
Papa's war, and other satires. + Garnett, Edward
The paper dolls. + Davies, L. P.
The papers of Andrew Melmoth. + Davies, Hugh Sykes
The parable. + Goethe, Johann Wolfgang von
The paradise game. + Stableford, Brian M.
Paradise is not enough. + Elder, Michael
The Paradise man. + Hale, John
The paradise of the north. + Johnstone, David Lawson
Paradise on Earth. + Hayes, Jeff W.
Paradox lost, and twelve other great science fiction stories. + Brown, Fredric
The paradox men. + Harness, Charles L.
A parallel case. + none
The paralyzing rays vs. the nuclears. + Nizzi, Guido
Paramind. + Willer, Jim
Pararobot. + Charles, Neil
The parasaurians. + Wells, Robert
The parasite. + Doyle, A. Conan
Parasite planet. + none
Pardon my fangs. + Hill, Elizabeth Starr
Paris prelude. + Howard, Christopher
Park. + Gray, John

Parsecs and parables. + Silverberg, Robert
The parting of Arwen. + Bradley, Marion Zimmer
The partisan leader. + Sidney, Edward William
The partisan leader. + Tucker, Beverly
Partners in wonder. + Ellison, Harlan, and others
Pasha the Persian. + Linden, Margaret
Pasquinade. + Walker, Earl
Passage to Pluto. + Walters, Hugh
Passage to Saturn. + (Harbottle, Philip)
The passing of the third floor back. + Houghton,
   Claude
The passing of the third floor back. + Jerome, Jerome
   K.
The passing of the third floor back, and other stories.
   + Jerome, Jerome K.
Passion-fruit. + Vivian, E. Charles
The passion stroke. + Fairweather, Mary
The passionate astrologer. + Griffiths, Alan
The passionate witch. + Matson, Norman & Smith, Thorne
Passport to eternity. + Ballard, J. G.
Passport to the supernatural. + Hurwood, Bernhardt J.
Past and future; and, The last generation. + Day,
   Bradford M.
Past master. + Lafferty, R. A.
Past, present, and future perfect. + Fitz Gerald,
   Gregory & Wolf, Jack C.
The past through tomorrow. + Heinlein, Robert A.
The Pastel City. + Harrison, M. John
Pastels in prose. + Merrill, Stuart
Pat Collins and the captive scientist. + Palmer,
   Bernard
Pat Collins and the hidden treasure. + Palmer, Bernard
Pat Collins and the mysterious orbiting rocket. +
   Palmer, Bernard
Pat Collins and the peculiar Dr. Brockton. + Palmer,
   Bernard
Pat Collins and the secret engine. + Palmer, Bernard
Pat Collins and the wingless plane. + Palmer, Bernard
The path beyond the stars. + Petaja, Emil
Path into the unknown. + none
The path of the great. + Gargilis, Stephen
The path of unreason. + Smith, George O.
Path to savagery. + Alter, Robert Edmond
The pathless trail. + Friel, Arthur O.
The patient dark. + Bulmer, Kenneth
Patron of the arts. + Rotsler, William
Pattern for conquest. + Smith, George O.
Pattern of a man. + Gottlieb, Seymour
Pattern of shadows. + Burke, Jonathan
The patterns of chaos. + Kapp, Colin
Patterns of unification in Sylvie & Bruno. + Berman,
   Ruth
Paul Rees. + Augustinus
Paul the minstrel, and other stories. + Benson, Art-
   hur Christopher
Pause to wonder. + Fischer, Marjorie & Humphries,
   Rolfe
Pavane. + Roberts, Keith
The paw of God. + Gordon, Rex
Pawn of time. + Carson, Robin
Pawns in ice. + Gibbs, Henry
Pawns of destiny. + Devito, John A.
The pawns of null-A. + van Vogt, A. E.
Peabody's mermaid. + Jones, Constance & Jones, Guy
   Pearce
Peace, my daughters. + Barker, Shirley
The peace of 1975. + Sterne, Richard E.
Peace under Earth. + Beaujon, Paul
A peaceful revolution. + "Gentle Joseph"
The Peacemaker. + Forester, C. S.
The peacemaker. + Remenham, John
The peacemakers. + Casewit, Curtis W.

The peacemakers. + Hayes, Hiram W.
Pearl-Maiden. + Haggard, H. Rider
Pearl of Patmos. + Lord, Jeffrey
Pebble in the sky. + Asimov, Isaac
Pecker's bad boy. + Lamont, Gil
The Peckster professorship. + Quincy, J. P.
The peculiar exploits of Brigadier Ffellowes. + Lanier,
   Sterling E.
The peculiar Major. + Howard, Keble
The pedestal. + Lanning, George
The pedestrian. + Bradbury, Ray
A peek at Heaven. + Bush, Lucius M.
Peggy the aeronaut. + Carter, J. L.
The Peking pornographer. + Knight, Mallory T.
Pellucidar. + Burroughs, Edgar Rice
The penal colony. + Kafka, Franz
The pencil of God. + Marcelin, Pierre & Thoby-Marce-
   lin, Philippe
Pender among the residents. + Reid, Forrest
The Pendragon legend. + Szerb, Antal
Pendulum. + Christopher, John
The pendulum of fate. + Alexander, Robert
Penelope. + Anderson, William C.
Penelope, the damp detective. + Anderson, William C.
Penelope's man. + Erskine, John
Penguin Island. + France, Anatole
Penguin science fiction. + Aldiss, Brian W.
The Penguin science fiction omnibus. + Aldiss, Brian
   W.
The penultimate adventure. + Davey, Norman
The penultimate truth. + Dick, Philip K.
People machines. + Williamson, Jack
The people maker. + Knight, Damon
People minus X. + Gallun, Raymond Z.
The People: no different flesh. + Henderson, Zenna
People of Asa. + Ashton, Marvin
The people of the abyss. + England, George Allan
The people of the ax. + Williams, Jay
The people of the black circle. + Howard, Robert E.
The people of the chasm. + Beck, Christopher
People of the comet. + Hall, Austin
People of the darkness. + Vivian, E. Charles
The people of the mist. + Haggard, H. Rider
The people of the Moon. + Carter, Tremlett
The people of the ruins. + Shanks, Edward
People of the South Pole. + Thomson, K. Graham
People of the Talisman. + Brackett, Leigh
People of the twilight. + Kaner, H.
The people of the wind. + Anderson, Poul
The people on other planets. + Fox, Richard A.
The people that time forgot. + Burroughs, Edgar Rice
The people trap, and other pitfalls. + Sheckley,
   Robert
Perchance to dream. + Knight, Damon
Percy. + Hitchcock, Raymond
Percy's progress. + Hitchcock, Raymond
Peregrine: primus. + Davidson, Avram
Perelandra. + Lewis, C. S.
The perfect planet. + Smith, Evelyn E.
The perfect world. + Scrymsour, Ella
Perfecting the Earth. + Wooldridge, C. W.
The perfume of the rainbow, and other stories. +
   Beck, L. Adams
The perfumed planet. + ·Elder, Michael
Perhaps. + Davey, Norman
Peril from space. + Maras, Karl
The peril of Barnabas Collins. + Ross, Marilyn
Peril of creation. + Burton, Edmund
The peril of Oliver Sargent. + Bliss, Edgar Janes
Peril of the starmen. + Neville, Kris
Peril on ice planet. + Perry Rhodan 23
Peril on Mars. + Moore, Patrick

Pioneer 1990. + Statten, Vargo
The piper of Arristoun. + Goldie, Mrs. Barre
Pippin's journal. + O'Grady, Rohan
The pirate aeroplane. + Gilson, Captain
Pirate of the Pacific. + Robeson, Kenneth
The pirate's ghost. + Robeson, Kenneth
Pirates of Cerebus. + Mistral, Bengo
The pirates of Shan. + Blaine, John
Pirates of the air. + Adams, Eustace L.
Pirates of the asteroids. + Asimov, Isaac
The pirates of the sky. + Gaillard, Stephen
Pirates of Venus. + Burroughs, Edgar Rice
The pirates of Venus; and, Lost on Venus. + Burroughs,
  Edgar Rice
The pirates of Zan. + Leinster, Murray
The pit and the pendulum. + Poe, Edgar Allan
The pit and the pendulum, and five other tales. +
  Poe, Edgar Allan
The pit and the pendulum, and other stories. + Poe,
  Edgar Allan
Pity about Earth. + Hill, Ernest
Pitzmaroon. + Beach, Charles A.
A pixie's adventures in humanland. + Delaire, Jean
The pixy. + Reynolds, George W. M.
A place named Hell. + Deer, M. J.
A place of demons. + Graat, Heinrich
The place of dreams. + Barry, William
A place of one's own. + Sitwell, Osbert
A place of sapphires. + Randall, Florence Engel
The place of the lion. + Williams, Charles
Plague from space. + Harrison, Harry
A plague of demons. + Laumer, Keith
The plague of oblivion. + Perry Rhodan 28
A plague of pythons. + Pohl, Frederik
The plague of silence. + Creasey, John
The plague of sound. + Steffanson, Con
The plague of the living dead, and more tales of the
  uncanny. + Singer, Kurt
Plague over London. + Thurlow Craig, (Charles)
Plague panic. + Hedges, Sid
Plague ship. + North, Andrew
Plan for conquest. + Glynn, A. A.
Planet Big Zero. + Hadley, Franklin
The planet buyer. + Smith, Cordwainer
A planet called Krishna. + de Camp, L. Sprague
A planet called Pavanne. + Wright, Lan
Planet explorer. + Leinster, Murray
Planet federation. + Shaw, David
Planet finders. + Dermott, Vern
A planet for Texans. + McGuire, John J. & Piper, H.
  Beam
Planet in peril. + Christopher, John
Planet in the eye of time. + Earnshaw, Brian
The planet killers. + Silverberg, Robert
The planet mappers. + Evans, E. Everett
A planet named Terra. + Wadey, Victor
Planet of adventure #1; City of the Chasch. + Vance,
  Jack
Planet of death. + Arch, E. L.
Planet of death. + Silverberg, Robert
Planet of doom, and other stories. + none
Planet of dread. + Kern, Gregory
Planet of exile. + Le Guin, Ursula K.
Planet of fear. + Detzer, Diane
Planet of fire. + Moore, P. A.
Planet of light. + Jones, Raymond F.
Planet of no return. + Anderson, Poul
The planet of peril. + Kline, Otis Adelbert
Planet of sex and orgies. + du Bomb, Bonnee
Planet of the apes. + Boulle, Pierre
Planet of the apes; Man the fugitive. + Effinger,
  George Alec

The planet of the blind. + Corey, Paul
The planet of the cross. + The Queen Norlatiadek
  Regime of Order 32
Planet of the damned. + Harrison, Harry
The planet of the double sun. + Jones, Neil R.
Planet of the Dreamers. + MacDonald, John D.
The planet of the dying sun. + Perry Rhodan #11
Planet of the gods. + Perry Rhodan 27
Planet of the Voles. + Platt, Charles
Planet of the whistlers. + Bamman, Henry & Odell,
  William & Whitehead, Robert
A planet of your own. + Brunner, John
The planet of youth. + Coblentz, Stanton A.
Planet plane. + Beynon, John
The planet poachers. + Lightner, A. M.
Planet probability. + Ball, Brian N.
Planet problems. + Henricksen, Henry C.
Planet run. + Dickson, Gordon R. & Laumer, Keith
The planet savers. + Bradley, Marion Zimmer
The planet seekers. + Barton, Erle
The planet strappers. + Gallun, Raymond Z.
Planet Tha. + Charles, Neil
Planet war. + Fysh
The planet wizard. + Jakes, John
Planet X. + Hunt, Gill
Planetary Agent X. + Reynolds, Mack
Planetary journeys and earthly sketches. + Raffalo-
  vich, George
The planeteers. + Campbell, John W.
Planetfall. + Hunt, Gill
Planetoid Disposals Ltd. + Gridban, Volsted
Planetoid 127; and, The Sweizer pump. + Wallace, Edgar
The planetoid peril. + Brown, George Sheldon
Planets and dimensions. + Smith, Clark Ashton
Planets for sale. + Hull, E. Mayne & van Vogt, A. E.
Planets in peril. + Hamilton, Edmond
Planets of adventure. + Wells, Basil
The planets of death. + Collins, Michael
Planets of peril. + Marfax, Clyde
The planned planethood caper. + Paul, F. W.
The plant from infinity. + Maras, Karl
The plant, The well, The angel. + Vassilikos, Vassilis
The Plantos affair. + Rankine, John
The plastic man. + Brent, Jeremy
Platonia. + L'Estrange, Henry
The platter. + Jong, A. M. de
The Plattner story, and others. + Wells, H. G.
Platypussy. + Allison, Clyde
A play of darkness. + Greenfield, Irving A.
The playactress; and, Mad Sir Uchtred of the hills. +
  Crockett, S. R.
The Playboy book of horror and the supernatural. +
  (Russell, Ray)
The Playboy book of science fiction and fantasy. +
  (Russell, Ray)
Playboy's stories of the sinister & strange. + (Rus-
  sell, Ray)
Player piano. + Vonnegut, Kurt
The players of Hell. + Van Arnam, Dave
The players of null-A. + van Vogt, A. E.
Pleasant dreams--nightmares. + Bloch, Robert
The pleasure mongers. + Sellers, Con
Pleasure planet. + George, Edward
Pleasures of Xanada. + Solo, Gabriello
Pleiades Club. + Hayes, Jeff W.
A plenteous seed. + Sims, D. N.
The plot against Earth. + Knox, Calvin M.
Plot and counterpoint. + Wheatley, Dennis
Plunder. + Goulart, Ron
A plunge into space. + Cromie, Robert
The pluperfect of love. + Crayder, Dorothy
Plus encore d'Angleterre. + (B., A. G. F.)

President Randolph as I knew him. + Goldsmith, John Francis
The president vanishes. + (Stout, Rex)
The presidential plot. + Johnson, Stanley
The prevalence of witches. + Menen, Aubrey
Priam's daughter. + Sallaska, Georgia
A pride of monsters. + Schmitz, James H.
Priest-Kings of Gor. + Norman, John
Priest or pagan. + Oliver, John Rathbone
Priestess and queen. + Reader, Emily E.
The priestess of Isis. + Schure, Edouard
Priestess of the damned. + Coffman, Virginia
The primal urge. + Aldiss, Brian W.
Prime number. + Harrison, Harry
Prince Bantam. + McNeer, May & Ward, Lynd
Prince Caspian. + Lewis, C. S.
Prince Charlie's bluff. + Thomas, Donald
Prince Hagen. + Sinclair, Upton
The Prince in Waiting. + Christopher, John
Prince Izon. + Kelly, James Paul
Prince Lucifer. + Staughton, Simon
Prince of Annwn. + Walton, Evangeline
The Prince of Argolis. + none
The prince of Atlantis. + Roy, Lillian Elizabeth
Prince of darkness. + Michaels, Barbara
Prince of darkness. + Russell, Ray
Prince of darkness. + (Verner, Gerald)
The Prince of Gravas. + Fleckenstein, Alfred C.
The prince of peril. + Kline, Otis Adelbert
Prince of Scorpio. + Akers, Alan Burt
Prince Pax. + Eldridge, Paul & Viereck, George Sylvester
Prince Prigio. + Lang, Andrew
Prince Ricardo. + Lang, Andrew
Prince Timoteo. + Foster, David Skaats
Prince Zaleski. + Shiel, M. P.
The princess and Curdie. + MacDonald, George [see Addendum]
The princess and the goblin. + MacDonald, George [see Addendum]
The princess Athura. + Odell, Samuel W.
The princess bride. + Goldman, William
The princess Daphne. + Heron-Allen, Edward & Delaro, Selina
The princess of Babylon. + Voltaire
A princess of Mars. + Burroughs, Edgar Rice
A princess of Mars; and, A fighting man of Mars. + Burroughs, Edgar Rice
The princess of the atom. + Cummings, Ray
The Princess of the Roses. + Motta, Luigi
The Princess Thora. + Burland, Harris
Princess Whoopee. + Cosper, Wilbert Le Roy
The priory of St. Clair. + Wilkinson, Sarah Scudgell
The Prism. + Petaja, Emil
Prison planet. + Heywood, Victor D.
The Prisoner. + Disch, Thomas M.
A prisoner in Fairyland. + Blackwood, Algernon
Prisoner in the skull. + Dye, Charles
The Prisoner #2; Number Two. + McDaniel, David
The Prisoner #3; A day in the life. + Stine, Hank
Prisoner of fire. + Cooper, Edmund
Prisoner of the Mound Builders. + Harnishfeger, Lloyd
Prisoner of time. + Perry Rhodan 56
Prisoners in serpent land. + Connell, Alan
Prisoners of chance. + Parrish, Randall
Prisoners of Saturn. + Suddaby, Donald
Prisoners of space. + del Rey, Lester
Prisoners of the sky. + MacApp, C. C.
The Pritcher Mass. + Dickson, Gordon R.
A private cosmos. + Farmer, Philip Jose
The private life of Adam and Eve. + Twain, Mark
The private life of Henry Perkins. + Reynolds, John Murray

The private lives of Adam and Eve. + Hill, Robert & Zugsmith, Albert
The private memoirs and confessions of a justified sinner. + Hogg, James
Private Selby. + Wallace, Edgar
A private volcano. + Sieveking, Lance
Private war with Russia. + May, Ernest R.
Prize science fiction. + Wollheim, Donald A.
Prize stories of space and time. + Wollheim, Donald A.
Pro patria. + Pemberton, Max
The Probability Man. + Ball, Brian N.
The probability pad. + Waters, T. A.
Probable tales. + Stebbing, W.
The proceedings; Discon. + Eney, Dick
Proceedings of the 20th World Science Fiction Convention--Chicon III. + Kemp, Earl
The prodigal sun. + High, Philip E.
The productions of time. + Brunner, John
The professional, and other psychic stories. + Goodrich-Freer, A.
The Professor Challenger stories. + Doyle, A. Conan
Professor Mmaa's lecture. + Themerson, Stefan
The professor on paws. + Cox, A. B.
Professor Peckam's adventures in a drop of water. + Malcolm-Smith, George
The professor's experiment. + Hungerford, Mrs.
The professor's last experiment. + Edmonds, Harry
The professor's last experiment. + Stewart, Ritson & Stewart, Stanley
The professor's poison. + Gordon, Neil
The professor's sister. + Hawthorne, Julian
The profit of doom. + Dirac, Hugh
Progeny of the adder. + Whitten, Leslie H.
The programmed man. + Sutton, Jean & Sutton, Jeff
The progress of the pilgrim. + Eleve
The Project. + Sinclair, Andrew
Project barrier. + Galouye, Daniel F.
Project Dracula. + Scott, Alan
Project: Earthsave. + Perry Rhodan 38
Project for a revolution in New York. + Robbe-Grillet, Alain
Project Jove. + Glasby, John
Project Jupiter. + Brown, Fredric
Project--Renaissance. + Williams, Eric C.
Project 12. + Grouling, Thomas E.
Projectile war. + Lang, King
Projection infinity. + Zeigfreid, Karl
Prologue to Analog. + Campbell, John W.
Prometheus and Epimetheus. + Spitteler, Carl
Promiscuous Philbert. + Stopeck, Philip
The promise. + Cram, Mildred
The promise of air. + Blackwood, Algernon
Promised land. + Stableford, Brian M.
A promising planet. + Strike, Jeremy
Propeller Island. + Verne, Jules
Prophecies and possibilities. + Whitenight, Cynthia S.
The prophet of fire. + Creasey, John
The prophetess. + Plym, Don & Plym, Thea
A prophetic romance. + The Lord Commissioner
Prose and poetry (1856-1870). + Morris, William
The prose tales by Edgar Allan Poe. + Poe, Edgar Allan
The prose tales of Edgar Allan Poe. + Poe, Edgar Allan
Prose tales of mystery and imagination. + Poe, Edgar Allan
Prostho plus. + Anthony, Piers
Protector. + Niven, Larry
The Proto papers. + Oakes, Philip
Protostars. + Gerrold, David & Goldin, Stephen
Prototype PZ-642. + Ford, Ken
The prots. + "Dudbroke"
Proud man. + Constantine, Murray
A proud taste for scarlet and miniver. + Koningsburg, E. L.

The quick and the dead. + Starrett, Vincent
Quicksand. + Brunner, John
The quincunx of time. + Blish, James
The Quisto-box. + Samuel, Horace B.
Quiver of horror. + Wheatley, Dennis
The Quy Effect. + Sellings, Arthur

REDCAP. + McCutchan, Philip
R is for rocket. + Bradbury, Ray
The R-Master. + Dickson, Gordon R.
R_x for tomorrow. + Nourse, Alan E.
Rabbits. + Philip, Alex J.
Race against time. + Anthony, Piers
Race to the stars. + Friend, Oscar J. & Margulies, Leo
Rachel Dyer. + Neal, John
Radar alert. + Zeigfreid, Karl
Radiana. + Crosby, Edward Harold
The radiant dome. + Perry Rhodan #2
A radical nightmare. + An Ex-M.P.
The radio beasts. + Farley, Ralph Milne
The radio boys seek the lost Atlantis. + Breckenridge, Gerald
The radio detective. + Reeve, Arthur B.
The radio gunner. + (Forbes, Alexander)
The radio man. + Farley, Ralph Milne
The radio planet. + Farley, Ralph Milne
Radio Rocketeers. + Quintero, Jorge
The radioactive camel affair. + Leslie, Peter
The radium casket. + Bourne, Lawrence R.
The radium king. + Burton, Edmund
The radium pool. + Repp, Ed Earl
The Radium Rebels. + Meredith, Geoffrey
The radium seekers. + Ash, Fenton
The radium terrors. + Dorrington, Albert
Rafnaland. + Wilson, William Huntington
Raga Six. + Lauria, Frank
The ragged edge. + Christopher, John
Ragnarok. + Desmond, Shaw
The raid of Dover. + (Ford, D. M.)
The raid of 'Le Vengeur,' and other stories. + Griffith, George
The raid of the Terribore. + Mackworth, John
Raiders from the Rings. + Nourse, Alan E.
Raiders of Gor. + Norman, John
Raiders of Mars. + Moore, Patrick
Raiders of Noomas. + Nuetzel, Charles
Rain before seven. + Brandel, Marc
Rain boat. + Stoutenburg, Adrien
Rain in the doorway. + Smith, Thorne
The Rainbow affair. + McDaniel, David
The rainbow in the valley. + Meredith, James Creed
The Rainbox. + Goodwin, John C.
The rajah's sapphire. + Shiel, M. P.
The rakehells of Heaven. + Boyd, John
The Raksha Rajah. + Kerruish, Jessie D.
Ralph 124C 41+. + Gernsback, Hugo
Rama retold. + Menen, Aubrey
Ramayana. + Menen, Aubrey
Ramola twice born. + Field, Ben
Ramsden. + Mundy, Talbot
The random factor. + Maine, Charles Eric
The ranger boys in space. + Clement, Hal
Rangers of the universe. + Law, Winifred
Rania. + Rudhyar, Dane
The ransom for London. + Fletcher, J. S.
Rape is a no-no. + Paul, F. W.
The rape of man. + Cowie, Donald
The rape of Sun Lee Fong. + Macao, Marshall
The rape of Tamar. + Jacobson, Dan
Rare earth. + Owen, Frank
Rare science fiction. + Howard, Ivan
Rashomon, and other stories. + Akutagawa, Ryunosuke

The rat race. + Franklin, Jay
Rational communism. + (Van Deusen, Alonzo)
Ratman's notebooks. + Gilbert, Stephen
The rats. + Herbert, James
Ravelette. + Randolph, P. B.
The raven. + Sudak, Eunice
The raven, The fall of the House of Usher, and other poems and tales. + Poe, Edgar Allan
Ravenna and her ghosts. + Lee, Vernon
Ravens' brood. + Benson, E. F.
The Ravenscroft affair. + Gull, C. Ranger
The Ravenscroft horror. + Gull, C. Ranger
Raw meat. + Geis, Richard E.
Raxl, voodoo priestess. + Daniels, Dorothy
Ray Bradbury review. + Nolan, William F.
Ray Ellis in the Green Mandarin mystery. + Malcom, Grant
The ray of doom. + Sykes, W. Stanley
Raymi. + Holland, Clive
Raymond Bury. + Keating, Eliza H.
Reach for tomorrow. + Clarke, Arthur C.
Reactor XK9. + Muller, John E.
Reader's guide to the Cthulhu Mythos, second revised edition. + Berglund, E. P. & Weinberg, Robert
The real Munchausen. + (Raspe, Rudolf)
Real-time world. + Priest, Christopher
Reality forbidden. + High, Philip E.
The Reality Trip, and other implausibilities. + Silverberg, Robert
The Realm of Light. + Hatfield, Frank
Realm of the alien. + Delray, Chester
Realm of the tri-planets. + Perry Rhodan 31
The realm of the wizard king. + Gilson, Charles
Realmah. + (Helps, Arthur)
The re-appearing. + Morice, Charles
The reassembled man. + Kastle, Herbert D.
The Rebel of Rhada. + Gilman, Robert Cham
The rebel passion. + Burdekin, Kay
The rebel worlds. + Anderson, Poul
The rebellers. + Roberts, Jane
The rebellion of the beasts. + Sprat, John
A rebellious heroine. + Bangs, John Kendrick
The rebellious stars. + Asimov, Isaac
Rebels of the red planet. + Fontenay, Charles L.
The rebels of Tuglan. + Perry Rhodan #12
Rebels' triumph. + Hannay, J. F. W.
Rebirth. + McClary, Thomas Calvert
Re-birth. + Wilson, Rathmell
Re-birth. + Wyndham, John
Recall not Earth. + MacApp, C. C.
Recalled to life. + Silverberg, Robert
The recess. + Grisewood, Harman
The recipe for diamonds. + Hyne, C. J. Cutcliffe
The recipe for rubber. + Stock, Ralph
The reckoning. + Conquest, Joan
Recoil. + Nunes, Claude & Nunes, Rhoda
The Recording Angel. + Brenholtz, Edwin Arnold
The recovered continent. + Mundo, Oto
Recreations of a psychologist. + Hall, G. Stanley
Recruit for Andromeda. + Lesser, Milton
The Red Brain, and other thrillers. + Hammett, Dashiell
The Red Chindvit conspiracy. + Holzer, Hans
The Red Court. + Vale, Rena M.
Red death of Mars. + none
The Red Demon. + Wright, A. J.
The red dust. + Baldwin, Bee
Red ending. + Sadler, Adam
Red England. + none
Red Eve. + Haggard, H. Rider
Red eye of Betelgeuse. + Perry Rhodan 40
The red feathers. + Roberts, Theodore

The return of Karl Marx. + Grey, Lynn
The return of Kavin. + Mason, David
The return of Peter Grimm. + Belasco, David
The return of Robinson Crusoe. + Pain, Barry
The return of She. + Haggard, H. Rider
Return of Sumuru. + Rohmer, Sax
The return of Tarzan. + Burroughs, Edgar Rice
Return of Tharn. + Browne, Howard
The return of the ceteosaurus, and other tales. + Radcliffe, Garnett
The return of the Half Moon. + Crayon, Diedrick Jr.
The return of the hero. + Figgis, Darrell
The return of the hero. + Ireland, Michael
The return of the King. + Tolkien, J. R. R.
The return of the Lloigor. + Wilson, Colin
Return of the Mucker. + Burroughs, Edgar Rice
Return of the opium wars. + Macao, Marshall
Return of the Shadow. + Gibson, Walter B.
The return of the starships. + de Reyna, Jorge
The return of the Time Machine. + Friedell, Egon
Return of the traveller. + Warner, Rex
The return of the Twelves. + Clarke, Pauline
The return of William Shakespeare. + Kingsmill, Hugh
Return of Zeus. + Muller, John E.
Return to Earth. + Berry, Bryan
Return to Elysium. + Grant, Joan
Return to Mars. + Johns, W. E.
Return to Mars. + Westward, Elton
Return to otherness. + Kuttner, Henry
Return to space. + Fear, W. H.
Return to the lost planet. + MacVicar, Angus
Return to the stars. + Hamilton, Edmond
Return to the wonderful farm. + Ayme, Marcel
Return to tomorrow. + Hubbard, L. Ron
Return trip. + Evain, Elaine
Returned empty. + Barclay, Florence L.
Revelation. + Wyndham, Eric
Revelations. + Malzberg, Barry N.
Revelations in black. + Jacobi, Carl
Revelations of the dead-alive. + (Banim, John)
Revelry in Hell. + Weinberg, Robert E.
The revels of Orsera. + Ross, Ronald
The revenge of Frankenstein. + Janes, H. Hurford
The revenge of Increase Sewell. + Graat, Heinrich
The revenge of Taurus. + Lory, Robert
The Rev. Annabel Lee. + Buchanan, Robert
Reverse universe. + Gridban, Volsted
Revi-Lona. + Cowan, Frank
The revised H. P. Lovecraft bibliography. + Chalker, Jack L. & Owings, Mark
Revised Hannes Bok checklist. + Brooks, C. W.
Revolt. + McMasters, William H.
Revolt! + Pendleton, Don
Revolt in Arcadia. + Larsson, Gosta
Revolt in 2100. + Heinlein, Robert A.
The revolt of man. + Besant, Walter
The revolt of the angels. + France, Anatole
The revolt of the bees. + (Morgan, John M.)
The revolt of the birds. + Post, Melville Davisson
The revolt of the brutes. + Kirk, Hyland C.
The revolt of the horses. + Perry, Walter Copland
Revolt of the humans. + Burke, Jonathan
The revolt of the oyster. + Marquis, Don
Revolt of the triffids. + Wyndham, John
Revolt on Alpha C. + Silverberg, Robert
The revolt on Venus. + Rockwell, Carey
Revolution. + Beresford, J. D.
The revolving boy. + Friedberg, Gertrude
Rewards and fairies. + Kipling, Rudyard
Rhapsody in black. + Stableford, Brian M.
Rhapsody in death. + Mauro, John F.
Rhode Island on Lovecraft. + Grant, Donald M. & Hadley, Thomas G.

The rhubarb tree. + Allott, Kenneth & Tait, Stephen
Rhythm of the spheres. + Merritt, A.
Rhythm rides the rocket. + Olsen, Bob
Riallaro, the archipelago of exiles. + Sweven, Godfrey
The Richardson story. + Williams, Francis
The richest corpse in show business. + Morgan, Dan
The riddle, and other tales. + de la Mare, Walter
The riddle of the Caid's jewels. + Frost, Kelman
The riddle of the Straits. + Edmonds, Harry
The riddle of the tower. + Beresford, J. D. & Wynne-Tyson, Esme
Riddle stories. + French, Joseph Lewis
Ride a wild horse. + Carlsen, Ruth Christoffer
A ride on a cyclone. + Ballou, William Hosea
Ride the east wind. + Berkeley, Edmund C.
Riders to the stars. + Smith, Robert
The rift in the lute. + Langley, Noel
Right-handed wilderness. + Wells, Robert
Right of reply. + Harris, John
The Rim gods. + Chandler, A. Bertram
The rim of morning. + Sloane, William M.
The Rim of space. + Chandler, A. Bertram
The rim of the unknown. + Long, Frank Belknap
The rim-world legacy. + Javor, F. A.
Rinehard. + Tweed, Thomas F.
The ring. + Anthony, Piers & Margroff, Robert E.
Ring around the Sun. + Simak, Clifford D.
The ring of Amasis. + Lytton, Robert Bulwer
The ring of Amasis. + Meredith, Owen
The Ring of Garamas. + Rankine, John
The ring of Gyges. + Lisle, Charles Wentworth
The Ring of Ritornel. + Harness, Charles L.
The ring of the Lowenskolds. + Lagerlof, Selma
The ring of Thoth, and other stories. + Doyle, A. Conan
The ring of Ug, and other weird tales. + Stock, E. Elliot
Ring of violence. + Mason, Douglas R.
Rings of ice. + Anthony, Piers
The rings of Saturn. + Asimov, Isaac
Ringstones. + Sarban
Ringstones, and other curious tales. + Sarban
Ringworld. + Niven, Larry
Riot '71. + Peters, Ludovic
Rip Foster in Ride the gray planet. + Savage, Blake
Rip Foster rides the gray planet. + Savage, Blake
Rip Van Winkle. + Irving, Washington
A Rip Van Winkle of the Kalahari, and other tales of South-West Africa. + Cornell, Fred C.
The rise and fall of the United States. + A Diplomat
The rise of the meritocracy. + Young, Michael
Rite of passage. + Panshin, Alexei
The rites of Ohe. + Brunner, John
The Rithian Terror. + Knight, Damon
The rituals of infinity. + Moorcock, Michael
The rival Rigelians. + Reynolds, Mack
The rival Rigelians; Planetary agent X. + Reynolds, Mack
The rival submarines. + Westerman, Percy F.
The river at Green Knowe. + Boston, L. M.
The river journey. + Nathan, Robert
The river of darkness. + Graydon, William Murray
River of ice. + Robeson, Kenneth
River of time. + West, Wallace
The rivet in Grandfather's neck. + Elliott, Bruce
Rivets and Sprockets. + Key, Alexander
Roach. + Lamont, Gil
The road goes ever on. + Tolkien, J. R. R.
Road of ages. + Nathan, Robert
The road to Avalon. + Dawson, Coningsby
Road to the Moon. + Carey, George W.
The road to the Rim. + Chandler, A. Bertram
Roads. + Quinn, Seabury

Roamin' circus. + Dauphine, Claude
Roar of the rocket. + Friend, Oscar J.
The roaring dove. + Kerby, Susan
Robert A. Heinlein: a bibliography. + Owings, Mark
Robert Bloch bibliography. + Hall, Graham M.
The Robert E. Howard fantasy biblio. + Weinberg,
   Robert
Robert Heinlein omnibus. + Heinlein, Robert A.
A Robert Heinlein omnibus. + Heinlein, Robert A.
The Robert Sheckley omnibus. + Sheckley, Robert
A Robert Silverberg omnibus. + Silverberg, Robert
Robin Ritchie. + Haynes, Dorothy K.
Robinson Christopher. + Noyes, Sherman A.
Robinson Crusoe's return. + Pain, Barry
Robinson the Great. + (Muir, Ramsay)
The robot and the man. + Greenberg, Martin
The robot Brains. + Bounds, Sydney J.
Robot hunt. + Vernon, Roger Lee
The robot novels. + Asimov, Isaac
The robot rocket. + Rockwell, Carey
The robot rulers. + Shirley, George E.
Robots and changelings. + del Rey, Lester
Robots have no tails. + Kuttner, Henry
Robots have no tails. + Padgett, Lewis
Robots of Saturn. + Greene, Joseph
Robur the Conqueror. + Verne, Jules
Robur the Conqueror; and, Master of the world. +
   Verne, Jules
Rocannon's World. + Le Guin, Ursula K.
The Rock. + Masters, John
Rock City rebels. + Stratton, Chris
The rock of Babylon. + Campbell, Austin
The rock of three planets. + Lightner, A. M.
Rock the big rock. + Peterson, John Victor
Rocket from infinity. + del Rey, Lester
Rocket invasion. + Lang, King
Rocket jockey. + St. John, Philip
Rocket jumper. + Blaine, John
Rocket man. + Correy, Lee
Rocket pilot. + St. John, Philip
Rocket rescue. + Halacy, D. S.
Rocket Riders across the ice. + Garis, Howard R.
Rocket Riders in stormy seas. + Garis, Howard R.
Rocket Riders in the air. + Garis, Howard R.
Rocket Riders over the desert. + Garis, Howard R.
Rocket ship Galileo. + Heinlein, Robert A.
Rocket to Limbo. + Nourse, Alan E.
Rocket to Luna. + Marsten, Richard
Rocket to the Moon. + Peril, Bruce
The rocket to the Moon. + von Harbou, Thea
Rocket to the morgue. + Boucher, Anthony
Rocket to the morgue. + Holmes, H. H.
Rockets in Ursa Major. + Hoyle, Fred & Hoyle, Geoffrey
The rockets (Operation Manhattan). + Edmonds, Harry
The rocket's shadow. + Blaine, John
Rockets to nowhere. + St. John, Philip
The Rod of the Snake. + Mathews, Frances & Shortt,
   Vere
Rod Serling's Devils and demons. + Serling, Rod
Rod Serling's The twilight zone. + Gibson, Walter B.
Rod Serling's Triple W. + Serling, Rod
Rodent mutation. + Fane, Bron
Rogue dragon. + Davidson, Avram
Rogue in space. + Brown, Fredric
Rogue Moon. + Budrys, Algis
Rogue Queen. + de Camp, L. Sprague
Rogue Reynard. + Norton, Andre
Rogue ship. + van Vogt, A. E.
Rogue star. + Pohl, Frederik & Williamson, Jack
Roller Ball Murder. + Harrison, William
Roller coaster world. + Bulmer, Kenneth
The Rolling Stones. + Heinlein, Robert A.

Roman holiday. + Sinclair, Upton
Romance in black. + Field, Gans T.
A romance in radium. + Harris, J. Henry
Romance in starland. + Glass, Mrs. Charles Wilder
Romance in starland, and other stories. + Glass, Mrs.
   Charles Wilder
Romance island. + Gale, Zona
The romance of a country. + Curtois, M. A.
The romance of a demon. + Malyn, Thomas
The romance of a mummy. + Gautier, Theophile
The romance of Elaine. + Reeve, Arthur B.
The romance of Golden Star... + Griffith, George
A romance of N'Shabe. + Anderson, A. A. & Wall, A.
The romance of Palombris and Pallogris. + Baker, G.
   P.
The romance of paradise. + Gunn, Edmund S.
Romance of politics. + Upward, Allen
The romance of the river. + Ponsot, Georges
The romance of the stars. + Leo, Bessie
A romance of two centuries. + Guthrie, Kenneth Sylvan
A romance of two worlds. + Corelli, Marie
The romances of Amosis Ra. + Thurstan, Frederic
The romances of Voltaire. + Voltaire
Romances, tales, and smaller pieces of M. de Voltaire.
   + Voltaire
A romantic story book. + Bishop, Morris
Romantic tales. + (Craik, D. M.)
Rondah. + Dieudonne, Florence Carpenter
The room beyond. + Carr, Robert Spencer
The room in the tower, and other stories. + Benson,
   E. F.
The room opposite, and other tales of mystery and ima-
   gination. + Mayor, F. M.
The roots of the mountains. + Morris, William
Rork! + Davidson, Avram
Rosa. + Pons, Maurice
The Rose. + Harness, Charles L.
The rose and the ring. + (Thackeray, William Make-
   peace) [see Addendum]
A rose for Ecclesiastes. + Zelazny, Roger
The rose rabbi. + Stern, Daniel
Rosemary's baby. + Levin, Ira
The Rosicrucian. + Thurston, Temple
The Rosicrucian's story. + Randolph, P. B.
Rosy cheeks. + Kanto, Peter
Rough passages. + Perrin, A.
Rough shooting. + Wren, Percival Christopher
Round the Moon. + Verne, Jules
Round the world in eighty days. + Verne, Jules
Round trip space ship. + Slobodkin, Louis
Round trip to Hell in a flying saucer. + Michael,
   Cecil
A round trip to the year 2000. + Cook, William Wallace
Rox Hall illuminated. + Paul, Phyllis
A royal enchantress. + Dessar, Leo Charles
Ru, the conqueror. + Gregory, Jackson
The ruby ray mystery. + Blaine, John
The ruby toad. + Raven, Anthony
Rudra. + Westermayr, Arthur J.
The ruin. + Sackville-West, Edward
The ruins of Earth. + Disch, Thomas M.
Rule Britannia. + du Maurier, Daphne
The rule of the beasts. + Murray, V. T.
The Rule of the Door, and other fanciful regulations.
   + Biggle, Lloyd Jr.
The rule of the pagbeasts. + McIntosh, J. T.
Ruled by radio. + Farncombe, Frank E. & Hadfield,
   R. L.
Rulers of men. + Santesson, Hans Stefan
The rumour in the forest. + Couppey, Madeleine
The runaway robot. + del Rey, Lester
The runaway world. + Coblentz, Stanton A.

The Runestaff. + Moorcock, Michael
The Running Man. + Holly, J. Hunter
Runts of 61 Cygni C. + Grazier, James
Rupert Piper and Megan, the valuable girl. + Parkinson, Ethelyn M.
A Russian princess; and, A Russian ghost story. + Turnerelli, Tracy
Russian science fiction. + Magidoff, Robert
Russian science fiction literature and criticism, 1956-1970. + Suvin, Darko
Russian science fiction, 1968. + Magidoff, Robert
Russian science fiction, 1969. + Magidoff, Robert
The "Russia's Hope." + none
Rusty's space ship. + Lampman, Evelyn
Ruth's marriage in Mars. + Glass, Mrs. Charles Wilder

SADISTO royale. + Allison, Clyde
The S.E.X. machine. + Key, David
SF. + Allinson, A. A. & Hotchin, F. E.
SF: a dream of other worlds. + Clareson, Thomas D.
SF: authors' choice. + Harrison, Harry
SF: authors' choice 4. + Harrison, Harry
SF: authors' choice 3. + Harrison, Harry
SF: authors' choice 2. + Harrison, Harry
SFBRI; science fiction book review index 1970. + Hall, H. W.
SFBRI; science fiction book review index 1971 (volume 2). + Hall, H. W.
SFBRI; science fiction book review index 1972, volume 3. + Hall, H. W.
SFBRI; science fiction book review index, volume 4, 1973. + Hall, H. W.
SF bibliographies. + Briney, Robert E. & Wood, Edward
SF: '57. + Merril, Judith
SF: '58. + Merril, Judith
SF: '59. + Merril, Judith
SF horizons--one. + Boardman, Tom
SF published in 1969. + Burger, Joanne
SF published in 1970. + Burger, Joanne
SF published in 1971. + Burger, Joanne
SF published in 1972. + Burger, Joanne
SF reprise 1. + Moorcock, Michael
SF reprise 2. + Moorcock, Michael
SF symposium; FC simposio. + Sanz, Jose
SF: the best of the best. + Merril, Judith
SF: the best of the best, part one. + Merril, Judith
SF: the best of the best, part two. + Merril, Judith
SF: the other side of realism. + Clareson, Thomas
S-F; the year's greatest science-fiction and fantasy stories and novelettes. + Merril, Judith
SF; the year's greatest science fiction and fantasy, fourth annual volume. + Merril, Judith
SF; the year's greatest science-fiction and fantasy, second annual volume. + Merril, Judith
SF; the year's greatest science-fiction and fantasy, third annual volume. + Merril, Judith
SF12. + Merril, Judith
S is for space. + Bradbury, Ray
SOS from Mars. + Cross, John Keir
S.O.S. from three worlds. + Leinster, Murray
SOS: spaceship Titan! + Perry Rhodan 34
S.S. San Pedro; and, The castaway. + Cozzens, James Gould
S.T.A.R. flight. + Tubb, E. C.
S-w-o-o-p. + Prince, Don
The sabertooth. + Kinder, Stephen
Sabotage in space. + Rockwell, Carey
The sack of London in the great French war of 1901. + none
Sacrament of death. + Esmond, Sidney
The sacred giraffe. + Madariaga, Salvador de
The sacred herb. + Hume, Fergus

Sacred Locomotive flies. + Lupoff, Richard
The Sacred Skull. + Griffith, George
Sacrilegious hands. + Warner, William Henry
Sadastor. + Smith, Clark Ashton
Safespace. + Miles, Robert
Saga of lost Earths. + Petaja, Emil
Sagittarius. + Russell, Ray
The saint and the hunchback. + Stauffer, Donald A.
St. Dingan's bones. + Callender, Julian
St. George and the witches. + Dunne, J. W.
St. Irvyne. + (Shelley, Percy Bysshe)
St. Leon. + Godwin, William
St. Mawr; and, The man who died. + Lawrence, D. H.
The saint of the Dragon's Dale. + Davis, William Stearns
Saint on holiday. + Dearmer, Geoffrey
The saintmaker's Christmas Eve. + Horgan, Paul
The Saint's choice of impossible crime. + Charteris, Leslie
The Salamander. + Smith, E. Oakes
Salamander war. + Carr, Charles
Salander and the dragon. + Shelton, Frederic William
Salathiel. + Croly, George
Salathiel the immortal. + Croly, George
Salathiel, the wandering Jew. + Croly, George
The sale of an appetite. + Lafargue, Paul
The saliva tree, and other strange growths. + Aldiss, Brian W.
Salome the wandering Jewess. + Eldridge, Paul & Viereck, George Sylvester
Salted almonds. + Anstey, F.
Saltflower. + Van Scyoc, Sydney
The Salzburg tales. + Stead, Christina
Sam Small flies again. + Knight, Eric
Sam Small, the flying Yorkshireman. + Knight, Eric
Sam Weskit on the planet Framingham. + Johnston, William
Samax, the gladiator. + Faraday, Robert
Sambo and Snitch. + Blackwood, Algernon
The same to you doubled, and other stories. + Sheckley, Robert
The Samsons. + Archambault, Alberic A.
San Salvador. + Tincker, Mary Agnes
Sanctuary in the sky. + Brunner, John
Sand and satin. + Rohmer, Sax
The sand bird. + Baker, Margaret J.
The sands of Karakorum. + Ullman, James Ramsey
The sands of Mars. + Clarke, Arthur C.
The sands of Mars, and other stories. + none
Sands of time. + Dagmar, Peter
Sannikov Land. + Obruchev, Vladimir
Santana morning. + Dolan, Mike
The Santaroga Barrier. + Herbert, Frank
The Sanyasi. + Penny, F. E.
Sar. + Russell, John Robert
Sara Hall's sea god. + DuBois, Theodora
The Saracen lamp. + Arthur, Ruth M.
The Saragossa manuscript. + Potocki, Jan
Sarah Mandrake. + Wadelton, Maggie-Owen
Saratoga in 1901. + Perkins, Eli
Sarchedon. + Whyte-Melville, G. J.
Sardonicus, and other stories. + Russell, Ray
Sargasso of space. + North, Andrew
Sargasso of space. + Norton, Andre
The Sargasso Ogre. + Robeson, Kenneth
Saronia. + Short, Richard
Satan in Goray. + Singer, Isaac Bashevis
Satan in the suburbs, and other stories. + Russell, Bertrand
Satan, Ltd. + Evans, Gwyn
The Satanic mill. + Preussler, Otfried
Satanic omnibus. + Singer, Kurt

The Satanic power. + Van der Elst, Violet
The Satanist. + Wheatley, Dennis
The Satanists. + Haining, Peter
Satan's child. + Saxon, Peter
Satan's circus. + Smith, Lady Eleanor
Satan's diary. + Andreev, Leonid
Satan's Drome. + Reeves, William
Satan's pets. + Ghidalia, Vic
Satan's realm. + Blum, Edgar C.
Satan's sabbath. + Valdez, Paul
Satan's stud. + Harrington, Len
Satan's world. + Anderson, Poul
Satellite. + Fanthorpe, R. Lionel
Satellite B.C. + Le Page, Rand
Satellite E One. + Castle, Jeffery Lloyd
Satellite 54-Zero. + Mason, Douglas R.
Satellite in space. + Low, A. M.
Satellite 7. + MacVicar, Angus
Satiric tales. + Lunatic, Nicholas
The Saturday evening post fantasy stories. + Fles,
  Barthold
The Saturday evening post reader of fantasy and science
  fiction. + none
Saturn over the water. + Priestley, J. B.
Saturn Patrol. + Lang, King
The satyr. + Knox, Hugh
Satyr trek. + Kainen, Ray
The saucer people. + Garver, Ronald G.
Saucers over the moor. + Saville, Malcolm
Saurus. + Phillpotts, Eden
Savage bride. + Woolrich, Cornell
Savage passions. + none
Savage Pellucidar. + Burroughs, Edgar Rice
Savaran and the Great Sand. + Newton, Douglas
Saving worlds. + Elwood, Roger & Kidd, Virginia
Saw. + Katz, Steve
Sax Rohmer: a bibliography. + Day, Bradford M.
Sax Rohmer omnibus. + Rohmer, Sax
Saxon's ghost. + Fisher, Steve
Say not good-night. + B., K.
The scapegoat. + Brooke, Jocelyn
Scarabaeus. + Harvey, James Clarence & Lanza, Clara
The scarecrow, and other stories. + de la Mare, Walter
The scarecrow, and other stories. + Wormser, G. Ranger
Scarlet arena 30303. + Moore, Silas
The Scarlet boy. + Calder-Marshall, Arthur
The scarlet empire. + Parry, David M.
Scarlet feather. + Grant, Joan
The scarlet hill. + Owen, Frank
The Scarlet Lake mystery. + Blaine, John
The scarlet plague. + London, Jack
The scarlet plague; and, Before Adam. + London, Jack
The scarlet plague; Love of life; The unexpected. +
  London, Jack
The scarlet tanager. + Tyson, J. Aubrey
The Scarlet Vampire. + Burke, Norah
The scars of Dracula. + Hall, Angus
A scatter of stardust. + Tubb, E. C.
Scavengers in space. + Nourse, Alan E.
The scene is changed. + Ray, James
Scenes in the spirit world. + Tuttle, Hudson
A scent of new-mown hay. + Blackburn, John
Schamyl. + Prest, Peckett
The scheme of things. + del Rey, Lester
School and society through science fiction. + Green-
  berg, Martin Harry & Olander, Joseph D. & Warrick,
  Patricia S.
School in space. + Browne, Reginald
The Schwartz index. + Weston, Kim
Science against man. + Cheetham, Anthony
Science and fiction. + Moore, Patrick
Science and literature. + Eastwood, W.

Science and literature, second series. + Eastwood, W.
Science and sorcery. + Ford, Garret
Science fantasy quintette. + none
Science fiction. + Brodkin, Sylvia Z. & Pearson, Eli-
  zabeth J.
Science fiction. + Burton, S. H.
Science fiction: a bibliography. + none
Science fiction adventure from way out. + Elwood,
  Roger
Science-fiction adventures in dimension. + Conklin,
  Groff
Science-fiction adventures in mutation. + Conklin,
  Groff
Science fiction: an introduction. + Allen, L. David
Science fiction and fantasy pseudonyms. + McGhan,
  Barry
Science fiction and fantasy pseudonyms, with 1973 supp-
  lement. + McGhan, Barry
Science fiction and utopian fantasy in Soviet literature.
  + Yershov, Peter
A science fiction argosy. + Knight, Damon
The science fiction bestiary. + Silverberg, Robert
Science fiction books published in 1967. + Burger,
  Joanne
Science fiction books published in 1968. + Burger,
  Joanne
Science fiction by gaslight. + Moskowitz, Sam
Science-fiction carnival. + Brown, Fredric & Reynolds,
  Mack
Science fiction collections index. + Collins, Len
Science fiction comes to college. + Williamson, Jack
Science fiction criticism. + Clareson, Thomas
Science fiction elsewhen. + Conklin, Groff
Science fiction elsewhere. + Conklin, Groff
Science fiction emphasis I. + Gerrold, David & Goldin,
  Stephen
Science fiction film. + Gifford, Denis
Science fiction for people who hate science fiction.
  + Carr, Terry
The science fiction galaxy. + Conklin, Groff
The science fiction hall of fame, volume one. + Sil-
  verberg, Robert
The science fiction hall of fame, volume three. +
  Bova, Ben
The science fiction hall of fame, volume 2. + Bova,
  Ben
Science fiction hall of fame, volume two. + Silver-
  berg, Robert
The science fiction hall of fame, volume 2A. + Bova,
  Ben
The science fiction hall of fame, volume 2B. + Bova,
  Ben
Science-fiction handbook. + de Camp, L. Sprague
Science fiction in college. + Williamson, Jack
Science fiction in the cinema. + Baxter, John
Science fiction inventions. + Knight, Damon
Science fiction: Jules Verne to Ray Bradbury. + Allen,
  Dick & Allen, Lori
Science-fiction library, no. 1. + none
Science-fiction library, no. 2. + none
The science-fiction magazine checklist, 1961-1972. +
  Desmond, William H.
The science fiction novel. + none
Science fiction oddities. + Conklin, Groff
Science fiction oddities, second series. + Conklin,
  Groff
The science fiction of Isaac Asimov. + Patrouch,
  Joseph F. Jr.
Science fiction omnibus. + Bleiler, Everett F. &
  Dikty, T. E.
Science fiction omnibus. + Conklin, Groff
A science fiction omnibus on pollution. + none

Science fiction on radio. + Frierson, Meade
A science fiction reader. + Harrison, Harry & Pugner, Carol
Science fiction reader. + Kingsbury, R. H.
Science fiction reader's guide. + Allen, L. David
Science fiction showcase. + Kornbluth, Mary
Science fiction special (8). + none
Science fiction special (11). + none
Science fiction special (5). + none
Science fiction special (4). + none
Science fiction special (9). + none
Science fiction special (1). + none
Science fiction special (7). + none
Science fiction special (6). + none
Science fiction special (10). + none
Science fiction special (3). + none
Science fiction special (2). + none
Science-fiction stories. + Elam, Richard M. Jr.
Science fiction story index, 1950-1968. + Siemon, Frederick
The science-fiction subtreasury. + Tucker, Wilson
Science fiction tales. + Elwood, Roger
Science fiction terror tales. + Conklin, Groff
Science fiction: the academic awakening. + McNelly, Willis E.
Science fiction: the classroom in orbit. + Friend, Beverly
Science fiction: the classroom in orbit; a supplement. + Friend, Beverly
Science fiction: the future. + Allen, Dick
Science fiction: the great years. + Pohl, Carol & Pohl, Frederik
Science-fiction thinking machines. + Conklin, Groff
Science fiction through the ages 1. + Evans, I. O.
Science fiction through the ages 2. + Evans, I. O.
Science fiction title changes. + Franson, Donald & Viggiano, Michael
Science fiction, today and tomorrow. + Bretnor, Reginald
Science fiction: what it's all about. + Lundwall, Sam
Science fiction worlds of Forrest J Ackerman & friends. + Ackerman, Forrest J
The science-fictional Sherlock Holmes. + (Peterson, Robert C.)
Science fictions. + Thompson, Arnold
Science in fiction. + Bayliss, A. E. M. & Bayliss, J. C.
Science metropolis. + Statten, Vargo
Scientific romances, first series. + Hinton, C. H.
The scientific romances of H. G. Wells. + Wells, H. G.
Scientific romances, second series. + Hinton, C. H.
The scorpion god. + Golding, William
The Scorpions. + Kelly, Robert
The Scorpius equation. + Townsend, Larry
Scotch on the rocks. + Hurd, Douglas & Osmond, Andrew
Scottish tales of terror. + Campbell, Angus
Scoundrel of the air. + Burrage, A. Harcourt
A scourge of screamers. + Galouye, Daniel F.
Scourge of the atom. + Gridban, Volsted
Scourge of the blood cult. + Smith, George H.
Scream along with me. + Hitchcock, Alfred
Scream and scream again. + Saxon, Peter
Scream at midnight. + Brennan, Joseph Payne
Scream from outer space. + Haynes, John Robert
The screaming dead balloons. + McCutchan, Philip
The screaming face. + Lymington, John
The screaming ghost, and other stories. + Carmer, Carl
The screaming lake. + Wright, S. Fowler
The screaming skull, and other stories. + Horler, Sydney
The Screwtape letters. + Lewis, C. S.

The Screwtape letters; &, Screwtape proposes a toast. + Lewis, C. S.
Screwtape proposes a toast, and other pieces. + Lewis, C. S.
Scribblings. + de Camp, L. Sprague
The scrolls of Lysis. + Ross, Barnaby
"Scrooge." + Donaldson, Elaine
The Sea Angel. + Robeson, Kenneth
The sea beasts. + Chandler, A. Bertram
Sea change. + Hunt, Barbara
Sea change. + Watters, Barbara H.
The sea demons. + Egbert, H. M.
The sea girl. + Cummings, Ray
Sea gods. + Baumgartl, I.
Sea gold. + Blaine, John
Sea-green magic. + Beresford, Elisabeth
The sea hath its pearls. + Blissett, Nellie K.
The sea horse. + Coon, Merlin J.
Sea-horse in the sky. + Cooper, Edmund
The sea is boiling hot. + Bamber, George
Sea kissed. + none
Sea kissed. + Bloch, Robert
The sea lady. + Wells, H. G.
The sea magician. + Robeson, Kenneth
The sea monarch. + Westerman, Percy F.
A sea of space. + Nolan, William F.
A sea of thighs. + Kainen, Ray
The sea people. + Lukens, Adam
The sea people. + Sizemore, Julius C. & Sizemore, Wilkie G.
The sea priestess. + Fortune, Dion
Sea siege. + Norton, Andre
The sea surrenders. + Potter, Martin H.
Sea tales of terror. + Strating, J. J.
The sea thing, and other stories. + Hull, E. Mayne & van Vogt, A. E.
The seagoing tank. + Snell, Roy J.
The seal of John Solomon. + Hawkwood, Allan
The seal-singing. + Harris, Rosemary
Seal woman. + Lockley, Ronald
Sealed entrance. + Voss-Bark, C.
Sealskin trousers, and other stories. + Linklater, Eric
The seance, and other stories. + Singer, Isaac Bashevis
The seance at Ridley Manor. + Drake, Katherine
Seaports in the Moon. + Starrett, Vincent
Search. + Weverka, Robert
The search for Joseph Tully. + Hallahan, William H.
A search for the king. + Vidal, Gore
The search for the silver city. + Otis, James
The search for Zei. + de Camp, L. Sprague
Search the dark stars. + Muller, John E.
Search the sky. + Kornbluth, C. M. & Pohl, Frederik
Season of ponies. + Snyder, Zilpha Keatley
Season of the witch. + Stine, Hank
The season to be wary. + Serling, Rod
Seaward for the foe. + Hill, Headon
Secession, coercion, and civil war. + (Jones, J. B.)
A second, and more strange voyage to the world in the Moon. + (Defoe, Daniel)
The second Armada. + (Hayward, Abraham)
The second Armada ghost book. + Bernard, Christine
The second Arrow book of horror stories. + (Lee, Elizabeth)
The second Astounding science fiction anthology. + Campbell, John W.
The second Atlantis. + Williams, Robert Moore
The 2nd Avon fantasy reader. + Ernsberger, George & Wollheim, Donald A.
Second book of horror stories. + Wheatley, Dennis
Second book of tales. + Field, Eugene

The second book of Tros of Samothrace; Helma. + Mundy, Talbot
A second century of creepy stories. + Walpole, Hugh
The second coming. + Janes, Henry P. & Kummer, Frederic Arnold
A second coming. + Marsh, Richard
The second conquest. + de Wohl, Louis
The second deluge. + Serviss, Garrett P.
Second ending. + White, James
The second experiment. + Jeppson, J. O.
The second face. + Ayme, Marcel
The second flight of the Starfire. + Mumford, Edwin
The second Fontana book of great ghost stories. + Aickman, Robert
The second Fontana book of great horror stories. + Bernard, Christine
Second Foundation. + Asimov, Isaac
2nd Foundation: galactic empire. + Asimov, Isaac
A second Franco-German war and its consequences for England. + none
The second Galaxy reader of science fiction. + Gold, H. L.
The second ghost book. + Asquith, Cynthia
Second ghost omnibus. + Singer, Kurt
The second Hammer horror film omnibus. + Burke, John
The second If reader of science fiction. + Pohl, Frederik
A second Isaac Asimov double. + Asimov, Isaac
The second jungle book. + Kipling, Rudyard
The second leopard. + Lambourne, John
The second man. + Roberts, C. B.
The second man. + Urbanek, Mae
The second Mayflower book of black magic stories. + Parry, Michel
The second omnibus of crime. + Sayers, Dorothy L.
Second orbit. + Doherty, G. D.
The second Pacific book of science fiction. + Baxter, John
The second Pan book of horror stories. + van Thal, Herbert
The second part of Armata. + (Erskine, Thomas)
The second part of The Abbey of Kilkhampton. + (Croft, Herbert)
The second rising. + Beresford, Leslie
Second satellite. + Richardson, Robert S.
Second stage Lensmen. + Smith, E. E.
Second storm. + Sutherland, Morris
The second trip. + Silverberg, Robert
The second world of If. + Quinn, James L. & Wulff, Eve
The second youth of Theodora Desanges. + Linton, Lynn
Secret agent of Terra. + Brunner, John
Secret barrier X. + Perry Rhodan 16
The secret battleplane. + Westerman, Percy F.
The secret city. + Doke, Joseph J.
The secret formula. + Peters, Alan
The secret formula. + Pollard, A. O.
The secret galactics. + van Vogt, A. E.
The Secret Glory. + Machen, Arthur
The secret in the sky. + Robeson, Kenneth
Secret in the Stlalakum Wild. + Harris, Christie
The secret kingdom. + Richardson, Frank
The secret Martians. + Sharkey, Jack
The secret masters. + Kersh, Gerald
Secret memoirs and manners of several persons of quality. + (Manley, Mary)
Secret memoirs and manners of several persons of quality, the second volume. + (Manley, Mary)
The secret mountain, and other tales. + Morris, Kenneth
The secret of a star. + Martin, Eva M.
The secret of Barnabas Collins. + Ross, Marilyn

The secret of Hidden Valley. + Hutchinson, Loring
The secret of Holm Peel, and other strange stories. + Rohmer, Sax
The secret of Josiah Black. + Payne, Charles
The secret of mankind. + none
The secret of Red Skull. + Stahl, Ben
The secret of Saturn's rings. + Wollheim, Donald A.
The secret of Sinharat. + Brackett, Leigh
The secret of the Australian desert. + Favenc, Ernest
Secret of the black planet. + Lesser, Milton
The secret of the court. + Moore, F. Frankfort
The secret of the crater. + Osborne, Duffield
The secret of the desert. + Fawcett, E. Douglas
The secret of the desert. + Turner, C. C.
The secret of the Dragon. + Pendered, Mary L.
The secret of the Earth. + Beale, Charles Willing
The secret of the island. + Verne, Jules
The secret of the lamas. + none
The secret of the League. + Bramah, Ernest
Secret of the lost planet. + MacVicar, Angus
Secret of the lost race. + Norton, Andre
The secret of the Magian. + Laurie, A.
Secret of the marauder satellite. + White, Ted
The secret of the Martian moons. + Wollheim, Donald A.
The secret of the ninth planet. + Wollheim, Donald A.
The secret of the plateau. + Westerman, Percy F.
Secret of the Red Spot. + Binder, Eando
The secret of the Runestaff. + Moorcock, Michael
The secret of the sacred lake. + Gammon, David
The secret of the Sargasso. + Macdonald, Robert M.
The secret of the south. + Gurdon, J. E.
The secret of the sphinx. + Carew, Henry
The secret of the sphinx. + Dreyer, Hans P.
The secret of the sphinx. + Smith, James & Sutton, John Wren
The secret of the Stradivarius, and other stories. + Conway, Hugh
Secret of the sunless world. + MacApp, C. C.
The secret of the time vault. + Perry Rhodan #6
The secret of the Zodiac. + Sterne, Julian
The secret of Tibet. + Bell, William Dixon
The secret of Wilhelm Storitz. + Verne, Jules
The secret of ZI. + Bulmer, Kenneth
The secret people. + Beynon, John
The secret people. + Harris, John Beynon
The secret people. + Holmes, F. Ratcliffe
The secret people. + Jones, Raymond F.
The secret people. + Wyndham, John
The secret power. + Corelli, Marie
The secret power. + Van der Elst, Violet
Secret sceptre. + Gerard, Francis
The secret sea-plane. + Thorne, Guy
The secret sex curse of Bertha T. + Short, Jackson
A secret sin. + Le Queux, William
Secret sisterhood. + Rheingold, Howard
The secret songs. + Leiber, Fritz
The secret speech. + Beal, John Robinson
Secret under Antarctica. + Dickson, Gordon R.
Secret under the Caribbean. + Dickson, Gordon R.
Secret under the sea. + Dickson, Gordon R.
The secret visitors. + White, James
The secret voyage. + Edmonds, Harry
The secret warrior. + Heeley, Maureen
Secret weapon. + Newman, Bernard
Secret weapons. + Walsh, J. M.
The secret world of Og. + Berton, Pierre
The secrets of Dr. Taverner. + Fortune, Dion
Secrets of Stardeep. + Jakes, John
The sedan-chair; and, Sir Wilfred's seven flights. + Chatelain, Madame de
Sedge. + Halle, Louis J.
The seed. + Thomas, Dan

The seed of Earth. + Silverberg, Robert
Seed of light. + Cooper, Edmund
Seed of stars. + Kippax, John & Morgan, Dan
Seed of the beast. + Morgan, Helene
Seed of the dreamers. + Petaja, Emil
Seed of the gods. + Hughes, Zach
The seedbearers. + Timlett, Peter Valentine
The seedling stars. + Blish, James
The seeds of enchantment. + Frankau, Gilbert
The seeds of frenzy. + Elder, Michael
Seeds of life. + Taine, John
Seeds of life; and, White Lily. + Taine, John
The seeds of time. + Wyndham, John
The seedy. + Ray, Robert
Seeker from the stars. + Coleman, James Nelson
Seeker to the dead. + Burrage, A. M.
The seekers. + Bates, H. E.
Seekers of tomorrow. + Moskowitz, Sam
The seen and the unseen. + Marsh, Richard
The seen and unseen at Stratford-on-Avon. + Howells,
W. D.
The seer. + Forrester, Mary
The seeress. + Lissenden, George B.
Seetee alert! + Kern, Gregory
Seetee ship. + Stewart, Will
Seetee ship. + Williamson, Jack
Seetee ship/Seetee shock. + Williamson, Jack
Seetee shock. + Stewart, Will
Seetee shock. + Williamson, Jack
Segaki. + Stacton, David
Sekhet. + Miller, Irene
A select bibliography of H. P. Lovecraft. + Brennan,
Joseph Payne
Select tales. + Poe, Edgar Allan
The select works of Edgar Allan Poe. + Poe, Edgar
Allan
Selected ghost stories of M. R. James. + James, M. R.
Selected letters, 1911-1924. + Lovecraft, H. P.
Selected letters, 1925-1929. + Lovecraft, H. P.
Selected letters, 1929-1931. + Lovecraft, H. P.
Selected poems and tales of Edgar Allan Poe. + Poe,
Edgar Allan
Selected poetry and prose of Edgar Allan Poe. + Poe,
Edgar Allan
Selected prose and poetry. + Poe, Edgar Allan
Selected prose, poetry, and Eureka. + Poe, Edgar Allan
Selected stories. + Benet, Stephen Vincent
Selected short stories. + Poe, Edgar Allan
Selected short stories. + Wells, H. G.
Selected short stories of Algernon Blackwood. + Black-
wood, Algernon
Selected short stories of Frank Kafka. + Kafka, Franz
Selected stories. + Poe, Edgar Allan
Selected stories. + "Q"
Selected stories and poems. + Poe, Edgar Allan
Selected stories from Science-fiction adventures in
mutation. + Conklin, Groff
Selected tales. + Poe, Edgar Allan
Selected tales and poems. + Poe, Edgar Allan
Selected tales and sketches. + Hawthorne, Nathaniel
Selected tales of Algernon Blackwood. + Blackwood,
Algernon
Selected tales of mystery. + Poe, Edgar Allan
Selected tales of the genii. + (Ridley, James)
Selected works of Stephen Vincent Benet, volume two.
+ Benet, Stephen Vincent
Selected writings. + Poe, Edgar Allan
Selected writings of E. T. A. Hoffmann. + Hoffmann,
E. T. A.
Selected writings of Edgar Allan Poe. + Poe, Edgar
Allan
Selections from Adventures in time and space. + Healy,
Raymond J. & McComas, J. Francis

Selections from Beyond human ken. + Merril, Judith
Selections from Deep space. + Russell, Eric Frank
Selections from Edgar Allan Poe. + Poe, Edgar Allan
Selections from Poe. + Poe, Edgar Allan
Selections from Science-fiction thinking machines. +
Conklin, Groff
Selections from the early prose works of H. G. Wells.
+ Wells, H. G.
Selections from The Pan book of horror stories #5. +
van Thal, Herbert
Selections from The Pan book of horror stories #4. +
van Thal, Herbert
Selections from The Pan book of horror stories #3. +
van Thal, Herbert
Selections from the prose tales of Edgar Allan Poe. +
Poe, Edgar Allan
Selections from the prose works of William Morris. +
Morris, William
Selections from the writings of Lord Dunsany. + Dun-
sany, Lord
Selestor's men of Atlantis. + von Ravn, Clara Iza
Sell England? + Balsdon, Dacre
Semiramis. + Peple, Edward
Send for Johnny Danger. + Patchett, M. E.
Send him victorious. + Hurd, Douglas & Osmond, Andrew
Senrac, the lion man. + Langford, George
A sensational trance. + Dawson, Forbes
Sense of obligation. + Harrison, Harry
A sense of reality. + Greene, Graham
The sense of the past. + James, Henry
A sense of wonder. + Moskowitz, Sam
The sensitives. + Charbonneau, Louis
The sentinel. + Konvitz, Jeffrey
The sentinel stars. + Charbonneau, Louis
Sentinels from space. + Russell, Eric Frank
Seola. + (Smith, Mrs. J. G.)
A sequel to Looking backward. + Michaelis, Richard
A sequel to the adventures of Baron Munchausen. +
(Raspe, Rudolf)
Seraph--or mortal? + Gardner, Celia E.
Seraph wings. + Lynch, Arthur
The Serapion Brethren. + Hoffmann, E. T. A.
Serenvs, & other stories of the past & present. +
Lemaitre, Jules
Sergeant Terry Bull. + Bull, Terry
Sermons by the devil. + Harris, W. S.
The serpent. + Gaskell, Jane
Servants of the Wankh. + Vance, Jack
The setting sun. + "X"
The seven agate devils. + Robeson, Kenneth
Seven come infinity. + Conklin, Groff
Seven conquests. + Anderson, Poul
Seven-day magic. + Eager, Edward
Seven days in May. + Bailey, Charles W. II & Knebel,
Fletcher
Seven days in New Crete. + Graves, Robert
Seven days to never. + Frank, Pat
Seven famous novels. + Wells, H. G.
7 footprints to Satan. + Merritt, A.
Seven footprints to Satan; and, Burn witch burn! +
Merritt, A.
Seven for murder. + Glenning, Raymond
Seven for the sea. + Cutt, W. Towrie
Seven from the stars. + Bradley, Marion Zimmer
Seven gothic tales. + Dinesen, Isak
Seven journeys. + Flatau, Dorota
Seven masterpieces of gothic horror. + Spector,
Robert Donald
Seven men. + Beerbohm, Max
Seven men, and two others. + Beerbohm, Max
The seven miracles of Gubbio, and the eighth. + Bruck-
berger, Raymond Leopold
Seven more strange stories. + Hardie, John L.

Seven out of time. + Zagat, Arthur Leo

The seven pillars. + Fernandez-Florez, Wenceslao

Seven science fiction novels. + Wells, H. G.

Seven select stories from Edgar Allan Poe. + Poe, Edgar Allan

The seven sexes. + Tenn, William

Seven sins. + Rohmer, Sax

The seven sleepers. + Beeding, Francis

The seven sons of Ballyhack. + Spivey, Thomas Sawyer

Seven stars for Catfish Bend. + Burman, Ben Lucien

Seven steps to the Sun. + Hoyle, Fred & Hoyle, Geoffrey

Seven stories. + Wells, H. G.

7 strange stories. + Hardie, John L.

Seven tales. + Poe, Edgar Allan

The seven that were hanged. + Andreev, Leonid

The seven that were hanged, and other stories. + Andreev, Leonid

Seven tickets to Hell. + Williams, Robert Moore

Seven trips through time and space. + Conklin, Groff

17 x infinity. + Conklin, Groff

7th annual edition, the year's best S-F. + Merril, Judith

The 7th annual of the year's best S-F. + Merril, Judith

The seventh bowl. + Bell, Neil

The seventh bowl. + Miles

The seventh day. + Kirst, Hans Hellmut

The seventh dimension. + La Salle, Victor

The seventh Fontana book of great ghost stories. + Aickman, Robert

The seventh Fontana book of great horror stories. + Danby, Mary

The seventh Galaxy reader. + Pohl, Frederik

The seventh ghost book. + Timperley, Rosemary

The seventh Pan book of horror stories. + van Thal, Herbert

The seventh swan. + Gray, Nicholas Stuart

Sever the Earth. + Spitz, Jacques

The several minds. + Morgan, Dan

The severed hand. + Lecale, Errol

Sex and the High Command. + Boyd, John

Sex burns like fire. + Harmon, Jim

The sex diary of Gerard Sorme. + Wilson, Colin

Sex, hypnosis, and the infinite. + Anex, Guy

The sex life of Hercules. + (Eagle, Robin)

Sex life of the gods. + Knerr, Michael

Sex life of the immortals. + Young, Red

The sex life of Ulysses. + (Kantor, Hal)

Sex machine. + (Camra, Roy)

The sex machine. + Conway, Troy

The sex machine. + Geis, Richard E.

The sex machine. + Mead, Shepherd

The sex magicians. + Wilson, Robert Anton

Sex 99. + Kullinger, J. L.

A sex odyssey. + von Grau, Wernher

The sex pill. + Williams, J. X.

The sex-ray. + Allison, Clyde

The sex-ray. + Mellows, Suzanne

The sex savages. + Anvic, Frank

The sex serum. + none

Sex slaves of the black mass. + Nathan, Richard

Sex teacher 2000 A.D. + Reeves, James

Sex trek. + Stephan, Peter

The sex triumphant. + Fox-Davies, A. C.

The sex war. + Merwin, Sam Jr.

The sexless dynasty. + Bolton, William W.

Sexmax. + Cooper, Hughes

Sexodus. + Jason, Jerry [see Addendum]

The sexorcist. + none

The sexorcist. + Cleve, John

The sexorcist. + Fedakh, Fatima

The sextuplets of Loqmaria. + Labry, Michel

Sexualis 1984. + Ramdagger, Geoffrey

Sexualis '95. + Sternberg, Jacques

A Shackleton called Sheila. + Mariner, David

A shade of difference. + Drury, Allen

The shades of time. + Darity, William A.

The Shadow and the voice of murder. + Grant, Maxwell

Shadow beware. + Grant, Maxwell

Shadow castle. + Cockrell, Marian

The Shadow: destination Moon. + Grant, Maxwell

Shadow forms. + Hall, Manly P.

The shadow girl. + Cummings, Ray

Shadow--go mad! + Grant, Maxwell

The shadow in the sea. + John, Owen

The Shadow laughs! + Grant, Maxwell

The shadow man. + Barton, Lee

The shadow of a dream. + Haldane, Charlotte

Shadow of authority. + Waller, Robert

Shadow of evil. + La Spina, Greye

Shadow of Fu Manchu. + Rohmer, Sax

The shadow of glory. + Kipling, Arthur Wellesley

Shadow of Heaven. + Shaw, Bob

The shadow of the moor. + Northumberland, Duke of

Shadow of the mutant master. + Perry Rhodan 47

The shadow of the unseen. + Blyth, James & Pain, Barry

Shadow of tomorrow. + Pohl, Frederik

The shadow on the blind, and other ghost stories. + Baldwin, Mrs. Alfred

Shadow on the hearth. + Merril, Judith

The shadow on the sea. + Pemberton, Max

The shadow on the sun. + Harris, Rosemary

The shadow out of time, and other tales of horror. + Derleth, August & Lovecraft, H. P.

The shadow over Innsmouth. + Lovecraft, H. P.

The shadow over Innsmouth, and other stories of horror. + Lovecraft, H. P.

Shadow over Mars. + Brackett, Leigh

Shadow over the Earth. + Wilding, Philip

The shadow people. + St. Clair, Margaret

Shadow play. + Beaumont, Charles

Shadow-shapes. + Annesley, Maude

The Shadow strikes. + Grant, Maxwell

Shadowed! + Belloc, Hilaire

Shadowings. + Hearn, Lafcadio

The shadowless man. + Chamisso, Adalbert von

Shadows in the sun. + Oliver, Chad

Shadows of ecstasy. + Williams, Charles

Shadows of Heaven. + Urang, Gunnar

Shadows of imagination. + Hillegas, Mark R.

The Shadow's revenge. + Grant, Maxwell

Shadows waiting. + Chilton, Eleanor Carroll

Shadows with eyes. + Leiber, Fritz

The shadowy thing. + Drake, H. B.

The shadowy third. + Glasgow, Ellen

The shadowy third, and other stories. + Glasgow, Ellen

Shafts of fear. + Wheatley, Dennis

The shaggy dog. + Griffen, Elizabeth L.

Shaggy planet. + Goulart, Ron

Shakespearian fantasias. + Singleton, Esther

Shambleau, and others. + Moore, C. L.

Shanadu. + Briney, Robert E.

Shanghaied socialists. + Ward, Will J.

The shape changer. + Laumer, Keith

The shape of fear, and other ghostly tales. + Peattie, Elia W.

The shape of further things. + Aldiss, Brian W.

The shape of space. + Niven, Larry

The shape of the war to come. + (Antheil, George)

The shape of things. + Knight, Damon

The shape of things to come. + Wells, H. G.

Shapes in the fire. + Shiel, M. P.

Shapes of the supernatural. + Lewis, Gogo & Manley, Seon
Shapes that haunt the dusk. + Alden, Henry Mills & Howells, William Dean
Shara-Li. + Castilla, Clyde Andre
Shardik. + Adams, Richard
Shards of space. + Sheckley, Robert
Shareworld. + Hershman, Morris
The shark in the window. + Lazarus, Keo Felker
The shattered ring. + Rose, Lois & Rose, Stephen
Shattering silence. + Dorman, Geoffrey
The shaving of Shagpat. + Meredith, George
The shawl of Solomon. + Hawkwood, Allan
She. + Haggard, H. Rider
She. + Haggard, H. Rider & Ward, Don
She and Allan. + Haggard, H. Rider
She; and, King Solomon's mines. + Haggard, H. Rider
She; and, The return of She. + Haggard, H. Rider
She of the holy light. + Claxton, John G.
Sheba visits Solomon. + Eliat, Helene
Shedding the years. + Bennett, James Clark
The sheep look up. + Brunner, John
The sheik's white slave. + Raife, Raimond
Shekinah. + Whitell, Evelyn
SheLa. + Menen, Aubrey
Shellbreak. + Groves, J. W.
Shelter. + Ljoka, Dan
The Shepherd is my Lord. + Gat, Dimitri V.
Sheridan La Fanu: the diabolic genius. + Le Fanu, J. Sheridan
Sherry and ghosts. + Ruck, Berta
The Sherwood ring. + Pope, Elizabeth Marie
Sheykh Hassan. + Hillam, S. A.
Shield. + Anderson, Poul
The shining east. + Hotson, Cornelia Hinkley
The shining pyramid. + Machen, Arthur
The shiny narrow grin. + Gaskell, Jane
Ship ashore. + Parkman, Sydney
The ship beautiful. + Allen, C. R.
The ship from Atlantis. + Munn, H. Warner
The ship from nowhere. + none
The ship from outside. + Chandler, A. Bertram
The ship of death. + Stilgebauer, Edward
Ship of destiny. + Slater, H. J.
The ship of flame. + Stone, William S.
The Ship of Ishtar. + Merritt, A.
The ship that flew. + Lewis, Hilda
The ship that sailed the time stream. + Edmondson, G. C.
The ship that sailed to Mars. + Timlin, William M.
The ship who sang. + McCaffrey, Anne
The ships of Durostorum. + Bulmer, Kenneth
The ships of Tarshish. + Mohoao
Ships of Vero. + Shaw, Brian
Ships to the stars. + Leiber, Fritz
Shipwrecked in the air. + Verne, Jules
Shivers. + none
Shock! + Allen, M. C.
Shock! + Matheson, Richard
The shock of battle. + Vaux, Patrick
Shock III. + Matheson, Richard
Shock II. + Matheson, Richard
Shock wave. + Richmond, Leigh & Richmond, Walt
Shock waves. + Matheson, Richard
A shocking thing. + Knight, Damon
Shocks. + Blackwood, Algernon
Shoot! + Newman, Bernard
Shoot at the Moon. + Temple, William F.
The shooting of the green. + Poyer, Joe
The shores beneath. + Sallis, James
The shores of another sea. + Oliver, Chad
The shores of death. + Moorcock, Michael

The shores of space. + Matheson, Richard
The shores of tomorrow. + Mason, David
The short fiction of Isaac Asimov. + Patrouch, Joseph F. Jr.
Short Friday, and other stories. + Singer, Isaac Bashevis
A short history of the future. + Churchill, R. C.
The short reign of Pippin IV. + Steinbeck, John
Short stories. + Dostoievski, Fiodor
Short stories. + Poe, Edgar Allan
The short stories. + Wells, H. G.
Short stories by H. G. Wells, first series. + Wells, H. G.
Short stories by H. G. Wells, second series. + Wells, H. G.
The short stories of H. G. Wells. + Wells, H. G.
The short stories of Robert Louis Stevenson. + Stevenson, Robert Louis
Short stories of Stephen Vincent Benet. + Benet, Stephen Vincent
Short stories of to-day and yesterday. + Blackwood, Algernon
Shorter novels, eighteenth century. + Henderson, Philip
Shot in the dark. + Merril, Judith
Showcase. + Elwood, Roger
The shrine of death, and other stories. + Dilke, Lady
The shrine of love, and other stories. + Dilke, Lady
The shrinking man. + Matheson, Richard
The shriveling murders. + Zorro
The shrouded planet. + Randall, Robert
The shrouded woman. + Bombal, Maria-Luisa
Shuddering castle. + Fawley, Wilbur
Shudders. + none
Shudders. + Asquith, Cynthia
Shudders and shakes. + Ingram, Anne Bower
Shuna and the lost tribe. + King, John
Shuna, white queen of the jungle. + King, John
The shunned house. + Lovecraft, H. P.
The shunned vicar of the Gilliflowers. + Herbert, Frederick William von
The shuttered room. + Withers, Julia
The shuttered room, and other pieces. + (Derleth, August)
The shuttered room, and other tales of horror. + Derleth, August & Lovecraft, H. P.
Shy leopardess. + Barringer, Leslie
The shy stegosaurus of Cricket Creek. + Lampman, Evelyn Sibley
The shy stegosaurus of Indian Springs. + Lampman, Evelyn Sibley [see Addendum]
Shylock Homes: his posthumous memoirs. + Bangs, John Kendrick
The Si-Fan mysteries. + Rohmer, Sax
The Siamese cat. + Underwood, Leon
The sibyl. + Lagerkvist, Par
Sibyl Sue Blue. + Brown, Rosel George
Sideslip. + Van Arnam, Dave & White, Ted
Sidewise in time, and other scientific adventures. + Leinster, Murray
Sidonia the sorceress. + Meinhold, Wilhelm
Siege. + Corley, Edwin
The siege of Bodike. + Lester, Edward
Siege of Earth. + Faucette, John M.
The siege of Harlem. + Miller, Warren
The siege of London. + M., J. W.
The siege of London. + Posteritas
Siege of the unseen. + van Vogt, A. E.
Siege perilous. + del Rey, Lester
Siegfried the mystic. + Wheeler, Ida Worden
The sign at six. + White, Stewart Edward
The sign of Taurus. + Fifield, William

The sign of the burning hart. + Keller, David H.
Sign of the Labrys. + St. Clair, Margaret
The sign of the salamander. + Miller, Eugenia
The sign of the seven seas. + Dawson, Carley
The sign of the spider. + Mitford, Bertram
A sign of the times. + Kee, Robert
Signor. + Mulier
Signs and portents. + Hine, Al
Signs & wonders. + Beresford, J. D.
Signs and wonders. + Elwood, Roger
Silence. + Poe, Edgar Allan
Silence in Heaven. + Erlanger, Michael
The silence of Gom. + Perry Rhodan 39
The silent bullet. + Reeve, Arthur B.
The Silent City. + Thorpe, Fred
The silent invaders. + Silverberg, Robert
The silent miaow. + Gallico, Paul
The silent multitude. + Compton, D. G.
The silent planet. + Briggs, Philip
Silent running. + Thompson, Harlan
The silent speakers. + Sellings, Arthur
The silent voice. + Dell, Berenice V.
Silent, white, and beautiful, and other stories. +
   Robbins, Tod
The Silkie. + van Vogt, A. E.
Silky. + Coatsworth, Elizabeth
Silver bells and cockle shells. + DuBreuil, Linda
The silver chair. + Lewis, C. S.
The silver city. + Ober, Frederick A.
The silver crown. + O'Brien, Robert C.
The silver crown. + Richards, Laura E.
The silver curlew. + Farjeon, Eleanor [see Addendum]
The Silver Death. + Gibbs, George
The silver eggheads. + Leiber, Fritz
The Silver God of the Orang Hutan. + Douglas, David
The silver locusts. + Bradbury, Ray
Silver nutmegs. + Knowles, Vernon
The Silver Peril. + Rutledge, Maryse
The Silver Stallion. + Cabell, James Branch
The silver unicorn. + Reid, Vera W.
The Silver Warriors. + Moorcock, Michael
Silverlock. + Myers, John Myers
Simbi and the satyr of the dark jungle. + Tutuola,
   Amos
Simiocracy. + (Brookfield, A. M.)
Simon Black and the spacemen. + Southall, Ivan
Simon Black in peril. + Southall, Ivan
Simon Black in space. + Southall, Ivan
Simon, king of the witches. + Hills, Baldwin
Simon Rack; Earth lies sleeping. + James, Laurence
Simon Rack; Starcross. + James, Laurence
The simulacra. + Dick, Philip K.
Simulacron-3. + Galouye, Daniel F.
The simultaneous man. + Blum, Ralph
The sin-eater, and other scientific impossibilities.
   + Walter, Elizabeth
The sin-eater, and other tales. + Macleod, Fiona
The sin-eater, The washer of the ford, and other legen-
   dary moralities. + Macleod, Fiona
The sin funnel. + Allison, Clyde
Sin in space. + Judd, Cyril
The sin of Atlantis. + Horniman, Roy
The sin veldt. + Dexter, John
Sindbad, Smith & Co. + Stearns, Albert
The sinful ones. + Leiber, Fritz
Sing for your supper. + Frankau, Pamela
The singing citadel. + Moorcock, Michael
The singing mouse stories. + Hough, Emerson
The singing stones. + Coulson, Juanita
Singoalla. + Rydberg, Viktor
The singular adventures of Baron Munchausen. + (Raspe,
   Rudolf)

Singular travels, campaigns, and adventures of Baron
   Munchausen. + (Raspe, Rudolf)
Singular travels, campaigns, voyages, and sporting ad-
   ventures of Baron Munnikhouson. + (Raspe, Rudolf)
Singularity station. + Ball, Brian N.
Sinister barrier. + Russell, Eric Frank
Sinister forces. + Westwood, Alvin
Sinister house. + Hall, Leland
Sinister madonna. + Rohmer, Sax
The sinister researches of C. P. Ransom. + Nearing,
   H. Jr.
Sinister stories. + John, Jasper
The sinners of HWANG. + Dexter, John
Sins of Severac Bablon. + Rohmer, Sax
Sins of Sumuru. + Rohmer, Sax
Sintram and his companions. + La Motte-Fouque,
   Friedrich de
Sintram and his companions; and, Undine. + La Motte-
   Fouque, Friedrich de
Sintram and his companions; Aslauga's knight. + La
   Motte-Fouque, Friedrich de
The Sioux Spaceman. + Norton, Andre
Sir Henry. + Nathan, Robert
Sir MacHinery. + McGowen, Tom
Sir Peter's arm. + Cobb, Michael
Sir Pulteney. + Ward, E. D.
Sir Rohan's ghost. + (Prescott, Harriet)
Sir Wilfrid's seven flights. + Chatelain, Clara de
The siren stars. + Carrigan, Richard & Carrigan,
   Nancy
Sirenia. + (Lumley, Benjamin)
The sirens of Titan. + Vonnegut, Kurt Jr.
Sirius. + Stapledon, Olaf
Sister Earth. + Brede, Arnold
Sivan the sleeper. + Adams, H. C.
The six. + Rocker, Rudolf
6 and the silent scream. + Howard, Ivan
The 6 fingers of time, and other stories. + none
6 from worlds beyond. + Dikty, T. E.
Six gates from Limbo. + McIntosh, J. T.
Six ghost stories. + Jackson, Thomas Graham
6 great short novels of science fiction. + Conklin,
   Groff
Six great short science fiction novels. + Conklin,
   Groff
The six greatest novels of Anatole France. + France,
   Anatole
Six-gun planet. + Jakes, John
666. + Kirban, Salem
Six moral tales from Jules Laforgue. + Laforgue, Jules
Six novels of the supernatural. + Wagenknecht, Edward
Six stories by Edgar Allan Poe. + Poe, Edgar Allan
6,000 tons of gold. + Chamberlain, H. R.
Six thousand years hence. + Ramsey, Milton W.
6 x H. + Heinlein, Robert A.
Six worlds yonder. + Russell, Eric Frank
6th annual edition, the year's best S-F. + Merril,
   Judith
The 6th annual of the year's best S-F. + Merril,
   Judith
The sixth Armada ghost book. + Danby, Mary
The sixth column. + Fleming, Peter
Sixth column. + Heinlein, Robert A.
The sixth Fontana book of great ghost stories. +
   Aickman, Robert
The sixth Fontana book of great horror stories. +
   Danby, Mary
The sixth Galaxy reader. + Gold, H. L.
The sixth ghost book. + Timperley, Rosemary
The sixth ghost book, book one. + Timperley, Rosemary
The sixth ghost book, book two. + Timperley, Rosemary
The sixth Pan book of horror stories. + van Thal,
   Herbert

The sixth seal. + Wesley, Mary
The sixth sense. + McKenna, Stephen
The sixth sense #2; In the steps of the Master. +
  Bradley, Marion Zimmer
The sixth speed. + Rath, E. J.
Sixty days to live. + Wheatley, Dennis
'68. + Scaevola, Peter
Sixty years hence. + (Henningsen, Charles)
The skeleton man. + Munn, Bertram
Skiffy. + Mayne, William
Skin and bones. + Smith, Thorne
Skrine. + Sully, Kathleen
A skull and two crystals. + Dick-Lauder, George
Skull-face, and others. + Howard, Robert E.
Skull face omnibus. + Howard, Robert E.
The skull of Kanaima. + Norwood, Victor
The skull of the Marquis de Sade, and other stories.
  + Bloch, Robert
The sky block. + Frazee, Steve
The sky blue. + Ross, Olin J.
The sky cage. + Prior, Ann
The sky is falling. + del Rey, Lester
The sky is filled with ships. + Meredith, Richard C.
The sky-man. + Webster, Henry Kitchell
Sky pirates of Callisto. + Carter, Lin
The sky walker. + Robeson, Kenneth
Skyjak. + ezra
Skylark DuQuesne. + Smith, E. E.
The Skylark of space. + Garby, Lee Hawkins & Smith,
  E. E.
Skylark of Valeron. + Smith, E. E.
Skylark Three. + Smith, E. E.
The skynappers. + Brunner, John
Skyport. + Siodmak, Curt
Skyprobe. + McCutchan, Philip
Skyraft. + Clark, Charles
The skyrocket. + Hader, Berta & Hader, Elmer
The skyscraper doom. + Zierold, Norman
The Skystone. + Hilzinger, J. Geo.
Skyward and Earthward. + Penrice, Arthur
Skyways for Doorian. + Van Tuyl, Zaara
Slan. + van Vogt, A. E.
Slanting Earth. + Haun, Blair A.
Slater's planet. + Moore, Harris
Slaughterhouse-five. + Vonnegut, Kurt Jr.
Slave island. + La Buque, Jean de
The slave of Ea. + Molnar, E. F.
Slave of Sarma. + Lord, Jeffrey
Slave planet. + Janifer, Laurence M.
Slave ship. + Pohl, Frederik
Slave ship from Sergan. + Kern, Gregory
Slave traders of the sky. + Future, Steve
Slavers of space. + Brunner, John
The slaves of Heaven. + Cooper, Edmund
Slaves of Ijax. + Fearn, John Russell
The slaves of Lomooro. + Augustus, Albert Jr.
Slaves of sleep. + Hubbard, L. Ron
Slaves of Sumuru. + Rohmer, Sax
Slaves of the Klau. + Vance, Jack
Slaves of the lamp. + Frankau, Pamela
Slaves of the spectrum. + Kent, Philip
The slayer of souls. + Chambers, Robert W.
The sleep. + Creasey, John
The Sleep Eaters. + Lymington, John
Sleep is death. + Kensch, Otto
Sleep no more. + Derleth, August
Sleep, two, three, four! + Neufeld, John
The sleeper awakes. + Wells, H. G.
The sleeper awakes; and, Men like gods. + Wells, H. G.
The sleeper awakes; Tales of the unexpected. + Wells,
  H. G.
The Sleepers. + Curry, Jane Louise

Sleepers of Mars. + Wyndham, John
The sleeping & the dead. + Derleth, August
The sleeping bomb. + Moffatt, James
A sleeping memory. + Oppenheim, E. Phillips
Sleeping planet. + Burkett, William R. Jr.
The sleeping sorceress. + Moorcock, Michael
Sleepwalker's world. + Dickson, Gordon R.
A slip in time. + Gibson, Floyd
A slip under the microscope. + Wells, H. G.
Slow Burner. + Haggard, William
The slowing down process. + Wessex, Martyn
A small armageddon. + Roshwald, Mordecai
The small assassin. + Bradbury, Ray
Small changes. + Clement, Hal
The small gods & Mr. Barnum. + Trell, Max
Small shadows creep. + Norton, Andre
The smashed world. + Slater, Henry J.
The smell of evil. + Birkin, Charles
The smile on the face of the tiger. + Hurd, Douglas
  & Osmond, Andrew
The smiler with the knife. + Blake, Nicholas
The smiling Kouros. + Soloviev, Mikhail
Smire. + Cabell, Branch
Smirt. + Cabell, Branch
Smith. + Cabell, Branch
Smith and the pharaohs, and other tales. + Haggard,
  H. Rider
Smith Minor on the Moon. + Hardy, Philip
Smith of Wootton Major. + Tolkien, J. R. R.
Smith of Wootton Major; and, Farmer Giles of Ham. +
  Tolkien, J. R. R.
The smog. + Creasey, John
Smoke from Cromwell's time, and other stories. +
  Aiken, Joan
The smoking leg, and other stories. + Metcalfe, John
The Smoky God. + Emerson, Willis George
Smoky-House. + Goudge, Elizabeth [see Addendum]
Smugglers' Reef. + Blaine, John
The snake. + Powell, F. Inglis
Snake-bite, and other stories. + Hichens, Robert
The snake horn. + Grosser, Morton
The Snake Lady, and other stories. + Lee, Vernon
Snapdragon. + Savill, Mervyn
Sneak preview. + Bloch, Robert
Sneaker Hill. + Little, Jane
Snoggle. + Priestley, J. B.
The snouters. + Stumpke, Harald
Snow fury. + Holden, Robert
The snow-image, and other tales. + Hawthorne, Natha-
  niel
Snow White and the giants. + McIntosh, J. T.
The Snow-White soliloquies. + MacLeod, Sheila
Snowfall, and other chilling events. + Walter, Eli-
  zabeth
Snowland. + Hale, Robert Beverly
Snowman in flames. + Perry Rhodan 25
The snows of Ganymede. + Anderson, Poul
The snowstorm. + Netherclift, Beryl
So a leader came. + Palmer, Frederick
So bright the vision. + Simak, Clifford D.
So close to home. + Blish, James
So fair a house. + Neill, Robert
So fast he ran. + Armour, Donald
So here then are dreams. + Schreiner, Olive
So love returns. + Nathan, Robert
So Moses was born. + Grant, Joan
So pale, so cold, so fair. + Birkin, Charles
Soaring sunward. + Adriel, Jeanne
The sociable ghost. + Harper, Olive
The social gangster. + Reeve, Arthur B.
Social integration. + Frank, Robert
The social war of the year 1900. + Landis, S. M.

The soul of a bishop, and three short stories. +
  Wells, H. G.
The soul of a mummy, and other stories. + Schleppey,
  Blanche Bloor
The soul of Countess Adrian. + Praed, Mrs. Campbell
The soul of Kol Nikon. + Farjeon, Eleanor
The soul of Lilith. + Corelli, Marie
The soul of Melicent. + Cabell, James Branch
The soul of the Orient. + Cavalier, Z. Langrana
Soul of the robot. + Bayley, Barrington J.
A soul on fire. + Marryat, Florence
A soul on fire. + Williams, Frances Fenwick
The soul scar. + Reeve, Arthur B.
The soul stealer. + Gull, C. Ranger-
The soul stealers. + Huntington, Charles
The soul that came back. + Wentworth-James, G. de S.
Soulless saints. + Leach, Bailey Kay
Soulmate. + Runyon, Charles W.
Soul's end. + Carroll, Joy
Souls in Hell. + O'Neill, John
Souls' judgment day. + Albano, M. W.
Souls on Fifth. + Granville Barker, (Harley)
The Sound-Machine. + Snell, Edmund
The sound of a voice that is still. + Campbell, Archie
A sound of chariots. + Hunter, Mollie
A sound of crying. + Sudbery, Rodie
The sound of his horn. + "Sarban"
A sour apple tree. + Blackburn, John
The South Pole terror. + Robeson, Kenneth
Southern exploration. + Dale, Adam
The Southlanders. + Fox, Lady Mary
The sovereign guide. + Miller, William Amos
Soviet science fiction. + none
Sown in the darkness. + Twiford, William Richard
Space. + Kerr, A. W.
Space Agent and the ancient peril. + MacVicar, Angus
Space Agent and the Isles of Fire. + MacVicar, Angus
Space Agent from the lost planet. + MacVicar, Angus
The space ark. + Lightner, A. M.
The space barbarians. + Godwin, Tom
The space barbarians. + Reynolds, Mack
Space beam. + Robb, John
The space-born. + Tubb, E. C.
Space born. + Wright, Lan
Space-borne. + Fanthorpe, R. Lionel
Space by the tale. + Bixby, Jerome
Space cadet. + Heinlein, Robert A.
Space captain. + Leinster, Murray
Space captives of the golden men. + Patchett, M. E.
Space cat. + Todd, Ruthven
Space cat and the kittens. + Todd, Ruthven
Space cat meets Mars. + Todd, Ruthven
Space cat visits Venus. + Todd, Ruthven
Space chantey. + Lafferty, R. A.
The space circus. + Steffanson, Con
The space dreamers. + Clarke, Arthur C.
Space Eagle; operation doomsday. + Pearl, Jack
Space Eagle; operation star voyage. + Pearl, Jack
The space egg. + Winterbotham, Russ
Space family Stone. + Heinlein, Robert A.
Space flight. + Hunt, Gill
Space flight 139. + Mistral, Bengo
Space for hire. + Nolan, William F.
The space frontiers. + Vernon, Roger Lee
Space fury. + Fanthorpe, R. L.
Space gypsies. + Leinster, Murray
The space gypsies. + Lightner, A. M.
Space Hawk. + Gilmore, Anthony
Space hostages. + Fisk, Nicholas
Space hunger. + Grey, Charles
Space intruder. + Muirden, James
Space lash. + Clement, Hal

Space lawyer. + Schachner, Nat
Space line. + Lang, King
Space lords. + Smith, Cordwainer
The space machine. + Daniel, Jerry C.
The space magicians. + Moskowitz, Sam & Norton,
  Alden H.
Space men. + Shaw, David
Space mercenaries. + Chandler, A. Bertram
The space merchants. + Kornbluth, C. M. & Pohl,
  Frederik
Space no barrier. + Torro, Pel
Space novels by Jules Verne. + Verne, Jules
The Space Olympics. + Lightner, A. M.
Space on my hands. + Brown, Fredric
Space 1. + Davis, Richard
Space opera. + Aldiss, Brian W.
Space opera. + Vance, Jack
Space pioneer. + Reynolds, Mack
Space pioneers. + Norton, Andre
The space pioneers. + Rockwell, Carey
Space pirate. + Bamman, Henry & Odell, William &
  Whitehead, Robert
The space pirate. + Vance, Jack
Space pirates. + Del Martia, Astron
The space plague. + Lightner, A. M.
The space plague. + Smith, George O.
Space Platform. + Leinster, Murray
Space police. + Norton, Andre
Space prison. + Godwin, Tom
Space probe. + Garner, Graham
Space Puppet. + Rackham, John
The space raiders. + Beverley, Barrington
Space ranger. + Asimov, Isaac
Space relations. + Barr, Donald
Space salvage. + Bulmer, H. K.
Space service. + Norton, Andre
Space sex. + Warren, Roy
The space ship in the park. + Slobodkin, Louis
The space ship returns to the apple tree. + Slobod-
  kin, Louis
Space ship to Venus. + Nicholson, John
The space ship under the apple tree. + Slobodkin,
  Louis
Space skimmer. + Gerrold, David
The space sorcerers. + McIntosh, J. T.
Space space space. + Sloane, William M.
Space stadium. + Bevis, H. U.
Space Station 42, and other stories. + none
Space Station 1. + Long, Frank Belknap
The space story omnibus. + none
Space swap, 1984-8612. + Piper, Walter
Space swappers. + James, Dolan
The Space Swimmers. + Dickson, Gordon R.
Space, time & crime. + deFord, Miriam Allen
Space, time, and Nathaniel. + Aldiss, Brian W.
The space-time journal. + Merril, Judith
The space-time juggler. + Brunner, John
Space-time task force. + Yorke, Preston
Space train. + Haile, Terence
Space trap. + Bell, Thornton
Space treason. + Bulmer, H. K. & Clarke, A. V.
Space Tug. + Leinster, Murray
Space 2. + Davis, Richard
Space Viking. + Piper, H. Beam
The space visitors. + Bell, Paul W. & Robinett,
  Ralph F.
Space void. + Johns, Marston
Space void. + Muller, John E.
Space war. + Jones, Neil R.
Space warp. + Statten, Vargo
The space willies. + Russell, Eric Frank
Space winners. + Dickson, Gordon R.

Star barbarian. + Van Arnam, Dave
The star beast. + Heinlein, Robert A.
Star-begotten. + Wells, H. G.
Star born. + Norton, Andre
Star bridge. + Gunn, James E. & Williamson, Jack
The star called Wormwood. + Bishop, Morchard
Star child. + Stewart, Fred Mustard
Star city. + Zetford, Tully
Star Cluster Seven. + Random, Alex
The star conquerors. + Bova, Ben
The star-crossed woman. + Cormack, Maribelle
Star dog. + Lightner, A. M.
The star dreamer. + Castle, Agnes & Castle, Edgerton
Star dust. + Vivian, E. Charles
The star dwellers. + Blish, James
Star fourteen. + Pohl, Frederik
The Star Fox. + Anderson, Poul
Star Gate. + Norton, Andre
Star giant. + Skinkle, Dorothy E.
Star girl. + Winterfeld, Henry
Star gladiator. + Van Arnam, Dave
Star guard. + Norton, Andre
Star hunter. + Norton, Andre
Star hunter; &, Voodoo planet. + Norton, Andre
The Star King. + Vance, Jack
The star kings. + Hamilton, Edmond
Star lady. + Webster, F. A. M.
Star light. + Clement, Hal
The star magicians. + Carter, Lin
Star Maker. + Stapledon, Olaf
Star man. + Byrne, Stuart J.
Star Man's son, 2250 A.D. + Norton, Andre
The star men. + Friend, Oscar J.
The star mill. + Petaja, Emil
Star of danger. + Bradley, Marion Zimmer
Star of ill-omen. + Wheatley, Dennis
The star of Les Baux. + Severin, Jean
The star of life. + Hamilton, Edmond
The star of Satan. + Bernanos, Georges [see Addendum]
Star of stars. + Pohl, Frederik
The star of the Incas. + Blundell, Peter
Star of the morning. + The Author of "The truth about man"
Star of the unborn. + Werfel, Franz
Star over the frontier. + Schaper, Edzard
Star quest. + Brockley, Fenton
Star quest. + Koontz, Dean R.
The star raiders. + Suddaby, Donald
Star-Raker. + Gordon, Donald
Star rangers. + Norton, Andre
Star rider. + Piserchia, Doris
The star road. + Dickson, Gordon R.
Star rogue. + Carter, Lin
The star rover. + London, Jack
The star rovers. + Bevis, H. U.
Star science fiction, no. 6. + Pohl, Frederik
Star science fiction stories. + Pohl, Frederik
Star science fiction stories, no. 5. + Pohl, Frederik
Star science fiction stories, no. 4. + Pohl, Frederik
Star science fiction stories, no. 1. + Pohl, Frederik
Star science fiction stories, no. 6. + Pohl, Frederik
Star science fiction stories, no. 3. + Pohl, Frederik
Star science fiction stories, no. 2. + Pohl, Frederik
The star seekers. + Lesser, Milton
The star seekers. + Rayer, Francis G.
Star shine. + Brown, Fredric
Star ship on Saddle Mountain. + Hallam, Atlantis
Star short novels. + Pohl, Frederik
Star smashers of the galaxy rangers. + Harrison, Harry
The star spangled crunch. + Congdon, Richard
Star surgeon. + Nourse, Alan E.

Star surgeon. + White, James
Star trail. + Crumley, Thomas W.
The star treasure. + Laumer, Keith
Star trek. + Blish, James
Star trek concordance. + Jones, Dorothy
Star trek 8. + Blish, James
Star trek 5. + Blish, James
Star trek 4. + Blish, James
Star trek, log one. + Foster, Alan Dean
Star trek, log two. + Foster, Alan Dean
Star trek: Mission to Horatius. + Reynolds, Mack
Star trek 9. + Blish, James
Star trek 7. + Blish, James
Star trek 6. + Blish, James
Star trek 10. + Blish, James
Star trek 3. + Blish, James
Star trek 2. + Blish, James
Star trove. + Bulmer, Kenneth
The star venturers. + Bulmer, Kenneth
The star virus. + Bayley, Barrington J.
The star wasps. + Williams, Robert Moore
Star Watchman. + Bova, Ben
Star ways. + Anderson, Poul
Star Well. + Panshin, Alexei
The star witches. + Lymington, John
Star wolf! + White, Ted
The Star Woman. + Bedford-Jones, H.
Starblood. + Koontz, Dean R.
Starboy. + Biemiller, Carl
Starbrat. + Morressy, John
Starbreed. + Clow, Martha deMey
Starburst. + Bester, Alfred
Starchild. + Pohl, Frederik
Stardreamer. + Smith, Cordwainer
Stardrift, and other fantastic flotsam. + Petaja, Emil
The stardroppers. + Brunner, John
Starfire. + Buckner, Robert
The Starfire. + Edgar, Ken
Starfire. + Richardson, Dale
Starflight 3000. + Mackelworth, R. W.
Starhaven. + Jorgenson, Ivar
Stark #2; The hounds of Skaith. + Brackett, Leigh
The Starkahn of Rhada. + Gilman, Robert Cham
The Starkenden quest. + Collins, Gilbert
The starlight barking. + Smith, Dodie
The starlit corridor. + Mansfield, Roger
Starman. + McWilliams, J. A.
Starman Jones. + Heinlein, Robert A.
Starman's quest. + Silverberg, Robert
Starmasters' gambit. + Klein, Gerard
The starmen. + Brackett, Leigh
Starmind. + Van Arnam, Dave
The stars and under. + Crispin, Edmund
The stars are ours. + Bulmer, H. K.
The stars are ours! + Norton, Andre
The stars are too high. + Bahnson, Agnew H. Jr.
The stars around us. + Hoskins, Robert
The stars came down. + Saxon, Richard
The stars incline. + Judson, Jeanne
The stars, like dust. + Asimov, Isaac
The stars my destination. + Bester, Alfred
The stars scream murder. + Reeve, Arthur B.
The stars will judge. + Greenfield, Irving A.
The stars will wait. + Hasse, Henry L.
The starseekers. + Garnett, Dav
Starshine. + Sturgeon, Theodore
Starship. + Aldiss, Brian W.
Starship Intercourse. + Wilhelm, Lambert
Starship through space. + Correy, Lee
Starship troopers. + Heinlein, Robert A.
Starswarm. + Aldiss, Brian W.

The story of Gosta Berling. + Lagerlof, Selma
The story of Gulliver's travels. + Swift, Jonathan
The story of Happinolande, and other legends. + Bunce, Oliver Bell
The story of Kastan. + Ekberg, C. Whitworth
The story of my village. + Stacpoole, H. deVere
The story of Scraggles. + James, George Wharton
The story of Sensa. + Collins, Mabel
The story of Sintram and his companions. + La Motte-Fouque, Friedrich de
The story of the amulet. + Nesbit, E.
The story of the bold Pecopin. + Hugo, Victor
The story of the Glittering Plain. + Morris, William
The story of the other wise man. + Van Dyke, Henry
The story of the unknown church; and, Lindenborg Pool. + Morris, William
The story of the unknown church, and other tales. + Morris, William
The story of Undine. + La Motte-Fouque, Friedrich de
The story of Venus and Tannhauser. + Beardsley, Aubrey
The story of Wan and the remarkable shrub; and, The story of Ching-Kwei and the destinies. + Bramah, Ernest
Stowaway to Mars. + Beynon, John
Stowaway to the Moon. + Shelton, William R.
Stowaway to the Mushroom Planet. + Cameron, Eleanor
Stranded in Heaven. + Crottet, Robert
Strange adventures in science fiction. + Conklin, Groff
Strange adventures in time. + Green, Roger Lancelyn
The strange adventures of Israel Pendray. + Hocking, Silas K.
The strange adventures of Mr. Middleton. + Curtis, Wardon Allan
Strange and fantastic stories. + Margolies, Joseph A.
Strange assembly. + Gawsworth, John
Strange awakening. + Quick, Dorothy
Strange beasts and unnatural monsters. + Stern, Philip Van Doren
Strange bedfellows. + Scortia, Thomas N.
The strange bedfellows of Montague Ames. + Parker, Norton
Strange caravan. + Lawrence, Margery
The strange case of Big Harry. + Johnson, Frosty
The strange case of Dr. Bruno. + Daniel, F. E.
Strange case of Dr. Jekyll and Mr. Hyde. + Stevenson, Robert Louis
The strange case of Dr. Jekyll and Mr. Hyde, and other fables. + Stevenson, Robert Louis
The strange case of Dr. Jekyll and Mr. Hyde, and other famous tales. + Stevenson, Robert Louis
The strange case of Dr. Jekyll and Mr. Hyde, and other macabre stories. + none
The strange case of Dr. Jekyll and Mr. Hyde, and other stories. + Stevenson, Robert Louis
The strange case of Dr. Jekyll and Mr. Hyde; and, The story of a lie. + Stevenson, Robert Louis
The strange case of Dr. Jekyll and Mr. Hyde, fables, other stories, and fragments. + Stevenson, Robert Louis
The strange case of Miss Annie Spragg. + Bromfield, Louis
The strange case of Mr. Pelham. + Armstrong, Anthony
The strange cases of Dr. Stanchon. + Bacon, Josephine Daskam
A strange conflict. + Batchelor, John M.
Strange conflict. + Wheatley, Dennis
Strange conquest. + Harvey, Walter
Strange daughter. + de Wohl, Louis
A strange destiny. + Dawe, Carlton
A strange discovery. + Dake, Charles Romyn
The strange doctor, and other mystic stories. + Van der Elst, Violet

Strange doings. + Lafferty, R. A.
Strange ecstasies. + Parry, Michel
Strange ends and discoveries. + Housman, Laurence
Strange evil. + Gaskell, Jane
The strange experiences of Mr. Verschoyle. + Speight, T. W.
The strange flight of Frank Shapar. + Milligan, Alfred L.
The strange friend of Tito Gil. + Alarcon, Pedro de
Strange gateways. + Price, E. Hoffmann
The strange genius of David Lindsay. + Pick, J. B. & Wilson, Colin & Visiak, E. H.
Strange gift. + Bushnell, Adelyn
Strange gods. + Elwood, Roger
Strange happenings. + none
Strange happenings. + Vitarelli, Robert
Strange harvest. + Wandrei, Donald
Strange houses. + Jarrett, Cora
Strange hunger. + Hervey, Michael
The strange invaders. + Llewellyn, Alun
The strange inventor. + Hyde, Mark Powell
Strange journey. + Cairnes, Maud
The strange journeys of Colonel Polders. + Dunsany, Lord
A strange land. + Ryark, Felix
Strange life of Ivan Osokin. + Ouspensky, P. D.
The strange light. + Reeves, James
Strange love stories. + none
Strange lust. + none
A strange manuscript found in a copper cylinder. + (De Mille, James)
Strange news from another star, and other tales. + Hesse, Hermann
Strange news from Heaven. + Griffiths, Alan
Strange offspring. + none
The strange old man. + Skaife, S. H.
The strange ones. + Torro, Pel
The strange papers of Dr. Blayre. + Blayre, Christopher
Strange paradise. + Daniels, Dorothy
Strange paradise #2; Island of evil. + Daniels, Dorothy
Strange paradise #3; Raxl, voodoo priestess. + Daniels, Dorothy
A strange people. + Batchelor, John M.
Strange ports of call. + Derleth, August
The strange quest. + Stables, Gordon
Strange relations. + Farmer, Philip Jose
Strange romance. + Herbert, Benson
Strange seas and shores. + Davidson, Avram
Strange secrets told by A. Conan Doyle and others. + none
Strange signposts. + Elwood, Roger & Moskowitz, Sam
Strange stories. + Blackwood, Algernon
Strange stories. + Jepson, R. W.
Strange stories. + Sorensen, Villy
Strange stories of coincidence and ghostly adventure. + none
Strange stories--the last seven. + Hardie, John L.
A strange story. + Lytton, Edward
A strange story; and, Eugene Aram. + Lytton, Edward
A strange story; and, The haunted and the haunters. + Lytton, Edward
The strange story of Ahrinziman. + Silvani, Anita
The strange story of Hester Wynne. + Colmore, G.
The strange story of William Hyde. + Casey, Patrick & Casey, Terence
Strange tales. + none
Strange tales. + Rathbone, Basil
Strange tales from "Blackwood." + none
Strange tales of the borders, old and new. + Boyd, Halbert J.
Strange tales, second selection. + none

Supernatural tales. + Lee, Vernon
Supernatural tales of terror and suspense. + Hitch-
  cock, Alfred
Supernatural tales I. + Grant, Gary
Supernatural tales II. + Grant, Gary
Superspill. + Becker, Mary Kay & Coburn, Patricia
Superstition. + McKenna, Stephen
Superstoe. + Borden, William
The supplemental checklist of fantastic literature.
  + Day, Bradford M.
The supreme mystery. + Symons, J. H.
The supreme rulers. + Houghton, J. A.
Sure-Dart. + Costello, Frederick H.
The surly sullen bell. + Kirk, Russell
The surprise of the Channel Tunnel. + Forth, C.
The surprising adventures of Baron Munchausen. +
  (Raspe, Rudolf)
The surprising adventures of Captain Gulliver in a
  voyage to the Kingdom of Lilliput. + Swift, Jona-
  than
The surprising adventures of the renowned Baron Mun-
  chausen abridged. + (Raspe, Rudolf)
The surprising adventures, singular travels, miraculous
  escapes, and wonderful voyages and campaigns of the
  renowned Baron Munchausen. + (Raspe, Rudolf)
The surprising travels and adventures of Baron Munchau-
  sen. + (Raspe, Rudolf)
Survival from infinity. + Elwood, Roger
Survival margin. + Maine, Charles Eric
Survival printout. + Allison, Leonard & Jenkin, Leo-
  nard & Perrault, Robert
Survival project. + Muller, John E.
Survival ship, and other stories. + Merril, Judith
Survival world. + Long, Frank Belknap
The survivor. + Parry, Dennis
The survivor, and others. + Derleth, August & Love-
  craft, H. P.
The survivors. + Godwin, Tom
The survivors. + Griffiths, John
The survivors. + Sibson, Francis H.
The survivors. + Tabori, Paul
Suspension. + Fane, Bron
Svend & his brethren. + Morris, William
Swallow. + Haggard, H. Rider
Swallowed by an earthquake. + Fawcett, E. D.
The swami's curse. + Penny, F. E.
Swampworld west. + Chapdelaine, Perry A.
Swapping with Satan. + Evans, Grant
The swarm. + Herzog, Arthur
Swastika night. + Constantine, Murray
Swear by Apollo. + Barker, Shirley
The sweat of fear. + Dennis, Robert C.
Sweeney's Island. + Christopher, John
Sweepers of the sea. + Wetmore, Claude H.
Sweet chariot. + Baker, Frank
Sweet dreams. + Frayn, Michael
Sweet illusions. + Regberg, S. L.
Sweet land of liberty. + Silberstang, Edwin
Sweet river in the morning. + Clewes, Winston
Sweet Rocket. + Johnston, Mary
A sweet, sweet summer. + Gaskell, Jane
The sweet taste of burning. + Andreota, Paul
Sweetwater. + Yep, Laurence
The swine-gods, and other visions. + Bloch, Regina
  Miriam
The swing in the summerhouse. + Langton, Jane
Switch bitch. + Dahl, Roald
Switch-off. + Smythe, R. John
Switch on the light. + Thomson, Christine Campbell
The swoop! + Wodehouse, P. G.
The swoop of the vulture. + Blyth, James
Swooping vengeance. + Dorman, Geoffrey

A sword above the night. + Lymington, John
The sword and the stallion. + Moorcock, Michael
Sword in the snow. + Tubb, E. C.
The sword in the stone. + White, T. H.
The Sword of Aldones. + Bradley, Marion Zimmer
The sword of Conan. + Howard, Robert E.
The sword of Culann. + Levin, Betty
The sword of Lankor. + Cory, Howard L.
The sword of Morning Star. + Meade, Richard
The sword of Rhiannon. + Brackett, Leigh
Sword of the dawn. + Moorcock, Michael
The sword of the Golem. + Rothberg, Abraham
The sword of the spirits. + Christopher, John
Sword of tomorrow. + Kuttner, Henry
The sword of Welleran, and other stories. + Dunsany,
  Lord
The sword of Welleran, and other tales of enchantment.
  + Dunsany, Lord
The sword swallower. + Goulart, Ron
Swordmen of Vistar. + Nuetzel, Charles
Swords against death. + Leiber, Fritz
Swords against tomorrow. + Hoskins, Robert
Swords against wizardry. + Leiber, Fritz
Swords and deviltry. + Leiber, Fritz
Swords and sorcery. + de Camp, L. Sprague
Swords in the mist. + Leiber, Fritz
The swords of Lankhmar. + Leiber, Fritz
Swords of Mars. + Burroughs, Edgar Rice
Swords of the barbarians. + Bulmer, Kenneth
Swordships of Scorpio. + Akers, Alan Burt
The swordsman of Mars. + Kline, Otis Adelbert
Swordsmen and supermen. + (Grant, Donald M.)
Swordsmen in the sky. + Wollheim, Donald A.
Sybaris, and other homes. + Hale, Edward E.
Sylva. + Vercors
The Symmetrians. + Harker, Kenneth
Symzonia. + Seaborn, Adam
Syn. + Jones, Raymond F.
The Syndic. + Kornbluth, C. M.
Synthajoy. + Compton, D. G.
The synthetic man. + Sturgeon, Theodore
Synthetic men of Mars. + Burroughs, Edgar Rice
The synthetic ones. + Roberts, Lionel
Syra. + Gay, William S.
A syrup of the bees. + Bain, F. W.
Syzygy. + Coney, Michael G.

The T. C. Bridges adventure book. + Bridges, T. C.
T.H.E.M. + Edmondson, G. C.
THX 1138. + Bova, Ben
t zero. + Calvino, Italo
Taash and the jesters. + McKenzie, Ellen Kindt
The table. + Curtis, Robert
Tabletop. + Phillpotts, Eden
Taboo. + none
Taboo. + Cabell, James Branch
Tactics of conquest. + Malzberg, Barry N.
The tactics of mistake. + Dickson, Gordon R.
The tadpole of an archangel, and other naval stories.
  + Drury, W. P.
The tadpole of an archangel, the petrified eye, and
  other naval stories. + Drury, W. P.
Tahara among African tribes. + Sherman, Harold M.
Tahara, boy king of the desert. + Sherman, Harold M.
Tahara, boy mystic of India. + Sherman, Harold M.
Tahara in the land of Yucatan. + Sherman, Harold M.
The tailors' cake. + Devaulx, Noel
Take away the flowers; &, Fuller's world. + Chilton,
  Irma
Take heed of loving me. + Conway, Laura
Take me to your leader. + Waller, Leslie & Waller,
  Louise [see Addendum]

Take me to your president. + Wibberley, Leonard
Take three witches. + Mian, Mary
Takeoff. + Kornbluth, C. M.
Takeover. + Goldman, Lawrence Louis
Take-over. + Rossetto, Louis Jr.
The taking of Dover. + Lester, H. F.
Talargain. + Gard, Joyce
Talargain, the seal's whelp. + Gard, Joyce
Talbot Mundy biblio. + Day, Bradford M.
The Talbott Agreement. + Addeo, Edmond G. & Garvin, Richard M.
The tale. + Goethe, Johann Wolfgang von
A tale of ancient Egypt. + Heckel, Frederick C.
The tale of Christopher. + Colton, Abigail
The tale of Lal. + Paton, Raymond
The tale of terror. + Birkhead, Edith
The tale of the big computer. + Johannesson, Olof
The tale of the future. + Clarke, I. F.
The tale of the future, second edition. + Clarke, I. F.
The tale of the House of the Wolfings. + Morris, William
The tale of the land of green ginger. + Langley, Noel
A tale of three lions. + Haggard, H. Rider
A tale of two clocks. + Schmitz, James H.
Tale of two futures. + Heyne, William P.
A talent for the invisible. + Goulart, Ron
The talent scout. + Gary, Romain
Talents, Incorporated. + Leinster, Murray
Tales. + Gautier, Theophile
Tales. + Hauff, Wilhelm
Tales. + Hunt, Leigh
The tales. + Poe, Edgar Allan
Tales and fantasies. + Stevenson, Robert Louis
Tales and poems. + Poe, Edgar Allan
Tales and romances. + Gautier, Theophile
Tales and sketches. + Poe, Edgar Allan
Tales; and, The raven and other poems. + Poe, Edgar Allan
Tales before midnight. + Benet, Stephen Vincent
Tales beyond time. + de Camp, L. Sprague & de Camp, Catherine Crook
Tales by three brothers. + Robinson, E. Kay & Robinson, Phil & Robinson, H. Perry
Tales, criticisms, poems. + Poe, Edgar Allan
Tales for a stormy night. + none
Tales for Christmas Eve. + Broughton, Rhoda
Tales from a mother-of-pearl casket. + France, Anatole
Tales from Gautier. + Gautier, Theophile
Tales from Gavagan's Bar. + de Camp, L. Sprague & Pratt, Fletcher
Tales from Gulliver's travels. + Swift, Jonathan
Tales from Hoffmann. + Hoffmann, E. T. A.
Tales from Jokai. + Jokai, Maurus
Tales from Nights black agents. + Leiber, Fritz
Tales from Not long for this world. + Derleth, August
Tales from the beyond. + Lloyd, John
Tales from the crypt. + Oleck, Jack
Tales from the galaxies. + Pearson, Michael & Williams-Ellis, Amabel
Tales from the German. + Feiling, C. A. & Oxenford, John
Tales from the House of mystery. + Oleck, Jack
Tales from the House of mystery, volume 2. + Oleck, Jack
Tales from the travels of Baron Munchausen. + (Raspe, Rudolf)
Tales from the White Hart. + Clarke, Arthur C.
Tales from Underwood. + Keller, David H.
Tales grotesque. + Poe, Edgar Allan

Tales grotesque and curious. + Akutagawa, Ryunosuke
Tales grotesque and weird. + Poe, Edgar Allan
Tales in a jugular vein. + Bloch, Robert
Tales in prose and verse, and dramas. + Heath, Thomas Edward
Tales, legends, and historical reminiscences of the Scottish Covenanters. + Guthrie, Ellen Jane
Tales of a Dalai Lama. + Delattre, Pierre
Tales of a voyager to the Arctic Ocean, vol. I. + (Gillies, R. P.)
Tales of a voyager to the Arctic Ocean, second series. + (Gillies, R. P.)
Tales of adventure, mystery, and imagination. + Poe, Edgar Allan
The tales of Algernon Blackwood. + Blackwood, Algernon
Tales of Chinatown. + Rohmer, Sax
The tales of Clark Ashton Smith. + Cockcroft, T. G. L.
Tales of Conan. + de Camp, L. Sprague & Howard, Robert E.
Tales of cosmic wisdom. + Theodamus
Tales of death. + none
Tales of destiny. + Mitchell, Edmund
Tales of dread. + none
Tales of E. T. A. Hoffmann. + Hoffmann, E. T. A.
Tales of east and west. + Rohmer, Sax
Tales of Edgar Allan Poe. + Poe, Edgar Allan
Tales of effect. + Poe, Edgar Allan
Tales of fantasy. + Jenks, Tudor
Tales of fantasy and fact. + Matthews, Brander
Tales of fear. + none
Tales of ghouls and ghosts. + Bierce, Ambrose
Tales of gooseflesh and laughter. + Wyndham, John
Tales of haunted houses. + Bierce, Ambrose
Tales of Hoffmann. + Hoffmann, E. T. A.
Tales of horror. + Higham, Charles
Tales of horror. + Riefe, Alan
Tales of horror and the supernatural. + Machen, Arthur
Tales of horror and the supernatural, volume one. + Machen, Arthur
Tales of horror and the supernatural, volume two. + Machen, Arthur
Tales of hypnotism and revenge. + Poe, Edgar Allan
Tales of imaginative science. + Poe, Edgar Allan
Tales of life and adventure. + Wells, H. G.
Tales of life and adventure; Tales of wonder. + Wells, H. G.
Tales of love and horror. + Congdon, Don
Tales of love, fantasy, and horror. + Peterson, Russell C.
Tales of moonlight and rain. + Ueda, Akinari
Tales of Mourne. + Rowley, Richard
Tales of mystery. + Poe, Edgar Allan
Tales of mystery. + Rhys, Ernest & Scott, C. A. Dawson
Tales of mystery. + Saintsbury, George
Tales of mystery and horror. + none
Tales of mystery and imagination. + Poe, Edgar Allan
Tales of mystery and imagination, and poems. + Poe, Edgar Allan
Tales of mystery and revenge. + Langley, Noel
Tales of mystery and surprise. + none
Tales of mystery and terror. + Poe, Edgar Allan
Tales of mystery, imagination, and humour. + Poe, Edgar Allan
Tales of mystery, imagination, and humour; and, Poems. + Poe, Edgar Allan
Tales of outer space. + Wollheim, Donald A.
Tales of piracy, crime, and ghosts. + Defoe, Daniel
Tales of science and sorcery. + Smith, Clark Ashton
Tales of science fiction. + Ball, Brian N.
Tales of secret Egypt. + Rohmer, Sax

Tales of soaring science fantasy from "...And some were human." + del Rey, Lester
Tales of soldiers and civilians. + Bierce, Ambrose
Tales of space and time. + Wells, H. G.
Tales of 'strange doings.' + Wheatley, Dennis
Tales of strange happenings. + Wheatley, Dennis
Tales of supernatural terror. + Maupassant, Guy de
Tales of ten worlds. + Clarke, Arthur C.
Tales of terror. + Donovan, Dick
Tales of terror. + French, Joseph Lewis
Tales of terror. + Higham, Charles
Tales of terror. + Karloff, Boris
Tales of terror. + Muspratt, Rosalie
Tales of terror. + Poe, Edgar Allan & Sudak, Eunice
Tales of terror. + St. Clair, Henry
Tales of terror. + Singer, Kurt
Tales of terror and fantasy. + Poe, Edgar Allan
Tales of terror and mystery. + Doyle, A. Conan
Tales of terror and of fantasy. + Poe, Edgar Allan
Tales of terror and surprise. + none
Tales of terror and suspense. + Benedict, Stewart H.
Tales of terror and the supernatural. + Collins, Wilkie
Tales of terror and the unknown. + none
Tales of terror and the unknown. + Blackwood, Algernon
Tales of the caliph. + al Arawiyah
Tales of the caravan, inn, and palace. + Hauff, Wilhelm
Tales of the Covenanters. + Guthrie, Ellen Jane
Tales of the Cthulhu Mythos. + Derleth, August
Tales of the Cthulhu Mythos, vol. 2. + Derleth, August
Tales of the dead. + (Utterson, Sarah)
Tales of the flying mountains. + Anderson, Poul
Tales of the frightened. + Avallone, Michael
The tales of the genii. + (Ridley, James)
Tales of the grotesque. + Lewis, L. A.
Tales of the grotesque and arabesque. + Poe, Edgar Allan
Tales of the grotesque and arabesque, with other stories. + Poe, Edgar Allan
Tales of the macabre. + Singer, Kurt
Tales of the masque. + Pearce, J. H.
Tales of the mysterious and macabre. + Blackwood, Algernon
Tales of the natural and supernatural. + Pei, Mario
The tales of the rat. + Wilis
Tales of the strange and supernatural. + Machen, Arthur
Tales of the supernatural. + none
Tales of the supernatural. + Dumas, Alexandre
Tales of the supernatural. + Greening, Frank
Tales of the supernatural. + Platt, James Junior
Tales of the two borders. + O'Meara, Walter
Tales of the uncanny. + none
Tales of the uncanny. + Singer, Kurt
Tales of the uncanny and supernatural. + Blackwood, Algernon
Tales of the undead. + Blaisdell, Elinore
Tales of the uneasy. + Hunt, Violet
Tales of the unexpected. + Wells, H. G.
Tales of the weird and the west countree. + St. Germain, Marie
Tales of the Wonder Club. + Dryasdust
Tales of the Wonder Club. + Halidom, M. Y.
Tales of the Wonder Club, second series. + Halidom, M. Y.
Tales of the Wonder Club, vol. II-III. + Dryasdust
Tales of three hemispheres. + Dunsany, Lord
Tales of three planets. + Burroughs, Edgar Rice
Tales of time and space. + Olney, Ross R.

The tales of Tusitala. + Stevenson, Robert Louis
Tales of unease. + Burke, John
Tales of wonder. + Dunsany, Lord
Tales of wonder. + Wells, H. G.
Tales out of the east. + Hearn, Lafcadio
Tales, poems, essays. + Poe, Edgar Allan
Tales psychological and gruesome. + Poe, Edgar Allan
Tales to be told in the dark. + Davenport, Basil
Tales to tremble by. + Sutton, Stephen P.
"Talk of the devil." + Butler, Ewan
The talkers. + Chambers, Robert W.
The talking horse. + Anstey, F.
The talking image of Urur. + Hartmann, Franz
The talking jewels. + Diderot, Denis
The talking parcel. + Durrell, Gerald
The talking pussy. + Diderot, Denis
Talking totem. + Chilton, H. Herman
The talking tree. + Tabori, Paul
Talks with a devil. + Ouspensky, P. D.
The tall villa. + Malet, Lucas
Talons of Time. + Twitchell, Paul [see Addendum]
Tam of the fire cave. + Garis, Howard R.
Tam, son of the tiger. + Kline, Otis Adelbert
Tama of the light country. + Cummings, Ray
Tama, princess of Mercury. + Cummings, Ray
Tamar Curze. + St. Luz, Berthe
The tamer of herds. + Rolt-Wheeler, Francis
The taming power. + W. W.
Tanar of Pellucidar. + Burroughs, Edgar Rice
The Tandar saga. + Hanna, W. C.
The Tandem book of ghost stories. + Birkin, Charles
The Tandem book of horror stories. + Birkin, Charles
Tandem horror 3. + Davis, Richard
Tandem horror 2. + Davis, Richard
The tapestry of time. + Crawford, Isabell C.
Tapiola's brave regiment. + Nathan, Robert
Tapster's tapestry. + Coppard, A. E.
The Tar-Aiym Krang. + Foster, Alan Dean
Taran Wanderer. + Alexander, Lloyd
Target: Terra. + Janifer, Laurence M. & Treibich, S. J.
Tarnished utopia. + Jameson, Malcolm
Tarnsman of Gor. + Norman, John
Tarrano, the Conqueror. + Cummings, Ray
Tarry, knight! + Allen, C. R.
Tarry thou till I come. + Croly, George
Tartarian tales. + Gueullette, Thomas
Tarzan alive. + Farmer, Philip Jose
Tarzan and the Abominable Snowmen. + Werper, Barton
Tarzan and the ant men. + Burroughs, Edgar Rice
Tarzan and the castaways. + Burroughs, Edgar Rice
Tarzan and the cave city. + Werper, Barton
Tarzan and the city of gold. + Burroughs, Edgar Rice
Tarzan and the Forbidden City. + Burroughs, Edgar Rice
Tarzan and "The Foreign Legion." + Burroughs, Edgar Rice
Tarzan and the golden lion. + Burroughs, Edgar Rice
Tarzan and the jewels of Opar. + Burroughs, Edgar Rice
Tarzan and the Leopard Men. + Burroughs, Edgar Rice
Tarzan and the lion man. + Burroughs, Edgar Rice
Tarzan and the lost empire. + Burroughs, Edgar Rice
Tarzan and the lost safari. + none
Tarzan and the madman. + Burroughs, Edgar Rice
Tarzan and the Silver Globe. + Werper, Barton
Tarzan and the snake people. + Werper, Barton
Tarzan and the Tarzan twins. + Burroughs, Edgar Rice
Tarzan and the Tarzan twins with Jad-Bal-Ja, the golden lion. + Burroughs, Edgar Rice
Tarzan and the valley of gold. + Leiber, Fritz
Tarzan and the winged invaders. + Werper, Barton

Tarzan at the Earth's core. + Burroughs, Edgar Rice
Tarzan in the forbidden city. + Burroughs, Edgar Rice
Tarzan, Lord of the Jungle. + Burroughs, Edgar Rice
Tarzan of the apes. + Burroughs, Edgar Rice
Tarzan of the movies. + Essoe, Gabe
Tarzan the invincible. + Burroughs, Edgar Rice
Tarzan the magnificent. + Burroughs, Edgar Rice
Tarzan the terrible. + Burroughs, Edgar Rice
Tarzan the untamed. + Burroughs, Edgar Rice
Tarzan triumphant. + Burroughs, Edgar Rice
The Tarzan twins. + Burroughs, Edgar Rice
Tarzan's jungle tales. + Burroughs, Edgar Rice
Tarzan's quest. + Burroughs, Edgar Rice
Tas and the postal rocket. + Eliott, E. C.
Tas and the space machine. + Eliott, E. C.
Task flight. + Lang, King
A taste for honey. + Heard, H. F.
A taste for murder. + Heard, H. F.
Tau zero. + Anderson, Poul
Le taureau blanc. + Voltaire
Taurus Four. + Vale, Rena
Tea at Crumbo Castle. + King-Hall, Magdalen
Teacher's guide; Flowers for Algernon. + Boyle, John
  Patrick
Teacher's guide; science fiction. + Bradbury, Ray &
  Olfson, Lewy
Teaching SF. + Williamson, Jack
Teaching tomorrow. + Calkins, Elizabeth & McGhan,
  Barry
Teach's light. + Wechter, Nell Wise
The Technicolor time machine. + Harrison, Harry
Technos. + Tubb, E. C.
Teddy in darkest Africa. + Coggs, Dr.
Tedious brief tales of Granta and Gramarye. + "Ingul-
  phus"
Teenage ghost stories, volume 1. + Hallinan, Tim
Teen-age outer space stories. + Furman, A. L.
Teen-age science fiction stories. + Elam, Richard M.
Teenage space adventures. + Furman, A. L.
Teen-age super science stories. + Elam, Richard M.
Teenocracy. + Shirley, Robert
The Teetotalitarian state. + De Chair, Somerset
Teg's 1994. + Scott, J. M. & Theobald, Robert
Telepath. + Sellings, Arthur
Telepathist. + Brunner, John
Telepower. + Hoffman, Lee
Tele-sex. + Malcolm, Ed
The television detective. + Keller, David H.
The television girl. + Wentworth-James, G. de S.
The tell-tale heart. + Poe, Edgar Allan
The tell-tale heart, and other stories. + Poe, Edgar
  Allan
The tell-tale picture gallery. + Blavatsky, H. P. &
  Judge, W. Q.
The Telsa raiders. + Bowen, Robert Sidney
The Telzey toy. + Schmitz, James H.
The temple of Amon Ra. + Gray, Mary
The temple of Demos. + Bower, B. M.
The Temple of Dreams. + Bo'ld, Paul
The temple of fire. + Ashley, Fred
The temple of fire. + Ramsden, Lewis
The temple of Sahr. + Pengreep, William
The temple of the dead. + Norwood, Victor
The temple of the past. + Wul, Stefan
The Temple of the Ten. + Bedford-Jones, H. & Robert-
  son, W. C.
Temple of the Winds. + Hyde, Christopher
The temple servant, and other stories. + Morrough,
  E. R.
The temptation of Friar Gonsol. + Field, Eugene
The temptation of Saint Antony. + Flaubert, Gustave

Ten days to oblivion. + Cooney, Michael
Ten days to the Moon. + Mingston, R. Gresham
Ten from infinity. + Jorgensen, Ivar
Ten from tomorrow. + Tubb, E. C.
Ten great mysteries. + Poe, Edgar Allan
Ten million years to Friday. + Lymington, John
Ten minute stories. + Blackwood, Algernon
Ten poplars. + Magriska, Helene
Ten tales. + Bierce, Ambrose
Ten tales. + Maginn, William
Ten tales calculated to give you shudders. + Olney,
  Ross R.
Ten thousand light-years from home. + Tiptree, James
  Jr.
10,000 years in a block of ice. + Boussenard, Louis
Ten times one is ten. + Ingham, Frederic
Ten tomorrows. + Elwood, Roger
Ten top stories. + Sohn, David A.
Ten years hence? + Coron, Hannah
Ten years to doomsday. + Anderson, Chester & Kurland,
  Michael
The tenant of Cromlech Cottage. + Hocking, Joseph
10th annual edition, the year's best SF. + Merril,
  Judith
10th annual S-F. + Merril, Judith
The tenth Fontana book of great ghost stories. +
  Chetwynd-Hayes, R.
The tenth Galaxy reader. + Pohl, Frederik
The tenth ghost book. + Chambers, Aidan
The tenth Pan book of horror stories. + van Thal,
  Herbert
The tenth planet. + Cooper, Edmund
The tenth planet. + Sterling, Brett
The tenth session. + Quilty, Rafe
The 10th victim. + Sheckley, Robert
Terminal beach. + Ballard, J. G.
The terminal man. + Crichton, Michael
Terminus. + Daventry, Leonard
Terminus. + Perkins, Michael
Termush. + Holm, Sven
Terra. + Lang, Gregor
Terra! + Lang, King
The terraces of night. + Lawrence, Margery
Terrania. + Bradford, Columbus
Terrenia. + Grahame, Edith
The terrible awakening. + Desmond, Hugh
The terrible churnadryne. + Cameron, Eleanor
The terrible sexy secret of Castle McNab. + Sterling,
  Barry
Terrible tales; French. + T., C. J.
Terrible tales; German. + T., C. J.
Terrible tales; Italian. + T., C. J.
Terrible tales; Spanish. + T., C. J.
The terrible ten. + Knight, Mallory T.
Terribly strange tales. + Sechrist, Elizabeth Hough
  & Woolsey, Janette
Terrifying tales. + Dark, James
The terror. + Creasey, John
The Terror. + Machen, Arthur
Terror! + Netherwood, Bryan
Terror! + Shaw, Larry T.
Terror at night. + Williams, Herbert
Terror by night. + Chetwynd-Hayes, R.
The terror by night. + Mattingly, Sidney
Terror by night. + Thomson, Christine Campbell
Terror by satellite. + Walters, Hugh
The terror catches up. + Kaner, H.
The terror from Timorkal. + Pragnell, Festus
Terror in the modern vein. + Wollheim, Donald A.
The terror in the Navy. + Robeson, Kenneth
The terror in the sky. + Mackenzie, Nigel
The Terror of the Air. + Le Queux, William

Terror of the seven crypts. + Aubin, Etienne
The terror of the Shape. + Jude, Christopher
The terror of Villadonga. + Household, Geoffrey
Terror on planet Ionus. + Adler, Allen
Terror strikes. + Firth, N. Wesley
Terror-trap! + Lazenby, Norman
Terror wears a feathered cloak. + Crawford, Thelmar
Terrors. + none
Terrors of the screen. + Manchel, Frank
The test-tube babies. + Jackson, Noel
Test tube baby. + Fuller, Sam
Testament XXI. + Snyder, Guy
The testing of Tertius. + Newman, Robert
Tetrasomy two. + Rossiter, Oscar
Texas, Brooklyn, and Heaven. + Benefield, Barry
The Texas-Israeli War: 1999. + Saunders, Jakes &
  Waldrop, Howard
The texts of Festival. + Farren, Mick
Thais. + France, Anatole
Thanks for the rubies, now please pass the Moon. +
  Schary, Jill
Thanks to Claudius. + Leeming, John F.
Tharkol, lord of the unknown. + Hamilton, Edmond
That first affair, and other sketches. + Mitchell,
  J. A.
That hideous strength. + Lewis, C. S.
That something. + Woodbridge, W. W.
"That very Mab." + (Kendall, May)
Their man in the White House. + Ardies, Tom
Their winged destiny. + Horner, Donald W.
Themes in science fiction. + Kelley, Leo P.
Then we shall hear singing. + Jameson, Storm
Theodora, a soul on fire. + Williams, Frances Fenwick
Theodore Savage. + Hamilton, Cicely
Theophile Gautier. + Gautier, Theophile
"Theory of flight." + Casolet, Jacques
There is another Heaven. + Nathan, Robert
There was a door. + Mundy, Talbot
There was a king in Egypt. + Lorimer, Norma
There was a little man. + Jones, Constance Bridges &
  Jones, Guy Pearce
There was once a city. + Turton, Godfrey
There were no Asper ladies. + Ascher, Eugene
There were two pirates. + Cabell, James Branch
There will be time. + Anderson, Poul
These mortals. + Irwin, Margaret
These restless heads. + Cabell, Branch
These savage futurians. + High, Philip E.
These will chill you. + Sheehan, Richard G. & Wright,
  Lee
They. + Kipling, Rudyard
They. + Mannes, Marya
'They'; and, The brushwood boy. + Kipling, Rudyard
They came from Mars. + Cockcroft, W. P.
They came from the sea. + Steele, Alex
They came, they saw. + Hallums, James R.
They chose to be birds. + Dearmer, Geoffrey
They found Atlantis. + Wheatley, Dennis
They never come back. + Brett, Leo
They return at evening. + Wakefield, H. R.
They shall have stars. + Blish, James
They shall not die. + Parkinson, H. F.
They used dark forces. + Wheatley, Dennis
They walk again. + de la Mare, Colin
They walked like men. + Simak, Clifford D.
They went. + Douglas, Norman
They went on together. + Nathan, Robert
They'd rather be right. + Clifton, Mark & Riley,
  Frank
The thief of Bagdad. + Abdullah, Achmed
Thief of Baghdad. + Wormser, Richard
Thief of Llarn. + Fox, Gardner F.

The thief of Thoth. + Carter, Lin
Thieves of the air. + Herbert, Benson & Pragnell,
  Festus
Thin air. + Jenkins, Alan C.
A thin ghost, and others. + James, M. R.
The thing. + Madison, J. J.
The thing, and other stories. + Campbell, John W.
The thing from another world. + Campbell, John W.
The Thing from the lake. + Ingram, Eleanor M.
The thing in B-3. + Powell, Talmage
The thing in the cellar. + Keller, David H.
The thing in the woods. + Williams, Harper
A thing of the past. + Gridban, Volsted
The thing that made love. + Reed, David V.
Things. + Howard, Ivan
Things...and other things. + Hartl, Harold W.
Things with claws. + Burnett, Whit & Burnett, Hallie
The thinking machine affair. + Bernard, Joel
The thinking seat. + Tate, Peter
The third Armada ghost book. + Danby, Mary
The third book of Tros of Samothrace; Liafail. +
  Mundy, Talbot
The third ear. + Siodmak, Curt
The third eye. + Cogswell, Theodore
The third flight of the Starfire. + Mumford, Edwin
The third Fontana book of great ghost stories. +
  Aickman, Robert
The third Fontana book of great horror stories. +
  Bernard, Christine
The third force. + Matheson, Hugh
Third from the Sun. + Matheson, Richard
The third Galaxy reader. + Gold, H. L.
The third ghost book. + Asquith, Cynthia
The third Isaac Asimov double. + Asimov, Isaac
The third level. + Finney, Jack
The Third Mutant. + Elliot, Lee
A third of life. + Maxwell, Perriton
The third omnibus of crime. + Sayers, Dorothy L.
The third Pan book of horror stories. + van Thal,
  Herbert
The third policeman. + O'Brien, Flann
The third road. + Bacon, Martha
The third season supplement to the Star trek concor-
  dance. + Jones, Dorothy & Trimble, Bjo
The third window. + Sedgwick, Anne Douglas
The third world. + Fairman, Henry Clay
The thirst quenchers. + Raphael, Rick
The thirsty sword. + Leighton, Robert
13. + Loraine, Philip
13 above the night. + Conklin, Groff
The thirteen bracelets. + Lory, Robert
The 13 clocks. + Thurber, James
The 13 clocks; and, The wonderful O. + Thurber, James
Thirteen French science-fiction stories. + Knight,
  Damon
13 ghostly tales. + Littledale, Freya
Thirteen ghostly yarns. + Sechrist, Elizabeth Hough
13 great stories of science fiction. + Conklin, Groff
13 more stories they wouldn't let me do on TV. +
  Hitchcock, Alfred
Thirteen o'clock. + Benet, Stephen Vincent
Thirteen o'clock, and other zero hours. + Kornbluth,
  C. M.
13 seconds that rocked the world. + Meyer, John J.
Thirteen uncanny tales. + Green, Roger Lancelyn
The 13th immortal. + Silverberg, Robert
The 13th Pan book of horror stories. + van Thal,
  Herbert
The thirtieth piece of silver. + Hayes, Lilian
30-day wonder. + Wilson, Richard
The thirty days. + Wales, Hubert
The thirty-first of February. + Bond, Nelson S.

The thirty-first of June. + Priestley, J. B.
Thirty million gas masks. + Campion, Sarah
Thirty pieces of silver. + Kelland, Clarence B.
Thirty seconds over New York. + Buchard, Robert
Thirty-six inches of adventure. + Arnac, Marcel
Thirty strange stories. + Wells, H. G.
30 tales of romance and adventure. + Shaw, Arnold
Thirty years of Arkham House. + Derleth, August
This above all. + Shiel, M. P.
This business of Bomfog. + Duke, Madelaine
This creeping evil. + 'Sea-Lion'
This delicate creature. + O'Leary, Con
This fortress world. + Gunn, James E.
This immortal. + Zelazny, Roger
This incredible adventure. + Macmillan, Armour
This inward light. + Warren, J. Russell
This is armageddon. + Howorth, Muriel K.
This is Moscow speaking, and other stories. + Daniel',
   Yuli
This is Sylvia. + Wilson, Sandy
This island Earth. + Jones, Raymond F.
This mortal coil. + Asquith, Cynthia
This mortal coil. + Warren, J. Russell
This perfect day. + Levin, Ira
This planet for sale. + Hay, George
This second Earth. + Bowers, R. L.
This side of infinity. + Carr, Terry
This side of Jordan. + Bradford, Roark
This siren song. + Elmore, Ernest
This star shall abide. + Engdahl, Sylvia Louise
This strange tomorrow. + Long, Frank Belknap
This suitcase is going to explode. + Ardies, Tom
This time tomorrow. + Paine, Lauran
This was Ivor Trent. + Houghton, Claude
This way out. + Littell, Philip
This witch. + Tucker, Wilson
This world is taboo. + Leinster, Murray
Thomas and the warlock. + Hunter, Mollie
Thomas Boobig. + Marshall, Luther
Thomasina. + Gallico, Paul
Thongor against the Gods. + Carter, Lin
Thongor and the dragon city. + Carter, Lin
Thongor and the Wizard of Lemuria. + Carter, Lin
Thongor at the end of time. + Carter, Lin
Thongor fights the Pirates of Tarakus. + Carter, Lin
Thongor in the City of Magicians. + Carter, Lin
Thongor of Lemuria. + Carter, Lin
The Thorne Smith three-bagger. + Smith, Thorne
The Thorne Smith 3-decker. + Smith, Thorne
The Thorne Smith triplets. + Smith, Thorne
Thorns. + Silverberg, Robert
Those idiots from Earth. + Wilson, Richard
Those who can. + Wilson, Robin Scott
Those who watch. + Silverberg, Robert
Thoth. + (Nicholson, Joseph Shield)
Thou hast a devil. + Hutchinson, R. C.
The thought projector. + Keller, David H.
The thought-reading machine. + Maurois, Andre
The thought-rope. + Coleridge, Christabel
The thought translator. + none
A thousand ages. + Ellis, D. E.
A thousand and one quarters of hours. + (Gueullette,
   Thomas Simon)
The thousand coffins affair. + Avallone, Michael
The Thousand-headed Man. + Robeson, Kenneth
A thousand miles an hour. + Givins, Robert C.
A thousand miles an hour. + Strang, Herbert
A thousand years a minute. + Claudy, Carl H.
A thousand years of yesterdays. + Lewis, H. Spencer
A 1,000 years on. + Muller, John E.
The thousandth frog. + Hubbard, Wynant Davis
The thrall of hypno. + Perry Rhodan 20

The thrall of Leif the Lucky. + Liljencrantz, Ottilie
   A.
Thrawn Janet; Markheim. + Stevenson, Robert Louis
Threads of time. + Silverberg, Robert
Threatened people. + Borodin, George
Three adventure novels. + Haggard, H. Rider
Three against the witch world. + Norton, Andre
The three brothers. + Pickersgill, Joshua
Three by Heinlein. + Heinlein, Robert A.
The three days' terror. + Fletcher, J. S.
Three eighteenth century romances. + Steeves,
   Harrison R.
The three eternals. + Binder, Eando
The three eyes. + Le Blanc, Maurice
The three eyes of evil; and, Earth's last fortress.
   + van Vogt, A. E.
Three faces of science fiction. + Lowndes, Robert W.
The three faces of time. + Long, Frank Belknap
Three faces of time. + Merwin, Sam Jr.
Three fantastic tales. + Houghton, Claude
Three for tomorrow. + none
Three from Catfish Bend. + Burman, Ben Lucien
3 from out there. + Margulies, Leo
Three ghosts. + Strode, William
Three go back. + Mitchell, J. Leslie
Three gothic novels. + Fairclough, Peter
3 great classics. + none
Three hearts and three lions. + Anderson, Poul
334. + Disch, Thomas M.
"333." + Crawford, Joseph H. Jr. & Donahue, James J.
   & Grant, Donald M.
Three hundred years hence. + Griffith, Mary
Three hundred years hence. + Hay, William Delisle
The three impostors. + Machen, Arthur
Three in one. + Margulies, Leo
Three in three. + Price, Roger
Three legends. + Gallico, Paul
Three lines of old French. + Merritt, A.
Three marchen. + Hoffmann, E. T. A.
Three Martian novels. + Burroughs, Edgar Rice
Three men and a maid. + Ludlow, Phill
Three men make a world. + Marvell, Andrew
The three Mulla-mulgars. + de la Mare, Walter
Three novels. + Capek, Karel
Three novels. + Knight, Damon
Three novels. + Peacock, Thomas Love
Three novels. + Wells, H. G.
Three paths. + Clifton, Wallace
Three prophetic novels. + Wells, H. G.
Three-quarters. + De Timms, Graeme
Three romances. + Gautier, Theophile
The three royal monkeys. + de la Mare, Walter
The three-seated space ship. + Slobodkin, Louis
Three sevens. + The Phelons
Three ships and three kings. + Sallaska, Georgia
Three steps spaceward. + Long, Frank Belknap
The three stigmata of Palmer Eldritch. + Dick, Philip
   K.
Three stories. + Gallico, Paul
Three stories. + (Moskowitz, Sam)
The three suns of Amara. + Temple, William F.
Three survived. + Silverberg, Robert
Three tales. + Hauff, Wilhelm
Three tales. + O'Connor, William Douglas
Three tales. + Poe, Edgar Allan
3 tales of horror. + Lovecraft, H. P.
Three thousand dollars a year. + Benefice
Three thousand years. + McClary, Thomas Calvert
3000 years of fantasy and science fiction. + de Camp,
   L. Sprague & de Camp, Catherine Crook
Three times infinity. + Margulies, Leo
Three to conquer. + Russell, Eric Frank

3 to the highest power. + Nolan, William F.
The three toymakers. + Williams, Ursula Moray [see Addendum]
Three trips in time and space. + none
Three works by William Morris. + Morris, William
Three worlds. + Griffiths, Isabel
Three worlds of futurity. + St. Clair, Margaret
Three worlds to conquer. + Anderson, Poul
Threshold of eternity. + Brunner, John
The threshold of fear. + Rees, Arthur J.
Threshold of the stars. + Berna, Paul
Thrill city. + Stine, Hank
The thrill seeker. + Damon, Ray
Thrillers. + none
Thrillers and more thrillers. + Arthur, Robert
Thrilling stories. + none
Thrilling tales of unusual interest. + none
Thrills. + none
Thrills, crimes, and mysteries. + none
Thro' space. + Rock, James
The throne of Eden. + Colville, W. J.
The throne of Saturn. + Drury, Allen
The throne of Saturn. + Wright, S. Fowler
Through a glass, clearly. + Asimov, Isaac
Through a glass darkly. + Norris, Kathleen
Through sea and sky. + Chatterton, E. Keble
Through space to Mars. + Rockwood, Roy
Through space to Planet T. + Goll, Reinhold W.
Through space to the planets. + Law, Winifred
Through the air to the North Pole. + Rockwood, Roy
Through the Alimentary Canal with gun and camera. + Chappell, George S.
Through the barrier. + Torro, Pel
Through the dark curtain. + Saxon, Peter
Through the Earth. + Fezandie, Clement
Through the invisible. + Tyner, Paul
Through the looking-glass. + Carroll, Lewis
Through the sun in an airship. + Mastin, John
Through the visograph. + Chancellor, J. W.
Through time and space with Ferdinand Feghoot. + Briarton, Grendel
The throwbacks. + Sarac, Roger
Thru the dragon glass. + Merritt, A.
Thuka of the Moon. + Hannan, Charles
Thundar. + Bloodstone, John
The thunder and lightning man. + Cooper, Colin
Thunder and roses. + Sturgeon, Theodore
The Thunder Dragon Gate. + Mundy, Talbot
Thunder of stars. + Kippax, John & Morgan, Dan
Thunder on the left. + Morley, Christopher
Thunderbirds. + Theydon, John
Thunderbirds are go. + Allan, Angus P.
Thunderbirds ring of fire. + Theydon, John
Thunderbolt and the rebel planet. + Ohlson, Hereward
Thunderbolt of the spaceways. + Ohlson, Hereward
Thunderclap. + Brophy, John
The Thurb revolution. + Panshin, Alexei
The Thursday toads. + Lightner, A. M.
Thus far. + Snaith, J. C.
Thuvia, maid of Mars. + Burroughs, Edgar Rice
Thuvia, maid of Mars; and, The chessmen of Mars. + Burroughs, Edgar Rice
Thyra. + Bennet, Robert Ames
Ti-Coyo and his shark. + Richer, Clement
Tibby. + Gilchrist, Rosette Luce
The ticket that exploded. + Burroughs, William S.
A ticket to nowhere. + Becher, Don
The ticking is in your head. + Daventry, Leonard
Tide. + Hughes, Zach
The tide. + Sheean, Vincent
A tide of terror. + Lamb, Hugh
The tide went out. + Maine, Charles Eric

The tides in the Bay of Fundy. + Xanthus, Xavier
Tiger by the tail, and other science fiction stories. + Nourse, Alan E.
Tiger girl. + none
Tiger girl. + Casserly, Gordon
Tiger in the kitchen, and other strange stories. + Sorensen, Villy
Tiger Mountain. + MacVicar, Angus
Tiger River. + Friel, Arthur O.
Tiger! Tiger! + Bester, Alfred
The tigerman of Terrahpur. + Lecale, Errol
Tigers and traitors. + Verne, Jules
Tigers of the sea. + Howard, Robert E.
Till we have faces. + Lewis, C. S.
Tiltangle. + Mackelworth, R. W.
Time and again. + Finney, Jack
Time and again. + Simak, Clifford D.
Time and Mr. Bass. + Cameron, Eleanor
Time and space. + Le Page, Rand
Time and stars. + Anderson, Poul
Time and the gods. + Dunsany, Lord
Time and the hunter. + Calvino, Italo
A time appointed. + Statten, Vargo
Time at the top. + Ormondroyd, Edward
The time axis. + Kuttner, Henry
The time bargain. + Anstey, F.
The time before this. + Monsarrat, Nicholas
The time bender. + Laumer, Keith
Time beyond time. + Green, I. G.
Time bomb. + Tucker, Wilson
The time bridge. + Statten, Vargo
The time button. + Chilton, Irma
Time cat. + Alexander, Lloyd
The time chariot. + Hickey, T. Earl
The time curve. + Elwood, Roger & Moskowitz, Sam
The time dissolver. + Sohl, Jerry
Time drug. + Casson, Miles
The Time Dweller. + Moorcock, Michael
Time echo. + Lionel, Robert
Time echo. + Roberts, Lionel
Time enough for love. + Heinlein, Robert A.
Time exile. + Millers, Reinhold
The time factor. + Gordon, Rex
Time flight. + Longstreth, T. Morris
Time for a change. + McIntosh, J. T.
A time for survival. + McCutchan, Philip
Time for the stars. + Heinlein, Robert A.
The time garden. + Eager, Edward
Time gate. + Jakes, John
Time gladiator. + Reynolds, Mack
Time has a door. + Kensch, Otto
The time-hoppers. + Silverberg, Robert
Time in advance. + Tenn, William
Time in eclipse. + Garnett, David S.
The time injection. + Williams, Eric C.
The time is coming. + Bolmer, W. B.
Time is the simplest thing. + Simak, Clifford D.
The time-journey of Dr. Barton. + Hodgson, John
Time-jump. + Brunner, John
The Time Kings. + Dexter, J. B.
The time-lockers. + West, Wallace
The time machine. + Wells, H. G.
The time machine, and other stories. + Wells, H. G.
The time machine; and, The invisible man. + Wells, H. G.
The time machine; and, The man who could work miracles. + Wells, H. G.
The time machine; and, The war of the worlds. + Wells, H. G.
The time machine that never got past first base. + Severance, Felix
The time machine; The first men in the Moon. + Wells, H. G.

The time machine, The wonderful visit, and other stories. + Wells, H. G.
Time machine to the rescue. + Keith, Donald
Time marches off. + de Wreder, Paul
Time marches sideways. + Finn, Ralph L.
The time masters. + Tucker, Wilson
The time maze. + Maddock, Reginald
The time mercenaries. + High, Philip E.
Time must have a stop. + Huxley, Aldous
A time of changes. + Silverberg, Robert
The time of infinity. + Derleth, August
A time of terror. + (Ford, Douglas)
The time of the crack. + Tennant, Emma
The time of the eye. + Ellison, Harlan
Time of the great death. + Skinner, Claude M.
Time of the great freeze. + Silverberg, Robert
The time of the hedrons. + Eckstrom, Jack Dennis
Time: 110100. + Kelley, Leo P.
Time out for tomorrow. + Wilson, Richard
Time out of joint. + Dick, Philip K.
Time out of mind. + Cowper, Richard
Time out of mind, and other stories. + Boulle, Pierre
A time piece. + Neill, Peter
Time probe. + Clarke, Arthur C.
Time rogue. + Kelley, Leo P.
The time shifters. + Merwin, Sam Jr.
Time story. + Gordon, Stuart
The time stream. + Taine, John
Time stream, and other stories. + Taine, John
The time stream; The greatest adventure; The purple sapphire. + Taine, John
Time swap. + Weldon, Rex
The time thief. + Valdez, Paul
Time thieves. + Koontz, Dean R.
A time to choose. + Parker, Richard
Time to come. + Derleth, August
Time to go back. + Allan, Mabel Esther
Time to live. + Rackham, John
Time to teleport. + Dickson, Gordon R.
The time traders. + Norton, Andre
Time transfer, and other stories. + Sellings, Arthur
Time trap. + Laumer, Keith
Time trap. + Phillips, Rog
The time trap. + Statten, Vargo
The time trap gambit. + Maddock, Larry
The time trap of Ming XIII. + Steffanson, Con
Time tunnel. + Leinster, Murray
The time twister. + Petaja, Emil
The time twisters. + Holly, J. Hunter
Time untamed. + none
Time waits for Winthrop, and four other short novels from Galaxy. + Pohl, Frederik
Time war. + Carter, Lin
Time will run back. + Hazlitt, Henry
The time winder. + Bevis, H. U.
Time: X. + Tucker, Wilson
The timeless ones. + Torro, Pel
Timeless stories for today and tomorrow. + Bradbury, Ray
Timeliner. + Maine, Charles Eric
Timepiece. + Ball, Brian N.
Timepit. + Ball, Brian N.
Timepivot. + Ball, Brian N.
Time's door. + Meynell, Esther
Times 4. + Allen, Virginia French
Time's last gift. + Farmer, Philip Jose
Time's lonely one. + Perry Rhodan 42
Times without number. + Brunner, John
Timescoop. + Brunner, John
Timeslip! + Leinster, Murray
Timeslip. + Stewart, Bruce
Timestop! + Farmer, Philip Jose

Timetracks. + Laumer, Keith
The tin angel. + Goulart, Ron
Tin gods. + Bryat, Edith
The tin men. + Frayn, Michael
Ting-a-ling. + Stockton, Frank R.
Ting-a-ling tales. + Stockton, Frank R.
The tinted Venus. + Anstey, F.
Tistou of the green fingers. + Druon, Maurice [see Addendum]
Tistou of the green thumbs. + Druon, Maurice [see Addendum]
The titan. + Miller, P. Schuyler
Titan and Volcan. + Gillet, A. F.
Titan, son of Saturn. + Burroughs, Joseph Birkbeck
Titania has a mother. + Brahms, Caryl & Simon, S. J.
Titan's daughter. + Blish, James
Titan's moon. + Charles, Neil
Tittivulus. + Ayrton, Michael
Titus alone. + Peake, Mervyn
Titus Groan. + Peake, Mervyn
To and again. + Brooks, Walter R.
To Arkon! + Perry Rhodan 30
To bear witness! + Clark, Susie C.
To bear witness! + StClair, Cecil
To bring the judgment. + Roberts, Paul K.
To challenge Chaos. + Stableford, Brian M.
To conquer chaos. + Brunner, John
To die in Italbar. + Zelazny, Roger
To dream of evil. + Comer, Ralph
To end all telescopes. + Williams, Eric C.
To here and the easel. + Sturgeon, Theodore
To Jupiter via Hell. + none
To kill a corpse. + Ascher, Eugene
To live again. + Silverberg, Robert
To live forever. + Vance, Jack
To Luna with love. + Bevis, H. U.
To Mars via the Moon. + Wicks, Mark
To meet Mr. Stanley. + Johnson, Dorothy
To open the sky. + Silverberg, Robert
To outer space. + Johns, W. E.
To outrun doomsday. + Bulmer, Kenneth
To play the devil. + Hall, Angus
To prime the pump. + Chandler, A. Bertram
To ride Pegasus. + McCaffrey, Anne
To the chapel perilous. + Mitchison, Naomi
To the devil--a daughter. + Wheatley, Dennis
To the end of time. + Stapledon, Olaf
To the end of time, and other stories. + Williams, Robert Moore
To the land of fair delight. + none
To the Moon! + Rapport, Samuel & Wright, Hamilton & Wright, Helen
To the Moon and back in ninety days. + Brown, John Young
To the poles by airship. + Wright, Allen Kendrick
To the stars. + Silverberg, Robert
To the Sun? + Verne, Jules
To the Tombaugh Station. + Tucker, Wilson
To the ultimate. + Statten, Vargo
To vanishing point. + Norman, Doreen
To Venus in five seconds. + Jane, Fred T.
To Venus! To Venus! + Grinnell, David
To walk the night. + Sloane, William
To whom it may concern. + Borgese, Elisabeth Mann
To whom it may concern, and other short stories. + Wright, Laura Jane
To worlds beyond. + Silverberg, Robert
To worlds unknown. + Johns, W. E.
To your scattered bodies go. + Farmer, Philip Jose
Toad. + Cronin, Bernard
Today we choose faces. + Zelazny, Roger
The toe, and other tales. + Harvey, Alexander

Toil and self. + (Caswell, Edward A.)
The token. + none
Told by the death's head. + Jokai, Maurus
Told in the dark. + van Thal, Herbert
Tolkien. + Carter, Lin
Tolkien and the critics. + Isaacs, Neil D. & Zimbardo, Rose A.
Tolkien criticism. + West, Richard C.
The Tolkien papers. + none
The Tolkien reader. + Tolkien, J. R. R.
The Tolkien relation. + Ready, William B.
Tolkien's world. + Helms, Randel
The toll of the sea. + Norton, Roy
Tom. + Prince, Don
Tom Ossington's ghost. + Marsh, Richard
Tom Swift among the diamond makers. + Appleton, Victor
Tom Swift among the fire fighters. + Appleton, Victor
Tom Swift and his aerial warship. + Appleton, Victor
Tom Swift and his air glider. + Appleton, Victor
Tom Swift and his air scout. + Appleton, Victor
Tom Swift and his airline express. + Appleton, Victor
Tom Swift and his airship. + Appleton, Victor
Tom Swift and his aquatomic tracker. + Appleton, Victor II
Tom Swift and his atomic earth blaster. + Appleton, Victor II
Tom Swift and his big dirigible. + Appleton, Victor
Tom Swift and his big tunnel. + Appleton, Victor
Tom Swift and his chest of secrets. + Appleton, Victor
Tom Swift and his Cosmotron Express. + Appleton, Victor II
Tom Swift and his deep-sea hydrodome. + Appleton, Victor II
Tom Swift and his diving seacopter. + Appleton, Victor II
Tom Swift and his Dyna-4 capsule. + Appleton, Victor II
Tom Swift and his electric locomotive. + Appleton, Victor
Tom Swift and his electric rifle. + Appleton, Victor
Tom Swift and his electric runabout. + Appleton, Victor
Tom Swift and his electronic retroscope. + Appleton, Victor II
Tom Swift and his flying boat. + Appleton, Victor
Tom Swift and his flying lab. + Appleton, Victor II
Tom Swift and his G-force inverter. + Appleton, Victor II
Tom Swift and his giant cannon. + Appleton, Victor
Tom Swift and his giant magnet. + Appleton, Victor
Tom Swift and his giant oil gusher. + Appleton, Victor
Tom Swift and his giant robot. + Appleton, Victor II
Tom Swift and his great searchlight. + Appleton, Victor
Tom Swift and his house on wheels. + Appleton, Victor
Tom Swift and his jetmarine. + Appleton, Victor II
Tom Swift and his megascope space prober. + Appleton, Victor II
Tom Swift and his motor-boat. + Appleton, Victor
Tom Swift and his motor-cycle. + Appleton, Victor
Tom Swift and his ocean airport. + Appleton, Victor
Tom Swift and his outpost in space. + Appleton, Victor II
Tom Swift and his photo telephone. + Appleton, Victor
Tom Swift and his planet stone. + Appleton, Victor
Tom Swift and his polar-ray dynasphere. + Appleton, Victor II
Tom Swift and his repelatron skyway. + Appleton, Victor II

Tom Swift and his rocket ship. + Appleton, Victor II
Tom Swift and his sky racer. + Appleton, Victor
Tom Swift and his sky train. + Appleton, Victor
Tom Swift and his sonic boom trap. + Appleton, Victor II
Tom Swift and his space solartron. + Appleton, Victor II
Tom Swift and his spectromarine selector. + Appleton, Victor II
Tom Swift and his submarine boat. + Appleton, Victor
Tom Swift and his subocean geotron. + Appleton, Victor II
Tom Swift and his talking pictures. + Appleton, Victor
Tom Swift and his television detector. + Appleton, Victor
Tom Swift and his 3-D telejector. + Appleton, Victor II
Tom Swift and his triphibian atomicar. + Appleton, Victor II
Tom Swift and his ultrasonic cycloplane. + Appleton, Victor II
Tom Swift and his undersea search. + Appleton, Victor
Tom Swift and his war tank. + Appleton, Victor
Tom Swift and his wireless message. + Appleton, Victor
Tom Swift and his wizard camera. + Appleton, Victor
Tom Swift and the asteroid pirates. + Appleton, Victor II
Tom Swift and the captive planetoid. + Appleton, Victor II
Tom Swift and the city of gold. + Appleton, Victor II
Tom Swift and the cosmic astronauts. + Appleton, Victor II
Tom Swift and the electronic hydrolung. + Appleton, Victor II
Tom Swift and the galaxy ghosts. + Appleton, Victor II
Tom Swift and the mystery comet. + Appleton, Victor II
Tom Swift and the visitor from Planet X. + Appleton, Victor II
Tom Swift circling the globe. + Appleton, Victor
Tom Swift in captivity. + Appleton, Victor
Tom Swift in the caves of fire. + Appleton, Victor
Tom Swift in the caves of nuclear fire. + Appleton, Victor II
Tom Swift in the city of gold. + Appleton, Victor
Tom Swift in the jungle of the Mayas. + Appleton, Victor II
Tom Swift in the land of wonders. + Appleton, Victor
Tom Swift in the race to the Moon. + Appleton, Victor II
Tom Swift on the phantom satellite. + Appleton, Victor II
The tomb, and other tales. + Lovecraft, H. P.
The tomb of the dark ones. + Mills, J. M. A.
The tombs of Atuan. + Le Guin, Ursula K.
To-morrow. + Ollivant, Alfred
Tomorrow! + Wylie, Philip
Tomorrow always comes. + Bartlett, Vernon
Tomorrow and a day. + Janson, Hank
Tomorrow and tomorrow. + Collins, Hunt
Tomorrow and tomorrow. + Eldershaw, M. Barnard
Tomorrow and tomorrow. + Knight, Damon
Tomorrow and tomorrow. + Padgett, Lewis
Tomorrow and tomorrow; and, The fairy chessmen. + Padgett, Lewis
Tomorrow came. + Cooper, Edmund
Tomorrow has arrived. + Knight, Randy
To-morrow is a new day. + Hubbard, T. O'B.

A traveller in time. + Uttley, Alison
Travellers by night. + Derleth, August
The traveller's return. + Bozman, E. F.
The travelling grave, and other stories. + Hartley, L. P.
Travelling magic. + Beresford, Elisabeth
The travels and adventures by sea and land of Baron Munchausen. + (Raspe, Rudolf)
The travels and adventures of James Massey. + Bayle, Monsieur
Travels and adventures of Little Baron Trump and his wonderful dog Bulger. + Lockwood, Ingersoll
The travels and adventures of William Bingfield, Esq. + Bingfield, William
The travels and surprising adventures of Baron Munchausen. + (Raspe, Rudolf)
Travels by sea and land of Alethitheras. + (Osborn, Laughton)
The travels by sea and land of the renowned Baron Munchausen. + (Raspe, Rudolf)
Travels in Nihilon. + Sillitoe, Alan
Travels in the interior. + Courteney, Luke Theophilus
Travels into several remote nations of the world. + (Swift, Jonathan)
Travels into several remote nations of the world, vol. III. + Gulliver, Lemuel
Travels into several remote nations of the world, vol. III, part II. + Gulliver, Lemuel
The travels of Baron Munchausen. + (Raspe, Rudolf)
Travels of Lemuel Gulliver into several remote nations of the world. + (Swift, Jonathan)
The travels of Mr. John Gulliver, son of Capt. Lemuel Gulliver. + (Desfontaines, Pierre)
The treacherous time machine. + Merlino, Merlin Mesmer
Treachery in outer space. + Rockwell, Carey
Treasure box. + Shanklin, Imelda Octavia
The treasure divers. + Holder, Charles Frederick
The treasure in the forest. + Wells, H. G.
The treasure in the forest, and other stories. + Wells, H. G.
The treasure of Atlantis. + Dunn, J. Allan
Treasure of Green Knowe. + Boston, L. M.
The treasure of Ho. + Beck, L. Adams
Treasure of Tau Ceti. + Rackham, John
Treasure of the Black Falcon. + Burroughs, John Coleman
The treasure of the golden crater. + Lounsberry, Lionel
The treasure of the ice. + Bisbee, Eugene Shade
The treasure of the Isle of Mist. + Tarn, W. W.
Treasure of the lake. + Haggard, H. Rider
The treasure trail. + Scott, T. H.
The treasure-train. + Reeve, Arthur B.
The treasure vault of Atlantis. + Anderson, Olof W.
The treasures of Asshur. + Dallas, Oswald
The treasures of Typhon. + Phillpotts, Eden
A treasury of great ghost stories. + Peck, Ira
A treasury of great science fiction. + Boucher, Anthony
A treasury of science fiction. + Conklin, Groff
The treasury of science fiction classics. + Kuebler, Harold W.
The tree. + Spiegelman, J. Marvin
Tree and leaf. + Tolkien, J. R. R.
The tree, and other stories. + Baughman, Grace
Tree by Tolkien. + Wilson, Colin
The tree lord of Imeten. + Purdom, Tom
The tree of Heaven. + Chambers, Robert W.
The tree of Heaven. + Sinclair, May
The tree that conquered the world. + Leek, Sybil
The trembling tower. + Yelnick, Claude
The trembling world. + Del Martia, Astron

The tremendous event. + LeBlanc, Maurice
Tremor. + Lederman, Frank
Trespass. + Knebel, Fletcher
Triad. + Leader, Mary
Triad. + van Vogt, A. E.
Triage. + Lewin, Leonard C.
The trial of Charles de Gaulle. + Fabre-Luce, Alfred
The trial of Gideon; and, Countess Almara's murder. + Hawthorne, Julian
The trial of John and Henry Norton. + Puccetti, Roland
The trial of man. + (Lawrence, Charles)
The trial of Mussolini. + "Cassius"
The trial of Terra. + Williamson, Jack
Triangle. + Asimov, Isaac
Tribal war. + Garron, Marco
The triffids. + Nobes, Patrick & Wyndham, John
Trilby. + du Maurier, George
Trillions. + Fisk, Nicholas
Trilogy of the future. + Wollheim, Donald A.
Trimblerigg. + Housman, Laurence
A trip around the world in a flying machine. + Verne, Jules
A trip to Mars. + Ash, Fenton
A trip to Mars. + Cobb, Weldon J.
A trip to Mars. + Rossi, Marcianus F.
A trip to Paradoxia, and other humours of the hour. + Escott, T. H. S.
A trip to the center of the Earth. + Verne, Jules
A trip to the Moon. + Lunatic, Sir Humphrey
A trip to the Moon. + McDermot, Murtagh
A trip to the North Pole. + Lindelof, O. J. S.
A trip to Venus. + Munro, John
Tri-planet. + Kellar, Von
Triplanetary. + Smith, E. E.
Triple detente. + Anthony, Piers
The triple man. + Fanthorpe, R. L.
0008 meets Gnatman. + Allison, Clyde
0008 meets Modesta Blaze. + Allison, Clyde
Triple W. + Serling, Rod
The triptych of the three kings. + Timmermans, Felix
Triton. + Hubbard, L. Ron
Tritonastra. + Donson, Cyril
The Tritonian ring, and other Pusadian tales. + de Camp, L. Sprague
Triumph. + Wylie, Philip
The triumph of death. + Ramuz, C. F.
The triumph of Elaine. + Reeve, Arthur B.
The triumph of socialism, and how it succeeded. + Mayne, John D.
The triumph of time. + Blish, James
The triumph of woman. + Rowcroft, Charles
The triuneverse. + (Kennedy, R. A.)
Trivana I. + Abel, R. Cox & Barren, Charles
The Troglodytes. + Rafcam, Nal
The Troika incident. + Brown, James Cooke
Tros. + Mundy, Talbot
Tros of Samothrace. + Mundy, Talbot
Trouble at the top. + Flood, Charles Bracelen
Trouble on Project Ceres. + White, Ted
Trouble on Titan. + Nourse, Alan E.
Trouble planet. + Steel, Mark
The trouble twisters. + Anderson, Poul
Trouble with lichen. + Wyndham, John
The trouble with tribbles. + Gerrold, David
The trouble with Tycho. + Simak, Clifford D.
Troubled star. + Smith, George O.
The troubling of the city. + Lloyd, Roger
Trout fishing in America; The pill "versus" the Springhill Mill Disaster; and, In watermelon sugar. + Brautigan, Richard
Trout's testament. + Fraser, Ronald

Troyana. + Meek, S. P.
The true dimension. + Dawson, Warrington
Trullion: Alastor 2262. + Vance, Jack
A trumpet in Zion. + Gruhn, Carrie E.
Trumpet of jubilee. + Lewisohn, Ludwig
The truth about dragons. + Adams, Hazard
The truth about Pyecraft, and other short stories. + Wells, H. G.
The truth about Pyecraft, and other stories. + Wells, H. G.
The truth about Stone Hollow. + Snyder, Zilpha Keatley
The truth about unicorns. + Reynolds, Bonnie Jones
Truth game. + Hurd, Douglas
Try another world. + Meyer, John J.
Tryst. + Thane, Elswyth
The Tsaddik of the seven wonders. + Haiblum, Isidore
Tsimmis in Tangier. + Knight, Mallory T.
Tucker's countryside. + Selden, George [see Addendum]
Tunc. + Durrell, Lawrence
Tuned for murder. + Robeson, Kenneth
The Tunnel. + Kellerman, Bernard
The tunnel, and other stories. + (Elwood, Roger)
Tunnel from Calais. + Divine, Arthur D.
Tunnel from Calais. + Rame, David
Tunnel in the sky. + Heinlein, Robert A.
Tunnel through the deeps. + Harrison, Harry
Tunnel through time. + del Rey, Lester
The tunnel thru the air. + Gann, W. D.
Turn left at Thursday. + Pohl, Frederik
The turn of the screw. + James, Henry
The turn of the screw; and, Daisy Miller. + James, Henry
The turn of the screw, and other short novels. + James, Henry
The turn of the screw, and other stories. + James, Henry
The turn of the screw; The Aspern papers. + James, Henry
The turn of the screw, The Aspern papers, and other stories. + James, Henry
The turn of the screw; The lesson of the master. + James, Henry
Turnabout. + Smith, Thorne
Turned loose on Irdra. + MacLennan, Phyllis
Turning on. + Knight, Damon
The turning wheel. + Creswick, Paul
The turquoise. + Seton, Anya
The turret. + Sharp, Margery
Tussles with time. + Romains, Jules
The twelfth. + Stanford, J. K.
The twelfth Pan book of horror stories. + van Thal, Herbert
The twelve adventurers, and other stories. + Bronte, Charlotte
12 adventures of the celebrated Baron Munchausen. + (Raspe, Rudolf)
The twelve and the genii. + Clarke, Pauline
12 great classics of science fiction. + Conklin, Groff
The twelve maidens. + Farrar, Stewart
12 must die. + Zorro
The twelve pictures. + Simon, Edith
Twelve ravens. + Rose, Howard
Twelve stories and a dream. + Wells, H. G.
12 stories for late at night. + Hitchcock, Alfred
Twelve stories from Deals with the devil. + Davenport, Basil
12 stories they wouldn't let me do on TV. + Hitchcock, Alfred
Twelve tales of suspense and the supernatural. + Grubb, Davis

12 to the Moon. + Wise, Robert A.
12:20 P.M. + Beymer, William Gilmore
"2894." + Browne, Walter
28 science fiction stories. + Wells, H. G.
The twenty-fifth hour. + Best, Herbert
21st century sub. + Herbert, Frank
Twenty-five ghost stories. + Holland, W. Bob
Twenty-five great ghost stories. + (Holland, W. Bob)
Twenty-five short stories. + Benet, Stephen Vincent
Twenty-four hours. + Charles, Neil
20 great ghost stories. + (Holland, W. Bob)
Twenty-nine kisses from Roald Dahl. + Dahl, Roald
The twenty-one balloons. + Du Bois, William Pene
Twenty-one billionth paradox. + Daventry, Leonard
2150. + Plym, Don & Plym, Thea
The twenty-second century. + Christopher, John
The twenty-seventh day. + Mantley, John
26 mystery stories old and new, by twenty and six authors. + Rhys, Ernest & Scott, C. A. Dawson-
2069. + Townsend, Larry
2069+1. + Townsend, Larry
2069+2. + Townsend, Larry
2010. + (Carrel, Frederic)
20,000 leagues under the sea. + Verne, Jules
20,000 trails under the universe with the cerebroscope. + Meyer, John J.
Twenty trillion light-years through space. + Virg, Leo [see Addendum]
2020 vision. + Pournelle, Jerry
22 Hallowfield. + Shannon, Doris
Twenty-two strange stories. + Hardie, John L.
"20 years of Analog/Astounding science fiction*science fact, 1952-1971." + Lorenzen, Jan A.
Twenty years of the Magazine of fantasy and science fiction. + Ferman, Edward L. & Mills, Robert P.
The twice=born. + A Late Associate of the Society for Psychical Research
Twice in time. + Wellman, Manly Wade
Twice they lived. + Ezra, I. B.
Twice-told tales. + Hawthorne, Nathaniel
Twice twenty-two. + Bradbury, Ray
Twice upon a time. + Fontenay, Charles L.
Twilight. + Danby, Frank
Twilight dreams. + Carpenter, W. B.
Twilight journey. + Davies, L. P.
The twilight man. + Moorcock, Michael
The twilight men. + Basil, Otto
The twilight of Briareus. + Cowper, Richard
The twilight of magic. + Lofting, Hugh [see Addendum]
Twilight of reason. + Burke, Jonathan
Twilight of the basilisks. + Transue, Jacob
The twilight of the gods, and other tales. + Garnett, Richard
The twilight of the Vilp. + Ableman, Paul
Twilight on the Betzy. + Dinesen, Thomas
Twilight stories. + Broughton, Rhoda
Twilight world. + Anderson, Poul
The twilight zone. + Gibson, Walter B.
Twilight Zone. + La Salle, Victor
Twilight zone revisited. + Gibson, Walter B.
Twin of the Amazon. + Fearn, John Russell
Twin orbs. + Vanden, Dirk
Twin planets. + High, Philip E.
Twin spell. + Lunn, Janet
Twin worlds. + Jones, Neil R.
Twinkle, twinkle, little star. + Barzman, Ben
A twist of sand. + Jenkins, Geoffrey
Twisted. + Conklin, Groff
The twisted men. + van Vogt, A. E.
The twisted tree. + Benedict, Lynn
The twisters. + Hansen, Vern
Twists in time. + Leinster, Murray

Two against the tide. + Clements, Bruce
Two and two is six. + Hatch, Eric
Two and two make five. + Knowles, Vernon
Two billions of miles. + Ramsey, Milton W.
Two bottles of relish. + Burnett, Whit
Two boys' trip to an unknown planet. + Montgomery, Richard R.
Two brothers. + Augustinus
Two by two. + Garnett, David
Two came to town. + Strunksky, Simeon
Two complete novels. + del Rey, Lester
Two complete novels. + Sturgeon, Theodore
Two complete novels. + Williamson, Jack
Two days of terror. + Sheldon, Roy
The two destinies. + Collins, Wilkie
Two dozen dragon eggs. + Wollheim, Donald A.
Two early stories. + Firbank, Ronald
Two-Eyes. + Gordon, Stuart
The two faces of Silenus. + Clarke, Pauline [see Addendum]
Two fantastic tales. + Poe, Edgar Allan
Two gods ride the hydrogen bomb. + Demonicus
Two great mystery stories. + O'Brien, Fitz-James
Two hours to darkness. + Trew, Antony
Two hundred million A.D. + van Vogt, A. E.
200 years to Christmas. + McIntosh, J. T.
The two jungle books. + Kipling, Rudyard
Two legends. + Feducha, Bertha
Two-Legs. + Ewald, Carl
Two-Legs, and other stories. + Ewald, Carl
Two lives in parenthesis. + Long, George
The two magics. + James, Henry
Two mediaeval tales. + Stevenson, Robert Louis
Two novels. + Hubbard, L. Ron
Two novels. + Knight, Damon
Two planets. + Lasswitz, Kurd
Two qualms & a quirk. + de Mille, Richard
Two rubles to Times Square. + Richards, Guy
Two short novels. + James, Henry
Two sought adventure. + Leiber, Fritz
Two stories of the seen and unseen. + (Oliphant, Mrs.)
Two tales. + Wells, H. G.
Two tales and 8 tomorrows. + Harrison, Harry
Two tales of the occult. + Eliade, Mircea
2001: a space odyssey. + Clarke, Arthur C.
"2002." + Fessenden, Laura Dayton
Two thousand years hence. + O'Neil, Henry
2000 years of space travel. + Freedman, Russell
2,000 years on. + Statten, Vargo
Two tickets for Tangier. + Mason, Van Wyck
The two-timers. + Shaw, Bob
The two towers. + Tolkien, J. R. R.
Two trillion immortals. + Cruso, Solomon
Two views of wonder. + Scortia, Thomas N. & Yarbro, Chelsea Quinn
Two voyages of Gulliver. + Swift, Jonathan
Two weird tails. + Tower, Harker [see Addendum]
Two worlds. + Haggard, Andrew C. P.
Two worlds. + Lorraine, Paul
Two young inventors. + Kerr, Alvah Milton
Tychiades. + Dickeson, Alfred
Tyopa. + Glanville, Ernest
Typewriter in the sky; Fear. + Hubbard, L. Ron
Typhon's beard. + Vasseur, John
The tyranny of the dark. + Garland, Hamlin
Tyrant of time. + Eshbach, Lloyd Arthur
The tyrants of Kool-Sim. + Cobban, J. Maclaren

UFO. + Miall, Robert
U.F.O. 517. + Fane, Bron
UFO-1. + Miall, Robert
UFO 2. + Miall, Robert

U.N. confidential--A.D. 2000. + Blake, Thomas
UNIAD. + Williams, Jay
UN-man, and other novellas. + Anderson, Poul
Ubik. + Dick, Philip K.
The Ugglians. + Fallaw, L. M.
The Ugglians at large. + Fallaw, L. M.
"Ugly," a hospital dog. + Dabbs, George H. R.
The ugly dachshund. + Stern, G. B.
The ugupu bird. + Mrozek, Slawomir
The ulcer culture. + Bulmer, Kenneth
Ulric the jarl. + Stoddard, William O.
Ulterior motives. + Garnett, David
The ultimate. + Fear, W. H.
The ultimate flower. + Serrano, Miguel
The ultimate invader, and other science-fiction. + Wollheim, Donald A.
The Ultimate Island. + Sieveking, L. de Giberne
The ultimate man. + Muller, John E.
The ultimate solution. + Norden, Eric
The ultimate threshold. + Ginsburg, Mirra
The ultimate weapon. + Campbell, John W.
Ultimate world. + Gernsback, Hugo
Ultimatum. + MacClure, Victor
Ultimatum. + Meyer, Bill
Ultimatum. + Rohmer, Richard H.
Ultimatum in 2050 A.D. + Sharkey, Jack
Ultimo. + Vassos, John & Vassos, Ruth
Ultra. + Hunt, Laura Shellabarger
Ultra spectrum. + Statten, Vargo
Ultra-violet tales. + Villa, Silvio
Ultus, the man from the dead. + Hodder, Reginald
The unaltered cat. + Lewis, Albert
The unbegotten. + Creasey, John
The unbidden. + Chetwynd-Hayes, R.
Unborn tomorrow. + Cooper, Edmund
Unborn tomorrow. + Frankau, Gilbert
Unborn to-morrow. + Kendall, John
Unbroken barriers. + Lindsay, Kathleen
Uncanny. + Bachelor, George C.
Uncanny. + Netherwood, Bryan A.
Uncanny adventures. + Ascher, Eugene
The uncanny house. + Pendered, Mary L.
Uncanny stories. + none
Uncanny stories. + Sinclair, May
Uncanny stories. + Sprigg, C. St. John
Uncanny tales. + Crawford, F. Marion
Uncanny tales. + Hopkins, R. Thurston
Uncanny tales. + Molesworth, Mrs.
Uncanny tales. + Poe, Edgar Allan
Uncanny tales 1. + Wheatley, Dennis
Uncanny tales 2. + Wheatley, Dennis
The uncensored man. + Sellings, Arthur
The uncertain element. + Dick, Kay
The uncertain midnight. + Cooper, Edmund
The uncharted planet. + Ranzetta, V.
Uncharted seas. + Wheatley, Dennis
Uncharted stars. + Norton, Andre
Unclay. + Powys, T. F.
Uncle Bijah's ghost. + Lee, Jennette
An uncle from India. + Pierson, Ernest de Lancey
Uncle Julius and the angel with heartburn. + Rosenberg, Ethel
Uncle Morgan's ghost. + Westreich, Alice & Westreich, Budd
Uncle Peter's fairy tale for the nineteenth century. + Sewell, Elizabeth M.
Uncle Sam in the eyes of his family. + Erskine, John
"Uncle Sam's" cabins. + Davenport, Benjamin Rush
The unconfined. + Fanthorpe, R. Lionel
The unconquerable survivor of 2055 A.D. + Lyons, Victor S.
Unconquered wings. + Westerman, Percy F.

The uncrowned king. + Wright, Harold Bell
The undead. + Dickie, James
The undefeated. + Laumer, Keith
Under compulsion. + Disch, Thomas M.
Under five lakes. + Quad, M.
Under home rule. + Palmer, William
Under old Earth, and other explorations. + Smith, Cordwainer
Under other conditions. + Lach-Szyrma, Wladislaw S.
Under Pike's Peak. + McKesson, Charles L.
Under pressure. + Herbert, Frank
Under the Auroras. + Shaw, W. J.
Under the desert stars. + Koester, Frank
Under the flag of the cross. + Sedberry, J. Hamilton
Under the green star. + Carter, Lin
Under the Hermes, and other stories. + Dehan, Richard
Under the hill, and other essays in prose and verse. + Beardsley, Aubrey
Under the influence. + Kerr, Geoffrey
Under the label. + Tombleson, J. B.
Under the moons of Mars. + Moskowitz, Sam
Under the ocean to the South Pole. + Rockwood, Roy
Under the red ensign. + Campbell, Spencer
Under the sea to the North Pole. + Mael, Peter
Under the sign of pain. + Mooney, Leo F.
Under the Sun. + Buck, Charles W.
Under the sun of Satan. + Bernanos, Georges [see Addendum]
Under the sunset. + Stoker, Bram
Under the triple suns. + Coblentz, Stanton A.
Under the witches's moon. + Gallizier, Nathan
Underground man. + Tarde, Gabriel de
The underground picnic. + Johnston, William
The underpeople. + Smith, Cordwainer
Undersea city. + Pohl, Frederik & Williamson, Jack
Undersea fleet. + Pohl, Frederik & Williamson, Jack
Undersea quest. + Pohl, Frederik & Williamson, Jack
Understanding Tolkien and the Lord of the Rings. + Ready, William
The undertaker's dozen. + Forrest, David
Underworld of Zello. + Deegan, Jon J.
The undesired princess. + de Camp, L. Sprague
The undine. + Carrel, Mark
Undine. + La Motte-Fouque, Friedrich de
Undine. + Young, Phyllis Brett
Undine; and, Aslauga's knight. + La Motte-Fouque, Friedrich de
Undine, and other tales. + La Motte-Fouque, Friedrich de
Undine; and, Sintram and his companions. + La Motte-Fouque, Friedrich de
Undine; and, The two captains. + La Motte-Fouque, Friedrich de
The undying fire. + Pratt, Fletcher
The undying fire. + Wells, H. G.
The undying fire; and, Philosophical and theological speculations. + Wells, H. G.
The undying monster. + Kerruish, Jessie Douglas
Undying world. + Lord, Jeffrey
The unearth people. + Neville, Kris
The unearthly kingdom. + Whitney, Verner Meurice
Unearthly neighbors. + Oliver, Chad
Uneasy freehold. + Macardle, Dorothy
The unending night. + Smith, George H.
The unexpected. + Cerf, Bennett
The unexpected. + Margulies, Leo
The unexpected dimension. + Budrys, Algis
The unexpected island. + Lin, Yutang
The unfair fare affair. + Leslie, Peter
Unfamiliar territory. + Silverberg, Robert
Unfinished business. + Erskine, John
The unforeseen. + Macardle, Dorothy

The unforgotten. + Conway, Laura
The unfortunate Fursey. + Wall, Mervyn
The unfortunate princess. + (Haywood, Eliza)
The unfriendly future. + Boardman, Tom Jr.
The unfrozen. + Dreyfuss, Ernst
An unholy alliance. + Tweedale, Violet
The unholy city. + Finney, Charles G.
Unholy crusade. + Wheatley, Dennis
Unholy depths. + Dunn, Gertrude
Unholy flame. + Rosmanith, Olga
Unholy relics, and other uncanny tales. + Dare, M. P.
Unholy trinity. + Russell, Ray
The unhumans. + Karp, Marvin Allen
The unicorn. + Buchanan, Thomas G.
The Unicorn Girl. + Kurland, Michael
The unicorn with silver shoes. + Young, Ella
The uninhabited house. + Riddell, Mrs. J. H.
The uninhabited house; and, The haunted river. + Riddell, Mrs. J. H.
The uninhibited. + Morgan, Dan
The uninvited. + Macardle, Dorothy
The uninvited. + Muller, John E.
The united planets. + Wadey, Victor
Universal Station. + Brown, Beth
The universal strike. + Oakhurst, William
The universal strike of 1899. + Oakhurst, William
Universe. + Heinlein, Robert A.
The universe against her. + Schmitz, James H.
The universe between. + Nourse, Alan E.
Universe day. + O'Donnell, K. M.
Universe 5. + Carr, Terry
Universe 4. + Carr, Terry
The universe maker. + van Vogt, A. E.
The universe makers. + Wollheim, Donald A.
Universe 1. + Carr, Terry
Universe 3. + Carr, Terry
Universe 2. + Carr, Terry
The universes of E. E. Smith. + Ellik, Ron & Evans, Bill
The University of Intelligence. + Eisenberg, Manuel
The unknown. + Bensen, D. R.
The unknown. + Leinster, Murray
The unknown country. + Dawson, Coningsby
Unknown danger. + Leinster, Murray
The unknown depths. + O'Donnell, Elliott
Unknown destiny. + Fane, Bron
The unknown five. + Bensen, D. R.
The unknown goddess. + Cross, Ruth
The unknown island. + Royal, Matthew J.
An unknown land. + Samuel, Viscount
Unknown Sector: Milky Way. + Perry Rhodan 45
The unknown soldier. + Dawson, Coningsby
The unknown to-morrow. + Le Queux, William
Unknown worlds. + Flanigan, Michael C. & Trout, Lawana
An unlaid ghost. + none
Unlawful. + Turner, Charles Cyril
The unlikely ghosts. + Turner, James
The unmeasured place. + Lambourne, John
An unofficial breath. + Buchanan, Marie
The unpardonable war. + Barnes, James
Unpath'd waters. + Harris, Frank
The unpleasant profession of Jonathan Hoag. + Heinlein, Robert A.
The unpossessed. + Muller, John E.
The unpredictable adventure. + Spotswood, Claire Myers
The unquiet corpse. + Sloane, William
The unquiet grave. + Derleth, August
The unquiet spirit. + Steen, Marguerite
The unreal people. + Siegel, Martin
Unrest of their time. + Kirkham, Nellie

The unrivalled adventures of that great aeronaut and Glum, Peter Wilkins. + Trueman, T.
The unseen. + Barton, Lee
The unseen assassin. + Janson, Hank
The unseen thing. + Dyllington, Anthony
The unsleep. + Gillon, Diana & Gillon, Meir
The unsleeping eye. + Compton, D. G.
The unspeakable people. + Haining, Peter
The untamed. + Norwood, Victor
The unteleported man. + Dick, Philip K.
Unthinkable. + Sibson, Francis H.
Untouched by human hands. + Sheckley, Robert
Untravelled worlds. + Barter, Alan Frank & Wilson, Raymond
Untrodden streets of time. + Falkner, John
Unveiling a parallel. + (Jones, Alice & Marchant, Ella)
Unweave a rainbow. + Johnson, Edgar
Unwise child. + Garrett, Randall
Up above. + Raphael, John N.
Up and out. + Powys, John Cowper
Up Jenkins! + Hingley, Ronald
Up the ladder of gold. + Oppenheim, E. Phillips
Up the line. + Silverberg, Robert
Up the Matterhorn in a boat. + Pope, Marion Manville
Up the pier. + Cresswell, Helen
Up-tight. + Winfield, Dick
The Upas tree. + Barclay, Florence L.
Upon the midnight. + Bull, R. C.
The upper berth. + Crawford, F. Marion
Upsidonia. + Marshall, Archibald
Urania. + Flammarion, Camille
Uranie. + Flammarion, Camille
The uranium seekers. + Zeigfried, Karl
Uranium 235. + Muller, John E.
Urban the Ninth. + Marshall, Bruce
Urien's voyage. + Gide, Andre
Ursus of Ultima Thule. + Davidson, Avram
Useless hands. + Farrere, Claude
Ush. + "Adelphos"
The usurping ghost, and other encounters and experiences. + Dickinson, Susan
Uther & Igraine. + Deeping, Warwick
Utinam. + Arkwright, William
The utmost island. + Myers, Henry
Utopia. + Cridge, Alfred Denton
Utopia. + Rosewater, Frank
Utopia achieved. + Brinsmade, Herman Hine
The utopia affair. + McDaniel, David
Utopia 14. + Vonnegut, Kurt Jr.
Utopia, Inc. + Gieske, Herman Everett
Utopia minus X. + Gordon, Rex
Utopia (the volcano island). + Dimondstein, Boris
Utopia 239. + Gordon, Rex
Utopian fantasy. + Gerber, Richard
The uttermost. + Stallard, Mrs. Arthur

VOR. + Blish, James
The Vaivaisukko's bride. + Scott-Moncrieff, David
Valdar the oft-born. + Griffith, George
Valdmer the Viking. + Nisbet, Hume
Valence and vision. + Jones, Rich & Roe, Richard L.
Valhalla. + Long, George
Valiant clay. + Bell, Neil
The Valkyries. + Benson, E. F.
Valley beyond time. + Silverberg, Robert
Valley beyond time. + Wilkins, Vaughan
The valley of Achor. + Champion de Crespigny, Mrs. Philip
The valley of creation. + Hamilton, Edmond
The Valley of Creeping Men. + Crawley, Rayburn
The valley of doom. + Richmond, Mary

Valley of doom. + Rutley, C. Bernard
The valley of eyes unseen. + Collins, Gilbert
The Valley of Josaphat. + Figueroa, Medardo
The valley of mystery. + Dallas, Oswald
Valley of pretenders. + Clive, Dennis
Valley of shadows. + Lyons, Delphine C.
The Valley of Song. + Goudge, Elizabeth [see Addendum]
The valley of spiders. + Wells, H. G.
The valley of spiders, and other stories. + Wells, H. G.
Valley of terror. + Rey, Russell
Valley of the damned. + Lambert, William J.
Valley of the Flame. + Kuttner, Henry
The valley of the gods. + Anderson, Andy
The valley of the great ray. + Black, Pansy E.
The valley where time stood still. + Carter, Lin
The vampire. + Horler, Sydney
The vampire. + Riva, Valeria & Volta, Ornella
The vampire affair. + McDaniel, David
A vampire, and other stories. + Leitch, Lavinia
The vampire, and sixteen other stories. + Fox, Leslie
The vampire contessa. + Ross, Marilyn
Vampire lovers, and other stories. + Le Fanu, J. Sheridan
The vampire of N'Gobi. + Cullum, Ridgwell
A vampire of souls. + P., H. M.
The vampire women. + Samuels, Victor
Vampires. + Tolstoi, Alexis
Vampires at midnight. + Haining, Peter
Vampires Ltd. + Nesvadba, Josef
Vampire's moon. + Saxon, Peter
The vampires of Finistere. + Saxon, Peter
The vampires of the Andes. + Carew, Henry
Vampires of Venus. + Mannheim, Karl
Vampires overhead. + Hyder, Alan
Vampires, werewolves, and other monsters. + Elwood, Roger
The vampyre. + (Polidori, John)
Ye vampyres. + The Spectre
Van. + Converse, Frank H.
Vandals of eternity. + Gibbard, T. S. J.
Vandals of the void. + Vance, Jack
Vandals of the void. + Walsh, J. M.
The Vandekkers. + Thorndike, Russell
Vandenberg. + Lange, Oliver
Vanessa. + Martin, Kay
Vanessa. + Ralli, Constantine
Vanguard from Alpha. + Aldiss, Brian W.
The vanguard of Venus. + Bartlett, Landell
Vanguard to Neptune. + Walsh, J. M.
Vanguard to Venus. + Castle, Jeffery Lloyd
Van Hoff. + Smythe, Alfred
The vanished empire. + Dunn, Waldo H.
The vanished jet. + Blish, James
The vanisher. + Robeson, Kenneth
The vanishing fleets. + Norton, Roy
The vanishing garden. + Beresford, Elisabeth
The vanishing island. + O'Connell, Charles C.
Vanishing men. + Winsor, G. McLeod
The vanishing professor. + MacIsaac, Fred
Vantage Hall. + Gluyas, Constance
A van Vogt omnibus. + van Vogt, A. E. & Hull, E. Mayne
van Vogt omnibus (2). + van Vogt, A. E. & Hull, E. Mayne
Var, the Stick. + Anthony, Piers
The variable man, and other stories. + Dick, Philip K.
Variation on a theme. + Collier, John
Varney the Vampyre. + none
Vassals of Venus. + Kent, Philip
Vathek. + Beckford, William

Voices prophesying war, 1763-1984. + Clarke, I. F.
The void beyond, and other stories. + Williams, Robert Moore
Volonor. + Winship, Glen B.
Voltaire. + Voltaire
Voltaire's romances. + Voltaire
Volteface. + Adlard, Mark
Voodoo drums. + Wilmot, Eileen
The voodoo goat. + Gaines, Audrey
Voodoo planet. + North, Andrew
Voodoo slave. + Daniels, Norman
Vornan-19. + Silverberg, Robert
Vortex. + Bearne, C. G.
The Vortex Blaster. + Smith, E. E.
The vortex blasters, and other stories. + Moskowitz, Sam
Votan. + James, John
Voyage into space. + Van Loden, Erle
The voyage of Captain Popanilla. + Disraeli, Benjamin
The voyage of Lemuel Gulliver to Lilliput and Brobding-nag. + Swift, Jonathan
The voyage of the Ark. + Allen, F. M.
The voyage of the Dawn Treader. + Lewis, C. S.
The voyage of the Luna I. + Craigie, David
The voyage of the Space Beagle. + van Vogt, A. E.
The voyage of the Starfire to Atlantis. + Mumford, Edwin
The voyage of Will Rogers to the South Pole. + Spots-wood, Christopher
A voyage to Arcturus. + Lindsay, David
A voyage to Brobdingnag. + Swift, Jonathan
A voyage to Cacklogallinia. + Brunt, Samuel
A voyage to Dari. + Wallace, Ian
Voyage to Faremido; Capillaria. + Karinthy, Frigyes
The voyage to Laputa. + Swift, Jonathan
The voyage to Lilliput. + Swift, Jonathan
A voyage to Purilia. + Rice, Elmer
Voyage to the bottom of the sea. + Jones, Raymond F.
Voyage to the bottom of the sea. + Sturgeon, Theodore
A voyage to the island of the Articoles. + Maurois, Andre
A voyage to the Moon. + Aratus
A voyage to the Moon. + Atterley, Joseph
A voyage to the Moon. + Verne, Jules
Voyage to the stars. + Bramwell, Frank
A voyage to the world in the centre of the Earth. + none
Voyage to Venus. + Healy, Dominic
Voyage to Venus. + Lewis, C. S.
Voyagers in time. + Silverberg, Robert
Voyages. + Sauer, Rob
The voyages and adventures of Captain Hatteras. + Verne, Jules
The voyages, shipwrecks, travels, distresses, strange adventures, and miraculous preservation of William Bingfield. + Bingfield, William
Voyages to the Moon. + Nicolson, Marjorie
Vril. + Lytton, Edward Bulwer
Vulcan's hammer. + Dick, Philip K.
The Vulture. + Noy, John
Vulture stew. + Zacherley
Vultures of the white death. + Hogan, Robert J.

WT50. + Weinberg, Robert
Wabeno, the magician. + Wright, Mabel Osgood [see Addendum]
The wagered world. + Janifer, Laurence M. & Treibich, S. J.
Wagner, the wehr-wolf. + Reynolds, George W. M.
The waif woman. + Stevenson, Robert Louis
The wailing asteroid. + Leinster, Murray
The wailing octopus. + Blaine, John

Waiters on the dance. + Savarin, Julian Jay
Waiting for the signal. + Morris, Henry O.
The waiting sands; and, The devil on Lammas Night. + Howatch, Susan
The Waiting World. + Fanthorpe, R. Lionel
Wake up, England! + Prince, Edward
Wake up screaming. + Sheehan, Richard G. & Wright, Lee
Waldo; and, Magic, Inc. + Heinlein, Robert A.
Waldo: genius in orbit. + Heinlein, Robert A.
Walk in dread. + none
Walk in dread. + Tomlinson, Dorothy
A walk out of the world. + Nichols, Ruth
Walk through to-morrow. + Zeigfreid, Karl
Walk to the end of the world. + Charnas, Suzy McKee
Walk up the sky. + Williams, Robert Moore
A walk with the beast. + Collins, Charles M.
The walker-through-walls. + Ayme, Marcel
The walking stones. + Hunter, Mollie
The Wall. + Grey, Charles
The wall around the world. + Cogswell, Theodore R.
Wall of serpents. + de Camp, L. Sprague & Pratt, Fletcher
The wallet of Kai Lung. + Bramah, Ernest
The Walter de la Mare omnibus. + de la Mare, Walter
The waltz of death. + Maxon, P. B.
The Wanderer. + Leiber, Fritz
Wanderer in space. + Moore, Patrick
Wanderer of space. + Statten, Vargo
The wanderers. + Johnston, Mary
The wanderer's necklace. + Haggard, H. Rider
Wanderers of time. + Wyndham, John
Wandering ghosts. + Crawford, F. Marion
Wandering heath. + (Quiller-Couch, A. T.)
The wandering Jew. + Sue, Eugene
The wandering Jew. + Thurston, Emily Temple
Wandering stars. + Dann, Jack
The wandering Tellurian. + Schwartz, Alan
The wandering variables. + Trimble, Louis
Wandl the invader. + Cummings, Ray
Wandor's ride. + Green, Roland
The wanting seed. + Burgess, Anthony
The war against the Rull. + van Vogt, A. E.
The war book. + Sallis, James
The war breakers. + Ganpat
The war for the Lot. + Lanier, Sterling E.
The war game. + Watkins, Peter
The war god walks again. + Austin, F. Britten
War in Heaven. + Williams, Charles
War in space. + Gastine, Louis
War in the air. + Helders, Major
The war in the air, and other war forebodings. + Wells, H. G.
The war in the air, and particularly how Mr. Bert Smallways fared while it lasted. + Wells, H. G.
The war in the air; In the days of the comet; The food of the gods. + Wells, H. G.
The war in the air, 1936. + Helders, Major
The war in the marshes. + Young, Robert
The war inevitable. + Burgoyne, Alan H.
War lords of space. + Hughes, Denis
War of Argos. + Le Page, Rand
The war of dreams. + Carter, Angela
The war of 1908 for the supremacy of the Pacific. + Crabapple, John
The war of 1938. + Wright, S. Fowler
The war of the ghosts. + Burtis, Thomson
War of the gurus. + Rheingold, Howard
The war of the sexes. + Young, F. E.
The war of the Wenuses. + Graves, C. L. & Lucas, E. V
War of the wing-men. + Anderson, Poul
The war of the wireless waves. + Westerman, Percy F.

The war of the worlds. + Robinson, Frederick
The war of the worlds. + Wells, H. G.
The war of the worlds; A dream of armageddon; The land ironclads. + Wells, H. G.
The war of the worlds; and, The time machine. + Wells, H. G.
The war of the worlds, The time machine, and selected short stories. + Wells, H. G.
War of the Xromatids. + Hunter-Blair, John
The war of time. + Carpentier, Alejo
The war of two worlds. + Anderson, Poul
War of two worlds. + Detre, L.
War on Aleph. + James, Laurence
War on Saturday week. + Adam, Ruth
War over England. + Charlton, L. E. O.
The war terror. + Reeve, Arthur B.
War under water. + none
War upon women. + Moseley, Maboth
War with the Gizmos. + Leinster, Murray
War with the Newts. + Capek, Karel
War with the robots. + Harrison, Harry
'Ware wolf!' + Forester, E. Lascelles
Warlock. + Koontz, Dean R.
The warlock in spite of himself. + Stasheff, Christopher
The Warlock of Night. + Ipcar, Dahlov
Warlock of the witch world. + Norton, Andre
Warlocks and warriors. + de Camp, L. Sprague
Warlocks and warriors. + Hill, Douglas
Warlord of Kor. + Carr, Terry
The Warlord of Mars. + Burroughs, Edgar Rice
The Warlord of the air. + Moorcock, Michael
A warning from Mars. + Whiteside, Edward
A warning to Earth. + Townsend, John
A warning to the curious, and other ghost stories. + James, M. R.
Warrior of Llarn. + Fox, Gardner F.
Warrior of Mars. + Fearn, John Russell
Warrior of Scorpio. + Akers, Alan Burt
Warrior of the dawn. + Browne, Howard
The warrior of world's end. + Carter, Lin
Warrior Scarlet. + Sutcliff, Rosemary
The Warriors of Day. + Blish, James
Warriors of Mars. + Bradbury, Edward P.
Warriors of Noomas. + Nuetzel, Charles
Warriors of serpent land. + Connell, Alan
The warriors of Terra. + Faucette, John M.
The Warstock. + Gerrare, Wirt
The washer of the ford. + Macleod, Fiona
Wasp. + Russell, Eric Frank
Wasp-waisted Arabella. + Bagley, John
The watch below. + White, James
Watch on Peter. + Rackham, John
Watch the northwind rise. + Graves, Robert
The watcher, and other weird stories. + Le Fanu, J. Sheridan
The watcher by the threshold. + Buchan, John
A watcher of the skies. + Mertins, Gustave Frederick
Watchers of the dark. + Biggle, Lloyd Jr.
The watchers out of time, and others. + Lovecraft, H. P. & Derleth, August
The watching world. + Fanthorpe, R. L.
The water ghost, and others. + Bangs, John Kendrick
The water of the Wondrous Isles. + Morris, William
The water of thought. + Saberhagen, Fred
Watermelon man. + Raucher, Herman
The waters of Aswan. + Heim, Michael
The waters of Centaurus. + Brown, Rosel George
The waters of death. + Greenfield, Irving A.
The waters of Kronos. + Richter, Conrad
Waters of Lethe. + Keller, David H.
Watership Down. + Adams, Richard

A wave of fear. + Lamb, Hugh
The wave that drowned a baby. + Beer, Richard C.
The way home. + Phipson, Joan
A way home. + Sturgeon, Theodore
The way of Ecben. + Cabell, James Branch
The way of Heaven, and other fantasies told in the manner of the Chinese. + Hall, Manly P.
The way of stars. + Beck, L. Adams
Way of the gods. + Kuttner, Henry
Way of the werewolf. + Hill, Douglas
The way of war. + Scot, Hew
Way out. + Howard, Ivan
The way out. + Lewis, Henry
Way Station. + Simak, Clifford D.
The ways of the lonely ones. + Hall, Manly P.
The wayward robot. + Bannon, Mark
We. + Zamyatin, Eugene
We all died at Breakaway Station. + Meredith, Richard C.
We are for the dark. + Aickman, Robert & Howard, Elizabeth Jane
We band of brothers. + 'Seaforth'
We can build you. + Dick, Philip K.
We claim these stars! + Anderson, Poul
We, people of America, and how we ended poverty. + Sinclair, Upton
We, the Venusians. + Rackham, John
We who survived. + Noel, Sterling
Wealth of the void. + Statten, Vargo
The Weans. + Nathan, Robert
The weapon from beyond. + Hamilton, Edmond
The weapon makers. + van Vogt, A. E.
The weapon shops of Isher. + van Vogt, A. E.
The weapons of mystery. + Hocking, Joseph
The weathermakers. + Bova, Ben
The weathermonger. + Dickinson, Peter
The web of Easter Island. + Wandrei, Donald
Web of everywhere. + Brunner, John
The web of the golden spider. + Bartlett, Frederick Orin
Web of the witch world. + Norton, Andre
The wedding garment. + Pendleton, Louis
The week-end book of ghost stories. + Carrington, Hereward
The weigher of souls. + Maurois, Andre
The weigher of souls; &, The Earth dwellers. + Maurois, Andre
Weightless in Gaza. + Shannon, Fred
The weightless mother. + Bell, Norman
The weird adventures of Professor Delapine of the Sorbonne. + Johnson, George Lindsay
The weird adventures of the Shadow. + Gibson, Walter B.
The weird adventures of the Shadow; Grove of doom. + Grant, Maxwell
Weird and uncanny stories. + Hopkins, R. Thurston
A weird gift. + Ohnet, Georges
Weird islands. + Bosschere, Jean de
The weird menace. + (Cazedessus, Camille)
The weird of the wanderer. + Prospero & Caliban
The weird ones. + (Howard, Ivan)
The weird Orient. + Iliowizi, Henry
The weird shadow over Innsmouth, and other stories of the supernatural. + Lovecraft, H. P.
Weird shadows from beyond. + Carnell, John
Weird shorts, first selection. + none
Weird show. + (Russell, Ray)
The weird sisters. + Blyth, James
Weird stories. + Higham, Charles
Weird stories. + Riddell, Mrs. J. H.
Weird tales. + none
Weird tales. + Hoffmann, E. T. A.

Weird tales. + Margulies, Leo
Weird tales. + Poe, Edgar Allan
Weird tales; American. + none
Weird tales; English. + none
Weird tales; German. + none
Weird tales in the thirties. + Smith, Reginald
Weird tales; Irish. + none
Weird tales of the supernatural. + Singer, Kurt
Weird tales; Scottish. + none
Weird tit-bits; American. + none
Weird tit-bits; English. + none
Weird tit-bits; German. + none
Weird tit-bits; Irish. + none
Weird tit-bits; Scottish. + none
A weird transformation. + Halidom, M. Y.
The weird witch's spell. + Vitarelli, Robert
Weirdest of weird tales. + Poe, Edgar Allan
Weirdies. + Hoke, Helen
The weirdstone. + Garner, Alan
The weirdstone of Brisingamen. + Garner, Alan
The Weirwoods. + Swann, Thomas Burnett
The Weisman experiment. + Rankine, John
Welcome, Stranger & Partners. + Pesin, Harry
Welcome to Mars. + Blish, James
Welcome to the monkey house. + Vonnegut, Kurt
The Well at the world's end. + Gunn, Neil M.
The Well at the world's end. + Morris, William
Well met by witchlight. + Beachcroft, Nina
The well of St. Clare. + France, Anatole
The Well of the Unicorn. + Fletcher, George U.
The Well of the Unicorn. + Pratt, Fletcher
The Well of the Worlds. + Kuttner, Henry
Well of the Worlds. + Padgett, Lewis
Welsh rarebit tales. + Cummins, Harle Oren
Welsh tales of terror. + Chetwynd-Hayes, R.
The were-wolf. + Housman, Clemence
A werewolf among us. + Koontz, Dean R.
Werewolf by moonlight. + Smith, Guy N.
The werewolf of Paris. + Endore, Guy
The werewolf of Ponkert. + Munn, H. Warner
The Werewolf Principle. + Simak, Clifford D.
The werewolf vs the vampire woman. + Scram, Arthur N.
West India lights. + Whitehead, Henry S.
West of the Moon. + Simpson, Howard
West of the Sun. + Pangborn, Edgar
West wind drift. + McCutcheon, George Barr
Wet magic. + Nesbit, E. [see Addendum]
The whale and the grasshopper, and other fables. + O'Brien, Seumas
The wham! bam! thank you, ma'am affair. + Conway, Troy
What a way to go! + O'Shea, Sean
What Didymus did. + Sinclair, Upton
What dreams may come. + Asquith, Cynthia
"What dreams may come..." + Beresford, J. D.
What entropy means to me. + Effinger, Geo. Alec
What Farrar saw. + Hanley, James
What Father Cuthbert knew. + Christmas, Grace V.
What happened after the Battle of Dorking. + none
What happened in the Ark. + Boumphrey, Geoffrey M. & Walker, Kenneth M.
What happened to Hammond? + Blayn, Hugo
What happened to the Corbetts. + Shute, Nevil
What has four wheels and flies? + Wallop, Douglass
What if He came? + Williams, Garfield Hodder
What mad universe. + Brown, Fredric
What may happen in the next 90 days. + none
What might have been. + (Bramah, Ernest)
What next? + Housman, Laurence
What not. + Macaulay, Rose
What strange stars and skies. + Davidson, Avram
What Timmy did. + Lowndes, Mrs. Belloc

What was it? and other stories. + O'Brien, Fitz-James
What we are coming to. + L'Estrange, Miles
What we did to father. + Lewis, Roy
What will Japan do? + Morris, J.
Whatever goes up. + Conway, Troy
What's become of Screwloose? and other inquiries. + Goulart, Ron
What's it like out there? and other stories. + Hamilton, Edmond
What's the world coming to? + Moffat, W. Graham & White, John
The wheel comes a turn. + Good, Charles H.
Wheel in space. + Moore, Patrick
The Wheel in the Sky. + Bernard, Rafe
The wheels of chance; The time machine. + Wells, H. G.
The wheels of chance; The world set free. + Wells, H. G.
The wheels of if, and other science-fiction. + de Camp, L. Sprague
When Adolf came. + Hawkin, Martin
When age grows young. + Kirk, Hyland C.
When all men starve. + Gleig, Charles
When and if. + Reynolds, Philip
When churchyards yawn. + Asquith, Cynthia
When England slept. + Curties, Henry
When evil wakes. + Derleth, August
When fortune dares. + Baker, Emerson
When graveyards yawn. + Derleth, August
When Gubbins ruled. + Joscelyne, Cyril
When Harlie was one. + Gerrold, David
When He shall appear. + Kampf, Harold
When it was light. + (Lang, Andrew)
When mammoths roamed the frozen Earth. + Schutz, Heinrich
When mankind was young. + Austin, F. Britten
When men talk truth, and other stories. + Swaffer, Hannen
When Shiloh came. + Jackson, Ambrose Lester
When Smuts goes. + Keppel-Jones, Arthur
When strange drums sound. + Webster, F. A. M.
When the bells rang. + Armstrong, Anthony & Graeme, Bruce
When the birds fly south. + Coblentz, Stanton A.
When the devil was sick. + Ross, Charles
When the Earth died. + Mannheim, Karl
When the Earth swung over. + Colbeck, Alfred
When the enemy is tired. + Braddon, Russell
When the Gods came. + Adams, John
When the great war came. + Navarchus
When the green star calls. + Carter, Lin
When the hurly-burly's done. + Clarke, Allen
When the kissing had to stop. + Fitz Gibbon, Constantine
When the Moon died. + Savage, Richard
When the Moon fell. + Colladay, Morrison
When the Moon ran wild. + Ainsbury, Ray
When the Red King awoke. + Kelleam, Joseph E.
When the saints are gone. + Serjeant, Constancia
When the sky burned. + Bova, Ben
When the Sleeper wakes. + Wells, H. G.
When the star kings die. + Jakes, John
When the Sun went out. + Stone, Leslie F.
When the whites went. + Bateman, Robert
When the women reign, 1930. + Wilson, J.
When the world reeled. + Thorne, Guy
When the world screamed, and other stories. + Doyle, A. Conan
When the world shook. + Haggard, H. Rider
When they come from space. + Clifton, Mark
When thoughts will soar. + Suttner, Bertha von
When Thunders spoke. + Sneve, Virginia Driving Hawk

When time stood still. + Orkow, Ben
When two worlds meet. + Williams, Robert Moore
When war breaks out. + White, A. & Wilson, H. W.
When William came. + Munro, H. H.
When woman reigns. + Anson, August
When woman rules. + A Well-Known Member of Parliament
When women rule. + Moskowitz, Sam
When worlds collide. + Balmer, Edwin & Wylie, Philip
When Yvonne was dictator. + Gresswell, Elise Kay
Where are the Russians? + Bentley, John
Where do we go from here? + Asimov, Isaac
Where do we go from here, book 1. + Asimov, Isaac
Where do we go from here, book 2. + Asimov, Isaac
Where eternity ends. + Binder, Eando
Where is the bird of fire? + Swann, Thomas Burnett
Where men have walked. + Rhodes, H. Henry
Where nightmares are. + Haining, Peter
Where Satan dwells. + Stevenson, Florence
Where terror stalked, and other stories. + Birkin, Charles
Where the blue begins. + Morley, Christopher
Where the needle points. + Finley, Harry T.
Where were you last Pluterday? + Van Herck, Paul
Which hath been. + McLaren, Mrs. Jack
While England slept. + James, Rowland
Whims. + Wanderer
Whims and oddities in prose and verse. + Hood, Thomas
Whipping star. + Herbert, Frank
The Whirling Shapes. + North, Joan
Whirlpool of stars. + Zetford, Tully
Whirlwind harvest. + Van Winkle, Monica F.
Whisper from the stars. + Sutton, Jeff
The whisper of Glocken. + Kendall, Carol
The whispering box mystery. + Blaine, John
The whispering Buddha. + Cowles, John Clifford
The whispering gorilla. + Reed, David V.
The whispering knights. + Lively, Penelope
The Whispering Mountain. + Aiken, Joan
Whispering walls. + Brennan, Elizabeth
The whistle of doom. + Ludwig, Boris
The Whistling Ancestors. + Goddard, Richard E.
The whistling boy. + Arthur, Ruth M.
The whistling whirligig. + Shecter, Ben
The White Angel. + Corbett, James
White August. + Boland, John
The white battalions. + White, F. M.
The white blackbird. + Musset, Alfred de
The white bull. + Voltaire
The white bull, with Saul, and various short pieces. + Voltaire
White city. + Sutton, Paralee S.
The white deer. + Thurber, James
The white fakir. + Huddleston, George
White Fang goes Dingo, and other funny s.f. stories. + Disch, Thomas M.
White fangs. + Garron, Marco
White fire. + W. W.
The white flame. + Cornelius, Mary
The white island. + Wood, Michael
White kimono. + Newton, Joseph Emerson
The white king of Manoa. + Hatton, Joseph
White Lotus. + Hersey, John
The white man's burden. + Hodge, T. Shirby
The white man's garden. + Skipper, Mervyn
The white mantle. + Owen, Maurice
The white morning. + Atherton, Gertrude
The White Mountains. + Christopher, John
The white owl. + Smithson, Annie M. P.
The White Owl. + Snell, Edmund
The White People. + Burnett, Frances Hodgson
White pills. + Carroll, Ted
The white pope. + Crockett, S. R.

The white princess of the hidden city. + Johnstone, David Lawson
White python. + Channing, Mark
The white robe. + Cabell, James Branch
The white room. + Coatsworth, Elizabeth
The white shield. + Mitford, Bertram
The white sybil; Men of Avalon. + none
The White Tiger. + Mitchell-Hedges, F. A.
The White Widows. + Merwin, Sam Jr.
The White Witch of Mayfair. + Griffith, George
The white witch of Rosehall. + de Lisser, Herbert G.
The white witnesses. + Spalding, Helen
The white wolf. + Gregory, Franklin
Who? + Budrys, Algis
Who can replace a man? + Aldiss, Brian W.
Who fears the devil? + Wellman, Manly Wade
Who goes there? + Campbell, John W.
Who has poisoned the sea? + Coppard, Audrey
Who is Julia? + Harris, Barbara S.
Who is Mary Stark? + Kropp, Lloyd
Who is Victoria? + Erwin, Betty K.
Who killed Enoch Powell? + Wise, Arthur
Who killed science fiction? + Kemp, Earl
Who knocks? + Derleth, August
Who needs men? + Cooper, Edmund
Who put the devil in Miss Jones? + Evans, Derek
Who shall condemn? and other stories. + Shannon, John C.
Who speaks of conquest? + Wright, Lan
Who walk in fear. + Bell, Neil
Who wants a green bottle? and other uneasy tales. + Robbins, Tod
Who will remember? + Irwin, Margaret
The whole man. + Brunner, John
Whom the gods destroy. + Bennett, Alfred Gordon
Whom the gods would slay. + Jorgensen, Ivar
The Whooping Crane. + Kreisheimer, H. C.
Who's that lady in the president's bed? + Ripley, B. K.
Who's who in science fiction fandom, 1961. + Broyles, L. D.
Whose name is legion. + Clarke, Isabel C.
Whose soul have I now? + Knapp, Mary Clay
Why call them back from Heaven? + Simak, Clifford D.
Why have the birds stopped singing? + Sherburne, Zoa
The wicked enchantment. + Benary-Isbert, Margot
The wicked pigeon ladies in the garden. + Chase, Mary
The wicked, wicked ladies in the haunted house. + Chase, Mary
The Widderburn horror. + Warner-Crozetti, R.
Widdershins. + Onions, Oliver
Wide white page. + Cunningham, Beall
Wife styles and life styles. + Darrow, Frank M.
Wiggins for president. + Brooks, Walter R.
Wild adventures round the Pole. + Stables, Gordon
Wild and outside. + Lang, Allen Kim
Wild and weird. + Campbell, Gilbert
The wild ass' skin, and other stories. + Balzac, Honore de
The wild ass skin; The quest of the absolute. + Balzac, Honore de
The wild ass's skin. + Balzac, Honore de
The wild boys. + Burroughs, William S.
Wild Card. + Bingham, Roger & Hawkey, Raymond
The Wild Goose Chase. + Warner, Rex
Wild harbour. + Macpherson, Ian
The wild hunt of Hagworthy. + Lively, Penelope
The wild hunt of the ghost hounds. + Lively, Penelope
The wild huntsman, and other tales. + Erckmann-Chatrian
Wild in the streets. + Thom, Robert
Wild Jack. + Christopher, John

The wild night company. + Haining, Peter
Wild Southern scenes. + Jones, J. B.
Wild talent. + Tucker, Wilson
The wild valley. + Severn, David
The wild white witch. + Stafford, Peter
The wilderness of ice. + Verne, Jules
A wilderness of stars. + Nolan, William F.
The wilderness-stone. + Nathan, Robert
Wildsmith. + Goulart, Ron
Wilkin's tooth. + Jones, Diana Wynne
Will it end this way? + Geigley, Vance A.
Will o' the mill; Markheim. + Stevenson, Robert Louis
Willard. + Gilbert, Stephen
William and Mary. + Farmer, Penelope
William and the Moon rocket. + Crompton, Richmal
William and the space animal. + Crompton, Richmal
William F. Nolan: a checklist. + Yenter, Charles E.
William Morris. + Morris, William
William Morris: selected writings and designs. + Morris, William
Willmoth, the wanderer. + Dail, C. C.
The willows, and other queer tales. + Blackwood, Algernon
The wind and the fire. + Osborne, Chester G.
The wind between the worlds. + Brown, Alice
The wind blows over. + de la Mare, Walter
The Wind Boy. + Eliot, Ethel Cook [see Addendum]
The wind from nowhere. + Ballard, J. G.
Wind from the north. + O'Neill, Joseph
The wind from the Sun. + Clarke, Arthur C.
A wind in the door. + L'Engle, Madeleine
The wind in the rose-bush, and other stories of the supernatural. + Wilkins, Mary E.
The wind in the sails. + Perret, Jacques
The wind in the willows. + Grahame, Kenneth [see Addendum]
The wind obeys Lama Toru. + Lee, Tung
The wind of liberty. + Bulmer, Kenneth
The wind on the Moon. + Linklater, Eric
The wind that tramps the world. + Owen, Frank
The wind whales of Ishmael. + Farmer, Philip Jose
Windmills. + Cannan, Gilbert
Window on the future. + Hill, Douglas
Windows into tomorrow. + Silverberg, Robert
The winds of Altair. + Bova, Ben
The winds of Darkover. + Bradley, Marion Zimmer
The winds of Gath. + Tubb, E. C.
The winds of Limbo. + Moorcock, Michael
Winds of the Heliopolis. + Fretland, Don J.
The winds of time. + Oliver, Chad
The windscreen weepers, and other tales of horror and suspense. + Aiken, Joan
Windsor Castle. + Ainsworth, W. Harrison
Windwagon Smith, and other yarns. + Schramm, Wilbur
The wine-ghosts of Bremen. + Hauff, Wilhelm
Wine of death. + Armstrong, Anthony
Wine of the Dreamers. + MacDonald, John D.
The winged bull. + Fortune, Dion
Winged heels. + Wood, S. Andrew
The winged man. + Hull, E. Mayne & van Vogt, A. E.
Winged pharoah. + Grant, Joan
Winged victory. + Macfarlane, Claire
Winged world. + Harper, Harry
Wings. + Abdullah, Achmed
Wings across the cosmos. + Fearn, John Russell
Wings across time. + Arnold, Frank Edward
Wings of danger. + Nelson, Arthur A.
The wings of Dr. Smidge. + Philbrook, Rose
The wings of peace. + Creasey, John
Wings of the morning. + Anderson, Adrienne
Wings over Eldorado. + Taylor, Malcolm
The wink. + Bennett, Kem

A winter amid the ice, and other stories. + Verne, Jules
Winter evening tales. + Hogg, James
Winter kills. + Condon, Richard
The winter of enchantment. + Walker, Victoria
Winter of madness. + Walker, David
The Winter People. + Phelps, Gilbert
Winter's children. + Coney, Michael G.
Winter's youth. + Gloag, John
Wintersol. + Earnshaw, A. & Thacker, Eric
Wipe your face, you just swallowed my soul. + Prather, Hugh
Ye wisdom of Confucius. + Gilhooley, Lord
Wisdom's daughter. + Haggard, H. Rider
The wise man's story. + Bailey, Albert Edward [see Addendum]
A wish a day. + Ruck, Berta
Wish goes to Slumber Land. + Cooper, Edmund
Wishes limited. + Darlington, W. A.
The wishful think. + Newman, Bernard
Wishing Smith. + Hyne, C. J. Cutcliffe
The wishing stone. + Penny, F. E.
Witch. + Michaels, Barbara
The witch and the priest. + Lewis, Hilda
The witch-baiter. + Birkin, Charles
The witch family. + Estes, Eleanor
Witch House. + Walton, Evangeline
The witch in the wood. + White, T. H.
The witch of Prague. + Crawford, F. Marion
Witch of the dark gate. + Jakes, John
A witch of the nineteenth century. + Phelon, W. P.
Witch of the sea. + Colby, Marie W.
The witch of Withyford. + Chanter, Gratiana
Witch power. + Forest, Salambo
Witch princess. + Johnson, Dorothy
The witch queen of Khem. + Fitzgerald, Ena
Witch Queen of Lochlann. + Smith, George Henry
The witch queen of Mongo. + Bingham, Carson
The witch-woman. + Cabell, James Branch
Witch world. + Norton, Andre
Witchcraft. + Sleigh, Bernard
The witchcraft reader. + Haining, Peter
The witchery of Rita; and, Waiting for Tonti. + Robinson, Will H.
The witchery of the serpent. + Barr, James
The witches of Karres. + Schmitz, James H.
Witches three. + none
Witches, warlocks, and ghosts. + Mason, J. Edward
Witches, wraiths, & warlocks. + Curran, Ronald
The witchfinder. + Hilliard, Maurice
The witchfinders. + Comer, Ralph
The witching hour. + Gunn, James E.
The witching hour. + Stevenson, Florence
The witching hour. + Thomas, Augustus
The witching night. + Cody, C. S.
The witching of Dracula. + Lory, Robert
The witching time. + Norman, Henry
Witch's blood. + Blain, William
Witch's business. + Jones, Diana Wynne
Witch's curse. + Ludlam, Harry
A witch's garden. + Young, Miriam
The witch's head; Allan's wife. + Haggard, H. Rider
A witch's mouth. + Mitchell, Linda
The witch's spell. + James, Gunthar
The Witchstone. + Graham, Victoria
With a finger in my I. + Gerrold, David
With a strange device. + Russell, Eric Frank
With airship and submarine. + Collingwood, Harry
With gyves of gold. + Athey, Henry & Bowers, A. Herbert
With my friends. + Mathews, Brander
With the immortals. + Crawford, F. Marion

With the night mail. + Kipling, Rudyard
With the revolutionists in Bolivia. + Craine, E. J.
With wings outspread. + Gouvrieux, Marc
Within the Temple of Isis. + Wagner, Belle M.
Without bloodshed. + Gorst, H. E.
Without sorcery. + Sturgeon, Theodore
The wizard. + Haggard, H. Rider
The wizard; and, Black Heart and White Heart. + Haggard, H. Rider
The wizard of Anharitte. + Kapp, Colin
The wizard of Berner's Abbey. + Hansom, Mark
A wizard of Earthsea. + Le Guin, Ursula K.
The Wizard of Lemuria. + Carter, Lin
The wizard of Linn. + van Vogt, A. E.
The wizard of Starship Poseidon. + Bulmer, Kenneth
Wizard of storms. + Van Arnam, Dave
The wizard of the Atlas. + Hawkwood, Allan
The wizard of the mountain. + Gilbert, William
The wizard of the sea. + Rockwood, Roy
The wizard of Venus. + Burroughs, Edgar Rice
The wizard of Zacna. + Willard, T. A.
The wizard priest and the witch. + Poynet, Quintin
Wizards and warlocks. + Ghidalia, Vic
The wizard's mantle. + Dryasdust
The wizard's mantle. + Halidom, M. Y.
The Wizards of Senchuria. + Bulmer, Kenneth
Wolf. + McCord, P. G.
The wolf in the garden. + Bill, Alfred H.
The wolf-leader. + Dumas, Alexandre
The wolf-men. + Powell, Frank
The wolf trail. + Pocock, Roger S.
Wolfbane. + Pohl, Frederik & Kornbluth, C. M.
Wolfling. + Dickson, Gordon R.
The wolf's bride. + Kallas, Aino
Wolfshead. + Howard, Robert E.
The wolf's-head and the queen. + John-Martin & Morris, William
Wolfwinter. + Swann, Thomas Burnett
The wolves of God, and other fey stories. + Blackwood, Algernon & Wilson, Wilfred
The wolves of Willoughby Chase. + Aiken, Joan [see Addendum]
A woman a day. + Farmer, Philip Jose
A woman against the world. + Griffith, George
Woman alive. + Ertz, Susan
A woman as great as the world, and other fables. + Hawkes, Jacquetta
Woman dominant. + Vivian, E. Charles
Woman from another planet. + Long, Frank Belknap
The woman from nowhere. + Brophy, John
The woman in the house. + Hichens, Robert S.
The woman marches. + Gainess, Arthur A.
A woman of the ice age. + Gratacap, L. P.
A woman of to-morrow. + Glyn, Coralie
The woman on the beast. + Simpson, Helen
A woman--or what? + Lee, Mrs. Norman
Woman unsexed. + Chilton, H. Herman
The woman who couldn't die. + Stringer, Arthur
The woman who saved the world. + Holt-White, W.
The woman who stopped war. + Cornwallis-West, G.
The woman who vowed. + Harding, Ellison
The woman who would not die. + Bauman, Carolyn Busey
The woman without a heart. + Burgin, G. B.
A woman's heart, and other stories. + Wells, H. G.
The Wombles. + Beresford, Elisabeth
Women of Landau. + Kent, Jim
The Wonder. + Beresford, J. D.
The wonder effect. + Kornbluth, C. M. & Pohl, Frederik
The wonder stick. + Coblentz, Stanton A.
The wonder war. + Janifer, Laurence M.
The wonderbolt. + Capon, Paul

The wonderful adventures of Arthur Gordon Pym. + Poe, Edgar Allan
The wonderful adventures of Phra the Phoenician. + Arnold, Edward Lester
The wonderful city. + Fletcher, J. S.
The wonderful electric elephant. + Montgomery, Frances Trego
The wonderful farm. + Ayme, Marcel
The wonderful flight to the mushroom planet. + Cameron, Eleanor
The wonderful history of Peter Schlemihl. + Chamisso, Adalbert von
The wonderful history of the shadowless man; The cold heart. + none
The wonderful O. + Thurber, James
The wonderful story of Ravalette; also, Tom Clark and his wife. + Randolph, P. B.
The wonderful travellers. + Verne, Jules
The wonderful visit. + Wells, H. G.
The wonderful voyages of Cap'n Penn. + Shumway, Harry Irving
The wonderful voyages of Gulliver. + Swift, Jonathan
Wondermakers. + Hoskins, Robert
Wondermakers 2. + Hoskins, Robert
The wonders of Mouseland. + Childs, Edward Earle
The wondrous tale of Alroy. + Disraeli, Benjamin
The wood beyond the world. + Morris, William
Wood magic. + Jefferies, Richard
The woodcutter's house. + Nathan, Robert
The wooden heads. + Hales, C. L.
The wooden star. + Tenn, William
The wooden woman. + Townsend, Alexander
The woodnymph's song. + (Mertens, Karl R.)
The Woodrow Wilson dime. + Finney, Jack
The wooings of Jezebel Pettyfer. + Macfall, Haldane
The word of the sorceress. + Mitford, Bertram
Workers in darkness. + Harris-Burland, J. B.
The works of Edgar Allan Poe. + Poe, Edgar Allan
The works of H. Rider Haggard. + Haggard, H. Rider
The works of M. P. Shiel. + Morse, A. Reynolds
The works of Satan. + Maher, Richard Aumerle
The works of Theophile Gautier. + Gautier, Theophile
The world a department store. + Peck, Bradford
The world above. + Crow, Martha Foote
World aflame. + Bulmer, H. K.
World aflame. + Engel, Leonard & Piller, Emanuel S.
A world aflame. + Kern, Gregory
The world at bay. + Capon, Paul
World at bay. + Tubb, E. C.
The world below. + Wright, S. Fowler
The world between, and other stories. + Vance, Jack
A world beyond. + Shirley, George E.
A world by the tale. + Cambpell, John W.
World D. + Trevarthen, Hal P.
The world ends. + Lamb, William
The world goes smash. + Adams, Samuel Hopkins
A world gone mad. + Perry Rhodan 29
The world grabbers. + Fairman, Paul W.
The world grown young. + Herbert, William
World in eclipse. + Dexter, William
The world in 1931. + Bruce, Stewart E.
The world in peril. + Chilton, Charles
The world in reverse. + Ranzetta, Luan
A world in spell. + Stevenson, D. E.
The world in winter. + Christopher, John
The world inside. + Silverberg, Robert
A world intervenes. + Viking, Otto
The world Jones made. + Dick, Philip K.
"The world makers." + Maxwell, John C.
The World Masters. + Griffith, George
The world menders. + Biggle, Lloyd Jr.
The world of Ā. + van Vogt, A. E.

World of chance. + Dick, Philip K.
A world of difference. + Conquest, Robert
The world of fanzines. + Wertham, Fredric
World of Gol. + Charles, Neil
World of if. + Phillips, Rog
World of mists. + Moore, Patrick
The world of null-A. + van Vogt, A. E.
World of Ptavvs. + Niven, Larry
The world of Star trek. + Gerrold, David
World of the future. + Zeigfreid, Karl
World of the gods. + Torro, Pel
World of the masterminds. + Williams, Robert Moore
World of the sleeper. + Wayman, Tony Russell
World of the Starwolves. + Hamilton, Edmond
The world of the wizard king. + Wood, Wallace
The world of Theda. + Wade, Tom
A world of their own. + Shirley, George E.
World of tomorrow. + Marshall, James & Marshall, Margaret
World of tomorrow. + Zeigfreid, Karl
A world of trouble. + Toomey, Robert E. Jr.
A world of women. + Beresford, J. D.
World of wonder. + Pratt, Fletcher
A world of wonders. + Peabody, Joel R.
World out of mind. + McIntosh, J. T.
The world peril of 1910. + Griffith, George
The world set free. + Wells, H. G.
The world set free, and other war papers. + Wells, H. G.
The world shuffler. + Laumer, Keith
The world stood still. + Holt-White, W.
The world swappers. + Brunner, John
The world that couldn't be, and 8 other novelets from Galaxy. + Gold, H. L.
The world that never was. + Zeigfreid, Karl
The world was mine. + Clarke, T. E. B.
World well lost. + Aiken, John
World well lost. + Paget, John
The world where sex was born. + Kanto, Peter
The world within. + Lukens, Adam
World without children; and, The Earth Quarter. + Knight, Damon
World without end. + Mackenzie, Nigel
World without men. + Maine, Charles Eric
World without raiment. + Dardenelle, Louise
World without stars. + Anderson, Poul
World without women. + Keene, Day & Pruyn, Leonard
The world without women. + Martini, Virgilio
The world wrecker. + Bounds, Sydney J.
The world wreckers. + Bradley, Marion Zimmer
World zero minus. + Chambers, Aidan & Chambers, Nancy
Worlds apart. + Cowper, Richard
Worlds apart. + Locke, George
Worlds apart. + McIntosh, J. T.
Worlds apart. + Owen, Mably & Williams-Ellis, Amabel
Worlds at war. + none
The world's awakening. + Navarchus
Worlds away. + Beemish, Cragg
Worlds beginning. + Ardrey, Robert
The world's best mystery stories. + none
World's best S.F., no. 1. + Carr, Terry & Wollheim, Donald A.
World's best science fiction: first series. + Carr, Terry & Wollheim, Donald A.
World's best science fiction: fourth series. + Carr, Terry & Wollheim, Donald A.
World's best science fiction: 1965. + Carr, Terry & Wollheim, Donald A.
World's best science fiction: 1966. + Carr, Terry & Wollheim, Donald A.
World's best science fiction: 1967. + Carr, Terry & Wollheim, Donald A.

World's best science fiction: 1968. + Carr, Terry & Wollheim, Donald A.
World's best science fiction: 1969. + Carr, Terry & Wollheim, Donald A.
World's best science fiction: 1970. + Carr, Terry & Wollheim, Donald A.
World's best science fiction: 1971. + Carr, Terry & Wollheim, Donald A.
World's best science fiction: second series. + Carr, Terry & Wollheim, Donald A.
World's best science fiction: third series. + Carr, Terry & Wollheim, Donald A.
The world's desire. + Haggard, H. Rider & Lang, Andrew
The world's double. + Horner, Donald W.
World's Fair goblin. + Robeson, Kenneth
World's Fair, 1992. + Silverberg, Robert
Worlds far from here. + Wheatley, Dennis
Worlds for the taking. + Bulmer, Kenneth
The world's great crime stories. + Sayers, Dorothy L.
World's great mystery stories. + Cuppy, Will
The world's greatest athlete. + Caruso, Dee & Gardner, Gerald
Worlds in balance. + Wallace, F. L.
Worlds near and far. + Carr, Terry
The worlds of A. E. van Vogt. + van Vogt, A. E.
The worlds of Clifford Simak. + Simak, Clifford D.
The worlds of Eclos. + Gordon, Rex
The worlds of Frank Herbert. + Herbert, Frank
The worlds of Jack Vance. + Vance, Jack
Worlds of maybe. + Silverberg, Robert
The worlds of Poul Anderson. + Anderson, Poul
The worlds of Robert A. Heinlein. + Heinlein, Robert A.
The worlds of Robert F. Young. + Young, Robert F.
The worlds of science fiction. + Mills, Robert P.
Worlds of the Imperium. + Laumer, Keith
Worlds of the Wall. + MacApp, C. C.
The worlds of Theodore Sturgeon. + Sturgeon, Theodore
Worlds of tomorrow. + Derleth, August
Worlds of Weird. + Margulies, Leo
Worlds of when. + Conklin, Groff
Worlds of wonder. + Harrison, Harry
Worlds of wonder. + Johns, W. E.
Worlds of wonder. + Stapledon, Olaf
The world's one hundred best short stories, volume nine. + Overton, Grant
Worlds to come. + Knight, Damon
Worlds to conquer. + Statten, Vargo
Worlds within. + Phillips, Rog
Worlds without end. + Baker, Denys Val
Worlds without end. + Simak, Clifford D.
The worm Ouroboros. + Eddison, E. R.
Worms of the Earth. + Howard, Robert E.
Worse things waiting. + Wellman, Manly Wade
The wounded planet. + Elwood, Roger & Kidd, Virginia
Woven in darkness. + Fenn, W. W.
The wrath of Fu Manchu, and other stories. + Rohmer, Sax
The wrath of grapes. + Wibberley, Leonard
Wrath of the shades. + Nicholson, C. A.
The wrath to come. + Mackenzie, Nigel
The wrath to come. + Oppenheim, E. Phillips
Wraxton Marne. + Ray, Rene
The wreck of a world. + Grove, W.
The wreck of the South Pole. + Hahn, Charles Curtz
The wreck of Westminster Abbey. + (Croft, Herbert)
The wrecking ray. + Wedlake, G. E. C.
The wrecks of time. + Moorcock, Michael
Wrexham's romance. + "Ganpat"
A wrinkle in the skin. + Christopher, John
A wrinkle in time. + L'Engle, Madeleine
The writing on the wall. + 'General Staff'

Written with my left hand. + Barker, Nugent
The wrong end of time. + Brunner, John
Wrong side of the Moon. + Ashton, Francis & Ashton, Stephen
Wulfheim. + Furey, Michael
Wulnoth the Wanderer. + Inman, H. Escott-
Wuthering heights. + Bronte, Emily
The Wyndcliffe. + Lawrence, Louise

X. + Sudak, Eunice
The X factor. + Norton, Andre
The X-machine. + Muller, John E.
The "X" People. + Brack, Vektis
X-ray menace. + Herscholt, Wolfe
Xenogenesis. + deFord, Miriam Allen
Xiccarph. + Smith, Clark Ashton
Xuan and the girl from the other side. + Bergin, Paul A.

A yank at Valhalla. + Hamilton, Edmond
A Yankee at the court of King Arthur. + Twain, Mark
A Yankee Napoleon. + Macpherson, John F.
Yankee viking. + Hartley, Livingston
The year after tomorrow. + Carmer, Carl & del Rey, Lester & Matschat, Cecile
The year dot. + Lymington, John
The year for love. + (Smith, George H.)
Year of consent. + Crossen, Kendell Foster
The year of miracle. + Hume, Fergus
The year of regeneration. + Lawrence, James Cooper
The year of the angry rabbit. + Braddon, Russell
The year of the cloud. + Thomas, Ted & Wilhelm, Kate
The year of the comet. + Christopher, John
The year of the last eagle. + Rienow, Leona Train & Rienow, Robert
The year of the quiet sun. + Tucker, Wilson
The year of the rats. + Ricci, Barbara Guignon
Year of the Unicorn. + Norton, Andre
Year of the yahoo. + Wartofsky, Victor
The year the Yankees lost the pennant. + Wallop, Douglass
Year 3097. + Hunger, Anna & Miller, R. DeWitt
Year 2018! + Blish, James
The year 2000. + Harrison, Harry
The year when stardust fell. + Jones, Raymond F.
The year's best horror stories, no. 1. + Davis, Richard
The year's best horror stories, no. 3. + Davis, Richard
The year's best horror stories, no. 2. + Davis, Richard
The year's best horror stories, series II. + Davis, Richard
The year's best S-F, 5th annual edition. + Merril, Judith
Year's best science fiction novels. + Bleiler, Everett F. & Dikty, T. E.
Year's best science fiction novels, 1952. + Bleiler, Everett F. & Dikty, T. E.
Year's best science fiction novels, 1953. + Bleiler, Everett F. & Dikty, T. E.
Year's best sicence fiction novels, 1954. + Bleiler, Everett F. & Dikty, T. E.
Year's best science fiction novels, second series. + Bleiler, Everett F. & Dikty, T. E.
The year's best science fiction, no. 5. + Aldiss, Brian W. & Harrison, Harry
The year's best science fiction, no. 4. + Aldiss, Brian W. & Harrison, Harry
The year's best science fiction, no. 1. + Aldiss, Brian W. & Harrison, Harry
The year's best science fiction, no. 6. + Aldiss, Brian W. & Harrison, Harry

The year's best science fiction, no. 2. + Aldiss, Brian W. & Harrison, Harry
The year's best science fiction 3. + Aldiss, Brian W. & Harrison, Harry
The yellow cloud. + Robeson, Kenneth
The yellow danger. + Shiel, M. P.
Yellow death. + Key, Uel
The Yellow fraction. + Gordon, Rex
The Yellow God. + Haggard, H. Rider
The yellow hand. + Upward, Allen
The yellow inferno. + Ranzetta, Luan
Yellow magic. + Thomas, Eugene
The yellow mistletoe. + Masterman, Walter S.
The yellow people. + Peterson, Margaret
The yellow peril. + Shiel, M. P.
The yellow peril in action. + Manson, Marsden
The yellow planet. + Brown, George Sheldon
The Yellow Room. + Shipway, George
The yellow scourge. + Steele, Curtis
The yellow wave. + Mackay, Kenneth
Yermah the Dorado. + Colburn, Frona Eunice Wait
Yesterday. + Davey, Norman
Yesterday and tomorrow. + Verne, Jules
Yesterday's children. + Gerrold, David
'Yet in my flesh--.' + Mitchell, M. E.
Yet more Penguin science fiction. + Aldiss, Brian W.
Yezad. + Babcock, George
The yngling. + Dalmas, John
The yoke. + Miller, Elizabeth
Yonder. + Beaumont, Charles
You can't hang the dead. + Carroll, Leslie
You can't keep murder out. + Valdez, Paul
You do take it with you. + MacDonald, Donald K. & Roberts, Alaric J.
You sane men. + Janifer, Laurence M.
You shall know them. + Vercors
You will never be the same. + Smith, Cordwainer
You'll need a night light. + Thomson, Christine Campbell
You'll see. + Larsen, Egon
Young demons. + Elwood, Roger & Ghidalia, Vic
The young Diana. + Corelli, Marie
Young folks' library, vol. IV. + Jenks, Tudor
Young Frankenstein. + Pearlman, Gilbert
The young magicians. + Carter, Lin
The Young Man from Lima. + Blackburn, John
The Young Men are coming! + Shiel, M. P.
Young readers' science fiction stories. + Elam, Richard M. Jr.
Young stowaways in space. + Elam, Richard M. Jr.
The young unicorns. + L'Engle, Madeleine
Young visitor to Mars. + Elam, Richard M. Jr.
Young visitor to the Moon. + Elam, Richard M. Jr.
Young West. + Schindler, Solomon
Your sins and mine. + Caldwell, Taylor
Your story, Zalea. + Langdon, Norman E.
You're all alone. + Leiber, Fritz
Yours truly, Jack the Ripper. + Bloch, Robert
Youth madness. + none
The youth monopoly. + Wobig, Ellen
The Yu-Chi Stone. + Snell, Edmund
Yu'an Hee See laughs. + Rohmer, Sax

The Z effect. + Laurens, Marshall
Z formations. + Shaw, Brian
ZR wins. + Green, Fitzhugh
The "Z" ray. + Snell, Edmund
Zacherleys midnight snacks. + Zacherley
Zacherley's vulture stew. + Zacherley
Zadig. + Voltaire
Zadig, and other romances. + Voltaire
Zag the Great and Zig the Big. + Young, Peter
Zalea. + Garland, Rufus Cummins

Zanoni. + Lytton, Edward Bulwer
Zanoni; Zicci. + Lytton, Edward Bulwer
Zanthar at Moon's madness. + Williams, Robert Moore
Zanthar at the edge of never. + Williams, Robert Moore
Zanthar at trip's end. + Williams, Robert Moore
Zanthar of the many worlds. + Williams, Robert Moore
The zap gun. + Dick, Philip K.
Zardoz. + Boorman, John & Stair, Bill
Zarlah, the Martian. + Grisewood, R. Norman
Zaudi (Princess of Abyssinia). + Ashley-Brown, W.
Zelma, the mystic. + Thurber, Alwyn M.
Zenia, the Vestal. + Peeke, Margaret B.
Zenith-D. + Lorraine, Paul
Zenya. + Tubb, E. C.
The Zeppelin destroyer. + Le Queux, William
Zero field. + Hunt, Gill
Zero gravity swap. + Pygaster, Cal I.
Zero hour. + Statten, Vargo
Zero minus X. + Zeigfreid, Karl
Zero Point. + Le Page, Rand
The zero ray terrors. + Portwin, E. T.
The zero stone. + Norton, Andre
Zero the slaver. + Fletcher, Lawrence
Zero to eighty. + Pseudoman, Akkad
Zeus Bentley. + Parker, Joseph D.
Zhorani (master of the universe). + Maras, Karl
Zig and Zag from planet ZV7. + Young, Peter
The Zilov bombs. + Barron, D. G.
Zip-Zip and his flying saucer. + Schealer, John M.
Zip-Zip and the red planet. + Schealer, John M.
Zip-Zip goes to Venus. + Schealer, John M.
Ziska. + Corelli, Marie
Zodiak. + Eidlitz, Walther
Zoe & Zaida. + Raffin, Alain
Zoe's revenge. + Halidom, M. Y.
Zofloya. + Dacre, Charlotte
The Zolotov affair. + Rimmer, Robert H.
Zone null. + Franke, Herbert W.
Zoo 2000. + Yolen, Jane
Zoraida. + Le Queux, William
Zorastro. + Thompson, Creswick J.
Zoroaster. + Crawford, F. Marion
Zothique. + Smith, Clark Ashton
Zotz! + Karig, Walter
Zozu the robot. + Carter, Angela
Zulu heart. + Du Bois, Shirley Graham
Zylgrahof, and other stories. + Shannon, John C.

Series Index

AANN SERIES (Alan Dean Foster)

#1 The Tar-Aiym Krang. (1972)
#2 Bloodhype. (1973)

ABBEY OF KILKHAMPTON (Sir Herbert Croft)

#1 The Abbey of Kilkhampton. (1780)
#2 The second part of The Abbey of Kilkhampton.
    (1780)

ABDALLAH SERIES (Katrina Dombrowski [K.O.S.])

#1 Abdallah and the donkey. (1928)
#2 The fat camel of Bagdad. (1929)

THE ADDAMS FAMILY (various authors)

#1 The Addams family. (1965) [by Jack Sharkey]
#2 The Addams family strikes back. (1965) [by
    William Miksch]

ADONIS TRILOGY (William J. Lambert III)

#1 Adonis. (1969)
#2 Adonis at Actum. (1970)
#3 Adonis at Bomasa. (1970)

ADVENTURES IN THE TIME MACHINE (Robert Faraday)

#1 The anytime rings. (1963)
#2 Samax, the gladiator. (1964)

ADVENTURES IN THE UNKNOWN (Carl H. Claudy)

#1 The mystery men of Mars. (1933)
#2 A thousand years a minute. (1933)
#3 The Land of No Shadow. (1933)
#4 The Blue Grotto terror. (1934)

ADVISE AND CONSENT (Allen Drury)

#1 Advise and consent. (1959)
#2 A shade of difference. (1962)
#3 Capable of honor. (1966)
#4 Preserve and protect. (1968)
#5A Come Nineveh, come Tyre. (1973)

AFTER SUCH KNOWLEDGE (James Blish)

#1 Doctor Mirabilis. (1964) [not SF]
#2 Black Easter. (1968)
#3 The day after judgment. (1971)
#4 A case of conscience. (1958)

THE AGENCY (David Meltzer)

#1 The Agency. (1968)
#2 The agent. (1968)
#3 How many blocks in the pile? (1968)

AGENT OF T.E.R.R.A. (Larry Maddock)

#1 The flying saucer gambit. (1966)
#2 The Golden Goddess gambit. (1967)
#3 The emerald elephant gambit. (1967)
#4 The time trap gambit. (1969)

AGENT 0008 (Clyde Allison)

#1 Our man from SADISTO. (1965)
#2 Our girl from MEPHISTO. (1965)
#3 Nautipuss. (1965)

#4 Go-go SADISTO. (1966)
#5 The Desdamona affair. (1966)
#6 Gamefinger. (1966)
#7 SADISTO royale. (1966)
#8 0008 meets Gnatman. (1966)
#9 For your sighs only. (1966)
#10 The lost bomb. (1966)
#11 Merciless mermaids. (1966)
#12 Mondo SADISTO. (1966)
#13 0008 meets Modesta Blaze. (1966)
#14 The sex-ray. (1966)
#15 Roburta the Conqueress. (1966)
#16 From rapture with love. (1966)
#17 The ice maiden. (1967)
#18 The sin funnel. (1967)
#19 Platypussy. (1968)
#20 The desert damsels. (1968)

AIA SEQUENCE (E. Charles Vivian)

#1 Fields of sleep. (1923)
#2 People of the darkness. (1924)

THE AIRPLANE BOYS [THE SKY BUDDIES] (E. J.
Craine)

#1 Airplane Boys on the border line. (1930)
#2 Airplane Boys at Cap Rock. (1930)
#3 Airplane Boys discover the secrets of Cuzco.
    (1930)
#4 Airplane Boys flying to Amy-Ran Fastness. (1930)
#5 Airplane Boys at Platinum River. (1931)
#6 Airplane Boys with the revolutionists in Bolivia.
    (1931)
#7 Airplane Boys in the Black Woods. (1932)
#8 Airplane Boys at Belize. (1932)
--Also issued as part of the Sky Buddies series
without the words "Airplane Boys" in the titles.

THE AIRSHIP BOYS (H. L. Sayler)

#1 The Airship Boys. (1909)
#2 The Airship Boys adrift. (1909)
#3 The Airship Boys due north. (1910)
#4 The Airship Boys in the barren lands. (1910)
#5 The Airship Boys in finance. (1911)
#6 The Airship Boys' ocean flyer. (1911)

ALICE SERIES (Lewis Carroll)

#1 Alice's adventures in Wonderland. (1865)
#2 Through the looking-glass. (1872)

SEQUELS AND PARODIES:

    Alice in Blunderland. (1907) [by John Kendrick
    Bangs]
#1 Clara in Blunderland. (1902) [by Harold Begbie,
    J. Stafford Ransome, & M. H. Temple writing
    as Caroline Lewis]
#2 Lost in Blunderland. (1903) [by Caroline Lewis]
    Davy and the goblin. (1885) [by Charles E.
    Carryl]
    Alice's adventures in Cambridge. (1913) [by R.
    C. Evarts]
    Alice in the Delighted States. (1928) [by Edward
    Hope]
#1 Alice in Orchestralia. (1925) [by Ernest La
    Prade]
#2 Marching notes. (1929) [by Ernest La Prade]
    Alice in Rankbustland. (1923) [by Edwin M. Otter-
    bourg]

ALICE SERIES (Lewis Carroll) [cont.]

SEQUELS AND PARODIES (cont.):

A new Alice in the old Wonderland. (1895) [by
   Anna M. Richards Jr.]
Blue Alice. (1972) [by Jackson Short]
More 'Alice.' (1959) [by Yates Wilson]
Malice in Kulturland. (1914) [by Horace Wyatt]

DIG ALLEN SPACE EXPLORER ADVENTURES (Joseph
Greene)

#1   The forgotten star. (1959)
#2   Captives in space. (1960)
#3   Journey to Jupiter. (1961)
#4   Trappers of Venus. (1961)
#5   Robots of Saturn. (1962)
#6   Lost city of Uranus. (1962)

AMARTUS SEQUENCE (Phyllis Cradock)

#1   Gateway to remembrance. (1949)
#2   The eternal echo. (1950)

AMBER SERIES (Roger Zelazny)

#1   Nine princes in Amber. (1970)
#2   The guns of Avalon. (1972)

CAPTAIN AMERICA (various authors)

#1   The Avengers battle the Earth-wrecker. (1967)
    [by Otto Binder]
#2   Captain America: the great gold steal. (1968)
    [by Ted White]

ANDREW AMES (Marie C. Farca)

#1   Earth. (1972)
#2   Complex man. (1973)

AMPHIBIANS SEQUENCE (S. Fowler Wright)

#1   The amphibians. (1925)
#2   The world below. (1951)
#s 1-2   The world below. (1929)

ANNABEL ANDREWS (Mary Rodgers)

#1   Freaky Friday. (1972)
#2   A billion for Boris. (1974)

ANDROMEDA SERIES (John Elliot & Fred Hoyle)

#1   A for Andromeda. (1962)
#2   Andromeda breakthrough. (1964)

BROTHER ANGELO (Rosalie Lieberman)

#1   The man who sold Christmas. (1951)
#2   The man who captivated New York. (1960)

ANGRIA SERIES (Charlotte Bronte)

The twelve adventurers, and other stories. (1925)
Legends of Angria. (1933)

ANJANI (Earl Titan [John Russell Fearn])

#1   The gold of Akada. (1951)
#2   Anjani the mighty. (1951)

ANNWN SERIES (George H. Smith)

#1   Scourge of the blood cult. (1961)
#2   Kar Kaballa. (1969)
#3   Witch Queen of Lochlann. (1969)

ANTHROPOL SERIES (Louis Trimble)

#1   Anthropol. (1968)
#2   The noblest experiment in the galaxy. (1970)

ANTIGEOS TRILOGY (Paul Capon)

#1   The other side of the Sun. (1950)
#2   The other half of the planet. (1952)
#3   Down to Earth. (1954)

ARCOT, WADE & MOREY SERIES (John W. Campbell)

#1   The black star passes. (1953)
#2   Islands of space. (1956)
#3   Invaders from the infinite. (1961)
#s 1-3   John W. Campbell anthology. (1973)

ARDEN SEQUENCE (E. Nesbit) [see Addendum]

#1   The house of Arden. (1908)
#2   Harding's luck. (1909)

SIMON ARK (Edward D. Hoch)

#1   The judges of Hades, and other Simon Ark stories.
    (1971)
#2   City of Brass. (1971)

ARMATA SEQUENCE (Thomas Erskine)

#1   Armata. (1817)
#2   The second part of Armata. (1817)

JAMES ARMITAGE (Franklyn Kelsey)

#1   The island in the mist. (1937)
#2   The children of the Sun. (1939)
#3   The prowlers of the deep. (1942)

KING ARTHUR (T. H. White)

#1   The sword in the stone. (1938)
#2   The witch in the wood. (1939)
#3   The ill-made knight. (1940)
#s 1-4   The once and future king. (1958)

ARWEN (Marion Zimmer Bradley)

#1   The jewel of Arwen. (1974)
#2   The parting of Arwen. (1974)

ASTRA SEQUENCE (Andre Norton)

#1   The stars are ours! (1954)
#2   Star born. (1957)

ATHALIE (Robert W. Chambers)

#1   Quick action. (1914)
#2   Athalie. (1915)

STEVE AUSTIN
   see: CYBORG

GEOFFREY AYLETT (Vivian Meik)

#1 Devils' drums. (1933)
#2 Veils of fear. (1934)

DUSTY AYRES AND HIS BATTLE BIRDS (Robert Sidney Bowen)

#1 Black lightning. (1966)
#2 Crimson doom. (1966)
#3 Purple tornado. (1966)
#4 The Telsa raiders. (1966)
#5 Black invaders vs. the Battle Birds. (1966)

AZAN THE APE MAN (Marco Gar(r)on)

#1 The missing safari. (1950)
#2 The lost city. (1950)
#3 Jungle fever. (1950?)
#4 White fangs. (1951?)
#5 Tribal war. (1951?)
#6 King hunters. (1951?)

BADSHAH SERIES (Gordon Casserly)

#1 The elephant god. (1920)
#2 The jungle girl. (1921)

LIJE BALEY
    see: ROBOT STORIES

BARCLAY SERIES (Michael Elder)

#1 Nowhere on Earth. (1972)
#2 The perfumed planet. (1973)
#3 Down to Earth. (1973)
#4 The seeds of frenzy. (1974)

BARNUM SYSTEM (Ron Goulart)

#1 The fire-eater. (1970)
#2 Shaggy planet. (1972)

JACK SUMNER STORIES:

#1 Death Cell. (1971)
#2 Plunder. (1972)

THE BARONESS (Paul Kenyon)

#1 The ecstasy connection. (1974)
#2 Diamonds are for dying. (1974)
#3 Death is a ruby light. (1974)
#4 Hard-core murder. (1974)
#5 Operation Doomsday. (1974)
#6 Sonic slave. (1974)
#7 Flicker of doom. (1974)

RON BARRON (Raymond F. Jones)

#1 Son of the stars. (1952)
#2 Planet of light. (1953)

THE BARSAC MISSION (Jules Verne)

#1 Into the Niger Bend. (1960)
#2 The city in the Sahara. (1960)

TYCHO BASS (Eleanor Cameron)

#1 The wonderful flight to the mushroom planet.
    (1954)

#2 Stowaway to the mushroom planet. (1956)
#3 Mr. Bass's planetoid. (1958)
#4 A mystery for Mr. Bass. (1960)
#5 Time and Mr. Bass. (1967)

OSWALD BASTABLE (Michael Moorcock)

#1 The Warlord of the air. (1971)
#2 The Land Leviathan. (1974)

BED-KNOB AND BROOMSTICK (Mary Norton)

#1 The magic bed-knob. (1943)
#2 Bonfires and broomsticks. (1947)
#s 1-2 Bed-knob and broomstick. (1957)

BEL SERIES (Charles Carr)

#1 Colonists of space. (1954)
#2 Salamander war. (1955)

BEN SERIES (various authors)

#1 Ratman's notebooks. (1968) [by Stephen Gilbert]
#2 Ben. (1972) [by Gilbert A. Ralston]

BERSERKER SERIES (Fred Saberhagen)

#1 Berserker. (1967)
#2 Brother assassin. (1969)

BEWITCHED (various authors)

    Bewitched. (1965) [by Al Hine]
    Bewitched; The opposite uncle. (1970) [by William Johnston]

MISS BIANCA (Margery Sharp)

#1 The rescuers. (1959)
#2 Miss Bianca. (1962)
#3 The turret. (1963)
#4 Miss Bianca in the salt mines. (1966)
#5 Miss Bianca in the Orient. (1970)
#6 Miss Bianca in the Antarctic. (1971)
#7 Miss Bianca and the bridesmaid. (1972)

CAPTAIN BLACK (Max Pemberton)

#1 The iron pirate. (1893)
#2 Captain Black. (1911)

GAVIN BLACK (John Jakes)

#1 Master of the dark gate. (1970)
#2 Witch of the dark gate. (1972)

BLACKBEARD (Ben Stahl)

#1 Blackbeard's ghost. (1965)
#2 The secret of Red Skull. (1971)

RICHARD BLADE (Jeffrey Lord, house pseud.)

#1 The bronze axe. (1969)
#2 The jade warrior. (1969)
#3 Jewel of Tharn. (1969)
#4 Slave of Sarma. (1970)
#5 Liberator of Jedd. (1971)
#6 Monster of the maze. (1972)
#7 Pearl of Patmos. (1973)
#8 Undying world. (1973)
#9 Kingdom of Royth. (1974)

RICHARD BLADE (Jeffrey Lord) [cont.]

#10 Ice dragon. (1974)
#11 Dimension of dreams. (1974)

BLIND SPOT SERIES (Austin Hall & Homer Eon Flint)

#1 The Blind Spot. (1951)
#2 The Spot of Life. (1965) [by Austin Hall]

SIBYL SUE BLUE (Rosel George Brown)

#1 Sibyl Sue Blue. (1966)
#2 The waters of Centaurus. (1970)

BOMBA THE JUNGLE BOY (Roy Rockwood)

#1 Bomba the jungle boy. (1926)
#2 Bomba the jungle boy at the moving mountain.
     (1926)
#3 Bomba the jungle boy at the giant cataract.
     (1926)
#4 Bomba the jungle boy on Jaguar Island. (1927)
#5 Bomba the jungle boy in the abandoned city.
     (1927)
#6 Bomba the jungle boy on terror trail. (1928)
#7 Bomba the jungle boy in the swamp of death.
     (1929)
#8 Bomba the jungle boy among the slaves. (1929)
#9 Bomba the jungle boy on the underground river.
     (1930)
#10 Bomba the jungle boy and the lost explorers.
     (1930)
#11 Bomba the jungle boy in a strange land. (1931)
#12 Bomba the jungle boy among the pygmies. (1931)
#13 Bomba the jungle boy and the cannibals. (1932)
#14 Bomba the jungle boy and the painted hunters.
     (1932)
#15 Bomba the jungle boy and the river demons.
     (1933)
#16 Bomba the jungle boy and the hostile chieftain.
     (1934)
#17 Bomba the jungle boy trapped by the cyclone.
     (1935)
#18 Bomba the jungle boy in the land of burning lava.
     (1936)
#19 Bomba the jungle boy in the perilous kingdom.
     (1937)
#20 Bomba the jungle boy in the steaming grotto.
     (1938)

THE BORROWERS (Mary Norton)

#1 The Borrowers. (1952)
#2 The Borrowers afield. (1955)
#3 The Borrowers afloat. (1959)
#4 The Borrowers aloft. (1961)
#s 1-4 The Borrowers omnibus. (1966)

THE BOY INVENTORS (Richard Bonner)

#1 The Boy Inventors' wireless triumph. (1912)
#2 The Boy Inventors and the vanishing gun. (1912)
#3 The Boy Inventors' diving torpedo. (1912)
#4 The Boy Inventors' flying ship. (1913)
#5 The Boy Inventors' electric hydroaeroplane.
     (1914)
#6 The Boy Inventors' radio-telephone. (1915)

BRAIN-PLANT QUATROLOGY (David Meltzer)

#1 Lovely. (1969)
#2 Healer. (1969)
#3 Out. (1969)
#4 Glue factory. (1969)

BRAK THE BARBARIAN (John Jakes)

#1 Brak the barbarian. (1968)
#2 Brak the barbarian versus the sorceress. (1969)
#3 Brak the barbarian versus the mark of the demons.
     (1969)

RICK BRANT SCIENCE-ADVENTURE STORIES (John Blaine)

#1 The rocket's shadow. (1947)
#2 The lost city. (1947)
#3 Sea gold. (1947)
#4 100 fathoms under. (1947)
#5 The whispering box mystery. (1948)
#6 The phantom shark. (1949)
#7 Smugglers' Reef. (1950)
#8 The Caves of Fear. (1951)
#9 Stairway to danger. (1952)
#10 The golden skull. (1954)
#11 The wailing octopus. (1956)
#12 The electronic mind reader. (1957)
#13 The Scarlet Lake mystery. (1958)
#14 The pirates of Shan. (1958)
#15 The blue ghost mystery. (1960)
#16 The Egyptian cat mystery. (1961)
#17 The flaming mountain. (1962)
#18 The flying stingaree. (1963)
#19 The ruby ray mystery. (1964)
#20 The veiled raiders. (1965)
#21 Rocket jumper. (1966)
#22 The deadly Dutchman. (1967)
#23 Danger below! (1968)

CASTLE BRASS
   see: RUNESTAFF

FRANK BRAUN (Hanns Heinz Ewers)

     The sorcerer's apprentice. (1927)
     Alraune. (1929)

THE BRITISH BARBARIANS (Grant Allen)

     The British barbarians. (1895)

SEQUELS AND PARODIES:

     The barbarous Britishers. (1896) [by H. D. Traill]

BRONSON BETA SERIES (Edwin Balmer & Philip Wylie)

#1 When worlds collide. (1933)
#2 After worlds collide. (1934)

REGGIE BROOKS (Donald Macpherson)

#1 Go home, unicorn. (1935)
#2 Men are like animals. (1937)

THE BUGALOOS (Chris Stratton)

#1 The Bugaloos and the vile Vibes. (1971)
#2 Rock City rebels. (1971)
#3 Benita's platter pollution. (1971)

MILES CABOT (Ralph Milne Farley)

#1 The radio man. (1948)
#2 The radio beasts. (1964)
#3 The radio planet. (1964)

TARL CABOT
  see: GOR SERIES

DOC CALIBAN (Philip Jose Farmer)

#1 A feast unknown. (1969)
#2 The mad goblin. (1970)

BEN CAMDEN (Heinrich Graat)

#1 The revenge of Increase Sewell. (1969)
#2 The devil and Ben Camden. (1970)
#3 A place of demons. (1972)

DON CAMILLO (Giovanni Guareschi)

#1 The little world of Don Camillo. (1950)
#2 Don Camillo and his flock. (1952)
#3 Don Camillo's dilemma. (1954)
#4 Don Camillo takes the devil by the tail. (1957)
#5 Comrade Don Camillo. (1964)
#6 Don Camillo meets the flower children. (1969)

CARBONEL (Barbara Sleigh)

#1 Carbonel. (1955)
#2 The kingdom of Carbonel. (1959)

LUCIAN CAROLUS (Eugene Ascher)

The grim caretaker. (1944)
There were no Asper ladies. (1944)

CASPAK SERIES (Edgar Rice Burroughs)

#1 The land that time forgot. (1963)
#2 The people that time forgot. (1963)
#3 Out of time's abyss. (1963)
#s 1-3 The land that time forgot. (1924)

CATFISH BEND (Ben Lucien Burman)

#1 High water at Catfish Bend. (1952)
#2 Seven stars for Catfish Bend. (1956)
#3 The owl hoots twice at Catfish Bend. (1961)
#s 1-3 Three from Catfish Bend. (1967)

PROFESSOR CHALLENGER (A. Conan Doyle)

#1 The lost world. (1912)
#2 The poison belt. (1913)
#3 The land of mist. (1926)
#s 1-3 The Professor Challenger stories. (1952)

THE CHAMELEON CORPS
  see: JOLSON, BEN

THE CHANGES (Peter Dickinson)

#1 The devil's children. (1970)
#2 Heartsease. (1969)
#3 The weathermonger. (1968)

FELIX CHARLOCK (Lawrence Durrell)

#1 Tunc. (1968)
#2 Nunquam. (1970)

HERALD CHILDE (Philip Jose Farmer)

#1 The image of the beast. (1968)
#2 Blown. (1969)
#3 Traitor to the living. (1973)

CHILDE CYCLE [DORSAI SERIES] (Gordon R. Dickson)

#1 The genetic general. (1960)
#2 Necromancer. (1962)
#3 Soldier, ask not. (1967)

A CHRISTMAS CAROL (Charles Dickens)

A Christmas carol. (1843)

SEQUELS AND PARODIES:

"Christmas Eve" with the spirits. (1869) [anonymously published]
"Scrooge." (1970) [by Elaine Donaldson]

CHRONICLES OF PRYDAIN (Lloyd Alexander)

#1 The Book of Three. (1964)
#2 The Black Cauldron. (1965)
#3 The Castle of Llyr. (1966)
#4 Taran Wanderer. (1967)
#5 The High King. (1968)

RELATED TITLES:

The foundling, and other tales of Prydain. (1973)

CIJA (Jane Gaskell)

#1 The serpent. (1963)
#2 Atlan. (1965)
#3 The City. (1966)

CITIES IN FLIGHT (James Blish)

#1 They shall have stars. (1956)
#2 A life for the stars. (1962)
#3 Earthman, come home. (1955)
#4 The triumph of time. (1958)
#s 1-4 Cities in flight. (1970)

CLARA
  see: ALICE

HORACE CLARKE (Irwin Lewis)

#1 The day they invaded New York. (1964)
#2 The day New York trembled. (1967)

CLAUDIUS THE BEE (John F. Leeming)

#1 Claudius the bee. (1936)
#2 Thanks to Claudius. (1937)

REX CLINTON (W. F. Johns)

#1 Kings of space. (1954)
#2 Return to Mars. (1955)
#3 Now to the stars. (1956)
#4 To outer space. (1957)

REX CLINTON (W. E. Johns) [cont.]

#5 The edge of beyond. (1958)
#6 The death rays of Ardilla. (1959)
#7 To worlds unknown. (1960)
#8 The quest for the perfect planet. (1961)
#9 Worlds of wonder. (1962)
#10 The man who vanished into space. (1963)

CLOTHES OF A KING'S SON (Pamela Frankau)

#1 Sing for your supper. (1963)
#2 Slaves of the lamp. (1965)
#3 Over the mountains. (1967) [not SF?]

CLUB OF THE ROUND TABLE (Margery Lawrence)

#1 Nights of the Round Table. (1926)
#2 The terraces of night. (1932)

GENGHIS COHN (Romain Gary)

#1 The dance of Genghis Cohn. (1968)
#2 The guilty head. (1969)

COLIN (E. F. Benson)

#1 Colin. (1923)
#2 Colin II. (1925)

COLIN AND SUSAN (Alan Garner)

#1 The weirdstone of Brisingamen. (1960)
#2 The moon of Gomrath. (1963)

PAT COLLINS (Bernard Palmer)

#1 Pat Collins and the peculiar Dr. Brockton.
    (1957)
#2 Pat Collins and the secret engine. (1957)
#3 Pat Collins and the hidden treasure. (1957)
#4 Pat Collins and the wingless plane. (1957)
#5 Pat Collins and the mysterious orbiting rocket.
    (1958)
#6 Pat Collins and the captive scientist. (1958)
--[see also JIM DUNLAP]

COLOSSUS SERIES (D. F. Jones)

#1 Colossus. (1966)
#2 The fall of Colossus. (1974)

CONAN (Robert E. Howard and others)

FIRST SERIES:

#1 Conan the Conqueror. (1950)
#2 The sword of Conan. (1952)
#3 The coming of Conan. (1953)
#4 King Conan. (1953)
#5 Conan the barbarian. (1954)
#6 Tales of Conan. (1955) [with L. Sprague de Camp]
#7 The return of Conan. (1957) [by L. Sprague de
    Camp and Bjorn Nyberg]

SECOND SERIES:

#1 Conan. (1967) [with Lin Carter & L. Sprague de
    Camp]
#2 Conan of Cimmeria. (1969) [with Lin Carter &
    L. Sprague de Camp]
#3 Conan the freebooter. (1968) [with L. Sprague
    de Camp]

#4 Conan the wanderer. (1968) [with Lin Carter &
    L. Sprague de Camp]
#5 Conan the adventurer. (1966) [with L. Sprague
    de Camp]
#6 Conan the buccaneer. (1971) [by Lin Carter &
    L. Sprague de Camp]
#7 Conan the warrior. (1967)
#8 Conan the usurper (1967) [with L. Sprague de
    Camp]
#9 Conan the Conqueror. (1967)
#10 Conan the avenger. (1968) [with L. Sprague de
    Camp and Bjorn Nyberg]
#11 (Conan of Aquilonia.)
#12 Conan of the Isles. (1968) [by Lin Carter &
    L. Sprague de Camp]

THIRD SERIES:

#1 The people of the black circle. (1974)

RELATED TITLES:

    The Conan reader. (1968) [edited by L. Sprague
    de Camp]
    The Conan swordbook. (1969) [edited by L. Sprague
    de Camp & George Scithers]
    The Conan grimoire. (1972) [edited by L. Sprague
    de Camp & George Scithers]

CONCEPTION SEQUENCE (R. John Smythe)

#1 The conception. (1969)
#2 The coming of Morikand. (1970)

THE CONQUEST OF THE UNITED STATES (H. Irving
Hancock)

#1 The invasion of the United States. (1916)
#2 In the battle for New York. (1916)
#3 At the defense of Pittsburgh. (1916)
#4 Making the stand for Old Glory. (1916)

TOM CORBETT, SPACE CADET (Carey Rockwell)

#1 Stand by for Mars! (1952)
#2 Danger in deep space. (1953)
#3 On the trail of space pirates. (1953)
#4 The space pioneers. (1953)
#5 The revolt on Venus. (1954)
#6 Treachery in outer space. (1954)
#7 Sabotage in space. (1955)
#8 The robot rocket. (1956)

JERRY CORNELIUS (Michael Moorcock)

#1 The final programme. (1968)
#2 A cure for cancer. (1971)
#3 The English assassin. (1972)

CORUM (Michael Moorcock)

#1 The Knight of the Swords. (1971)
#2 The Queen of the Swords. (1971)
#3 The King of the Swords. (1971)
#4 The bull and the spear. (1973)
#5 The oak and the ram. (1973)
#6 The sword and the stallion. (1974)

CORY (Curt Siodmak)

#1 Donovan's brain. (1943)
#2 Hauser's memory. (1968)

CRAB ISLAND SERIES (Freda Hurt)

#1 Crab Island. (1965) [not SF?]
#2 Benny and the dolphin. (1968)
#3 Benny and the space boy. (1970)

CRAGHOLD SERIES (Edwina Noone [Michael Avallone])

#1 The Craghold legacy. (1971)
#2 The Craghold curse. (1972)
#3 The Craghold creatures. (1972)
#4 The Craghold crypt. (1973)

COMMANDER CRAIG GALACTIC ADVENTURES (Bart Somers [Gardner F. Fox])

#1 Beyond the black Enigma. (1965)
#2 Abandon galaxy! (1967)

MARGUERITE CRANLEIGH (S. Fowler Wright)

#1 Dream. (1931)
#2 Spiders' war. (1954)

HOMER CRAWFORD (Mack Reynolds)

#1 Blackman's burden. (1972)
#2 Border, breed, nor birth. (1972)

JASON CROFT (J. U. Giesy)

#1 Palos the Dog Star Pack. (1965)
#2 The Mouthpiece of Zitu. (1965)
#3 Jason, son of Jason. (1966)

CROYD (Ian Wallace)

#1 Croyd. (1967)
#2 Deathstar voyage. (1969)
#3 A voyage to Dari. (1974)

CURDIE (George MacDonald) [see Addendum]

#1 The princess and the goblin. (1871)
#2 The princess and Curdie. (1883)

THE CURIOUS LOBSTER (Richard W. Hatch)

#1 The curious lobster. (1937)
#2 The curious lobster's island. (1939)
#s 1-2 The lobster books. (1951)

CYBORG [STEVE AUSTIN] (Martin Caidin)

#1 Cyborg. (1972)
#2 Operation Nuke. (1973)
#3 High crystal. (1974)

THE DANCERS AT THE END OF TIME (Michael Moorcock)

#1 An alien heat. (1972)
#2 The hollow lands. (1974)

THE DARK IS RISING (Susan Cooper)

#1 Over sea, under stone. (1965)
#2 The dark is rising. (1973)
#3 Greenwitch. (1974)

DARK SHADOWS (Marilyn Ross)

#1 Dark shadows. (1966)
#2 Victoria Winters. (1967)
#3 Strangers at Collins House. (1967)
#4 The mystery of Collinwood. (1967)
#5 The curse of Collinwood. (1968)
#6 Barnabas Collins. (1968)
#7 The secret of Barnabas Collins. (1969)
#8 The demon of Barnabas Collins. (1969)
#9 The foe of Barnabas Collins. (1969)
#10 The phantom and Barnabas Collins. (1969)
#11 Barnabas Collins versus the warlock. (1969)
#12 The peril of Barnabas Collins. (1969)
#13 Barnabas Collins and the mysterious ghost.
     (1970)
#14 Barnabas Collins and Quentin's demon. (1970)
#15 Barnabas Collins and the gypsy witch. (1970)
#16 Barnabas, Quentin, and the mummy's curse. (1970)
#17 Barnabas, Quentin, and the avenging ghost.
     (1970)
#18 Barnabas, Quentin, and the nightmare assassin.
     (1970)
#19 Barnabas, Quentin, and the crystal coffin.
     (1970)
#20 Barnabas, Quentin, and the witch's curse. (1970)
#21 Barnabas, Quentin, and the haunted cave. (1970)
#22 Barnabas, Quentin, and the frightened bride.
     (1970)
#23 Barnabas, Quentin, and the Scorpio curse. (1970)
#24 Barnabas, Quentin, and the serpent. (1970)
#25 Barnabas, Quentin, and the magic potion. (1971)
#26 Barnabas, Quentin, and the body snatchers.
     (1971)
#27 Barnabas, Quentin, and Dr. Jekyll's son. (1971)
#28 Barnabas, Quentin, and the grave robbers. (1971)
#29 Barnabas, Quentin, and the sea ghost. (1971)
#30 Barnabas, Quentin, and the mad magician. (1971)
#31 Barnabas, Quentin, and the hidden tomb. (1971)
#32 Barnabas, Quentin, and the vampire beauty.
     (1972)

RELATED TITLE:

     House of dark shadows. (1970)

DARKNESS AND DAWN (George Allen England)

#1 Darkness and dawn. (1964)
#2 Beyond the great oblivion. (1965)
#3 The people of the abyss. (1966)
#4 Out of the abyss. (1967)
#5 The afterglow. (1967)
#s 1-5 Darkness and dawn. (1914)

DARKOVER SERIES (Marion Zimmer Bradley)

#1 Darkover landfall. (1972)
#2 The spell sword. (1974)
#3 Star of danger. (1965)
#4 The winds of Darkover. (1970)
#5 The bloody sun. (1964)
#6 (The heritage of Hastur.)
#7 The Sword of Aldones. (1962)
#8 The planet savers. (1962)
#9 The world wreckers. (1971)

PERCY DARROW (Stewart Edward White)

#1 The mystery. (1907) [with Samuel Hopkins Adams]
#2 The sign at six. (1912)

JAN DARZEK (Lloyd Biggle Jr.)

#1 All the colors of darkness. (1963)
#2 Watchers of the dark. (1966)

DR. DEATH (Zorro)

#1 12 must die. (1966)
#2 The gray creatures. (1966)
#3 The shriveling murders. (1966)

THE DEATHWORLD TRILOGY (Harry Harrison)

#1 Deathworld. (1960)
#2 Deathworld 2. (1964)
#3 Deathworld 3. (1968)
#s 1-3 The Deathworld trilogy. (1974)

MIKE DELANEY (Charles Eric Maine)

#1 The isotope man. (1957)
#2 Subterfuge. (1959)
#3 Never let up. (1964)

DEMON SERIES (William J. Lambert III)

#1 Demon's stalk. (1970)
#2 Demon's coronation. (1971)

DEMON PRINCE SERIES (Jack Vance)

#1 The Star King. (1964)
#2 The Killing Machine. (1964)
#3 The Palace of Love. (1967)

DERYNI CYCLE (Katherine Kurtz)

#1 Deryni rising. (1970)
#2 Deryni checkmate. (1972)
#3 High Deryni. (1973)

DESTINY SEQUENCE (David Grinnell [Donald A. Wollheim])

#1 Destiny's orbit. (1961)
#2 Destination: Saturn. (1967) [with Lin Carter]

THE DEVIL UPON TWO STICKS (Alain Rene Le Sage)

The devil upon crutches. (1750)

SEQUELS AND PARODIES:

The devil upon crutches in England. (1755)
The devil upon two sticks in England. (1790)
[by William Combe]

DEVILDAY SEQUENCE (Angus Hall)

#1 Devilday. (1969)
#2 To play the devil. (1971)

DIES IRAE (Brian M. Stableford)

#1 The days of glory. (1971)
#2 In the kingdom of the Beasts. (1971)
#3 Day of wrath. (1971)

SLIPPERY JIM DiGRIZ (Harry Harrison)

#1 The Stainless Steel Rat. (1961)
#2 The Stainless Steel Rat's revenge. (1970)
#3 The Stainless Steel Rat saves the world. (1972)

DILBIA SERIES (Gordon R. Dickson)

#1 Spacial delivery. (1961)
#2 Spacepaw. (1969)

MATTHEW DILKE (Lindsay Gutteridge)

#1 Cold war in a country garden. (1971)
#2 Killer pine. (1973)

DIPPLE SERIES (Andre Norton)

#1 Catseye. (1961)
#2 Judgment on Janus. (1963)
#3 Night of masks. (1964)

ANGELO DiSTEFANO (Laurence M. Janifer & S. J. Treibich)

#1 Target: Terra. (1968)
#2 The high hex. (1969)
#3 The wagered world. (1969)

DOLPHIN CYCLE (Roy Meyers)

#1 Dolphin boy. (1967)
#2 Daughters of the dolphin. (1968)
#3 Destiny and the dolphins. (1969)

DORKING (Sir George Chesney)

The Battle of Dorking. (1871)

SEQUELS AND PARODIES:

After the Battle of Dorking. (1871)
The Battle of Dorking a myth. (1871)
The battle off Worthing. (1887) [by a Captain
of the Royal Navy]
The cruise of the anti-torpedo. (1871)
The second Armada. (1871) [by Abraham Hayward]
The hens who tried to crow. (1871)
The new Battle of Dorking. (1900) [by F. N.
Maude]
The other side at the Battle of Dorking. (1871)
[by Maximilian Moltruhn]
The official despatches and correspondence rela-
to the Battle of Dorking. (1871)
Our hero. (1871)
Mrs. Brown on the Battle of Dorking. (1871) [by
Arthur Sketchley]
What happened after the Battle of Dorking. (1871)

RELATED TITLE:

The Battle of Dorking controversy. (1972) [edi-
ted by I. F. Clarke]

DORSAI CYCLE
see: CHILDE CYCLE

DRACULA (Bram Stoker)

Dracula. (1897)

SEQUELS AND PARODIES:

Dracula and the virgins of the undead. (1974)
[by Etienne Aubin]
The scars of Dracula. (1971) [by Angus Hall]
The adult version of Dracula. (1970) [by Hal
Kantor]
Dracutwig. (1969) [by Mallory T. Knight]

DRACULA (Bram Stoker) [cont.]

   SEQUELS AND PARODIES (cont.):

      The brides of Dracula. (1960) [by Dean Owen]
      Countess Dracula. (1971) [by Michel Parry]
      The Dracula archives. (1971) [by Raymond Ru-
        dorff]
      The vampire women. (1973) [by Victor Samuels]

   DRACULA HORROR SERIES (Robert Lory):

   #1 Dracula returns. (1973)
   #2 The hand of Dracula. (1973)
   #3 Dracula's brother. (1973)
   #4 Dracula's gold. (1973)
   #5 Drums of Dracula. (1974)
   #6 The witching of Dracula. (1974)
   #7 Dracula's lost world. (1974)

DRAGONFALL 5 (Brian Earnshaw)

   #1 Dragonfall 5 and the space cowboys. (1972)
   #2 Dragonfall 5 and the Royal Beast. (1972)
   #3 Dragonfall 5 and the empty planet. (1973)
   #4 Dragonfall 5 and the hijackers. (1974)

DRAGONRIDERS OF PERN (Anne McCaffrey)

   #1 Dragonflight. (1968)
   #2 Dragonquest. (1971)

DRALE SEQUENCE (Ben Aronin)

   #1 The lost tribe. (1934)
   #2 Cavern of destiny. (1943)

THE DREAMHOUSE (Tony Russell Wayman)

   #1 World of the sleeper. (1967)
   #2 Ads infinitum. (1971)

CLAYTON DREW (John Russell Fearn)

   #1 Emperor of Mars. (1950)
   #2 Warrior of Mars. (1950)
   #3 Red men of Mars. (1950)
   #4 Goddess of Mars. (1950)

EARL DUMAREST (E. C. Tubb)

   #1 The winds of Gath. (1967)
   #2 Derai. (1968)
   #3 Toyman. (1969)
   #4 Kalin. (1969)
   #5 The jester at Scar. (1970)
   #6 Lallia. (1971)
   #7 Technos. (1972)
   #8 Mayenne. (1973)
   #9 Veruchia. (1973)
   #10 Jondelle. (1973)
   #11 Zenya. (1974)

DUNE (Frank Herbert)

   #1 Dune. (1965)
   #2 Dune messiah. (1969)

JIM DUNLAP [PAT COLLINS] (Bernard Palmer)

   #1 Jim Dunlap and the strange Dr. Brockton. (1967)
   #2 Jim Dunlap and the secret rocket formula. (1967)
   #3 Jim Dunlap and the wingless plane. (1968)

   #4 Jim Dunlap and the mysterious orbiting rocket.
      (1968)
   #5? Jim Dunlap and the long lunar walk. (1974)
   #6? Jim Dunlap and the mysterious spy. (1974)

DANNY DUNN (Raymond Abrashkin & Jay Williams)

   #1 Danny Dunn and the anti-gravity paint. (1956)
   #2 Danny Dunn on a desert island. (1957)
   #3 Danny Dunn and the homework machine. (1958)
   #4 Danny Dunn and the weather machine. (1959)
   #5 Danny Dunn on the ocean floor. (1960)
   #6 Danny Dunn and the fossil cave. (1961)
   #7 Danny Dunn and the heat ray. (1962)
   #8 Danny Dunn, time traveller. (1963)
   #9 Danny Dunn and the automatic house. (1965)
   #10 Danny Dunn and the voice from space. (1967)
   #11 Danny Dunn and the smallifying machine. (1969)
   #12 Danny Dunn and the swamp monster. (1971)
   #13 Danny Dunn, invisible boy. (1974)

DURDANE TRILOGY (Jack Vance)

   #1 The Anome. (1973)
   #2 The Brave Free Men. (1973)
   #3 The Asutra. (1974)

THE DYING EARTH (Jack Vance)

   #1 The dying Earth. (1950)
   #2 The Eyes of the Overworld. (1966)

   SEQUELS AND PARODIES:

      A quest for Simbilis. (1974) [by Michael Shea]

DYSART TRILOGY (Jon J. Deegan)

   #1 Corridors of time. (1953)
   #2 Beyond the fourth door. (1954)
   #3 Exiles in time. (1954)

EARTH'S END SERIES (Fred Saberhagen)

   #1 The Broken Lands. (1968)
   #2 The Black Mountains. (1971)
   #3 Changeling Earth. (1973)

EARTHSEA TRILOGY (Ursula K. Le Guin)

   #1 A wizard of Earthsea. (1968)
   #2 The tombs of Atuan. (1971)
   #3 The farthest shore. (1972)

EDEN SERIES (Frederik Pohl & Jack Williamson)

   #1 Undersea quest. (1954)
   #2 Undersea fleet. (1956)
   #3 Undersea city. (1958)

ELANA SEQUENCE (Sylvia Louise Engdahl)

   #1 Enchantress from the stars. (1970)
   #2 The far side of evil. (1971)

ELEANOR (Jane Langton) [see Addendum]

   #1 The diamond in the window. (1962)
   #2 The swing in the summerhouse. (1967)
   #3 The astonishing stereoscope. (1971)

THE ELECTRIC ELEPHANT (Frances Trego Montgomery)

#1   The wonderful electric elephant. (1903)
#2   On a lark to the planets. (1904)

ELRIC (Michael Moorcock)

#1   Elric of Melnibone. (1972)
#2   The stealer of souls, and other stories. (1963)
#3   The sleeping sorceress. (1971)
#4   Stormbringer. (1965)
#5   The singing citadel. (1970)

RELATED TITLE:

The Jade Man's eyes.

EMMA (Penelope Farmer)

#1   The summer birds. (1962)
#2   Emma in winter. (1966)
#3   Charlotte sometimes. (1969)

THE EMPRESS OF OUTER SPACE (A. Bertram Chandler)

#1   Empress of outer space. (1965)
#2   Space mercenaries. (1965)

THE ENFORCER (Andrew Sugar)

#1   The enforcer. (1973)
#2   Calling Doctor Kill! (1973)
#3   Kill city. (1973)
#4   Kill deadline. (1973)

EREWHON (Samuel Butler)

#1   Erewhon. (1872)
#2   Erewhon revisited. (1901)
#s 1-2 Erewhon; and, Erewhon revisited. (1927)

THE ETERNAL CHAMPION (Michael Moorcock)

#1   The Eternal Champion. (1970)
#2   Phoenix in obsidian. (1970)

EUNOSTOS (Thomas Burnett Swann)

#1   Day of the minotaur. (1966)
#2   The forest of forever. (1971)

EXILES SEQUENCE (Ben Bova)

#1   Exiled from Earth. (1971)
#2   Flight of exiles. (1972)

THE EXORCIST (William Peter Blatty)

The exorcist. (1971)

SEQUELS AND PARODIES:

The Exerciser. (1974) [by Howard Albrecht &
Sol Weinstein]

EYES SERIES (Stuart Gordon)

#1   One-Eye. (1973)
#2   Two-Eyes. (1974)

FAFHRD AND THE GRAY MOUSER (Fritz Leiber)

#1   Swords and deviltry. (1970)
#2   Swords against death. (1970)
#3   Swords in the mist. (1968)
#4   Swords against wizardry. (1968)
#5   The swords of Lankhmar. (1968)

RELATED TITLE:

Two sought adventure. (1957)

THE FALL OF THE TOWERS (Samuel R. Delany)

#1   Captives of the Flame. (1963)
#2   The towers of Toron. (1964)
#3   City of a thousand suns. (1965)
#s 1-3 The fall of the towers. (1970)

FLATLAND (Edwin A. Abbott)

Flatland. (1884)

SEQUELS AND PARODIES:

Sphereland. (1965) [by Dionys Burger]
An episode of Flatland. (1907) [by C. H. Hinton]

DAG FLETCHER (John Rankine [Douglas R. Mason])

#1   The Ring of Garamas. (1972)
#2   Interstellar Two-Five. (1966)
#3   The Plantos affair. (1971)
#4   The Bromius phenomenon. (1973)
#5   One is one. (1968)

RELATED TITLE:

The blockade of Sinitron. (1966)

THE FLOATING CITY (Jules Verne)

#1   A floating city. (1876)
#2   The blockade runners. (1876)
#s 1-2 A floating city; and, The blockade runners.
(1874)

THE FLYING FISH (Harry Collingwood)

#1   The log of the "Flying Fish." (1886)
#2   With airship and submarine. (1907)
#3   The cruise of the "Flying Fish." (1924)

THE FLYING NUN (Tere Rios)

The fifteenth pelican. (1965) [later reissued
as The flying nun]

THE FLYING NUN [TV series] (William Johnston):

#1   Miracle at San Tanco. (1968)
#2   The littlest rebels. (1968)
#3   Mother of invention. (1969)
#4   The little green men. (1969)
#5   The underground picnic. (1970)

VALENTINE FLYNN (Sean O'Shea [Robert Tralins])

#1   What a way to go! (1966)
#2   Operation Boudoir. (1967)
#3   Win with sin. (1967) [not SF]
#4   The nymph island affair. (1967)
#5   Invasion of the nymphomaniacs. (1967?) [not SF]

PHILEAS FOGG (Jules Verne)

Around the world in eighty days. (1874)

SEQUELS AND PARODIES:

The other log of Phileas Fogg. (1973) [by
Philip Jose Farmer]

THE FOUNDATION TRILOGY (Isaac Asimov)

#1 Foundation. (1951)
#2 Foundation and empire. (1952)
#3 Second Foundation. (1953)
#s 1-3 The Foundation trilogy. (1963)

FRAMES SERIES (Brian N. Ball)

#1 The Probability Man. (1972)
#2 Planet probability. (1973)

FRANCIS (David Stern)

#1 Francis...the Army mule. (1945) [as Peter
      Sterling]
#2 Francis. (1946)
#3 Francis goes to Washington. (1948)

FRANKENSTEIN (Mary Wollstonecraft Shelley)

Frankenstein. (1818)

SEQUELS AND PARODIES:

Frankenstein unbound. (1973) [by Brian W.
  Aldiss]
Frankenstein. (1968) [an adaptation by Dale
  Carlson]
The bride of Frankenstein. (1935) [by Michael
  Egremont]
The Frankenstein Wheel. (1972) [by Paul W.
  Fairman]
The revenge of Frankenstein. (1958) [by H.
  Hurford Janes]
The adult version of Frankenstein. (1970) [by
  Hal Kantor]
Frankenstein '69. (1969) [by Ed Martin]

RELATED TITLE:

The Frankenstein legend. (1973) [by Donald F.
  Flut]

FREDDY (Walter R. Brooks)

#1 To and again. (1927)
#2 More to and again. (1930)
#3 Freddy the detective. (1932)
#4 Wiggins for president. (1939)
#5 Freddy's cousin Weedly. (1940)
#6 Freddy and the ignoramus. (1941)
#7 Freddy and the perilous adventure. (1942)
#8 Freddy and the Bean home news. (1943)
#9 Freddy and Mr. Camphor. (1944)
#10 Freddy and the popinjay. (1945)
#11 Freddy the pied piper. (1946)
#12 Freddy the magician. (1947)
#13 Freddy goes camping. (1948)
#14 Freddy plays football. (1949)
#15 Freddy the cowboy. (1950)
#16 Freddy rides again. (1951)
#17 Freddy the pilot. (1952)

#18 Freddy and the space ship. (1953)
#19 Freddy and the men from Mars. (1954)
#20 Freddy and the baseball team from Mars. (1955)
#21 Freddy and Simon the dictator. (1956)
#22 Freddy and the flying saucer plans. (1957)
#23 Freddy and the dragon. (1958)

FU MANCHU (Sax Rohmer)

#1 The mystery of Dr. Fu-Manchu. (1913)
#2 The devil doctor. (1916)
#3 The Si-Fan mysteries. (1917)
#4 The golden scorpion. (1919)
#5 Daughter of Fu Manchu. (1931)
#6 The mask of Fu Manchu. (1932)
#7 Fu Manchu's bride. (1933)
#8 The trail of Fu Manchu. (1934)
#9 President Fu Manchu. (1936)
#10 The drums of Fu Manchu. (1939)
#11 The island of Fu Manchu. (1941)
#12 Shadow of Fu Manchu. (1948)
#13 Re-enter Fu Manchu. (1957)
#14 Emperor Fu Manchu. (1959)

FURSEY (Mervyn Wall)

#1 The unfortunate Fursey. (1946)
#2 The return of Fursey. (1948)

CAPTAIN FUTURE (various authors)

#1 Danger planet. (1968) [by Brett Sterling (Ed-
      mond Hamilton)]
#2 The Solar invasion. (1968) [by Manly Wade Well-
      man]
#3 Outlaw World. (1969) [by Edmond Hamilton]
#4 Quest beyond the stars. (1969) [by Edmond Hamil-
      ton]
#5 Outlaws of the Moon. (1969) [by Edmond Hamilton]
#6 The comet kings. (1969) [by Edmond Hamilton]
#7 Planets in peril. (1969) [by Edmond Hamilton]
#8 Calling Captain Future. (1969) [by Edmond Hamil-
      ton]
#9 Captain Future's challenge. (1969) [by Edmond
      Hamilton]
#10 Galaxy mission. (1969) [by Edmond Hamilton]
#11 The Magician of Mars. (1969) [by Edmond Hamil-
      ton]
#12 The tenth planet. (1969) [by Brett Sterling
      (Joseph Samachson)]
#13 Captain Future and the Space Emperor. (1969)
      [by Edmond Hamilton]

FUTURE HISTORY (Poul Anderson)

The day of their return. (1973)
Let the spacemen beware! (1963)
The people of the wind. (1973)

DAVID FALKAYN:

The trouble twisters. (1966)

DOMINIC FLANDRY:

Agent of the Terran Empire. (1965)
A circus of hells. (1970)
Earthman, go home! (1960)
Ensign Flandry. (1966)
Flandry of Terra. (1965)
A knight of ghosts and shadows. (1974)
Mayday orbit. (1961)

FUTURE HISTORY (Poul Anderson) [cont.]

DOMINIC FLANDRY (cont.):

The rebel worlds. (1969)
We claim these stars! (1959)

NICHOLAS van RIJN:

Satan's world. (1969)
Trader to the stars. (1964)
War of the wing-men. (1958)

FUTURE HISTORY (Robert A. Heinlein)

The green hills of Earth. (1951)
The man who sold the Moon. (1950)
Universe. (1951)
Orphans of the sky [includes Universe]. (1963)
The past through tomorrow. (1973) [an omnibus volume]

LAZARUS LONG:

#1 Methuselah's children. (1958)
#2 Time enough for love. (1973)

FUTURE HISTORY [HAINISH NOVELS] (Ursula K. Le Guin)

#1 The lathe of Heaven. (1971)
#2 The dispossessed. (1974)
#3 "Vaster than empires, and more slow."
#4 (The word for world is forest.)
#5 Rocannon's world. (1966)
#6 Planet of exile. (1966)
#7 City of illusions. (1967)
#8 The left hand of darkness. (1969)

FUZZY SERIES (H. Beam Piper)

#1 Little Fuzzy. (1962)
#2 The other human race. (1964)

G-8 AND HIS BATTLE ACES (Robert J. Hogan)

#1 The bat staffel. (1969)
#2 Purple Aces. (1970)
#3 Ace of the white death. (1970)
#4 Bombs from the murder wolves. (1971)
#5 Vultures of the white death. (1971)
#6 Flight from the grave. (1971)
#7 Fangs of the sky leopard. (1971)
#8 The mark of the vulture. (1971)

GALLOWGLASS (Christopher Stasheff)

#1 The warlock in spite of himself. (1969)
#2 King Kobold. (1971)

GANYMEDE SERIES (Michael D. Resnick)

#1 The Goddess of Ganymede. (1967)
#2 Pursuit on Ganymede. (1968)

GARNETT (Clive Egleton)

#1 A piece of resistance. (1970)
#2 Last post for a partisan. (1971)
#3 The Judas mandate. (1972)

GEES (Jack Mann [E. Charles Vivian])

#1 Gees' first case. (1936) [not SF]
#2 Nightmare farm. (1937)
#3 Grey shapes. (1937)
#4 Maker of shadows. (1938)
#5 The Kleinert case. (1938) [not SF]
#6 The ninth life. (1939)
#7 The glass too many. (1940)
#8 Her ways are death. (1941)

GET SMART (William Johnston)

#1 Get Smart! (1965)
#2 Sorry, Chief... (1966)
#3 Get Smart once again! (1966)
#4 Max Smart and the perilous pellets. (1966)
#5 Missed it by that much! (1967)
#6 And loving it! (1967)
#7 Max Smart--the spy who went out to the cold. (1968)
#8 Max Smart loses Control. (1968)
#9 Max Smart and the ghastly ghost affair. (1969)

THE GIRL FROM U.N.C.L.E. (various authors)

U.S. SERIES:

#1 The birds-of-a-feather affair. (1966) [by Michael Avallone]
#2 The blazing affair. (1966) [by Michael Avallone]

U.K. SERIES:

#1 The global globules affair. (1967) [by Simon Latter]
#2 The birds-of-a-feather affair. (1967) [by Michael Avallone]
#3 The golden boats of Taradata affair. (1967) [by Simon Latter]
#4 The Cornish pixie affair. (1967) [by Peter Leslie]

MIKE GLENN (Robert C. Lee)

#1 The iron arm of Michael Glenn. (1965)
#2 The day it rained forever. (1968)

KARL GLOGAUER (Michael Moorcock)

#1 Behold the man. (1969)
#2 Breakfast in the ruins. (1972)

THE GNOMOBILE (Upton Sinclair)

The gnomobile. (1936)

SEQUELS AND PARODIES:

The gnome-mobile. (1967) [by Mary Carey]

CHRIS GODFREY (Hugh Walters)

#1 Blast off at Woomera. (1957)
#2 The domes of Pico. (1958)
#3 Operation Columbus. (1960)
#4 Moon Base One. (1961)
#5 Expedition Venus. (1962)
#6 Destination Mars. (1963)
#7 Terror by satellite. (1964)
#8 Journey to Jupiter. (1965)
#9 Mission to Mercury. (1965)

CHRIS GODFREY (Hugh Walters) [cont.]

#10 Spaceship to Saturn. (1967)
#11 The Mohole mystery. (1968)
#12 Nearly Neptune. (1969)
#13 First contact? (1971)
#14 Passage to Pluto. (1973)
#15 Tony Hale, space detective. (1973)

THE GOLDEN AMAZON (John Russell Fearn)

#1 The Golden Amazon. (1944)
#2 The Golden Amazon returns. (1948)
#3 The Golden Amazon's triumph. (1953)
#4 The Amazon's diamond quest. (1953)
#5 The Amazon strikes again. (1954)
#6 Twin of the Amazon. (1954)
#7 Conquest of the Amazon. (1973)

DR. GOODWIN (A. Merritt)

#1 The Moon Pool. (1919)
#2 The Metal Monster. (1946)

GOR SERIES (John Norman)

#1 Tarnsman of Gor. (1966)
#2 Outlaw of Gor. (1967)
#3 Priest-Kings of Gor. (1968)
#4 Nomads of Gor. (1969)
#5 Assassin of Gor. (1970)
#6 Raiders of Gor. (1971)
#7 Captive of Gor. (1972)
#8 Hunters of Gor. (1974)

FLASH GORDON (various authors)

#1 The lion men of Mongo. (1974) [Con Steffanson]
#2 The plague of sound. (1974) [by Con Steffanson]
#3 The space circus. (1974) [by Con Steffanson]
#4 The time trap of Ming XIII. (1974) [by Con Steffanson]
#5 The witch queen of Mongo. (1974) [by Carson Bingham]

RELATED TITLE:

Flash Gordon in the caverns of Mongo. (1937) [by Alex Raymond]

GORMENGHAST TRILOGY (Mervyn Peake)

#1 Titus Groan. (1946)
#2 Gormenghast. (1950)
#3 Titus alone. (1959)
#3A Titus alone (revised ed.). (1970)

KING GOSHAWK (Eimar O'Duffy)

#1 King Goshawk and the birds. (1926)
#2 Asses in clover. (1933)

DENIS GRAFTON (William Dexter)

#1 World in eclipse. (1954)
#2 Children of the void. (1955)

STAR-PILOT GRAINGER (Brian M. Stableford)

#1 The Halcyon Drift. (1972)
#2 Rhapsody in black. (1973)
#3 Promised land. (1974)

#4 The paradise game. (1974)
#5 The Fenris device. (1974)

GRAND FENWICK SERIES (Leonard Wibberley)

#1 Beware of the mouse. (1958)
#2 The mouse that roared. (1955)
#3 The mouse on the Moon. (1962)
#4 The mouse on Wall Street. (1969)

LORD GRANDITH (Philip Jose Farmer)

#1 A feast unknown. (1969)
#2 Lord of the trees. (1970)

GRANDON TRILOGY (Otis Adelbert Kline)

#1 The planet of peril. (1929)
#2 The prince of peril. (1930)
#3 The port of peril. (1949)

JEREMY GRANT (Angus MacVicar)

#1 The lost planet. (1953)
#2 Return to the lost planet. (1954)
#3 Secret of the lost planet. (1955)
#4 Red fire on the lost planet. (1959)
#5 Peril on the lost planet. (1960)
#6 Space agent from the lost planet. (1961)
#7 Space agent and the Isles of Fire. (1962)
#8 Space agent and the ancient peril. (1964)

COLIN GRAY (Mark Channing)

#1 King Cobra. (1933)
#2 White python. (1934)
#3 The poisoned mountain. (1935)
#4 Nine lives. (1937)

MAURICE GRAY (Patrick Moore)

#1 Mission to Mars. (1955)
#2 The domes of Mars. (1956)
#3 The voices of Mars. (1957)
#4 Peril on Mars. (1958)
#5 Raiders of Mars. (1959)

GRAY LANDS SERIES (Richard Meade)

#1 The sword of Morning Star. (1969)
#2 Exile's quest. (1970)

GREAT MARVEL SERIES (Roy Rockwood)

#1 Through the air to the North Pole. (1906)
#2 Under the ocean to the South Pole. (1907)
#3 Five thousand miles underground. (1908)
#4 Through space to Mars. (1910)
#5 Lost on the Moon. (1911)
#6 On a torn-away world. (1913)
#7 The city beyond the clouds. (1925)
#8 By air express to Venus. (1929)
#9 By space ship to Saturn. (1935)

GREEN HORNET (various authors)

The Green Hornet in The infernal light. (1966) [by Ed Friend (Richard Wormser)]
The case of the disappearing doctor. (1966) [by Brandon Keith]

GREEN KNOWE SERIES (L. M. Boston)

#1 The children of Green Knowe. (1954)
#2 The chimneys of Green Knowe. (1958)
#3 The river at Green Knowe. (1959)
#4 A stranger at Green Knowe. (1961)
#5 An enemy at Green Knowe. (1964)

GREEN PLANET SEQUENCE (Emil Petaja)

#1 Lord of the Green Planet. (1967)
#2 Doom of the Green Planet. (1968)

GREEN STAR SERIES (Lin Carter)

#1 Under the green star. (1972)
#2 When the green star calls. (1973)
#3 By the light of the green star. (1974)

GREENWICH VILLAGE TRILOGY (various authors)

#1 The Butterfly Kid. (1967) [by Chester Anderson]
#2 The Unicorn Girl. (1969) [by Michael Kurland]
#3 The probability pad. (1970) [by T. A. Waters]

THE GREENWOOD TALES (G. P. Baker)

#1 The magic tale of Harvanger and Yolande. (1914)
#2 The romance of Palombris and Pallogris. (1915)

GRENFELL & WRIGHT (Patrick Moore)

#1 The master of the Moon. (1952)
#2 The island of fear. (1954)

DICK GRENVILLE (Lawrence Fletcher)

#1 Into the unknown. (1892)
#2 Zero the slaver. (1892)

GUARDIANS SERIES (Peter Saxon)

U.S. SERIES:

#1 The killing bone. (1969)
#2 Dark ways to death. (1968)
#3 The haunting of Alan Mais. (1969)
#4 The vampires of Finistere. (1970)

OTHER TITLES:

The curse of Rathlaw. (1968)
The Guardians. (1967) [by W. Howard Baker]
Through the dark curtain. (1968)

GULLIVER (Jonathan Swift)

Travels into several remote nations of the
    world. (1726)

SEQUELS AND PARODIES:

An account of the state of learning in the Em-
    pire of Lilliput. (1728) [by John Arbuthnot]
A cursory view of the history of Lilliput for
    these last forty three years. (1727)
The travels of Mr. John Gulliver, son to Capt.
    Lemuel Gulliver. (1731) [by Pierre Desfon-
    taines]
The new Gulliver. (1898) [by Wendell Garrison]
Memoirs of the court of Lilliput. (1727) [by
    Captain Gulliver]

Travels into several remote nations of the world,
    vol. III. (1727) [by Capt. Lemuel Gulliver]
Lilliput. (1796) [by Lemuel Gulliver Jun.]
In the Sealed Cave. (1935) [by Louis Herrman]
A new voyage to the country of the Houyhnhnms.
    (1969) [by Matthew Hodgart]
Voyage to Faremido; Capillaria. (1965) [by
    Frigyes Karinthy]
Laputa. (1905)
Gulliver Joi. (1851) [by Elbert Perce]
Mistress Masham's repose. (1946) [by T. H.
    White]
Modern Lilliput. (1924) [by David Alec Wilson]
Castaways in Lilliput. (1960) [by Henry Winter-
    feld]

RELATED TITLES:

Gulliveriana: I. (1970) [edited by George E.
    Bush Jr. & Jeanne K. Welcher]
Gulliveriana: II. (1971) [Bush & Welcher]
Gulliveriana III. (1972) [Bush & Welcher]
Gulliveriana IV. (1973) [Buch & Welcher]
Gulliveriana V. (1974) [Bush & Welcher]

GUN CLUB SERIES (Jules Verne)

#1 From the Earth to the Moon direct in 97 hours
    20 minutes; and, A trip around it. (1873)
#2 The purchase of the North Pole. (1890)

GWALCHMAI SEQUENCE (H. Warner Munn)

#1 King of the world's edge. (1966)
#2 The ship from Atlantis. (1967)
#3 Merlin's ring. (1974)

HADES (Frederic Arnold Kummer)

#1 Ladies in Hades. (1928)
#2 Gentlemen in Hades. (1930)

HAINISH NOVELS
see: FUTURE HISTORY (Ursula K. Le Guin)

GREGG HALJAN (Ray Cummings)

#1 Brigands of the Moon. (1931)
#2 Wandl the invader. (1961)

GEORGE HANLON (E. Everett Evans)

#1 Man of many minds. (1953)
#2 Alien minds. (1955)

RALPH HANNON (Winifred Law)

#1 Through space to the planets. (1944)
#2 Rangers of the universe. (1945)

KAY HARKER (John Masefield)

#1 The midnight folk. (1927)
#2 The box of delights. (1935)

CAPTAIN HATTERAS (Jules Verne)

#1 The English at the North Pole. (1874)
#2 The field of ice. (1876)
#s 1-2 The adventures of Captain Hatteras. (1876)

HAVENGORE (Mark S. Geston)

#1 Lords of the starship. (1967)
#2 Out of the mouth of the dragon. (1969)

HEAVEN AND HELL (Harry Blamires)

#1 The devil's hunting-ground. (1954)
#2 Cold war in Hell. (1955)
#3 Blessing unbounded. (1955)

HER-BAK SERIES (Isha Schwaller De Lubicz)

#1 Her-Bak "Chick-Pea." (1954)
#2 Her-Bak, Egyptian initiate. (1967)

HERBERT (Volsted Gridban [John Russell Fearn])

#1 A thing of the past. (1953)
#2 The genial dinosaur. (1954)

HERBIE (Mel Cebulash)

#1 The love bug. (1969)
#2 Herbie rides again. (1974)

HIDDEN PEOPLE (Leo E. Miller)

#1 The hidden people. (1920)
#2 In the tiger's lair. (1921)

ALF HIGGINS (W. A. Darlington)

#1 Alf's button. (1919)
#2 Alf's carpet. (1928)
#3 Alf's new button. (1940)

HISTORY OF THE GREAT IMPERIUM (Lin Carter)

#1 The man without a planet. (1966)
#2 Star rogue. (1970)
#3 Outworlder. (1971)

THE HIVE (T. J. Bass)

#1 Half past human. (1971)
#2 The Godwhale. (1974)

ROBBY HOENIG (Gordon R. Dickson)

#1 Secret under the sea. (1960)
#2 Secret under Antarctica. (1963)
#3 Secret under the Caribbean. (1964)

HOOK (Tully Zetford [Kenneth Bulmer])

#1 Whirlpool of stars. (1974)
#2 The boosted man. (1974)
#3 Star city. (1974)

BENJAMIN HOOKER (Arthur Train & Robert W. Wood)

#1 The man who rocked the Earth. (1915)
#2 The Moon maker. (1958)

HORRORSCOPE SERIES (Robert Lory)

#1 The green flames of Aries. (1974)
#2 The revenge of Taurus. (1974)
#3 The curse of Leo. (1974)

HOUSE-BOAT ON THE STYX (John Kendrick Bangs)

#1 A house-boat on the Styx. (1895)
#2 The pursuit of the house-boat. (1897)

THE HUB (James H. Schmitz)

The demon breed. (1968)
A nice day for screaming, and other tales of the Hub. (1965)
A pride of monsters. (1970)
A tale of two clocks. (1962)

TELZEY SERIES:

#1 The universe against her. (1964)
#2 The Lion Game. (1973)
#3 The Telzey toy. (1973)

THE HUMAN AGE (Wyndham Lewis)

#1 The Childermass. (1928)
#2 Monstre gai. (1965)
#3 Malign fiesta. (1966)
#s 2-3 The human age, books two-three. (1955)

THE HUMAN BAT (Edward R. Home-Gall)

#1 The Human Bat. (1950)
#2 The Human Bat v. the robot gangster. (1950)

THE HUNTERS (Paul Tabori)

#1 The doomsday brain. (1967)
#2 The invisible eye. (1967)
#3 The torture machine. (1969)

HYDRONAUTS (Carl L. Biemiller)

#1 The hydronauts. (1970)
#2 Follow the whales. (1973)
#3 Escape from the Crater. (1974)

IMPERIUM (Keith Laumer)

#1 Worlds of the Imperium. (1962)
#2 The other side of time. (1965)
#3 Assignment in nowhere. (1968)

INSTRUMENTALITY (Cordwainer Smith)

The planet buyer. (1964)
Quest of the three worlds. (1966)
Space lords. (1965)
Stardreamer. (1971)
Under old Earth, and other explorations. (1970)
The underpeople. (1968)
You will never be the same. (1963)

INTERSTELLAR PATROL (Edmond Hamilton)

#1 Outside the universe. (1964)
#2 Crashing suns. (1965)

THE INVADERS (various authors)

U.S. SERIES:

#1 The Invaders. (1967) [by Keith Laumer]
#2 Enemies from beyond. (1967) [by Keith Laumer]
#3 Army of the undead. (1967) [by Rafe Bernard]

THE INVADERS (various authors) [cont.]

U.K. SERIES:

#1   The halo highway. (1967) [by Rafe Bernard]
#2   The meteor men. (1968) [by Anthony LeBaron]
#3   The night of the Trilobites. (1968) [by Peter
       Leslie]
#4   The autumn accelerator. (1969) [by Peter
       Leslie]

RELATED TITLE:

     The Invaders; Dam of death. (1967) [by J. Pearl]

THE INVISIBLES (Bernhardt J. Hurwood)

#1   The invisibles. (1971)
#2   The mind master. (1973)

IRONBARK BILL (Dal Stivens)

#1   The gambling ghost, and other tales. (1953)
#2   Ironbark Bill. (1955)

ISHER (A. E. van Vogt)

#1   The weapon makers. (1947)
#2   The weapon shops of Isher. (1951)

ISLANDIA (Austin Tappan Wright)

     Islandia. (1942)

SEQUELS AND PARODIES:

     The Islar. (1969) [by Mark Saxton]

IT HAPPENED IN FLORIDA (James Branch Cabell)

#1   The St. Johns. (1943) [nonf.]
#2   There were two pirates. (1946)
#3   The devil's own dear son. (1949)

JACARE (Victor Norwood)

#1   The untamed. (1951)
#2   Caves of death. (1951)
#3   The temple of the dead. (1951)
#4   The skull of Kanaima. (1951)
#5   The island of creeping death. (1952)
#6? Cry of the beast. (1953)
#7? Drums along the Amazon. (1953)

PROFESSOR JAMESON SPACE ADVENTURES (Neil R.
Jones)

#1   The planet of the double sun. (1967)
#2   Space war. (1967)
#3   The sunless world. (1967)
#4   Twin worlds. (1967)
#5   Doomsday on Ajiat. (1968)

JAMNAR (Dave Van Arnam)

#1   Star barbarian. (1969)
#2   Lord of blood. (1970)

JAN (Otis Adelbert Kline)

#1   Call of the savage. (1937)
#2   Jan in India. (1974)

JANDAR SERIES (Lin Carter)

#1   Jandar of Callisto. (1972)
#2   Black Legion of Callisto. (1972)
#3   Sky pirates of Callisto. (1973)

DR. JEKYLL AND MR. HYDE (Robert Louis Stevenson)

     Strange case of Dr. Jekyll and Mr. Hyde. (1886)

SEQUELS AND PARODIES:

     The adult version of Dr. Jekyll and Mr. Hyde.
       (1970) [by Terry Stacy]

JENNIFER (Thorne Smith & Norman Matson)

#1   The passionate witch. (1941)
#2   Bats in the belfry. (1943) [by Norman Matson]

MURDOC JERN (Andre Norton)

#1   The zero stone. (1968)
#2   Uncharted stars. (1969)

BEN JOLSON [THE CHAMELEON CORPS] (Ron Goulart)

#1   The sword swallower. (1968)
#2   The Chameleon Corps, & other shape changers.
       (1972)
#3   Flux. (1974)

COYOTE JONES (Suzette Haden Elgin)

#1   The Communipaths. (1970)
#2   Furthest. (1971)
#3   At the Seventh Level. (1972)

JONGOR (Robert Moore Williams)

#1   Jongor of Lost Land. (1970)
#2   The return of Jongor. (1970)
#3   Jongor fights back. (1970)

JONNY (Carl L. Biemiller)

#1   The magic ball from Mars. (1953)
#2   Starboy. (1956)

JORIAN (L. Sprague de Camp)

#1   The Goblin Tower. (1968)
#2   The clocks of Iraz. (1971)

JORKENS (Lord Dunsany)

#1   The travel tales of Mr. Joseph Jorkens. (1931)
#2   Mr. Jorkens remembers Africa. (1934)
#3   Jorkens has a large whiskey. (1940)
#4   The fourth book of Jorkens. (1948)
#5   Jorkens borrows another whiskey. (1954)

MICHAEL JOUSSE (Paul Berna)

#1   Threshold of the stars. (1958)
#2   Continent in the sky. (1959)

KAI LUNG (Ernest Bramah)

#1   The wallet of Kai Lung. (1900)
#2   Kai Lung's golden hours. (1922)

KAI LUNG (Ernest Bramah) [cont.]

#3 Kai Lung unrolls his mat. (1928)
#4 The moon of much gladness. (1932)
#5 Kai Lung beneath the mulberry-tree. (1940)
#6 Kai Lung: six. (1974)

RELATED TITLES:

Kin Weng and the miraculous tusk. (1941)
The transmutation of Ling. (1911)

KALEVALA SERIES (Emil Petaja)

#1 Saga of lost Earths. (1966)
#2 The star mill. (1966)
#3 The stolen sun. (1967)
#4 Tramontane. (1967)

KANE (Karl Edward Wagner)

#1 Darkness weaves with many shades... (1970)
#2 Death Angel's Shadow. (1973)

MICHAEL KANE (Edward P. Bradbury [Michael Moorcock])

#1 Warriors of Mars. (1965)
#2 Blades of Mars. (1965)
#3 Barbarians of Mars. (1965)

REISSUED UNDER THE NAME MICHAEL MOORCOCK:

#1 The city of the beast. (1970)
#2 The lord of the spiders. (1971)
#3 The masters of the pit. (1971)

SOLOMON KANE (Robert E. Howard)

#1 The moon of skulls. (1969)
#2 The hand of Kane. (1970)
#3 Solomon Kane. (1971)
#s 1-3 Red shadows. (1968)

KAR-CHEE SERIES (Avram Davidson)

#1 Rogue dragon. (1965)
#2 The Kar-chee reign. (1966)

KARMIC DESTINY TRILOGY (Marjorie Livingston)

#1 Island sonata. (1944)
#2 Muted strings. (1946)
#3 Delphic echo. (1948)

KASPA THE LION MAN (C. T. Stoneham)

#1 The lion's way. (1931)
#2 Kaspa, the lion man. (1933)

KAVIN (David Mason)

#1 Kavin's world. (1969)
#2 The return of Kavin. (1972)

KEMLO (E. C. Eliott)

#1 Kemlo and the Crazy Planet. (1954)
#2 Kemlo and the Zones of Silence. (1954)
#3 Kemlo and the sky horse. (1954)
#4 Kemlo and the Martian ghosts. (1954)
#5 Kemlo and the craters of the Moon. (1955)

#6 Kemlo and the space lanes. (1955)
#7 Kemlo and the star men. (1955)
#8 Kemlo and the gravity rays. (1956)
#9 Kemlo and the purple dawn. (1957)
#10 Kemlo and the end of time. (1957)
#11 Kemlo and the zombie men. (1958)
#12 Kemlo and the space men. (1959)
#13 Kemlo and the satellite builders. (1960)
#14 Kemlo and the space invaders. (1961)
#15 Kemlo and the masters of space. (1963)

JOE KENMORE (Murray Leinster)

#1 Space Platform. (1953)
#2 Space Tug. (1953)
#3 City on the Moon. (1957)

CAP KENNEDY (Gregory Kern [E. C. Tubb])

#1 Galaxy of the lost. (1973)
#2 Slave ship from Sergan. (1973)
#3 Monster of Metelaze. (1973)
#4 Enemy within the skull. (1974)
#5 Jewel of Jarhen. (1974)
#6 Seetee alert! (1974)
#7 The Gholan Gate. (1974)
#8 The eater of worlds. (1974)
#9 Earth enslaved. (1974)
#10 Planet of dread. (1974)
#11 Spawn of Laban. (1974)
#12 The genetic buccaneer. (1974)
#13 A world aflame. (1974)

CRAIG KENNEDY (Arthur B. Reeve)

#1 The silent bullet. (1912)
#2 The poisoned pen. (1913)
#3 The dream doctor. (1914)
#4 The war terror. (1915)
#5 The gold of the gods. (1915)
#6 The exploits of Elaine. (1915) [Elaine #1]
#7 The social gangster. (1916)
#8 The ear in the wall. (1916)
#9 The romance of Elaine. (1916) [Elaine #2]
#10 The triumph of Elaine. (1916) [Elaine #3]
#11 The treasure-train. (1917)
#12 The adventuress. (1917)
#13 The Panama plot. (1918)
#14 The soul scar. (1919)
#15 The film mystery. (1921)
#16 Craig Kennedy listens in. (1923)
#17 Atavar. (1924)
#18 The fourteen points. (1925)
#19 The Boy Scouts' Craig Kennedy. (1925)
#20 Craig Kennedy on the farm. (1925)
#21 The radio detective. (1926)
#22 Pandora. (1926)
#23 The kidnap club. (1932)
#24 The Clutching Hand. (1934)
#25 Enter Craig Kennedy. (1935) [with Ashley Locke]
#26 The stars scream murder. (1936)

KENNET TRILOGY (Rolf Garner [Bryan Berry])

#1 Resurgent dust. (1953)
#2 The Immortals. (1953)
#3 The indestructible. (1954)

KEYS SERIES (Michael Cooney)

#1 Doomsday England. (1967)
#2 Ten days to oblivion. (1968)

KEYS TO THE DIMENSIONS (Kenneth Bulmer)

#1 The key to Irunium. (1967)
#2 The key to Venudine. (1968)
#3 The Wizards of Senchuria. (1969)
#4 The ships of Durostorum. (1970)
#5 The Hunters of Jundagai. (1971)
#6 The Chariots of Ra. (1972)

K'ING KUNG FU (Marshall Macao)

#1 Son of the flying tiger. (1973)
#2 Return of the opium wars. (1973)
#3 The rape of Sun Lee Fong. (1973)
#4 The Kak-Abdullah conspiracy. (1973)
#5 Red plague in Bolivia. (1974)
#6 New York necromancy. (1974)
#7 Mark of the vulture. (1974)

RANDY KNOWLES (Hans Holzer)

#1 The Red Chindvit conspiracy. (1970)
#2 The alchemy deception. (1973)

KOLCHAK (Jeff Rice)

#1 The night stalker. (1973)
#2 The night strangler. (1974)

KONARR (Dave Van Arnam)

#1 The players of Hell. (1968)
#2 Wizard of storms. (1970)

KOTHAR (Gardner F. Fox)

#1 Kothar, barbarian swordsman. (1969)
#2 Kothar of the magic sword! (1969)
#3 Kothar and the demon queen. (1969)
#4 Kothar and the conjurer's curse. (1970)
#5 Kothar and the wizard slayer. (1970)

ROI KUNZER (Richard E. Geis)

#1 The sex machine. (1967)
#2 The endless orgy. (1968)

LAND OF THE GIANTS (various authors)

U.S. SERIES:

#1 Land of the giants. (1968) [by Murray Leinster]
#2 The hot spot. (1969) [by Murray Leinster]
#3 Unknown danger. (1969) [by Murray Leinster]

OTHER TITLES:

The mean city. (1969) [by James Bradwell]
Flight of fear. (1969) [by Carl Henry Rathjen]

LA NOIRE SERIES (Bron Fane [R. L. Fanthorpe])

#1 The intruders. (1963)
#2 Somewhere out there. (1963)
#3 Softly by moonlight. (1963)
#4 Unknown destiny. (1964)
#5 Nemesis. (1964)
#6 Suspension. (1964)
#7 The macabre ones. (1964)
#8 U.F.O. 517. (1966?)

LAST MEN (Olaf Stapledon)

#1 Last and first men. (1930)
#2 Last men in London. (1932)
#s 1-2 Last and first men; and, Last men in London.
     (1972)

LATIMER BROTHERS (Manning Coles)

#1 Brief candles. (1954)
#2 Happy returns. (1955)
#3 Come and go. (1958)

ROBERT LAWSON (Ralph Comer)

#1 The witchfinders. (1968)
#2 The mirror of Dionysos. (1969)

LEGION OF SPACE (Jack Williamson)

#1 The Legion of Space. (1947)
#2 The Cometeers. (1967)
#3 One against the Legion. (1967)
#4 "Nowhere near." (1967)

LEGION OF TIME (Jack Williamson)

#1 The legion of time. (1961)
#2 After world's end. (1961)
#s 1-2 The legion of time. (1952)

LENSMAN SERIES (E. E. Smith)

#1 Triplanetary. (1948)
#2 First Lensman. (1950)
#3 Galactic Patrol. (1950)
#4 Gray Lensman. (1951)
#5 Second stage Lensmen. (1953)
#6 Children of the Lens. (1954)
#7 The Vortex Blaster. (1960)

JULIUS LeVALLON (Algernon Blackwood)

#1 Julius LeVallon. (1916)
#2 The bright messenger. (1921)

PRINCE LINCOAS (Jane Louise Curry)

#1 The daybreakers. (1970)
#2 Over the sea's edge. (1971)

ADAM LINK (Eando Binder)

Adam Link in the past. (1950)
Adam Link--robot. (1965)

LINN SERIES (A. E. van Vogt)

#1 Empire of the atom. (1956)
#2 The wizard of Linn. (1962)

THE LISTENER (Taylor Caldwell)

#1 The listener. (1960)
#2 No one hears but Him. (1966)

THE LONG JOURNEY (Johannes V. Jensen)

#1 Fire and ice. (1923)
#2 The Cimbrians. (1923)
#3 Christopher Columbus. (1924)
#s 1-3 The long journey. (1933)

LOOKING BACKWARD [JULIAN WEST] (Edward Bellamy)

#1 Looking backward, 2000-1887. (1888)
#2 Equality. (1897)

SEQUELS AND PARODIES:

Looking forward. (1899) [by Arthur Bird]
Looking beyond. (1891) [by L. A. Geissler]
Looking further forward. (1890) [by Richard
    Michaelis]
Looking ahead. (1892) [by Alfred Morris]
Looking backward, from the year 2000. (1973)
    [by Mack Reynolds]
Looking within. (1893) [by J. W. Roberts]
One of "Berrian's" novels. (1890) [by Mrs. C.
    H. Stone]
Looking further backward. (1890) [by Arthur
    Dudley Vinton]
My afterdream. (1900) [by Julian West]
Christopher Brand. (1934) [by Cuthbert Yerex]

MATTHEW LOONEY (Jerome Beatty Jr.)

#1 Matthew Looney's voyage to the Earth. (1961)
#2 Matthew Looney's invasion of the Earth. (1965)
#3 Matthew Looney in the outback. (1969)
#4 Matthew Looney and the space pirates. (1972)

LORD OF THE RINGS (J. R. R. Tolkien)

#1 The Fellowship of the Ring. (1954)
#2 The two towers. (1954)
#3 The return of the King. (1955)
#s 1-3 The Lord of the Rings. (1968)

A PREQUEL:

The hobbit. (1937)

SEQUELS AND PARODIES:

Bored of the rings. (1969) [by Henry N. Beard
    & Douglas C. Kenney]

ARWEN SERIES (Marion Zimmer Bradley):

#1 The jewel of Arwen. (1974)
#2 The parting of Arwen. (1974)

LINDA LOVELACE (D. M. Perkins)

#1 Deep throat. (1973)
#2 Deep throat, part II. (1974)

DR. LOWELL (A. Merritt)

#1 Burn witch burn! (1933)
#2 Creep, shadow! (1934)

LUCIFER COVE SERIES (Virginia Coffman)

#1 The devil's mistress. (1970)
#2 Priestess of the damned. (1970)
#3 The devil's virgin. (1971)
#4 Masque of Satan. (1971)
#5 Chalet Diabolique. (1971)
#6 From Satan, with love. (1971)

LUCIFRAM SERIES (Edith Allonby)

#1 Jewel sowers. (1903)
#2 Marigold. (1905)

LUKE TRILOGY (John Christopher)

#1 The Prince in Waiting. (1970)
#2 Beyond the Burning Lands. (1971)
#3 The sword of the spirits. (1972)

LYDIS SEQUENCE (Andre Norton)

#1 Moon of three rings. (1966)
#2 Exiles of the stars. (1971)

STEPHEN MacFARLANE (John Keir Cross)

#1 The angry planet. (1945)
#2 SOS from Mars. (1954)

MABINOGION CYCLE (Evangeline Walton)

#1 Prince of Annwn. (1974)
#2 The children of Llyr. (1971)
#3 The song of Rhiannon. (1972)
#4 The virgin and the swine. (1936)

MAGDAH (Roy Sheldon [H. J. Campbell])

#1 Mammoth man. (1952)
#2 Two days of terror. (1952)

MAGI SERIES (A. van der Naillen)

#1 On the heights of Himalay. (1890)
#2 In the sanctuary. (1895)
#3 Balthazar the Magus. (1904)

MAGIC STORIES (Edward Eager)

#1 Half magic. (1954)
#2 Knight's castle. (1956)
#3 Magic by the lake. (1957)
#4 The time garden. (1958)

MARTIN MAGNUS (William F. Temple)

#1 Martin Magnus, planet rover. (1955)
#2 Martin Magnus on Venus. (1955)
#3 Martin Magnus on Mars. (1956)

FANTAZIUS MALLARE (Ben Hecht)

#1 Fantazius Mallare. (1922)
#2 The Kingdom of Evil. (1924)

KEN MALONE (Mark Phillips [Randall Garrett &
Laurence M. Janifer])

#1 Brain twister. (1962)
#2 The impossibles. (1963)
#3 Supermind. (1963)

THE MAN FROM T.O.M.C.A.T. (Mallory T. Knight)

#1 The dozen deadly dragons of joy. (1967)
#2 The million missing maidens. (1967)
#3 The terrible ten. (1967)
#4 The dirty rotten depriving ray. (1967)
#5 Tsimmis in Tangier. (1968)
#6 The malignant metaphysical menace. (1968)

THE MAN FROM T.O.M.C.A.T. (Mallory T. Knight)
[cont.]

#7 The ominous orgy. (1969)
#8 The Peking pornographer. (1969)
#9 The bra-burner's brigade. (1971)

THE MAN FROM U.N.C.L.E. (various authors)

U.S. SERIES:

#1 The man from U.N.C.L.E. (1965) [by Michael
      Avallone]
#2 The doomsday affair. (1965) [by Harry Whitting-
      ton]
#3 The Copenhagen affair. (1965) [by John Oram]
#4 The Dagger affair. (1965) [by David McDaniel]
#5 The mad scientist affair. (1966) [by John T.
      Phillifent]
#6 The vampire affair. (1966) [by David McDaniel]
#7 The radioactive camel affair. (1966) [by Peter
      Leslie]
#8 The monster wheel affair. (1967) [by David
      McDaniel]
#9 The diving dames affair. (1967) [by Peter
      Leslie]
#10 The assassination affair. (1967) [by J. Hunter
      Holly]
#11 The invisibility affair. (1967) [by Thomas
      Stratton]
#12 The mind-twisters affair. (1967) [by Thomas
      Stratton]
#13 The Rainbow affair. (1967) [by David McDaniel]
#14 The cross of gold affair. (1968) [by Fredric
      Davies]
#15 The utopia affair. (1968) [by David McDaniel]
#16 The splintered sunglasses affair. (1968) [by
      Peter Leslie]
#17 The hollow crown affair. (1969) [by David
      McDaniel]
#18 The unfair fare affair. (1969) [by Peter Leslie]
#19 The power cube affair. (1969) [by John T. Phil-
      lifent]
#20 The Corfu affair. (1970) [by John T. Phillifent]
#21 The thinking machine affair. (1970) [by Joel
      Bernard]
#22 The stone-cold dead in the market affair. (1970)
      [by John Oram]
#23 The finger in the sky affair. (1971) [by Peter
      Leslie]

U.K. SERIES:

#1 The man from U.N.C.L.E. (1965) [by Michael Aval-
      lone]
#2 The doomsday affair. (1966) [by Harry Whitting-
      ton]
#3 The Copenhagen affair. (1966) [by John Oram]
#4 The stone-cold dead in the market affair. (1966)
      [by John Oram]
#5 The finger in the sky affair. (1966) [by Peter
      Leslie]
#6 The Dagger affair. (1966) [by David McDaniel]
#7 The radioactive camel affair. (1966) [by Peter
      Leslie]
#8 The mad scientist affair. (1966) [by John T.
      Phillifent]
#9 The vampire affair. (1966) [by David McDaniel]
#10 The diving dames affair. (1967) [by Peter Les-
      lie]
#11 The thinking machine affair. (1967) [by Joel
      Bernard]

#12 The monster wheel affair. (1967) [by David Mc-
      Daniel]
#13 The Corfu affair. (1967) [by John T. Phillifent]
#14 The splintered sunglasses affair. (1968) [by
      Peter Leslie]
#15 The power cube affair. (1968) [by John T. Phil-
      lifent]
#16 The unfair fare affair. (1968) [by Peter Leslie]

RELATED TITLE:

    The man from U.N.C.L.E. and the affair of the
    gentle saboteur. (1966) [by Brandon Keith]

THE MANATITLANS (R. Elton Smile)

#1 The Manatitlans. (1877)
#2 Investigations and experience of M. Shawtinbach
      at Saar Soong, Sumatra. (1879)

BIOGRAPHY OF MANUEL (James Branch Cabell)

#1 Beyond life. (1919) [not SF]
#2 Figures of Earth. (1921)
#3 The Silver Stallion. (1926)
#4 The witch-woman. (1948)
#4A The music from behind the Moon. (1926)
#4B The way of Ecben. (1929)
#4C The white robe. (1928)
#5 The soul of Melicent [Domnei]. (1913)
#6 Chivalry. (1921) [not SF]
#7 Jurgen. (1919)
#8 The line of love. (1905)
#9 The high place. (1923)
#10 Gallantry. (1907) [not SF]
#11 Something about Eve. (1927)
#12 The certain hour. (1916)
#13 The cords of vanity. (1920) [not SF]
#14 From the hidden way. (1916) [not SF]
#15 The jewel merchants. (1921) [not SF]
#16 The rivet in grandfather's neck. (1915) [not SF]
#17 The Eagle's shadow. (1904) [not SF]
#18 The cream of the jest. (1917)
#19 The lineage of Lichfield. (1922)
#20 Straws and prayer-books. (1924) [not SF]
#21 Townsend of Lichfield. (1930)
#22 Preface to the past. (1936) [nonf.]
#23 Sonnets from Antan. (1930) [not SF]

RELATED TITLE:

    The judging of Jurgen. (1920)

MARIS SEQUENCE (Sheila Moon)

#1 Knee-deep in thunder. (1967)
#2 Hunt down the prize. (1971)

LAWRENCE MARLEY (Jerry Walker)

#1 Mission accomplished. (1947)
#2 A date with destiny. (1949)

MAROONED IN ORBIT (Arthur W. Ballou)

#1 Marooned in orbit. (1968)
#2 Bound for Mars. (1970)

ELSPETH MARRINER (Sam Merwin Jr.)

#1 The house of many worlds. (1951)
#2 Three faces of time. (1955)

MIKE MARS (Donald A. Wollheim)

    #1 Mike Mars, astronaut. (1961)
    #2 Mike Mars flies the X-15. (1961)
    #3 Mike Mars at Cape Canaveral. (1961)
    #4 Mike Mars in orbit. (1961)
    #5 Mike Mars flies the Dyna-Soar. (1962)
    #6 Mike Mars, South Pole spaceman. (1962)
    #7 Mike Mars and the mystery satellite. (1963)
    #8 Mike Mars around the Moon. (1964)

MARS SERIES (Leigh Brackett)

        Shadow over Mars. (1951)
        The sword of Rhiannon. (1953)
        The coming of the Terrans. (1967)

    ERIC JOHN STARK:

        The secret of Sinharat. (1964)
        People of the Talisman. (1964)

MARS SERIES (Edgar Rice Burroughs)

    #1 A princess of Mars. (1917)
    #2 The gods of Mars. (1918)
    #3 The Warlord of Mars. (1919)
    #4 Thuvia, maid of Mars. (1920)
    #5 The chessmen of Mars. (1922)
    #6 The master mind of Mars. (1928)
    #7 A fighting man of Mars. (1931)
    #8 Swords of Mars. (1936)
    #9 Synthetic men of Mars. (1940)
    #10 Llana of Gathol. (1948)
    #11 John Carter of Mars. (1964)

    SEQUELS AND PARODIES:

        The forgotten sea of Mars. (1965) [by Michael
            Resnick]
    #1 The Goddess of Ganymede. (1967) [by Michael
            Resnick]
    #2 Pursuit on Ganymede. (1968) [by Michael Res-
            nick]

MARS SERIES (Otis Adelbert Kline)

    #1 The swordsman of Mars. (1960)
    #2 The outlaws of Mars. (1960)

JOE MAUSER (Mack Reynolds)

    #1 Mercenary from tomorrow. (1968)
    #2 The Earth war. (1963)
    #3 Time gladiator. (1966)

McKAY, KNOWLTON & RYAN (Arthur O. Friel)

    #1 The pathless trail. (1922)
    #2 Tiger River. (1923)
    #3 The King of No Man's Land. (1924)
    #4 Mountains of mystery. (1925)

MED SERVICE SERIES (Murray Leinster)

    #1 The mutant weapon. (1959)
    #2 This world is taboo. (1961)
    #3 Doctor to the stars. (1964)
    #4 S.O.S. from three worlds. (1967)

MEMOIRS OF A PHYSICIAN (Alexandre Dumas)

    #1 Joseph Balsamo. (1846)
    #2 Memoirs of a physician. (1847)
    #3 The queen's necklace. (1847)
    --See main entry for variant titles.

MERLIN (Mary Stewart)

    #1 The crystal cave. (1970)
    #2 The hollow hills. (1973)

MESKLIN SERIES (Hal Clement)

    #1 Mission of gravity. (1954)
    #2 Close to critical. (1964)
    #3 Star light. (1971)

THE MIND BROTHERS (Peter Heath)

    #1 The Mind Brothers. (1967)
    #2 Assassins from tomorrow. (1967)
    #3 Men who die twice. (1968)

MINDY (Jane Louise Curry)

    #1 Mindy's mysterious miniature. (1970)
    #2 The lost farm. (1974)

MINNIPINS (Carol Kendall)

    #1 The Gammage cup. (1959)
    #2 The whisper of Glocken. (1965)

MONELLA (Frank Aubrey)

    #1 The devil-tree of El Dorado. (1897)
    #2 A queen of Atlantis. (1899)
    #3 King of the dead. (1903)

MOON SERIES (Edgar Rice Burroughs)

    #1 The Moon maid. (1962)
    #2 The Moon men. (1962)
    #s 1-2 The Moon maid. (1926)

MOON SERIES (Lester del Rey)

    #1 Step to the stars. (1954)
    #2 Mission to the Moon. (1956)
    #3 Moon of mutiny. (1961)

ALAN MORGAN (Gardner F. Fox)

    #1 Warrior of Llarn. (1964)
    #2 Thief of Llarn. (1966)

JET MORGAN (Charles Chilton)

    #1 Journey into space. (1954)
    #2 The Red Planet. (1956)

THE MOTOR PIRATE (G. Sidney Paternoster)

    #1 The motor pirate. (1903)
    #2 The cruise of the Conqueror. (1906)

THE MOUSE THAT ROARED
    see: GRAND FENWICK

THE MUCKER (Edgar Rice Burroughs)

#1 The mucker. (1921)
#2 The man without a soul. (1922)
#s 1-2 The mucker. (1921)

BARON MUNCHAUSEN (Rudolf Erich Raspe)

    Baron Munchausen's narrative of his marvellous
    travels and campaigns in Russia. [the first
    edition; see main entry for title variations
    and later editions]

    SEQUELS AND PARODIES:

    Mr. Munchausen. (1901) [by John Kendrick Bangs]
    The extraordinary exploits and experiences of
    Munchausen, M.D. (1924) [by Julian Walter
    Brandeis]
    Munchausen at the Pole. (1819) [by Capt. Mun-
    chausen]
    Munchausen XX. (1904) [by W. G. Worfel]

AARN MUNRO (John W. Campbell)

#1 The mightiest machine. (1947)
#2 The incredible planet. (1949)

THE MUNSTERS (various authors)

    The Munsters. (1964) [by Morton Cooper]
    The Munsters and the great camera caper. (1965)
      [by William Johnston]
    The last resort. (1966) [by William Johnston]

MEG MURRY (Madeleine L'Engle)

#1 A wrinkle in time. (1962)
#2 A wind in the door. (1973)

MR. MYCROFT (H. F. Heard)

#1 A taste for honey. (1941)
#2 Reply paid. (1942)

NARNIAN CHRONICLES (C. S. Lewis)

#1 The lion, the witch, and the wardrobe. (1950)
#2 Prince Caspian. (1951)
#3 The voyage of the Dawn Treader. (1952)
#4 The silver chair. (1953)
#5 The horse and his boy. (1954)
#6 The magician's nephew. (1955)
#7 The last battle. (1956)
#s 1-7 The Chronicles of Narnia; with, The Lion of
      Judah in Never-Never Land. (1973)

GILBERT NASH (Wilson Tucker)

#1 The time masters. (1953)
#2 Time bomb. (1955)

THE NATURAL MAN (J. William Lloyd)

#1 The natural man. (1902)
#2 The dwellers in Vale Sunrise. (1904)

CAPT. NEMO (Jules Verne)

#1 20,000 leagues under the sea. (1872)
#2 The mysterious island. (1875)
#2A Abandoned. (1875)

#2B Shipwrecked in the air. (1874)
#2C The secret of the island. (1875)

NEUSTRIAN CYCLE (Leslie Barringer)

#1 Gerfalcon. (1927)
#2 Joris of the Rock. (1928)
#3 Shy leopardess. (1948)

NEW ATALANTIS (Mary Manley)

#1 Secret memoirs and manners of several persons
      of quality. (1709)
#2 Secret memoirs and manners of several persons
      of quality, the second volume. (1709)
#3 Memoirs of Europe. (1710)
#4 Memoirs of Europe, vol. II. (1710)
#5 Court intrigues in a collection of original
      letters. (1711)
#6 The modern Atalantis. (1784)

NIDOR SEQUENCE (Robert Randall [Robert Silverberg & Randall Garrett])

#1 The shrouded planet. (1957)
#2 The dawning light. (1959)

THE NIGHTMARE HAS TRIPLETS (Branch Cabell)

#1 Smirt. (1934)
#2 Smith. (1935)
#3 Smire. (1937)
#s 1-3 The nightmare has triplets. (1972)

    RELATED TITLE:

    The nightmare has triplets; an author's note on
      Smire. (1937)

DR. NIKOLA (Guy Boothby)

#1 A bid for fortune. (1895)
#2 Doctor Nikola. (1896)
#3 The lust of hate. (1898)
#4 Dr. Nikola's experiment. (1899)
#5 "Farewell, Nikola!" (1901)

NOIBLA (Sir Humphrey Lunatic)

#1 A trip to the Moon. (1764)
#2 A trip to the Moon, volume II. (1765)

NOOMAS SERIES (Charles Nuetzel)

#1 Warriors of Noomas. (1969)
#2 Raiders of Noomas. (1969)

NOREN SEQUENCE (Sylvia Louise Engdahl)

#1 This star shall abide. (1972)
#2 Beyond the Tomorrow Mountains. (1973)

ROBIN NORTH (Patrick Moore)

#1 Wanderer in space. (1961)
#2 Crater of fear. (1962)
#3 Invader from space. (1963)
#4 Caverns of the Moon. (1964)

NOVA CYCLE (William S. Burroughs)

#1 The ticket that exploded. (1962)
#2 Nova express. (1964)

NULL-A SERIES (A. E. van Vogt)

    #1 The world of null-A. (1948)
    #2 The pawns of null-A. (1956)

SHAMRYKE ODELL (Robert Lory)

    #1 Masters of the lamp. (1970)
    #2 The veiled world. (1972)

JACK ODIN (Joseph E. Kelleam)

    #1 The little men. (1960)
    #2 Hunters of space. (1960)

OG SERIES (Irving Crump)

    #1 Og--son of fire. (1922)
    #2 Og--boy of battle. (1925)
    #3 Og of the cave people. (1935)
    #4 Og, son of Og. (1965)

ALOYSIUS O'KENNEDY (Eimar O'Duffy)

    #1 The spacious adventures of the man in the street.
        (1928)
    #2 Asses in clover. (1933)

OLD GROWLER SERIES (Jon J. Deegan)

    #1 Amateurs in alchemy. (1952)
    #2 Antro, the life-giver. (1953)
    #3 The Great Ones. (1953)

THE OLEANDRE TRILOGY (D. John Fretland)

    #1 The Persimmon Sequence. (1971)
    #2 Winds of the Heliopolis. (1972)
    #3 The Oleandre solution. (never issued)

COLIN O'LEARY (C. E. Scoggins)

    #1 The house of dawn. (1935)
    #2 Lost road. (1941)

LAFAYETTE O'LEARY (Keith Laumer)

    #1 The time bender. (1966)
    #2 The world shuffler. (1970)
    #3 The shape changer. (1972)

OMINA SEQUENCE (Roland Starr [Donald S. Row-
land])

    #1 Operation Omina. (1970)
    #2 Omina uncharted. (1974)

OMNIVORE SERIES (Piers Anthony)

    #1 Omnivore. (1968)
    #2 Orn. (1970)

THE ONCE AND FUTURE KING
    see: KING ARTHUR

THE 101 DALMATIANS (Dodie Smith)

    #1 The hundred and one dalmatians. (1956)
    #2 The starlight barking. (1967)

OPERATOR 5 (Curtis Steele)

    FIRST SERIES:

    #1 Legions of the death master. (1966)
    #2 The army of the dead. (1966)
    #3 The invisible empire. (1966)
    #4 Master of broken men. (1966)
    #5 Hosts of the flaming death. (1966)
    #6 Blood reign of the dictator. (1966)
    #7 March of the flame marauders. (1966)
    #8 Invasion of the yellow warlords. (1966)

    SECOND SERIES:

    #1 The masked invasion. (1974)
    #2 The invisible empire. (1974)
    #3 The yellow scourge. (1974)

DR. ORIENT (Frank Lauria)

    #1 Doctor Orient. (1970)
    #2 Raga Six. (1972)
    #3 Lady Sativa. (1973)
    #4 Baron Orgaz. (1974)

THE HANDS OF ORLAC (Maurice Renard)

        The hands of Orlac. (1929)

    MOVIE ADAPTATION:

        The hands of Orlac. (1961) [by Robert Bateman]

OUTLANDER SERIES (Stanton A. Coblentz)

    #1 The Moon People. (1964)
    #2 The crimson capsule. (1967)
    #3 The island people. (1971)

DR. PALFREY (John Creasey)

    NON-SF TITLES:

    #1 Traitors' doom. (1942)
    #2 The valley of fear. (1943)
    #3 The legion of the lost. (1943)
    #4 Dangerous quest. (1944)
    #5 The hounds of vengeance. (1944)
    #6 Death in the rising sun. (1945)
    #7 Shadow of doom. (1946)
    #8 The house of the bears. (1947)

    SF TITLES:

    #9   Dark harvest. (1947)
    #10 Sons of Satan. (1947)
    #11 The wings of peace. (1948)
    #12 The dawn of darkness. (1949)
    #13 The league of light. (1949)
    #14 The man who shook the world. (1950)
    #15 The prophet of fire. (1951)
    #16 The children of hate. (1952)
    #17 The touch of death. (1954)
    #18 The mists of fear. (1955)
    #19 The flood. (1956)
    #20 The plague of silence. (1958)
    #21 The drought. (1959)
    #22 The terror. (1962)
    #23 The depths. (1963)
    #24 The sleep. (1964)
    #25 The inferno. (1965)

DR. PALFREY (John Creasey) [cont.]

#26 The famine. (1967)
#27 The blight. (1968)
#28 The oasis. (1969)
#29 The smog. (1970)
#30 The unbegotten. (1971)
#31 The insulators. (1972)
#32 The voiceless ones. (1973)

PETER PAN (J. M. Barrie)

#1 Peter Pan in Kensington Gardens. (1906)
#2 Peter and Wendy. (1911)

PAN SAGITTARIUS (Ian Wallace)

#1 Deathstar voyage. (1969)
#2 Pan Sagittarius. (1973)
#3 A voyage to Dari. (1974)

PANTOUFLIA (Andrew Lang)

#1 Prince Prigio. (1889)
#2 Prince Ricardo. (1893)
#s 1-2 My own fairy book. (1895)

PARALYZING RAY SERIES (Guido "Skipper" Nizzi)

#1 The victor. (1946)
#2 The paralyzing rays vs. the nuclears. (1964)
#3 The daring trip to the Moon. (1968)

UNCLE PAUL (Algernon Blackwood)

#1 The education of Uncle Paul. (1909)
#2 A prisoner in Fairyland. (1913)

THE PEACEMAKERS (John M. Faucette)

#1 The warriors of Terra. (1970)
#2 Siege of Earth. (1971)

PELLUCIDAR SERIES (Edgar Rice Burroughs)

#1 At the Earth's core. (1922)
#2 Pellucidar. (1923)
#3 Tanar of Pellucidar. (1930)
#4 Tarzan at the Earth's core. (1930)
#5 Back to the Stone Age. (1937)
#6 Land of terror. (1944)
#7 Savage Pellucidar. (1963)

PENELOPE (William C. Anderson)

#1 Penelope. (1963)
#2 Penelope, the damp detective. (1974)

THE PEOPLE (Zenna Henderson)

#1 Pilgrimage: the book of the People. (1961)
#2 The People: no different flesh. (1966)

PERCY (Raymond Hitchcock)

#1 Percy. (1969)
#2 Percy's progress. (1974)

PETER (Stephen Mogridge)

#1 Peter and the flying saucers. (1954)
#2 Peter and the atomic valley. (1955)
#3 Peter and the Moon bomb. (1956)

DR. PHIBES (William Goldstein)

#1 Dr. Phibes. (1971)
#2 Dr. Phibes rises again. (1973)

PIC (George Langford)

#1 Pic, the weapon-maker. (1920)
#2 Kutnar, son of Pic. (1921)

MISS PICKERELL (Ellen MacGregor)

#1 Miss Pickerell goes to Mars. (1951)
#2 Miss Pickerell and the geiger counter. (1953)
#3 Miss Pickerell goes undersea. (1953)
#4 Miss Pickerell goes to the Arctic. (1954)
#5 Miss Pickerell on the Moon. (1965) [with Dora
      Pantell]
#6 Miss Pickerell goes on a dig. (1966) [with Dora
      Pantell]
#7 Miss Pickerell harvests the sea. (1968) [with
      Dora Pantell]
#8 Miss Pickerell and the weather satellite. (1971)
      [with Dora Pantell]
#9 Miss Pickerell meets Mr. H.U.M. (1974) [with
      Dora Pantell]

MARTIN PIPPIN (Eleanor Farjeon)

#1 Martin Pippin in the apple-orchard. (1921)
#2 Martin Pippin in the daisy-field. (1937)

PLANET OF ADVENTURE
   see: TSCHAI CYCLE

PLANET OF THE APES (various authors)

#1 Planet of the apes. (1963) [by Pierre Boulle]

MOVIE SERIES:

#2 Beneath the planet of the apes. (1970) [by
      Michael Avallone]
#3 Escape from the planet of the apes. (1974) [by
      Jerry Pournelle]
#4 Conquest of the planet of the apes. (1974) [by
      John Jakes]
#5 Battle for the planet of the apes. (1973) [by
      David Gerrold]

TV SERIES:

#1 Man the fugitive. (1974) [by George Alec Effin-
      ger]

PLANETARY AGENT SERIES (Mack Reynolds)

#1 Planetary Agent X. (1965)
#2 Dawnman planet. (1966)
#3 The rival Rigelians. (1967)
#4 Code duello. (1968)

POLARIS TRILOGY (Charles B. Stilson)

#1 Polaris--of the Snows. (1965)
#2 Minos of Sardanes. (1966)
#3 Polaris and the immortals. (1968)

MARY POPPINS (P. L. Travers)

#1 Mary Poppins. (1934)
#2 Mary Poppins comes back. (1935)

MARY POPPINS (P. L. Travers) [cont.]

    #3 Mary Poppins opens the door. (1943)
    #4 Mary Poppins in the park. (1952)

DRAY PRESCOT [SCORPIO] (Alan Burt Akers [Kenneth Bulmer])

    #1 Transit to Scorpio. (1972)
    #2 The suns of Scorpio. (1973)
    #3 Warrior of Scorpio. (1973)
    #4 Swordships of Scorpio. (1973)
    #5 Prince of Scorpio. (1974)
    #6 Manhounds of Antares. (1974)
    #7 Arena of Antares. (1974)

PRESTER JOHN (Norvell W. Page]

    #1 Flame Winds. (1969)
    #2 Sons of the Bear-God. (1969)

THE PRISONER (various authors)

    #1 The prisoner. (1969) [by Thomas M. Disch]
    #2 Number Two. (1969) [by David McDaniel]
    #3 A day in the life. (1970) [by Hank Stine]

CHARLES PRY (E. C. Large)

    #1 Asleep in the afternoon. (1938)
    #2 Sugar in the air. (1937)

PRYDAIN CHRONICLES
    see: CHRONICLES OF PRYDAIN

PSAMMAED SERIES (E. Nesbit)

    #1 Five children and it. (1902)
    #2 The phoenix and the carpet. (1904)
    #3 The story of the amulet. (1906)
    #s 1-3 The five children. (1930)

PUCK (Rudyard Kipling)

    #1 Puck of Pook's Hill. (1906)
    #2 Rewards and fairies. (1910)

ARTHUR GORDON PYM (Edgar Allan Poe)

    The narrative of Arthur Gordon Pym of Nantucket.
      (1838)

    SEQUELS AND PARODIES:

        A strange discovery. (1899) [by Charles Dake]
        An Antarctic mystery. (1898) [by Jules Verne]
        The mystery of Arthur Gordon Pym. (1960) [includes Poe's original and Verne's sequel]

QANAR SEQUENCE (Ted White)

    #1 Phoenix prime. (1966)
    #2 The Sorceress of Qar. (1966)
    #3 Star wolf! (1971)

QFWFQ SERIES (Italo Calvino)

    #1 Cosmicomics. (1968)
    #2 t zero. (1969)

QHE (William Bloom writing as W.W.)

    #1 The taming power. (1974)

    #2 White fire. (1974)

ALLAN QUATERMAIN (H. Rider Haggard)

    #1   Marie. (1912)
    #2   Allan's wife. (1887)
    #3   Child of storm. (1913)
    #4   A tale of three lions. (1887)
    #5   Maiwa's revenge. (1888)
    #6   "Allan the hunter." (1889)
    #7   "Long odds." (1889)
    #8   The Holy Flower. (1915)
    #9   Heu-Heu. (1924)
    #10 She and Allan. (1921)
    #11 Treasure of the lake. (1926)
    #12 The ivory child. (1916)
    #13 Finished. (1916)
    #14 "Magepa the Buck." (1920)
    #15 King Solomon's mines. (1885)
    #16 The ancient Allan. (1920)
    #17 Allan and the ice-gods. (1927)
    #18 Allan Quatermain. (1887)

    RELATED TITLES:

        Allan the hunter; A tale of three lions. (1898)
          [Allan Quatermain #s 6, 4]
        Allan's wife, and other tales. (1889) [includes
          "Allan's wife" (#2), "Hunter Quatermain's
          story" (#6), "A tale of three lions" (#4),
          and "Long odds" (#7)]
        King Solomon's mines. (1950) [rewritten from
          the movie version by Jean Francis Webb]

    SEQUELS AND PARODIES:

        King Solomon's treasures. (1887) [by John De
          Morgan]
        King Solomon's wives. (1887) [by John De Morgan]
        King Solomon's wives. (1887) [by Hyder Ragged]

GREGORY QUEST (Patrick Moore)

    #1 Quest of the spaceways. (1955)
    #2 World of mists. (1956)

HAUTLEY QUICKSILVER (Lin Carter)

    #1 The thief of Thoth. (1968)
    #2 The purloined planet. (1969)

ADAM QUIRKE (Volsted Gridban [John Russell Fearn])

    #1 The Master must die. (1953)
    #2 The lonely astronomer. (1954)

RA-AB HOTEP (Joan Grant)

    #1 Eyes of Horus. (1942)
    #2 Lord of the horizon. (1943)

RACK (Laurence James)

    #1 Earth lies sleeping. (1974)
    #2 War on Aleph. (1974)

RADIO SERIES
    see: MILES CABOT

RAGNAROK (Tom Godwin)

    #1 The survivors. (1958)
    #2 The space barbarians. (1964)

RANSOM TRILOGY (C. S. Lewis)

    #1   Out of the silent planet. (1938)
    #2   Perelandra. (1943)
    #3   That hideous strength. (1945)

PAUL REEDER (Robert C. Dennis)

    #1   The sweat of fear. (1973)
    #2   Conversations with a corpse. (1974)

REGINA SERIES (John Mastin)

    #1   The stolen planet. (1905)
    #2   Through the Sun in an airship. (1909)

NAILL RENFRO (Andre Norton)

    #1   Judgment on Janus. (1963)
    #2   Victory on Janus. (1966)

RETIEF (Keith Laumer)

    #1   Envoy to new worlds. (1963)
    #2   Galactic diplomat. (1965)
    #3   Retief's war. (1966)
    #4   Retief and the warlords. (1968)
    #5   Retief: ambassador to space. (1969)
    #6   Retief's ransom. (1971)
    #7   Retief of the CDT. (1971)

JUSTIN RETIEF (Joseph J. Doke)

    #1   The secret city. (1913)
    #2   The queen of the secret city. (1916)

REUBEN (Rosemary Harris)

    #1   The Moon in the cloud. (1968)
    #2   The shadow on the Sun. (1970)
    #3   The bright and morning star. (1972)

RHADA SEQUENCE (Robert Cham Gilman [Alfred Coppel])

    #1   The Rebel of Rhada. (1968)
    #2   The navigator of Rhada. (1969)
    #3   The Starkahn of Rhada. (1970)

PROFESSOR RHYMER (Uel Key)

    #1   The broken fang, and other experiences of a
           specialist in spooks. (1920)
    #2   Yellow death. (1921)

ROY RICKMAN (David Craig)

    #1   The alias man. (1968)
    #2   Message ends. (1969)
    #3   Contact lost. (1970)

RIM SERIES [GRIMES] (A. Bertram Chandler)

    #1   The road to the Rim. (1967)
    #2   To prime the pump. (1971)
    #3   The hard way up. (1972)
    #4   False fatherland. (1968)
    #5   The inheritors. (1972)
    #6   (The broken cycle.)
    #7   (The big black mark.)
    #8   Catch the star winds. (1969)
    #9   Into the alternate universe. (1964)

    #10 Contraband from otherspace. (1967)
    #11 The Rim gods. (1969)
    #12 Alternate orbits. (1971)
    #13 Nebula alert. (1967)
    #14 The gateway to never. (1972)
    #15 The dark dimensions. (1971)

    OTHER RIM STORIES:

        Beyond the galactic Rim. (1963)
        The deep reaches of space. (1964)
        Rendezvous on a lost world. (1961)
        The Rim of space. (1961)
        The ship from outside. (1963)

RIVERWORLD SERIES (Philip Jose Farmer)

    #1   To your scattered bodies go. (1971)
    #2   The fabulous Riverboat. (1971)

ROBOT SERIES (Isaac Asimov)

    #1   I, robot. (1950)
    #2   The rest of the robots. (1964)

    LIJE BALEY SERIES:

    #1   The caves of steel. (1954)
    #2   The naked sun. (1957)

ROBUR (Jules Verne)

    #1   The clipper of the clouds. (1887)
    #2   The master of the world. (1914)
    #s 1-2 Robur the conqueror; and, Master of the
              world. (1951)

ROCK SERIES (A. M. Lightner)

    #1   The rock of three planets. (1963)
    #2   The planet poachers. (1965)
    #3   The space ark. (1968)

ROCKET RIDERS (Howard R. Garis)

    #1   Rocket Riders across the ice. (1933)
    #2   Rocket Riders over the desert. (1933)
    #3   Rocket Riders in stormy seas. (1933)
    #4   Rocket Riders in the air. (1934)

ROMANOFF SERIES (George Griffith)

    #1   The angel of the revolution. (1893)
    #2   Olga Romanoff. (1894)

RUDI (Ursula Moray Williams) [see Addendum]

    #1   The three toymakers. (1945)
    #2   Malkin's mountain. (1948)

RUNESTAFF [COUNT BRASS] (Michael Moorcock)

    #1   The jewel in the skull. (1967)
    #2   Sorcerer's amulet. (1968)
    #3   Sword of the dawn. (1968)
    #4   The secret of the Runestaff. (1969)

    CASTLE BRASS:

    #1   Count Brass. (1973)
    #2   The Champion of Garathorm. (1973)

CLAUDINE ST. CYR (Ian Wallace)

#1 Dr. Orpheus. (1968)
#2 The purloined prince. (1971)

SAKAELAND (Ganpat)

#1 Harilek. (1923)
#2 Wrexham's romance. (1935)

SARAGOSSA MANUSCRIPT (Jan Potocki)

#1 The Saragossa manuscript. (1960)
#2 The new Decameron. (1967)

SAUCER SERIES (Eando Binder)

#1 Menace of the saucers. (1969)
#2 Night of the saucers. (1971)

DOC SAVAGE (Kenneth Robeson)

FIRST SERIES:

#1 The man of bronze. (1933)
#2 The land of terror. (1933)
#3 Quest of the Spider. (1933)

SECOND SERIES:

#1 The man of bronze. (1964)
#2 The Thousand-Headed Man. (1964)
#3 Meteor menace. (1964)
#4 The polar treasure. (1965)
#5 Brand of the werewolf. (1965)
#6 The lost oasis. (1965)
#7 The monsters. (1965)
#8 The land of terror. (1965)
#9 The Mystic Mullah. (1965)
#10 The Phantom City. (1966)
#11 Fear Cay. (1966)
#12 Quest of Qui. (1966)
#13 Land of always-night. (1966)
#14 The fantastic island. (1966)
#15 Murder melody. (1967)
#16 The spook legion. (1967)
#17 The red skull. (1967)
#18 The Sargasso Ogre. (1967)
#19 Pirate of the Pacific. (1967)
#20 The secret in the sky. (1967)
#21 Cold death. (1968)
#22 The czar of fear. (1968)
#23 Fortress of Solitude. (1968)
#24 The green eagle. (1968)
#25 The devil's playground. (1968)
#26 Death in silver. (1968)
#27 Mystery under the sea. (1968)
#28 The deadly dwarf. (1968)
#29 The other world. (1968)
#30 The flaming falcons. (1968)
#31 The Annihilist. (1968)
#32 Dust of death. (1969)
#33 The terror in the Navy. (1969)
#34 Mad eyes. (1969)
#35 The Squeaking Goblin. (1969)
#36 Resurrection day. (1969)
#37 Hex. (1969)
#38 Red snow. (1969)
#39 World's Fair goblin. (1969)
#40 The dagger in the sky. (1969)
#41 Merchants of disaster. (1969)
#42 The gold ogre. (1969)

#43 The man who shook the Earth. (1969)
#44 The sea magician. (1970)
#45 The men who smiled no more. (1970)
#46 The Midas man. (1970)
#47 Land of long juju. (1970)
#48 The Feathered Octopus. (1970)
#49 The Sea Angel. (1970)
#50 Devil on the Moon. (1970)
#51 Haunted ocean. (1970)
#52 The vanisher. (1970)
#53 The mental wizard. (1970)
#54 He could stop the world. (1970)
#55 The golden peril. (1970)
#56 The giggling ghosts. (1971)
#57 Poison island. (1971)
#58 The munitions master. (1971)
#59 The yellow cloud. (1971)
#60 The Majii. (1971)
#61 The living-fire menace. (1971)
#62 The pirate's ghost. (1971)
#63 The submarine mystery. (1971)
#64 The motion menace. (1971)
#65 The green death. (1971)
#66 Mad Mesa. (1972)
#67 The freckled shark. (1972)
#68 Quest of the Spider. (1972)
#69 The mystery on the snow. (1972)
#70 Spook Hole. (1972)
#71 Murder mirage. (1972)
#72 The Metal Master. (1973)
#73 The seven agate devils. (1973)
#74 The derrick devil. (1973)
#75 The land of fear. (1973)
#76 The black spot. (1974)
#77 The South Pole terror. (1974)
#78 The crimson serpent. (1974)
#79 The devil Genghis. (1974)

SEQUELS AND PARODIES:

    The living toilets. (1973) [by Kin I. Disrobeson]

DOC CALIBAN (Philip Jose Farmer):

#1 A feast unknown. (1969)
#2 The mad goblin. (1970)

SAVAGE REPORT (Howard Rheingold)

#1 Jack Anderson against Dr. Tek! (1974)
#2 War of the gurus. (1974)

CAPT. SCARLET (John Theydon)

#1 Captain Scarlet and the Mysterons. (1967)
#2 Captain Scarlet and the silent saboteur. (1967)

PETER SCHLEMIHL (Adalbert von Chamisso)

    Peter Schlemihl. (1823)

SEQUELS AND PARODIES:

    Future life. (1858) [by George Wood]
    Peter Schlemihl in America. (1848) [by Wood]

SCORPIO SERIES
    see: DRAY PRESCOT

SCREWTAPE (C. S. Lewis)

#1 The Screwtape letters. (1942)

SCREWTAPE (C. S. Lewis) [cont.]

#2 Screwtape proposes a toast, and other pieces.
    (1965)
#s 1-2 The Screwtape letters; &, Screwtape proposes
    a toast. (1961)

JONATHAN LIVINGSTON SEAGULL (Richard Bach)

    Jonathan Livingston Seagull. (1970)

SEQUELS AND PARODIES:

    Jonathan Livingston Fliegle. (1973) [by Hubert
      Bermont]
    Jonathan Segal Chicken. (1973) [by Howard Al-
      brecht & Sol Weinstein]
    Ludwig von Wolfgang Vulture. (1973) [by Dolph
      Sharp]

SEARCH (Robert Weverka)

#1 Search. (1973)
#2 Moonrock. (1973)

SECTOR GENERAL SERIES (James White)

#1 Hospital station. (1962)
#2 Star surgeon. (1963)
#3 Major operation. (1971)

SEETEE SERIES (Jack Williamson)

#1 Seetee ship. (1951)
#2 Seetee shock. (1950)
#s 1-2 Seetee ship/Seetee shock. (1972)

SERPENT LAND (Alan Connell)

#1 Lords of serpent land. (1945)
#2 Prisoners in serpent land. (1945)
#3 Warriors of serpent land. (1945)

HECTOR SERVADAC (Jules Verne)

#1 Hector Servadac. (1877)
#2 Off on a comet! (1878)
#s 1-2 Hector Servadac. (1878)

NED SHACKLETON (Rayburn Crawley)

#1 The Valley of Creeping Men. (1930)
#2 Chattering gods. (1931)

THE SHADOW (Maxwell Grant)

BANTAM SERIES:

#1 The living Shadow. (1969)
#2 The eyes of the Shadow. (1969)
#3 The Shadow laughs! (1969)
#4 The death tower. (1969)
#5 The ghost makers. (1970)
#6 Hidden death. (1970)
#7 Gangdom's doom. (1970)

PYRAMID SERIES:

#1 The living Shadow. (1974)
#2 The black master. (1974)
#3 The mobsmen on the spot. (1974)

NEW SHADOW SERIES:

#1 Return of the Shadow. (1963) [by Walter Gibson]
#2 The Shadow strikes. (1964)
#3 Shadow beware. (1965)
#4 Cry Shadow! (1965)
#5 The Shadow's revenge. (1965)
#6 Mark of the Shadow. (1966)
#7 Shadow--go mad! (1966)
#8 The night of the Shadow. (1966)
#9 The Shadow: destination: Moon. (1967)

OTHER TITLES:

    The Shadow and the voice of murder. (1940)
    The weird adventures of the Shadow. (1966) [by
      Walter B. Gibson]
    The weird adventures of the Shadow; Grove of doom.
      (1969)

SHE (H. Rider Haggard)

#1 Wisdom's daughter. (1923)
#2 She and Allan. (1921)
#3 She. (1886)
#4 Ayesha. (1905)

SEQUELS AND PARODIES:

#1 He, a companion to She. (1887) [by John De Mor-
      gan]
#2 "It." (1887) [by John De Morgan]
    He. (1887) [by Andrew Lang & Walter Pollock]
    The king of Kor. (1903) [by Sidney J. Marshall]
    She, the story retold. (1949) [adapted by
      Don Ward]
    Her. (1967) [by J. X. Williams]

HAROLD SHEA (L. Sprague de Camp & Fletcher
Pratt)

#1 The incomplete enchanter. (1941)
#2 The castle of iron. (1950)
#3 Wall of serpents. (1960)

SHINY SPEAR SERIES (Roy Sheldon [H. J. Camp-
bell])

#1 Atoms in action. (1953)
#2 House of entropy. (1953)

SHUNA (John King)

#1 Shuna, white queen of the jungle. (1951)
#2 Shuna and the lost tribe. (1951)

THE SHY STEGOSAURUS (Evelyn Sibley Lampman)

#1 The shy stegosaurus of Cricket Creek. (1955)
#2 The shy stegosaurus of Indian Springs. (1962)

SISTERHOOD TRILOGY (Howard Rheingold)

#1 Mama Liz drinks deep. (1973)
#2 Mama Liz tastes flesh. (1973)
#3 Secret sisterhood. (1973)

SIXTH PERCEPTION SERIES (Dan Morgan)

#1 The new minds. (1967)
#2 The several minds. (1969)
#3 Mind trap. (1970)

SKY BUDDIES
   see: AIRPLANE BOYS

SKYLARK SERIES (E. E. Smith)

  #1 The Skylark of space. (1946) [with Lee Hawkins
      Garby]
  #2 Skylark Three. (1948)
  #3 Skylark of Valeron. (1949)
  #4 Skylark DuQuesne. (1966)

SAM SMALL (Eric Knight)

  #1 The flying Yorkshireman. (1940)
  #2 Sam Small flies again. (1942)

SMITH MINOR (Philip Hardy)

  #1 The buried country. (1945?)
  #2 Smith Minor on the Moon. (1945?)

SNOWBIRD SERIES (Gordon Stables)

  #1 The cruise of the Snowbird. (1882)
  #2 Wild adventures round the Pole. (1883)

SOCIOLAND (Albert Chavannes)

  #1 The future commonwealth. (1892)
  #2 In brighter climes. (1895)

SOLAR QUEEN (Andrew North [Andre Norton])

  #1 Sargasso of space. (1955)
  #2 Plague ship. (1956)
  #3 Voodoo planet. (1959)
  #4 Postmarked the stars. (1969)

SORAK (Harvey D. Richards)

  #1 Sorak of the Malay jungle. (1934)
  #2 Sorak and the clouded tiger. (1934)
  #3 Sorak and the Sultan's ankus. (1934)
  #4 Sorak and the tree-men. (1936)

THE SORCERESS (Nathan Gallizier)

  #1 Castel del Monte. (1905) [not SF?]
  #2 The sorceress of Rome. (1907)
  #3 The court of Lucifer. (1910)

GERARD SORME (Colin Wilson)

  #1 Ritual in the dark. (1960) [not SF]
  #2 Man without a shadow. (1963)
  #3 The god of the labyrinth. (1970)

SOS (Piers Anthony)

  #1 Sos, the rope. (1968)
  #2 Var, the stick. (1972)

SPACE CAT (Ruthven Todd)

  #1 Space cat. (1952)
  #2 Space cat visits Venus. (1955)
  #3 Space cat meets Mars. (1957)
  #4 Space cat and the kittens. (1958)

SPACE CORPORATION (John Rankine [Douglas Mason])

  #1 Never the same door. (1968)

  #2 Moons of Triopus. (1968)

SPACE PROBE 6 (Charles Huntington)

  #1 The soul stealers. (1973)
  #2 Nightmare on Vega 3. (1973)

SPACE PUPPET (John Rackham)

  #1 Space Puppet. (1954)
  #2 The master weed. (1954)
  #3 Jupiter equilateral. (1954)
  #4 Alien virus. (1954)

SPACE SHIP SERIES (Louis Slobodkin)

  #1 The space ship under the apple tree. (1952)
  #2 The space ship returns to the apple tree. (1958)
  #3 The three-seated space ship. (1962)
  #4 Round trip space ship. (1968)
  #5 The space ship in the park. (1972)

THE SPECIALIST (Errol Lecale)

  #1 The tigerman of Terrahpur. (1973)
  #2 Castledoom. (1974)
  #3 The severed hand. (1974)
  #4 The death box. (1974)

SPROCKETS (Alexander Key)

  #1 Sprockets, a little robot. (1963)
  #2 Rivets and Sprockets. (1964)
  #3 Bolts, a robot dog. (1966)

THE STAINLESS STEEL RAT
   see: SLIPPERY JIM DiGRIZ

STAR KINGS (Edmond Hamilton)

  #1 The star kings. (1949)
  #2 Return to the stars. (1970)

STAR TREK (various authors)

  TV ADAPTATIONS (James Blish):

  #1 Star trek. (1967)
  #2 Star trek 2. (1968)
  #3 Star trek 3. (1969)
  #4 Star trek 4. (1971)
  #5 Star trek 5. (1972)
  #6 Star trek 6. (1972)
  #7 Star trek 7. (1972)
  #8 Star trek 8. (1972)
  #9 Star trek 9. (1973)
  #10 Star trek 10. (1974)

  ANIMATED SERIES ADAPTATIONS (Alan Dean Foster):

  #1 Star trek, log one. (1974)
  #2 Star trek, log two. (1974)

  OTHER TITLES:

    Spock must die! (1970) [by James Blish]
    Star trek: mission to Horatius. (1968) [by Mack
    Reynolds]

STARCHILD TRILOGY (Frederik Pohl & Jack Williamson)

  #1 The Reefs of Space. (1964)

STARCHILD TRILOGY (Frederik Pohl & Jack Williamson) [cont.]

#2   Starchild.   (1965)
#3   Rogue star.   (1969)

STARFIRE SERIES (Edwin Mumford)

#1   Flight of the Starfire.   (1972)
#2   The second flight of the Starfire.   (1972)
#3   The third flight of the Starfire.   (1972)
#4   The fourth flight of the Starfire.   (1972)
#5   The voyage of the Starfire to Atlantis.   (1973)
#s 1-5   The five flights of the Starfire.   (1974)

ERIC JOHN STARK (Leigh Brackett)

    FIRST SERIES:

       People of the Talisman.   (1964)
       The secret of Sinharat.   (1964)

    SECOND SERIES:

    #1   The ginger star.   (1974)
    #2   The hounds of Skaith.   (1974)

LUCKY STARR (Paul French [Isaac Asimov])

#1   David Starr, Space Ranger.   (1952)
#2   Lucky Starr and the pirates of the asteroids. (1953)
#3   Lucky Starr and the oceans of Venus.   (1954)
#4   Lucky Starr and the big sun of Mercury.   (1956)
#5   Lucky Starr and the moons of Jupiter.   (1957)
#6   Lucky Starr and the rings of Saturn.   (1958)

STARWOLF (Edmond Hamilton)

#1   The weapon from beyond.   (1967)
#2   The Closed Worlds.   (1968)
#3   World of the Starwolves.   (1968)

STEAM HOUSE SERIES (Jules Verne)

#1   The demon of Cawnpore.   (1881)
#2   Tigers and traitors.   (1881)

STINGRAY (John Theydon)

#1   Stingray.   (1965)
#2   Stingray and the monster.   (1966)

HOSTEEN STORM (Andre Norton)

#1   The Beast Master.   (1959)
#2   Lord of Thunder.   (1962)

STRANGE PARADISE (Dorothy Daniels)

#1   Strange paradise.   (1969)
#2   Island of evil.   (1970)
#3   Raxl, voodoo priestess.   (1970)

JASON STRIKER (Piers Anthony & Roberto Fuentes)

#1   Kiai!   (1974)
#2   Mistress of death.   (1974)
#3   The bamboo bloodbath.   (1974)

JACK SUMNER
    see: BARNUM SYSTEM

MATTHEW SUMNER (Norman Davey)

#s 1-2   The pilgrim of a smile.   (1921)
#2   The penultimate adventure.   (1924)

SUMURU (Sax Rohmer)

#1   Nude in mink.   (1950)
#2   Sumuru.   (1951)
#3   Virgin in flames.   (1953)
#4   Return of Sumuru.   (1954)
#5   Sinister madonna.   (1956)

SUPER NOVA (Angus MacVicar)

#1   'Super Nova' and the rogue satellite.   (1969)
#2   'Super Nova' and the frozen man.   (1970)

THE SURVIVORS (Francis H. Sibson)

#1   The survivors.   (1932)
#2   The stolen continent.   (1934)

TOM SWIFT (Victor Appleton)

#1   Tom Swift and his motor-cycle.   (1910)
#2   Tom Swift and his motor-boat.   (1910)
#3   Tom Swift and his airship.   (1910)
#4   Tom Swift and his submarine boat.   (1910)
#5   Tom Swift and his electric runabout.   (1910)
#6   Tom Swift and his wireless message.   (1911)
#7   Tom Swift among the diamond makers.   (1911)
#8   Tom Swift in the caves of ice.   (1911)
#9   Tom Swift and his sky racer.   (1911)
#10   Tom Swift and his electric rifle.   (1911)
#11   Tom Swift in the city of gold.   (1912)
#12   Tom Swift and his air glider.   (1912)
#13   Tom Swift in captivity.   (1912)
#14   Tom Swift and his wizard camera.   (1912)
#15   Tom Swift and his great searchlight.   (1912)
#16   Tom Swift and his giant cannon.   (1913)
#17   Tom Swift and his photo telephone.   (1914)
#18   Tom Swift and his aerial warship.   (1915)
#19   Tom Swift and his big tunnel.   (1916)
#20   Tom Swift in the land of wonders.   (1917)
#21   Tom Swift and his war tank.   (1918)
#22   Tom Swift and his air scout.   (1919)
#23   Tom Swift and his undersea search.   (1920)
#24   Tom Swift among the fire fighters.   (1921)
#25   Tom Swift and his electric locomotive.   (1922)
#26   Tom Swift and his flying boat.   (1923)
#27   Tom Swift and his giant oil gusher.   (1924)
#28   Tom Swift and his chest of secrets.   (1925)
#29   Tom Swift and his airline express.   (1926)
#30   Tom Swift circling the globe.   (1927)
#31   Tom Swift and his talking pictures.   (1928)
#32   Tom Swift and his house on wheels.   (1929)
#33   Tom Swift and his big dirigible.   (1930)
#34   Tom Swift and his sky train.   (1931)
#35   Tom Swift and his giant magnet.   (1932)
#36   Tom Swift and his television detector.   (1933)
#37   Tom Swift and his ocean airport.   (1934)
#38   Tom Swift and his planet stone.   (1935)

TOM SWIFT JR. (Victor Appleton II)

#1   Tom Swift and his flying lab.   (1954)
#2   Tom Swift and his jetmarine.   (1954)
#3   Tom Swift and his rocket ship.   (1954)
#4   Tom Swift and his giant robot.   (1954)
#5   Tom Swift and his atomic earth blaster.   (1954)
#6   Tom Swift and his outpost in space.   (1955)
#7   Tom Swift and his diving seacopter.   (1956)

TOM SWIFT JR. (Victor Appleton II) [cont.]

#8 Tom Swift in the caves of nuclear fire. (1956)
#9 Tom Swift on the phantom satellite. (1957)
#10 Tom Swift and his ultrasonic cycloplane. (1957)
#11 Tom Swift and his deep-sea hydrodome. (1958)
#12 Tom Swift in the race to the Moon. (1958)
#13 Tom Swift and his space solartron. (1958)
#14 Tom Swift and his electronic retroscope. (1959)
#15 Tom Swift and his spectromarine selector. (1960)
#16 Tom Swift and the cosmic astronauts. (1960)
#17 Tom Swift and the visitor from Planet X. (1961)
#18 Tom Swift and the electronic hydrolung. (1961)
#19 Tom Swift and his triphibian atomicar. (1962)
#20 Tom Swift and his megascope space prober. (1962)
#21 Tom Swift and the asteroid pirates. (1963)
#22 Tom Swift and his repelatron skyway. (1963)
#23 Tom Swift and his aquatomic tracker. (1964)
#24 Tom Swift and his 3-D telejector. (1964)
#25 Tom Swift and his polar-ray dynasphere. (1965)
#26 Tom Swift and his sonic boom trap. (1965)
#27 Tom Swift and his subocean geotron. (1966)
#28 Tom Swift and the mystery comet. (1966)
#29 Tom Swift and the captive planetoid. (1967)
#30 Tom Swift and his G-force inverter. (1968)
#31 Tom Swift and his Dyna-4 capsule. (1969)
#32 Tom Swift and his Cosmotron Express. (1970)
#33 Tom Swift and the galaxy ghosts. (1971)

T-CITY TRILOGY (Mark Adlard)

#1 Interface. (1971)
#2 Volteface. (1972)

TAHARA (Harold M. Sherman)

#1 Tahara, boy king of the desert. (1933)
#2 Tahara among African tribes. (1933)
#3 Tahara, boy mystic of India. (1933)
#4 Tahara in the land of Yucatan. (1933)

CANON TALLIS (Madeleine L'Engle)

#1 The arm of the starfish. (1965)
#2 The young unicorns. (1968)

TAMA (Ray Cummings)

#1 Tama of the light country. (1965)
#2 Tama, princess of Mercury. (1966)

TAPIOLA (Robert Nathan)

#1 Journey of Tapiola. (1938)
#2 Tapiola's brave regiment. (1941)
#s 1-2 The adventures of Tapiola. (1950)

TARZAN (Edgar Rice Burroughs)

#1 Tarzan of the apes. (1914)
#2 The return of Tarzan. (1915)
#3 The beasts of Tarzan. (1916)
#4 The son of Tarzan. (1917)
#5 Tarzan and the jewels of Opar. (1918)
#6 Jungle tales of Tarzan. (1919)
#7 Tarzan the untamed. (1920)
#8 Tarzan the terrible. (1921)
#9 Tarzan and the golden lion. (1923)
#10 Tarzan and the ant men. (1924)
#11 Tarzan, Lord of the Jungle. (1928)
#12 Tarzan and the lost empire. (1929)
#13 Tarzan at the Earth's core. (1930)
#14 Tarzan the invincible. (1931)

#15 Tarzan triumphant. (1932)
#16 Tarzan and the city of gold. (1933)
#17 Tarzan and the lion man. (1934)
#18 Tarzan and the Leopard Men. (1935)
#19 Tarzan's quest. (1936)
#20 Tarzan and the Forbidden City. (1938)
#21 Tarzan the magnificent. (1939)
#22 Tarzan and "The Foreign Legion." (1947)
#23 Tarzan and the madman. (1964)
#24 Tarzan and the castaways. (1965)

OTHER TITLES:

#25 Tarzan and the valley of gold. (1966) [by Fritz
      Leiber]
#1 The Tarzan Twins. (1927)
#2 Tarzan and the Tarzan Twins with Jad-Bal-Ja, the
      golden lion. (1936)
#s 1-2 Tarzan and the Tarzan Twins. (1963)
      The eternal lover. (1925)

SEQUELS AND PARODIES:

The adventure of the peerless peer. (1974) [by
   Philip Jose Farmer]
Hadon of ancient Opar. (1974) [by Farmer]
Lord Tyger. (1970) [by Farmer]
Tarzan alive. (1972) [by Farmer]
Tarzan and the lost safari. (1966) [anonymous]
Her. (1967) [by J. X. Williams]

NEW TARZAN SERIES (Barton Werper):

#1 Tarzan and the Silver Globe. (1964)
#2 Tarzan and the cave city. (1964)
#3 Tarzan and the snake people. (1964)
#4 Tarzan and the Abominable Snowmen. (1965)
#5 Tarzan and the winged invaders. (1965)
--See also: ANJANI, AZAN, BOMBA, LORD GRANDITH,
KASPA, SHUNA, SORAK.

TAS (E. C. Eliott)

Tas and the postal rocket. (1955)
Tas and the space machine. (1955)

KITTY TELFAIR (Florence Stevenson)

#1 The witching hour. (1971)
#2 Where Satan dwells. (1971)
#3 Altar of evil. (1973)
#4 Mistress of Devil's Manor. (1973)
#5 The sorcerer of the castle. (1974)

TELZEY
  see: THE HUB

TERRAN EMPIRE SERIES (various authors)

Cosmic Echelon. (1952) [by Arthur Roberts &
   John Glasby writing as Berl Cameron]
Time and space. (1952) [by Arthur Roberts &
   John Glasby writing as Rand Le Page]

TERTIUS (Robert Newman)

#1 Merlin's mistake. (1970)
#2 The testing of Tertius. (1973)

THARN (Howard Browne)

#1 Warrior of the dawn. (1943)
#2 Return of Tharn. (1956)

THONGOR (Lin Carter)

#1   The Wizard of Lemuria. (1965)
#2   Thongor of Lemuria. (1966)
#3   Thongor against the Gods. (1967)
#4   Thongor in the City of Magicians. (1968)
#5   Thongor at the end of time. (1968)
#6   Thongor fights the pirates of Tarakus. (1970)

DANE THORSON
see: SOLAR QUEEN

THE THREE IMMORTALS (Paul Eldridge & George Sylvester Viereck)

#1   My first two thousand years. (1928)
#2   Salome, the wandering Jewess. (1930)
#3   The invincible Adam. (1932)

THUNDERBIRDS (various authors)

#1   Thunderbirds. (1966) [by John Theydon]
#2   Calling Thunderbirds. (1966) [by John Theydon]
#3   Thunderbirds ring of fire. (1966) [by John Theydon]
#4   Thunderbirds are go. (1966) [by Angus P. Allan]
#5   Lady Penelope: the Albanian affair. (1967) [by John Theydon]

OTHER TITLE:

Lost world. (1966) [by John W. Jennison]

THUNDERBOLT (Hereward Ohlson)

#1   Thunderbolt of the spaceways. (1954)
#2   Thunderbolt and the rebel planet. (1954)

TI-COYO (Clement Richer)

#1   Ti-Coyo and his shark. (1951)
#2   Son of Ti-Coyo. (1954)

TIME AGENTS SERIES (Andre Norton)

#1   The time traders. (1958)
#2   Galactic derelict. (1959)
#3   The defiant agents. (1962)
#4   Key out of time. (1963)

TIME MACHINE (Donald Keith)

#1   Mutiny in the time machine. (1963)
#2   Time machine to the rescue. (1967)

TIME MACHINE (H. G. Wells)

The time machine. (1895)

SEQUELS AND PARODIES:

The return of the time machine. (1972) [by Egon Friedell]

TIME TUNNEL (Murray Leinster)

#1   The Time Tunnel. (1967)
#2   Timeslip! (1967)

TLEN SEQUENCE (William J. Lambert III)

#1   Five roads to Tlen. (1970)

#2   The gods of Tlen. (1970)

THE TOMORROW PEOPLE (Roger Price)

#1   The Tomorrow People in The visitor. (1973) [with Julian R. Gregory]
#2   The Tomorrow People in Three in three. (1974)

MR. TOMPKINS (George Gamow)

#1   Mr. Tompkins in Wonderland. (1939)
#2   Mr. Tompkins explores the atom. (1944)
#3   Mr. Tompkins learns the facts of life. (1953)
#4   Mr. Tompkins inside himself. (1967) [with Martynas Ycas]

TOPPER (Thorne Smith)

#1   Topper. (1926)
#2   Topper takes a trip. (1932)

TRANTORIAN EMPIRE SERIES (Isaac Asimov)

#1   Pebble in the sky. (1950)
#2   The stars, like dust. (1951)
#3   The currents of space. (1952)
#s 1-3   Triangle. (1961)

SCOBEE TRENT (Frank Owen)

#1   Rare earth. (1931)
#2   The house mother. (1929)

TRIPODS SEQUENCE (John Christopher)

#1   The White Mountains. (1967)
#2   The city of gold and lead. (1967)
#3   The pool of fire. (1968)

TROS OF SAMOTHRACE (Talbot Mundy)

#1   Tros. (1967)
#2   Helma. (1967)
#3   Liafail. (1967)
#4   Helene. (1967)
#s 1-4   Tros of Samothrace. (1934)
#5   Queen Cleopatra. (1929)
#6   The purple pirate. (1935)

TROVO (Robert Lory)

#1   The eyes of Bolsk. (1969)
#2   Master of the Etrax. (1970)

TROYANA (S. P. Meek)

#1   The Drums of Tapajos. (1961)
#2   Troyana. (1961)

BARON TRUMP (Ingersoll Lockwood)

#1   Travels and adventures of Little Baron Trump and his wonderful dog Bulger. (1890)
#2   Baron Trump's marvellous underground journey. (1893)

TSCHAI CYCLE [PLANET OF ADVENTURE] (Jack Vance)

#1   City of the Chasch. (1968)
#2   Servants of the Wankh. (1969)
#3   The Dirdir. (1969)
#4   The Pnume. (1970)

TUCKER & HARRY (George Selden)

#1 The cricket in Time's Square. (1960)
#2 Tucker's countryside. (1969)
#3 Harry Cat's pet puppy. (1974)

THE TURN OF THE SCREW (Henry James)

The turn of the screw. (1898)

SEQUELS AND PARODIES:

The nightcomers. (1972) [by Michael Hastings]

2069 TRILOGY (Larry Townsend)

#1 2069. (1969)
#2 2069+1. (1970)
#3 2069+2. (1970)

NATE TWITCHELL (Oliver Butterworth)

#1 The enormous egg. (1956)
#2 The narrow passage. (1973)

II GALAXY SERIES (John Jakes)

#1 When the star kings die. (1967)
#2 The planet wizard. (1969)
#3 Tonight we steal the stars. (1969)

UFO (Robert Miall [John Burke])

#1 UFO. (1970)
#2 UFO 2. (1971)

THE UGGLIANS (L. M. Fallaw)

#1 The Ugglians. (1957)
#2 The Ugglians at large. (1959)

UNIVERSITY OF COSMOPOLI SERIES (Christopher Blayre [Edward Heron-Allen])

#1 The Purple Sapphire, and other posthumous papers. (1921)
#1A The cheetah girl. (1923)
#2 The strange papers of Dr. Blayre. (1932) [incorporates #1, with additions]
#3 Some women of the university. (1934)

UNTUSWA (Bertram Mitford)

#1 The King's Assegai. (1894)
#2 The white shield. (1895)
#3 The word of the sorceress. (1902)

VANSITTART (Louis Tracy)

#1 An American emperor. (1897)
#2 The lost provinces. (1898)

VELTAKIN (Cristabel)

#1 Manalacor of Veltakin. (1970)
#2 The Cruachan and the Killane. (1970)

VENTURER TWELVE SERIES (Dan Morgan & John Kippax)

#1 Thunder of stars. (1968)
#2 Seed of stars. (1972)
#3 The neutral stars. (1973)

VENUS SERIES (Edgar Rice Burroughs)

#1 Pirates of Venus. (1934)
#2 Lost on Venus. (1935)
#3 Carson of Venus. (1939)
#4 Escape on Venus. (1946)
#5 The wizard of Venus. (1970)

VENUS SERIES (Ronald Fraser)

#1 A visit to Venus. (1958)
#2 Jupiter in the chair. (1958)
#3 Trout's testament. (1960)
#4 City of the sun. (1961)

VENUS SERIES (W. S. Lach-Szyrma)

#1 A voice from another world. (1874)
#2 Under other conditions. (1892)

VETA SERIES (Reinhold W. Goll)

#1 The visitors from planet Veta. (1961)
#2 Spaceship to planet Veta. (1962)

VIAGENS INTERPLANETARIAS [KRISHNA SERIES] (L. Sprague de Camp)

#1 Rogue Queen. (1951)
#2 The continent makers, and other tales of the Viagens. (1953)
#3 Cosmic manhunt. (1954)
#4 The tower of Zanid. (1958)
#5 The search for Zei. (1962)
#6 The hand of Zei. (1963)

ANTHONY VILLIERS (Alexei Panshin)

#1 Star Well. (1968)
#2 The Thurb revolution. (1968)
#3 Masque world. (1969)

VOYAGE TO THE BOTTOM OF THE SEA (various authors)

#1 Voyage to the bottom of the sea. (1961) [by Theodore Sturgeon)
#2 City under the sea. (1965) [by Paul W. Fairman] Voyage to the bottom of the sea. (1965) [by Raymond F. Jones]

BLAKE WALKER (Andre Norton)

#1 The crossroads of time. (1956)
#2 Quest crosstime. (1965)

THE WANDERING JEW (Eugene Sue)

The wandering Jew. (1844)

SEQUELS AND PARODIES:

The ships of Tarshish. (1867) [by Mohoao]

THE WAR OF 1938 (S. Fowler Wright)

#1 Prelude in Prague. (1935)
#2 Four days war. (1936)
#3 Meggido's Ridge. (1937)

THE WAR OF THE WORLDS (H. G. Wells)

The war of the worlds. (1898)

THE WAR OF THE WORLDS (H. G. Wells) [cont.]

    SEQUELS AND PARODIES:

        The war of the Wenuses. (1898) [by C. L. Graves
          & E. V. Lucas]
        Edison's conquest of Mars. (1947) [by Garrett
          P. Serviss]

WARLOCK SERIES (Andre Norton)

  #1 Storm over Warlock. (1960)
  #2 Ordeal in otherwhere. (1964)

WATER WAGON SERIES (W. C. Gibson & Bert Leston Taylor)

  #1 The log of the Water Wagon. (1905)
  #2 Extra dry. (1906)

MARTIN WEBSTER (S. Fowler Wright)

  #1 Deluge. (1927)
  #2 Dawn. (1929)

JULIAN WEST
    see: LOOKING BACKWARD, 2000-1887

WHEN WORLDS COLLIDE
    see: BRONSON BETA

DEL WHITBY (John Morressy)

  #1 Starbrat. (1972)
  #2 Nail down the stars. (1973)

DR. WHO (various authors)

  #1 Doctor Who in an exciting adventure with the
      Daleks. (1964) [by David Whitaker]
  #2 Doctor Who and the Zarbi. (1965) [by Bill Strutton]
  #3 Doctor Who and the crusaders. (1965) [by David
      Whitaker]
  #4 Doctor Who and the Auton invasion. (1974) [by
      Terrance Dicks]
  #5 Doctor Who and the cave-monsters. (1974) [by
      Malcolm Hulke]
  #6 Doctor Who and the doomsday weapon. (1974)
      [by Malcolm Hulke]
  #7 Doctor Who and the day of the Daleks. (1974)
      [by Terrance Dicks]
  #8 Doctor Who and the Daemons. (1974) [by Barry
      Letts]
  #9 Doctor Who and the Sea-Devils. (1974) [by
      Malcolm Hulke]
 #10 Doctor Who and the abominable snowmen. (1974)
      [by Terrance Dicks]
 #11 Doctor Who and the Cybermen. (1974) [by Gerry
      Davis]
 #12 Doctor Who and the curse of Peladon. (1974)
      [by Brian Hayles]

MR. WICKER (Carley Dawson)

  #1 Mr. Wicker's window. (1952)
  #2 The sign of the seven seas. (1954)

WILLOUGHBY CHASE (Joan Aiken)

  #1 The wolves of Willoughby Chase. (1962)

  #2 Black hearts in Battersea. (1964)
  #3 Nightbirds on Nantucket. (1966)
  #4 The Whispering Mountain. (1968)
  #5 The cuckoo tree. (1971)

WINTERSOL (A. Earnshaw & Eric Thacker)

  #1 Musrum. (1968)
  #2 Wintersol. (1971)

WITCH WORLD SERIES (Andre Norton)

    ESTCARP CYCLE:

  #1 Witch world. (1963)
  #2 Web of the witch world. (1964)
  #3 Three against the witch world. (1965)
  #4 Warlock of the witch world. (1967)
  #5 Sorceress of the witch world. (1968)

    HIGH HALLACK CYCLE:

  #1 The crystal gryphon. (1972)
  #2 Spell of the witch world. (1972)
  #3 Year of the Unicorn. (1965)
  #4 The jargoon pard. (1974)

THE WONDERFUL FARM (Marcel Ayme)

  #1 The wonderful farm. (1951)
  #2 The magic pictures. (1954)

WORLD OF TIERS (Philip Jose Farmer)

  #1 The maker of universes. (1965)
  #2 The gates of creation. (1966)
  #3 A private cosmos. (1968)
  #4 Behind the walls of Terra. (1970)

WORLD WITHOUT MEN (Charles Eric Maine)

  #1 World without men. (1958)
  #2 Alph. (1972)

ZALMA (Phylos the Thibetan)

  #1 A dweller on two planets. (1905)
  #2 An Earth dweller's return. (1940)

ZANTHAR (Robert Moore Williams)

  #1 Zanthar of the many worlds. (1967)
  #2 Zanthar at the edge of never. (1968)
  #3 Zanthar at Moon's madness. (1968)
  #4 Zanthar at trip's end. (1969)

ZANZIBAR SERIES (John Brunner)

  #1 Stand on Zanzibar. (1968)
  #2 The sheep look up. (1972)

ZIG & ZAG (Peter Young)

  #1 Zig and Zag from planet ZV7. (1966)
  #2 Zag the Great and Zig the Big. (1966)

ZIMIAMVIAN TRILOGY (E. R. Eddison)

  #1 Mistress of mistresses. (1935)
  #2 A fish dinner in Memison. (1941)
  #3 The Mezentian gate. (1958)
      The worm Ouroboros. (1922) [prequel]

ZIP-ZIP (John M. Schealer)

   #1 Zip-Zip and his flying saucer. (1956)
   #2 Zip-Zip goes to Venus. (1958)
   #3 Zip-Zip and the red planet. (1961)

ZULU NATION CYCLE (H. Rider Haggard)

   #1 Nada the Lily. (1892)
   #2 Marie. (1912)
   #3 Child of storm. (1913)
   #4 Finished. (1917)

Awards Index

WORLD SCIENCE FICTION CONVENTIONS

Number	Date	Title	Place	Guests of Honor
1st	1939	NyCon I	New York	Frank R. Paul
2nd	1940	Chicon I	Chicago	Edward E. Smith
3rd	1941	Denvention	Denver	Robert A. Heinlein
4th	1946	Pacificon I	Los Angeles	A. E. van Vogt; E. Mayne Hull
5th	1947	Philcon I	Philadelphia	John W. Campbell, Jr.
6th	1948	Torcon I	Toronto	Robert Bloch
7th	1949	Cinvention	Cincinnati	Lloyd A. Eshbach
8th	1950	Norwescon	Portland	Anthony Boucher
9th	1951	Nolacon	New Orleans	Fritz Leiber
10th	1952	Chicon II	Chicago	Hugo Gernsback
11th	1953	Philcon II	Philadelphia	Willy Ley
12th	1954	SFCon	San Francisco	John W. Campbell, Jr.
13th	1955	Clevention	Cleveland	Isaac Asimov
14th	1956	Newyorcon (2)	New York	Arthur C. Clarke
15th	1957	Loncon I	London	John W. Campbell, Jr.
16th	1958	Solacon	Los Angeles	Richard Matheson
17th	1959	Detention	Denver	Poul Anderson
18th	1960	Pittcon	Pittsburgh	James Blish
19th	1961	Seacon	Seattle	Robert A. Heinlein
20th	1962	Chicon III	Chicago	Theodore Sturgeon
21st	1963	DisCon I	Washington	Murray Leinster
22nd	1964	Pacificon II	Oakland	Edmond Hamilton; Leigh Brackett; Forrest J. Ackerman (fan)
23rd	1965	Loncon II	London	Brian W. Aldiss
24th	1966	Tricon	Cleveland	L. Sprague de Camp
25th	1967	NyCon 3	New York	Lester del Rey; Wilson Tucker (fan)
26th	1968	Baycon	Oakland	Philip Jose Farmer; Walter Daugherty (fan)
27th	1969	St. Louiscon	St. Louis	Jack Gaughan; Eddie Jones (fan)
28th	1970	Heicon '70	Heidelberg	Robert Silverberg; E. C. Tubb; Herbert W. Franke; Elliot K. Shorter (fan)
29th	1971	Noreascon	Boston	Clifford D. Simak; Harry Warner, Jr. (fan)
30th	1972	L.A.Con	Los Angeles	Frederik Pohl; Robert Coulson (fan); Juanita Coulson (fan)
31st	1973	Torcon 2	Toronto	Robert Bloch; William Rotsler (fan)
32nd	1974	Discon 2	Washington	Roger Zelazny; J. K. Klein (fan)
33rd	1975	Aussiecon	Sydney	Ursula K. Le Guin; Donald H. Tuck (Australian)
34th	1976	Midamericon	Kansas City	Robert A. Heinlein; George Barr (fan)
35th	1977	Suncon	Orlando	Jack Williamson; Bob Madle (fan)
36th	1978	IguanaCon	Phoenix	Harlan Ellison; Bill Bowers (fan)

SCIENCE FICTION WRITERS OF AMERICA OFFICERS

1965-1966
President.................Damon Knight
Vice President............Harlan Ellison
Secretary/Treasurer.......Lloyd Biggle, Jr.

1966-1967
President.................Damon Knight
Vice President............James Blish
Secretary/Treasurer.......Lloyd Biggle, Jr.

1967-1968
President.................Robert Silverberg
Vice President............James Blish
Secretary/Treasurer.......Roger Zelazny

1968-1969
President.................Alan E. Nourse
Vice President............Harry Harrison
Secretary/Treasurer.......Anne McCaffrey

1969-1970
President.................Gordon R. Dickson
Vice President............Ron Goulart
Secretary/Treasurer.......Anne McCaffrey

1970-1971
President.................Gordon R. Dickson
Vice President............Tom Purdom
Secretary................Chelsea Quinn Yarbro
Treasurer................Joe Haldeman

1971-1972
President.................James E. Gunn
Vice President............Tom Purdom
Secretary................Chelsea Quinn Yarbro
Treasurer................Joe Haldeman

1972-1973
President.................Poul Anderson
Vice President............Norman Spinrad
Secretary................Robert Coulson
Treasurer................Joe Haldeman

1973-1974
President.................Jerry Pournelle
Vice President............Norman Spinrad
Secretary................Robert Coulson
Treasurer................Andrew Offutt

1974-1975
President.................Frederik Pohl
Vice President............F. M. Busby
Secretary................Theodore R. Cogswell
Treasurer................Andrew Offutt

1975-1976
President.................Frederik Pohl
Vice President............F. M. Busby
Secretary................Thomas F. Monteleone
Treasurer................Andrew Offutt

1976-1977
President.................Andrew Offutt
Vice President............Mildred Downey Broxon
Secretary................Thomas F. Monteleone
Treasurer................Joan Hunter Holly

1977-1978
President.................Andrew Offutt
Vice President............Mildred Downey Broxon
Secretary................Thomas F. Monteleone
Treasurer................Joan Hunter Holly

1978-1979
President.................Jack Williamson
Vice President............Marion Zimmer Bradley
Secretary................David F. Bischoff
Treasurer................Joan Hunter Holly

Executive Secretaries
C. L. Grant..............1975-1977
Peter D. Pautz...........1977-

AWARMS

August Derleth Awards (British Fantasy Awards)

1972 (1973).....*The Knight of the Swords*, by Michael
Moorcock

1973 (1974).....*The King of the Swords*, by Michael
Moorcock

1974 (1975).....*Hrolf Kraki's Saga*, by Poul Anderson

1975 (1976).....*The Hollow Lands*, by Michael Moorcock

1976 (1977).....*The Dragon and the George*, by Gordon
R. Dickson

Hugo Awards (World Science Fiction Convention)

1952 (1953)
Novel---*The Demolished Man*, by Alfred Bester
Professional Magazine---*Galaxy* (H. L. Gold, Editor);
Astounding (John W. Campbell, Editor) [tie]
Cover Artist--Ed Emshwiller; Hannes Bok [tie]
New Science Fiction Author or Artist---Philip Jose Far-
mer
Excellence in Fact Articles---Willy Ley
Interior Illustrator---Virgil Finlay
Number 1 Fan Personality---Forrest J Ackerman

1954 (1955)
Novel---*They'd Rather Be Right*, by Frank Riley & Mark
Clifton
Novelette---"The Darfstellar," by Walter M. Miller, Jr.
Short Story---"Allamagoosa," by Eric Frank Russell
Professional Magazine---*Astounding* (John W. Campbell,
Editor)
Illustrator--Frank Kelly Freas
Amateur Publication--*Fantasy Times* (James V. Taurasi &
Ray Van Houten, Editors)
Special Plaque---to Sam Moskowitz, for *The Immortal
Storm*

1955 (1956)
Novel---*Double Star*, by Robert A. Heinlein
Novelette---"Exploration Team," by Murray Leinster
Short Story---"The Star," by Arthur C. Clarke
Feature Writer---Willy Ley
Professional Magazine---*Astounding* (John W. Campbell,
Editor)
Illustrator---Frank Kelly Freas
Most Promising New Author---Robert Silverberg
Amateur Publication---*Inside & Science Fiction Adver-
tiser* (Ron Smith, Editor)
Critic---Damon Knight

1956 (1957)
Professional Magazine, American---*Astounding* (John W.
Campbell, Editor)
Professional Magazine, British---*New Worlds* (Edward
Carnell, Editor)
Amateur Publication---*Science Fiction Times* (James V.
Taurasi, Ray Van Houten, & Frank Prieto, Editors)

1957 (1958)
Novel---*The Big Time*, by Fritz Leiber
Short Story---"Or All the Seas with Oysters," by Avram
Davidson
Professional Magazine---*The Magazine of Fantasy and
Science Fiction* (Anthony Boucher, Editor)
Illustrator---Frank Kelly Freas
Motion Picture---*The Incredible Shrinking Man* (written
by Richard Matheson)
Most Outstanding Actifan---Walter A. Willis

1958 (1959)
Novel---*A Case of Conscience*, by James Blish
Novelette--"The Big Front Yard," by Clifford D. Simak
Short Story---"The Hell-Bound Train," by Robert Bloch
Illustrator---Frank Kelly Freas
Professional Magazine---*The Magazine of Fantasy and
Science Fiction* (Anthony Boucher & Robert P. Mills,
Editors)
Amateur Publication---*Fanac* (Terry Carr & Ron Ellik,
Editors)
Most Promising New Author---no award [Brian W. Aldiss,
who received the most votes, was given a plaque]

1959 (1960)
Novel---*Starship Troopers*, by Robert A. Heinlein
Short Fiction---"Flowers for Algernon," by Daniel Keyes
Professional Magazine---*The Magazine of Fantasy and
Science Fiction* (Robert P. Mills, Editor)
Amateur Publication---*Cry of the Nameless* (F. M. Busby,
Editor)
Illustrator---Ed Emshwiller
Dramatic Presentation---*The Twilight Zone* (created by
Rod Serling)
Special Award---to Hugo Gernsback as "The Father of
Magazine Science Fiction"

1960 (1961)
Novel---*A Canticle for Leibowitz*, by Walter M. Miller,
Jr.
Short Story---"The Longest Voyage," by Poul Anderson
Professional Magazine---*Analog (Astounding)* (John W.
Campbell, Editor)
Amateur Publication---*Who Killed Science Fiction?* (Earl
Kemp, Editor)
Illustrator---Ed Emshwiller
Dramatic Presentation---*The Twilight Zone* (created by
Rod Serling)

1961 (1962)
Novel---*Stranger in a Strange Land*, by Robert A. Hein-
lein
Short Fiction---The "Hothouse" Series, by Brian W. Al-
diss
Professional Magazine---*Analog* (John W. Campbell, Edi-
tor)
Amateur Magazine---*Warhoon* (Richard Bergeron, Editor)
Professional Artist--Ed Emshwiller
Dramatic Presentation---*The Twilight Zone* (created by
Rod Serling)
Special Plaque---to Cele Goldsmith, Editor of *Amazing*
and *Fantastic*
Special Plaque---to Don Tuck, for *The Handbook of Sci-
ence Fiction*

1962 (1963)
Novel---*The Man in the High Castle*, by Philip K. Dick
Short Fiction---"The Dragon Masters," by Jack Vance
Dramatic Presentation---no award
Professional Magazine---*The Magazine of Fantasy and
Science Fiction* (Robert P. Mills & Avram Davidson,
Editors)
Amateur Magazine---*Xero* (Richard Lupoff, Editor)
Professional Artist---Roy G. Krenkel

Hugo Awards (cont.)

1962 (1963), continued

Special Plaque---to P. Schuyler Miller, for the "Reference Library" in *Analog*

Special Plaque---to Isaac Asimov, for his distinguished contributions to the field

1963 (1964)

Novel---*Way Station*, by Clifford D. Simak

Short Fiction---"No Truce with Kings," by Poul Anderson

Professional Magazine---*Analog* (John W. Campbell, Editor)

Professional Artist---Ed Emshwiller

Book Publisher---Ace Books (Donald A. Wollheim, Editor)

Amateur Publication---*Amra* (George Scithers, Editor)

1964 (1965)

Novel---*The Wanderer*, by Fritz Leiber

Short Fiction---"Soldier, Ask Not," by Gordon R. Dickson

Professional Magazine---*Analog* (John W. Campbell, Editor)

Professional Artist---John Schoenherr

Book Publisher---Ballantine Books (Ian & Betty Ballantine, Editors)

Amateur Publication---*Yandro* (Robert & Juanita Coulson, Editors)

Dramatic Presentation---*Dr. Strangelove* (written by Stanley Kubrick and Peter George)

1965 (1966)

Novel---*And Call Me Conrad*, by Roger Zelazny; *Dune*, by Frank Herbert [tie]

Short Fiction---"'Repent, Harlequin!' Said the Ticktockman," by Harlan Ellison

Professional Magazine---*Worlds of If* (Frederik Pohl, Editor)

Professional Artist---Frank Frazetta

Amateur Magazine---*ERB-dom* (Camille Cazedessus, Jr., Editor)

Best All-Time Series---*The Foundation Trilogy*, by Isaac Asimov

1966 (1967)

Novel---*The Moon Is a Harsh Mistress*, by Robert A. Heinlein

Novelette---"The Last Castle," by Jack Vance

Short Story---"Neutron Star," by Larry Niven

Professional Magazine---*Worlds of If* (Frederik Pohl, Editor)

Professional Artist---Jack Gaughan

Dramatic Presentation---"The Menagerie," an episode of *Star Trek* (written by Gene Roddenberry)

Amateur Publication---*Niekas* (Ed Meskys & Felice Rolfe, Editors)

Fan Artist---Jack Gaughan

Fan Writer---Alexei Panshin

Special Plaque---to CBS for *The 21st Century*

1967 (1968)

Novel---*Lord of Light*, by Roger Zelazny

Novella---"Weyr Search," by Anne McCaffrey; "Riders of the Purple Wage," by Philip Jose Farmer [tie]

Novelette---"Gonna Roll the Bones," by Fritz Leiber

Short Story---"I Have no Mouth, and I Must Scream," by Harlan Ellison

Dramatic Presentation---"City at the Edge of Forever," an episode of *Star Trek* (written by Harlan Ellison)

Professional Magazine---*Worlds of If* (Frederik Pohl, Editor)

Professional Artist---Jack Gaughan

Amateur Publication---*Amra* (George Scithers, Editor)

Fan Artist---George Barr

Fan Writer---Ted White

Special Plaque---to Harlan Ellison for *Dangerous Visions*

Special Plaque---to Gene Roddenberry for *Star Trek*

1968 (1969)

Novel---*Stand on Zanzibar*, by John Brunner

Novella---"Nightwings," by Robert Silverberg

Novelette---"The Sharing of Flesh," by Poul Anderson

Short Story---"The Beast That Shouted Love at the Heart of the World," by Harlan Ellison

Drama---*2001: A Space Odyssey* (written by Arthur C. Clarke and Stanley Kubrick)

Professional Magazine---*The Magazine of Fantasy and Science Fiction* (Edward L. Ferman, Editor)

Professional Artist---Jack Gaughan

Amateur Publication---*Psychotic (Science Fiction Review)* (Richard E. Geis, Editor)

Fan Writer---Harry Warner, Jr.

Fan Artist---Vaughn Bode

Special Award---to Neil Armstrong, Buzz Aldrin, and Michael Collins for "Best Moon Landing Ever"

1969 (1970)

Novel---*The Left Hand of Darkness*, by Ursula K. Le Guin

Novella---"Ship of Shadows," by Fritz Leiber

Short Story---"Time Considered As a Helix of Semi-Precious Stones," by Samuel R. Delany

Dramatic Presentation---television coverage of "Apollo XI" flight

Professional Magazine---*The Magazine of Fantasy and Science Fiction* (Edward L. Ferman, Editor)

Professional Artist---Frank Kelly Freas

Amateur Magazine---*Science Fiction Review* (Richard E. Geis, Editor)

Fan Writer---Wilson Tucker

Fan Artist---Tim Kirk

1970 (1971)

Novel---*Ringworld*, by Larry Niven

Novella---"Ill Met in Lankhmar," by Fritz Leiber

Short Story---"Slow Sculpture," by Theodore Sturgeon

Dramatic Presentation---no award

Professional Artist---Leo & Diane Dillon

Professional Magazine---*The Magazine of Fantasy and Science Fiction* (Edward L. Ferman, Editor)

Amateur Magazine---*Locus* (Charles & Dena Brown, Editors)

Fan Writer---Richard E. Geis

Fan Artist---Alicia Austin

1971 (1972)

Novel---*To Your Scattered Bodies Go*, by Philip Jose Farmer

Novella---"The Queen of Air and Darkness," by Poul Anderson

Short Story---"Inconstant Moon," by Larry Niven

Dramatic Presentation---*A Clockwork Orange* (written by Anthony Burgess and Stanley Kubrick)

Amateur Magazine---*Locus* (Charles & Dena Brown, Editors)

Professional Magazine---*The Magazine of Fantasy and Science Fiction* (Edward L. Ferman, Editor)

Professional Artist---Frank Kelly Freas

Fan Writer---Harry Warner, Jr.

Fan Artist---Tim Kirk

Special Plaque---to France's Club du Livre d'Anticipation for Excellence in Book Production

Special Plaque---to Harlan Ellison for *Again, Dangerous Visions*

Special Plaque---to *Nueva Dimension* for Excellence in Magazine Production

Hugo Awards (cont.)

1972 (1973)
Novel---*The Gods Themselves*, by Isaac Asimov
Novella---"The Word for World Is Forest," by Ursula K. Le Guin
Novelette---"Goat Song," by Poul Anderson
Short Story---"Eurema's Dam," by R. A. Lafferty; "The Meeting," by Frederik Pohl & C. M. Kornbluth [tie]
Dramatic Presentation---*Slaughterhouse-5* (written by Kurt Vonnegut, Jr.)
Best Editor---Ben Bova
Professional Artist---Frank Kelly Freas
Fanzine---*Energumen* (Michael & Susan Glicksohn, Editors)
Fan Writer---Terry Carr
Fan Artist---Tim Kirk
John W. Campbell Award for Best New Writer---Jerry Pournelle
Special Plaque---to Pierre Versins for *Encyclopedie de l'Utopie et de la Science-Fiction*

1973 (1974)
Novel---*Rendezvous with Rama*, by Arthur C. Clarke
Novella---"The Girl Who Was Plugged In," by James Tiptree, Jr.
Novelette---"The Deathbird," by Harlan Ellison
Short Story---"The Ones Who Walk Away from Omelas," by Ursula K. Le Guin
Professional Editor---Ben Bova
Professional Artist---Frank Kelly Freas
Dramatic Presentation---*Sleeper* (written by Woody Allen)
Fanzine---*Algol* (Andrew Porter, Editor); *Alien Critic* (Richard E. Geis, Editor) [tie]
Fan Writer---Susan Wood
Fan Artist---Tim Kirk
Special Hugo---to Chesley Bonestell
John W. Campbell Award for Best New Writer---Spider Robinson; Lisa Tuttle [tie]
Gandalf Award, Grand Master of Fantasy---J. R. R. Tolkien

1974 (1975)
Novel---*The Dispossessed*, by Ursula K. Le Guin
Novella---"A Song for Lya," by George R. R. Martin
Novelette---"Adrift, Just Off the Islets of Langerhans," by Harlan Ellison
Short Story---"The Hole Man," by Larry Niven
Professional Editor---Ben Bova
Professional Artist---Frank Kelly Freas
Dramatic Presentation---*Young Frankenstein* (written by Mel Brooks and Gene Wilder)
Fanzine---*Alien Critic* (Richard E. Geis, Editor)
Fan Writer---Richard E. Geis
Fan Artist---Bill Rotsler
John W. Campbell Award for Best New Writer---P. J. Plauger
Gandalf Award, Grand Master of Fantasy---Fritz Leiber
Special Plaque---to Donald A. Wollheim, "The Fan Who Has Done Everything"
Special Plaque---to Walt Lee, for *The Reference Guide to Fantastic Films*

1975 (1976)
Novel---*The Forever War*, by Joe Haldeman
Novella---"Home Is the Hangman," by Roger Zelazny
Novelette---"Borderland of Sol," by Larry Niven
Short Story---"Catch That Zeppelin," by Fritz Leiber
Dramatic Presentation---*A Boy and His Dog* (written by Harlan Ellison)
Fanzine---*Locus* (Charles & Dena Brown, Editors)
Professional Artist---Frank Kelly Freas
Professional Editor---Ben Bova

Fan Writer---Richard E. Geis
Fan Artist---Tim Kirk
Gandalf Award, Grand Master of Fantasy---L. Sprague de Camp
John W. Campbell Award for Best New Writer---Tom Reamy

1976 (1977)
Novel---*Where Late the Sweet Birds Sang*, by Kate Wilhelm
Novella---"Houston, Houston, Do You Read?" by James Tiptree, Jr.; "By Any Other Name," by Spider Robinson [tie]
Novelette---"The Bicentennial Man," by Isaac Asimov
Short Story---"Tricentennial," by Joe Haldeman
Dramatic Presentation---no award
Fanzine---*Science Fiction Review* (Richard E. Geis, Editor)
Professional Artist---Rick Sternbach
Fan Writer---Susan Wood; Richard E. Geis [tie]
Fan Artist---Phil Foglio
Gandalf Award, Grand Master of Fantasy---Andre Norton
John W. Campbell Award, Best New Writer---C. J. Cherryh
Professional Editor---Ben Bova
Special Plaque---to *Star Wars* (written by George Lucas)

1977 (1978)
Novel---*Gateway*, by Frederik Pohl
Novella---"Stardance," by Spider & Jean Robinson
Novelette---"Eyes of Amber," by Joan Vinge
Short Story---"Jeffty Is Five," by Harlan Ellison
Dramatic Presentation---*Star Wars* (written by George Lucas)
Professional Artist---Rick Sternbach
Professional Editor---George Scithers
Fanzine---*Locus* (Charles & Dena Brown, Editors)
Fan Writer---Richard E. Geis
Fan Artist---Phil Foglio
Gandalf Award, Grand Master of Fantasy---Poul Anderson
Gandalf Award, Best Fantasy Novel---*The Silmarillion*, by J. R. R. Tolkien
John W. Campbell Award for Best New Writer---Orson Scott Card

International Fantasy Awards

1951   Fiction---*Earth Abides*, by George R. Stewart
Nonfiction---*The Conquest of Space*, by Willy Ley & Chesley Bonestell

1952   Fiction---*Fancies and Goodnights*, by John Collier
Nonfiction---*The Exploration of Space*, by Arthur C. Clarke

1953   Fiction---*City*, by Clifford D. Simak
Nonfiction---*Lands Beyond*, by Willy Ley & L. Sprague de Camp

1954   *More Than Human*, by Theodore Sturgeon

1955   *A Mirror for Observors*, by Edgar Pangborn

1956   no award

1957   *The Lord of the Rings*, by J. R. R. Tolkien

Discontinued in 1958.

John W. Campbell Memorial Award for Best Science Fiction Novel of the Year

1972 (1973)   *Beyond Apollo*, by Barry N. Malzberg

1973 (1974)   *Rendezvous with Rama*, by Arthur C. Clarke; *Malevil*, by Robert Merle [tie]
               Special Award---*The Cosmic Connection*, by Carl Sagan

1974 (1975)   *Flow My Tears, the Policeman Said*, by Philip K. Dick

1975 (1976)   no award; a special retrospective prize was given to Wilson Tucker for his novel *The Year of the Quiet Sun*

1976 (1977)   *The Alteration*, by Kingsley Amis

1977 (1978)   *Gateway*, by Frederik Pohl

Jupiter Awards (Instructors of Science Fiction in Higher Education)

1973 (1974)
Novel---*Rendezvous with Rama*, by Arthur C. Clarke
Novella---"The Feast of St. Dionysus," by Robert Silverberg
Novelette---"The Deathbird," by Harlan Ellison
Short Story---"A Supplicant in Space," by Robert Sheckley

1974 (1975)
Novel---*The Dispossessed*, by Ursula K. Le Guin
Novella---"Riding the Torch," by Norman Spinrad
Novelette---"The Seventeen Virgins," by Jack Vance
Short Story---"The Day Before the Revolution," by Ursula K. Le Guin

1975 (1976)
no awards

1976 (1977)
Novel---*Where Late the Sweet Birds Sang*, by Kate Wilhelm
Novella---"Houston, Houston, Do You Read?" by James Tiptree, Jr.
Novelette---"The Diary of the Rose," by Ursula K. Le Guin
Short Story---"I See You," by Damon Knight

1977 (1978)
Novel---*A Heritage of Stars*, by Clifford D. Simak
Novella---"In the Hall of the Martian Kings," by John Varley
Novelette---"Time Storm," by Gordon R. Dickson
Short Story---"Jeffty Is Five," by Harlan Ellison

Locus Awards (an annual readers' survey conducted by Locus)

1970 (1971)
Novel---*Ringworld*, by Larry Niven
Short Fiction---"The Region Between," by Harlan Ellison
Anthology/Collection---*Science Fiction Hall of Fame, Volume One*, edited by Robert Silverberg
Magazine---*The Magazine of Fantasy and Science Fiction* (Edward L. Ferman, Editor)

Paperback Cover Illustrator---Leo & Diane Dillon
Fanzine---*Locus* (Charles & Dena Brown, Editors)
Single Issue of a Fanzine---*Locus #70* (Charles & Dena Brown, Editors)
Fan Artist---Alicia Austin
Fan Cartoonist---Bill Rotsler
Fan Writer---Harry Warner, Jr.
Fan Critic---Ted Pauls

1971 (1972)
Novel---*The Lathe of Heaven*, by Ursula K. Le Guin
Short Fiction---"The Queen of Air and Darkness," by Poul Anderson
Original Anthology---*Universe 1*, edited by Terry Carr
Reprint Anthology/Collection---*World's Best Science Fiction: 1971*, edited by Donald A. Wollheim & Terry Carr
Book Publisher---Ballantine Books (Betty Ballantine, Ed.)
Magazine---*The Magazine of Fantasy and Science Fiction* (Edward L. Ferman, Editor)
Paperback Artist---Gene Szafran
Magazine Artist---Frank Kelly Freas
Fanzine---*Locus* (Charles & Dena Brown, Editors)
Fan Writer---Charles Brown
Fan Artist---Bill Rotsler
Best Convention---Noreascon

1972 (1973)
Novel---*The Gods Themselves*, by Isaac Asimov
Novella---"The Gold at the Starbow's End," by Frederik Pohl
Short Fiction---"Basilisk," by Harlan Ellison
Reprint Anthology/Collection---*The Best Science Fiction of the Year*, edited by Terry Carr
Original Anthology/Collection---*Again, Dangerous Visions*, edited by Harlan Ellison
Magazine---*The Magazine of Fantasy and Science Fiction* (Edward L. Ferman, Editor)
Book Publisher---Ballantine Books (Betty Ballantine, Editor)
Paperback Cover Artist---Frank Kelly Freas
Magazine Artist---Frank Kelly Freas
All-Time Favorite Author---Robert A. Heinlein
Fanzine---*Locus* (Charles & Dena Brown, Editors)
Fan Artist---Bill Rostler
Fan Writer---Terry Carr

1973 (1974)
Novel---*Rendezvous with Rama*, by Arthur C. Clarke
Novella---"The Death of Doctor Island," by Gene Wolfe
Short Fiction---"The Deathbird," by Harlan Ellison
Original Anthology---*Astounding*, edited by Harry Harrison
Reprint Anthology---*The Best Science Fiction of the Year #2*, edited by Terry Carr
Magazine---*The Magazine of Fantasy and Science Fiction* (Edward L. Ferman, Editor)
Book Publisher---Ballantine Books (Betty Ballantine & Judy-Lynn del Rey, Editors)
Professional Artist---Frank Kelly Freas
Fanzine---*Locus* (Charles & Dena Brown, Editors)
Fan Artist---Tim Kirk
Critic---Richard E. Geis

1974 (1975)
Novel---*The Dispossessed*, by Ursula K. Le Guin
Novella---"Born with the Dead," by Robert Silverberg
Novelette---"Adrift, Just Off the Islets of Langerhans...," by Harlan Ellison
Short Story---"The Day Before the Revolution," by Ursula K. Le Guin

Locus Awards (cont.)

1974 (1975), continued

Magazine---*The Magazine of Fantasy and Science Fiction* (Edward L. Ferman, Editor)

Book Publisher---Ballantine Books (Judy-Lynn del Rey, Editor)

Original Anthology---*Universe 4*, edited by Terry Carr

Reprint Anthology---*Before the Golden Age*, edited by Isaac Asimov

Professional Artist---Frank Kelly Freas

All-Time Best Novel---*Dune*, by Frank Herbert

Fanzine---*Outworlds* (Bill Bowers, Editor)

Fan Artist---Tim Kirk

Critic---P. Schuyler Miller

1975 (1976)

Novel---*The Forever War*, by Joe Haldeman

Novella---"The Storms of Windhaven," by George R. R. Martin & Lisa Tuttle

Novelette---"The New Atlantis," by Ursula K. Le Guin

Short Story---"Croatoan," by Harlan Ellison

Anthology---*Epoch*, edited by Roger Elwood & Robert Silverberg

Collection---*The Wind's Twelve Quarters*, by Ursula K. Le Guin

Associational Item---*Alternate Worlds*, by James Gunn

Magazine---*The Magazine of Fantasy and Science Fiction* (Edward L. Ferman, Editor)

Hardcover Publisher---Science Fiction Book Club

Paperback Publisher---Ballantine Books (Judy-Lynn del Rey, Editor)

Artist---Rick Sternbach

Critic---Richard E. Geis

Fanzine---*Locus* (Charles & Dena Brown, Editors)

1976 (1977)

Novel---*Where Late the Sweet Birds Sang*, by Kate Wilhelm

Novella---"The Samurai and the Willows," by Michael Bishop

Novelette---"The Bicentennial Man," by Isaac Asimov

Short Story---"Tricentennial," by Joe Haldeman

Collection---*A Song for Lya*, by George R. R. Martin

Reprint Anthology---*The Best Science Fiction of the Year #5*, edited by Terry Carr

Original Anthology---*Stellar #2*, edited by Judy-Lynn del Rey

Publisher---Ballantine Books (Judy-Lynn del Rey, Editor)

Magazine---*The Magazine of Fantasy and Science Fiction* (Edward L. Ferman, Editor)

Artist---Rick Sternbach

Fanzine---*Locus* (Charles & Dena Brown, Editors)

Critic---Spider Robinson

Best All-Time Author---Robert A. Heinlein

Special Award---John Varley

Special Award---Peter Weston, for *Andromeda*

1977 (1978)

Novel---*Gateway*, by Frederik Pohl

Novella---"Stardance," by Jeanne & Spider Robinson

Short Fiction---"Jeffty Is Five," by Harlan Ellison

Fantasy Novel---*The Silmarillion*, by J. R. R. Tolkien

Publisher---Del Rey Books (Judy-Lynn & Lester del Rey, Editors)

Magazine---*The Magazine of Fantasy and Science Fiction* (Edward L. Ferman, Editor)

Nebula Awards (Science Fiction Writers of America)

1965 (1966)

Novel---*Dune*, by Frank Herbert

Novella---"He Who Shapes," by Roger Zelazny; "The Saliva Tree," by Brian Aldiss [tie]

Novelette---"The Doors of His Face, the Lamps of His Mouth," by Roger Zelazny

Short Story---"'Repent, Harlequin!' Said the Ticktockman," by Harlan Ellison

1966 (1967)

Novel---*Babel-17*, by Samuel R. Delany; *Flowers for Algernon*, by Daniel Keyes [tie]

Novella---"The Last Castle," by Jack Vance

Novelette---"Call Him Lord," by Gordon R. Dickson

Short Story---"The Secret Place," by Richard McKenna

1967 (1968)

Novel---*The Einstein Intersection*, by Samuel R. Delany

Novella---"Behold the Man," by Michael Moorcock

Novelette---"Gonna Roll the Bones," by Fritz Leiber

Short Story---"Aye, and Gomorrah," by Samuel R. Delany

1968 (1969)

Novel---*Rite of Passage*, by Alexei Panshin

Novella---"Dragon Rider," by Anne McCaffrey

Novelette---"Mother to the World," by Richard Wilson

Short Story---"The Planners," by Kate Wilhelm

1969 (1970)

Novel---*The Left Hand of Darkness*, by Ursula K. Le Guin

Novella---"A Boy and His Dog," by Harlan Ellison

Novelette---"Time Considered As a Helix of Semi-Precious Stones," by Samuel R. Delany

Short Story---"Passengers," by Robert Silverberg

1970 (1971)

Novel---*Ringworld*, by Larry Niven

Novella---"Ill Met in Lankhmar," by Fritz Leiber

Novelette---"Slow Sculpture," by Theodore Sturgeon

Short Story---no award

1971 (1972)

Novel---*A Time of Changes*, by Robert Silverberg

Novella---"The Missing Man," by Katherine MacLean

Novelette---"The Queen of Air and Darkness," by Poul Anderson

Short Story---"Good News from the Vatican," by Robert Silverberg

1972 (1973)

Novel---*The Gods Themselves*, by Isaac Asimov

Novella---"A Meeting with Medusa," by Arthur C. Clarke

Novelette---"Goat Song," by Poul Anderson

Short Story---"When It Changed," by Joanna Russ

1973 (1974)

Novel---*Rendezvous with Rama*, by Arthur C. Clarke

Novella---"The Death of Dr. Island," by Gene Wolfe

Novelette---"Of Mist, and Grass, and Sand," by Vonda N. McIntyre

Short Story---"Love Is the Plan, the Plan Is Death," by James Tiptree, Jr.

Dramatic Presentation---*Soylent Green*, from the novel *Make Room! Make Room!* by Harry Harrison

Nebula Awards (cont.)

1974 (1975)
Novel---*The Dispossessed*, by Ursula K. Le Guin
Novella---"Born with the Dead," by Robert Silverberg
Novelette---"The Stars Are Gods," by Gregory Benford
Short Story---"The Day Before the Revolution," by
  Ursula K. Le Guin
Dramatic Presentation---*Sleeper* (written by Woody Allen)
Grand Master Award---Robert A. Heinlein

1975 (1976)
Novel---*The Forever War*, by Joe Haldeman
Novella---"Home Is the Hangman," by Roger Zelazny
Novelette---"San Diego Light Foot Sue," by Tom Reamy
Short Story---"Catch That Zeppelin," by Fritz Leiber
Dramatic Writing---*Young Frankenstein* (written by Mel
  Brooks & Gene Wilder)
Grand Master Award---Jack Williamson
Special Plaque---to George Pal, for his film work

1976 (1977)
Novel---*Man Plus*, by Frederik Pohl
Novella---"Houston, Houston, Do You Read?" by James
  Tiptree, Jr.
Novelette---"The Bicentennial Man," by Isaac Asimov
Short Story---"A Crowd of Shadows," by Charles L. Grant
Dramatic Presentation---no award
Grand Master Award---Clifford D. Simak

1977 (1978)
Novel---*Gateway*, by Frederik Pohl
Novella---"Stardance," by Jeanne & Spider Robinson
Novelette---"The Screwfly Solution," by Raccoona Shel-
  don (James Tiptree Jr.)
Short Story---"Jeffty Is Five," by Harlan Ellison
Special Plaque to George Lucas, for *Star Wars*.

Pilgrim Awards (Science Fiction Research Association)

1970......J. O. Bailey
1971......Marjorie Nicholson
1972......Julius Kagarlitski
1973......Jack Williamson
1974......I. F. Clarke
1975......Damon Knight
1976......James Gunn
1977......Thomas Clareson
1978......Brian W. Aldiss

World Fantasy Awards (World Fantasy Convention)

1973/1974 (1975)
Novel---*The Forgotten Beasts of Eld*, by Patricia Mc-
  Killip
Short Fiction Work---"Pages from a Young Girl's Diary,"
  by Robert Aickman
Single Author Collection or Anthology---*Worse Things
  Waiting*, by Manly Wade Wellman
Artist---Lee Brown Coye
Life Award---Robert Bloch
Special Award, Professional---Ian & Betty Ballantine
Special Award, Non-Professional---Stuart David Schiff

1975 (1976)
Novel---*Bid Time Return*, by Richard Matheson
Short Fiction---"Belsen Express," by Fritz Leiber
Collection---*The Enquiries of Dr. Esterhazy*, by Avram

Davidson
Artist---Frank Frazetta
Life Award---Fritz Leiber
Special Award (Professional)---Donald M. Grant
Special Award (Non-Professional)---Carcosa Publishers

1976 (1977)
Novel---*Doctor Rat*, by William Kotzwinkle
Short Fiction---"There's a Long, Long Trail A-Winding,"
  by Russell Kirk
Collection---*Frights*, edited by Kirby McCauley
Artist---Roger Dean
Life Achievement---Ray Bradbury
Special Award (Professional)---Alternate World Recor-
  dings
Special Award (Non-Professional)---*Whispers* (Stuart
  Schiff, Editor)

NAME INDEX

Ace Books---Hugo Award, Best Book Publisher, 1963 (1964)

Ackerman, Forrest J---Fan Guest of Honor, 22nd World Science Fiction Convention (Pacificon II), Oakland, 1964; Hugo Award, Number One Fan Personality, 1952 (1953).

Aickman, Robert---World Fantasy Award, Short Fiction Work, 1973/74 (1975), "Pages from a Young Girl's Diary."

Aldiss, Brian W.---Guest of Honor, 23rd World Science Fiction Convention (Loncon II), London, 1965; Nebula Award, Best Novella, 1965 (1966), "The Saliva Tree"; Special Plaque, 17th World Science Fiction Convention, 1959, as Most Promising New Author; Hugo Award, Best Short Fiction, 1961 (1962), The "Hothouse" Series; Pilgrim Award, 1978.

Aldrin, Buzz---Special Plaque, 27th World Science Fiction Convention, 1969, for "Best Moon Landing Ever"

Allen, Woody--Nebula Award, Best Dramatic Presentation, 1974 (1975), *Sleeper*; Hugo Award, Best Dramatic Presentation, 1973 (1974), *Sleeper*.

Alternate World Records---World Fantasy Award, Special Award (Professional), 1976 (1977).

Amis, Kingsley---John W. Campbell Memorial Award for Best Science Fiction Novel of the Year, 1976 (1977), *The Alteration*.

Analog (Astounding)---Hugo Award, Best Professional Magazine, 1952 (1953); 1954 (1955); 1955 (1956); 1960 (1961); 1961 (1962); 1963 (1964); 1964 (1965); Hugo Award, Best Professional Magazine, American, 1956 (1957).

Anderson, Poul---President, SFWA, 1972-1973; Guest of Honor, 17th World Science Fiction Convention (Detention), Detroit, 1959; Nebula Award, Best Novelette, 1971 (1972), "The Queen of Air and Darkness; Best Novelette, 1972 (1973), "Goat Song"; Hugo Award, Best Short Story, 1960 (1961), "The Longest Voyage"; Best Short Story, 1963 (1964), "No Truce with Kings"; Best Novelette, 1968 (1969), "The Sharing of Flesh"; Best Novella, 1971 (1972), "The Queen of Air and Darkness"; Best Novelette, 1972 (1973), "Goat Song"; August Derleth Award, 1974 (1975), *Hrolf Kraki's Saga*; Locus Award, Best Short Fiction, 1971 (1972), "The Queen of Air and Darkness"; Gandalf Award, Grand Master of Fantasy, 1978.

Apollo XI Flight---Hugo Award, Best Dramatic Presentation, 1969 (1970).

Armstrong, Neil---Special Plaque, 27th World Science Fiction Convention, 1969, for "Best Moon Landing Ever"

Asimov, Isaac---Guest of Honor, 13th World Science Fiction Convention (Clevention), Cleveland, 1955; Nebula Award, Best Novel, 1972 (1973), *The Gods Themselves*; Novelette, 1976 (1977), "The Bicentennial Man"; Hugo Award, Best All-Time Series, 1966, *The Foundation Trilogy*; Best Novel, 1972 (1973), *The Gods Themselves*; Best Novelette, 1976 (1977), "The Bicentennial Man"; Special Plaque, 21st World Science Fiction Convention, 1963, for Distinguished Contributions to the Field; Locus Award, Best Novel, 1972

(1973), *The Gods Themselves*; Best Reprint Anthology, 1974 (1975), *Before the Golden Age*; Best Novelette, 1976 (1977), "The Bicentennial Man."

Astounding
SEE: *Analog*

Austin, Alicia---Hugo Award, Best Fan Artist, 1970 (1971); Locus Award, Best Fan Artist, 1970 (1971).

Bailey, J. O.---Pilgrim Award, 1970.

Ballantine, Betty & Ian---Hugo Award, Best Book Publisher, 1964 (1965), Ballantine Books; World Fantasy Award, Special Award (Professional), 1973/74 (1975); Locus Award, Best Book Publisher, 1971 (1972), 1972 (1973), 1973 (1974), Ballantine Books.

Ballantine Books---Hugo Award, Best Book Publisher, 1964 (1965); Locus Award, Best Book Publisher, 1971 (1972), 1972 (1973), 1973 (1974), 1974 (1975); Best Paperback Publisher, 1975 (1976); Best Publisher, 1976 (1977), 1977 (1978).

Barr, George---Fan Guest of Honor, 34th World Science Fiction Convention (Midamericon), Kansas City, 1976; Hugo Award, Best Fan Artist, 1967 (1968).

Benford, Gregory---Nebula Award, Best Novelette, 1974 (1975), "The Stars Are Gods."

Bergeron, Richard---Hugo Award, Best Amateur Magazine, 1961 (1962), *Warhoon*.

Bester, Alfred---Hugo Award, Best Novel, 1952 (1953), *The Demolished Man*.

Biggle, Lloyd---Secretary/Treasurer, SFWA, 1965-1967.

Bischoff, David F.---Secretary, SFWA, 1978-

Bishop, Michael---Locus Award, Best Novella, 1976 (1977), "The Samurai and the Willows."

Blish, James---Vice President, SFWA, 1966-1968; Guest of Honor, 18th World Science Fiction Convention (Pittcon), Pittsburgh, 1960; Hugo Award, Best Novel, 1958 (1959), *A Case of Conscience*.

Bloch, Robert---Guest of Honor, 6th World Science Fiction Convention (Torcon I), Toronto, 1948; Guest of Honor, 31st World Science Fiction Convention (Torcon 2), Toronto, 1973; Hugo Award, Best Short Story, 1958 (1959), "The Hell-Bound Train"; World Fantasy Award, Life Award, 1975.

Bode, Vaughn---Hugo Award, Best Fan Artist, 1968 (1969).

Bok, Hannes---Hugo Award, Best Cover Artist, 1952 (1953).

Bonestell, Chesley---International Fantasy Award, Nonfiction, 1951, *The Conquest of Space* (with Willy Ley); Hugo Award, Special Award, 1974, for his art work.

Boucher, Anthony---Guest of Honor, 8th World Science Fiction Convention (Norwescon), Portland, 1950; Hugo Award, Best Professional Magazine, 1957 (1958), 1958 (1959), *The Magazine of Fantasy and Science Fiction*.

Bova, Ben---Hugo Award, Best Editor, 1972 (1973), 1973 (1974), 1974 (1975), 1975 (1976), 1976 (1977).

Bowers, Bill---Fan Guest of Honor, 36th World Science Fiction Convention (IguanaCon), Phoenix, 1978; Locus Award, Best Fanzine, 1974 (1975), *Outworlds*.

Brackett, Leigh---Guest of Honor, 22nd World Science Fiction Convention (Pacificon II), Oakland, 1964.

Bradbury, Ray---World Fantasy Award, Life Achievement, 1977.

Bradley, Marion Zimmer---Vice President, SFWA, 1978-

Brooks, Mel---Nebula Award, Best Dramatic Presentation, 1975 (1976), *Young Frankenstein* (with Gene Wilder); Hugo Award, Best Dramatic Presentation, 1974 (1975), *Young Frankenstein* (with Gene Wilder).

Brown, Charles & Dena---Hugo Award, Best Amateur Magazine, 1970 (1971), *Locus*; Best Fanzine, 1975 (1976), 1977 (1978), *Locus*; Locus Award, Best Fanzine, 1970 (1971), 1971 (1972), 1972 (1973), 1973 (1974), 1975 (1976), 1976 (1977), *Locus*.

Brown, Lee Coye---World Fantasy Award, Best Artist, 1973/74 (1975).

Broxon, Mildred Downey---Vice President, SFWA, 1976-1978.

Brunner, John---Hugo Award, Best Novel, 1968 (1969), *Stand on Zanzibar*.

Burgess, Anthony---Hugo Award, Best Dramatic Presentation, 1971 (1972), *A Clockwork Orange* (with Stanley Kubrick).

Busby, F. M.---Vice President, SFWA, 1974-1976; Hugo Award, Best Amateur Publication, 1959 (1960), *Cry of the Nameless*.

CBS---Special Plaque, 25th World Science Fiction Convention, 1967, for *The 21st Century*.

Campbell, John W.---Guest of Honor, 5th World Science Fiction Convention (Philcon I), Philadelphia, 1947; Guest of Honor, 12th World Science Fiction Convention (SFCon), San Francisco, 1954; Guest of Honor, 15th World Science Fiction Convention (Loncon I), London, 1957; Hugo Award, Best Professional Magazine, 1952 (1953), 1954 (1955), 1955 (1956), 1960 (1961), *Astounding*; Best Professional Magazine, American, 1956 (1957), *Astounding*; Best Professional Magazine, 1961 (1962), 1963 (1964), 1964 (1965), *Analog*.

Carcosa Publishers---World Fantasy Award, Special Award, Non-Professional, 1975 (1976).

Card, Orson Scott---John W. Campbell Award for Best New Writer, 1977 (1978).

Carnell, E. J.---Hugo Award, Best Professional Magazine, British, 1956 (1957), *New Worlds*.

Carr, Terry---Hugo Award, Best Amateur Publication, 1958 (1959), *Fanac* (with Ron Ellik); Best Fan Writer, 1972 (1973); Locus Award, Best Original Anthology, 1971 (1972), *Universe 1*; Best Reprint Anthology/Collection, 1971 (1972), *World's Best Science Fiction: 1971* (with Donald A. Wollheim); Best Reprint Antholo-

gy/Collection, 1972 (1973), *The Best Science Fiction of the Year*; Best Fan Writer, 1972 (1973); Best Reprint Anthology, 1973 (1974), *The Best Science Fiction of the Year #2*; Best Original Anthology, 1974 (1975), *Universe 4*; Best Reprint Anthology, 1976 (1977), *The Best Science Fiction of the Year #5*.

Cazedessus, Camille Jr.---Hugo Award, Best Amateur Magazine, 1965 (1966), *ERB-dom*.

Cherryh, C. J.---John W. Campbell Award for Best New Writer, 1976 (1977).

Clareson, Thomas---Pilgrim Award, 1977.

Clarke, Arthur C.---Guest of Honor, 14th World Science Fiction Convention (Newyorcon), New York, 1956; Nebula Award, Best Novella, 1972 (1973), "A Meeting with Medusa"; Best Novel, 1973 (1974), *Rendezvous with Rama*; Hugo Award, Best Short Story, 1955 (1956), "The Star"; Best Drama, 1968 (1969), *2001: A Space Odyssey* (with Stanley Kubrick); Best Novel, 1973 (1974), *Rendezvous with Rama*; John W. Campbell Memorial Award for Best Science Fiction Novel of the Year, 1973 (1974), *Rendezvous with Rama*; International Fantasy Award, Nonfiction, 1952, *The Exploration of Space*; Jupiter Award, Best Novel, 1973 (1974), *Rendezvous with Rama*; Locus Award, Best Novel, 1973 (1974), *Rendezvous with Rama*.

Clarke, I. F.---Pilgrim Award, 1974.

Clifton, Mark ---Hugo Award, Best Novel, 1954 (1955), *They'd Rather Be Right* (with Frank Riley).

Club du Livre d'Anticipation---Special Plaque, 30th World Science Fiction Convention, 1972, for Excellence in Book Production.

Cogswell, Theodore R.---Secretary, SFWA, 1974-1975.

Collier, John---International Fantasy Award, Fiction, 1952, *Fancies and Goodnights*.

Collins, Michael---Special Plaque, 27th World Science Fiction Convention, 1969, for "Best Moon Landing Ever."

Coulson, Juanita---Fan Guest of Honor, 30th World Science Fiction Convention (L.A.Con), Los Angeles, 1972; Hugo Award, Best Amateur Publication, 1964 (1965), *Yandro* (with Robert Coulson).

Coulson, Robert S.---Secretary, SFWA, 1972-1974; Fan Guest of Honor, 30th World Science Fiction Convention (L.A.Con), Los Angeles, 1972; Hugo Award, Best Amateur Publication, 1964 (1965); *Yandro* (with Juanita Coulson).

Daugherty, Walter---Fan Guest of Honor, 26th World Science Fiction Convention (Baycon), Oakland, 1968.

Davidson, Avram---Hugo Award, Best Short Story, 1957 (1958), "Or All the Seas with Oysters"; Best Professional Magazine, 1962 (1963), *The Magazine of Fantasy and Science Fiction* (with Robert P. Mills); World Fantasy Award, Best Collection, 1975 (1976), *The Enquiries of Dr. Esterhazy*.

Dean, Roger---World Fantasy Award, Best Artist, 1976 (1977).

de Camp, L. Sprague---Guest of Honor, 24th World Science Fiction Convention (Tricon), Cleveland, 1966; International Fantasy Award, Nonfiction, 1953, *Lands Beyond* (with Willy Ley); Gandalf Award, Grand Master of Fantasy, 1976.

Delany, Samuel R.---Nebula Award, Best Novel, 1966 (1967), *Babel-17*; Best Novel, 1967 (1968), *The Einstein Intersection*; Best Short Story, 1967 (1968), "Aye, and Gomorrah"; Best Novelette, 1969 (1970), "Time Considered As a Helix of Semi-Precious Stones"; Hugo Award, Best Short Story, 1969 (1970), "Time Considered As a Helix of Semi-Precious Stones."

del Rey, Judy-Lynn---Locus Award, Best Book Publisher, 1973 (1974), 1974 (1975), 1975 (1976), 1976 (1977), Ballantine Books; Best Book Publisher, 1977 (1978), Del Rey Books; Best Original Anthology, 1976 (1977), *Stellar #2*.

del Rey, Lester---Guest of Honor, 25th World Science Fiction Convention (NyCon 3), New York, 1967; Locus Award, Best Publisher, 1977 (1978), Del Rey Books.

Dick, Philip K.---Hugo Award, Best Novel, 1962 (1963), *The Man in the High Castle*; John W. Campbell Memorial Award for Best Science Fiction Novel of the Year, 1974 (1975), *Flow My Tears, the Policeman Said*.

Dickson, Gordon R.---President, SFWA, 1969-1971; Nebula Award, Best Novelette, 1966 (1967), "Call Him Lord"; Hugo Award, Best Short Fiction, 1964 (1965), "Soldier, Ask Not"; August Derleth Award, Best Novel, 1976 (1977), *The Dragon and the George*; Jupiter Award, Best Novelette, 1977 (1978), "Time Storm."

Dillon, Leo & Diane---Hugo Award, Best Professional Artist, 1970 (1971); Locus Award, Best Paperback Cover Illustrator, 1970 (1971).

Ellik, Ron---Hugo Award, Best Amateur Publication, 1958 (1959), *Fanac* (with Terry Carr).

Ellison, Harlan---Vice President, SFWA, 1965-1966; Nebula Award, Best Short Story, 1965 (1966), "'Repent, Harlequin!' Said the Ticktockman"; Best Novella, 1969 (1970), "A Boy and His Dog"; Best Short Story, 1977 (1978), "Jeffty Is Five"; Hugo Award, Best Short Fiction, 1965 (1966), "'Repent, Harlequin!' Said the Ticktockman"; Best Short Story, 1967 (1968), "I Have No Mouth, and I Must Scream"; Best Dramatic Presentation, 1967 (1968), "City at the Edge of Forever" (an episode of *Star Trek*); Best Short Story, 1968 (1969), "The Beast That Shouted Love at the Heart of the World"; Best Novelette, 1973 (1974), "The Deathbird"; Best Novelette, 1974 (1975), "Adrift, Just Off the Islets of Langerhans..."; Best Dramatic Presentation, 1975 (1976), *A Boy and His Dog*; Best Short Story, 1977 (1978), "Jeffty Is Five"; Jupiter Award, Best Novelette, 1973 (1974), "The Deathbird"; Best Short Story, 1977 (1978), "Jeffty Is Five"; Locus Award, Best Short Fiction, 1970 (1971), "The Region Between"; Best Short Fiction, 1972 (1973), "Basilisk"; Best Original Anthology/Collection, 1972 (1973), *Again, Dangerous Visions*; Best Short Fiction, 1973 (1974), "The Deathbird"; Best Novelette, 1974 (1975), "Adrift, Just Off the Islets of Langerhans..."; Best Short Story, 1975 (1976), "Croatoan"; Best Short Fiction, 1977 (1978), "Jeffty Is Five"; Special Plaque, 26th World Science Fiction Convention, 1968, for *Dangerous Visions*; Special Plaque, 30th World Science Fiction Convention, 1972, for *Again, Dangerous Visions*.

Elwood, Roger---Locus Award, Best Anthology, 1975 (1976), *Epoch* (with Robert Silverberg).

Emshwiller, Ed---Hugo Award, Best Cover Artist, 1952 (1953); Best Illustrator, 1959 (1960), 1960 (1961); Best Professional Artist, 1961 (1962), 1963 (1964).

Eshbach, Lloyd A.---Guest of Honor, 7th World Science Fiction Convention (Cinvention), Cincinnati, 1949.

Farmer, Philip Jose---Guest of Honor, 26th World Science Fiction Convention (Baycon), Oakland, 1968; Hugo Award, Best New Science Fiction Author or Artist, 1952 (1953); Best Novella, 1967 (1968), "Riders of the Purple Wage"; Best Novel, 1971 (1972), *To Your Scattered Bodies Go*.

Ferman, Edward L.---Hugo Award, Best Professional Magazine, 1968 (1969), 1969 (1970), 1970 (1971), 1971 (1972), *The Magazine of Fantasy and Science Fiction*; Locus Award, Best Magazine, 1970 (1971), 1971 (1972), 1972 (1973), 1973 (1974), 1974 (1975), 1975 (1976), 1976 (1977), 1977 (1978), *The Magazine of Fantasy and Science Fiction*.

Finlay, Virgil---Hugo Award, Best Interior Illustrator, 1952 (1953).

Foglio, Phil---Hugo Award, Best Fan Artist, 1976 (1977), 1977 (1978).

Franke, Herbert W.---Guest of Honor, 28th World Science Fiction Convention (Heicon '70), Heidelberg, 1970.

Frazetta, Frank---Hugo Award, Best Professional Artist, 1965 (1966); World Fantasy Award, Best Artist, 1975 (1976).

Freas, Frank Kelly---Hugo Award, Best Illustrator, 1954 (1955), 1955 (1956), 1957 (1958), 1958 (1959); Best Professional Artist, 1969 (1970), 1971 (1972), 1972 (1973), 1973 (1974), 1974 (1975), 1975 (1976); Locus Award, Best Magazine Artist, 1971 (1972), 1972 (1973); Best Paperback Artist, 1972 (1973); Best Professional Artist, 1973 (1974), 1974 (1975).

Galaxy Magazine---Hugo Award, Best Professional Magazine, 1952 (1953).

Gaughan, Jack---Guest of Honor, 27th World Science Fiction Convention (St. Louiscon), St. Louis, 1969; Hugo Award, Best Professional Artist, 1966 (1967), 1967 (1968), 1968 (1969).

Geis, Richard E.---Hugo Award, Best Amateur Publication, 1968 (1969), *Psychotic*; 1969 (1970), *Science Fiction Review*; Best Fan Writer, 1970 (1971), Best Fanzine, 1973 (1974), 1974 (1975), *The Alien Critic*; Best Fan Writer, 1974 (1975), 1975 (1976), 1976 (1977), 1977 (1978); Best Fanzine, 1976 (1977), *Science Fiction Review*; Locus Award, Best Critic, 1973 (1974), 1975 (1976).

George, Peter---Hugo Award, Best Dramatic Presentation, 1964 (1965), *Dr. Strangelove* (with Stanley Kubrick).

Gernsback, Hugo---Guest of Honor, 10th World Science Fiction Convention (Chicon II), Chicago, 1952; Special Award, 18th World Science Fiction Convention, 1960, as "The Father of Magazine Science Fiction."

Glicksohn, Michael & Susan---Hugo Award, Best Fanzine, 1972 (1973), *Energumen*.

Gold, H. L.---Hugo Award, Best Professional Magazine, 1952 (1953), *Galaxy*.

Goldsmith, Cele---Special Plaque, 20th World Science Fiction Convention, 1962, for her work in editing *Amazing* and *Fantastic*.

Goulart, Ron---Vice President, SFWA, 1969-1970.

Grant, C. L.---Executive Secretary, SFWA, 1975-1977; Nebula Award, Best Short Story, 1976 (1977), "A Crowd of Shadows."

Grant, Donald M.---World Fantasy Award, Special Award, Professional, 1975 (1976).

Gunn, James E.---President, SFWA, 1971-1972; Pilgrim Award, 1976; Locus Award, Best Associational Item, 1975 (1976), *Alternate Worlds*.

Haldeman, Joe---Treasurer, SFWA, 1970-1973; Nebula Award, Best Novel, 1975 (1976), *The Forever War*; Hugo Award, Best Novel, 1975 (1976), *The Forever War*; Best Short Story, 1976 (1977), "Tricentennial"; Locus Award, Best Novel, 1975 (1976), *The Forever War*; Best Short Story, 1976 (1977), "Tricentennial."

Hamilton, Edmond---Guest of Honor, 22nd World Science Fiction Convention (Pacificon II), Oakland, 1964.

Harrison, Harry---Vice President, SFWA, 1968-1969; Nebula Award, Best Dramatic Presentation, 1973 (1974), *Soylent Green* (from his novel *Make Room! Make Room!*); Locus Award, Best Original Anthology, 1973 (1974), *Astounding*.

Heinlein, Robert A.---Guest of Honor, 3rd World Science Fiction Convention (Denvention), Denver, 1941; Guest of Honor, 19th World Science Fiction Convention (Seacon), Seattle, 1961; Guest of Honor, 34th World Science Fiction Convention (Midamericon), Kansas City, 1976; Nebula Award, Grand Master Award, 1975; Hugo Award, Best Novel, 1955 (1956), *Double Star*; Best Novel, 1959 (1960), *Starship Troopers*; Best Novel, 1961 (1962), *Stranger in a Strange Land*; Best Novel, 1966 (1967), *The Moon Is a Harsh Mistress*; Locus Award, Best All-Time Favorite Author, 1973; Best All-Time Author, 1977.

Herbert, Frank---Nebula Award, Best Novel, 1965 (1966), *Dune*; Hugo Award, Best Novel, 1965 (1966), *Dune*; Locus Award, Best All-Time Novel, 1975, *Dune*.

Holly, Joan Hunter---Treasurer, SFWA, 1976-

Hull, E. Mayne---Guest of Honor, 4th World Science Fiction Convention (Pacificon I), Los Angeles, 1946.

If---Hugo Award, Best Professional Magazine, 1965 (1966), 1966 (1967), 1967 (1968).

Jones, Eddie---Fan Guest of Honor, 27th World Science Fiction Convention (St. Louiscon), St. Louis, 1969.

Kagarlitski, Julius---Pilgrim Award, 1972.

Kemp, Earl---Hugo Award, Best Amateur Publication, 1960 (1961), *Who Killed Science Fiction?*

Keyes, Daniel---Nebula Award, Best Novel, 1966 (1967), *Flowers for Algernon*; Hugo Award, Best Short Fiction, 1959 (1960), "Flowers for Algernon."

Kirk, Russell---World Fantasy Award, Best Short Fiction, 1976 (1977), "There's a Long, Long Trail A-Winding."

Kirk, Tim---Hugo Award, Best Fan Artist, 1969 (1970), 1971 (1972), 1972 (1973), 1973 (1974), 1975 (1976); Locus Award, Best Fan Artist, 1973 (1974), 1974 (1975).

Klein, J. K.---Fan Guest of Honor, 32nd World Science Fiction Convention (Discon 2), Washington, 1974.

Knight, Damon---Founding President, SFWA, 1965-1967; Pilgrim Award, 1975; Hugo Award, Best Critic, 1955 (1956); Jupiter Award, Best Short Story, 1976 (1977), "I See You."

Kornbluth, C. M.---Hugo Award, Best Short Story, 1972 (1973), "The Meeting" (with Frederik Pohl).

Kotzwinkle, William---World Fantasy Award, Best Novel, 1976 (1977), *Doctor Rat*.

Krenkel, Roy G.---Hugo Award, Best Professional Artist, 1962 (1963).

Kubrick, Stanley---Hugo Award, Best Dramatic Presentation, 1964 (1965), *Dr. Strangelove* (with Peter George); Best Drama, 1968 (1969), *2001: A Space Odyssey* (with Arthur C. Clarke); Best Dramatic Presentation, 1971 (1972), *A Clockwork Orange* (with Anthony Burgess).

Lafferty, R. A.---Hugo Award, Best Short Story, 1972 (1973), "Eurema's Dam."

Lee, Walt---Special Plaque, 33rd World Science Fiction Convention, 1975, for *The Reference Guide to Fantastic Films*.

Le Guin, Ursula K.---Guest of Honor, 33rd World Science Fiction Convention (Aussiecon), Sydney, 1975; Nebula Award, Best Novel, 1969 (1970), *The Left Hand of Darkness*; Best Novel, 1974 (1975), *The Dispossessed*; Best Short Story, 1974 (1975), "The Day Before the Revolution"; Hugo Award, Best Novel, 1969 (1970), *The Left Hand of Darkness*; Best Novella, 1972 (1973), "The Word for World Is Forest"; Best Short Story, 1973 (1974), "The Ones Who Walk Away from Omelas"; Best Novel, 1974 (1975), *The Dispossessed*; Jupiter Award, Best Novel, 1974 (1975), *The Dispossessed*; Best Short Story, 1974 (1975), "The Day Before the Revolution"; Best Novelette, 1976 (1977), "The Diary of the Rose"; Locus Award, Best Novel, 1971 (1972), *The Lathe of Heaven*; Best Novel, 1974 (1975), *The Dispossessed*; Best Short Story, 1974 (1975), "The Day Before the Revolution"; Best Novelette, 1975 (1976), "The New Atlantis"; Best Collection, 1975 (1976), *The Wind's Twelve Quarters*.

Leiber, Fritz---Guest of Honor, 9th World Science Fiction Convention (Nolacon), New Orleans, 1951; Nebula Award, Best Novelette, 1967 (1968), "Gonna Roll the Bones"; Best Novella, 1970 (1971), "Ill Met in Lankhmar"; Best Short Story, 1975 (1976), "Catch That Zeppelin"; Hugo Award, Best Novel, 1957 (1958), *The Big Time*; Best Novel, 1964 (1965), *The Wanderer*; Best Novelette, 1967 (1968), "Gonna Roll the Bones"; Best Novella, 1969 (1970), "Ship of Shadows" Best Novella, 1970 (1971), "Ill Met in Lankhmar"; Best Short Story, 1975 (1976), "Catch That Zeppelin"; Gandalf Award, Grand Master of Fantasy, 1975; World Fantasy Award, Best Short Fiction, 1975 (1976), "Belsen Express"; World Fantasy Award, Life Award, 1976.

Leinster, Murray---Guest of Honor, 21st World Science Fiction Convention (DisCon I), Washington, 1963; Hugo Award, Best Short Story, 1955 (1956), "Exploration Team."

Ley, Willy---Guest of Honor, 11th World Science Fiction Convention (Philcon II), Philadelphia, 1953; International Fantasy Award, Nonfiction, 1951, *The Conquest of Space*; International Fantasy Award, Nonfiction, 1953, *Lands Beyond* (with L. Sprague de Camp); Hugo Award, Excellence in Fact Articles, 1952 (1953); Best Feature Writer, 1955 (1956).

Lucas, George---Hugo Award, Best Dramatic Presentation, 1977 (1978), *Star Wars*; Special Nebula Plaque, 1977 (1978), for *Star Wars*; Special Plaque, 35th World Science Fiction Convention, 1977, for *Star Wars*.

Lupoff, Richard A.---Hugo Award, Best Amateur Magazine, 1962 (1963), *Xero*.

MacLean, Katherine---Nebula Award, Best Novella, 1971 (1972), "The Missing Man."

The Magazine of Fantasy and Science Fiction---Hugo Award, Best Professional Magazine, 1957 (1958), 1958 (1959), 1959 (1960), 1962 (1963), 1968 (1969), 1969 (1970), 1970 (1971), 1971 (1972); Locus Award, Best Magazine, 1970 (1971), 1971 (1972), 1972 (1973), 1973 (1974), 1974 (1975), 1975 (1976), 1976 (1977), 1977 (1978).

Malzberg, Barry N.---John W. Campbell Memorial Award for Best Science Fiction Novel of the Year, 1972 (1973), *Beyond Apollo*.

Martin, George R. R.---Hugo Award, Best Novella, 1974 (1975), "A Song for Lya"; Locus Award, Best Novella, 1975 (1976), "The Storms of Windhaven" (with Lisa Tuttle); Best Collection, 1976 (1977), *A Song for Lya*.

Matheson, Richard---Guest of Honor, 16th World Science Fiction Convention (Solacon), Los Angeles, 1958; Hugo Award, Best Motion Picture, 1957 (1958), *The Incredible Shrinking Man*; World Fantasy Award, Best Novel, 1975 (1976), *Bid Time Return*.

McCaffrey, Anne---Secretary/Treasurer, SFWA, 1968-1970; Nebula Award, Best Novella, 1968 (1969), "Dragon Rider"; Hugo Award, Best Novella, 1967 (1968), "Weyr Search."

McCauley, Kirby---World Fantasy Award, Best Collection, 1976 (1977), *Frights*.

McIntyre, Vonda N.---Nebula Award, Best Novelette, 1973 (1974), "Of Mist, and Grass, and Sand."

McKenna, Richard---Nebula Award, Best Short Story, 1966 (1967), "The Secret Place."

McKillip, Patricia---World Fantasy Award, Best Novel, 1973/74 (1975), *The Forgotten Beasts of Eld*.

Merle, Robert---John W. Campbell Memorial Award for Best Science Fiction Novel of the Year, 1973 (1974), *Malevil*.

Meskys, Ed---Hugo Award, Best Amateur Publication, 1966 (1967), *Niekas* (with Felice Rolfe).

Miller, P. Schuyler---Special Plaque, 21st World Science Fiction Convention, 1963, for "The Reference Library" in *Analog*; Locus Award, Best Critic, 1974 (1975).

Miller, Walter M. Jr.---Hugo Award, Best Novelette, 1954 (1955), "The Darfstellar"; Best Novel, 1960 (1961), *A Canticle for Leibowitz*.

Mills, Robert P.---Hugo Award, Best Professional Magazine, 1958 (1959), 1959 (1960), 1962 (1963), *The Magazine of Fantasy and Science Fiction*.

Monteleone, Thomas F.---Secretary, SFWA, 1975-1978.

Moorcock, Michael---Nebula Award, Best Novelette, 1967 (1968), "Behold the Man"; August Derleth Award, 1972 (1973), *The Knight of the Swords*; 1973 (1974), *The King of the Swords*; 1975 (1976), *The Hollow Lands*.

Moskowitz, Sam---Special Plaque, 13th World Science Fiction Convention, 1955, for *The Immortal Storm*.

New Worlds---Hugo Award, Best Professional Magazine, British, 1956 (1957).

Nicholson, Marjorie---Pilgrim Award, 1971.

Niven, Larry---Nebula Award, Best Novel, 1970 (1971), *Ringworld*; Hugo Award, Best Short Story, 1966 (1967), "Neutron Star"; Best Novel, 1970 (1971), *Ringworld*; Best Short Story, 1971 (1972), "Inconstant Moon"; Best Short Story, 1974 (1975), "The Hole Man"; Best Novelette, 1975 (1976), "Borderland of Sol"; Locus Award, Best Novel, 1970 (1971), *Ringworld*.

Norton, Andre---Gandalf Award, Grand Master of Fantasy, 1977.

Nourse, Alan E.---President, SFWA, 1968-1969.

Offutt, Andrew---Treasurer, SFWA, 1973-1976; President, 1976-1978.

Pal, George---Special Nebula Plaque, 1976, for his film work.

Pangborn, Edgar---International Fantasy Award, 1955, *A Mirror for Observers*.

Panshin, Alexei---Nebula Award, Best Novel, 1968 (1969), *Rite of Passage*; Hugo Award, Best Fan Writer, 1966 (1967).

Paul, Frank R.---Guest of Honor, 1st World Science Fiction Convention (NyCon I), New York, 1939.

Pauls, Ted---Locus Award, Best Fan Critic, 1970 (1971).

Pautz, Peter D.---Executive Secretary, SFWA, 1977-

Plauger, P. J.---John W. Campbell Award for Best New Writer, 1974 (1975).

Pohl, Frederik---President, SFWA, 1974-1976; Guest of Honor, 30th World Science Fiction Convention (L.A.Con), Los Angeles, 1972; Nebula Award, Best Novel, 1976 (1977), *Man Plus*; Best Novel, 1977 (1978), *Gateway*; Hugo Award, Best Professional Magazine, 1965 (1966), 1966 (1967), 1967 (1968), *Worlds of If*; Best Short Story, 1972 (1973), "The Meeting" (with C. M. Kornbluth); Best Novel, 1977 (1978), *Gateway*; John W.

Campbell Memorial Award for Best Science Fiction Novel of the Year, 1977 (1978), *Gateway*; Locus Award, Best Novella, 1972 (1973), "The Gold at the Starbow's End"; Best Novel, 1977 (1978), *Gateway*.

Porter, Andrew---Hugo Award, Best Fanzine, 1973 (1974), *Algol*.

Pournelle, Jerry---President, SFWA, 1973-1974; John W. Campbell Award for Best New Writer, 1972 (1973).

Prieto, Frank---Hugo Award, Best Amateur Publication, 1956 (1957), *Science Fiction Times* (with James V. Taurasi & Ray Van Houten).

Purdom, Tom---Vice President, SFWA, 1970-1972.

Reamy, Tom---Nebula Award, Best Novelette, 1975 (1976), "San Diego Light Foot Sue"; John W. Campbell Award for Best New Writer, 1975 (1976).

Riley, Frank--Hugo Award, Best Novel, 1954 (1955), *They'd Rather Be Right* (with Mark Clifton).

Robinson, Jeanne---Nebula Award, Best Novella, 1977 (1978), "Stardance" (with Spider Robinson); Hugo Award, Best Novella, 1977 (1978), "Stardance" (with Spider Robinson); Locus Award, Best Novella, 1977 (1978), "Stardance" (with Spider Robinson).

Robinson, Spider---John W. Campbell Award for Best New Writer, 1973 (1974); Nebula Award, Best Novella, 1977 (1978), "Stardance" (with Jeanne Robinson); Hugo Award, Best Novella, 1976 (1977), "By Any Other Name"; Best Novella, 1977 (1978), "Stardance" (with Jeanne Robinson); Locus Award, Best Critic, 1976 (1977); Best Novella, 1977 (1978), "Stardance" (with Jeanne Robinson).

Roddenberry, Gene---Hugo Award, Best Dramatic Presentation, 1966 (1967), "The Menagerie" (an episode of *Star Trek*); Special Plaque, 26th World Science Fiction Convention, 1968, for *Star Trek*.

Rolfe, Felice---Hugo Award, Best Amateur Publication, 1966 (1967), *Niekas* (with Ed Meskys).

Rotsler, William---Fan Guest of Honor, 31st World Science Fiction Convention (Torcon 2), Toronto, 1973; Hugo Award, Best Fan Artist, 1974 (1975); Locus Award, Best Fan Cartoonist, 1970 (1971); Best Fan Artist, 1971 (1972), 1972 (1973).

Russ, Joanna---Nebula Award, Best Short Story, 1972 (1973), "When It Changed."

Russell, Eric Frank---Hugo Award, Best Short Story, 1954 (1955), "Allamagoosa."

Sagan, Carl---Special Nonfiction Award, John W. Campbell Memorial Award, 1973 (1974), for *The Cosmic Connection*.

Schiff, Stuart David---World Fantasy Award, Special Award, Non-Professional, 1973/74 (1975), 1976 (1977), *Whispers*.

Schoenherr, John---Hugo Award, Best Professional Artist, 1964 (1965).

Science Fiction Book Club---Locus Award, Best Hardcover Publisher, 1975 (1976).

Scithers, George---Hugo Award, Best Amateur Publication, 1963 (1964), 1967 (1968), *Amra*; Best Professional Editor, 1977 (1978).

Serling, Rod---Hugo Award, Best Dramatic Presentation, 1959 (1960), 1960 (1961), 1961 (1962), *The Twilight Zone*.

Sheckley, Robert---Jupiter Award, Best Short Story, 1973 (1974), "A Supplicant in Space."

Sheldon, Raccoona
  SEE: Tiptree, James Jr.

Shorter, Elliot K.---Fan Guest of Honor, 28th World Science Fiction Convention (Heicon '70), Heidelberg, 1970.

Silverberg, Robert---President, SFWA, 1967-1968; Guest of Honor, 28th World Science Fiction Convention (Heicon '70), Heidelberg, 1970; Nebula Award, Best Short Story, 1969 (1970), "Passengers"; Best Novel, 1971 (1972), *A Time of Changes*; Best Short Story, 1971 (1972), "Good News from the Vatican"; Best Novella, 1974 (1975), "Born with the Dead"; Hugo Award, Most Promising New Author, 1955 (1956); Best Novella, 1968 (1969), "Nightwings"; Jupiter Award, Best Novella, 1973 (1974), "The Feast of St. Dionysus"; Locus Award, Best Anthology/Collection, 1970 (1971), *The Science Fiction Hall of Fame, Volume One*; Best Novella, 1974 (1975), "Born with the Dead"; Best Anthology, 1975 (1976), *Epoch* (with Roger Elwood).

Simak, Clifford D.---Guest of Honor, 29th World Science Fiction Convention (Noreascon), Boston, 1971; International Fantasy Award, Fiction, 1953, *City*; Nebula Award, Grand Master Award, 1977; Hugo Award, Best Novelette, 1958 (1959), "The Big Front Yard"; Best Novel, 1963 (1964), *Way Station*; Jupiter Award, Best Novel, 1977 (1978), *A Heritage of Stars*.

Smith, Edward E.---Guest of Honor, 2nd World Science Fiction Convention (Chicon I), Chicago, 1940.

Smith, Ron---Hugo Award, Best Amateur Publication, 1955 (1956), *Inside & Science Fiction Advertiser*.

Spinrad, Norman---Vice President, SFWA, 1972-1974; Jupiter Award, Best Novella, 1974 (1975), "Riding the Torch."

Sternback, Rick---Hugo Award, Best Professional Artist, 1976 (1977), 1977 (1978); Locus Award, Best Artist, 1975 (1976), 1976 (1977).

Stewart, George R.---International Fantasy Award, Fiction, 1951, *Earth Abides*.

Sturgeon, Theodore---Guest of Honor, 20th World Science Fiction Convention (Chicon III), Chicago, 1962); Nebula Award, Best Novelette, 1970 (1971), "Slow Sculpture"; International Fantasy Award, 1954, *More Than Human*; Hugo Award, Best Short Story, 1970 (1971), "Slow Sculpture."

Szafran, Gene---Locus Award, Best Paperback Artist, 1971 (1972).

Taurasi, James V.---Hugo Award, Best Amateur Publication, 1954 (1955), *Fantasy Times* (with Ray Van Houten); 1956 (1957), *Science Fiction Times* (with Ray Van Houten & Frank Prieto).

Tiptree, James Jr.---Nebula Award, Best Short Story, 1973 (1974), "Love Is the Plan, the Plan Is Death"; Best Novella, 1976 (1977), "Houston, Houston, Do You Read?"; Best Novelette, 1977 (1978), "The Screwfly Solution" (as Raccoona Sheldon); Hugo Award, Best Novella, 1973 (1974), "The Girl Who Was Plugged In"; Best Novella, 1976 (1977), "Houston, Houston, Do You Read?"; Jupiter Award, Best Novella, 1976 (1977), "Houston, Houston, Do You Read?"

Tolkien, J. R. R.---International Fantasy Award, 1957, *The Lord of the Rings*; Gandalf Award, Grand Master of Fantasy, 1974; Gandalf Award, Best Fantasy Novel, 1977 (1978), *The Silmarillion*; Locus Award, Best Fantasy Novel, 1977 (1978), *The Silmarillion*.

Tubb, E. C.---Guest of Honor, 28th World Science Fiction Convention (Heicon '70), Heidelberg, 1970.

Tuck, Donald H.---Fan Guest of Honor, 33rd World Science Fiction Convention (Aussiecon), Sydney, 1975; Special Plaque, 20th World Science Fiction Convention, 1962, for *The Handbook of Science Fiction*.

Tucker, Wilson---Fan Guest of Honor, 25th World Science Fiction Convention (NyCon 3), New York, 1967; Hugo Award, Best Fan Writer, 1969 (1970); John W. Campbell Memorial Award for Best Science Fiction Novel of the Year, Retrospective Award, 1976, for *The Year of the Quiet Sun*.

Tuttle, Lisa---John W. Campbell Award for Best New Writer, 1973 (1974); Locus Award, Best Novella, 1975 (1976), "The Storms of Windhaven" (with George R. R. Martin).

Vance, Jack---Nebula Award, Best Novelette, 1966 (1967), "The Last Castle"; Hugo Award, Best Short Fiction, 1962 (1963), "The Dragon Masters"; Best Novelette, 1966 (1967), "The Last Castle"; Jupiter Award, Best Novelette, 1974 (1975), "The Seventeen Virgins."

Van Houten, Ray---Hugo Award, Best Amateur Publication, 1954 (1955), *Fantasy Times* (with James V. Taurasi); 1956 (1957), *Science Fiction Times* (with James V. Taurasi & Frank Prieto).

van Vogt, A. E.---Guest of Honor, 4th World Science Fiction Convention (Pacificon I), Los Angeles, 1946.

Varley, John---Jupiter Award, Best Novella, 1977 (1978), "In the Hall of the Martian Kings"; Locus Award, Special Award, 1976 (1977).

Versins, Pierre---Special Plaque, 31st World Science Fiction Convention, 1973, for *Encyclopedie de l'Utopie et de la Science-Fiction*.

Vinge, Joan---Hugo Award, Best Novelette, 1977 (1978), "Eyes of Amber."

Vonnegut, Kurt---Hugo Award, Best Dramatic Presentation, 1972 (1973), *Slaughterhouse-5*.

Warner, Harry Jr.---Fan Guest of Honor, 29th World Science Fiction Convention (Noreascon), Boston, 1971; Hugo Award, Best Fan Writer, 1968 (1969), 1971 (1972); Locus Award, Best Fan Writer, 1970 (1971).

Wellman, Manly Wade---World Fantasy Award, Best Single Author Collection or Anthology, 1973/74 (1975), *Worse Things Waiting*.

Weston, Peter---Locus Award, Special Award, 1977, for *Andromeda*.

White, Ted---Hugo Award, Best Fan Writer, 1967 (1968).

Wilder, Gene---Nebula Award, Best Dramatic Presentation, 1975 (1976), *Young Frankenstein* (with Mel Brooks); Hugo Award, Best Dramatic Presentation, 1974 (1975), *Young Frankenstein* (with Mel Brooks).

Wilhelm, Kate---Nebula Award, Best Short Story, 1968 (1969), "The Planners"; Hugo Award, Best Novel, 1976 (1977), *Where Late the Sweet Birds Sang*; Jupiter Award, Best Novel, 1976 (1977), *Where Late the Sweet Birds Sang*; Locus Award, Best Novel, 1976 (1977), *Where Late the Sweet Birds Sang*.

Williamson, Jack---Nebula Award, Grand Master Award, 1976; Pilgrim Award, 1973; President, SFWA, 1978-

Willis, Walter A.---Hugo Award, Most Outstanding Actifan, 1957 (1958).

Wilson, Richard---Nebula Award, Best Novelette, 1968 (1969), "Mother to the World."

Wolfe, Gene---Nebula Award, Best Novella, 1973 (1974), "The Death of Dr. Island"; Locus Award, Best Novella, 1973 (1974), "The Death of Dr. Island."

Wollheim, Donald A.---Hugo Award, Best Book Publisher, 1963 (1964), Ace Books; Special Plaque, 33rd World Science Fiction Convention, 1975, for "The Fan Who Has Done Everything."

Wood, Susan---Hugo Award, Best Fan Writer, 1973 (1974), 1976 (1977).

Worlds of If---Hugo Award, Best Professional Magazine, 1965 (1966), 1966 (1967), 1967 (1968).

Yarbro, Chelsea Quinn---Secretary, SFWA, 1970-1972.

Zelazny, Roger---Secretary/Treasurer, SFWA, 1967-1968; Guest of Honor, 32nd World Science Fiction Convention (Discon 2), Washington, 1974; Nebula Award, Best Novella, 1965 (1966), "He Who Shapes"; Best Novelette, 1965 (1966), "The Doors of His Face, the Lamps of his Mouth"; Best Novella, 1975 (1976), "Home Is the Hangman"; Hugo Award, Best Novel, 1965 (1966), *And Call Me Conrad*; Best Novel, 1967 (1968), *Lord of Light*; Best Novella, 1975 (1976), "Home Is the Hangman."

STATISTICAL TABLES

Award Winners (Fiction) by Number of Awards

Winner	Nebulas	Hugos	Jupiters	Locus	Others	Total
Ellison	3	8	2	7	2	22
Le Guin	3	4	3	5		15
Leiber	3	6			3	12
Anderson	2	5		1	2	10
Pohl	2	5		2	1	10
Silverberg	4	2	1	3		10
Asimov	2	3		3	1	9
Clarke	2	3	1	1	2	9
Heinlein	1	4		2		7
Niven	1	5		1		7
Robinson	1	2		2	1	6
Tiptree	3	2	1			6
Zelazny	3	3				6
Delany	4	1				5
Haldeman	1	2		2		5
Simak	1	2	1		1	5
Aldiss	1	1			2	4
Dickson	1	1			2	4
Moorcock	1				3	4
Tolkien				1	3	4
Vance	1	2	1			4
Wilhelm	1	1	1	1		4

Award Winners in All Categories by Number

Winner	Nebulas	Hugos	Locus	Others	Honors	Total
Ellison	3	8	7	4	1	23
Le Guin	3	4	5	3	1	16
Freas		10	5			15
Leiber	3	6		3	1	13
Ferman		4	8			12
Geis		10	2			12
Anderson	2	5	1	2	1	11
Campbell		8			3	11
Pohl	2	5	2	1	1	11
Silverberg	4	2	3	1	1	11
Asimov	2	3	3	1	1	10
Brown		4	6			10
Clarke	2	3	1	3	1	10
Heinlein	1	4	2		3	10
Carr		2	7			9
Kirk		5	2			7
Niven	1	5	1			7
Zelazny	3	3			1	7
del Rey, J.			6			6
Robinson	1	2	2	1		6
Simak	1	2		2	1	6
Tiptree	3	2		1		6
Aldiss	1	1		2	1	5
Ballantine		1	3	1		5
Bova		5				5
Delany	4	1				5
Emshwiller		5				5
Haldeman	1	2	2			5
Ley		2		2	1	5
Rotsler		1	3		1	5
Bloch		1		1	2	4
Dickson	1	1		2		4
Farmer		3			1	4
Gaughan		3			1	4
Moorcock	1			3		4
Sternback		2	2			4
Sturgeon	1	1		1	1	4
Tolkien			1	3		4
Vance	1	2		1		4
Warner		2	1		1	4
Wilhelm	1	1	1	1		4

Hugo Award Winners by Number of Awards

Winner	Novel	Novella	Novelette	Story	Other	Total
Freas					10	10
Geis					10	10
Campbell					8	8
Ellison			2	4	2	8
Leiber	2	2	1	1		6
Anderson		1	2	2		5
Bova					5	5
Emshwiller					5	5
Kirk					5	5
Niven	1		1	3		5
Pohl	1			1	3	5
Brown					4	4
Ferman					4	4
Heinlein	4					4
Le Guin	2	1		1		4
Asimov	1		1		1	3
Clarke	1			1	1	3
Farmer	1	1			1	3
Gaughan					3	3
Kubrick					3	3
Mills					3	3
Scithers					3	3
Serling					3	3
Zelazny	2	1				3

Nebula Award Winners by Number of Awards

Winner	Novel	Novella	Novelette	Story	Other	Total
Delany	2			1	1	4
Silverberg	1	1			2	4
Ellison		1			2	3
Le Guin	2				1	3
Leiber		1		1	1	3
Tiptree		1		1	1	3
Zelazny		2		1		3
Anderson				2		2
Asimov	1			1		2
Clarke	1	1				2
Pohl	2					2

Ace and Belmont Doubles Index

D-303   1958   *The snows of Ganymede.* + Poul Anderson
                  War of the wing-men. + Poul Anderson

D-311   1958   *Stepsons of Terra.* + Robert Silverberg
                  A man called destiny. + Lan Wright

D-315   1958   *Six worlds yonder.* + Eric Frank Russell
                  The space willies. + Eric Frank Russell

D-322   1958   *The void beyond, and other stories.* +
                  Robert Moore Williams
                  The Blue Atom. + Robert Moore Williams

D-331   1958   *The secret of ZI.* + Kenneth Bulmer
                  Beyond the vanishing point. + Ray Cummings

D-335   1959   *The war of two worlds.* + Poul Anderson
                  Threshold of eternity. + John Brunner

D-345   1959   *Plague ship.* + Andrew North
                  Voodoo planet. + Andrew North

D-351   1959   *The sun smasher.* + Edmond Hamilton
                  Starhaven. + Ivar Jorgenson

D-358   1959   *Recruit for Andromeda.* + Milton Lesser
                  The plot against Earth. + Calvin M. Knox

D-362   1959   *The 100th millennium.* + John Brunner
                  Edge of time. + David Grinnell

D-369   1959   *The changeling worlds.* + Kenneth Bulmer
                  Vanguard from Alpha. + Brian W. Aldiss

D-375   1959   *Masters of evolution.* + Damon Knight
                  Fire in the heavens. + George O. Smith

D-381   1959   *Secret of the lost race.* + Andre Norton
                  One against Herculum. + Jerry Sohl

D-385   1959   *Echo in the skull.* + John Brunner
                  Rocket to limbo. + Alan E. Nourse

D-391   1959   *Siege of the unseen.* + A. E. van Vogt
                  The world swappers. + John Brunner

D-403   1959   *The pirates of Zan.* + Murray Leinster
                  The mutant weapon. + Murray Leinster

D-407   1959   *The planet killers.* + Robert Silverberg
                  We claim these stars! + Poul Anderson

D-413   1960   *The man with nine lives.* + Harlan Ellison
                  A touch of infinity. + Harlan Ellison

D-421   1960   *Slavers of space.* + John Brunner
                  Dr. Futurity. + Philip K. Dick

D-427   1960   *World of the masterminds.* + Robert Moore Williams
                  To the end of time, and other stories. + Robert Moore Williams

D-431   1960   *Earth's last fortress.* + A. E. van Vogt
                  Lost in space. + George O. Smith

D-437   1960   *The Sioux spaceman.* + Andre Norton
                  And then the town took off. + Richard Wilson

D-443   1960   *Bow down to nul.* + Brian W. Aldiss
                  The dark destroyers. + Manly Wade Wellman

D-449   1960   *Time to teleport.* + Gordon R. Dickson
                  The genetic general. + Gordon R. Dickson

D-453   1960   *The Earth gods are coming.* + Kenneth Bulmer
                  The games of Neith. + Margaret St. Clair

D-457   1960   *Vulcan's hammer.* + Philip K. Dick
                  The skynappers. + John Brunner

D-465   1960   *The Martian missile.* + David Grinnell
                  The Atlantic abomination. + John Brunner

D-471   1960   *Sanctuary in the sky.* + John Brunner
                  The secret Martians. + Jack Sharkey

D-479   1960   *To the Tombaugh Station.* + Wilson Tucker
                  Earthman, go home! + Poul Anderson

D-485   1961   *The puzzle planet.* + Robert A. W. Lowndes
                  The angry espers. + Lloyd Biggle, Jr.

D-491   1961   *The mind spider, and other stories.* + Fritz Leiber
                  The Big Time. + Fritz Leiber

D-497   1961   *Wandl the invader.* + Ray Cummings
                  I speak for Earth. + Keith Woodcott

D-507   1961   *Beyond the silver sky.* + Kenneth Bulmer
                  Meeting at infinity. + John Brunner

D-509   1961   *Star hunter.* + Andre Norton
                  The beast master. + Andre Norton

D-517   1961   *Bring back yesterday.* + A. Bertram Chandler
                  The trouble with Tycho. + Clifford Simak

F-104   1961   *Mayday orbit.* + Poul Anderson
                  No man's world. + Kenneth Bulmer

F-108   1961   *The light of Lilith.* + G. McDonald Wallis
                  The sun saboteurs. + Damon Knight

F-113   1961   *Rebels of the red planet.* + Charles L. Fontenay
                  200 years to Christmas. + J. T. McIntosh

F-117   1961   *The door through space.* + Marion Zimmer Bradley
                  Rendezvous on a lost world. + A. Bertram Chandler

F-119   1961   *Spacial delivery.* + Gordon R. Dickson
                  Delusion world. + Gordon R. Dickson

F-123   1961   *The nemesis from Terra.* Leigh Brackett
                  Collision course. + Robert Silverberg

M-111	1965	*Fugitive of the stars.* + Edmond Hamilton *Land beyond the map.* + Kenneth Bulmer
M-113	1965	*The Rithian terror.* + Damon Knight *Off center.* + Damon Knight
M-115	1965	*The repairmen of Cyclops.* + John Brunner *Enigma from Tantalus.* + John Brunner
M-117	1965	*Our man in space.* + Bruce W. Ronald *Ultimatum in 2050 A.D.* + Jack Sharkey
M-121	1965	*The ballad of Beta-2.* + Samuel R. Delany *Alpha yes, Terra no!* + Emil Petaja
M-123	1965	*Android avenger.* + Ted White *The altar on Asconel.* + John Brunner
M-125	1965	*The world between, and other stories.* + Jack Vance *Monsters in orbit.* + Jack Vance
M-127	1965	*The water of thought.* + Fred Saberhagen *We, the Venusians.* + John Rackham
M-129	1965	*Empress of outer space.* + A. Bertram Chandler *The alternate Martians.* + A. Bertram Chandler
M-131	1965	*Planetary agent X.* + Mack Reynolds *Behold the stars.* + Kenneth Bulmer
M-133	1965	*The caves of Mars.* + Emil Petaja *Space mercenaries.* + A. Bertram Chandler
M-135	1966	*The mad metropolis.* + Philip E. High *Space captain.* + Murray Leinster
M-139	1966	*Empire star.* + Samuel R. Delany *The tree lord of Imeten.* + Tom Purdom
M-141	1966	*The brains of Earth.* + Jack Vance *The many worlds of Magnus Ridolph.* + Jack Vance
G-574	1966	*The Kar-chee reign.* + Avram Davidson *Rocannon's world.* + Ursula K. Le Guin
G-576	1966	*Clash of star-kings.* + Avram Davidson *Danger from Vega.* + John Rackham
G-580	1966	*Inherit the Earth.* + Claude Nunes *Dawnman planet.* + Mack Reynolds
G-585	1966	*The ultimate weapon.* + John W. Campbell *The planeteers.* + John W. Campbell
G-588	1966	*The star magicians.* + Lin Carter *The off-worlders.* + John Baxter
G-592	1966	*A planet of your own.* + John Brunner *The beasts of Kohl.* + John Rackham
G-597	1966	*Planet of exile.* + Ursula K. Le Guin *Mankind under the leash.* + Thomas M. Disch
G-602	1966	*The unteleported man.* + Philip K. Dick *The mind monsters.* + Howard L. Cory
G-606	1966	*The man without a planet.* + Lin Carter *Time to live.* + John Rackham
G-609	1967	*Contraband from otherspace.* + A. Bertram Chandler *Reality forbidden.* + Philip E. High
G-614	1967	*Envoy to the Dog Star.* + Frederick L. Shaw, Jr. *Shock wave.* + Walt & Leigh Richmond
G-618	1967	*The ship from Atlantis.* + H. Warner Munn *The stolen sun.* + Emil Petaja
G-623	1967	*The double invaders.* + John Rackham *These savage futurians.* + Philip E. High
G-632	1967	*The rival Rigelians.* + Mack Reynolds *Nebula alert.* + A. Bertram Chandler
H-20	1967	*The wandering Tellurian.* + Alan Schwartz *The key to Irunium.* + Kenneth Bulmer
H-21	1967	*The last castle.* + Jack Vance *World of the sleeper.* + Tony Russell Wayman
H-22	1967	*Lord of the green planet.* + Emil Petaja *Five against Arlane.* + Tom Purdom
H-27	1967	*The winds of Gath.* + E. C. Tubb *Crisis on Cheiron.* + Juanita Coulson
H-29	1967	*The lost millennium.* + Walt & Leigh Richmond *The road to the Rim.* A. Bertram Chandler
H-34	1967	*Death is a dream.* + E. C. Tubb *Computer war.* + Mack Reynolds
H-36	1967	*Tramontane.* + Emil Petaja *The wrecks of time.* + Michael Moorcock
H-40	1968	*Alien sea.* + John Rackham *C.O.D. Mars.* + E. C. Tubb
H-48	1968	*The pictures of Pavanne.* + Lan Wright *The youth monopoly.* + Ellen Wobig
H-51	1968	*Crown of infinity.* + John M. Faucette *The prism.* + Emil Petaja
H-56	1968	*Pity about Earth.* + Ernest Hill *Space chantey.* + R. A. Lafferty
H-59	1968	*The time mercenaries.* + Philip E. High *Anthropol.* + Louis Trimble.
H-65	1968	*Mercenary from tomorrow.* + Mack Reynolds *The key to Venudine.* + Kenneth Bulmer
H-70	1968	*Star quest.* + Dean R. Koontz *Doom of the green planet.* + Emil Petaja

58880   1971   *Alice's world.* + Sam J. Lundwall
               No time for heroes. + Sam J. Lundwall

66160   1969   *Phoenix ship.* + Walt & Leigh Richmond
               Earthrim. + Nick Kamin

66525   1971   *The pirates of Zan.* + Murray Leinster
               The mutant weapon. + Murray Leinster

68310   1971   *Project Jove.* + John Glasby
               The hunters of Jundagai. + Kenneth Bulmer

71082   1971   *Recoil.* + Claude & Rhoda Nunes
               Lallia. + E. C. Tubb

72400   1969   *The Rim gods.* + A. Bertram Chandler
               The high hex. + Laurence M. Janifer
                 & S. J. Treibich

75781   1971   *The secret of Sinharat.* + Leigh Brackett
               People of the Talisman. + Leigh Brackett

76096   1970   *The ships of Durostorum.* + Kenneth Bulmer
               Alton's unguessable. + Jeff Sutton

76380   1973   *Battle on Venus.* + William F. Temple
               The three suns of Amara. + William F. Temple

76960   1973   *Badge of infamy.* + Lester del Rey
               The sky is falling. + Lester del Rey

77525   1971   *Son of the tree.* + Jack Vance
               The houses of Iszm. + Jack Vance

77710   1969   *The space barbarians.* + Mack Reynolds
               The eyes of Bolsk. + Robert Lory

77785   1971   *The space willies.* + Eric Frank Russell
               Six worlds yonder. + Eric Frank Russell

78400   1970   *The star virus.* + Barrington J. Bayley
               Mask of chaos. + John Jakes

79975   1972   *Technos.* + E. C. Tubb
               A scatter of stardust. + E. C. Tubb

81610   1970   *To Venus! To Venus!* + David Grinnell
               The jester at Scar. + E. C. Tubb

81680   1969   *The wagered world.* + Laurence M. Janifer & S. J. Treibich
               Tonight we steal the stars. + John Jakes

89250   1970   *The winds of Darkover.* + Marion Zimmer Bradley
               The anything Tree. + John Rackham

89301   1973   *Derai.* + E. C. Tubb
               The winds of Gath. + E. C. Tubb

93900   1973   *The sun destroyers.* + Ross Rocklynne
               A yank at Valhalla. + Edmond Hamilton

<u>BELMONT DOUBLES NUMBER INDEX</u>

B50-759   1967   *The Flame of Iridar.* + Lin Carter
                 Peril of the starmen. + Kris Neville

B50-779   1967   *Doomsman.* + Harlan Ellison
                 Telepower. + Lee Hoffman

B50-788   1967   *Special delivery.* + Kris Neville
                 Star gladiator. + Dave Van Arnam

B50-809   1968   *The thief of Thoth.* + Lin Carter
                 ...And others shall be born. + Frank Belknap Long

B60-077   1968   *A lamp for Medusa.* + William Tenn
                 The players of Hell. + Dave Van Arnam

B60-080   1968   *Ladies' day.* + Robert Bloch
                 This crowded Earth. + Robert Bloch

B60-081   1968   *Father of lies.* + John Brunner
                 Mirror image. + Bruce Duncan

B60-1010 1969   *The evil that men do.* + John Brunner
                 The purloined planet. + Lin Carter

50244   1972   *Doomsman.* + Harlan Ellison
               The thief of Thoth. + Lin Carter

50787   1975   *The evil that men do.* + John Brunner
               The purloined planet. + Lin Carter